THE
MACMILLAN
VISUAL
DICTIONARY

THE
MACMILLAN
VISUAL
DICTIONARY

Edición Español/Inglés
Spanish/English Edition

MACMILLAN
A Simon & Schuster Macmillan Company
1633 Broadway
New York, NY 10019-6785

Library of Congress Cataloging-in-Publication Data available

ISBN 0-02-861434-8

Created and produced
by Québec/Amérique International
a division of
Éditions Québec/Amérique Inc.
425, rue Saint-Jean-Baptiste, Montréal, Québec H2Y 2Z7
Tel. : (514) 393-1450 Fax : (514) 866-2430

MACMILLAN is a registered trademark of Macmillan, Inc.

Printed in U.S.A.

10 9 8 7 6 5 4 3 2 1

EDICIÓN INGLÉS/ENGLISH LANGUAGE EDITION
Natalie Chapman - *Publisher*
John Michel - *Executive Editor*
Beth Jordan - *Production Director*
Kevin Hanek - *Production Editor*

**EQUIPO EDITORIAL PARA LA PRIMERA EDICIÓN/
EDITORIAL STAFF FOR THE ORIGINAL EDITION**
Jacques Fortin - *Publisher*
Jean-Claude Corbeil - *Editor-in-chief*
Ariane Archambault - *Assistant Editor*
François Fortin - *Illustrations Editor*
Jean-Louis Martin - *Art Director*

**ARTISTAS DE DISEÑO POR ORDENADOR/
COMPUTER GRAPHIC ARTISTS**
Jacques Perrault
Anne Tremblay
Jocelyn Gardner
Christiane Beauregard
Michel Blais
Rielle Lévesque
Marc Lalumière
Stéphane Roy
Alice Comtois
Jean-Yves Ahern
Benoît Bourdeau

EDICIÓN DE TEXTO/COMPUTER COPYEDITING
Daniel Beaulieu
Yves Ferland

INVESTIGACIÓN/RESEARCH EDITOR
Serge D'Amico

MAQUETACIÓN/PAGE SETUP
Pascal Goyette
Lucie Mc Brearty
Martin Langlois

PRODUCCIÓN/PRODUCTION
Tony O'Riley

DISEÑO GRÁFICO/GRAPHIC DESIGN
Emmanuel Blanc

AGRADECIMIENTOS/ACKNOWLEDGMENTS

Los creadores de la primera edición quieren agradecer la contribución de las siguientes personas e instituciones:
The creators of the original edition wish to thank the following persons and institutions for their contributions:

A.C. Delco
Aérospatiale (France)
Aérospatiale Canada (ACI) Inc.
Air Canada (Linguistic Policy and Services)
Amity-Leather Products Company
Animat Inc.
Archambault Musique
International Association of Lighthouse
  Authorities (Marie-Hélène Grillet)
Association des groupes d'astronomes amateurs
  (Jean-Marc Richard)
Atlas Copco
Atomic Energy of Canada Ltd. (Pierre Giguère)
Bell Canada
Bell Helicopter Textron
Bellefontaine
Benoît, Richard
Beretta
Black & Decker
Bombardier Inc.
Boutique de harnais Pépin
British Hovercraft Corporation Ltd. (Division of
  Westland Aerospace)
C. Plath North American Division
Caloritech Inc.
Cambridge Instruments (Canada) Inc.
CAMIF (Direction relations extérieures)
Canada Billard & Bowling Inc. (Bernard Monsec)
Canadian National (Information and Linguistic
  Services)
Canadian Kenworth Company
Canadian Coleman Supply Inc.
Canadian Liquid Air Ltd.
Canadian Curling Association
Canadian Coast Guard
Canadian Broadcasting Corporation (Gilles
  Amyot, Pierre Beaucage, Claude L'Hérault,
  Pierre Laroche)
Carpentier, Jean-Marc
Casavant Frères Limitée (Gilbert Lemieux)
Centre de Tissage Leclerc Inc.
Chromalox Inc.
Clerc, Redjean
Club de tir à l'arc de Montréal
Club de planeur Champlain
Collège Jean de Brébeuf (Paul-Émile Tremblay)
Collège militaire royal de Saint-Jean
Communauté urbaine de Montréal (Bureau de
  transport métropolitain)
Complexe sportif Claude-Robillard
Control Data Canada Ltd.
Cycles Performance
David M. Stewart Museum (Philippe Butler)
Department of National Defence of Canada
  (Public Relations)
Detson
Direction des constructions navales
  (Programmes internationaux) (France)
Distributions TTI Inc.
Energy, Mines and Resources Canada (Canada
  Centre for Remote Sensing)
Environment Canada (Atmospheric Environment
  Service, Gilles Sanscartier)
FACOM
Fédération québécoise des échecs
Fédération québécoise de tennis
Fédération québécoise de luge et bobsleigh
Fédération québécoise de canot-camping
Fédération québécoise de boxe olympique
Fédération québécoise de badminton
Fédération québécoise d'haltérophilie

Fédération québécoise d'escrime
Fédération québécoise de patinage de vitesse du Québec
Festival des Montolfières du Haut-Richelieu
Fincantieri Naval Shipbuilding Division
Fisher Scientific Ltd.
Ford New-Holland Inc.
Gadbois, Alain
GAM Pro Plongée
G.E. Astro-Space Division
G.T.E. Sylvania Canada Ltd.
General Electric Canada Inc. (Dominion
  Engineering Works, Mony Schinasi)
General Motors of Canada Ltd.
GIAT Industries
Government of Canada Terminology Bank
Gym Plus
Harrison (1985) Inc.
Hewitt Equipment Ltd.
Hippodrome Blue Bonnets (Robert Perez)
Honeywell Ltd.
Hortipro
Hughes Aircraft Company
Hydro-Québec (Centre de documentation, Anne
  Crépeau)
IBM Canada Ltd.
Imperial Oil Ltd.
Institut de recherche d'Hydro-Québec (IREQ)
International Telecommunications Satellite
  Organization (Intelsat)
International Civil Aviation Organization (IATA)
Jardin Botanique de Montréal
John Deere Ltd.
Johnson & Johnson Inc.
La Maison Olympique (Sylvia Doucette)
La Cordée
Le Beau Voyage
Le Coz, Jean-Pierre
Lee Valley Tools Ltd.
Leica Camera
Les Manufacturiers Draco ltée
Les Instruments de Musique Twigg Inc.
Les Équipements Chalin ltée
Les Appareils orthopédiques BBG Inc.
Leviton Manufacturing of Canada Ltd.
Liebherr-Québec
Manac Inc.
Manutan
Marcoux, Jean-Marie
Marrazza Musique
MATRA S.A.
Matra Défense (Direction de la communication)
Mazda Canada
Médiatel
Mendes Inc. (François Caron)
Michelin
MIL Tracy (Henri Vacher)
Ministère des transports du Québec (Sécurité
  routière, Signalisation routière)
Monette Sport Inc.
Moto Internationale
National Oceanic and Atmospheric
  Administration (NOAA) — National
  Environmental Satellite and Information
  Service (Frank Lepore)
National Aeronautics and Space Administration
  (NASA)
Nikon Canada Inc.
Northern Telecom Canada Ltd.
Office de la langue française du Québec
  (Chantal Robinson)
Ogilvie Mills Ltd. (Michel Ladouceur)

Olivetti Systems and Networks Canada Ltd.
Ontario Hydro
Paterson Darkroom Necessities
Petro-Canada (Calgary)
Philips Electronics Ltd. (Philips Lighting)
Philips Electronics Ltd. (Scientific and Analytical
  Equipment)
Pierre-Olivier Decor
Planétarium Dow (Pierre Lacombe)
Plastimo
Port of Montreal (Public Affairs)
Pratt & Whitney Canada Inc.
Quincaillerie A.C.L. Inc.
Radio-Québec
Remington Products (Canada) Inc.
Russell Rinfret
Rodriguez Cantieri navali S.p.A.
S.A. Redoute Catalogue (Relations extérieures)
Samsonite
Secretary of State of Canada (Translation
  Bureau)
Shell Canada
SIAL Poterie
Smith-Corona (Canada) Ltd.
SNC Defence Products Ltd.
Société Nationale des Chemins de Fer français
  (S.N.C.F.) (Direction de la communication)
Société de transport de la Communauté urbaine
  de Montréal
Spalding Canada
Spar Aerospace Ltd. (Hélène Lapierre)
St. Lawrence Seaway Authority (Normand
  Dodier)
Sunbeam Corporation (Canada) Ltd.
Swimming Canada
Teleglobe Canada Inc. (Roger Leblanc)
Telesat Canada (Yves Comtois)
The Coal Association of Canada
The British Petroleum Company p.l.c.
  (Photographic Services)
Thibault
Tideland Signal Canada Ltd.
Transport Canada (Montreal Airports, Gilbert
  L'Espérance, Koos R. Van der Peijl)
Ultramar Canada Inc.
United States Department of Defense
  (Department of the Navy, Office of
  Information)
Université du Québec à Montréal (Module des
  arts, Michel Fournier)
Université du Québec (Institut national de la
  recherche scientifique, Benoît Jean)
Varin, Claude
Via Rail Canada Inc.
Viala L.R. Inc. (Jean Beaudin)
Ville de Montréal (Bureau du cinéma; Service de
  l'habitation et du développement urbain;
  Service de la prévention des incendies,
  Robert Gilbert, Réal Audet; Service des
  travaux publics)
Volcano Inc.
Volkswagen Canada Inc.
Volvo Canada Ltd.
Water Ski Canada
Weider
Wild Leitz Canada ltée
Xerox Canada Inc.
Yamaha Canada Music Ltd.

Este exhaustivo trabajo de renombre internacional es el primer diccionario visual a todo color en cuatro idiomas. Con una cobertura de más de 600 materias, identifica más de 25,000 términos sirviéndose de miles de ilustraciones detalladas y precisas. El *Diccionario Visual* nos permite conocer, a simple vista, el vocabulario de un tema en dos idiomas: español e inglés.

UN DICCIONARIO DE IMÁGENES Y PALABRAS

El *Diccionario Visual español/inglés* relaciona palabras con imágenes.

A través de las imágenes se describe y analiza el mundo de hoy: los objetos que empleamos en la vida cotidiana, el medio físico que nos rodea, la flora y la fauna, las técnicas de comunicación y de trabajo que están modificando nuestro estilo de vida, las armas que nos preocupan, los medios de transporte que están borrando las barreras geográficas, las fuentes de energía de las que dependemos, etc.

Las ilustraciones desempeñan un papel específico en este diccionario: sirven para definir palabras, de manera que el usuario del diccionario pueda "ver" inmediatamente el significado de cada término. Así el usuario puede reconocer los objetos que busca y, con una sola mirada, encontrar el vocabulario correspondiente.

El *Diccionario Visual* proporciona a los usuarios las palabras que necesitan para nombrar con precisión los objetos que forman parte del mundo que los rodea.

Los términos de este diccionario han sido cuidadosamente seleccionados utilizando material actualizado sobre cada materia escrito por expertos. Cuando ha surgido alguna duda, los expertos en la materia correspondiente han examinado el vocabulario, que luego hemos comprobado y contrastado consultando enciclopedias y diccionarios de la lengua. Hemos hecho estas comprobaciones con el fin de garantizar la exactitud de cada palabra empleada, así como un alto nivel de estandarización.

UN DICCIONARIO PARA TODOS

El *Diccionario Visual* se dirige a todo el que participa de un modo u otro en la civilización actual y que, por consiguiente, necesita conocer y utilizar un número elevado de términos técnicos de una gran variedad de materias.

Este diccionario cubre las necesidades de cada uno de nosotros, y no se dirige necesariamente o exclusivamente a los expertos.

La profundidad del análisis varía según el tema. En lugar de hacer una subdivisión arbitraria de cada tema, los autores han reconocido que el nivel de conocimientos de los usuarios varía enormemente de un tema a otro, y que la complejidad con la que han de tratarse también

ha de ser diferente. Por ejemplo, la mayoría de los usuarios está más familiarizada con el mundo del vestuario o de los automóviles que con el de la energía atómica o de las telecomunicaciones por satélite, y encuentran aquellos más sencillos que éstas. Por otro lado, para describir, por ejemplo, la anatomía humana, hemos tenido que utilizar la terminología médica a pesar de que ésta resulte más complicada que la que hemos utilizado para describir las frutas y las verduras. Además, el mundo que nos rodea cambia constantemente: el vocabulario del mundo de la fotografía, por ejemplo, es cada vez más complejo debido a la automatización de la cámara. De forma similar, y aunque hoy día hay numerosos aficionados a la microinformática que conocen la terminología del campo, éste sigue siendo un misterio para la mayor parte de la población.

UN DICCIONARIO FÁCIL DE CONSULTAR

Gracias a la Lista de los Capítulos (página xxxi), el índice de materias (página xv) y el índice analítico (página 833), los usuarios de este diccionario podrán consultarlo y utilizarlo de formas diferentes.

Este diccionario puede consultarse de las formas siguientes:

De la idea a la palabra. Si el usuario está familiarizado con el objeto y lo visualiza, pero no conoce la palabra, debe acudir al índice de materias, que se organiza según un sistema de clasificación fácil de consultar. El *Diccionario Visual* es el único que permite a los usuarios encontrar la palabra a partir de su significado.

De la palabra a la idea. El usuario desea consultar el significado de una palabra. El índice analítico lo remite a las ilustraciones, en las que encontrará la descripción de los nombres que recibe cada parte o componente del objeto.

Una ojeada rápida. El usuario puede utilizar la Lista de Capítulos para encontrar rápidamente los capítulos que le interesa consultar. Para facilitar esta tarea, cada capítulo está marcado con un color diferente, que aparece en el margen de la página.

Por el placer de la consulta. El usuario puede consultar el diccionario simplemente por placer, saltando de una ilustración a otra o de una palabra a otra, con el fin de mirar las ilustraciones y enriquecer sus conocimientos.

ILUSTRACIONES REALIZADAS POR ORDENADOR

Las ilustraciones del *Diccionario Visual* se han realizado por ordenador utilizando material actual y fotografías originales.

El uso del ordenador ha dado un aspecto realista y casi fotográfico a las ilustraciones, al tiempo que ha permitido destacar las características fundamentales del vocabulario descrito. La precisión gráfica del *Diccionario Visual* es una de las fuentes principales de su elevada calidad como herramienta de consulta enciclopédica y lexicográfica.

VOCABULARIO CUIDADOSAMENTE SELECCIONADO Y ESTABLECIDO

Para la creación del *Diccionario Visual* se ha utilizado el método de investigación terminológica sistemático y comparativo, que es hoy práctica generalizada entre los profesionales que elaboran este tipo de obras:

Delimitación de campo

En primer lugar, y de acuerdo con los objetivos planteados, se definieron el alcance y los contenidos de la obra propuesta, eligiendo los capítulos que pensamos se debían cubrir. A continuación, dividimos cada capítulo en materias y sub-materias, intentando siempre atenernos a nuestra línea editorial y evitar tanto una excesiva especialización como la tentación de cubrir todas las materias con detalle. Esta etapa dio como resultado la elaboración del índice de los contenidos y el marco u organización del diccionario. Éste sirvió para guiar las etapas siguientes, y se afinó a medida que la obra avanzaba. El índice de materias es el resultado final de este proceso.

Investigación y documentación

Para garantizar la máxima fiabilidad, nos documentamos de las siguientes fuentes:

• Artículos y libros escritos por expertos en las distintas materias y en el idioma original, con un nivel aceptable de especialización. Las traducciones de los textos proporcionan información valiosa en cuanto al uso del vocabulario, pero deben ser utilizadas con la debida prudencia.

• Documentos técnicos, como estándares nacionales o las líneas propuestas por la Organización Estándar Internacional (OEI), instrucciones de productos, documentos técnicos proporcionados por fabricantes e industriales, publicaciones oficiales gubernamentales, etc.

• Catálogos, textos comerciales, anuncios de revistas especializadas y periódicos de amplia difusión.

• Enciclopedias, diccionarios enciclopédicos y diccionarios de léxico monolingües.

• Vocabularios y diccionarios especializados monolingües, bilingües y multilingües. La calidad y fiabilidad de estas obras debe, sin embargo, evaluarse cuidadosamente.

• Diccionarios de léxico monolingües y multilingües. En todos ellos consultamos de cuatro a cinco mil referencias. De la bibliografía seleccionada e incluida en este diccionario se indican únicamente las fuentes de documentación general, pero no las fuentes especializadas.

Comprobación de la documentación y la terminología

Un editor experto en terminología examinó la documentación de cada materia, en busca de conceptos específicos y de las palabras que los diferentes autores utilizaron para expresarlos. La organización o marco del diccionario se fue estableciendo gradualmente, a medida que el editor "terminólogo" observaba el uso del mismo término para un concepto determinado de una fuente a otra o, al contrario, el uso de términos diferentes para expresar la misma idea. En este último caso, el editor "terminólogo" continuó su investigación hasta poder emitir una opinión adecuadamente documentada sobre cada término y sus variantes. Todo este proceso se registró a través de notas.

Creación de archivos de terminología

El paso anterior nos permitió reunir todos los elementos necesarios para crear archivos de terminología.

Cada concepto, identificado y definido mediante una imagen, va acompañado del término que los autores principales o las fuentes más fiables utilizan con mayor frecuencia para describirlo. Cuando en el material de consulta se encontraron varios términos alternativos, se procedió a la consulta, discusión y consenso entre el editor experto en terminología y el director científico, para elegir al fin uno de los términos.

Variantes de un término

A menudo se pueden utilizar varias palabras para designar el mismo concepto.

Esta situación se ha resuelto de la manera siguiente:

• En algunos casos, un término aparecía una sola vez en la documentación o lo utilizaba un solo autor. En este caso hemos mantenido el término que se utilizaba con mayor frecuencia.

• Los términos técnicos son a menudo palabras compuestas separadas o no por un guión, o incluso una expresión compuesta de varias palabras. Esto resulta en al menos dos tipos de variantes terminológicas:

a) El término técnico compuesto puede abreviarse con la supresión de uno o más de sus elementos, sobre todo cuando el significado se entiende por el contexto. La expresión abreviada puede incluso convertirse en el término normal para el concepto. En estos casos hemos decidido mantener las formas compuestas, de manera que el usuario pueda o no abreviarlas libremente según el contexto.

b) Uno de los elementos del compuesto puede tener equivalentes (casi siempre sinónimos de uso corriente en la lengua hablada). En este caso hemos mantenido la forma utilizada con mayor frecuencia.

Las variantes pueden surgir de la evolución de la lengua sin tener consecuencias terminológicas. Por ello hemos mantenido la forma más actual o difundida.

T*he Macmillan Visual Dictionary Spanish/English Edition* is quite unlike other dictionaries with respect to both contents and presentation. Given its uniqueness, a few words of explanation will help you appreciate its usefulness and the quality of the information it contains. The following introduction explains how and why *The Macmillan Visual Dictionary Spanish/English Edition* differs from language dictionaries and encyclopedias.

A PICTURE/WORD DICTIONARY

The Macmillan Visual Dictionary Spanish/English Edition closely links pictures and words.

The pictures describe and analyze today's world: the objects of everyday life, our physical environment, the animal and vegetable life that surrounds us, the communication and work techniques that are changing our lifestyles, the weapons that preoccupy us, the means of transportation that are breaking down geographical barriers, the sources of energy on which we depend, etc.

Illustrations play a specific role in our dictionary: they serve to define words, enabling dictionary users to "see" immediately the meaning of each term. Users can thus recognize the objects they are looking for and, at a single glance, find the corresponding vocabulary. *The Macmillan Visual Dictionary Spanish/English Edition* provides users with the words they need to accurately name the objects that make up the world around them.

The terms in the dictionary have been carefully selected from current documents written by experts in each area. In case of doubt, the vocabulary has been studied by specialists in the corresponding field and cross-checked in encyclopedias and language dictionaries. We have taken these precautions to ensure the accuracy of each word and a high level of standardization.

A DICTIONARY FOR ONE AND ALL

The Macmillan Visual Dictionary Spanish/English Edition is aimed at all persons who participate in one way or another in contemporary civilization and, as a consequence, need to know and use a great number of technical terms from a wide range of fields.

It thus addresses the needs and curiosity of each and every one of us. It is not designed only for specialists.

The depth of analysis varies according to the subject. Rather than arbitrarily providing a uniform breakdown of each subject, the authors have acknowledged that people's degrees of knowledge differ from one field to another, and that the complexity of the topics dealt with varies widely. For example, more people are familiar with clothing and automobiles than with atomic energy or telecommunications satellites, and find the former subjects simpler than the latter. Another aspect of the same problem is that, in describing human anatomy, we are obliged to use medical terminology, even though the terms seem more complicated than those for fruits and vegetables. In addi-

tion, our world is changing: photographic vocabulary, for example, has become much more complicated due to camera automation. Similarly, although microcomputer fans are familiar with computer terminology, the field remains a mystery for much of the rest of the population. *The Macmillan Visual Dictionary Spanish/English Edition* allows for these phenomena, and thus reflects the specialized vocabulary commonly used in each field.

AN EASY-TO-CONSULT DICTIONARY

People may use *The Macmillan Visual Dictionary Spanish/English Edition* in several different ways, thanks to the List of Chapters (page xxxi), the detailed table of contents (page xv), and the index (page 867).

Users may consult the dictionary:

By going from an idea to a word, if they are familiar with an object and can clearly visualize it, but cannot find or do not know the name for it. The table of contents breaks down each subject according to an easy-to-consult, stratified classification system. *The Macmillan Visual Dictionary Spanish/English Edition* is the only dictionary that allows users to find a word from its meaning.

By going from a word to an idea, if they want to check the meaning of a term. The index refers users to the illustrations, which provide the names for the individual features.

At a glance, by using the List of Chapters. The colored page edges help users find the chapters they are looking for.

For foreign language equivalents, by browsing through the book or going into depth for particular themes. The objects of the modern world are clearly identified at a glance in four languages.

For sheer pleasure, by flipping from one illustration to another, or from one word to another, for the sole purpose of enjoying the illustrations and enriching their knowledge.

COMPUTER-PRODUCED ILLUSTRATIONS

The illustrations in *The Macmillan Visual Dictionary Spanish/English Edition* have been created by computer from recent documents and original photographs.

The use of computers has given the illustrations a highly realistic, almost photographic look, while allowing us to highlight the essential features corresponding to the vocabulary. The graphic precision of *The Macmillan Visual Dictionary Spanish/English Edition* is one of the main sources of its excellence as an encyclopedic and lexicographical reference tool.

CAREFULLY ESTABLISHED VOCABULARY

In creating *The Macmillan Visual Dictionary Spanish/English Edition*, we have used the method of systematic and comparative terminological research, which is standard practice among professionals who prepare works of this type.

Field delimitation

First of all, on the basis of our objectives, we defined the scope and contents of the proposed work.

We began by choosing the chapters we felt it necessary to cover. We then divided each chapter into fields and sub-fields, taking care to abide by our editorial policy and avoiding overspecialization and the temptation to cover all subjects in detail. This step resulted in a working table of contents, the dictionary framework, which guided our subsequent steps and was refined as the work progressed. The detailed table of contents is the end result of this process.

Documentary research

In order of reliability, our documentary sources were as follows:

• Articles and books by experts in the various fields, written in their native language, with an acceptable degree of specialization. Translations of such texts provide revealing information about vocabulary usage, but must be used with due caution;

• Technical documents, such as national standards or the guidelines of the International Standard Organization (ISO), product instructions, technical documents provided by manufacturers, official government publications, etc.;

• Catalogs, commercial texts, advertisements from specialized magazines and major newspapers;

• Encyclopedias, encyclopedic dictionaries, and unilingual language dictionaries;

• Unilingual, bilingual, and multilingual specialized vocabularies and dictionaries. The quality and reliability of these works, however, must be carefully assessed;

• Bilingual and multilingual language dictionaries.

In all, we consulted four to five thousand references. The selected bibliography included in the dictionary indicates only the general documentary sources consulted, and does not include specialized sources.

Sifting through the documents

A terminologist went through the documents for each subject, in search of specific concepts and the words used to express them by different authors and works.

Gradually, a framework was established, as the terminologist noted the use of the same term for a given concept from one source to another, or, on the contrary, the use of several terms for the same idea. In the latter case, the terminologist continued his research until he was able to form a well-documented opinion of each competing term. All of this research was recorded, with reference notes.

Creation of a multilingual terminology base

The English terminology is based on standard North American usage and the Spanish terminology on Castilian usage. Nothing in this dictionary is the result of translation; all languages have been prepared by renowned specialists and verified by major dictionary houses. Because of this, errors frequently found in other multilingual dictionaries based exclusively on a translation approach have been avoided.

Creation of terminological files

The preceding step enabled us to assemble all of the elements for our terminological files.

Each concept identified and defined by an illustration has been paired with the term most frequently used to describe it by the leading authors or in the most reliable sources. Where several competing terms were found in the reference material, following discussion and consensus between the terminologist and the scientific director, a single term was chosen.

Terminological variants

Frequently, several words may be used to designate virtually the same concept.

We dealt with such situations as follows:

• In some cases, a term was used by a single author or appeared only once in our documentary sources. We retained the most frequently used competing term.

• Technical terms are often compound words with or without a hyphen, or several-word expressions. This results in at least two types of terminological variants:

a) The compound technical term may be shortened by the deletion of one or more of its elements, especially where the meaning is clear in the context. The shortened expression may even become the normal term for the concept. In such cases, we retained the compound form, leaving users the freedom to abbreviate it according to the context.

b) An element of the compound term may itself have equivalents (most often synonyms from the commonly spoken language). We retained the most frequently used form.

Variants may stem from the evolution of the language, without terminological consequences. We therefore retained the most contemporary or well-known form.

JEAN-CLAUDE CORBEIL
ARIANE ARCHAMBAULT

EL TÍTULO/HEADING •
identifica el contenido de cada
página/identifies the topic of each page

EL SUBTÍTULO/SUBHEADING •
indica el objeto que aparece en la
ilustración/indicates the object depicted

EL TEMA/CHAPTER •
de cada sección del diccionario
aparece claramente indicado en cada
página/of the dictionary is shown in
the side margin of each page

**Si quiere averiguar el nombre de
un objeto, consulte el índice de
materias, que contiene los temas,
títulos y subtítulos con sus corres-
pondientes referencias a la página
de cada título.**

**To find the correct term for some-
thing, start by turning to the table
of contents, which lists the dictionary's chapters, headings, and
subheadings, with the first page
reference for each heading.**

**LAS ILUSTRACIONES
A COLOR/COLOR
ILLUSTRATIONS** •
muestran de forma realista todos
los elementos relevantes/realistically
depict the objects and their
component parts

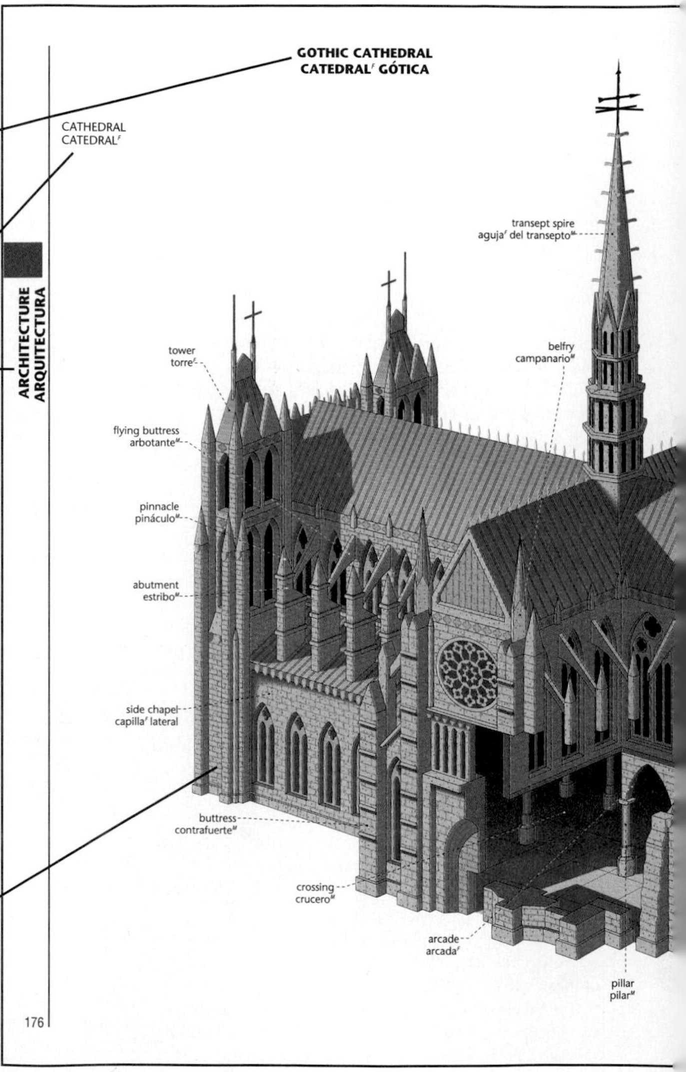

GOTHIC CATHEDRAL
CATEDRAL' GÓTICA

CATHEDRAL
CATEDRAL'

ARCHITECTURE
ARQUITECTURA

transept spire
aguja' del transepto"

tower
torre'

belfry
campanario"

flying buttress
arbotante"

pinnacle
pináculo"

abutment
estribo"

side chapel
capilla' lateral

buttress
contrafuerte"

crossing
crucero"

arcade
arcada'

pillar
pilar"

176

XII

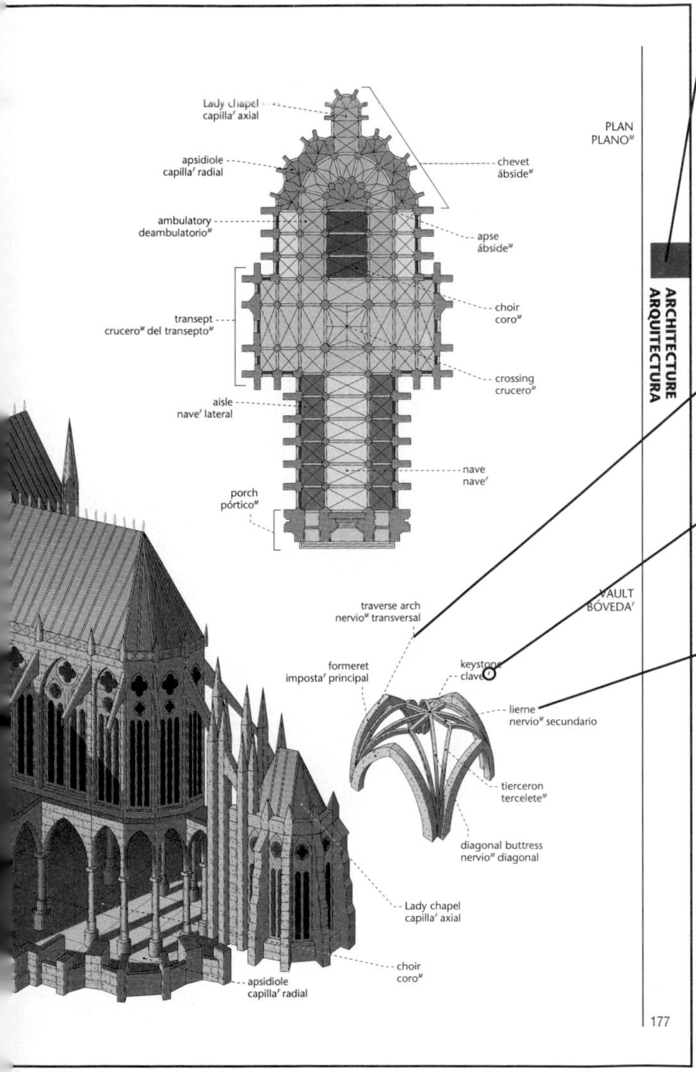

COMO UTILIZAR EL DICCIONARIO/USAGE GUIDE

Lady chapel
capilla' axial

apsidiole
capilla' radial

ambulatory
deambulatorio"

transept
crucero" del transepto"

aisle
nave' lateral

porch
pórtico"

chevet
ábside"

apse
ábside"

choir
coro"

crossing
crucero"

nave
nave'

PLAN
PLANO"

traverse arch
nervio" transversal

formeret
imposta' principal

keystone
clave'

lierne
nervio" secundario

tierceron
tercelete"

diagonal buttress
nervio" diagonal

Lady chapel
capilla' axial

choir
coro"

apsidiole
capilla' radial

VAULT
BÓVEDA'

ARCHITECTURE
ARQUITECTURA

177

• LA ETIQUETA DE COLOR/ COLORED TAB

corresponde a cada uno de los temas, y permite localizarlos rápidamente/ on the edge of the page corresponds to the chapter as shown in the List of Chapters. This color-coding allows you to find, at a glance, the subject you are looking for

• LAS LINEAS DE PUNTOS/ DOTTED LINES

unen los términos con los objetos que designan/link the terms with the objects they describe

• INDICACIÓN DE GÉNERO/ GENDER

f: femenino/feminine
m: masculino/masculine
n: neutro/neuter

• CADA PALABRA/TERMS

aparece en el índice analítico con su correspondiente referencia a la página en la que figura/are included in the index, with references to all pages on which they appear

Si quiere ver una ilustración que corresponde a un término que conoce, consulte el índice analítico.

To see an illustration depicting a term that you know, consult the index.

XIII

DICCIONARIOS/DICTIONARIES

- *Gage Canadian Dictionary*. Toronto: Gage Publishing Limited, 1983, 1313 p.
- *The New Britannica/Webster Dictionary and Reference Guide*. Chicago, Toronto: Encyclopedia Britannica, 1981, 1505 p.
- *The Oxford English Dictionary*. Second edition. Oxford: Clarendon Press, 1989, 20 vol.
- *The New Shorter Oxford English Dictionary*, 1994, 2 vols.
- *Concise Oxford Dictionary*, 1995, 1673 p.
- *The Oxford Illustrated Dictionary*. Oxford: Clarendon Press, 1967, 974 p.
- *Oxford American Dictionary*. Eugene Ehrlich, et al. New York, Oxford: Oxford University Press, 1980, 816 p.
- *The Random House Dictionary of the English Language*. Second edition. New York: Random House 1983, 2059 p.
- *Webster's Encyclopedic Unabridged Dictionary of the English Language*. New York: Portland House, 1989, 2078 p.
- *Webster's Third New International Dictionary*. Springfield: Merriam-Webster, 1986, 2662 p.
- *Webster's Ninth New Collegiate Dictionary*. Springfield: Merriam-Webster, 1984, 1563 p.
- *Webster's New World Dictionary of American Language*. New York: The World Pub., 1953.

ENCICLOPEDIAS/ENCYCLOPEDIAS

- *Academic American Encyclopedia*. Princeton: Arete Publishing Company, 1980, 21 vol.
- *Architectural Graphic Standards*. Eighth edition. New York: John Wiley & Sons, 1988, 854 p.
- *Chamber's Encyclopedia*. New rev. edition. London: International Learning System, 1989.
- *Collier's Encyclopedia*. New York: Macmillan Educational Company, 1984, 24 vol.
- *Compton's Encyclopedia*. Chicago: F.E. Compton Company, Division of Encyclopedia Britannica Inc., 1982, 26 vol.
- *Encyclopedia Americana*. International Edition, Danbury: Grolier, 1981, 30 vol.
- *How It Works, The Illustrated Science and Invention Encyclopedia*. New York: H.S. Stuttman, 1977, 21 vol.
- *McGraw-Hill Encyclopedia of Science & Technology*. New York: McGraw-Hill Book Company, 1982, 15 vol.
- *Merit Students Encyclopedia*. New York: Macmillan Educational Company, 1984, 20 vol.
- *New Encyclopedia Britannica*. Chicago, Toronto: Encyclopedia Britannica, 1985, 32 vol.
- *The Joy of Knowledge Encyclopedia*. London: Mitchell Beazley Encyclopedias, 1976, 7 vol.
- *The Random House Encyclopedia*. New York: Random House, 1977, 2 vol.
- *The World Book Encyclopedia*. Chicago: Field Enterprises Educational Corporation, 1973.

ÍNDICE DE MATERIAS

ÍNDICE DE MATERIAS

ÍNDICE DE MATERIAS

ÍNDICE DE MATERIAS

CONTENTS

CONTENTS

CONTENTS

CONTENTS

CONTENTS

CONTENTS

CONTENTS

CONTENTS

LIST OF CHAPTERS

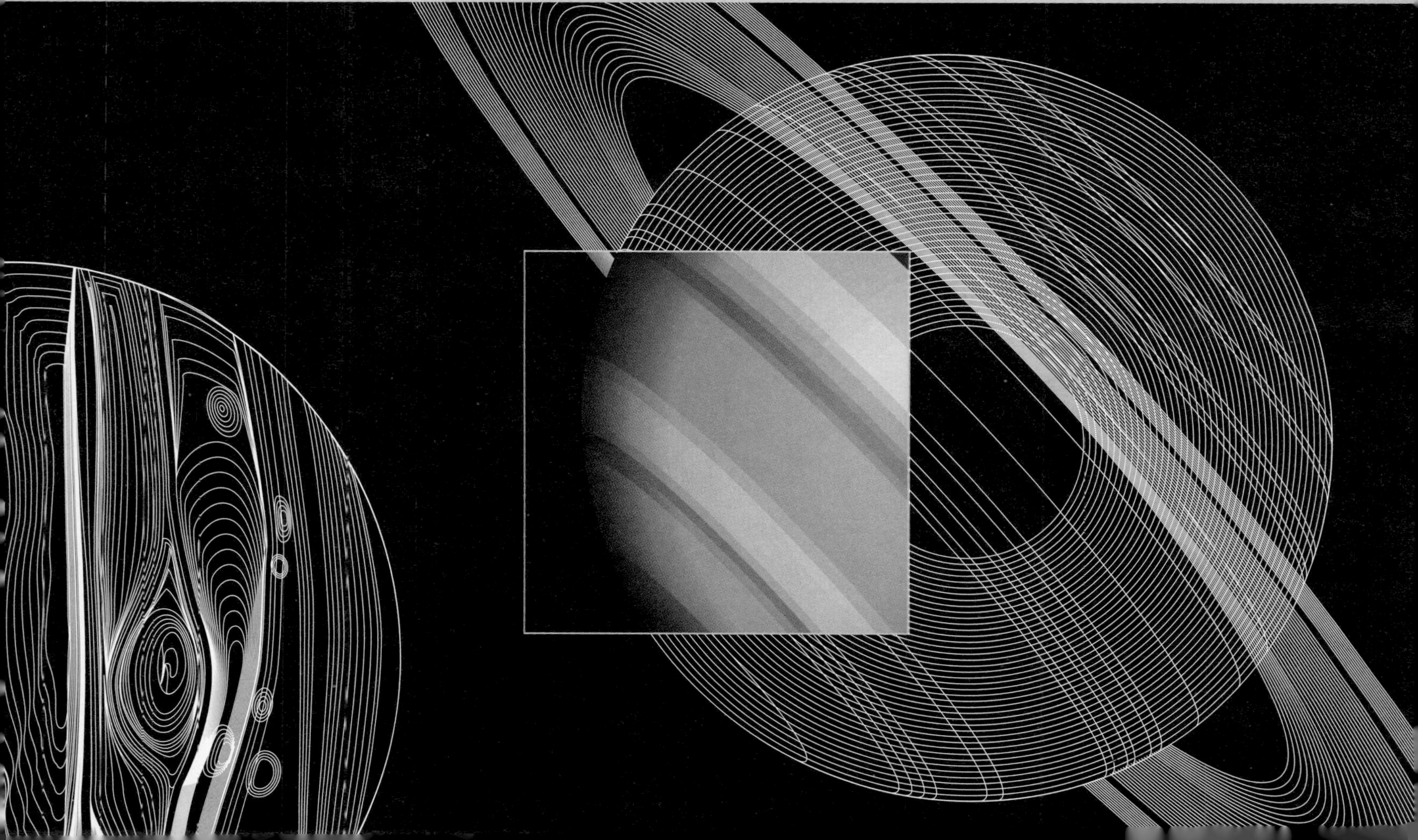

CONTENTS

CELESTIAL COORDINATE SYSTEM
COORDENADAS^F ASTRONÓMICAS

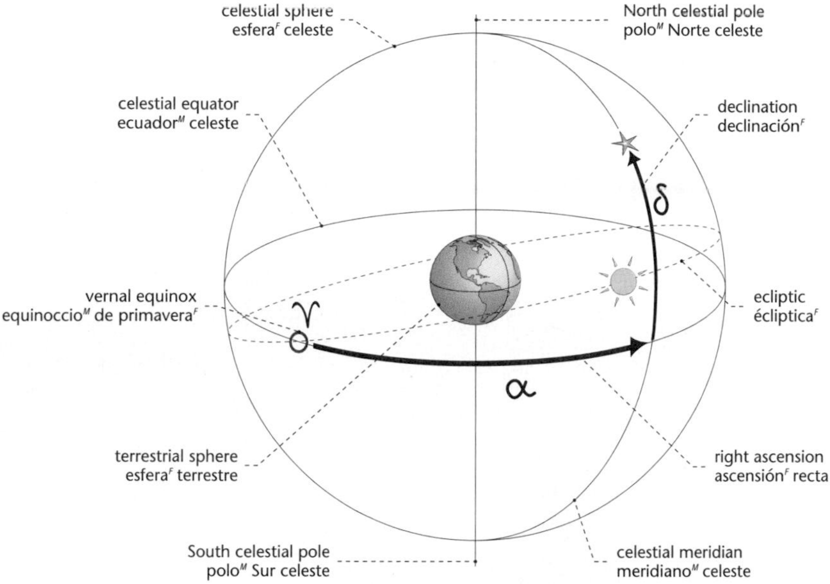

celestial sphere
esfera^F celeste

North celestial pole
polo^M Norte celeste

celestial equator
ecuador^M celeste

declination
declinación^F

vernal equinox
equinoccio^M de primavera^F

ecliptic
écliptica^F

terrestrial sphere
esfera^F terrestre

right ascension
ascensión^F recta

South celestial pole
polo^M Sur celeste

celestial meridian
meridiano^M celeste

EARTH COORDINATE SYSTEM
COORDENADAS^F GEOGRÁFICAS

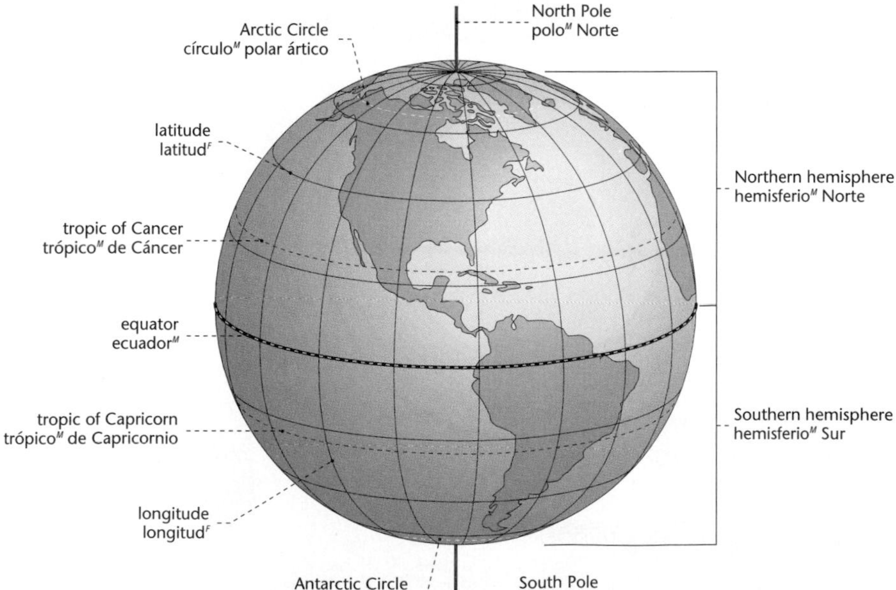

Arctic Circle
círculo^M polar ártico

North Pole
polo^M Norte

latitude
latitud^F

Northern hemisphere
hemisferio^M Norte

tropic of Cancer
trópico^M de Cáncer

equator
ecuador^M

tropic of Capricorn
trópico^M de Capricornio

Southern hemisphere
hemisferio^M Sur

longitude
longitud^F

Antarctic Circle
círculo^M polar antártico

South Pole
polo^M Sur

SOLAR SYSTEM
SISTEMA^M SOLAR

PLANETS AND MOONS
PLANETAS^M Y LUNAS^F

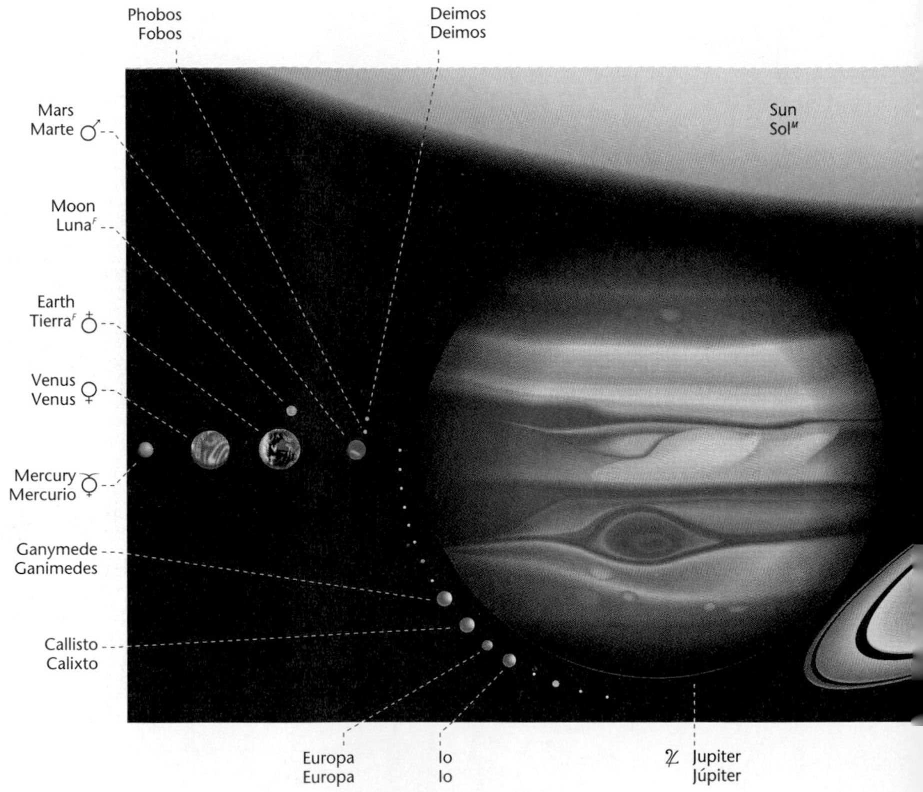

Phobos
Fobos

Deimos
Deimos

Mars
Marte ♂

Sun
Sol^M

Moon
Luna^F

Earth
Tierra^F ♁

Venus
Venus ♀

Mercury ☿
Mercurio ☿

Ganymede
Ganimedes

Callisto
Calixto

Europa
Europa

Io
Io

♃ Jupiter
Júpiter

ORBITS OF THE PLANETS
ÓRBITAS^F DE LOS PLANETAS^M

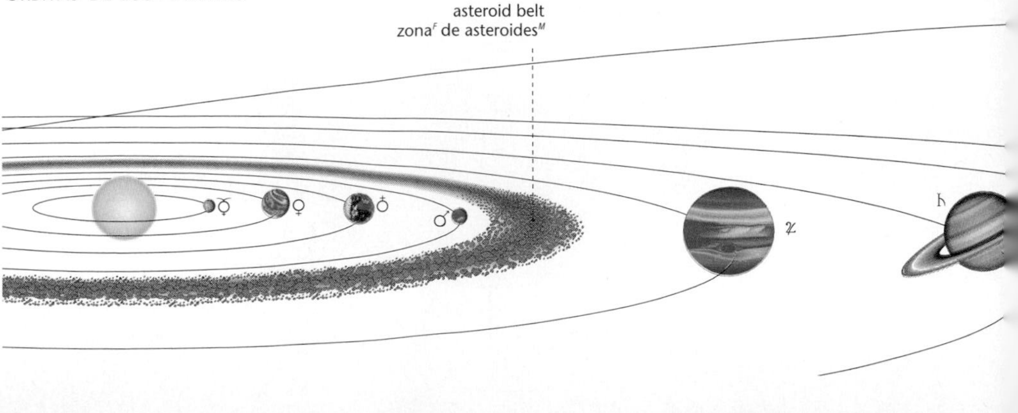

asteroid belt
zona^F de asteroides^M

♃

♄

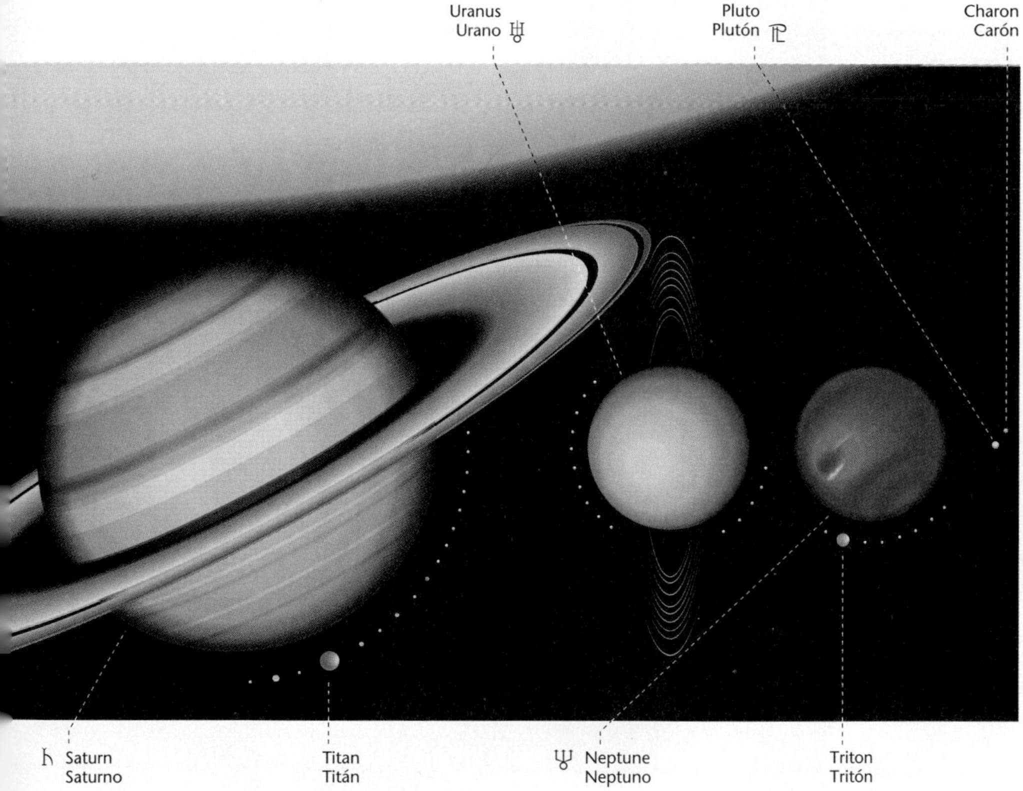

Uranus
Urano ♅

Pluto
Plutón ♇

Charon
Carón

♄ Saturn
Saturno

Titan
Titán

♆ Neptune
Neptuno

Triton
Tritón

5

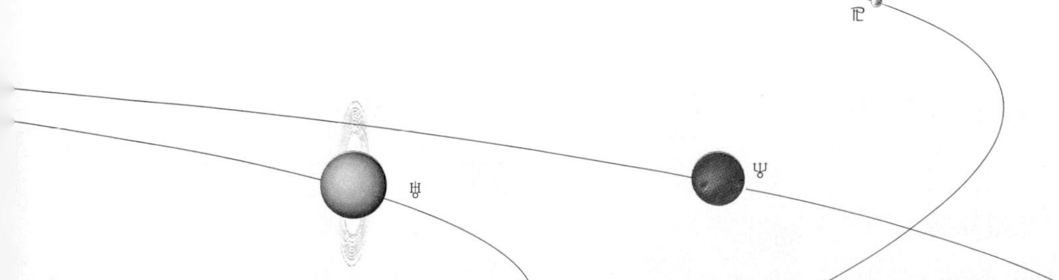

SUN
SOL^M

STRUCTURE OF THE SUN
ESTRUCTURA^F DEL SOL^M

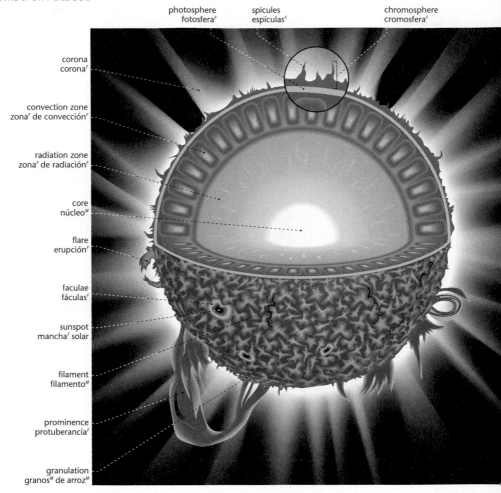

photosphere
fotosfera^F

spicules
espículas^F

chromosphere
cromosfera^F

corona
corona^F

convection zone
zona^F de convección^F

radiation zone
zona^F de radiación^F

core
núcleo^M

flare
erupción^F

faculae
fáculas^F

sunspot
mancha^F solar

filament
filamento^M

prominence
protuberancia^F

granulation
granos^M de arroz^M

PHASES OF THE MOON
FASES^F DE LA LUNA^F

new moon
Luna^F nueva

new crescent
creciente^M

first quarter
cuarto^M creciente

waxing gibbous
quinto^M octante

MOON
LUNA[F]

LUNAR FEATURES
SUPERFICIE[F] LUNAR

bay
bahía[F]

cliff
risco[M]

ocean
océano[M]

lake
lago[M]

sea
mar[M]

mountain range
cordillera[F]

crater
cráter[M]

wall
muro[M]

cirque
circo[M]

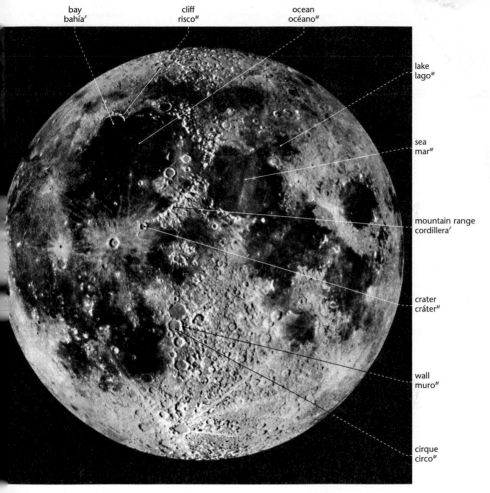

full moon
Luna[F] llena

waning gibbous
tercer[M] octante

last quarter
cuarto[M] menguante

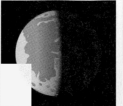

old crescent
menguante[M]

SOLAR ECLIPSE
ECLIPSE^M DE SOL^M

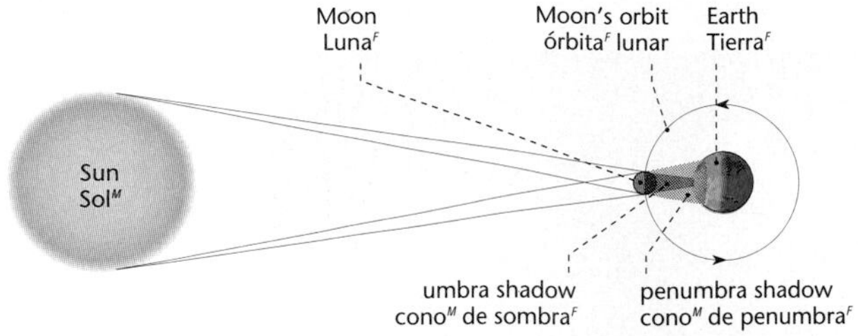

Moon
Luna^F

Moon's orbit
órbita^F lunar

Earth
Tierra^F

Sun
Sol^M

umbra shadow
cono^M de sombra^F

penumbra shadow
cono^M de penumbra^F

TYPES OF ECLIPSES
TIPOS^M DE ECLIPSES^M

total eclipse
eclipse^M total

annular eclipse
eclipse^M anular

partial eclipse
eclipse^M parcial

LUNAR ECLIPSE
ECLIPSE^M DE LUNA^F

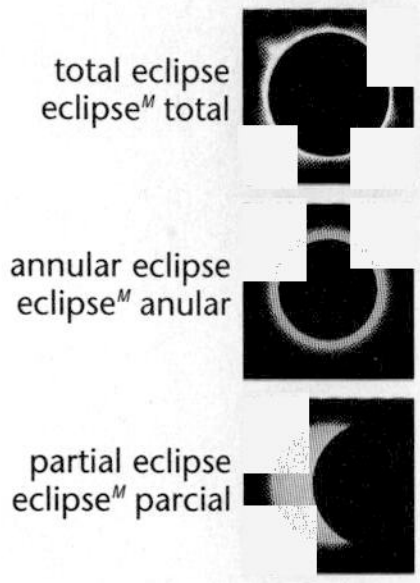

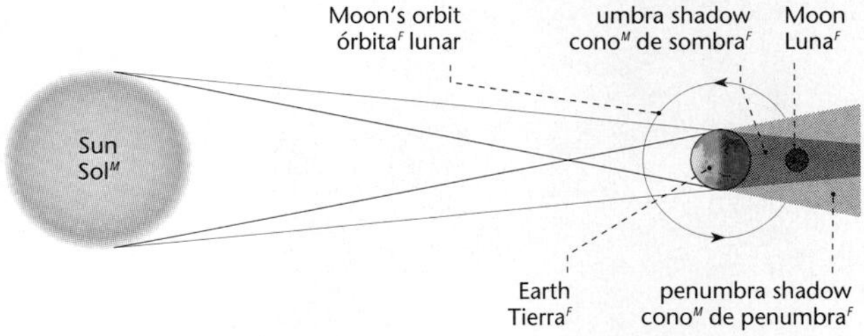

Moon's orbit
órbita^F lunar

umbra shadow
cono^M de sombra^F

Moon
Luna^F

Sun
Sol^M

Earth
Tierra^F

penumbra shadow
cono^M de penumbra^F

TYPES OF ECLIPSES
TIPOS^M DE ECLIPSES^M

partial eclipse
eclipse^M parcial

total eclipse
eclipse^M total

SEASONS OF THE YEAR
ESTACIONES^F DEL AÑO^M

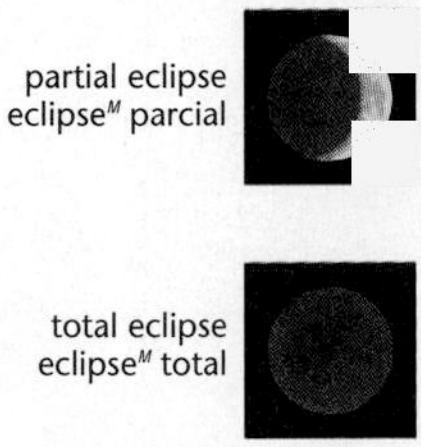

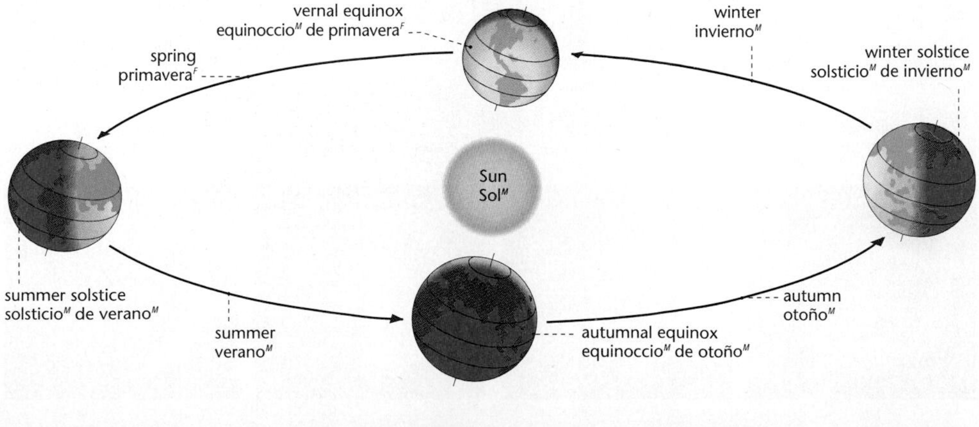

vernal equinox
equinoccio^M de primavera^F

winter
invierno^M

spring
primavera^F

winter solstice
solsticio^M de invierno^M

Sun
Sol^M

summer solstice
solsticio^M de verano^M

summer
verano^M

autumn
otoño^M

autumnal equinox
equinoccio^M de otoño^M

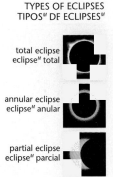

COMET
COMETA[M]

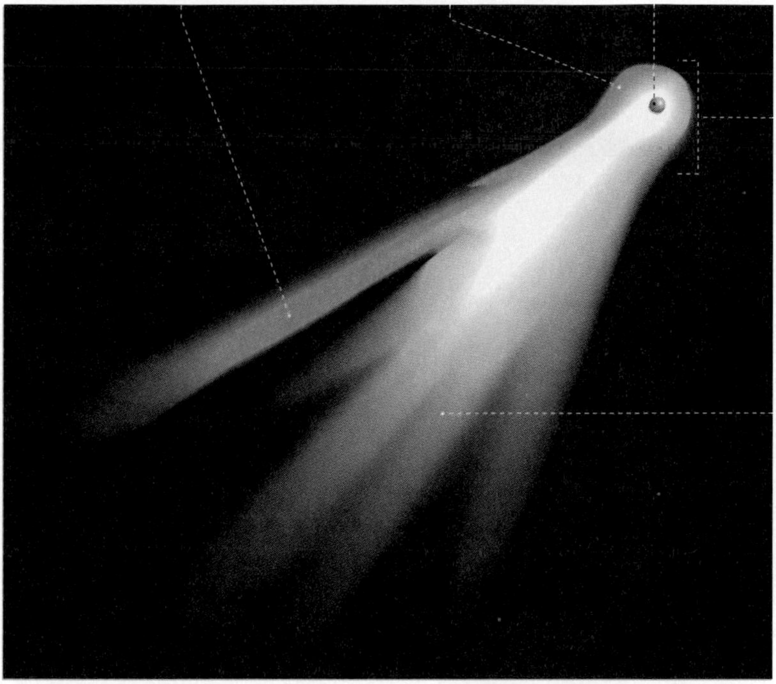

gas tail
cola[f] gaseosa

coma
cabellera[f]

nucleus
núcleo[M]

head
cabeza[f]

dust tail
cola[f] de polvo[M]

GALAXY
GALAXIA[F]

HUBBLE'S CLASSIFICATION
CLASIFICACIÓN[F] DE HUBBLE

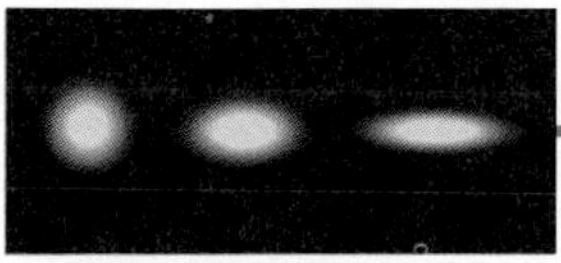

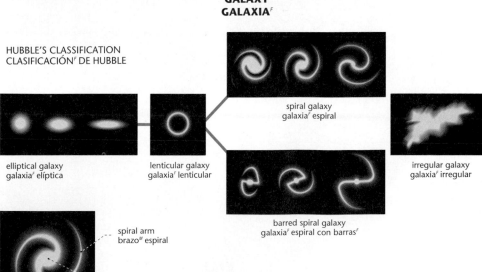

elliptical galaxy
galaxia[f] elíptica

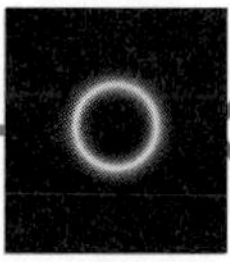

lenticular galaxy
galaxia[f] lenticular

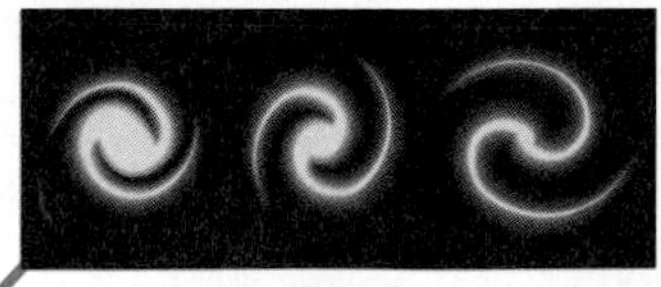

spiral galaxy
galaxia[f] espiral

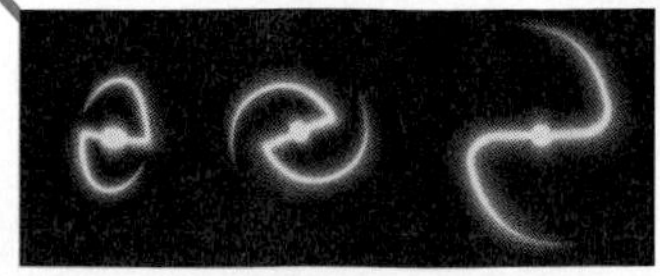

barred spiral galaxy
galaxia[f] espiral con barras[f]

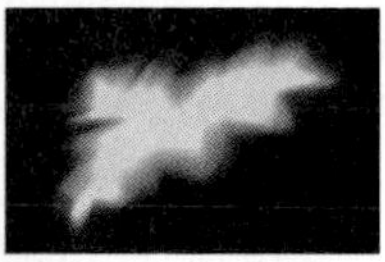

irregular galaxy
galaxia[f] irregular

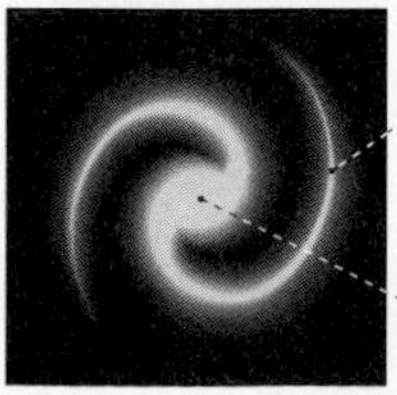

spiral arm
brazo[M] espiral

nucleus
núcleo[M]

CONSTELLATIONS OF THE NORTHERN HEMISPHERE
CONSTELACIONES[F] EN EL HEMISFERIO[M] BOREAL

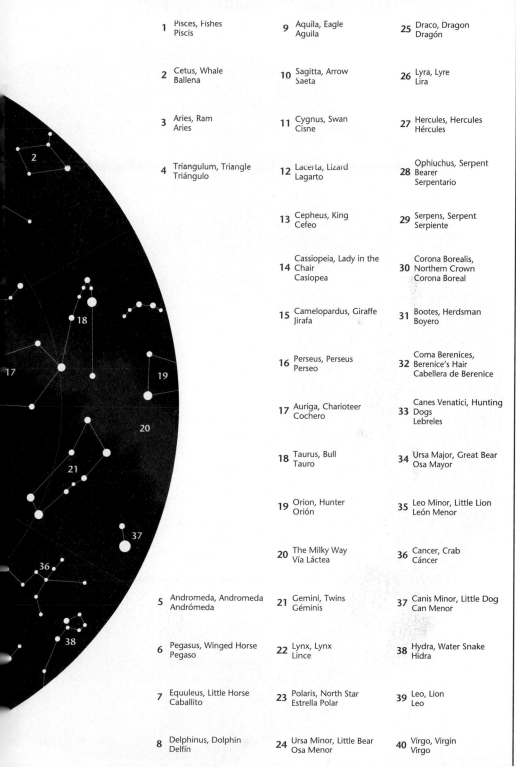

1 Pisces, Fishes
Piscis

2 Cetus, Whale
Ballena

3 Aries, Ram
Aries

4 Triangulum, Triangle
Triángulo

5 Andromeda, Andromeda
Andrómeda

6 Pegasus, Winged Horse
Pegaso

7 Equuleus, Little Horse
Caballito

8 Delphinus, Dolphin
Delfín

9 Aquila, Eagle
Aguila

10 Sagitta, Arrow
Saeta

11 Cygnus, Swan
Cisne

12 Lacerta, Lizard
Lagarto

13 Cepheus, King
Cefeo

14 Cassiopeia, Lady in the
Chair
Casiopea

15 Camelopardus, Giraffe
Jirafa

16 Perseus, Perseus
Perseo

17 Auriga, Charioteer
Cochero

18 Taurus, Bull
Tauro

19 Orion, Hunter
Orión

20 The Milky Way
Vía Láctea

21 Gemini, Twins
Géminis

22 Lynx, Lynx
Lince

23 Polaris, North Star
Estrella Polar

24 Ursa Minor, Little Bear
Osa Menor

25 Draco, Dragon
Dragón

26 Lyra, Lyre
Lira

27 Hercules, Hercules
Hércules

28 Ophiuchus, Serpent
Bearer
Serpentario

29 Serpens, Serpent
Serpiente

30 Corona Borealis,
Northern Crown
Corona Boreal

31 Bootes, Herdsman
Boyero

32 Coma Berenices,
Berenice's Hair
Cabellera de Berenice

33 Canes Venatici, Hunting
Dogs
Lebreles

34 Ursa Major, Great Bear
Osa Mayor

35 Leo Minor, Little Lion
León Menor

36 Cancer, Crab
Cáncer

37 Canis Minor, Little Dog
Can Menor

38 Hydra, Water Snake
Hidra

39 Leo, Lion
Leo

40 Virgo, Virgin
Virgo

CONSTELLATIONS OF THE SOUTHERN HEMISPHERE
CONSTELACIONES^F DEL HEMISFERIO^M AUSTRAL

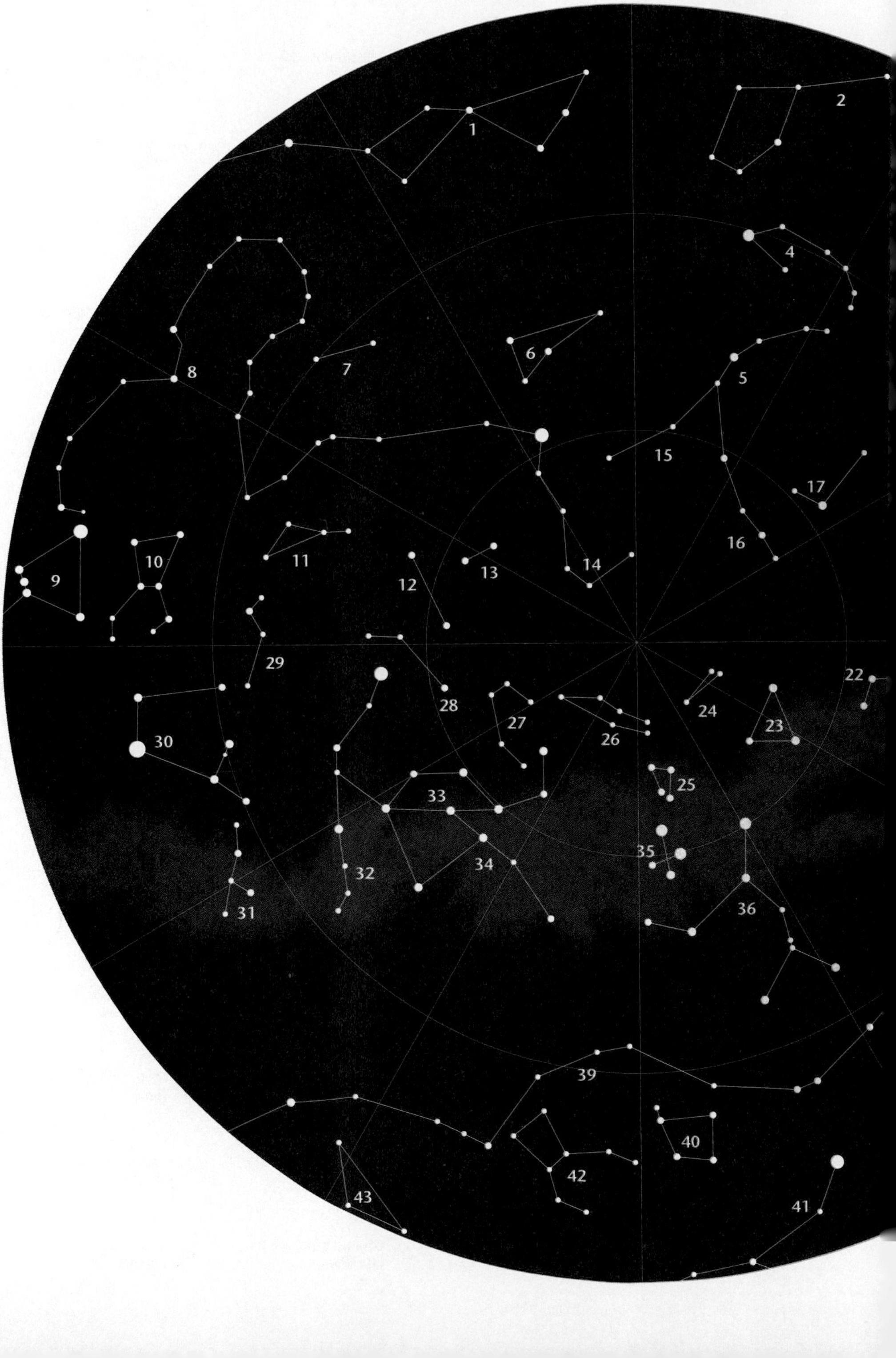

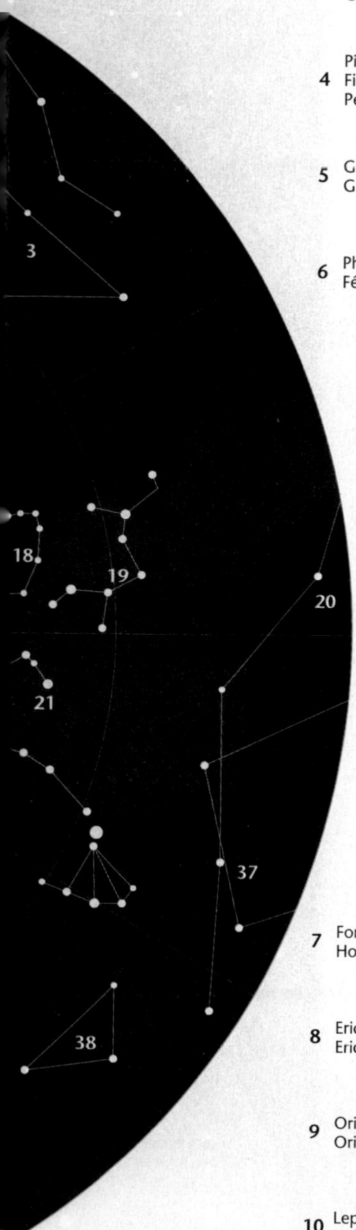

1 Cetus, Whale
Ballena

2 Aquarius, Water Bearer
Acuario

12 Dorado, Swordfish
Pez Dorado

28 Pictor, Painter's Easel
Caballete del pintor

3 Capricornus, Goat
Capricornlo

13 Reticulum, Net
Reticulo

29 Columba, Dove
Paloma

4 Piscis Austrinus, Southern
Fish
Pez Austral

14 Hydrus, Sea-Serpent
Hidra macho

30 Canis Major, Great Dog
Can Mayor

5 Grus, Crane
Grulla

15 Tucana, Toucan
Tucán

31 Puppis, Ship's Stern
Popa

6 Phoenix, Phoenix
Fénix

16 Pavo, Peacock
Pavo

32 Pyxis, Ship's Compass
Brújula

17 Indus, Indian
Indio

33 Carina, Ship's Keel
Quilla

18 Corona Australis,
Southern Crown
Corona Austral

34 Vela, Ship's Sails
Velas

19 Sagittarius, Archer
Sagitario

35 Crux, Southern Cross
Cruz del Sur

20 Serpens, Serpent
Serpiente

36 Centaurus, Centaur
Centauro

21 Scorpius, Scorpion
Escorpión

37 Ophiuchus, Serpent
Bearer
Ofiuco

22 Ara, Altar
Altar

38 Libra, Scales
Libra

7 Fornax, Furnace
Horno

23 Triangulum Australe,
Southern Triangle
Triángulo Austral

39 Hydra, Water Snake
Hidra

8 Eridanus, River Eridanus
Eridano

24 Apus, Bird of Paradise
Ave del Paraíso

40 Corvus, Crow
Cuervo

9 Orion, Hunter
Orión

25 Musca, Fly
Mosca

41 Virgo, Virgin
Virgo

10 Lepus, Hare
Liebre

26 Chamaeleon, Chameleon
Camaleón

42 Crater, Cup
Cráter

11 Caelum, Chisel
Buril

27 Volans, Flying Fish
Pez Volador

43 Sextans, Sextant
Sextante

ASTRONOMICAL OBSERVATORY
OBSERVATORIO*ᴹ* ASTRONÓMICO

TELESCOPE
TELESCOPIO*ᴹ*

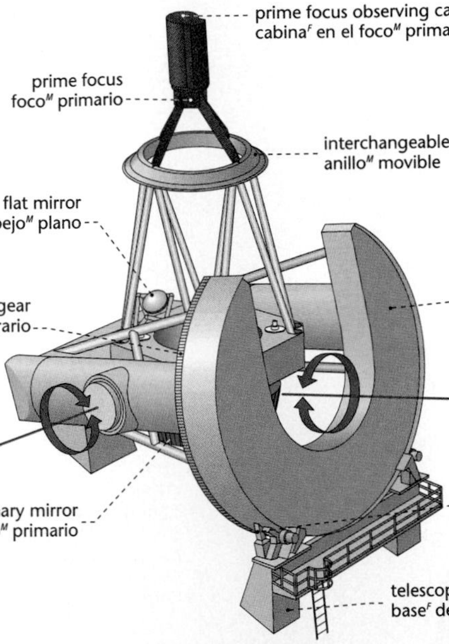

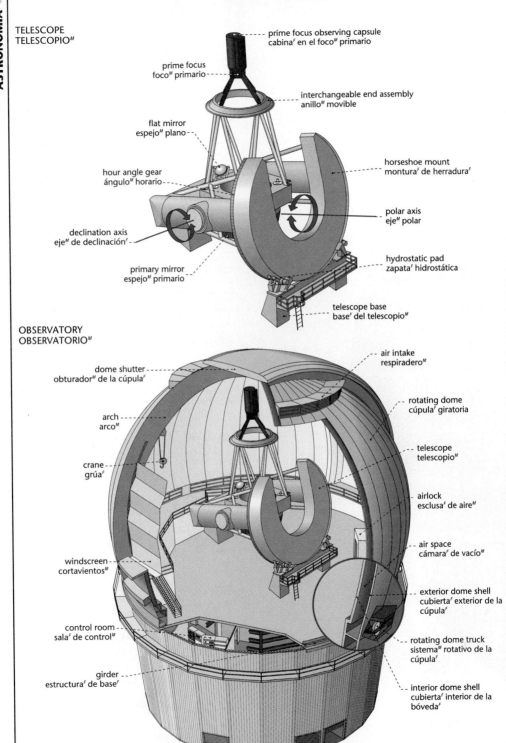

prime focus observing capsule
cabina*ᶠ* en el foco*ᴹ* primario

prime focus
foco*ᴹ* primario

interchangeable end assembly
anillo*ᴹ* movible

flat mirror
espejo*ᴹ* plano

hour angle gear
ángulo*ᴹ* horario

horseshoe mount
montura*ᶠ* de herradura*ᶠ*

declination axis
eje*ᴹ* de declinación*ᶠ*

polar axis
eje*ᴹ* polar

primary mirror
espejo*ᴹ* primario

hydrostatic pad
zapata*ᶠ* hidrostática

telescope base
base*ᶠ* del telescopio*ᴹ*

OBSERVATORY
OBSERVATORIO*ᴹ*

dome shutter
obturador*ᴹ* de la cúpula*ᶠ*

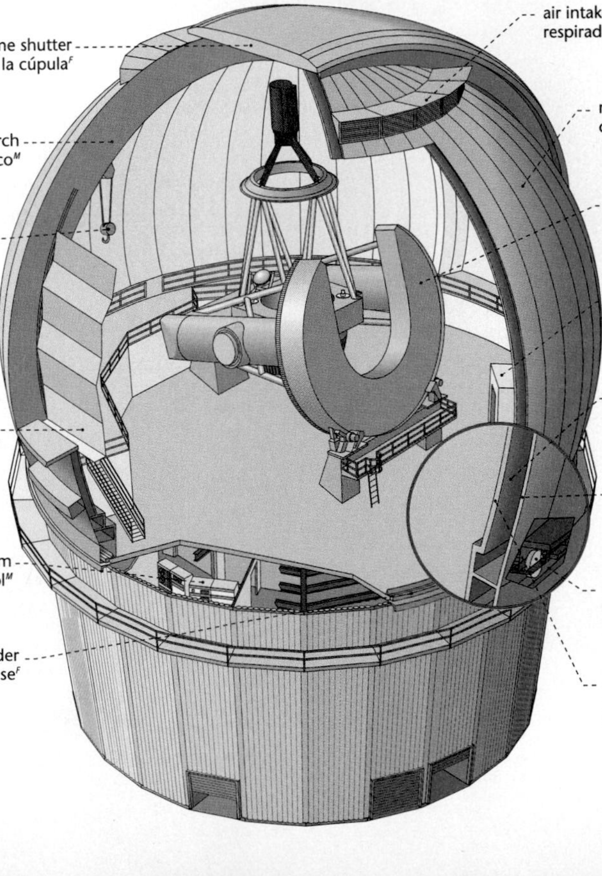

air intake
respiradero*ᴹ*

arch
arco*ᴹ*

rotating dome
cúpula*ᶠ* giratoria

crane
grúa*ᶠ*

telescope
telescopio*ᴹ*

airlock
esclusa*ᶠ* de aire*ᴹ*

air space
cámara*ᶠ* de vacío*ᴹ*

windscreen
cortavientos*ᴹ*

exterior dome shell
cubierta*ᶠ* exterior de la
cúpula*ᶠ*

control room
sala*ᶠ* de control*ᴹ*

rotating dome truck
sistema*ᴹ* rotativo de la
cúpula*ᶠ*

girder
estructura*ᶠ* de base*ᶠ*

interior dome shell
cubierta*ᶠ* interior de la
bóveda*ᶠ*

RADIO TELESCOPE
RADIOTELESCOPIO^M

ALTAZIMUTH MOUNTING
MONTURA^F ACIMUTAL

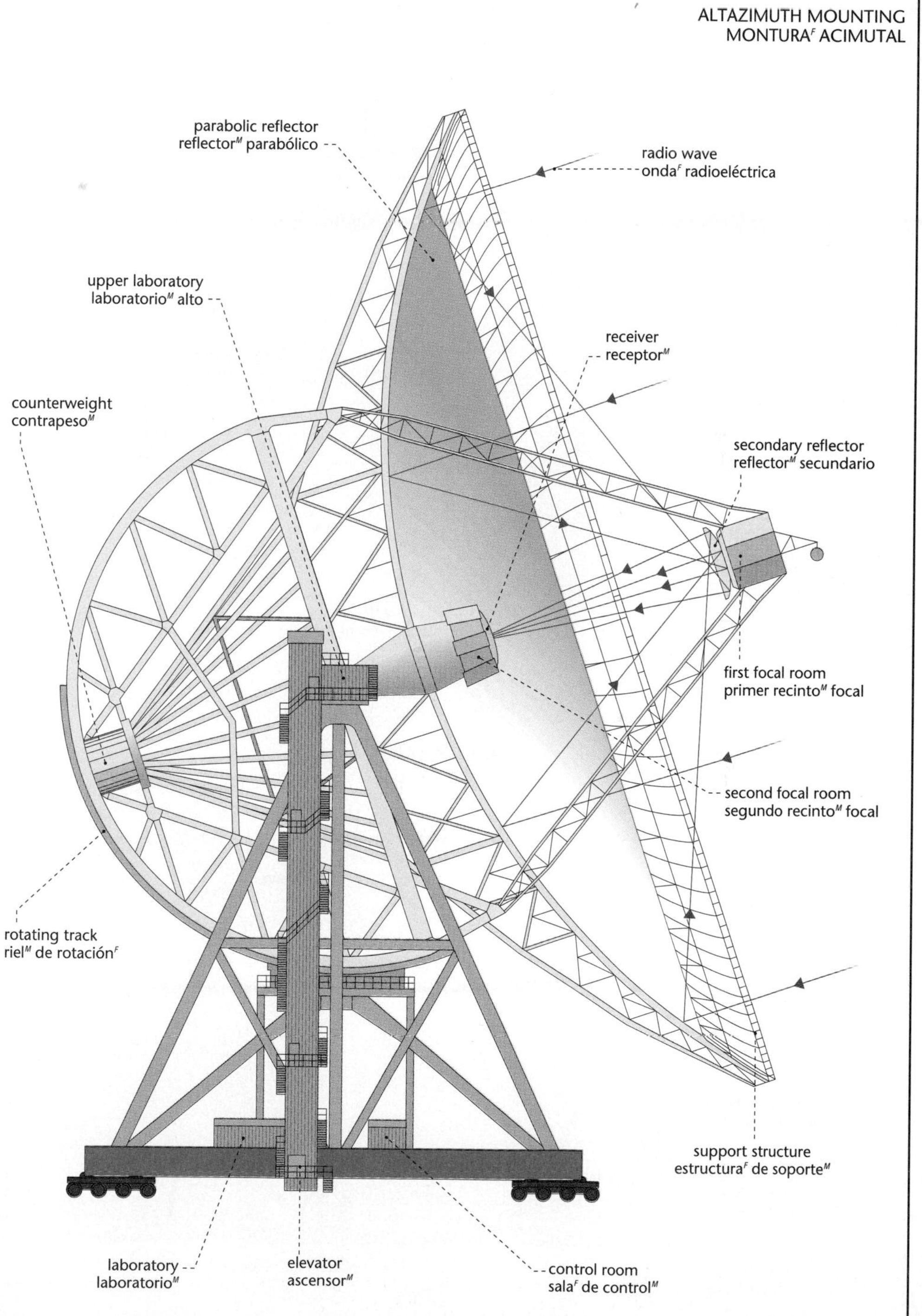

parabolic reflector
reflector^M parabólico

radio wave
onda^F radioeléctrica

upper laboratory
laboratorio^M alto

receiver
receptor^M

counterweight
contrapeso^M

secondary reflector
reflector^M secundario

first focal room
primer recinto^M focal

second focal room
segundo recinto^M focal

rotating track
riel^M de rotación^F

support structure
estructura^F de soporte^M

laboratory
laboratorio^M

elevator
ascensor^M

control room
sala^F de control^M

HUBBLE SPACE TELESCOPE
TELESCOPIO^M ESPACIAL HUBBLE

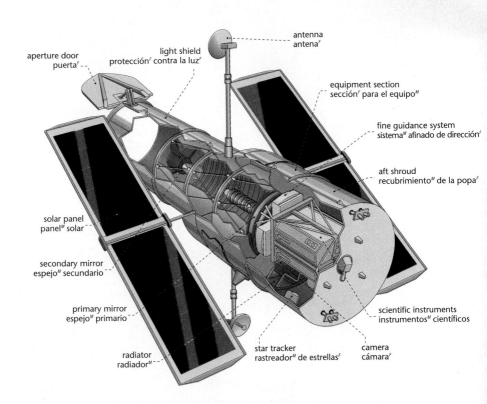

antenna
antena^F

aperture door
puerta^F

light shield
protección^F contra la luz^F

equipment section
sección^F para el equipo^M

fine guidance system
sistema^M afinado de dirección^F

aft shroud
recubrimiento^M de la popa^F

solar panel
panel^M solar

secondary mirror
espejo^M secundario

primary mirror
espejo^M primario

scientific instruments
instrumentos^M científicos

radiator
radiador^M

star tracker
rastreador^M de estrellas^F

camera
cámara^F

PLANETARIUM
PLANETARIO^M

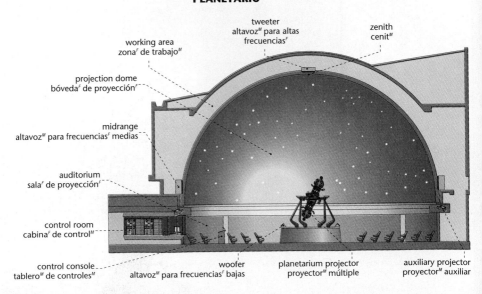

tweeter
altavoz^M para altas
frecuencias^F

zenith
cenit^M

working area
zona^F de trabajo^M

projection dome
bóveda^F de proyección^F

midrange
altavoz^M para frecuencias^F medias

auditorium
sala^F de proyección^F

control room
cabina^F de control^M

control console
tablero^M de controles^M

woofer
altavoz^M para frecuencias^F bajas

planetarium projector
proyector^M múltiple

auxiliary projector
proyector^M auxiliar

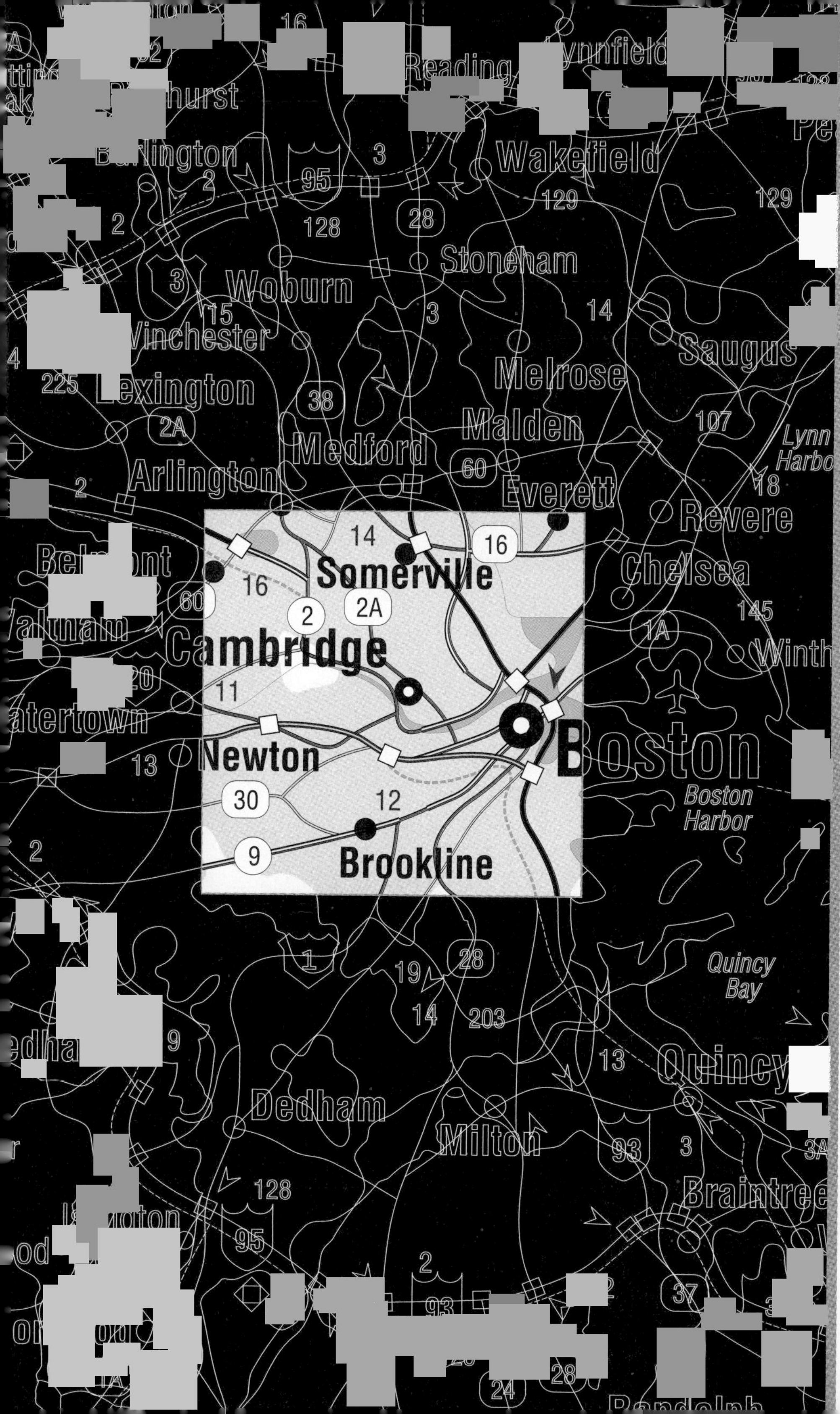
Reading
Wakefield
Burlington
Woburn
Stoneham
Winchester
Melrose
Saugus
Lexington
Medford
Malden
Arlington
Everett
Revere
Lynn
Harbor
Chelsea
Somerville
Cambridge
Newton
Brookline
Boston
Boston
Harbor
Quincy
Bay
Quincy
Dedham
Milton
Braintree

CONTENTS

PROFILE OF THE EARTH'S ATMOSPHERE
CORTE^M DE LA ATMÓSFERA^F TERRESTRE

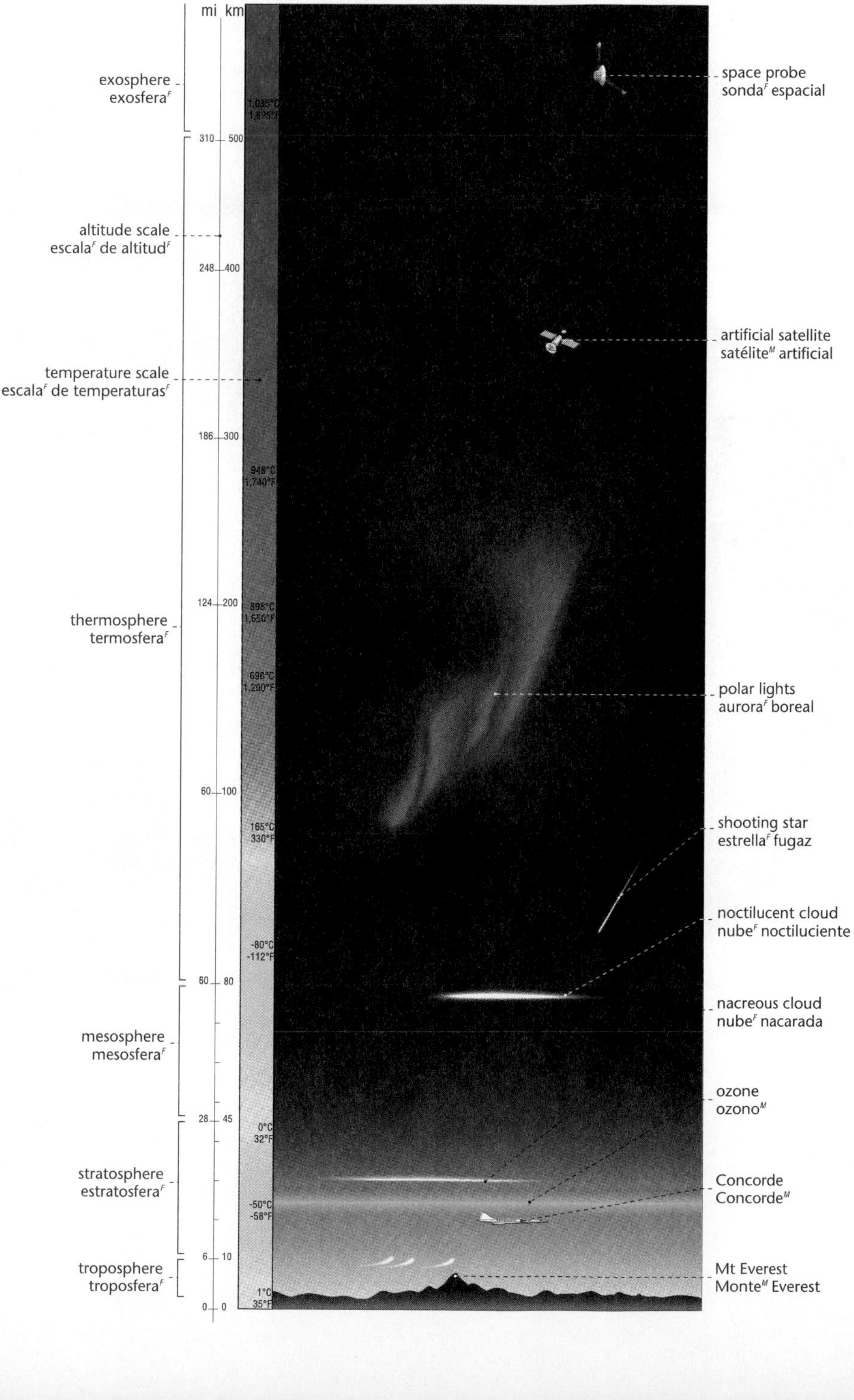

mi km

exosphere
exosfera^F

1,035°C
1,898°F

310 — 500

altitude scale
escala^F de altitud^F

248 — 400

temperature scale
escala^F de temperaturas^F

186 — 300

948°C
1,740°F

124 — 200   898°C
1,650°F

thermosphere
termosfera^F

698°C
1,290°F

60 — 100

165°C
330°F

−80°C
−112°F

60 — 80

mesosphere
mesosfera^F

28 — 45   0°C
32°F

stratosphere
estratosfera^F   −50°C
−58°F

troposphere
troposfera^F   6 — 10

1°C
35°F

0 — 0

space probe
sonda^F espacial

artificial satellite
satélite^M artificial

polar lights
aurora^F boreal

shooting star
estrella^F fugaz

noctilucent cloud
nube^F noctiluciente

nacreous cloud
nube^F nacarada

ozone
ozono^M

Concorde
Concorde^M

Mt Everest
Monte^M Everest

CONFIGURATION OF THE CONTINENTS
CONFIGURACIÓN^F DE LOS CONTINENTES^M

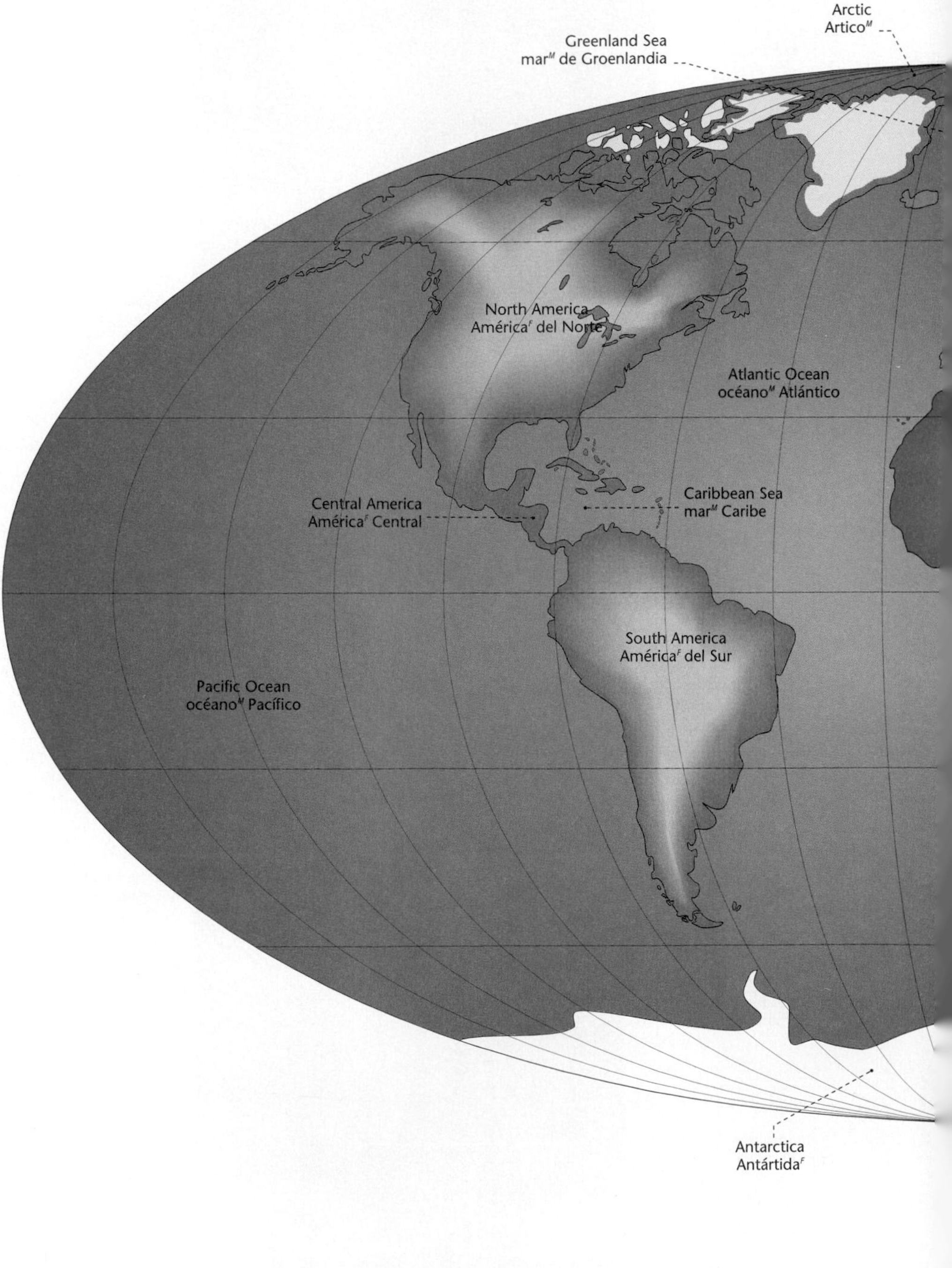

Arctic
Ártico^M

Greenland Sea
mar^M de Groenlandia

North America
América^F del Norte

Atlantic Ocean
océano^M Atlántico

Central America
América^F Central

Caribbean Sea
mar^M Caribe

South America
América^F del Sur

Pacific Ocean
océano^M Pacífico

Antarctica
Antártida^F

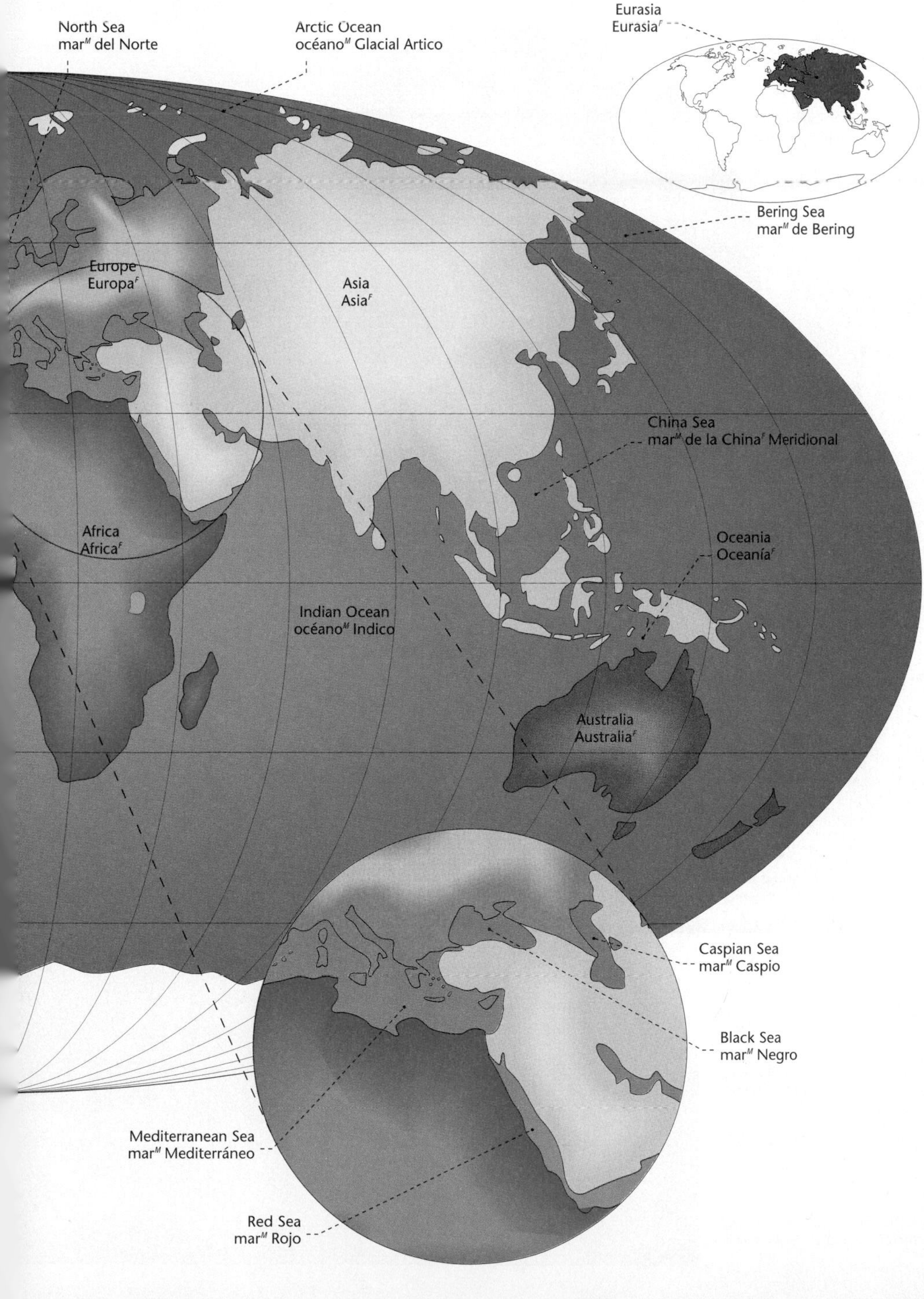

North Sea
mar^M del Norte

Arctic Ocean
océano^M Glacial Ártico

Eurasia
Eurasia^F

Bering Sea
mar^M de Bering

Europe
Europa^F

Asia
Asia^F

China Sea
mar^M de la China^F Meridional

Africa
Africa^F

Oceania
Oceanía^F

Indian Ocean
océano^M Índico

Australia
Australia^F

Caspian Sea
mar^M Caspio

Black Sea
mar^M Negro

Mediterranean Sea
mar^M Mediterráneo

Red Sea
mar^M Rojo

21

STRUCTURE OF THE EARTH
ESTRUCTURA^F DE LA TIERRA^F

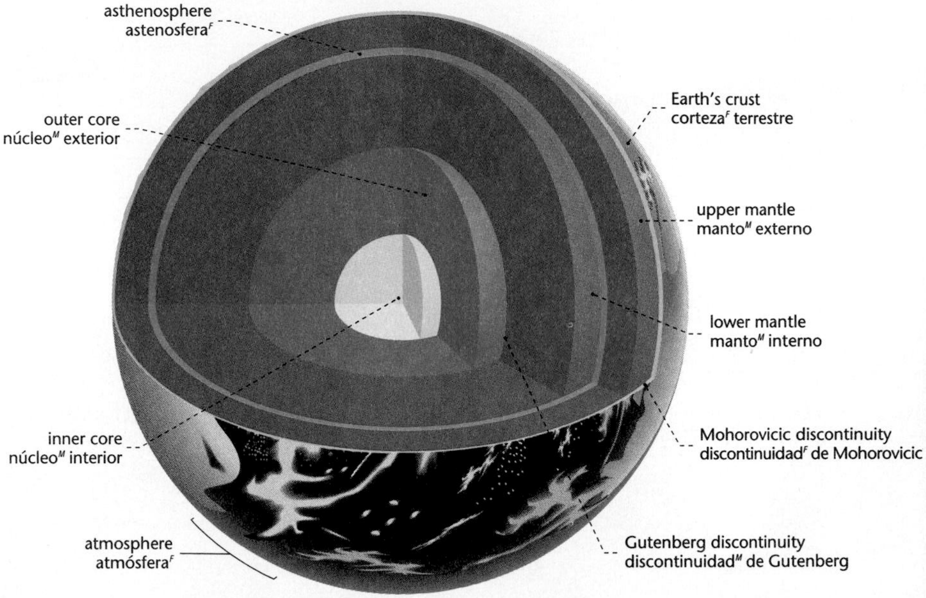

asthenosphere
astenosfera^F

outer core
núcleo^M exterior

inner core
núcleo^M interior

atmosphere
atmósfera^F

Earth's crust
corteza^F terrestre

upper mantle
manto^M externo

lower mantle
manto^M interno

Mohorovicic discontinuity
discontinuidad^F de Mohorovicic

Gutenberg discontinuity
discontinuidad^M de Gutenberg

SECTION OF THE EARTH'S CRUST
CORTE^M DE LA CORTEZA^F TERRESTRE

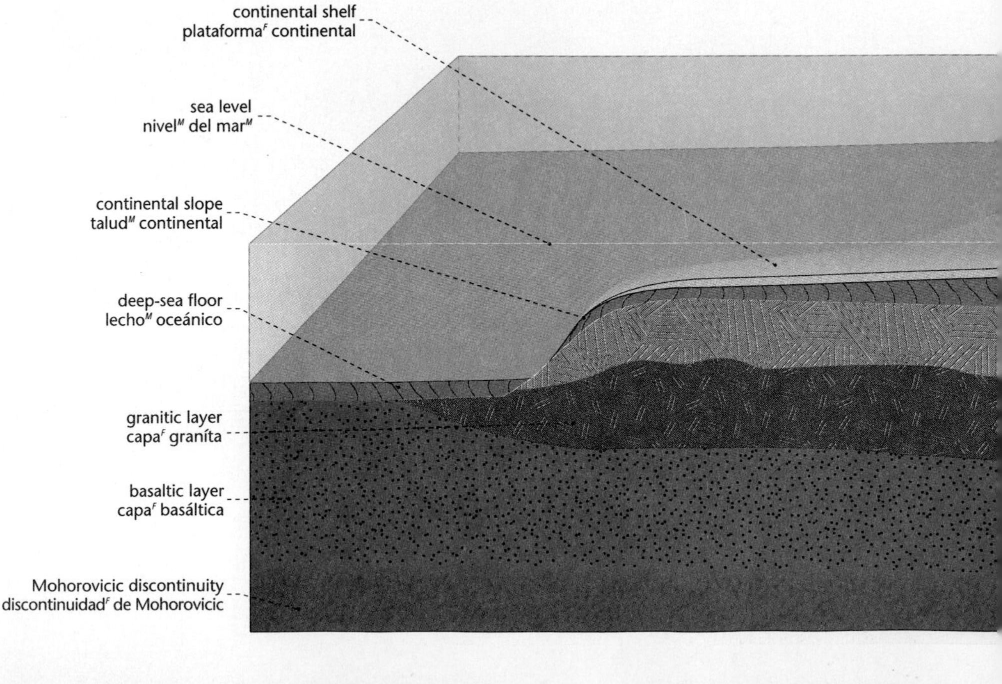

continental shelf
plataforma^F continental

sea level
nivel^M del mar^M

continental slope
talud^M continental

deep-sea floor
lecho^M oceánico

granitic layer
capa^F graníta

basaltic layer
capa^F basáltica

Mohorovicic discontinuity
discontinuidad^F de Mohorovicic

EARTHQUAKE
TERREMOTO[M]

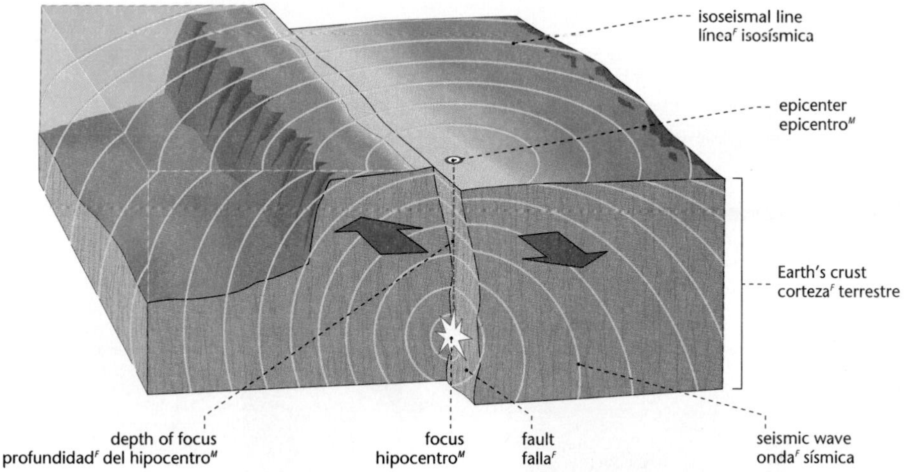

isoseismal line
línea[f] isosísmica

epicenter
epicentro[M]

Earth's crust
corteza[f] terrestre

seismic wave
onda[f] sísmica

fault
falla[f]

focus
hipocentro[M]

depth of focus
profundidad[f] del hipocentro[M]

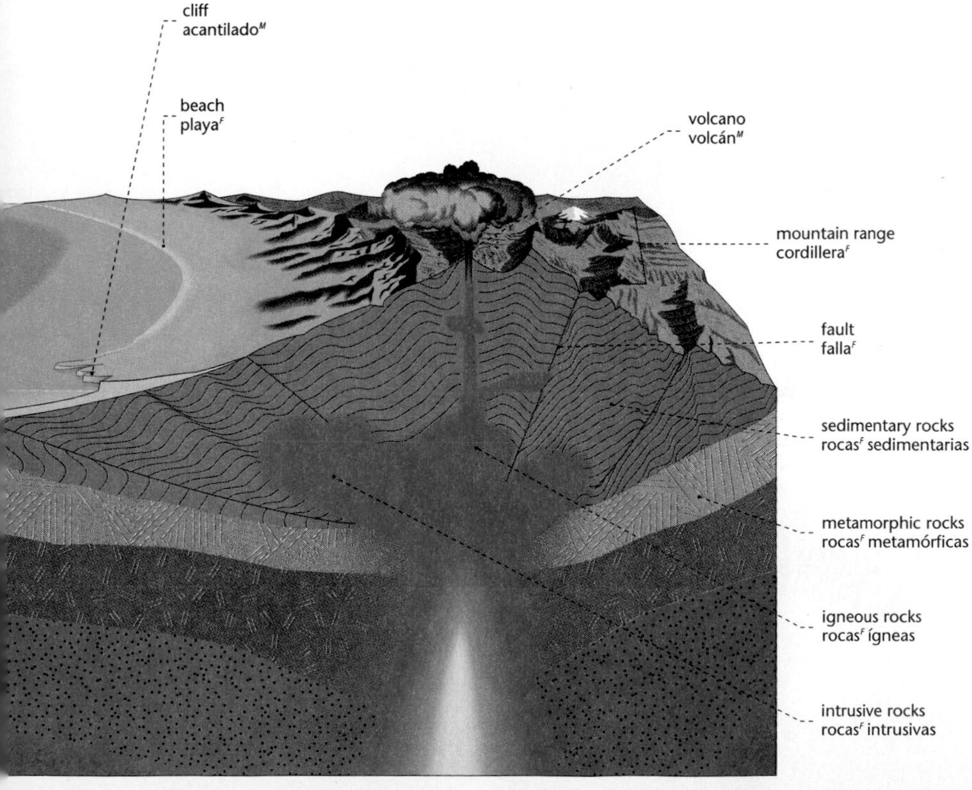

cliff
acantilado[M]

beach
playa[f]

volcano
volcán[M]

mountain range
cordillera[f]

fault
falla[f]

sedimentary rocks
rocas[f] sedimentarias

metamorphic rocks
rocas[f] metamórficas

igneous rocks
rocas[f] ígneas

intrusive rocks
rocas[f] intrusivas

CAVE
GRUTA[F]

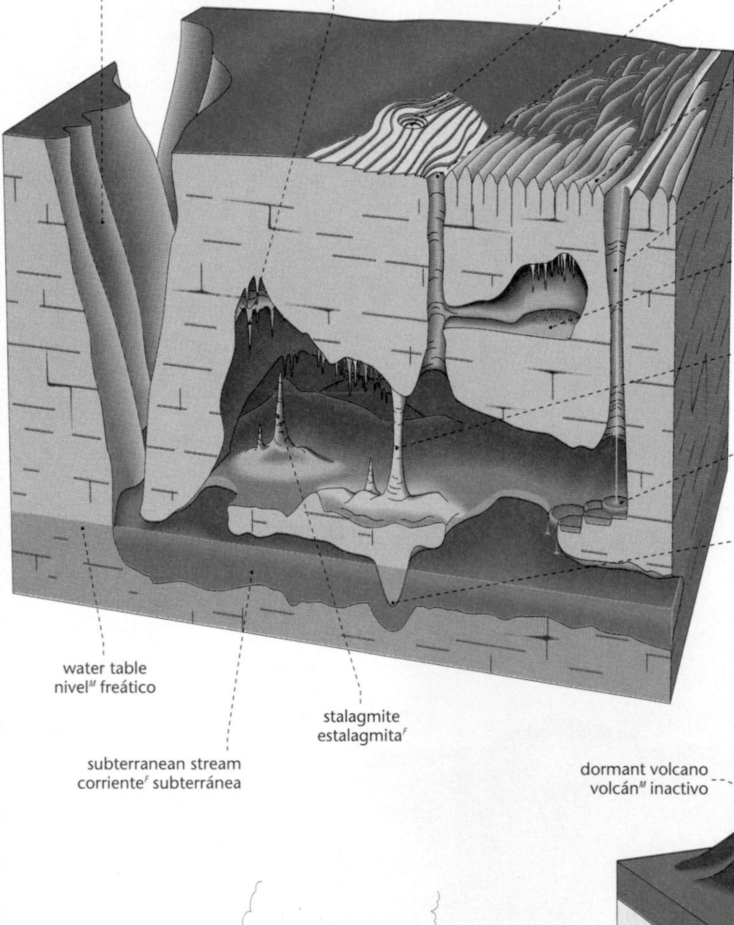

gorge
desfiladero[M]

stalactite
estalactita[F]

sinkhole
sumidero[M]

pothole
hoyo[M]

lapiaz
lapiaz[M]

swallow hole
tragadero[M]

dry gallery
galería[F] seca

column
columna[F]

gour
derrubios[M]

siphon
sifón[M]

water table
nivel[M] freático

subterranean stream
corriente[F] subterránea

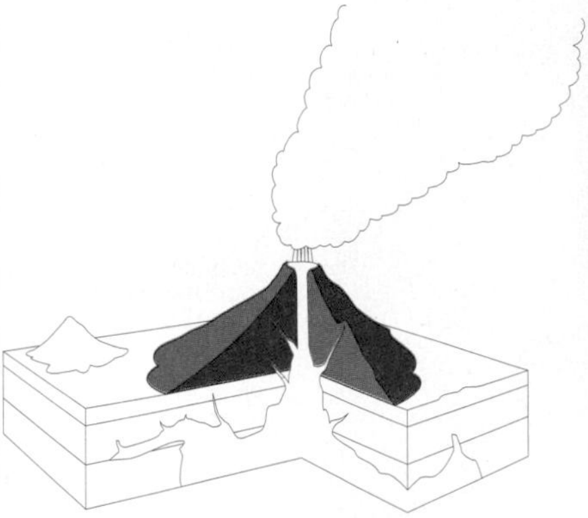

stalagmite
estalagmita[F]

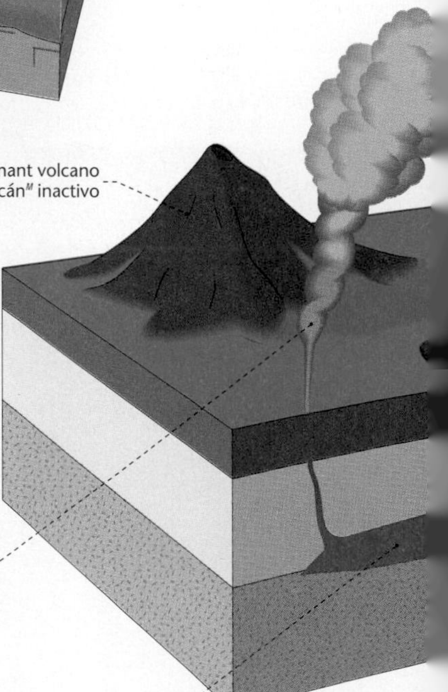

dormant volcano
volcán[M] inactivo

fumarole
fumarola[F]

cone
cono[M]

sill
reborde[M]

VOLCANO
VOLCÁN[M]

VOLCANO DURING ERUPTION
VOLCÁN[M] EN ERUPCIÓN[F]

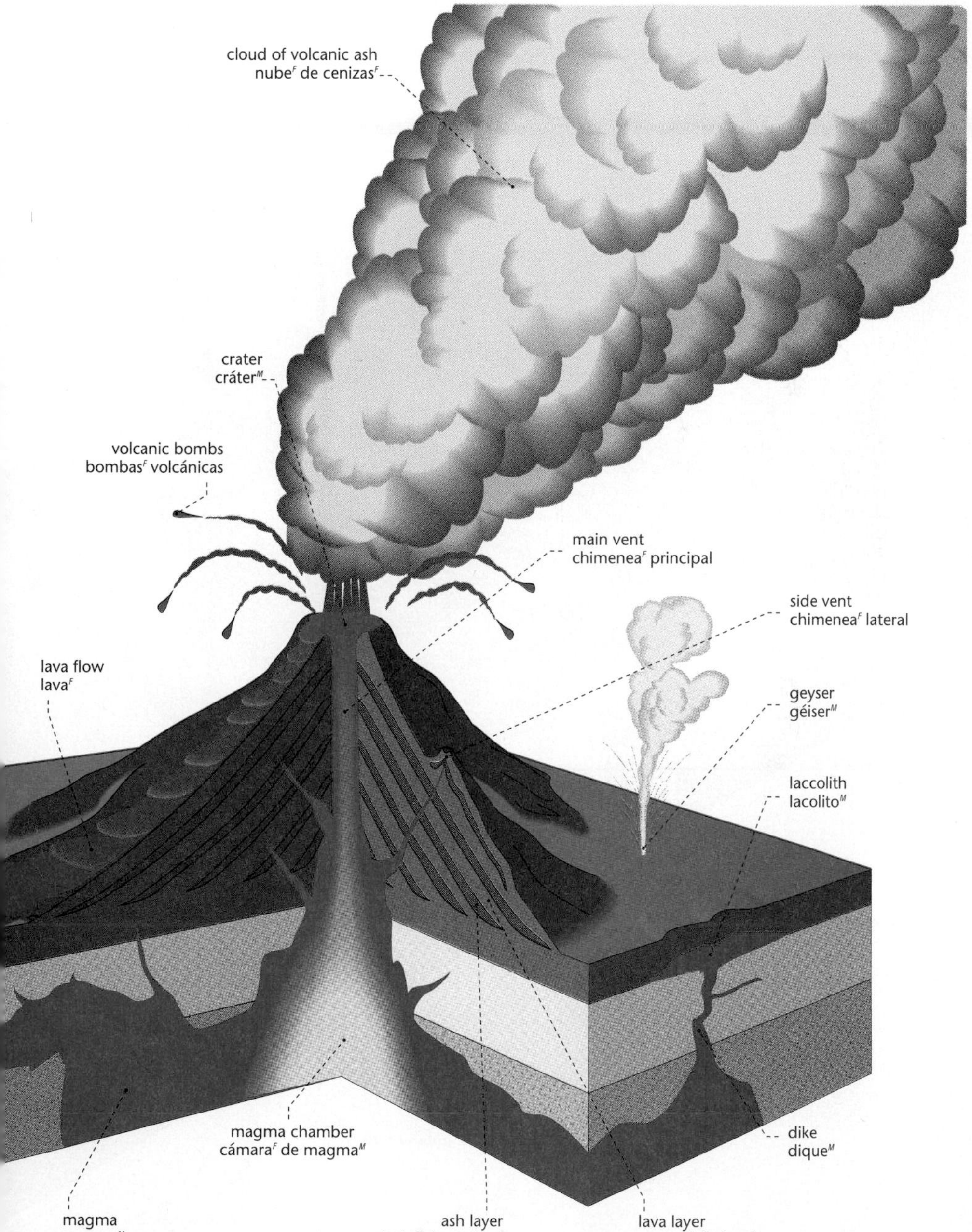

cloud of volcanic ash
nube[F] de cenizas[F]

crater
cráter[M]

volcanic bombs
bombas[F] volcánicas

main vent
chimenea[F] principal

side vent
chimenea[F] lateral

lava flow
lava[F]

geyser
géiser[M]

laccolith
lacolito[M]

magma chamber
cámara[F] de magma[M]

dike
dique[M]

magma
magma[M]

ash layer
estrato[M] de cenizas[F]

lava layer
estrato[M] de lava[F]

25

GLACIER
GLACIAR^M

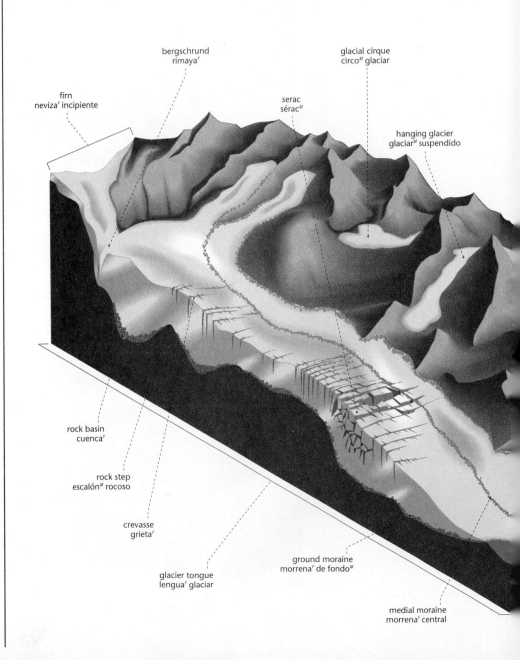

firn
neviza^F incipiente

bergschrund
rimaya^F

serac
sérac^M

glacial cirque
circo^M glaciar

hanging glacier
glaciar^M suspendido

rock basin
cuenca^F

rock step
escalón^M rocoso

crevasse
grieta^F

glacier tongue
lengua^F glaciar

ground moraine
morrena^F de fondo^M

medial moraine
morrena^F central

MOUNTAIN
MONTAÑA[F]

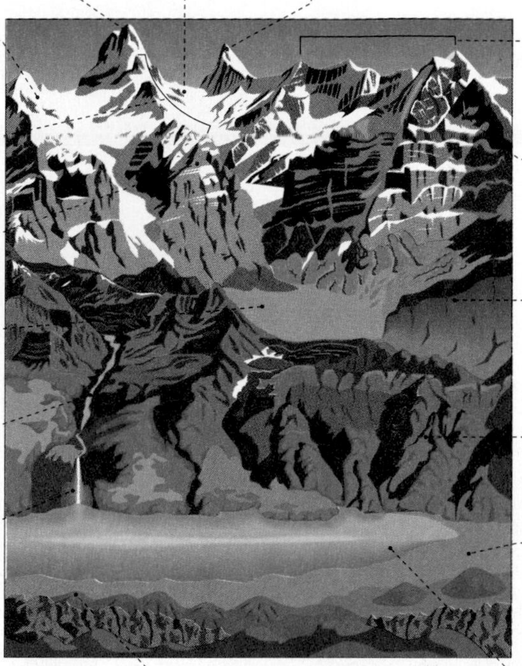

summit
cima[F]

pass
paso[M]

peak
pico[M]

perpetual snows
nieves[F] perpetuas

ridge
cresta[F]

spur
plcacho[M]

crest
cresta[F]

mountain slope
ladera[F]

cliff
acantilado[M]

plateau
meseta[F]

mountain torrent
torrente[M] de montaña[F]

forest
bosque[M]

waterfall
cascada[F]

valley
valle[M]

lake
lago[M]

hill
colina[F]

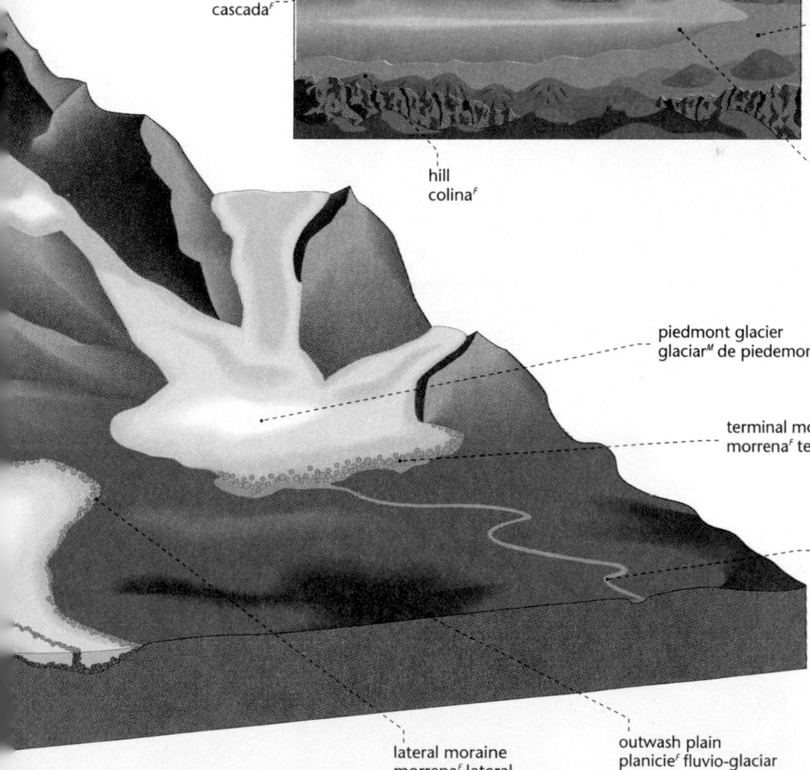

piedmont glacier
glaciar[M] de piedemonte[M]

terminal moraine
morrena[F] terminal

meltwater
agua[F] de deshielo[M]

lateral moraine
morrena[F] lateral

outwash plain
planicie[F] fluvio-glaciar

GEOGRAPHY
GEOGRAFÍA

MID-OCEAN RIDGE
DORSAL^F OCEÁNICA

TOPOGRAPHIC FEATURES
CONFIGURACIÓN^F TOPOGRÁFICA

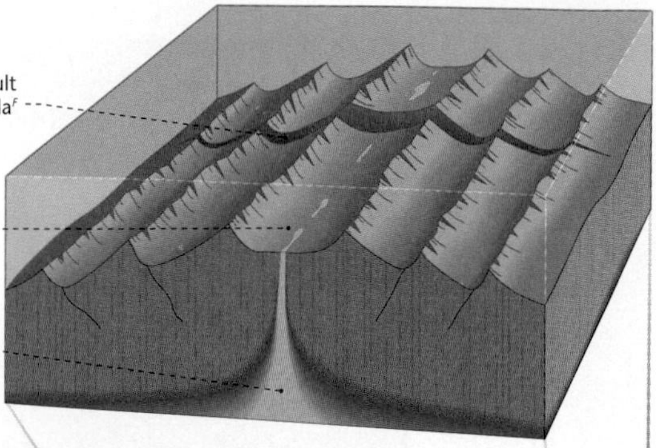

transform fault
falla^F

rift
hendidura^F

magma
magma^M

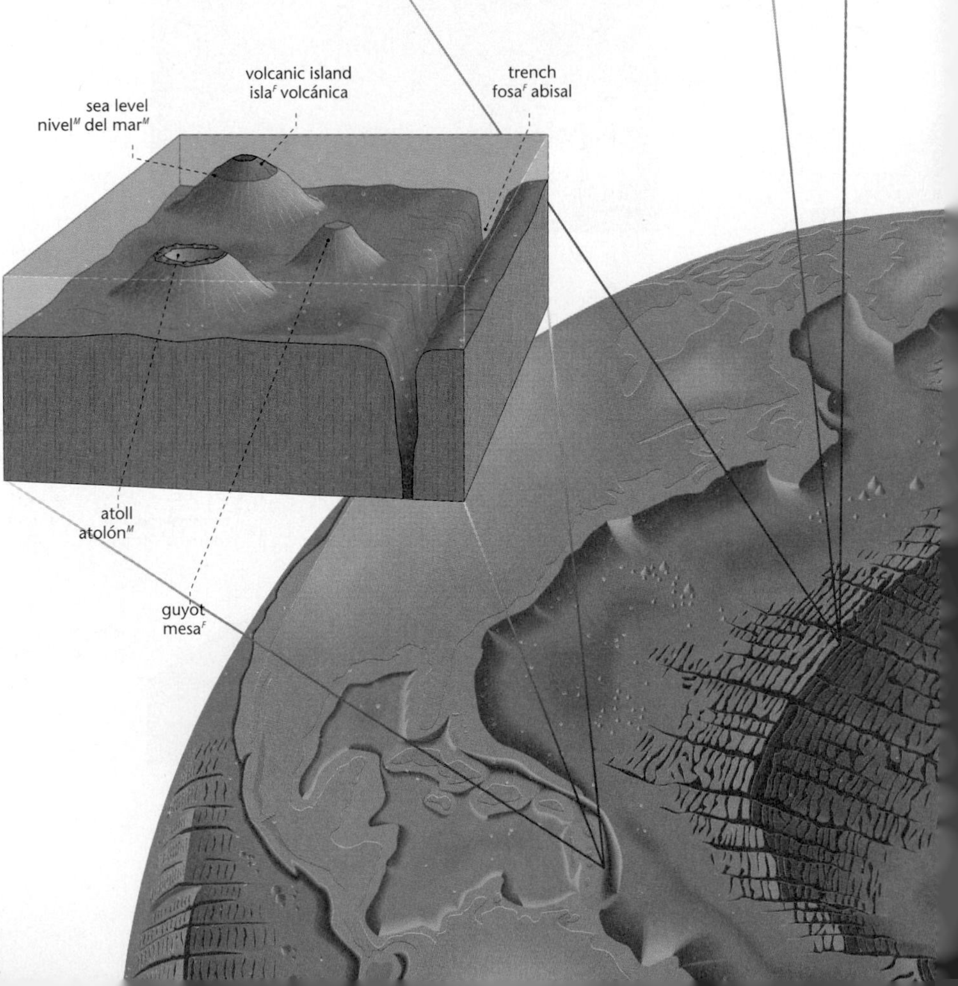

volcanic island
isla^F volcánica

trench
fosa^F abisal

sea level
nivel^M del mar^M

atoll
atolón^M

guyot
mesa^F

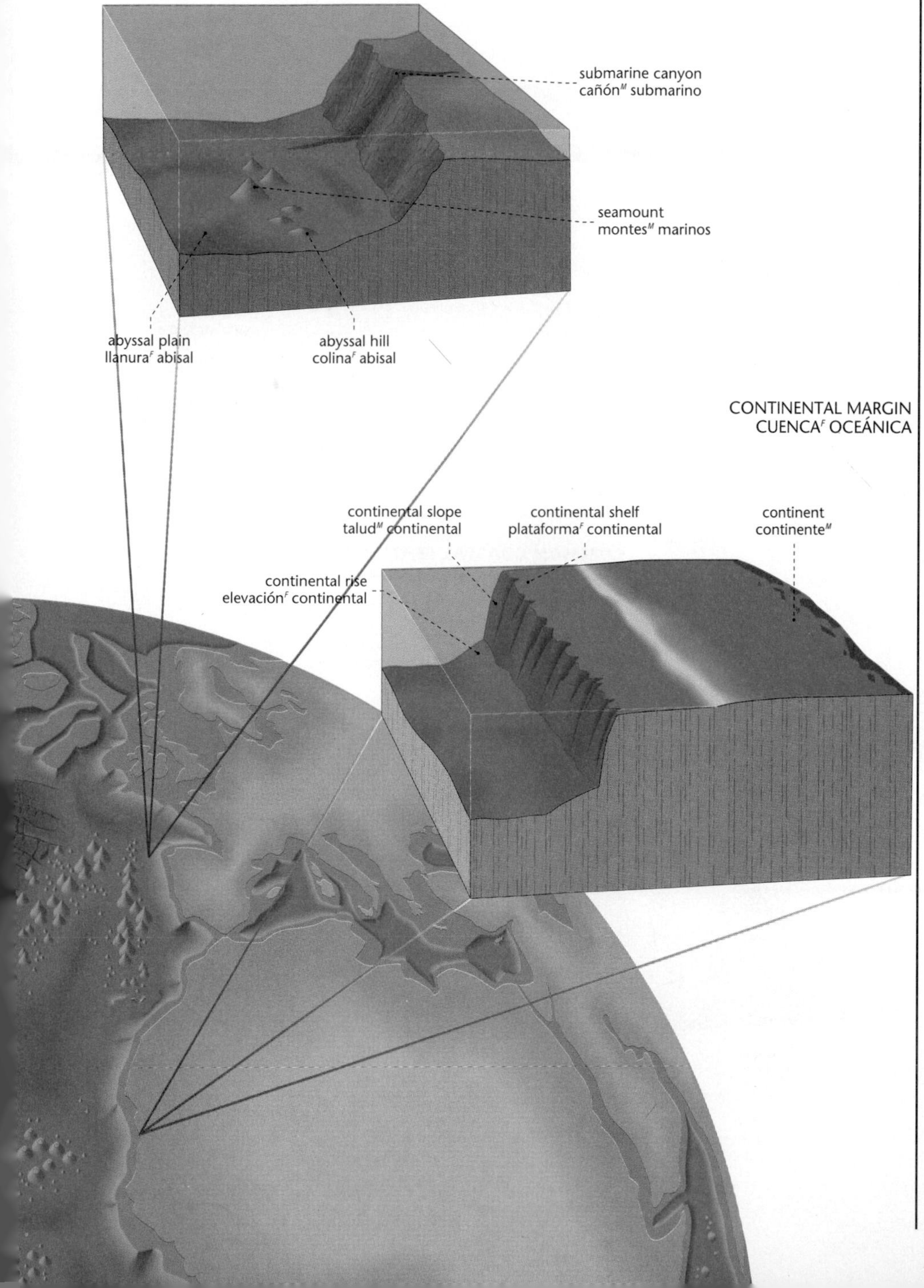

ABYSSAL PLAIN
LLANURA^F ABISAL

submarine canyon
cañón^M submarino

seamount
montes^M marinos

abyssal plain
llanura^F abisal

abyssal hill
colina^F abisal

CONTINENTAL MARGIN
CUENCA^F OCEÁNICA

continental slope
talud^M continental

continental shelf
plataforma^F continental

continent
continente^M

continental rise
elevación^F continental

WAVE
OLA[F]

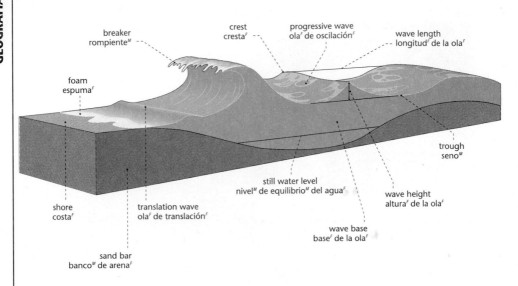

breaker
rompiente[M]

crest
cresta[F]

progressive wave
ola[F] de oscilación[F]

wave length
longitud[F] de la ola[F]

foam
espuma[F]

trough
seno[M]

still water level
nivel[M] de equilibrio[M] del agua[F]

wave height
altura[F] de la ola[F]

shore
costa[F]

translation wave
ola[F] de translación[F]

wave base
base[F] de la ola[F]

sand bar
banco[M] de arena[F]

COMMON COASTAL FEATURES
CONFIGURACIÓN[F] DEL LITORAL[M]

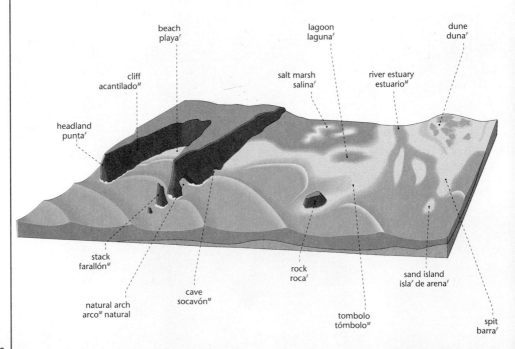

beach
playa[F]

lagoon
laguna[F]

dune
duna[F]

cliff
acantilado[M]

salt marsh
salina[F]

river estuary
estuario[M]

headland
punta[F]

stack
farallón[M]

rock
roca[F]

sand island
isla[F] de arena[F]

natural arch
arco[M] natural

cave
socavón[M]

tombolo
tómbolo[M]

spit
barra[F]

ECOLOGY
ECOLOGÍA*f*

STRUCTURE OF THE BIOSPHERE
ESTRUCTURA*f* DE LA BIOSFERA*f*

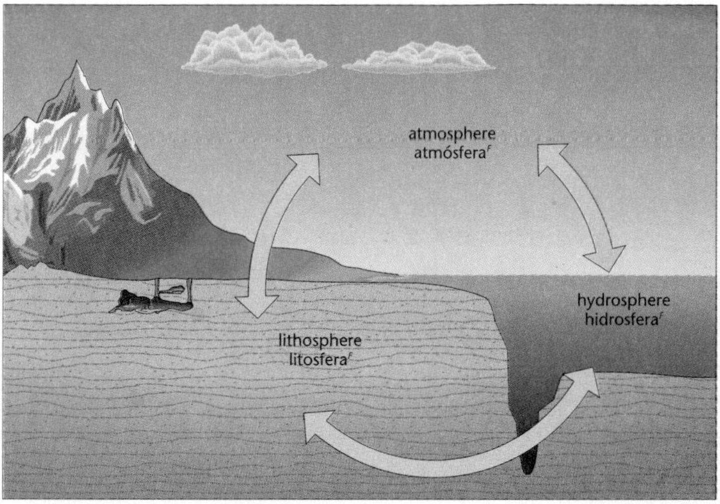

atmosphere
atmósfera*f*

hydrosphere
hidrosfera*f*

lithosphere
litosfera*f*

FOOD CHAIN
CADENA*f* ALIMENTICIA

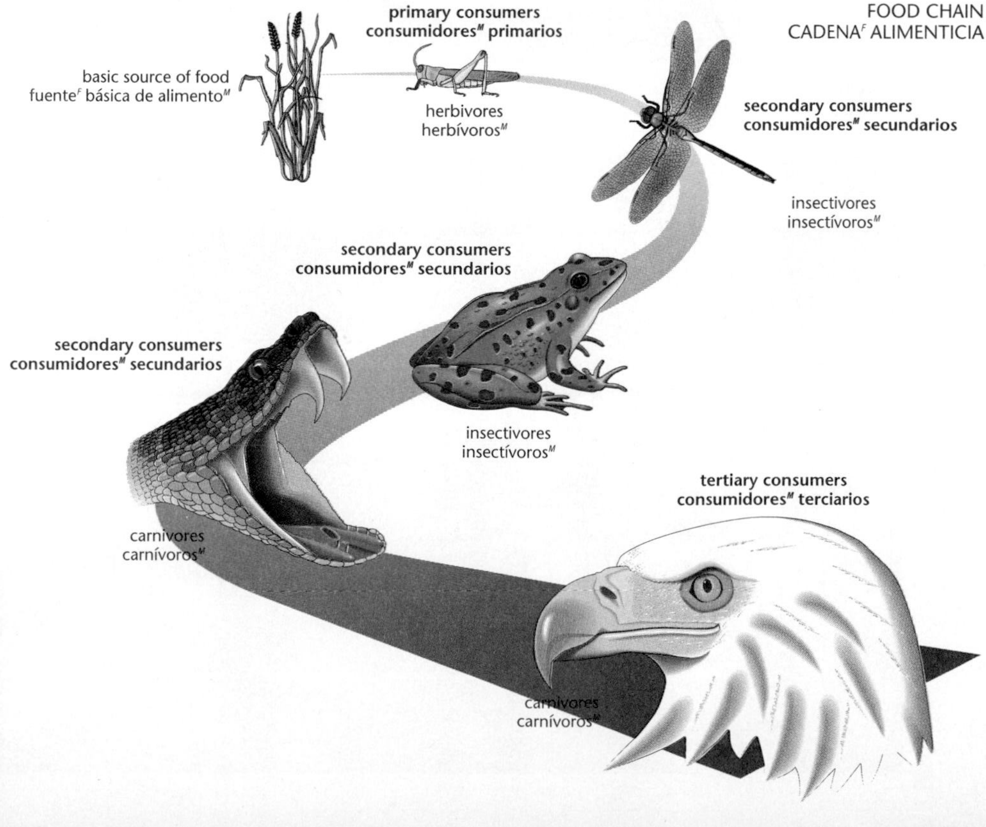

primary consumers
consumidores*M* primarios

basic source of food
fuente*f* básica de alimento*M*

herbivores
herbívoros*M*

secondary consumers
consumidores*M* secundarios

insectivores
insectívoros*M*

secondary consumers
consumidores*M* secundarios

secondary consumers
consumidores*M* secundarios

insectivores
insectívoros*M*

tertiary consumers
consumidores*M* terciarios

carnivores
carnívoros*M*

carnivores
carnívoros*M*

31

ECOLOGY
ECOLOGÍA*F*

POLLUTION OF FOOD ON GROUND
CONTAMINACIÓN*F* DE ALIMENTOS*M* EN LA TIERRA*F*

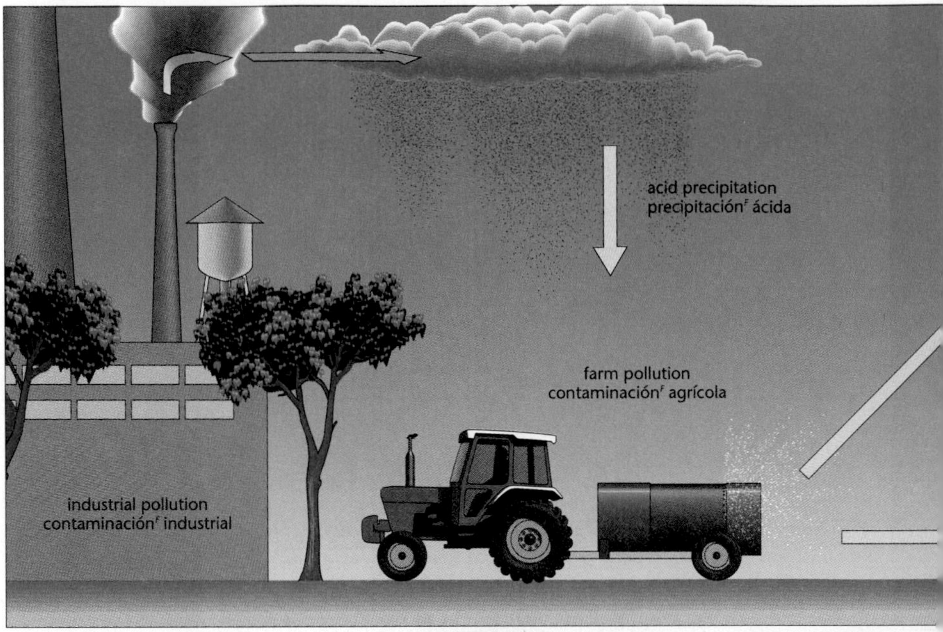

acid precipitation
precipitación*F* ácida

farm pollution
contaminación*F* agrícola

industrial pollution
contaminación*F* industrial

POLLUTION OF FOOD IN WATER
CONTAMINACIÓN*F* DE ALIMENTOS*M* EN EL AGUA*F*

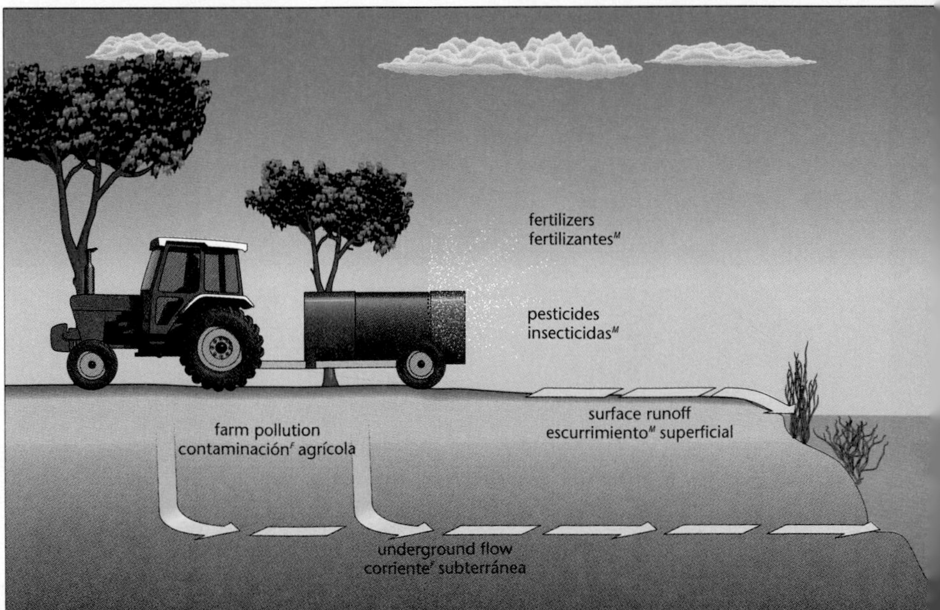

fertilizers
fertilizantes*M*

pesticides
insecticidas*M*

surface runoff
escurrimiento*M* superficial

farm pollution
contaminación*F* agrícola

underground flow
corriente*F* subterránea

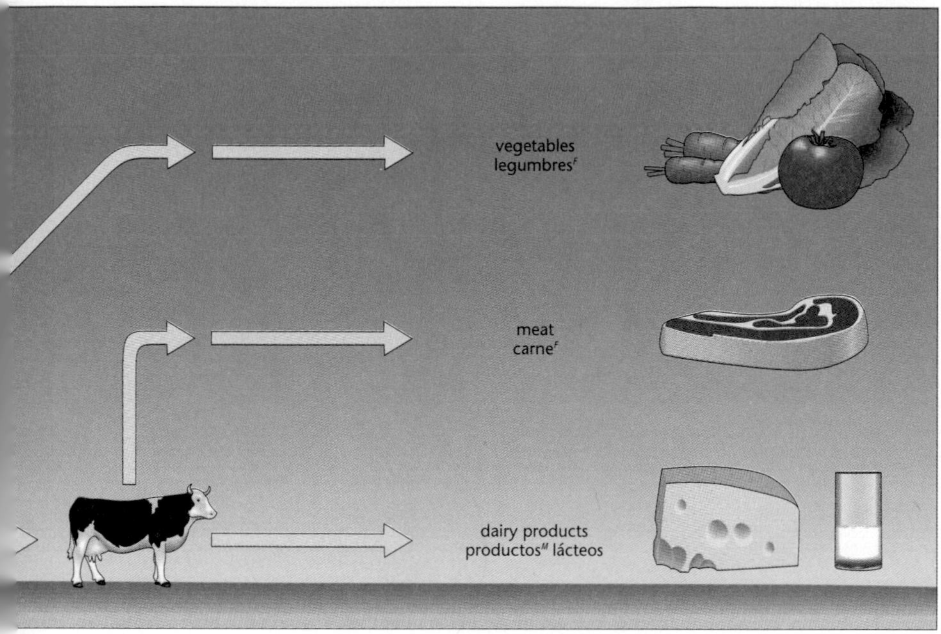

vegetables
legumbres^f

meat
carne^f

dairy products
productos^M lácteos

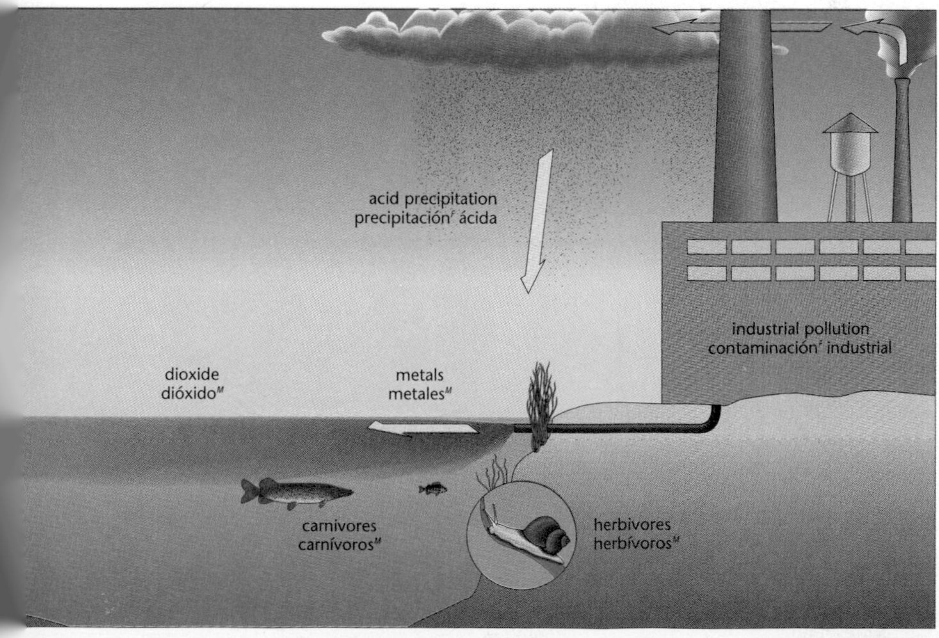

acid precipitation
precipitación^f ácida

industrial pollution
contaminación^f industrial

dioxide
dióxido^M

metals
metales^M

carnivores
carnívoros^M

herbivores
herbívoros^M

ECOLOGY
ECOLOGÍA^F

ATMOSPHERIC POLLUTION
CONTAMINACIÓN^F ATMOSFÉRICA

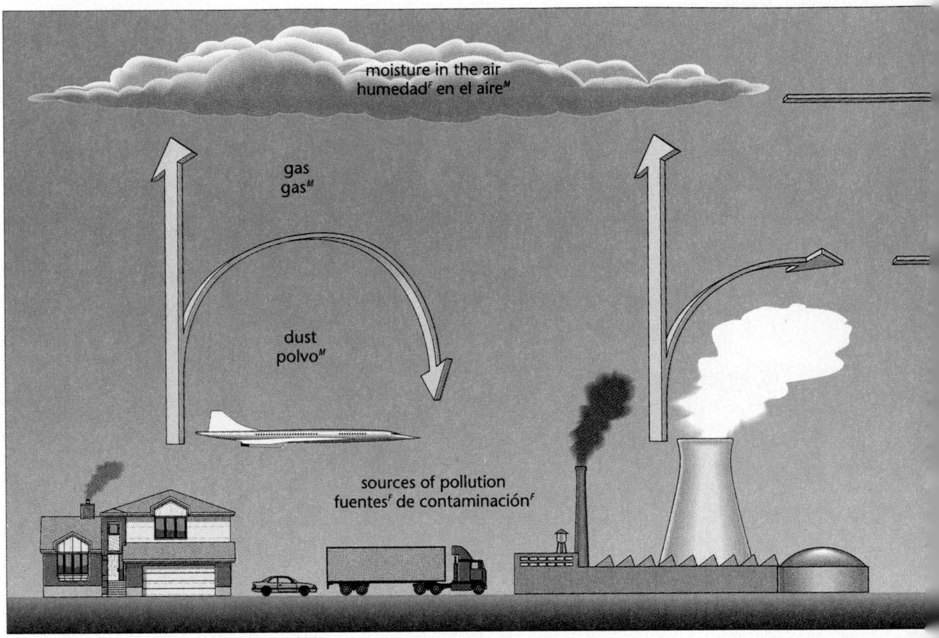

HYDROLOGIC CYCLE
CICLO^M HIDROLÓGICO

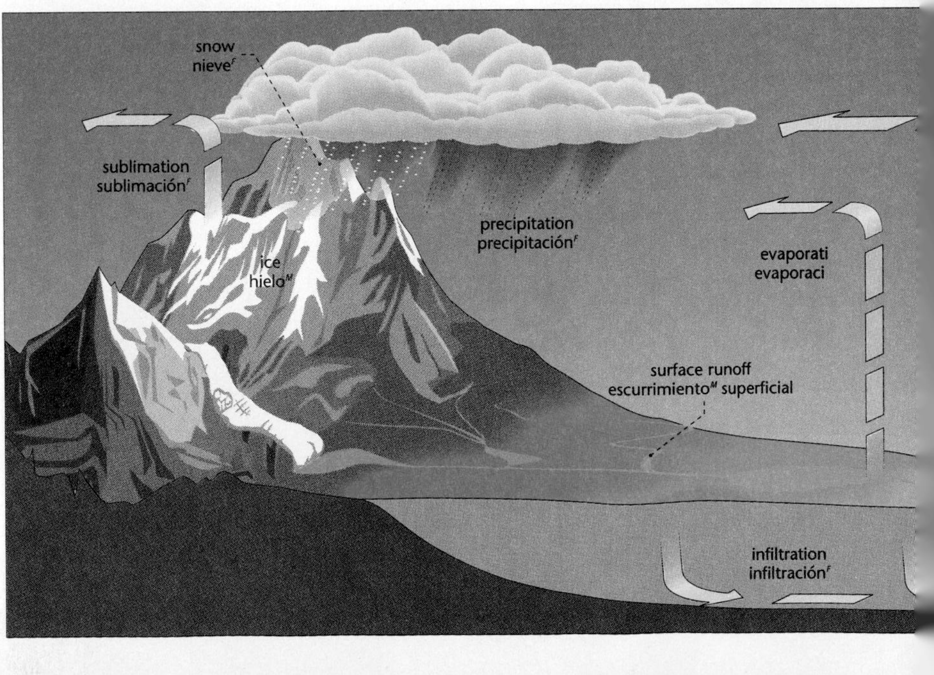

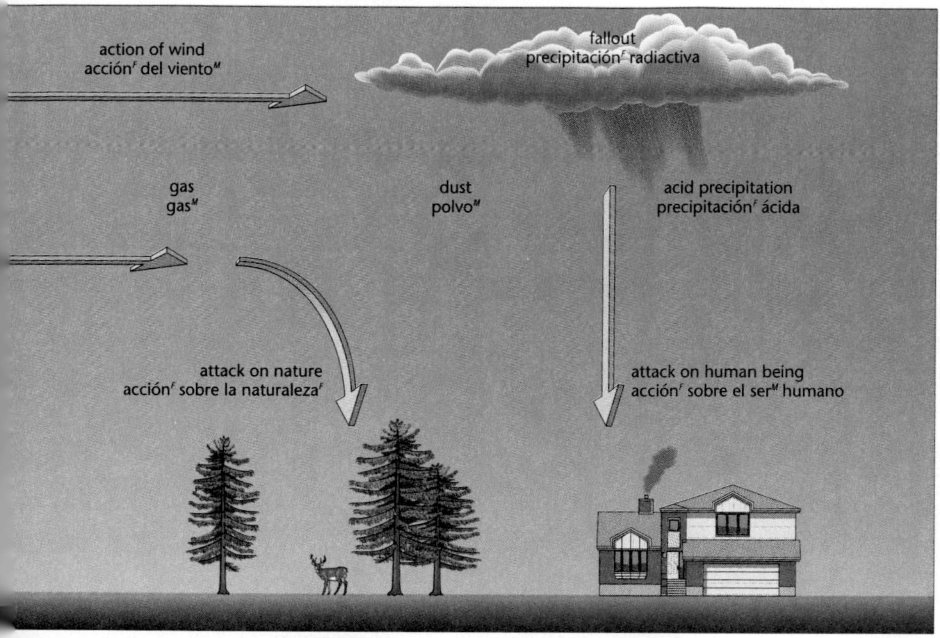

action of wind
acción^f del viento^M

fallout
precipitación^f radiactiva

gas
gas^M

dust
polvo^M

acid precipitation
precipitación^f ácida

attack on nature
acción^f sobre la naturaleza^f

attack on human being
acción^f sobre el ser^M humano

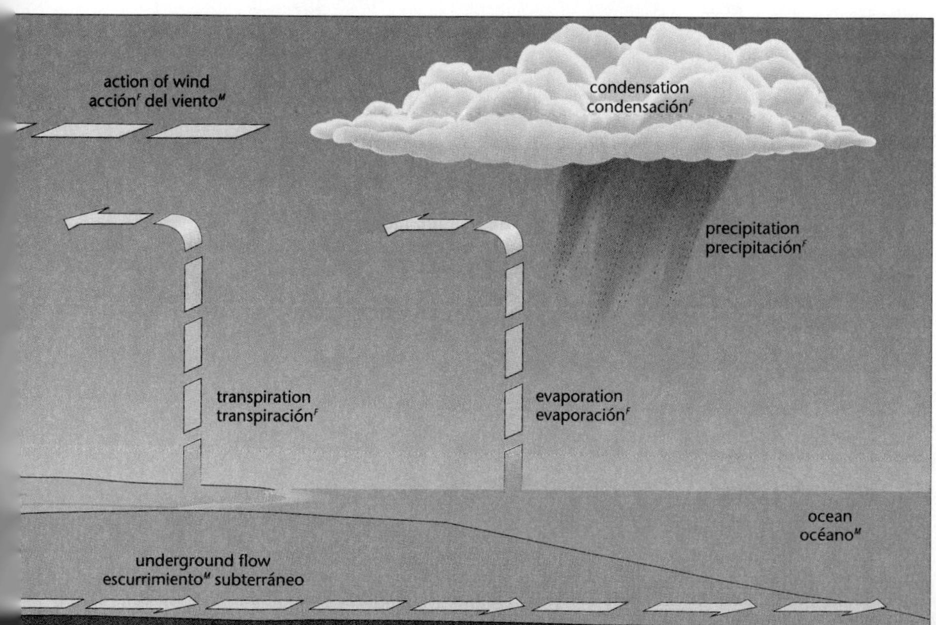

action of wind
acción^f del viento^M

condensation
condensación^f

precipitation
precipitación^f

transpiration
transpiración^f

evaporation
evaporación^f

ocean
océano^M

underground flow
escurrimiento^M subterráneo

PRECIPITATIONS
PRECIPITACIONES^F

STORMY SKY
CIELO^M TURBULENTO

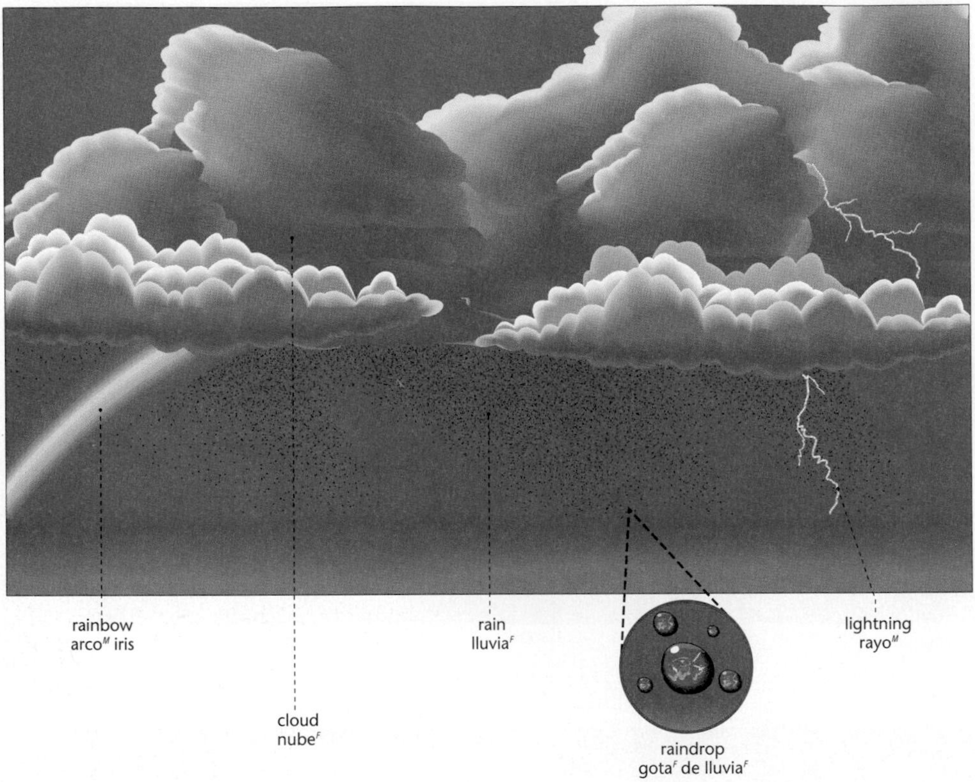

rainbow
arco^M iris

cloud
nube^F

rain
lluvia^F

raindrop
gota^F de lluvia^F

lightning
rayo^M

CLASSIFICATION OF SNOW CRYSTALS
CLASIFICACIÓN^F DE LOS CRISTALES^M DE NIEVE^F

plate crystal
plaquita^F de hielo^M

stellar crystal
estrella^F

column
columna^F

needle
aguja^F

spatial dendrite
dendrita^F espacial

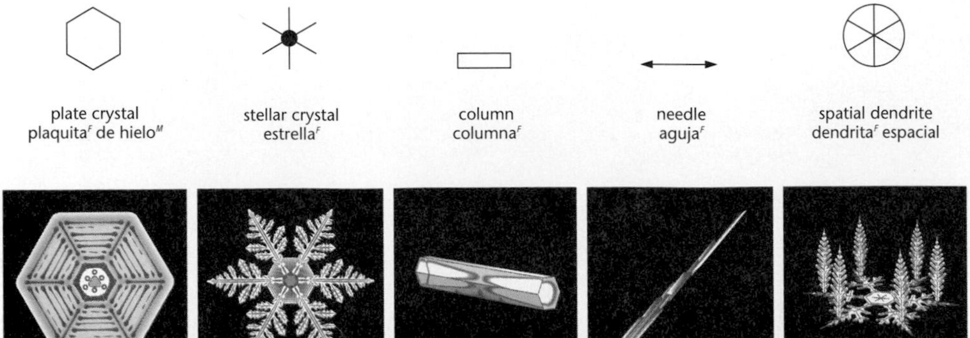

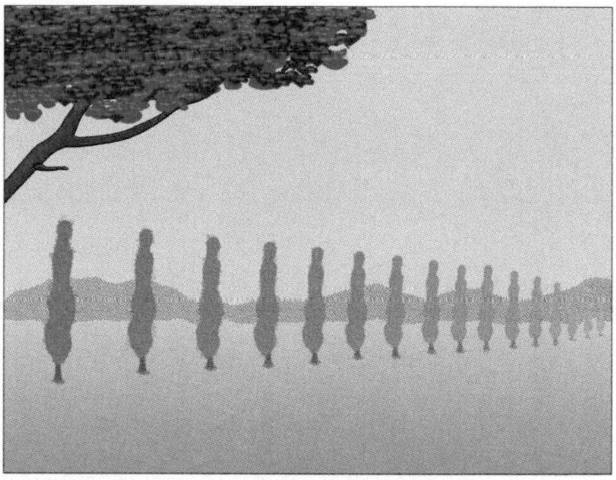

mist
neblina^F

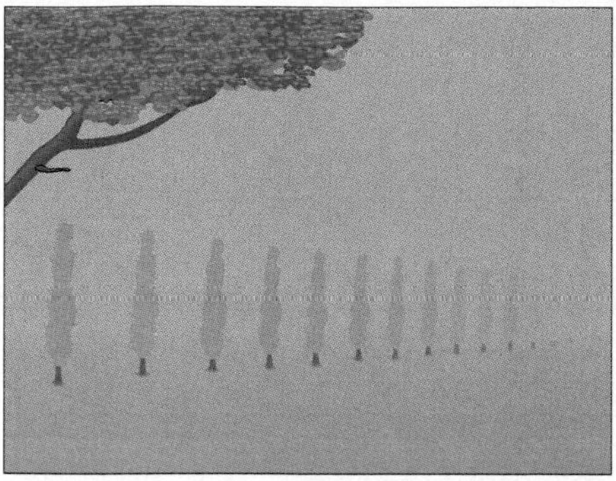

fog
niebla^F

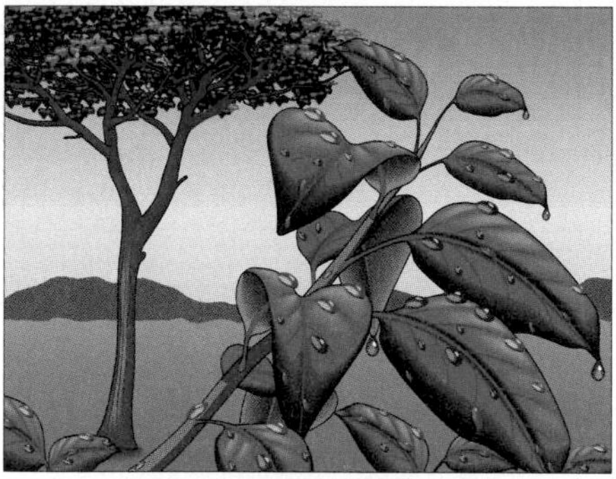

dew
rocío^M

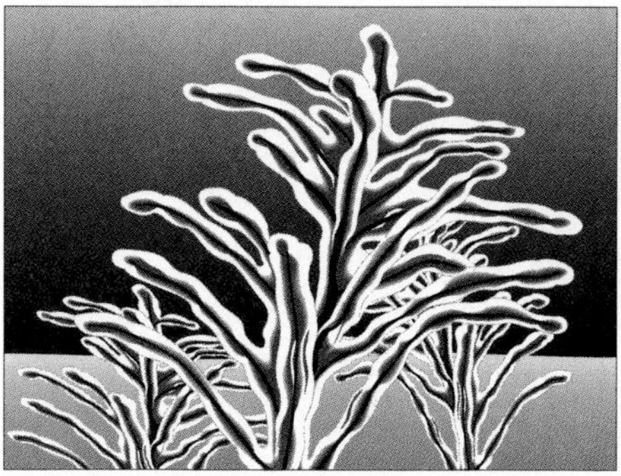

frost
escarcha^F

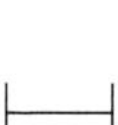

capped column
columna^F con capuchon^M

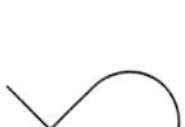

irregular crystal
cristales^M irregulares

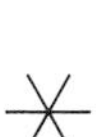

snow pellet
copo^M de nieve^F

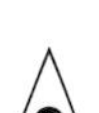

sleet
cellisca^F

hail
granizo^M

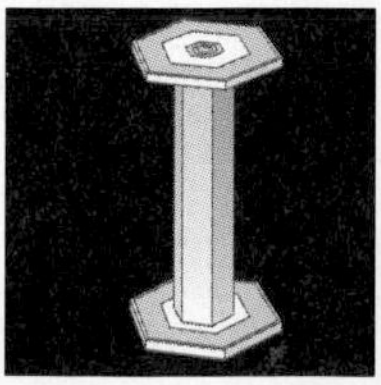

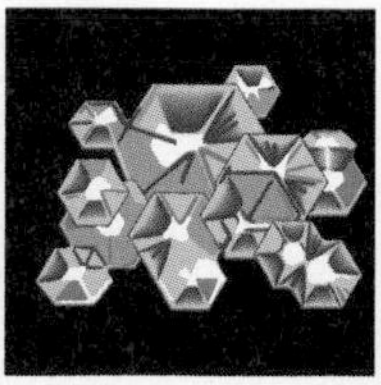

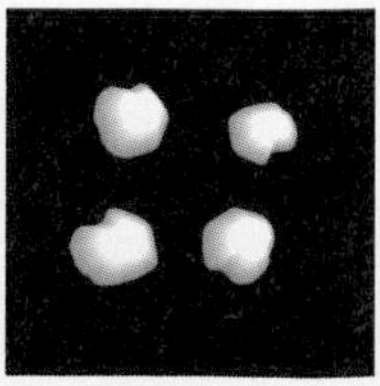

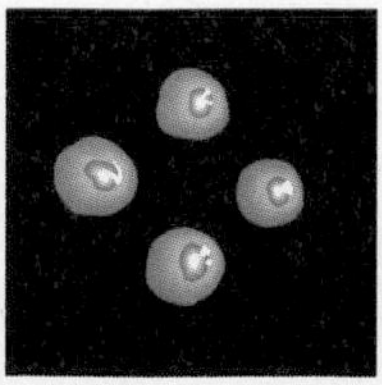

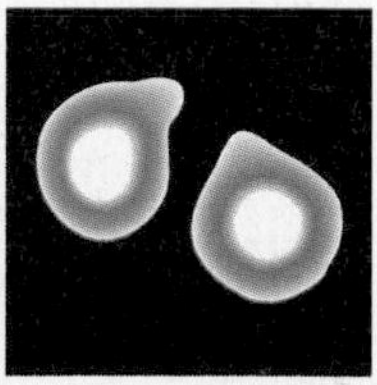

METEOROLOGY
METEOROLOGÍA*F*

WEATHER MAP
CARTA*F* DEL TIEMPO*M*

wind direction and speed
dirección*F* y velocidad*F* del viento*M*

barometric pressure
presión*F* barométrica

isobar
isobara*F*

low pressure center
zona*F* de baja presión*F*

precipitation area
zona*F* de precipitación*F*

trough
depresión*F* barométrica

type of the air mass
masa*F* de aire*M*

high pressure center
zona*F* de alta presión*F*

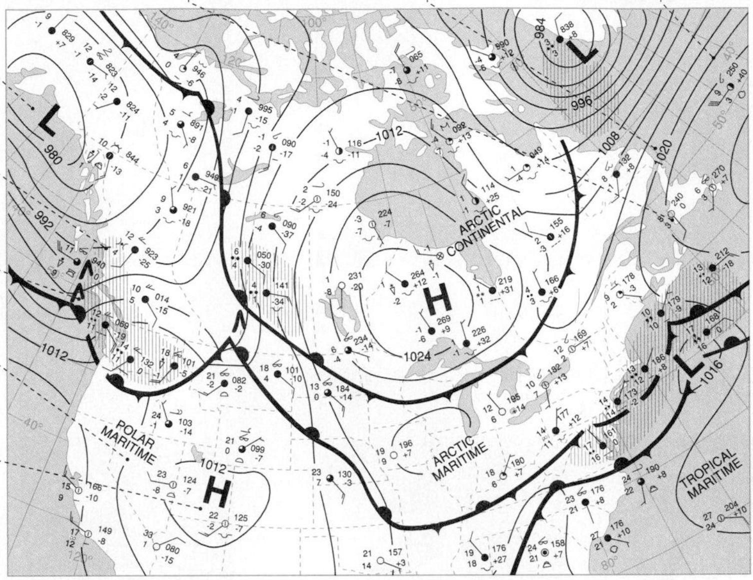

ARCTIC
CONTINENTAL

POLAR
MARITIME

ARCTIC
MARITIME

TROPICAL
MARITIME

STATION MODEL
MODELO*M* DE CLAVE*F*

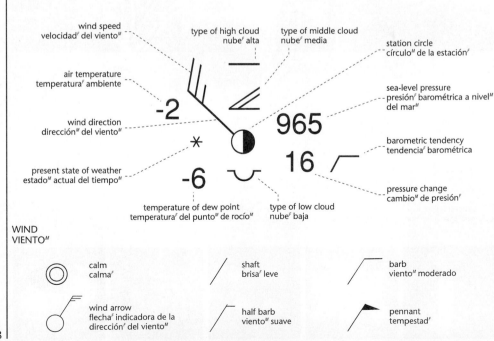

wind speed
velocidad*F* del viento*M*

type of high cloud
nube*F* alta

type of middle cloud
nube*F* media

station circle
círculo*M* de la estación*F*

air temperature
temperatura*F* ambiente

sea-level pressure
presión*F* barométrica a nivel*M*
del mar*M*

-2

wind direction
dirección*M* del viento*M*

965

barometric tendency
tendencia*F* barométrica

present state of weather
estado*M* actual del tiempo*M*

16

pressure change
cambio*M* de presión*F*

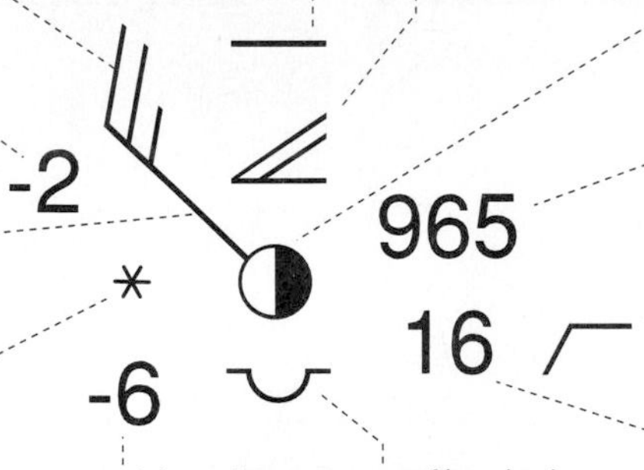

-6

temperature of dew point
temperatura*F* del punto*M* de rocío*M*

type of low cloud
nube*F* baja

WIND
VIENTO*M*

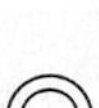

calm
calma*F*

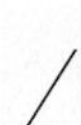

shaft
brisa*F* leve

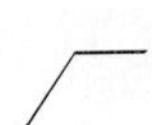

barb
viento*M* moderado

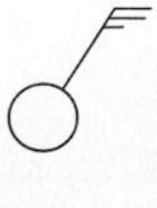

wind arrow
flecha*F* indicadora de la
dirección*F* del viento*M*

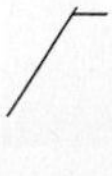

half barb
viento*M* suave

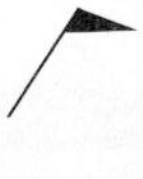

pennant
tempestad*F*

INTERNATIONAL WEATHER SYMBOLS
SÍMBOLOS^M METEOROLÓGICOS INTERNACIONALES

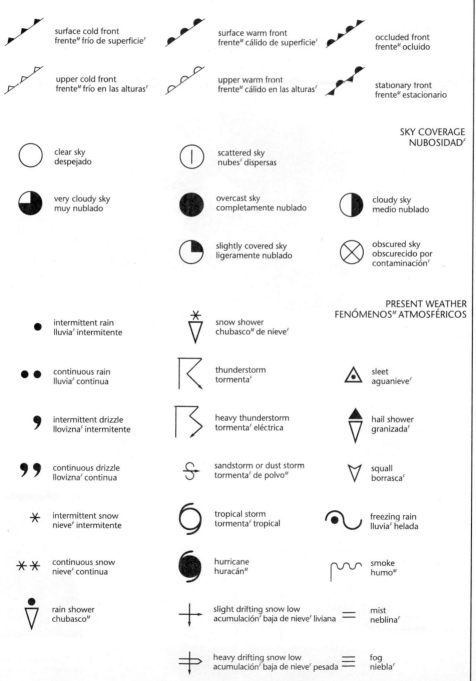

FRONTS
FRENTES^M

surface cold front
frente^M frío de superficie^F

surface warm front
frente^M cálido de superficie^F

occluded front
frente^M ocluido

upper cold front
frente^M frío en las alturas^F

upper warm front
frente^M cálido en las alturas^F

stationary front
frente^M estacionario

SKY COVERAGE
NUBOSIDAD^F

clear sky
despejado

scattered sky
nubes^F dispersas

very cloudy sky
muy nublado

overcast sky
completamente nublado

cloudy sky
medio nublado

slightly covered sky
ligeramente nublado

obscured sky
obscurecido por
contaminación^F

PRESENT WEATHER
FENÓMENOS^M **ATMOSFÉRICOS**

intermittent rain
lluvia^F intermitente

snow shower
chubasco^M de nieve^F

continuous rain
lluvia^F continua

thunderstorm
tormenta^F

sleet
aguanieve^F

intermittent drizzle
llovizna^F intermitente

heavy thunderstorm
tormenta^F eléctrica

hail shower
granizada^F

continuous drizzle
llovizna^F continua

sandstorm or dust storm
tormenta^F de polvo^M

squall
borrasca^F

intermittent snow
nieve^F intermitente

tropical storm
tormenta^F tropical

freezing rain
lluvia^F helada

continuous snow
nieve^F continua

hurricane
huracán^M

smoke
humo^M

rain shower
chubasco^M

slight drifting snow low
acumulación^F baja de nieve^F liviana

mist
neblina^F

heavy drifting snow low
acumulación^F baja de nieve^F pesada

fog
niebla^F

MEASURE OF SUNSHINE
MEDICIÓN*F* DE LA LUZ*F* SOLAR

sunshine recorder
actinómetro*M*

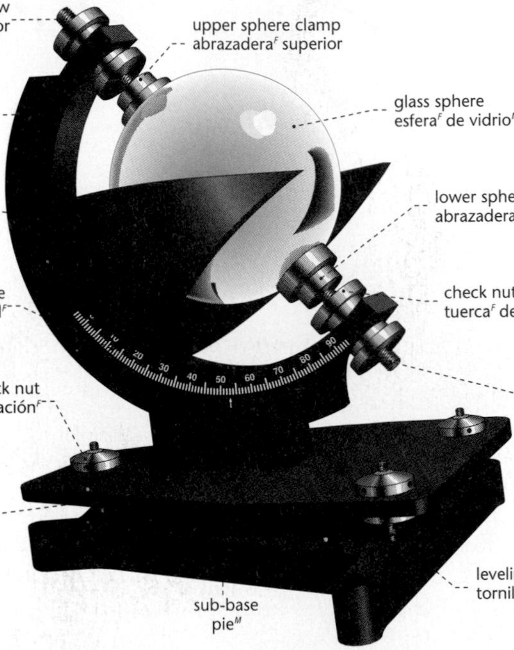

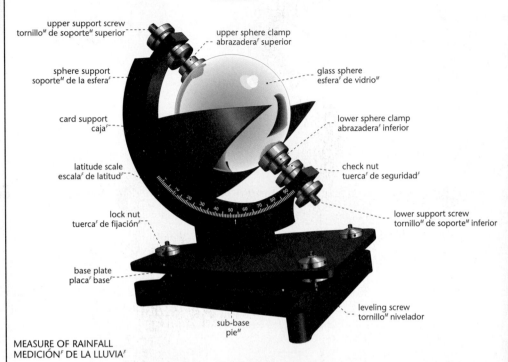

upper support screw
tornillo*M* de soporte*M* superior

upper sphere clamp
abrazadera*F* superior

sphere support
soporte*M* de la esfera*F*

glass sphere
esfera*F* de vidrio*M*

card support
caja*F*

lower sphere clamp
abrazadera*F* inferior

latitude scale
escala*F* de latitud*F*

check nut
tuerca*F* de seguridad*F*

lock nut
tuerca*F* de fijación*F*

lower support screw
tornillo*M* de soporte*M* inferior

base plate
placa*F* base*F*

leveling screw
tornillo*M* nivelador

sub-base
pie*M*

MEASURE OF RAINFALL
MEDICIÓN*F* DE LA LLUVIA*F*

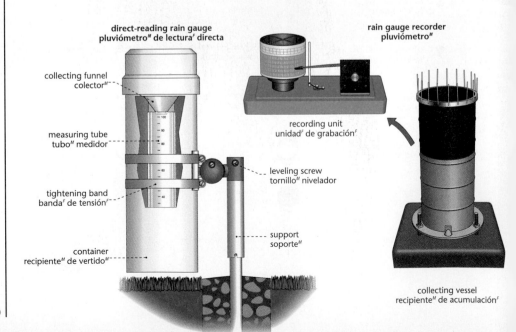

direct-reading rain gauge
pluviómetro*M* de lectura*F* directa

rain gauge recorder
pluviómetro*M*

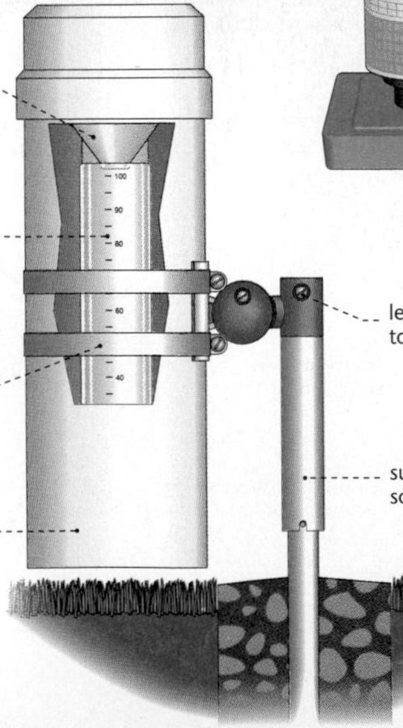

collecting funnel
colector*M*

measuring tube
tubo*M* medidor

tightening band
banda*F* de tensión*F*

container
recipiente*M* de vertido*M*

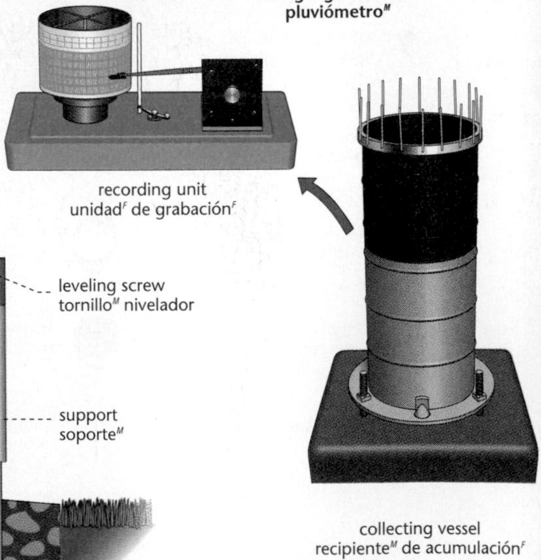

recording unit
unidad*F* de grabación*F*

leveling screw
tornillo*M* nivelador

support
soporte*M*

collecting vessel
recipiente*M* de acumulación*F*

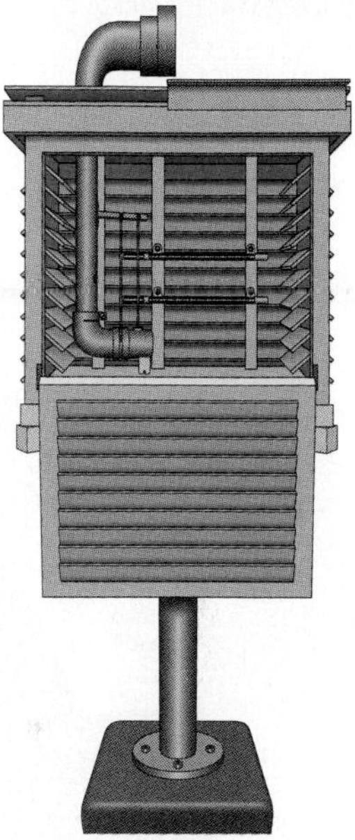

MEASURE OF TEMPERATURE
MEDICIÓN^F DE LA TEMPERATURA^F

INSTRUMENT SHELTER
CASETA^F DE INSTRUMENTOS^M METEOROLÓGICOS

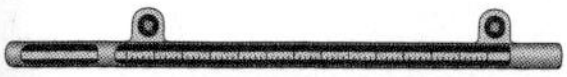

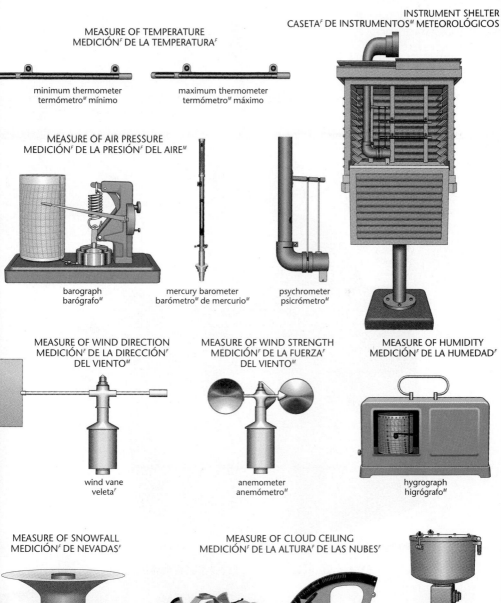

minimum thermometer
termómetro^M mínimo

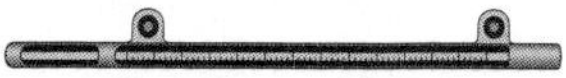

maximum thermometer
termómetro^M máximo

MEASURE OF AIR PRESSURE
MEDICIÓN^F DE LA PRESIÓN^F DEL AIRE^M

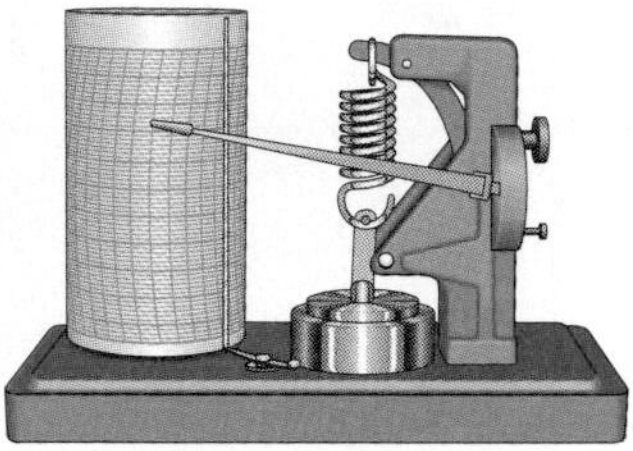

barograph
barógrafo^M

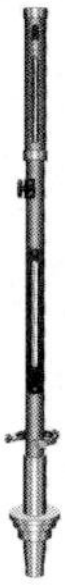

mercury barometer
barómetro^M de mercurio^M

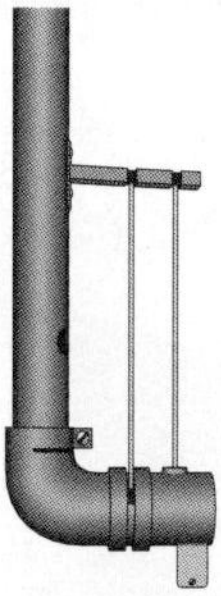

psychrometer
psicrómetro^M

MEASURE OF WIND DIRECTION
MEDICIÓN^F DE LA DIRECCIÓN^F
DEL VIENTO^M

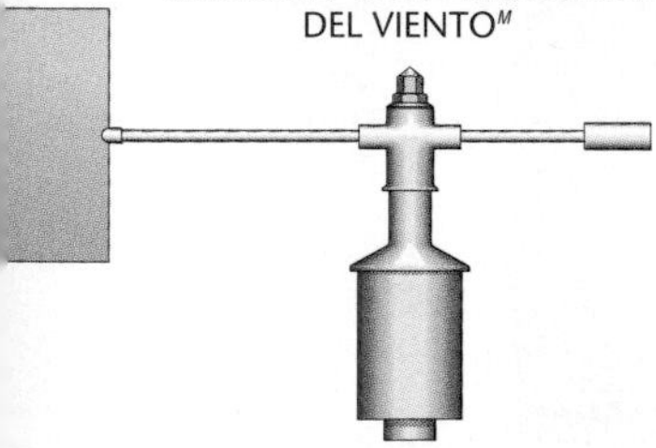

MEASURE OF WIND STRENGTH
MEDICIÓN^F DE LA FUERZA^F
DEL VIENTO^M

MEASURE OF HUMIDITY
MEDICIÓN^F DE LA HUMEDAD^F

wind vane
veleta^F

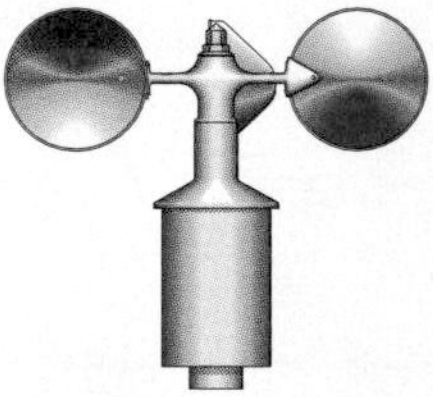

anemometer
anemómetro^M

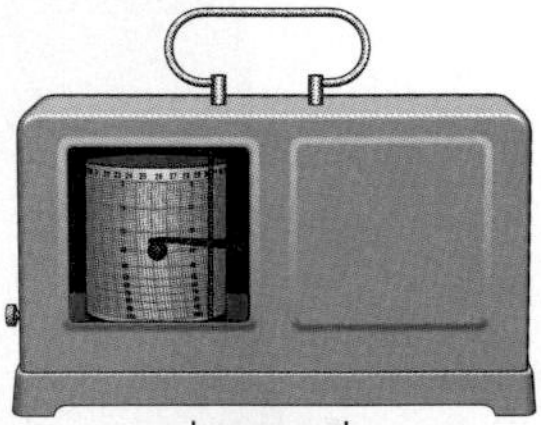

hygrograph
higrógrafo^M

MEASURE OF SNOWFALL
MEDICIÓN^F DE NEVADAS^F

MEASURE OF CLOUD CEILING
MEDICIÓN^F DE LA ALTURA^F DE LAS NUBES^F

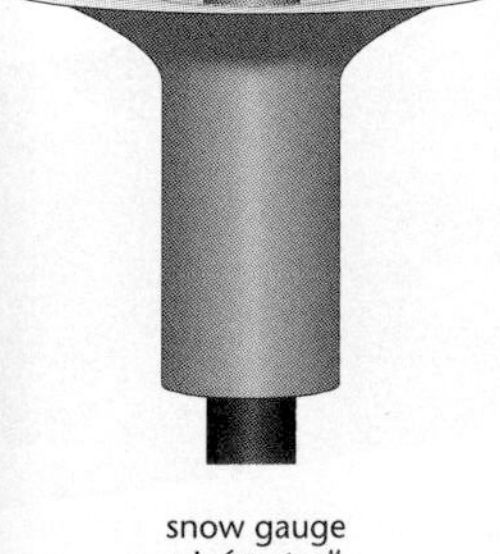

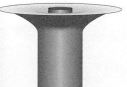

snow gauge
nivómetro^M

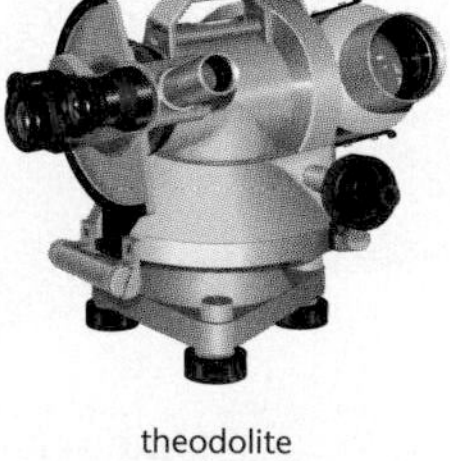

theodolite
teodolito^M

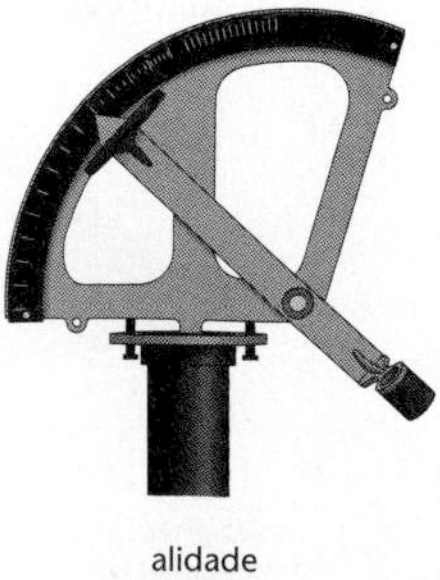

alidade
alidada^F

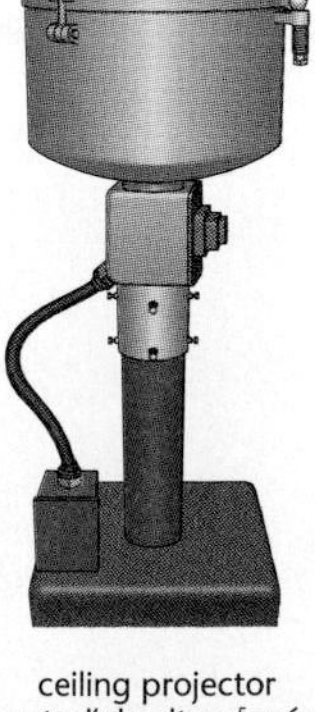

ceiling projector
proyector^M de altura^F máxima

WEATHER SATELLITE
SATÉLITE^M METEOROLÓGICO

GEOSTATIONARY SATELLITE
SATÉLITE^M GEOESTACIONARIO

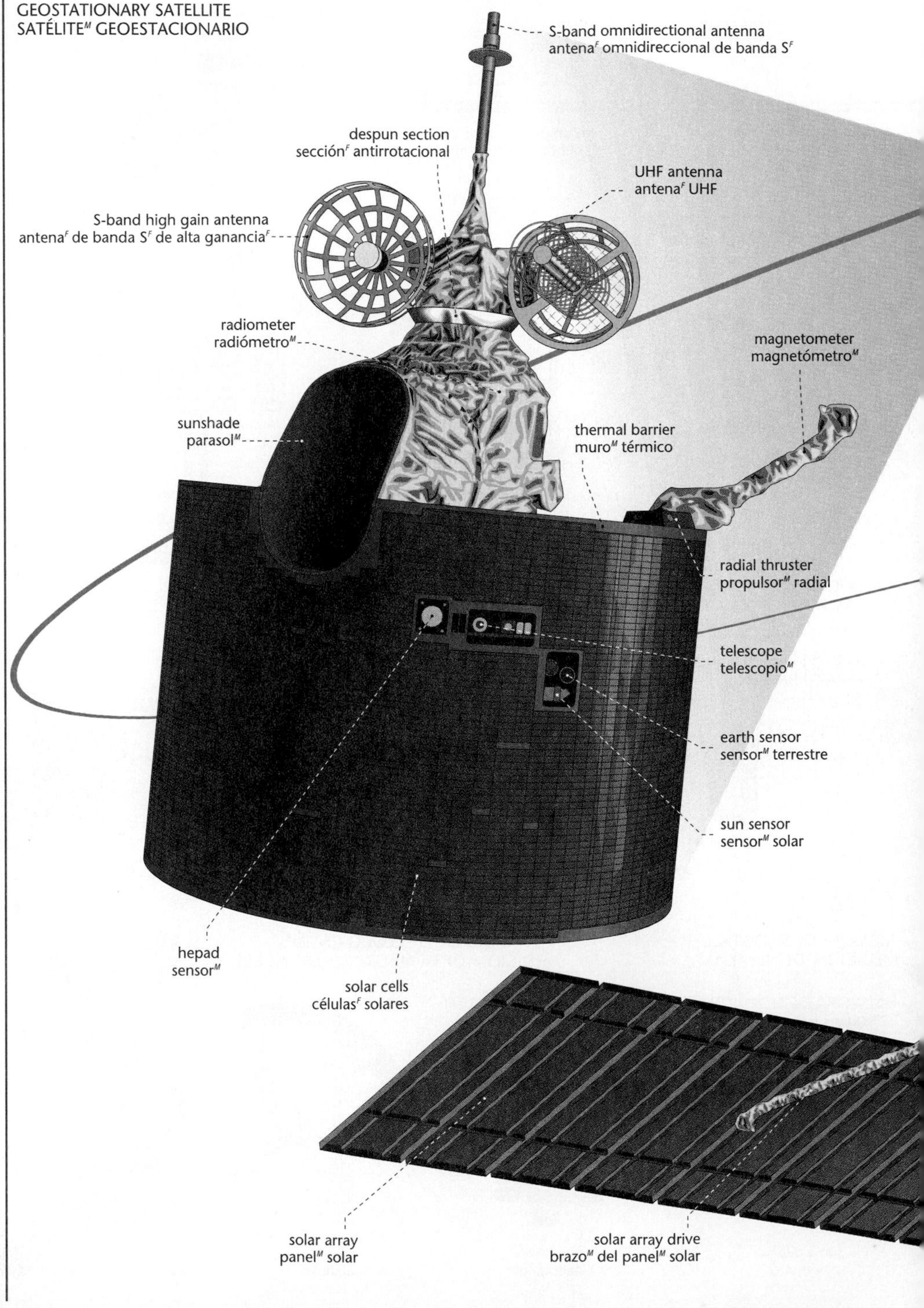

S-band omnidirectional antenna
antena^F omnidireccional de banda S^F

despun section
sección^F antirrotacional

UHF antenna
antena^F UHF

S-band high gain antenna
antena^F de banda S^F de alta ganancia^F

radiometer
radiómetro^M

magnetometer
magnetómetro^M

sunshade
parasol^M

thermal barrier
muro^M térmico

radial thruster
propulsor^M radial

telescope
telescopio^M

earth sensor
sensor^M terrestre

sun sensor
sensor^M solar

hepad
sensor^M

solar cells
células^F solares

solar array
panel^M solar

solar array drive
brazo^M del panel^M solar

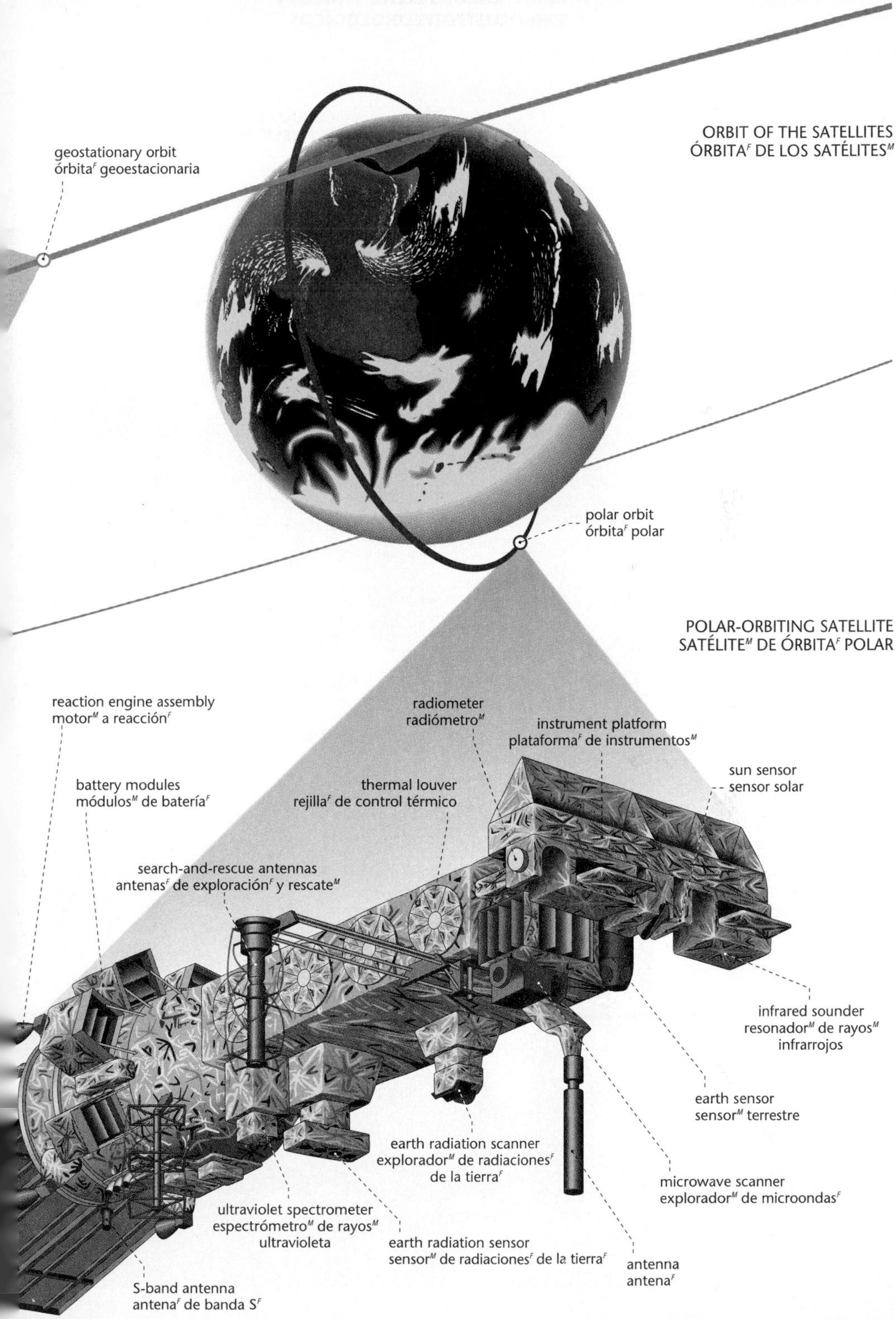

geostationary orbit
órbita^F geoestacionaria

ORBIT OF THE SATELLITES
ÓRBITA^F DE LOS SATÉLITES^M

polar orbit
órbita^F polar

POLAR-ORBITING SATELLITE
SATÉLITE^M DE ÓRBITA^F POLAR

reaction engine assembly
motor^M a reacción^F

radiometer
radiómetro^M

instrument platform
plataforma^F de instrumentos^M

sun sensor
sensor solar

battery modules
módulos^M de batería^F

thermal louver
rejilla^F de control térmico

search-and-rescue antennas
antenas^F de exploración^F y rescate^M

infrared sounder
resonador^M de rayos^M
infrarrojos

earth sensor
sensor^M terrestre

earth radiation scanner
explorador^M de radiaciones^F
de la tierra^F

microwave scanner
explorador^M de microondas^F

ultraviolet spectrometer
espectrómetro^M de rayos^M
ultravioleta

earth radiation sensor
sensor^M de radiaciones^F de la tierra^F

antenna
antena^F

S-band antenna
antena^F de banda S^F

43

CLOUDS AND METEOROLOGICAL SYMBOLS
NUBES^F Y SÍMBOLOS^M METEOROLÓGICOS

HIGH CLOUDS
NUBES^F ALTAS

CLOUDS OF VERTICAL DEVELOPMENT
NUBES^F DE DESARROLLO^M VERTICAL

cirrus
cirros^M

cumulonimbus
cumulonimbos^M

cirrocumulus
cirrocúmulos^M

cirrostratus
cirrostratos^M

MIDDLE CLOUDS
NUBES^F MEDIAS

altostratus
altostratos^M

altocumulus
altocúmulos^M

stratocumulus
estratocúmulos^M

LOW CLOUDS
NUBES^F BAJAS

nimbostratus
nimbostratos^M

stratus
estratos^M

cumulus
cúmulos^M

CLIMATES OF THE WORLD
CLIMAS^M DEL MUNDO^M

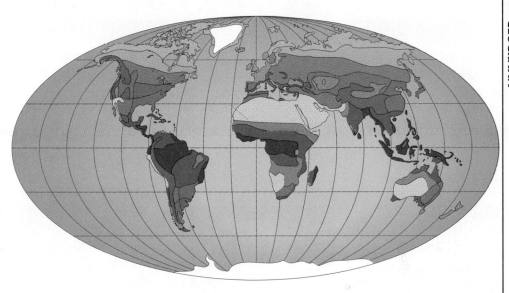

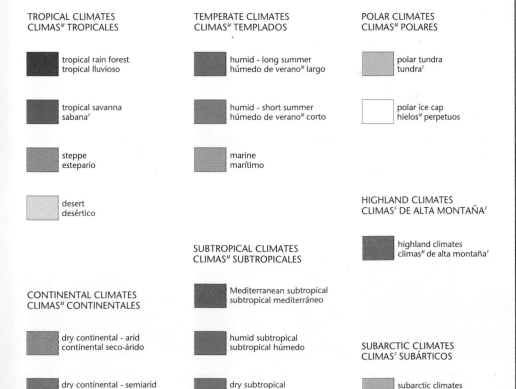

TROPICAL CLIMATES
CLIMAS^M TROPICALES

tropical rain forest
tropical lluvioso

tropical savanna
sabana^F

steppe
estepario

desert
desértico

CONTINENTAL CLIMATES
CLIMAS^M CONTINENTALES

dry continental - arid
continental seco-árido

dry continental - semiarid
continental seco-semiárido

TEMPERATE CLIMATES
CLIMAS^M TEMPLADOS

humid - long summer
húmedo de verano^M largo

humid - short summer
húmedo de verano^M corto

marine
marítimo

SUBTROPICAL CLIMATES
CLIMAS^M SUBTROPICALES

Mediterranean subtropical
subtropical mediterráneo

humid subtropical
subtropical húmedo

dry subtropical
subtropical seco

POLAR CLIMATES
CLIMAS^M POLARES

polar tundra
tundra^F

polar ice cap
hielos^M perpetuos

HIGHLAND CLIMATES
CLIMAS^F DE ALTA MONTAÑA^F

highland climates
climas^M de alta montaña^F

SUBARCTIC CLIMATES
CLIMAS^F SUBÁRTICOS

subarctic climates
climas^M subárticos

DESERT
DESIERTO^M

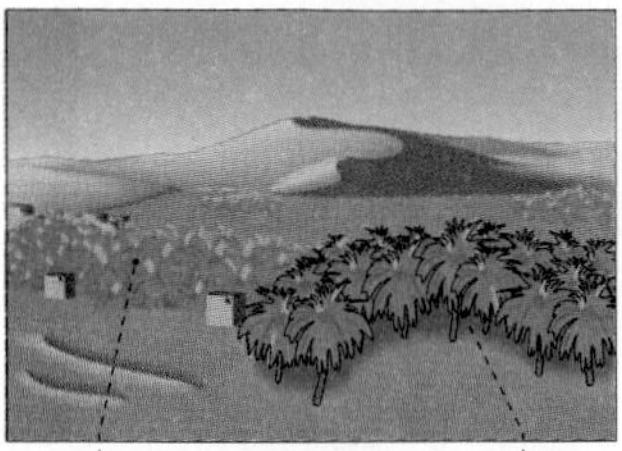

oasis
oasis^M

palm grove
palmar^M

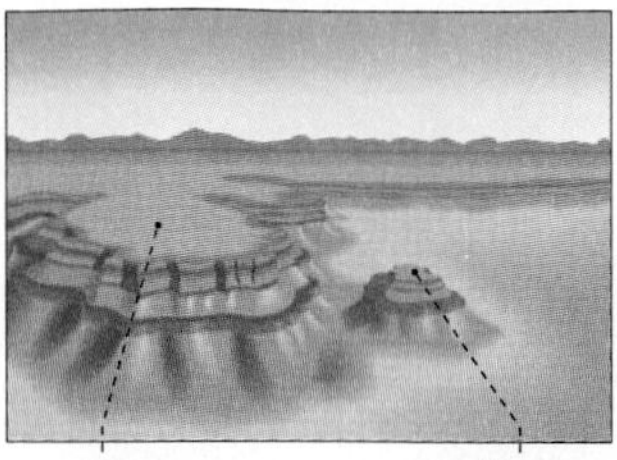

mesa
otero^M

butte
hamada^F

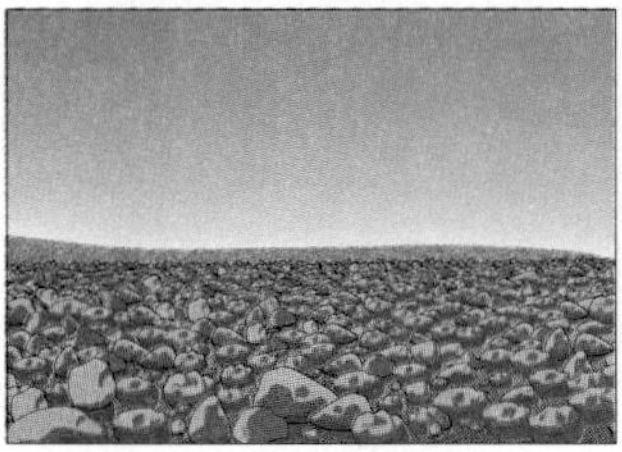

rocky desert
desierto^M rocoso

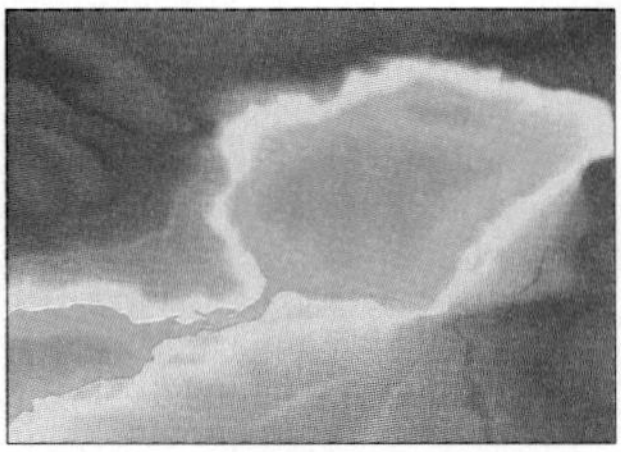

saline lake
laguna^F salada

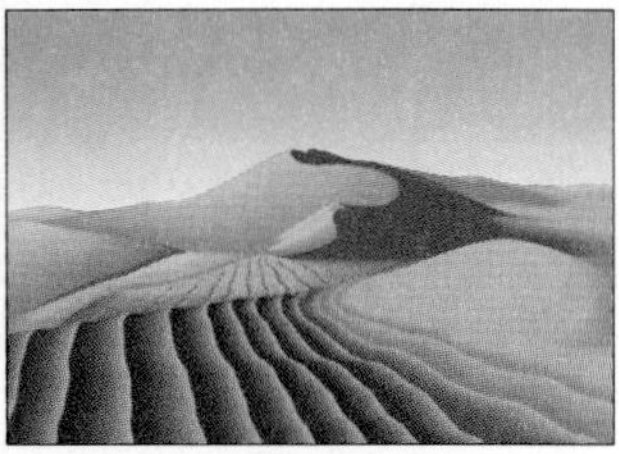

sandy desert
desierto^M arenoso

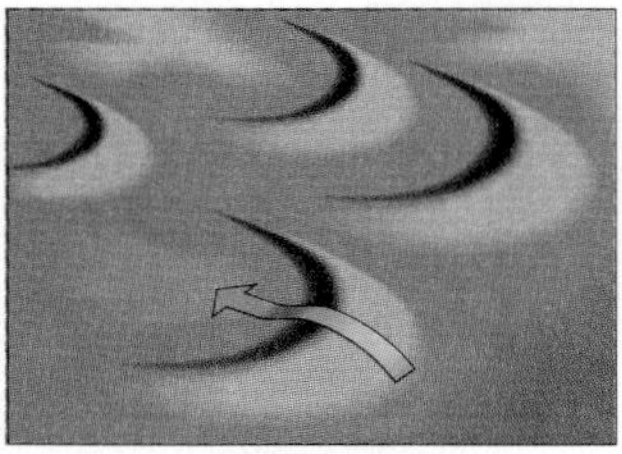

crescentic dune
barjana^F

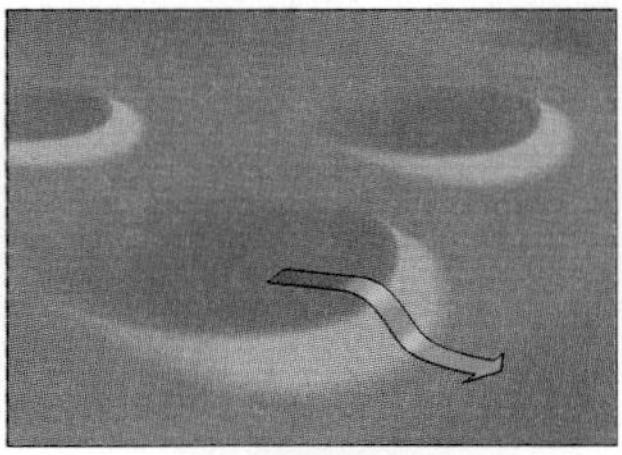

parabolic dune
duna^F parabólica

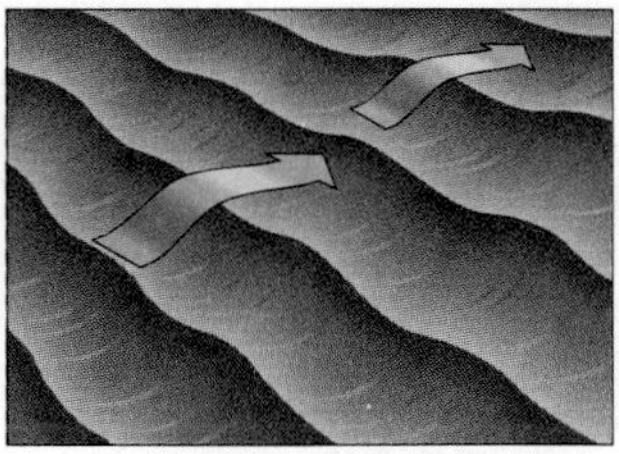

transverse dunes
dunas^F paralelas

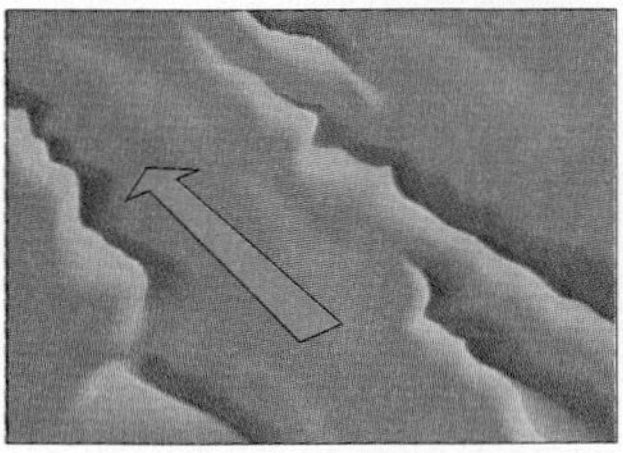

chain of dunes
cadena^F de dunas^F

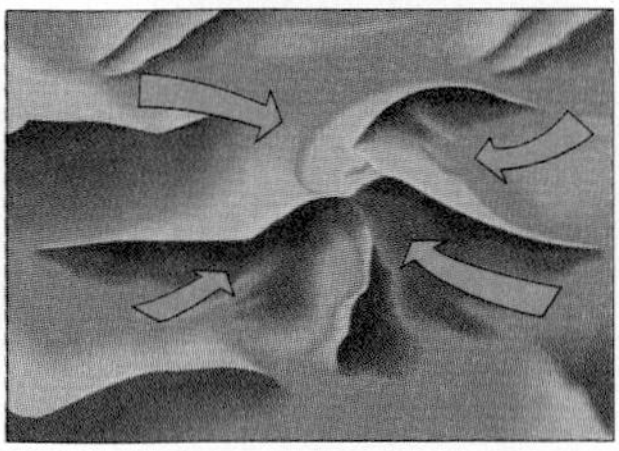

complex dune
duna^F compleja

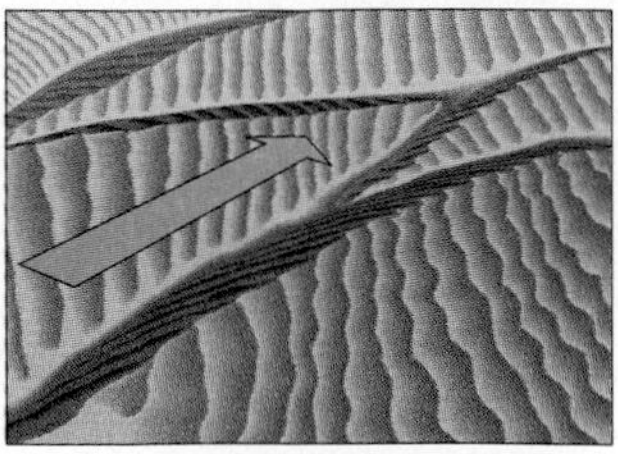

longitudinal dunes
dunas^F longitudinales

CARTOGRAPHY
CARTOGRAFÍA^F

HEMISPHERES
HEMISFERIOS^M

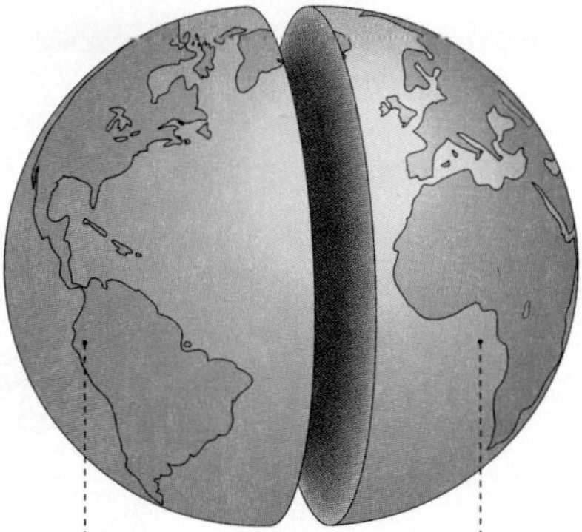

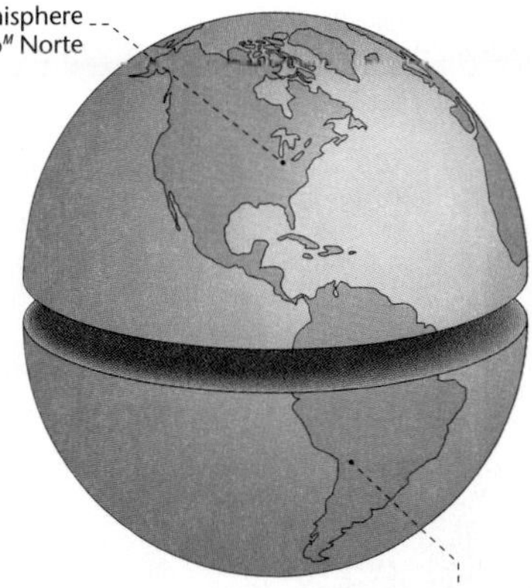

Northern hemisphere
hemisferio^M Norte

Western hemisphere
hemisferio^M occidental

Eastern hemisphere
hemisferio^M oriental

Southern hemisphere
hemisferio^M Sur

GRID SYSTEM
SISTEMA^M DE REJILLA^F

lines of latitude
líneas^F de latitud^F

lines of longitude
líneas^F de longitud^F

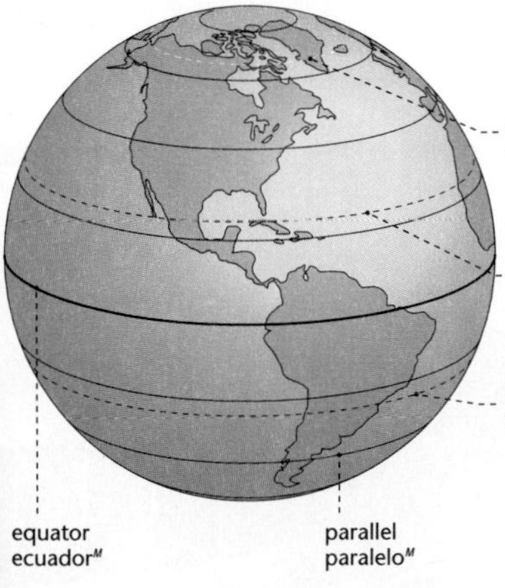

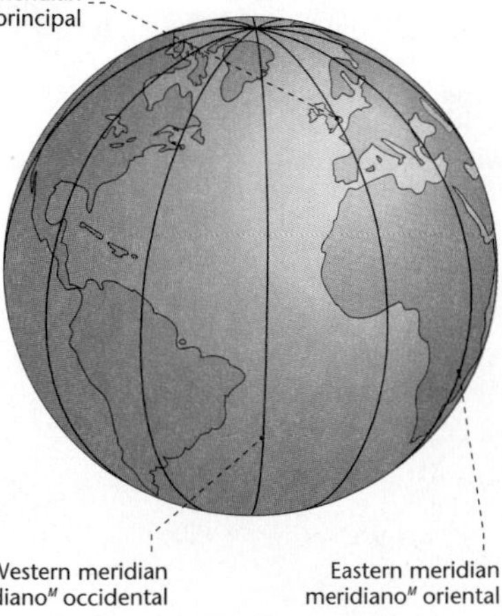

prime meridian
meridiano^M principal

Arctic Circle
círculo^M polar ártico

tropic of Cancer
trópico^M de Cáncer

tropic of Capricorn
trópico^M de Capricornio

equator
ecuador^M

parallel
paralelo^M

Western meridian
meridiano^M occidental

Eastern meridian
meridiano^M oriental

REMOTE DETECTION SATELLITE
SATÉLITE^M DE DETECCIÓN^F A LARGA DISTANCIA^F

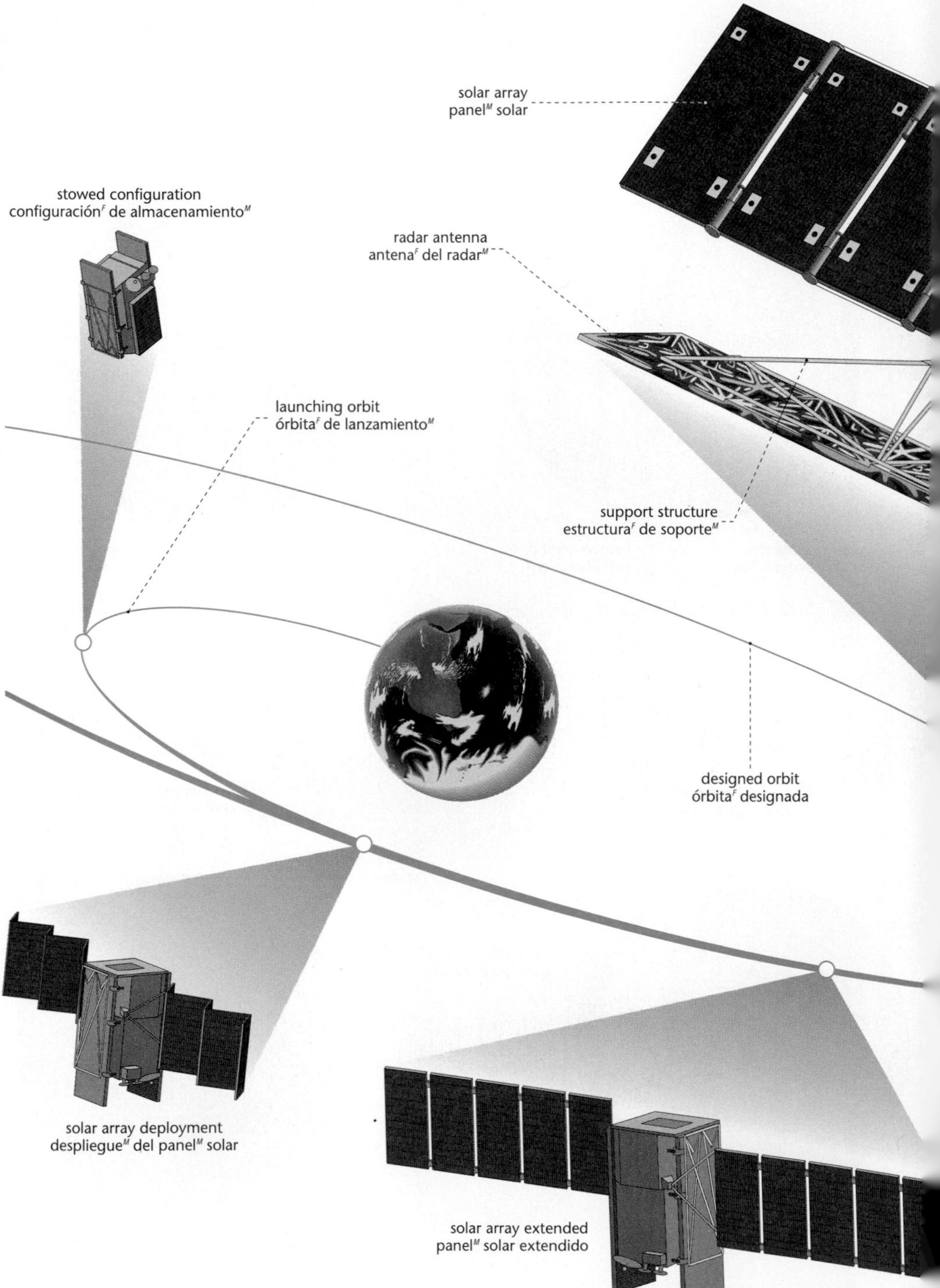

solar array
panel^M solar

stowed configuration
configuración^F de almacenamiento^M

radar antenna
antena^F del radar^M

launching orbit
órbita^F de lanzamiento^M

support structure
estructura^F de soporte^M

designed orbit
órbita^F designada

solar array deployment
despliegue^M del panel^M solar

solar array extended
panel^M solar extendido

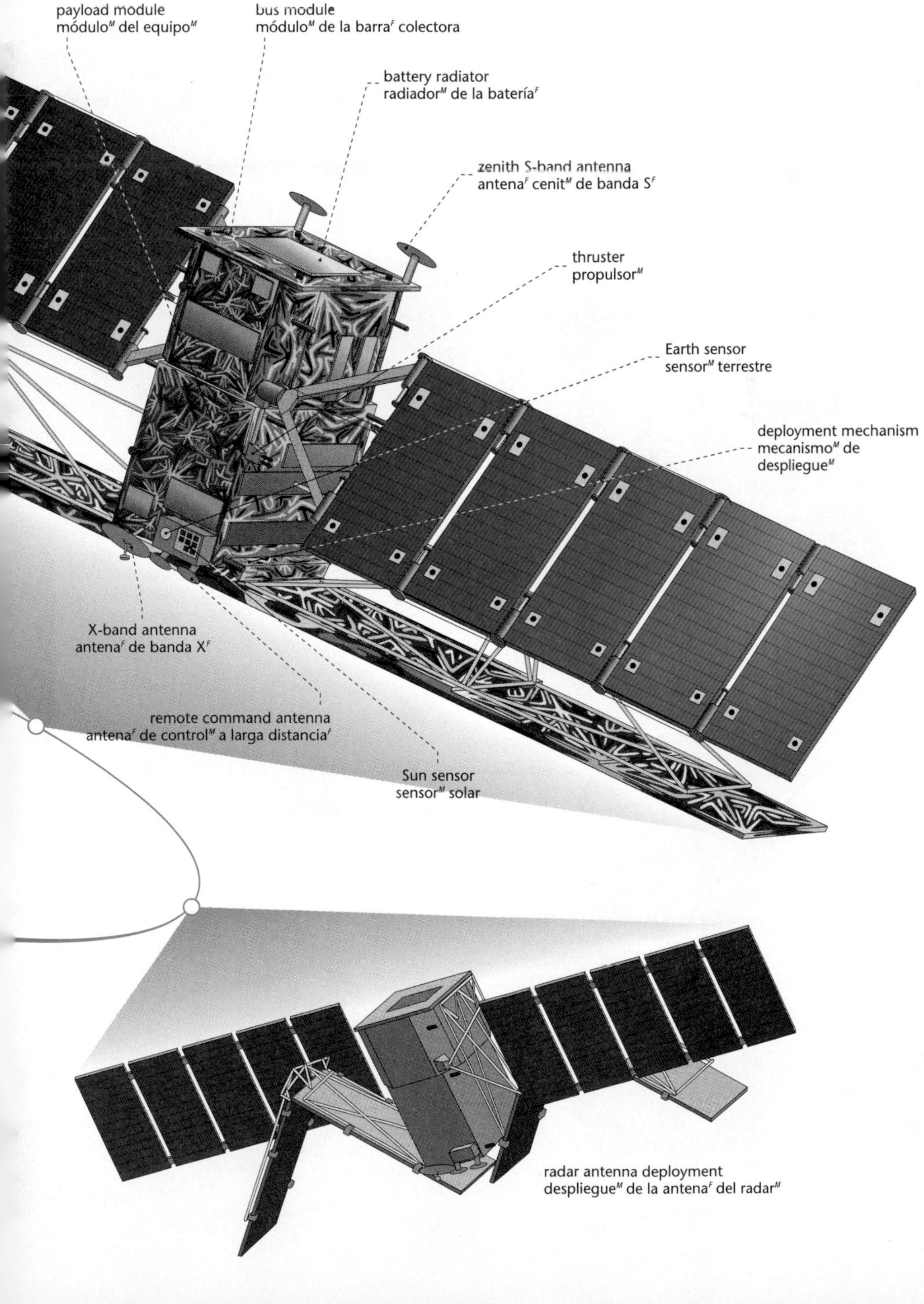

payload module
módulo*M* del equipo*M*

bus module
módulo*M* de la barra*F* colectora

battery radiator
radiador*M* de la batería*F*

zenith S-band antenna
antena*F* cenit*M* de banda S*F*

thruster
propulsor*M*

Earth sensor
sensor*M* terrestre

deployment mechanism
mecanismo*M* de
despliegue*M*

X-band antenna
antena*F* de banda X*F*

remote command antenna
antena*F* de control*M* a larga distancia*F*

Sun sensor
sensor*M* solar

radar antenna deployment
despliegue*M* de la antena*F* del radar*M*

MAP PROJECTIONS
PROYECCIONES*F* DEL MAPA*M*

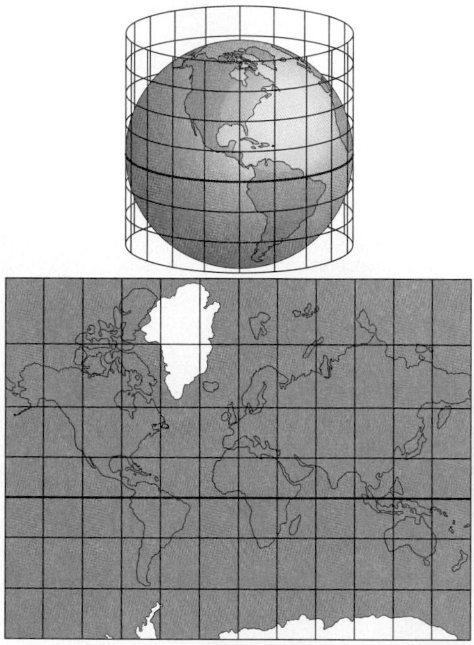

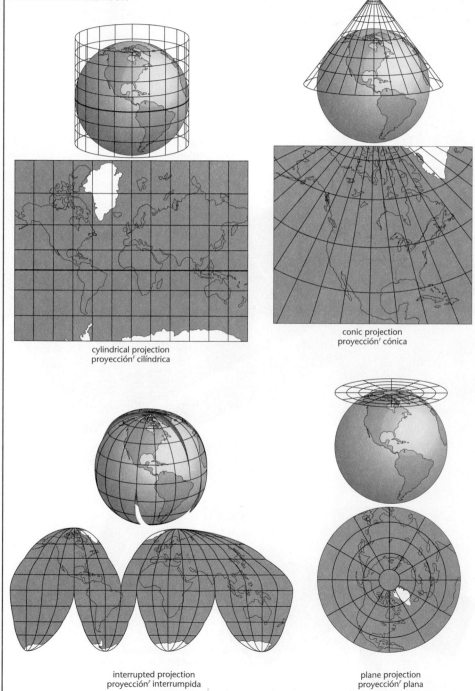

cylindrical projection
proyección*F* cilíndrica

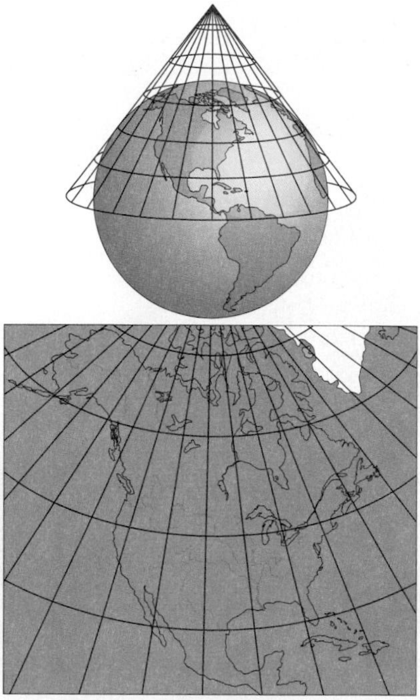

conic projection
proyección*F* cónica

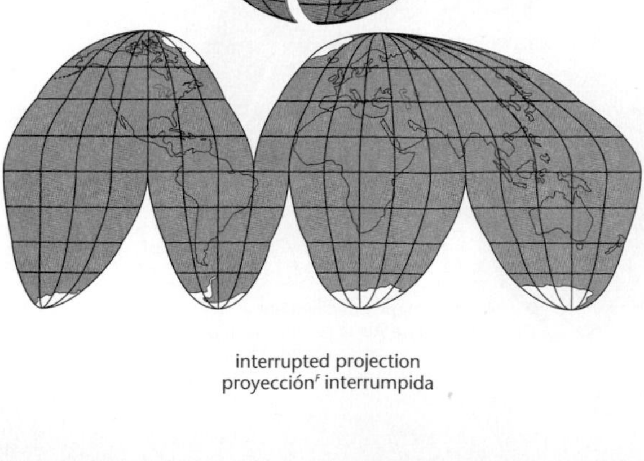

interrupted projection
proyección*F* interrumpida

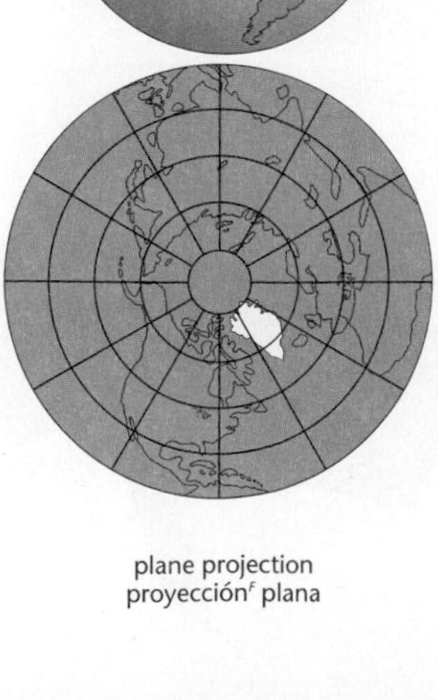

plane projection
proyección*F* plana

POLITICAL MAP
MAPA^M POLÍTICO

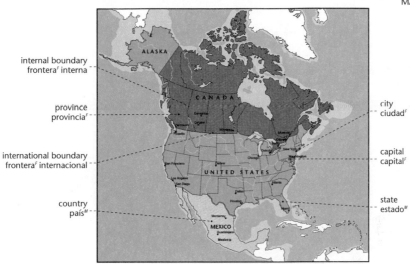

internal boundary
frontera^F interna

province
provincia^F

international boundary
frontera^F internacional

country
país^M

city
ciudad^F

capital
capital^F

state
estado^M

ALASKA

CANADA

UNITED STATES

MEXICO

PHYSICAL MAP
MAPA^M FÍSICO

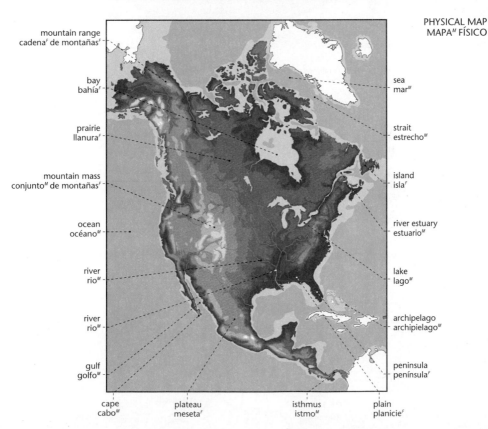

mountain range
cadena^F de montañas^F

bay
bahía^F

prairie
llanura^F

mountain mass
conjunto^M de montañas^F

ocean
océano^M

river
río^M

river
río^M

gulf
golfo^M

sea
mar^M

strait
estrecho^M

island
isla^F

river estuary
estuario^M

lake
lago^M

archipelago
archipielago^M

peninsula
península^F

cape
cabo^M

plateau
meseta^F

isthmus
istmo^M

plain
planicie^F

CARTOGRAPHY
CARTOGRAFÍA^F

URBAN MAP
MAPA^M URBANO

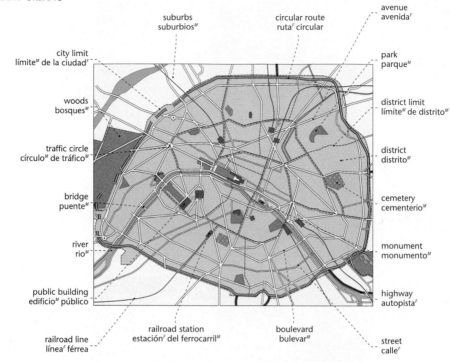

suburbs
suburbios^M

circular route
ruta^F circular

avenue
avenida^F

city limit
límite^M de la ciudad^F

park
parque^M

woods
bosques^M

district limit
límite^M de distrito^M

traffic circle
círculo^M de tráfico^M

district
distrito^M

bridge
puente^M

cemetery
cementerio^M

river
río^M

monument
monumento^M

public building
edificio^M público

highway
autopista^F

railroad line
línea^F férrea

railroad station
estación^F del ferrocarril^M

boulevard
bulevar^M

street
calle^F

ROAD MAP
MAPA^M DE CARRETERAS^F

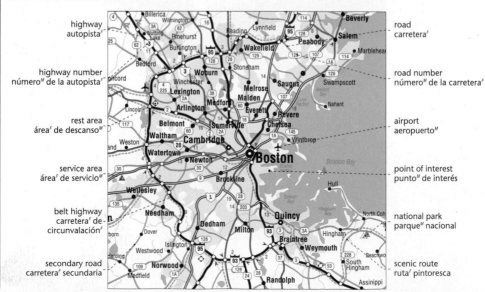

highway
autopista^F

road
carretera^F

highway number
número^M de la autopista^F

road number
número^M de la carretera^F

rest area
área^F de descanso^M

airport
aeropuerto^M

service area
área^F de servicio^M

point of interest
punto^M de interés

belt highway
carretera^F de
circunvalación^F

national park
parque^M nacional

secondary road
carretera^F secundaria

scenic route
ruta^F pintoresca

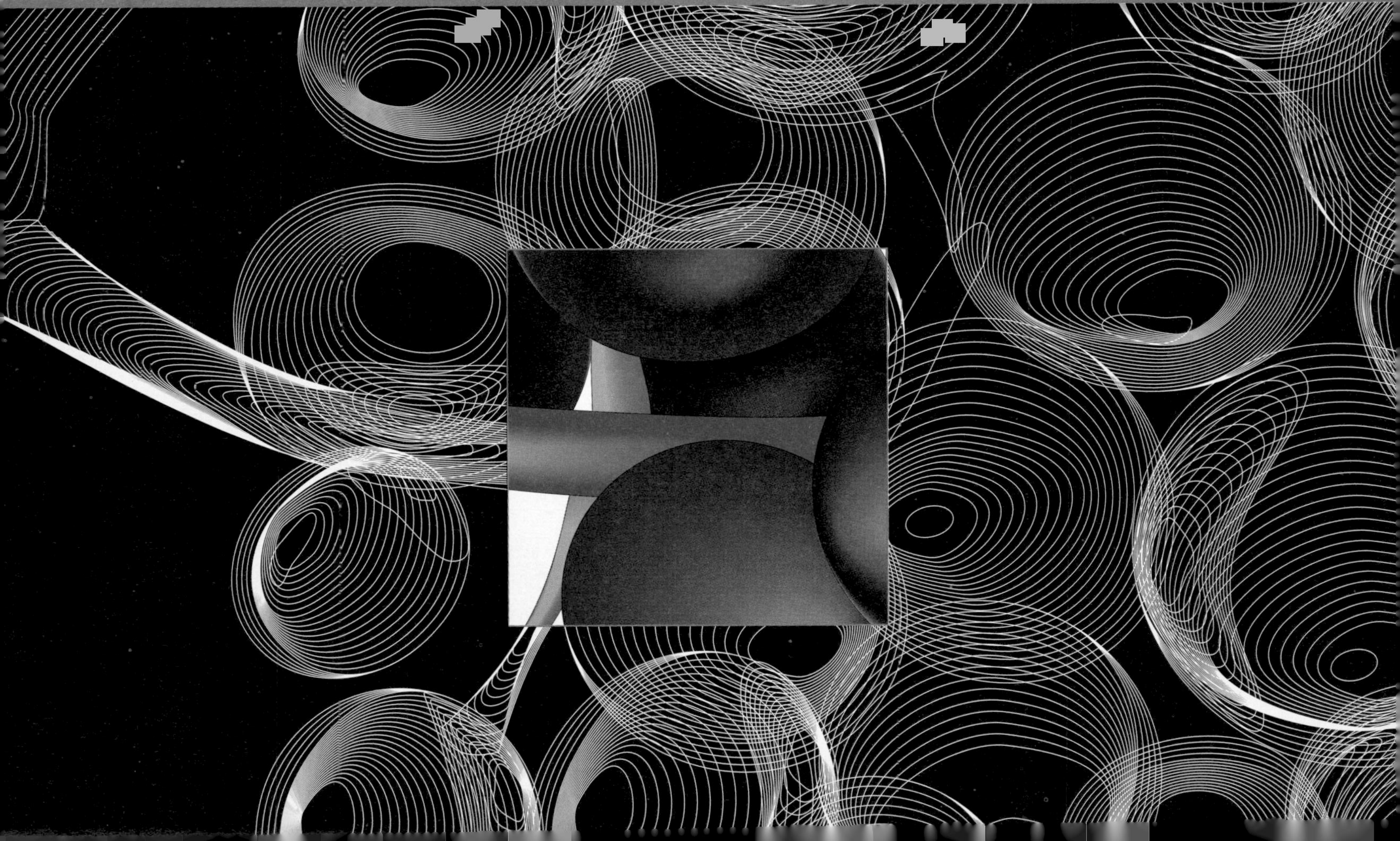

CONTENTS

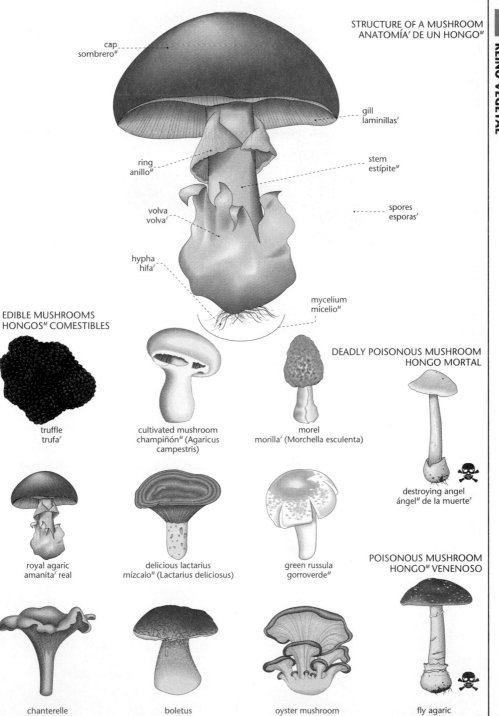

STRUCTURE OF A MUSHROOM
ANATOMÍA^F DE UN HONGO^M

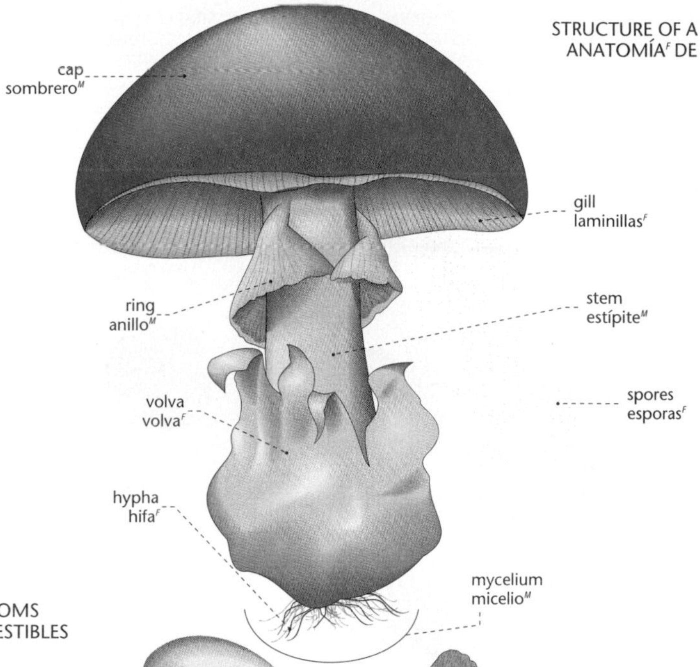

cap
sombrero^M

gill
laminillas^F

ring
anillo^M

stem
estípite^M

volva
volva^F

spores
esporas^F

hypha
hifa^F

mycelium
micelio^M

EDIBLE MUSHROOMS
HONGOS^M COMESTIBLES

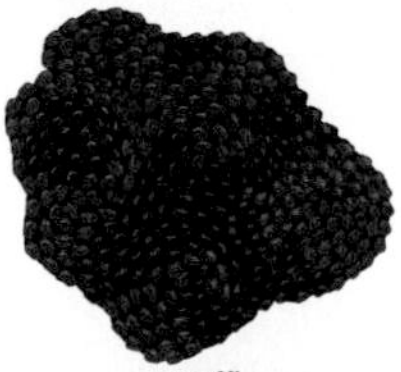

truffle
trufa^F

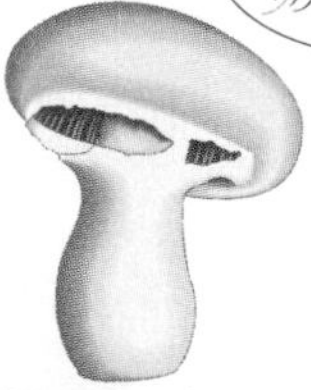

cultivated mushroom
champiñón^M (Agaricus
campestris)

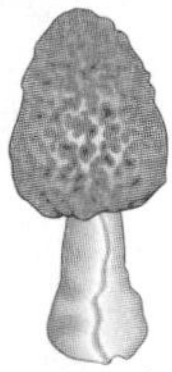

morel
morilla^F (Morchella esculenta)

DEADLY POISONOUS MUSHROOM
HONGO MORTAL

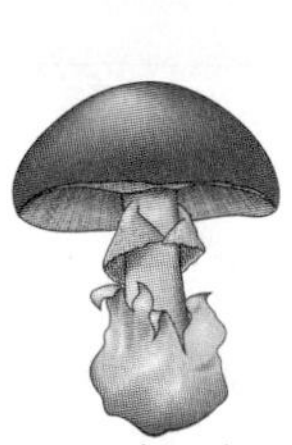

royal agaric
amanita^F real

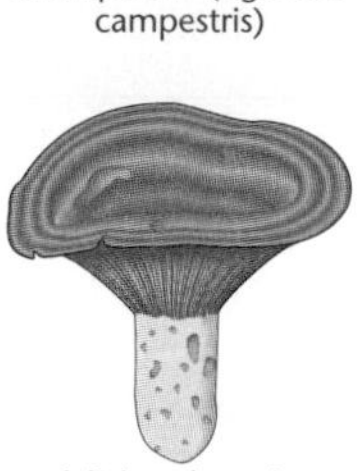

delicious lactarius
mízcalo^M (Lactarius deliciosus)

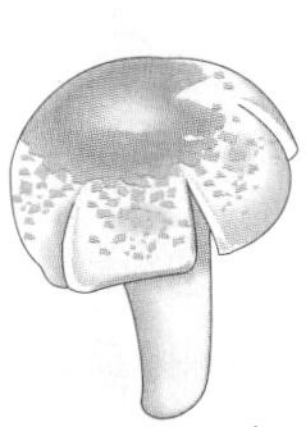

green russula
gorroverde^M

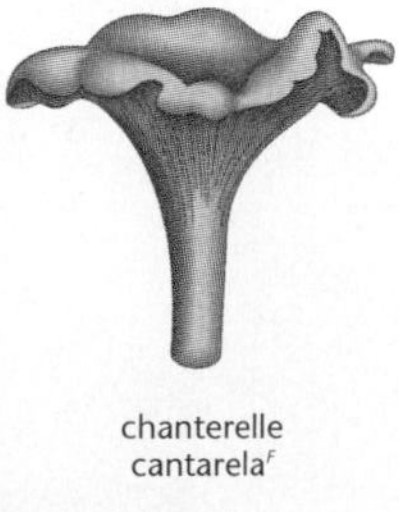

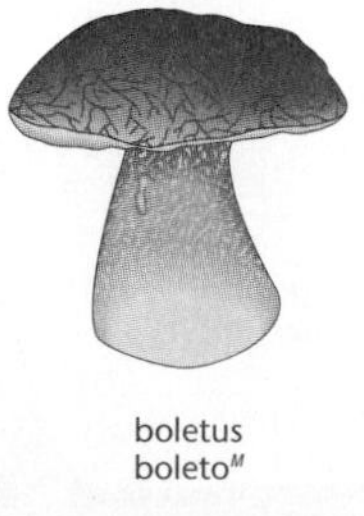

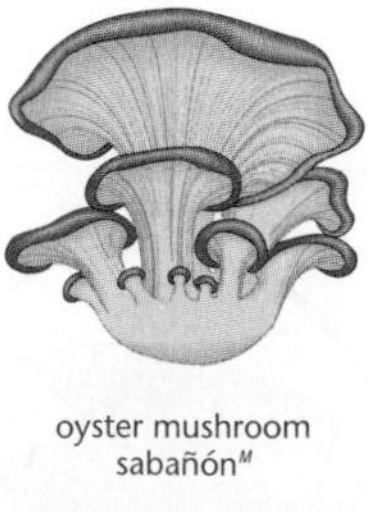

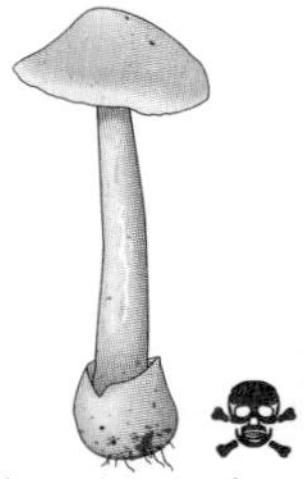

destroying angel
ángel^M de la muerte^F

POISONOUS MUSHROOM
HONGO^M VENENOSO

chanterelle
cantarela^F

boletus
boleto^M

oyster mushroom
sabañón^M

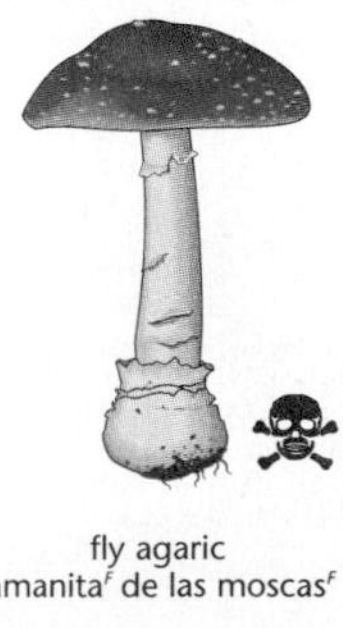

fly agaric
amanita^F de las moscas^F

TYPES OF LEAVES
LA HOJA^F SEGÚN SU LIMBO^M

LEAF MARGIN
LA HOJA^F SEGÚN SU BORDE^M

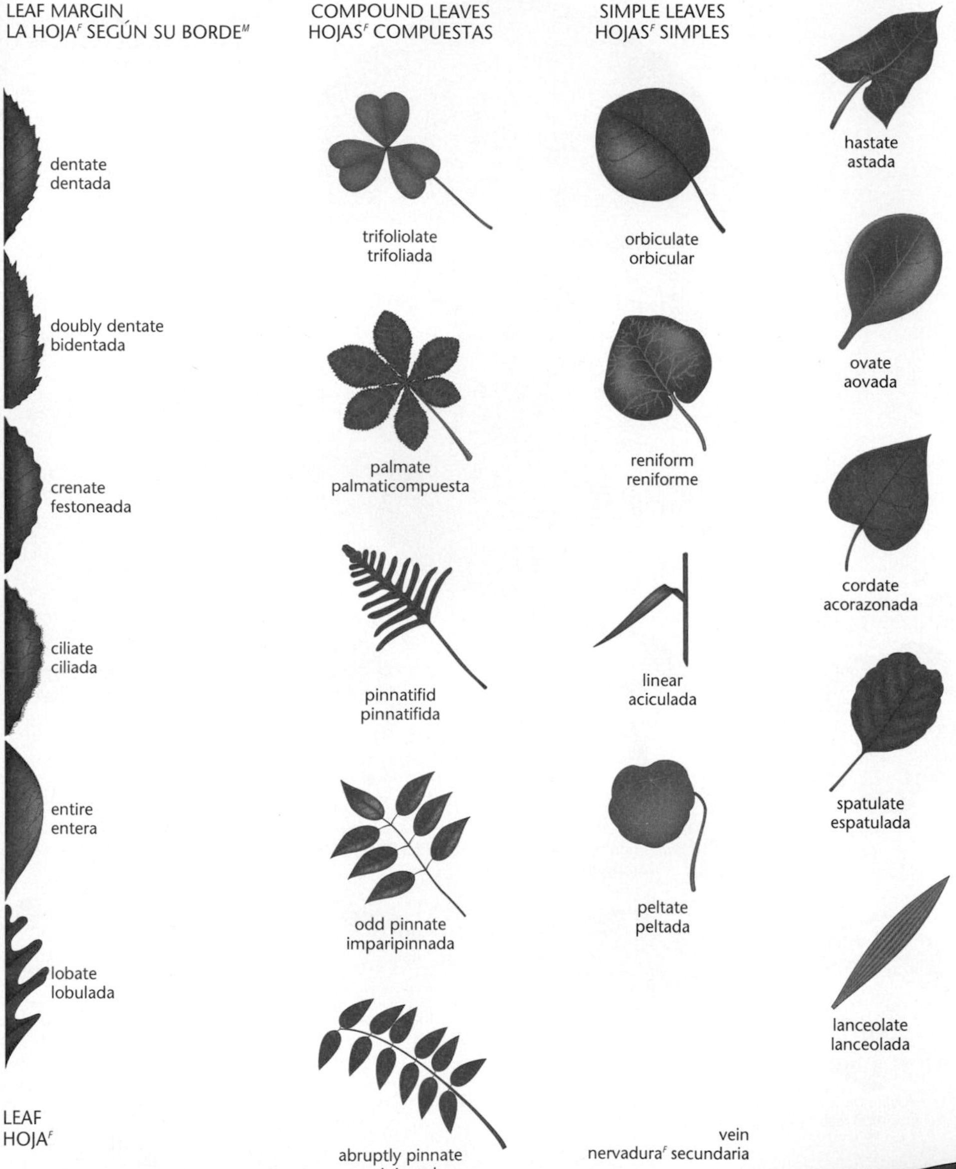

dentate
dentada

doubly dentate
bidentada

crenate
festoneada

ciliate
ciliada

entire
entera

lobate
lobulada

LEAF
HOJA^F

COMPOUND LEAVES
HOJAS^F COMPUESTAS

trifoliolate
trifoliada

palmate
palmaticompuesta

pinnatifid
pinnatifida

odd pinnate
imparipinnada

abruptly pinnate
paripinnada

SIMPLE LEAVES
HOJAS^F SIMPLES

orbiculate
orbicular

reniform
reniforme

linear
aciculada

peltate
peltada

hastate
astada

ovate
aovada

cordate
acorazonada

spatulate
espatulada

lanceolate
lanceolada

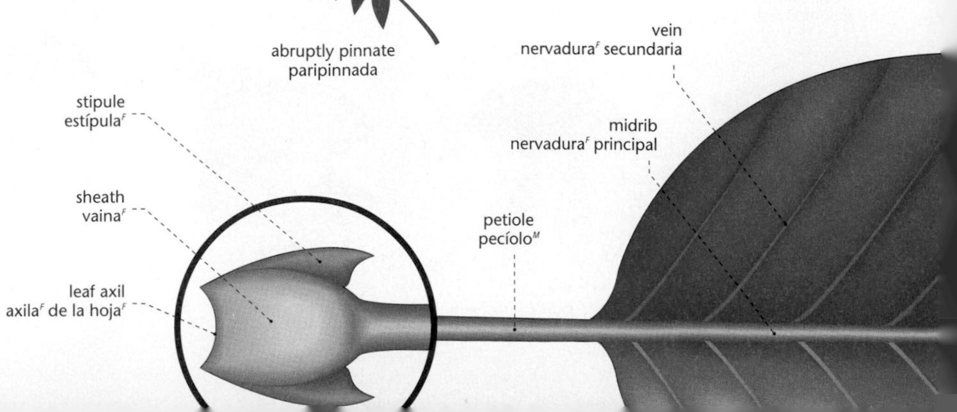

vein
nervadura^F secundaria

midrib
nervadura^F principal

stipule
estípula^F

sheath
vaina^F

petiole
pecíolo^M

leaf axil
axila^F de la hoja^F

STRUCTURE OF A PLANT
ANATOMÍA^F DE UNA PLANTA^F

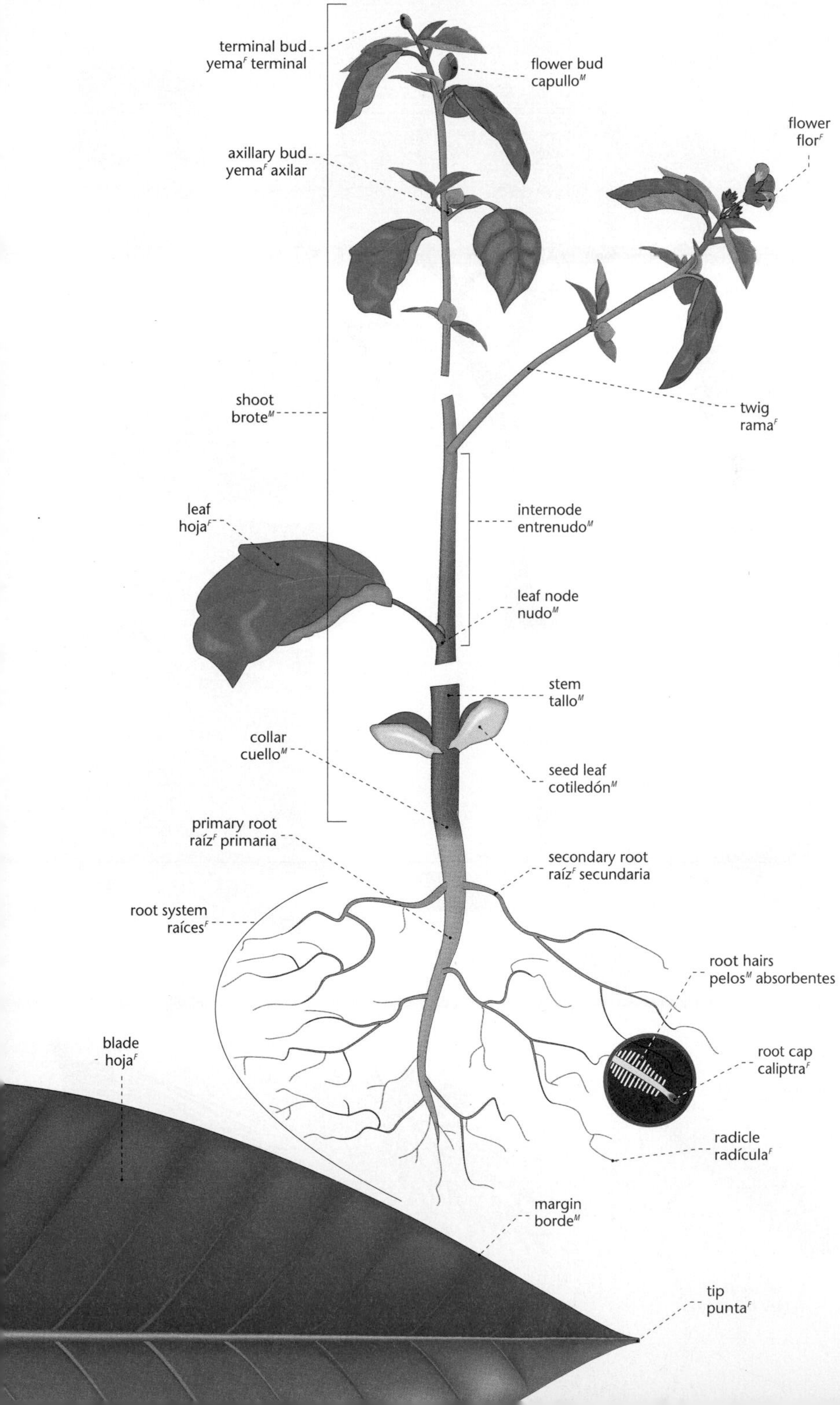

terminal bud
yema^F terminal

flower bud
capullo^M

flower
flor^F

axillary bud
yema^F axilar

shoot
brote^M

twig
rama^F

internode
entrenudo^M

leaf
hoja^F

leaf node
nudo^M

stem
tallo^M

collar
cuello^M

seed leaf
cotiledón^M

primary root
raíz^F primaria

secondary root
raíz^F secundaria

root system
raíces^F

root hairs
pelos^M absorbentes

root cap
caliptra^F

blade
hoja^F

radicle
radícula^F

margin
borde^M

tip
punta^F

57

CONIFER
CONÍFERA^F

cone
piña^F

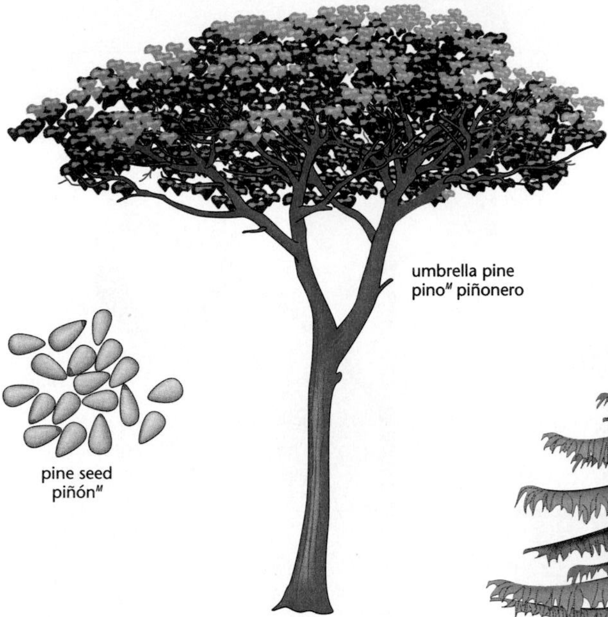

umbrella pine
pino^M piñonero

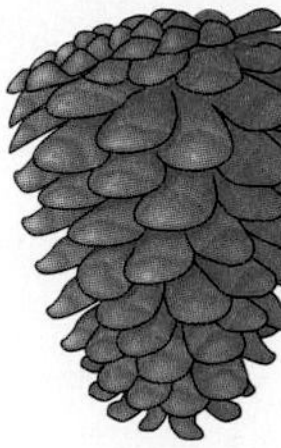

pine seed
piñón^M

BRANCH
RAMA^F

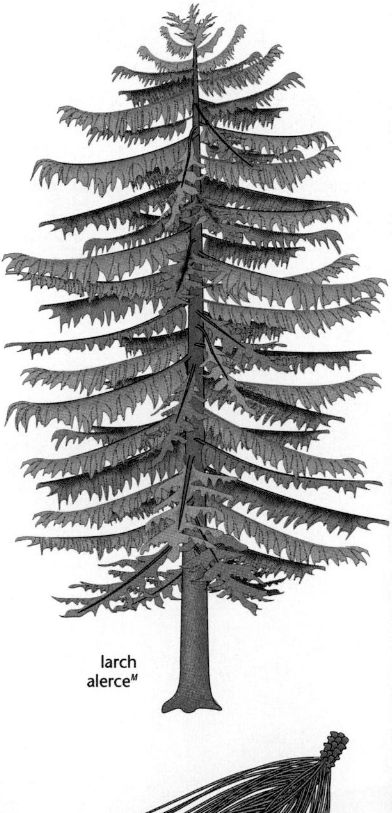

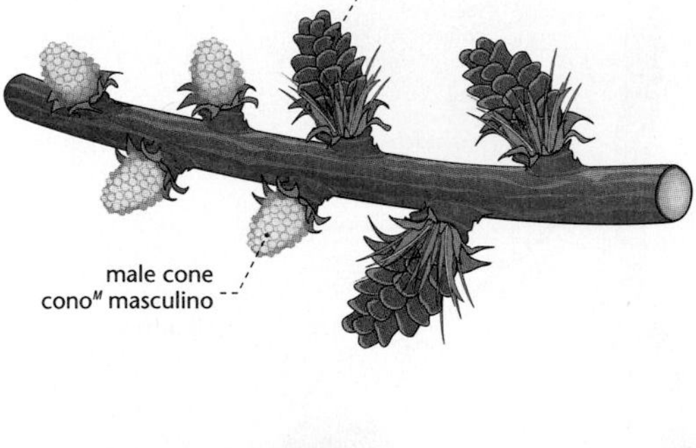

female cone
cono^M femenino

male cone
cono^M masculino

larch
alerce^M

TYPES OF LEAVES
VARIEDADES^F DE AGUJAS^F

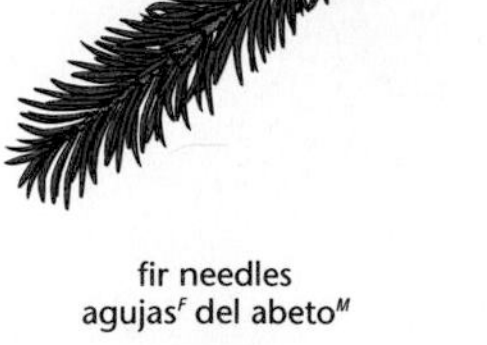

fir needles
agujas^F del abeto^M

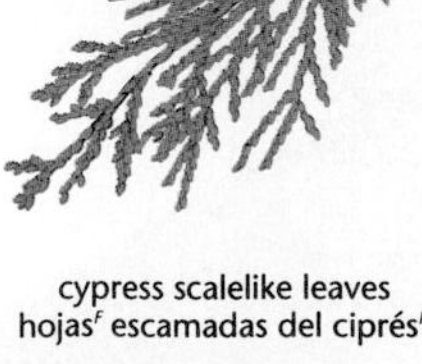

cypress scalelike leaves
hojas^F escamadas del ciprés^M

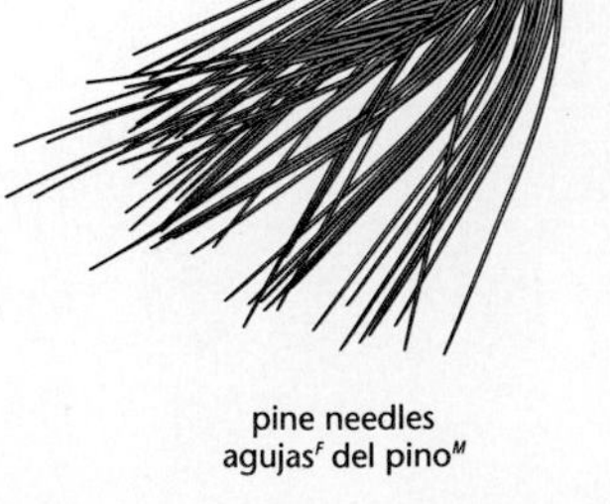

pine needles
agujas^F del pino^M

STRUCTURE OF A TREE
ANATOMÍA*F* DE UN ÁRBOL*M*

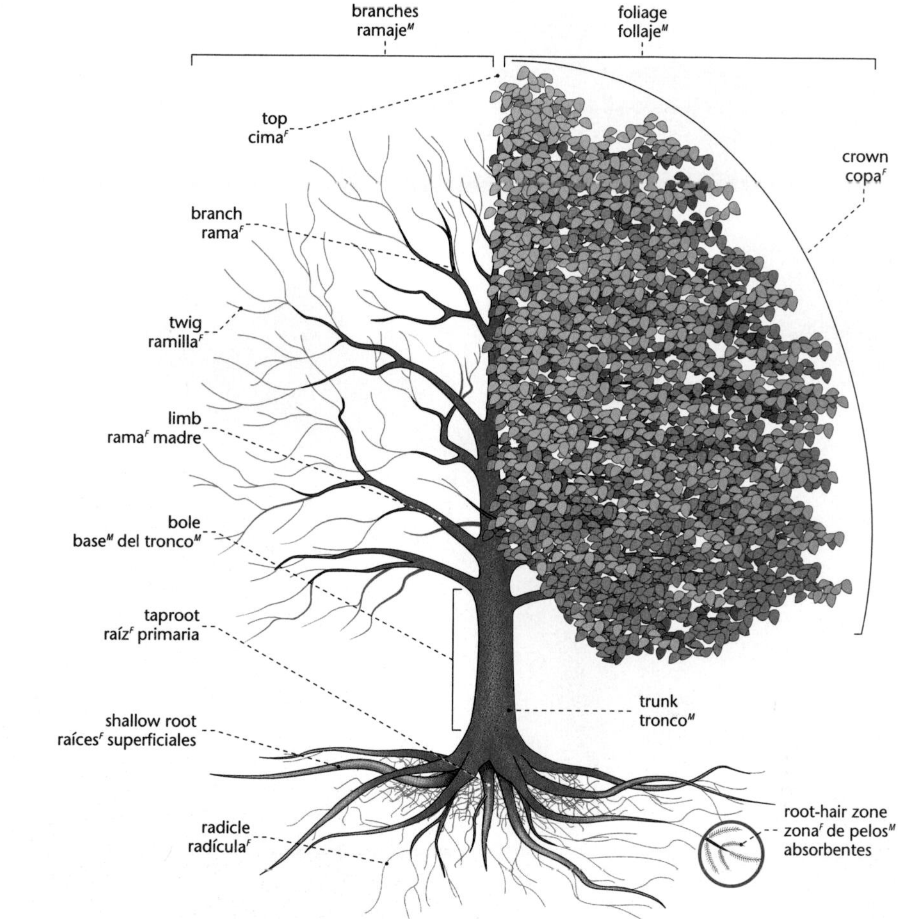

branches
ramaje*M*

foliage
follaje*M*

top
cima*F*

crown
copa*F*

branch
rama*F*

twig
ramilla*F*

limb
rama*F* madre

bole
base*M* del tronco*M*

taproot
raíz*F* primaria

shallow root
raíces*F* superficiales

trunk
tronco*M*

root-hair zone
zona*F* de pelos*M*
absorbentes

radicle
radícula*F*

CROSS SECTION OF A TRUNK
CORTE*M* TRANSVERSAL DE UN TRONCO*M*

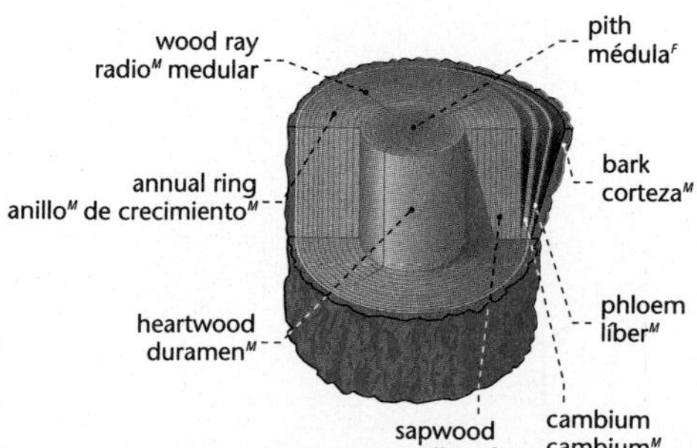

wood ray
radio*M* medular

pith
médula*F*

annual ring
anillo*M* de crecimiento*M*

bark
corteza*M*

heartwood
duramen*M*

phloem
líber*M*

sapwood
albura*F*

cambium
cambium*M*

STUMP
TOCÓN*M*

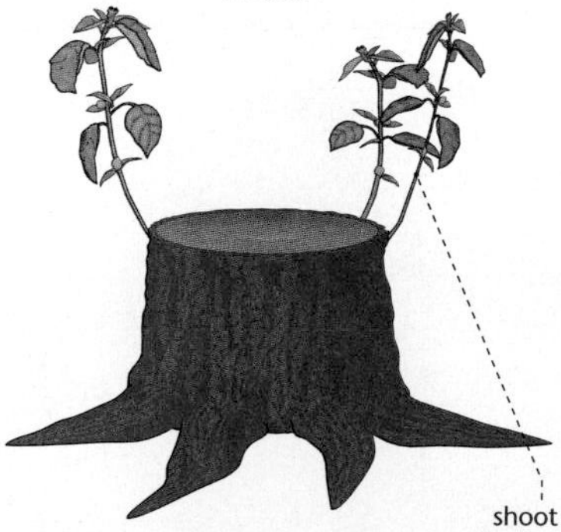

shoot
retoño*M*

STRUCTURE OF A FLOWER
ANATOMÍA^F DE UNA FLOR^F

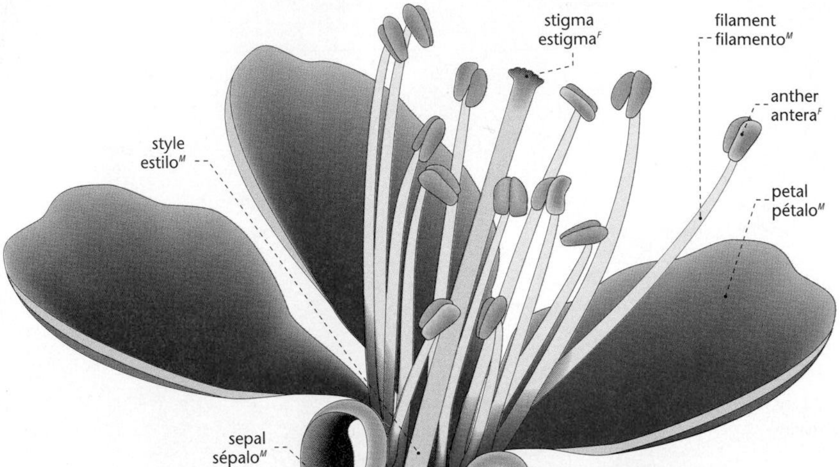

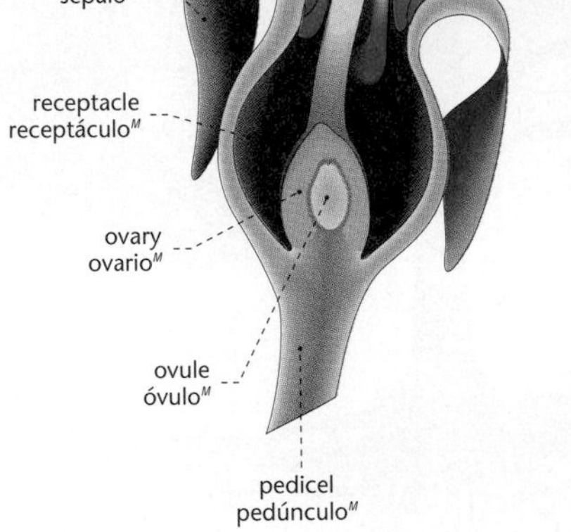

stigma
estigma^F

filament
filamento^M

anther
antera^F

style
estilo^M

petal
pétalo^M

sepal
sépalo^M

receptacle
receptáculo^M

ovary
ovario^M

ovule
óvulo^M

pedicel
pedúnculo^M

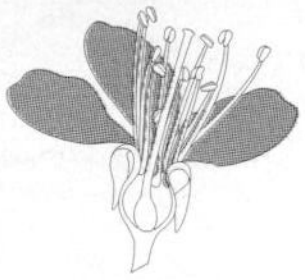

corolla
corola^F

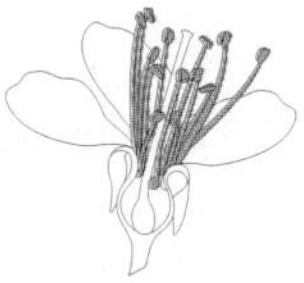

stamen
estambre^M

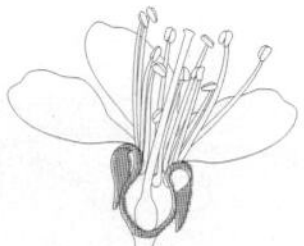

calyx
cáliz^M

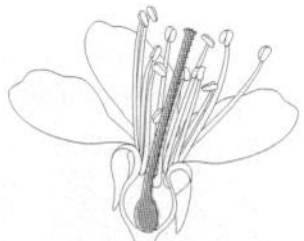

pistil
pistilo^M

TYPES OF INFLORESCENCES
VARIEDADES^F DE INFLORESCENCIAS^F

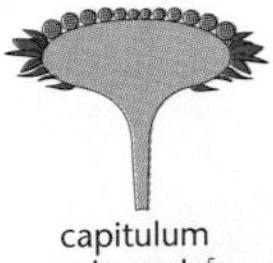

capitulum
cabezuela^F

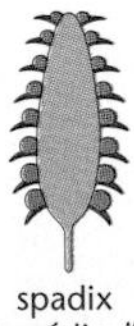

spadix
espádice^M

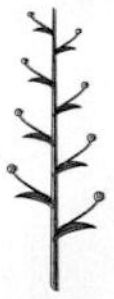

raceme
racimo^M

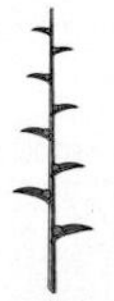

spike
espiga^F

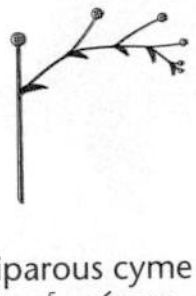

uniparous cyme
cima^F unípara

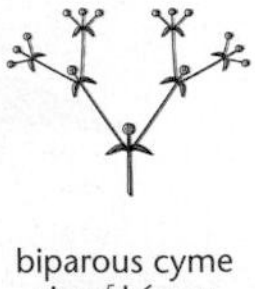

biparous cyme
cima^F bípara

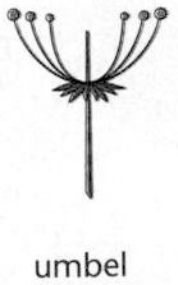

umbel
umbela^F

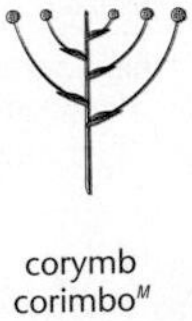

corymb
corimbo^M

GRAPE
UVA^F

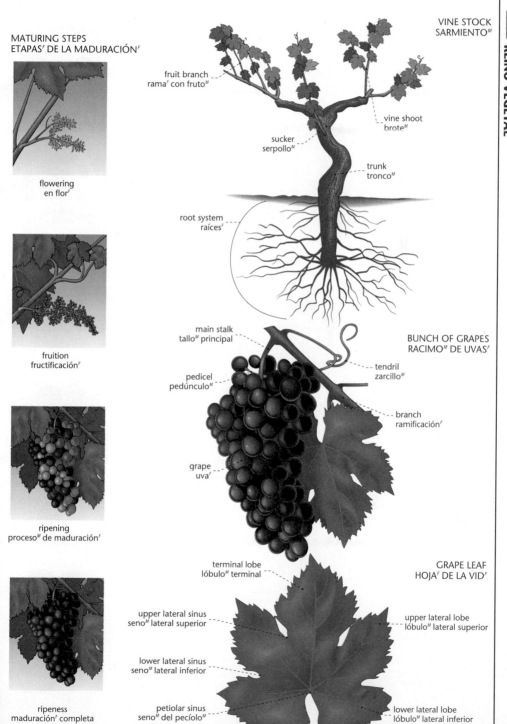

VINE STOCK
SARMIENTO^M

MATURING STEPS
ETAPAS^F DE LA MADURACIÓN^F

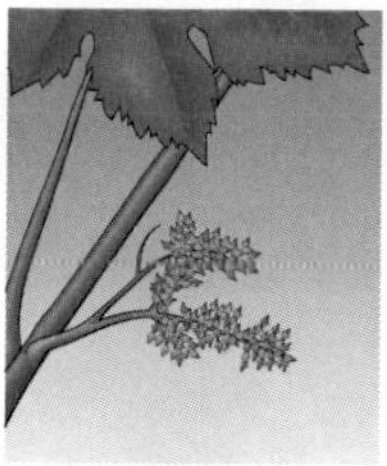

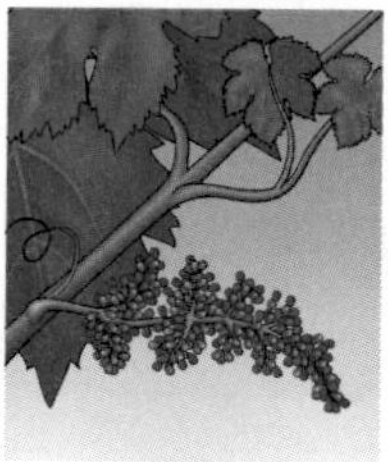

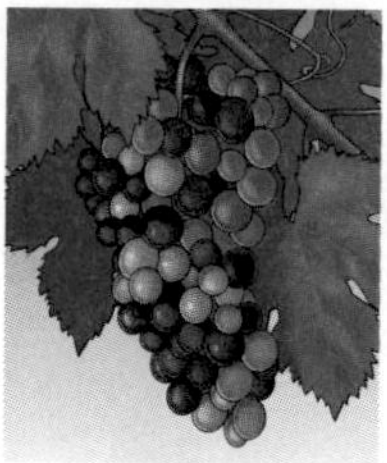

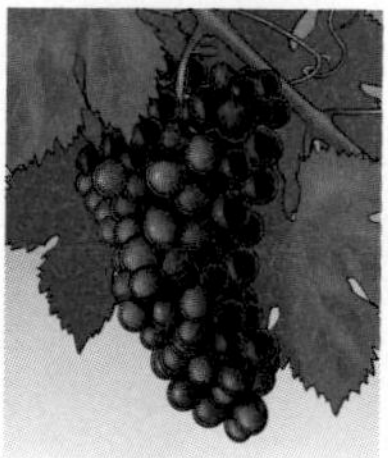

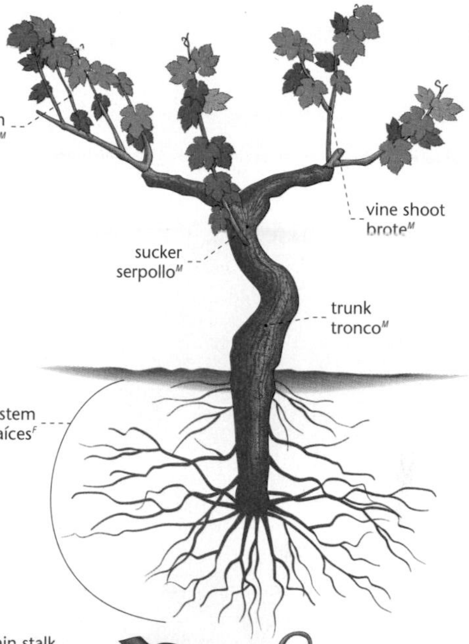

fruit branch
rama^F con fruto^M

vine shoot
brote^M

sucker
serpollo^M

trunk
tronco^M

flowering
en flor^F

root system
raíces^F

fruition
fructificación^F

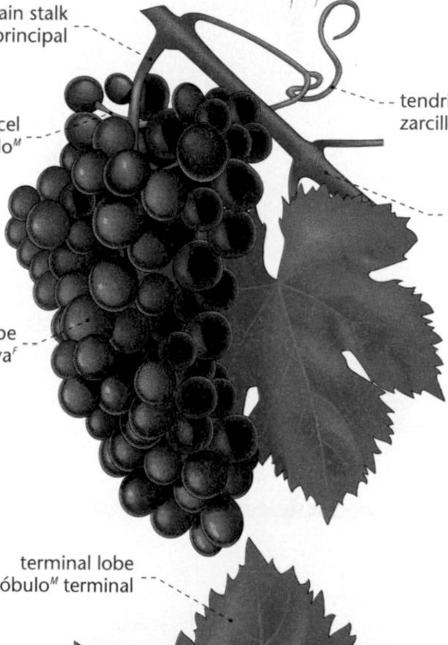

main stalk
tallo^M principal

BUNCH OF GRAPES
RACIMO^M DE UVAS^F

tendril
zarcillo^M

pedicel
pedúnculo^M

branch
ramificación^F

grape
uva^F

ripening
proceso^M de maduración^F

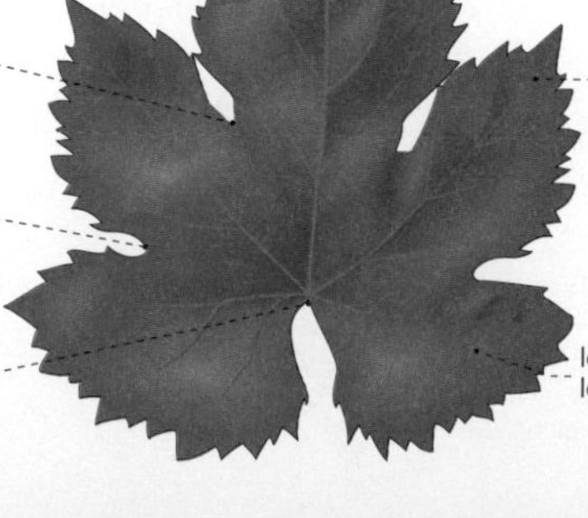

terminal lobe
lóbulo^M terminal

GRAPE LEAF
HOJA^F DE LA VID^F

upper lateral sinus
seno^M lateral superior

upper lateral lobe
lóbulo^M lateral superior

lower lateral sinus
seno^M lateral inferior

petiolar sinus
seno^M del pecíolo^M

lower lateral lobe
lóbulo^M lateral inferior

ripeness
maduración^F completa

VEGETABLE KINGDOM / REINO VEGETAL

SECTION OF A BERRY
CORTE^M DE UNA BAYA^F

MAJOR TYPES OF BERRIES
PRINCIPALES VARIEDADES^F DE BAYAS^F

GRAPE
UVA^F

usual terms
términos familiares

technical terms
términos técnicos

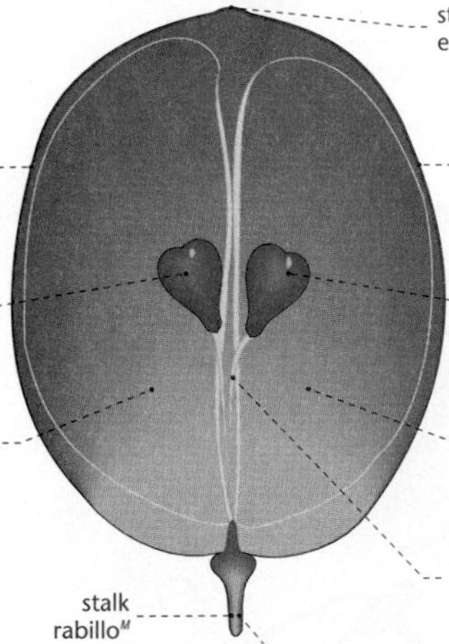

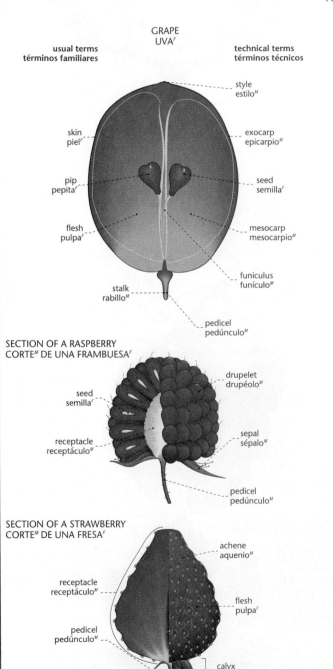

style
estilo^M

skin
piel^F

exocarp
epicarpio^M

pip
pepita^F

seed
semilla^F

flesh
pulpa^F

mesocarp
mesocarpio^M

funiculus
funículo^M

stalk
rabillo^M

pedicel
pedúnculo^M

SECTION OF A RASPBERRY
CORTE^M DE UNA FRAMBUESA^F

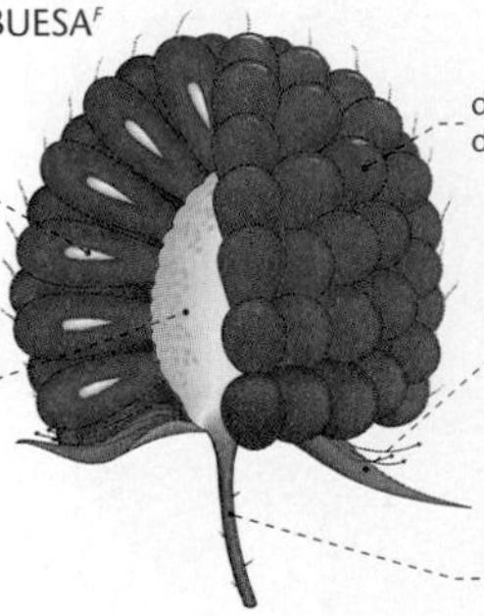

drupelet
drupéolo^M

seed
semilla^F

receptacle
receptáculo^M

sepal
sépalo^M

pedicel
pedúnculo^M

SECTION OF A STRAWBERRY
CORTE^M DE UNA FRESA^F

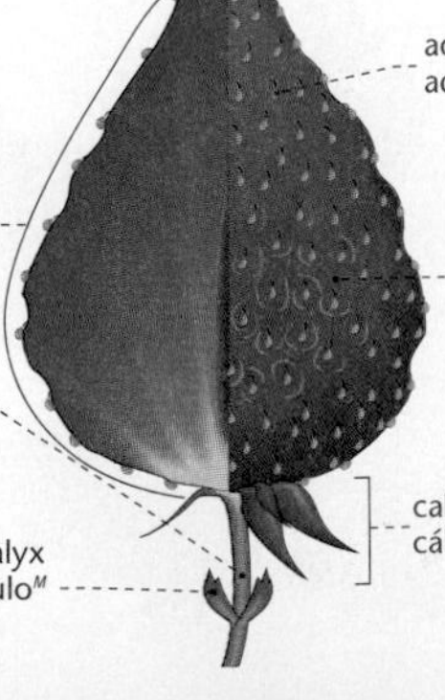

achene
aquenio^M

receptacle
receptáculo^M

flesh
pulpa^F

pedicel
pedúnculo^M

calyx
cáliz^M

epicalyx
calículo^M

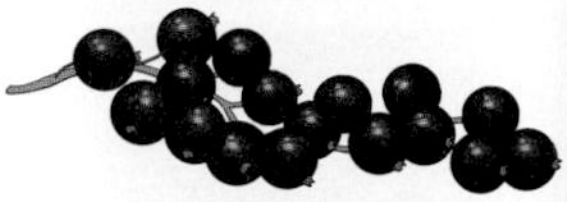

black currant
grosella^F negra

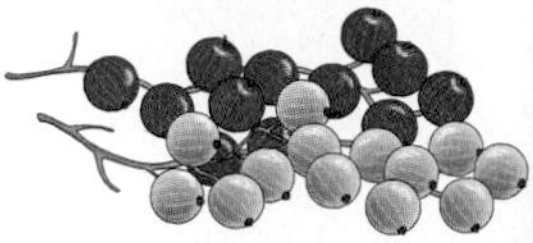

currant
grosella^F

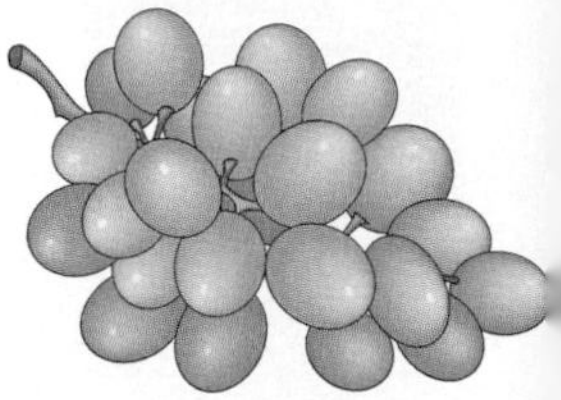

grape
uva^F

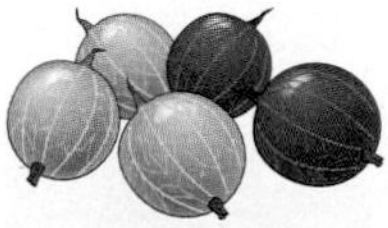

gooseberry
grosella^F espinosa

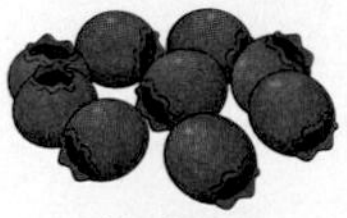

blueberry
arándano^M

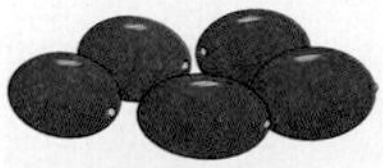

huckleberry
ráspano^M

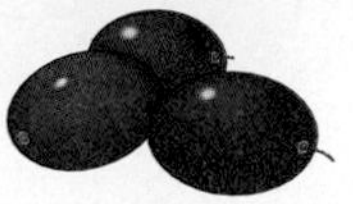

cranberry
arándano^M agrio

STONE FLESHY FRUITS
FRUTOS^M CARNOSOS CON HUESO^M

SECTION OF A STONE FRUIT
CORTE^M DE UN FRUTO^M CARNOSO CON
HUESO^M

PEACH
MELOCOTÓN^M

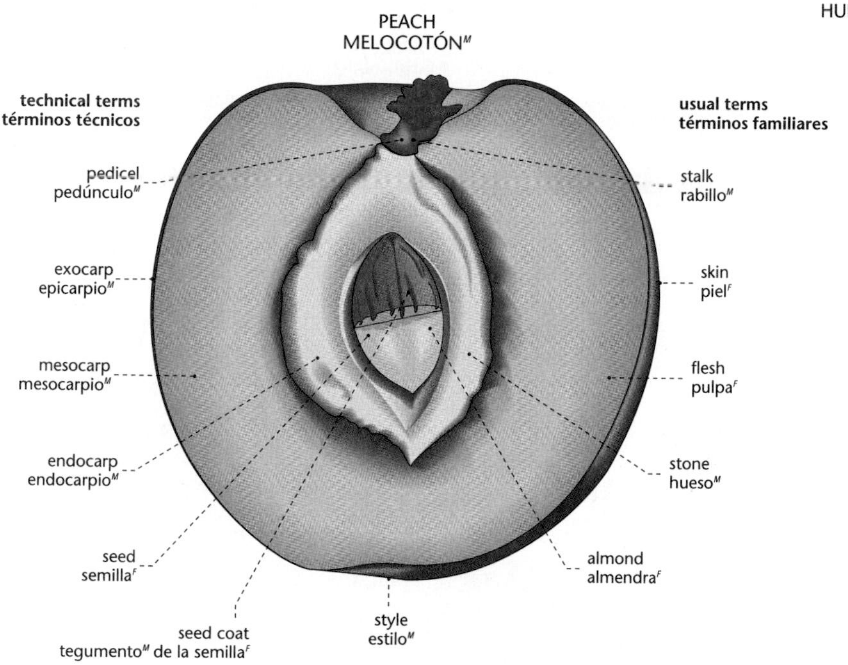

technical terms
términos técnicos

usual terms
términos familiares

pedicel
pedúnculo^M

stalk
rabillo^M

exocarp
epicarpio^M

skin
piel^F

mesocarp
mesocarpio^M

flesh
pulpa^F

endocarp
endocarpio^M

stone
hueso^M

seed
semilla^F

almond
almendra^F

seed coat
tegumento^M de la semilla^F

style
estilo^M

MAJOR TYPES OF STONE FRUITS
PRINCIPALES VARIEDADES^F DE FRUTOS^M CARNOSOS CON HUESO^M

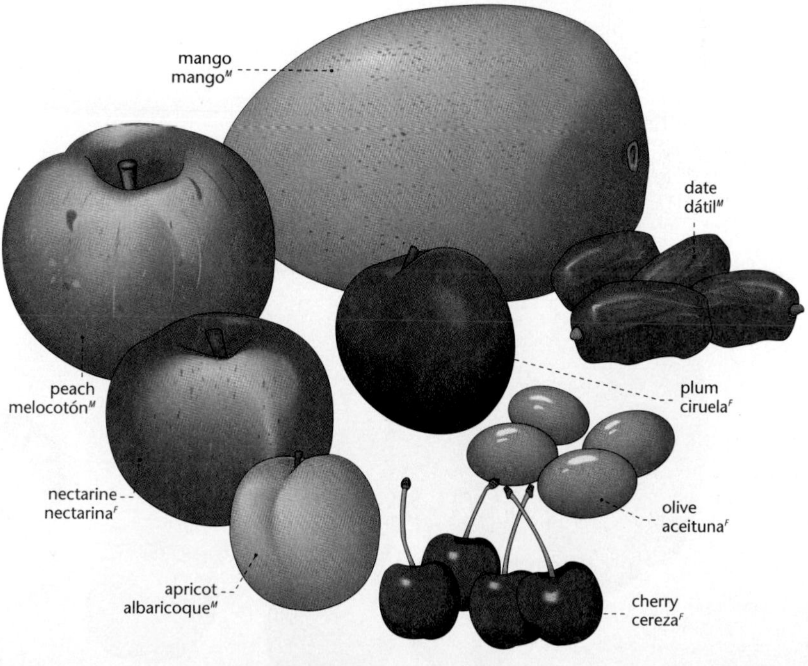

mango
mango^M

date
dátil^M

peach
melocotón^M

plum
ciruela^F

nectarine
nectarina^F

olive
aceituna^F

apricot
albaricoque^M

cherry
cereza^F

SECTION OF A POME FRUIT
CORTE^M DE UN FRUTO^M CARNOSO CON SEMILLAS^F

APPLE
MANZANA^F

technical terms
términos técnicos

usual terms
términos familiares

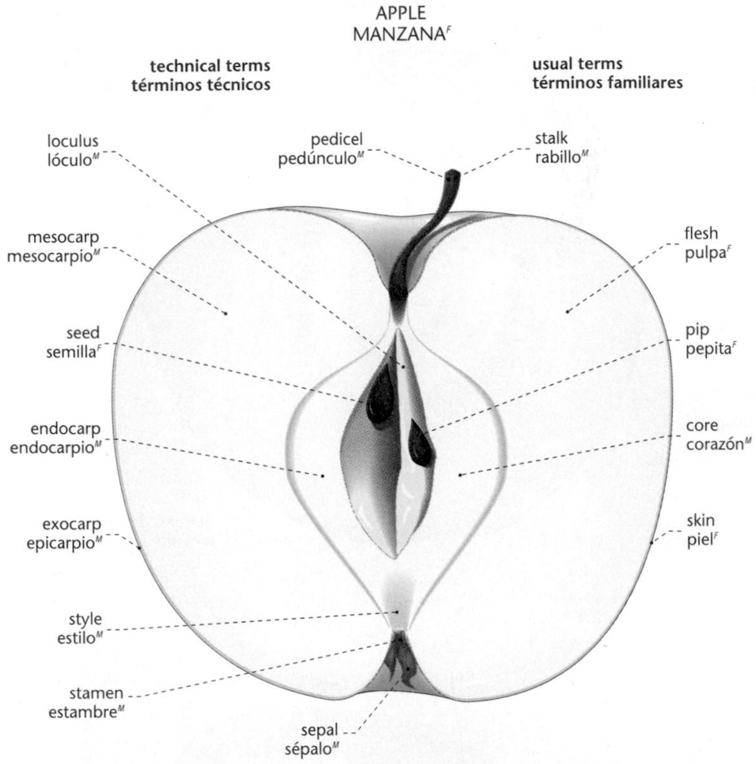

loculus
lóculo^M

pedicel
pedúnculo^M

stalk
rabillo^M

mesocarp
mesocarpio^M

flesh
pulpa^F

seed
semilla^F

pip
pepita^F

endocarp
endocarpio^M

core
corazón^M

exocarp
epicarpio^M

skin
piel^F

style
estilo^M

stamen
estambre^M

sepal
sépalo^M

MAJOR TYPES OF POME FRUITS
PRINCIPALES VARIEDADES^F DE FRUTOS^M
CARNOSOS CON SEMILLAS^F

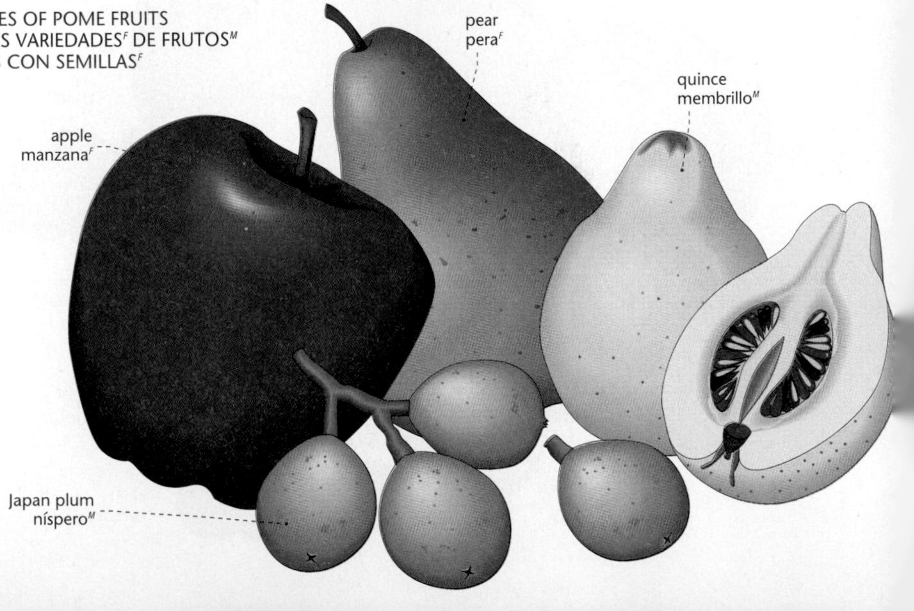

pear
pera^F

quince
membrillo^M

apple
manzana^F

Japan plum
níspero^M

FLESHY FRUITS: CITRUS FRUITS
FRUTOS^M CARNOSOS: CÍTRICOS^M

SECTION OF A CITRUS FRUIT
CORTE^M DE UN CÍTRICO^M

ORANGE
NARANJA^F

technical terms
términos técnicos

usual terms
términos familiares

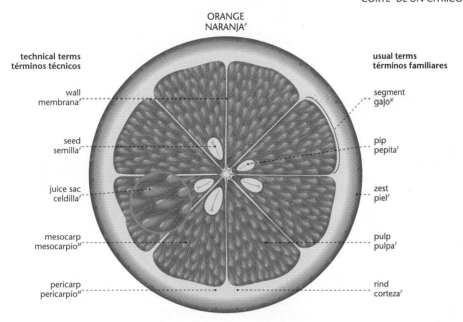

wall
membrana^F

seed
semilla^F

juice sac
celdilla^F

mesocarp
mesocarpio^M

pericarp
pericarpio^M

segment
gajo^M

pip
pepita^F

zest
piel^F

pulp
pulpa^F

rind
corteza^F

MAJOR TYPES OF CITRUS FRUITS
PRINCIPALES VARIEDADES^F DE CÍTRICOS^M

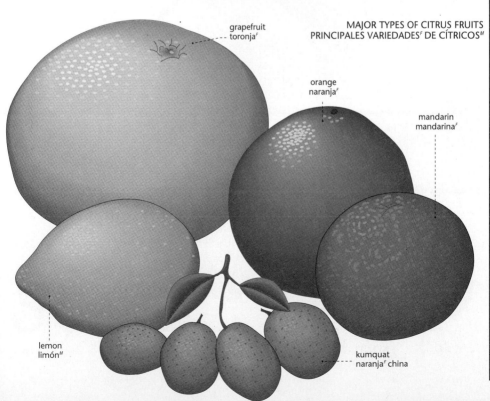

grapefruit
toronja^F

orange
naranja^F

mandarin
mandarina^F

lemon
limón^M

kumquat
naranja^F china

VEGETABLE KINGDOM
REINO VEGETAL

SECTION OF A HAZELNUT
CORTE^M DE UNA AVELLANA^F

SECTION OF A WALNUT
CORTE^M DE UNA NUEZ^F

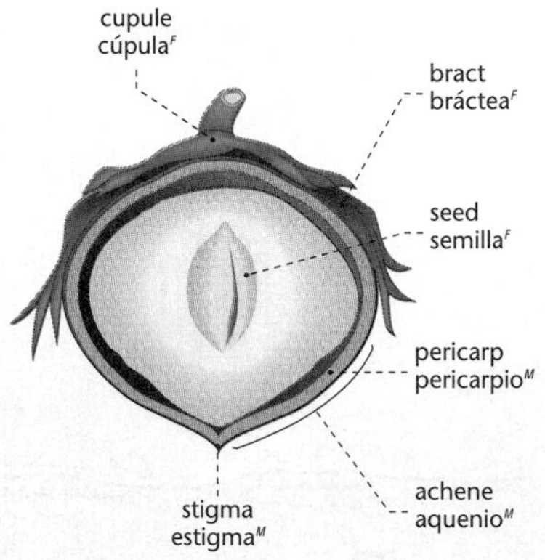

cupule
cúpula^F

bract
bráctea^F

seed
semilla^F

pericarp
pericarpio^M

stigma
estigma^M

achene
aquenio^M

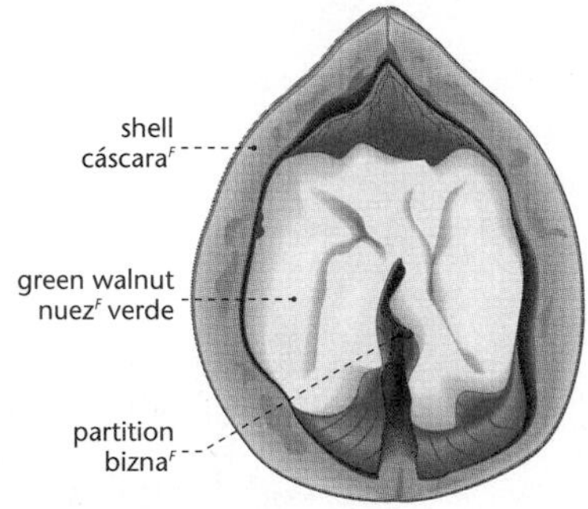

shell
cáscara^F

green walnut
nuez^F verde

partition
bizna^F

HUSK
CÁSCARA^F

MAJOR TYPES OF NUTS
PRINCIPALES VARIEDADES^F DE FRUTOS^M SECOS

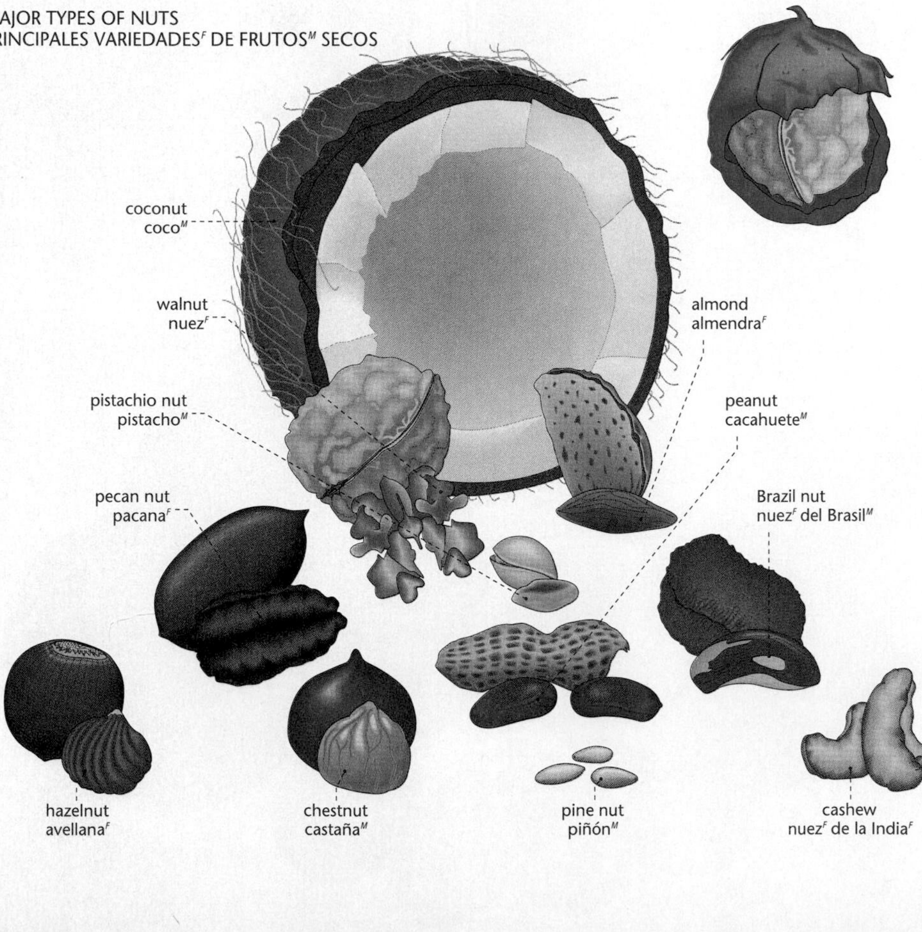

coconut
coco^M

walnut
nuez^F

pistachio nut
pistacho^M

pecan nut
pacana^F

hazelnut
avellana^F

chestnut
castaña^M

pine nut
piñón^M

almond
almendra^F

peanut
cacahuete^M

Brazil nut
nuez^F del Brasil^M

cashew
nuez^F de la India^F

SECTION OF A FOLLICLE
CORTE^M DE UN FOLÍCULO^M

star anise
anís^M estrellado

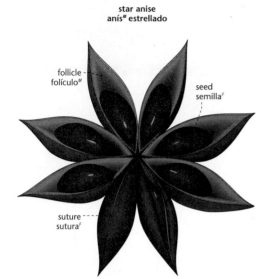

follicle
folículo^M

seed
semilla^F

suture
sutura^F

SECTION OF A SILIQUE
CORTE^M DE UNA SILICUA^F

mustard
mostaza^F

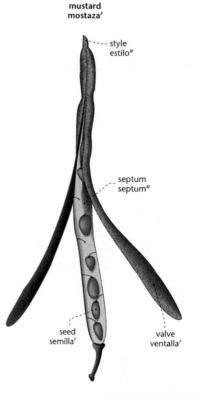

style
estilo^M

septum
septum^M

seed
semilla^F

valve
ventalla^F

SECTION OF A LEGUME
CORTE^M DE UNA LEGUMBRE^F

pea
guisante^M

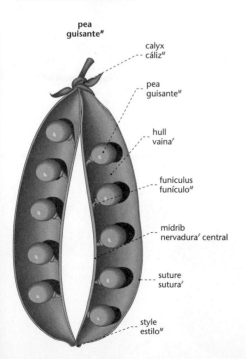

calyx
cáliz^M

pea
guisante^M

hull
vaina^F

funiculus
funículo^M

midrib
nervadura^F central

suture
sutura^F

style
estilo^M

SECTION OF A CAPSULE
CORTE^M DE UNA CÁPSULA^F

poppy
amapola^F

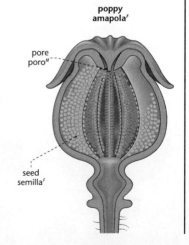

pore
poro^M

seed
semilla^F

67

VEGETABLE KINGDOM
REINO VEGETAL

MAJOR TYPES OF TROPICAL FRUITS
PRINCIPALES VARIEDADES^F DE FRUTAS^F TROPICALES

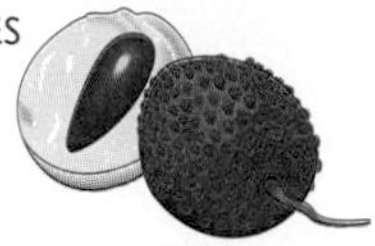

litchi
litchi^M

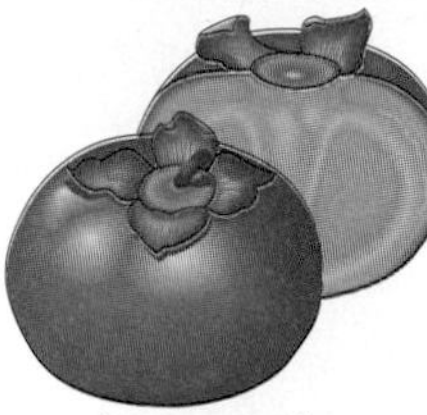

Japanese persimmon
caqui^M

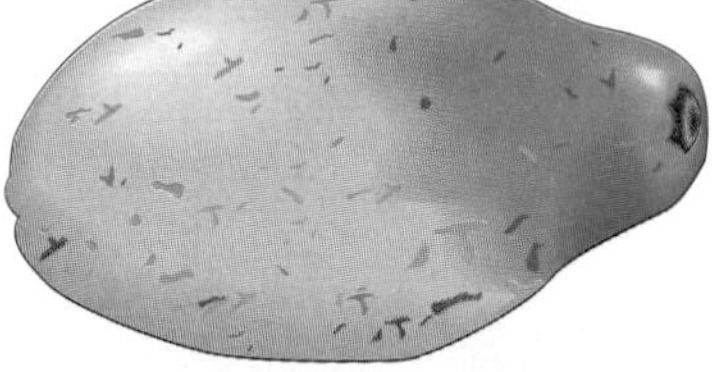

papaya
papaya^F

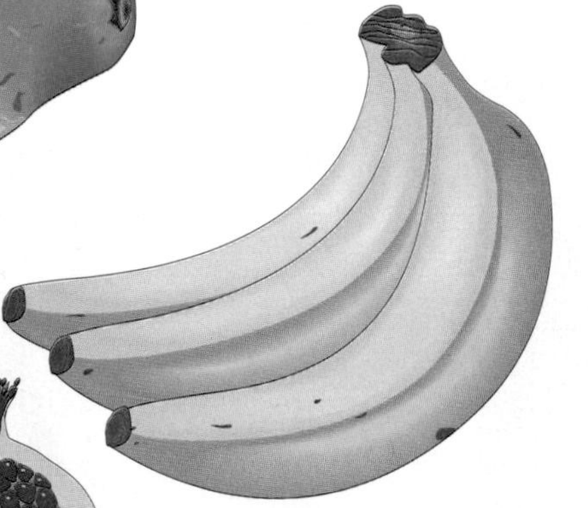

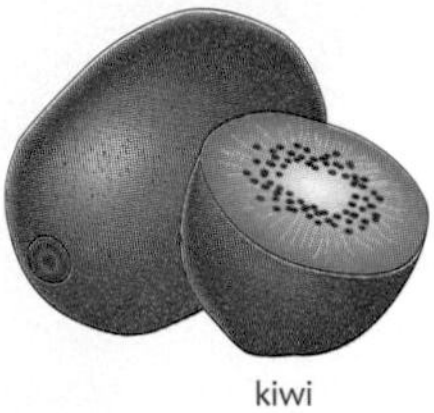

kiwi
kiwi^M

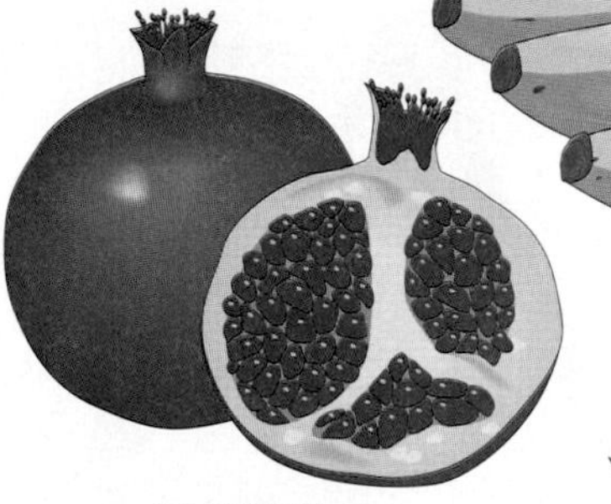

pomegranate
granada^F

banana
plátano^M

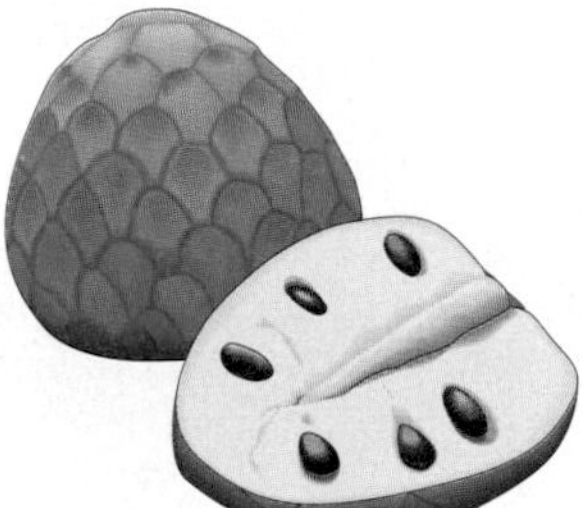

cherimoya
chirimoya^F

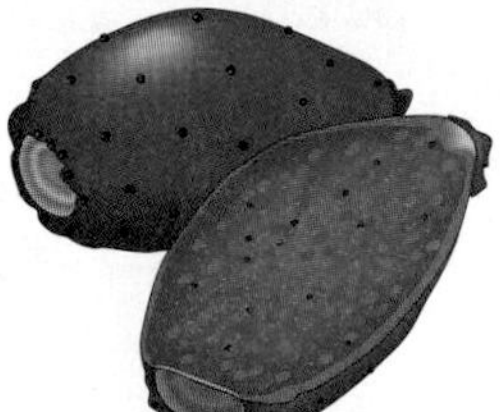

Indian fig
higo chumbo^M

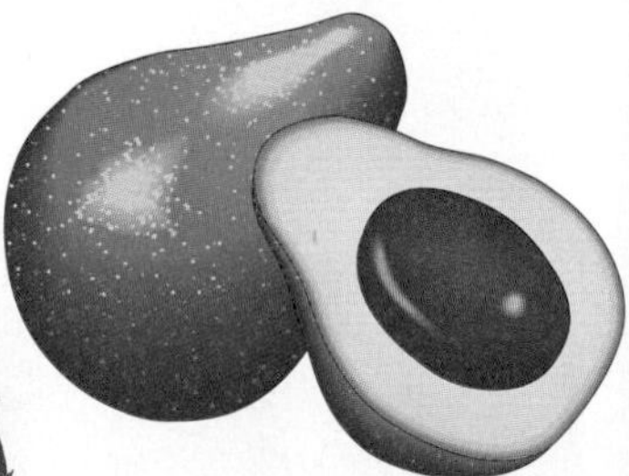

avocado
aguacate^M

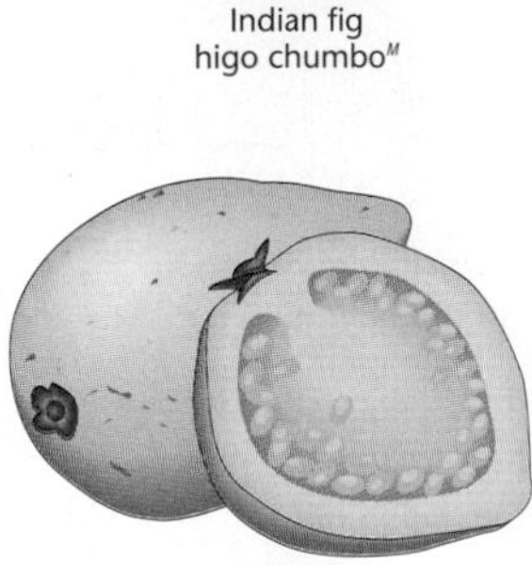

guava
guayaba^F

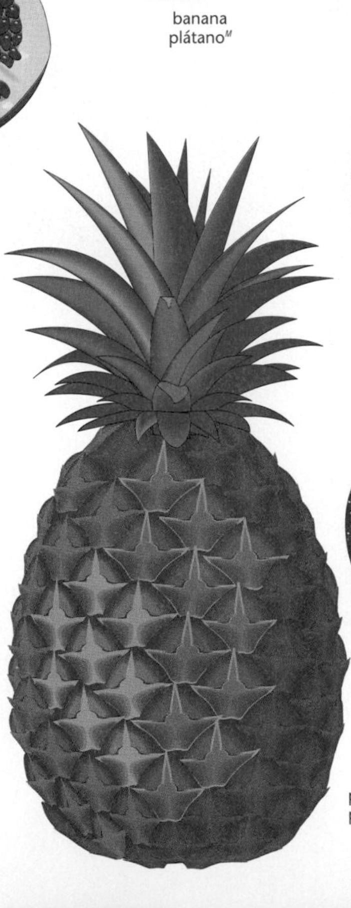

pineapple
piña^F

VEGETABLES
HORTALIZAS^F

FRUIT VEGETABLES
FRUTOS^M

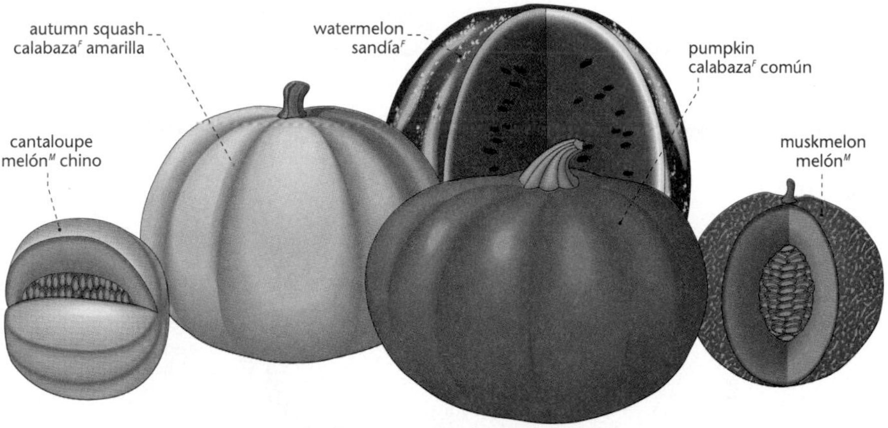

autumn squash
calabaza^F amarilla

watermelon
sandía^F

pumpkin
calabaza^F común

cantaloupe
melón^M chino

muskmelon
melón^M

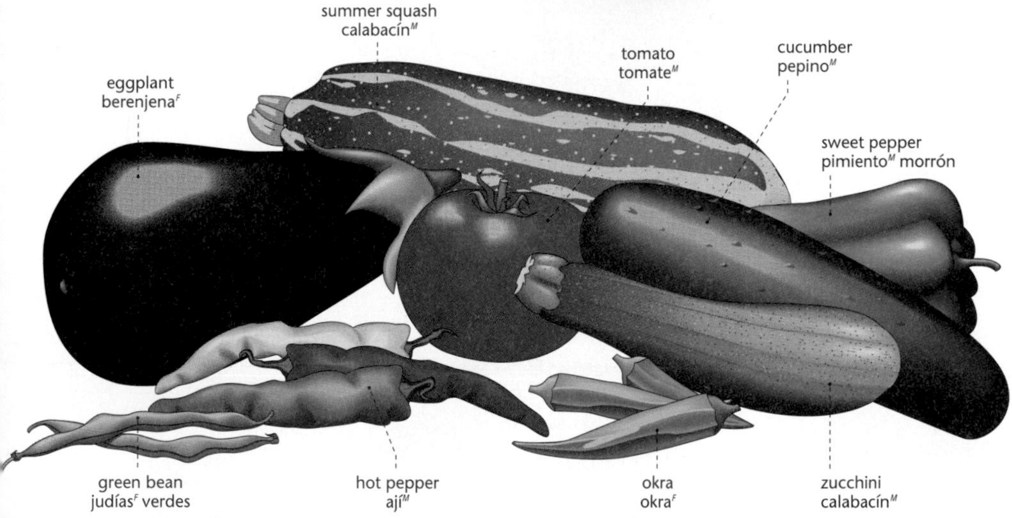

summer squash
calabacín^M

tomato
tomate^M

cucumber
pepino^M

eggplant
berenjena^F

sweet pepper
pimiento^M morrón

green bean
judías^F verdes

hot pepper
ají^M

okra
okra^F

zucchini
calabacín^M

INFLORESCENT VEGETABLES
INFLORESCENCIAS^F

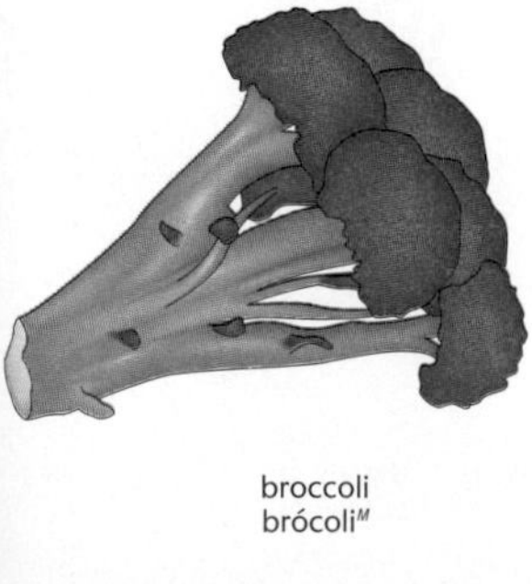

broccoli
brócoli^M

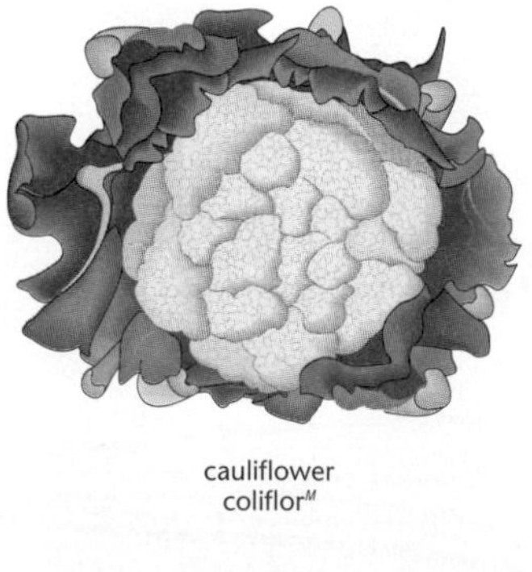

cauliflower
coliflor^M

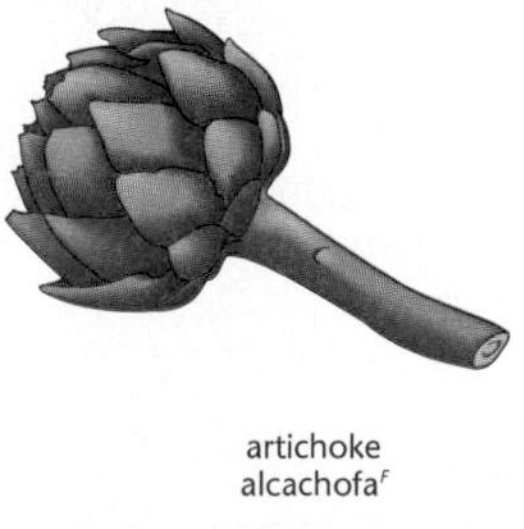

artichoke
alcachofa^F

SECTION OF A BULB
CORTE*M* DE UN BULBO*M*

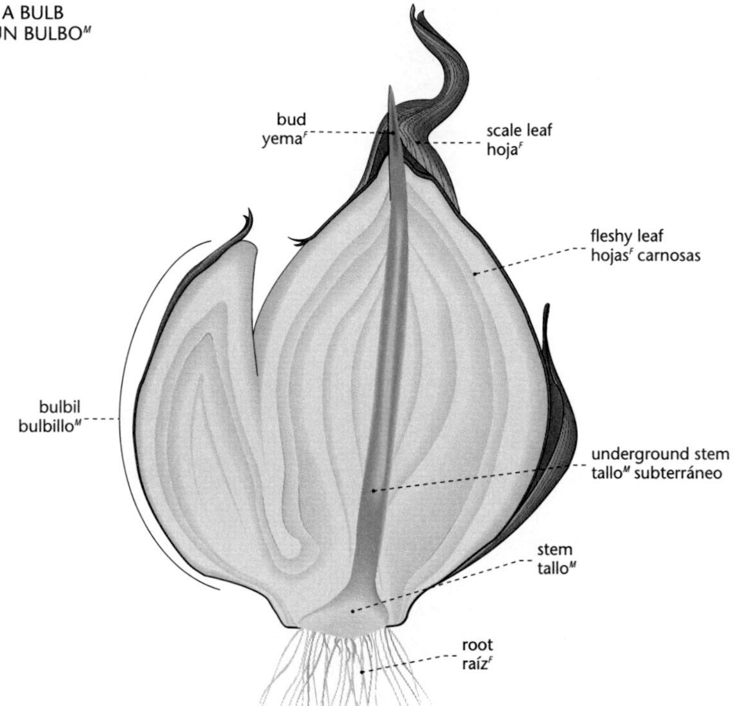

bud
yema*F*

scale leaf
hoja*F*

fleshy leaf
hojas*F* carnosas

bulbil
bulbillo*M*

underground stem
tallo*M* subterráneo

stem
tallo*M*

root
raíz*F*

BULB VEGETABLES
BULBOS*M*

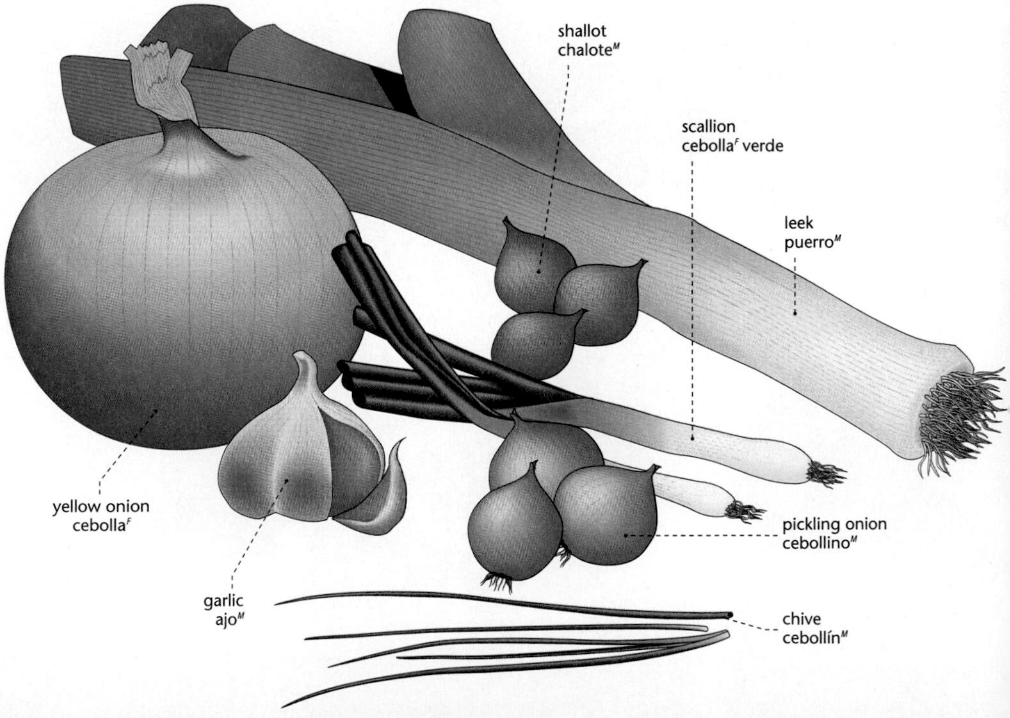

shallot
chalote*M*

scallion
cebolla*F* verde

leek
puerro*M*

yellow onion
cebolla*F*

garlic
ajo*M*

pickling onion
cebollino*M*

chive
cebollín*M*

VEGETABLES
HORTALIZAS[F]

TUBER VEGETABLES
TUBÉRCULOS[M]

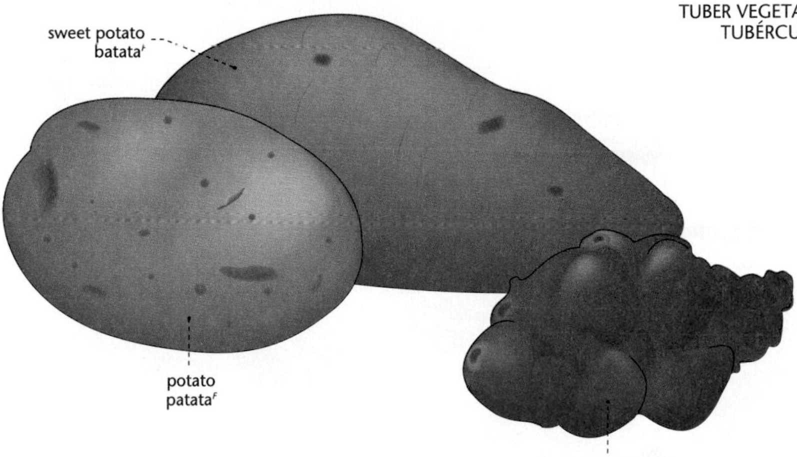

sweet potato
batata[F]

potato
patata[F]

Jerusalem artichoke
cotufa[F]

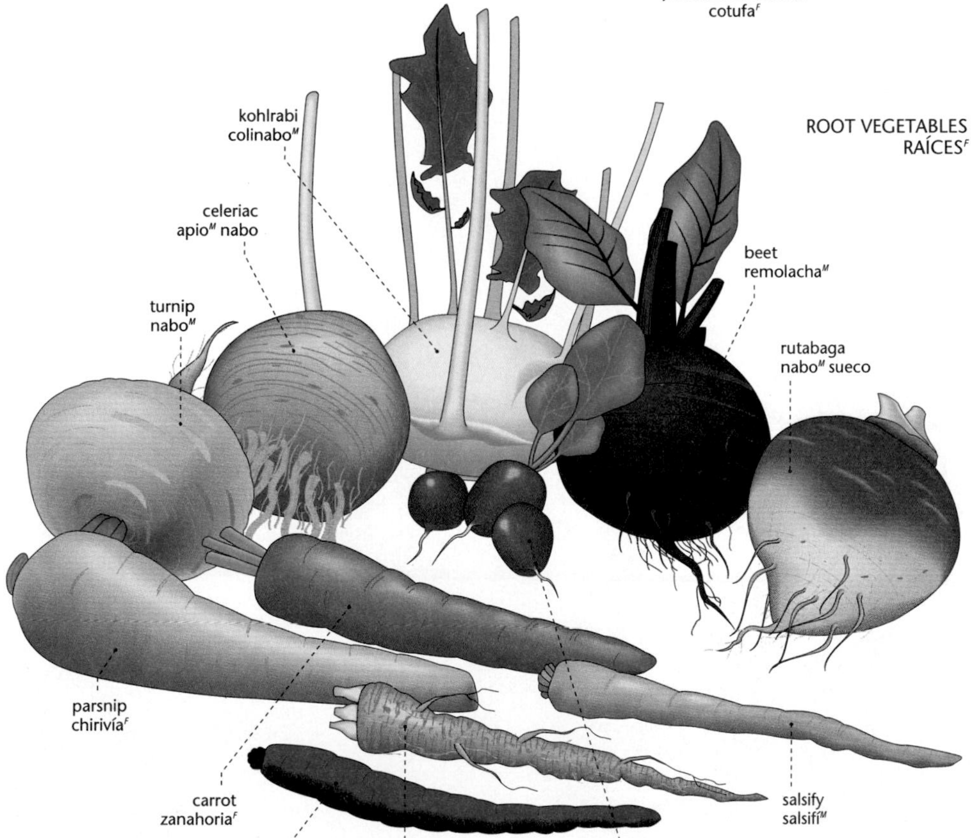

kohlrabi
colinabo[M]

ROOT VEGETABLES
RAÍCES[F]

celeriac
apio[M] nabo

beet
remolacha[M]

turnip
nabo[M]

rutabaga
nabo[M] sueco

parsnip
chirivía[F]

carrot
zanahoria[F]

black salsify
escorzonera[F]

horseradish
rábano[M] blanco

radish
rábano[M]

salsify
salsifí[M]

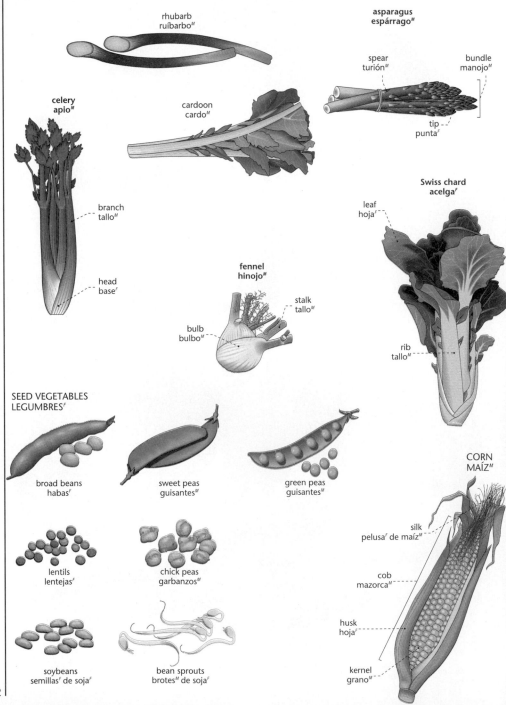

STALK VEGETABLES
TALLOS^M

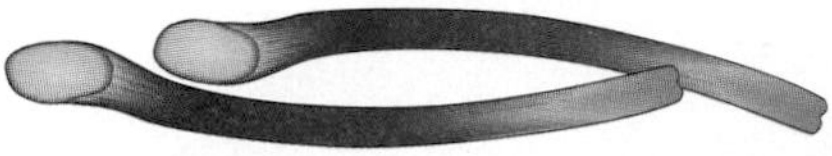

rhubarb
ruíbarbo^M

asparagus
espárrago^M

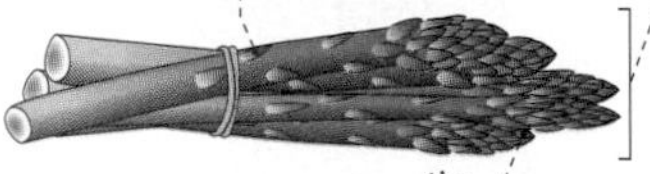

spear
turión^M

bundle
manojo^M

tip
punta^F

celery
apio^M

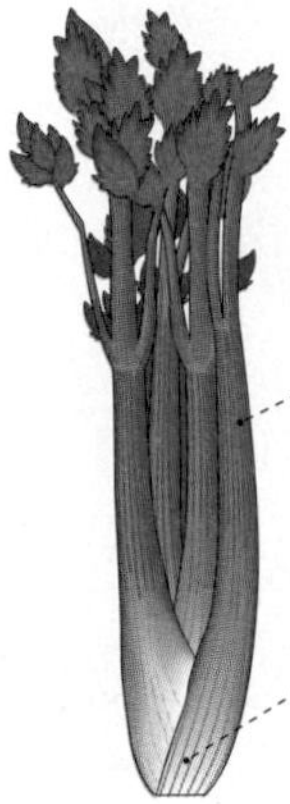

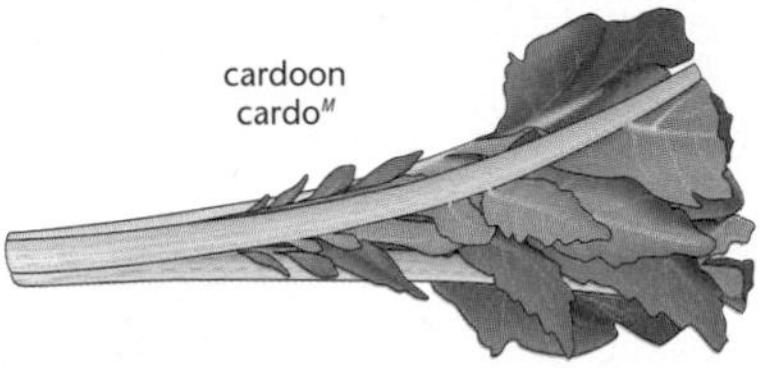

cardoon
cardo^M

Swiss chard
acelga^F

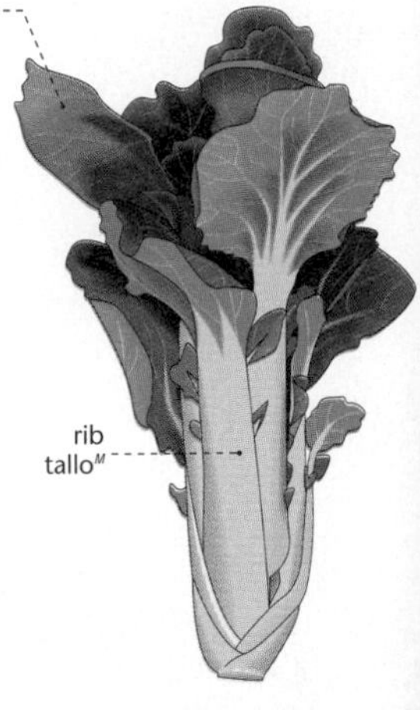

leaf
hoja^F

branch
tallo^M

head
base^F

fennel
hinojo^M

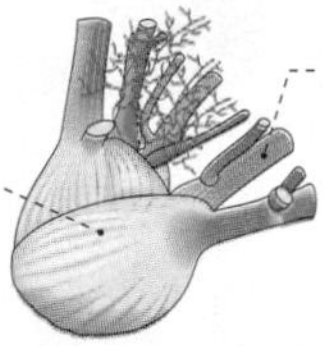

stalk
tallo^M

bulb
bulbo^M

rib
tallo^M

SEED VEGETABLES
LEGUMBRES^F

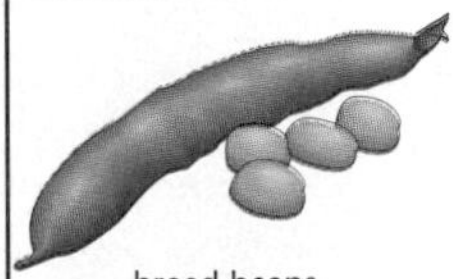

broad beans
habas^F

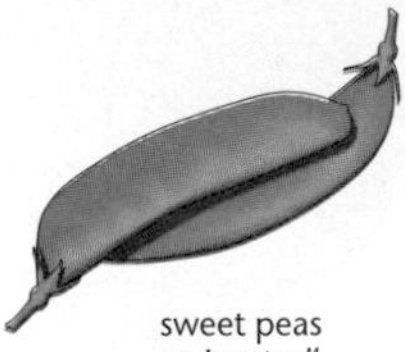

sweet peas
guisantes^M

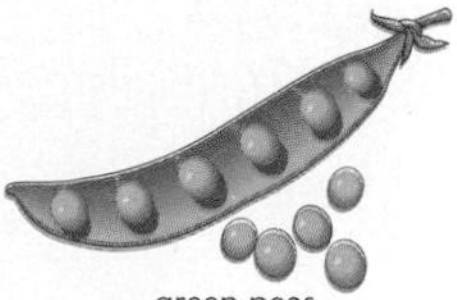

green peas
guisantes^M

CORN
MAÍZ^M

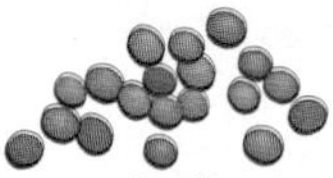

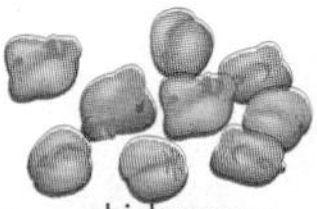

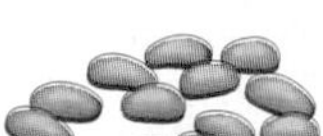

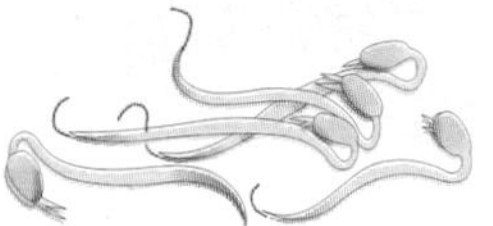

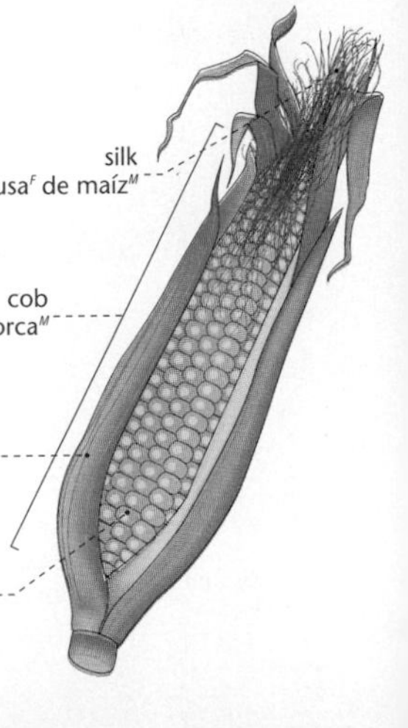

silk
pelusa^F de maíz^M

lentils
lentejas^F

chick peas
garbanzos^M

cob
mazorca^M

husk
hoja^F

soybeans
semillas^F de soja^F

bean sprouts
brotes^M de soja^F

kernel
grano^M

72

LEAF VEGETABLES
VERDURAS^F DE HOJAS^F

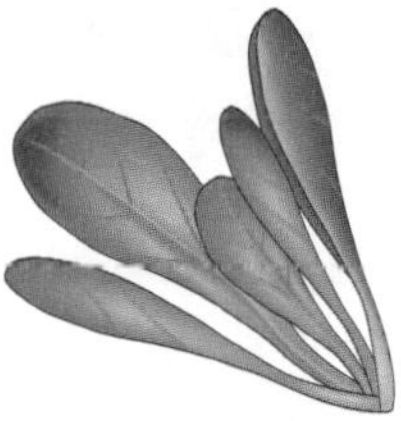

corn salad
colleja^F

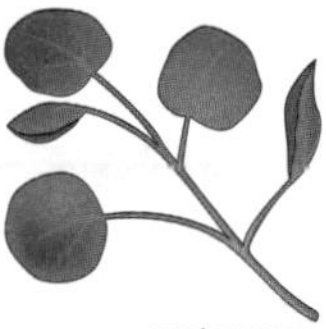

watercress
berro^M

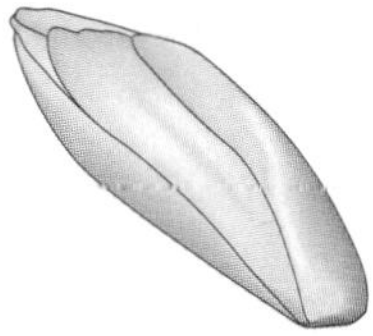

chicory
achicoria^F

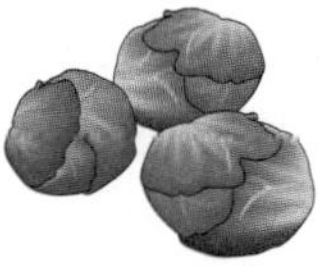

Brussels sprouts
coles^F de Bruselas

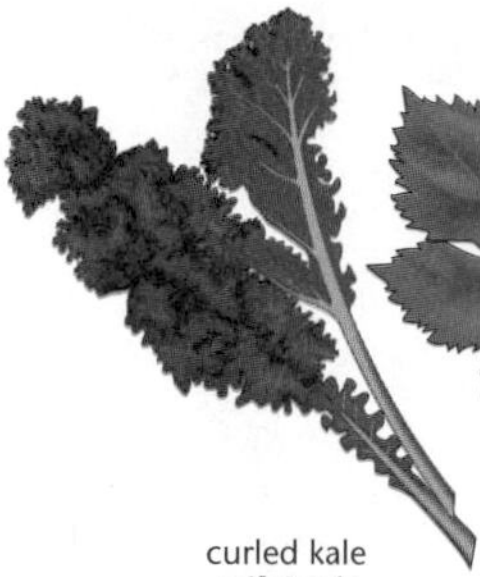

curled kale
col^F rizada

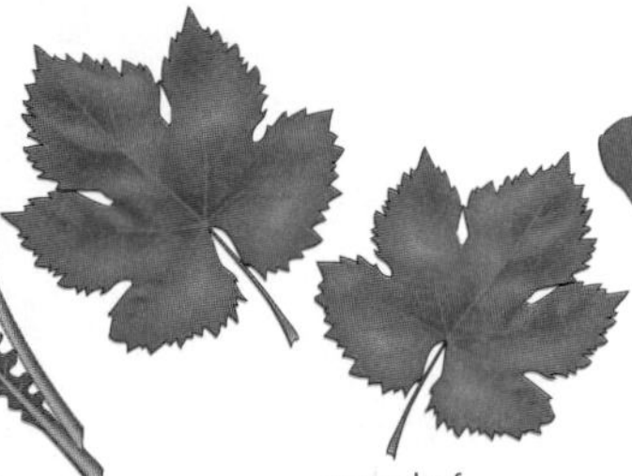

grape leaf
hoja^F de parra^F

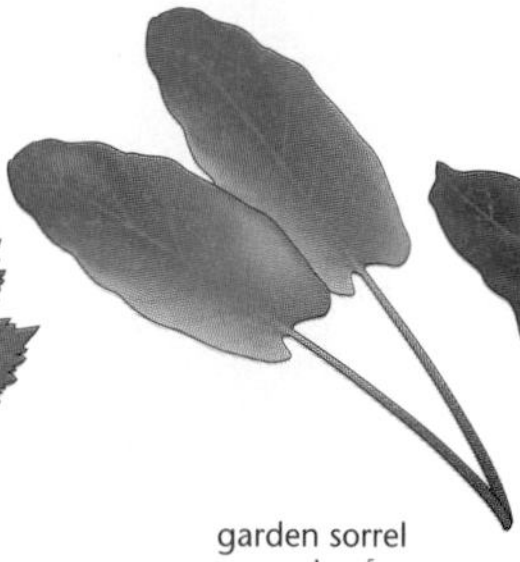

garden sorrel
acedera^F

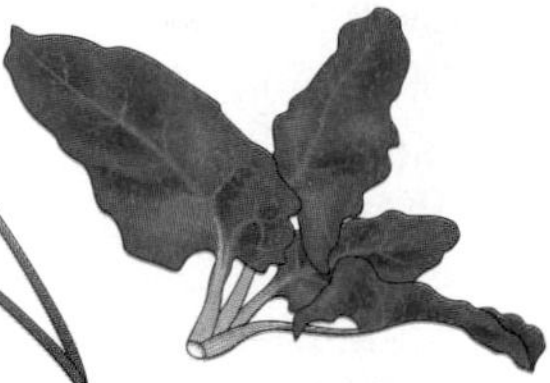

spinach
espinaca^F

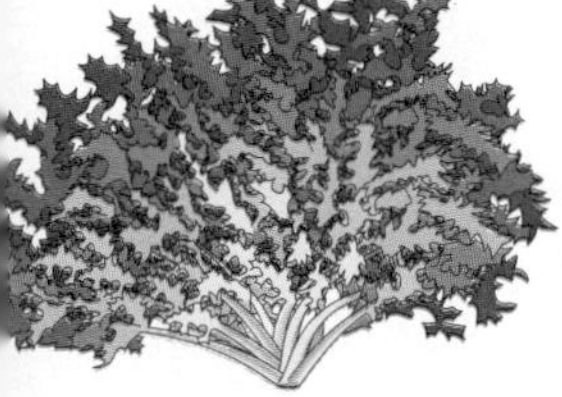

curled endive
escarola^F rizada

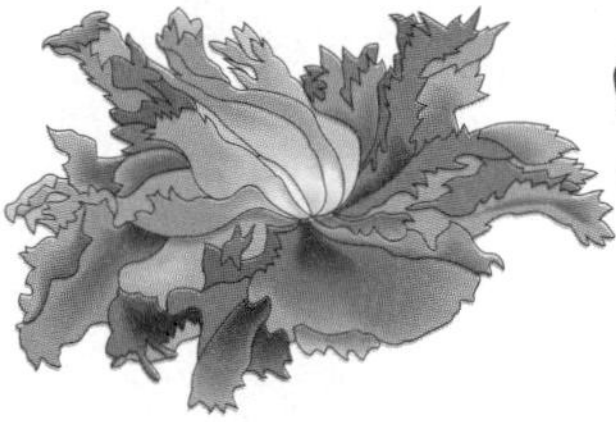

broad-leaved endive
escarola^F

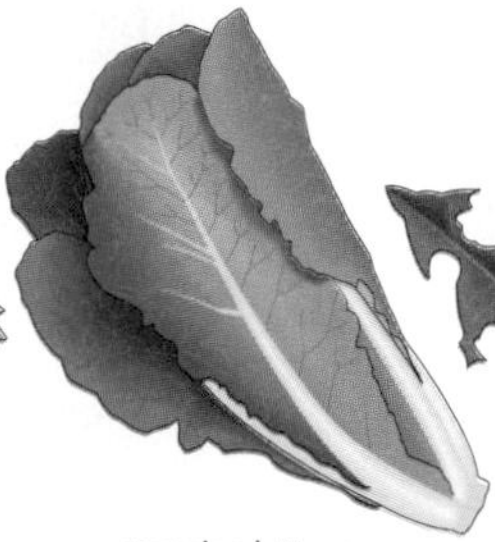

romaine lettuce
lechuga^F romana

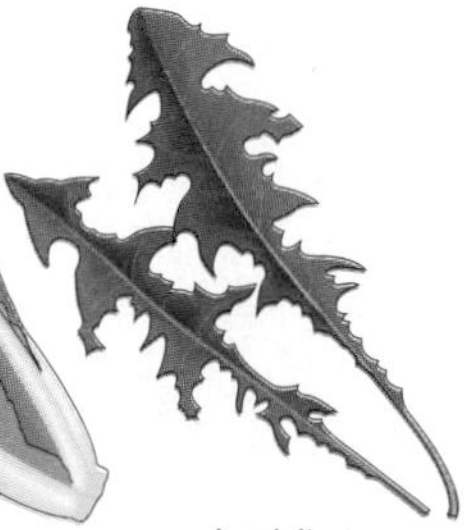

dandelion
diente^M de león^M

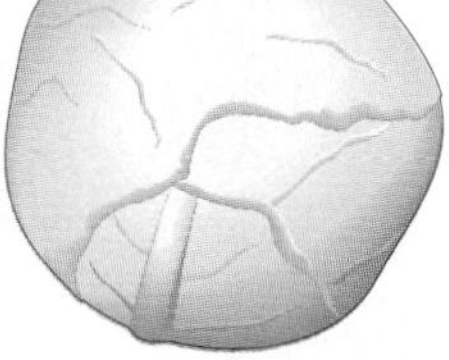

white cabbage
repollo^M

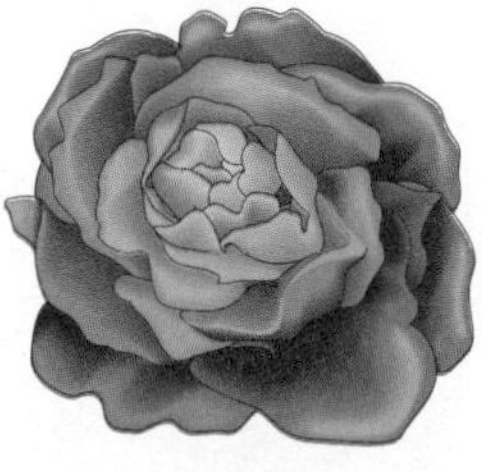

cabbage lettuce
lechuga^F francesa

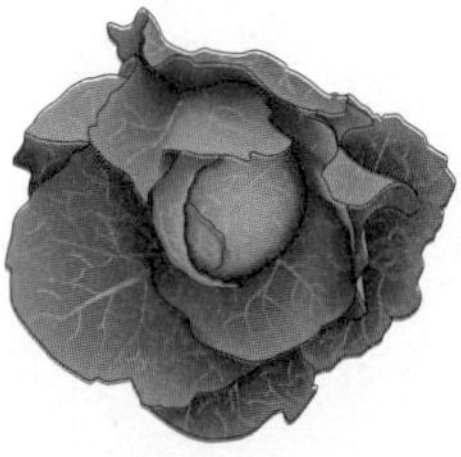

green cabbage
repollo^M verde

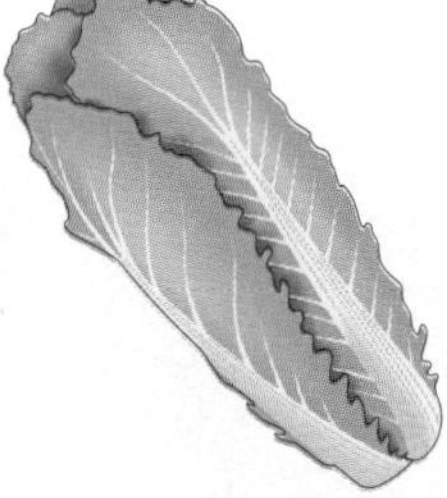

Chinese cabbage
col^F de China^F

HERBS
HIERBAS^F AROMÁTICAS

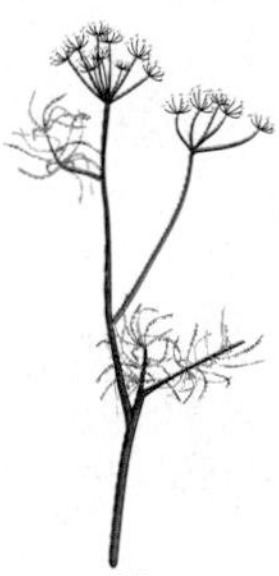

dill
eneldo^M

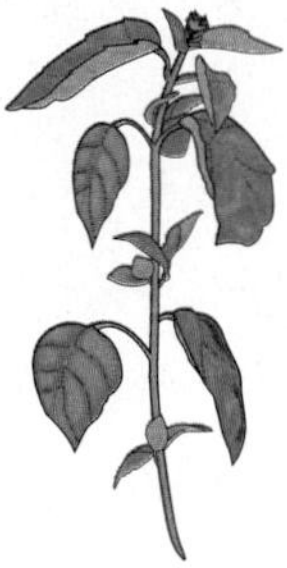

basil
albahaca^F

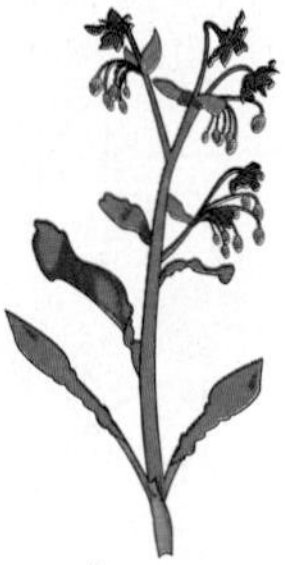

borage
borraja^F

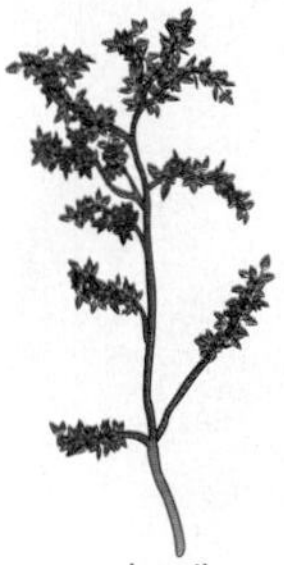

chervil
perifollo^M

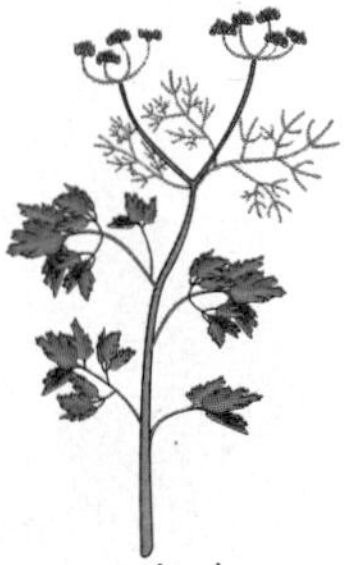

coriander
cilantro^M

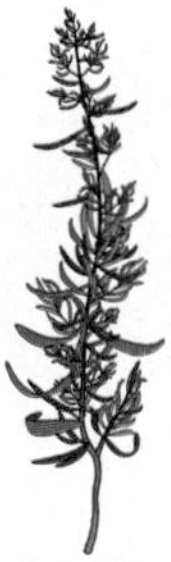

tarragon
estragón^M

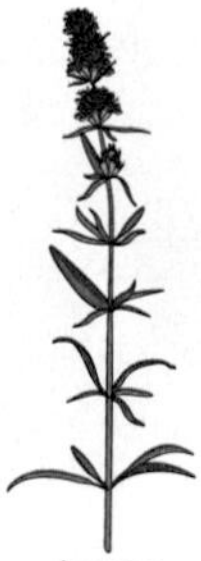

hyssop
hisopo^M

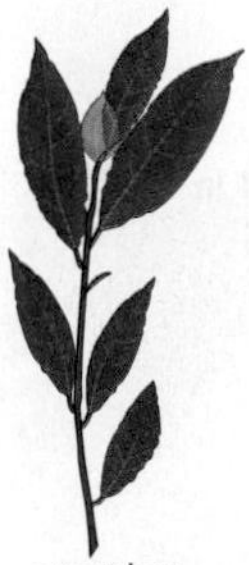

sweet bay
laurel^M

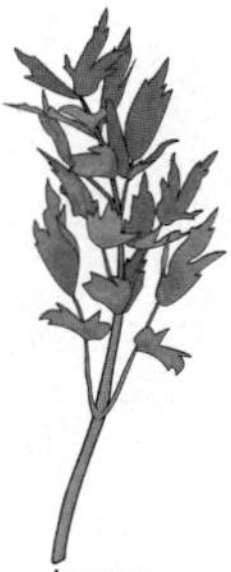

lovage
ligústico^M

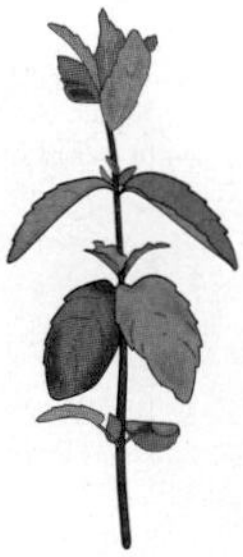

mint
hierbabuena^F

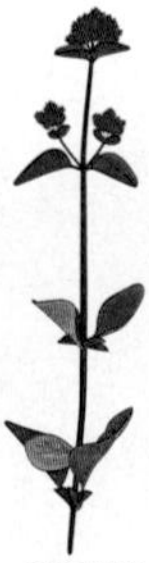

oregano
orégano^M

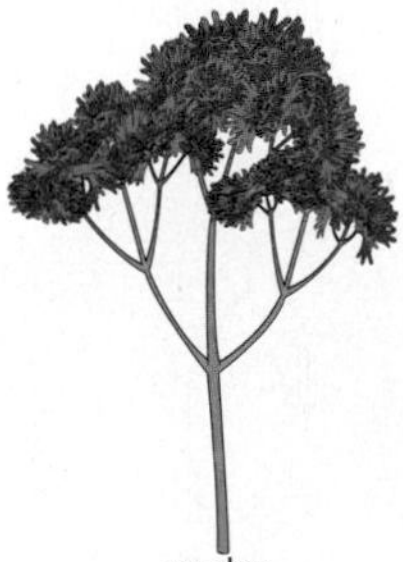

parsley
perejil^M

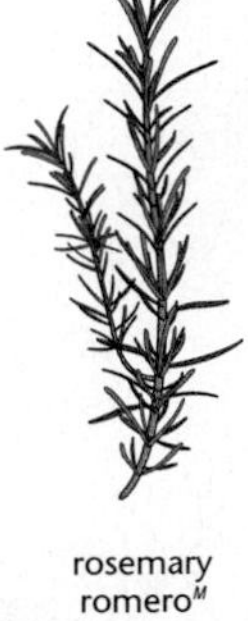

rosemary
romero^M

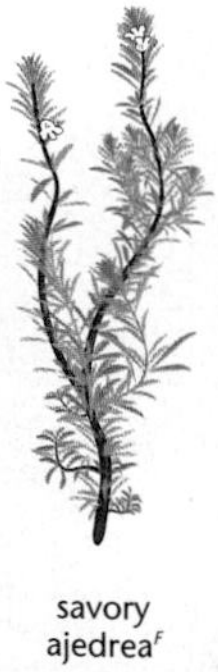

savory
ajedrea^F

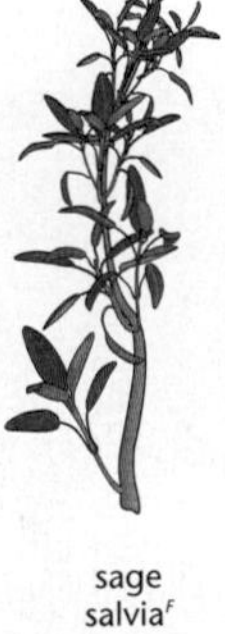

sage
salvia^F

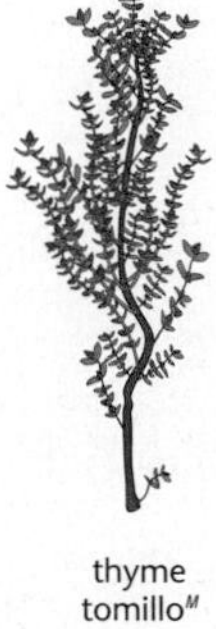

thyme
tomillo^M

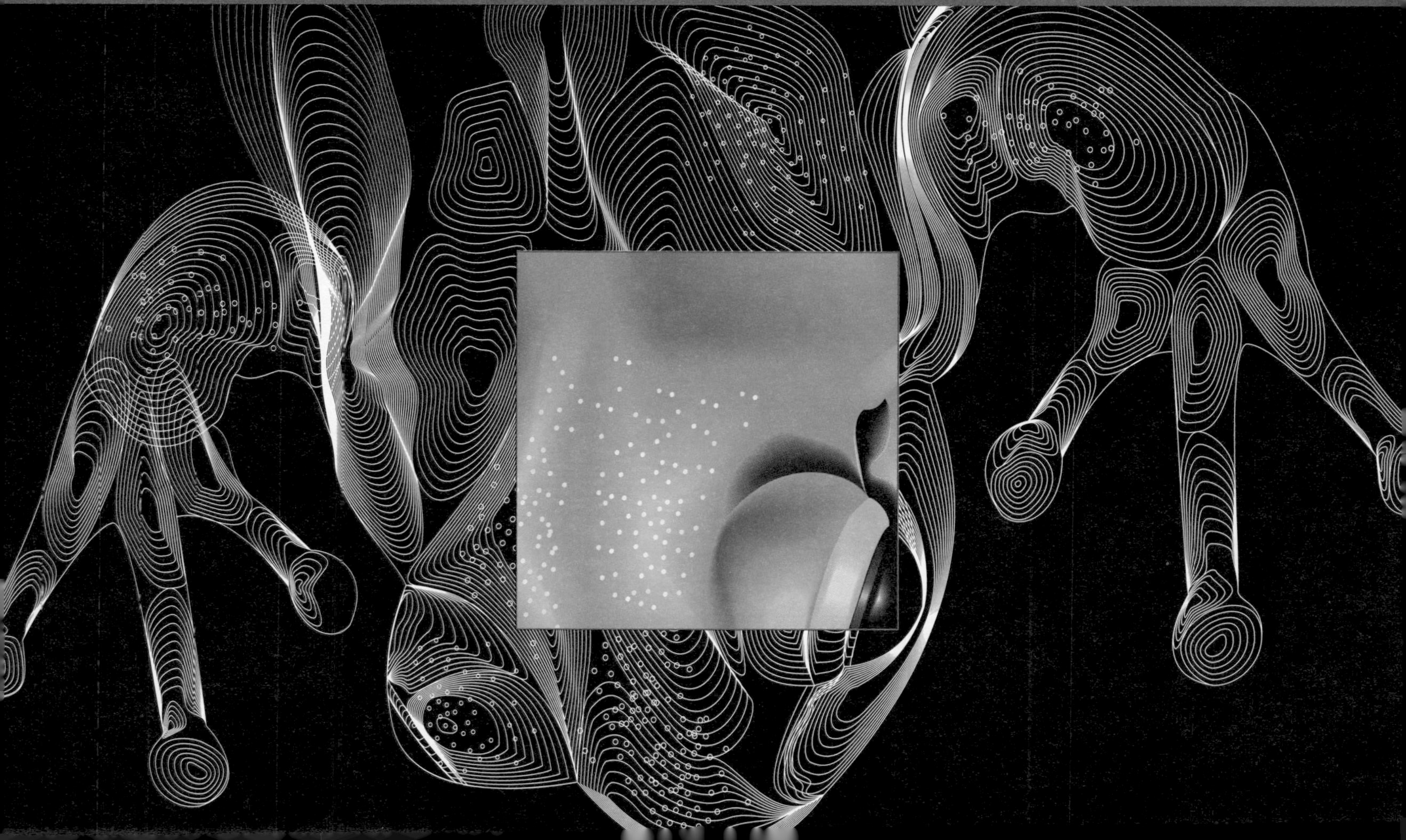

CONTENTS

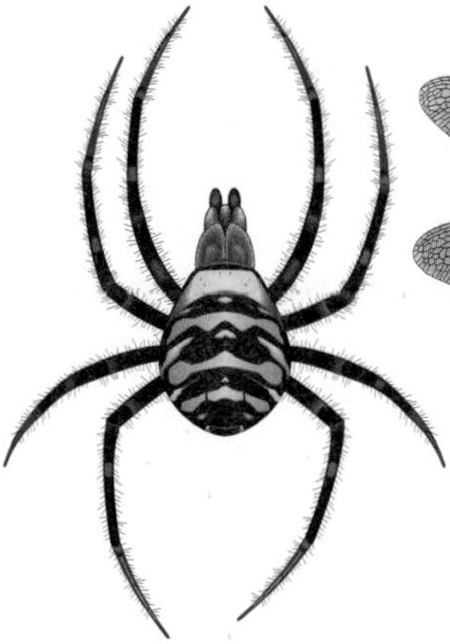

spider
araña^F

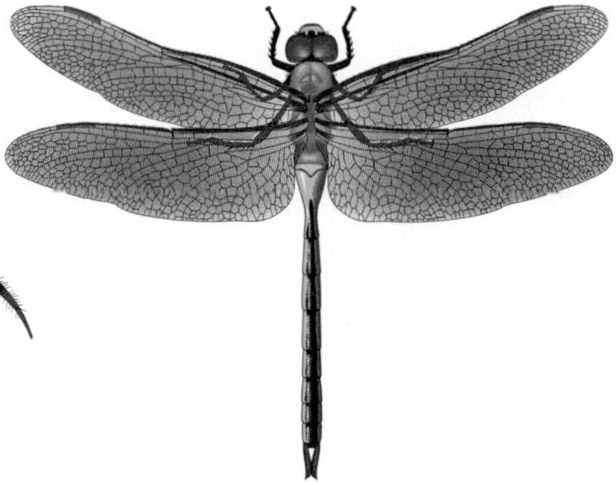

dragonfly
libélula^F

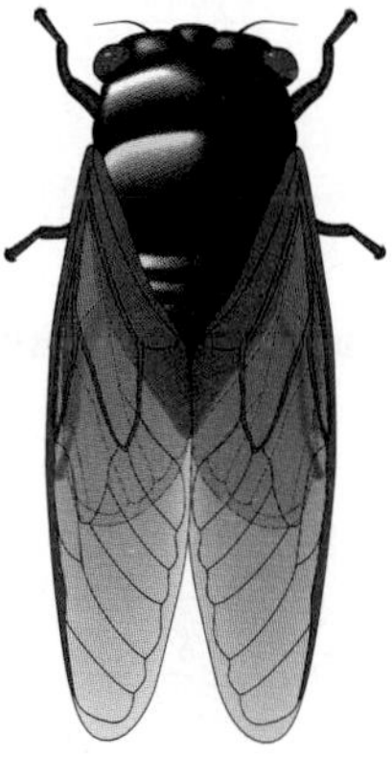

cicada
cigarra^F

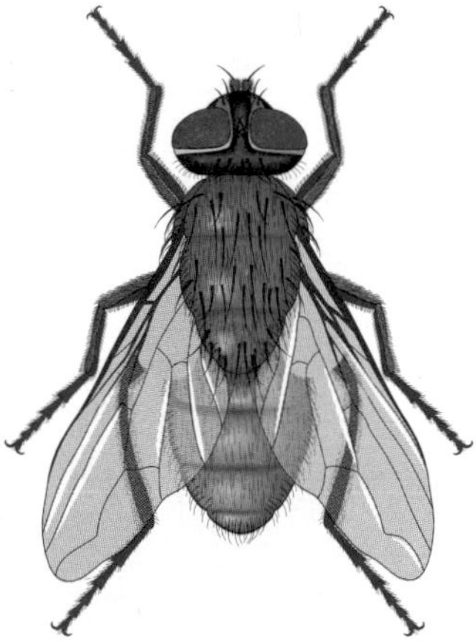

fly
mosca^F

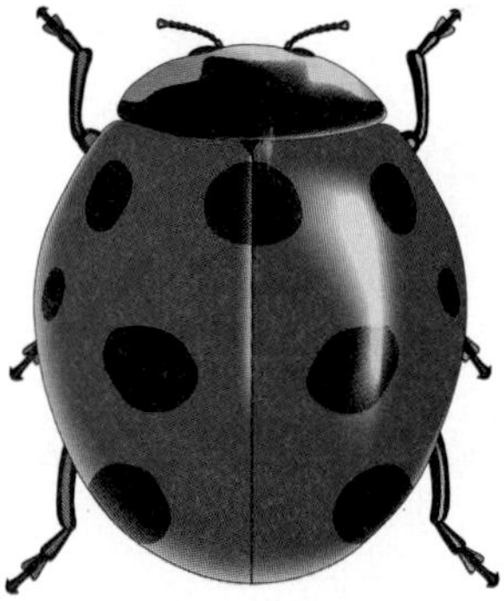

ladybug
cochinilla^F

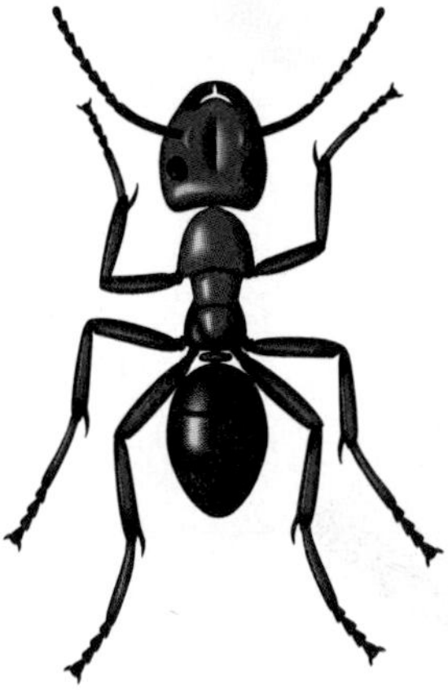

ant
hormiga^F

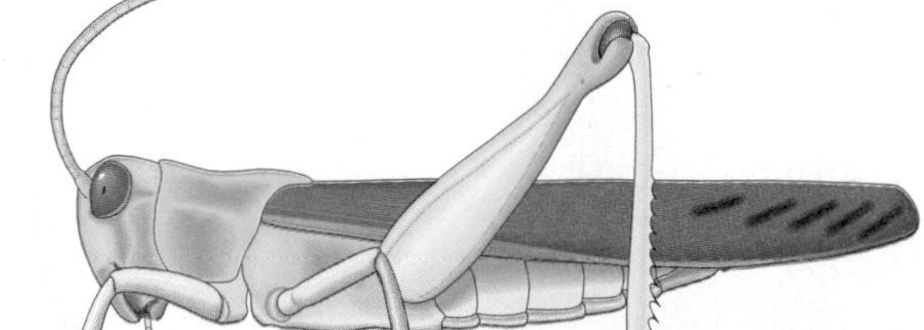

grasshopper
saltamontes^M

**BUTTERFLY
MARIPOSA**^F

CATERPILLAR
ORUGA^F

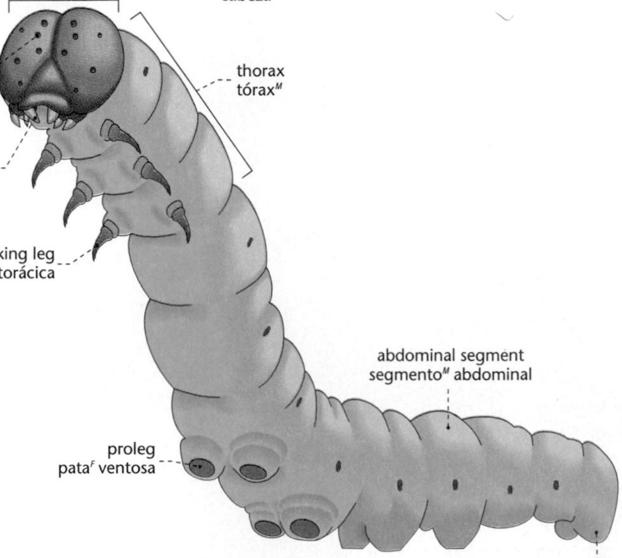

head
cabeza^F

simple eye
ocelo^M

thorax
tórax^M

mandible
mandíbula^F

walking leg
pata^F torácica

abdominal segment
segmento^M abdominal

proleg
pata^F ventosa

anal proleg
pata^F anal

CHRYSALIS
CRISÁLIDA^F

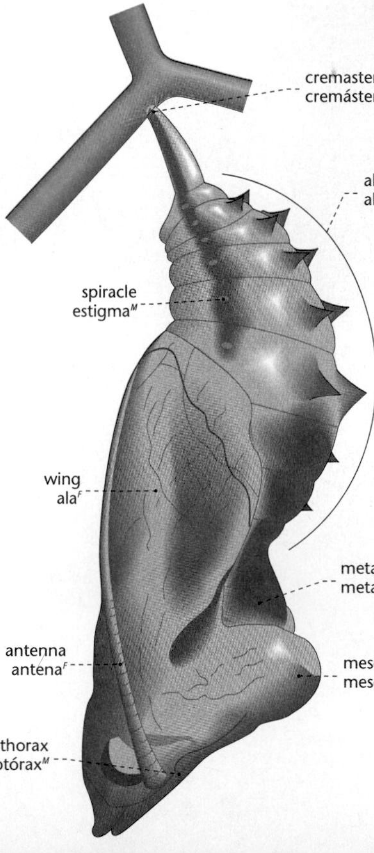

cremaster
cremáster^M

abdomen
abdomen^M

HIND LEG
PATA^F POSTERIOR

spiracle
estigma^M

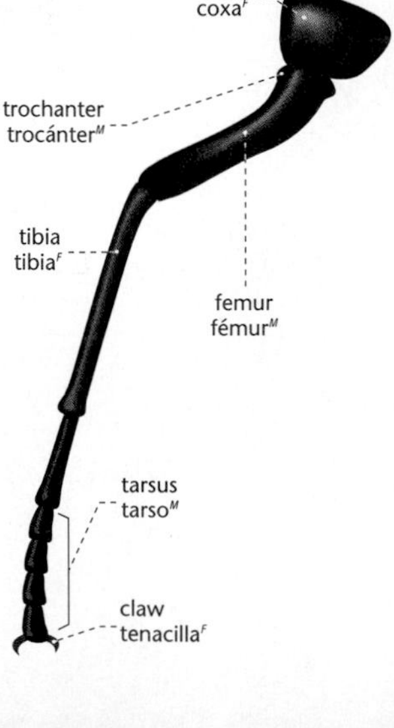

coxa
coxa^F

trochanter
trocánter^M

wing
ala^F

tibia
tibia^F

femur
fémur^M

metathorax
metatórax^M

antenna
antena^F

mesothorax
mesotórax^M

tarsus
tarso^M

prothorax
protórax^M

claw
tenacilla^F

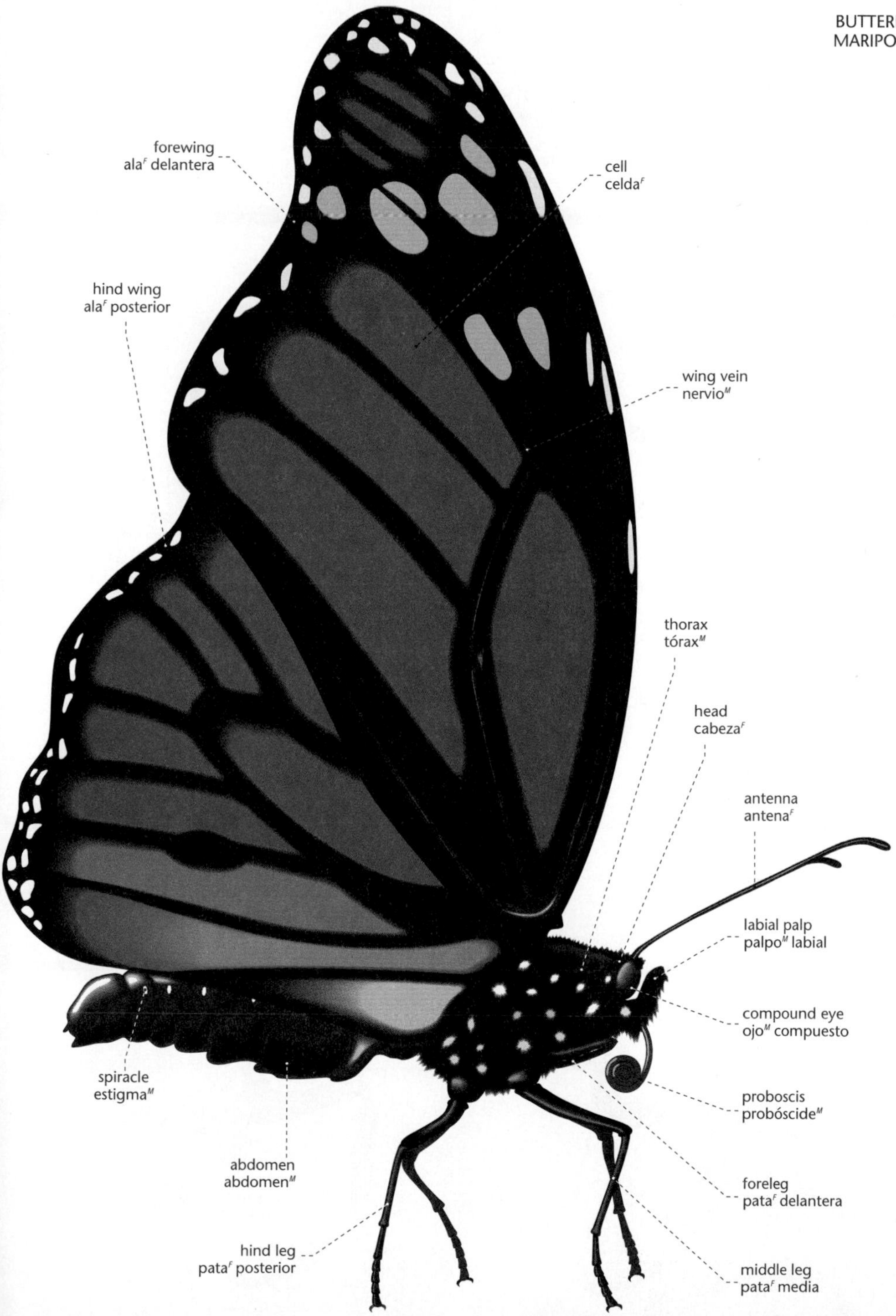

BUTTERFLY
MARIPOSA^F

forewing
ala^F delantera

cell
celda^F

hind wing
ala^F posterior

wing vein
nervio^M

thorax
tórax^M

head
cabeza^F

antenna
antena^F

labial palp
palpo^M labial

compound eye
ojo^M compuesto

proboscis
probóscide^M

foreleg
pata^F delantera

middle leg
pata^F media

hind leg
pata^F posterior

abdomen
abdomen^M

spiracle
estigma^M

WORKER
OBRERA[F]

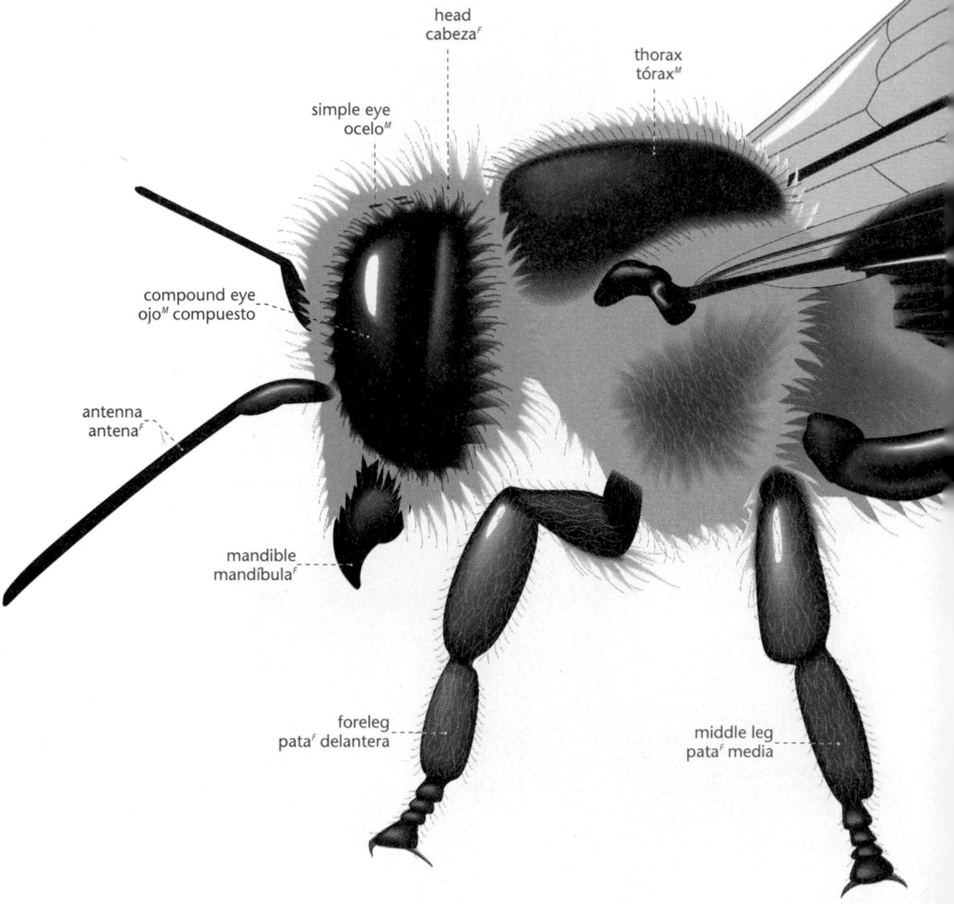

head
cabeza[F]

thorax
tórax[M]

simple eye
ocelo[M]

compound eye
ojo[M] compuesto

antenna
antena[F]

mandible
mandíbula[F]

foreleg
pata[F] delantera

middle leg
pata[F] media

FORELEG (OUTER SURFACE)
PATA[F] DELANTERA (SUPERFICIE[F] EXTERIOR)

MIDDLE LEG (OUTER SURFACE)
PATA[F] MEDIA (SUPERFICIE[F] EXTERIOR)

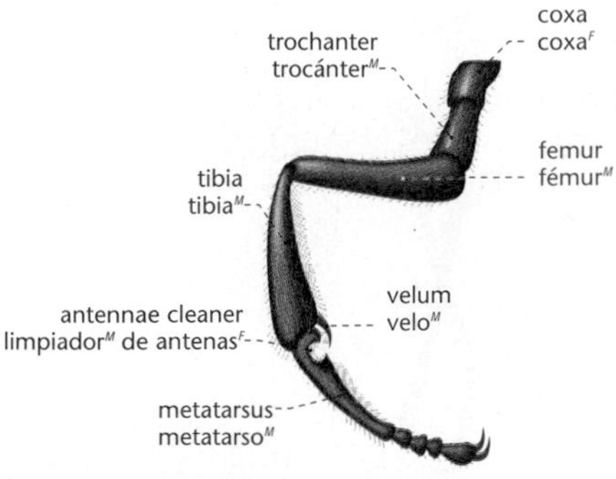

coxa
coxa[F]

trochanter
trocánter[M]

femur
fémur[M]

tibia
tibia[M]

antennae cleaner
limpiador[M] de antenas[F]

velum
velo[M]

metatarsus
metatarso[M]

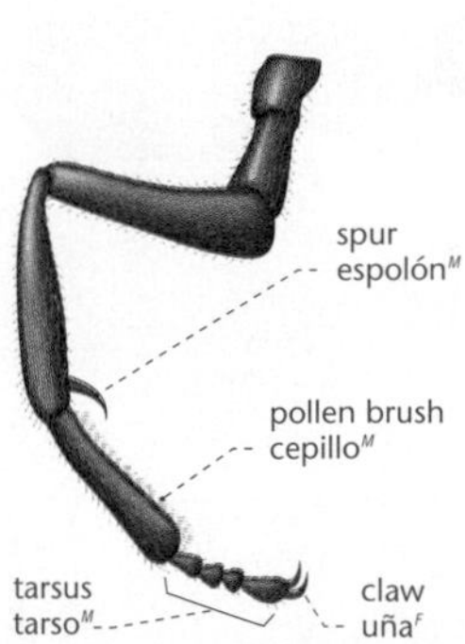

spur
espolón[M]

pollen brush
cepillo[M]

tarsus
tarso[M]

claw
uña[F]

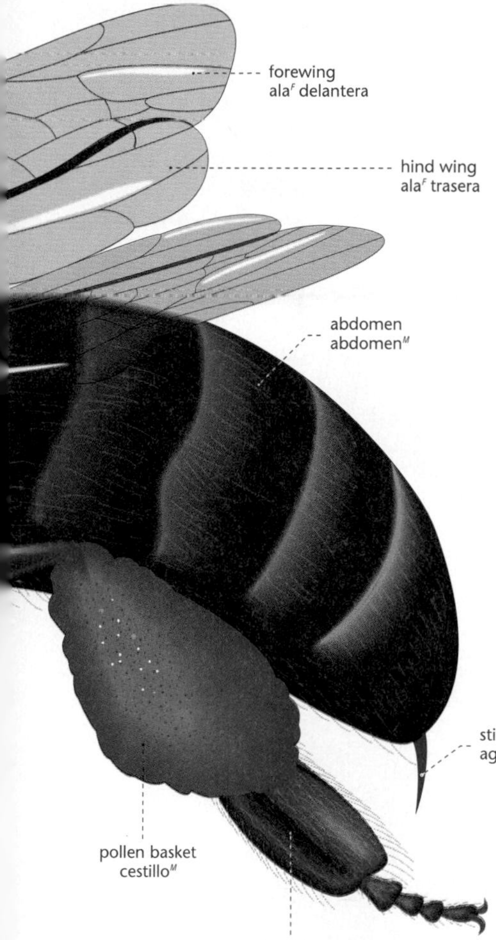

forewing
ala^F delantera

hind wing
ala^F trasera

abdomen
abdomen^M

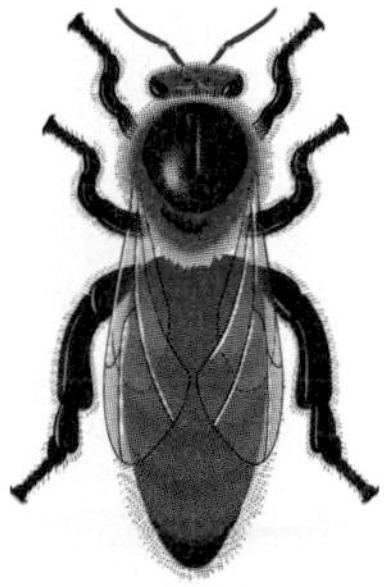

queen
reina^F

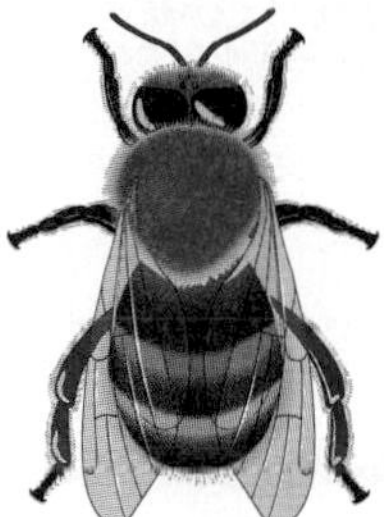

drone
zángano^M

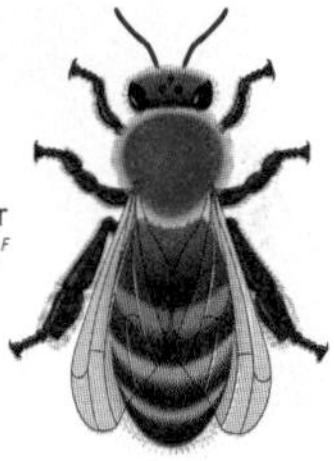

worker
obrera^F

stinger
aguijón^M

pollen basket
cestillo^M

hind leg
pata^F trasera

MOUTHPARTS
APÉNDICES^M BUCALES

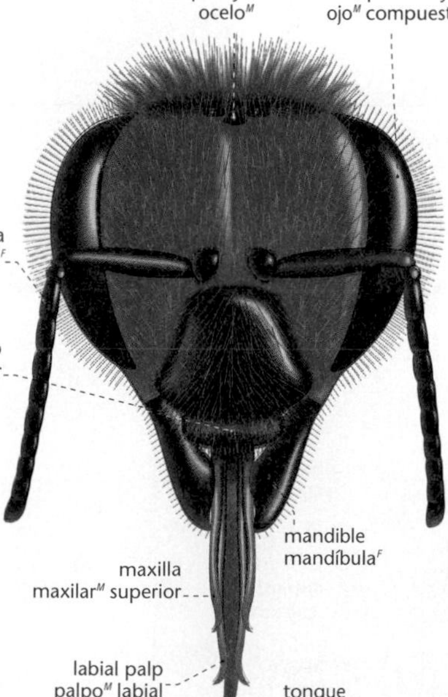

simple eye
ocelo^M

compound eye
ojo^M compuesto

antenna
antena^F

HIND LEG (INNER SURFACE)
PATA^F TRASERA (SUPERFICIE^F INTERIOR)

upper lip
labio^M superior

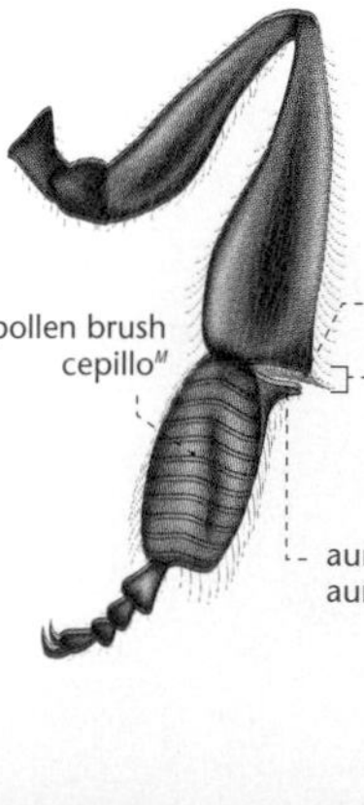

pecten
pectén^M

pollen brush
cepillo^M

pollen packer
pinza^F tibiotarsiana

mandible
mandíbula^F

maxilla
maxilar^M superior

auricle
aurícula^F

labial palp
palpo^M labial

tongue
lengua^F

81

HONEYBEE
ABEJA^F DE COLMENA^F

HONEYCOMB SECTION
CORTE^M DE UN PANAL^M

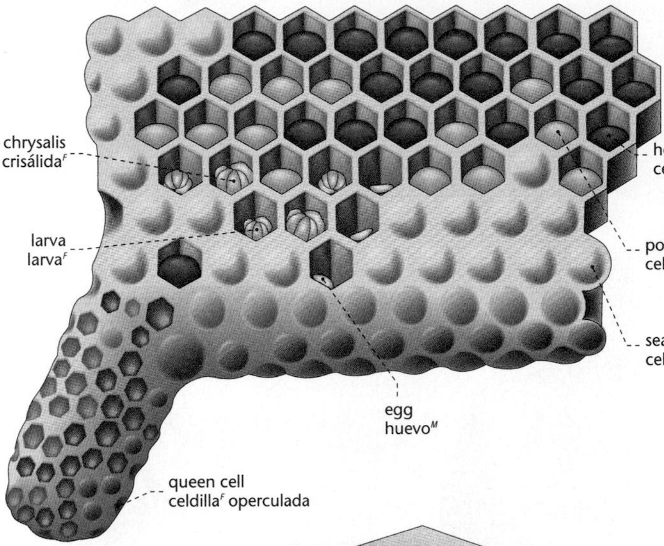

chrysalis
crisálida^F

larva
larva^F

honey cell
celdilla^F de la miel^F

pollen cell
celdilla^F del polen^M

sealed cell
celdilla^F sellada

egg
huevo^M

queen cell
celdilla^F operculada

HIVE
COLMENA^F

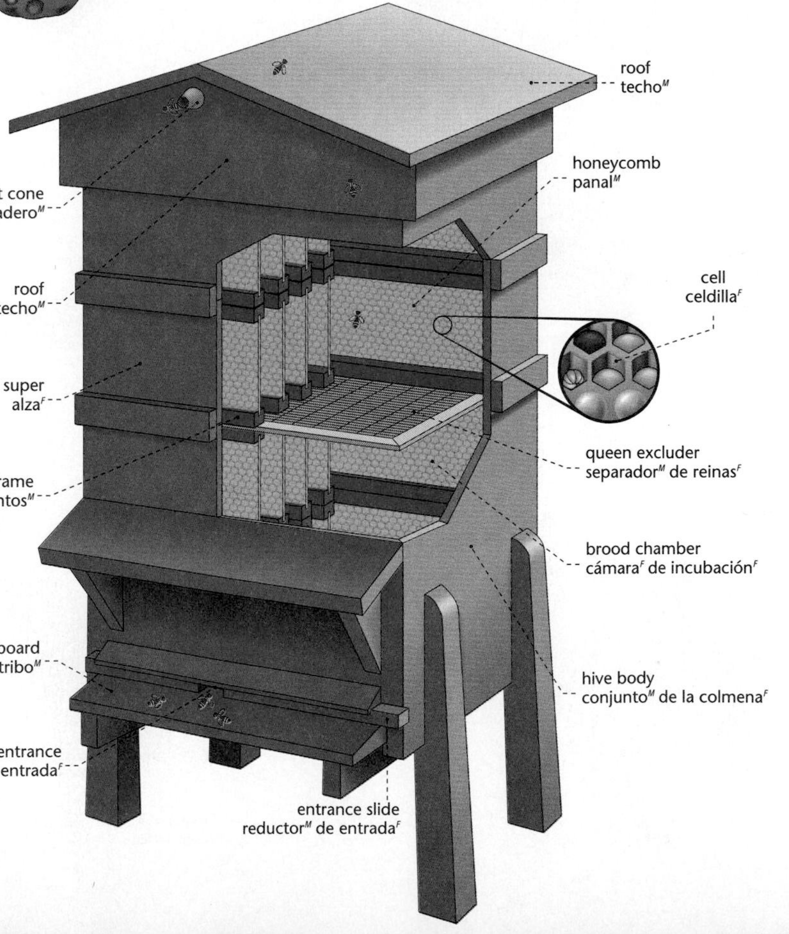

roof
techo^M

honeycomb
panal^M

cell
celdilla^F

exit cone
respiradero^M

roof
techo^M

super
alza^F

frame
compartimentos^M

queen excluder
separador^M de reinas^F

brood chamber
cámara^F de incubación^F

alighting board
estribo^M

entrance
entrada^F

entrance slide
reductor^M de entrada^F

hive body
conjunto^M de la colmena^F

GASTROPOD
MOLUSCO^M GASTERÓPODO

SNAIL
CARACOL^M TERRESTRE

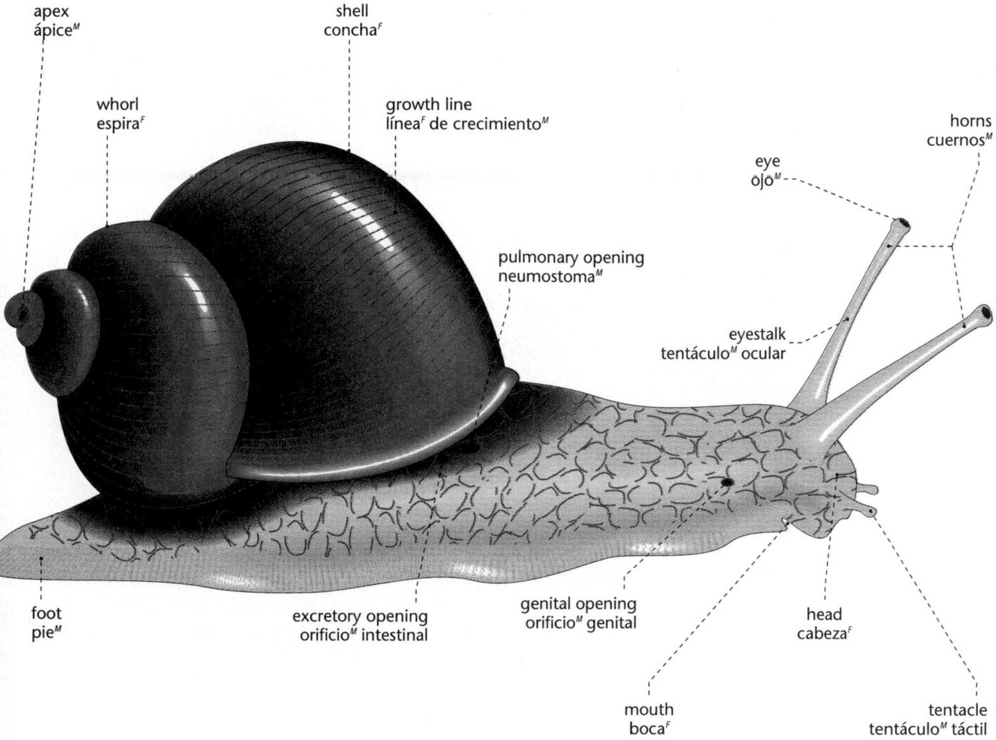

apex
ápice^M

shell
concha^F

whorl
espira^F

growth line
línea^F de crecimiento^M

horns
cuernos^M

eye
ojo^M

pulmonary opening
neumostoma^M

eyestalk
tentáculo^M ocular

foot
pie^M

excretory opening
orificio^M intestinal

genital opening
orificio^M genital

head
cabeza^F

mouth
boca^F

tentacle
tentáculo^M táctil

MAJOR EDIBLE GASTROPODS
GASTERÓPODOS^M COMESTIBLES

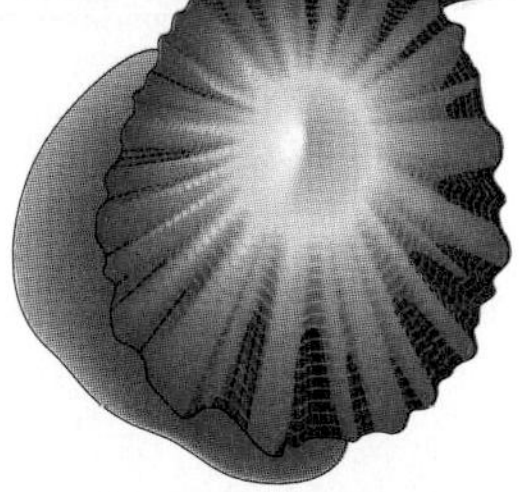

limpet
lapa^F

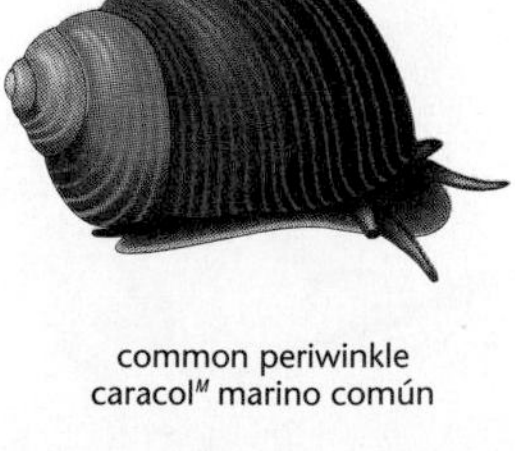

common periwinkle
caracol^M marino común

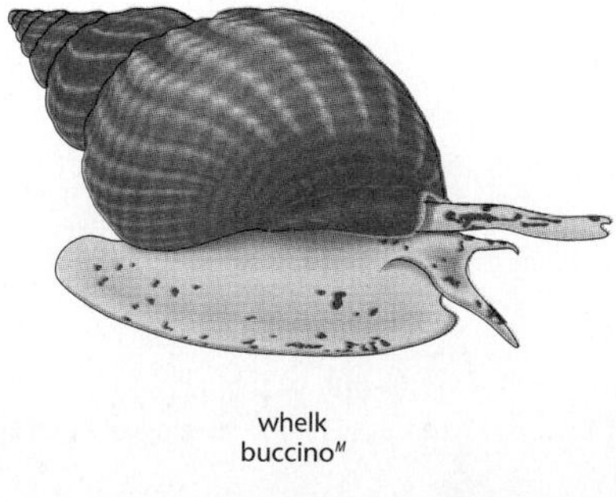

whelk
buccino^M

ANIMAL KINGDOM
REINO ANIMAL

FROG
RANA^F

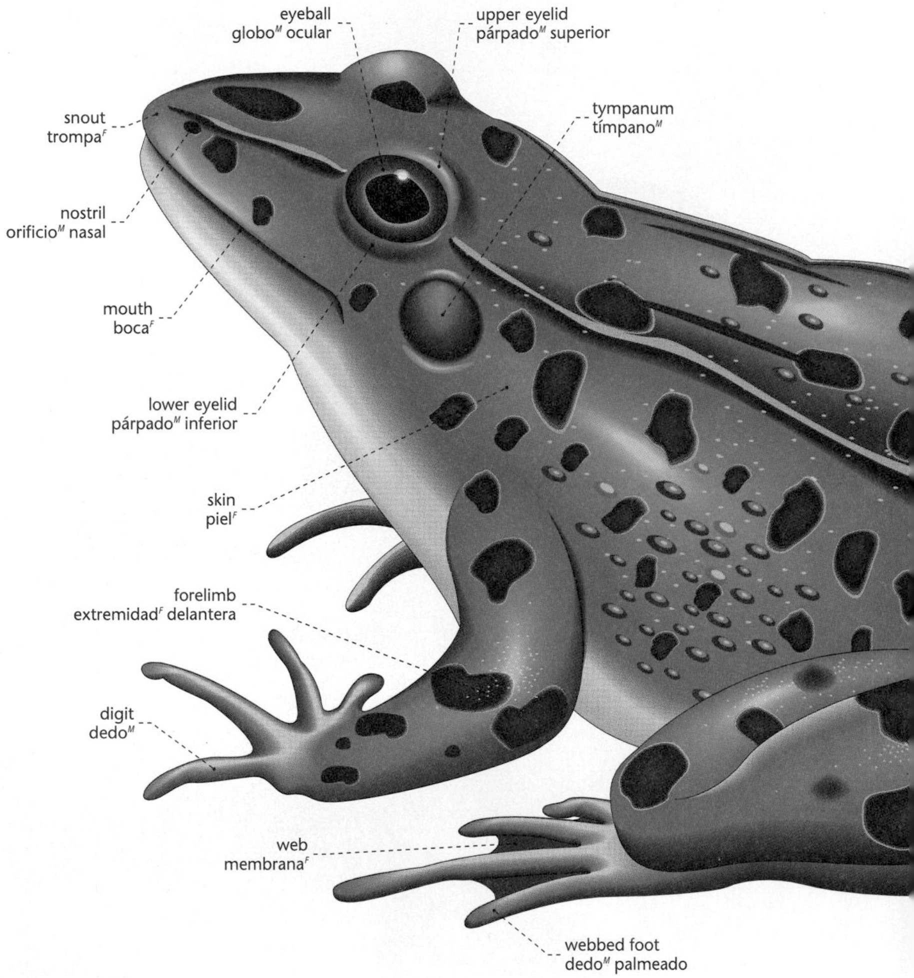

eyeball
globo^M ocular

upper eyelid
párpado^M superior

tympanum
tímpano^M

snout
trompa^F

nostril
orificio^M nasal

mouth
boca^F

lower eyelid
párpado^M inferior

skin
piel^F

forelimb
extremidad^F delantera

digit
dedo^M

web
membrana^F

webbed foot
dedo^M palmeado

LIFE CYCLE OF THE FROG
METAMÓRFOSIS^F DE LA RANA^F

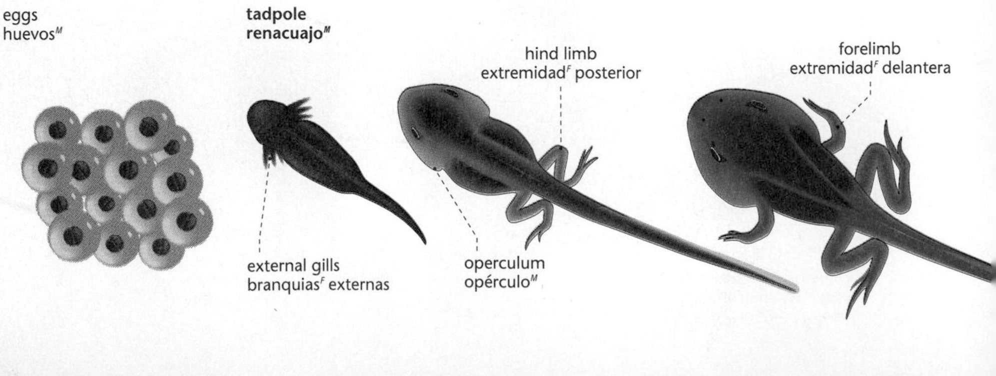

eggs
huevos^M

tadpole
renacuajo^M

hind limb
extremidad^F posterior

forelimb
extremidad^F delantera

external gills
branquias^F externas

operculum
opérculo^M

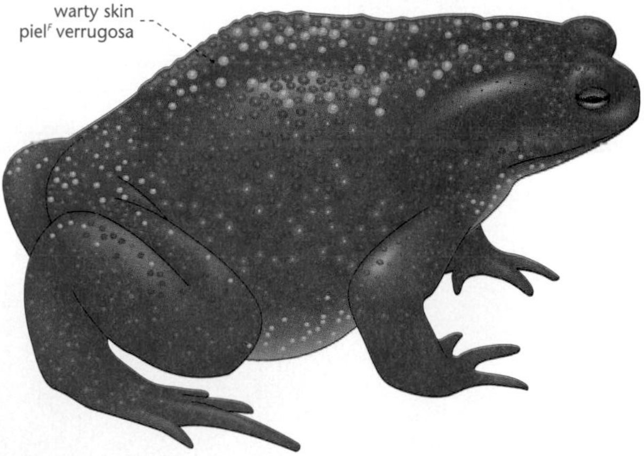

toad
sapo^M

warty skin
piel^F verrugosa

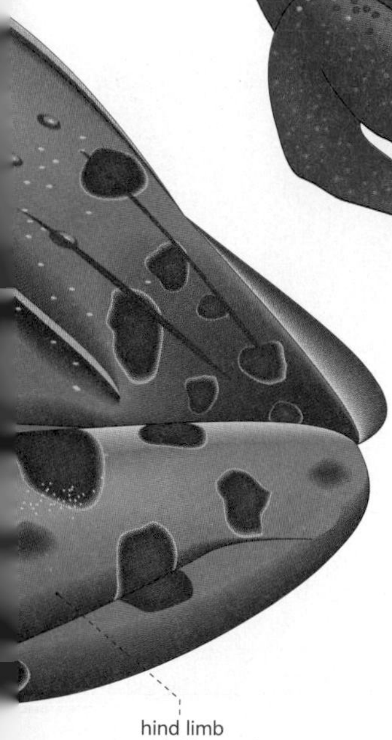

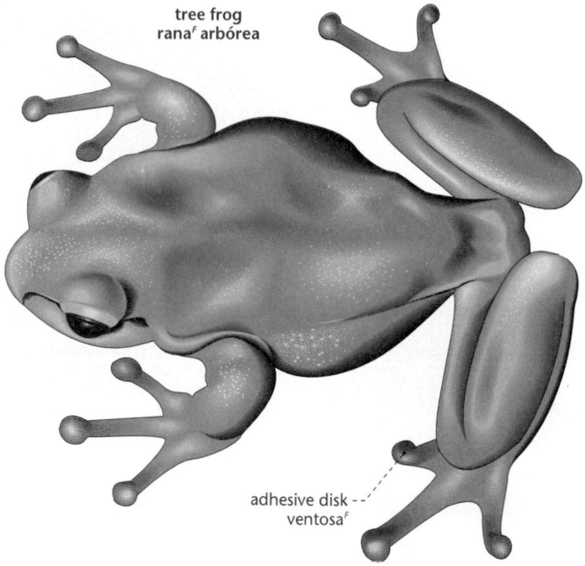

tree frog
rana^F arbórea

hind limb
extremidad^F posterior

adhesive disk
ventosa^F

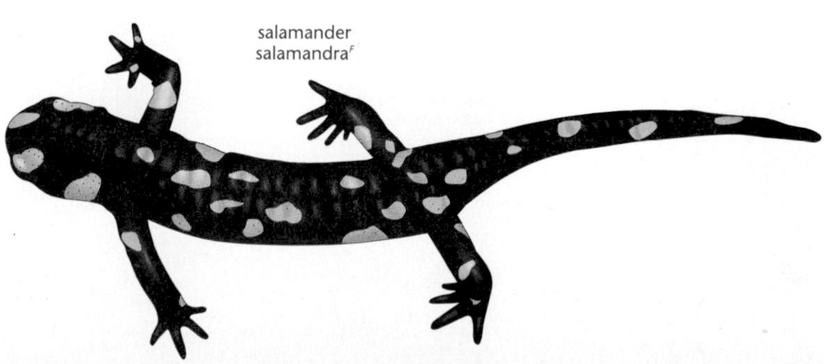

salamander
salamandra^F

MORPHOLOGY
MORFOLOGÍA^F

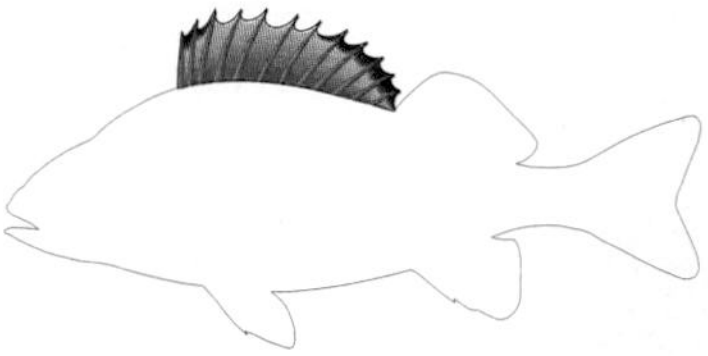

first dorsal fin
aleta^F dorsal anterior

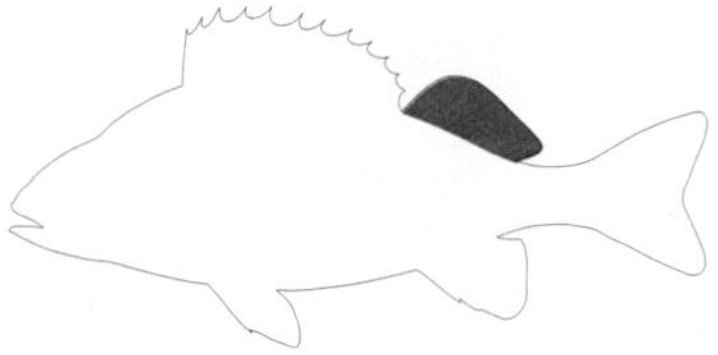

second dorsal fin
aleta^F dorsal posterior

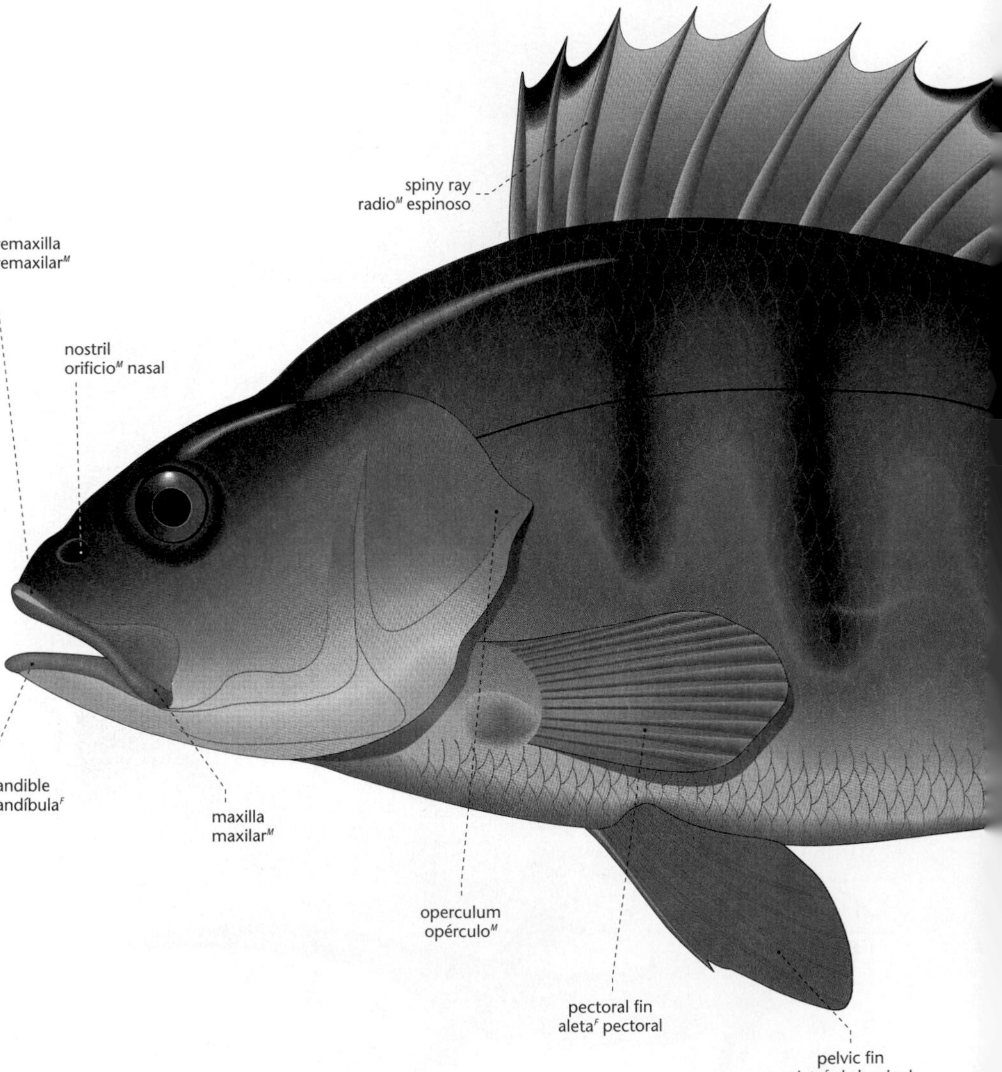

spiny ray
radio^M espinoso

premaxilla
premaxilar^M

nostril
orificio^M nasal

mandible
mandíbula^F

maxilla
maxilar^M

operculum
opérculo^M

pectoral fin
aleta^F pectoral

pelvic fin
aleta^F abdominal

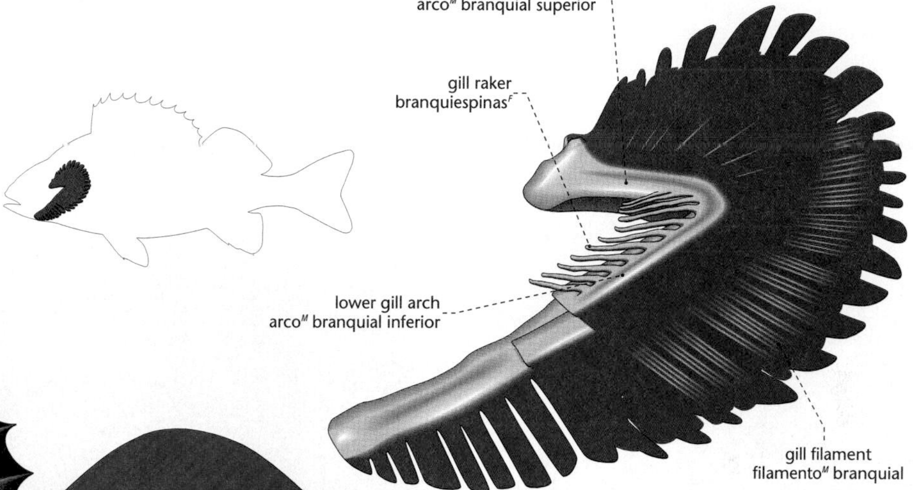

upper gill arch
arco^M branquial superior

gill raker
branquiespinas^F

lower gill arch
arco^M branquial inferior

gill filament
filamento^M branquial

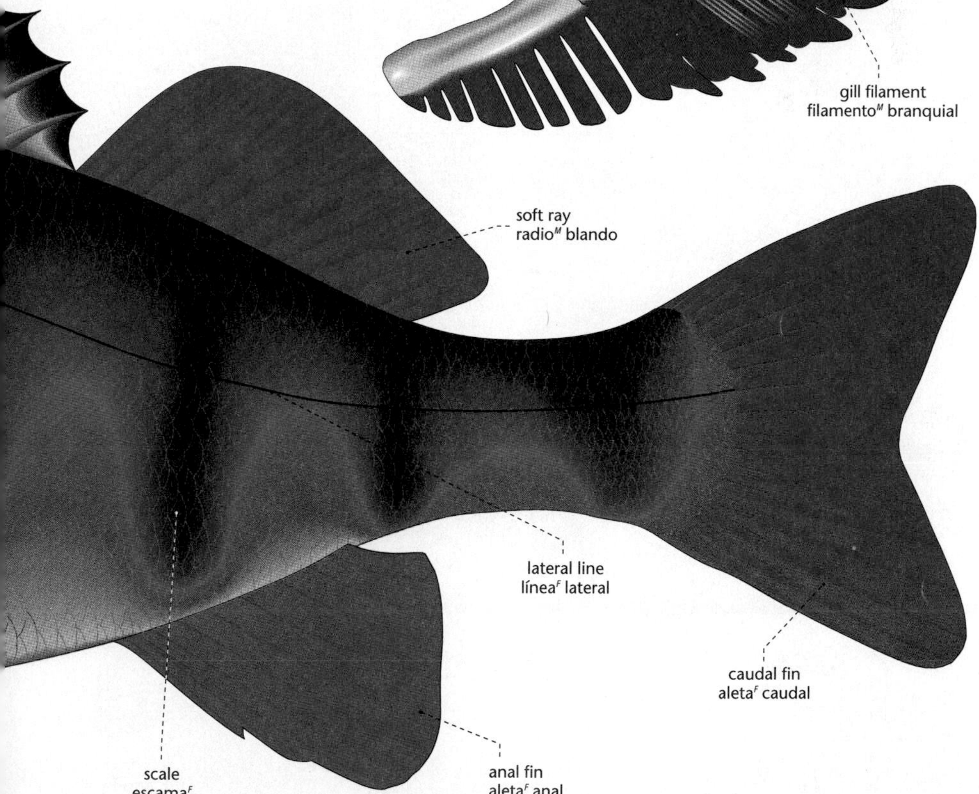

soft ray
radio^M blando

lateral line
línea^F lateral

caudal fin
aleta^F caudal

scale
escama^F

anal fin
aleta^F anal

ANIMAL KINGDOM
REINO ANIMAL

ANATOMY
ANATOMÍA^F

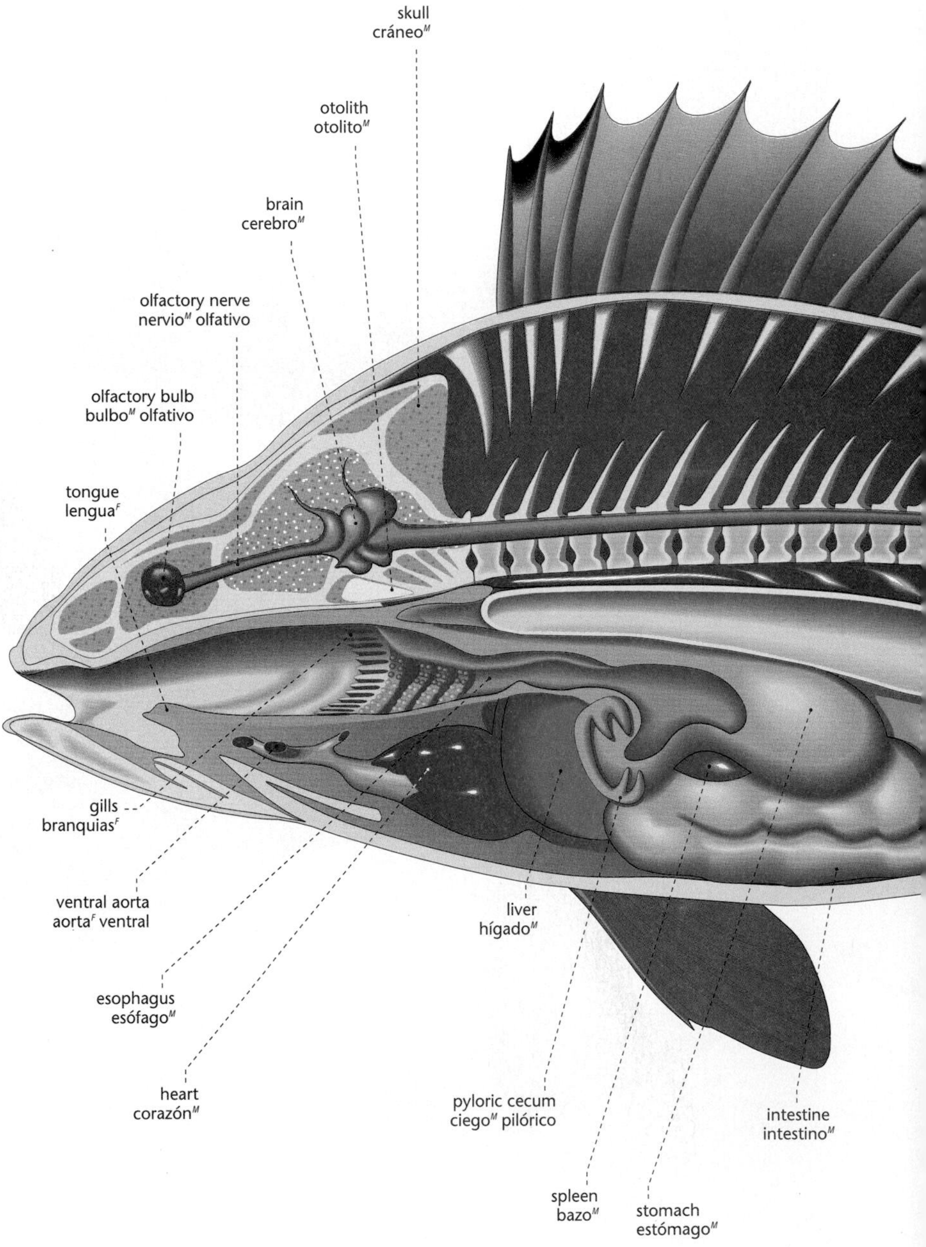

skull
cráneo^M

otolith
otolito^M

brain
cerebro^M

olfactory nerve
nervio^M olfativo

olfactory bulb
bulbo^M olfativo

tongue
lengua^F

gills
branquias^F

ventral aorta
aorta^F ventral

esophagus
esófago^M

heart
corazón^M

liver
hígado^M

pyloric cecum
ciego^M pilórico

intestine
intestino^M

spleen
bazo^M

stomach
estómago^M

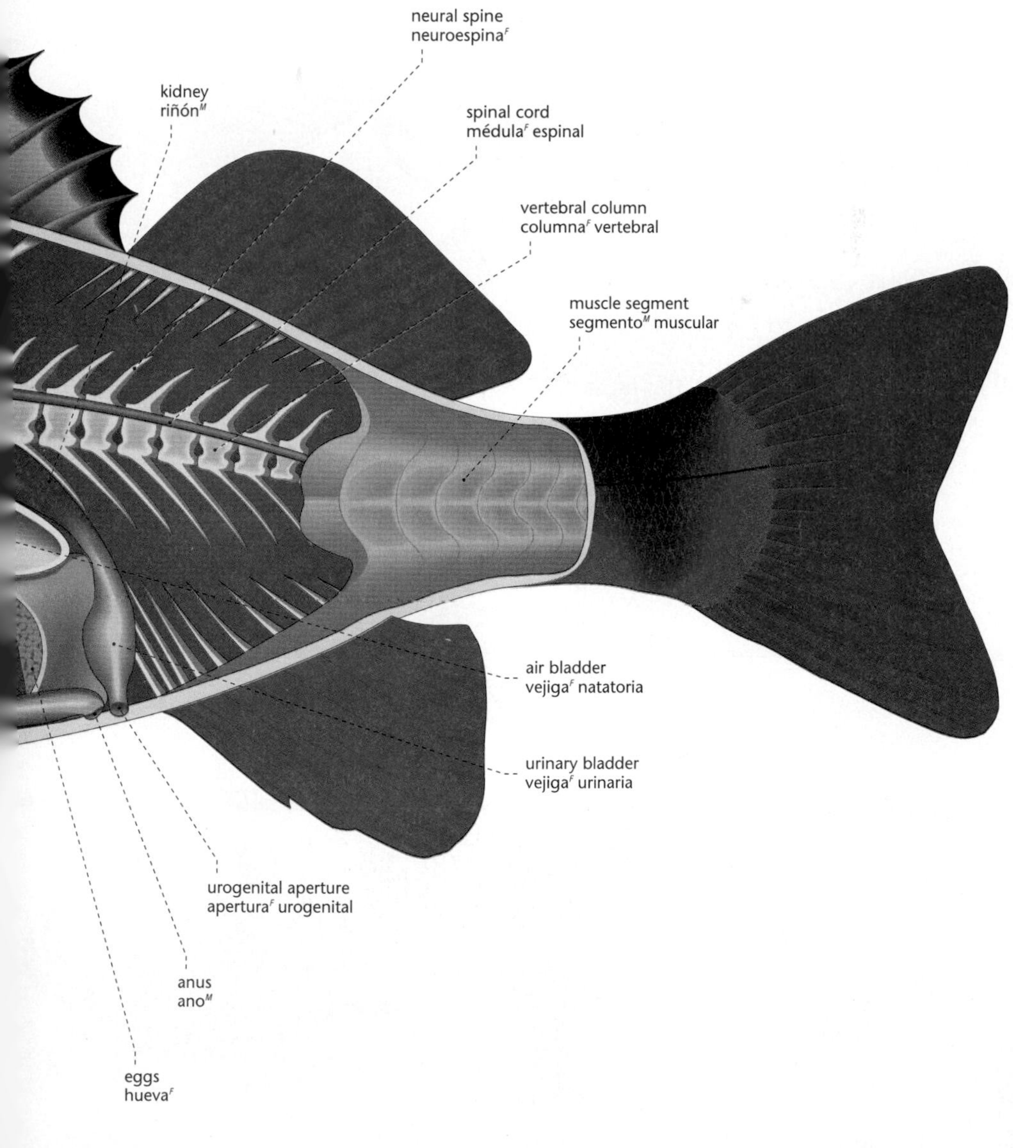

neural spine
neuroespina^F

kidney
riñón^M

spinal cord
médula^F espinal

vertebral column
columna^F vertebral

muscle segment
segmento^M muscular

air bladder
vejiga^F natatoria

urinary bladder
vejiga^F urinaria

urogenital aperture
apertura^F urogenital

anus
ano^M

eggs
hueva^F

CRUSTACEAN
CRUSTÁCEO[M]

LOBSTER
LANGOSTA[F]

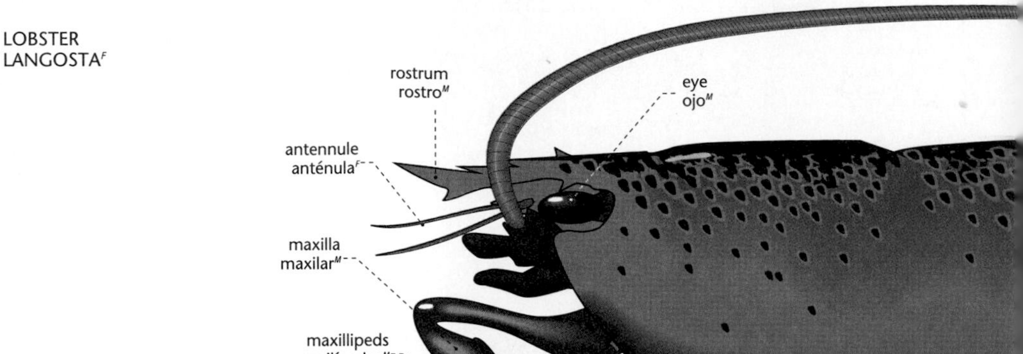

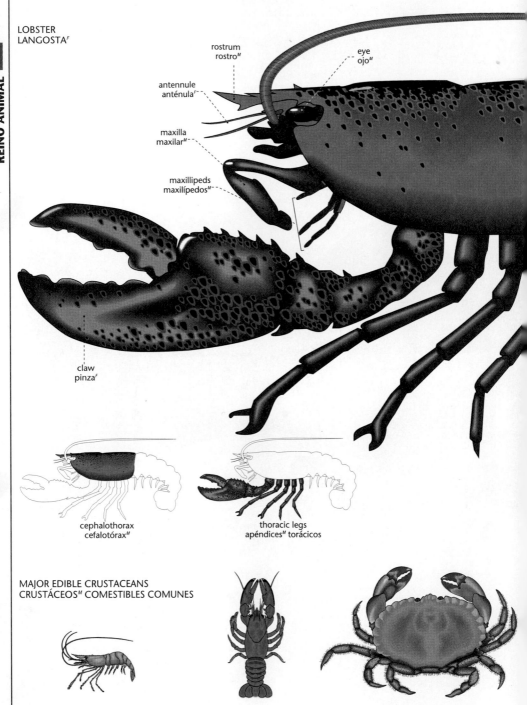

rostrum
rostro[M]

eye
ojo[M]

antennule
anténula[F]

maxilla
maxilar[M]

maxillipeds
maxilípedos[M]

claw
pinza[F]

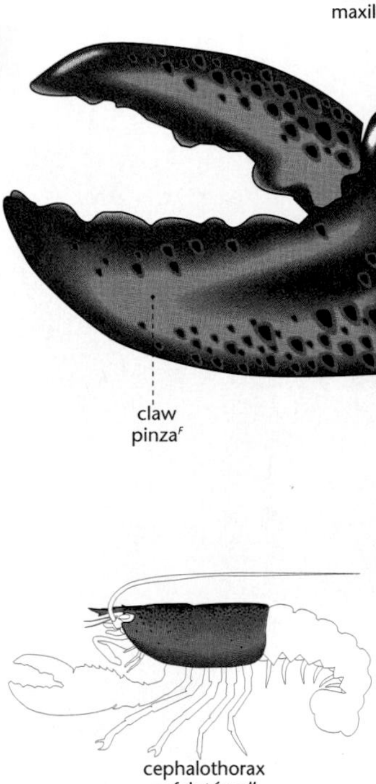

cephalothorax
cefalotórax[M]

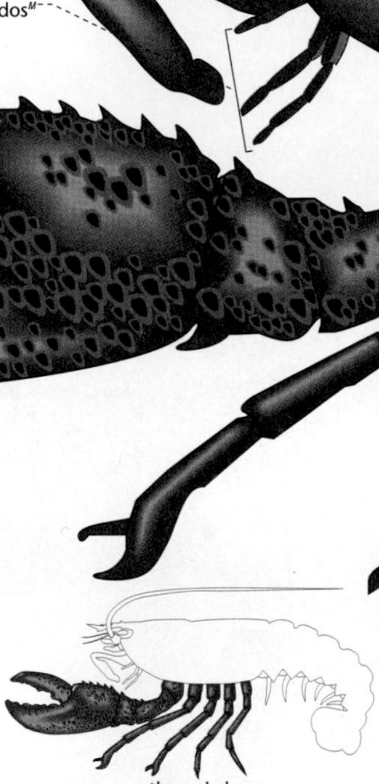

thoracic legs
apéndices[M] torácicos

MAJOR EDIBLE CRUSTACEANS
CRUSTÁCEOS[M] COMESTIBLES COMUNES

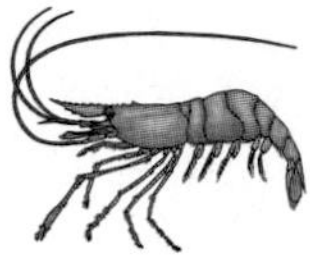

shrimp
gamba[F]

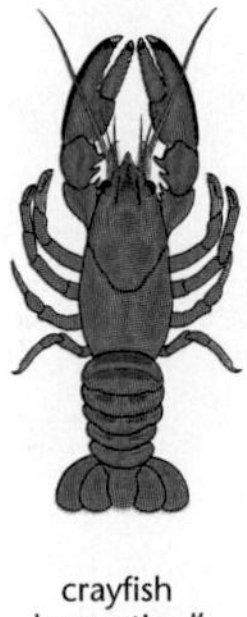

crayfish
langostino[M]

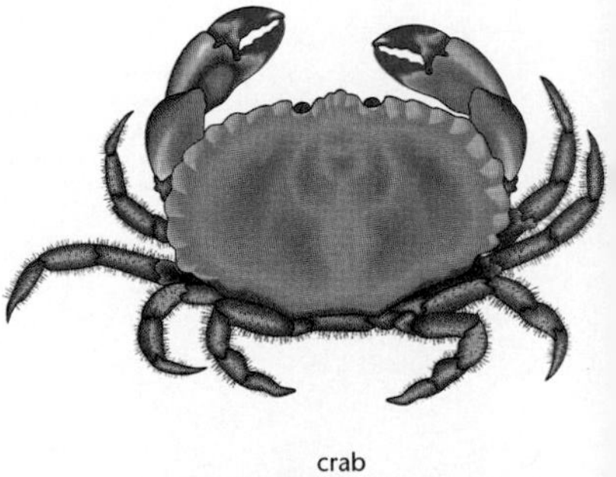

crab
cangrejo[M]

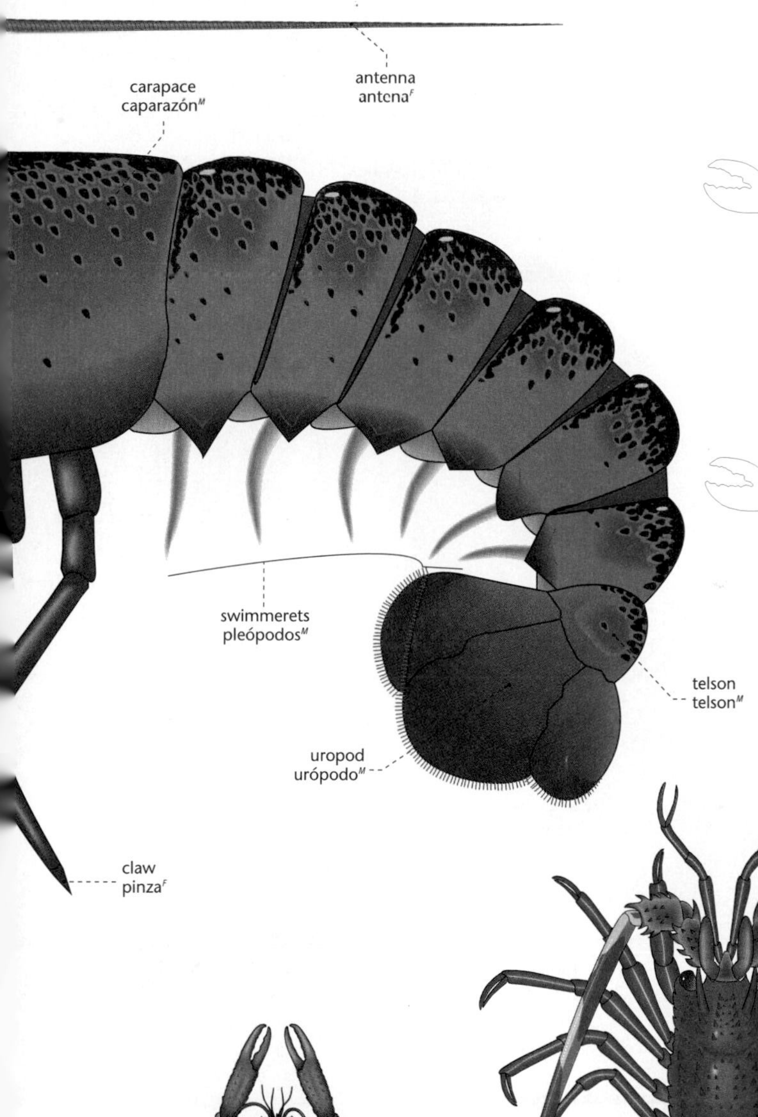

carapace
caparazón[M]

antenna
antena[F]

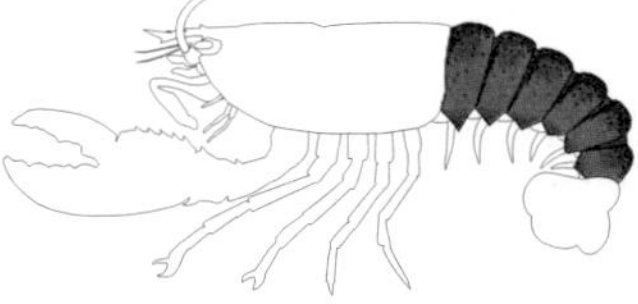

abdomen
abdomen[M]

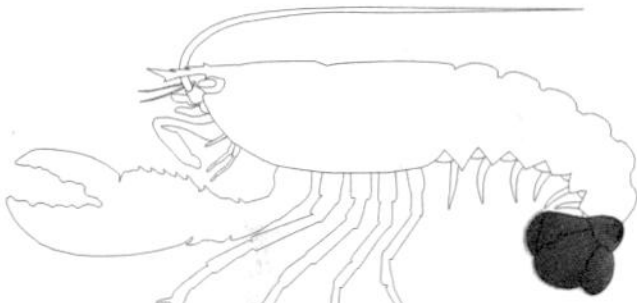

tail
cola[F]

swimmerets
pleópodos[M]

telson
telson[M]

uropod
urópodo[M]

claw
pinza[F]

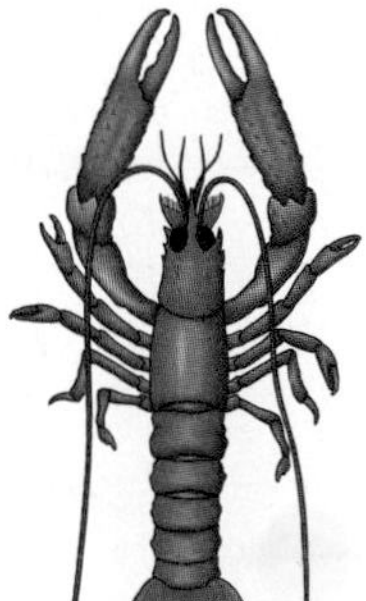

scampi
cigala[F]

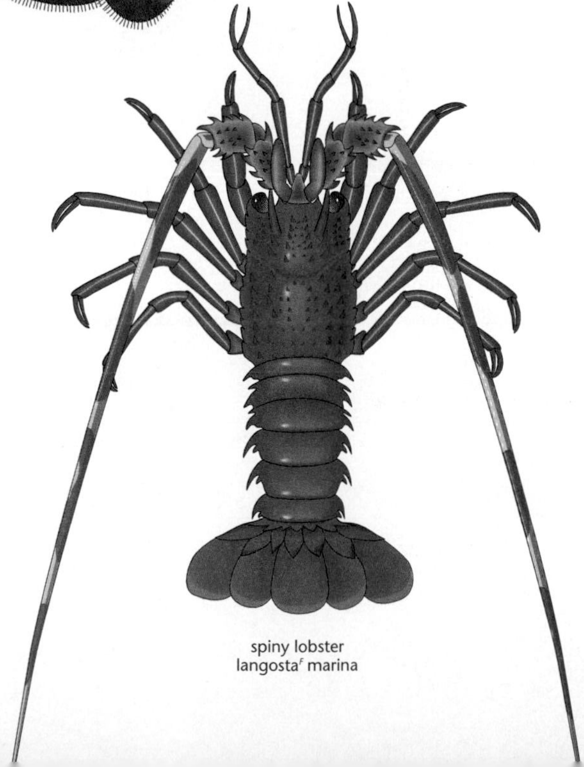

spiny lobster
langosta[F] marina

ANIMAL KINGDOM
REINO ANIMAL

OYSTER
OSTRA^F

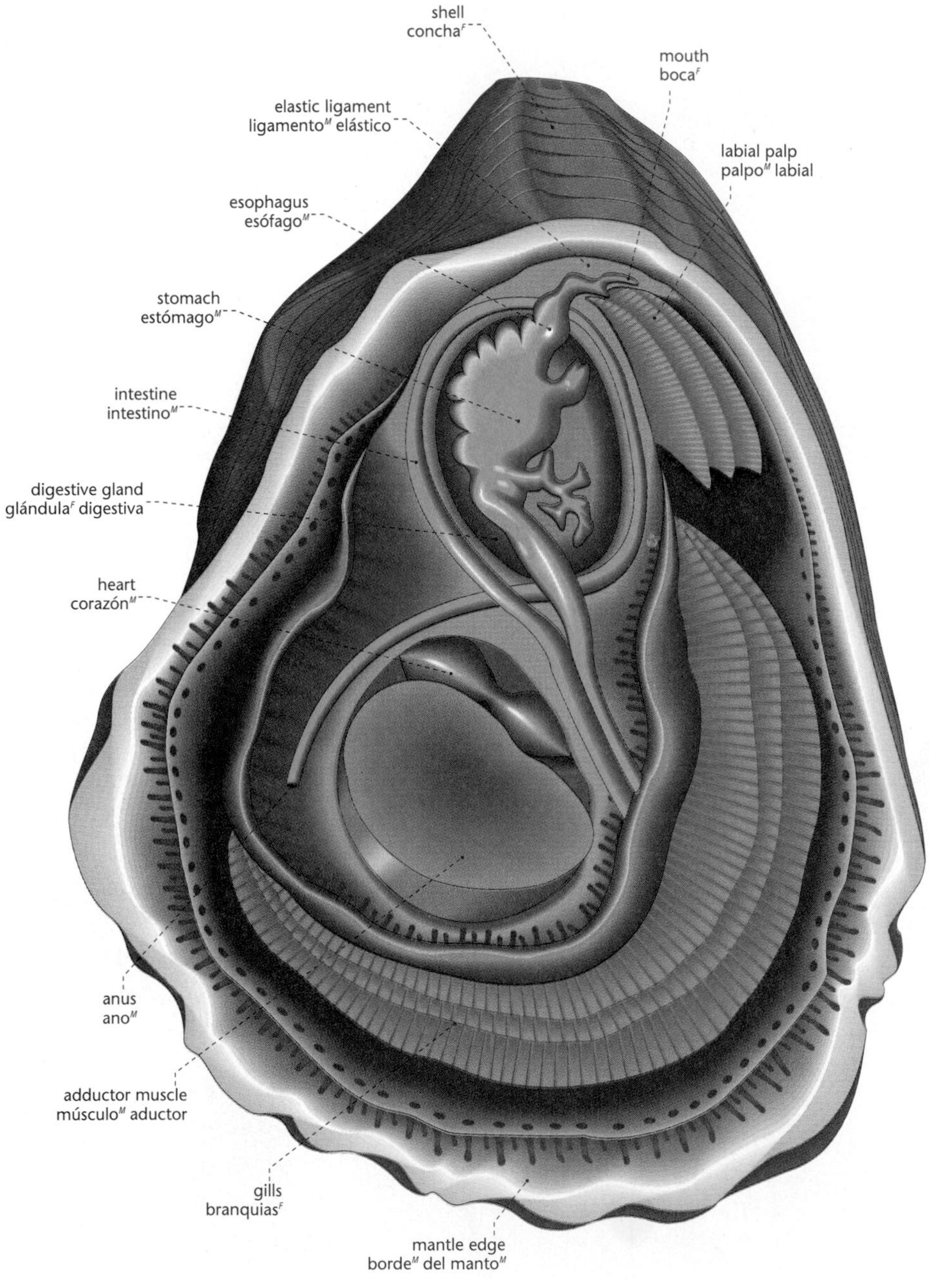

shell
concha^F

mouth
boca^F

elastic ligament
ligamento^M elástico

labial palp
palpo^M labial

esophagus
esófago^M

stomach
estómago^M

intestine
intestino^M

digestive gland
glándula^F digestiva

heart
corazón^M

anus
ano^M

adductor muscle
músculo^M aductor

gills
branquias^F

mantle edge
borde^M del manto^M

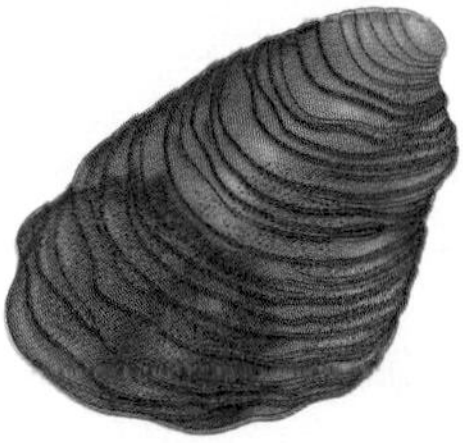

oyster
ostra^F

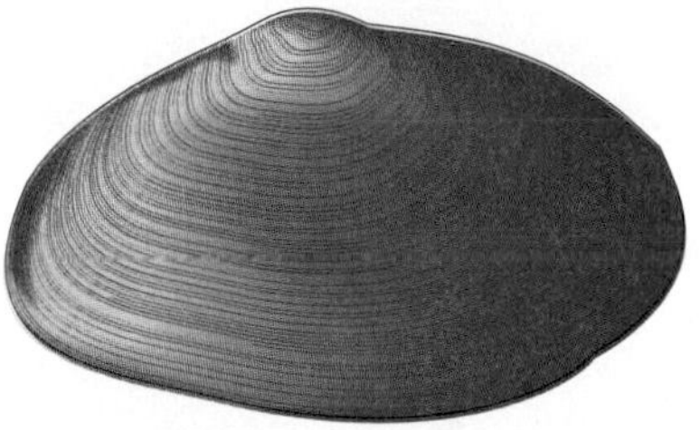

soft shell clam
coquina^F

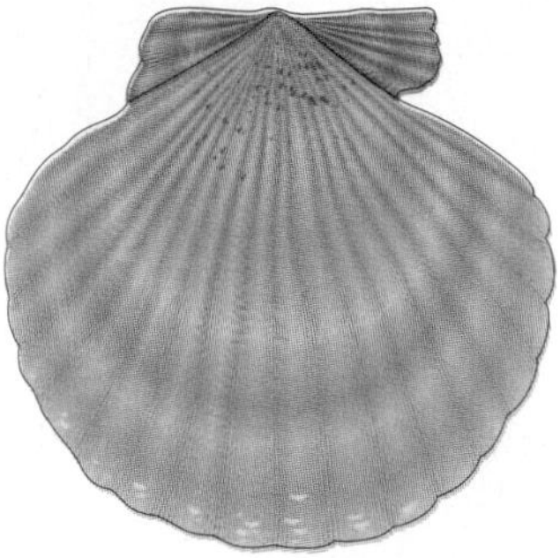

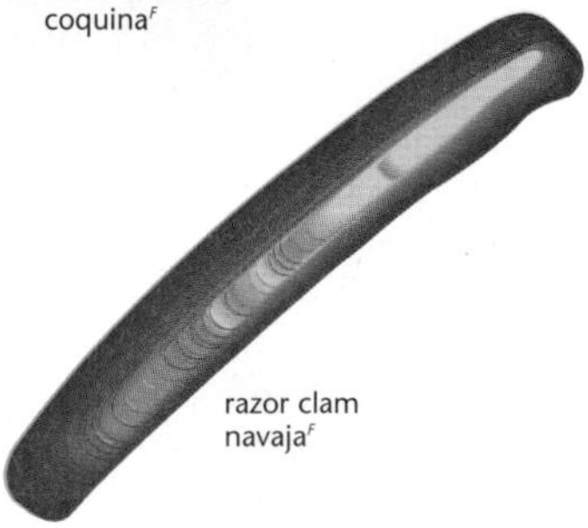

razor clam
navaja^F

scallop
venera^F

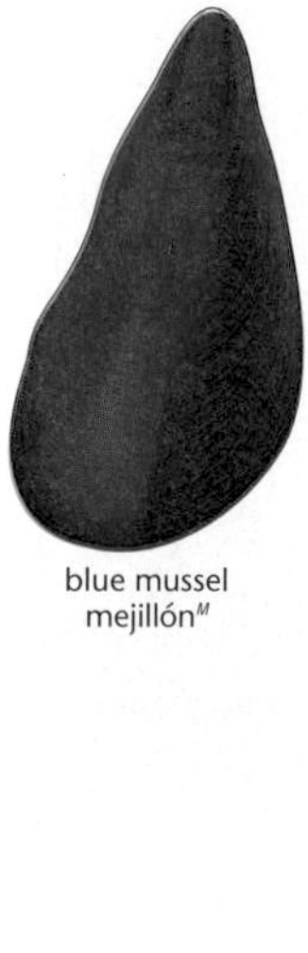

blue mussel
mejillón^M

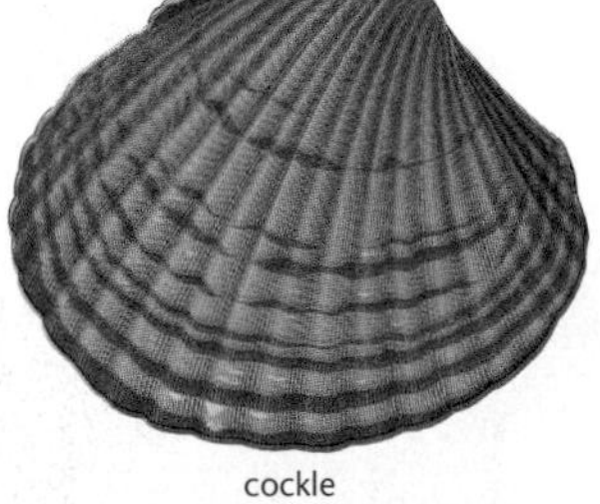

cockle
berberecho^M

clam
almeja^F

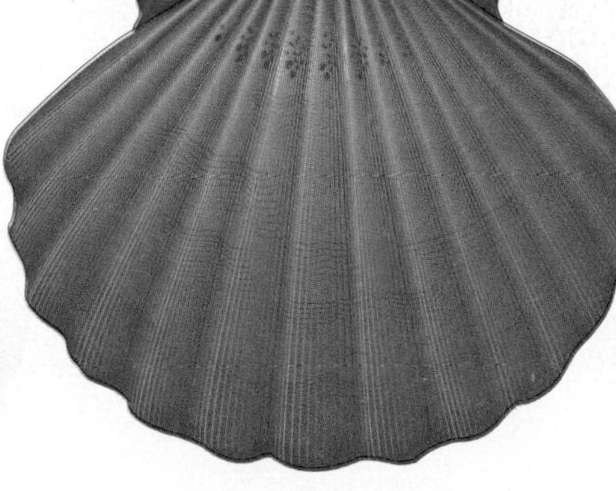

great scallop
vieira^F

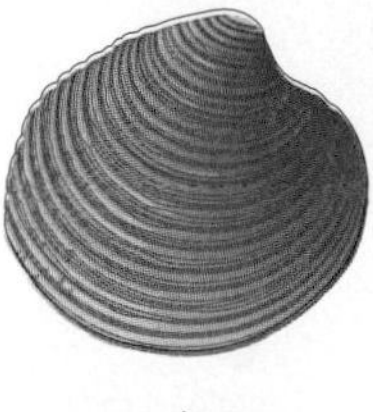

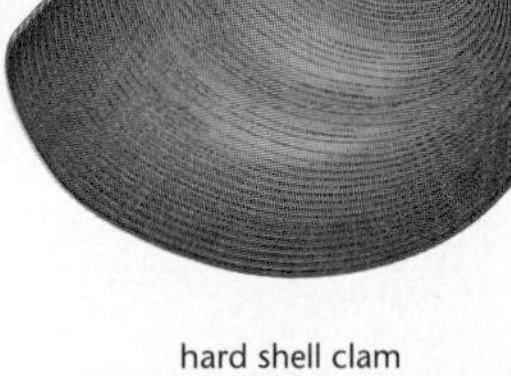

hard shell clam
almeja^F de concha^F dura

UNIVALVE SHELL
CONCHA^F UNIVALVA

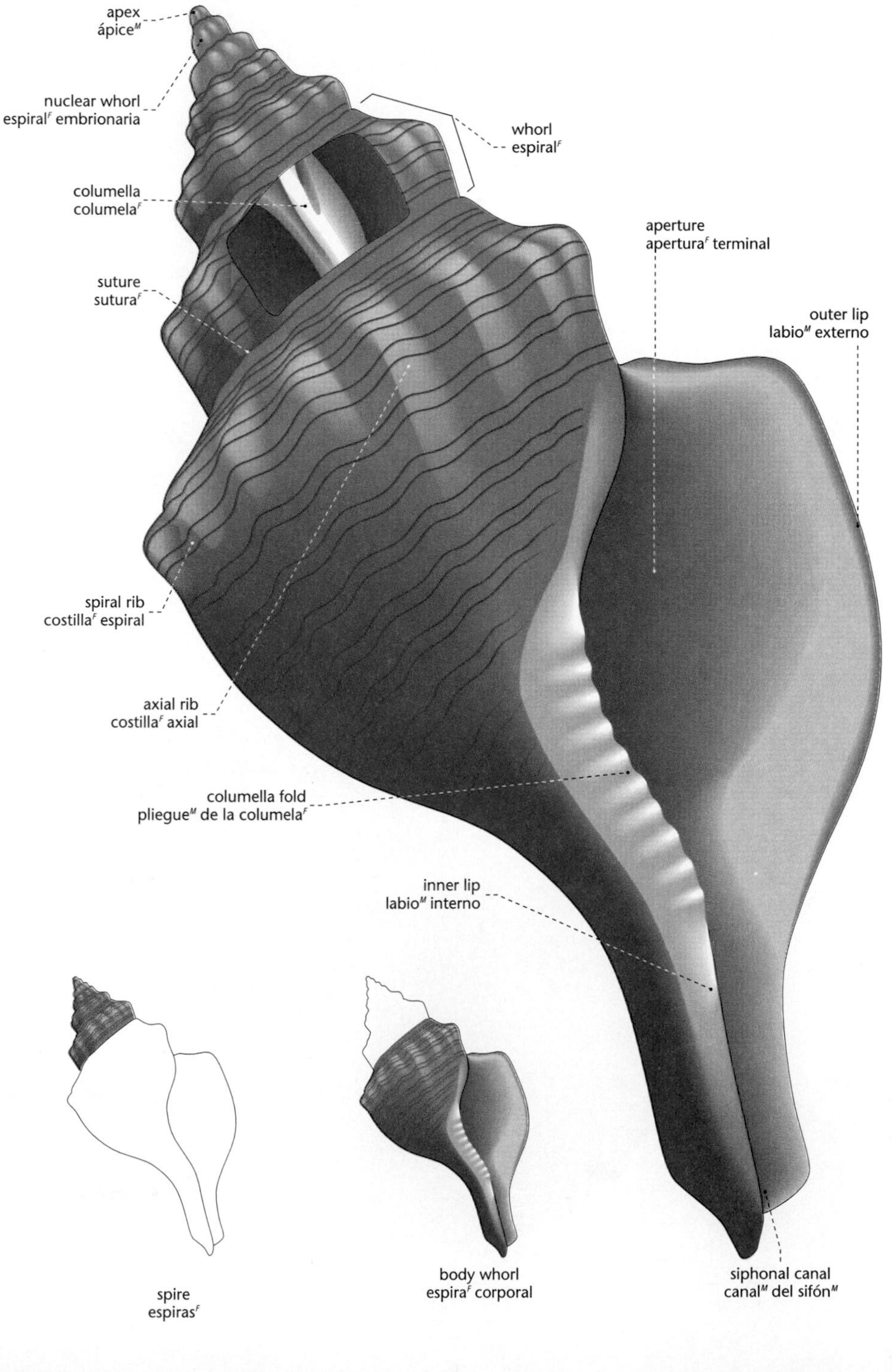

apex
ápice^M

nuclear whorl
espiral^F embrionaria

whorl
espiral^F

columella
columela^F

aperture
apertura^F terminal

suture
sutura^F

outer lip
labio^M externo

spiral rib
costilla^F espiral

axial rib
costilla^F axial

columella fold
pliegue^M de la columela^F

inner lip
labio^M interno

spire
espiras^F

body whorl
espira^F corporal

siphonal canal
canal^M del sifón^M

BIVALVE SHELL
CONCHA^F BIVALVA

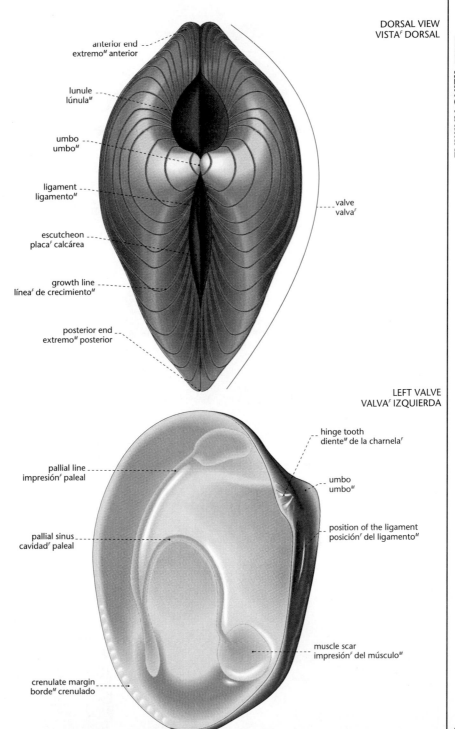

DORSAL VIEW
VISTA^F DORSAL

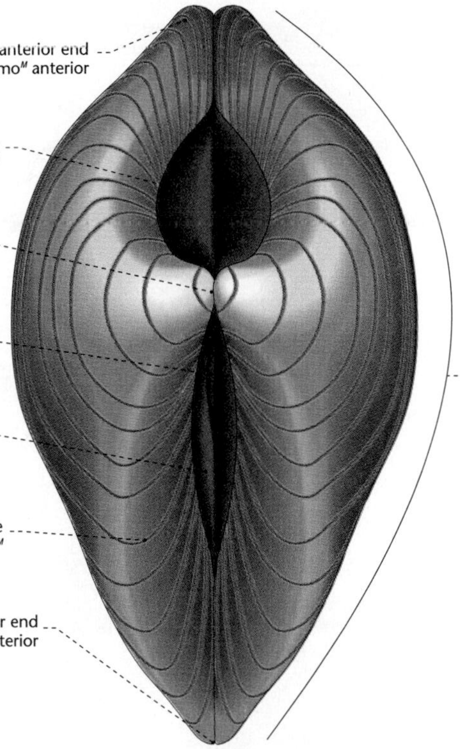

anterior end
extremo^M anterior

lunule
lúnula^M

umbo
umbo^M

ligament
ligamento^M

escutcheon
placa^F calcárea

growth line
línea^F de crecimiento^M

posterior end
extremo^M posterior

valve
valva^F

LEFT VALVE
VALVA^F IZQUIERDA

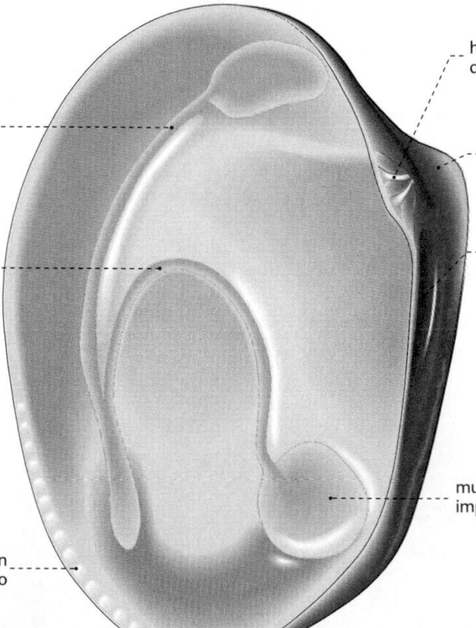

hinge tooth
diente^M de la charnela^F

pallial line
impresión^F paleal

umbo
umbo^M

position of the ligament
posición^F del ligamento^M

pallial sinus
cavidad^F paleal

muscle scar
impresión^F del músculo^M

crenulate margin
borde^M crenulado

95

ANIMAL KINGDOM
REINO ANIMAL

VENOMOUS SNAKE'S HEAD
CABEZA^F DE SERPIENTE^F VENENOSA

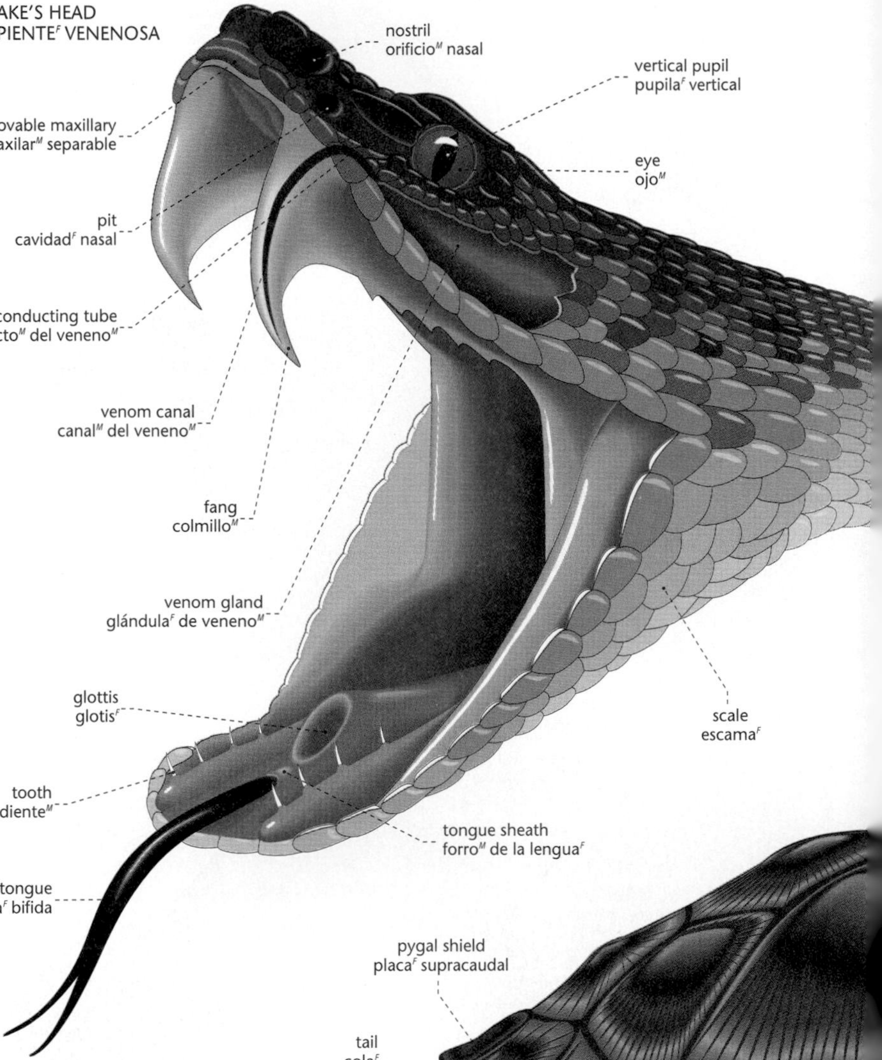

nostril
orificio^M nasal

vertical pupil
pupila^F vertical

movable maxillary
maxilar^M separable

eye
ojo^M

pit
cavidad^F nasal

venom-conducting tube
conducto^M del veneno^M

venom canal
canal^M del veneno^M

fang
colmillo^M

venom gland
glándula^F de veneno^M

glottis
glotis^F

scale
escama^F

tooth
diente^M

tongue sheath
forro^M de la lengua^F

forked tongue
lengua^F bífida

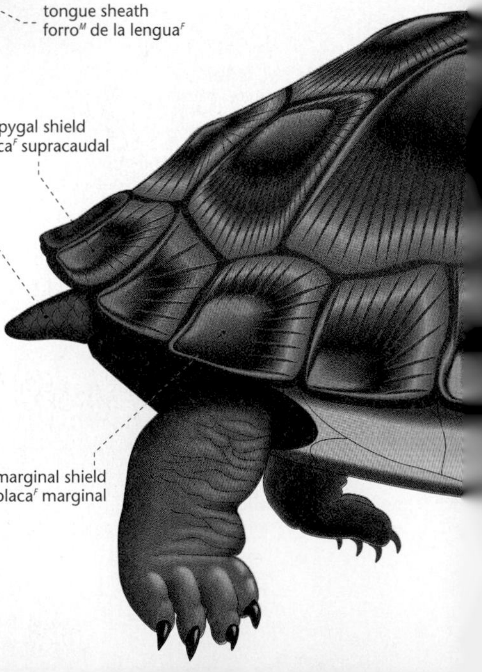

pygal shield
placa^F supracaudal

tail
cola^F

SHELL
CAPARAZÓN^M

carapace
espaldar^M

marginal shield
placa^F marginal

plastron
plastrón^M

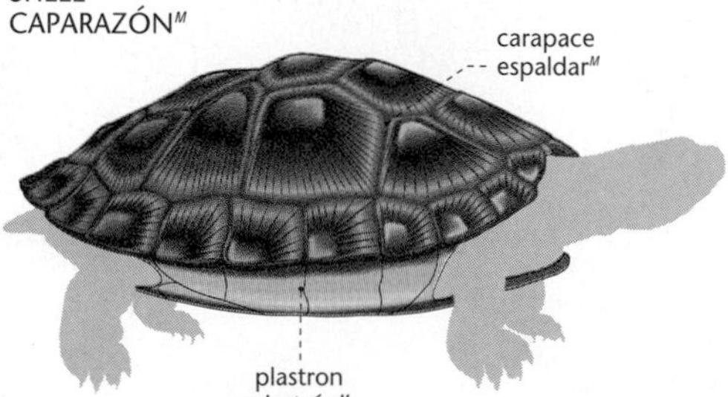

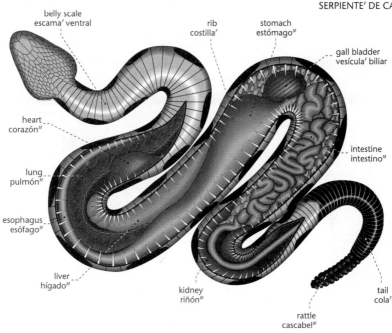

RATTLESNAKE
SERPIENTE^F DE CASCABEL^M

belly scale
escama^F ventral

rib
costilla^F

stomach
estómago^M

gall bladder
vesícula^F biliar

heart
corazón^M

intestine
intestino^M

lung
pulmón^M

esophagus
esófago^M

liver
hígado^M

kidney
riñón^M

rattle
cascabel^M

tail
cola^F

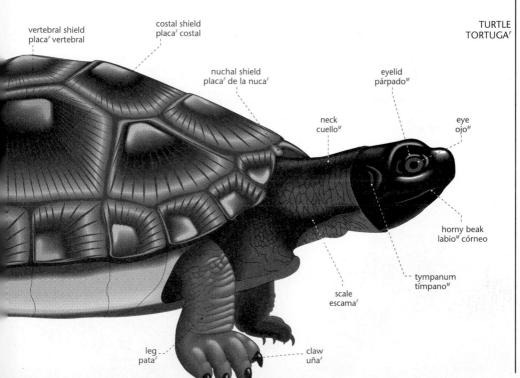

TURTLE
TORTUGA^F

vertebral shield
placa^F vertebral

costal shield
placa^F costal

nuchal shield
placa^F de la nuca^F

eyelid
párpado^M

neck
cuello^M

eye
ojo^M

horny beak
labio^M córneo

tympanum
tímpano^M

scale
escama^F

leg
pata^F

claw
uña^F

ANIMAL KINGDOM
REINO ANIMAL

BEAVER
CASTOR^M

RODENT'S JAW
MANDÍBULA^F DE ROEDOR^M

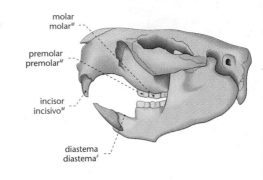

molar
molar^M

premolar
premolar^M

incisor
incisivo^M

diastema
diastema^F

LION
LEÓN^M

CARNIVORE'S JAW
MANDÍBULA^F DE CARNÍVORO^M

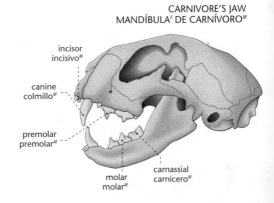

incisor
incisivo^M

canine
colmillo^M

premolar
premolar^M

molar
molar^M

carnassial
carnicero^M

HORSE
CABALLO^M

HERBIVORE'S JAW
MANDÍBULA^F DE HERBÍVORO^M

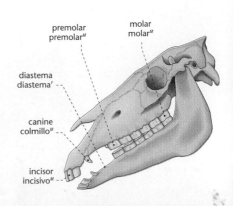

premolar
premolar^M

molar
molar^M

diastema
diastema^F

canine
colmillo^M

incisor
incisivo^M

MAJOR TYPES OF HORNS
CUERNOS^M: TIPOS^M MÁS COMUNES

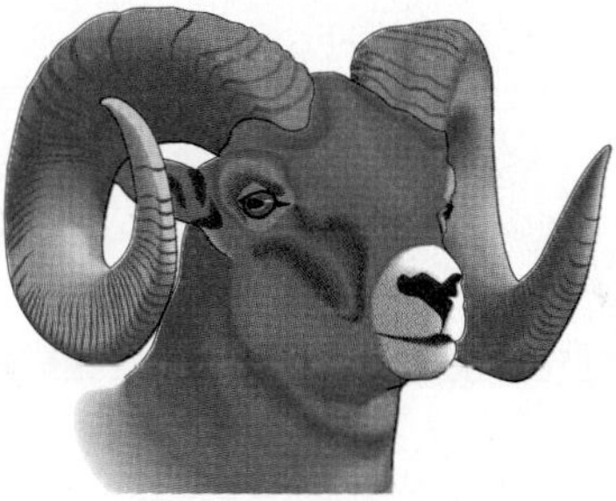

horns of mouflon
cuernos^M de muflón^M

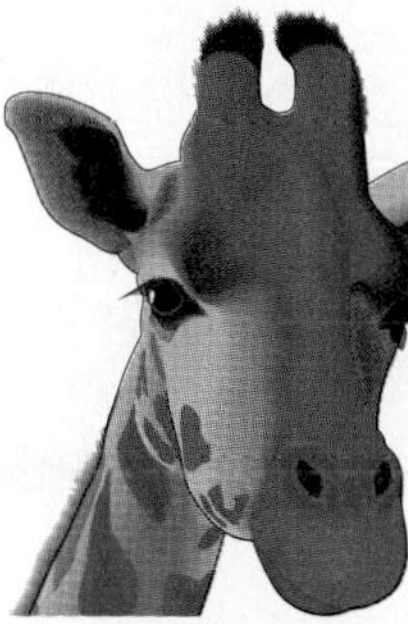

horns of giraffe
cuernos^M de jirafa^F

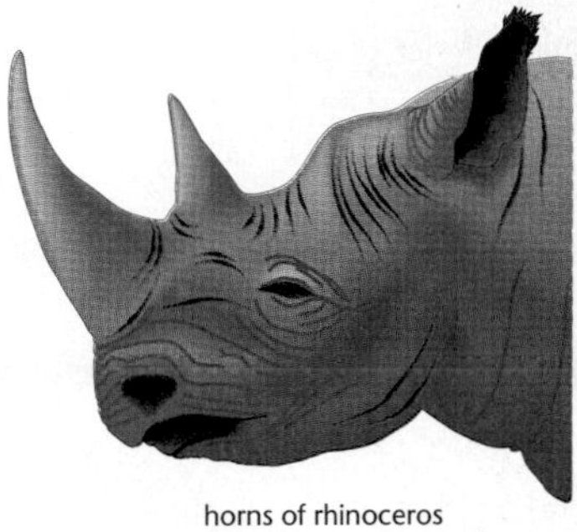

horns of rhinoceros
cuernos^M de rinoceronte^M

MAJOR TYPES OF TUSKS
COLMILLOS^M: TIPOS^M MÁS COMUNES

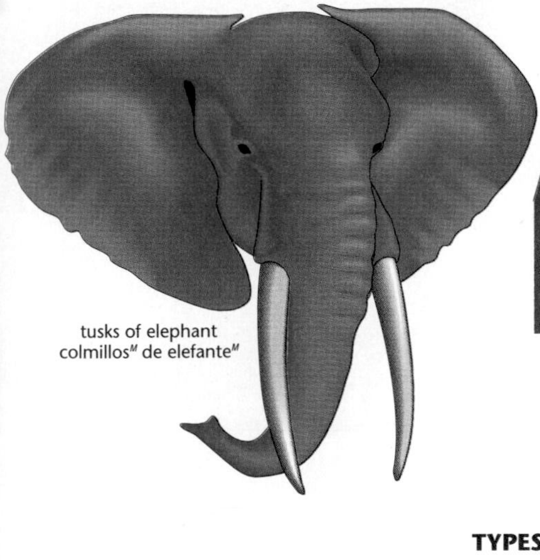

tusks of elephant
colmillos^M de elefante^M

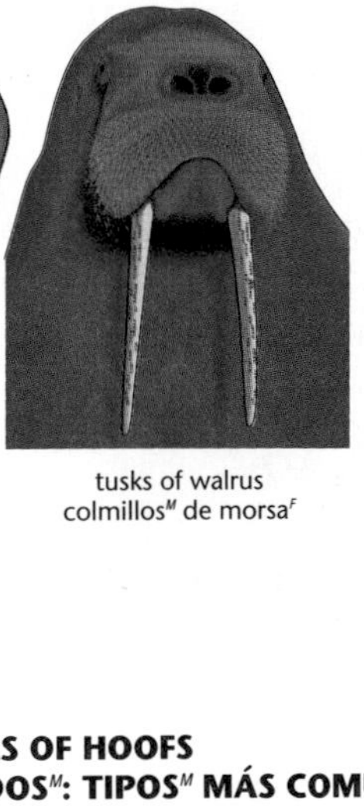

tusks of walrus
colmillos^M de morsa^F

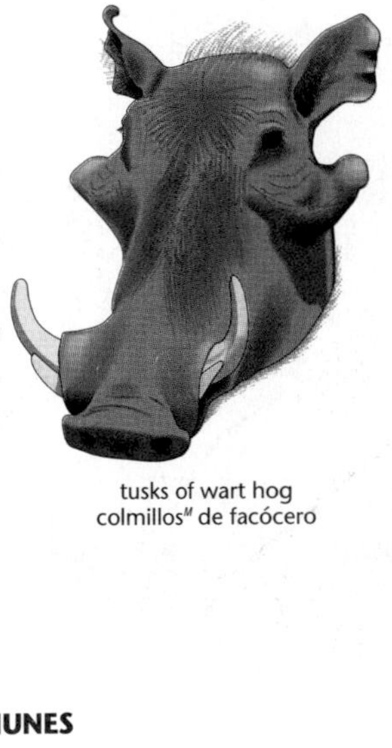

tusks of wart hog
colmillos^M de facócero

TYPES OF HOOFS
PATAS^F DE UNGULADOS^M: TIPOS^M MÁS COMUNES

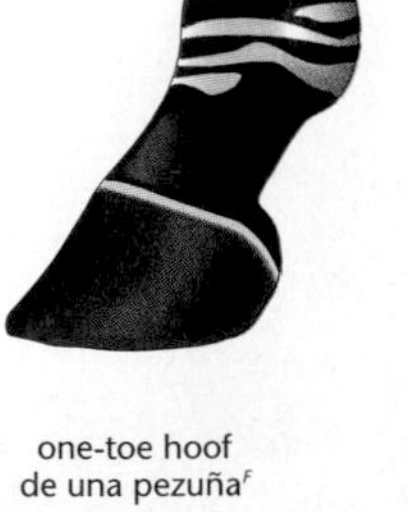

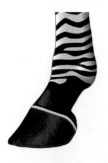

one-toe hoof
de una pezuña^F

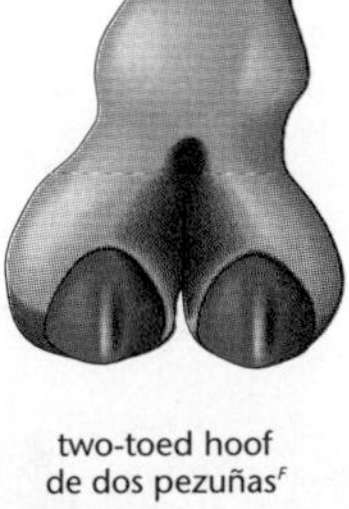

two-toed hoof
de dos pezuñas^F

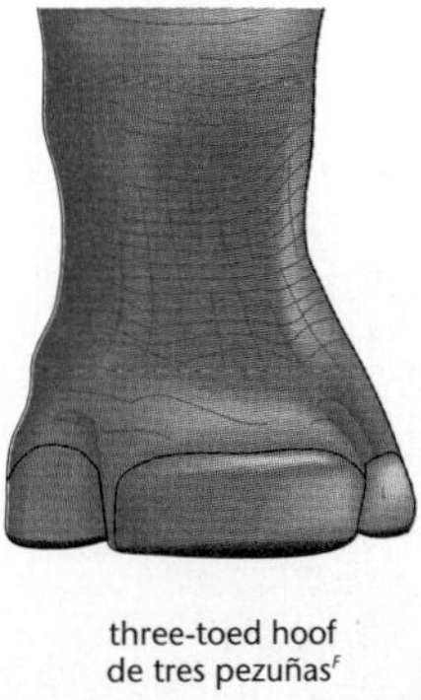

three-toed hoof
de tres pezuñas^F

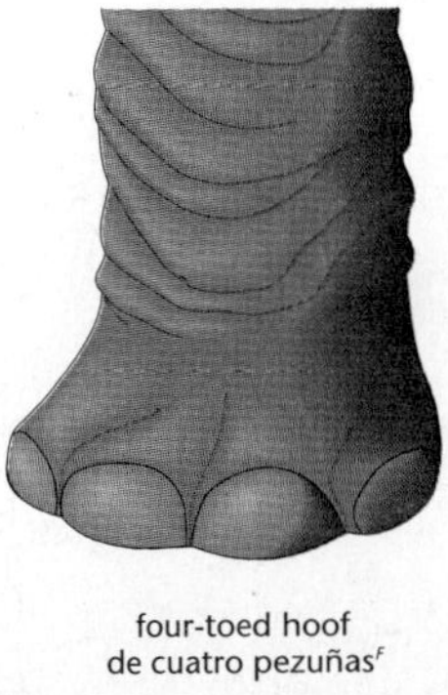

four-toed hoof
de cuatro pezuñas^F

HORSE
CABALLO[M]

MORPHOLOGY
MORFOLOGÍA[F]

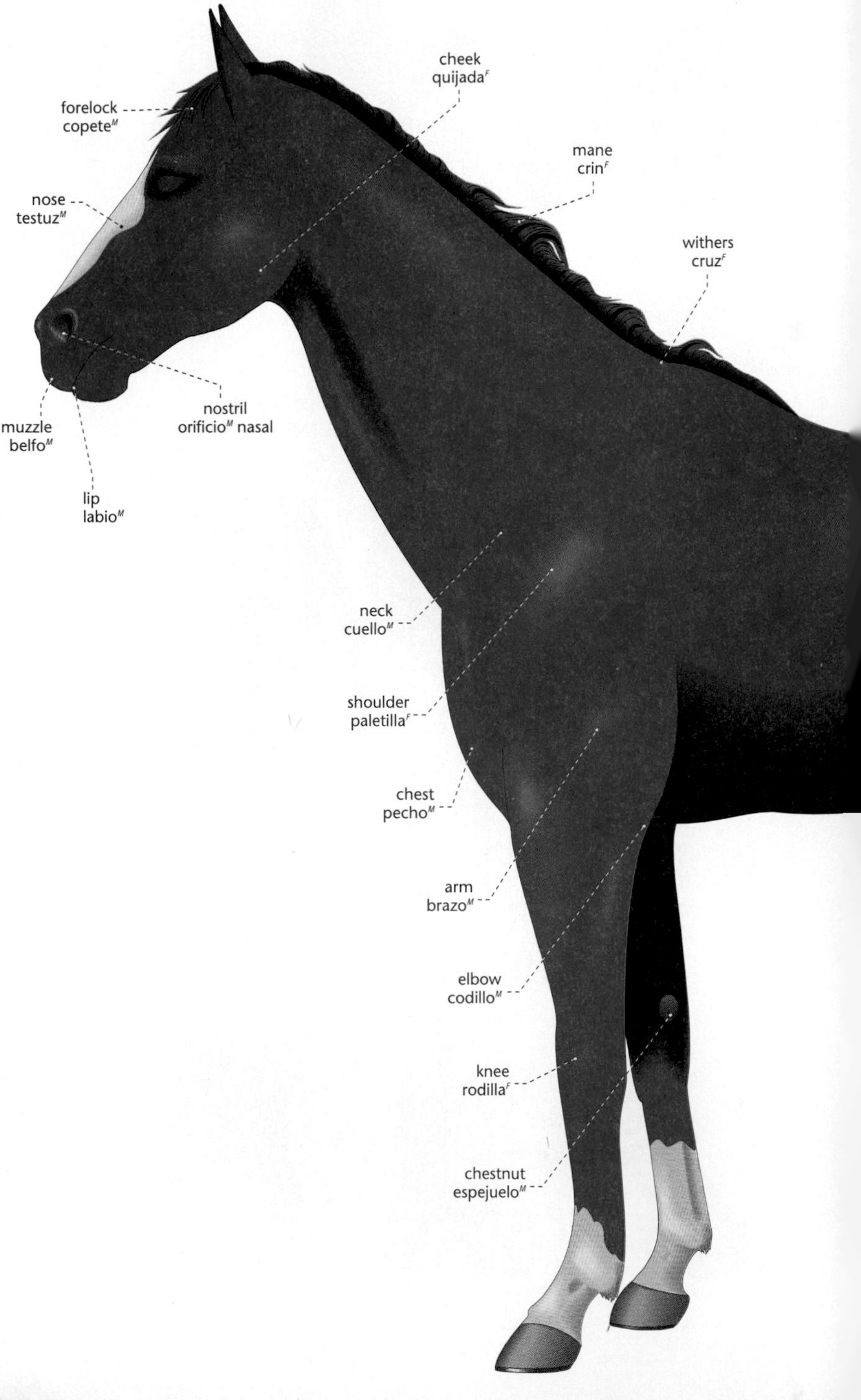

forelock
copete[M]

cheek
quijada[F]

mane
crin[F]

withers
cruz[F]

nose
testuz[M]

muzzle
belfo[M]

nostril
orificio[M] nasal

lip
labio[M]

neck
cuello[M]

shoulder
paletilla[F]

chest
pecho[M]

arm
brazo[M]

elbow
codillo[M]

knee
rodilla[F]

chestnut
espejuelo[M]

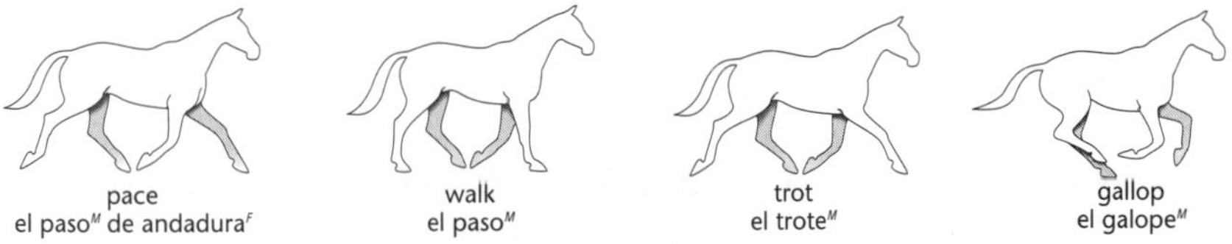

pace
el paso^M de andadura^F

walk
el paso^M

trot
el trote^M

gallop
el galope^M

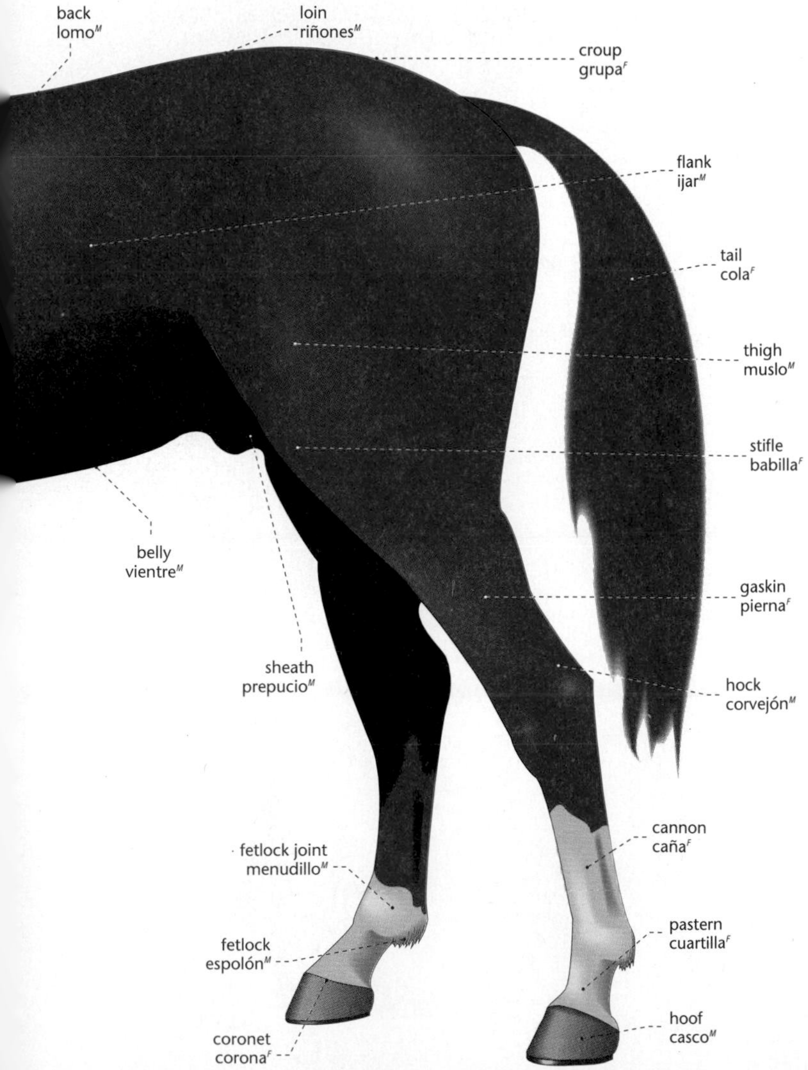

back
lomo^M

loin
riñones^M

croup
grupa^F

flank
ijar^M

tail
cola^F

thigh
muslo^M

stifle
babilla^F

belly
vientre^M

sheath
prepucio^M

gaskin
pierna^F

hock
corvejón^M

fetlock joint
menudillo^M

cannon
caña^F

fetlock
espolón^M

pastern
cuartilla^F

coronet
corona^F

hoof
casco^M

101

SKELETON
ESQUELETO^M

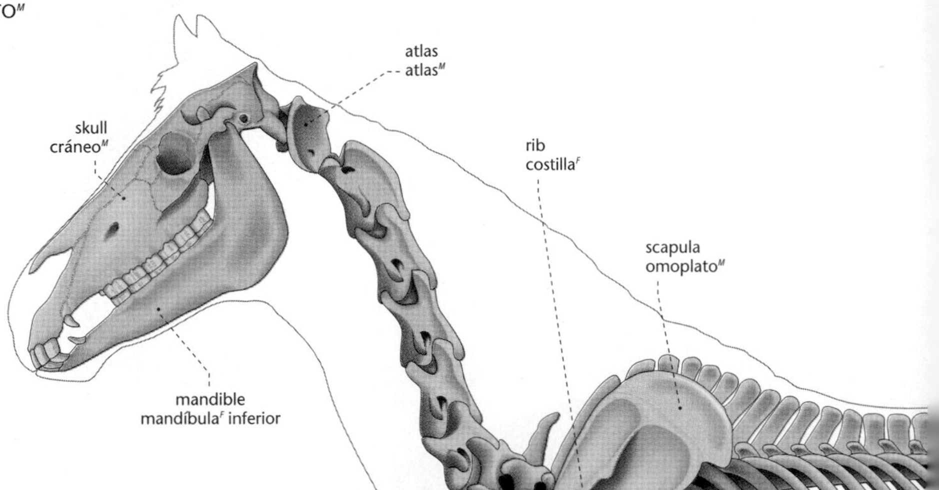

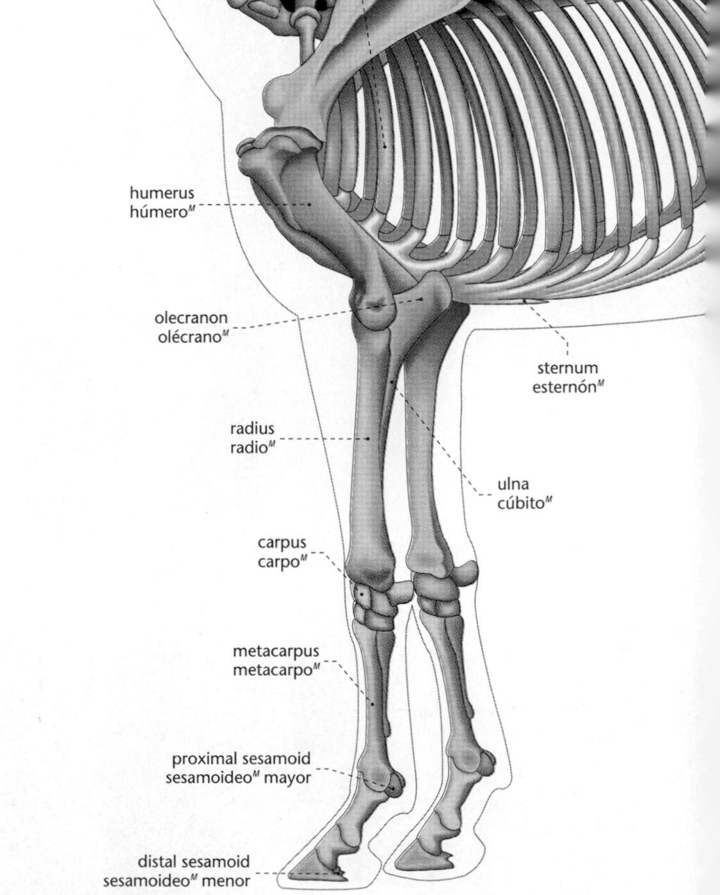

atlas
atlas^M

skull
cráneo^M

rib
costilla^F

scapula
omoplato^M

mandible
mandíbula^F inferior

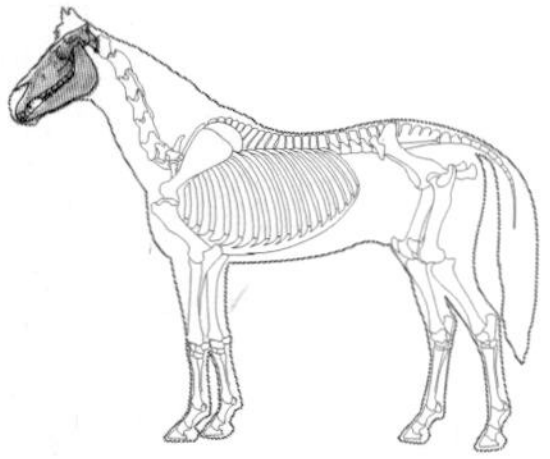

skull
cráneo^M

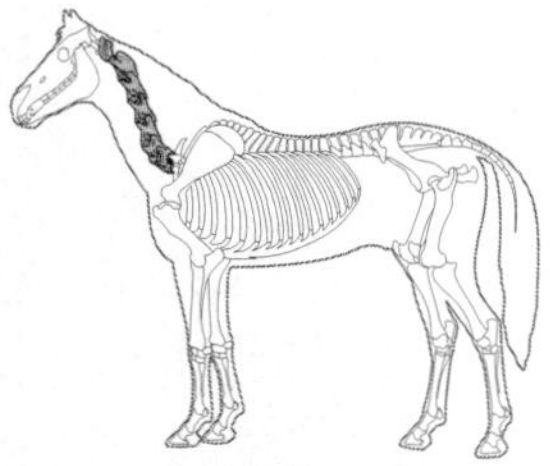

cervical vertebrae
vértebras^F cervicales

thoracic vertebrae
vértebras^F torácicas

humerus
húmero^M

olecranon
olécrano^M

sternum
esternón^M

radius
radio^M

ulna
cúbito^M

carpus
carpo^M

metacarpus
metacarpo^M

proximal sesamoid
sesamoideo^M mayor

distal sesamoid
sesamoideo^M menor

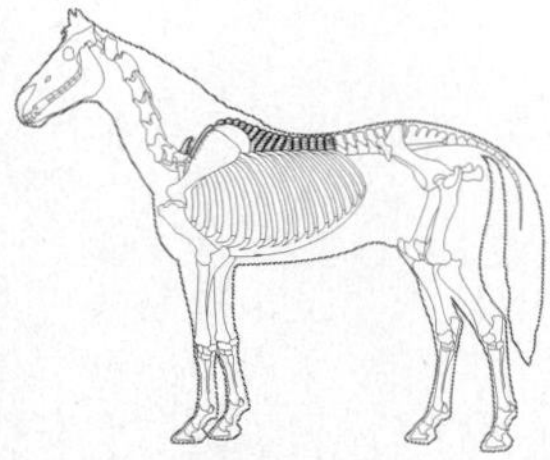

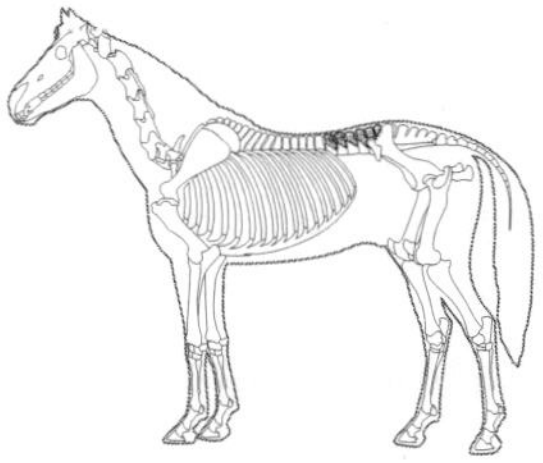

lumbar vertebrae
vértebras^F lumbares

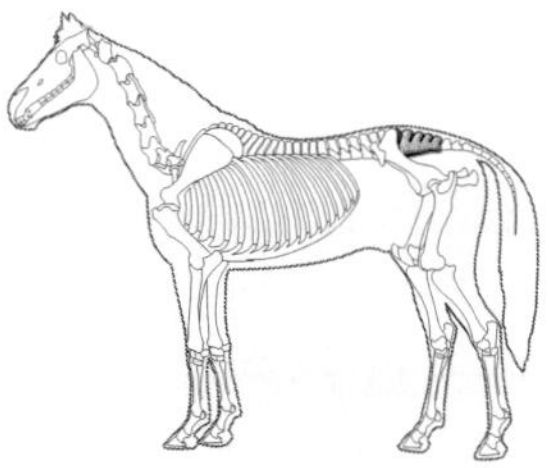

sacral vertebrae
vértebras^F sacras

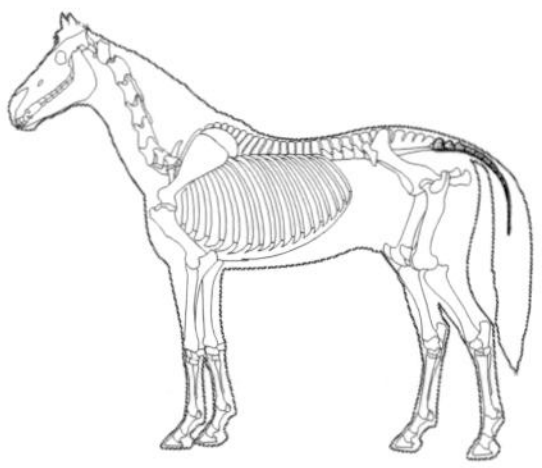

caudal vertebrae
vértebras^F caudales

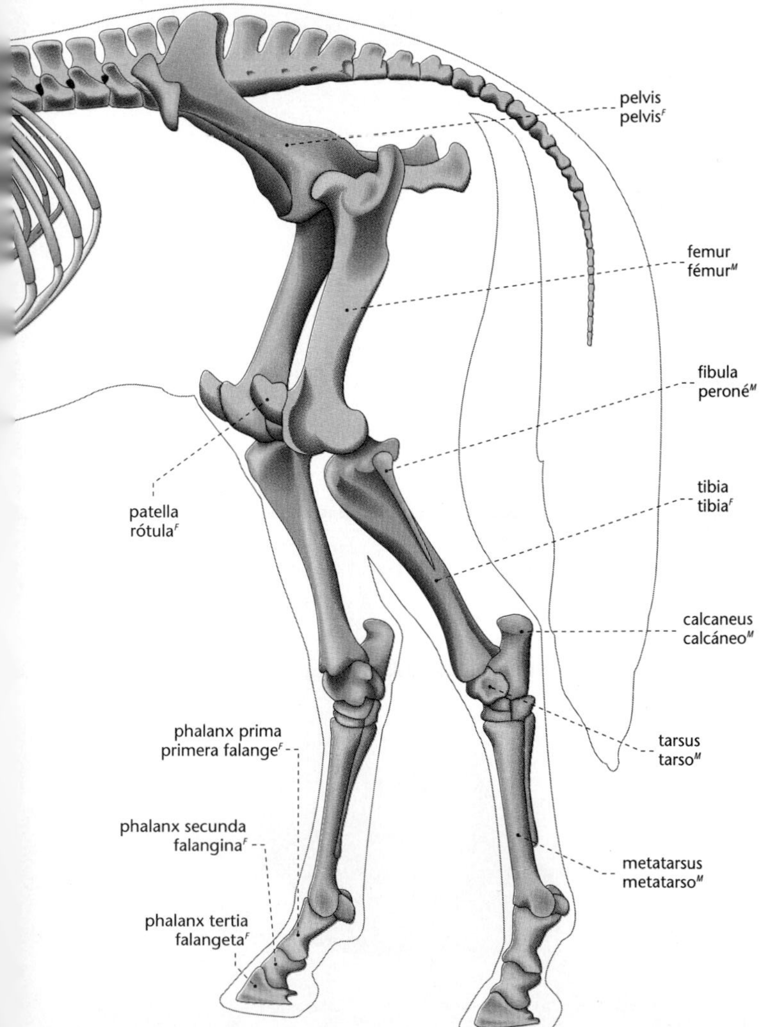

pelvis
pelvis^F

femur
fémur^M

fibula
peroné^M

tibia
tibia^F

patella
rótula^F

calcaneus
calcáneo^M

phalanx prima
primera falange^F

tarsus
tarso^M

phalanx secunda
falangina^F

metatarsus
metatarso^M

phalanx tertia
falangeta^F

103

PLANTAR SURFACE OF THE HOOF
SUPERFICIE^F PLANTAR DEL CASCO^M

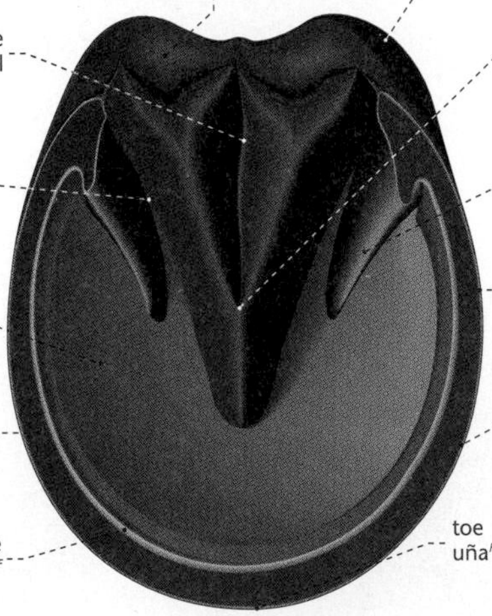

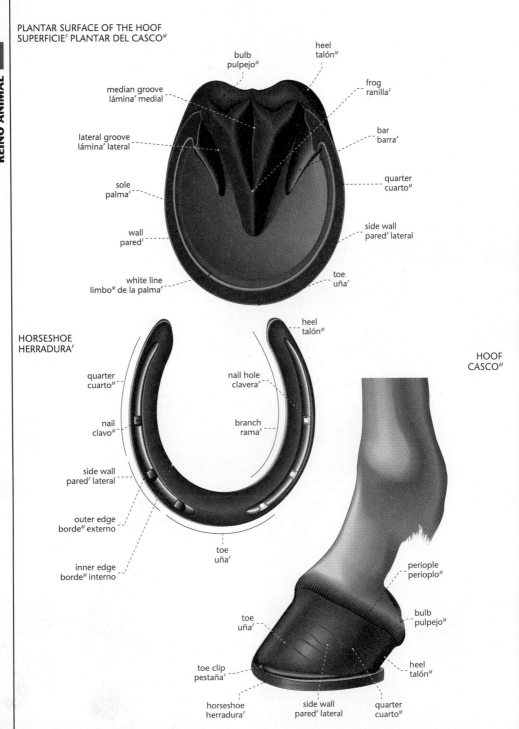

bulb
pulpejo^M

heel
talón^M

median groove
lámina^F medial

frog
ranilla^F

lateral groove
lámina^F lateral

bar
barra^F

sole
palma^F

quarter
cuarto^M

wall
pared^F

side wall
pared^F lateral

white line
limbo^M de la palma^F

toe
uña^F

HORSESHOE
HERRADURA^F

heel
talón^M

HOOF
CASCO^M

quarter
cuarto^M

nail hole
clavera^F

nail
clavo^M

branch
rama^F

side wall
pared^F lateral

outer edge
borde^M externo

toe
uña^F

inner edge
borde^M interno

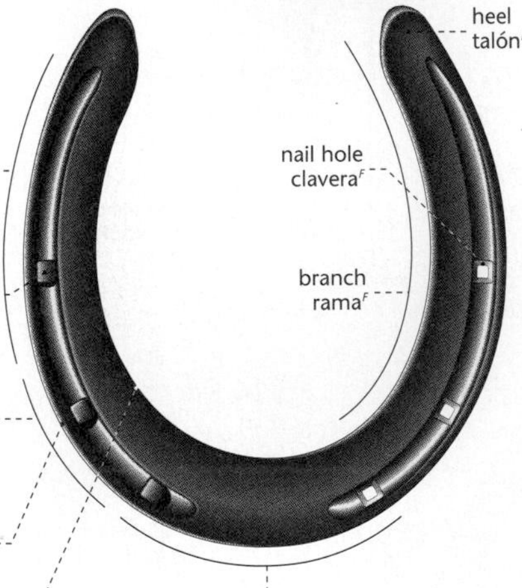

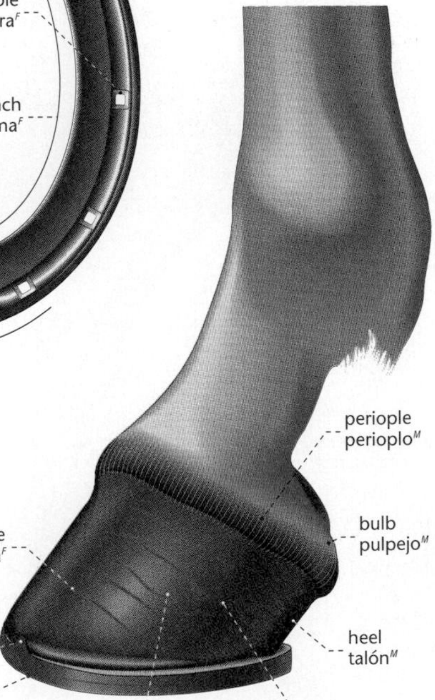

periople
perioplo^M

toe
uña^F

bulb
pulpejo^M

toe clip
pestaña^F

heel
talón^M

horseshoe
herradura^F

side wall
pared^F lateral

quarter
cuarto^M

DEER FAMILY
CÉRVIDOS^M

DEER ANTLERS
CORNAMENTA^F

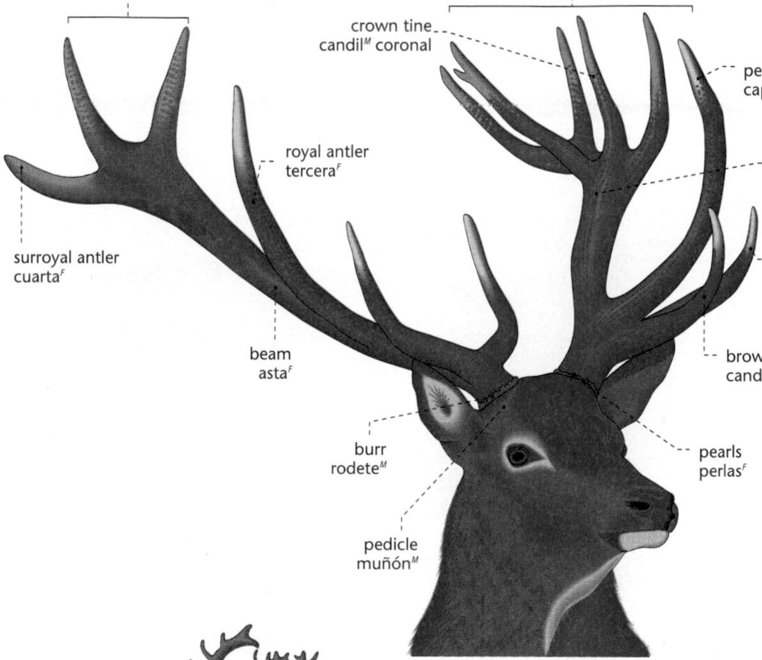

fork
horquilla^F

palm
palma^F

crown tine
candil^M coronal

pearl
capa^F córnea

royal antler
tercera^F

gutter
canalón^M

surroyal antler
cuarta^F

bay antler
baya^F

beam
asta^F

brow tine
candil^M frontal

burr
rodete^M

pearls
perlas^F

pedicle
muñón^M

KINDS OF DEER
PRINCIPALES CÉRVIDOS^M

caribou
caribú^M

white-tailed deer
ciervo^M de Virginia

moose
alce^M

wapiti
wapití^M

105

DOG
PERRO^M

MORPHOLOGY
MORFOLOGÍA^F

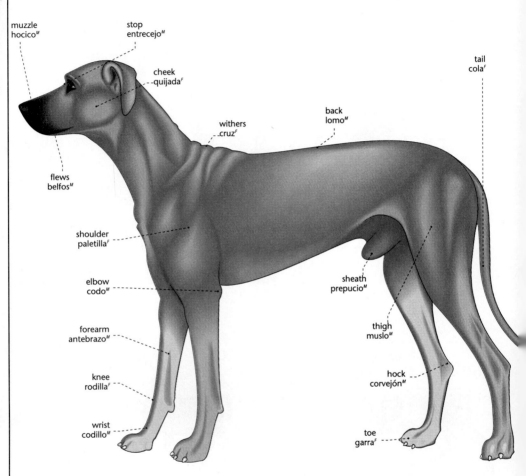

muzzle
hocico^M

stop
entrecejo^M

cheek
quijada^F

tail
cola^F

back
lomo^M

withers
cruz^F

flews
belfos^M

shoulder
paletilla^F

sheath
prepucio^M

elbow
codo^M

thigh
muslo^M

forearm
antebrazo^M

hock
corvejón^M

knee
rodilla^F

wrist
codillo^M

toe
garra^F

DOG'S FOREPAW
PATA^F DELANTERA DEL PERRO^M

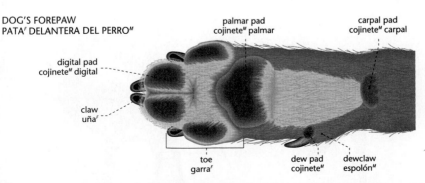

palmar pad
cojinete^M palmar

carpal pad
cojinete^M carpal

digital pad
cojinete^M digital

claw
uña^F

toe
garra^F

dew pad
cojinete^M

dewclaw
espolón^M

CAT
GATO^M DOMÉSTICO

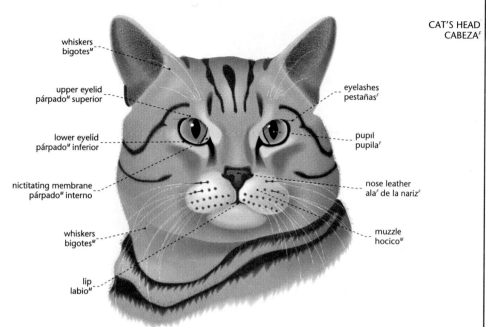

CAT'S HEAD
CABEZA^F

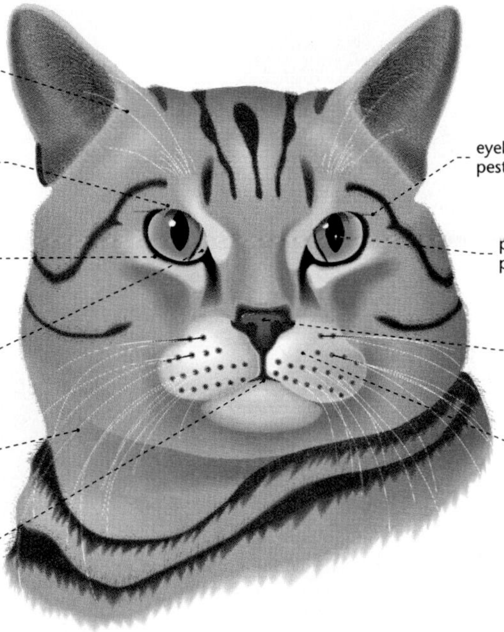

whiskers
bigotes^M

upper eyelid
párpado^M superior

lower eyelid
párpado^M inferior

nictitating membrane
párpado^M interno

whiskers
bigotes^M

lip
labio^M

eyelashes
pestañas^F

pupil
pupila^F

nose leather
ala^F de la nariz^F

muzzle
hocico^M

EXTENDED CLAW
UÑA^F EXTENDIDA

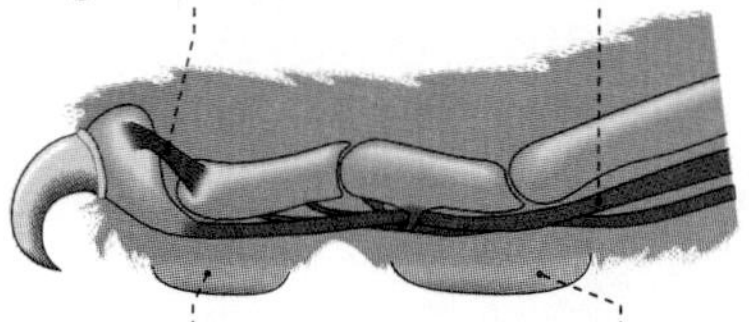

elastic ligament
ligamento^M elástico

tendon
tendón^M

digital pad
cojinete^M digital

plantar pad
cojinete^M plantar

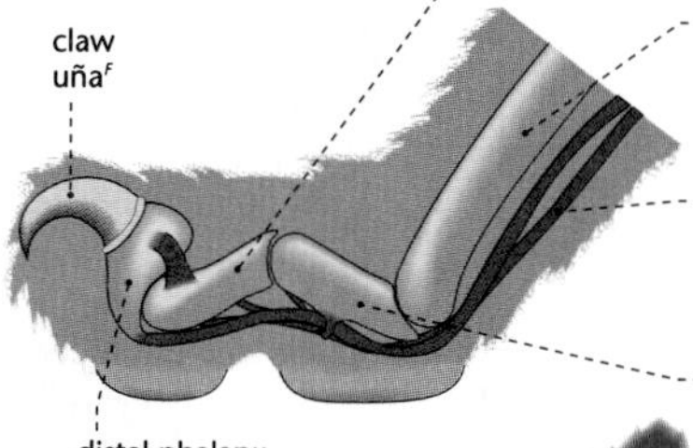

middle phalanx
falangina^F

RETRACTED CLAW
UÑA^F CONTRAIDA

claw
uña^F

metacarpus
metacarpo^M

tendon
tendón^M

proximal phalanx
falange^F

distal phalanx
falangeta^F

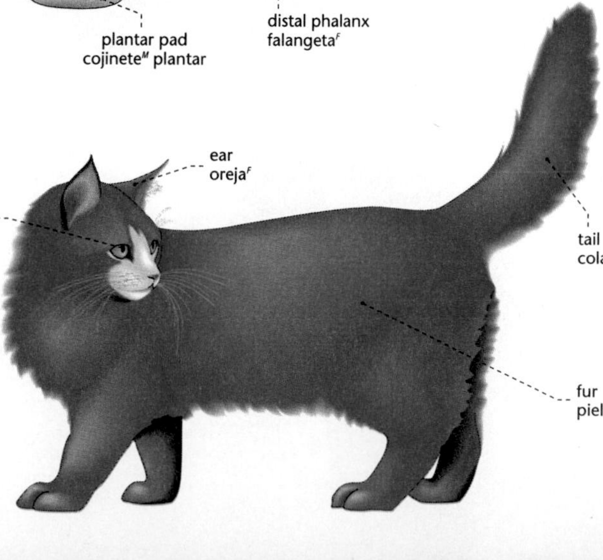

ear
oreja^F

eye
ojo^M

tail
cola^F

fur
piel^F

MORPHOLOGY
MORFOLOGÍA^F

ANIMAL KINGDOM
REINO ANIMAL

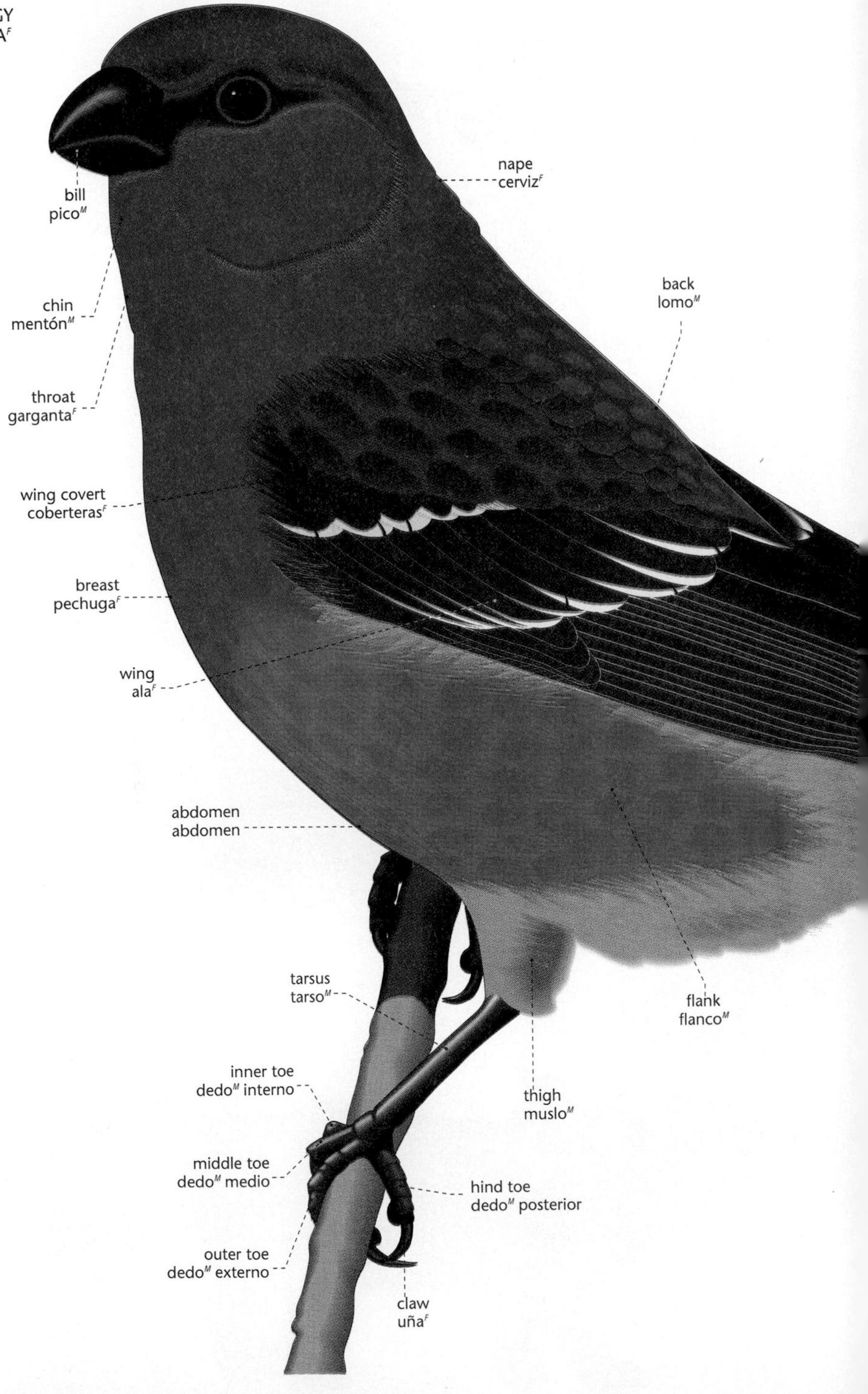

bill
pico^M

nape
cerviz^F

back
lomo^M

chin
mentón^M

throat
garganta^F

wing covert
coberteras^F

breast
pechuga^F

wing
ala^F

abdomen
abdomen

tarsus
tarso^M

flank
flanco^M

inner toe
dedo^M interno

thigh
muslo^M

middle toe
dedo^M medio

hind toe
dedo^M posterior

outer toe
dedo^M externo

claw
uña^F

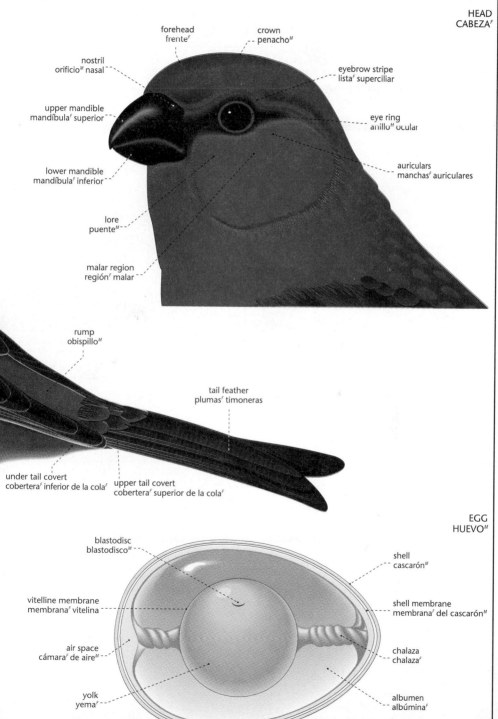

HEAD
CABEZA^F

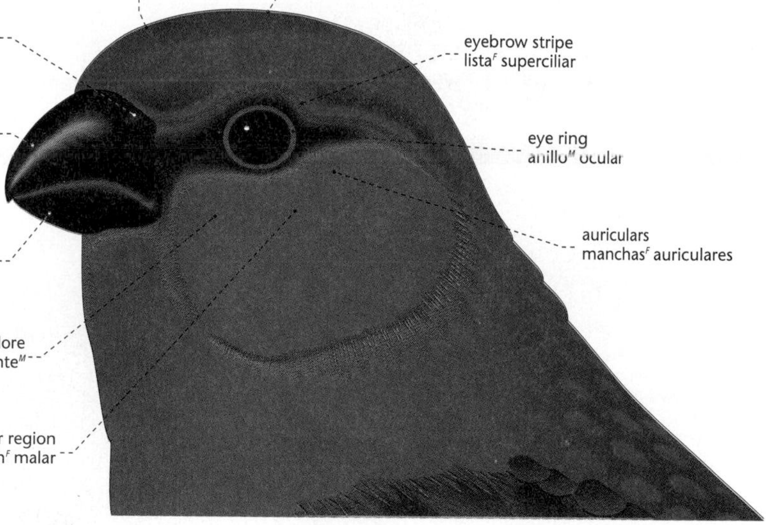

forehead
frente^F

crown
penacho^M

nostril
orificio^M nasal

eyebrow stripe
lista^F superciliar

upper mandible
mandíbula^F superior

eye ring
anillo^M ocular

lower mandible
mandíbula^F inferior

auriculars
manchas^F auriculares

lore
puente^M

malar region
región^F malar

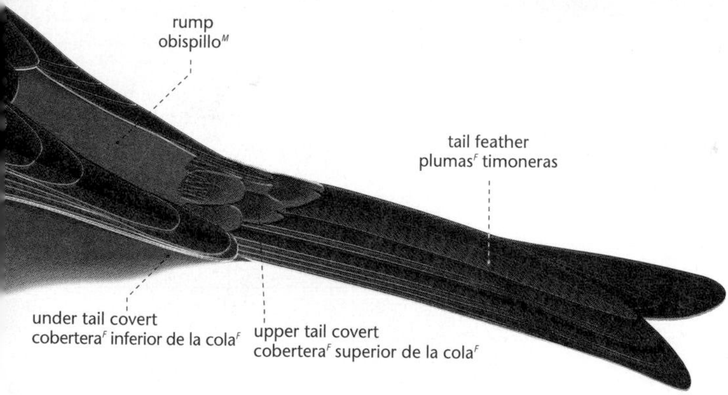

rump
obispillo^M

tail feather
plumas^F timoneras

under tail covert
cobertera^F inferior de la cola^F

upper tail covert
cobertera^F superior de la cola^F

EGG
HUEVO^M

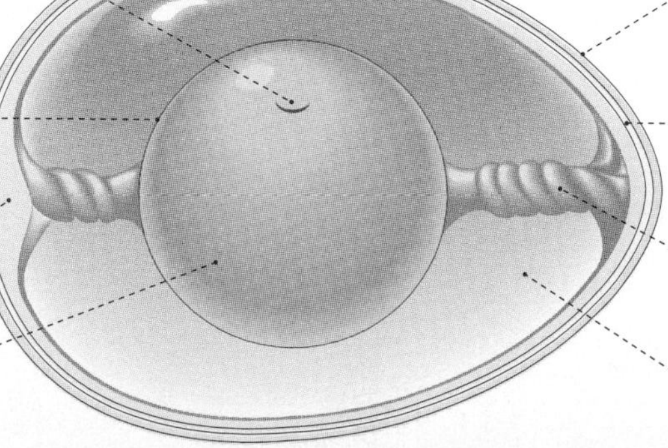

blastodisc
blastodisco^M

shell
cascarón^M

vitelline membrane
membrana^F vitelina

shell membrane
membrana^F del cascarón^M

air space
cámara^F de aire^M

chalaza
chalaza^F

yolk
yema^F

albumen
albúmina^F

ANIMAL KINGDOM
REINO ANIMAL

WING
ALA^F

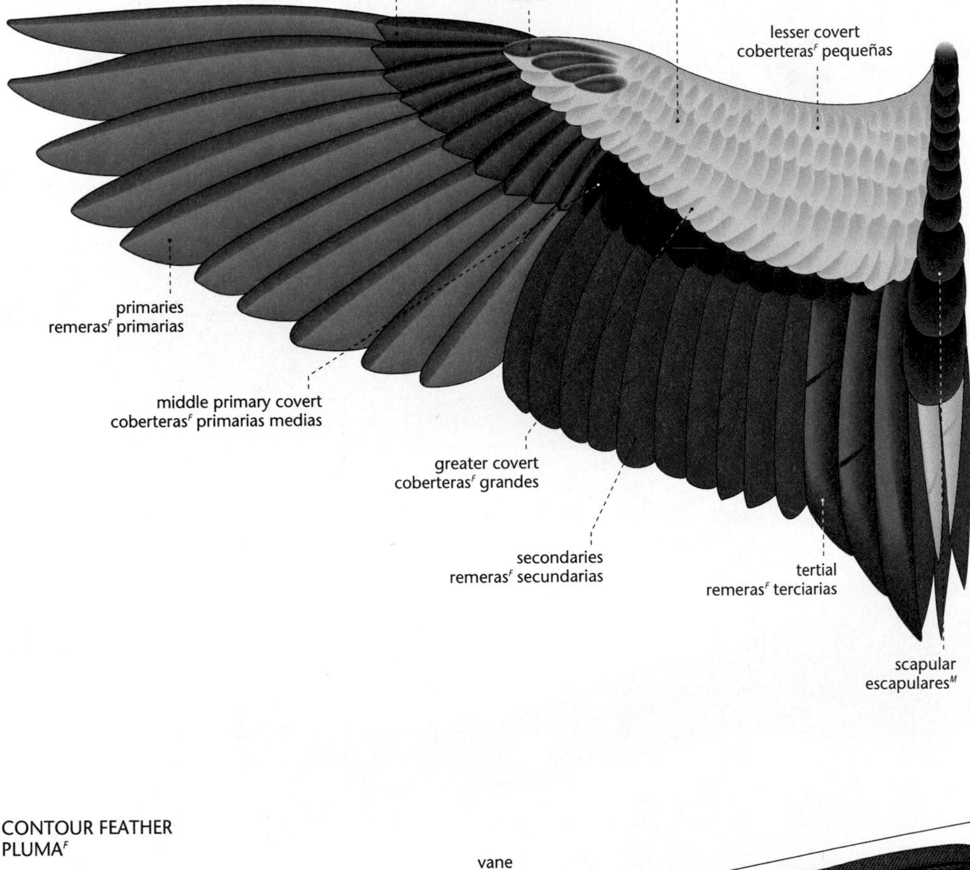

primary covert
coberteras^F primarias

alula
álula^F

middle covert
coberteras^F medias

lesser covert
coberteras^F pequeñas

primaries
remeras^F primarias

middle primary covert
coberteras^F primarias medias

greater covert
coberteras^F grandes

secondaries
remeras^F secundarias

tertial
remeras^F terciarias

scapular
escapulares^M

CONTOUR FEATHER
PLUMA^F

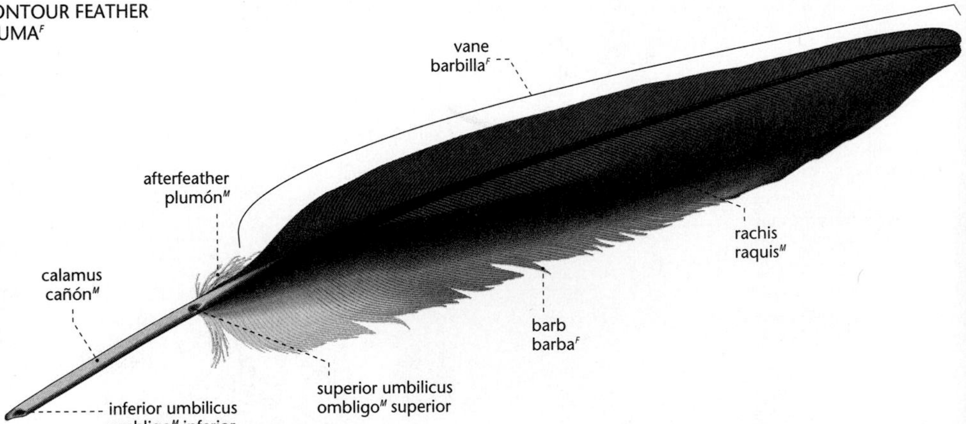

vane
barbilla^F

afterfeather
plumón^M

rachis
raquis^M

calamus
cañón^M

barb
barba^F

inferior umbilicus
ombligo^M inferior

superior umbilicus
ombligo^M superior

110

PRINCIPAL TYPES OF BILLS
PRINCIPALES TIPOS^M DE PICOS^M

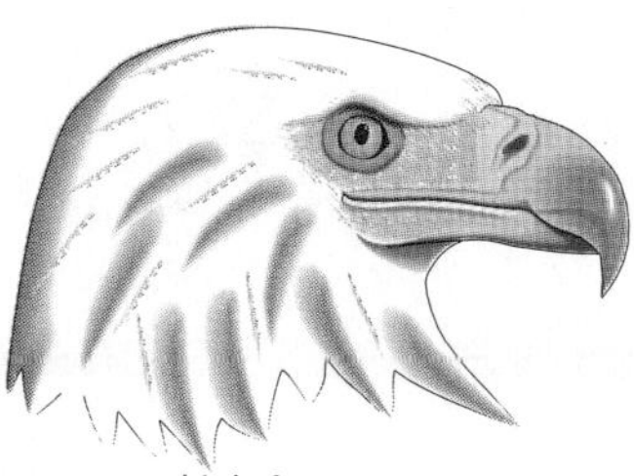

bird of prey
ave^F de rapiña

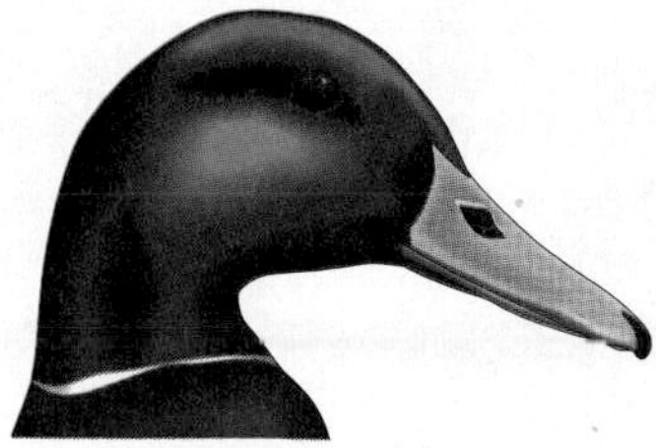

aquatic bird
ave^F acuática

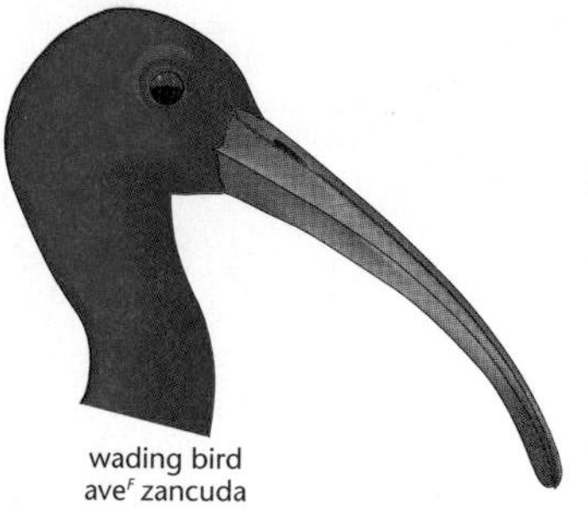

wading bird
ave^F zancuda

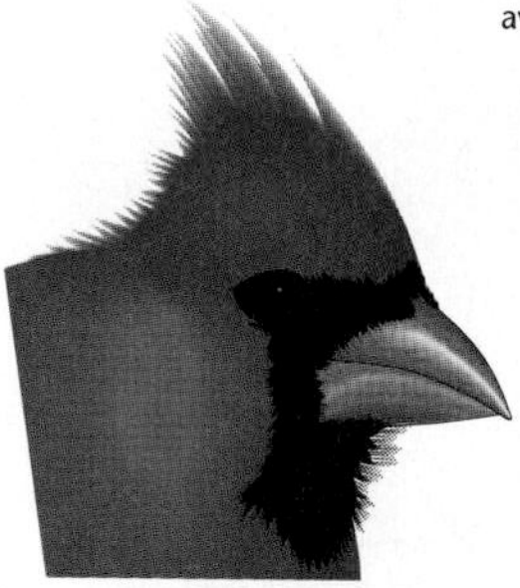

granivorous bird
ave^F granívora

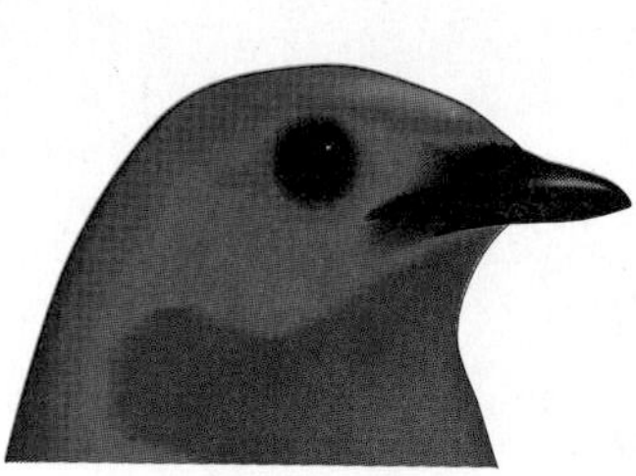

insectivorous bird
ave^F insectívora

PRINCIPAL TYPES OF FEET
PRINCIPALES TIPOS^M DE PATAS^F

**perching bird
aves^F trepadoras**

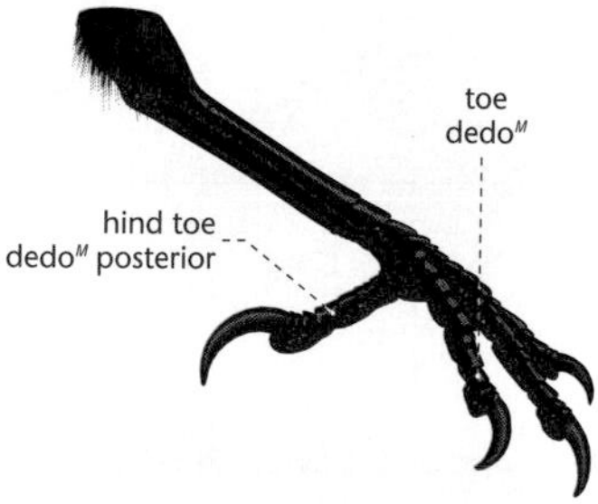

toe
dedo^M

hind toe
dedo^M posterior

**bird of prey
aves^F de rapiña**

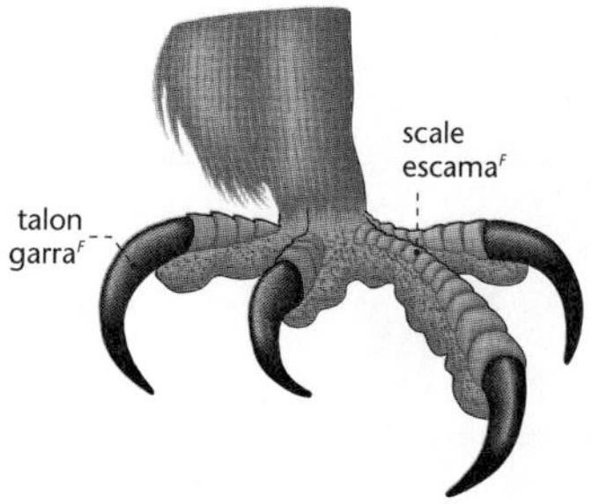

scale
escama^F

talon
garra^F

**aquatic bird
aves^F acuáticas**

**aquatic bird
aves^F acuáticas**

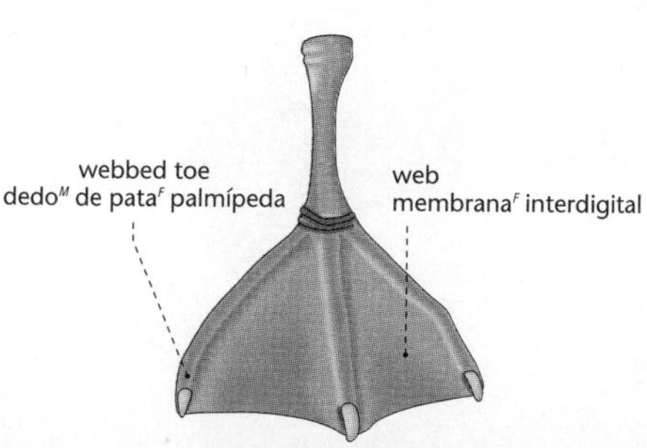

webbed toe
dedo^M de pata^F palmípeda

web
membrana^F interdigital

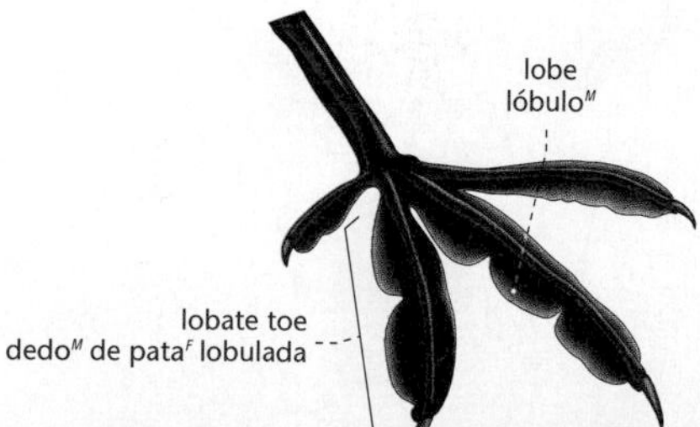

lobe
lóbulo^M

lobate toe
dedo^M de pata^F lobulada

111

BAT
MURCIÉLAGO^M

BAT'S HEAD
CABEZA^F DEL MURCIÉLAGO^M

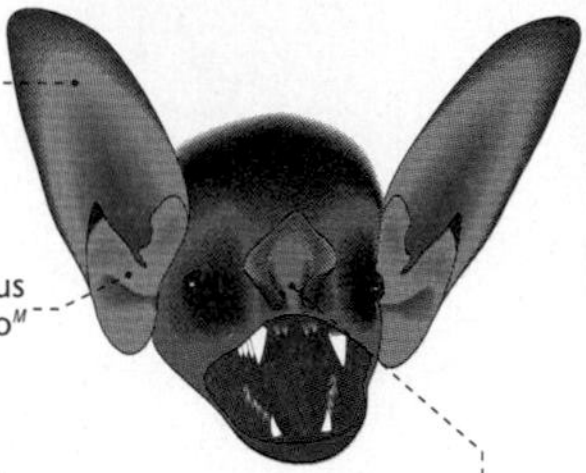

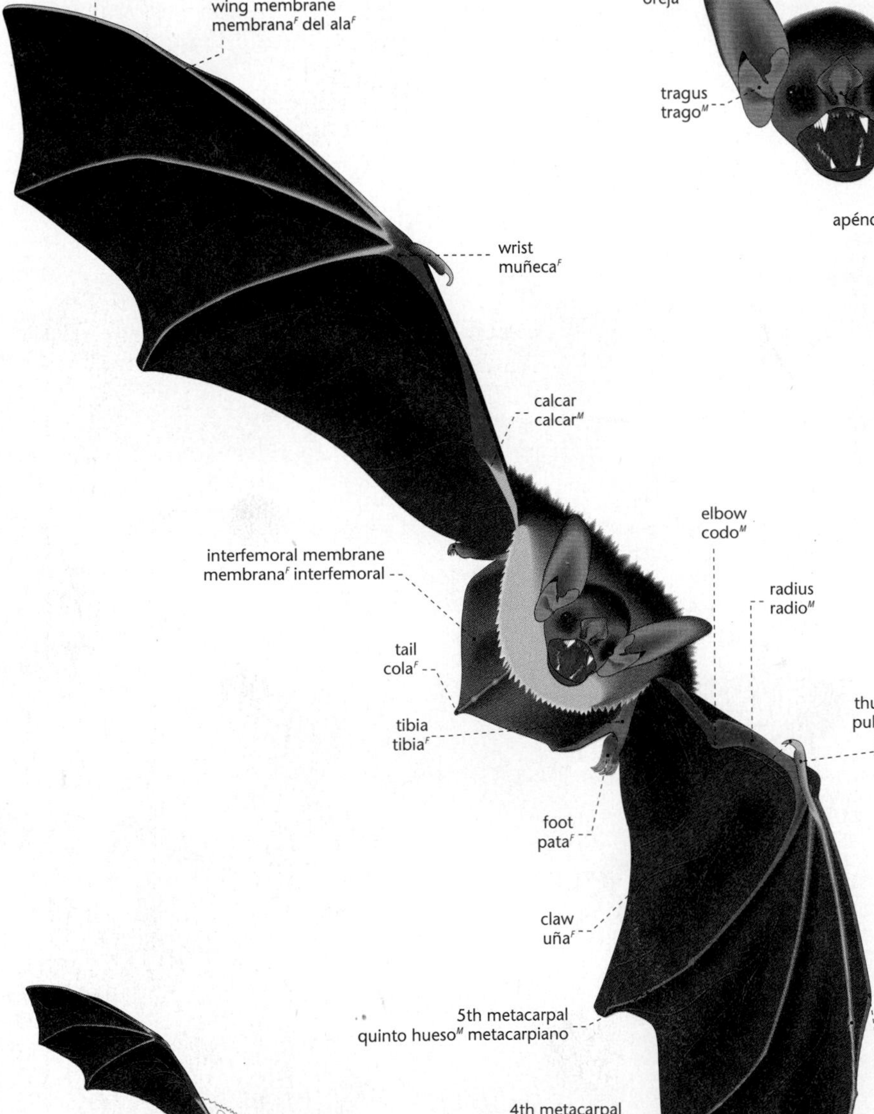

blood vessels
vasos^M sanguíneos

wing membrane
membrana^F del ala^F

ear
oreja^F

tragus
trago^M

nose leaf
apéndice^M nasal

wrist
muñeca^F

calcar
calcar^M

elbow
codo^M

radius
radio^M

interfemoral membrane
membrana^F interfemoral

tail
cola^F

thumb
pulgar^M

tibia
tibia^F

foot
pata^F

claw
uña^F

5th metacarpal
quinto hueso^M metacarpiano

4th metacarpal
cuarto hueso^M metacarpiano

3rd metacarpal
tercer hueso^M metacarpiano

2nd metacarpal
segundo hueso^M metacarpiano

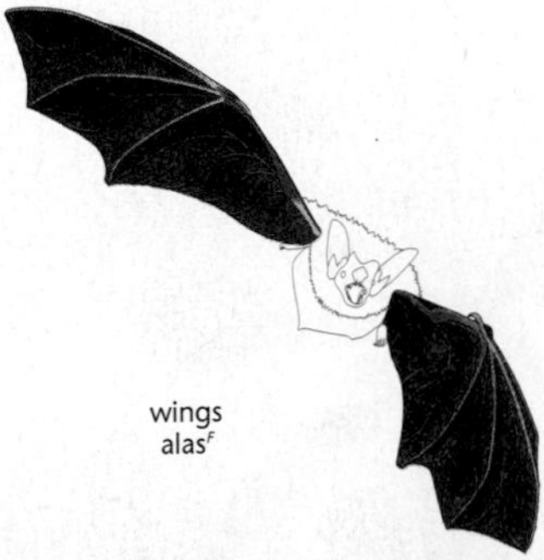

wings
alas^F

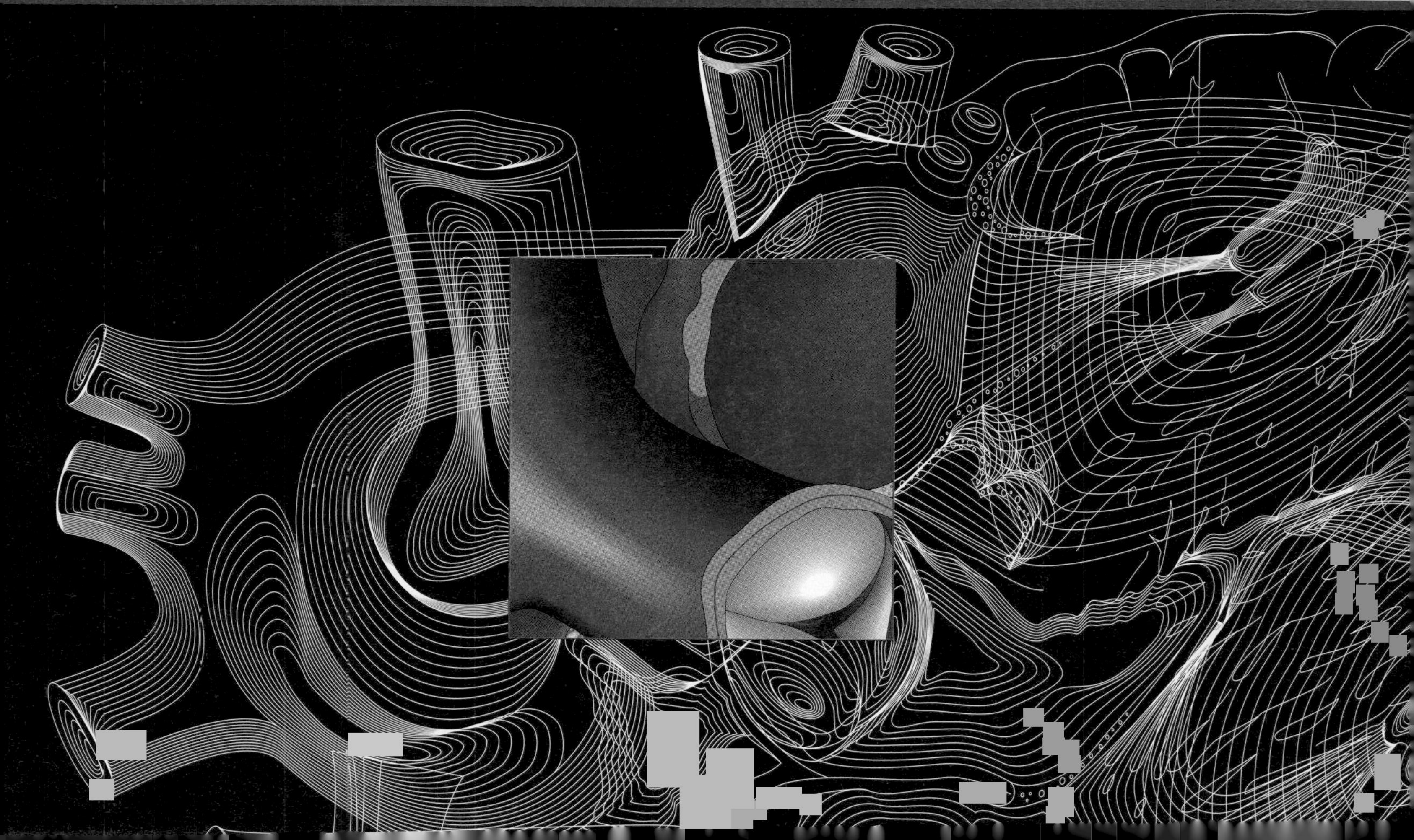

CONTENTS

PLANT CELL
CÉLULA^F VEGETAL

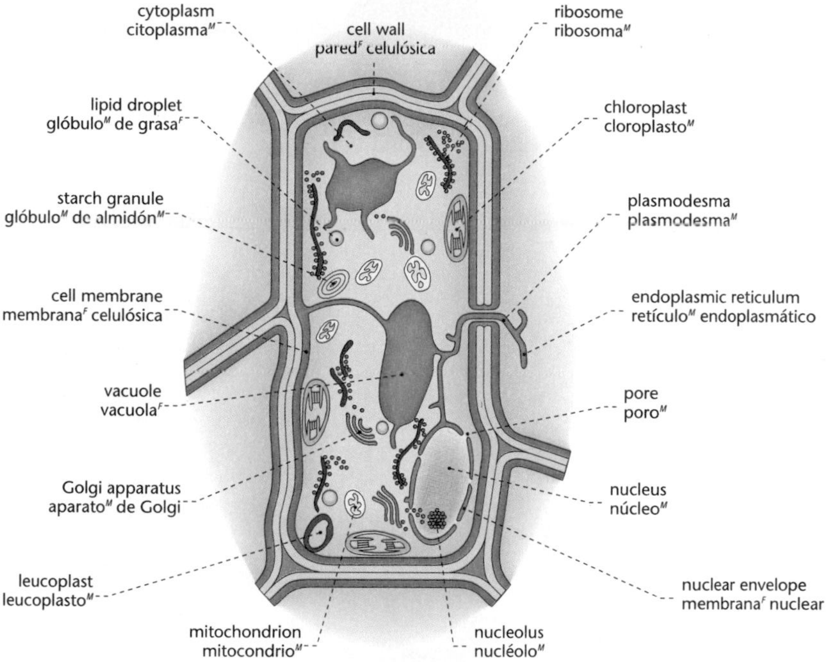

cytoplasm
citoplasma^M

cell wall
pared^F celulósica

ribosome
ribosoma^M

lipid droplet
glóbulo^M de grasa^F

chloroplast
cloroplasto^M

starch granule
glóbulo^M de almidón^M

plasmodesma
plasmodesma^M

cell membrane
membrana^F celulósica

endoplasmic reticulum
retículo^M endoplasmático

vacuole
vacuola^F

pore
poro^M

Golgi apparatus
aparato^M de Golgi

nucleus
núcleo^M

leucoplast
leucoplasto^M

nuclear envelope
membrana^F nuclear

mitochondrion
mitocondrio^M

nucleolus
nucléolo^M

ANIMAL CELL
CÉLULA^F ANIMAL

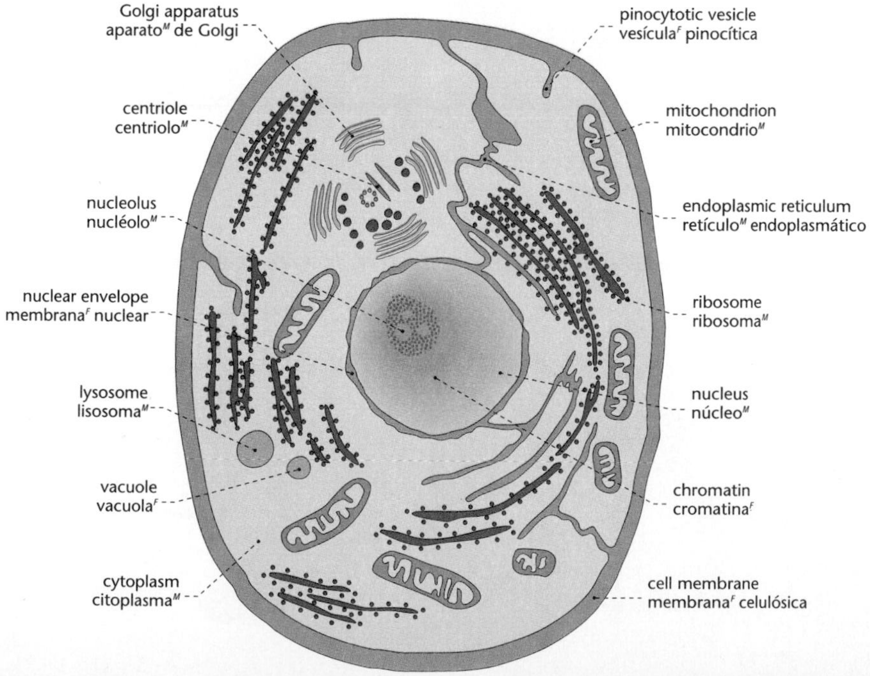

Golgi apparatus
aparato^M de Golgi

pinocytotic vesicle
vesícula^F pinocítica

centriole
centriolo^M

mitochondrion
mitocondrio^M

nucleolus
nucléolo^M

endoplasmic reticulum
retículo^M endoplasmático

nuclear envelope
membrana^F nuclear

ribosome
ribosoma^M

lysosome
lisosoma^M

nucleus
núcleo^M

vacuole
vacuola^F

chromatin
cromatina^F

cytoplasm
citoplasma^M

cell membrane
membrana^F celulósica

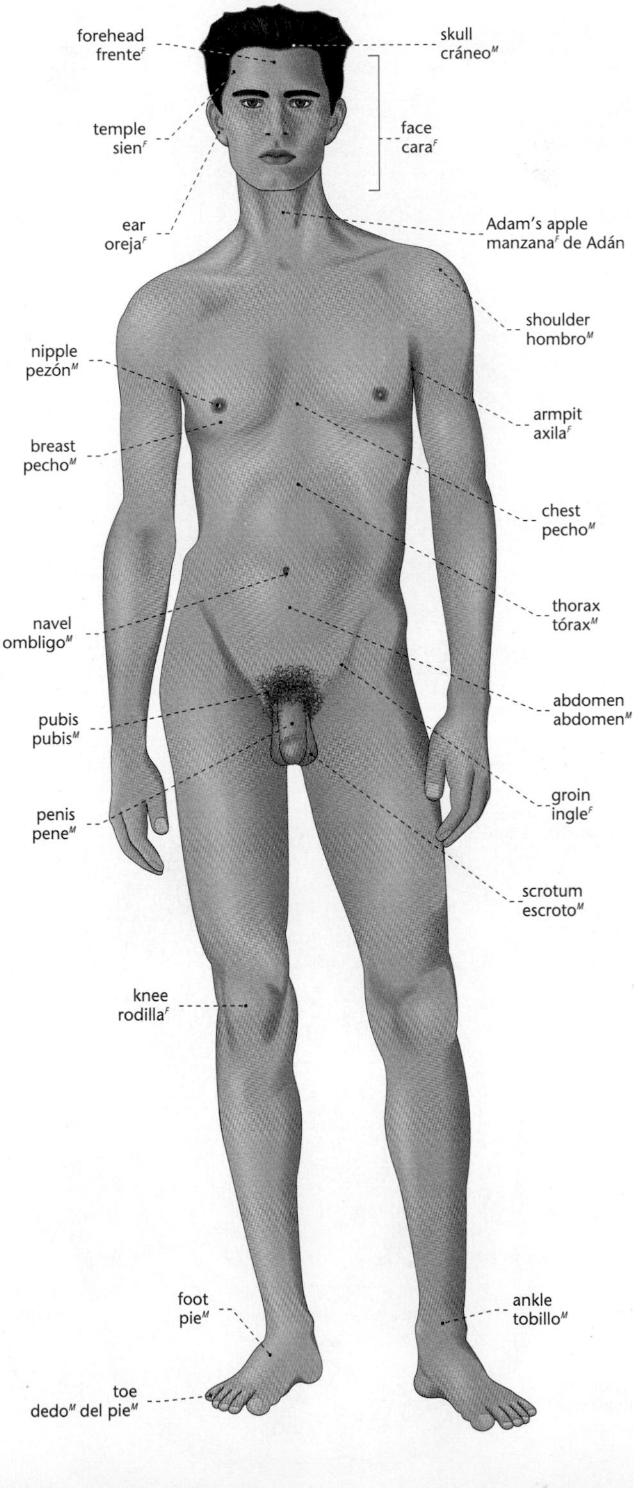

forehead
frente^F

skull
cráneo^M

temple
sien^F

face
cara^F

ear
oreja^F

Adam's apple
manzana^F de Adán

shoulder
hombro^M

nipple
pezón^M

armpit
axila^F

breast
pecho^M

chest
pecho^M

navel
ombligo^M

thorax
tórax^M

pubis
pubis^M

abdomen
abdomen^M

penis
pene^M

groin
ingle^F

scrotum
escroto^M

knee
rodilla^F

foot
pie^M

ankle
tobillo^M

toe
dedo^M del pie^M

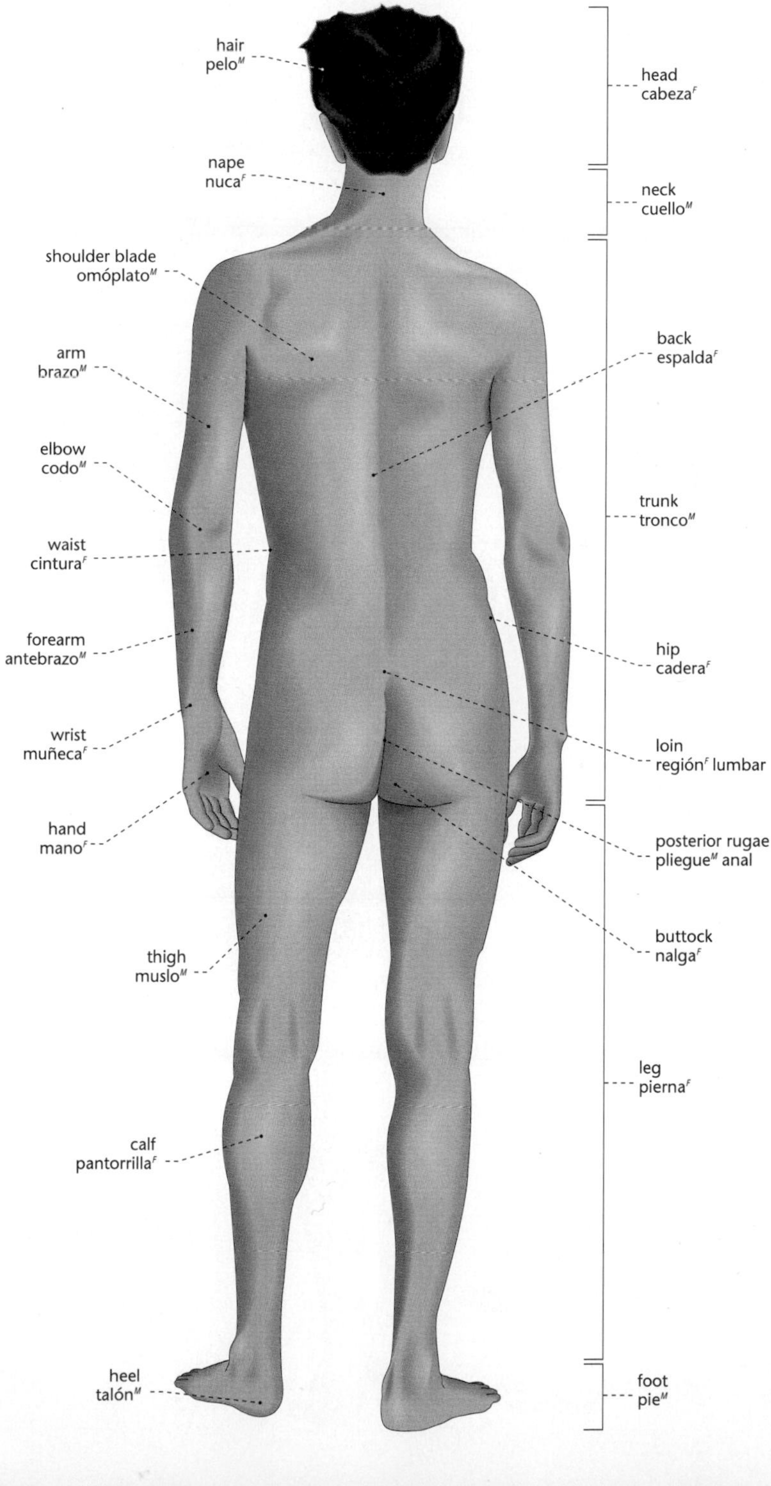

hair
pelo^M

nape
nuca^F

shoulder blade
omóplato^M

arm
brazo^M

elbow
codo^M

waist
cintura^F

forearm
antebrazo^M

wrist
muñeca^F

hand
mano^F

thigh
muslo^M

calf
pantorrilla^F

heel
talón^M

head
cabeza^F

neck
cuello^M

back
espalda^F

trunk
tronco^M

hip
cadera^F

loin
región^F lumbar

posterior rugae
pliegue^M anal

buttock
nalga^F

leg
pierna^F

foot
pie^M

HUMAN BODY
CUERPO^M HUMANO

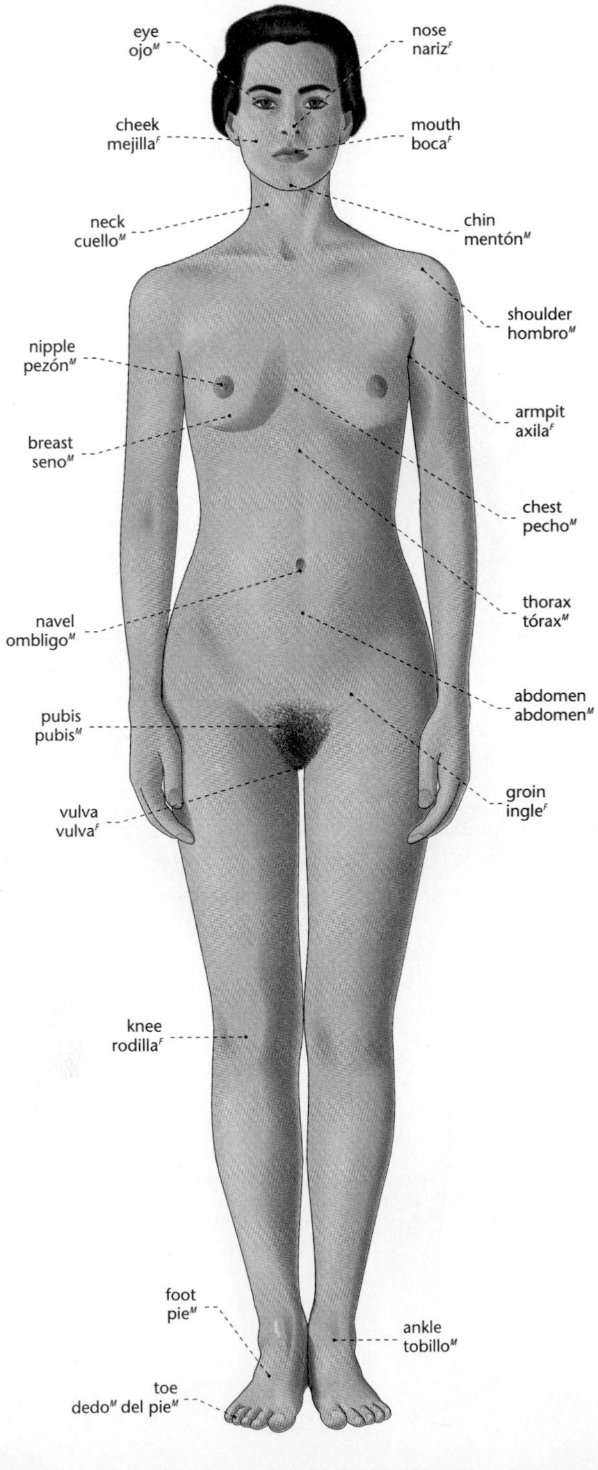

eye
ojo^M

nose
nariz^F

cheek
mejilla^F

mouth
boca^F

neck
cuello^M

chin
mentón^M

shoulder
hombro^M

nipple
pezón^M

armpit
axila^F

breast
seno^M

chest
pecho^M

navel
ombligo^M

thorax
tórax^M

abdomen
abdomen^M

pubis
pubis^M

vulva
vulva^F

groin
ingle^F

knee
rodilla^F

foot
pie^M

ankle
tobillo^M

toe
dedo^M del pie^M

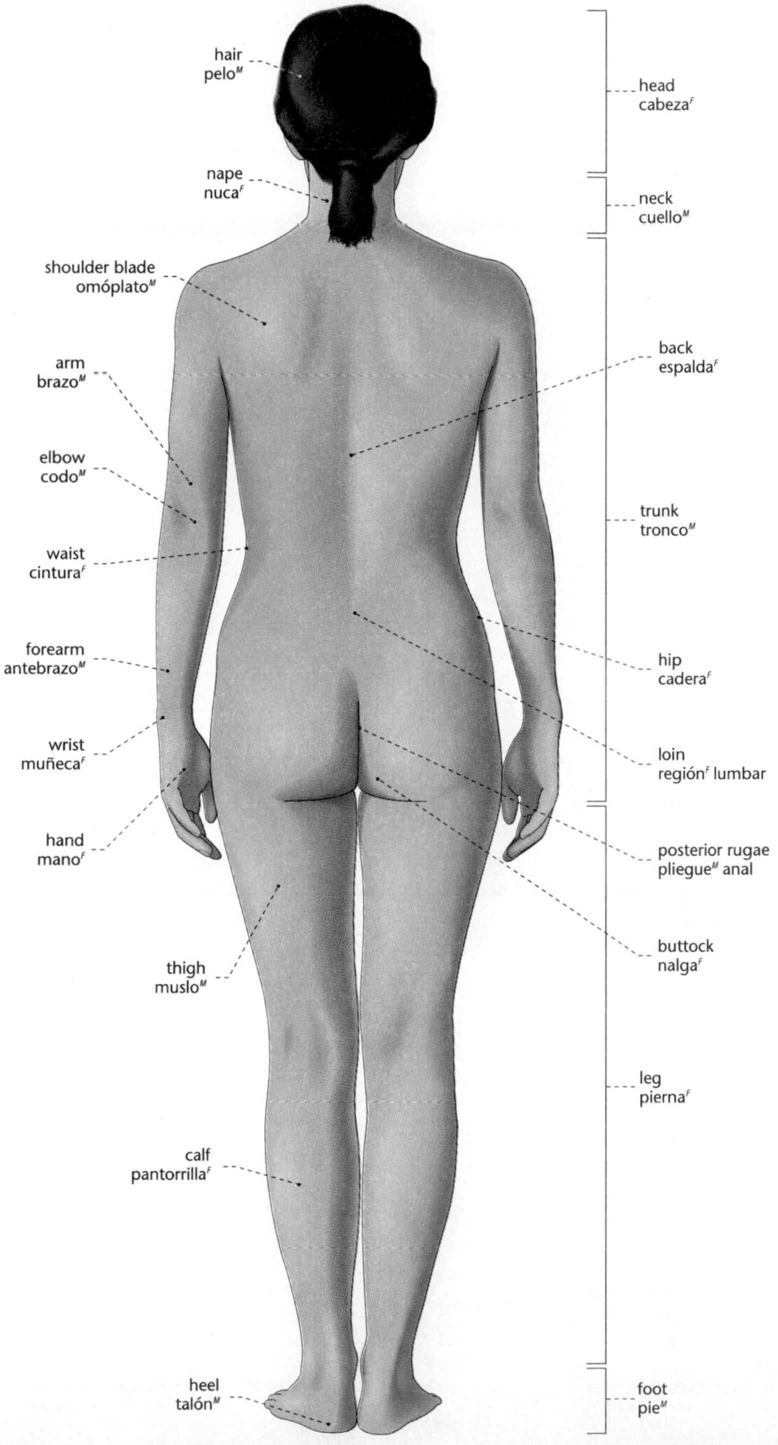

hair
pelo^M

nape
nuca^F

shoulder blade
omóplato^M

arm
brazo^M

elbow
codo^M

waist
cintura^F

forearm
antebrazo^M

wrist
muñeca^F

hand
mano^F

thigh
muslo^M

calf
pantorrilla^F

heel
talón^M

head
cabeza^F

neck
cuello^M

back
espalda^F

trunk
tronco^M

hip
cadera^F

loin
región^F lumbar

posterior rugae
pliegue^M anal

buttock
nalga^F

leg
pierna^F

foot
pie^M

MUSCLES
MÚSCULOS^M

ANTERIOR VIEW
VISTA^F ANTERIOR

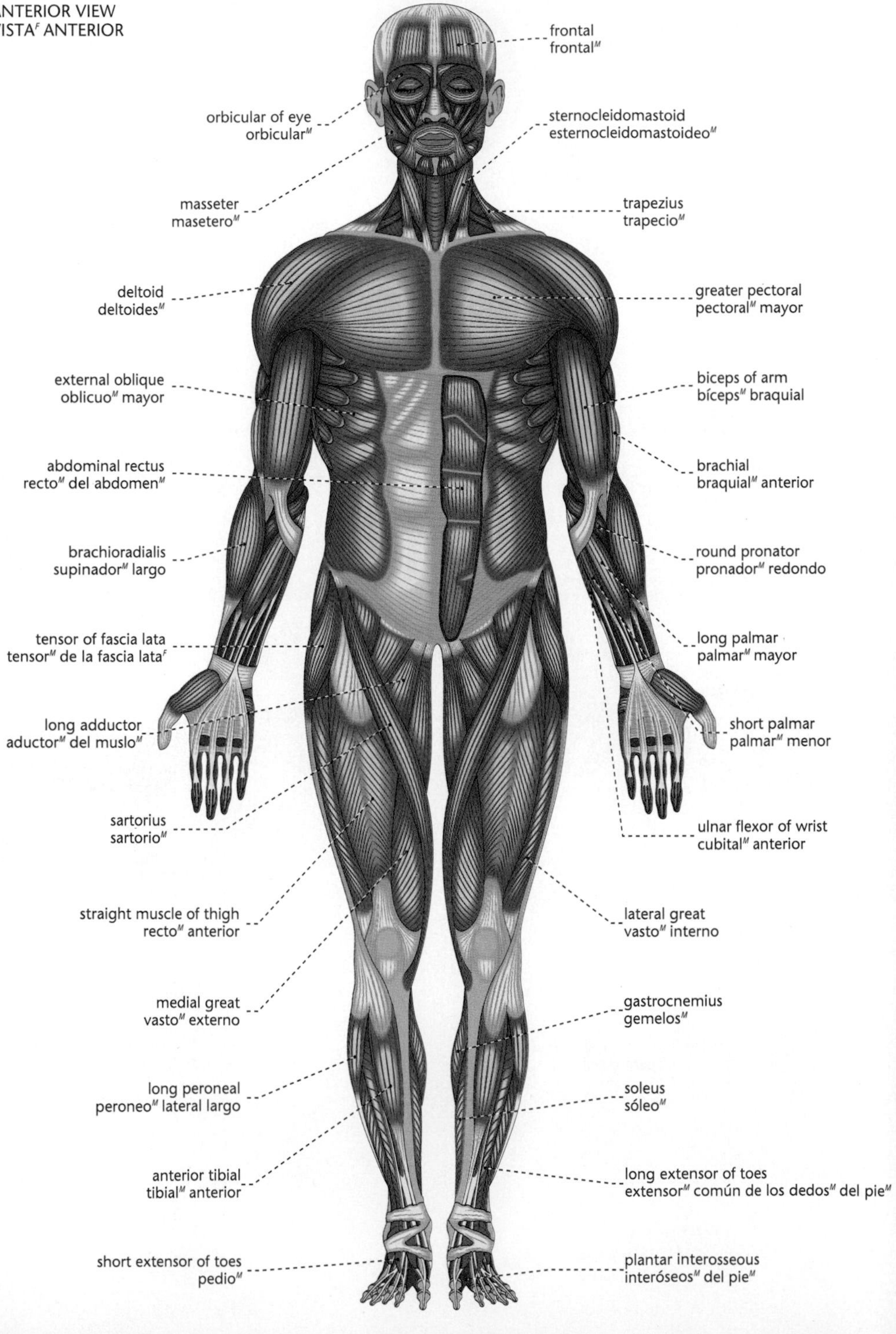

orbicular of eye
orbicular^M

masseter
masetero^M

deltoid
deltoides^M

external oblique
oblicuo^M mayor

abdominal rectus
recto^M del abdomen^M

brachioradialis
supinador^M largo

tensor of fascia lata
tensor^M de la fascia lata^F

long adductor
aductor^M del muslo^M

sartorius
sartorio^M

straight muscle of thigh
recto^M anterior

medial great
vasto^M externo

long peroneal
peroneo^M lateral largo

anterior tibial
tibial^M anterior

short extensor of toes
pedio^M

frontal
frontal^M

sternocleidomastoid
esternocleidomastoideo^M

trapezius
trapecio^M

greater pectoral
pectoral^M mayor

biceps of arm
bíceps^M braquial

brachial
braquial^M anterior

round pronator
pronador^M redondo

long palmar
palmar^M mayor

short palmar
palmar^M menor

ulnar flexor of wrist
cubital^M anterior

lateral great
vasto^M interno

gastrocnemius
gemelos^M

soleus
sóleo^M

long extensor of toes
extensor^M común de los dedos^M del pie^M

plantar interosseous
interóseos^M del pie^M

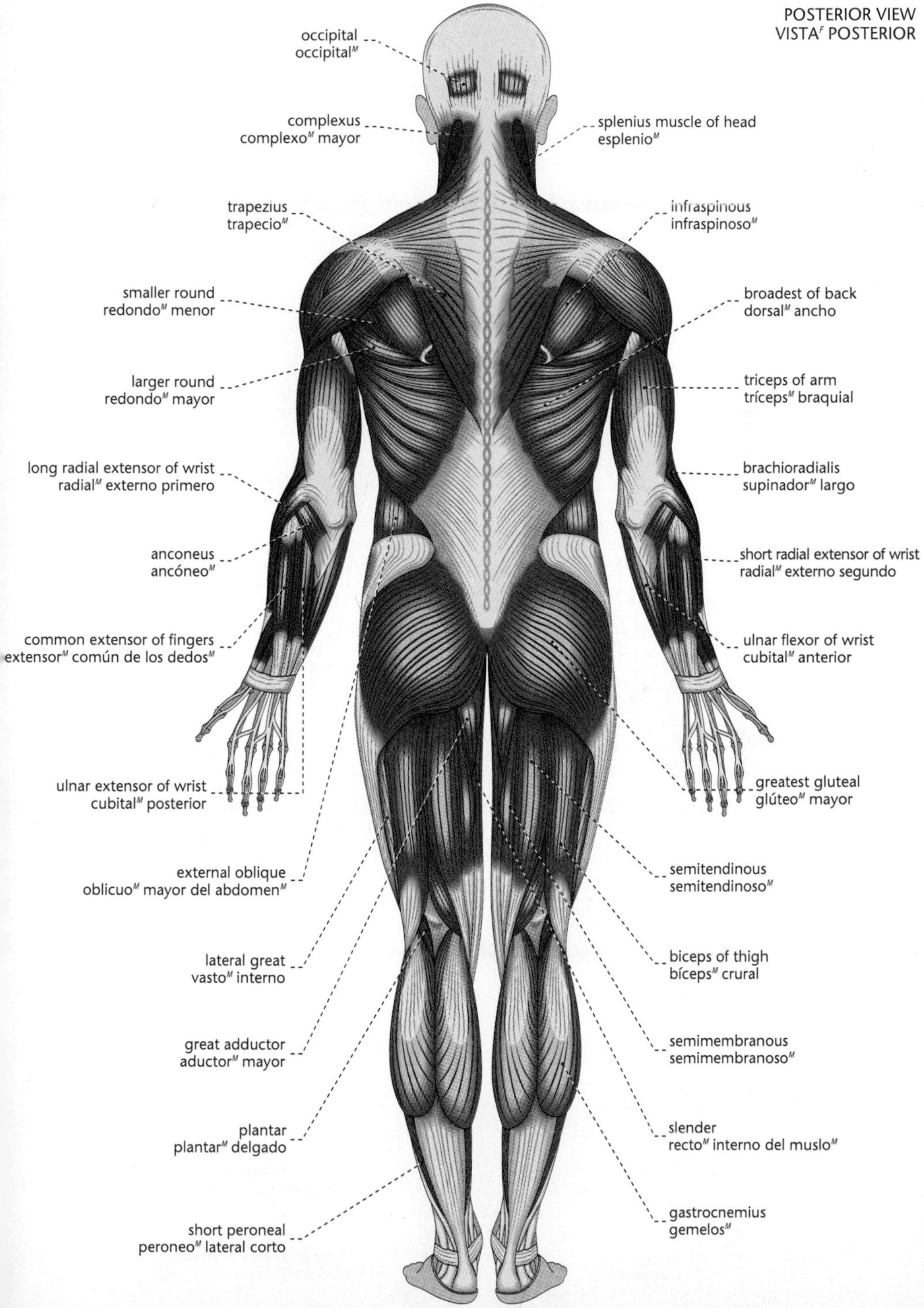

occipital
occipital^M

complexus
complexo^M mayor

trapezius
trapecio^M

smaller round
redondo^M menor

larger round
redondo^M mayor

long radial extensor of wrist
radial^M externo primero

anconeus
ancóneo^M

common extensor of fingers
extensor^M común de los dedos^M

ulnar extensor of wrist
cubital^M posterior

external oblique
oblicuo^M mayor del abdomen^M

lateral great
vasto^M interno

great adductor
aductor^M mayor

plantar
plantar^M delgado

short peroneal
peroneo^M lateral corto

splenius muscle of head
esplenio^M

infraspinous
infraspinoso^M

broadest of back
dorsal^M ancho

triceps of arm
tríceps^M braquial

brachioradialis
supinador^M largo

short radial extensor of wrist
radial^M externo segundo

ulnar flexor of wrist
cubital^M anterior

greatest gluteal
glúteo^M mayor

semitendinous
semitendinoso^M

biceps of thigh
bíceps^M crural

semimembranous
semimembranoso^M

slender
recto^M interno del muslo^M

gastrocnemius
gemelos^M

SKELETON
ESQUELETO^M

ANTERIOR VIEW
VISTA^F ANTERIOR

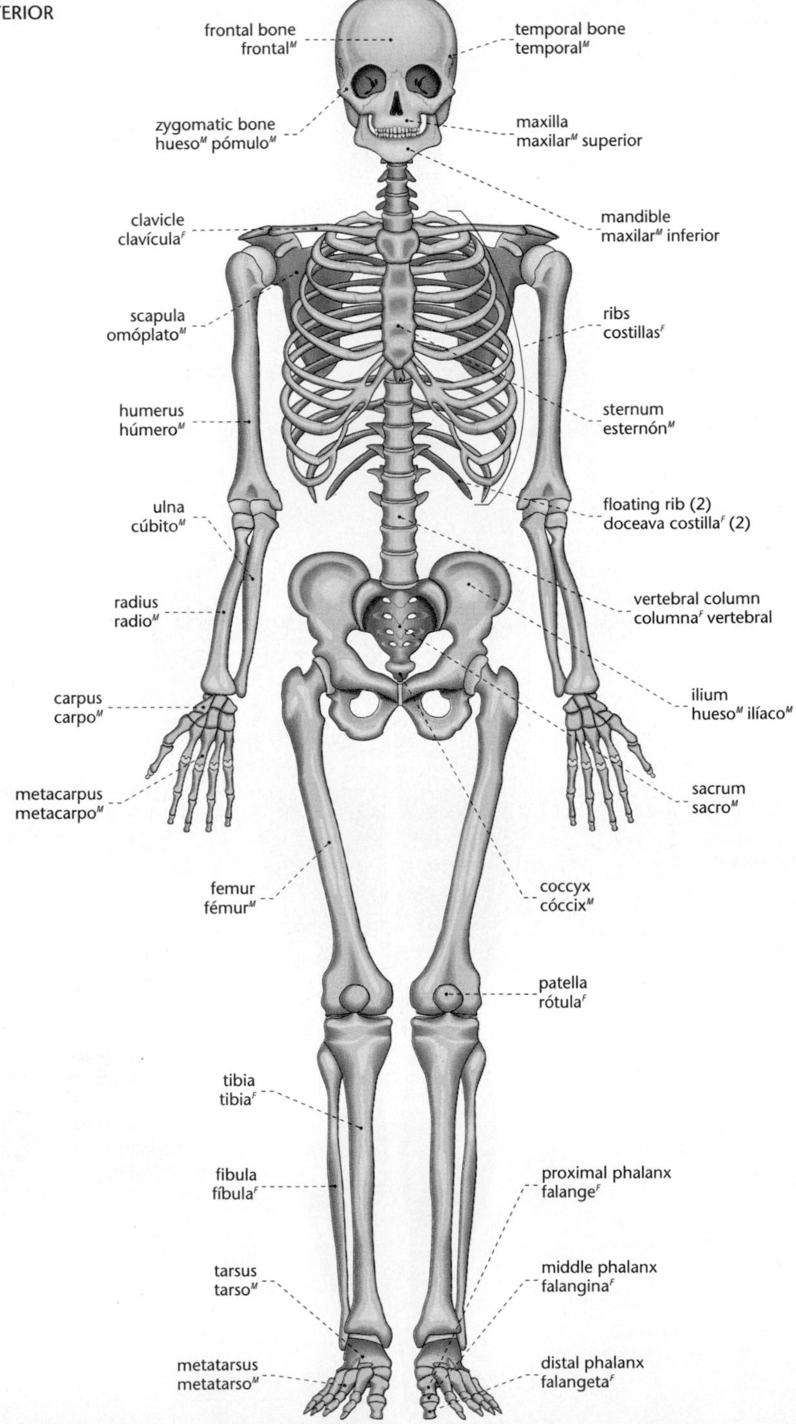

frontal bone
frontal^M

temporal bone
temporal^M

zygomatic bone
hueso^M pómulo^M

maxilla
maxilar^M superior

clavicle
clavícula^F

mandible
maxilar^M inferior

scapula
omóplato^M

ribs
costillas^F

humerus
húmero^M

sternum
esternón^M

ulna
cúbito^M

floating rib (2)
doceava costilla^F (2)

radius
radio^M

vertebral column
columna^F vertebral

carpus
carpo^M

ilium
hueso^M ilíaco^M

metacarpus
metacarpo^M

sacrum
sacro^M

femur
fémur^M

coccyx
cóccix^M

patella
rótula^F

tibia
tibia^F

fibula
fíbula^F

proximal phalanx
falange^F

tarsus
tarso^M

middle phalanx
falangina^F

metatarsus
metatarso^M

distal phalanx
falangeta^F

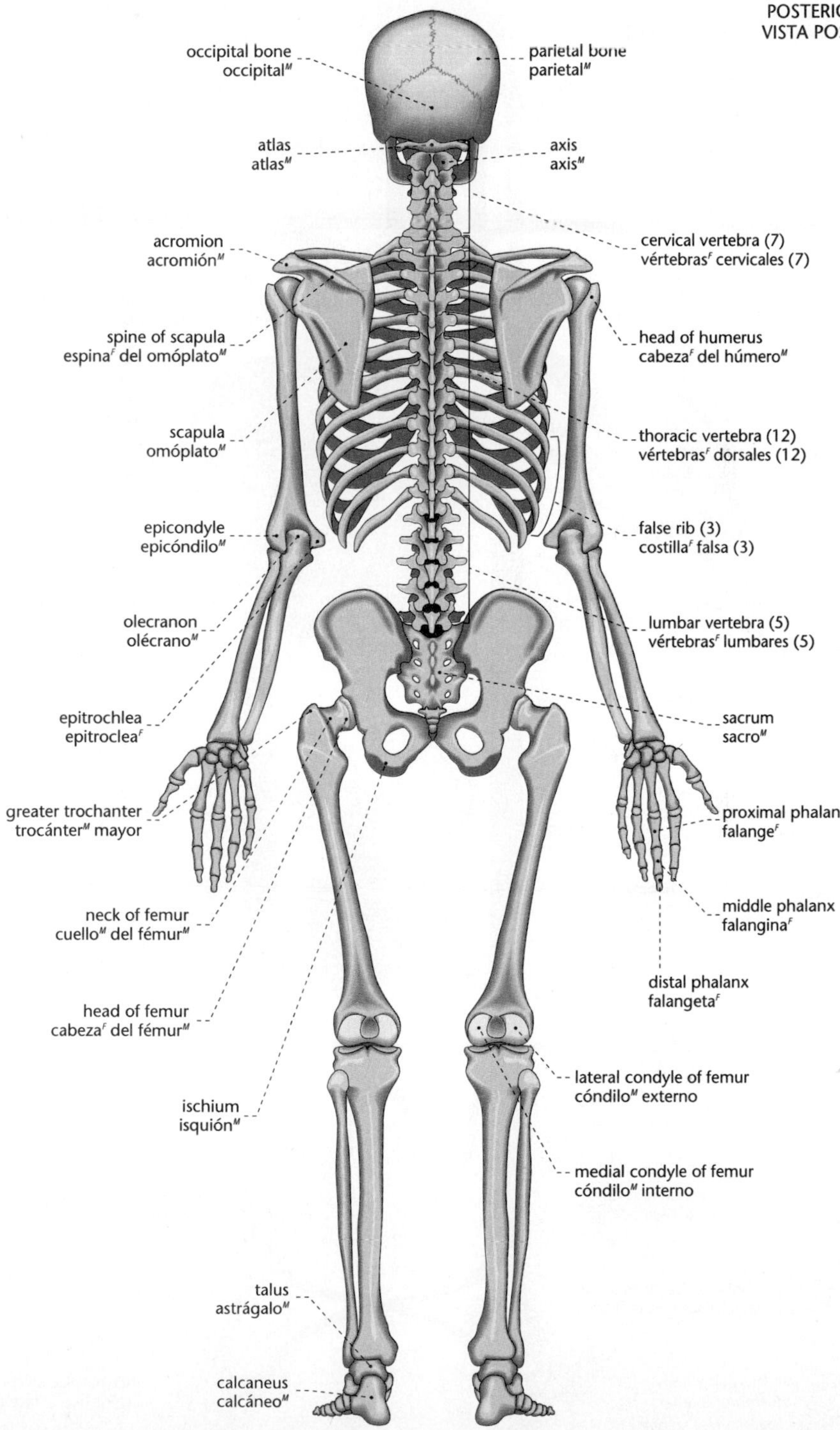

HUMAN BEING
SER HUMANO

occipital bone
occipital^M

parietal bone
parietal^M

atlas
atlas^M

axis
axis^M

acromion
acromión^M

cervical vertebra (7)
vértebras^F cervicales (7)

spine of scapula
espina^F del omóplato^M

head of humerus
cabeza^F del húmero^M

scapula
omóplato^M

thoracic vertebra (12)
vértebras^F dorsales (12)

epicondyle
epicóndilo^M

false rib (3)
costilla^F falsa (3)

olecranon
olécrano^M

lumbar vertebra (5)
vértebras^F lumbares (5)

epitrochlea
epitroclea^F

sacrum
sacro^M

greater trochanter
trocánter^M mayor

proximal phalanx
falange^F

neck of femur
cuello^M del fémur^M

middle phalanx
falangina^F

head of femur
cabeza^F del fémur^M

distal phalanx
falangeta^F

lateral condyle of femur
cóndilo^M externo

ischium
isquión^M

medial condyle of femur
cóndilo^M interno

talus
astrágalo^M

calcaneus
calcáneo^M

SCHEMA OF CIRCULATION
DIAGRAMA_M_ DE LA CIRCULACIÓN_F_

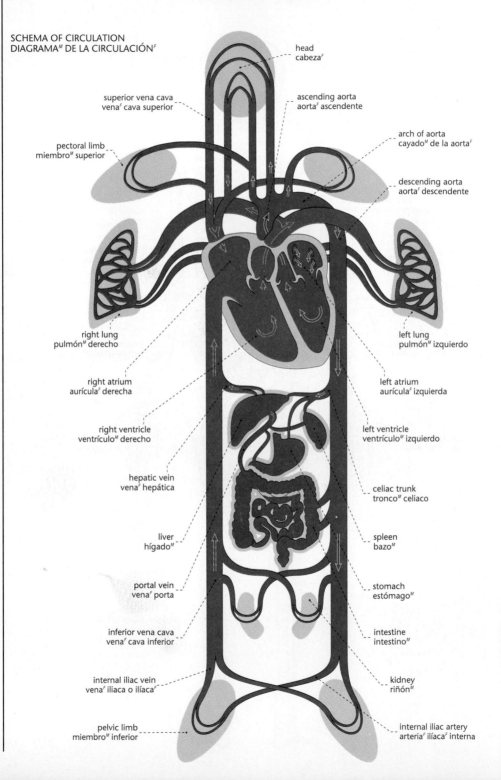

head
cabeza_F_

superior vena cava
vena_F_ cava superior

ascending aorta
aorta_F_ ascendente

arch of aorta
cayado_M_ de la aorta_F_

pectoral limb
miembro_M_ superior

descending aorta
aorta_F_ descendente

right lung
pulmón_M_ derecho

left lung
pulmón_M_ izquierdo

right atrium
aurícula_F_ derecha

left atrium
aurícula_F_ izquierda

right ventricle
ventrículo_M_ derecho

left ventricle
ventrículo_M_ izquierdo

hepatic vein
vena_F_ hepática

celiac trunk
tronco_M_ celiaco

liver
hígado_M_

spleen
bazo_M_

portal vein
vena_F_ porta

stomach
estómago_M_

inferior vena cava
vena_F_ cava inferior

intestine
intestino_M_

internal iliac vein
vena_F_ iliaca o ilíaca_F_

kidney
riñón_M_

pelvic limb
miembro_M_ inferior

internal iliac artery
arteria_F_ ilíaca_F_ interna

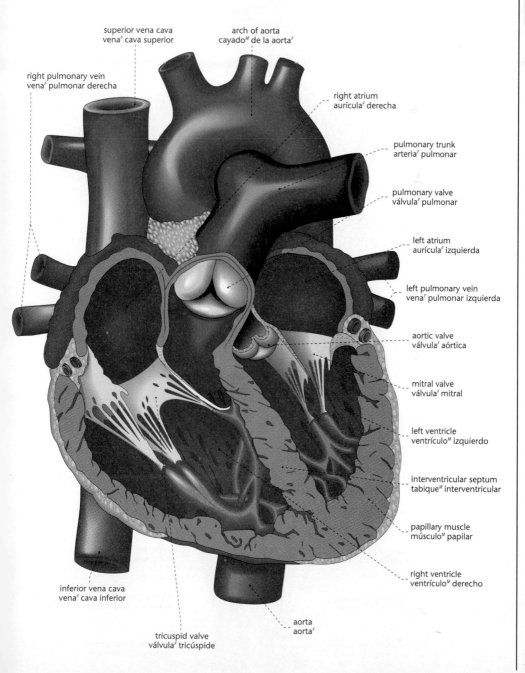

superior vena cava
vena^f cava superior

arch of aorta
cayado^M de la aorta^f

right pulmonary vein
vena^f pulmonar derecha

right atrium
aurícula^f derecha

pulmonary trunk
arteria^f pulmonar

pulmonary valve
válvula^f pulmonar

left atrium
aurícula^f izquierda

left pulmonary vein
vena^f pulmonar izquierda

aortic valve
válvula^f aórtica

mitral valve
válvula^f mitral

left ventricle
ventrículo^M izquierdo

interventricular septum
tabique^M interventricular

papillary muscle
músculo^M papilar

right ventricle
ventrículo^M derecho

inferior vena cava
vena^f cava inferior

aorta
aorta^f

tricuspid valve
válvula^f tricúspide

BLOOD CIRCULATION
CIRCULACIÓN^F SANGUÍNEA

PRINCIPAL VEINS AND ARTERIES
PRINCIPALES VENAS^F Y ARTERIAS^F

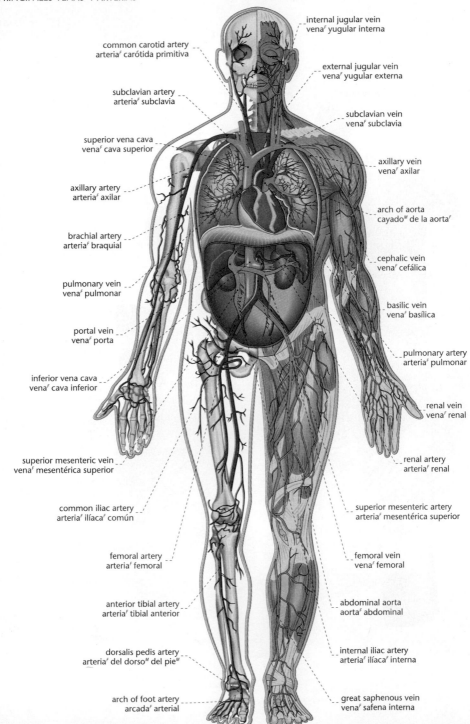

common carotid artery
arteria^F carótida primitiva

subclavian artery
arteria^F subclavia

superior vena cava
vena^F cava superior

axillary artery
arteria^F axilar

brachial artery
arteria^F braquial

pulmonary vein
vena^F pulmonar

portal vein
vena^F porta

inferior vena cava
vena^F cava inferior

superior mesenteric vein
vena^F mesentérica superior

common iliac artery
arteria^F ilíaca^F común

femoral artery
arteria^F femoral

anterior tibial artery
arteria^F tibial anterior

dorsalis pedis artery
arteria^F del dorso^M del pie^M

arch of foot artery
arcada^F arterial

internal jugular vein
vena^F yugular interna

external jugular vein
vena^F yugular externa

subclavian vein
vena^F subclavia

axillary vein
vena^F axilar

arch of aorta
cayado^M de la aorta^F

cephalic vein
vena^F cefálica

basilic vein
vena^F basílica

pulmonary artery
arteria^F pulmonar

renal vein
vena^F renal

renal artery
arteria^F renal

superior mesenteric artery
arteria^F mesentérica superior

femoral vein
vena^F femoral

abdominal aorta
aorta^F abdominal

internal iliac artery
arteria^F ilíaca^F interna

great saphenous vein
vena^F safena interna

MALE GENITAL ORGANS
ÓRGANOS^M GENITALES MASCULINOS

SAGITTAL SECTION
CORTE^M SAGITAL

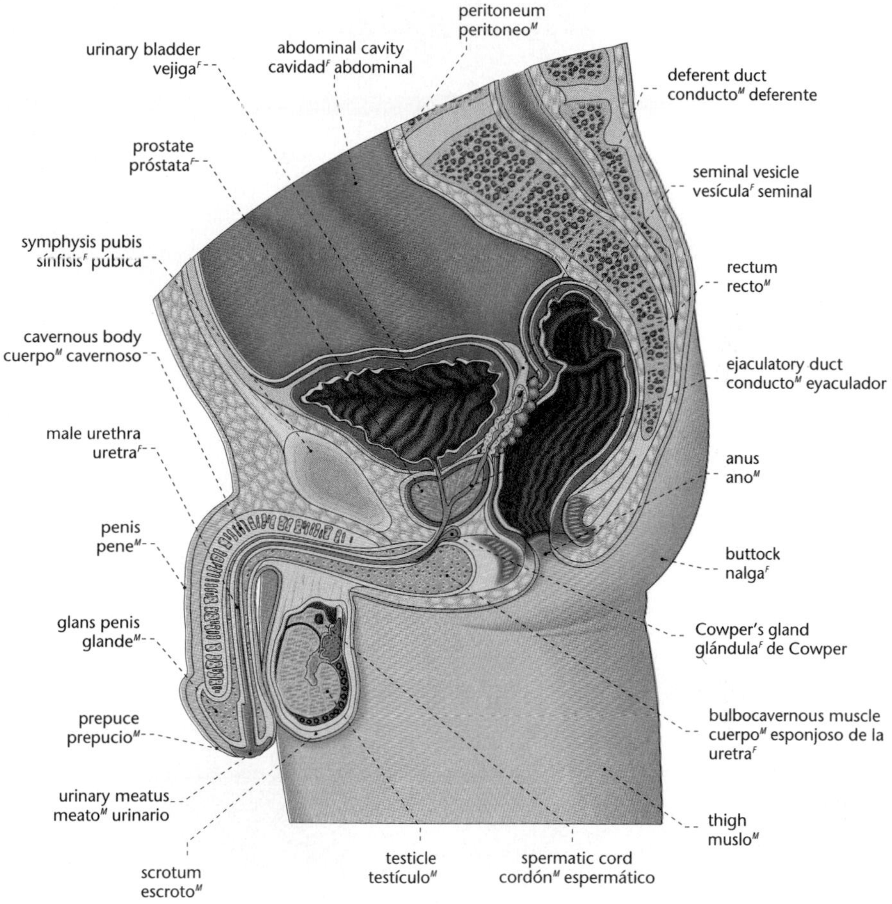

urinary bladder
vejiga^F

abdominal cavity
cavidad^F abdominal

peritoneum
peritoneo^M

deferent duct
conducto^M deferente

prostate
próstata^F

seminal vesicle
vesícula^F seminal

symphysis pubis
sínfisis^F púbica

rectum
recto^M

cavernous body
cuerpo^M cavernoso

ejaculatory duct
conducto^M eyaculador

male urethra
uretra^F

anus
ano^M

penis
pene^M

buttock
nalga^F

glans penis
glande^M

Cowper's gland
glándula^F de Cowper

prepuce
prepucio^M

bulbocavernous muscle
cuerpo^M esponjoso de la
uretra^F

urinary meatus
meato^M urinario

thigh
muslo^M

scrotum
escroto^M

testicle
testículo^M

spermatic cord
cordón^M espermático

SPERMATOZOON
ESPERMATOZOIDE^M

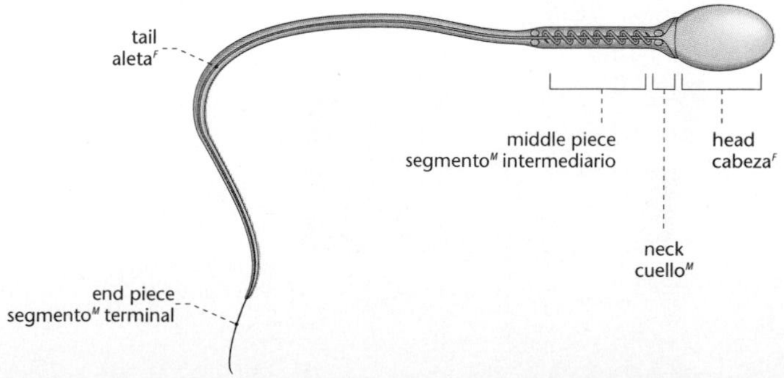

tail
aleta^F

middle piece
segmento^M intermediario

head
cabeza^F

neck
cuello^M

end piece
segmento^M terminal

127

FEMALE GENITAL ORGANS
ÓRGANOS^M GENITALES FEMENINOS

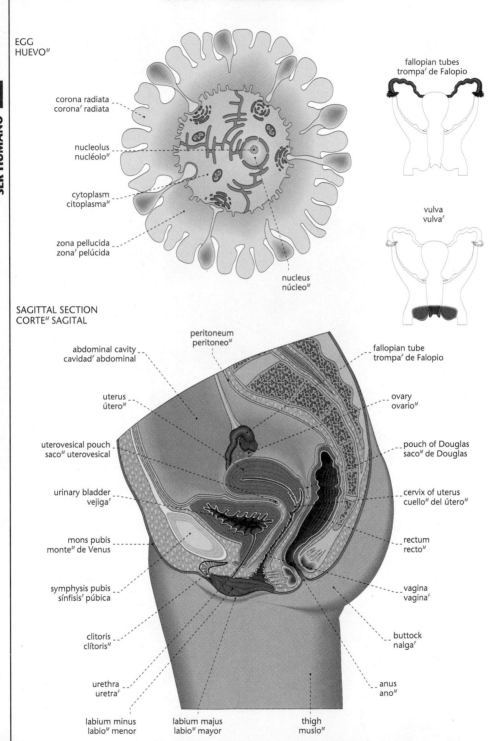

EGG
HUEVO^M

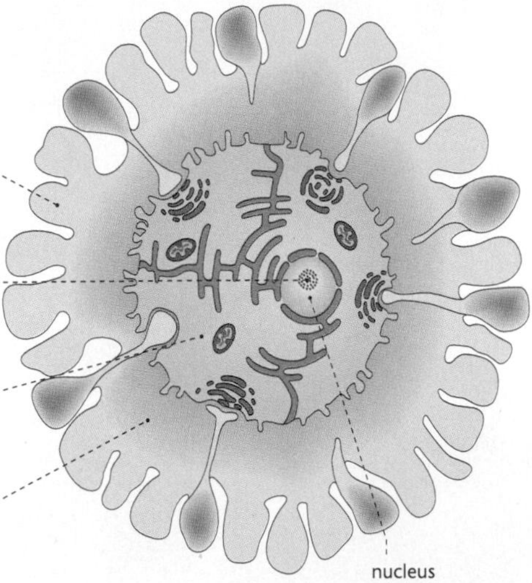

corona radiata
corona^F radiata

nucleolus
nucléolo^M

cytoplasm
citoplasma^M

zona pellucida
zona^F pelúcida

nucleus
núcleo^M

fallopian tubes
trompa^F de Falopio

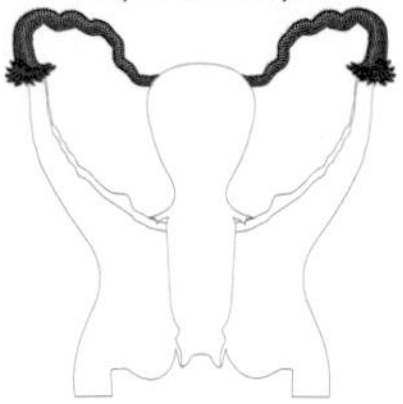

vulva
vulva^F

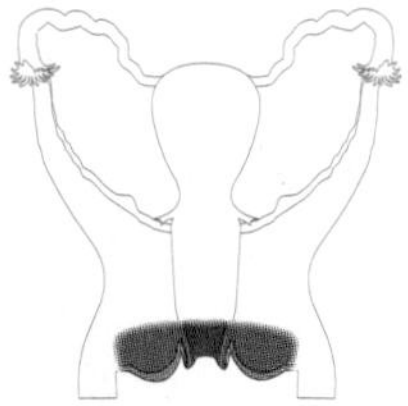

SAGITTAL SECTION
CORTE^M SAGITAL

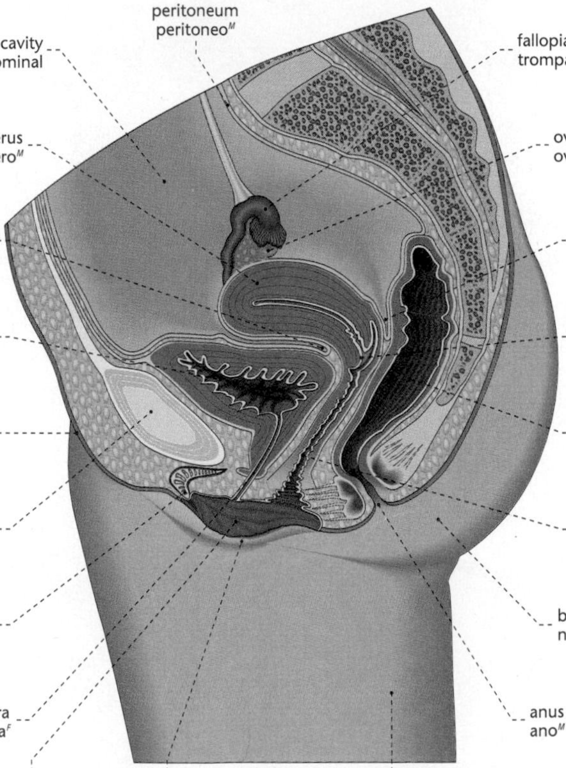

peritoneum
peritoneo^M

abdominal cavity
cavidad^F abdominal

uterus
útero^M

uterovesical pouch
saco^M uterovesical

urinary bladder
vejiga^F

mons pubis
monte^M de Venus

symphysis pubis
sínfisis^F púbica

clitoris
clítoris^M

urethra
uretra^F

labium minus
labio^M menor

labium majus
labio^M mayor

thigh
muslo^M

fallopian tube
trompa^F de Falopio

ovary
ovario^M

pouch of Douglas
saco^M de Douglas

cervix of uterus
cuello^M del útero^M

rectum
recto^M

vagina
vagina^F

buttock
nalga^F

anus
ano^M

FEMALE GENITAL ORGANS
ÓRGANOS^M GENITALES FEMENINOS

POSTERIOR VIEW
VISTA^F POSTERIOR

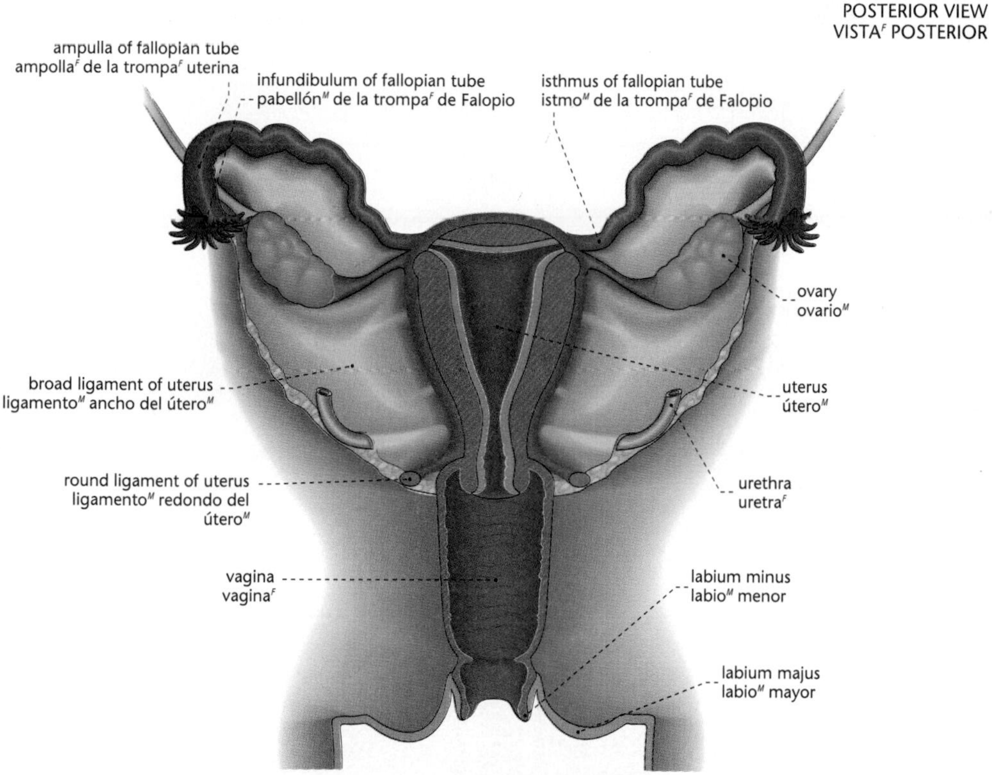

ampulla of fallopian tube
ampolla^F de la trompa^F uterina

infundibulum of fallopian tube
pabellón^M de la trompa^F de Falopio

isthmus of fallopian tube
istmo^M de la trompa^F de Falopio

ovary
ovario^M

broad ligament of uterus
ligamento^M ancho del útero^M

uterus
útero^M

round ligament of uterus
ligamento^M redondo del
útero^M

urethra
uretra^F

vagina
vagina^F

labium minus
labio^M menor

labium majus
labio^M mayor

BREAST
SENO^M

SAGITTAL SECTION
CORTE^M SAGITAL

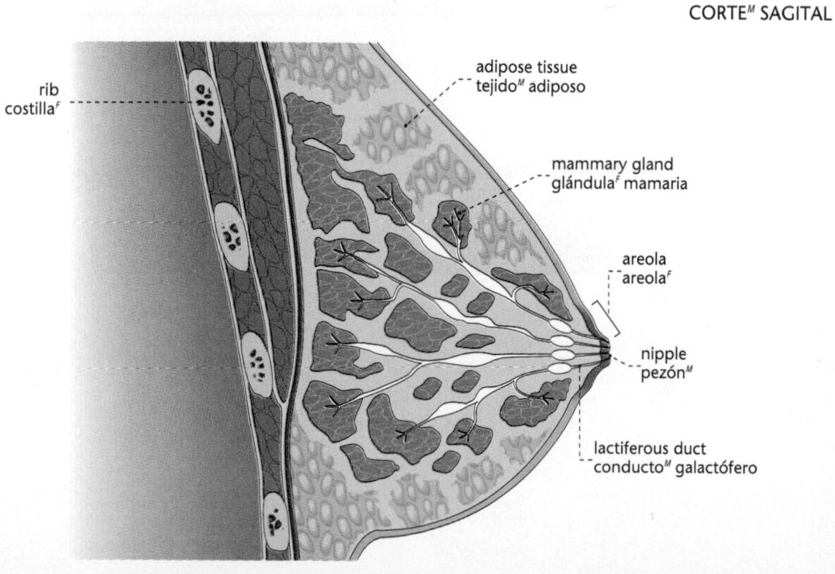

rib
costilla^F

adipose tissue
tejido^M adiposo

mammary gland
glándula^F mamaria

areola
areola^F

nipple
pezón^M

lactiferous duct
conducto^M galactófero

129

RESPIRATORY SYSTEM
APARATO^M RESPIRATORIO

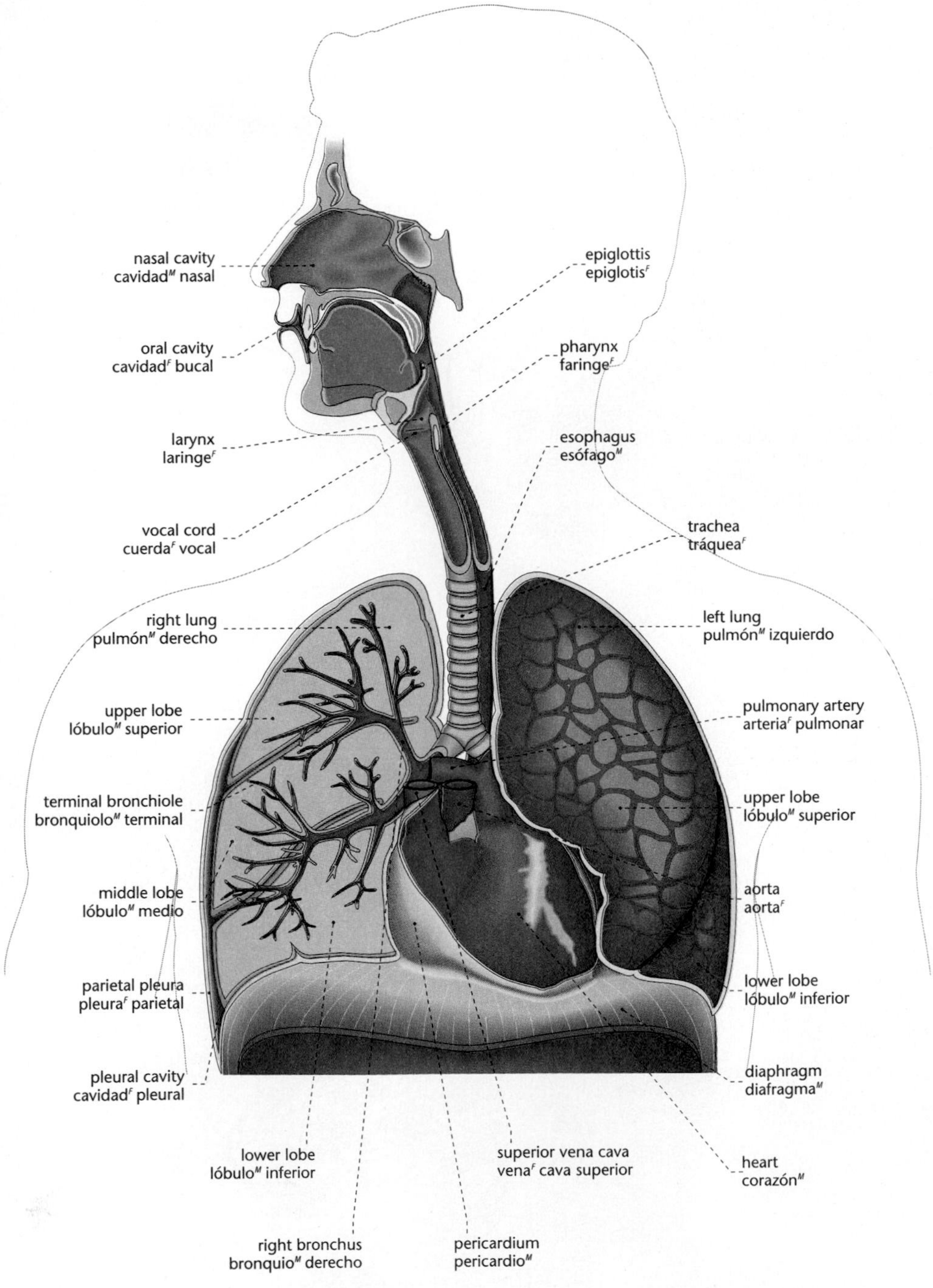

nasal cavity
cavidad^M nasal

oral cavity
cavidad^F bucal

larynx
laringe^F

vocal cord
cuerda^F vocal

right lung
pulmón^M derecho

upper lobe
lóbulo^M superior

terminal bronchiole
bronquiolo^M terminal

middle lobe
lóbulo^M medio

parietal pleura
pleura^F parietal

pleural cavity
cavidad^F pleural

lower lobe
lóbulo^M inferior

right bronchus
bronquio^M derecho

pericardium
pericardio^M

superior vena cava
vena^F cava superior

epiglottis
epiglotis^F

pharynx
faringe^F

esophagus
esófago^M

trachea
tráquea^F

left lung
pulmón^M izquierdo

pulmonary artery
arteria^F pulmonar

upper lobe
lóbulo^M superior

aorta
aorta^F

lower lobe
lóbulo^M inferior

diaphragm
diafragma^M

heart
corazón^M

DIGESTIVE SYSTEM
APARATO^M DIGESTIVO

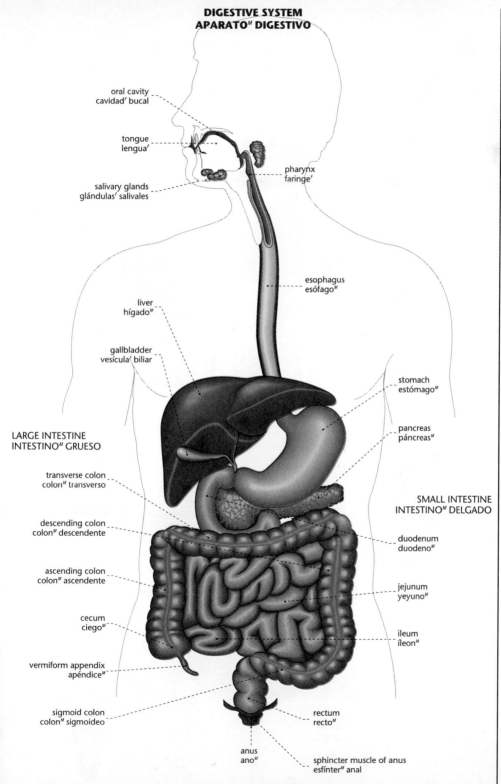

oral cavity
cavidad^F bucal

tongue
lengua^F

salivary glands
glándulas^F salivales

pharynx
faringe^F

esophagus
esófago^M

liver
hígado^M

gallbladder
vesícula^F biliar

stomach
estómago^M

pancreas
páncreas^M

LARGE INTESTINE
INTESTINO^M GRUESO

transverse colon
colon^M transverso

descending colon
colon^M descendente

ascending colon
colon^M ascendente

cecum
ciego^M

vermiform appendix
apéndice^M

sigmoid colon
colon^M sigmoideo

SMALL INTESTINE
INTESTINO^M DELGADO

duodenum
duodeno^M

jejunum
yeyuno^M

ileum
íleon^M

rectum
recto^M

anus
ano^M

sphincter muscle of anus
esfínter^M anal

131

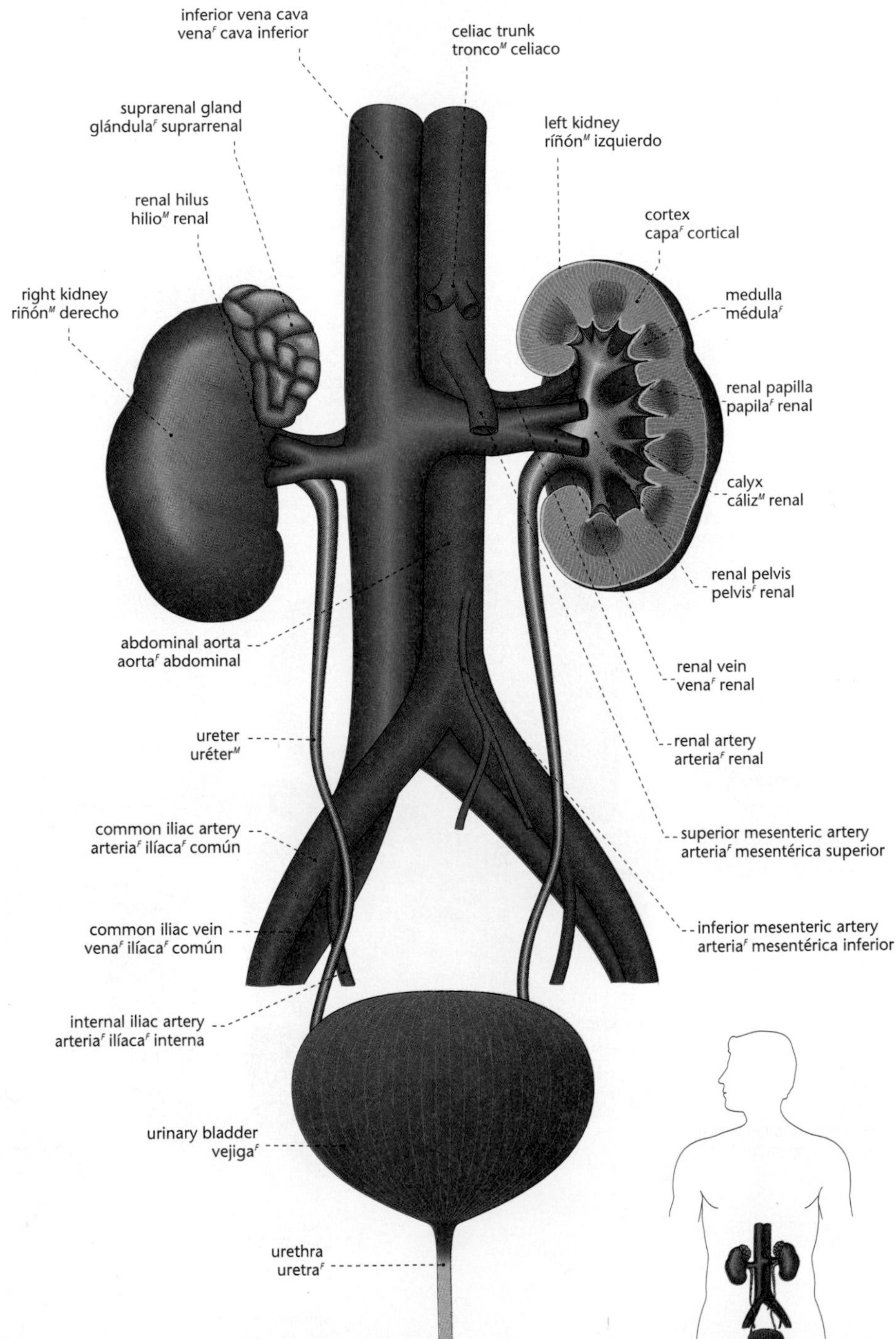

inferior vena cava
vena^F cava inferior

celiac trunk
tronco^M celiaco

suprarenal gland
glándula^F suprarrenal

left kidney
ríñón^M izquierdo

renal hilus
hilio^M renal

cortex
capa^F cortical

right kidney
riñón^M derecho

medulla
médula^F

renal papilla
papila^F renal

calyx
cáliz^M renal

renal pelvis
pelvis^F renal

abdominal aorta
aorta^F abdominal

renal vein
vena^F renal

ureter
uréter^M

renal artery
arteria^F renal

common iliac artery
arteria^F ilíaca^F común

superior mesenteric artery
arteria^F mesentérica superior

common iliac vein
vena^F ilíaca^F común

inferior mesenteric artery
arteria^F mesentérica inferior

internal iliac artery
arteria^F ilíaca^F interna

urinary bladder
vejiga^F

urethra
uretra^F

132

PERIPHERAL NERVOUS SYSTEM
SISTEMA^M NERVIOSO PERIFÉRICO

HUMAN BEING
SER HUMANO

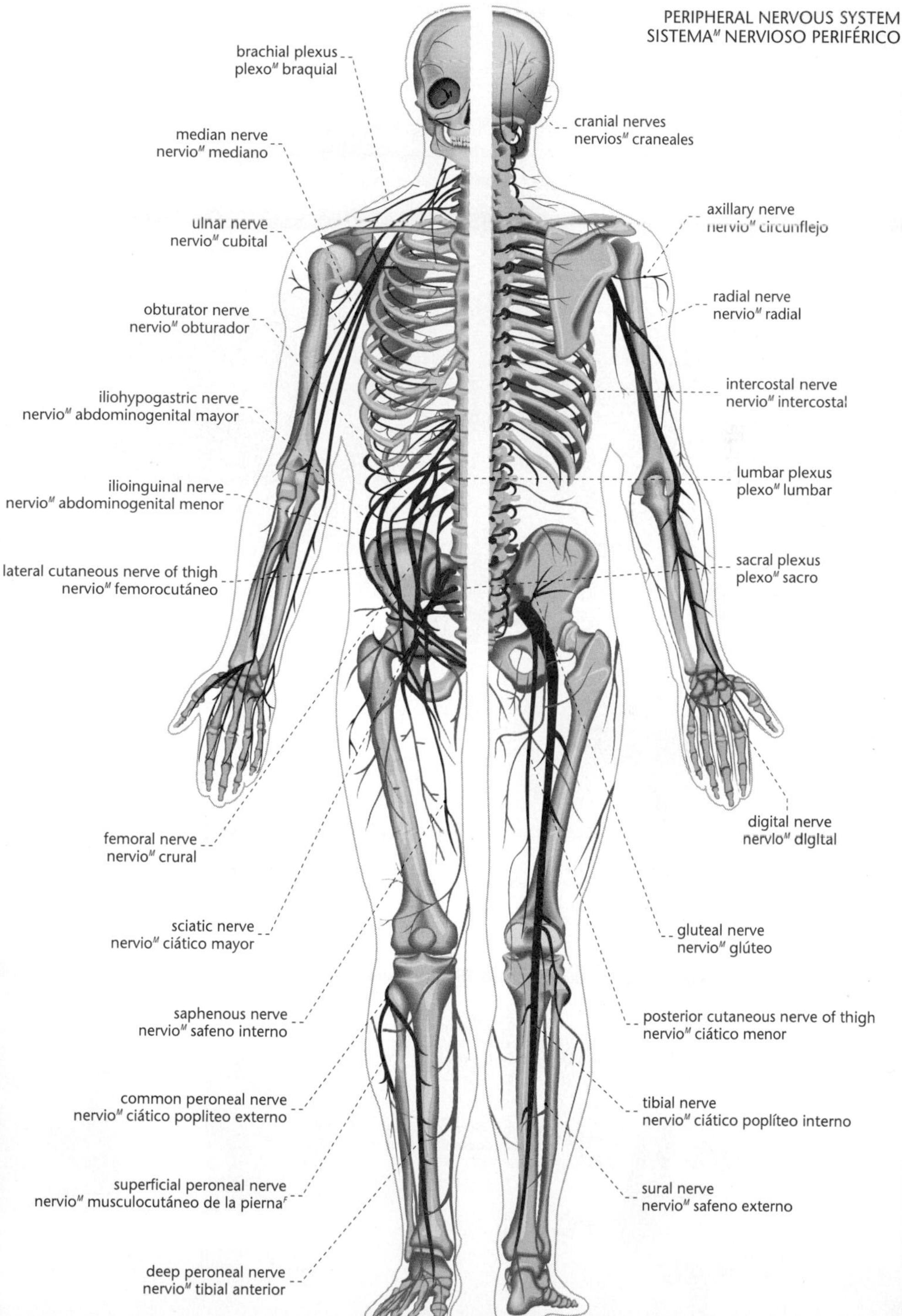

brachial plexus
plexo^M braquial

median nerve
nervio^M mediano

ulnar nerve
nervio^M cubital

obturator nerve
nervio^M obturador

iliohypogastric nerve
nervio^M abdominogenital mayor

ilioinguinal nerve
nervio^M abdominogenital menor

lateral cutaneous nerve of thigh
nervio^M femorocutáneo

femoral nerve
nervio^M crural

sciatic nerve
nervio^M ciático mayor

saphenous nerve
nervio^M safeno interno

common peroneal nerve
nervio^M ciático poplíteo externo

superficial peroneal nerve
nervio^M musculocutáneo de la pierna^F

deep peroneal nerve
nervio^M tibial anterior

cranial nerves
nervios^M craneales

axillary nerve
nervio^M circunflejo

radial nerve
nervio^M radial

intercostal nerve
nervio^M intercostal

lumbar plexus
plexo^M lumbar

sacral plexus
plexo^M sacro

digital nerve
nervio^M digital

gluteal nerve
nervio^M glúteo

posterior cutaneous nerve of thigh
nervio^M ciático menor

tibial nerve
nervio^M ciático poplíteo interno

sural nerve
nervio^M safeno externo

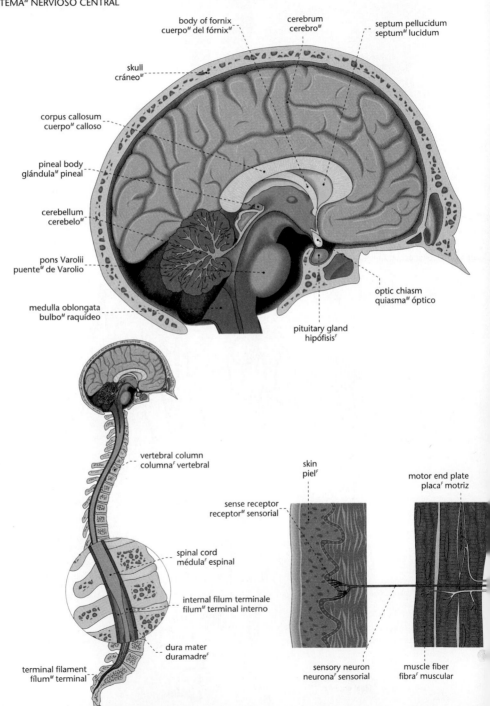

CENTRAL NERVOUS SYSTEM
SISTEMA^M NERVIOSO CENTRAL

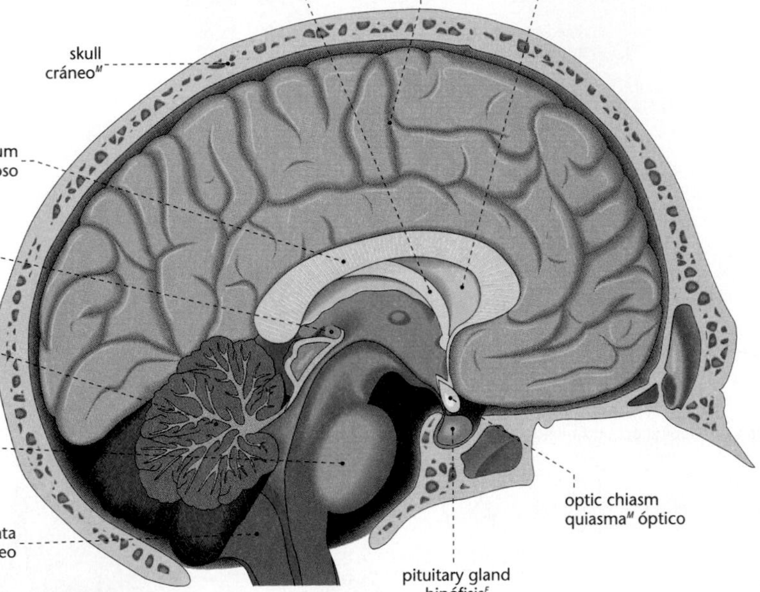

body of fornix
cuerpo^M del fórnix^M

cerebrum
cerebro^M

septum pellucidum
septum^M lucidum

skull
cráneo^M

corpus callosum
cuerpo^M calloso

pineal body
glándula^M pineal

cerebellum
cerebelo^M

pons Varolii
puente^M de Varolio

medulla oblongata
bulbo^M raquídeo

optic chiasm
quiasma^M óptico

pituitary gland
hipófisis^F

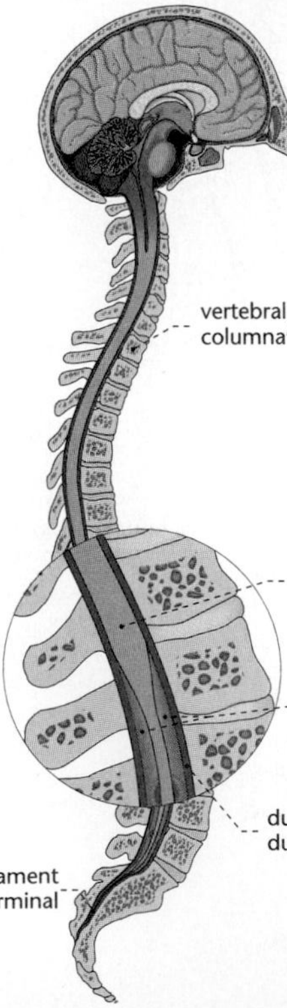

vertebral column
columna^F vertebral

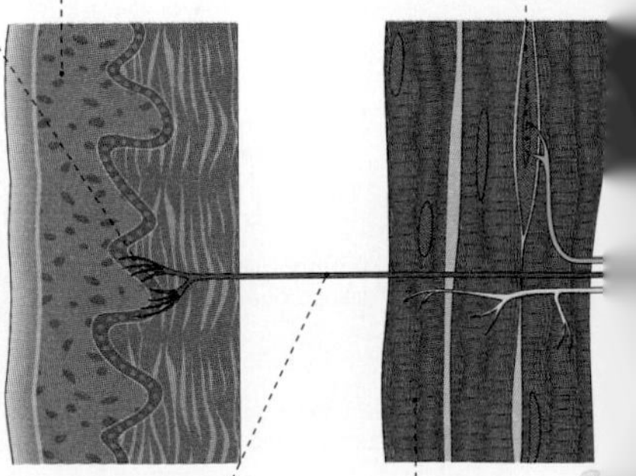

skin
piel^F

motor end plate
placa^F motriz

sense receptor
receptor^M sensorial

spinal cord
médula^F espinal

internal filum terminale
filum^M terminal interno

dura mater
duramadre^F

terminal filament
fílum^M terminal

sensory neuron
neurona^F sensorial

muscle fiber
fibra^F muscular

HUMAN BEING
SER HUMANO

LUMBAR VERTEBRA
VÉRTEBRA^F LUMBAR

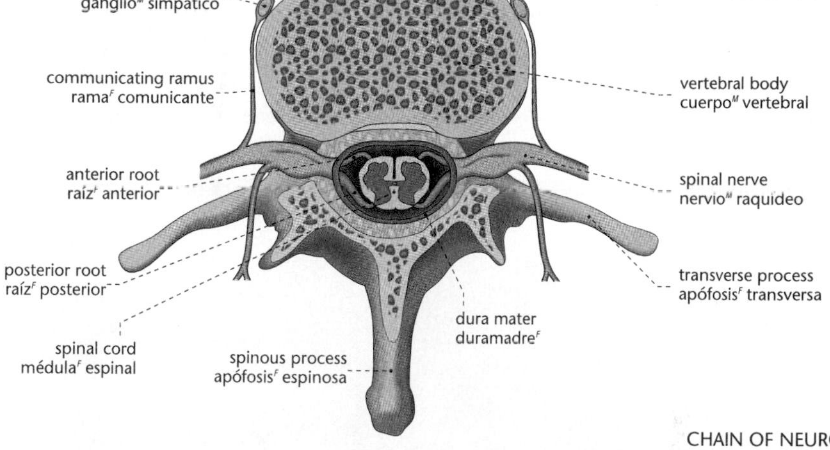

sympathetic ganglion
ganglio^M simpático

communicating ramus
rama^F comunicante

anterior root
raíz^F anterior

posterior root
raíz^F posterior

spinal cord
médula^F espinal

spinous process
apófosis^F espinosa

dura mater
duramadre^F

vertebral body
cuerpo^M vertebral

spinal nerve
nervio^M raquídeo

transverse process
apófosis^F transversa

CHAIN OF NEURONS
ENCADENAMIENTO^M DE NEURONAS^F

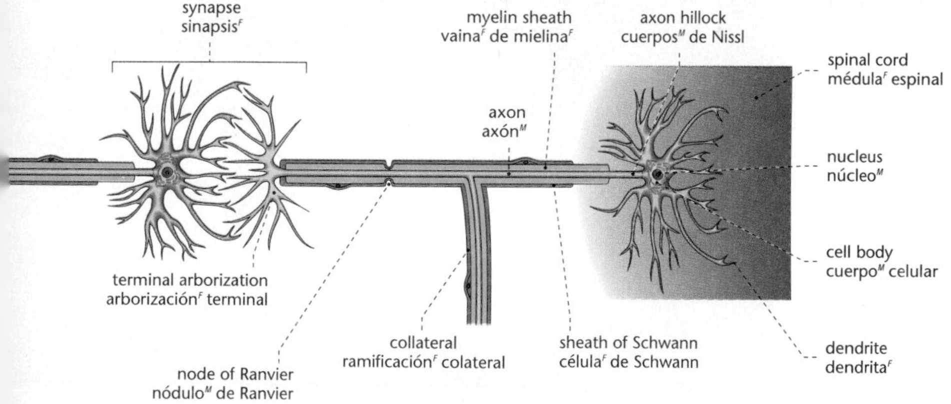

synapse
sinapsis^F

myelin sheath
vaina^F de mielina^F

axon hillock
cuerpos^M de Nissl

spinal cord
médula^F espinal

axon
axón^M

nucleus
núcleo^M

cell body
cuerpo^M celular

terminal arborization
arborización^F terminal

collateral
ramificación^F colateral

sheath of Schwann
célula^F de Schwann

dendrite
dendrita^F

node of Ranvier
nódulo^M de Ranvier

SENSORY IMPULSE
IMPULSO^M NERVIOSO

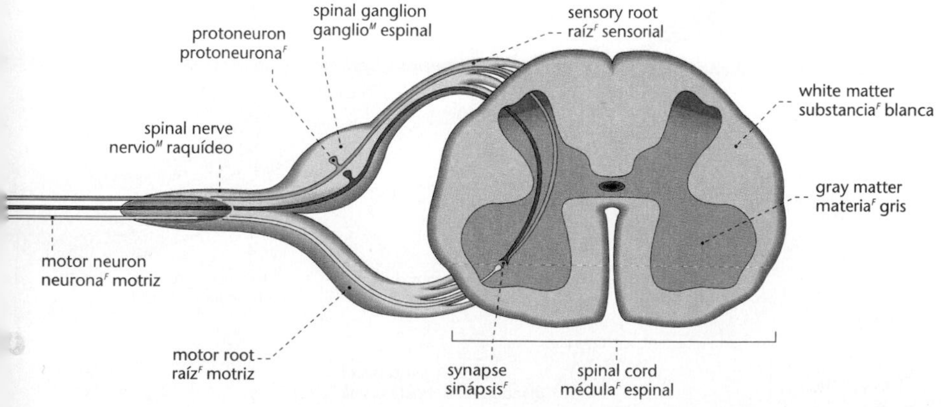

protoneuron
protoneurona^F

spinal ganglion
ganglio^M espinal

sensory root
raíz^F sensorial

white matter
substancia^F blanca

spinal nerve
nervio^M raquídeo

gray matter
materia^F gris

motor neuron
neurona^F motriz

motor root
raíz^F motriz

synapse
sinápsis^F

spinal cord
médula^F espinal

SENSE ORGANS: TOUCH
TACTO^M

SKIN
PIEL^F

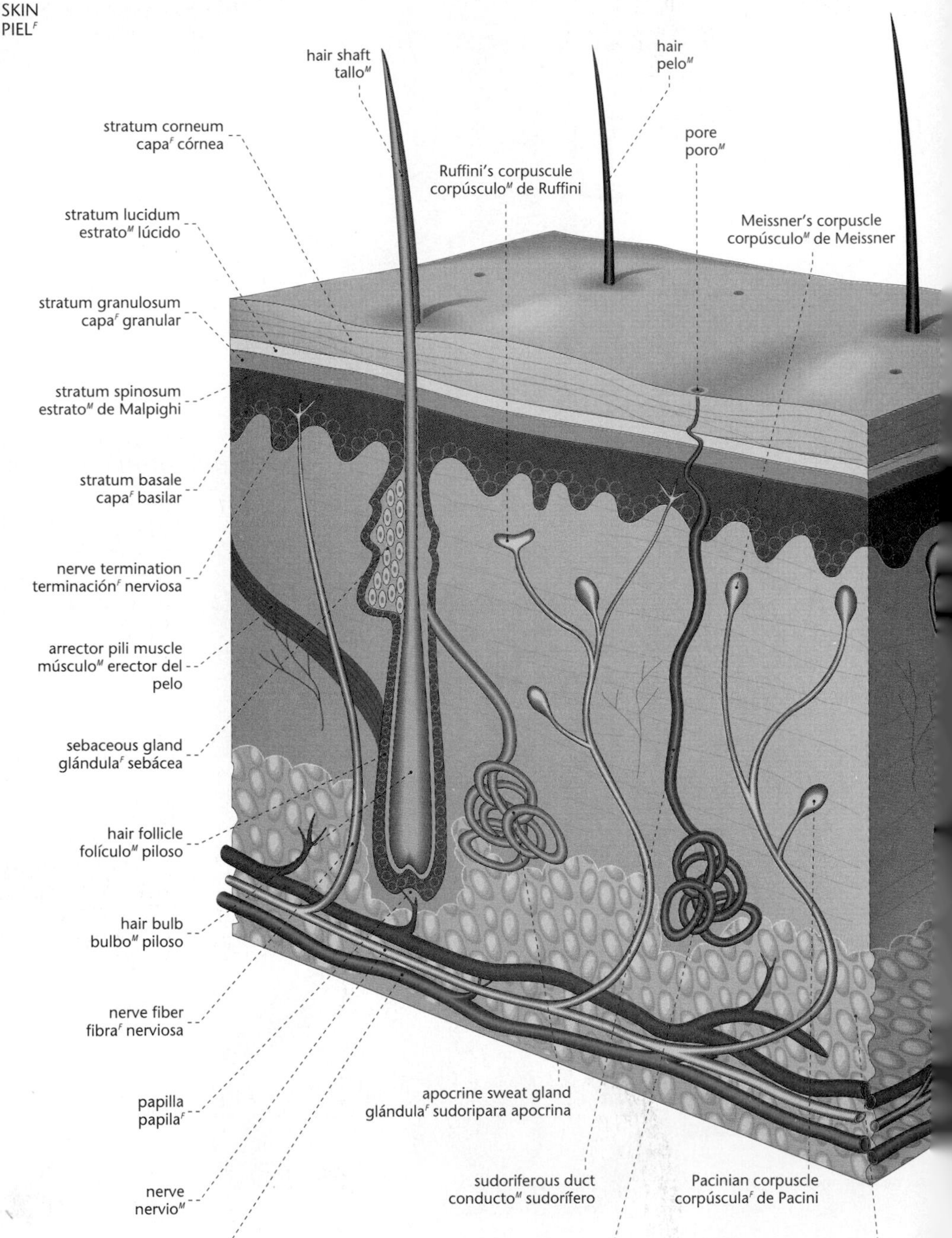

hair shaft
tallo^M

hair
pelo^M

stratum corneum
capa^F córnea

Ruffini's corpuscle
corpúsculo^M de Ruffini

pore
poro^M

stratum lucidum
estrato^M lúcido

Meissner's corpuscle
corpúsculo^M de Meissner

stratum granulosum
capa^F granular

stratum spinosum
estrato^M de Malpighi

stratum basale
capa^F basilar

nerve termination
terminación^F nerviosa

arrector pili muscle
músculo^M erector del
pelo

sebaceous gland
glándula^F sebácea

hair follicle
folículo^M piloso

hair bulb
bulbo^M piloso

nerve fiber
fibra^F nerviosa

papilla
papila^F

apocrine sweat gland
glándula^F sudoripara apocrina

nerve
nervio^M

sudoriferous duct
conducto^M sudorífero

Pacinian corpuscle
corpúscula^F de Pacini

blood vessel
vaso^M sanguíneo

eccrine sweat gland
glándula^F sudorípara ecrina

adipose tissue
tejido^M adiposo

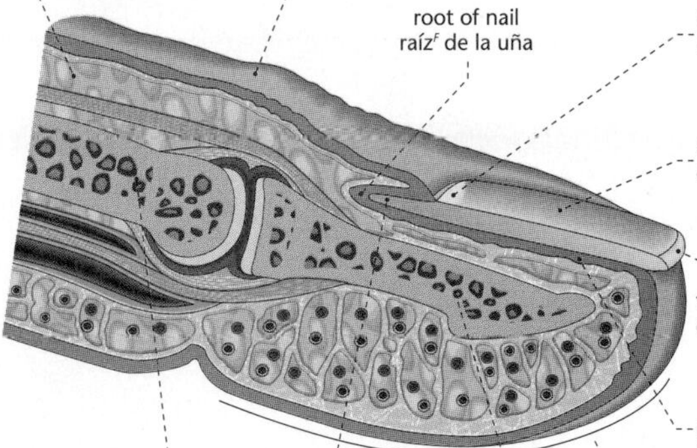

dermis
dermis^F

epidermis
epidermis^F

root of nail
raíz^F de la uña

lunula
lúnula^F

body of nail
cuerpo^M de la uña^F

free margin
extremo^M libre

nail bed
lecho^M ungular

digital pulp
yema^F

nail matrix
matriz^F ungular

distal phalanx
falangeta^F

middle phalanx
falangina^F

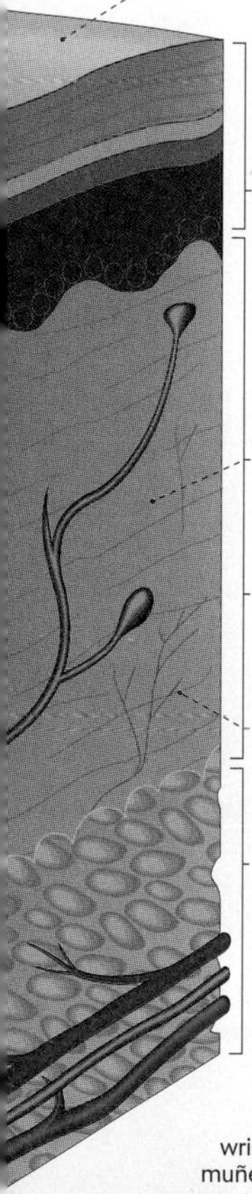

skin surface
superficie^F de la piel^F

epidermis
epidermis^F

connective tissue
tejido^M conjuntivo

dermis
dermis^F

capillary blood vessel
vaso^M capilar

subcutaneous tissue
tejido^M subcutáneo

HAND
MANO^F

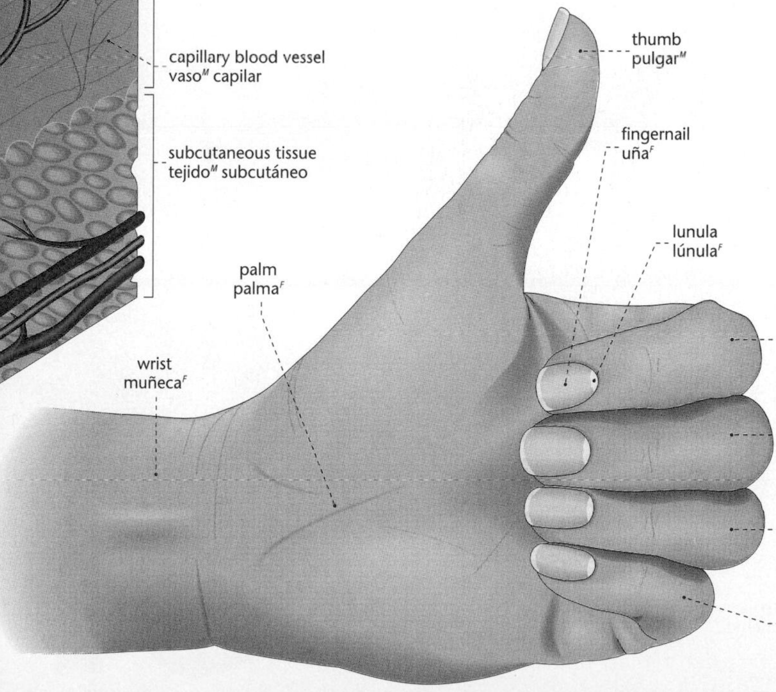

thumb
pulgar^M

fingernail
uña^F

lunula
lúnula^F

index finger
dedo^M índice

middle finger
dedo^M del corazón^M

third finger
dedo^M anular

little finger
dedo^M meñique

palm
palma^F

wrist
muñeca^F

PARTS OF THE EAR
PARTES*F* DEL OÍDO*M*

AUDITORY OSSICLES
HUESECILLOS*M* AUDITIVOS

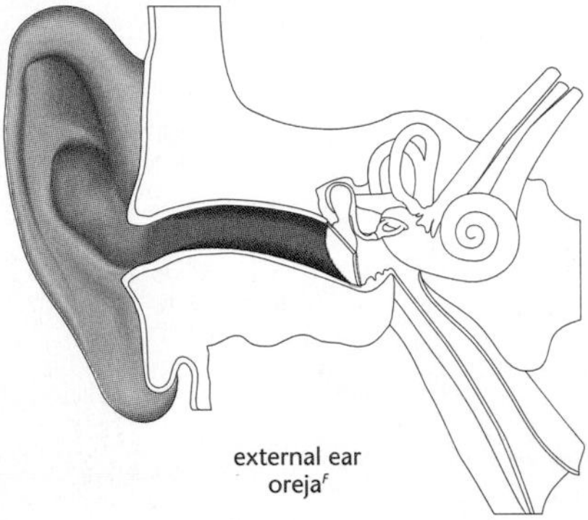

incus
yunque*M*

malleus
martillo*M*

stapes
estribo*M*

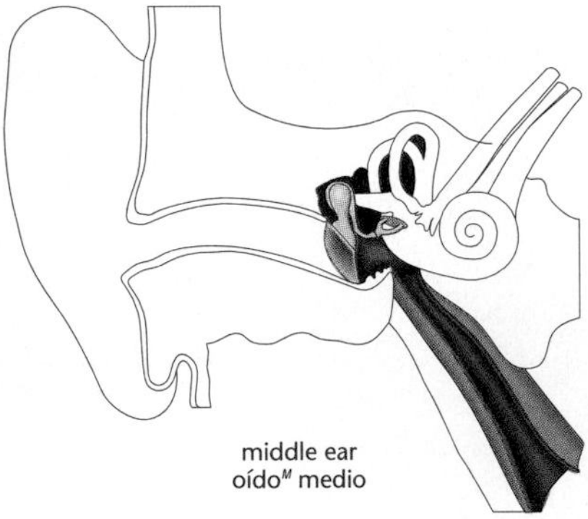

external ear
oreja*F*

auricle
pabellón*M* de la oreja*F*

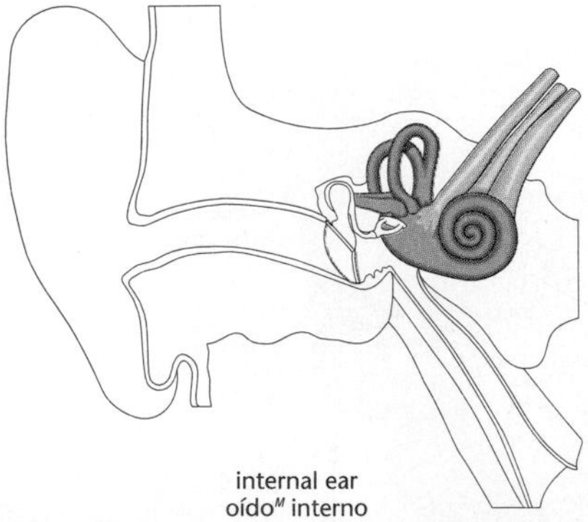

middle ear
oído*M* medio

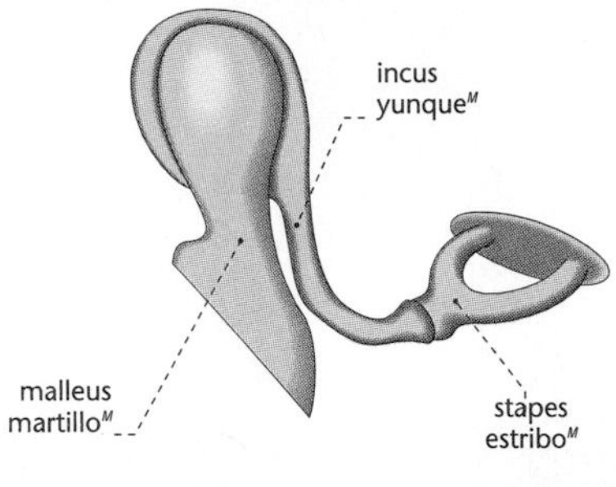

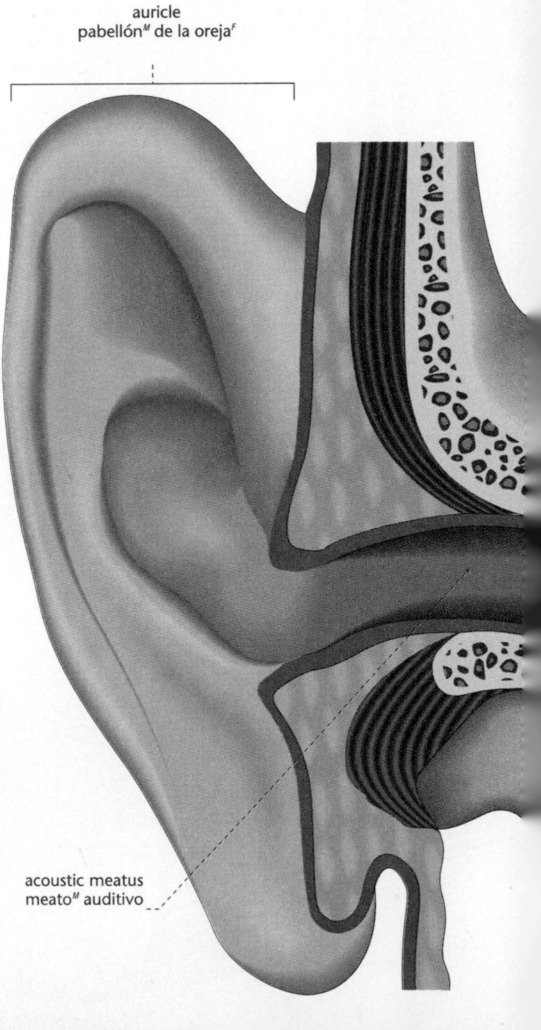

internal ear
oído*M* interno

acoustic meatus
meato*M* auditivo

138

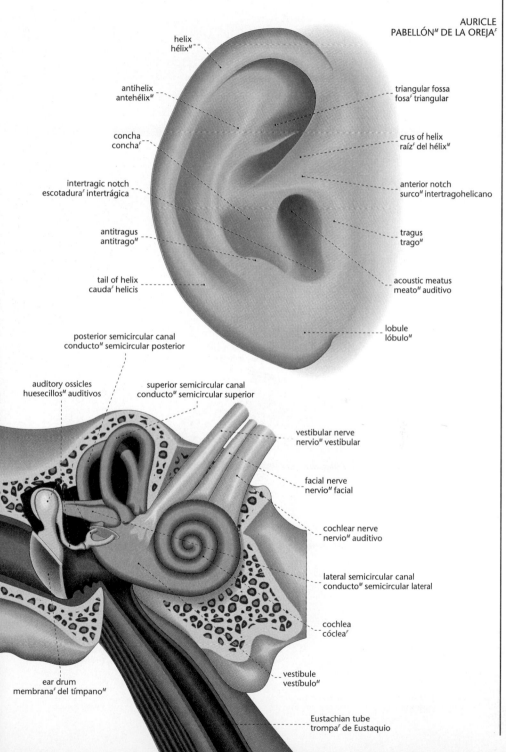

AURICLE
PABELLÓN^M DE LA OREJA^F

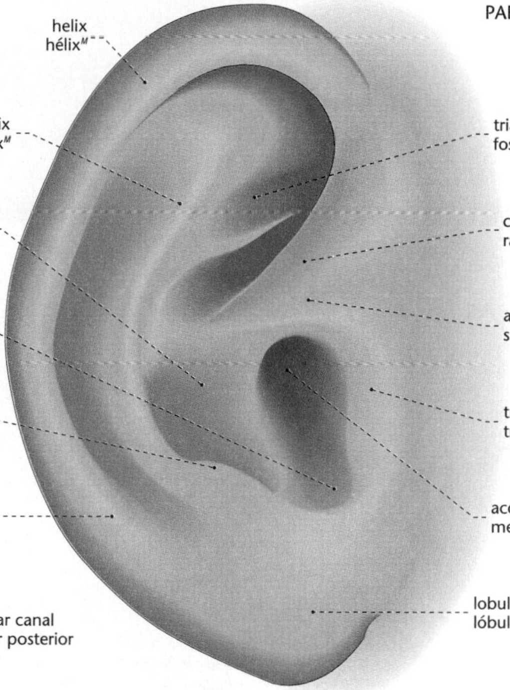

helix
hélix^M

antihelix
antehélix^M

concha
concha^F

intertragic notch
escotadura^F intertrágica

antitragus
antitrago^M

tail of helix
cauda^F helicis

triangular fossa
fosa^F triangular

crus of helix
raíz^F del hélix^M

anterior notch
surco^M intertragohelicano

tragus
trago^M

acoustic meatus
meato^M auditivo

lobule
lóbulo^M

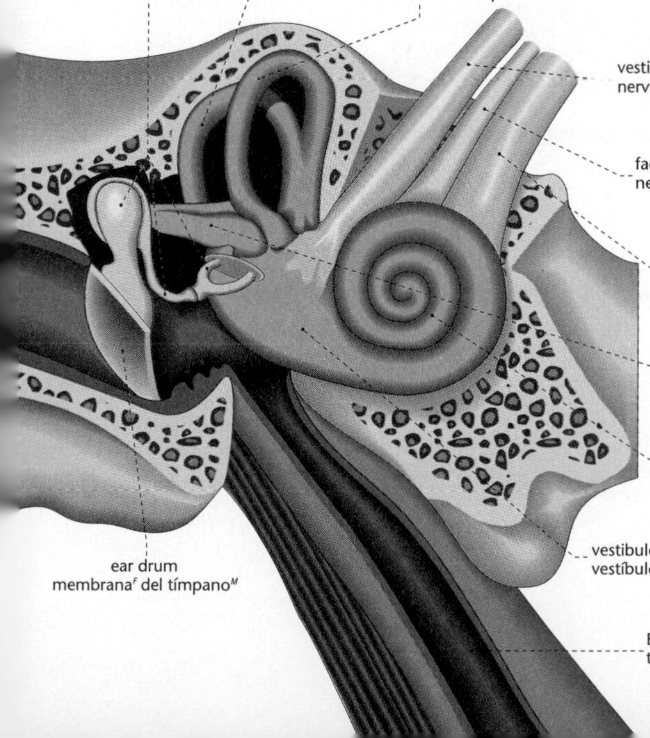

posterior semicircular canal
conducto^M semicircular posterior

auditory ossicles
huesecillos^M auditivos

superior semicircular canal
conducto^M semicircular superior

vestibular nerve
nervio^M vestibular

facial nerve
nervio^M facial

cochlear nerve
nervio^M auditivo

lateral semicircular canal
conducto^M semicircular lateral

cochlea
cóclea^F

ear drum
membrana^F del tímpano^M

vestibule
vestíbulo^M

Eustachian tube
trompa^F de Eustaquio

**HUMAN BEING
SER HUMANO**

EYE
OJO^M

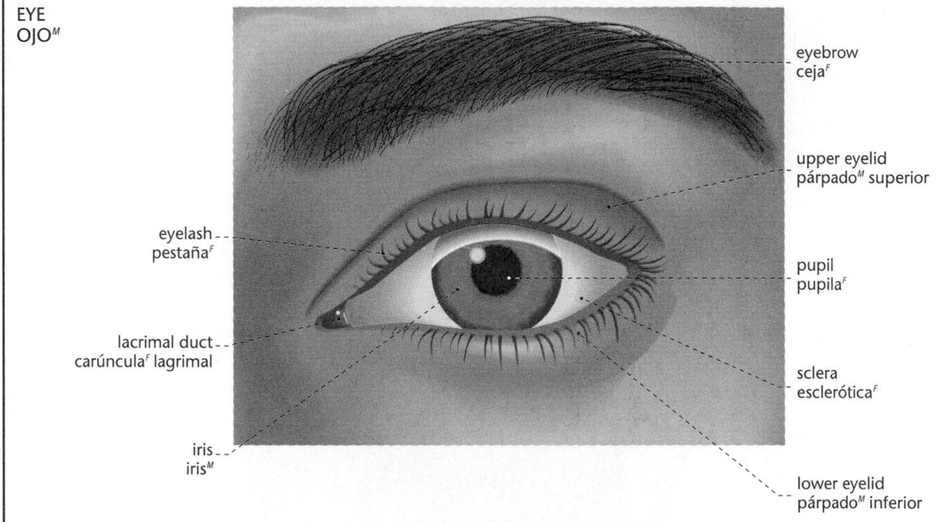

eyebrow
ceja^F

upper eyelid
párpado^M superior

pupil
pupila^F

sclera
esclerótica^F

lower eyelid
párpado^M inferior

eyelash
pestaña^F

lacrimal duct
carúncula^F lagrimal

iris
iris^M

EYEBALL
GLOBO^M OCULAR

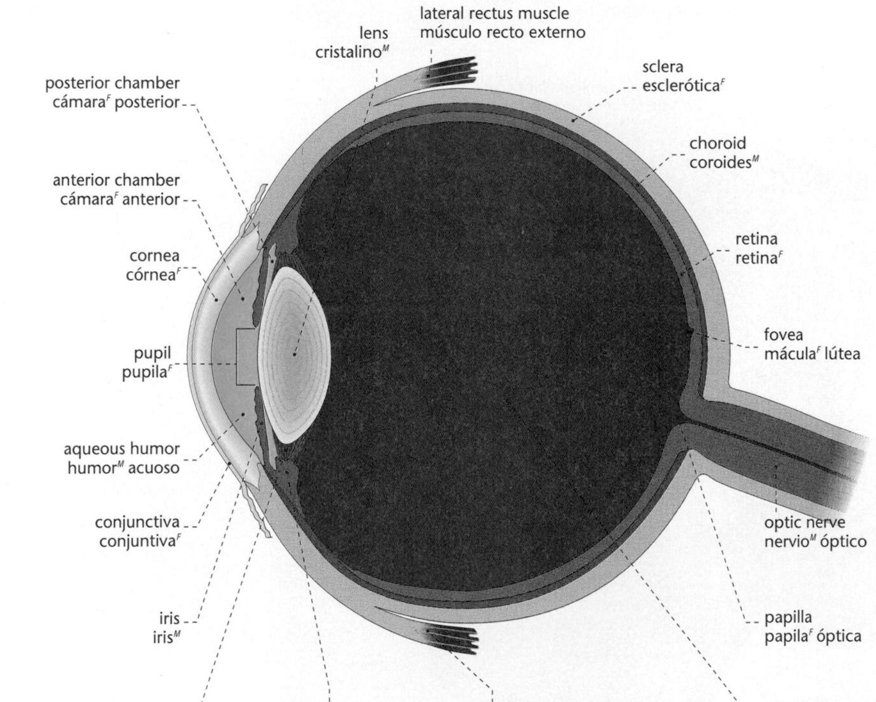

lens
cristalino^M

lateral rectus muscle
músculo recto externo

sclera
esclerótica^F

choroid
coroides^M

retina
retina^F

fovea
mácula^F lútea

posterior chamber
cámara^F posterior

anterior chamber
cámara^F anterior

cornea
córnea^F

pupil
pupila^F

aqueous humor
humor^M acuoso

conjunctiva
conjuntiva^F

iris
iris^M

optic nerve
nervio^M óptico

papilla
papila^F óptica

vitreous body
humor^M vitreo

suspensory ligament
ligamento^M suspensorio

ciliary body
procesos^M ciliares

medial rectus muscle
músculo recto interno

HUMAN BEING
SER HUMANO

EXTERNAL NOSE
NARIZ^F

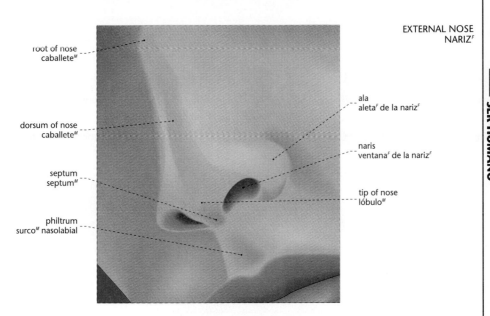

root of nose
caballete^M

dorsum of nose
caballete^M

septum
septum^M

philtrum
surco^M nasolabial

ala
aleta^F de la nariz^F

naris
ventana^F de la nariz^F

tip of nose
lóbulo^M

NASAL FOSSAE
FOSAS^F NASALES

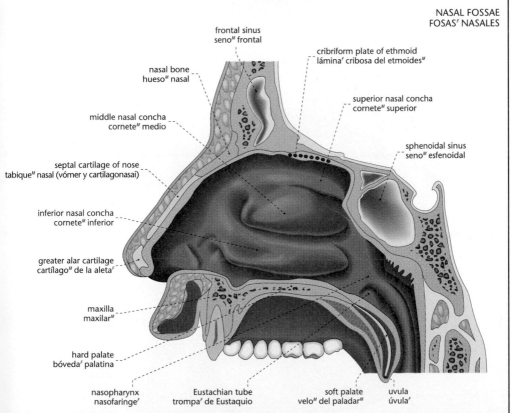

frontal sinus
seno^M frontal

cribriform plate of ethmoid
lámina^F cribosa del etmoides^M

nasal bone
hueso^M nasal

superior nasal concha
cornete^M superior

middle nasal concha
cornete^M medio

sphenoidal sinus
seno^M esfenoidal

septal cartilage of nose
tabique^M nasal (vómer y cartilagonasai)

inferior nasal concha
cornete^M inferior

greater alar cartilage
cartílago^M de la aleta^F

maxilla
maxilar^M

hard palate
bóveda^F palatina

nasopharynx
nasofaringe^F

Eustachian tube
trompa^F de Eustaquio

soft palate
velo^M del paladar^M

uvula
úvula^F

141

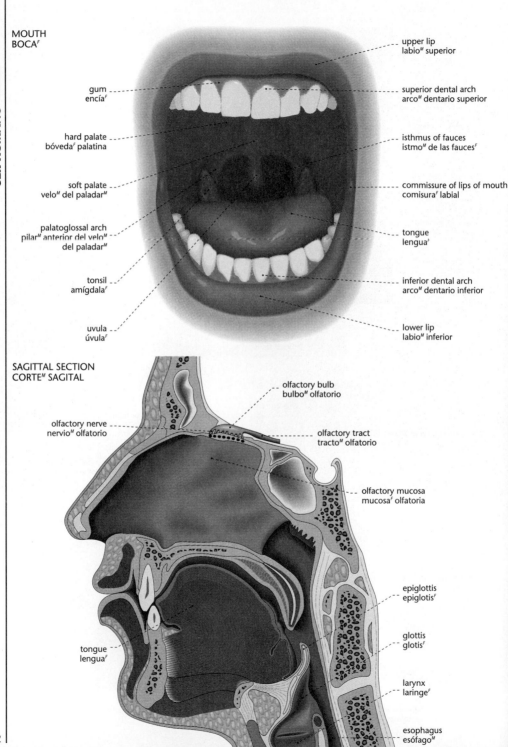

MOUTH
BOCA^F

gum
encía^F

hard palate
bóveda^F palatina

soft palate
velo^M del paladar^M

palatoglossal arch
pilar^M anterior del velo^M
del paladar^M

tonsil
amígdala^F

uvula
úvula^F

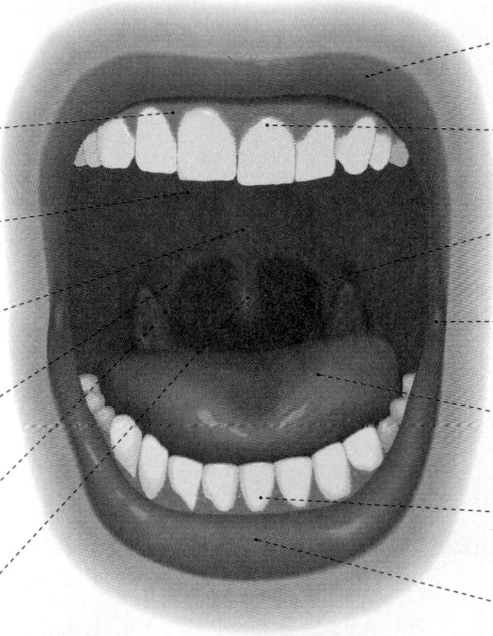

upper lip
labio^M superior

superior dental arch
arco^M dentario superior

isthmus of fauces
istmo^M de las fauces^F

commissure of lips of mouth
comisura^F labial

tongue
lengua^F

inferior dental arch
arco^M dentario inferior

lower lip
labio^M inferior

SAGITTAL SECTION
CORTE^M SAGITAL

olfactory nerve
nervio^M olfatorio

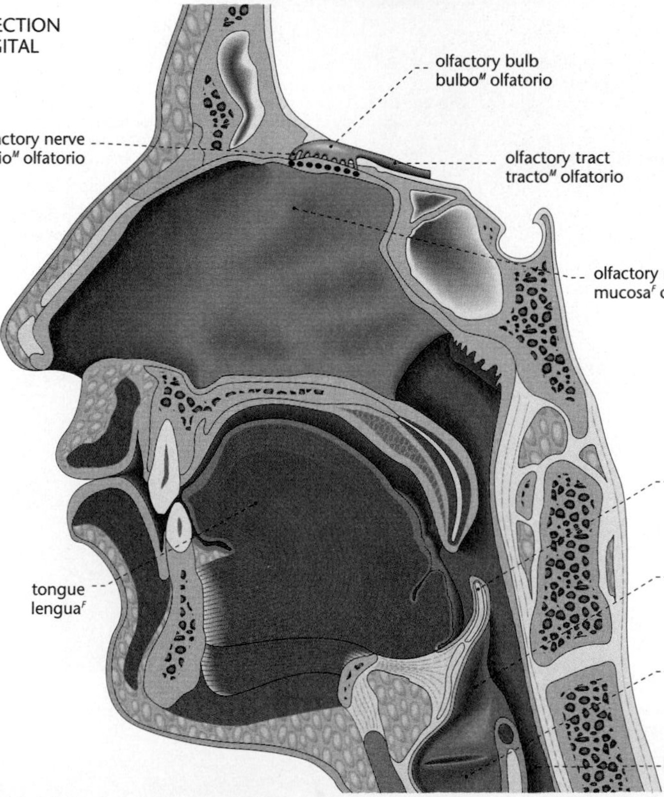

olfactory bulb
bulbo^M olfatorio

olfactory tract
tracto^M olfatorio

olfactory mucosa
mucosa^F olfatoria

tongue
lengua^F

epiglottis
epiglotis^F

glottis
glotis^F

larynx
laringe^F

esophagus
esófago^M

HUMAN BEING
SER HUMANO

DORSUM OF TONGUE
LENGUA^F

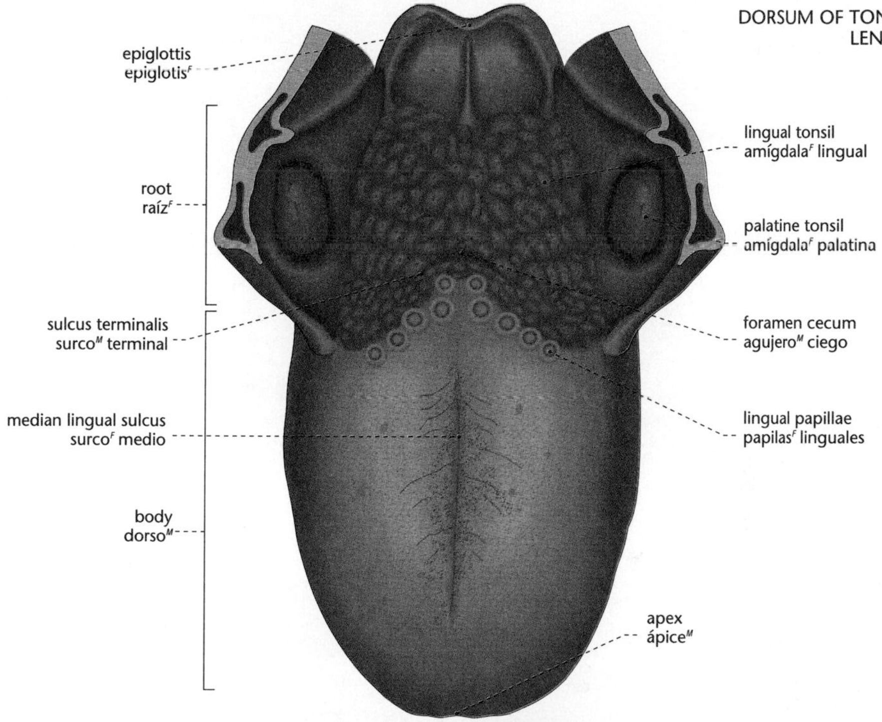

epiglottis
epiglotis^F

lingual tonsil
amígdala^F lingual

root
raíz^F

palatine tonsil
amígdala^F palatina

sulcus terminalis
surco^M terminal

foramen cecum
agujero^M ciego

median lingual sulcus
surco^F medio

lingual papillae
papilas^F linguales

body
dorso^M

apex
ápice^M

TASTE SENSATIONS
SABORES^M

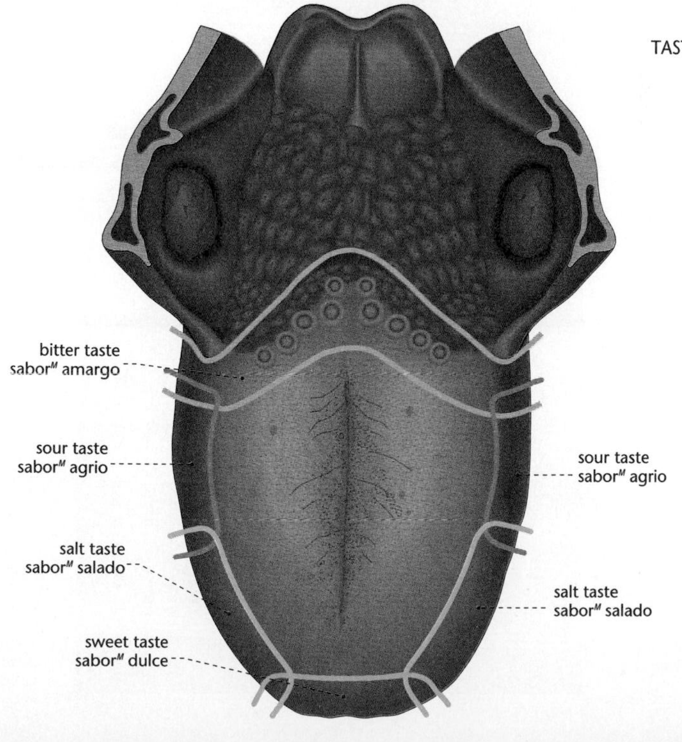

bitter taste
sabor^M amargo

sour taste
sabor^M agrio

sour taste
sabor^M agrio

salt taste
sabor^M salado

salt taste
sabor^M salado

sweet taste
sabor^M dulce

HUMAN DENTURE
DENTADURA_F_ HUMANA

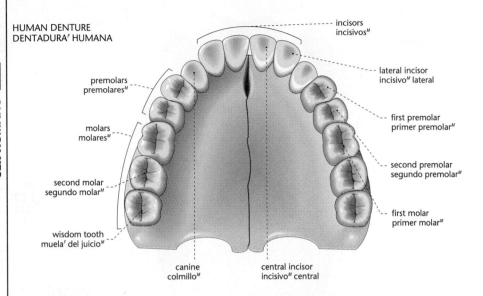

incisors
incisivos_M_

lateral incisor
incisivo_M_ lateral

premolars
premolares_M_

first premolar
primer premolar_M_

molars
molares_M_

second premolar
segundo premolar_M_

second molar
segundo molar_M_

first molar
primer molar_M_

wisdom tooth
muela_F_ del juicio_M_

canine
colmillo_M_

central incisor
incisivo_M_ central

CROSS SECTION OF A MOLAR
CORTE_M_ TRANSVERSAL DE UN MOLAR_M_

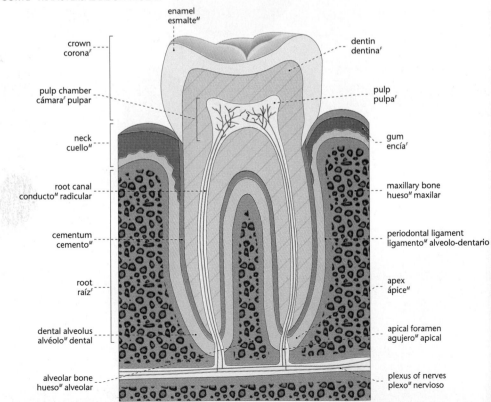

enamel
esmalte_M_

crown
corona_F_

dentin
dentina_F_

pulp chamber
cámara_F_ pulpar

pulp
pulpa_F_

neck
cuello_M_

gum
encía_F_

root canal
conducto_M_ radicular

maxillary bone
hueso_M_ maxilar

cementum
cemento_M_

periodontal ligament
ligamento_M_ alveolo-dentario

root
raíz_F_

apex
ápice_M_

dental alveolus
alvéolo_M_ dental

apical foramen
agujero_M_ apical

alveolar bone
hueso_M_ alveolar

plexus of nerves
plexo_M_ nervioso

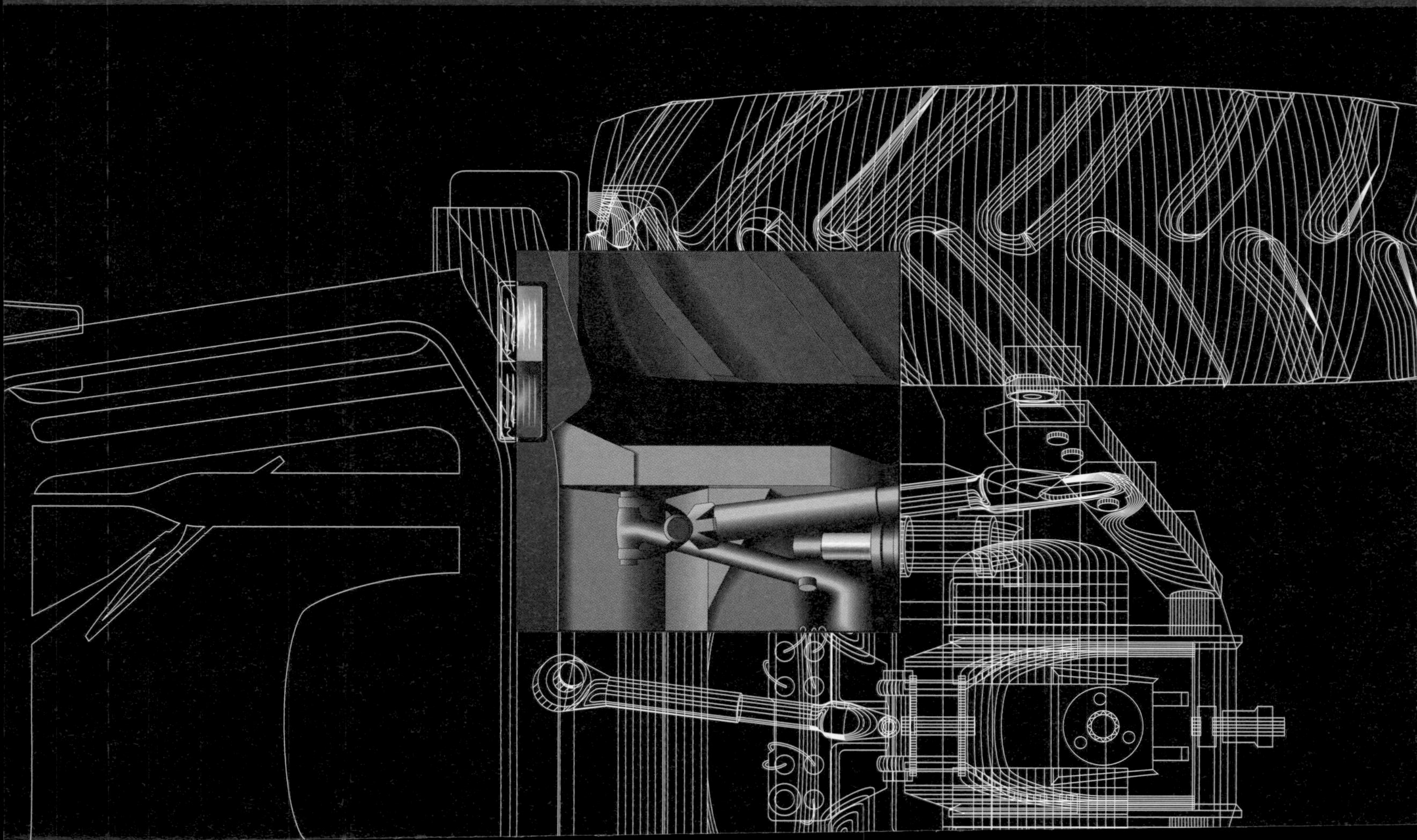

CONTENTS

TRACTOR
TRACTOR^M

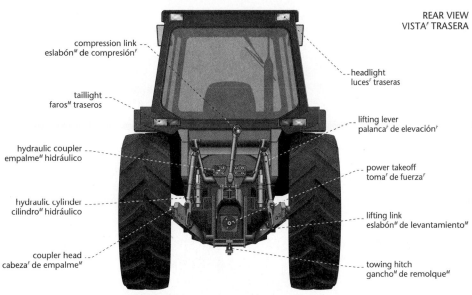

REAR VIEW
VISTA^F TRASERA

compression link
eslabón^M de compresión^F

headlight
luces^F traseras

taillight
faros^M traseros

lifting lever
palanca^F de elevación^F

hydraulic coupler
empalme^M hidráulico

power takeoff
toma^F de fuerza^F

hydraulic cylinder
cilindro^M hidráulico

lifting link
eslabón^M de levantamiento^M

coupler head
cabeza^F de empalme^M

towing hitch
gancho^M de remolque^M

FRONT VIEW
VISTA^F FRONTAL

steering wheel
volante^M

cab
cabina^F

exhaust stack
tubo^M de escape^M

mudguard
guardabarros^M

headlight
faro^F delantero

rim
llanta^F

step
peldaño^M

counterweight
contrapeso^M

driving wheel
rueda^F motriz

front wheel
rueda^F delantera

tread bar
banda^F de rodamiento^M

engine
motor^M

FARMSTEAD
GRANJA^F

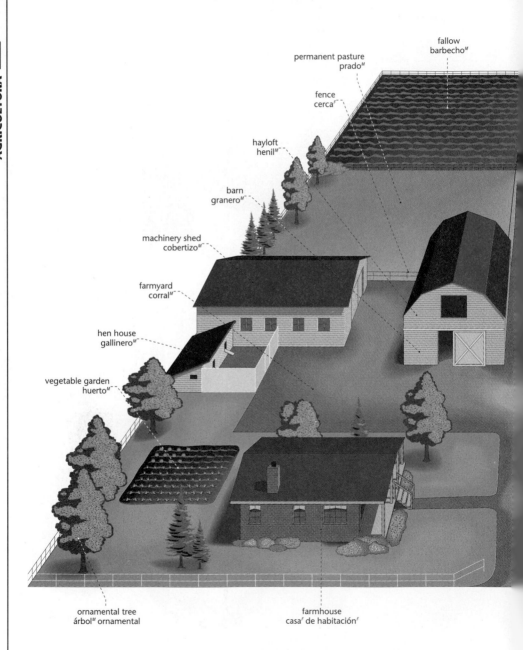

permanent pasture
prado^M

fallow
barbecho^M

fence
cerca^F

hayloft
henil^M

barn
granero^M

machinery shed
cobertizo^M

farmyard
corral^M

hen house
gallinero^M

vegetable garden
huerto^M

ornamental tree
árbol^M ornamental

farmhouse
casa^F de habitación^F

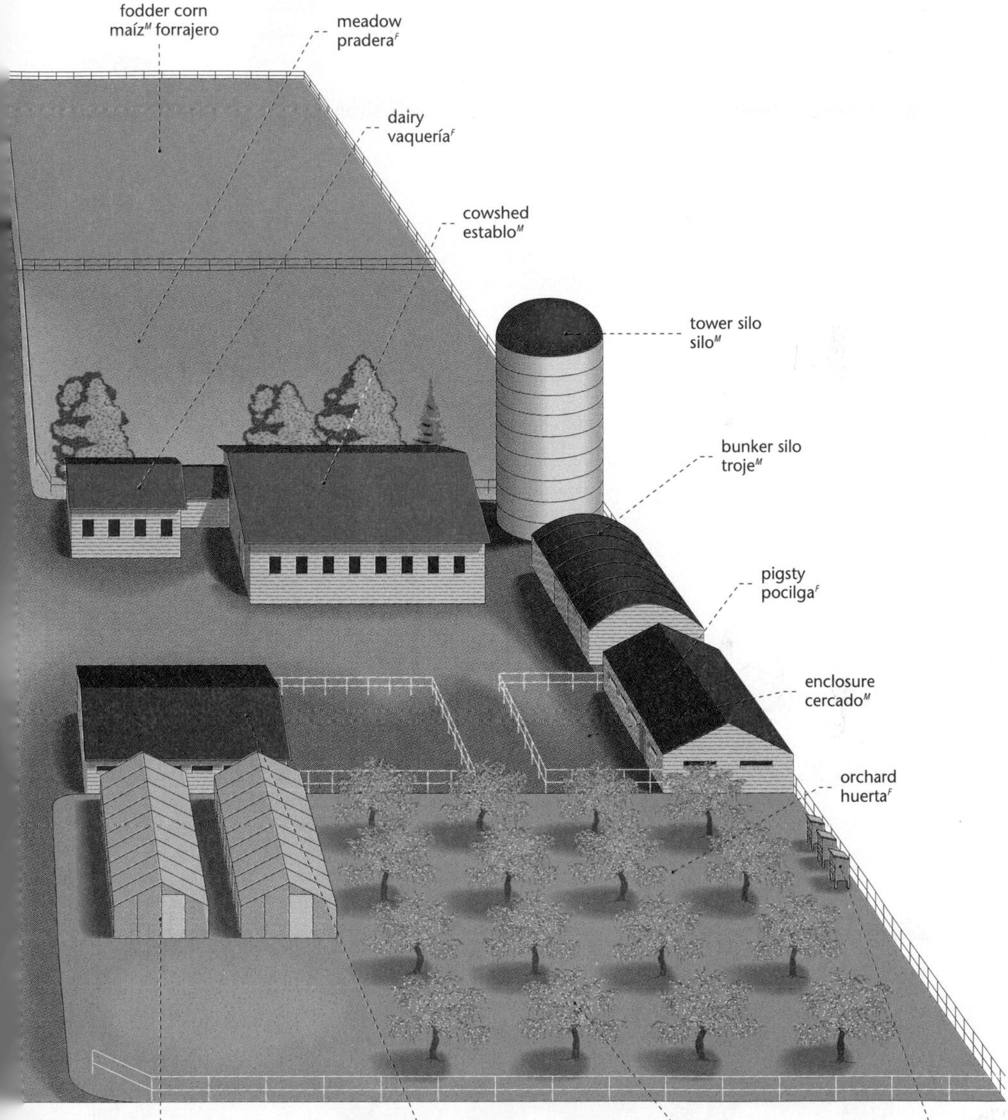

fodder corn
maíz^M forrajero

meadow
pradera^F

dairy
vaquería^F

cowshed
establo^M

tower silo
silo^M

bunker silo
troje^M

pigsty
pocilga^F

enclosure
cercado^M

orchard
huerta^F

greenhouse
invernadero^M

sheep shelter
cobertizo^M para ovejas^F

fruit tree
árbol^M frutal

hive
colmena^F

FARMING
AGRICULTURA

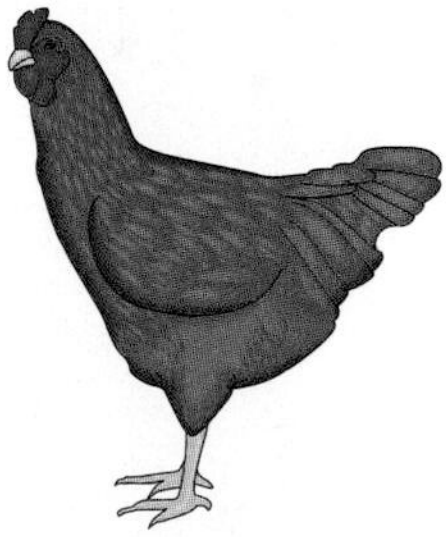

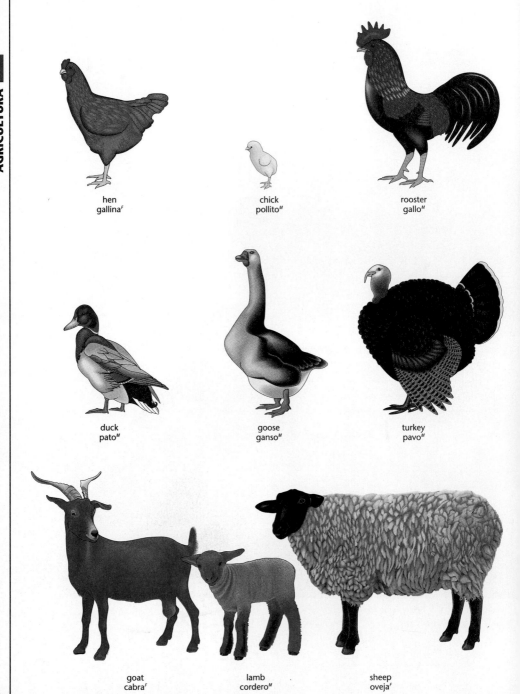

hen
gallina^F

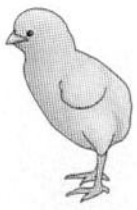

chick
pollito^M

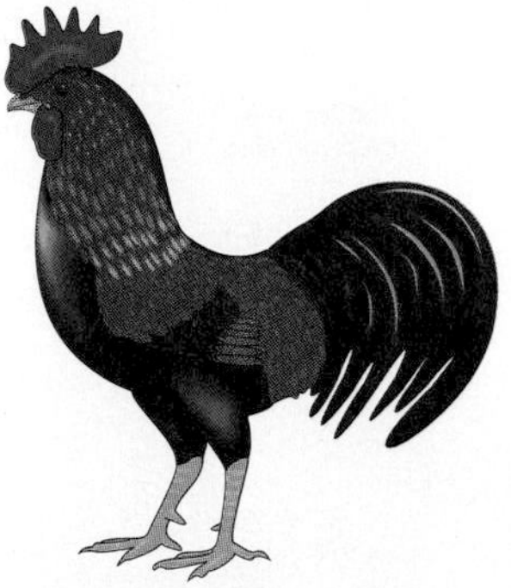

rooster
gallo^M

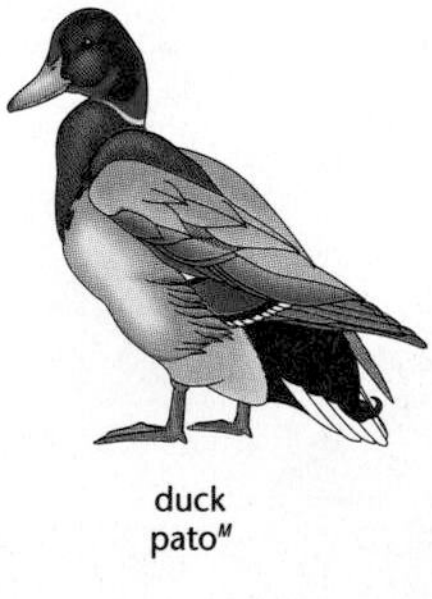

duck
pato^M

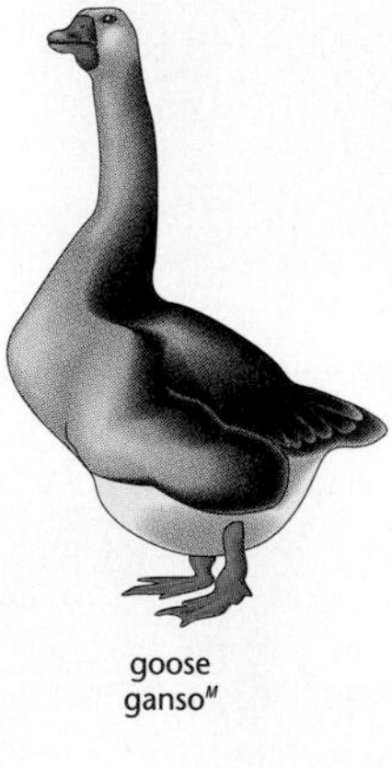

goose
ganso^M

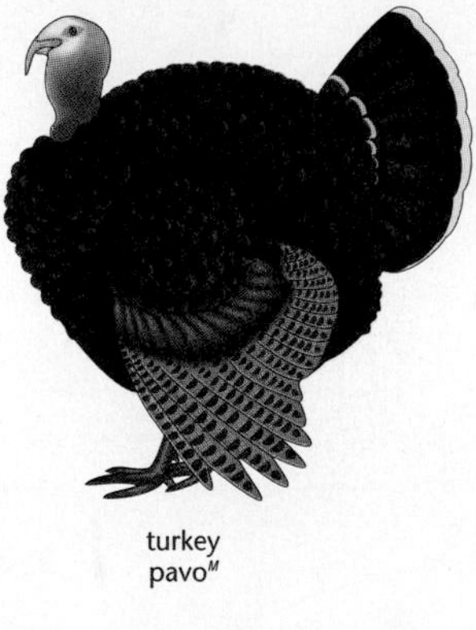

turkey
pavo^M

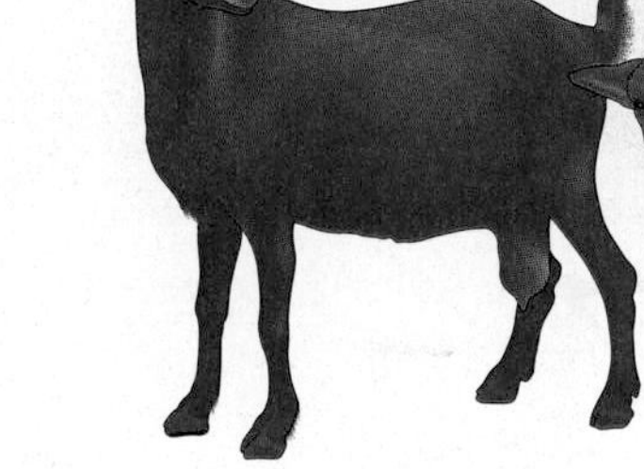

goat
cabra^F

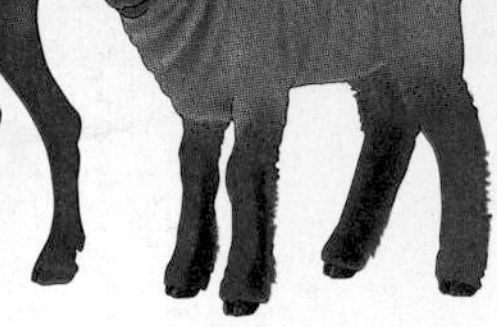

lamb
cordero^M

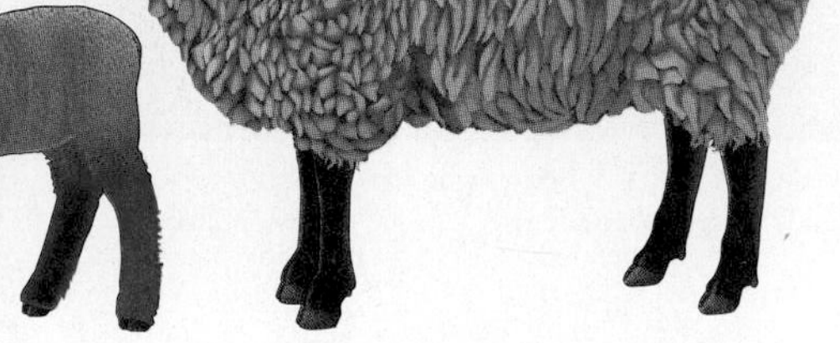

sheep
oveja^F

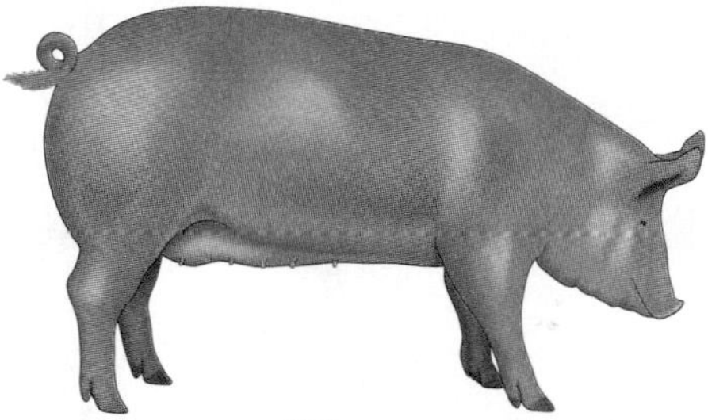

sow
cerda*F*

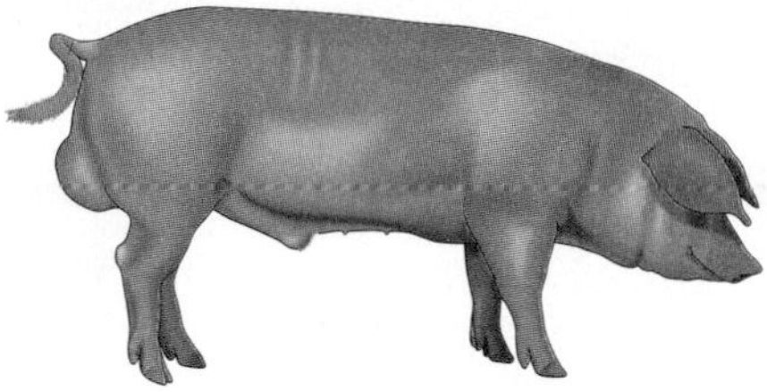

pig
cerdo*M*

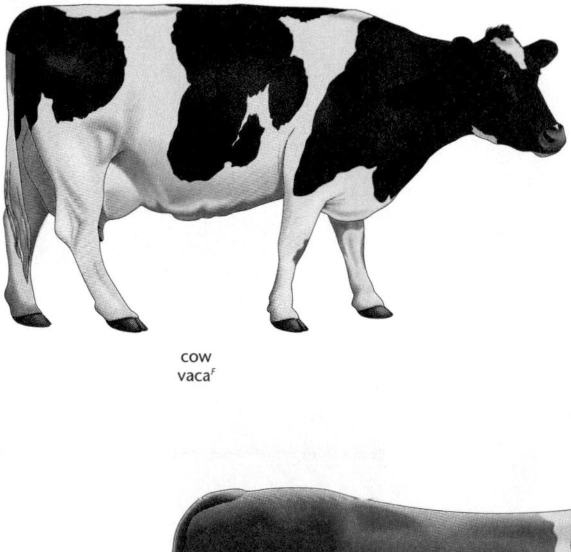

cow
vaca*F*

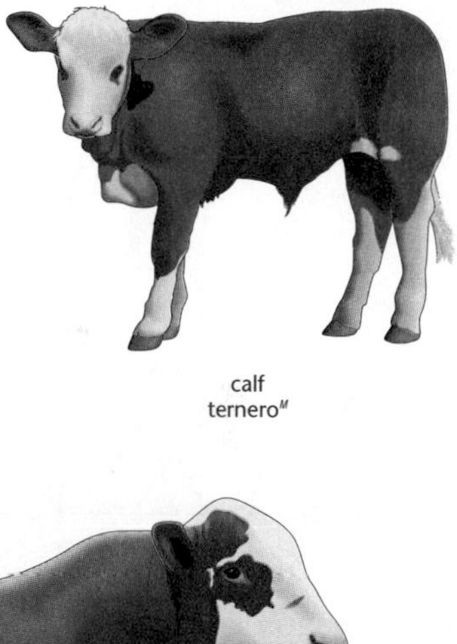

calf
ternero*M*

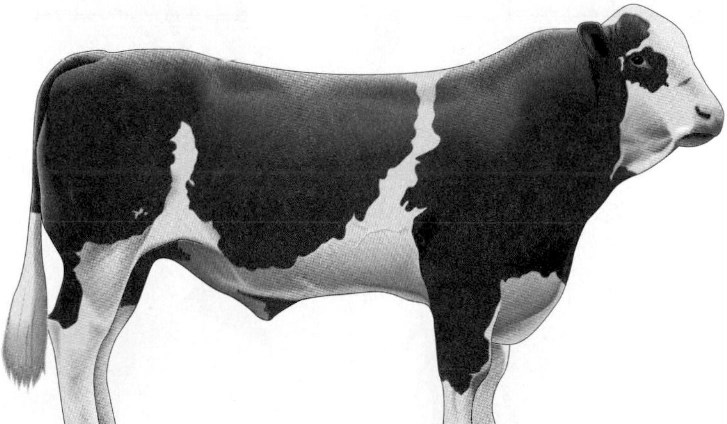

ox
buey*M*

SECTION OF A GRAIN OF WHEAT
CORTE^M DE UN GRANO^M DE
TRIGO^M

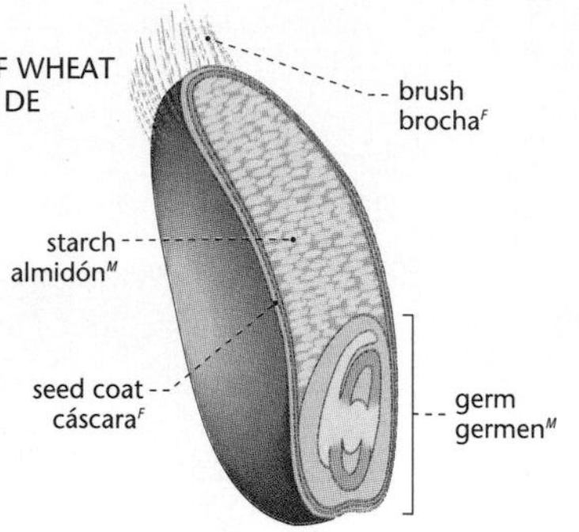

brush
brocha^F

starch
almidón^M

seed coat
cáscara^F

germ
germen^M

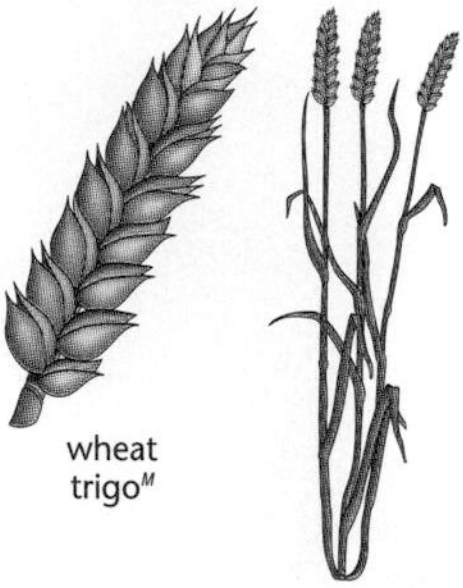

wheat
trigo^M

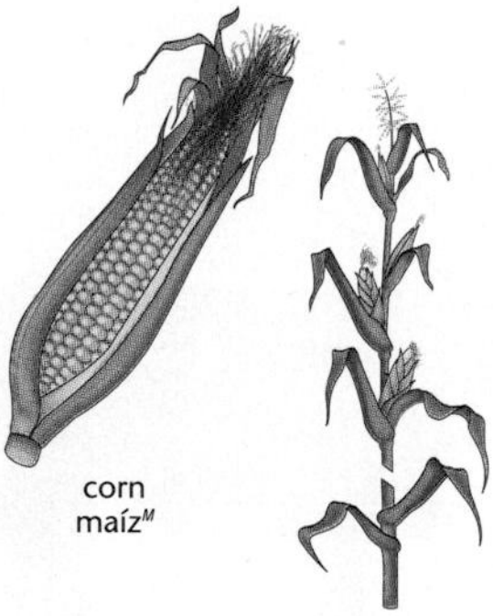

corn
maíz^M

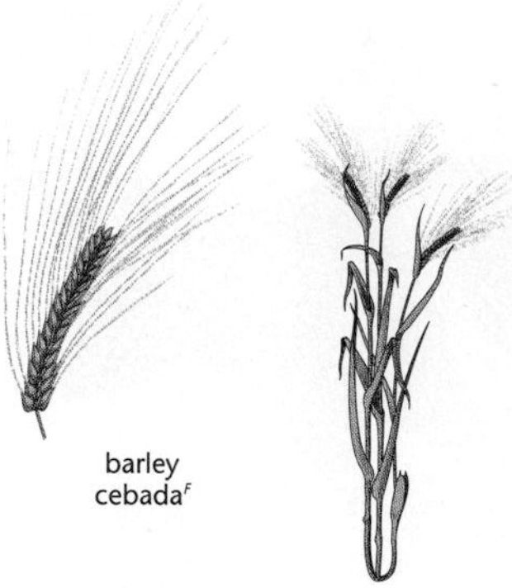

barley
cebada^F

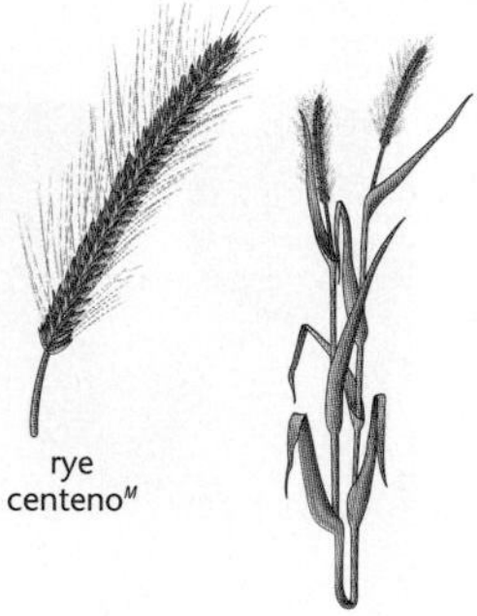

rye
centeno^M

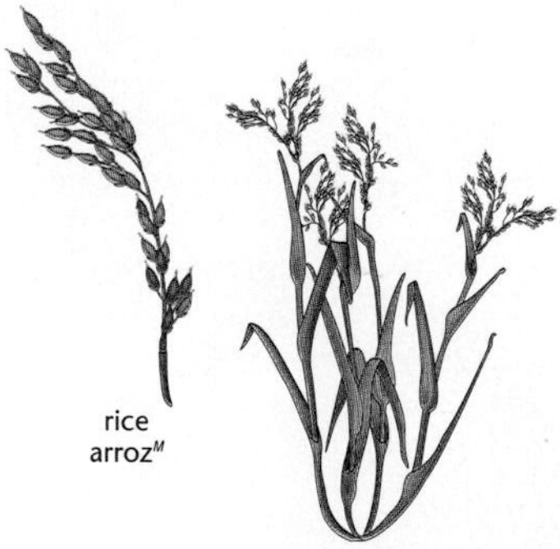

rice
arroz^M

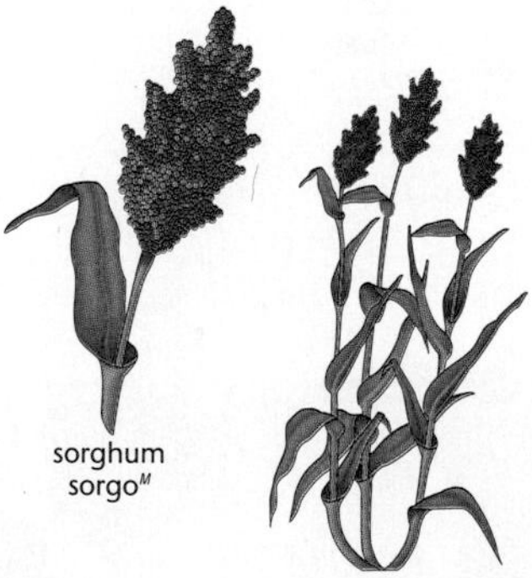

sorghum
sorgo^M

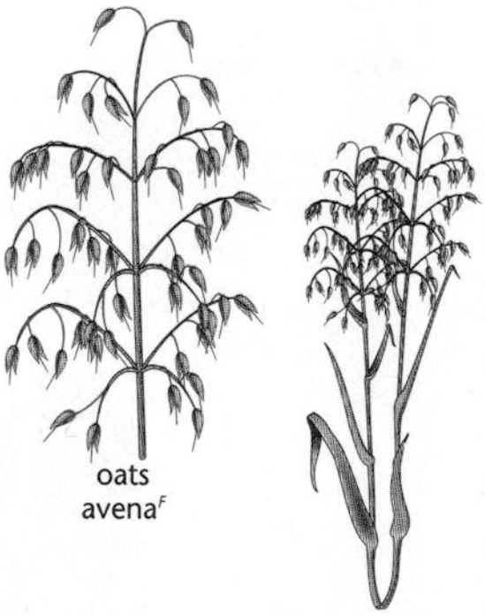

oats
avena^F

millet
mijo^M

buckwheat
trigo^M sarraceno

FARMING
AGRICULTURA

152

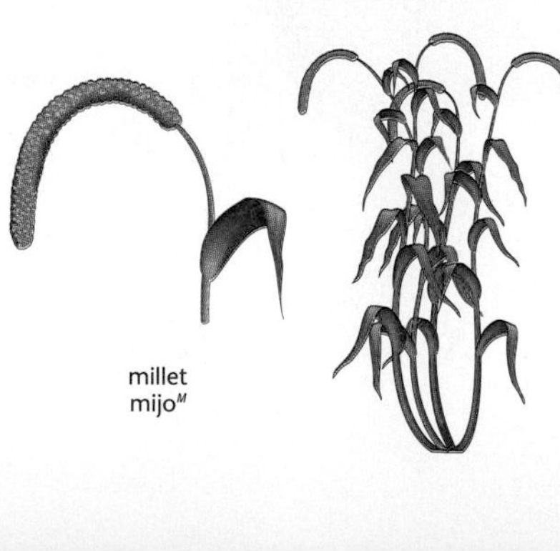

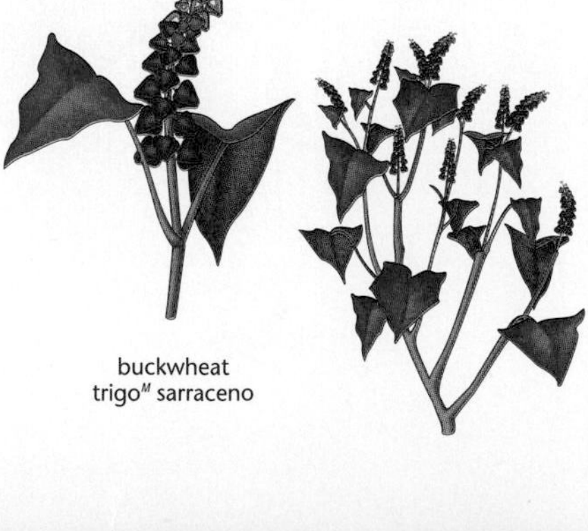

BREAD
PAN^M

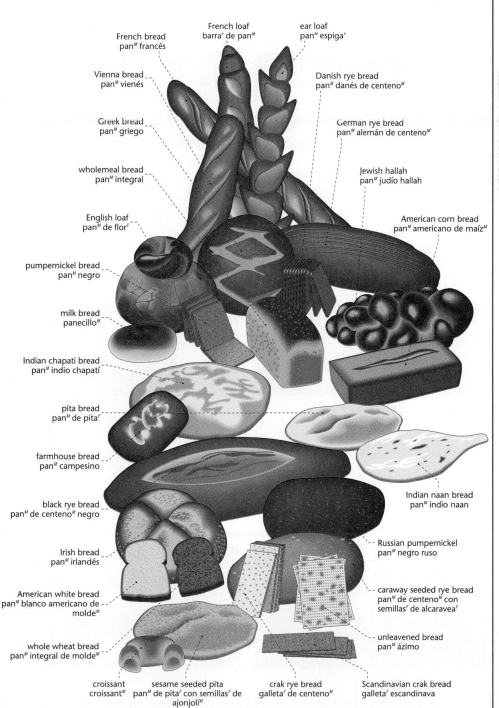

French bread
pan^M francés

French loaf
barra^F de pan^M

ear loaf
pan^M espiga^F

Vienna bread
pan^M vienés

Danish rye bread
pan^M danés de centeno^M

Greek bread
pan^M griego

German rye bread
pan^M alemán de centeno^M

wholemeal bread
pan^M integral

Jewish hallah
pan^M judío hallah

English loaf
pan^M de flor^F

American corn bread
pan^M americano de maíz^M

pumpernickel bread
pan^M negro

milk bread
panecillo^M

Indian chapati bread
pan^M indio chapatí

pita bread
pan^M de pita^F

farmhouse bread
pan^M campesino

Indian naan bread
pan^M indio naan

black rye bread
pan^M de centeno^M negro

Irish bread
pan^M irlandés

Russian pumpernickel
pan^M negro ruso

American white bread
pan^M blanco americano de
molde^M

caraway seeded rye bread
pan^M de centeno^M con
semillas^F de alcaravea^F

whole wheat bread
pan^M integral de molde^M

unleavened bread
pan^M ázimo

croissant
croissant^M

sesame seeded pita
pan^M de pita^F con semillas^F de
ajonjolí^M

crak rye bread
galleta^F de centeno^M

Scandinavian crak bread
galleta^F escandinava

STEPS FOR CULTIVATING SOIL
PASOS^M PARA EL CULTIVO^M DEL SUELO^M

PLOWING SOIL
ARADO^M

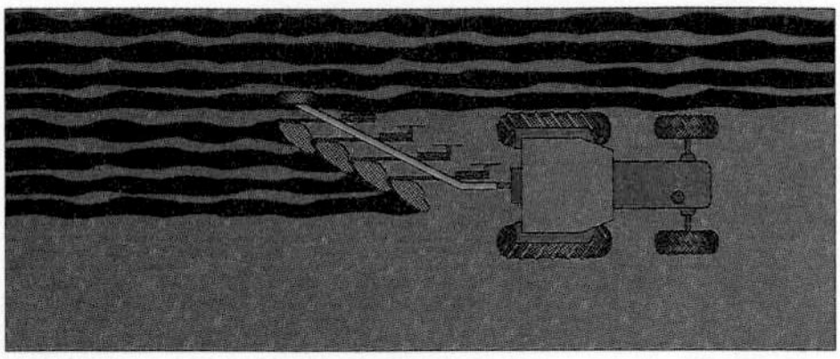

ribbing plow
arado^M de vertedera^F

FERTILIZING SOIL
ABONADO^M

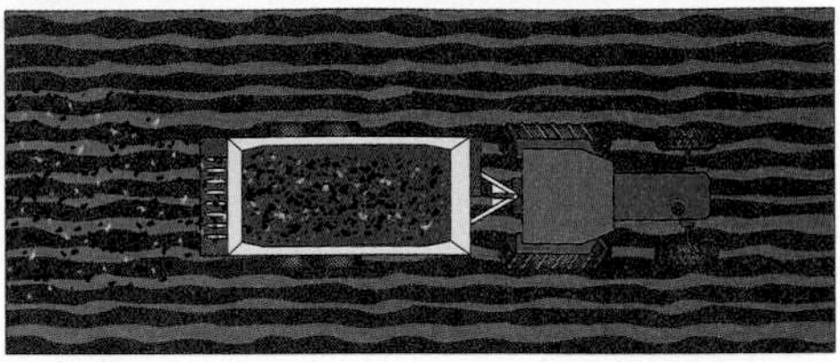

manure spreader
esparcidora^F de estiércol^M

PULVERIZING SOIL
PULVERIZACIÓN^F

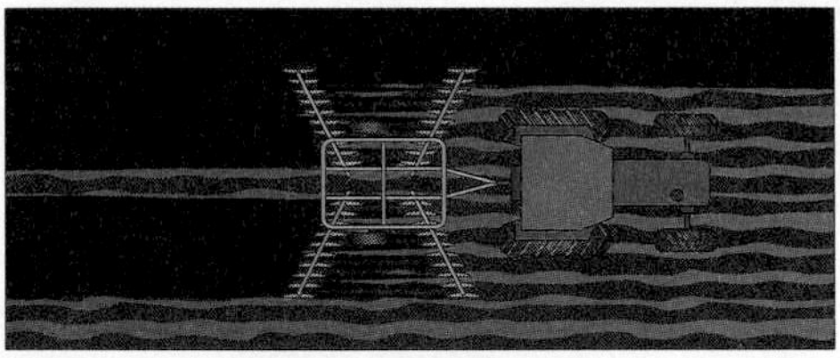

tandem disk harrow
pulverizador^M de discos^M

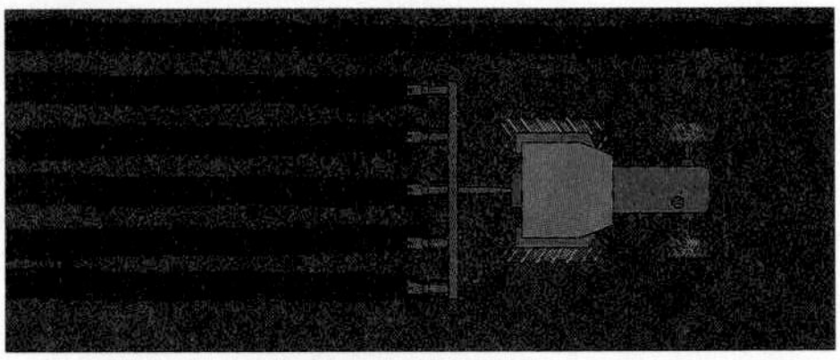

cultivator
cultivador^M

PLANTING
SIEMBRA^F

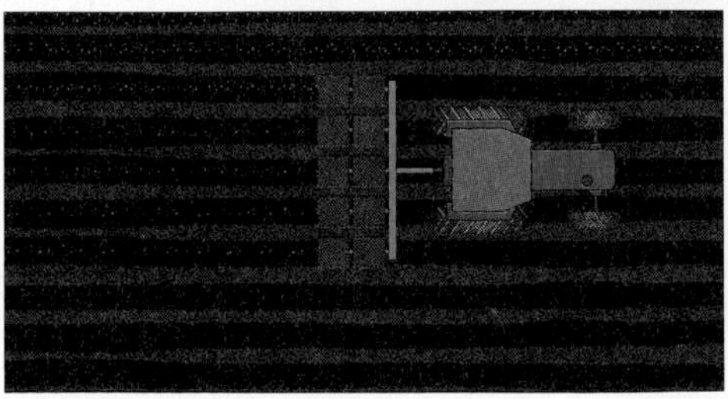

seed drill
sembradora^F a chorrillo^M

MOWING
SIEGA^F

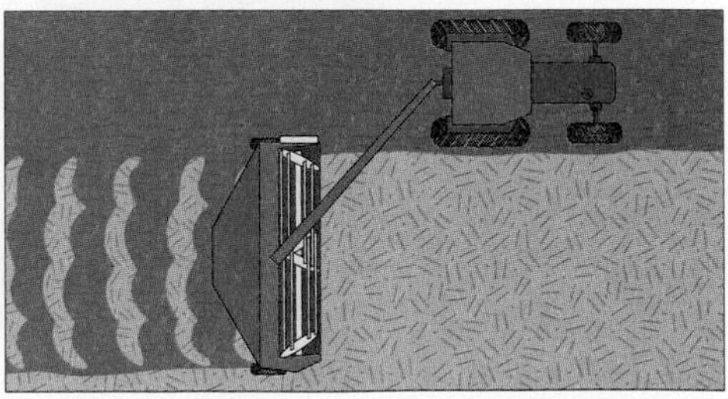

flail mower
segadora^F

TEDDING
HENIFICACIÓN^F

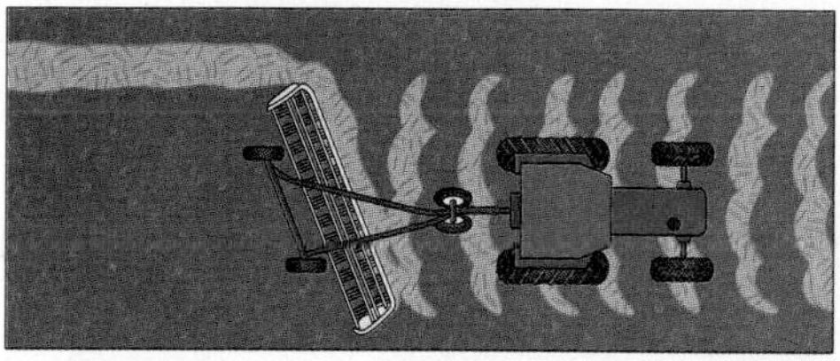

rake
rastrillo^M

HARVESTING
COSECHA^F

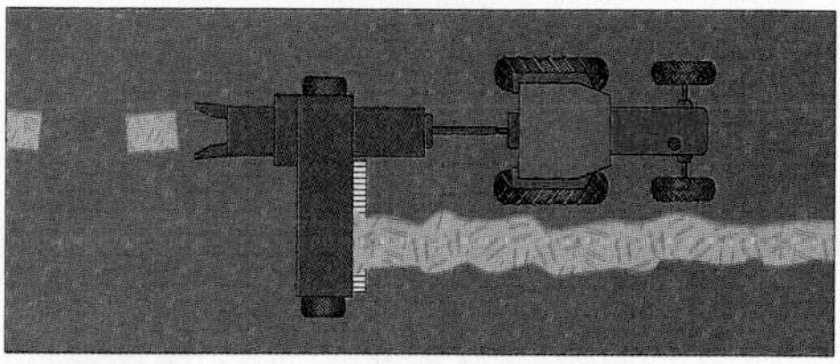

hay baler
empacadora^F de heno^M

HARVESTING
COSECHA^F

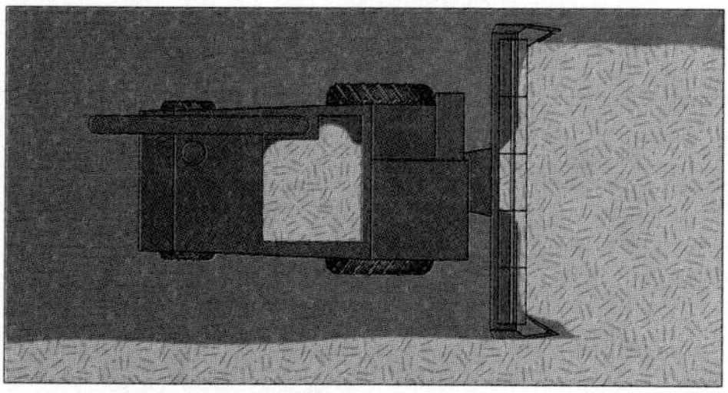

combine harvester
cosechadora^F trilladora^F

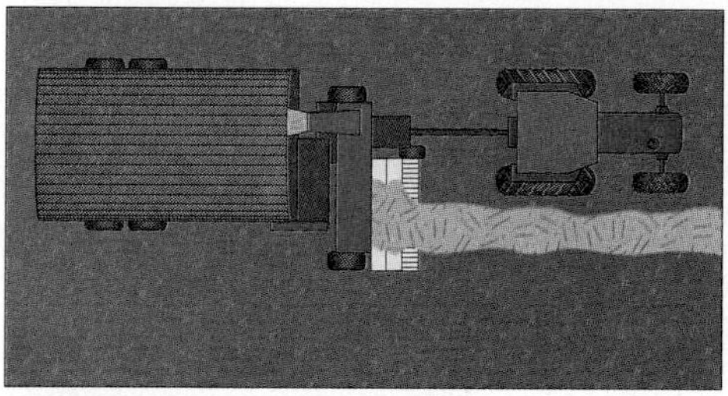

forage harvester
cosechadora^F de forraje^M

ENSILING
ENSILAJE^M

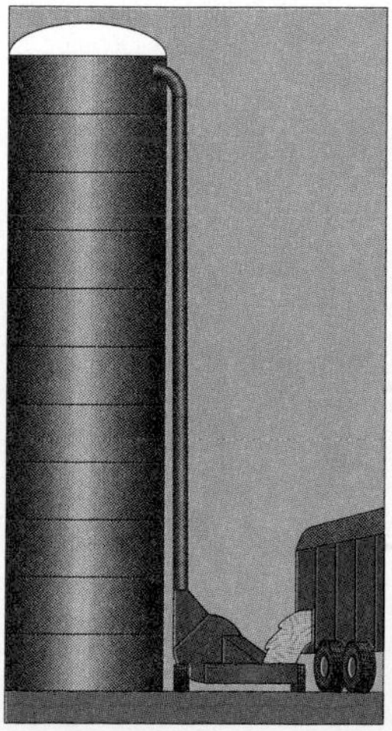

forage blower
aventador^M de frorraje^M

PLOWING SOIL
ARADO^M

RIBBING PLOW
ARADO^M DE VERTEDERA^F

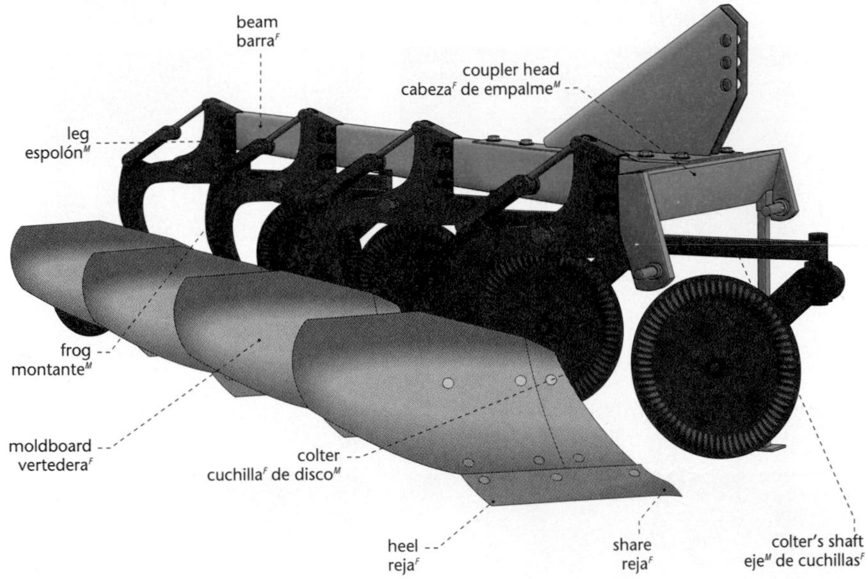

beam
barra^F

coupler head
cabeza^F de empalme^M

leg
espolón^M

frog
montante^M

moldboard
vertedera^F

colter
cuchilla^F de disco^M

heel
reja^F

share
reja^F

colter's shaft
eje^M de cuchillas^F

FERTILIZING SOIL
ABONADO^M

MANURE SPREADER
ESPARCIDORA^M DE ESTIÉRCOL^M

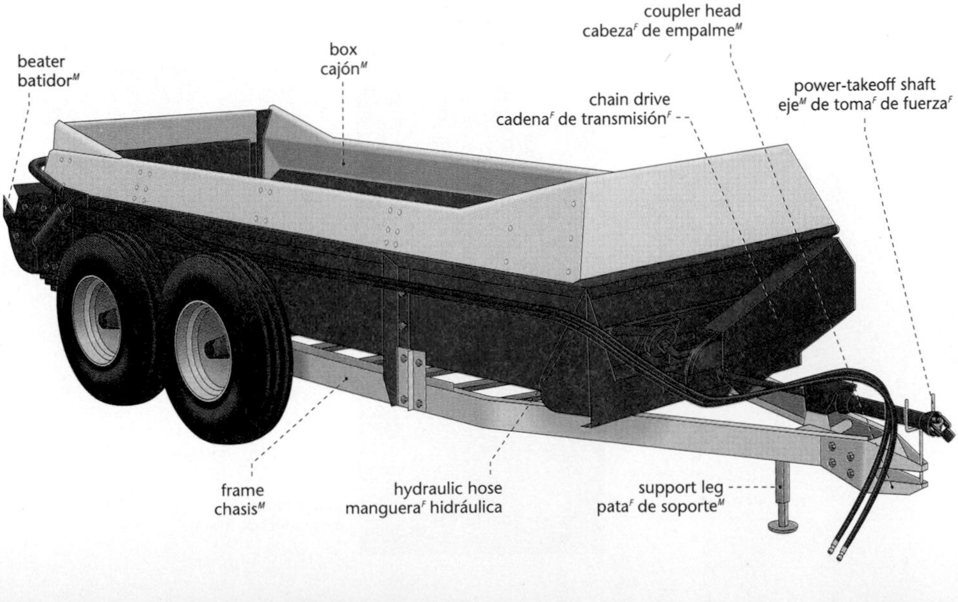

beater
batidor^M

box
cajón^M

coupler head
cabeza^F de empalme^M

chain drive
cadena^F de transmisión^F

power-takeoff shaft
eje^M de toma^F de fuerza^F

frame
chasis^M

hydraulic hose
manguera^F hidráulica

support leg
pata^F de soporte^M

PULVERIZING SOIL
PULVERIZACIÓN^F

TANDEM DISK HARROW
PULVERIZADOR^M DE DISCOS^M

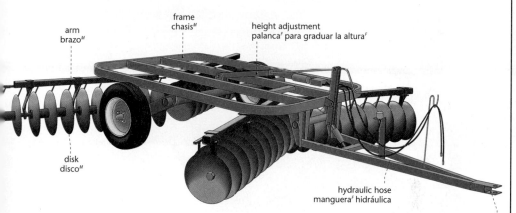

arm
brazo^M

frame
chasis^M

height adjustment
palanca^F para graduar la altura^F

disk
disco^M

hydraulic hose
manguera^F hidráulica

coupler head
cabeza^F de emplame^M

CULTIVATOR
CULTIVADOR^M

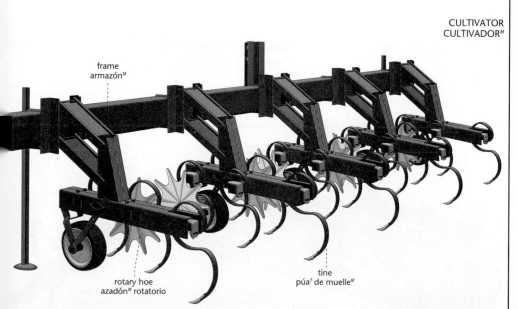

frame
armazón^M

rotary hoe
azadón^M rotatorio

tine
púa^F de muelle^M

157

PLANTING
SIEMBRA*F*

SEED DRILL
SEMBRADORA*F* A CHORRILLO*M*

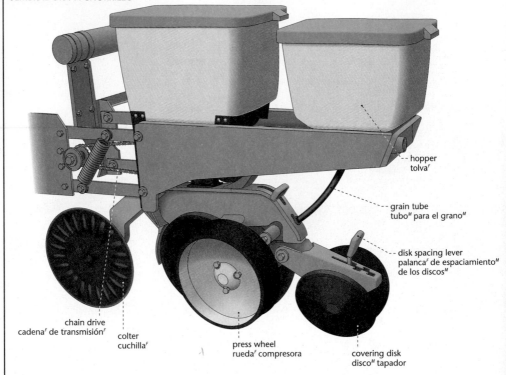

hopper
tolva*F*

grain tube
tubo*M* para el grano*M*

disk spacing lever
palanca*F* de espaciamiento*M*
de los discos*M*

chain drive
cadena*F* de transmisión*F*

colter
cuchilla*F*

press wheel
rueda*F* compresora

covering disk
disco*M* tapador

MOWING
SIEGA*F*

FLAIL MOWER
SEGADORA*F*

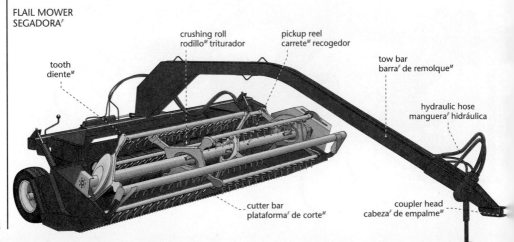

crushing roll
rodillo*M* triturador

pickup reel
carrete*M* recogedor

tooth
diente*M*

tow bar
barra*F* de remolque*M*

hydraulic hose
manguera*F* hidráulica

cutter bar
plataforma*F* de corte*M*

coupler head
cabeza*F* de empalme*M*

TEDDING
HENIFICACIÓN^M

RAKE
RASTRILLO^M

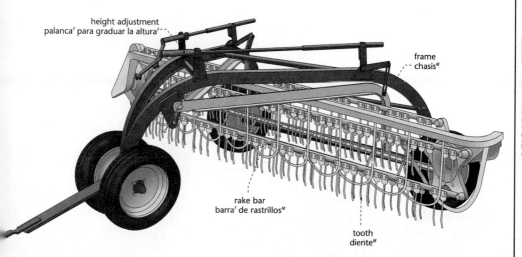

height adjustment
palanca^F para graduar la altura^F

frame
chasis^M

rake bar
barra^F de rastrillos^M

tooth
diente^M

HARVESTING
COSECHA^F

HAY BALER
EMPACADORA^F DE HENO^M

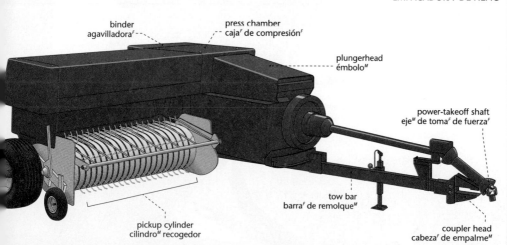

binder
agavilladora^F

press chamber
caja^F de compresión^F

plungerhead
émbolo^M

power-takeoff shaft
eje^M de toma^F de fuerza^F

pickup cylinder
cilindro^M recogedor

tow bar
barra^F de remolque^M

coupler head
cabeza^F de empalme^M

159

COMBINE HARVESTER
COSECHADORA[F] TRILLADORA[F]

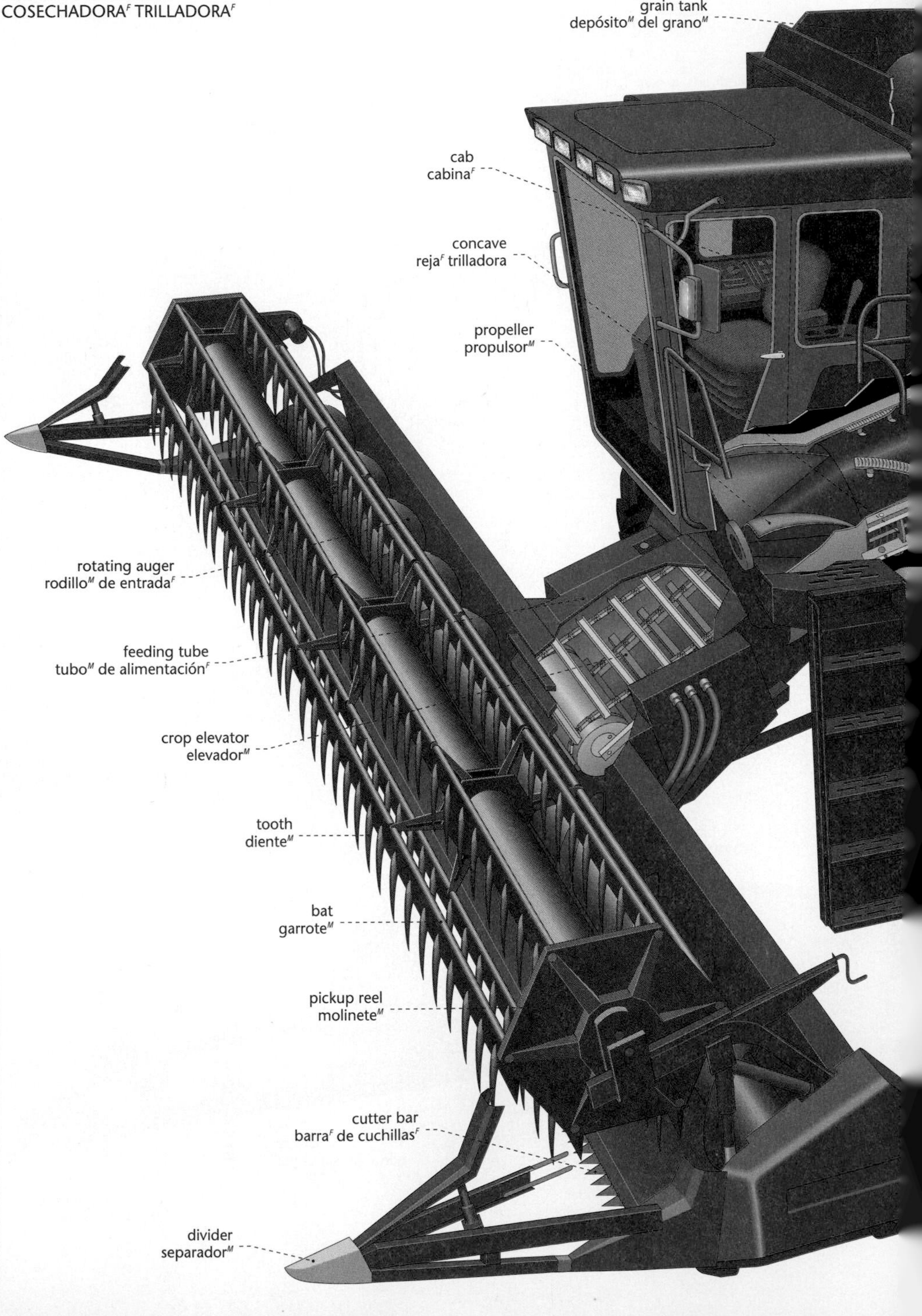

grain tank
depósito[M] del grano[M]

cab
cabina[F]

concave
reja[F] trilladora

propeller
propulsor[M]

rotating auger
rodillo[M] de entrada[F]

feeding tube
tubo[M] de alimentación[F]

crop elevator
elevador[M]

tooth
diente[M]

bat
garrote[M]

pickup reel
molinete[M]

cutter bar
barra[F] de cuchillas[F]

divider
separador[M]

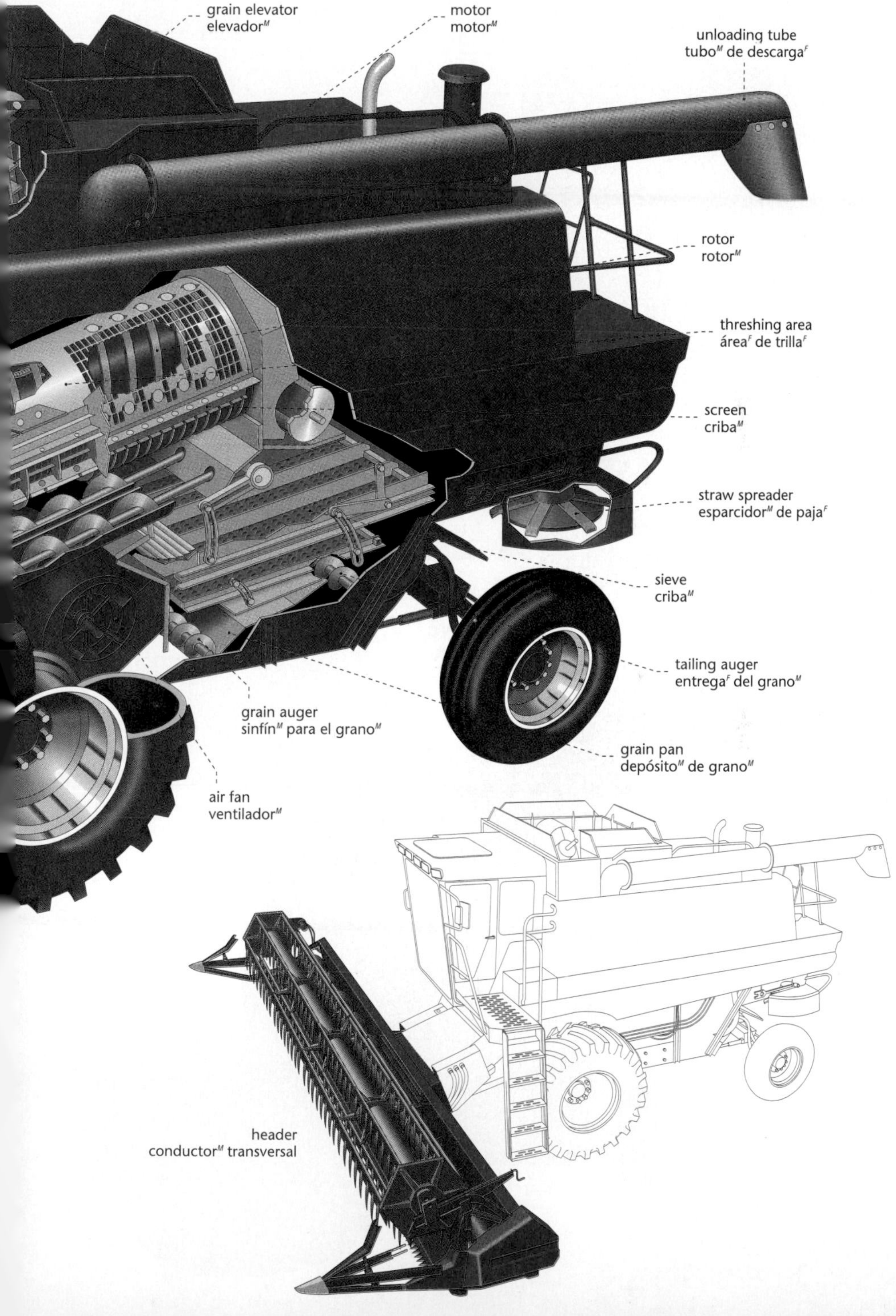

grain elevator
elevador^M

motor
motor^M

unloading tube
tubo^M de descarga^F

rotor
rotor^M

threshing area
área^F de trilla^F

screen
criba^M

straw spreader
esparcidor^M de paja^F

sieve
criba^M

tailing auger
entrega^F del grano^M

grain pan
depósito^M de grano^M

grain auger
sinfín^M para el grano^M

air fan
ventilador^M

header
conductor^M transversal

FARMING
AGRICULTURA

FORAGE HARVESTER
COSECHERA^F DE FORRAJE^M

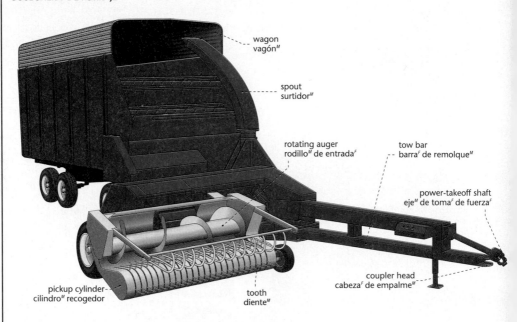

wagon
vagón^M

spout
surtidor^M

rotating auger
rodillo^M de entrada^F

tow bar
barra^F de remolque^M

power-takeoff shaft
eje^M de toma^F de fuerza^F

coupler head
cabeza^F de empalme^M

pickup cylinder
cilindro^M recogedor

tooth
diente^M

ENSILING
ENSILAJE^M

FORAGE BLOWER
AVENTADOR^M DE FORRAJE^M

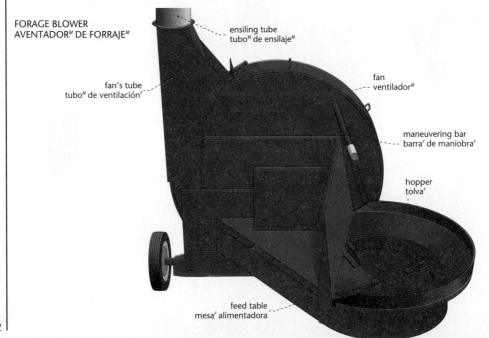

ensiling tube
tubo^M de ensilaje^M

fan
ventilador^M

fan's tube
tubo^M de ventilación^F

maneuvering bar
barra^F de maniobra^F

hopper
tolva^F

feed table
mesa^F alimentadora

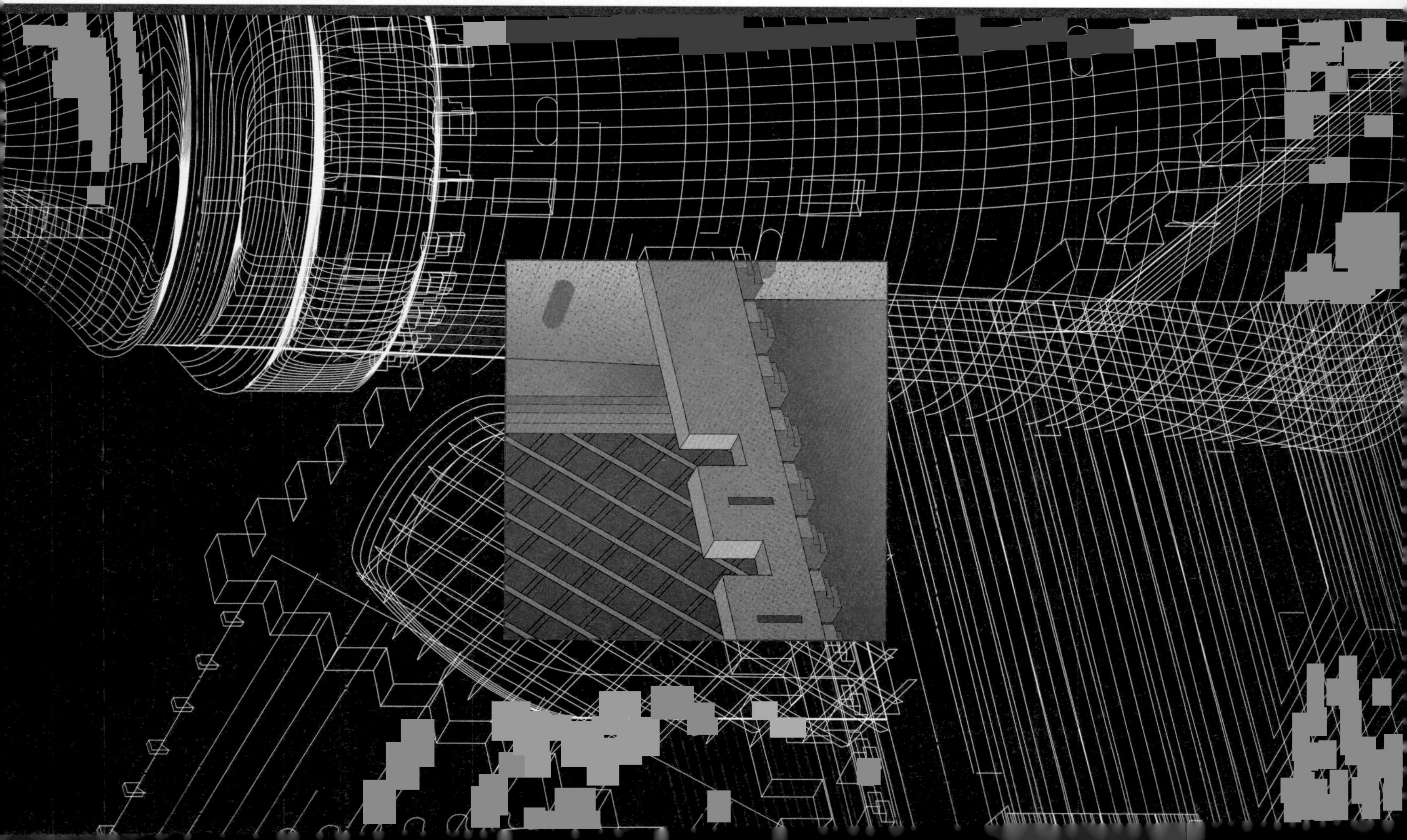

CONTENTS

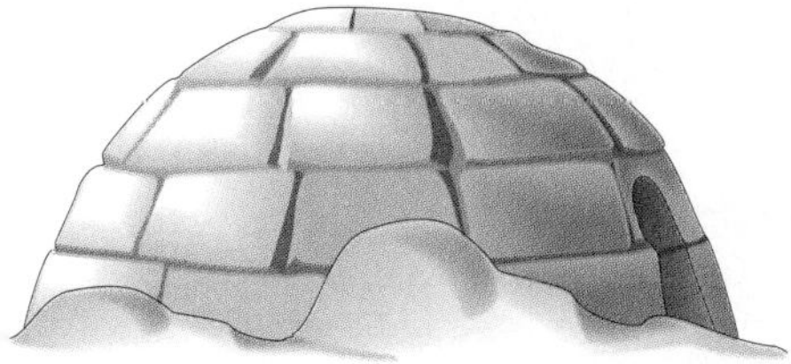

igloo
iglú^M

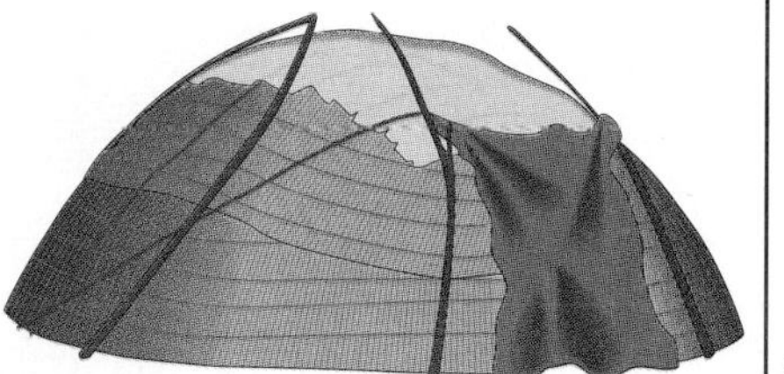

wigwam
wigwam^M

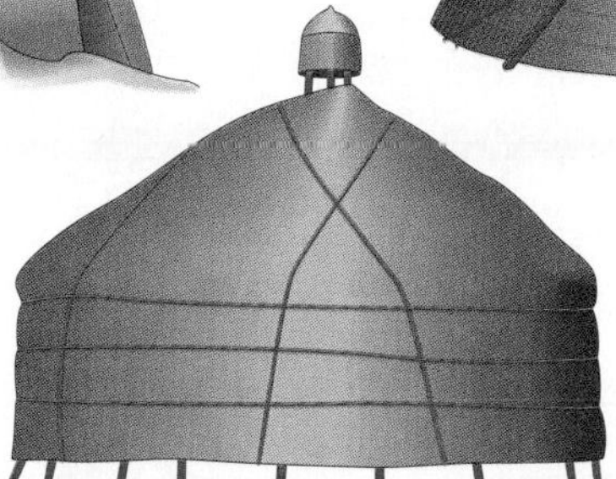

yurt
yurta^F

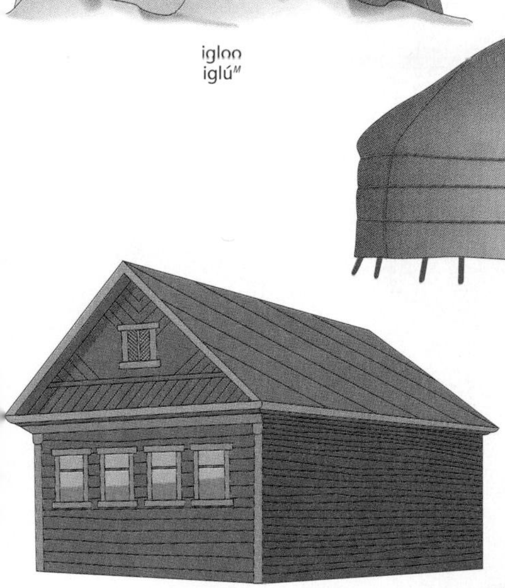

isba
isba^F

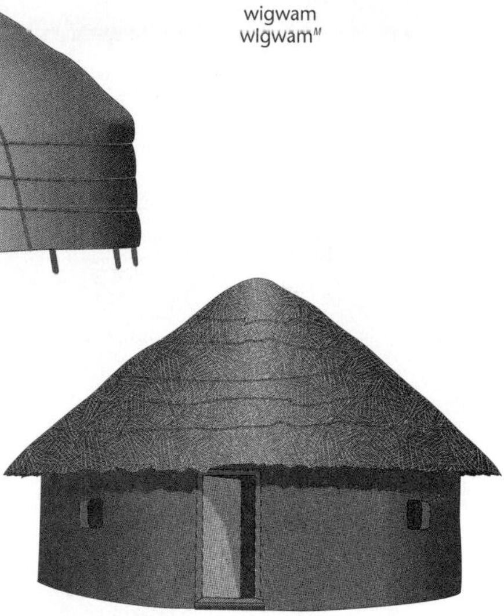

hut
chabola^F

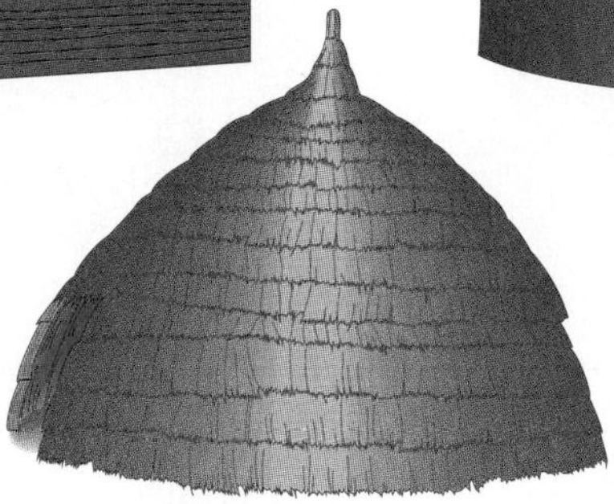

hut
choza^F indígena

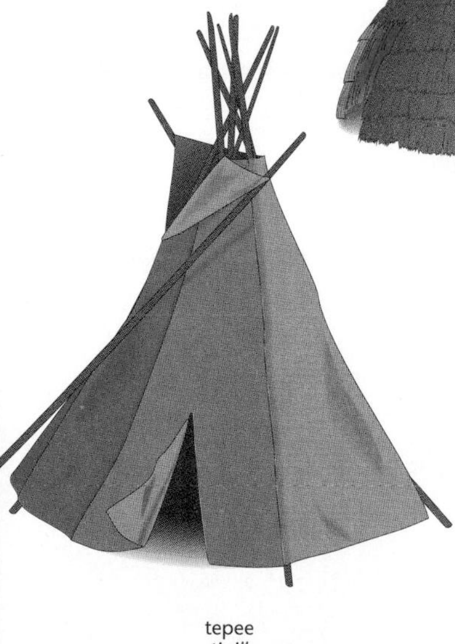

tepee
tipi^M

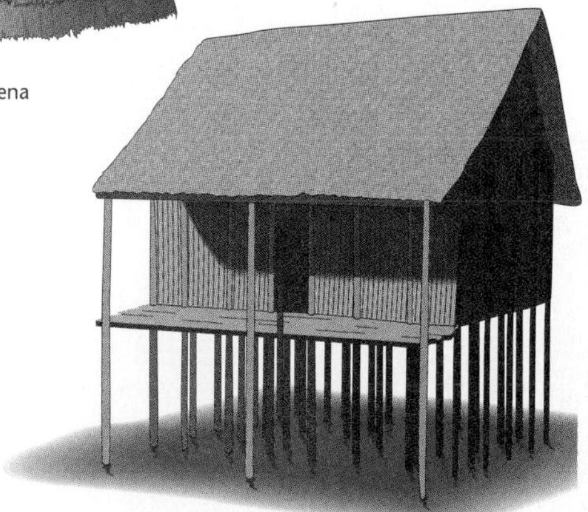

pile dwelling
habitación^F lacustre

ARCHITECTURE
ARQUITECTURA

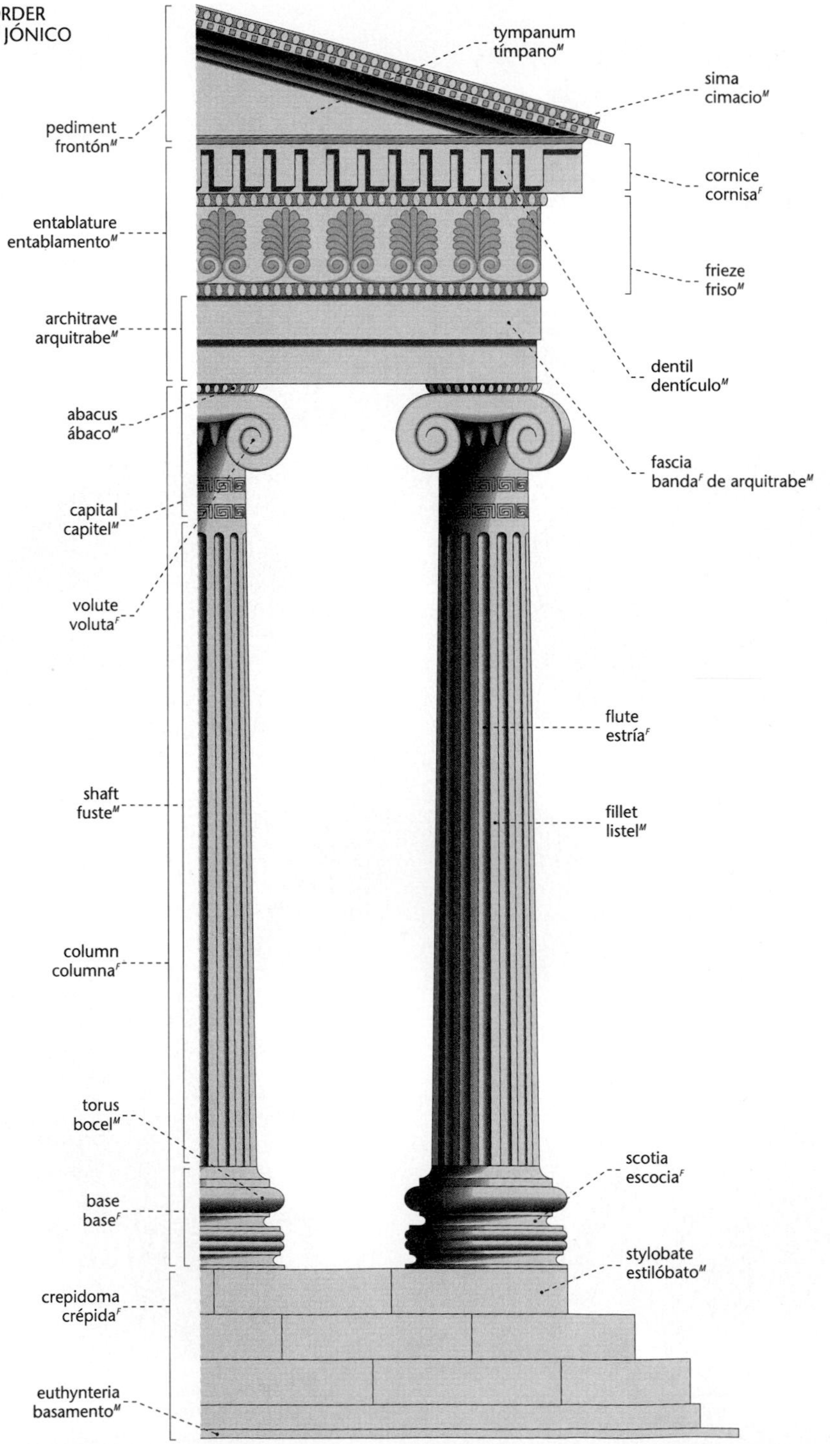

IONIC ORDER
ORDEN^M JÓNICO

pediment
frontón^M

entablature
entablamento^M

architrave
arquitrabe^M

abacus
ábaco^M

capital
capitel^M

volute
voluta^F

shaft
fuste^M

column
columna^F

torus
bocel^M

base
base^F

crepidoma
crépida^F

euthynteria
basamento^M

tympanum
tímpano^M

sima
cimacio^M

cornice
cornisa^F

frieze
friso^M

dentil
dentículo^M

fascia
banda^F de arquitrabe^M

flute
estría^F

fillet
listel^M

scotia
escocia^F

stylobate
estilóbato^M

166

DORIC ORDER
ORDEN^M DÓRICO

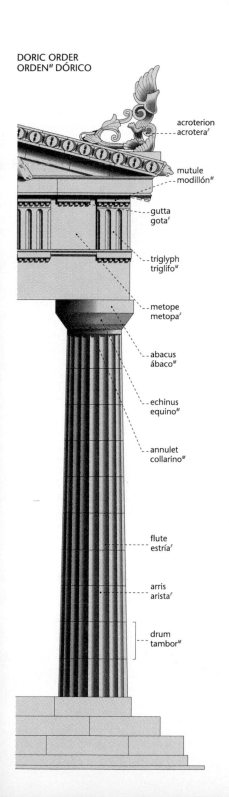

acroterion
acrotera^F

mutule
modillón^M

gutta
gota^F

triglyph
triglifo^M

metope
metopa^F

abacus
ábaco^M

echinus
equino^M

annulet
collarino^M

flute
estría^F

arris
arista^F

drum
tambor^M

CORINTHIAN ORDER
ORDEN^M CORINTIO

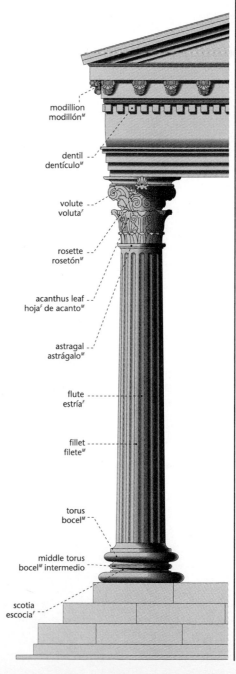

modillion
modillón^M

dentil
dentículo^M

volute
voluta^F

rosette
rosetón^M

acanthus leaf
hoja^F de acanto^M

astragal
astrágalo^M

flute
estría^F

fillet
filete^M

torus
bocel^M

middle torus
bocel^M intermedio

scotia
escocia^F

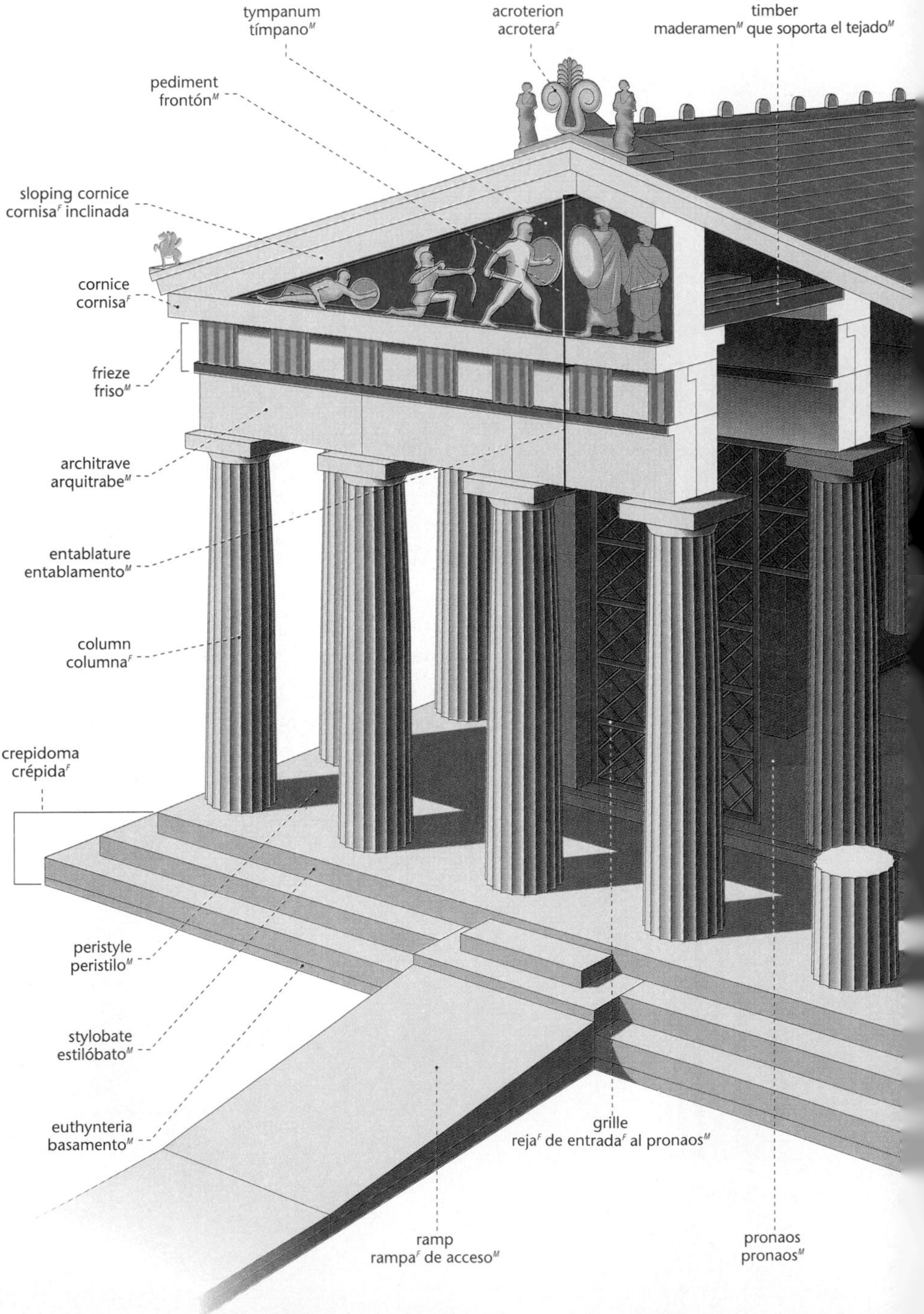

tympanum
tímpano^M

acroterion
acrotera^F

timber
maderamen^M que soporta el tejado^M

pediment
frontón^M

sloping cornice
cornisa^F inclinada

cornice
cornisa^F

frieze
friso^M

architrave
arquitrabe^M

entablature
entablamento^M

column
columna^F

crepidoma
crépida^F

peristyle
peristilo^M

stylobate
estilóbato^M

euthynteria
basamento^M

grille
reja^F de entrada^F al pronaos^M

ramp
rampa^F de acceso^M

pronaos
pronaos^M

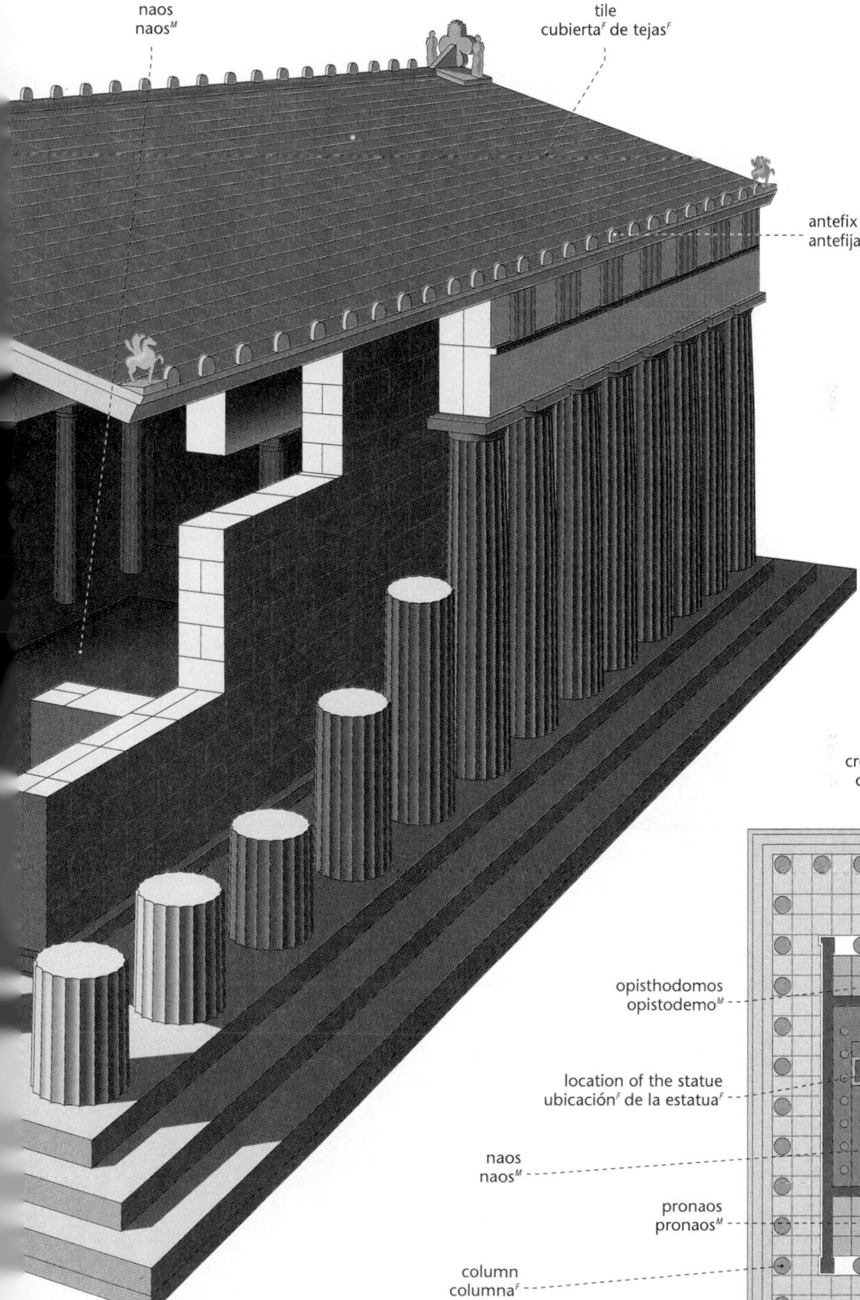

naos
naos^M

tile
cubierta^F de tejas^F

antefix
antefijas^F de la cumbrera^F

PLAN
PLANO^M

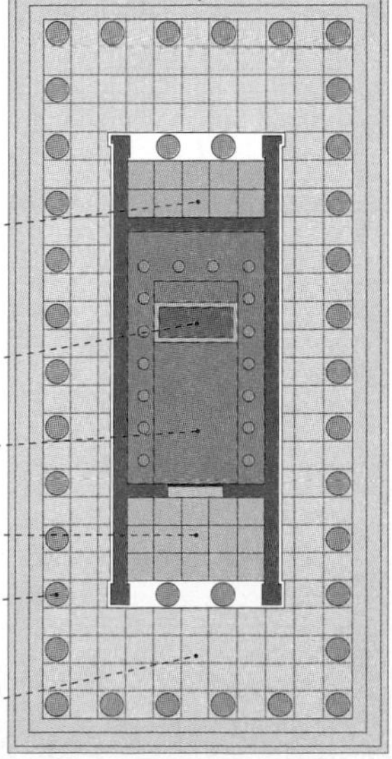

crepidoma
crépida^F

opisthodomos
opistodemo^M

location of the statue
ubicación^F de la estatua^F

naos
naos^M

pronaos
pronaos^M

column
columna^F

peristyle
peristilo^M

169

ROMAN HOUSE
CASA^F ROMANA

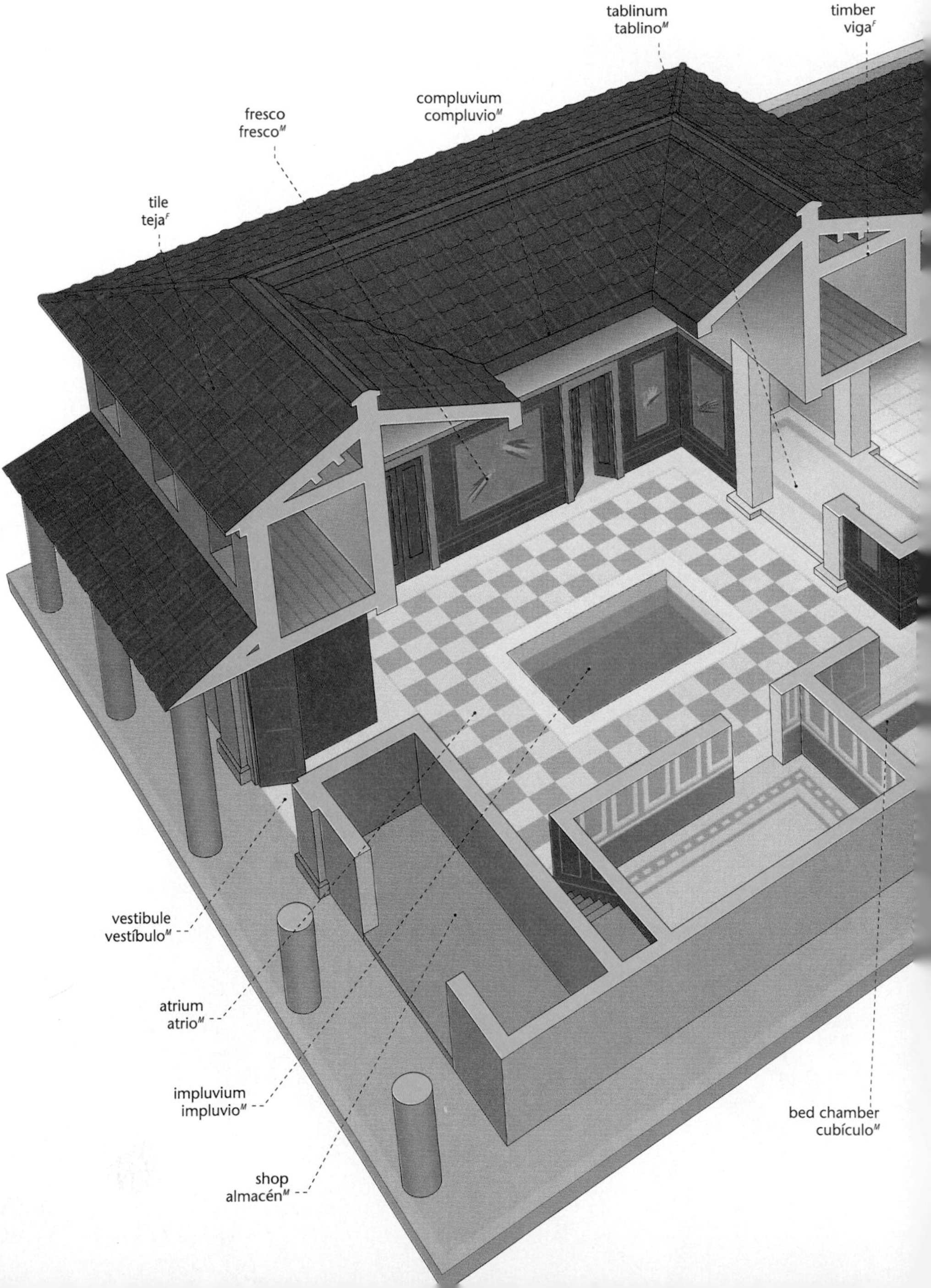

tablinum
tablino^M

timber
viga^F

fresco
fresco^M

compluvium
compluvio^M

tile
teja^F

vestibule
vestíbulo^M

atrium
atrio^M

impluvium
impluvio^M

shop
almacén^M

bed chamber
cubículo^M

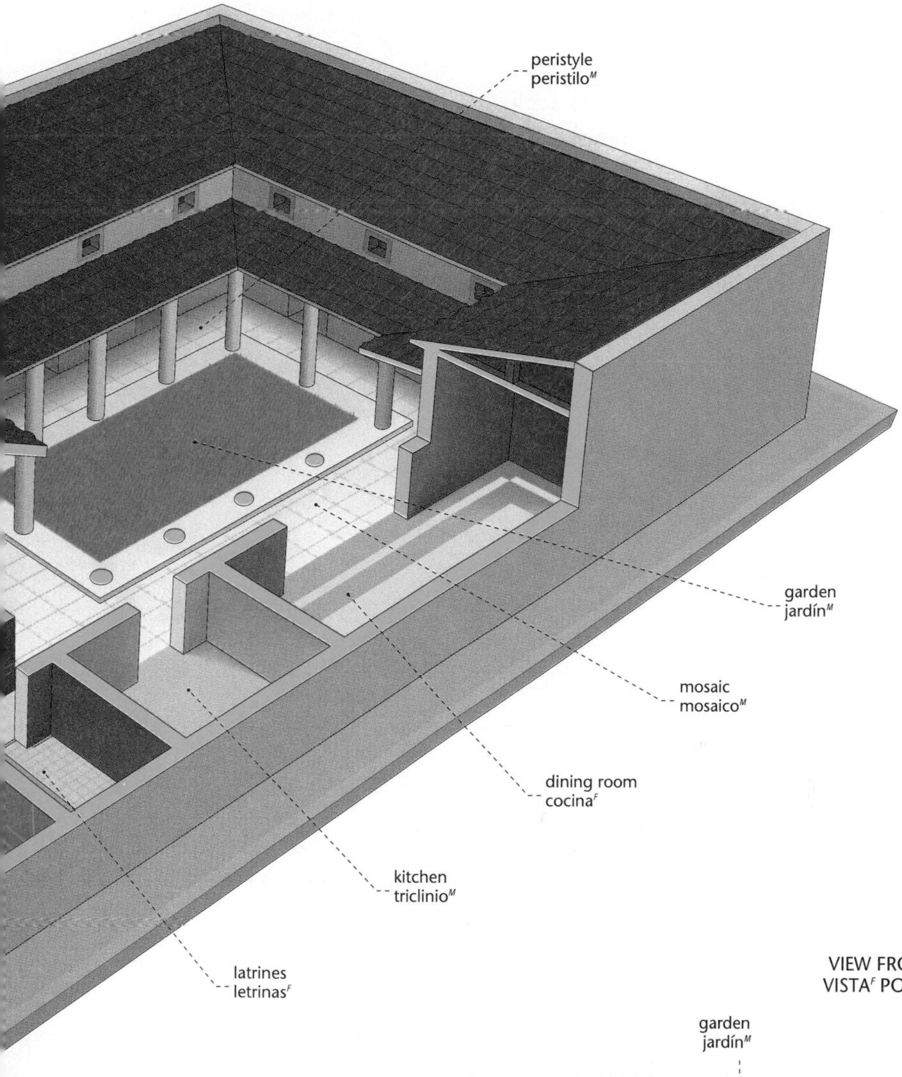

peristyle
peristilo[M]

garden
jardín[M]

mosaic
mosaico[M]

dining room
cocina[F]

kitchen
triclinio[M]

latrines
letrinas[F]

VIEW FROM ABOVE
VISTA[F] POR ENCIMA

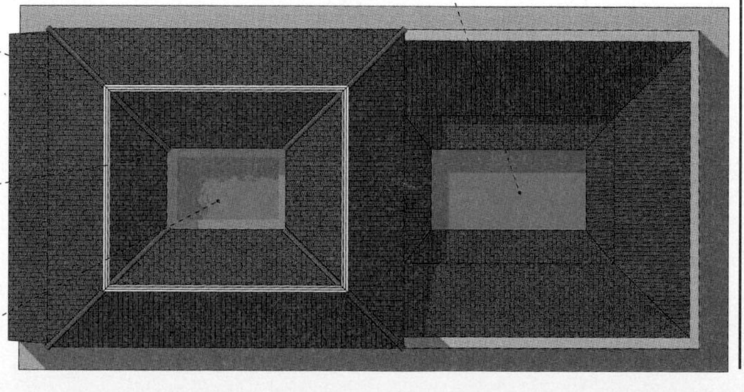

garden
jardín[M]

roof
techo[M]

compluvium
compluvio[M]

impluvium
impluvio[M]

171

MOSQUE
MEZQUITA^F

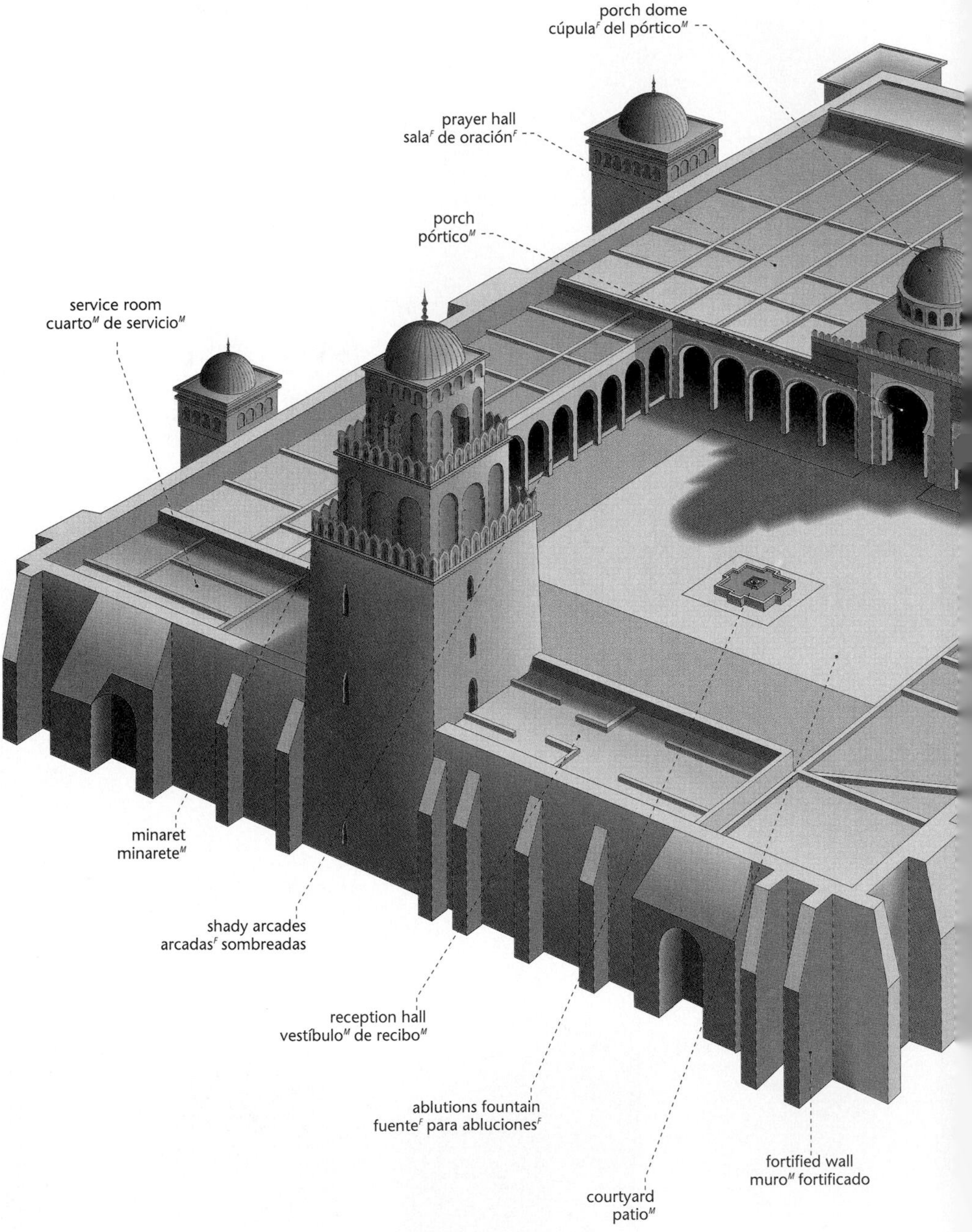

porch dome
cúpula^F del pórtico^M

prayer hall
sala^F de oración^F

porch
pórtico^M

service room
cuarto^M de servicio^M

minaret
minarete^M

shady arcades
arcadas^F sombreadas

reception hall
vestíbulo^M de recibo^M

ablutions fountain
fuente^F para abluciones^F

courtyard
patio^M

fortified wall
muro^M fortificado

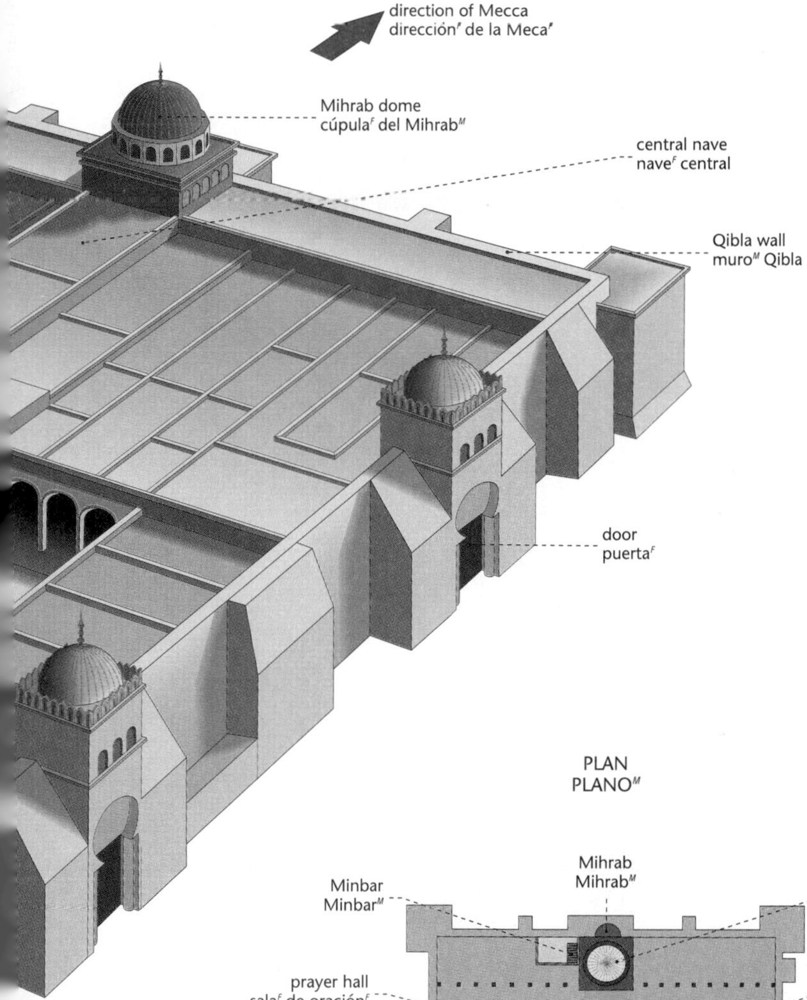

direction of Mecca
dirección^F de la Meca^F

Mihrab dome
cúpula^F del Mihrab^M

central nave
nave^F central

Qibla wall
muro^M Qibla

door
puerta^F

PLAN
PLANO^M

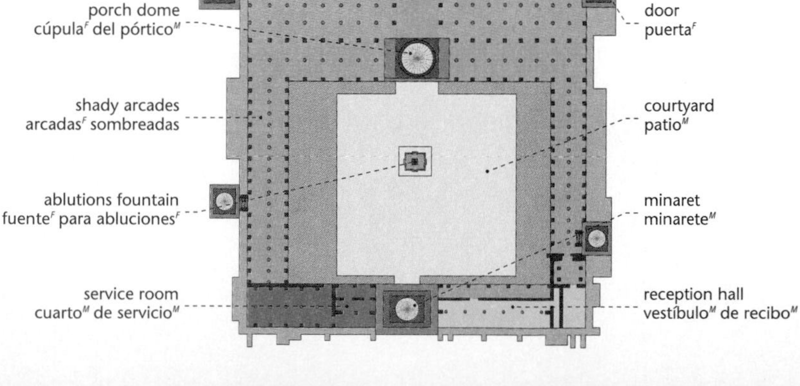

Minbar
Minbar^M

Mihrab
Mihrab^M

Mihrab dome
cúpula^F del Mihrab^M

prayer hall
sala^F de oración^F

central nave
nave^F central

porch dome
cúpula^F del pórtico^M

door
puerta^F

shady arcades
arcadas^F sombreadas

courtyard
patio^M

ablutions fountain
fuente^F para abluciones^F

minaret
minarete^M

service room
cuarto^M de servicio^M

reception hall
vestíbulo^M de recibo^M

173

ARCH
ARCO^M

SEMICIRCULAR ARCH
ARCO^M DE MEDIO PUNTO^M

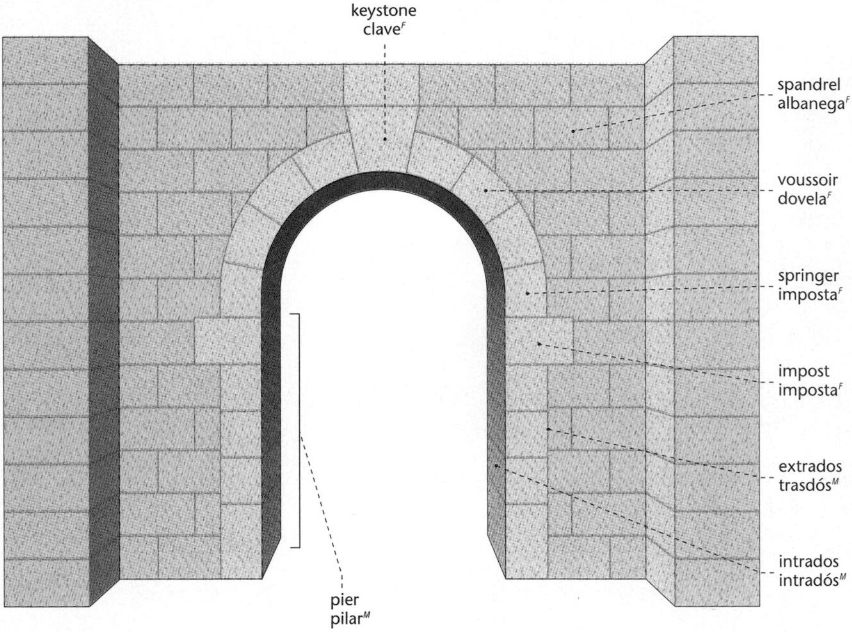

keystone
clave^F

spandrel
albanega^F

voussoir
dovela^F

springer
imposta^F

impost
imposta^F

extrados
trasdós^M

intrados
intradós^M

pier
pilar^M

TYPES OF ARCHES
TIPOS^M DE ARCOS^M

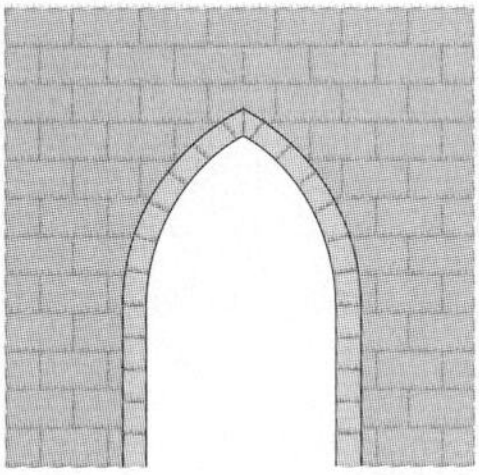

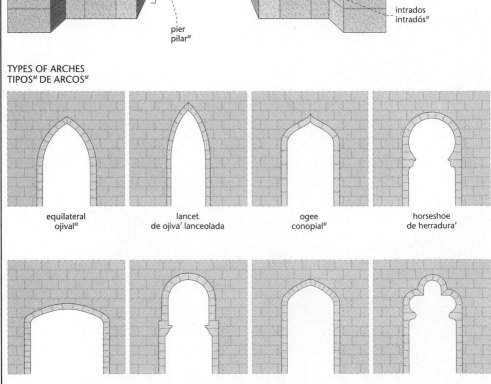

equilateral
ojival^M

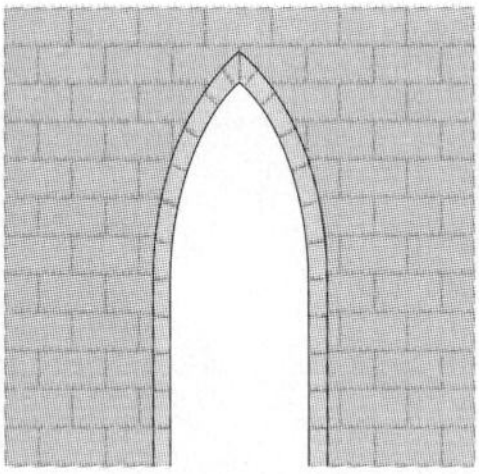

lancet
de ojiva^F lanceolada

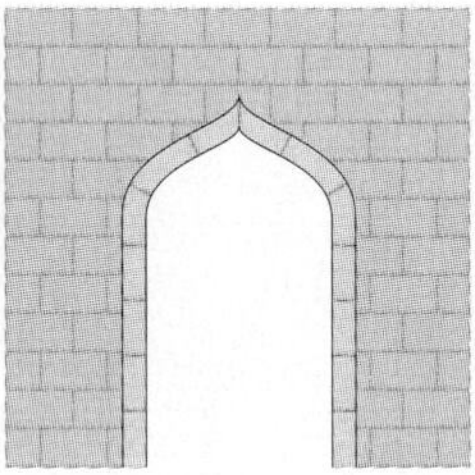

ogee
conopial^M

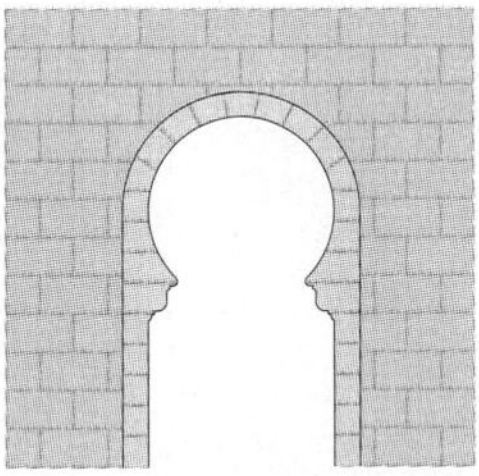

horseshoe
de herradura^F

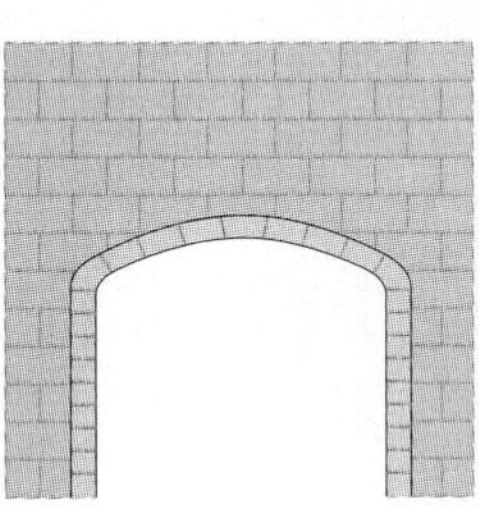

basket handle
adintelado^M

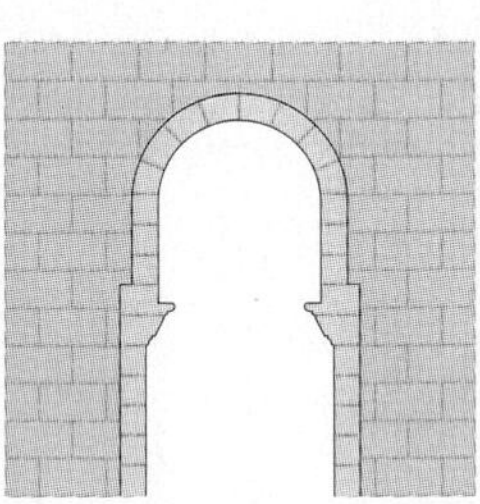

stilted
peraltado^M

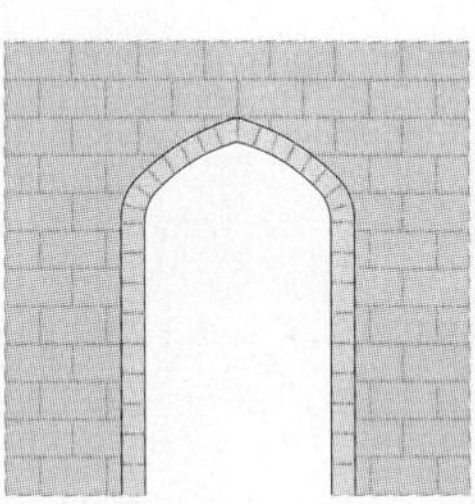

Tudor
Tudor

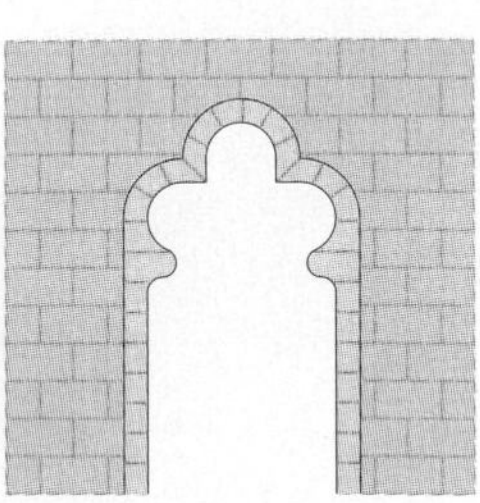

trefoil
trebolado^M

GOTHIC CATHEDRAL
CATEDRAL^F GÓTICA

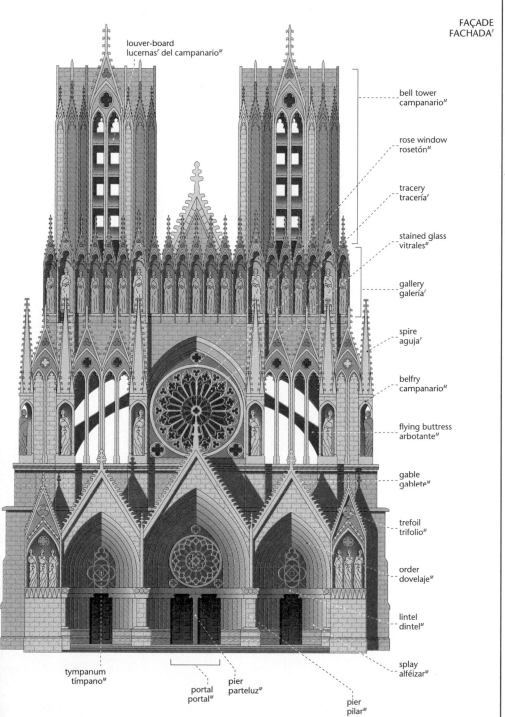

louver-board
lucernas^F del campanario^M

bell tower
campanario^M

rose window
rosetón^M

tracery
tracería^F

stained glass
vitrales^M

gallery
galería^F

spire
aguja^F

belfry
campanario^M

flying buttress
arbotante^M

gable
gablete^M

trefoil
trifolio^M

order
dovelaje^M

lintel
dintel^M

splay
alféizar^M

tympanum
tímpano^M

portal
portal^M

pier
parteluz^M

pier
pilar^M

175

GOTHIC CATHEDRAL
CATEDRAL*F* GÓTICA

CATHEDRAL
CATEDRAL*F*

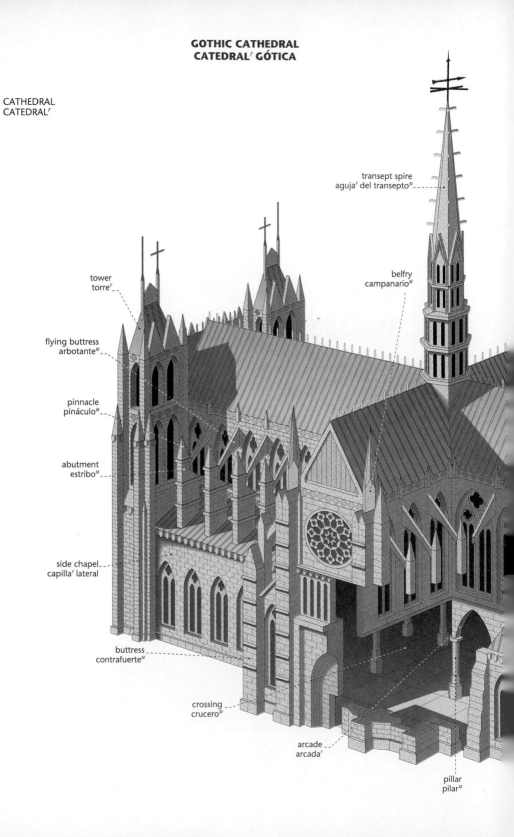

transept spire
aguja*F* del transepto*M*

belfry
campanario*M*

tower
torre*F*

flying buttress
arbotante*M*

pinnacle
pináculo*M*

abutment
estribo*M*

side chapel
capilla*F* lateral

buttress
contrafuerte*M*

crossing
crucero*M*

arcade
arcada*F*

pillar
pilar*M*

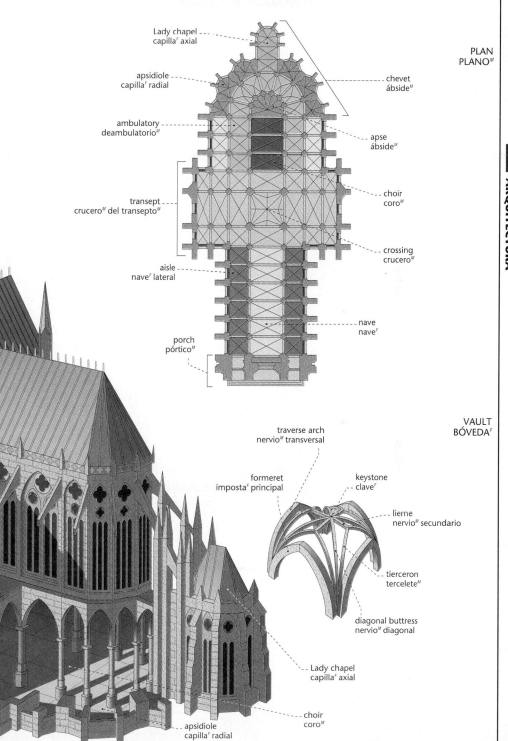

PLAN
PLANO^M

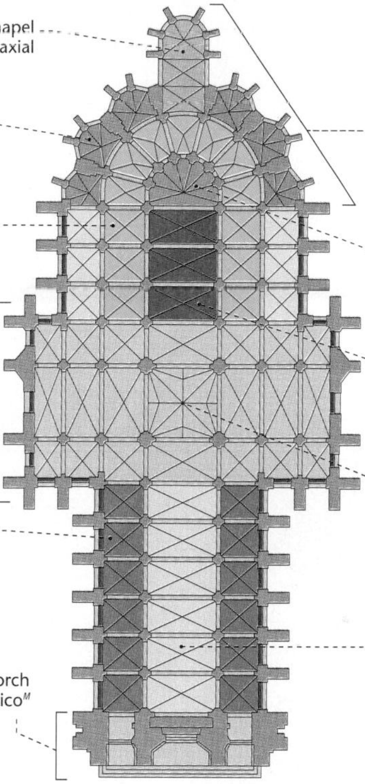

Lady chapel
capilla^F axial

apsidiole
capilla^F radial

ambulatory
deambulatorio^M

transept
crucero^M del transepto^M

aisle
nave^F lateral

porch
pórtico^M

chevet
ábside^M

apse
ábside^M

choir
coro^M

crossing
crucero^M

nave
nave^F

VAULT
BÓVEDA^F

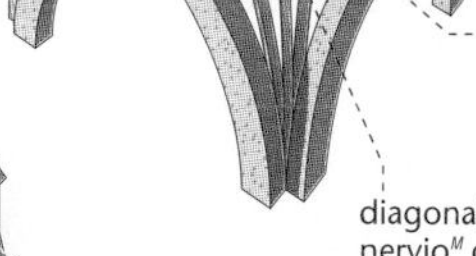

traverse arch
nervio^M transversal

formeret
imposta^F principal

keystone
clave^F

lierne
nervio^M secundario

tierceron
tercelete^M

diagonal buttress
nervio^M diagonal

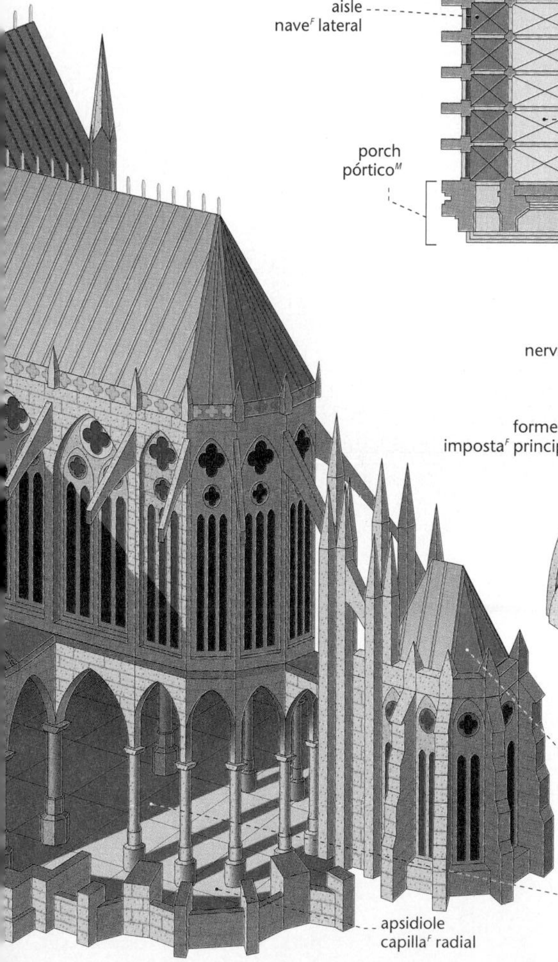

Lady chapel
capilla^F axial

choir
coro^M

apsidiole
capilla^F radial

VAUBAN FORTIFICATION
FORTIFICACIÓN^F DE VAUBAN

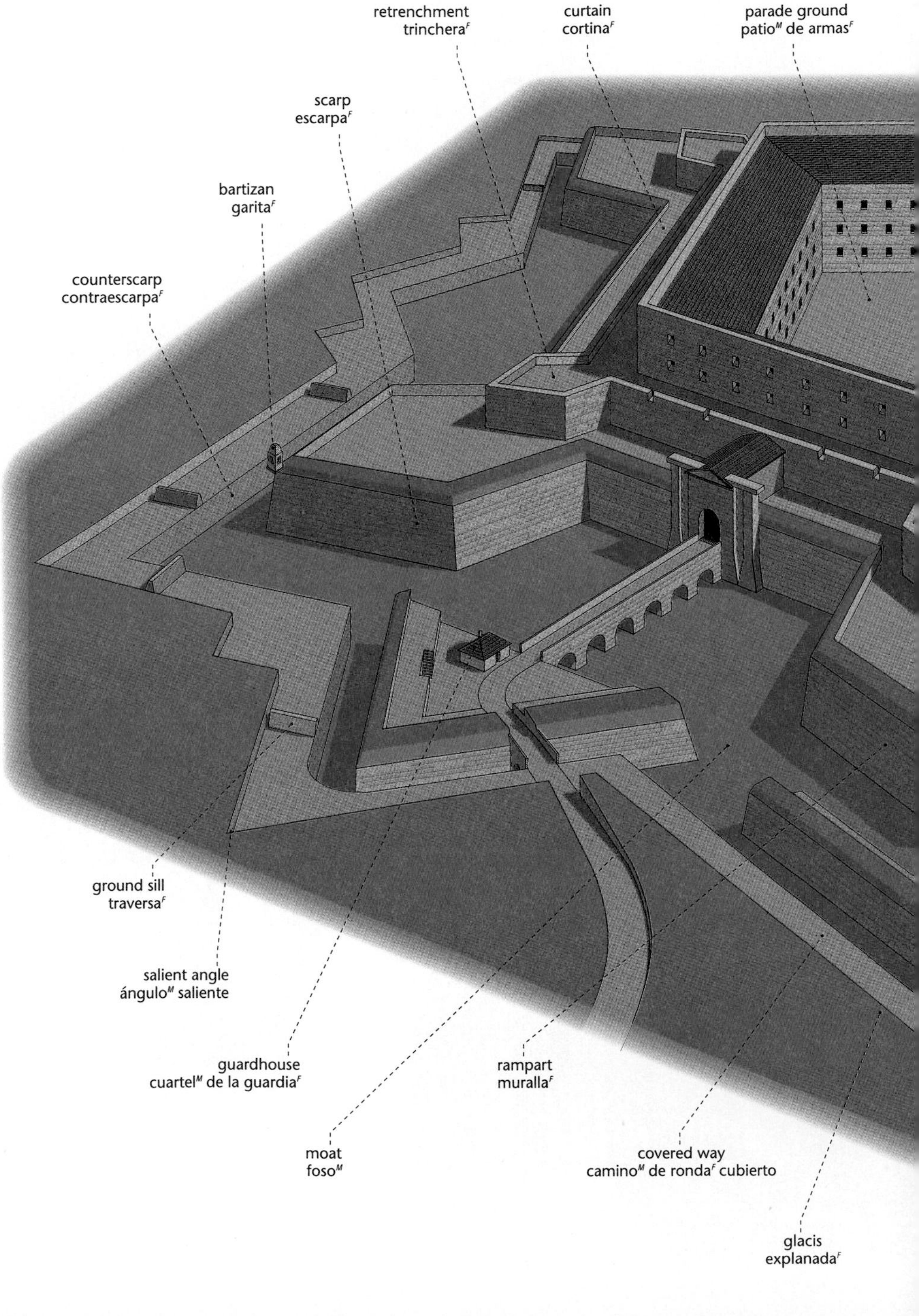

retrenchment
trinchera^F

curtain
cortina^F

parade ground
patio^M de armas^F

scarp
escarpa^F

bartizan
garita^F

counterscarp
contraescarpa^F

ground sill
traversa^F

salient angle
ángulo^M saliente

guardhouse
cuartel^M de la guardia^F

rampart
muralla^F

moat
foso^M

covered way
camino^M de ronda^F cubierto

glacis
explanada^F

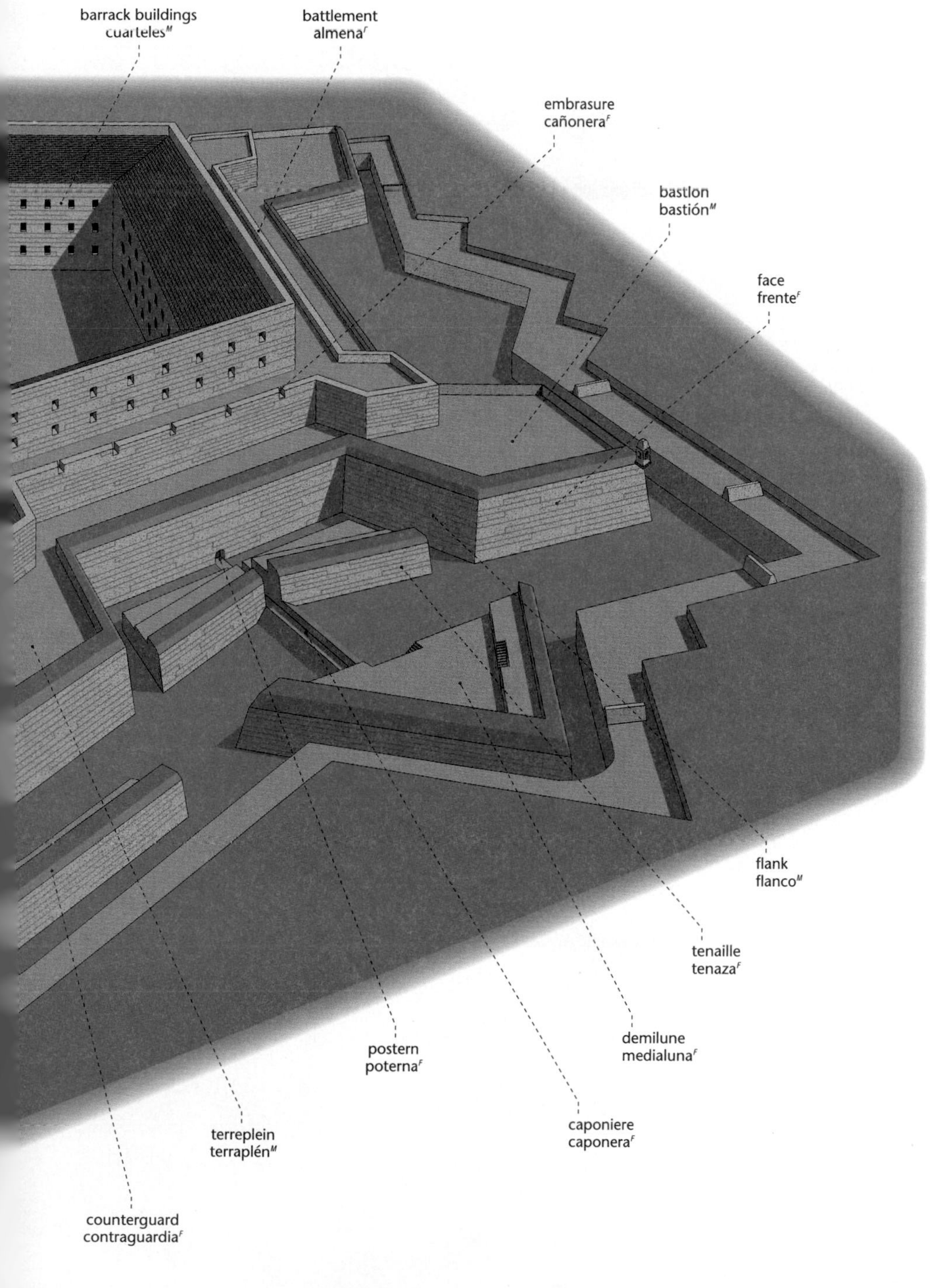

barrack buildings
cuarteles^M

battlement
almena^F

embrasure
cañonera^F

bastlon
bastión^M

face
frente^F

flank
flanco^M

tenaille
tenaza^F

demilune
medialuna^F

caponiere
caponera^F

postern
poterna^F

terreplein
terraplén^M

counterguard
contraguardia^F

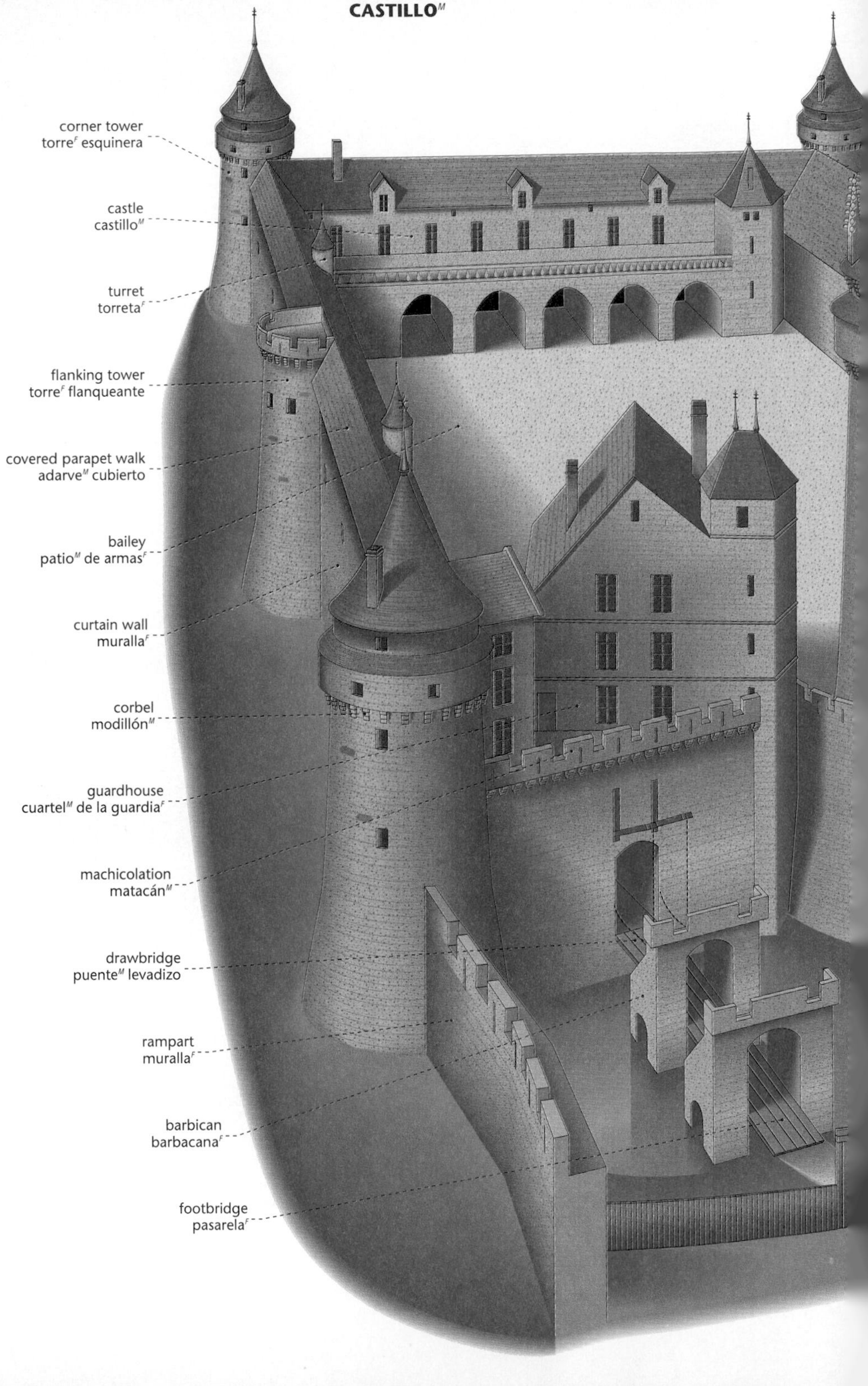

corner tower
torre^F esquinera

castle
castillo^M

turret
torreta^F

flanking tower
torre^F flanqueante

covered parapet walk
adarve^M cubierto

bailey
patio^M de armas^F

curtain wall
muralla^F

corbel
modillón^M

guardhouse
cuartel^M de la guardia^F

machicolation
matacán^M

drawbridge
puente^M levadizo

rampart
muralla^F

barbican
barbacana^F

footbridge
pasarela^F

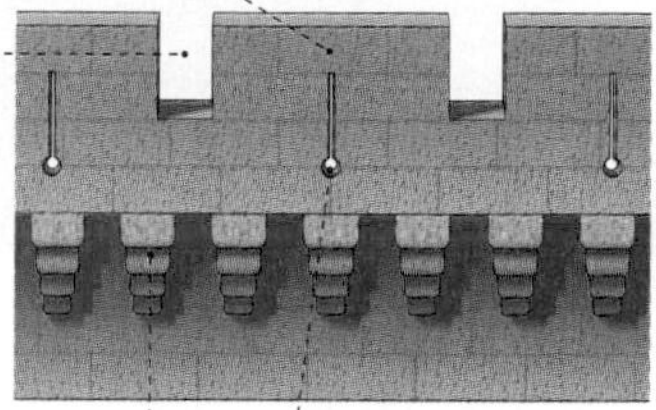

merlon
merlón^M

crenel
aspillera^F

loophole
tronera^F

corbel
modillón^M

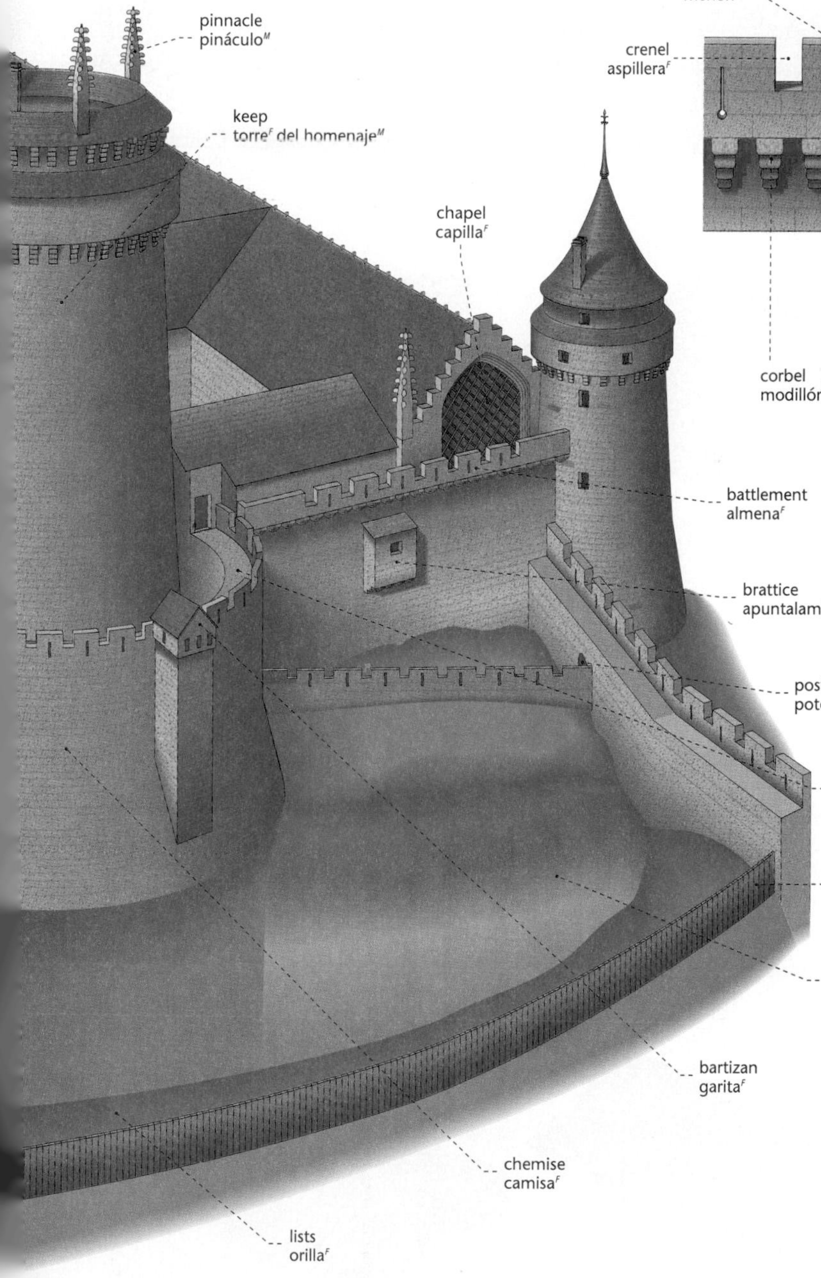

pinnacle
pináculo^M

keep
torre^F del homenaje^M

chapel
capilla^F

battlement
almena^F

brattice
apuntalamiento^M

postern
poterna^F

parapet walk
camino^M de ronda^F

stockade
empalizada^F

moat
foso^M

bartizan
garita^F

chemise
camisa^F

lists
orilla^F

181

ARCHITECTURE
ARQUITECTURA

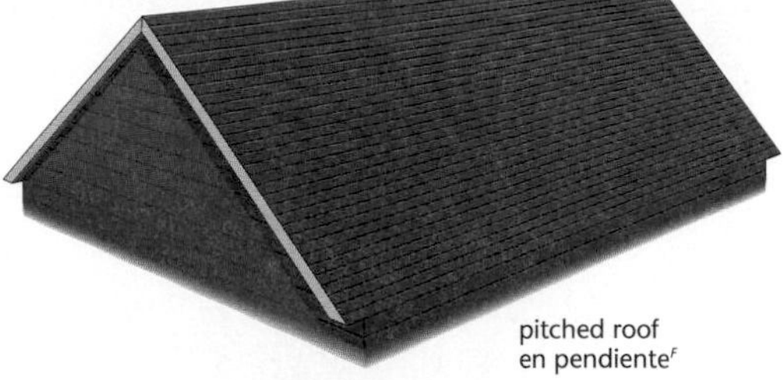

pitched roof
en pendiente^F

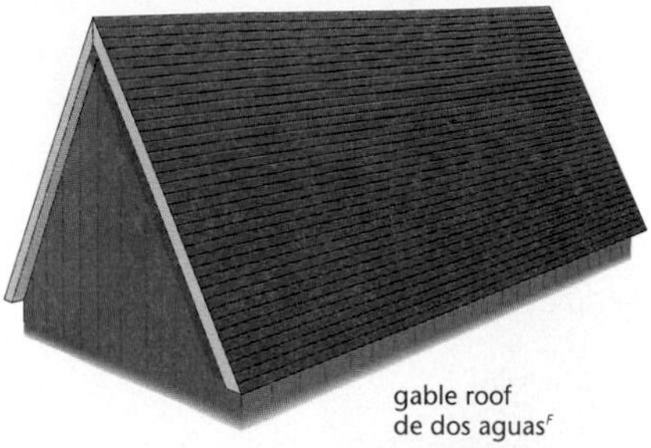

gable roof
de dos aguas^F

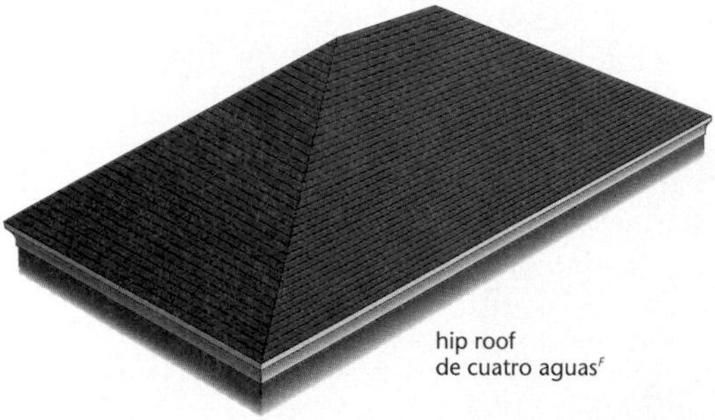

hip roof
de cuatro aguas^F

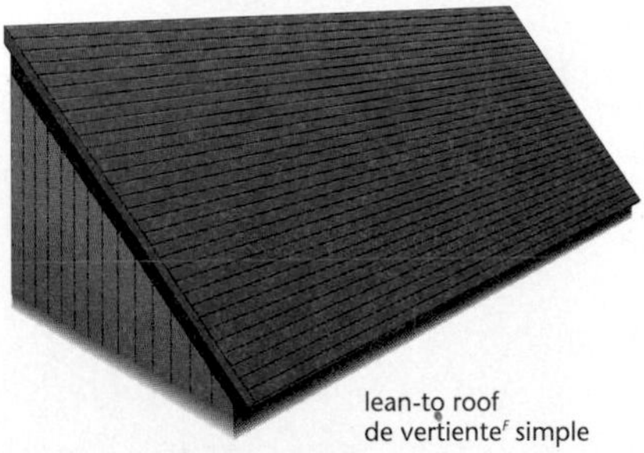

lean-to roof
de vertiente^F simple

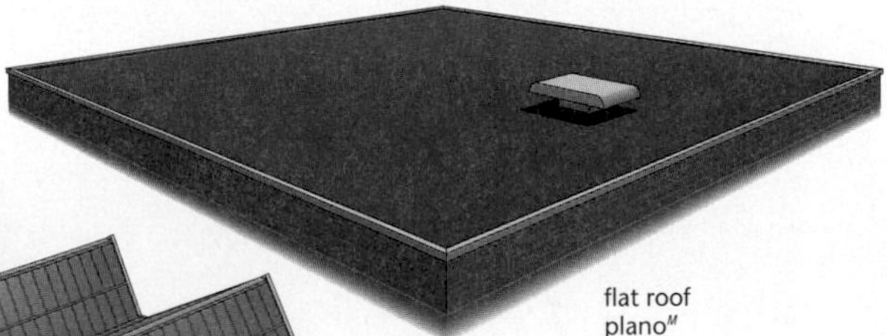

flat roof
plano^M

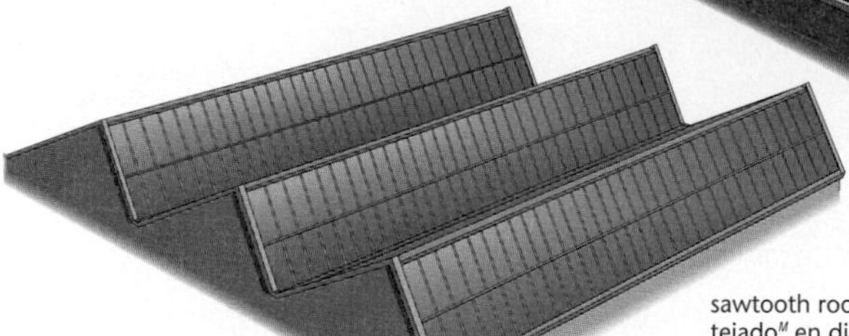

sawtooth roof
tejado^M en diente^M de sierra^F

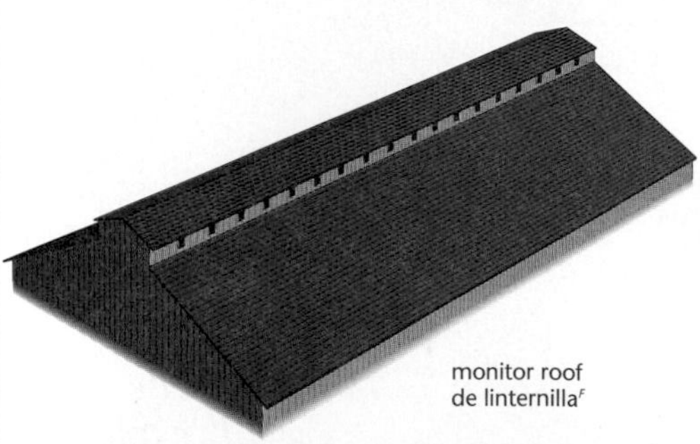

monitor roof
de linternilla^F

ogee roof
de arco^M conopial

182

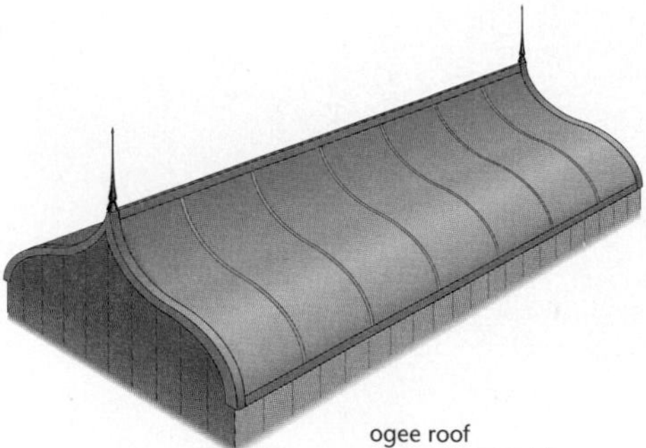

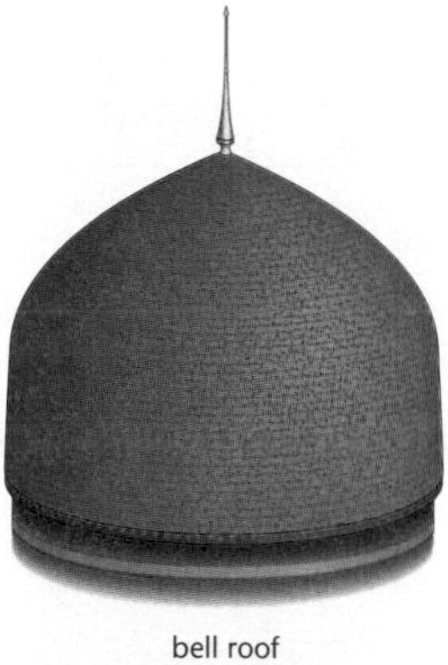

bell roof
de cúpula^F

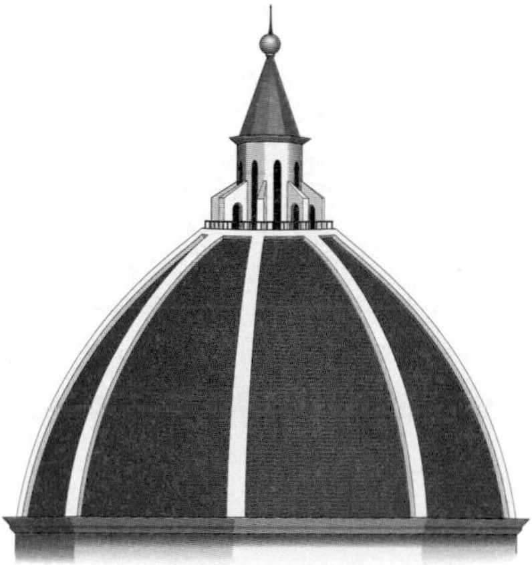

dome roof
cúpula^F

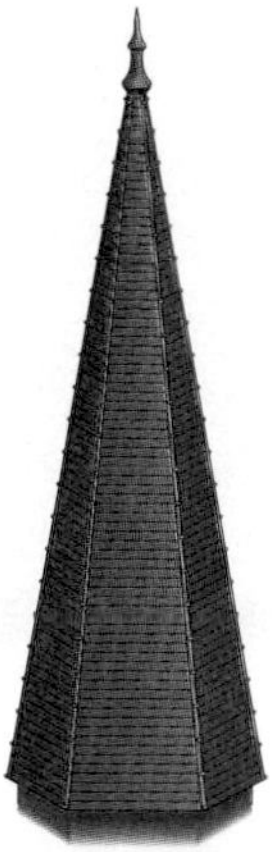

helm roof
de aguja^F

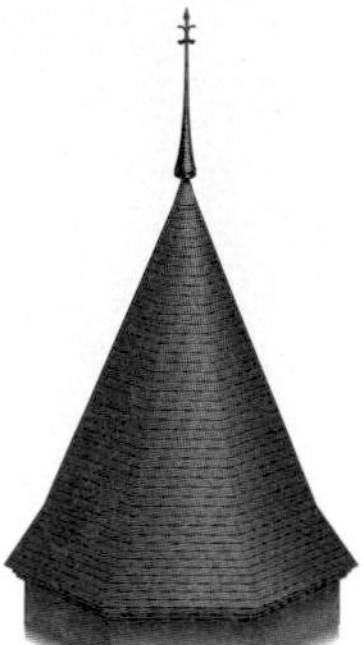

sloped turret
de torrecilla^F

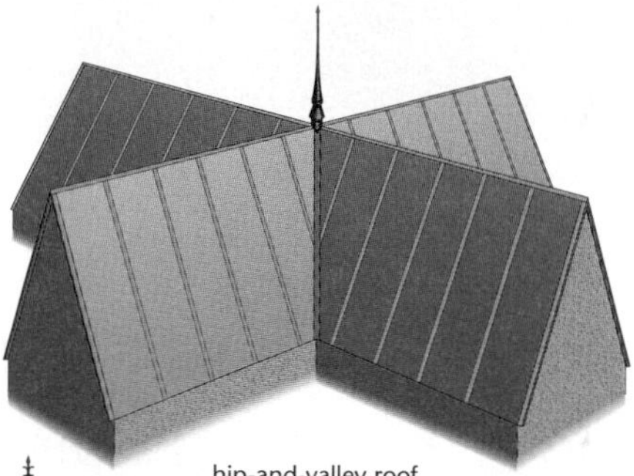

hip-and-valley roof
de cuatro aguas^F con canalera^F

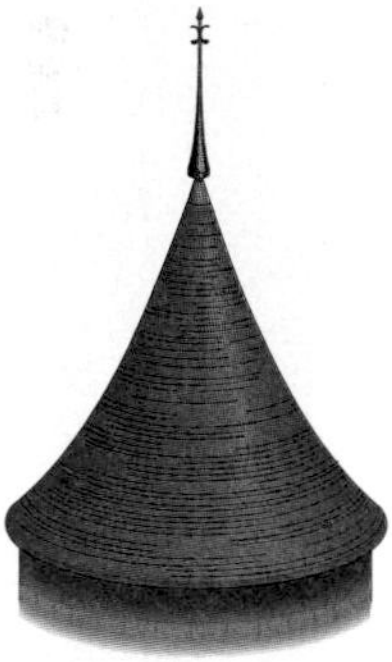

conical broach roof
cónico

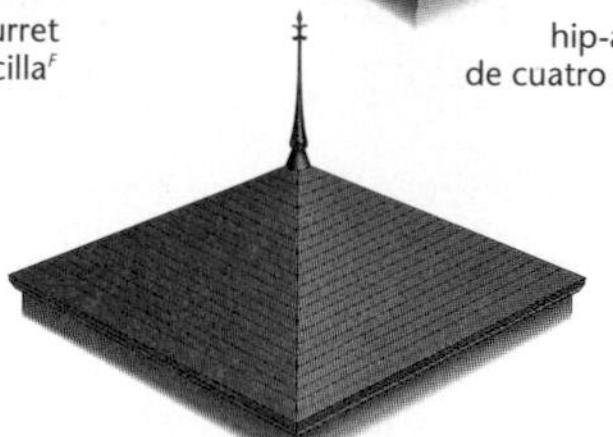

pavilion roof
de pabellón^M

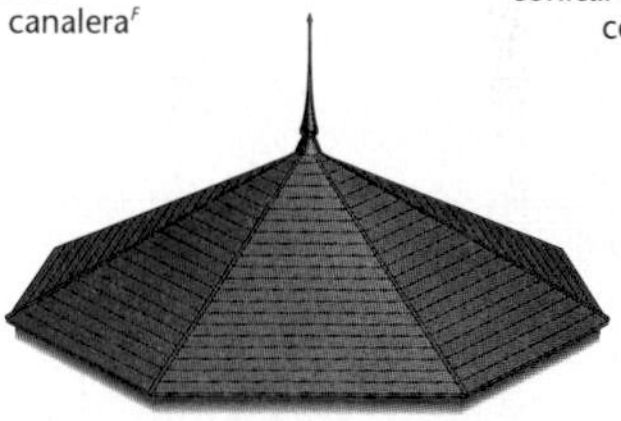

rotunda roof
de rotonda^F

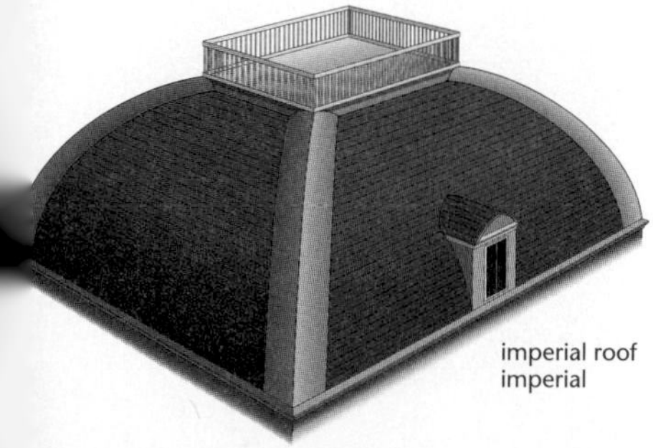

imperial roof
imperial

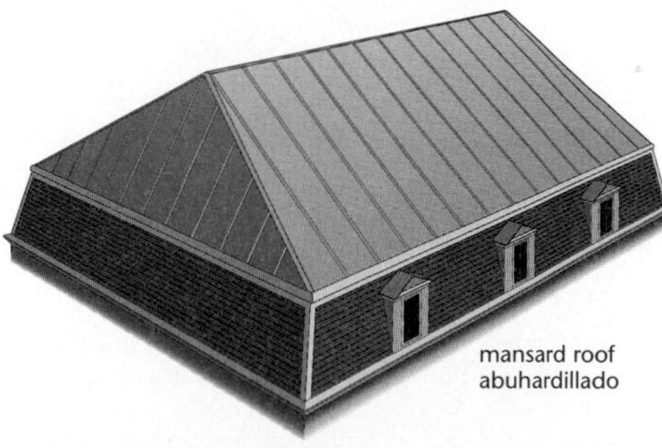

mansard roof
abuhardillado

ARCHITECTURE
ARQUITECTURA

park
parque^M

convention center
centro^M de congresos^M

office tower
edificio^M de oficinas^F

square
zona^F verde

cathedral
catedral^F

passenger station
estación^M de ferrocarril^M

median strip
separador^M

planetarium
planetario^M

railroad
vía^F férrea

traffic island
separador^M

boulevard
avenida^F

street
calle^F

delivery ramp
rampa^F para mercancías^F

freeway
autopista^F

hotel
hotel^M

skyscraper
rascacielos^M

restaurant
restaurante^M

church
iglesia^F

high-rise apartment
edificio^M de apartamentos^M

street light
farol^M

parking lot
estacionamiento^M

trade building
edificio^M comercial

office building
edificio^M de oficinas^F

museum
museo^M

stadium
estadio^M

CROSS SECTION OF A STREET
VISTA^F TRANSVERSAL DE UNA CALLE^F

street light
farol^M

sidewalk
acera^F

roadway
calzada^F

traffic light
semáforo^M

manhole
boca^F de acceso^M

center divider strip
separador^M central

curb
guarnición^F

fire hydrant
boca^F de agua^F para incendios^M

pedestrian crossing
paso^M de peatones^M

storm sewer
tubo^M drenaje^Mde tormenta^F

bus stop
parada^F de autobús^M

barrier
valla^F

bus shelter
cobertizo^M de la parada^F

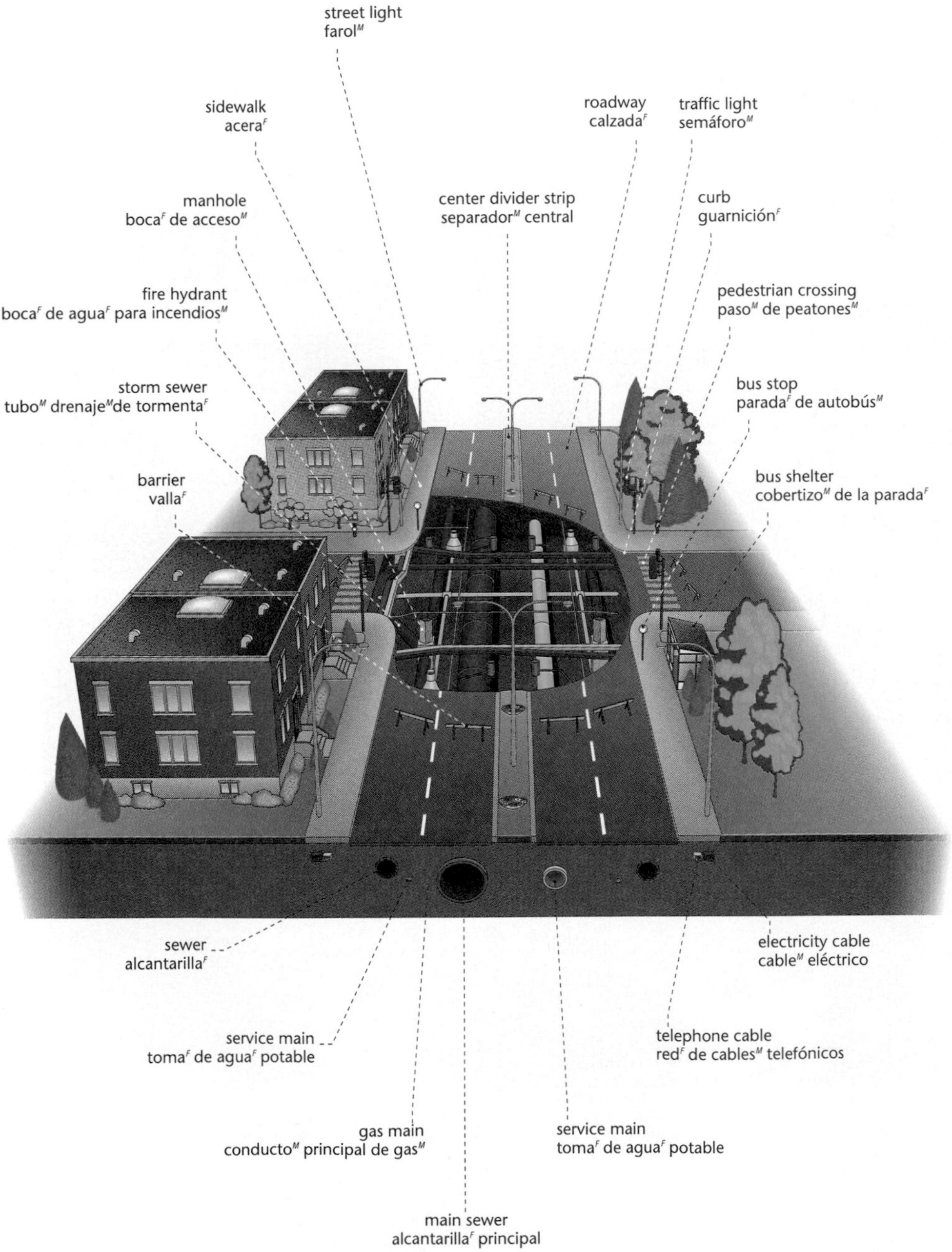

sewer
alcantarilla^F

electricity cable
cable^M eléctrico

service main
toma^F de agua^F potable

telephone cable
red^F de cables^M telefónicos

gas main
conducto^M principal de gas^M

service main
toma^F de agua^F potable

main sewer
alcantarilla^F principal

CITY HOUSES
VIVIENDAS^F URBANAS

cottage
casa^F de campo^M

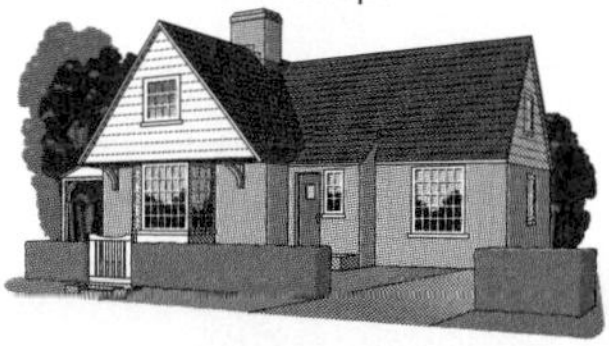

single-famIly home
casas^F independientes

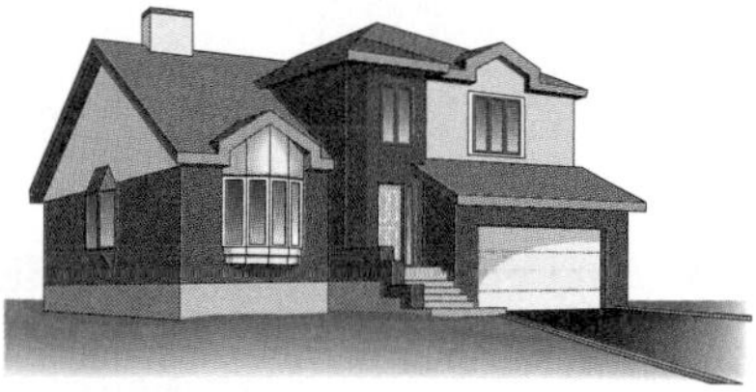

apartment building
condominios^M

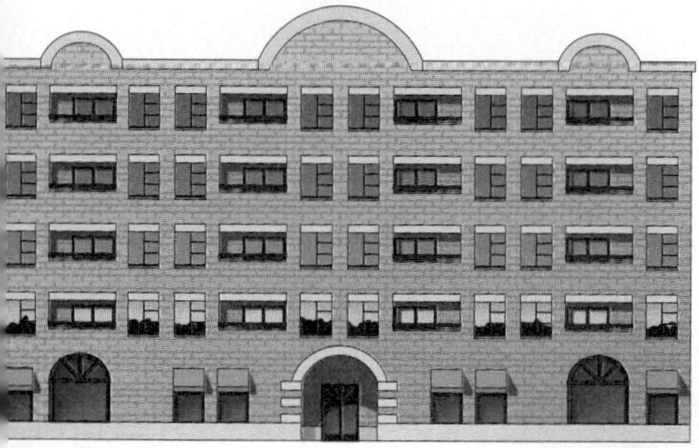

semi-detached cottage
casas^F gemelas

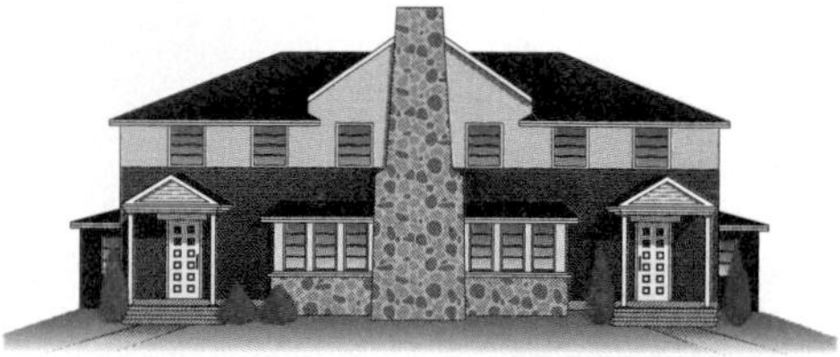

town houses
casas^F en serie^F

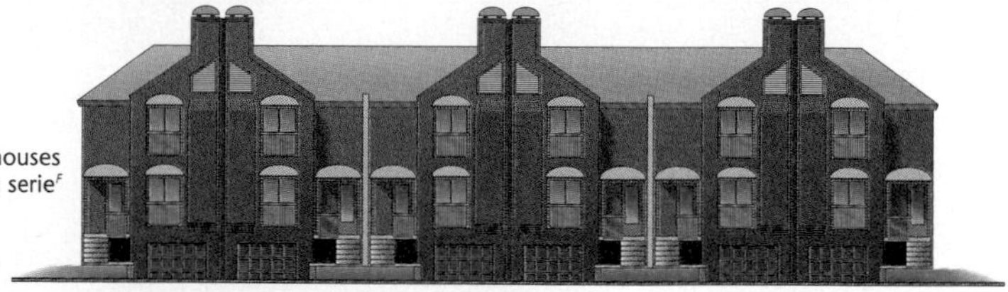

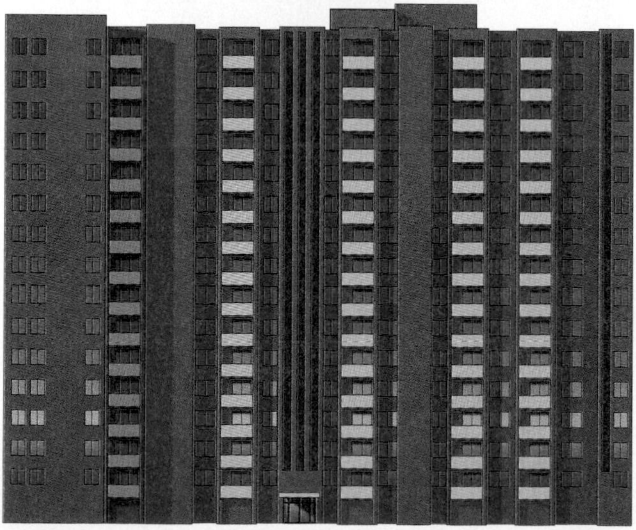

high-rise apartment
edificio^M de apartamentos^M

ARCHITECTURE
ARQUITECTURA

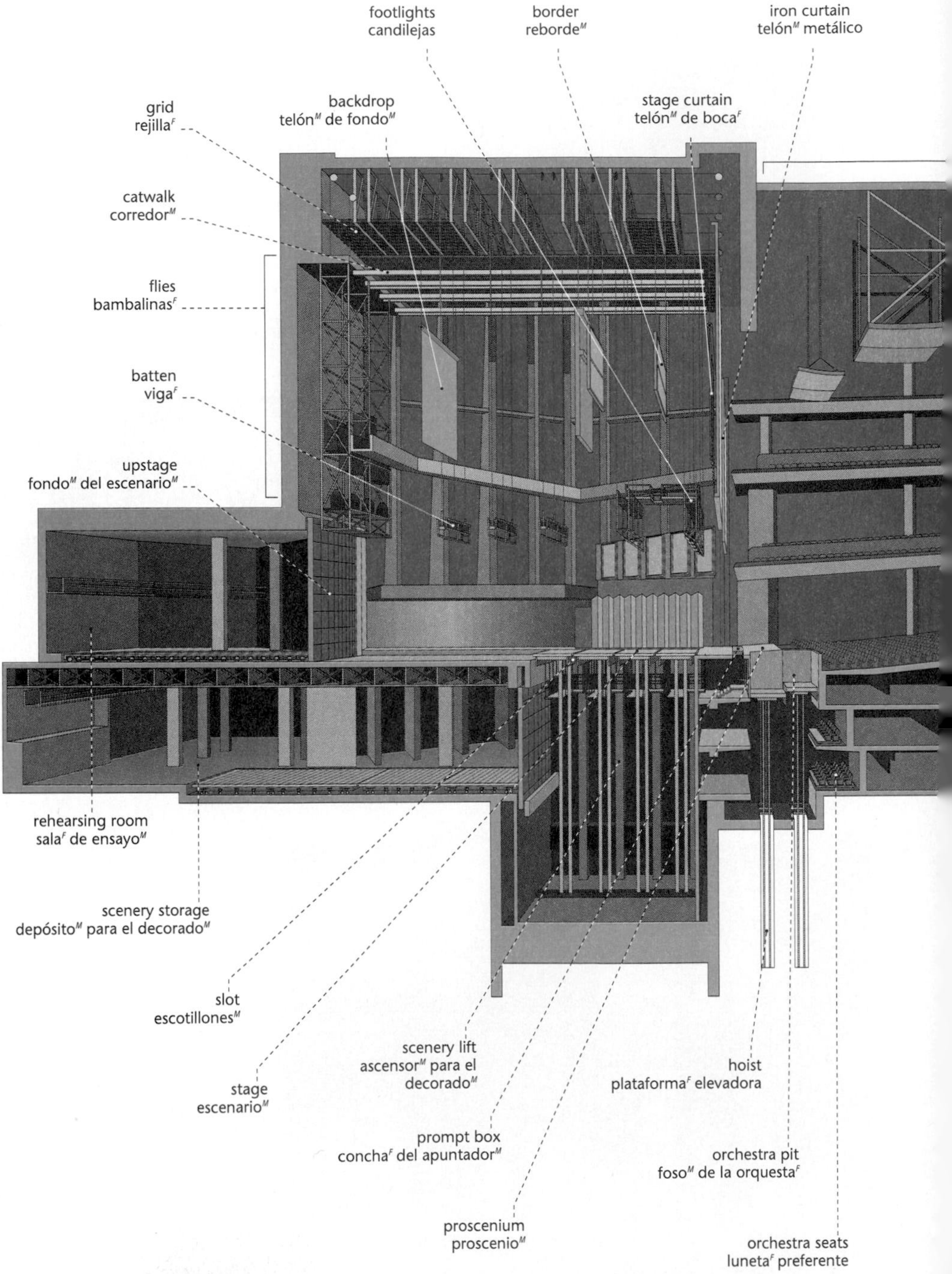

footlights
candilejas

border
reborde^M

iron curtain
telón^M metálico

grid
rejilla^F

backdrop
telón^M de fondo^M

stage curtain
telón^M de boca^F

catwalk
corredor^M

flies
bambalinas^F

batten
viga^F

upstage
fondo^M del escenario^M

rehearsing room
sala^F de ensayo^M

scenery storage
depósito^M para el decorado^M

slot
escotillones^M

stage
escenario^M

scenery lift
ascensor^M para el
decorado^M

prompt box
concha^F del apuntador^M

proscenium
proscenio^M

hoist
plataforma^F elevadora

orchestra pit
foso^M de la orquesta^F

orchestra seats
luneta^F preferente

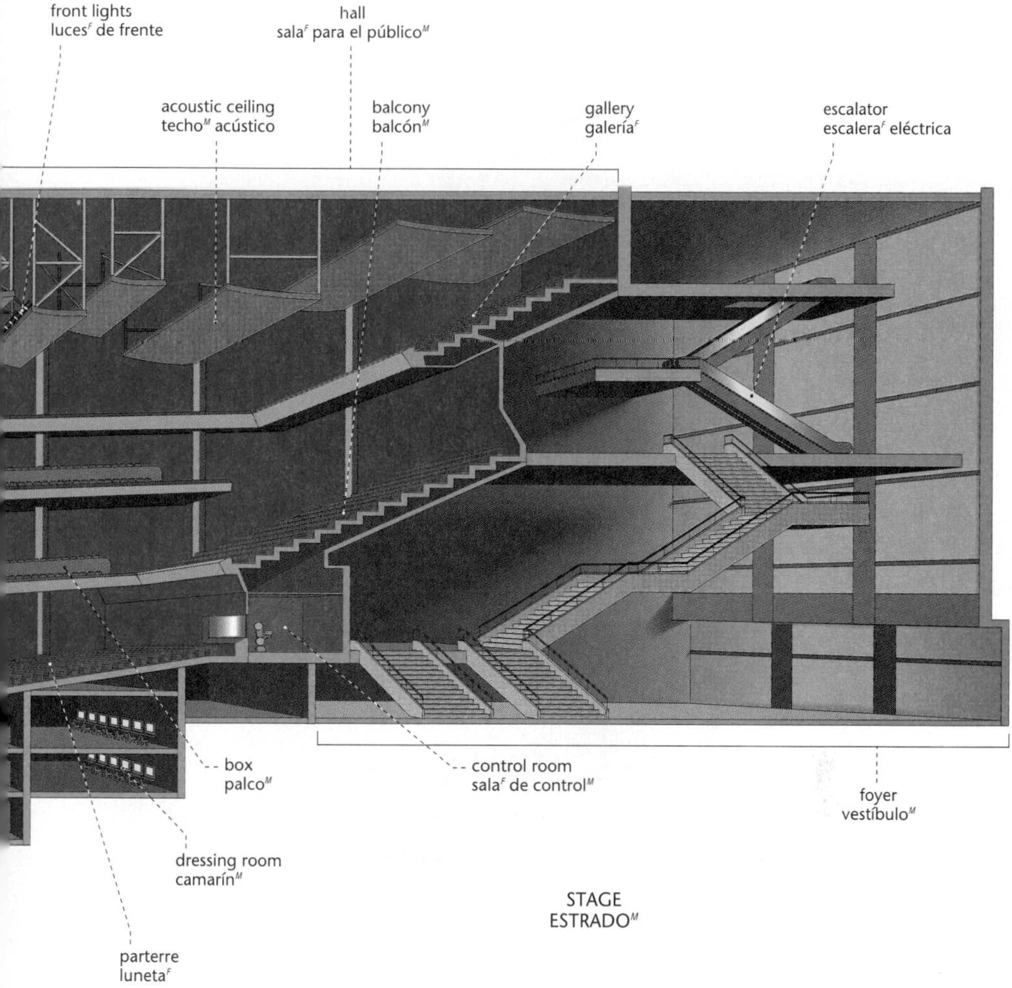

front lights
luces^F de frente

hall
sala^F para el público^M

acoustic ceiling
techo^M acústico

balcony
balcón^M

gallery
galería^F

escalator
escalera^F eléctrica

box
palco^M

control room
sala^F de control^M

foyer
vestíbulo^M

dressing room
camarín^M

parterre
luneta^F

STAGE
ESTRADO^M

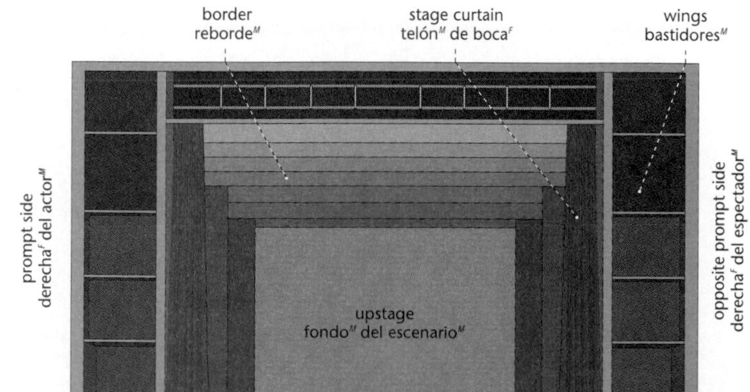

border
reborde^M

stage curtain
telón^M de boca^F

wings
bastidores^M

prompt side
derecha^F del actor^M

opposite prompt side
derecha^F del espectador^M

upstage
fondo^M del escenario^M

OFFICE BUILDING
EDIFICIO*ᴹ* DE OFICINAS*ᶠ*

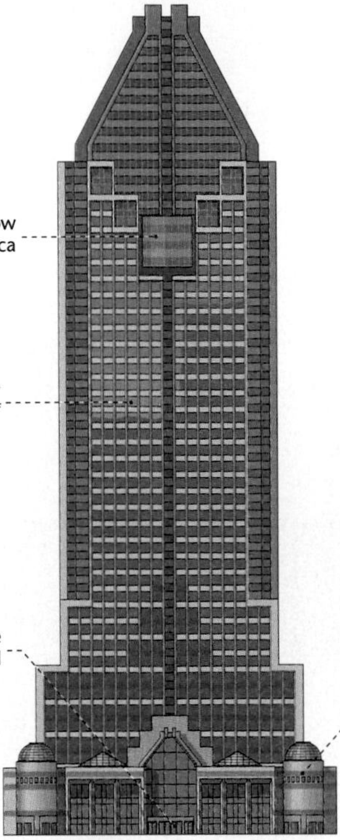

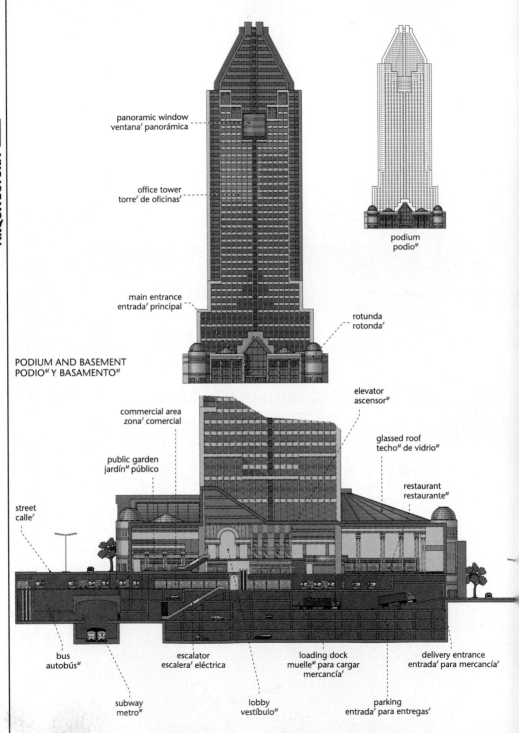

panoramic window
ventana*ᶠ* panorámica

office tower
torre*ᶠ* de oficinas*ᶠ*

main entrance
entrada*ᶠ* principal

rotunda
rotonda*ᶠ*

PODIUM AND BASEMENT
PODIO*ᴹ* Y BASAMENTO*ᴹ*

podium
podio*ᴹ*

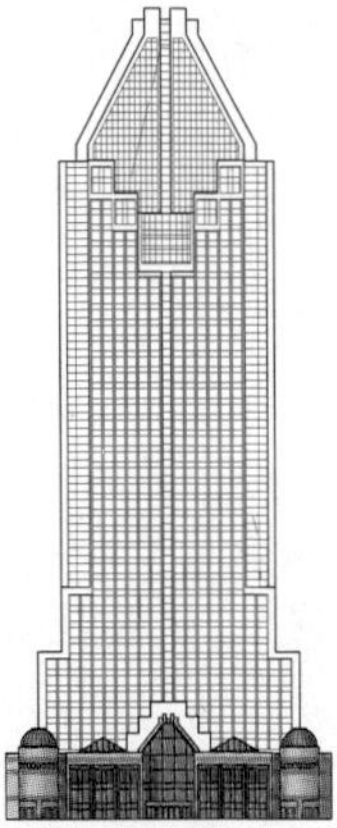

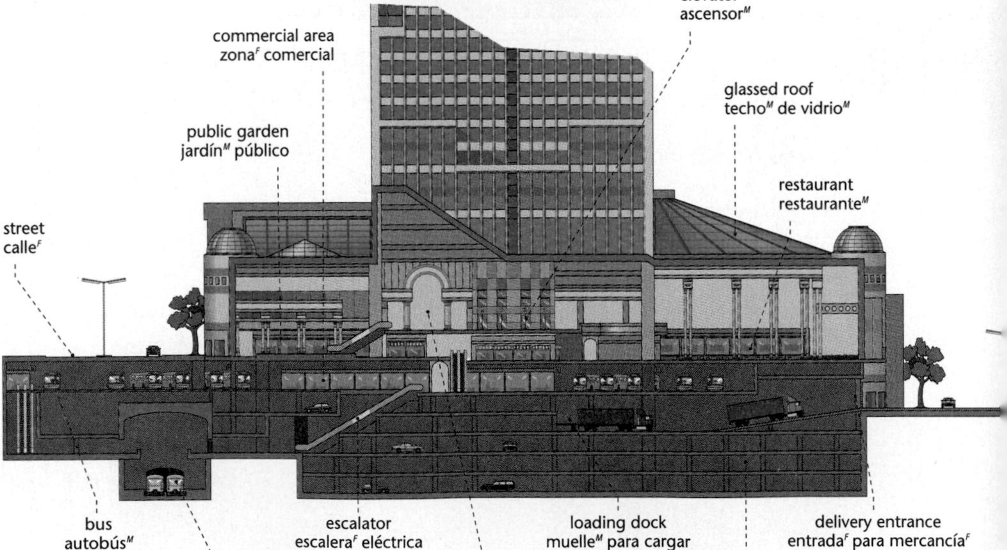

elevator
ascensor*ᴹ*

commercial area
zona*ᶠ* comercial

glassed roof
techo*ᴹ* de vidrio*ᴹ*

public garden
jardín*ᴹ* público

restaurant
restaurante*ᴹ*

street
calle*ᶠ*

bus
autobús*ᴹ*

escalator
escalera*ᶠ* eléctrica

loading dock
muelle*ᴹ* para cargar
mercancía*ᶠ*

delivery entrance
entrada*ᶠ* para mercancía*ᶠ*

subway
metro*ᴹ*

lobby
vestíbulo*ᴹ*

parking
entrada*ᶠ* para entregas*ᶠ*

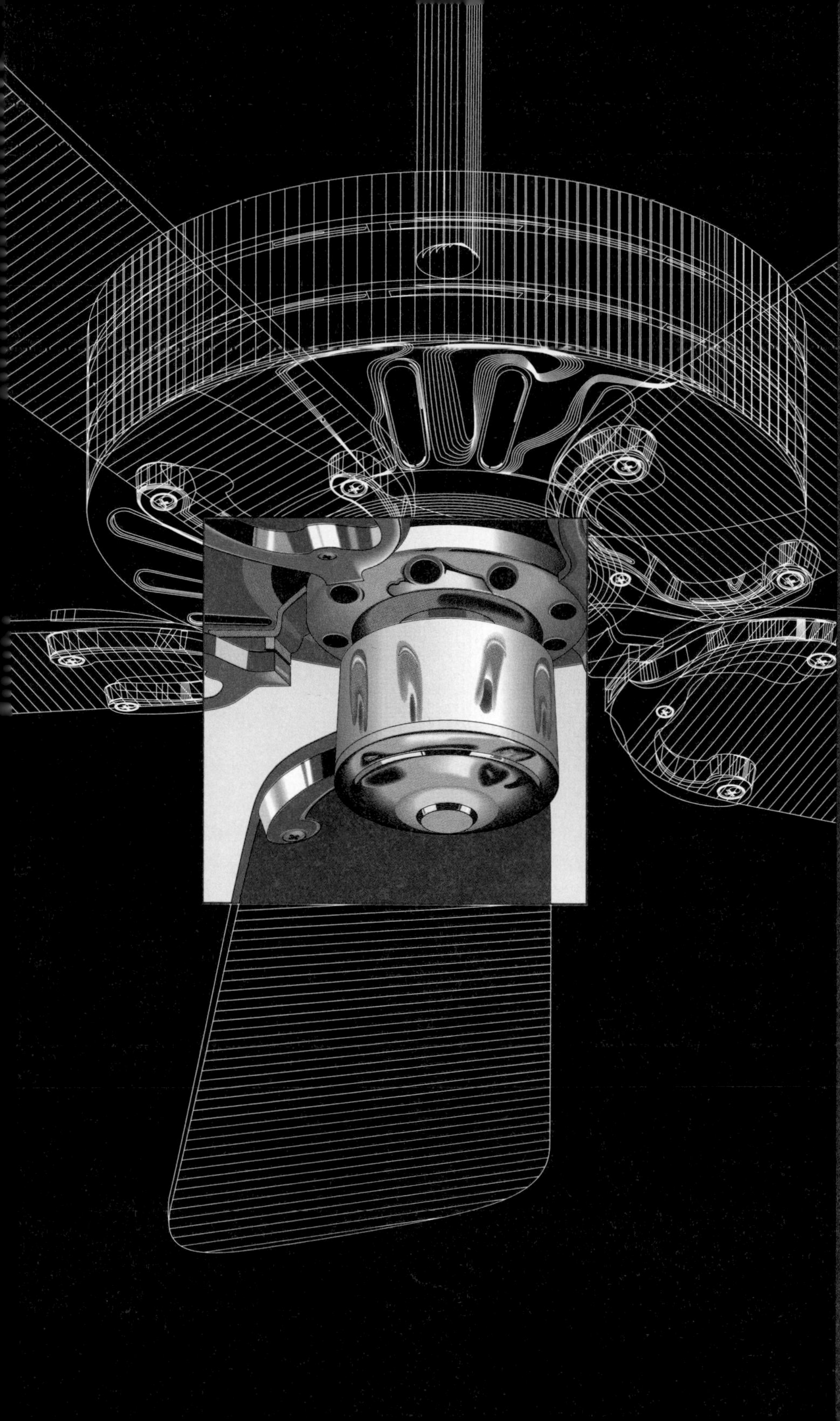

CONTENTS

HOUSE
CASA

BLUEPRINT READING
PLANO^M DE UNA CASA

ELEVATION
ELEVACIÓN^F

SITE PLAN
PLANO^M DEL TERRENO

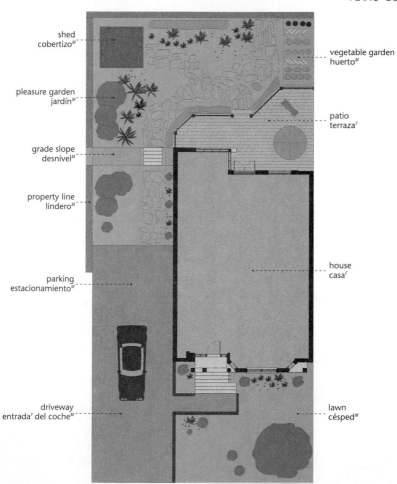

shed
cobertizo^M

vegetable garden
huerto^M

pleasure garden
jardín^M

patio
terraza^F

grade slope
desnivel^M

property line
lindero^M

house
casa^F

parking
estacionamiento^M

driveway
entrada^F del coche^M

lawn
césped^M

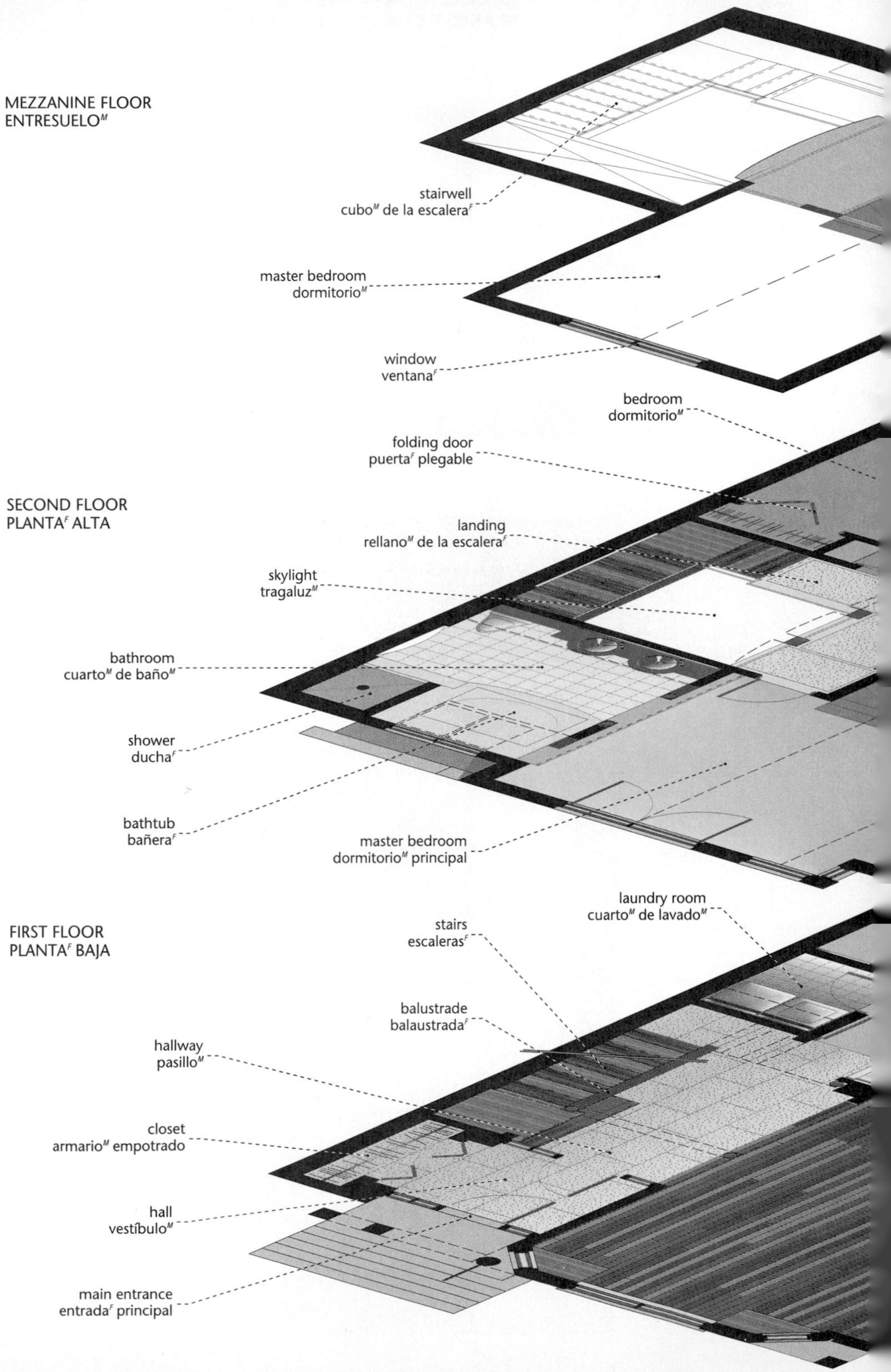

MEZZANINE FLOOR
ENTRESUELO^M

stairwell
cubo^M de la escalera^F

master bedroom
dormitorio^M

window
ventana^F

bedroom
dormitorio^M

folding door
puerta^F plegable

SECOND FLOOR
PLANTA^F **ALTA**

landing
rellano^M de la escalera^F

skylight
tragaluz^M

bathroom
cuarto^M de baño^M

shower
ducha^F

bathtub
bañera^F

master bedroom
dormitorio^M principal

laundry room
cuarto^M de lavado^M

stairs
escaleras^F

FIRST FLOOR
PLANTA^F **BAJA**

balustrade
balaustrada^F

hallway
pasillo^M

closet
armario^M empotrado

hall
vestíbulo^M

main entrance
entrada^F principal

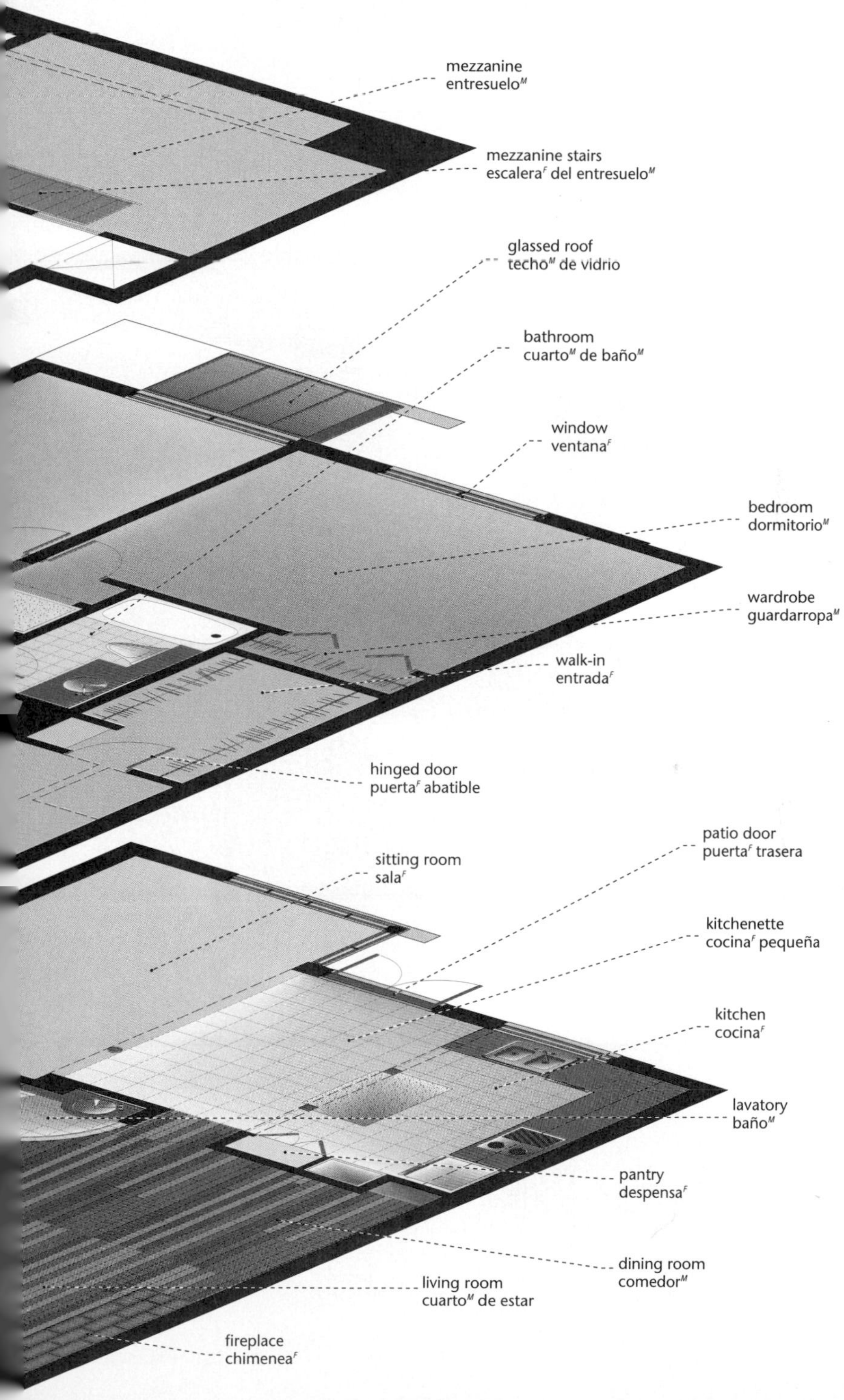

mezzanine
entresuelo^M

mezzanine stairs
escalera^f del entresuelo^M

glassed roof
techo^M de vidrio

bathroom
cuarto^M de baño^M

window
ventana^f

bedroom
dormitorio^M

wardrobe
guardarropa^M

walk-in
entrada^f

hinged door
puerta^f abatible

patio door
puerta^f trasera

sitting room
sala^f

kitchenette
cocina^f pequeña

kitchen
cocina^f

lavatory
baño^M

pantry
despensa^f

dining room
comedor^M

living room
cuarto^M de estar

fireplace
chimenea^f

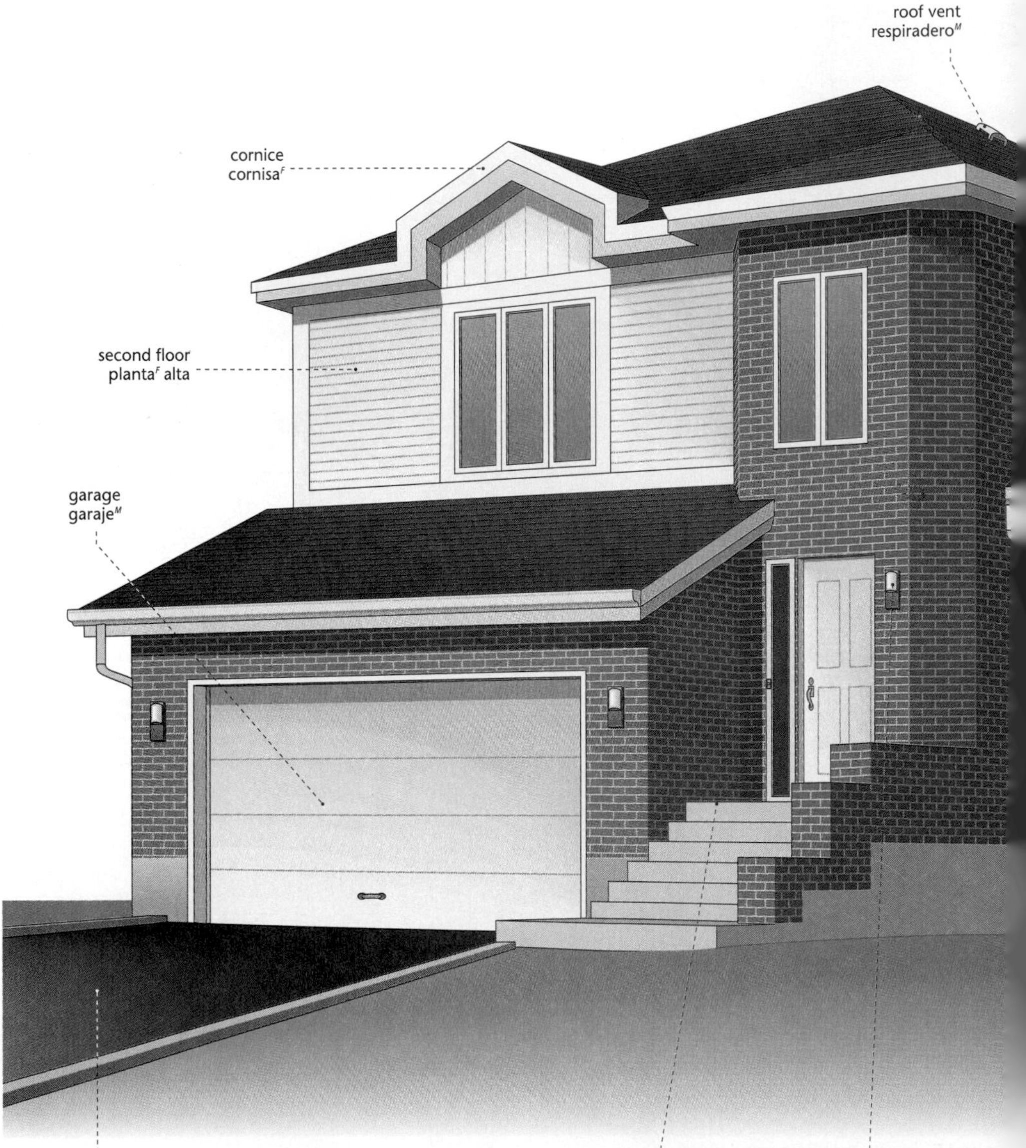

roof vent
respiradero^M

cornice
cornisa^F

second floor
planta^F alta

garage
garaje^M

driveway
entrada^F del coche^M

perron
escalinata^F

outdoor light
luz^F exterior

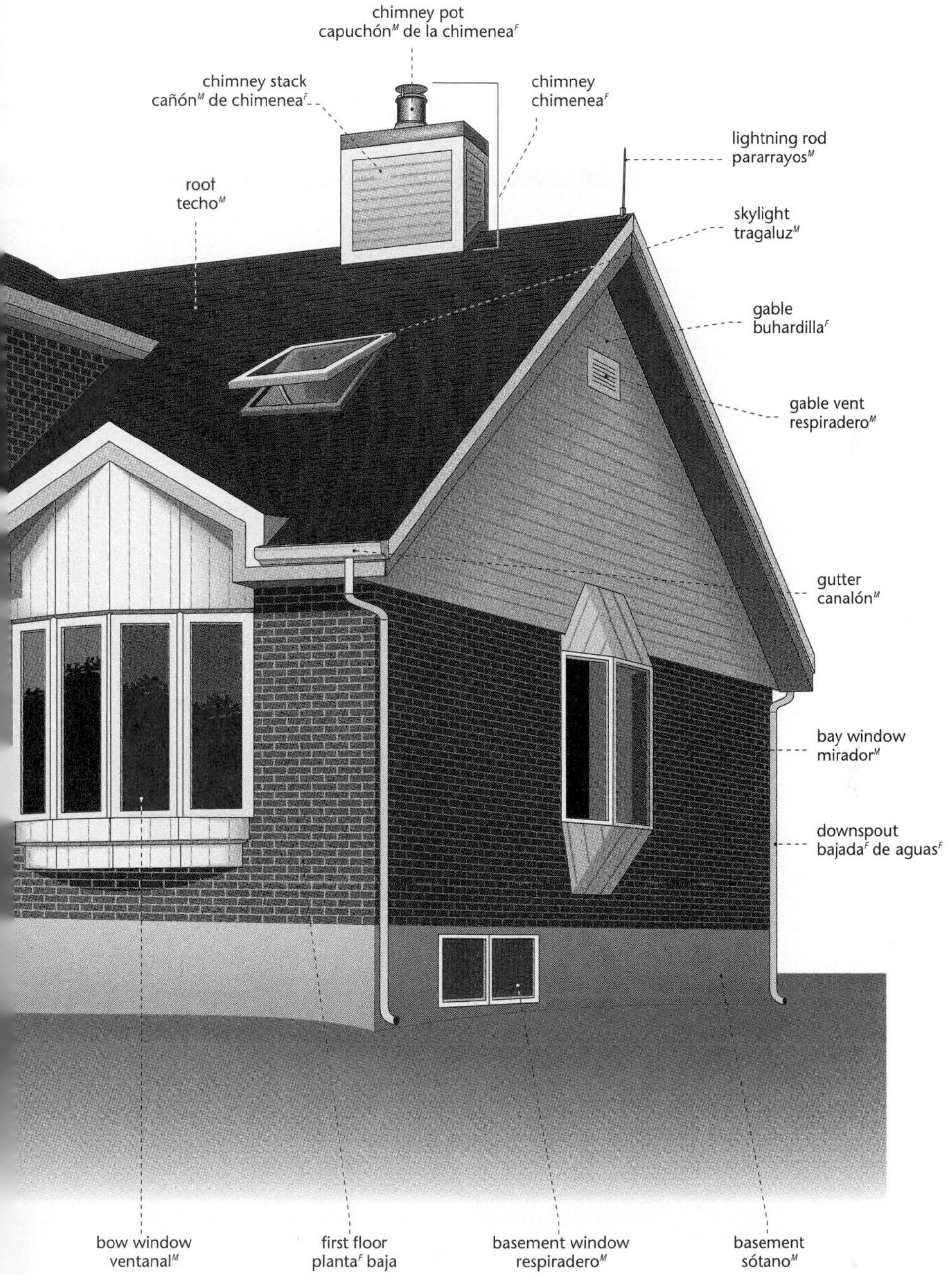

chimney pot
capuchón^M de la chimenea^F

chimney stack
cañón^M de chimenea^F

chimney
chimenea^F

roof
techo^M

lightning rod
pararrayos^M

skylight
tragaluz^M

gable
buhardilla^F

gable vent
respiradero^M

gutter
canalón^M

bay window
mirador^M

downspout
bajada^F de aguas^F

bow window
ventanal^M

first floor
planta^F baja

basement window
respiradero^M

basement
sótano^M

FRAME
ARMAZÓN^M

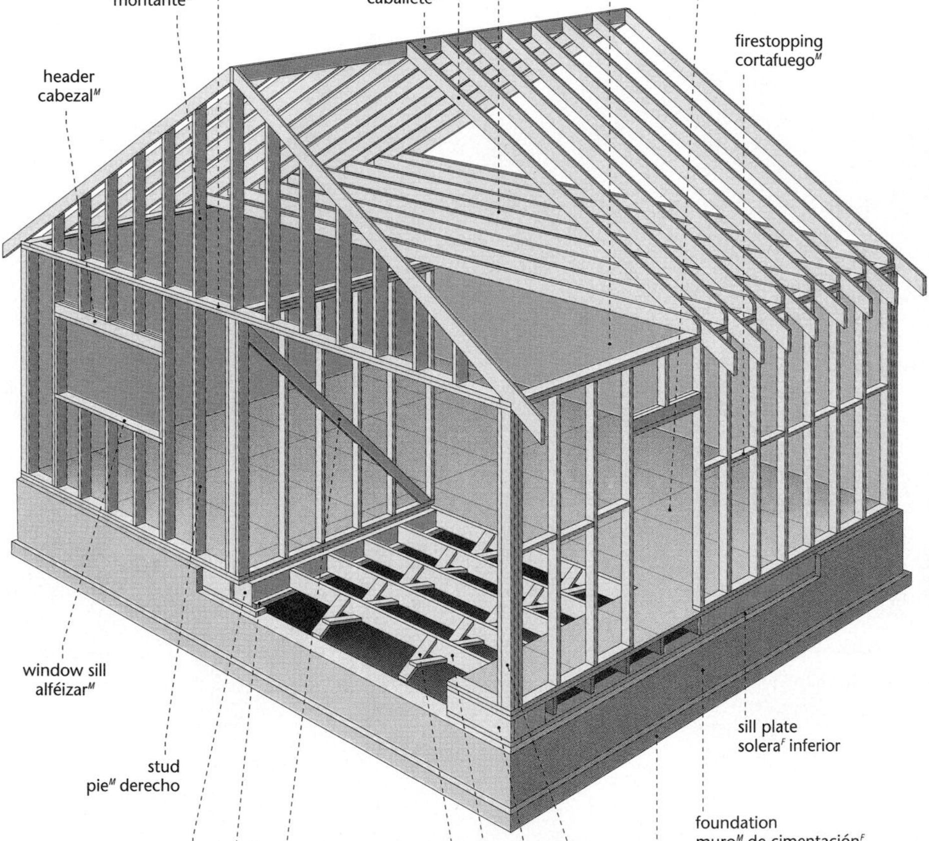

ceiling joist
vigueta^F del techo^M

sheathing
entablado^M

double plate
sofera^F doble

rafter
cabrio^M

subfloor
contrapiso^M

gable stud
montante^M

tie beam
caballete^M

firestopping
cortafuego^M

header
cabezal^M

window sill
alféizar^M

sill plate
solera^F inferior

stud
pie^M derecho

foundation
muro^M de cimentación^F

girder
viga^F maestra

footing
zarpa^F

ledger
travesaño^M

bridging
puntales^M de refuerzo^M

corner stud
montante^M esquinero

brace
tirante^M

floor joist
vigueta^F del piso^M

end joist
vigueta^F esquinera

ROOF TRUSS
ARMADURA^F DEL TECHO^M

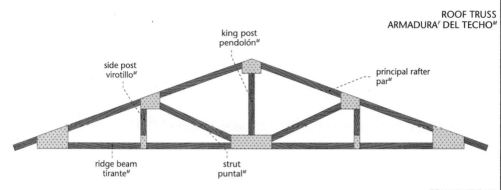

king post
pendolón^M

side post
virotillo^M

principal rafter
par^M

ridge beam
tirante^M

strut
puntal^M

FOUNDATIONS
CIMIENTOS^M

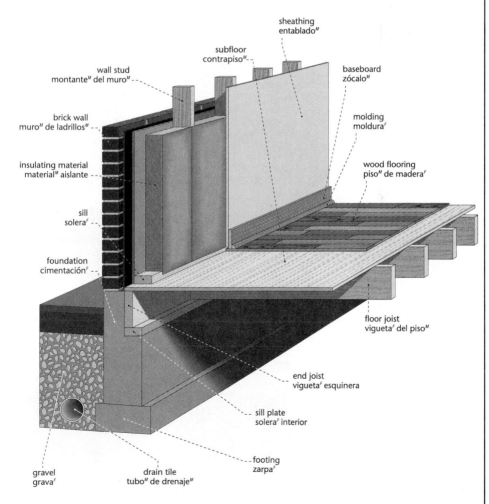

sheathing
entablado^M

subfloor
contrapiso^M·

wall stud
montante^M del muro^M·

baseboard
zócalo^M

brick wall
muro^M de ladrillos^M ·

molding
moldura^F

insulating material
material^M aislante

wood flooring
piso^M de madera^F

sill
solera^F ·

foundation
cimentación^F ·

floor joist
vigueta^F del piso^M

end joist
vigueta^F esquinera

sill plate
solera^F interior

footing
zarpa^F

gravel
grava^F

drain tile
tubo^M de drenaje^M

WOOD FLOORING ON CEMENT SCREED
PARQUÉ^M SOBRE BASE^F DE CEMENTO^M

WOOD FLOORING ON WOODEN STRUCTURE
ENTARIMADO^M SOBRE ESTRUCTURA^F DE MADERA^F

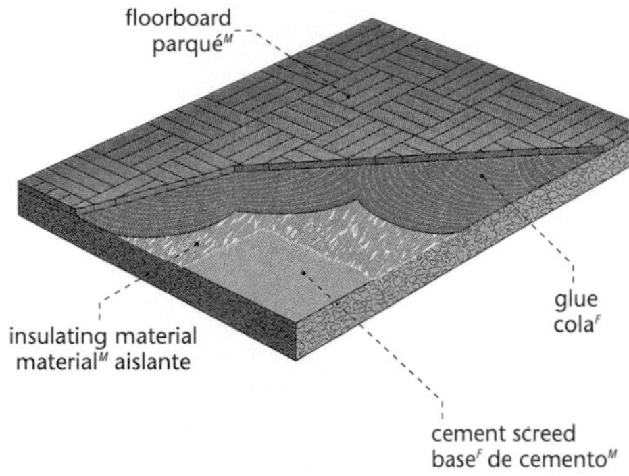

floorboard
parqué^M

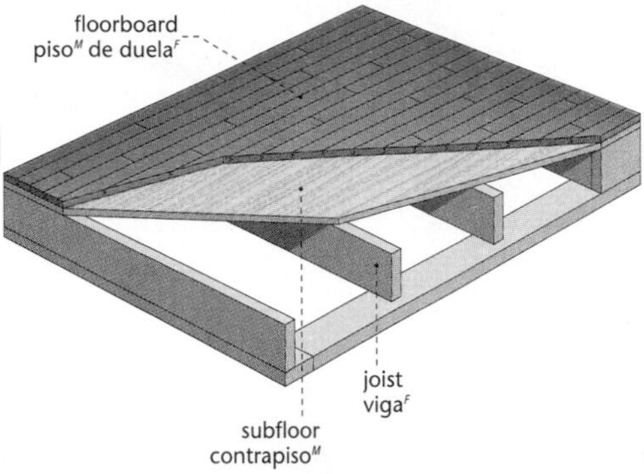

floorboard
piso^M de duela^F

glue
cola^F

insulating material
material^M aislante

cement screed
base^F de cemento^M

joist
viga^F

subfloor
contrapiso^M

WOOD FLOORING ARRANGEMENTS
TIPOS^M DE PARQUÉ^M

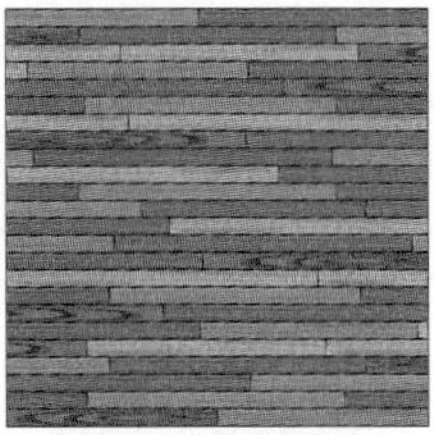

overlay flooring
parqué^M sobrepuesto

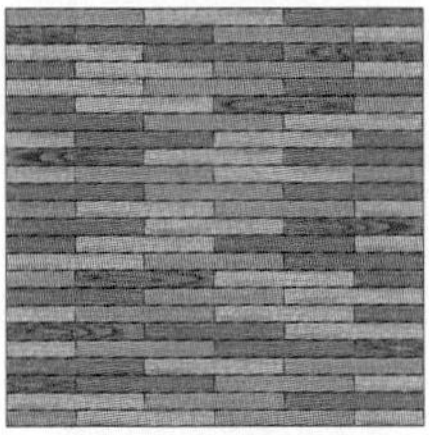

strip flooring with alternate joints
parqué^M alternado a la inglesa

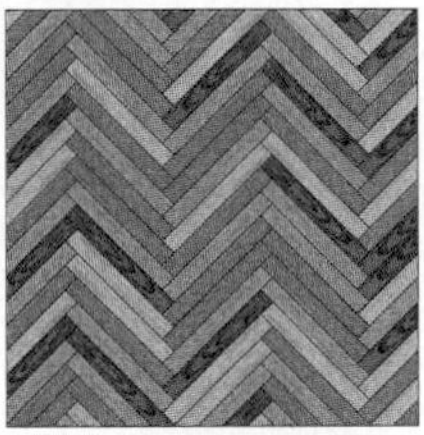

herringbone parquet
parqué^M espinapez^M

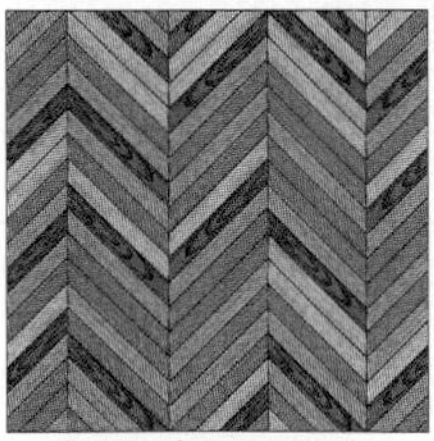

herringbone pattern
espinapez^M

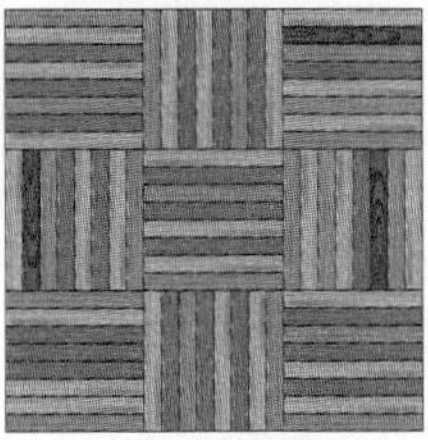

inlaid parquet
parqué^M entretejido

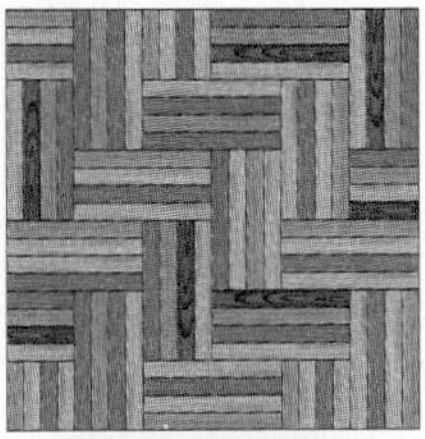

basket weave pattern
parqué^M de cestería^F

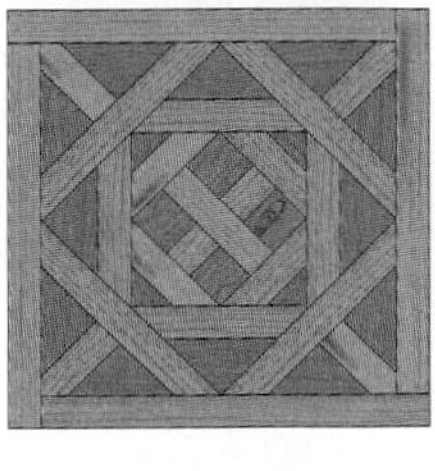

Arenberg parquet
parqué^M Arenberg

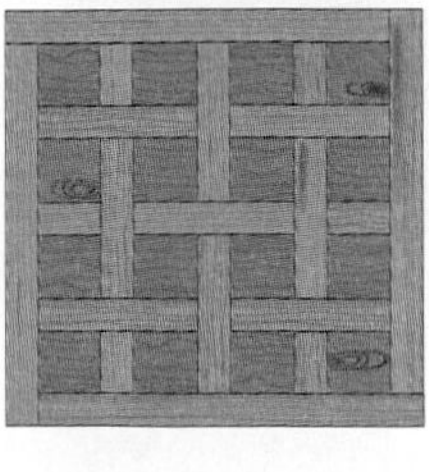

Chantilly parquet
parqué^M Chantilly

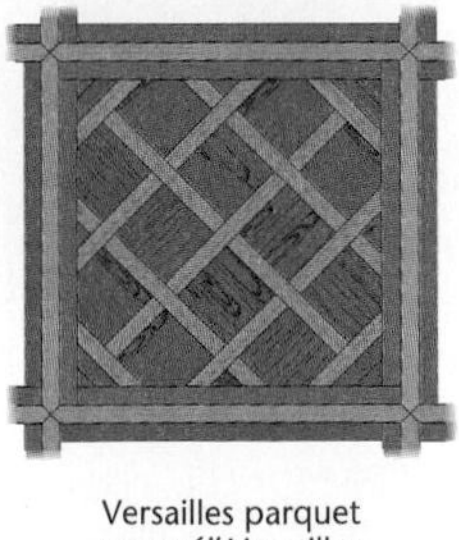

Versailles parquet
parqué^M Versailles

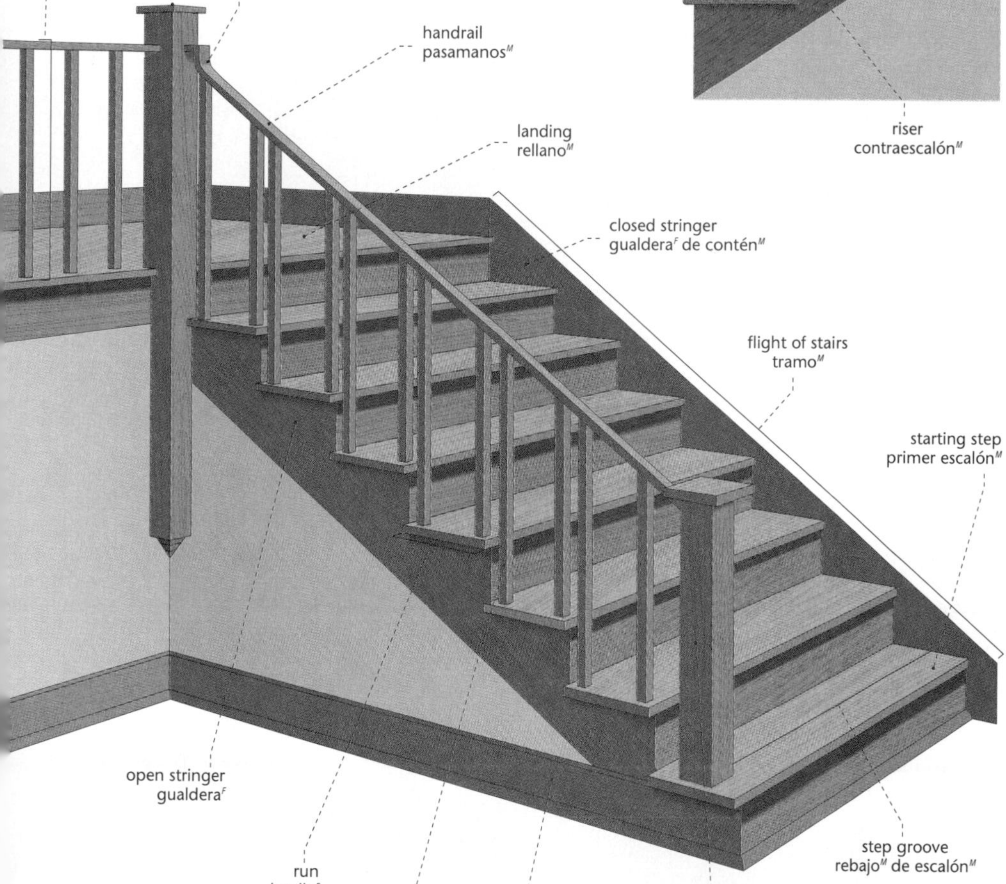

guard
barandilla*F*

cap
remate*M*

goose-neck
cuello*M* de cisne*M*

handrail
pasamanos*M*

landing
rellano*M*

closed stringer
gualdera*F* de contén*M*

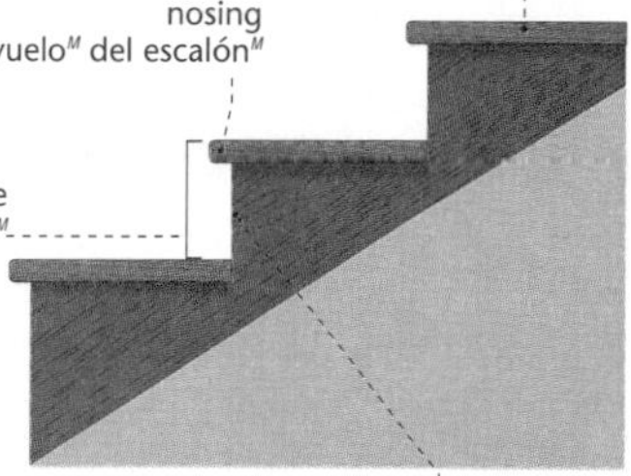

tread
escalón*M*

nosing
vuelo*M* del escalón*M*

rise
altura*F* del escalón*M*

riser
contraescalón*M*

flight of stairs
tramo*M*

starting step
primer escalón*M*

step groove
rebajo*M* de escalón*M*

newel post
poste*M*

baseboard
zócalo*M*

banister
balaustre*M*

run
huella*F*

open stringer
gualdera*F*

HOUSE
CASA

201

DOOR
PUERTA^F

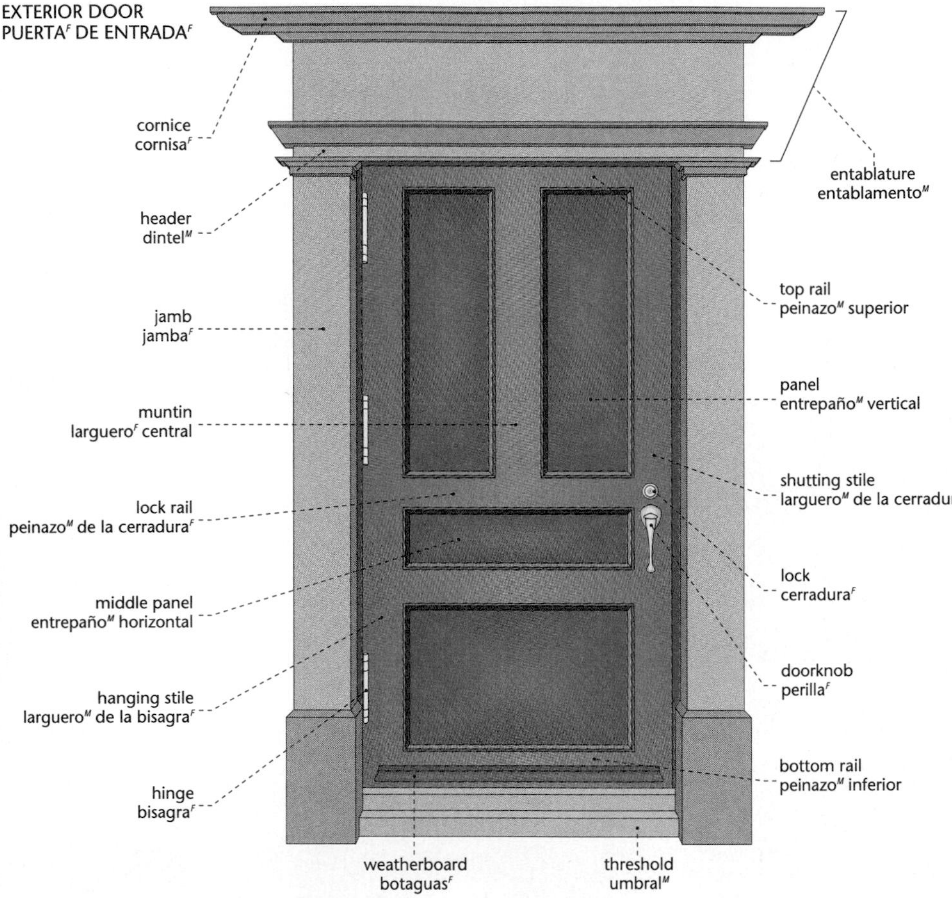

EXTERIOR DOOR
PUERTA^F DE ENTRADA^F

cornice
cornisa^F

header
dintel^M

jamb
jamba^F

muntin
larguero^F central

lock rail
peinazo^M de la cerradura^F

middle panel
entrepaño^M horizontal

hanging stile
larguero^M de la bisagra^F

hinge
bisagra^F

entablature
entablamento^M

top rail
peinazo^M superior

panel
entrepaño^M vertical

shutting stile
larguero^M de la cerradura^F

lock
cerradura^F

doorknob
perilla^F

bottom rail
peinazo^M inferior

weatherboard
botaguas^F

threshold
umbral^M

**HOUSE
CASA**

TYPES OF DOORS
TIPOS^M DE PUERTAS^F

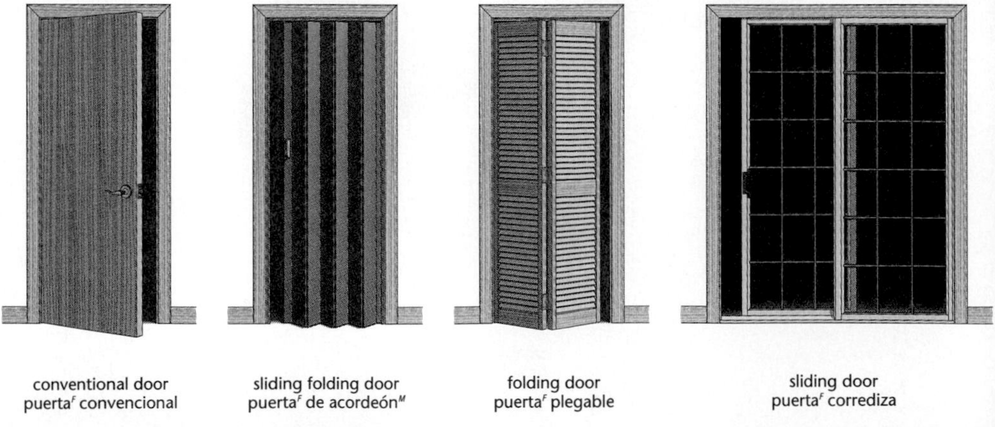

conventional door
puerta^F convencional

sliding folding door
puerta^F de acordeón^M

folding door
puerta^F plegable

sliding door
puerta^F corrediza

WINDOW
VENTANA^F

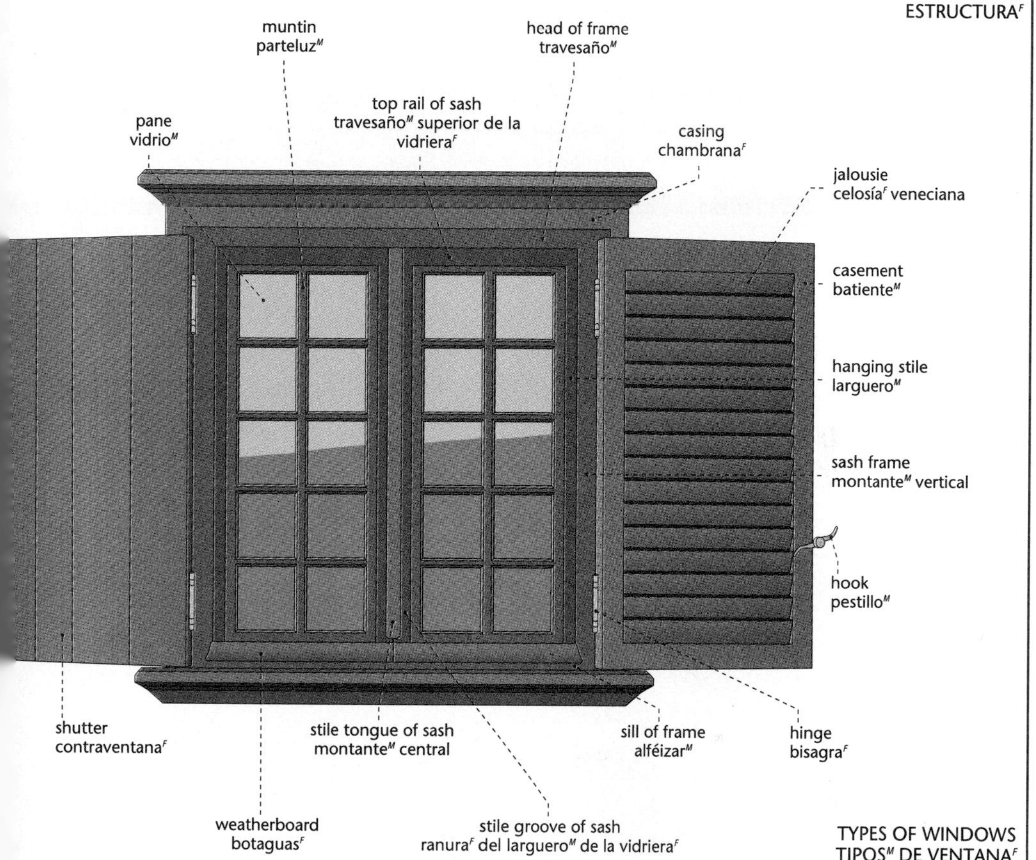

muntin
parteluz^M

head of frame
travesaño^M

top rail of sash
travesaño^M superior de la
vidriera^F

casing
chambrana^F

pane
vidrio^M

jalousie
celosía^F veneciana

casement
batiente^M

hanging stile
larguero^M

sash frame
montante^M vertical

hook
pestillo^M

shutter
contraventana^F

stile tongue of sash
montante^M central

sill of frame
alféizar^M

hinge
bisagra^F

weatherboard
botaguas^F

stile groove of sash
ranura^F del larguero^M de la vidriera^F

**HOUSE
CASA**

TYPES OF WINDOWS
TIPOS^M DE VENTANA^F

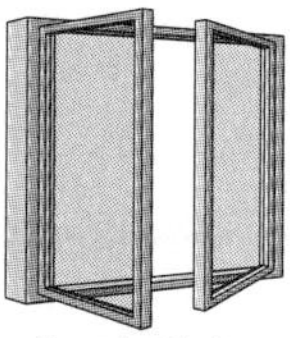

French window
ventana^F francesa

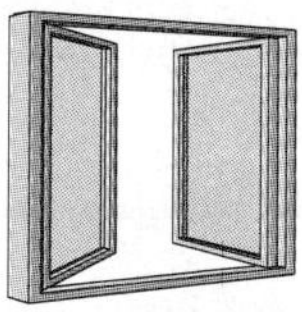

casement window
ventana^F de dos hojas^F

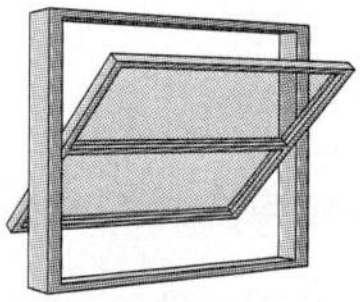

horizontal pivoting window
ventana^F basculante

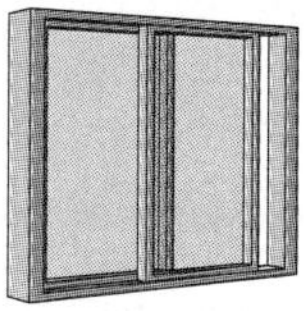

sliding window
ventana^F corrediza

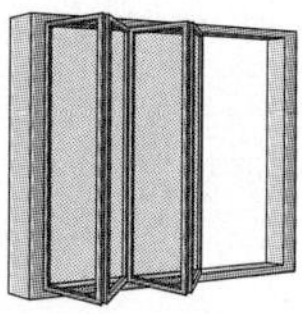

sliding folding window
ventana^F de acordeón^M

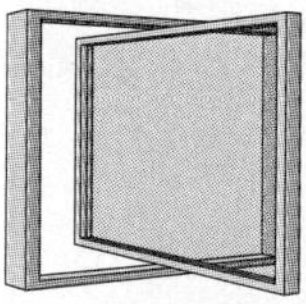

vertical pivoting window
ventana^F giratoria

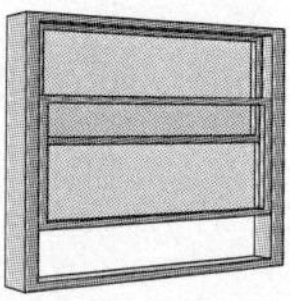

sash window
ventana^F de guillotina^F

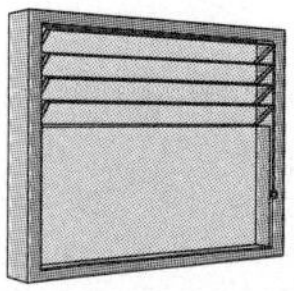

louvered window
ventana^F de celosía^F

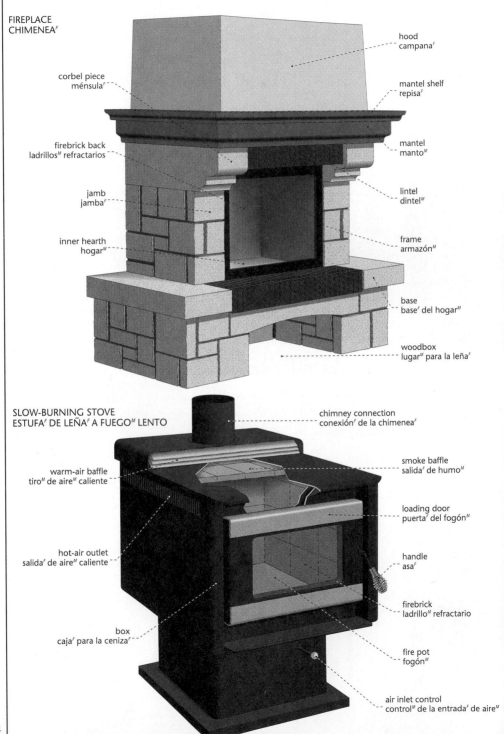

FIREPLACE
CHIMENEA[F]

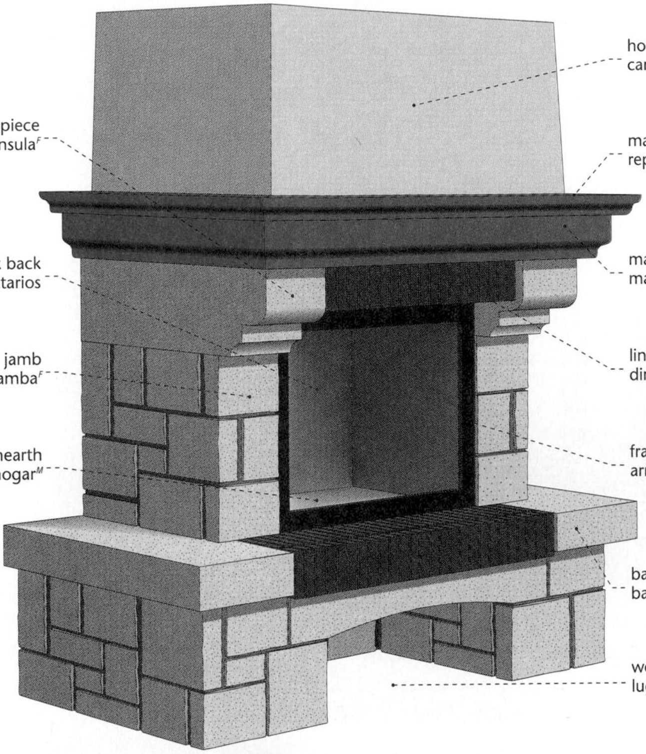

hood
campana[F]

corbel piece
ménsula[F]

mantel shelf
repisa[F]

firebrick back
ladrillos[M] refractarios

mantel
manto[M]

jamb
jamba[F]

lintel
dintel[M]

inner hearth
hogar[M]

frame
armazón[M]

base
base[F] del hogar[M]

woodbox
lugar[M] para la leña[F]

SLOW-BURNING STOVE
ESTUFA[F] DE LEÑA[F] A FUEGO[M] LENTO

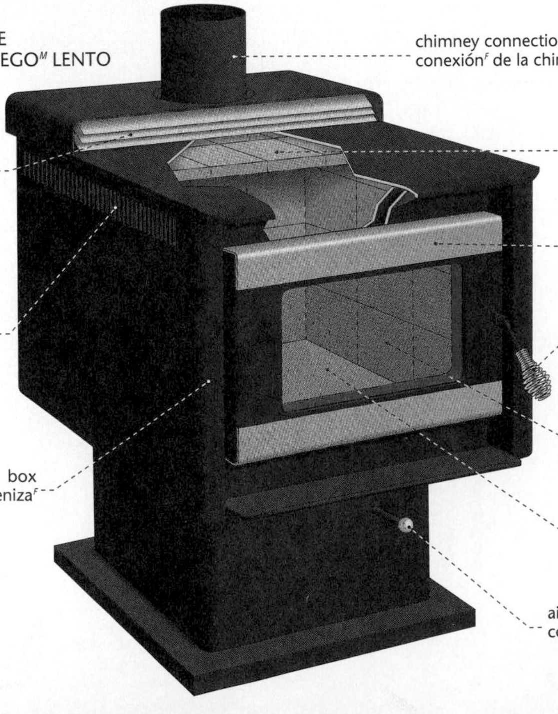

chimney connection
conexión[F] de la chimenea[F]

warm-air baffle
tiro[M] de aire[M] caliente

smoke baffle
salida[F] de humo[M]

loading door
puerta[F] del fogón[M]

hot-air outlet
salida[F] de aire[M] caliente

handle
asa[F]

firebrick
ladrillo[M] refractario

box
caja[F] para la ceniza[F]

fire pot
fogón[M]

air inlet control
control[M] de la entrada[F] de aire[M]

CHIMNEY
CHIMENEA^F

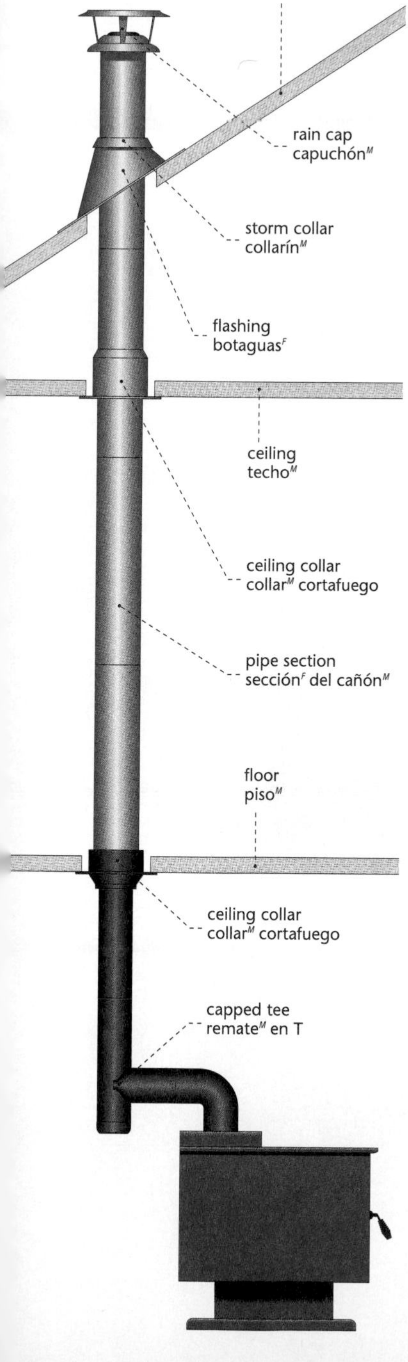

roof
tejado^M

rain cap
capuchón^M

storm collar
collarín^M

flashing
botaguas^F

ceiling
techo^M

ceiling collar
collar^M cortafuego

pipe section
sección^F del cañón^M

floor
piso^M

ceiling collar
collar^M cortafuego

capped tee
remate^M en T

FIRE IRONS
UTENSILIOS^M PARA LA CHIMENEA^F

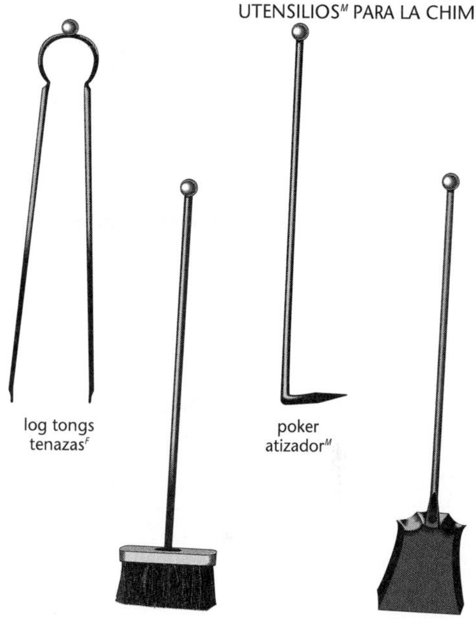

log tongs
tenazas^F

poker
atizador^M

broom
escobilla^F

shovel
pala^F

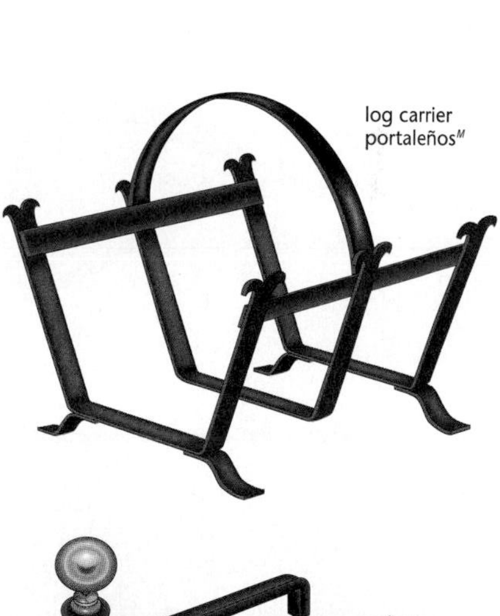

log carrier
portaleños^M

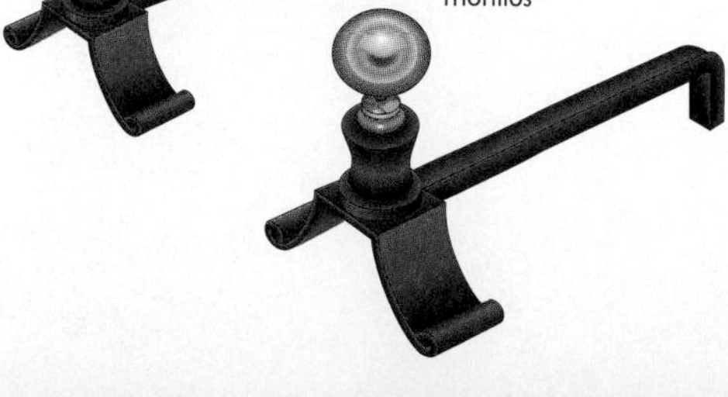

andirons
morillos^M

FORCED WARM-AIR SYSTEM
SISTEMA^M DE AIRE^M CALIENTE A PRESIÓN^F

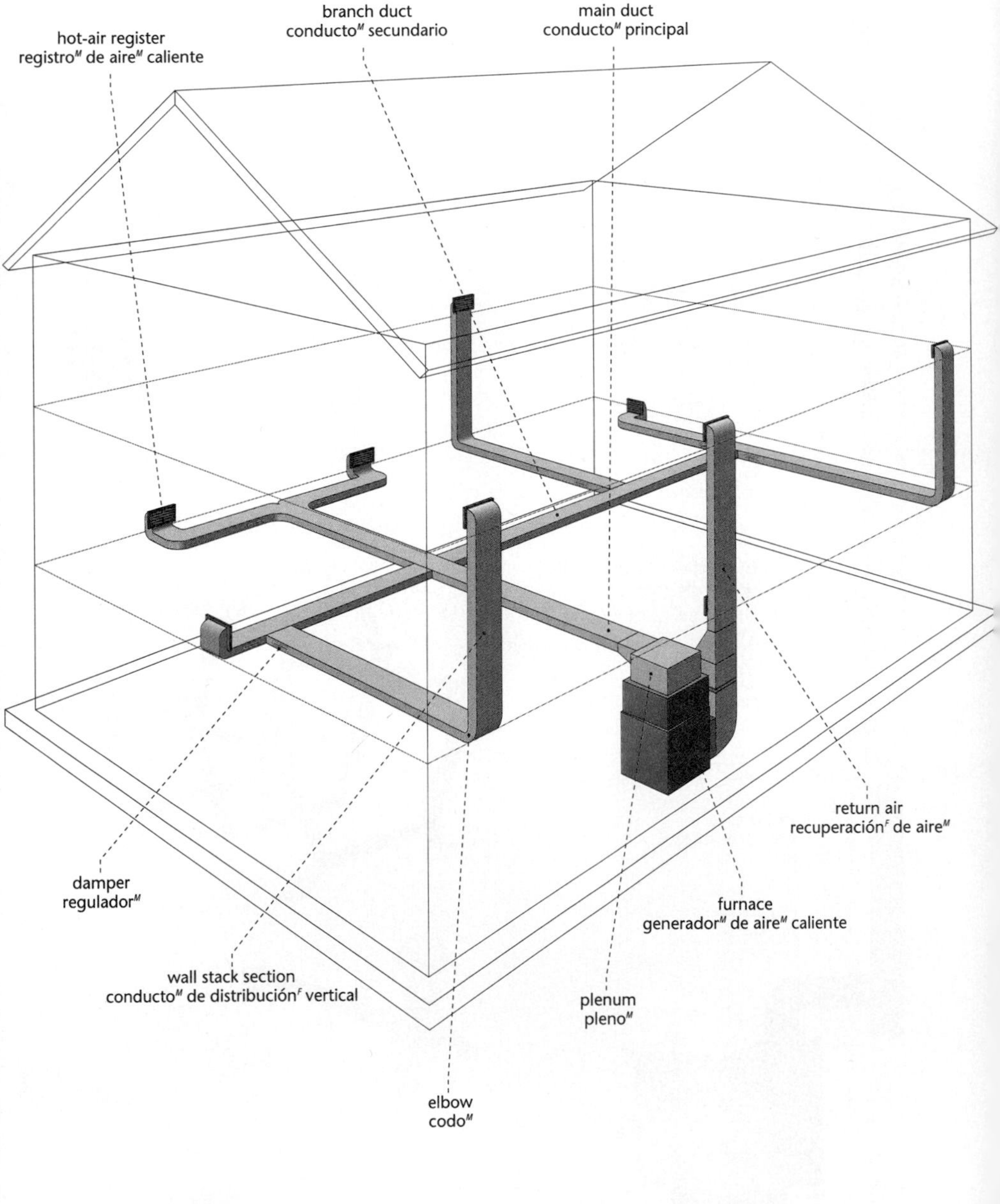

hot-air register
registro^M de aire^M caliente

branch duct
conducto^M secundario

main duct
conducto^M principal

damper
regulador^M

wall stack section
conducto^M de distribución^F vertical

elbow
codo^M

plenum
pleno^M

furnace
generador^M de aire^M caliente

return air
recuperación^F de aire^M

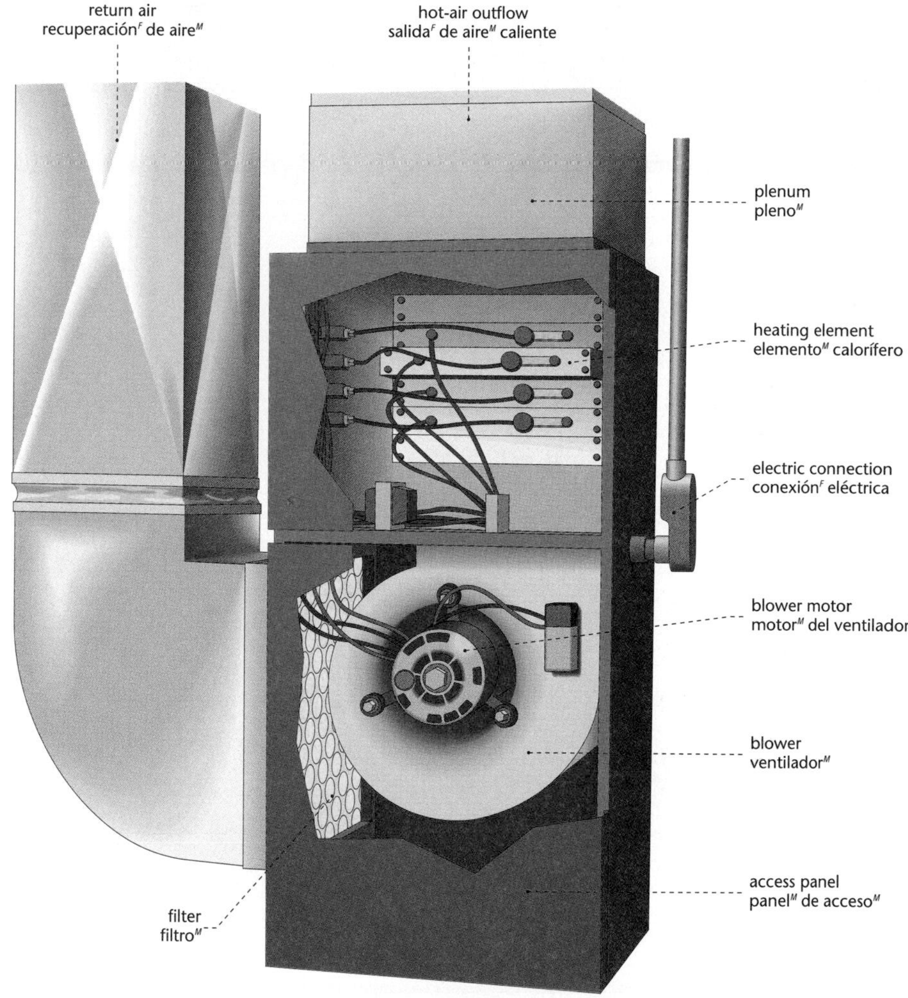

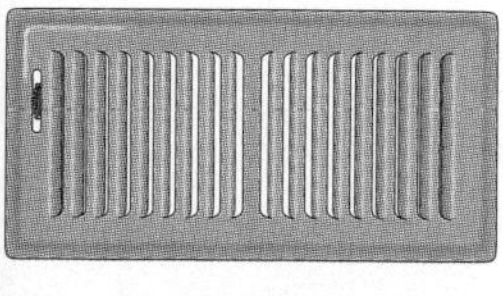

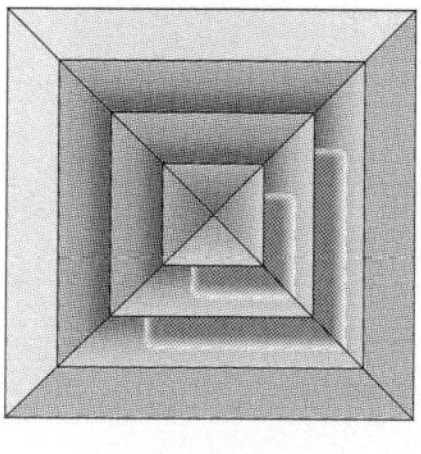

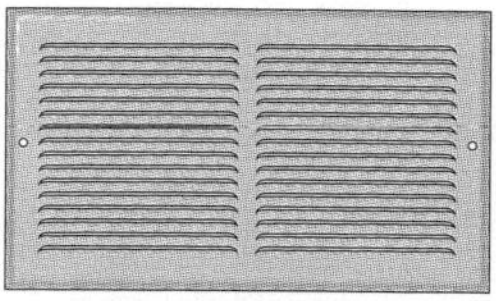

return air
recuperación^F de aire^M

hot-air outflow
salida^F de aire^M caliente

plenum
pleno^M

heating element
elemento^M calorífero

electric connection
conexión^F eléctrica

blower motor
motor^M del ventilador^M

blower
ventilador^M

access panel
panel^M de acceso^M

filter
filtro^M

TYPES OF REGISTERS
REJILLAS^F

baseboard register
rejilla^F de piso^M

ceiling register
rejilla^F de techo^M

wall register
rejilla^F de pared^F

HEADING
CALEFACCIÓN[F]

FORCED HOT-WATER SYSTEM
SISTEMA[M] DE AGUA[F] CALIENTE A PRESIÓN[F]

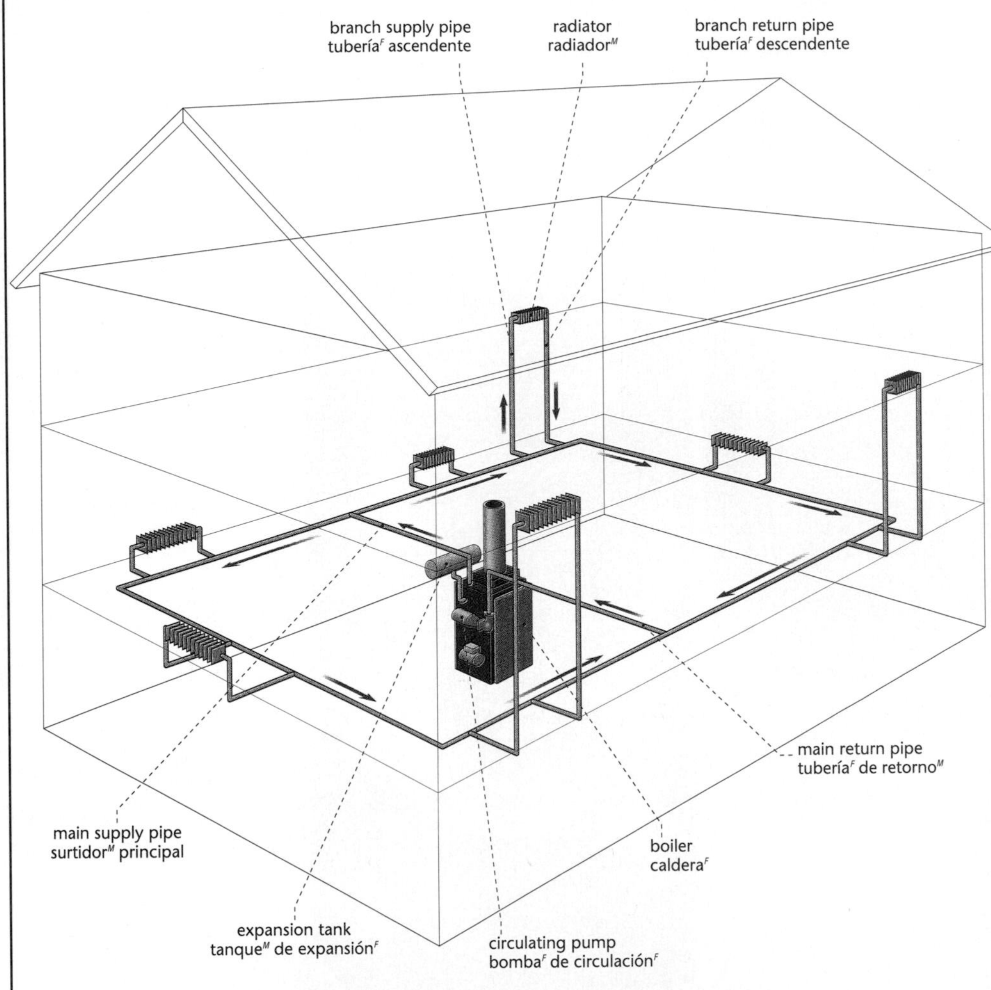

branch supply pipe
tubería[F] ascendente

radiator
radiador[M]

branch return pipe
tubería[F] descendente

main return pipe
tubería[F] de retorno[M]

main supply pipe
surtidor[M] principal

boiler
caldera[F]

expansion tank
tanque[M] de expansión[F]

circulating pump
bomba[F] de circulación[F]

COLUMN RADIATOR
RADIADOR[M] TUBULAR

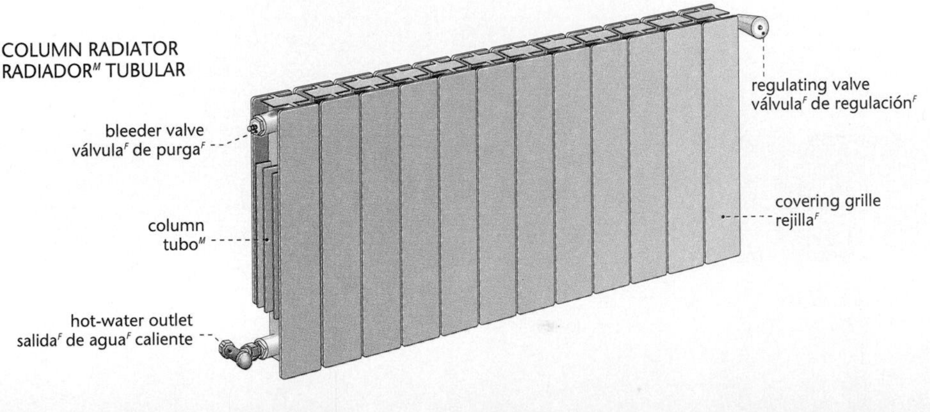

regulating valve
válvula[F] de regulación[F]

bleeder valve
válvula[F] de purga[F]

covering grille
rejilla[F]

column
tubo[M]

hot-water outlet
salida[F] de agua[F] caliente

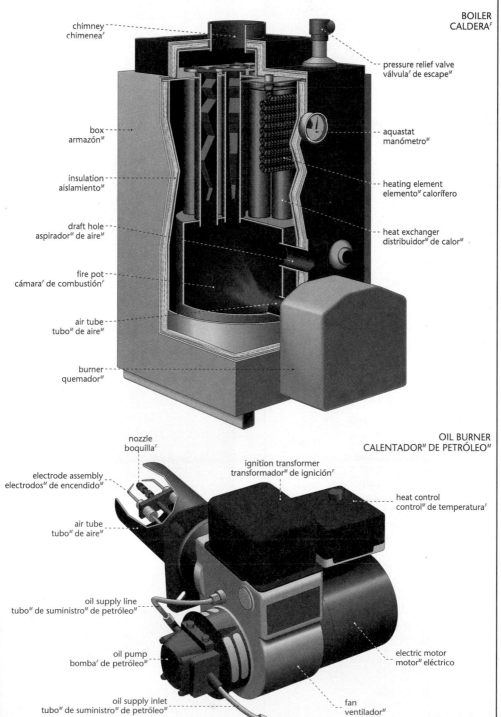

BOILER
CALDERA^F

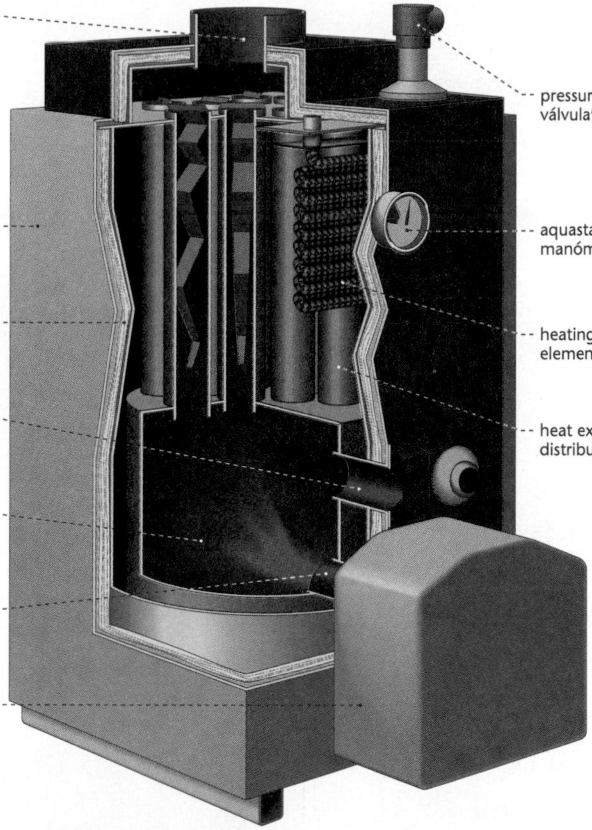

chimney
chimenea^F

pressure relief valve
válvula^F de escape^M

box
armazón^M

aquastat
manómetro^M

insulation
aislamiento^M

heating element
elemento^M calorífero

draft hole
aspirador^M de aire^M

heat exchanger
distribuidor^M de calor^M

fire pot
cámara^F de combustión^F

air tube
tubo^M de aire^M

burner
quemador^M

OIL BURNER
CALENTADOR^M DE PETRÓLEO^M

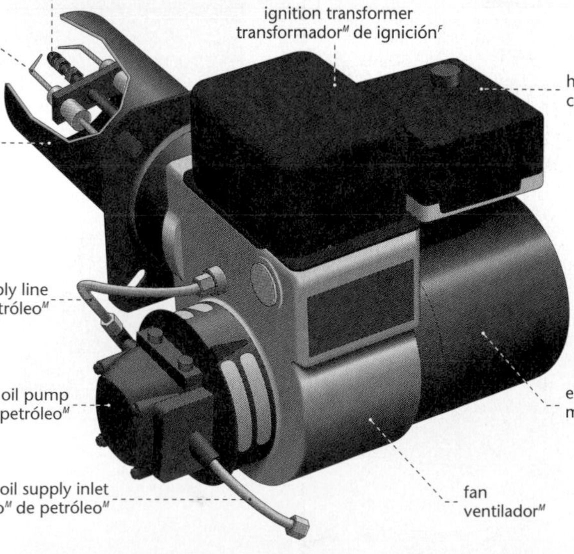

nozzle
boquilla^F

ignition transformer
transformador^M de ignición^F

electrode assembly
electrodos^M de encendido^M

heat control
control^M de temperatura^F

air tube
tubo^M de aire^M

oil supply line
tubo^M de suministro^M de petróleo^M

oil pump
bomba^F de petróleo^M

electric motor
motor^M eléctrico

oil supply inlet
tubo^M de suministro^M de petróleo^M

fan
ventilador^M

HEATING
CALEFACCIÓN^F

HUMIDIFIER
HUMIDIFICADOR^M

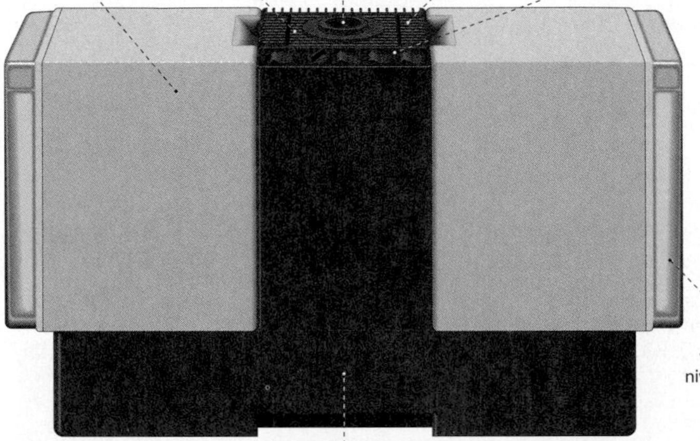

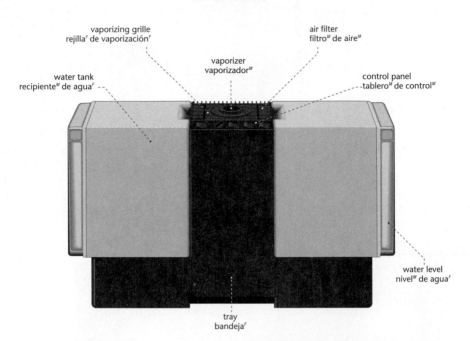

vaporizing grille
rejilla^F de vaporización^F

air filter
filtro^M de aire^M

vaporizer
vaporizador^M

water tank
recipiente^M de agua^F

control panel
tablero^M de control^M

water level
nivel^M de agua^F

tray
bandeja^F

HYGROMETER
HIGRÓMETRO^M

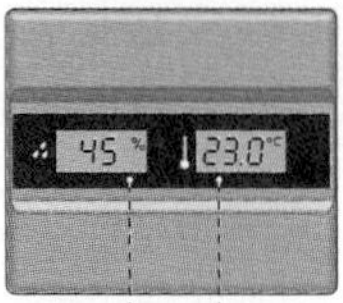

humidity
humedad^F del aire^M

temperature
temperatura^F

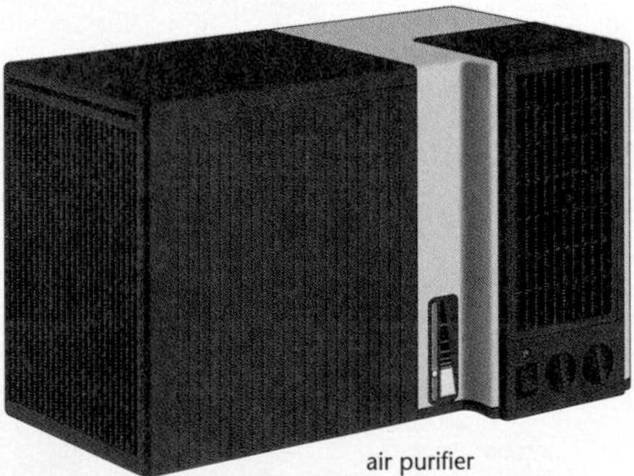

air purifier
purificador^M de aire^M

ELECTRIC BASEBOARD RADIATOR
RADIADOR^M ELÉCTRICO

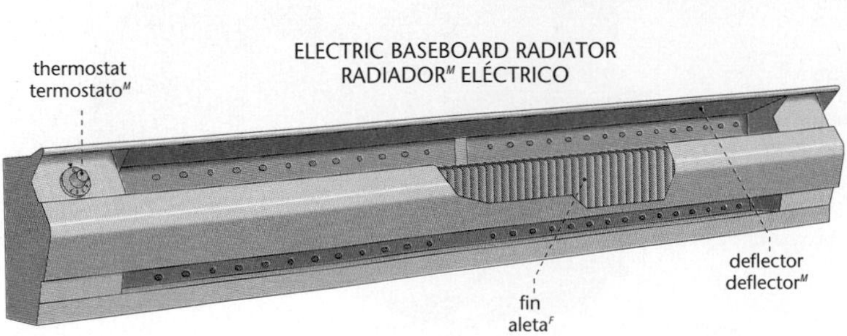

thermostat
termostato^M

deflector
deflector^M

fin
aleta^F

CONVECTOR
RADIADOR^M DE CONVEXIÓN^F

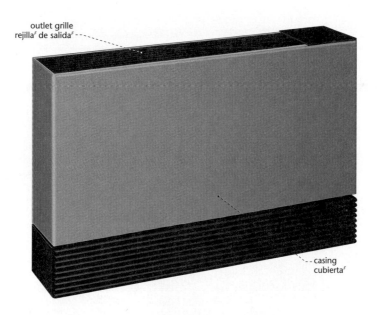

outlet grille
rejilla^F de salida^F

casing
cubierta^F

AUXILIARY HEATING
CALEFACCIÓN^F AUXILIAR

radiant heater
calentador^M eléctrico

oil-filled heater
calentador^M de aceite^M

fan heater
ventilador^M de aire^M caliente

HEAT PUMP
SISTEMA[M] DE BOMBA[F] DE CALOR[M]

OUTDOOR UNIT
UNIDAD[F] EXTERIOR

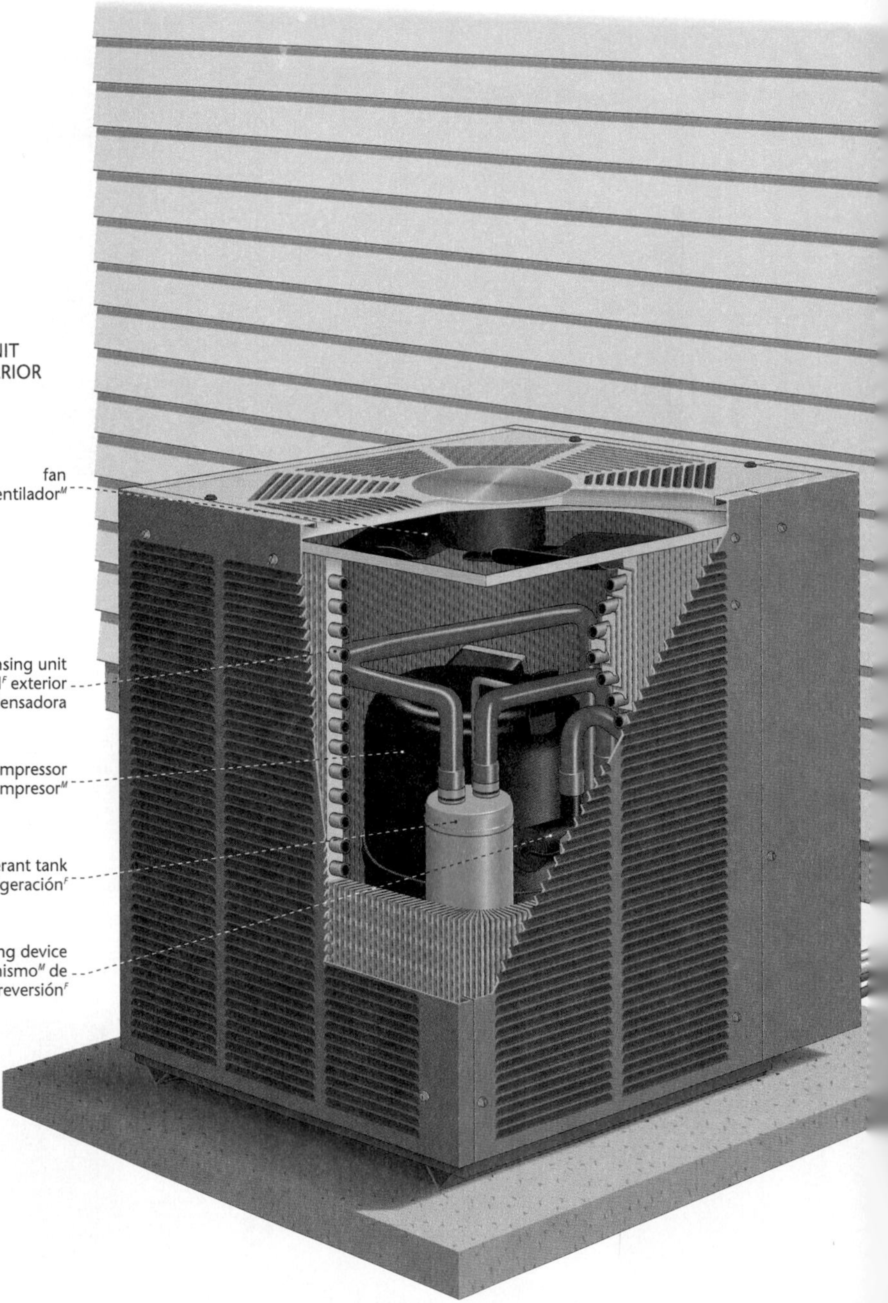

fan
ventilador[M]

outdoor condensing unit
unidad[F] exterior
condensadora

compressor
compresor[M]

refrigerant tank
tanque[M] de refrigeración[F]

reversing device
mecanismo[M] de
reversión[F]

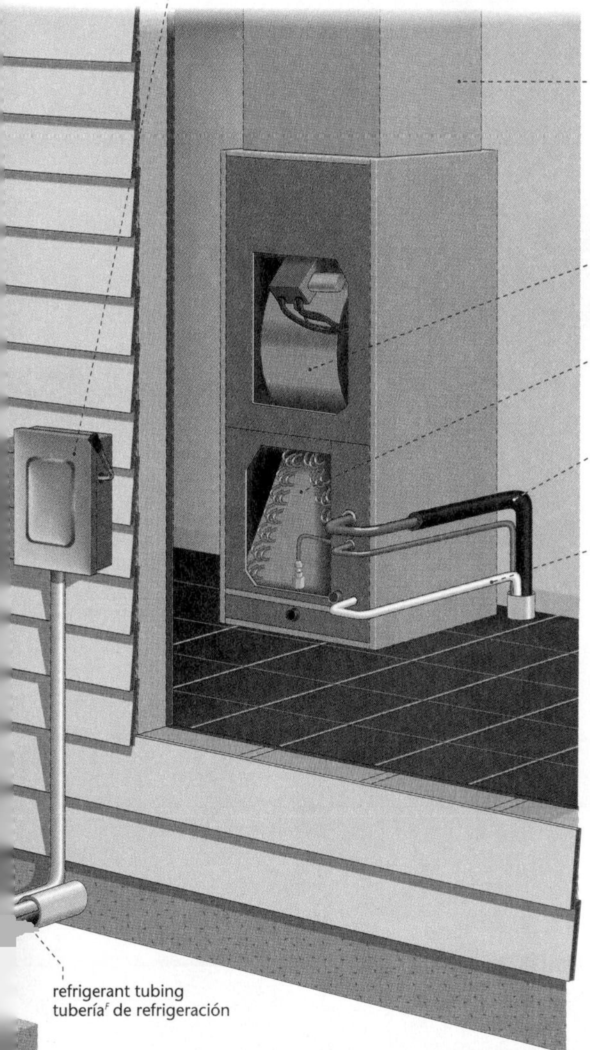

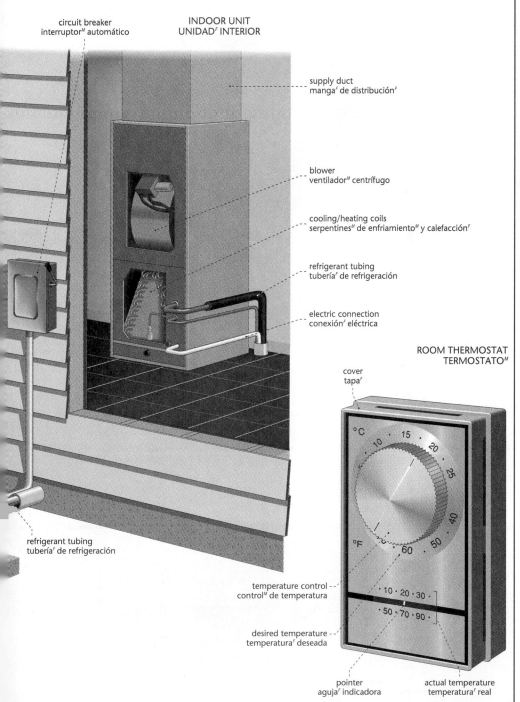

circuit breaker
interruptor^M automático

INDOOR UNIT
UNIDAD^F INTERIOR

supply duct
manga^F de distribución^F

blower
ventilador^M centrífugo

cooling/heating coils
serpentines^M de enfriamiento^M y calefacción^F

refrigerant tubing
tubería^F de refrigeración

electric connection
conexión^F eléctrica

ROOM THERMOSTAT
TERMOSTATO^M

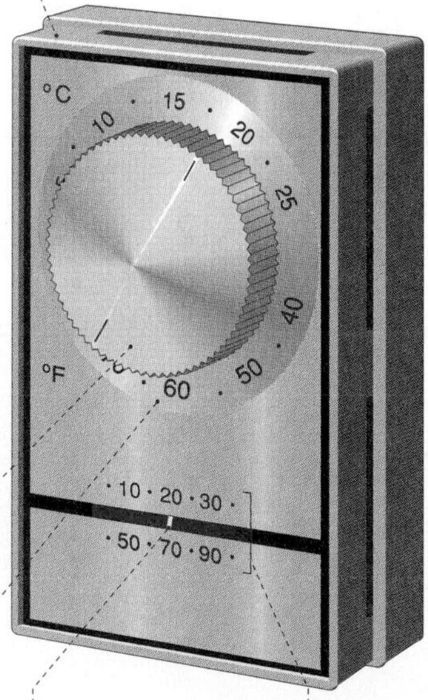

cover
tapa^F

refrigerant tubing
tubería^F de refrigeración

temperature control
control^M de temperatura

desired temperature
temperatura^F deseada

pointer
aguja^F indicadora

actual temperature
temperatura^F real

HOUSE
CASA

AIR CONDITIONING
AIRE^M ACONDICIONADO

CEILING FAN
VENTILADOR^M DE TECHO^M

rod
flecha^F

motor
motor^M

blade
aspa^F

ROOM AIR CONDITIONER
ACONDICIONADOR^M DE AIRE^M

condenser fan
ventilador^M del
condensador^M

condenser coil
serpentín^M del
condensador^M

casing
cubierta^F

fan motor
motor^M del ventilador^M

evaporator blower
ventilador^M del evaporador^M

louver
rejilla^F de ventilación^F

thermostat
termostato^M

fan control
control^M del ventilador^M

function selector
selector^M

control panel
tablero^M de control^M

grille
rejilla^F

evaporator coils
serpentines^M del evaporador^M

blower motor
motor^M del ventilador^M

vent
respiradero^M

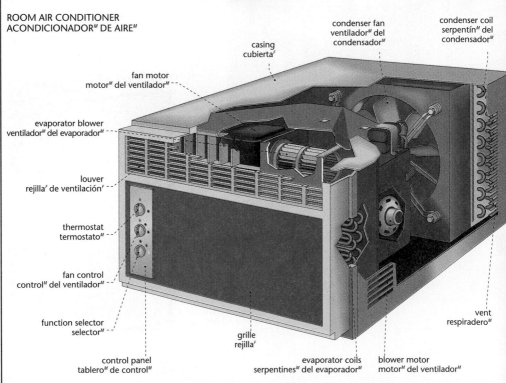

214

PLUMBING SYSTEM
CAÑERÍAS*F*

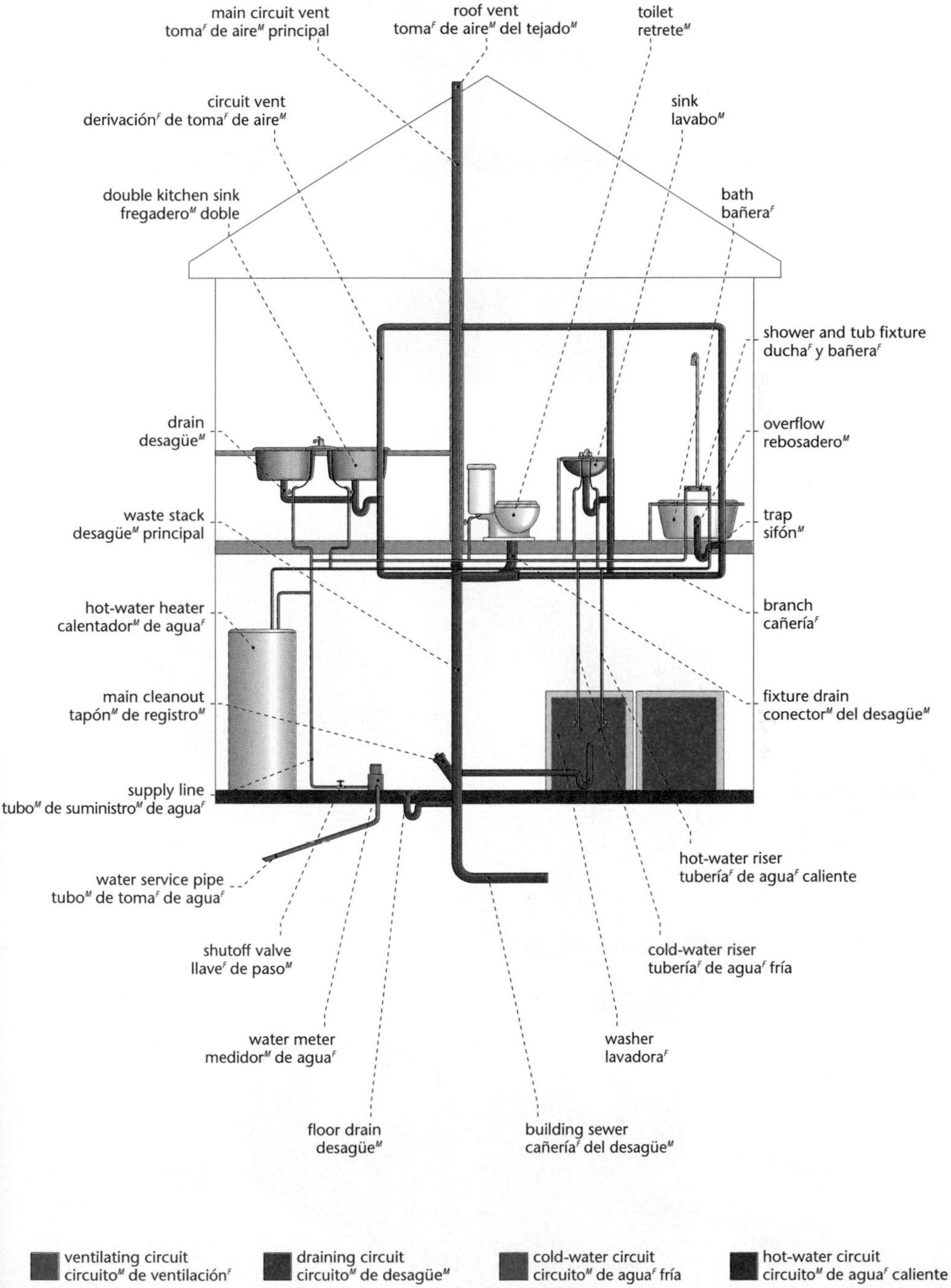

main circuit vent
toma*F* de aire*M* principal

roof vent
toma*F* de aire*M* del tejado*M*

toilet
retrete*M*

circuit vent
derivación*F* de toma*F* de aire*M*

sink
lavabo*M*

double kitchen sink
fregadero*M* doble

bath
bañera*F*

shower and tub fixture
ducha*F* y bañera*F*

drain
desagüe*M*

overflow
rebosadero*M*

waste stack
desagüe*M* principal

trap
sifón*M*

hot-water heater
calentador*M* de agua*F*

branch
cañería*F*

main cleanout
tapón*M* de registro*M*

fixture drain
conector*M* del desagüe*M*

supply line
tubo*M* de suministro*M* de agua*F*

water service pipe
tubo*M* de toma*F* de agua*F*

hot-water riser
tubería*F* de agua*F* caliente

shutoff valve
llave*F* de paso*M*

cold-water riser
tubería*F* de agua*F* fría

water meter
medidor*M* de agua*F*

washer
lavadora*F*

floor drain
desagüe*M*

building sewer
cañería*F* del desagüe*M*

■ ventilating circuit
circuito*M* de ventilación*F*

■ draining circuit
circuito*M* de desagüe*M*

■ cold-water circuit
circuito*M* de agua*F* fría

■ hot-water circuit
circuito*M* de agua*F* caliente

PEDESTAL-TYPE SUMP PUMP
BOMBA^F TIPO^M PEDESTAL^M PARA SUMIDERO^M

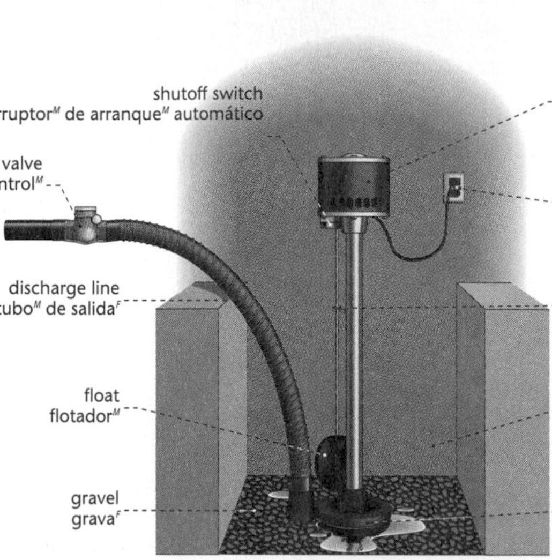

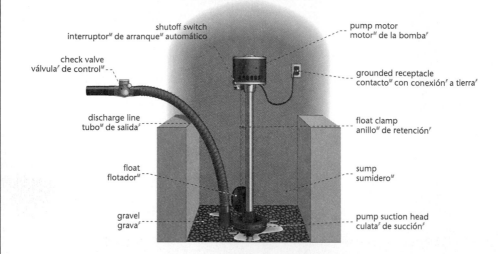

shutoff switch
interruptor^M de arranque^M automático

pump motor
motor^M de la bomba^F

check valve
válvula^F de control^M

grounded receptacle
contacto^M con conexión^F a tierra^F

discharge line
tubo^M de salida^F

float clamp
anillo^M de retención^F

float
flotador^M

sump
sumidero^M

gravel
grava^F

pump suction head
culata^F de succión^F

SEPTIC TANK
FOSA^F SÉPTICA

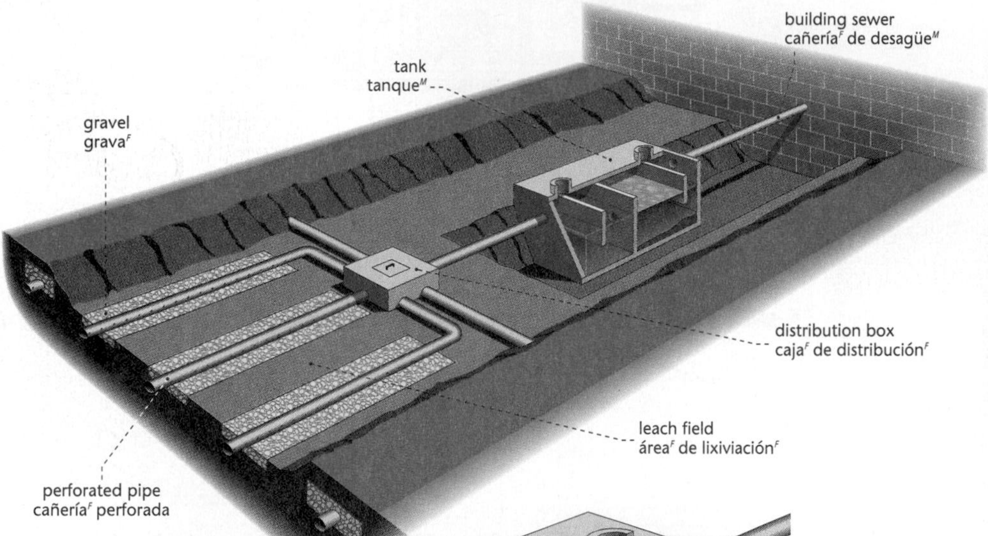

building sewer
cañería^F de desagüe^M

tank
tanque^M

gravel
grava^F

distribution box
caja^F de distribución^F

leach field
área^F de lixiviación^F

perforated pipe
cañería^F perforada

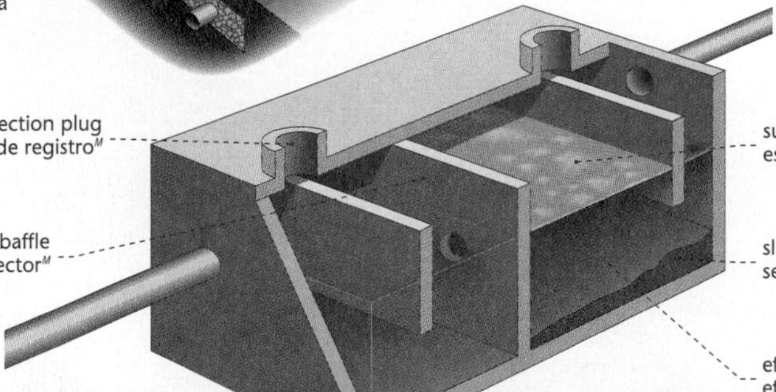

inspection plug
tapón^M de registro^M

surface scum
espuma^F

baffle
deflector^M

sludge
sedimento^M

effluent
efluvio^M

HOUSE
CASA

216

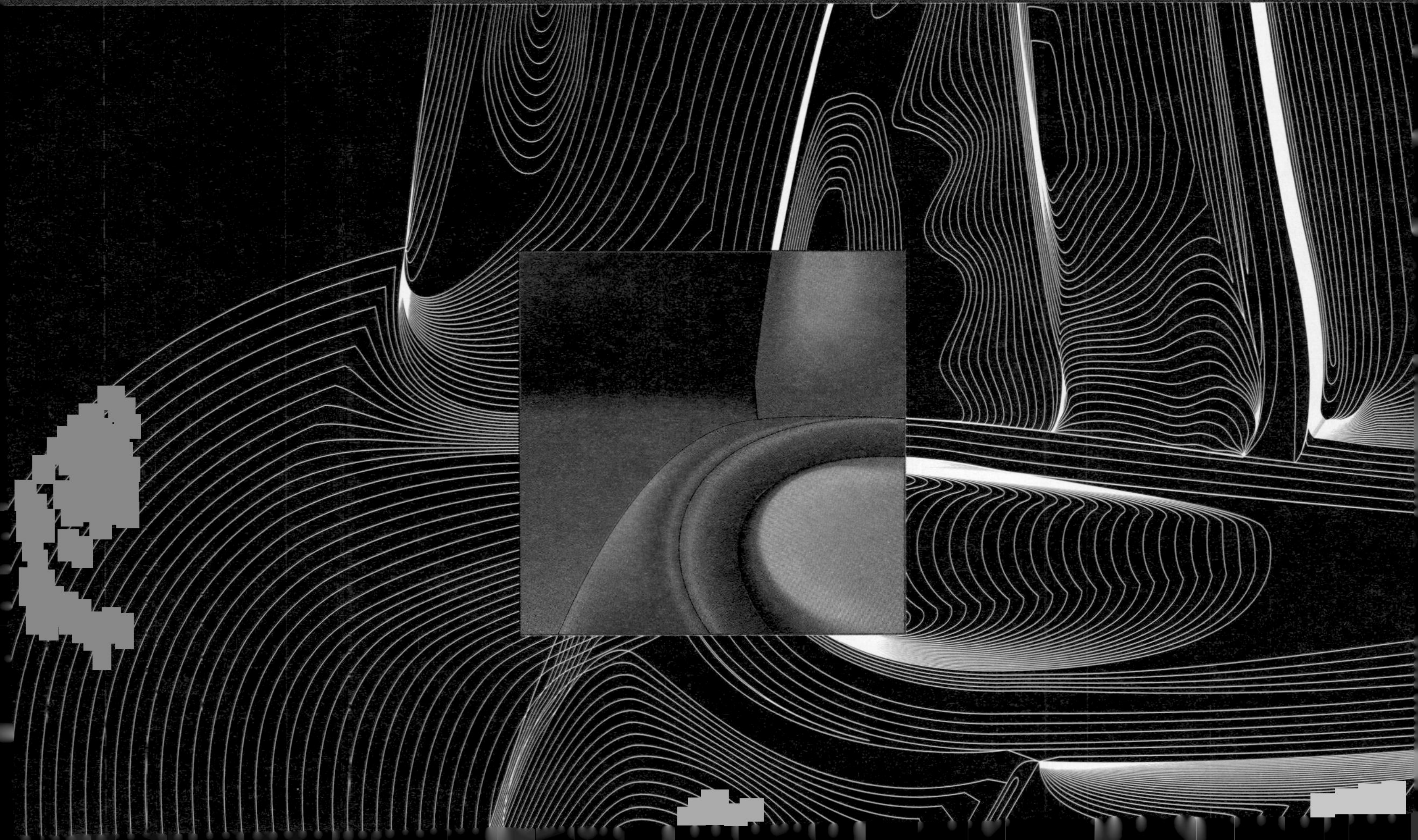

HOUSE FURNITURE • ENSERES DOMÈSTICS

CONTENTS

HOUSE FURNITURE
ENSERES DOMÉSTICOS

TABLE
MESA^F

GATE-LEG TABLE
MESA^F DE HOJAS^F ABATIBLES

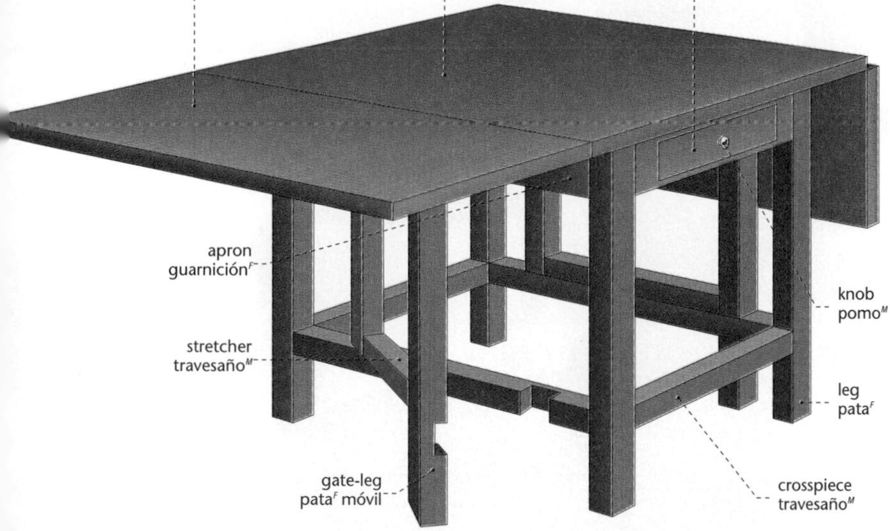

drop-leaf
extensión^F plegable

top
tablero^M

drawer
cajón^M

apron
guarnición^F

knob
pomo^M

stretcher
travesaño^M

leg
pata^F

gate-leg
pata^F móvil

crosspiece
travesaño^M

TYPES OF TABLES
TIPOS^M DE MESAS^F

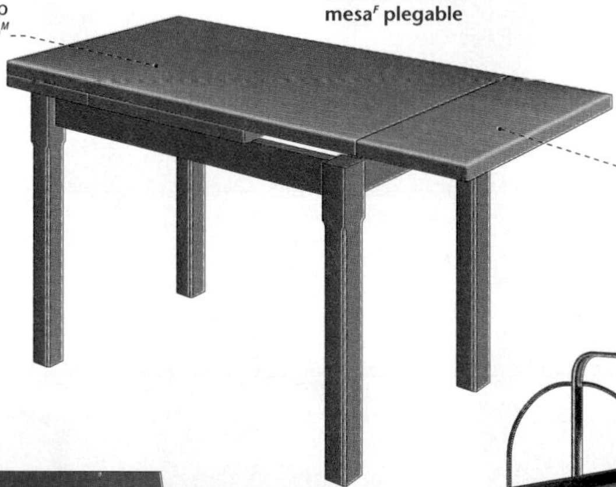

extension table
mesa^F plegable

top
tablero^M

extension
extensión^F

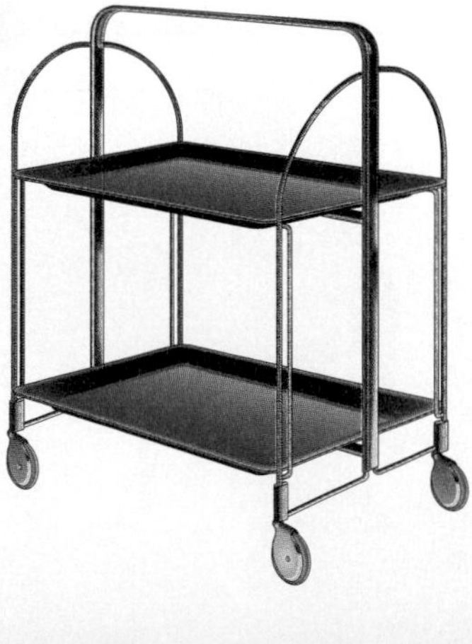

serving cart
mesita^F de servicio^M

nest of tables
juego^M de mesas^F

219

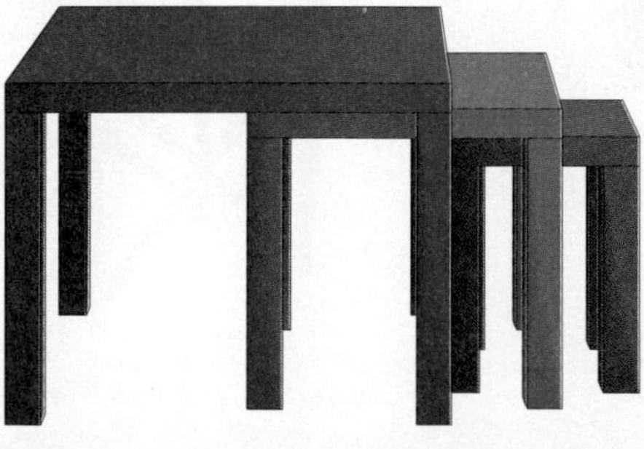

ARMCHAIR
SILLA^F DE BRAZOS^M

PARTS
PARTES^F

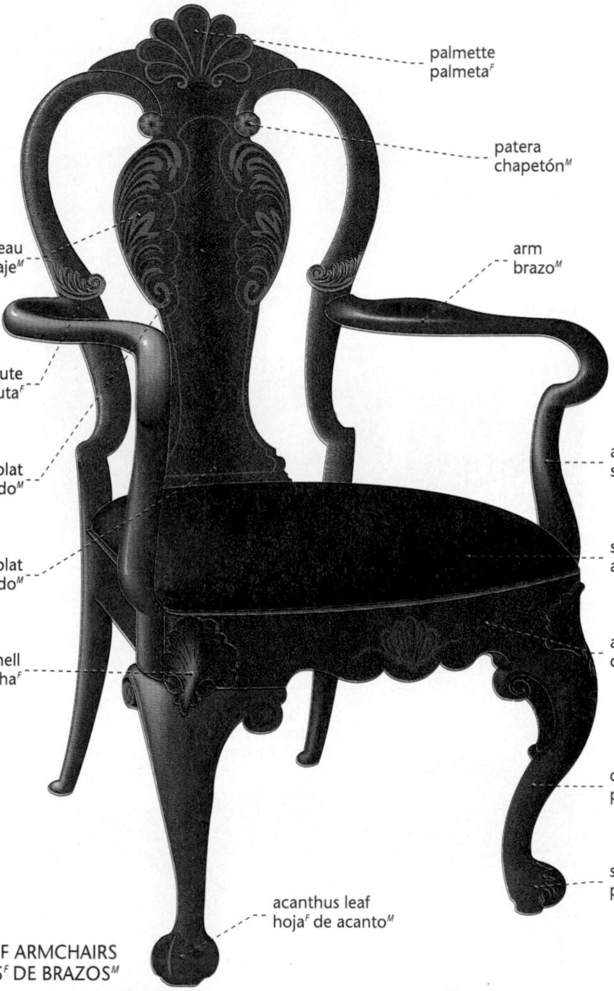

palmette
palmeta^F

patera
chapetón^M

rinceau
follaje^M

arm
brazo^M

volute
voluta^F

arm stump
soporte^M del brazo^M

splat
respaldo^M

seat
asiento^M

base of splat
base^F del respaldo^M

apron
cortina^F

cockleshell
concha^F

cabriole leg
pata^F curvada

scroll foot
pie^M de voluta^F

acanthus leaf
hoja^F de acanto^M

PRINCIPAL TYPES OF ARMCHAIRS
PRINCIPALES SILLAS^F DE BRAZOS^M

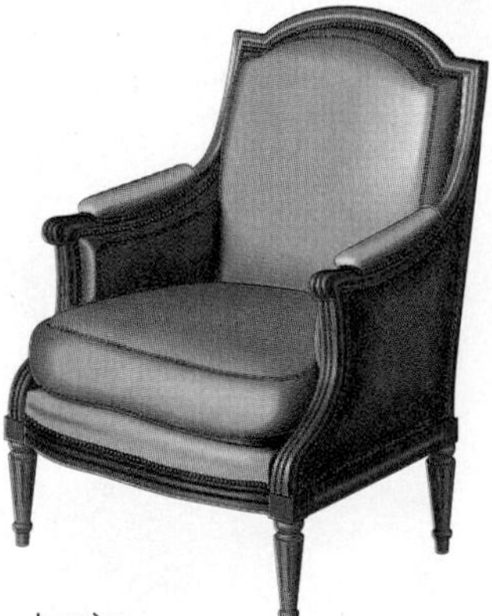

bergère
silla^F poltrona

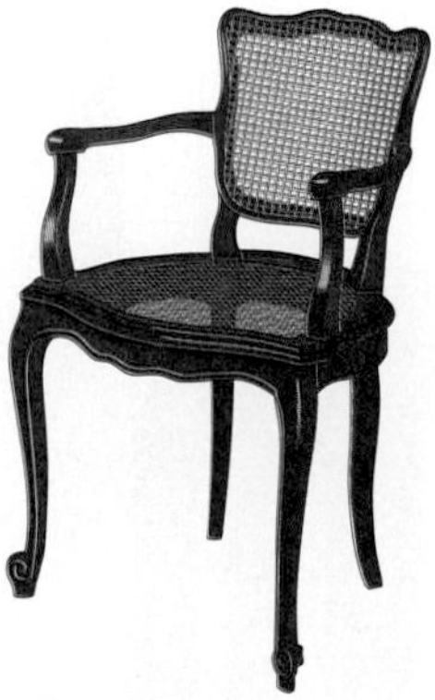

cabriolet
silla^F cabriolé

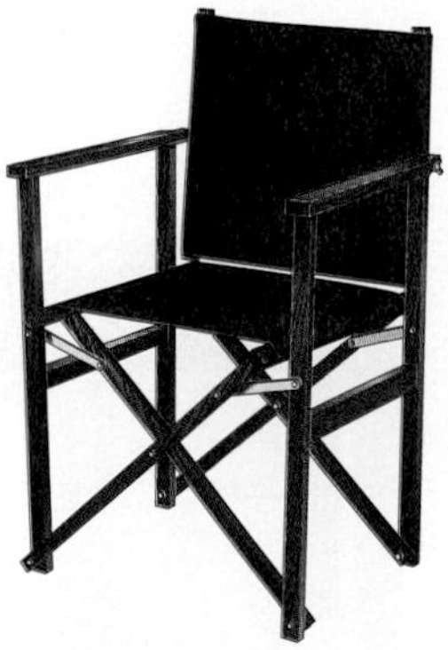

director's chair
silla^F plegable de lona^F

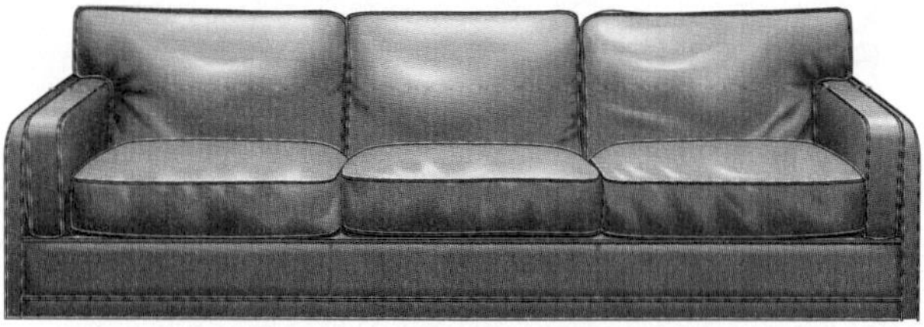

sofa
sofá^F

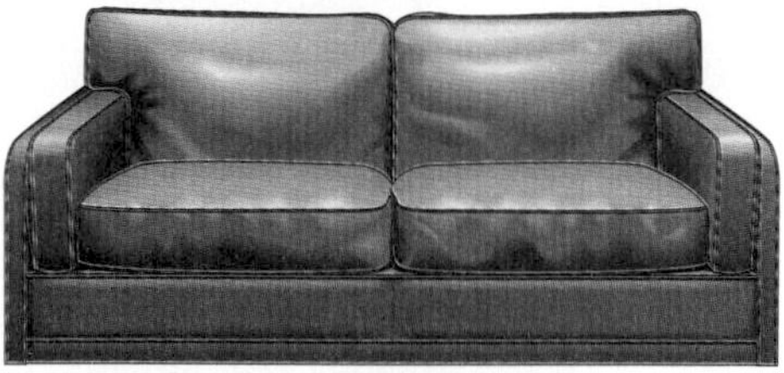

love seat
confidente^M

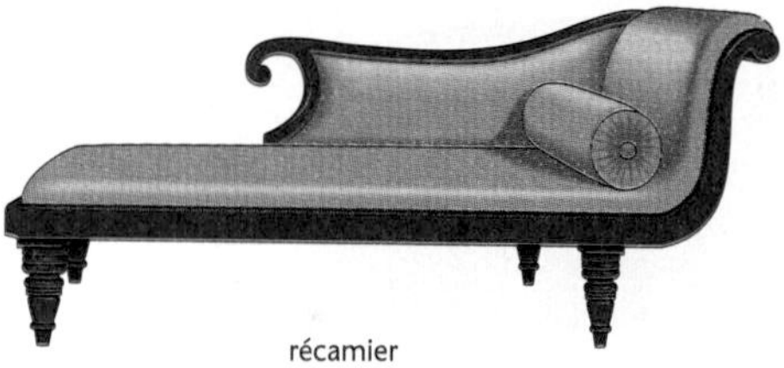

récamier
sofá^M tipo^M imperio

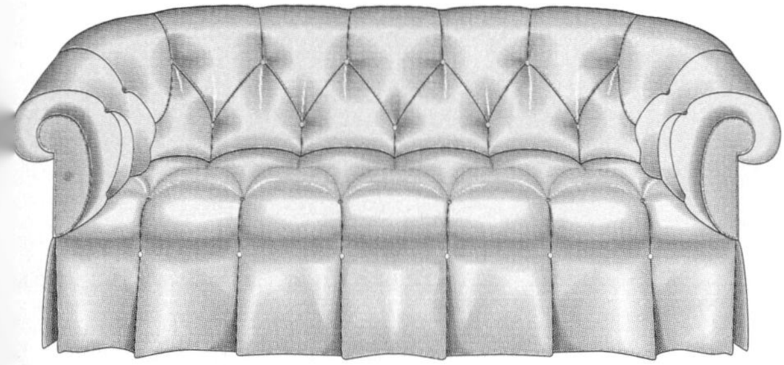

chesterfield
chesterfield^M

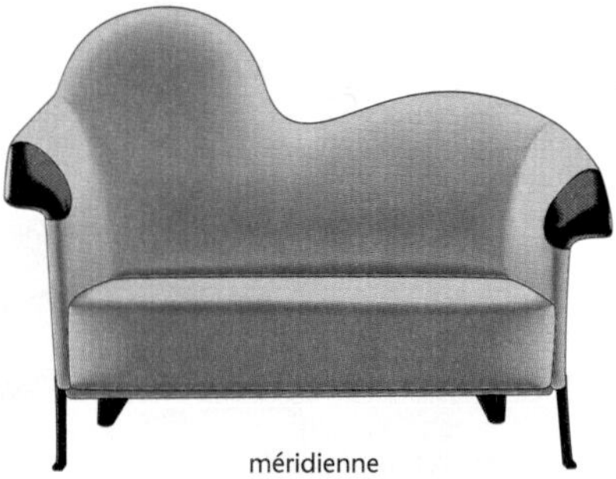

méridienne
meridiana^F

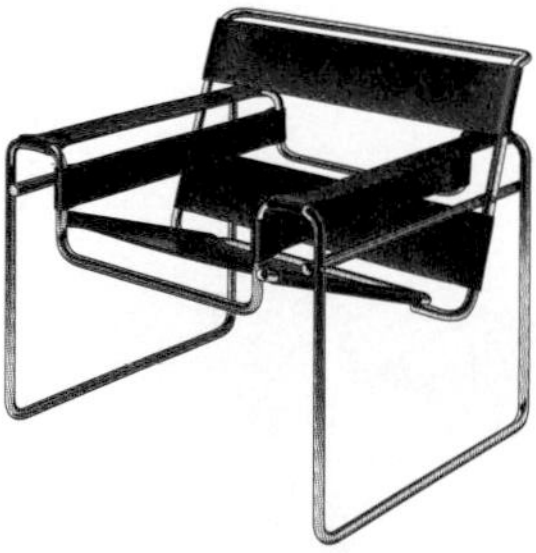

Wassily chair
silla^F Wassily

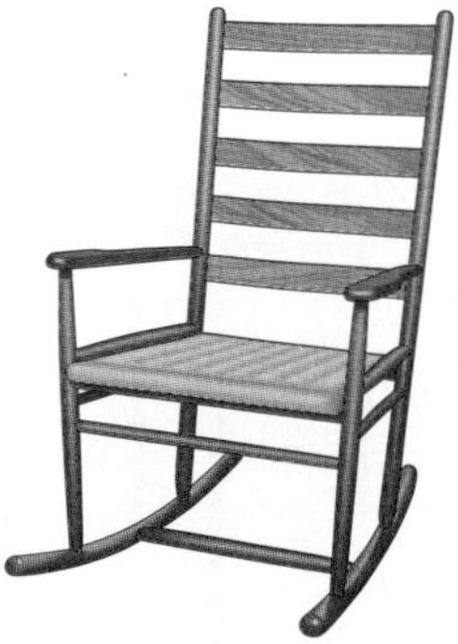

rocking chair
mecedora^F

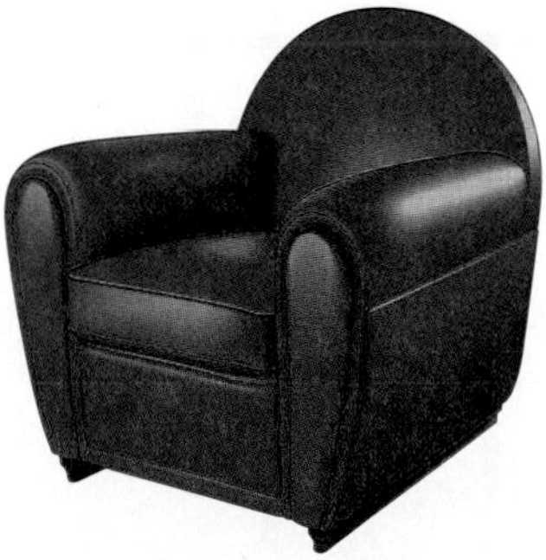

club chair
butaca^F

HOUSE FURNITURE
ENSERES DOMÉSTICOS

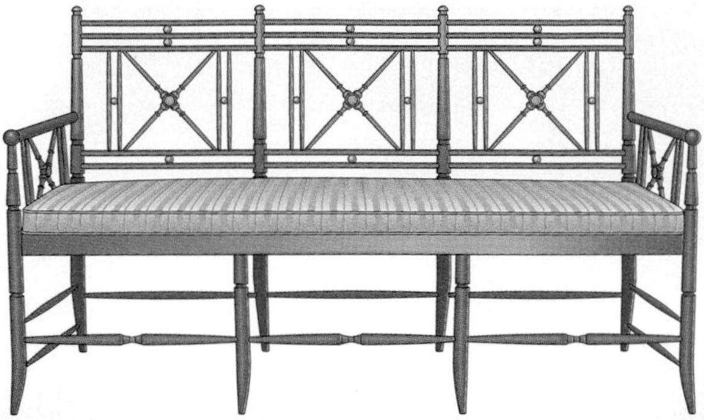

banquette
banco^M

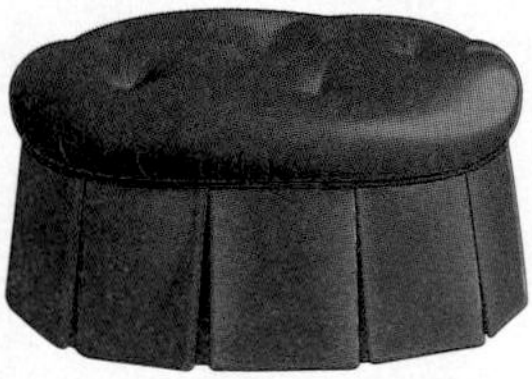

ottoman
taburete^M

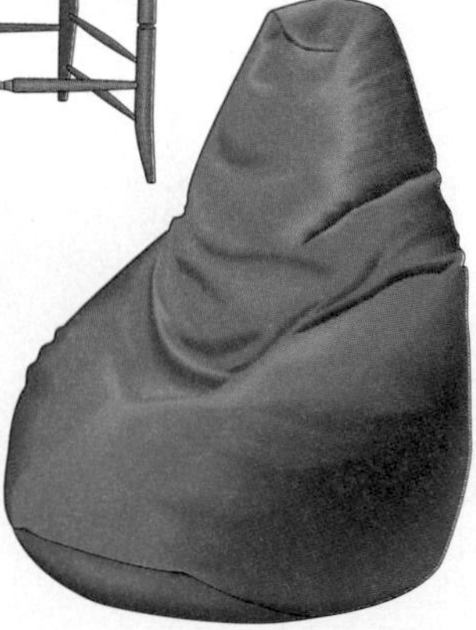

bean bag chair
silla^F cojín^M

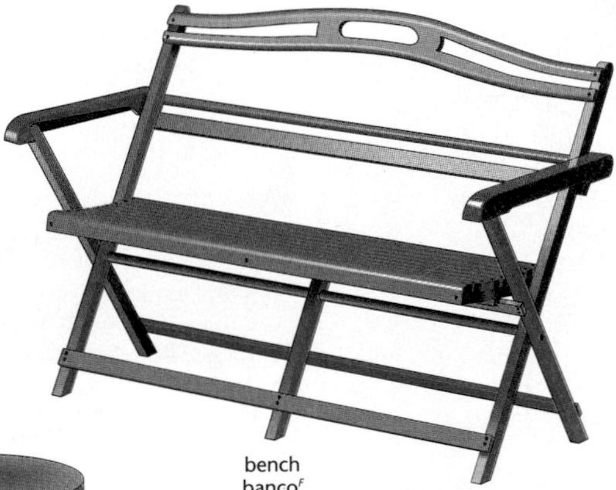

bench
banco^F

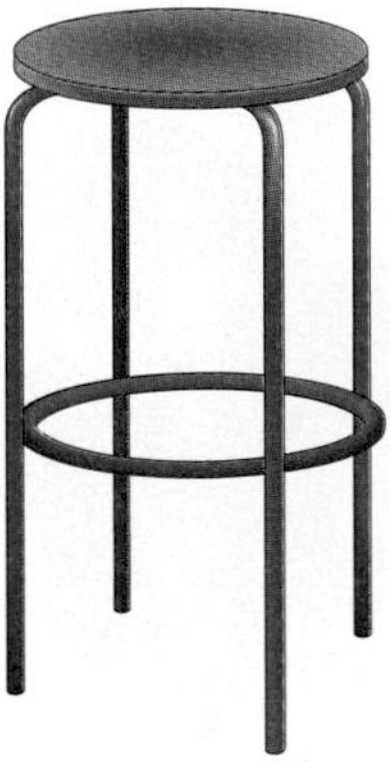

bar stool
taburete^M

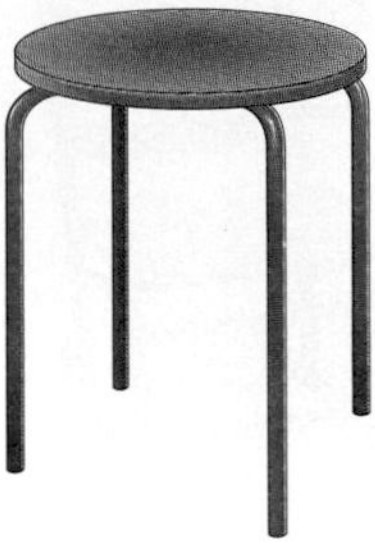

footstool
escabel^M

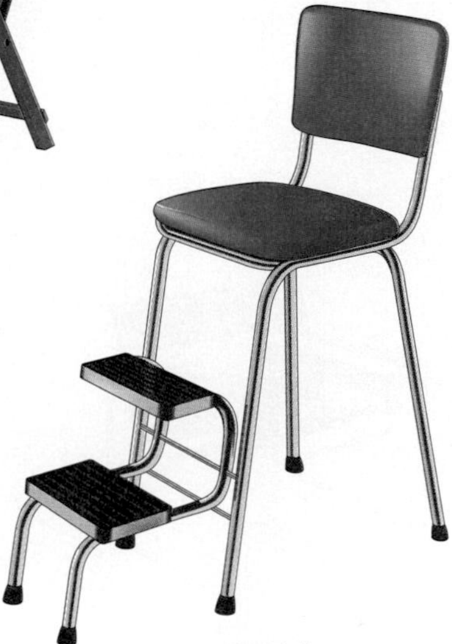

step chair
banco^M escalera^F

SIDE CHAIR
SILLA^F SIN BRAZOS^M

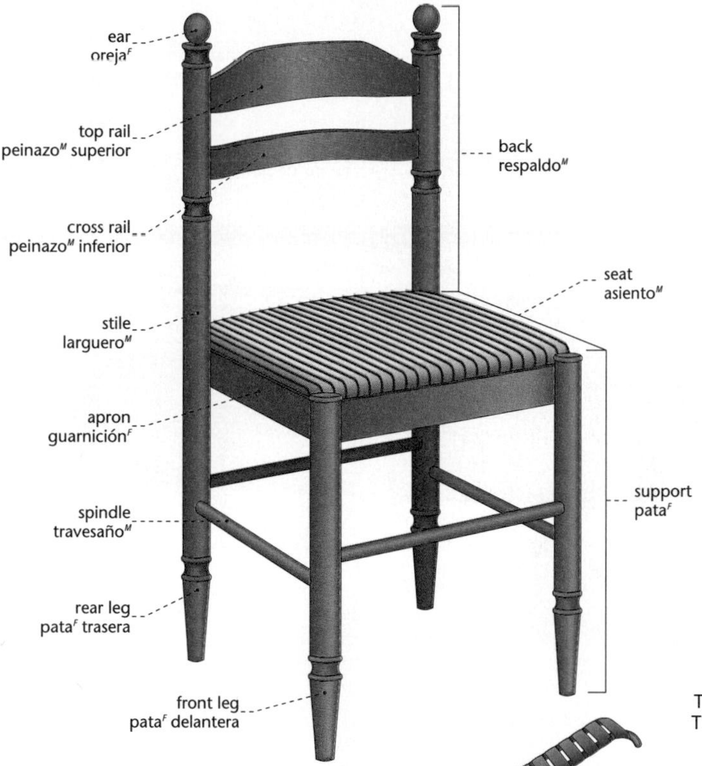

ear
oreja^F

top rail
peinazo^M superior

cross rail
peinazo^M inferior

stile
larguero^M

apron
guarnición^F

spindle
travesaño^M

rear leg
pata^F trasera

front leg
pata^F delantera

back
respaldo^M

seat
asiento^M

support
pata^F

TYPES OF CHAIRS
TIPOS^M DE SILLAS^F

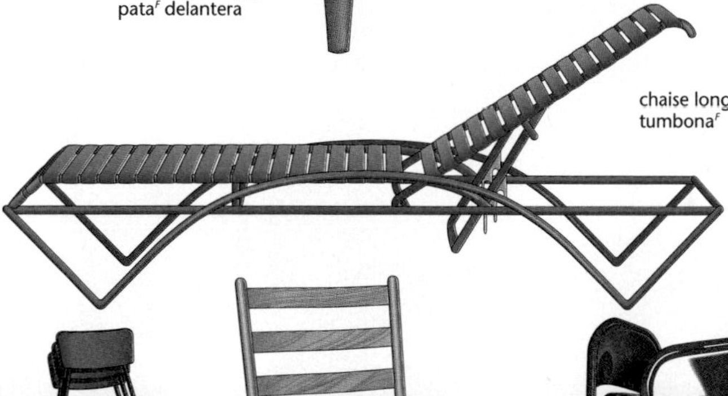

chaise longue
tumbona^F

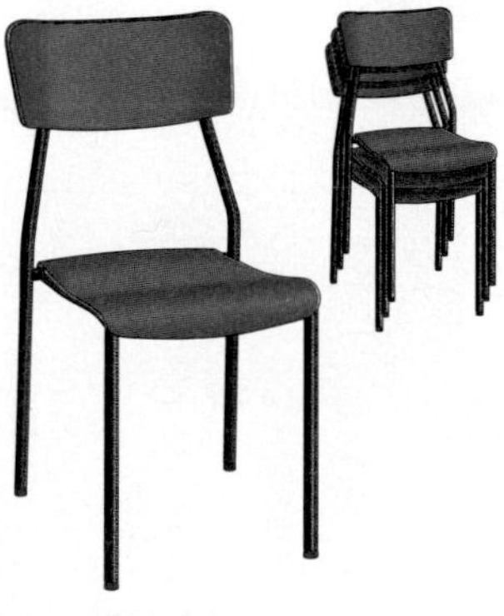

stacking chairs
sillas^F apilables

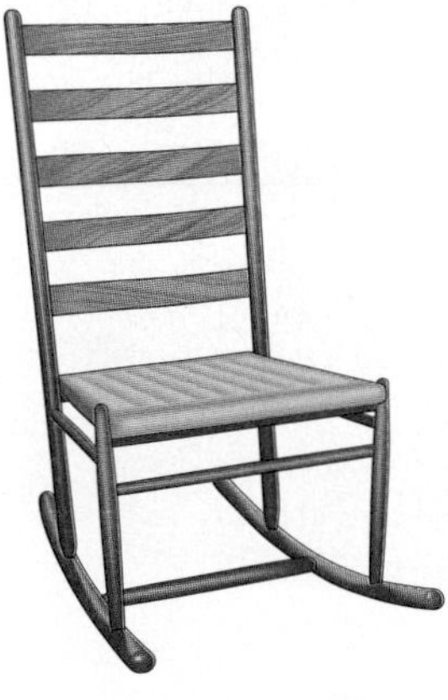

rocking chair
mecedora^F

folding chair
silla^F plegable

HOUSE FURNITURE
ENSERES DOMÉSTICOS

223

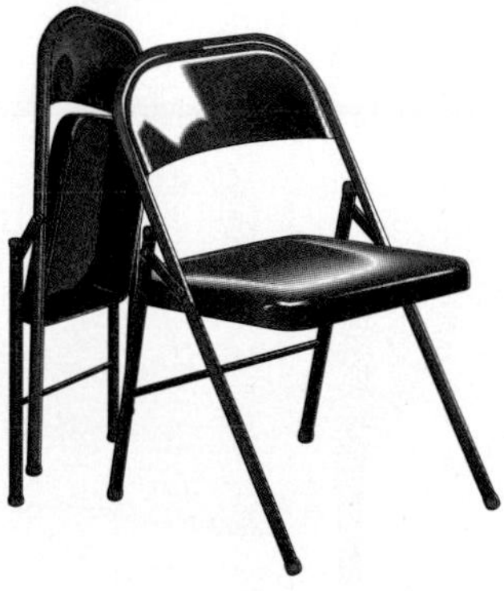

BED
CAMA^F

PARTS
PARTES^F

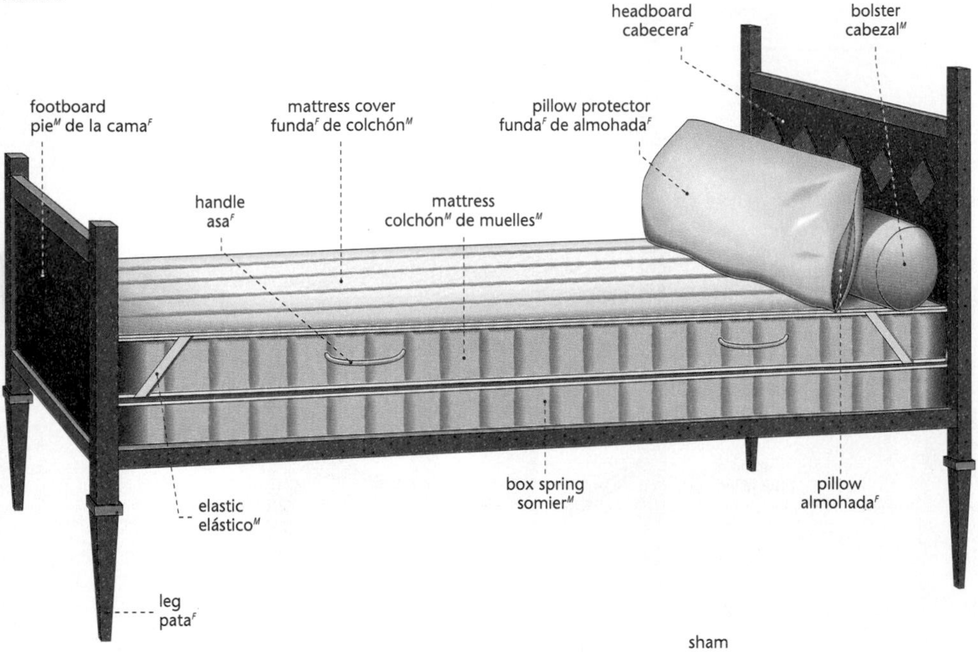

headboard
cabecera^F

bolster
cabezal^M

footboard
pie^M de la cama^F

mattress cover
funda^F de colchón^M

pillow protector
funda^F de almohada^F

handle
asa^F

mattress
colchón^M de muelles^M

elastic
elástico^M

box spring
somier^M

pillow
almohada^F

leg
pata^F

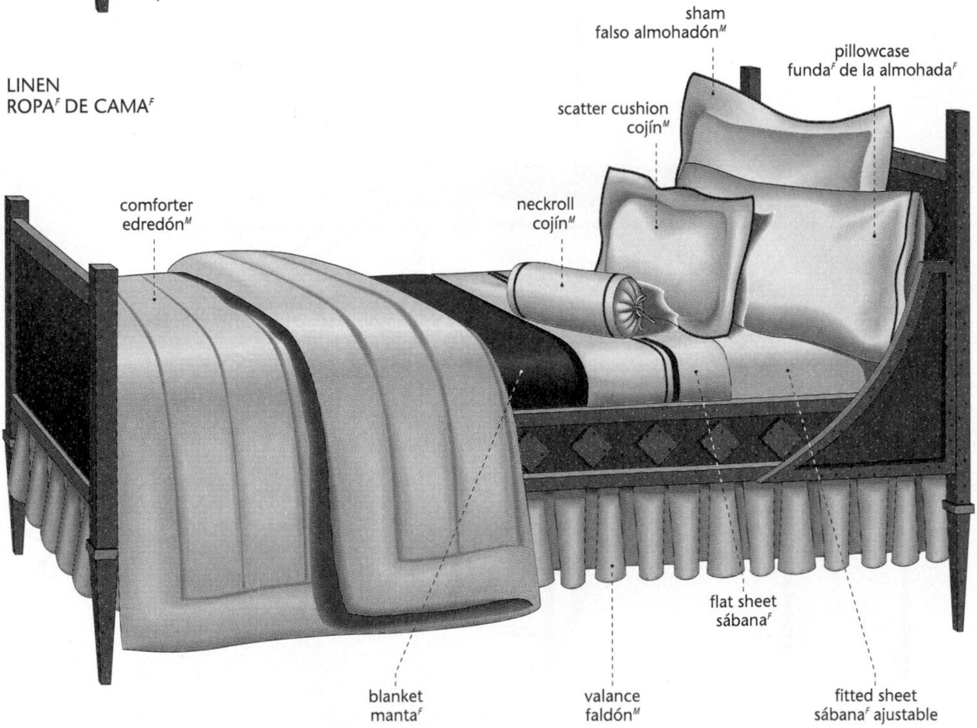

sham
falso almohadón^M

pillowcase
funda^F de la almohada^F

scatter cushion
cojín^M

LINEN
ROPA^F DE CAMA^F

comforter
edredón^M

neckroll
cojín^M

blanket
manta^F

valance
faldón^M

flat sheet
sábana^F

fitted sheet
sábana^F ajustable

ARMOIRE
ARMARIO^M

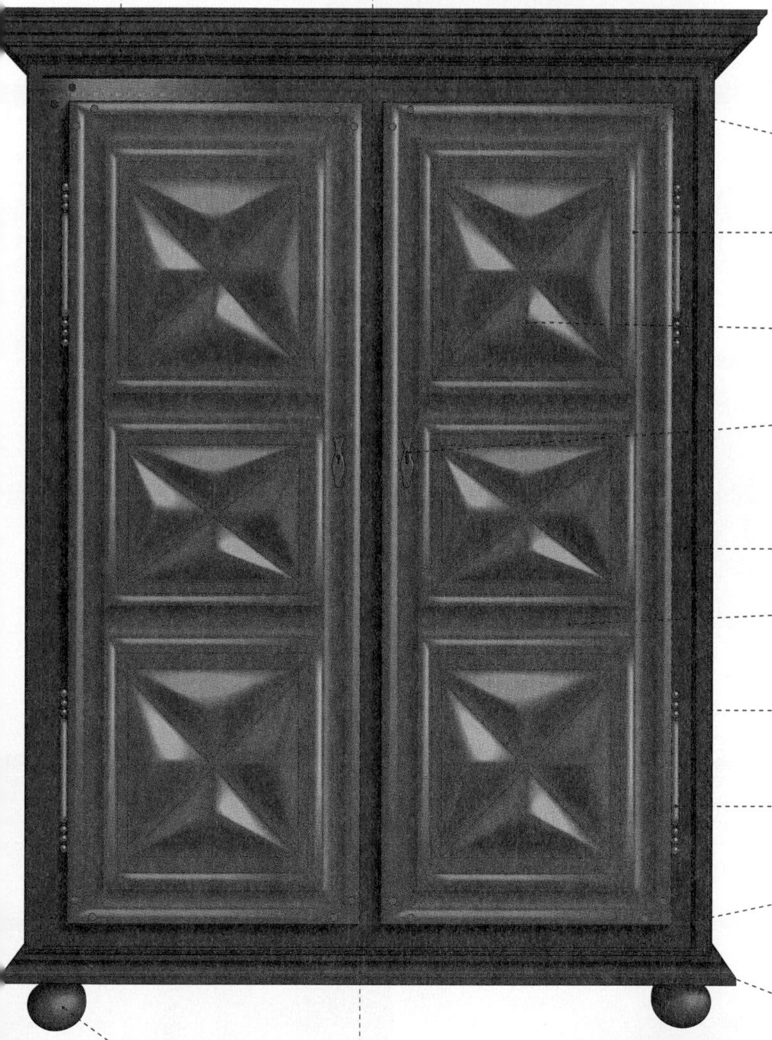

frieze
friso^M

center post
montante^M central

cornice
cornisa^F

top rail
peinazo^M superior

door panel
entrepaño^M

diamond point
punta^F de diamante^M

lock
cerradura^F

hanging stile
larguero^M de la bisagra^F

rail
peinazo^M

frame stile
larguero^M del marco^M

hinge
bisagra^F

peg
espiga^F

bottom rail
peinazo^M inferior

foot
pata^F

bracket base
rodapié^M

frame
armazón^M

door
puerta^F

HOUSE FURNITURE
ENSERES DOMÉSTICOS

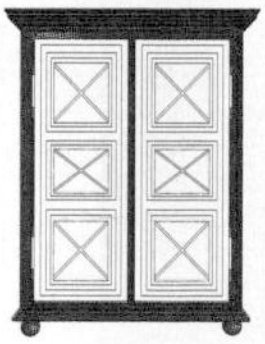

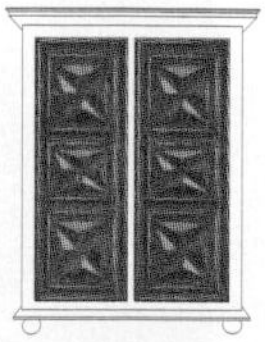

HOUSE FURNITURE
ENSERES DOMÉSTICOS

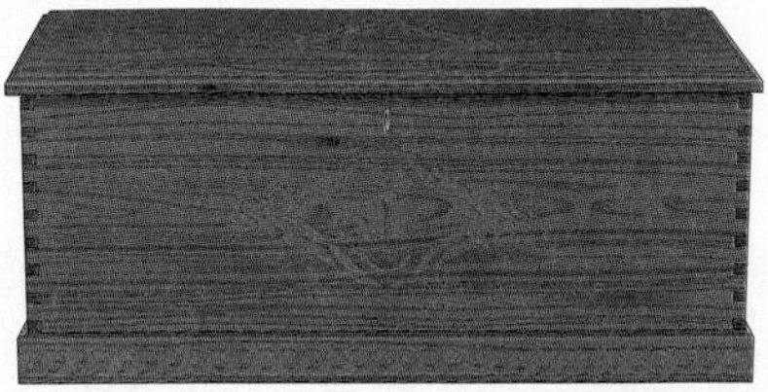

linen chest
baúl^M

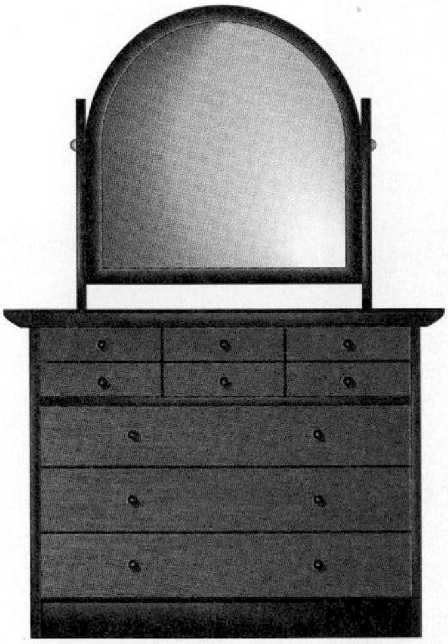

dresser
tocador^M

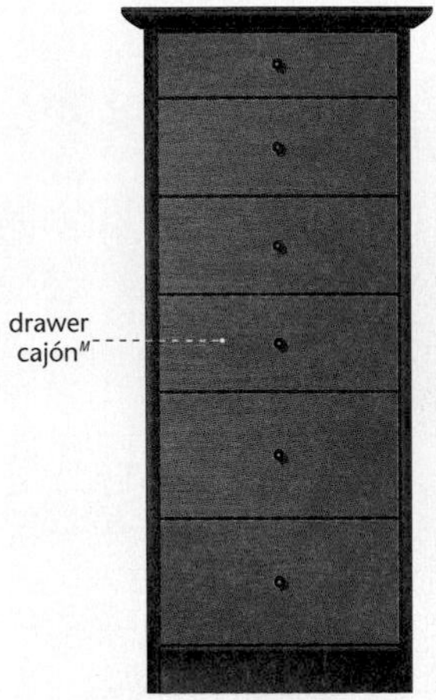

drawer
cajón^M

chiffonier
chifonier^M

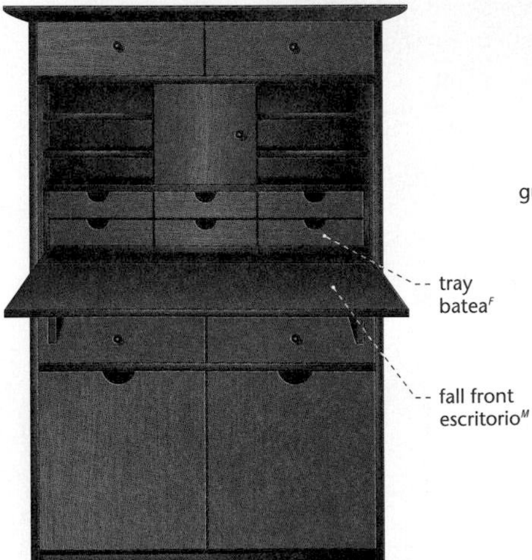

tray
batea^F

fall front
escritorio^M

secretary
bufete^M

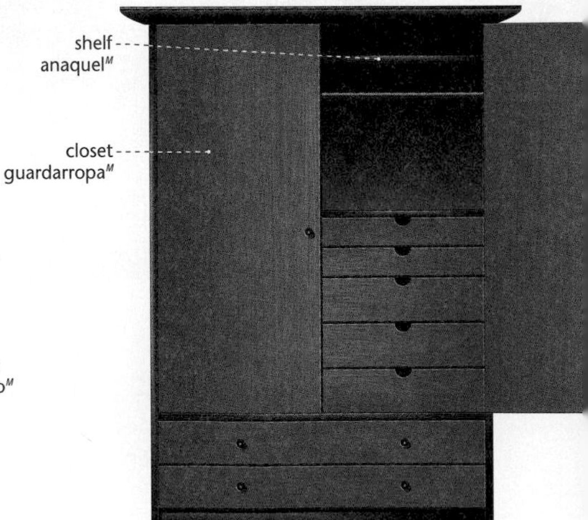

shelf
anaquel^M

closet
guardarropa^M

wardrobe
ropero^M

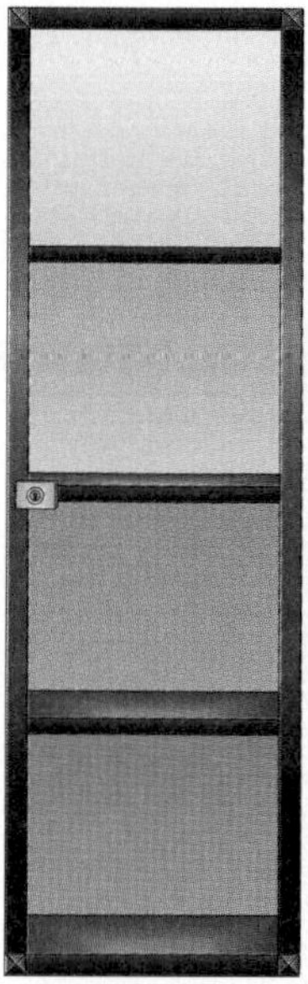

display cabinet
vitrina^F

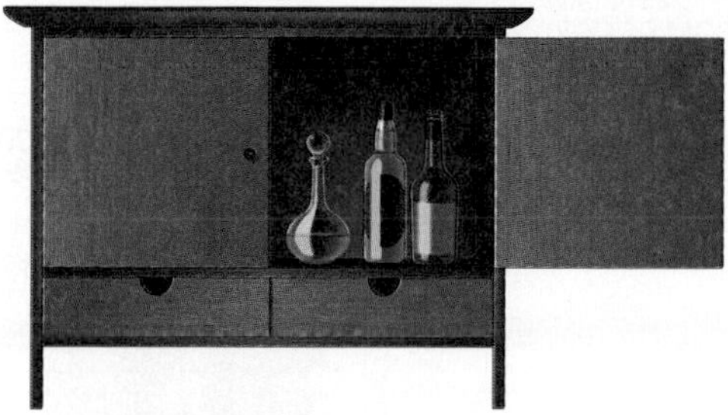

cocktail cabinet
mueble^M bar^M

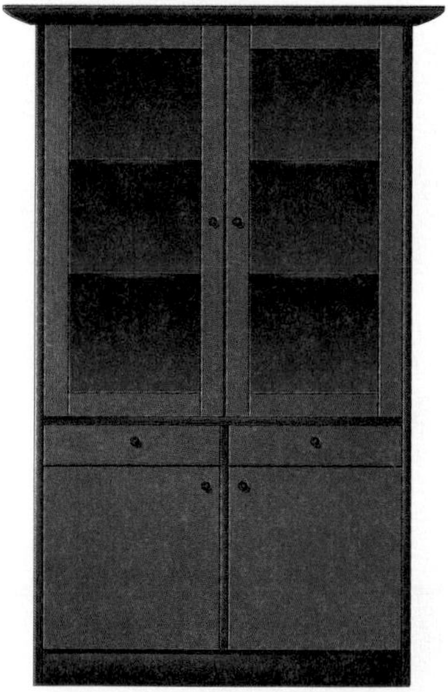

glass-fronted display cabinet
armario^M de vajilla^F

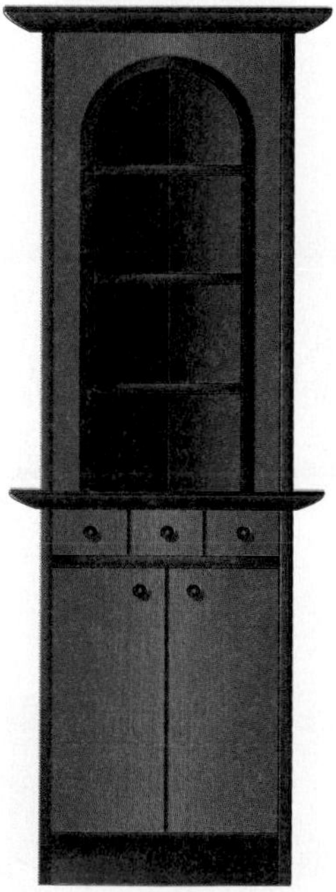

corner cupboard
rinconera^F

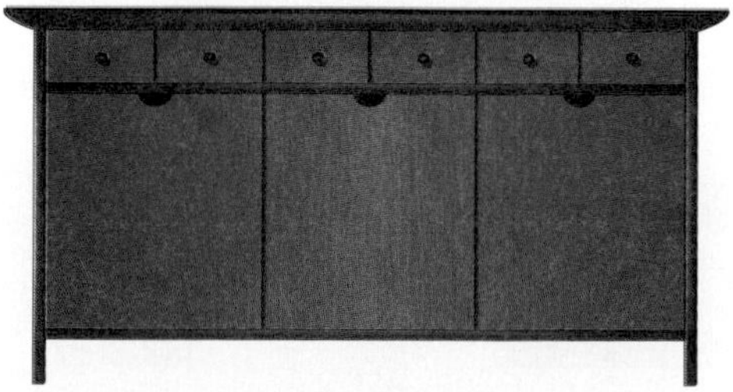

buffet
aparador^M

TYPES OF CURTAINS
TIPOS*M* DE CORTINAS*F*

GLASS CURTAIN
CORTINA*F* DE VENTANA*F*

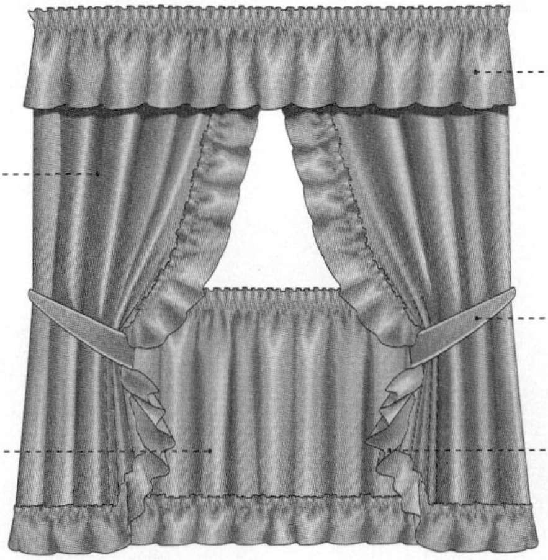

valance
doselera*F*

cottage curtain
visillos*M* recogidos

tieback
lazo*M*

café curtain
visillo*M*

ruffle
volante*M*

ATTACHED CURTAIN
CORTINA*F* SUJETA DE DOBLE BARRA*F*

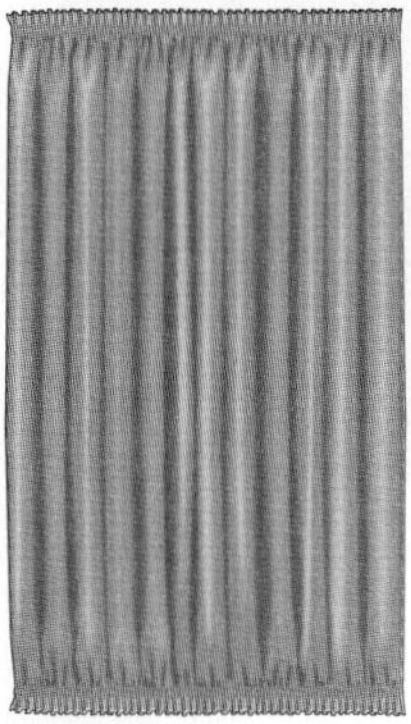

LOOSE CURTAIN
CORTINA*F* SUELTA CORREDIZA

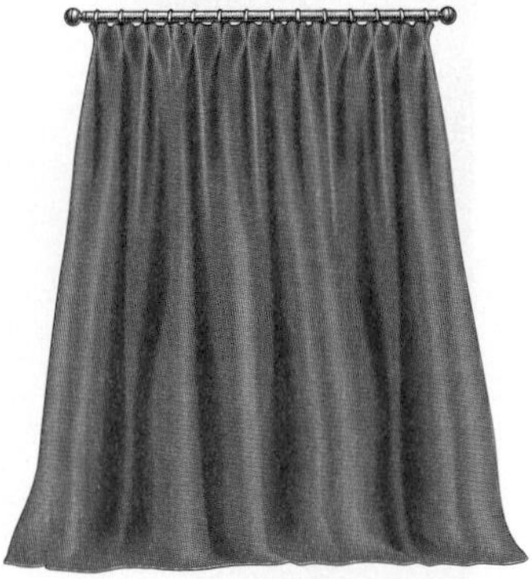

TYPES OF PLEATS
TIPOS*M* DE CENEFAS*F*

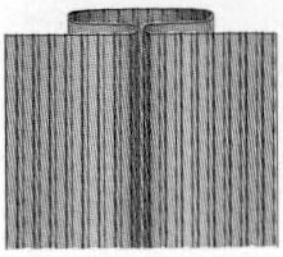

box pleat
pliegue*M* de cajón*M*

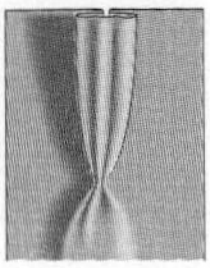

pinch pleat
pliegue*M* de pinza*F*

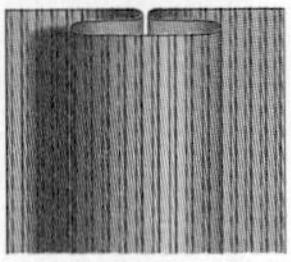

inverted pleat
pliegue*M* de cajón*M* invertido

CURTAIN
CORTINA^F

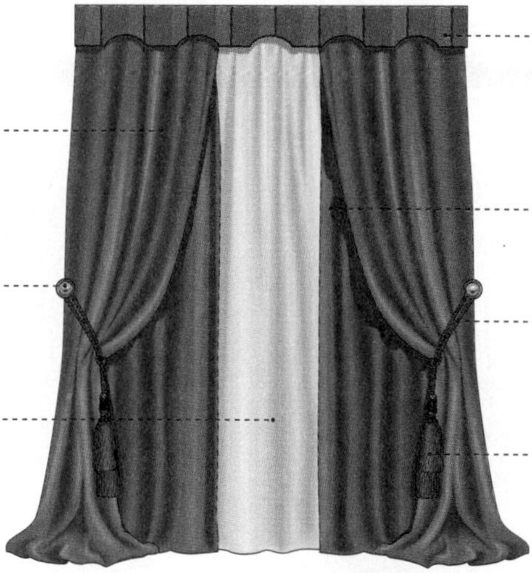

cornice
dosel^M

overdrapery
sobrecortina^F

draw drapery
cortinas^F corredizas

holdback
anilla^F del cordón^M

cord tieback
cordón^M

sheer curtain
visillos^M sencillos

tassel
borla^F

BALLOON CURTAIN
CORTINA^F ABOMBADA

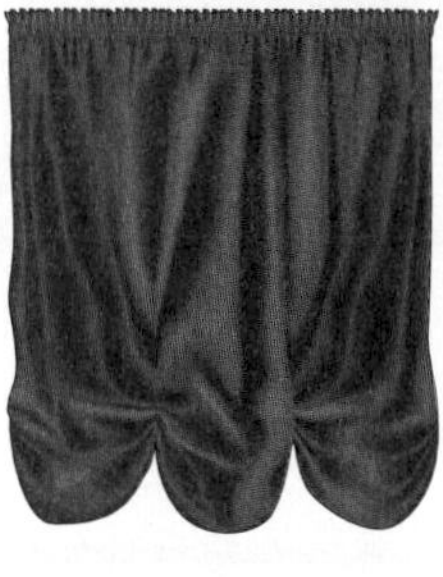

CRISSCROSS CURTAINS
CORTINAS^F CRUZADAS

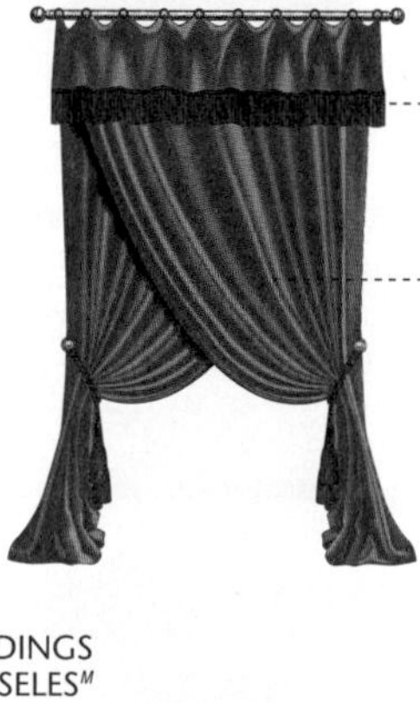

fringe trimming
cenefa^F con flecos^M

panel
cortina^F

TYPES OF HEADINGS
TIPOS^M DE DOSELES^M

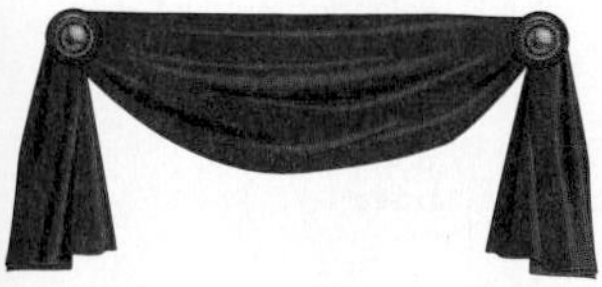

draped swag
festón^M colgado

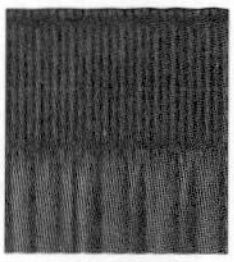

pencil pleat heading
dosel^M plisado de canotillo^M

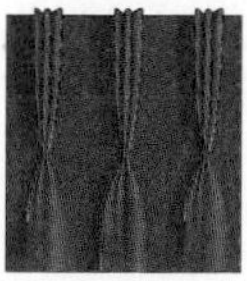

pleated heading
dosel^M plisado

shirred heading
dosel^M fruncido

229

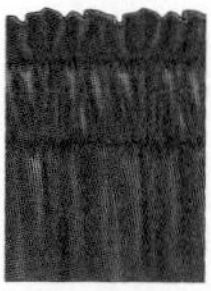

HOUSE FURNITURE
ENSERES DOMÉSTICOS

CURTAIN POLE
PALO^M DE CORTINA^F

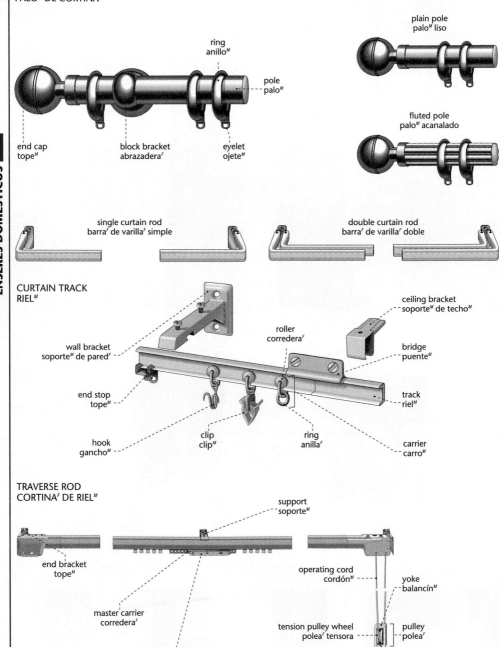

plain pole
palo^M liso

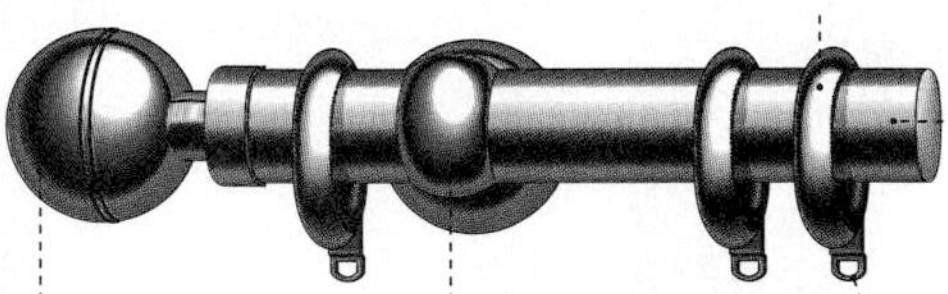

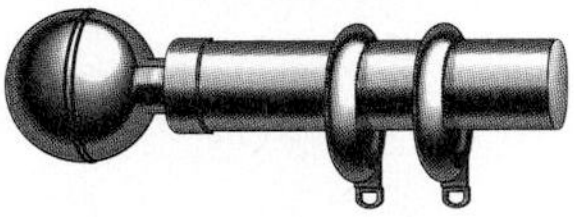

fluted pole
palo^M acanalado

ring
anillo^M

pole
palo^M

end cap
tope^M

block bracket
abrazadera^F

eyelet
ojete^M

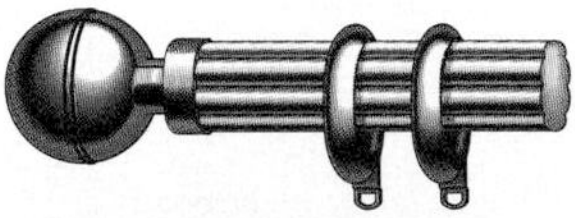

single curtain rod
barra^F de varilla^F simple

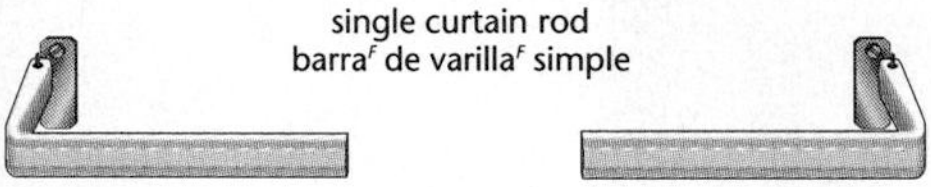

double curtain rod
barra^F de varilla^F doble

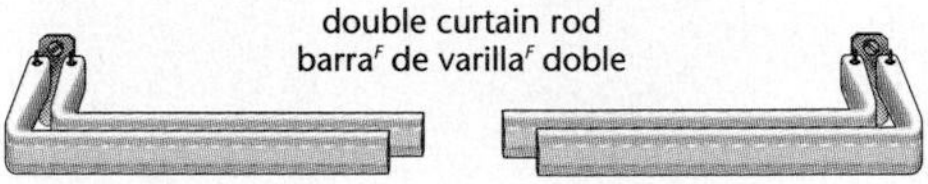

CURTAIN TRACK
RIEL^M

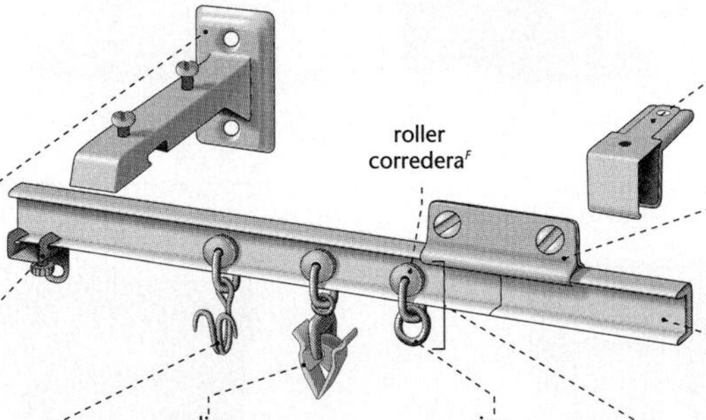

ceiling bracket
soporte^M de techo^M

roller
corredera^F

wall bracket
soporte^M de pared^F

bridge
puente^M

end stop
tope^M

track
riel^M

hook
gancho^M

clip
clip^M

ring
anilla^F

carrier
carro^M

TRAVERSE ROD
CORTINA^F DE RIEL^M

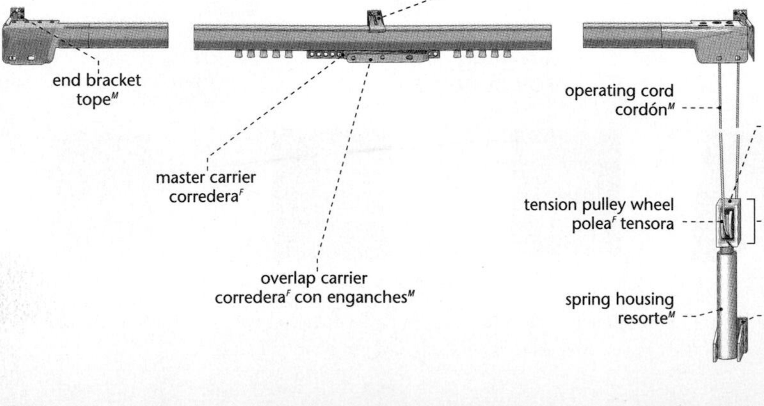

support
soporte^M

end bracket
tope^M

operating cord
cordón^M

yoke
balancín^M

master carrier
corredera^F

tension pulley wheel
polea^F tensora

pulley
polea^F

overlap carrier
corredera^F con enganches^M

spring housing
resorte^M

fastening device
sujeción^F

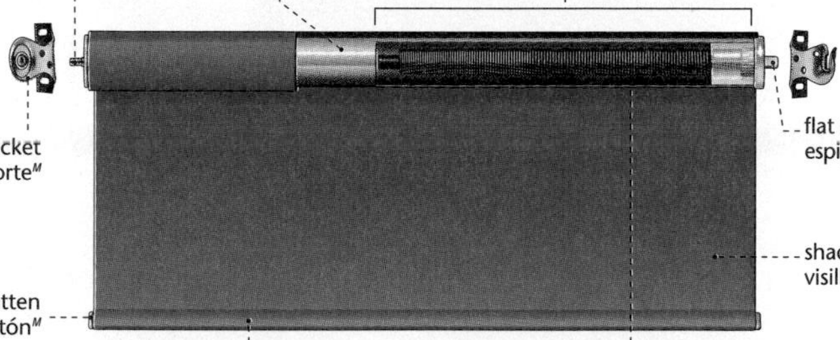

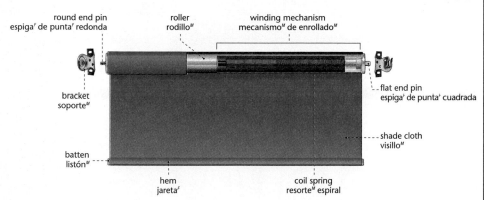

round end pin
espiga*f* de punta*f* redonda

roller
rodillo*M*

winding mechanism
mecanismo*M* de enrollado*M*

bracket
soporte*M*

flat end pin
espiga*f* de punta*f* cuadrada

shade cloth
visillo*M*

batten
listón*M*

hem
jareta*f*

coil spring
resorte*M* espiral

VENETIAN BLIND
PERSIANA*f* VENECIANA

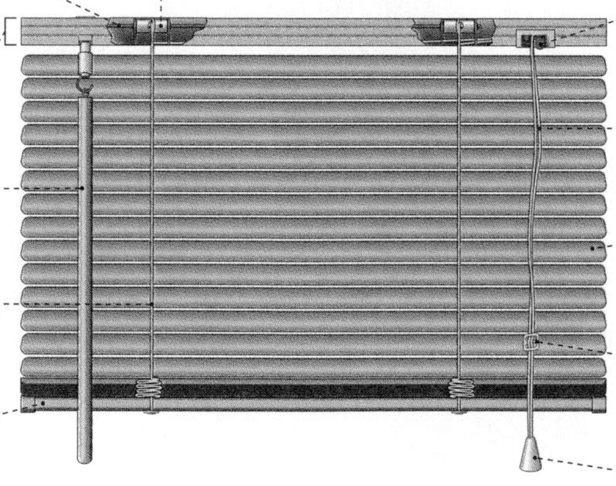

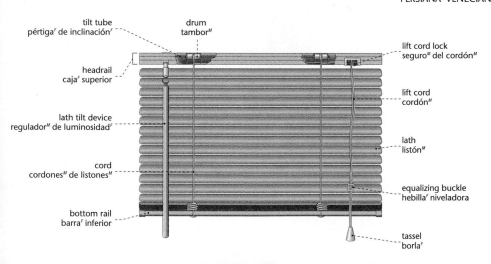

tilt tube
pértiga*f* de inclinación*f*

drum
tambor*M*

lift cord lock
seguro*M* del cordón*M*

headrail
caja*f* superior

lift cord
cordón*M*

lath tilt device
regulador*M* de luminosidad*f*

lath
listón*M*

cord
cordones*M* de listones*M*

equalizing buckle
hebilla*f* niveladora

bottom rail
barra*f* inferior

tassel
borla*f*

roll-up blind
persiana*f* enrollable

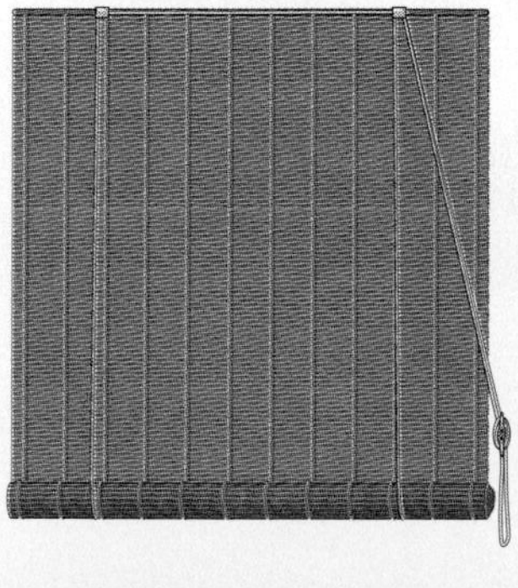

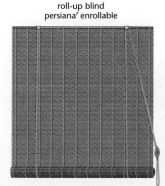

roman shade
persianas*f* romana

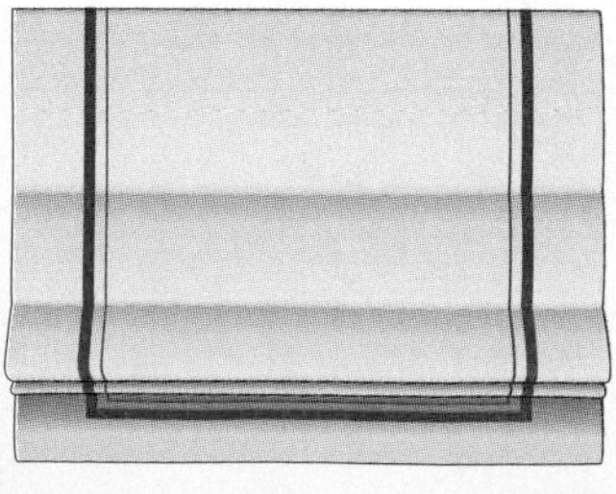

indoor shutters
postigos*M* interiores

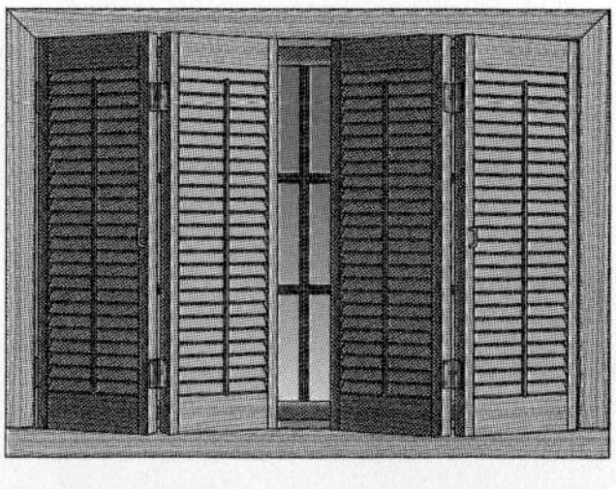

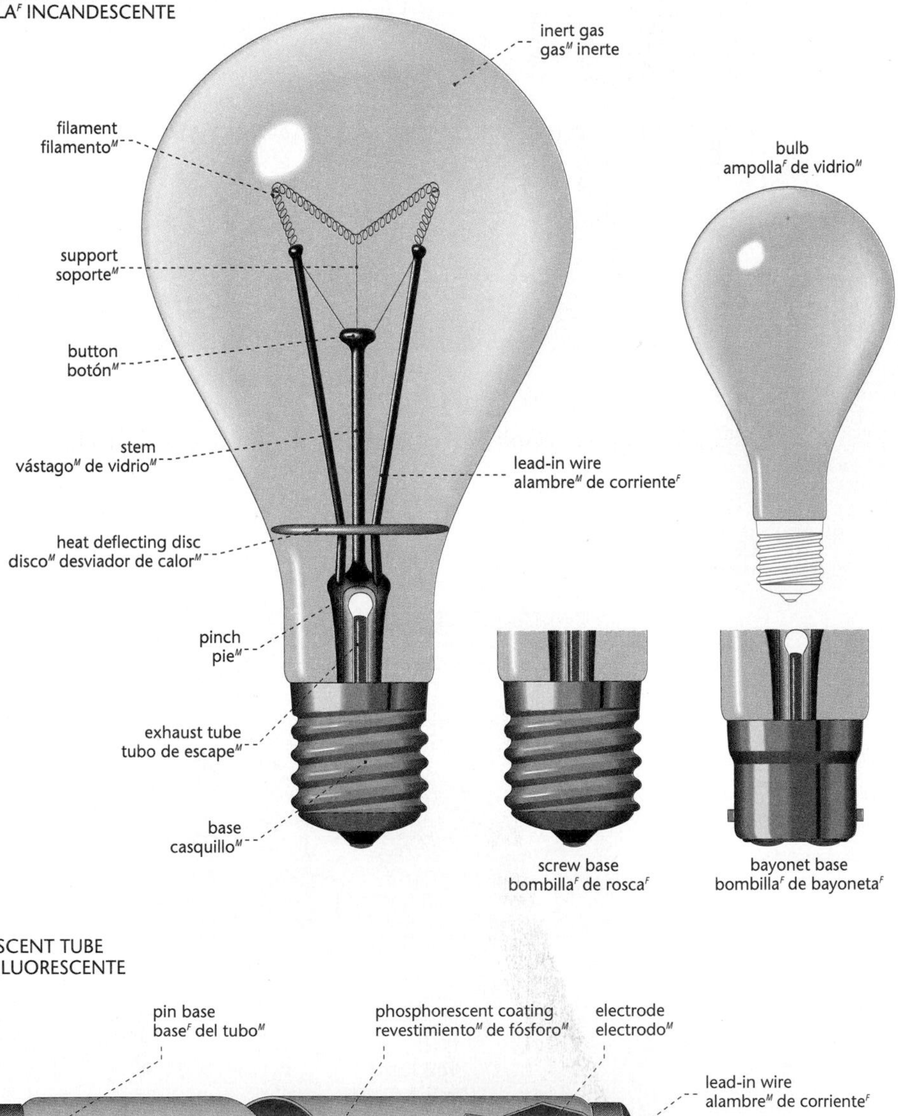

**HOUSE FURNITURE
ENSERES DOMÉSTICOS**

INCANDESCENT LAMP
BOMBILLA^F INCANDESCENTE

inert gas
gas^M inerte

filament
filamento^M

support
soporte^M

button
botón^M

stem
vástago^M de vidrio^M

heat deflecting disc
disco^M desviador de calor^M

pinch
pie^M

exhaust tube
tubo de escape^M

base
casquillo^M

lead-in wire
alambre^M de corriente^F

bulb
ampolla^F de vidrio^M

screw base
bombilla^F de rosca^F

bayonet base
bombilla^F de bayoneta^F

FLUORESCENT TUBE
TUBO^M FLUORESCENTE

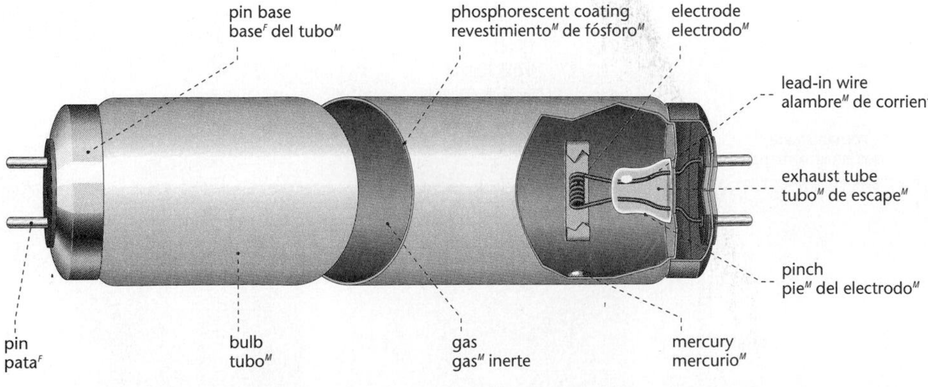

pin base
base^F del tubo^M

phosphorescent coating
revestimiento^M de fósforo^M

electrode
electrodo^M

lead-in wire
alambre^M de corriente^F

exhaust tube
tubo^M de escape^M

pinch
pie^M del electrodo^M

pin
pata^F

bulb
tubo^M

gas
gas^M inerte

mercury
mercurio^M

TUNGSTEN-HALOGEN LAMP
LÁMPARA^F HALÓGENA

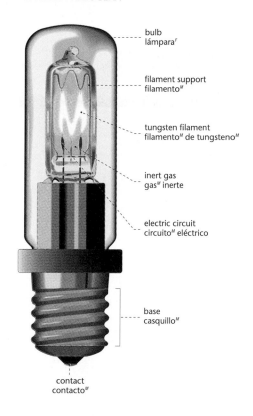

bulb
lámpara^F

filament support
filamento^M

tungsten filament
filamento^M de tungsteno^M

inert gas
gas^M inerte

electric circuit
circuito^M eléctrico

base
casquillo^M

contact
contacto^M

TUNGSTEN-HALOGEN LAMP
LÁMPARA^F HALÓGENA

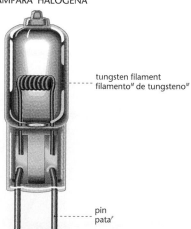

tungsten filament
filamento^M de tungsteno^M

pin
pata^F

ENERGY SAVING BULB
BOMBILLA^F ECONÓMICA

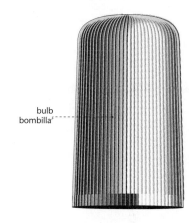

bulb
bombilla^F

fluorescent tube
tubo^M fluorescente

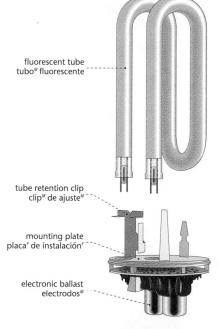

tube retention clip
clip^M de ajuste^M

mounting plate
placa^F de instalación^F

electronic ballast
electrodos^M

housing
pantalla^F

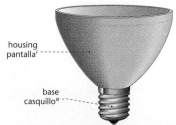

base
casquillo^M

HOUSE FURNITURE
ENSERES DOMÉSTICOS

wall fitting
aplique^M

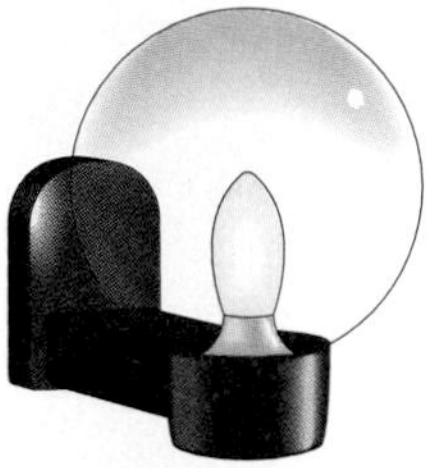

swivel wall lamp
lámpara^F orientable de pared^F

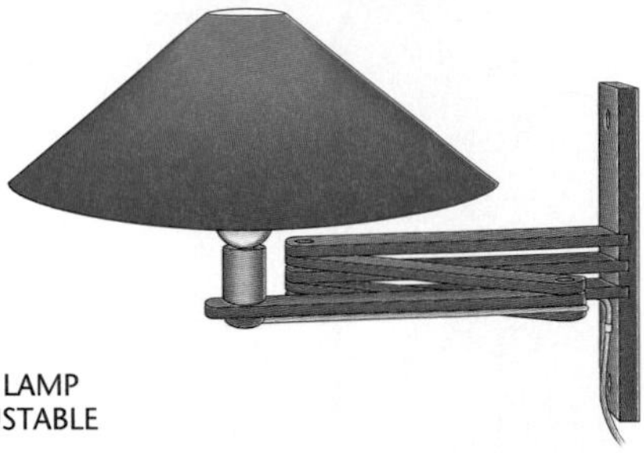

ADJUSTABLE LAMP
LÁMPARA^F AJUSTABLE

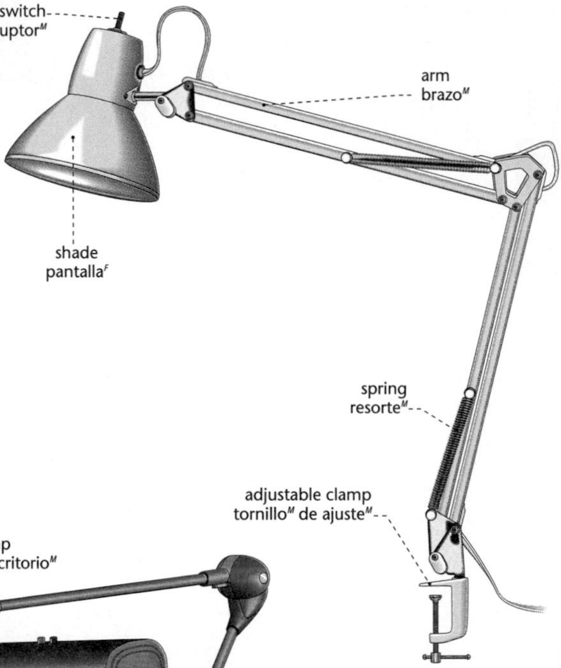

on-off switch
interruptor^M

arm
brazo^M

shade
pantalla^F

spring
resorte^M

adjustable clamp
tornillo^M de ajuste^M

desk lamp
lámpara^F de escritorio^M

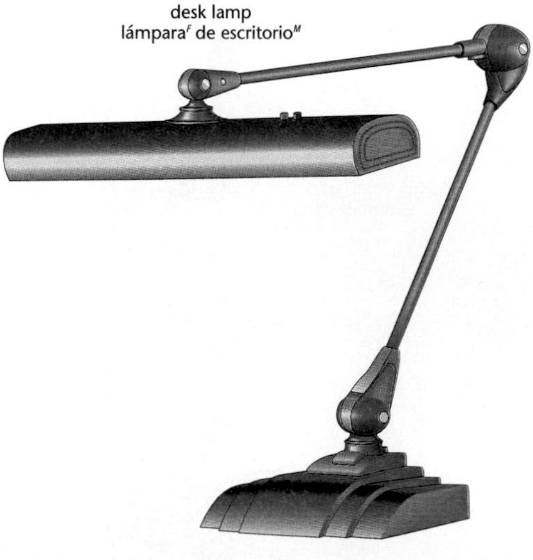

bed lamp
lámpara^F de cabecera^F

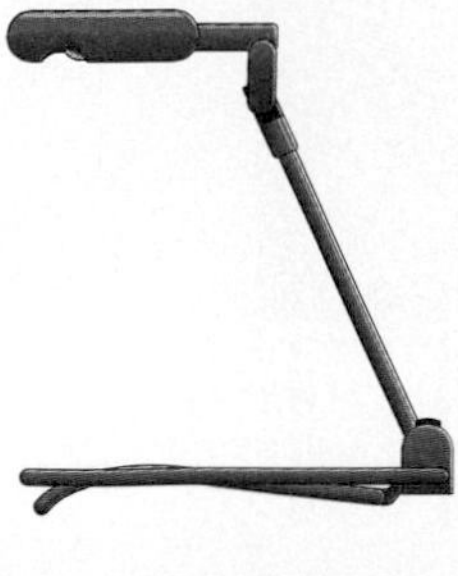

TRACK LIGHTING
RIEL^M DE ILUMINACIÓN^F

bar frame
armazón^M

transformer
transformador^M

contact lever
interruptor^M

spot
foco^M

post lantern
farola^F

clamp spotlight
lámpara de pinza^F

wall lantern
farol^M

strip light
lámparas^F en serie^F

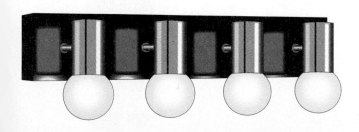

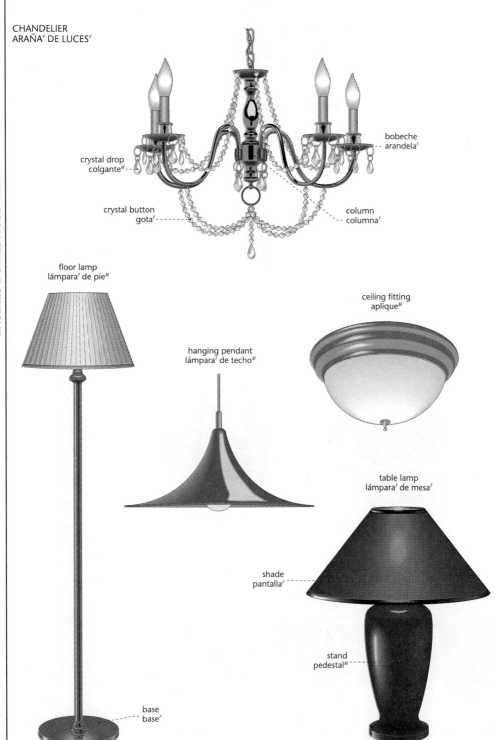

CHANDELIER
ARAÑA*F* DE LUCES*F*

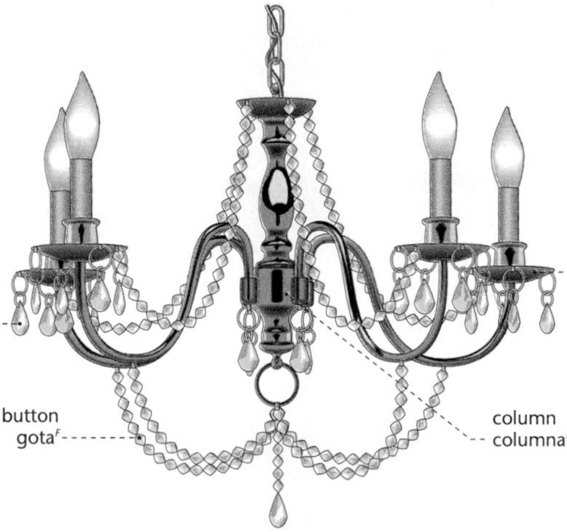

bobeche
arandela*F*

crystal drop
colgante*M*

column
columna*F*

crystal button
gota*F*

floor lamp
lámpara*F* de pie*M*

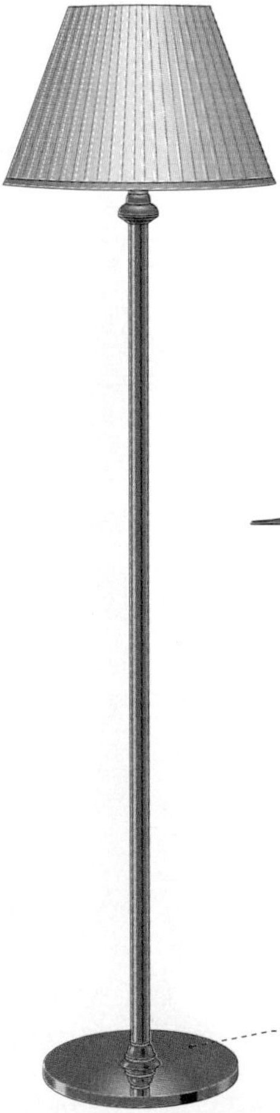

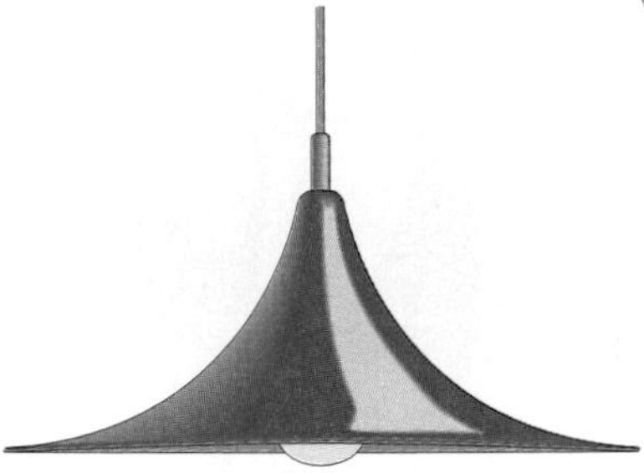

ceiling fitting
aplique*M*

hanging pendant
lámpara*F* de techo*M*

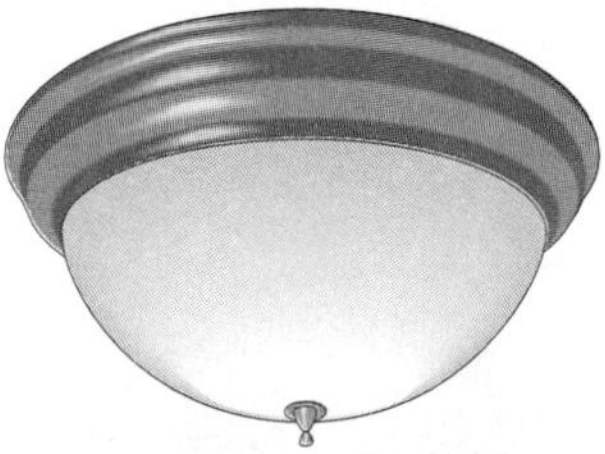

table lamp
lámpara*F* de mesa*F*

shade
pantalla*F*

stand
pedestal*M*

base
base*F*

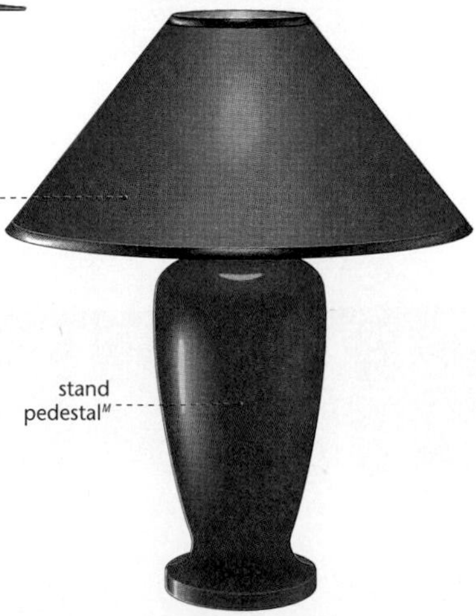

GLASSWARE
CRISTALERÍA^F

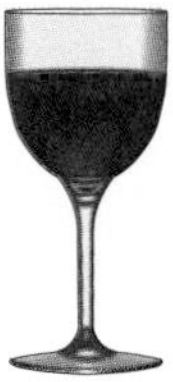

port glass
copa^F para oporto^M

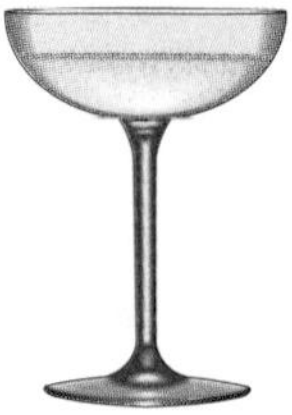

sparkling wine glass
copa^F de cava^F

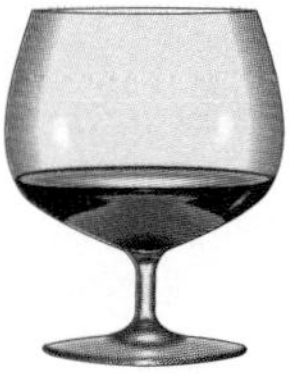

brandy snifter
copa^F de coñac^M

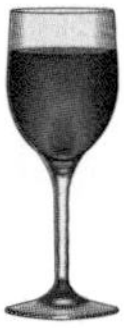

liqueur glass
copa^F para licores^M

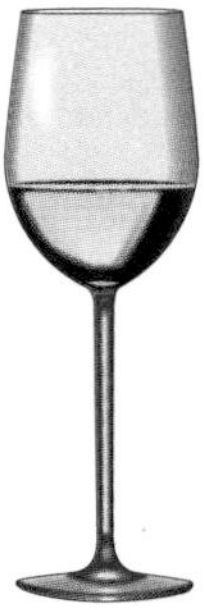

white wine glass
copa^F de vino^M blanco

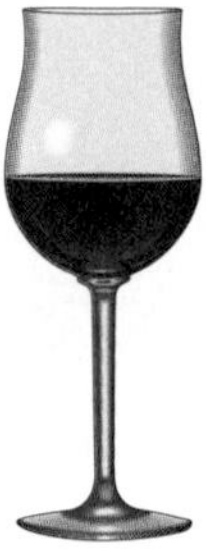

bordeaux glass
copa^F para vinos^M de Burdeos

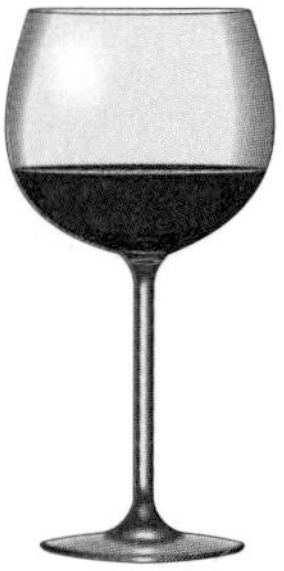

burgundy glass
copa^F para vinos^M de Borgoña

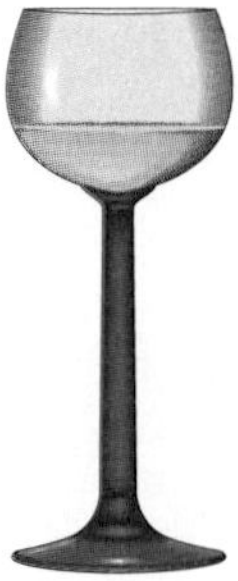

Alsace glass
copa^F para vino^M de Alsacia

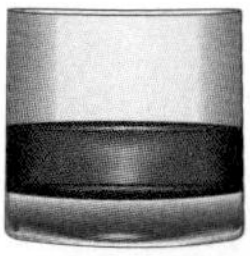

old-fashioned glass
vaso^M corto

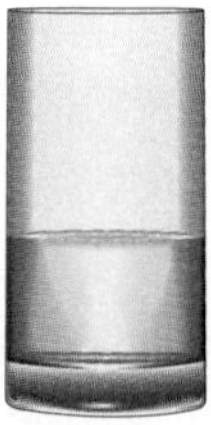

highball glass
vaso^M largo

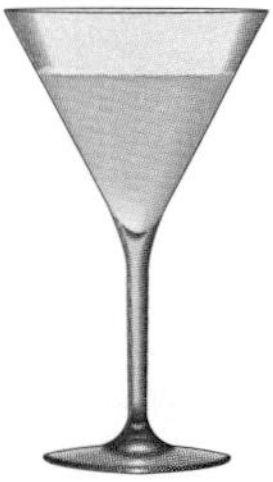

cocktail glass
copa^F de cóctel^M

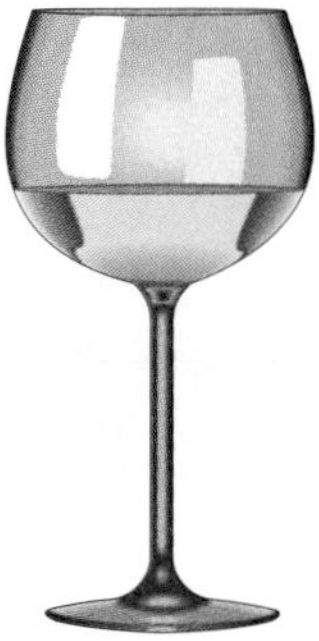

water goblet
copa^F para agua^F

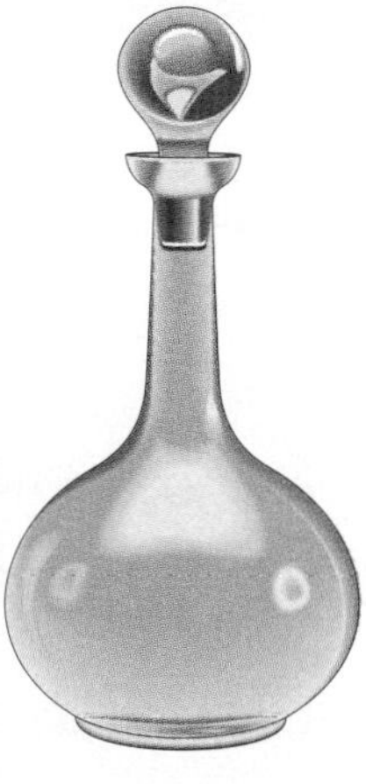

decanter
garrafa^F

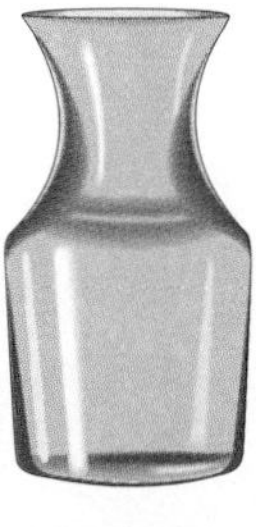

small decanter
garrafita^F

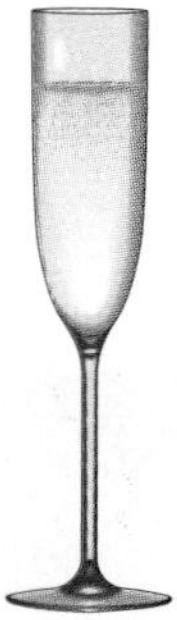

champagne flute
copa^F de champaña^F

beer mug
jarra^M para cerveza^F

237

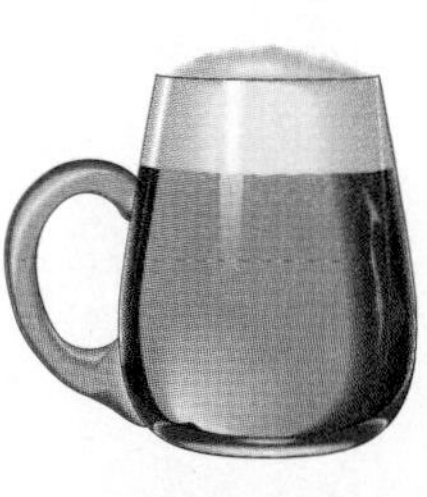

HOUSE FURNITURE
ENSERES DOMÉSTICOS

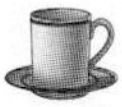

demitasse
tacita*F* de café*M*

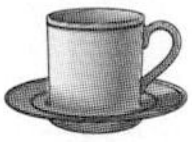

cup
taza*F*

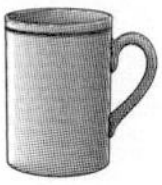

coffee mug
jarra*F* para café*M*

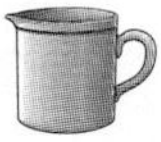

creamer
jarrito*M* de la leche*F*

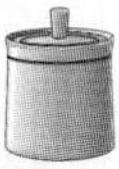

sugar bowl
azucarero*M*

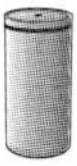

pepper shaker
pimentera*F*

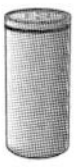

salt shaker
salero*M*

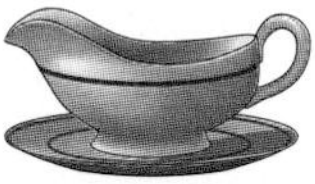

gravy boat
salsera*F*

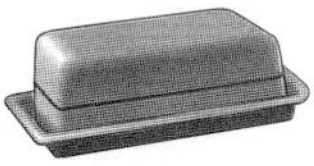

butter dish
mantequera*F*

ramekin
cuenco*M* de queso*M*
blando

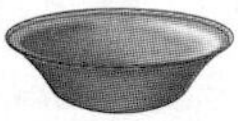

soup bowl
bol*M* para sopa*F*

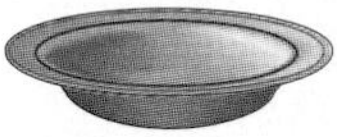

rim soup bowl
plato*M* sopero

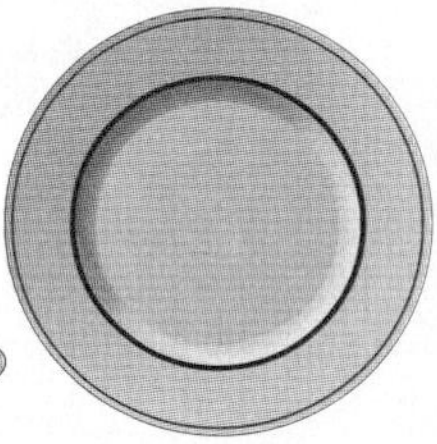

dinner plate
plato*M* llano

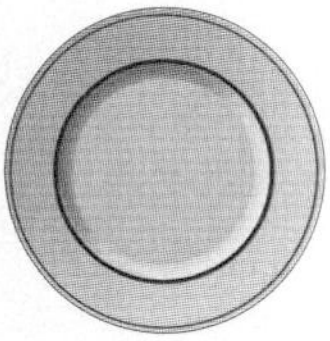

salad plate
plato*M* para ensalada*F*

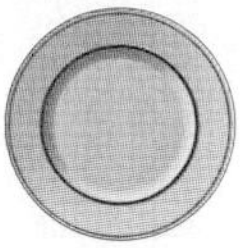

bread and butter plate
plato*M* para pan*M* y
mantequilla*F*

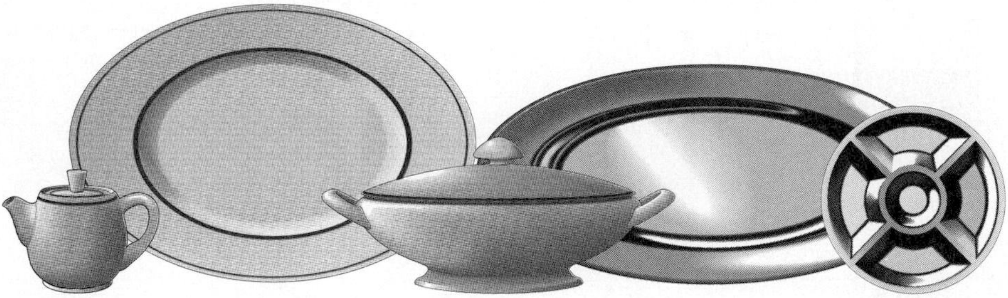

teapot
tetera*F*

platter
fuente*F* de servir

vegetable bowl
fuente*F* de verdura*F*

fish platter
fuente*F* para pescado*M*

hors d'oeuvre dish
bandeja*F* para canapés*M*

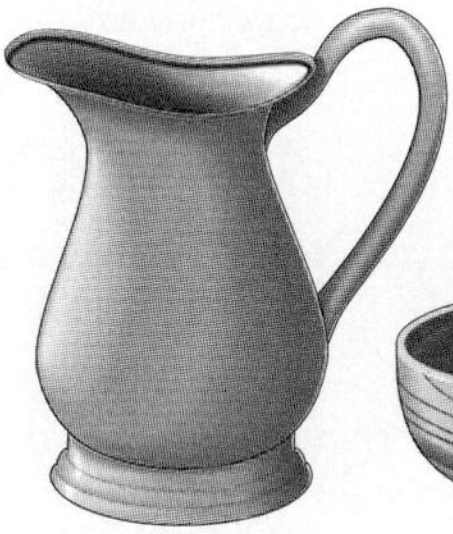

water pitcher
jarra*F* para agua*F*

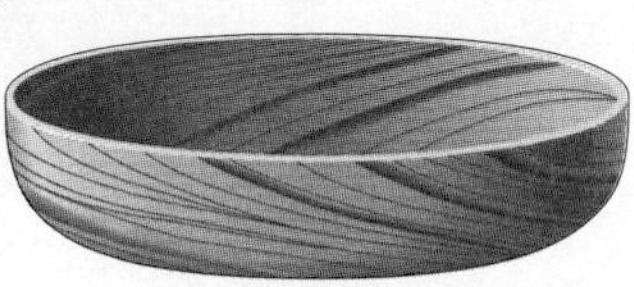

salad bowl
ensaladera*F*

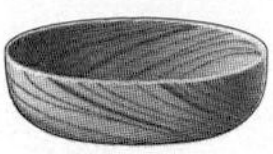

salad dish
bol*M* para ensalada*F*

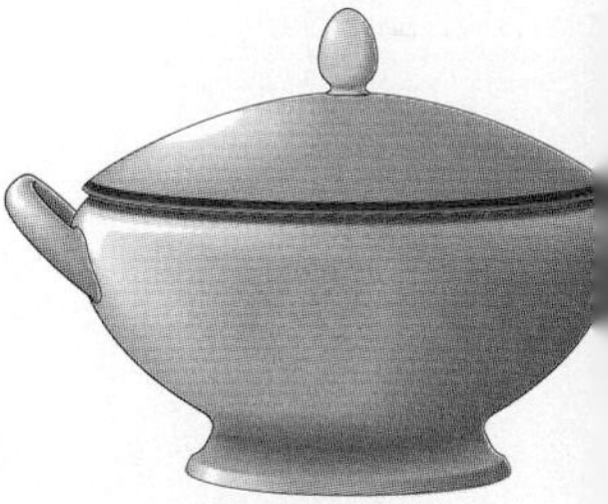

soup tureen
sopera*F*

SILVERWARE
CUBERTERÍA^F

KNIFE
CUCHILLO^M

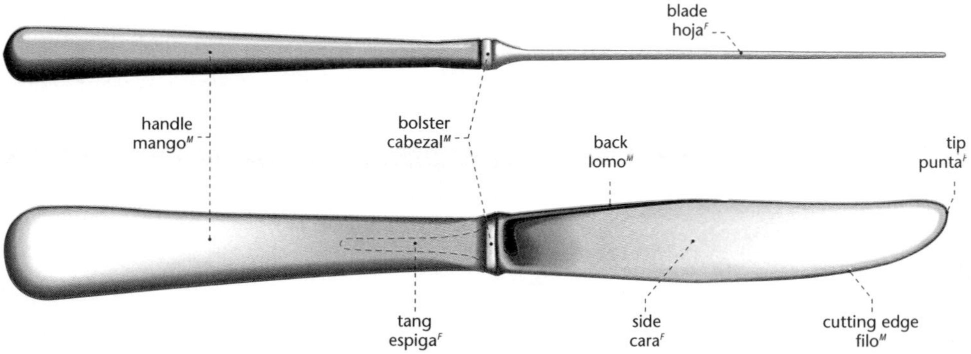

blade
hoja^F

handle
mango^M

bolster
cabezal^M

back
lomo^M

tip
punta^F

tang
espiga^F

side
cara^F

cutting edge
filo^M

PRINCIPAL TYPES OF KNIVES
TIPOS^M DE CUCHILLOS^M

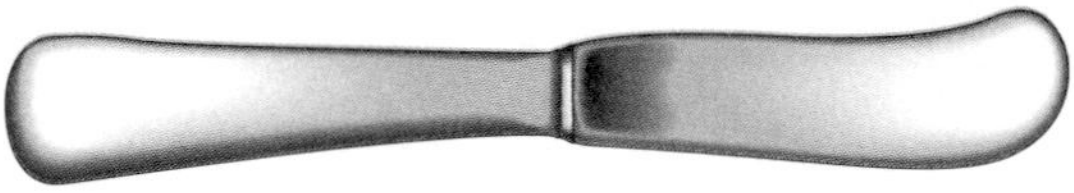

butter knife
cuchillo^M para mantequilla^F

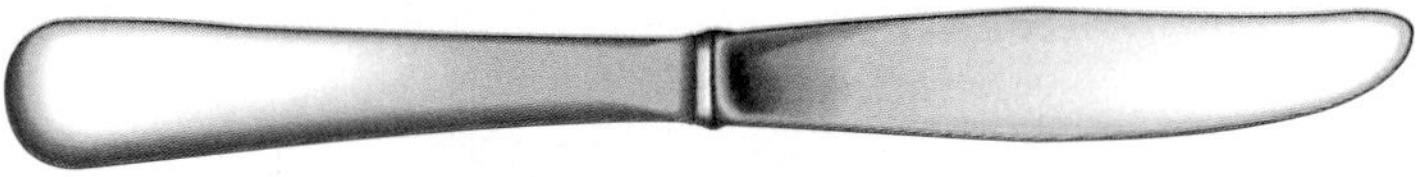

dessert knife
cuchillo^M para postre^M

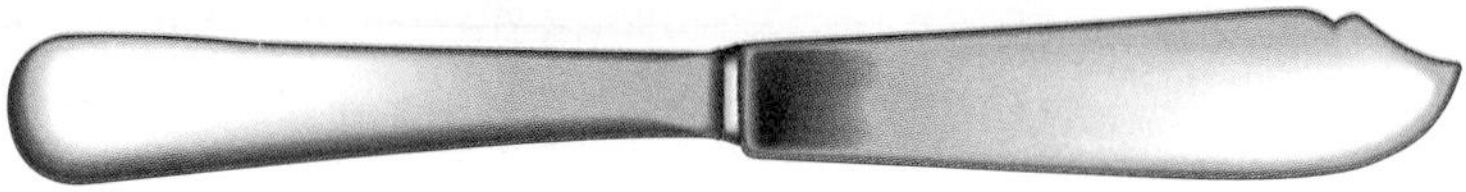

fish knife
cuchillo^M para pescado^M

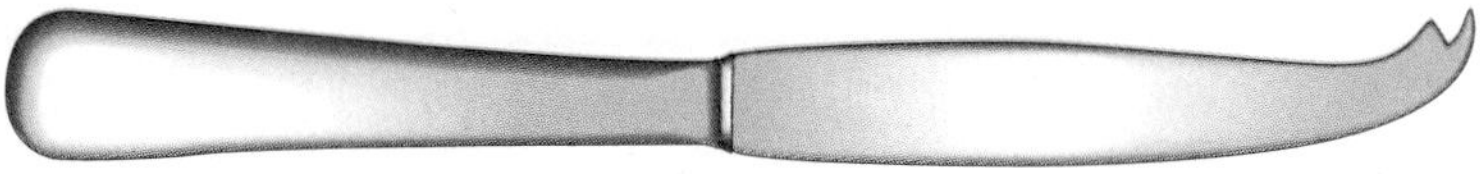

cheese knife
cuchillo^M para queso^M

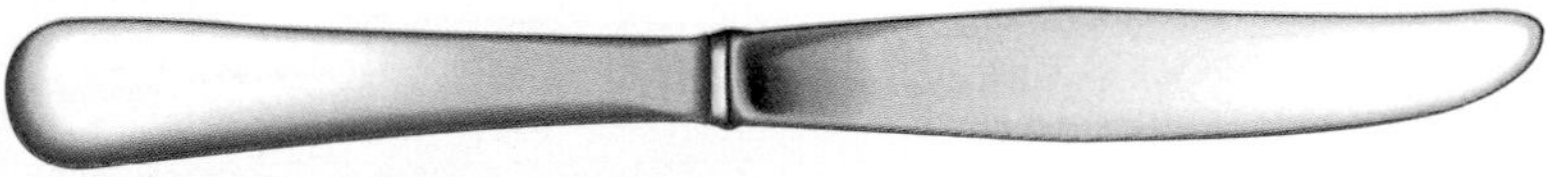

dinner knife
cuchillo^M de mesa^F

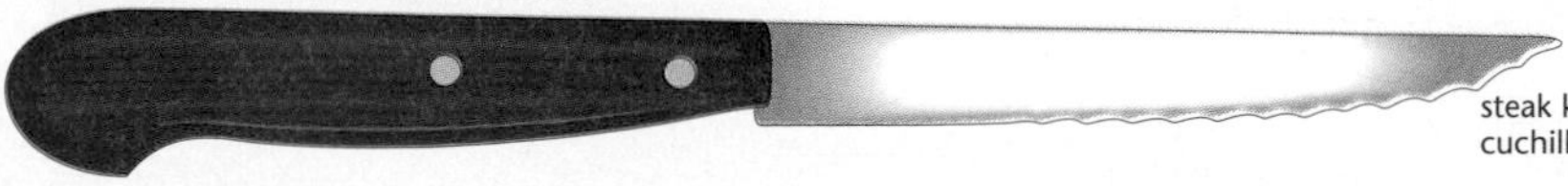

steak knife
cuchillo^M para carne^F

FORK
TENEDOR^M

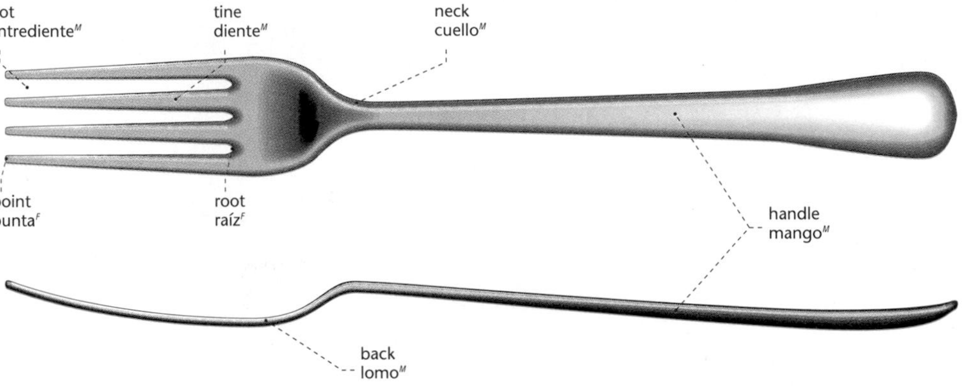

slot
entrediente^M

tine
diente^M

neck
cuello^M

point
punta^F

root
raíz^F

handle
mango^M

back
lomo^M

PRINCIPAL TYPES OF FORKS
TIPOS^M DE TENEDORES^M

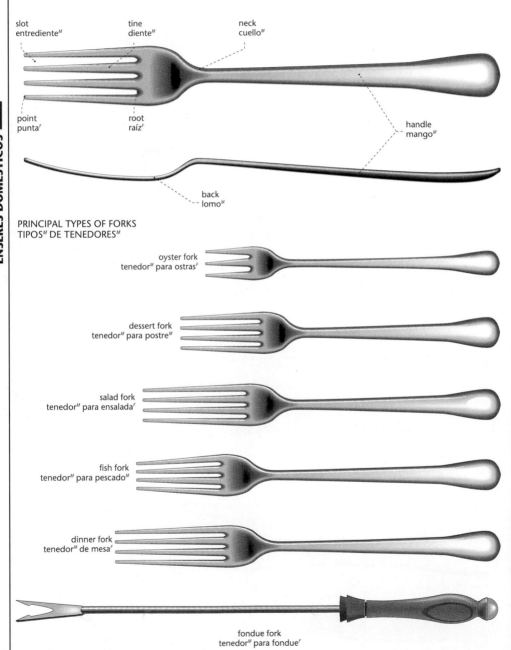

oyster fork
tenedor^M para ostras^F

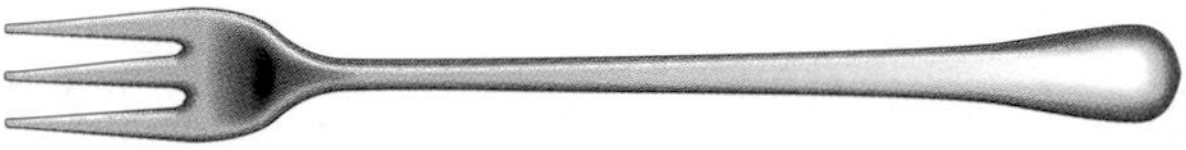

dessert fork
tenedor^M para postre^M

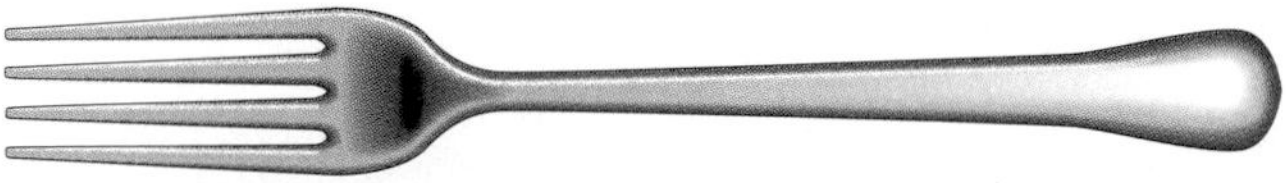

salad fork
tenedor^M para ensalada^F

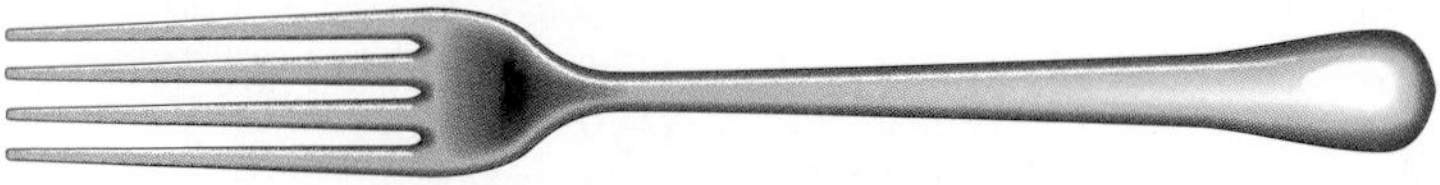

fish fork
tenedor^M para pescado^M

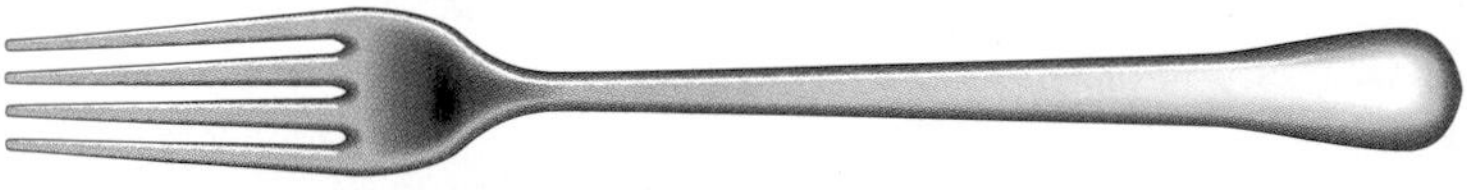

dinner fork
tenedor^M de mesa^F

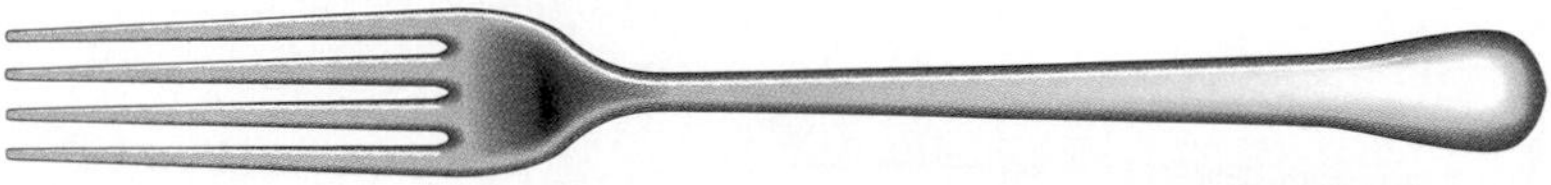

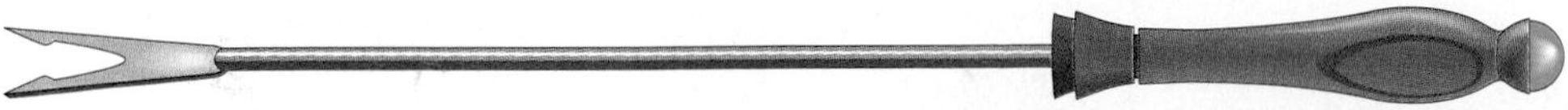

fondue fork
tenedor^M para fondue^F

SPOON
CUCHARA^F

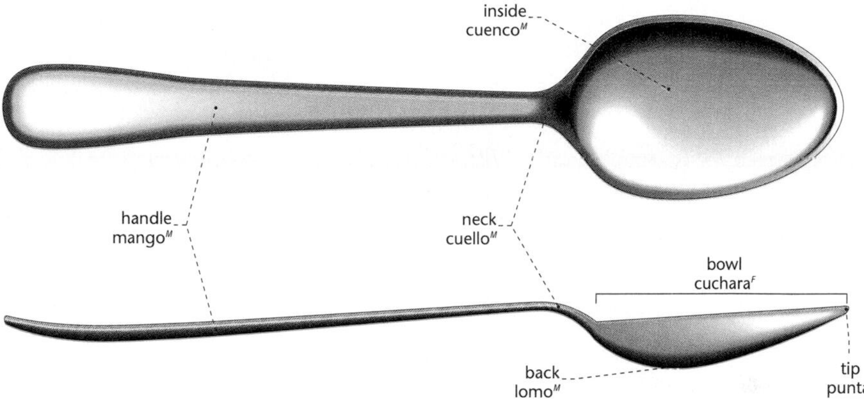

inside
cuenco^M

handle
mango^M

neck
cuello^M

bowl
cuchara^F

back
lomo^M

tip
punta^F

PRINCIPAL TYPES OF SPOONS
TIPOS^M DE CUCHARAS^F

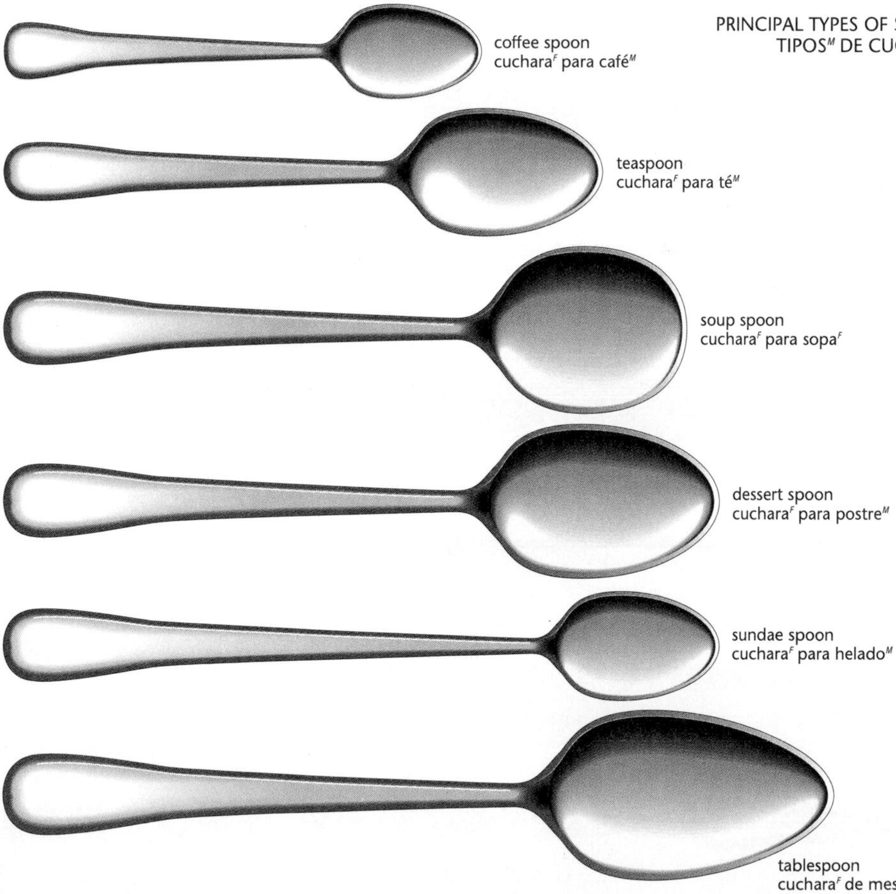

coffee spoon
cuchara^F para café^M

teaspoon
cuchara^F para té^M

soup spoon
cuchara^F para sopa^F

dessert spoon
cuchara^F para postre^M

sundae spoon
cuchara^F para helado^M

tablespoon
cuchara^F de mesa^F

241

KITCHEN UTENSILS
UTENSILIOS^M DE COCINA^F

KITCHEN KNIFE
CUCHILLO^M DE COCINA^F

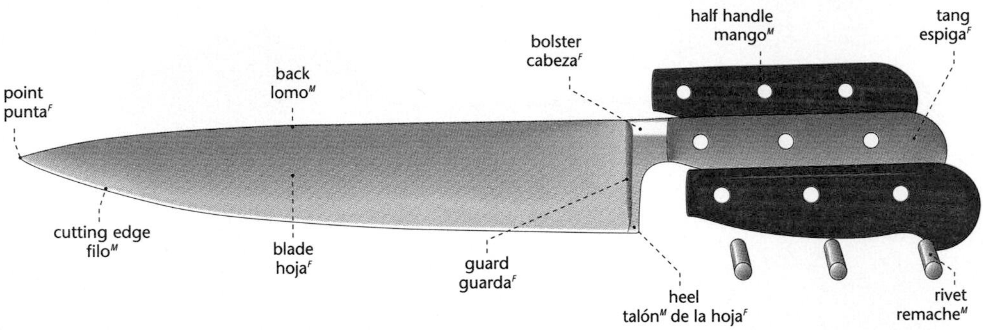

half handle
mango^M

tang
espiga^F

bolster
cabeza^F

point
punta^F

back
lomo^M

cutting edge
filo^M

blade
hoja^F

guard
guarda^F

heel
talón^M de la hoja^F

rivet
remache^M

TYPES OF KITCHEN KNIVES
TIPOS^M DE CUCHILLOS^M DE COCINA^F

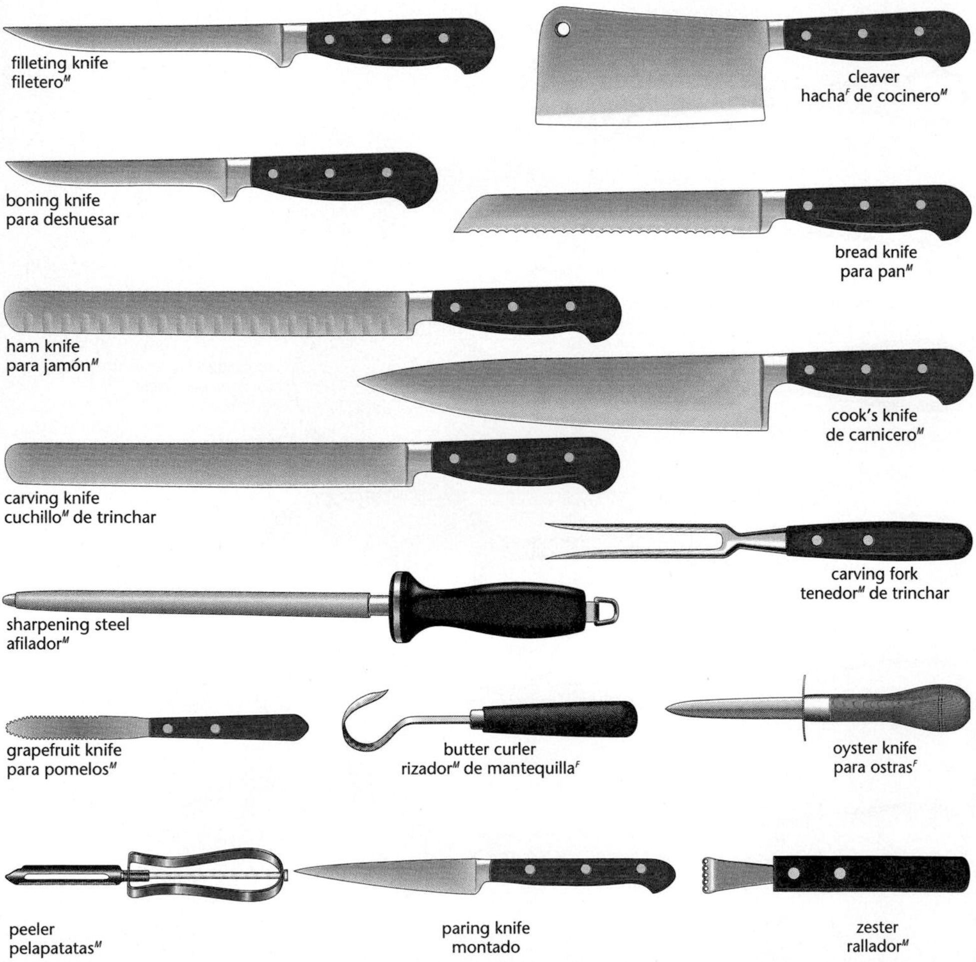

filleting knife
filetero^M

cleaver
hacha^F de cocinero^M

boning knife
para deshuesar

bread knife
para pan^M

ham knife
para jamón^M

cook's knife
de carnicero^M

carving knife
cuchillo^M de trinchar

carving fork
tenedor^M de trinchar

sharpening steel
afilador^M

grapefruit knife
para pomelos^M

butter curler
rizador^M de mantequilla^F

oyster knife
para ostras^F

peeler
pelapatatas^M

paring knife
montado

zester
rallador^M

242

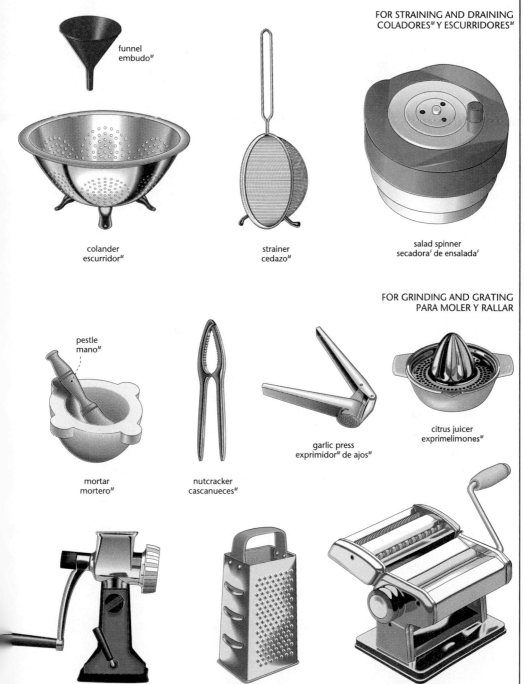

funnel
embudo^M

FOR STRAINING AND DRAINING
COLADORES^M Y ESCURRIDORES^M

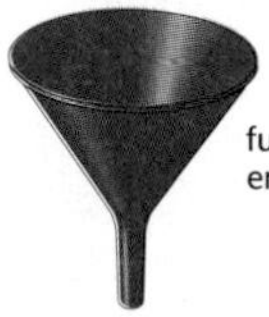

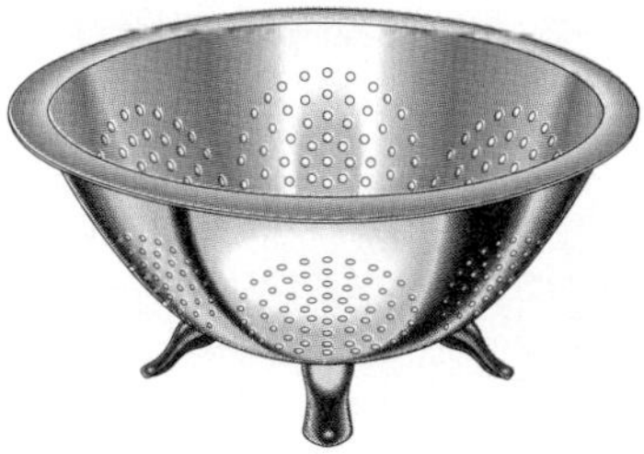

colander
escurridor^M

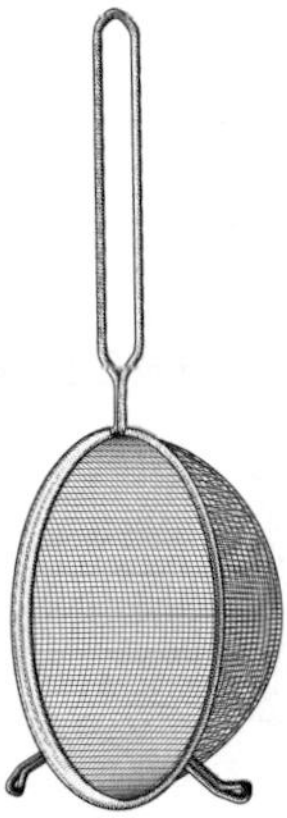

strainer
cedazo^M

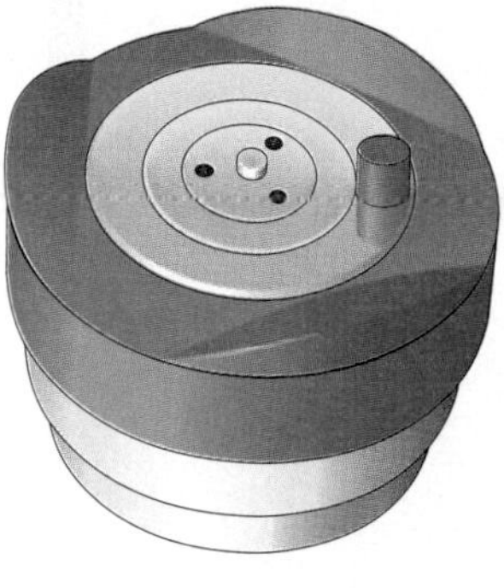

salad spinner
secadora^F de ensalada^F

FOR GRINDING AND GRATING
PARA MOLER Y RALLAR

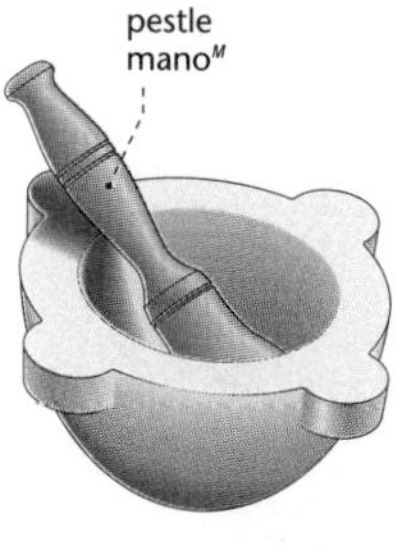

pestle
mano^M

mortar
mortero^M

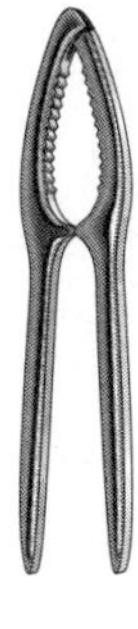

nutcracker
cascanueces^M

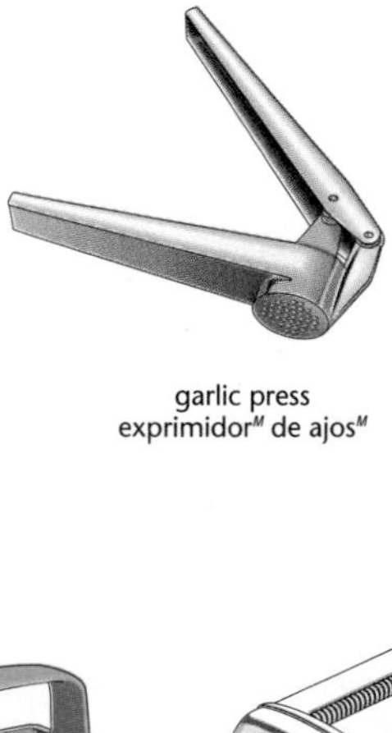

garlic press
exprimidor^M de ajos^M

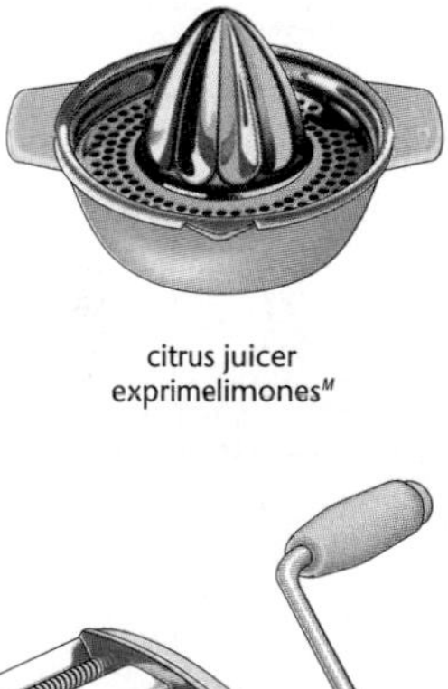

citrus juicer
exprimelimones^M

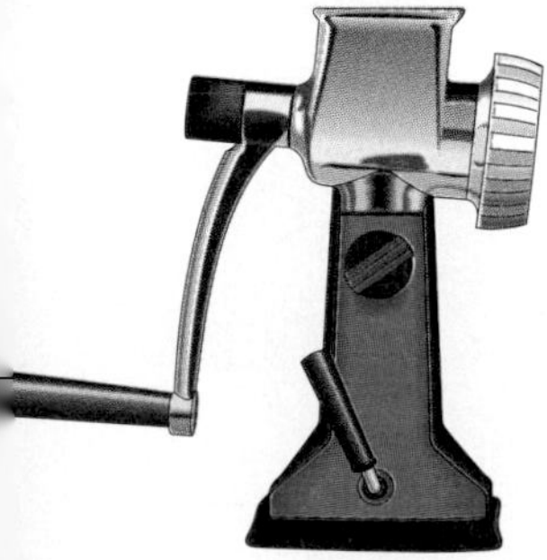

meat grinder
máquina de picar carne^F

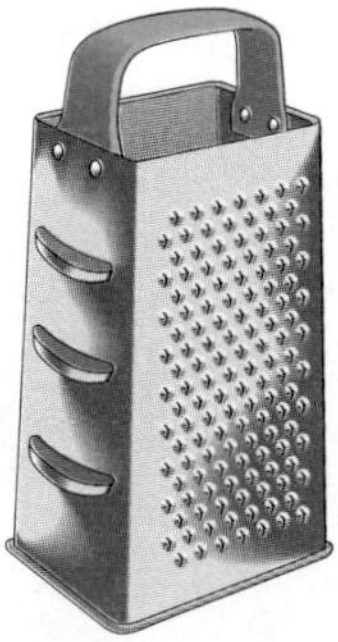

grater
rallador^M

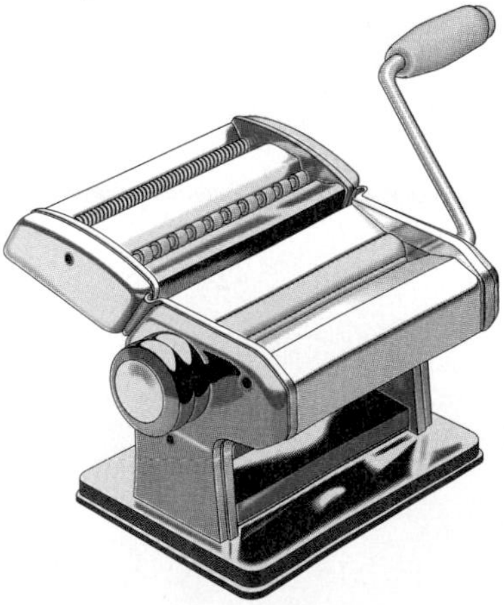

pasta maker
máquina^F para hacer pasta^F italiana

KITCHEN UTENSILS
UTENSILIOS^M DE COCINA^F

SET OF UTENSILS
JUEGO^M DE UTENSILIOS^M

potato masher
pasapuré^M

spatula
espátula^F

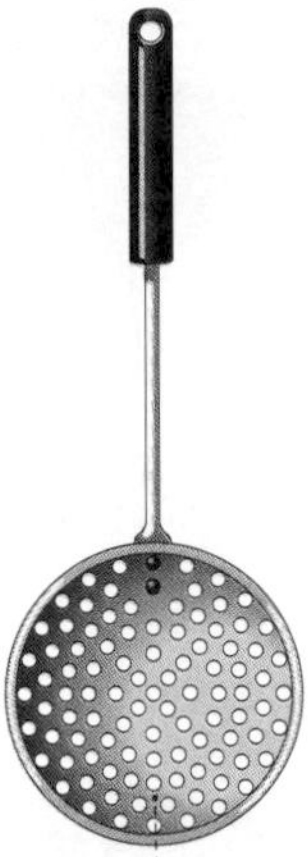

skimmer
espumadera^F

ladle
cucharón^M

turner
paleta^F

draining spoon
escurridera^F

FOR OPENING
UTENSILIOS^M PARA ABRIR Y DESCORCHAR

FOR MEASURING
UTENSILIOS^M PARA MEDIR

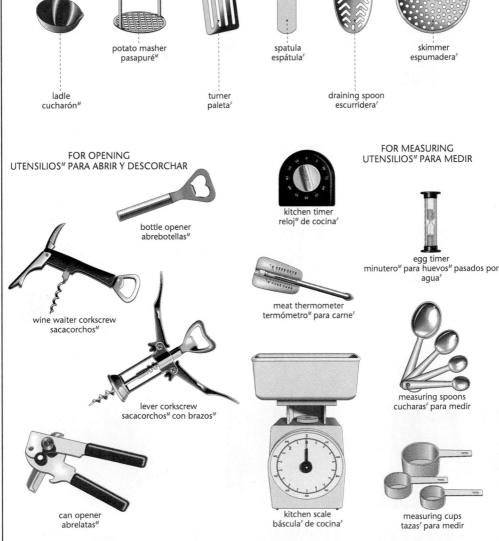

bottle opener
abrebotellas^M

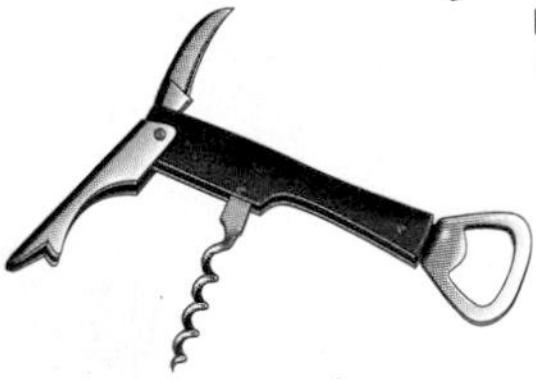

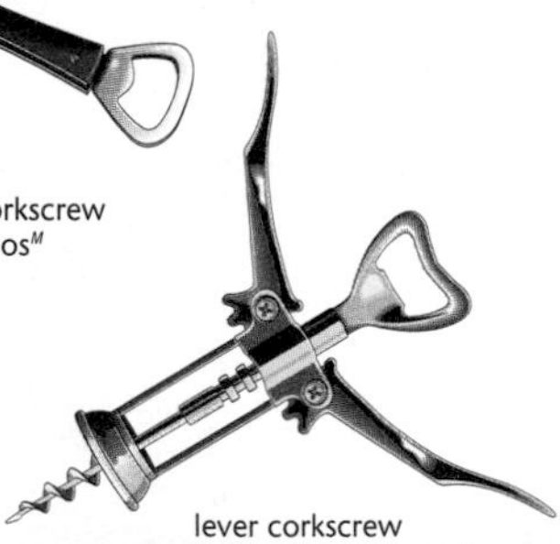

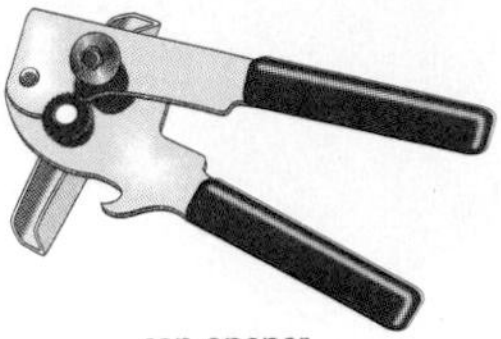

kitchen timer
reloj^M de cocina^F

egg timer
minutero^M para huevos^M pasados por
agua^F

wine waiter corkscrew
sacacorchos^M

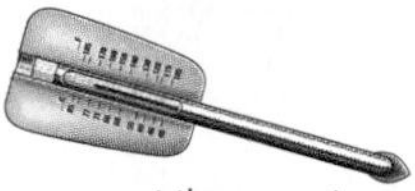

meat thermometer
termómetro^M para carne^F

lever corkscrew
sacacorchos^M con brazos^M

measuring spoons
cucharas^F para medir

can opener
abrelatas^M

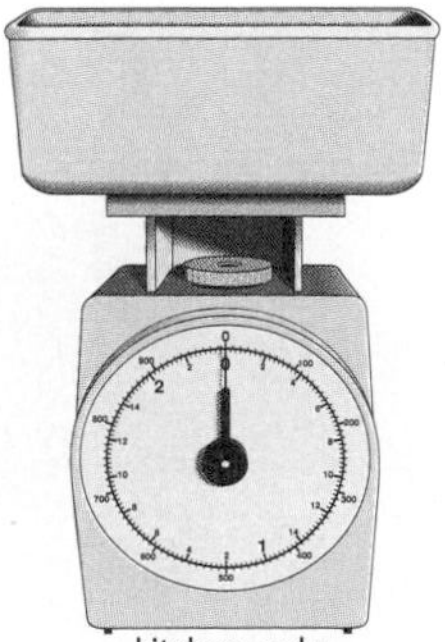

kitchen scale
báscula^F de cocina^F

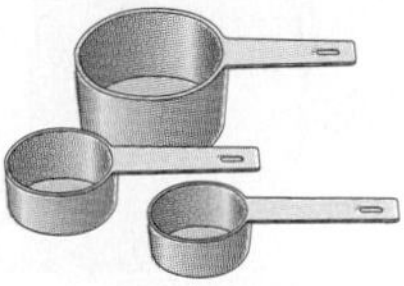

measuring cups
tazas^F para medir

pastry brush
pincel*M* de repostería*F*

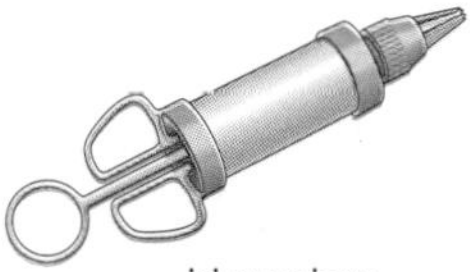

icing syringe
tubito*M* de decoración*F*

whisk
batidor*M*

egg beater
batidor*M* mecánico

sifter
tamiz*M*

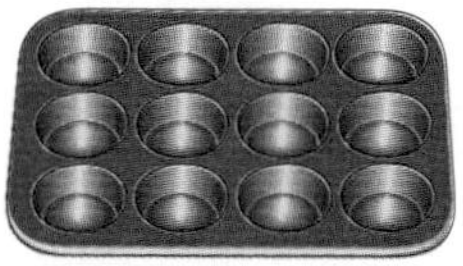

muffin pan
molde*M* para magdalenas*F*

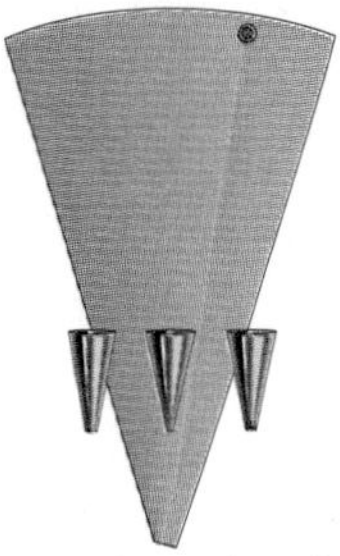

pastry bag and nozzles
manga*F* y boquillas*F*

pastry cutting wheel
cortapastas*M*

cookie sheet
bandeja*F* para hornear galletas*F*

rolling pin
rodillo*M*

mixing bowls
boles*M* para batir

cookie cutters
moldes*M* de pastas*F*

removable-bottomed pan
molde*M* redondo con muelles*M*

pie pan
molde*M* para tartas*F*

quiche plate
molde*M* acanalado

cake pan
molde*M* para bizcocho*M*

245

MISCELLANEOUS UTENSILS
UTENSILIOS*M* DIVERSOS

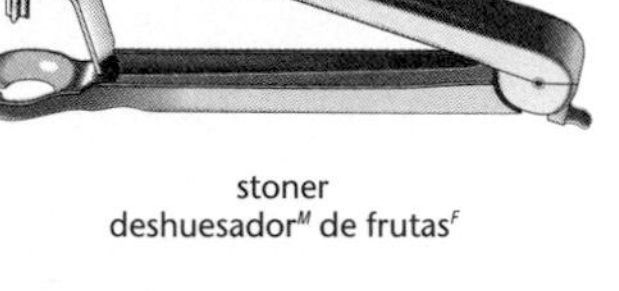

stoner
deshuesador*M* de frutas*F*

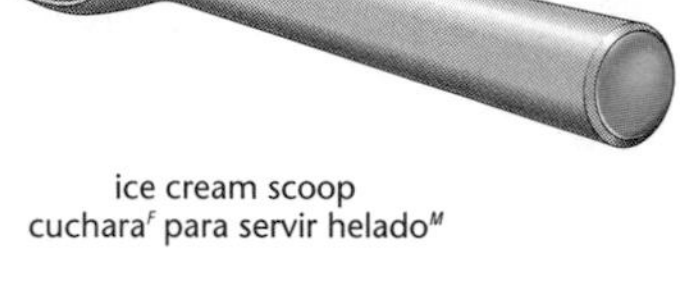

ice cream scoop
cuchara*F* para servir helado*M*

poultry shears
tijeras*F* para aves*F*

spaghetti tongs
tenacillas*F* para espagueti*M*

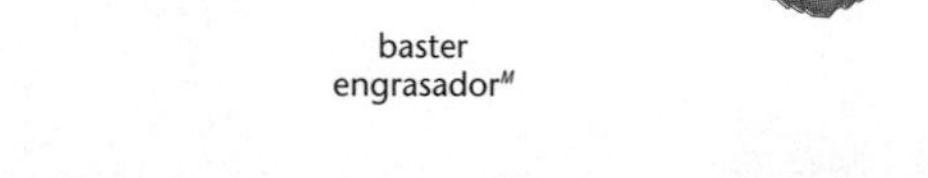

baster
engrasador*M*

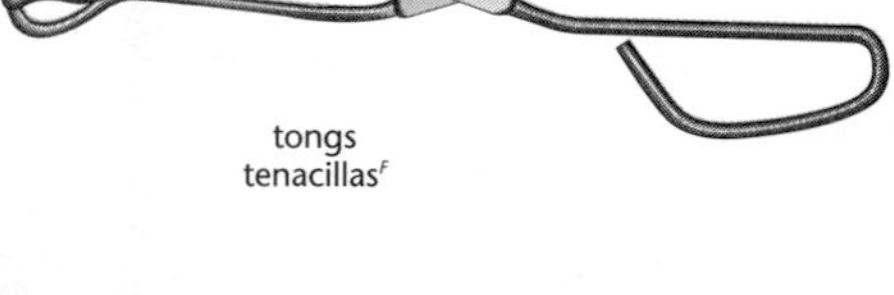

tongs
tenacillas*F*

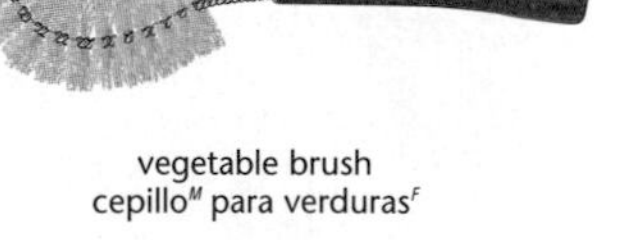

vegetable brush
cepillo*M* para verduras*F*

tea ball
esfera*F* de té*M*

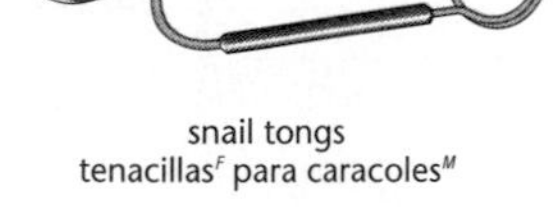

snail tongs
tenacillas*F* para caracoles*M*

dredger
espolvoreador*M*

egg slicer
cortador*M* de huevos*M* duros

snail dish
plato*M* para caracoles*M*

COFFEE MAKERS
CAFETERAS^F

AUTOMATIC DRIP COFFEE MAKER
CAFETERA^F DE FILTRO^M AUTOMÁTICA

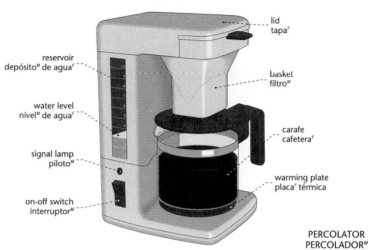

lid
tapa^F

reservoir
depósito^M de agua^F

basket
filtro^M

water level
nivel^M de agua^F

carafe
cafetera^F

signal lamp
piloto^M

warming plate
placa^F térmica

on-off switch
interruptor^M

PERCOLATOR
PERCOLADOR^M

VACUUM COFFEE MAKER
CAFETERA^F DE INFUSIÓN^F

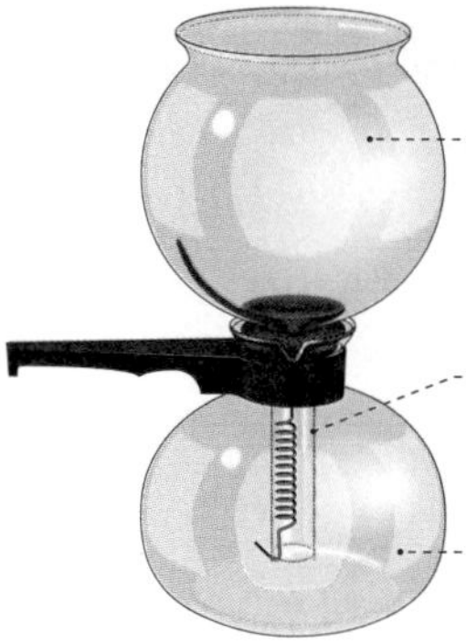

upper bowl
recipiente^M superior

stem
tubo^M de subida^F del agua^F

lower bowl
recipiente^M inferior

spout
pitorro^M

signal lamp
piloto^M

PLUNGER
CAFETERA^F DE ÉMBOLO^M

NEAPOLITAN COFFEE MAKER
CAFETERA^F NAPOLITANA

ESPRESSO COFFEE MAKER
CAFETERA^F ITALIANA

COOKING UTENSILS
UTENSILIOS^M DE COCINA^F

WOK SET
WOK^M

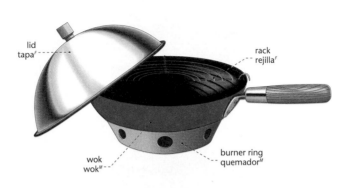

lid
tapa^F

rack
rejilla^F

wok
wok^M

burner ring
quemador^M

FISH POACHER
BESUGUERA^F

rack
rejilla^F desmontable

lid
tapa^F

FONDUE SET
JUEGO^M PARA FONDUE^F

fondue pot
cacerola^F para fondue^F

stand
soporte^M

burner
quemador^M

roasting pans
asadores^M

PRESSURE COOKER
OLLA^F A PRESIÓN^F

pressure regulator
regulador^M de presión^F

safety valve
válvula^F de seguridad^F

Dutch oven
cacerola^F refractaria

stock pot
olla^F

frying pan
sartén^F

pancake pan
sartén^F para crepas^F

couscous kettle
olla^F para alcuzcuz^M

egg poacher
escalfador^M de huevos^M

sauté pan
sartén^F honda

vegetable steamer
alcachofa^F para vegetales^M

double boiler
cacerola^F para baño^M de María

saucepan
cacerola^F

249

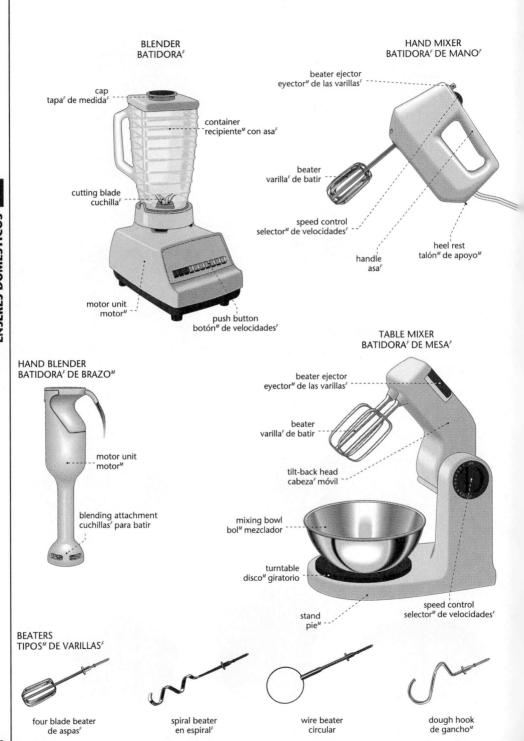

HOUSE FURNITURE
ENSERES DOMÉSTICOS

BLENDER
BATIDORA^F

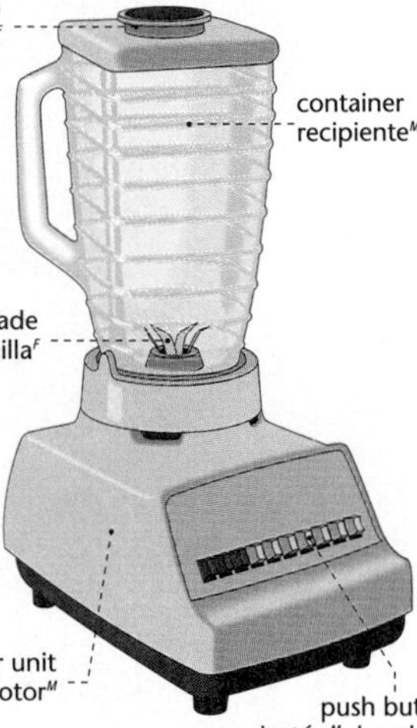

cap
tapa^F de medida^F

container
recipiente^M con asa^F

cutting blade
cuchilla^F

motor unit
motor^M

push button
botón^M de velocidades^F

HAND MIXER
BATIDORA^F DE MANO^F

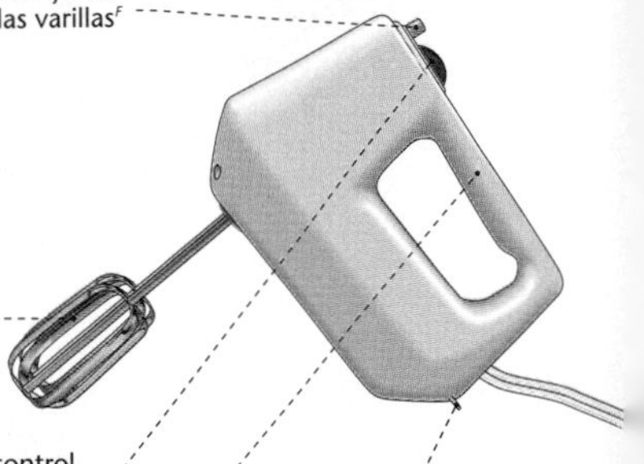

beater ejector
eyector^M de las varillas^F

beater
varilla^F de batir

speed control
selector^M de velocidades^F

handle
asa^F

heel rest
talón^M de apoyo^M

HAND BLENDER
BATIDORA^F DE BRAZO^M

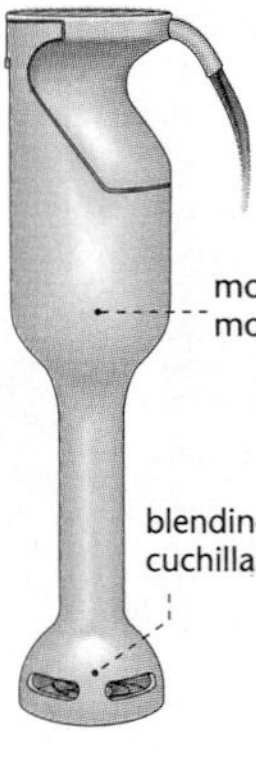

motor unit
motor^M

blending attachment
cuchillas^F para batir

TABLE MIXER
BATIDORA^F DE MESA^F

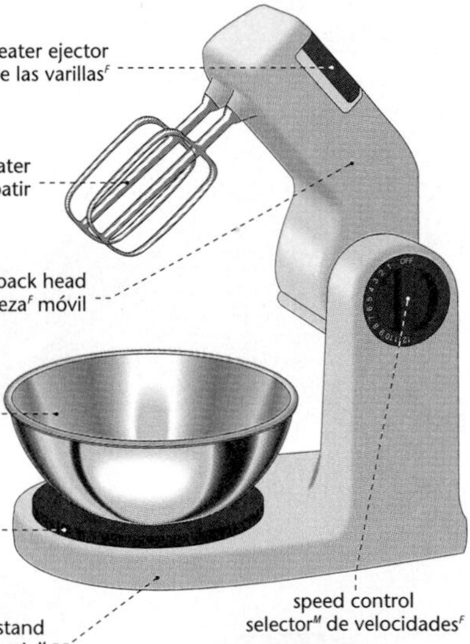

beater ejector
eyector^M de las varillas^F

beater
varilla^F de batir

tilt-back head
cabeza^F móvil

mixing bowl
bol^M mezclador

turntable
disco^M giratorio

stand
pie^M

speed control
selector^M de velocidades^F

BEATERS
TIPOS^M DE VARILLAS^F

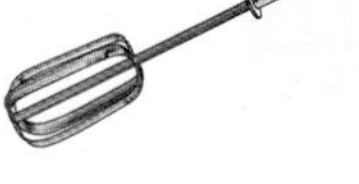

four blade beater
de aspas^F

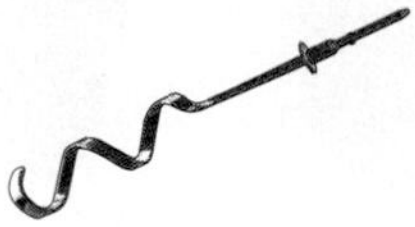

spiral beater
en espiral^F

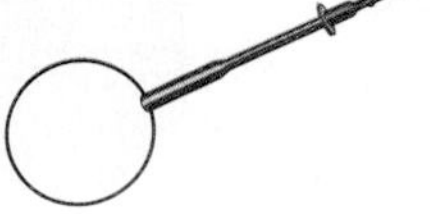

wire beater
circular

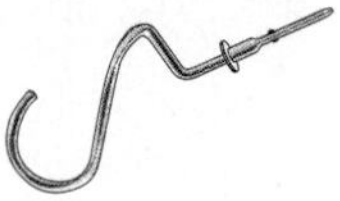

dough hook
de gancho^M

FOOD PROCESSOR
ROBOT^M DE COCINA^F

DISKS
DISCO^M

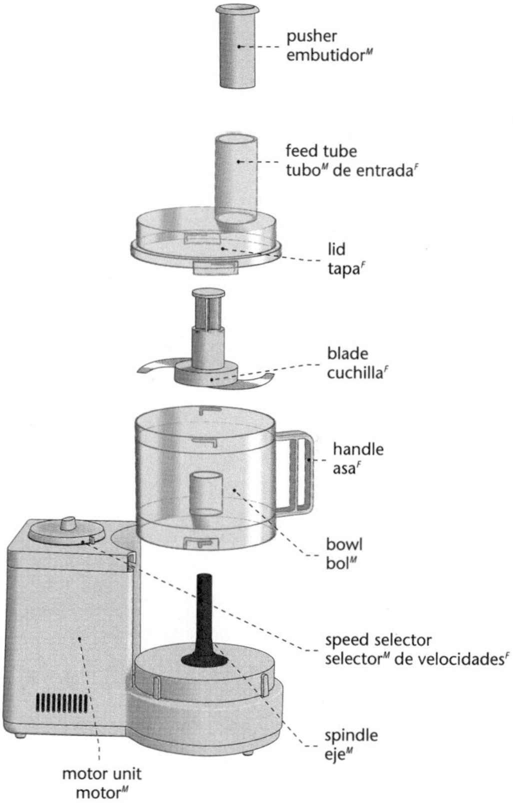

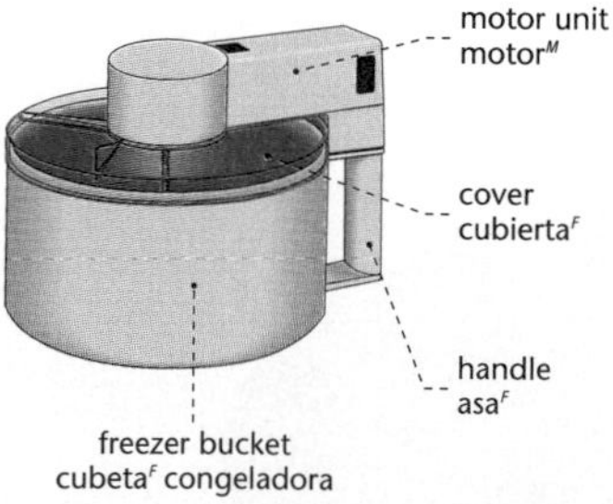

pusher
embutidor^M

feed tube
tubo^M de entrada^F

lid
tapa^F

blade
cuchilla^F

handle
asa^F

bowl
bol^M

speed selector
selector^M de velocidades^F

spindle
eje^M

motor unit
motor^M

CITRUS JUICER
EXPRIMIDOR^M DE CÍTRICOS^M

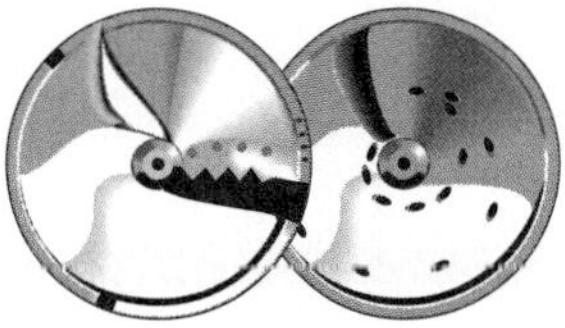

strainer
colador^M

reamer
exprimidero^M

bowl with serving spout
recipiente^M con vertedor^M

motor unit
motor^M

JUICER
EXTRACTOR^M DE JUGOS^M

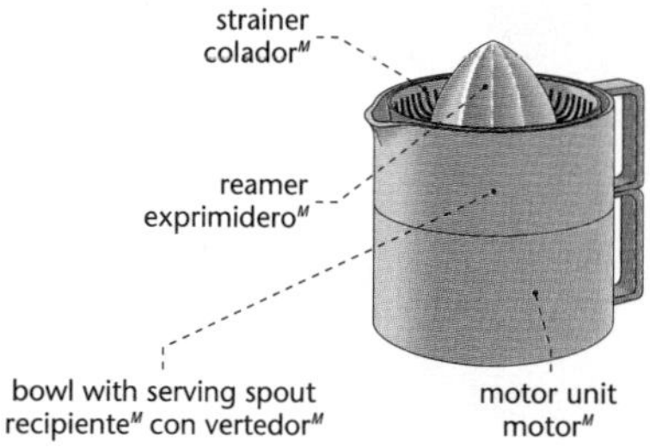

pusher
embutidor^M

feed tube
tubo^M alimentador

lid
tapa^F

strainer
colador^M

motor unit
motor^M

bowl
recipiente^M

ICE CREAM FREEZER
HELADERA^F

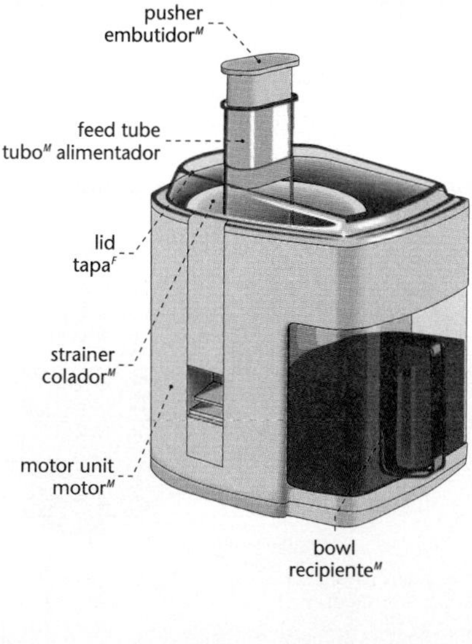

motor unit
motor^M

cover
cubierta^F

handle
asa^F

freezer bucket
cubeta^F congeladora

KETTLE
HERVIDOR*M* DE SILBATO*M*

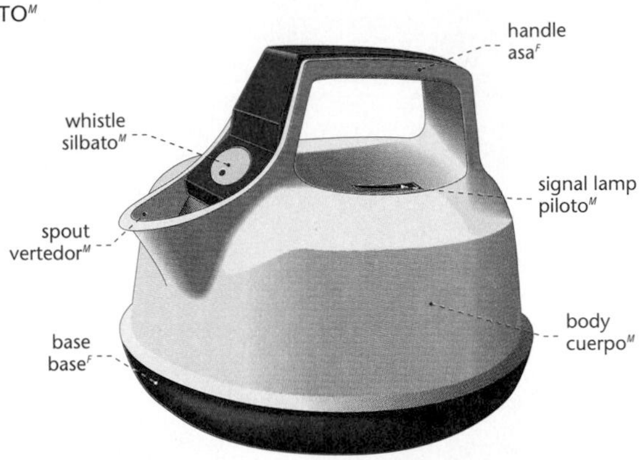

handle
asa*F*

whistle
silbato*M*

signal lamp
piloto*M*

spout
vertedor*M*

base
base*F*

body
cuerpo*M*

TOASTER
TOSTADOR*M*

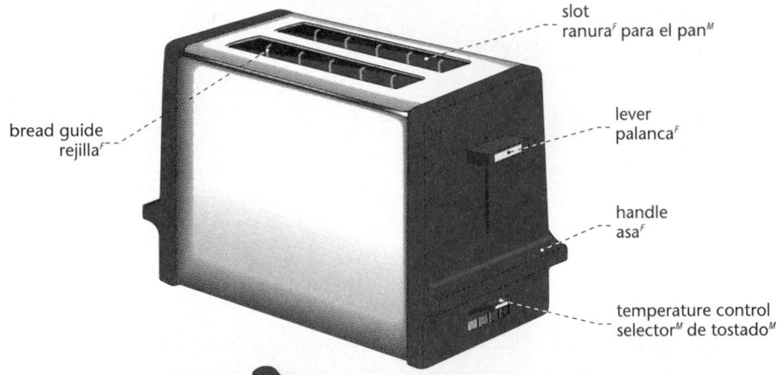

slot
ranura*F* para el pan*M*

bread guide
rejilla*F*

lever
palanca*F*

handle
asa*F*

temperature control
selector*M* de tostado*M*

DEEP FRYER
FREIDORA*F*

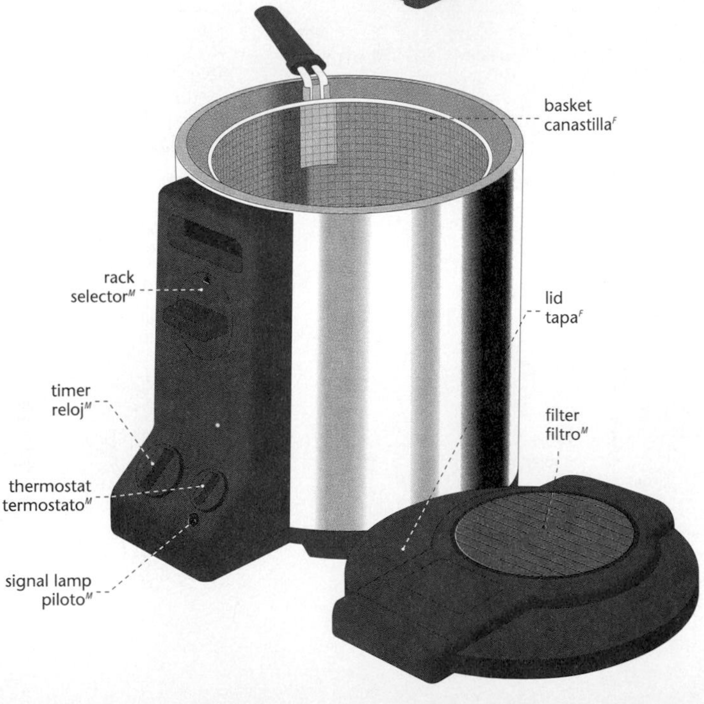

basket
canastilla*F*

rack
selector*M*

lid
tapa*F*

timer
reloj*M*

filter
filtro*M*

thermostat
termostato*M*

signal lamp
piloto*M*

WAFFLE IRON
BARQUILLERO*M* ELÉCTRICO

handle
asa*f*

lid
plancha*f* superior

plate
parrilla*f*

hinge
blsagra*f*

plate
parrilla*f*

temperature selector
selector*M* de temperatura*f*

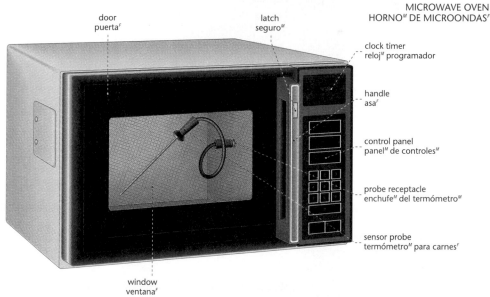

MICROWAVE OVEN
HORNO*M* DE MICROONDAS*F*

door
puerta*f*

latch
seguro*M*

clock timer
reloj*M* programador

handle
asa*f*

control panel
panel*M* de controles*M*

probe receptacle
enchufe*M* del termómetro*M*

sensor probe
termómetro*M* para carnes*f*

window
ventana*f*

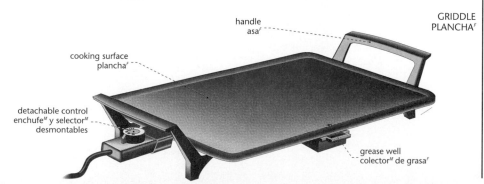

GRIDDLE
PLANCHA*F*

handle
asa*f*

cooking surface
plancha*f*

detachable control
enchufe*M* y selector*M*
desmontables

grease well
colector*M* de grasa*f*

253

REFRIGERATOR
FRIGORÍFICO^M

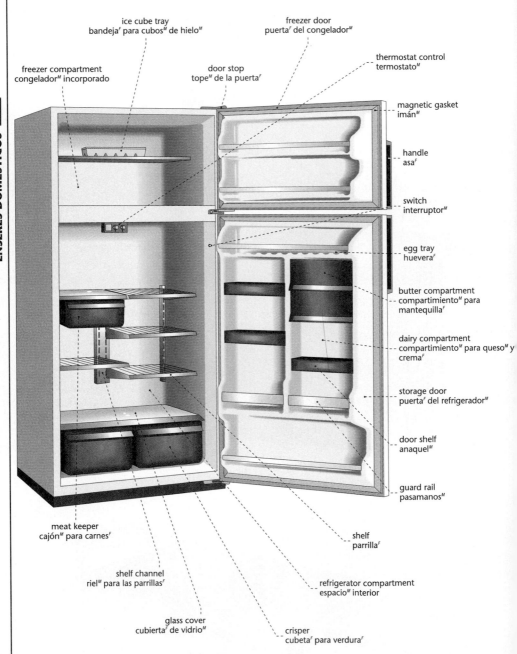

ice cube tray
bandeja^f para cubos^M de hielo^M

freezer door
puerta^f del congelador^M

thermostat control
termostato^M

freezer compartment
congelador^M incorporado

door stop
tope^M de la puerta^f

magnetic gasket
imán^M

handle
asa^f

switch
interruptor^M

egg tray
huevera^f

butter compartment
compartimiento^M para
mantequilla^f

dairy compartment
compartimiento^M para queso^M y
crema^f

storage door
puerta^f del refrigerador^M

door shelf
anaquel^M

guard rail
pasamanos^M

meat keeper
cajón^M para carnes^f

shelf
parrilla^f

shelf channel
riel^M para las parrillas^f

refrigerator compartment
espacio^M interior

glass cover
cubierta^f de vidrio^M

crisper
cubeta^f para verdura^f

254

RANGE HOOD
CAMPANA^F

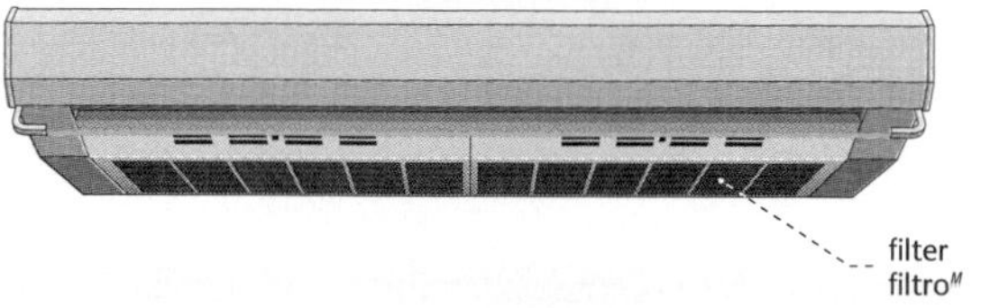

filter
filtro^M

ELECTRIC RANGE
COCINA^F ELÉCTRICA

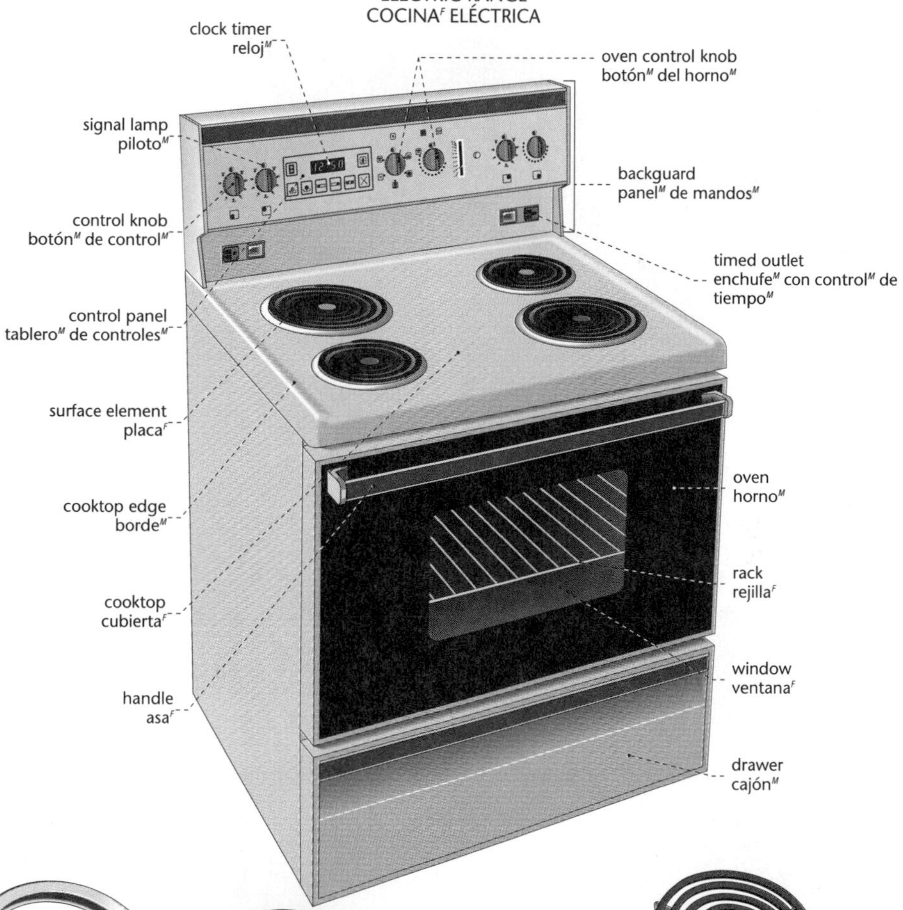

clock timer
reloj^M

oven control knob
botón^M del horno^M

signal lamp
piloto^M

backguard
panel^M de mandos^M

control knob
botón^M de control^M

timed outlet
enchufe^M con control^M de
tiempo^M

control panel
tablero^M de controles^M

surface element
placa^F

oven
horno^M

cooktop edge
borde^M

rack
rejilla^F

cooktop
cubierta^F

window
ventana^F

handle
asa^F

drawer
cajón^M

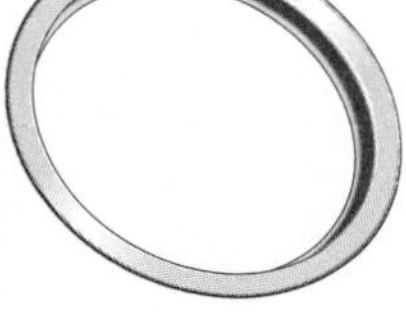

trim ring
arandela^F

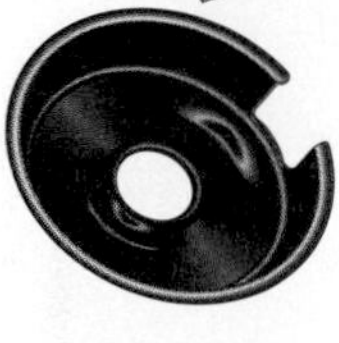

drip bowl
protector^M

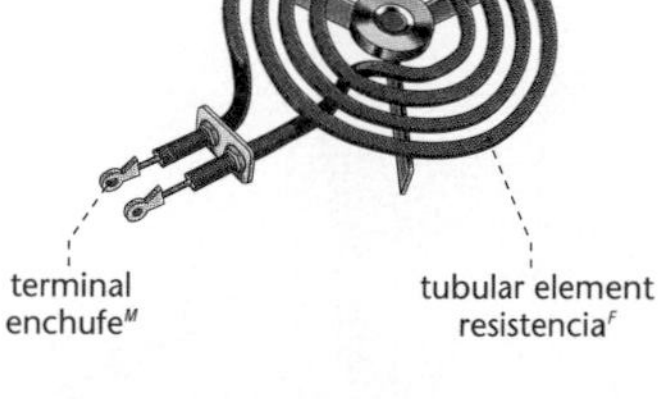

terminal
enchufe^M

tubular element
resistencia^F

DOMESTIC APPLIANCES
APARATOS^M ELECTRODOMÉSTICOS

STEAM IRON
PLANCHA^F DE VAPOR^M

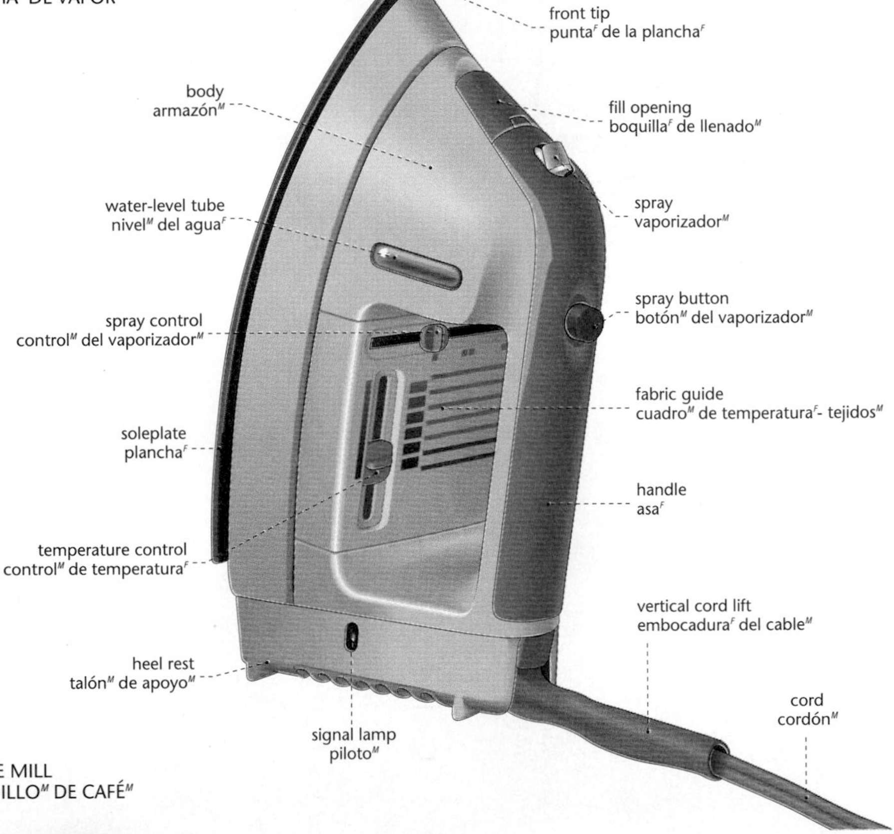

front tip
punta^F de la plancha^F

body
armazón^M

fill opening
boquilla^F de llenado^M

water-level tube
nivel^M del agua^F

spray
vaporizador^M

spray control
control^M del vaporizador^M

spray button
botón^M del vaporizador^M

fabric guide
cuadro^M de temperatura^F- tejidos^M

soleplate
plancha^F

handle
asa^F

temperature control
control^M de temperatura^F

vertical cord lift
embocadura^F del cable^M

heel rest
talón^M de apoyo^M

cord
cordón^M

signal lamp
piloto^M

COFFEE MILL
MOLINILLO^M DE CAFÉ^M

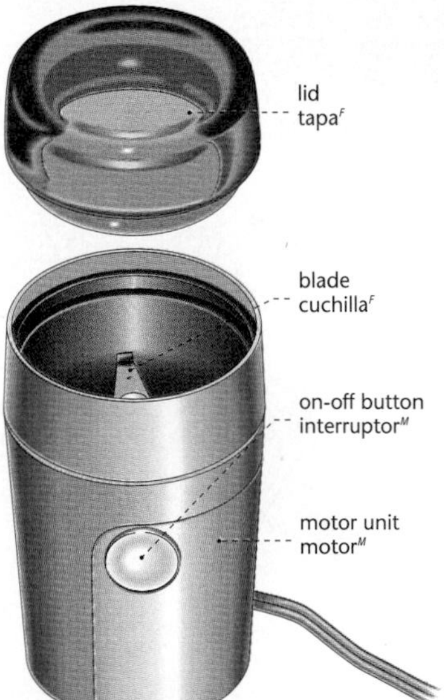

CAN OPENER
ABRELATAS^M

lid
tapa^F

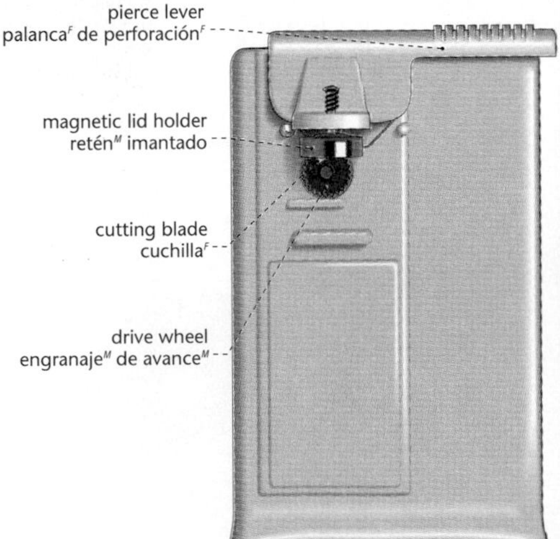

pierce lever
palanca^F de perforación^F

magnetic lid holder
retén^M imantado

blade
cuchilla^F

cutting blade
cuchilla^F

on-off button
interruptor^M

drive wheel
engranaje^M de avance^M

motor unit
motor^M

DOMESTIC APPLIANCES
APARATOS^M ELECTRODOMÉSTICOS

CONTROL PANEL
PANEL^M DE MANDOS^M

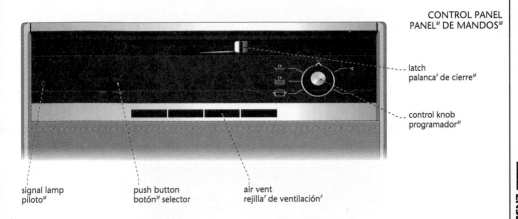

latch
palanca^F de cierre^M

control knob
programador^M

signal lamp
piloto^M

push button
botón^M selector

air vent
rejilla^F de ventilación^F

DISHWASHER
LAVAVAJILLAS^M

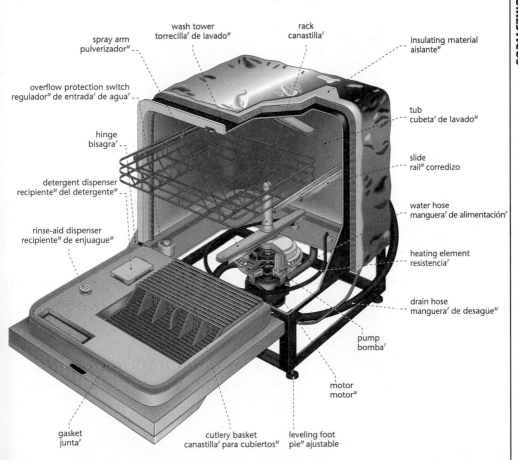

wash tower
torrecilla^F de lavado^M

rack
canastilla^F

spray arm
pulverizador^M

insulating material
aislante^M

overflow protection switch
regulador^M de entrada^F de agua^F

tub
cubeta^F de lavado^M

hinge
bisagra^F

slide
rail^M corredizo

detergent dispenser
recipiente^M del detergente^M

water hose
manguera^F de alimentación^F

rinse-aid dispenser
recipiente^M de enjuague^M

heating element
resistencia^F

drain hose
manguera^F de desagüe^M

pump
bomba^F

motor
motor^M

gasket
junta^F

cutlery basket
canastilla^F para cubiertos^M

leveling foot
pie^M ajustable

WASHER
LAVADORA^F

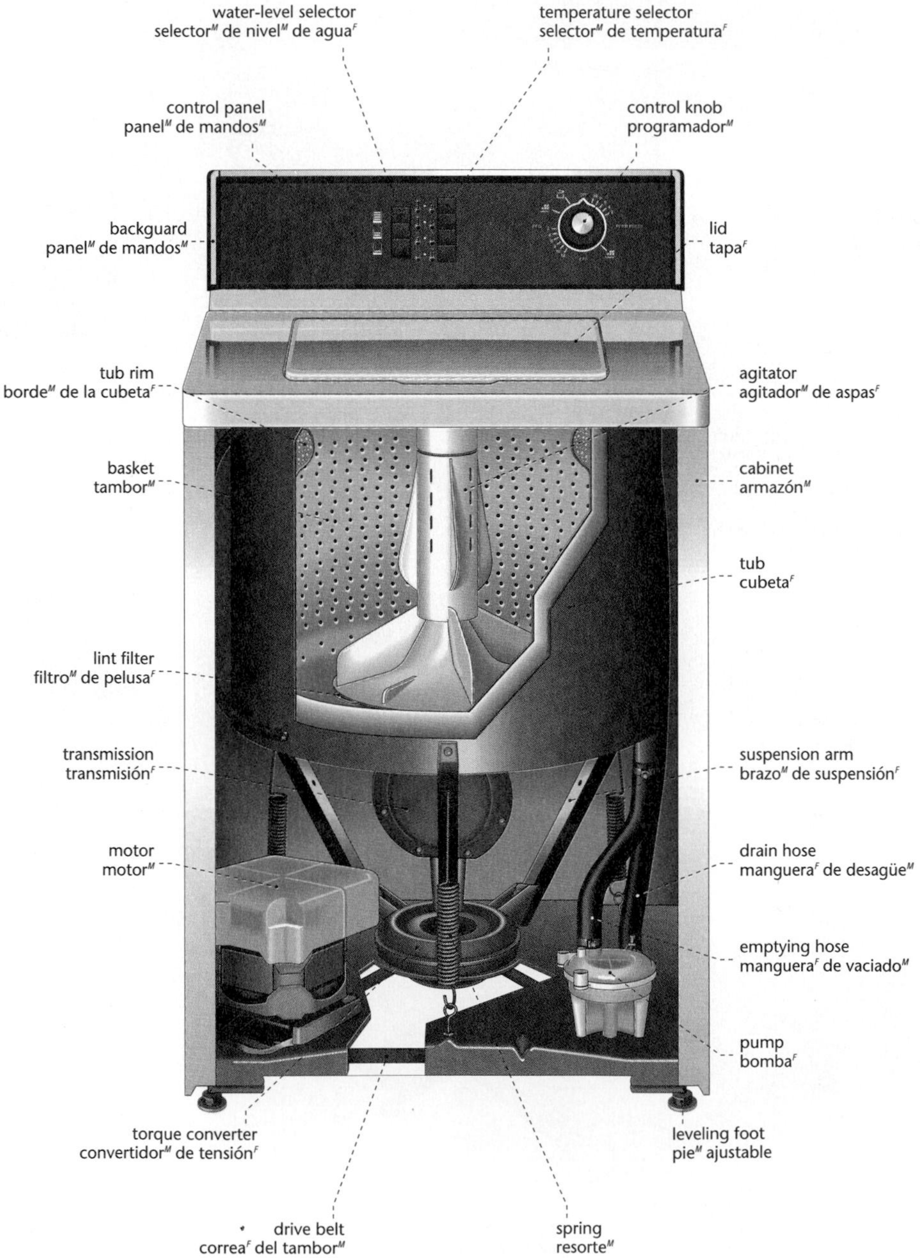

water-level selector
selector^M de nivel^M de agua^F

temperature selector
selector^M de temperatura^F

control panel
panel^M de mandos^M

control knob
programador^M

backguard
panel^M de mandos^M

lid
tapa^F

tub rim
borde^M de la cubeta^F

agitator
agitador^M de aspas^F

basket
tambor^M

cabinet
armazón^M

tub
cubeta^F

lint filter
filtro^M de pelusa^F

transmission
transmisión^F

suspension arm
brazo^M de suspensión^F

motor
motor^M

drain hose
manguera^F de desagüe^M

emptying hose
manguera^F de vaciado^M

pump
bomba^F

torque converter
convertidor^M de tensión^F

leveling foot
pie^M ajustable

drive belt
correa^F del tambor^M

spring
resorte^M

start switch
interruptor^M

temperature selector
selector^M de temperatura^F

control knob
programador^M

drum
tambor^M

control panel
tablero^M de control^M

heating duct
conducto^M de aire^M caliente

vane
aleta^F

backguard
panel^M de mandos^M

door switch
interruptor^M de la puerta^F

lint trap
filtro^M de pelusa^F

door
puerta^F

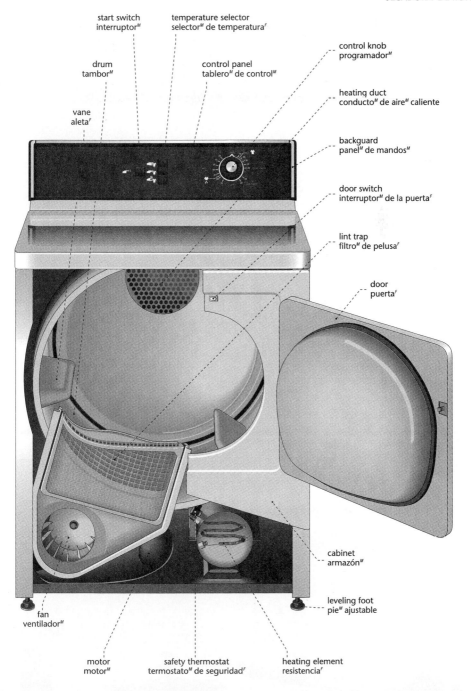

cabinet
armazón^M

leveling foot
pie^M ajustable

fan
ventilador^M

motor
motor^M

safety thermostat
termostato^M de seguridad^F

heating element
resistencia^F

**HOUSE FURNITURE
ENSERES DOMÉSTICOS**

HAND VACUUM CLEANER
ASPIRADOR^M MANUAL

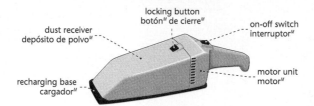

dust receiver
depósito de polvo^M

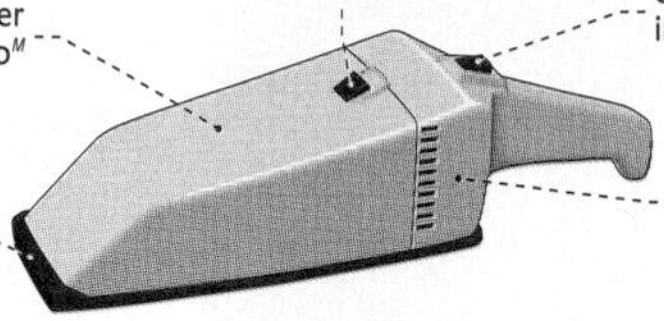

locking button
botón^M de cierre^M

on-off switch
interruptor^M

recharging base
cargador^M

motor unit
motor^M

CANISTER VACUUM CLEANER
ASPIRADOR^M

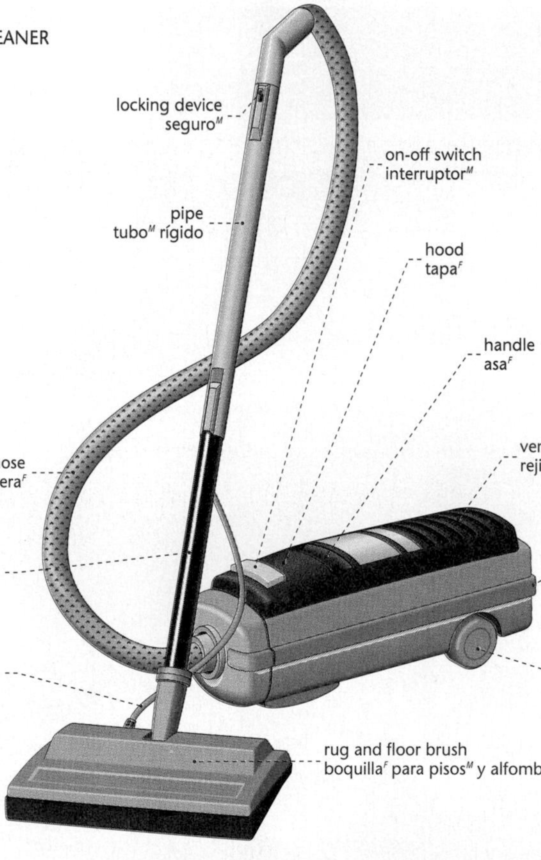

locking device
seguro^M

on-off switch
interruptor^M

pipe
tubo^M rígido

hood
tapa^F

handle
asa^F

flexible hose
manguera^F

ventilating grille
rejilla^F del ventilador^M

extension pipe
tubo^M de extensión^F

bumper
tope^M amortiguador

cord
cordón^M

caster
ruedecilla^F

rug and floor brush
boquilla^F para pisos^M y alfombras^F

CLEANING TOOLS
ACCESORIOS^M

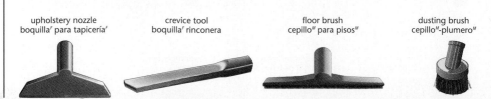

upholstery nozzle
boquilla^F para tapicería^F

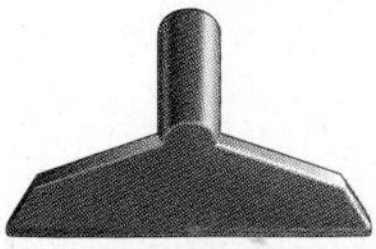

crevice tool
boquilla^F rinconera

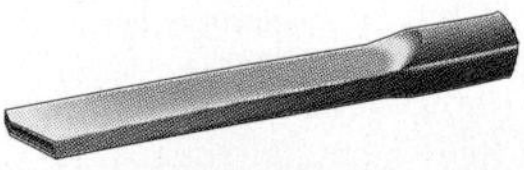

floor brush
cepillo^M para pisos^M

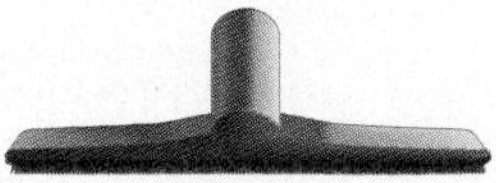

dusting brush
cepillo^M-plumero^M

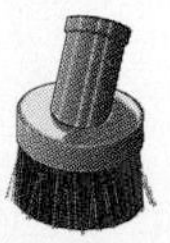

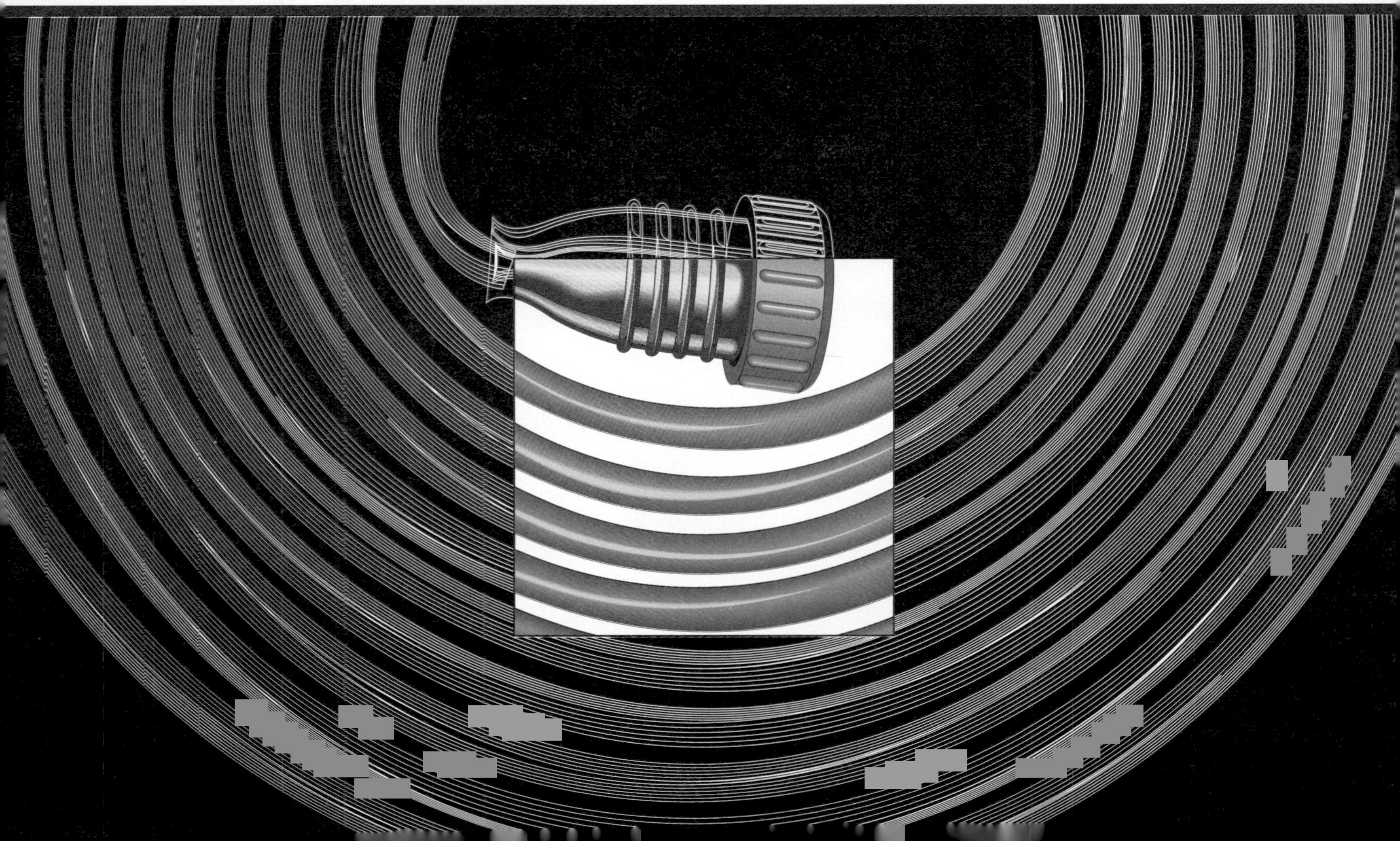

CONTENTS

GARDENING
JARDINERÍA

PLEASURE GARDEN
JARDÍN^M

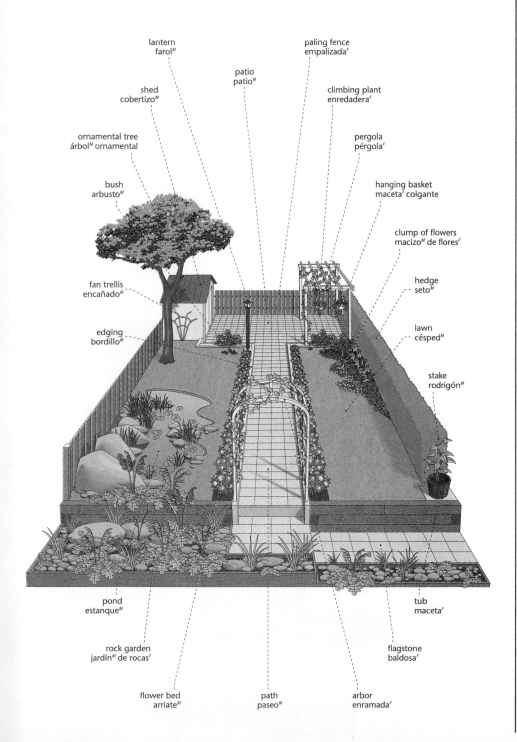

lantern
farol^M

patio
patio^M

paling fence
empalizada^F

climbing plant
enredadera^F

shed
cobertizo^M

pergola
pérgola^F

ornamental tree
árbol^M ornamental

hanging basket
maceta^F colgante

bush
arbusto^M

clump of flowers
macizo^M de flores^F

fan trellis
encañado^M

hedge
seto^M

lawn
césped^M

edging
bordillo^M

stake
rodrigón^M

pond
estanque^M

tub
maceta^F

rock garden
jardín^M de rocas^F

flagstone
baldosa^F

flower bed
arriate^M

path
paseo^M

arbor
enramada^F

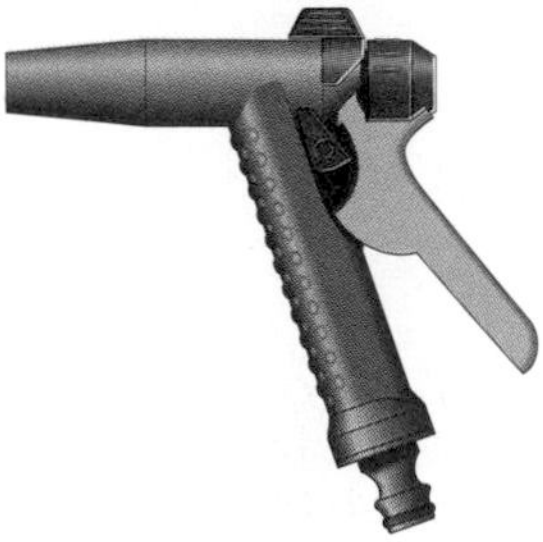

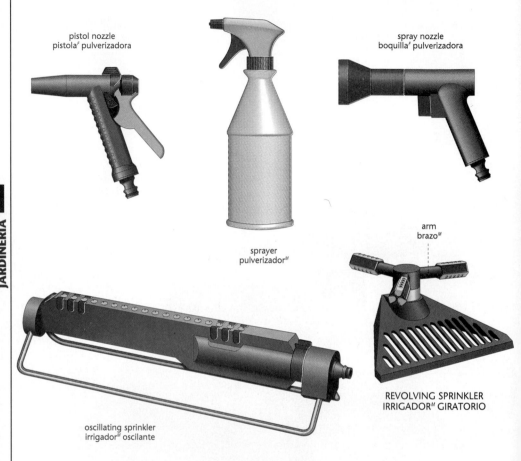

pistol nozzle
pistola^F pulverizadora

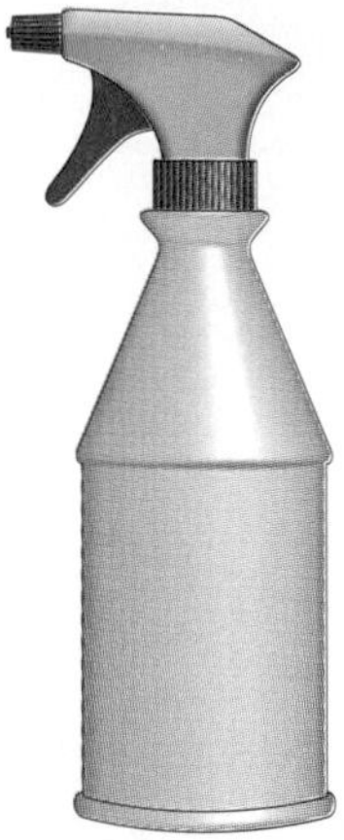

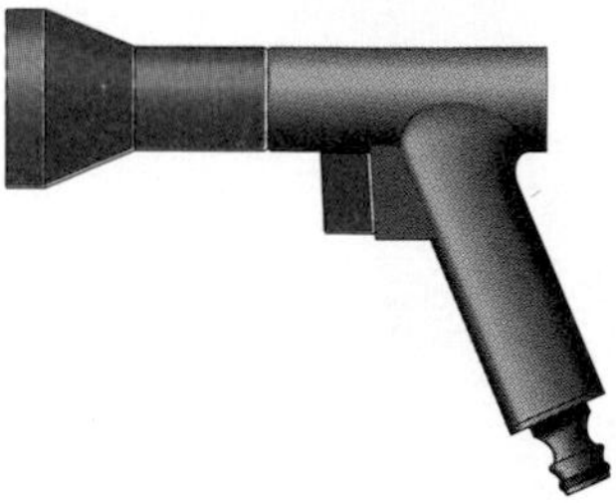

spray nozzle
boquilla^F pulverizadora

sprayer
pulverizador^M

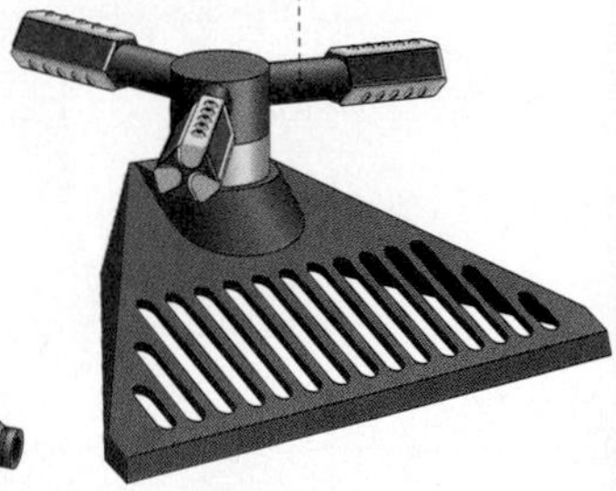

arm
brazo^M

REVOLVING SPRINKLER
IRRIGADOR^M GIRATORIO

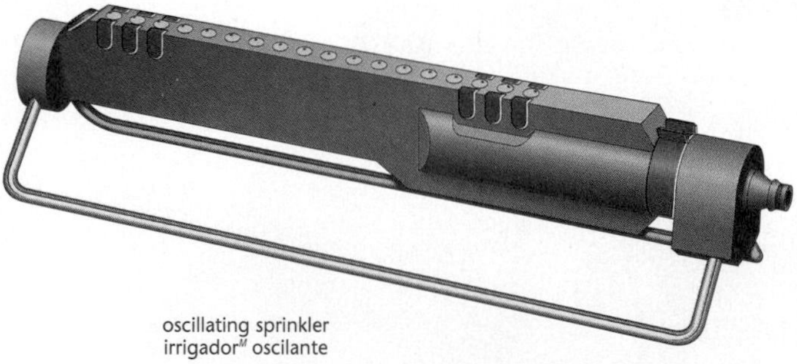

oscillating sprinkler
irrigador^M oscilante

IMPULSE SPRINKLER
IRRIGADOR^M DE IMPULSO^M

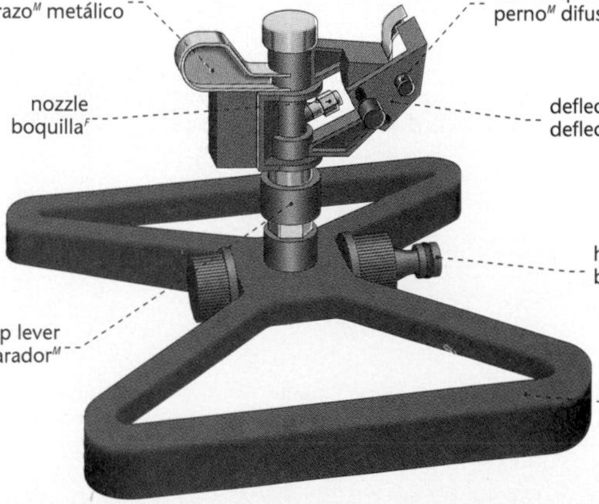

metal arm
brazo^M metálico

diffuser pin
perno^M difusor

nozzle
boquilla^F

deflector
deflector^M

hose connector
boca^F para la manguera^F

trip lever
disparador^M

sled
soporte^M

HOSE TROLLEY
CARRETILLA^F PARA MANGUERA^F

sprinkler hose
manguera^F de riego^M

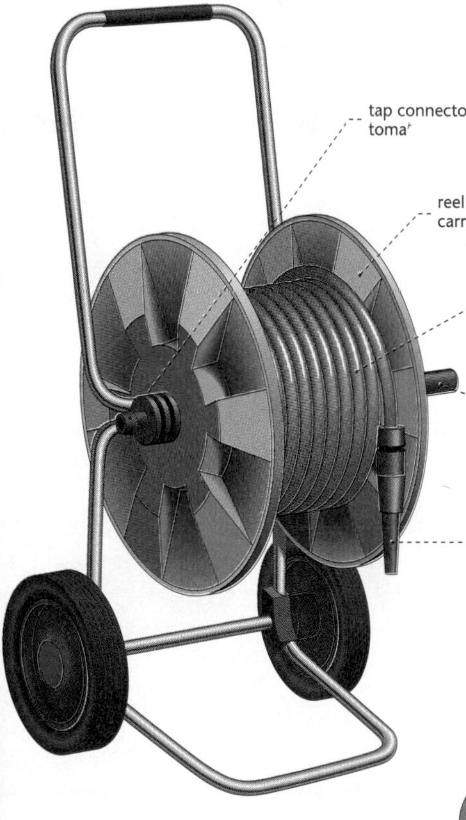

tap connector
toma^F

reel
carrete^M

garden hose
manguera^F

trolley crank
manivela^F del carrete^M

hose nozzle
boquilla^F

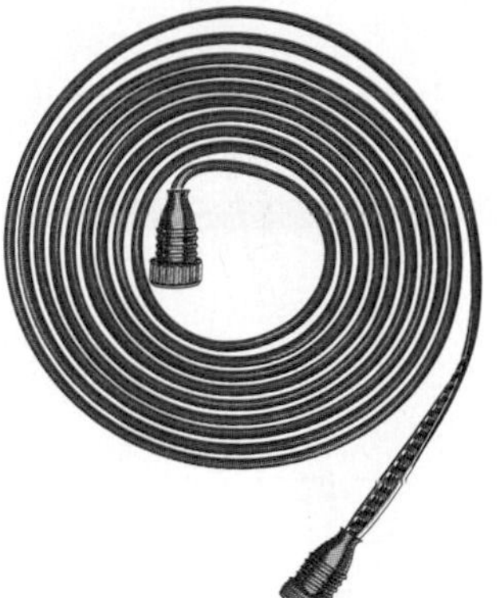

tank sprayer
pulverizador^M

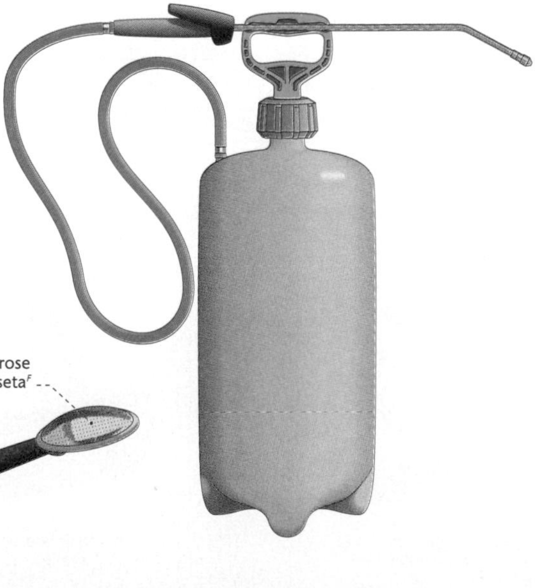

WATERING CAN
REGADERA^F

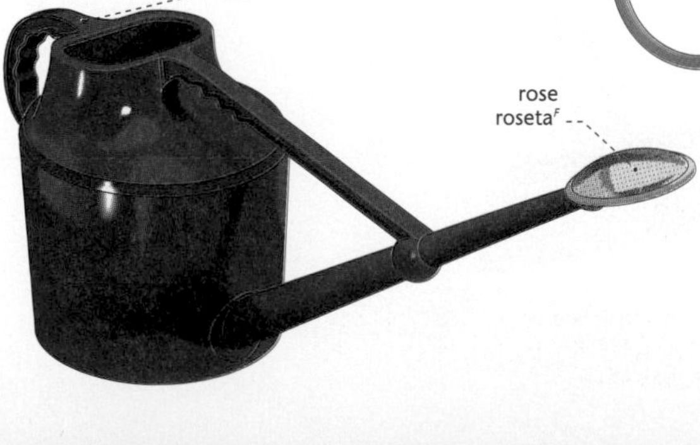

handle
asa^F

rose
roseta^F

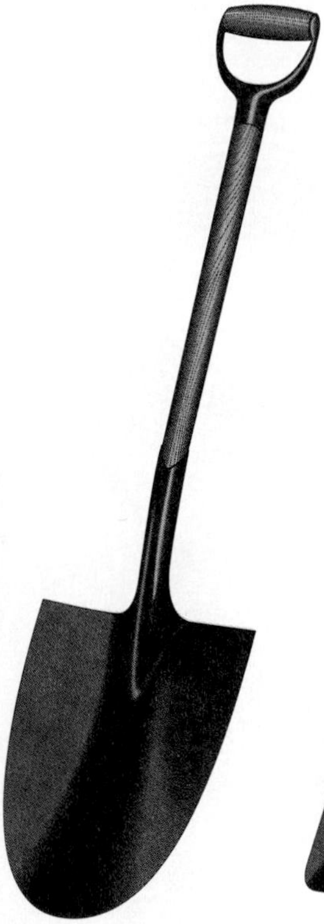

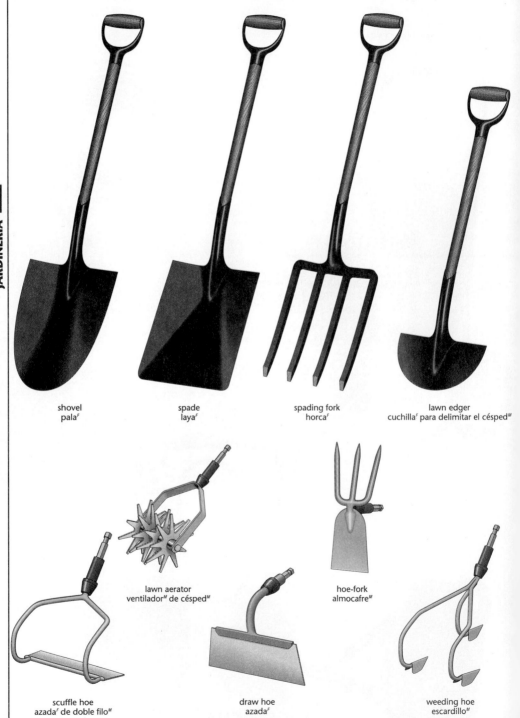

shovel
pala^F

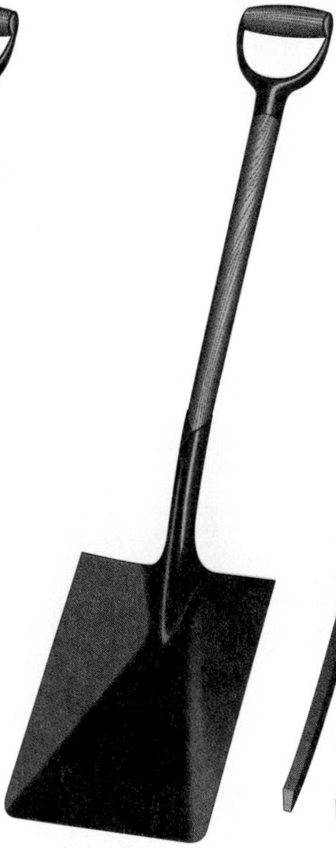

spade
laya^F

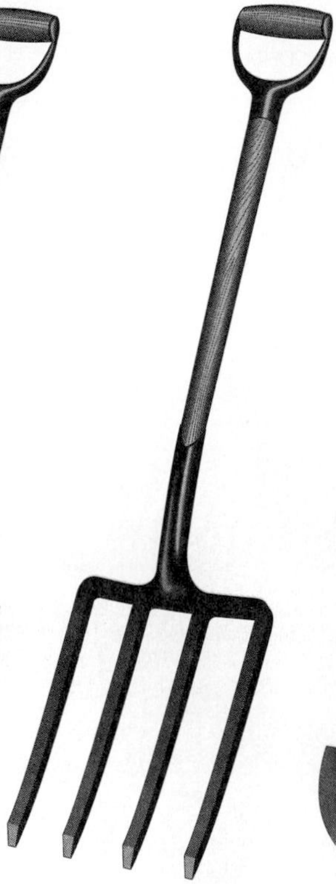

spading fork
horca^F

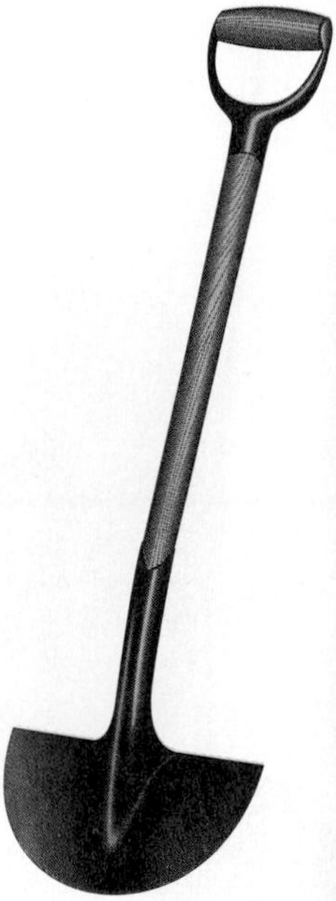

lawn edger
cuchilla^F para delimitar el césped^M

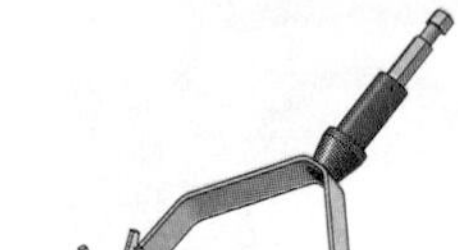

lawn aerator
ventilador^M de césped^M

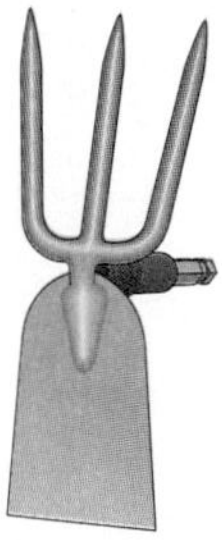

hoe-fork
almocafre^M

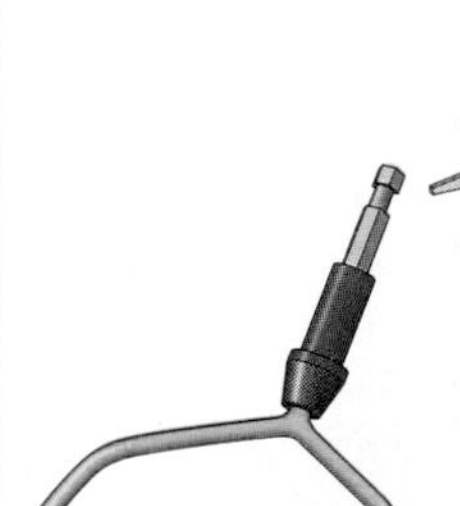

scuffle hoe
azada^F de doble filo^M

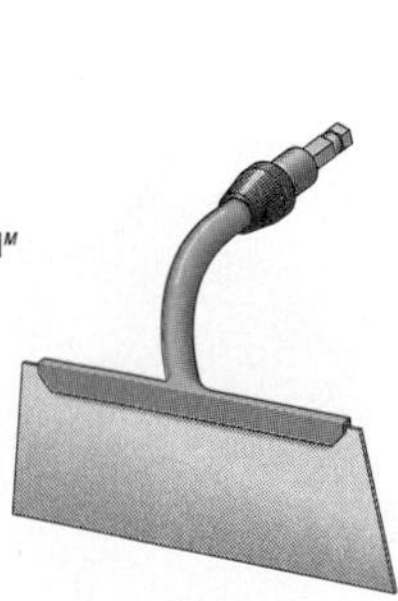

draw hoe
azada^F

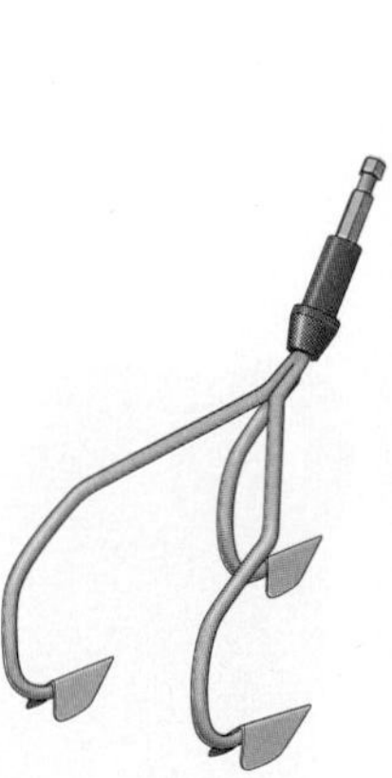

weeding hoe
escardillo^M

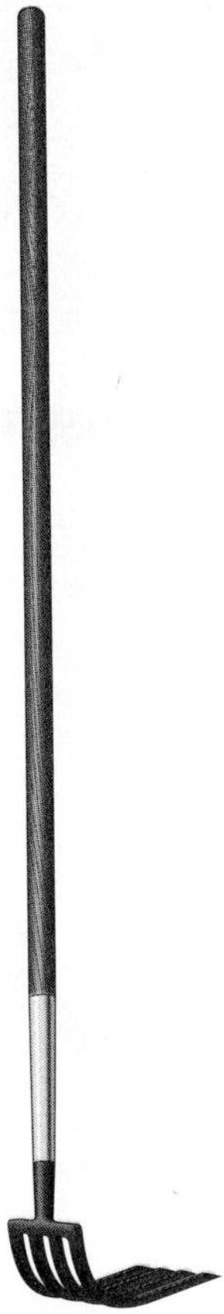

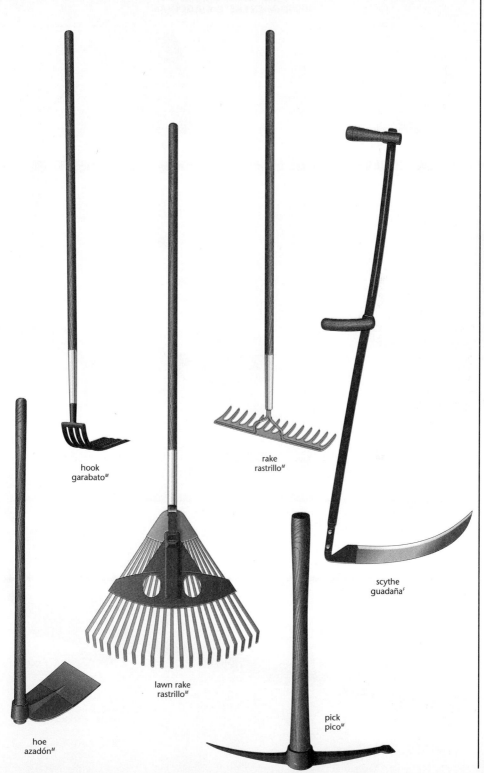

hook
garabato[M]

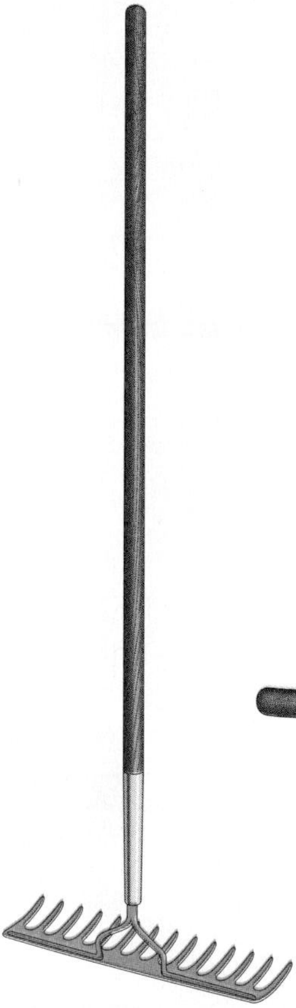

rake
rastrillo[M]

scythe
guadaña[F]

lawn rake
rastrillo[M]

pick
pico[M]

hoe
azadón[M]

267

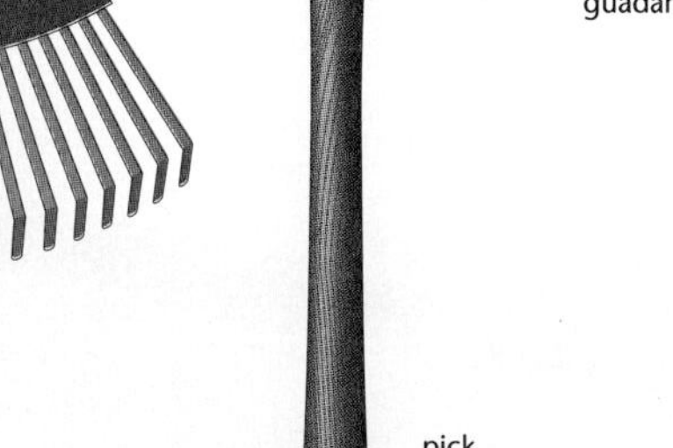

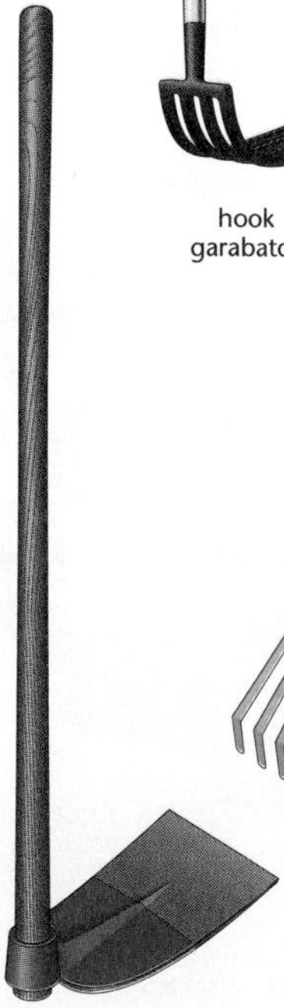

TOOLS AND EQUIPMENT
HERRAMIENTAS^F Y MÁQUINAS^F

hand fork
horquilla^F de mano^F

weeder
desyerbador^M

trowel
desplantador^M

small hand cultivator
cultivador^M de mano^F

seeder
sembradora^F de mano^F

garden line
instrumento^M para alinear el jardín^M

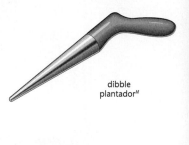

dibble
plantador^M

bulb dibble
plantador^M de bulbos^M

HEDGE TRIMMER
CORTASETOS^M ELÉCTRICO

cord
cable^M

hand protector
protector^M

trigger
gatillo^M

tooth
diente^M

blade
cuchilla^F

electric motor
motor^M eléctrico

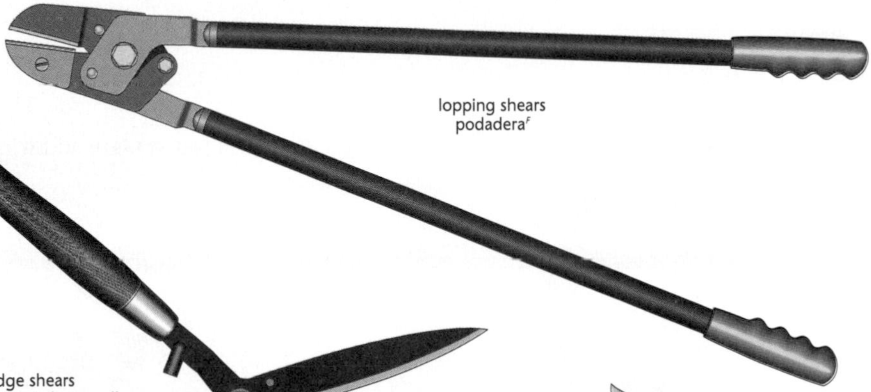

lopping shears
podadera^F

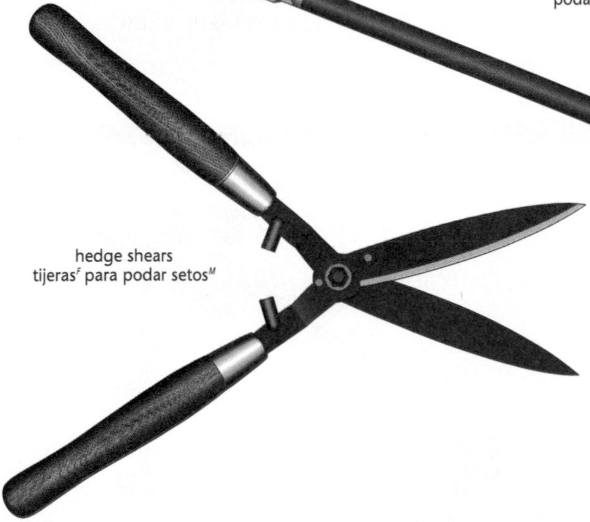

hedge shears
tijeras^F para podar setos^M

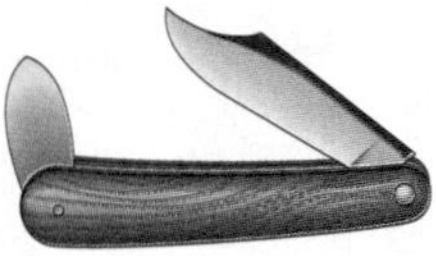

grafting knife
navaja^F de injertar

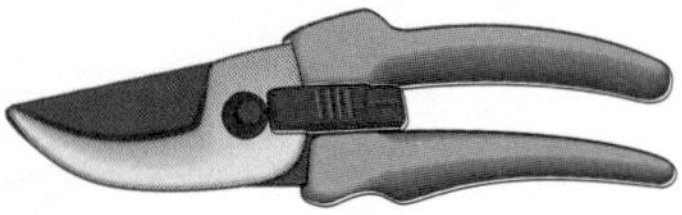

pruning shears
tijeras^F de podar

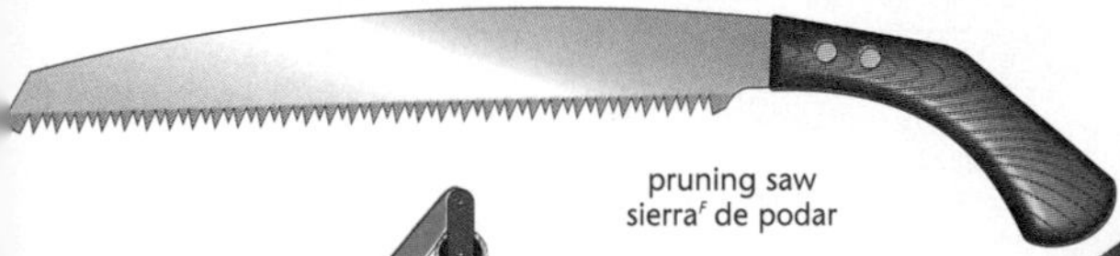

pruning saw
sierra^F de podar

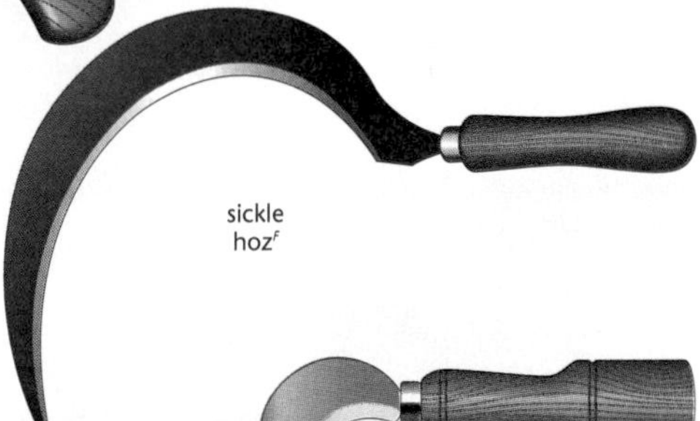

sickle
hoz^F

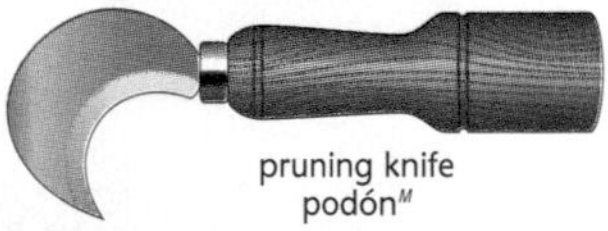

pruning knife
podón^M

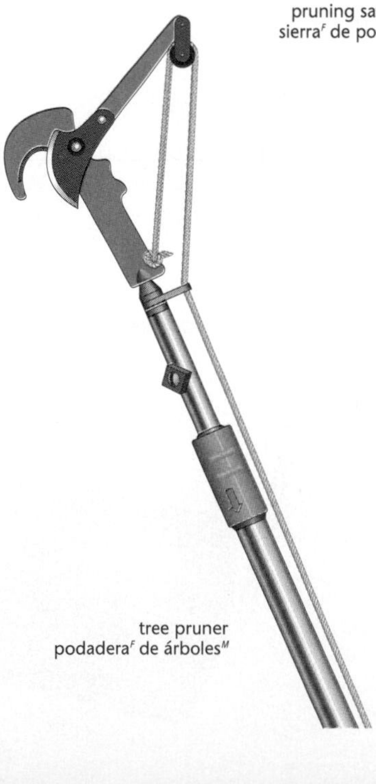

tree pruner
podadera^F de árboles^M

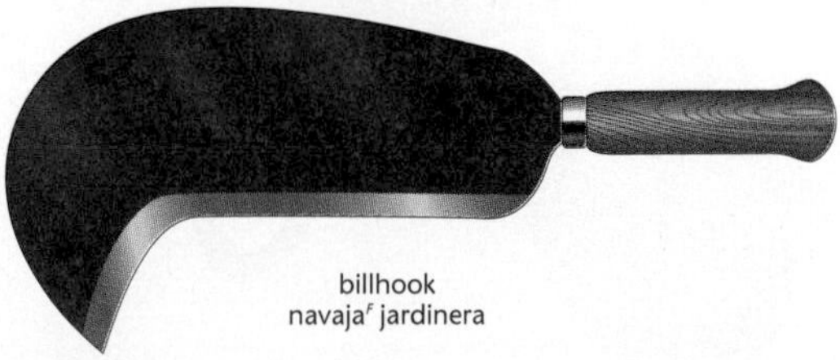

billhook
navaja^F jardinera

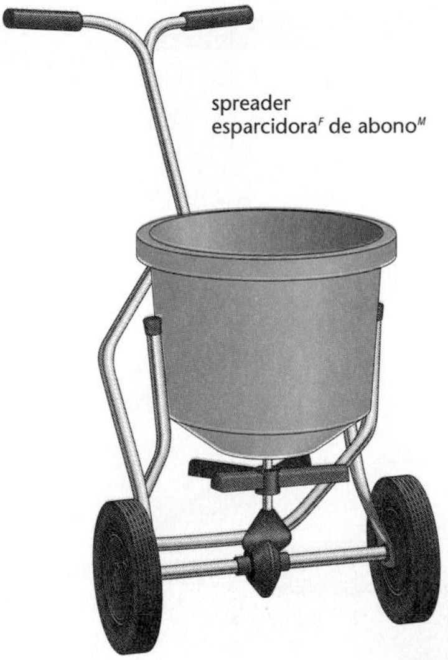

spreader
esparcidora*F* de abono*M*

MOTORIZED EARTH AUGER
TALADRO*M* DE MOTOR*M*

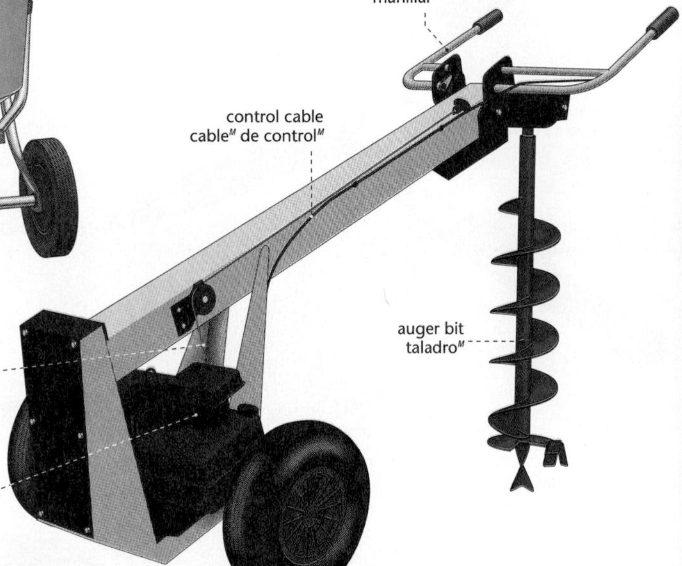

handle
manillar*M*

control cable
cable*M* de control*M*

auger bit
taladro*M*

starting cable
cable*M* de arranque*M*

motor
motor*M*

WHEELBARROW
CARRETILLA*F*

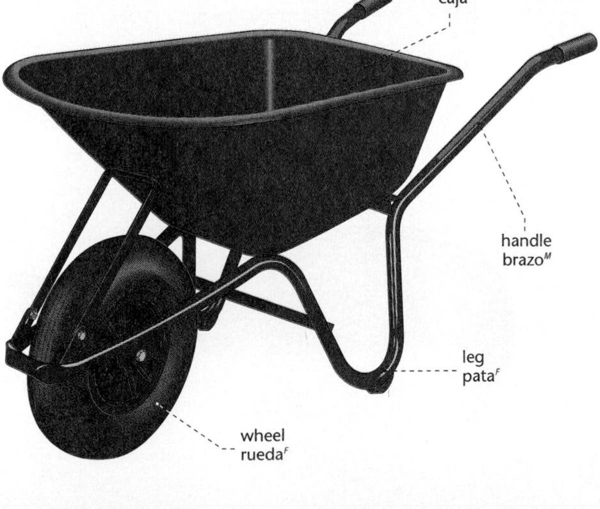

tray
caja*F*

roller
rodillo*M*

handle
brazo*M*

leg
pata*F*

wheel
rueda*F*

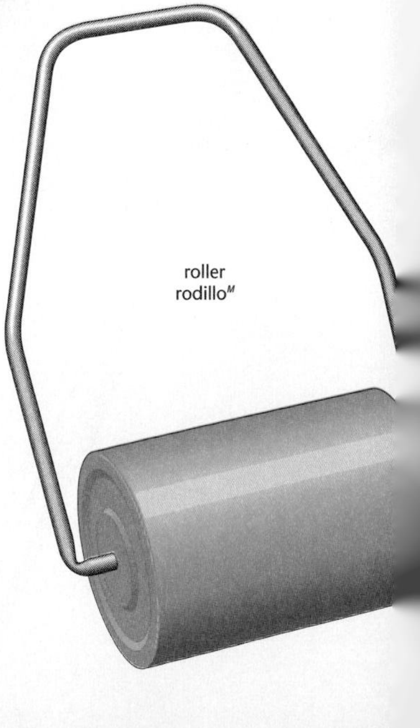

HAND MOWER
CORTACÉSPED^M

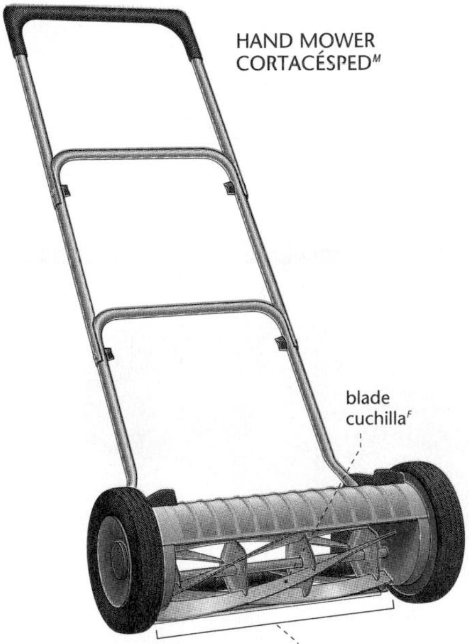

blade
cuchilla^F

cutting cylinder
cilindro^M de corte^M

EDGER
PODADORA^F DE BORDES^M

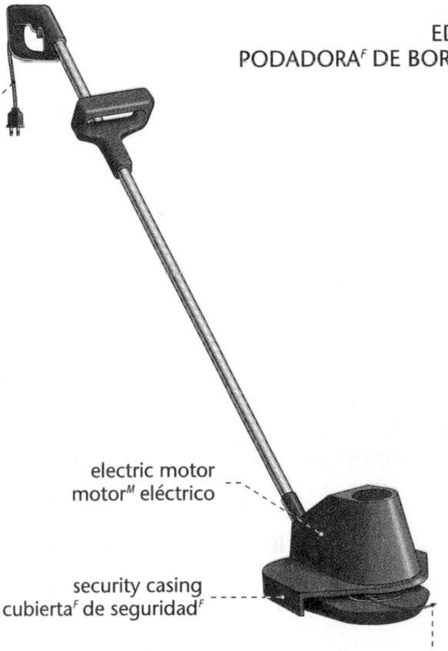

cord
cable^M

electric motor
motor^M eléctrico

security casing
cubierta^F de seguridad^F

nylon yarn
hilo^M de nilón^M

POWER MOWER
CORTACÉSPED^M ELÉCTRICO

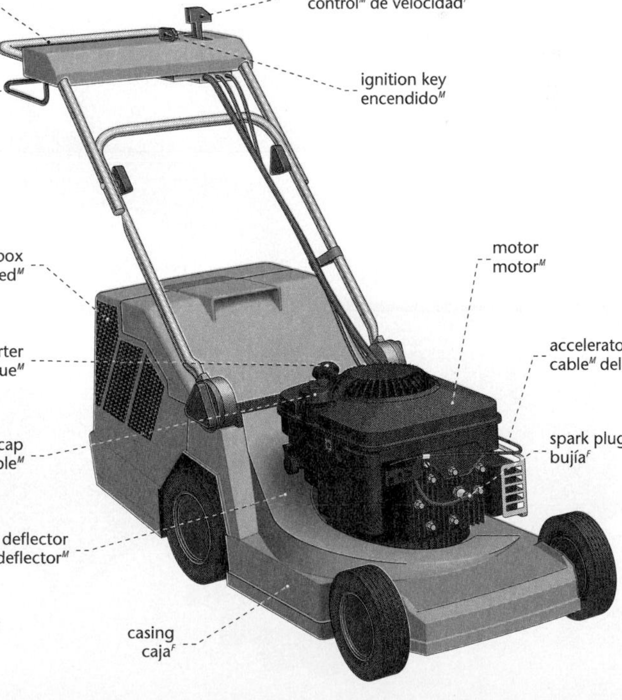

handle
barra^F

speed control
control^M de velocidad^F

safety handle
palanca^F de seguridad^F

ignition key
encendido^M

grassbox
caja^F para el césped^M

motor
motor^M

starter
motor^M de arranque^M

accelerator cable
cable^M del acelerador^M

filler cap
boca^F del tanque^M de combustible^M

spark plug
bujía^F

deflector
deflector^M

casing
caja^F

CHAINSAW
SIERRA*F* DE CADENA*F*

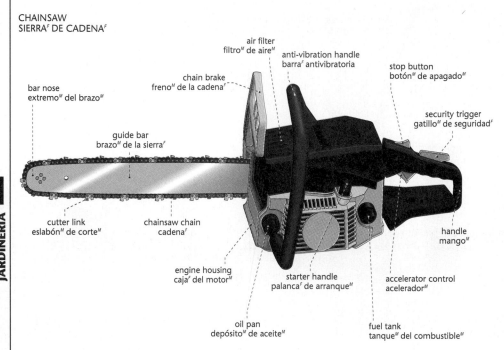

air filter
filtro*M* de aire*M*

anti-vibration handle
barra*F* antivibratoria

stop button
botón*M* de apagado*M*

chain brake
freno*M* de la cadena*F*

bar nose
extremo*M* del brazo*M*

security trigger
gatillo*M* de seguridad*F*

guide bar
brazo*M* de la sierra*F*

cutter link
eslabón*M* de corte*M*

chainsaw chain
cadena*F*

handle
mango*M*

engine housing
caja*F* del motor*M*

starter handle
palanca*F* de arranque*M*

accelerator control
acelerador*M*

oil pan
depósito*M* de aceite*M*

fuel tank
tanque*M* del combustible*M*

TILLER
CULTIVADORA*F*

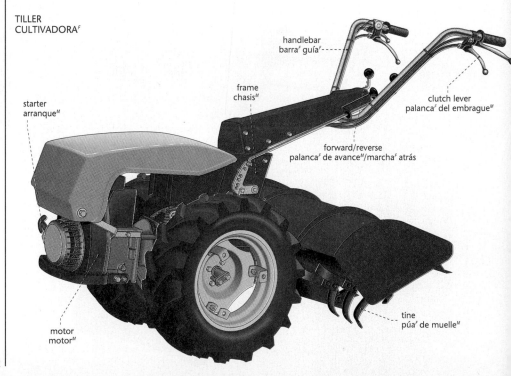

handlebar
barra*F* guía*F*

frame
chasis*M*

clutch lever
palanca*F* del embrague*M*

starter
arranque*M*

forward/reverse
palanca*F* de avance*M*/marcha*F* atrás

motor
motor*M*

tine
púa*F* de muelle*M*

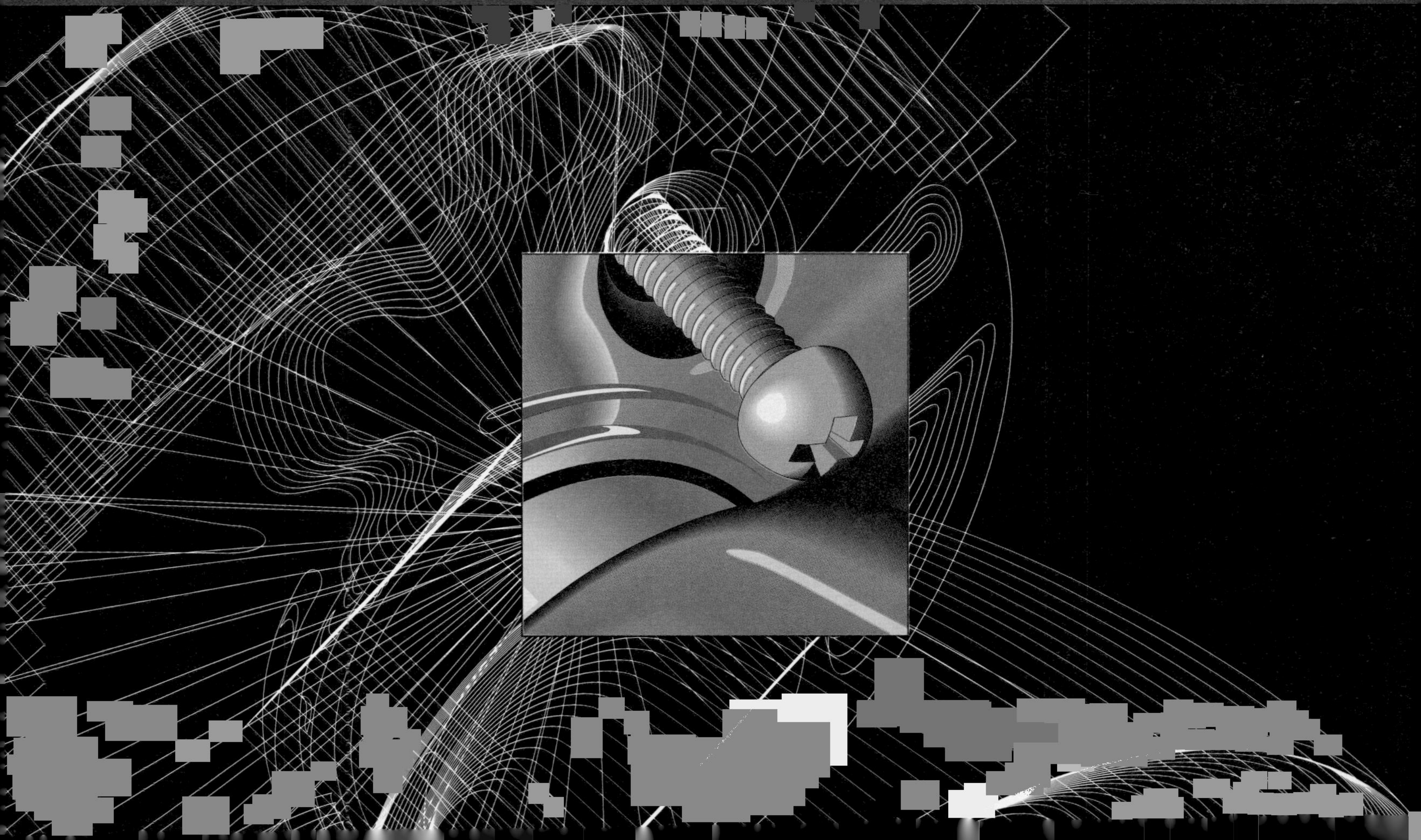

CONTENTS

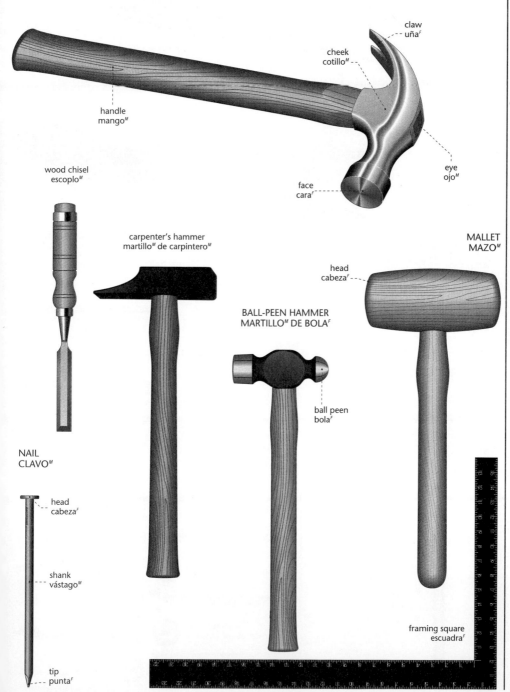

CLAW HAMMER
MARTILLO^M DE UÑA^F

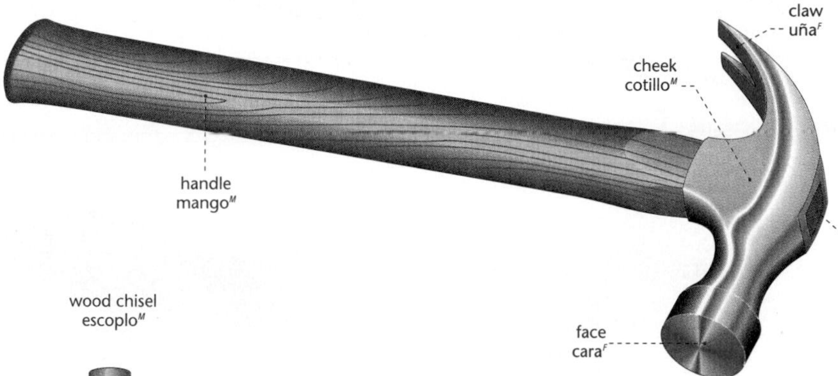

claw
uña^F

cheek
cotillo^M

handle
mango^M

eye
ojo^M

wood chisel
escoplo^M

face
cara^F

carpenter's hammer
martillo^M de carpintero^M

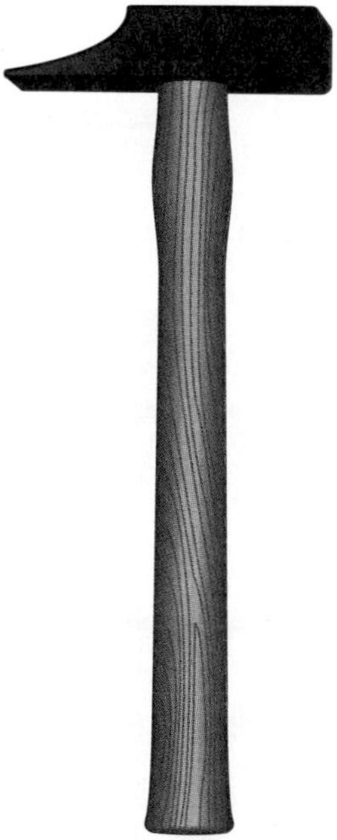

MALLET
MAZO^M

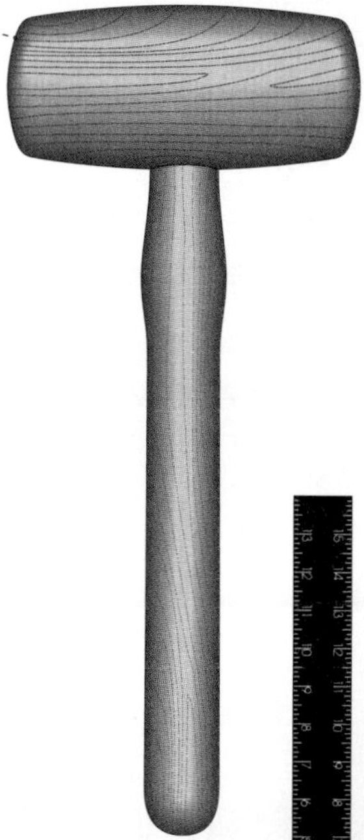

head
cabeza^F

BALL-PEEN HAMMER
MARTILLO^M DE BOLA^F

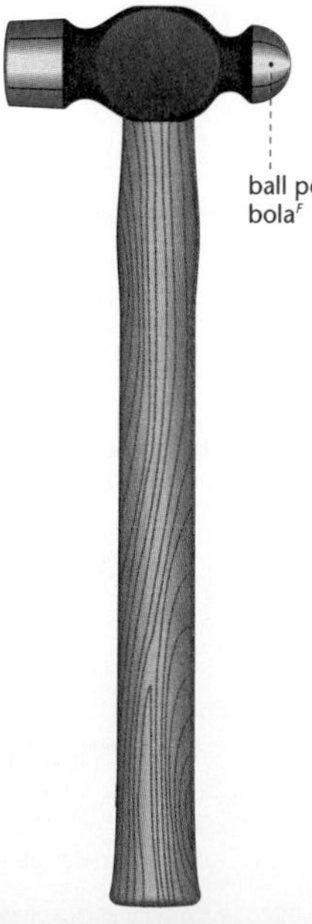

ball peen
bola^F

NAIL
CLAVO^M

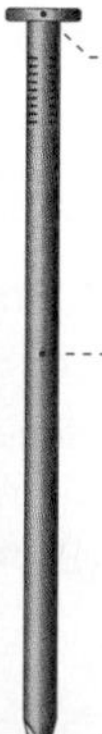

head
cabeza^F

shank
vástago^M

framing square
escuadra^F

tip
punta^F

DO-IT-YOURSELF
REPARACIONES CASERAS

275

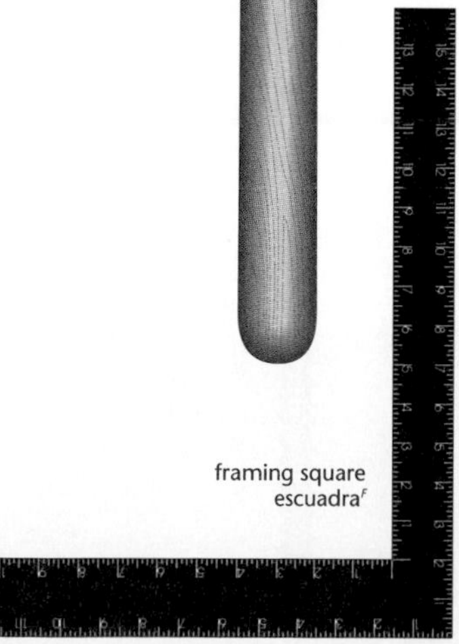

DO-IT-YOURSELF
REPARACIONES CASERAS

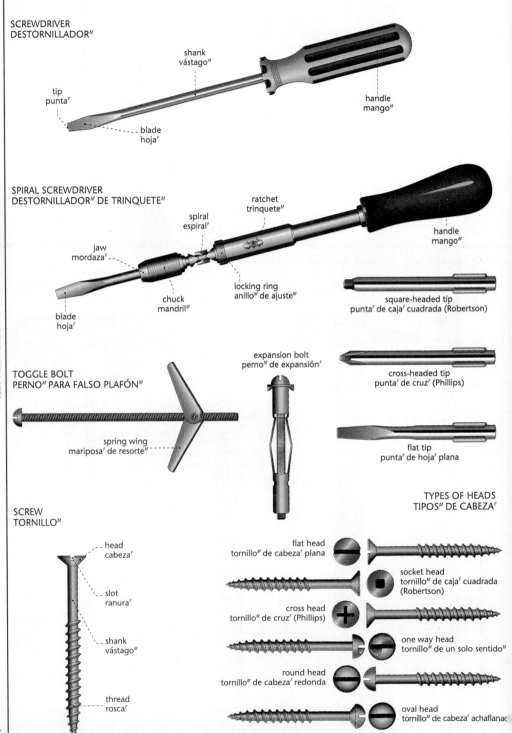

SCREWDRIVER
DESTORNILLADOR*ᴹ*

shank
vástago*ᴹ*

tip
punta*ᶠ*

handle
mango*ᴹ*

blade
hoja*ᶠ*

SPIRAL SCREWDRIVER
DESTORNILLADOR*ᴹ* DE TRINQUETE*ᴹ*

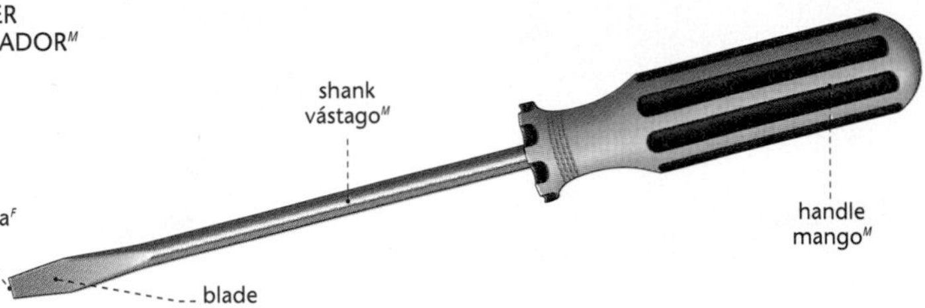

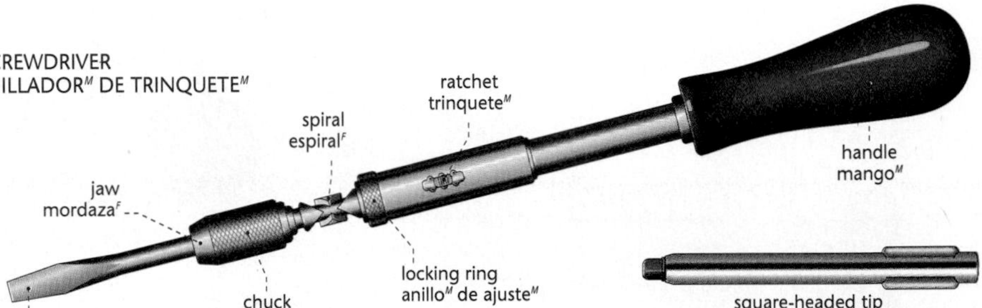

ratchet
trinquete*ᴹ*

spiral
espiral*ᶠ*

jaw
mordaza*ᶠ*

handle
mango*ᴹ*

locking ring
anillo*ᴹ* de ajuste*ᴹ*

chuck
mandril*ᴹ*

blade
hoja*ᶠ*

square-headed tip
punta*ᶠ* de caja*ᶠ* cuadrada (Robertson)

TOGGLE BOLT
PERNO*ᴹ* PARA FALSO PLAFÓN*ᴹ*

expansion bolt
perno*ᴹ* de expansión*ᶠ*

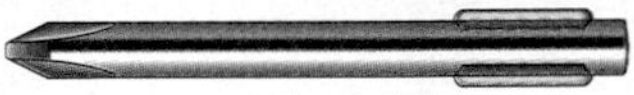

cross-headed tip
punta*ᶠ* de cruz*ᶠ* (Phillips)

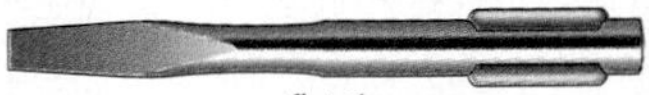

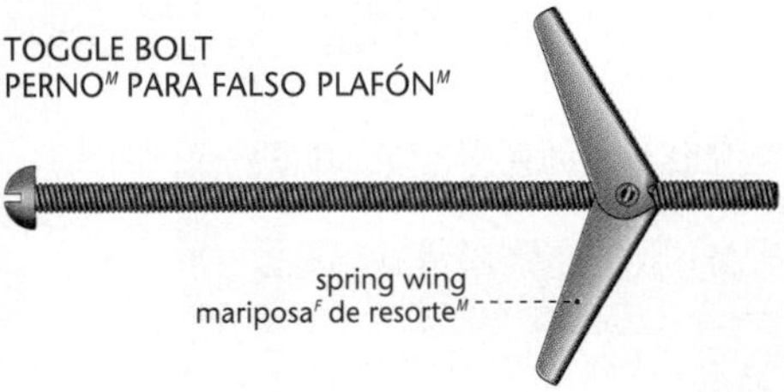

spring wing
mariposa*ᶠ* de resorte*ᴹ*

flat tip
punta*ᶠ* de hoja*ᶠ* plana

TYPES OF HEADS
TIPOS*ᴹ* DE CABEZA*ᶠ*

SCREW
TORNILLO*ᴹ*

head
cabeza*ᶠ*

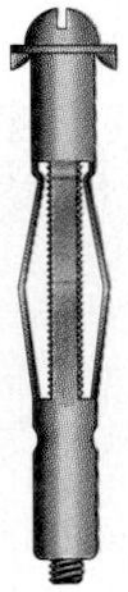

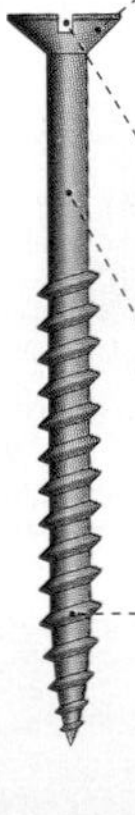

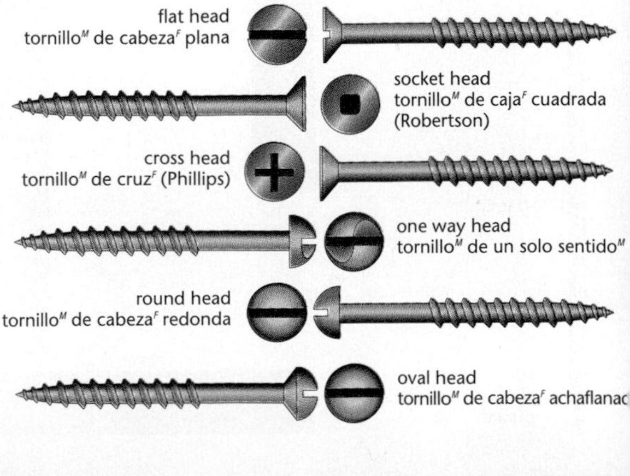

flat head
tornillo*ᴹ* de cabeza*ᶠ* plana

socket head
tornillo*ᴹ* de caja*ᶠ* cuadrada
(Robertson)

slot
ranura*ᶠ*

cross head
tornillo*ᴹ* de cruz*ᶠ* (Phillips)

shank
vástago*ᴹ*

one way head
tornillo*ᴹ* de un solo sentido*ᴹ*

round head
tornillo*ᴹ* de cabeza*ᶠ* redonda

thread
rosca*ᶠ*

oval head
tornillo*ᴹ* de cabeza*ᶠ* achaflanac

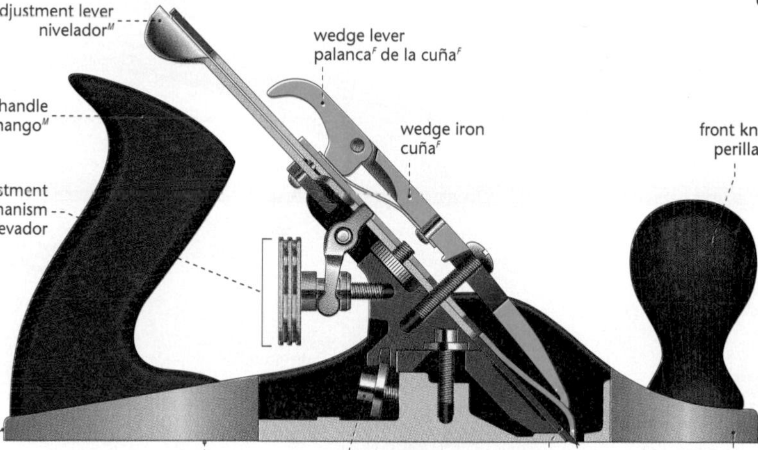

lateral-adjustment lever
nivelador^M

wedge lever
palanca^F de la cuña^F

handle
mango^M

wedge iron
cuña^F

front knob
perilla^F

depth adjustment
mechanism
tornillo^M elevador

heel
talón^M

face
base^F

blade
hoja^F

toe
puntera^F

frog-adjustment screw
ajustador^M de ranilla^F

cap iron
contrahoja^F

HACKSAW
SIERRA^F PARA METALES^M

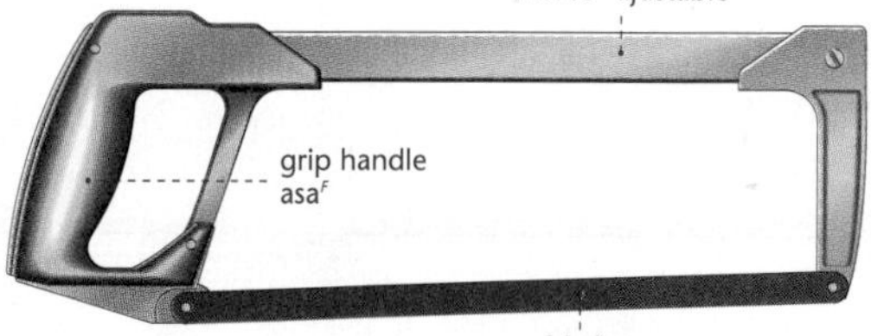

adjustable frame
marco^M ajustable

grip handle
asa^F

file
lima^F

blade
hoja^F

HANDSAW
SERRUCHO^M

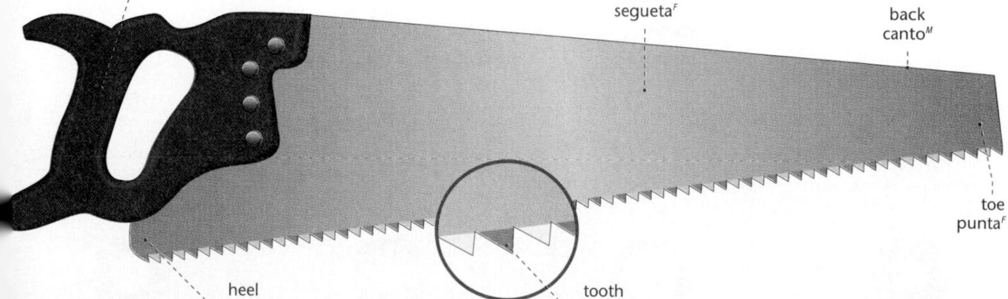

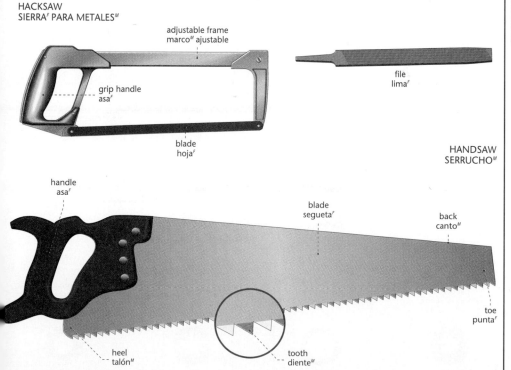

handle
asa^F

blade
segueta^F

back
canto^M

toe
punta^F

heel
talón^M

tooth
diente^M

SLIP JOINT PLIERS
ALICATES^M DE PIVOTE^M MÓVIL

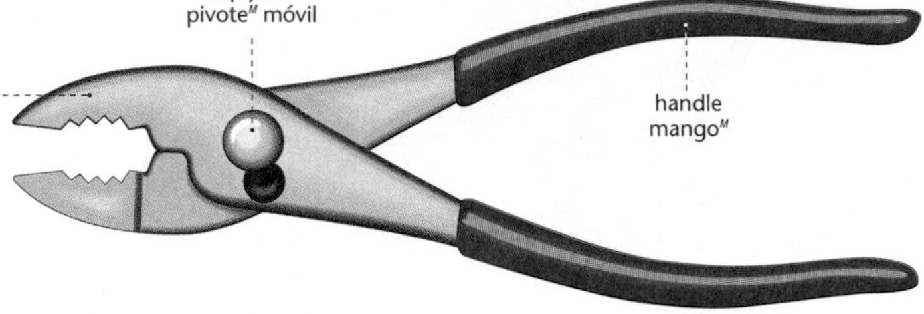

slip joint
pivote^M móvil

curved jaw
mordaza^F curva

handle
mango^M

RIB JOINT PLIERS
ALICATES^M DE EXTENSIÓN^F

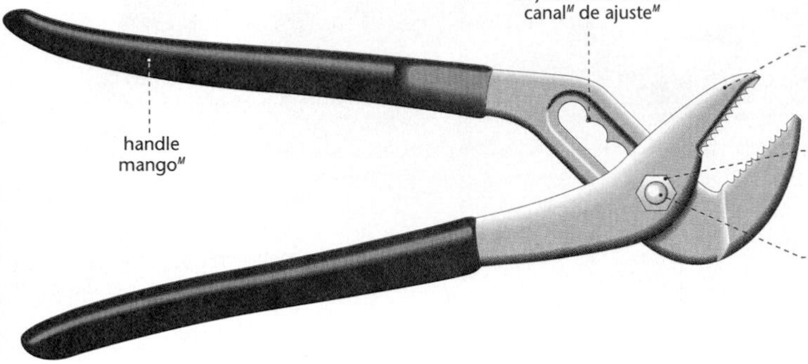

adjustable channel
canal^M de ajuste^M

straight jaw
mordaza^F recta

handle
mango^M

nut
tuerca^F

bolt
perno^M

LOCKING PLIERS
ALICATES^M DE PRESIÓN^F

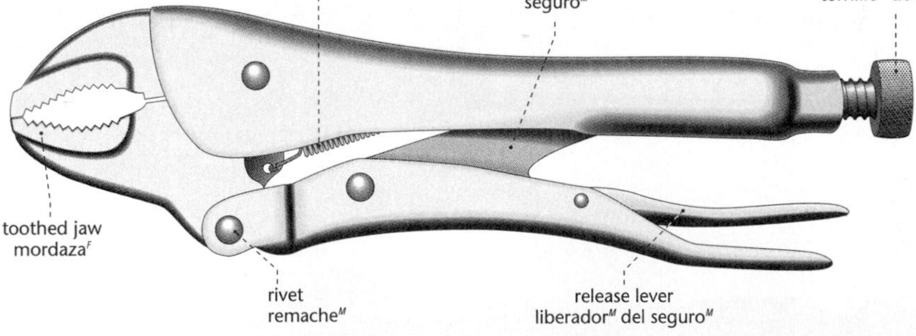

spring
resorte^M

lever
seguro^M

adjusting screw
tornillo^M de ajuste^M

toothed jaw
mordaza^F

rivet
remache^M

release lever
liberador^M del seguro^M

WASHERS
ARANDELAS^F

flat washer	lock washer	internal tooth lock washer	external tooth lock washer
arandela^F simple	arandela^F de presión^F común	arandela^F de presión^F con dientes^M internos	arandela^F de presión^F con dientes^M externos

DO-IT-YOURSELF
REPARACIONES CASERAS

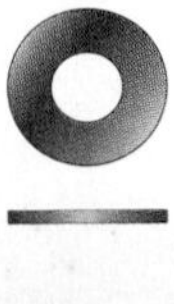

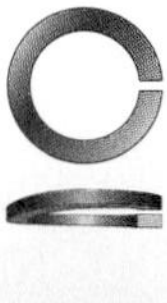

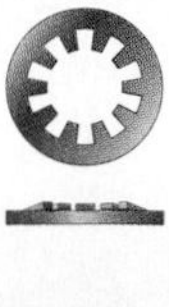

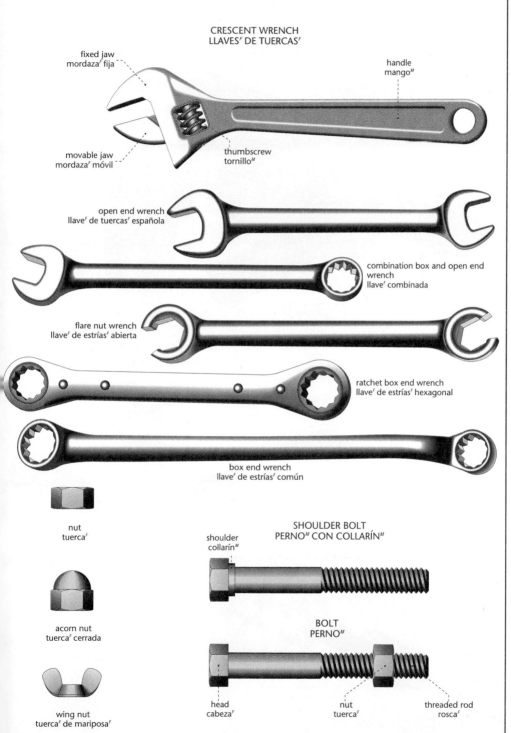

CRESCENT WRENCH
LLAVES^F DE TUERCAS^F

fixed jaw
mordaza^F fija

handle
mango^M

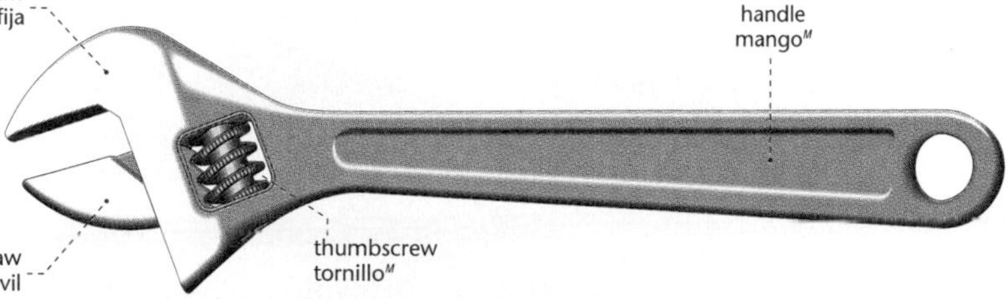

movable jaw
mordaza^F móvil

thumbscrew
tornillo^M

open end wrench
llave^F de tuercas^F española

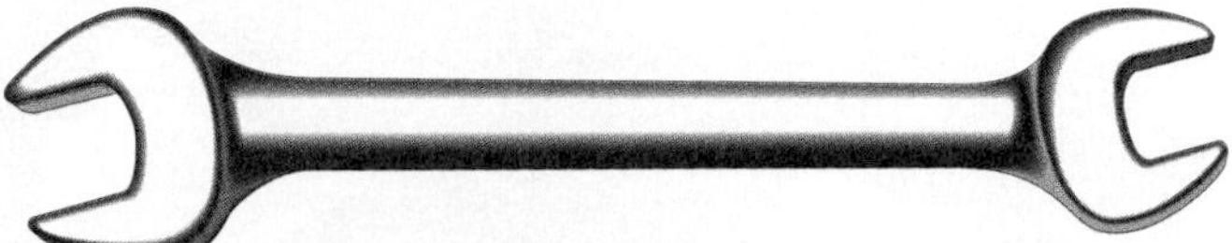

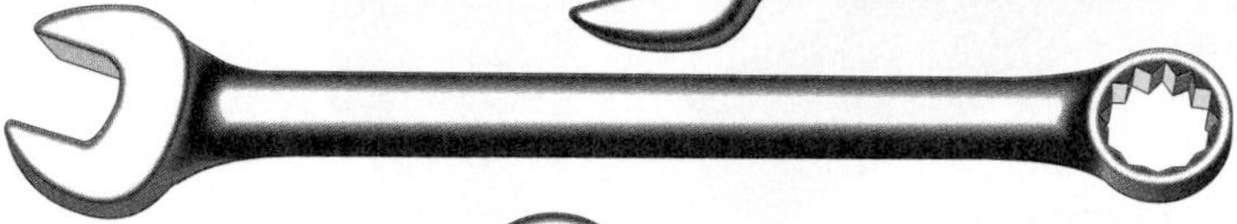

combination box and open end
wrench
llave^F combinada

flare nut wrench
llave^F de estrías^F abierta

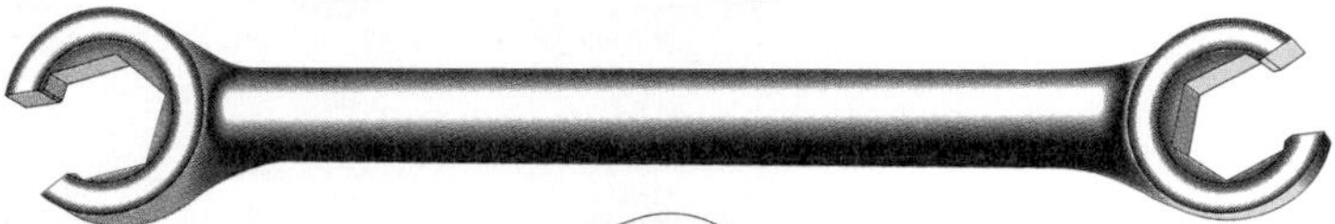

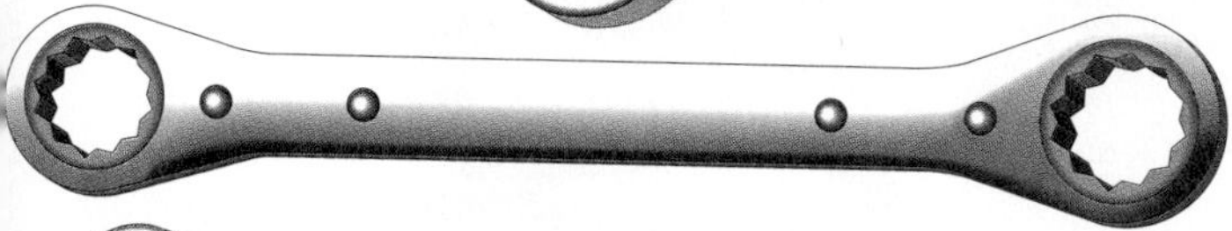

ratchet box end wrench
llave^F de estrías^F hexagonal

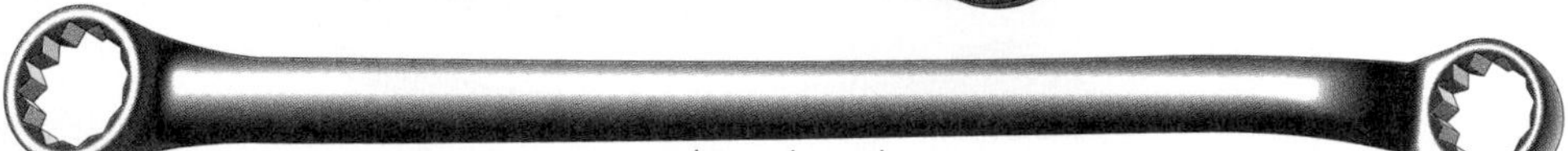

box end wrench
llave^F de estrías^F común

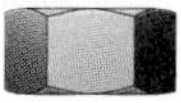

nut
tuerca^F

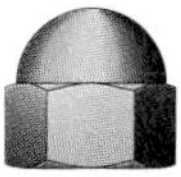

acorn nut
tuerca^F cerrada

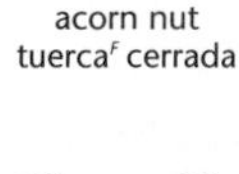

wing nut
tuerca^F de mariposa^F

SHOULDER BOLT
PERNO^M CON COLLARÍN^M

shoulder
collarín^M

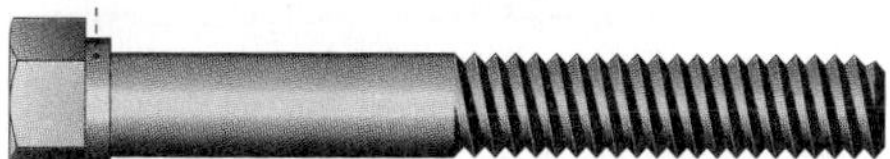

BOLT
PERNO^M

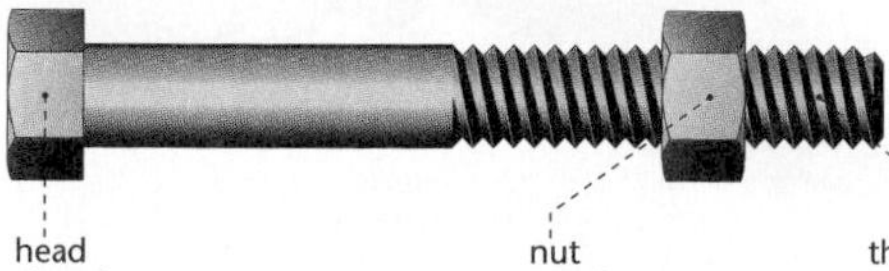

head
cabeza^F

nut
tuerca^F

threaded rod
rosca^F

DO-IT-YOURSELF
REPARACIONES CASERAS

ELECTRIC DRILL
TALADRO*M* ELÉCTRICO

name plate
placa*F* de especificaciones*F*

warning plate
placa*F* de advertencias*F*

switch lock
seguro*M* del interruptor*M*

housing
caja*F*

switch
interruptor*M*

chuck
mandril*M*

jaw
mordaza*F*

auxiliary handle
mango*M* auxiliar

pistol grip handle
mango*M*

cable sleeve
protector*M* del cable*M*

cable
cable*M* de corriente*F*

plug
enchufe*M*

HAND DRILL
TALADRO*M* DE MANO*F*

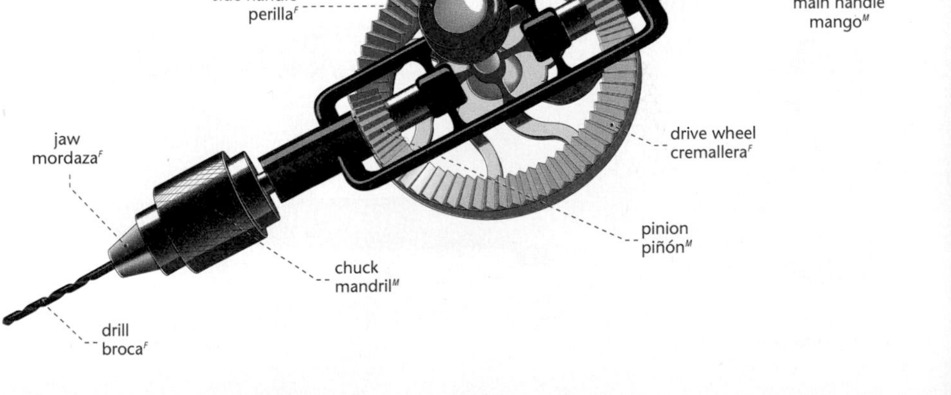

turning handle
manivela*F*

side handle
perilla*F*

main handle
mango*M*

jaw
mordaza*F*

drive wheel
cremallera*F*

pinion
piñón*M*

chuck
mandril*M*

drill
broca*F*

280

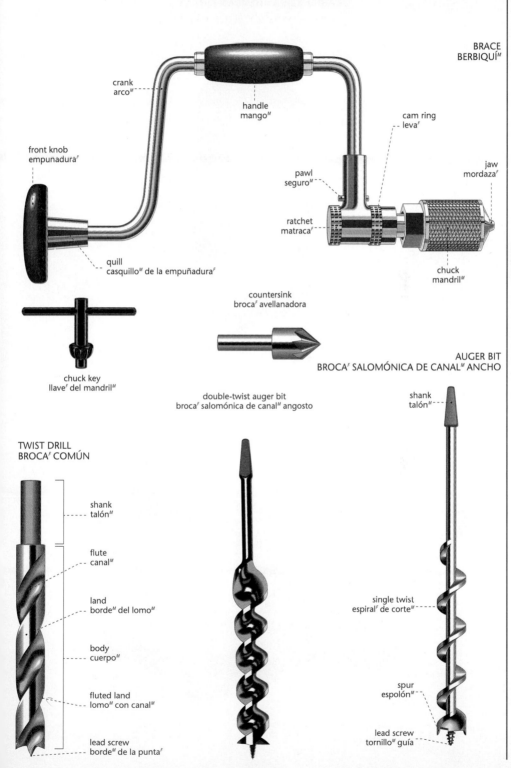

BRACE
BERBIQUÍ^M

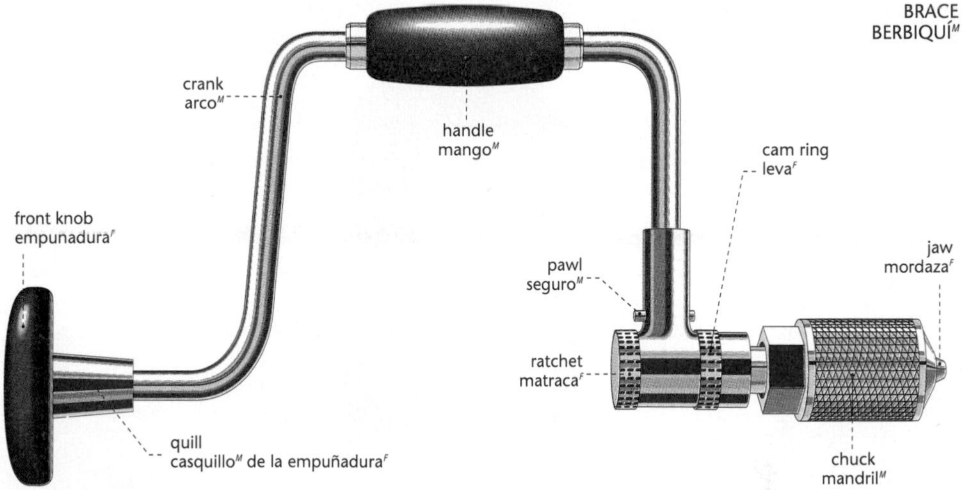

crank
arco^M

handle
mango^M

cam ring
leva^F

front knob
empunadura^F

jaw
mordaza^F

pawl
seguro^M

ratchet
matraca^F

chuck
mandril^M

quill
casquillo^M de la empuñadura^F

countersink
broca^F avellanadora

chuck key
llave^F del mandril^M

AUGER BIT
BROCA^F SALOMÓNICA DE CANAL^M ANCHO

double-twist auger bit
broca^F salomónica de canal^M angosto

shank
talón^M

TWIST DRILL
BROCA^F COMÚN

shank
talón^M

flute
canal^M

land
borde^M del lomo^M

single twist
espiral^F de corte^M

body
cuerpo^M

fluted land
lomo^M con canal^M

spur
espolón^M

lead screw
borde^M de la punta^F

lead screw
tornillo^M guía

C-CLAMP
PRENSA^F EN C

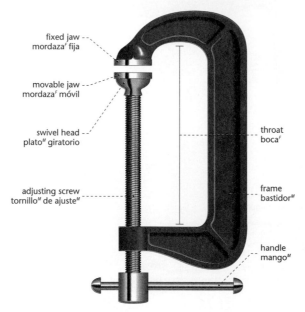

fixed jaw
mordaza^F fija

movable jaw
mordaza^F móvil

swivel head
plato^M giratorio

adjusting screw
tornillo^M de ajuste^M

throat
boca^F

frame
bastidor^M

handle
mango^M

VISE
TORNO^M DE BANCO^M

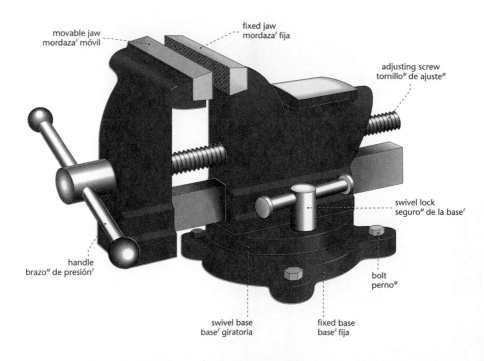

movable jaw
mordaza^F móvil

fixed jaw
mordaza^F fija

adjusting screw
tornillo^M de ajuste^M

swivel lock
seguro^M de la base^F

handle
brazo^M de presión^F

bolt
perno^M

swivel base
base^F giratoria

fixed base
base^F fija

DO-IT-YOURSELF
REPARACIONES CASERAS

ROUTER
ACANALADOR^M

head
parche^M

motor
motor^M

cord sleeve
protector^M del cable^M

switch
interruptor^M

guide handle
asa^F

depth adjustment
ajuste^M de profundidad^F

collet
collarín^M

tool holder
mordaza^F

base
base^F

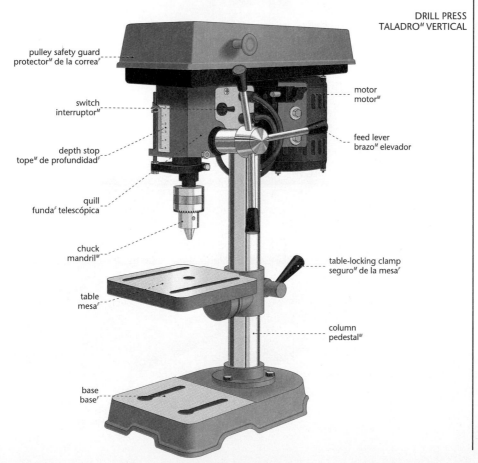

DRILL PRESS
TALADRO^M VERTICAL

pulley safety guard
protector^M de la correa^F

motor
motor^M

switch
interruptor^M

feed lever
brazo^M elevador

depth stop
tope^M de profundidad^F

quill
funda^F telescópica

chuck
mandril^M

table-locking clamp
seguro^M de la mesa^F

table
mesa^F

column
pedestal^M

base
base^F

CIRCULAR SAW BLADE
DISCO*

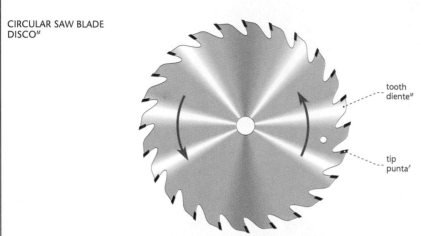

tooth
diente*

tip
punta*

CIRCULAR SAW
SIERRA* CIRCULAR DE MANO*

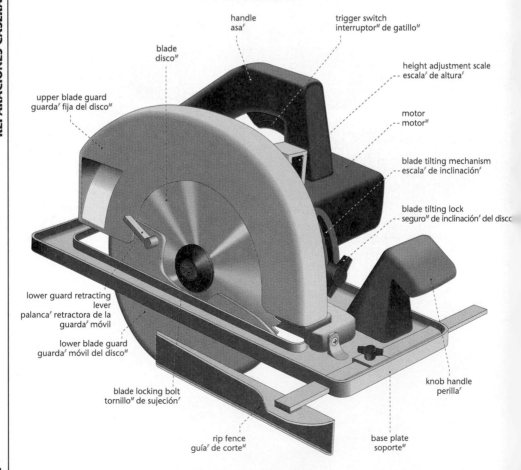

handle
asa*

trigger switch
interruptor* de gatillo*

blade
disco*

height adjustment scale
escala* de altura*

upper blade guard
guarda* fija del disco*

motor
motor*

blade tilting mechanism
escala* de inclinación*

blade tilting lock
seguro* de inclinación* del disco

lower guard retracting
lever
palanca* retractora de la
guarda* móvil

lower blade guard
guarda* móvil del disco*

blade locking bolt
tornillo* de sujeción*

knob handle
perilla*

rip fence
guía* de corte*

base plate
soporte*

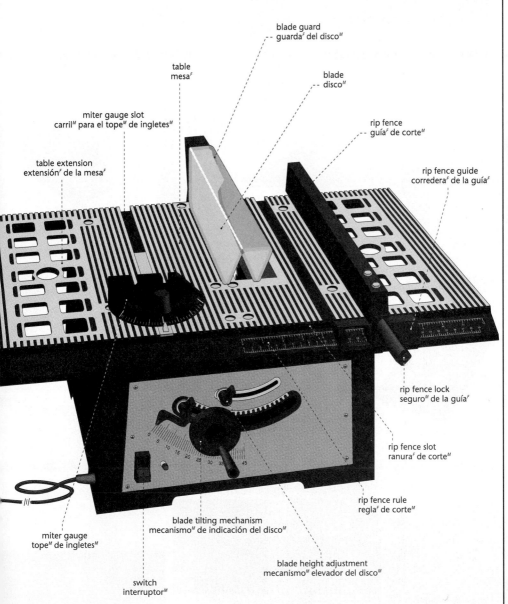

blade guard
guarda^F del disco^M

table
mesa^F

blade
disco^M

miter gauge slot
carril^M para el tope^M de ingletes^M

rip fence
guía^F de corte^M

table extension
extensión^F de la mesa^F

rip fence guide
corredera^F de la guía^F

rip fence lock
seguro^M de la guía^F

rip fence slot
ranura^F de corte^M

rip fence rule
regla^F de corte^M

miter gauge
tope^M de ingletes^M

blade tilting mechanism
mecanismo^M de indicación del disco^M

blade height adjustment
mecanismo^M elevador del disco^M

switch
interruptor^M

DO-IT-YOURSELF
REPARACIONES CASERAS

285

BUILDING MATERIALS
MATERIALES^M DE CONSTRUCCIÓN^F

DO-IT-YOURSELF
REPARACIONES CASERAS

BASIC BUILDING MATERIALS
MATERIALES^M BÁSICOS

brick
ladrillo^M

steel
acero^M

stone
piedra^F

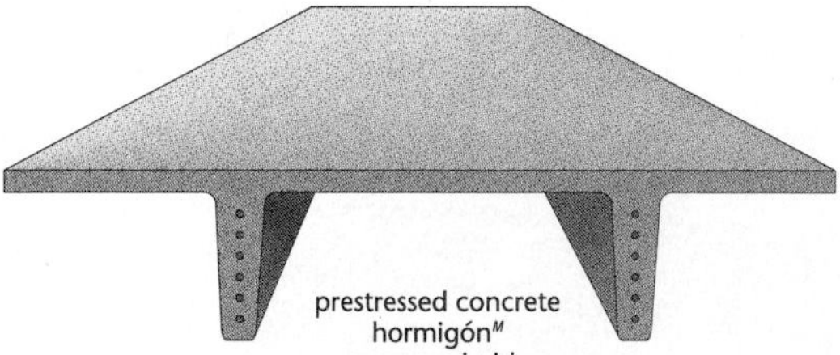

prestressed concrete
hormigón^M
precomprimido

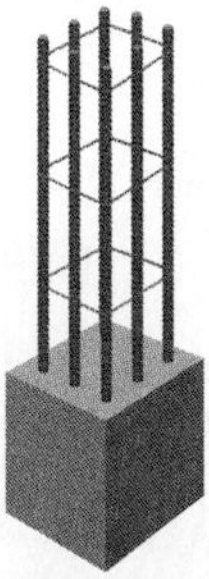

reinforced concrete
hormigón^M armado

concrete block
bloque^M de hormigón^M

COVERING MATERIALS
MATERIALES^M DE REVESTIMIENTO^M

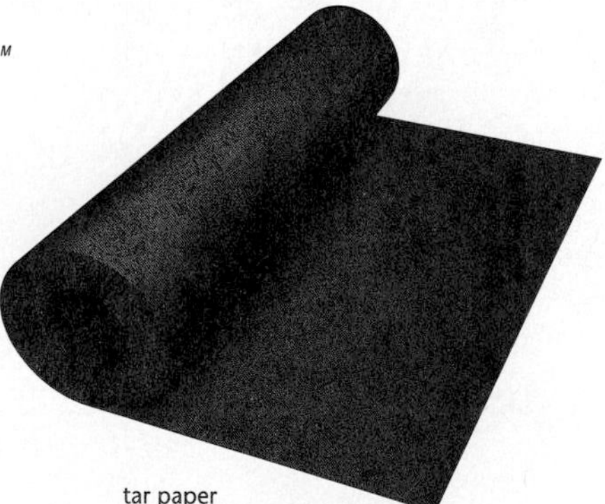

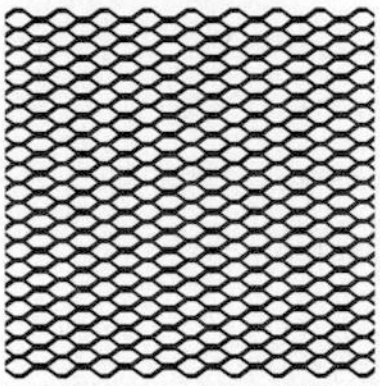

diamond mesh metal lath
hoja^F de lámina^F diamantada

tile
teja^F

tar paper
papel^M de brea^F

shingle
ripia^F

gypsum tile
tablero^M de yeso^M

plain gypsum lath
hoja^F de yeso^M liso

floor tile
baldosa^F

asphalt shingle
teja^F de asfalto^M

286

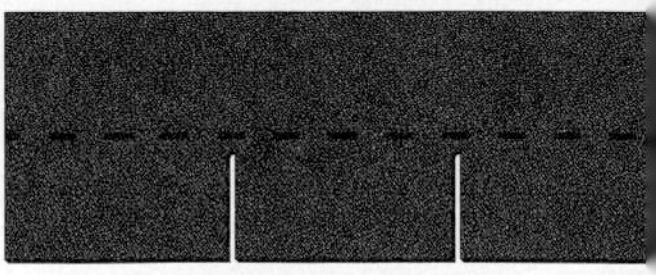

spring-metal insulation
aislante^M metálico

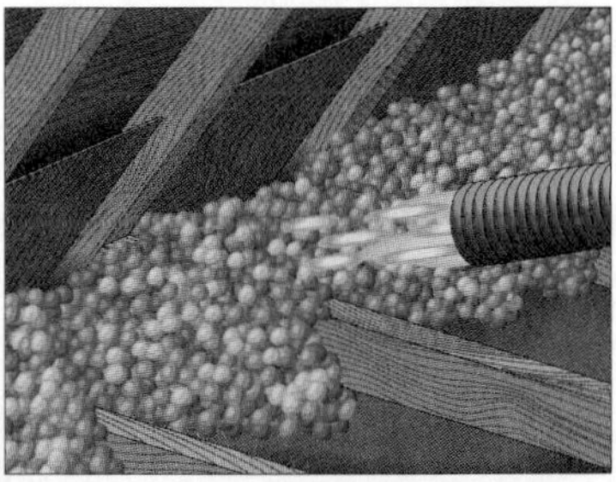

foam insulation
aislante^M de espuma^F

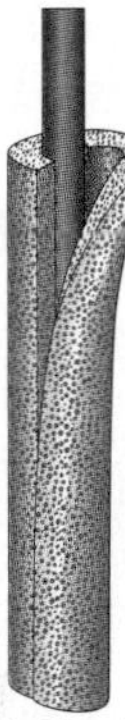

molded insulation
aislante^M premoldeado

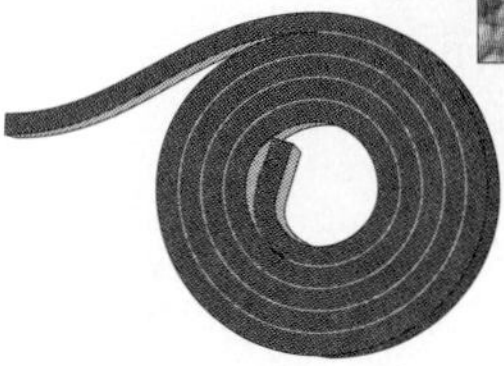

foam-rubber insulation
aislante^M de esponja^F

vinyl insulation
aislante^M vinílico

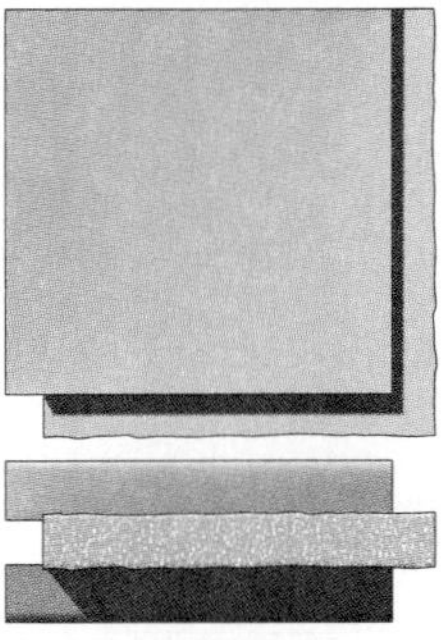

board insulation
tablero^M rígido aislante

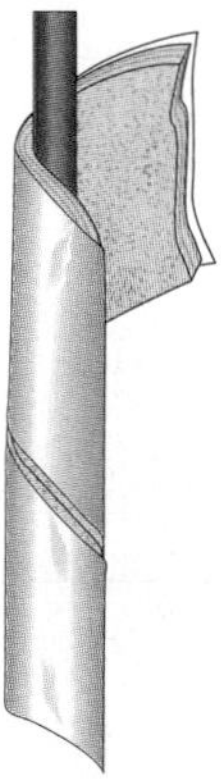

pipe-wrapping insulation
cinta^F aislante para tubería^F

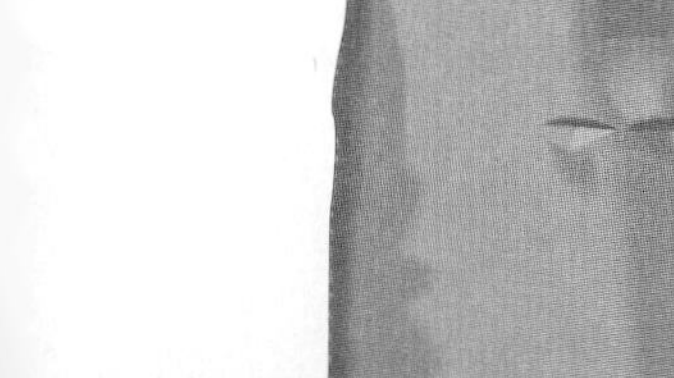

loose fill insulation
aislante^M a granel

blanket insulation
rollo^M para recubrimiento^M impermeabilizante

WOOD
MADERA^F

SECTION OF A LOG
CORTE^M DE UN TRONCO^M

slab
costero^M

log
tronco^M

board
tabla^F

BOARD
TABLA^F

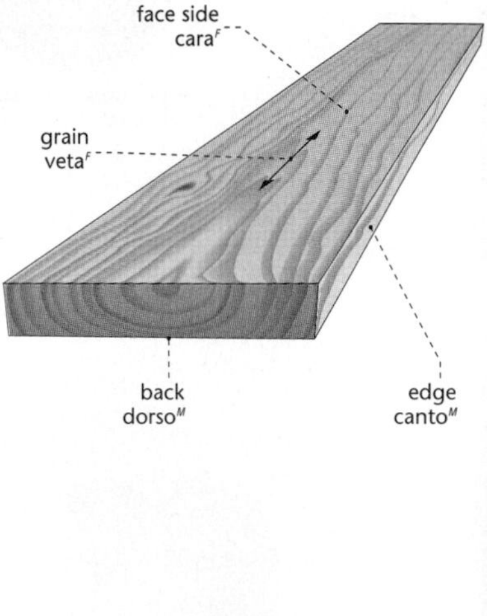

face side
cara^F

grain
veta^F

end grain
cabeza^F

back
dorso^M

edge
canto^M

WOOD-BASED MATERIALS
LÁMINAS^F Y TABLEROS^M

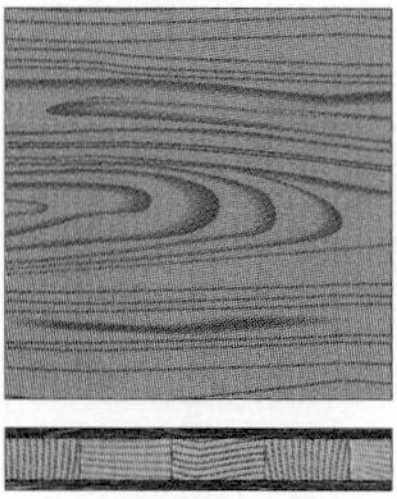

blockboard
panel^M de listones^M

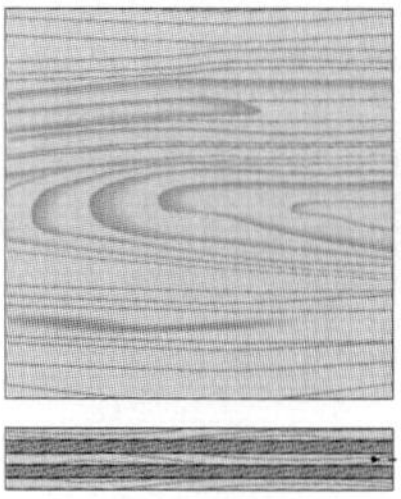

ply
contrachapado^M

multi-ply plywood
contrachapado^M múltiple

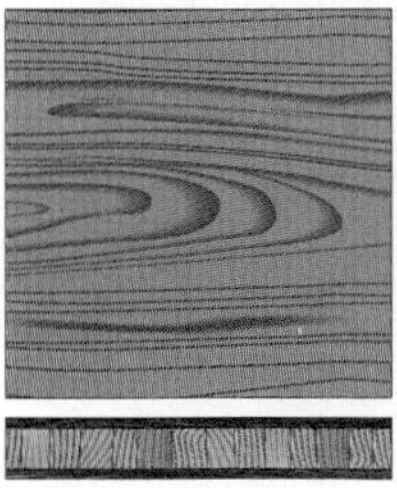

laminboard
panel^M laminado

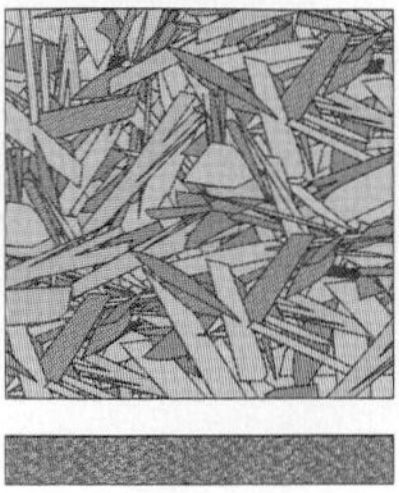

waferboard
aglomerado^M

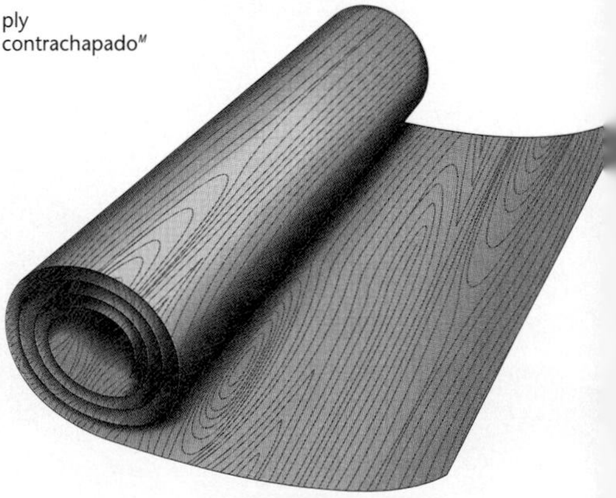

peeled veneer
chapa^F de madera^F

hardboard
tablero^M de fibra^F de madera^F

perforated hardboard
tablero^M de fibra^F de madera^F
perforada

plastic-laminated particle board
tablero^M de aglomerado^M con
laminado^M de plástico^M

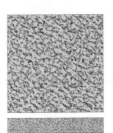

particle board
tablero^M de aglomerado^M

LOCK
CERRAJERÍA^F

GENERAL VIEW
VISTA^F GENERAL

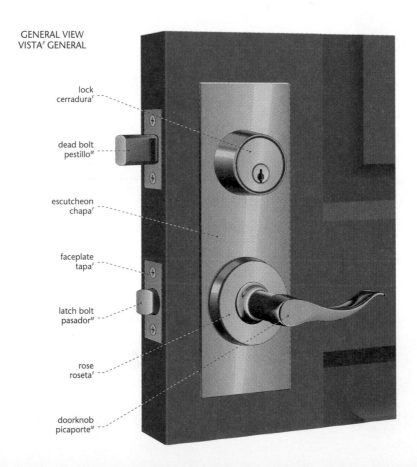

lock
cerradura^F

dead bolt
pestillo^M

escutcheon
chapa^F

faceplate
tapa^F

latch bolt
pasador^M

rose
roseta^F

doorknob
picaporte^M

DO-IT-YOURSELF
REPARACIONES CASERAS

289

MORTISE LOCK
CERRADURA^F EMBUTIDA

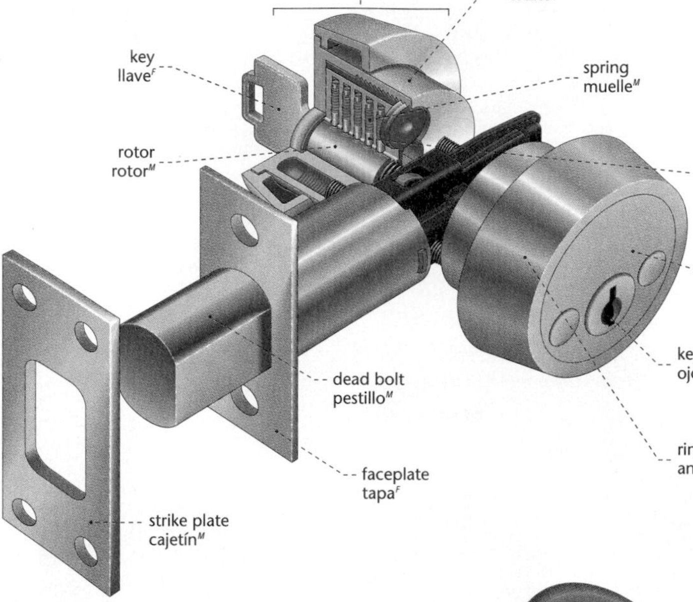

cylinder
cilindro^M

stator
estator^M

key
llave^F

spring
muelle^M

rotor
rotor^M

cotter pin
clavija^F hendida

cylinder case
caja^F del cilindro^M

keyway
ojo^M

dead bolt
pestillo^M

ring
anillo^M

faceplate
tapa^F

strike plate
cajetín^M

TUBULAR LOCK
CERRADURA^F DE POMO^M CON SEGURO^M

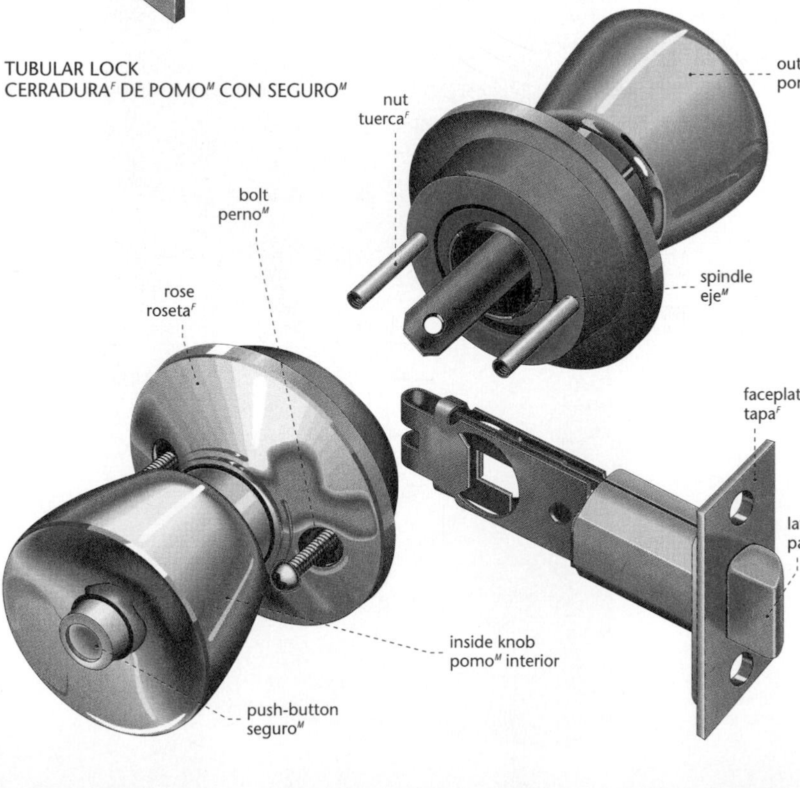

outside knob
pomo^M exterior

nut
tuerca^F

bolt
perno^M

rose
roseta^F

spindle
eje^M

faceplate
tapa^F

latch bolt
pasador^M

inside knob
pomo^M interior

push-button
seguro^M

MASONRY
HERRAMIENTAS^F DE ALBAÑIL^M

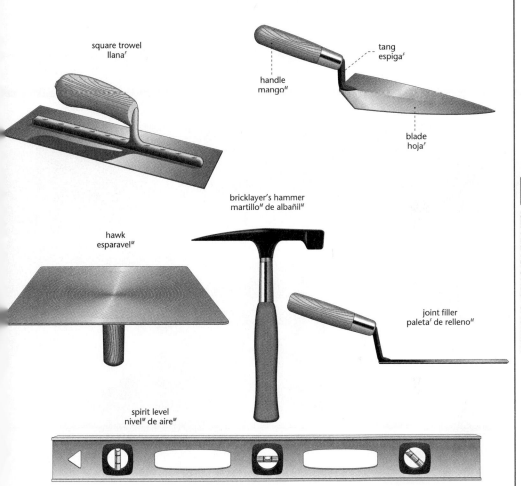

MASON'S TROWEL
PALETA^F DE ALBAÑIL^M

square trowel
llana^f

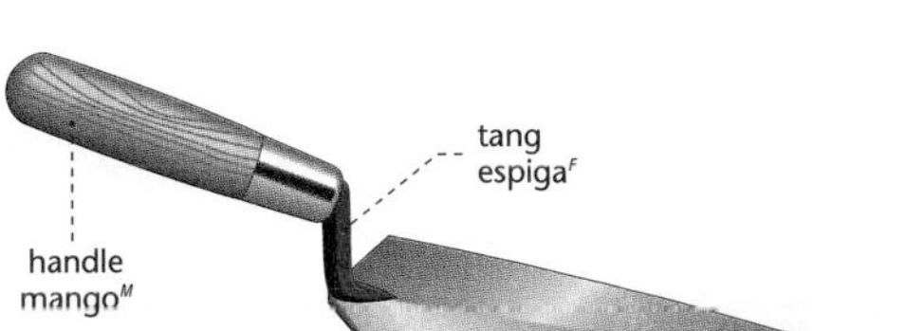

tang
espiga^f

handle
mango^M

blade
hoja^f

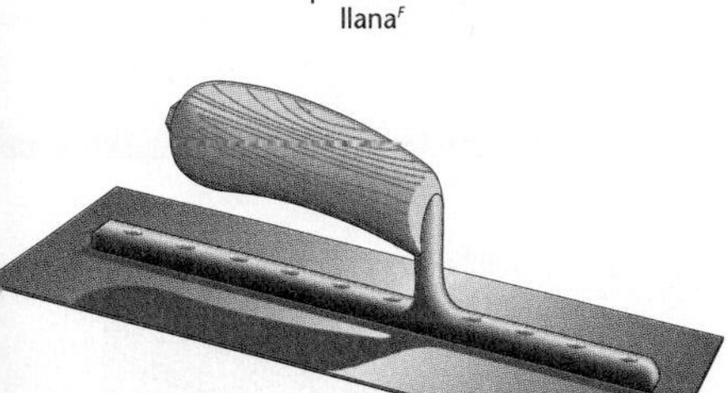

bricklayer's hammer
martillo^M de albañil^M

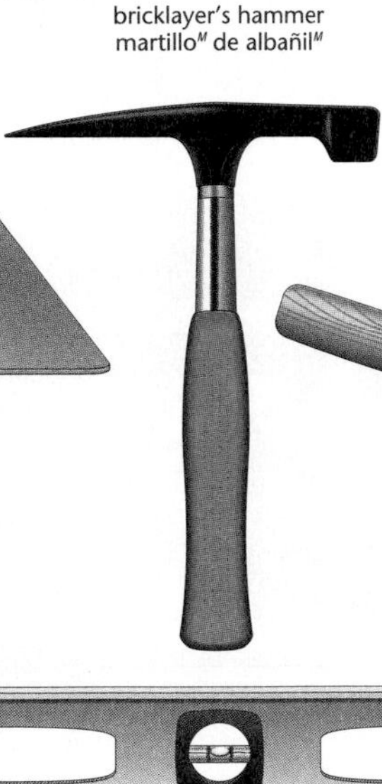

hawk
esparavel^M

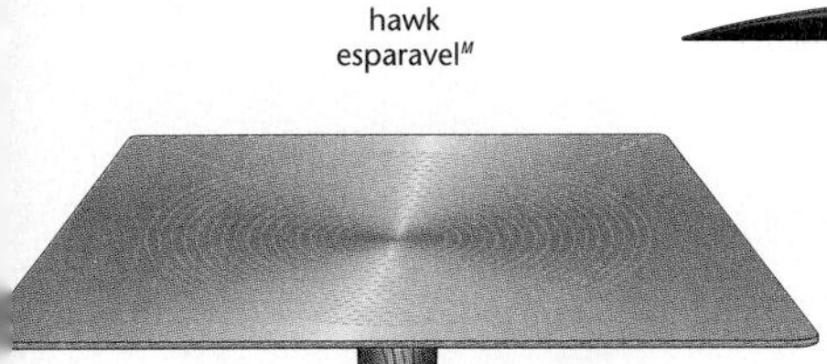

joint filler
paleta^f de relleno^M

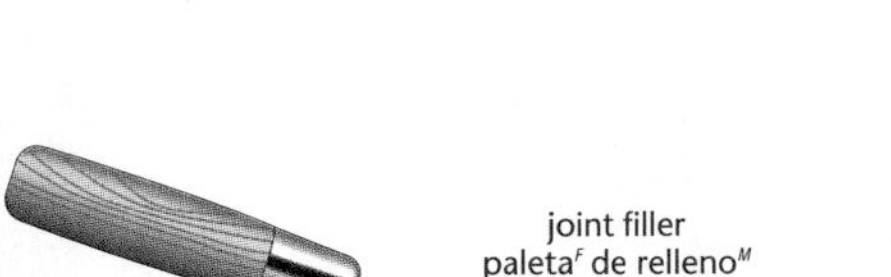

spirit level
nivel^M de aire^M

DO-IT-YOURSELF
REPARACIONES CASERAS

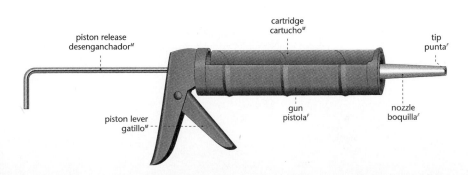

CAULKING GUN
PISTOLA^F PARA CALAFATEO^M

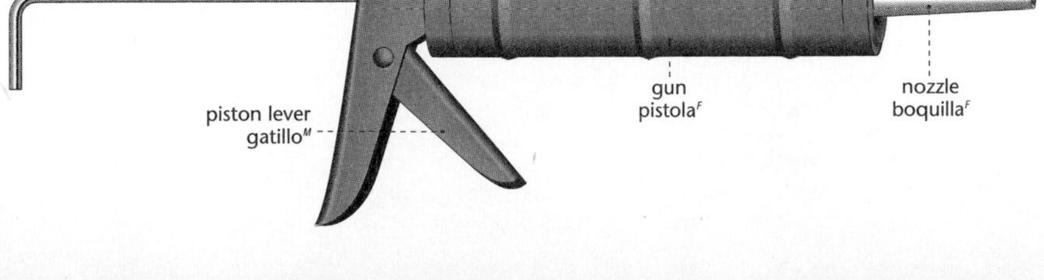

cartridge
cartucho^M

piston release
desenganchador^M

tip
punta^f

piston lever
gatillo^M

gun
pistola^f

nozzle
boquilla^f

291

sliding door
puerta^F plegable

shower stall
cubículo^M de la ducha^F

spray hose
manguera^F

portable shower head
ducha^F de teléfono^M

overflow
desagüe^M

shower head
alcachofa^F de la ducha^F

faucet
grifo^M

mirror
espejo^M

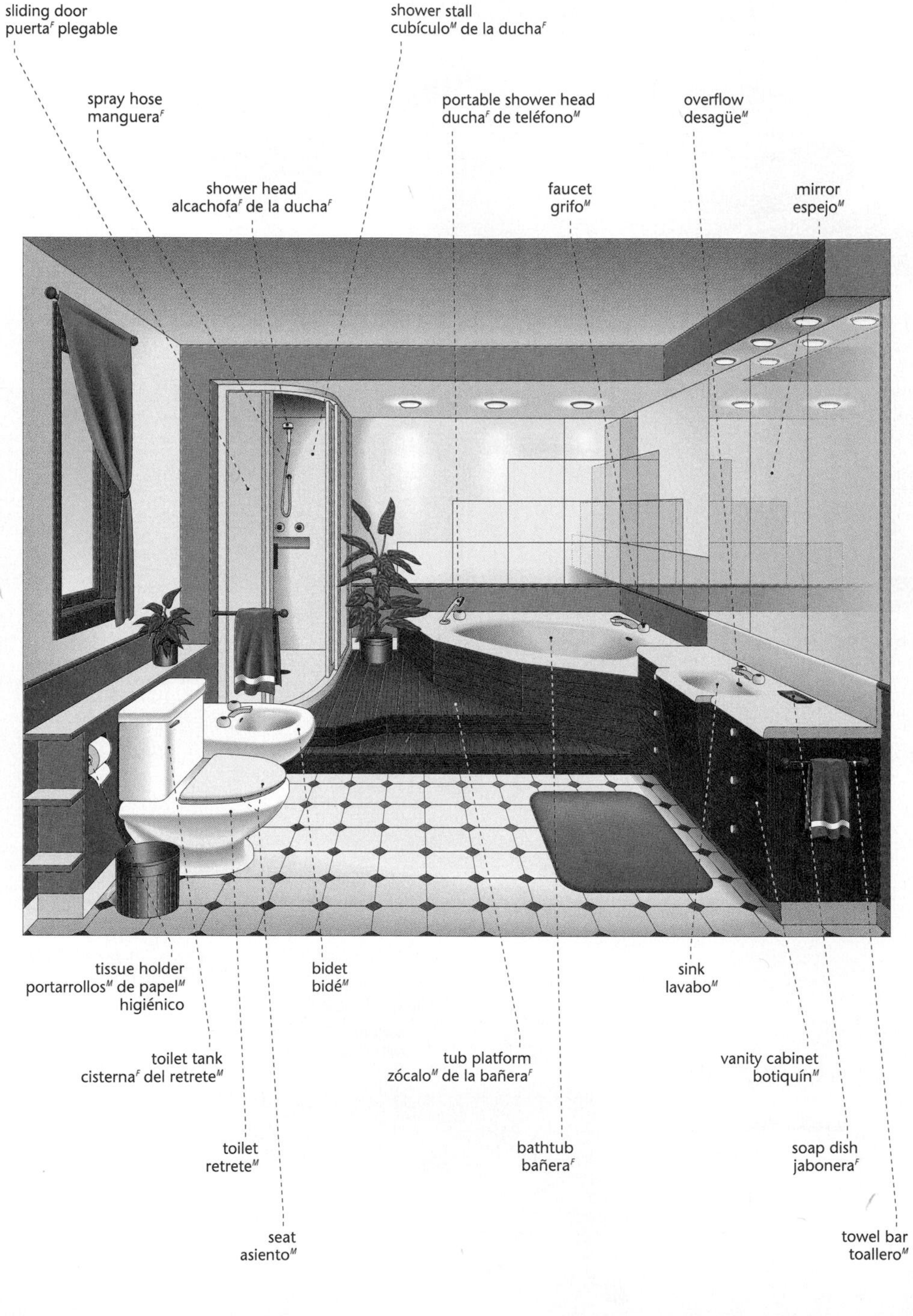

tissue holder
portarrollos^M de papel^M
higiénico

bidet
bidé^M

sink
lavabo^M

toilet tank
cisterna^F del retrete^M

tub platform
zócalo^M de la bañera^F

vanity cabinet
botiquín^M

toilet
retrete^M

bathtub
bañera^F

soap dish
jabonera^F

seat
asiento^M

towel bar
toallero^M

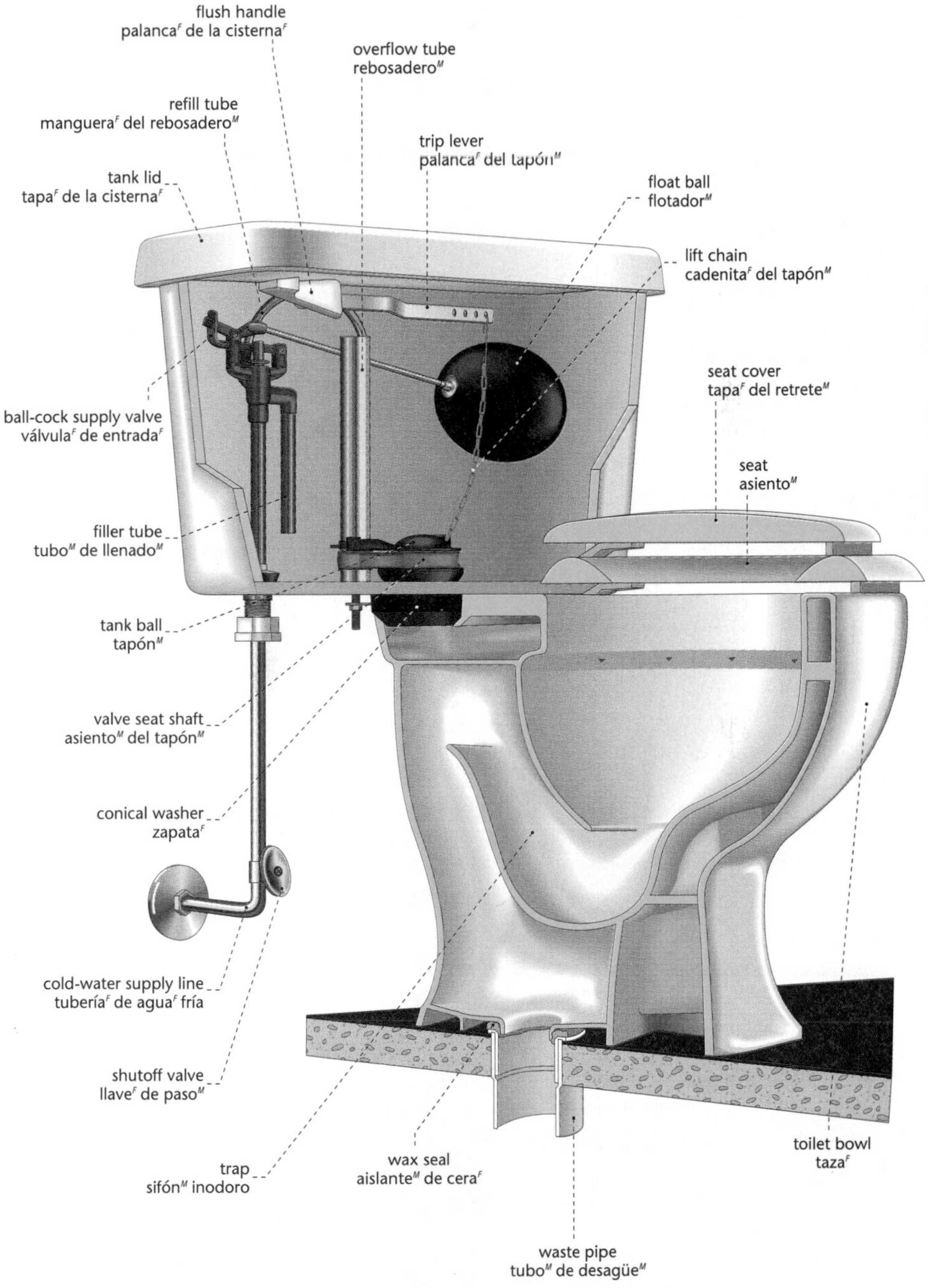

flush handle
palanca^F de la cisterna^F

overflow tube
rebosadero^M

refill tube
manguera^F del rebosadero^M

trip lever
palanca^F del tapón^M

tank lid
tapa^F de la cisterna^F

float ball
flotador^M

lift chain
cadenita^F del tapón^M

ball-cock supply valve
válvula^F de entrada^F

seat cover
tapa^F del retrete^M

seat
asiento^M

filler tube
tubo^M de llenado^M

tank ball
tapón^M

valve seat shaft
asiento^M del tapón^M

conical washer
zapata^F

cold-water supply line
tubería^F de agua^F fría

shutoff valve
llave^F de paso^M

trap
sifón^M inodoro

wax seal
aislante^M de cera^F

toilet bowl
taza^F

waste pipe
tubo^M de desagüe^M

DO-IT-YOURSELF
REPARACIONES CASERAS

293

STEM FAUCET
GRIFO^M

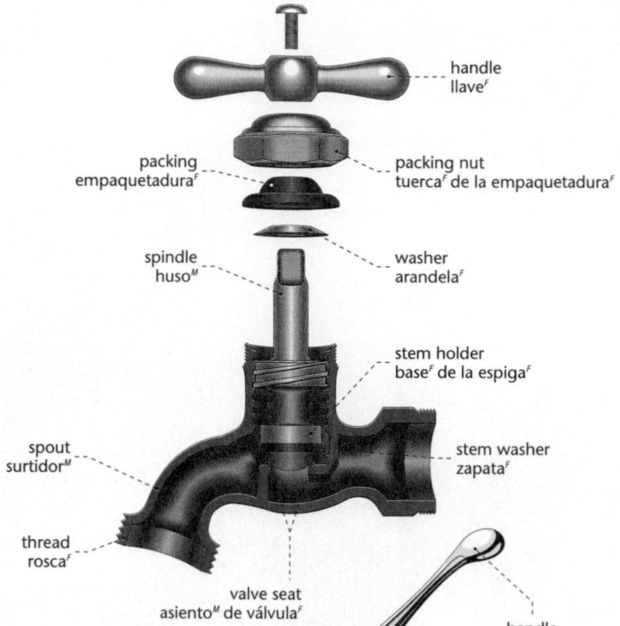

handle
llave^F

packing
empaquetadura^F

packing nut
tuerca^F de la empaquetadura^F

washer
arandela^F

spindle
huso^M

stem holder
base^F de la espiga^F

spout
surtidor^M

stem washer
zapata^F

thread
rosca^F

valve seat
asiento^M de válvula^F

handle
palanca^F

BALL-TYPE FAUCET
GRIFO^M DE BOLA^F

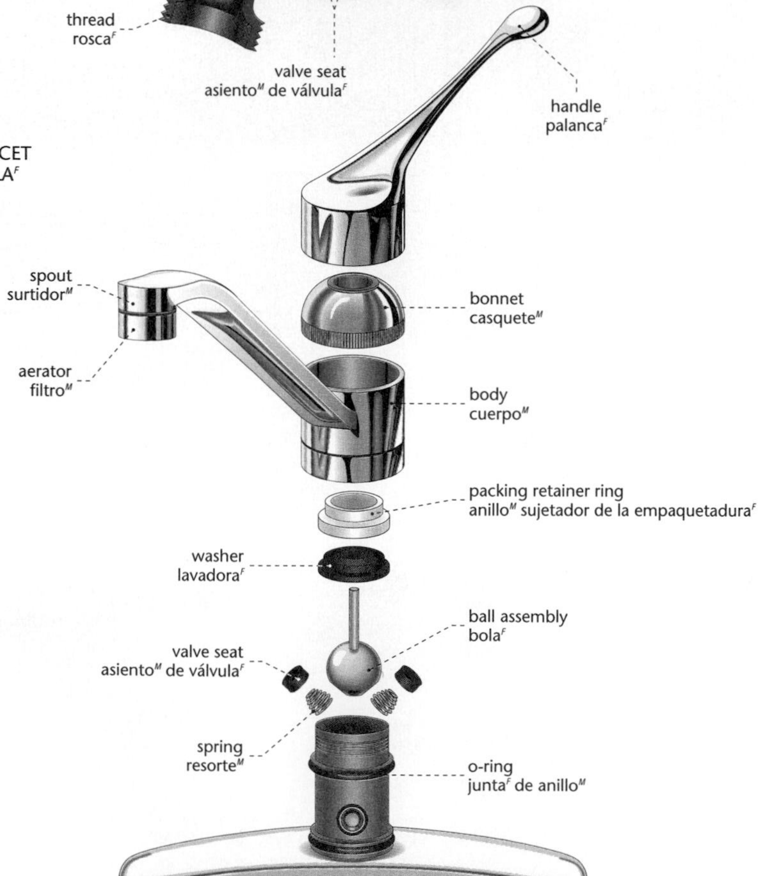

spout
surtidor^M

bonnet
casquete^M

aerator
filtro^M

body
cuerpo^M

packing retainer ring
anillo^M sujetador de la empaquetadura^F

washer
lavadora^F

ball assembly
bola^F

valve seat
asiento^M de válvula^F

spring
resorte^M

o-ring
junta^F de anillo^M

DISC FAUCET
GRIFO*M* DE DISCO*M*

handle
palanca*F*

bonnet
casquete*M*

cylinder
cilindro*M*

seal
zapata*F*

spout
surtidor*M*

water inlet
entrada*F* de agua*F*

aerator
flitro*M*

escutcheon
placa*F*

CARTRIDGE FAUCET
GRIFO*M* DE CARTUCHO*M*

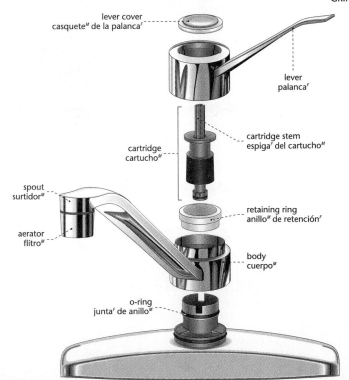

lever cover
casquete*M* de la palanca*F*

lever
palanca*F*

cartridge stem
espiga*F* del cartucho*M*

cartridge
cartucho*M*

spout
surtidor*M*

retaining ring
anillo*M* de retención*F*

aerator
flitro*M*

body
cuerpo*M*

o-ring
junta*F* de anillo*M*

DO-IT-YOURSELF
REPARACIONES CASERAS

295

GARBAGE DISPOSAL SINK
FREGADERO^M CON TRITURADOR^M DE BASURA^F

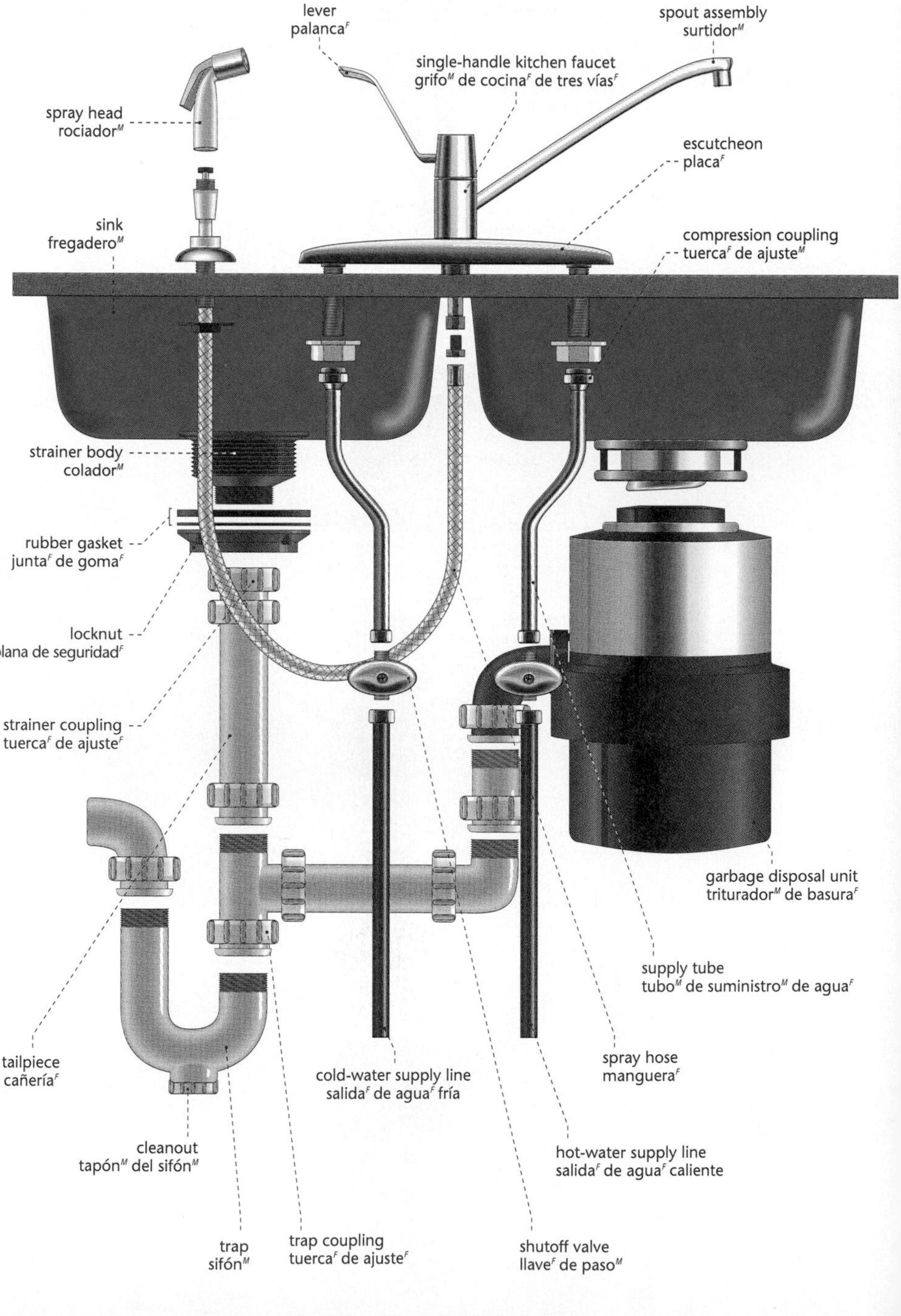

lever
palanca^F

spout assembly
surtidor^M

single-handle kitchen faucet
grifo^M de cocina^F de tres vías^F

spray head
rociador^M

escutcheon
placa^F

sink
fregadero^M

compression coupling
tuerca^F de ajuste^M

strainer body
colador^M

rubber gasket
junta^F de goma^F

locknut
tuerca^F plana de seguridad^F

strainer coupling
tuerca^F de ajuste^F

garbage disposal unit
triturador^M de basura^F

supply tube
tubo^M de suministro^M de agua^F

tailpiece
cañería^F

cold-water supply line
salida^F de agua^F fría

spray hose
manguera^F

cleanout
tapón^M del sifón^M

hot-water supply line
salida^F de agua^F caliente

trap
sifón^M

trap coupling
tuerca^F de ajuste^F

shutoff valve
llave^F de paso^M

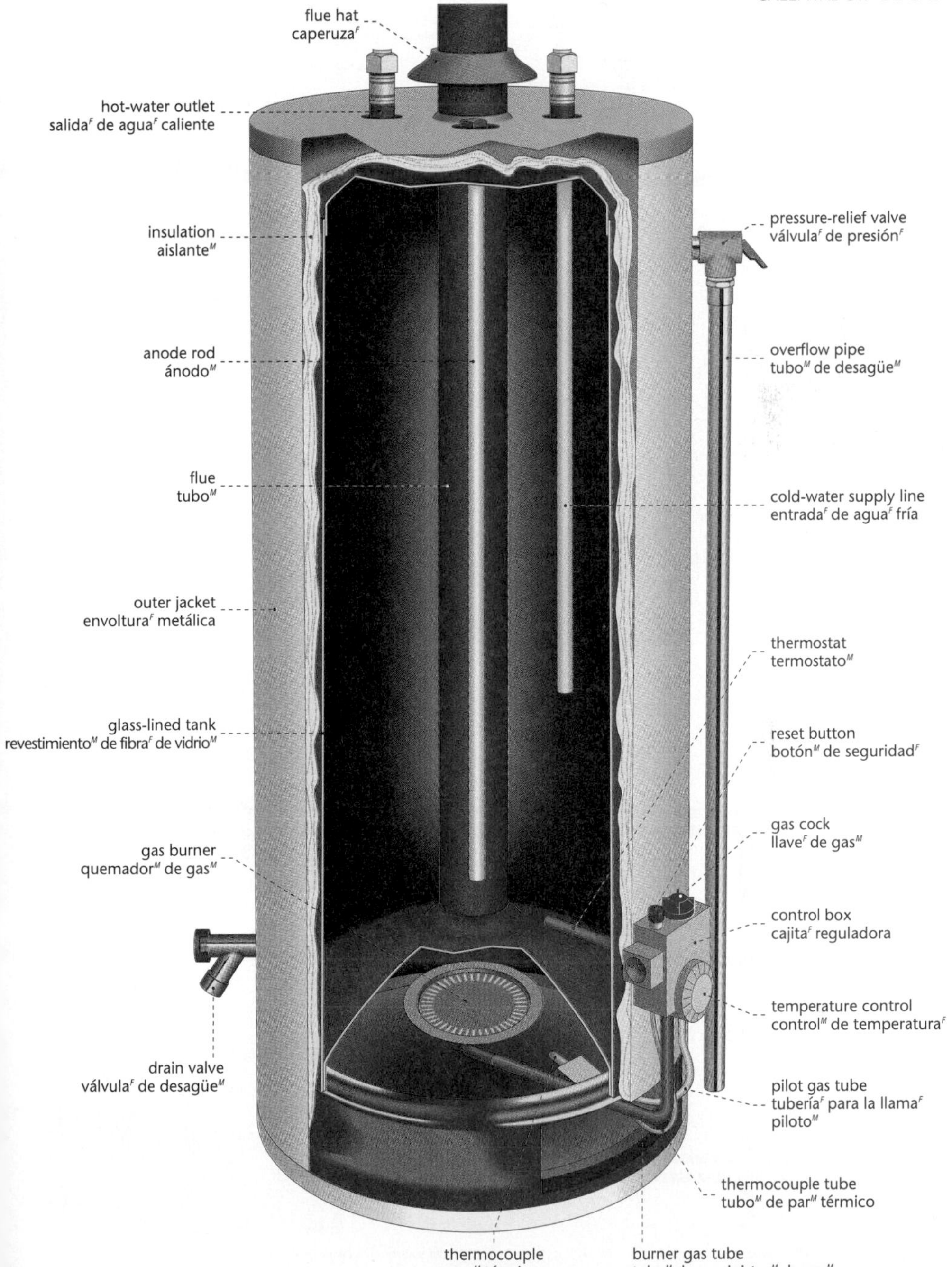

GAS WATER-HEATER TANK
CALENTADOR^M DE GAS^M

flue hat
caperuza^F

hot-water outlet
salida^F de agua^F caliente

insulation
aislante^M

anode rod
ánodo^M

flue
tubo^M

outer jacket
envoltura^F metálica

glass-lined tank
revestimiento^M de fibra^F de vidrio^M

gas burner
quemador^M de gas^M

drain valve
válvula^F de desagüe^M

pressure-relief valve
válvula^F de presión^F

overflow pipe
tubo^M de desagüe^M

cold-water supply line
entrada^F de agua^F fría

thermostat
termostato^M

reset button
botón^M de seguridad^F

gas cock
llave^F de gas^M

control box
cajita^F reguladora

temperature control
control^M de temperatura^F

pilot gas tube
tubería^F para la llama^F
piloto^M

thermocouple tube
tubo^M de par^M térmico

thermocouple
par^M térmico

burner gas tube
tubo^M de suministro^M de gas^M

PLUMBING: EXAMPLES OF BRANCHING
FONTANERÍA^F: CONEXIONES^F

WASHER
LAVADORA^F

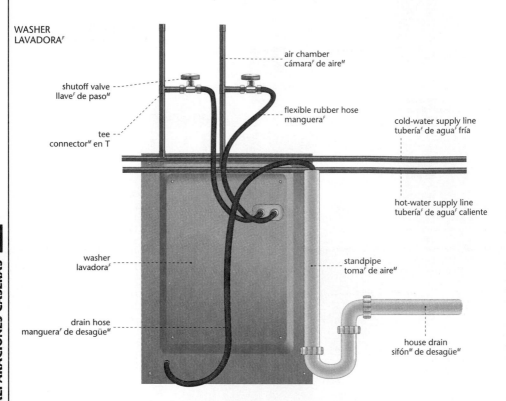

air chamber
cámara^F de aire^M

shutoff valve
llave^F de paso^M

flexible rubber hose
manguera^F

tee
connector^M en T

cold-water supply line
tubería^F de agua^F fría

hot-water supply line
tubería^F de agua^F caliente

washer
lavadora^F

standpipe
toma^F de aire^M

drain hose
manguera^F de desagüe^M

house drain
sifón^M de desagüe^M

DISHWASHER
MÁQUINA^F LAVAPLATOS^M

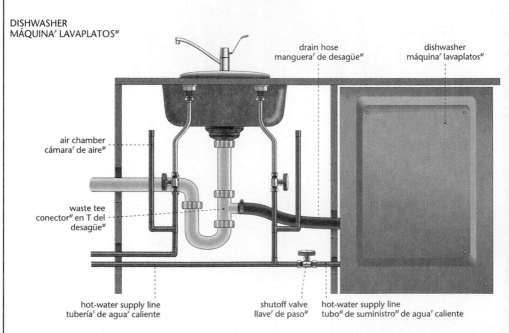

drain hose
manguera^F de desagüe^M

dishwasher
máquina^F lavaplatos^M

air chamber
cámara^F de aire^M

waste tee
conector^M en T del
desagüe^M

hot-water supply line
tubería^F de agua^F caliente

shutoff valve
llave^F de paso^M

hot-water supply line
tubo^M de suministro^M de agua^F caliente

PLUMBING
FONTANERÍA*F*

PLUMBING TOOLS
HERRAMIENTAS*F* DE FONTANERO*M*

tube cutter
cortatubos*M*

soldering torch
soplete*M*

pencil point tip
boquilla*F* del soplete*M*

pipe wrench
llave*F* inglesa

adjustable spud wrench
llave*F* ajustable

strap wrench
llave*F* de cincho*M*

disposable fuel cylinder
bombona*F* de gas*M*

chain pipe wrench
llave*F* de cadena*F*

pipe threader
terraja*F*

plumber's snake
sonda*F* destapacaños*M*

tube flaring tool
avellanadora*F* de tubos*M*

basin wrench
llave*F* pico*M* de ganso*M*

plunger
desatrancador*M*

hacksaw
sierra*F* para metales*M*

valve seat wrench
llave*F* de asientos*M* de válvula*F*

MECHANICAL CONNECTORS
CONEXIONES[F] MECÁNICAS

compression fitting
ensamblaje[M] por compresión[F]

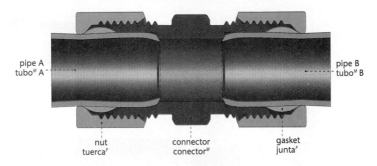

pipe A
tubo[M] A

pipe B
tubo[M] B

nut
tuerca[F]

connector
conector[M]

gasket
junta[F]

flare joint
ensamblaje[M] abocinado

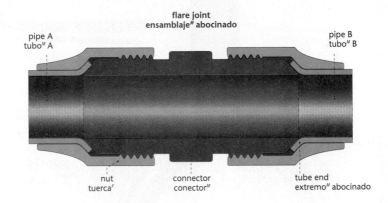

pipe A
tubo[M] A

pipe B
tubo[M] B

nut
tuerca[F]

connector
conector[M]

tube end
extremo[M] abocinado

union
unión[F]

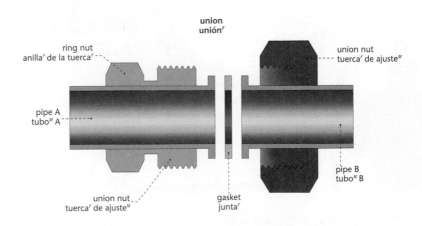

ring nut
anilla[F] de la tuerca[F]

union nut
tuerca[F] de ajuste[M]

pipe A
tubo[M] A

union nut
tuerca[F] de ajuste[M]

gasket
junta[F]

pipe B
tubo[M] B

TRANSITION FITTINGS
CONEXIONES^F DE TRANSICIÓN^F

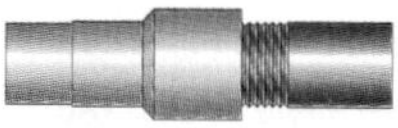

steel to plastic
de acero^M a plástico^M

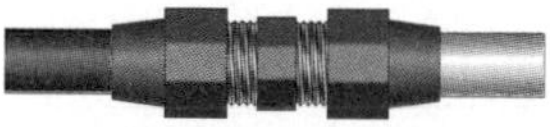

copper to plastic
de cobre^M a plástico^M

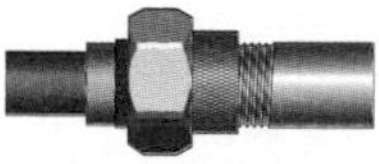

copper to steel
de cobre^M a acero^M

FITTINGS
CONEXIONES^F

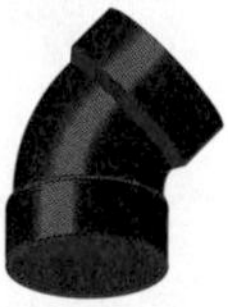

45° elbow
codo^M de 45 grados^M

elbow
codo^M de 90 grados^M

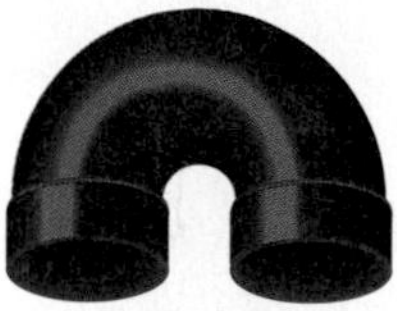

U-bend
conexión^F en U

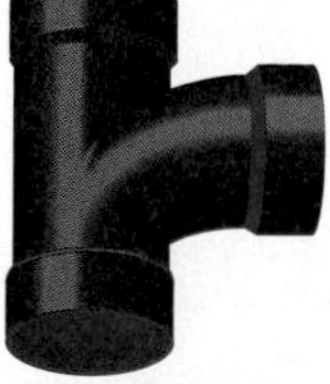

tee
conexión^F en T

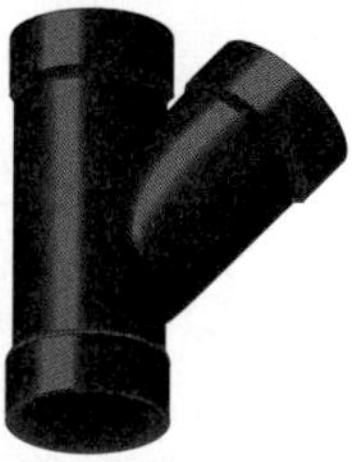

Y-branch
conexión^F en Y

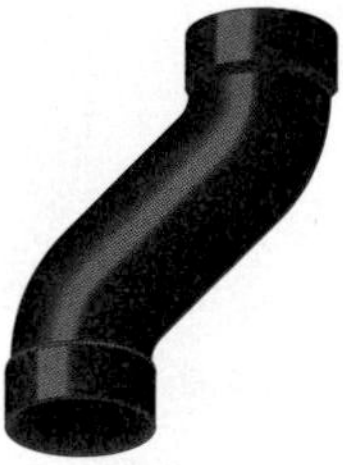

offset
desviación^F

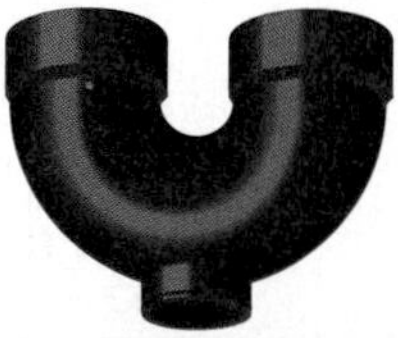

trap
sifón^M

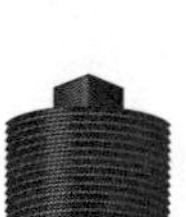

square head plug
tapón^M macho^M

cap
tapón^M

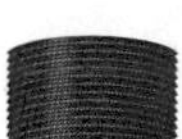

flush bushing
boquilla^F de reducir

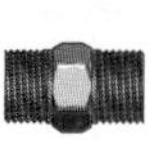

nipple
boquilla^F

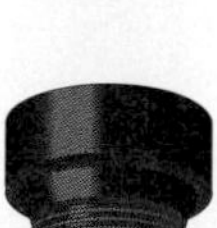

reducing coupling
reductor^M de calibre^M

threaded cap
tapón^M hembra^F

pipe coupling
unión^F

hexagon bushing
boquilla^F de reducir con
cabeza^F hexagonal

LADDERS AND STEPLADDERS
ESCALERAS^F DE MANO^F

STEPLADDER
ESCALERA^F DE TIJERA^F

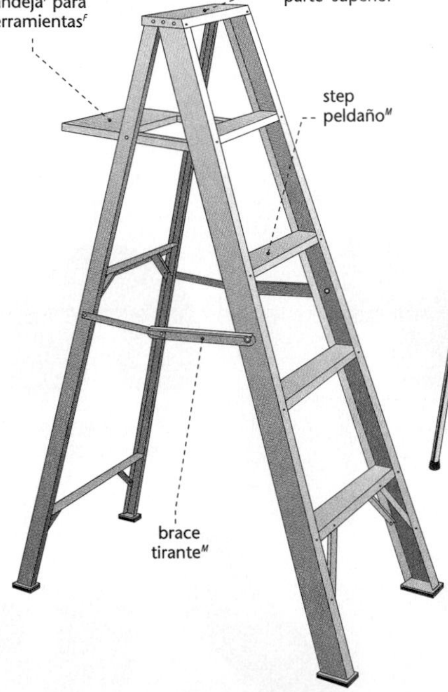

tool shelf
bandeja^F para
herramientas^F

top
parte^F superior

step
peldaño^M

brace
tirante^M

step stool
escalerilla^F

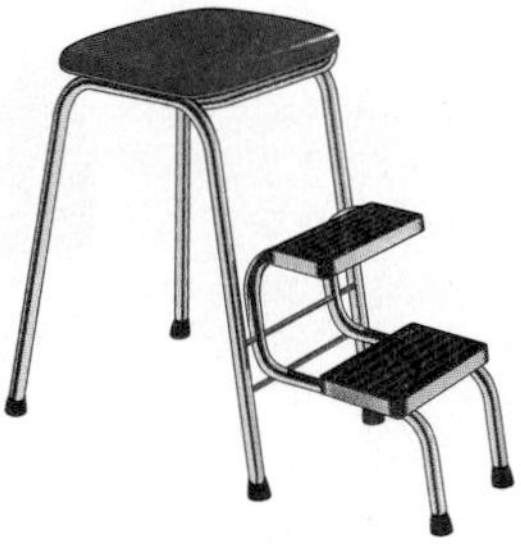

EXTENSION LADDER
ESCALERA^F DE EXTENSIÓN^F

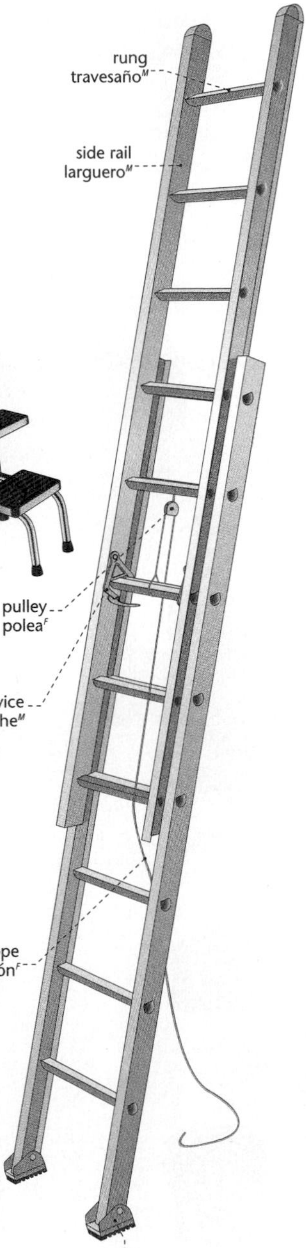

rung
travesaño^M

side rail
larguero^M

pulley
polea^F

locking device
broche^M

PLATFORM LADDER
ESCALERA^F DE PLATAFORMA^F

shelf
entrepaño^M

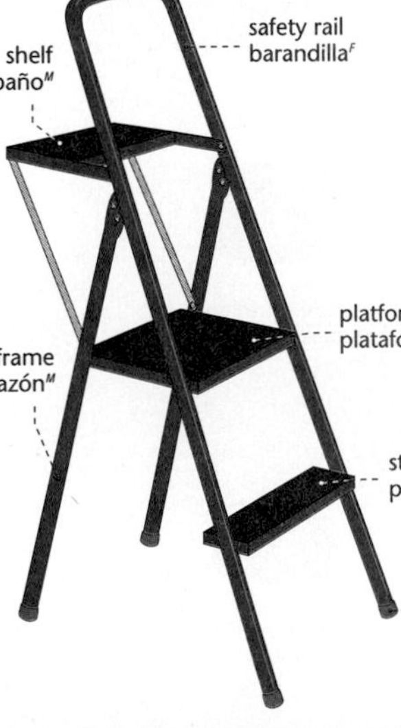

safety rail
barandilla^F

frame
armazón^M

platform
plataforma^F

step
peldaño^M

hoisting rope
cuerda^F de elevación^F

rubber tip
zapata^F de goma^F

anti-slip shoe
zapata^F antideslizante

straight ladder
escalera^F común

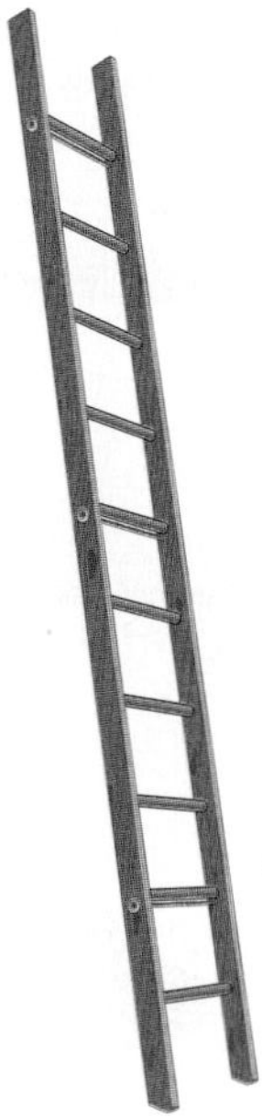

foldaway ladder
escalera^F de guardilla^F

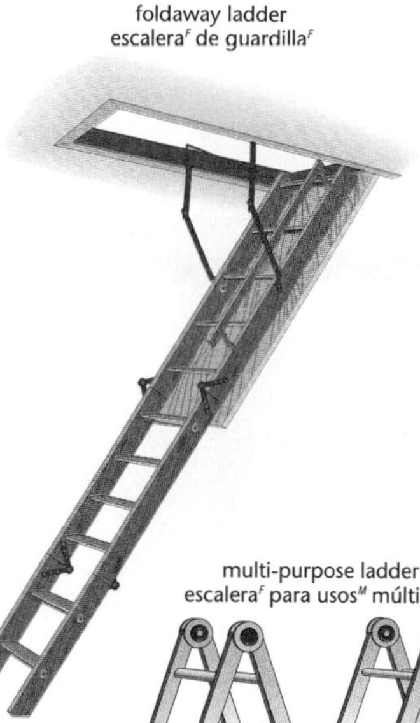

hook ladder
escalera^F de gancho^M

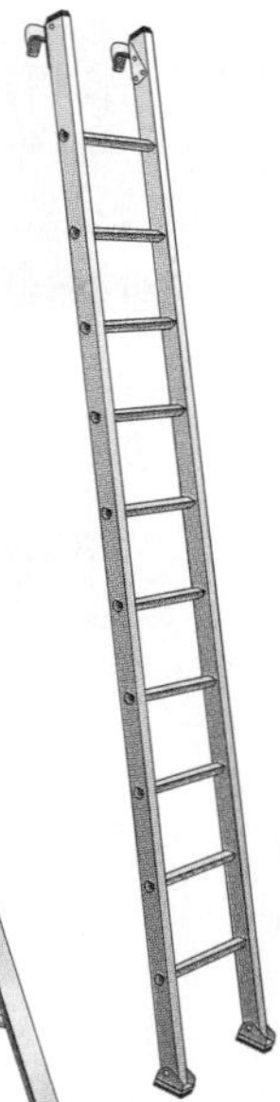

rope ladder
escalera^F de cuerda^F

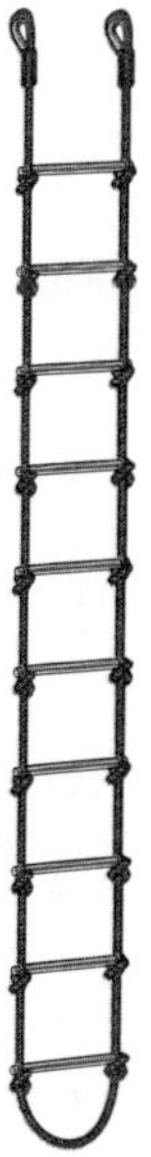

multi-purpose ladder
escalera^F para usos^M múltiples

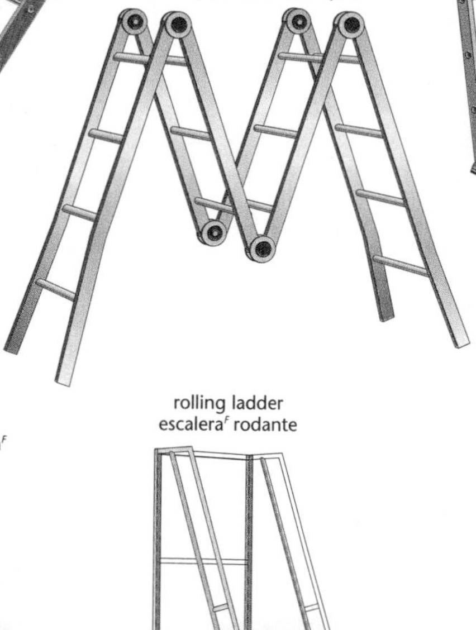

ladder scaffold
andamio^M sobre ruedas^F

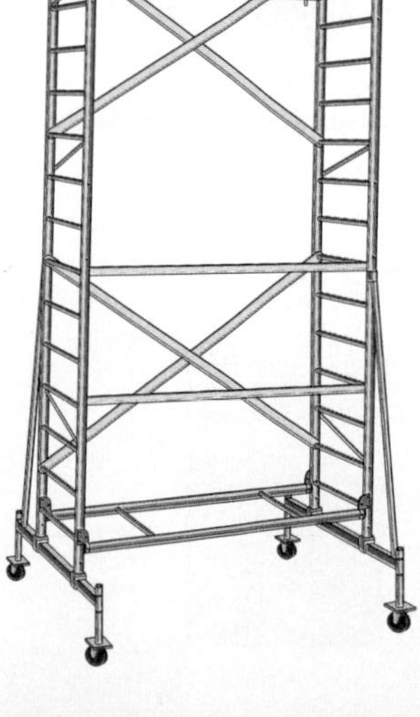

fruit-picking ladder
escalera^F de recolección^F de fruta^F

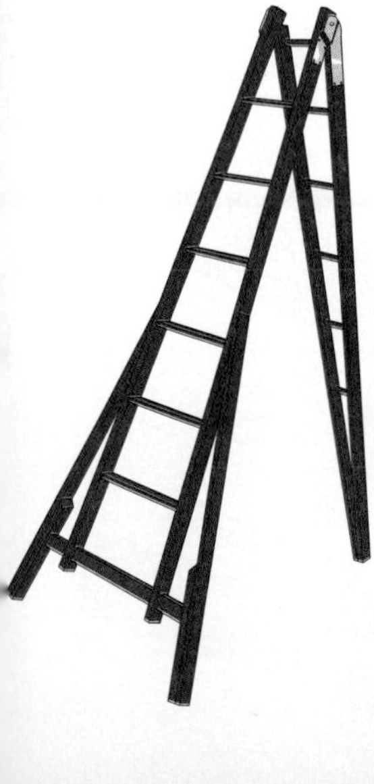

rolling ladder
escalera^F rodante

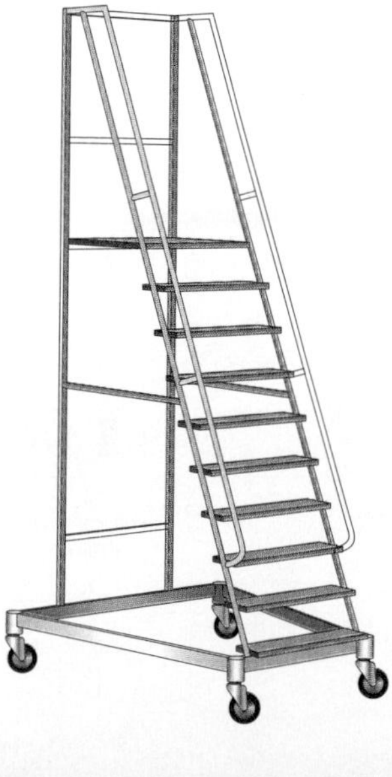

PAINTING UPKEEP
HERRAMIENTAS^F PARA PINTAR

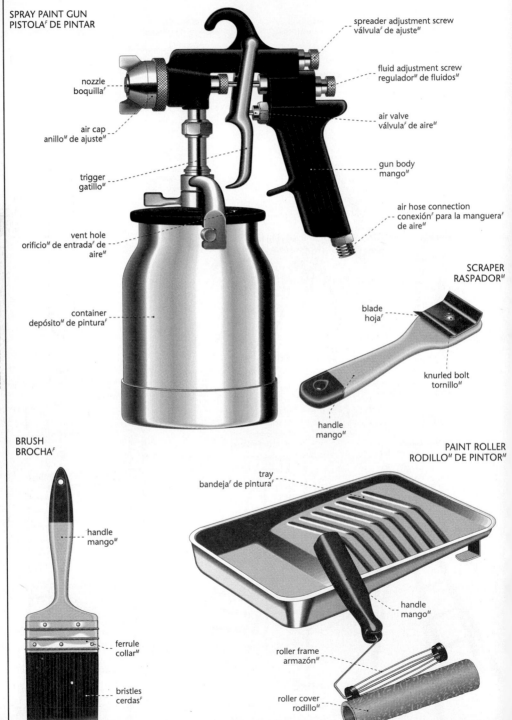

SPRAY PAINT GUN
PISTOLA^F DE PINTAR

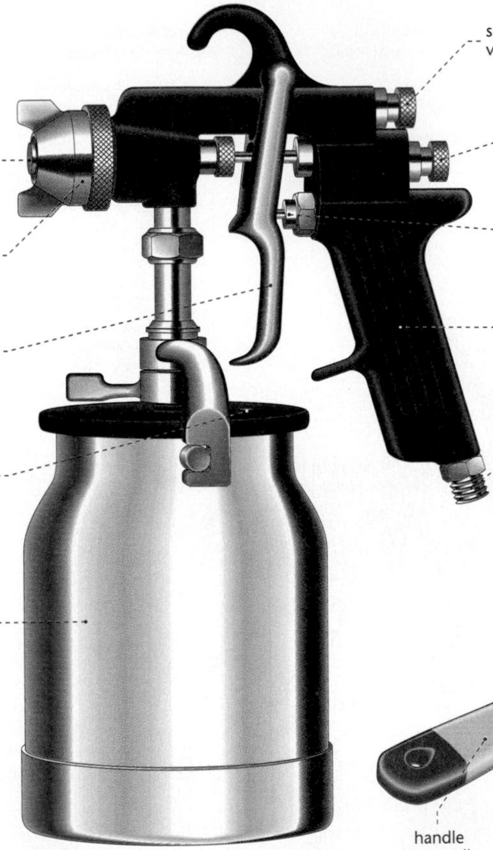

spreader adjustment screw
válvula^F de ajuste^M

fluid adjustment screw
regulador^M de fluidos^M

nozzle
boquilla^F

air valve
válvula^F de aire^M

air cap
anillo^M de ajuste^M

gun body
mango^M

trigger
gatillo^M

air hose connection
conexión^F para la manguera^F
de aire^M

vent hole
orificio^M de entrada^F de
aire^M

SCRAPER
RASPADOR^M

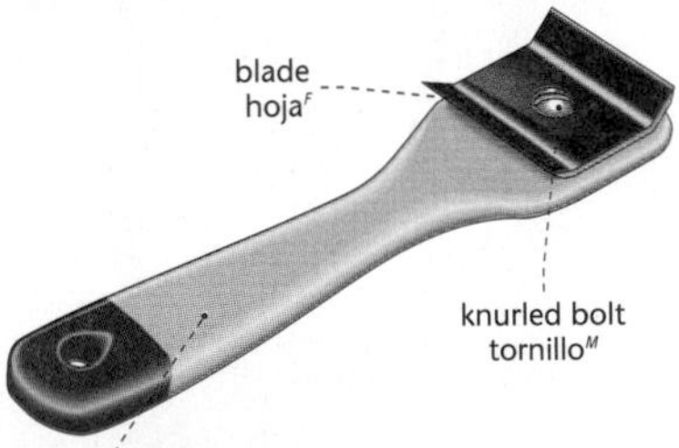

blade
hoja^F

container
depósito^M de pintura^F

knurled bolt
tornillo^M

handle
mango^M

BRUSH
BROCHA^F

PAINT ROLLER
RODILLO^M DE PINTOR^M

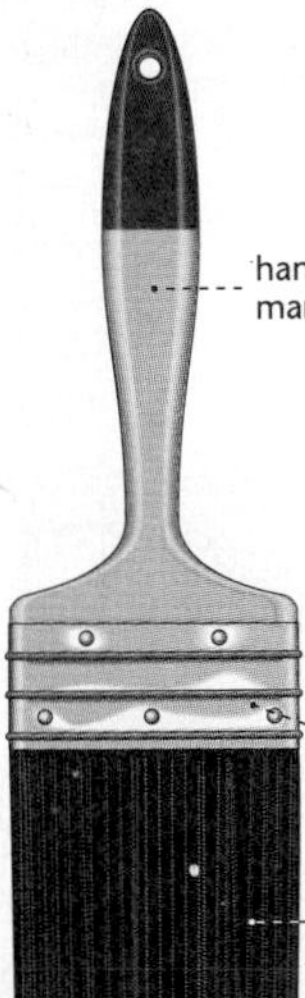

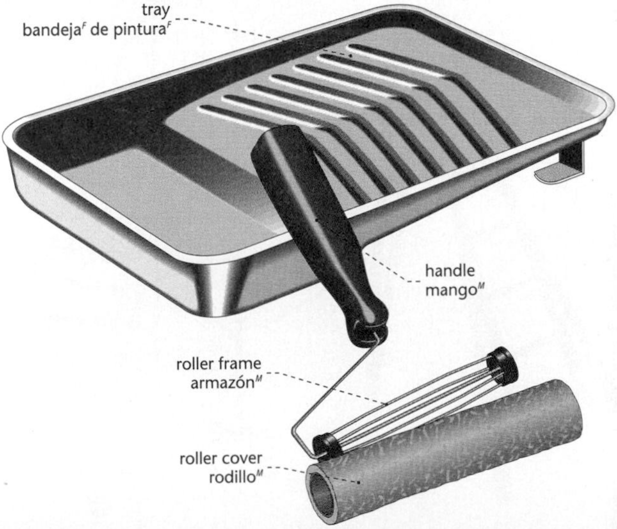

tray
bandeja^F de pintura^F

handle
mango^M

handle
mango^M

ferrule
collar^M

roller frame
armazón^M

bristles
cerdas^F

roller cover
rodillo^M

304

SOLDERING AND WELDING
SOLDADURA^F

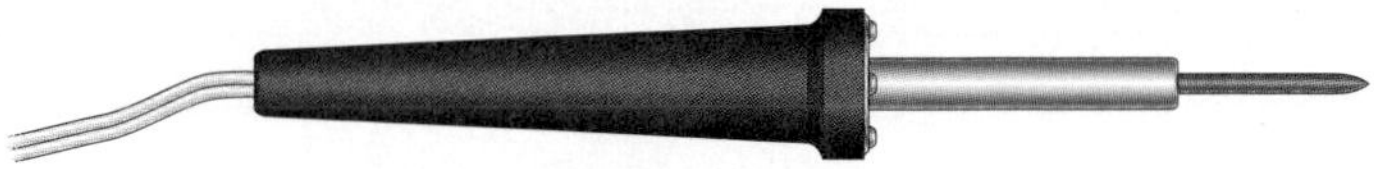

soldering iron
hierro^M para soldar

SOLDERING GUN
PISTOLA^F PARA SOLDAR

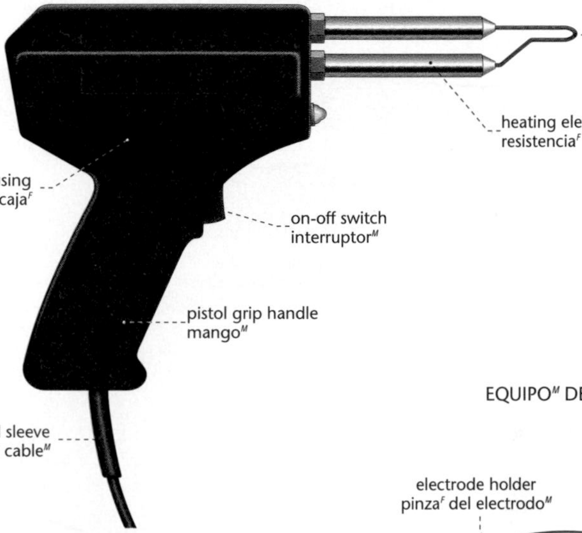

tip
punta^F

heating element
resistencia^F

housing
caja^F

on-off switch
interruptor^M

pistol grip handle
mango^M

cord sleeve
protector^M del cable^M

ARC WELDING
EQUIPO^M DE SOLDADURA^F ELÉCTRICA

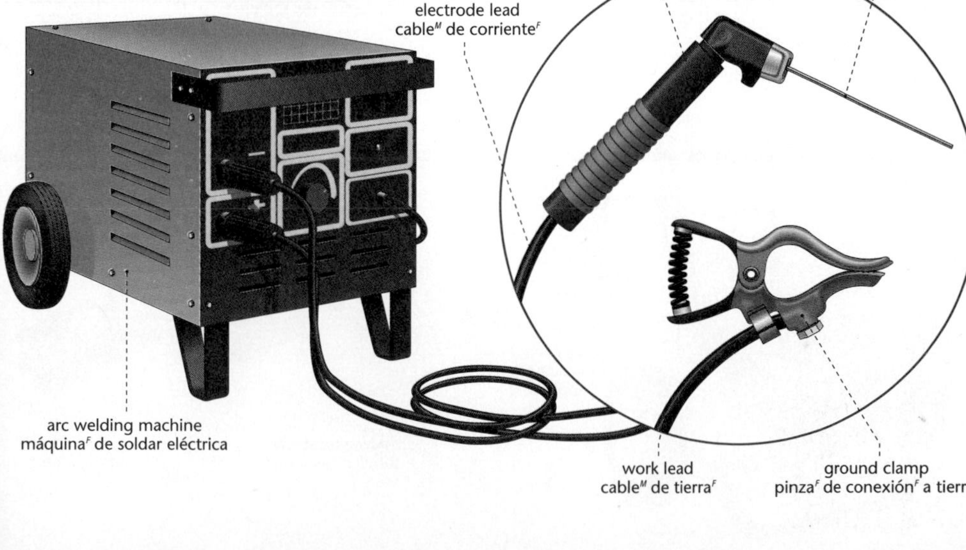

electrode holder
pinza^F del electrodo^M

electrode
electrodo^M

electrode lead
cable^M de corriente^F

arc welding machine
máquina^F de soldar eléctrica

work lead
cable^M de tierra^F

ground clamp
pinza^F de conexión^F a tierra^F

DO-IT-YOURSELF
REPARACIONES CASERAS

SOLDERING AND WELDING
SOLDADURA^F

CUTTING TORCH
SOPLETE^M DE CORTE^M

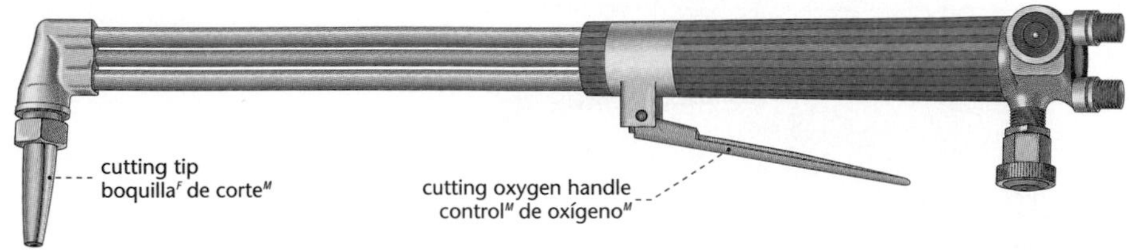

cutting tip
boquilla^F de corte^M

cutting oxygen handle
control^M de oxígeno^M

WELDING TORCH
SOPLETE^M DE SOLDADURA^F
AUTÓGENA

head tube
cuello^M

handle
mango^M

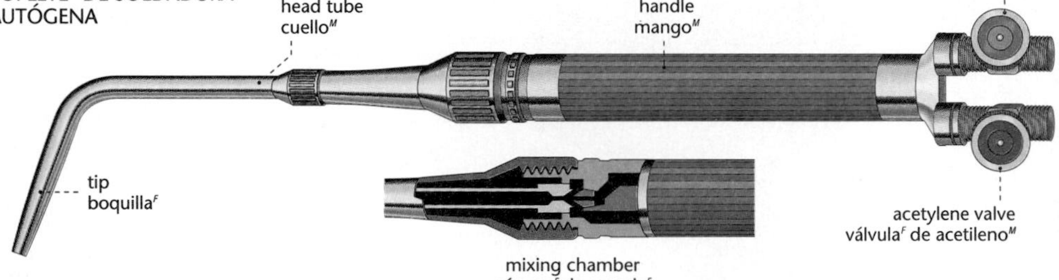

oxygen valve
válvula^F de oxígeno^M

tip
boquilla^F

acetylene valve
válvula^F de acetileno^M

mixing chamber
cámara^F de mezcla^F

OXYACETYLENE WELDING
EQUIPO^M DE SOLDADURA^F AUTÓGENA

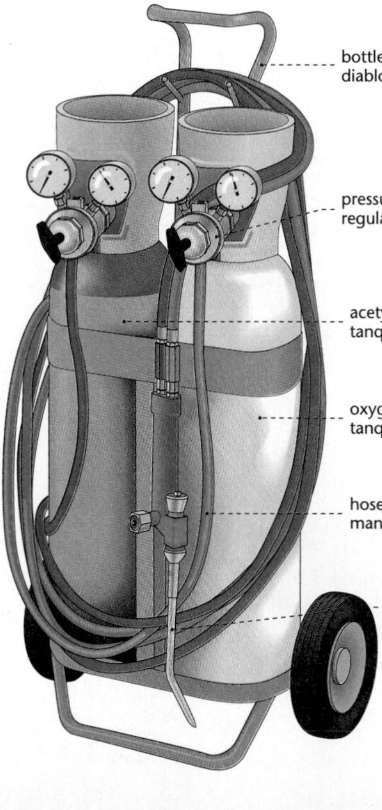

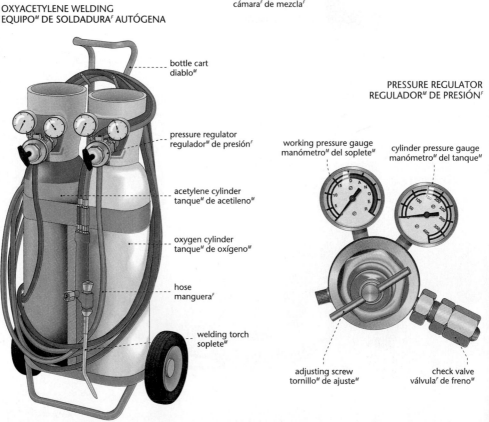

bottle cart
diablo^M

PRESSURE REGULATOR
REGULADOR^M DE PRESIÓN^F

pressure regulator
regulador^M de presión^F

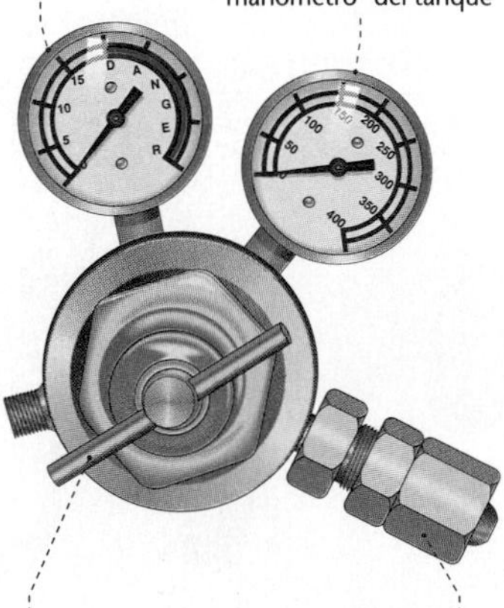

working pressure gauge
manómetro^M del soplete^M

cylinder pressure gauge
manómetro^M del tanque^M

acetylene cylinder
tanque^M de acetileno^M

oxygen cylinder
tanque^M de oxígeno^M

hose
manguera^F

welding torch
soplete^M

adjusting screw
tornillo^M de ajuste^M

check valve
válvula^F de freno^M

BUTT WELDING
SOLDADURA*F* A TOPE*M*

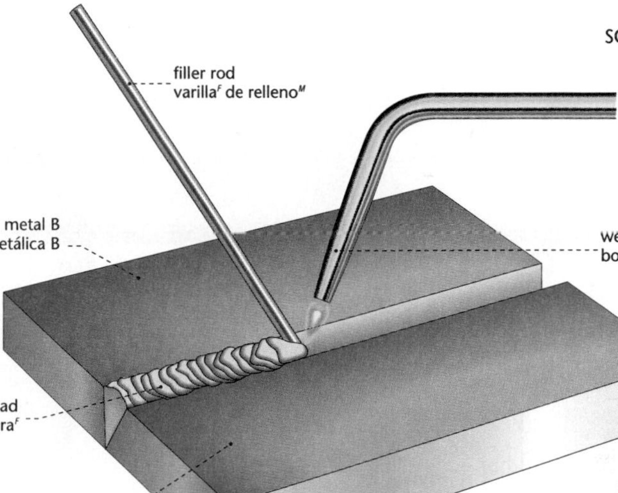

filler rod
varilla*F* de relleno*M*

metal B
placa*F* metálica B

welding torch
boquilla*F* del soplete*M*

weld bead
soldadura*F*

metal A
placa*F* metálica A

SOLDERING TORCH
SOPLETE*M*

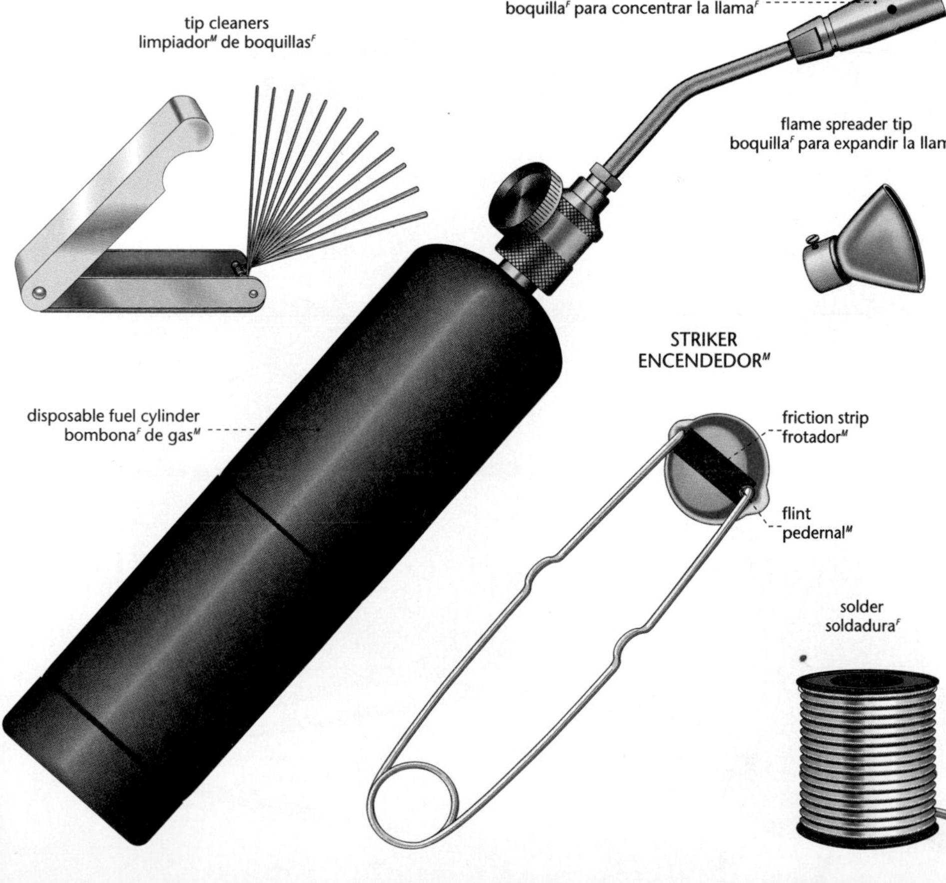

pencil point tip
boquilla*F* para concentrar la llama*F*

tip cleaners
limpiador*M* de boquillas*F*

flame spreader tip
boquilla*F* para expandir la llama*F*

STRIKER
ENCENDEDOR*M*

disposable fuel cylinder
bombona*F* de gas*M*

friction strip
frotador*M*

flint
pedernal*M*

solder
soldadura*F*

goggles
anteojos^M protectores

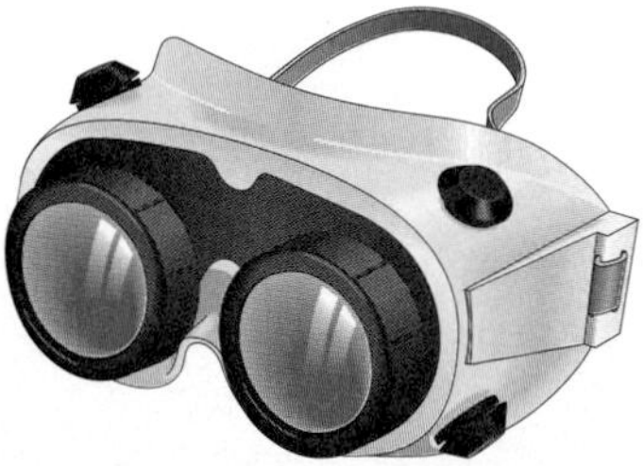

hand shield
careta^F de mano^F

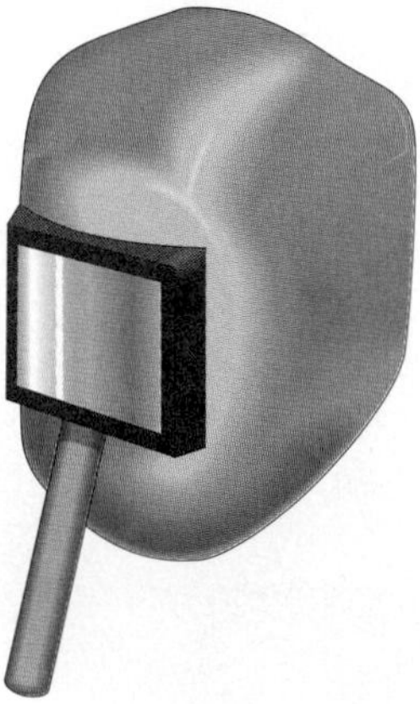

face shield
careta^F

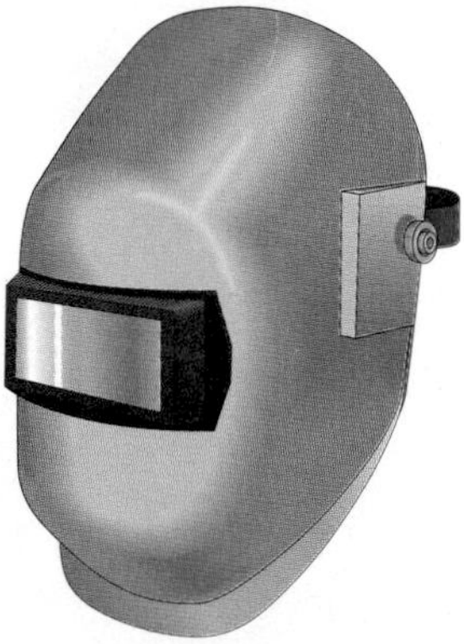

gauntlet
guantes^M

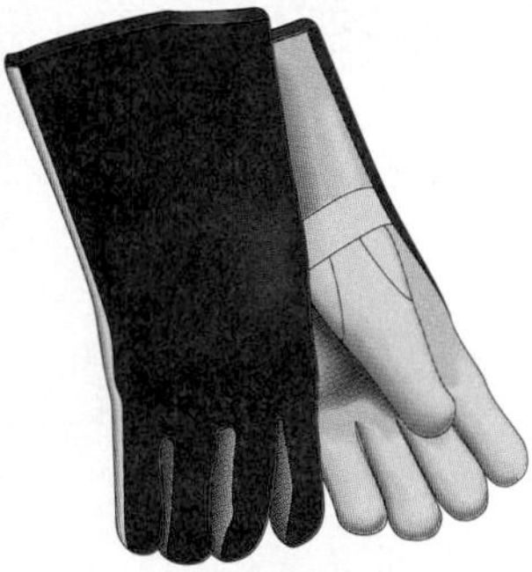

welding curtain
biombo^M para soldar

mitten
manoplas^F

DO-IT-YOURSELF
REPARACIONES CASERAS

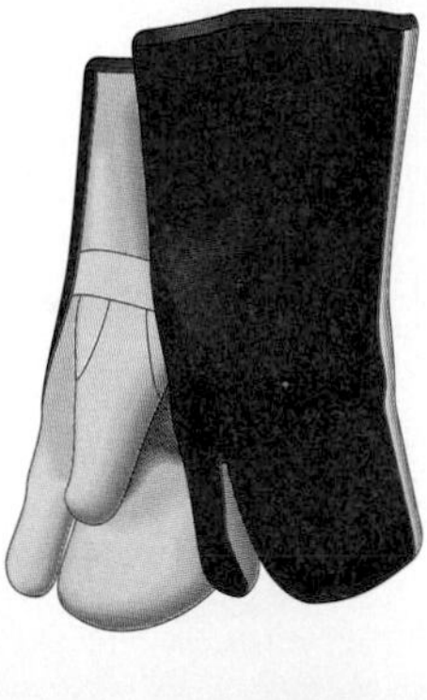

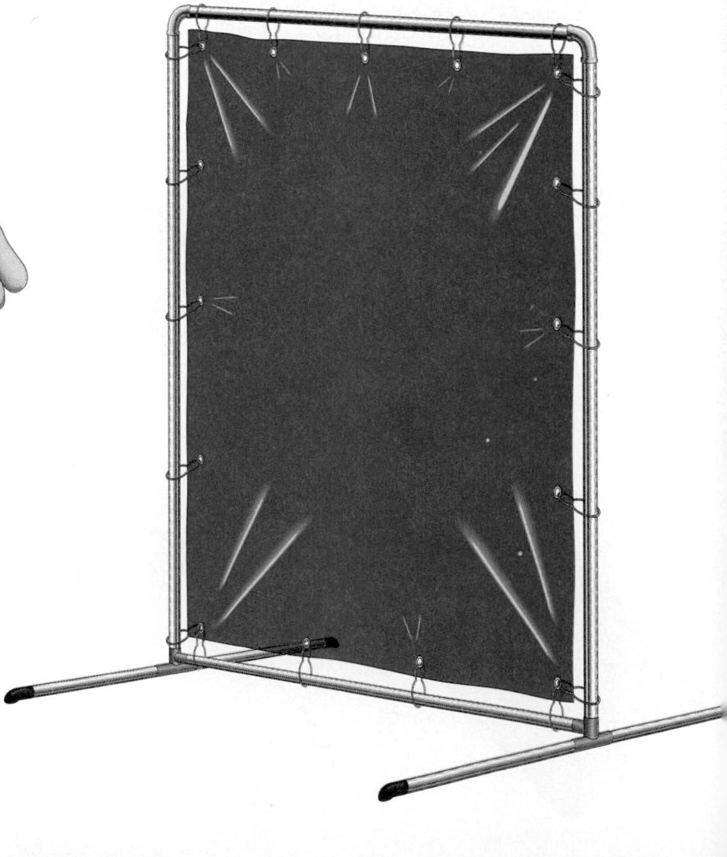

ELECTRICITY
ELECTRICIDAD^F

dimmer switch
conmutador^M de intensidad^F

switch plate
placa^F del interruptor^M

LAMP SOCKET
PORTALÁMPARAS^M

cap
tapa^F

socket
casquillo^M

insulating sleeve
manga^F de aislamiento^M

outer shell
cubierta^F

switch
interruptor^M

electrical box
caja^F de conexiones^F

outlet
enchufe^M

AMERICAN PLUG
ENCHUFE^M DE TIPO^M AMERICANO

blade
pata^F

grounding prong
pata^F de conexión^F a tierra^F

EUROPEAN PLUG
ENCHUFE^M DE TIPO^M EUROPEO

terminal
terminal^M

grounding prong
terminal^M de tierra^F

clamp
abrazadera^F

blade
pata^F

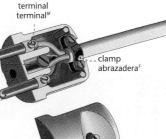

cover
tapa^F

ELECTRICIAN'S TOOLS
HERRAMIENTAS^F DE ELECTRICISTA^M

multimeter
voltímetro^M

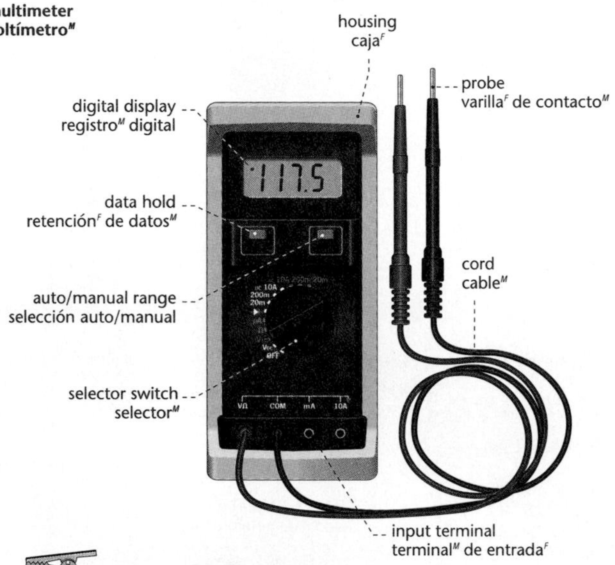

housing
caja^F

probe
varilla^F de contacto^M

digital display
registro^M digital

data hold
retención^F de datos^M

auto/manual range
selección auto/manual

cord
cable^M

selector switch
selector^M

input terminal
terminal^M de entrada^F

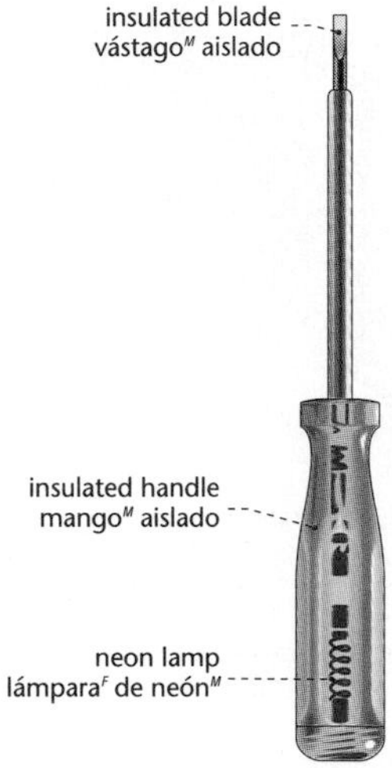

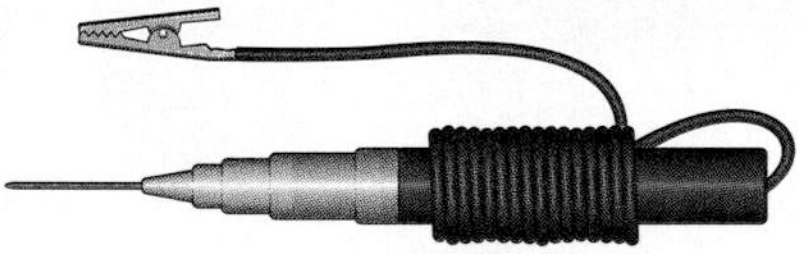

continuity tester
detector^M de continuidad^F

voltage tester
detector^M de tensión^F

insulated blade
vástago^M aislado

insulated handle
mango^M aislado

neon lamp
lámpara^F de neón^M

drop light
linterna^F movible

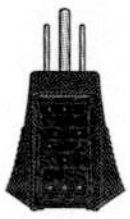

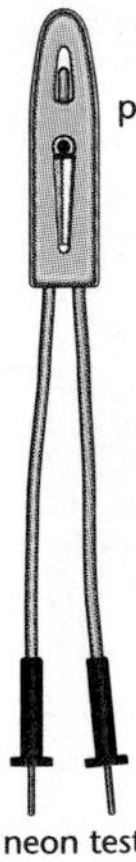

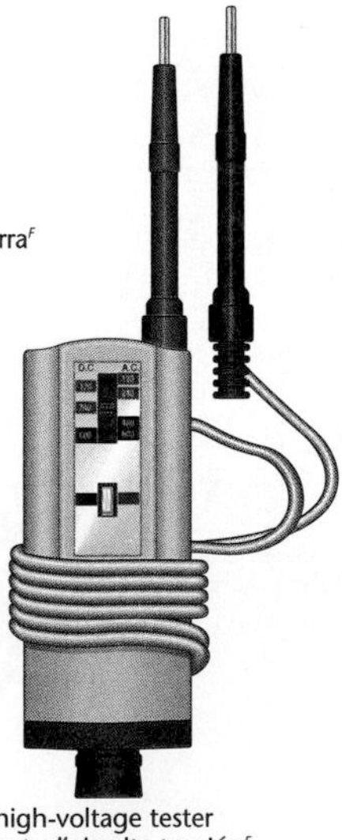

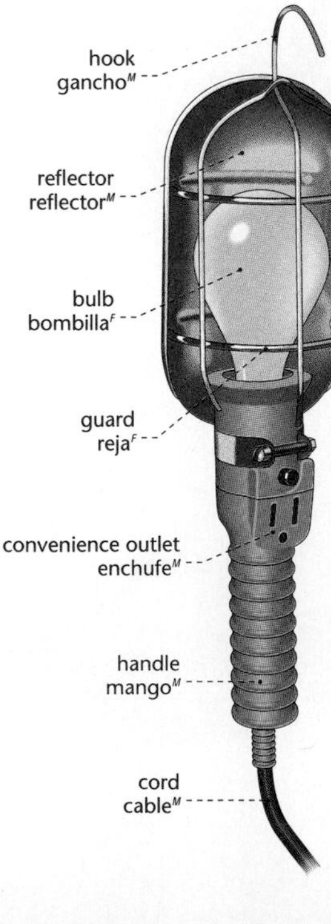

hook
gancho^M

reflector
reflector^M

bulb
bombilla^F

guard
reja^F

convenience outlet
enchufe^M

handle
mango^M

cord
cable^M

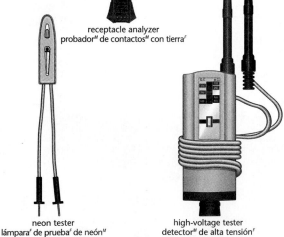

receptacle analyzer
probador^M de contactos^M con tierra^F

neon tester
lámpara^F de prueba^F de neón^M

high-voltage tester
detector^M de alta tensión^F

DO-IT-YOURSELF
REPARACIONES CASERAS

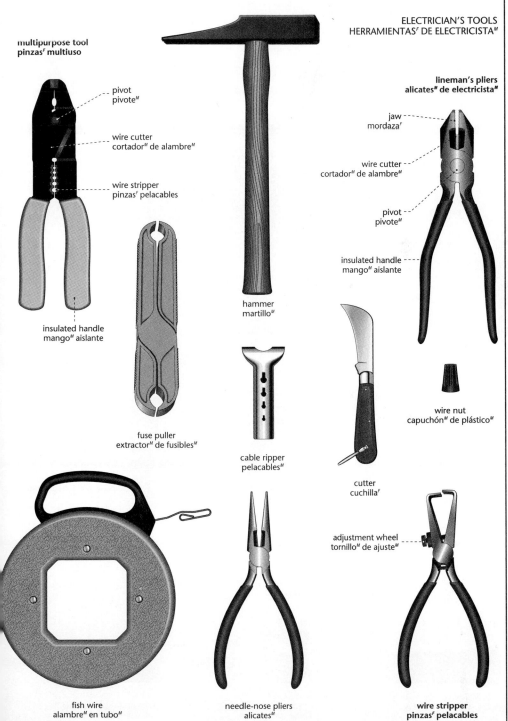

multipurpose tool
pinzas^F multiuso

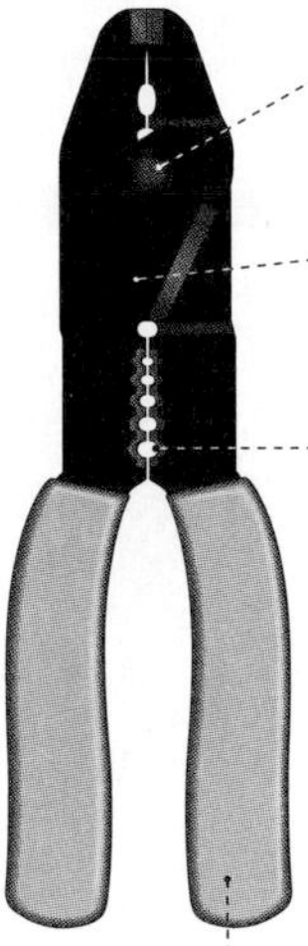

pivot
pivote^M

wire cutter
cortador^M de alambre^M

wire stripper
pinzas^F pelacables

insulated handle
mango^M aislante

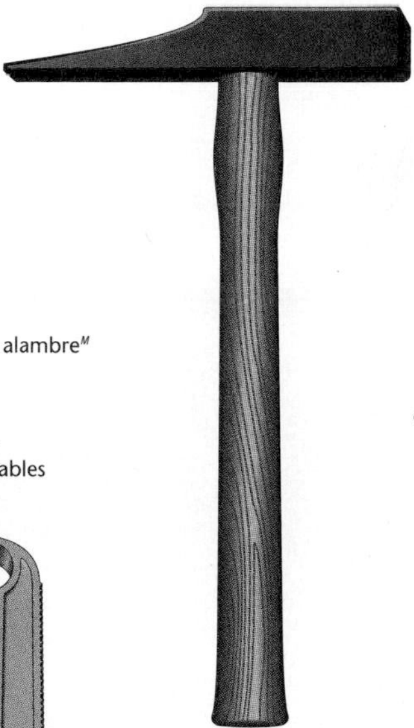

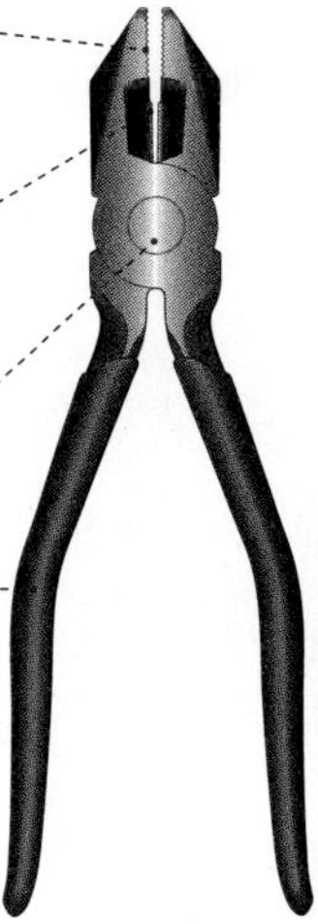

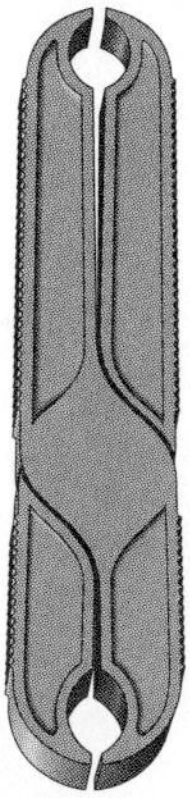

fuse puller
extractor^M de fusibles^M

hammer
martillo^M

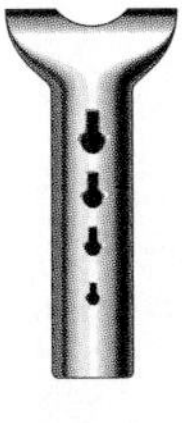

cable ripper
pelacables^M

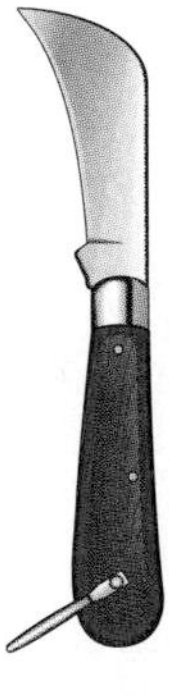

cutter
cuchilla^F

ELECTRICIAN'S TOOLS
HERRAMIENTAS^F DE ELECTRICISTA^M

lineman's pliers
alicates^M de electricista^M

jaw
mordaza^F

wire cutter
cortador^M de alambre^M

pivot
pivote^M

insulated handle
mango^M aislante

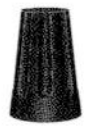

wire nut
capuchón^M de plástico^M

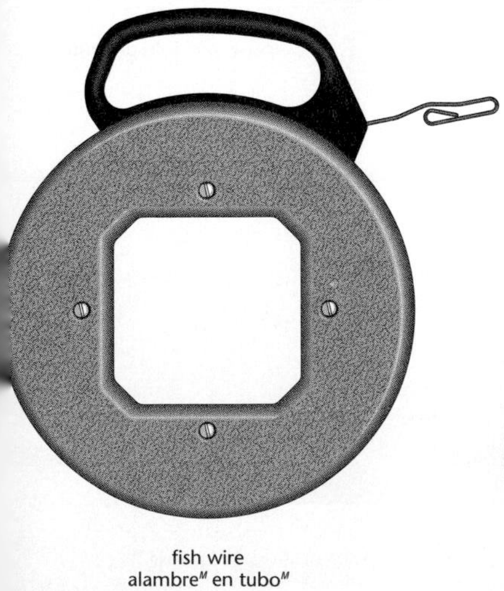

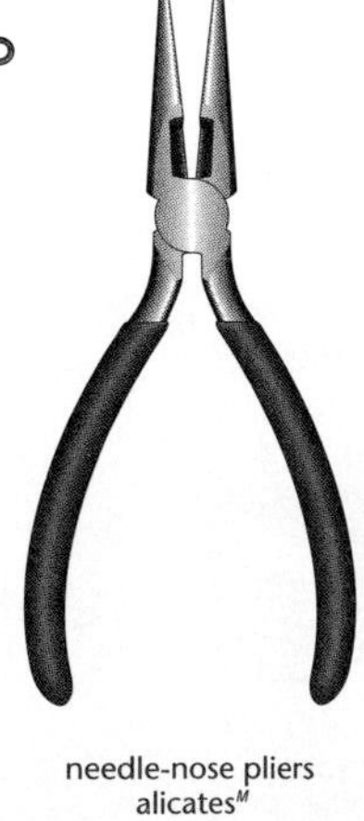

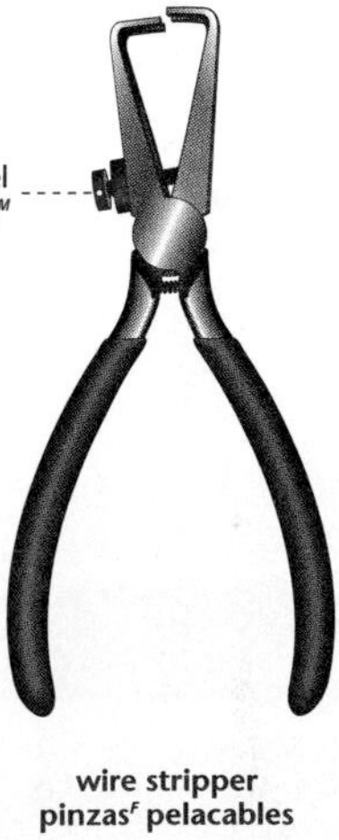

adjustment wheel
tornillo^M de ajuste^M

fish wire
alambre^M en tubo^M

needle-nose pliers
alicates^M

wire stripper
pinzas^F pelacables

DO-IT-YOURSELF
REPARACIONES CASERAS

311

FUSE BOX
CAJETÍN^M DE FUSIBLES^M

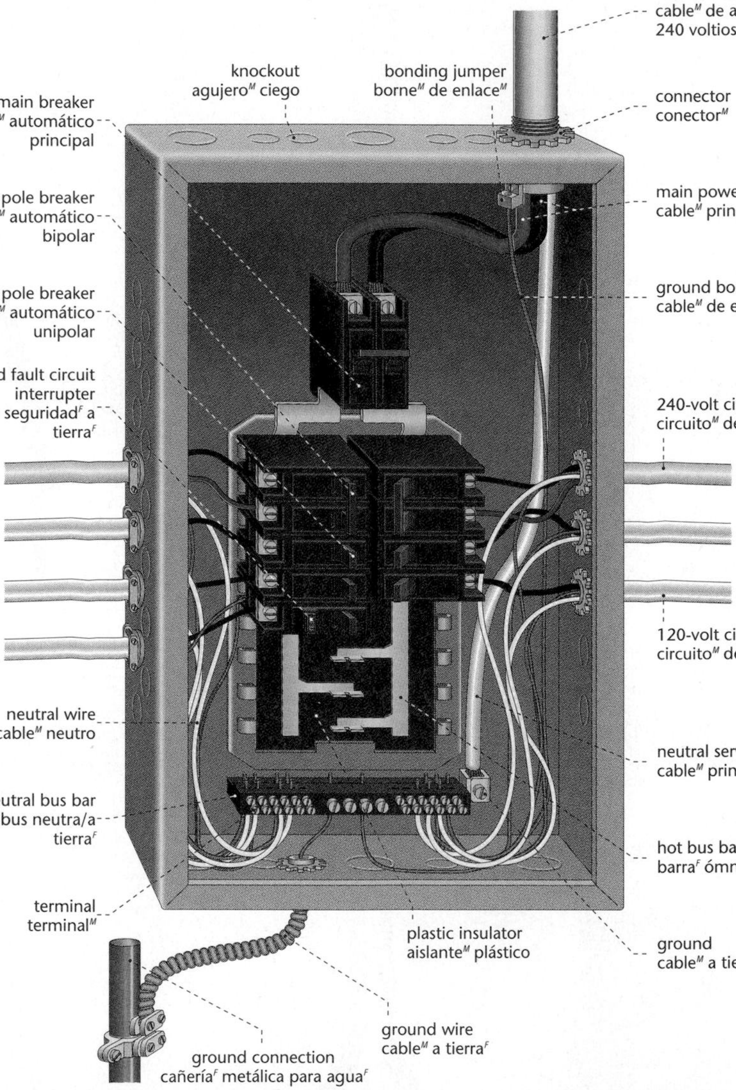

240-volt feeder cable
cable^M de alimentación^F de
240 voltios

knockout
agujero^M ciego

bonding jumper
borne^M de enlace^M

connector
conector^M

main breaker
interruptor^M automático
principal

main power cable
cable^M principal

double pole breaker
interruptor^M automático
bipolar

ground bond
cable^M de enlace^M

single pole breaker
interruptor^M automático
unipolar

ground fault circuit
interrupter
fusible^M de seguridad^F a
tierra^F

240-volt circuit
circuito^M de 240 voltios

120-volt circuit
circuito^M de 120 voltios

neutral wire
cable^M neutro

neutral service wire
cable^M principal neutro

ground/neutral bus bar
barra^F ómnibus neutra/a
tierra^F

hot bus bar
barra^F ómnibus de carga^F

terminal
terminal^M

plastic insulator
aislante^M plástico

ground
cable^M a tierra^F

ground wire
cable^M a tierra^F

ground connection
cañería^F metálica para agua^F

FUSES
FUSIBLES^M

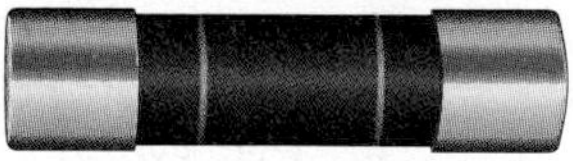

cartridge fuse
fusible^M de cartucho^M

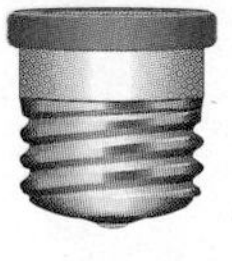

plug fuse
fusible^M de rosca^F

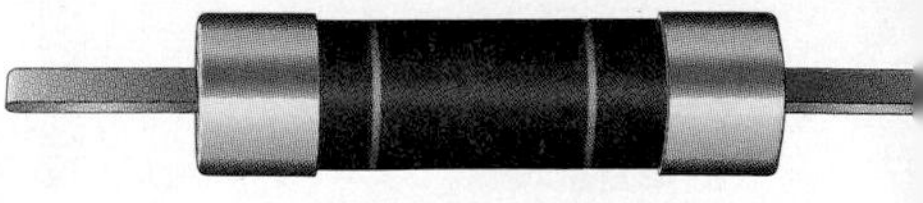

knife-blade cartridge fuse
fusible^M de bayoneta^F

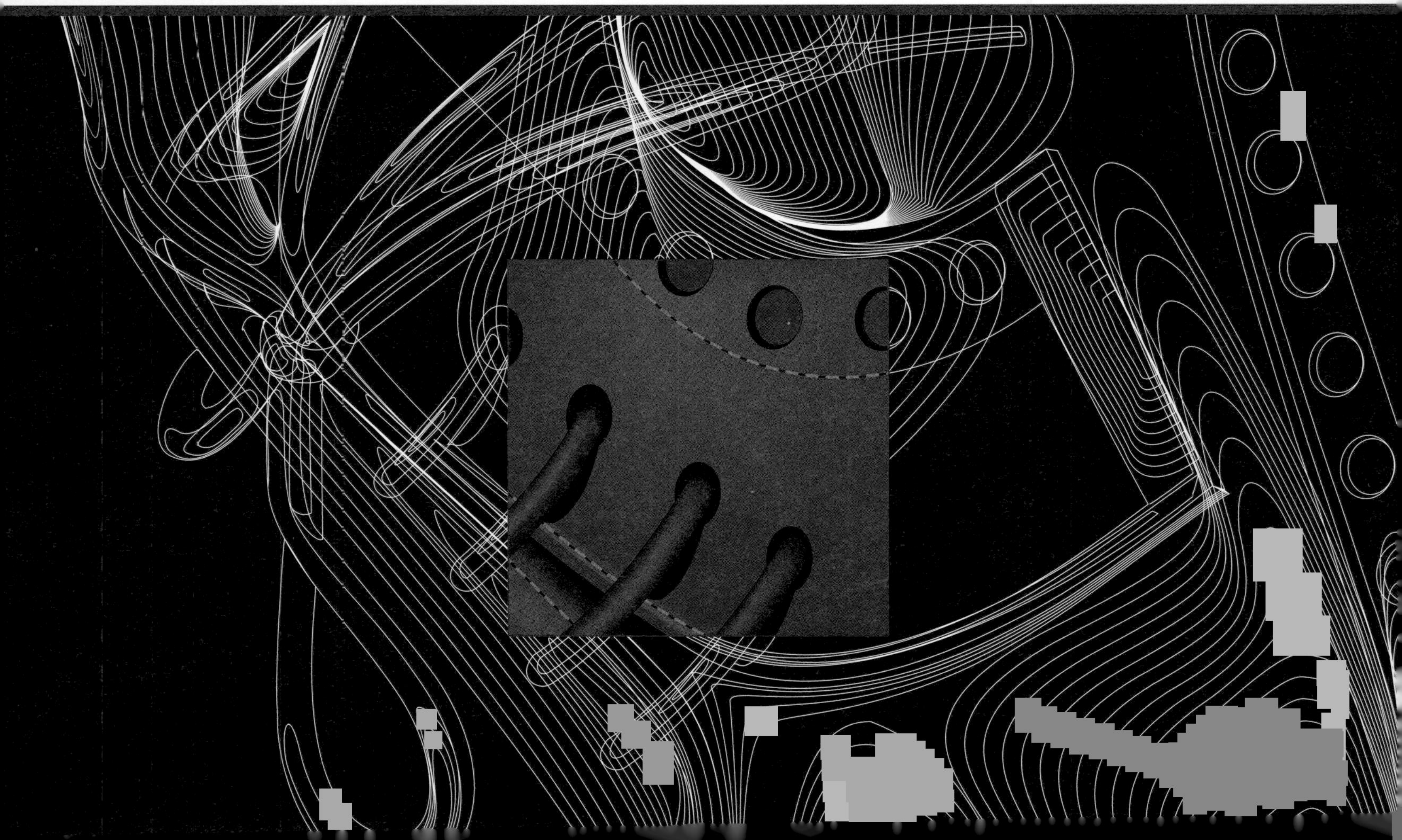

CONTENTS

CLOTHING
VESTIDO

ELEMENTS OF ANCIENT COSTUME
VESTIDURAS^F ANTIGUAS

PEPLOS
PEPLO^M

TOGA
TOGA^F

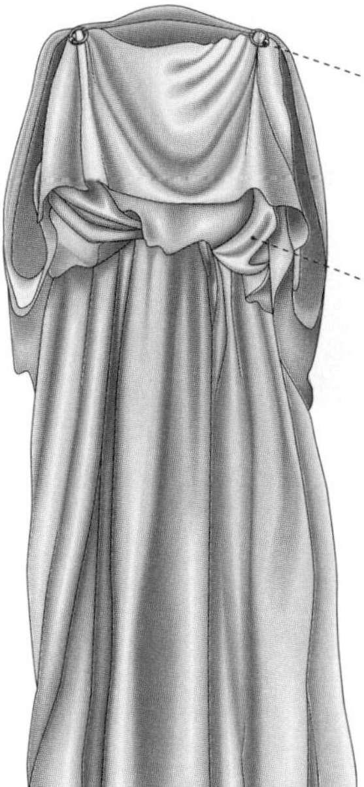

fibula
fíbula^F

fold
pliegue^M

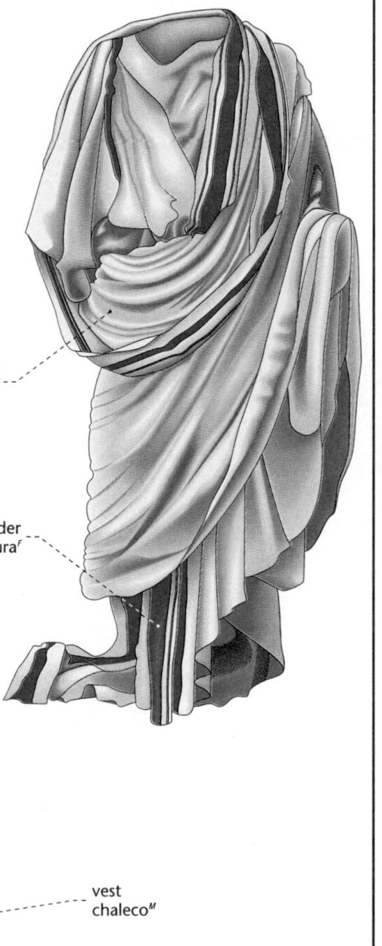

sinus
seno^M

purple border
orla^F de púrpura^F

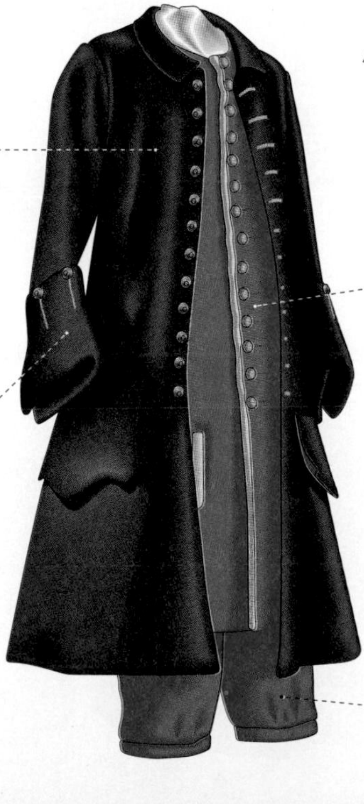

justaucorps
casaca^F

vest
chaleco^M

cuff
puño^M

breeches
calzas^F

ELEMENTS OF ANCIENT COSTUME
VESTIDURAS^F ANTIGUAS

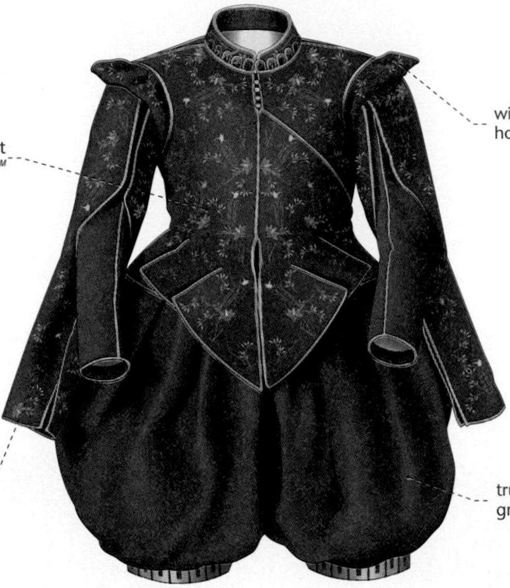

doublet
jubón^M

wing
hombrera^F

hanging sleeve
manga^F colgante

trunk hose
gregüescos^M

COTEHARDIE
TÚNICA^F DE MANGA^F LARGA

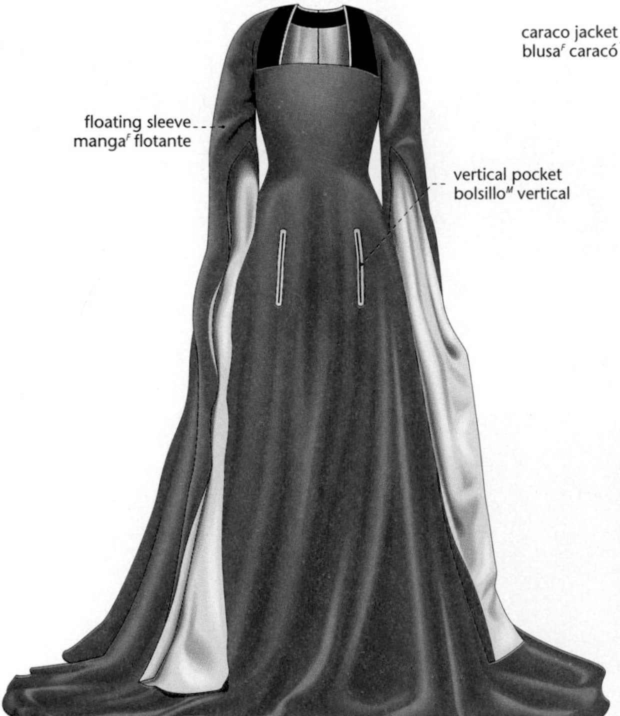

floating sleeve
manga^F flotante

vertical pocket
bolsillo^M vertical

DRESS WITH BUSTLE
VESTIDO^M CON POLISÓN^M

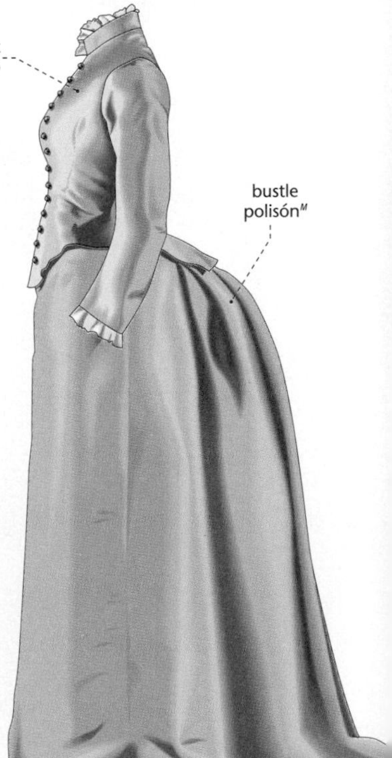

caraco jacket
blusa^F caracó

bustle
polisón^M

HOUPPELANDE
TOGA*F*

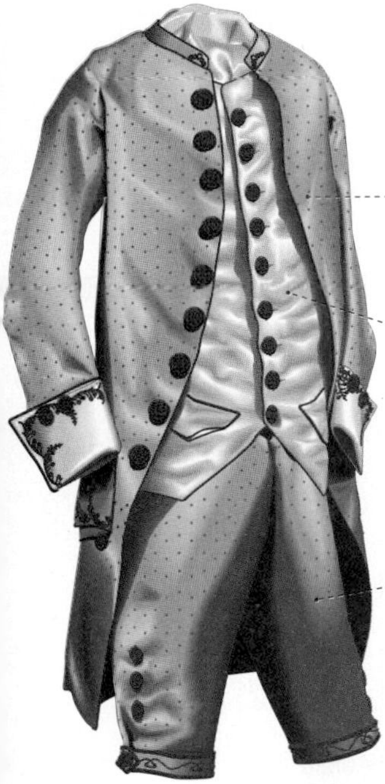

frock coat
levita*F*

waistcoat
chaleco*M*

breeches
calzas*F*

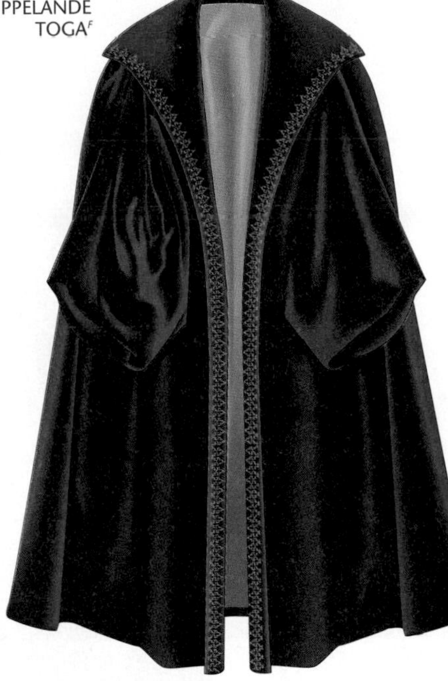

DRESS WITH PANNIERS
GUARDAINFANTE*M*

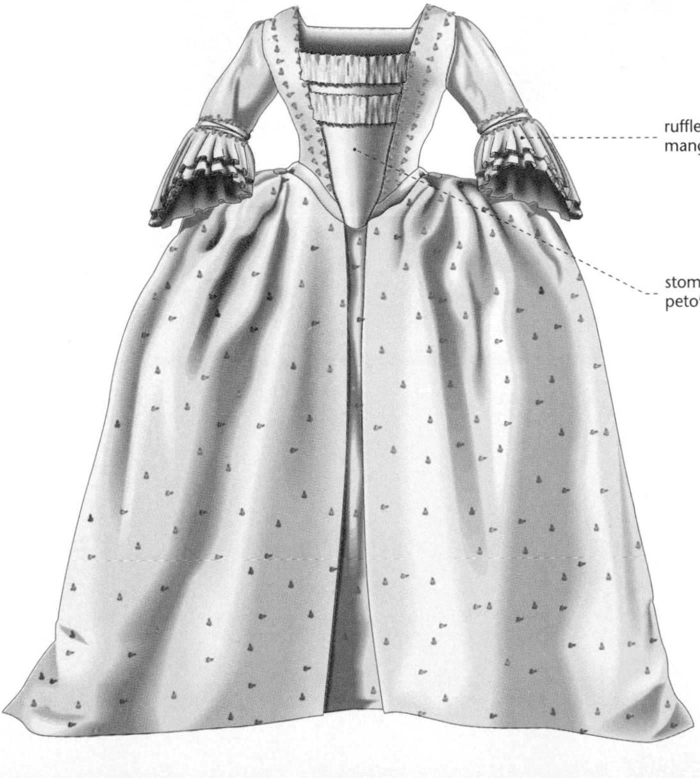

ruffle
manga*F* de volante*M*

stomacker
peto*M*

DRESS WITH CRINOLINE
MIRIÑAQUE^M

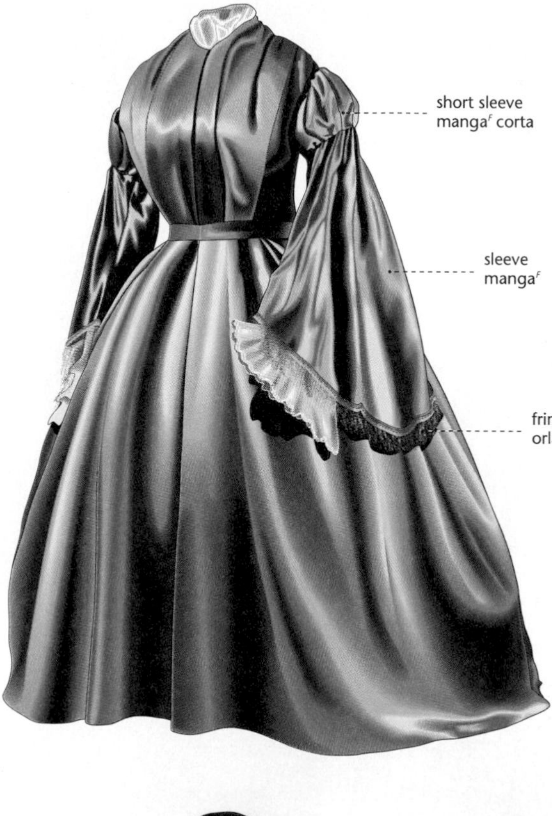

short sleeve
manga^f corta

sleeve
manga^f

fringe
orla^f

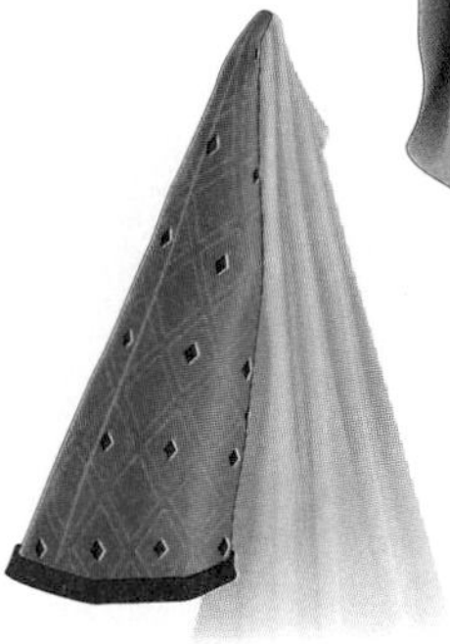

hennin
cofia^f cónica

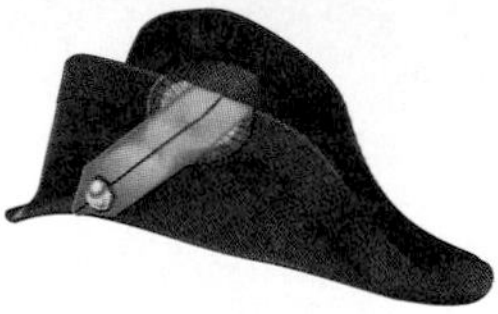

bicorne
bicornio^M

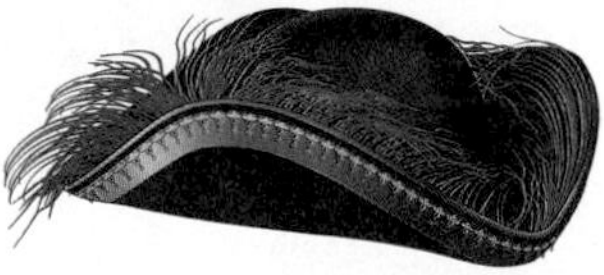

tricorne
tricornio^M

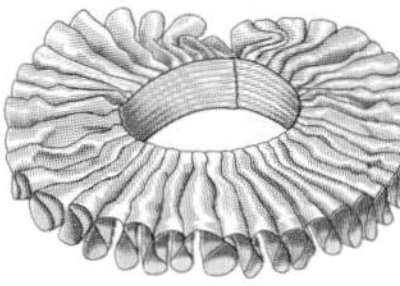

fraise
gorguera^f

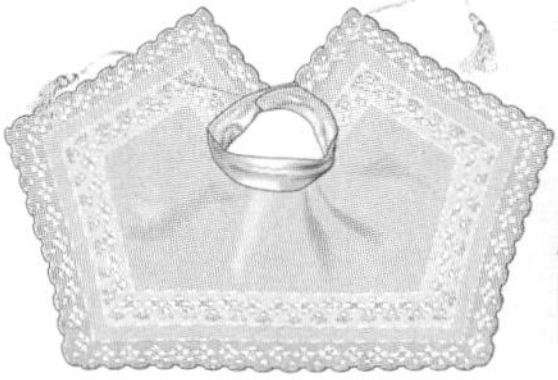

collaret
cuello^M de Holanda

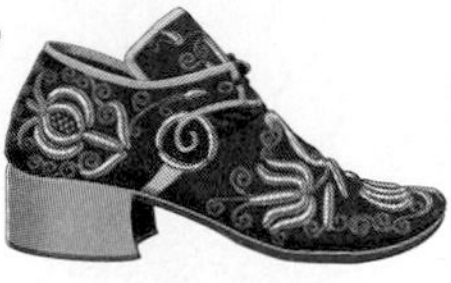

heeled shoe
zapato^M de tacón^M

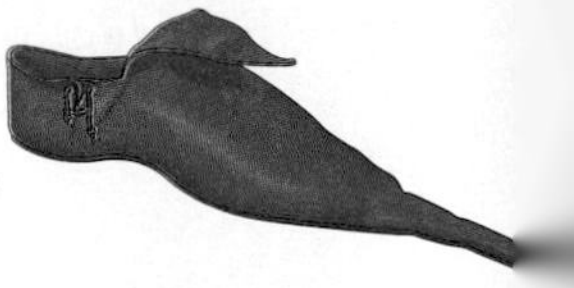

crakow
zapato^M a la polaca

RAINCOAT
IMPERMEABLE^M

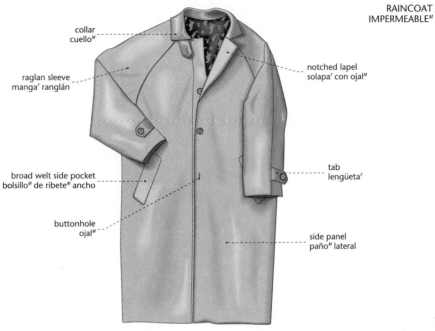

collar
cuello^M

notched lapel
solapa^F con ojal^M

raglan sleeve
manga^F ranglán

broad welt side pocket
bolsillo^M de ribete^M ancho

tab
lengüeta^F

buttonhole
ojal^M

side panel
paño^M lateral

TRENCH COAT
TRINCHERA^F

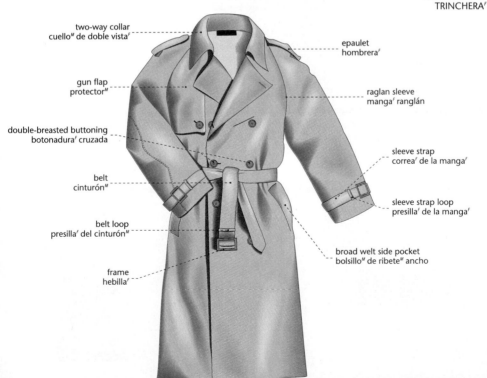

two-way collar
cuello^M de doble vista^F

epaulet
hombrera^F

gun flap
protector^M

raglan sleeve
manga^F ranglán

double-breasted buttoning
botonadura^F cruzada

sleeve strap
correa^F de la manga^F

belt
cinturón^M

sleeve strap loop
presilla^F de la manga^F

belt loop
presilla^F del cinturón^M

broad welt side pocket
bolsillo^M de ribete^M ancho

frame
hebilla^F

CLOTHING
VESTIDO

DUFFLE COAT
CAZADORA^F DE TRES CUARTOS

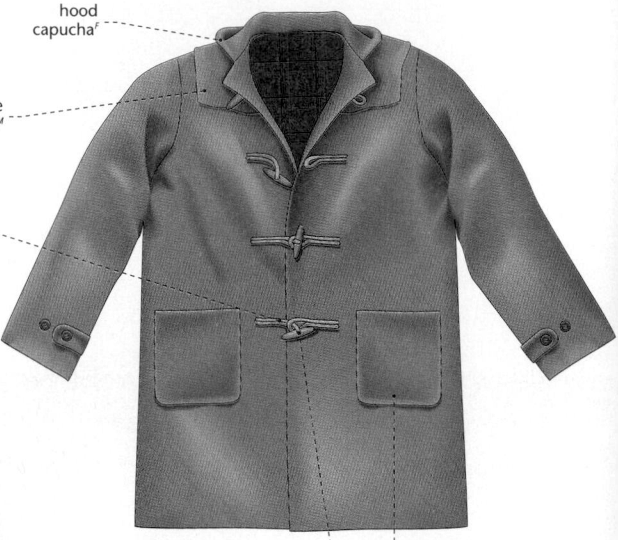

hood
capucha^F

yoke
hombrillo^M

frog
alamar^M

OVERCOAT
ABRIGO^M

patch pocket
bolsillo^M de parche^M

toggle fastening
botón^M de madera^F

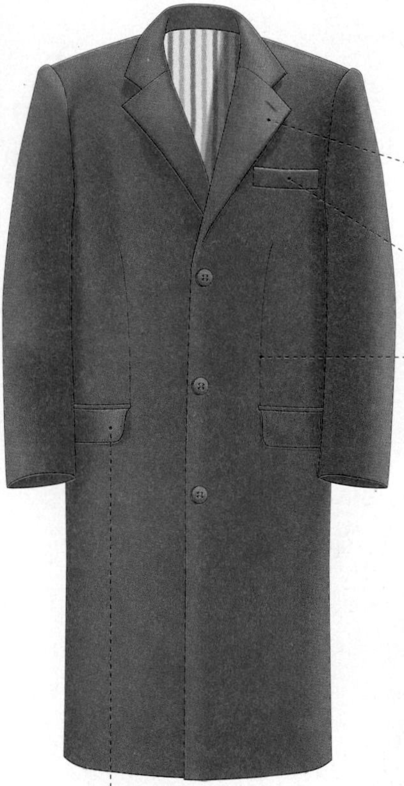

notched lapel
solapa^F con ojal^M

breast pocket
bolsillo^M superior

breast dart
pinza^F

WINDBREAKER
CAZADORA^F

flap pocket
bolsillo^M con cartera^F

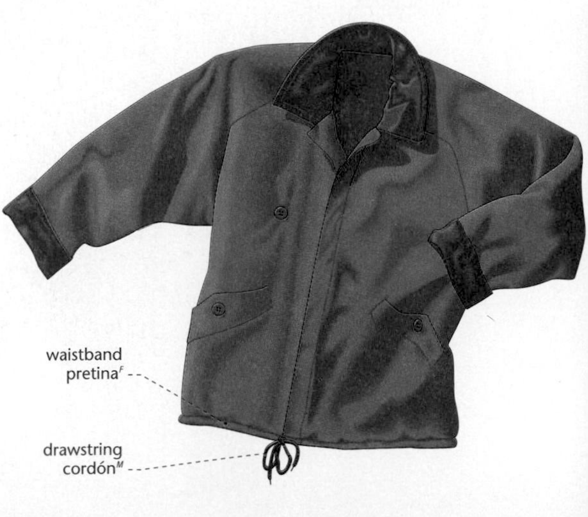

waistband
pretina^F

drawstring
cordón^M

three-quarter coat
abrigo^M de tres cuartos

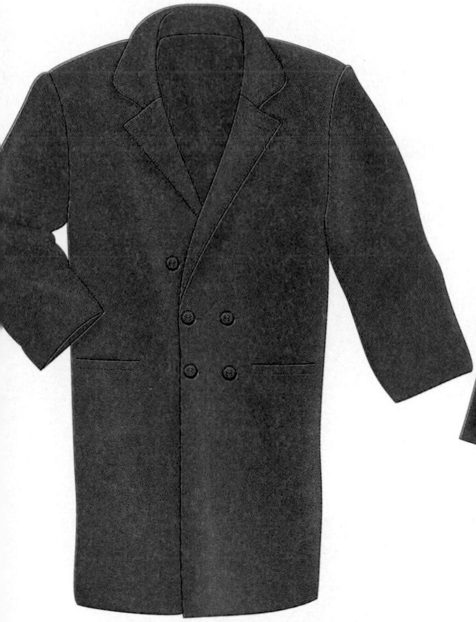

PARKA
PARKA^M

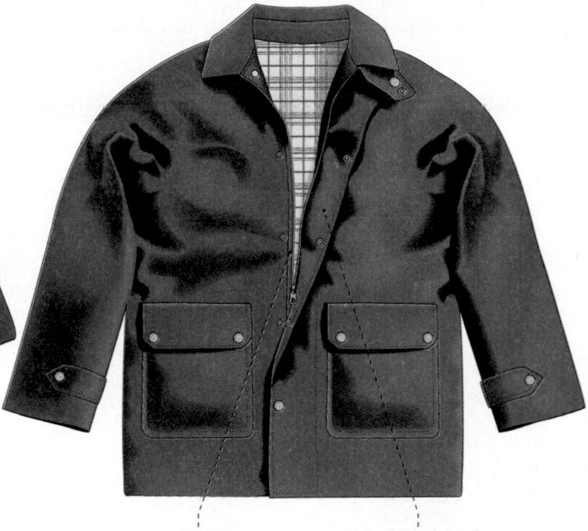

zipper
cremallera^F

snap-fastening tab
corchete^M de presión^F

JACKET
CAZADORA^F

sheepskin jacket
zamarra^F

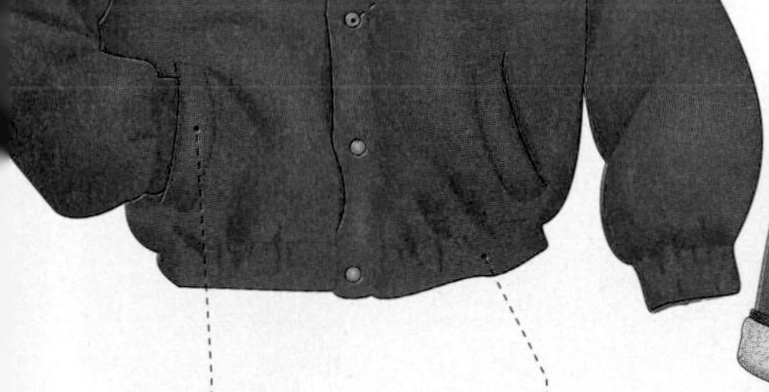

snap fastener
broche^M de presión^F

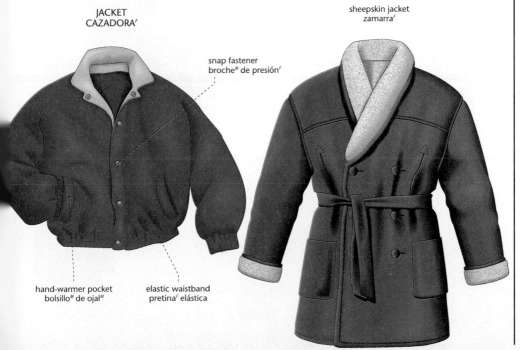

hand-warmer pocket
bolsillo^M de ojal^M

elastic waistband
pretina^F elástica

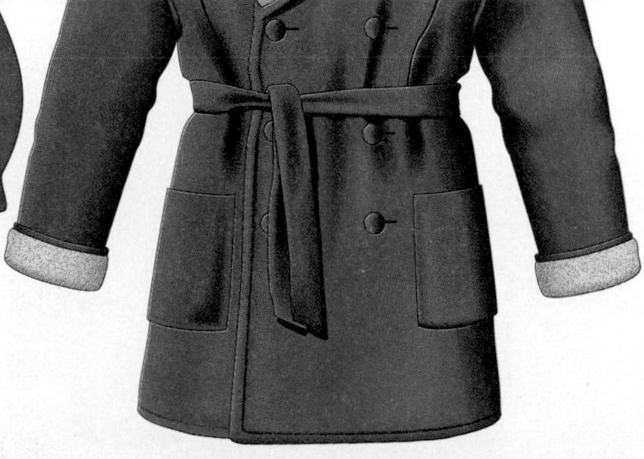

CLOTHING
VESTIDO

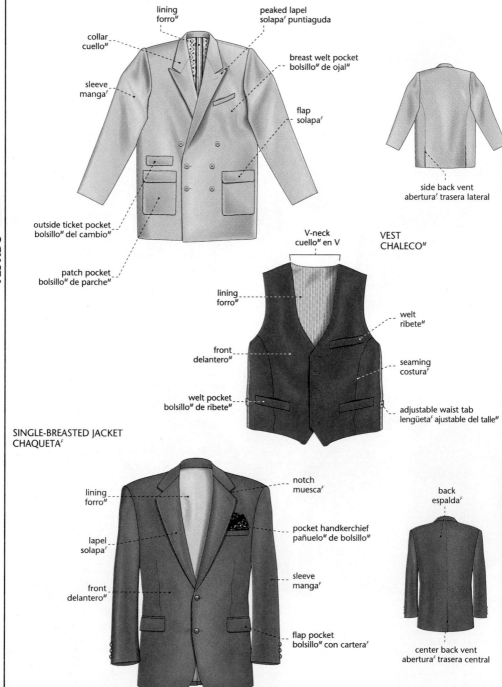

DOUBLE-BREASTED JACKET
CHAQUETA^F CRUZADA

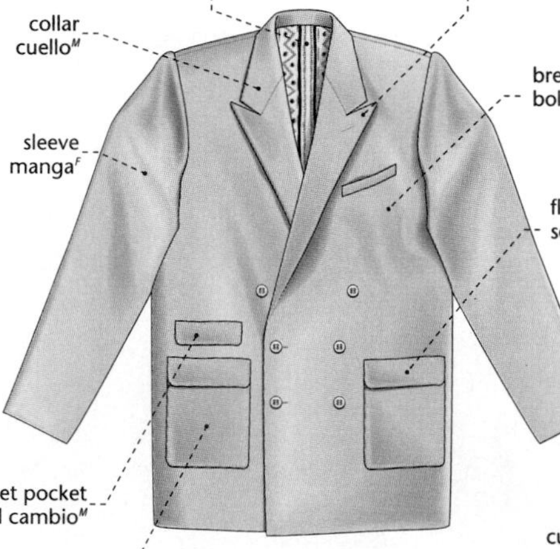

lining
forro^M

peaked lapel
solapa^F puntiaguda

collar
cuello^M

breast welt pocket
bolsillo^M de ojal^M

sleeve
manga^F

flap
solapa^F

outside ticket pocket
bolsillo^M del cambio^M

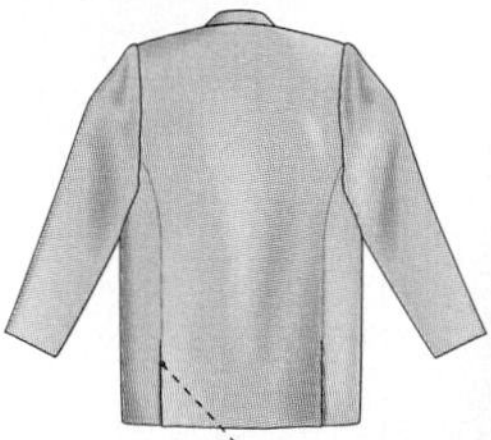

side back vent
abertura^F trasera lateral

patch pocket
bolsillo^M de parche^M

V-neck
cuello^M en V

VEST
CHALECO^M

lining
forro^M

welt
ribete^M

front
delantero^M

seaming
costura^F

welt pocket
bolsillo^M de ribete^M

adjustable waist tab
lengüeta^F ajustable del talle^M

SINGLE-BREASTED JACKET
CHAQUETA^F

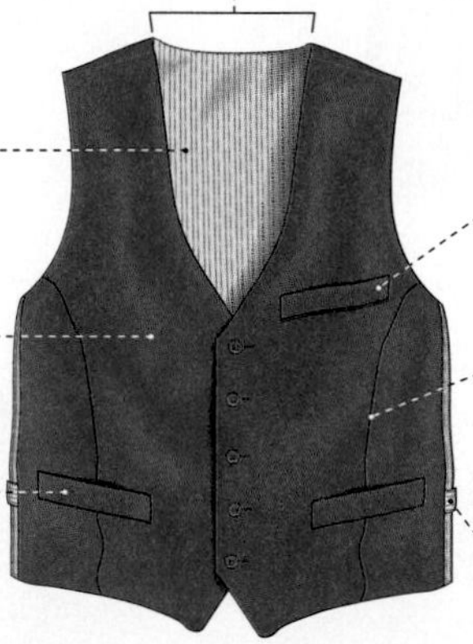

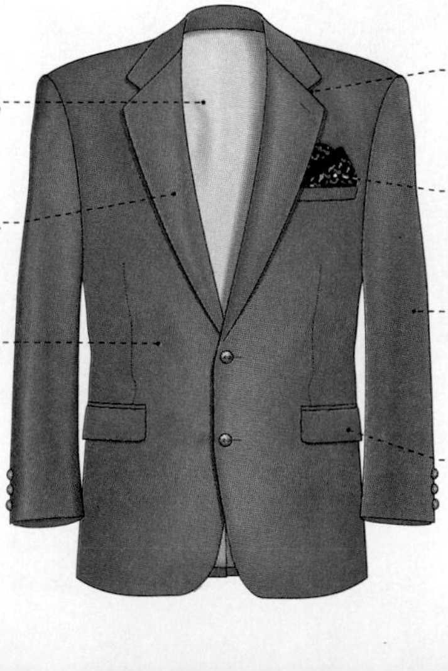

lining
forro^M

notch
muesca^F

back
espalda^F

pocket handkerchief
pañuelo^M de bolsillo^M

lapel
solapa^F

sleeve
manga^F

front
delantero^M

flap pocket
bolsillo^M con cartera^F

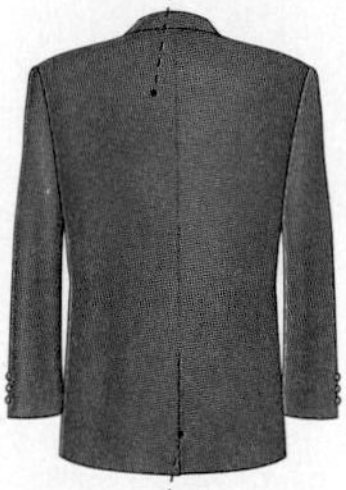

center back vent
abertura^F trasera central

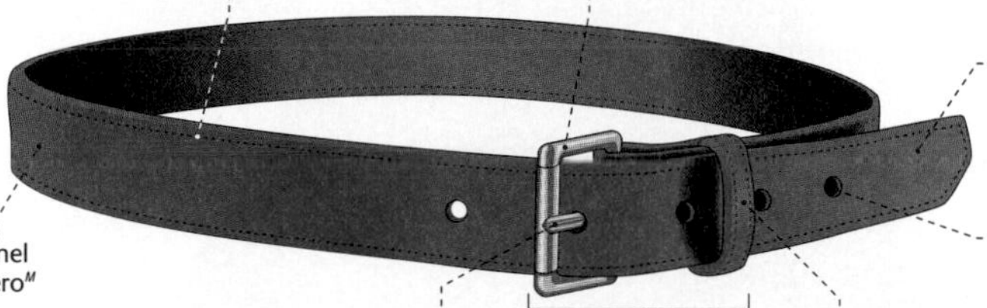

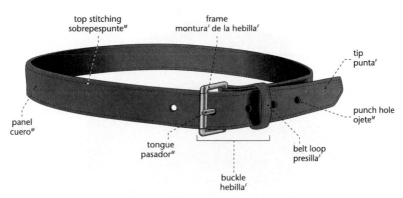

top stitching
sobrepespunte^M

frame
montura^F de la hebilla^F

tip
punta^F

panel
cuero^M

punch hole
ojete^M

tongue
pasador^M

belt loop
presilla^F

buckle
hebilla^F

CLOTHING
VESTIDO

SUSPENDERS
TIRANTES^M

PANTS
PANTALONES^M

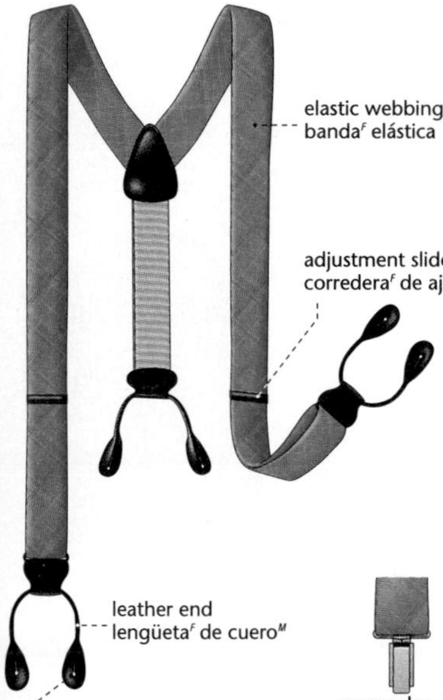

elastic webbing
banda^F elástica

adjustment slide
corredera^F de ajuste^M

leather end
lengüeta^F de cuero^M

button loop
presilla^F

suspender clip
sujetador^M

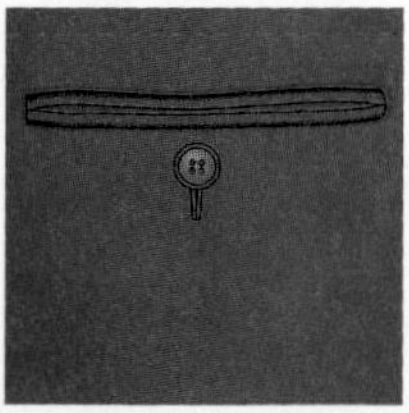

back pocket
bolsillo^M trasero

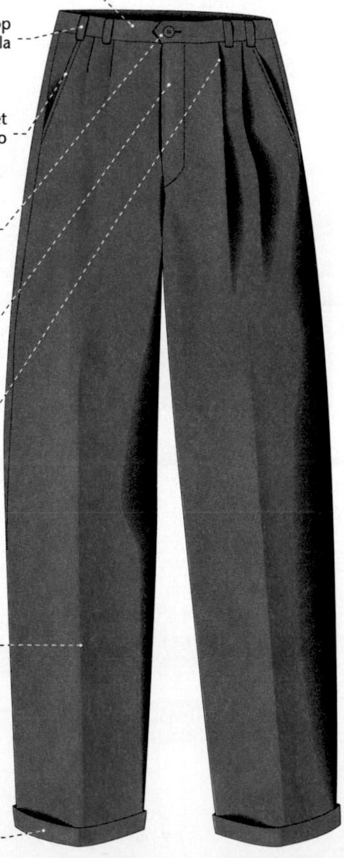

waistband
pretina^F

belt loop
trabilla

front top pocket
bolsillo^M delantero

waistband extension
traslape^M de la pretina^F

fly
brageta^F

knife pleat
pliegue^M

crease
raya^F

cuff
vuelta^F

CLOTHING
VESTIDO

SHIRT
CAMISA^F

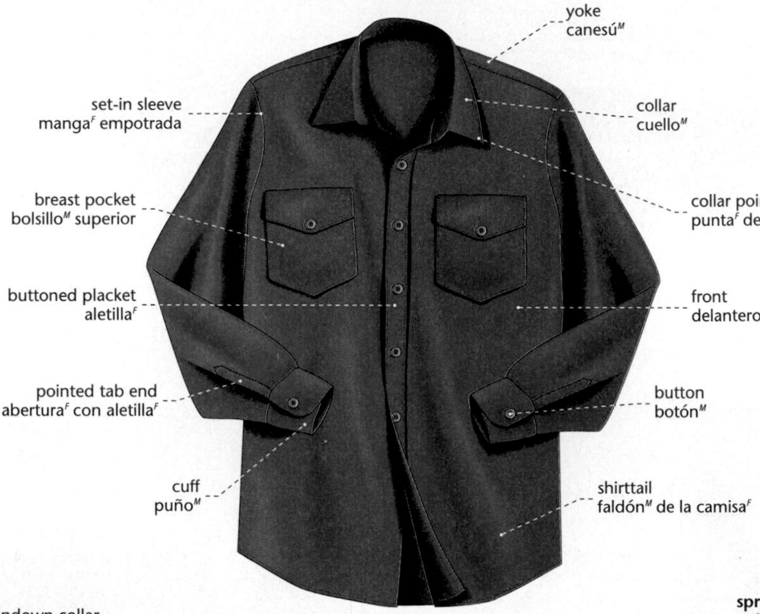

yoke
canesú^M

set-in sleeve
manga^F empotrada

collar
cuello^M

breast pocket
bolsillo^M superior

collar point
punta^F del cuello^M

buttoned placket
aletilla^F

front
delantero^M

pointed tab end
abertura^F con aletilla^F

button
botón^M

cuff
puño^M

shirttail
faldón^M de la camisa^F

buttondown collar
cuello^M con botones^M

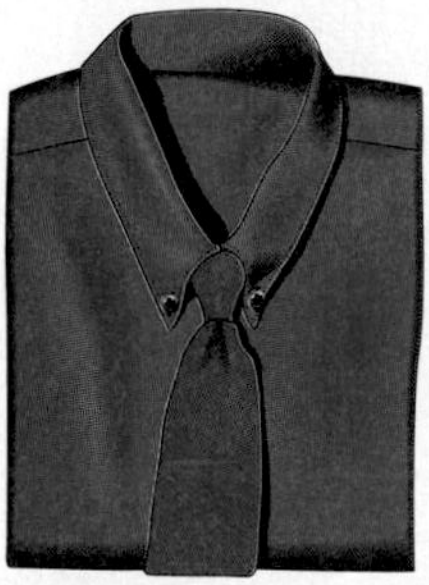

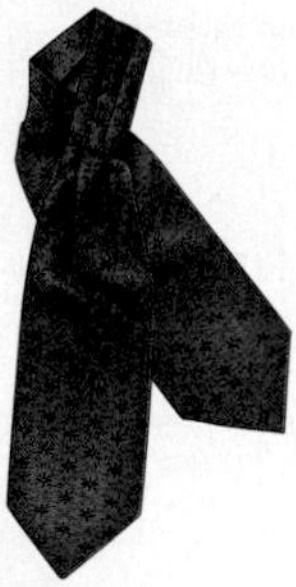

spread collar
cuello^M italiano

ascot tie
corbata^F inglesa

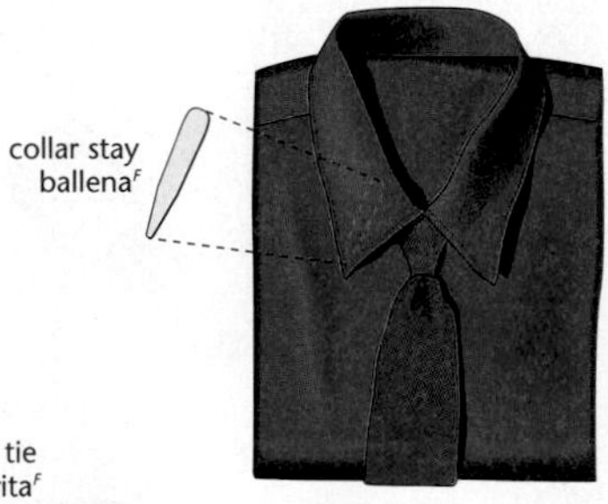

collar stay
ballena^F

bow tie
pajarita^F

NECKTIE
CORBATA^F

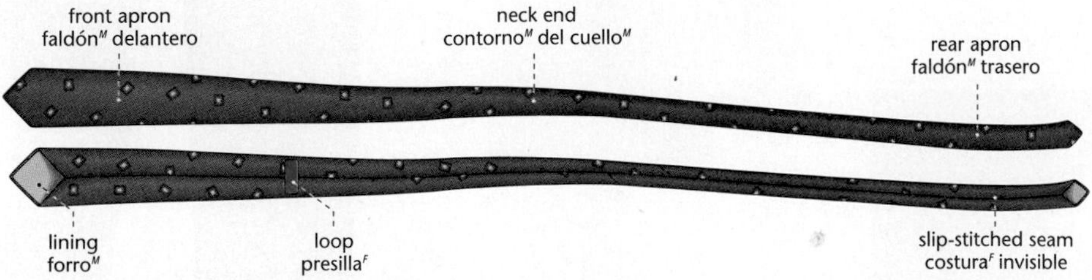

front apron
faldón^M delantero

neck end
contorno^M del cuello^M

rear apron
faldón^M trasero

lining
forro^M

loop
presilla^F

slip-stitched seam
costura^F invisible

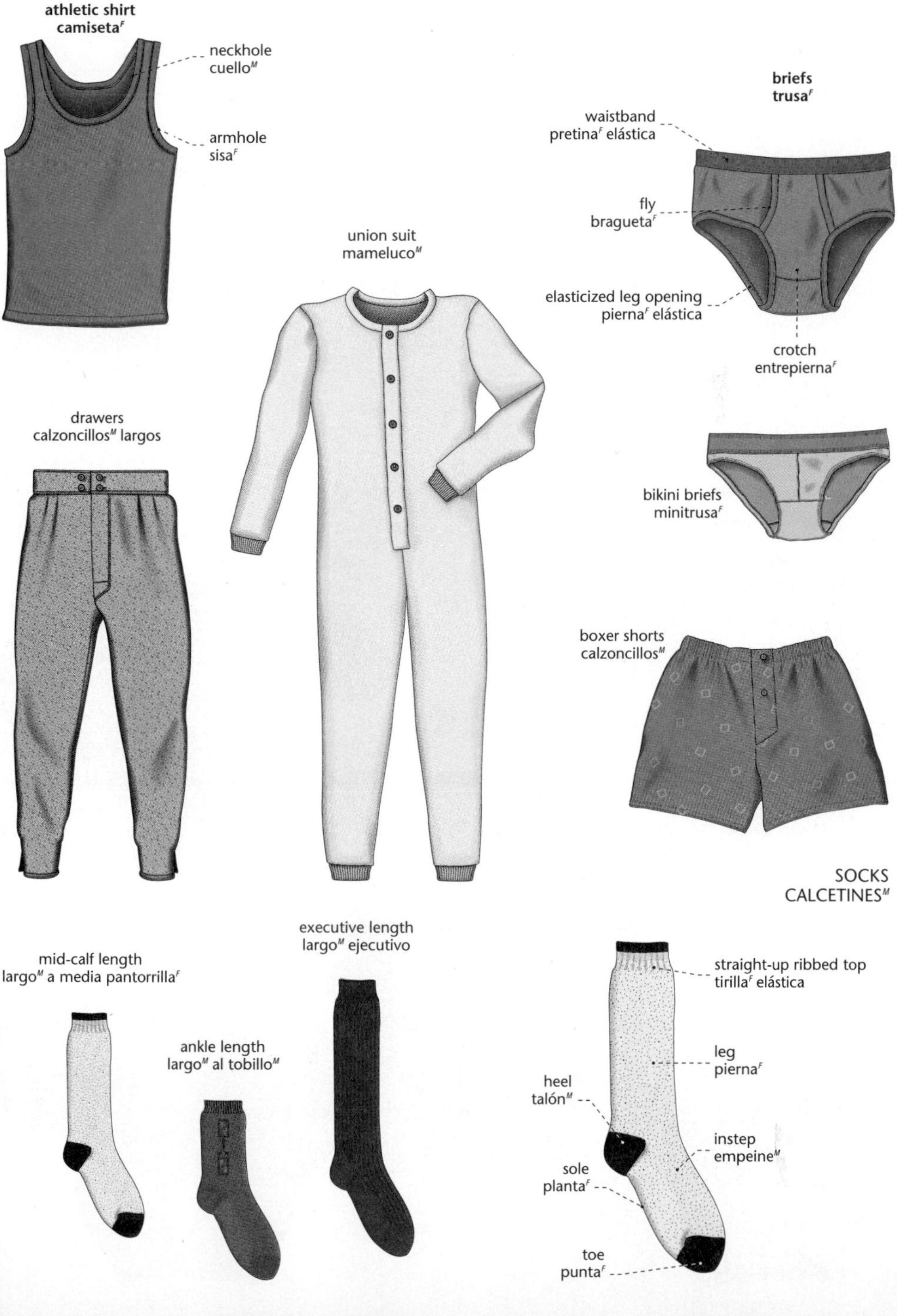

**athletic shirt
camiseta**^F

neckhole
cuello^M

armhole
sisa^F

union suit
mameluco^M

**briefs
trusa**^F

waistband
pretina^F elástica

fly
bragueta^F

elasticized leg opening
pierna^F elástica

crotch
entrepierna^F

drawers
calzoncillos^M largos

bikini briefs
minitrusa^F

boxer shorts
calzoncillos^M

CLOTHING
VESTIDO

SOCKS
CALCETINES^M

mid-calf length
largo^M a media pantorrilla^F

executive length
largo^M ejecutivo

straight-up ribbed top
tirilla^F elástica

ankle length
largo^M al tobillo^M

leg
pierna^F

heel
talón^M

instep
empeine^M

sole
planta^F

toe
punta^F

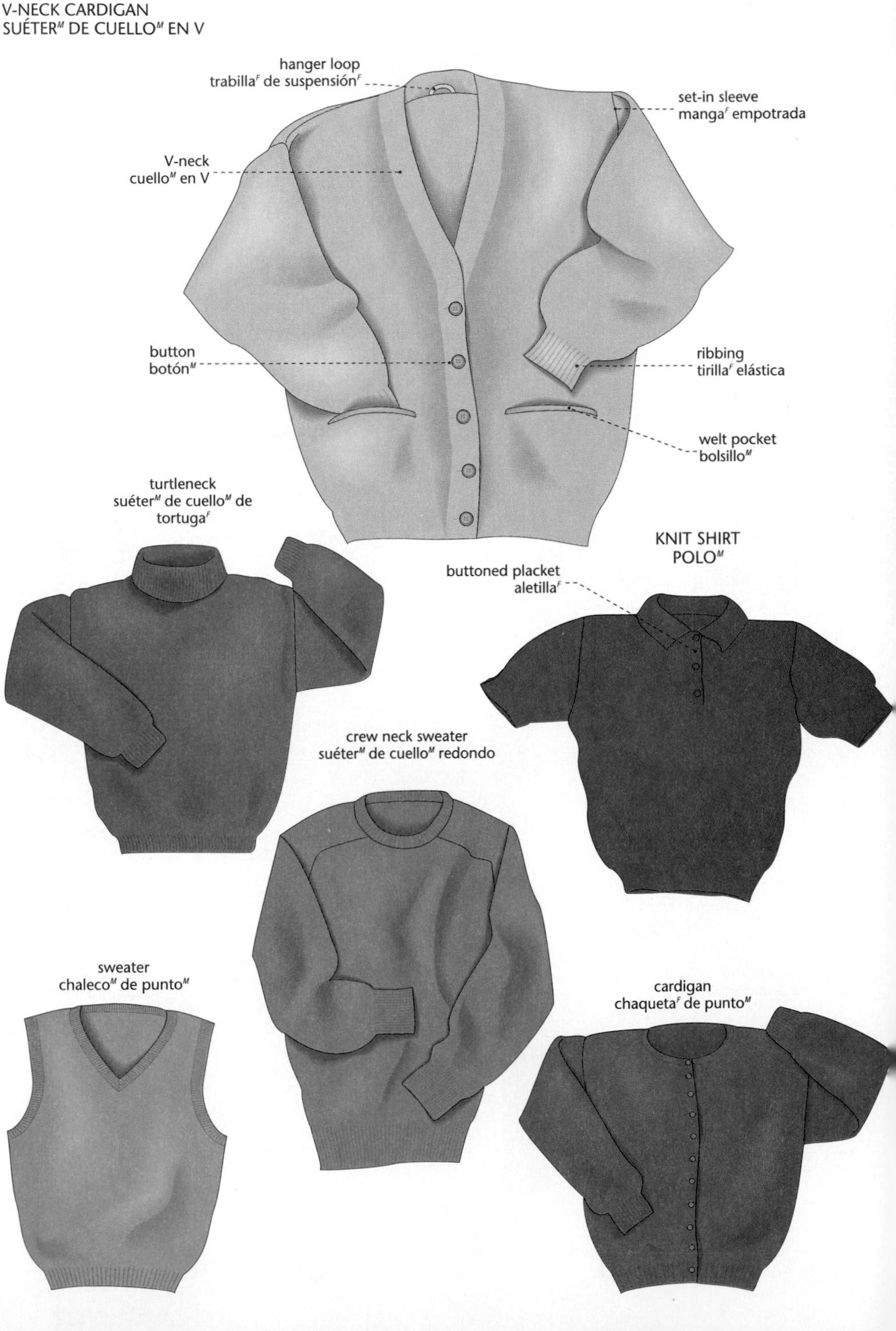

V-NECK CARDIGAN
SUÉTER^M DE CUELLO^M EN V

hanger loop
trabilla^F de suspensión^F

set-in sleeve
manga^F empotrada

V-neck
cuello^M en V

button
botón^M

ribbing
tirilla^F elástica

welt pocket
bolsillo^M

turtleneck
suéter^M de cuello^M de
tortuga^F

KNIT SHIRT
POLO^M

buttoned placket
aletilla^F

crew neck sweater
suéter^M de cuello^M redondo

sweater
chaleco^M de punto^M

cardigan
chaqueta^F de punto^M

GLOVES
GUANTES^M

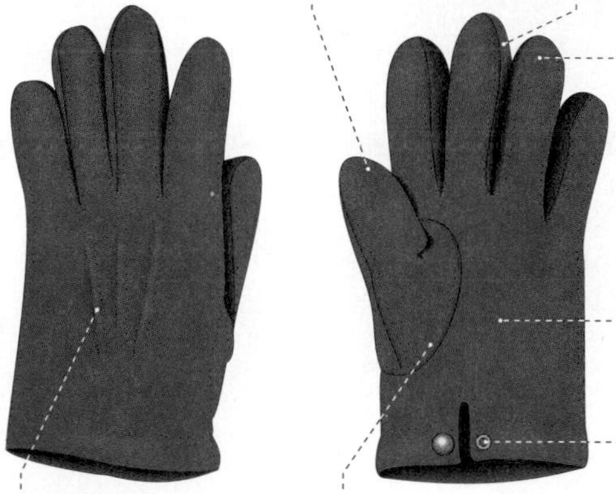

thumb
pulgar^M

fourchette
horquilla^F

glove finger
dedo^M

palm
palma^F

snap fastener
broche^M de presión^F

stitching
sobrepespunte^M

seam
costura^F

DRIVING GLOVE
GUANTE^M PARA CONDUCIR

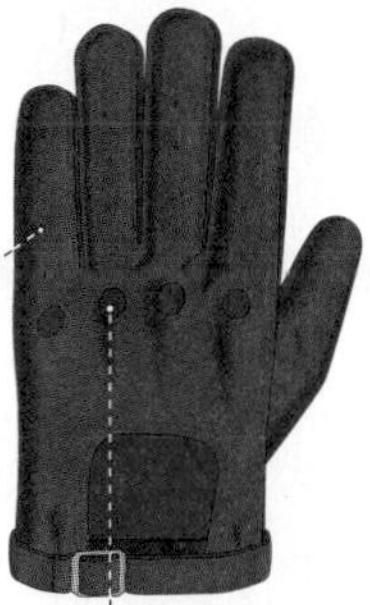

perforation
perforaciones^F

opening
aberturas^F para los nudillos^M

MITT
MITÓN^M SIN DEDOS^M

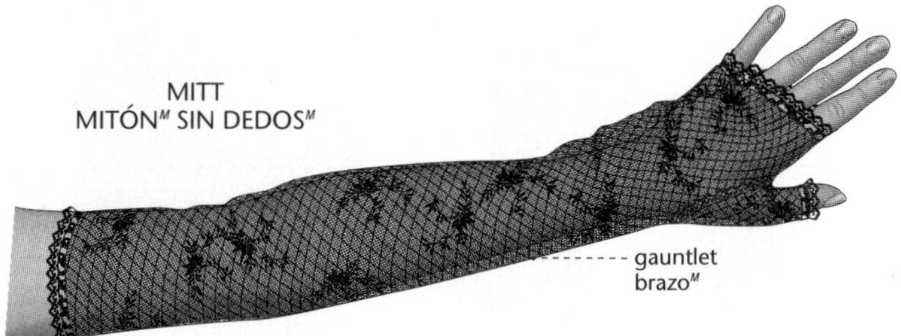

gauntlet
brazo^M

mitten
manopla^F

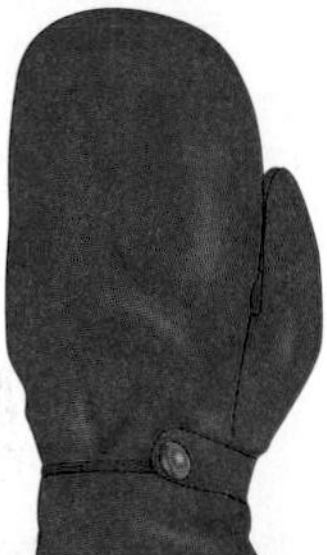

evening glove
guante^M de brazo^M largo

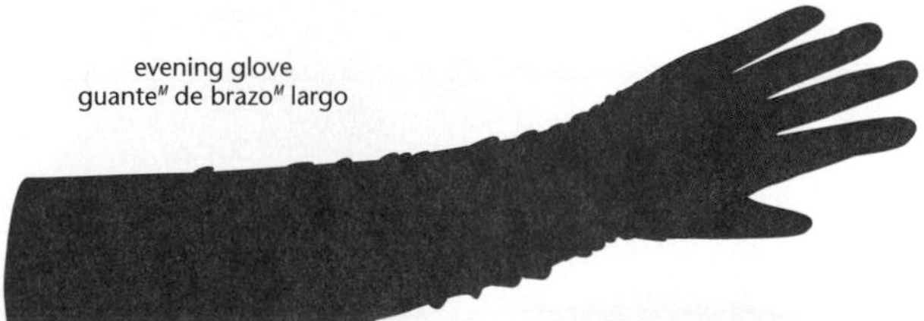

wrist-length glove
guante^M a la muñeca^F

short glove
guante^M corto

gauntlet
manopla^F

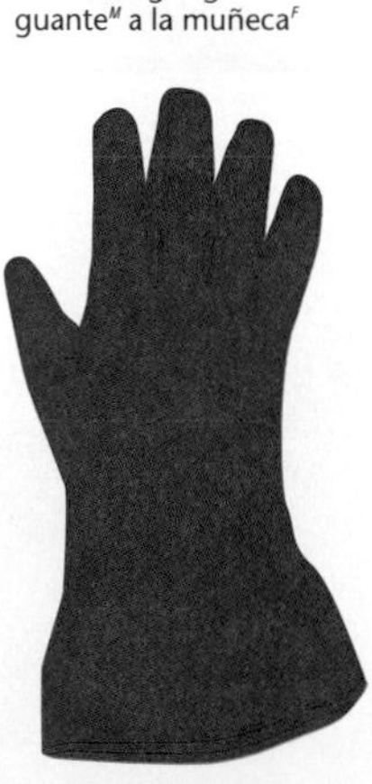

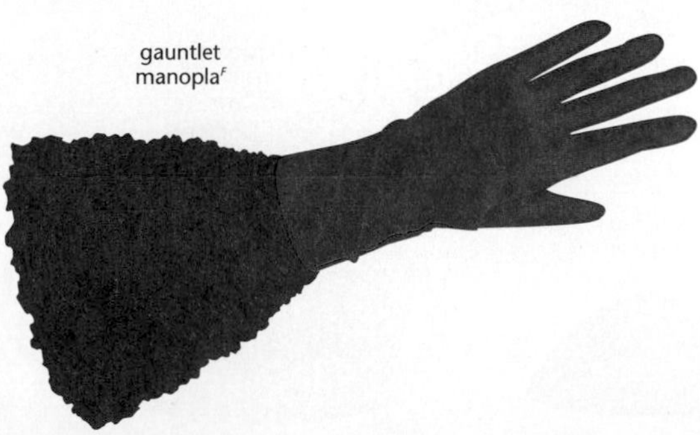

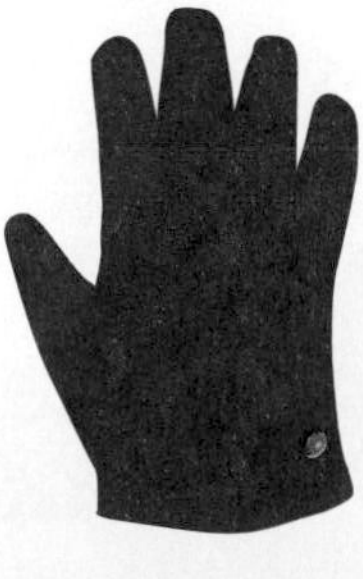

HEADGEAR
SOMBREROS[M]

FELT HAT
SOMBRERO[M] DE FIELTRO[M]

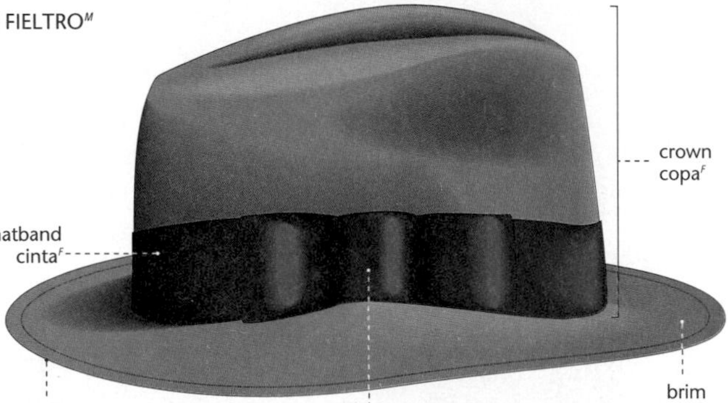

crown
copa[F]

hatband
cinta[F]

binding
ribete[M]

bow
lazo[M]

brim
ala[F]

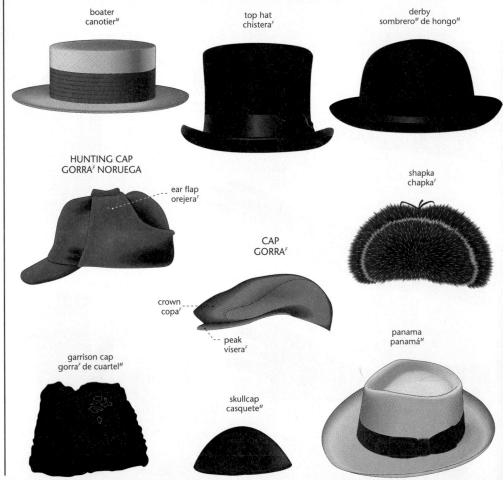

boater
canotier[M]

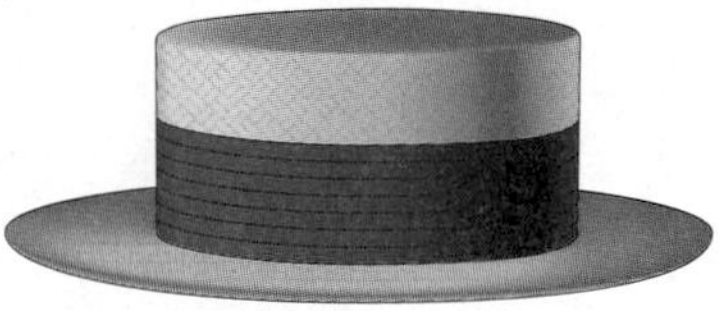

top hat
chistera[F]

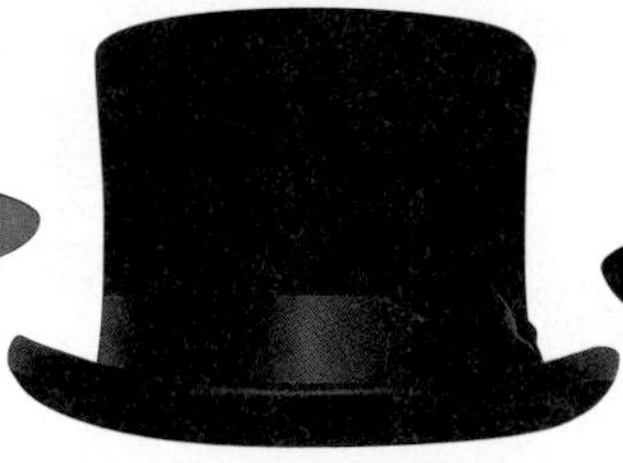

derby
sombrero[M] de hongo[M]

HUNTING CAP
GORRA[F] NORUEGA

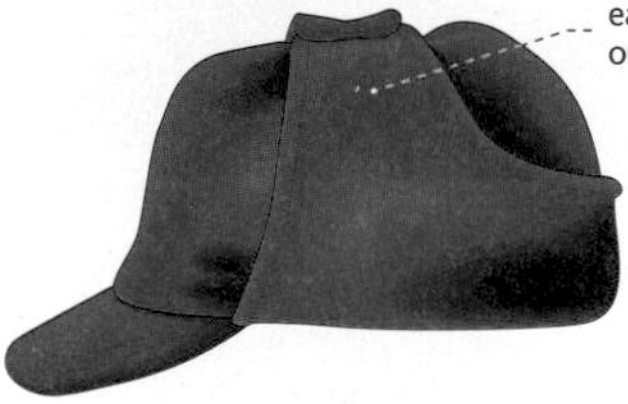

ear flap
orejera[F]

shapka
chapka[F]

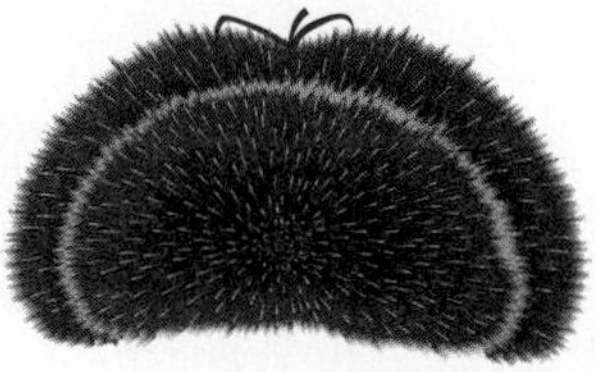

CAP
GORRA[F]

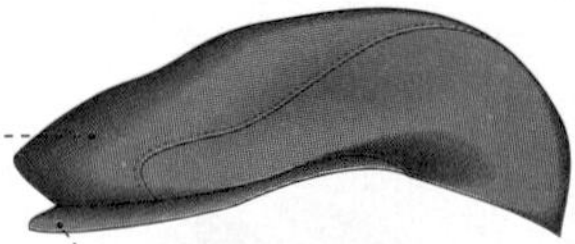

crown
copa[F]

peak
visera[F]

panama
panamá[M]

garrison cap
gorra[F] de cuartel[M]

skullcap
casquete[M]

328

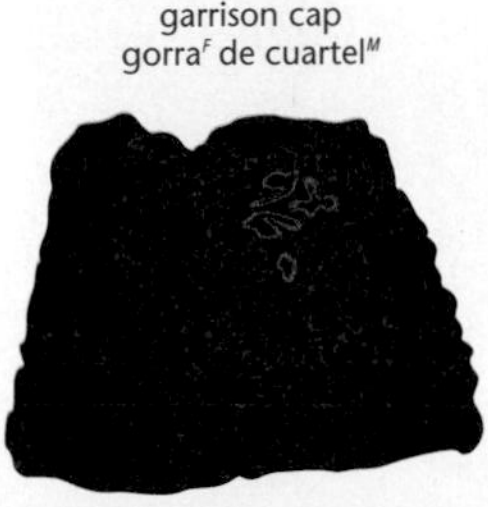

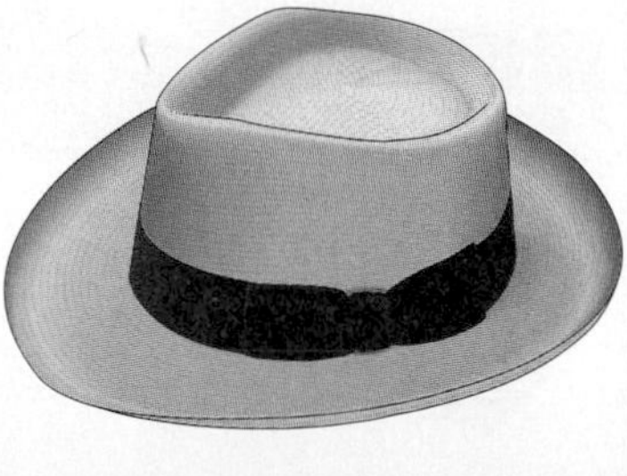

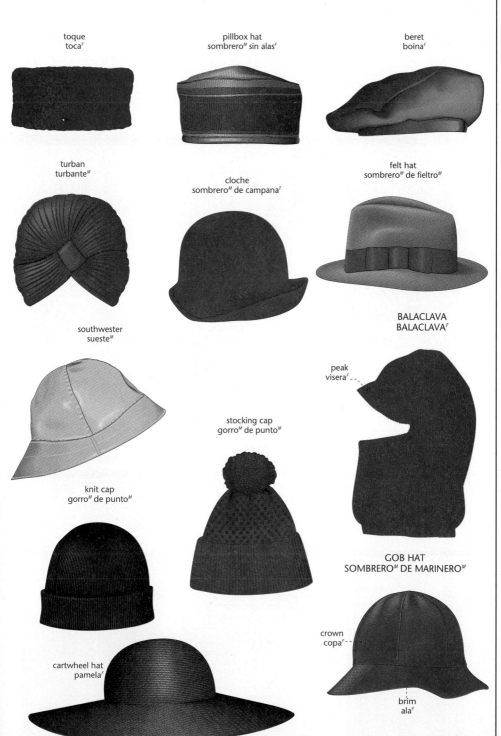

toque
toca^F

pillbox hat
sombrero^M sin alas^F

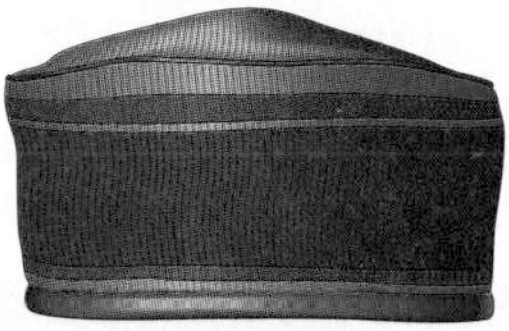

beret
boina^F

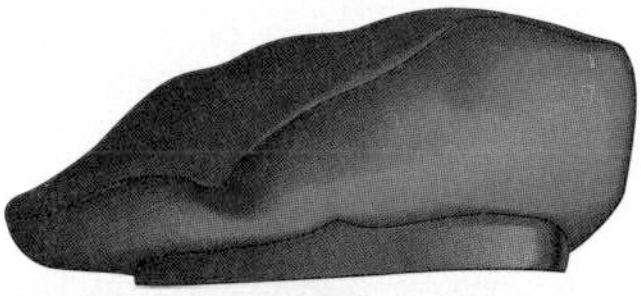

turban
turbante^M

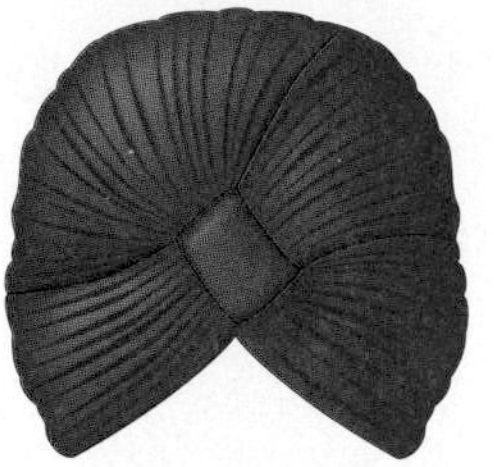

cloche
sombrero^M de campana^F

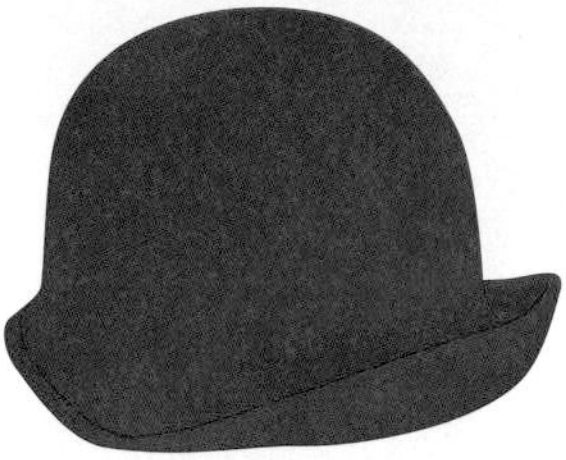

felt hat
sombrero^M de fieltro^M

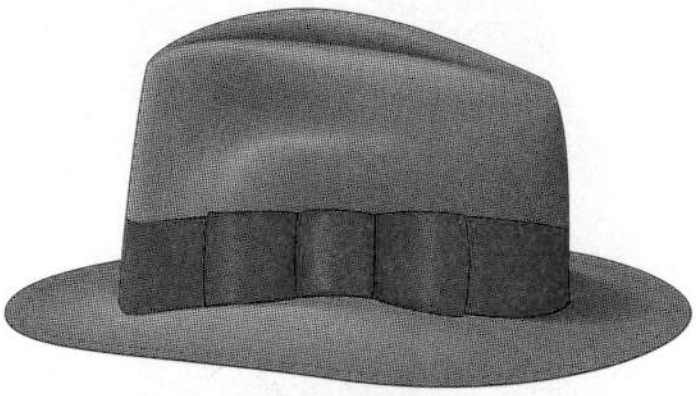

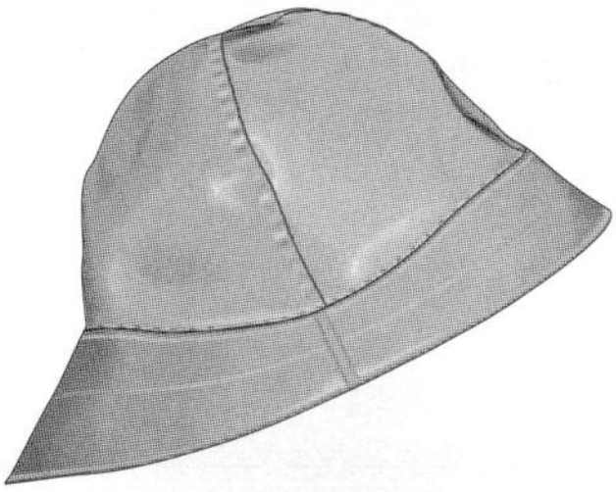

BALACLAVA
BALACLAVA^F

southwester
sueste^M

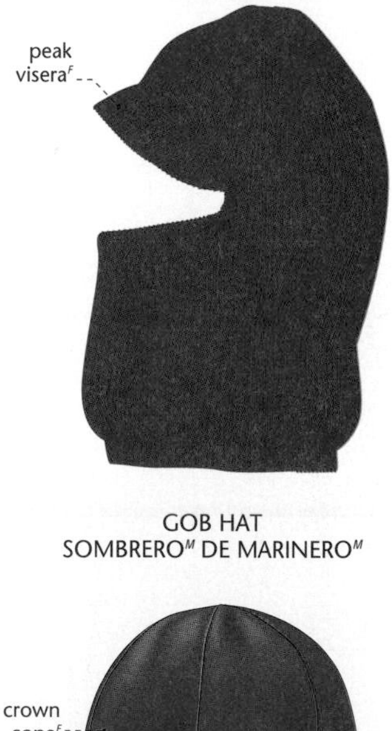

peak
visera^F

stocking cap
gorro^M de punto^M

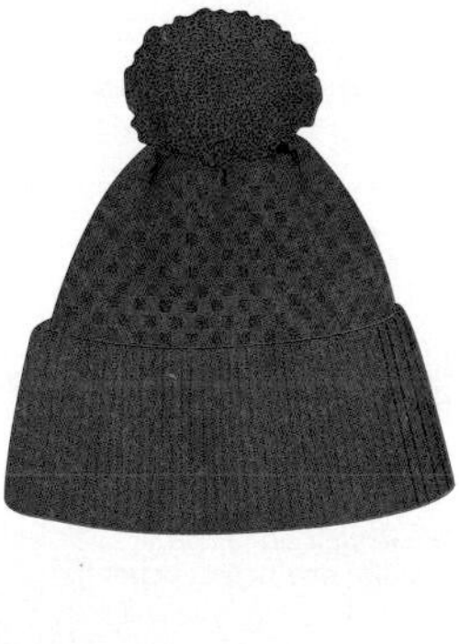

knit cap
gorro^M de punto^M

GOB HAT
SOMBRERO^M DE MARINERO^M

crown
copa^F

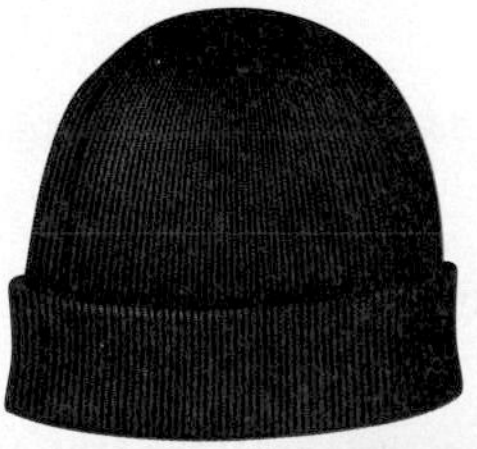

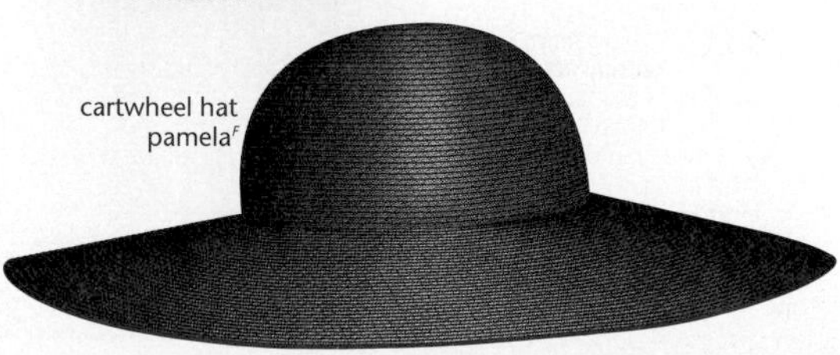

cartwheel hat
pamela^F

brim
ala^F

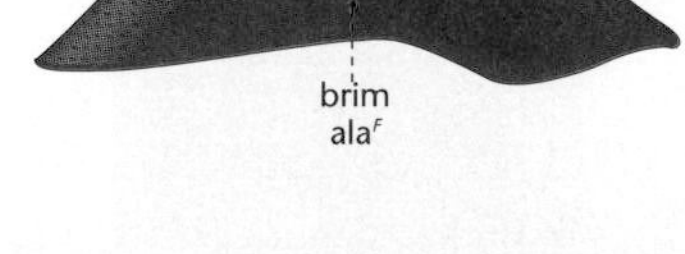

TYPES OF COATS
ABRIGOS^M Y CHAQUETAS^F

car coat
chaquetón^M

**pea jacket
chaquetón^M marinero**

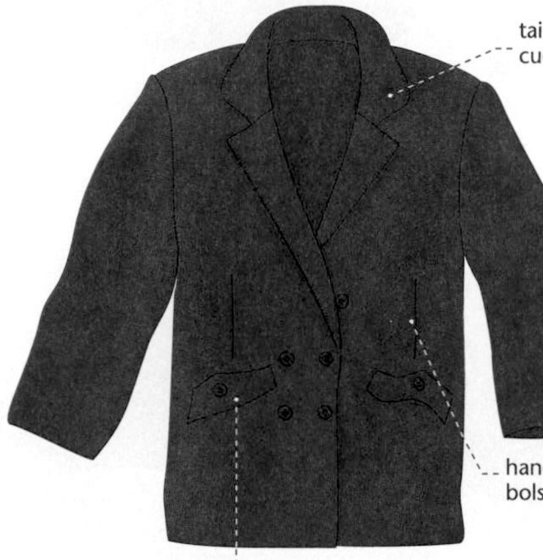

tailored collar
cuello^M hechura^F sastre^M

hand warmer pocket
bolsillo^M de ojal^M

mock pocket
bolsillo^M simulado

**raglan
abrigo^M corto**

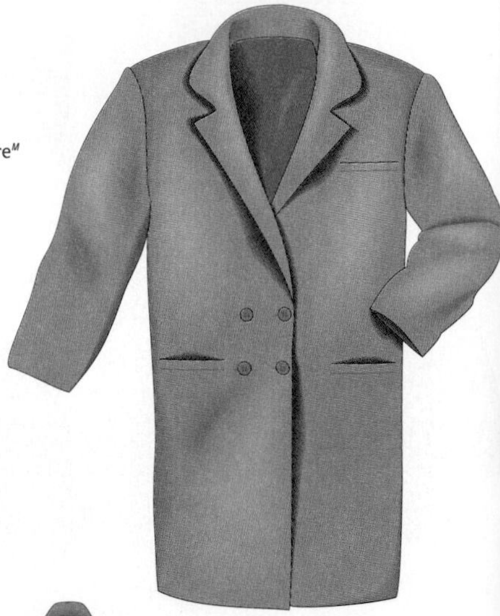

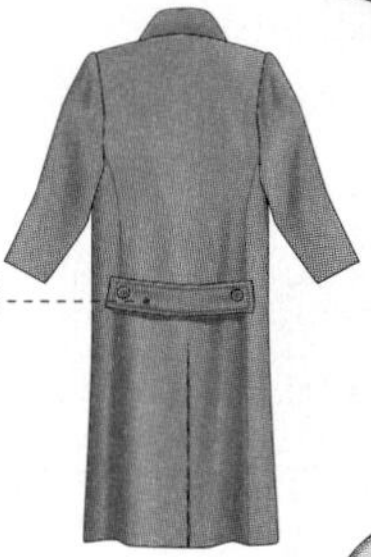

back belt
cinturón^M trasero^M

**pelerine
abrigo^M con esclavina^F**

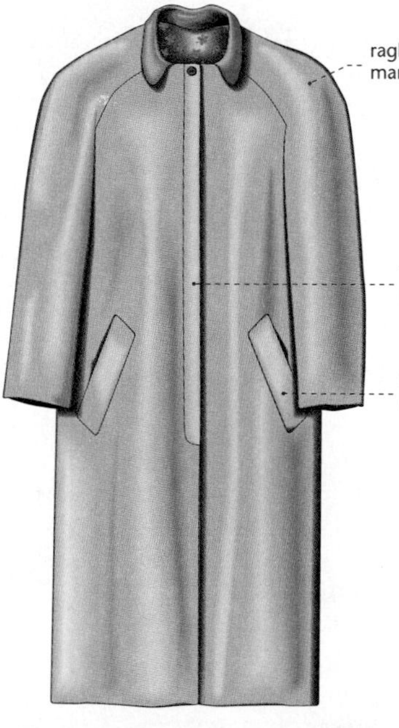

raglan sleeve
manga^F ranglán

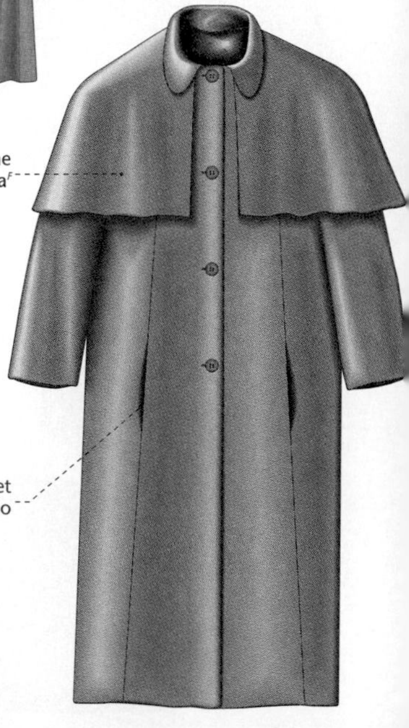

pelerine
esclavina^F

fly front closing
pestaña^F

broad welt side pocket
bolsillo^M de ribete^M ancho

seam pocket
bolsillo^M disimulado

CLOTHING
VESTIDO

330

cape
capa^F

overcoat
abrigo^M

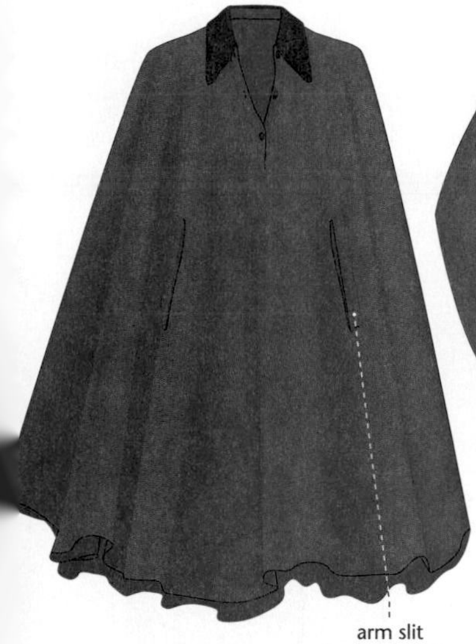

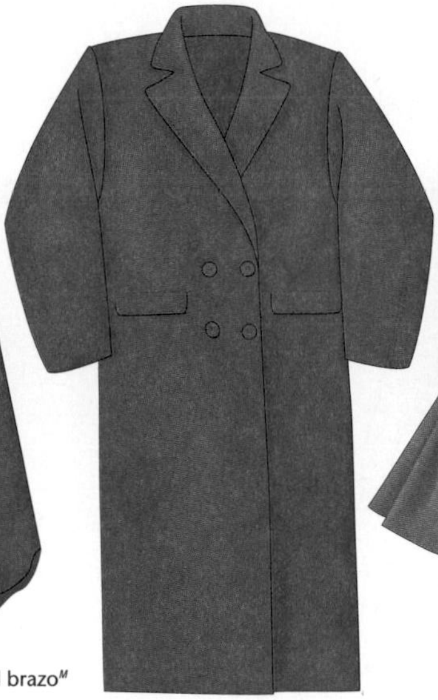

top coat
abrigo^M cruzado

arm slit
abertura^F para el brazo^M

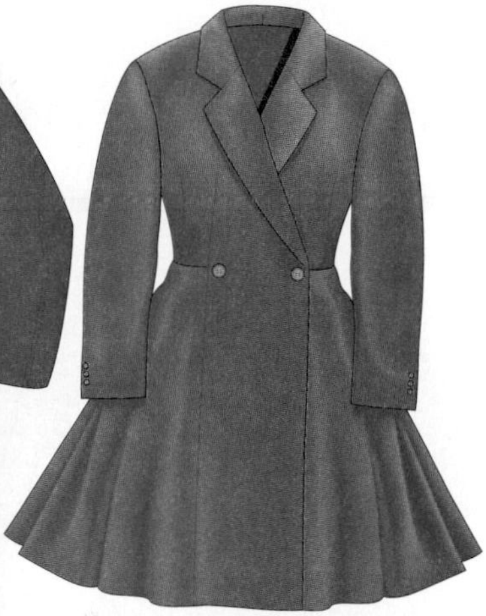

poncho
poncho^M

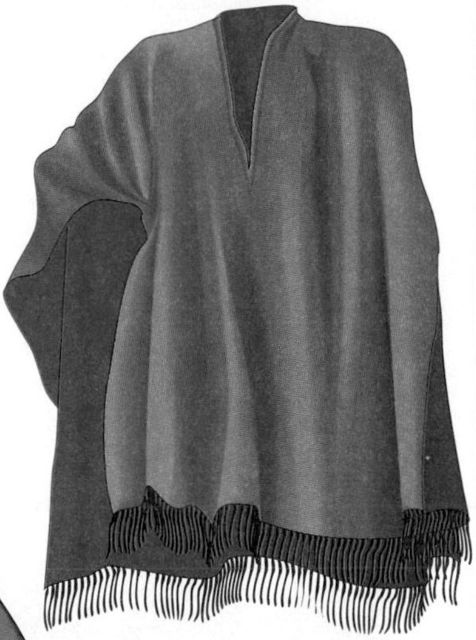

suit
traje^M

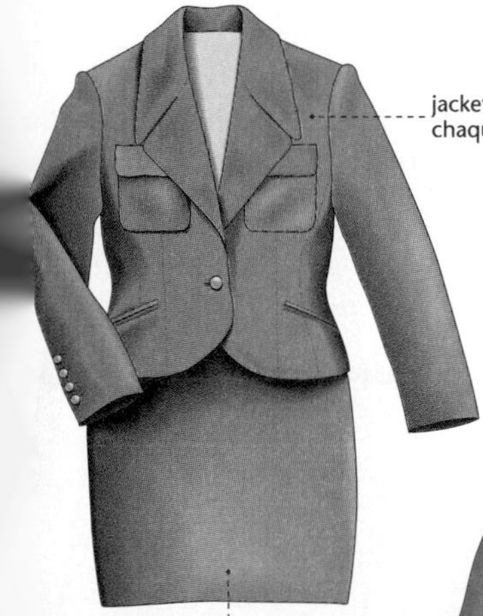

jacket
chaqueta^F

skirt
falda^F

jacket
chaquetón^M

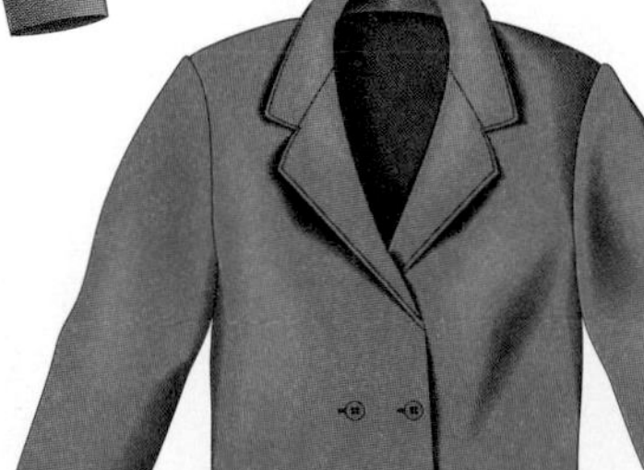

TYPES OF DRESSES
TIPOS^M DE VESTIDO^M

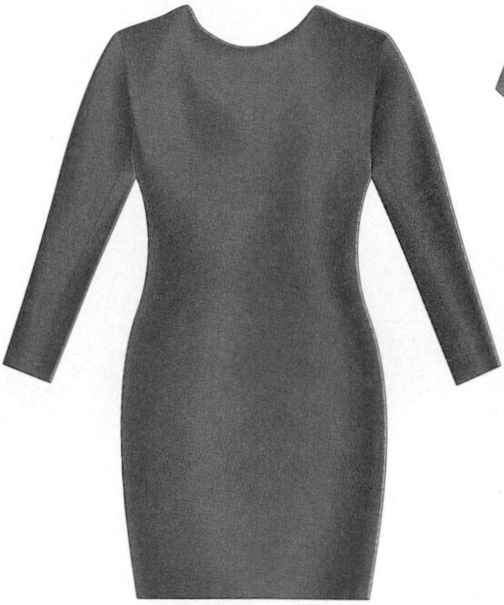

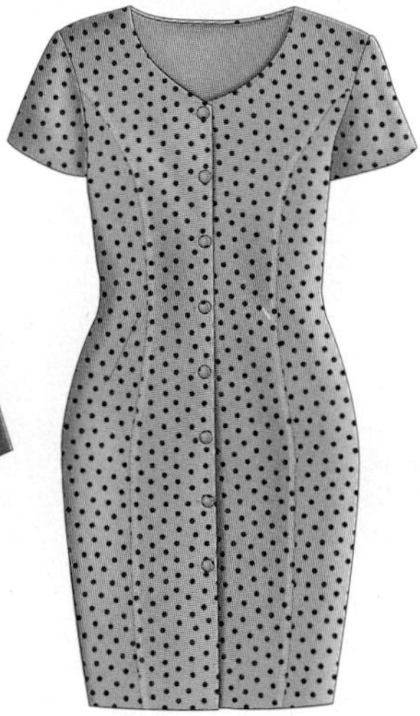

coat dress
vestido^M abrigo

princess dress
corte^M princesa^F

sheath dress
recto entallado

CLOTHING
VESTIDO

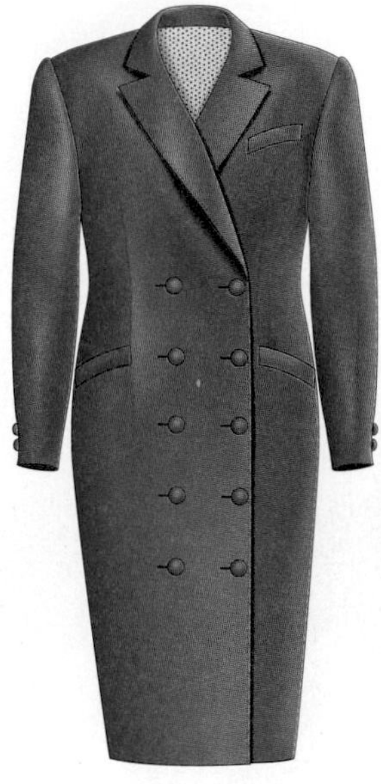

drop waist dress
de talle^M largo

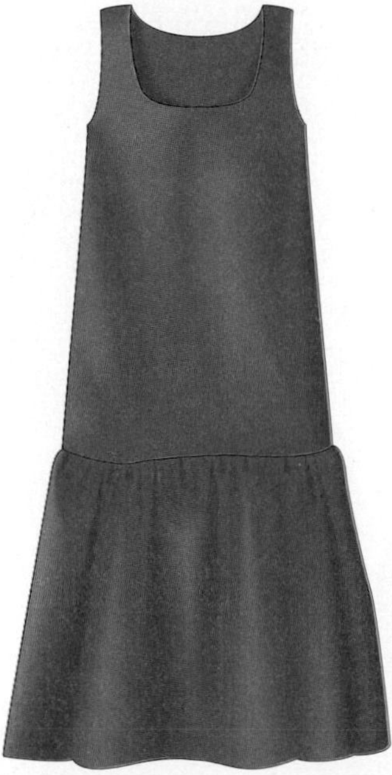

trapeze dress
de campana^F

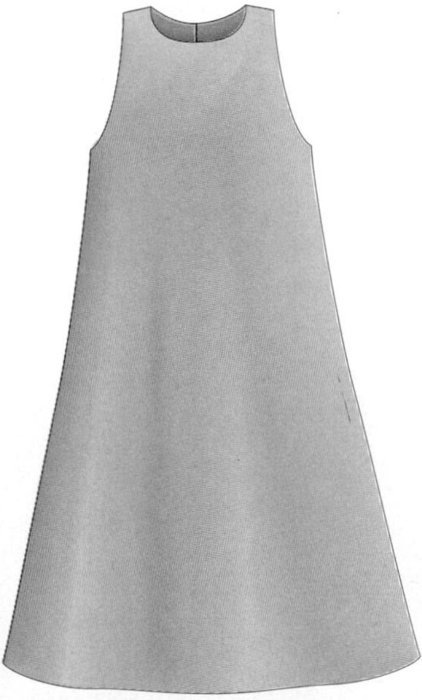

sundress
de verano^M

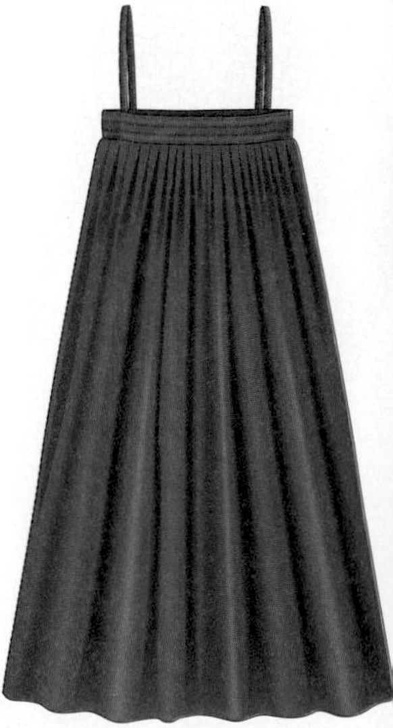

polo dress
de camiseta^F

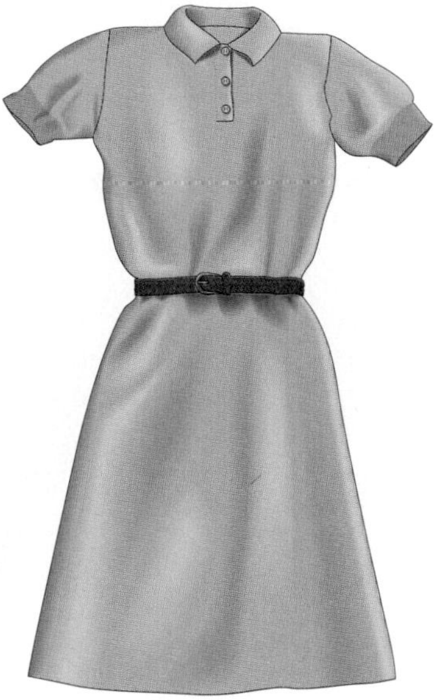

house dress
casero

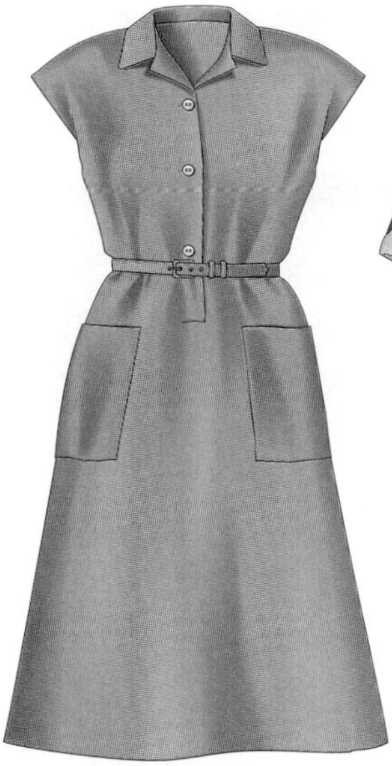

shirtwaist dress
camisero^M

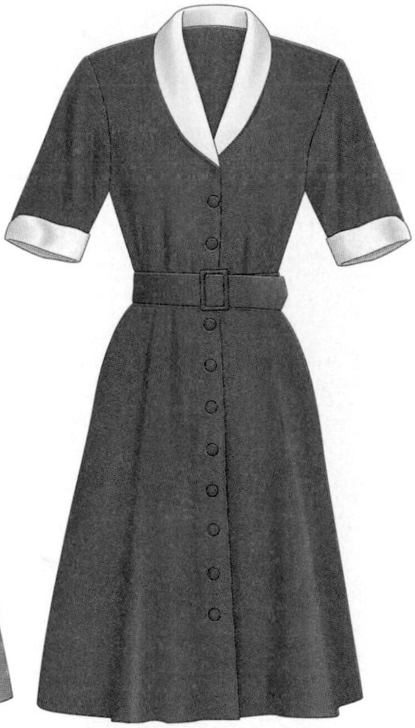

jumper
jumper^M

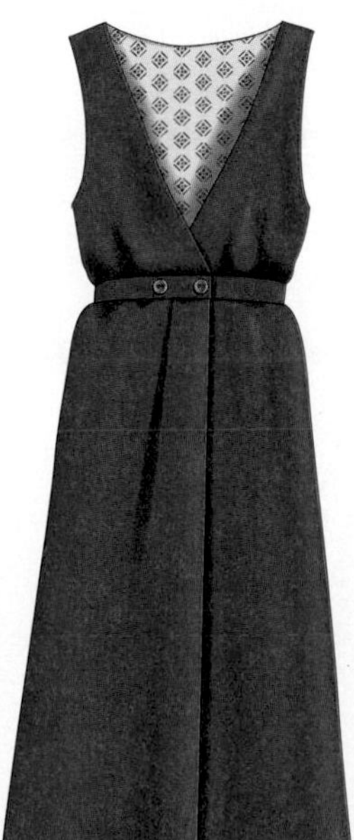

wraparound dress
cruzado

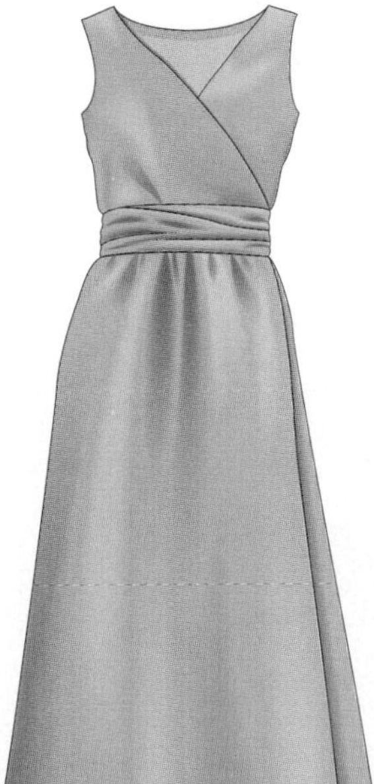

tunic dress
túnica^F

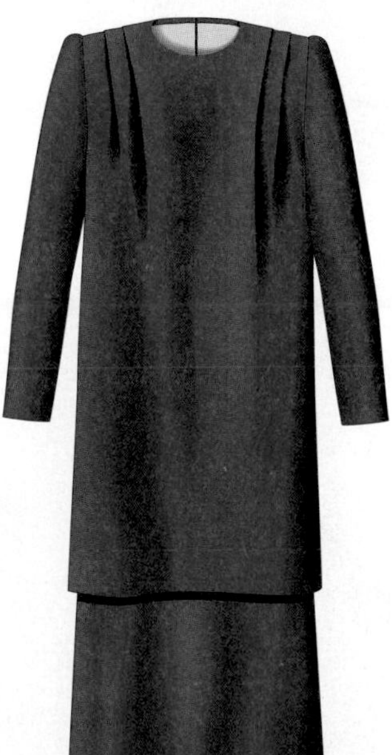

TYPES OF SKIRTS
TIPOS^M DE FALDA^F

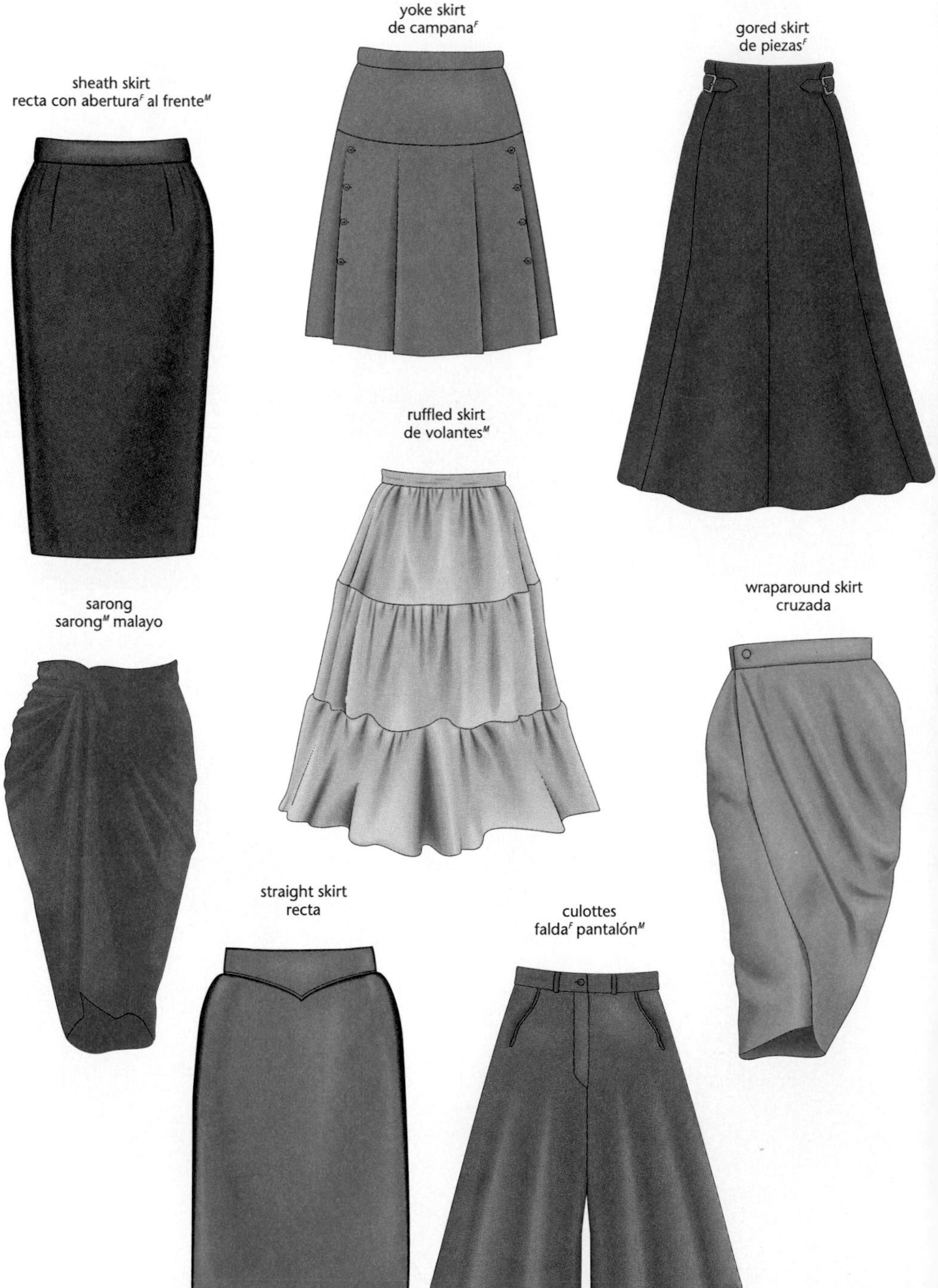

yoke skirt
de campana^F

gored skirt
de piezas^F

sheath skirt
recta con abertura^F al frente^M

ruffled skirt
de volantes^M

sarong
sarong^M malayo

wraparound skirt
cruzada

straight skirt
recta

culottes
falda^F pantalón^M

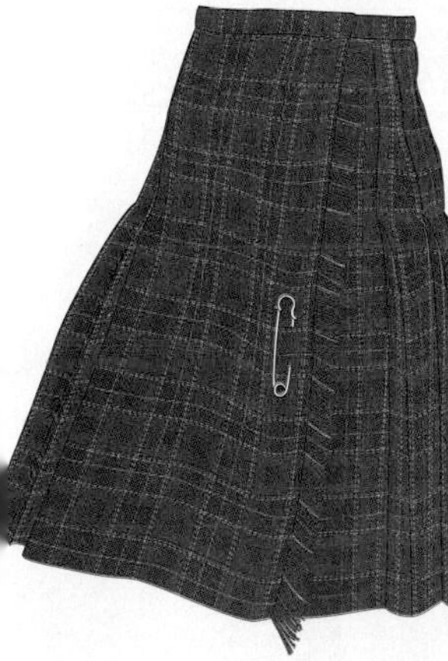

kilt
escocesa

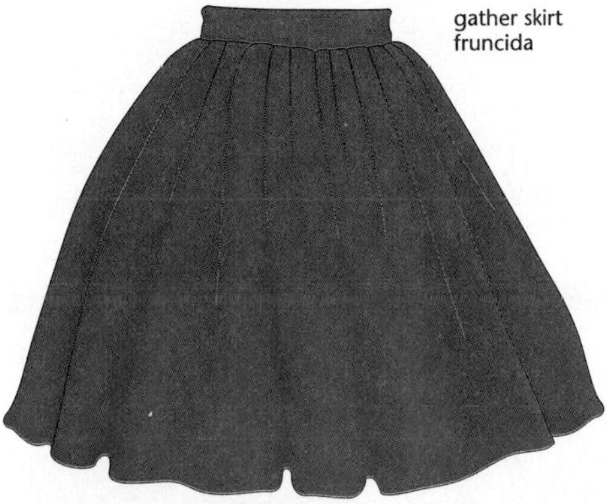

gather skirt
fruncida

inverted pleat
tablón^M delantero

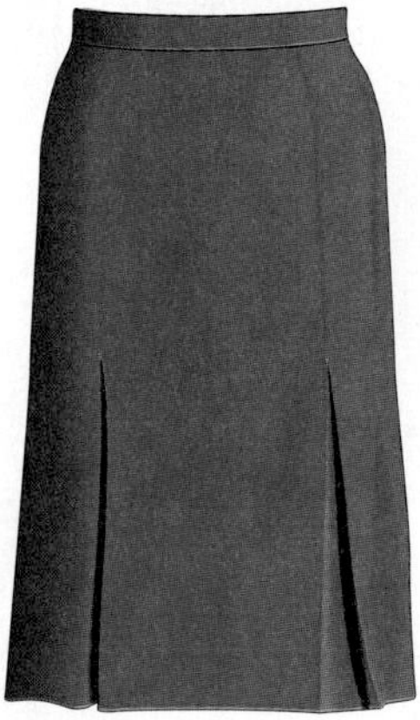

kick pleat
tabla^F abierta

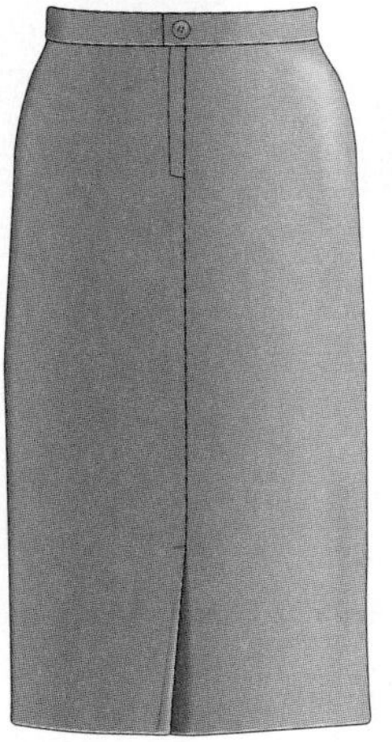

accordion pleat
plisada

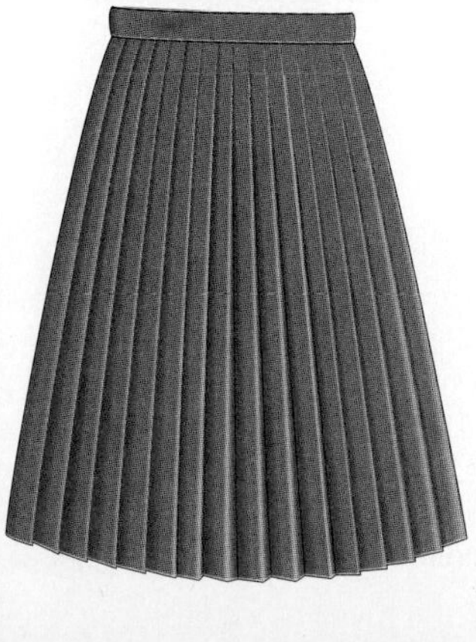

knife pleat
tablas^F

top stitched pleat
sobrepespunteada^F

335

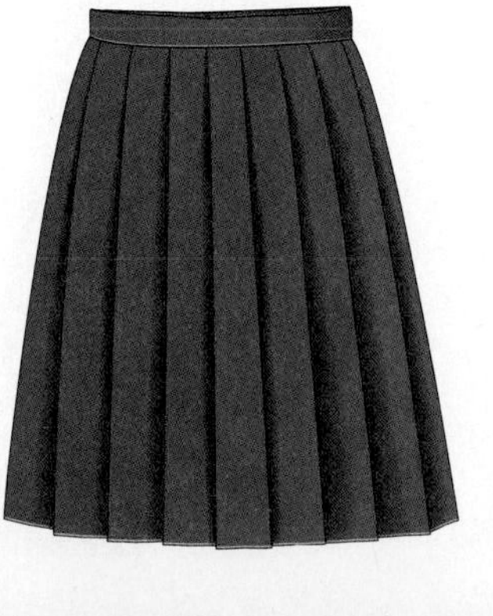

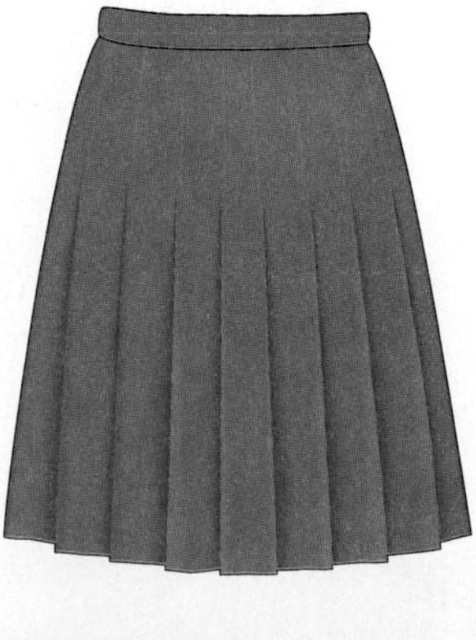

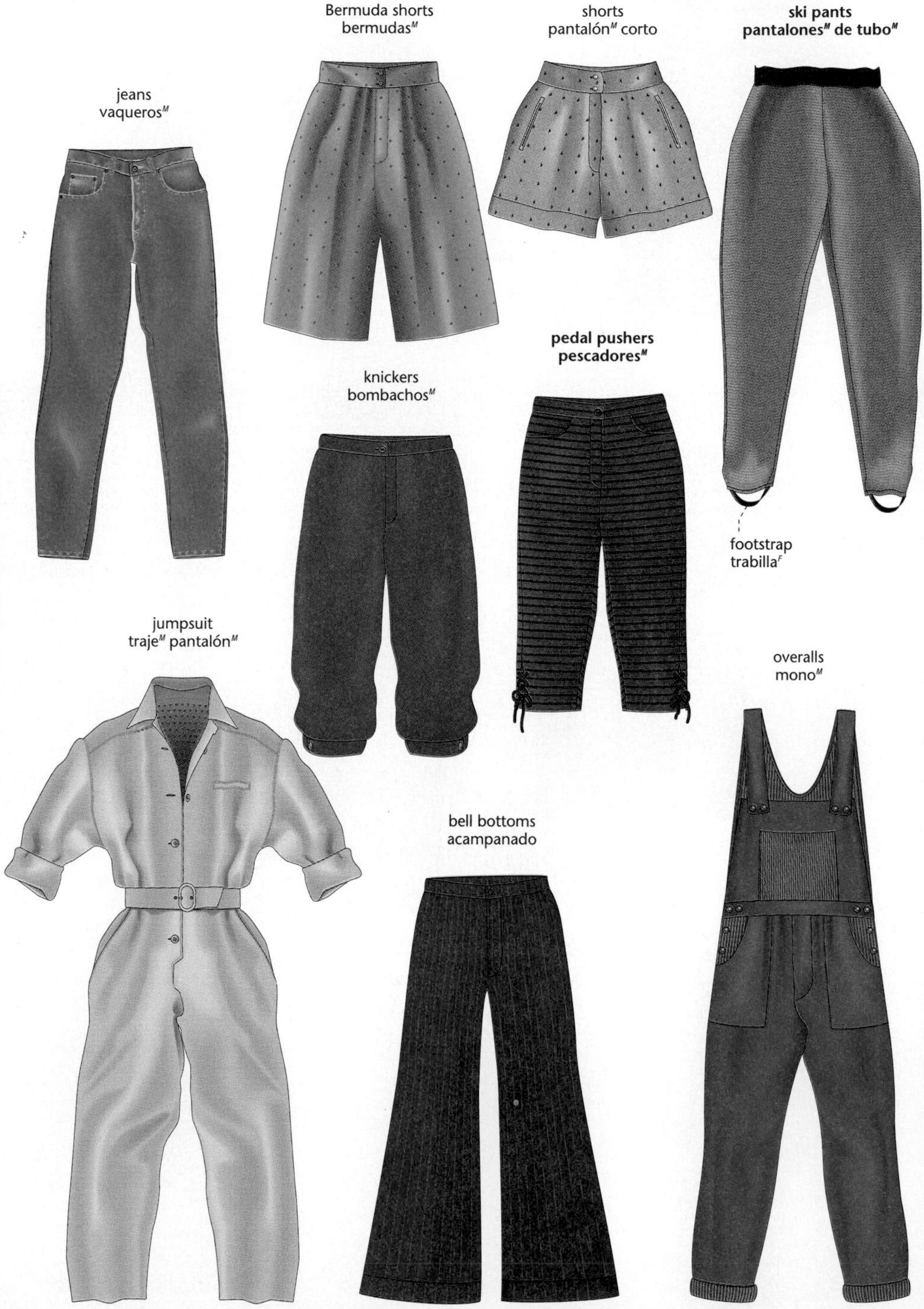

TYPES OF PANTS
PANTALONES^M

jeans
vaqueros^M

Bermuda shorts
bermudas^M

shorts
pantalón^M corto

**ski pants
pantalones^M de tubo^M**

knickers
bombachos^M

**pedal pushers
pescadores^M**

footstrap
trabilla^F

jumpsuit
traje^M pantalón^M

overalls
mono^M

bell bottoms
acampanado

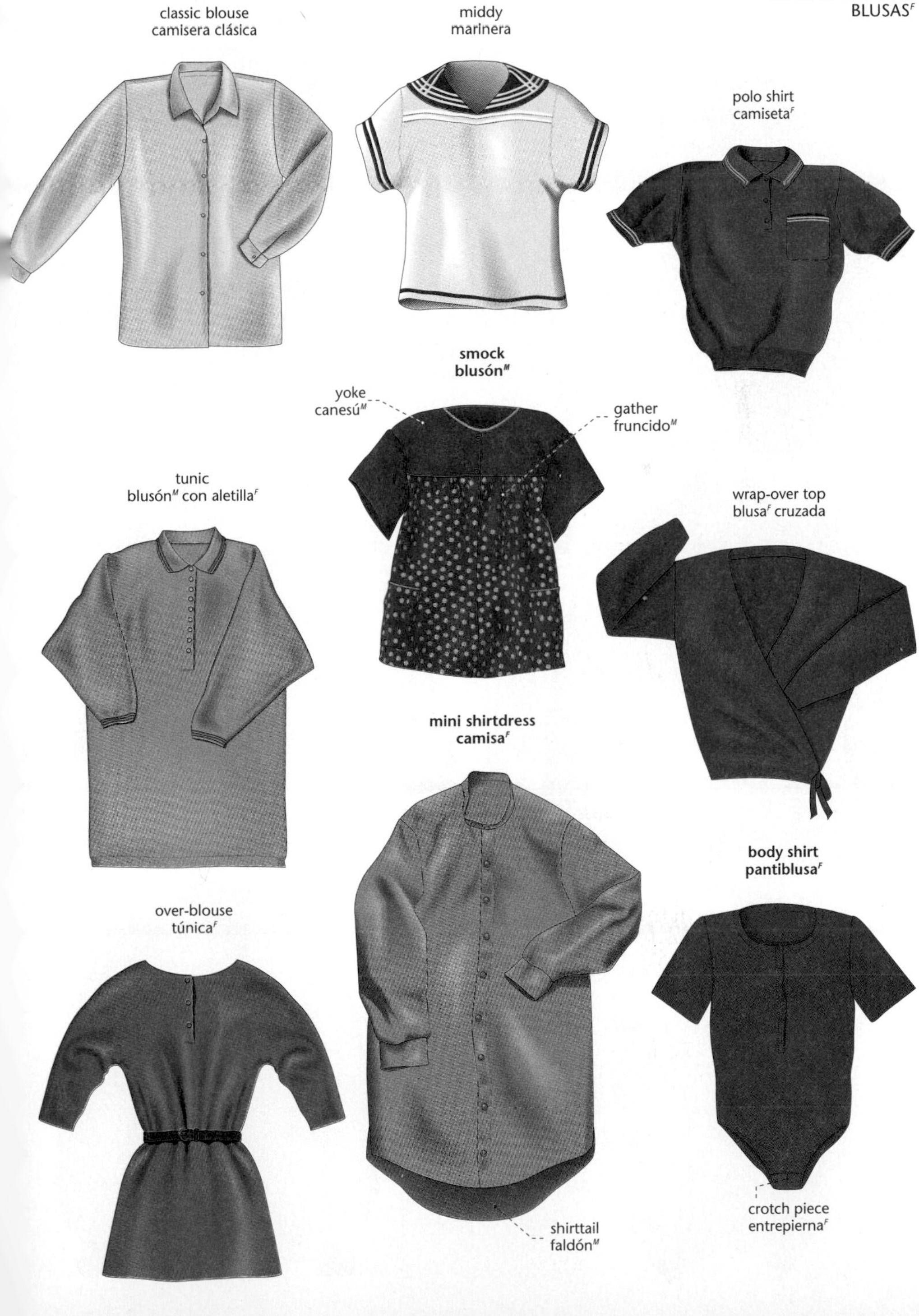

classic blouse
camisera clásica

middy
marinera

polo shirt
camiseta^F

smock
blusón^M

yoke
canesú^M

gather
fruncido^M

tunic
blusón^M con aletilla^F

wrap-over top
blusa^F cruzada

mini shirtdress
camisa^F

over-blouse
túnica^F

body shirt
pantiblusa^F

shirttail
faldón^M

crotch piece
entrepierna^F

**CLOTHING
VESTIDO**

337

JACKETS, VEST AND SWEATERS
CHALECOS^M, SUÉTERES^M Y CHAQUETAS^F

safari jacket
cazadora^F

blazer
blazer^M

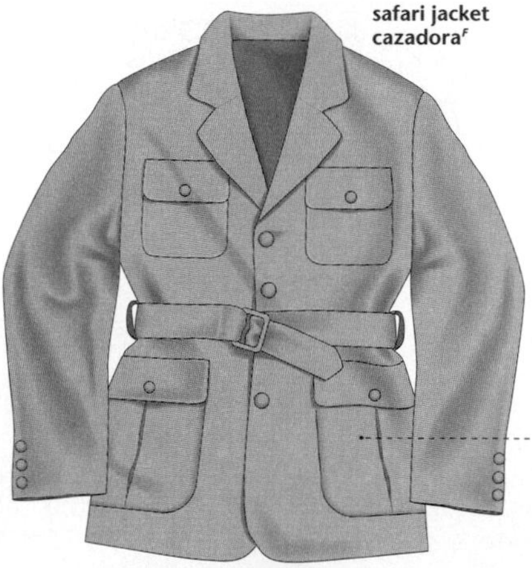

gusset pocket
bolsillo^M de fuelle^M

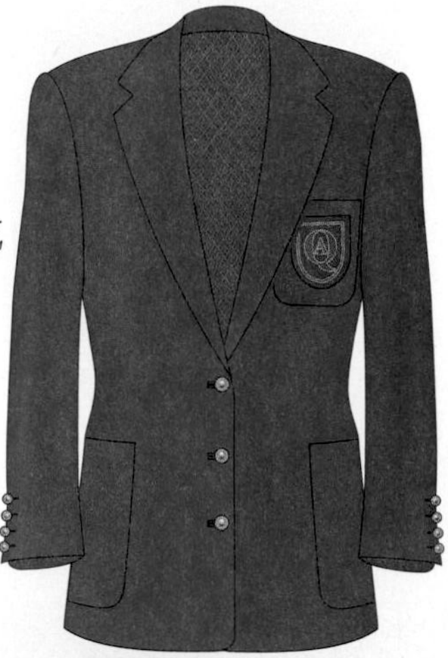

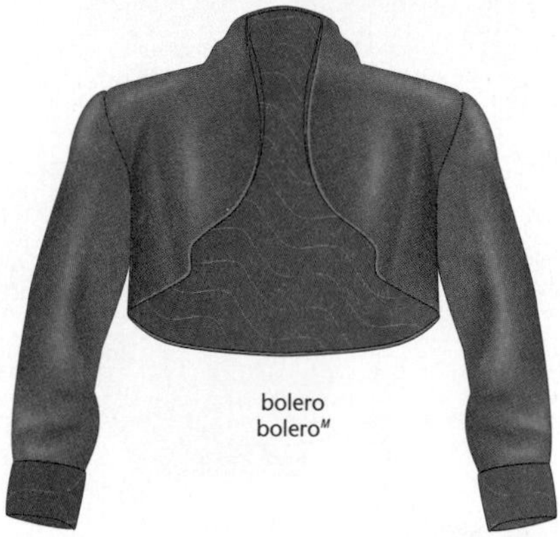

bolero
bolero^M

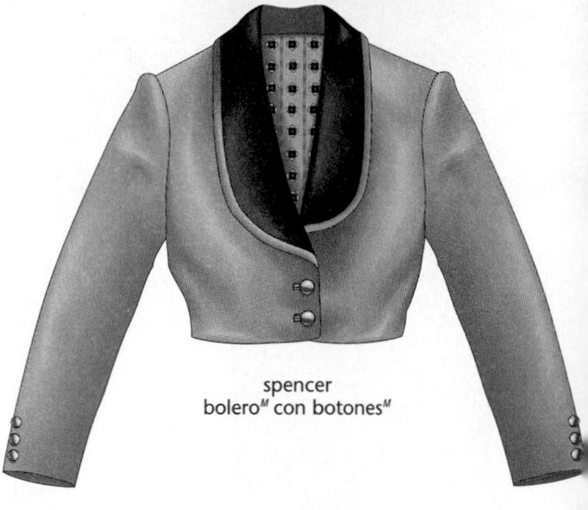

spencer
bolero^M con botones^M

vest
chaleco^M

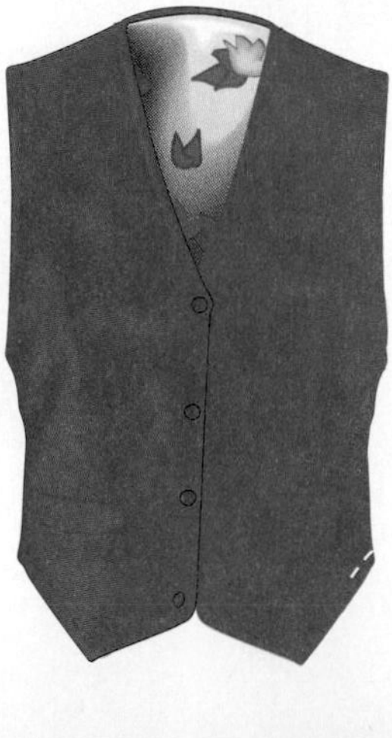

twin-set
suéteres^M combinados

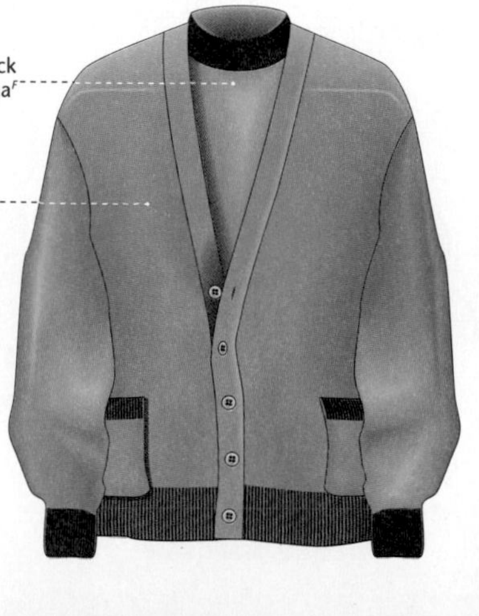

turtleneck
de tortuga^F

V-neck cardigan
suéter^M abierto de cuello^M en V

CLOTHING
VESTIDO

338

inset pocket
simulado

seam pocket
bolsillo*M* disimulado

broad welt side pocket
de ojal*M* con ribete*M*

hand warmer pouch
de manguito*M*

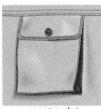

gusset pocket
de fuelle*M*

flap pocket
bolsa*F* de parche*M* con cartera*F*

patch pocket
de parche*M*

welt pocket
de ojal*M* de sastre*M*

CLOTHING
VESTIDO

French cuff
puño*M* para gemelos*M*

pointed tab end
aletilla*F*

cuff link
gemelos*M*

three-quarter sleeve
recta de tres cuartos*M*

batwing sleeve
de murciélago*M*

cap sleeve
corta sencilla

339

TYPES OF SLEEVES
TIPOS*M* DE MANGA*F*

**CLOTHING
VESTIDO**

bishop sleeve
común fruncida

leg-of-mutton sleeve
de jamón*M*

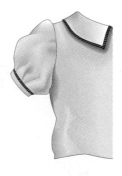

puff sleeve
de globo*M*

tailored sleeve
hechura*F* sastre*M*

epaulet sleeve
con hombrera*F*

kimono sleeve
kimono*M*

shirt sleeve
camisera*F*

raglan sleeve
manga*F* ranglán

pagoda sleeve
de pagoda*F*

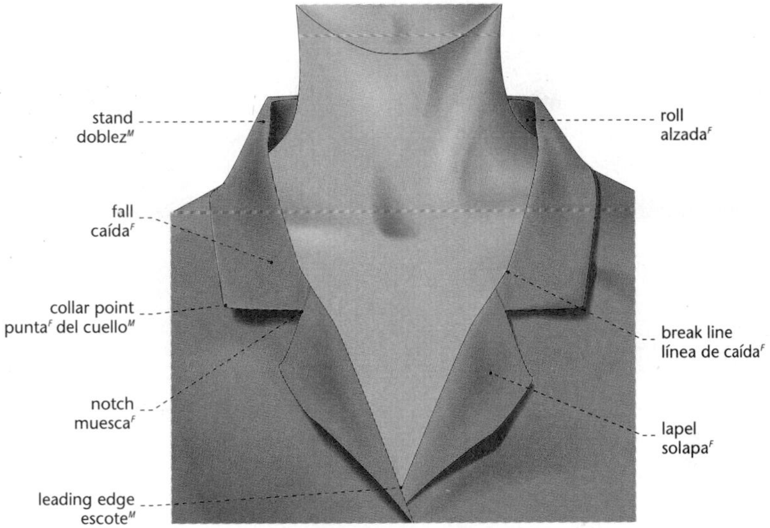

stand
doblez^M

roll
alzada^F

fall
caída^F

collar point
punta^F del cuello^M

break line
línea de caída^F

notch
muesca^F

lapel
solapa^F

leading edge
escote^M

TYPES OF COLLARS
CUELLOS^M

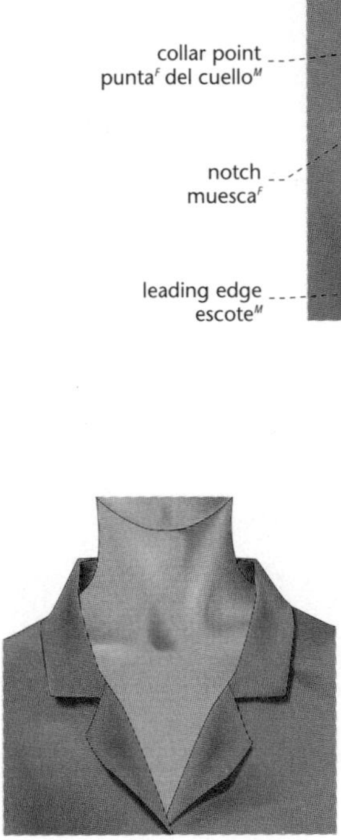

shirt collar
camisero

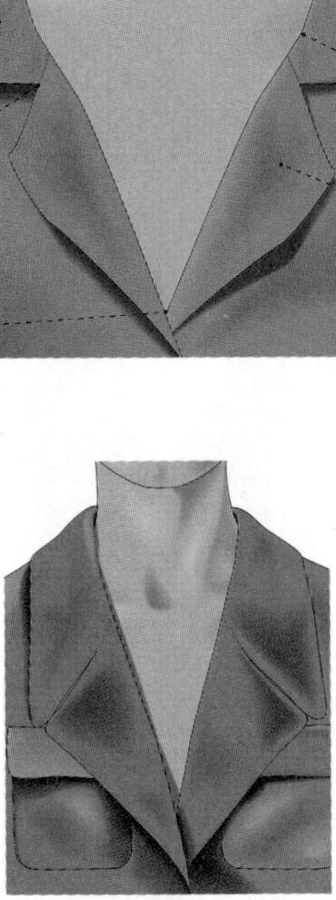

tailored collar
hechura^F de sastre^M

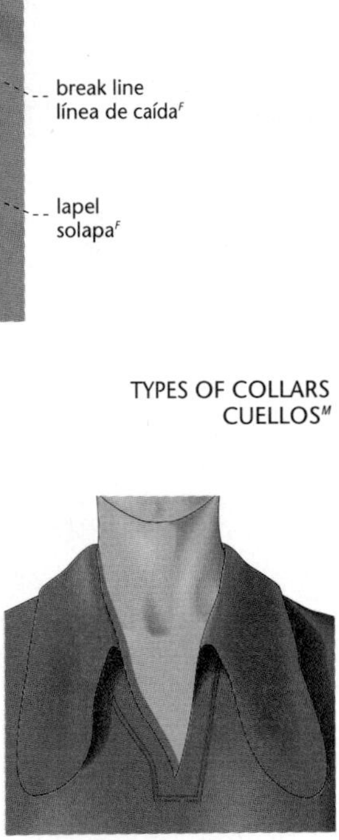

dog ear collar
plano con orejas^F

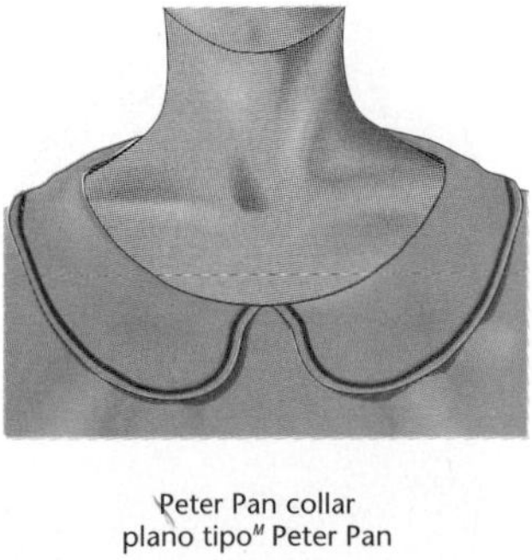

Peter Pan collar
plano tipo^M Peter Pan

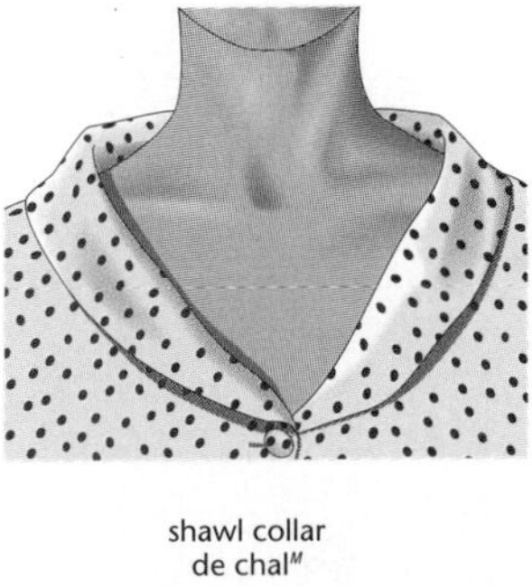

shawl collar
de chal^M

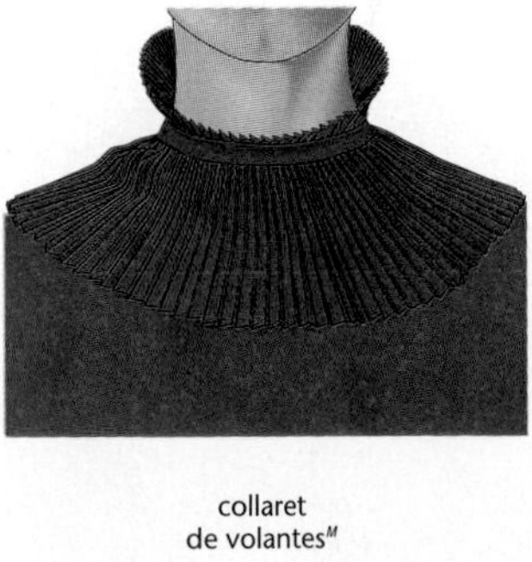

collaret
de volantes^M

TYPES OF COLLARS
CUELLOS*M*

CLOTHING
VESTIDO

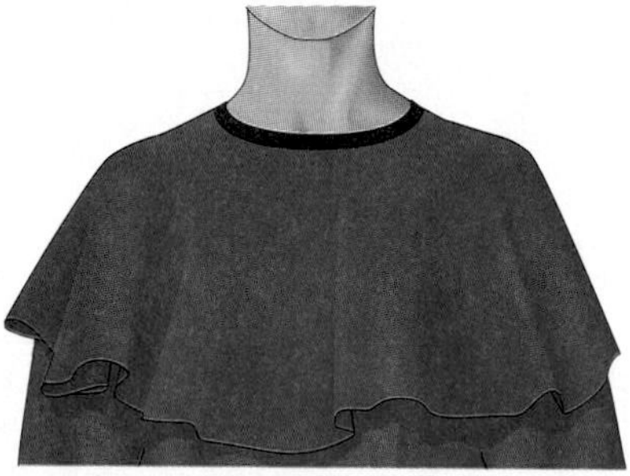

bertha collar
Berta

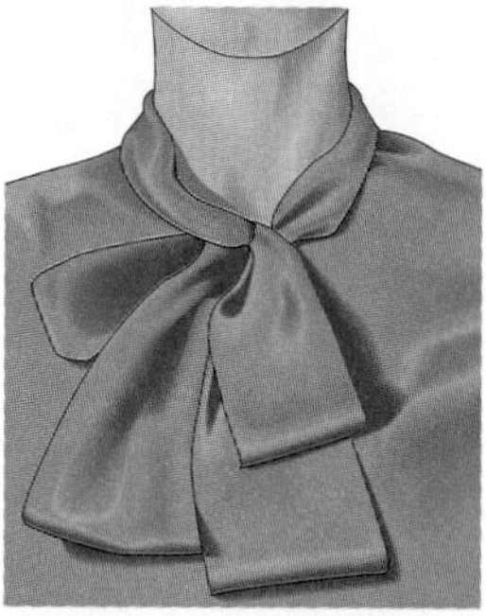

bow collar
de lazo*M*

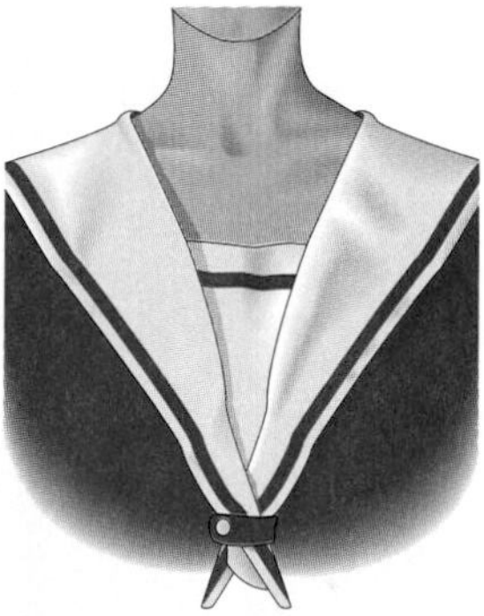

sailor collar
marinero

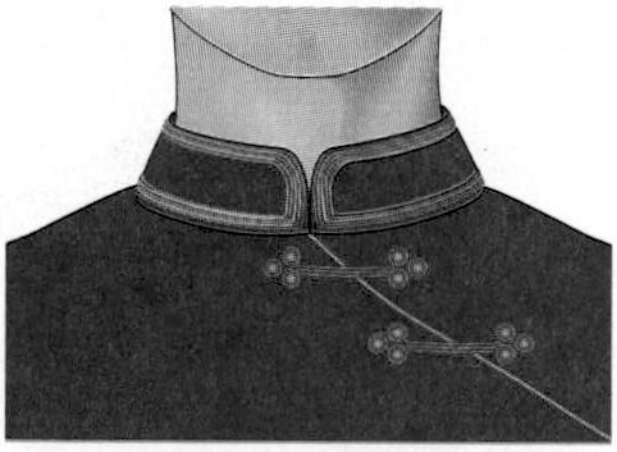

mandarin collar
chino

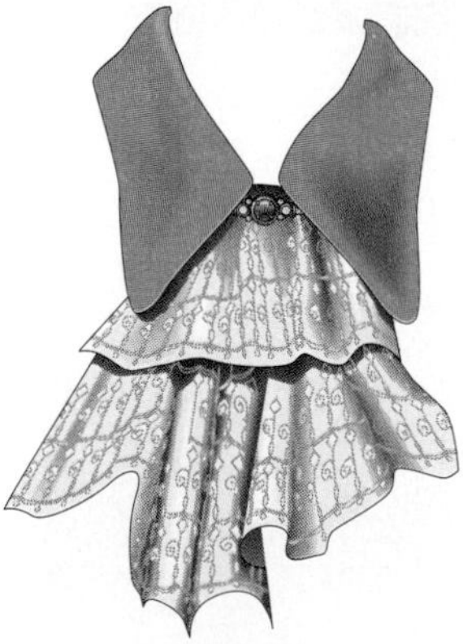

jabot
con chorrera*F*

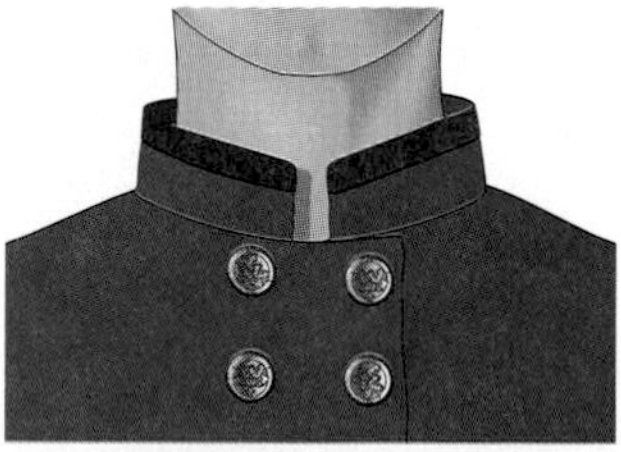

stand-up collar
Mao

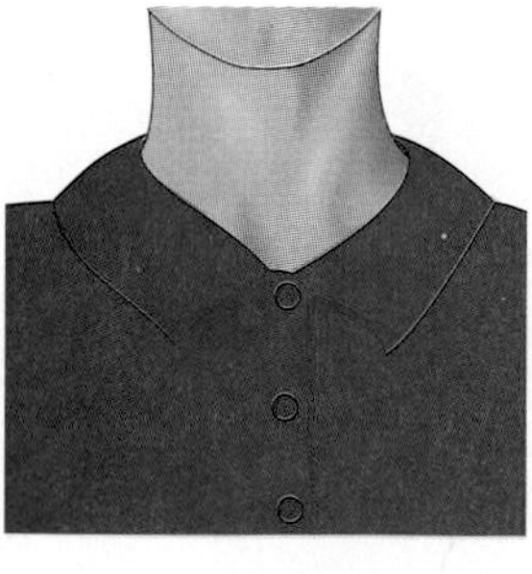

polo collar
con aletilla*F*

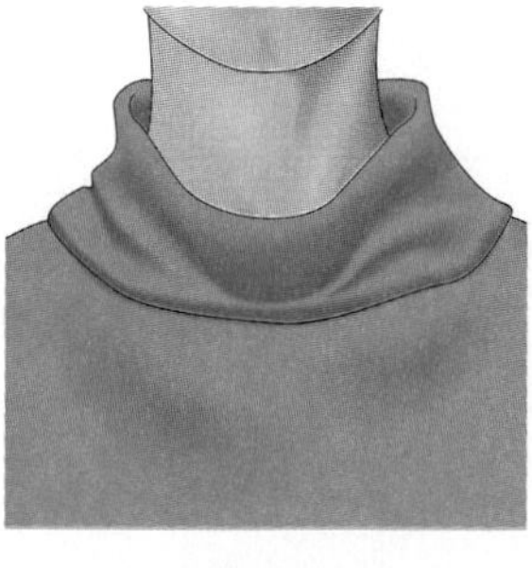

cowl neck
tipo*M* cogulla*F*

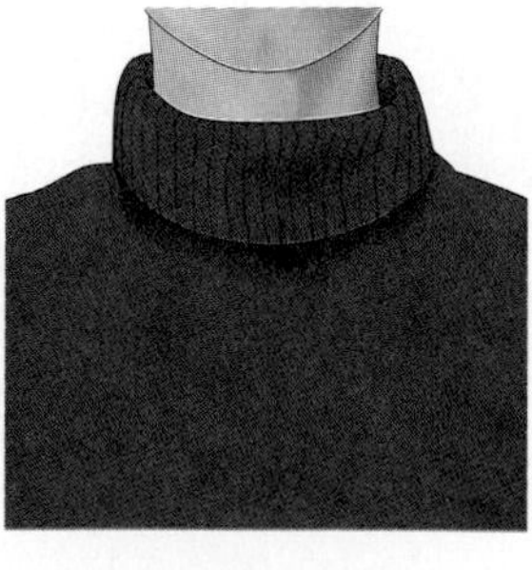

turtleneck
de tortuga*F*

plunging neckline
bajo

bateau neck
de ojal[M]

square neck
cuadrado

draped neck
drapeado

round neck
redondo

sweetheart neckline
de corazón[M]

draped neckline
drapeado

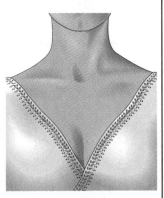

V-shaped neck
en V

343

HOSE
MEDIAS[F]

short sock
calcetín[M]

anklet
tobillera[F]

sock
calcetín[M] largo

knee-high sock
calceta[F]

panty hose
pantimedias[F]

stocking
medias[F]

thigh-high stocking
media[F] tres-cuartos

net stocking
medias[F] de malla[F]

body suit
corpiño^M

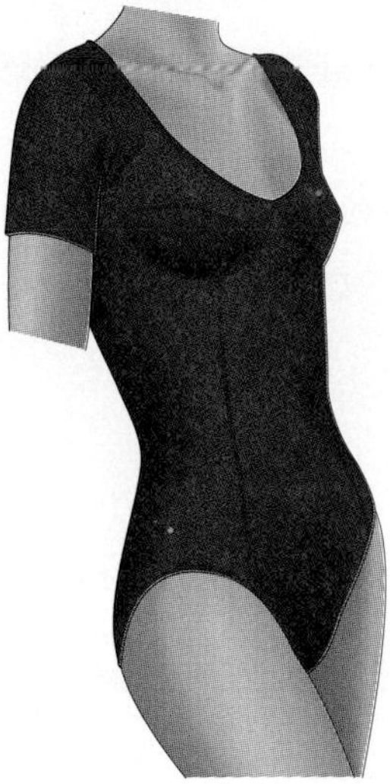

teddy
canesú^M

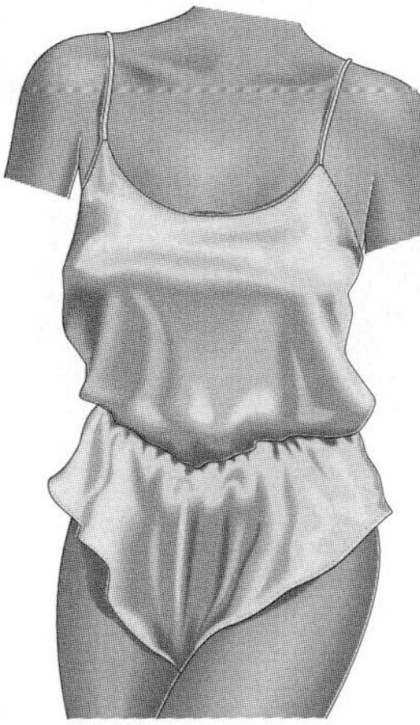

camisole
camisola^F

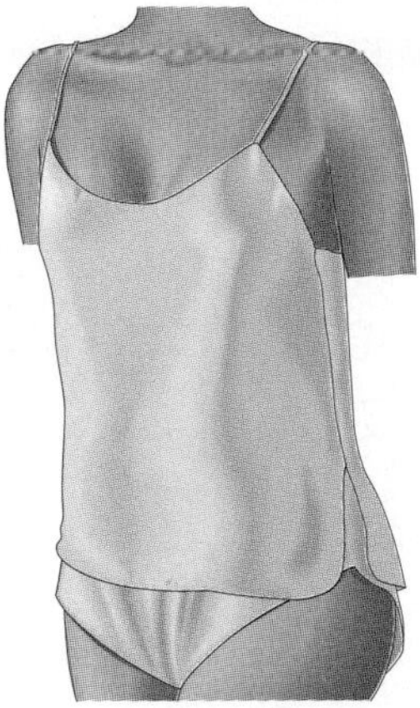

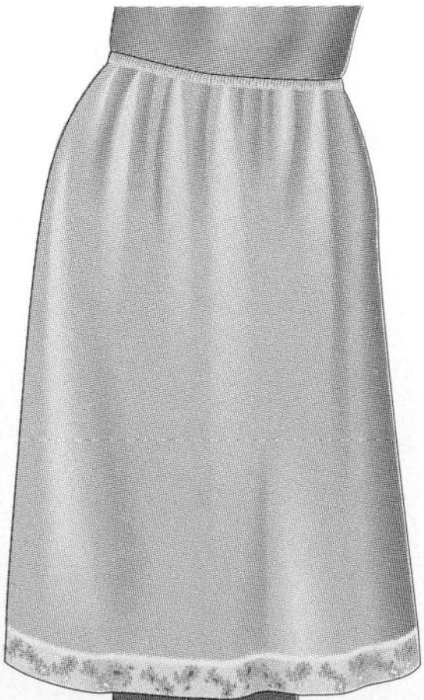

**foundation slip
combinación^F**

slip
combinación^F con sostén^M

princess seaming
costura^F de corte^M princesa^F

half-slip
media combinación^F

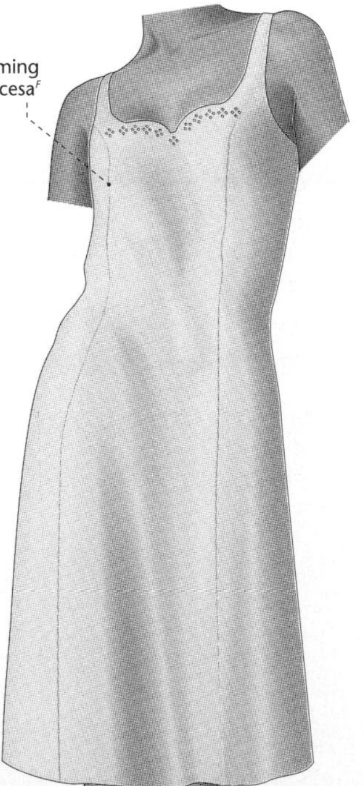

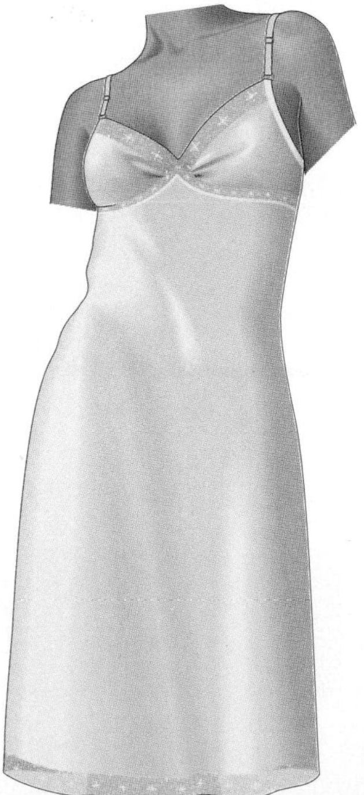

UNDERWEAR
ROPA^F^ INTERIOR

décolleté bra
sostén^M^ de escote^M^ bajo

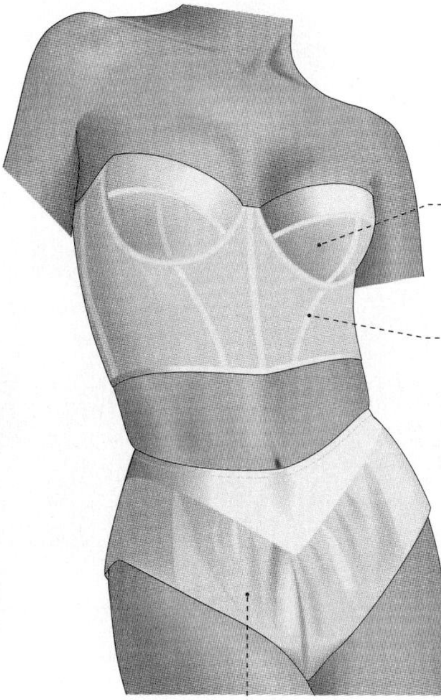

strapless brassiere
sostén^M^ sin tirantes^M^

steel
varilla^F^

briefs
bragas^F^

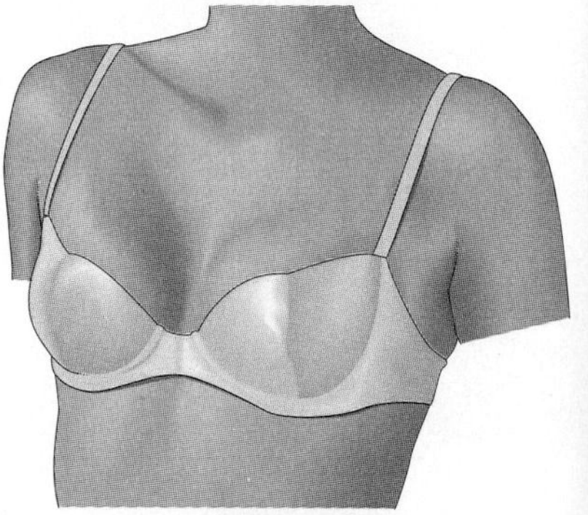

bra
sostén^M^

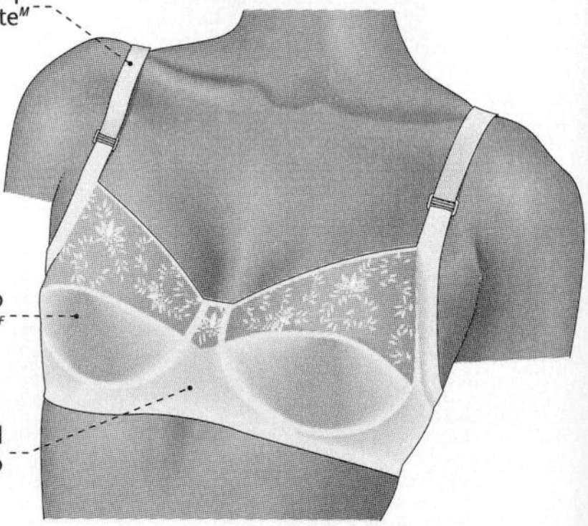

shoulder strap
tirante^M^

brassiere cup
copa^F^

midriff band
talle^M^ corto

girdle
faja^F^

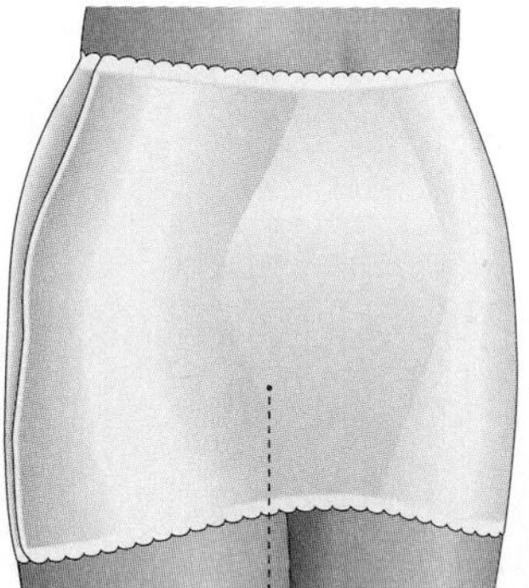

panty girdle
pantifaja^F^

corset
faja^F^ con sostén^M^

panel
refuerzo^M^

CLOTHING
VESTIDO

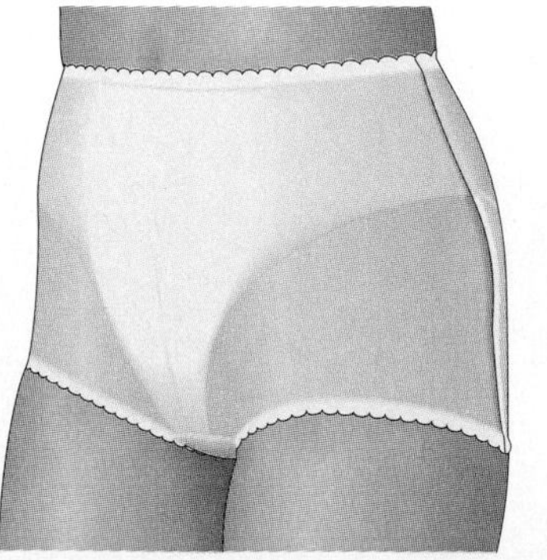

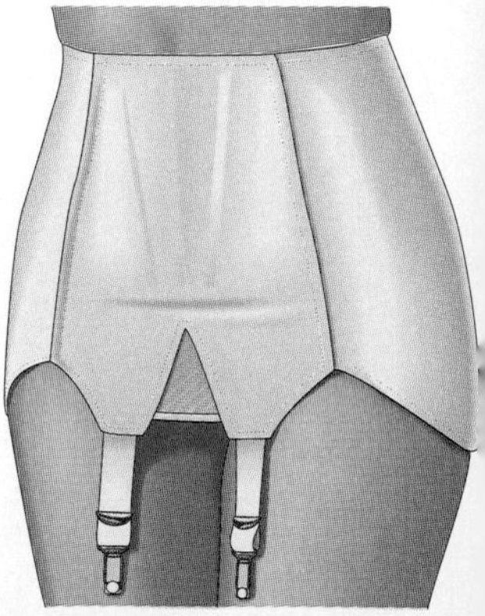

corselette
faja^F con sostén^M

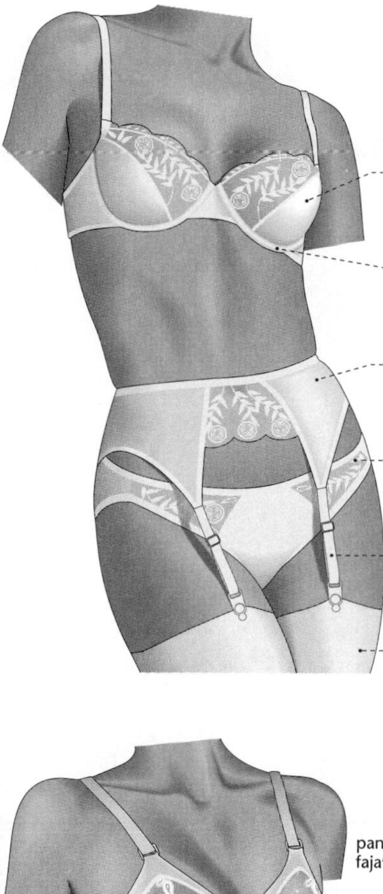

push-up bra
sostén^M con talle^M reforzado

underwiring
varilla^F

garter belt
liguero^M

bikini
slip^M

garter
liga^F

hose
medias^F

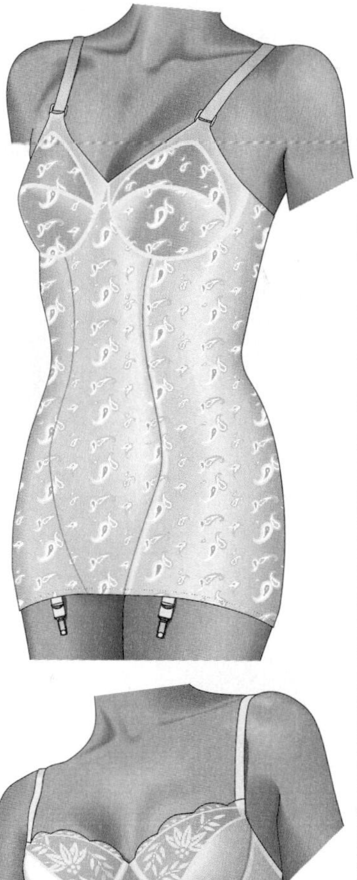

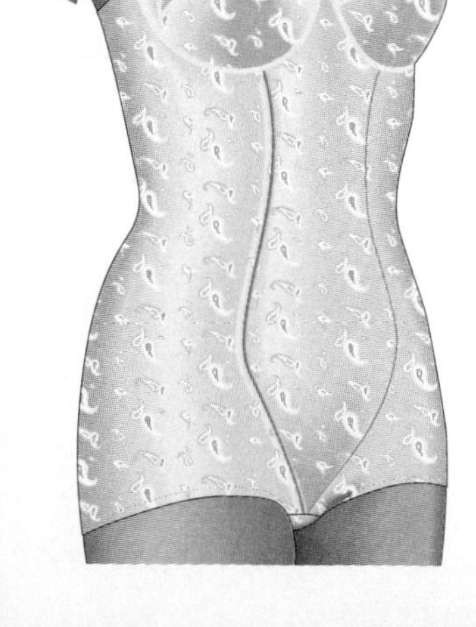

panty corselette
faja^F corsé^M

wasp-waisted corset
corsé^M de cinturón^M de avispa^F

347

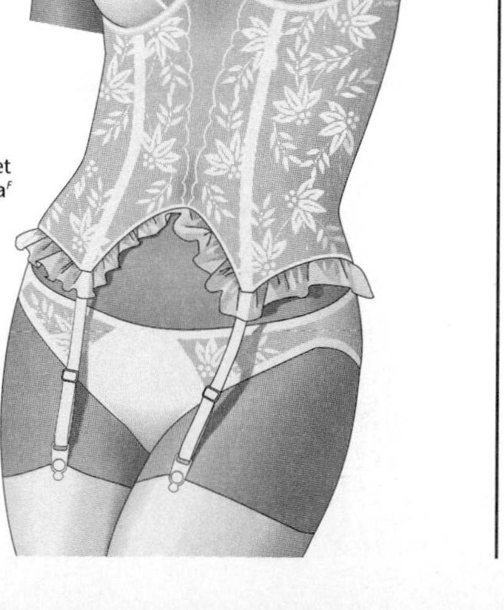

NIGHTWEAR
LENCERÍA^F

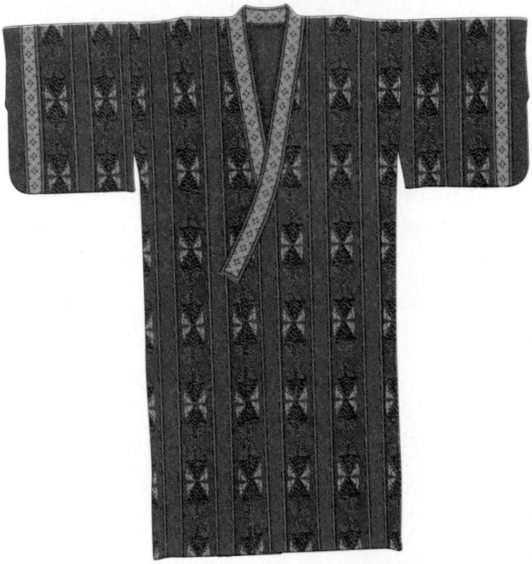

nightgown
camisón^M

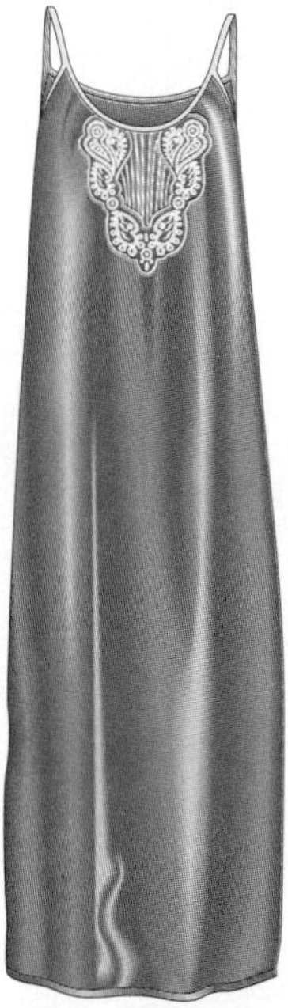

baby doll
camisón^M corto

kimono
kimono^M

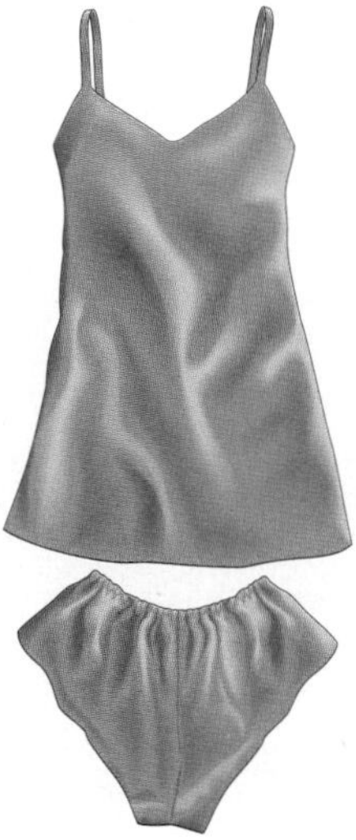

pajamas
pijama^M

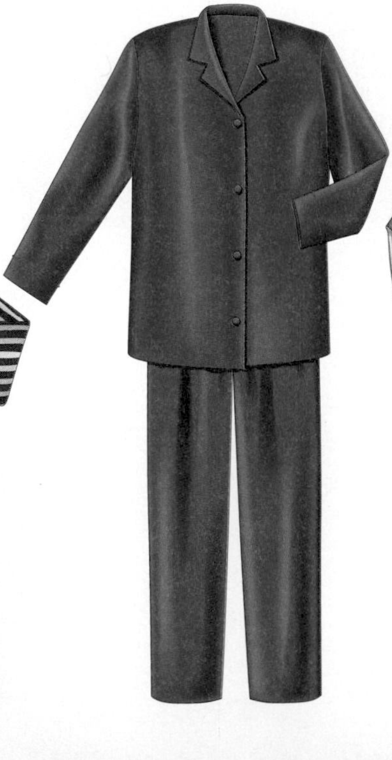

negligee
salto^M de cama^F

bathrobe
bata^F de baño^M

CLOTHING
VESTIDO

348

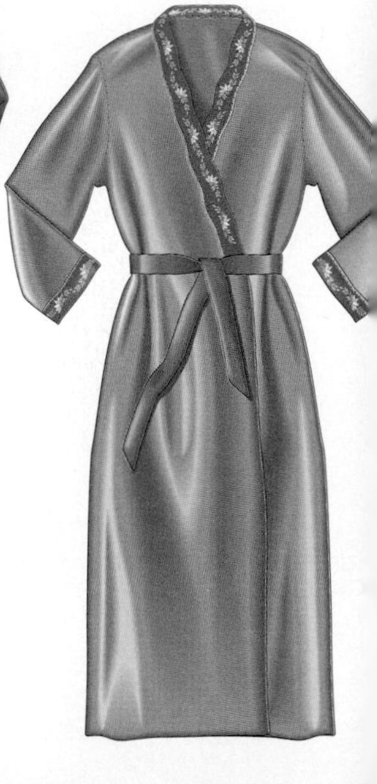

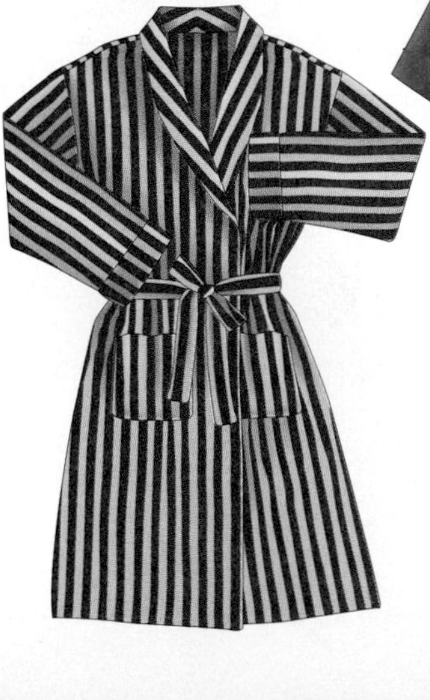

CHILDREN'S CLOTHING
ROPA^F DE NIÑOS^M

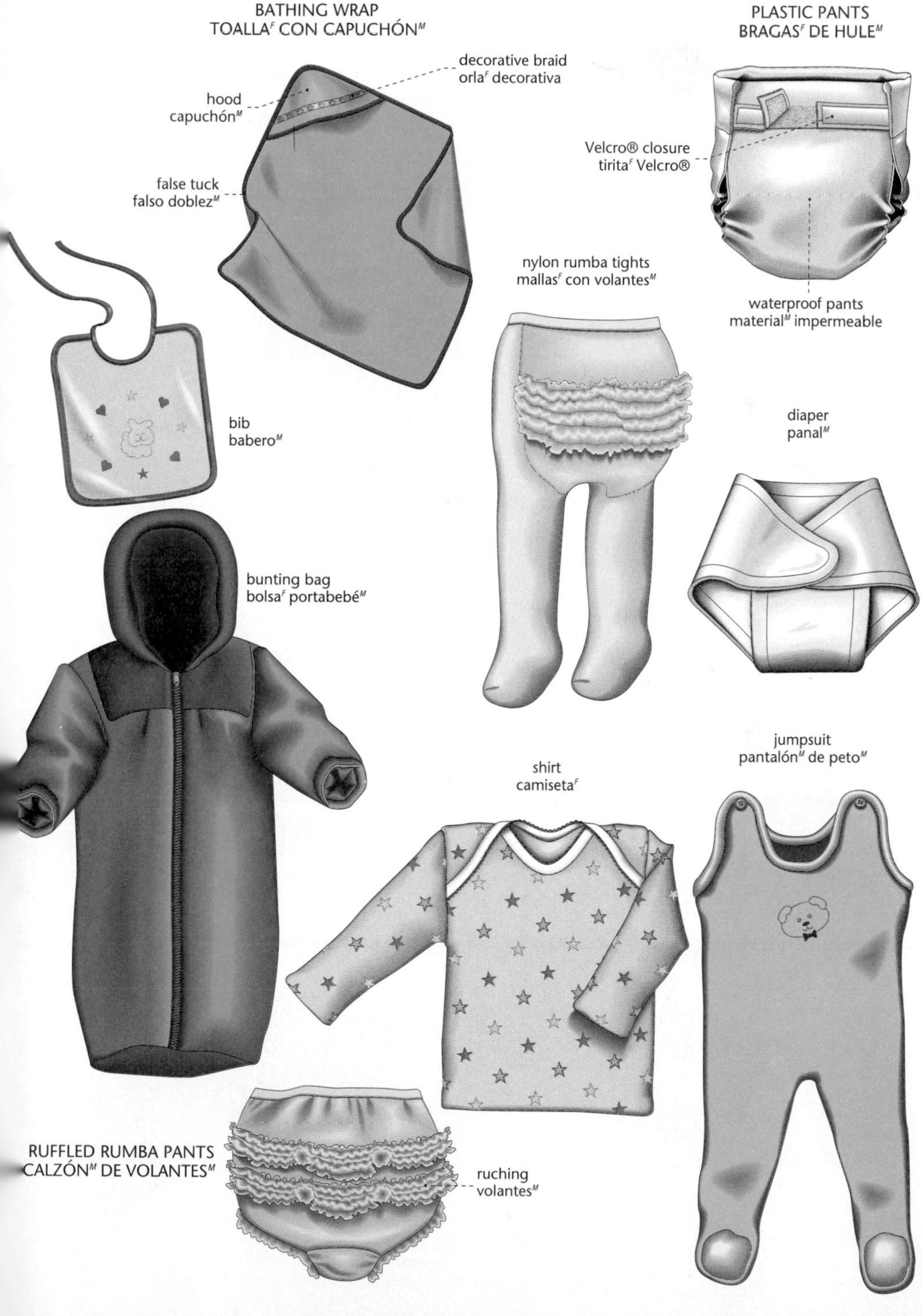

BATHING WRAP
TOALLA^F CON CAPUCHÓN^M

decorative braid
orla^F decorativa

hood
capuchón^M

false tuck
falso doblez^M

bib
babero^M

bunting bag
bolsa^F portabebé^M

PLASTIC PANTS
BRAGAS^F DE HULE^M

Velcro® closure
tirita^F Velcro®

nylon rumba tights
mallas^F con volantes^M

waterproof pants
material^M impermeable

diaper
pañal^M

jumpsuit
pantalón^M de peto^M

shirt
camiseta^F

RUFFLED RUMBA PANTS
CALZÓN^M DE VOLANTES^M

ruching
volantes^M

CLOTHING
VESTIDO

349

CLOTHING VESTIDO

BLANKET SLEEPERS
MAMELUCO^M

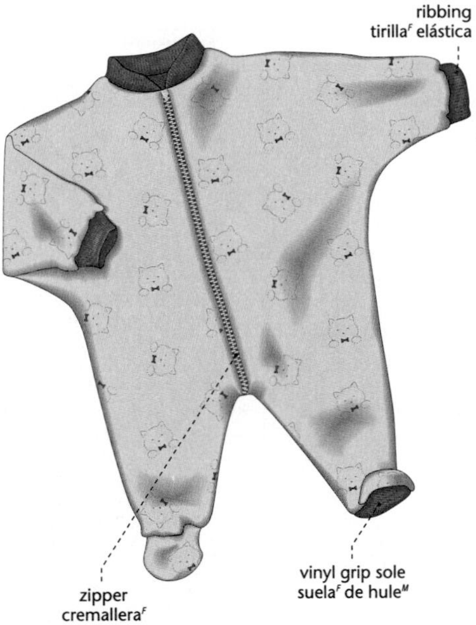

ribbing
tirilla^F elástica

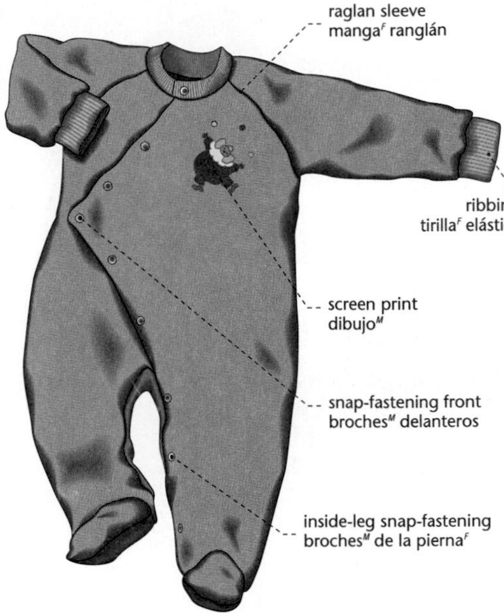

raglan sleeve
manga^F ranglán

ribbing
tirilla^F elástica

screen print
dibujo^M

snap-fastening front
broches^M delanteros

inside-leg snap-fastening
broches^M de la pierna^F

zipper
cremallera^F

vinyl grip sole
suela^F de hule^M

SLEEPERS
MAMELUCOS^M

HIGH-BACK OVERALLS
PANTALÓN^M CON TIRANTES^M

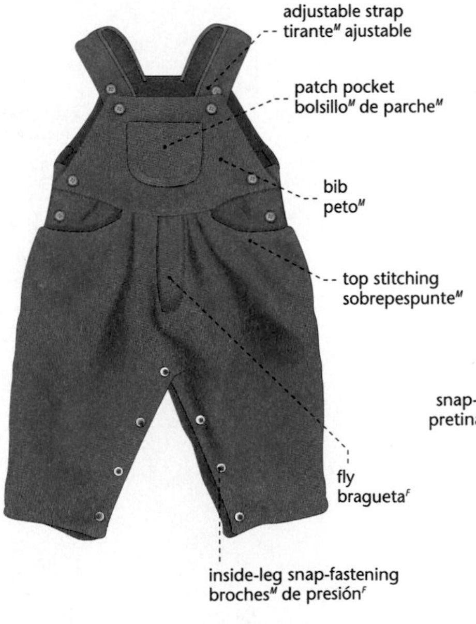

adjustable strap
tirante^M ajustable

patch pocket
bolsillo^M de parche^M

bib
peto^M

top stitching
sobrepespunte^M

fly
bragueta^F

inside-leg snap-fastening
broches^M de presión^F

GROW SLEEPERS
MAMELUCOS^M DE DOS PIEZAS^F

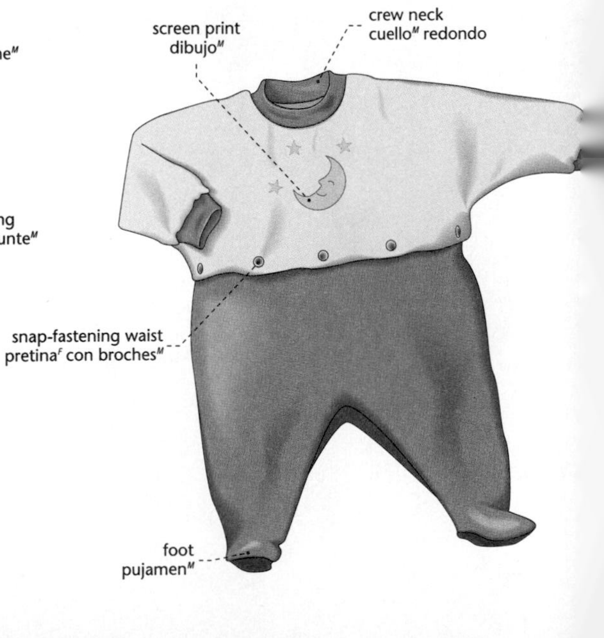

screen print
dibujo^M

crew neck
cuello^M redondo

snap-fastening waist
pretina^F con broches^M

foot
pujamen^M

TRAINING SET
CONJUNTO^M DEPORTIVO

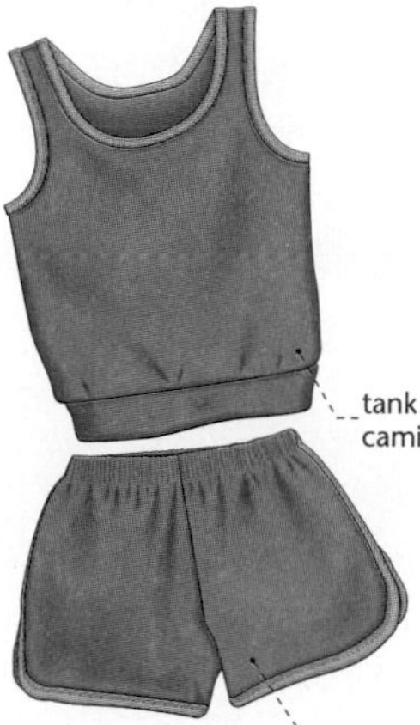

tank top
camiseta^F

shorts
pantalón^M corto

CROSSOVER BACK STRAPS OVERALLS
MONO^M DE TIRANTES CRUZADOS ATRÁS

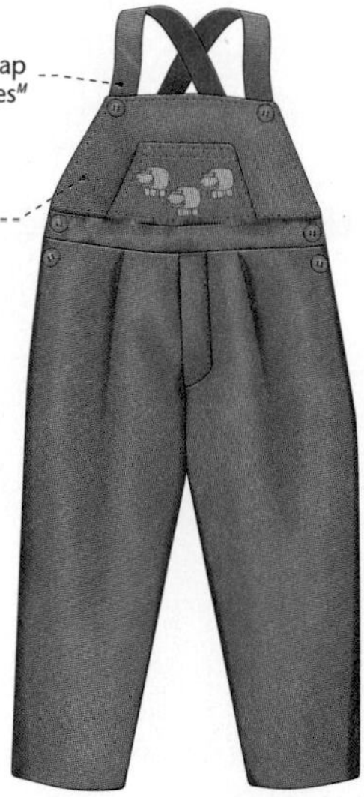

button strap
tirante^M con botones^M

bib
peto^M

polojama
pijama^M

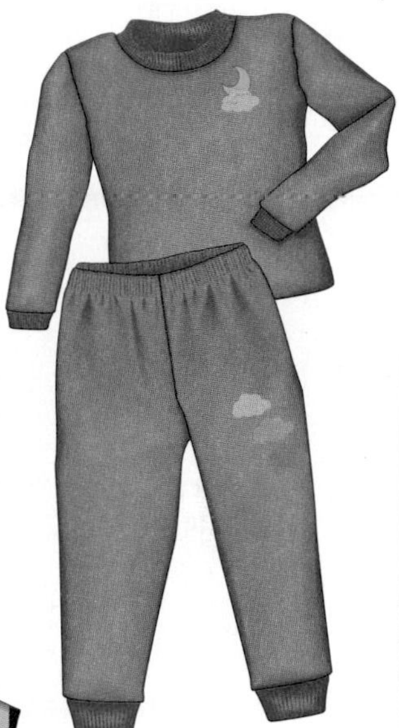

SNOWSUIT
TRAJE^M DE INVIERNO^M CON CAPUCHÓN^M

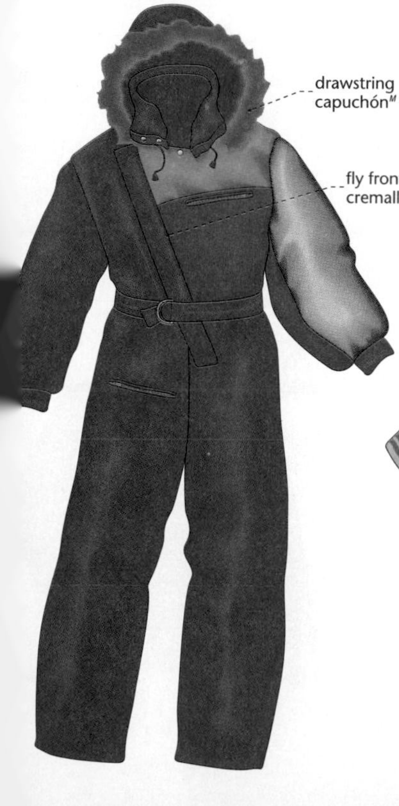

drawstring hood
capuchón^M con cordón^M

fly front closing
cremallera^F

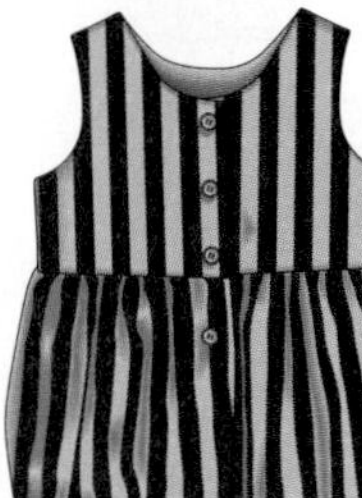

rompers
pelele^M

jumpsuit
traje^M pantalón^M

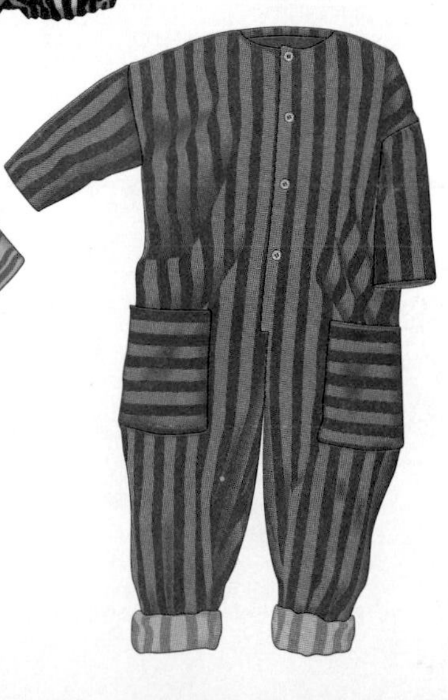

T-shirt dress
camiseta^F de cuerpo^M entero

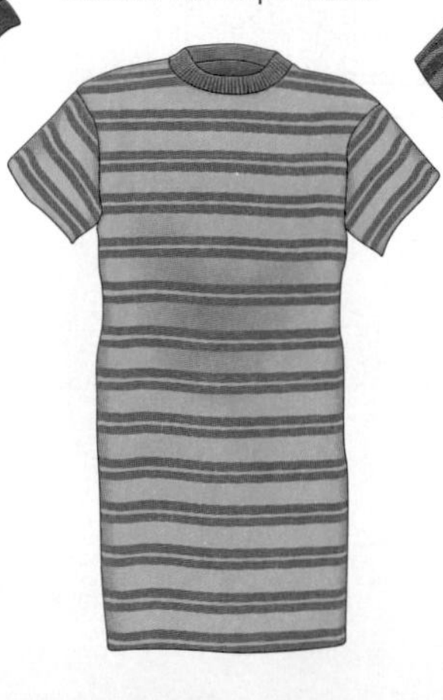

CLOTHING
VESTIDO

RUNNING SHOE
ZAPATO^M DEPORTIVO

tongue
lengüeta^F

nose of the quarter
ala^F del cuarto^M

collar
ribete^M

lining
forro^M

counter
contrafuerte^M

quarter
cuarto^M

stitch
pespunteado^M

heel
talón^M

middle sole
cambrillón^M

air unit
cámara^F de aire^M

aglet
herrete^M

shoelace
cordón^M

TRAINING SUIT
TRAJE^M DE ENTRENAMIENTO^M

hooded sweat shirt
camisa^F de entrenamiento^M con capucha^F

sweat pants
pantalones^M de entrenamiento^M

sweat shirt
camisa^F de entrenamiento^M

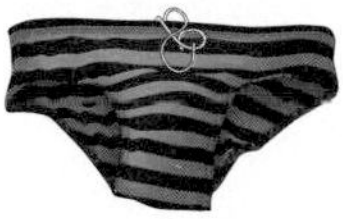

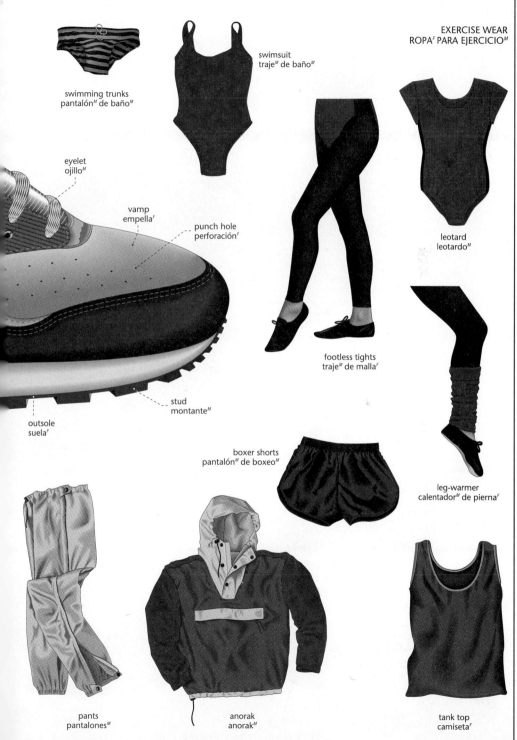

swimming trunks
pantalón^M de baño^M

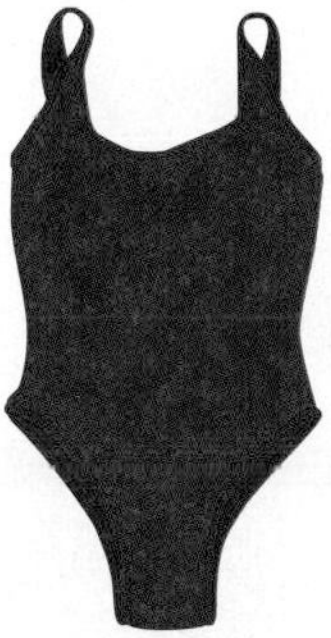

swimsuit
traje^M de baño^M

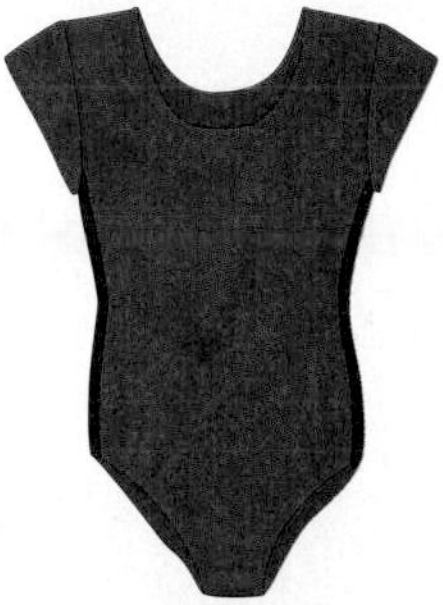

leotard
leotardo^M

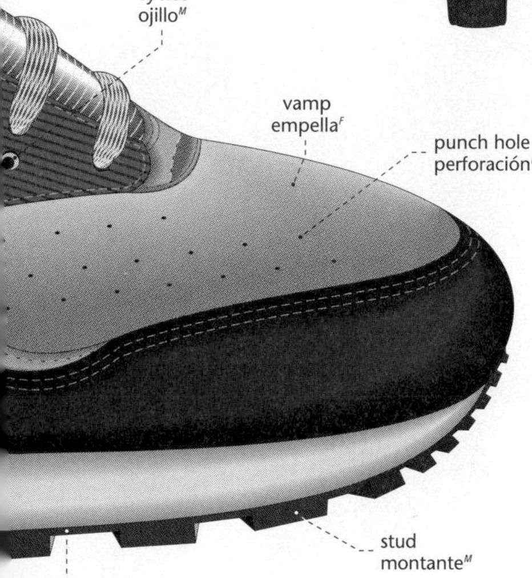

eyelet
ojillo^M

vamp
empella^F

punch hole
perforación^F

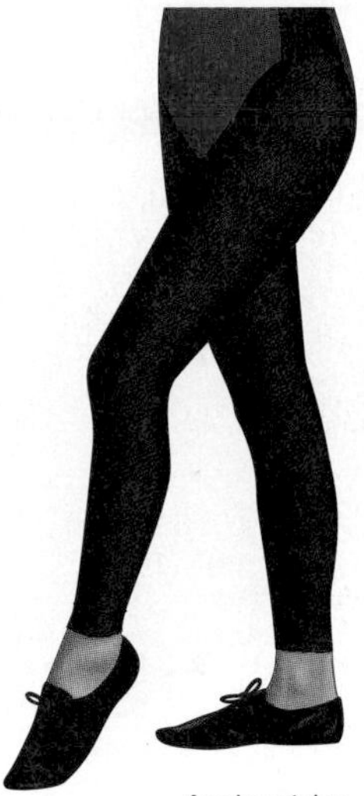

footless tights
traje^M de malla^F

stud
montante^M

outsole
suela^F

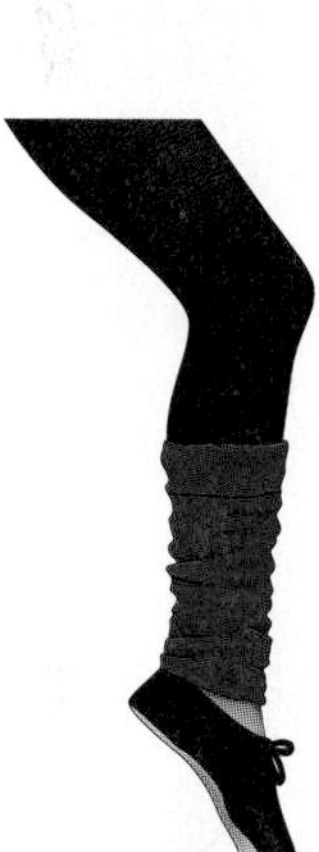

leg-warmer
calentador^M de pierna^F

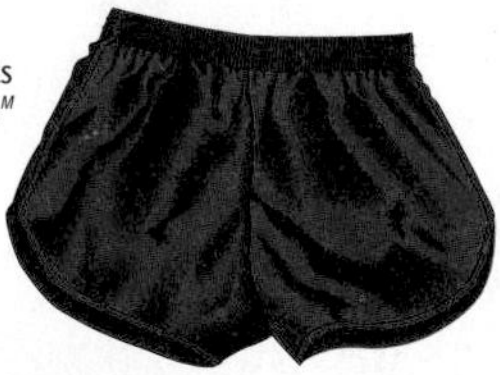

boxer shorts
pantalón^M de boxeo^M

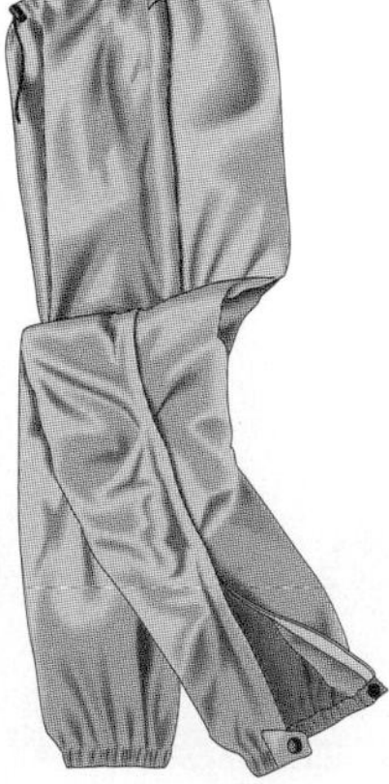

pants
pantalones^M

anorak
anorak^M

tank top
camiseta^F

CLOTHING
VESTIDO

353

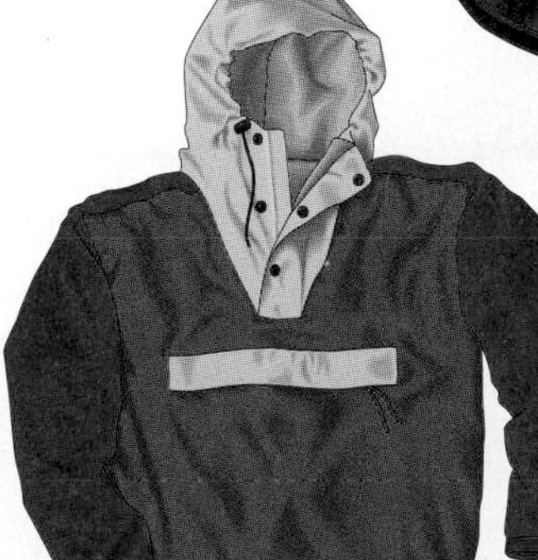

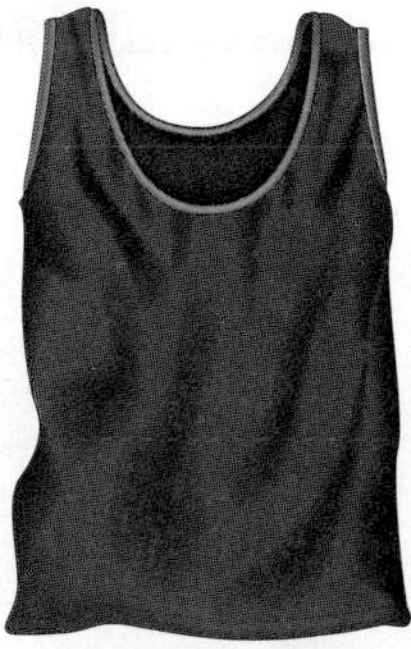

PARTS OF A SHOE
PARTES^F DE UN ZAPATO^M

lining
forro^M

tongue
lengüeta^F

cuff
ribete^M

shoelace
cordón^M

heel grip
refuerzo^M del talón^M

quarter
cuarto^M

outside counter
contrafuerte^M del talón^M

heel
talón^M

top lift
tapa^F

waist
cintura^F

nose of the quarter
ala^F del cuarto^M

aglet
herrete^M

eyelet
ojillo^M

eyelet tab
oreja^F

MAJOR TYPES OF SHOES
TIPOS^M DE CALZADO^M

oxford shoe
zapato^M de cordones^M

chukka
media bota^F

bootee
botina^F

CLOTHING
VESTIDO

354

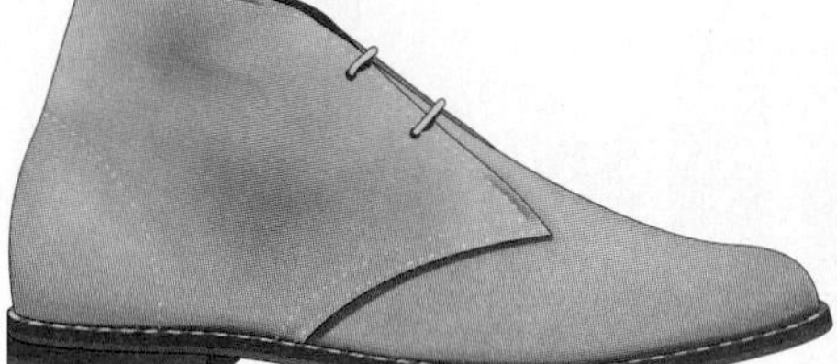

tennis shoe
zapato^M de tenis^M

blucher oxford
zapato^M de vestir

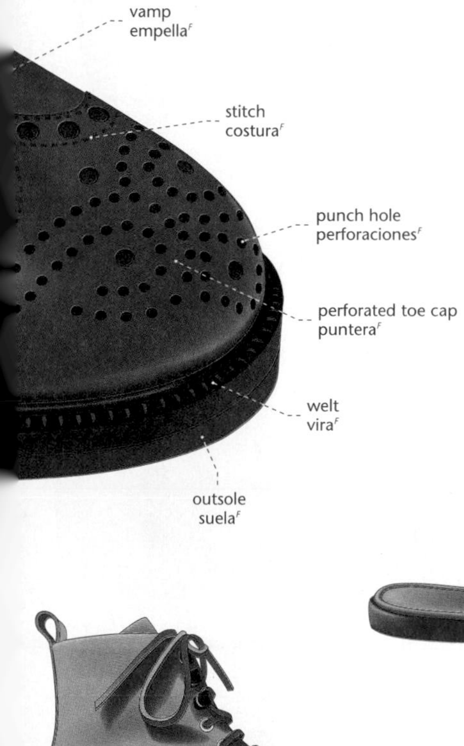

vamp
empella^F

stitch
costura^F

punch hole
perforaciones^F

perforated toe cap
puntera^F

welt
vira^F

outsole
suela^F

moccasin
mocasín^M

loafer
zapato^M de calle^F

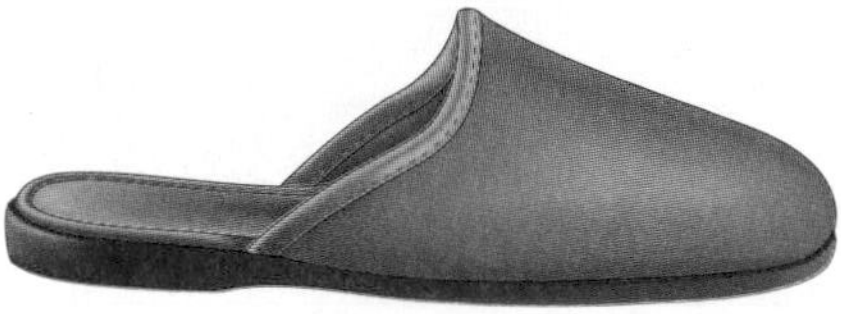

mule
pantufla^F

heavy duty boot
bota^F de trabajo^M

rubber
chanclo^M de goma^F

CLOTHING
VESTIDO

355

MAJOR TYPES OF SHOES
TIPOS^M DE CALZADO^M

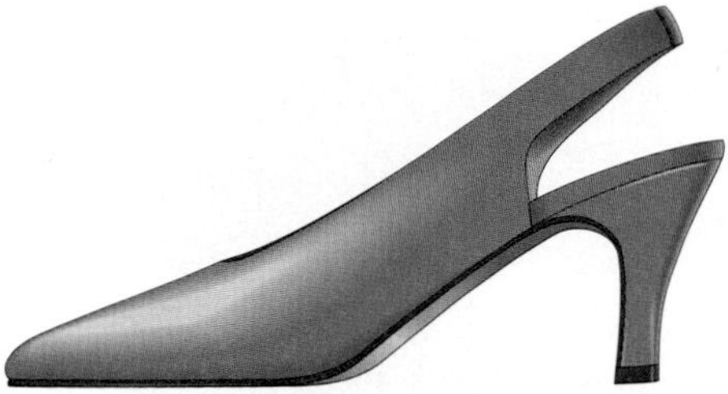

sling back shoe
zapato^M de tacón^M alto con presillas^F

pump
zapato^M de tacón^M alto

sandal
sandalia^F

T-strap shoe
zapato^M de correa^F

one-bar shoe
escarpín^M con correa^F

ballerina
zapatilla^F de ballet^M

casual shoe
zapato^M de calle^F

boot
bota^F

CLOTHING
VESTIDO

356

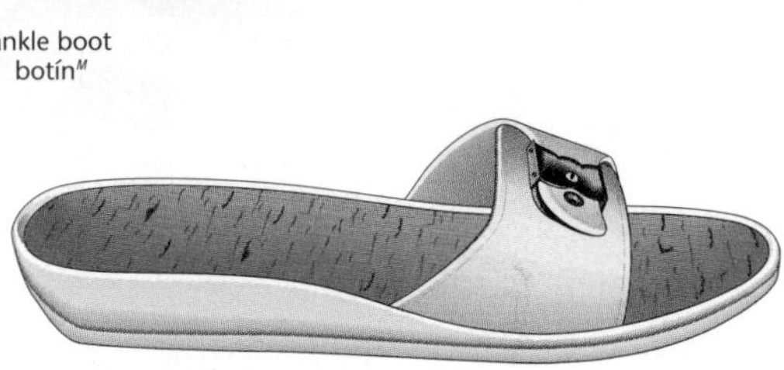

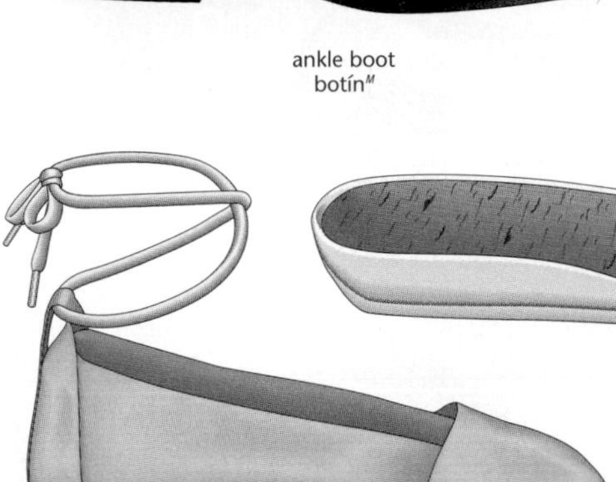

sandal
sandalia^F

thong
chancleta^F

ankle boot
botín^M

clog
chanclo^M

espadrille
alpargata^F

thigh-boot
bota^F de medio muslo^M

sandal
sandalia^F

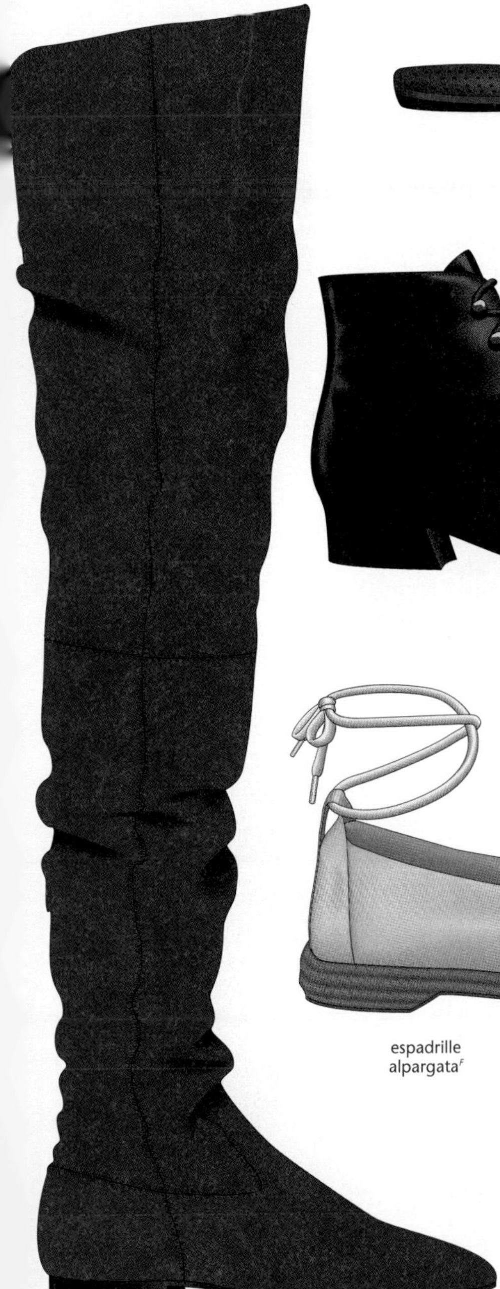

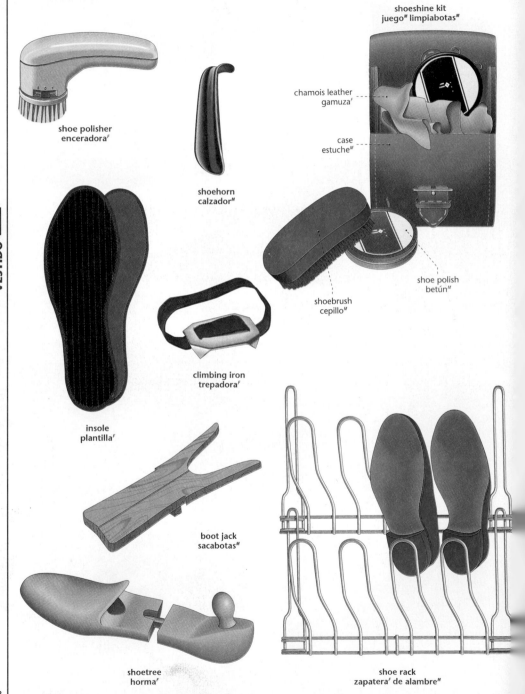

ACCESSORIES
ACCESORIOS*M*

shoeshine kit
juego*M* limpiabotas*M*

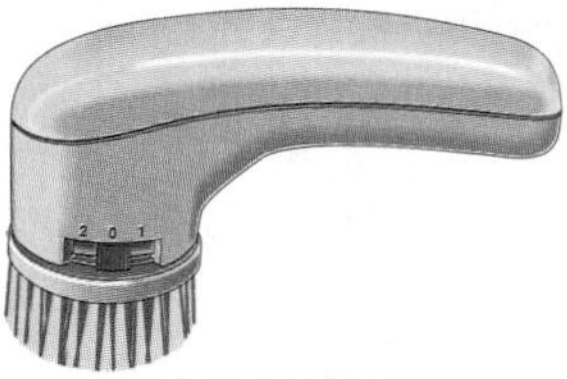

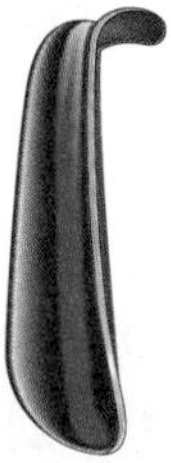

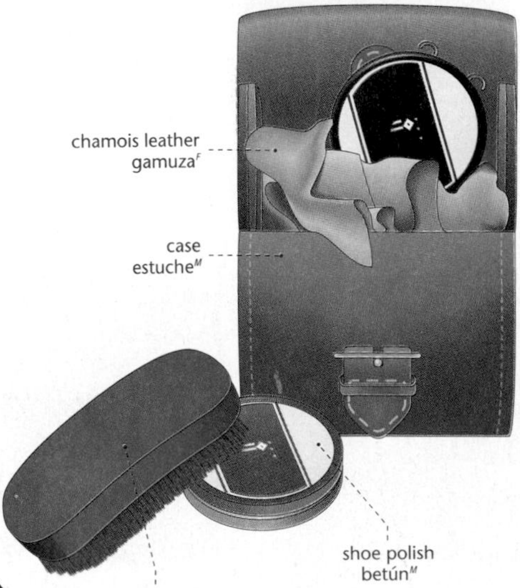

chamois leather
gamuza*F*

case
estuche*M*

shoe polisher
enceradora*F*

shoehorn
calzador*M*

shoe polish
betún*M*

shoebrush
cepillo*M*

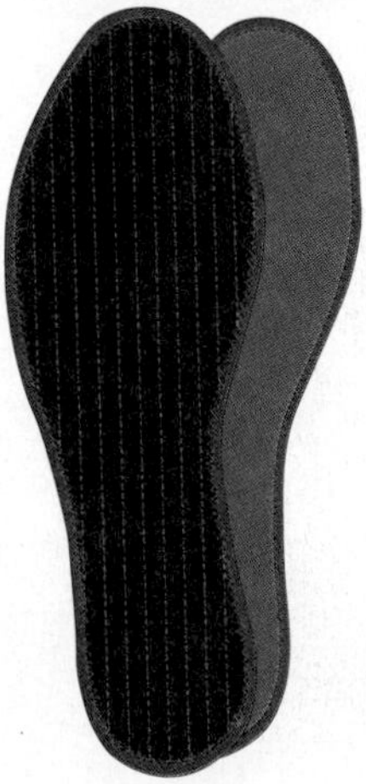

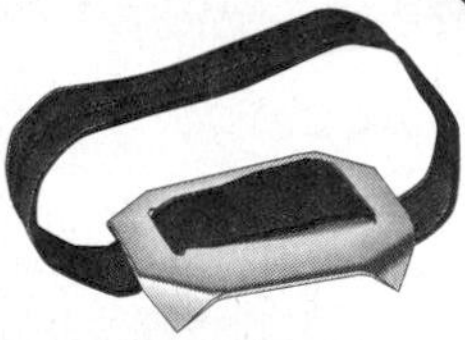

climbing iron
trepadora*F*

insole
plantilla*F*

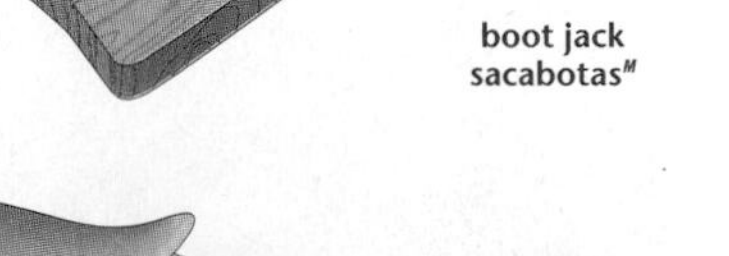

boot jack
sacabotas*M*

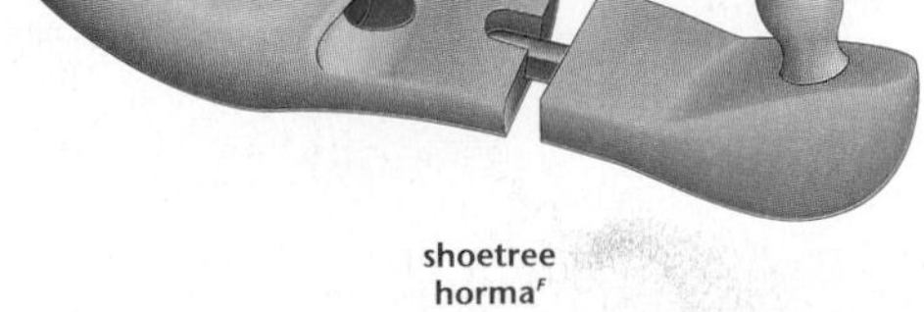

shoetree
horma*F*

shoe rack
zapatera*F* de alambre*M*

358

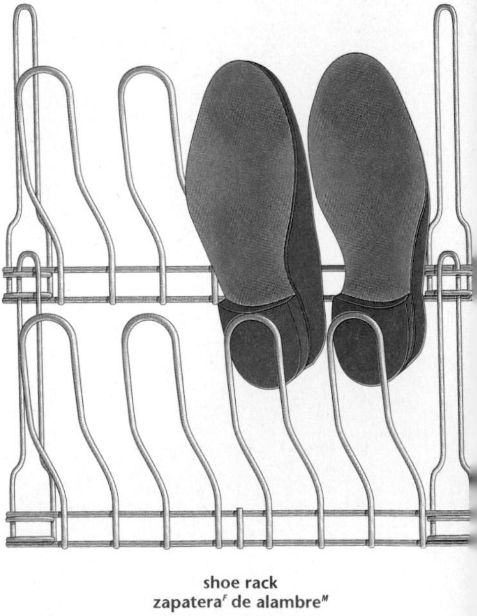

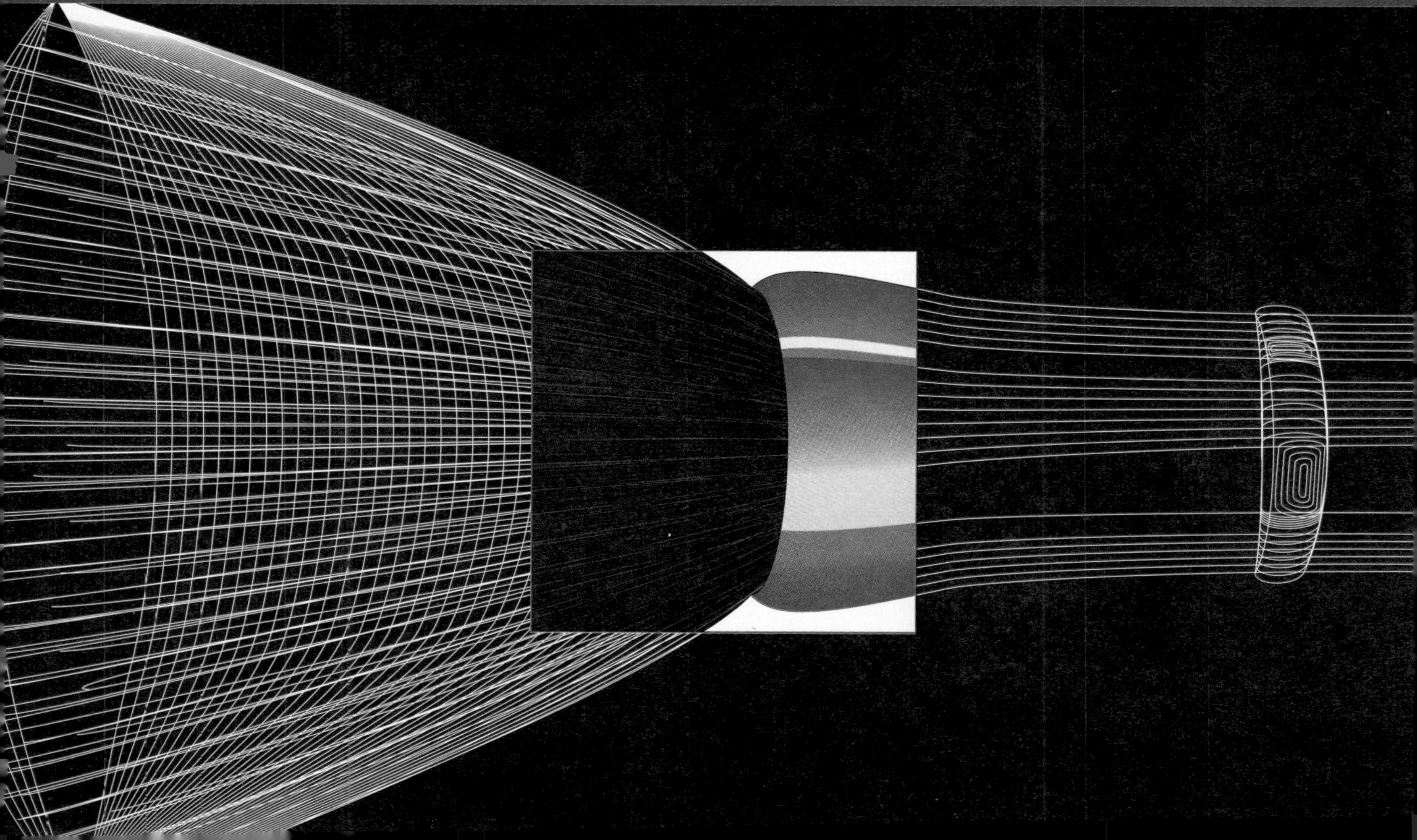

CONTENTS

PERSONAL ADORNMENT
ADORNOS PERSONALES

JEWELRY
JOYERÍA^F

EARRINGS
PENDIENTES^M

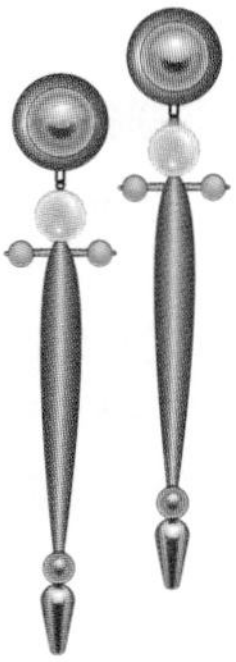

drop earrings
pendientes^M

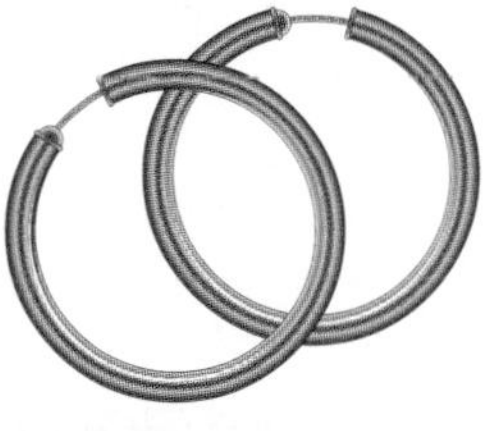

hoop earrings
zarcillos^M de aro^M

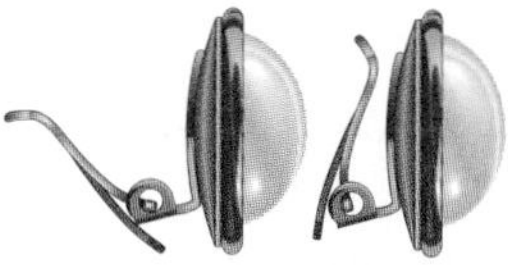

clip earrings
pendientes^M de clip^M

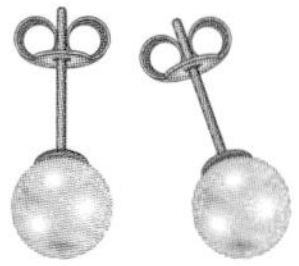

post earrings
pendientes^M de espiga^F

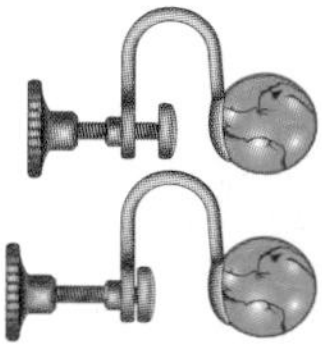

screw earrings
pendientes^M de tornillo^M

NECKLACES
COLLARES^M

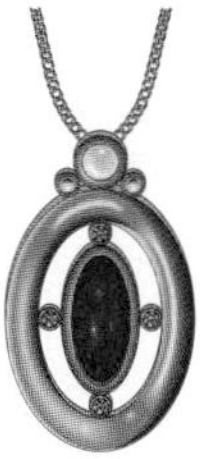

pendant
pendiente^M

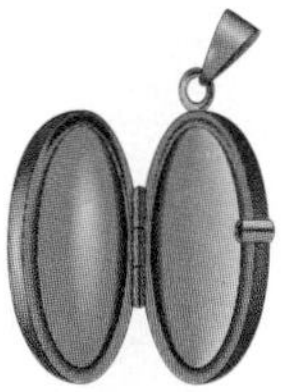

locket
relicario^M

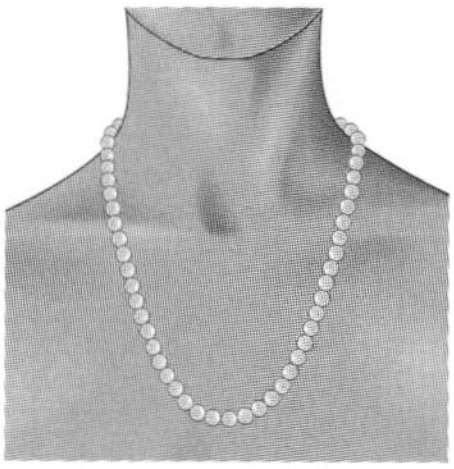

matinee-length necklace
collar^M de una vuelta^F

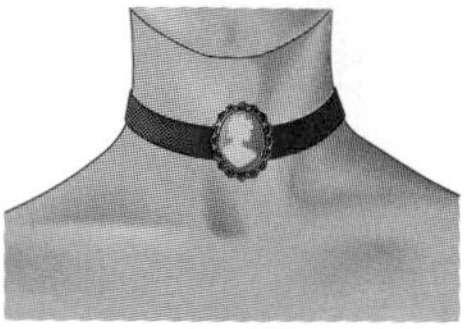

velvet-band choker
garagantilla^F de terciopelo^M

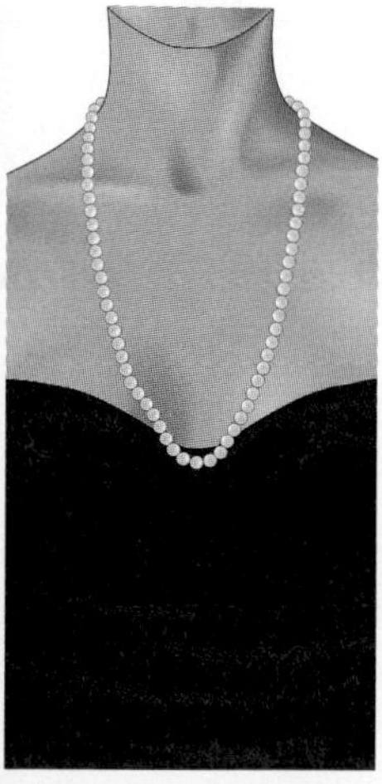

opera-length necklace
collar^M de una vuelta^F

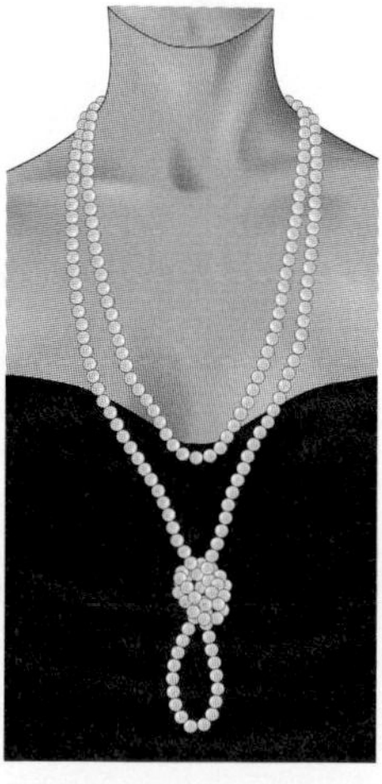

rope
sarta^F

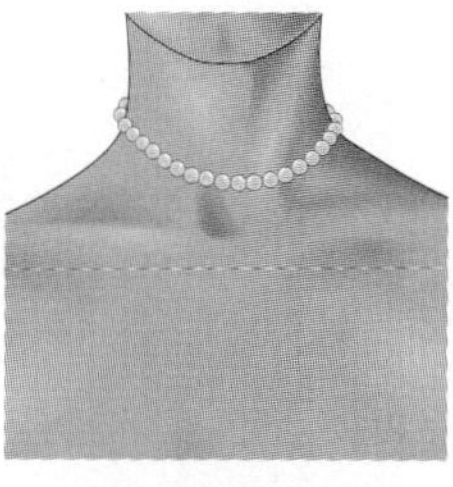

choker
gargantilla^F

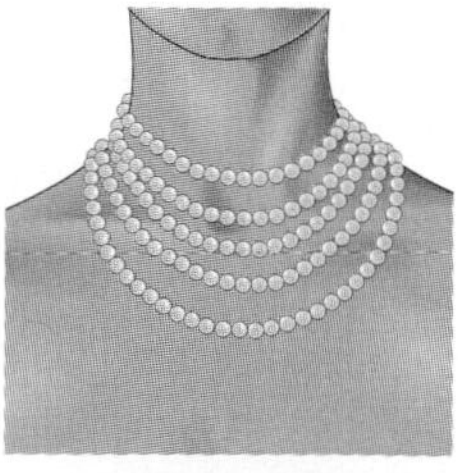

bib necklace
collar^M de 5 hilos^M

CUT FOR GEMSTONES
TALLAS[F] DE PIEDRAS[F] PRECIOSAS

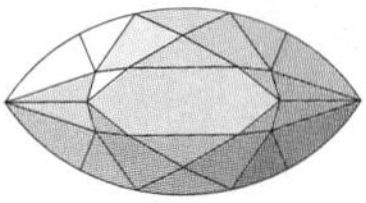

navette cut
marquesa[F]

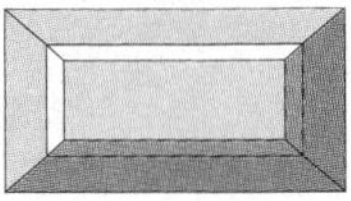

baguette cut
baguette[F]

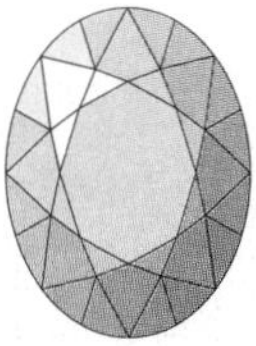

oval cut
oval

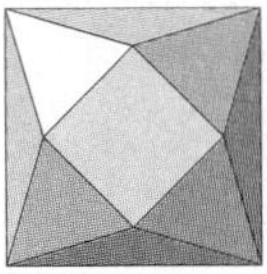

French cut
francés

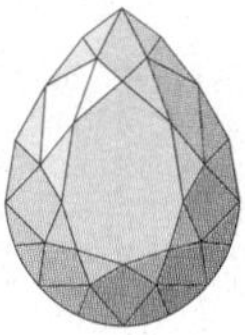

pear-shaped cut
pera[F]

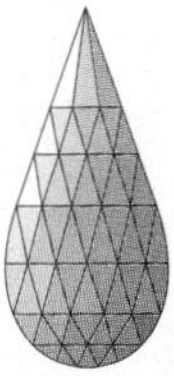

briolette cut
gota[F]

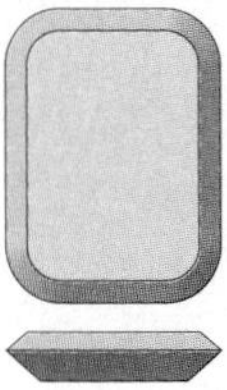

table cut
tabla[F]

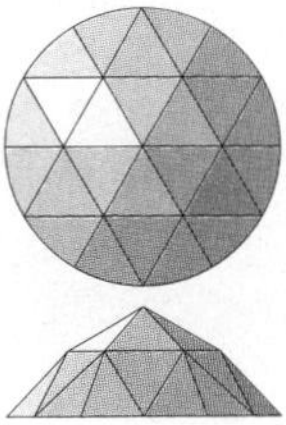

rose cut
rosa[F] holandesa

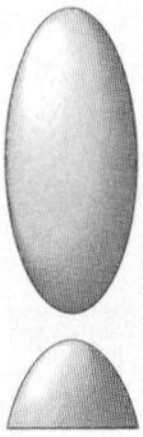

cabochon cut
cabujón[M]

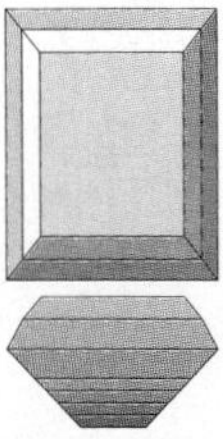

step cut
en escalera[F]

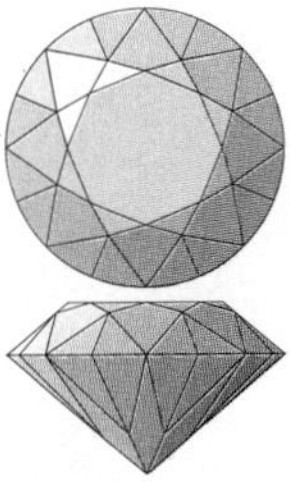

brilliant full cut
brillante[M]

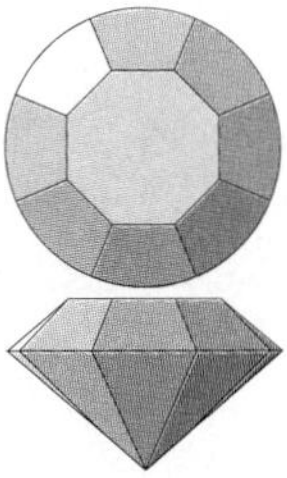

eight cut
ocho facetas[F]

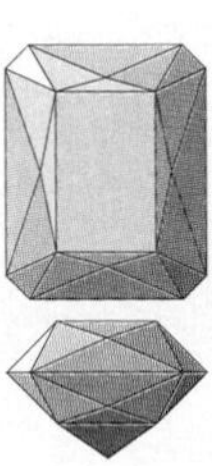

scissors cut
en tijera[F]

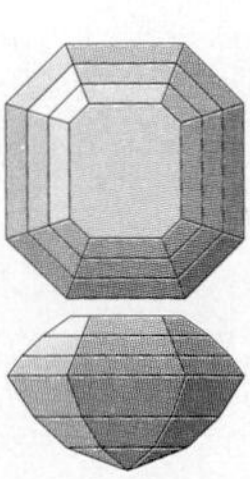

emerald cut
esmeralda[F]

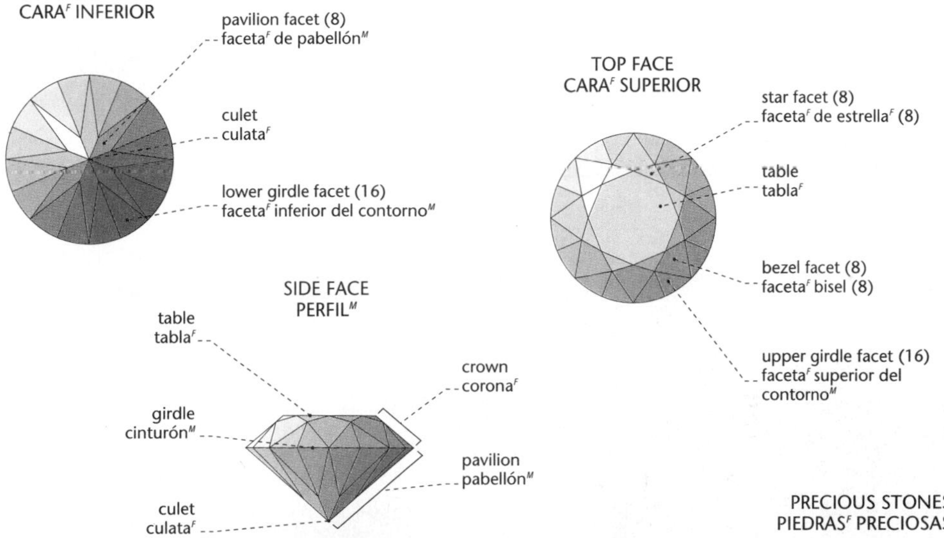

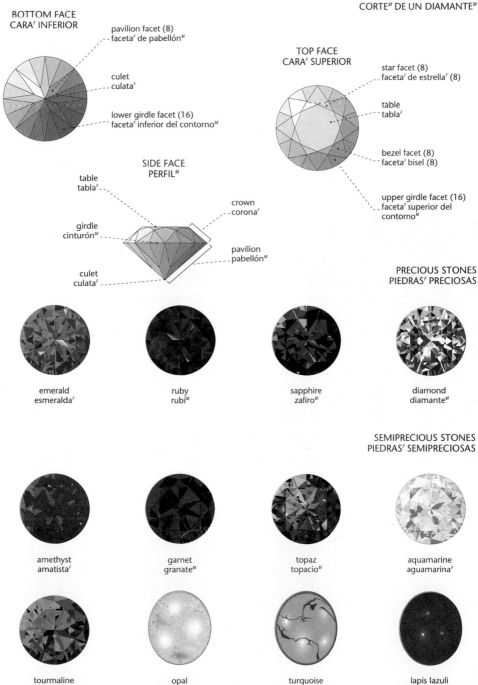

BOTTOM FACE
CARA^F INFERIOR

pavilion facet (8)
faceta^F de pabellón^M

culet
culata^F

lower girdle facet (16)
faceta^F inferior del contorno^M

BRILLIANT CUT FACETS
CORTE^M DE UN DIAMANTE^M

TOP FACE
CARA^F SUPERIOR

star facet (8)
faceta^F de estrella^F (8)

table
tabla^F

bezel facet (8)
faceta^F bisel (8)

upper girdle facet (16)
faceta^F superior del
contorno^M

SIDE FACE
PERFIL^M

table
tabla^F

crown
corona^F

girdle
cinturón^M

pavilion
pabellón^M

culet
culata^F

PRECIOUS STONES
PIEDRAS^F PRECIOSAS

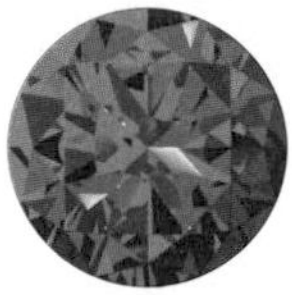

emerald
esmeralda^F

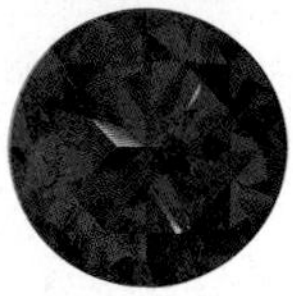

ruby
rubí^M

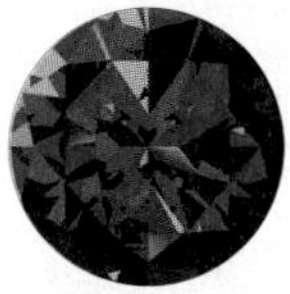

sapphire
zafiro^M

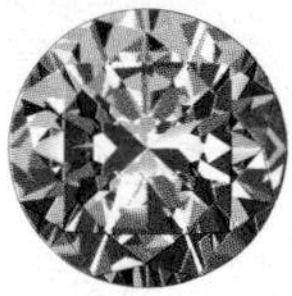

diamond
diamante^M

SEMIPRECIOUS STONES
PIEDRAS^F SEMIPRECIOSAS

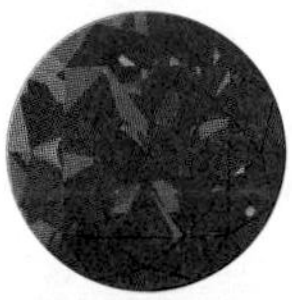

amethyst
amatista^F

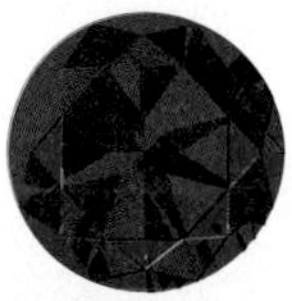

garnet
granate^M

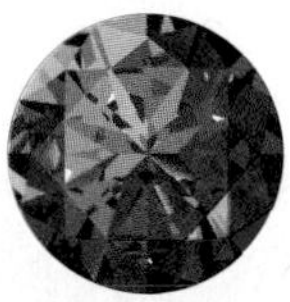

topaz
topacio^M

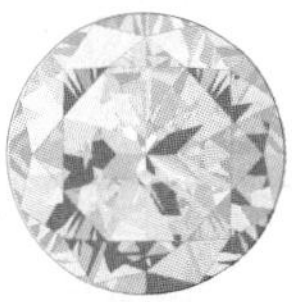

aquamarine
aguamarina^F

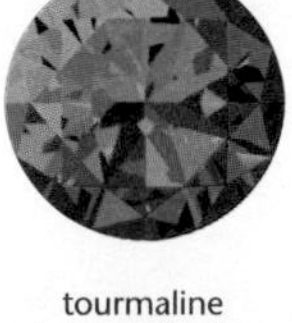

tourmaline
turmalina^F

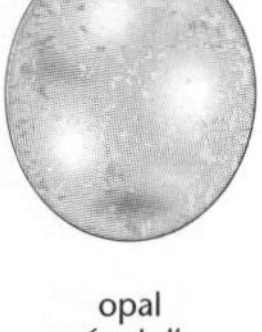

opal
ópalo^M

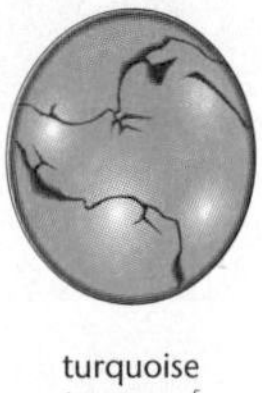

turquoise
turquesa^F

lapis lazuli
lapislázuli^M

PERSONAL ADORNMENT
ADORNOS PERSONALES

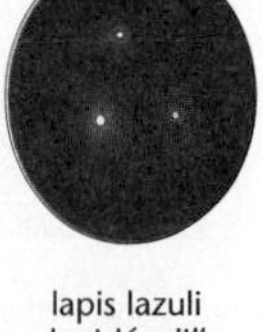

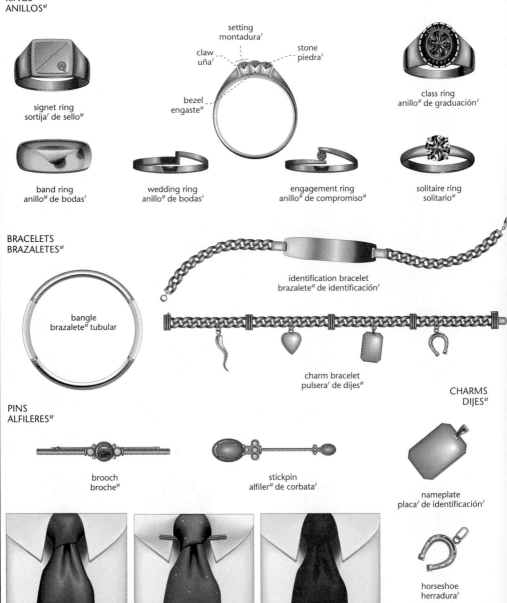

PERSONAL ADORNMENT / ADORNOS PERSONALES

RINGS
ANILLOS^M

signet ring
sortija^F de sello^M

setting
montadura^F

claw
uña^F

stone
piedra^F

bezel
engaste^M

class ring
anillo^M de graduación^F

band ring
anillo^M de bodas^F

wedding ring
anillo^M de bodas^F

engagement ring
anillo^M de compromiso^M

solitaire ring
solitario^M

BRACELETS
BRAZALETES^M

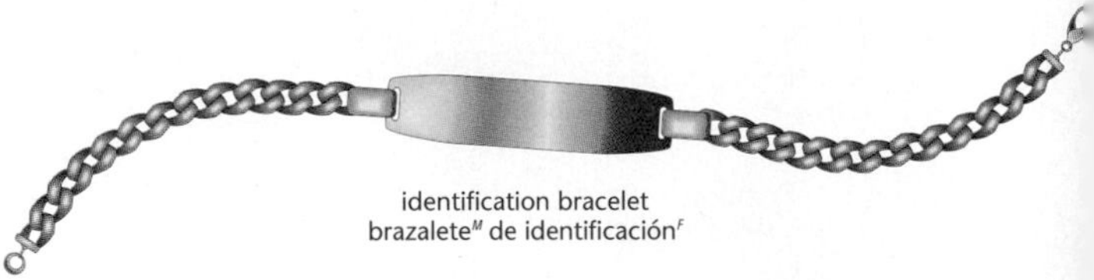

identification bracelet
brazalete^M de identificación^F

bangle
brazalete^M tubular

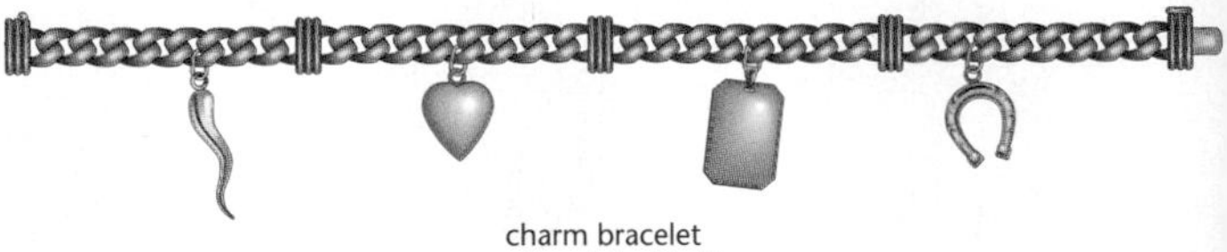

charm bracelet
pulsera^F de dijes^M

CHARMS
DIJES^M

PINS
ALFILERES^M

brooch
broche^M

stickpin
alfiler^M de corbata^F

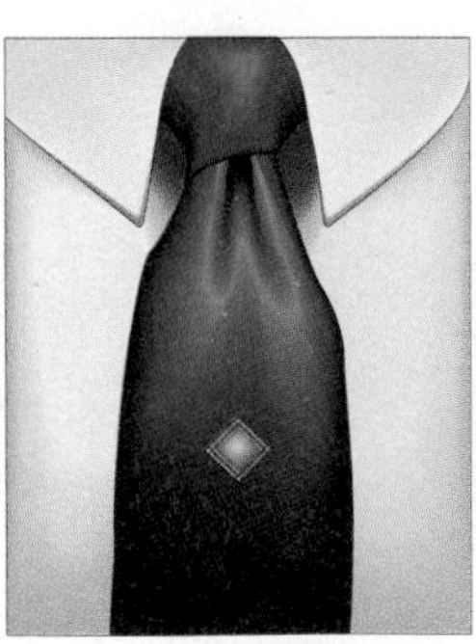

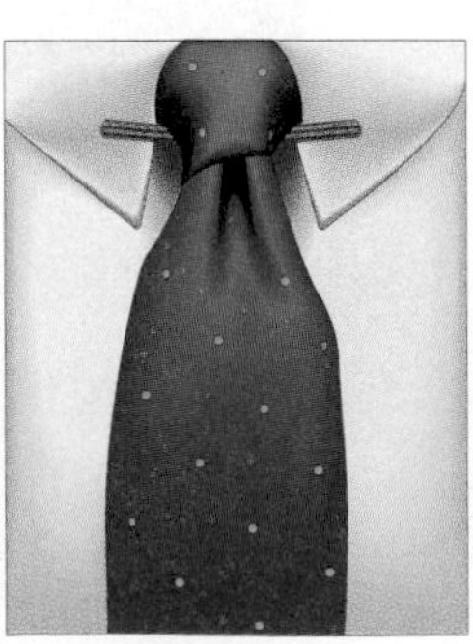

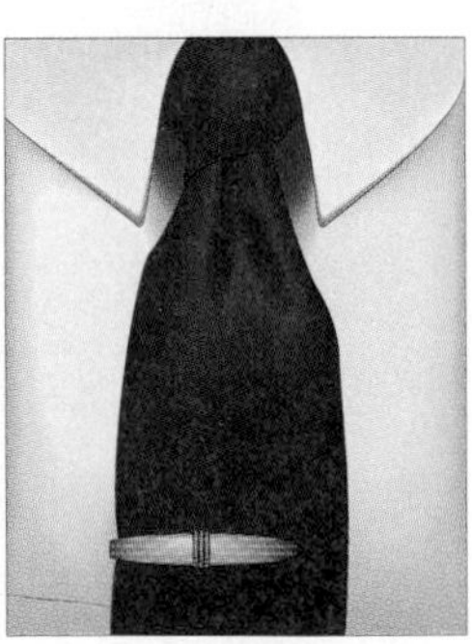

nameplate
placa^F de identificación^F

tiepin
alfiler^M de corbata^F

collar bar
yugo^M

tie bar
pisacorbatas^M

horseshoe
herradura^F

horn
cuerno^M

MANICURE
MANICURA^F

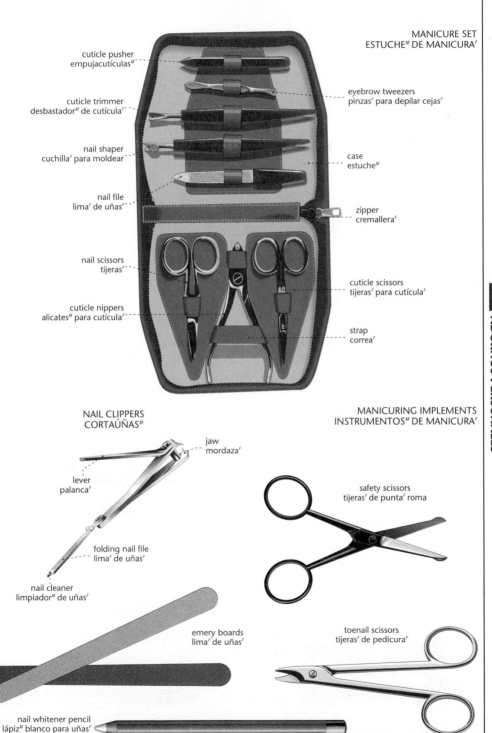

MANICURE SET
ESTUCHE^M DE MANICURA^F

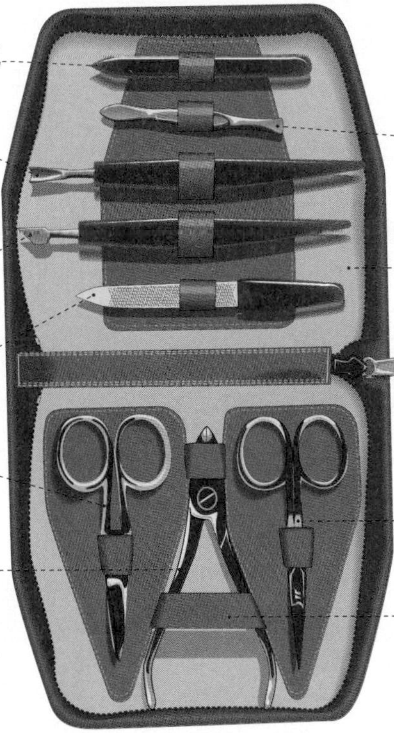

cuticle pusher
empujacutículas^M

eyebrow tweezers
pinzas^F para depilar cejas^F

cuticle trimmer
desbastador^M de cutícula^F

nail shaper
cuchilla^F para moldear

case
estuche^M

nail file
lima^F de uñas^F

zipper
cremallera^F

nail scissors
tijeras^F

cuticle scissors
tijeras^F para cutícula^F

cuticle nippers
alicates^M para cutícula^F

strap
correa^F

NAIL CLIPPERS
CORTAÚÑAS^M

MANICURING IMPLEMENTS
INSTRUMENTOS^M DE MANICURA^F

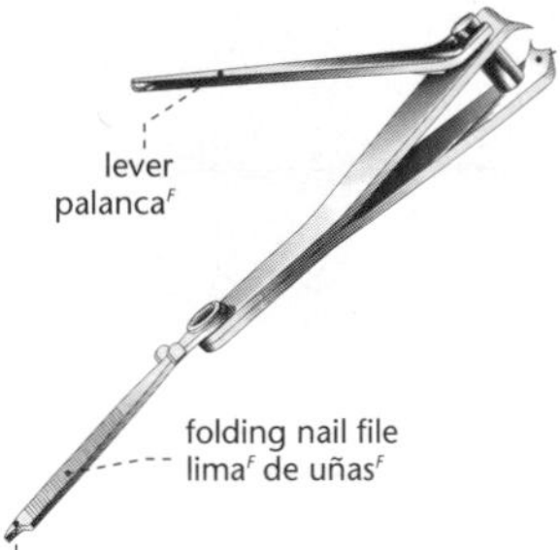

jaw
mordaza^F

lever
palanca^F

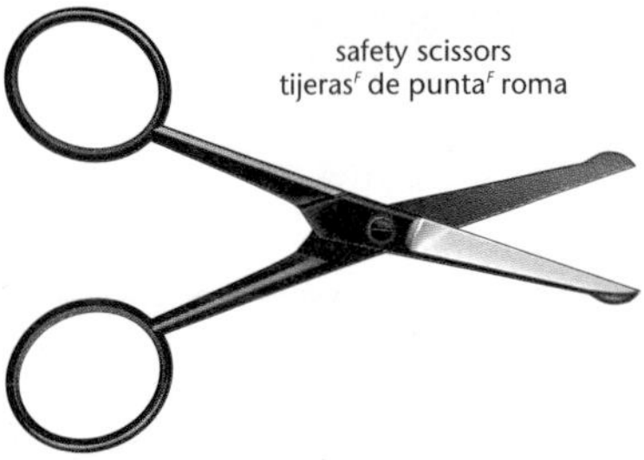

safety scissors
tijeras^F de punta^F roma

folding nail file
lima^F de uñas^F

nail cleaner
limpiador^M de uñas^F

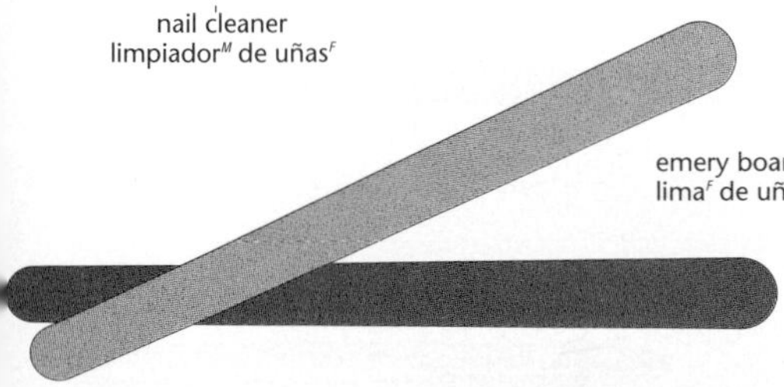

emery boards
lima^F de uñas^F

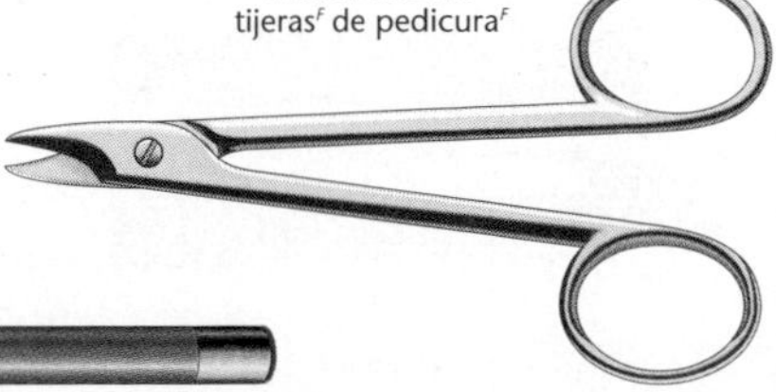

toenail scissors
tijeras^F de pedicura^F

nail whitener pencil
lápiz^M blanco para uñas^F

MAKEUP
MAQUILLAJE^M

FACIAL MAKEUP
MAQUILLAJE^M FACIAL

fan brush
brocha^F en forma^F de abanico^M

loose powder
polvos^M sueltos

loose powder brush
brocha^F

liquid foundation
base^F líquida

powder puff
borla^F

blusher brush
brocha^F aplicadora de rubor^M

compact
polvera^F

pressed powder
polvo^M compacto

powder blusher
rubor^M en polvo^M

LIP MAKEUP
MAQUILLAJE^M LABIAL

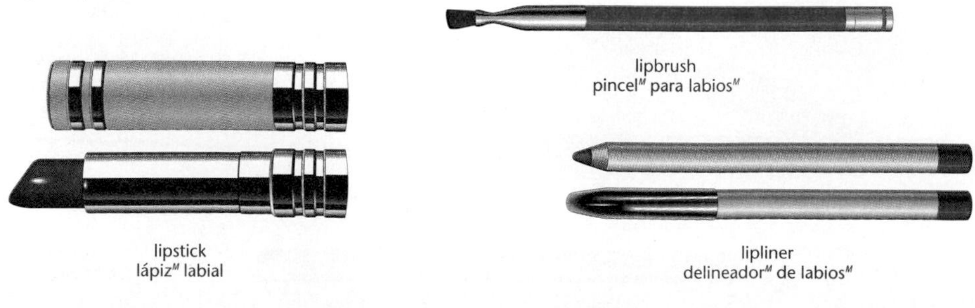

lipbrush
pincel^M para labios^M

lipstick
lápiz^M labial

lipliner
delineador^M de labios^M

366

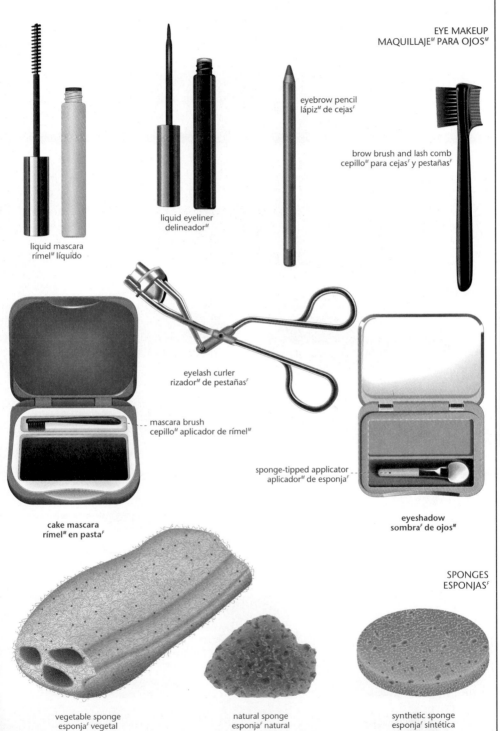

eyebrow pencil
lápiz^M de cejas^F

brow brush and lash comb
cepillo^M para cejas^F y pestañas^F

liquid eyeliner
delineador^M

liquid mascara
rímel^M líquido

eyelash curler
rizador^M de pestañas^F

mascara brush
cepillo^M aplicador de rímel^M

sponge-tipped applicator
aplicador^M de esponja^F

cake mascara
rímel^M en pasta^F

eyeshadow
sombra^F de ojos^M

SPONGES
ESPONJAS^F

vegetable sponge
esponja^F vegetal

natural sponge
esponja^F natural

synthetic sponge
esponja^F sintética

PERSONAL ADORNMENT
ADORNOS PERSONALES

367

eyebrow pencil
lápiz[M] de cejas[F]

brow brush and lash comb
cepillo[M] para cejas[F] y pestañas[F]

liquid eyeliner
delineador[M]

liquid mascara
rímel[M] líquido

eyelash curler
rizador[M] de pestañas[F]

mascara brush
cepillo[M] aplicador de rímel[M]

sponge-tipped applicator
aplicador[M] de esponja[F]

cake mascara
rímel[M] en pasta[F]

eyeshadow
sombra[F] de ojos[M]

SPONGES
ESPONJAS[F]

vegetable sponge
esponja[F] vegetal

natural sponge
esponja[F] natural

synthetic sponge
esponja[F] sintética

PERSONAL ADORNMENT
ADORNOS PERSONALES

367

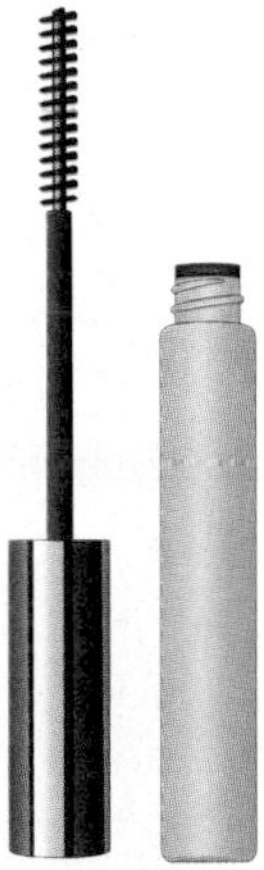

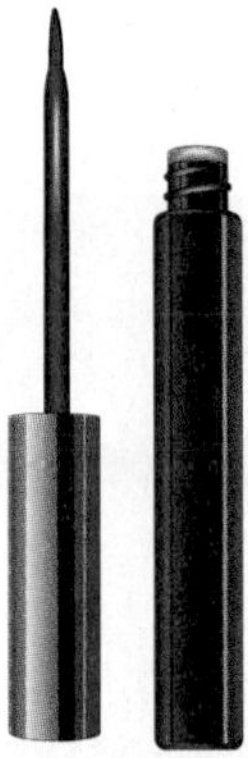

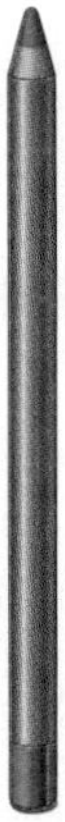

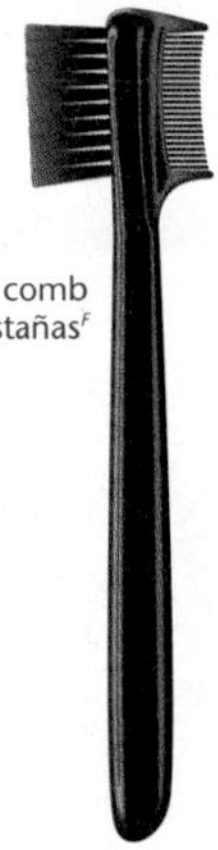

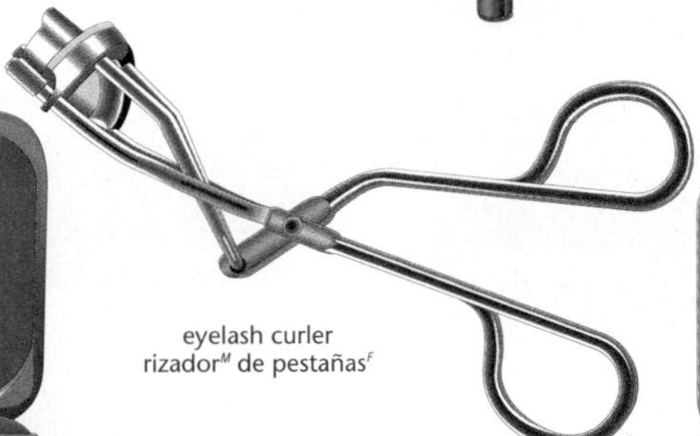

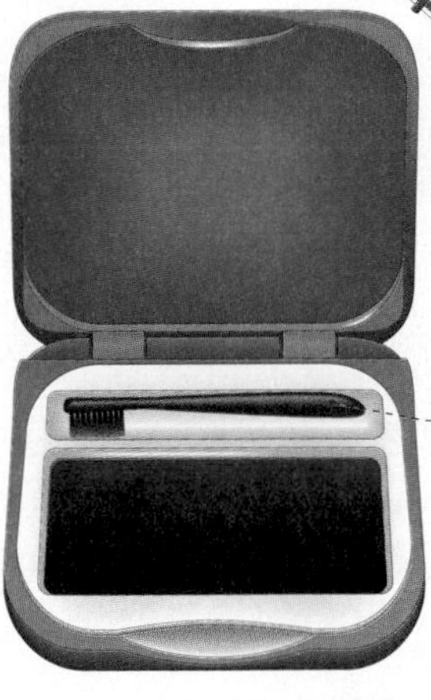

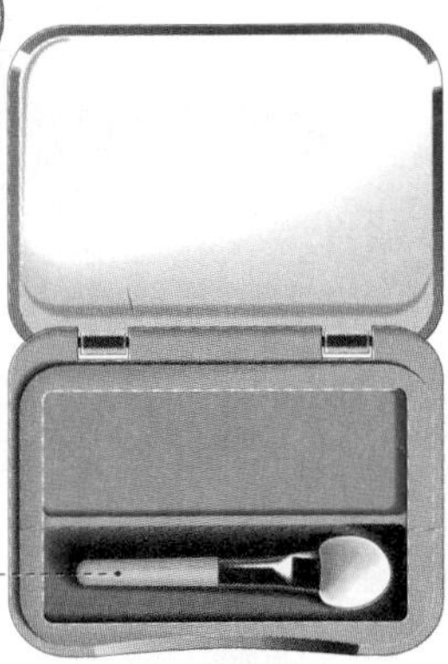

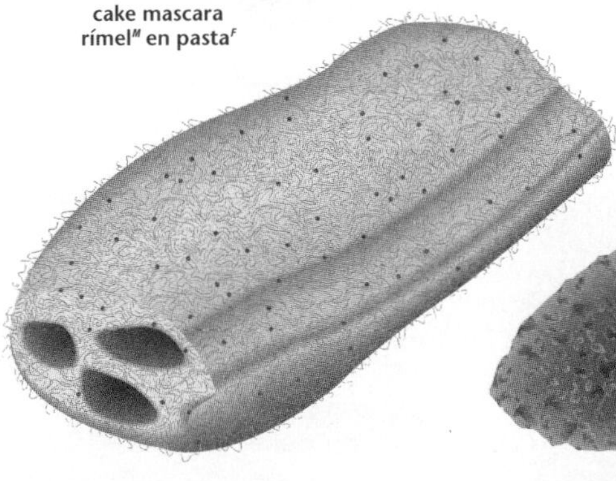

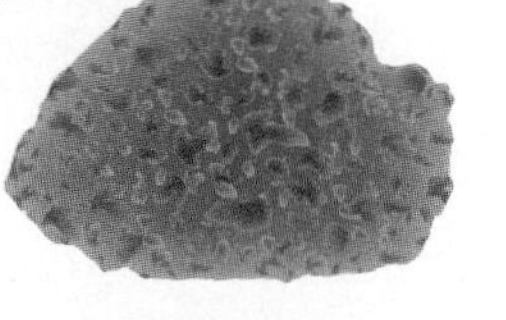

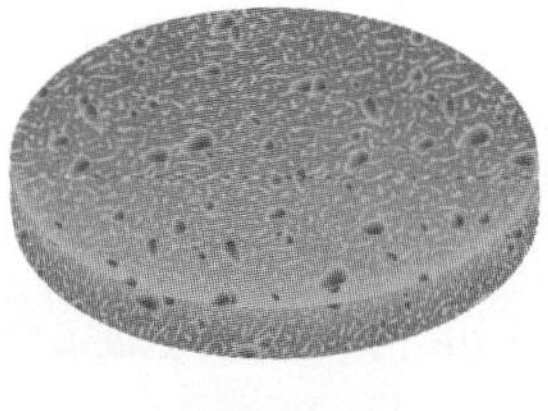

HAIRDRESSING
PEINADO^M

LIGHTED MIRROR
ESPEJO^M LUMINOSO

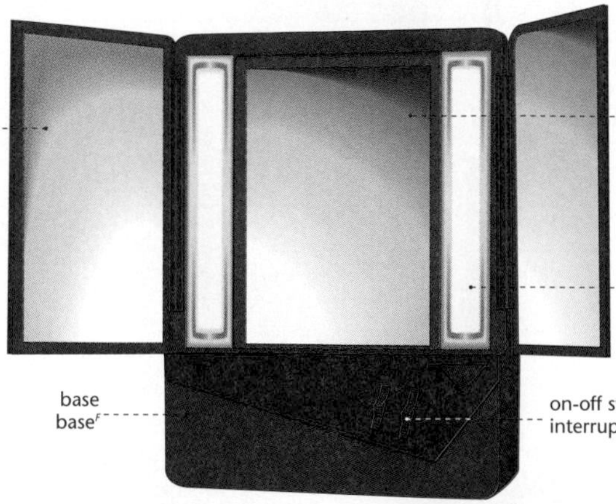

side mirror
espejo^M lateral

dual swivel mirror
espejo^M doble giratorio

lighting
iluminación^F

base
base^F

on-off switch
interruptor^M

HAIRBRUSHES
CEPILLOS^M

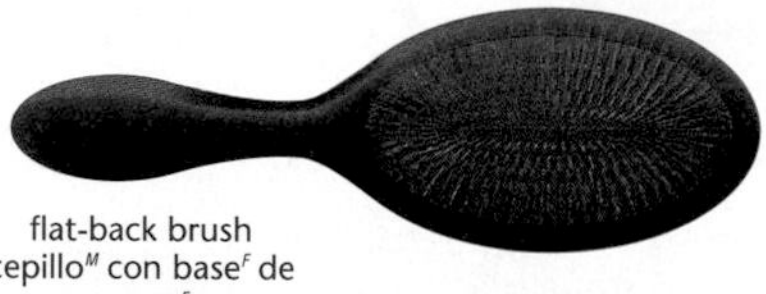

flat-back brush
cepillo^M con base^F de
goma^F

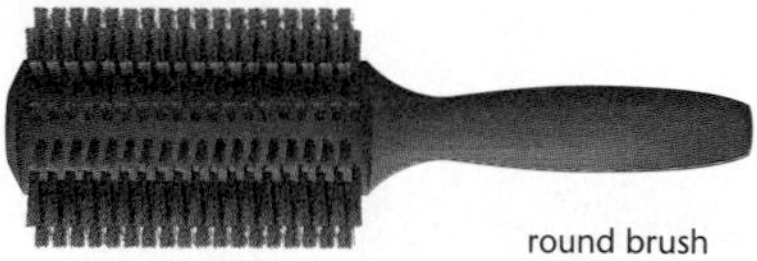

round brush
cepillo^M redondo

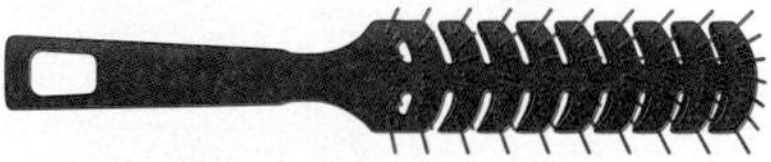

vent brush
cepillo^M metálico

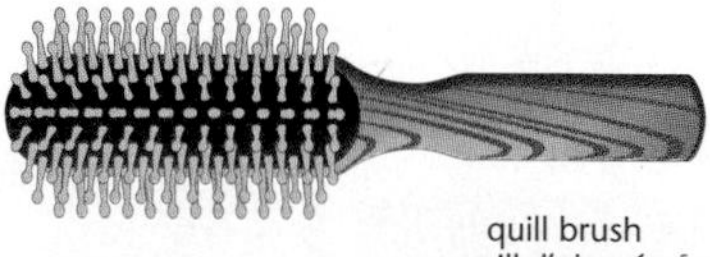

quill brush
cepillo^M de púas^F

COMBS
PEINES^M

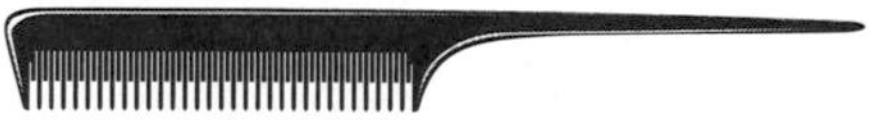

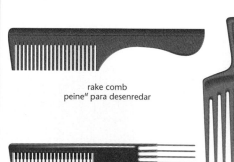

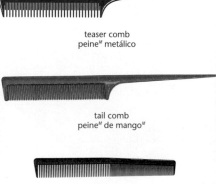

teaser comb
peine^M metálico

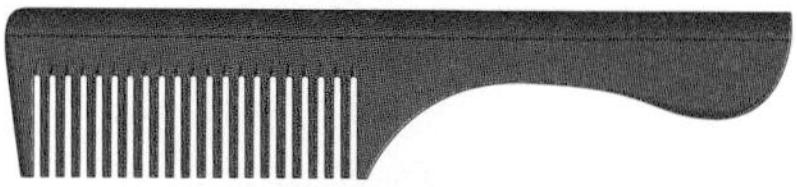

rake comb
peine^M para desenredar

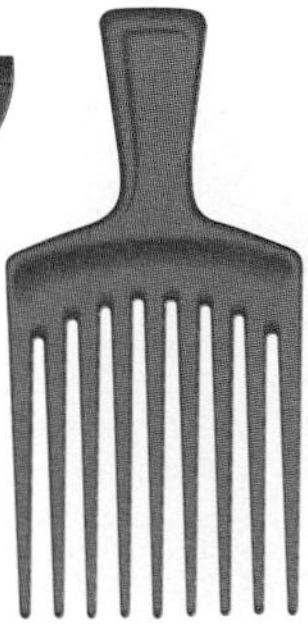

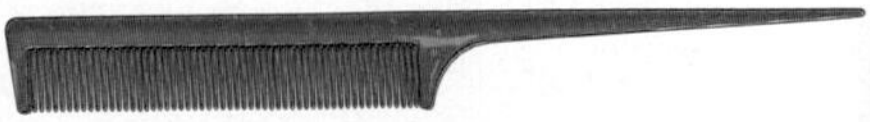

tail comb
peine^M de mango^M

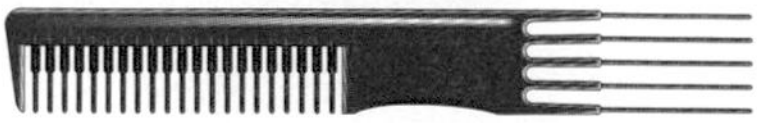

pitchfork comb
peine^M combinado^M

Afro pick
peine^M tenedor^M

barber comb
peine^M de peluquero^M

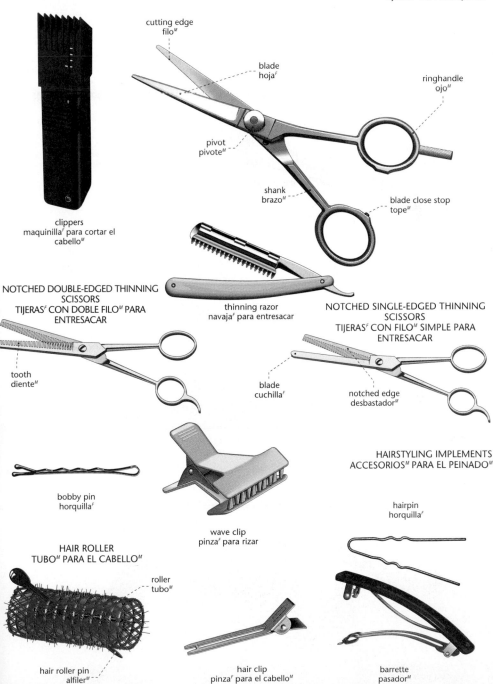

HAIRCUTTING SCISSORS
TIJERAS^F DE PELUQUERO^M

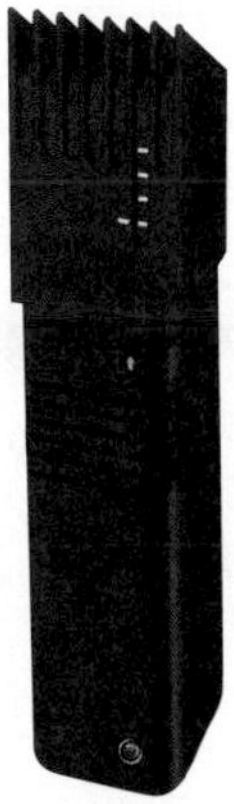

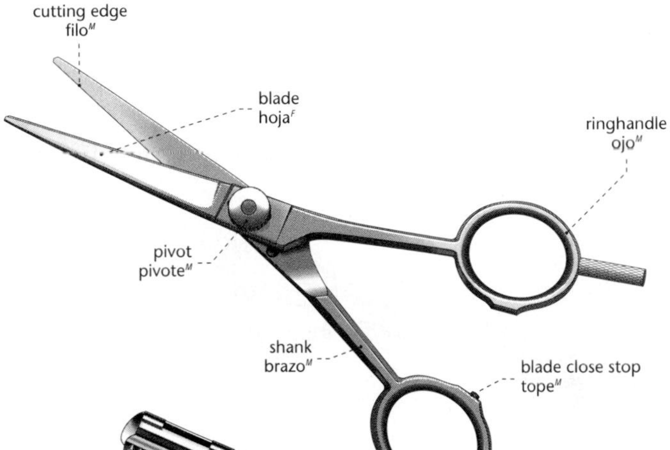

cutting edge
filo^M

blade
hoja^F

ringhandle
ojo^M

pivot
pivote^M

shank
brazo^M

blade close stop
tope^M

clippers
maquinilla^F para cortar el
cabello^M

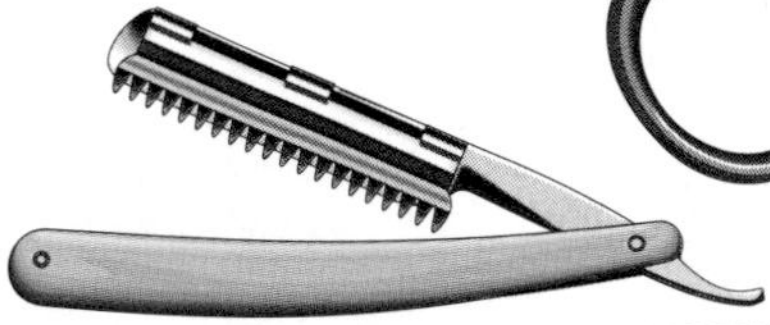

thinning razor
navaja^F para entresacar

NOTCHED DOUBLE-EDGED THINNING
SCISSORS
TIJERAS^F CON DOBLE FILO^M PARA
ENTRESACAR

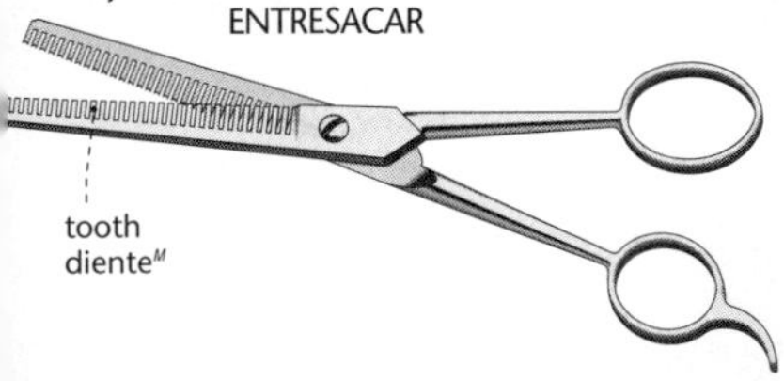

NOTCHED SINGLE-EDGED THINNING
SCISSORS
TIJERAS^F CON FILO^M SIMPLE PARA
ENTRESACAR

tooth
diente^M

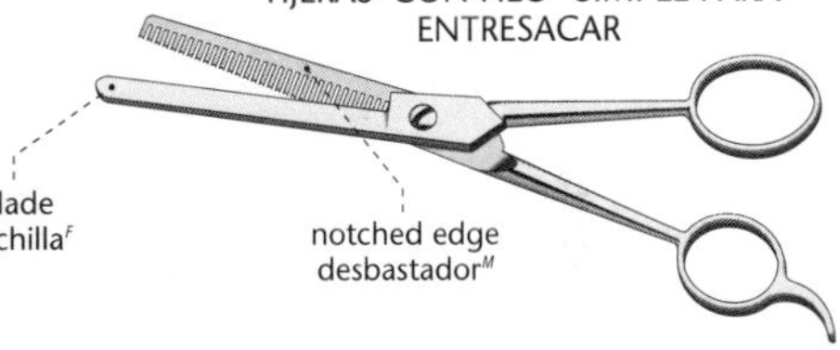

blade
cuchilla^F

notched edge
desbastador^M

HAIRSTYLING IMPLEMENTS
ACCESORIOS^M PARA EL PEINADO^M

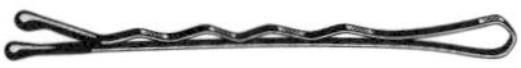

bobby pin
horquilla^F

hairpin
horquilla^F

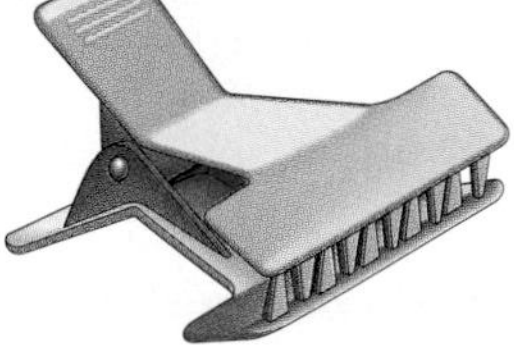

wave clip
pinza^F para rizar

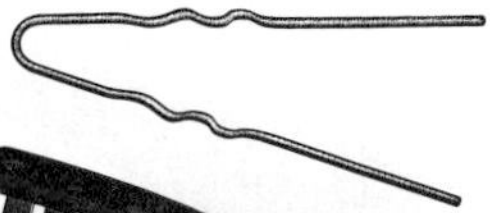

HAIR ROLLER
TUBO^M PARA EL CABELLO^M

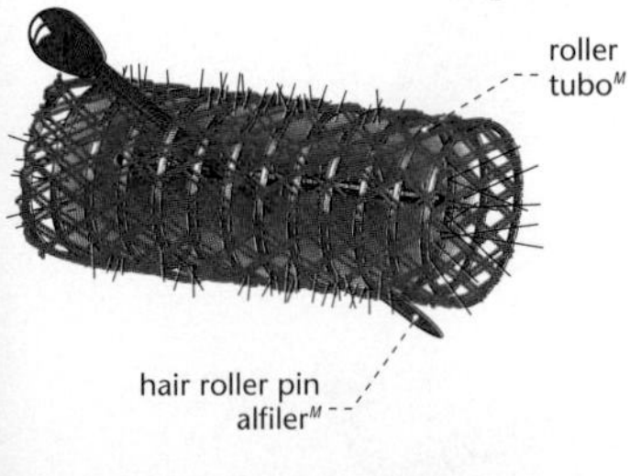

roller
tubo^M

hair roller pin
alfiler^M

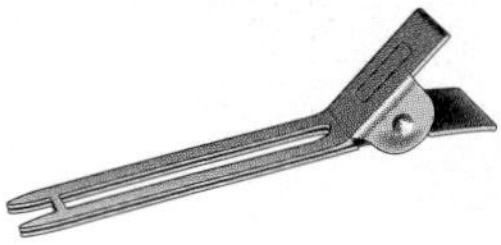

hair clip
pinza^F para el cabello^M

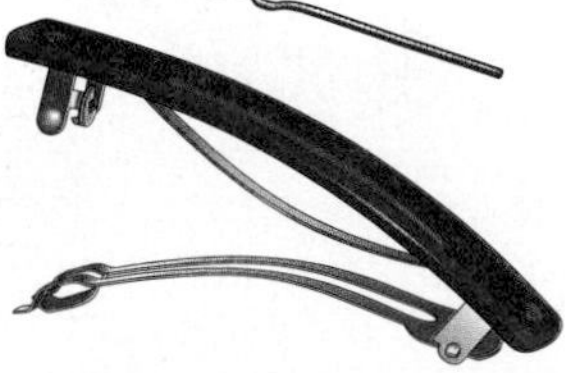

barrette
pasador^M

CURLING IRON
PINZA^F RIZADORA

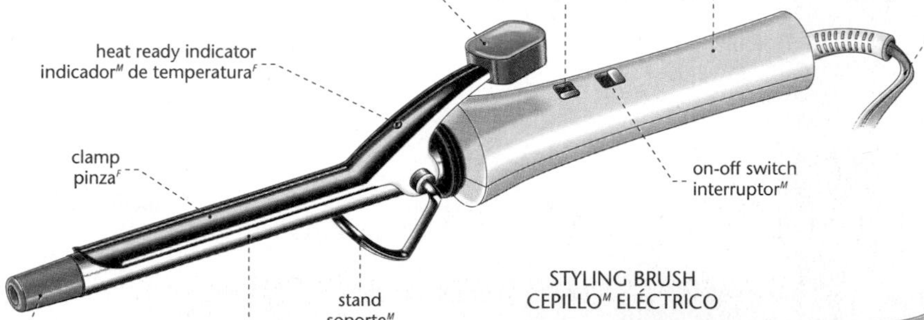

handle
mango^M

clamp lever
palanca^F

on-off indicator
luz^F piloto^M

swivel cord
cable^M giratorio

heat ready indicator
indicador^M de temperatura^F

clamp
pinza^F

on-off switch
interruptor^M

cool tip
punta^F de plástico^M

stand
soporte^M

STYLING BRUSH
CEPILLO^M ELÉCTRICO

barrel
varilla^F rizadora

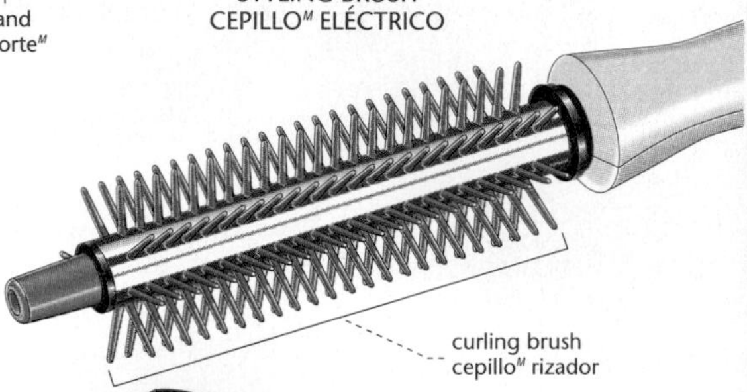

curling brush
cepillo^M rizador

HAIR DRYER
SECADOR^F MANUAL

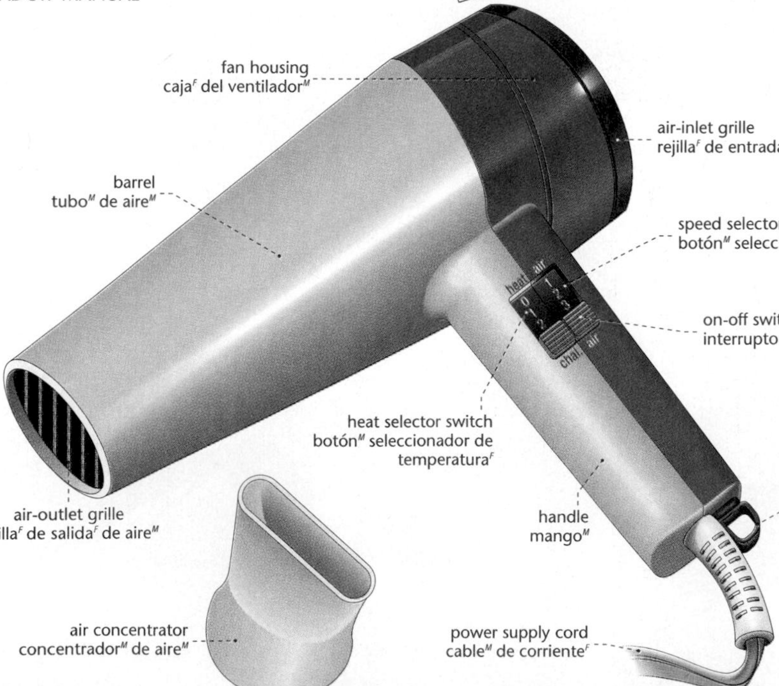

fan housing
caja^F del ventilador^M

air-inlet grille
rejilla^F de entrada^F de aire^M

barrel
tubo^M de aire^M

speed selector switch
botón^M seleccionador de velocidad^F

on-off switch
interruptor^M

heat selector switch
botón^M seleccionador de
temperatura^F

hang-up ring
trabilla^F

air-outlet grille
rejilla^F de salida^F de aire^M

handle
mango^M

air concentrator
concentrador^M de aire^M

power supply cord
cable^M de corriente^F

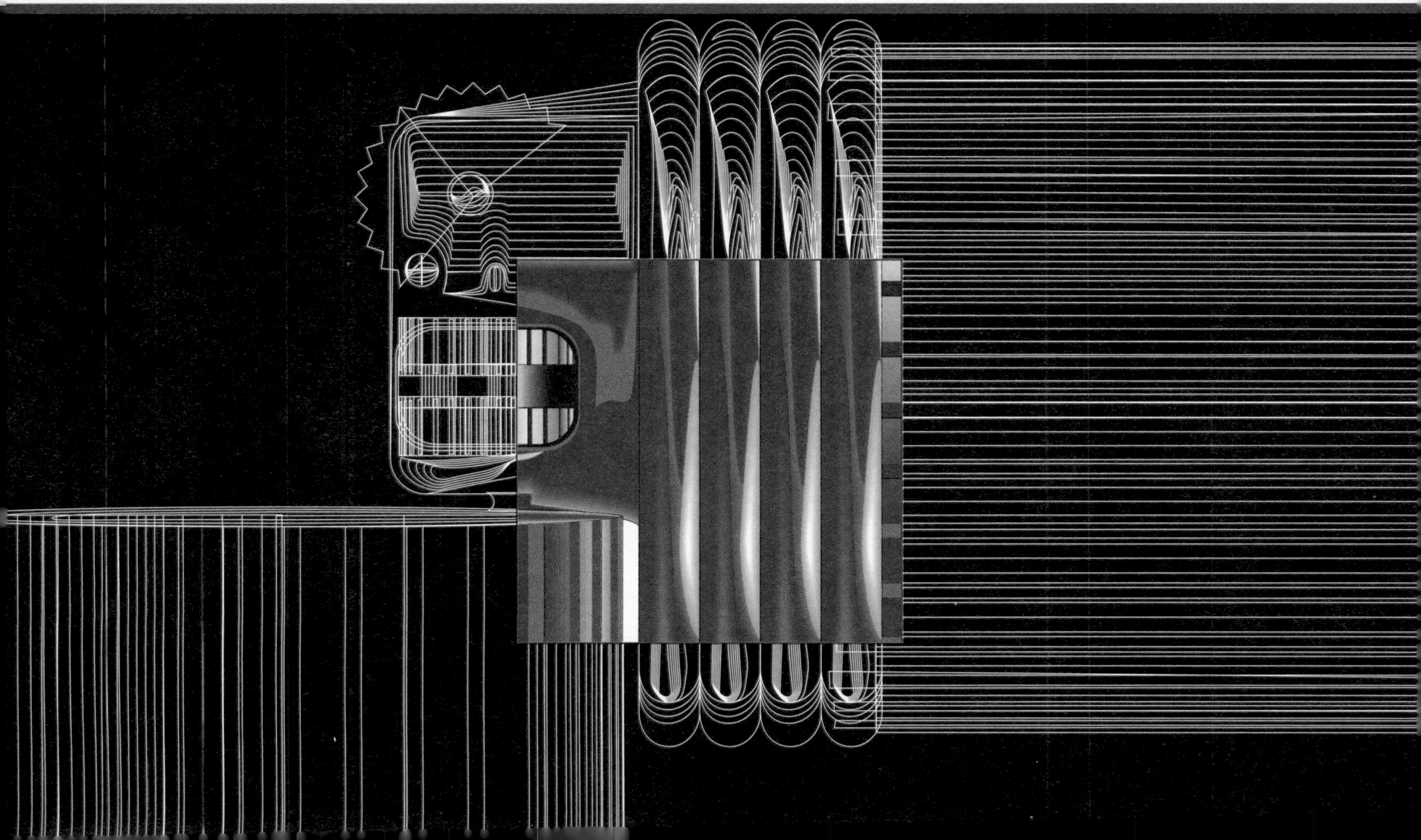

CONTENTS

**PERSONAL ARTICLES
ARTÍCULOS PERSONALES**

DENTAL CARE
HIGIENE^F DENTAL

TOOTHBRUSH
CEPILLO^M DE DIENTES^M

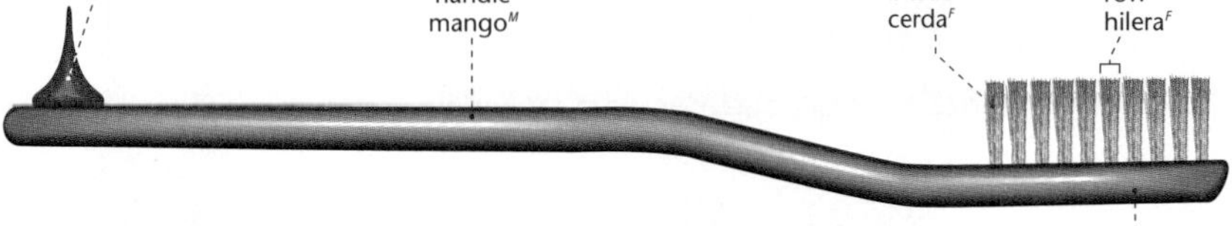

stimulator tip
estimulador^M de encías^F

handle
mango^M

bristle
cerda^F

row
hilera^F

head
cabeza^F hexagonal

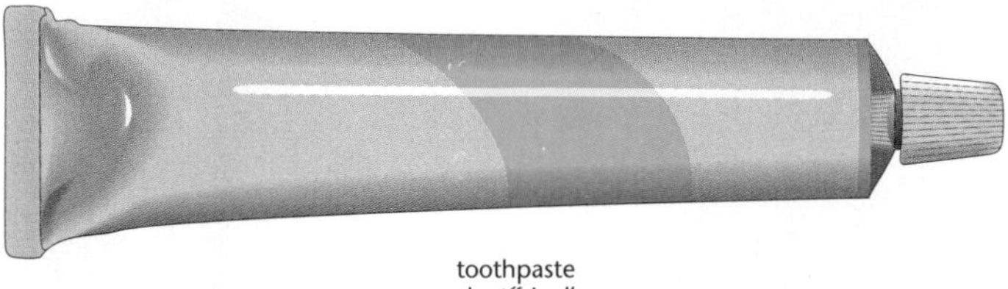

toothpaste
dentífrico^M

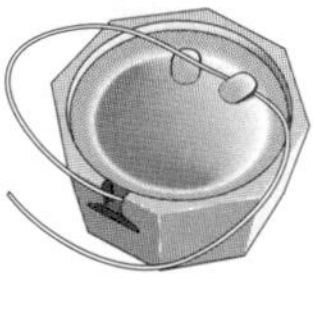

dental floss
hilo^M dental

ORAL HYGIENE CENTER
CEPILLO^M DE DIENTES^M ELÉCTRICO

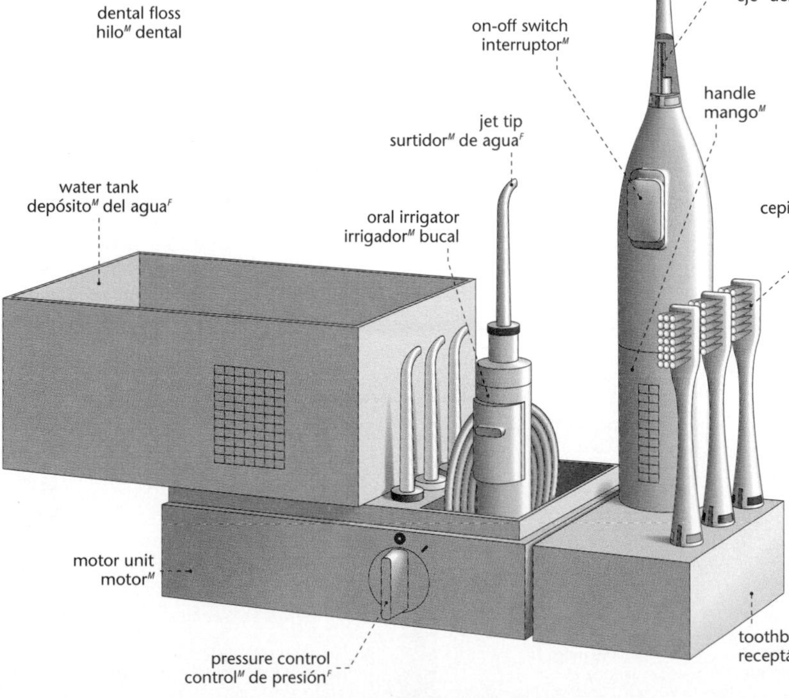

brush
cepillo^M

toothbrush shaft
eje^M del cepillo^M

on-off switch
interruptor^M

handle
mango^M

jet tip
surtidor^M de agua^F

toothbrush
cepillo^M de dientes^M

water tank
depósito^M del agua^F

oral irrigator
irrigador^M bucal

motor unit
motor^M

pressure control
control^M de presión^F

toothbrush well
receptáculo^M del cepillo^M

PERSONAL ARTICLES
ARTÍCULOS PERSONALES

373

RAZORS
RASURADORAS^F

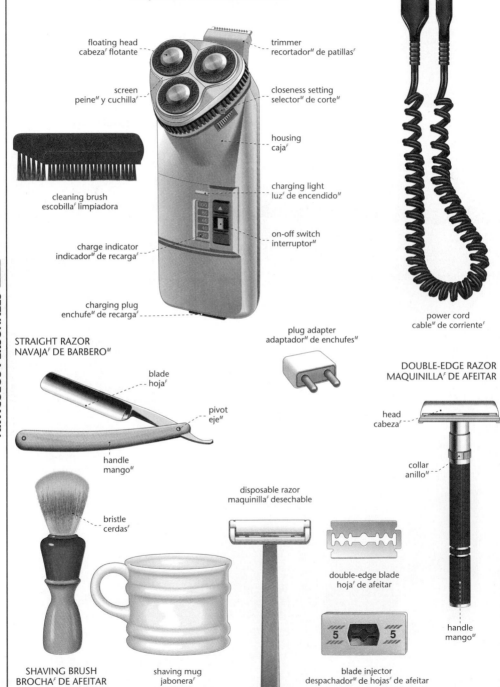

ELECTRIC RAZOR
MAQUINILLA^F DE AFEITAR ELÉCTRICA

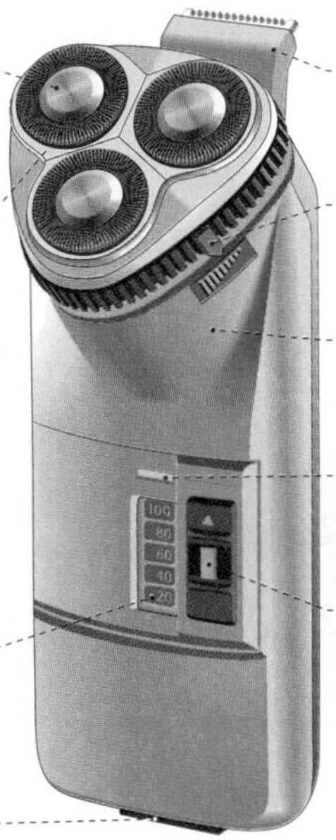

floating head
cabeza^F flotante

trimmer
recortador^M de patillas^F

screen
peine^M y cuchilla^F

closeness setting
selector^M de corte^M

housing
caja^F

charging light
luz^F de encendido^M

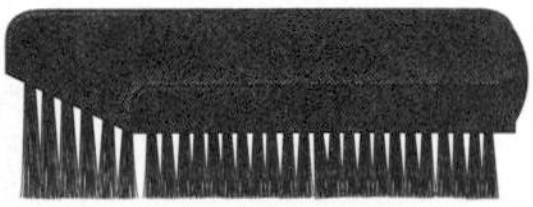

cleaning brush
escobilla^F limpiadora

on-off switch
interruptor^M

charge indicator
indicador^M de recarga^F

charging plug
enchufe^M de recarga^F

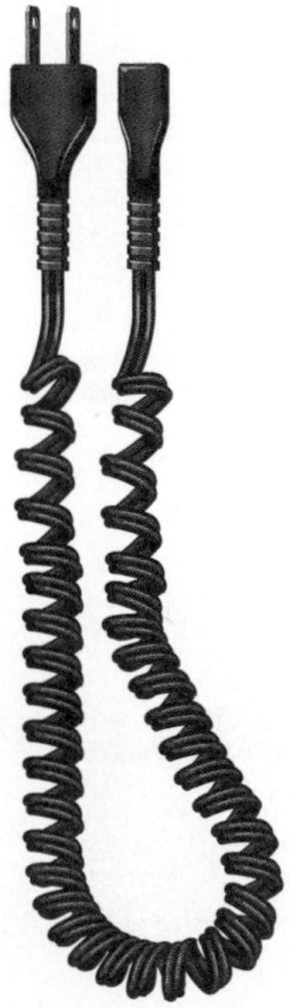

power cord
cable^M de corriente^F

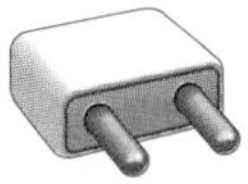

STRAIGHT RAZOR
NAVAJA^F DE BARBERO^M

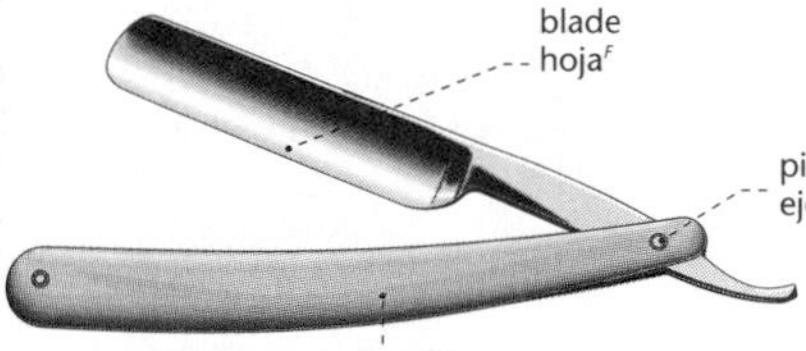

blade
hoja^F

pivot
eje^M

handle
mango^M

plug adapter
adaptador^M de enchufes^M

DOUBLE-EDGE RAZOR
MAQUINILLA^F DE AFEITAR

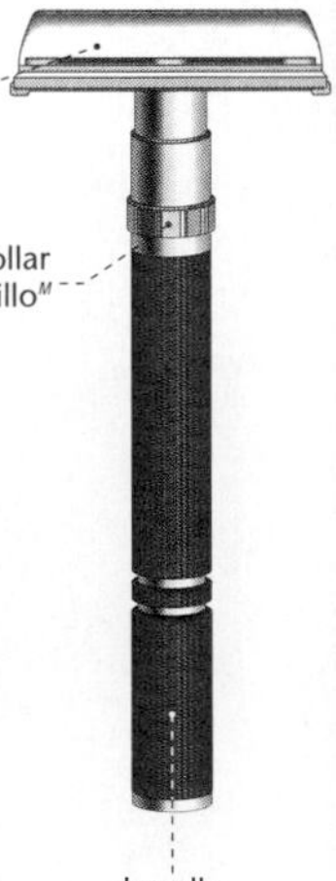

head
cabeza^F

collar
anillo^M

bristle
cerdas^F

disposable razor
maquinilla^F desechable

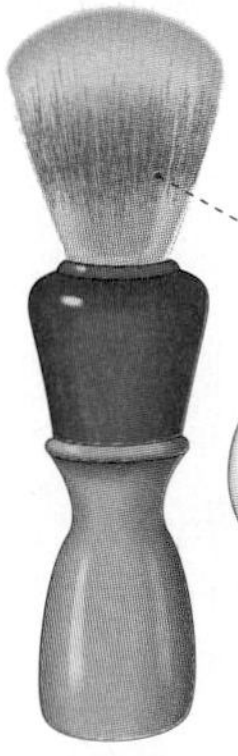

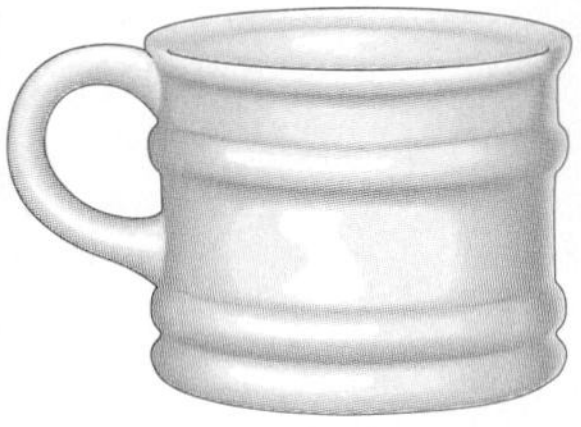

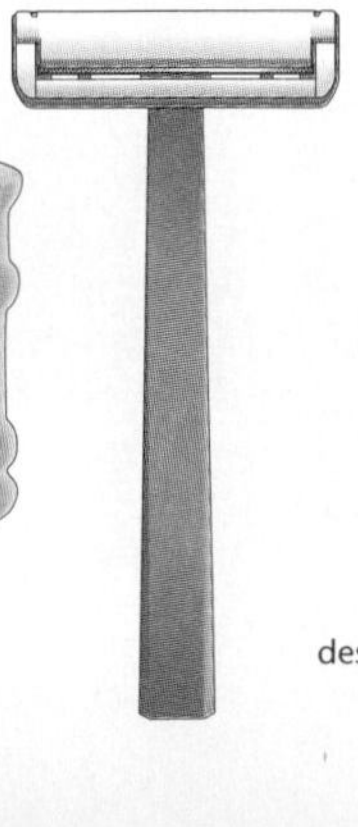

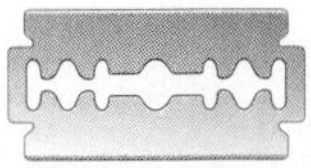

double-edge blade
hoja^F de afeitar

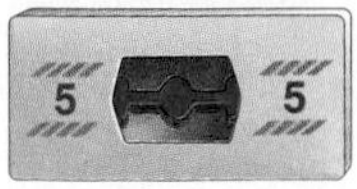

handle
mango^M

SHAVING BRUSH
BROCHA^F DE AFEITAR

shaving mug
jabonera^F

blade injector
despachador^M de hojas^F de afeitar

UMBRELLA AND STICK
PARAGUAS^M Y BASTONES^M

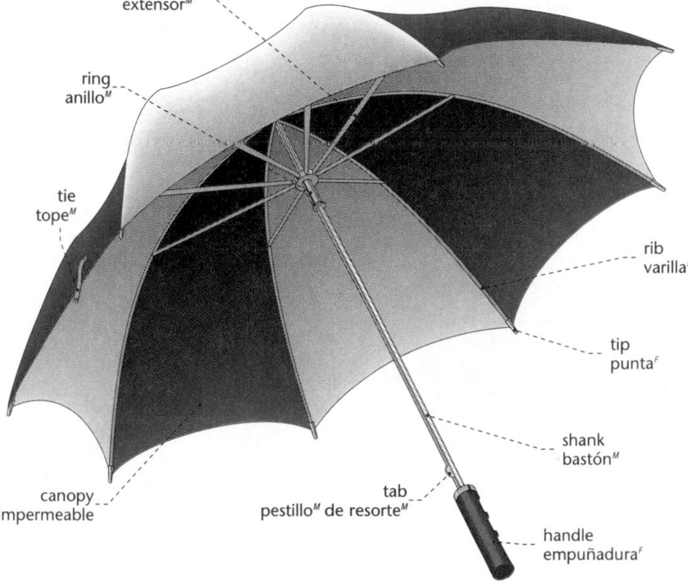

spreader
extensor^M

ring
anillo^M

tie
tope^M

rib
varilla^F

tip
punta^F

shank
bastón^M

canopy
tela^F impermeable

tab
pestillo^M de resorte^M

handle
empuñadura^F

TELESCOPIC UMBRELLA
PARAGUAS^M PLEGABLE

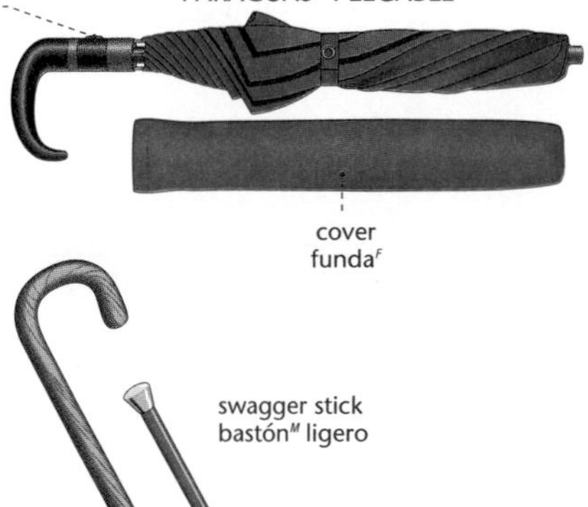

push button
botón^M de presión^F

STICK UMBRELLA
PARAGUAS^M DE BASTÓN^M

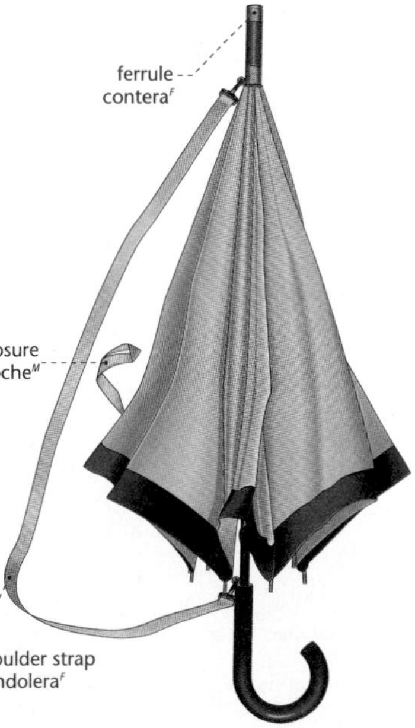

cover
funda^F

ferrule
contera^F

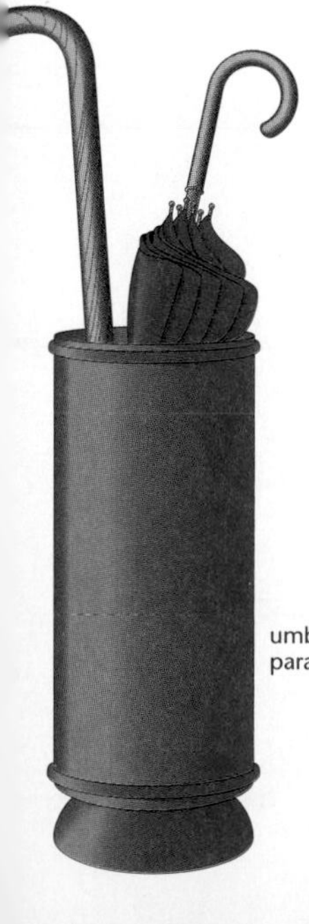

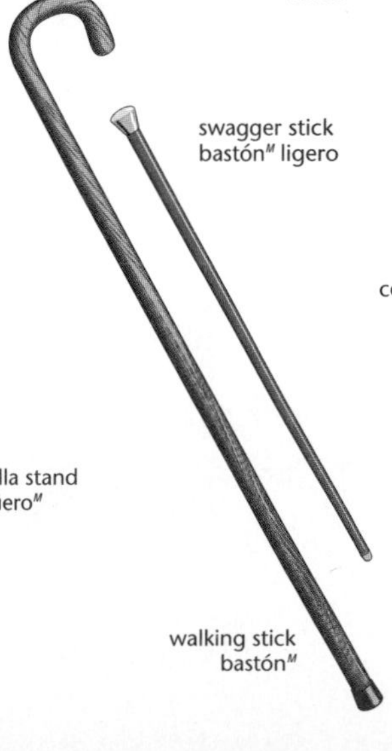

swagger stick
bastón^M ligero

tie closure
correa^F con broche^M

umbrella stand
paragüero^M

shoulder strap
bandolera^F

walking stick
bastón^M

375

EYEGLASSES
GAFAS^F

EYEGLASSES PARTS
GAFAS^F: PARTES^F

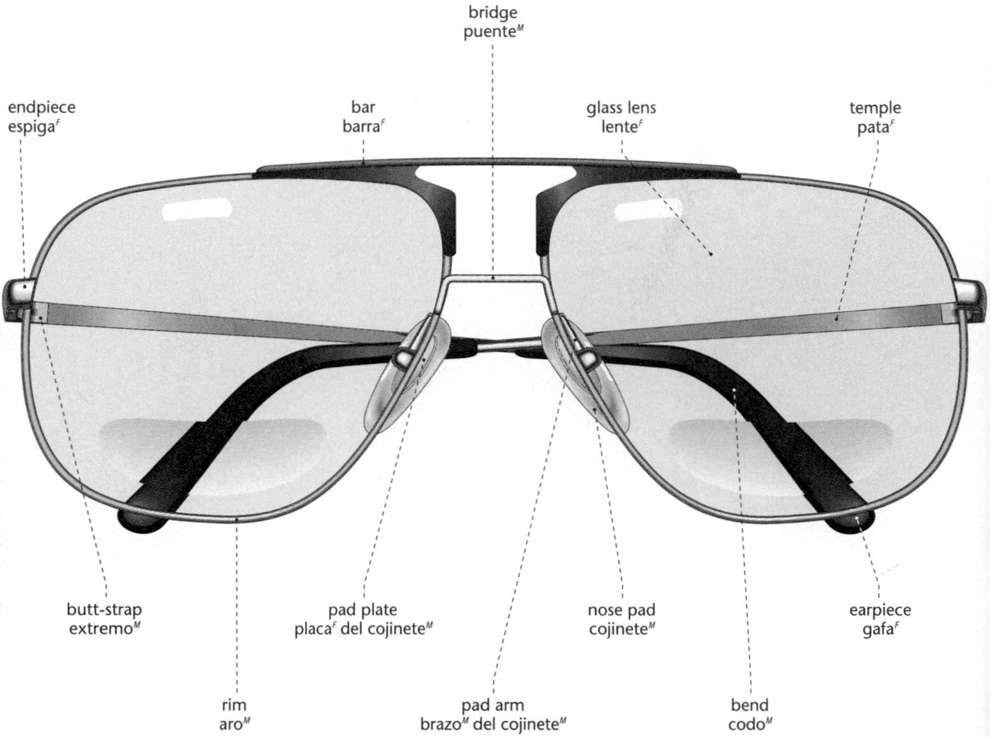

bridge
puente^M

endpiece
espiga^F

bar
barra^F

glass lens
lente^F

temple
pata^F

butt-strap
extremo^M

pad plate
placa^F del cojinete^M

nose pad
cojinete^M

earpiece
gafa^F

rim
aro^M

pad arm
brazo^M del cojinete^M

bend
codo^M

BIFOCAL LENS
LENTE^F BIFOCAL

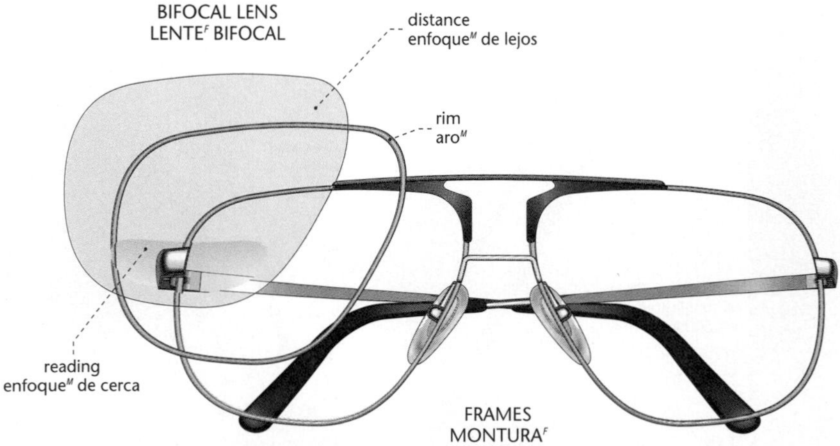

distance
enfoque^M de lejos

rim
aro^M

reading
enfoque^M de cerca

FRAMES
MONTURA^F

376

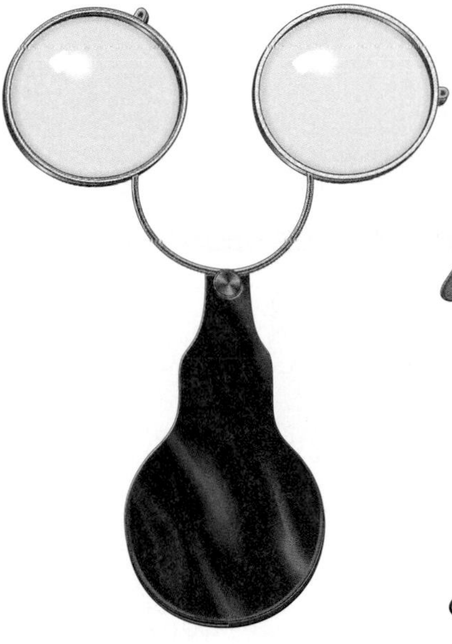

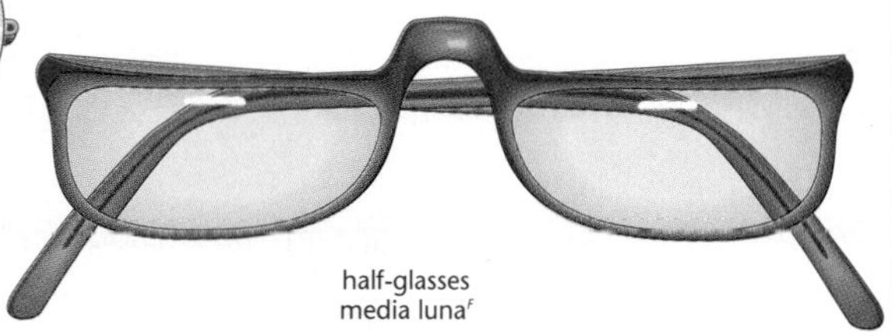

half-glasses
media luna^F

scissors-glasses
binóculos^M de tijera^F

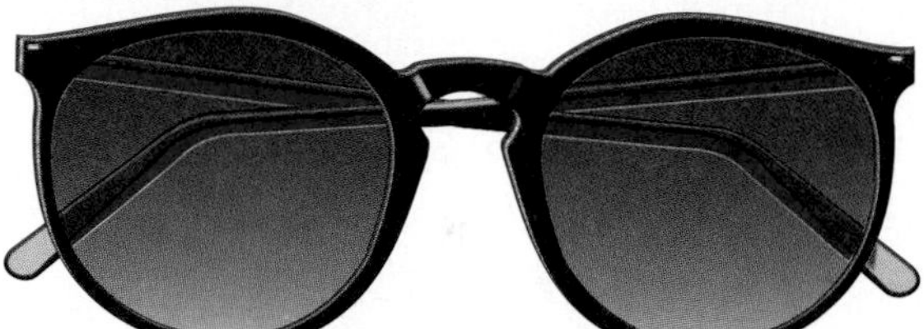

sunglasses
gafas^F de sol^M

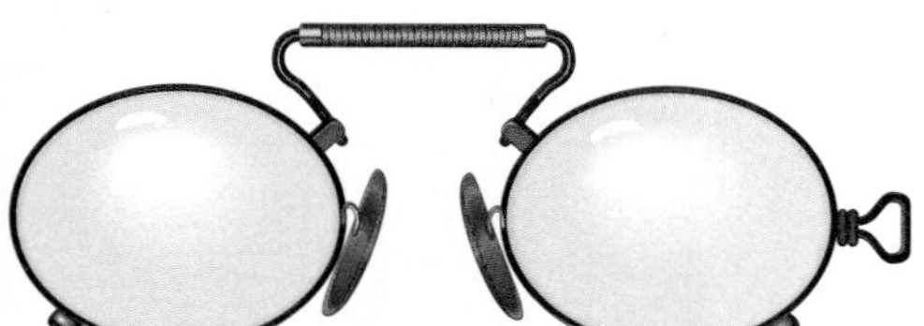

pince-nez
quevedos^M

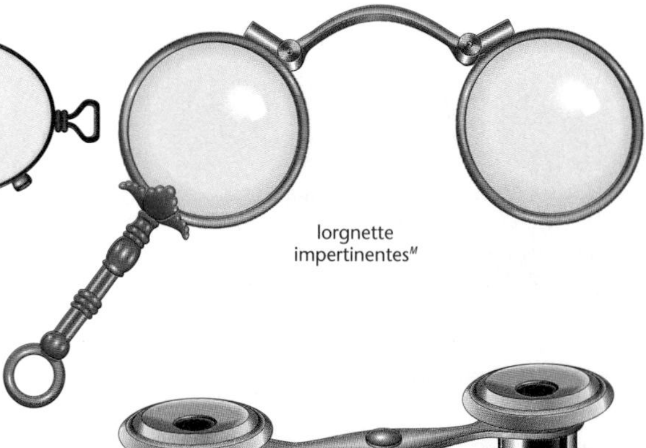

lorgnette
impertinentes^M

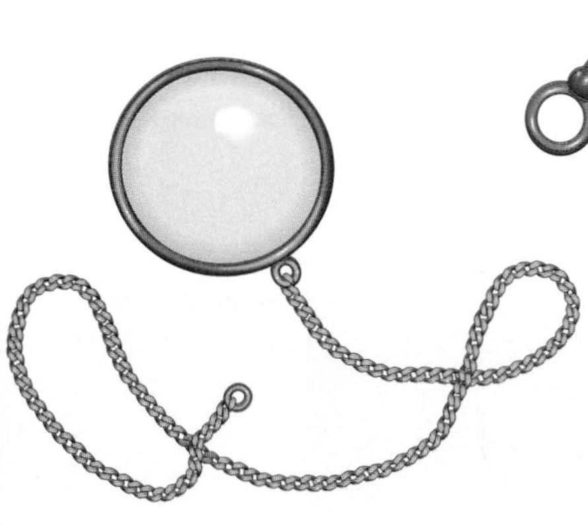

monocle
monóculo^M

opera glasses
gemelos^M de teatro^M

PERSONAL ARTICLES
ARTÍCULOS PERSONALES

377

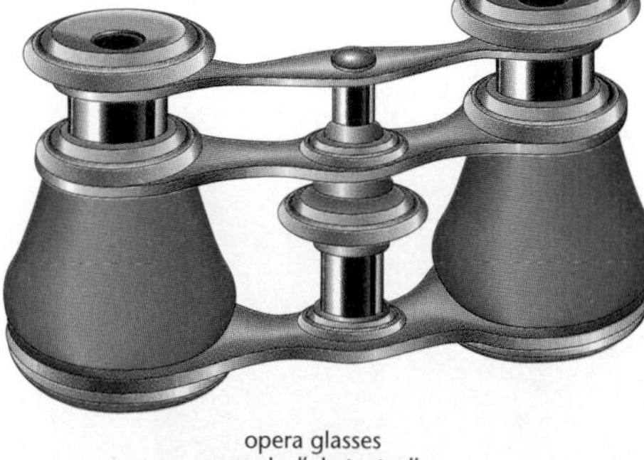

LEATHER GOODS
ARTÍCULOS^M DE PIEL^F

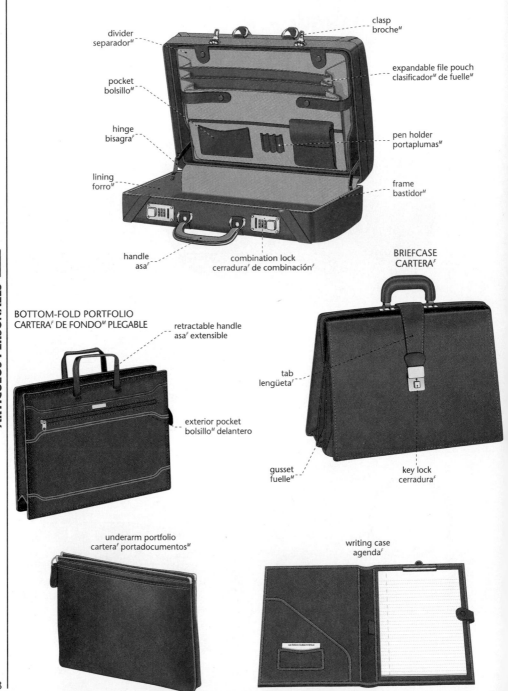

ATTACHÉ CASE
MALETÍN^M

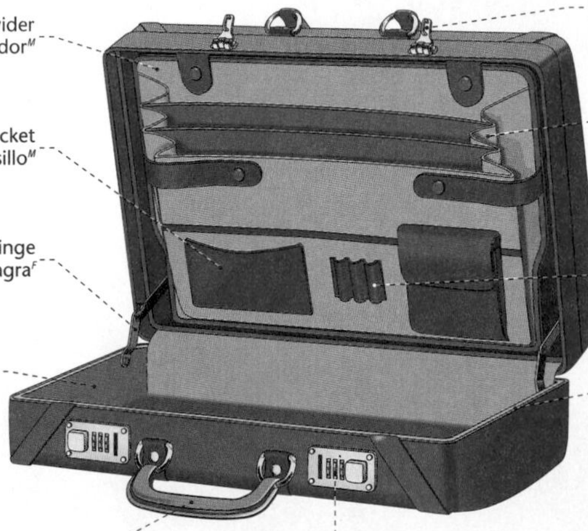

divider
separador^M

clasp
broche^M

pocket
bolsillo^M

expandable file pouch
clasificador^M de fuelle^M

hinge
bisagra^F

pen holder
portaplumas^M

lining
forro^M

frame
bastidor^M

handle
asa^F

combination lock
cerradura^F de combinación^F

BRIEFCASE
CARTERA^F

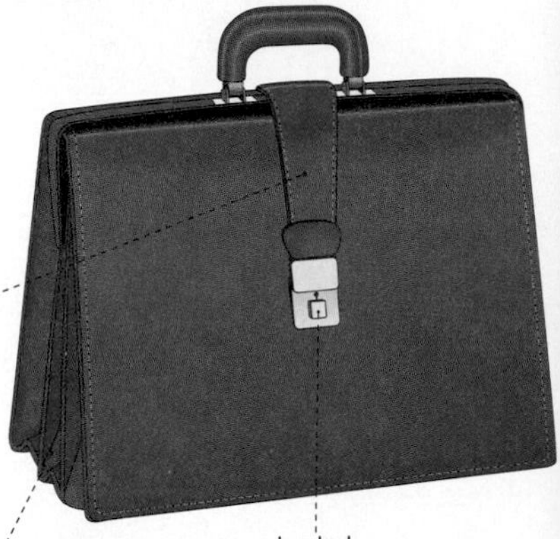

BOTTOM-FOLD PORTFOLIO
CARTERA^F DE FONDO^M PLEGABLE

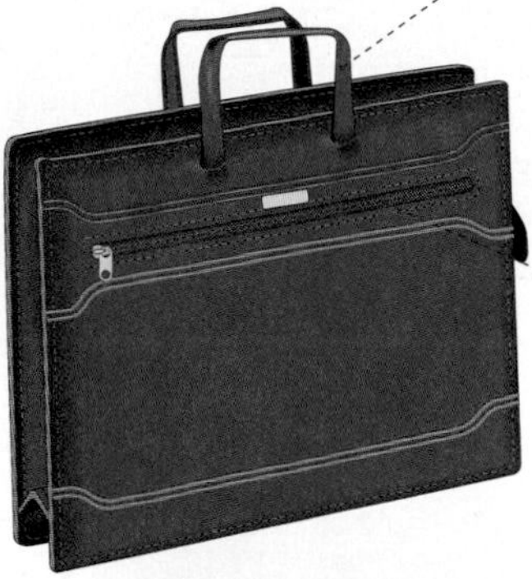

retractable handle
asa^F extensible

tab
lengüeta^F

exterior pocket
bolsillo^M delantero

gusset
fuelle^M

key lock
cerradura^F

underarm portfolio
cartera^F portadocumentos^M

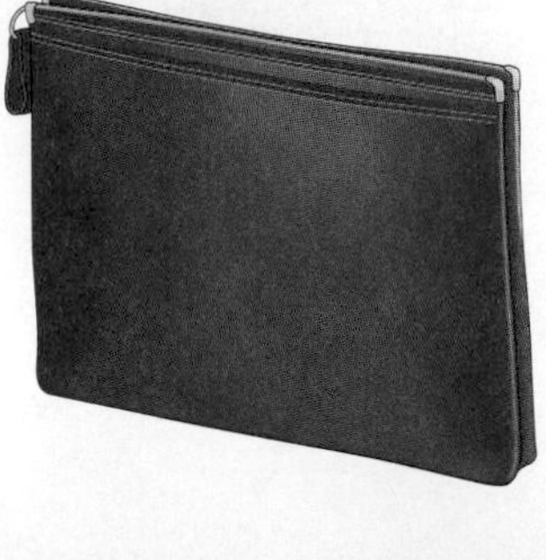

writing case
agenda^F

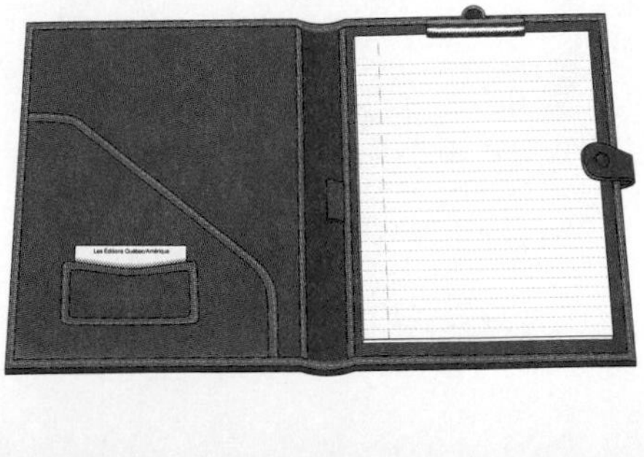

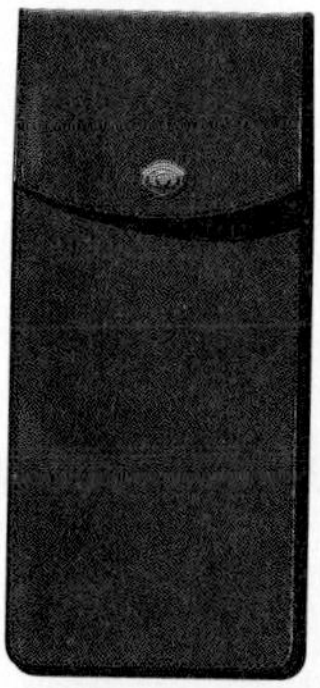

eyeglasses case
fundaᶠ para gafasᶠ

trimming
fileteᴹ

card case
tarjeteroᴹ

calculator
calculadoraᶠ

pen holder
portaplumasᴹ

hidden pocket
bolsilloᴹ secreto

checkbook
talonarioᴹ de chequesᴹ

CARD CASE
TARJETEROᴹ

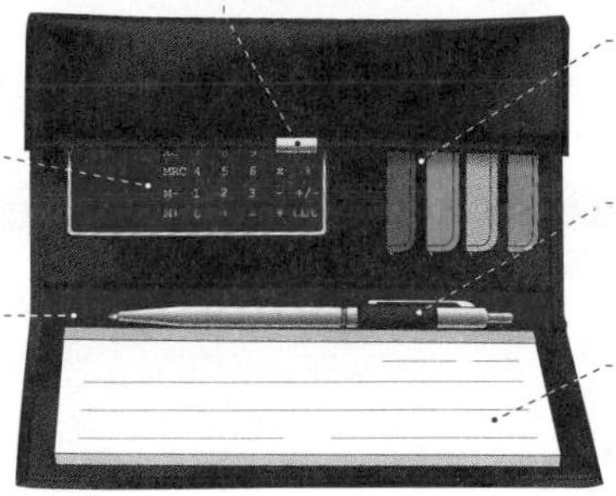

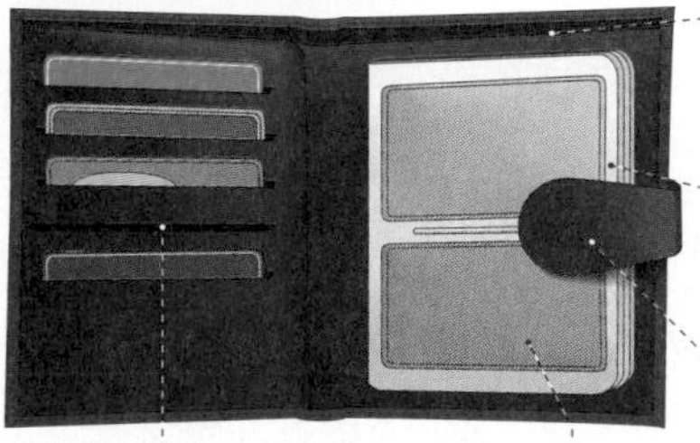

bill compartment
billeteraᶠ

key case
llaveroᴹ

windows
plásticosᴹ transparentes

tab
lengüetaᶠ

slot
ranuraᶠ

window
plásticoᴹ transparente

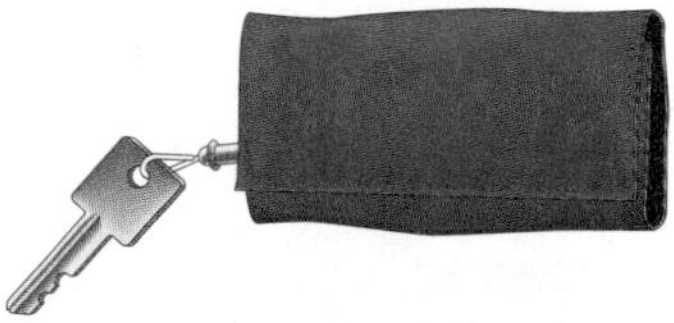

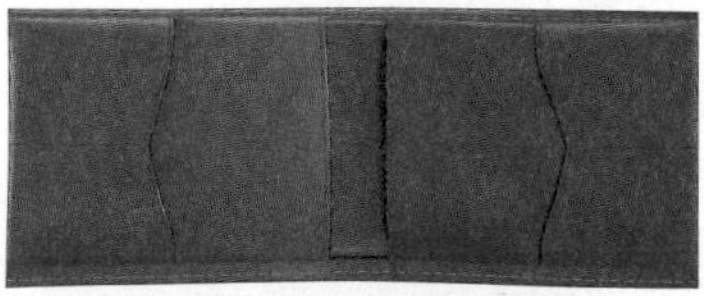

billfold
billeteraᶠ

purse
monederoᴹ

wallet
billeteraᶠ

checkbook
talonarioᴹ de chequesᴹ

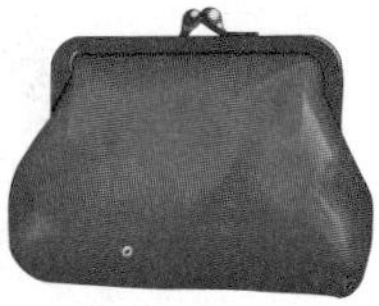

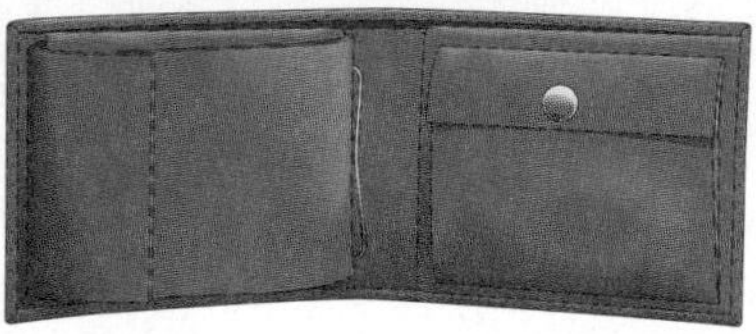

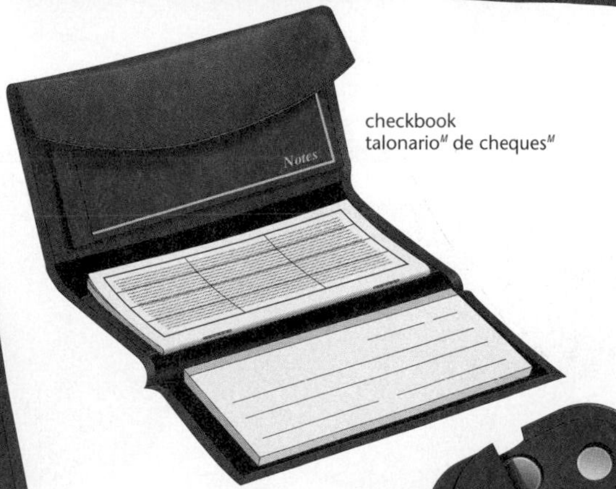

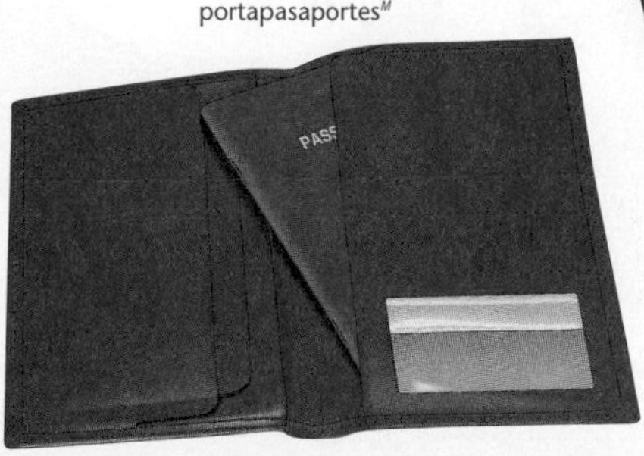

passport case
portapasaportesᴹ

coin purse
portamonedasᴹ

PERSONAL ARTICLES
ARTÍCULOS PERSONALES

379

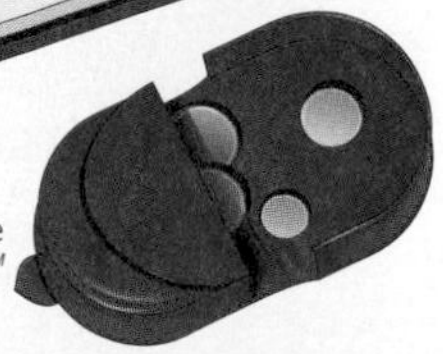

men's bag
bolso^M de hombre^M

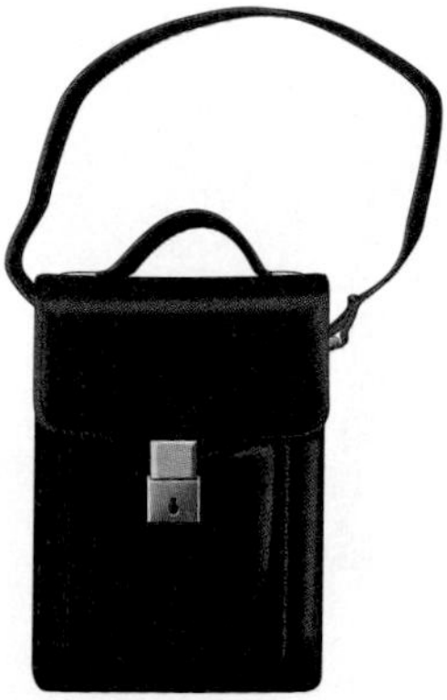

SATCHEL BAG
BOLSO^M CLÁSICO

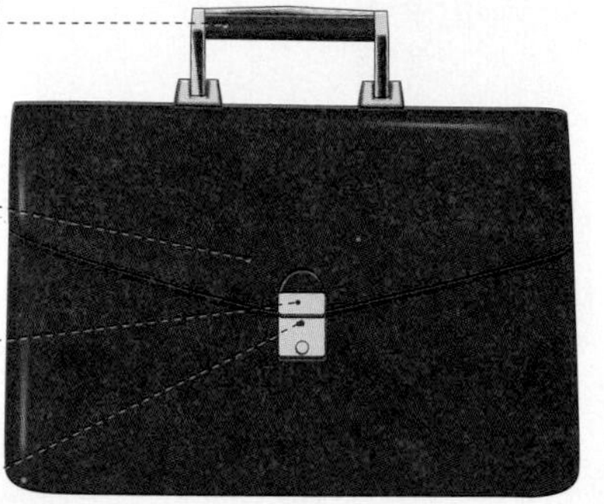

handle
mango^M

flap
ala^F

clasp
broche^M

lock
cierre^M

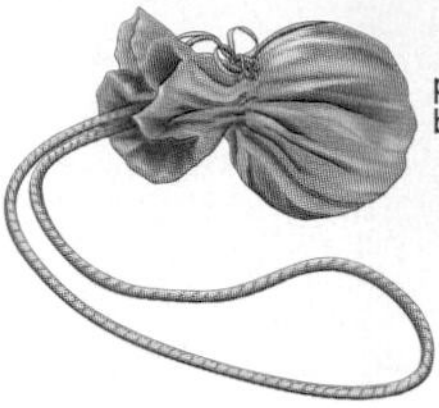

pouch
bolsita^F de cordones^M

SHOULDER BAG
BOLSO^M

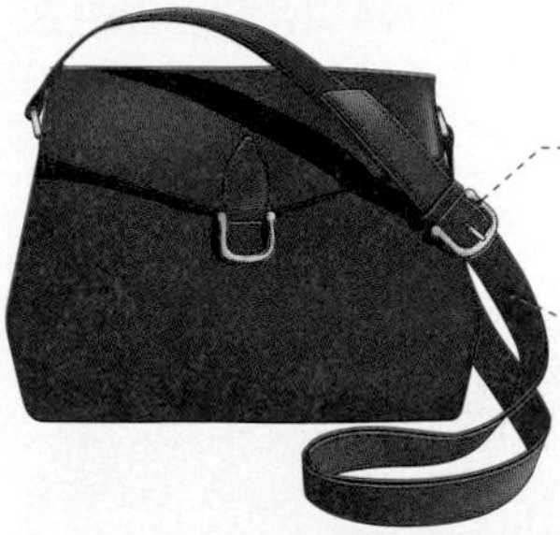

buckle
hebilla^F

shoulder strap
bandolera^F

ACCORDION BAG
BOLSA^F DE ACORDEÓN^M

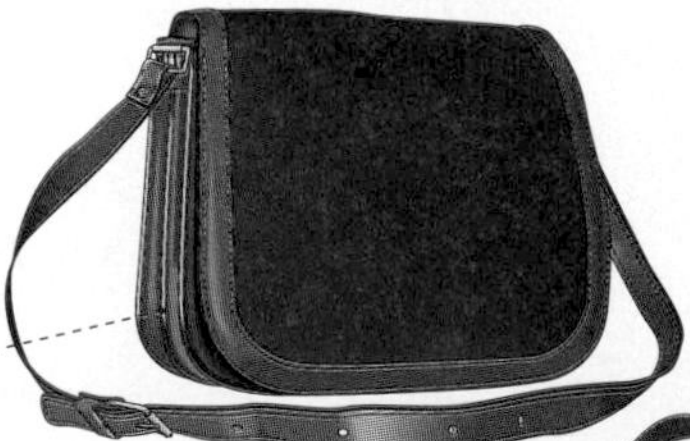

gusset
fuelle^M

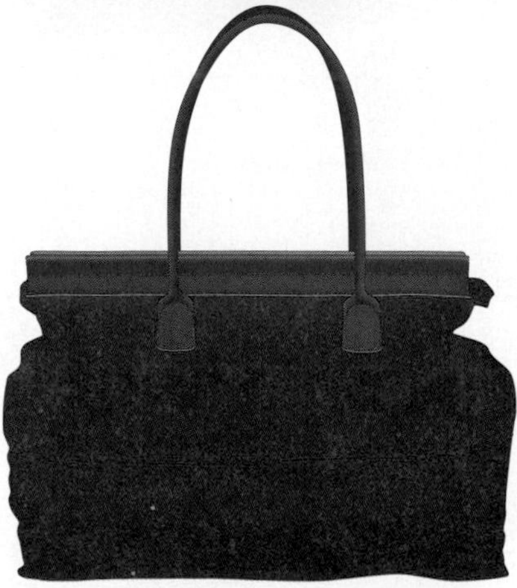

tote bag
bolsa^F de paja^F

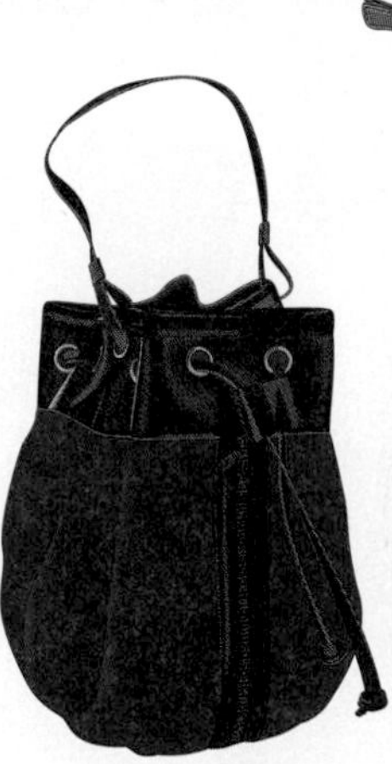

duffel bag
saco^M de viaje^M

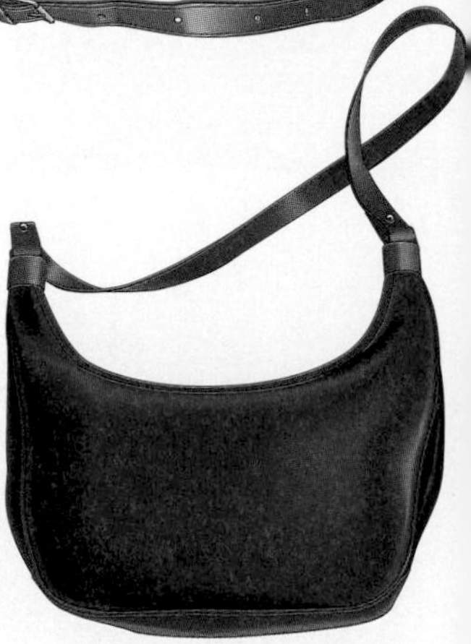

hobo bag
morral^M

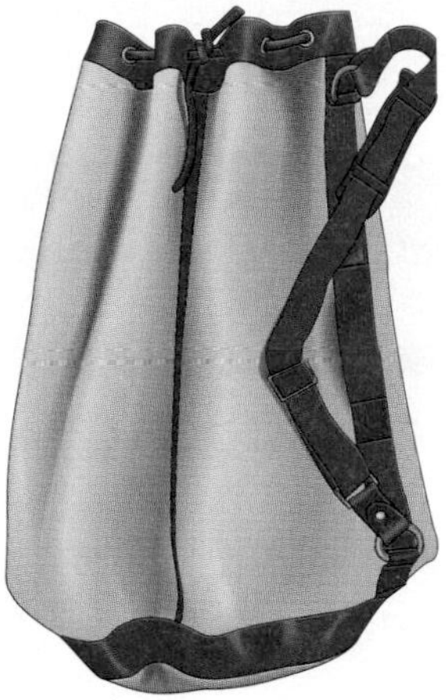

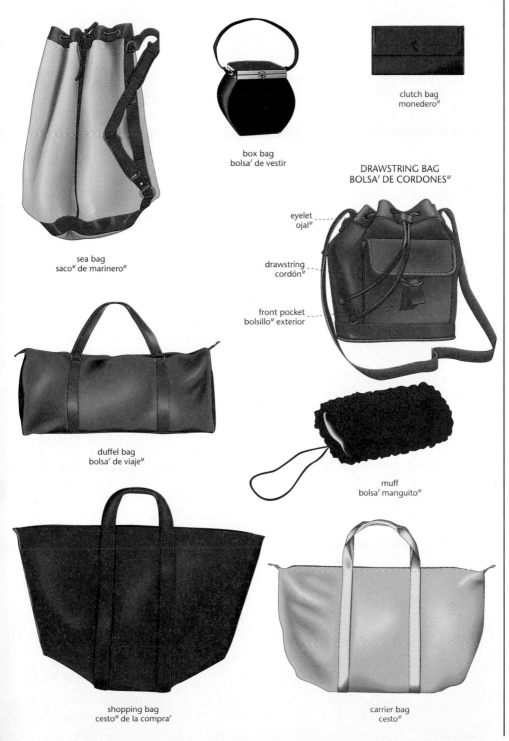

sea bag
saco^M de marinero^M

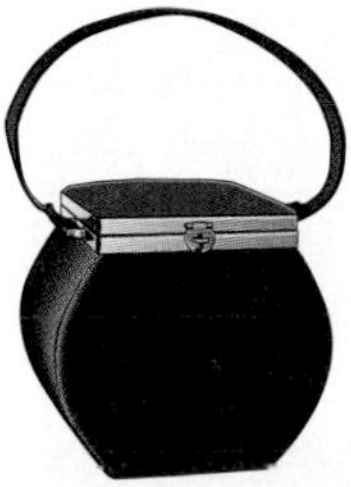

box bag
bolsa^F de vestir

clutch bag
monedero^M

DRAWSTRING BAG
BOLSA^F DE CORDONES^M

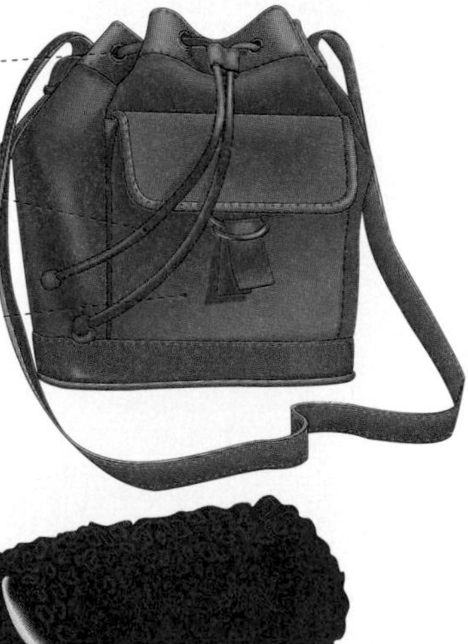

eyelet
ojal^M

drawstring
cordón^M

front pocket
bolsillo^M exterior

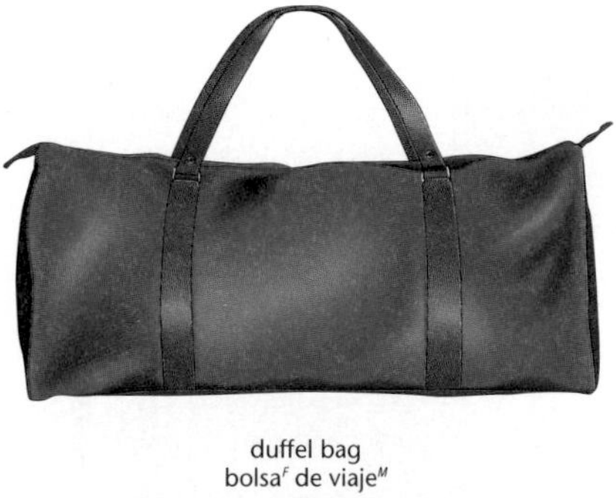

duffel bag
bolsa^F de viaje^M

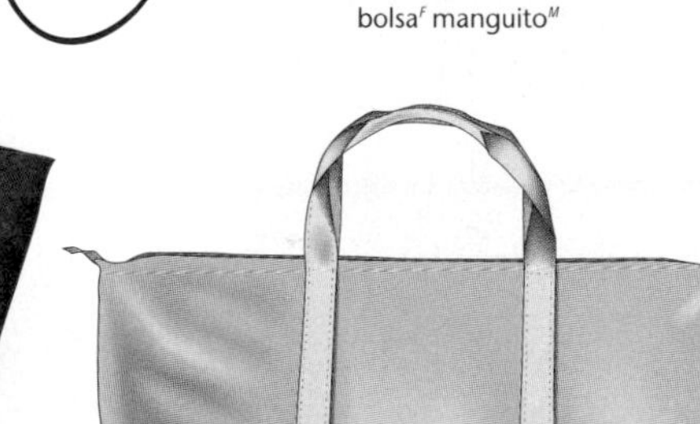

muff
bolsa^F manguito^M

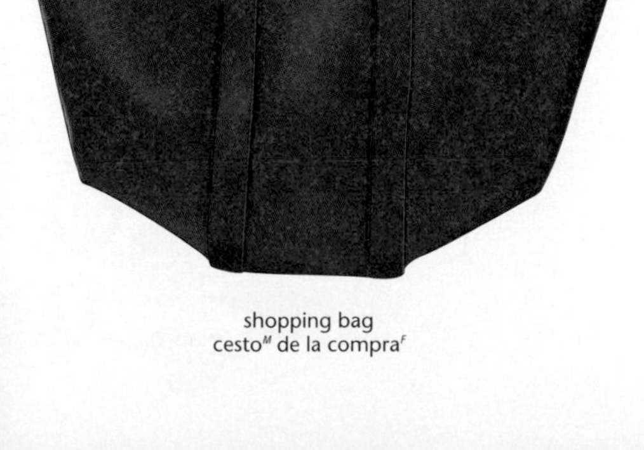

shopping bag
cesto^M de la compra^F

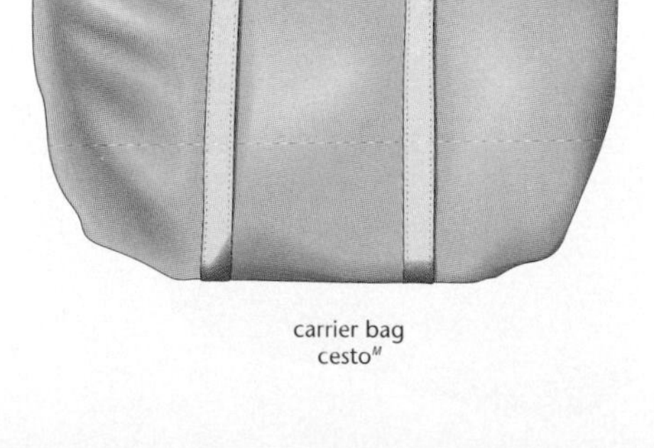

carrier bag
cesto^M

LUGGAGE
EQUIPAJE^M

CARRY-ON BAG
BOLSA^F DE VIAJE^M

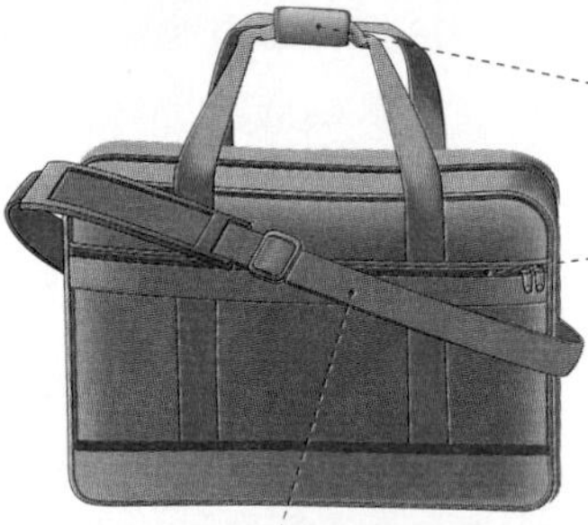

handle
asa^F

exterior pocket
bolsillo^M exterior

shoulder strap
bandolera^F

tote bag
maletín^M

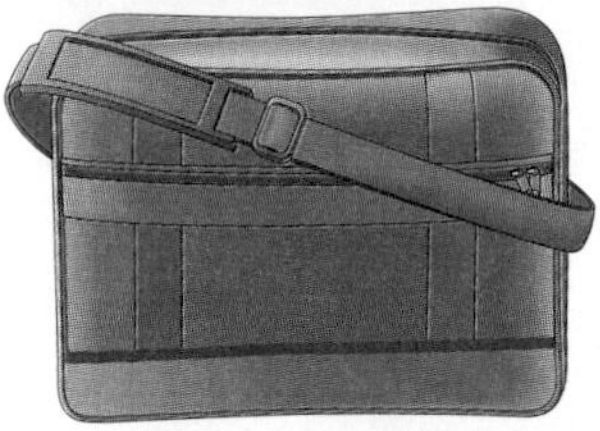

VANITY CASE
NECESER^M

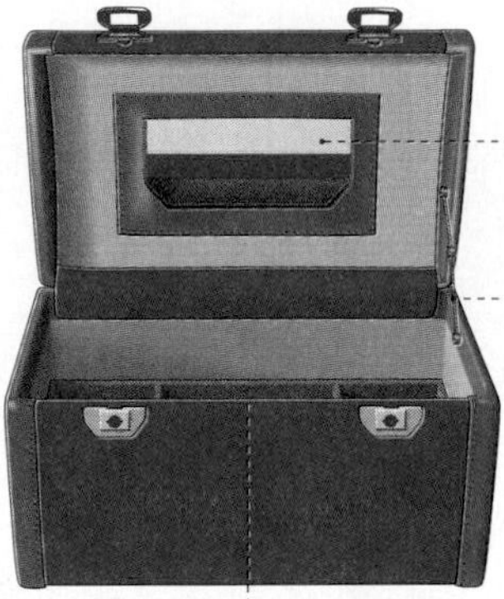

mirror
espejo^M

hinge
bisagra^F

GARMENT BAG
BOLSA^F PARA TRAJES^M

cosmetic tray
bandeja^F para cosméticos^M

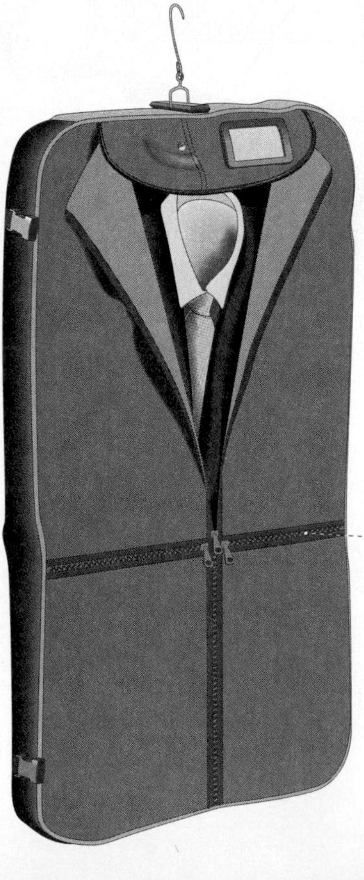

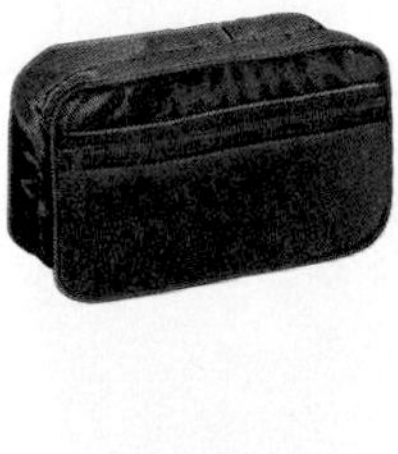

LUGGAGE CARRIER
CARRITO^M PORTAMALETAS^M

utility case
estuche^M de tocador^M

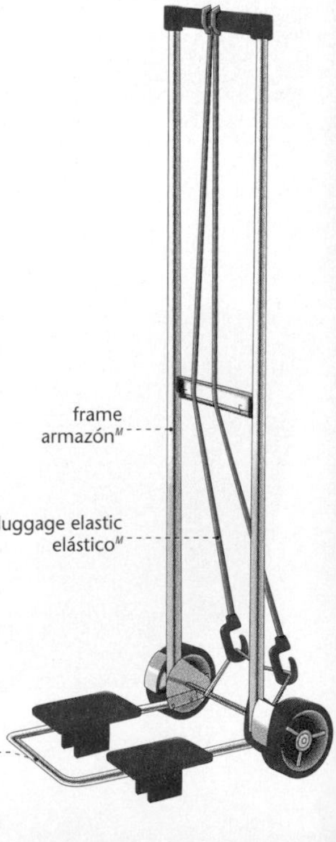

frame
armazón^M

luggage elastic
elástico^M

zipper
cremallera^F

stand
soporte^M

PULLMAN CASE
MALETA^F CLÁSICA

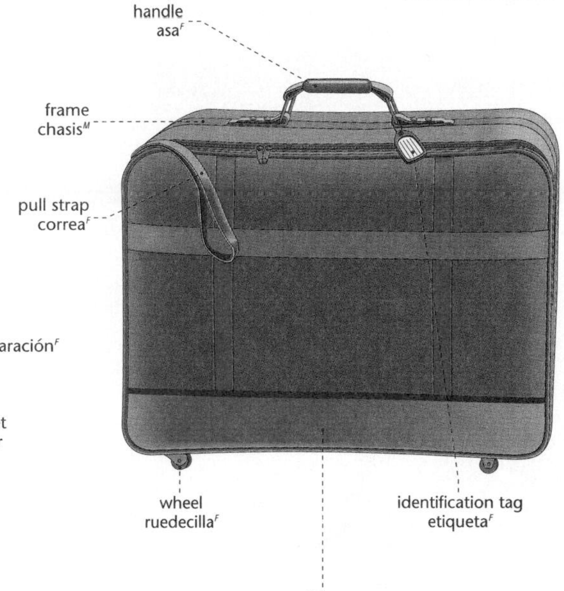

handle
asa^F

frame
chasis^M

pull strap
correa^F

WEEKENDER
MALETA^F DE FIN^M DE SEMANA^F

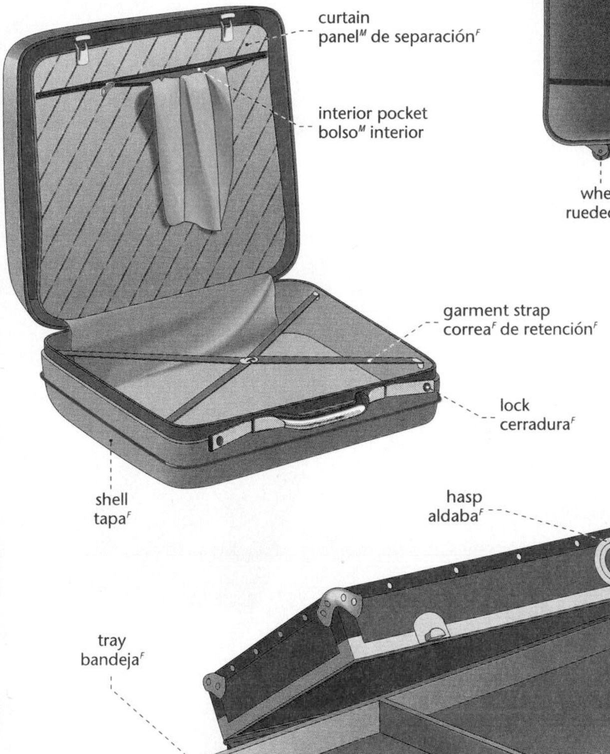

curtain
panel^M de separación^F

interior pocket
bolso^M interior

wheel
ruedecilla^F

identification tag
etiqueta^F

trim
guarnición^F

garment strap
correa^F de retención^F

lock
cerradura^F

shell
tapa^F

TRUNK
BAÚL^M

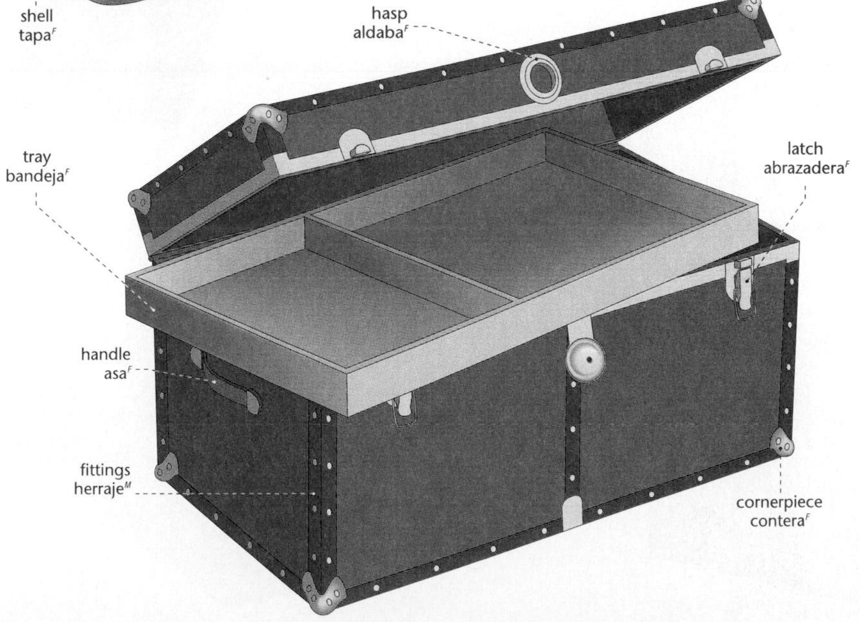

hasp
aldaba^F

latch
abrazadera^F

tray
bandeja^F

handle
asa^F

fittings
herraje^M

cornerpiece
contera^F

SMOKING ACCESSORIES
ACCESORIOS^M PARA FUMAR

CIGAR
PURO^M

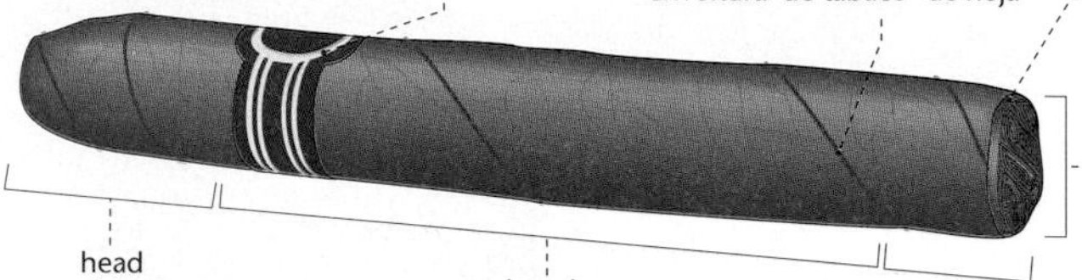

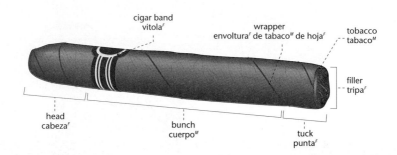

cigar band
vitola^F

wrapper
envoltura^F de tabaco^M de hoja^F

tobacco
tabaco^M

filler
tripa^F

head
cabeza^F

bunch
cuerpo^M

tuck
punta^F

CIGARETTE
CIGARRILLO^M

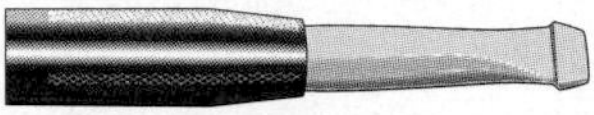

cigarette holder
boquilla^F

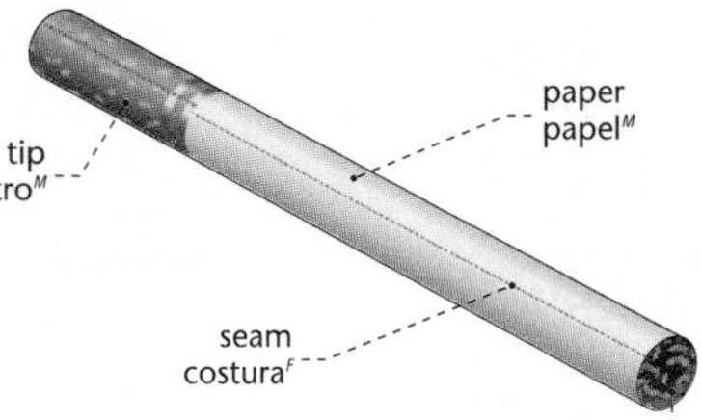

paper
papel^M

filter tip
filtro^M

seam
costura^F

tobacco
tabaco^M

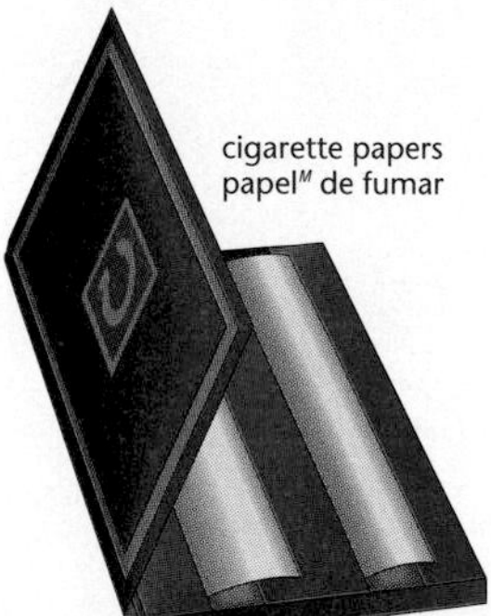

cigarette papers
papel^M de fumar

CIGARETTE PACK
PAQUETE^M DE CIGARRILLOS^M

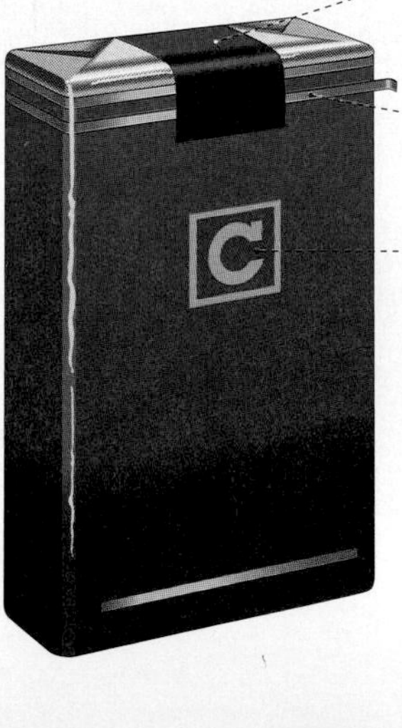

stamp
timbre^M

tear tape
tira^F para rasgar la envoltura^F

trade name
marca^F registrada

carton
cartón^M de cigarrillos^M

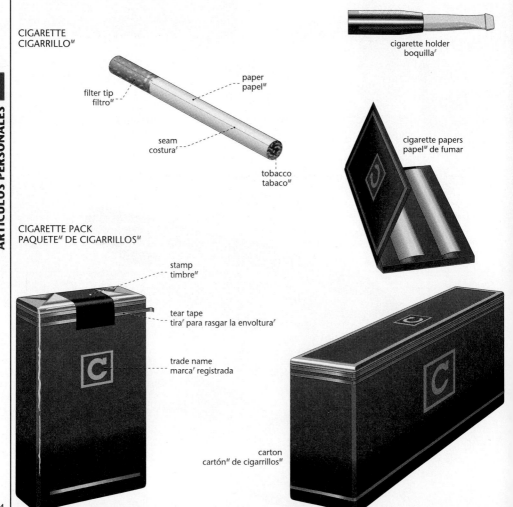

384

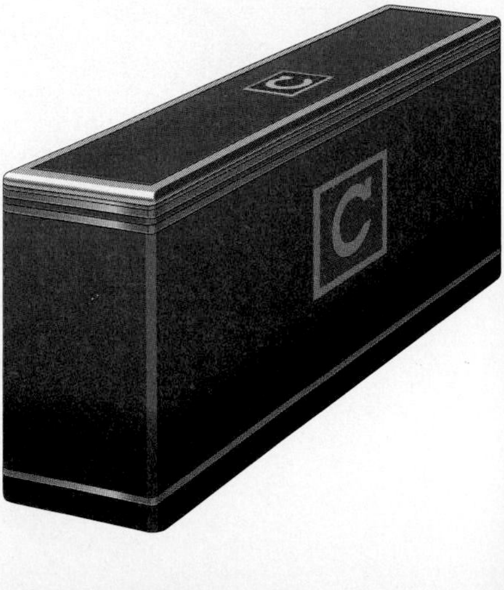

PIPE
PIPA^F

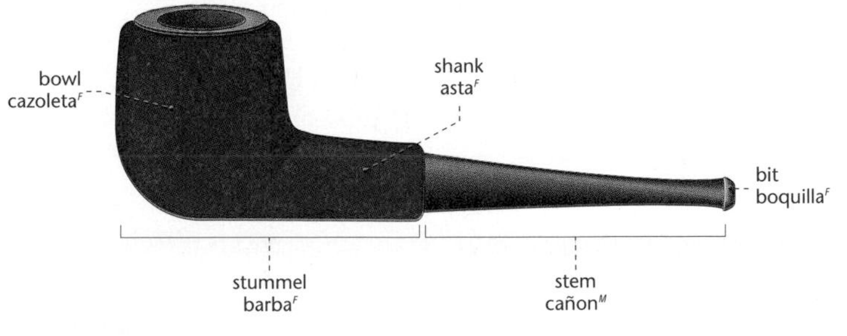

bowl
cazoleta^F

shank
asta^F

bit
boquilla^F

stummel
barba^F

stem
cañon^M

CROSS SECTION OF A PIPE
CORTE^M TRANSVERSAL DE UNA PIPA^F

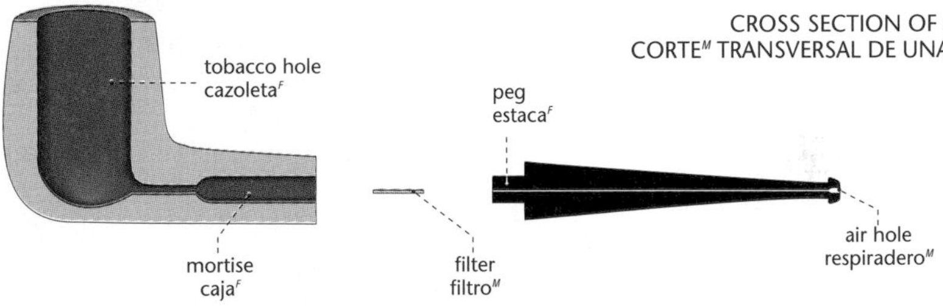

tobacco hole
cazoleta^F

peg
estaca^F

air hole
respiradero^M

mortise
caja^F

filter
filtro^M

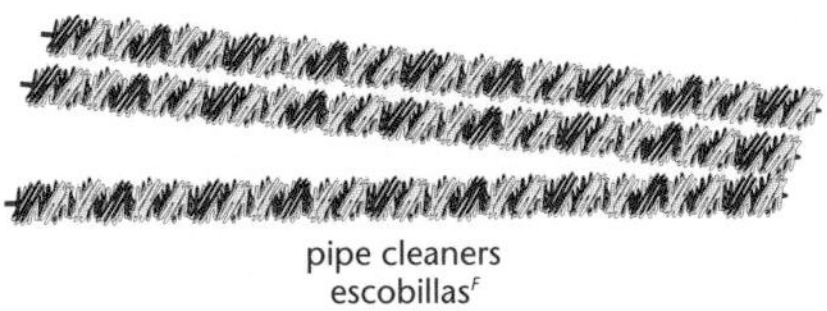

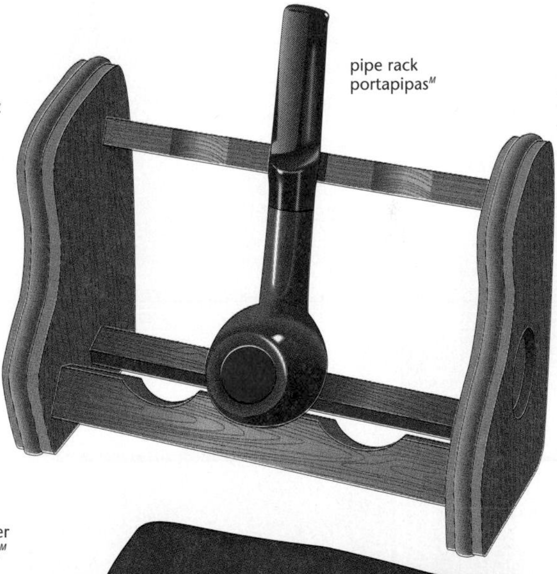

pipe rack
portapipas^M

pipe cleaners
escobillas^F

PIPE TOOLS
ACCESORIOS^M PARA LA PIPA^F

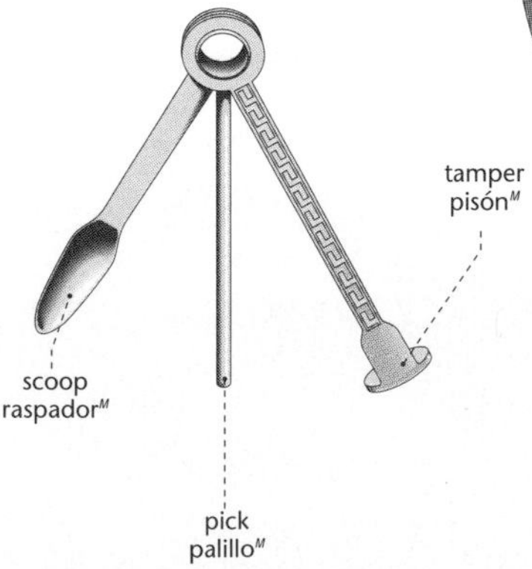

tamper
pisón^M

scoop
raspador^M

pick
palillo^M

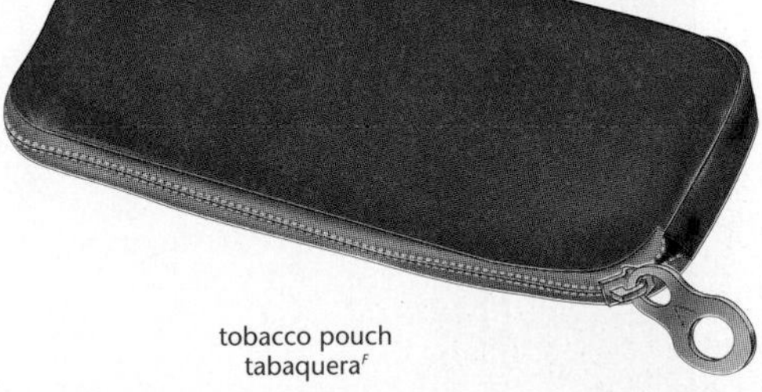

tobacco pouch
tabaquera^F

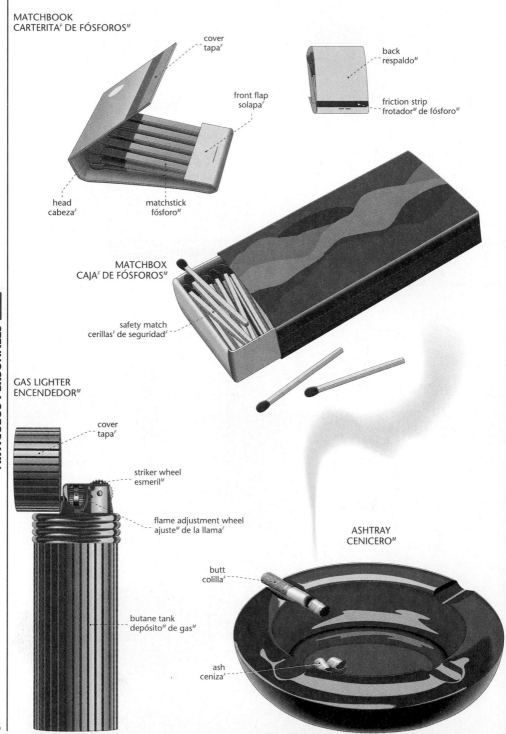

MATCHBOOK
CARTERITA^F DE FÓSFOROS^M

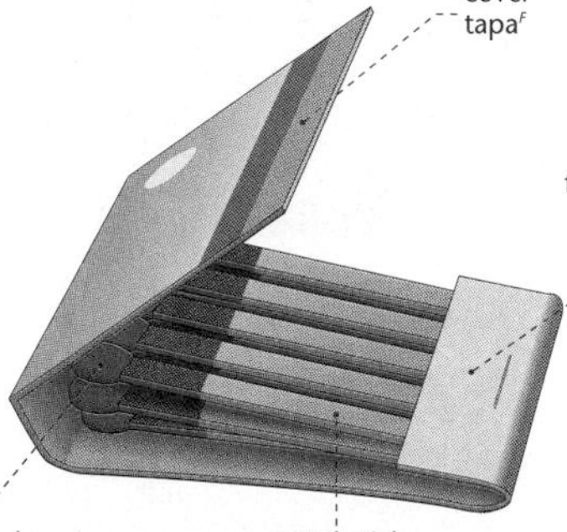

cover
tapa^F

back
respaldo^M

front flap
solapa^F

friction strip
frotador^M de fósforo^M

head
cabeza^F

matchstick
fósforo^M

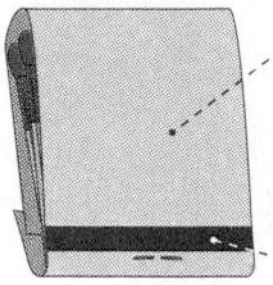

MATCHBOX
CAJA^F DE FÓSFOROS^M

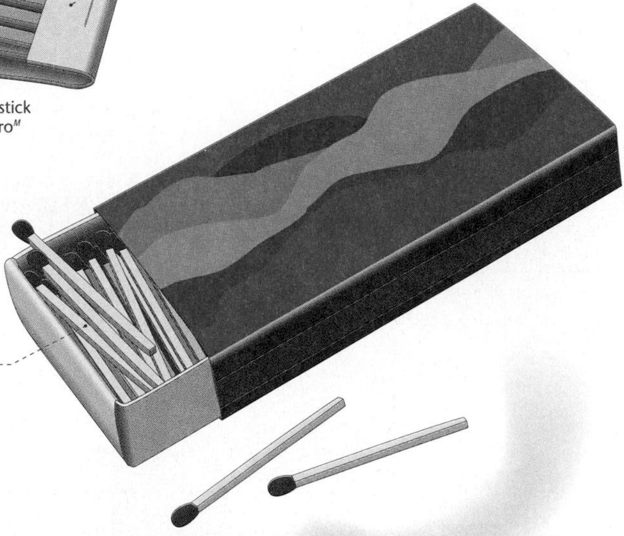

safety match
cerillas^F de seguridad^F

GAS LIGHTER
ENCENDEDOR^M

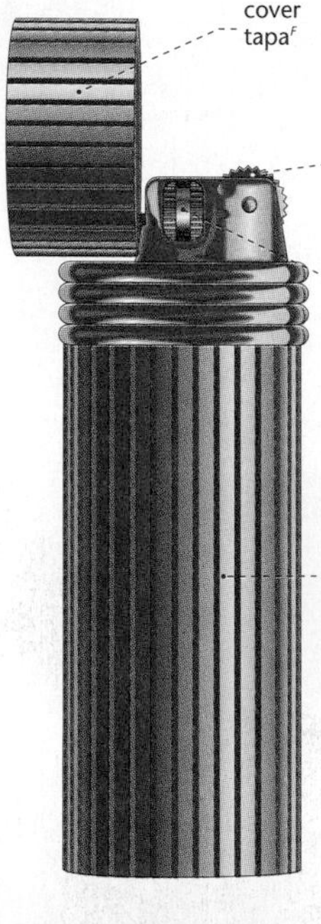

cover
tapa^F

striker wheel
esmeril^M

flame adjustment wheel
ajuste^M de la llama^F

ASHTRAY
CENICERO^M

butt
colilla^F

butane tank
depósito^M de gas^M

ash
ceniza^F

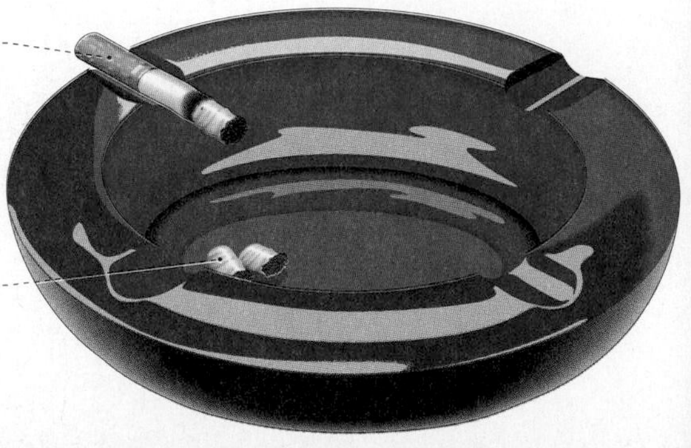

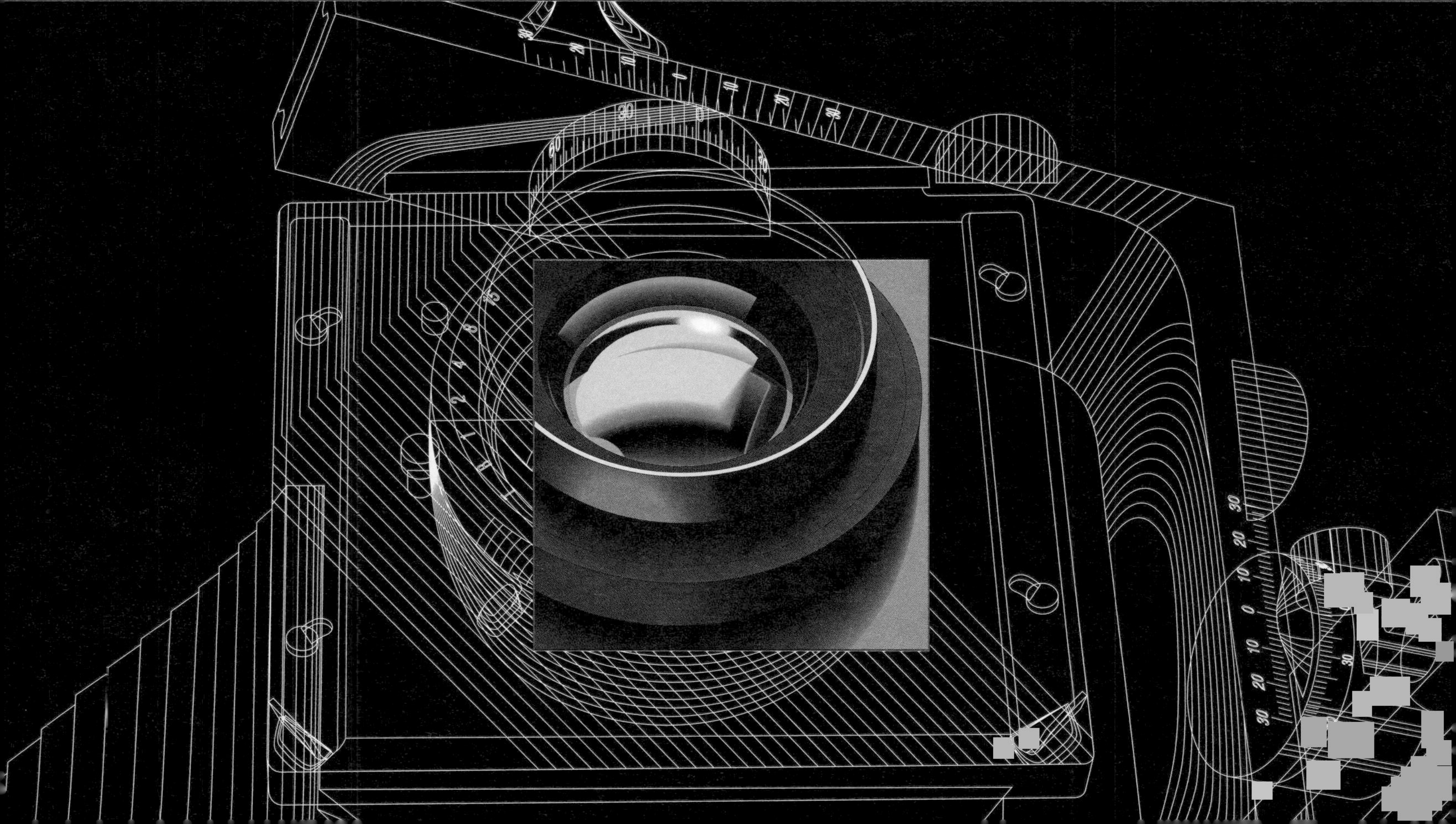

CONTENTS

**COMMUNICATIONS
COMUNICACIONES**

WRITING INSTRUMENTS
INSTRUMENTOS^M PARA ESCRIBIR

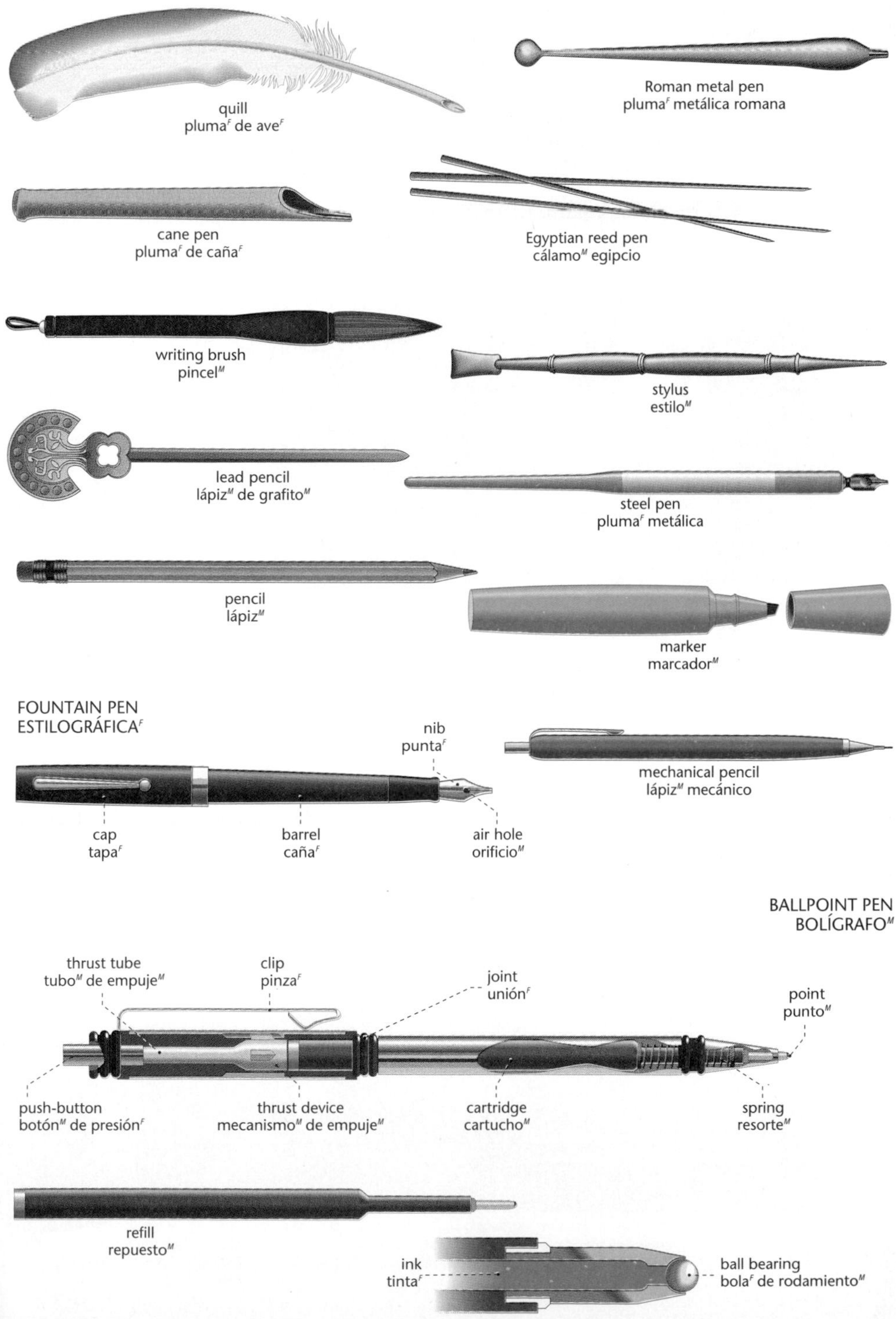

quill
pluma^F de ave^F

Roman metal pen
pluma^F metálica romana

cane pen
pluma^F de caña^F

Egyptian reed pen
cálamo^M egipcio

writing brush
pincel^M

stylus
estilo^M

lead pencil
lápiz^M de grafito^M

steel pen
pluma^F metálica

pencil
lápiz^M

marker
marcador^M

FOUNTAIN PEN
ESTILOGRÁFICA^F

nib
punta^F

mechanical pencil
lápiz^M mecánico

cap
tapa^F

barrel
caña^F

air hole
orificio^M

BALLPOINT PEN
BOLÍGRAFO^M

thrust tube
tubo^M de empuje^M

clip
pinza^F

joint
unión^F

point
punto^M

push-button
botón^M de presión^F

thrust device
mecanismo^M de empuje^M

cartridge
cartucho^M

spring
resorte^M

refill
repuesto^M

ink
tinta^F

ball bearing
bola^F de rodamiento^M

CROSS SECTION OF A REFLEX CAMERA
CORTE^M TRANSVERSAL DE UNA CÁMARA^F REFLEX

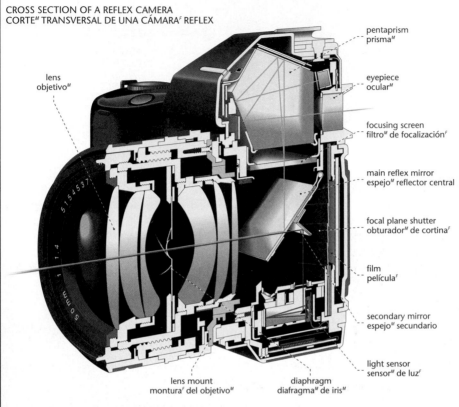

lens
objetivo^M

pentaprism
prisma^M

eyepiece
ocular^M

focusing screen
filtro^M de focalización^F

main reflex mirror
espejo^M reflector central

focal plane shutter
obturador^M de cortina^F

film
película^F

secondary mirror
espejo^M secundario

light sensor
sensor^M de luz^F

lens mount
montura^F del objetivo^M

diaphragm
diafragma^M de iris^M

CAMERA BACK
PARTE^F TRASERA DE UNA CÁMARA^F

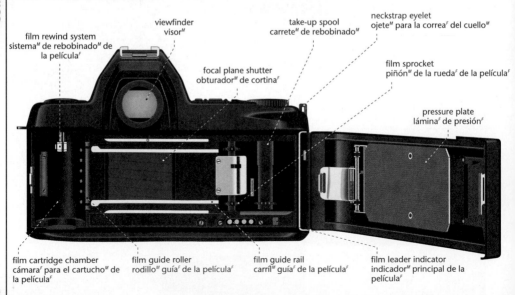

film rewind system
sistema^M de rebobinado^M de
la película^F

viewfinder
visor^M

take-up spool
carrete^M de rebobinado^M

neckstrap eyelet
ojete^M para la correa^F del cuello^M

focal plane shutter
obturador^M de cortina^F

film sprocket
piñón^M de la rueda^F de la película^F

pressure plate
lámina^F de presión^F

film cartridge chamber
cámara^F para el cartucho^M de
la película^F

film guide roller
rodillo^M guía^F de la película^F

film guide rail
carril^M guía^F de la película^F

film leader indicator
indicador^M principal de la
película^F

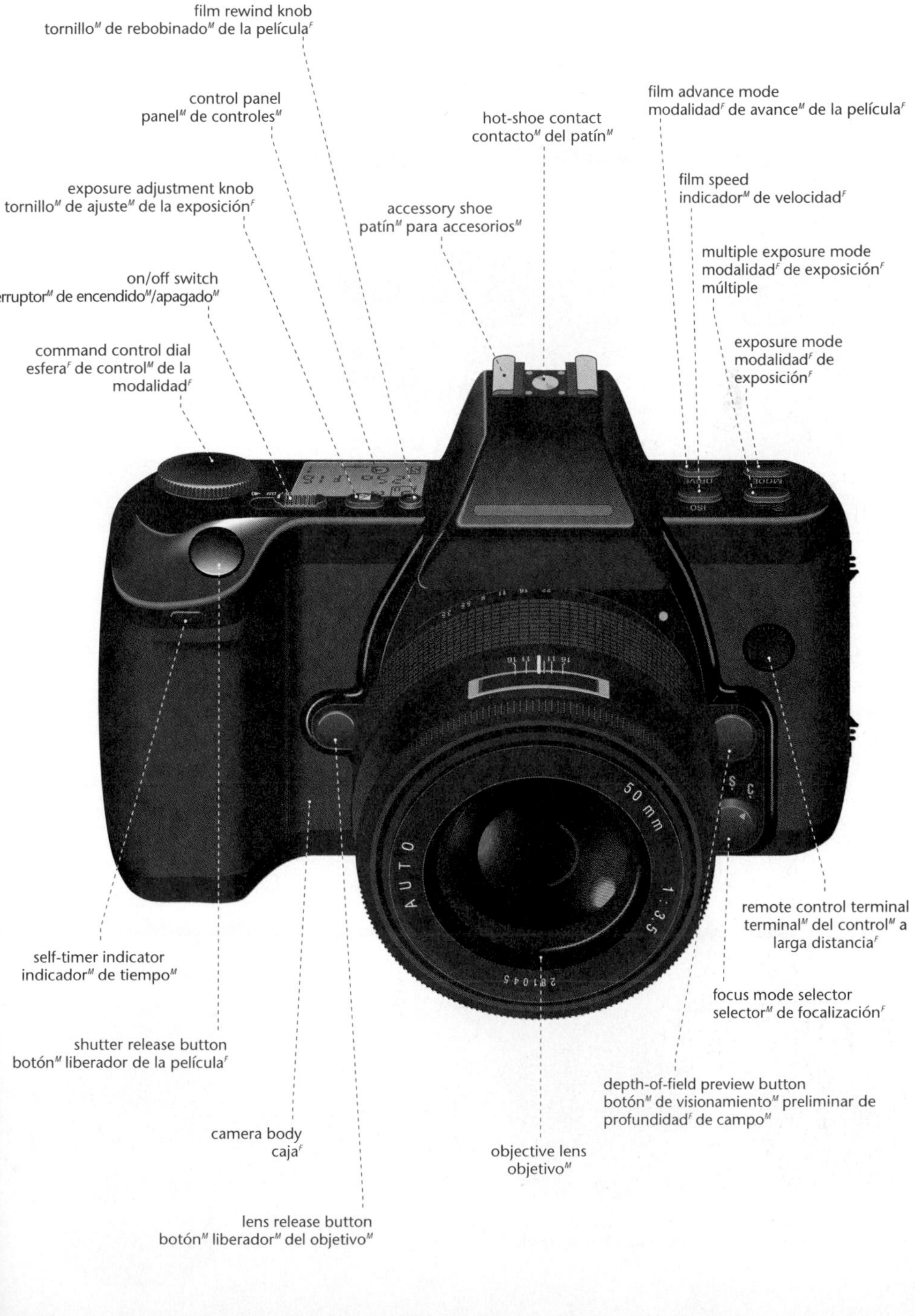

film rewind knob
tornillo^M de rebobinado^M de la película^F

control panel
panel^M de controles^M

exposure adjustment knob
tornillo^M de ajuste^M de la exposición^F

on/off switch
interruptor^M de encendido^M/apagado^M

command control dial
esfera^F de control^M de la
modalidad^F

hot-shoe contact
contacto^M del patín^M

accessory shoe
patín^M para accesorios^M

film advance mode
modalidad^F de avance^M de la película^F

film speed
indicador^M de velocidad^F

multiple exposure mode
modalidad^F de exposición^F
múltiple

exposure mode
modalidad^F de
exposición^F

self-timer indicator
indicador^M de tiempo^M

shutter release button
botón^M liberador de la película^F

camera body
caja^F

lens release button
botón^M liberador^M del objetivo^M

objective lens
objetivo^M

depth-of-field preview button
botón^M de visionamiento^M preliminar de
profundidad^F de campo^M

focus mode selector
selector^M de focalización^F

remote control terminal
terminal^M del control^M a
larga distancia^F

LENSES
OBJETIVOS^M

**standard lens
objetivo^M normal**

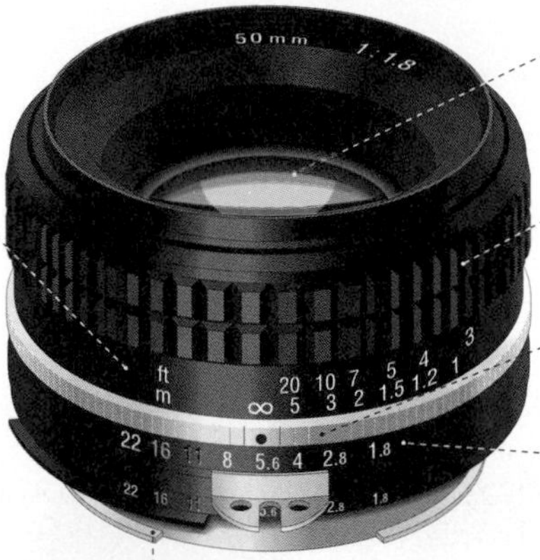

lens
objetivo^M

distance scale
escala^F de distancia^F

focus setting ring
anillo^M de ajuste^M del enfoque^M

depth-of-field scale
escala^F de profundidad^F de
campo^M de visión^F

lens aperture scale
escala^F de abertura^F del
diafragma^M

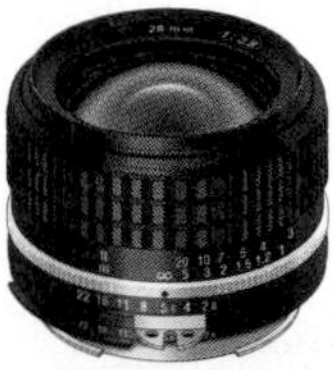

wide-angle lens
gran angular^M

bayonet mount
montura^F de bayoneta^F

LENS ACCESSORIES
OBJETIVOS^M Y ACCESORIOS^M

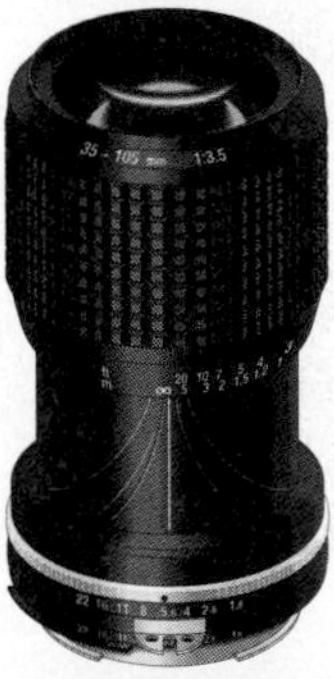

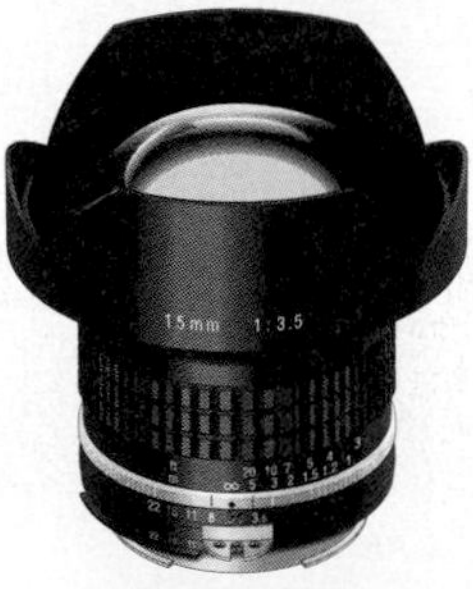

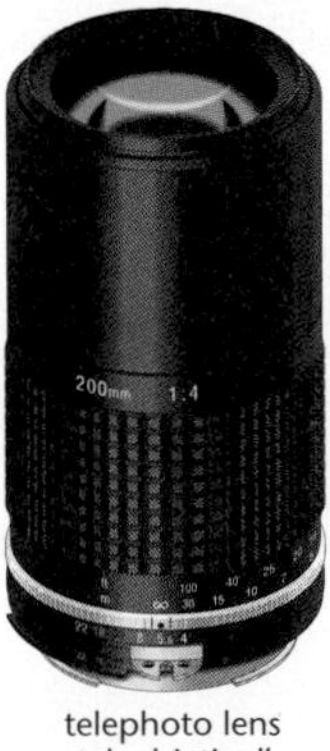

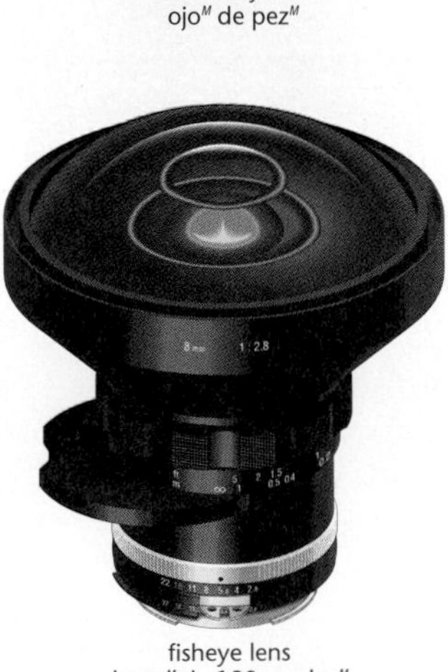

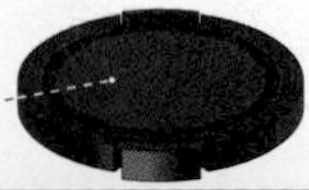

lens cap
tapa^F del objetivo^M

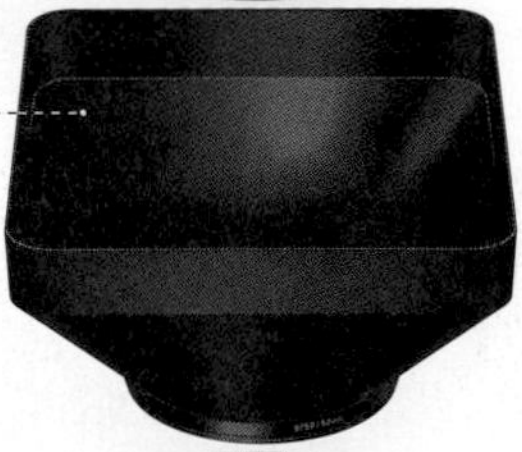

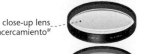

lens hood
capuchón^M

zoom lens
zoom^M

semi-fisheye lens
ojo^M de pez^M

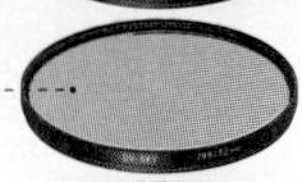

color filter
filtro^M de color^M

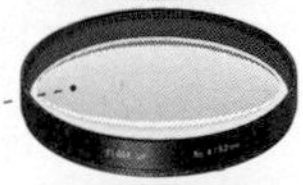

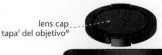

close-up lens
lente^M de acercamiento^M

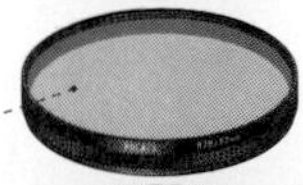

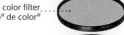

polarizing filter
filtro^M de polarización^F

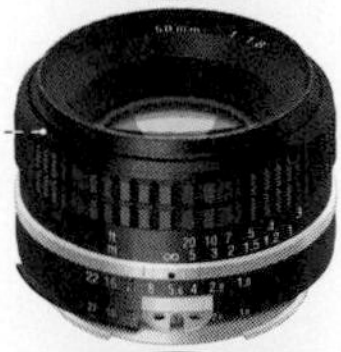

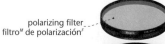

objective lens
objetivo^M normal

telephoto lens
teleobjetivo^M

fisheye lens
lente^M de 180 grados^M

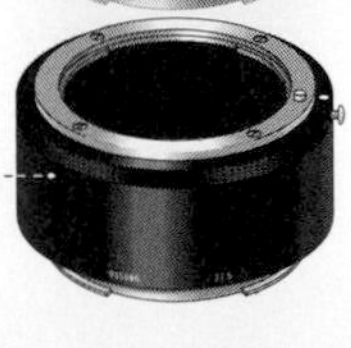

tele-converter
teleconvertidor^M

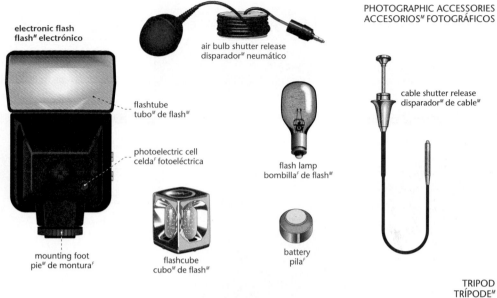

electronic flash
flash*M* electrónico

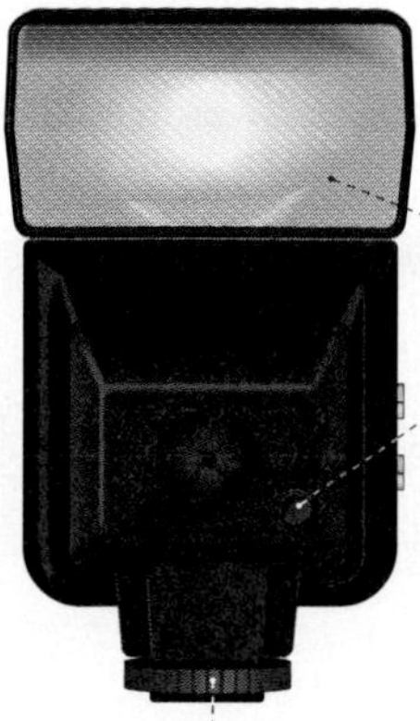

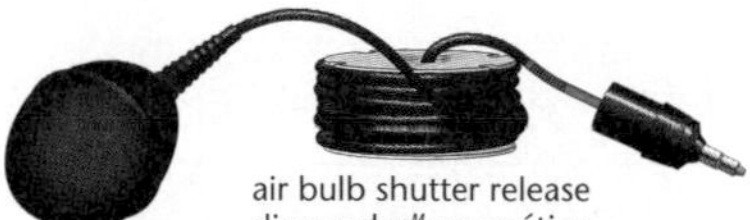

air bulb shutter release
disparador*M* neumático

flashtube
tubo*M* de flash*M*

photoelectric cell
celda*F* fotoeléctrica

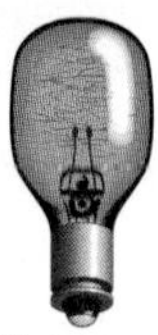

flash lamp
bombilla*F* de flash*M*

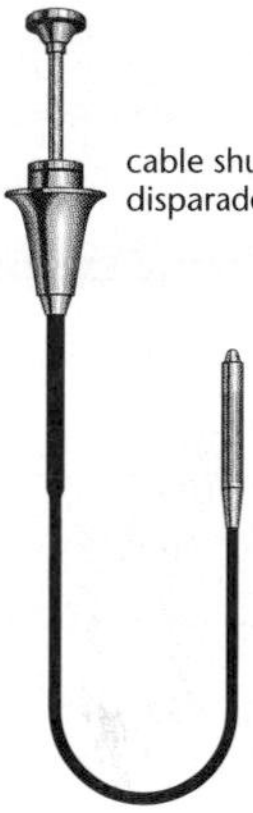

cable shutter release
disparador*M* de cable*M*

mounting foot
pie*M* de montura*F*

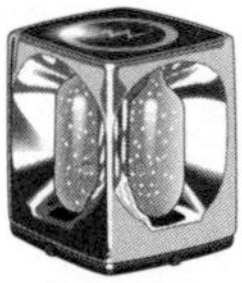

flashcube
cubo*M* de flash*M*

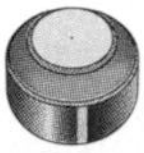

battery
pila*F*

TRIPOD
TRÍPODE*M*

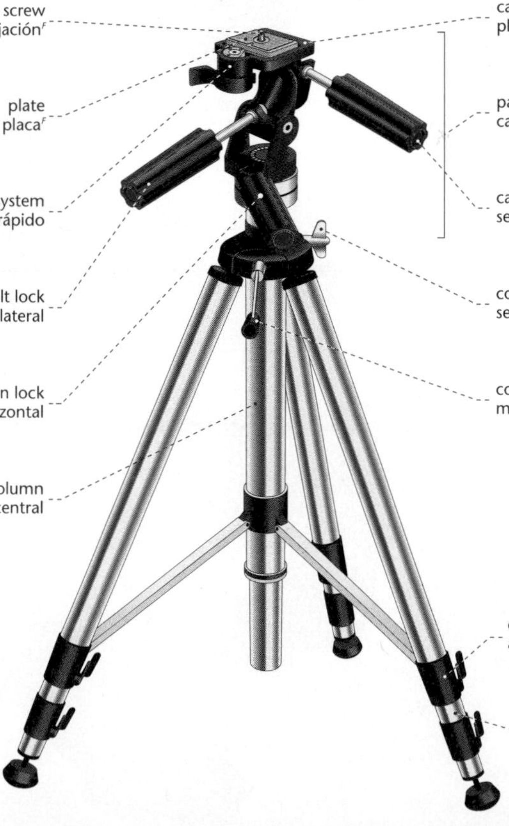

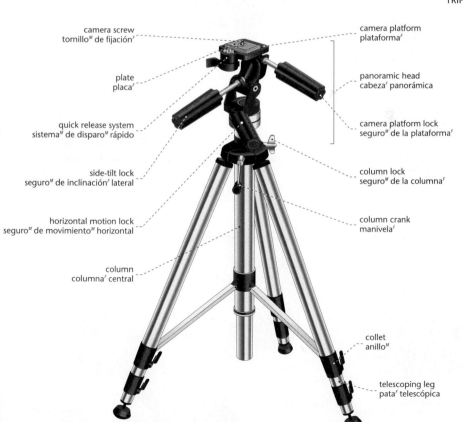

camera screw
tornillo*M* de fijación*F*

camera platform
plataforma*F*

plate
placa*F*

panoramic head
cabeza*F* panorámica

quick release system
sistema*M* de disparo*M* rápido

camera platform lock
seguro*M* de la plataforma*F*

side-tilt lock
seguro*M* de inclinación*F* lateral

column lock
seguro*M* de la columna*F*

horizontal motion lock
seguro*M* de movimiento*M* horizontal

column crank
manivela*F*

column
columna*F* central

collet
anillo*M*

telescoping leg
pata*F* telescópica

STILL CAMERAS
CÁMARAS^M FIJAS

rangefinder
telémetro^M

underwater camera
cámara^F submarina

Polaroid® Land camera
cámara^F Polaroid Land

disposable camera
cámara^F desechable

single-lens reflex camera
cámara^F reflex con objetivo^M
simple

twin-lens reflex camera
cámara^F tipo^M réflex con dos objetivos^M

view camera
cámara^F de enfoque^M

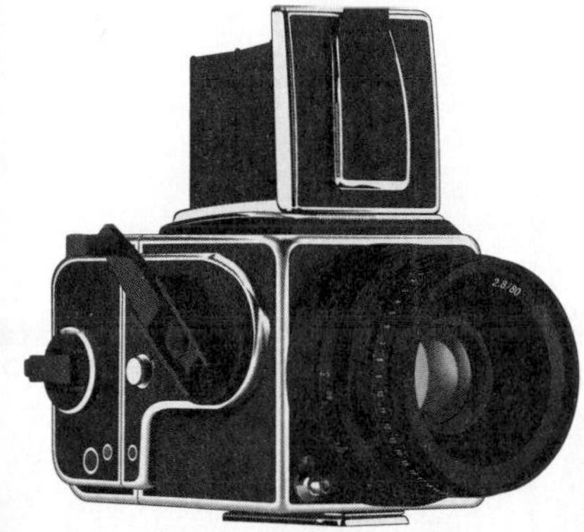

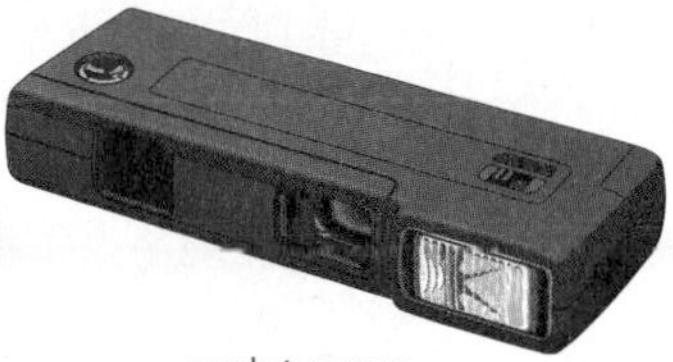

pocket camera
cámara^F de bolsillo^M

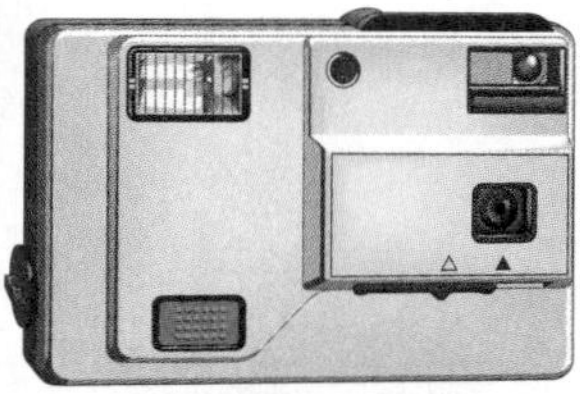

disk camera
cámara^F de disco^M

medium format SLR (6 x 6)
formato^M mediano SLR (6x6)

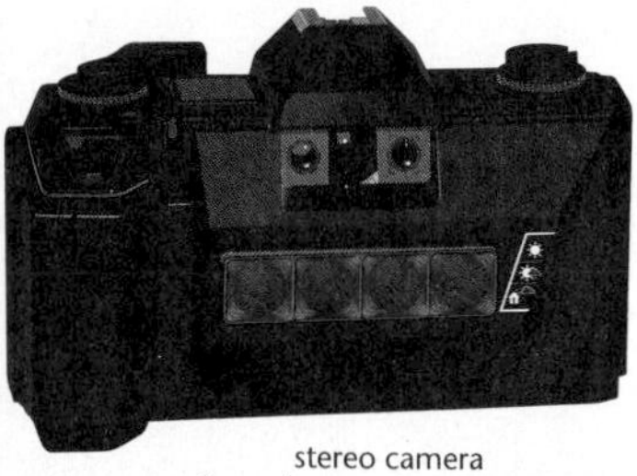

stereo camera
cámara^F estereofotogramétrica

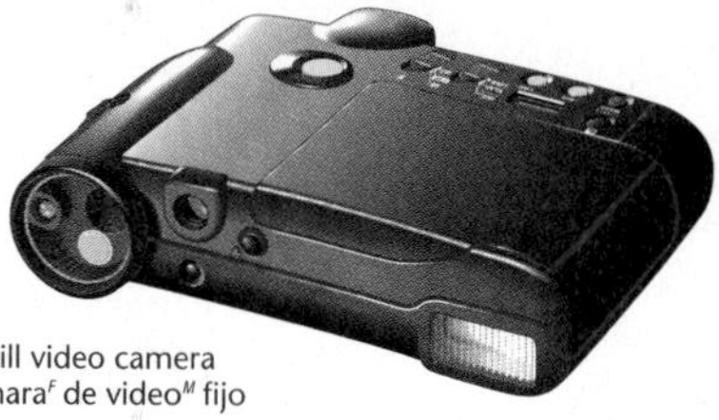

still video camera
cámara^F de video^M fijo

film leader
principio^M de la película^F

perforation
perforación^F

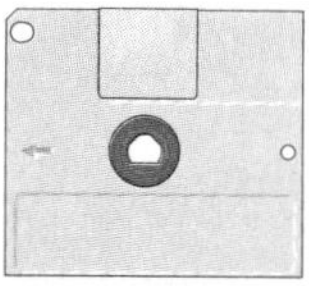

still video film disk
película^F de disco^M para video^M fijo

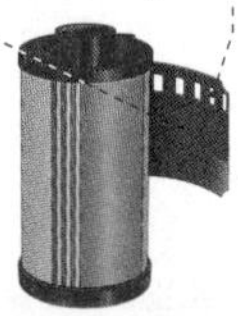

cassette film
cartucho^M de la película^F

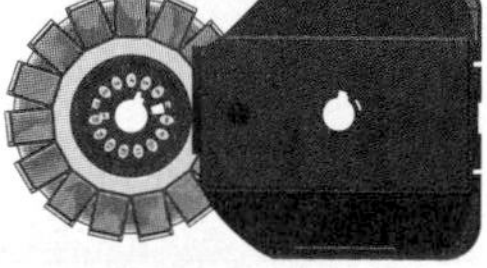

film disk
película^F de disco^M

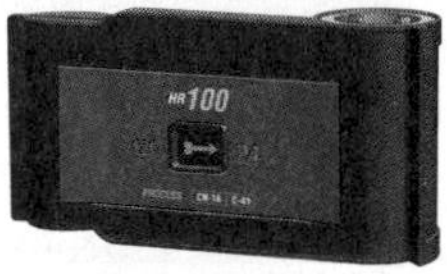

cartridge film
cartucho^M de la película^F

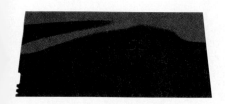

sheet film
hoja^F de la película^F

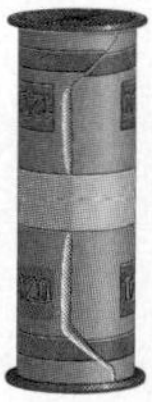

roll film
rollo^M de la película^F

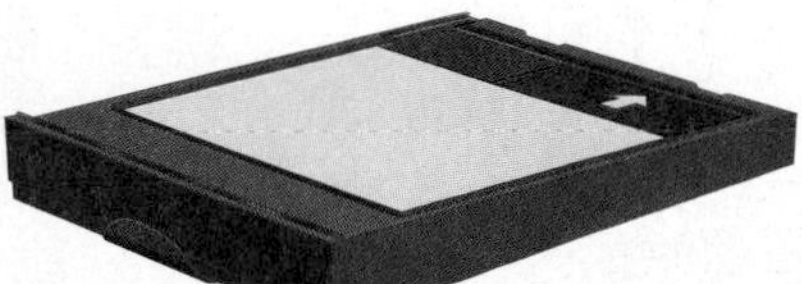

film pack
paquete^M de placas^F fotográficas

PHOTOGRAPHY
FOTOGRAFÍA^F

EXPOSURE METER
FOTÓMETRO^M

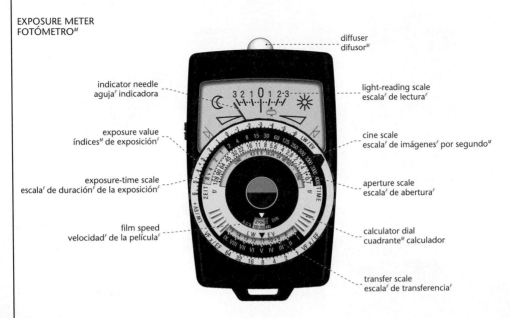

diffuser
difusor^M

indicator needle
aguja^F indicadora

light-reading scale
escala^F de lectura^F

exposure value
índices^M de exposición^F

cine scale
escala^F de imágenes^F por segundo^M

exposure-time scale
escala^F de duración^F de la exposición^F

aperture scale
escala^F de abertura^F

film speed
velocidad^F de la película^F

calculator dial
cuadrante^M calculador

transfer scale
escala^F de transferencia^F

SPOTMETER
FOTÓMETRO^M ELECTRÓNICO

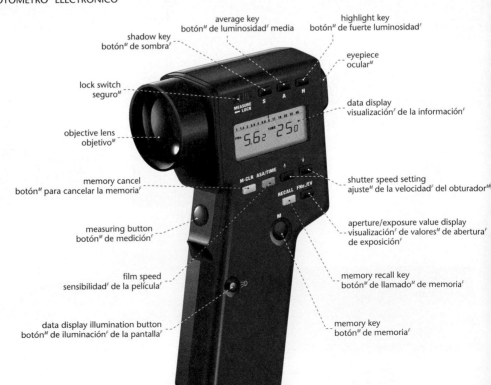

average key
botón^M de luminosidad^F media

highlight key
botón^M de fuerte luminosidad^F

shadow key
botón^M de sombra^F

eyepiece
ocular^M

lock switch
seguro^M

data display
visualización^F de la información^F

objective lens
objetivo^M

memory cancel
botón^M para cancelar la memoria^F

shutter speed setting
ajuste^M de la velocidad^F del obturador^M

measuring button
botón^M de medición^F

aperture/exposure value display
visualización^F de valores^M de abertura^F
de exposición^F

film speed
sensibilidad^F de la película^F

memory recall key
botón^M de llamado^M de memoria^F

data display illumination button
botón^M de iluminación^F de la pantalla^F

memory key
botón^M de memoria^F

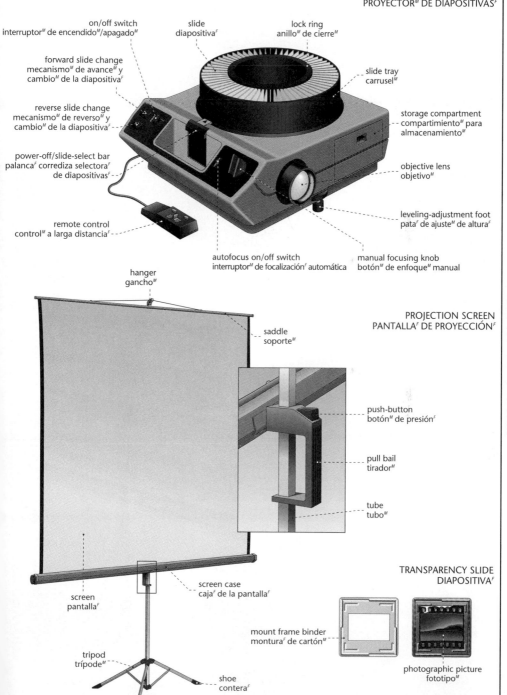

SLIDE PROJECTOR
PROYECTOR^M DE DIAPOSITIVAS^F

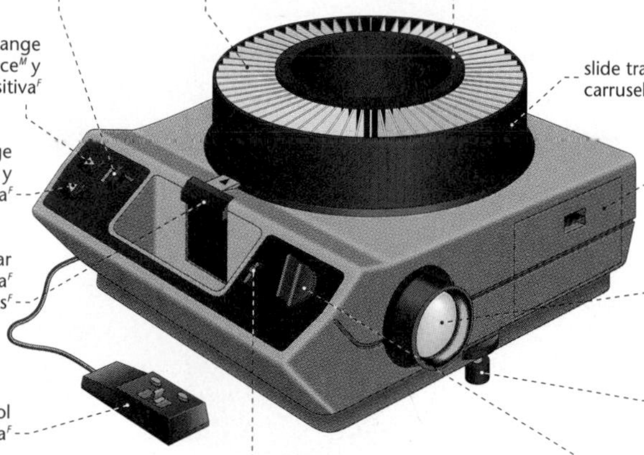

on/off switch
interruptor^M de encendido^M/apagado^M

slide
diapositiva^F

lock ring
anillo^M de cierre^M

forward slide change
mecanismo^M de avance^M y
cambio^M de la diapositiva^F

slide tray
carrusel^M

reverse slide change
mecanismo^M de reverso^M y
cambio^M de la diapositiva^F

storage compartment
compartimiento^M para
almacenamiento^M

power-off/slide-select bar
palanca^F corrediza selectora^F
de diapositivas^F

objective lens
objetivo^M

remote control
control^M a larga distancia^F

leveling-adjustment foot
pata^F de ajuste^M de altura^F

autofocus on/off switch
interruptor^M de focalización^F automática

manual focusing knob
botón^M de enfoque^M manual

hanger
gancho^M

PROJECTION SCREEN
PANTALLA^F DE PROYECCIÓN^F

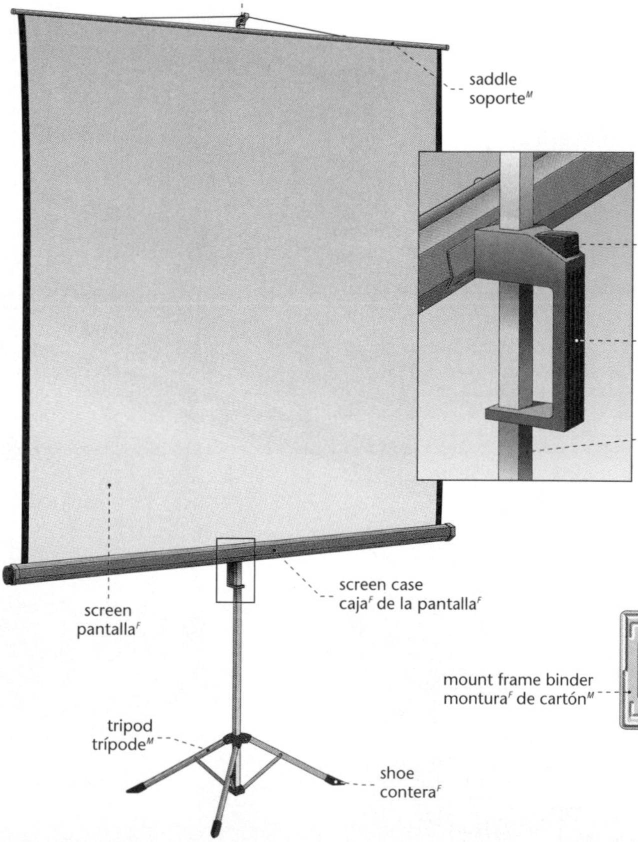

saddle
soporte^M

push-button
botón^M de presión^F

pull bail
tirador^M

tube
tubo^M

screen case
caja^F de la pantalla^F

TRANSPARENCY SLIDE
DIAPOSITIVA^F

screen
pantalla^F

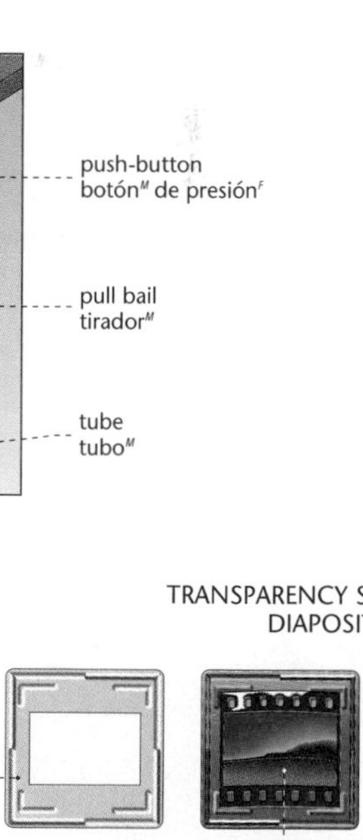

mount frame binder
montura^F de cartón^M

tripod
trípode^M

shoe
contera^F

photographic picture
fototipo^M

DEVELOPING TANK
TANQUE^M DE REVELADO^M

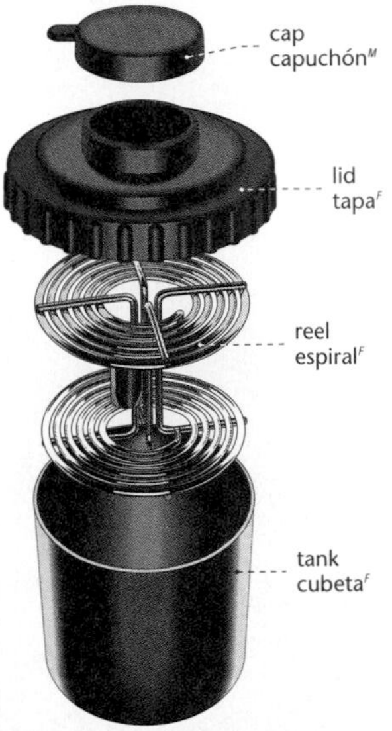

cap
capuchón^M

lid
tapa^F

reel
espiral^F

tank
cubeta^F

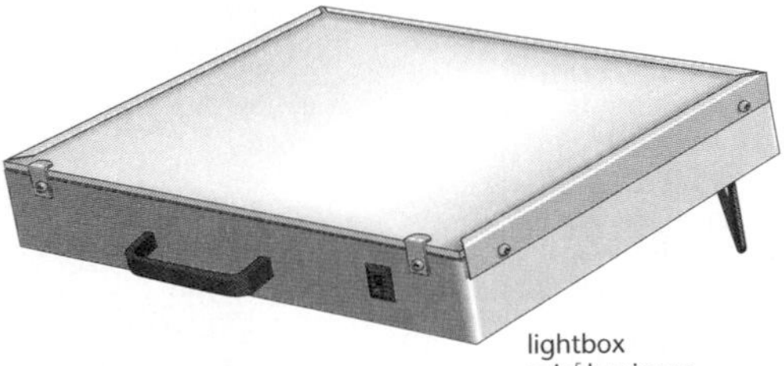

lightbox
caja^F luminosa

timer
reloj^M

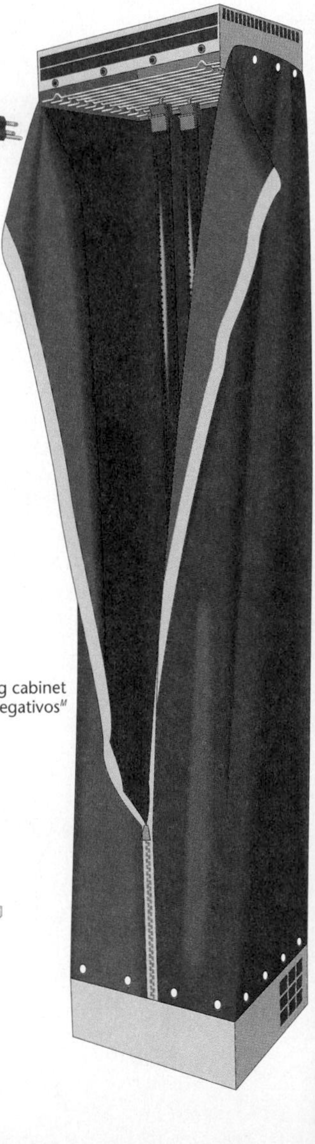

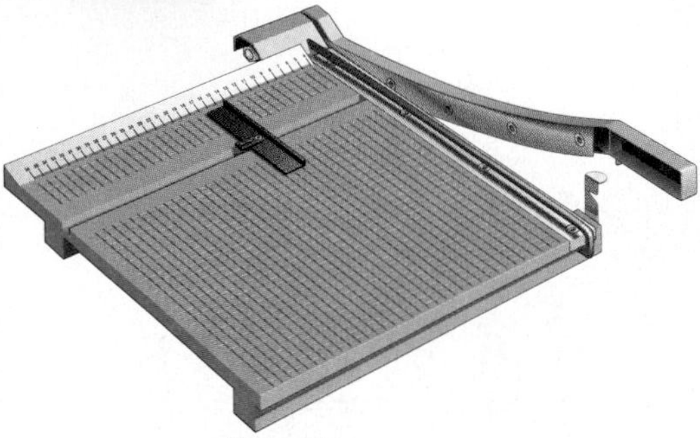

safelight
luz^F inactínica

guillotine trimmer
guillotina^F

film drying cabinet
armario^M de secado^M de negativos^M

easel
marginadora^F

contact printer
prensa^F de contactos^M

**COMMUNICATIONS
COMUNICACIONES**

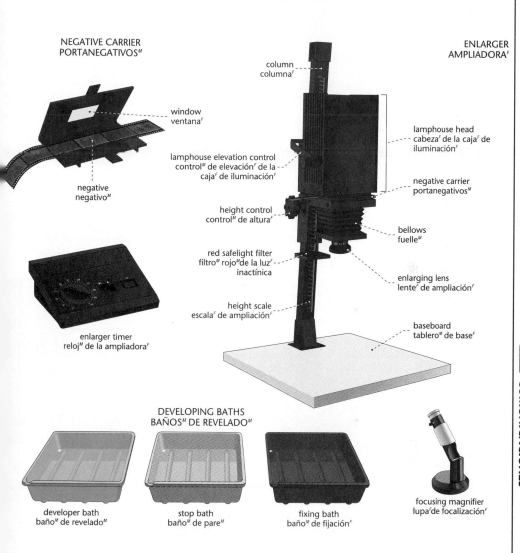

NEGATIVE CARRIER
PORTANEGATIVOS^M

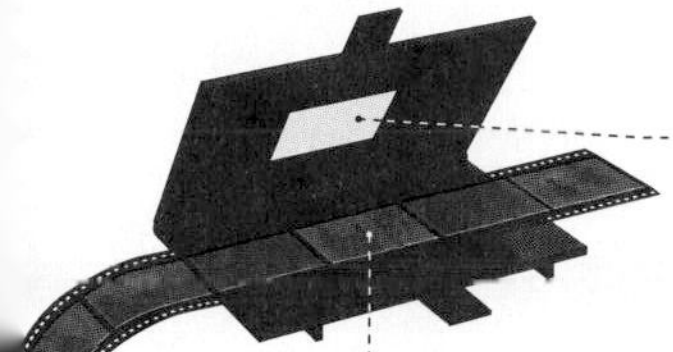

window
ventana^F

negative
negativo^M

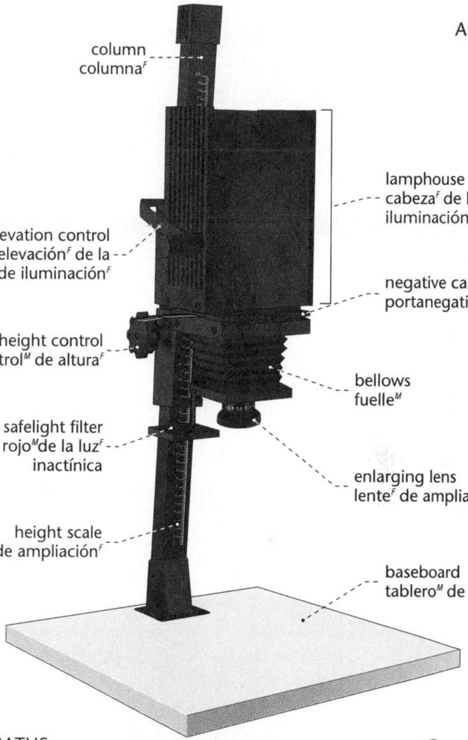

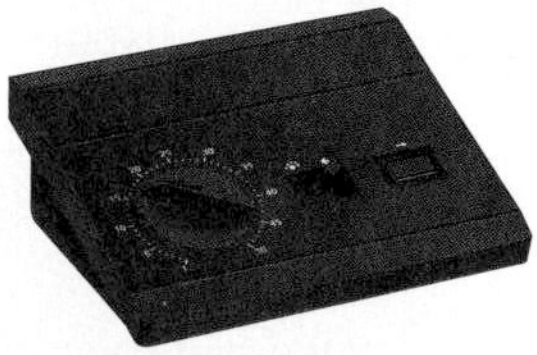

enlarger timer
reloj^M de la ampliadora^F

column
columna^F

lamphouse elevation control
control^M de elevación^F de la
caja^F de iluminación^F

height control
control^M de altura^F

red safelight filter
filtro^M rojo^M de la luz^F
inactínica

height scale
escala^F de ampliación^F

ENLARGER
AMPLIADORA^F

lamphouse head
cabeza^F de la caja^F de
iluminación^F

negative carrier
portanegativos^M

bellows
fuelle^M

enlarging lens
lente^F de ampliación^F

baseboard
tablero^M de base^F

DEVELOPING BATHS
BAÑOS^M DE REVELADO^M

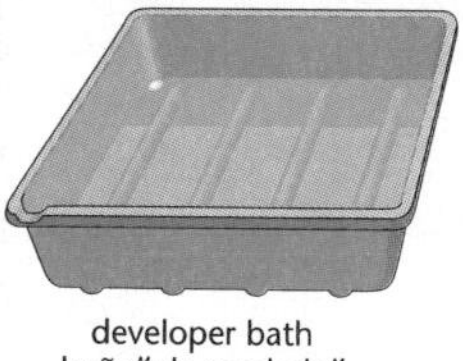

developer bath
baño^M de revelado^M

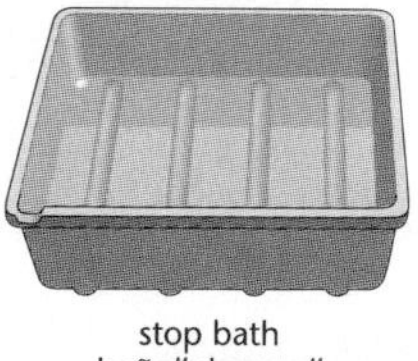

stop bath
baño^M de pare^M

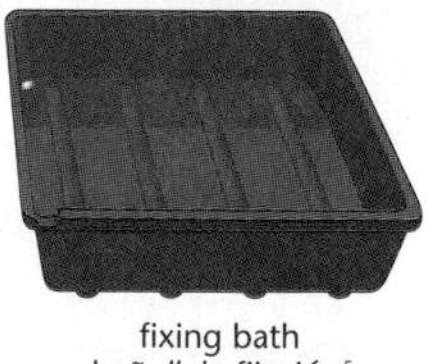

fixing bath
baño^M de fijación^F

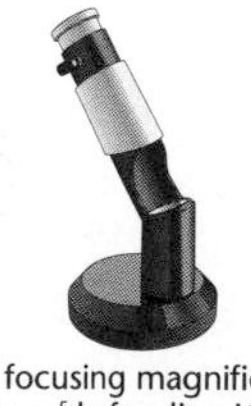

focusing magnifier
lupa^F de focalización^F

PRINT WASHER
CUBETA^F PARA LAVAR IMPRESIONES^F

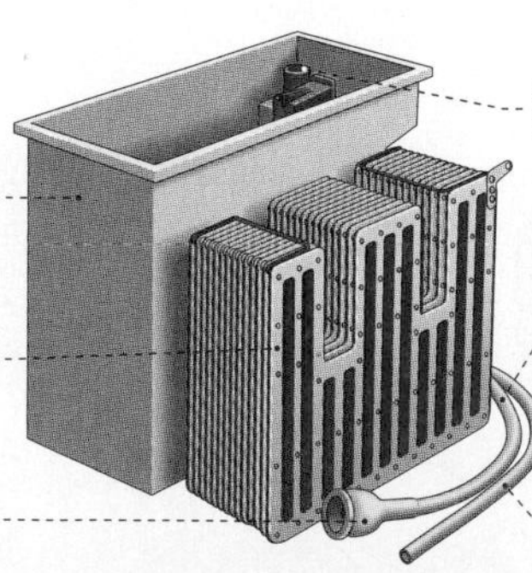

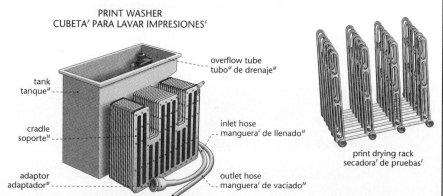

overflow tube
tubo^M de drenaje^M

tank
tanque^M

cradle
soporte^M

adaptor
adaptador^M

inlet hose
manguera^F de llenado^M

outlet hose
manguera^F de vaciado^M

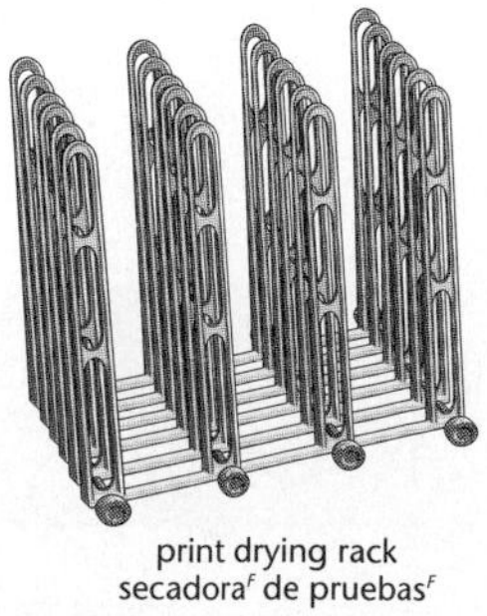

print drying rack
secadora^F de pruebas^F

SOUND REPRODUCING SYSTEM
EQUIPO^M ESTEREOFÓNICO

SYSTEM COMPONENTS
COMPONENTES^M

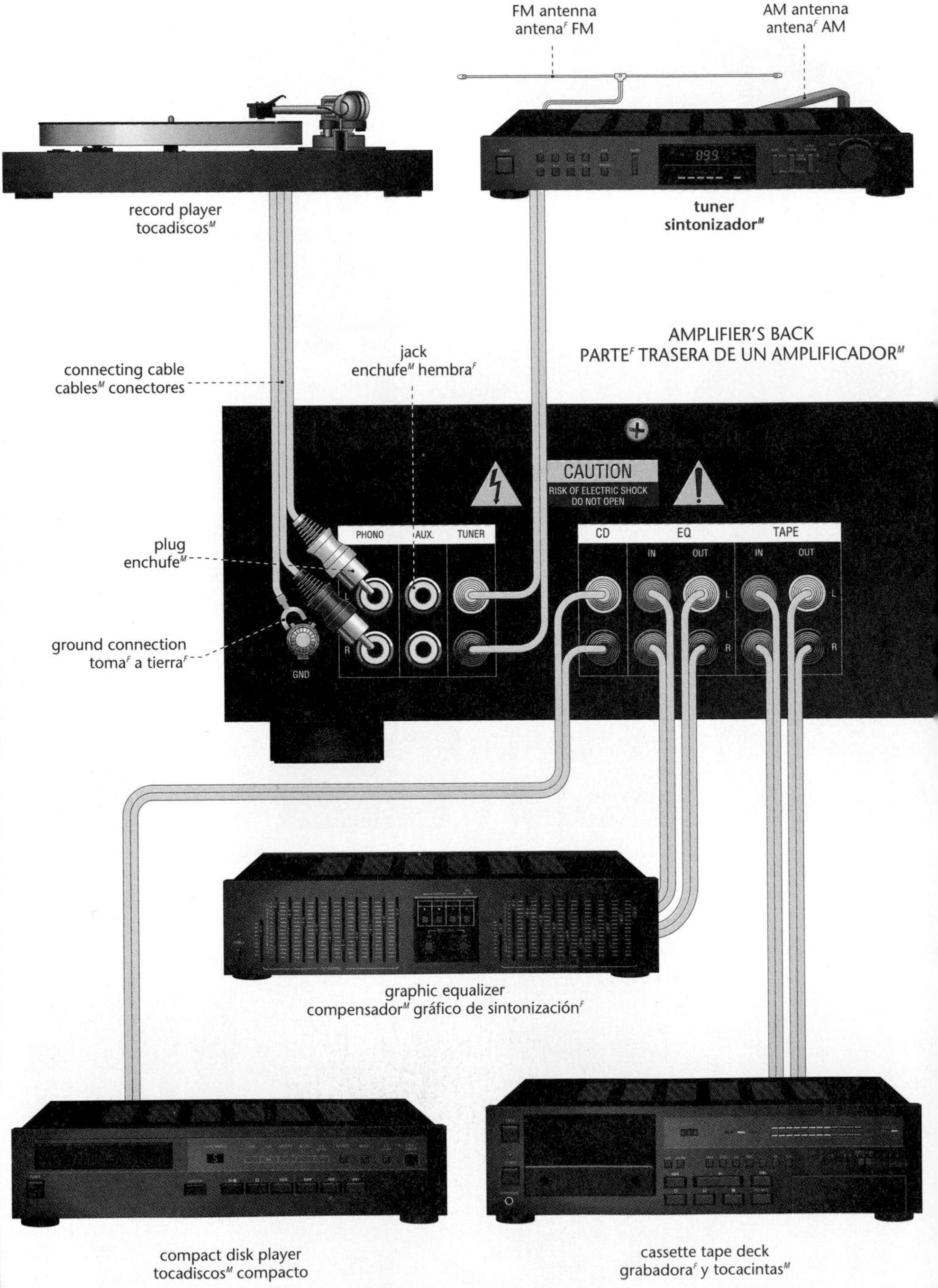

FM antenna
antena^F FM

AM antenna
antena^F AM

record player
tocadiscos^M

tuner
sintonizador^M

AMPLIFIER'S BACK
PARTE^F TRASERA DE UN AMPLIFICADOR^M

connecting cable
cables^M conectores

jack
enchufe^M hembra^F

plug
enchufe^M

ground connection
toma^F a tierra^F

CAUTION
RISK OF ELECTRIC SHOCK
DO NOT OPEN

PHONO   AUX.   TUNER   CD   EQ   TAPE
                                  IN OUT   IN OUT

L   L

R   R

GND

graphic equalizer
compensador^M gráfico de sintonización^F

compact disk player
tocadiscos^M compacto

cassette tape deck
grabadora^F y tocacintas^M

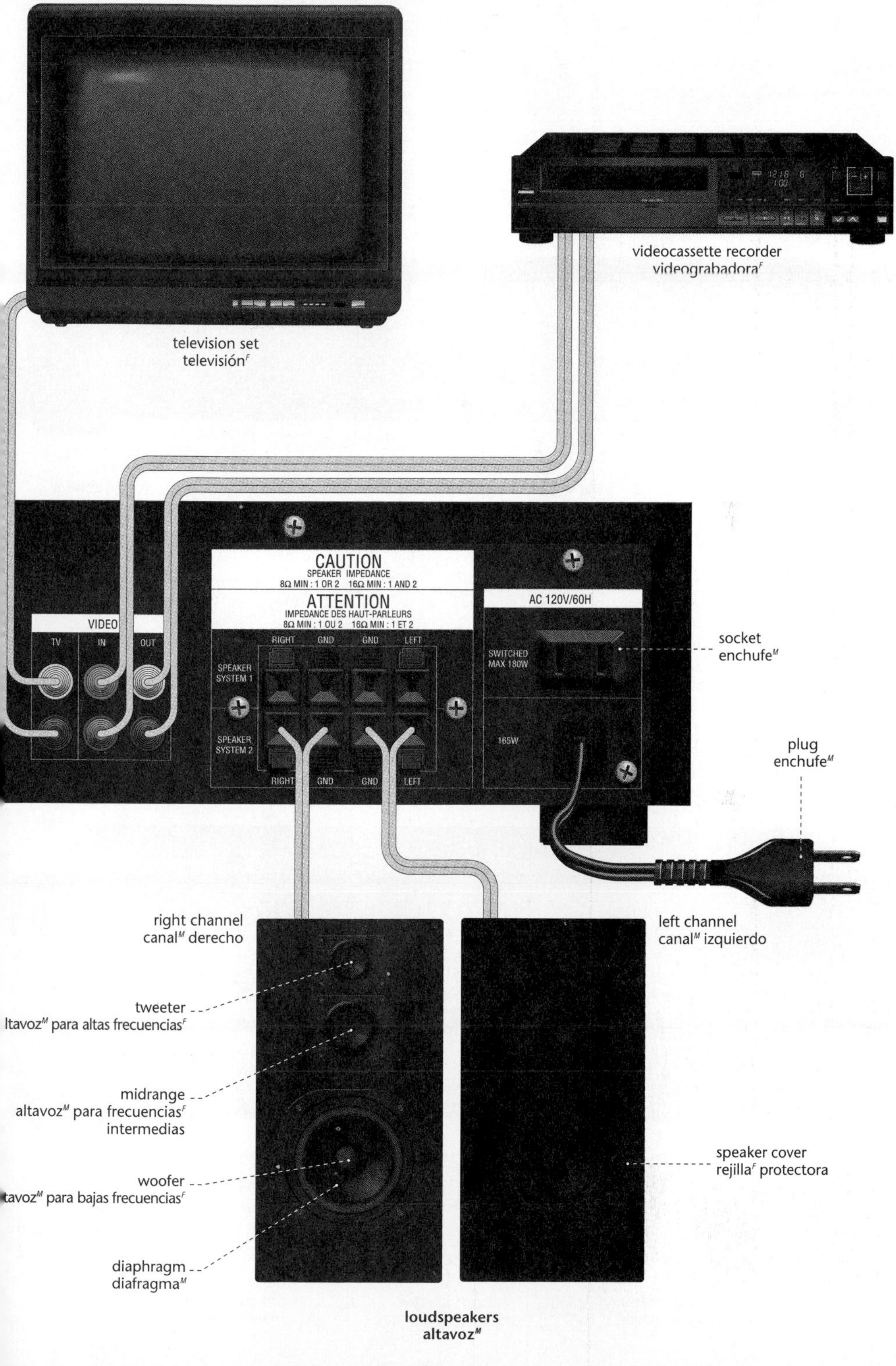

videocassette recorder
videograbadora^F

television set
televisión^F

CAUTION
SPEAKER IMPEDANCE
8Ω MIN : 1 OR 2   16Ω MIN : 1 AND 2

ATTENTION
IMPEDANCE DES HAUT-PARLEURS
8Ω MIN : 1 OU 2   16Ω MIN : 1 ET 2

AC 120V/60H

VIDEO

TV   IN   OUT

RIGHT   GND   GND   LEFT

SPEAKER
SYSTEM 1

SWITCHED
MAX 180W

SPEAKER
SYSTEM 2

165W

RIGHT   GND   GND   LEFT

socket
enchufe^M

plug
enchufe^M

right channel
canal^M derecho

left channel
canal^M izquierdo

tweeter
ltavoz^M para altas frecuencias^F

midrange
altavoz^M para frecuencias^F
intermedias

woofer
tavoz^M para bajas frecuencias^F

diaphragm
diafragma^M

speaker cover
rejilla^F protectora

**loudspeakers
altavoz^M**

401

SOUND REPRODUCING SYSTEM
EQUIPO^M ESTEREOFÓNICO

TUNER
SINTONIZADOR^M

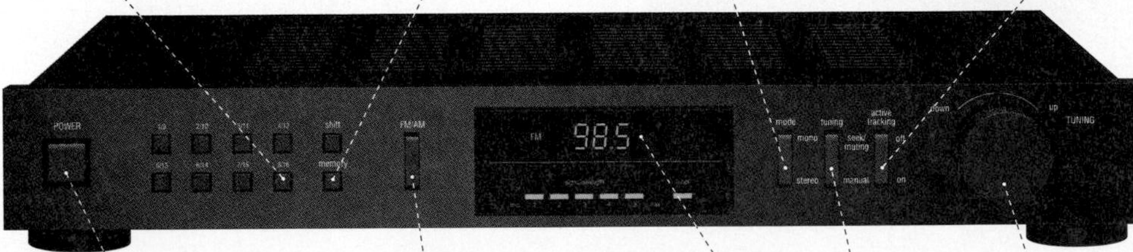

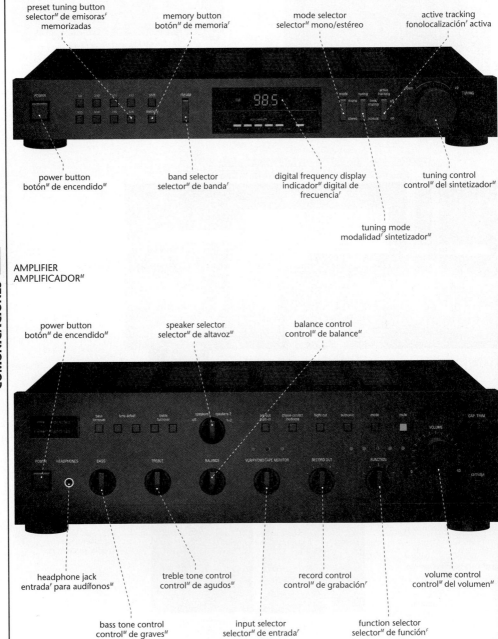

preset tuning button
selector^M de emisoras^F
memorizadas

memory button
botón^M de memoria^F

mode selector
selector^M mono/estéreo

active tracking
fonolocalización^F activa

power button
botón^M de encendido^M

band selector
selector^M de banda^F

digital frequency display
indicador^M digital de
frecuencia^F

tuning control
control^M del sintetizador^M

tuning mode
modalidad^F sintetizador^M

AMPLIFIER
AMPLIFICADOR^M

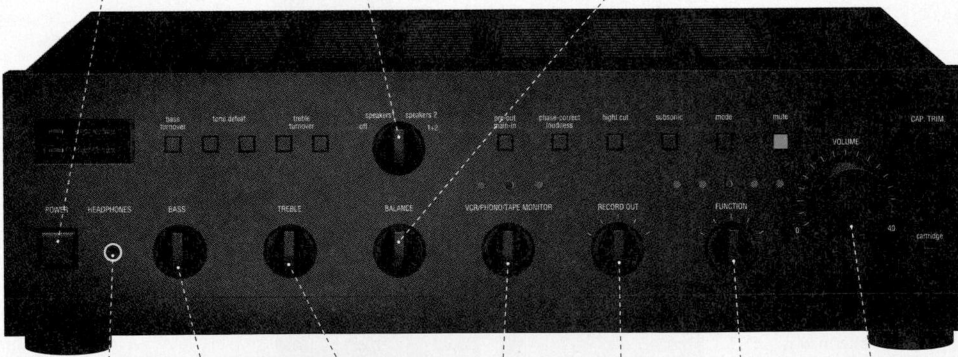

power button
botón^M de encendido^M

speaker selector
selector^M de altavoz^M

balance control
control^M de balance^M

headphone jack
entrada^F para audífonos^M

treble tone control
control^M de agudos^M

record control
control^M de grabación^F

volume control
control^M del volumen^M

bass tone control
control^M de graves^M

input selector
selector^M de entrada^F

function selector
selector^M de función^F

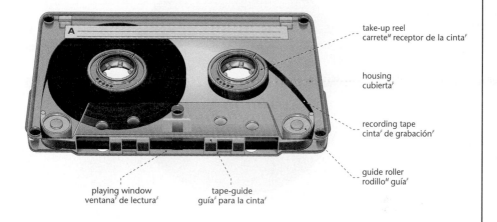

take-up reel
carrete^M receptor de la cinta^F

housing
cubierta^F

recording tape
cinta^F de grabación^F

guide roller
rodillo^M guía^F

playing window
ventana^F de lectura^F

tape-guide
guía^F para la cinta^F

CASSETTE TAPE DECK
GRABADORA^F Y TOCACINTAS^M

counter reset button
botón^M del contador^M a ceros^M

tape selector
selector^M de tipo^M de cinta^F

fast-forward button
botón^M de avance^M rápido

eject button
botón^M de expulsión^F

tape counter
contador^M

play button
botón^M de reproducción^F

peak level meter
medidor^M de altos niveles^M
de frecuencia^F

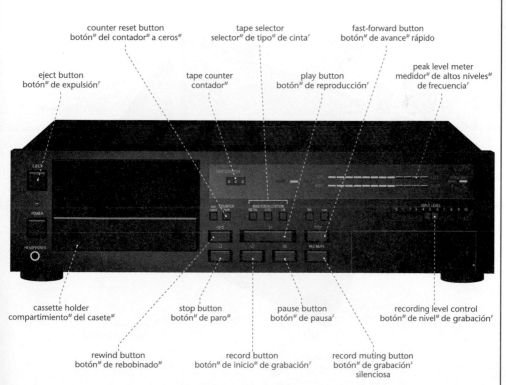

cassette holder
compartimiento^M del casete^M

stop button
botón^M de paro^M

pause button
botón^M de pausa^F

recording level control
botón^M de nivel^M de grabación^F

rewind button
botón^M de rebobinado^M

record button
botón^M de inicio^M de grabación^F

record muting button
botón^M de grabación^F
silenciosa

SOUND REPRODUCING SYSTEM
EQUIPO^M ESTEREOFÓNICO

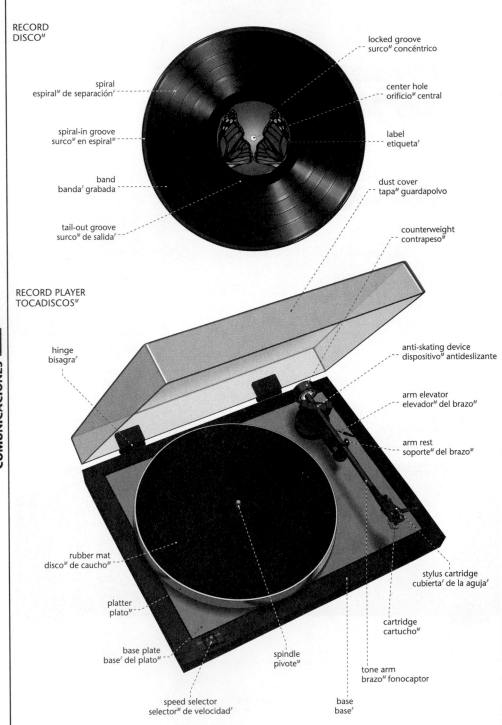

RECORD
DISCO^M

locked groove
surco^M concéntrico

spiral
espiral^M de separación^F

center hole
orificio^M central

spiral-in groove
surco^M en espiral^M

label
etiqueta^F

band
banda^F grabada

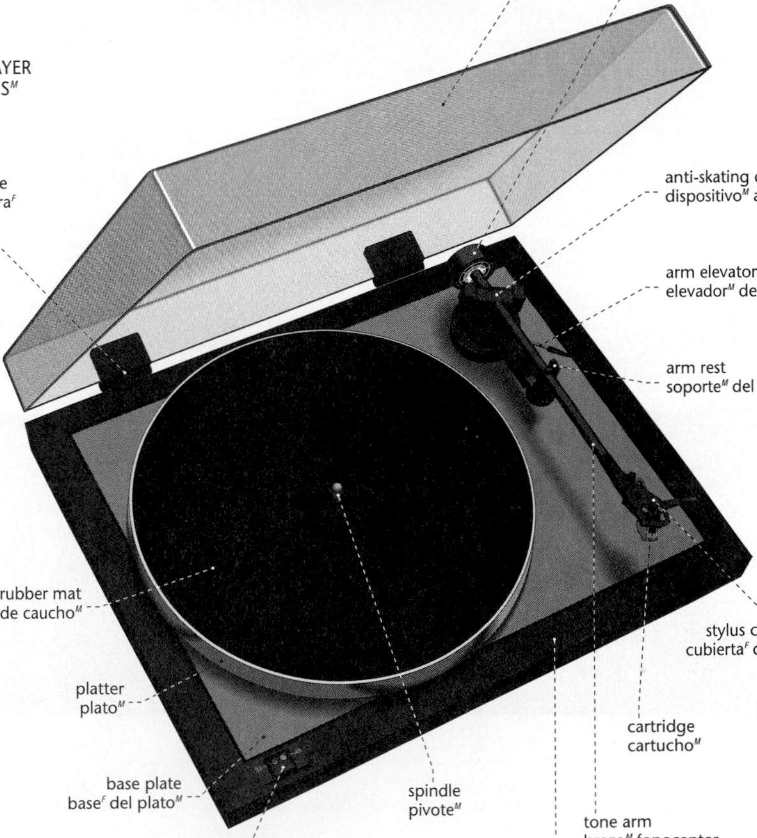

dust cover
tapa^M guardapolvo

tail-out groove
surco^M de salida^F

counterweight
contrapeso^M

RECORD PLAYER
TOCADISCOS^M

hinge
bisagra^F

anti-skating device
dispositivo^M antideslizante

arm elevator
elevador^M del brazo^M

arm rest
soporte^M del brazo^M

rubber mat
disco^M de caucho^M

stylus cartridge
cubierta^F de la aguja^F

platter
plato^M

cartridge
cartucho^M

base plate
base^F del plato^M

spindle
pivote^M

tone arm
brazo^M fonocaptor

speed selector
selector^M de velocidad^F

base
base^F

COMPACT DISK
DISCO^M COMPACTO

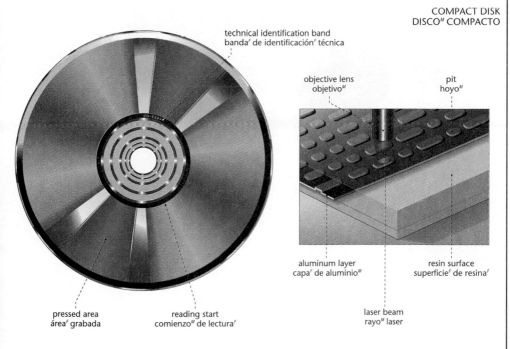

technical identification band
banda^F de identificación^F técnica

objective lens
objetivo^M

pit
hoyo^M

aluminum layer
capa^F de aluminio^M

resin surface
superficie^F de resina^F

pressed area
área^F grabada

reading start
comienzo^M de lectura^F

laser beam
rayo^M laser

COMPACT DISK PLAYER
LECTOR^M DE DISCO^M COMPACTO

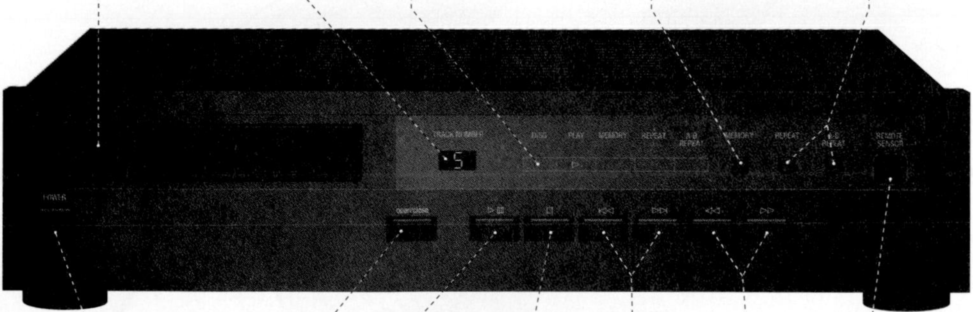

track number
número^M de pista^F

disk compartment
compartimiento^M para el disco^M

indicators
indicadores^M

memory key
botón^M de la memoria^F

repeat keys
tecla^F de repetición^F

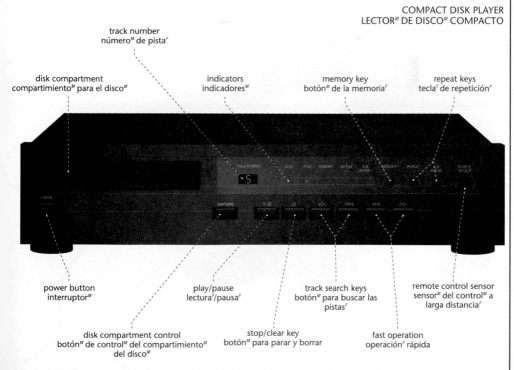

power button
interruptor^M

play/pause
lectura^F/pausa^F

track search keys
botón^M para buscar las
pistas^F

remote control sensor
sensor^M del control^M a
larga distancia^F

disk compartment control
botón^M de control^M del compartimiento^M
del disco^M

stop/clear key
botón^M para parar y borrar

fast operation
operación^F rápida

DYNAMIC MICROPHONE
MICRÓFONO^M ELECTRODINÁMICO

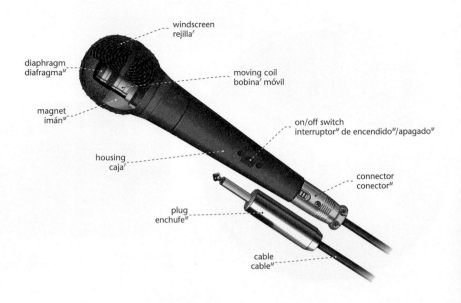

windscreen
rejilla^F

diaphragm
diafragma^M

moving coil
bobina^F móvil

magnet
imán^M

on/off switch
interruptor^M de encendido^M/apagado^M

housing
caja^F

connector
conector^M

plug
enchufe^M

cable
cable^M

HEADPHONES
AURICULARES^M

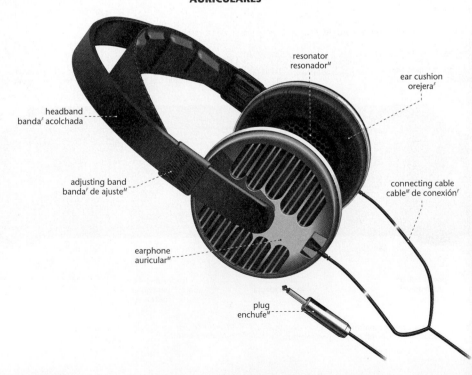

resonator
resonador^M

ear cushion
orejera^F

headband
banda^F acolchada

adjusting band
banda^F de ajuste^M

connecting cable
cable^M de conexión^F

earphone
auricular^M

plug
enchufe^M

studio
estudio^M

tone leader generator
generador^M principal de tono^M

cartridge tape recorder
cartucho^M de la cinta^F grabadora^F

microphone
micrófono^M

clock
reloj^M

digital audio tape recorder
cinta^F digital grabadora^F

announcer turret
torre^F del locutor^M

volume unit meters
unidad^F de medición^F de
volumen^M

compact disk player
tocadiscos^M para discos^M
compactos

on-air warning light
luz^F de advertencia^F de
emisión^F

audio monitor
monitor^M de sonido^M

cassette deck
grabadora^F y tocacintas^M

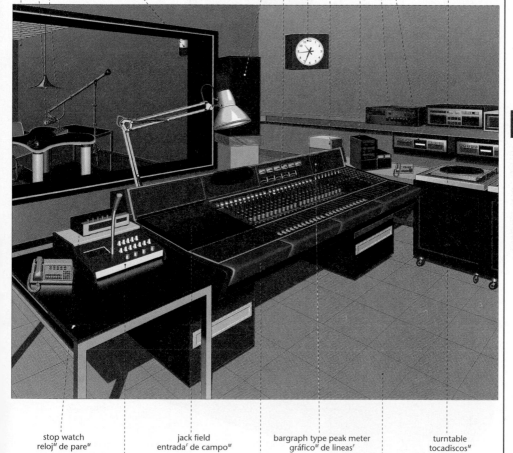

stop watch
reloj^M de pare^M

jack field
entrada^F de campo^M

bargraph type peak meter
gráfico^M de lineas^F

turntable
tocadiscos^M

producer turret
torre^F del productor^M

audio console
consola^F de sonido^M

control room
sala^F de control^M

PORTABLE SOUND SYSTEMS
SISTEMAS^M DE SONIDO^M PORTÁTILES

PERSONAL RADIO CASSETTE PLAYER
RADIO AM \ FM Y LECTOR^M DE CASETES^M PERSONAL

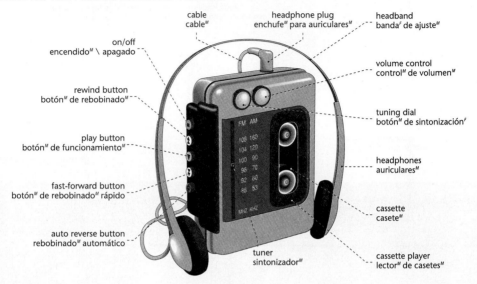

cable
cable^M

headphone plug
enchufe^M para auriculares^M

headband
banda^F de ajuste^M

on/off
encendido^M \ apagado

volume control
control^M de volumen^M

rewind button
botón^M de rebobinado^M

tuning dial
botón^M de sintonización^F

play button
botón^M de funcionamiento^M

headphones
auriculares^M

fast-forward button
botón^M de rebobinado^M rápido

cassette
casete^M

auto reverse button
rebobinado^M automático

tuner
sintonizador^M

cassette player
lector^M de casetes^M

PORTABLE CD RADIO CASSETTE RECORDER
GRABADORA^F PORTÁTIL

stereo control
control^M estereo

handle
asa^F

mode selectors
selectores^M de modalidad^F

antenna
antena^F

on/off/volume
encendido^M \ apagado^M
\ volumen^M

compact disk player
lector^M de discos^M compacto

headphone jack
toma^F para auriculares^M

compact disk
disco^M compacto

compact disk player control
controles^M del lector^M de
discos^M compactos

speaker
altavoz^M

tuner
sintonizador^M

tuning control
control^M de sintonización^F

power plug
enchufe^M

cassette
casete^M

cassette player
lector^M de casetes^M

cassette player controls
controles^M del lector^M de casetes^M

VIDEO CAMERA
CÁMARA^F DE VIDEO^M

eyepiece
adaptador^M al ojo^M

power zoom button
botón^M de funcionamiento^M del zoom^M

electronic viewfinder
visor^M electrónico

white balance sensor
captor^M de luz^F

accessory shoe
patín^M para accesorios^M

cassette eject switch
botón^M de eyección^F del casete^M

videotape operation controls
controles^M del video^M casete^M

viewfinder adjustment keys
botones^M de ajuste^M del visor^M

built-in microphone
micrófono^M integrado

DATA SET   ZERO MEM

ADJUST   RESET

SELECT

SPEED   EXPOSURE   EDIT SEARCH

AUTO LOCK   FOCUS   WHITE BAL   FADER

BATT

macro set button
botón^M de acercamiento^M

cassette compartment
compartimento^M para el casete^M

zoom lens
lente^F zoom^M

data display
visualización^F de la información^F

battery eject switch
botón^M para sacar la pila^F

lens hood
capuchón^M

shooting adjustment keys
botones^M de ajuste^M del rodaje^M

battery
pila^F

edit/search buttons
botones de montaje^M y búsqueda^F

COMMUNICATIONS
COMUNICACIONES

TELEVISION SET
TELEVISOR^M

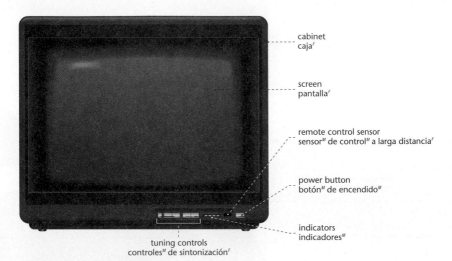

cabinet
caja^F

screen
pantalla^F

remote control sensor
sensor^M de control^M a larga distancia^F

power button
botón^M de encendido^M

indicators
indicadores^M

tuning controls
controles^M de sintonización^F

PICTURE TUBE
TUBO^M DE PANTALLA^F

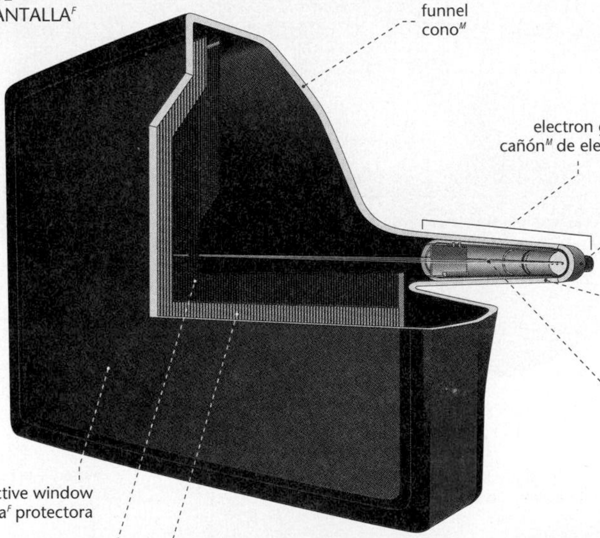

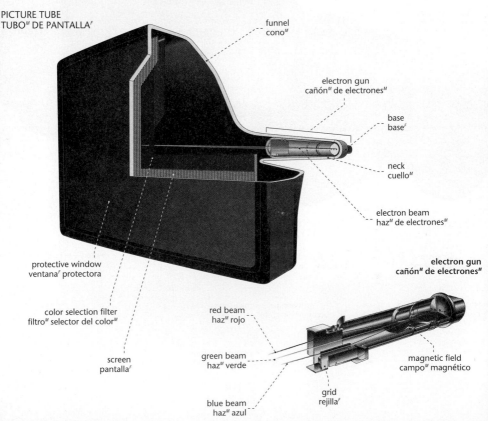

funnel
cono^M

electron gun
cañón^M de electrones^M

base
base^F

neck
cuello^M

electron beam
haz^M de electrones^M

protective window
ventana^F protectora

color selection filter
filtro^M selector del color^M

screen
pantalla^F

**electron gun
cañón^M de electrones^M**

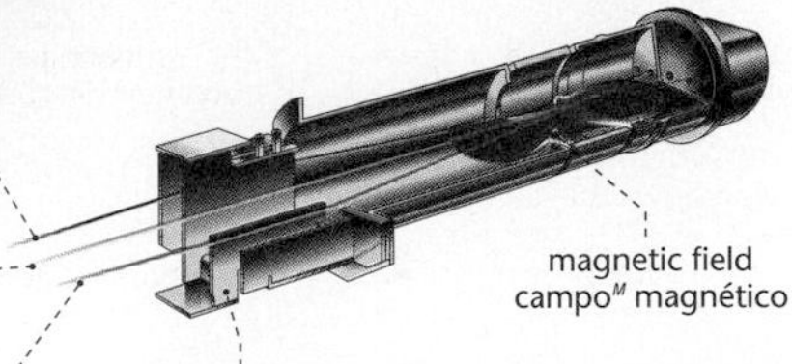

red beam
haz^M rojo

green beam
haz^M verde

blue beam
haz^M azul

grid
rejilla^F

magnetic field
campo^M magnético

**COMMUNICATIONS
COMUNICACIONES**

REMOTE CONTROL
CONTROL^M A LARGA DISTANCIA^F

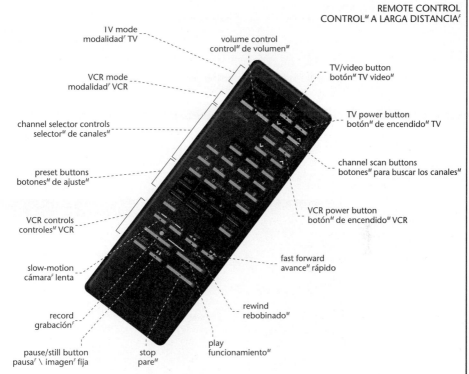

I V mode
modalidad^F TV

volume control
control^M de volumen^M

VCR mode
modalidad^F VCR

TV/video button
botón^M TV video^M

channel selector controls
selector^M de canales^M

TV power button
botón^M de encendido^M TV

preset buttons
botones^M de ajuste^M

channel scan buttons
botones^M para buscar los canales^M

VCR controls
controles^M VCR

VCR power button
botón^M de encendido^M VCR

slow-motion
cámara^F lenta

fast forward
avance^M rápido

record
grabación^F

rewind
rebobinado^M

pause/still button
pausa^F \ imagen^F fija

stop
pare^M

play
funcionamiento^M

VIDEOCASSETTE RECORDER
VIDEOGRABADORA^F

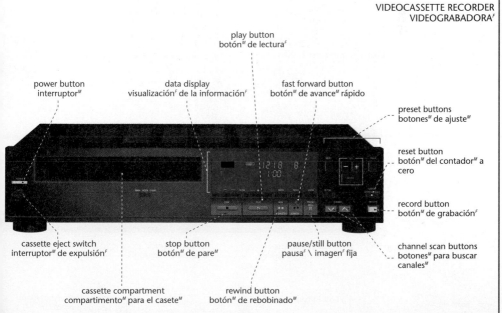

play button
botón^M de lectura^F

power button
interruptor^M

data display
visualización^F de la información^F

fast forward button
botón^M de avance^M rápido

preset buttons
botones^M de ajuste^M

reset button
botón^M del contador^M a cero

record button
botón^M de grabación^F

cassette eject switch
interruptor^M de expulsión^F

stop button
botón^M de pare^M

pause/still button
pausa^F \ imagen^F fija

channel scan buttons
botones^M para buscar canales^M

cassette compartment
compartimento^M para el casete^M

rewind button
botón^M de rebobinado^M

STUDIO AND CONTROL ROOMS
ESTUDIO^M DE TELEVISIÓN^F Y CABINAS^F DE CONTROL^M

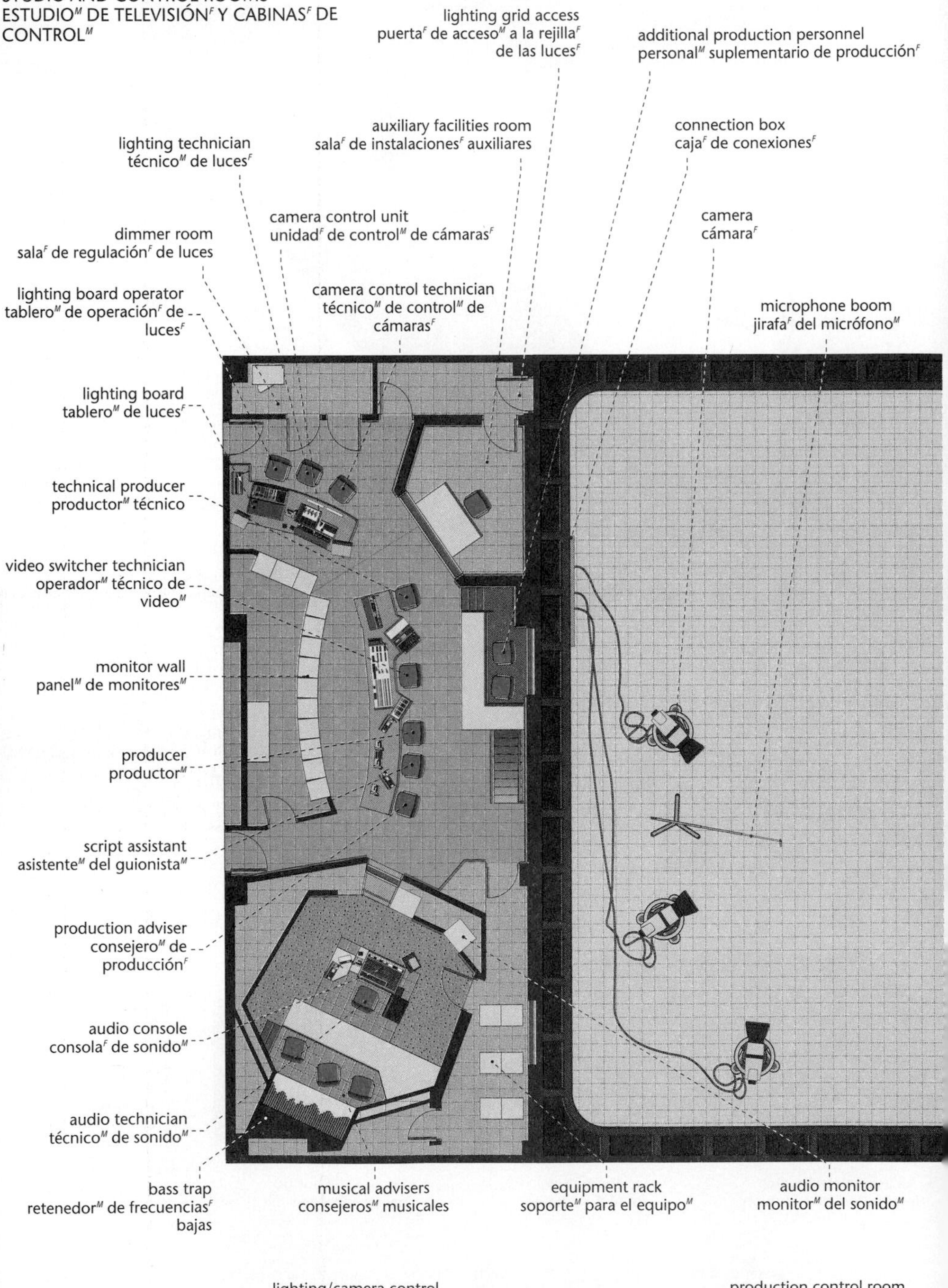

lighting grid access
puerta^F de acceso^M a la rejilla^F de las luces^F

additional production personnel
personal^M suplementario de producción^F

lighting technician
técnico^M de luces^F

auxiliary facilities room
sala^F de instalaciones^F auxiliares

connection box
caja^F de conexiones^F

dimmer room
sala^F de regulación^F de luces

camera control unit
unidad^F de control^M de cámaras^F

camera
cámara^F

lighting board operator
tablero^M de operación^F de luces^F

camera control technician
técnico^M de control^M de cámaras^F

microphone boom
jirafa^F del micrófono^M

lighting board
tablero^M de luces^F

technical producer
productor^M técnico

video switcher technician
operador^M técnico de video^M

monitor wall
panel^M de monitores^M

producer
productor^M

script assistant
asistente^M del guionista^M

production adviser
consejero^M de producción^F

audio console
consola^F de sonido^M

audio technician
técnico^M de sonido^M

bass trap
retenedor^M de frecuencias^F bajas

musical advisers
consejeros^M musicales

equipment rack
soporte^M para el equipo^M

audio monitor
monitor^M del sonido^M

studio floor
estudio^M

lighting/camera control area
sala^F de control^M de luces^F

audio control room
control^M de sonido^M

production control room
sala^F de producción^F y control^M

audio/video preview unit
unidad de visualización de imagen*F* \ sonido

stereo phase monitor
control*M* del sonido*M* estereofónico

monitor wall
panel*M* de monitores*M*

preview monitors
monitores*M* de visualización*F* previa

vector/waveform monitor
control*M* del vector*M* de vibraciones*F*

input monitors
monitores*M* de entrada*F*

digital video effects monitor
monitor*M* de efectos*M*
video\digitales

technical producer monitor
monitor*M* de la producción*F*
técnica

audio monitor
monitor*M* de sonido*M*

clock
reloj*M*

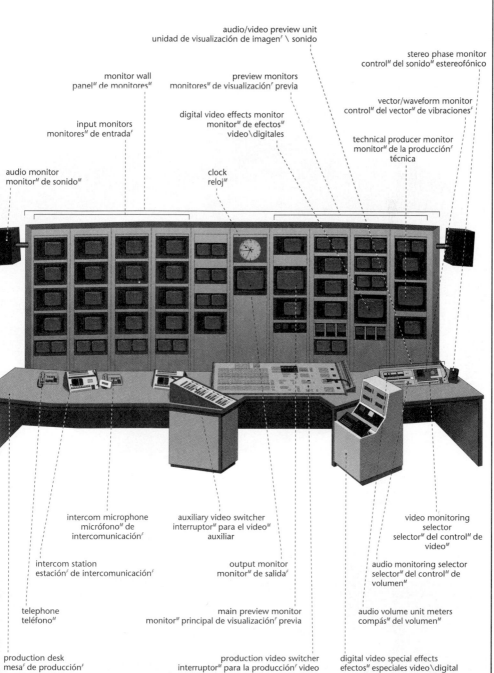

intercom microphone
micrófono*M* de
intercomunicación*F*

auxiliary video switcher
interruptor*M* para el video*M*
auxiliar

video monitoring
selector
selector*M* del control*M* de
video*M*

intercom station
estación*F* de intercomunicación*F*

output monitor
monitor*M* de salida*F*

audio monitoring selector
selector*M* del control*M* de
volumen*M*

telephone
teléfono*M*

main preview monitor
monitor*M* principal de visualización*F* previa

audio volume unit meters
compás*M* del volumen*M*

production desk
mesa*F* de producción*F*

production video switcher
interruptor*M* para la producción*F* video

digital video special effects
efectos*M* especiales video\digital

STUDIO FLOOR
ESTUDIO^M

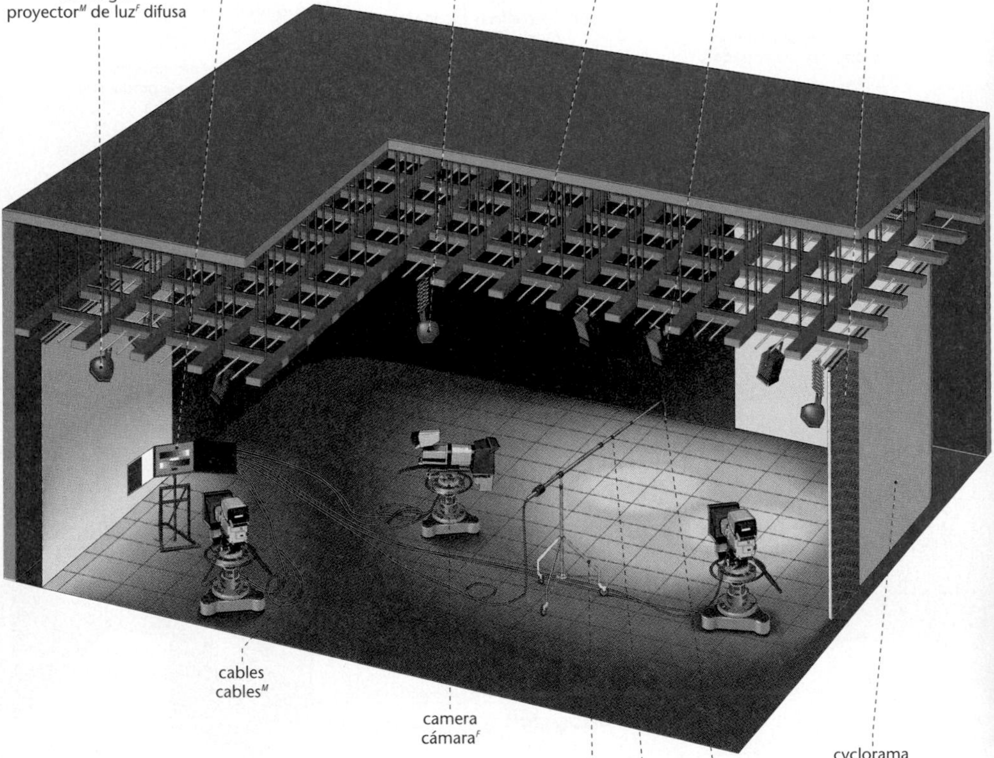

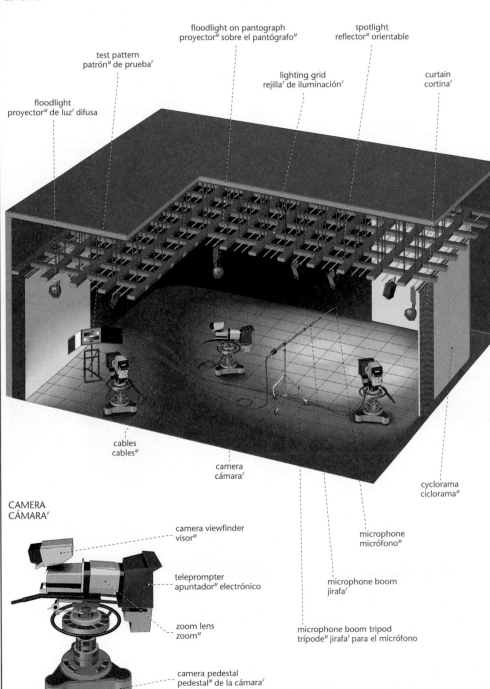

floodlight on pantograph
proyector^M sobre el pantógrafo^M

spotlight
reflector^M orientable

test pattern
patrón^M de prueba^F

lighting grid
rejilla^F de iluminación^F

curtain
cortina^F

floodlight
proyector^M de luz^F difusa

cables
cables^M

camera
cámara^F

cyclorama
ciclorama^M

CAMERA
CÁMARA^F

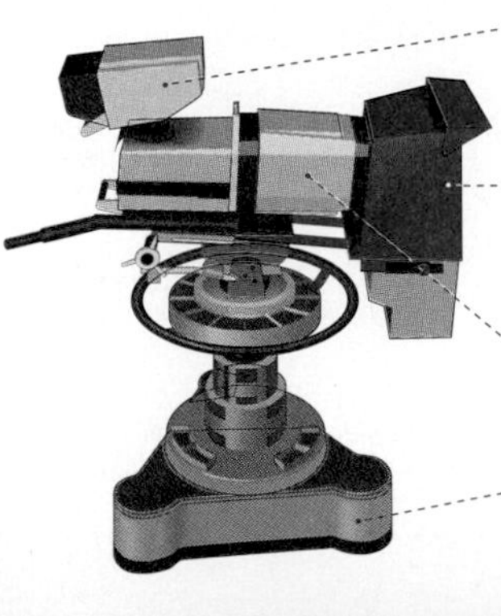

camera viewfinder
visor^M

teleprompter
apuntador^M electrónico

zoom lens
zoom^M

camera pedestal
pedestal^M de la cámara^F

microphone
micrófono^M

microphone boom
jirafa^F

microphone boom tripod
trípode^M jirafa^F para el micrófono

414

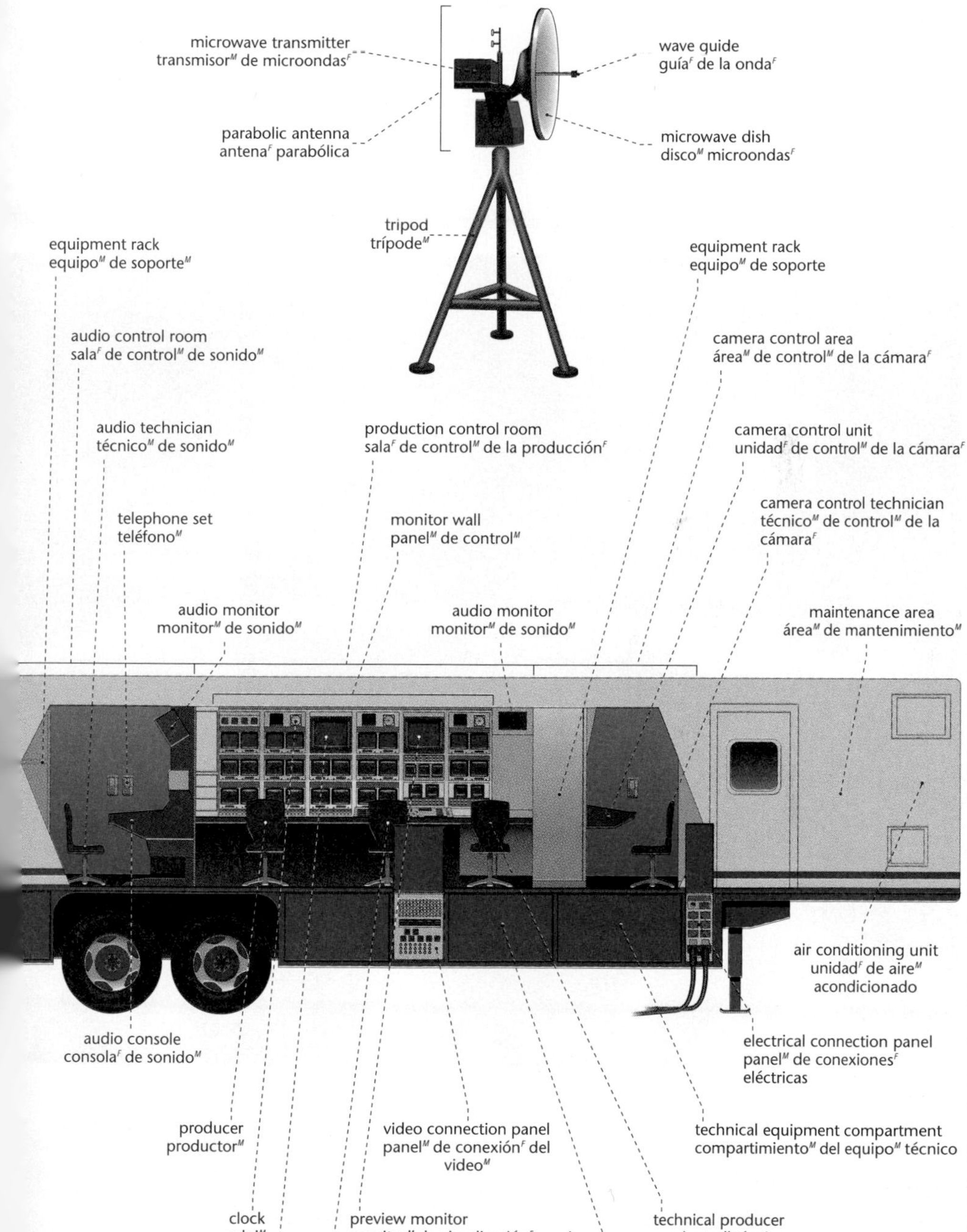

microwave transmitter
transmisor^M de microondas^F

wave guide
guía^F de la onda^F

parabolic antenna
antena^F parabólica

microwave dish
disco^M microondas^F

tripod
trípode^M

equipment rack
equipo^M de soporte^M

equipment rack
equipo^M de soporte

audio control room
sala^F de control^M de sonido^M

camera control area
área^F de control^M de la cámara^F

audio technician
técnico^M de sonido^M

production control room
sala^F de control^M de la producción^F

camera control unit
unidad^F de control^M de la cámara^F

telephone set
teléfono^M

monitor wall
panel^M de control^M

camera control technician
técnico^M de control^M de la cámara^F

audio monitor
monitor^M de sonido^M

audio monitor
monitor^M de sonido^M

maintenance area
área^M de mantenimiento^M

audio console
consola^F de sonido^M

air conditioning unit
unidad^F de aire^M
acondicionado

electrical connection panel
panel^M de conexiones^F
eléctricas

producer
productor^M

video connection panel
panel^M de conexión^F del
video^M

technical equipment compartment
compartimiento^M del equipo^M técnico

clock
reloj^M

preview monitor
monitor^M de visualización^F previa

technical producer
productor^M técnico

output monitor
monitor^M de producción^F

video switcher technician
operador^M técnico de video^M

cable drum compartment
compartimiento^M del cable^M de la batería^F

415

COMMUNICATIONS
COMUNICACIONES

cable distributor
cable^M distribuidor

satellite
satélite^M

local station
estación^F local

private broadcasting network
red^F de transmisión^F privada

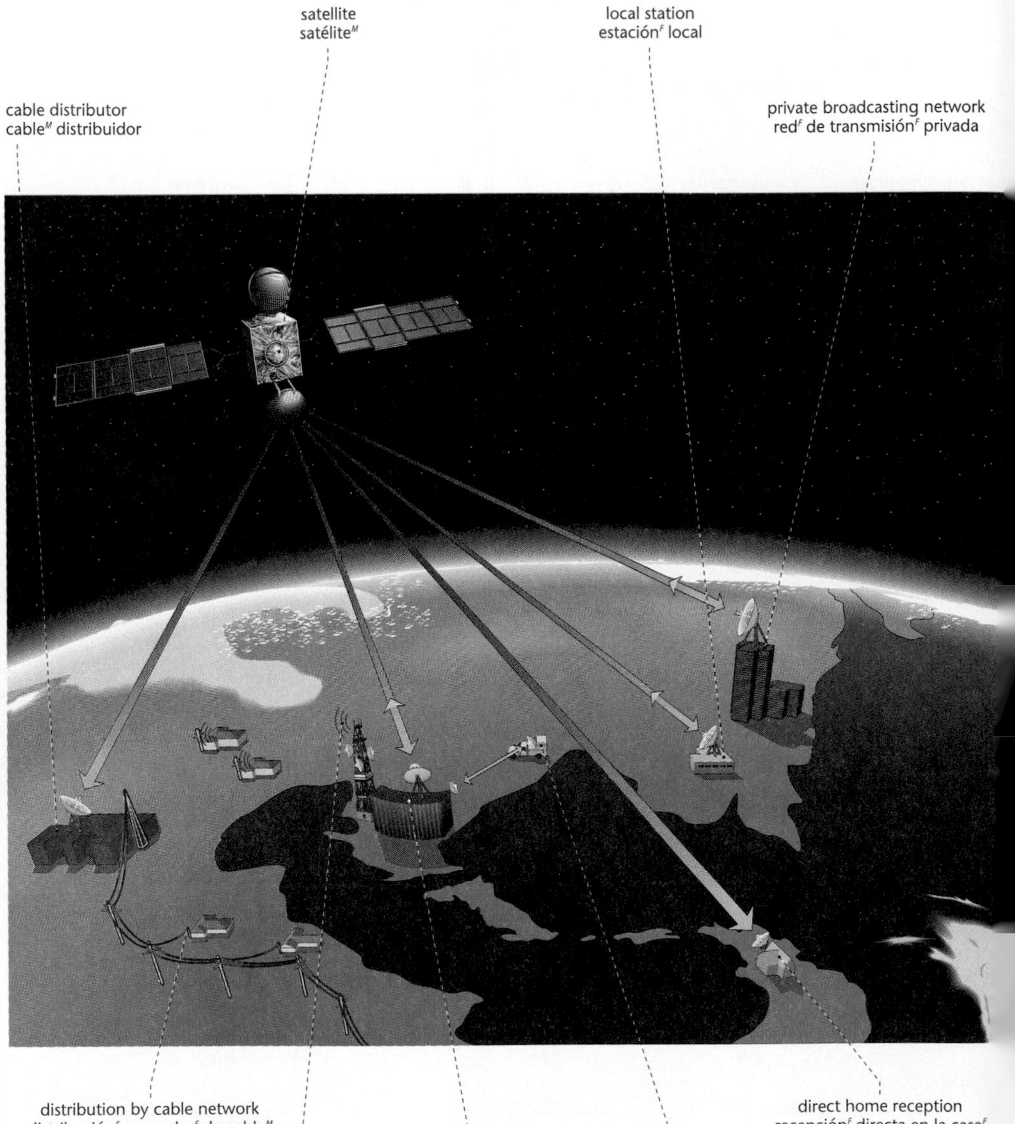

distribution by cable network
distribución^F por redes^F de cable^M

Hertzian wave transmission
transmisión^F de ondas^F Hertzianas

national broadcasting network
red^F nacional de transmisión^F

mobile unit
unidad^F móvil

direct home reception
recepción^F directa en la casa^F

TELECOMMUNICATIONS BY SATELLITE
TELECOMUNICACIONES^F POR SATÉLITE^M

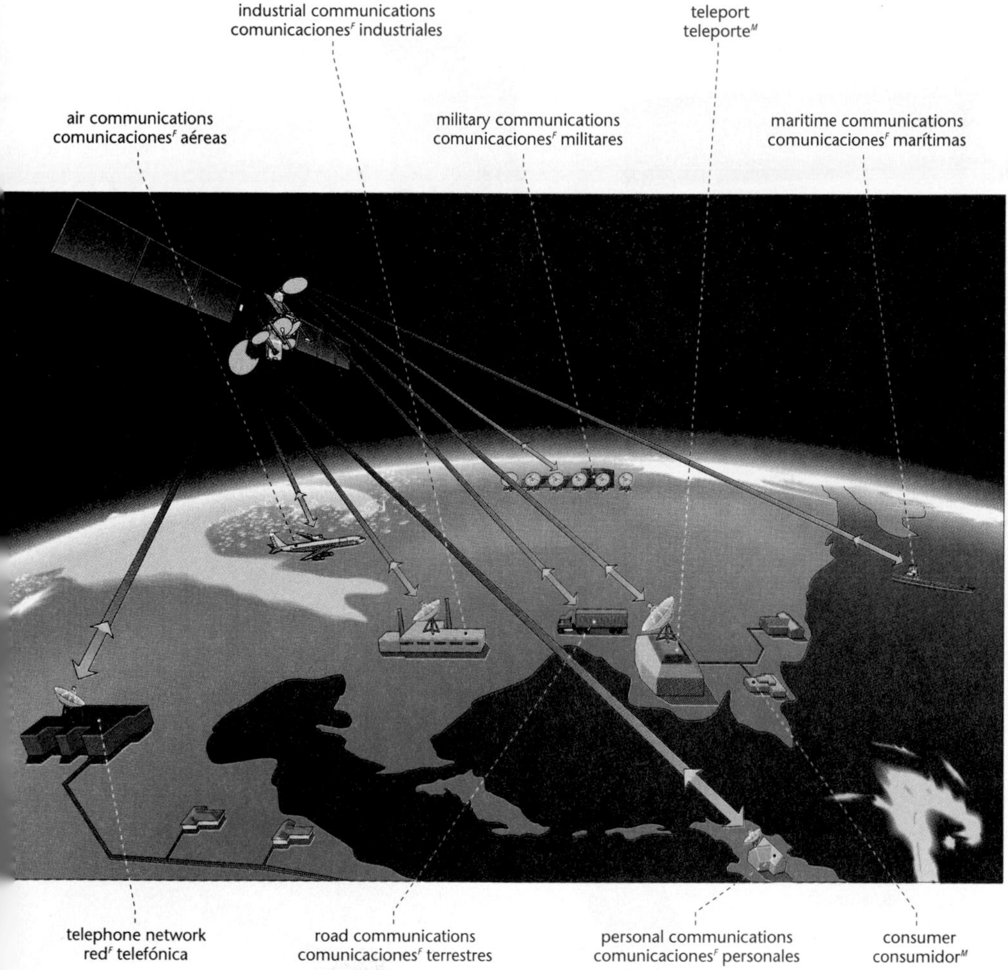

industrial communications
comunicaciones^F industriales

teleport
teleporte^M

air communications
comunicaciones^F aéreas

military communications
comunicaciones^F militares

maritime communications
comunicaciones^F marítimas

telephone network
red^F telefónica

road communications
comunicaciones^F terrestres

personal communications
comunicaciones^F personales

consumer
consumidor^M

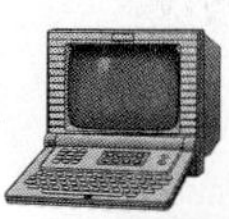

computer communication
comunicación^F por computador^M

TELECOMMUNICATIONS BY TELEPHONE NETWORK
TELECOMUNICACIONES^F POR RED^F TELEFÓNICA

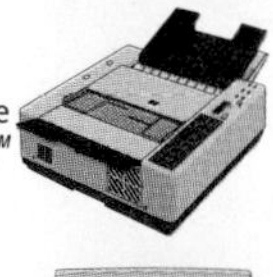

facsimile machine
facsímil^M

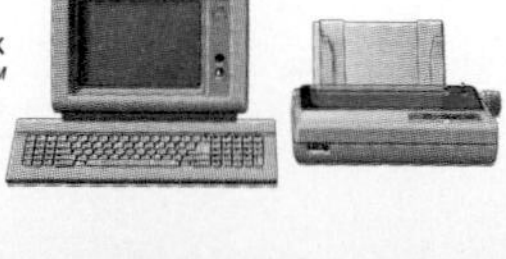

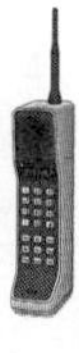

cellular telephone
teléfono^M celular

telex
télex^M

telephone set
teléfono^M

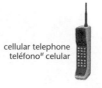

417

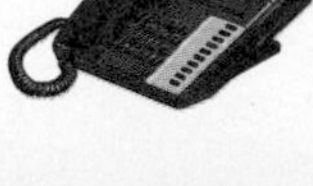

TELECOMMUNICATION SATELLITES
SATÉLITES^M DE TELECOMUNICACIONES^F

EXAMPLES OF SATELLITES
EJEMPLOS^M DE SATÉLITES^M

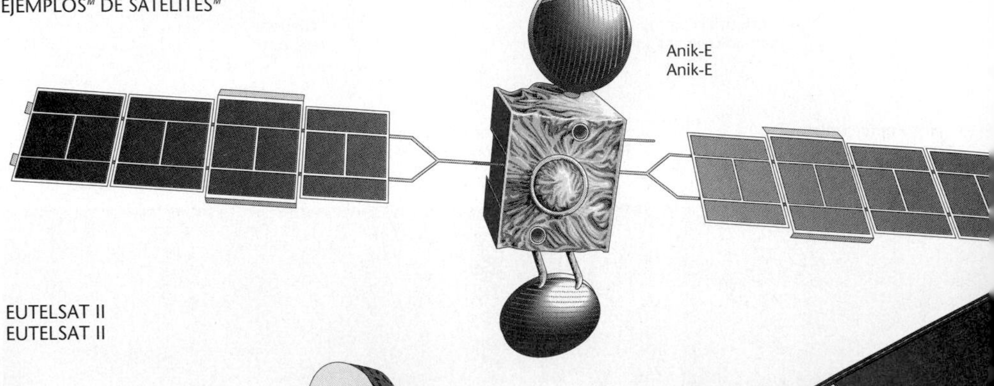

Anik-E
Anik-E

EUTELSAT II
EUTELSAT II

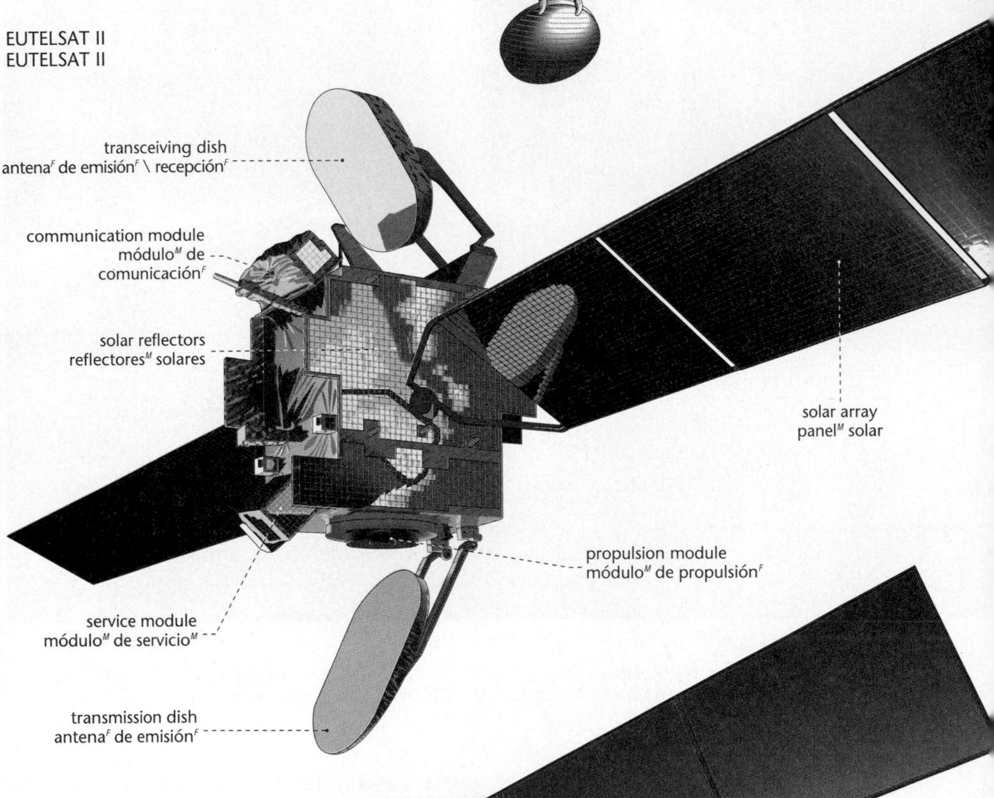

transceiving dish
antena^F de emisión^F \ recepción^F

communication module
módulo^M de
comunicación^F

solar reflectors
reflectores^M solares

solar array
panel^M solar

propulsion module
módulo^M de propulsión^F

service module
módulo^M de servicio^M

transmission dish
antena^F de emisión^F

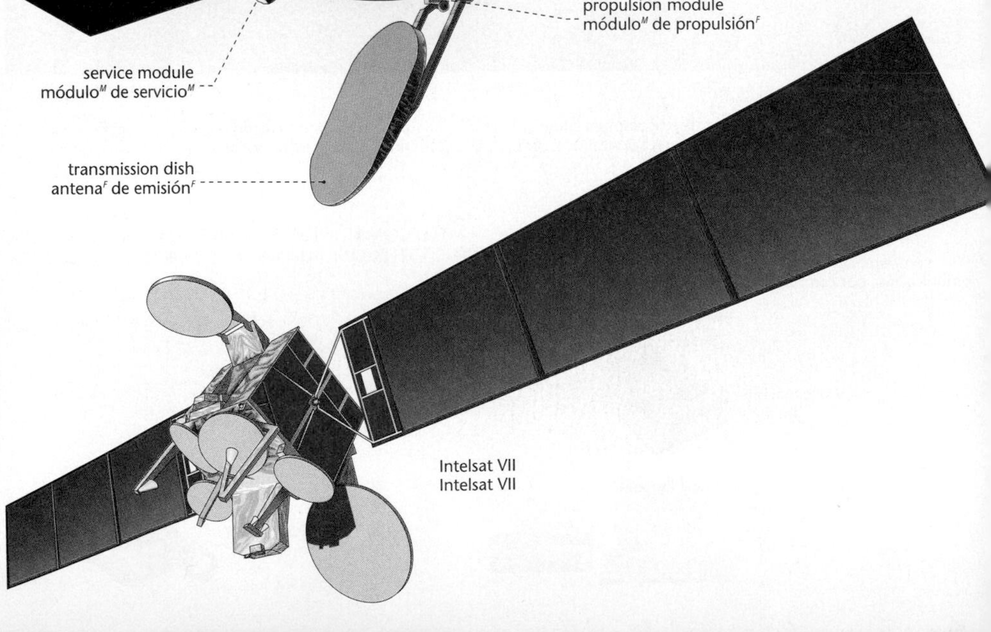

Intelsat VII
Intelsat VII

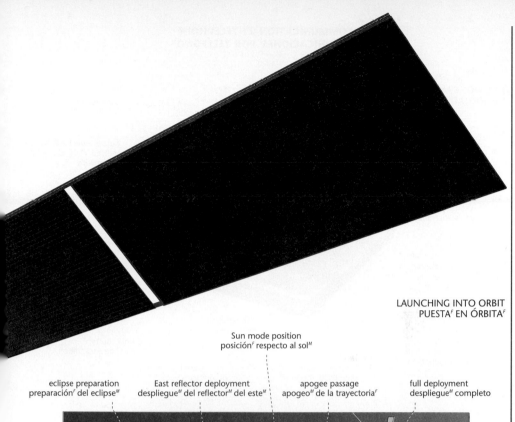

LAUNCHING INTO ORBIT
PUESTA^F EN ÓRBITA^F

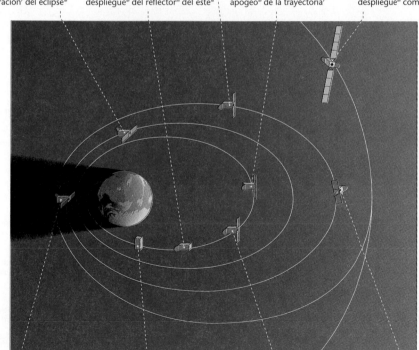

Sun mode position
posición^F respecto al sol^M

eclipse preparation
preparación^F del eclipse^M

East reflector deployment
despliegue^M del reflector^M del este^M

apogee passage
apogeo^M de la trayectoria^F

full deployment
despliegue^M completo

eclipse crossing
cruce^M del eclipse^M

launcher/satellite separation
separación^F del lanzador^M de satélites^M

solar array deployment
despliegue^M del panel solar

apogee motor firing
apogeo^M de encendido^M del
motor^M

TELEPHONE ANSWERING MACHINE
CONTESTADORA*F* AUTOMÁTICA

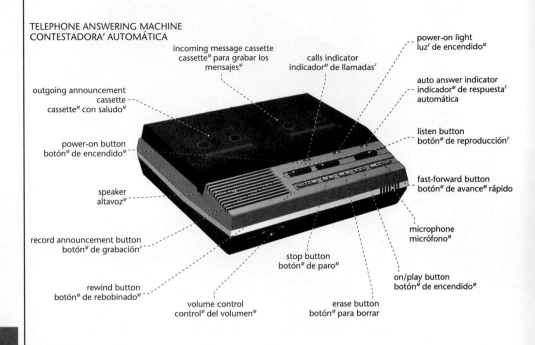

incoming message cassette
cassette*M* para grabar los
mensajes*M*

calls indicator
indicador*M* de llamadas*F*

power-on light
luz*F* de encendido*M*

auto answer indicator
indicador*M* de respuesta*F*
automática

outgoing announcement
cassette
cassette*M* con saludo*M*

power-on button
botón*M* de encendido*M*

listen button
botón*M* de reproducción*F*

fast-forward button
botón*M* de avance*M* rápido

speaker
altavoz*M*

microphone
micrófono*M*

record announcement button
botón*M* de grabación*F*

stop button
botón*M* de paro*M*

on/play button
botón*M* de encendido*M*

rewind button
botón*M* de rebobinado*M*

volume control
control*M* del volumen*M*

erase button
botón*M* para borrar

TELEPHONE SET
TELÉFONO*M*

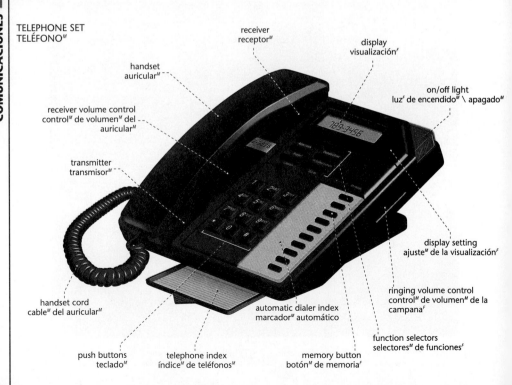

receiver
receptor*M*

display
visualización*F*

handset
auricular*M*

on/off light
luz*F* de encendido*M* \ apagado*M*

receiver volume control
control*M* de volumen*M* del
auricular*M*

transmitter
transmisor*M*

display setting
ajuste*M* de la visualización*F*

handset cord
cable*M* del auricular*M*

automatic dialer index
marcador*M* automático

ringing volume control
control*M* de volumen*M* de la
campana*F*

function selectors
selectores*M* de funciones*F*

push buttons
teclado*M*

telephone index
índice*M* de teléfonos*M*

memory button
botón*M* de memoria*F*

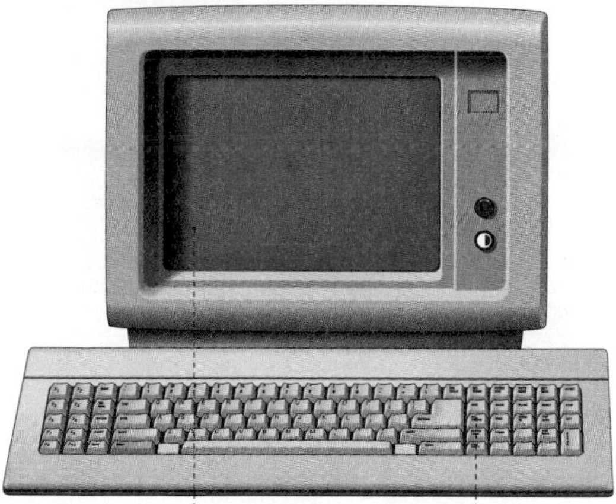

terminal
terminal^M

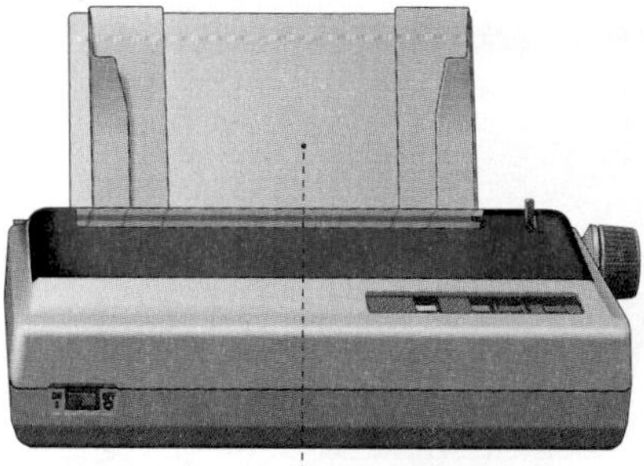

printer
impresora^F

visual display unit
pantalla^F

transmission/reception of messages
recepción^F y transmisión de mensajes^M

printing of messages
impresión^F de mensajes

FACSIMILE MACHINE
FACSIMIL^M

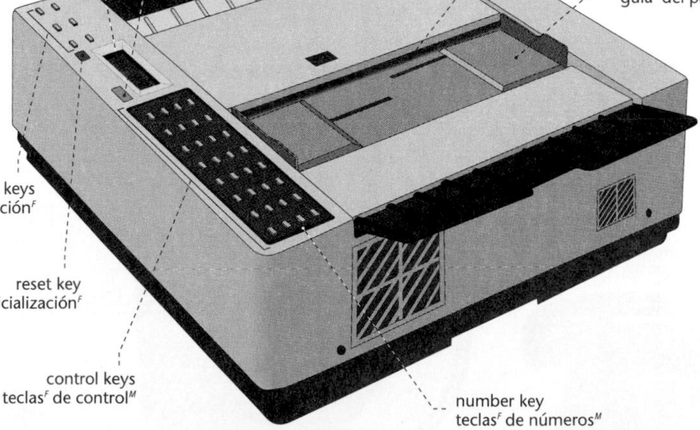

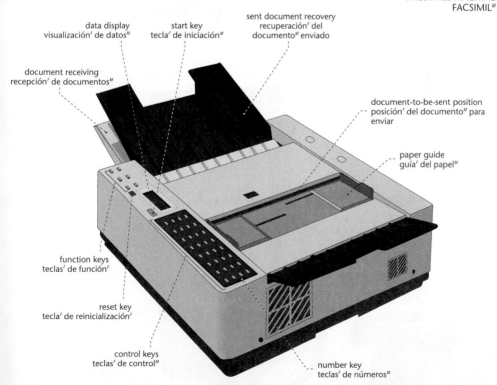

data display
visualización^F de datos^M

start key
tecla^F de iniciación^M

sent document recovery
recuperación^F del
documento^M enviado

document receiving
recepción^F de documentos^M

document-to-be-sent position
posición^F del documento^M para
enviar

paper guide
guía^F del papel^M

function keys
teclas^F de función^F

reset key
tecla^F de reinicialización^F

control keys
teclas^F de control^M

number key
teclas^F de números^M

TYPES OF TELEPHONES
TELÉFONOS^M

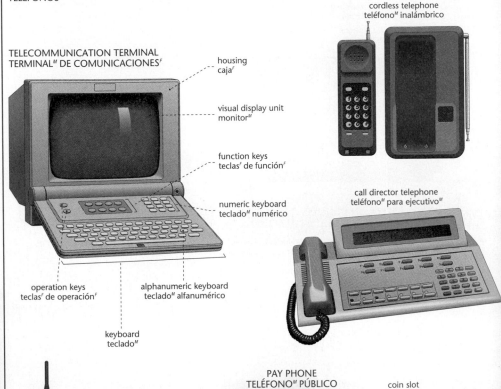

cordless telephone
teléfono^M inalámbrico

TELECOMMUNICATION TERMINAL
TERMINAL^M DE COMUNICACIONES^F

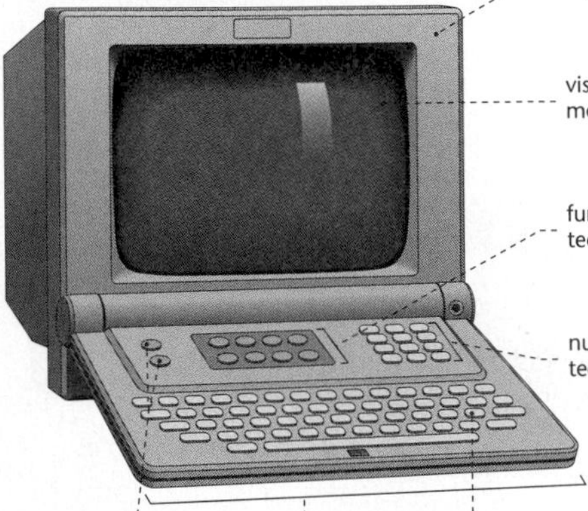

housing
caja^F

visual display unit
monitor^M

function keys
teclas^F de función^F

numeric keyboard
teclado^M numérico

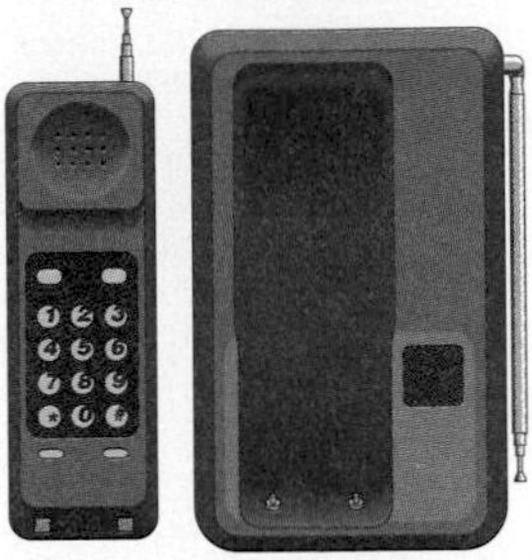

call director telephone
teléfono^M para ejecutivo^M

operation keys
teclas^F de operación^F

alphanumeric keyboard
teclado^M alfanumérico

keyboard
teclado^M

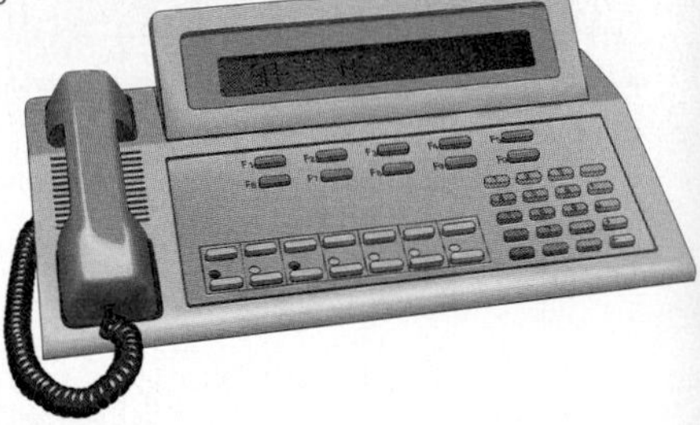

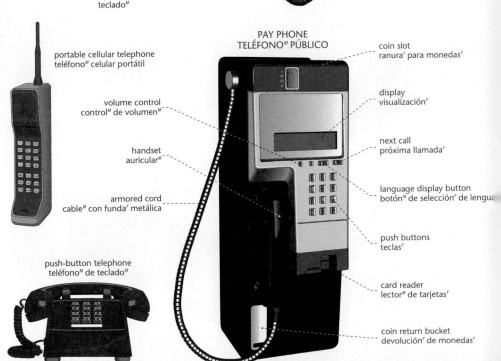

portable cellular telephone
teléfono^M celular portátil

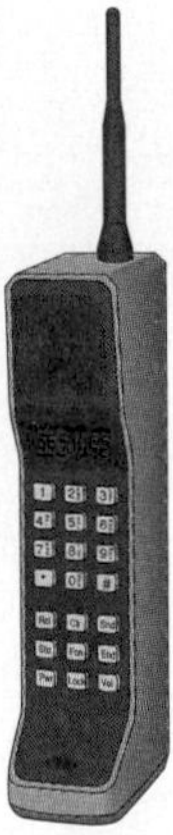

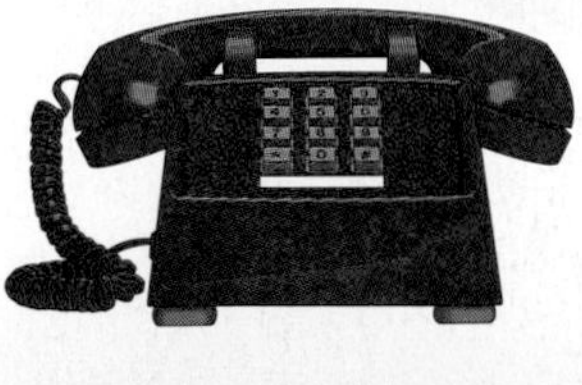

PAY PHONE
TELÉFONO^M PÚBLICO

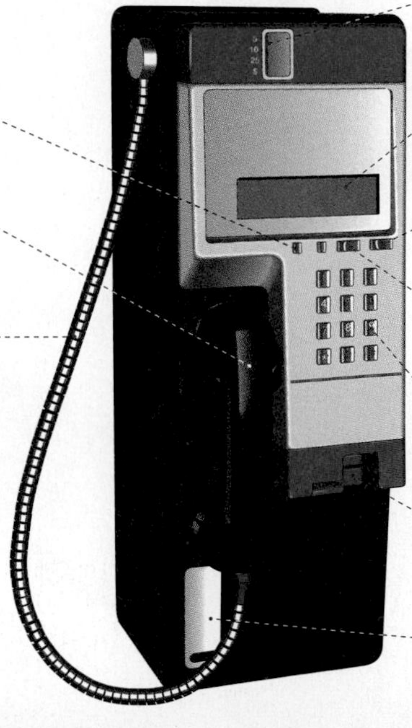

coin slot
ranura^F para monedas^F

volume control
control^M de volumen^M

display
visualización^F

handset
auricular^M

next call
próxima llamada^F

armored cord
cable^M con funda^F metálica

language display button
botón^M de selección^F de lengua

push buttons
teclas^F

push-button telephone
teléfono^M de teclado^M

card reader
lector^M de tarjetas^F

coin return bucket
devolución^F de monedas^F

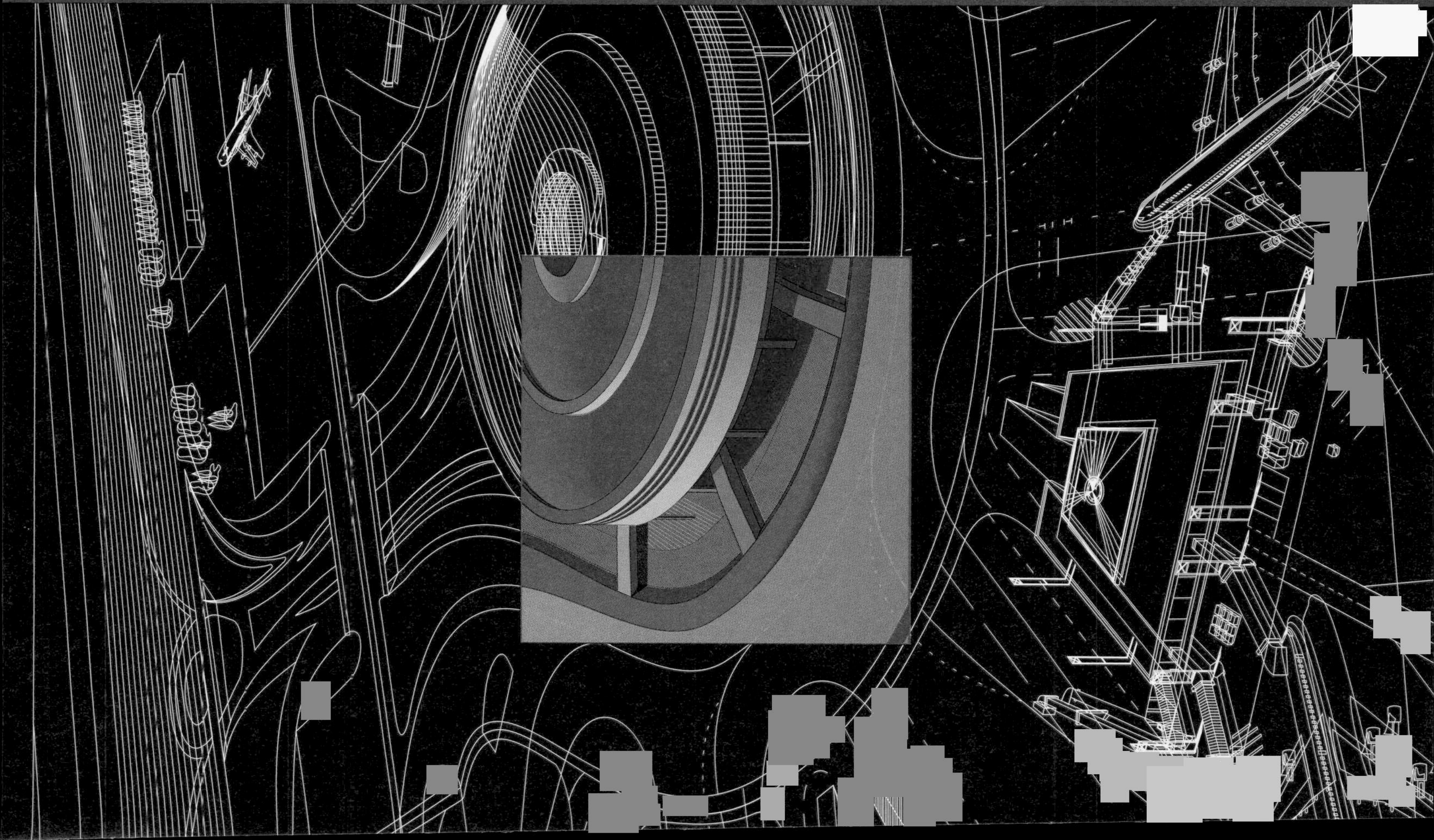

CONTENTS

TRANSPORT
TRANSPORTE

AUTOMOBILE
AUTOMÓVIL^M

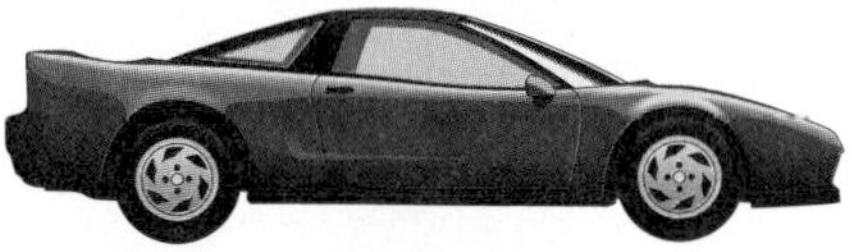

sports car
deportivo^M

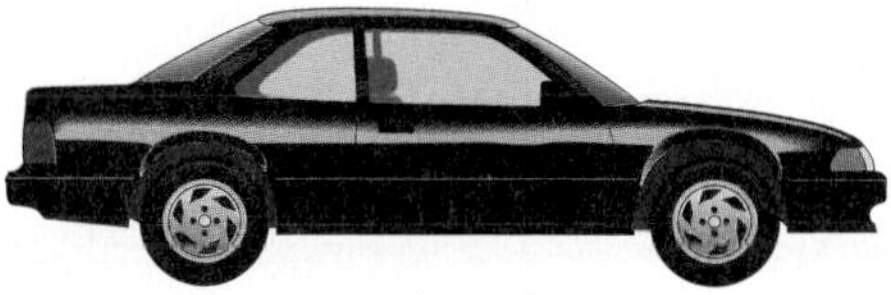

two-door sedan
turismo^M de dos puertas^F

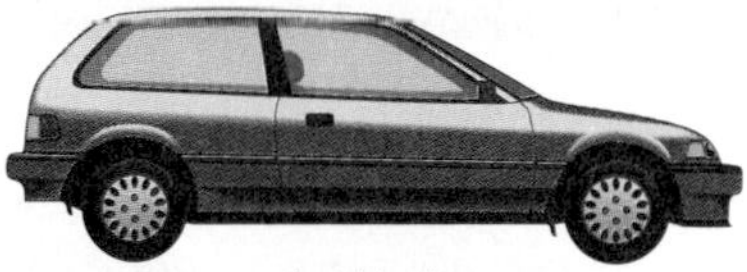

hatchback
turismo^M de tres puertas^F

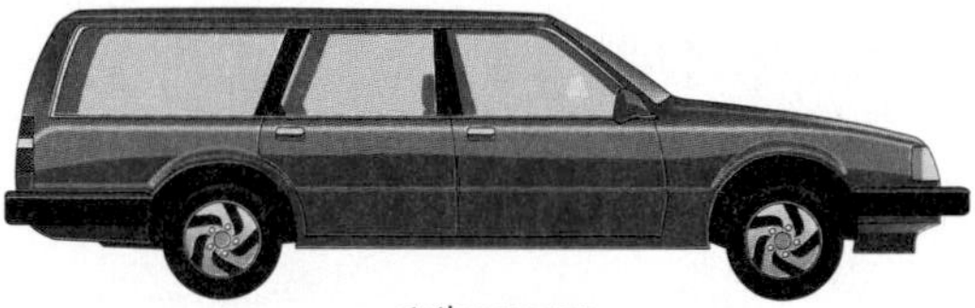

station wagon
rubia^F

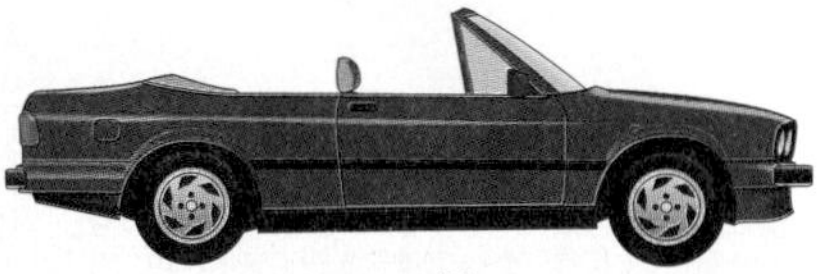

convertible
descapotable^M

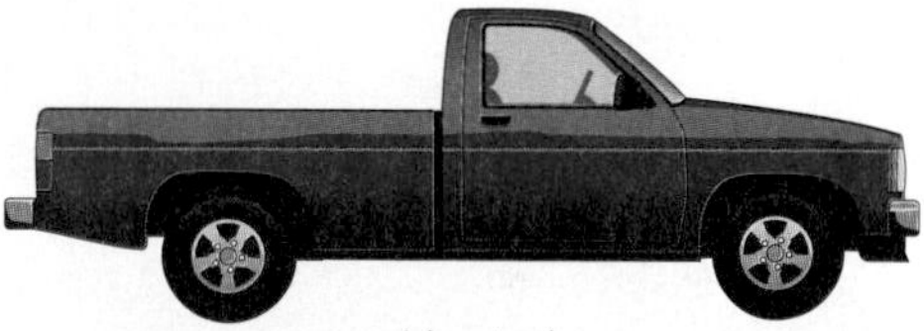

pickup truck
camioneta^F

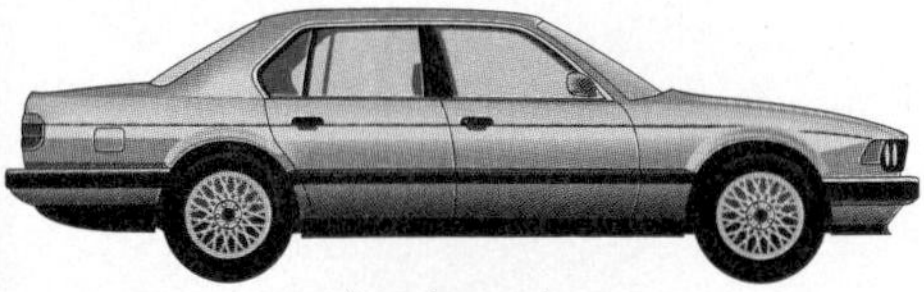

four-door sedan
sedán^M de cuatro puertas^F

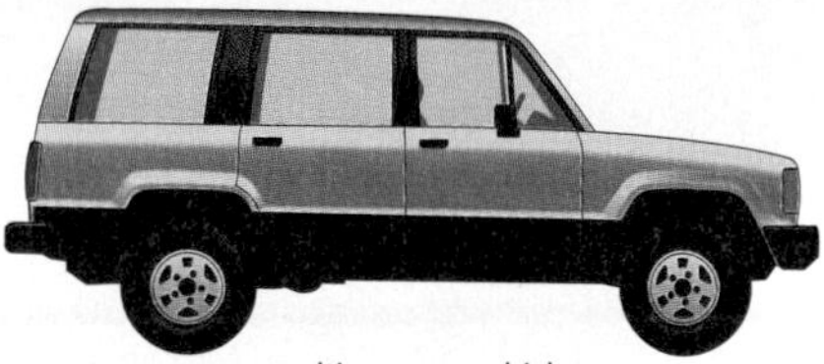

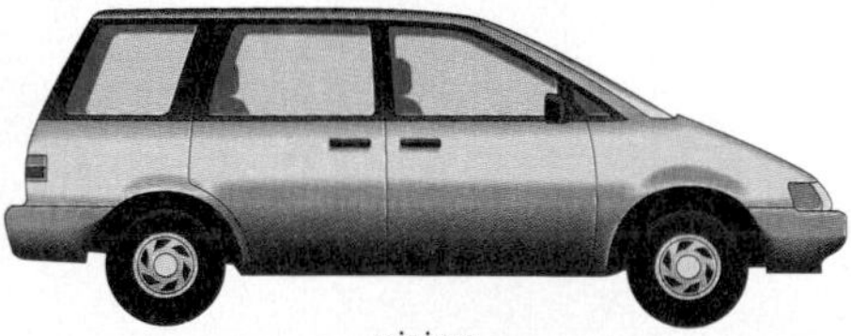

minivan
camioneta^F cubierta

multipurpose vehicle
vehículo^M todo terreno^M

limousine
pullman^M de ocho plazas^F

ROAD TRANSPORT
TRANSPORTE TERRESTRE

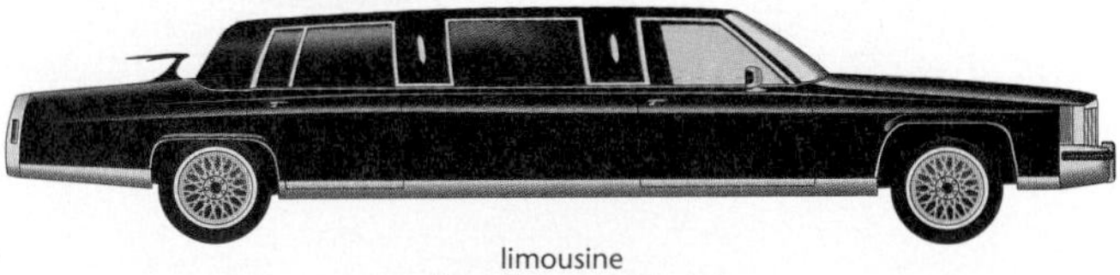

BODY
CARROCERÍA^F

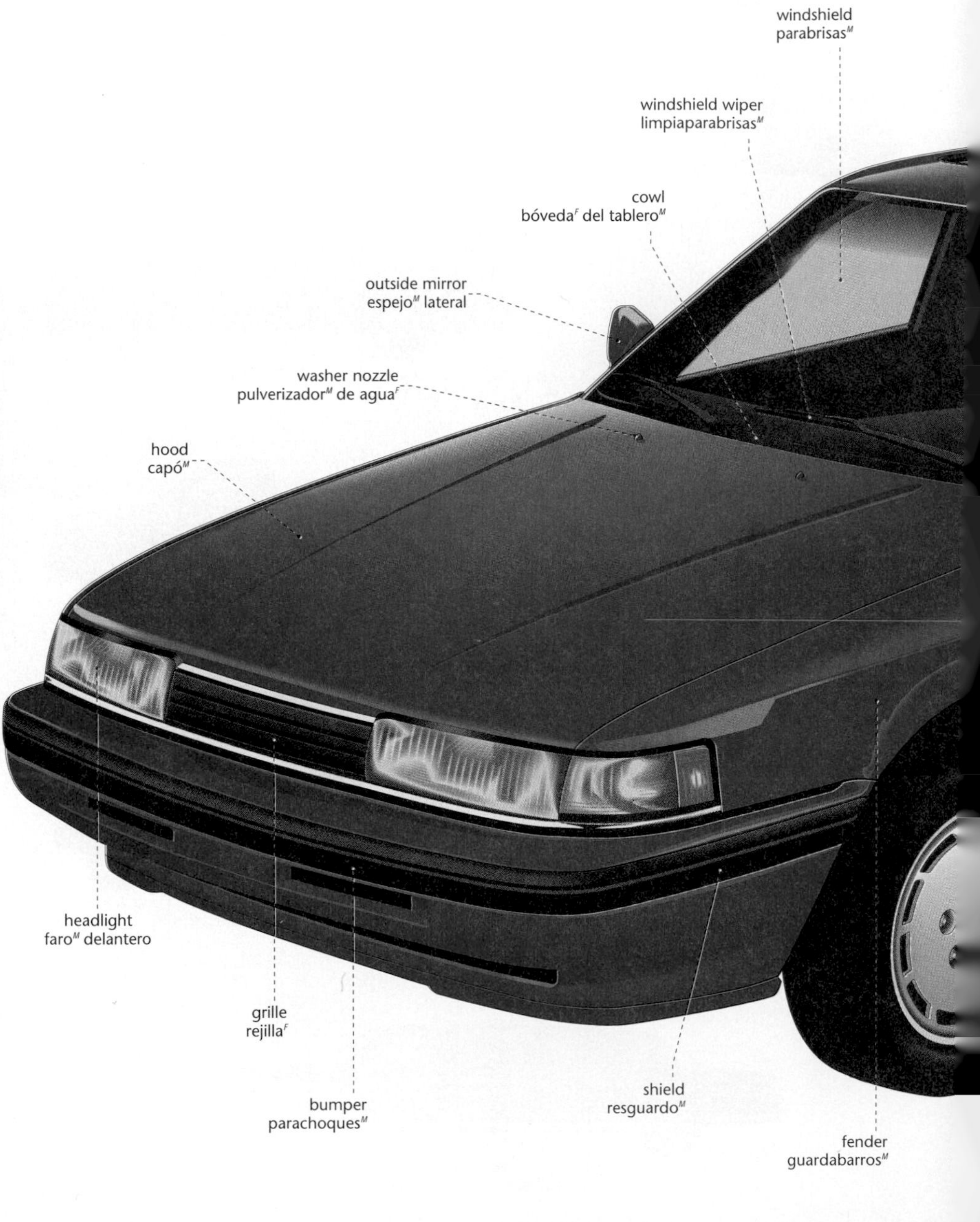

windshield
parabrisas^M

windshield wiper
limpiaparabrisas^M

cowl
bóveda^F del tablero^M

outside mirror
espejo^M lateral

washer nozzle
pulverizador^M de agua^F

hood
capó^M

headlight
faro^M delantero

grille
rejilla^F

bumper
parachoques^M

shield
resguardo^M

fender
guardabarros^M

antenna
antena^F

roof
techo^M

sliding sunroof
techo^M corredizo

center post
montante^M central

drip molding
canal^M de escurrimiento^M

quarter window
ventanilla^F trasera

trunk
portaequipaje^M

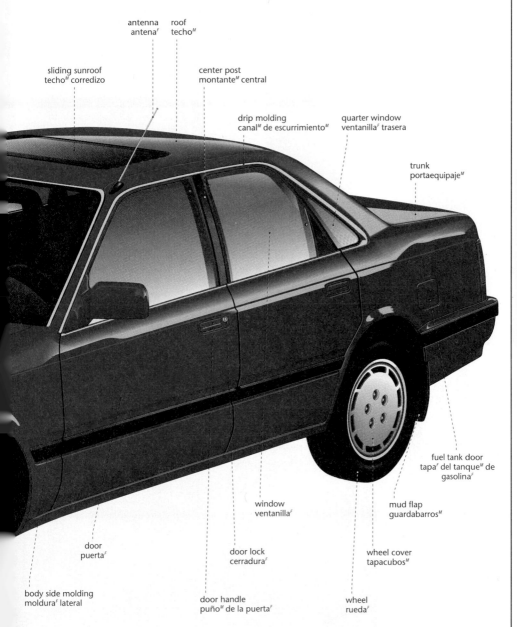

fuel tank door
tapa^F del tanque^M de
gasolina^F

window
ventanilla^F

mud flap
guardabarros^M

door
puerta^F

door lock
cerradura^F

wheel cover
tapacubos^M

body side molding
moldura^F lateral

door handle
puño^M de la puerta^F

wheel
rueda^F

ROAD TRANSPORT
TRANSPORTE TERRESTRE

BUCKET SEAT
ASIENTO^M RECLINABLE

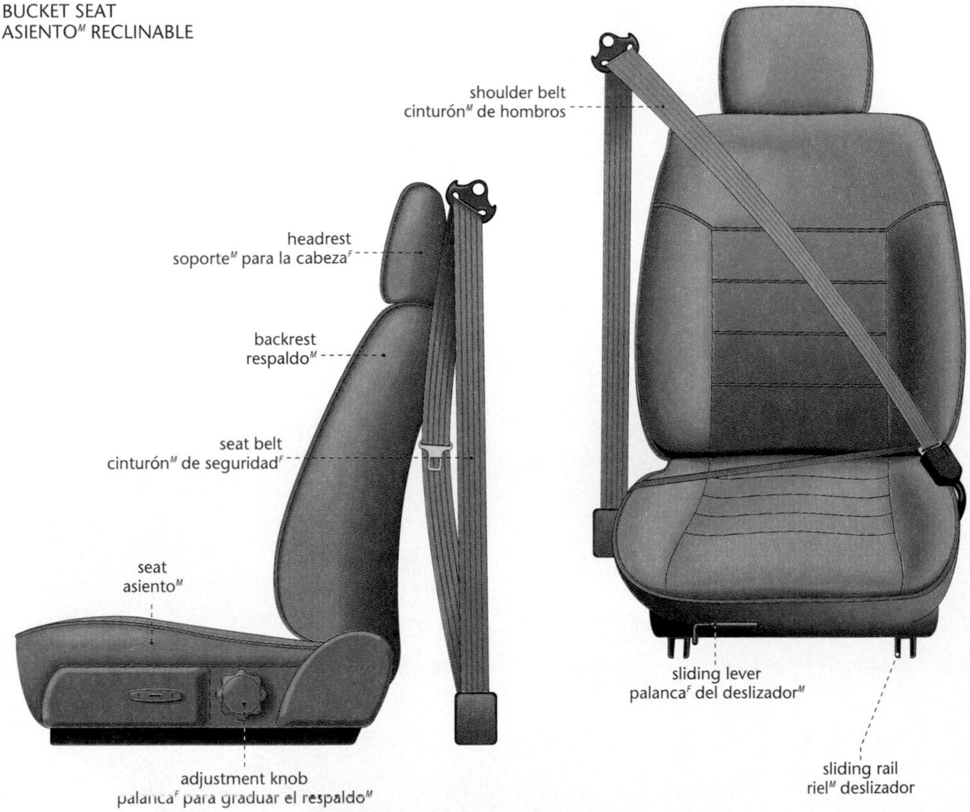

shoulder belt
cinturón^M de hombros

headrest
soporte^M para la cabeza^F

backrest
respaldo^M

seat belt
cinturón^M de seguridad^F

seat
asiento^M

adjustment knob
palanca^F para graduar el respaldo^M

sliding lever
palanca^F del deslizador^M

sliding rail
riel^M deslizador

REAR SEAT
ASIENTO^M TRASERO

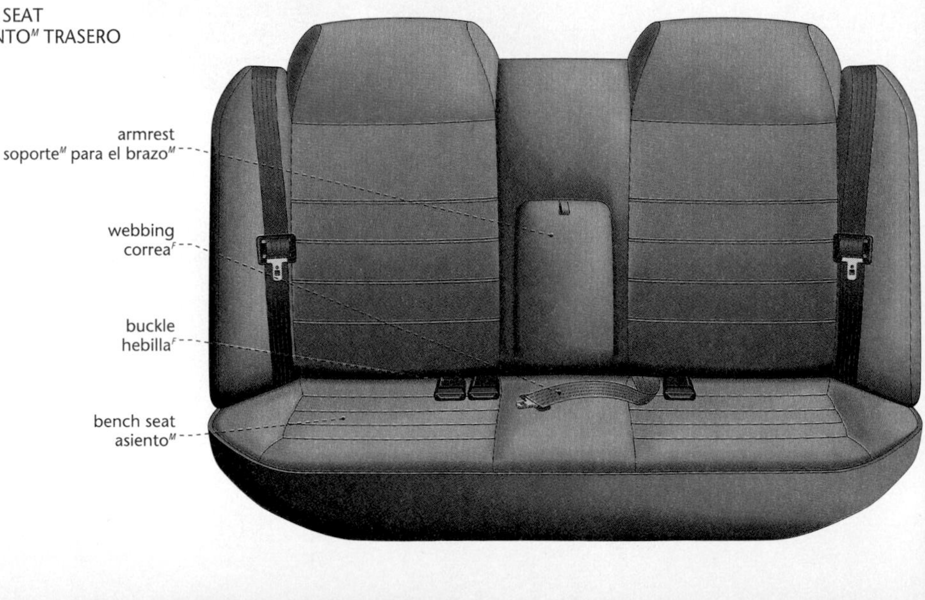

armrest
soporte^M para el brazo^M

webbing
correa^F

buckle
hebilla^F

bench seat
asiento^M

interior door handle
puño^M interior de la puerta^F

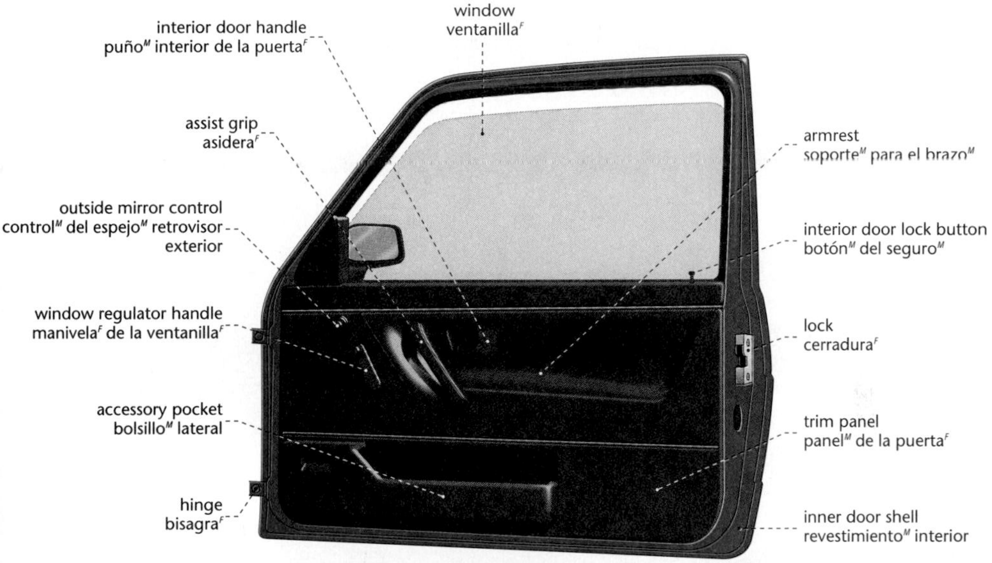

window
ventanilla^F

armrest
soporte^M para el brazo^M

assist grip
asidera^F

outside mirror control
control^M del espejo^M retrovisor
exterior

interior door lock button
botón^M del seguro^M

window regulator handle
manivela^F de la ventanilla^F

lock
cerradura^F

accessory pocket
bolsillo^M lateral

trim panel
panel^M de la puerta^F

hinge
bisagra^F

inner door shell
revestimiento^M interior

**headlights
faros^M delanteros**

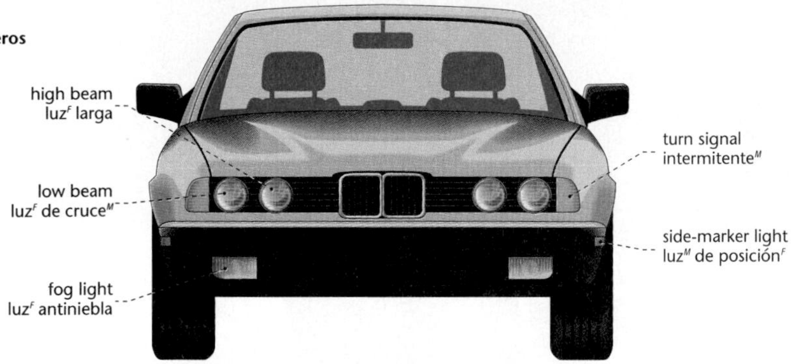

high beam
luz^F larga

turn signal
intermitente^M

low beam
luz^F de cruce^M

side-marker light
luz^M de posición^F

fog light
luz^F antiniebla

**taillights
luces^F traseras**

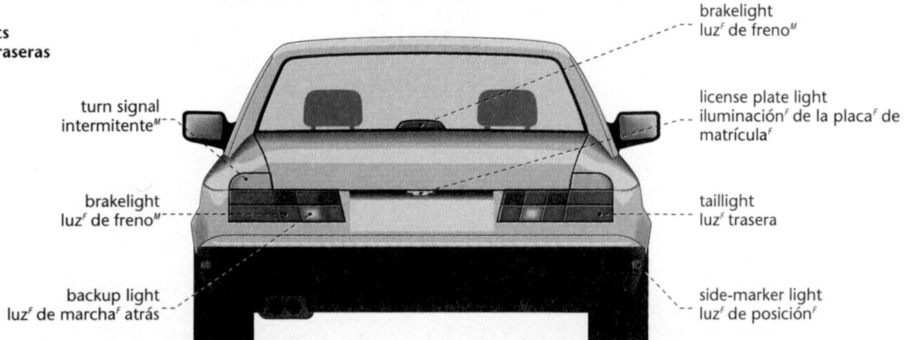

brakelight
luz^F de freno^M

turn signal
intermitente^M

license plate light
iluminación^F de la placa^F de
matrícula^F

brakelight
luz^F de freno^M

taillight
luz^F trasera

backup light
luz^F de marcha^F atrás

side-marker light
luz^F de posición^F

DASHBOARD
TABLERO^M

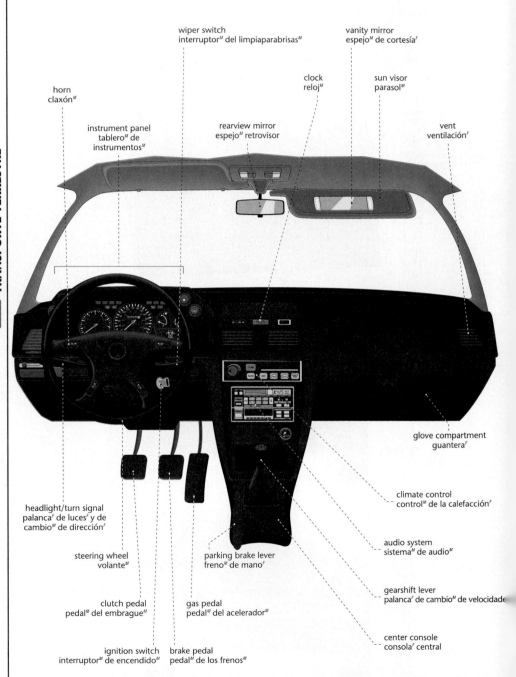

wiper switch
interruptor^M del limpiaparabrisas^M

vanity mirror
espejo^M de cortesía^F

clock
reloj^M

sun visor
parasol^M

horn
claxón^M

vent
ventilación^F

instrument panel
tablero^M de
instrumentos^M

rearview mirror
espejo^M retrovisor

glove compartment
guantera^F

headlight/turn signal
palanca^F de luces^F y de
cambio^M de dirección^F

climate control
control^M de la calefacción^F

steering wheel
volante^M

parking brake lever
freno^M de mano^F

audio system
sistema^M de audio^M

clutch pedal
pedal^M del embrague^M

gas pedal
pedal^M del acelerador^M

gearshift lever
palanca^F de cambio^M de velocidade

ignition switch
interruptor^M de encendido^M

brake pedal
pedal^M de los frenos^M

center console
consola^F central

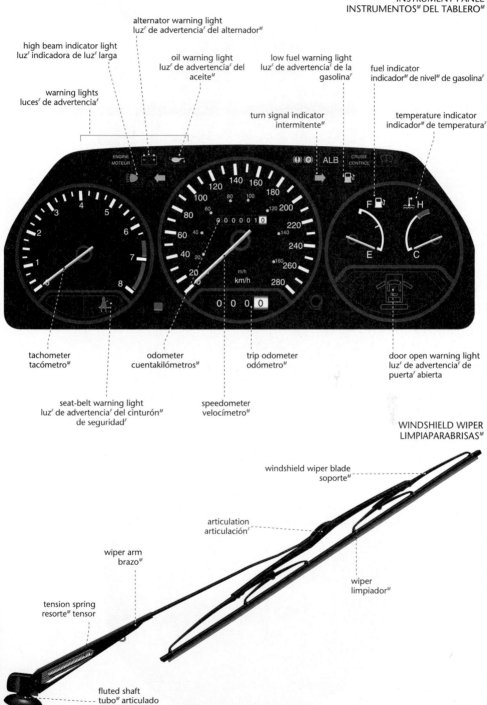

high beam indicator light
luz^F indicadora de luz^F larga

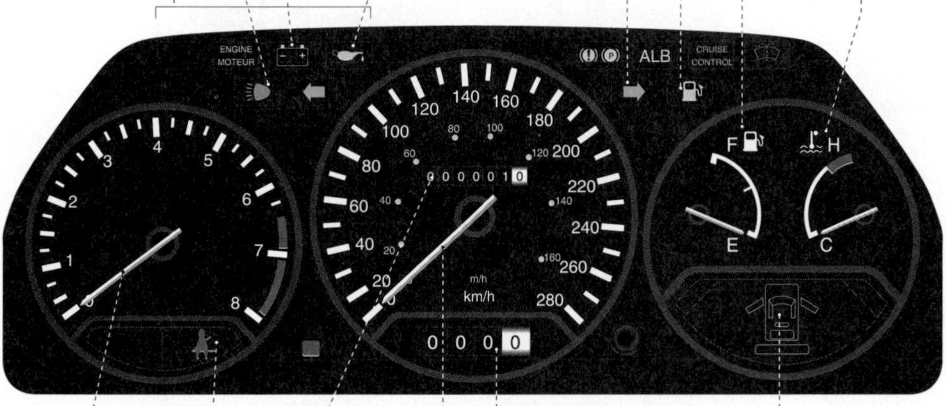

alternator warning light
luz^F de advertencia^F del alternador^M

oil warning light
luz^F de advertencia^F del
aceite^M

low fuel warning light
luz^F de advertencia^F de la
gasolina^F

fuel indicator
indicador^M de nivel^M de gasolina^F

warning lights
luces^F de advertencia^F

turn signal indicator
intermitente^M

temperature indicator
indicador^M de temperatura^F

tachometer
tacómetro^M

odometer
cuentakilómetros^M

trip odometer
odómetro^M

door open warning light
luz^F de advertencia^F de
puerta^F abierta

seat-belt warning light
luz^F de advertencia^F del cinturón^M
de seguridad^F

speedometer
velocímetro^M

WINDSHIELD WIPER
LIMPIAPARABRISAS^M

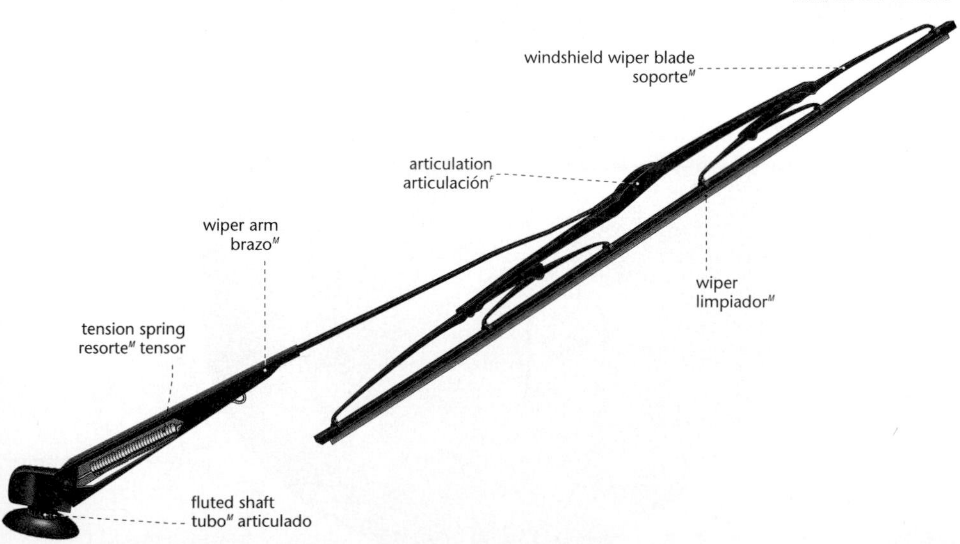

windshield wiper blade
soporte^M

articulation
articulación^F

wiper arm
brazo^M

wiper
limpiador^M

tension spring
resorte^M tensor

fluted shaft
tubo^M articulado

DISK BRAKE
FRENO^M DE DISCO^M

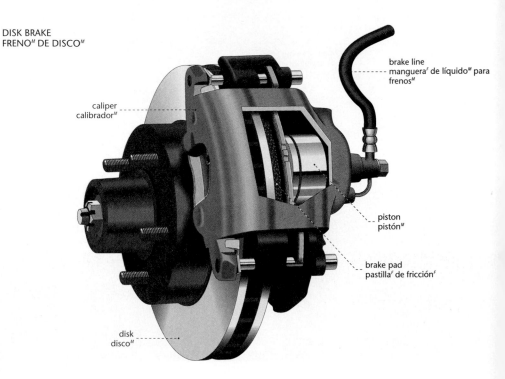

brake line
manguera^F de líquido^M para
frenos^M

caliper
calibrador^M

piston
pistón^M

brake pad
pastilla^F de fricción^F

disk
disco^M

DRUM BRAKE
FRENO^M DE TAMBOR^M

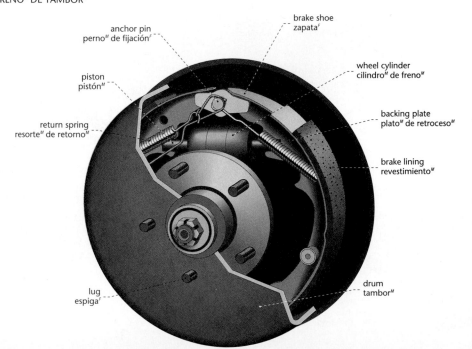

brake shoe
zapata^F

anchor pin
perno^M de fijación^F

wheel cylinder
cilindro^M de freno^M

piston
pistón^M

backing plate
plato^M de retroceso^M

return spring
resorte^M de retorno^M

brake lining
revestimiento^M

lug
espiga^F

drum
tambor^M

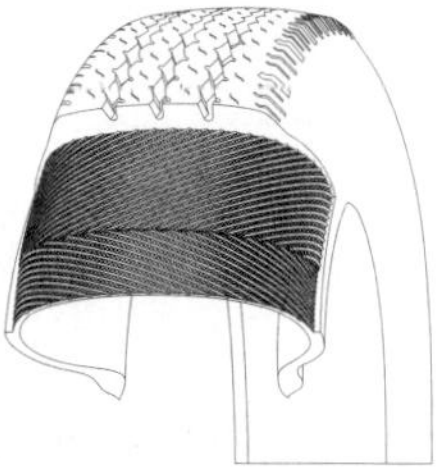

bias-ply tire
neumático[M] de capas[F] al sesgo[M]

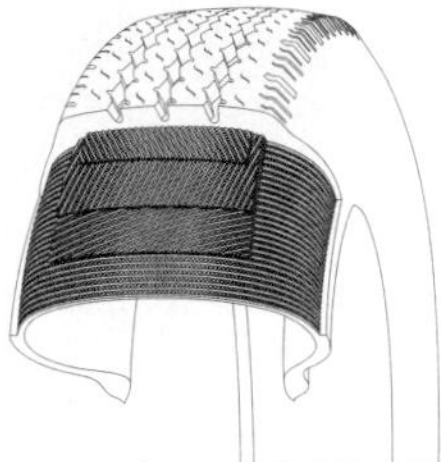

radial tire
neumático[M] radial

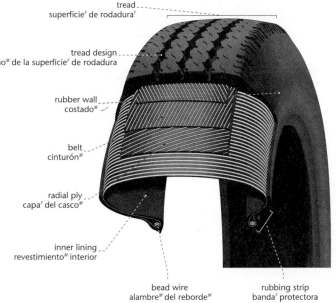

STEEL BELTED RADIAL TIRE
NEUMÁTICO[M] RADIAL CON CINTURONES[M]

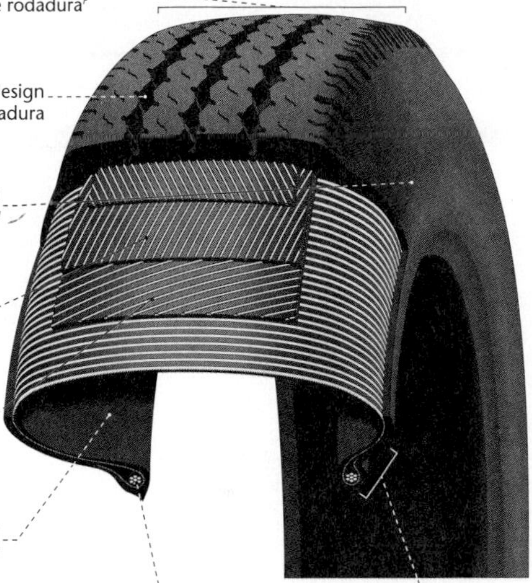

tread
superficie[F] de rodadura[F]

tread design
diseño[M] de la superficie[F] de rodadura

rubber wall
costado[M]

belt
cinturón[M]

radial ply
capa[F] del casco[M]

inner lining
revestimiento[M] interior

bead wire
alambre[M] del reborde[M]

rubbing strip
banda[F] protectora

TIRE
NEUMÁTICO[M]

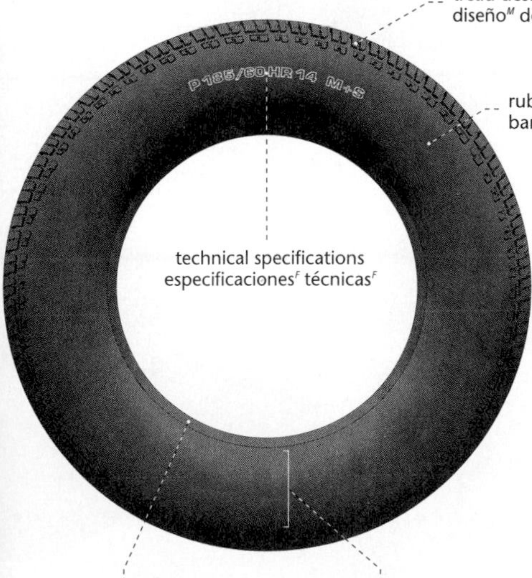

tread design
diseño[M] de la superficie[F] de rodadura[F]

rubbing strip
banda[F] protectora

P-185/60HR-14 M+S

technical specifications
especificaciones[F] técnicas[F]

bead
moldura[F]

rubber wall
costado[M]

WHEEL
RUEDA[F]

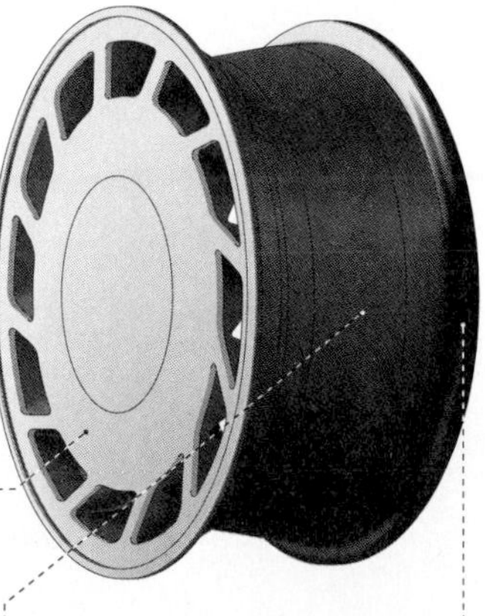

disk
disco[M]

rim
llanta[F]

rim flange
pestaña[F] de la llanta[F]

ROAD TRANSPORT
TRANSPORTE TERRESTRE

433

GASOLINE ENGINE
MOTOR^M DE GASOLINA^F

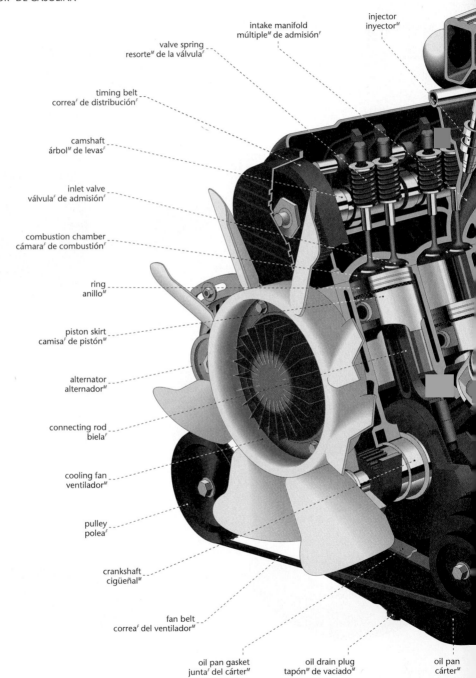

intake manifold
múltiple^M de admisión^F

injector
inyector^M

valve spring
resorte^M de la válvula^F

timing belt
correa^F de distribución^F

camshaft
árbol^M de levas^F

inlet valve
válvula^F de admisión^F

combustion chamber
cámara^F de combustión^F

ring
anillo^M

piston skirt
camisa^F de pistón^M

alternator
alternador^M

connecting rod
biela^F

cooling fan
ventilador^M

pulley
polea^F

crankshaft
cigüeñal^M

fan belt
correa^F del ventilador^M

oil pan gasket
junta^F del cárter^M

oil drain plug
tapón^M de vaciado^M

oil pan
cárter^M

GASOLINE ENGINE
MOTOR[M] DE GASOLINA[F]

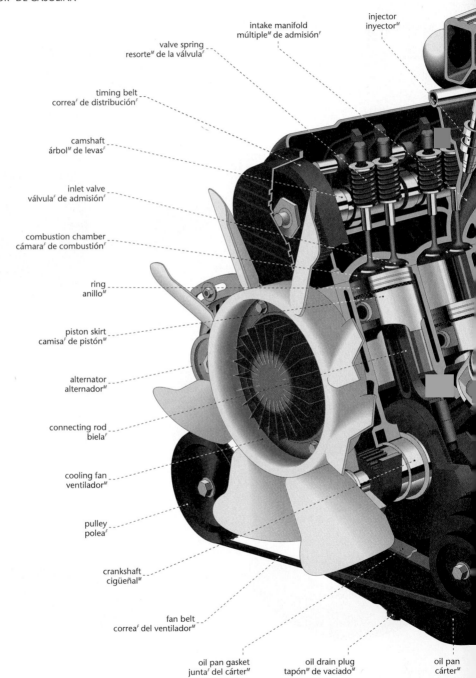

intake manifold
múltiple[M] de admisión[F]

injector
inyector[M]

valve spring
resorte[M] de la válvula[F]

timing belt
correa[F] de distribución[F]

camshaft
árbol[M] de levas[F]

inlet valve
válvula[F] de admisión[F]

combustion chamber
cámara[F] de combustión[F]

ring
anillo[M]

piston skirt
camisa[F] de pistón[M]

alternator
alternador[M]

connecting rod
biela[F]

cooling fan
ventilador[M]

pulley
polea[F]

crankshaft
cigüeñal[M]

fan belt
correa[F] del ventilador[M]

oil pan gasket
junta[F] del cárter[M]

oil drain plug
tapón[M] de vaciado[M]

oil pan
cárter[M]

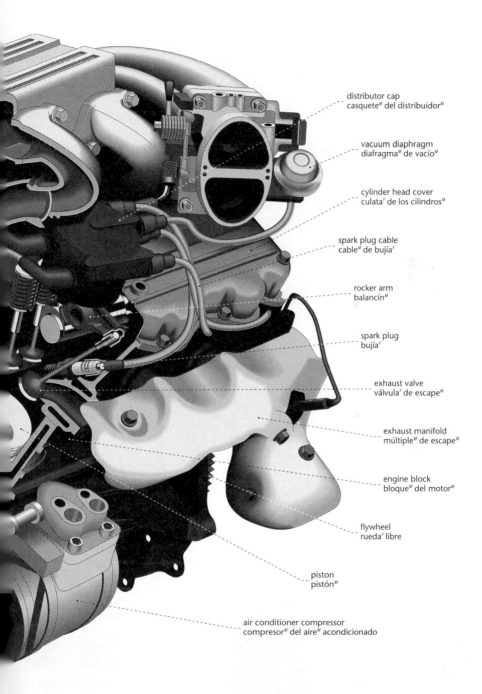

distributor cap
casquete^M del distribuidor^M

vacuum diaphragm
diafragma^M de vacío^M

cylinder head cover
culata^F de los cilindros^M

spark plug cable
cable^M de bujía^F

rocker arm
balancín^M

spark plug
bujía^F

exhaust valve
válvula^F de escape^M

exhaust manifold
múltiple^M de escape^M

engine block
bloque^M del motor^M

flywheel
rueda^F libre

piston
pistón^M

air conditioner compressor
compresor^M del aire^M acondicionado

TYPES OF ENGINES
TIPOS^M DE MOTORES^M

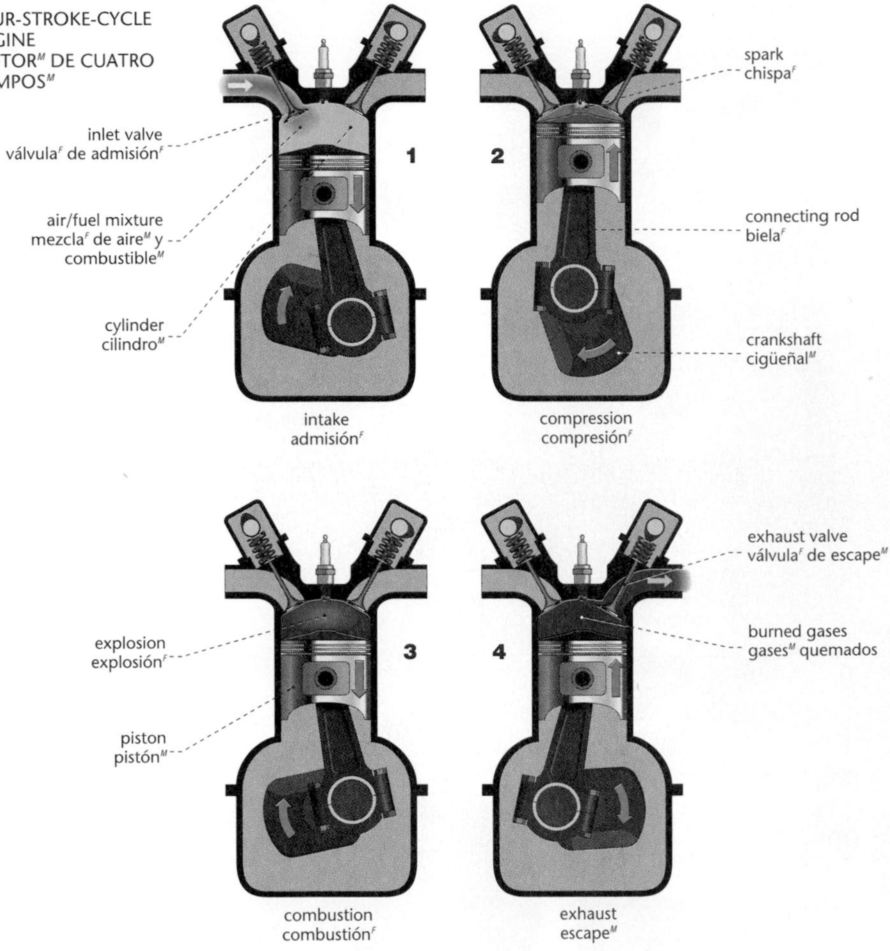

FOUR-STROKE-CYCLE ENGINE
MOTOR^M DE CUATRO TIEMPOS^M

inlet valve
válvula^F de admisión^F

air/fuel mixture
mezcla^F de aire^M y combustible^M

cylinder
cilindro^M

spark
chispa^F

connecting rod
biela^F

crankshaft
cigüeñal^M

1 · intake
admisión^F

2 · compression
compresión^F

explosion
explosión^F

piston
pistón^M

exhaust valve
válvula^F de escape^M

burned gases
gases^M quemados

3 · combustion
combustión^F

4 · exhaust
escape^M

TWO-STROKE-CYCLE ENGINE
MOTOR^M DE DOS TIEMPOS^M

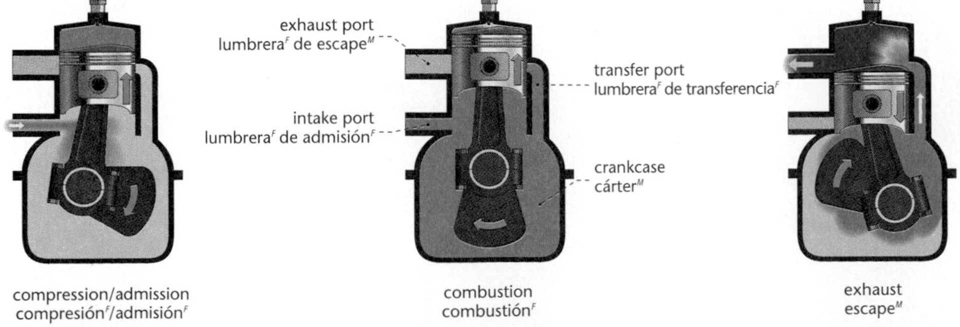

exhaust port
lumbrera^F de escape^M

intake port
lumbrera^F de admisión^F

transfer port
lumbrera^F de transferencia^F

crankcase
cárter^M

compression/admission
compresión^F/admisión^F

combustion
combustión^F

exhaust
escape^M

DIESEL ENGINE
MOTOR^M DIESEL

air
aire^M

injection/explosion
injección^F/explosión^F

fuel injector
injector^M de combustible^M

intake
admisión^F

compression
compresión^F

combustion
combustión^F

exhaust
escape^M

ROTARY ENGINE
MOTOR^M ROTATORIO

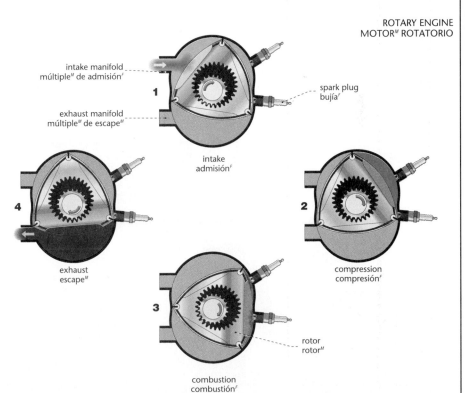

intake manifold
múltiple^M de admisión^F

spark plug
bujía^F

1

exhaust manifold
múltiple^M de escape^M

intake
admisión^F

4

exhaust
escape^M

2

compression
compresión^F

3

rotor
rotor^M

combustion
combustión^F

RADIATOR
RADIADOR^M

filler cap
tapa^F

grille
rejilla^F

cooling fan
ventilador^M

fan thermostat
termostato^M del
ventilador^M

electric motor
motor^M eléctrico

radiator hose
manguera^F

TURBO-COMPRESSOR ENGINE
MOTOR^M TURBO COMPRESOR

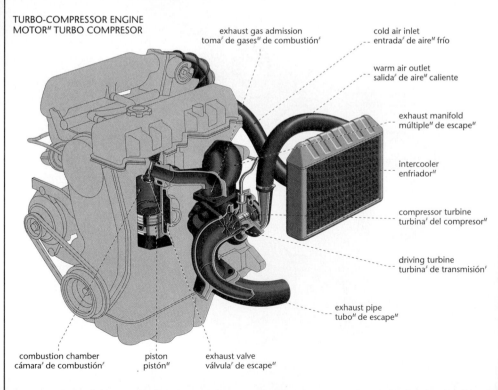

exhaust gas admission
toma^F de gases^M de combustión^F

cold air inlet
entrada^F de aire^M frío

warm air outlet
salida^F de aire^M caliente

exhaust manifold
múltiple^M de escape^M

intercooler
enfriador^M

compressor turbine
turbina^F del compresor^M

driving turbine
turbina^F de transmisión^F

exhaust pipe
tubo^M de escape^M

combustion chamber
cámara^F de combustión^F

piston
pistón^M

exhaust valve
válvula^F de escape^M

SPARK PLUG
BUJÍA^F

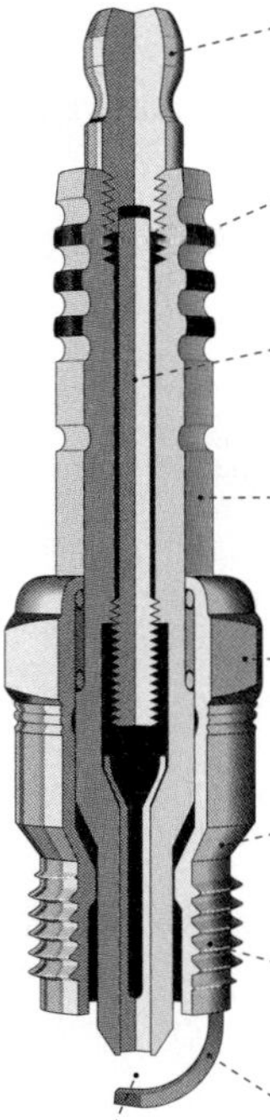

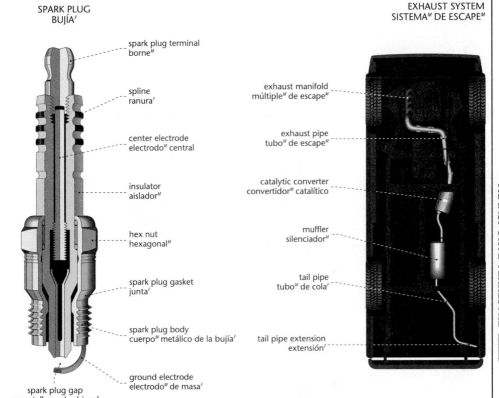

spark plug terminal
borne^M

spline
ranura^F

center electrode
electrodo^M central

insulator
aislador^M

hex nut
hexagonal^M

spark plug gasket
junta^F

spark plug body
cuerpo^M metálico de la bujía^F

ground electrode
electrodo^M de masa^F

spark plug gap
espacio^M para la chispa^F

EXHAUST SYSTEM
SISTEMA^M DE ESCAPE^M

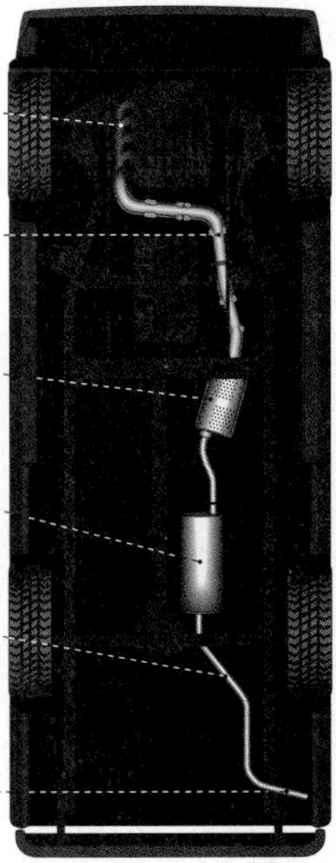

exhaust manifold
múltiple^M de escape^M

exhaust pipe
tubo^M de escape^M

catalytic converter
convertidor^M catalítico

muffler
silenciador^M

tail pipe
tubo^M de cola^F

tail pipe extension
extensión^F

BATTERY
BATERÍA^F

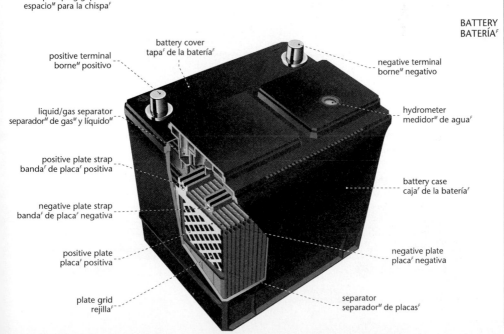

positive terminal
borne^M positivo

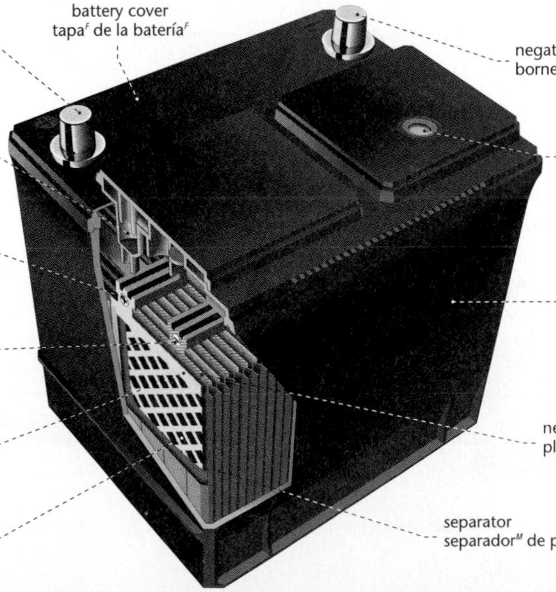

battery cover
tapa^F de la batería^F

negative terminal
borne^M negativo

liquid/gas separator
separador^M de gas^M y líquido^M

hydrometer
medidor^M de agua^F

positive plate strap
banda^F de placa^F positiva

negative plate strap
banda^F de placa^F negativa

battery case
caja^F de la batería^F

positive plate
placa^F positiva

negative plate
placa^F negativa

plate grid
rejilla^F

separator
separador^M de placas^F

TRUCK TRACTOR
CAMIÓN^M TRACTOR^M

ROAD TRANSPORT
TRANSPORTE TERRESTRE

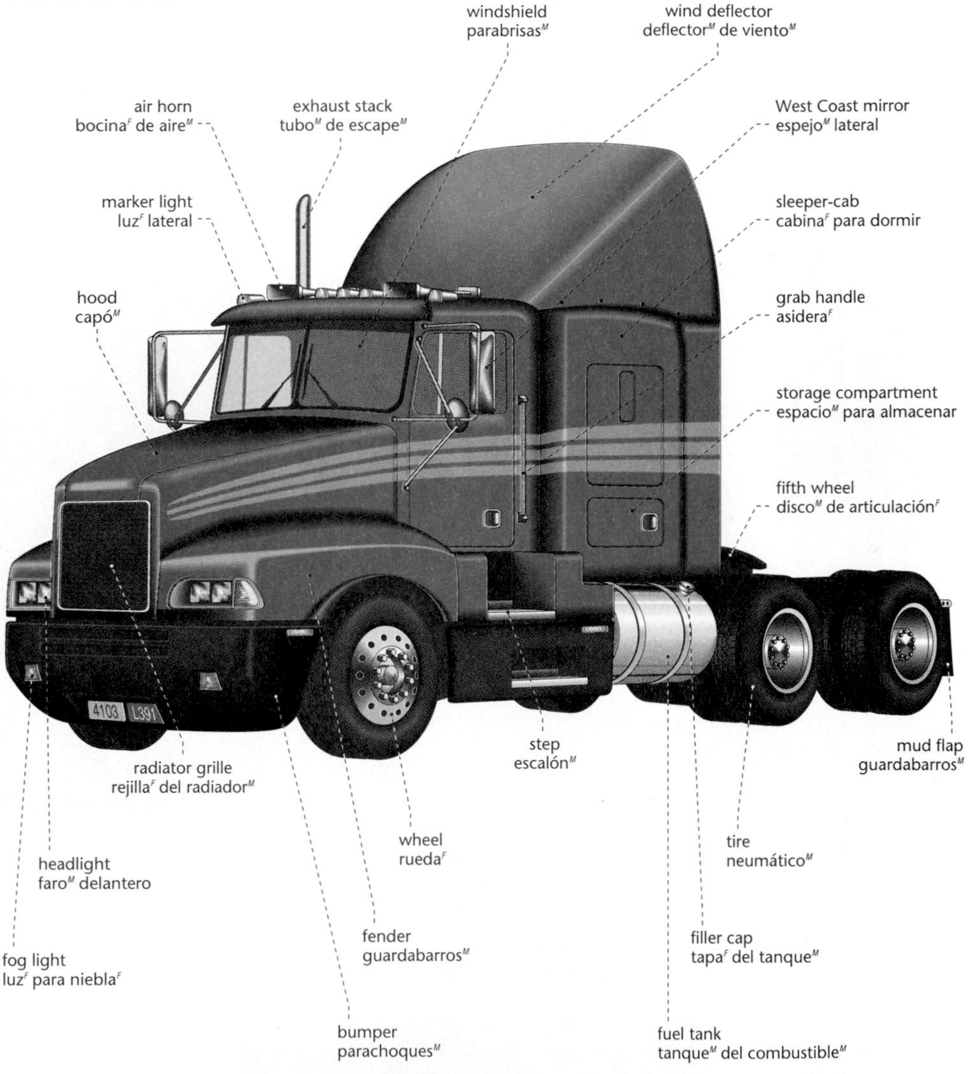

windshield
parabrisas^M

wind deflector
deflector^M de viento^M

air horn
bocina^F de aire^M

exhaust stack
tubo^M de escape^M

West Coast mirror
espejo^M lateral

marker light
luz^F lateral

sleeper-cab
cabina^F para dormir

hood
capó^M

grab handle
asidera^F

storage compartment
espacio^M para almacenar

fifth wheel
disco^M de articulación^F

step
escalón^M

mud flap
guardabarros^M

radiator grille
rejilla^F del radiador^M

wheel
rueda^F

tire
neumático^M

headlight
faro^M delantero

fender
guardabarros^M

filler cap
tapa^F del tanque^M

fog light
luz^F para niebla^F

bumper
parachoques^M

fuel tank
tanque^M del combustible^M

TANDEM TRACTOR TRAILER
CAMIÓN^M TRACTOR^M CON DOBLE CAJA^F

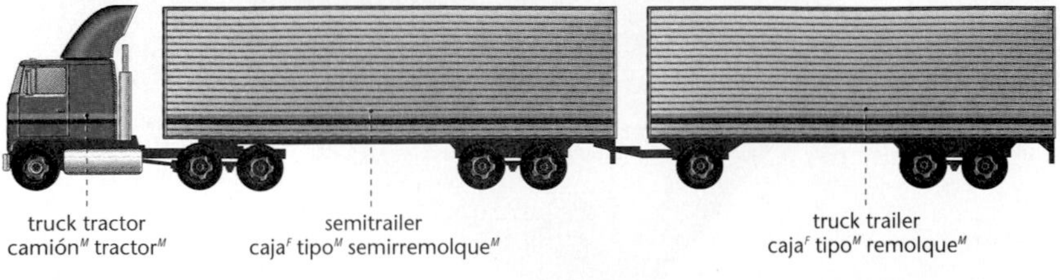

truck tractor
camión^M tractor^M

semitrailer
caja^F tipo^M semirremolque^M

truck trailer
caja^F tipo^M remolque^M

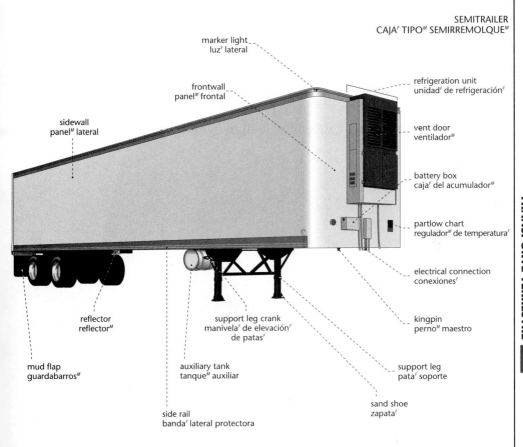

SEMITRAILER
CAJA^F TIPO^M SEMIRREMOLQUE^M

marker light
luz^F lateral

frontwall
panel^M frontal

sidewall
panel^M lateral

refrigeration unit
unidad^F de refrigeración^F

vent door
ventilador^M

battery box
caja^F del acumulador^M

partlow chart
regulador^M de temperatura^F

electrical connection
conexiones^F

kingpin
perno^M maestro

reflector
reflector^M

support leg crank
manivela^F de elevación^F
de patas^F

support leg
pata^F soporte

mud flap
guardabarros^M

auxiliary tank
tanque^M auxiliar

sand shoe
zapata^F

side rail
banda^F lateral protectora

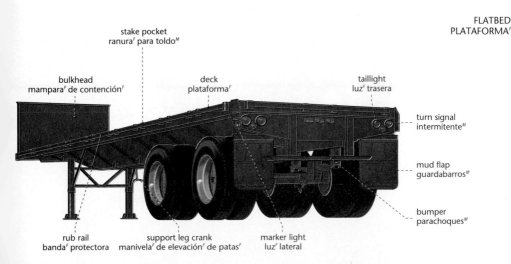

FLATBED
PLATAFORMA^F

stake pocket
ranura^F para toldo^M

bulkhead
mampara^F de contención^F

deck
plataforma^F

taillight
luz^F trasera

turn signal
intermitente^M

mud flap
guardabarros^M

bumper
parachoques^M

rub rail
banda^F protectora

support leg crank
manivela^F de elevación^F de patas^F

marker light
luz^F lateral

MOTORCYCLE
MOTOCICLETA^F

SIDE VIEW
VISTA^F LATERAL

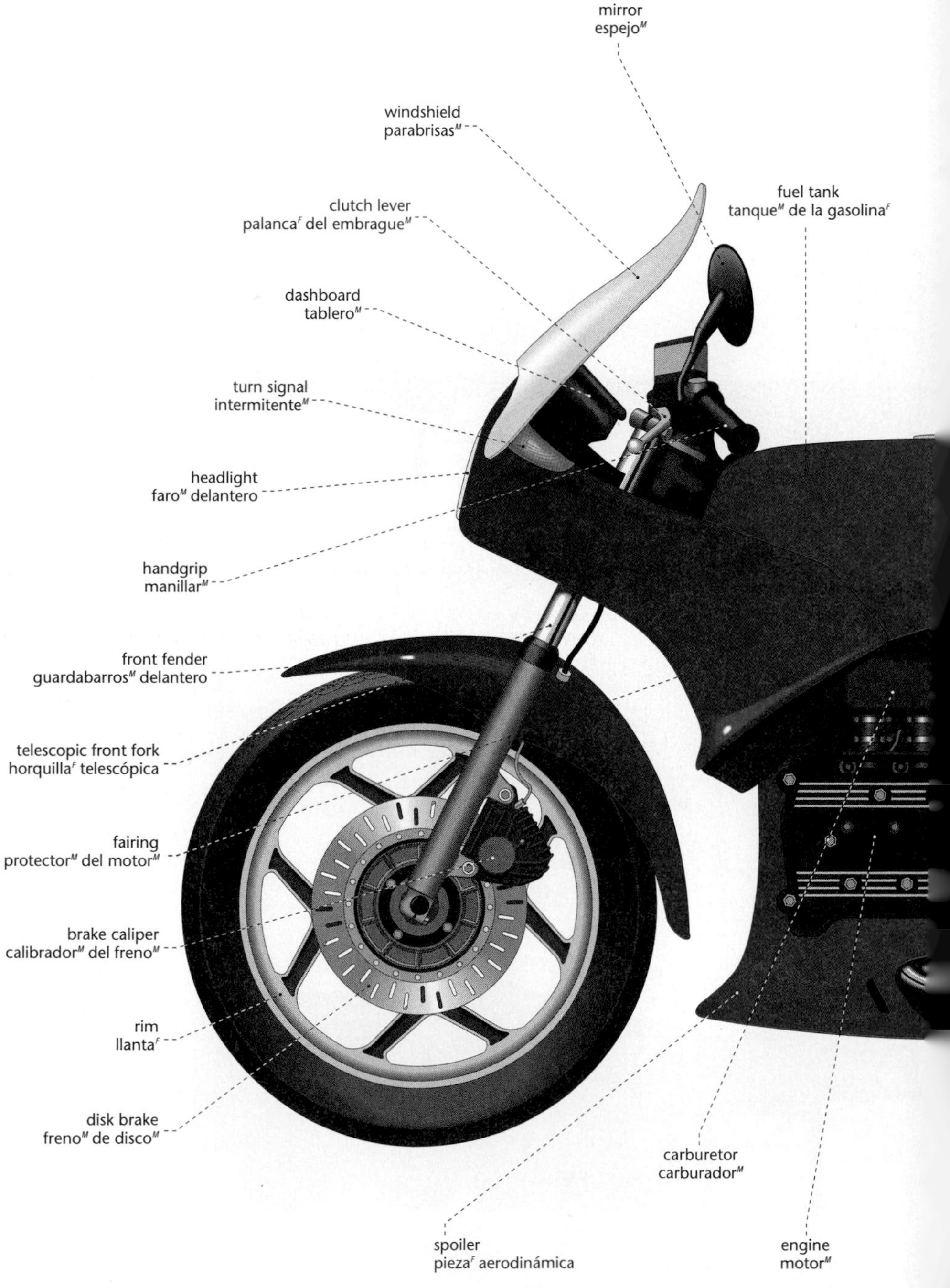

mirror
espejo^M

windshield
parabrisas^M

fuel tank
tanque^M de la gasolina^F

clutch lever
palanca^F del embrague^M

dashboard
tablero^M

turn signal
intermitente^M

headlight
faro^M delantero

handgrip
manillar^M

front fender
guardabarros^M delantero

telescopic front fork
horquilla^F telescópica

fairing
protector^M del motor^M

brake caliper
calibrador^M del freno^M

rim
llanta^F

disk brake
freno^M de disco^M

carburetor
carburador^M

spoiler
pieza^F aerodinámica

engine
motor^M

PROTECTIVE HELMET
CASCO^M PROTECTOR

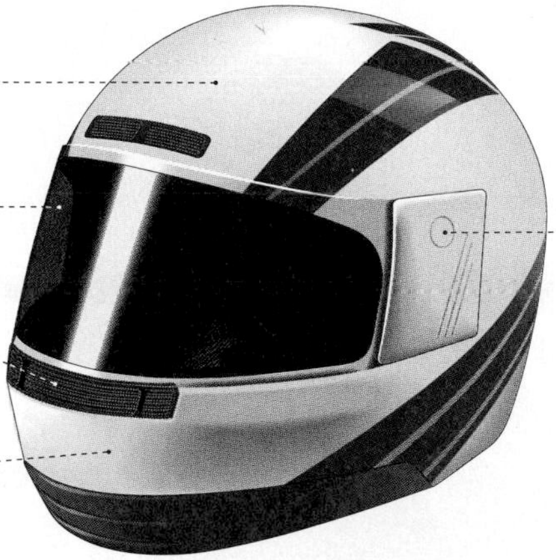

bubble
casco^M

visor
visera^F

visor hinge
visor^M lateral

air inlet
respiradero^M

chin protector
protector^M de la barbilla^F

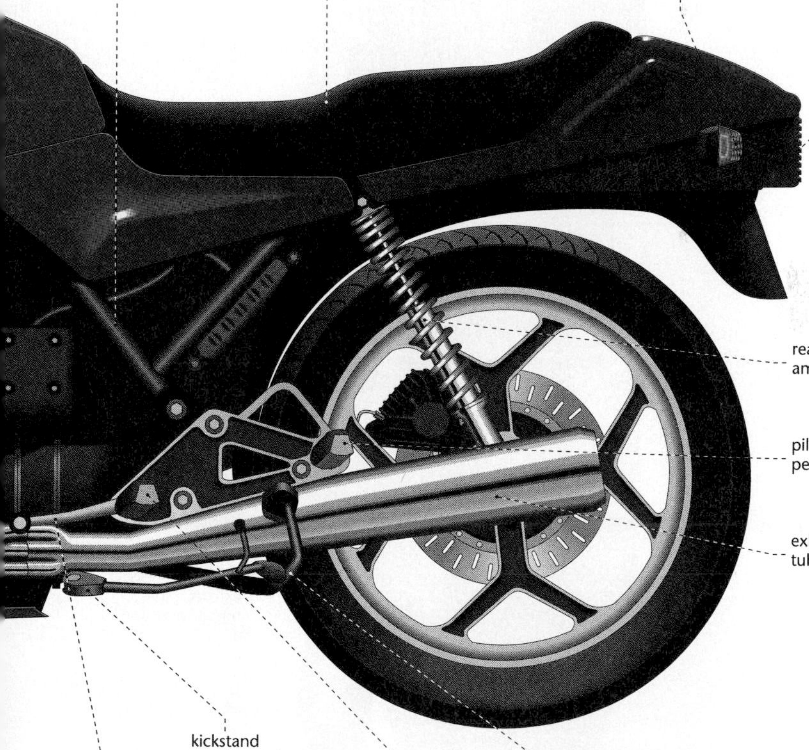

frame
bastidor^M

dual seat
sillín^M doble

turn signal
intermitente^M

taillight
luz^F trasera

rear shock absorber
amortiguador^M

pillion footrest
pedal^M trasero

exhaust pipe
tubo^M de escape^M

kickstand
soporte^M lateral

main stand
soporte^M principal

gearshift lever
lanca^F de cambio^M de velocidades^F

front footrest
pedal^M delantero

443

MOTORCYCLE
MOTOCICLETA^F

VIEW FROM ABOVE
VISTA^F POR ENCIMA

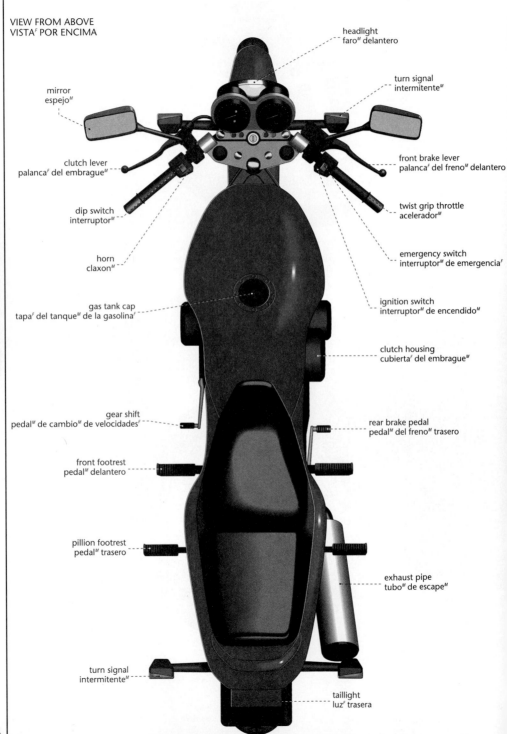

headlight
faro^M delantero

turn signal
intermitente^M

mirror
espejo^M

clutch lever
palanca^F del embrague^M

front brake lever
palanca^F del freno^M delantero

dip switch
interruptor^M

twist grip throttle
acelerador^M

horn
claxon^M

emergency switch
interruptor^M de emergencia^F

gas tank cap
tapa^F del tanque^M de la gasolina^F

ignition switch
interruptor^M de encendido^M

clutch housing
cubierta^F del embrague^M

gear shift
pedal^M de cambio^M de velocidades^F

rear brake pedal
pedal^M del freno^M trasero

front footrest
pedal^M delantero

pillion footrest
pedal^M trasero

exhaust pipe
tubo^M de escape^M

turn signal
intermitente^M

taillight
luz^F trasera

444

MOTORCYCLE DASHBOARD
TABLERO^M

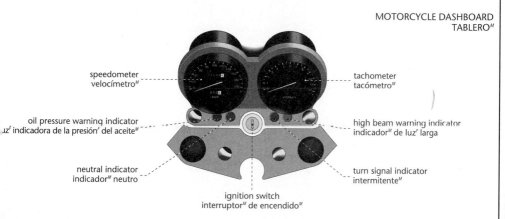

speedometer
velocímetro^M

tachometer
tacómetro^M

oil pressure warning indicator
luz^F indicadora de la presión^F del aceite^M

high beam warning indicator
indicador^M de luz^F larga

neutral indicator
indicador^M neutro

turn signal indicator
intermitente^M

ignition switch
interruptor^M de encendido^M

SNOWMOBILE
TRINEO^M MOTORIZADO

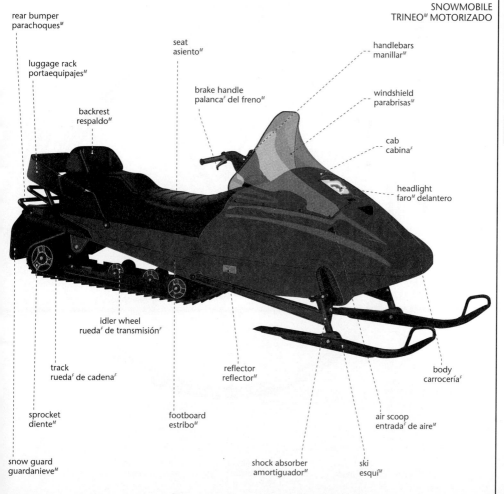

rear bumper
parachoques^M

seat
asiento^M

handlebars
manillar^M

luggage rack
portaequipajes^M

brake handle
palanca^F del freno^M

windshield
parabrisas^M

backrest
respaldo^M

cab
cabina^F

headlight
faro^M delantero

idler wheel
rueda^F de transmisión^F

track
rueda^F de cadena^F

reflector
reflector^M

body
carrocería^F

sprocket
diente^M

footboard
estribo^M

air scoop
entrada^F de aire^M

snow guard
guardanieve^M

shock absorber
amortiguador^M

ski
esquí^M

445

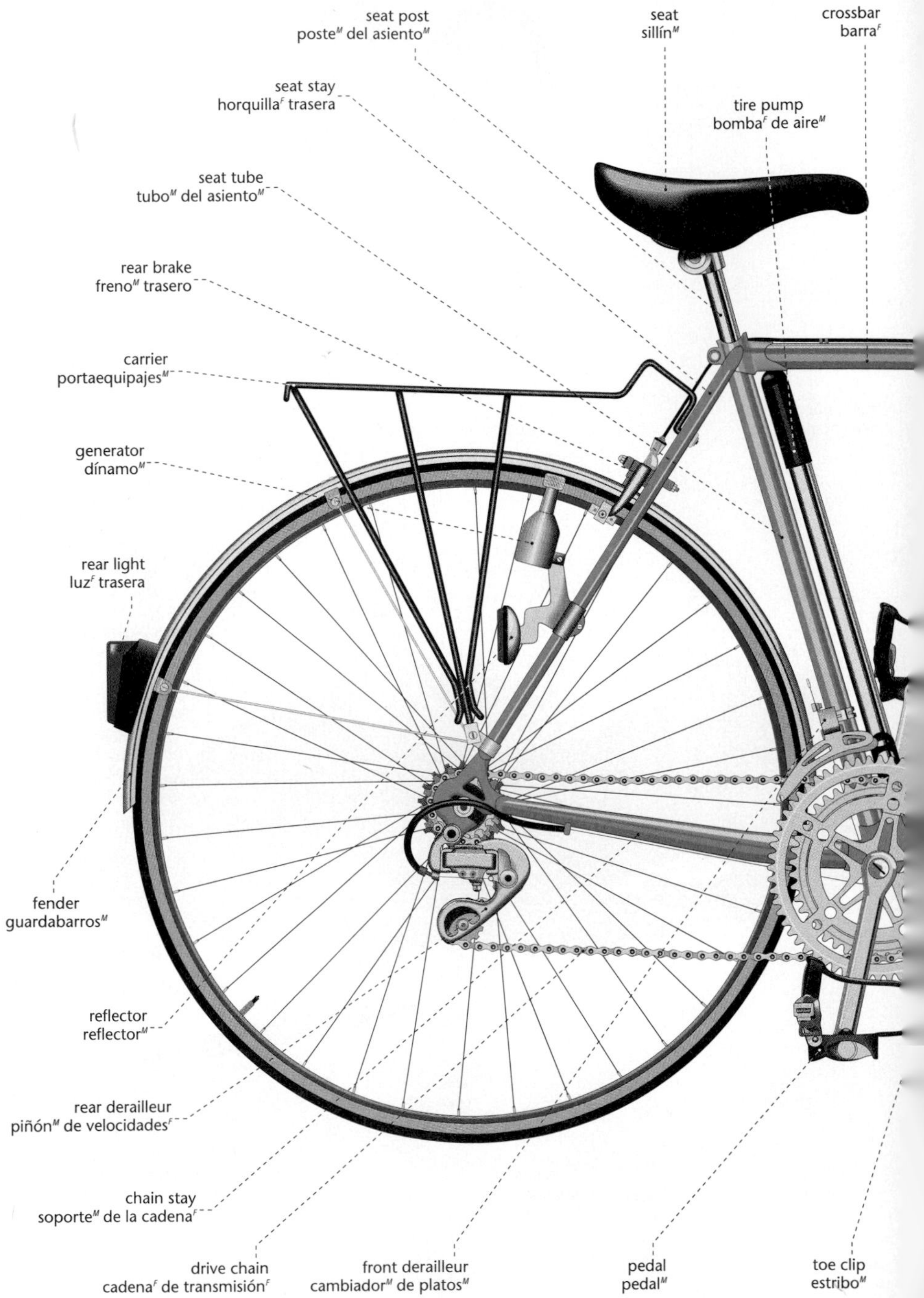

ROAD TRANSPORT
TRANSPORTE TERRESTRE

seat post
poste^M del asiento^M

seat stay
horquilla^F trasera

seat tube
tubo^M del asiento^M

rear brake
freno^M trasero

carrier
portaequipajes^M

generator
dínamo^M

rear light
luz^F trasera

fender
guardabarros^M

reflector
reflector^M

rear derailleur
piñón^M de velocidades^F

chain stay
soporte^M de la cadena^F

drive chain
cadena^F de transmisión^F

front derailleur
cambiador^M de platos^M

pedal
pedal^M

toe clip
estribo^M

seat
sillín^M

crossbar
barra^F

tire pump
bomba^F de aire^M

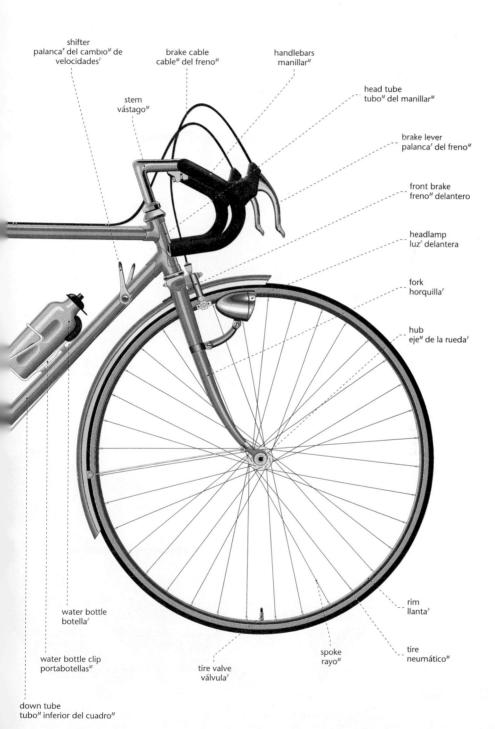

shifter
palanca^F del cambıo^M de
velocidades^F

brake cable
cable^M del freno^M

handlebars
manillar^M

head tube
tubo^M del manillar^M

stem
vástago^M

brake lever
palanca^F del freno^M

front brake
freno^M delantero

headlamp
luz^F delantera

fork
horquilla^F

hub
eje^M de la rueda^F

rim
llanta^F

water bottle
botella^F

tire
neumático^M

water bottle clip
portabotellas^M

tire valve
válvula^F

spoke
rayo^M

down tube
tubo^M inferior del cuadro^M

BICYCLE
BICICLETA^F

ROAD TRANSPORT
TRANSPORTE TERRESTRE

POWER TRAIN
TRANSMISIÓN^F DE CADENA^F

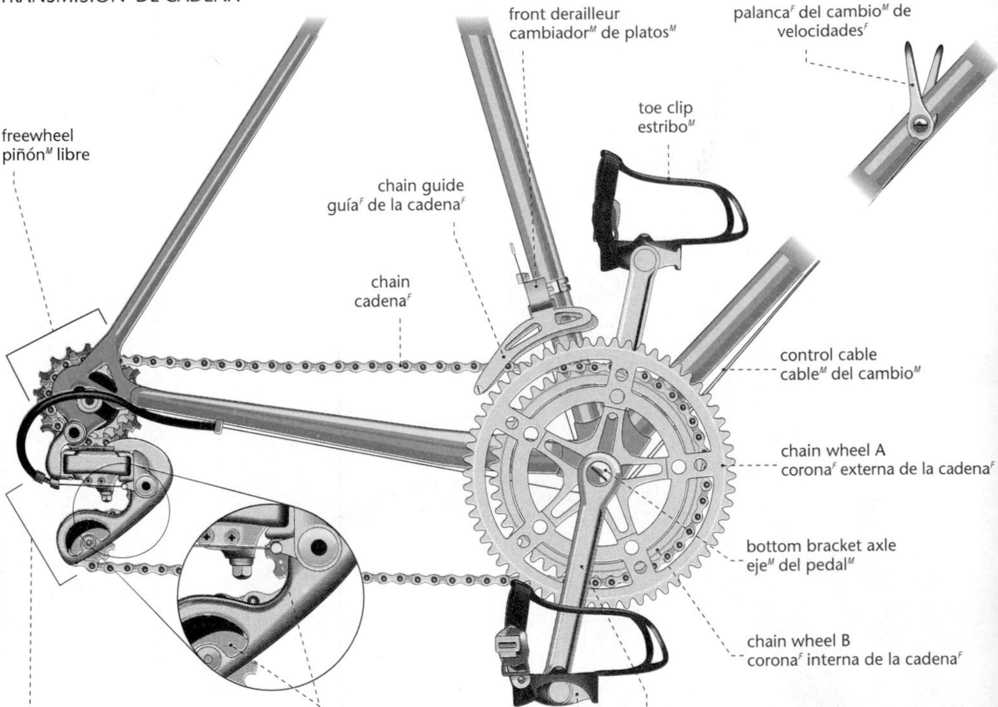

front derailleur
cambiador^M de platos^M

shifter
palanca^F del cambio^M de
velocidades^F

freewheel
piñón^M libre

toe clip
estribo^M

chain guide
guía^F de la cadena^F

chain
cadena^F

control cable
cable^M del cambio^M

chain wheel A
corona^F externa de la cadena^F

bottom bracket axle
eje^M del pedal^M

chain wheel B
corona^F interna de la cadena^F

jockey rollers
poleas^F de tensión^F

crank
manivela^F

rear derailleur
piñón^M de velocidades^F

pedal
pedal^M

ACCESSORIES
ACCESORIOS^M

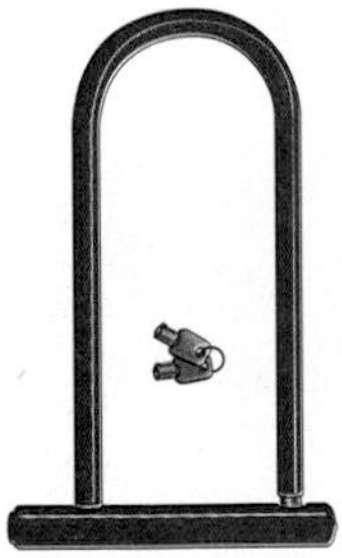

lock
candado^M para bicicleta^F

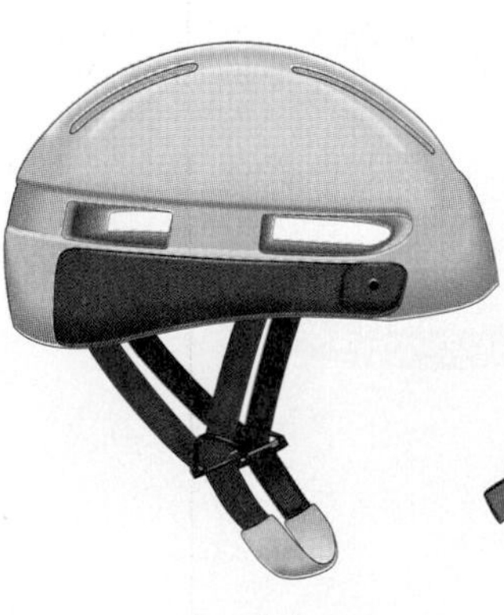

protective helmet
casco^M protector

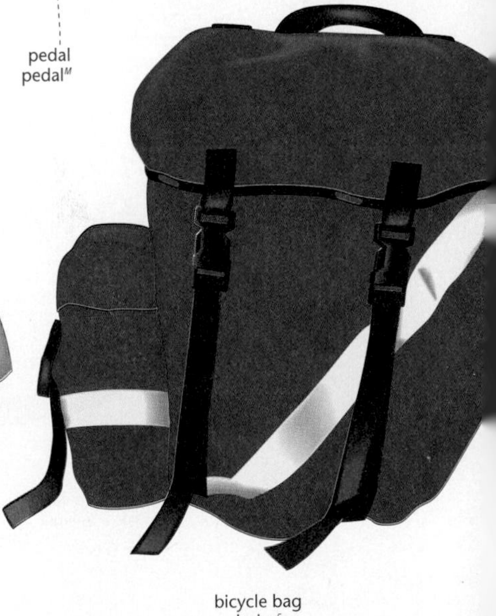

bicycle bag
bolsa^F

CARAVAN
CARAVANA*F*

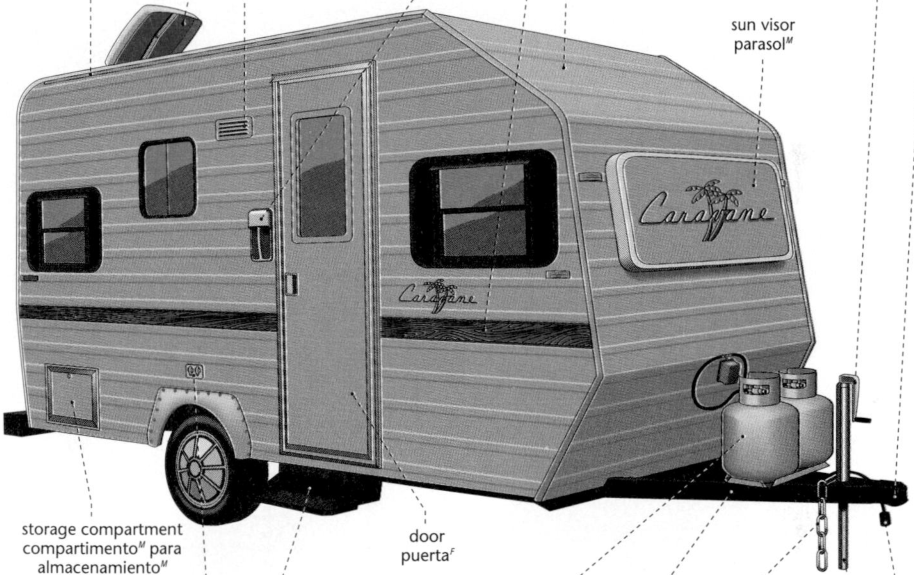

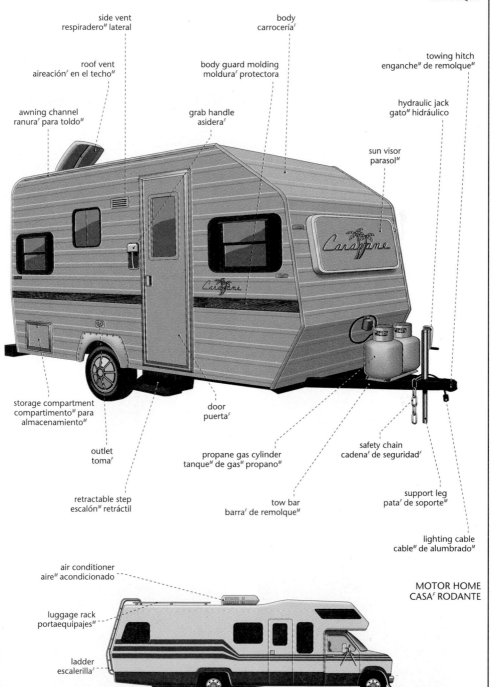

side vent
respiradero*M* lateral

body
carrocería*F*

roof vent
aireación*F* en el techo*M*

body guard molding
moldura*F* protectora

towing hitch
enganche*M* de remolque*M*

awning channel
ranura*F* para toldo*M*

grab handle
asidera*F*

hydraulic jack
gato*M* hidráulico

sun visor
parasol*M*

storage compartment
compartimento*M* para
almacenamiento*M*

door
puerta*F*

outlet
toma*F*

propane gas cylinder
tanque*M* de gas*M* propano*M*

safety chain
cadena*F* de seguridad*F*

retractable step
escalón*M* retráctil

tow bar
barra*F* de remolque*M*

support leg
pata*F* de soporte*M*

lighting cable
cable*M* de alumbrado*M*

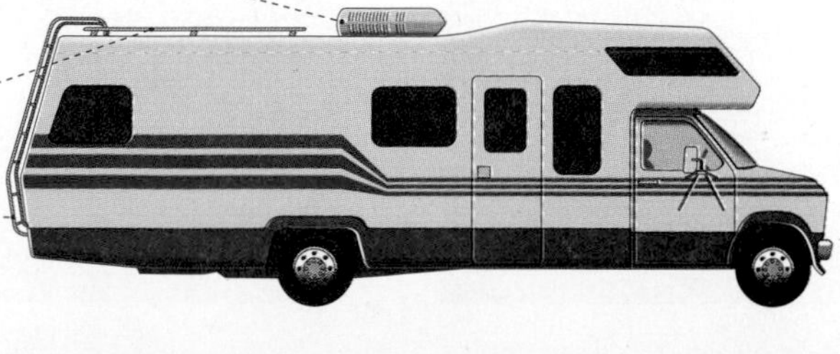

air conditioner
aire*M* acondicionado

MOTOR HOME
CASA*F* RODANTE

luggage rack
portaequipajes*M*

ladder
escalerilla*F*

449

ROAD SYSTEM
SISTEMA^M DE CARRETERAS^F

CROSS SECTION OF A ROAD
VISTA^F TRANSVERSAL DE UNA CARRETERA^F

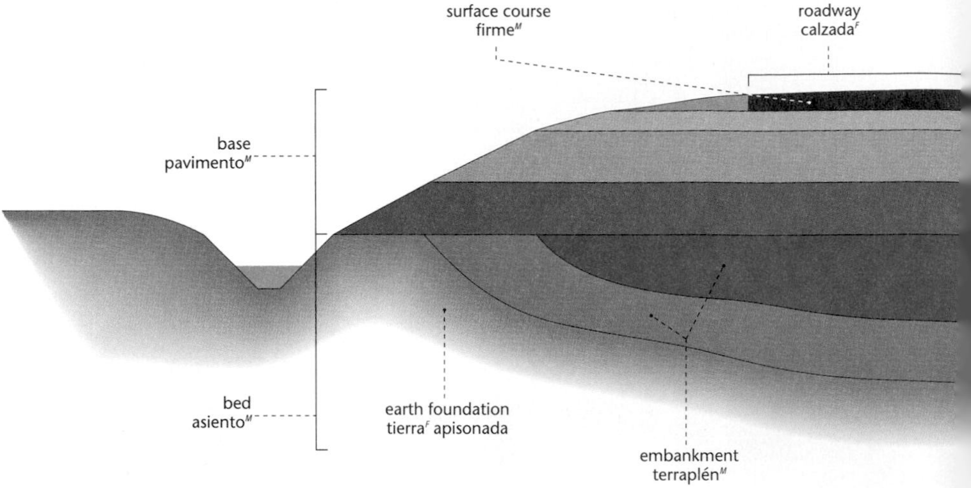

surface course
firme^M

roadway
calzada^F

base
pavimento^M

bed
asiento^M

earth foundation
tierra^F apisonada

embankment
terraplén^M

MAJOR TYPES OF INTERCHANGES
PRINCIPALES TIPOS^M DE INTERCAMBIOS^M

cloverleaf
trébol^M

traffic circle
glorieta^F

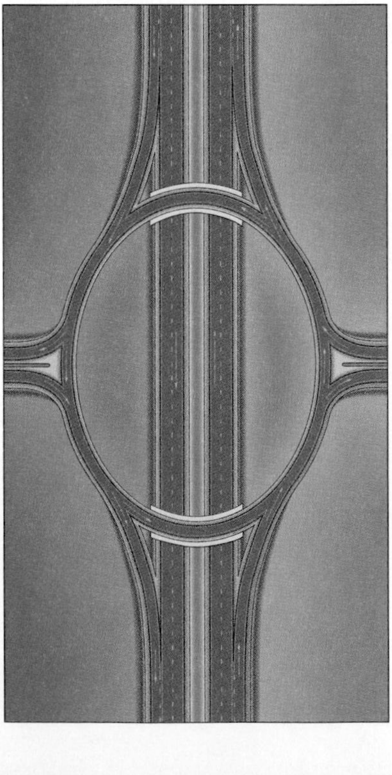

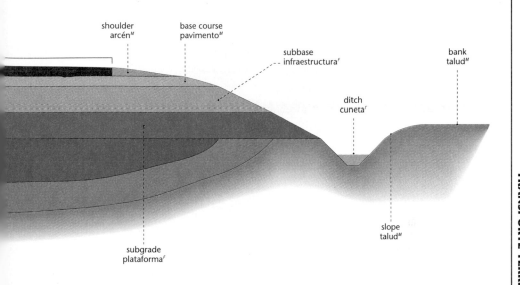

shoulder
arcén^M

base course
pavimento^M

subbase
infraestructura^F

bank
talud^M

ditch
cuneta^F

slope
talud^M

subgrade
plataforma^F

diamond interchange
diamante^M

trumpet interchange
trompeta^F

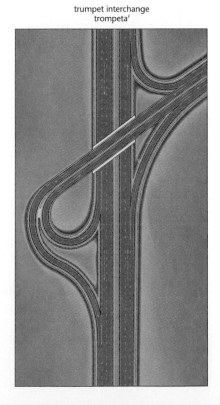

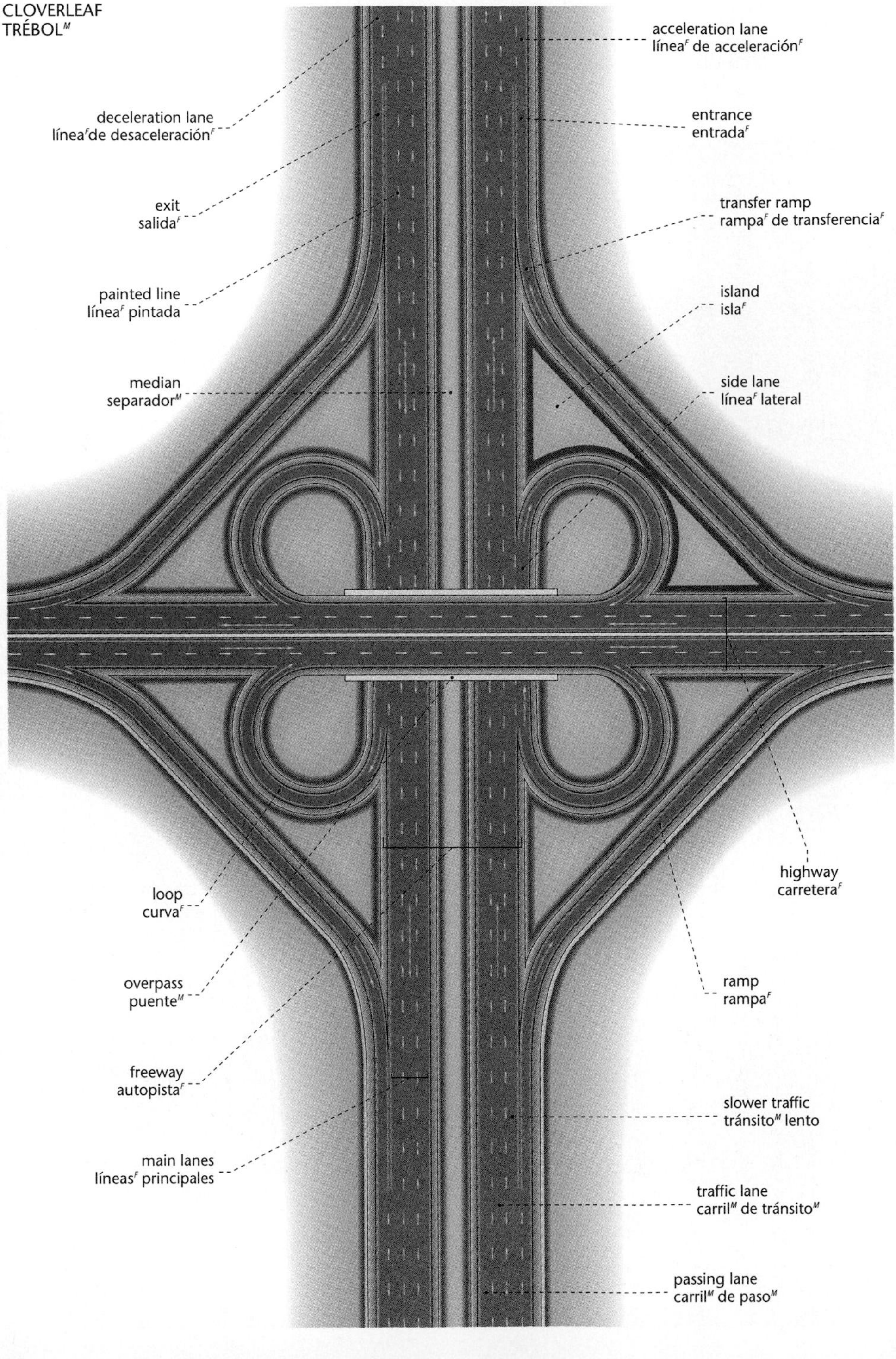

CLOVERLEAF
TRÉBOL^M

acceleration lane
línea^F de aceleración^F

deceleration lane
línea^F de desaceleración^F

entrance
entrada^F

exit
salida^F

transfer ramp
rampa^F de transferencia^F

painted line
línea^F pintada

island
isla^F

median
separador^M

side lane
línea^F lateral

ROAD TRANSPORT
TRANSPORTE TERRESTRE

highway
carretera^F

loop
curva^F

overpass
puente^M

ramp
rampa^F

freeway
autopista^F

slower traffic
tránsito^M lento

main lanes
líneas^F principales

traffic lane
carril^M de tránsito^M

passing lane
carril^M de paso^M

GASOLINE PUMP
SURTIDOR^M DE GASOLINA^F

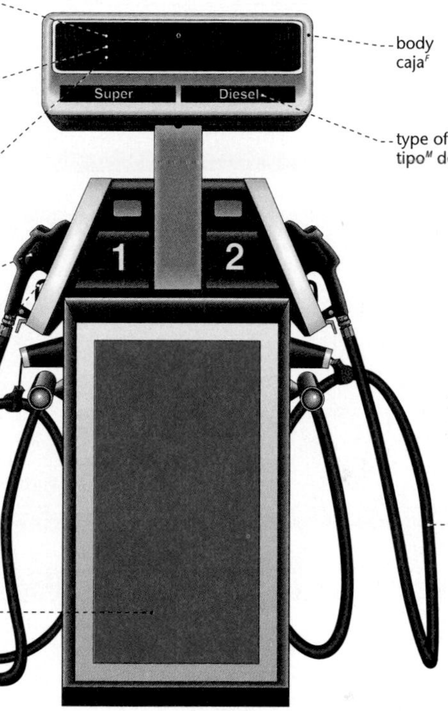

cash readout
indicador^M del importe^M total^M

body
caja^F

volume readout
cuentalitros^M

Super   Diesel

type of fuel
tipo^M de combustible^M

price per gallon/liter
indicador^M del precio^M por litro^M/galón^M

pump nozzle
pistola^F del surtidor^M

1   2

lever
palanca^F

gasoline pump hose
manguera^F de servicio^M

pedestal
base^F

SERVICE STATION
ESTACIÓN^F DE SERVICIO^M

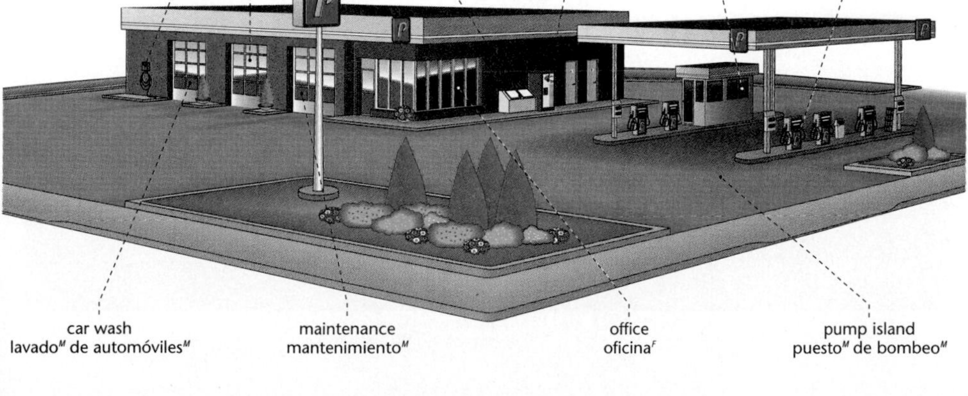

mechanics
taller^M de mecánica^F

kiosk
kiosco^M

air pump
toma^F de aire^M

ice dispenser
nevera^F

soft-drink dispenser
refrigerador^M

gasoline pump
surtidor^M de gasolina^F

car wash
lavado^M de automóviles^M

maintenance
mantenimiento^M

office
oficina^F

pump island
puesto^M de bombeo^M

FIXED BRIDGES
PUENTES^M FIJOS

BEAM BRIDGE
PUENTE^M DE VIGA^F

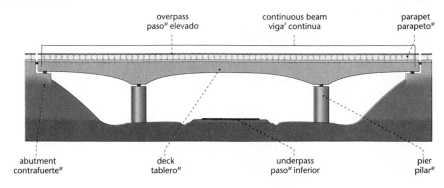

overpass
paso^M elevado

continuous beam
viga^F continua

parapet
parapeto^M

abutment
contrafuerte^M

deck
tablero^M

underpass
paso^M inferior

pier
pilar^M

TYPES OF BEAM BRIDGES
TIPOS^M DE PUENTES^M DE VIGA^F

multiple-span beam bridge
puente^M de viga^F de varios tramos^M

simple-span beam bridge
puente^M de viga^F de un tramo^M

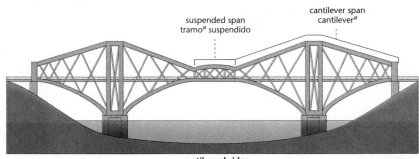

suspended span
tramo^M suspendido

cantilever span
cantilever^M

cantilever bridge
puente^M de cantilever

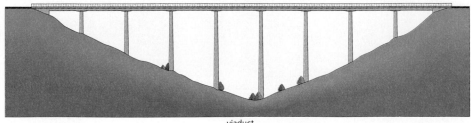

viaduct
viaducto^M

ARCH BRIDGE
PUENTE^M DE ARCO^M

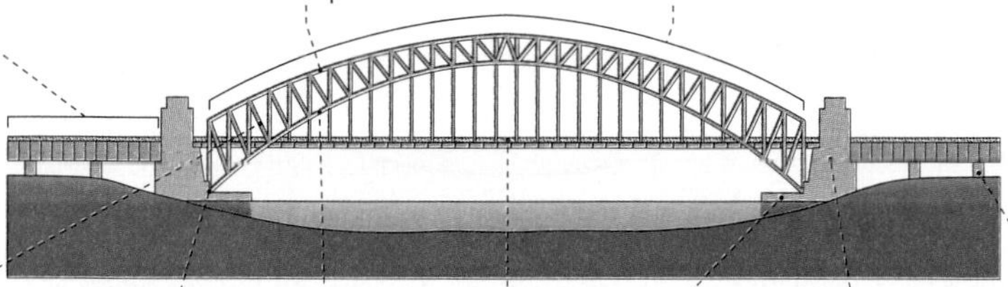

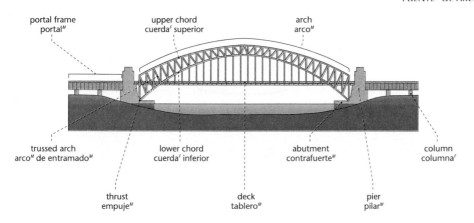

portal frame
portal^M

upper chord
cuerda^F superior

arch
arco^M

trussed arch
arco^M de entramado^M

lower chord
cuerda^F inferior

abutment
contrafuerte^M

column
columna^F

thrust
empuje^M

deck
tablero^M

pier
pilar^M

TYPES OF ARCH BRIDGES
TIPOS^M DE PUENTES^M DE ARCO^M

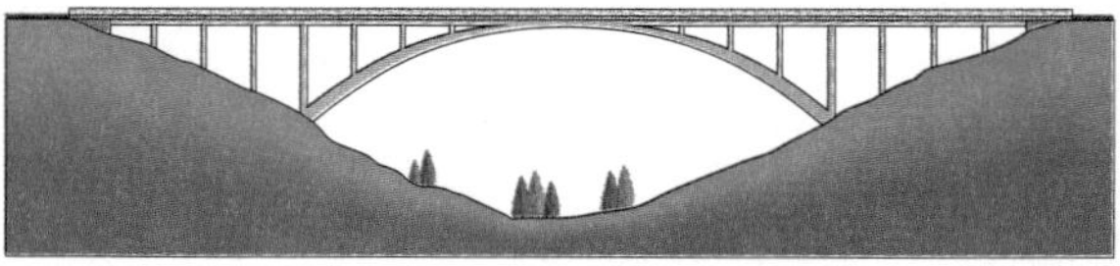

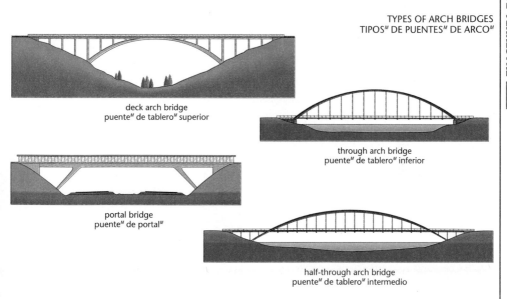

deck arch bridge
puente^M de tablero^M superior

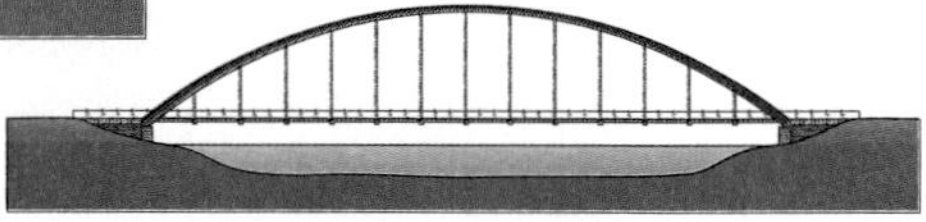

through arch bridge
puente^M de tablero^M inferior

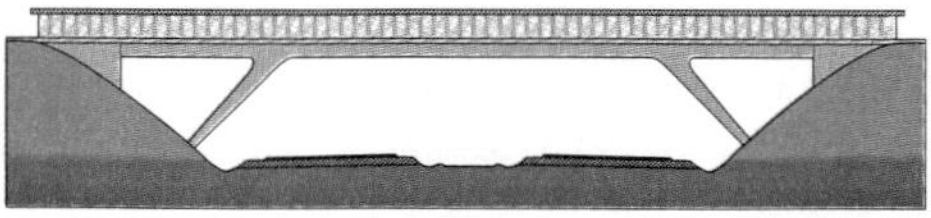

portal bridge
puente^M de portal^M

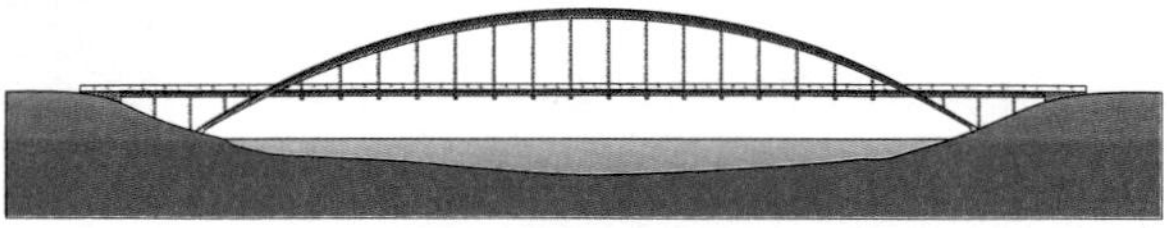

half-through arch bridge
puente^M de tablero^M intermedio

TYPES OF ARCHES
VARIEDADES^F DE ARCOS^M

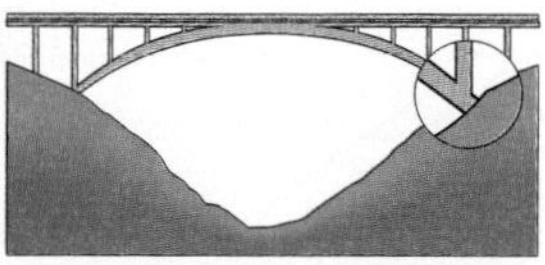

fixed arch
arco^M fijo

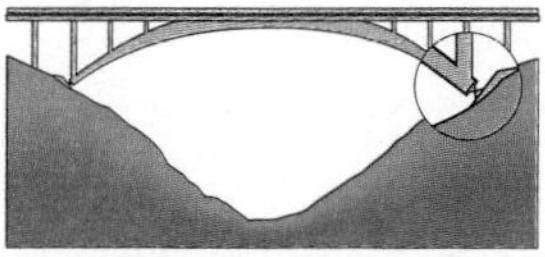

two-hinged arch
arco^M de dos articulaciones^F

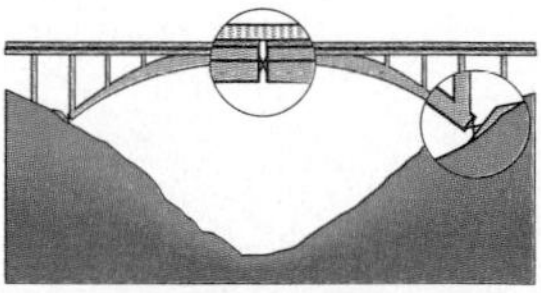

three-hinged arch
arco^M de tres articulaciones^F

FIXED BRIDGES
PUENTES^M FIJOS

SUSPENSION BRIDGE
PUENTE^M COLGANTE

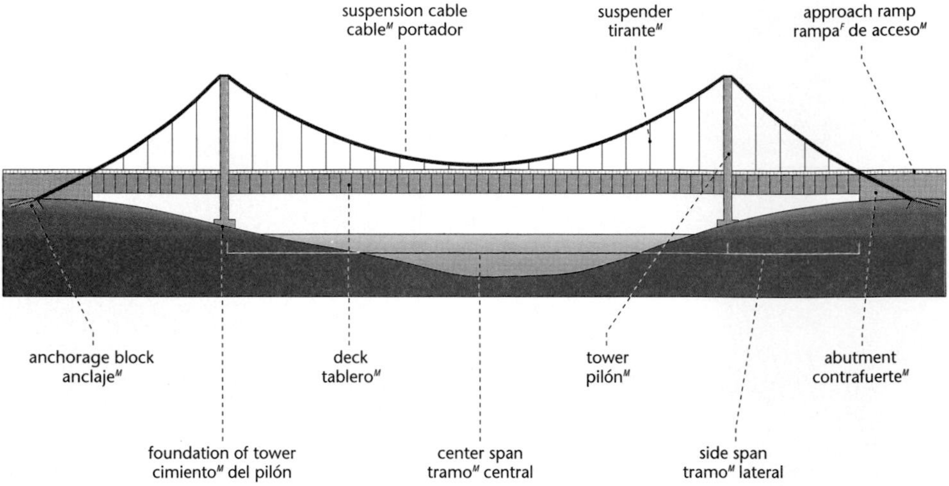

suspension cable
cable^M portador

suspender
tirante^M

approach ramp
rampa^F de acceso^M

anchorage block
anclaje^M

deck
tablero^M

tower
pilón^M

abutment
contrafuerte^M

foundation of tower
cimiento^M del pilón

center span
tramo^M central

side span
tramo^M lateral

CABLE-STAYED BRIDGES
PUENTES^M DE TIRANTES^M

fan cable stays
tirantes^M en abanico^M

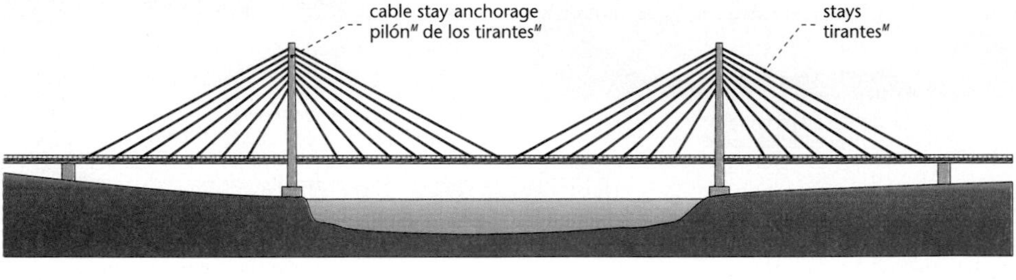

cable stay anchorage
pilón^M de los tirantes^M

stays
tirantes^M

harp cable stays
tirantes^M en forma^F de arpa^F

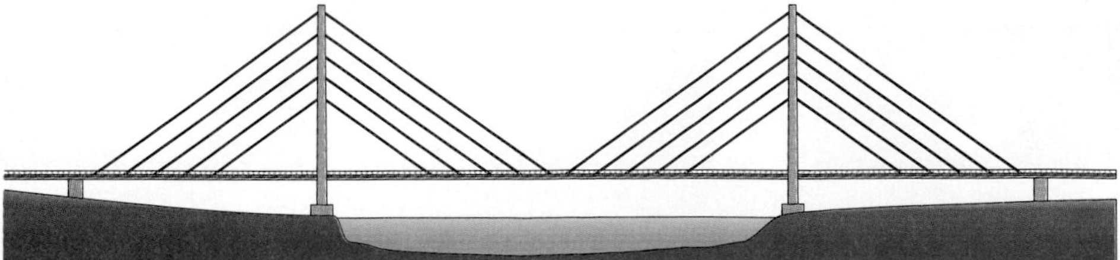

MOVABLE BRIDGES
PUENTES^M MOVIBLES

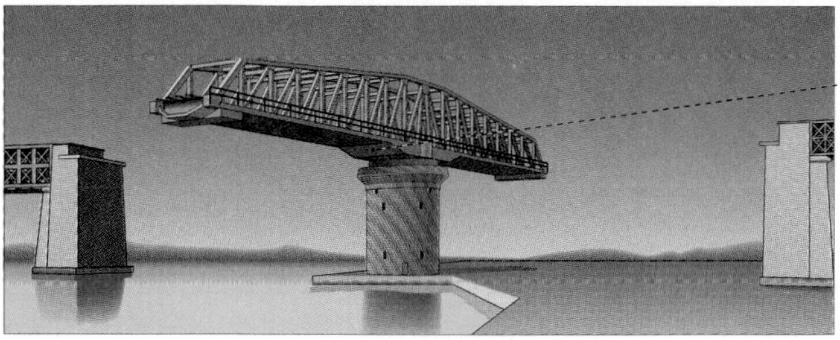

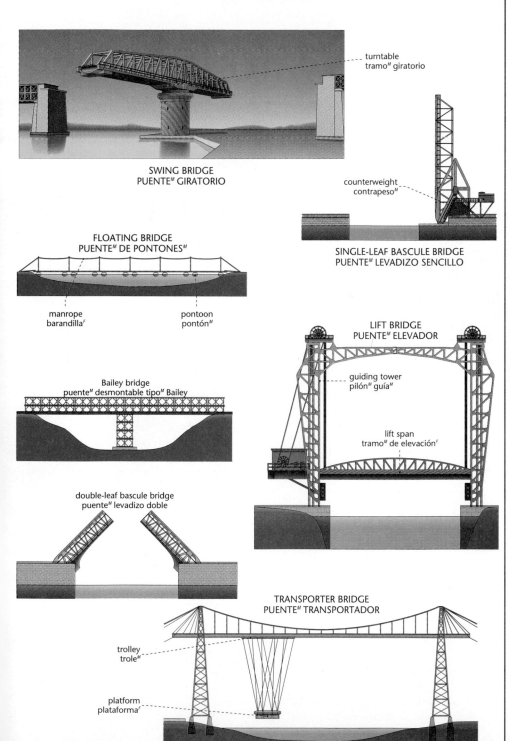

turntable
tramo^M giratorio

SWING BRIDGE
PUENTE^M GIRATORIO

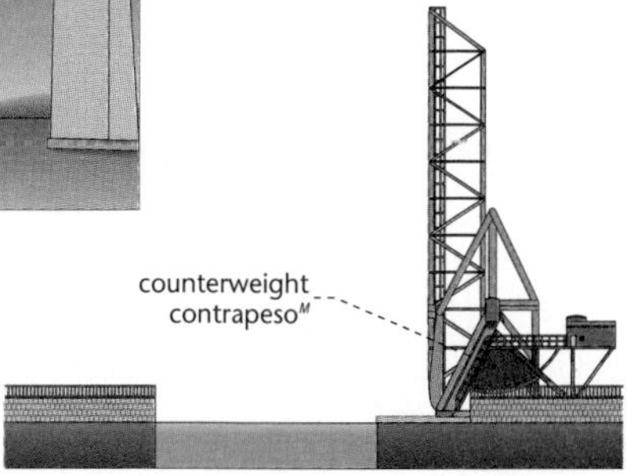

counterweight
contrapeso^M

SINGLE-LEAF BASCULE BRIDGE
PUENTE^M LEVADIZO SENCILLO

FLOATING BRIDGE
PUENTE^M DE PONTONES^M

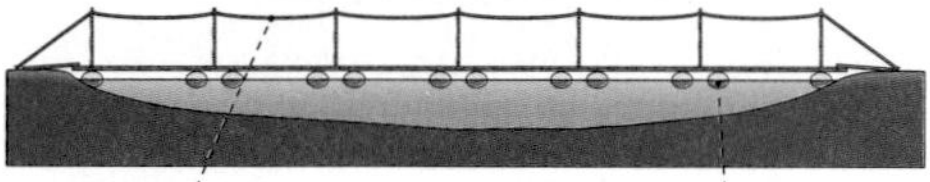

manrope
barandilla^F

pontoon
pontón^M

LIFT BRIDGE
PUENTE^M ELEVADOR

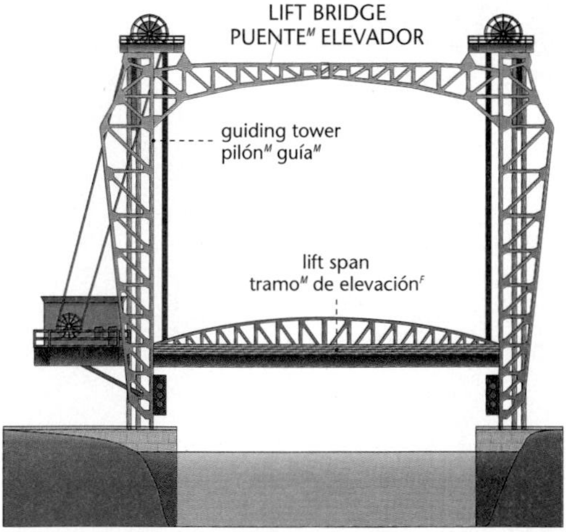

guiding tower
pilón^M guía^M

lift span
tramo^M de elevación^F

Bailey bridge
puente^M desmontable tipo^M Bailey

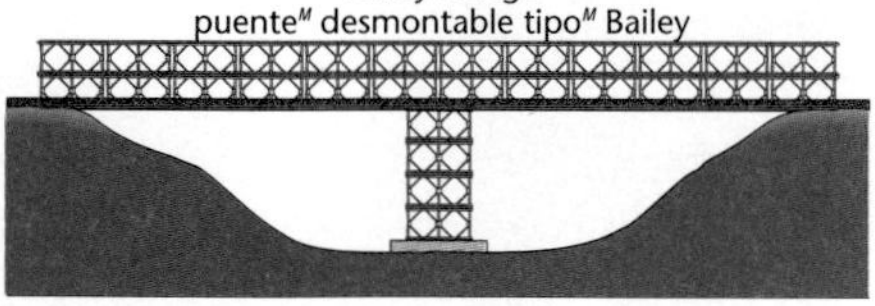

double-leaf bascule bridge
puente^M levadizo doble

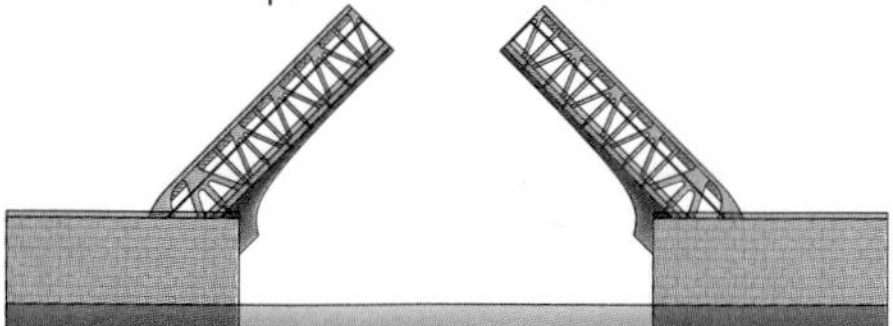

TRANSPORTER BRIDGE
PUENTE^M TRANSPORTADOR

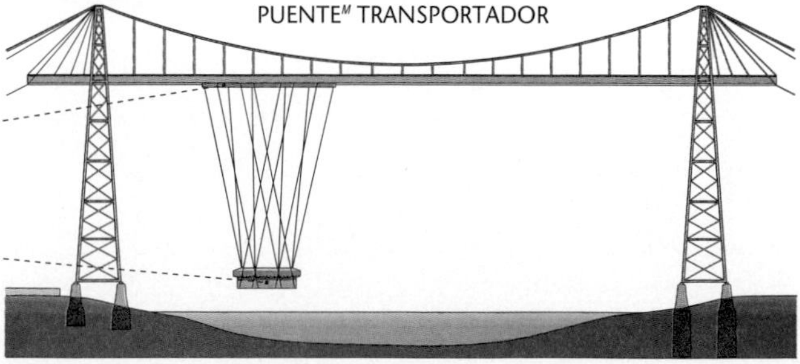

trolley
trole^M

platform
plataforma^F

HIGH-SPEED TRAIN
TREN^M DE ALTA VELOCIDAD^F

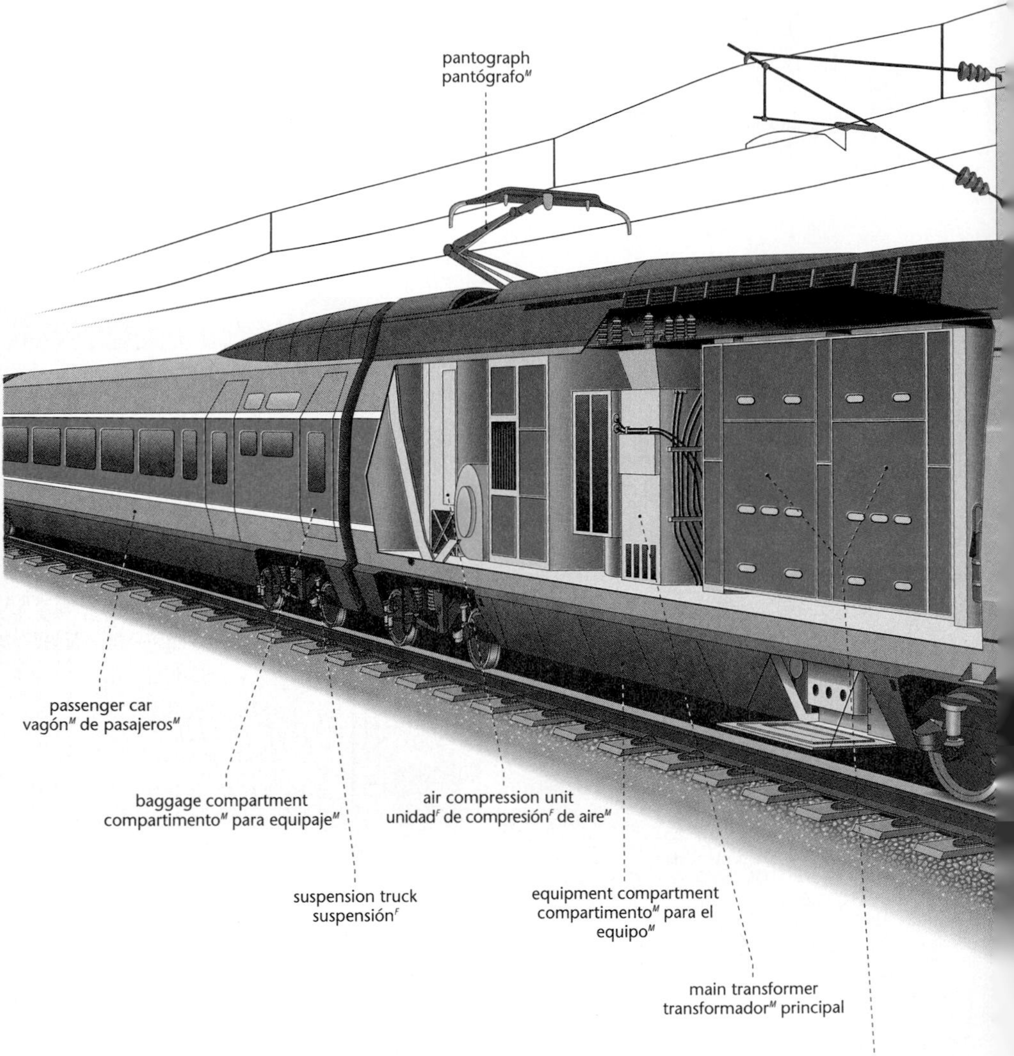

pantograph
pantógrafo^M

passenger car
vagón^M de pasajeros^M

baggage compartment
compartimento^M para equipaje^M

air compression unit
unidad^F de compresión^F de aire^M

suspension truck
suspensión^F

equipment compartment
compartimento^M para el
equipo^M

main transformer
transformador^M principal

motor unit
grupo^M motor^M

catenary
moderador^M

headlight
faro^M delantero

driver's cab
cabina^F del maquinista^M

power car
locomotora^F

headlight
faro^M delantero

position light
luz^F de posición^F

motor truck
carretilla^F del motor^M

pilot
quitapiedras^M

coupling guide device
guía^F de enganche^M

TYPES OF PASSENGER CARS
VAGONES*ᴹ* DE PASAJEROS*ᴹ*

COACH CAR
VAGÓN*ᴹ* DE PASAJEROS*ᴹ*

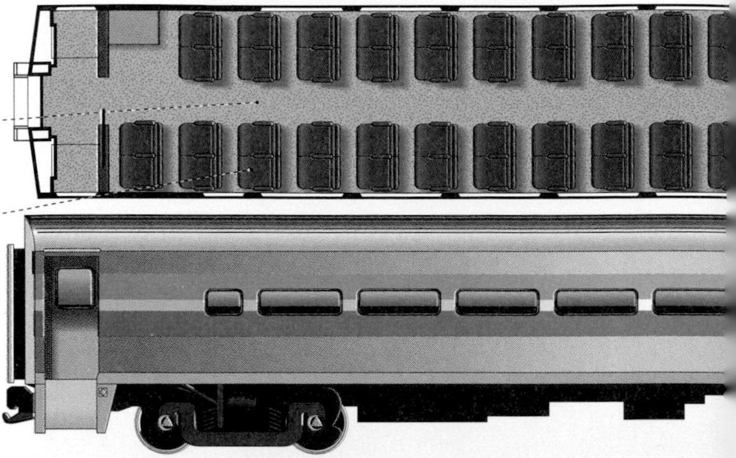

center aisle
pasillo*ᴹ* central

adjustable seat
asiento*ᴹ* ajustable

SLEEPING CAR
COCHE*ᴹ* CAMA*ᶠ*

berth
litera*ᶠ*

linen
lencería*ᶠ*

sleeping compartment
dormitorio*ᴹ*

DINING CAR
VAGÓN*ᴹ* COMEDOR*ᴹ*

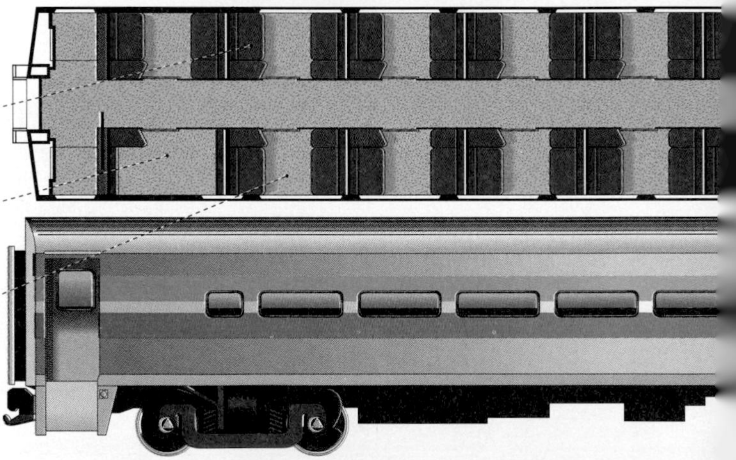

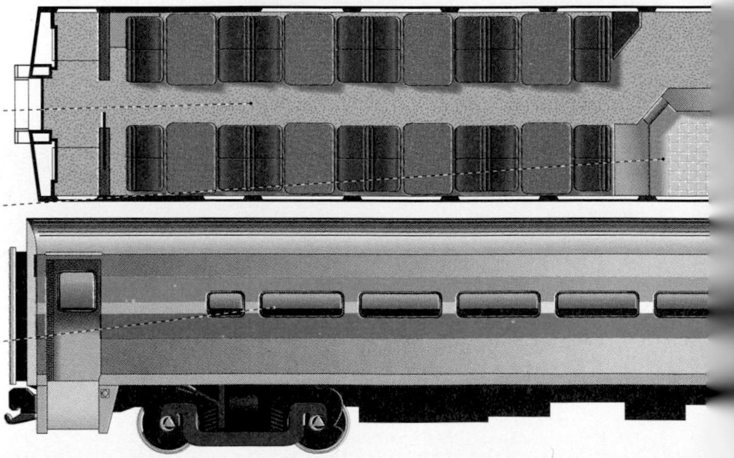

dining section
comedor*ᴹ*

kitchen
cocina*ᶠ*

panoramic window
ventanilla*ᶠ* panorámica

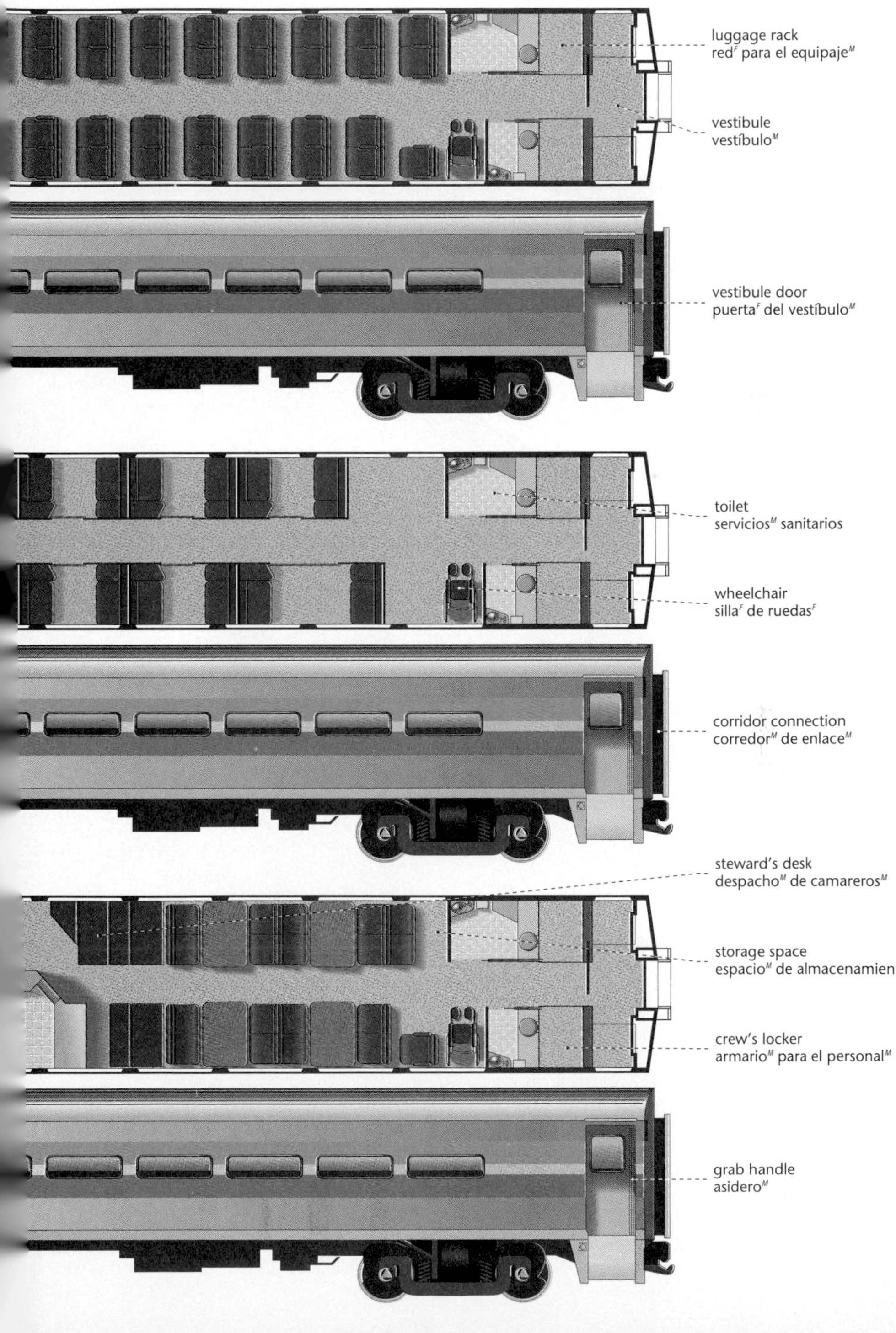

luggage rack
red^F para el equipaje^M

vestibule
vestíbulo^M

vestibule door
puerta^F del vestíbulo^M

toilet
servicios^M sanitarios

wheelchair
silla^F de ruedas^F

corridor connection
corredor^M de enlace^M

steward's desk
despacho^M de camareros^M

storage space
espacio^M de almacenamiento^M

crew's locker
armario^M para el personal^M

grab handle
asidero^M

RAIL TRANSPORT
TRANSPORTE FERROVIARIO

office
oficina^F

glassed roof
techo^M de vidiro^M

indicator board
pizarra^F de información^F

parcels office
consigna^F

baggage room
sala^F de equipajes^M

passenger train
tren^M de pasajeros^M

platform edge
borde^M del andén^M

passenger platform
andén^M de pasajeros^M

gate
barrera^F

booking hall
vestíbulo^M

platform number
indicador^M de número^M de andén^M

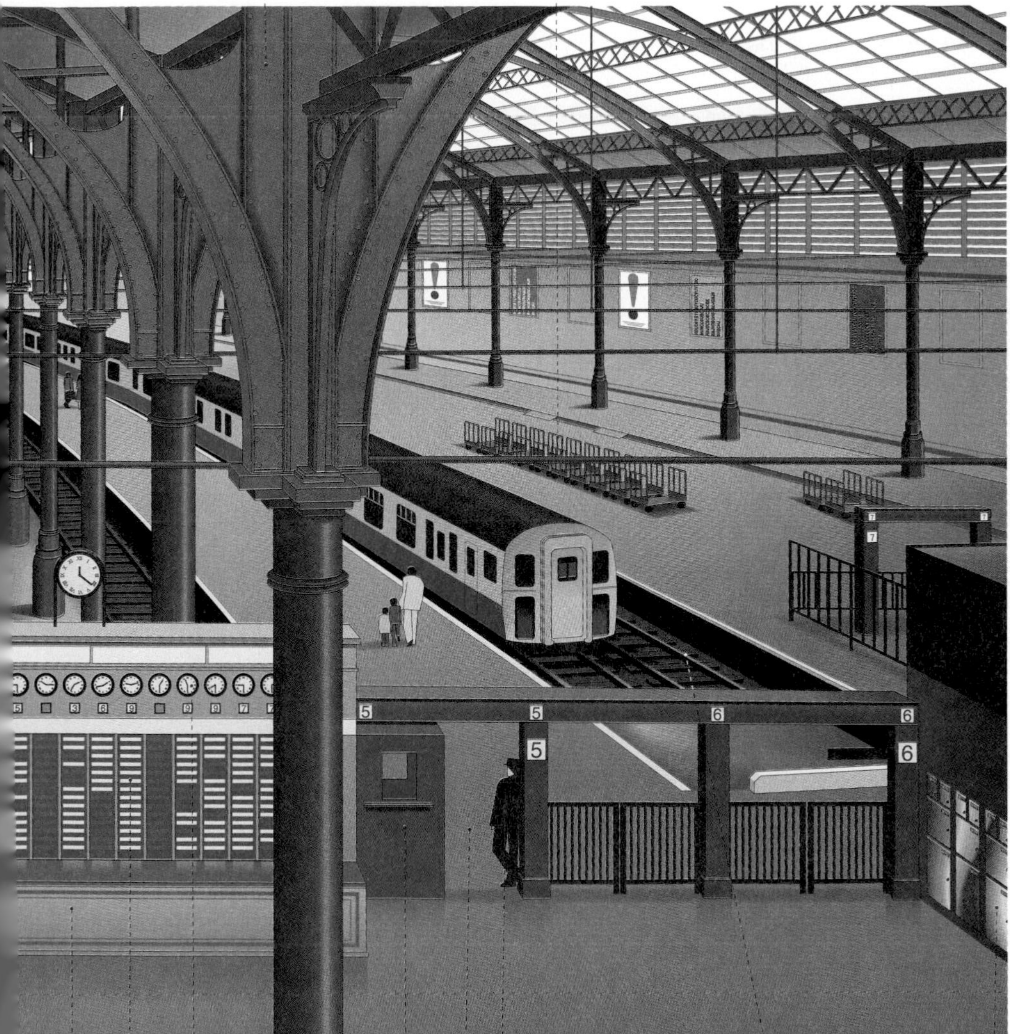

metal structure
estrucutra^F de metal^M

baggage cart
carro^M portaequipaje

departure time indicator
indicador^M de hora^F de salida^F

ticket collector
colector^M de billetes^M

baggage lockers
casillas^F de consigna^F
automática

destination
destinos^M

platform entrance
acceso^M a los andenes^M

track
vía^F

schedules
horarios^M

ticket control
control^M de billetes^M

RAILROAD STATION
ESTACIÓN^F DE FERROCARRIL^M

station platform
andén^M

passenger station
estación^F de ferrocarril^M

suburban commuter railroad
vía^F de tren^M suburbano

parking
estacionamiento^M

footbridge
puente^M peatonal

commuter train
tren^M suburbano

subsidiary track
vía^F subsidiaria

platform shelter
cobertizo^M del andén^M

main line
vía^F principal

level crossing
paso^M a nivel^M

semaphore
semáforo^M

bumper
tope^M

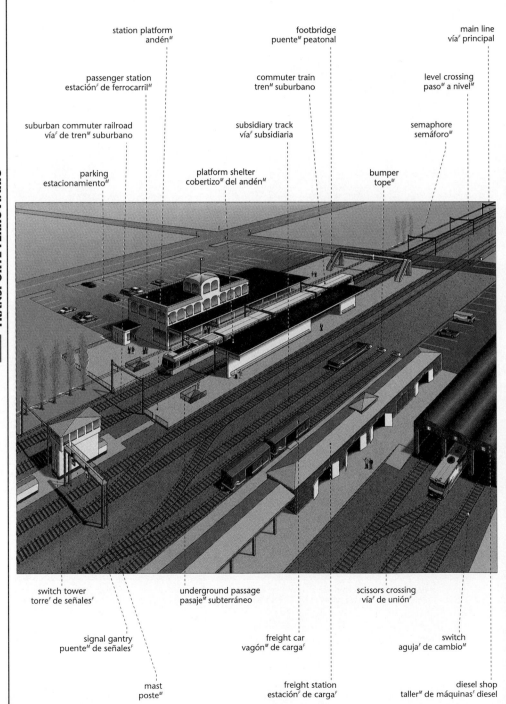

switch tower
torre^F de señales^F

signal gantry
puente^M de señales^F

mast
poste^M

underground passage
pasaje^M subterráneo

freight car
vagón^M de carga^F

freight station
estación^F de carga^F

scissors crossing
vía^F de unión^F

switch
aguja^F de cambio^M

diesel shop
taller^M de máquinas^F diesel

YARD
TALLERES^M DE FERROCARRIL^M

classification yard
patio^M de clasificación^F

outbound track
vía^F de salida^F

car repair shop
taller^M de reparación^F de
vagones^M

receiving yard
patio^M de recepción^F

second classification track
segunda vía^F de clasificación^F

car cleaning yard
patio^M de lavado^M de vagones^M

water tower
tanque^M de agua^F

locomotive track
vía^F locomotriz

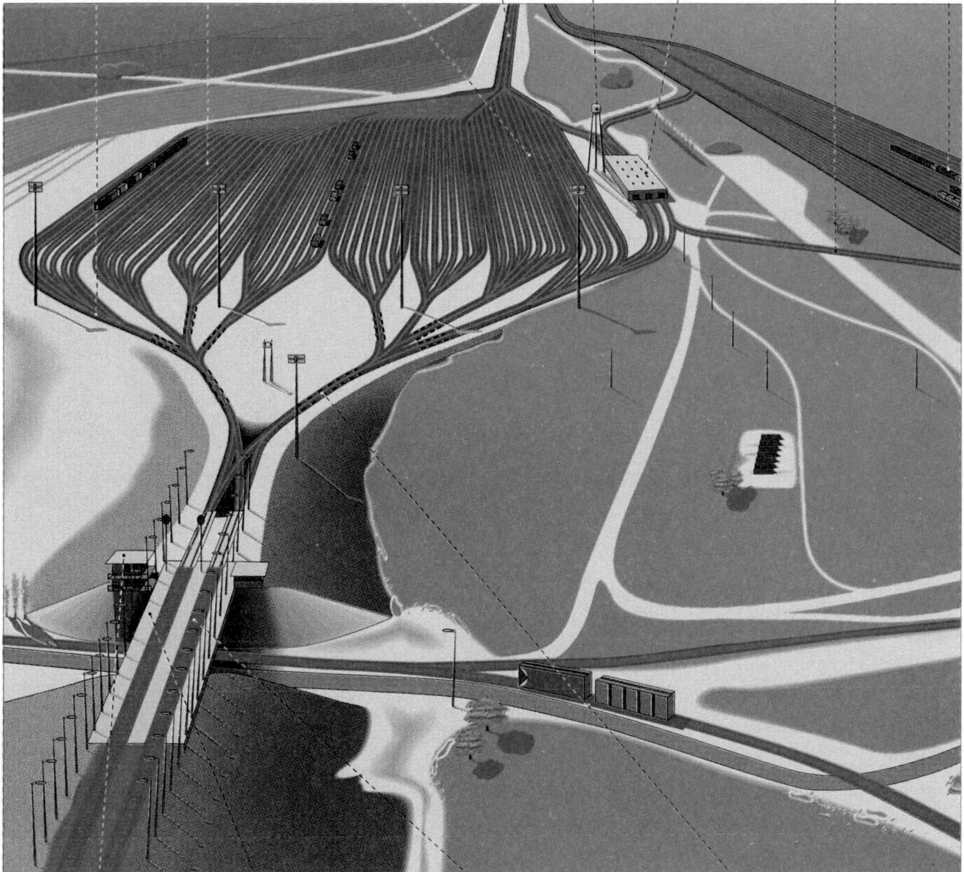

hump office
oficina^F

hump
lomo^M de maniobra^F

hump lead
dirección^F

first classification track
primera vía^F de clasificación^F

RAIL TRANSPORT
TRANSPORTE FERROVIARIO

RAIL JOINT
EMPALME^M DE RIELES^M

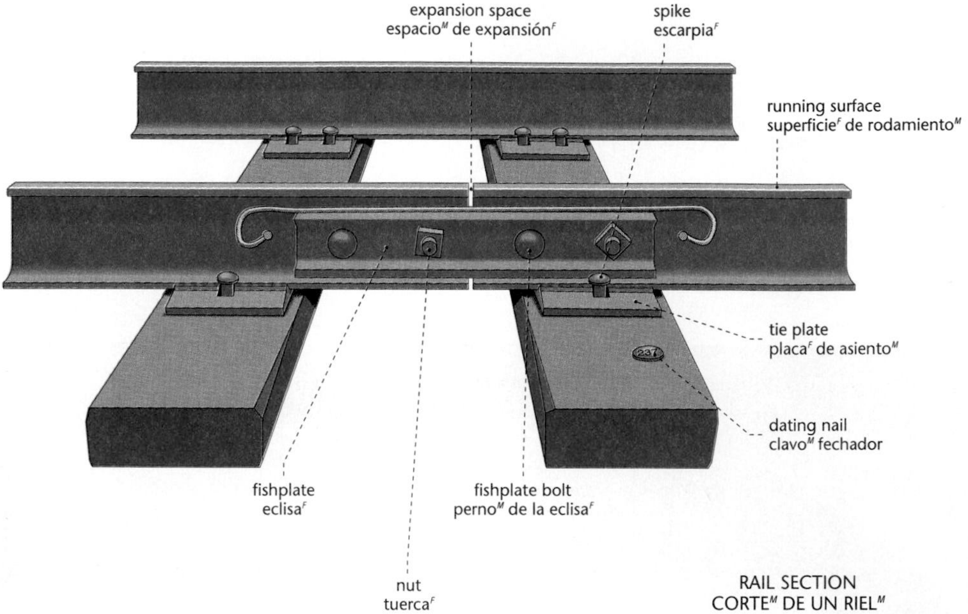

expansion space
espacio^M de expansión^F

spike
escarpia^F

running surface
superficie^F de rodamiento^M

tie plate
placa^F de asiento^M

dating nail
clavo^M fechador

fishplate
eclisa^F

fishplate bolt
perno^M de la eclisa^F

nut
tuerca^F

RAIL SECTION
CORTE^M DE UN RIEL^M

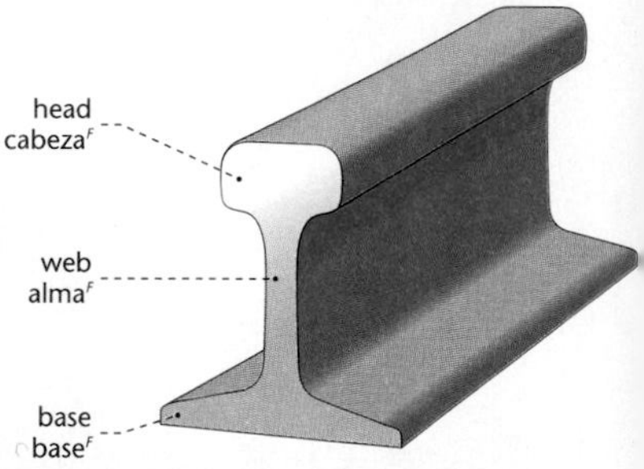

head
cabeza^F

web
alma^F

base
base^F

RAILROAD TRACK
VÍA^F FÉRREA

tie
traviesa^F

rail
riel^M

ballast
balasto^M

466

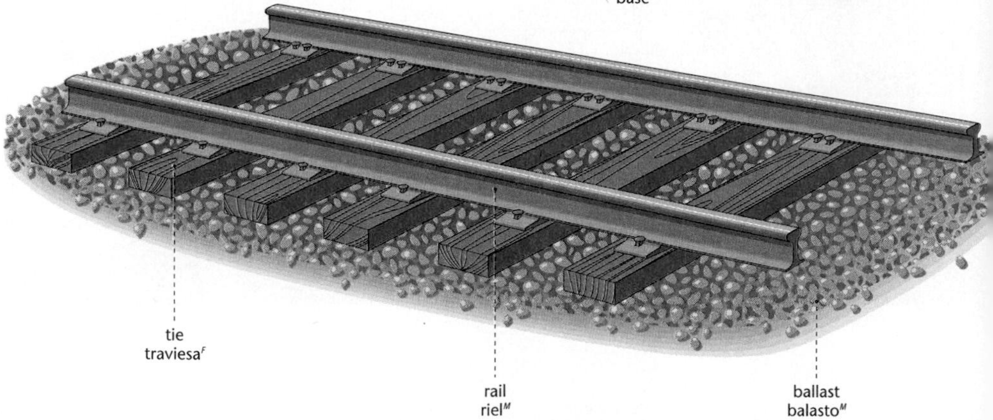

REMOTE-CONTROLLED SWITCH
AGUJA^F DE CONTROL^M A LARGA DISTANCIA^F

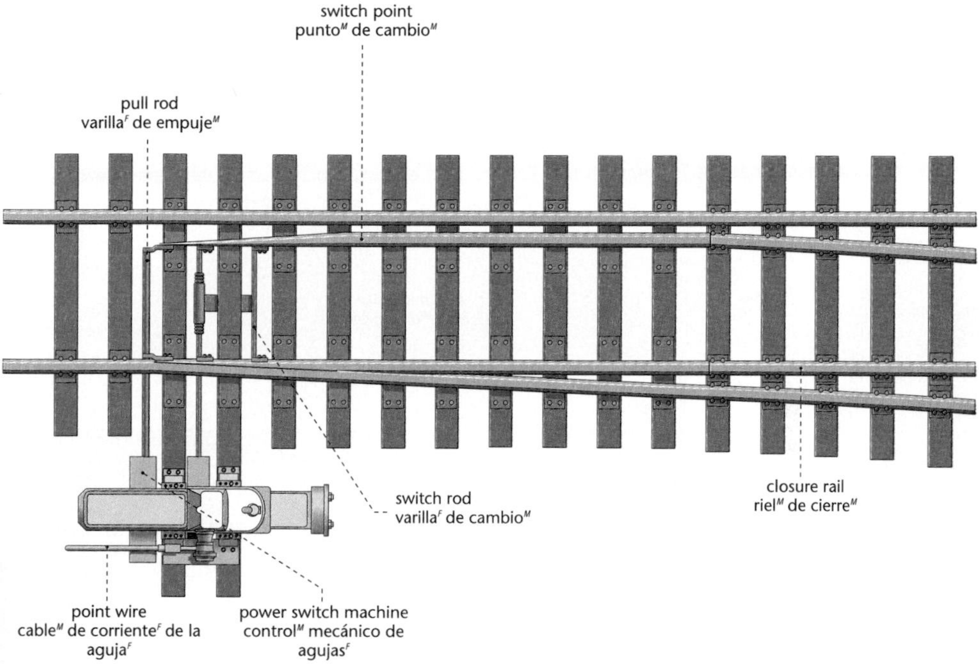

switch point
punto^M de cambio^M

pull rod
varilla^F de empuje^M

switch rod
varilla^F de cambio^M

closure rail
riel^M de cierre^M

point wire
cable^M de corriente^F de la
aguja^F

power switch machine
control^M mecánico de
agujas^F

MANUALLY-OPERATED SWITCH
CAMBIADOR^M MANUAL DE VÍA^F

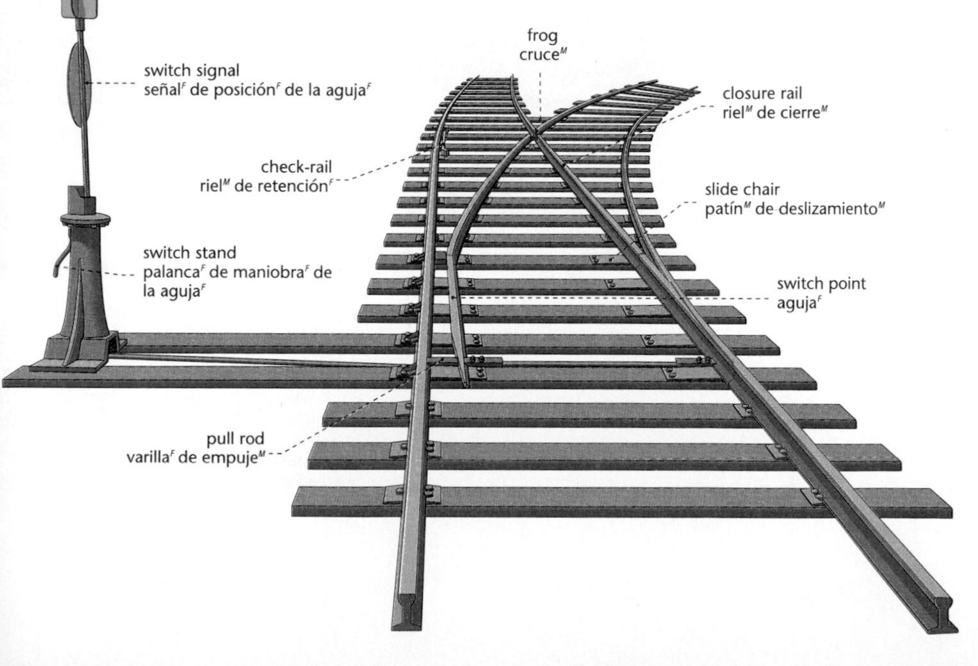

frog
cruce^M

closure rail
riel^M de cierre^M

switch signal
señal^F de posición^F de la aguja^F

check-rail
riel^M de retención^F

slide chair
patín^M de deslizamiento^M

switch stand
palanca^F de maniobra^F de
la aguja^F

switch point
aguja^F

pull rod
varilla^F de empuje^M

DIESEL-ELECTRIC LOCOMOTIVE
LOCOMOTORA^F DIESEL ELÉCTRICA

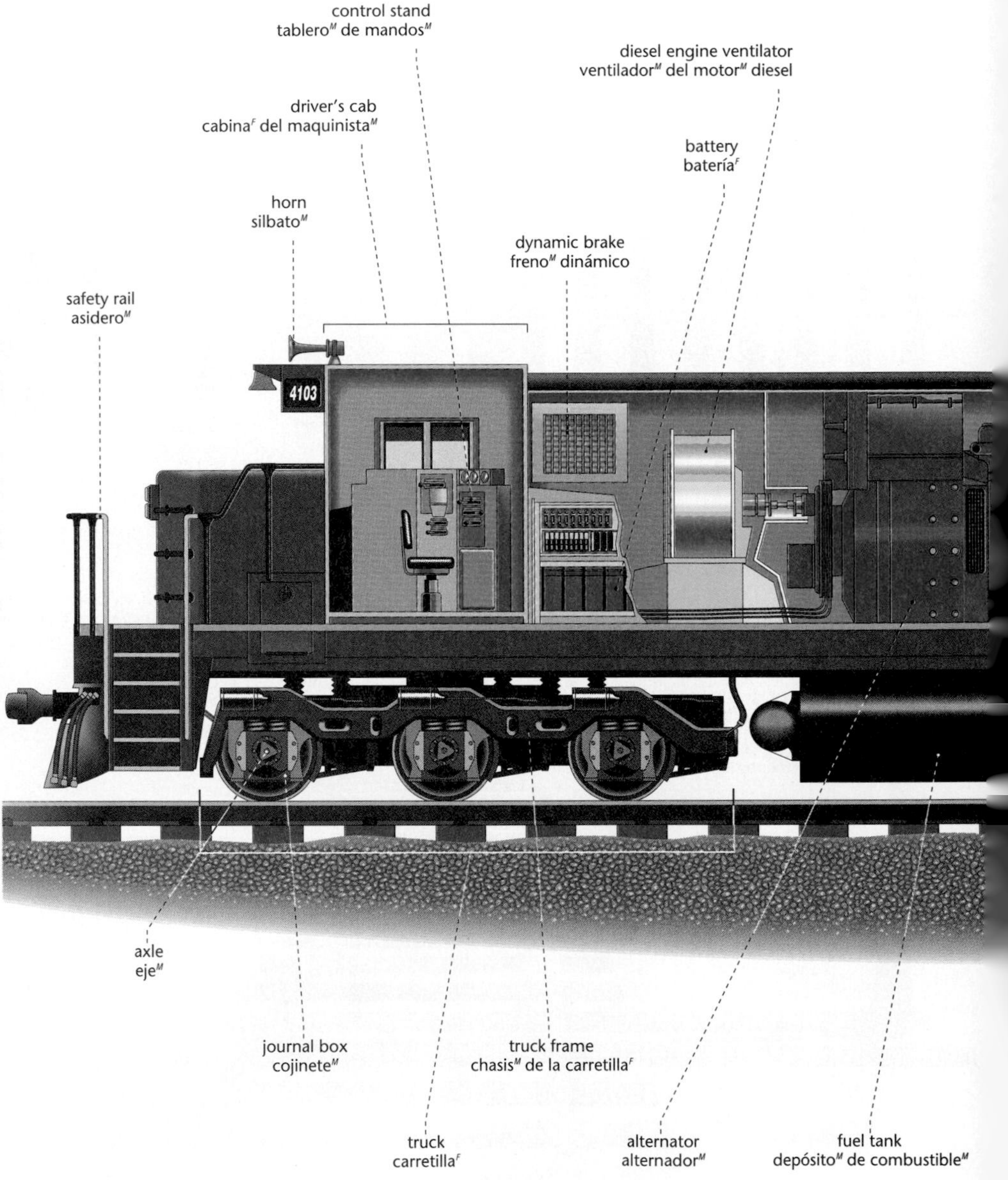

control stand
tablero^M de mandos^M

diesel engine ventilator
ventilador^M del motor^M diesel

driver's cab
cabina^F del maquinista^M

battery
batería^F

horn
silbato^M

dynamic brake
freno^M dinámico

safety rail
asidero^M

axle
eje^M

journal box
cojinete^M

truck frame
chasis^M de la carretilla^F

truck
carretilla^F

alternator
alternador^M

fuel tank
depósito^M de combustible^M

air compressor
compresor^M de aire^M

ventilating fan
ventilador^M

air filter
filtro^M de aire^M

radiator
radiador^M

diesel engine
motor^M diesel

water tank
depósito^M de agua^F

headlight
faro^M delantero

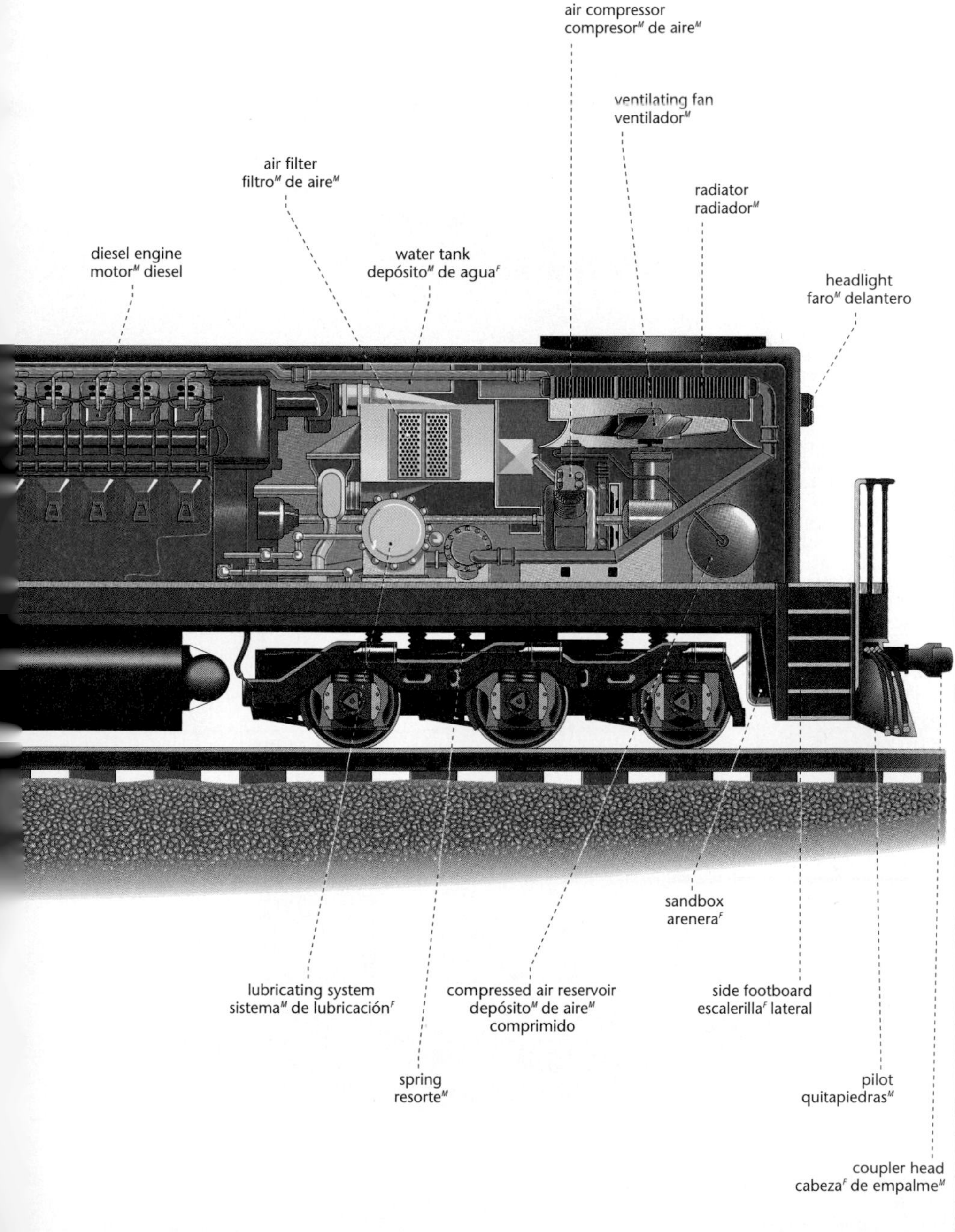

sandbox
arenera^F

lubricating system
sistema^M de lubricación^F

compressed air reservoir
depósito^M de aire^M
comprimido

side footboard
escalerilla^F lateral

spring
resorte^M

pilot
quitapiedras^M

coupler head
cabeza^F de empalme^M

CAR
VAGÓN^M

BOX CAR
FURGÓN^M

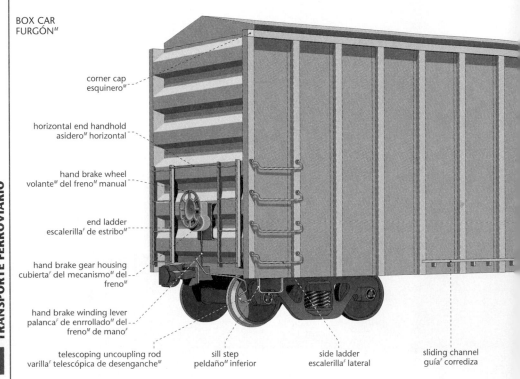

corner cap
esquinero^M

horizontal end handhold
asidero^M horizontal

hand brake wheel
volante^M del freno^M manual

end ladder
escalerilla^F de estribo^M

hand brake gear housing
cubierta^F del mecanismo^M del
freno^M

hand brake winding lever
palanca^F de enrrollado^M del
freno^M de mano^F

telescoping uncoupling rod
varilla^F telescópica de desenganche^M

sill step
peldaño^M inferior

side ladder
escalerilla^F lateral

sliding channel
guía^F corrediza

CONTAINER
CONTENEDOR^M

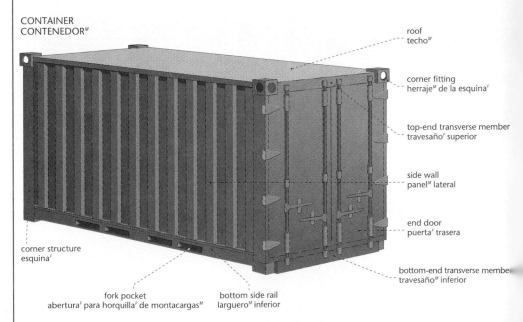

roof
techo^M

corner fitting
herraje^M de la esquina^F

top-end transverse member
travesaño^F superior

side wall
panel^M lateral

end door
puerta^F trasera

bottom-end transverse member
travesaño^M inferior

corner structure
esquina^F

fork pocket
abertura^F para horquilla^F de montacargas^M

bottom side rail
larguero^M inferior

COUPLER HEAD
CABEZA^F DE ENGANCHE^M

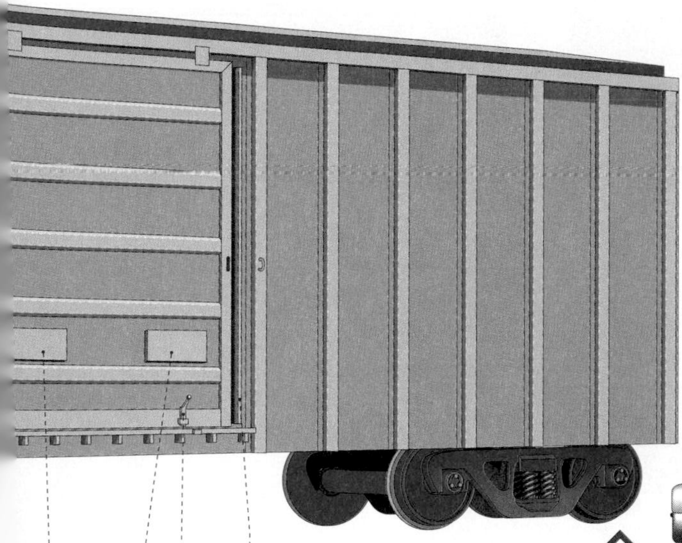

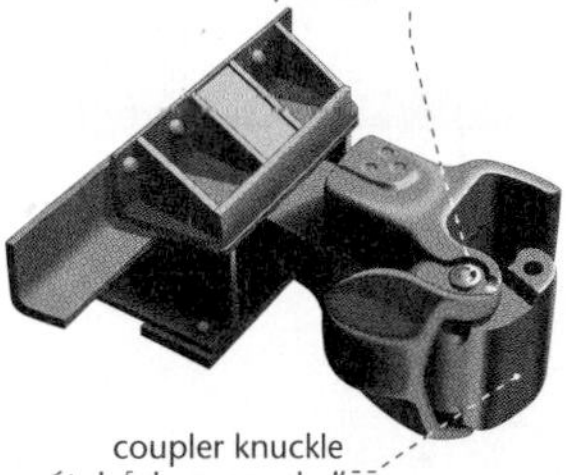

coupler knuckle pin
pivote^M de la rótula^F

coupler knuckle
rótula^F de enganche^M

HIGHWAY CROSSING
PASO^M A NIVEL^M

door stop
tope^M de la puerta^F

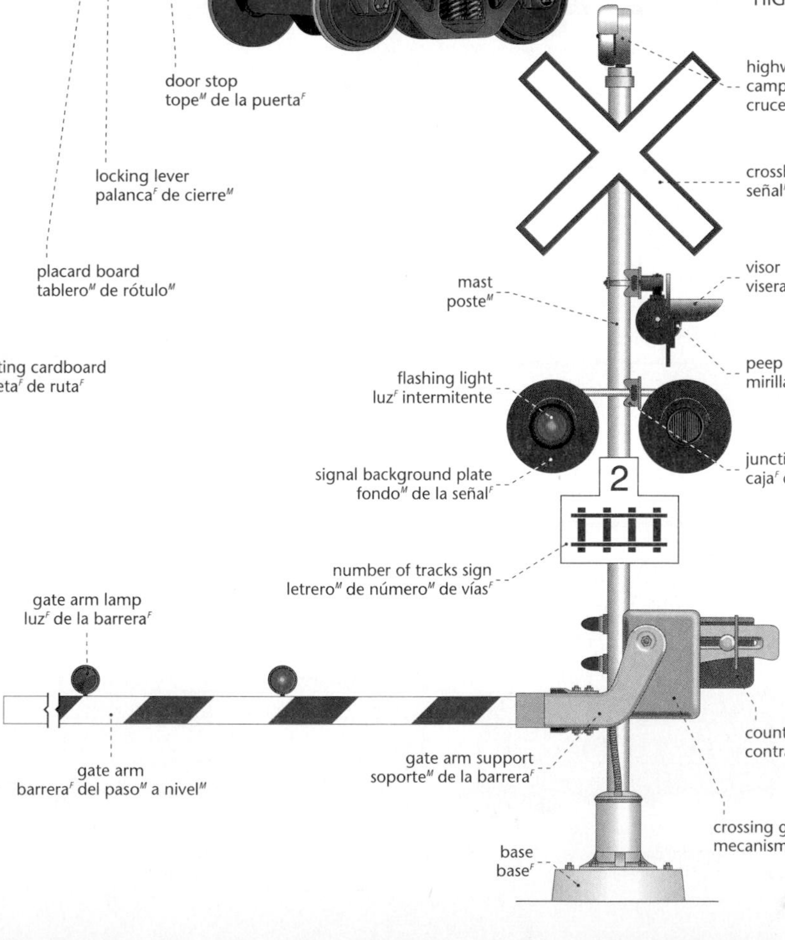

highway crossing bell
campana^F de aviso^M de
cruce^M

locking lever
palanca^F de cierre^M

crossbuck sign
señal^F de cruce^M

placard board
tablero^M de rótulo^M

visor
visera^F

mast
poste^M

routing cardboard
tarjeta^F de ruta^F

peep hole
mirilla^F

flashing light
luz^F intermitente

signal background plate
fondo^M de la señal^F

junction box
caja^F de empalmes^M

number of tracks sign
letrero^M de número^M de vías^F

gate arm lamp
luz^F de la barrera^F

gate arm
barrera^F del paso^M a nivel^M

gate arm support
soporte^M de la barrera^F

counterweight
contrapeso^M

crossing gate mechanism
mecanismo^M de la barrera^F

base
base^F

RAIL TRANSPORT
TRANSPORTE FERROVIARIO

box car
vagón^M cerrado

tank car
vagón^M cisterna^F

wood chip car
vagón^M para madera^F

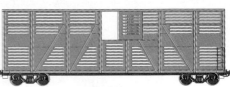

livestock car
vagón^M para ganado^M

hopper car
vagón^M tolva^F

hard top gondola
vagón^M con cubierta^F alquitranada

hopper ore car
vagón^M tolva^F para minerales^M

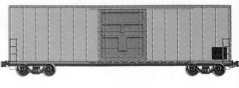

refrigerator car
vagón^M frigorífico

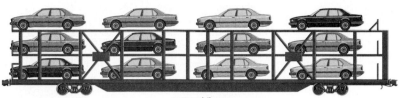

automobile car
vagón^M para automóviles^M

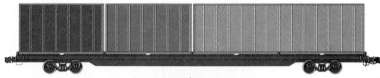

container car
vagón^M para contenedores^M

piggyback car
plataforma^F para transportar vagones^M

flat car
plataforma^F

bulkhead flat car
vagón^M plano con retenedores^M

gondola car
vagón^M de mercancías^F

depressed-center flat car
plataforma^F de piso^M bajo

caboose
furgón^M de cola^F

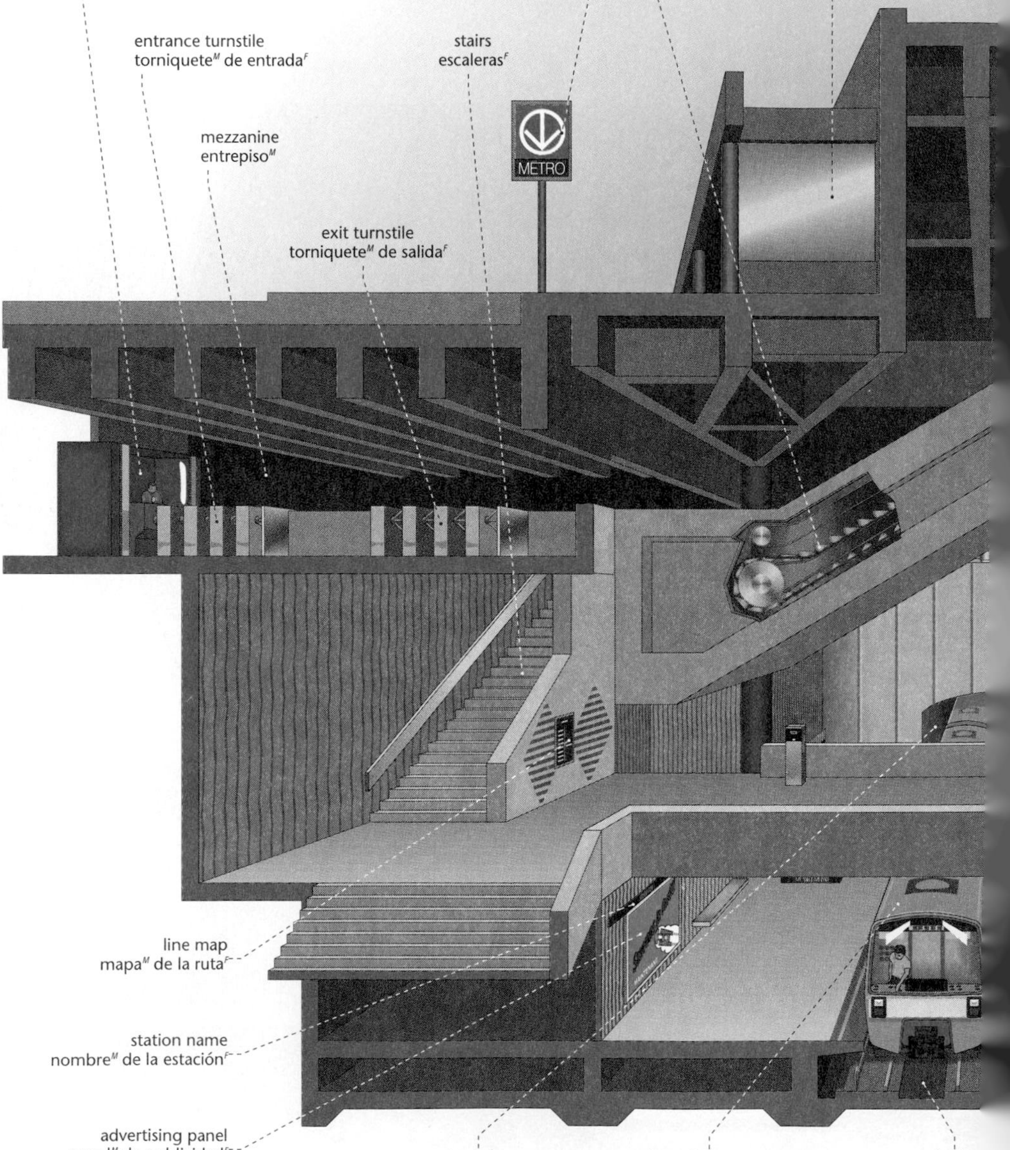

SUBWAY STATION
ESTACIÓN^F DE METRO^M

ticket collector's booth
cabina^F del colector^M de billetes^M

entrance turnstile
torniquete^M de entrada^F

mezzanine
entrepiso^M

exit turnstile
torniquete^M de salida^F

escalator
escalera^F eléctrica

exterior sign
señal^F exterior

station entrance
entrada^F de la estación^F

stairs
escaleras^F

METRO

line map
mapa^M de la ruta^F

station name
nombre^M de la estación^F

advertising panel
panel^M de publicidad^F

tunnel
túnel^M

subway train
tren^M subterráneo

track
vía^F

SUBWAY TRANSPORT
TRANSPORTE SUBTERRÁNEO

474

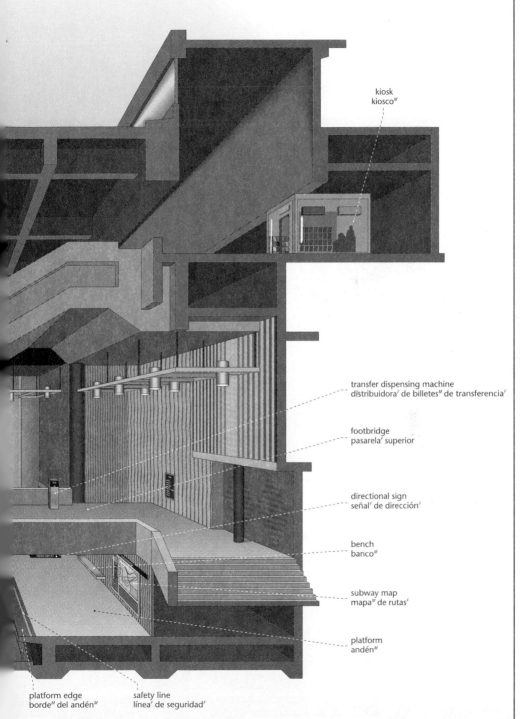

kiosk
kiosco[M]

transfer dispensing machine
distribuidora[F] de billetes[M] de transferencia[F]

footbridge
pasarela[F] superior

directional sign
señal[F] de dirección[F]

bench
banco[M]

subway map
mapa[M] de rutas[F]

platform
andén[M]

platform edge
borde[M] del andén[M]

safety line
línea[F] de seguridad[F]

TRUCK AND TRACK
CARRETILLA^F Y VÍA^F

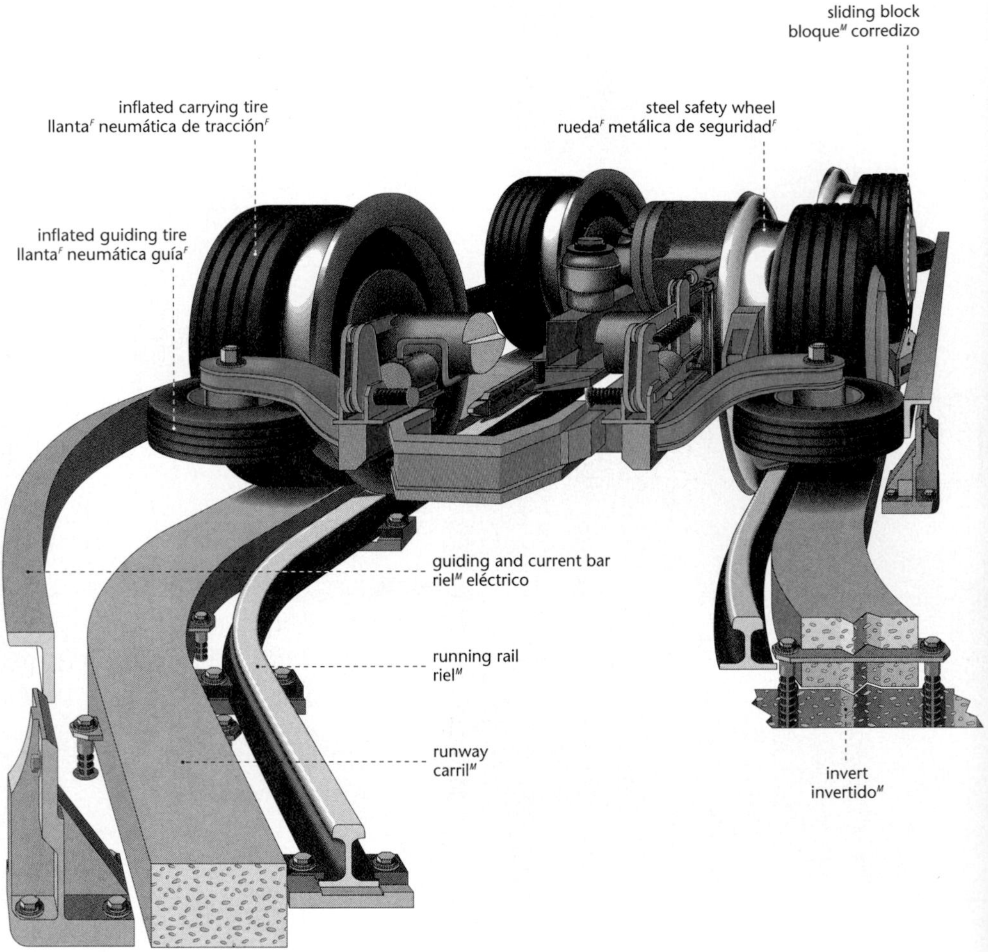

sliding block
bloque^M corredizo

inflated carrying tire
llanta^F neumática de tracción^F

steel safety wheel
rueda^F metálica de seguridad^F

inflated guiding tire
llanta^F neumática guía^F

guiding and current bar
riel^M eléctrico

running rail
riel^M

runway
carril^M

invert
invertido^M

SUBWAY TRAIN
TREN^M SUBTERRÁNEO

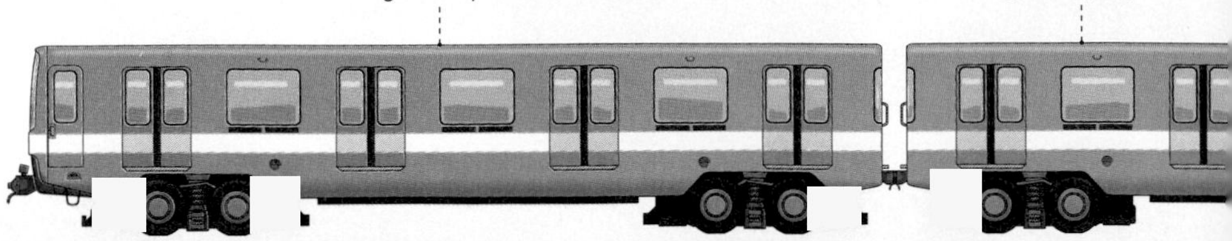

motor car
vagón^M máquina^F

passenger car
vagón^M de pasajeros^M

PASSENGER CAR
VAGÓN^M DE PASAJEROS^M

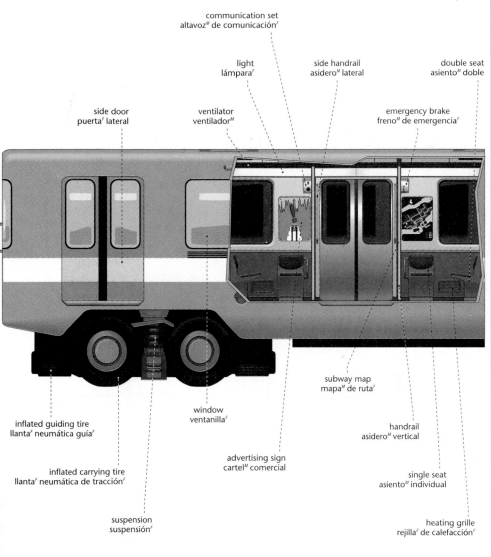

communication set
altavoz^M de comunicación^F

light
lámpara^F

side handrail
asidero^M lateral

double seat
asiento^M doble

side door
puerta^F lateral

ventilator
ventilador^M

emergency brake
freno^M de emergencia^F

inflated guiding tire
llanta^F neumática guía^F

window
ventanilla^F

subway map
mapa^M de ruta^F

handrail
asidero^M vertical

inflated carrying tire
llanta^F neumática de tracción^F

advertising sign
cartel^M comercial

single seat
asiento^M individual

suspension
suspensión^F

heating grille
rejilla^F de calefacción^F

motor car
vagón^M máquina^F

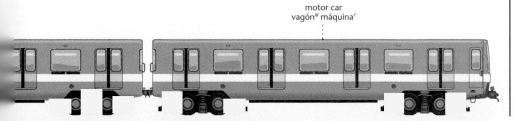

477

FOUR-MASTED BARK
BARCO^M DE VELA^F DE CUATRO PALOS^M

MASTING AND RIGGING
ARBOLADURA^F Y APAREJOS^M

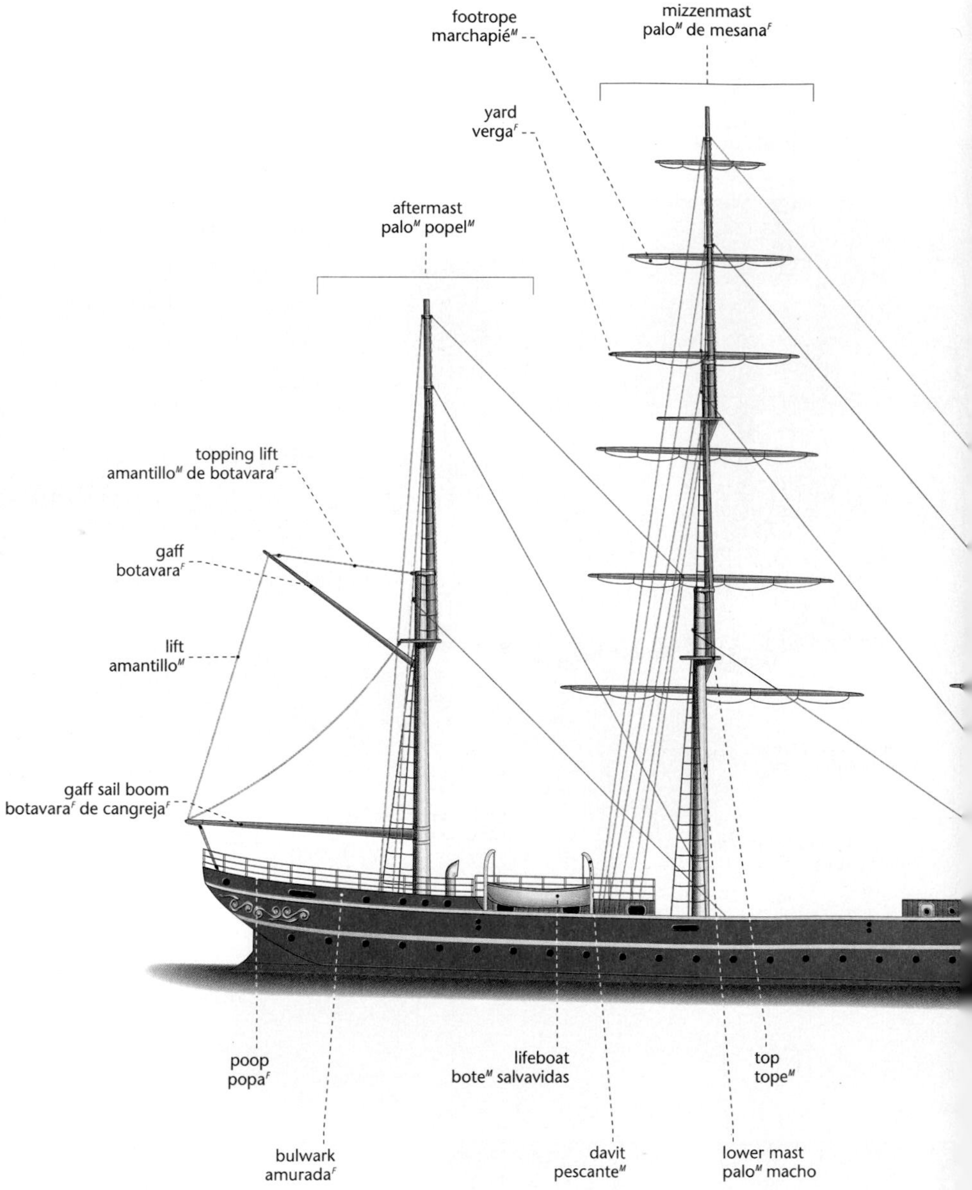

footrope
marchapié^M

mizzenmast
palo^M de mesana^F

yard
verga^F

aftermast
palo^M popel^M

topping lift
amantillo^M de botavara^F

gaff
botavara^F

lift
amantillo^M

gaff sail boom
botavara^F de cangreja^F

poop
popa^F

lifeboat
bote^M salvavidas

top
tope^M

bulwark
amurada^F

davit
pescante^M

lower mast
palo^M macho

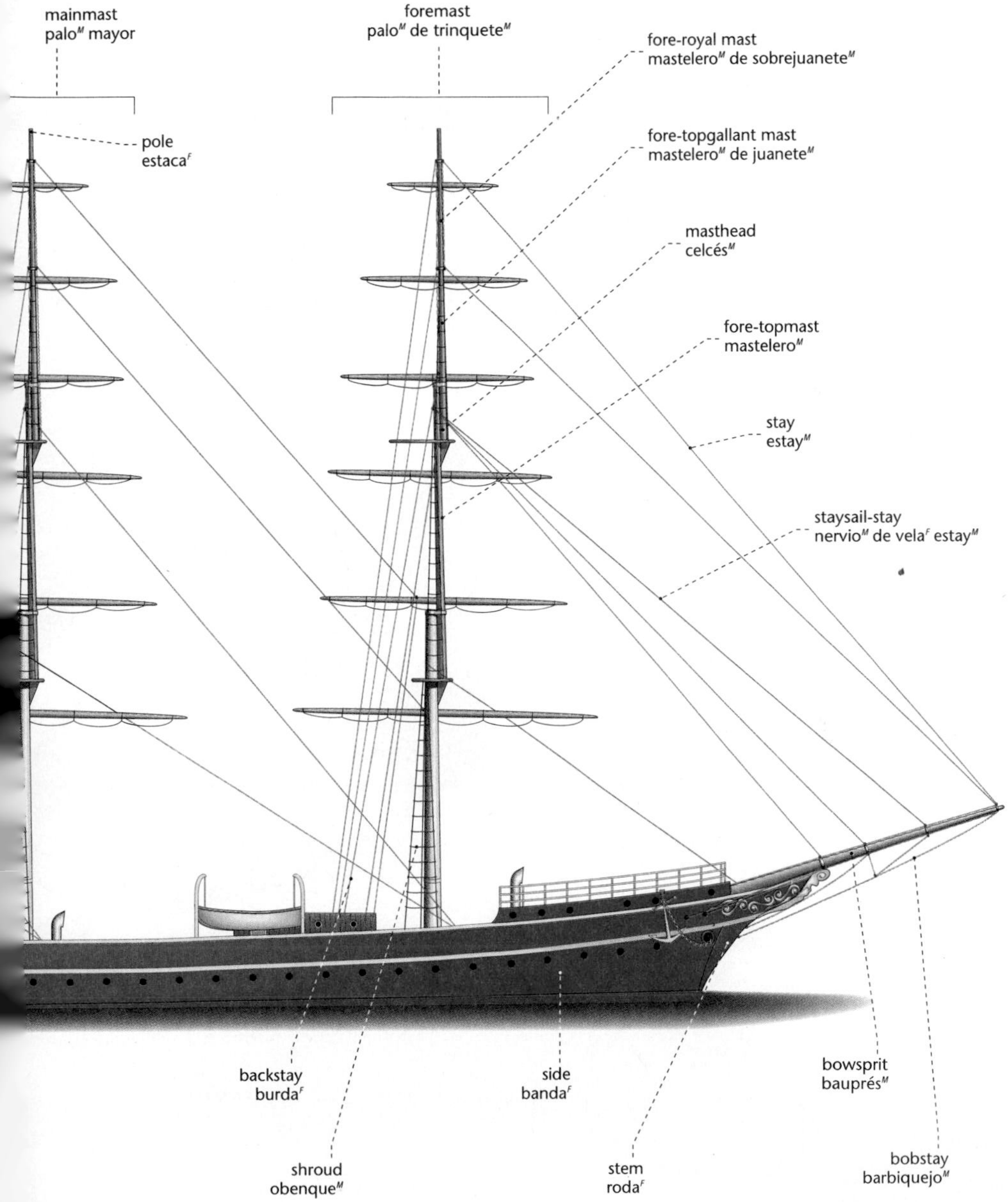

mainmast
palo^M mayor

foremast
palo^M de trinquete^M

fore-royal mast
mastelero^M de sobrejuanete^M

fore-topgallant mast
mastelero^M de juanete^M

pole
estaca^F

masthead
celcés^M

fore-topmast
mastelero^M

stay
estay^M

staysail-stay
nervio^M de vela^F estay^M

backstay
burda^F

side
banda^F

bowsprit
bauprés^M

shroud
obenque^M

stem
roda^F

bobstay
barbiquejo^M

FOUR-MASTED BARK
BARCO^M DE VELA^F DE CUATRO PALOS^M

SAILS
VELAMEN^M

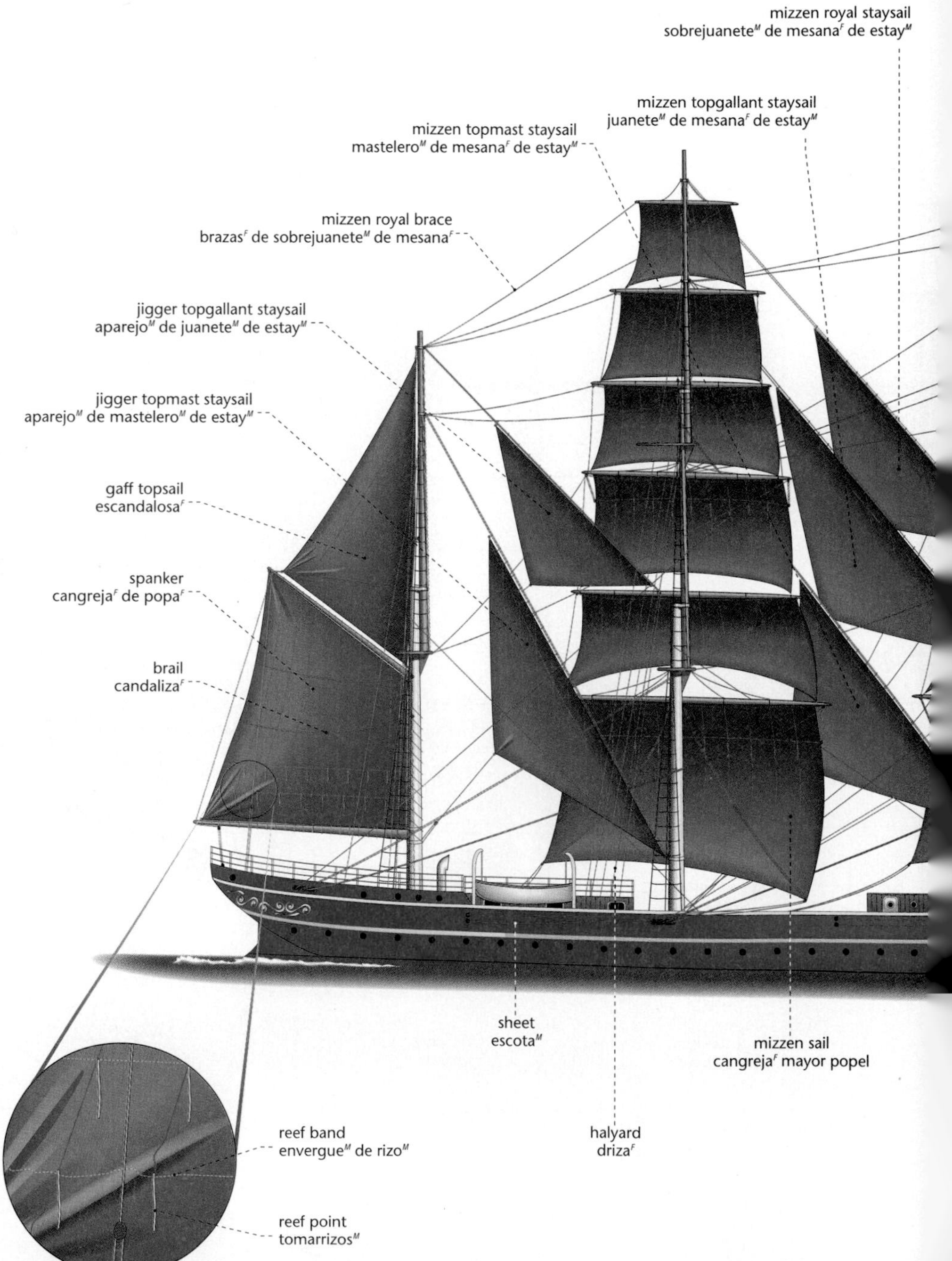

mizzen royal staysail
sobrejuanete^M de mesana^F de estay^M

mizzen topgallant staysail
juanete^M de mesana^F de estay^M

mizzen topmast staysail
mastelero^M de mesana^F de estay^M

mizzen royal brace
brazas^F de sobrejuanete^M de mesana^F

jigger topgallant staysail
aparejo^M de juanete^M de estay^M

jigger topmast staysail
aparejo^M de mastelero^M de estay^M

gaff topsail
escandalosa^F

spanker
cangreja^F de popa^F

brail
candaliza^F

sheet
escota^M

mizzen sail
cangreja^F mayor popel

reef band
envergue^M de rizo^M

halyard
driza^F

reef point
tomarrizos^M

480

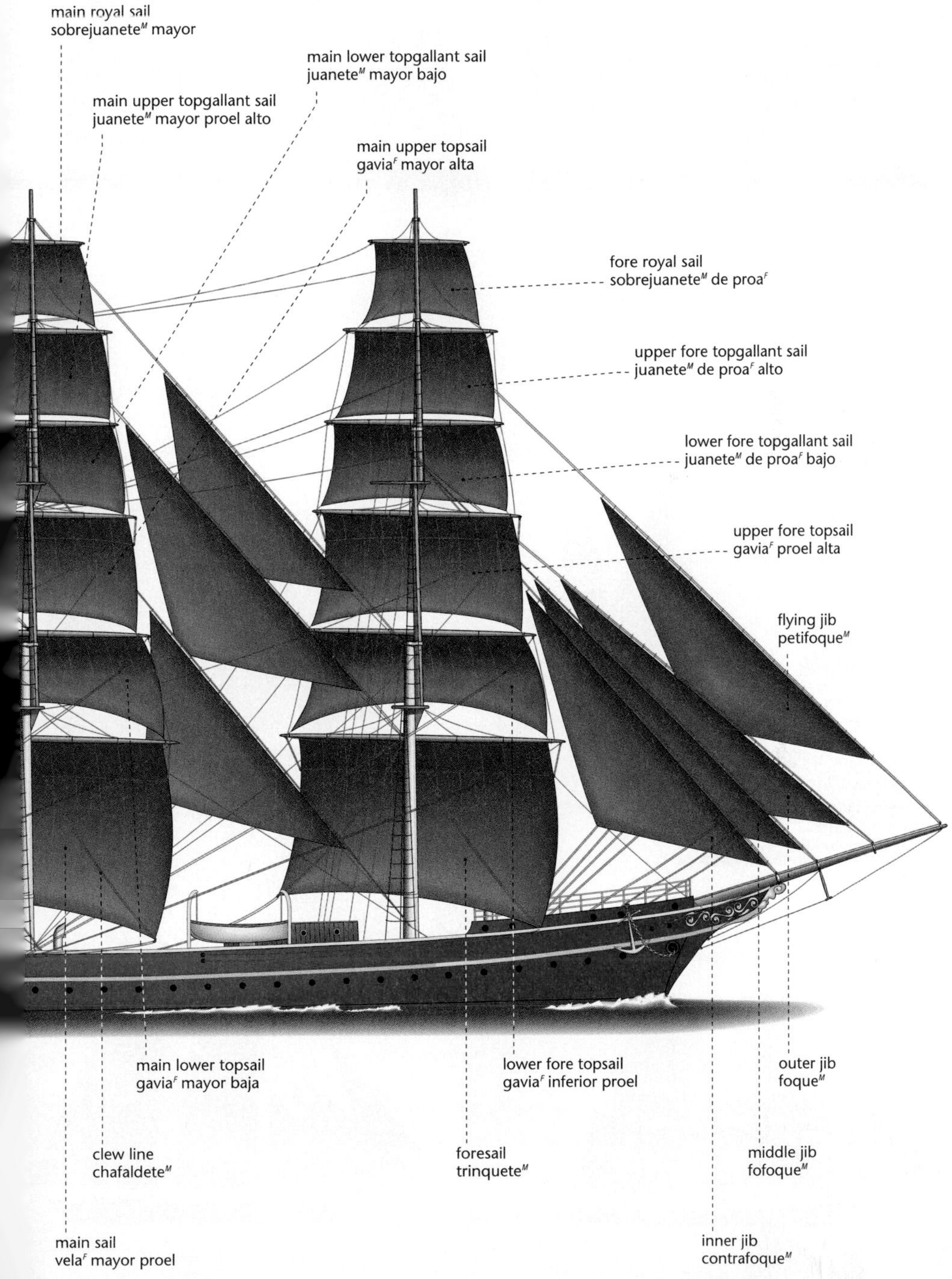

main royal sail
sobrejuanete^M mayor

main lower topgallant sail
juanete^M mayor bajo

main upper topgallant sail
juanete^M mayor proel alto

main upper topsail
gavia^F mayor alta

fore royal sail
sobrejuanete^M de proa^F

upper fore topgallant sail
juanete^M de proa^F alto

lower fore topgallant sail
juanete^M de proa^F bajo

upper fore topsail
gavia^F proel alta

flying jib
petifoque^M

main lower topsail
gavia^F mayor baja

lower fore topsail
gavia^F inferior proel

outer jib
foque^M

clew line
chafaldete^M

foresail
trinquete^M

middle jib
fofoque^M

main sail
vela^F mayor proel

inner jib
contrafoque^M

TYPES OF SAILS
TIPOS^M DE VELAS^F

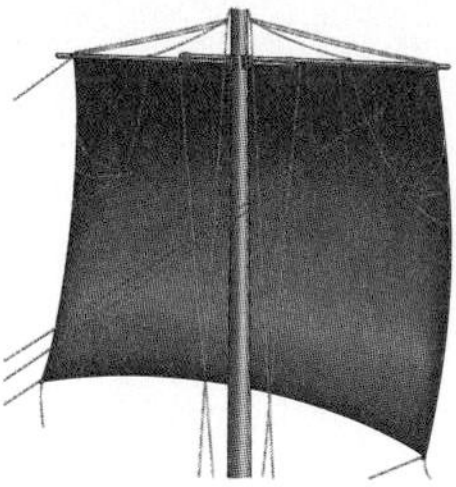

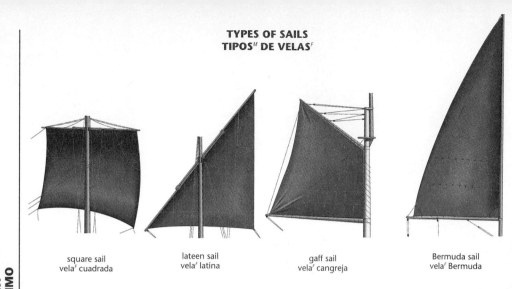

square sail
vela^F cuadrada

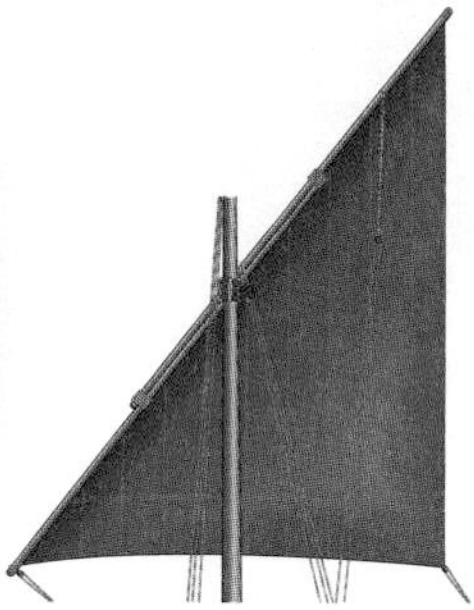

lateen sail
vela^F latina

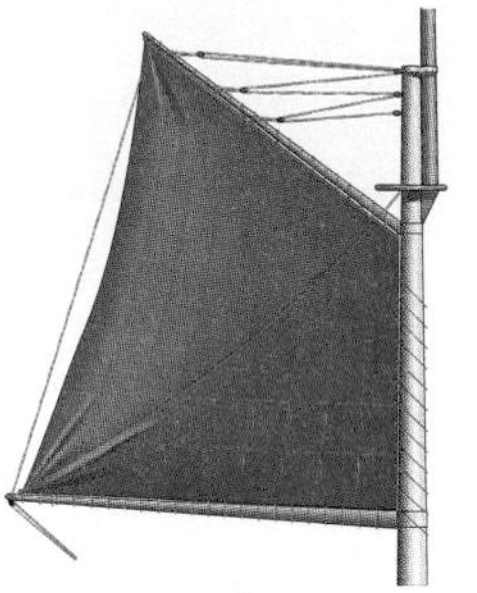

gaff sail
vela^F cangreja

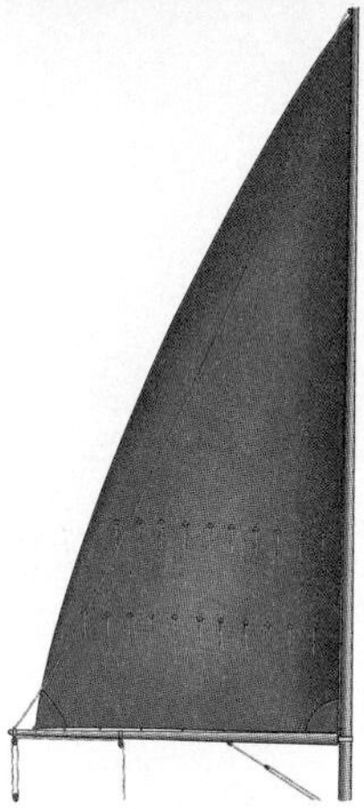

Bermuda sail
vela^F Bermuda

TYPES OF RIGS
TIPOS^M DE APAREJOS^M

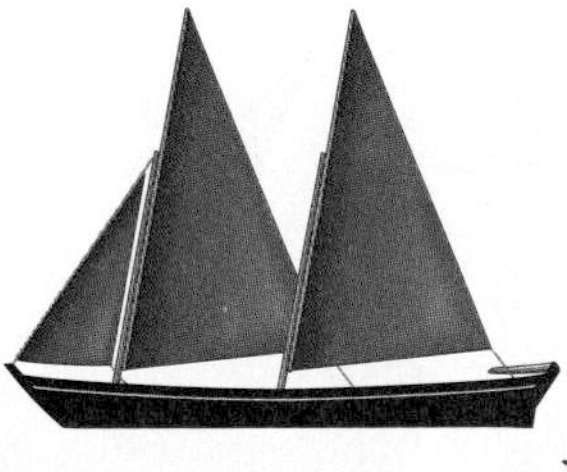

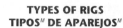

whale boat
ballenera^F

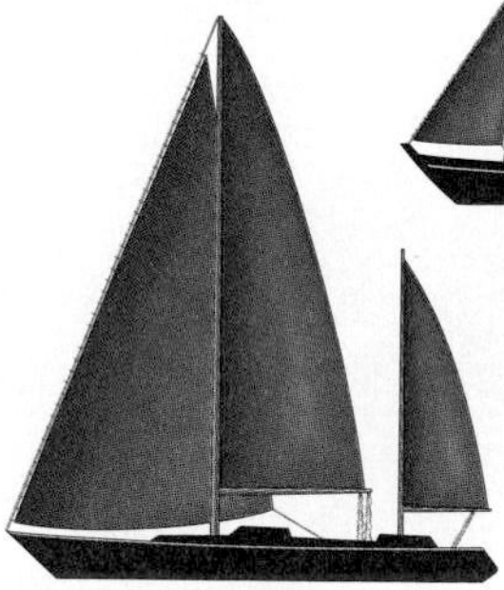

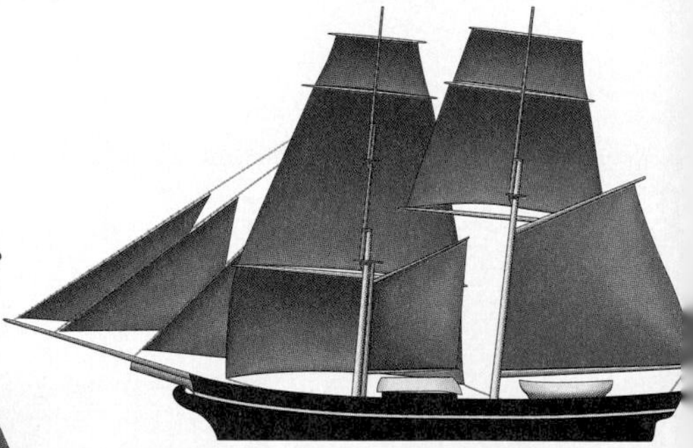

brigantine
bergantín^M goleta^F

ketch
queche^M

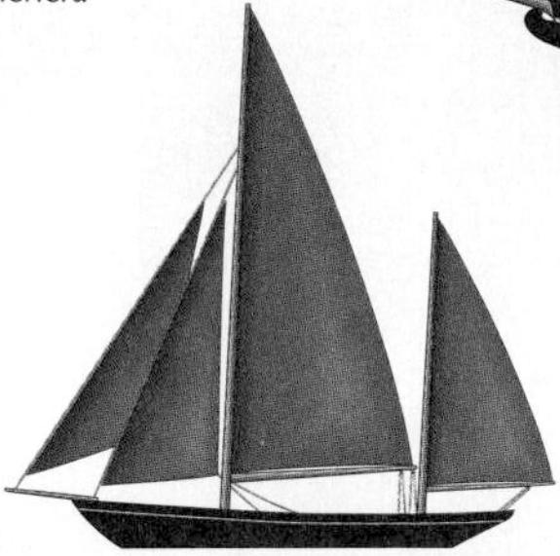

Marconi cutter
cúter^M Marconi

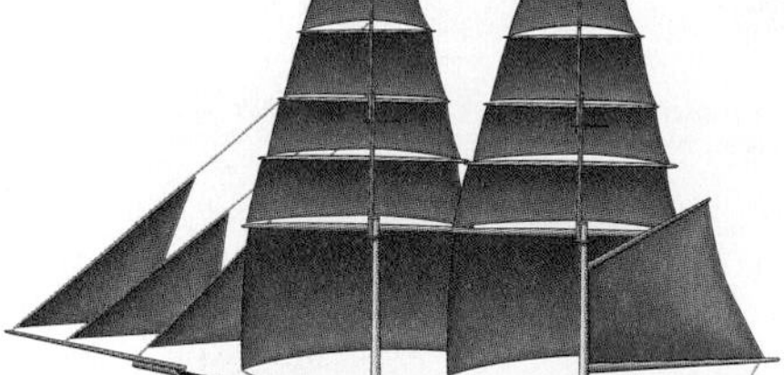

brig
bergantín^M

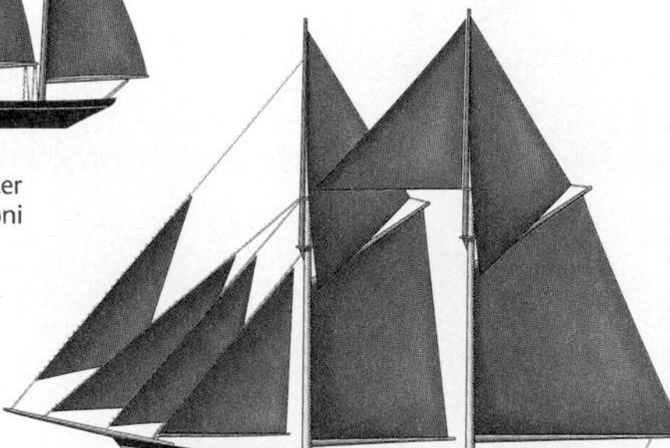

schooner
goleta^F

ANCHOR
ANCLA^F

SHIP'S ANCHOR
ANCLA^F DE BUQUE^M

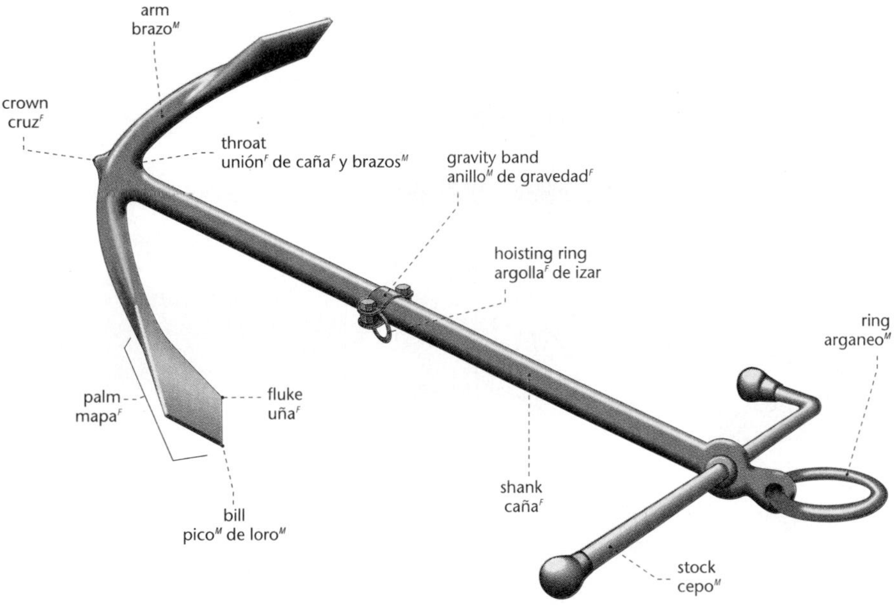

arm
brazo^M

crown
cruz^F

throat
unión^F de caña^F y brazos^M

gravity band
anillo^M de gravedad^F

hoisting ring
argolla^F de izar

ring
arganeo^M

palm
mapa^F

fluke
uña^F

shank
caña^F

bill
pico^M de loro^M

stock
cepo^M

TYPES OF ANCHORS
TIPOS^M DE ANCLAS^F

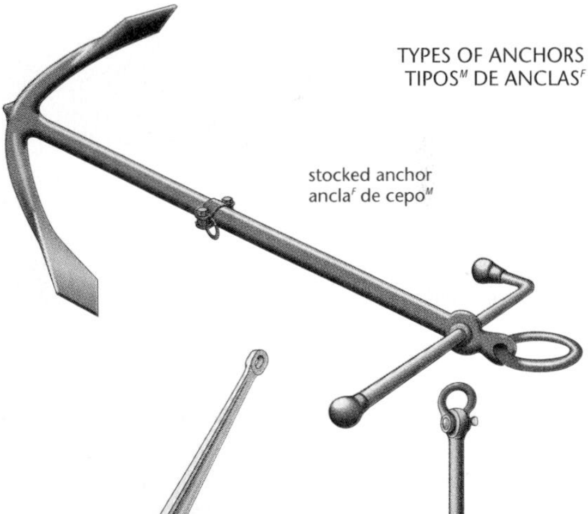

stocked anchor
ancla^F de cepo^M

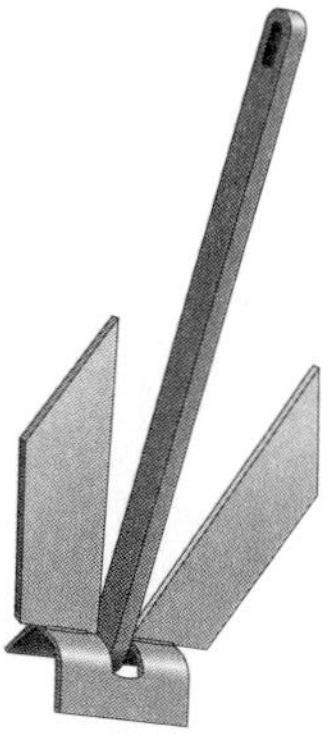

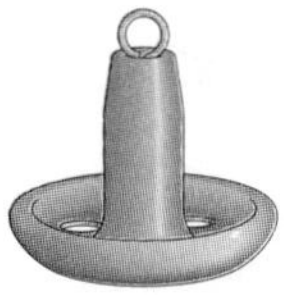

mushroom anchor
ancla^F de hongo^M

stockless anchor
ancla^F sin cepo^M

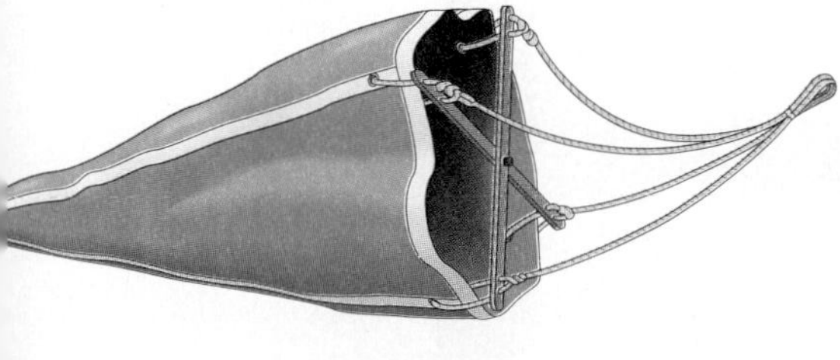

sea anchor
ancla^F flotante

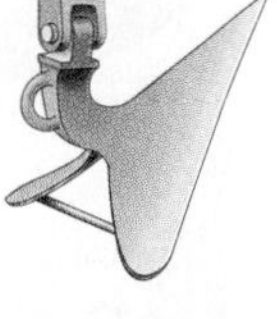

plow anchor
ancla^F de arado^M

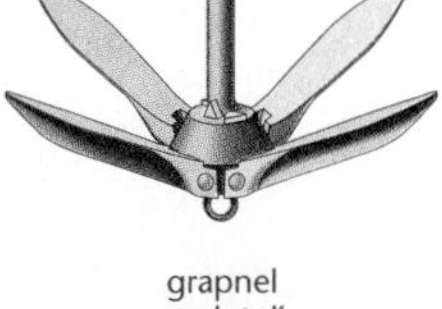

grapnel
anclote^M

SEXTANT
SEXTANTE^M

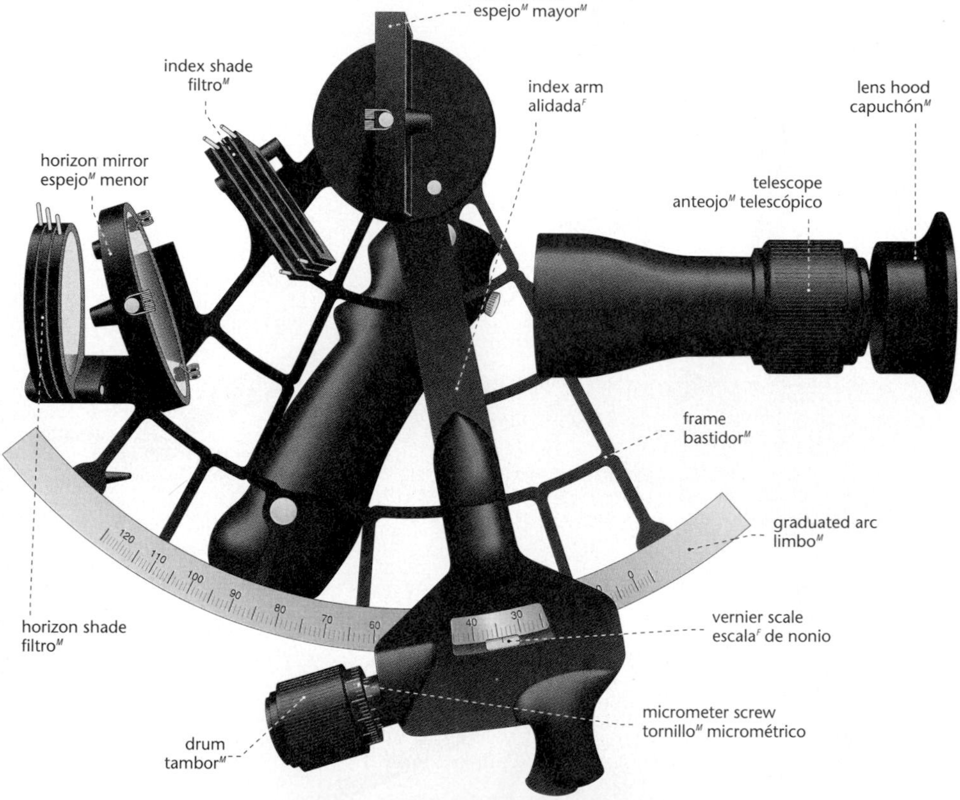

index mirror
espejo^M mayor^M

index shade
filtro^M

index arm
alidada^F

lens hood
capuchón^M

horizon mirror
espejo^M menor

telescope
anteojo^M telescópico

frame
bastidor^M

graduated arc
limbo^M

horizon shade
filtro^M

vernier scale
escala^F de nonio

drum
tambor^M

micrometer screw
tornillo^M micrométrico

LIQUID COMPASS
BRÚJULA^F LÍQUIDA

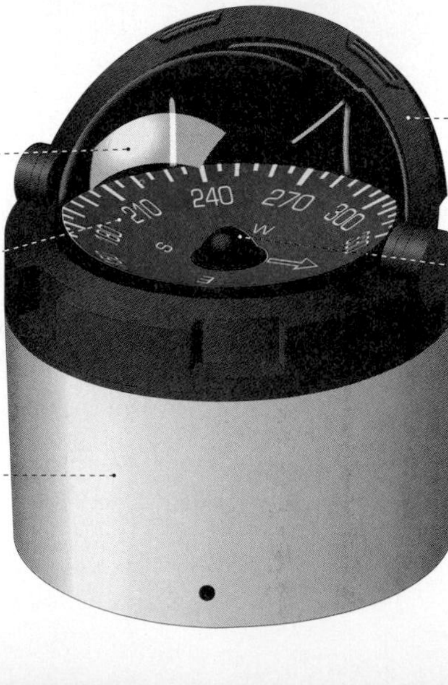

sliding cover
cubierta^F deslizable

glass dome
domo^M de vidrio^M

compass card
rosa^F de los vientos^M

pivot
pivote^M

bowl
mortero^M

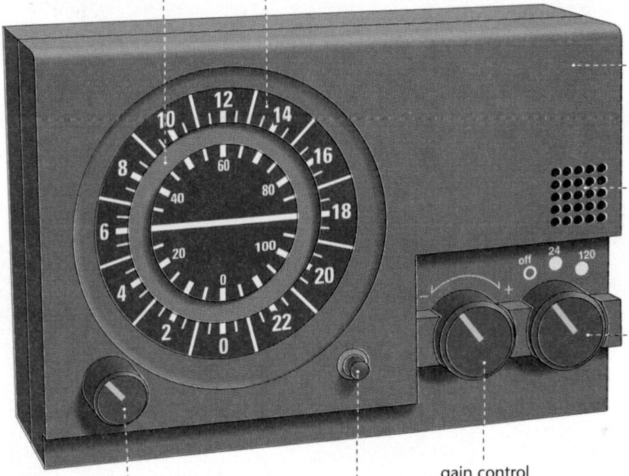

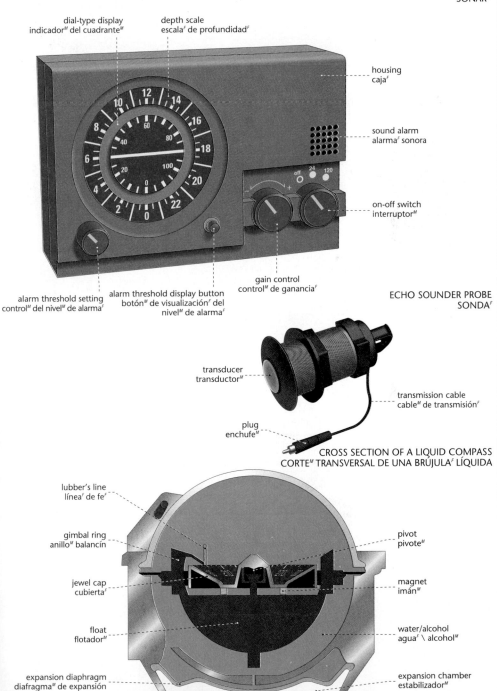

dial-type display
indicador^M del cuadrante^M

depth scale
escala^F de profundidad^F

housing
caja^F

sound alarm
alarma^F sonora

off   24   120

on-off switch
interruptor^M

gain control
control^M de ganancia^F

alarm threshold setting
control^M del nivel^M de alarma^F

alarm threshold display button
botón^M de visualización^F del
nivel^M de alarma^F

ECHO SOUNDER PROBE
SONDA^F

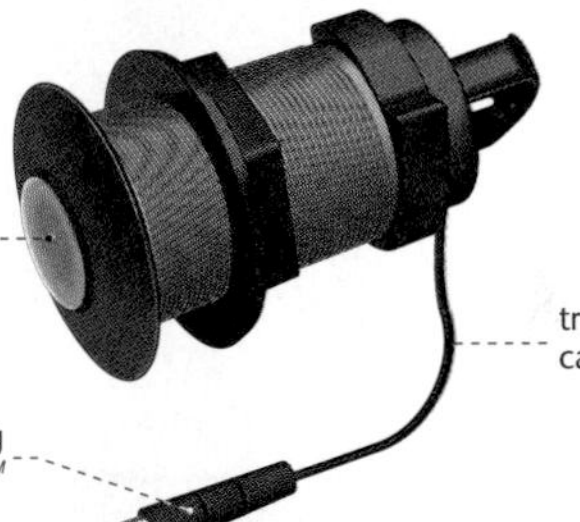

transducer
transductor^M

transmission cable
cable^M de transmisión^F

plug
enchufe^M

CROSS SECTION OF A LIQUID COMPASS
CORTE^M TRANSVERSAL DE UNA BRÚJULA^F LÍQUIDA

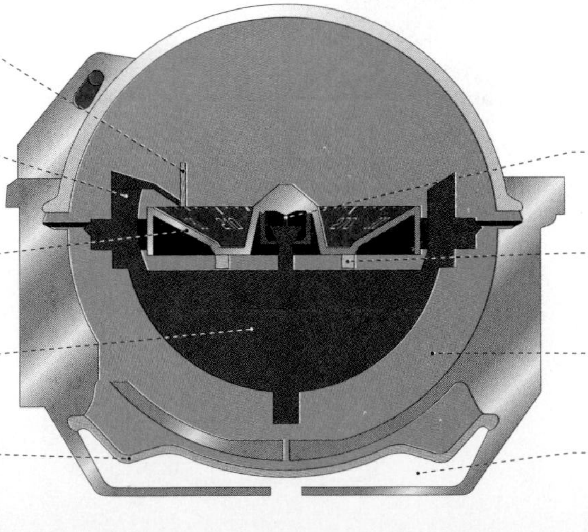

lubber's line
línea^F de fe^F

gimbal ring
anillo^M balancín

jewel cap
cubierta^F

float
flotador^M

expansion diaphragm
diafragma^M de expansión

pivot
pivote^M

magnet
imán^M

water/alcohol
agua^F \ alcohol^M

expansion chamber
estabilizador^M

485

LIGHTHOUSE LANTERN
LINTERNA^F DEL FARO^M

LIGHTHOUSE
FARO^M MARÍTIMO

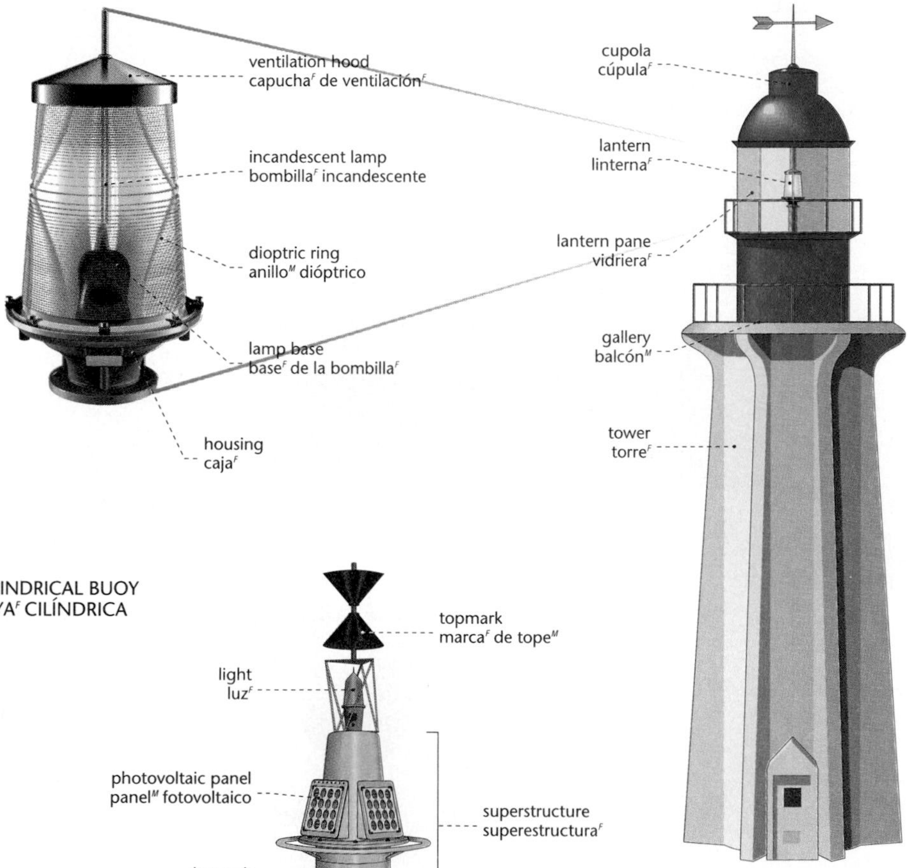

ventilation hood
capucha^F de ventilación^F

incandescent lamp
bombilla^F incandescente

dioptric ring
anillo^M dióptrico

lamp base
base^F de la bombilla^F

housing
caja^F

cupola
cúpula^F

lantern
linterna^F

lantern pane
vidriera^F

gallery
balcón^M

tower
torre^F

CYLINDRICAL BUOY
BOYA^F CILÍNDRICA

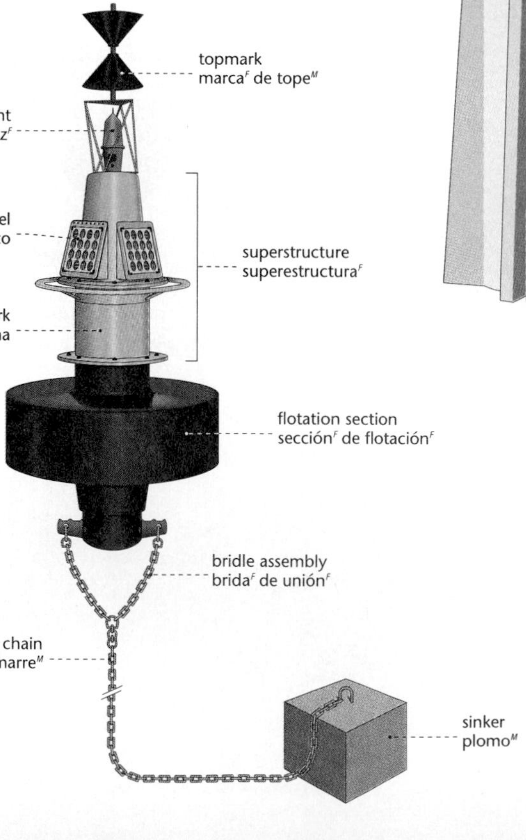

topmark
marca^F de tope^M

light
luz^F

photovoltaic panel
panel^M fotovoltaico

superstructure
superestructura^F

daymark
señal^F diurna

flotation section
sección^F de flotación^F

bridle assembly
brida^F de unión^F

mooring chain
cadena^F de amarre^M

sinker
plomo^M

light
luz^F

HIGH FOCAL PLANE BUOY
BOYA^F DE PLANO^M FOCAL ELEVADO

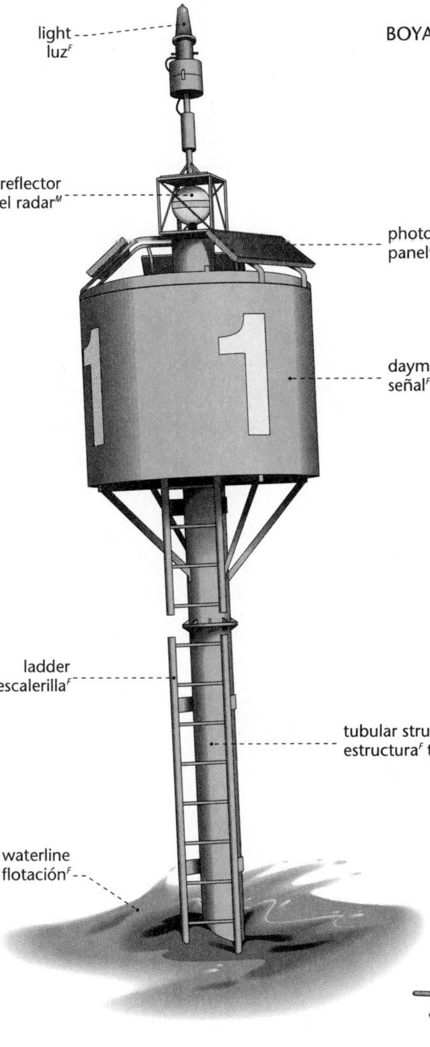

radar reflector
reflector^M del radar^M

photovoltaic panel
panel^M fotovoltaico

daymark
señal^F diurna

ladder
escalerilla^F

tubular structure
estructura^F tubular

waterline
línea^F de flotación^F

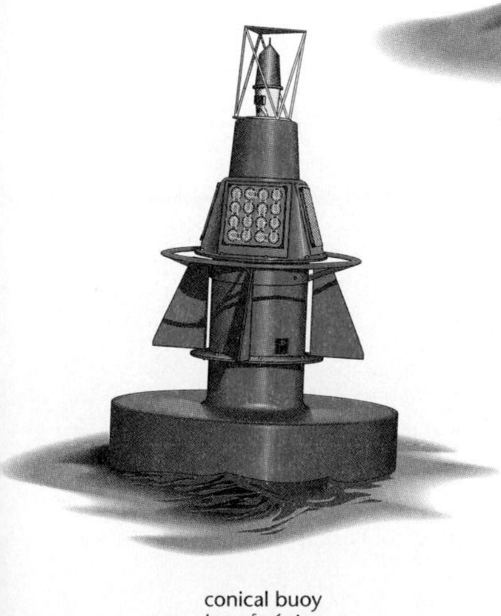

conical buoy
boya^F cónica

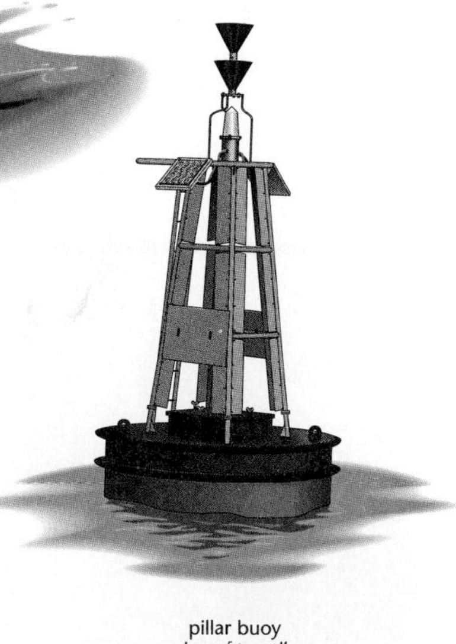

pillar buoy
boya^F torre^M

MARITIME BUOYAGE SYSTEM
SISTEMA^M DE BOYAS^F MARITIMAS

CARDINAL MARKS
SEÑALES^F DE LOS PUNTOS^M CARDINALES

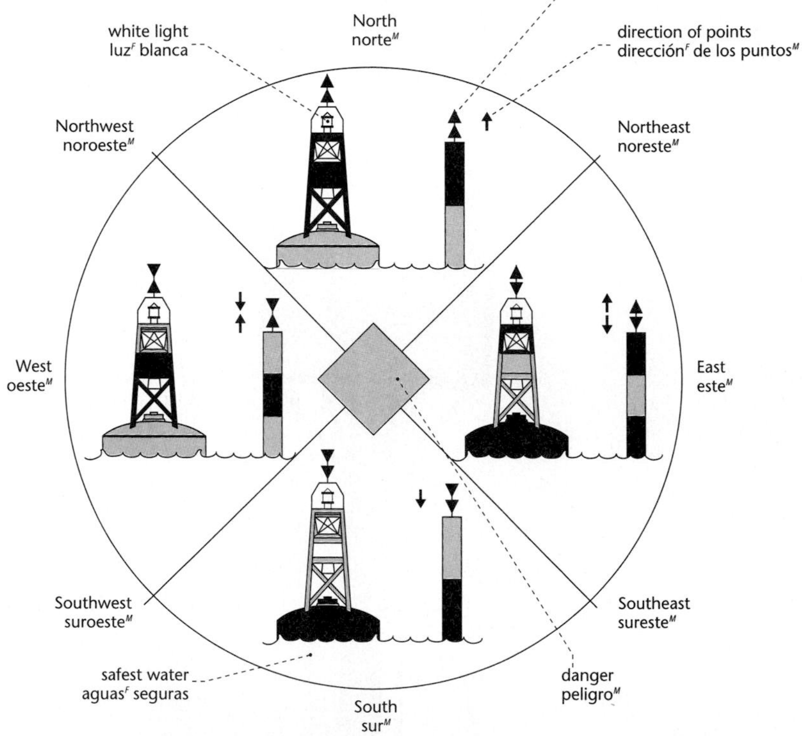

topmark
marca^F de tope^M

white light
luz^F blanca

North
norte^M

direction of points
dirección^F de los puntos^M

Northwest
noroeste^M

Northeast
noreste^M

West
oeste^M

East
este^M

Southwest
suroeste^M

Southeast
sureste^M

safest water
aguas^F seguras

danger
peligro^M

South
sur^M

BUOYAGE REGIONS
REGIONES^F DE BOYAS^F

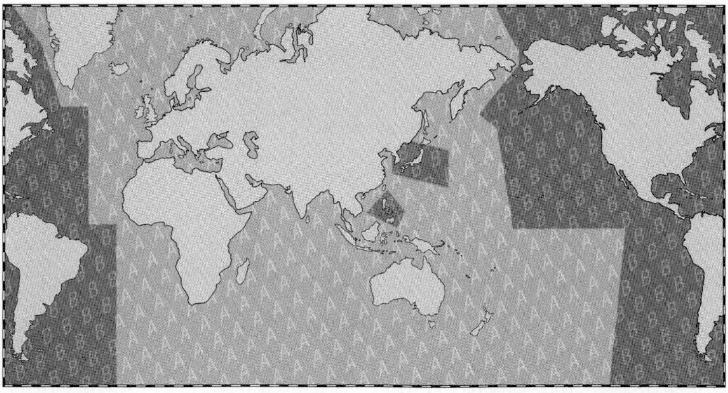

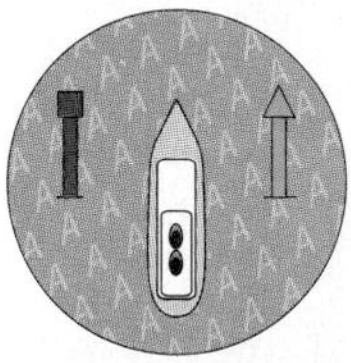

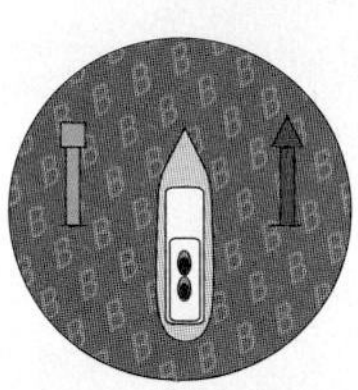

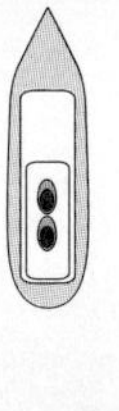

port hand
babor^M

starboard hand
estribor^M

RHYTHM OF MARKS BY NIGHT
RITMO^M DE LAS SEÑALES^F NOCTURNAS

RHYTHM OF MARKS BY NIGHT
RITMO^M DE LAS SEÑALES^F NOCTURNAS

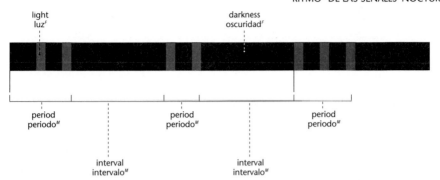

light
luz^F

darkness
oscuridad^F

period
periodo^M

period
periodo^M

period
periodo^M

interval
intervalo^M

interval
intervalo^M

DAYMARKS (REGION B)
SEÑALES^F DIURNAS (REGIÓN^F B)

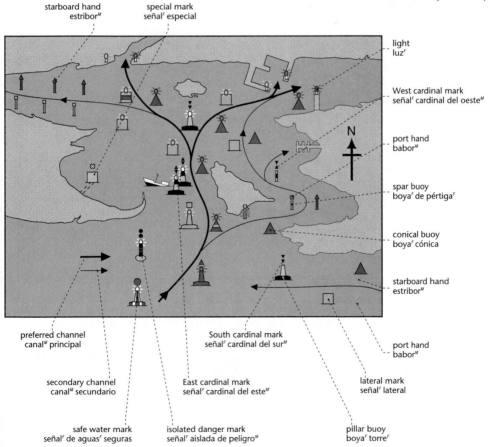

starboard hand
estribor^M

special mark
señal^F especial

light
luz^F

West cardinal mark
señal^F cardinal del oeste^M

port hand
babor^M

spar buoy
boya^F de pértiga^F

conical buoy
boya^F cónica

starboard hand
estribor^M

port hand
babor^M

preferred channel
canal^M principal

South cardinal mark
señal^F cardinal del sur^M

lateral mark
señal^F lateral

secondary channel
canal^M secundario

East cardinal mark
señal^F cardinal del este^M

safe water mark
señal^F de aguas^F seguras

isolated danger mark
señal^F aislada de peligro^M

pillar buoy
boya^F torre^F

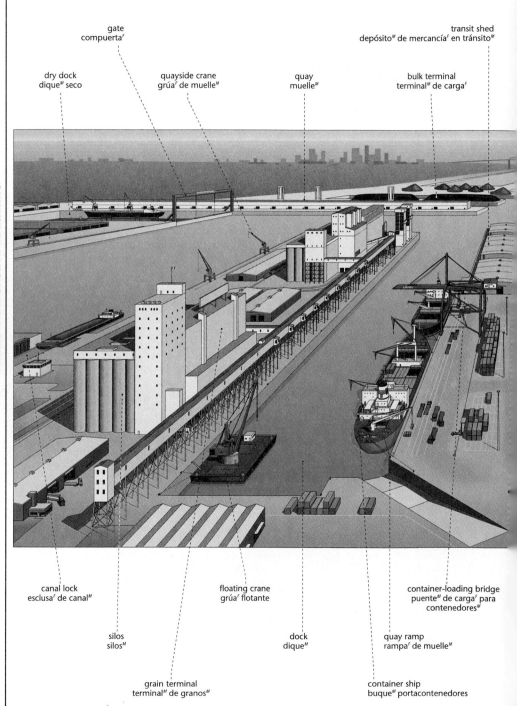

gate
compuerta^F

transit shed
depósito^M de mercancía^F en tránsito^M

dry dock
dique^M seco

quayside crane
grúa^F de muelle^M

quay
muelle^M

bulk terminal
terminal^F de carga^F

canal lock
esclusa^F de canal^M

floating crane
grúa^F flotante

container-loading bridge
puente^M de carga^F para
contenedores^M

silos
silos^M

dock
dique^M

quay ramp
rampa^F de muelle^M

grain terminal
terminal^M de granos^M

container ship
buque^M portacontenedores

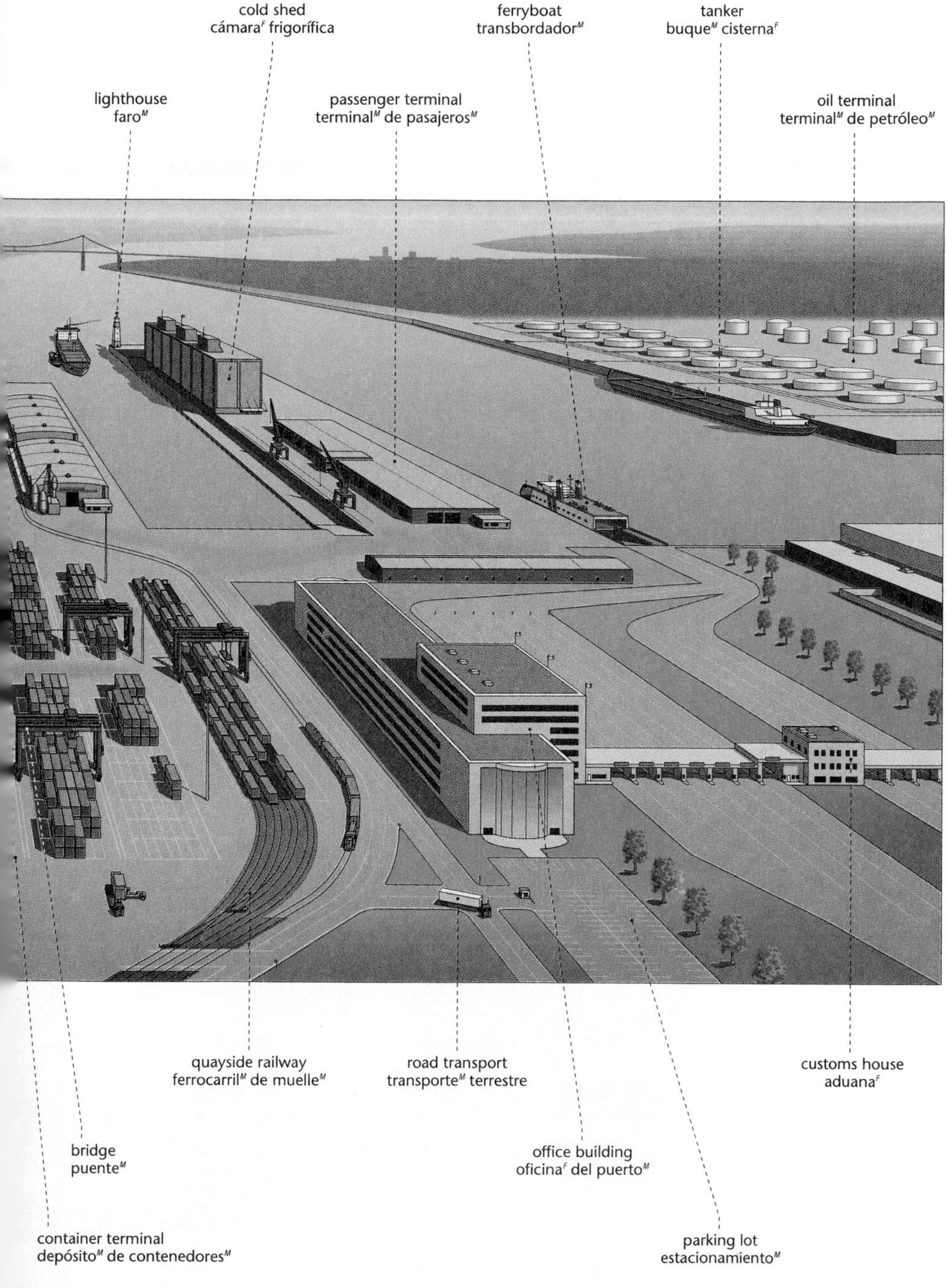

cold shed
cámara^F frigorífica

ferryboat
transbordador^M

tanker
buque^M cisterna^F

lighthouse
faro^M

passenger terminal
terminal^M de pasajeros^M

oil terminal
terminal^M de petróleo^M

quayside railway
ferrocarril^M de muelle^M

road transport
transporte^M terrestre

customs house
aduana^F

bridge
puente^M

office building
oficina^F del puerto^M

container terminal
depósito^M de contenedores^M

parking lot
estacionamiento^M

CANAL LOCK
ESCLUSA^F DE CANAL^M

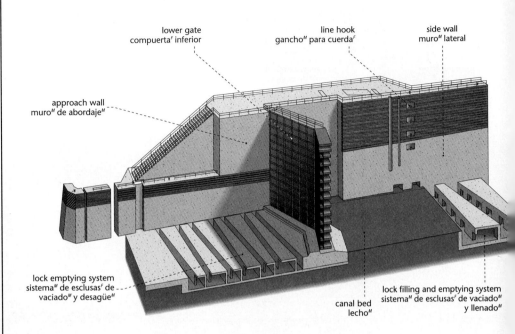

lower gate
compuerta^F inferior

line hook
gancho^M para cuerda^F

side wall
muro^M lateral

approach wall
muro^M de abordaje^M

lock emptying system
sistema^M de esclusas^F de
vaciado^M y desagüe^M

canal bed
lecho^M

lock filling and emptying system
sistema^M de esclusas^F de vaciado^M
y llenado^M

HOVERCRAFT
AERODESLIZADOR^M (HOVERCRAFT^M)

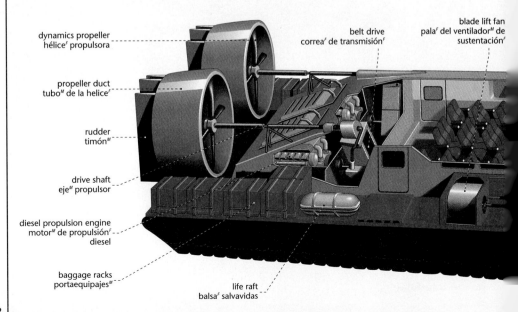

dynamics propeller
hélice^F propulsora

belt drive
correa^F de transmisión^F

blade lift fan
pala^F del ventilador^M de
sustentación^F

propeller duct
tubo^M de la helice^F

rudder
timón^M

drive shaft
eje^M propulsor

diesel propulsion engine
motor^M de propulsión^F
diesel

baggage racks
portaequipajes^M

life raft
balsa^F salvavidas

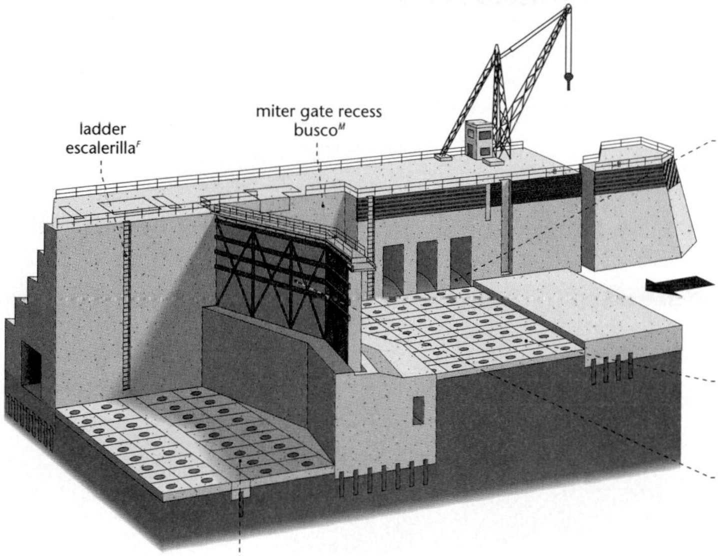

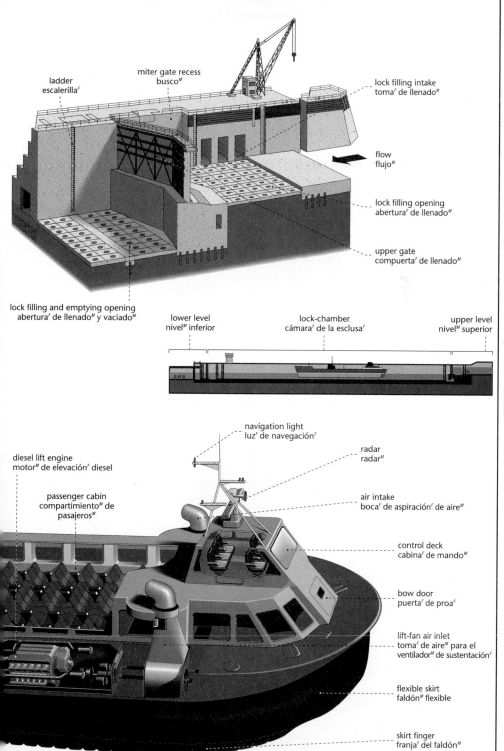

ladder
escalerilla^F

miter gate recess
busco^M

lock filling intake
toma^F de llenado^M

flow
flujo^M

lock filling opening
abertura^F de llenado^M

upper gate
compuerta^F de llenado^M

lock filling and emptying opening
abertura^F de llenado^M y vaciado^M

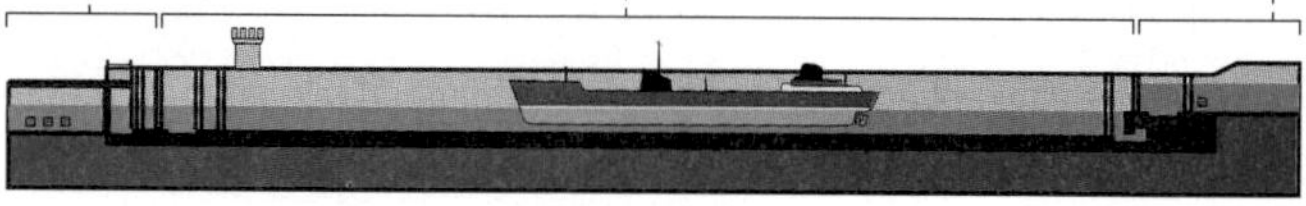

lower level
nivel^M inferior

lock-chamber
cámara^F de la esclusa^F

upper level
nivel^M superior

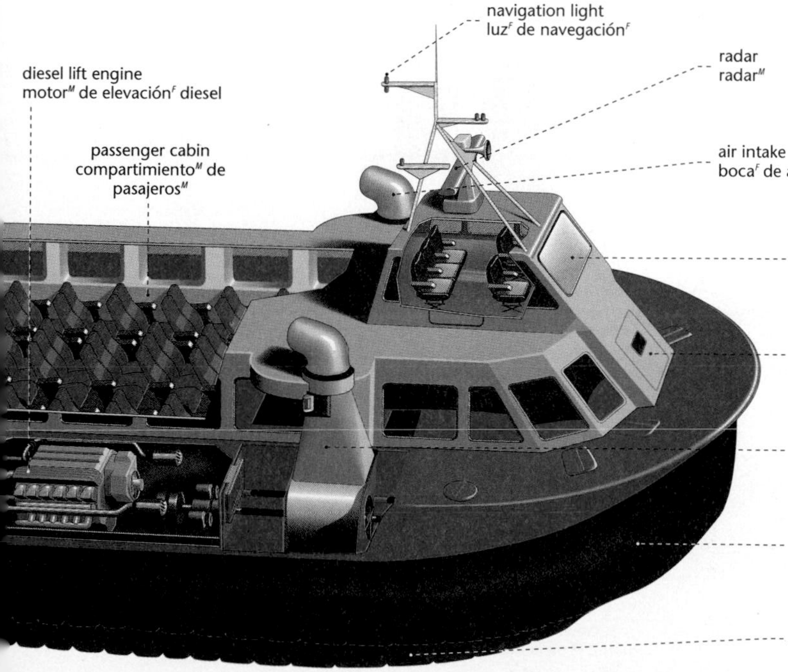

navigation light
luz^F de navegación^F

radar
radar^M

diesel lift engine
motor^M de elevación^F diesel

passenger cabin
compartimiento^M de
pasajeros^M

air intake
boca^F de aspiración^F de aire^M

control deck
cabina^F de mando^M

bow door
puerta^F de proa^F

lift-fan air inlet
toma^F de aire^M para el
ventilador^M de sustentación^F

flexible skirt
faldón^M flexible

skirt finger
franja^F del faldón^M

FERRY
TRANSBORDADOR^M

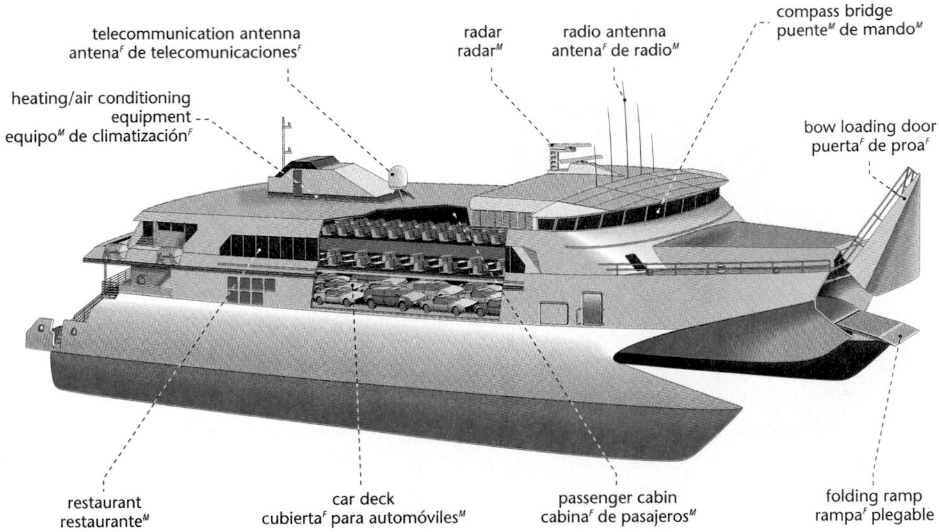

telecommunication antenna
antena^f de telecomunicaciones^f

heating/air conditioning
equipment
equipo^M de climatización^f

radar
radar^M

radio antenna
antena^f de radio^M

compass bridge
puente^M de mando^M

bow loading door
puerta^f de proa^f

restaurant
restaurante^M

car deck
cubierta^f para automóviles^M

passenger cabin
cabina^f de pasajeros^M

folding ramp
rampa^f plegable

CONTAINER SHIP
CARGUERO^M PORTACONTENEDORES

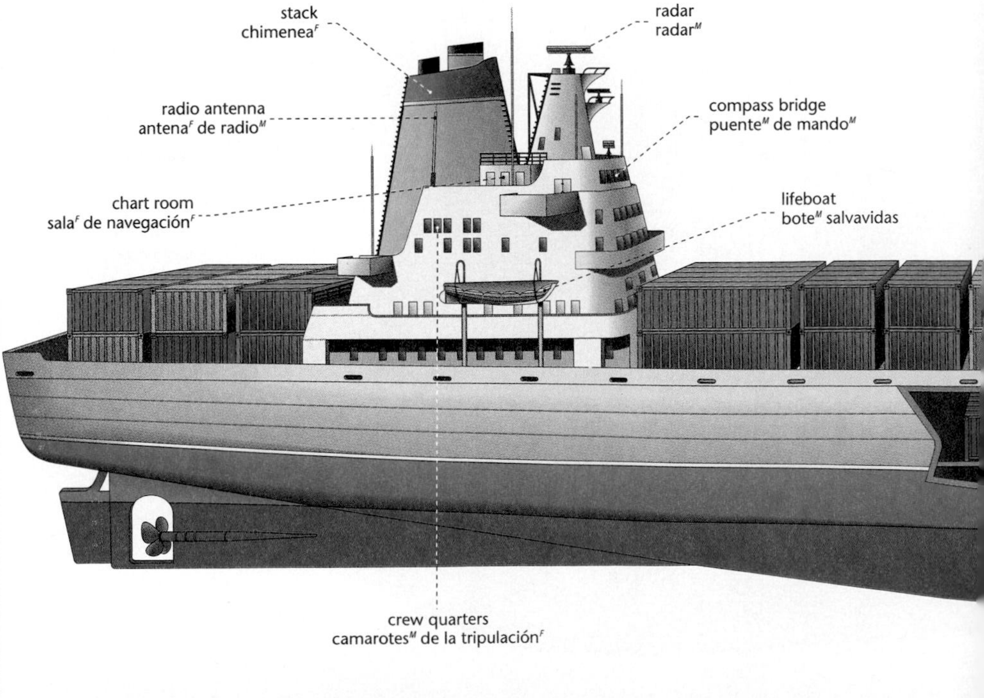

stack
chimenea^f

radio antenna
antena^f de radio^M

chart room
sala^f de navegación^f

radar
radar^M

compass bridge
puente^M de mando^M

lifeboat
bote^M salvavidas

crew quarters
camarotes^M de la tripulación^f

HYDROFOIL BOAT
AERODESLIZADOR^M

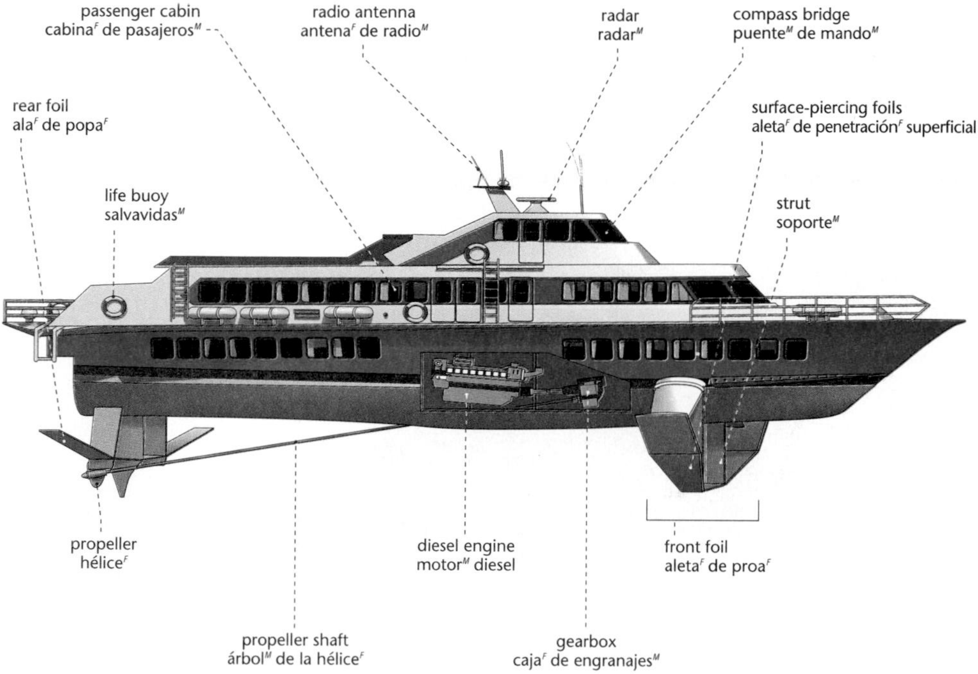

passenger cabin
cabina^F de pasajeros^M

radio antenna
antena^F de radio^M

radar
radar^M

compass bridge
puente^M de mando^M

rear foil
ala^F de popa^F

surface-piercing foils
aleta^F de penetración^F superficial

life buoy
salvavidas^M

strut
soporte^M

propeller
hélice^F

diesel engine
motor^M diesel

front foil
aleta^F de proa^F

propeller shaft
árbol^M de la hélice^F

gearbox
caja^F de engranajes^M

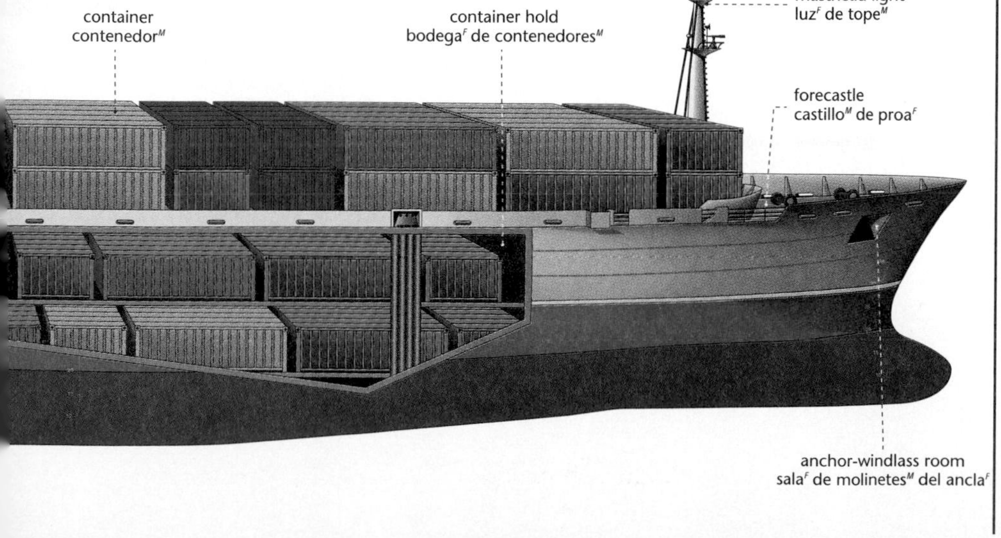

container
contenedor^M

container hold
bodega^F de contenedores^M

masthead light
luz^F de tope^M

forecastle
castillo^M de proa^F

anchor-windlass room
sala^F de molinetes^M del ancla^F

PASSENGER LINER
BUQUE^M TRASATLÁNTICO

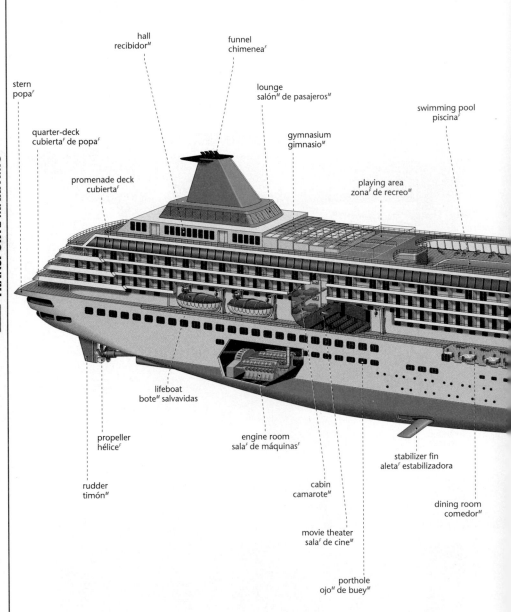

hall
recibidor^M

funnel
chimenea^F

stern
popa^F

lounge
salón^M de pasajeros^M

swimming pool
piscina^F

quarter-deck
cubierta^F de popa^F

gymnasium
gimnasio^M

promenade deck
cubierta^F

playing area
zona^F de recreo^M

lifeboat
bote^M salvavidas

propeller
hélice^F

engine room
sala^F de máquinas^F

stabilizer fin
aleta^F estabilizadora

rudder
timón^M

cabin
camarote^M

dining room
comedor^M

movie theater
sala^F de cine^M

porthole
ojo^M de buey^M

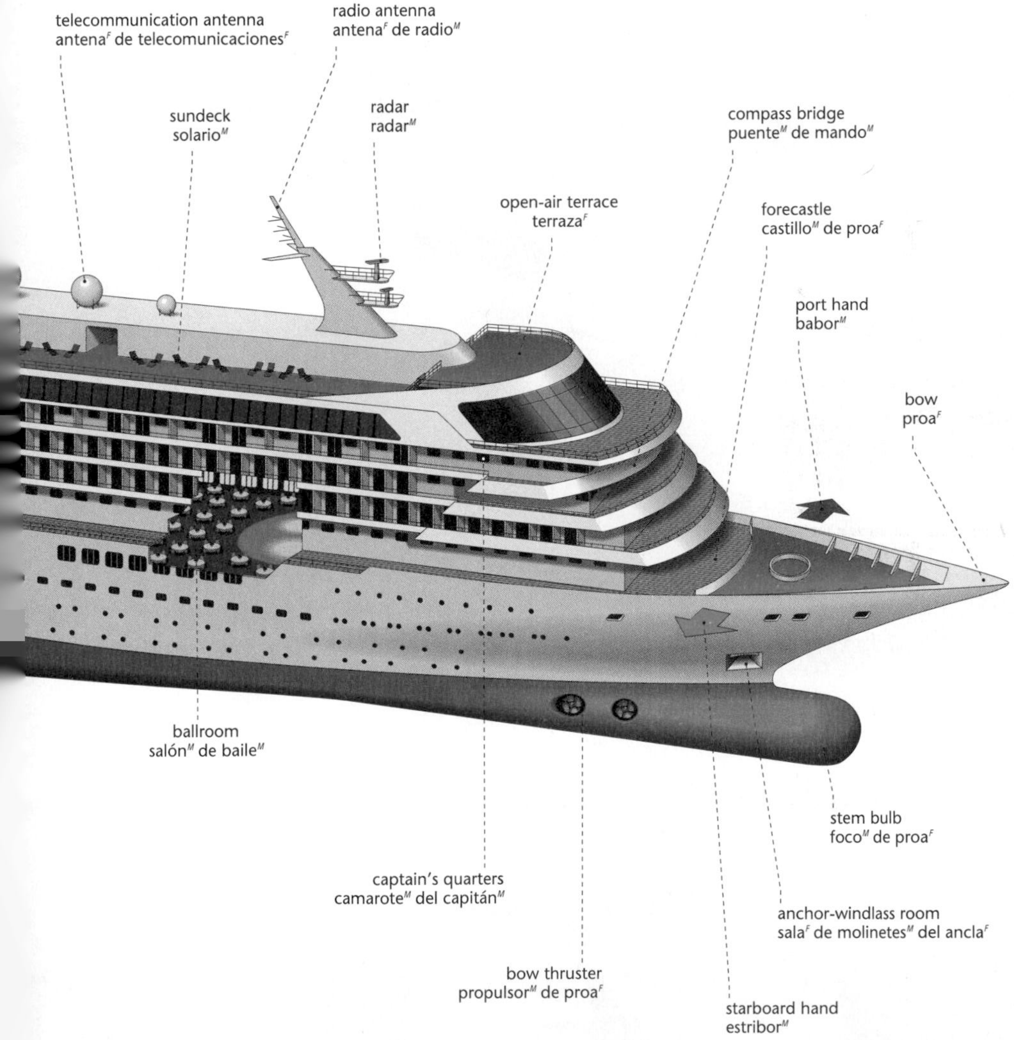

telecommunication antenna
antena^F de telecomunicaciones^F

radio antenna
antena^F de radio^M

sundeck
solario^M

radar
radar^M

compass bridge
puente^M de mando^M

open-air terrace
terraza^F

forecastle
castillo^M de proa^F

port hand
babor^M

bow
proa^F

ballroom
salón^M de baile^M

stem bulb
foco^M de proa^F

captain's quarters
camarote^M del capitán^M

anchor-windlass room
sala^F de molinetes^M del ancla^F

bow thruster
propulsor^M de proa^F

starboard hand
estribor^M

LONG-RANGE JET
AVIÓN^M TURBORREACTOR DE PASAJEROS^M

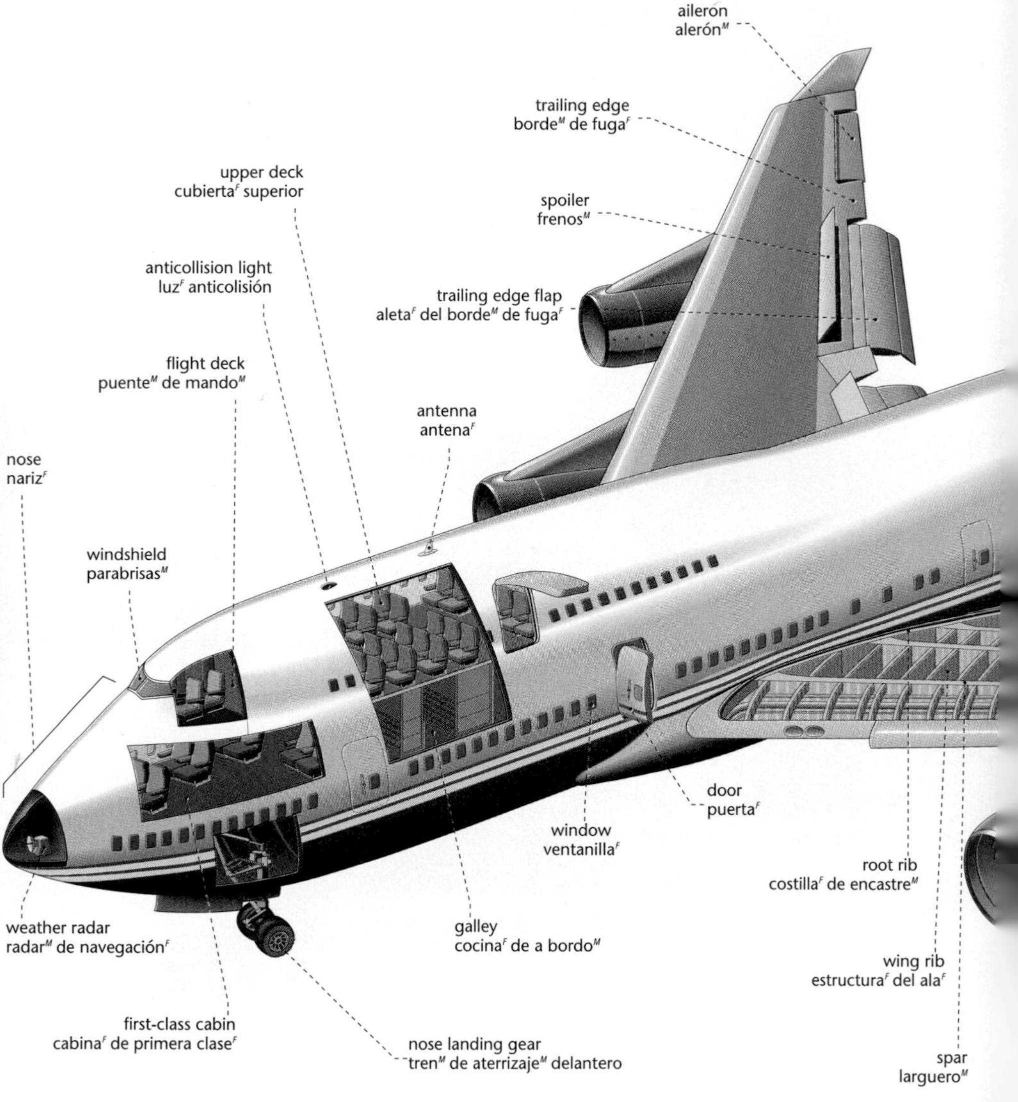

aileron
alerón^M

trailing edge
borde^M de fuga^F

upper deck
cubierta^F superior

spoiler
frenos^M

anticollision light
luz^F anticolisión

trailing edge flap
aleta^F del borde^M de fuga^F

flight deck
puente^M de mando^M

antenna
antena^F

nose
nariz^F

windshield
parabrisas^M

door
puerta^F

window
ventanilla^F

weather radar
radar^M de navegación^F

galley
cocina^F de a bordo^M

root rib
costilla^F de encastre^M

first-class cabin
cabina^F de primera clase^F

nose landing gear
tren^M de aterrizaje^M delantero

wing rib
estructura^F del ala^F

spar
larguero^M

TYPES OF TAIL SHAPES
TIPOS^M DE COLAS^F

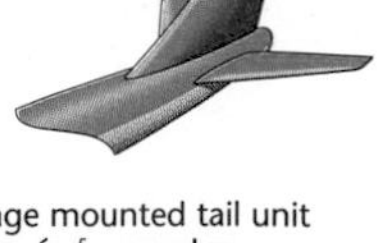

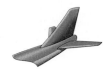

fuselage mounted tail unit
guías^F normales

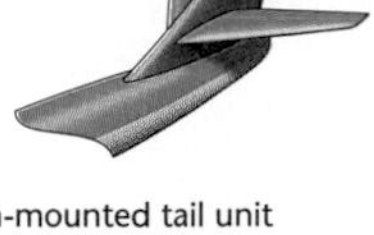

fin-mounted tail unit
unidad^F cruciforme

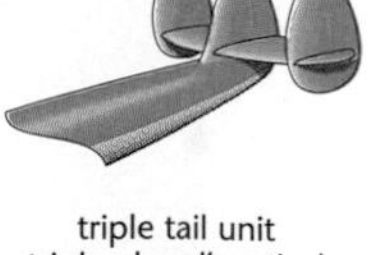

triple tail unit
triple plano^M vertical

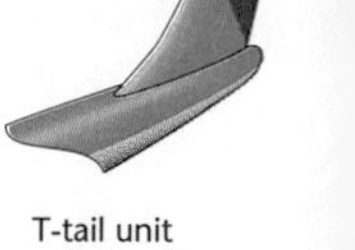

T-tail unit
guías^F en T

fin
plano*M* de deriva*F*

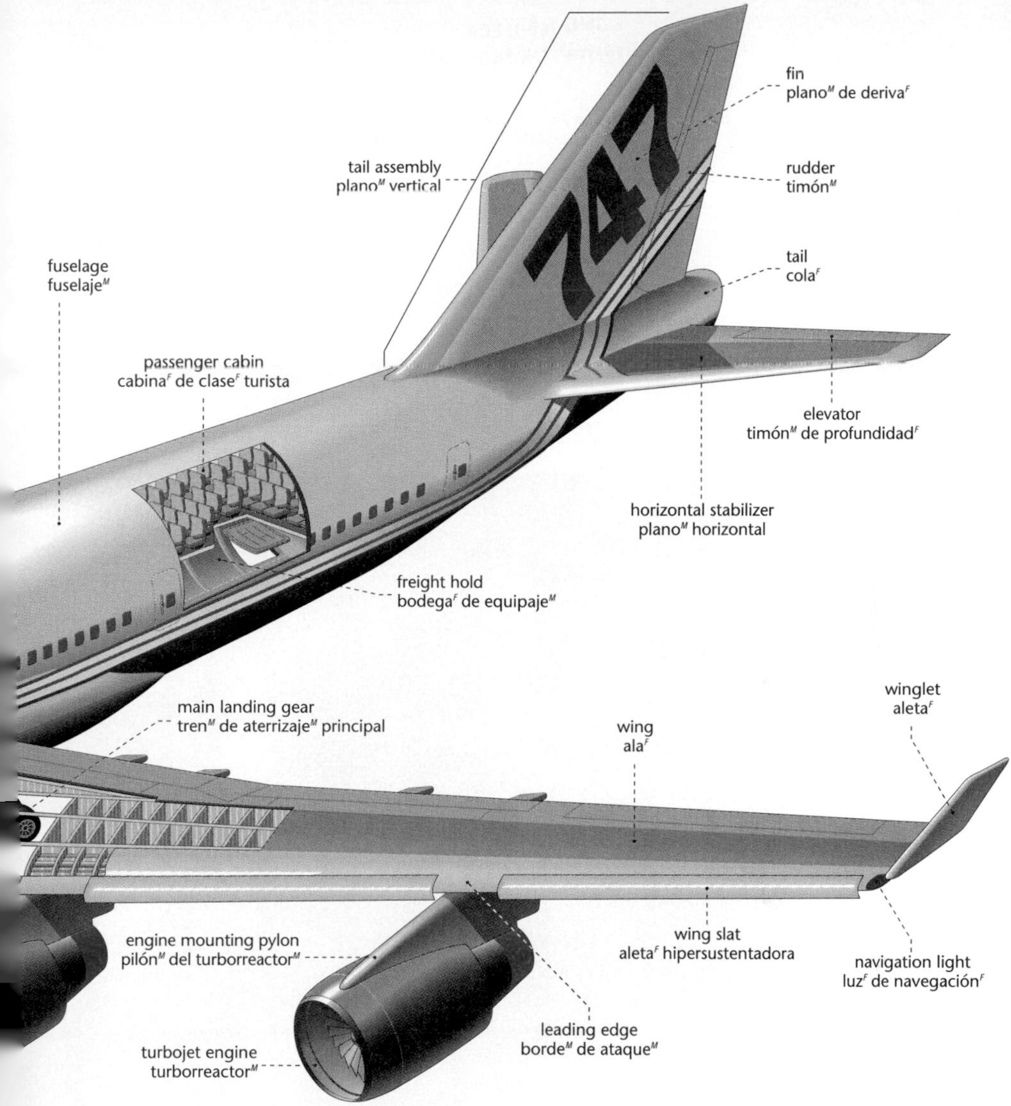

tail assembly
plano*M* vertical

rudder
timón*M*

fuselage
fuselaje*M*

tail
cola*F*

passenger cabin
cabina*F* de clase*F* turista

elevator
timón*M* de profundidad*F*

horizontal stabilizer
plano*M* horizontal

freight hold
bodega*F* de equipaje*M*

main landing gear
tren*M* de aterrizaje*M* principal

wing
ala*F*

winglet
aleta*F*

engine mounting pylon
pilón*M* del turborreactor*M*

wing slat
aleta*F* hipersustentadora

navigation light
luz*F* de navegación*F*

turbojet engine
turborreactor*M*

leading edge
borde*M* de ataque*M*

TYPES OF WING SHAPES
DIFERENTES FORMAS*F* DE ALAS*F*

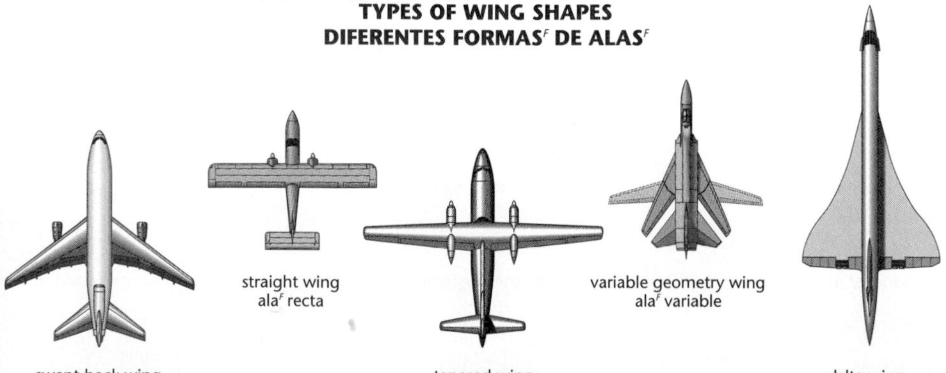

straight wing
ala*F* recta

variable geometry wing
ala*F* variable

swept-back wing
ala*F* en flecha*F*

tapered wing
ala*F* trapezoidal

delta wing
ala*F* en delta

FLIGHT DECK
PUENTE^M DE MANDO^M

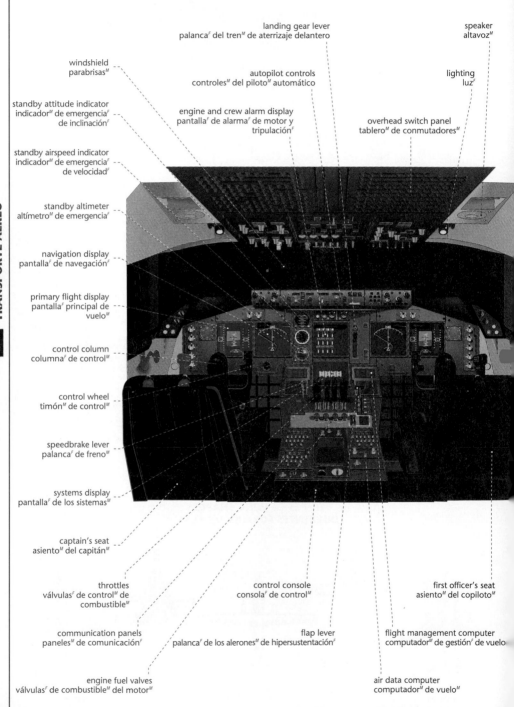

landing gear lever
palanca^F del tren^M de aterrizaje delantero

speaker
altavoz^M

windshield
parabrisas^M

autopilot controls
controles^M del piloto^M automático

lighting
luz^F

standby attitude indicator
indicador^M de emergencia^F
de inclinación^F

engine and crew alarm display
pantalla^F de alarma^F de motor y
tripulación^F

overhead switch panel
tablero^M de conmutadores^M

standby airspeed indicator
indicador^M de emergencia^F
de velocidad^F

standby altimeter
altímetro^M de emergencia^F

navigation display
pantalla^F de navegación^F

primary flight display
pantalla^F principal de
vuelo^M

control column
columna^F de control^M

control wheel
timón^M de control^M

speedbrake lever
palanca^F de freno^M

systems display
pantalla^F de los sistemas^M

captain's seat
asiento^M del capitán^M

throttles
válvulas^F de control^M de
combustible^M

control console
consola^F de control^M

first officer's seat
asiento^M del copiloto^M

communication panels
paneles^M de comunicación^F

flap lever
palanca^F de los alerones^M de hipersustentación^F

flight management computer
computador^M de gestión^F de vuelo^M

engine fuel valves
válvulas^F de combustible^M del motor^M

air data computer
computador^M de vuelo^M

TURBOFAN ENGINE
TURBOREACTOR^M

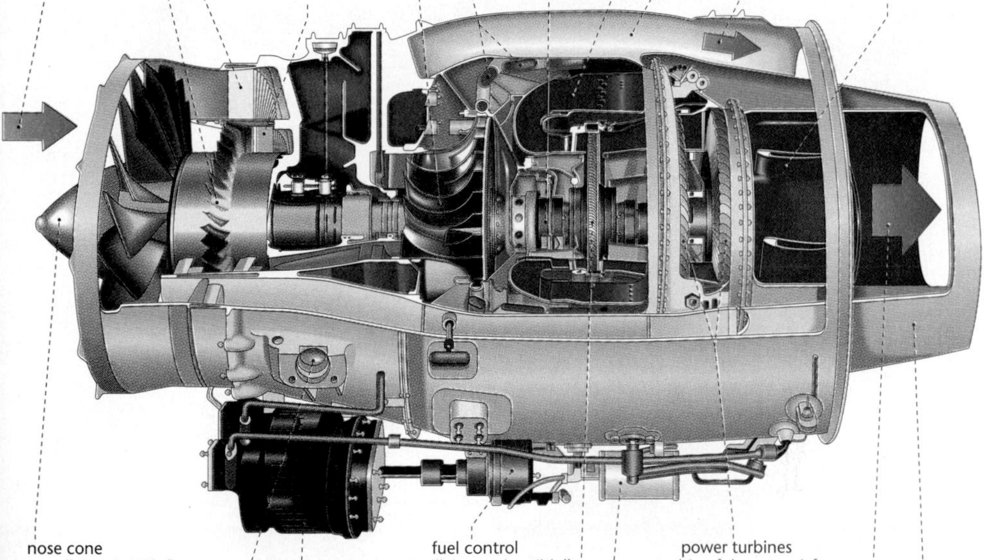

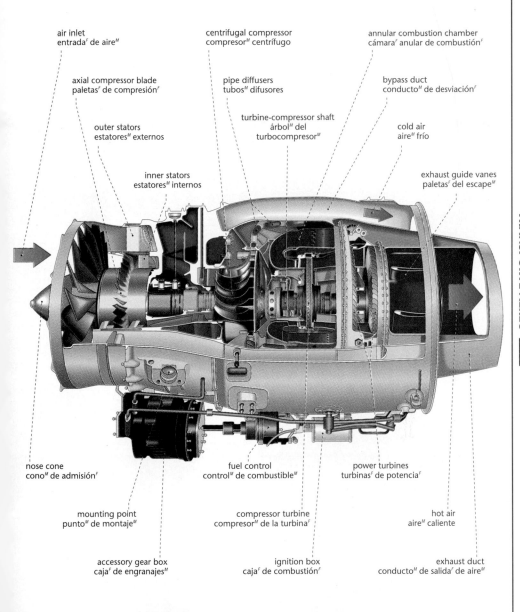

air inlet
entrada^F de aire^M

centrifugal compressor
compresor^M centrífugo

annular combustion chamber
cámara^F anular de combustión^F

axial compressor blade
paletas^F de compresión^F

pipe diffusers
tubos^M difusores

bypass duct
conducto^M de desviación^F

outer stators
estatores^M externos

turbine-compressor shaft
árbol^M del
turbocompresor^M

cold air
aire^M frío

inner stators
estatores^M internos

exhaust guide vanes
paletas^F del escape^M

nose cone
cono^M de admisión^F

fuel control
control^M de combustible^M

power turbines
turbinas^F de potencia^F

mounting point
punto^M de montaje^M

compressor turbine
compresor^M de la turbina^F

hot air
aire^M caliente

accessory gear box
caja^F de engranajes^M

ignition box
caja^F de combustión^F

exhaust duct
conducto^M de salida^F de aire^M

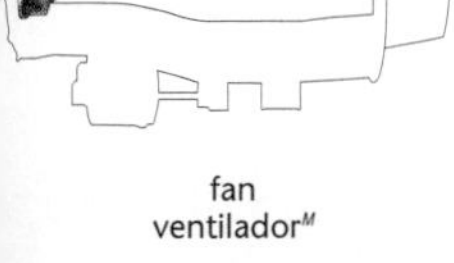

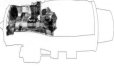

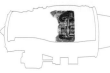

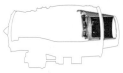

fan
ventilador^M

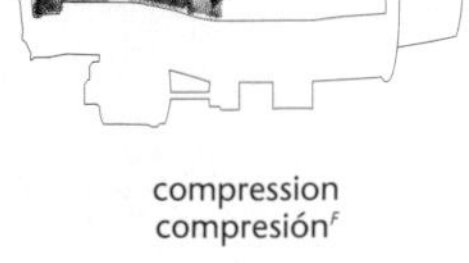

compression
compresión^F

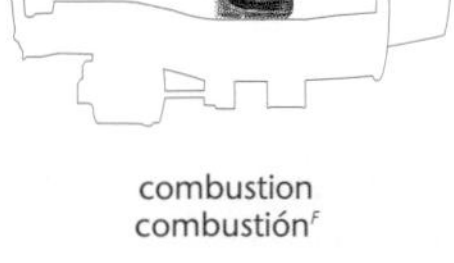

combustion
combustión^F

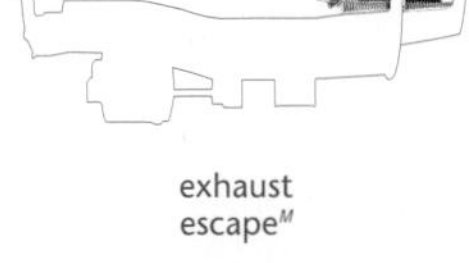

exhaust
escape^M

AIRPORT
AEROPUERTO^M

control tower cab
cabina^F de la torre^F de control^M

access road
carretera^F de acceso^M

high-speed exit taxiway
salida^F de la pista^F de alta velocidad^F

control tower
torre^F de control^M

taxiway
pista^F de maniobras^F

by-pass taxiway
pista^F de enlace^M

apron
pista^F de estacionamiento^M

apron
zona^F de circulación^F

taxiway
pista^F de maniobras^F

service road
ruta^F de servicio^M

maintenance hangar
hangar^M de mantenimiento^M

passenger terminal
terminal^M de pasajeros^M

parking area
zona^F de estacionamiento^M

telescopic corridor
corredor^M telescópico

boarding walkway
túnel^M de embarque^M

radial passenger loading area
terminal^M radial de pasajeros^M

service area
zona^F de servicio^M

taxiway line
línea^F de pista^F

AIRPORT
AEROPUERTO^M

PASSENGER TERMINAL
TERMINAL^M DE PASAJEROS^M

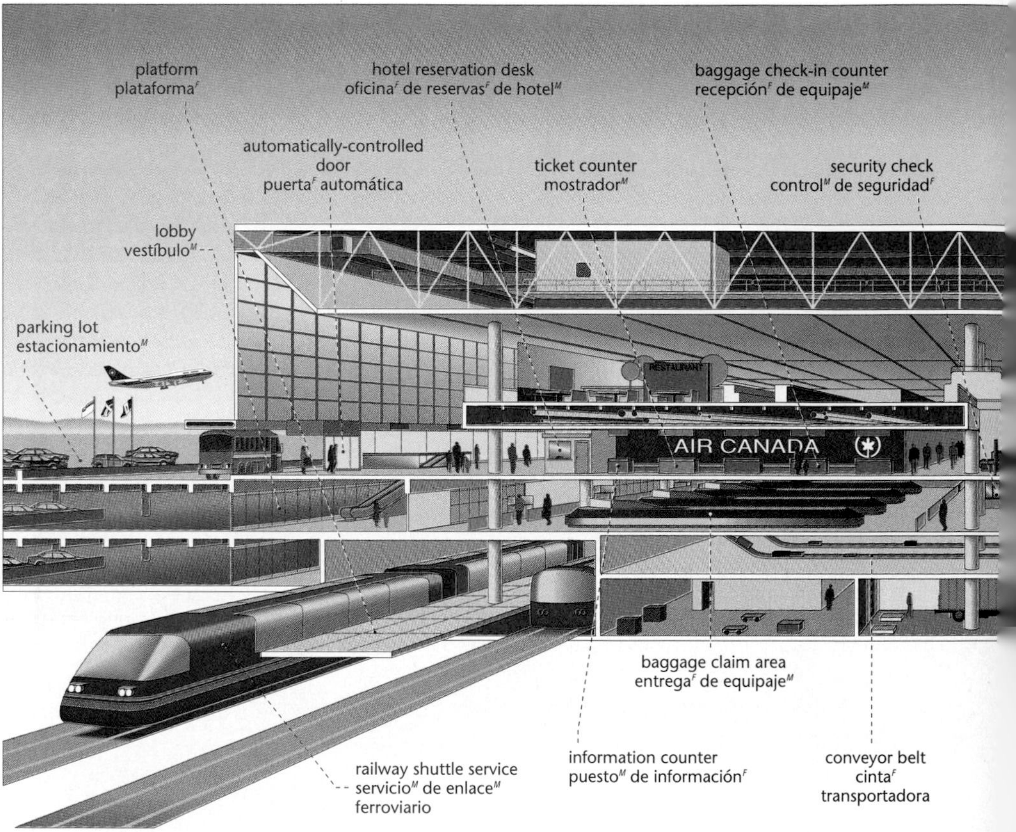

platform
plataforma^F

hotel reservation desk
oficina^F de reservas^F de hotel^M

baggage check-in counter
recepción^F de equipaje^M

automatically-controlled
door
puerta^F automática

ticket counter
mostrador^M

security check
control^M de seguridad^F

lobby
vestíbulo^M

parking lot
estacionamiento^M

baggage claim area
entrega^F de equipaje^M

railway shuttle service
servicio^M de enlace^M
ferroviario

information counter
puesto^M de información^F

conveyor belt
cinta^F
transportadora

RUNWAY
PISTA^F DE ATERRIZAJE^M Y DESPEGUE^M

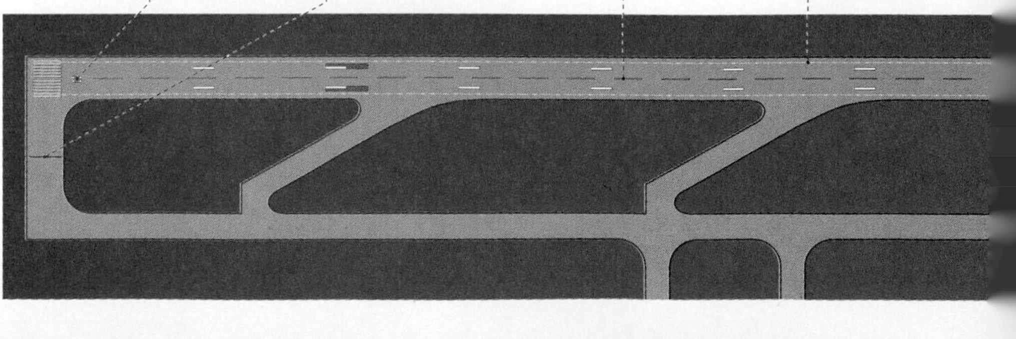

runway center line markings
señal^F de eje^M de pista^F

runway designation marking
señal^F de identificación^F de pista^F

holding area marking
señal^F de zona^F de espera^F

runway side stripe markings
señales^F laterales de pista^F

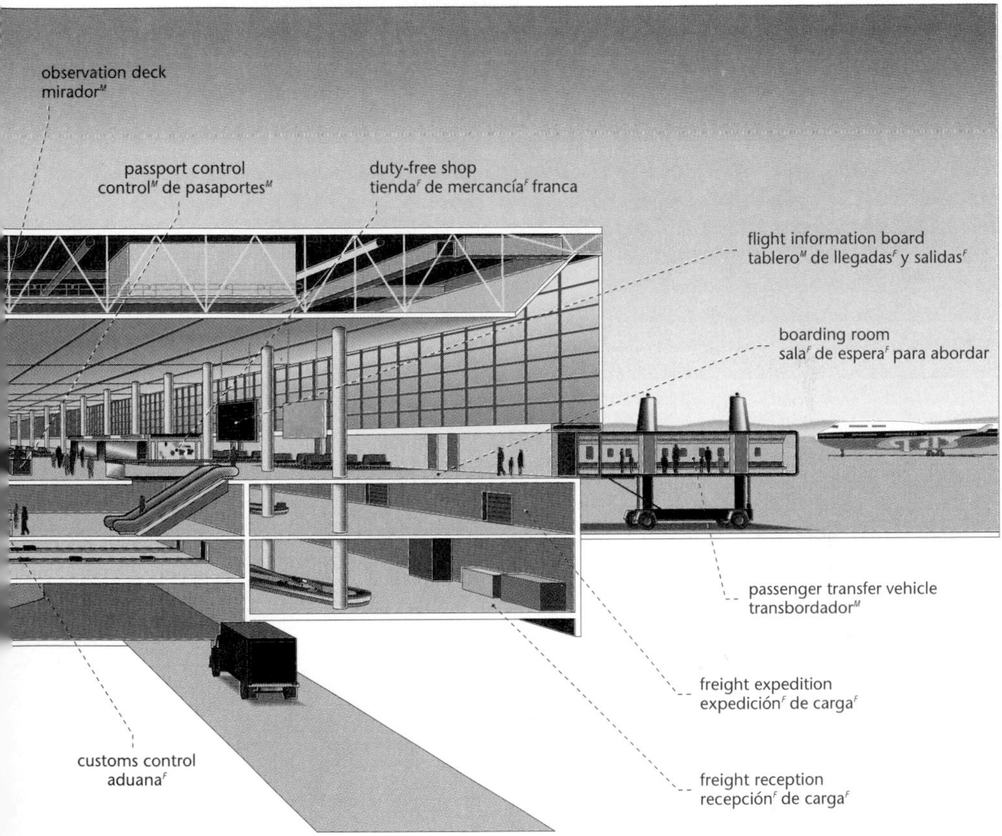

observation deck
mirador^M

passport control
control^M de pasaportes^M

duty-free shop
tienda^F de mercancía^F franca

flight information board
tablero^M de llegadas^F y salidas^F

boarding room
sala^F de espera^F para abordar

passenger transfer vehicle
transbordador^M

freight expedition
expedición^F de carga^F

customs control
aduana^F

freight reception
recepción^F de carga^F

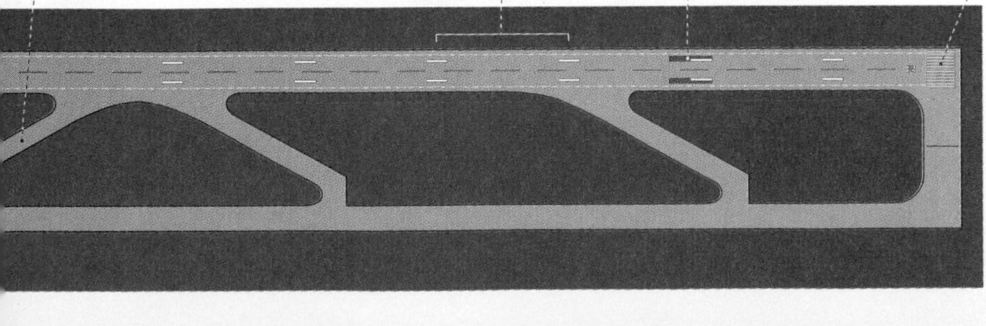

runway touchdown zone marking
señal^F de zona^F de contacto^M de pista^F

exit taxiway
salida^F de la pista^F

fixed distance marking
señal^F de distancia^F fija

runway threshold markings
señales de limite^M de la pista^F

AIR TRANSPORT
TRANSPORTE AÉREO

GROUND AIRPORT EQUIPMENT
EQUIPO^M DE TIERRA^F

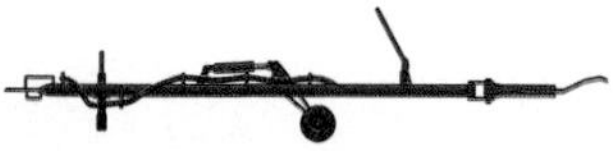

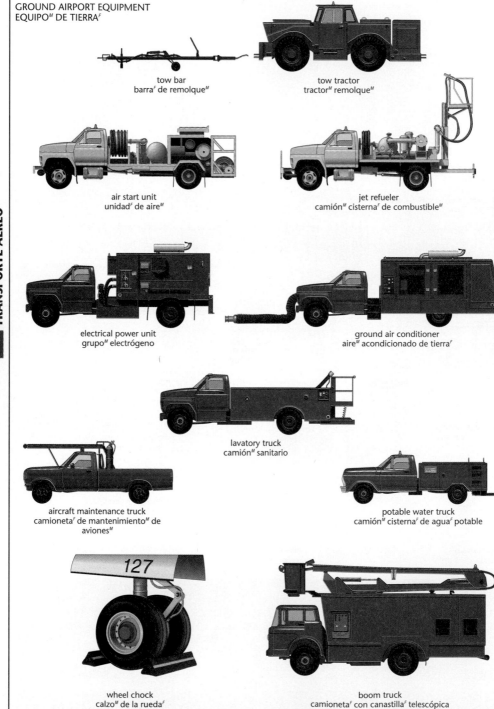

tow bar
barra^F de remolque^M

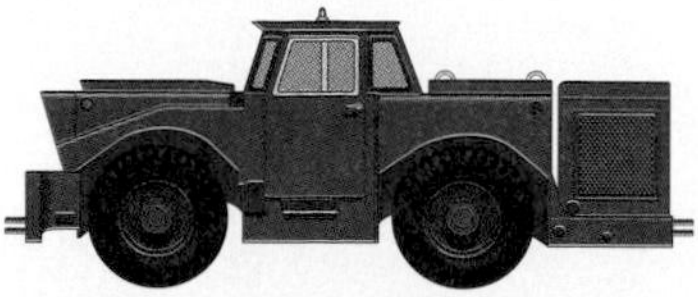

tow tractor
tractor^M remolque^M

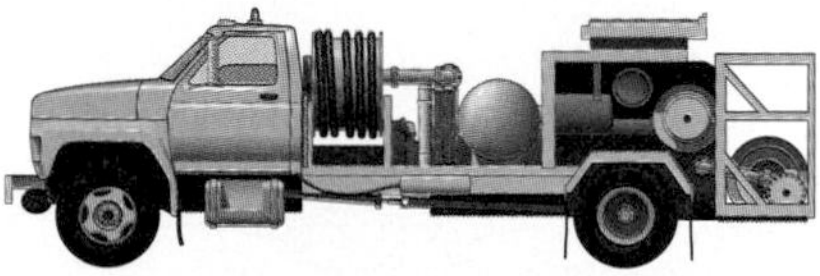

air start unit
unidad^F de aire^M

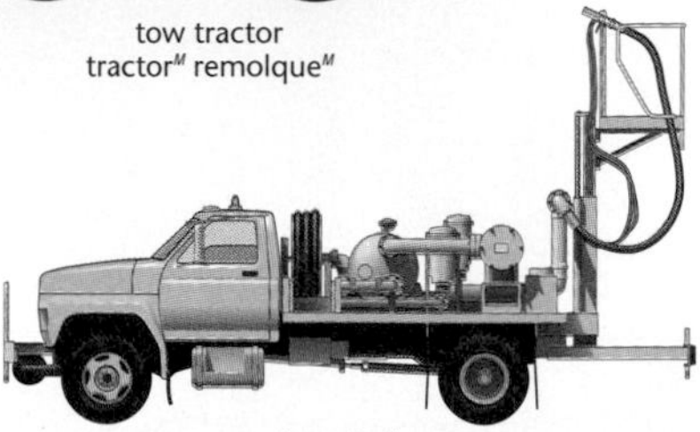

jet refueler
camión^M cisterna^F de combustible^M

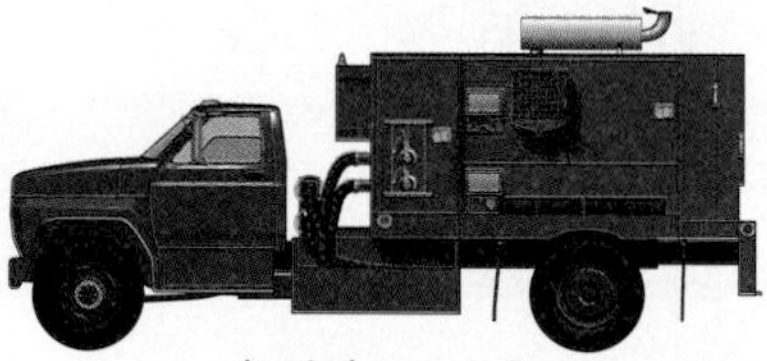

electrical power unit
grupo^M electrógeno

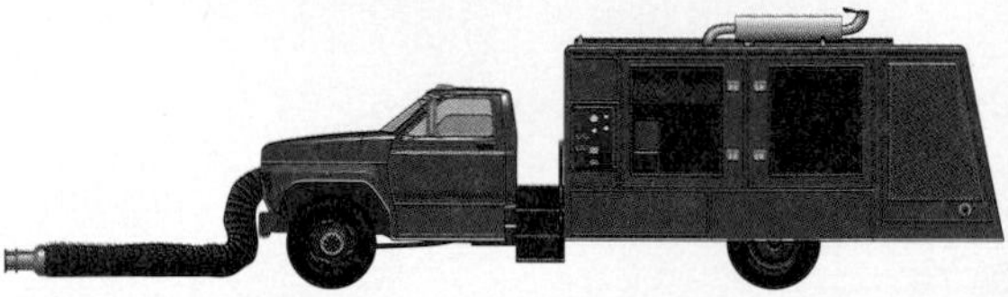

ground air conditioner
aire^M acondicionado de tierra^F

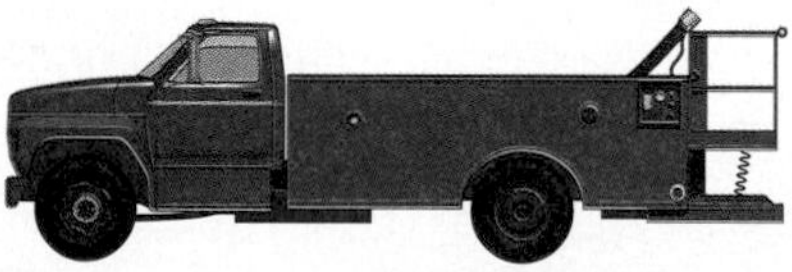

lavatory truck
camión^M sanitario

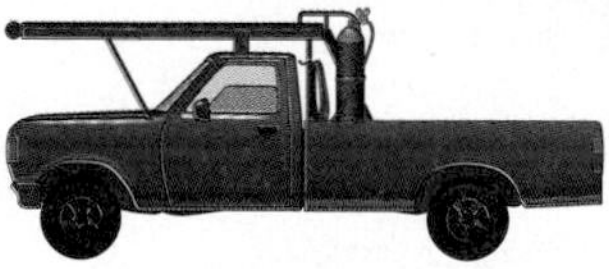

aircraft maintenance truck
camioneta^F de mantenimiento^M de
aviones^M

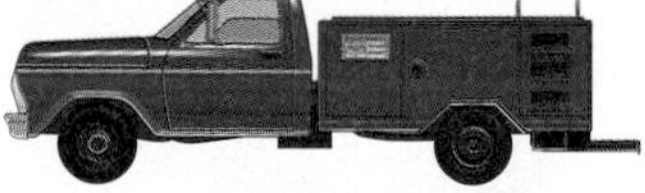

potable water truck
camión^M cisterna^F de agua^F potable

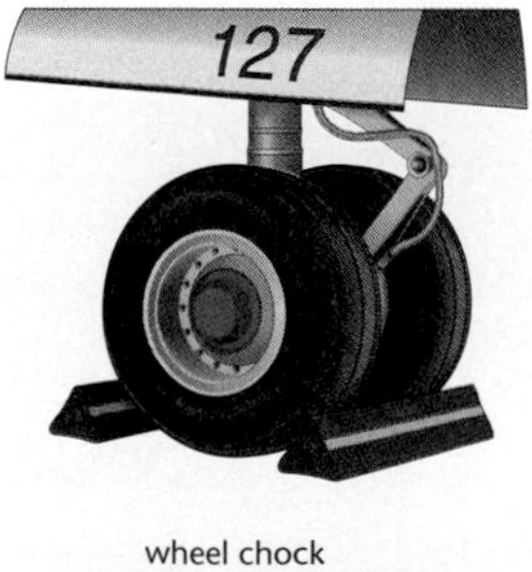

wheel chock
calzo^M de la rueda^F

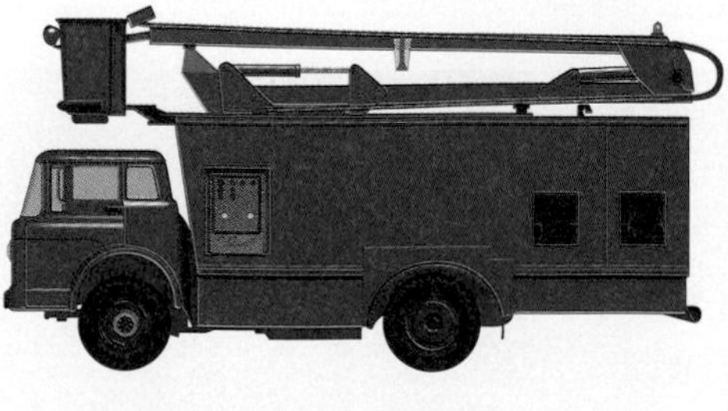

boom truck
camioneta^F con canastilla^F telescópica

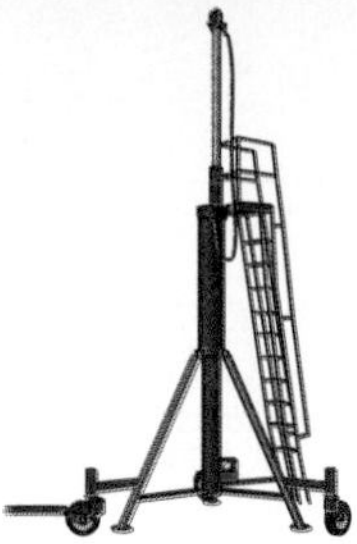

tripod tail support
soporte^M trípode de cola^F

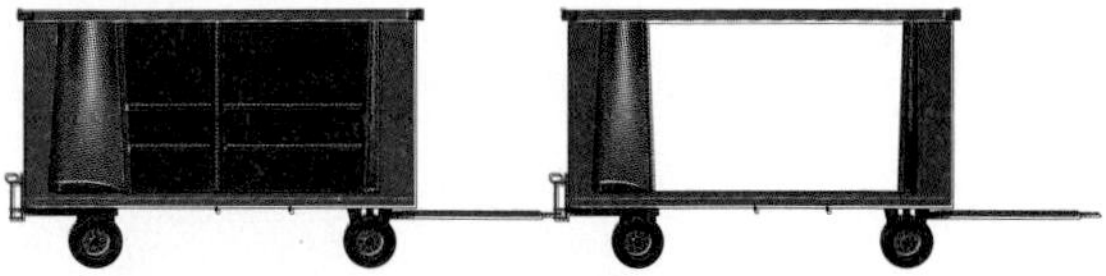

baggage trailer
remolque^M

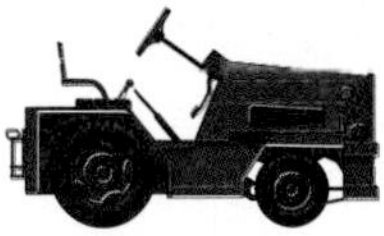

tow tractor
tractor^M remolcador

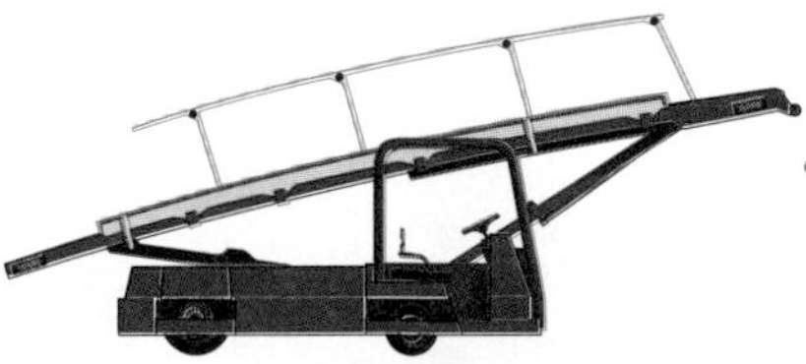

baggage conveyor
transportador^M de equipaje^M

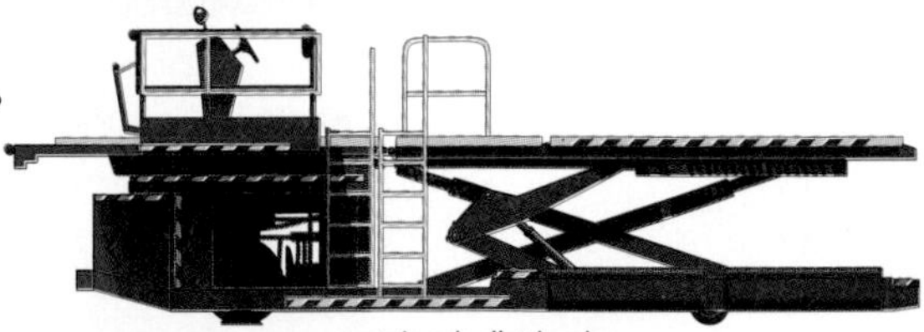

container/pallet loader
cargador^M de contenedores^M y plataformas^F

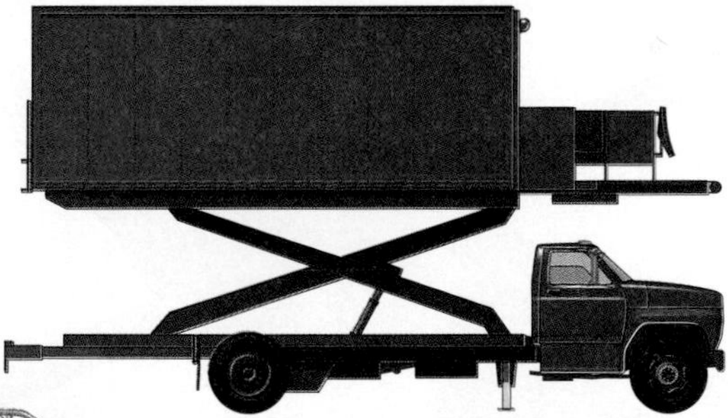

catering vehicle
camión^M de aprovisionamiento^M

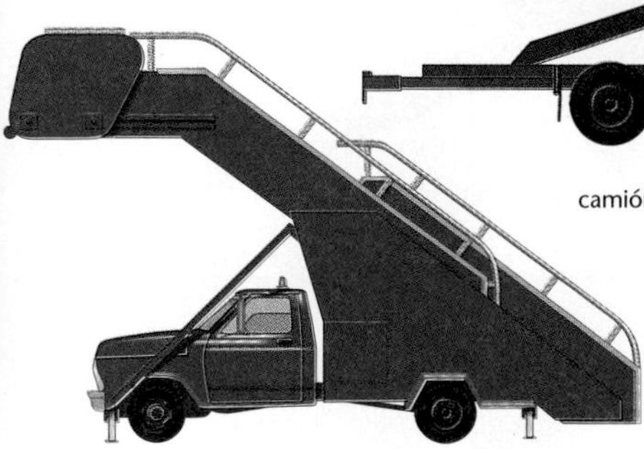

mobile passenger stairs
escalerilla^F transportable

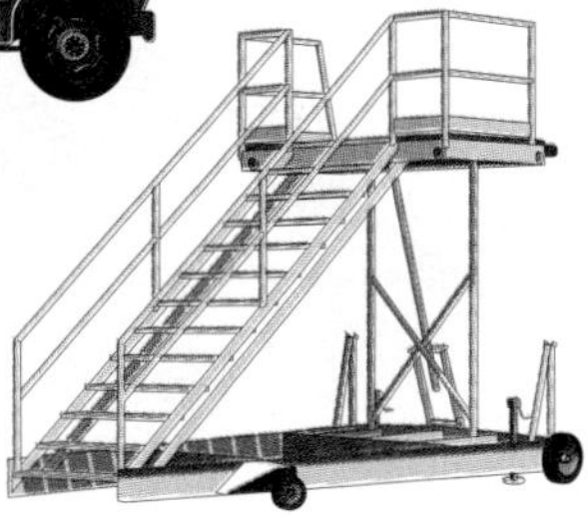

universal step
escalerilla^F rodante

passenger transfer vehicle
trasbordador^M

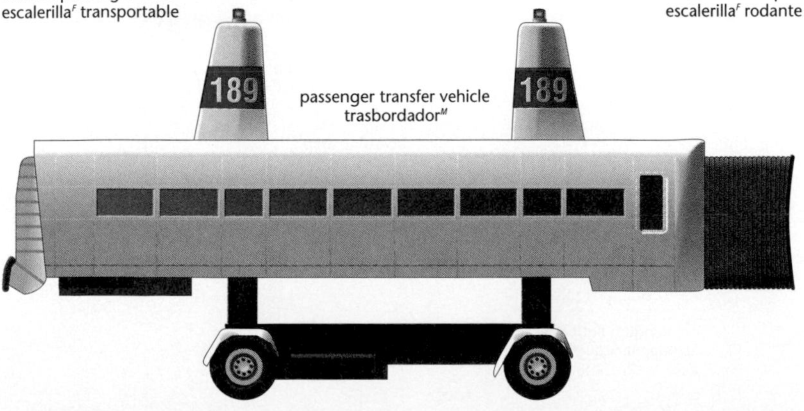

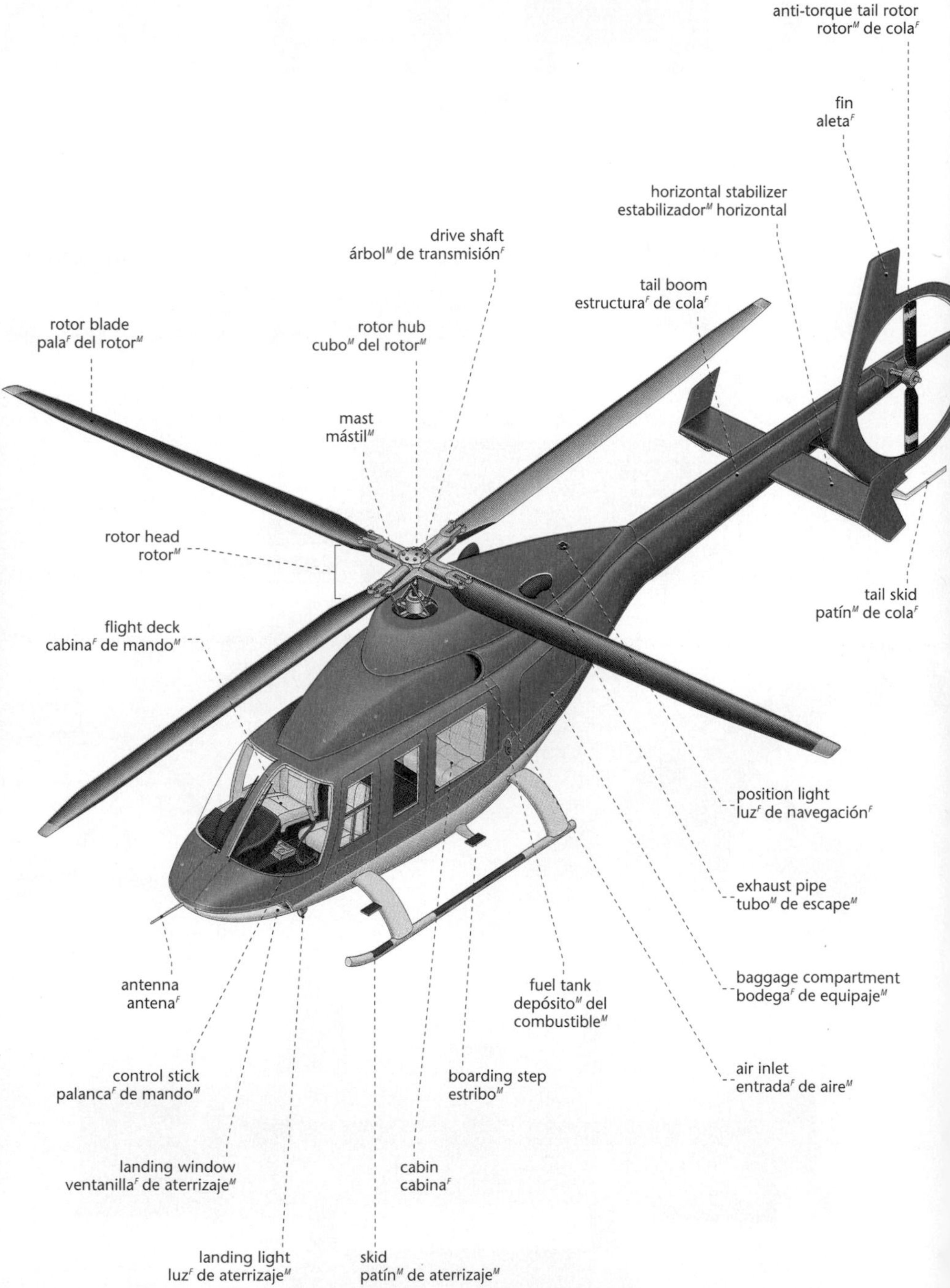

anti-torque tail rotor
rotor^M de cola^F

fin
aleta^F

horizontal stabilizer
estabilizador^M horizontal

drive shaft
árbol^M de transmisión^F

tail boom
estructura^F de cola^F

rotor blade
pala^F del rotor^M

rotor hub
cubo^M del rotor^M

mast
mástil^M

rotor head
rotor^M

tail skid
patín^M de cola^F

flight deck
cabina^F de mando^M

position light
luz^F de navegación^F

exhaust pipe
tubo^M de escape^M

antenna
antena^F

baggage compartment
bodega^F de equipaje^M

fuel tank
depósito^M del
combustible^M

control stick
palanca^F de mando^M

boarding step
estribo^M

air inlet
entrada^F de aire^M

landing window
ventanilla^F de aterrizaje^M

cabin
cabina^F

landing light
luz^F de aterrizaje^M

skid
patín^M de aterrizaje^M

ROCKET
COHETE^M

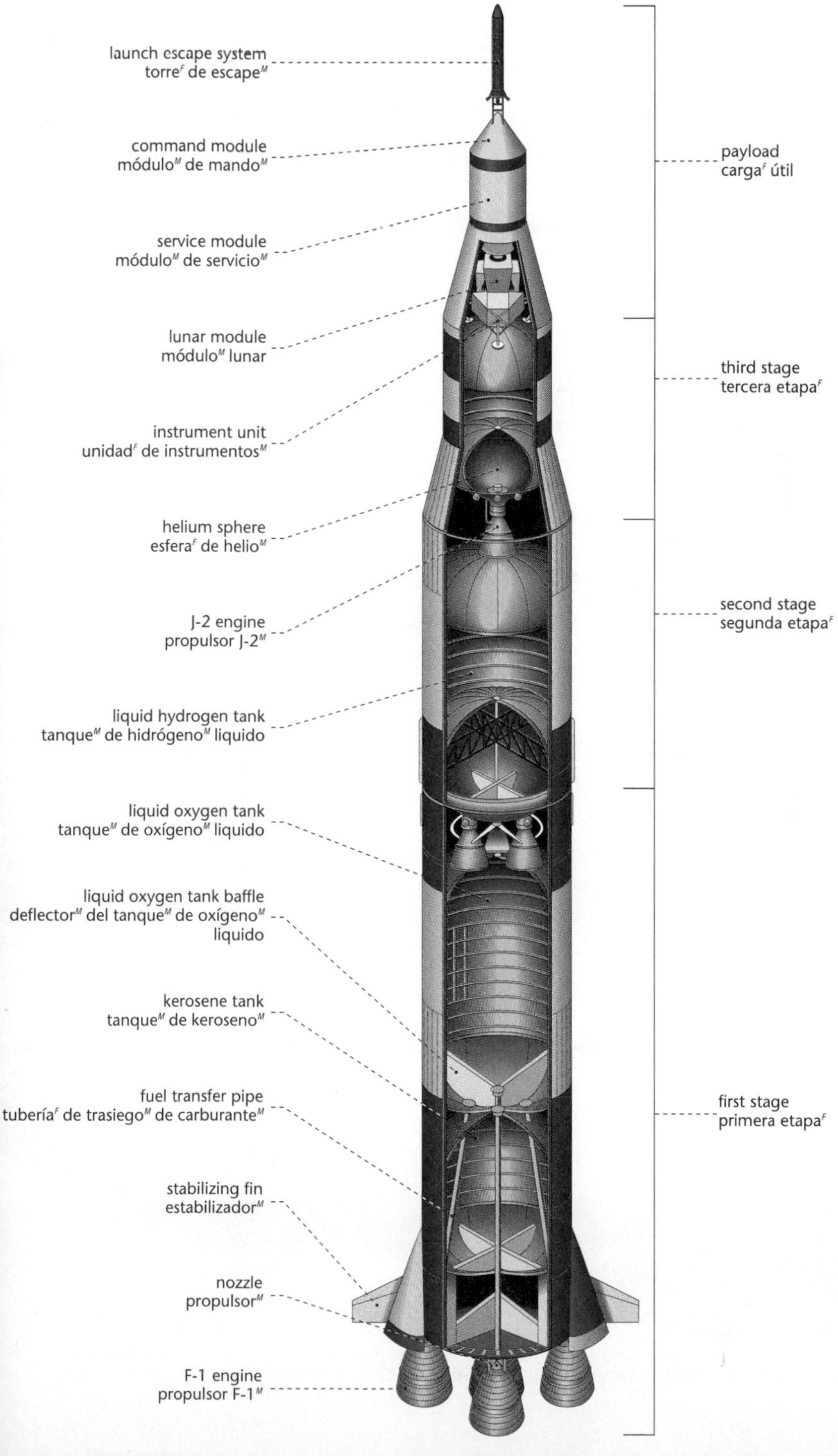

launch escape system
torre^F de escape^M

command module
módulo^M de mando^M

service module
módulo^M de servicio^M

lunar module
módulo^M lunar

instrument unit
unidad^F de instrumentos^M

helium sphere
esfera^F de helio^M

J-2 engine
propulsor J-2^M

liquid hydrogen tank
tanque^M de hidrógeno^M líquido

liquid oxygen tank
tanque^M de oxígeno^M líquido

liquid oxygen tank baffle
deflector^M del tanque^M de oxígeno^M
líquido

kerosene tank
tanque^M de keroseno^M

fuel transfer pipe
tubería^F de trasiego^M de carburante^M

stabilizing fin
estabilizador^M

nozzle
propulsor^M

F-1 engine
propulsor F-1^M

payload
carga^F útil

third stage
tercera etapa^F

second stage
segunda etapa^F

first stage
primera etapa^F

SPACE SHUTTLE
TRANSBORDADOR*^M* ESPACIAL

SPACE SHUTTLE AT TAKEOFF
TRANSBORDADOR*^M* ESPACIAL EN
POSICIÓN*^F* DE LANZAMIENTO*^M*

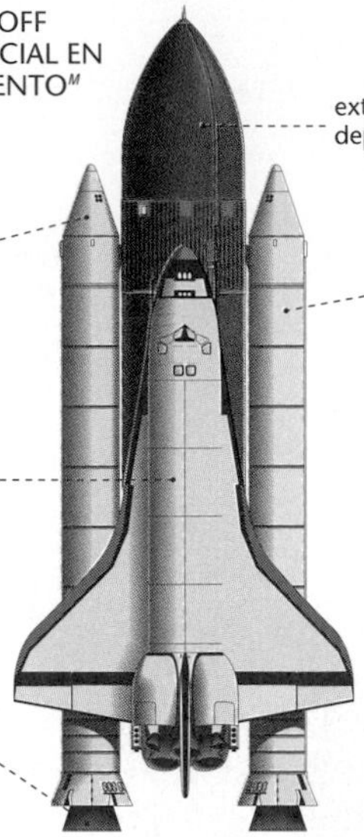

external fuel tank
depósito*^M* externo de combustible*^M*

booster parachute
paracaídas*^F* auxiliar

solid-rocket booster
cohetes*^M* impulsores

shuttle
lanzadera*^F*

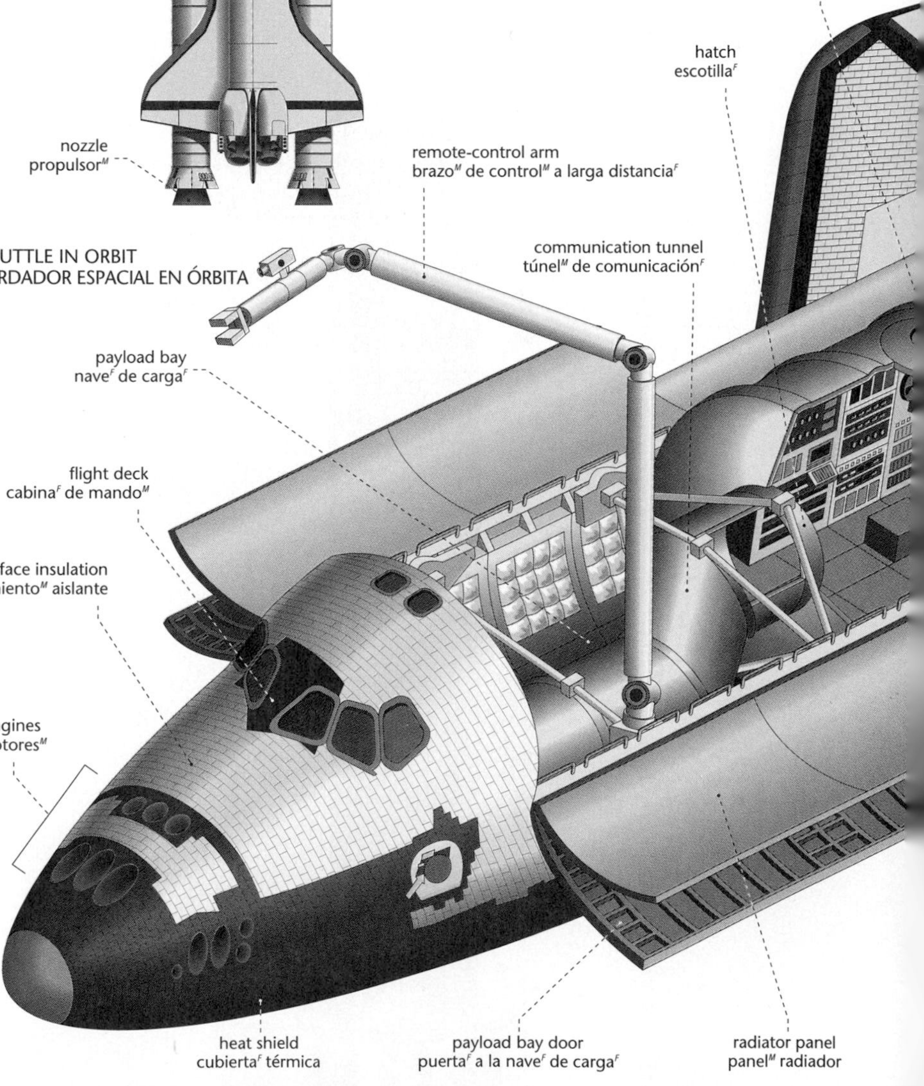

observation window
ventanilla*^F* de observación*^F*

hatch
escotilla*^F*

nozzle
propulsor*^M*

remote-control arm
brazo*^M* de control*^M* a larga distancia*^F*

communication tunnel
túnel*^M* de comunicación*^F*

SPACE SHUTTLE IN ORBIT
TRANSBORDADOR ESPACIAL EN ÓRBITA

payload bay
nave*^F* de carga*^F*

flight deck
cabina*^F* de mando*^M*

surface insulation
recubrimiento*^M* aislante

engines
motores*^M*

heat shield
cubierta*^F* térmica

payload bay door
puerta*^F* a la nave*^F* de carga*^F*

radiator panel
panel*^M* radiador

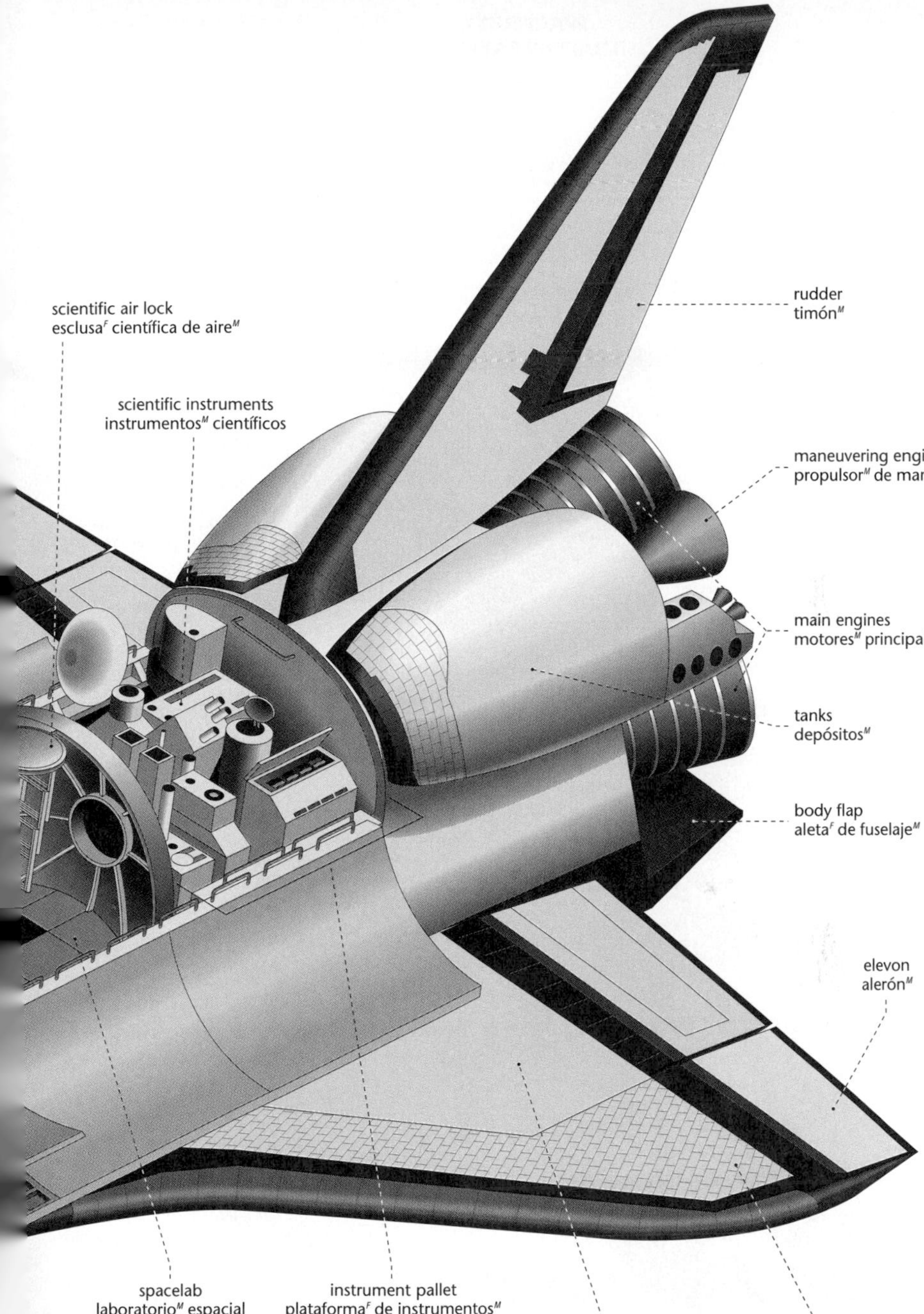

scientific air lock
esclusa^F científica de aire^M

scientific instruments
instrumentos^M científicos

rudder
timón^M

maneuvering engine
propulsor^M de maniobras^F

main engines
motores^M principales

tanks
depósitos^M

body flap
aleta^F de fuselaje^M

elevon
alerón^M

spacelab
laboratorio^M espacial

instrument pallet
plataforma^F de instrumentos^M

wing
ala^F

tile
teja^F

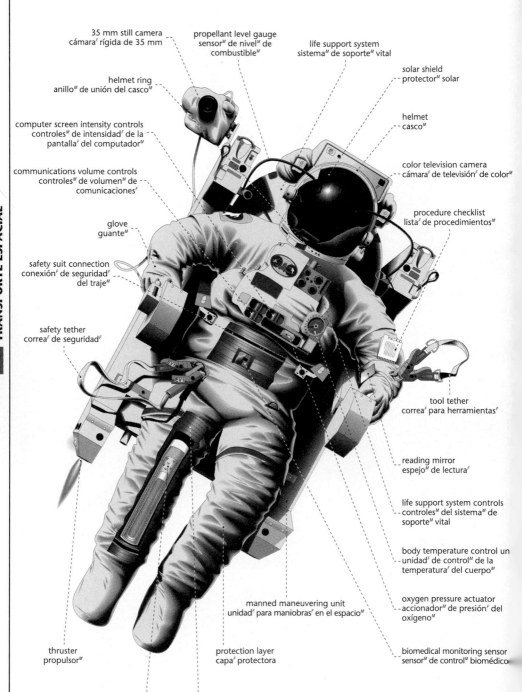

35 mm still camera
cámara^F rígida de 35 mm

propellant level gauge
sensor^M de nivel^M de
combustible^M

life support system
sistema^M de soporte^M vital

solar shield
protector^M solar

helmet ring
anillo^M de unión del casco^M

helmet
casco^M

computer screen intensity controls
controles^M de intensidad^F de la
pantalla^F del computador^M

color television camera
cámara^F de televisión^F de color^M

communications volume controls
controles^M de volumen^M de
comunicaciones^F

procedure checklist
lista^F de procedimientos^M

glove
guante^M

safety suit connection
conexión^F de seguridad^F
del traje^M

safety tether
correa^F de seguridad^F

tool tether
correa^F para herramientas^F

reading mirror
espejo^M de lectura^F

life support system controls
controles^M del sistema^M de
soporte^M vital

body temperature control un
unidad^F de control^M de la
temperatura^F del cuerpo^M

oxygen pressure actuator
accionador^M de presión^F del
oxígeno^M

thruster
propulsor^M

manned maneuvering unit
unidad^F para maniobras^F en el espacio^M

protection layer
capa^F protectora

biomedical monitoring sensor
sensor^M de control^M biomédico

liquid cooling and ventilation garment
liquido^M de enfriamiento^M y ventilación^F
del traje^M

insulation layers
capas^F aislantes

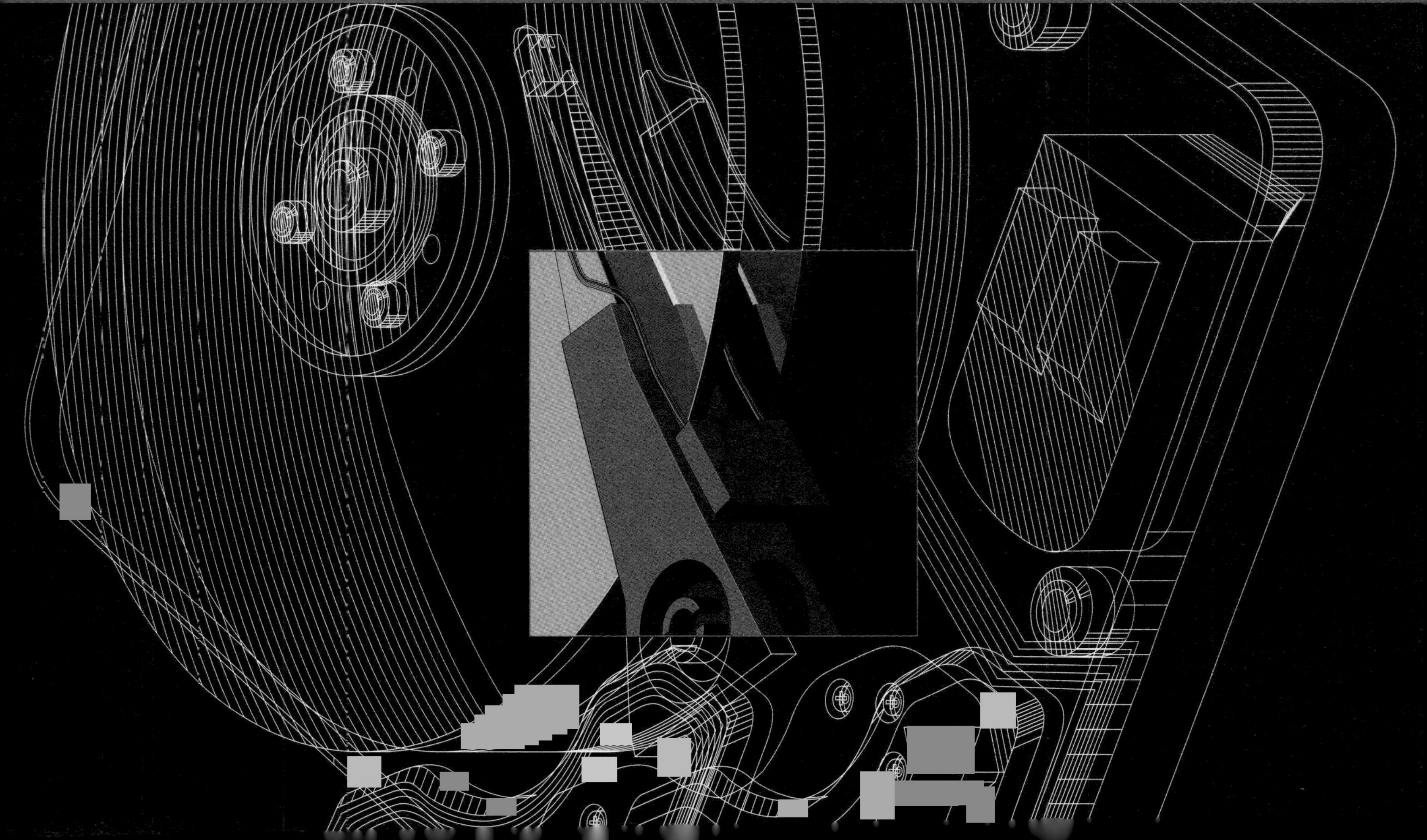

CONTENTS

OFFICE SUPPLIES
EQUIPO DE OFICINA

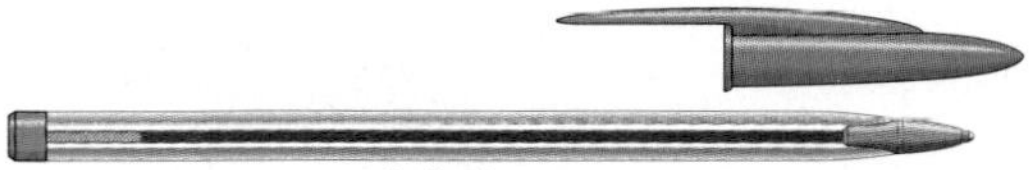

ballpoint pen
bolígrafo^M

mechanical pencil
lapicero^M

fountain pen
estilográfica^F

pencil
lápiz^M

eraser holder
portaborrador^M

stick eraser
lápiz^M borrador^M

marker
marcador^M

eraser
borrador^M

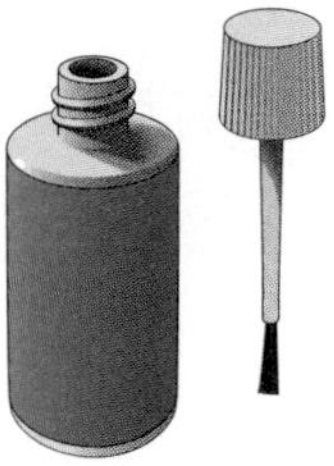

highlighter pen
destacador^M

glue stick
lápiz^M adhesivo

correction fluid
corrector^M líquido

clip
pinza^F

paper clips
presillas^F

stapler
engrapadora^F

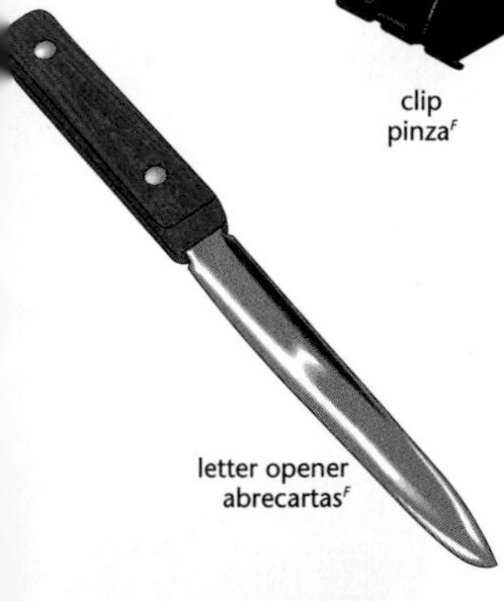

letter opener
abrecartas^F

paper fasteners
tachuelas^F para papel^M

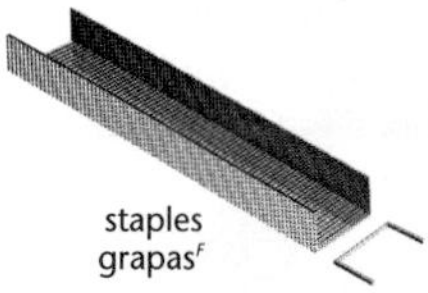

staples
grapas^F

thumb tacks
chinches^M

pencil sharpener
sacapuntas^M

correction paper
papel^M corrector

staple remover
uñas^F

OFFICE SUPPLIES
EQUIPO DE OFICINA

515

**OFFICE SUPPLIES
EQUIPO DE OFICINA**

rubber stamp
sello^M de goma^F

stamp pad
cojín^M para sellos^M

tape dispenser
carrete^M de cinta^F adhesiva

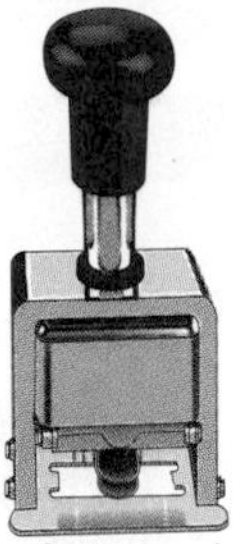

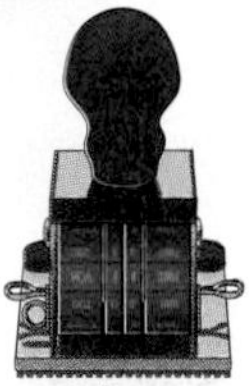

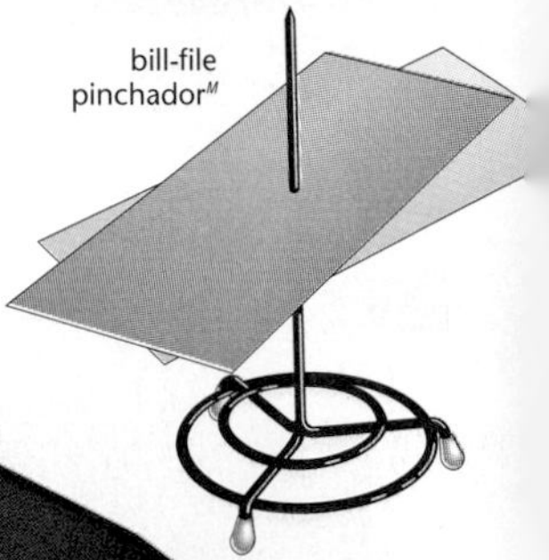

bill-file
pinchador^M

dater
fechador^M

numbering machine
foliador^M

stamp rack
portasellos^M

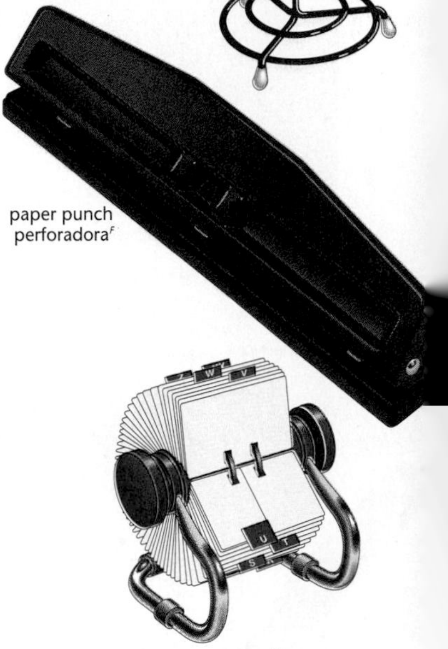

paper punch
perforadora^F

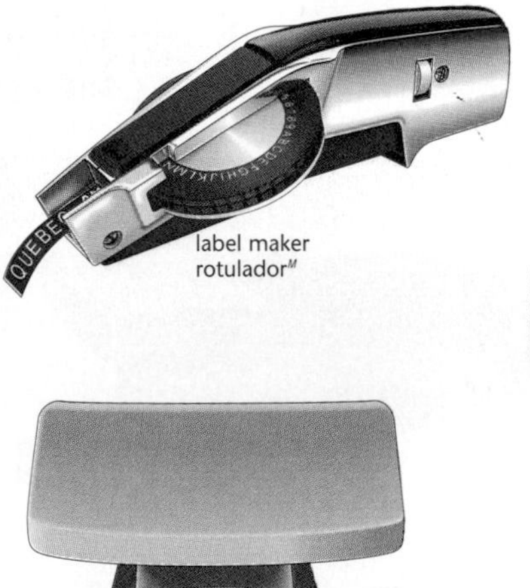

label maker
rotulador^M

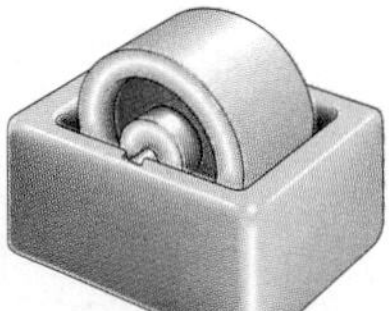

moistener
rueda^F humedecedora

rotary file
fichero^M giratorio

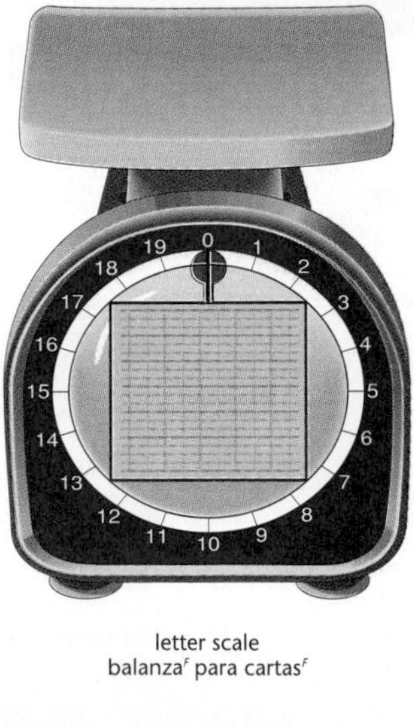

letter scale
balanza^F para cartas^F

pencil sharpener
sacapuntas^M

telephone index
directorio^M telefónico

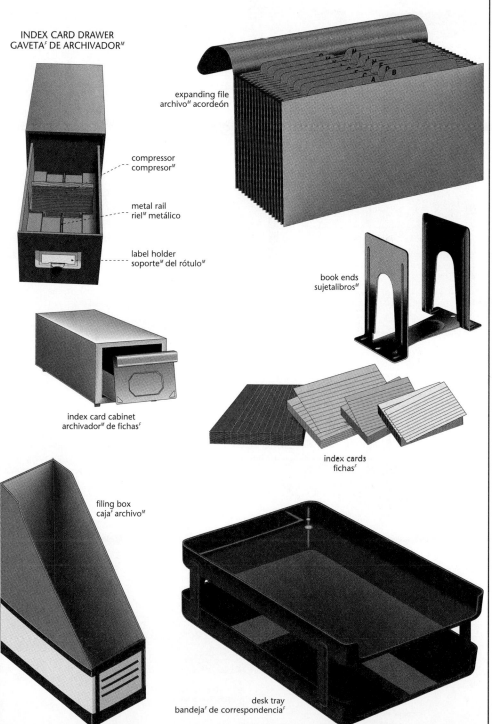

INDEX CARD DRAWER
GAVETA^F DE ARCHIVADOR^M

expanding file
archivo^M acordeón

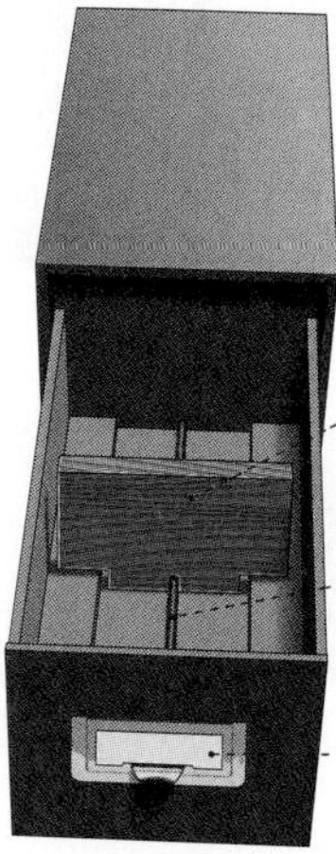

compressor
compresor^M

metal rail
riel^M metálico

label holder
soporte^M del rótulo^M

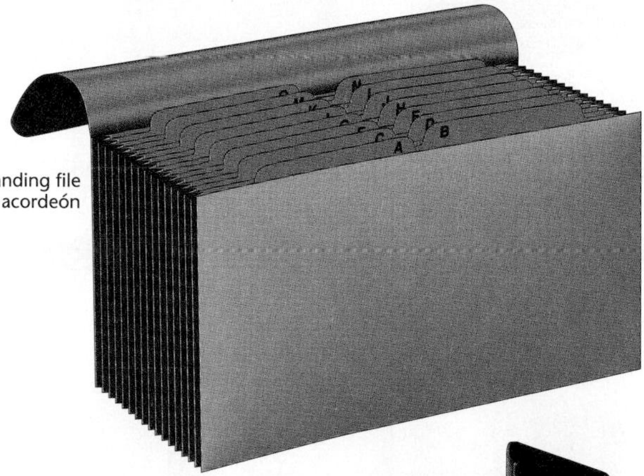

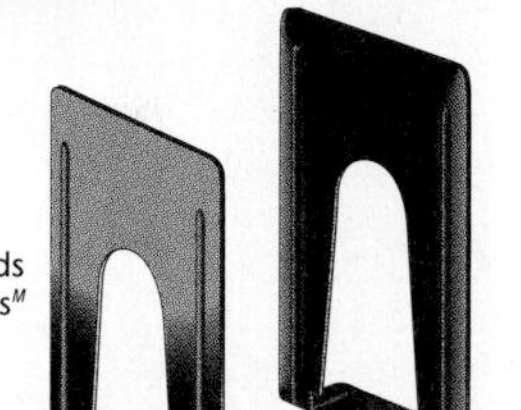

book ends
sujetalibros^M

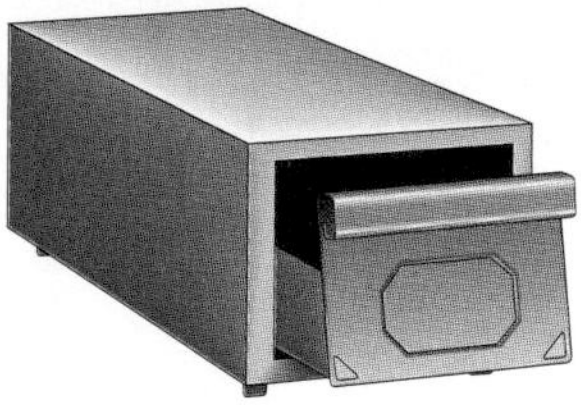

index card cabinet
archivador^M de fichas^F

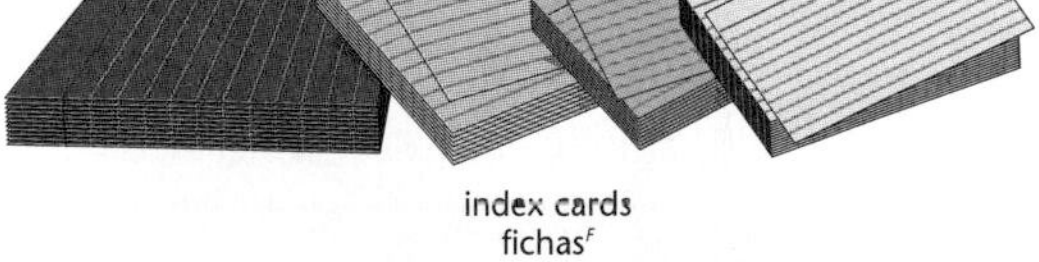

index cards
fichas^F

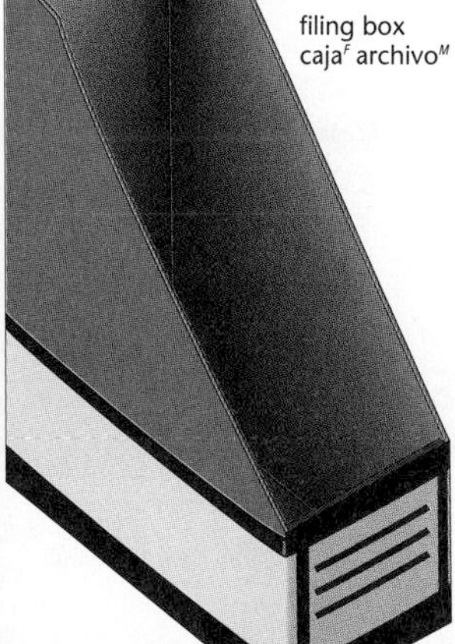

filing box
caja^F archivo^M

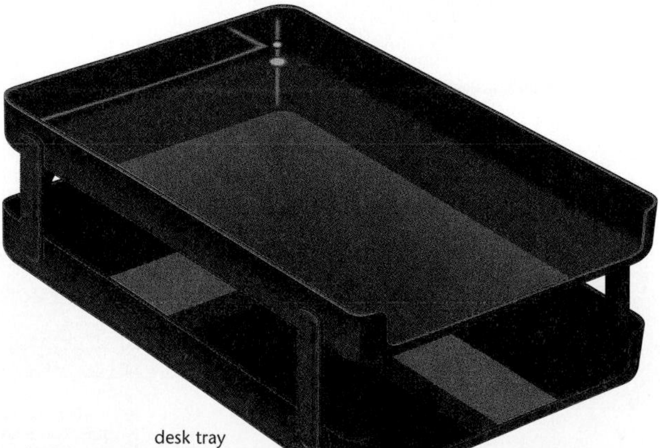

desk tray
bandeja^F de correspondencia^F

STATIONERY
ARTÍCULOS^M DE ESCRITORIO^M

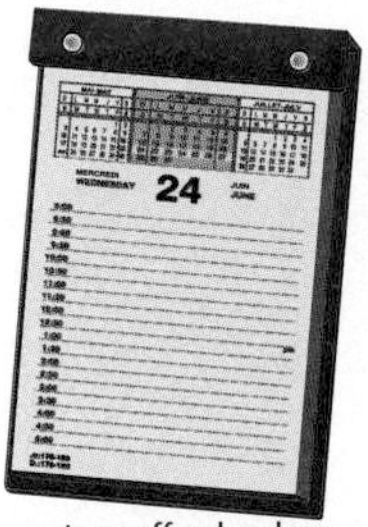

tear-off calendar
calendario^M de pared^F

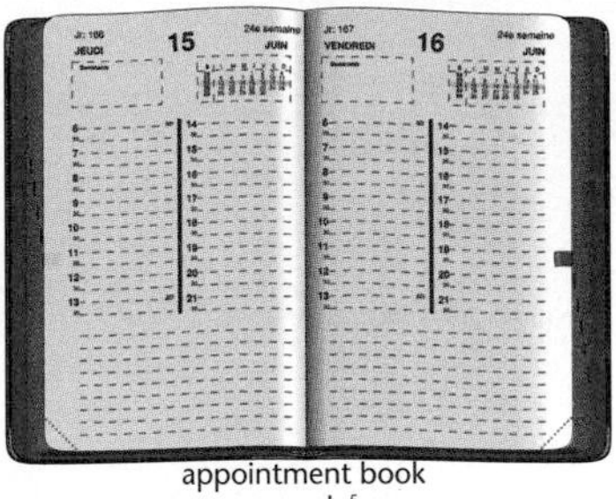

appointment book
agenda^F

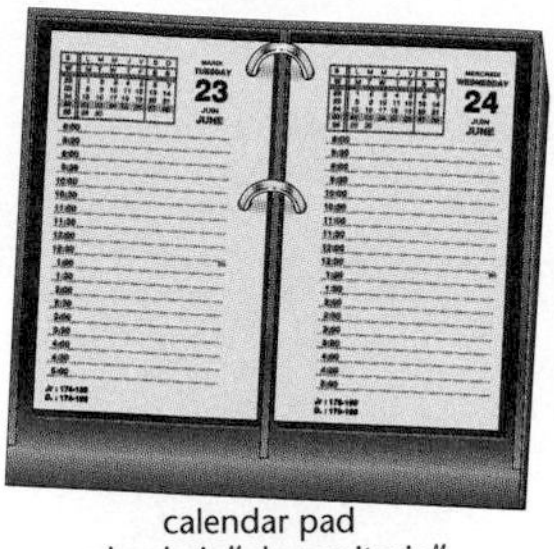

calendar pad
calendario^M de escritorio^M

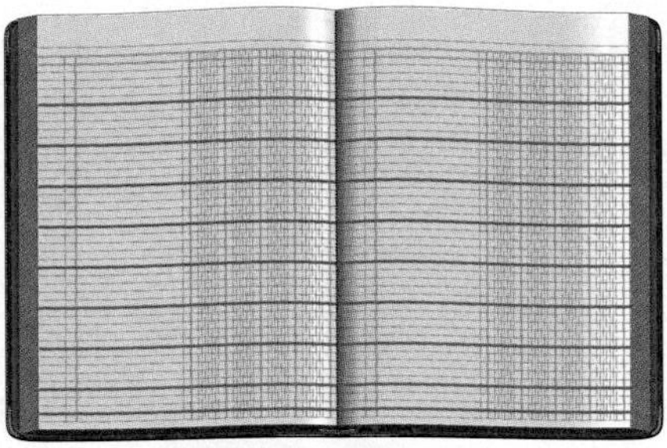

account book
agenda^F de caja^F

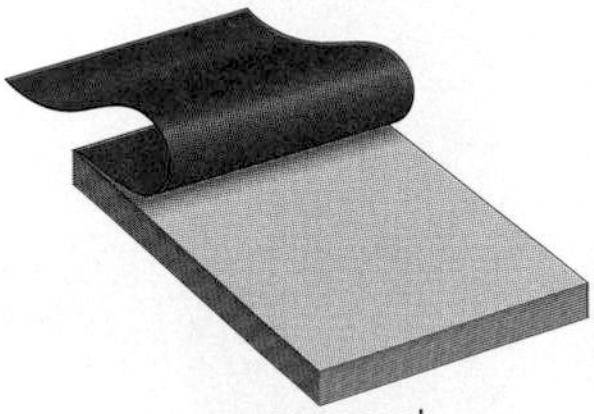

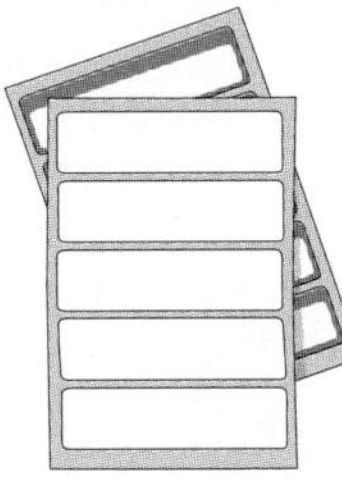

self-adhesive labels
etiquetas^F adhesivas

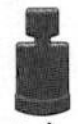

memo pad
libreta^F

tab
indicador^M

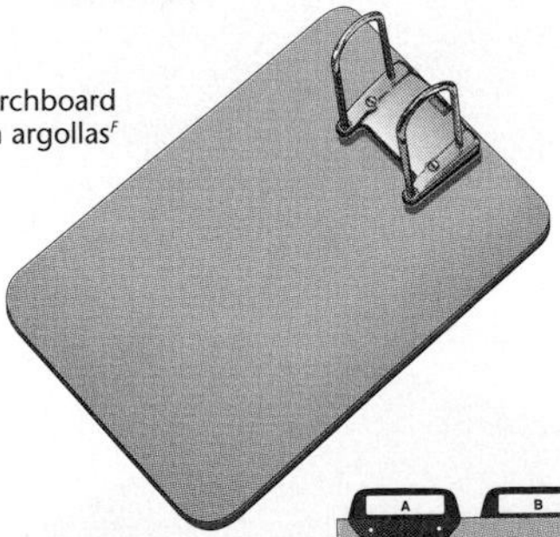

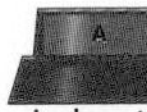

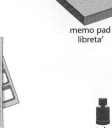

window tab
indicador^M transparente

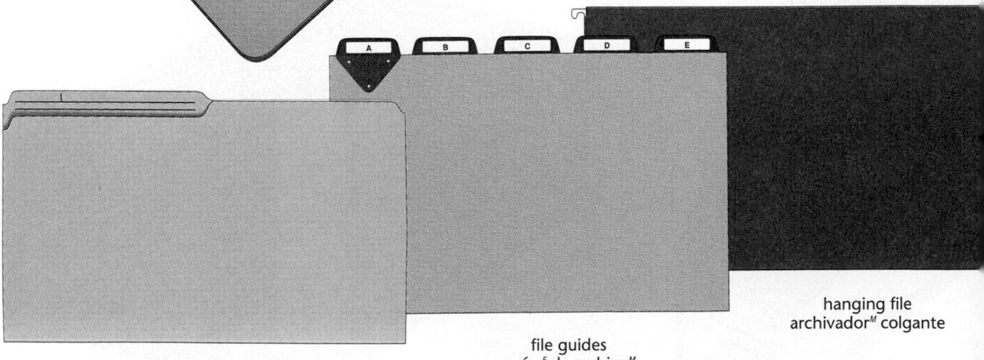

archboard
tabla^F con argollas^F

hanging file
archivador^M colgante

file guides
guías^F de archivo^M

folder
carpeta^F de archivo^M

518

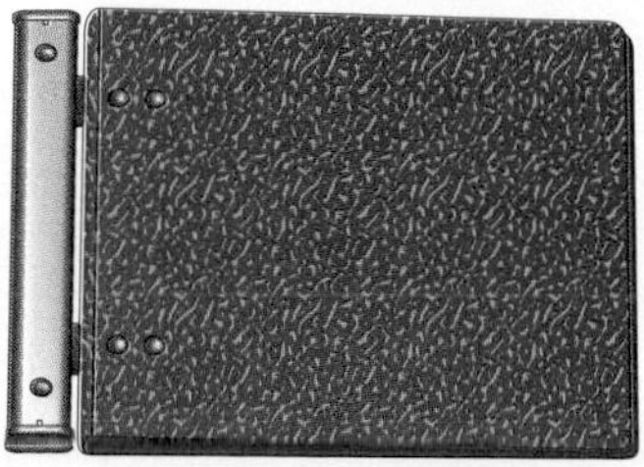

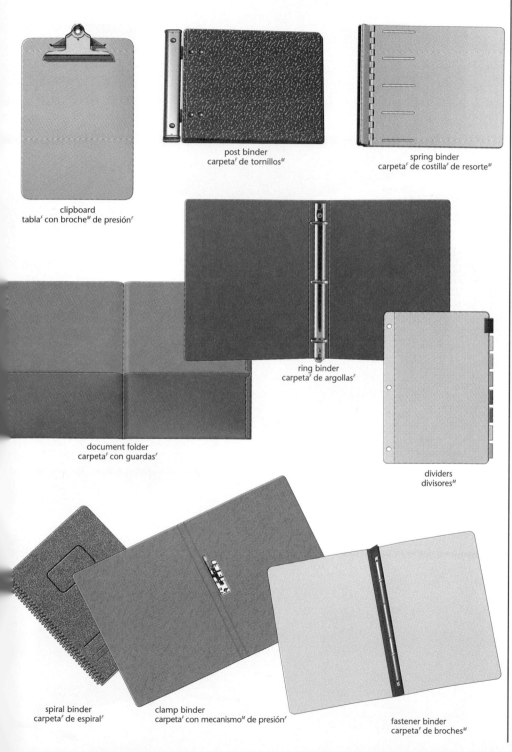

post binder
carpeta^F de tornillos^M

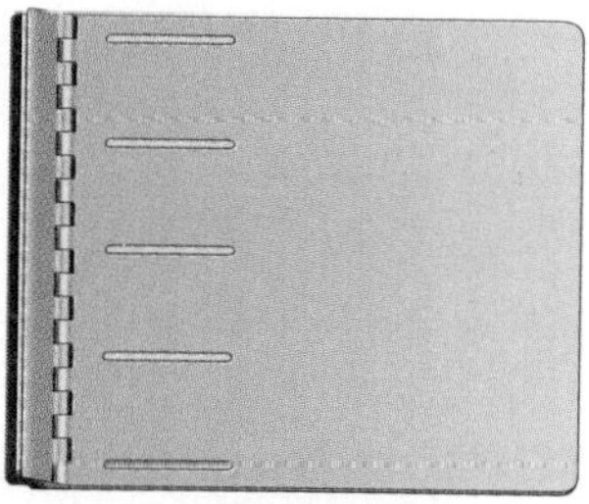

spring binder
carpeta^F de costilla^F de resorte^M

clipboard
tabla^F con broche^M de presión^F

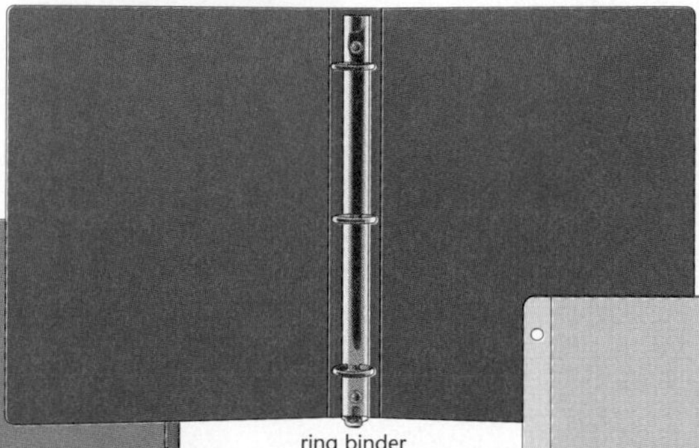

ring binder
carpeta^F de argollas^F

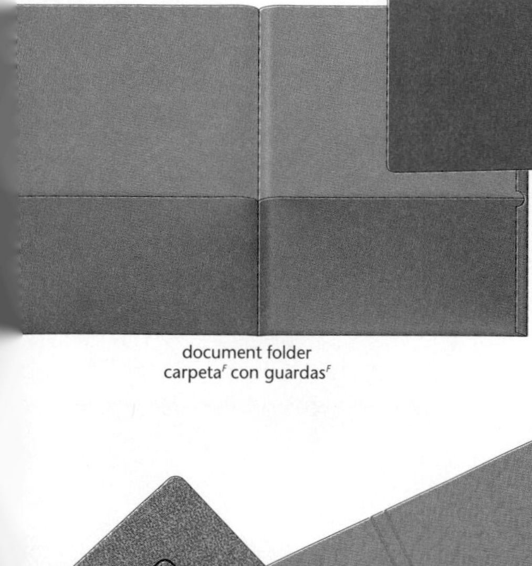

document folder
carpeta^F con guardas^F

dividers
divisores^M

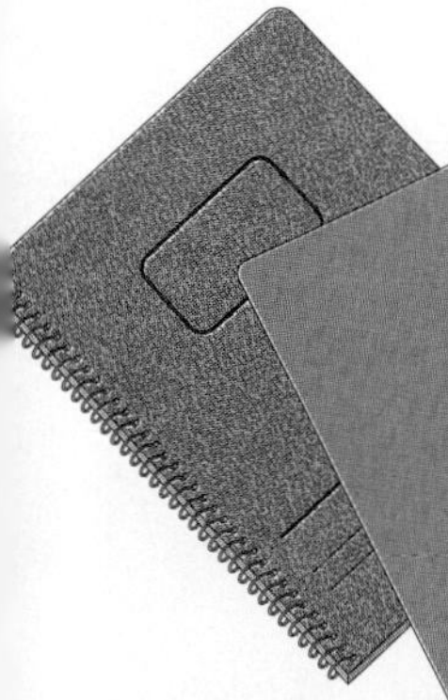

spiral binder
carpeta^F de espiral^F

clamp binder
carpeta^F con mecanismo^M de presión^F

fastener binder
carpeta^F de broches^M

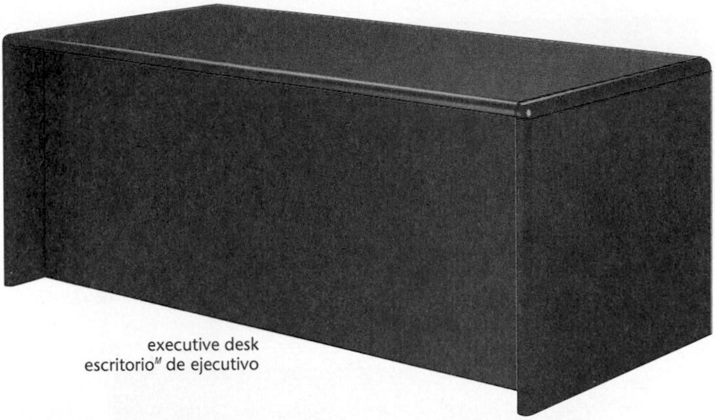

executive desk
escritorio^M de ejecutivo

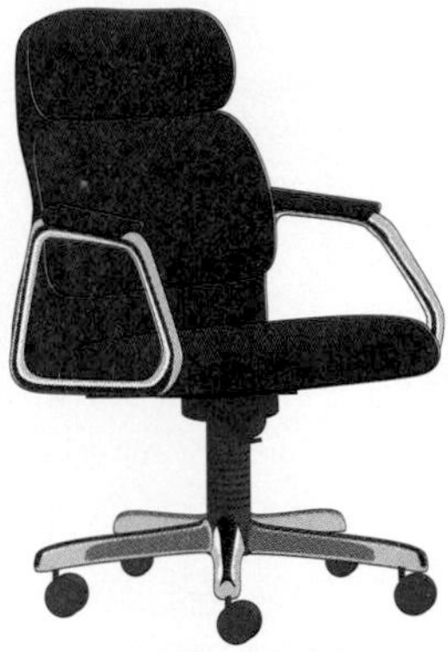

swivel-tilter armchair
sillón^M giratorio

desk mat
carpeta^F

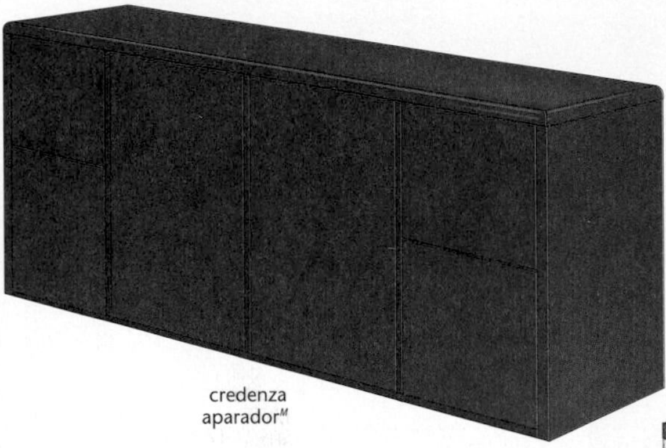

credenza
aparador^M

partition
biombo^M

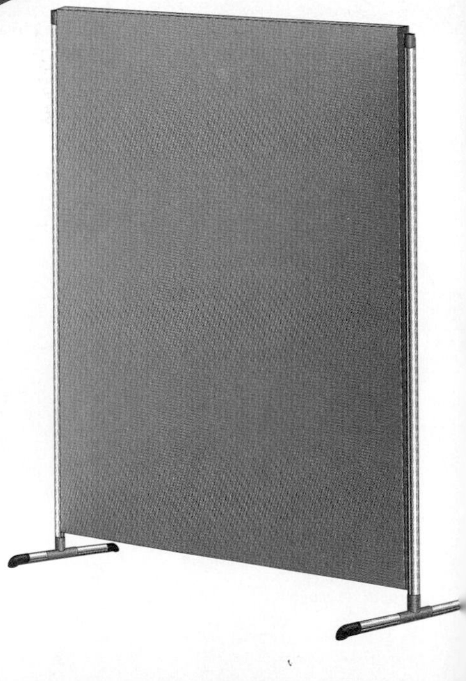

lateral filing cabinet
archivero^M lateral

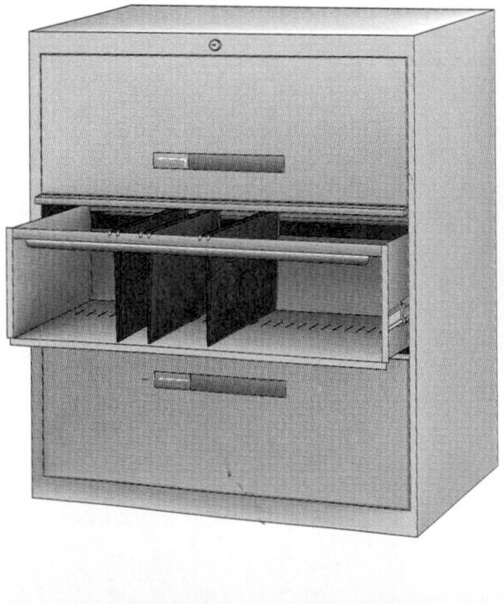

COMPUTER TABLE
MESA^F DEL COMPUTADOR^M

PRINTER TABLE
MESA^F DE LA IMPRESORA^F

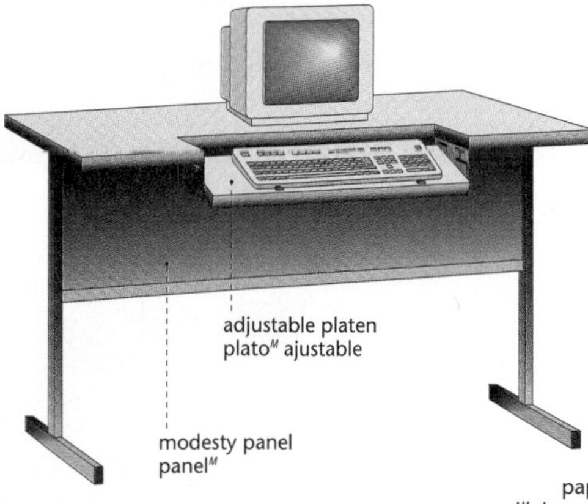

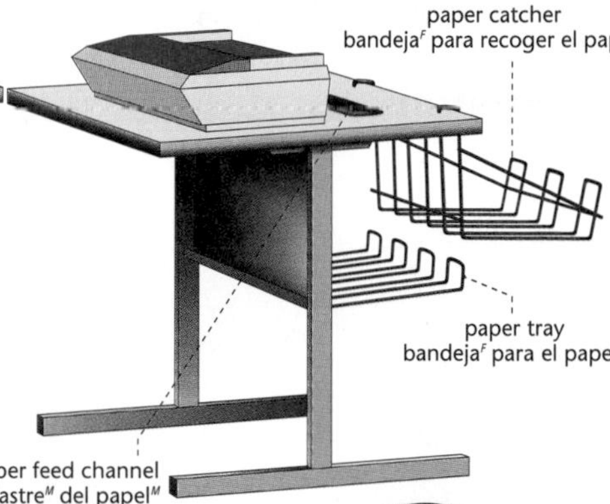

paper catcher
bandeja^F para recoger el papel^M

adjustable platen
plato^M ajustable

modesty panel
panel^M

paper feed channel
canal^M de arrastre^M del papel^M

paper tray
bandeja^F para el papel^M

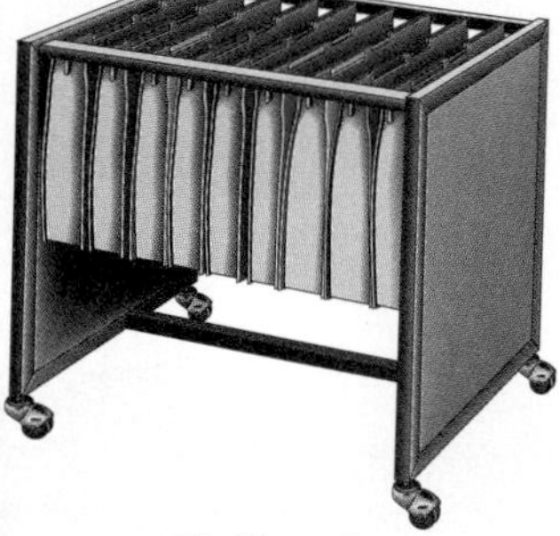

mobile filing unit
archivo^M movible

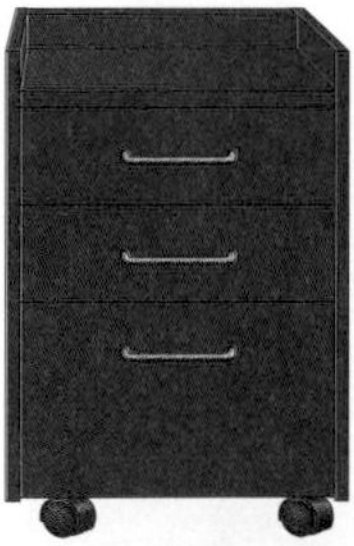

mobile drawer unit
archivador^M movible con cajones^M

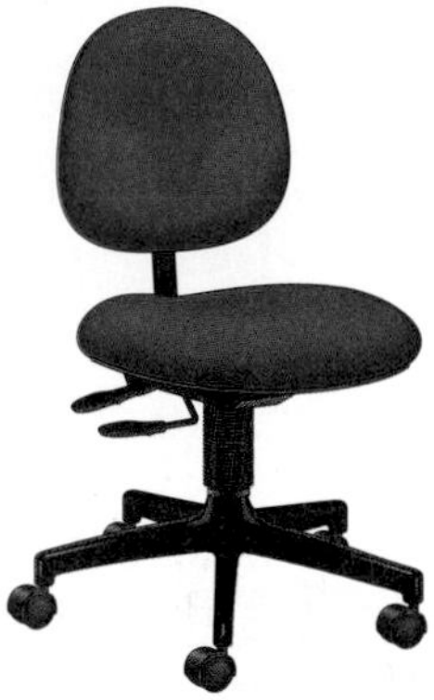

typist's chair
silla^F de secretaria^F

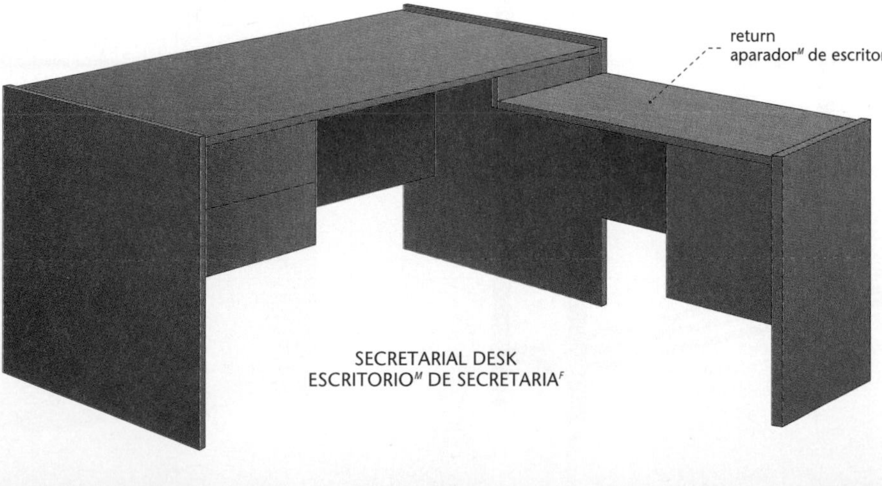

return
aparador^M de escritorio^M

SECRETARIAL DESK
ESCRITORIO^M DE SECRETARIA^F

display cabinet
estante^M para revistas^F

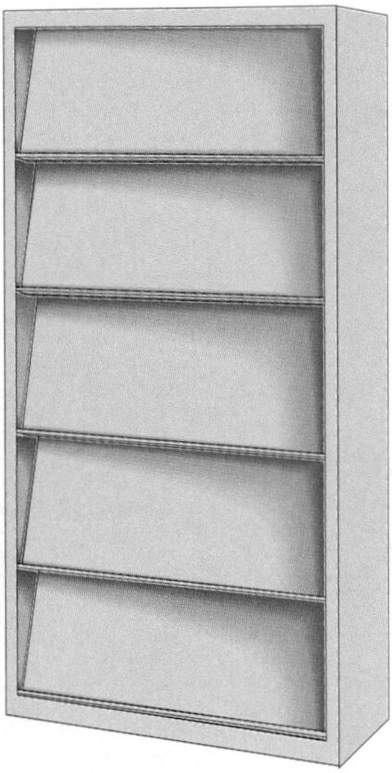

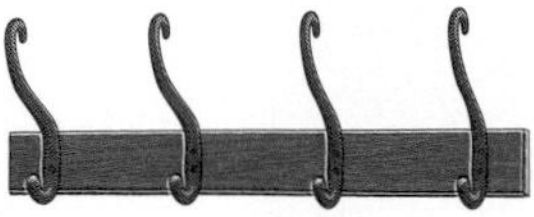

coat hook
perchero^M de pared^F

stationery cabinet
gabinete^M para papelería^F

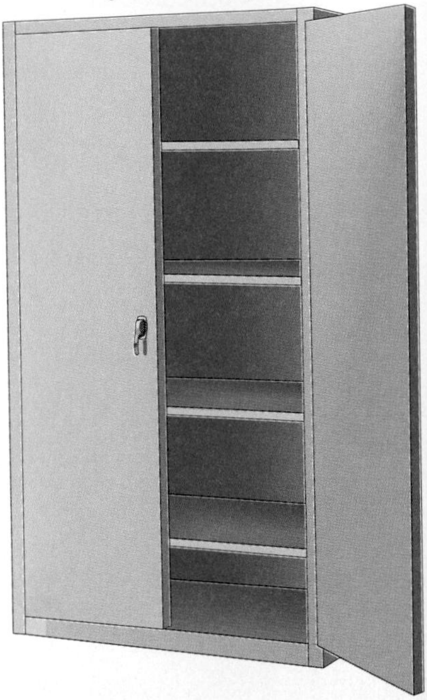

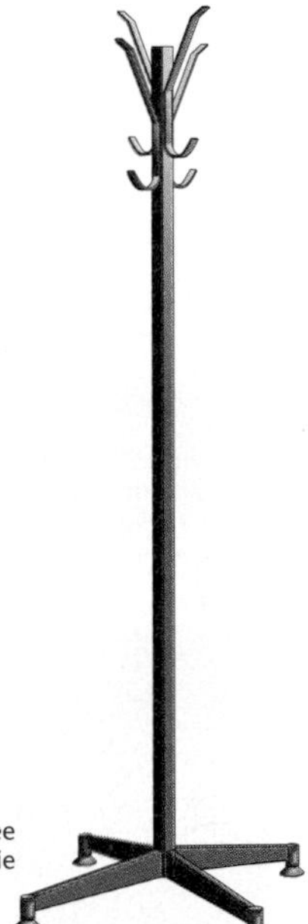

coat tree
perchero^M de pie

locker
armario^M

coat rack
perchero^M

522

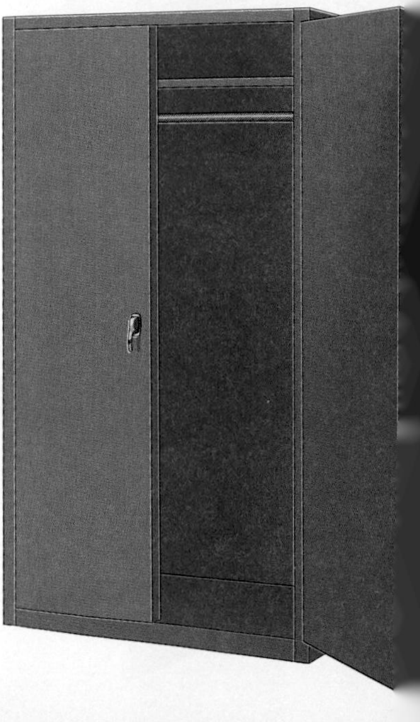

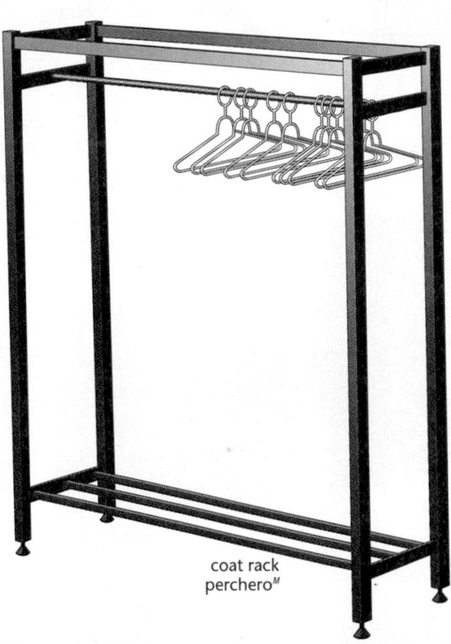

CALCULATOR
CALCULADORAS^F

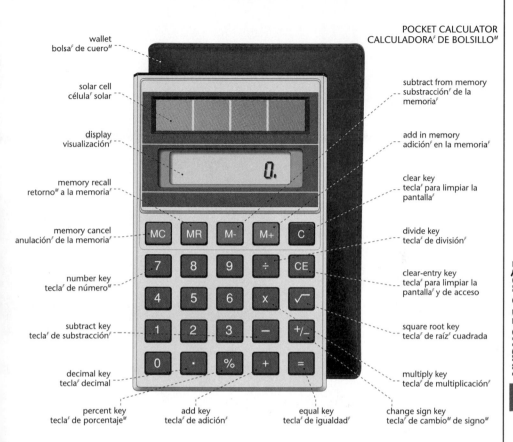

wallet
bolsa^F de cuero^M

solar cell
célula^F solar

display
visualización^F

memory recall
retorno^M a la memoria^F

memory cancel
anulación^F de la memoria^F

number key
tecla^F de número^M

subtract key
tecla^F de substracción^F

decimal key
tecla^F decimal

subtract from memory
substracción^F de la memoria^F

add in memory
adición^F en la memoria^F

clear key
tecla^F para limpiar la pantalla^F

divide key
tecla^F de división^F

clear-entry key
tecla^F para limpiar la pantalla^F y de acceso

square root key
tecla^F de raíz^F cuadrada

multiply key
tecla^F de multiplicación^F

percent key
tecla^F de porcentaje^M

add key
tecla^F de adición^F

equal key
tecla^F de igualdad^F

change sign key
tecla^F de cambio^M de signo^M

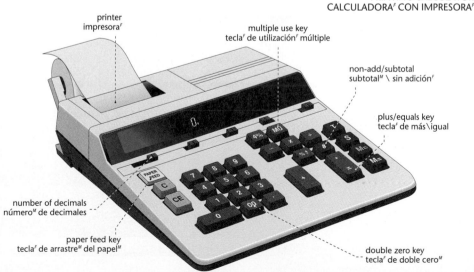

printer
impresora^F

multiple use key
tecla^F de utilización^F múltiple

non-add/subtotal
subtotal^M \ sin adición^F

plus/equals key
tecla^F de más\igual

number of decimals
número^M de decimales

paper feed key
tecla^F de arrastre^M del papel^M

double zero key
tecla^F de doble cero^M

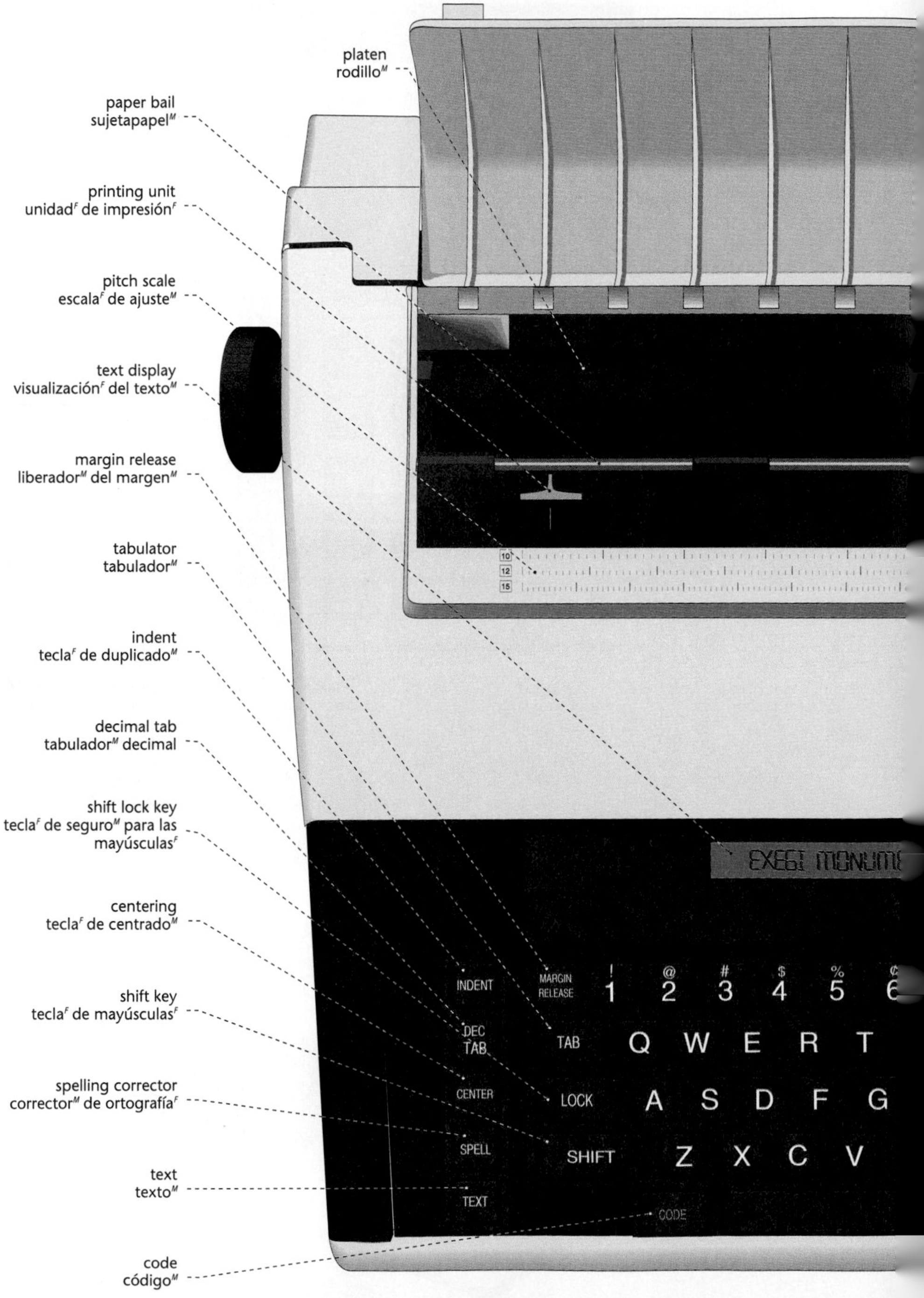

platen
rodillo^M

paper bail
sujetapapel^M

printing unit
unidad^F de impresión^F

pitch scale
escala^F de ajuste^M

text display
visualización^F del texto^M

margin release
liberador^M del margen^M

tabulator
tabulador^M

indent
tecla^F de duplicado^M

decimal tab
tabulador^M decimal

shift lock key
tecla^F de seguro^M para las
mayúsculas^F

centering
tecla^F de centrado^M

shift key
tecla^F de mayúsculas^F

spelling corrector
corrector^M de ortografía^F

text
texto^M

code
código^M

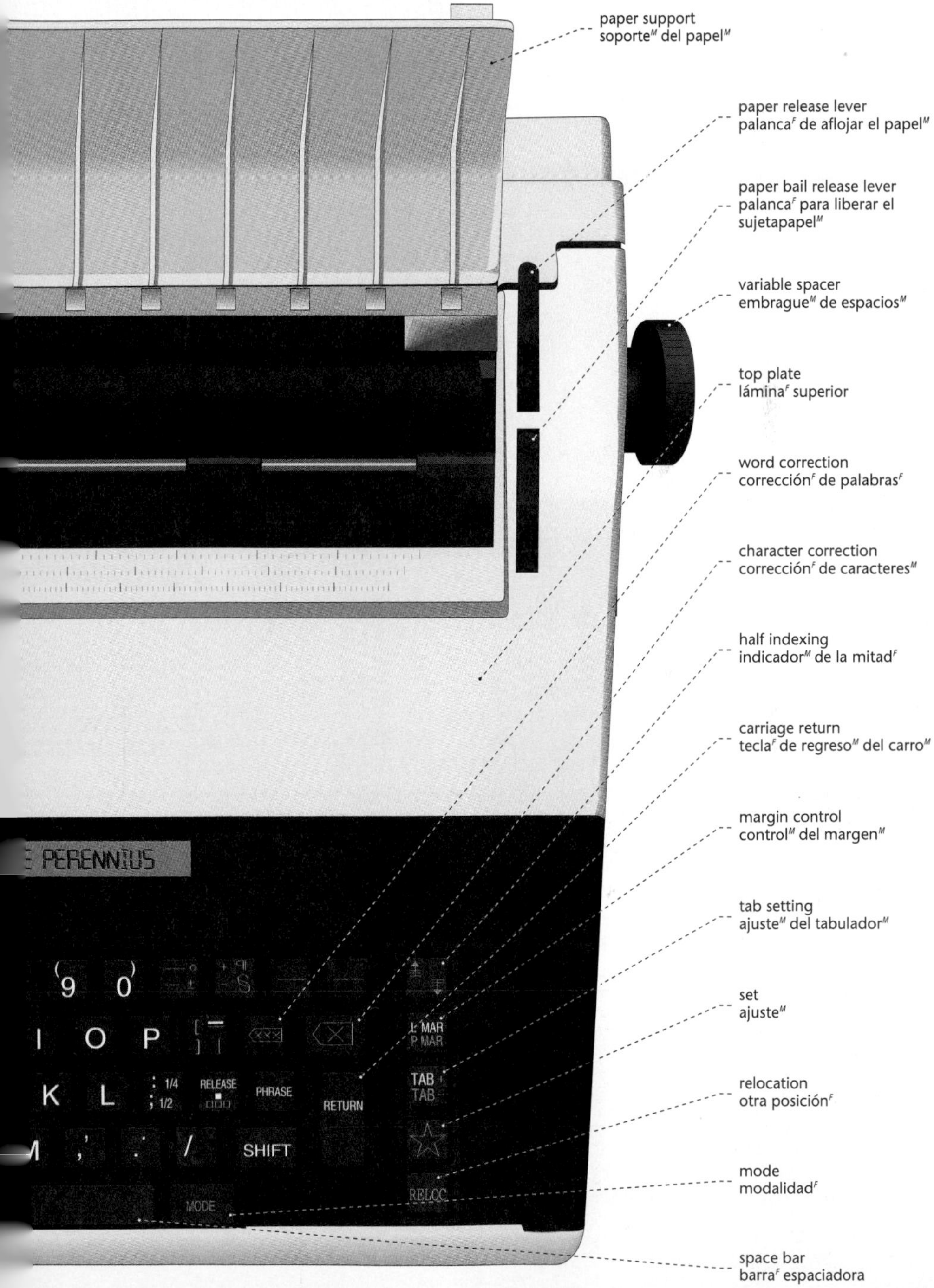

paper support
soporte^M del papel^M

paper release lever
palanca^F de aflojar el papel^M

paper bail release lever
palanca^F para liberar el
sujetapapel^M

variable spacer
embrague^M de espacios^M

top plate
lámina^F superior

word correction
corrección^F de palabras^F

character correction
corrección^F de caracteres^M

half indexing
indicador^M de la mitad^F

carriage return
tecla^F de regreso^M del carro^M

margin control
control^M del margen^M

tab setting
ajuste^M del tabulador^M

set
ajuste^M

relocation
otra posición^F

mode
modalidad^F

space bar
barra^F espaciadora

PERENNIUS

CONFIGURATION OF AN OFFICE AUTOMATION SYSTEM
CONFIGURACIÓN*F* DEL SISTEMA*M* DE UNA OFICINA*F* AUTOMATIZADA

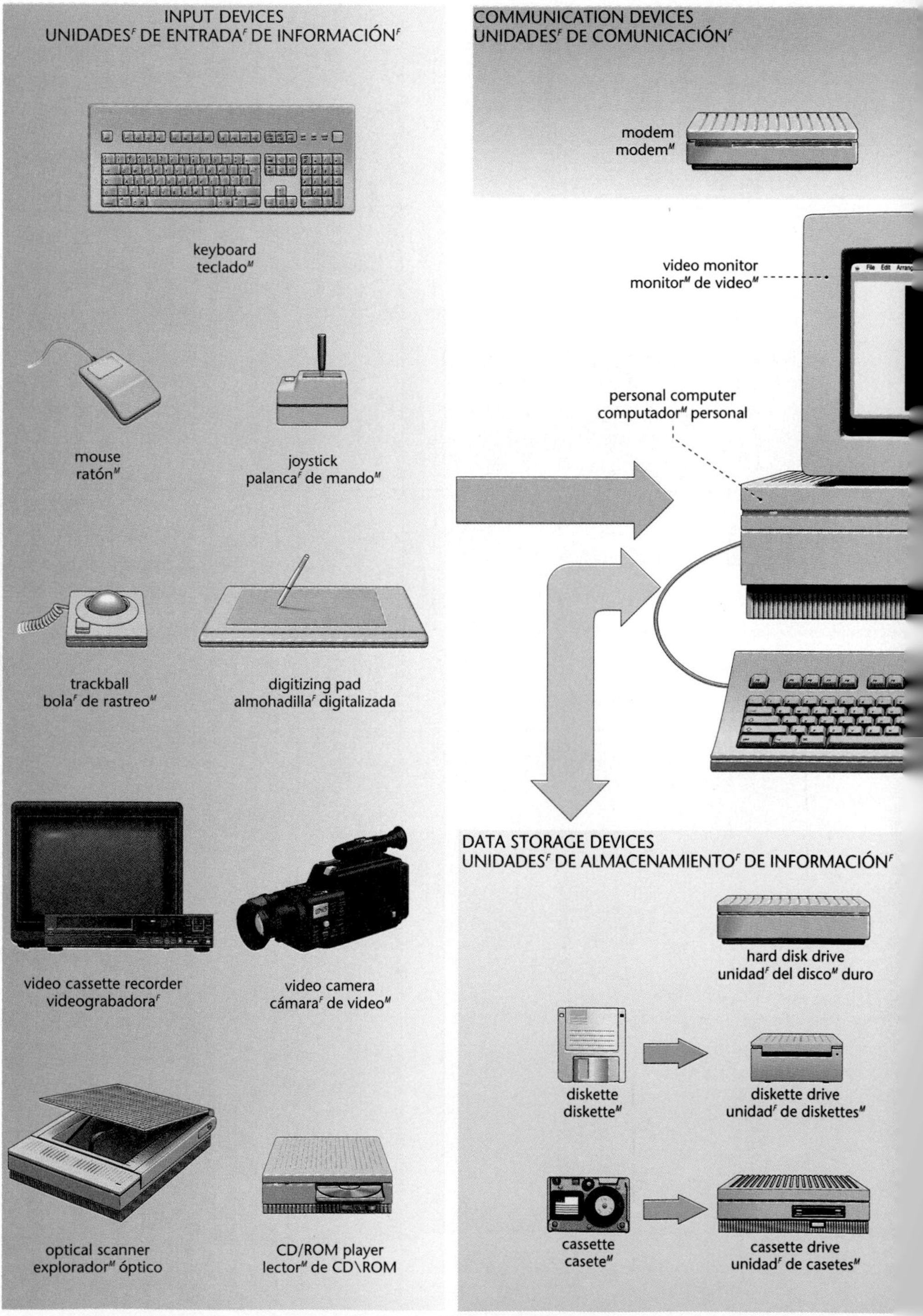

OFFICE AUTOMATION
AUTOMATIZACIÓN DE LA OFICINA

INPUT DEVICES
UNIDADES*F* DE ENTRADA*F* DE INFORMACIÓN*F*

keyboard
teclado*M*

mouse
ratón*M*

joystick
palanca*F* de mando*M*

trackball
bola*F* de rastreo*M*

digitizing pad
almohadilla*F* digitalizada

video cassette recorder
videograbadora*F*

video camera
cámara*F* de video*M*

optical scanner
explorador*M* óptico

CD/ROM player
lector*M* de CD\ROM

COMMUNICATION DEVICES
UNIDADES*F* DE COMUNICACIÓN*F*

modem
modem*M*

video monitor
monitor*M* de video*M*

personal computer
computador*M* personal

DATA STORAGE DEVICES
UNIDADES*F* DE ALMACENAMIENTO*F* DE INFORMACIÓN*F*

hard disk drive
unidad*F* del disco*M* duro

diskette
diskette*M*

diskette drive
unidad*F* de diskettes*M*

cassette
casete*M*

cassette drive
unidad*F* de casetes*M*

526

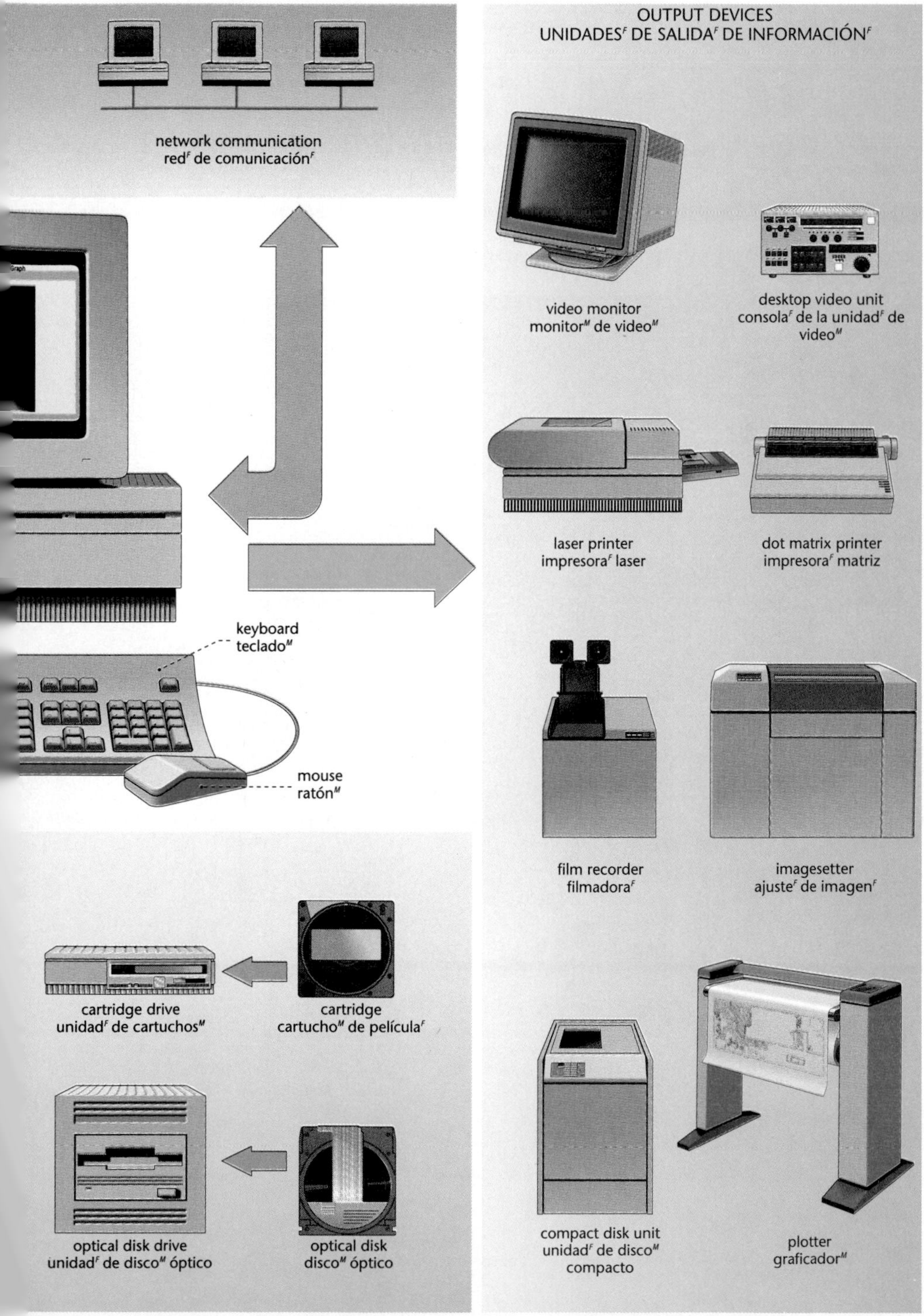

network communication
red^F de comunicación^F

OUTPUT DEVICES
UNIDADES^F DE SALIDA^F DE INFORMACIÓN^F

video monitor
monitor^M de video^M

desktop video unit
consola^F de la unidad^F de video^M

laser printer
impresora^F laser

dot matrix printer
impresora^F matriz

keyboard
teclado^M

mouse
ratón^M

film recorder
filmadora^F

imagesetter
ajuste^F de imagen^F

cartridge drive
unidad^F de cartuchos^M

cartridge
cartucho^M de película^F

optical disk drive
unidad^F de disco^M óptico

optical disk
disco^M óptico

compact disk unit
unidad^F de disco^M compacto

plotter
graficador^M

527

BASIC COMPONENTS
COMPONENTES^M BÁSICOS

PERSONAL COMPUTER (VIEW FROM ABOVE)
VISTA^F POR ENCIMA DE UN COMPUTADOR^M PERSONAL

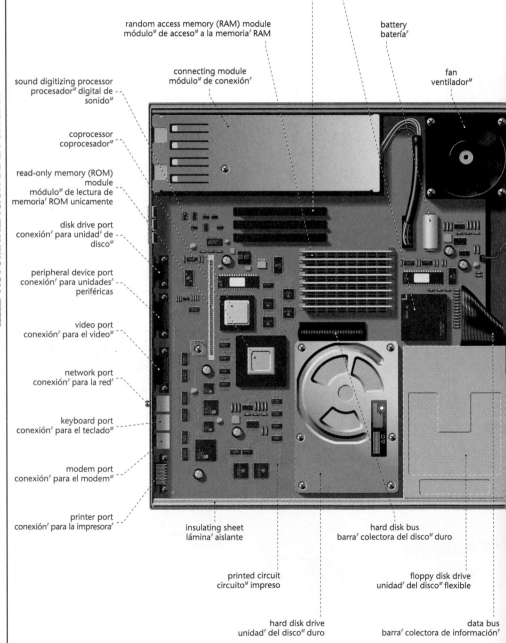

expansion connector
conector^M de expansión^F

microprocessor
microprocesador^M

random access memory (RAM) module
módulo^M de acceso^M a la memoria^F RAM

battery
batería^F

connecting module
módulo^M de conexión^F

fan
ventilador^M

sound digitizing processor
procesador^M digital de
sonido^M

coprocessor
coprocesador^M

read-only memory (ROM)
module
módulo^M de lectura de
memoria^F ROM unicamente

disk drive port
conexión^F para unidad^F de
disco^M

peripheral device port
conexión^F para unidades^F
periféricas

video port
conexión^F para el video^M

network port
conexión^F para la red^F

keyboard port
conexión^F para el teclado^M

modem port
conexión^F para el modem^M

printer port
conexión^F para la impresora^F

insulating sheet
lámina^F aislante

hard disk bus
barra^F colectora del disco^M duro

printed circuit
circuito^M impreso

floppy disk drive
unidad^F del disco^M flexible

hard disk drive
unidad^F del disco^M duro

data bus
barra^F colectora de información^F

528

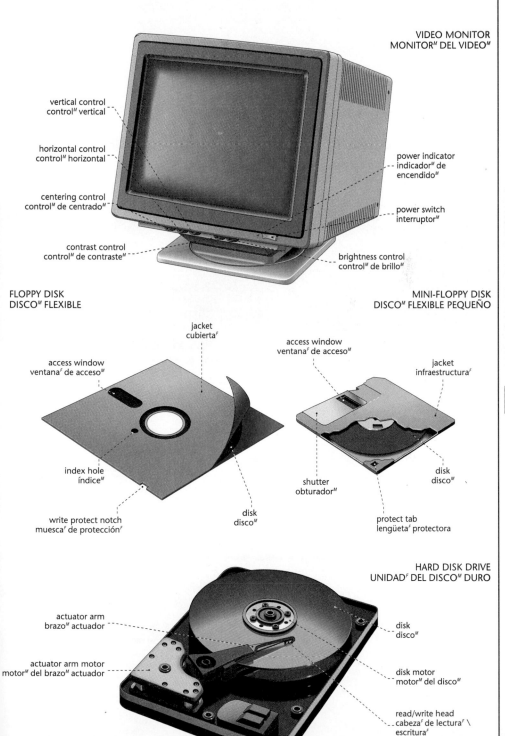

VIDEO MONITOR
MONITOR^M DEL VIDEO^M

vertical control
control^M vertical

horizontal control
control^M horizontal

centering control
control^M de centrado^M

contrast control
control^M de contraste^M

power indicator
indicador^M de
encendido^M

power switch
interruptor^M

brightness control
control^M de brillo^M

FLOPPY DISK
DISCO^M FLEXIBLE

MINI-FLOPPY DISK
DISCO^M FLEXIBLE PEQUEÑO

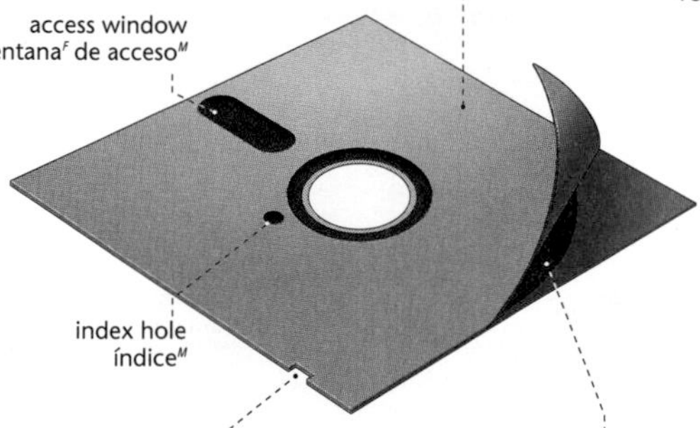

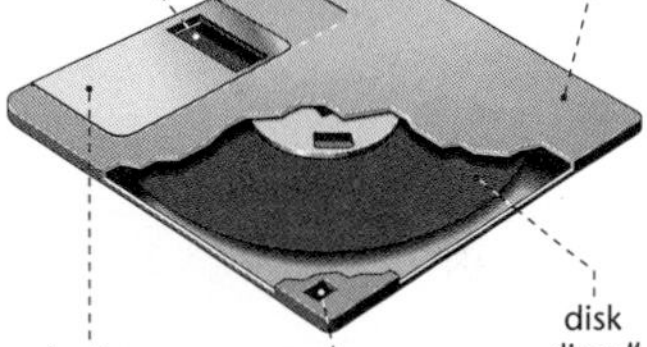

jacket
cubierta^F

access window
ventana^F de acceso^M

access window
ventana^F de acceso^M

jacket
infraestructura^F

index hole
índice^M

disk
disco^M

shutter
obturador^M

write protect notch
muesca^F de protección^F

disk
disco^M

protect tab
lengüeta^F protectora

HARD DISK DRIVE
UNIDAD^F DEL DISCO^M DURO

actuator arm
brazo^M actuador

disk
disco^M

actuator arm motor
motor^M del brazo^M actuador

disk motor
motor^M del disco^M

read/write head
cabeza^F de lectura^F \
escritura^F

529

BASIC COMPONENTS
COMPONENTES^M BÁSICOS

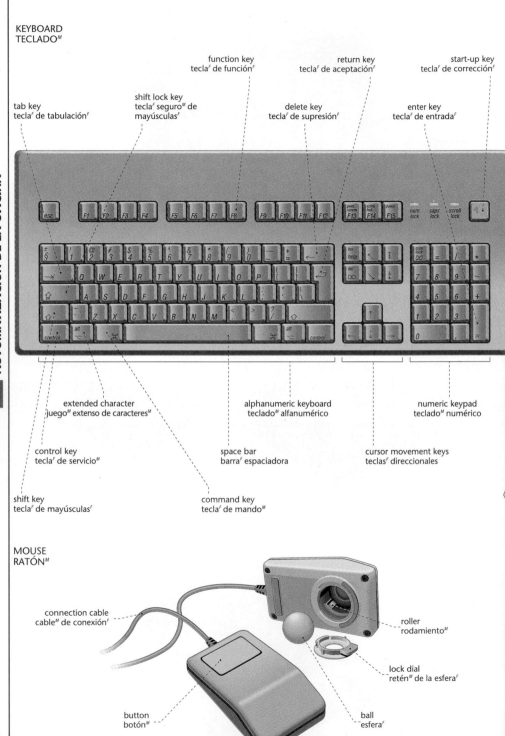

KEYBOARD
TECLADO^M

function key
tecla^F de función^F

return key
tecla^F de aceptación^F

start-up key
tecla^F de corrección^F

shift lock key
tecla^F seguro^M de
mayúsculas^F

delete key
tecla^F de supresión^F

enter key
tecla^F de entrada^F

tab key
tecla^F de tabulación^F

extended character
juego^M extenso de caracteres^M

alphanumeric keyboard
teclado^M alfanumérico

numeric keypad
teclado^M numérico

control key
tecla^F de servicio^M

space bar
barra^F espaciadora

cursor movement keys
teclas^F direccionales

shift key
tecla^F de mayúsculas^F

command key
tecla^F de mando^M

MOUSE
RATÓN^M

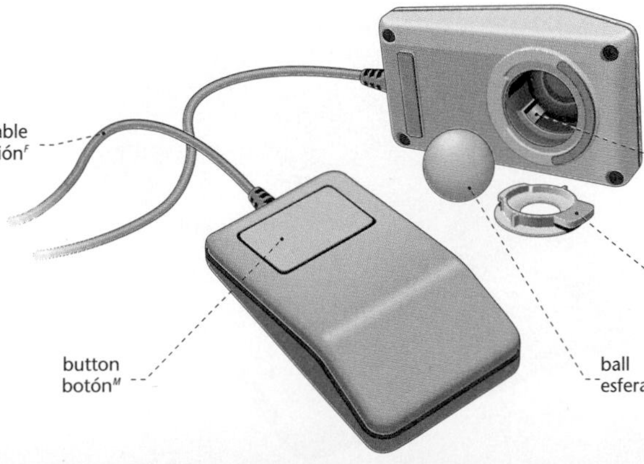

connection cable
cable^M de conexión^F

roller
rodamiento^M

lock dial
retén^M de la esfera^F

button
botón^M

ball
esfera^F

530

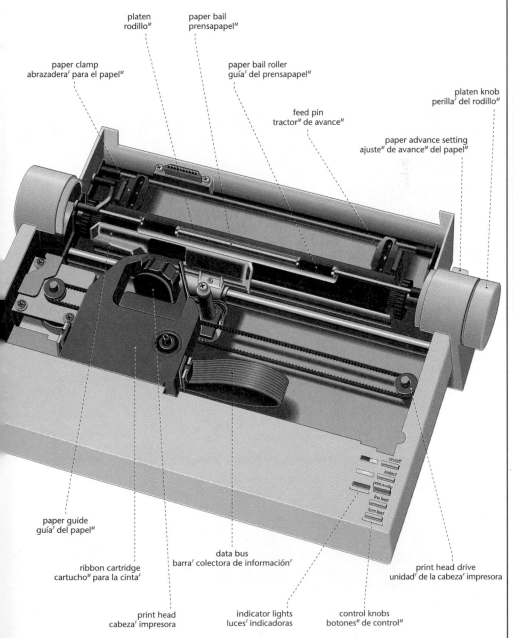

platen
rodillo^M

paper bail
prensapapel^M

paper clamp
abrazadera^F para el papel^M

paper bail roller
guía^F del prensapapel^M

platen knob
perilla^F del rodillo^M

feed pin
tractor^M de avance^M

paper advance setting
ajuste^M de avance^M del papel^M

on/off

select

print quality

line feed

form feed

paper guide
guía^F del papel^M

data bus
barra^F colectora de información^F

print head drive
unidad^F de la cabeza^F impresora

ribbon cartridge
cartucho^M para la cinta^F

print head
cabeza^F impresora

indicator lights
luces^F indicadoras

control knobs
botones^M de control^M

PHOTOCOPIER
FOTOCOPIADORA^F

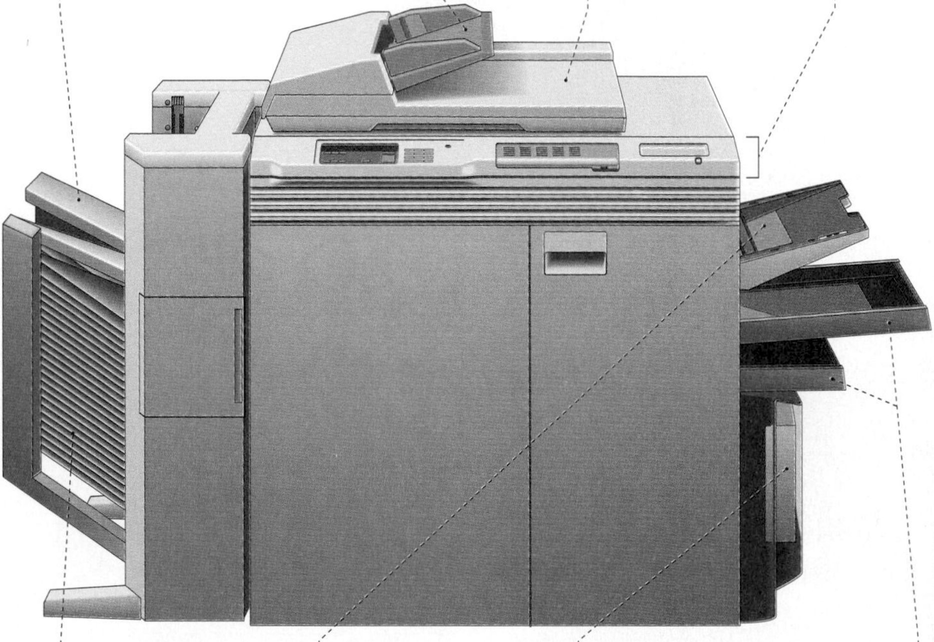

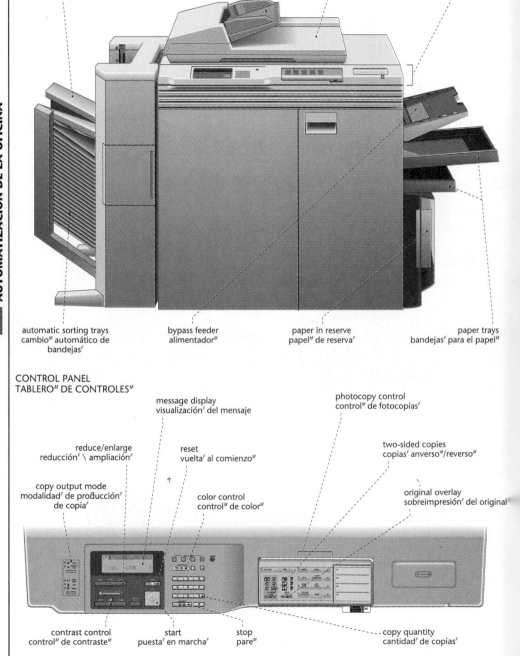

feeder output tray
bandeja^F de arrastre^M de
la producción^F

document handler
manipulador^M de documentos^M

cover
tapa^F

control panel
tablero^M de controles^M

automatic sorting trays
cambio^M automático de
bandejas^F

bypass feeder
alimentador^M

paper in reserve
papel^M de reserva^F

paper trays
bandejas^F para el papel^M

CONTROL PANEL
TABLERO^M DE CONTROLES^M

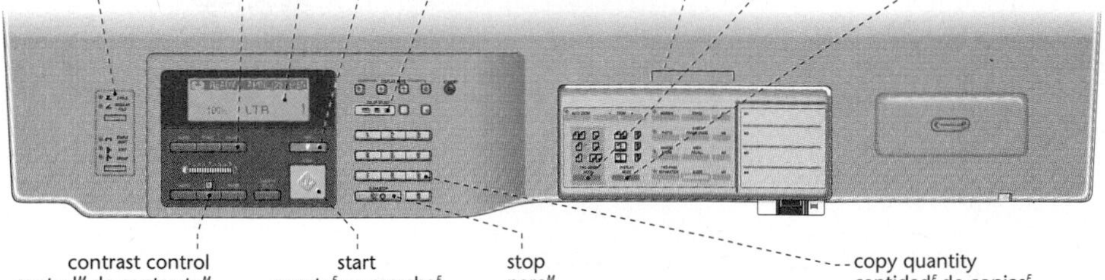

message display
visualización^F del mensaje

photocopy control
control^M de fotocopias^F

reduce/enlarge
reducción^F \ ampliación^F

reset
vuelta^F al comienzo^M

two-sided copies
copias^F anverso^M/reverso^M

copy output mode
modalidad^F de producción^F
de copia^F

color control
control^M de color^M

original overlay
sobreimpresión^F del original^M

contrast control
control^M de contraste^M

start
puesta^F en marcha^F

stop
pare^M

copy quantity
cantidad^F de copias^F

532

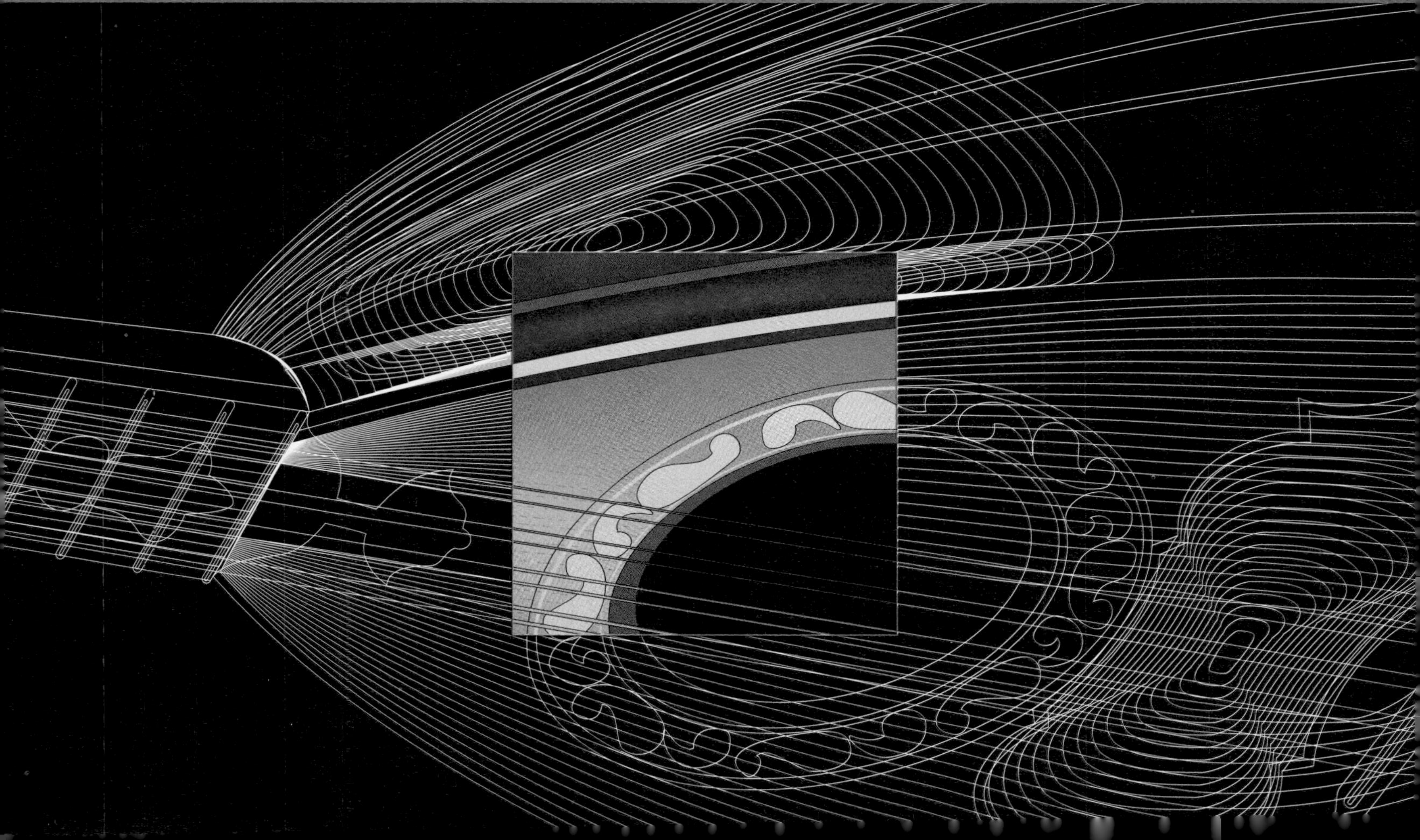

CONTENTS

MUSIC
MÚSICA

TRADITIONAL MUSICAL INSTRUMENTS
INSTRUMENTOS^M MUSICALES TRADICIONALES

ZITHER
CÍTARA^F

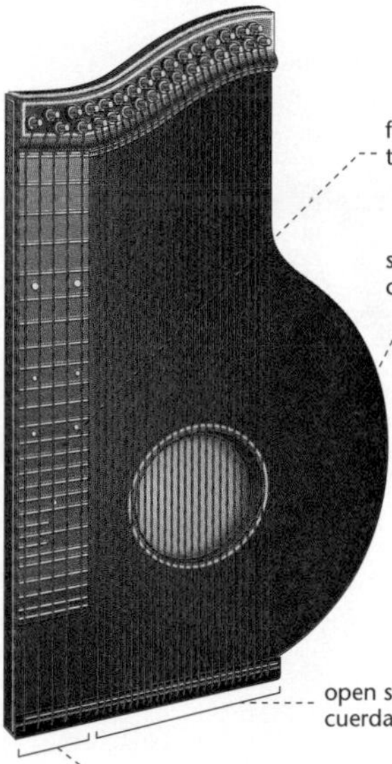

finger board
traste^M

soundboard
caja^F sonora

open strings
cuerdas^F de acompañamiento^M

melody strings
cuerdas^F melódicas

LYRE
LIRA^F

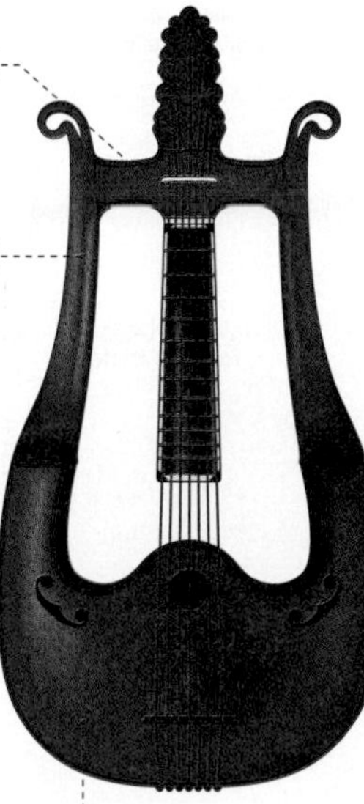

crossbar
travesaño^M

arm
brazo^M

soundboard
caja^F sonora

BALALAIKA
BALALAIKA^F

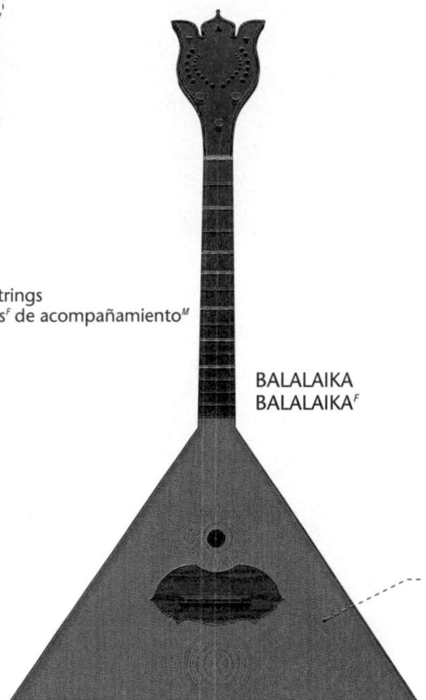

triangular body
caja^F triangular

MANDOLIN
MANDOLINA^F

BANJO
BANJO^M

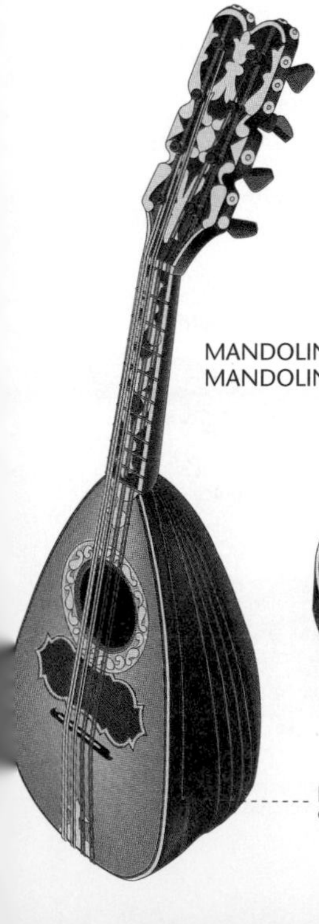

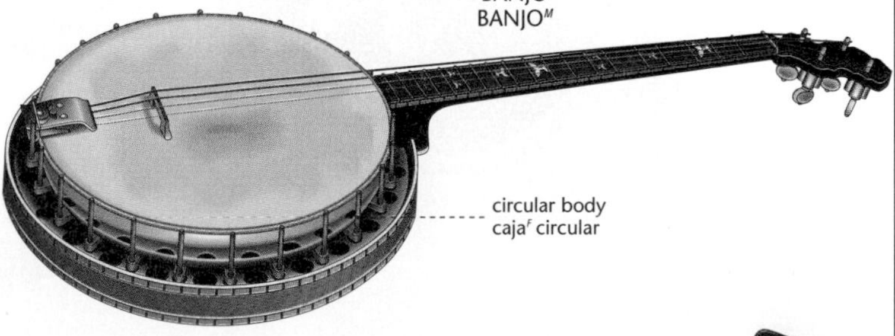

circular body
caja^F circular

pear-shaped body
caja^F media pera^F

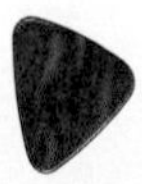

plectrum
plectro^M

ACCORDION
ACORDEÓN*M*

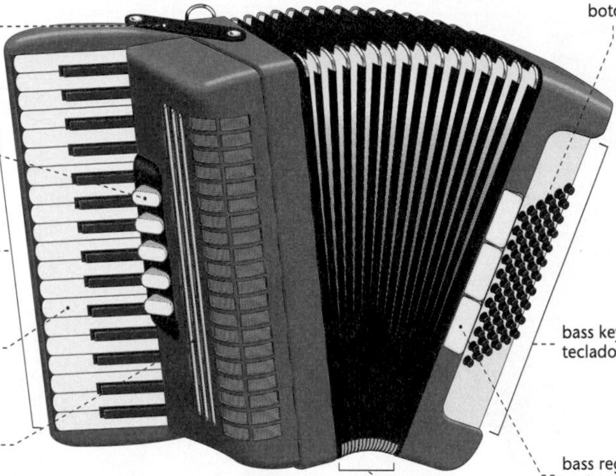

bellows strap
seguro*M* del fuelle*M*

button
botón*M*

treble register
registro*M* de altos*M*

treble keyboard
teclado*M* triple

key
tecla*F*

grille
rejilla*F*

bass keyboard
teclado*M* de los bajos*M*

bass register
registros*M* de los bajos*M*

bellows
doble fuelle*M*

BAGPIPES
GAITA*F*

JEW'S HARP
BIRIMBAO*M*

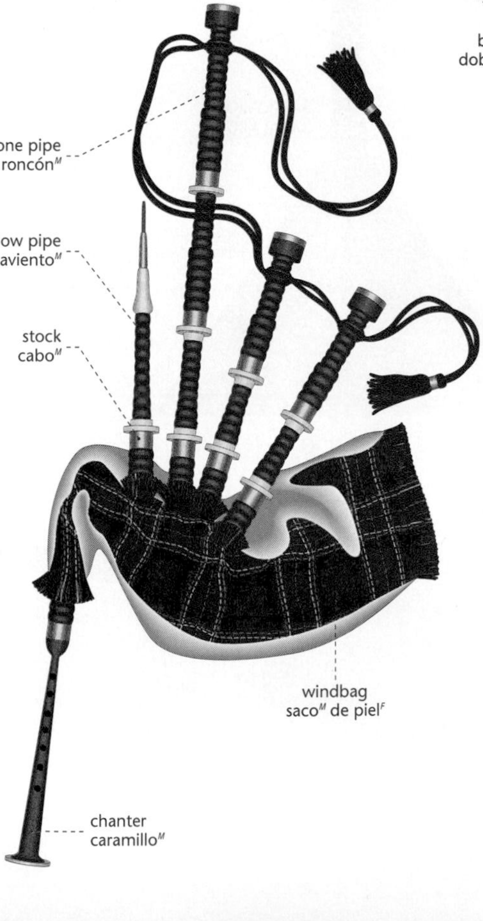

drone pipe
gran roncón*M*

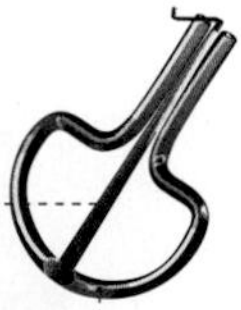

tongue
lengüeta*F* de la caña*F*

blow pipe
portaviento*M*

frame
estructura*F*

stock
cabo*M*

harmonica
armónica*F*

windbag
saco*M* de piel*F*

panpipe
zampoña*F*

chanter
caramillo*M*

MUSIC
MÚSICA

536

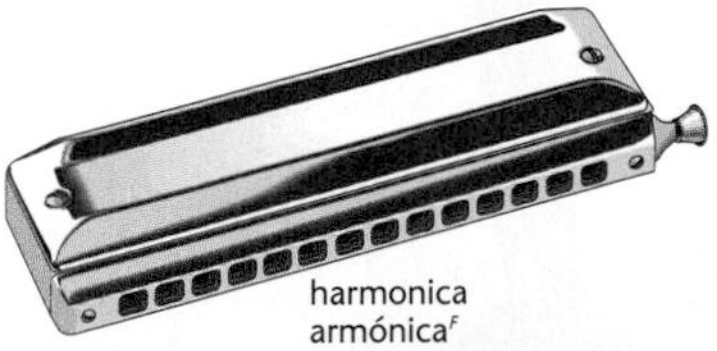

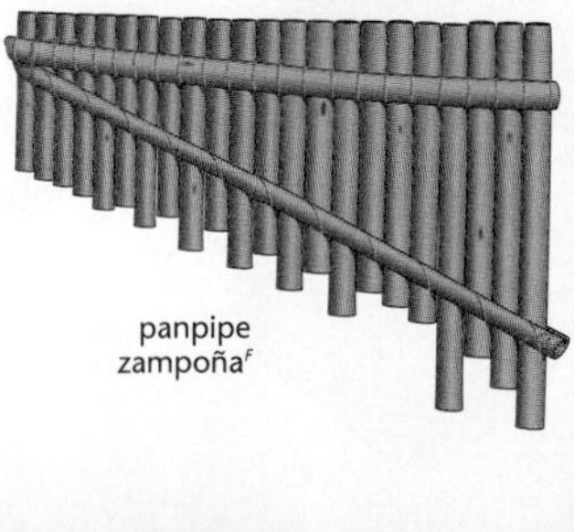

MUSICAL NOTATION
NOTACIÓN^F MUSICAL

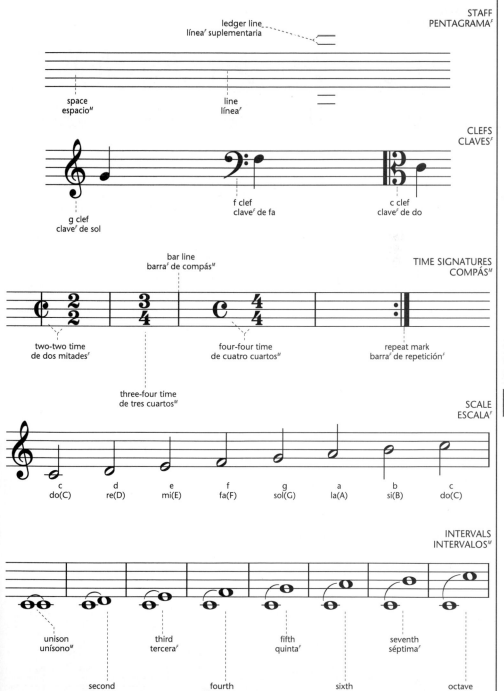

STAFF
PENTAGRAMA^F

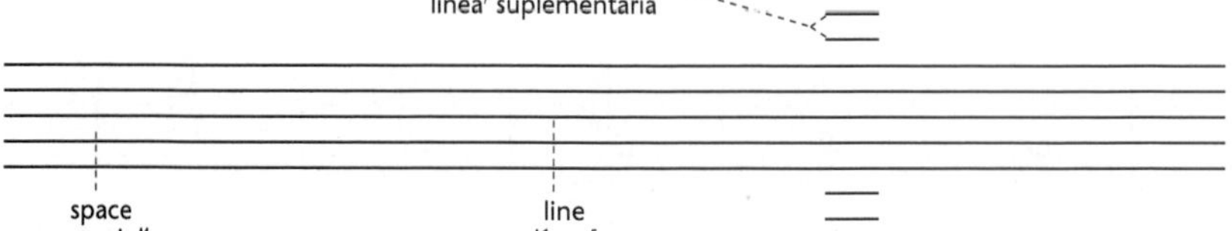

ledger line
línea^F suplementaria

space
espacio^M

line
línea^F

CLEFS
CLAVES^F

f clef
clave^F de fa

c clef
clave^F de do

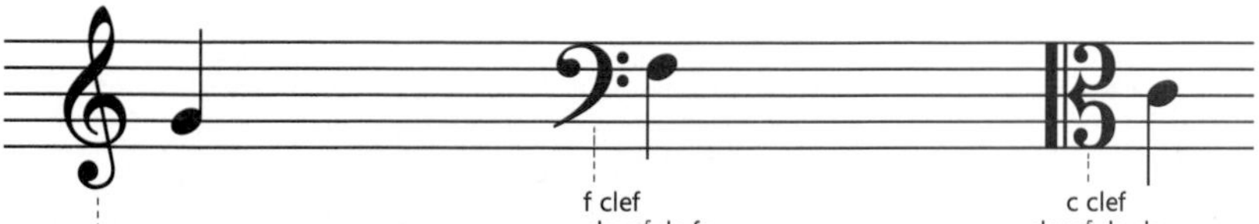

g clef
clave^F de sol

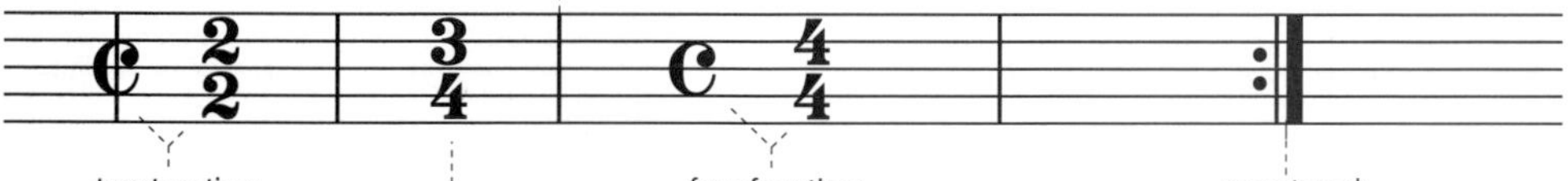

bar line
barra^F de compás^M

TIME SIGNATURES
COMPÁS^M

two-two time
de dos mitades^F

four-four time
de cuatro cuartos^M

repeat mark
barra^F de repetición^F

three-four time
de tres cuartos^M

SCALE
ESCALA^F

c	d	e	f	g	a	b	c
do(C)	re(D)	mi(E)	fa(F)	sol(G)	la(A)	si(B)	do(C)

INTERVALS
INTERVALOS^M

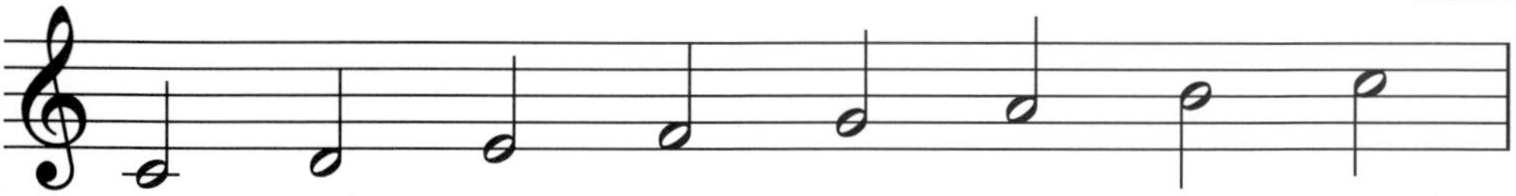

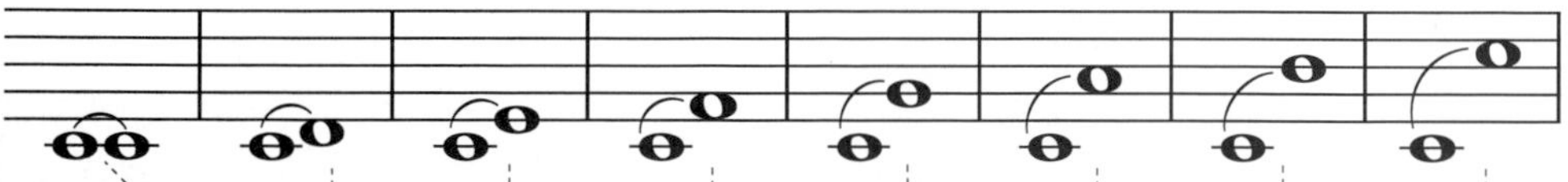

unison
unísono^M

third
tercera^F

fifth
quinta^F

seventh
séptima^F

second
segunda^F

fourth
cuarta^F

sixth
sexta^F

octave
octava^F

MUSICAL NOTATION
NOTACIÓN^F MUSICAL^F

NOTE SYMBOLS
VALORES^M DE LAS NOTAS^F MUSICALES

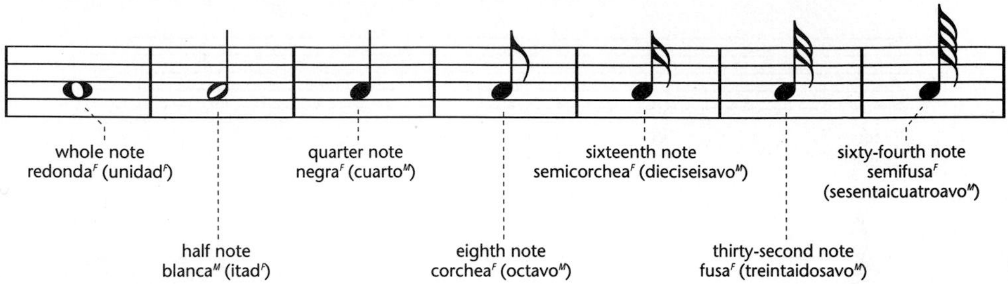

whole note
redonda^F (unidad^F)

quarter note
negra^F (cuarto^M)

sixteenth note
semicorchea^F (dieciseisavo^M)

sixty-fourth note
semifusa^F
(sesentaicuatroavo^M)

half note
blanca^M (itad^F)

eighth note
corchea^F (octavo^M)

thirty-second note
fusa^F (treintaidosavo^M)

REST SYMBOLS
VALORES^M DE LOS SILENCIOS^M

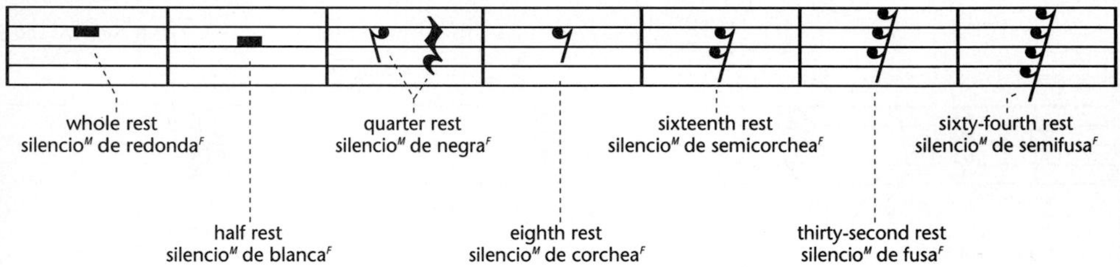

whole rest
silencio^M de redonda^F

quarter rest
silencio^M de negra^F

sixteenth rest
silencio^M de semicorchea^F

sixty-fourth rest
silencio^M de semifusa^F

half rest
silencio^M de blanca^F

eighth rest
silencio^M de corchea^F

thirty-second rest
silencio^M de fusa^F

ACCIDENTALS
ACCIDENTALES^M

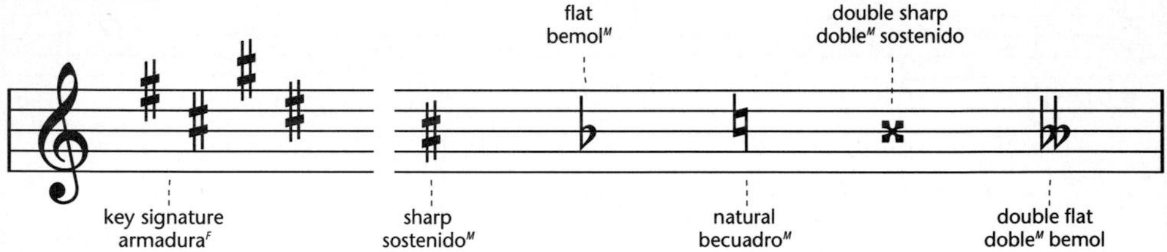

flat
bemol^M

double sharp
doble^M sostenido

key signature
armadura^F

sharp
sostenido^M

natural
becuadro^M

double flat
doble^M bemol

ORNAMENTS
ADORNOS^M

appoggiatura
apoyatura^F

trill
trino^M

turn
grupeto^M

mordent
mordente^M

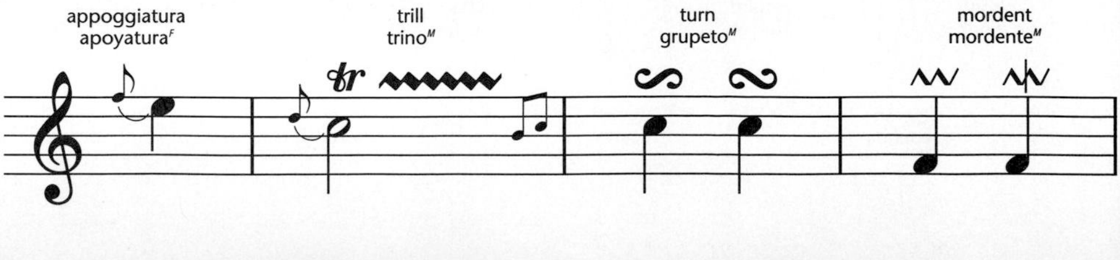

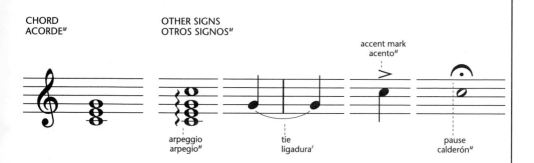

CHORD
ACORDE^M

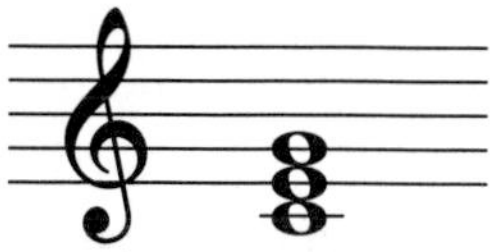

OTHER SIGNS
OTROS SIGNOS^M

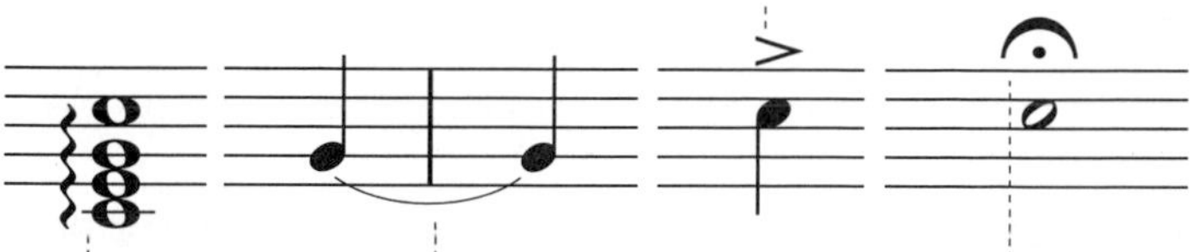

accent mark
acento^M

arpeggio
arpegio^M

tie
ligadura^F

pause
calderón^M

MUSICAL ACCESSORIES
ACCESORIOS^M MUSICALES

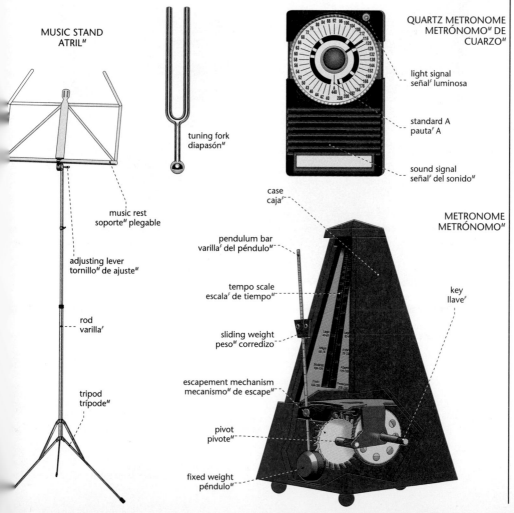

MUSIC STAND
ATRIL^M

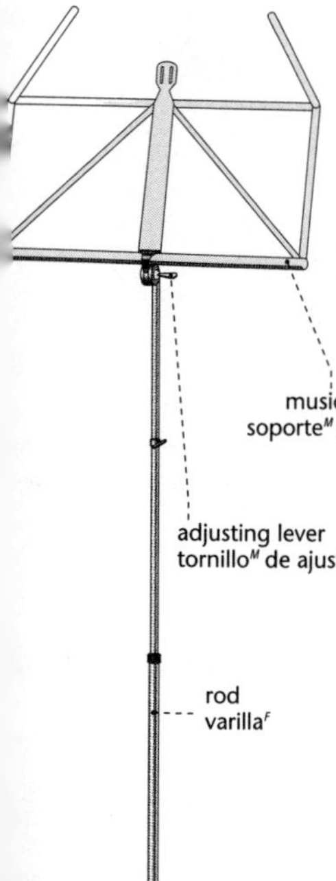

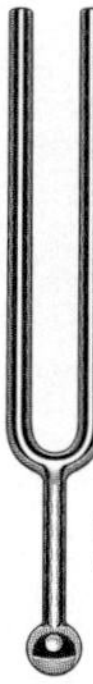

tuning fork
diapasón^M

QUARTZ METRONOME
METRÓNOMO^M DE
CUARZO^M

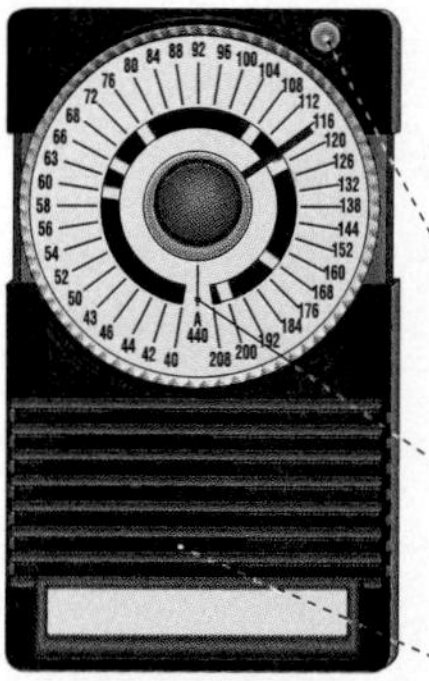

light signal
señal^F luminosa

standard A
pauta^F A

sound signal
señal^F del sonido^M

music rest
soporte^M plegable

case
caja^F

METRONOME
METRÓNOMO^M

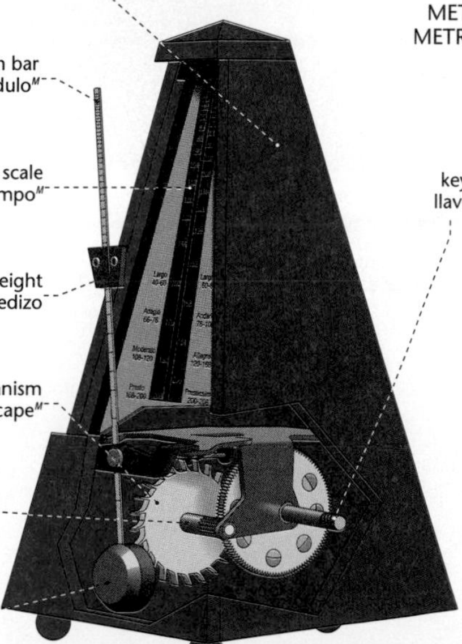

pendulum bar
varilla^F del péndulo^M

adjusting lever
tornillo^M de ajuste^M

tempo scale
escala^F de tiempo^M

key
llave^F

sliding weight
peso^M corredizo

rod
varilla^F

escapement mechanism
mecanismo^M de escape^M

tripod
trípode^M

pivot
pivote^M

fixed weight
péndulo^M

UPRIGHT PIANO
PIANO*M* VERTICAL

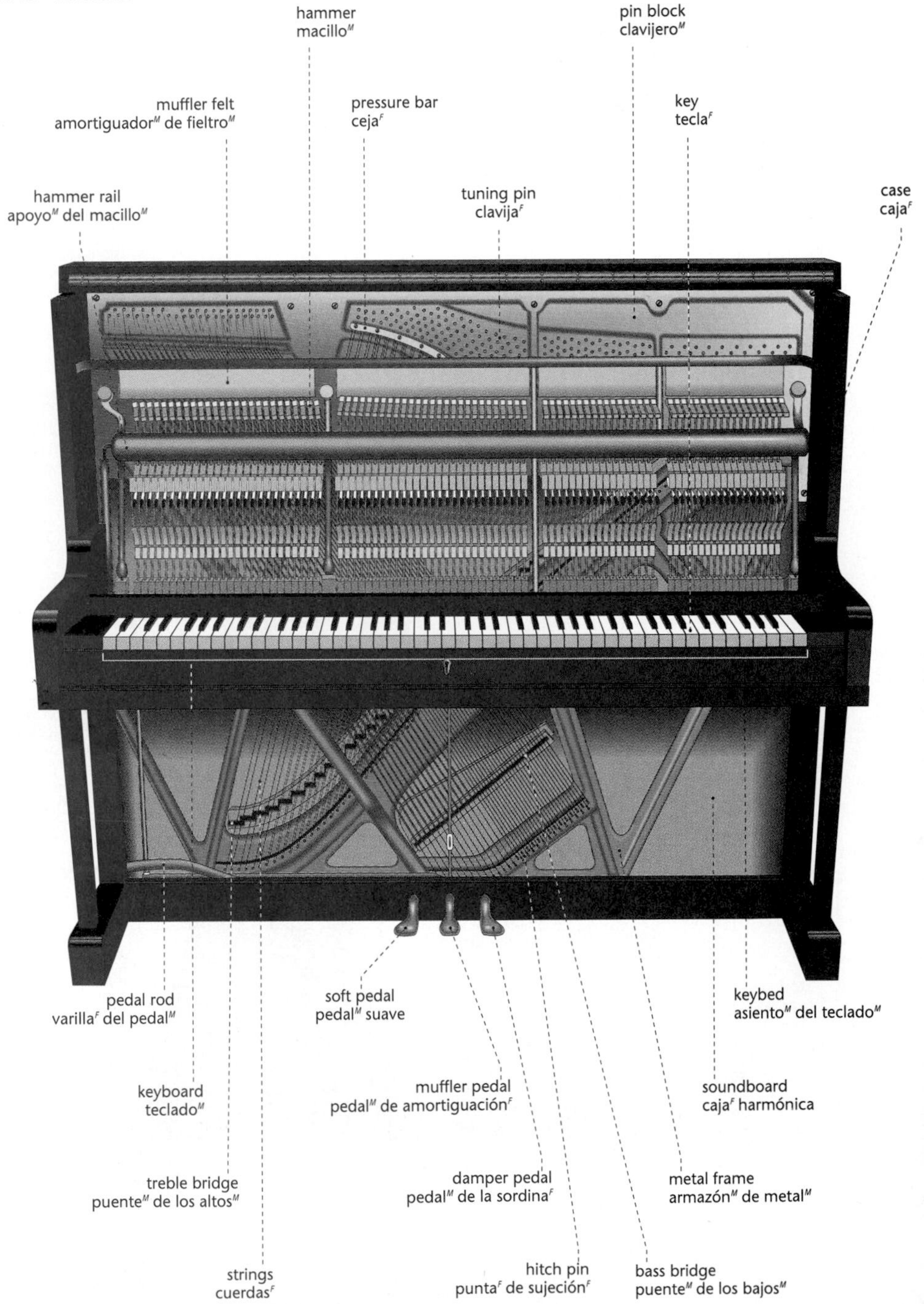

hammer
macillo*M*

pin block
clavijero*M*

muffler felt
amortiguador*M* de fieltro*M*

pressure bar
ceja*F*

key
tecla*F*

hammer rail
apoyo*M* del macillo*M*

tuning pin
clavija*F*

case
caja*F*

pedal rod
varilla*F* del pedal*M*

soft pedal
pedal*M* suave

keybed
asiento*M* del teclado*M*

keyboard
teclado*M*

muffler pedal
pedal*M* de amortiguación*F*

soundboard
caja*F* harmónica

treble bridge
puente*M* de los altos*M*

damper pedal
pedal*M* de la sordina*F*

metal frame
armazón*M* de metal*M*

strings
cuerdas*F*

hitch pin
punta*F* de sujeción*F*

bass bridge
puente*M* de los bajos*M*

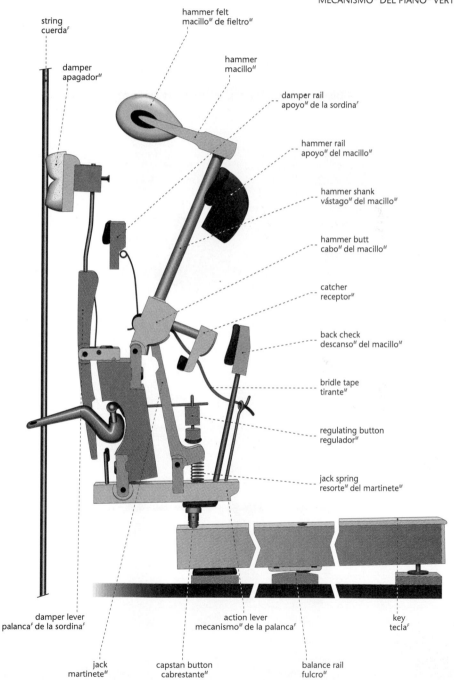

string
cuerda^F

damper
apagador^M

hammer felt
macillo^M de fieltro^M

hammer
macillo^M

damper rail
apoyo^M de la sordina^F

hammer rail
apoyo^M del macillo^M

hammer shank
vástago^M del macillo^M

hammer butt
cabo^M del macillo^M

catcher
receptor^M

back check
descanso^M del macillo^M

bridle tape
tirante^M

regulating button
regulador^M

jack spring
resorte^M del martinete^M

damper lever
palanca^F de la sordina^F

action lever
mecanismo^M de la palanca^F

key
tecla^F

jack
martinete^M

capstan button
cabrestante^M

balance rail
fulcro^M

MUSIC
MÚSICA

ORGAN
ÓRGANO^M ELECTRONEUMÁTICO

ORGAN CONSOLE
CONSOLA^F

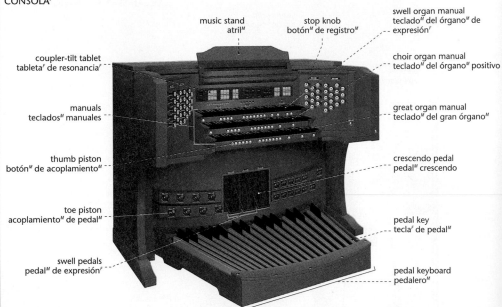

music stand
atril^M

stop knob
botón^M de registro^M

swell organ manual
teclado^M del órgano^M de
expresión^F

coupler-tilt tablet
tableta^F de resonancia^F

choir organ manual
teclado^M del órgano^M positivo

manuals
teclados^M manuales

great organ manual
teclado^M del gran órgano^M

thumb piston
botón^M de acoplamiento^M

crescendo pedal
pedal^M crescendo

toe piston
acoplamiento^M de pedal^M

pedal key
tecla^F de pedal^M

swell pedals
pedal^M de expresión^F

pedal keyboard
pedalero^M

REED PIPE
TUBO^M DE LENGÜETA^F

FLUE PIPE
CAÑO^M DEL ÓRGANO^M

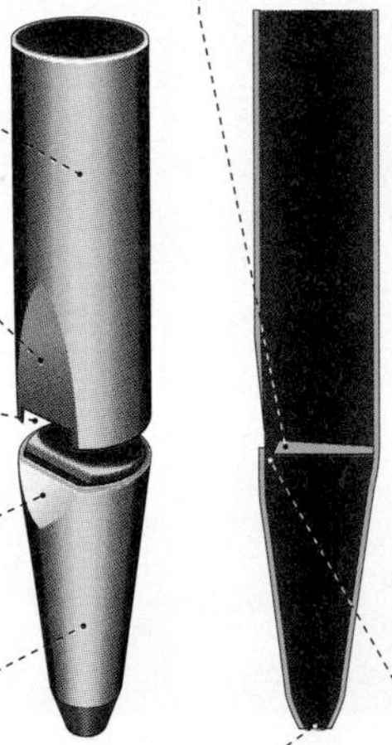

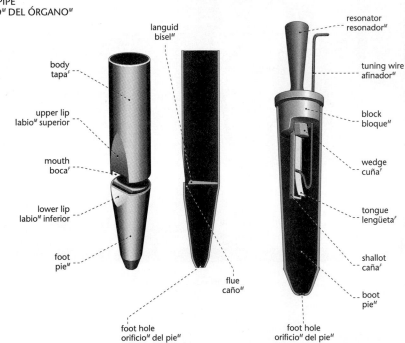

languid
bisel^M

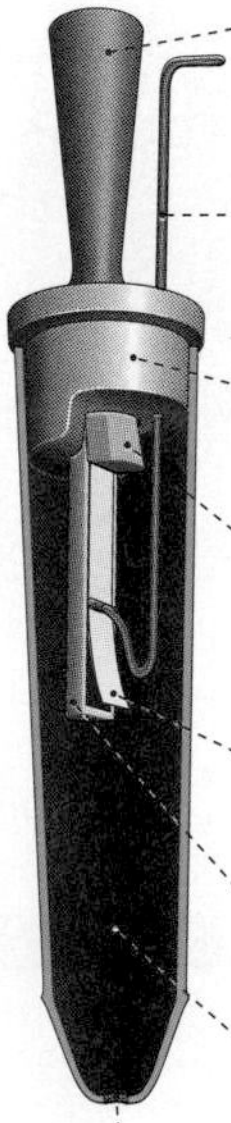

resonator
resonador^M

body
tapa^F

tuning wire
afinador^M

upper lip
labio^M superior

block
bloque^M

mouth
boca^F

wedge
cuña^F

lower lip
labio^M inferior

tongue
lengüeta^F

foot
pie^M

shallot
caña^F

flue
caño^M

boot
pie^M

foot hole
orificio^M del pie^M

foot hole
orificio^M del pie^M

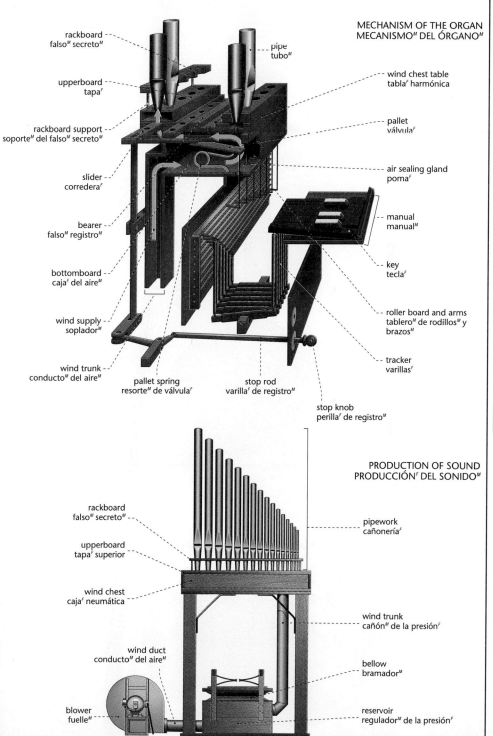

rackboard
falso^M secreto^M

pipe
tubo^M

MECHANISM OF THE ORGAN
MECANISMO^M DEL ÓRGANO^M

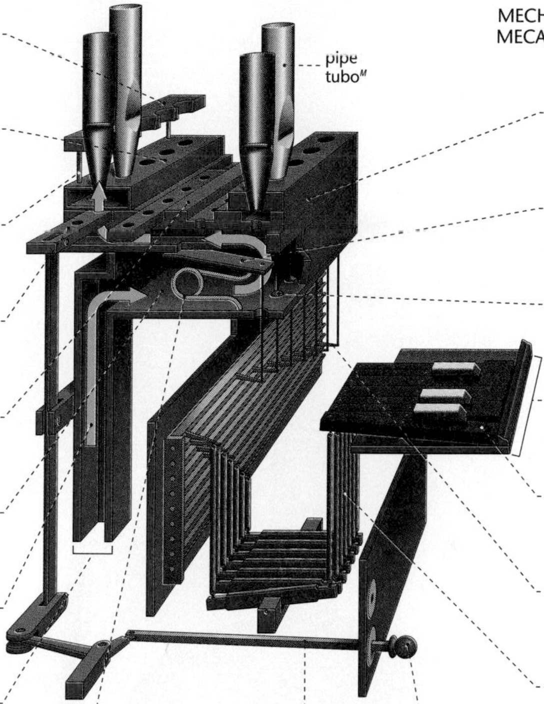

wind chest table
tabla^F harmónica

upperboard
tapa^F

pallet
válvula^F

rackboard support
soporte^M del falso^M secreto^M

air sealing gland
poma^F

slider
corredera^F

manual
manual^M

bearer
falso^M registro^M

key
tecla^F

bottomboard
caja^F del aire^M

wind supply
soplador^M

roller board and arms
tablero^M de rodillos^M y
brazos^M

tracker
varillas^F

wind trunk
conducto^M del aire^M

pallet spring
resorte^M de válvula^F

stop rod
varilla^F de registro^M

stop knob
perilla^F de registro^M

PRODUCTION OF SOUND
PRODUCCIÓN^F DEL SONIDO^M

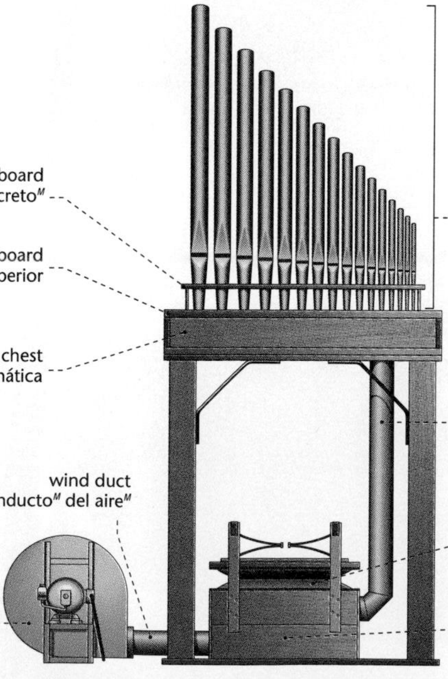

rackboard
falso^M secreto^M

pipework
cañonería^F

upperboard
tapa^F superior

wind chest
caja^F neumática

wind trunk
cañón^M de la presión^F

wind duct
conducto^M del aire^M

bellow
bramador^M

blower
fuelle^M

reservoir
regulador^M de la presión^F

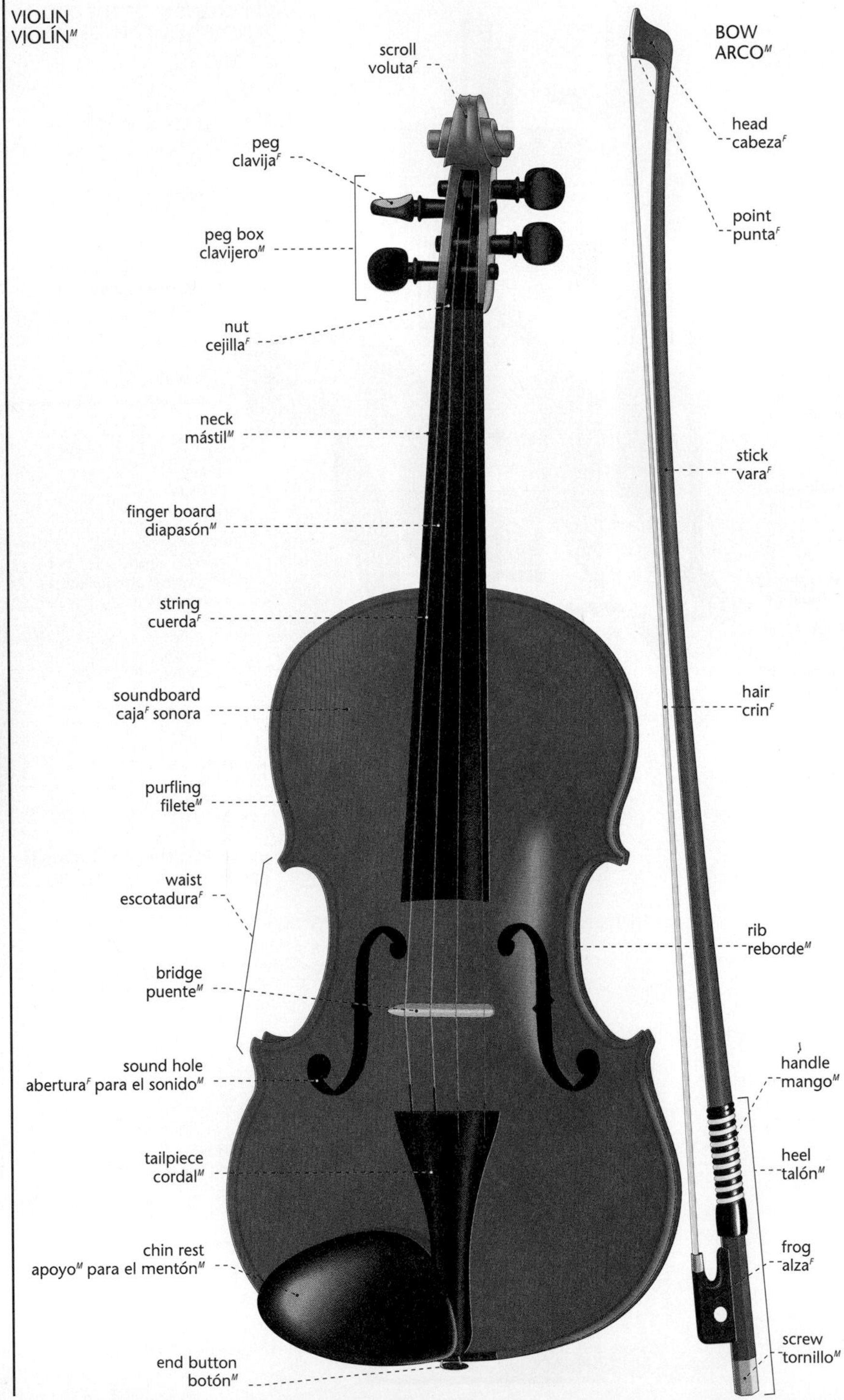

VIOLIN
VIOLÍN^M

BOW
ARCO^M

scroll
voluta^F

peg
clavija^F

peg box
clavijero^M

nut
cejilla^F

neck
mástil^M

finger board
diapasón^M

string
cuerda^F

soundboard
caja^F sonora

purfling
filete^M

waist
escotadura^F

bridge
puente^M

sound hole
abertura^F para el sonido^M

tailpiece
cordal^M

chin rest
apoyo^M para el mentón^M

end button
botón^M

head
cabeza^F

point
punta^F

stick
vara^F

hair
crin^F

rib
reborde^M

handle
mango^M

heel
talón^M

frog
alza^F

screw
tornillo^M

MUSIC
MÚSICA

544

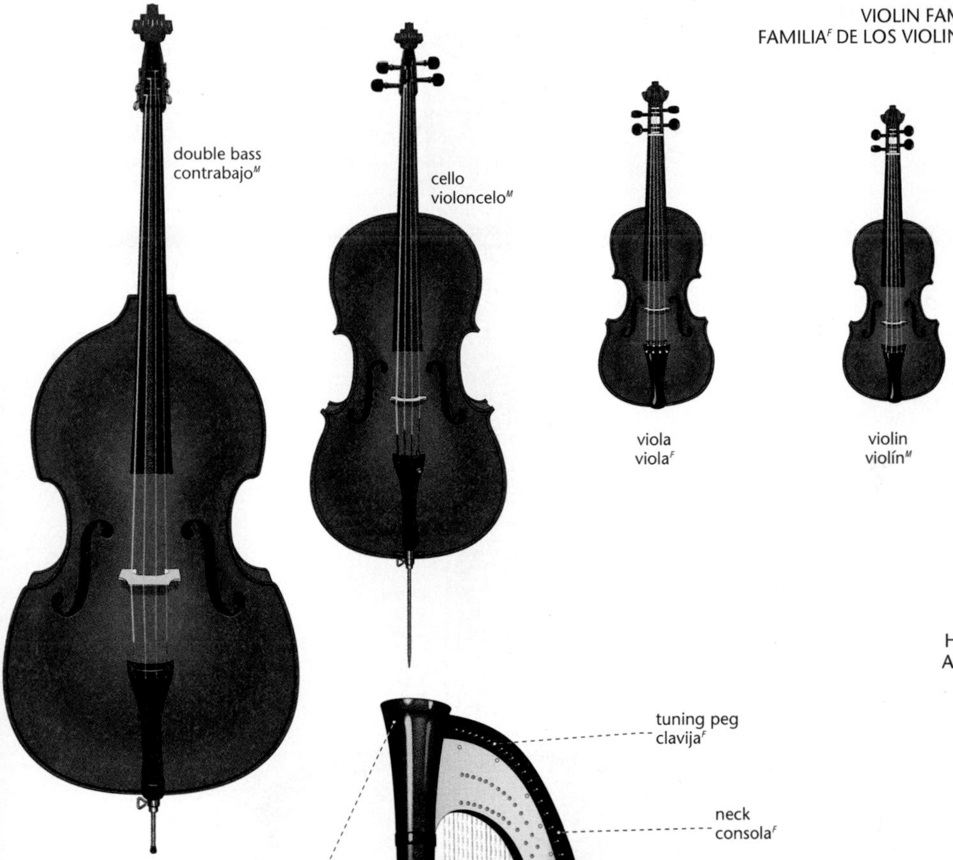

double bass
contrabajo*M*

cello
violoncelo*M*

viola
viola*F*

violin
violín*M*

HARP
ARPA*F*

**MUSIC
MÚSICA**

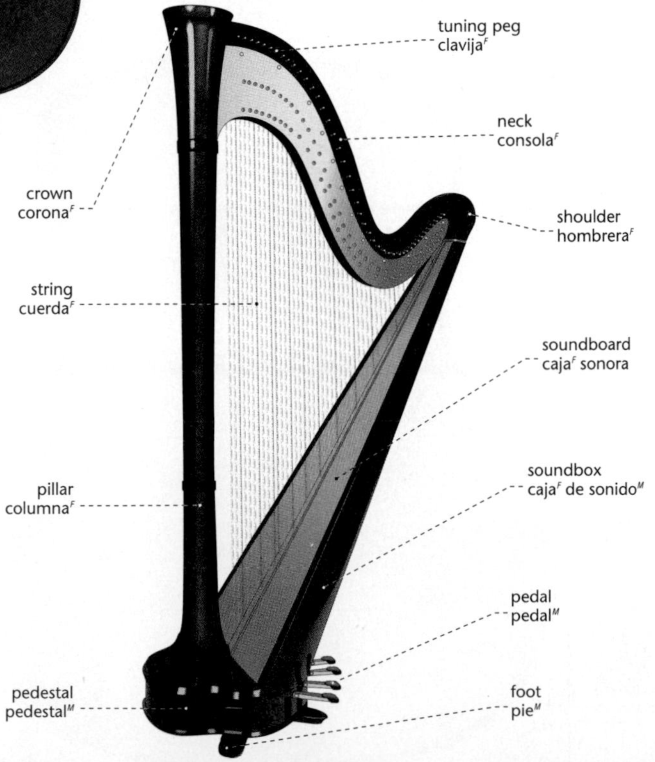

tuning peg
clavija*F*

neck
consola*F*

crown
corona*F*

shoulder
hombrera*F*

string
cuerda*F*

soundboard
caja*F* sonora

soundbox
caja*F* de sonido*M*

pillar
columna*F*

pedal
pedal*M*

pedestal
pedestal*M*

foot
pie*M*

ACOUSTIC GUITAR
GUITARRA^F CLÁSICA

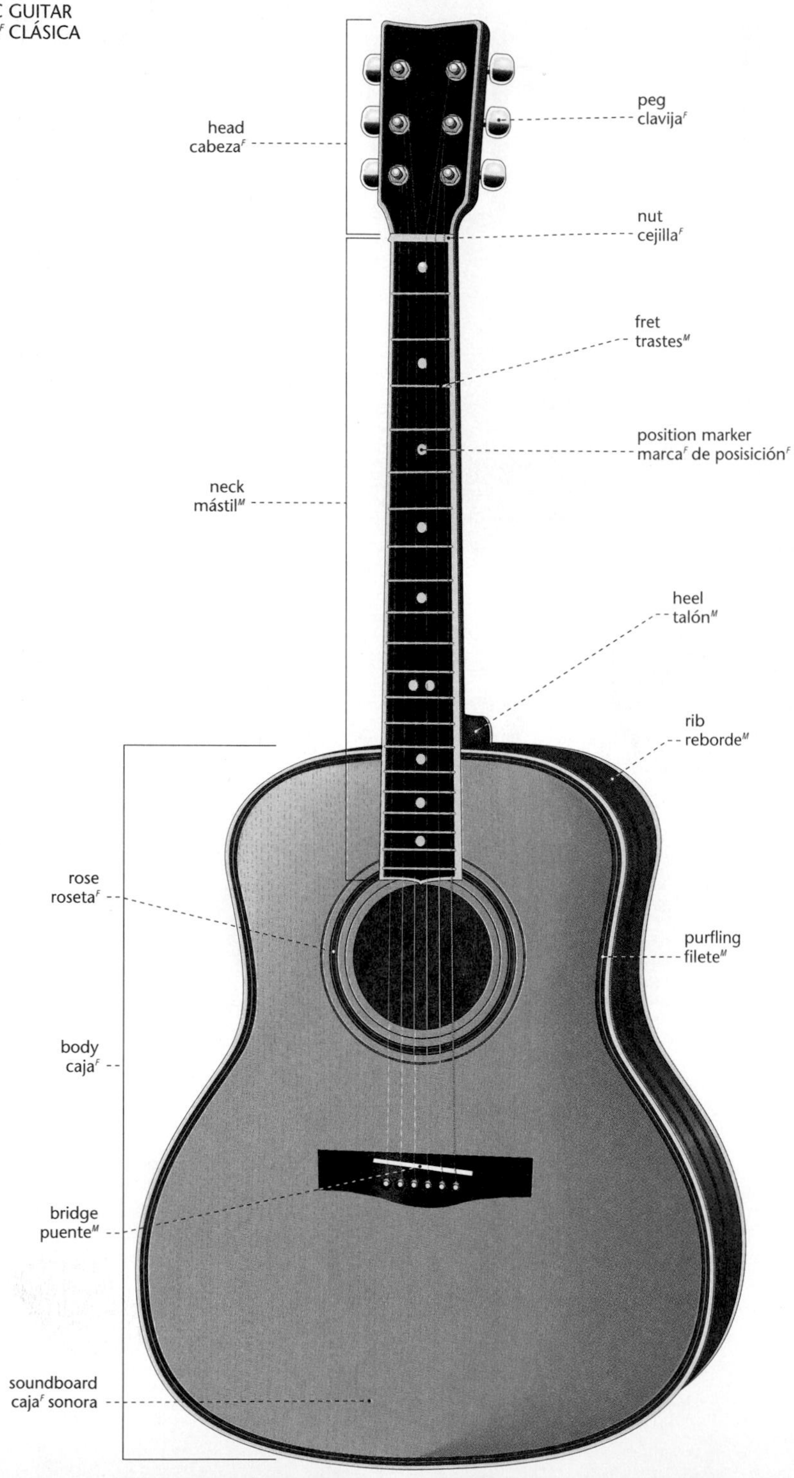

head
cabeza^F

peg
clavija^F

nut
cejilla^F

fret
trastes^M

position marker
marca^F de posisición^F

neck
mástil^M

heel
talón^M

rib
reborde^M

rose
roseta^F

purfling
filete^M

body
caja^F

bridge
puente^M

soundboard
caja^F sonora

tuning peg
clavija^F de afinación^F

head
cabeza^F

nut
cejilla^F

finger board
diapasón^M

position marker
marca^F de posición^F

fret
traste^M

neck
mástil^M

pickguard
guardacaptores^M

bass pickup
receptor^M de los bajos^M

vibrato arm
palanca^F de vibración^F

midrange pickup
fonocaptor^M de los intermedios^M

pickup selector
selector^M de la recepción^F

treble pickup
receptor^M triple

volume control
control^M de volumen^M

bridge assembly
puente^M de asamblaje^M

tone control
control^M del sonido^M

solid body
cuerpo^M sólido

output jack
conector^M de salida^F

SAXOPHONE
SAXOFÓN^M

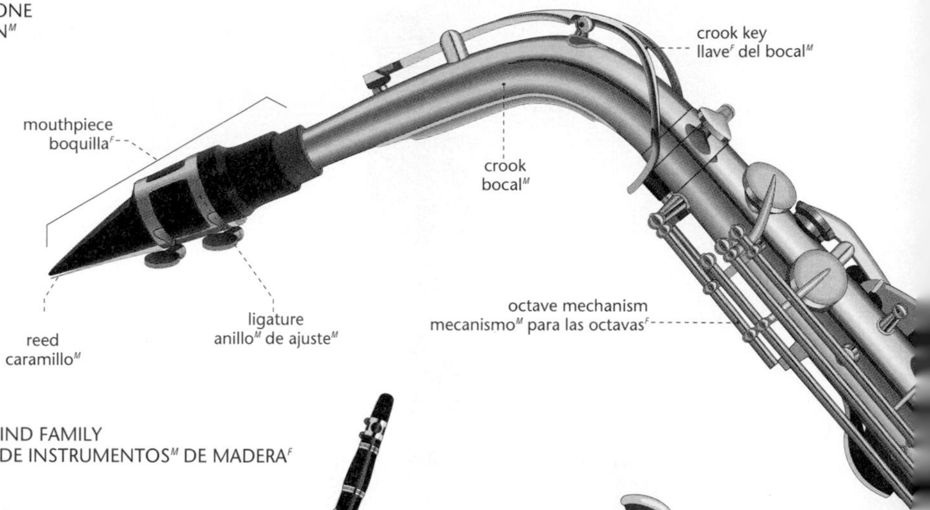

crook key
llave^F del bocal^M

mouthpiece
boquilla^F

crook
bocal^M

reed
caramillo^M

ligature
anillo^M de ajuste^M

octave mechanism
mecanismo^M para las octavas^F

WOODWIND FAMILY
FAMILIA^F DE INSTRUMENTOS^M DE MADERA^F

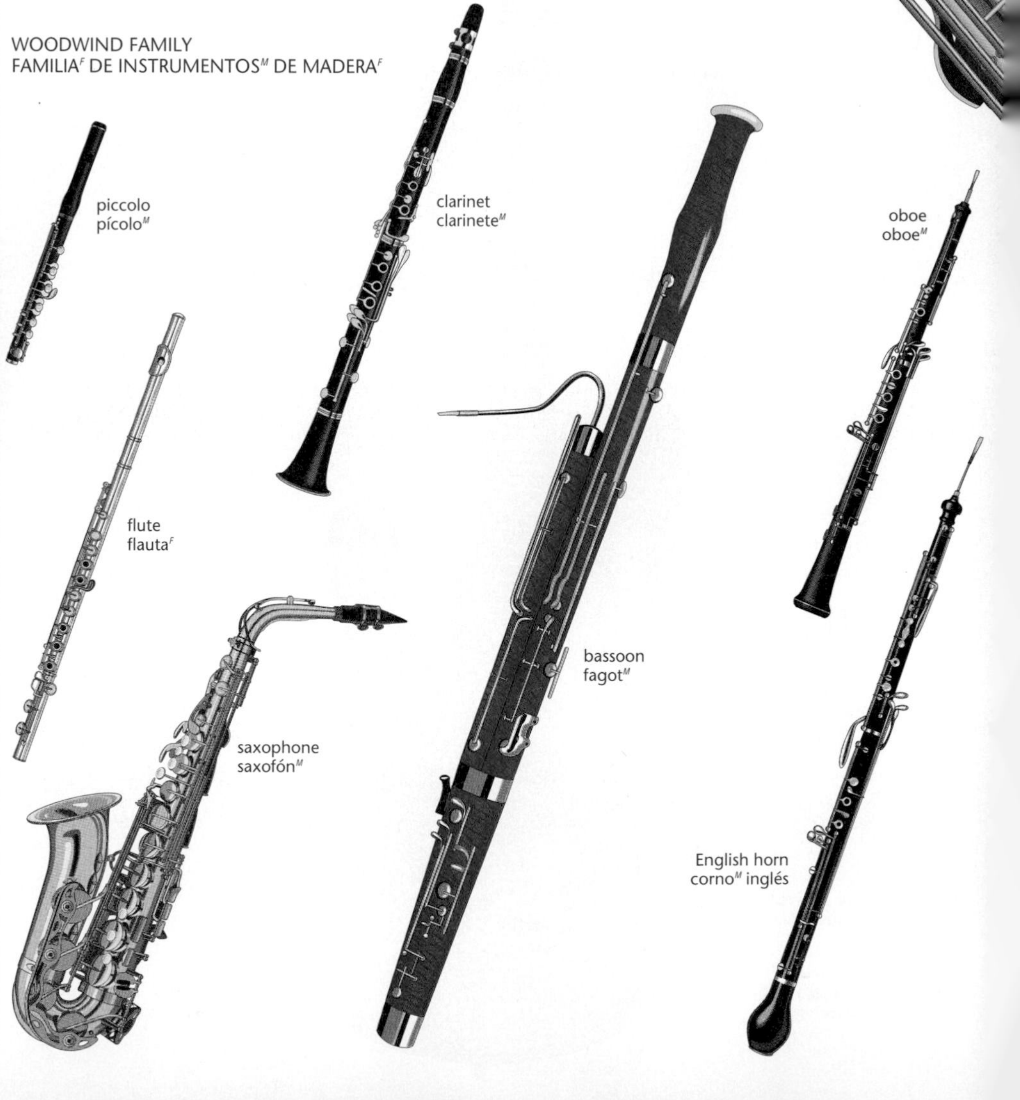

piccolo
pícolo^M

clarinet
clarinete^M

oboe
oboe^M

flute
flauta^F

saxophone
saxofón^M

bassoon
fagot^M

English horn
corno^M inglés

MUSIC
MÚSICA

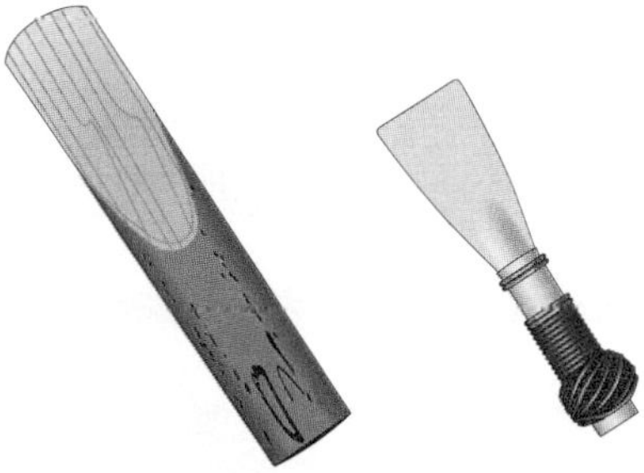

REEDS
CAÑAS^F

single reed
caña^F simple

double reed
doble caña^F

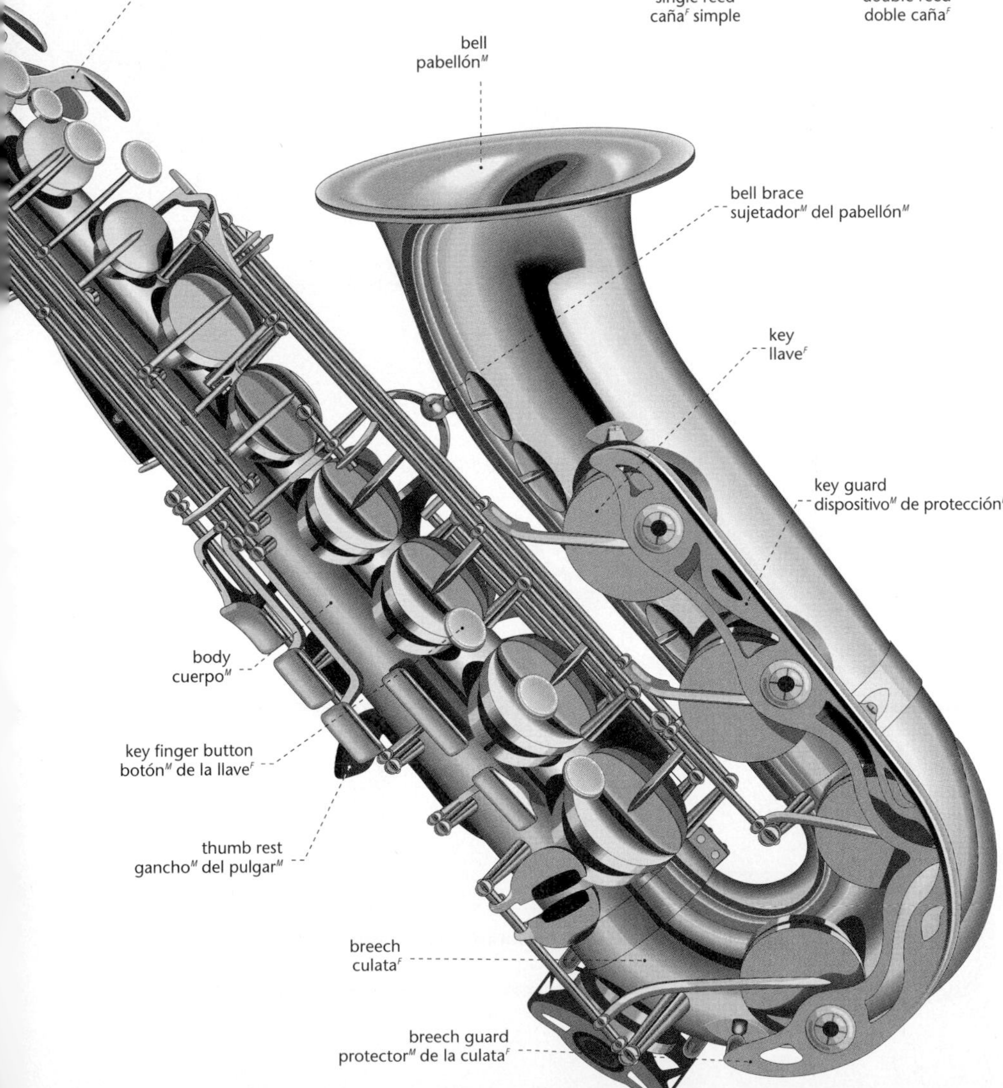

key lever
palanca^F

bell
pabellón^M

bell brace
sujetador^M del pabellón^M

key
llave^F

key guard
dispositivo^M de protección^F

body
cuerpo^M

key finger button
botón^M de la llave^F

thumb rest
gancho^M del pulgar^M

breech
culata^F

breech guard
protector^M de la culata^F

MUSIC
MÚSICA

TRUMPET
TROMPETA^F

mouthpiece
boquilla^F

mouthpiece receiver
empate^M de la boquilla^F

mouthpipe
tubo^M

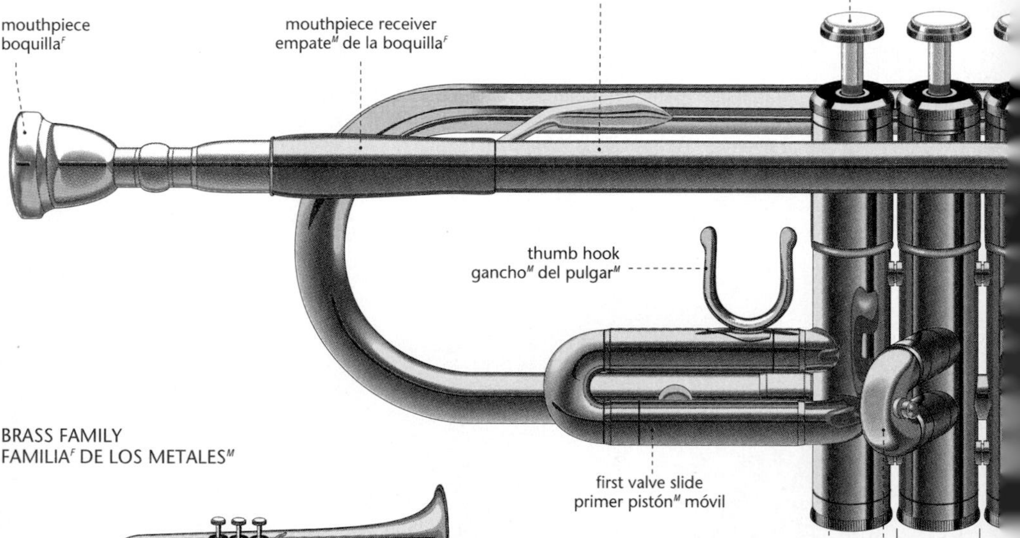

finger button
llave^F

thumb hook
gancho^M del pulgar^M

first valve slide
primer pistón^M móvil

valve casing
tubo^M del pistón^M

second valve slide
segundo pistón^M móvil

valve
pistón^M

BRASS FAMILY
FAMILIA^F DE LOS METALES^M

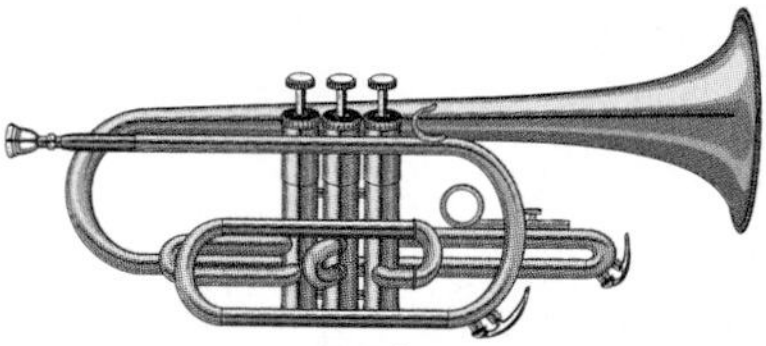

cornet
cornetín^M

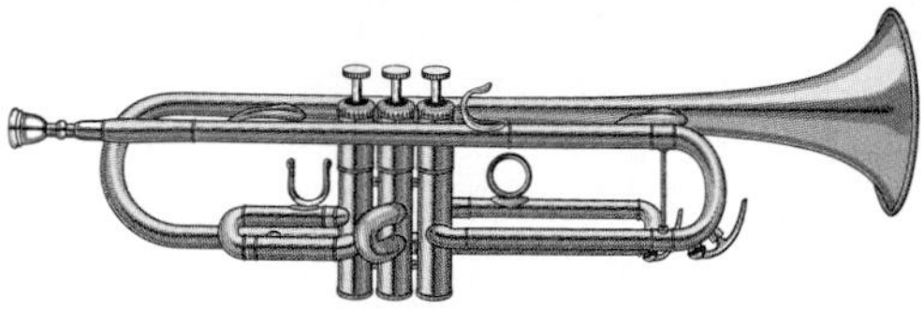

trumpet
trompeta^F

bugle
clarín^M

trombone
trombón^M

MUSIC
MÚSICA

550

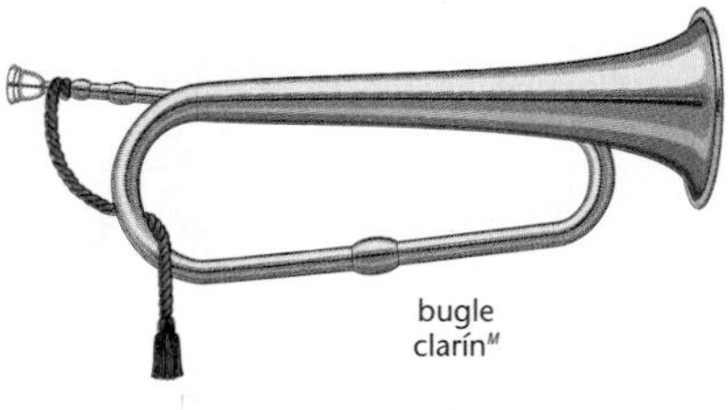

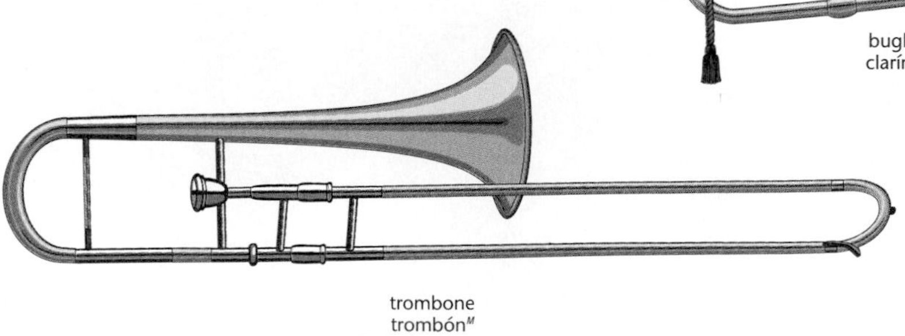

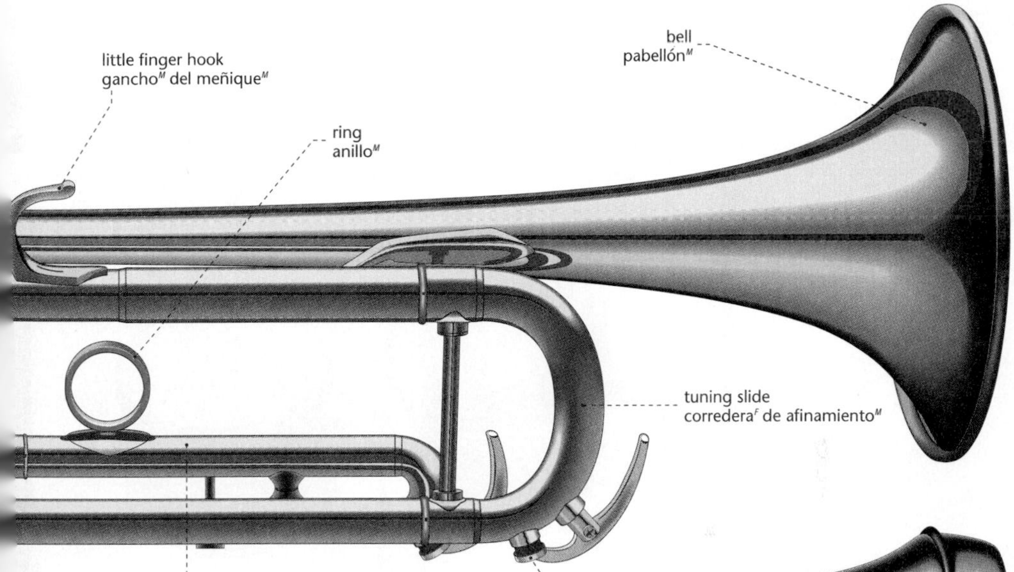

little finger hook
gancho^M del meñique^M

ring
anillo^M

bell
pabellón^M

tuning slide
corredera^F de afinamiento^M

third valve slide
tercer pistón^M móvil

water key
llave^F para agua^F

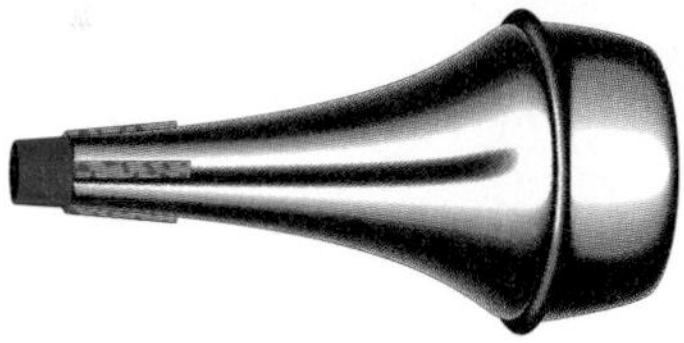

mute
sordina^F

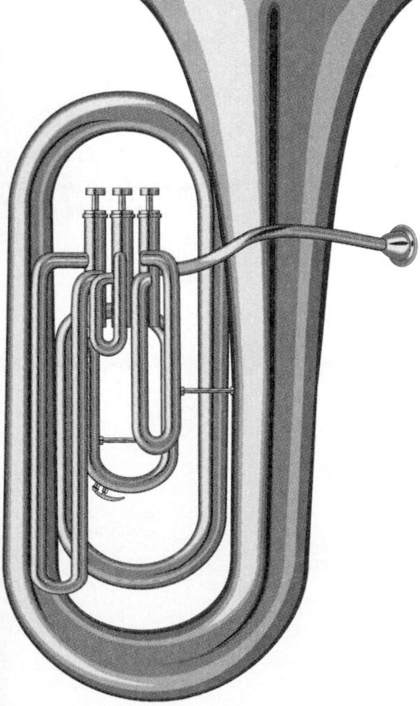

tuba
tuba^F

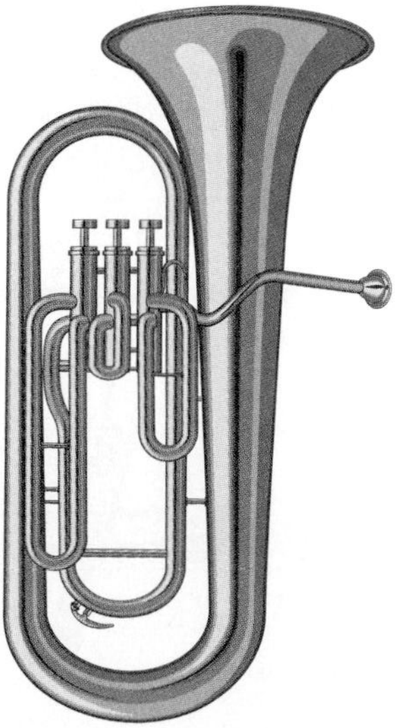

saxhorn
bombardino^M

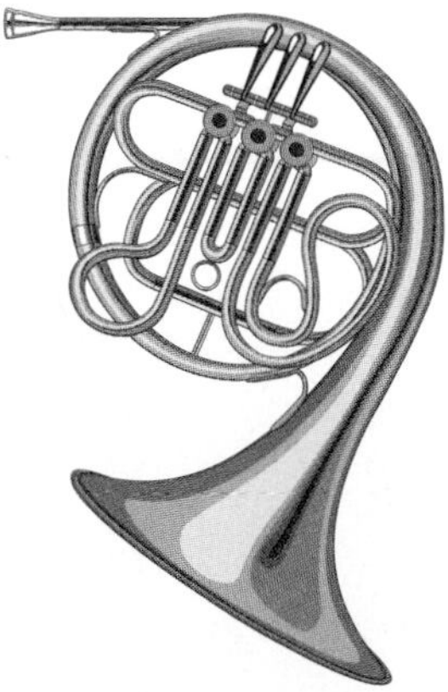

French horn
corno^M francés

DRUMS
TAMBORES^M

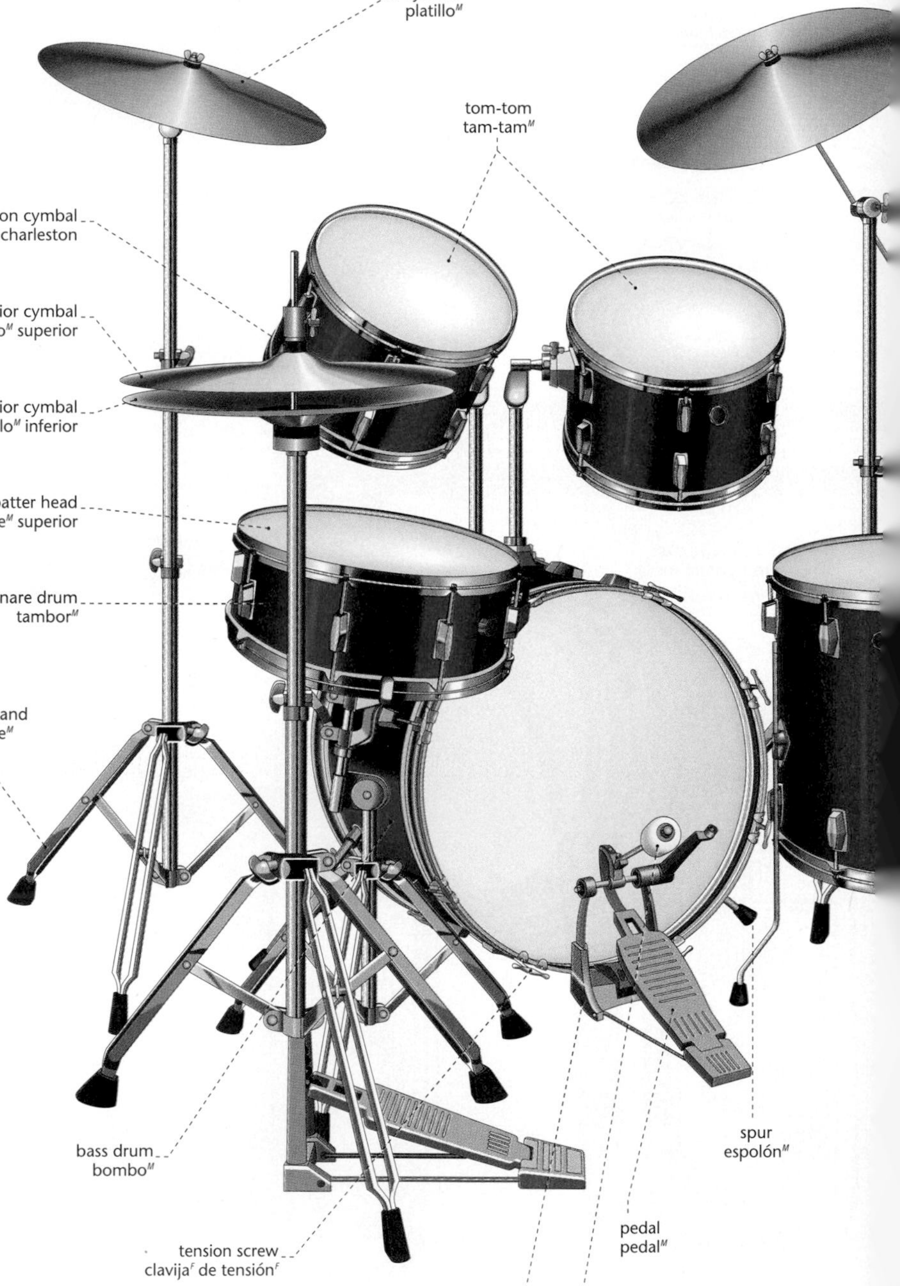

cymbal
platillo^M

tom-tom
tam-tam^M

Charleston cymbal
platillo^M charleston

superior cymbal
platillo^M superior

inferior cymbal
platillo^M inferior

batter head
parche^M superior

snare drum
tambor^M

tripod stand
trípode^M

bass drum
bombo^M

tension screw
clavija^F de tensión^F

spur
espolón^M

pedal
pedal^M

stand
soporte^M

mallet
palillo^M

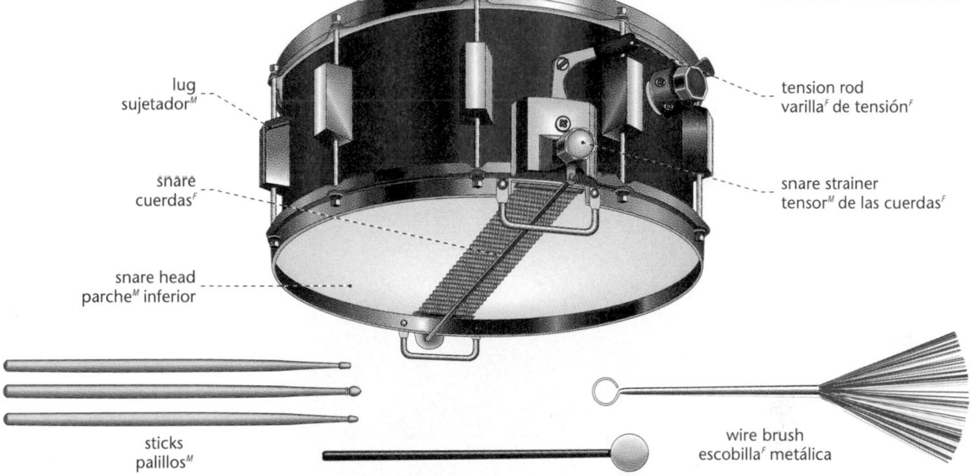

lug
sujetador^M

tension rod
varilla^F de tensión^F

snare
cuerdas^F

snare strainer
tensor^M de las cuerdas^F

snare head
parche^M inferior

sticks
palillos^M

wire brush
escobilla^F metálica

mallets
maza^F

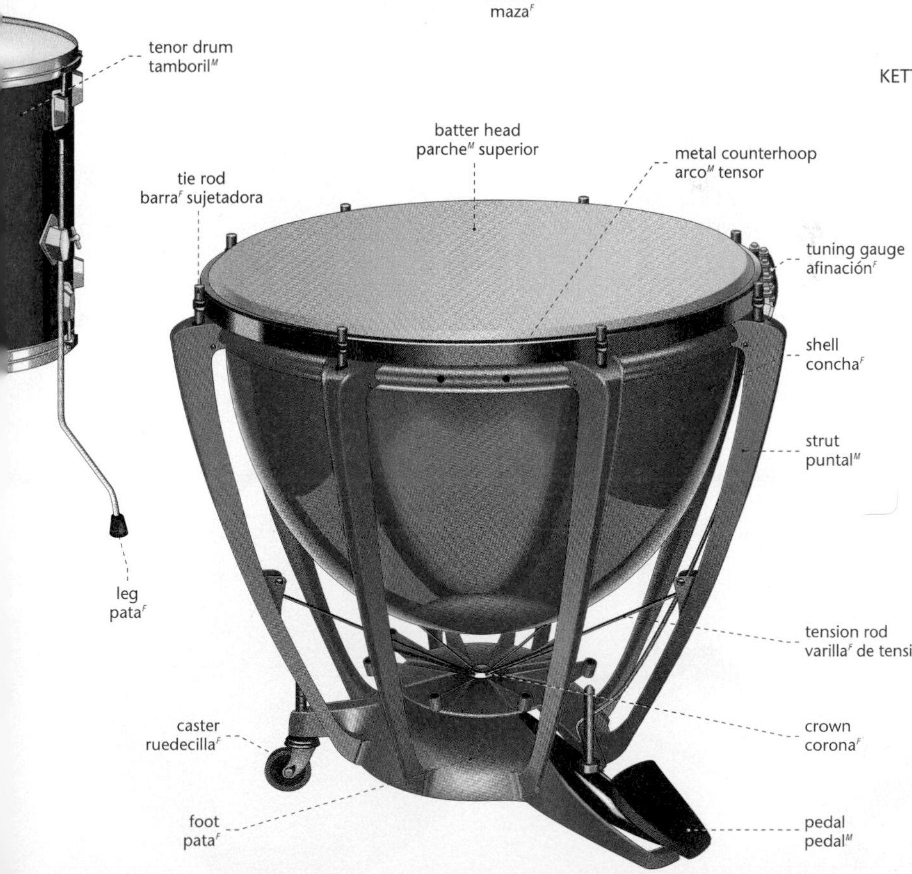

tenor drum
tamboril^M

KETTLEDRUM
TIMBAL^M

batter head
parche^M superior

metal counterhoop
arco^M tensor

tie rod
barra^F sujetadora

tuning gauge
afinación^F

shell
concha^F

strut
puntal^M

leg
pata^F

tension rod
varilla^F de tensión^F

caster
ruedecilla^F

crown
corona^F

foot
pata^F

pedal
pedal^M

TRIANGLE
TRIÁNGULO*M*

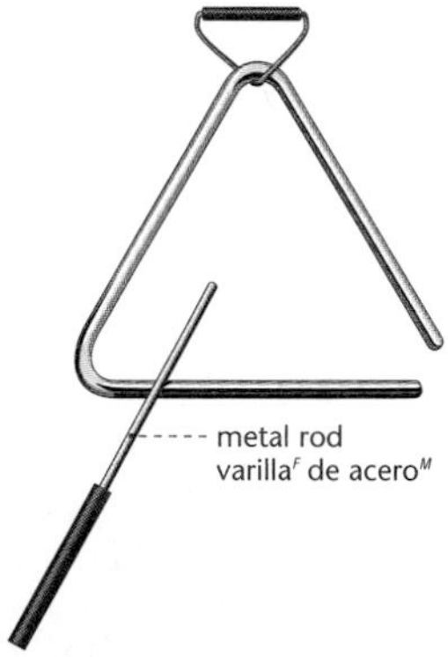

metal rod
varilla*F* de acero*M*

castanets
castañuelas*F*

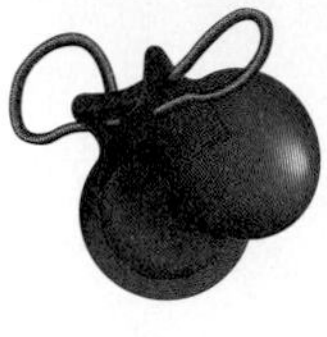

TAMBOURINE
PANDERETA*F*

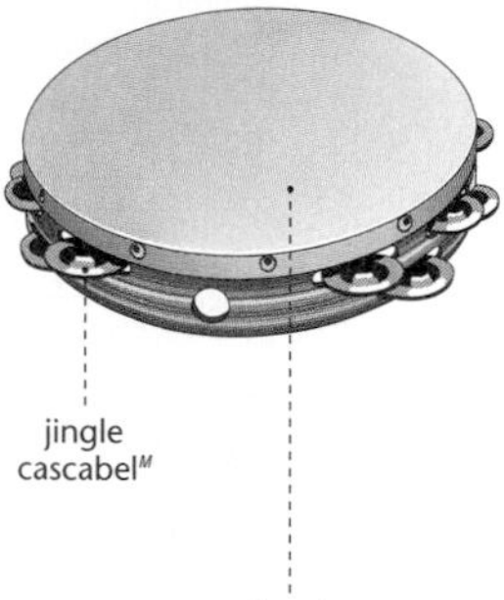

jingle
cascabel*M*

head
parche*M*

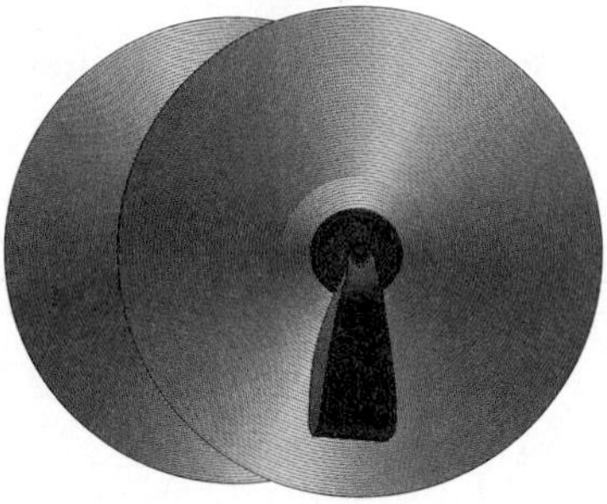

cymbals
platillos*M*

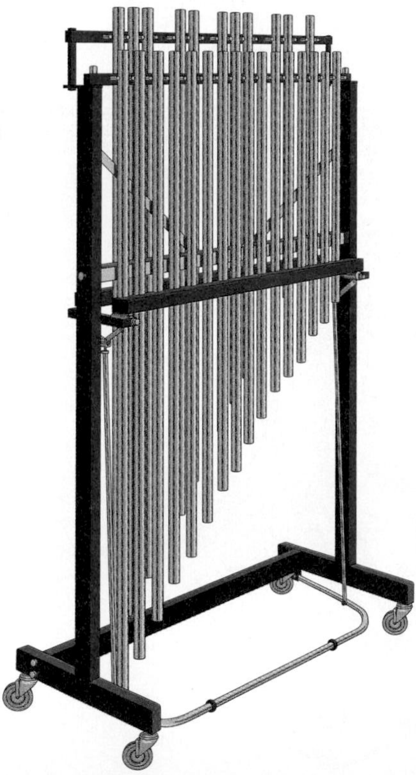

XYLOPHONE
XILÓFONO*M*

tubular bells
campanas*F* tubulares

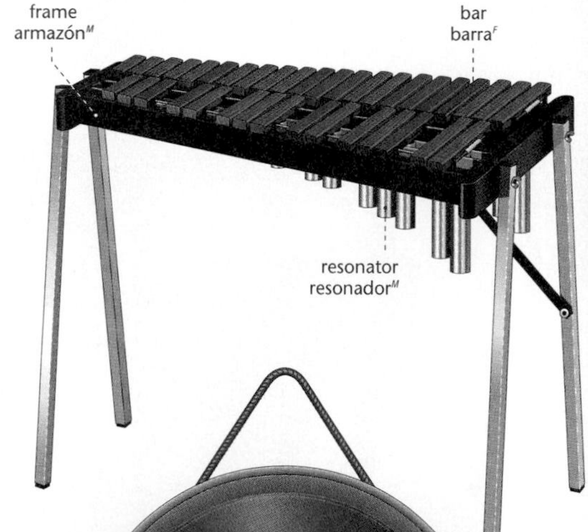

frame
armazón*M*

bar
barra*F*

resonator
resonador*M*

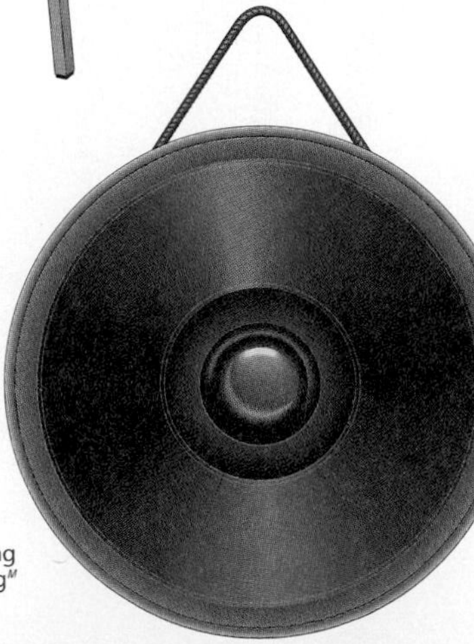

gong
gong*M*

ELECTRONIC INSTRUMENTS
INSTRUMENTOS^M ELECTRÓNICOS

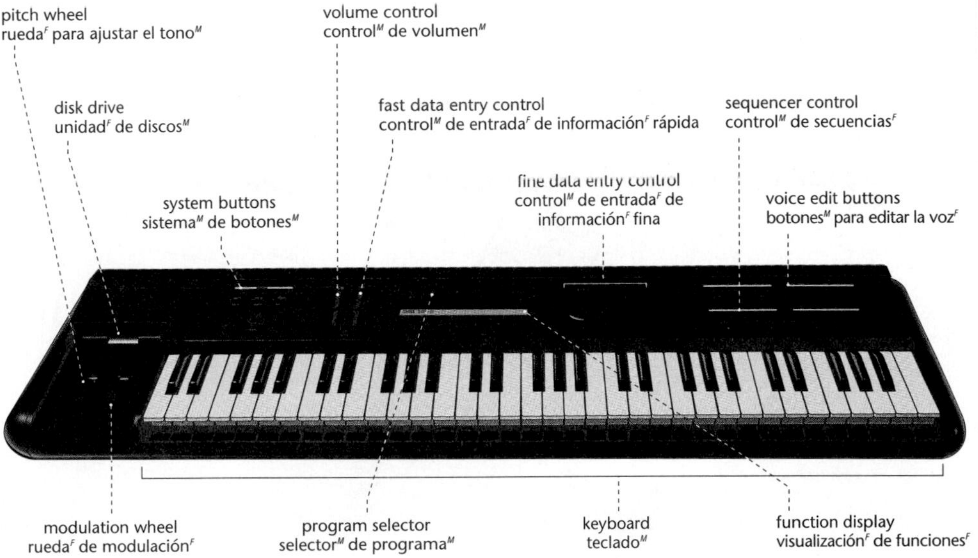

SYNTHESIZER
SINTETIZADOR^M

pitch wheel
rueda^F para ajustar el tono^M

volume control
control^M de volumen^M

disk drive
unidad^F de discos^M

fast data entry control
control^M de entrada^F de información^F rápida

sequencer control
control^M de secuencias^F

system buttons
sistema^M de botones^M

fine data entry control
control^M de entrada^F de información^F fina

voice edit buttons
botones^M para editar la voz^F

modulation wheel
rueda^F de modulación^F

program selector
selector^M de programa^M

keyboard
teclado^M

function display
visualización^F de funciones^F

ELECTRONIC PIANO
PIANO^M ELECTRÓNICO

power switch
interruptor^M

music stand
atril^M

rhythm selector
selector^M del rítmo^M

voice selector
selector^M de la voz^F

volume control
control^M de volumen^M

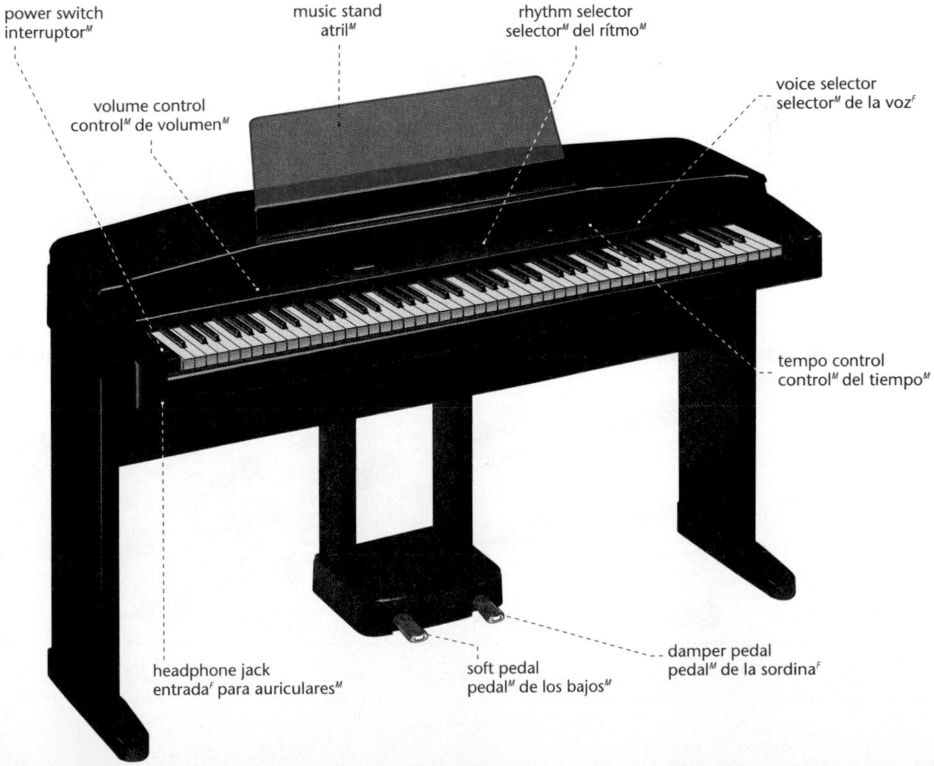

tempo control
control^M del tiempo^M

headphone jack
entrada^F para auriculares^M

soft pedal
pedal^M de los bajos^M

damper pedal
pedal^M de la sordina^F

MUSIC
MÚSICA

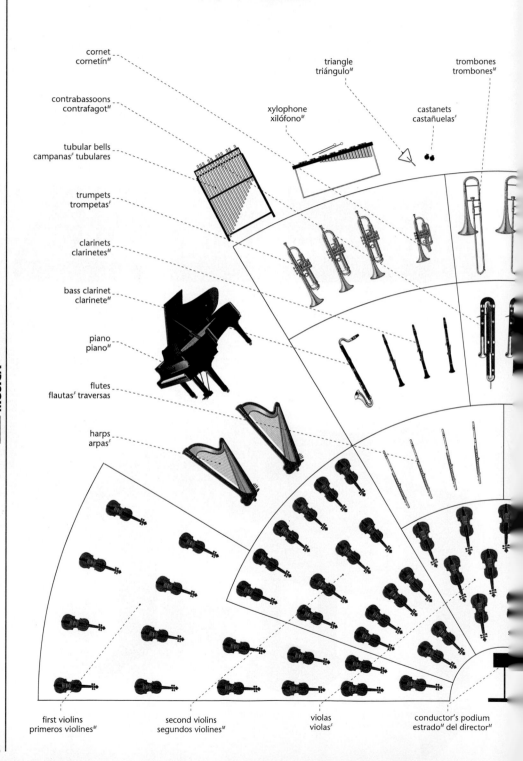

SYMPHONY ORCHESTRA
ORQUESTA[F] SINFÓNICA

cornet
cornetín[M]

triangle
triángulo[M]

trombones
trombones[M]

contrabassoons
contrafagot[M]

xylophone
xilófono[M]

castanets
castañuelas[F]

tubular bells
campanas[F] tubulares

trumpets
trompetas[F]

clarinets
clarinetes[M]

bass clarinet
clarinete[M]

piano
piano[M]

flutes
flautas[F] traversas

harps
arpas[F]

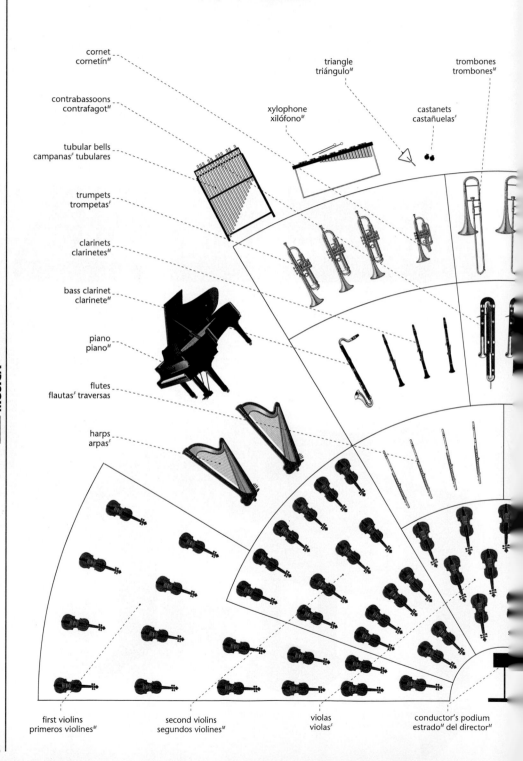

first violins
primeros violines[M]

second violins
segundos violines[M]

violas
violas[F]

conductor's podium
estrado[M] del director[M]

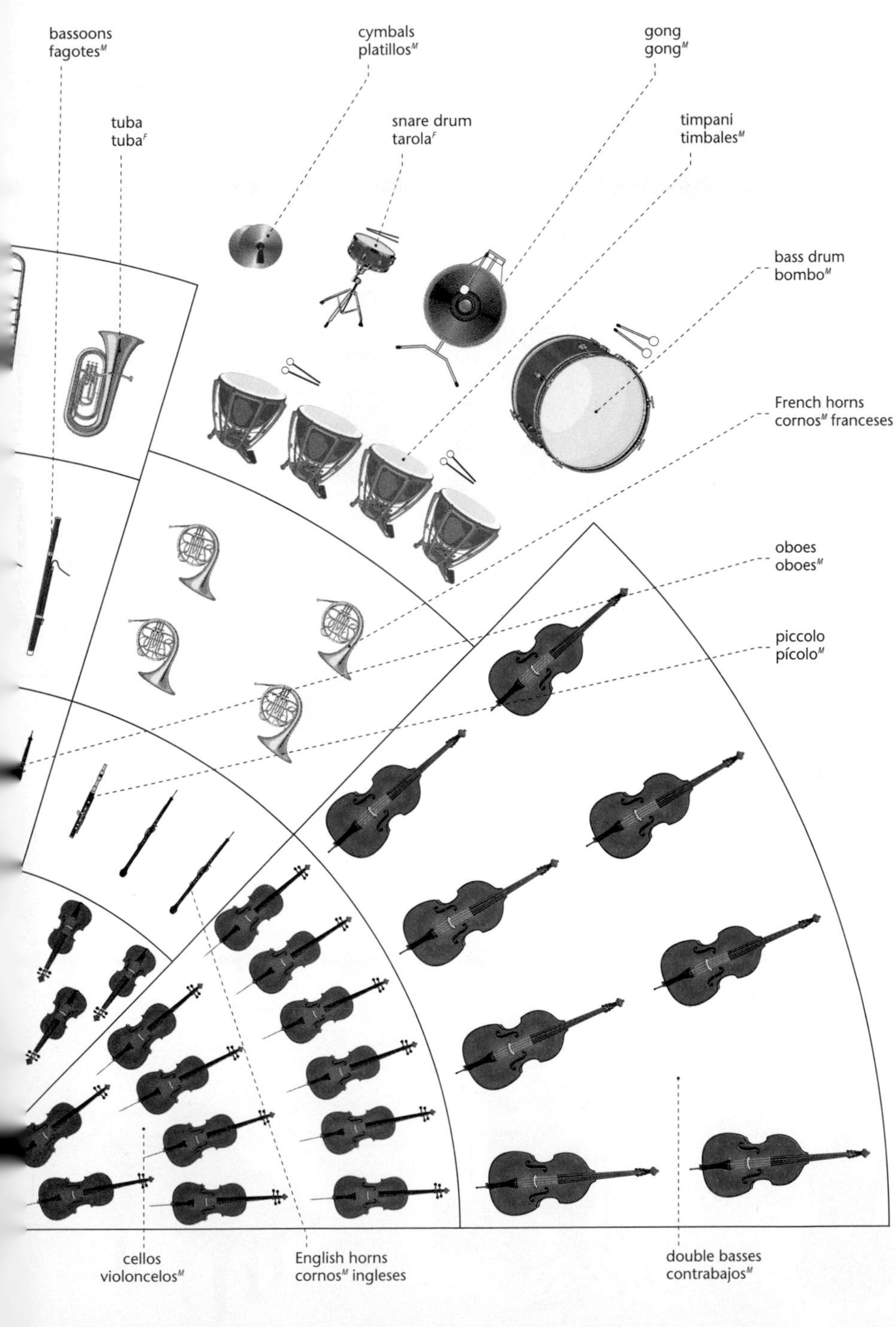

bassoons
fagotes^M

cymbals
platillos^M

gong
gong^M

tuba
tuba^F

snare drum
tarola^F

timpani
timbales^M

bass drum
bombo^M

French horns
cornos^M franceses

oboes
oboes^M

piccolo
pícolo^M

cellos
violoncelos^M

English horns
cornos^M ingleses

double basses
contrabajos^M

duo
dúo^M

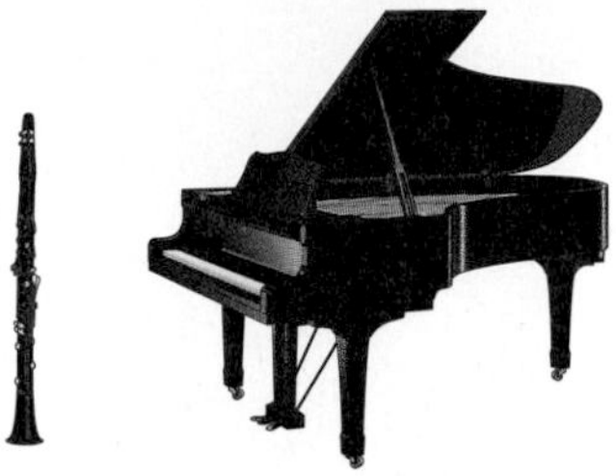

trio
trio^M

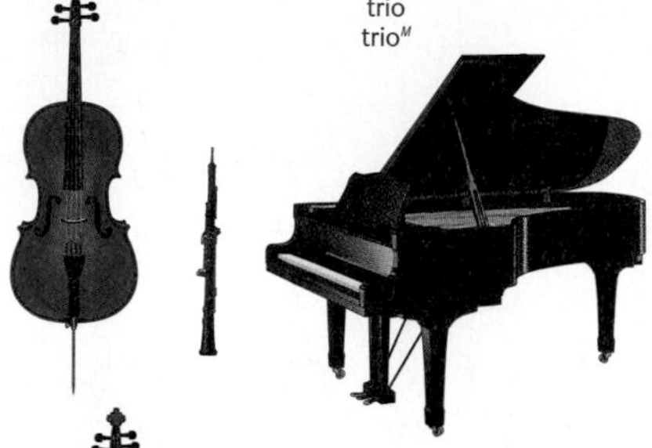

quartet
cuarteto^M

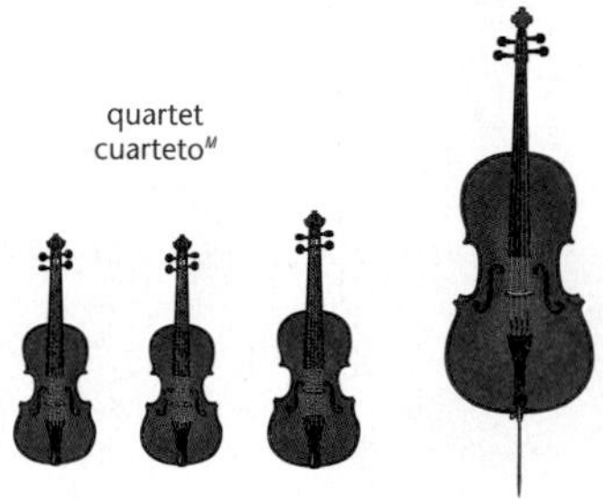

quintet
quinteto^M

sextet
sexteto^M

jazz band
banda^F de jazz^M

MUSIC
MÚSICA

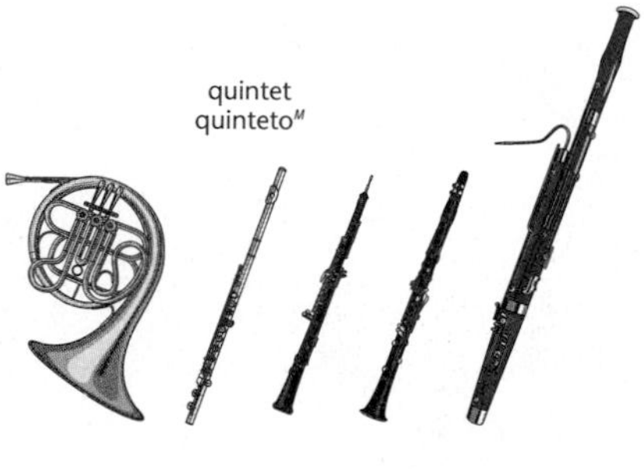

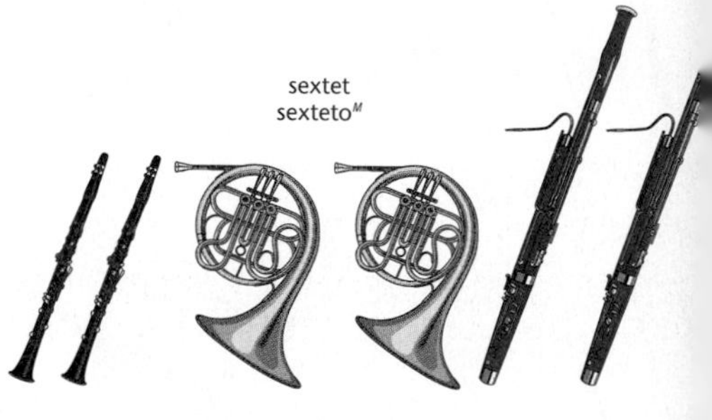

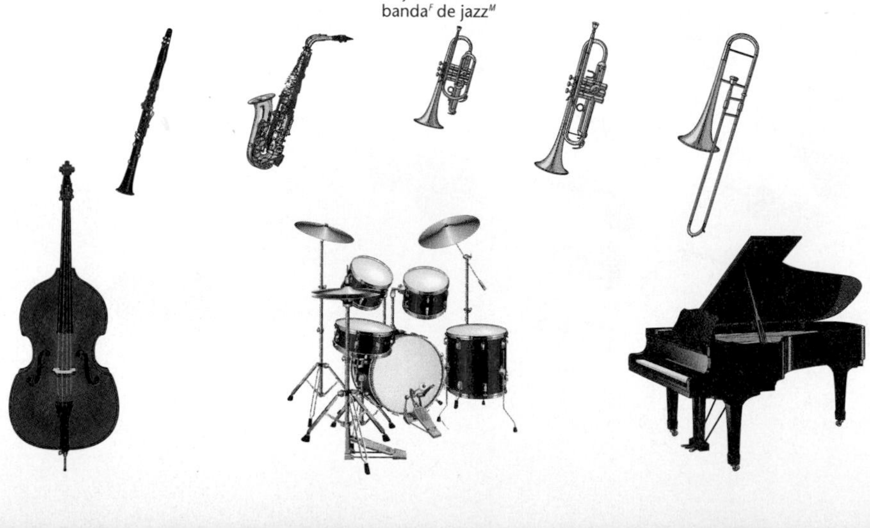

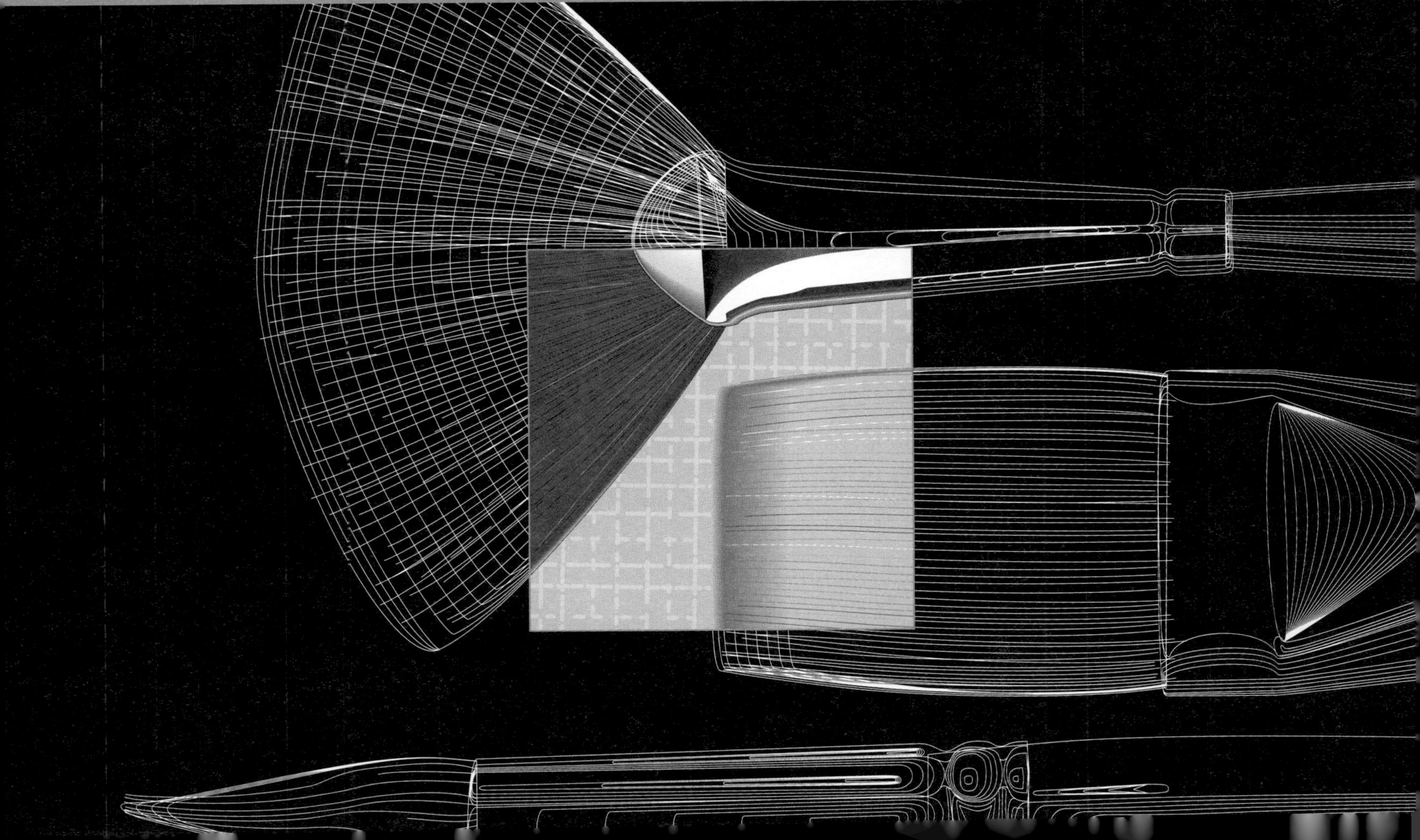

CONTENTS

SEWING
COSTURA^F

SEWING MACHINE
MÁQUINA^F DE COSER

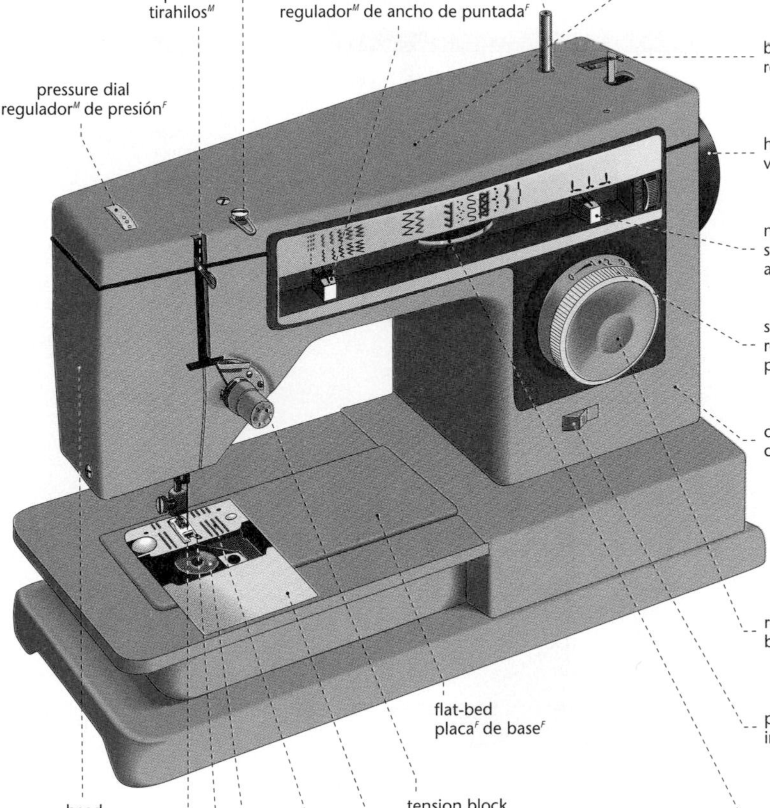

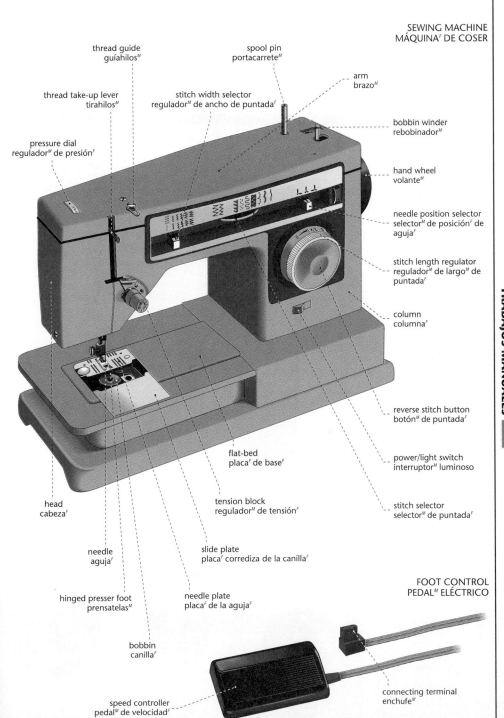

thread guide
guíahilos^M

spool pin
portacarrete^M

arm
brazo^M

thread take-up lever
tirahilos^M

stitch width selector
regulador^M de ancho de puntada^F

bobbin winder
rebobinador^M

pressure dial
regulador^M de presión^F

hand wheel
volante^M

needle position selector
selector^M de posición^F de aguja^F

stitch length regulator
regulador^M de largo^M de puntada^F

column
columna^F

reverse stitch button
botón^M de puntada^F

flat-bed
placa^F de base^F

power/light switch
interruptor^M luminoso

head
cabeza^F

tension block
regulador^M de tensión^F

stitch selector
selector^M de puntada^F

needle
aguja^F

slide plate
placa^F corrediza de la canilla^F

hinged presser foot
prensatelas^M

needle plate
placa^F de la aguja^F

FOOT CONTROL
PEDAL^M ELÉCTRICO

bobbin
canilla^F

speed controller
pedal^M de velocidad^F

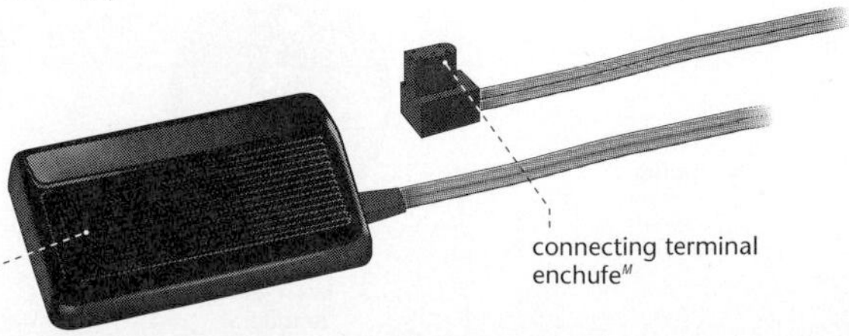

connecting terminal
enchufe^M

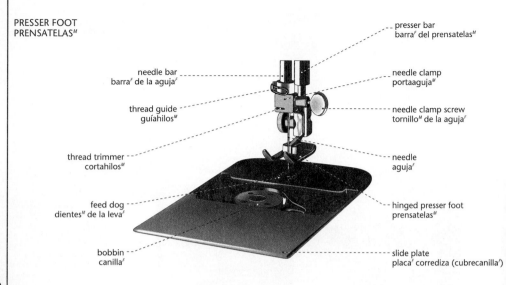

PRESSER FOOT
PRENSATELAS^M

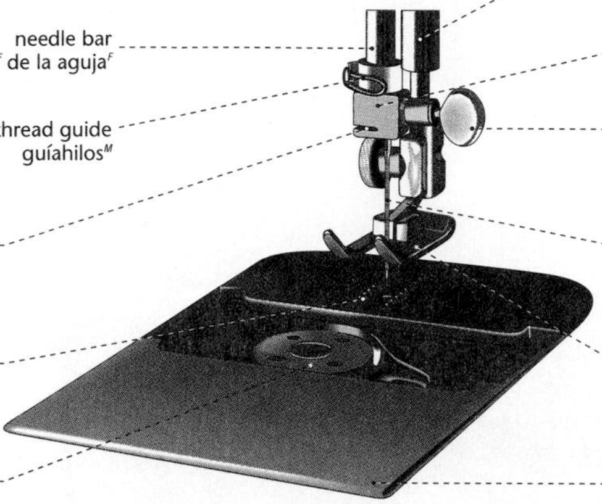

needle bar
barra^F de la aguja^F

thread guide
guíahilos^M

thread trimmer
cortahilos^M

feed dog
dientes^M de la leva^F

bobbin
canilla^F

presser bar
barra^F del prensatelas^M

needle clamp
portaaguja^M

needle clamp screw
tornillo^M de la aguja^F

needle
aguja^F

hinged presser foot
prensatelas^M

slide plate
placa^F corrediza (cubrecanilla^F)

NEEDLE
AGUJA^F

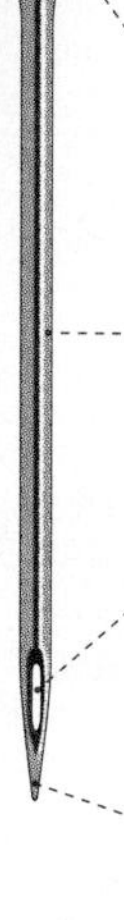

shank
talón^M de aguja^F

groove
ranura^F

blade
aguja^F

eye
ojo^M

point
punta^F

TENSION BLOCK
COLUMNA^F DE TENSIÓN^F

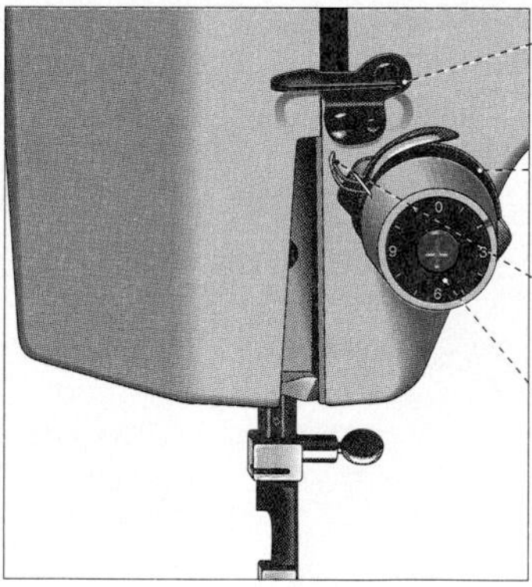

thread guide
guíahilos^M

tension disk
disco^M de tensión^F

tension spring
resorte^M de tensión^F

tension dial
regulador^M de tamaño^M de pun

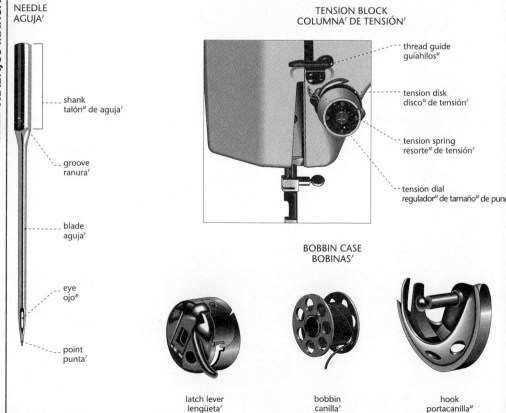

BOBBIN CASE
BOBINAS^F

latch lever
lengüeta^F

bobbin
canilla^F

hook
portacanilla^M

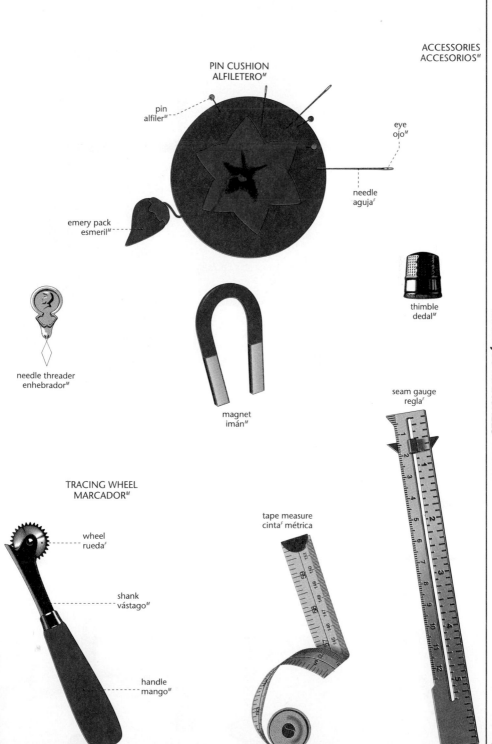

PIN CUSHION
ALFILETERO^M

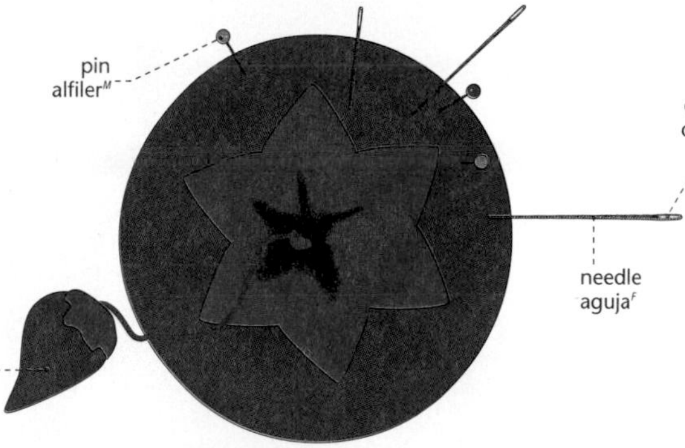

pin
alfiler^M

eye
ojo^M

needle
aguja^F

emery pack
esmeril^M

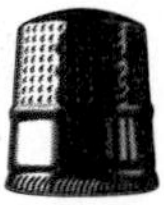

thimble
dedal^M

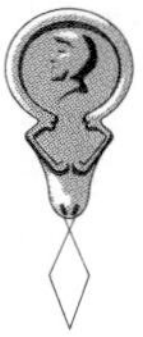

needle threader
enhebrador^M

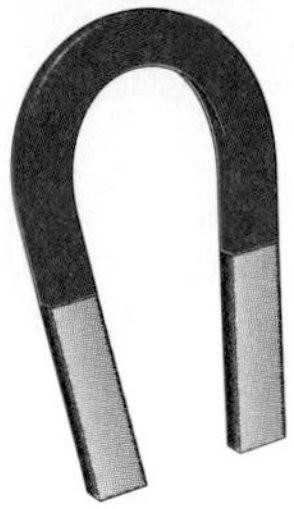

magnet
imán^M

seam gauge
regla^F

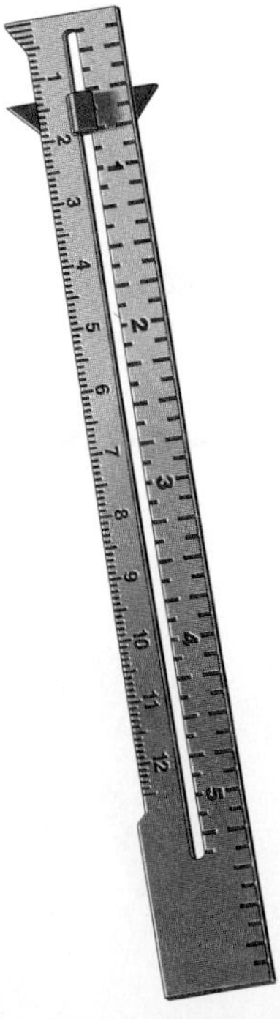

TRACING WHEEL
MARCADOR^M

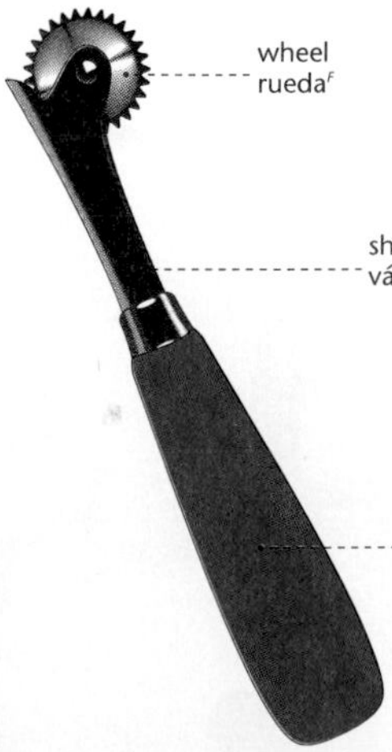

wheel
rueda^F

tape measure
cinta^F métrica

shank
vástago^M

handle
mango^M

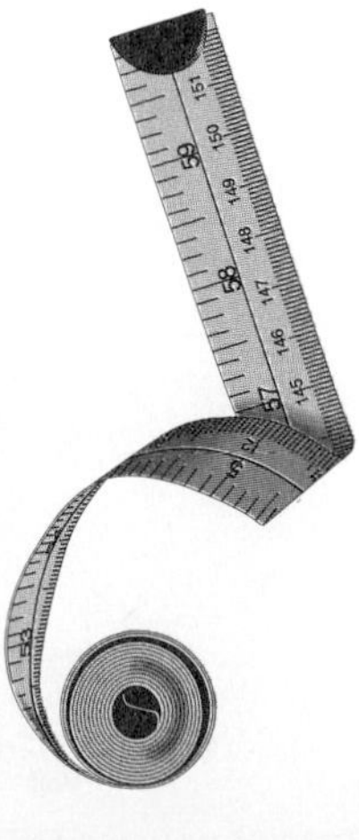

ACCESSORIES
ACCESORIOS^M DE COSTURA^F

scissors
tijeras^F de modista^F

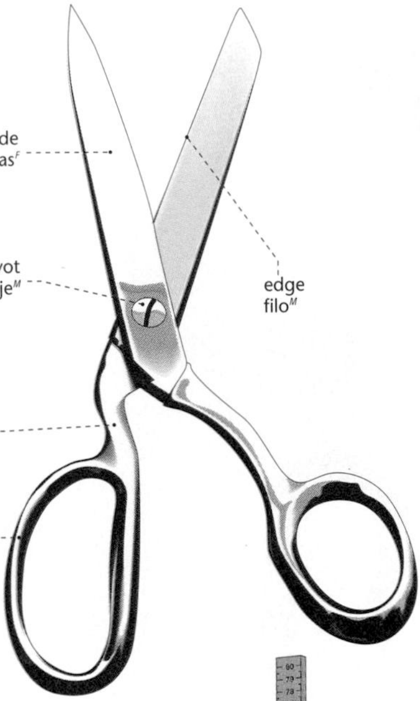

blade
hoja^F de las tijeras^F

pivot
eje^M

edge
filo^M

shank
mango^M

handle
ojo^M

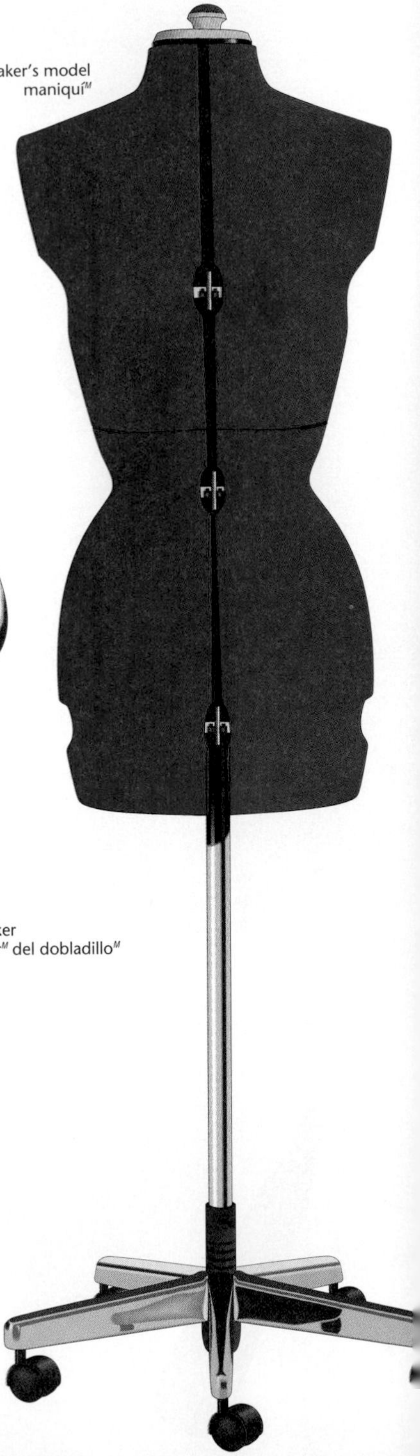

dressmaker's model
maniquí^M

pinking shears
tijeras^F para rematar

skirt marker
marcador^M del dobladillo^M

CREATIVE LEISURE ACTIVITIES
TRABAJOS MANUALES

564

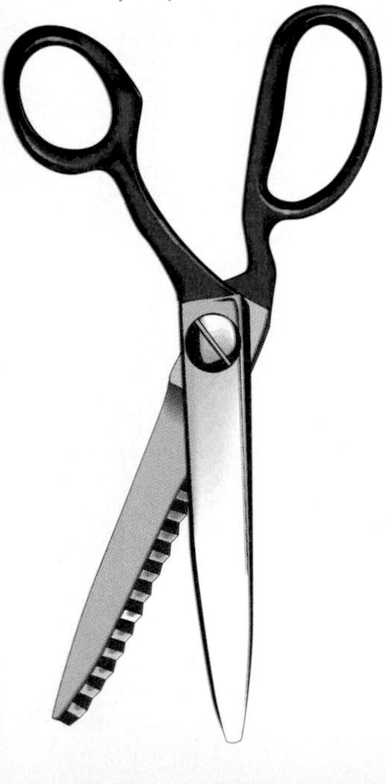

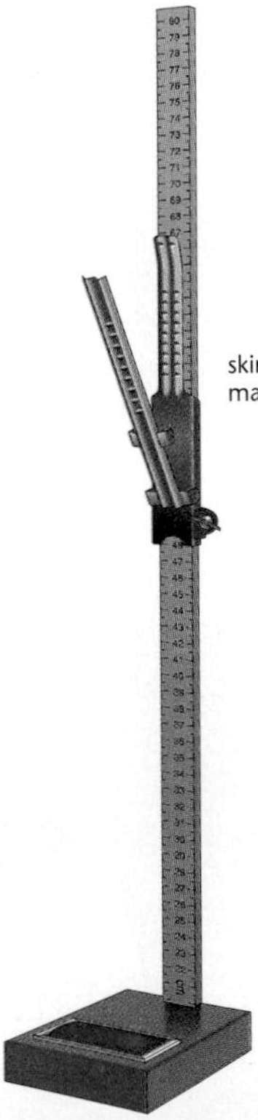

UNDERLYING FABRICS
FORRO^M Y ENTRETELAS^F

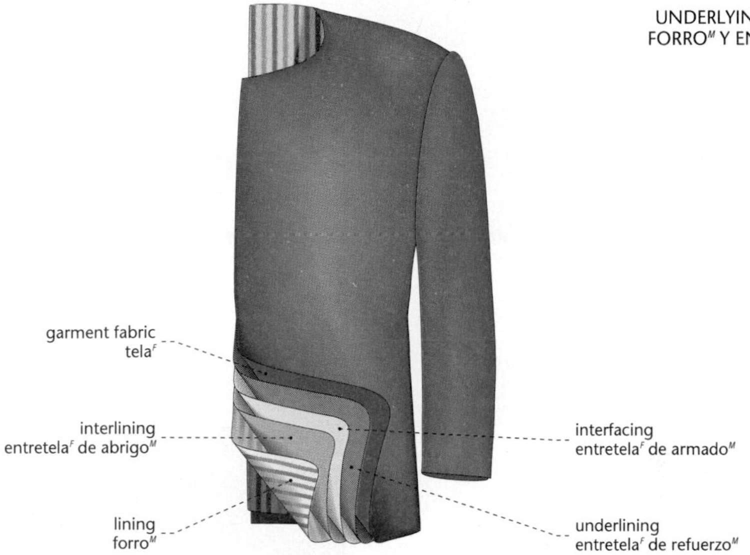

garment fabric
tela^F

interlining
entretela^F de abrigo^M

lining
forro^M

interfacing
entretela^F de armado^M

underlining
entretela^F de refuerzo^M

PATTERN
PATRÓN^M

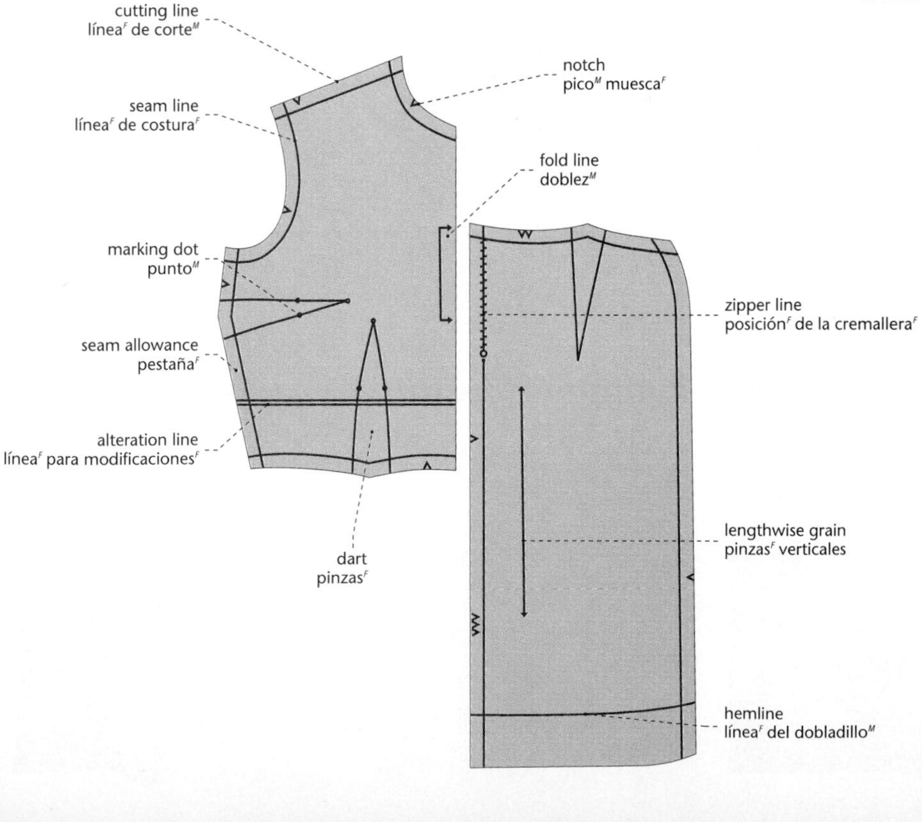

cutting line
línea^F de corte^M

notch
pico^M muesca^F

seam line
línea^F de costura^F

fold line
doblez^M

marking dot
punto^M

zipper line
posición^F de la cremallera^F

seam allowance
pestaña^F

alteration line
línea^F para modificaciones^F

lengthwise grain
pinzas^F verticales

dart
pinzas^F

hemline
línea^F del dobladillo^M

SEWING
COSTURA^F

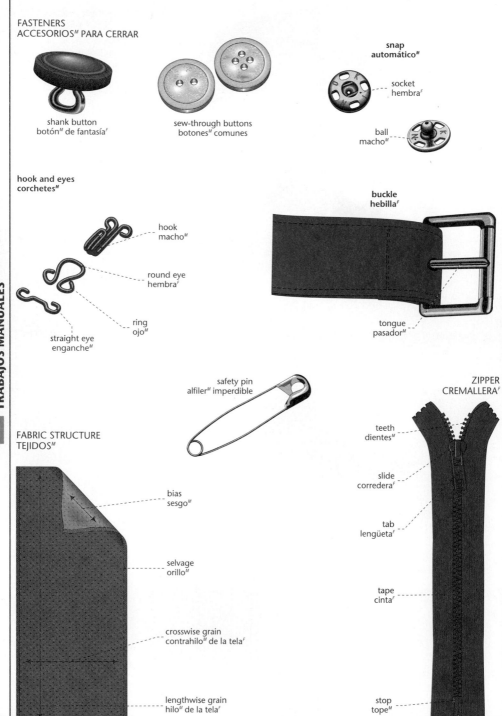

CREATIVE LEISURE ACTIVITIES
TRABAJOS MANUALES

FASTENERS
ACCESORIOS^M **PARA CERRAR**

snap
automático^M

socket
hembra^F

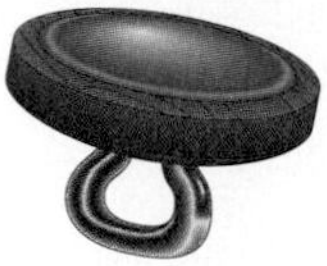

shank button
botón^M de fantasía^F

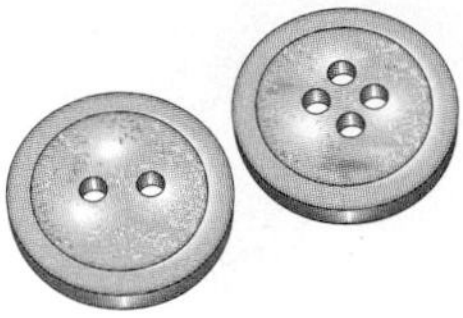

sew-through buttons
botones^M comunes

ball
macho^M

hook and eyes
corchetes^M

buckle
hebilla^F

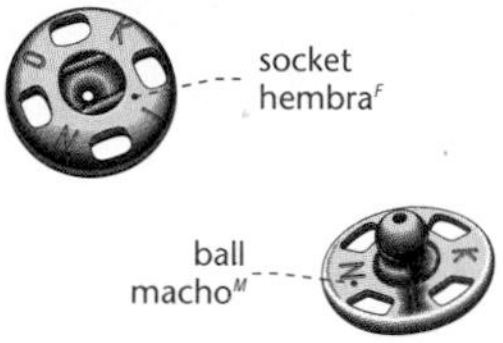

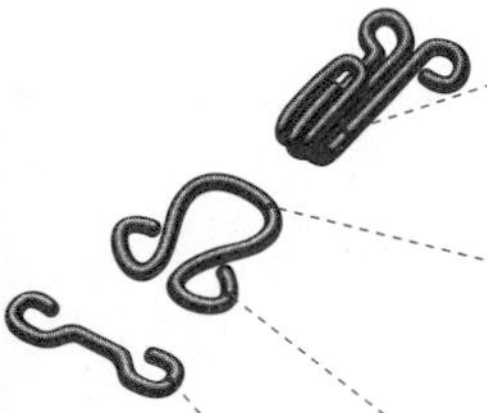

hook
macho^M

round eye
hembra^F

ring
ojo^M

straight eye
enganche^M

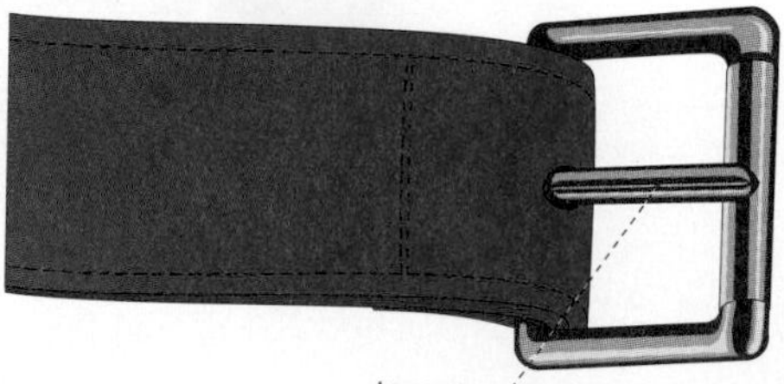

tongue
pasador^M

safety pin
alfiler^M imperdible

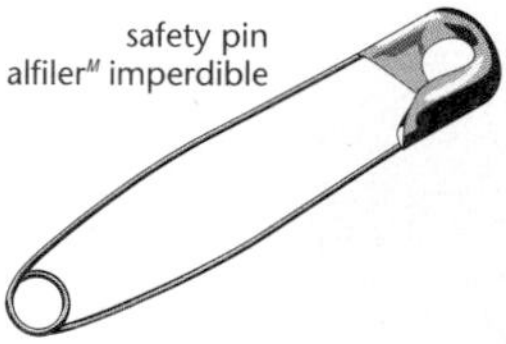

ZIPPER
CREMALLERA^F

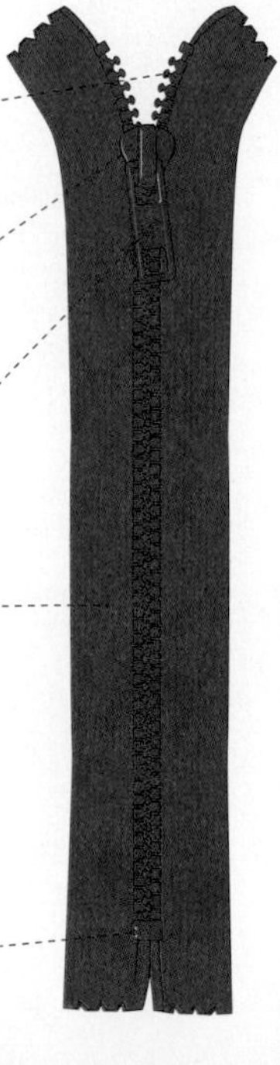

teeth
dientes^M

FABRIC STRUCTURE
TEJIDOS^M

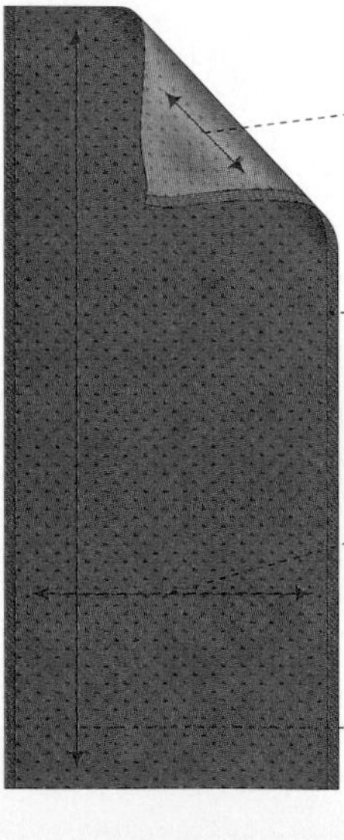

slide
corredera^F

bias
sesgo^M

tab
lengüeta^F

selvage
orillo^M

crosswise grain
contrahilo^M de la tela^F

tape
cinta^F

lengthwise grain
hilo^M de la tela^F

stop
tope^M

KNITTING
TEJIDO^M DE PUNTO^M

KNITTING NEEDLES
AGUJAS^F PARA TEJER

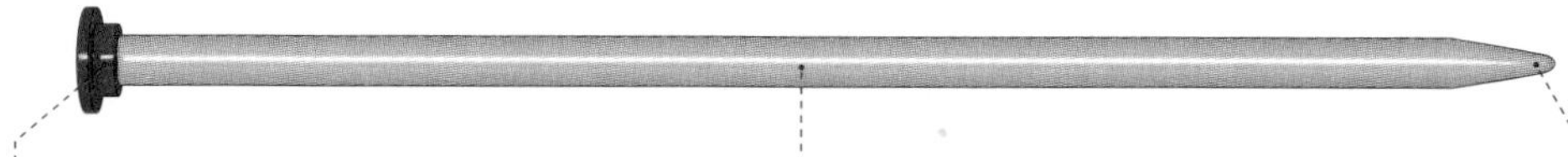

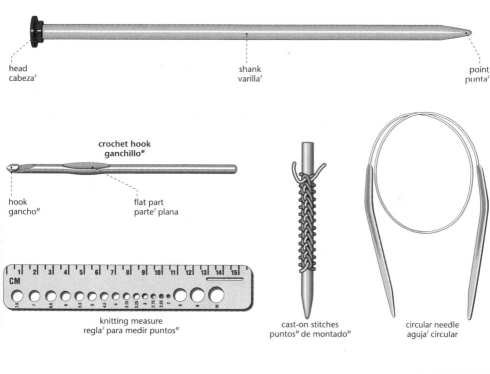

head
cabeza^F

shank
varilla^F

point
punta^F

crochet hook
ganchillo^M

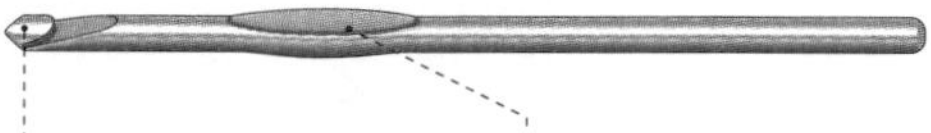

hook
gancho^M

flat part
parte^F plana

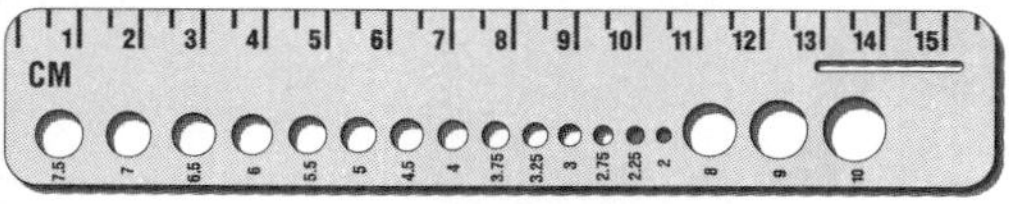

knitting measure
regla^F para medir puntos^M

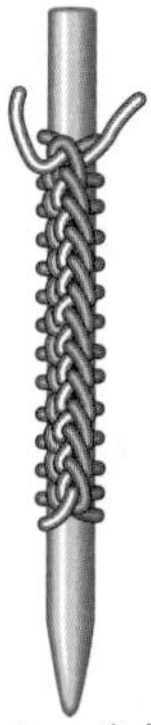

cast-on stitches
puntos^M de montado^M

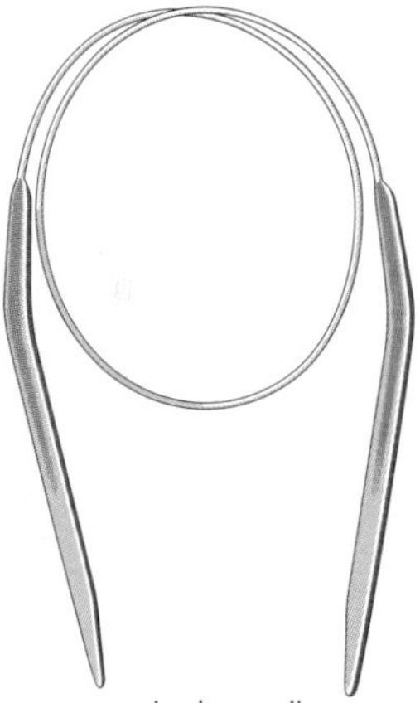

circular needle
aguja^F circular

STITCH PATTERNS
TIPOS^M DE PUNTO^M

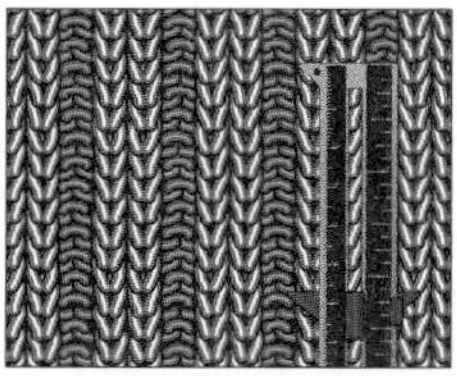

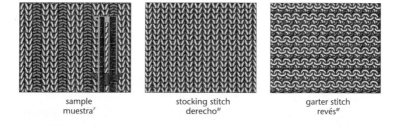

sample
muestra^F

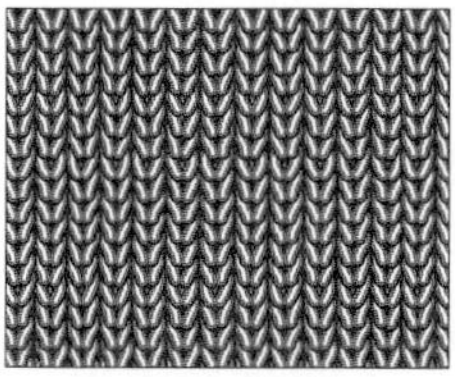

stocking stitch
derecho^M

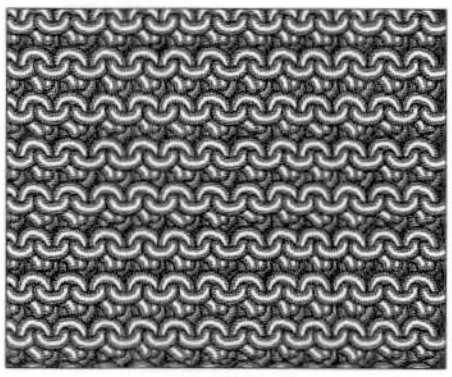

garter stitch
revés^M

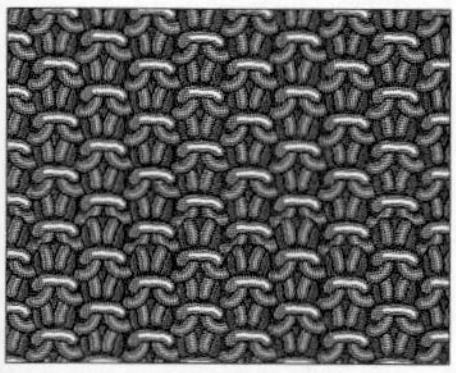

moss stitch
punto^M de musgo^M

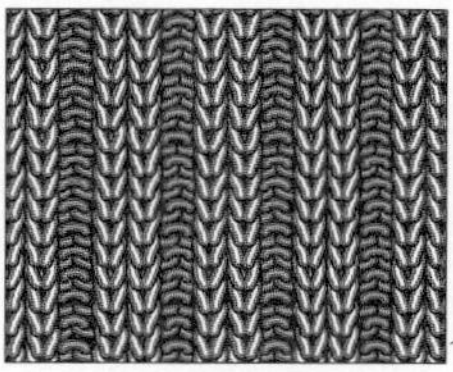

rib stitch
punto^M de respiguilla^F

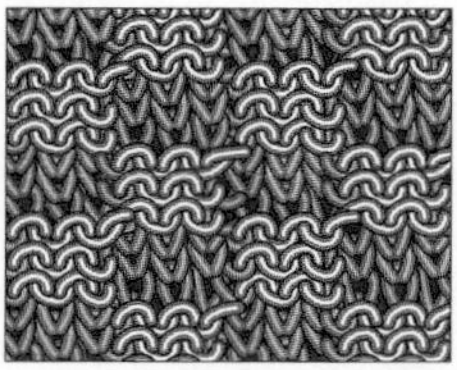

basket stitch
punto^M de malla^F

cable stitch
punto^M de ochos^M

567

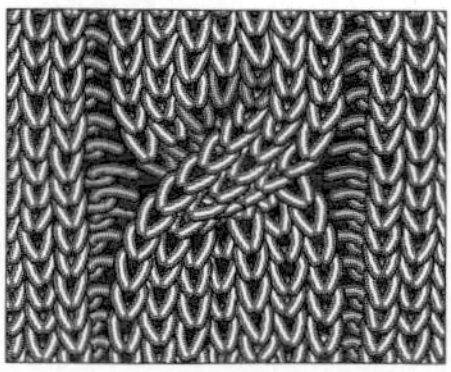

KNITTING MACHINE
MÁQUINA DE TRICOTAR

NEEDLE BED AND CARRIAGES
TRICOTADORAS*F*

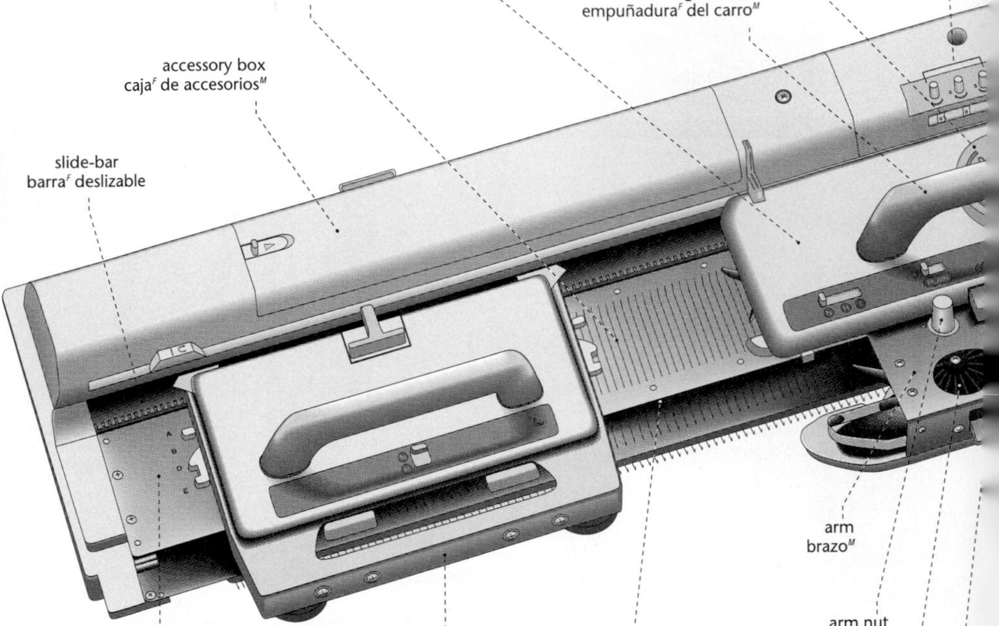

row counter
contador*M* de pasadas*F*

main carriage
carro*M* principal deslizante

tension dial
regulador*M* de tensión*F*

needle bed groove
placa*F* de agujas*F*

carriage handle
empuñadura*F* del carro*M*

accessory box
caja*F* de accesorios*M*

slide-bar
barra*F* deslizable

arm
brazo*M*

arm nut
seguro*M* del brazo*M*

needle bed
lecho*M* de agujas*F*

lace carriage
carro*M* de encaje*M*

weaving pattern brush
selector*M* para regular el tamaño*M*
de los puntos*M*

rail
guía*F*

weaving pattern lever
palanca*F* conmutadora de puntos*M*

LATCH NEEDLE
AGUJA*F* CON LENGÜETA*F*

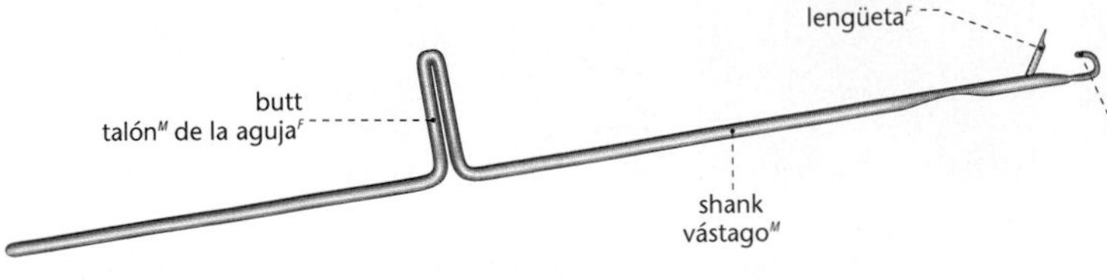

latch
lengüeta*F*

butt
talón*M* de la aguja*F*

shank
vástago*M*

hook
gancho*M*

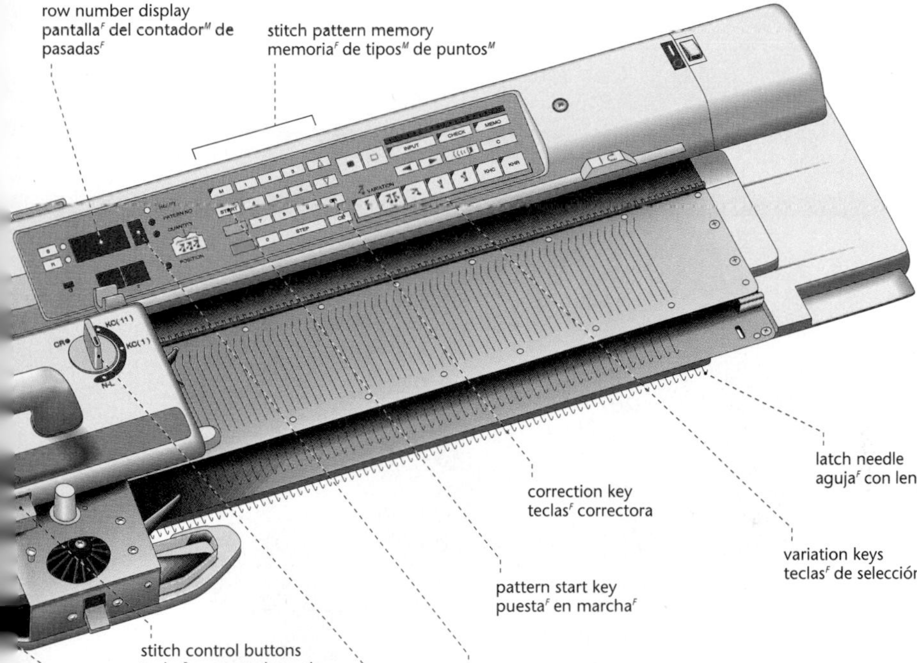

row number display
pantalla^F del contador^M de pasadas^F

stitch pattern memory
memoria^F de tipos^M de puntos^M

latch needle
aguja^F con lengüeta^F

correction key
teclas^F correctora

variation keys
teclas^F de selección^F

pattern start key
puesta^F en marcha^F

stitch control buttons
teclas^F conmutadoras de puntos^M

color display
pantalla^F de colores^M

yarn feeder
cerrojo^M

carriage control dial
mando^M de control^M del carro^M

TENSION BLOCK
SISTEMA^M DE TENSIÓN^F

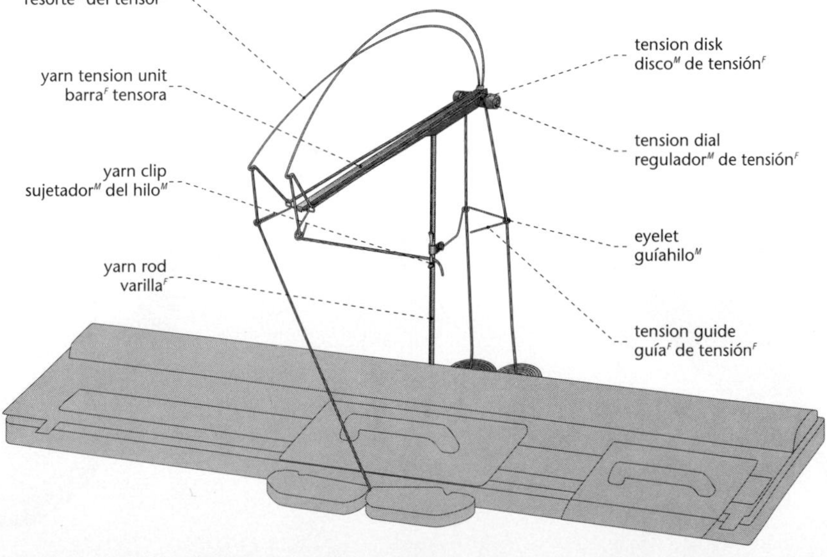

tension spring
resorte^M del tensor^M

yarn tension unit
barra^F tensora

yarn clip
sujetador^M del hilo^M

yarn rod
varilla^F

tension disk
disco^M de tensión^F

tension dial
regulador^M de tensión^F

eyelet
guíahilo^M

tension guide
guía^F de tensión^F

BOBBIN LACE
ENCAJE^M DE BOLILLOS^M

PILLOW
ALMOHADILLA^F

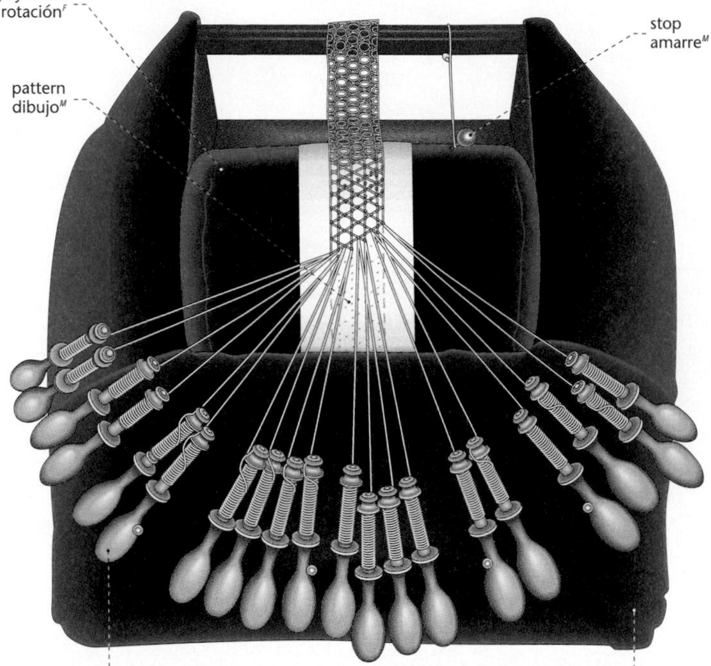

revolving cylinder
cilindro^M de rotación^F

pattern
dibujo^M

stop
amarre^M

bobbin
bolillo^M

pillow
almohadilla^F

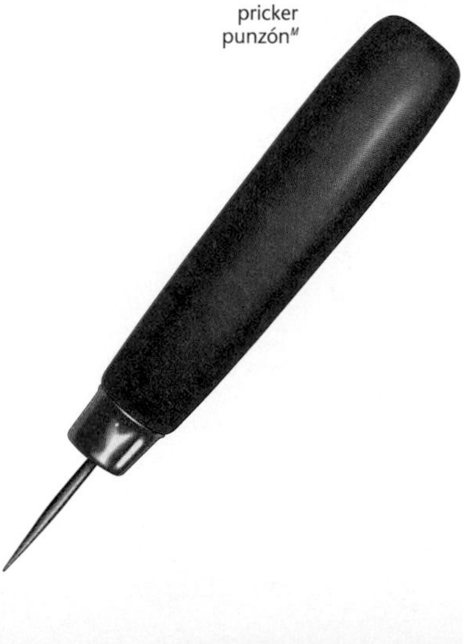

pricker
punzón^M

BOBBIN
BOLILLO^M

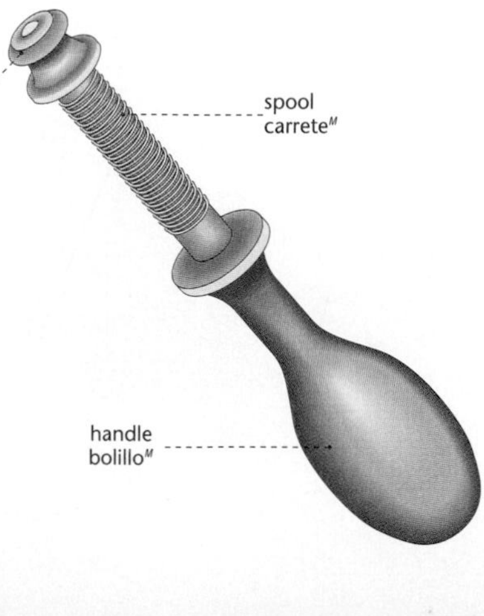

spool
carrete^M

head
cabeza^F

handle
bolillo^M

EMBROIDERY
BORDADO^M

FRAME
BASTIDOR^M

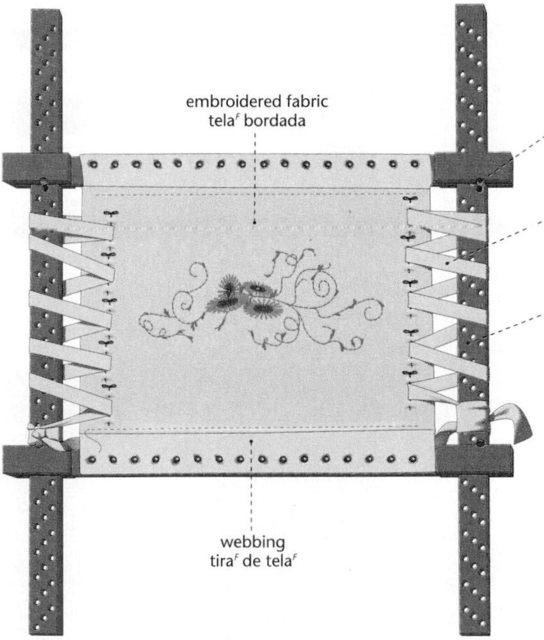

embroidered fabric
tela^F bordada

peg
espiga^F

tape
cinta^F

slat
listón^M de madera^F

webbing
tira^F de tela^F

hoop
lanzadera^F

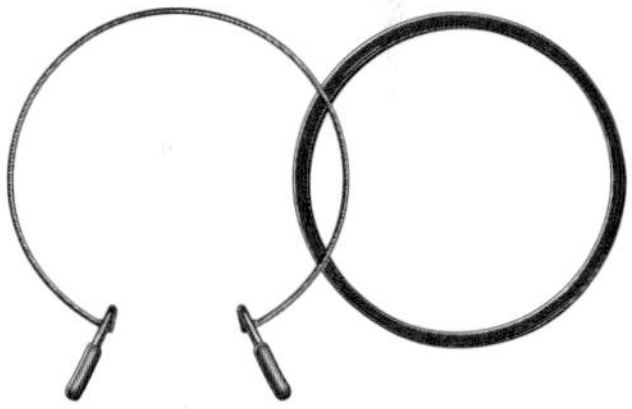

STITCHES
TIPOS^M DE PUNTOS^M

cross stitches
puntos^M de cruz^F

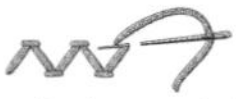

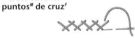

herringbone stitch
punto^M de escapulario^M

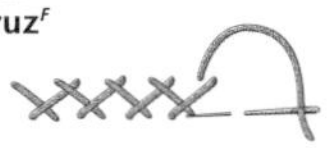

chevron stitch
punto^M de cruz^F

flat stitches
puntos^M de relleno^M

couched stitches
bordados^M planos

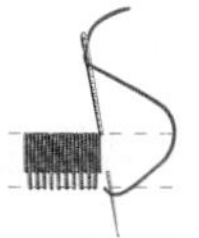

long and short stitch
lanzado^M desigual

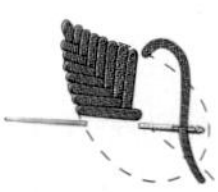

fishbone stitch
punto^M de espiga^F

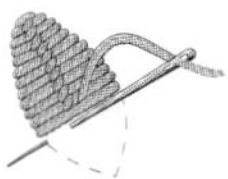

Romanian couching stitch
bordado^M plano

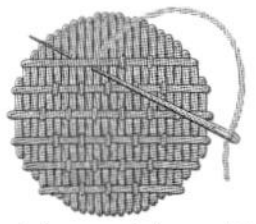

Oriental couching stitch
relleno^M alternado

knot stitches
puntos^M de relleno^M sueltos

loop stitches
puntos^M de malla^F

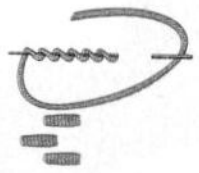

bullion stitch
pespunte^M

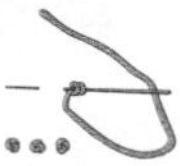

French knot stitch
punto^M de nudos^M

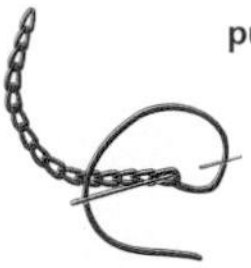

chain stitch
cadeneta^F

feather stitch
pata^F de gallo^M

571

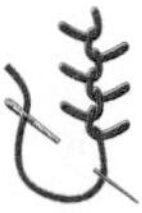

WEAVING
TELAR^M

LOW WARP LOOM
TELAR^M DE CUATRO MARCOS^M

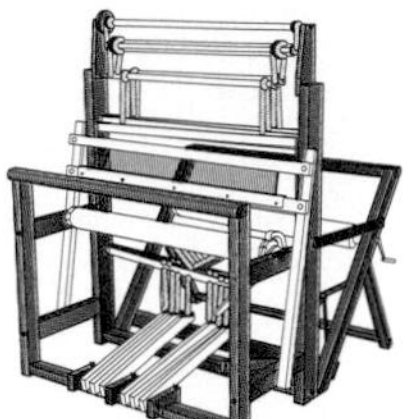

frame
armazón^M

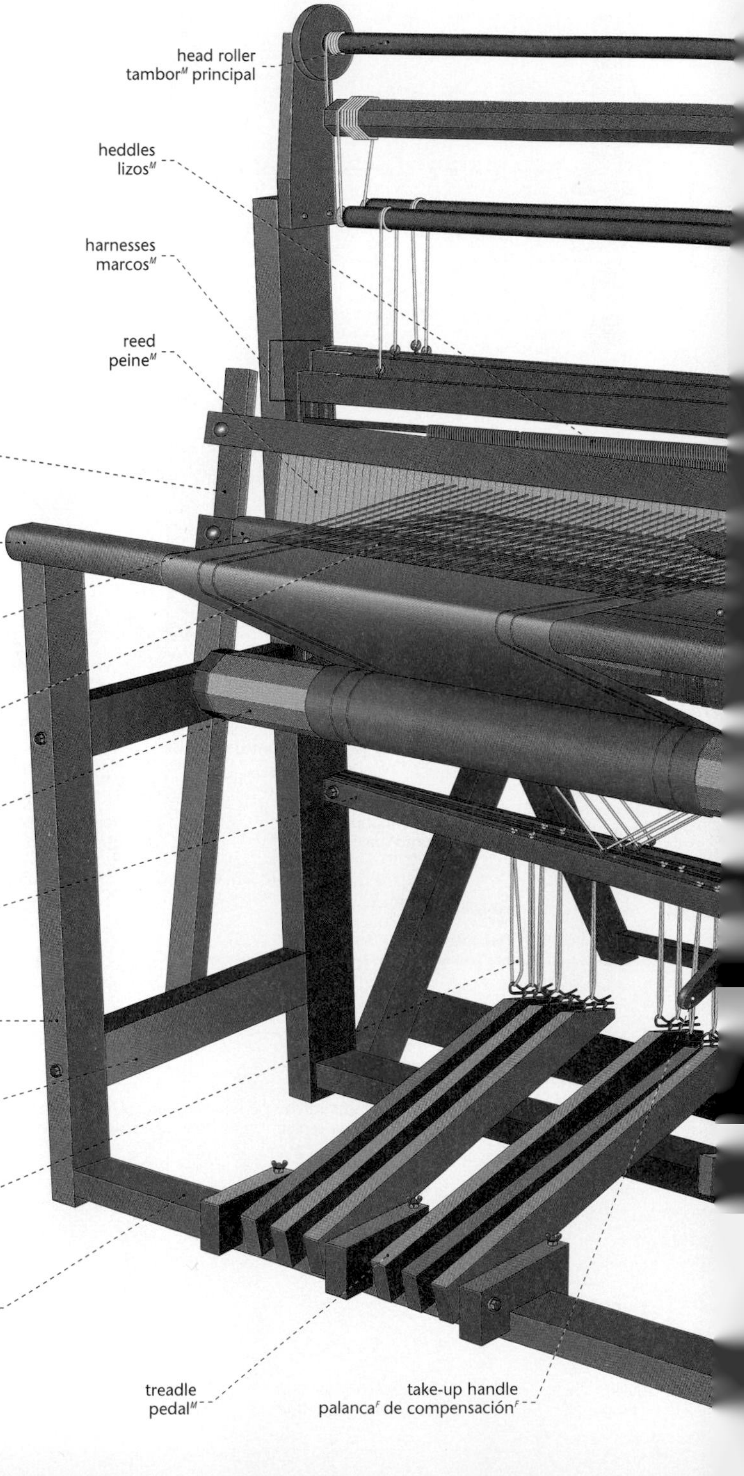

head roller
tambor^M principal

heddles
lizos^M

harnesses
marcos^M

reed
peine^M

beater
batán^M

breast beam
travesaño^M frontal

beater sley
travesaño^M intermedio del
batán^M

weft
trama^f

cloth roller
plegador^M del tejido^M

lam
travesaño^M

post
montante^M

crosspiece
travesaño^M

treadle cord
cordón^M del pedal^M

crossbeam
travesaño^M frontal interior

treadle
pedal^M

take-up handle
palanca^f de compensación^f

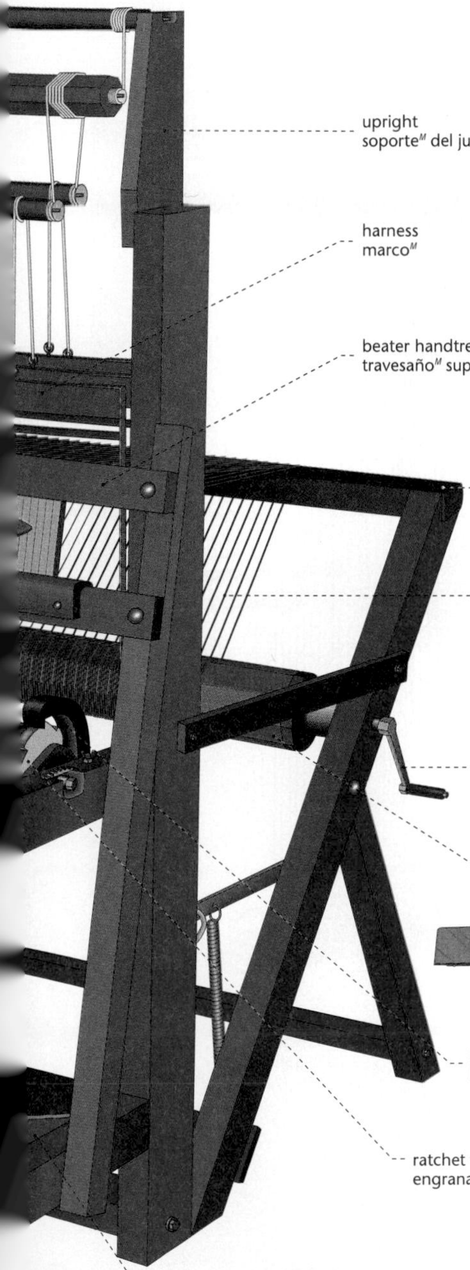

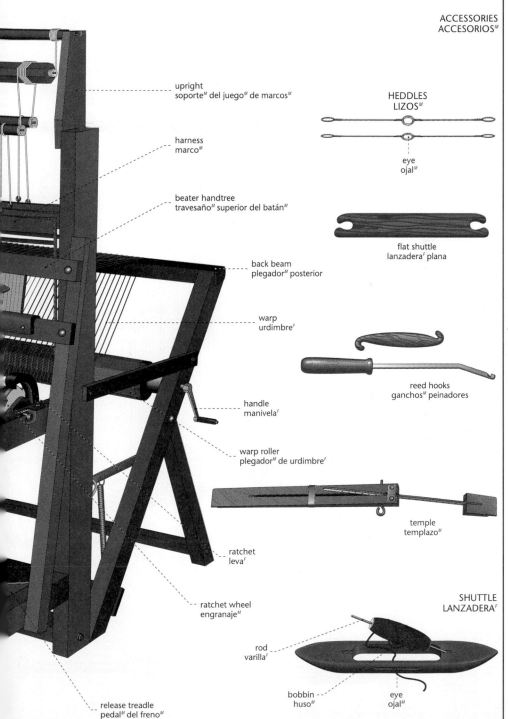

upright
soporte^M del juego^M de marcos^M

HEDDLES
LIZOS^M

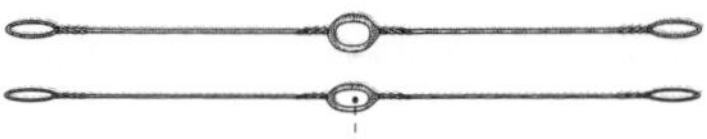

harness
marco^M

eye
ojal^M

beater handtree
travesaño^M superior del batán^M

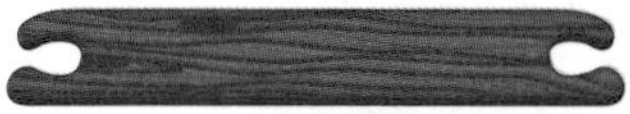

flat shuttle
lanzadera^F plana

back beam
plegador^M posterior

warp
urdimbre^F

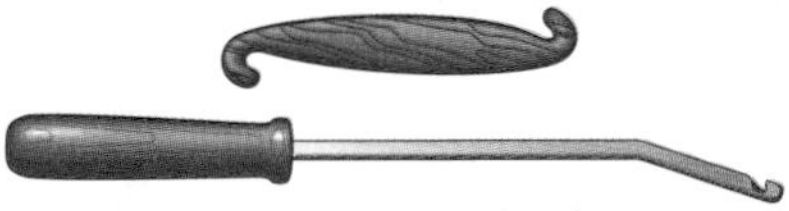

reed hooks
ganchos^M peinadores

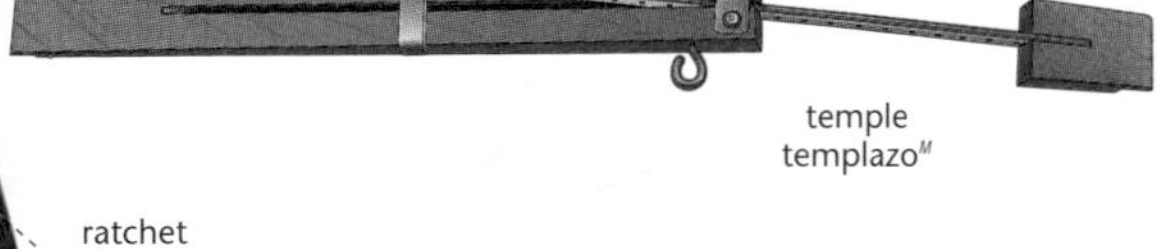

handle
manivela^F

warp roller
plegador^M de urdimbre^F

temple
templazo^M

ratchet
leva^F

ratchet wheel
engranaje^M

SHUTTLE
LANZADERA^F

rod
varilla^F

release treadle
pedal^M del freno^M

bobbin
huso^M

eye
ojal^M

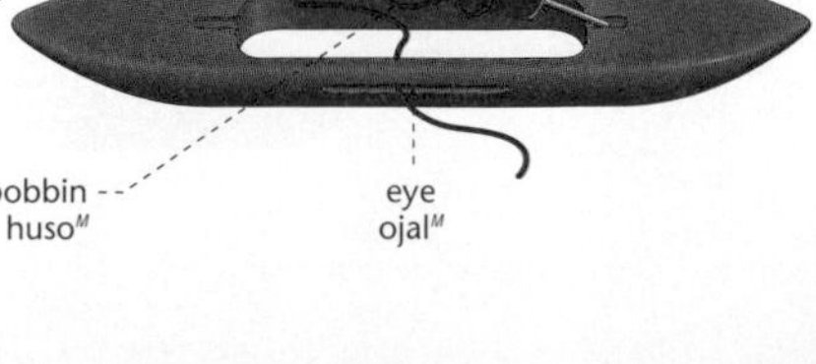

HIGH WARP LOOM
TELAR^M DE TAPICERÍA^F

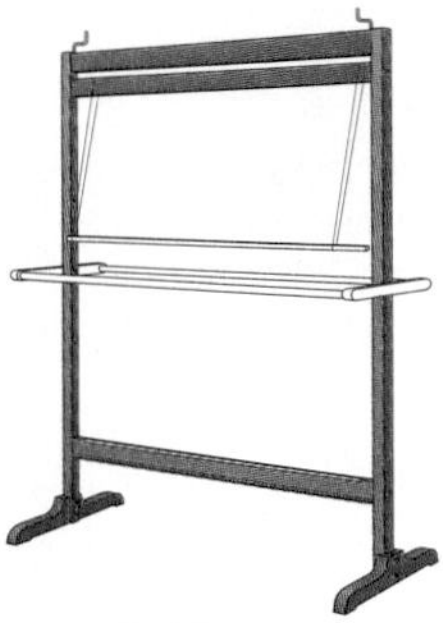

vertical frame
marco^M vertical

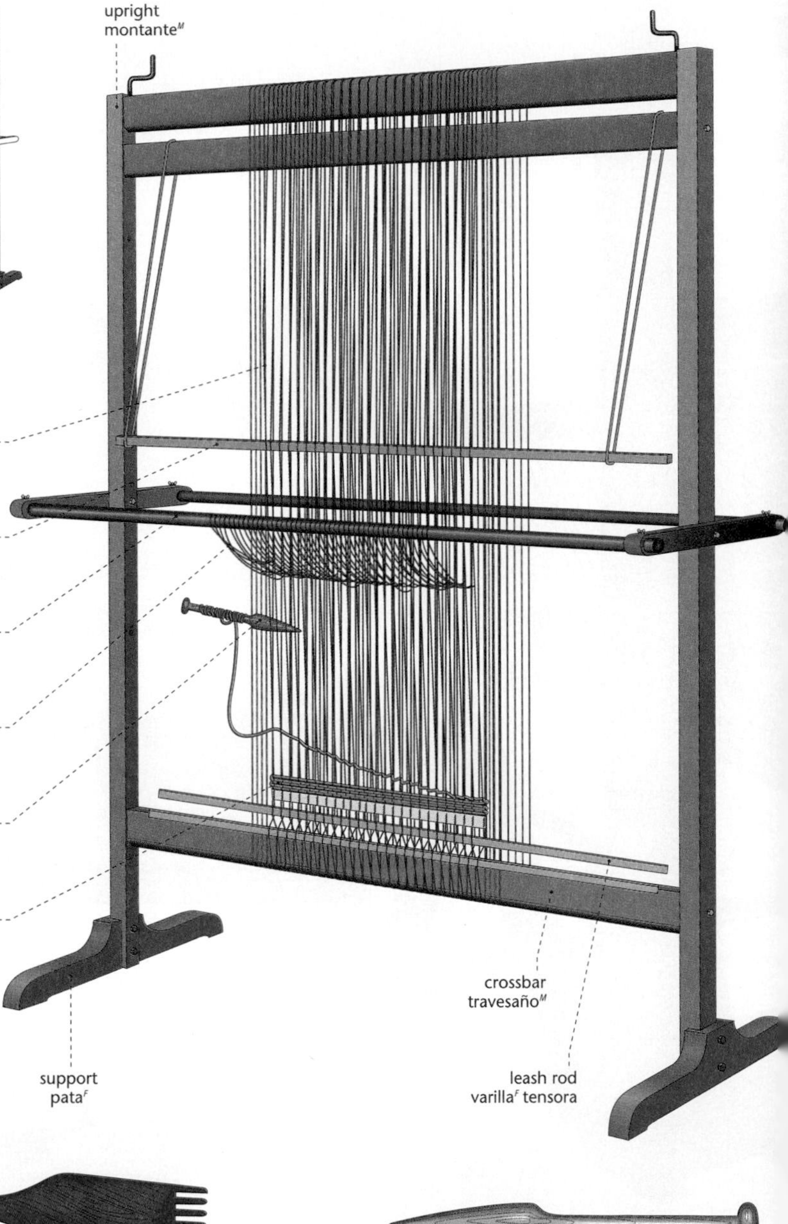

upright
montante^M

warp
urdimbre^F

shed stick
varilla^F de calada^F

heddle rod
varilla^F de lizos^M

heddles
lizos^M

tapestry bobbin
lanzadera^F

weft
trama^F

support
pata^F

crossbar
travesaño^M

leash rod
varilla^F tensora

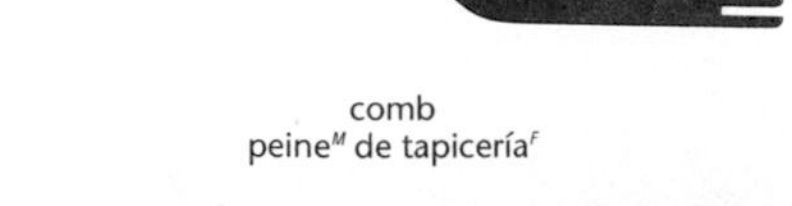

comb
peine^M de tapicería^F

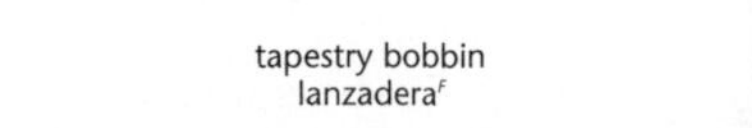

tapestry bobbin
lanzadera^F

bobbin winder
devanador^M de bobinas^F

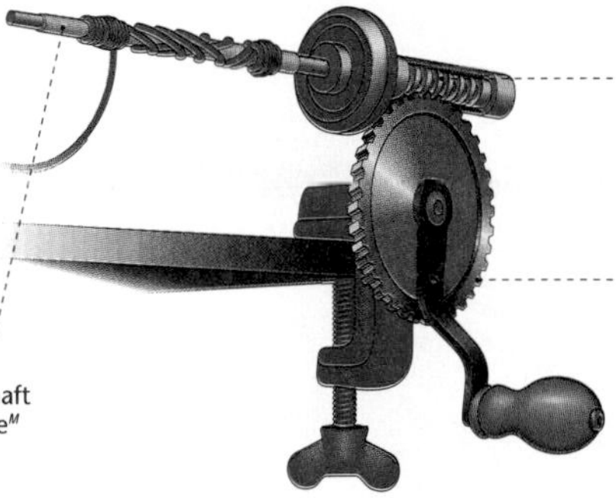

worm
tornillo^M sinfín

gear
engranaje^M

shaft
eje^M

ball winder
devanador^M

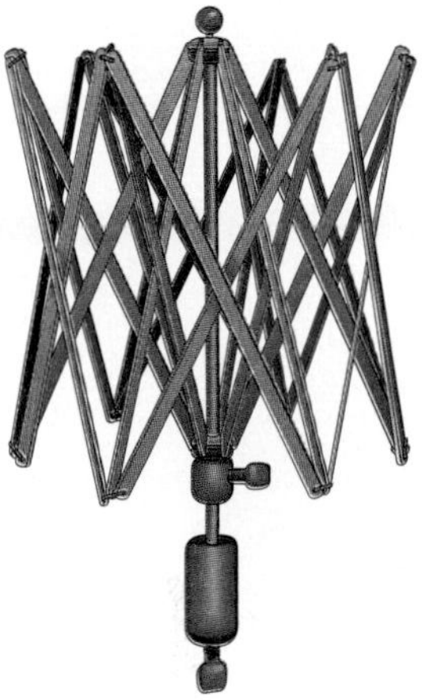

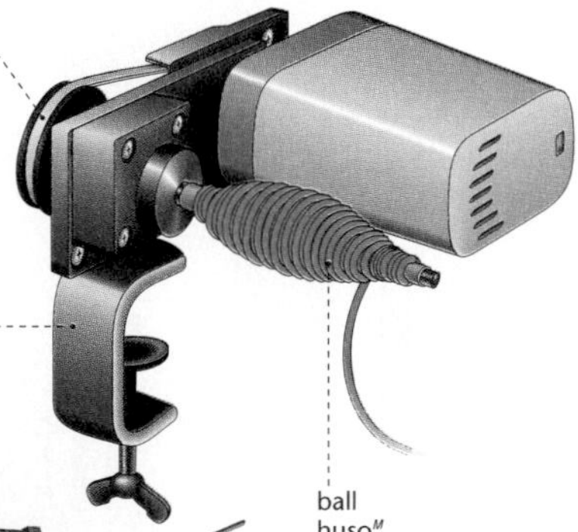

driving wheel
polea^F de transmisión^F

clamp
abrazadera^F

ball
huso^M

swift
devanadera^F

warping frame
urdidor^M

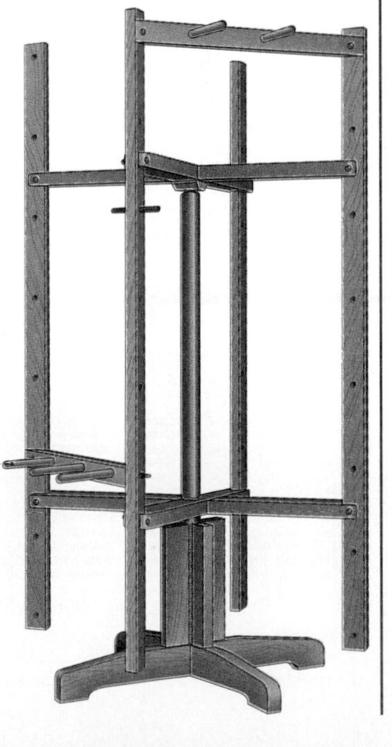

peg
espiga^F

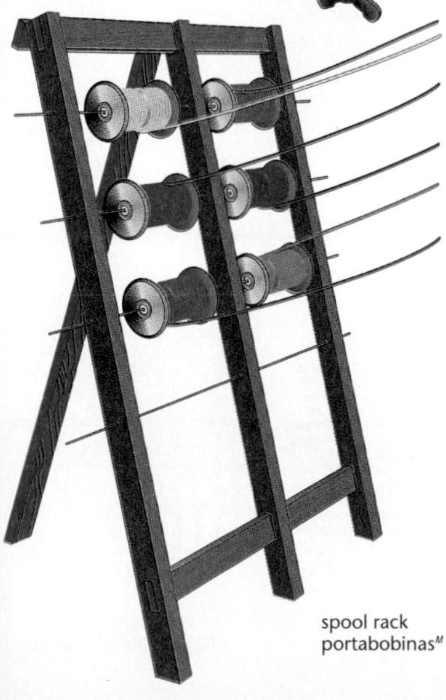

spool rack
portabobinas^M

DIAGRAM OF WEAVING PRINCIPLE
DIAGRAMAS^M DE TEJIDOS^M

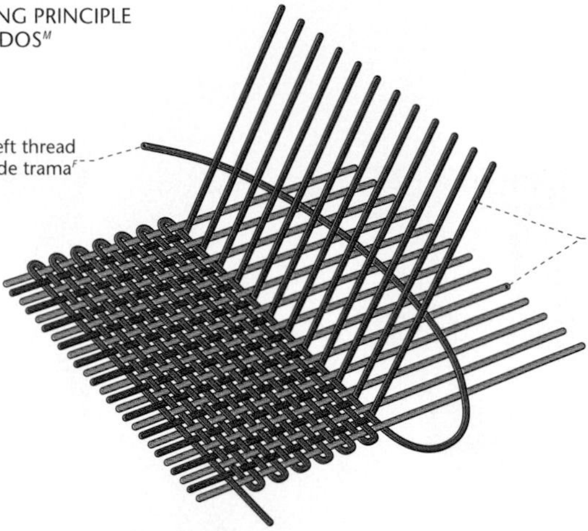

weft thread
hilo^M de trama^F

warp thread
hilo^M de urdimbre^F

BASIC WEAVES
LIGAMENTOS^M TEXTILES BÁSICOS

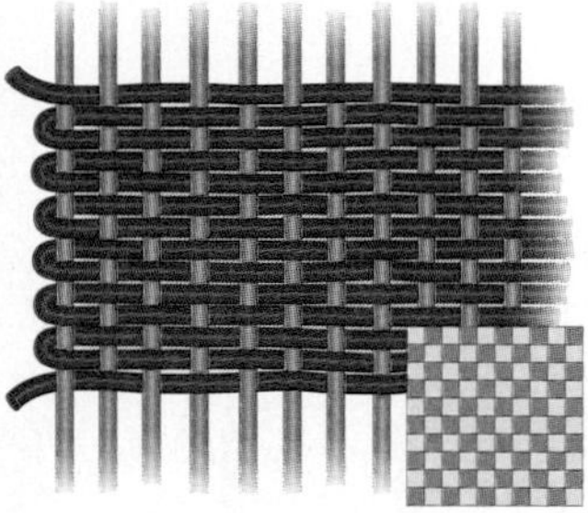

plain weave
tafetán^M

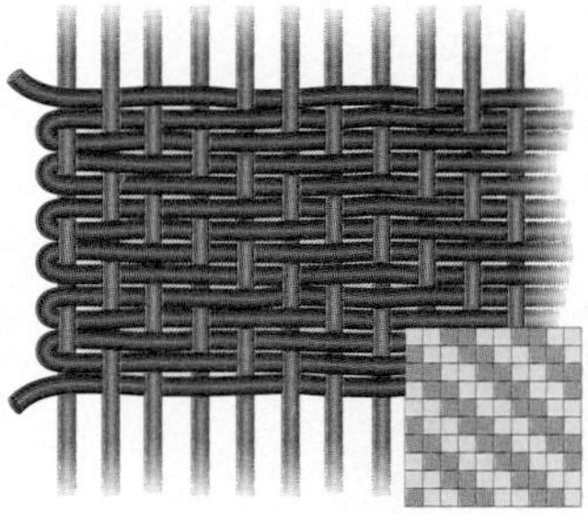

twill weave
sarga^F

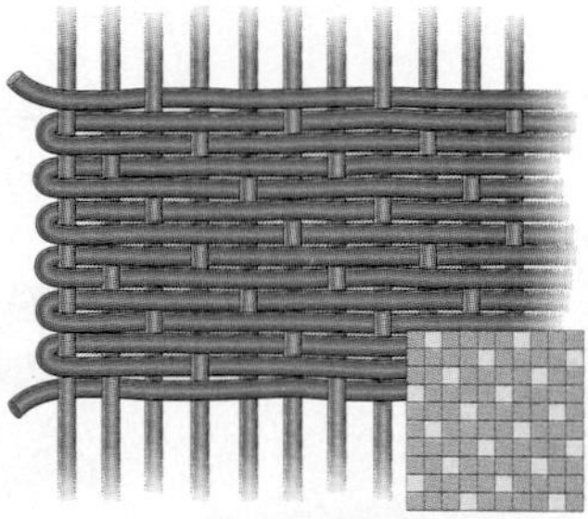

satin weave
satén^M

OTHER TECHNIQUES
OTROS LIGAMENTOS^M TEXTILES

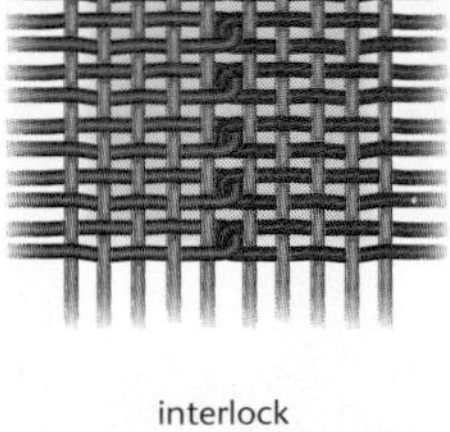

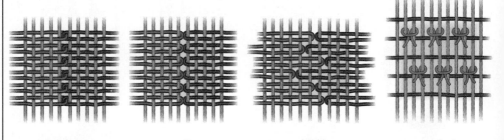

interlock
ligamento^M entrecruzado

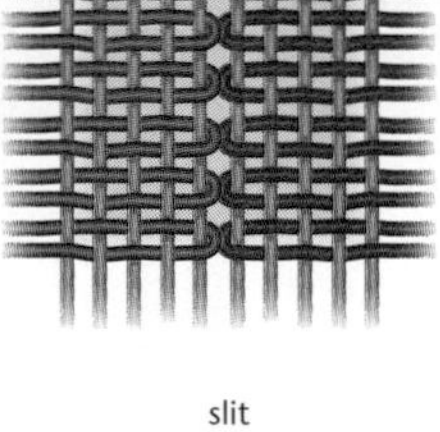

slit
ligamento^M vertical

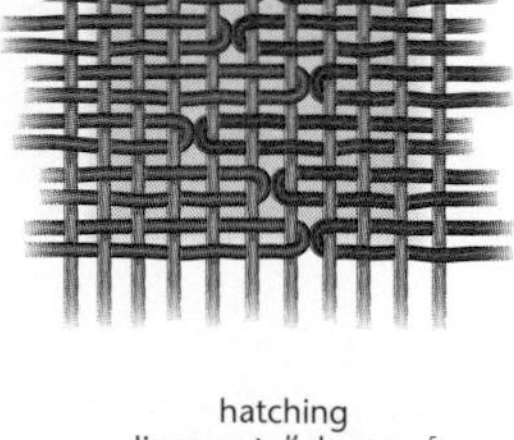

hatching
ligamento^M de rayas^F

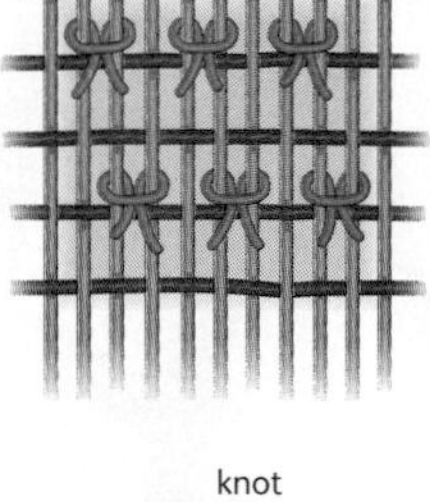

knot
ligamento^M de nudos^M

FINE BOOKBINDING
ENCUADERNACIÓN^F ARTÍSTICA^F

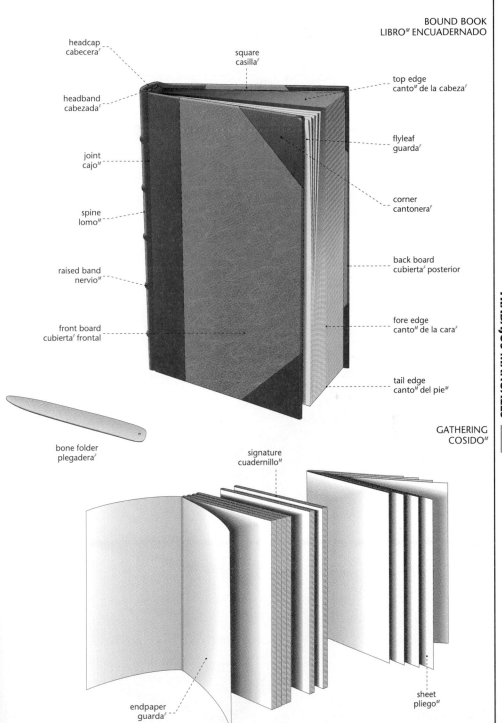

BOUND BOOK
LIBRO^M ENCUADERNADO

headcap
cabecera^F

square
casilla^F

top edge
canto^M de la cabeza^F

headband
cabezada^F

flyleaf
guarda^F

joint
cajo^M

corner
cantonera^F

spine
lomo^M

back board
cubierta^F posterior

raised band
nervio^M

fore edge
canto^M de la cara^F

front board
cubierta^F frontal

tail edge
canto^M del pie^M

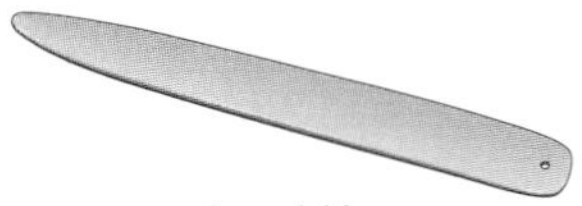

bone folder
plegadera^F

GATHERING
COSIDO^M

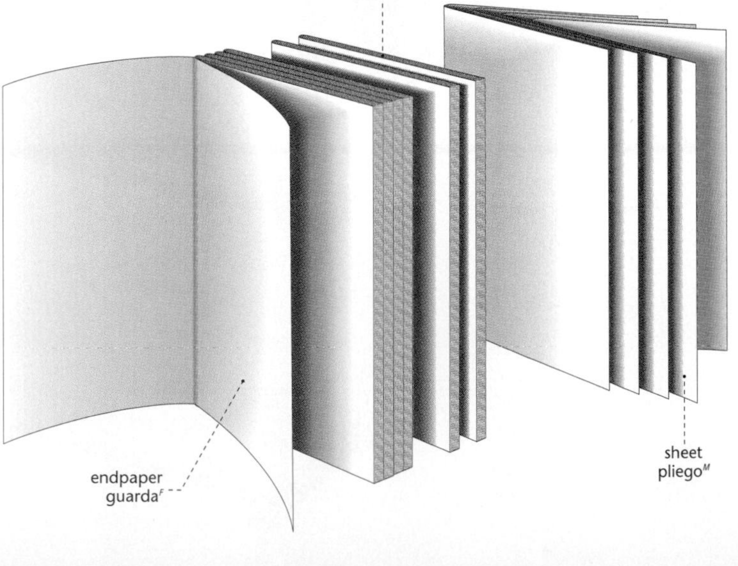

signature
cuadernillo^M

endpaper
guarda^F

sheet
pliego^M

TRIMMING
GUILLOTINA^F

board cutter
cizalla^F

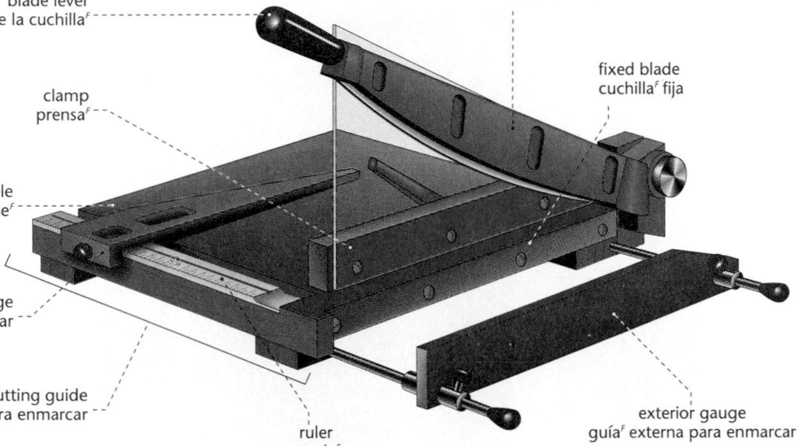

blade lever
palanca^F de la cuchilla^F

cutting blade
cuchilla^F móvil

fixed blade
cuchilla^F fija

clamp
prensa^F

table
base^F

gauge
guía^F para enmarcar

cutting guide
dispositivo^M para enmarcar

ruler
regla^F

exterior gauge
guía^F externa para enmarcar

SAWING-IN
ENSAMBLAJE^M A ESPIGA^F

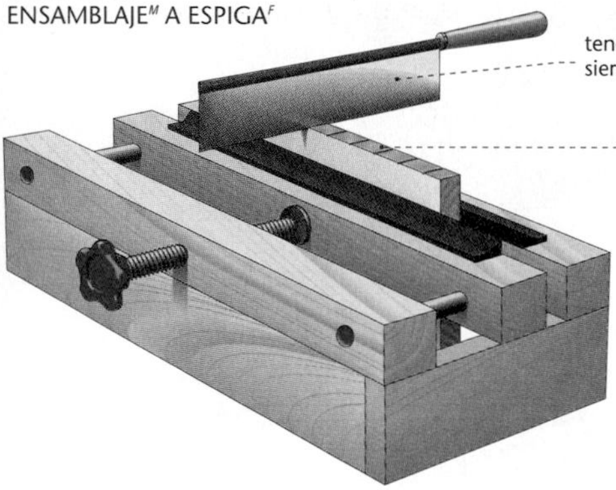

tenon saw
sierra^F de ensamblar

groove
muescas^F

SEWING
ENCUADERNACIÓN^F EN RÚSTICA

sewing frame
bastidor^M de coser

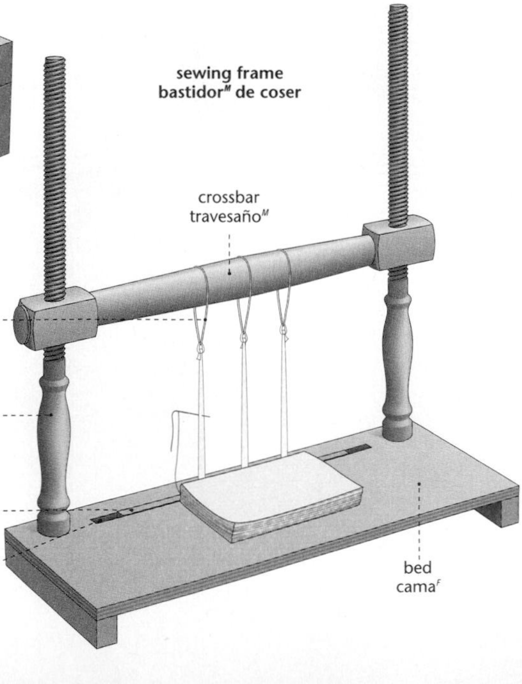

crossbar
travesaño^M

cord
cuerda^F para el cosido^M

upright
montante^M

temple
templador^M

slot
hendidura^F

bed
cama^F

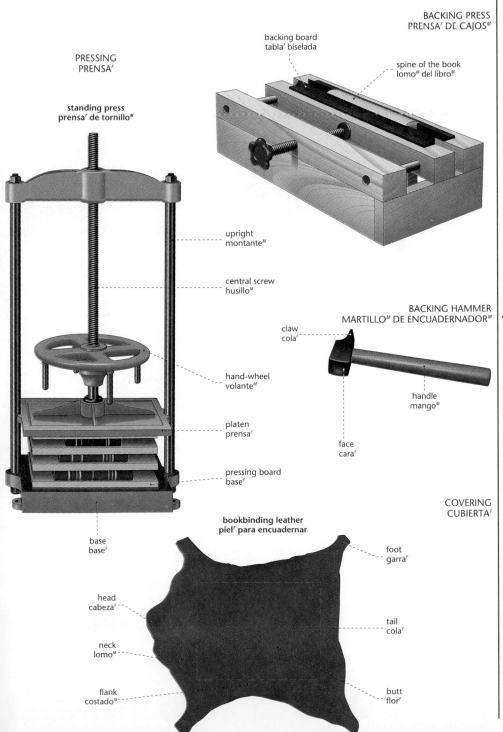

BACKING
REDONDEO^M

BACKING PRESS
PRENSA^F DE CAJOS^M

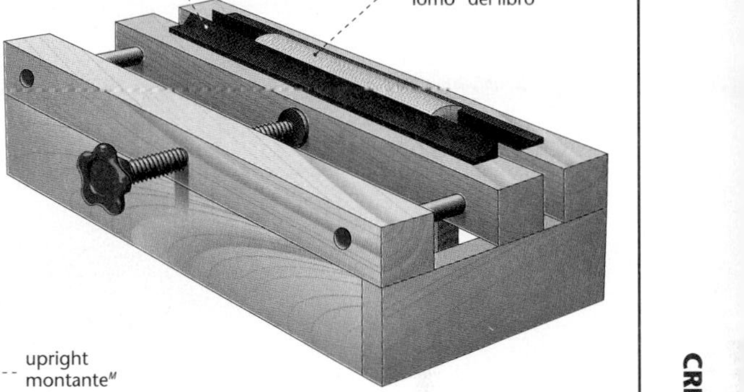

backing board
tabla^F biselada

spine of the book
lomo^M del libro^M

PRESSING
PRENSA^F

standing press
prensa^F de tornillo^M

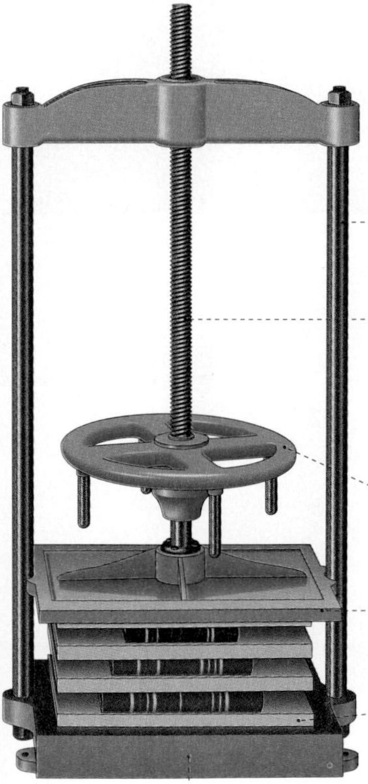

upright
montante^M

central screw
husillo^M

BACKING HAMMER
MARTILLO^M DE ENCUADERNADOR^M

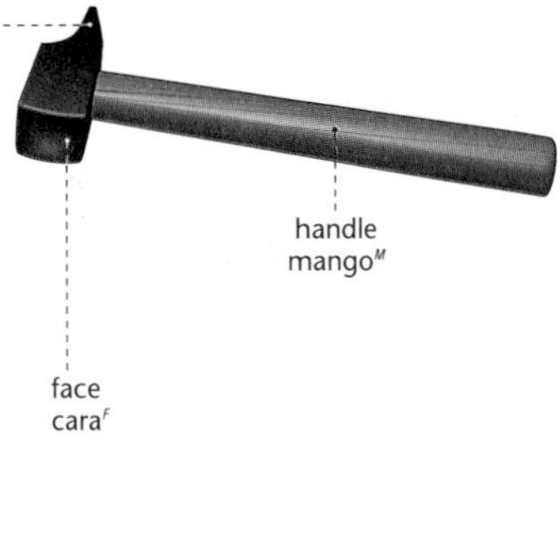

claw
cola^F

hand-wheel
volante^M

handle
mango^M

platen
prensa^F

face
cara^F

pressing board
base^F

COVERING
CUBIERTA^F

bookbinding leather
piel^F para encuadernar

base
base^F

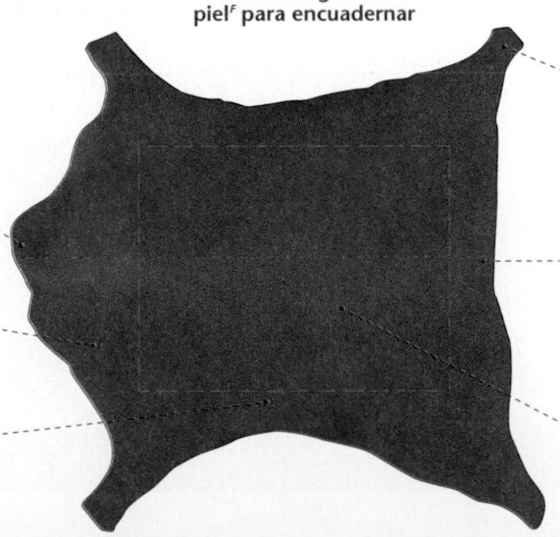

foot
garra^F

head
cabeza^F

tail
cola^F

neck
lomo^M

flank
costado^M

butt
flor^F

RELIEF PRINTING
IMPRESIÓN^F EN RELIEVE^M

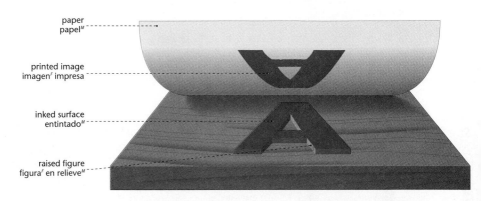

paper
papel^M

printed image
imagen^F impresa

inked surface
entintado^M

raised figure
figura^F en relieve^M

INTAGLIO PRINTING
HUECOGRABADO^M

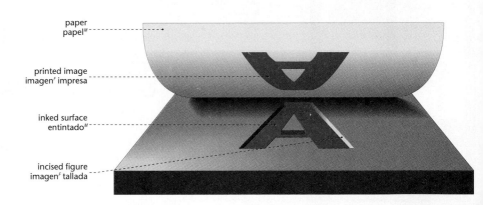

paper
papel^M

printed image
imagen^F impresa

inked surface
entintado^M

incised figure
imagen^F tallada

LITHOGRAPHIC PRINTING
IMPRESIÓN LITOGRÁFICA

printed image
imagen^F impresa

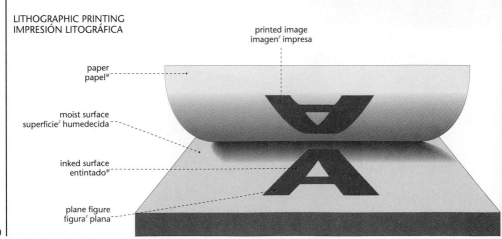

paper
papel^M

moist surface
superficie^F humedecida

inked surface
entintado^M

plane figure
figura^F plana

RELIEF PRINTING PROCESS
IMPRESIÓN^F EN RELIEVE^M

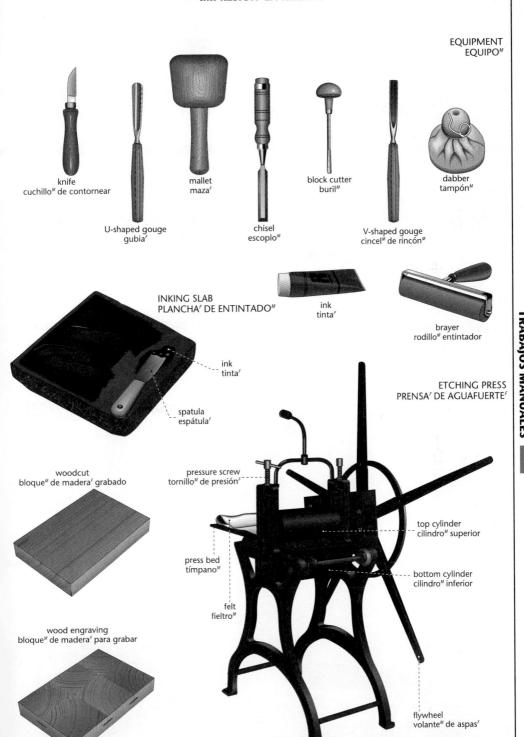

EQUIPMENT
EQUIPO^M

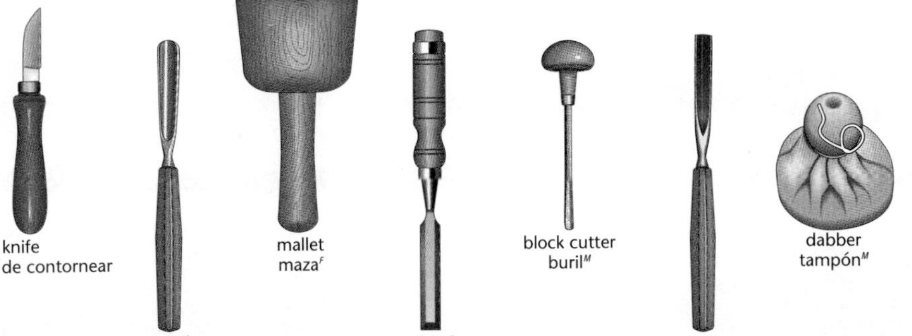

knife
cuchillo^M de contornear

U-shaped gouge
gubia^F

mallet
maza^F

chisel
escoplo^M

block cutter
buril^M

V-shaped gouge
cincel^M de rincón^M

dabber
tampón^M

INKING SLAB
PLANCHA^F DE ENTINTADO^M

ink
tinta^F

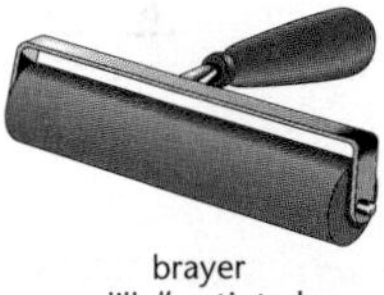

brayer
rodillo^M entintador

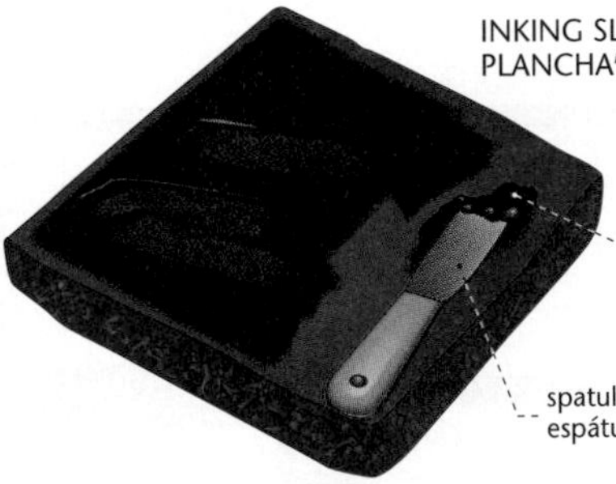

ink
tinta^F

spatula
espátula^F

ETCHING PRESS
PRENSA^F DE AGUAFUERTE^F

woodcut
bloque^M de madera^F grabado

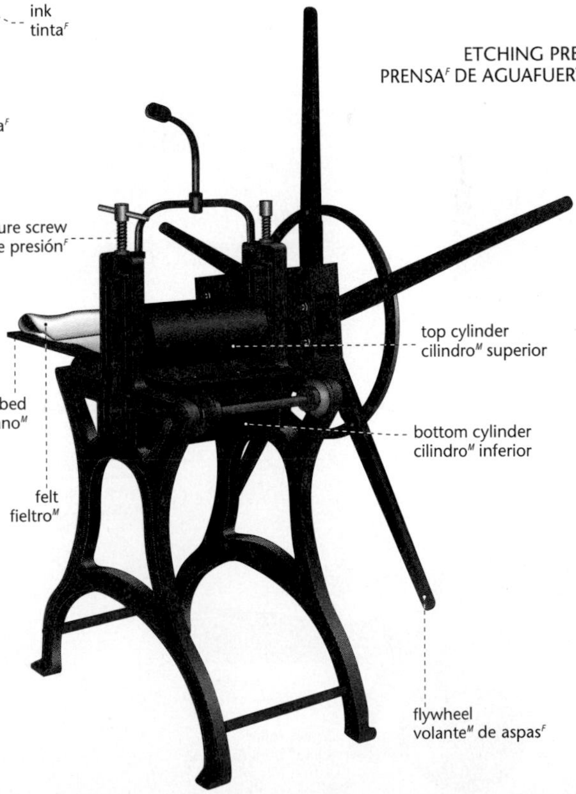

pressure screw
tornillo^M de presión^F

top cylinder
cilindro^M superior

press bed
tímpano^M

bottom cylinder
cilindro^M inferior

felt
fieltro^M

wood engraving
bloque^M de madera^F para grabar

flywheel
volante^M de aspas^F

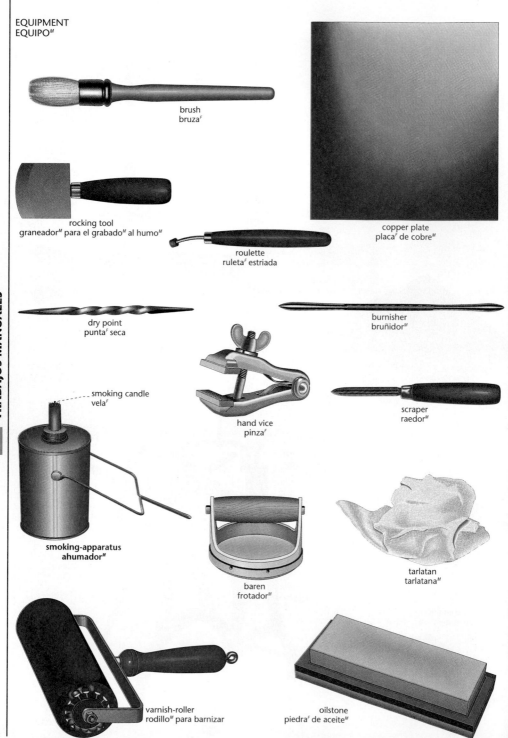

**CREATIVE LEISURE ACTIVITIES
TRABAJOS MANUALES**

EQUIPMENT
EQUIPO^M

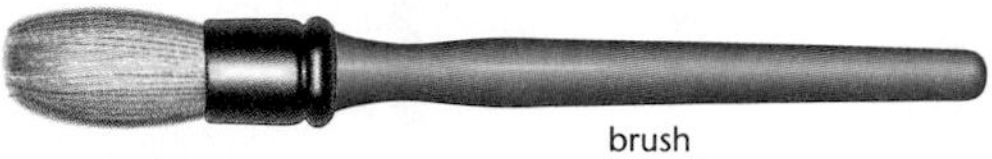

brush
bruza^F

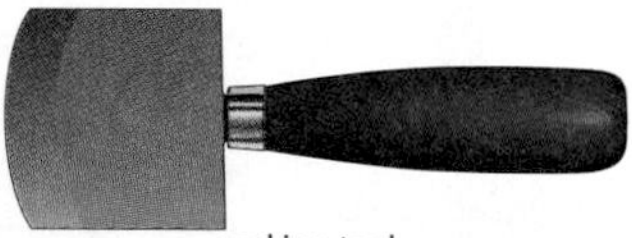

rocking tool
graneador^M para el grabado^M al humo^M

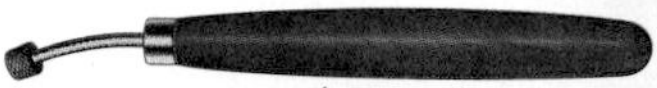

roulette
ruleta^F estriada

copper plate
placa^F de cobre^M

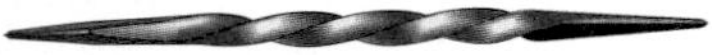

dry point
punta^F seca

burnisher
bruñidor^M

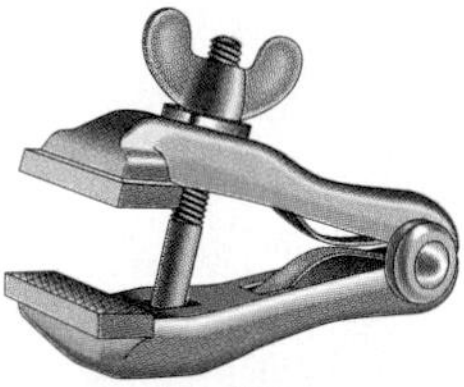

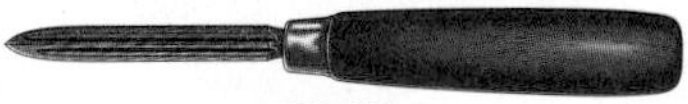

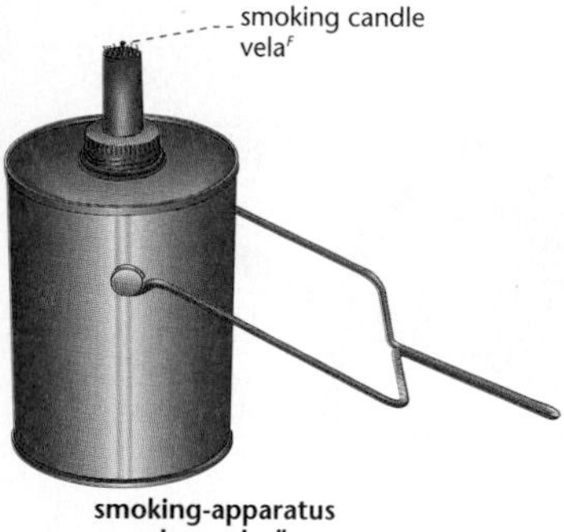

smoking candle
vela^F

hand vice
pinza^F

scraper
raedor^M

**smoking-apparatus
ahumador^M**

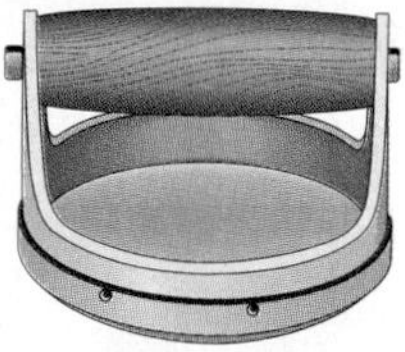

baren
frotador^M

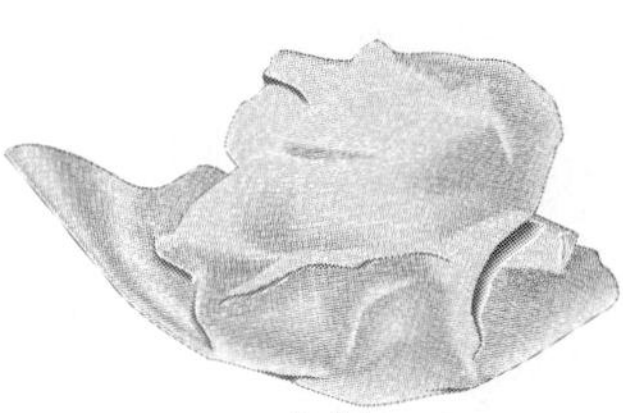

tarlatan
tarlatana^M

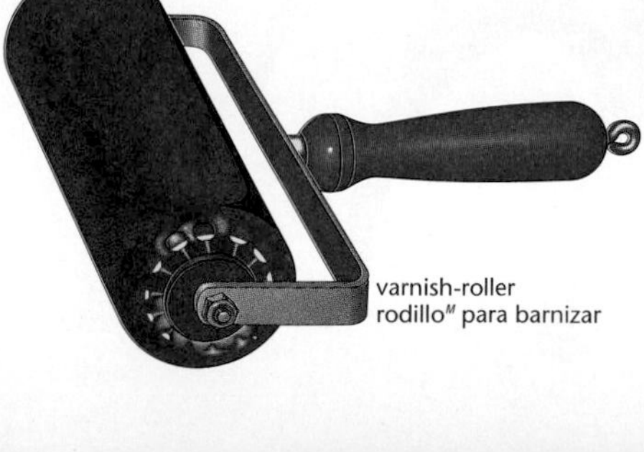

varnish-roller
rodillo^M para barnizar

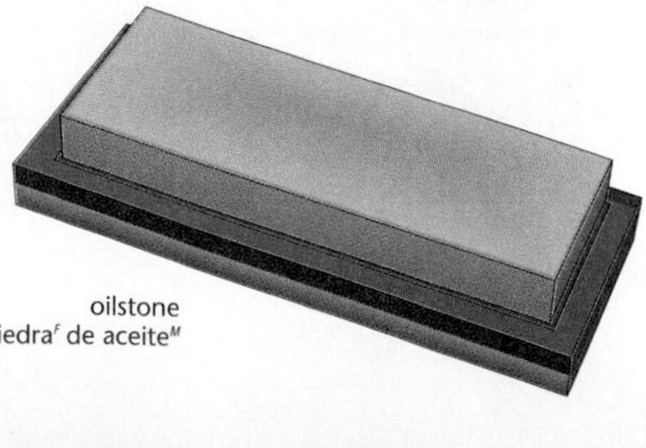

oilstone
piedra^F de aceite^M

LITHOGRAPHY
LITOGRAFÍA^F

EQUIPMENT
EQUIPO^M

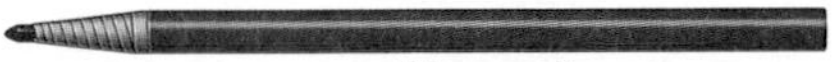

litho pencil
lápiz^M litográfico

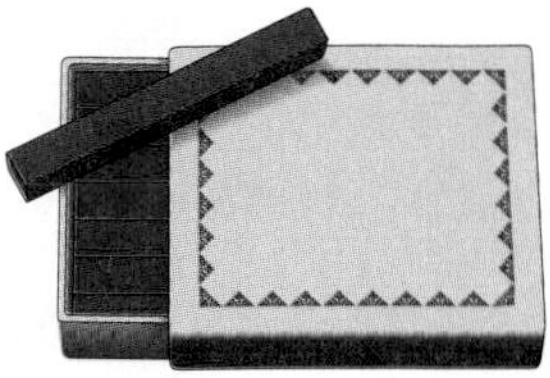

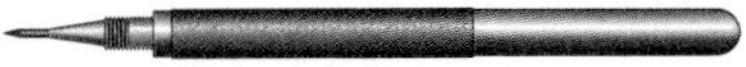

drypoint
punta^F seca

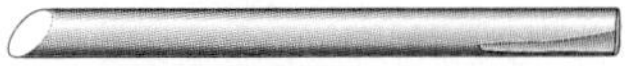

pumice correcting pencil
lápiz^M corrector de piedra^F pómez

litho crayon
jaboncillo^M litográfico

LEVIGATOR
BARRIQUETE^M

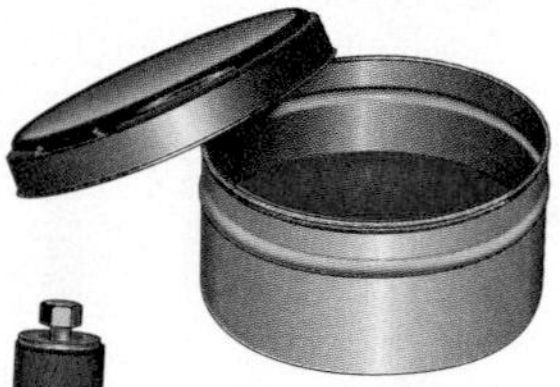

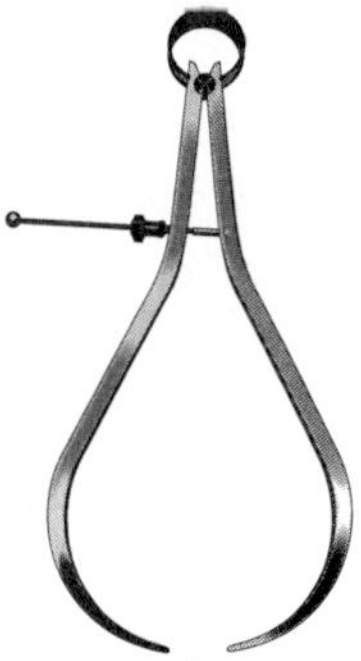

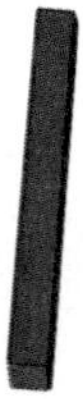

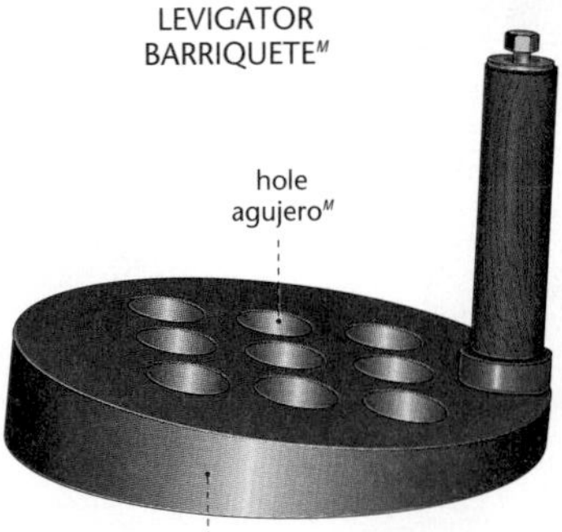

lithographic tusche
barra^F diluida al agua^F

red ocher pencil
lápiz^M corrector de ocre^M
rojo

hole
agujero^M

caliper
calibrador^M

disk
disco^M

LITHOGRAPHIC PRESS
PRENSA^F LITOGRÁFICA

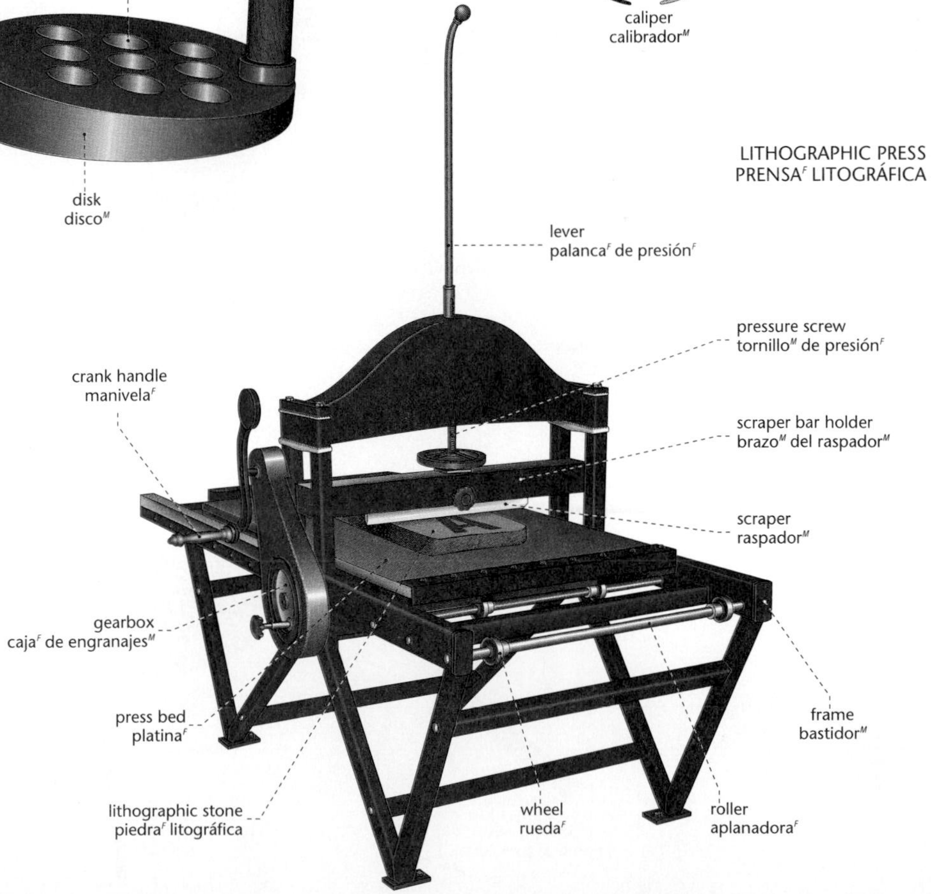

lever
palanca^F de presión^F

pressure screw
tornillo^M de presión^F

crank handle
manivela^F

scraper bar holder
brazo^M del raspador^M

scraper
raspador^M

gearbox
caja^F de engranajes^M

press bed
platina^F

frame
bastidor^M

lithographic stone
piedra^F litográfica

wheel
rueda^F

roller
aplanadora^F

TURNING
TORNO^M

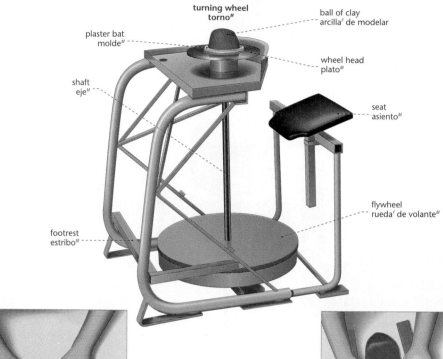

turning wheel
torno^M

ball of clay
arcilla^F de modelar

plaster bat
molde^M

wheel head
plato^M

shaft
eje^M

seat
asiento^M

flywheel
rueda^F de volante^M

footrest
estribo^M

COILING
CORDÓN^M PARA ESPIRALES^F

SLAB BUILDING
RODILLO^M

TOOLS
HERRAMIENTAS^F

ribs
costillar^M

cutting wire
alambre^M para cortar

banding wheel
torneta^F

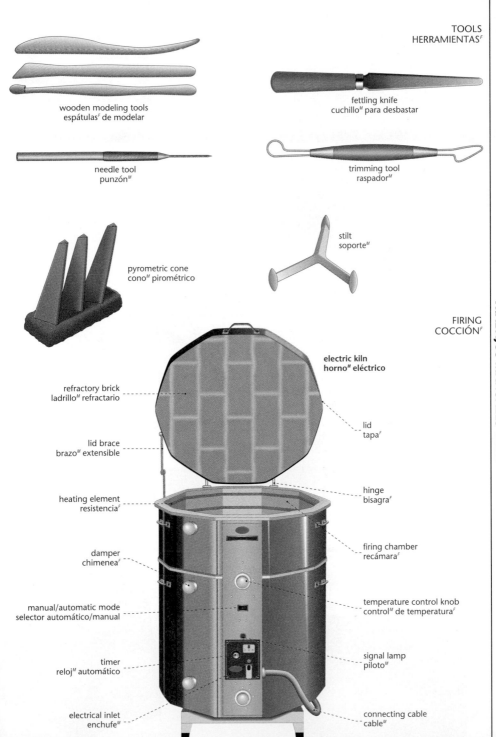

**TOOLS
HERRAMIENTAS**F

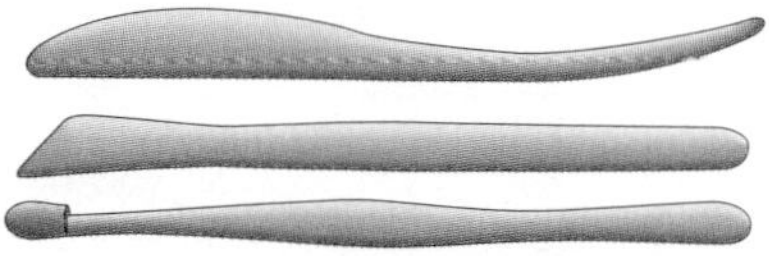

wooden modeling tools
espátulasF de modelar

needle tool
punzónM

fettling knife
cuchilloM para desbastar

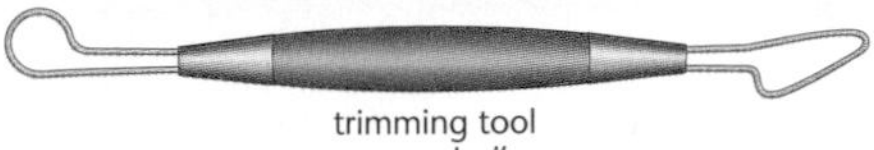

trimming tool
raspadorM

pyrometric cone
conoM pirométrico

stilt
soporteM

**FIRING
COCCIÓN**F

**electric kiln
hornoM eléctrico**

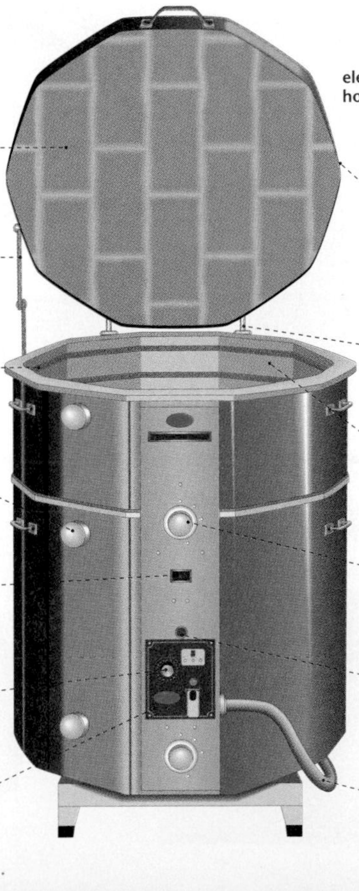

refractory brick
ladrilloM refractario

lid brace
brazoM extensible

heating element
resistenciaF

damper
chimeneaF

manual/automatic mode
selector automático/manual

timer
relojM automático

electrical inlet
enchufeM

lid
tapaF

hinge
bisagraF

firing chamber
recámaraF

temperature control knob
controlM de temperaturaF

signal lamp
pilotoM

connecting cable
cableM

**CREATIVE LEISURE ACTIVITIES
TRABAJOS MANUALES**

STEPS
ETAPAS^F

drawing
diseño^M

roughing out
desbaste^M

carving
talla^F

finishing
acabado^M

ACCESSORIES
ACCESORIOS^M

carver's bench screw
tornillo^M

mallet
mazo^M

stand
tarima^F

punch and pattern
punteo^M

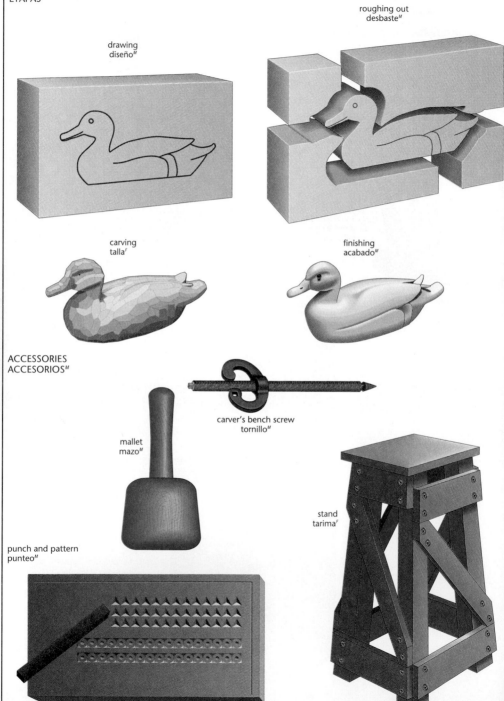

586

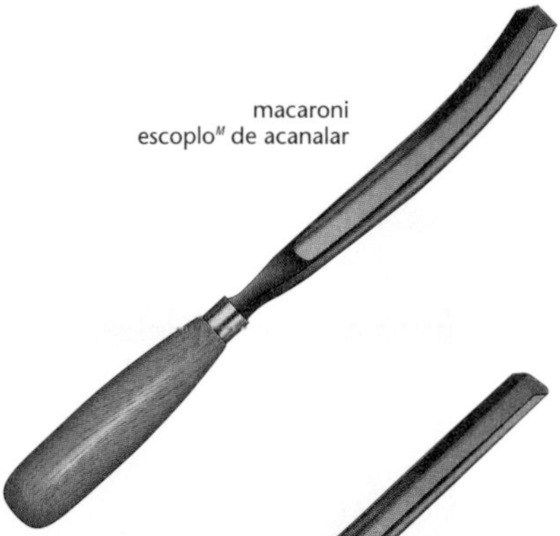

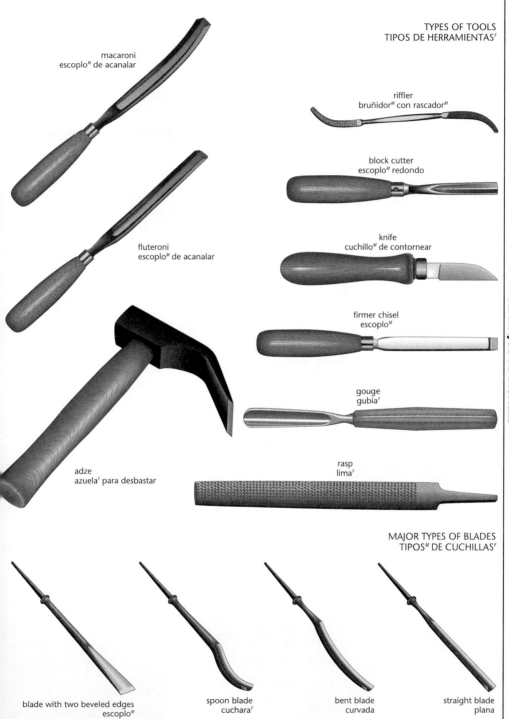

macaroni
escoplo[M] de acanalar

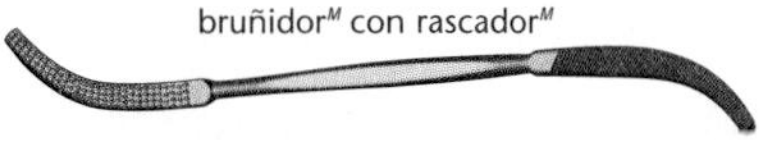

riffler
bruñidor[M] con rascador[M]

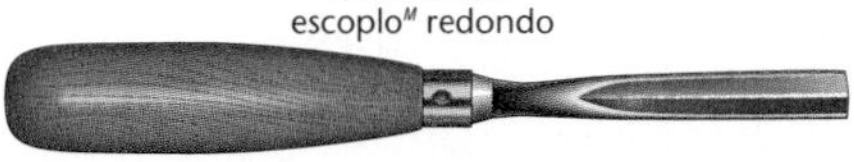

block cutter
escoplo[M] redondo

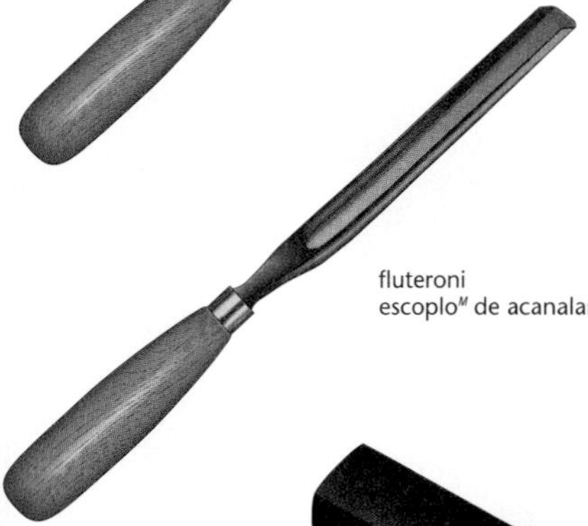

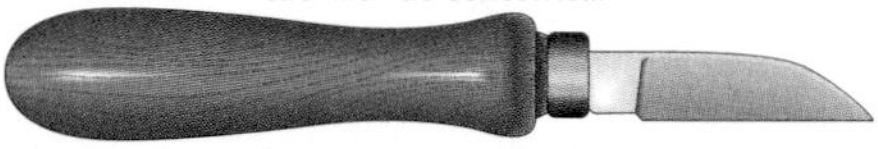

knife
cuchillo[M] de contornear

fluteroni
escoplo[M] de acanalar

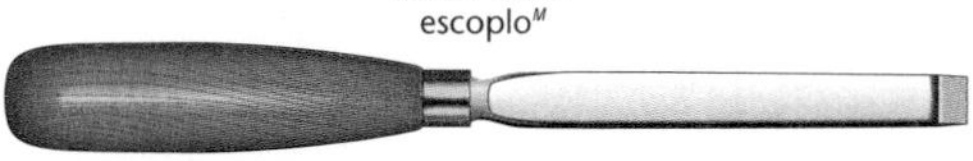

firmer chisel
escoplo[M]

gouge
gubia[F]

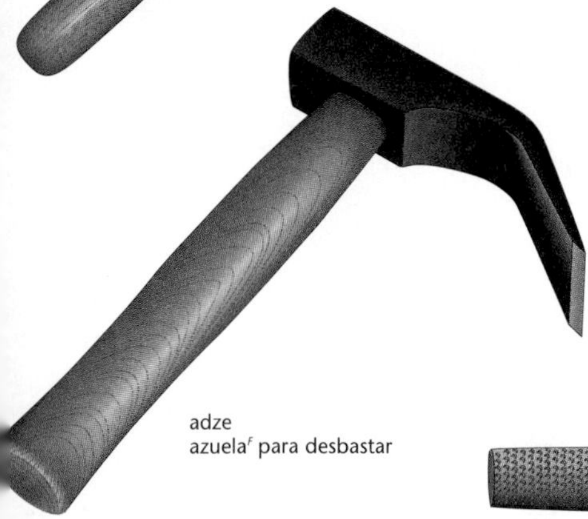

adze
azuela[F] para desbastar

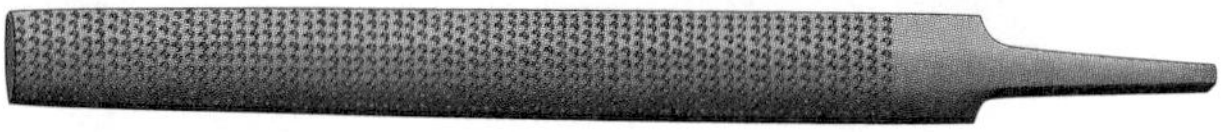

rasp
lima[F]

MAJOR TYPES OF BLADES
TIPOS[M] DE CUCHILLAS[F]

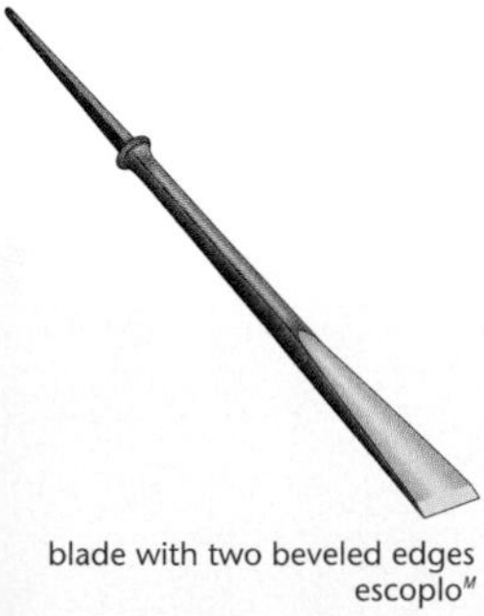

blade with two beveled edges
escoplo[M]

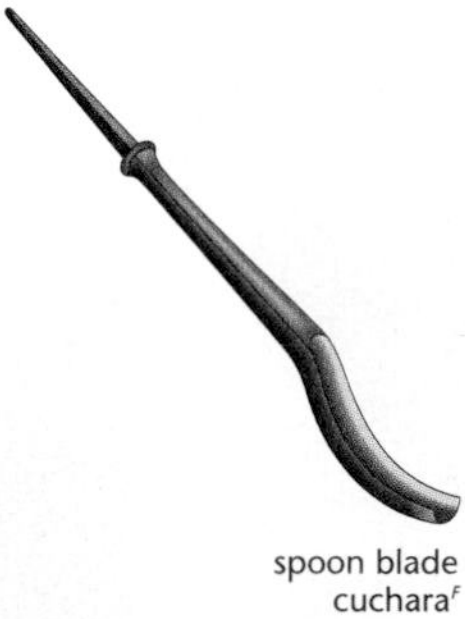

spoon blade
cuchara[F]

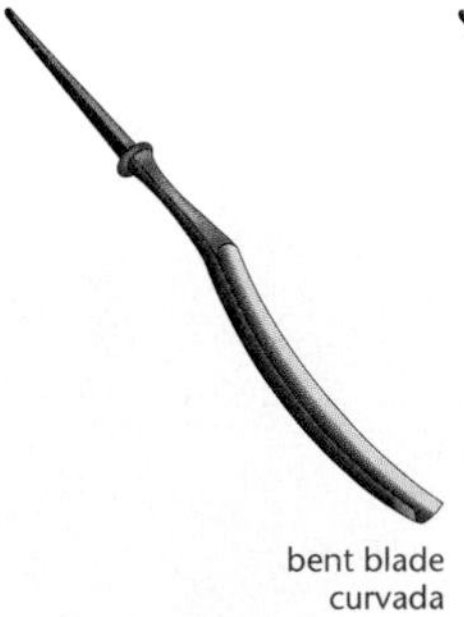

bent blade
curvada

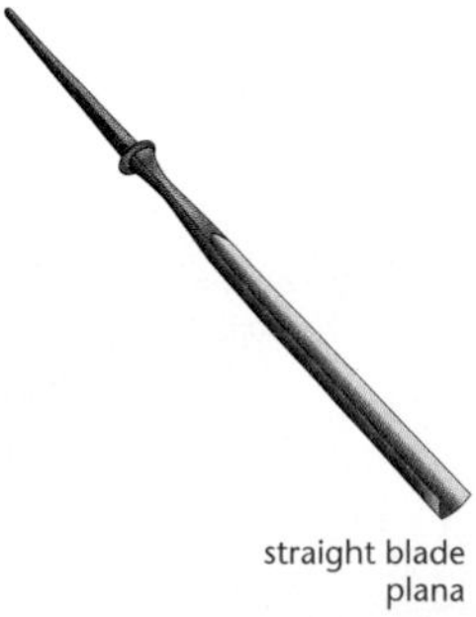

straight blade
plana

MAJOR TECHNIQUES
TÉCNICAS PRINCIPALES

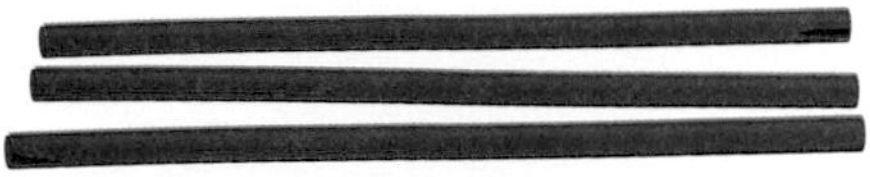

charcoal
carboncillo^M

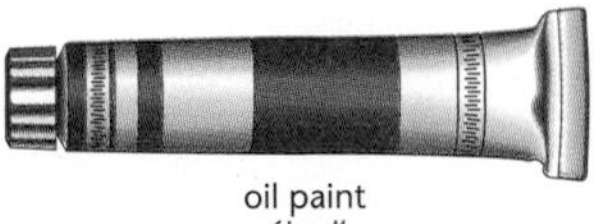

oil paint
óleo^M

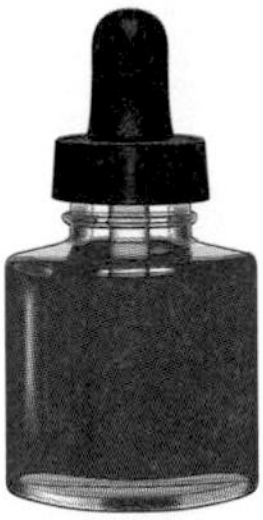

ink
tinta^F china

watercolor and gouache
acuarela^F y aguazo^M

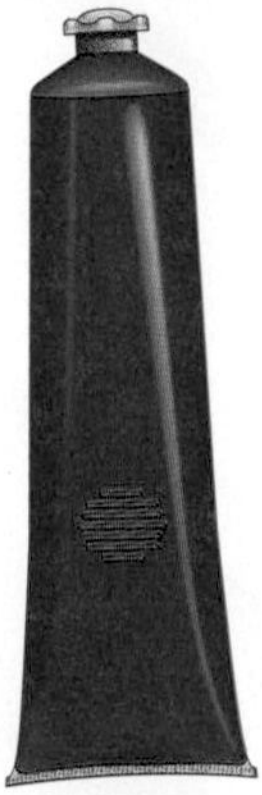

tube
tubo^M

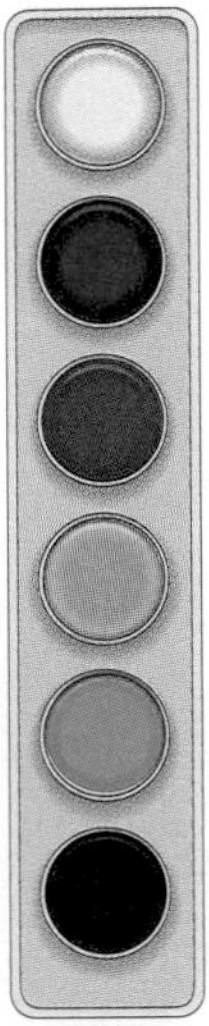

cakes
caja^F de acuarelas^F

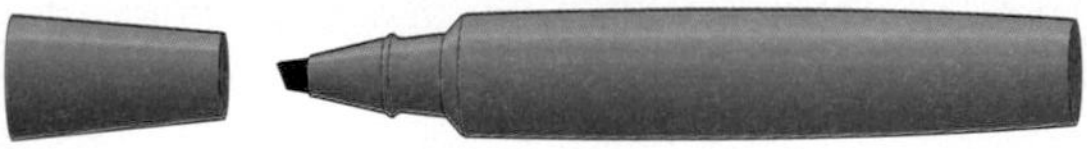

marker pen
rotulador^M

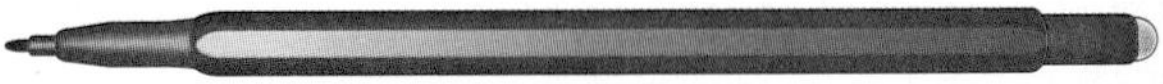

felt tip pen
rotulador^M

soft pastel
pastel^M

oil pastel
pastel^M de óleo^M

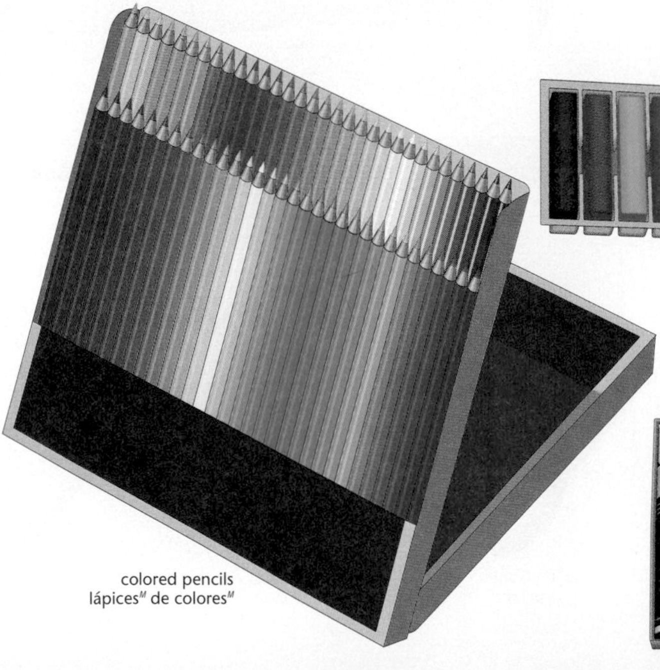

colored pencils
lápices^M de colores^M

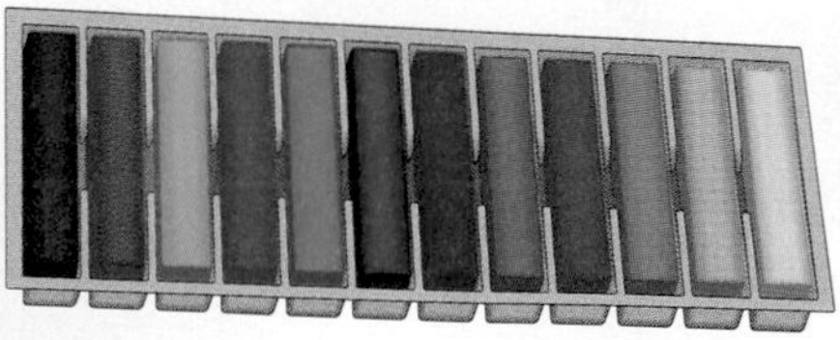

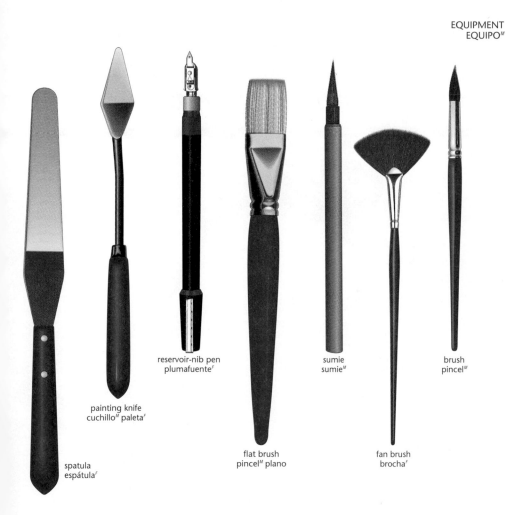

reservoir-nib pen
plumafuente^F

sumie
sumie^M

brush
pincel^M

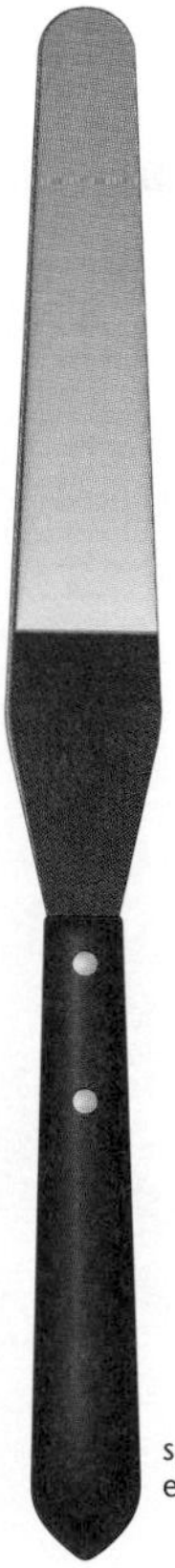

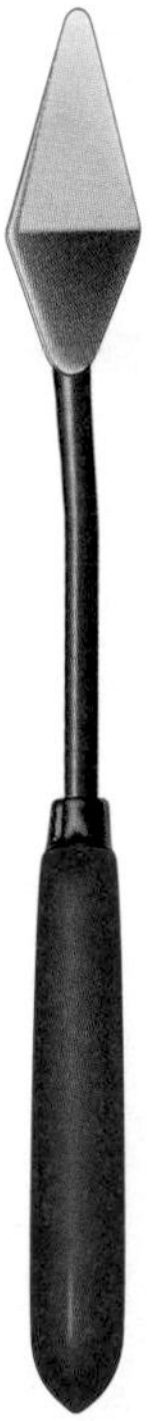

painting knife
cuchillo^M paleta^F

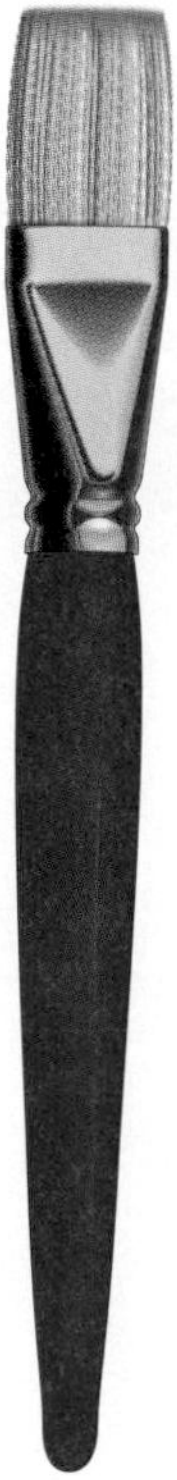

flat brush
pincel^M plano

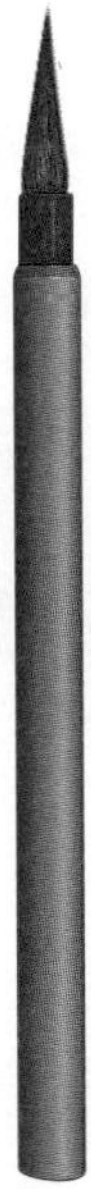

fan brush
brocha^F

spatula
espátula^F

SUPPORTS
LIENZOS^M

paper
papel^M

cardboard
cartón^M

canvas
lienzo^M

panel
tabla^F

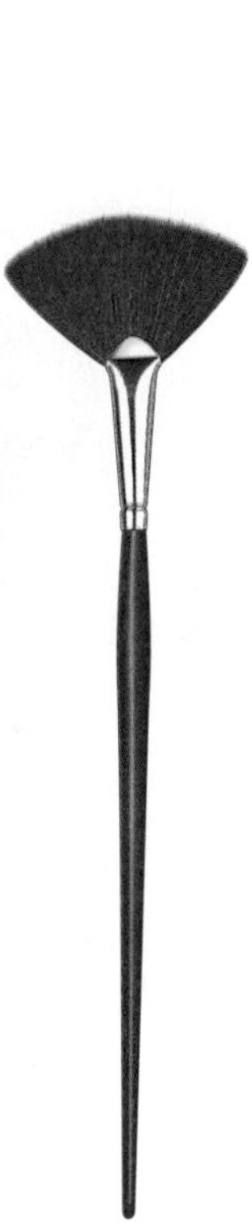

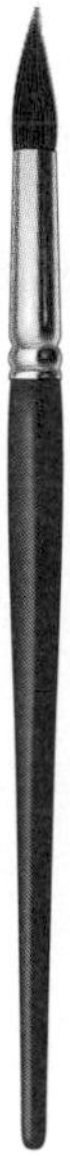

AIRBRUSH
PISTOLA*F* DE PINTAR

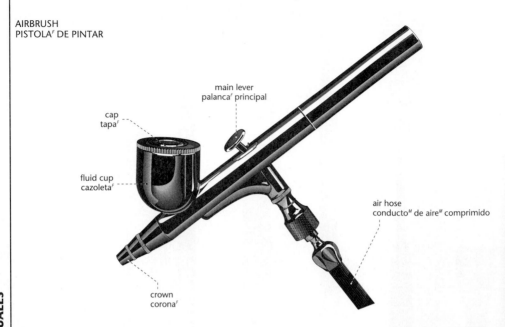

main lever
palanca*F* principal

cap
tapa*F*

fluid cup
cazoleta*F*

air hose
conducto*M* de aire*M* comprimido

crown
corona*F*

CROSS SECTION OF AN AIRBRUSH
CORTE*M* TRANSVERSAL DE UNA PISTOLA*F* DE PINTAR

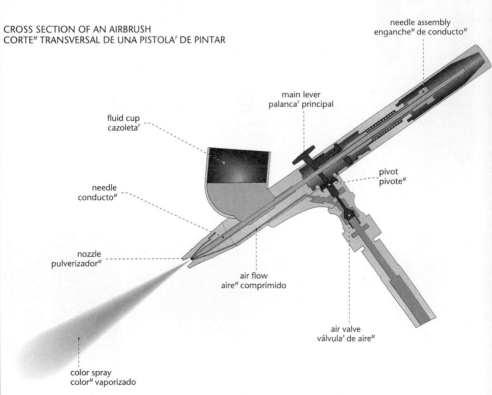

needle assembly
enganche*M* de conducto*M*

main lever
palanca*F* principal

fluid cup
cazoleta*F*

pivot
pivote*M*

needle
conducto*M*

nozzle
pulverizador*M*

air flow
aire*M* comprimido

air valve
válvula*F* de aire*M*

color spray
color*M* vaporizado

DRAFTING TABLE
TABLERO^M DE DIBUJO^M

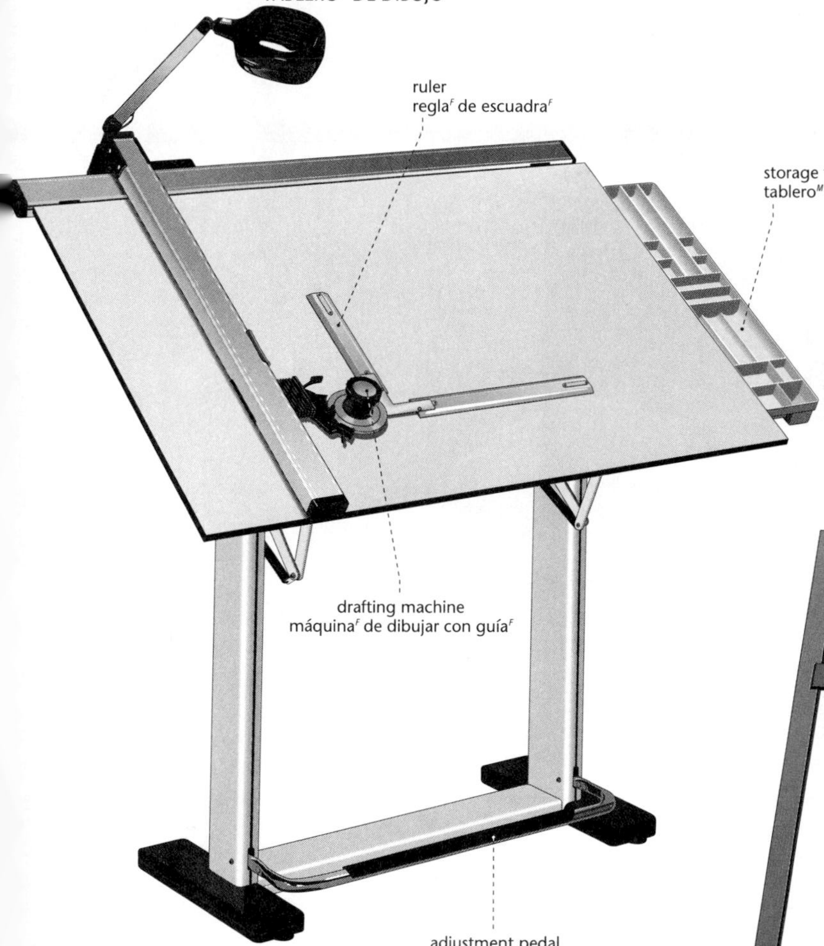

ruler
regla^F de escuadra^F

storage tray
tablero^M de accesorios^M

drafting machine
máquina^F de dibujar con guía^F

adjustment pedal
pedal^M de ajuste^M

maulstick
tiento^M

easel
caballete^M

CREATIVE LEISURE ACTIVITIES
TRABAJOS MANUALES

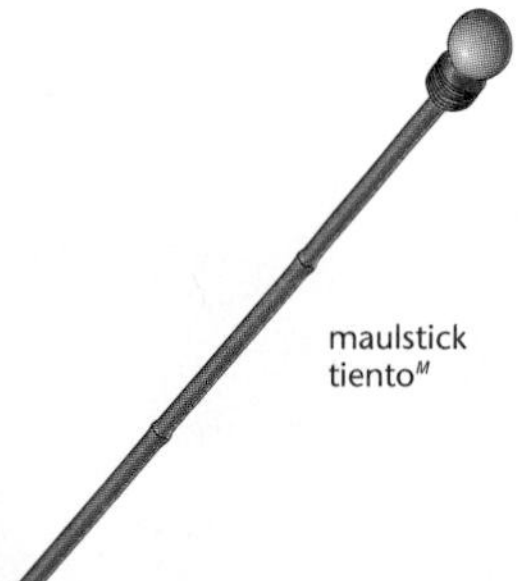

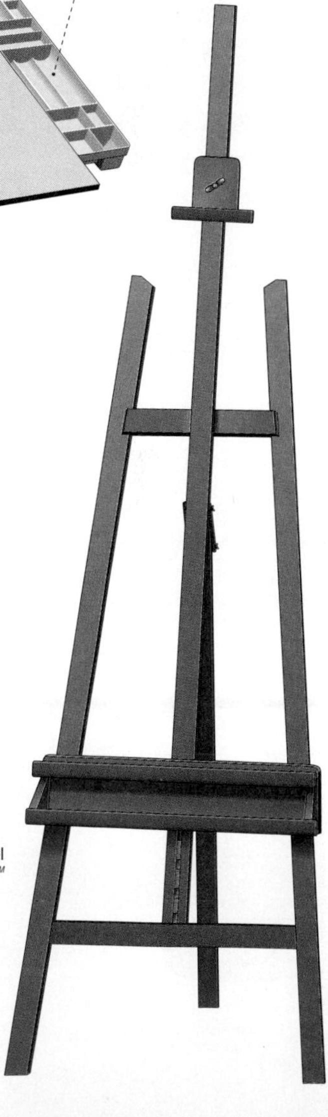

ACCESSORIES
ACCESORIOS^M

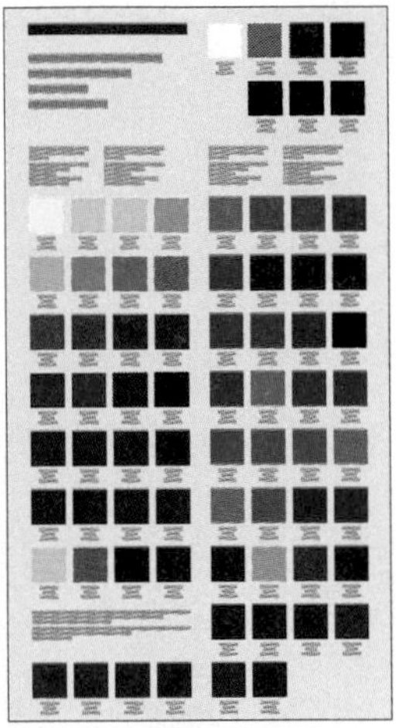

color chart
gama^F de colores^M

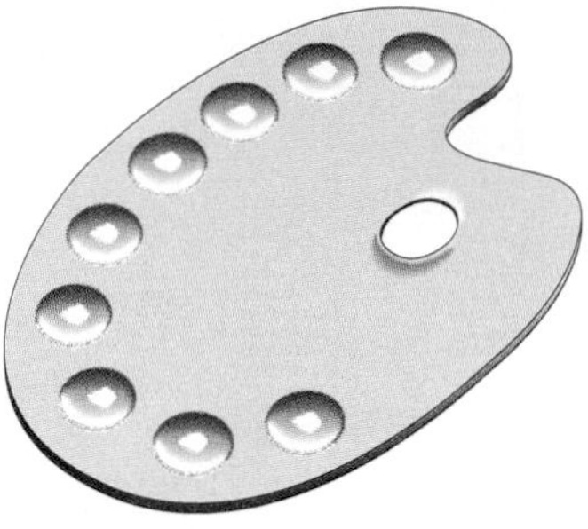

palette with hollows
paleta^F con huecos^M para pintura^F

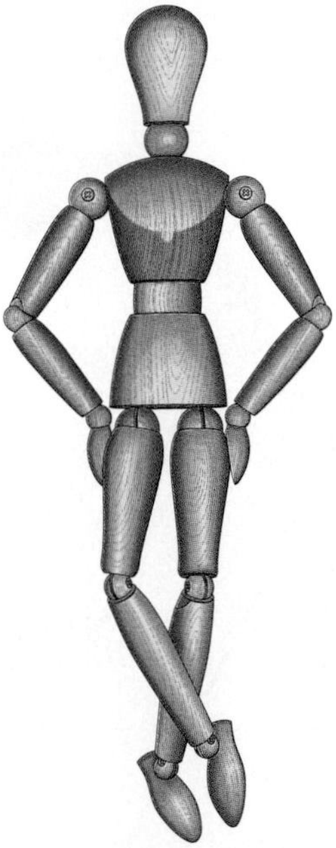

articulated mannequin
maniquí^M

dipper
tarrito^M para pincel^M

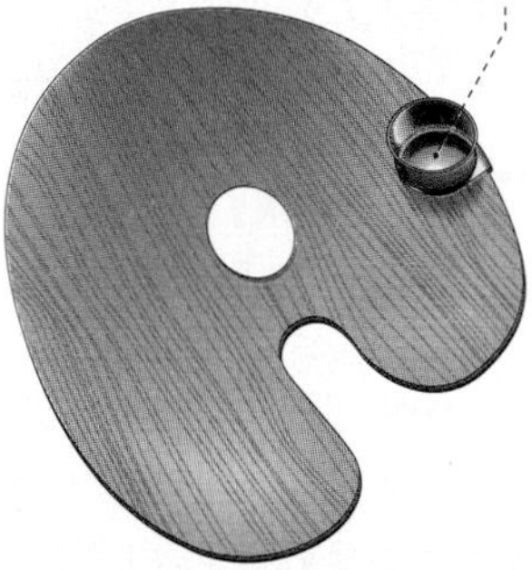

palette with dipper
paleta^F con tarrito^M

UTILITY LIQUIDS
LÍQUIDOS^M ACCESORIOS

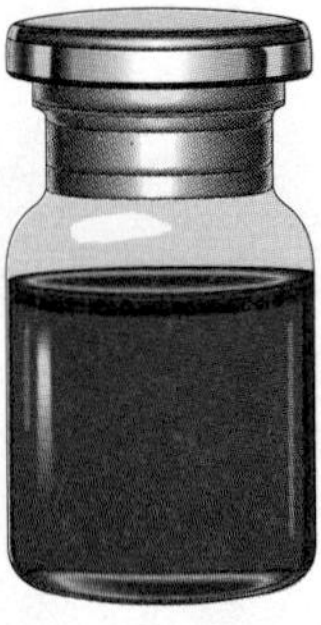

varnish
barniz^M

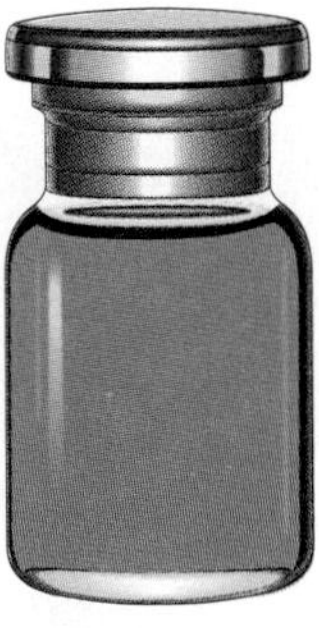

linseed oil
aceite^M de linaza^F

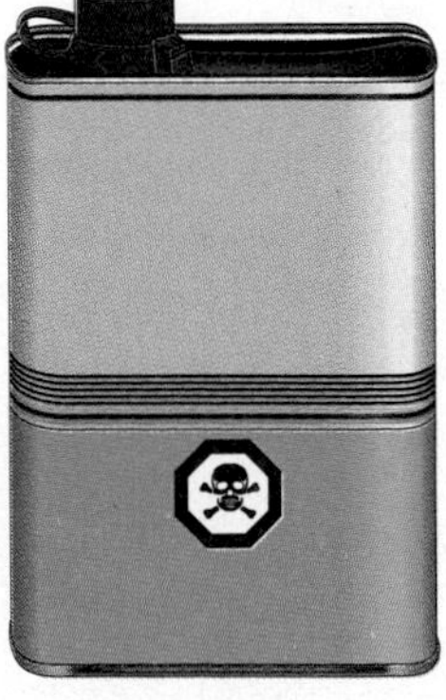

turpentine
aguarrás^M

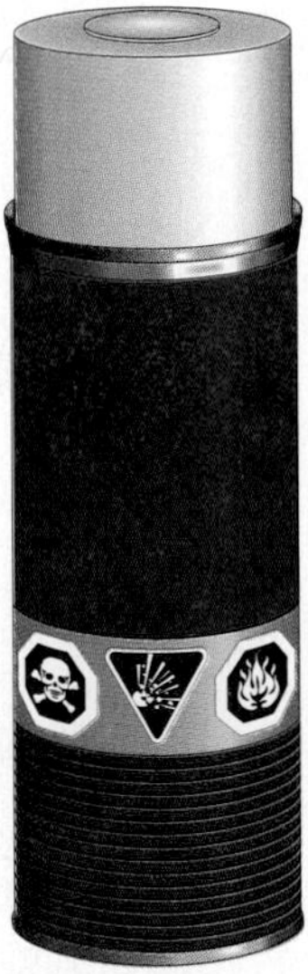

fixative
fijador^M

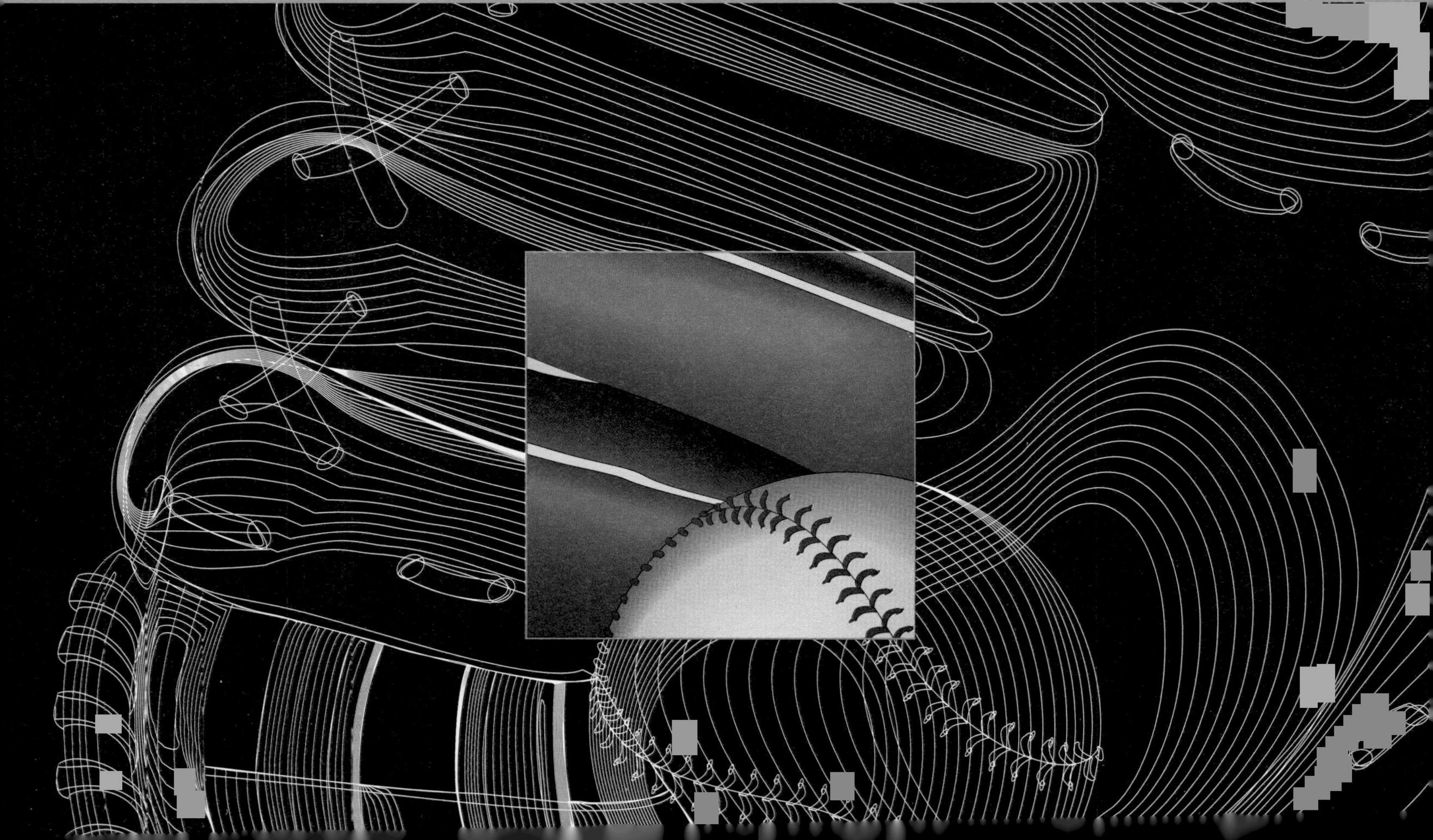

CONTENTS

TEAM GAMES

WATER SPORTS

AERIAL SPORTS

WINTER SPORTS

EQUESTRIAN SPORTS

ATHLETICS

COMBAT SPORTS

LEISURE SPORTS

CAMPING

BASEBALL
BÉISBOL^M

CATCHER
RECEPTOR^M

frame
armazón^M de la máscara^F

mask
máscara^F

throat protector
protector^M de la garganta^F

batter's helmet
casco^M del bateador^M

team shirt
camiseta^F

bat
bate^M

batting glove
guante^M de bateo^M

catcher's glove
guante^M del receptor^M

undershirt
camiseta^F interior

shin guard
espinillera^F

chest protector
peto^M

stirrup sock
calcetín^M con tirante^M

toe guard
protector^M del pie^M

knee pad
rodillera^F

pants
pantalón^M

spiked shoe
zapatilla^F con tacos^M

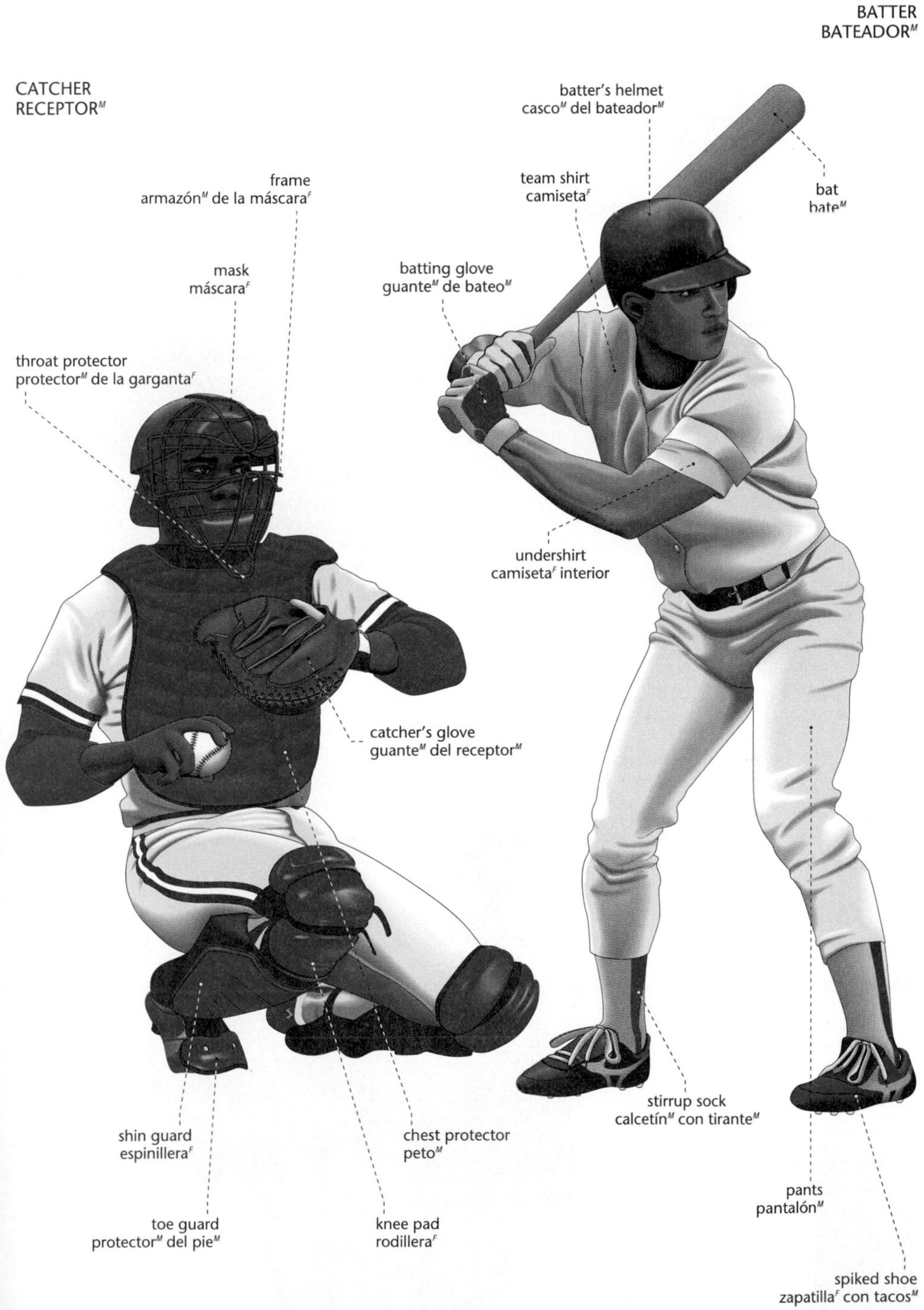

TEAM GAMES
DEPORTES DE EQUIPO

595

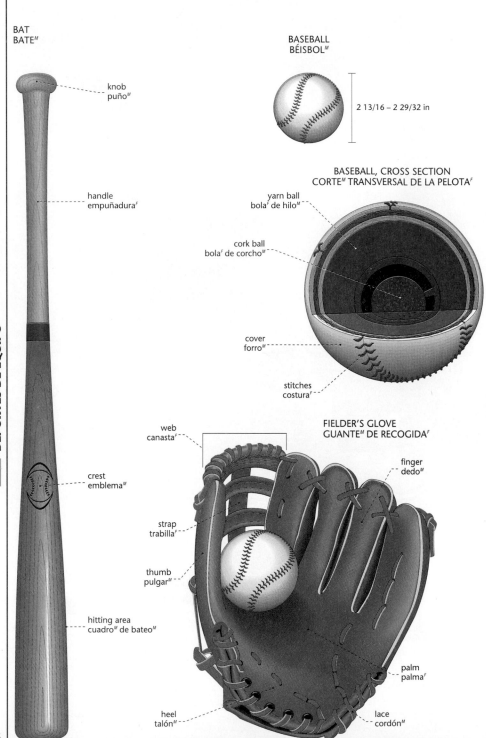

BAT
BATEᴹ

knob
puñoᴹ

handle
empuñaduraᶠ

crest
emblemaᴹ

hitting area
cuadroᴹ de bateoᴹ

BASEBALL
BÉISBOLᴹ

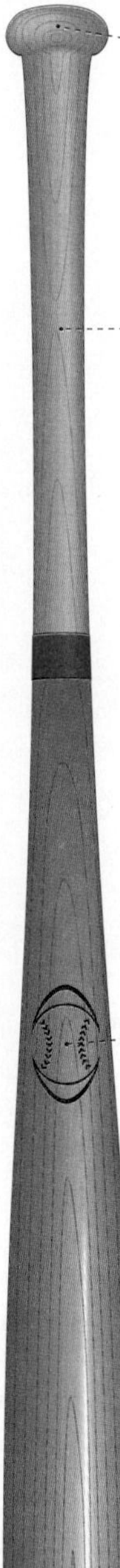

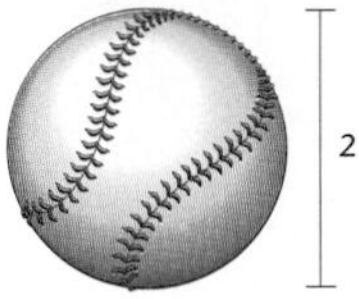

2 13/16 – 2 29/32 in

BASEBALL, CROSS SECTION
CORTEᴹ TRANSVERSAL DE LA PELOTAᶠ

yarn ball
bolaᶠ de hiloᴹ

cork ball
bolaᶠ de corchoᴹ

cover
forroᴹ

stitches
costuraᶠ

FIELDER'S GLOVE
GUANTEᴹ DE RECOGIDAᶠ

web
canastaᶠ

finger
dedoᴹ

strap
trabillaᶠ

thumb
pulgarᴹ

palm
palmaᶠ

heel
talónᴹ

lace
cordónᴹ

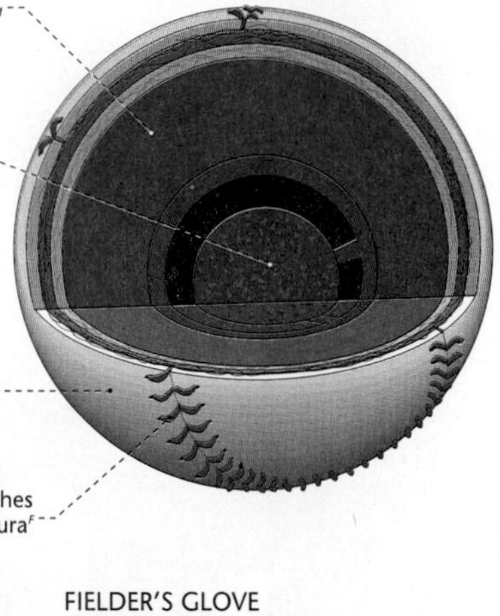

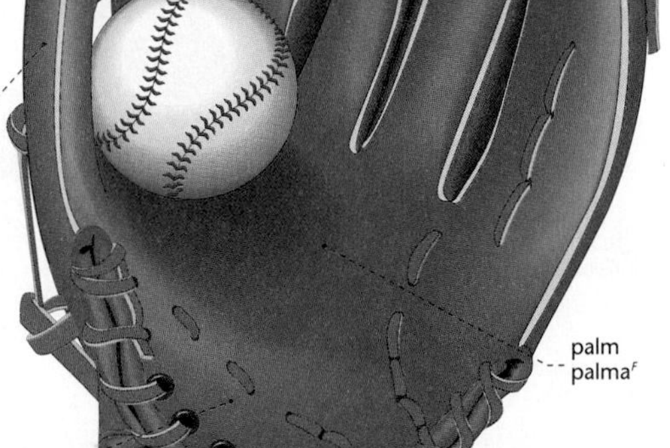

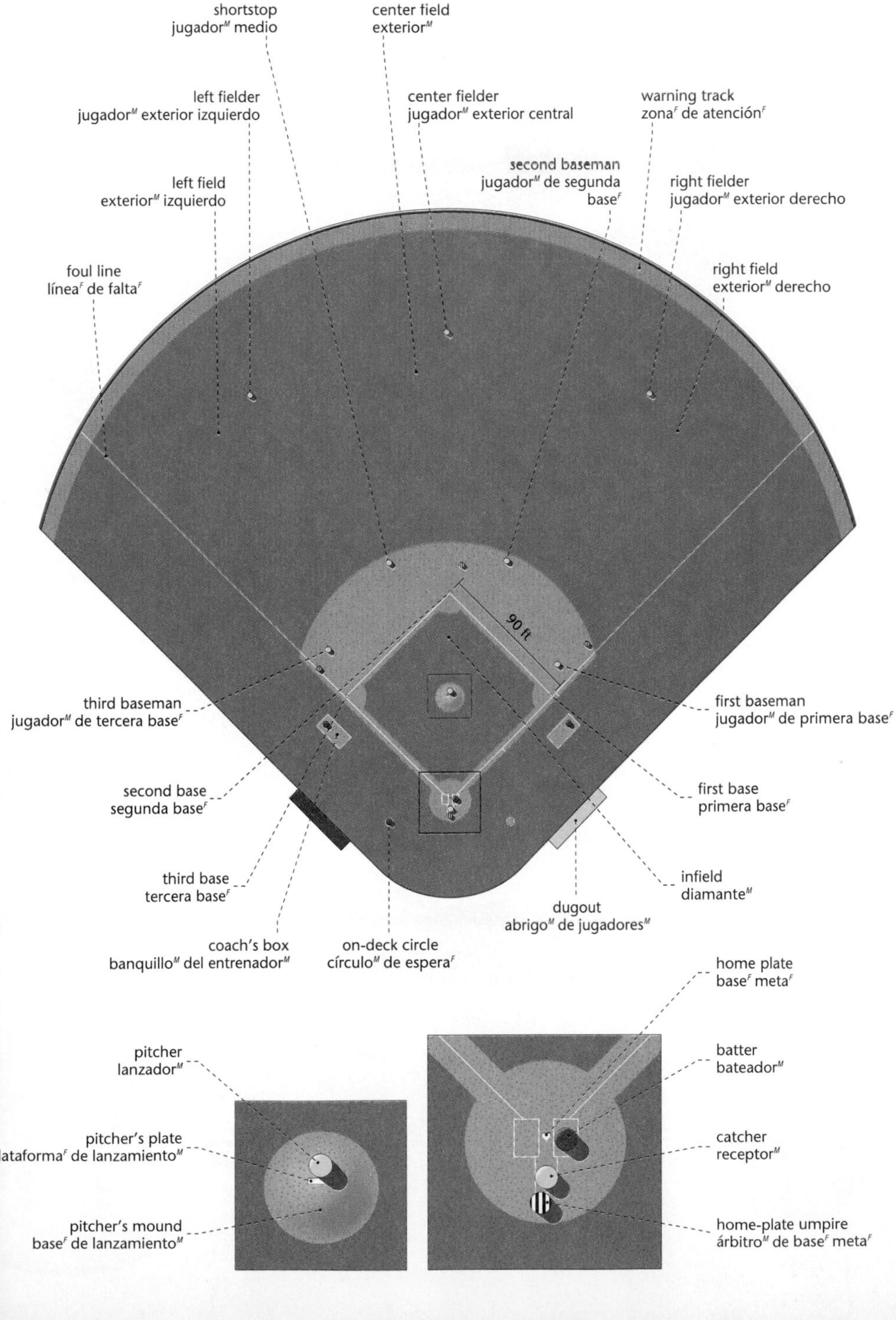

shortstop
jugador^M medio

center field
exterior^M

left fielder
jugador^M exterior izquierdo

center fielder
jugador^M exterior central

warning track
zona^F de atención^F

left field
exterior^M izquierdo

second baseman
jugador^M de segunda
base^F

right fielder
jugador^M exterior derecho

foul line
línea^F de falta^F

right field
exterior^M derecho

90 ft

third baseman
jugador^M de tercera base^F

first baseman
jugador^M de primera base^F

second base
segunda base^F

first base
primera base^F

third base
tercera base^F

infield
diamante^M

coach's box
banquillo^M del entrenador^M

on-deck circle
círculo^M de espera^F

dugout
abrigo^M de jugadores^M

home plate
base^F meta^F

pitcher
lanzador^M

batter
bateador^M

pitcher's plate
plataforma^F de lanzamiento^M

catcher
receptor^M

pitcher's mound
base^F de lanzamiento^M

home-plate umpire
árbitro^M de base^F meta^F

597

CRICKET
CRICKET^M

CRICKET^M

CRICKET PLAYER
JUGADOR^M DE CRICKET^M

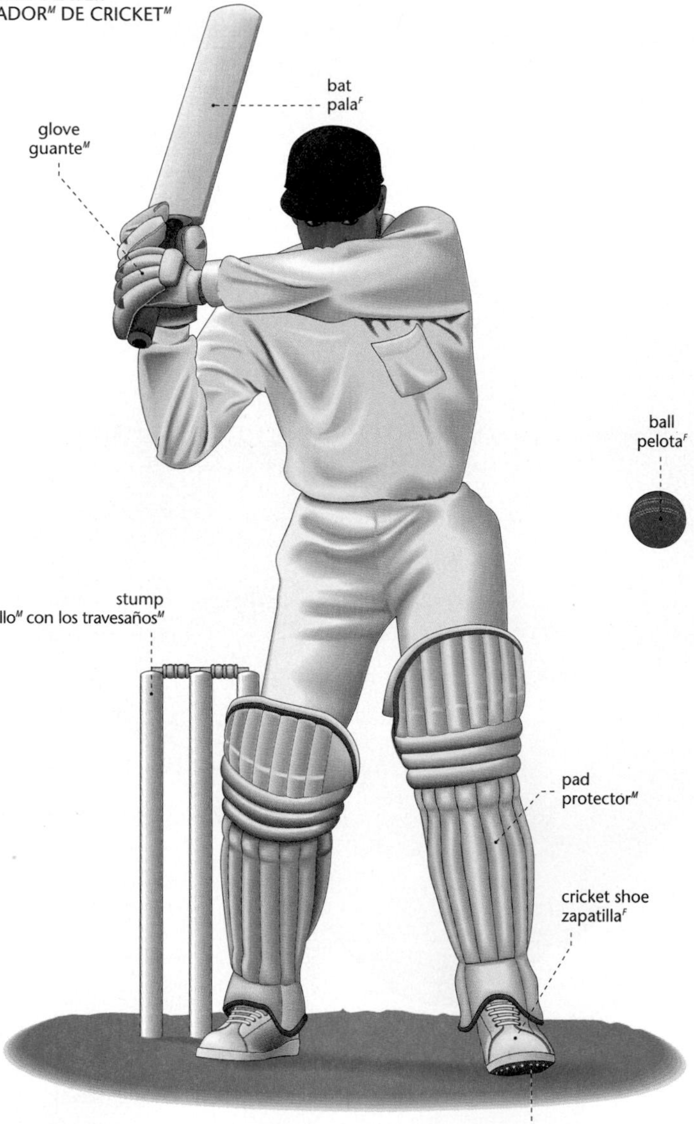

glove
guante^M

bat
pala^F

BAT
PALA^F

handle
mango^M

ball
pelota^F

stump
rastrillo^M con los travesaños^M

willow
pala^F

pad
protector^M

cricket shoe
zapatilla^F

studs
tacos^M

CRICKET BALL
PELOTA^F DE CRICKET^M

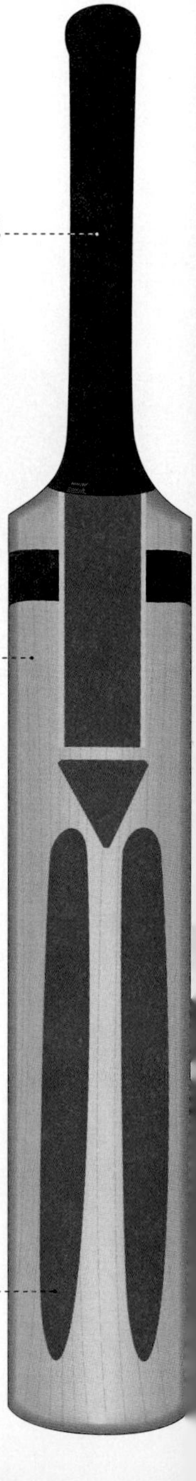

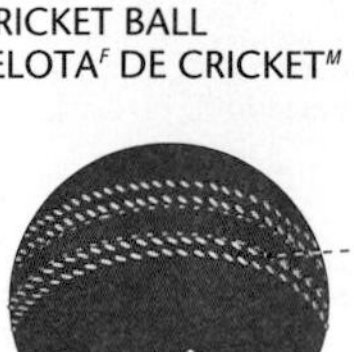

seam
costura^F

leather skin
forro^M de cuero^M

groove
ranura^F guía^F

2 13/16 – 2 7/8 in

TEAM GAMES
DEPORTES DE EQUIPO

598

WICKET
RASTRILLO^M CON LOS TRAVESAÑOS^M

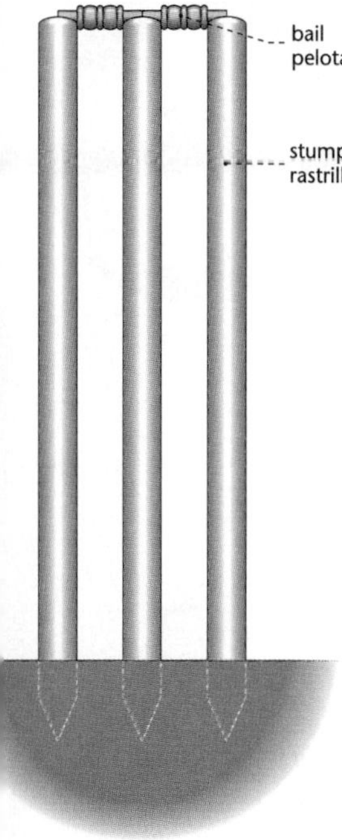

bail
pelota^F

stump
rastrillo^M

FIELD
CAMPO^M

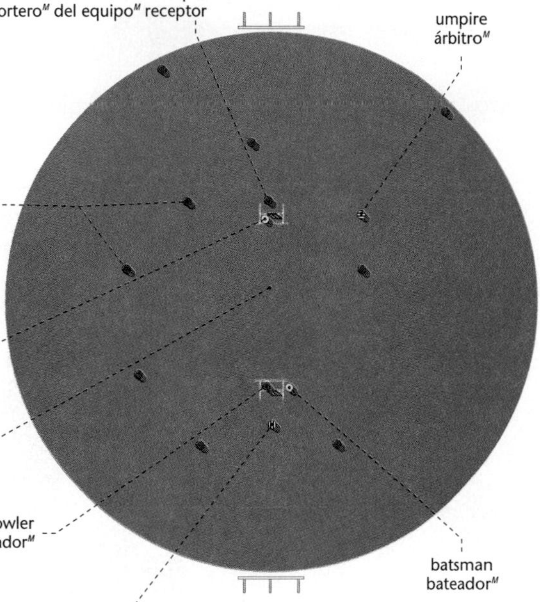

wicketkeeper
portero^M del equipo^M receptor

umpire
árbitro^M

fielders
equipo^M receptor

batsman
bateador^M

pitch
terreno^M de juego^M

bowler
lanzador^M

batsman
bateador^M

umpire
árbitro^M

TEAM GAMES
DEPORTES DE EQUIPO

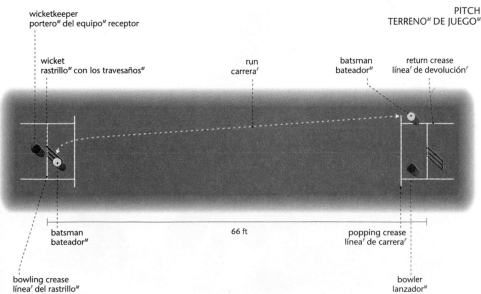

PITCH
TERRENO^M DE JUEGO^M

wicketkeeper
portero^M del equipo^M receptor

wicket
rastrillo^M con los travesaños^M

run
carrera^F

batsman
bateador^M

return crease
línea^F de devolución^F

batsman
bateador^M

66 ft

popping crease
línea^F de carrera^F

bowling crease
línea^F del rastrillo^M

bowler
lanzador^M

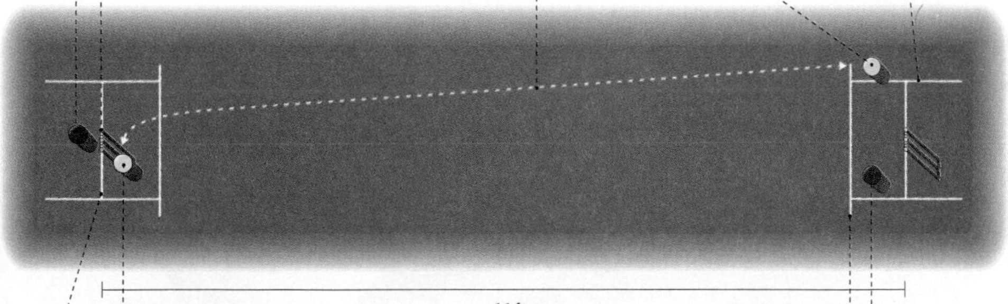

SOCCER
FÚTBOL^M

SOCCER PLAYER
FUTBOLISTA^{M/F}

SOCCER BALL
BALÓN^M

8 1/2 in

team shirt
camiseta^F de equipo^M

shorts
pantalones^M

shin guard
espinillera^F

soccer shoe
bota^F

interchangeable studs
tacos^M de rosca^F

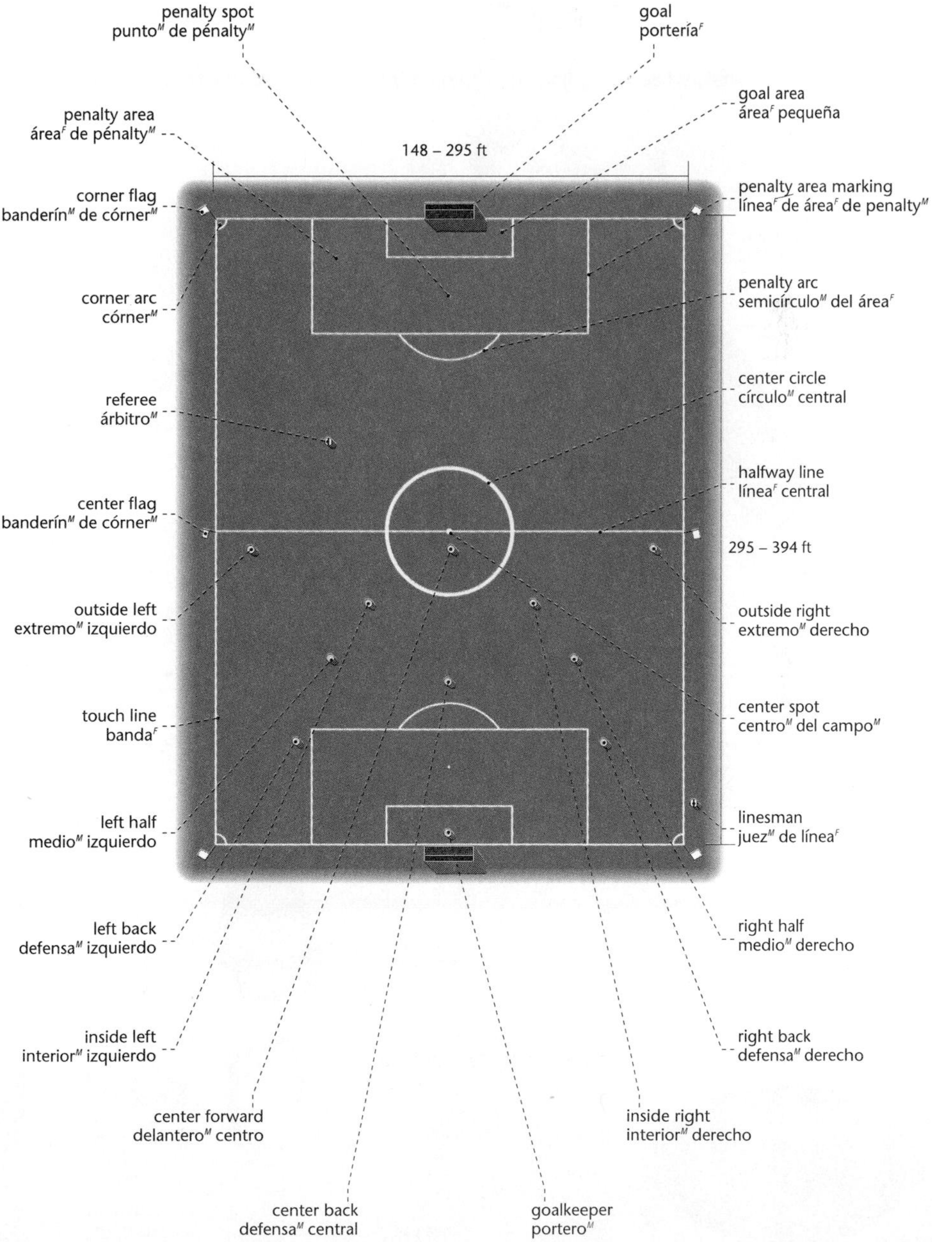

penalty spot
punto^M de pénalty^M

goal
portería^F

goal area
área^F pequeña

penalty area
área^F de pénalty^M

148 – 295 ft

penalty area marking
línea^F de área^F de penalty^M

corner flag
banderín^M de córner^M

corner arc
córner^M

penalty arc
semicírculo^M del área^F

referee
árbitro^M

center circle
círculo^M central

center flag
banderín^M de córner^M

halfway line
línea^F central

295 – 394 ft

outside left
extremo^M izquierdo

outside right
extremo^M derecho

touch line
banda^F

center spot
centro^M del campo^M

left half
medio^M izquierdo

linesman
juez^M de línea^F

left back
defensa^M izquierdo

right half
medio^M derecho

inside left
interior^M izquierdo

right back
defensa^M derecho

center forward
delantero^M centro

inside right
interior^M derecho

center back
defensa^M central

goalkeeper
portero^M

TEAM GAMES
DEPORTES DE EQUIPO

FOOTBALL PLAYER
JUGADOR^M

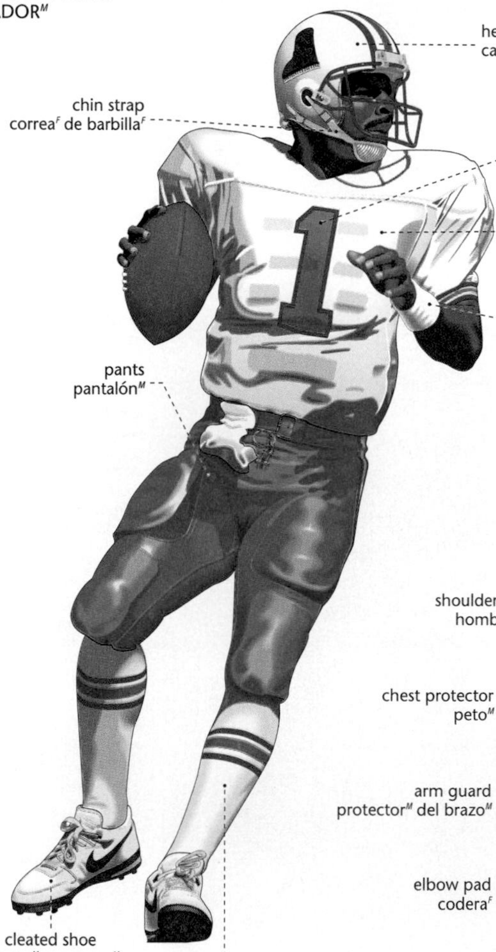

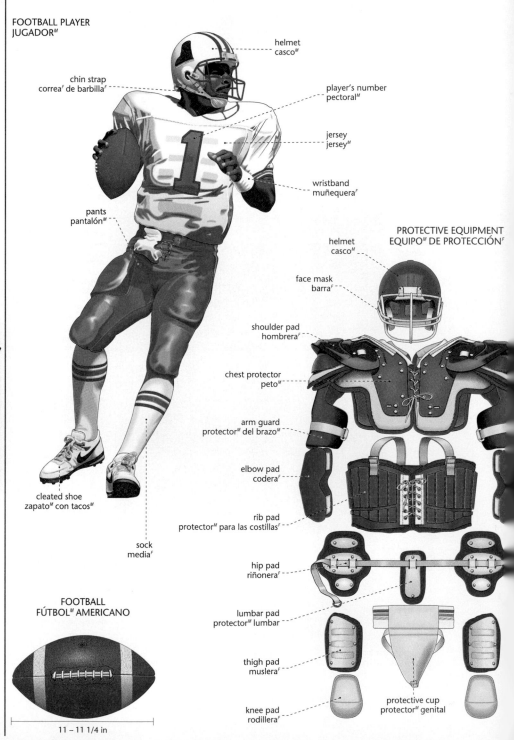

helmet
casco^M

chin strap
correa^F de barbilla^F

player's number
pectoral^M

jersey
jersey^M

wristband
muñequera^F

pants
pantalón^M

PROTECTIVE EQUIPMENT
EQUIPO^M DE PROTECCIÓN^F

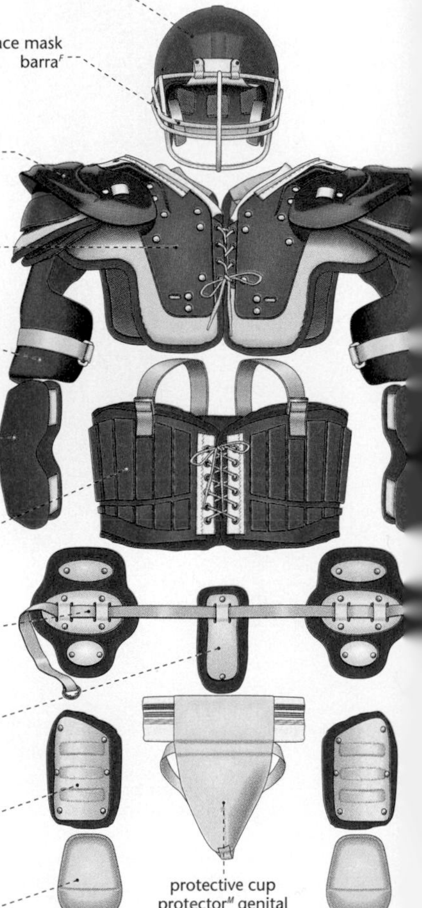

helmet
casco^M

face mask
barra^F

shoulder pad
hombrera^F

chest protector
peto^M

arm guard
protector^M del brazo^M

elbow pad
codera^F

rib pad
protector^M para las costillas^F

cleated shoe
zapato^M con tacos^M

sock
media^F

hip pad
riñonera^F

lumbar pad
protector^M lumbar

FOOTBALL
FÚTBOL^M AMERICANO

thigh pad
muslera^F

protective cup
protector^M genital

knee pad
rodillera^F

11 – 11 1/4 in

TEAM GAMES
DEPORTES DE EQUIPO

602

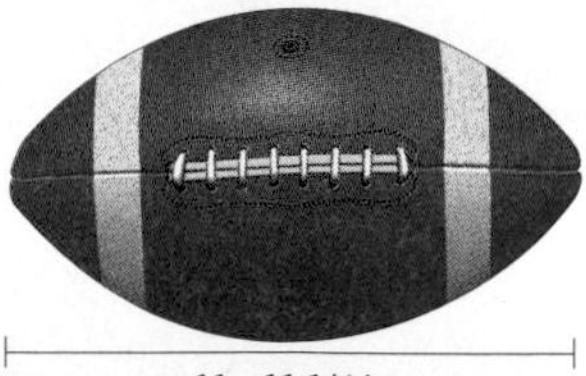

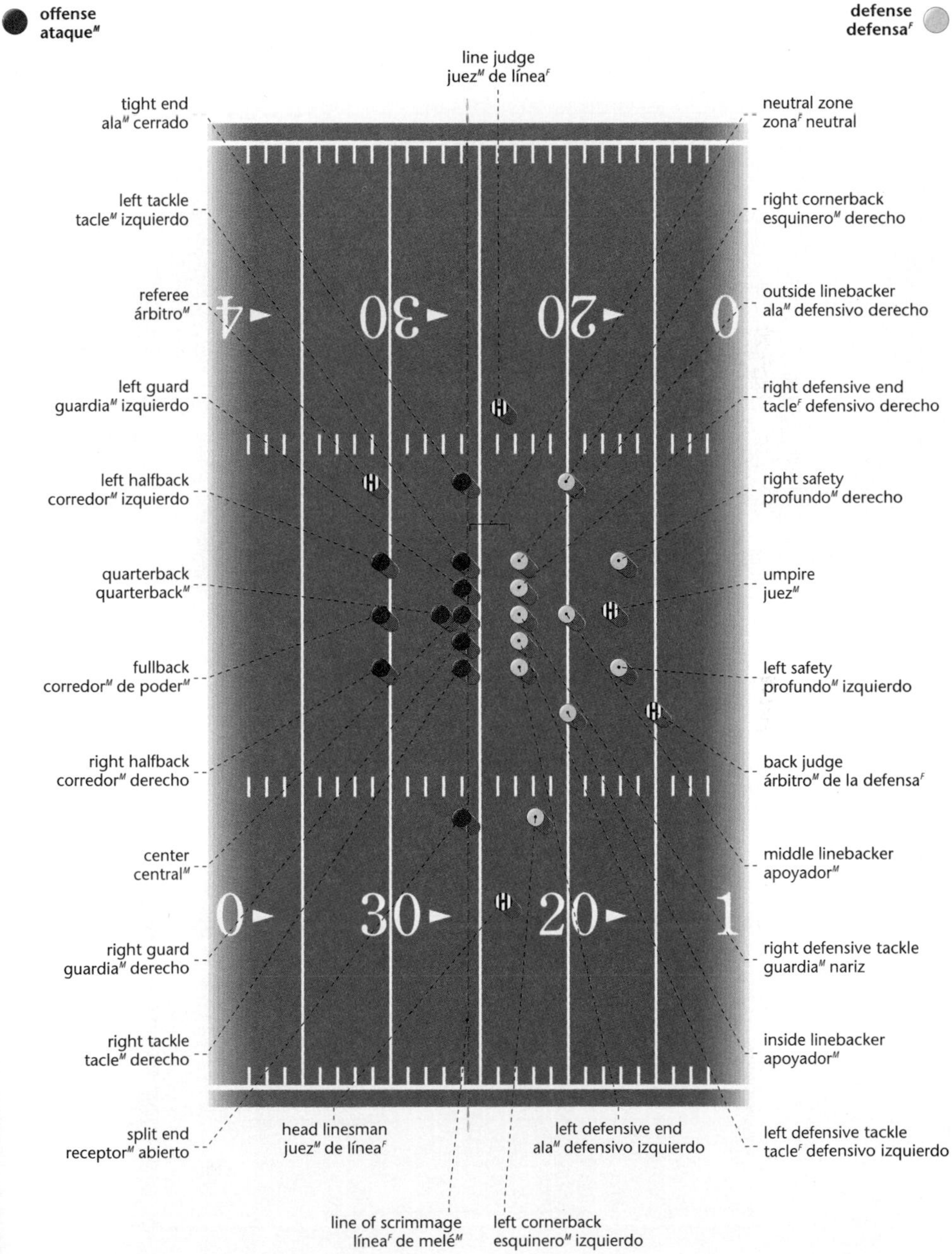

offense
ataque^M

defense
defensa^F

line judge
juez^M de línea^F

tight end
ala^M cerrado

neutral zone
zona^F neutral

left tackle
tacle^M izquierdo

right cornerback
esquinero^M derecho

referee
árbitro^M

outside linebacker
ala^M defensivo derecho

left guard
guardia^M izquierdo

right defensive end
tacle^F defensivo derecho

left halfback
corredor^M izquierdo

right safety
profundo^M derecho

quarterback
quarterback^M

umpire
juez^M

fullback
corredor^M de poder^M

left safety
profundo^M izquierdo

right halfback
corredor^M derecho

back judge
árbitro^M de la defensa^F

center
central^M

middle linebacker
apoyador^M

right guard
guardia^M derecho

right defensive tackle
guardia^M nariz

right tackle
tacle^M derecho

inside linebacker
apoyador^M

split end
receptor^M abierto

head linesman
juez^M de línea^F

left defensive end
ala^M defensivo izquierdo

left defensive tackle
tacle^F defensivo izquierdo

line of scrimmage
línea^F de melé^M

left cornerback
esquinero^M izquierdo

**TEAM GAMES
DEPORTES DE EQUIPO**

FOOTBALL
FÚTBOL^M AMERICANO

PLAYING FIELD FOR AMERICAN FOOTBALL
CAMPO^M DE JUEGO^M PARA FÚTBOL^M AMERICANO

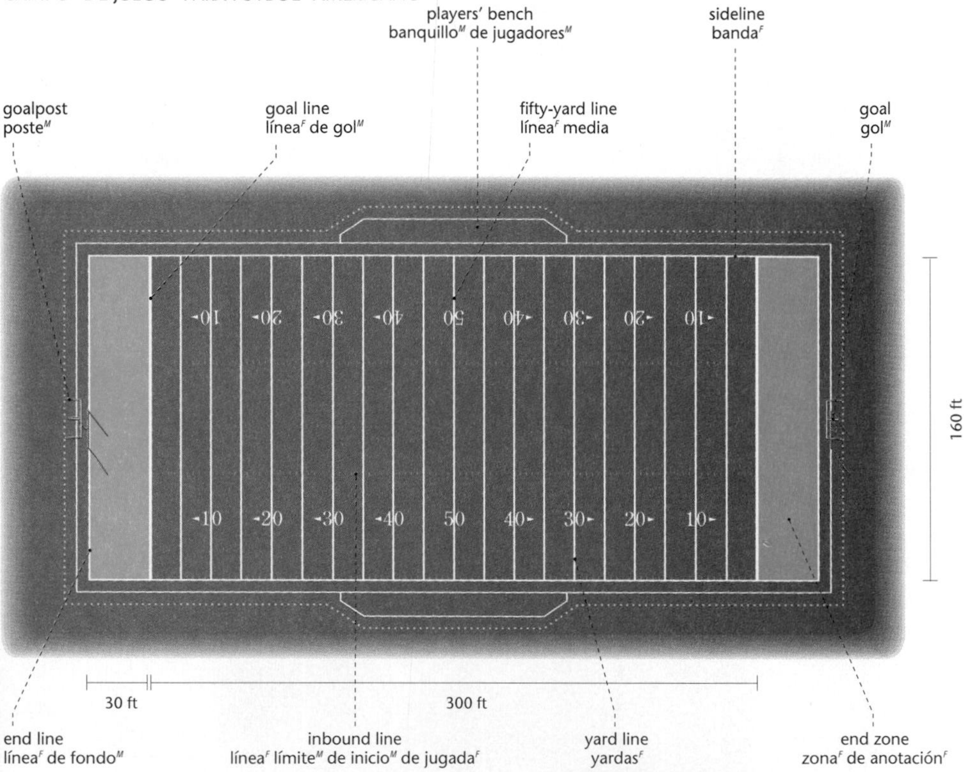

players' bench
banquillo^M de jugadores^M

sideline
banda^F

goalpost
poste^M

goal line
línea^F de gol^M

fifty-yard line
línea^F media

goal
gol^M

160 ft

30 ft

300 ft

end line
línea^F de fondo^M

inbound line
línea^F límite^M de inicio^M de jugada^F

yard line
yardas^F

end zone
zona^F de anotación^F

PLAYING FIELD FOR CANADIAN FOOTBALL
CAMPO^M DE JUEGO^M PARA FÚTBOL^M CANADIENSE

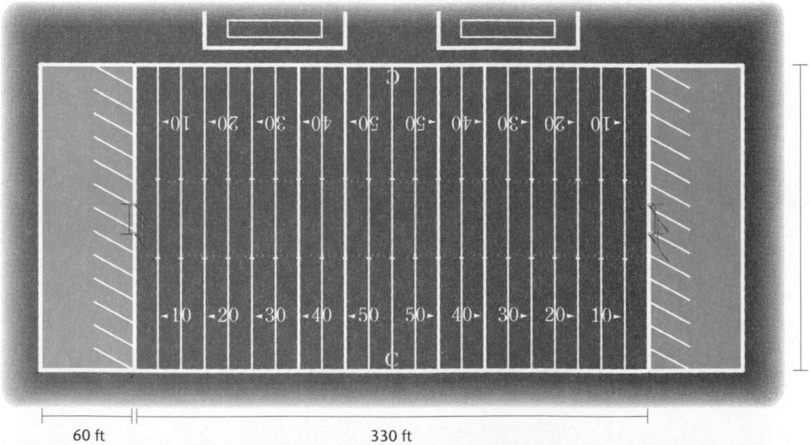

197 ft

60 ft

330 ft

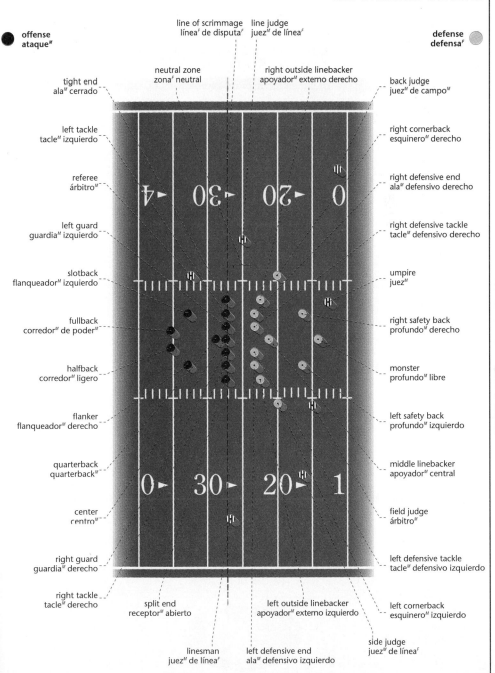

offense
ataque^M

defense
defensa^F

tight end
ala^M cerrado

line of scrimmage
línea^F de disputa^F

line judge
juez^M de línea^F

neutral zone
zona^F neutral

right outside linebacker
apoyador^M externo derecho

back judge
juez^M de campo^M

left tackle
tacle^M izquierdo

right cornerback
esquinero^M derecho

referee
árbitro^M

right defensive end
ala^M defensivo derecho

left guard
guardia^M izquierdo

right defensive tackle
tacle^M defensivo derecho

slotback
flanqueador^M izquierdo

umpire
juez^M

fullback
corredor^M de poder^M

right safety back
profundo^M derecho

halfback
corredor^M ligero

monster
profundo^M libre

flanker
flanqueador^M derecho

left safety back
profundo^M izquierdo

quarterback
quarterback^M

middle linebacker
apoyador^M central

center
centro^M

field judge
árbitro^M

right guard
guardia^M derecho

left defensive tackle
tacle^M defensivo izquierdo

right tackle
tacle^M derecho

split end
receptor^M abierto

left outside linebacker
apoyador^M externo izquierdo

left cornerback
esquinero^M izquierdo

linesman
juez^M de línea^F

left defensive end
ala^M defensivo izquierdo

side judge
juez^M de línea^F

TEAM GAMES
DEPORTES DE EQUIPO

605

RUGBY
RUGBY^M

RUGBY^M

FIELD
CAMPO^M DE JUEGO^M

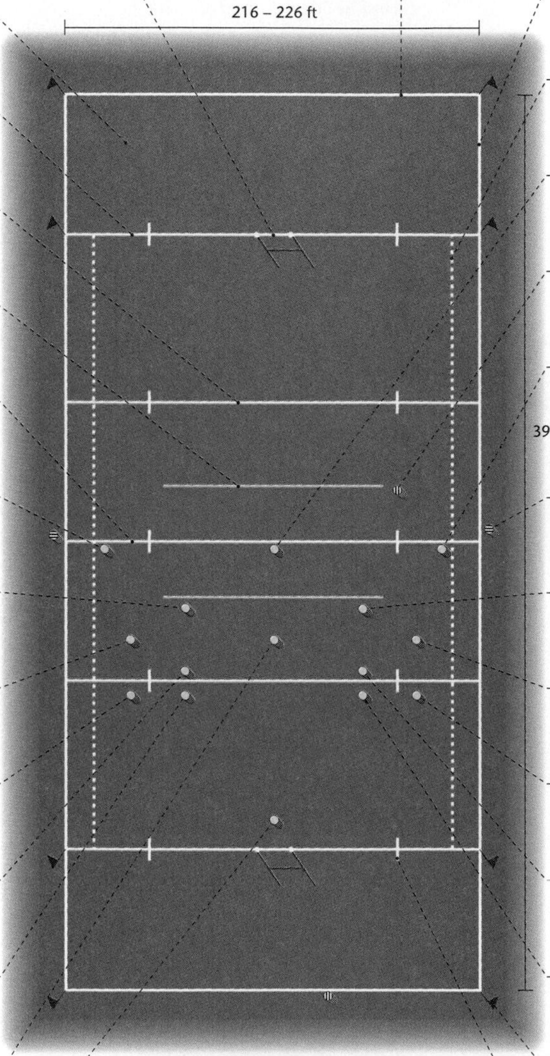

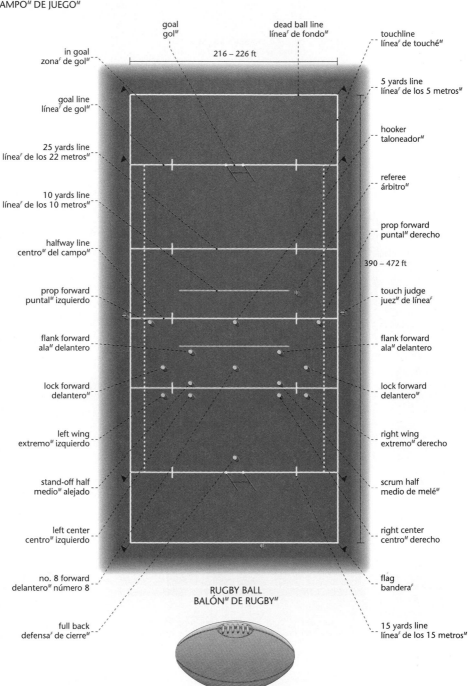

goal
gol^M

dead ball line
línea^F de fondo^M

touchline
línea^F de touché^M

in goal
zona^F de gol^M

216 – 226 ft

5 yards line
línea^F de los 5 metros^M

goal line
línea^F de gol^M

hooker
taloneador^M

25 yards line
línea^F de los 22 metros^M

referee
árbitro^M

10 yards line
línea^F de los 10 metros^M

prop forward
puntal^M derecho

halfway line
centro^M del campo^M

390 – 472 ft

prop forward
puntal^M izquierdo

touch judge
juez^M de línea^F

flank forward
ala^M delantero

flank forward
ala^M delantero

lock forward
delantero^M

lock forward
delantero^M

left wing
extremo^M izquierdo

right wing
extremo^M derecho

stand-off half
medio^M alejado

scrum half
medio de melé^M

left center
centro^M izquierdo

right center
centro^M derecho

no. 8 forward
delantero^M número 8

flag
bandera^F

RUGBY BALL
BALÓN^M DE RUGBY^M

full back
defensa^F de cierre^M

15 yards line
línea^F de los 15 metros^M

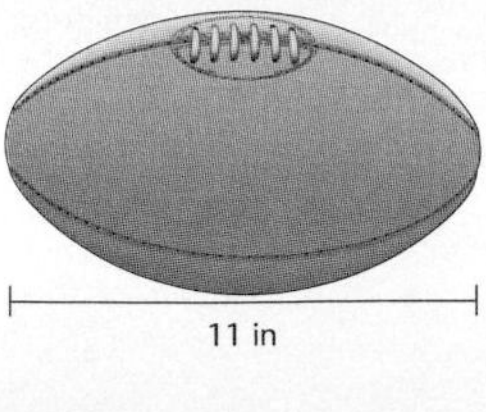

11 in

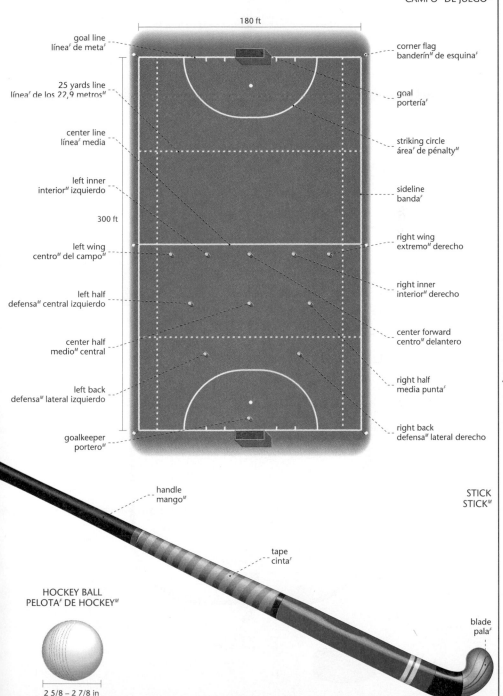

FIELD HOCKEY
HOCKEY^M SOBRE HIERBA^F

PLAYING FIELD
CAMPO^M DE JUEGO^M

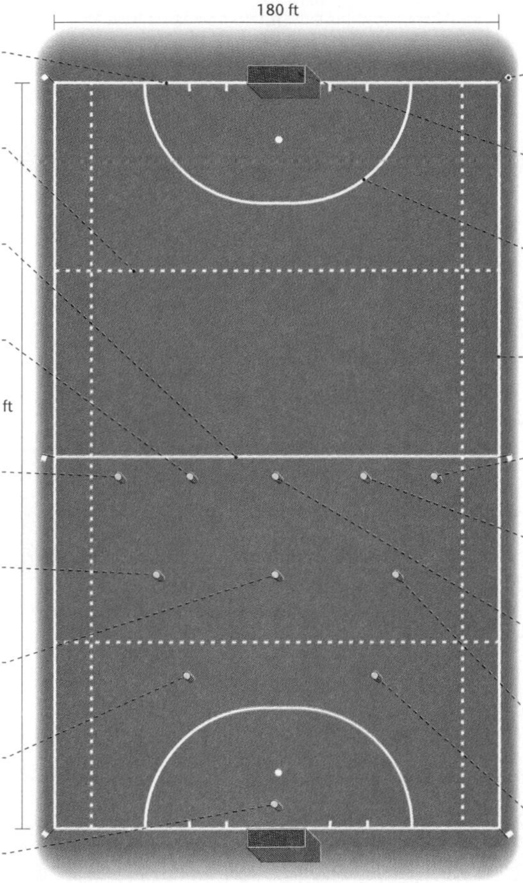

180 ft

goal line
línea^F de meta^F

corner flag
banderín^M de esquina^F

25 yards line
línea^F de los 22,9 metros^M

goal
portería^F

center line
línea^F media

striking circle
área^F de pénalty^M

left inner
interior^M izquierdo

sideline
banda^F

300 ft

left wing
centro^M del campo^M

right wing
extremo^M derecho

right inner
interior^M derecho

left half
defensa^M central izquierdo

center half
medio^M central

center forward
centro^M delantero

left back
defensa^M lateral izquierdo

right half
media punta^F

goalkeeper
portero^M

right back
defensa^M lateral derecho

handle
mango^M

STICK
STICK^M

tape
cinta^F

HOCKEY BALL
PELOTA^F DE HOCKEY^M

blade
pala^F

2 5/8 – 2 7/8 in

TEAM GAMES
DEPORTES DE EQUIPO

607

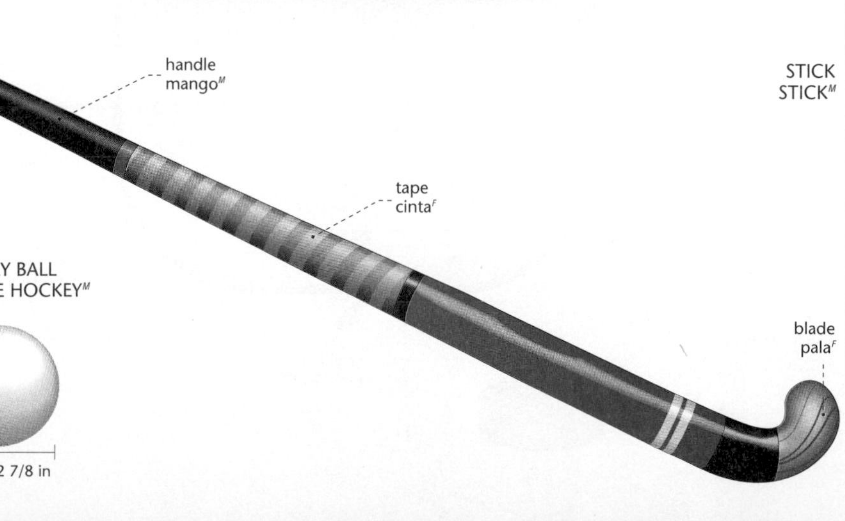

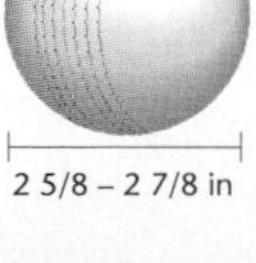

ICE HOCKEY
HOCKEY^M SOBRE HIELO

RINK
PISTA^F

RINK
PISTA^F

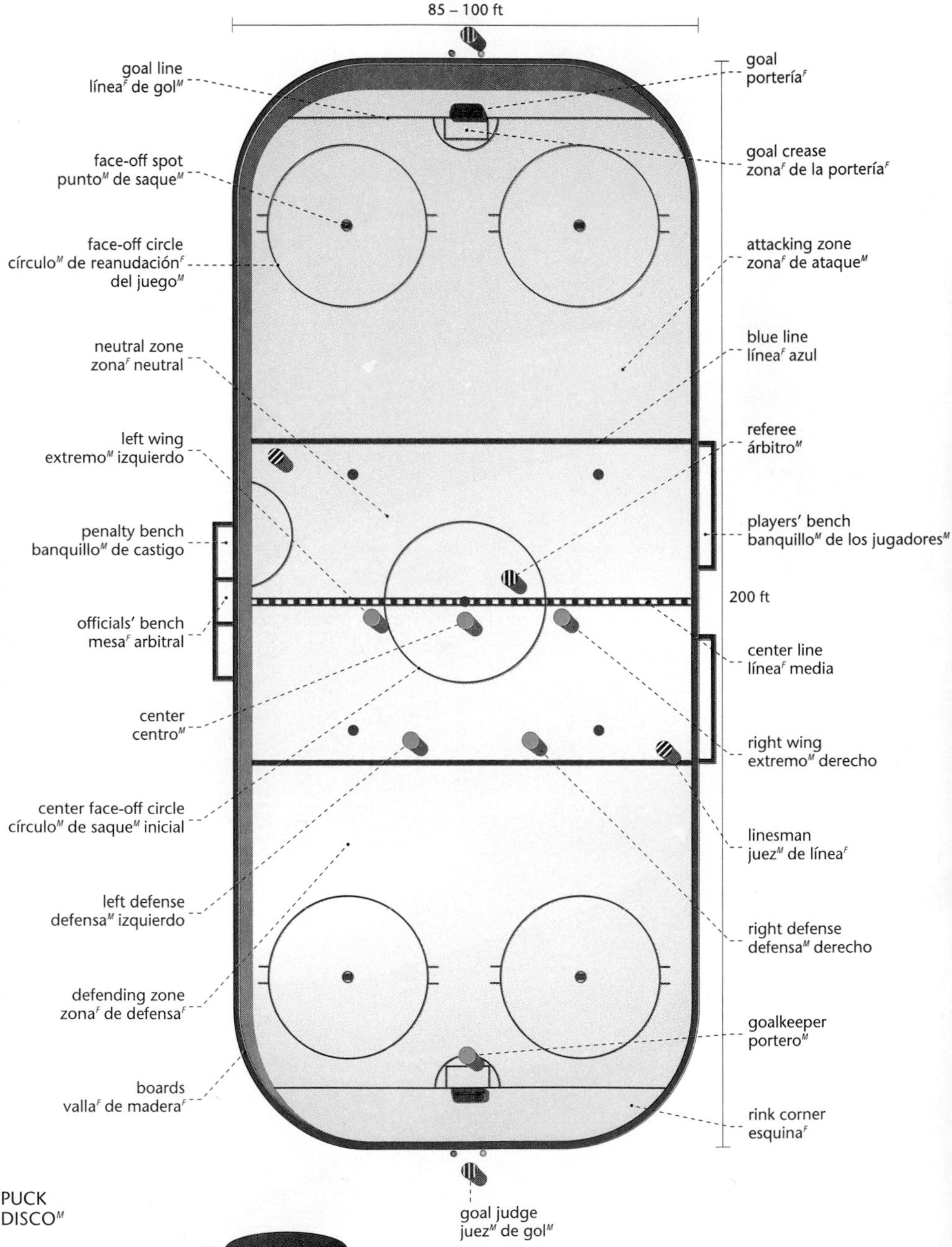

85 – 100 ft

goal line
línea^F de gol^M

goal
portería^F

face-off spot
punto^M de saque^M

goal crease
zona^F de la portería^F

face-off circle
círculo^M de reanudación^F
del juego^M

attacking zone
zona^F de ataque^M

neutral zone
zona^F neutral

blue line
línea^F azul

left wing
extremo^M izquierdo

referee
árbitro^M

penalty bench
banquillo^M de castigo

players' bench
banquillo^M de los jugadores^M

200 ft

officials' bench
mesa^F arbitral

center line
línea^F media

center
centro^M

right wing
extremo^M derecho

center face-off circle
círculo^M de saque^M inicial

linesman
juez^M de línea^F

left defense
defensa^M izquierdo

right defense
defensa^M derecho

defending zone
zona^F de defensa^F

goalkeeper
portero^M

boards
valla^F de madera^F

rink corner
esquina^F

PUCK
DISCO^M

goal judge
juez^M de gol^M

1 in

3 in

TEAM GAMES
DEPORTES DE EQUIPO

608

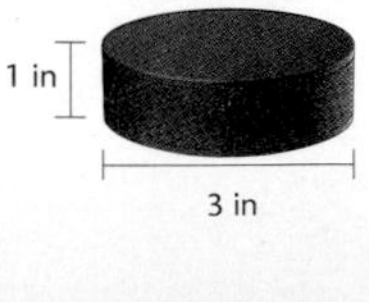

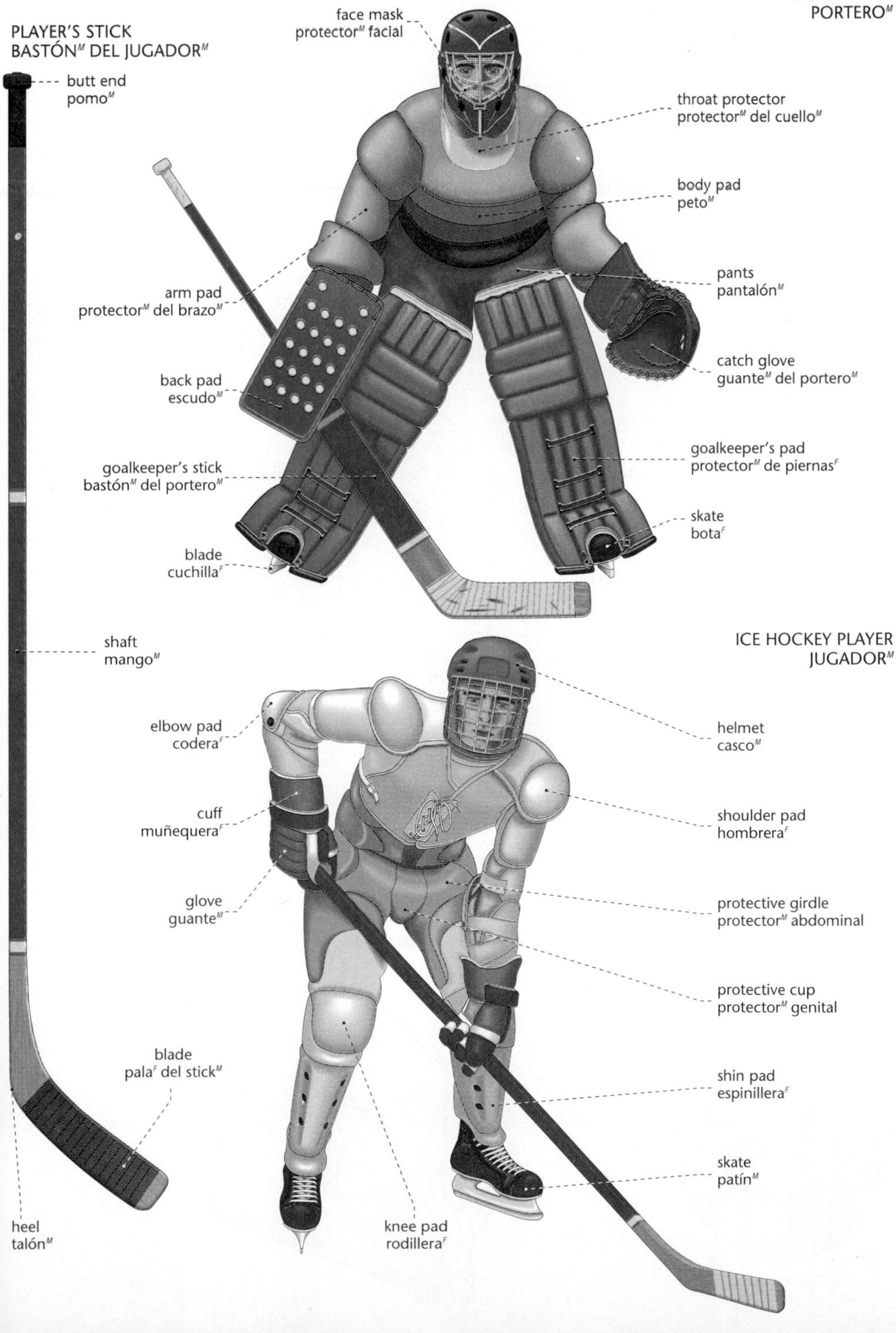

PLAYER'S STICK
BASTÓN^M DEL JUGADOR^M

butt end
pomo^M

face mask
protector^M facial

throat protector
protector^M del cuello^M

body pad
peto^M

pants
pantalón^M

arm pad
protector^M del brazo^M

catch glove
guante^M del portero^M

back pad
escudo^M

goalkeeper's stick
bastón^M del portero^M

goalkeeper's pad
protector^M de piernas^F

skate
bota^F

blade
cuchilla^F

shaft
mango^M

ICE HOCKEY PLAYER
JUGADOR^M

elbow pad
codera^F

helmet
casco^M

cuff
muñequera^F

shoulder pad
hombrera^F

glove
guante^M

protective girdle
protector^M abdominal

protective cup
protector^M genital

blade
pala^F del stick^M

shin pad
espinillera^F

skate
patín^M

heel
talón^M

knee pad
rodillera^F

BASKETBALL
BALONCESTO^M

COURT
CANCHA^F

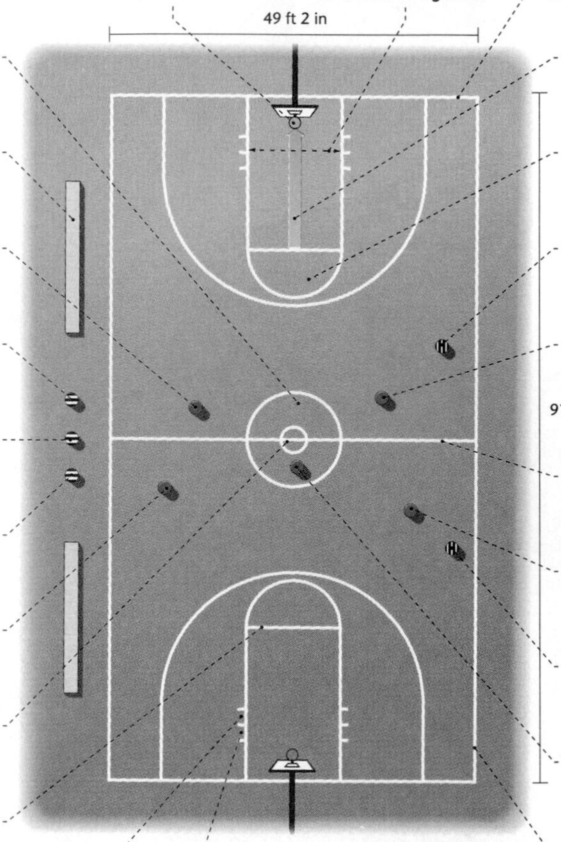

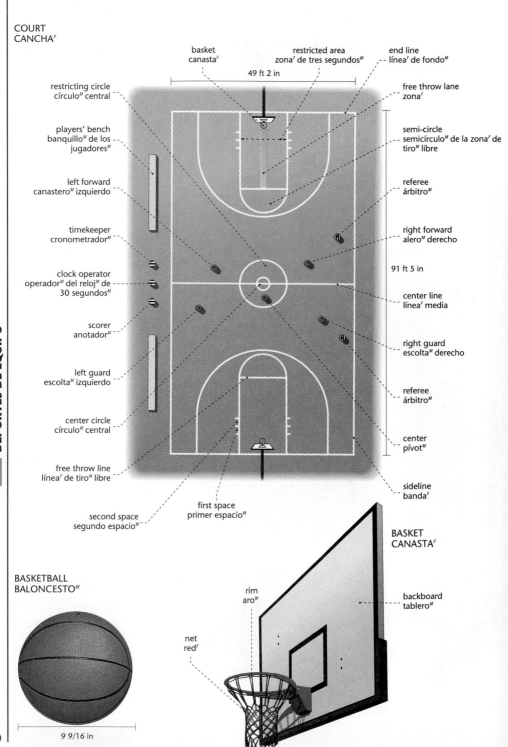

basket
canasta^F

restricted area
zona^F de tres segundos^M

end line
línea^F de fondo^M

49 ft 2 in

restricting circle
círculo^M central

free throw lane
zona^F

players' bench
banquillo^M de los
jugadores^M

semi-circle
semicírculo^M de la zona^F de
tiro^M libre

left forward
canastero^M izquierdo

referee
árbitro^M

timekeeper
cronometrador^M

right forward
alero^M derecho

91 ft 5 in

clock operator
operador^M del reloj^M de
30 segundos^M

center line
línea^F media

scorer
anotador^M

right guard
escolta^M derecho

left guard
escolta^M izquierdo

referee
árbitro^M

center circle
círculo^M central

center
pívot^M

free throw line
línea^F de tiro^M libre

sideline
banda^F

second space
segundo espacio^M

first space
primer espacio^M

BASKET
CANASTA^F

BASKETBALL
BALONCESTO^M

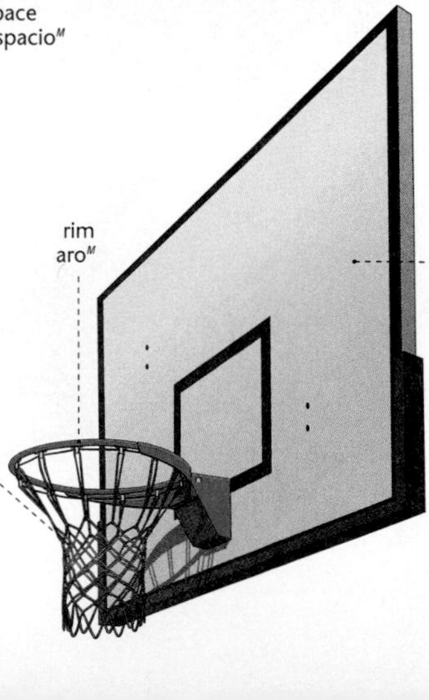

rim
aro^M

backboard
tablero^M

net
red^F

610

9 9/16 in

TEAM GAMES
DEPORTES DE EQUIPO

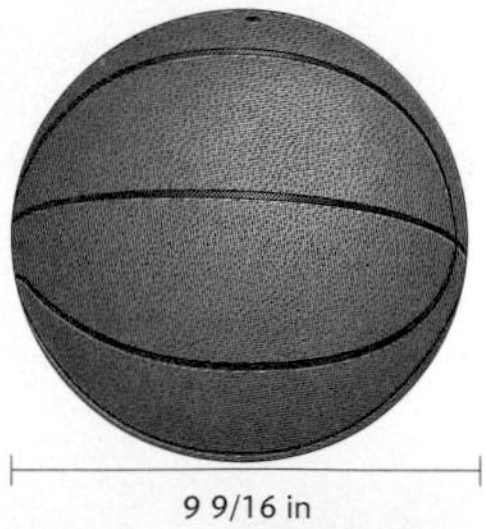

NETBALL
BALONCESTO^M DE MUJERES^F

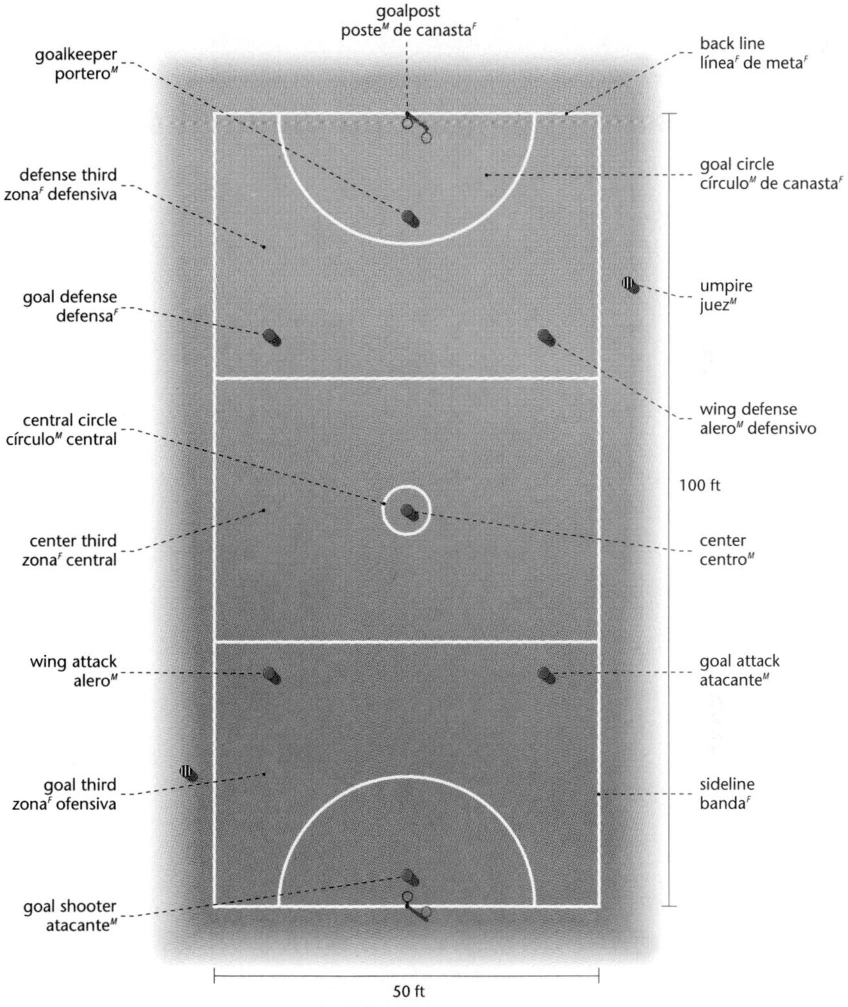

goalpost
poste^M de canasta^F

goalkeeper
portero^M

back line
línea^F de meta^F

defense third
zona^F defensiva

goal circle
círculo^M de canasta^F

goal defense
defensa^F

umpire
juez^M

central circle
círculo^M central

wing defense
alero^M defensivo

100 ft

center third
zona^F central

center
centro^M

wing attack
alero^M

goal attack
atacante^M

goal third
zona^F ofensiva

sideline
banda^F

goal shooter
atacante^M

50 ft

NETBALL
BALÓN^M

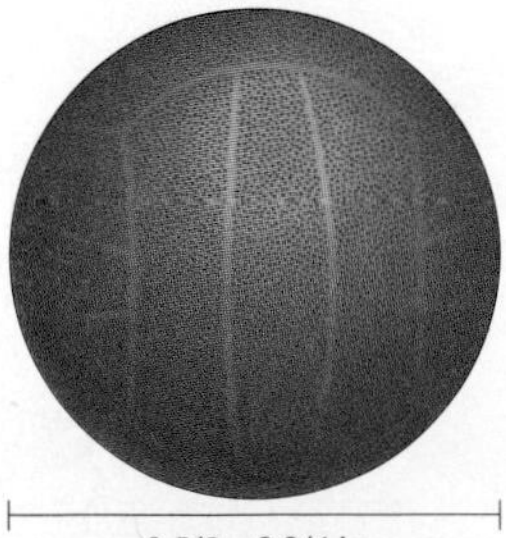

8 5/8 – 8 3/4 in

HANDBALL
BALÓN^M

COURT
CANCHA^F

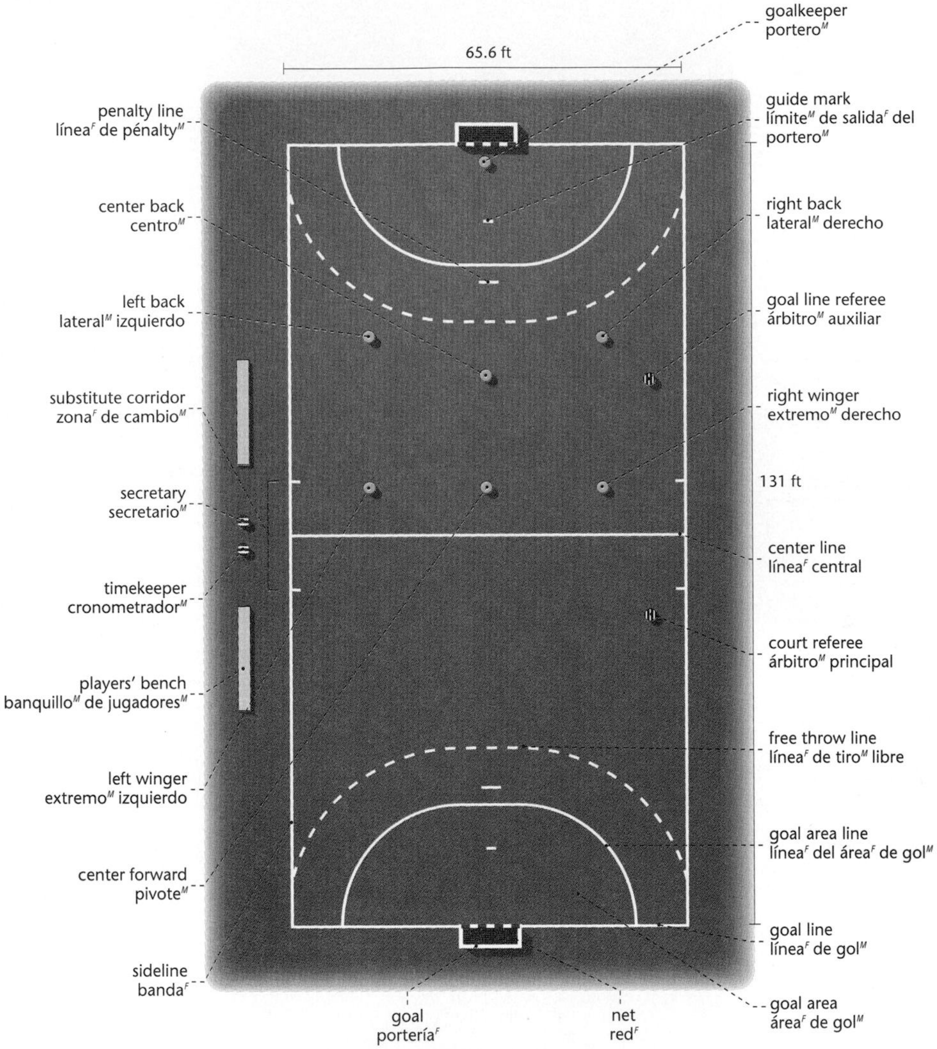

goalkeeper
portero^M

penalty line
línea^F de pénalty^M

guide mark
límite^M de salida^F del
portero^M

center back
centro^M

right back
lateral^M derecho

left back
lateral^M izquierdo

goal line referee
árbitro^M auxiliar

substitute corridor
zona^F de cambio^M

right winger
extremo^M derecho

secretary
secretario^M

131 ft

timekeeper
cronometrador^M

center line
línea^F central

players' bench
banquillo^M de jugadores^M

court referee
árbitro^M principal

left winger
extremo^M izquierdo

free throw line
línea^F de tiro^M libre

center forward
pivote^M

goal area line
línea^F del área^F de gol^M

sideline
banda^F

goal line
línea^F de gol^M

goal
portería^F

net
red^F

goal area
área^F de gol^M

65.6 ft

HANDBALL
BALONMANO^M

♀

6 11/16 – 7 in

♂

7 5/16 – 7 5/8 in

612

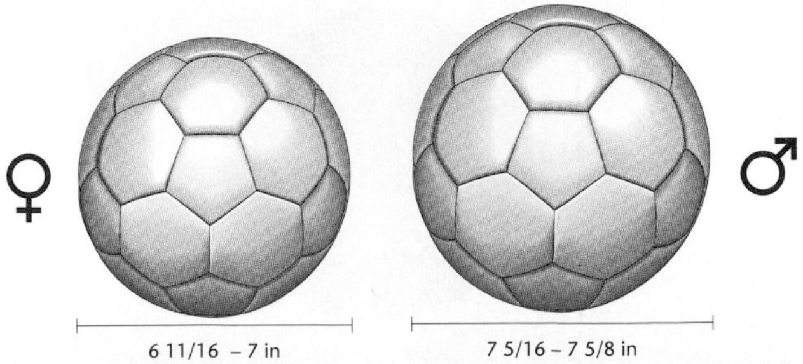

VOLLEYBALL
BALÓN^M VOLEA

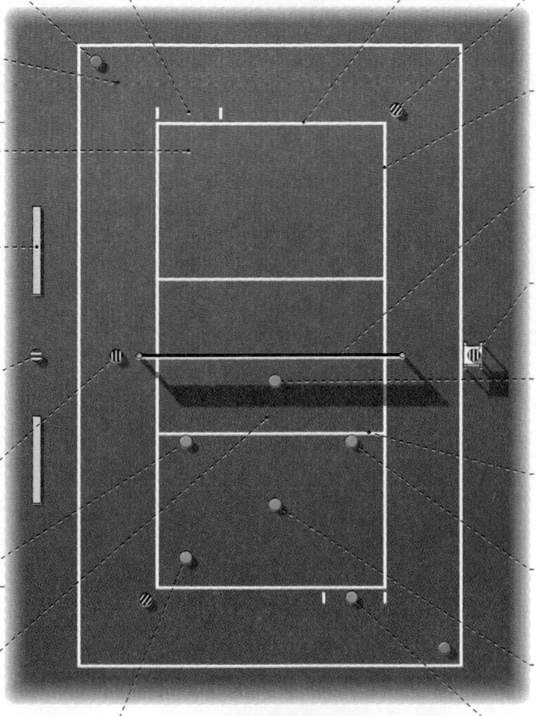

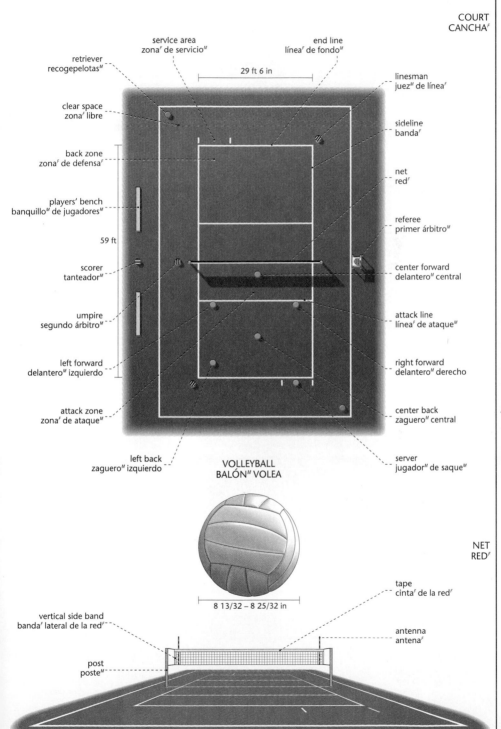

service area
zona^F de servicio^M

end line
línea^F de fondo^M

retriever
recogepelotas^M

29 ft 6 in

linesman
juez^M de línea^F

clear space
zona^F libre

sideline
banda^F

back zone
zona^F de defensa^F

net
red^F

players' bench
banquillo^M de jugadores^M

referee
primer árbitro^M

59 ft

scorer
tanteador^M

center forward
delantero^M central

umpire
segundo árbitro^M

attack line
línea^F de ataque^M

left forward
delantero^M izquierdo

right forward
delantero^M derecho

attack zone
zona^F de ataque^M

center back
zaguero^M central

left back
zaguero^M izquierdo

server
jugador^M de saque^M

VOLLEYBALL
BALÓN^M VOLEA

8 13/32 – 8 25/32 in

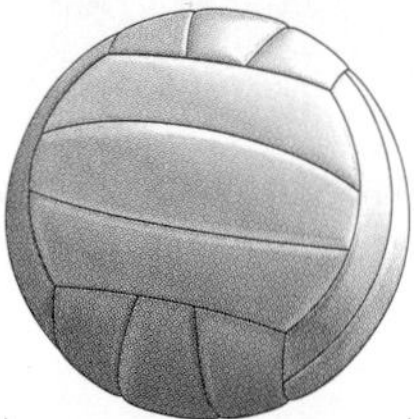

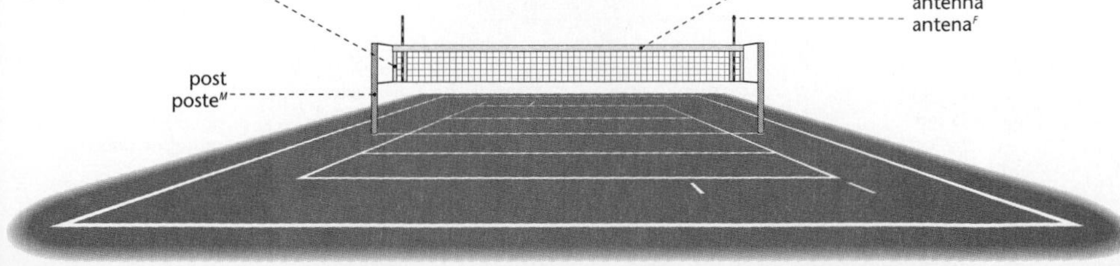

tape
cinta^F de la red^F

vertical side band
banda^F lateral de la red^F

antenna
antena^F

post
poste^M

TENNIS
TENIS^M

COURT
CANCHA^F

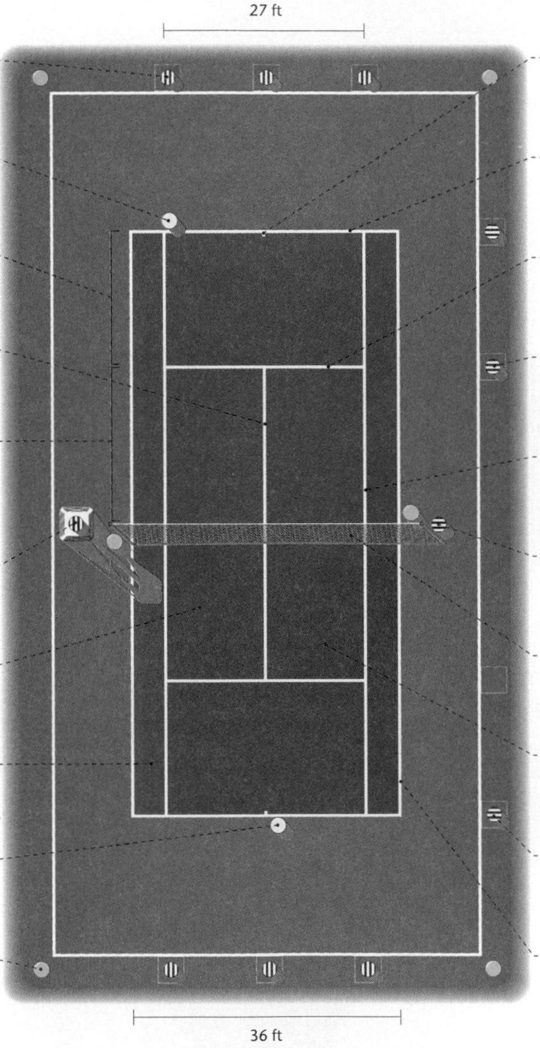

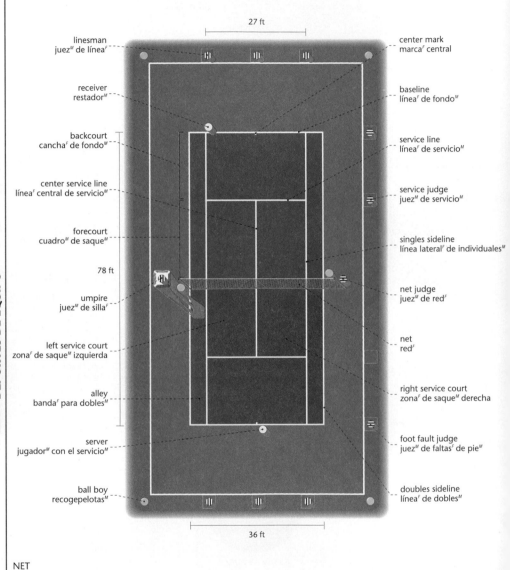

27 ft

linesman
juez^M de línea^F

center mark
marca^F central

receiver
restador^M

baseline
línea^F de fondo^M

backcourt
cancha^F de fondo^M

service line
línea^F de servicio^M

center service line
línea^F central de servicio^M

service judge
juez^M de servicio^M

forecourt
cuadro^M de saque^M

singles sideline
línea lateral^F de individuales^M

78 ft

umpire
juez^M de silla^F

net judge
juez^M de red^F

left service court
zona^F de saque^M izquierda

net
red^F

alley
banda^F para dobles^M

right service court
zona^F de saque^M derecha

server
jugador^M con el servicio^M

foot fault judge
juez^M de faltas^F de pie^M

ball boy
recogepelotas^M

doubles sideline
línea^F de dobles^M

36 ft

NET
RED^F

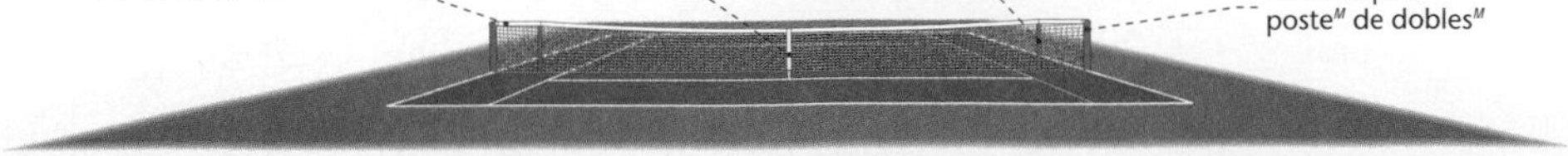

net band
cinta^F de la red^F

center strap
cinta^F central

singles pole
poste^M de individuales^M

doubles pole
poste^M de dobles^M

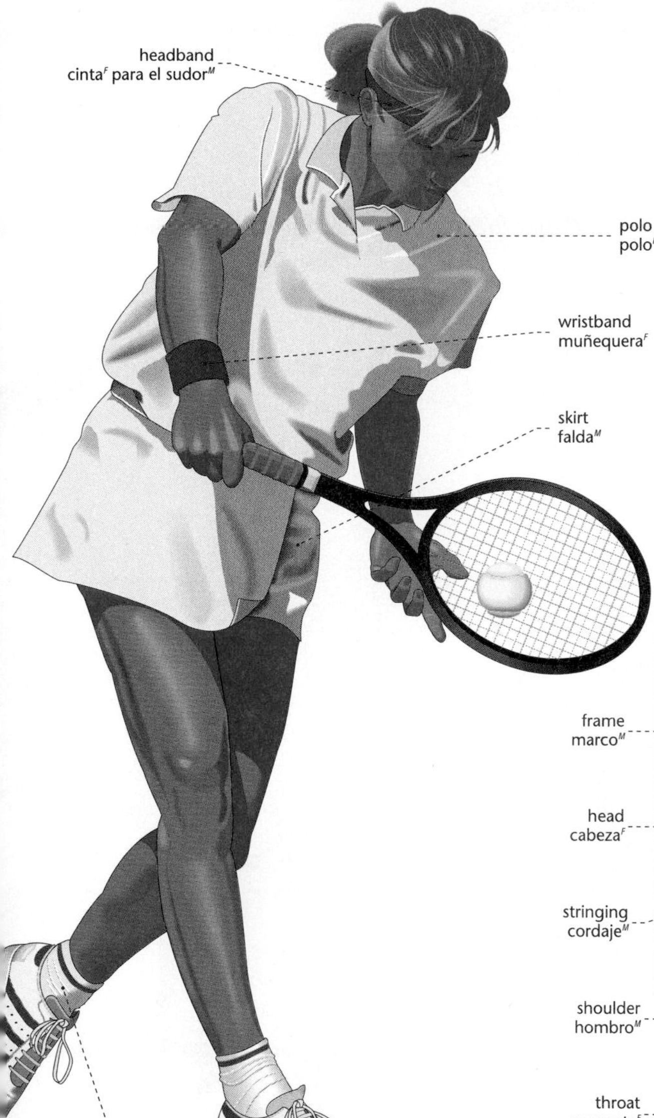

headband
cinta*F* para el sudor*M*

polo shirt
polo*M*

wristband
muñequera*F*

skirt
falda*M*

TENNIS RACKET
RAQUETA*F* DE TENIS*M*

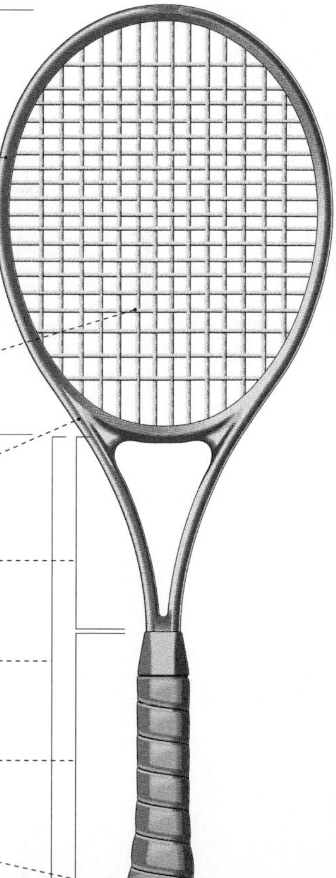

frame
marco*M*

head
cabeza*F*

stringing
cordaje*M*

shoulder
hombro*M*

throat
garganta*F*

shaft
mango*M*

handle
empuñadura*F*

butt
puño*M*

sock
calcetín*M*

tennis shoe
zapato*M* de tenis*M*

TENNIS BALL
PELOTA*F* DE TENIS*M*

2 1/2 – 2 5/8 in

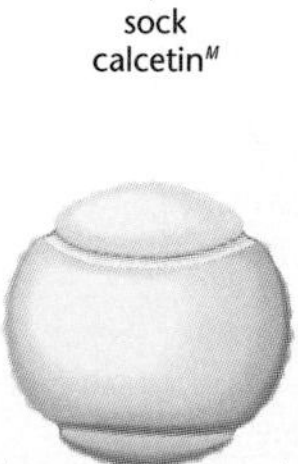

SQUASH
SQUASH^M

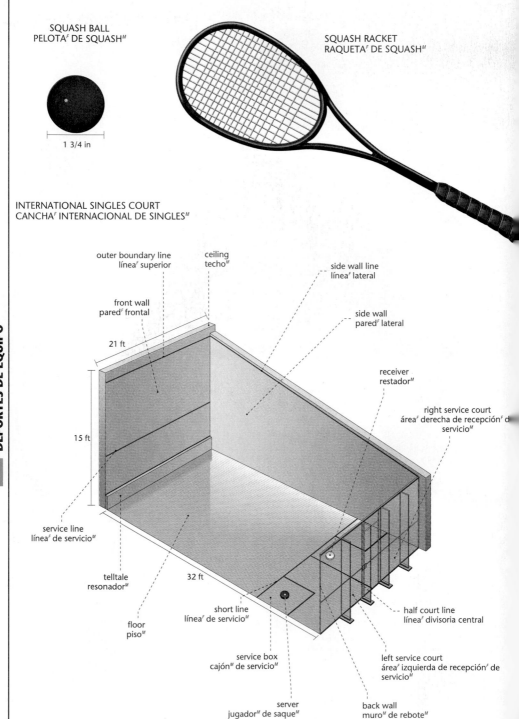

SQUASH BALL
PELOTA^F DE SQUASH^M

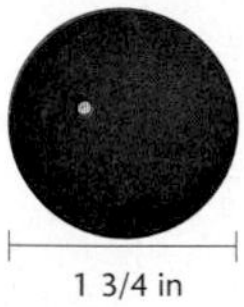

1 3/4 in

SQUASH RACKET
RAQUETA^F DE SQUASH^M

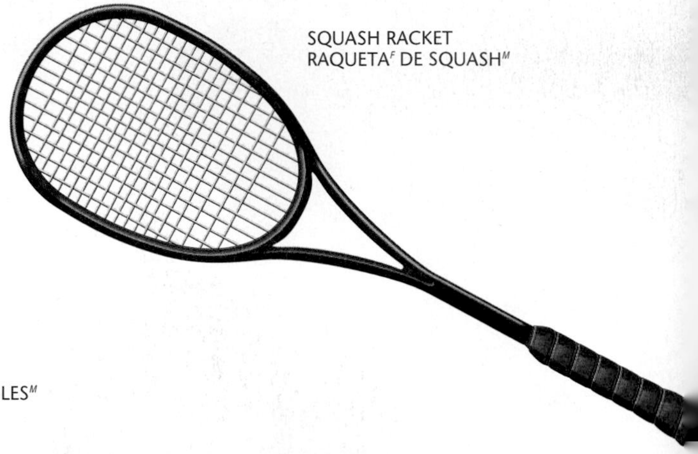

INTERNATIONAL SINGLES COURT
CANCHA^F INTERNACIONAL DE SINGLES^M

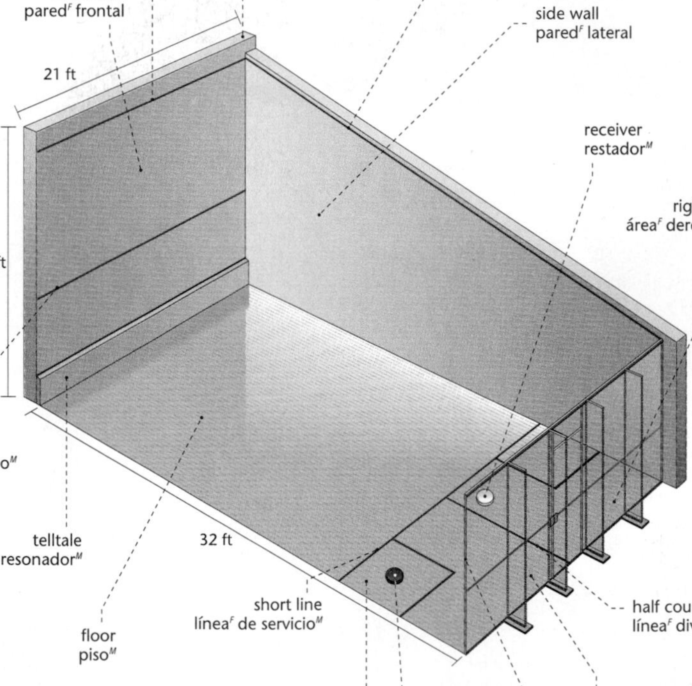

outer boundary line
línea^F superior

ceiling
techo^M

side wall line
línea^F lateral

front wall
pared^F frontal

side wall
pared^F lateral

21 ft

receiver
restador^M

right service court
área^F derecha de recepción^F d
servicio^M

15 ft

service line
línea^F de servicio^M

telltale
resonador^M

32 ft

half court line
línea^F divisoria central

floor
piso^M

short line
línea^F de servicio^M

service box
cajón^M de servicio^M

left service court
área^F izquierda de recepción^F de
servicio^M

server
jugador^M de saque^M

back wall
muro^M de rebote^M

TEAM GAMES
DEPORTES DE EQUIPO

RACQUETBALL
RAQUETBOL^M

RACQUETBALL RACKET
RAQUETA^F DE RAQUETBOL^M

RACQUETBALL
PELOTA^F DE RAQUETBOL^M

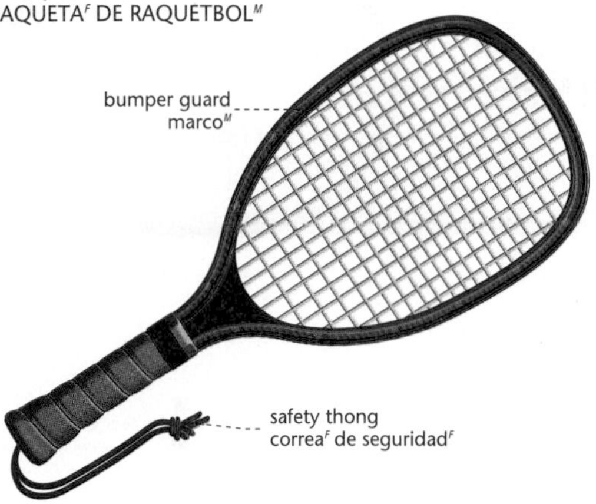

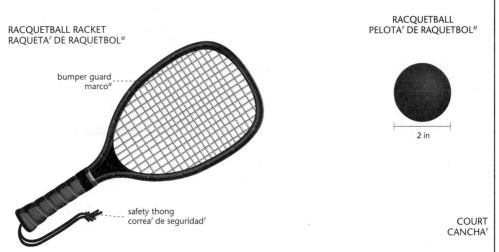

bumper guard
marco^M

safety thong
correa^F de seguridad^F

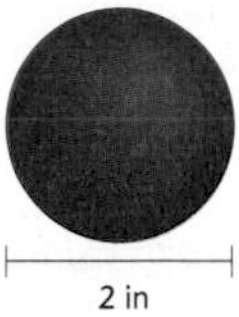

2 in

COURT
CANCHA^F

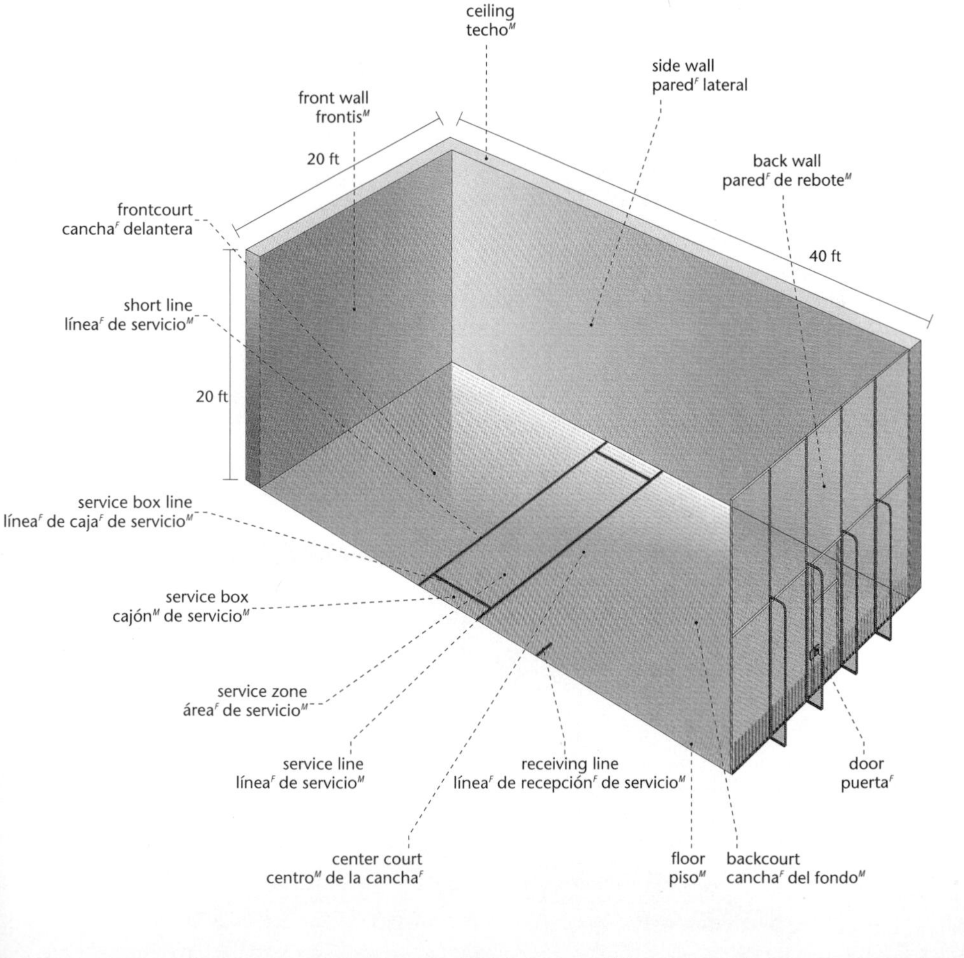

ceiling
techo^M

side wall
pared^F lateral

front wall
frontis^M

back wall
pared^F de rebote^M

20 ft

frontcourt
cancha^F delantera

40 ft

short line
línea^F de servicio^M

20 ft

service box line
línea^F de caja^F de servicio^M

service box
cajón^M de servicio^M

service zone
área^F de servicio^M

service line
línea^F de servicio^M

receiving line
línea^F de recepción^F de servicio^M

door
puerta^F

center court
centro^M de la cancha^F

floor
piso^M

backcourt
cancha^F del fondo^M

BADMINTON
BÁDMINTON*M*

BADMINTON RACKET
RAQUETA*F* DE BÁDMINTON*M*

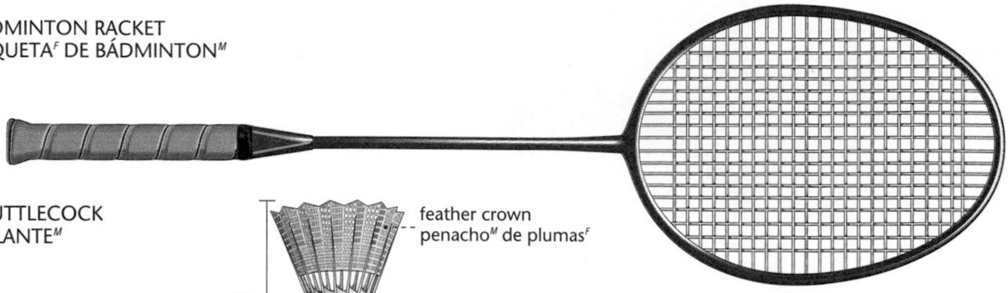

SHUTTLECOCK
VOLANTE*M*

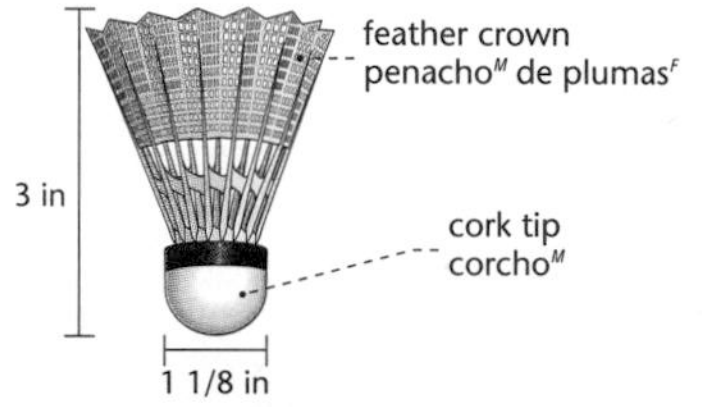

feather crown
penacho*M* de plumas*F*

3 in

cork tip
corcho*M*

1 1/8 in

COURT
CANCHA*F*

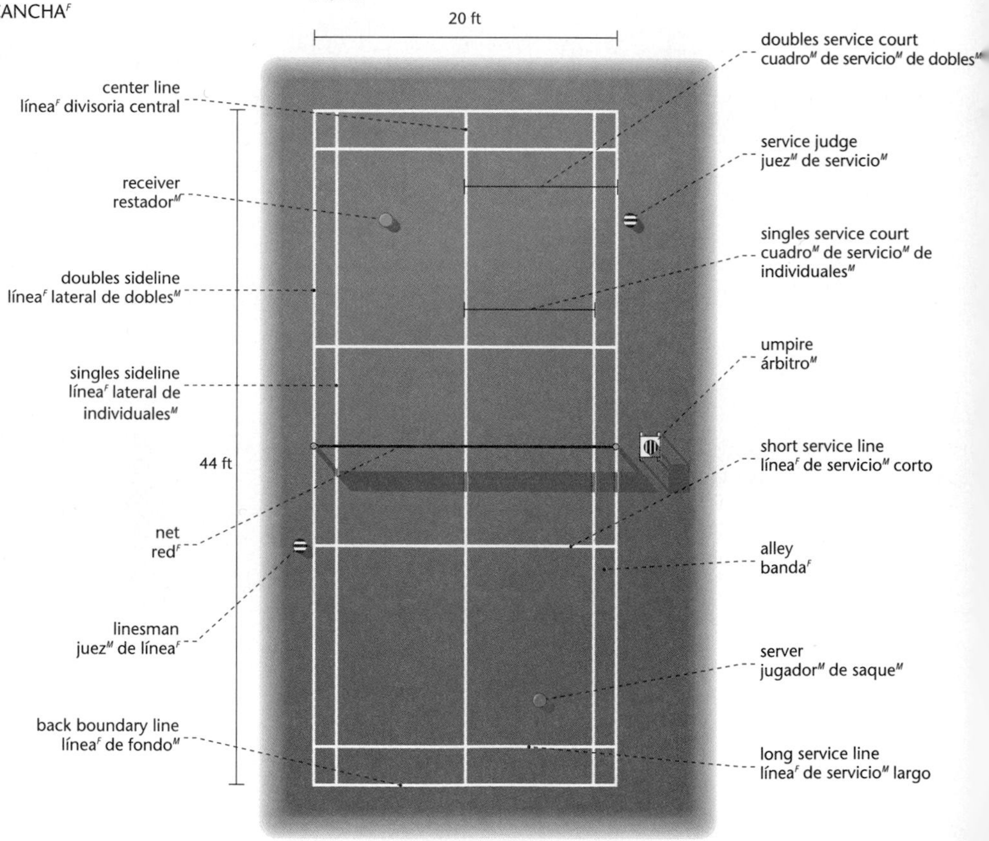

20 ft

doubles service court
cuadro*M* de servicio*M* de dobles*M*

center line
línea*F* divisoria central

service judge
juez*M* de servicio*M*

receiver
restador*M*

singles service court
cuadro*M* de servicio*M* de
individuales*M*

doubles sideline
línea*F* lateral de dobles*M*

umpire
árbitro*M*

singles sideline
línea*F* lateral de
individuales*M*

44 ft

short service line
línea*F* de servicio*M* corto

net
red*F*

alley
banda*F*

linesman
juez*M* de línea*F*

server
jugador*M* de saque*M*

back boundary line
línea*F* de fondo*M*

long service line
línea*F* de servicio*M* largo

NET
RED*F*

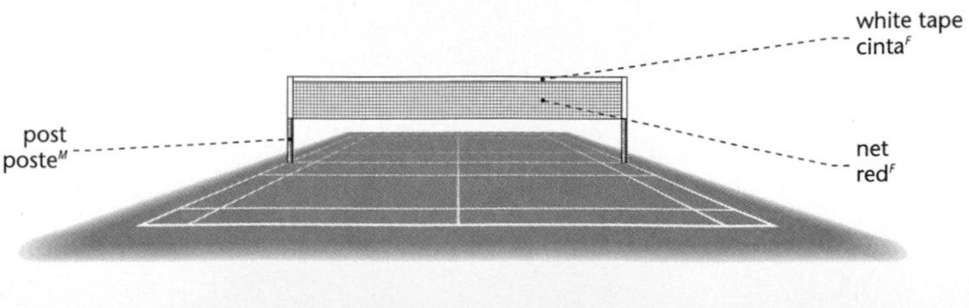

white tape
cinta*F*

post
poste*M*

net
red*F*

TABLE TENNIS
PING PONG^M

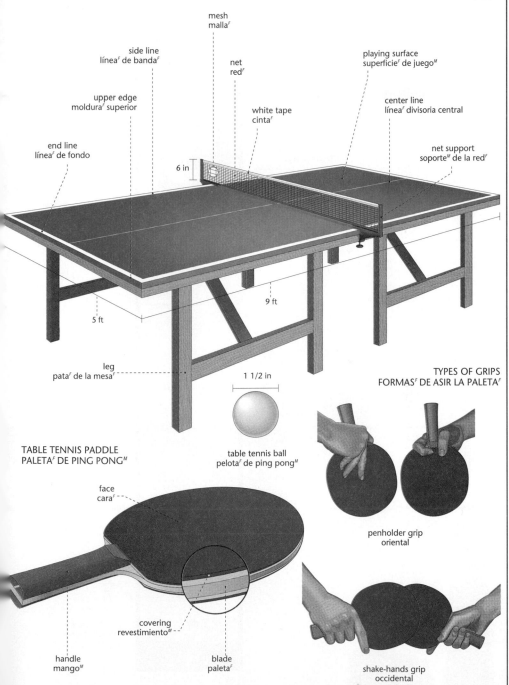

TABLE
MESA^F

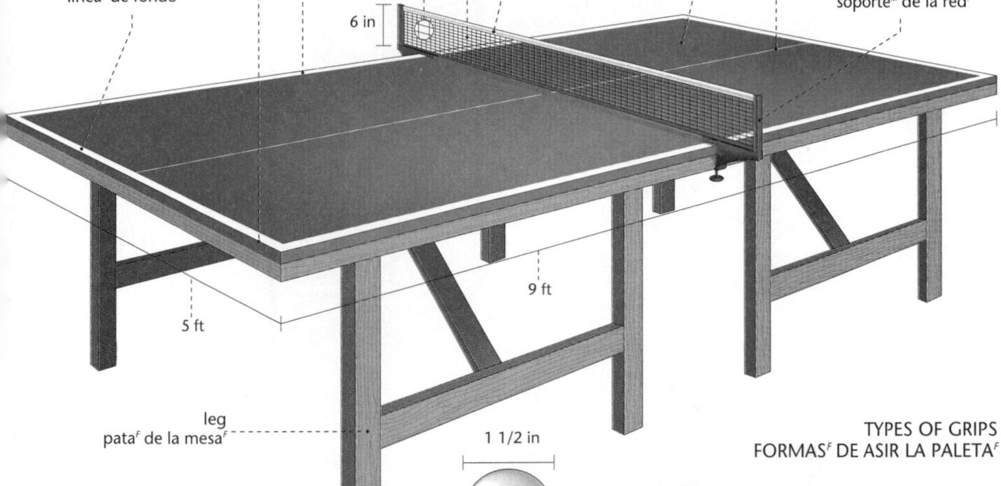

mesh
malla^F

side line
línea^F de banda^F

net
red^F

playing surface
superficie^F de juego^M

upper edge
moldura^F superior

white tape
cinta^F

center line
línea^F divisoria central

end line
línea^F de fondo

net support
soporte^M de la red^F

6 in

9 ft

5 ft

leg
pata^F de la mesa^F

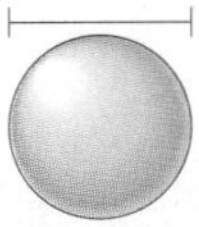

1 1/2 in

TYPES OF GRIPS
FORMAS^F DE ASIR LA PALETA^F

TABLE TENNIS PADDLE
PALETA^F DE PING PONG^M

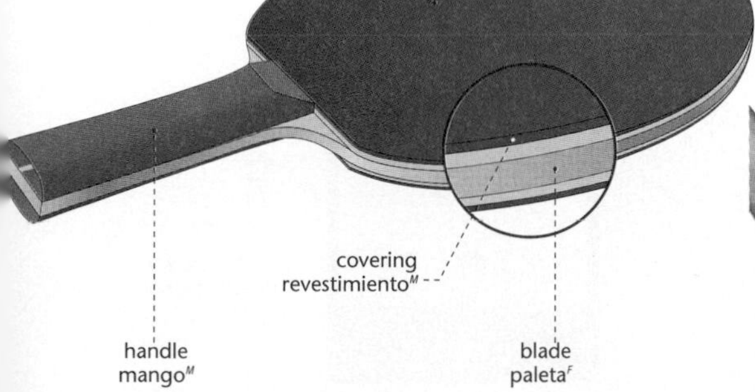

table tennis ball
pelota^F de ping pong^M

face
cara^F

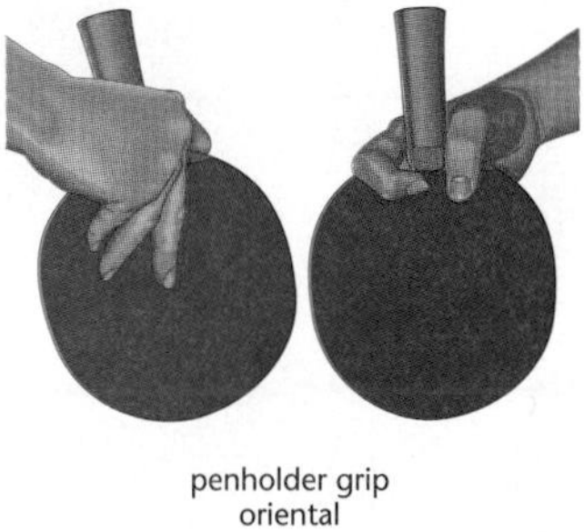

penholder grip
oriental

covering
revestimiento^M

handle
mango^M

blade
paleta^F

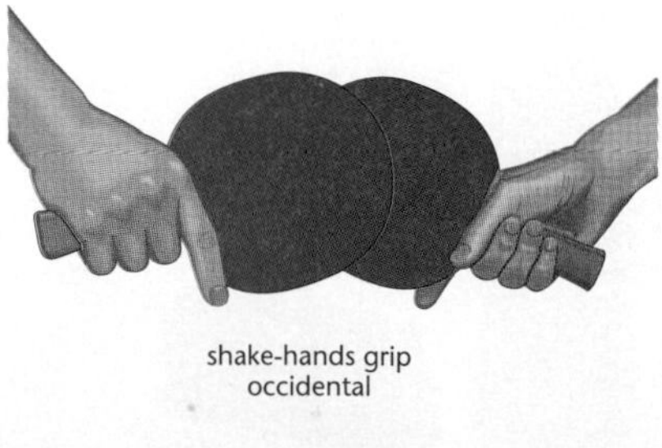

shake-hands grip
occidental

CURLING STONE
PIEDRA^F DE CURLING^M

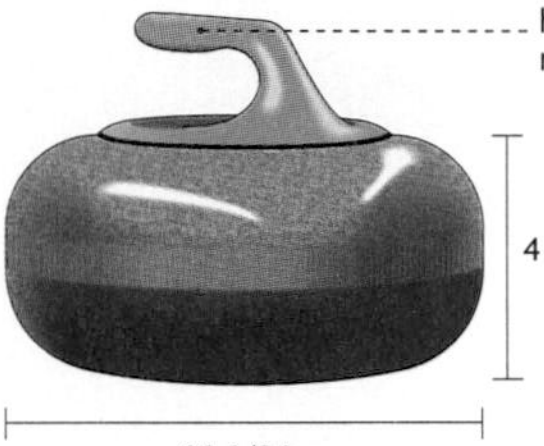

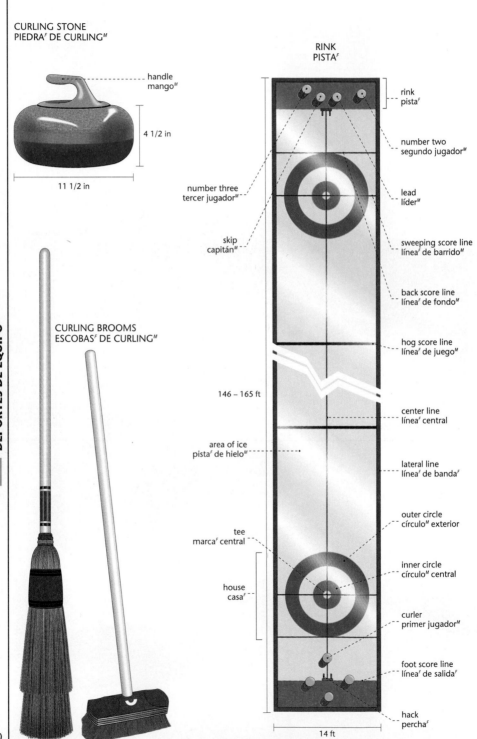

handle
mango^M

4 1/2 in

11 1/2 in

CURLING BROOMS
ESCOBAS^F DE CURLING^M

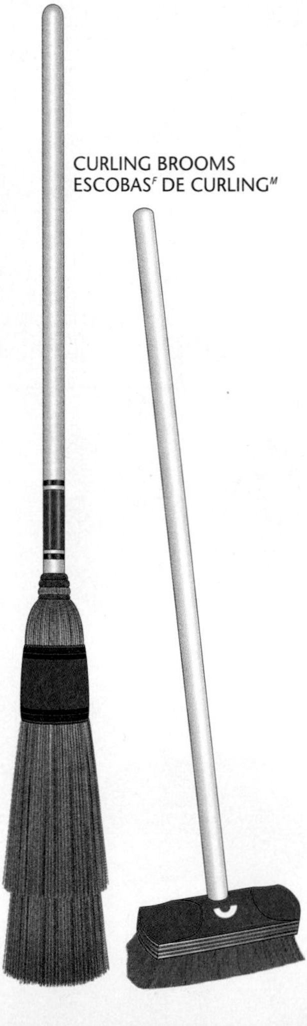

RINK
PISTA^F

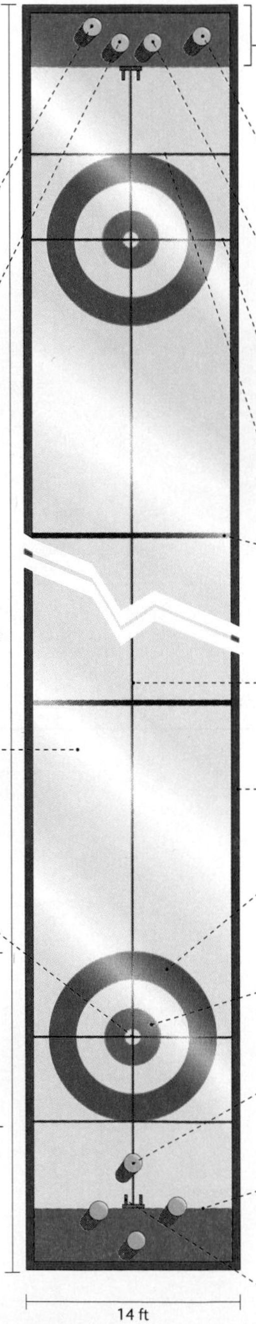

rink
pista^F

number two
segundo jugador^M

number three
tercer jugador^M

lead
líder^M

skip
capitán^M

sweeping score line
línea^F de barrido^M

back score line
línea^F de fondo^M

hog score line
línea^F de juego^M

146 – 165 ft

center line
línea^F central

area of ice
pista^F de hielo^M

lateral line
línea^F de banda^F

outer circle
círculo^M exterior

tee
marca^F central

inner circle
círculo^M central

house
casa^F

curler
primer jugador^M

foot score line
línea^F de salida^F

hack
percha^F

14 ft

TEAM GAMES
DEPORTES DE EQUIPO

620

SWIMMING
NATACIÓN^F

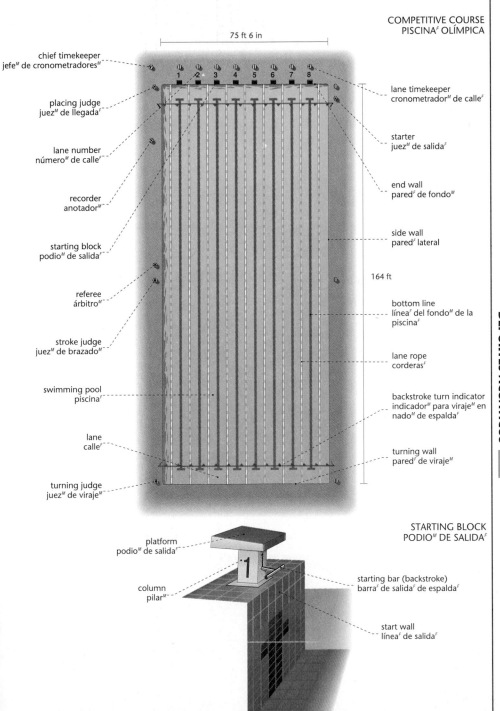

75 ft 6 in

chief timekeeper
jefe^M de cronometradores^M

lane timekeeper
cronometrador^M de calle^F

placing judge
juez^M de llegada^F

starter
juez^M de salida^F

lane number
número^M de calle^F

end wall
pared^F de fondo^M

recorder
anotador^M

side wall
pared^F lateral

starting block
podio^M de salida^F

164 ft

referee
árbitro^M

bottom line
línea^F del fondo^M de la
piscina^F

stroke judge
juez^M de brazado^M

lane rope
corderas^F

swimming pool
piscina^F

backstroke turn indicator
indicador^M para viraje^M en
nado^M de espalda^F

lane
calle^F

turning wall
pared^F de viraje^M

turning judge
juez^M de viraje^M

STARTING BLOCK
PODIO^M DE SALIDA^F

platform
podio^M de salida^F

starting bar (backstroke)
barra^F de salida^F de espalda^F

column
pilar^M

start wall
línea^F de salida^F

WATER SPORTS
DEPORTES ACUÁTICOS

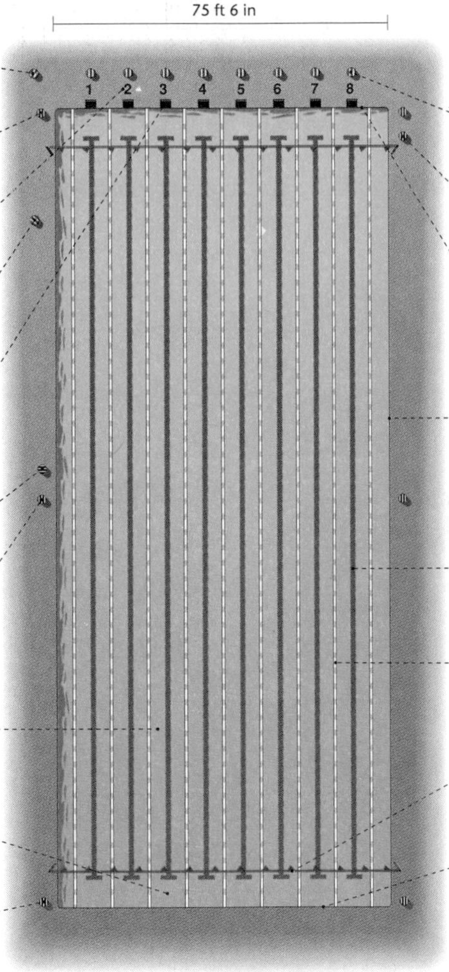

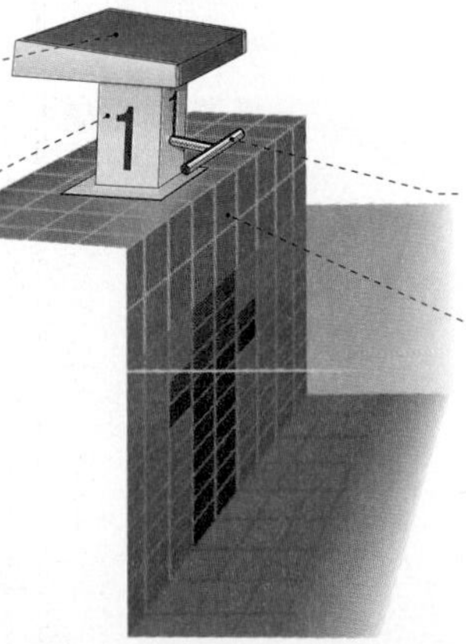

SWIMMING
NATACIÓN^F

TYPES OF STROKES
ESTILOS^M DE NATACIÓN^F

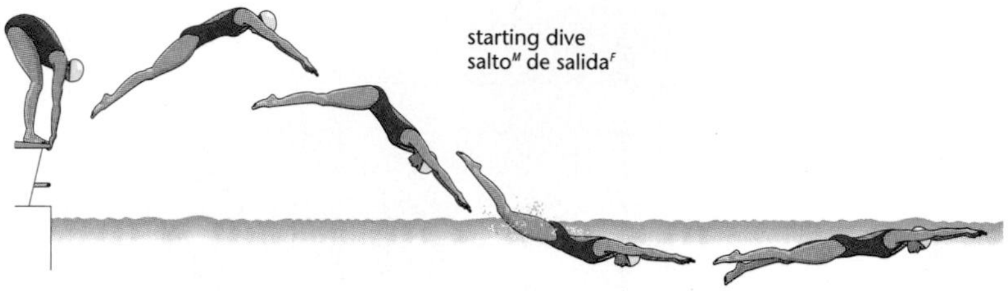

starting dive
salto^M de salida^F

FRONT CRAWL STROKE
BRAZADA^F DE CROL^M

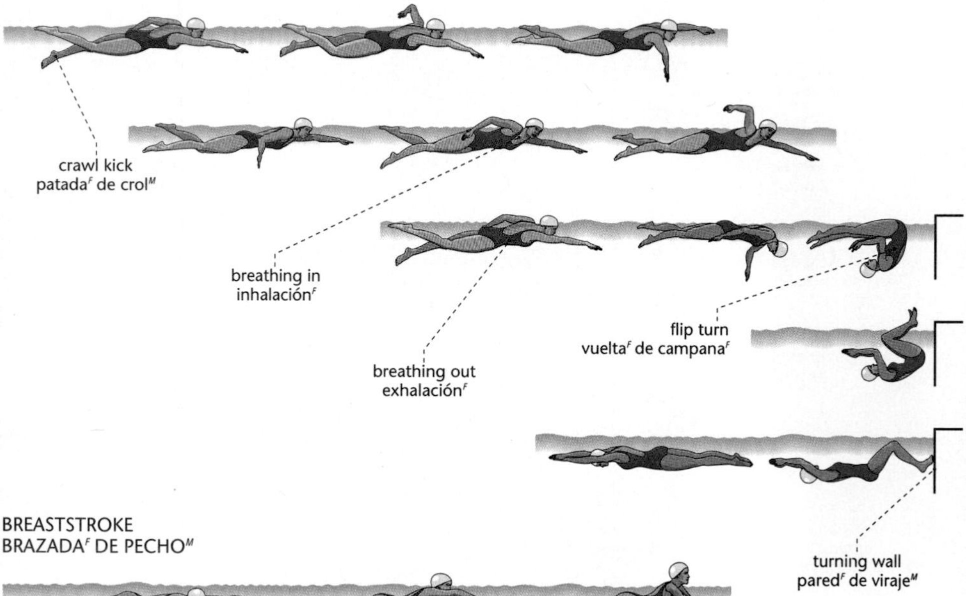

crawl kick
patada^F de crol^M

breathing in
inhalación^F

flip turn
vuelta^F de campana^F

breathing out
exhalación^F

turning wall
pared^F de viraje^M

BREASTSTROKE
BRAZADA^F DE PECHO^M

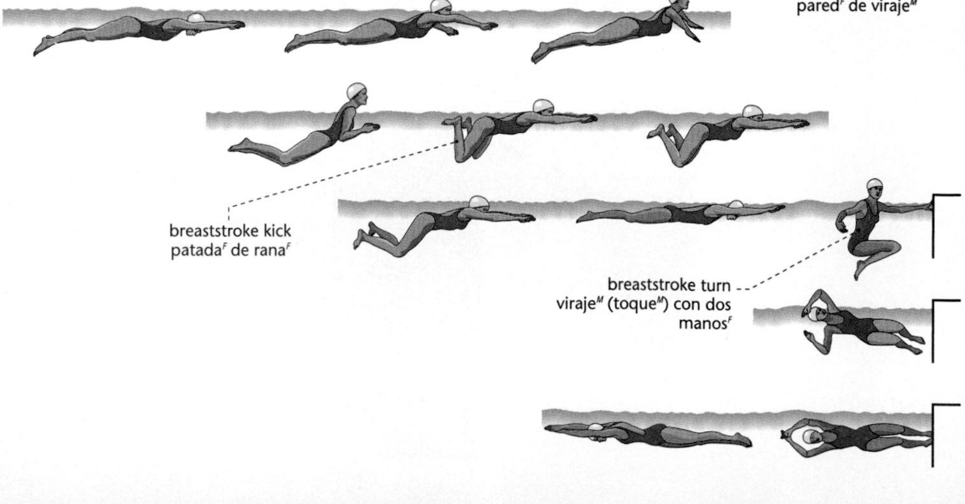

breaststroke kick
patada^F de rana^F

breaststroke turn
viraje^M (toque^M) con dos
manos^F

WATER SPORTS
DEPORTES ACUÁTICOS

BUTTERFLY STROKE
BRAZADA^F DE MARIPOSA^F

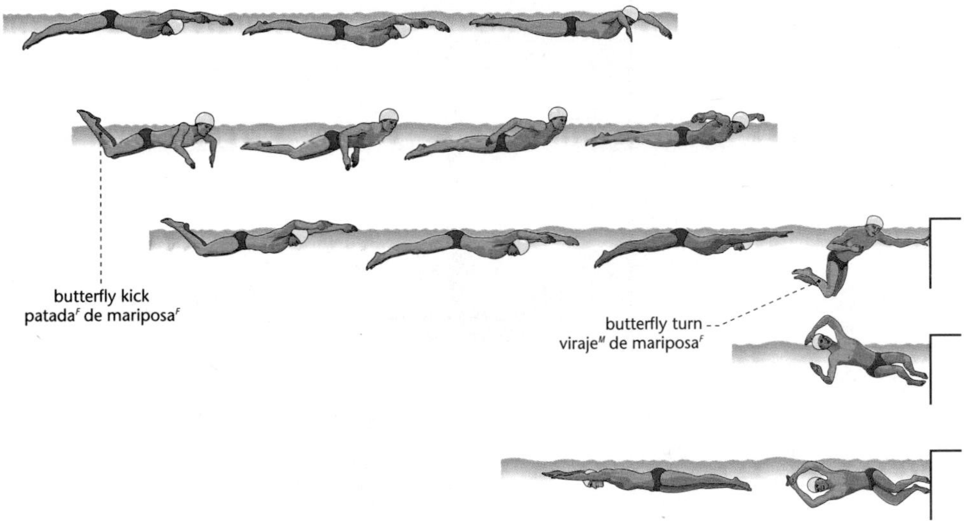

butterfly kick
patada^f de mariposa^f

butterfly turn
viraje^M de mariposa^f

BACKSTROKE START
POSICIÓN^F DE SALIDA^F DE ESPALDA^F

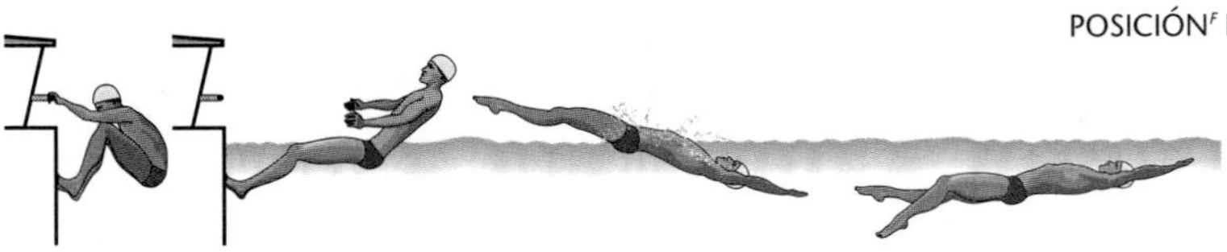

BACKSTROKE
BRAZADA^F DE ESPALDA^F

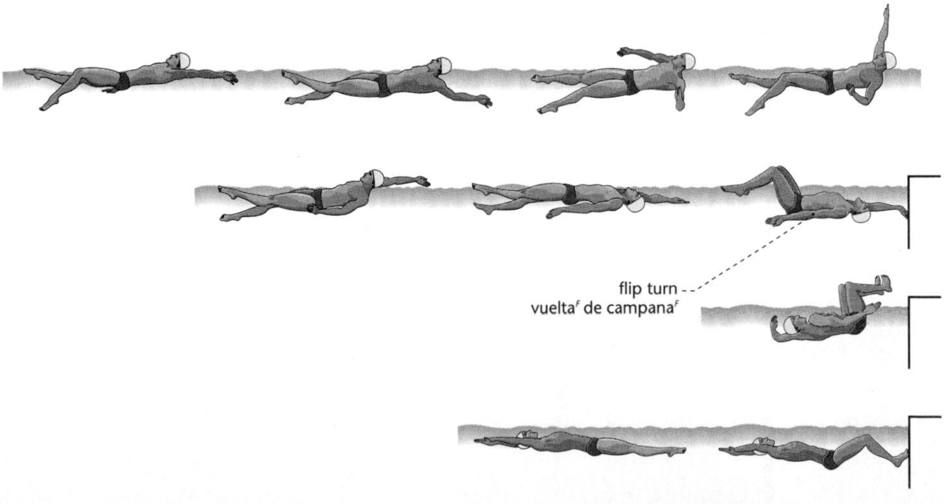

flip turn
vuelta^f de campana^f

DIVING
SALTO^M

DIVING
SALTO^M

DIVING INSTALLATIONS
TORRE^F DE SALTOS^M

diving tower
torre^F de saltos^M

3 m platform
palanca^F de 3 m

surface of the water
superficie^F del agua^F

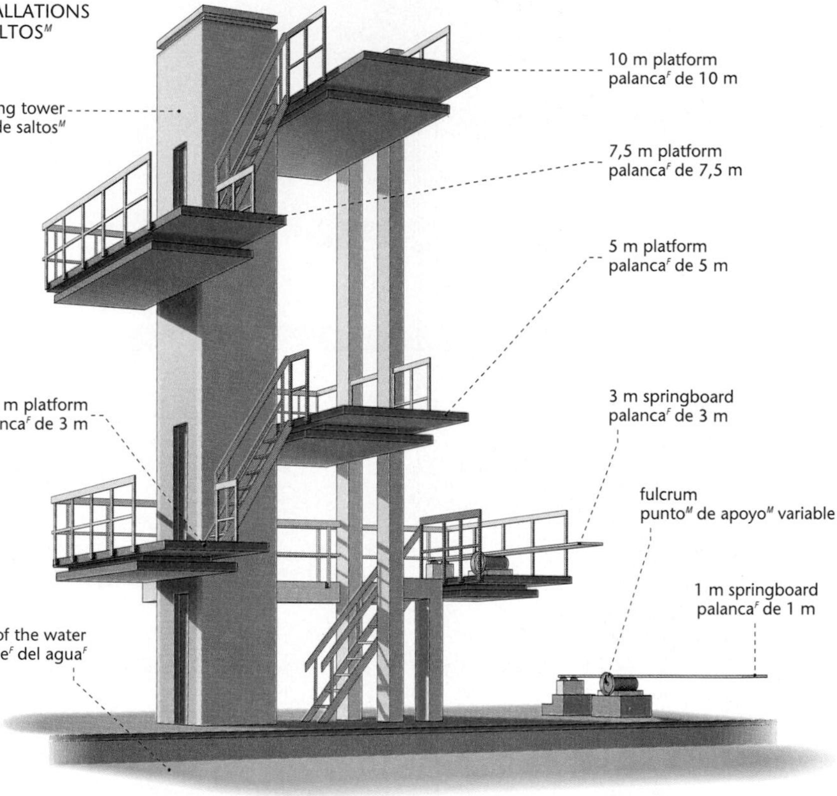

10 m platform
palanca^F de 10 m

7,5 m platform
palanca^F de 7,5 m

5 m platform
palanca^F de 5 m

3 m springboard
palanca^F de 3 m

fulcrum
punto^M de apoyo^M variable

1 m springboard
palanca^F de 1 m

WATER SPORTS
DEPORTES ACUÁTICOS

STARTING POSITIONS
POSICIONES^F DE SALTO^M

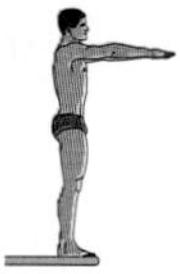

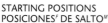

forward
salto^M al frente^M

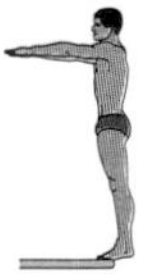

backward
salto^M atrás

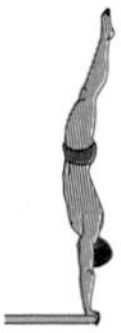

armstand
equilibrio^M

FLIGHTS
SALTOS^M

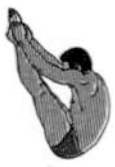

pike position
posición^F B - hacer la carpa^F

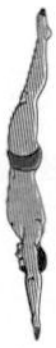

straight position
posición^F A - derecho

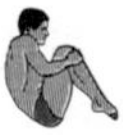

tuck position
posición^F C - cuerpo^M encogi

ENTRIES
ENTRADAS^F AL AGUA^F

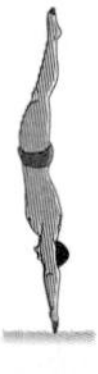

head-first entry
entrada^F de cabeza^F

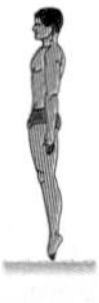

feet-first entry
entrada^F de pie^M

FORWARD DIVE
SALTO^M AL FRENTE^M EN POSICIÓN^F A

BACKWARD DIVE
SALTO^M ATRÁS EN POSICIÓN^F A

ARMSTAND DIVE
SALTO^M EN EQUILIBRIO^M

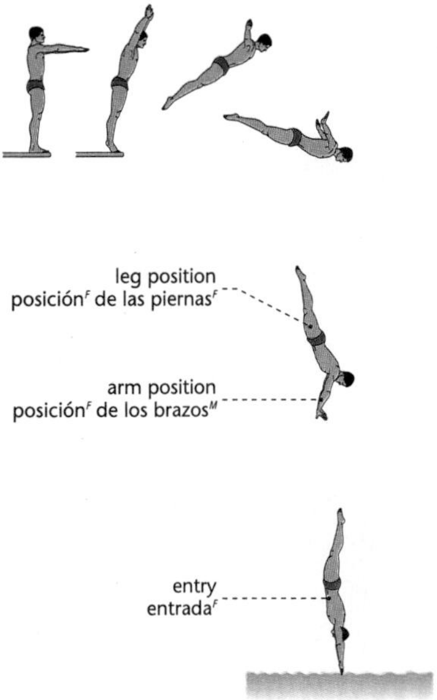

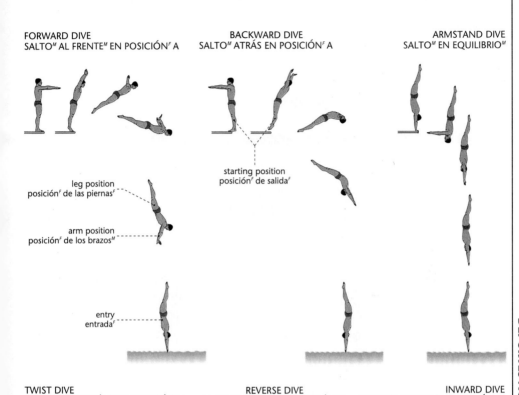

leg position
posición^F de las piernas^F

arm position
posición^F de los brazos^M

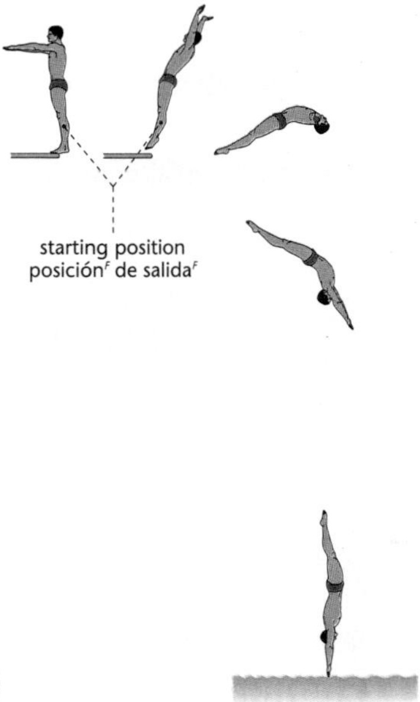

starting position
posición^F de salida^F

entry
entrada^F

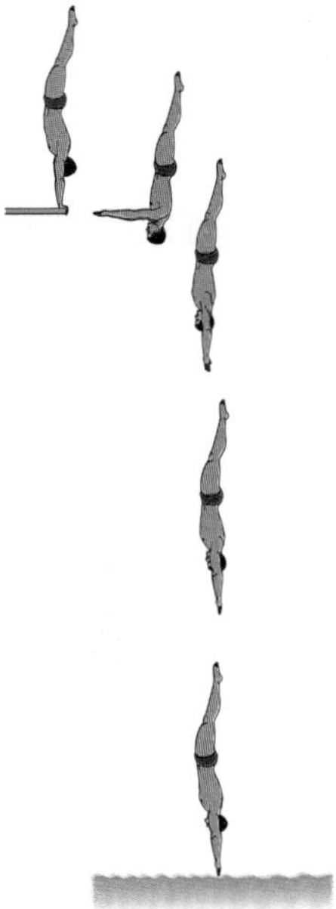

TWIST DIVE
SALTO^M TIRABUZÓN^M EN POSICIÓN^F A

REVERSE DIVE
SALTO^M INVERSO EN POSICIÓN^F B

INWARD DIVE
SALTO^M INTERIOR EN POSICIÓN^F B

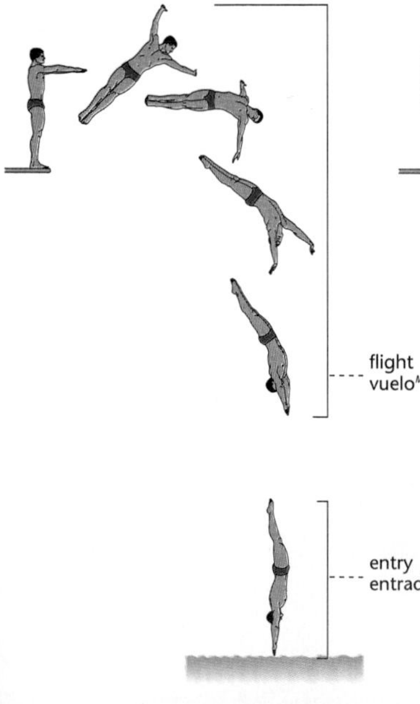

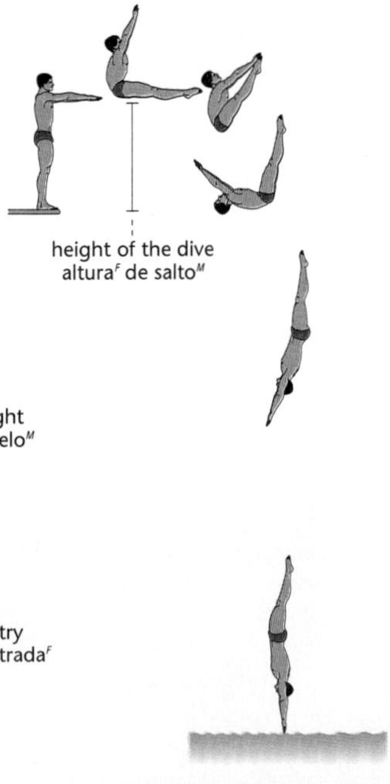

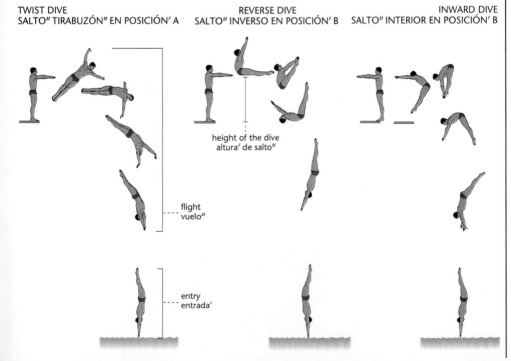

height of the dive
altura^F de salto^M

flight
vuelo^M

entry
entrada^F

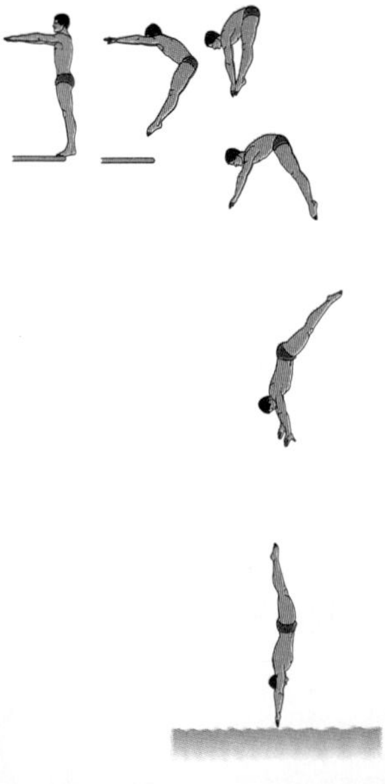

WATER POLO
WATERPOLO^M

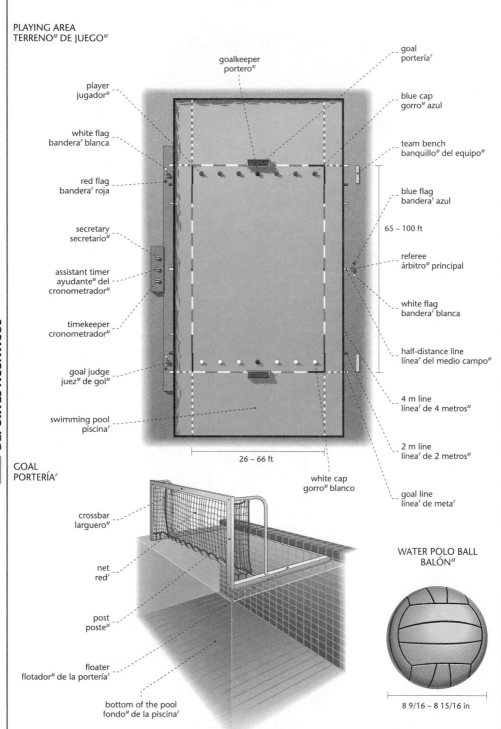

PLAYING AREA
TERRENO^M DE JUEGO^M

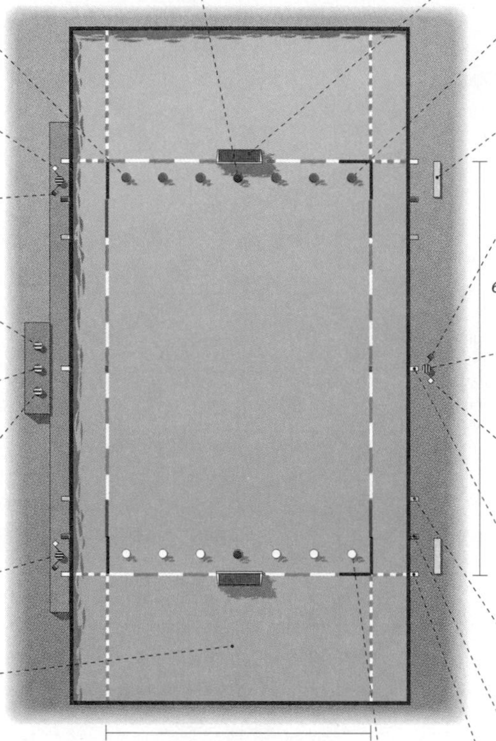

goalkeeper
portero^M

goal
portería^F

player
jugador^M

blue cap
gorro^M azul

white flag
bandera^F blanca

team bench
banquillo^M del equipo^M

red flag
bandera^F roja

blue flag
bandera^F azul

65 – 100 ft

secretary
secretario^M

referee
árbitro^M principal

assistant timer
ayudante^M del
cronometrador^M

white flag
bandera^F blanca

timekeeper
cronometrador^M

half-distance line
línea^F del medio campo^M

goal judge
juez^M de gol^M

4 m line
línea^F de 4 metros^M

swimming pool
piscina^F

2 m line
línea^F de 2 metros^M

26 – 66 ft

white cap
gorro^M blanco

goal line
línea^F de meta^F

GOAL
PORTERÍA^F

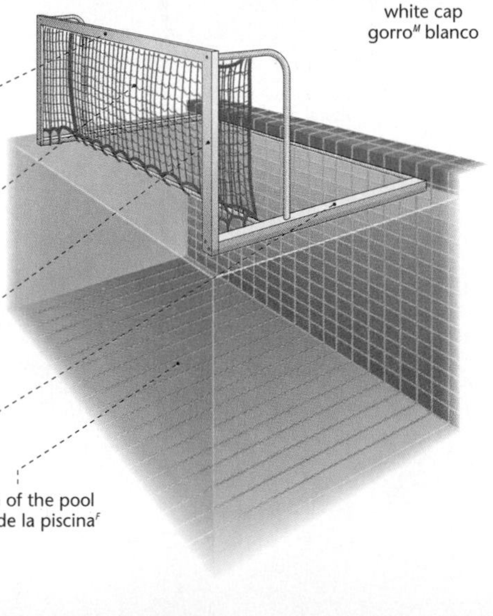

crossbar
larguero^M

WATER POLO BALL
BALÓN^M

net
red^F

post
poste^M

floater
flotador^M de la portería^F

bottom of the pool
fondo^M de la piscina^F

8 9/16 – 8 15/16 in

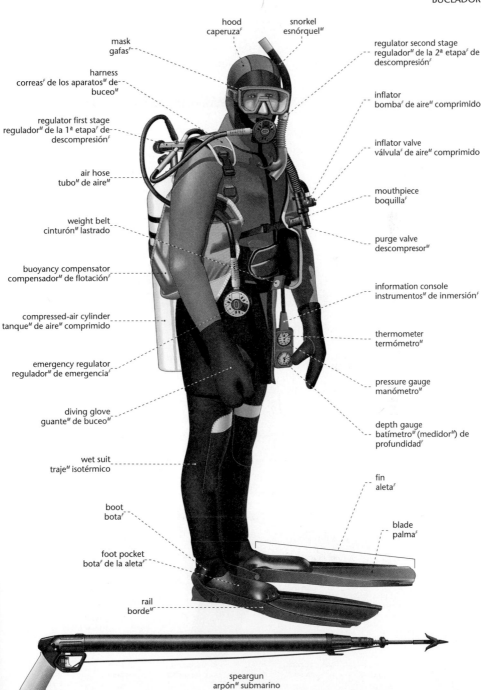

SCUBA DIVER
BUCEADOR^M

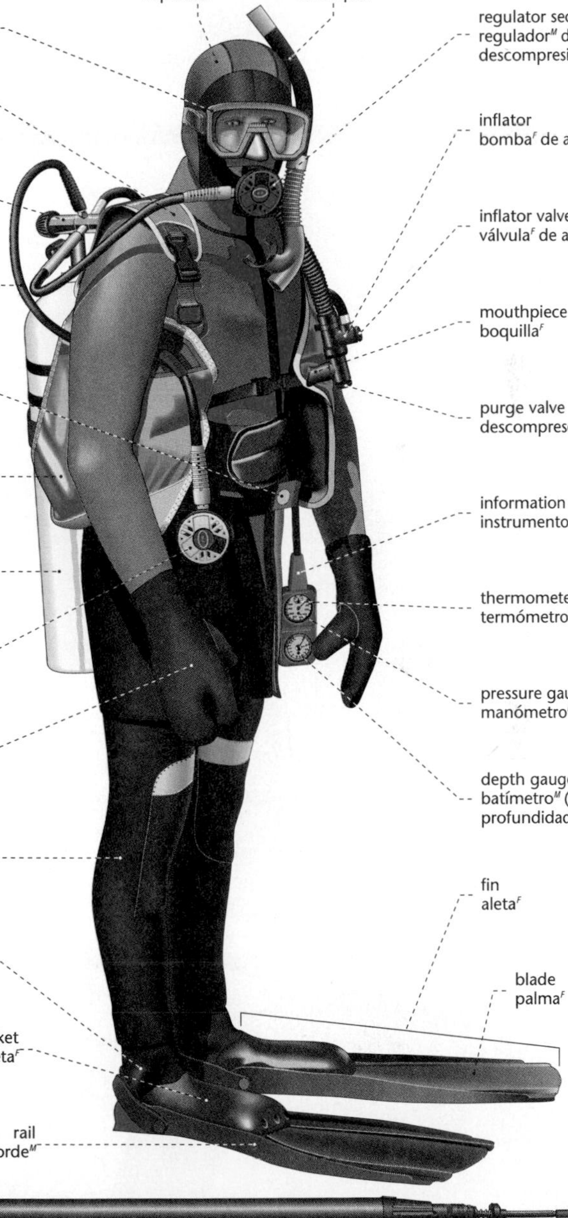

hood
caperuza^F

snorkel
esnórquel^M

mask
gafas^F

harness
correas^F de los aparatos^M de
buceo^M

regulator first stage
regulador^M de la 1ª etapa^F de
descompresión^F

air hose
tubo^M de aire^M

weight belt
cinturón^M lastrado

buoyancy compensator
compensador^M de flotación^F

compressed-air cylinder
tanque^M de aire^M comprimido

emergency regulator
regulador^M de emergencia^F

diving glove
guante^M de buceo^M

wet suit
traje^M isotérmico

boot
bota^F

foot pocket
bota^F de la aleta^F

rail
borde^M

regulator second stage
regulador^M de la 2ª etapa^F de
descompresión^F

inflator
bomba^F de aire^M comprimido

inflator valve
válvula^F de aire^M comprimido

mouthpiece
boquilla^F

purge valve
descompresor^M

information console
instrumentos^M de inmersión^F

thermometer
termómetro^M

pressure gauge
manómetro^M

depth gauge
batímetro^M (medidor^M) de
profundidad^F

fin
aleta^F

blade
palma^F

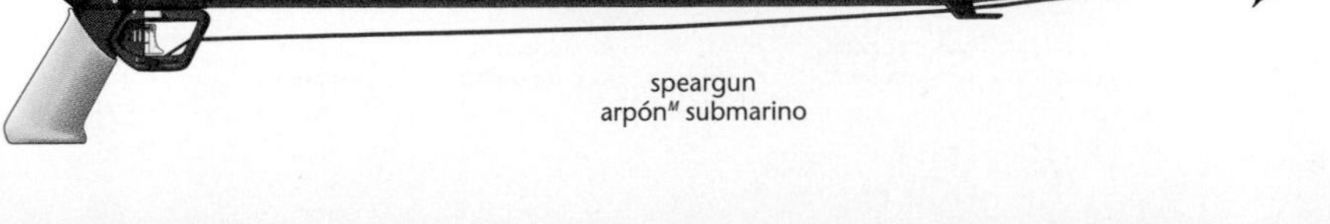

speargun
arpón^M submarino

SAILING
VELA^F

SAILBOAT
VELERO^M

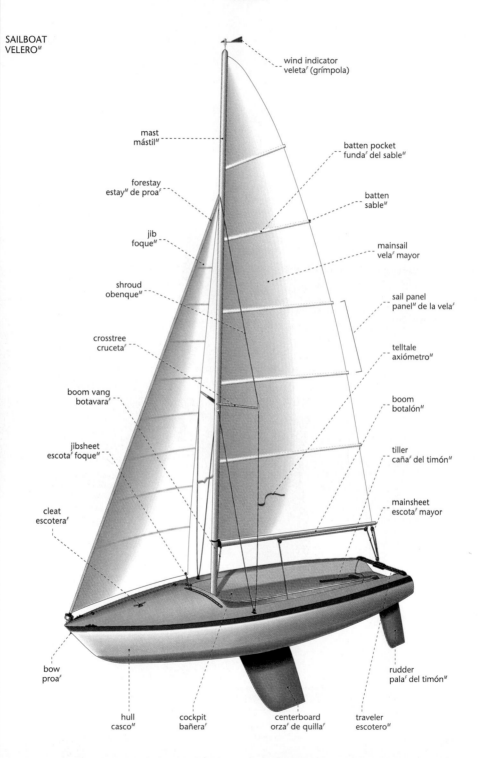

wind indicator
veleta^F (grímpola)

mast
mástil^M

batten pocket
funda^F del sable^M

forestay
estay^M de proa^F

batten
sable^M

jib
foque^M

mainsail
vela^F mayor

shroud
obenque^M

sail panel
panel^M de la vela^F

crosstree
cruceta^F

telltale
axiómetro^M

boom vang
botavara^F

boom
botalón^M

jibsheet
escota^F foque^M

tiller
caña^F del timón^M

cleat
escotera^F

mainsheet
escota^F mayor

bow
proa^F

rudder
pala^F del timón^M

hull
casco^M

cockpit
bañera^F

centerboard
orza^F de quilla^F

traveler
escotero^M

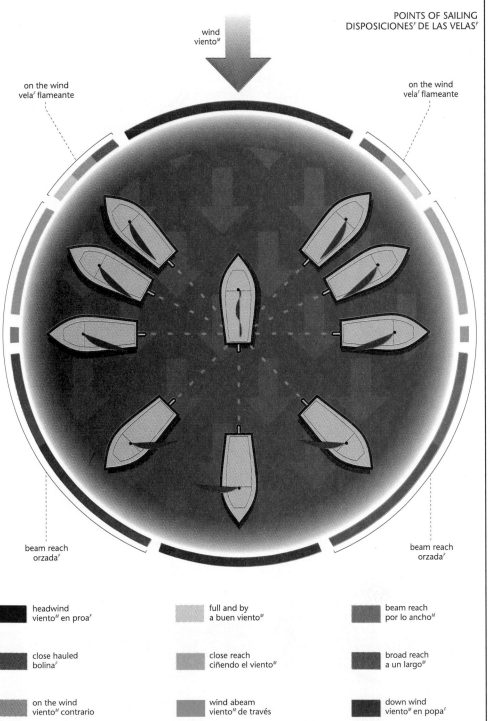

wind
viento^M

on the wind
vela^F flameante

on the wind
vela^F flameante

beam reach
orzada^F

beam reach
orzada^F

**WATER SPORTS
DEPORTES ACUÁTICOS**

headwind
viento^M en proa^F

full and by
a buen viento^M

beam reach
por lo ancho^M

close hauled
bolina^F

close reach
ciñendo el viento^M

broad reach
a un largo^M

on the wind
viento^M contrario

wind abeam
viento^M de través

down wind
viento^M en popa^F

629

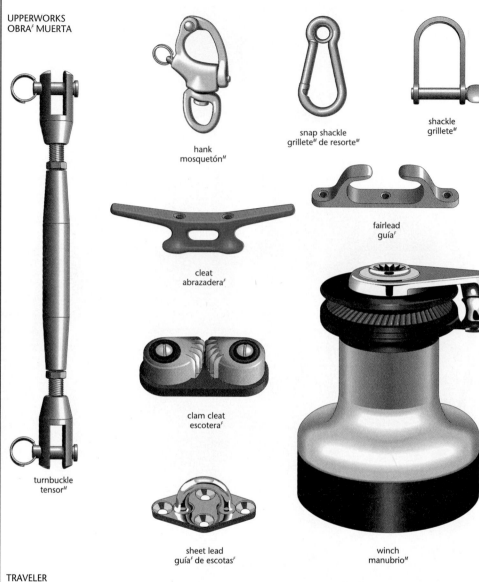

UPPERWORKS
OBRA^F MUERTA

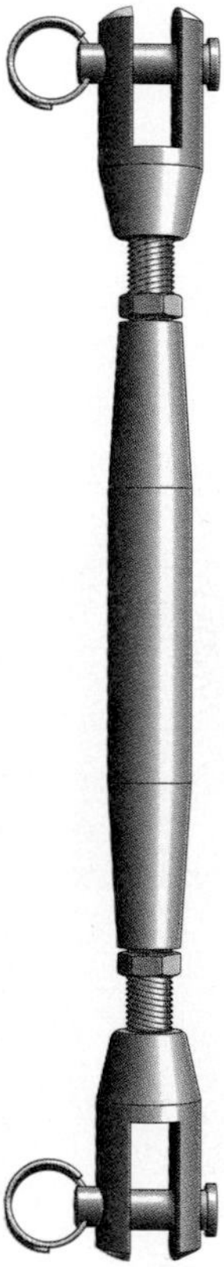

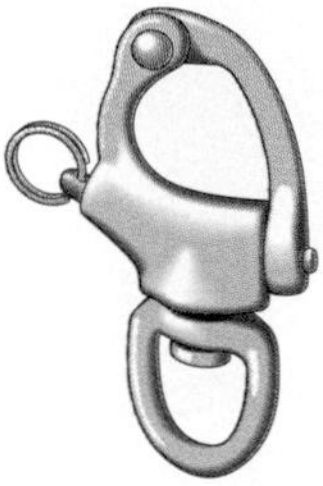

hank
mosquetón^M

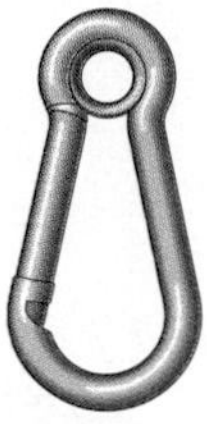

snap shackle
grillete^M de resorte^M

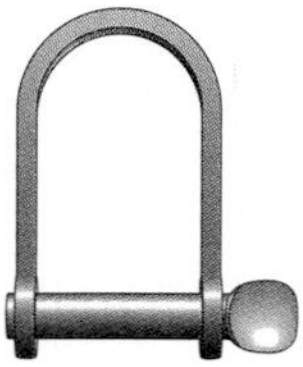

shackle
grillete^M

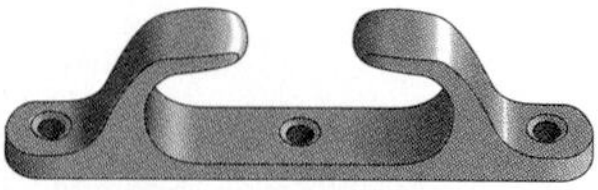

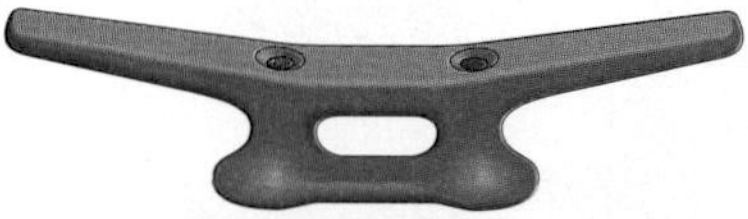

cleat
abrazadera^F

fairlead
guía^F

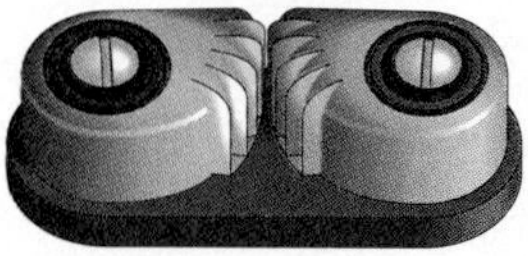

clam cleat
escotera^F

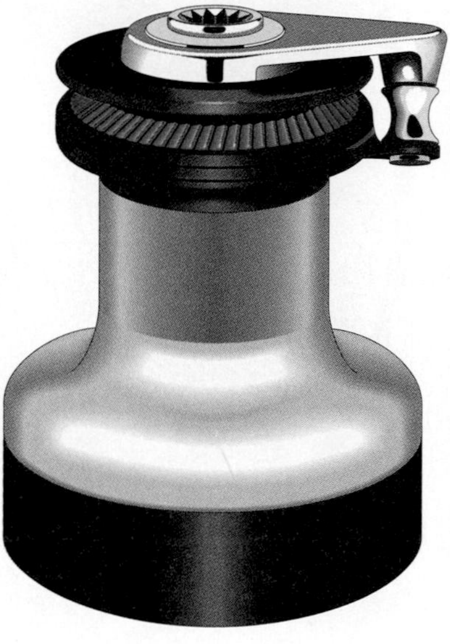

turnbuckle
tensor^M

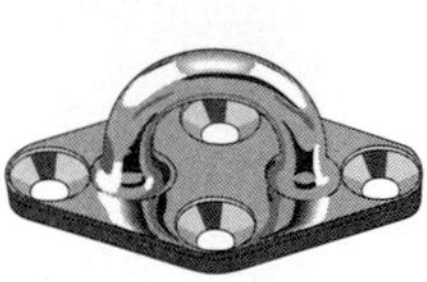

sheet lead
guía^F de escotas^F

winch
manubrio^M

TRAVELER
BARRA^F DE ESCOTAS^F

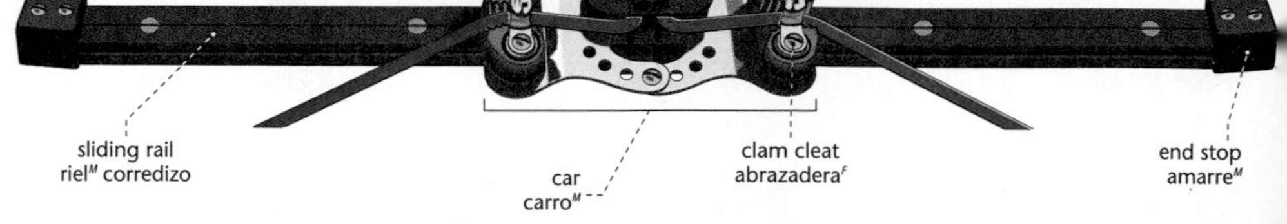

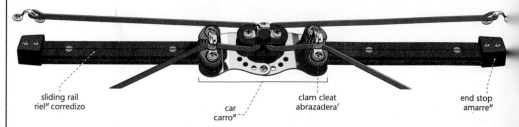

sliding rail
riel^M corredizo

car
carro^M

clam cleat
abrazadera^F

end stop
amarre^M

SAILBOARD
PLANCHA^F DE WINDSURF^M

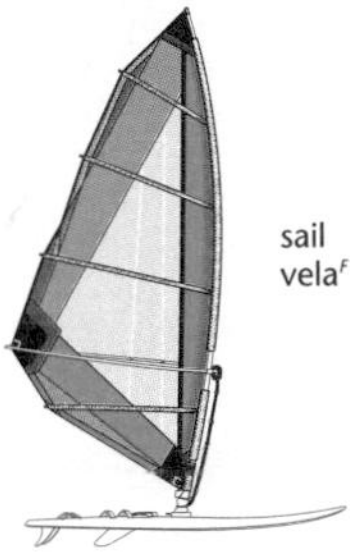

sail
vela^F

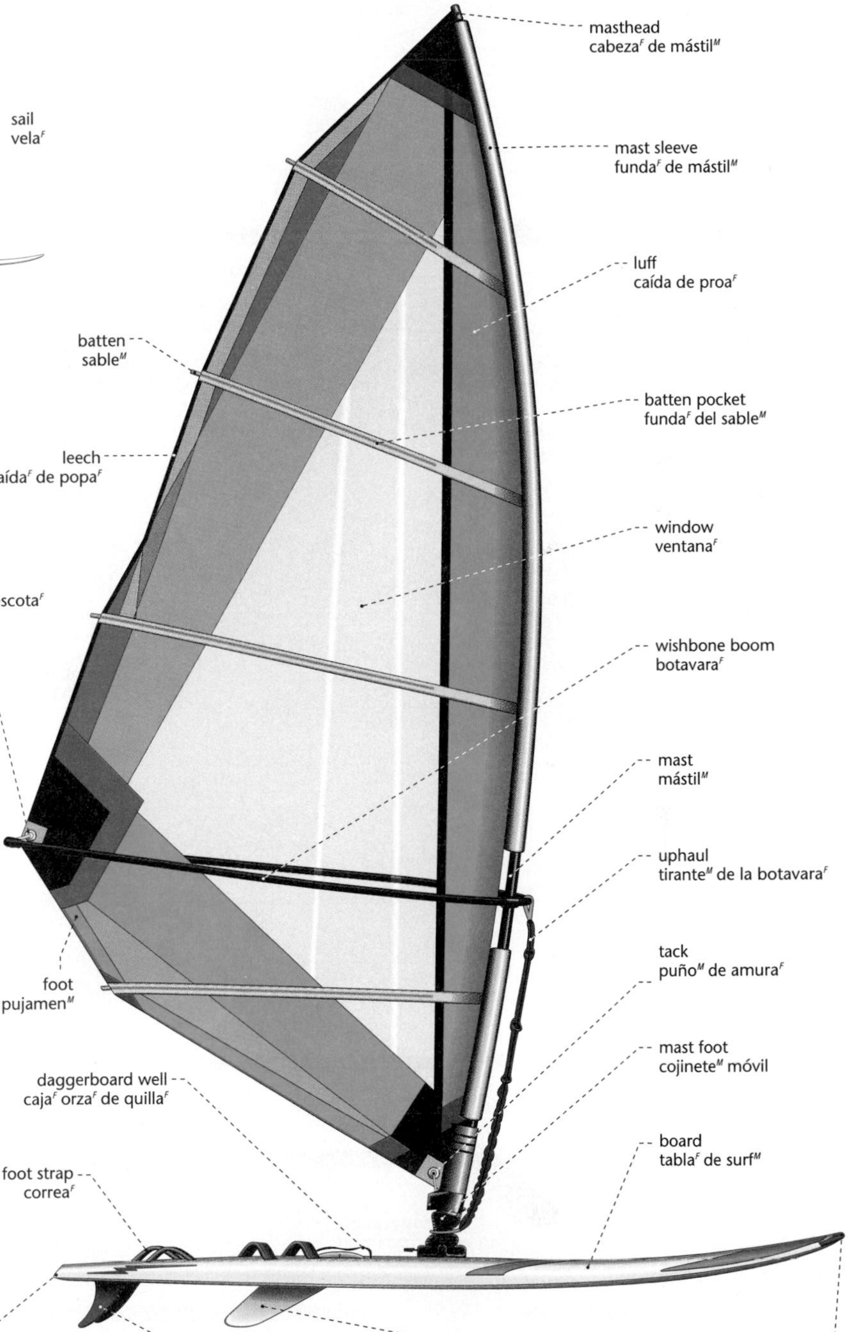

masthead
cabeza^F de mástil^M

mast sleeve
funda^F de mástil^M

luff
caída de proa^F

batten
sable^M

batten pocket
funda^F del sable^M

leech
caída^F de popa^F

window
ventana^F

clew
puño^M de escota^F

wishbone boom
botavara^F

mast
mástil^M

uphaul
tirante^M de la botavara^F

tack
puño^M de amura^F

foot
pujamen^M

mast foot
cojinete^M móvil

daggerboard well
caja^F orza^F de quilla^F

board
tabla^F de surf^M

foot strap
correa^F

stern
popa^F

skeg
orza^F de popa^F

daggerboard
orza^F de quilla^F

bow
proa^F

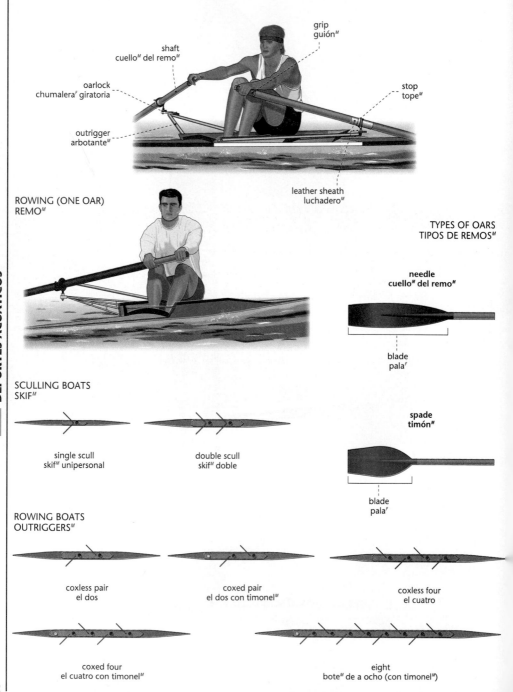

SCULLING (TWO OARS)
SKIF^M

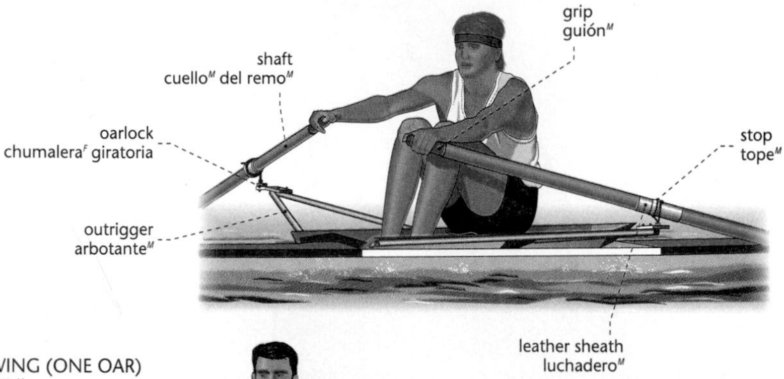

grip
guión^M

shaft
cuello^M del remo^M

oarlock
chumalera^F giratoria

stop
tope^M

outrigger
arbotante^M

leather sheath
luchadero^M

ROWING (ONE OAR)
REMO^M

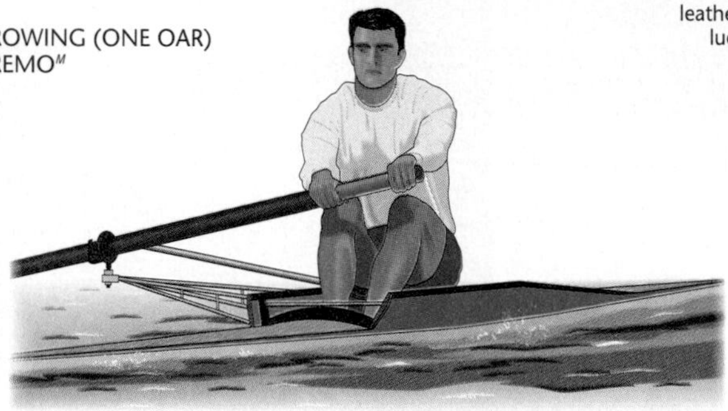

TYPES OF OARS
TIPOS DE REMOS^M

needle
cuello^M del remo^M

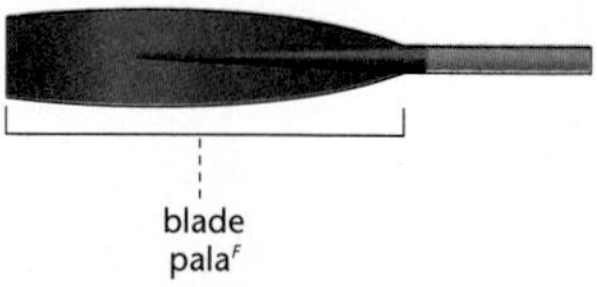

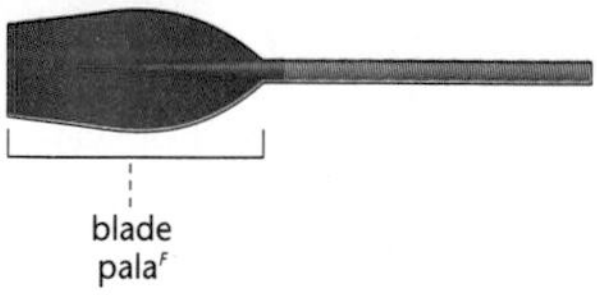

blade
pala^F

SCULLING BOATS
SKIF^M

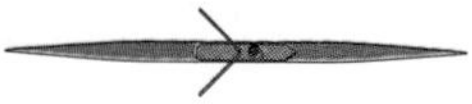

single scull
skif^M unipersonal

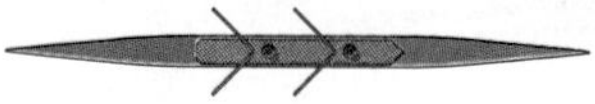

double scull
skif^M doble

spade
timón^M

blade
pala^F

ROWING BOATS
OUTRIGGERS^M

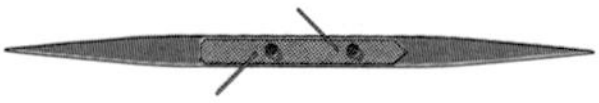

coxless pair
el dos

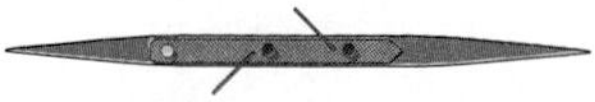

coxed pair
el dos con timonel^M

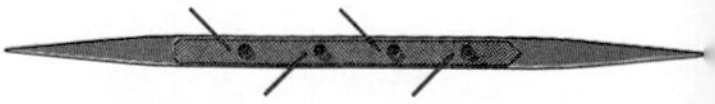

coxless four
el cuatro

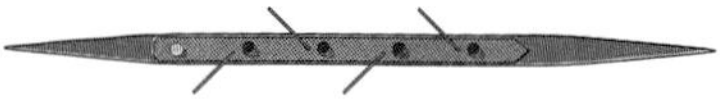

coxed four
el cuatro con timonel^M

eight
bote^M de a ocho (con timonel^M)

**WATER SPORTS
DEPORTES ACUÁTICOS**

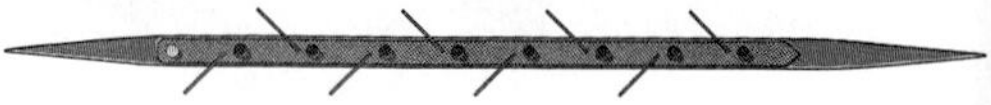

WATER SKIING
ESQUÍ^M ACUÁTICO

twin skis
esquí^M normal

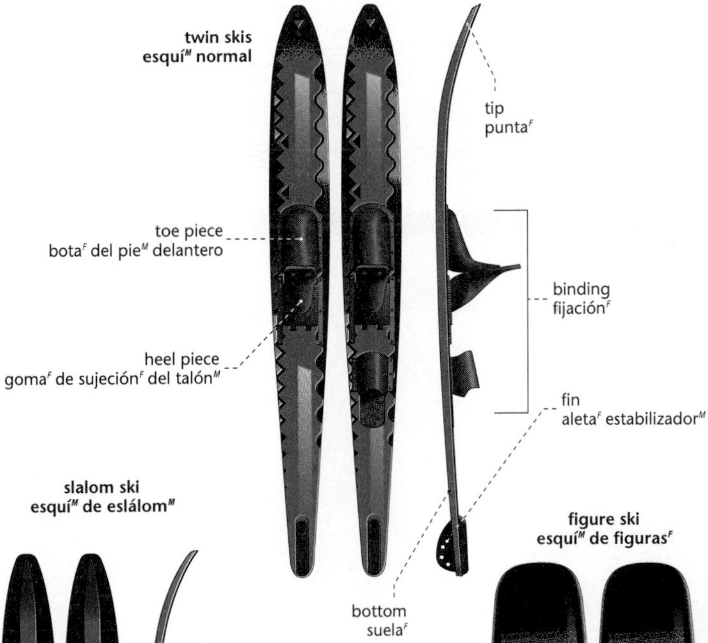

tip
punta^F

jump ski
esquí^M de salto^M

toe piece
bota^F del pie^M delantero

binding
fijación^F

heel piece
goma^F de sujeción^F del talón^M

fin
aleta^F estabilizador^M

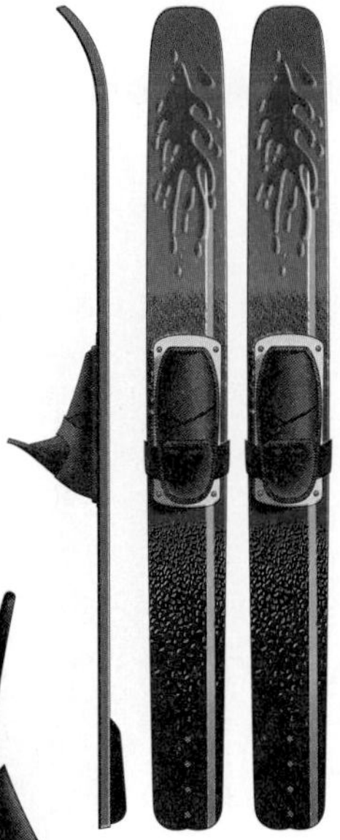

slalom ski
esquí^M de eslálom^M

figure ski
esquí^M de figuras^F

bottom
suela^F

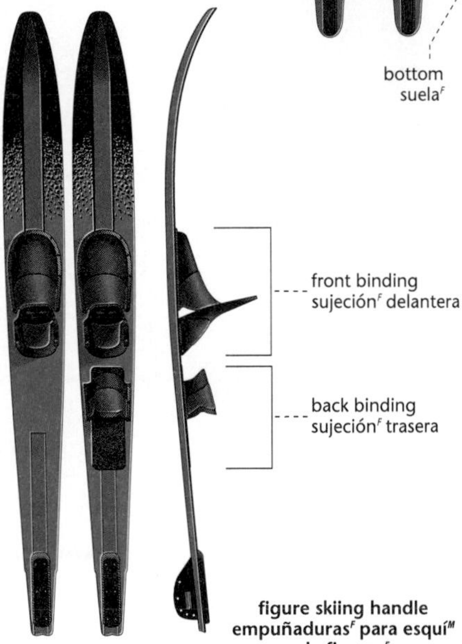

front binding
sujeción^F delantera

back binding
sujeción^F trasera

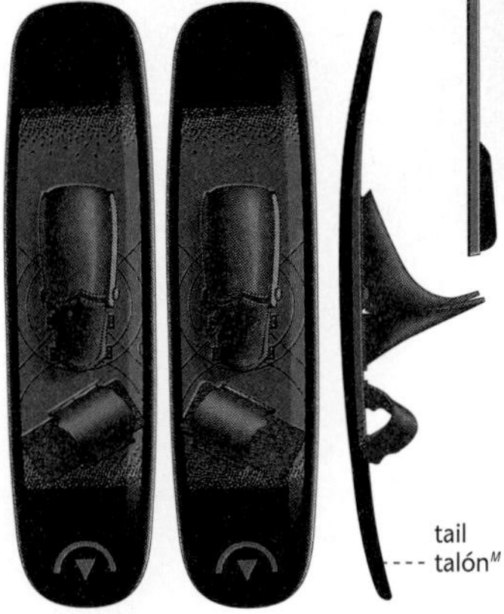

tail
talón^M

TYPES OF HANDLES
EMPUÑADURAS^F PARA ESQUÍ^M

figure skiing handle
empuñaduras^F para esquí^M
de figuras^F

double handles
cuerdas^F para eslálom^M

handle
empuñadura^F

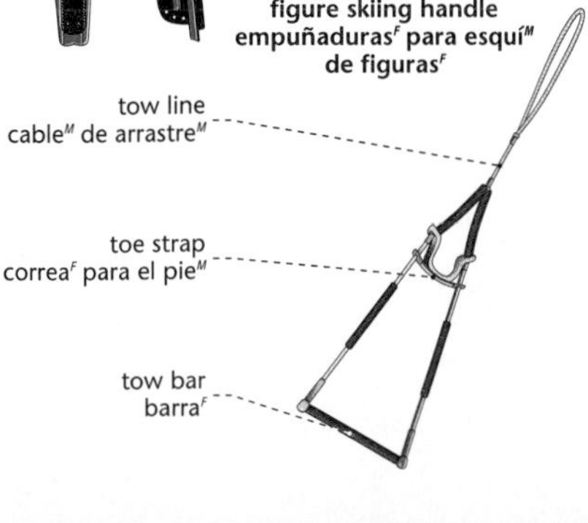

tow line
cable^M de arrastre^M

toe strap
correa^F para el pie^M

tow bar
barra^F

WATER SPORTS
DEPORTES ACUÁTICOS

633

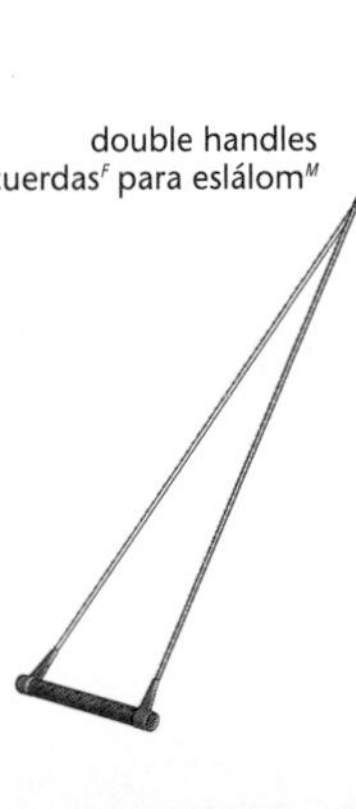

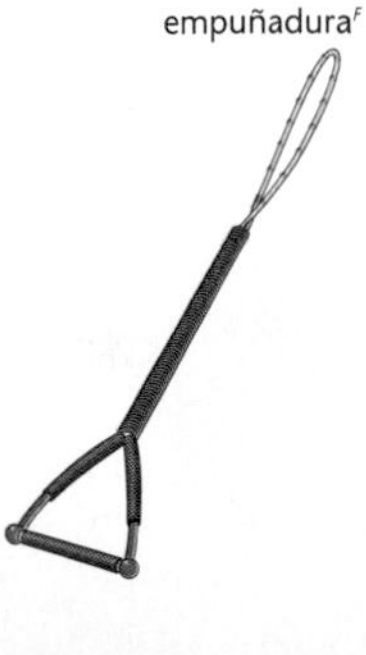

BALLOON
GLOBO*ᴹ* AEROSTÁTICO

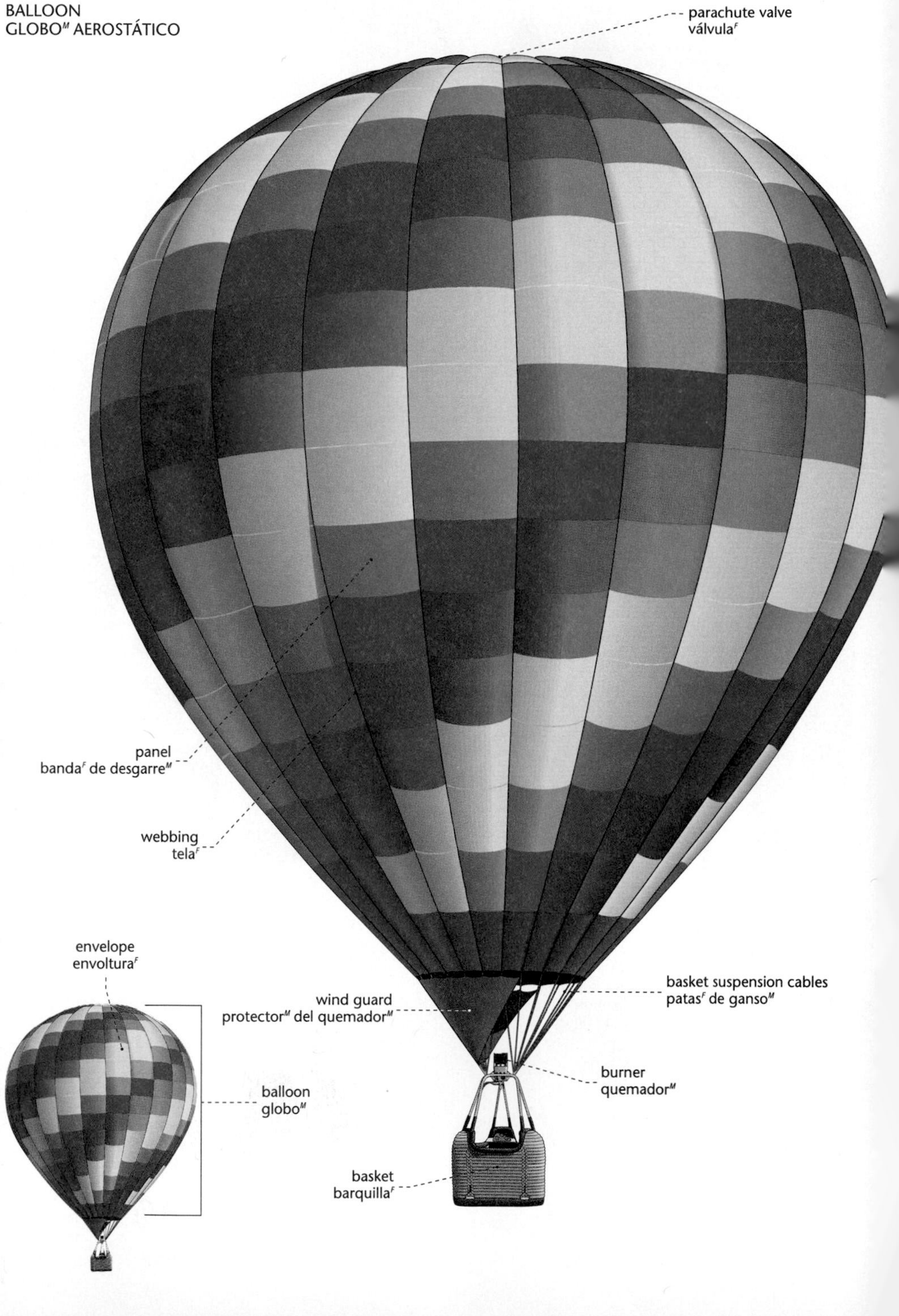

parachute valve
válvula*ꟳ*

panel
banda*ꟳ* de desgarre*ᴹ*

webbing
tela*ꟳ*

envelope
envoltura*ꟳ*

wind guard
protector*ᴹ* del quemador*ᴹ*

balloon
globo*ᴹ*

basket
barquilla*ꟳ*

basket suspension cables
patas*ꟳ* de ganso*ᴹ*

burner
quemador*ᴹ*

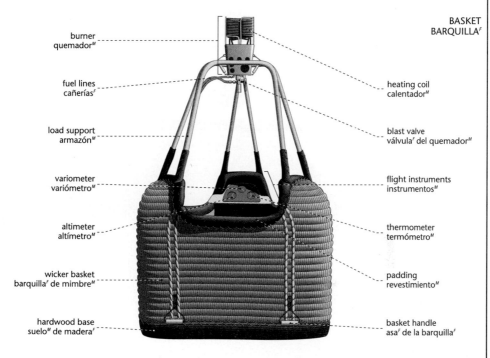

BASKET
BARQUILLA^F

burner
quemador^M

fuel lines
cañerías^F

load support
armazón^M

variometer
variómetro^M

altimeter
altímetro^M

wicker basket
barquilla^F de mimbre^M

hardwood base
suelo^M de madera^F

heating coil
calentador^M

blast valve
válvula^F del quemador^M

flight instruments
instrumentos^M

thermometer
termómetro^M

padding
revestimiento^M

basket handle
asa^F de la barquilla^F

**SKY DIVING
PARACAIDISMO^M**

SKY DIVER
PARACAIDISTA^{M/F}

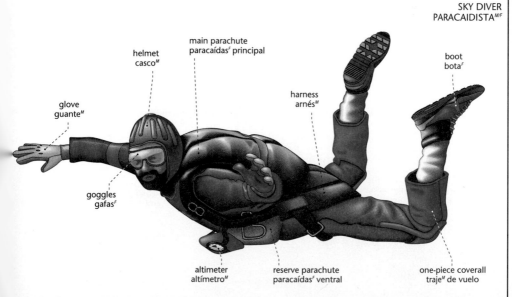

helmet
casco^M

main parachute
paracaídas^F principal

boot
bota^F

glove
guante^M

harness
arnés^M

goggles
gafas^F

altimeter
altímetro^M

reserve parachute
paracaídas^F ventral

one-piece coverall
traje^M de vuelo

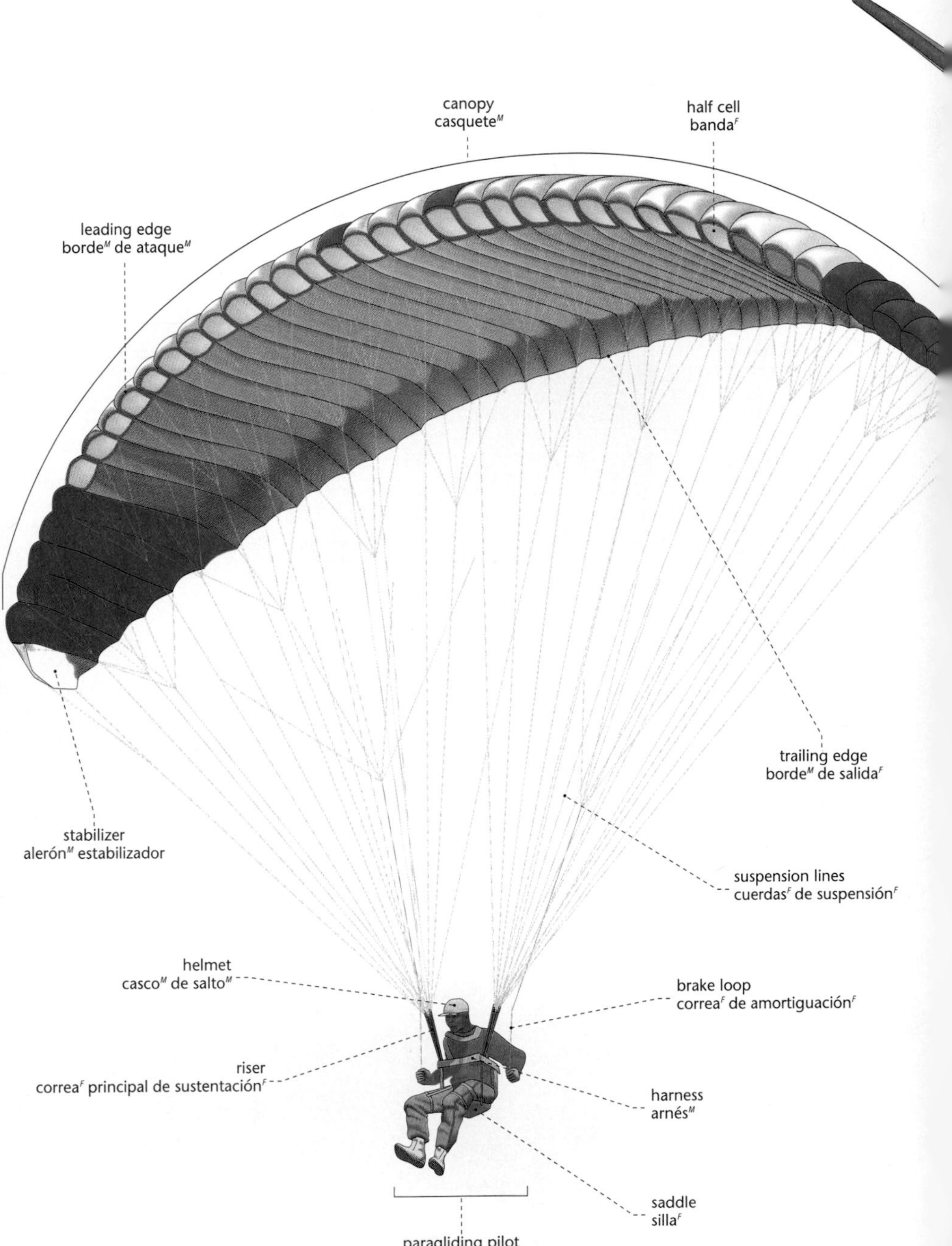

CANOPY
CASQUETE^M

canopy
casquete^M

half cell
banda^F

leading edge
borde^M de ataque^M

trailing edge
borde^M de salida^F

suspension lines
cuerdas^F de suspensión^F

stabilizer
alerón^M estabilizador

helmet
casco^M de salto^M

brake loop
correa^F de amortiguación^F

riser
correa^F principal de sustentación^F

harness
arnés^M

saddle
silla^F

paragliding pilot
piloto^M de planeador^M

HANG GLIDER
AERODESLIZADOR^M

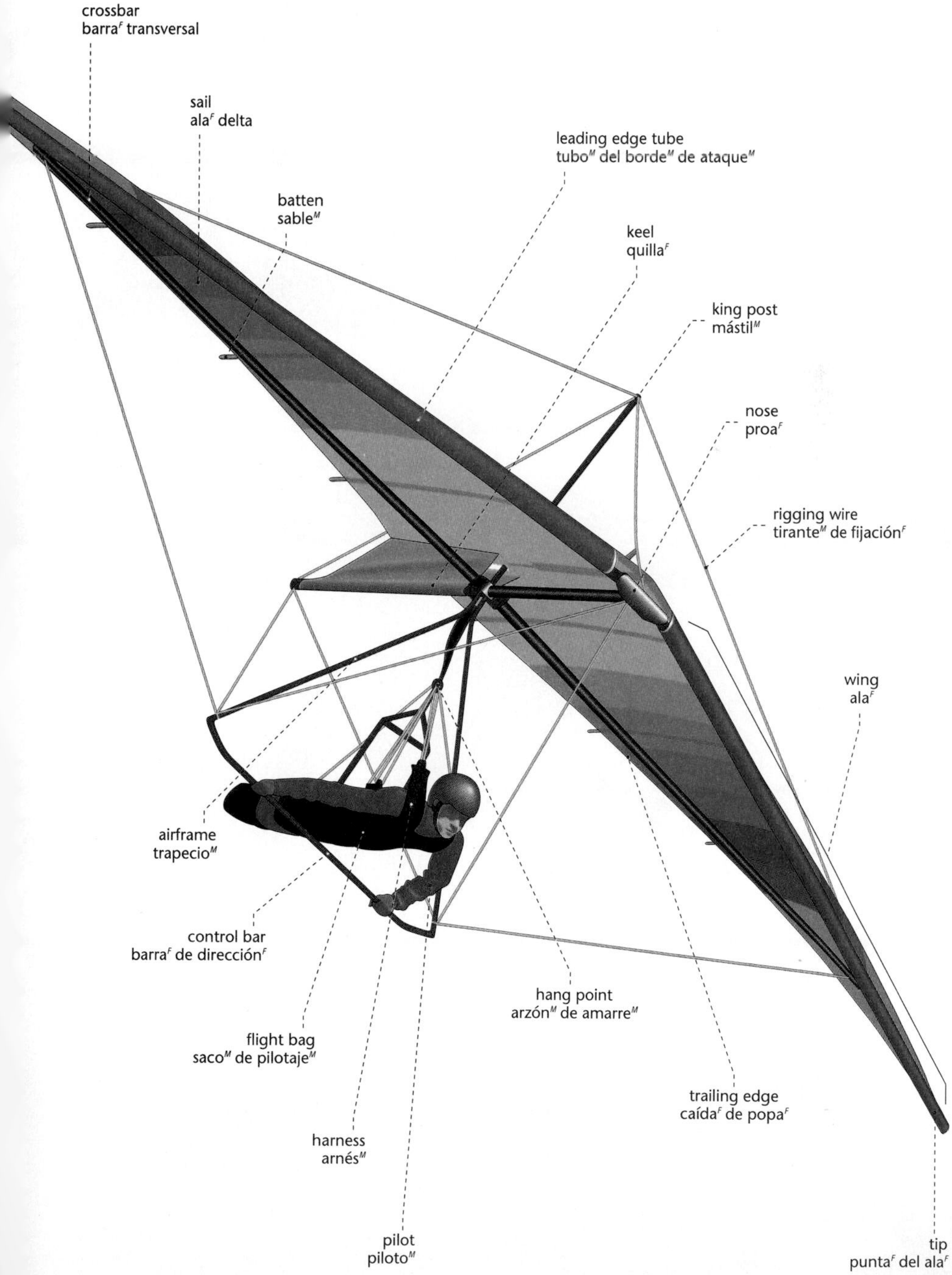

crossbar
barra^F transversal

sail
ala^F delta

batten
sable^M

leading edge tube
tubo^M del borde^M de ataque^M

keel
quilla^F

king post
mástil^M

nose
proa^F

rigging wire
tirante^M de fijación^F

wing
ala^F

airframe
trapecio^M

control bar
barra^F de dirección^F

hang point
arzón^M de amarre^M

flight bag
saco^M de pilotaje^M

trailing edge
caída^F de popa^F

harness
arnés^M

pilot
piloto^M

tip
punta^F del ala^F

AERIAL SPORTS
DEPORTES AÉREOS

GLIDING
VUELO^M SIN MOTOR^M

GLIDER
PLANEADOR^M

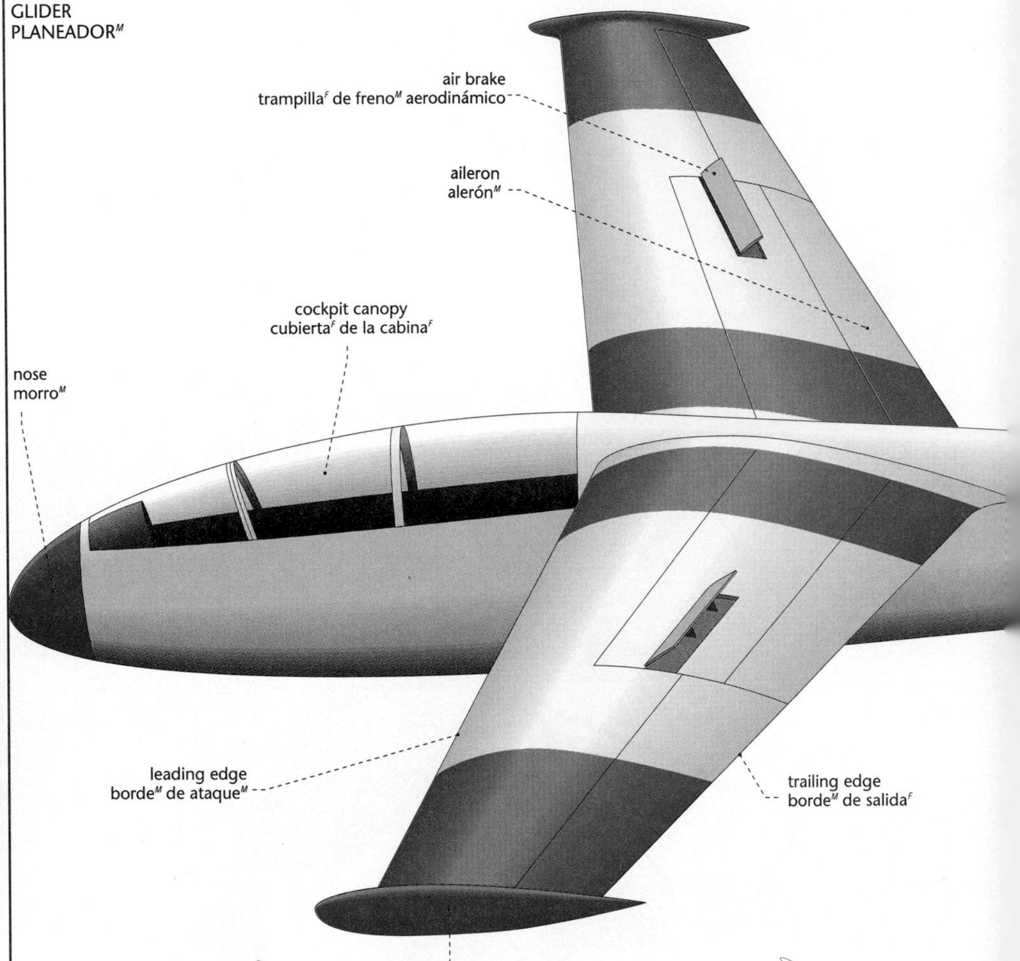

air brake
trampilla^F de freno^M aerodinámico

aileron
alerón^M

cockpit canopy
cubierta^F de la cabina^F

nose
morro^M

leading edge
borde^M de ataque^M

trailing edge
borde^M de salida^F

wing tip
borde^M marginal

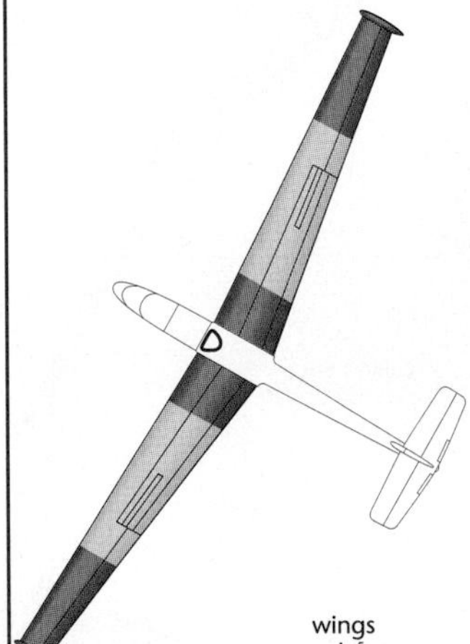

wings
ala^F

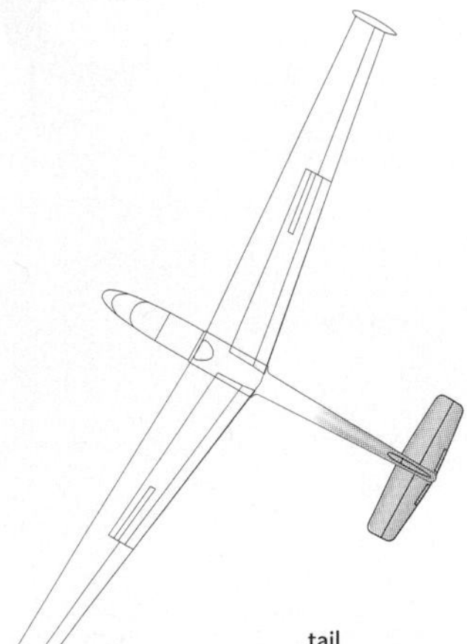

tail
grupo^M de cola^F

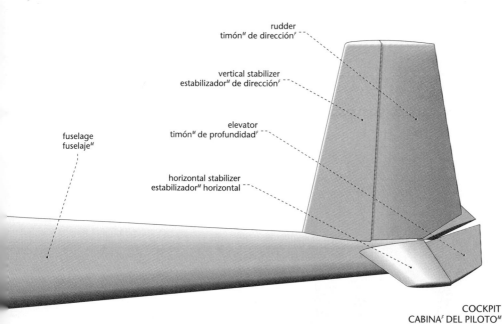

rudder
timón^M de dirección^F

vertical stabilizer
estabilizador^M de dirección^F

elevator
timón^M de profundidad^F

fuselage
fuselaje^M

horizontal stabilizer
estabilizador^M horizontal

COCKPIT
CABINA^F DEL PILOTO^M

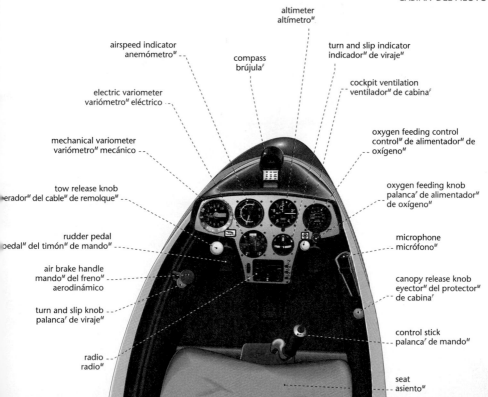

altimeter
altímetro^M

airspeed indicator
anemómetro^M

compass
brújula^F

turn and slip indicator
indicador^M de viraje^M

electric variometer
variómetro^M eléctrico

cockpit ventilation
ventilador^M de cabina^F

mechanical variometer
variómetro^M mecánico

oxygen feeding control
control^M de alimentador^M de oxígeno^M

tow release knob
...erador^M del cable^M de remolque^M

oxygen feeding knob
palanca^F de alimentador^M de oxígeno^M

rudder pedal
...pedal^M del timón^M de mando^M

microphone
micrófono^M

air brake handle
mando^M del freno^M aerodinámico

canopy release knob
eyector^M del protector^M de cabina^F

turn and slip knob
palanca^F de viraje^M

control stick
palanca^F de mando^M

radio
radio^M

seat
asiento^M

639

ALPINE SKIING
ESQUÍ^M ALPINO

ALPINE SKIER
ESQUIADOR^M ALPINO

ski hat
gorro^M de esquí^M

ski goggles
gafas^F de esquí^M

ski suit
traje^M para esquiar

ski glove
guante^M de esquí^M

handle
puño^M

wrist strap
correa^F para la mano^F

ski pole
bastón^M de esquí^M

bottom
superficie^F de deslizamiento^M

ski stop
freno^M del esquí^M

shovel
pala^F

edge
canto^M

heel piece
pieza^F automática del talón^M

ski boot
bota^F

tip
punta^F

toe piece
pieza^F de sujeción^F de la punta^F del pie^M

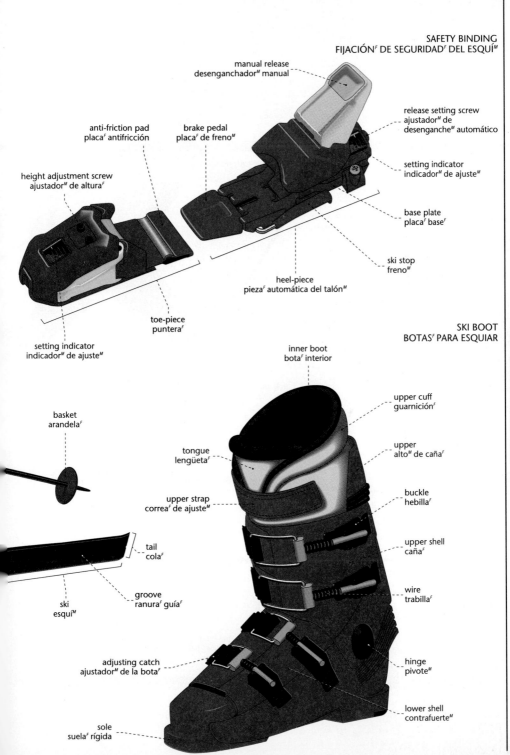

SAFETY BINDING
FIJACIÓN^F DE SEGURIDAD^F DEL ESQUÍ^M

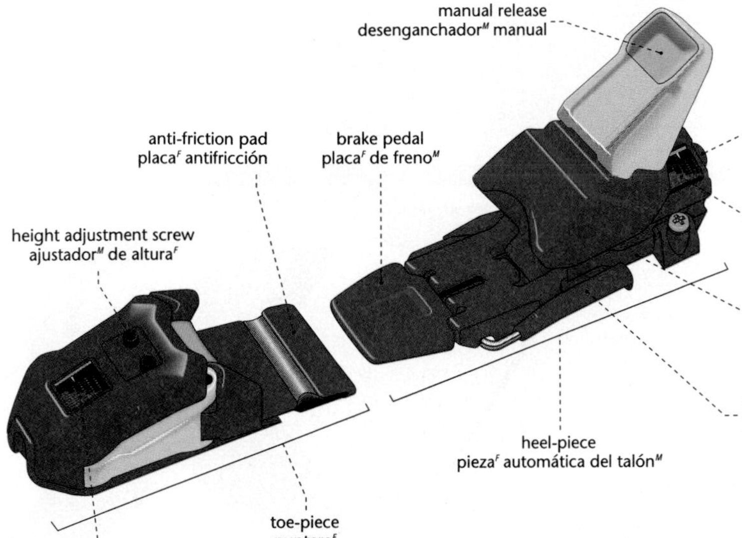

manual release
desenganchador^M manual

release setting screw
ajustador^M de
desenganche^M automático

anti-friction pad
placa^F antifricción

brake pedal
placa^F de freno^M

setting indicator
indicador^M de ajuste^M

height adjustment screw
ajustador^M de altura^F

base plate
placa^F base^F

ski stop
freno^M

heel-piece
pieza^F automática del talón^M

toe-piece
puntera^F

setting indicator
indicador^M de ajuste^M

SKI BOOT
BOTAS^F PARA ESQUIAR

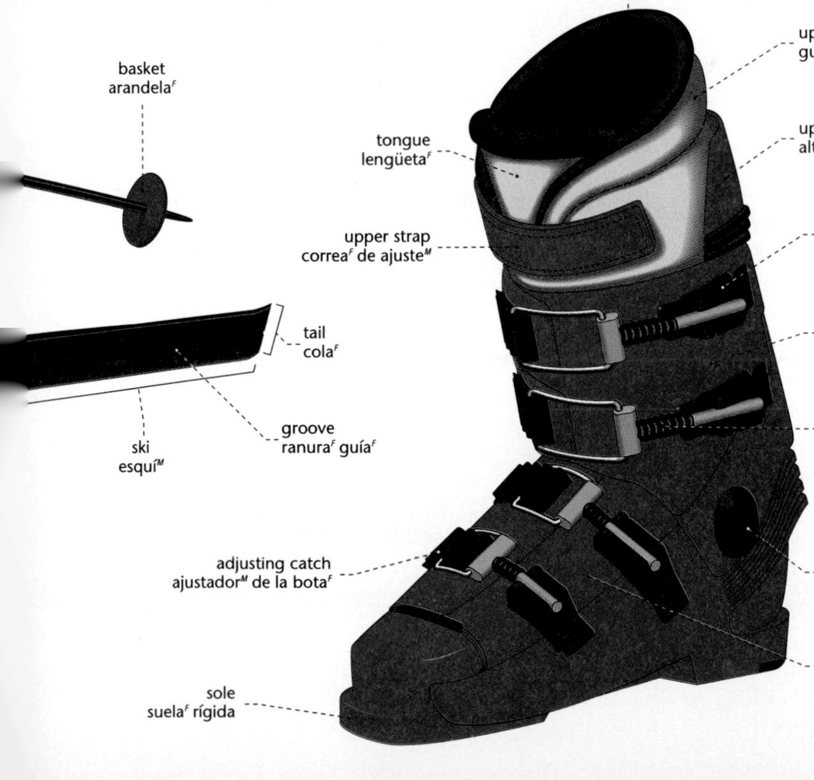

inner boot
bota^F interior

basket
arandela^F

upper cuff
guarnición^F

tongue
lengüeta^F

upper
alto^M de caña^F

upper strap
correa^F de ajuste^M

buckle
hebilla^F

tail
cola^F

upper shell
caña^F

groove
ranura^F guía^F

wire
trabilla^F

ski
esquí^M

adjusting catch
ajustador^M de la bota^F

hinge
pivote^M

lower shell
contrafuerte^M

sole
suela^F rígida

641

CROSS-COUNTRY SKIING
ESQUÍ^M DE FONDO^M

CROSS-COUNTRY SKIER
ESQUIADORA^F DE CAMPO^M TRAVIESA

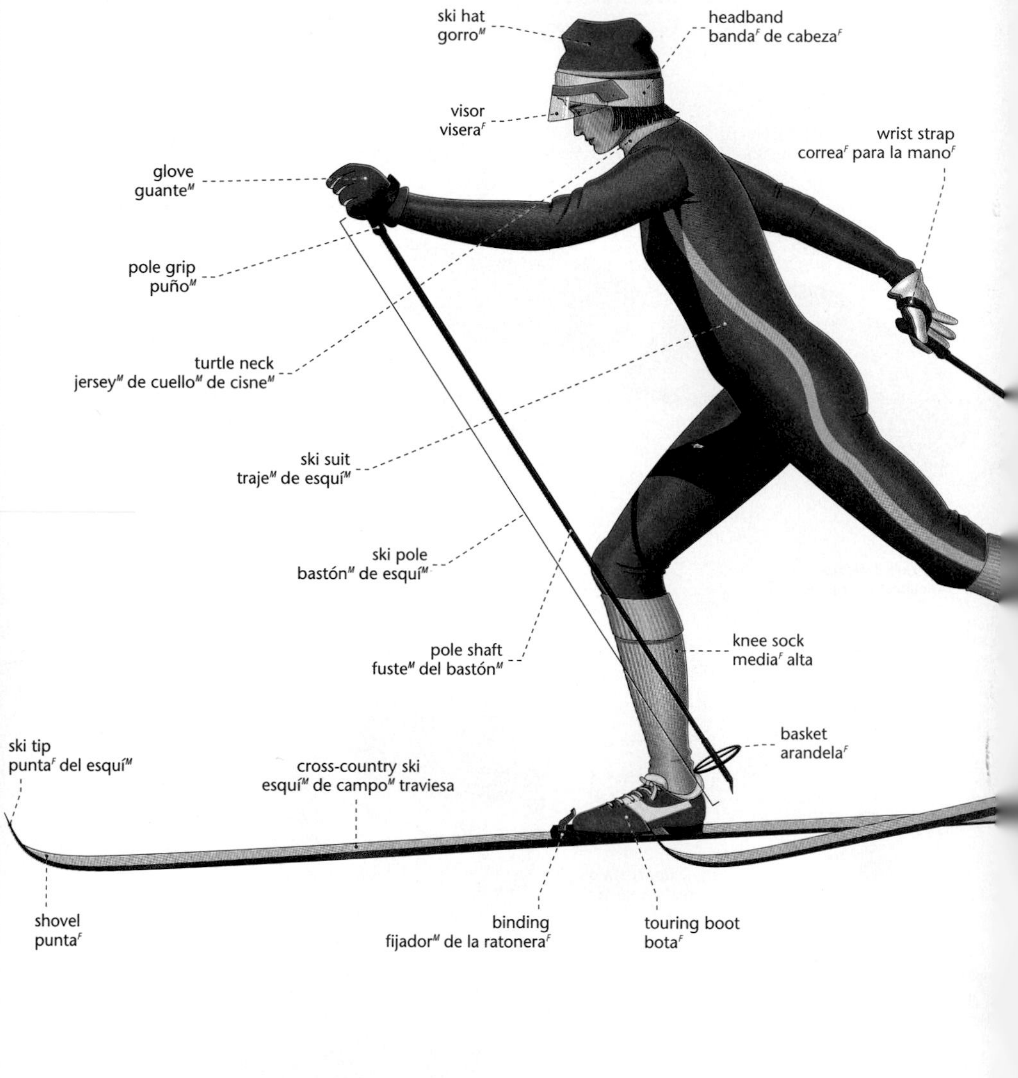

ski hat
gorro^M

headband
banda^F de cabeza^F

visor
visera^F

wrist strap
correa^F para la mano^F

glove
guante^M

pole grip
puño^M

turtle neck
jersey^M de cuello^M de cisne^M

ski suit
traje^M de esquí^M

ski pole
bastón^M de esquí^M

knee sock
media^F alta

pole shaft
fuste^M del bastón^M

basket
arandela^F

ski tip
punta^F del esquí^M

cross-country ski
esquí^M de campo^M traviesa

shovel
punta^F

binding
fijador^M de la ratonera^F

touring boot
bota^F

CROSS-COUNTRY SKI
ESQUÍ^M DE CAMPO^M TRAVIESA

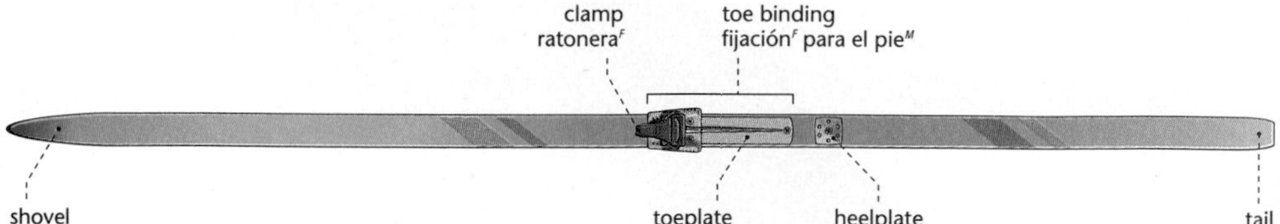

clamp
ratonera^F

toe binding
fijación^F para el pie^M

shovel
punta^F

toeplate
apoyo^M pie^M

heelplate
pieza^F de talón^M

tail
cola^F

LUGE
LUGE^M

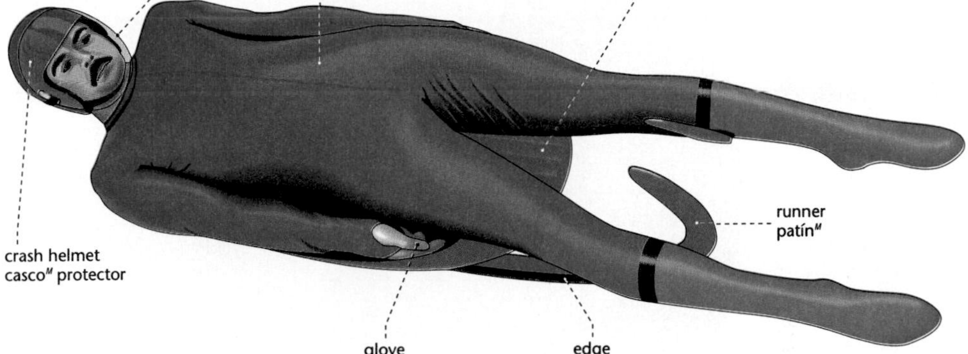

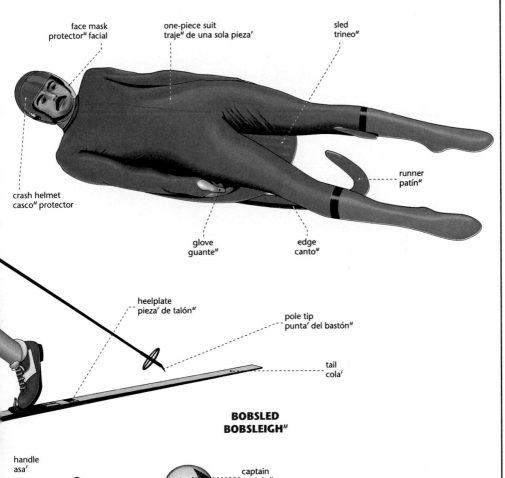

face mask
protector^M facial

one-piece suit
traje^M de una sola pieza^F

sled
trineo^M

crash helmet
casco^M protector

glove
guante^M

edge
canto^M

runner
patín^M

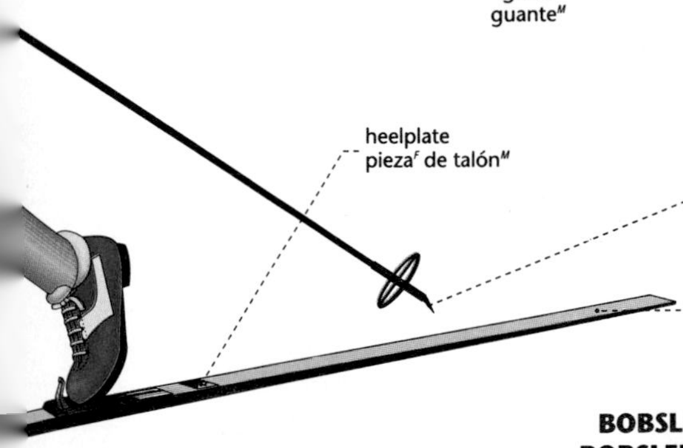

heelplate
pieza^F de talón^M

pole tip
punta^F del bastón^M

tail
cola^F

BOBSLED
BOBSLEIGH^M

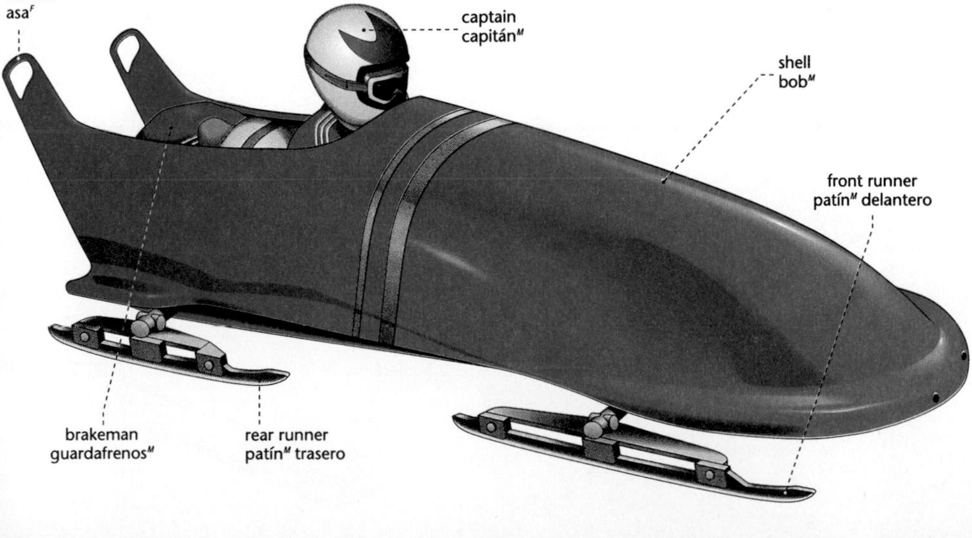

handle
asa^F

captain
capitán^M

shell
bob^M

front runner
patín^M delantero

brakeman
guardafrenos^M

rear runner
patín^M trasero

643

FIGURE SKATE
PATÍN^M PARA FIGURAS^F

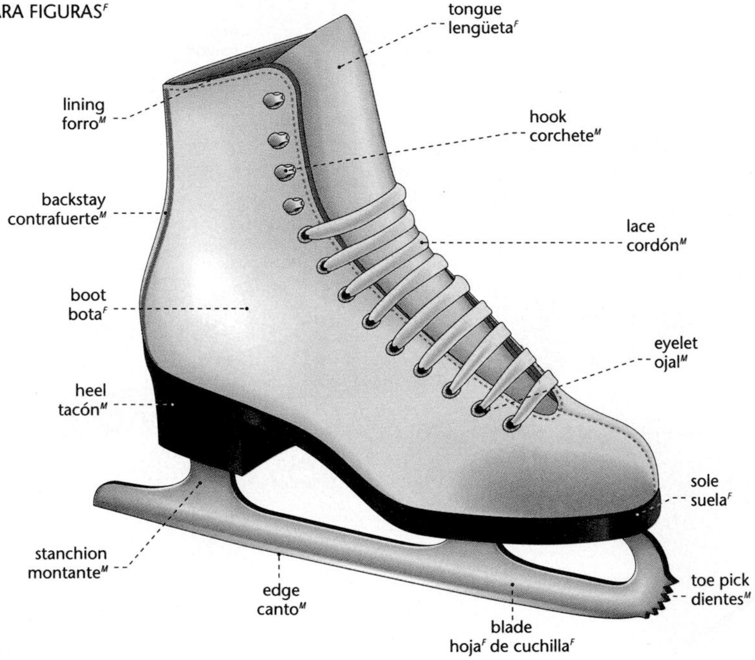

tongue
lengüeta^F

lining
forro^M

hook
corchete^M

backstay
contrafuerte^M

lace
cordón^M

boot
bota^F

eyelet
ojal^M

heel
tacón^M

sole
suela^F

stanchion
montante^M

toe pick
dientes^M

edge
canto^M

blade
hoja^F de cuchilla^F

HOCKEY SKATE
PATÍN^M DE HOCKEY^M

speed skate
patín^M de velocidad^F

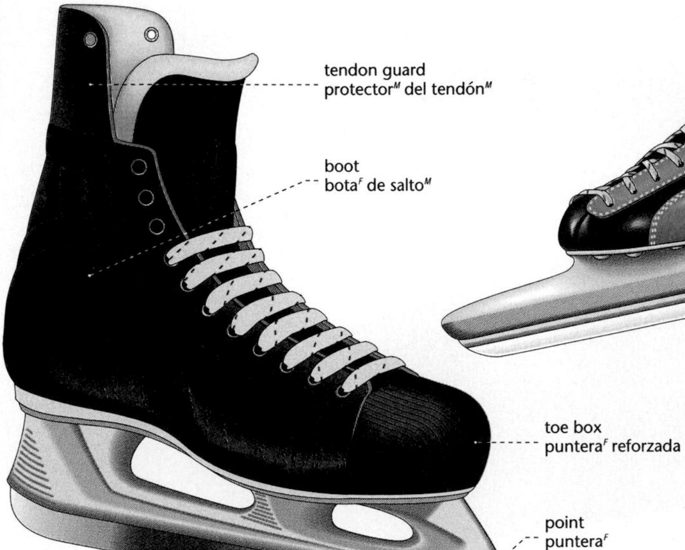

tendon guard
protector^M del tendón^M

boot
bota^F de salto^M

toe box
puntera^F reforzada

skate guard
funda^F protectora de la cuchilla^F

point
puntera^F

blade
hoja^F de cuchilla^F

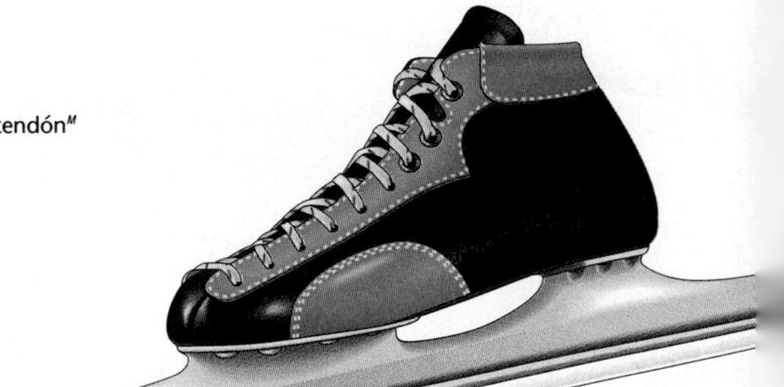

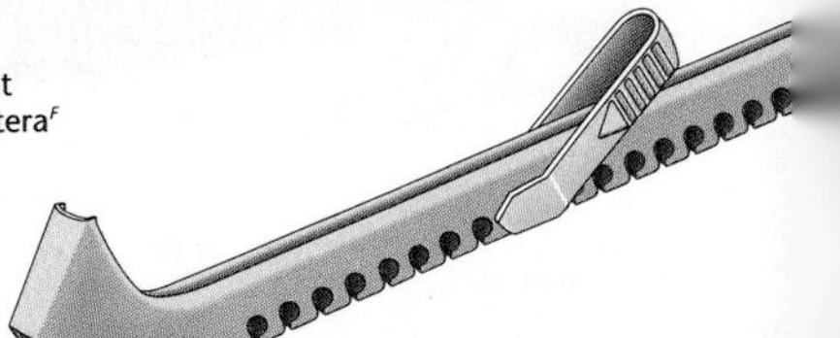

SNOWSHOE
RAQUETA^F

MICHIGAN SNOWSHOE
TIPO^M MICHIGAN

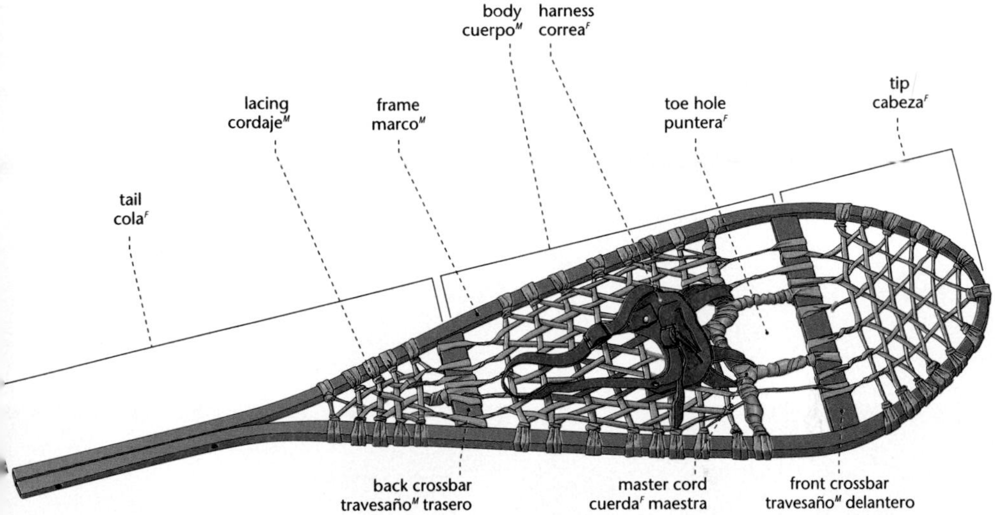

body
cuerpo^M

harness
correa^F

lacing
cordaje^M

frame
marco^M

toe hole
puntera^F

tip
cabeza^F

tail
cola^F

back crossbar
travesaño^M trasero

master cord
cuerda^F maestra

front crossbar
travesaño^M delantero

ROLLER SKATE
PATÍN^M DE RUEDAS^F

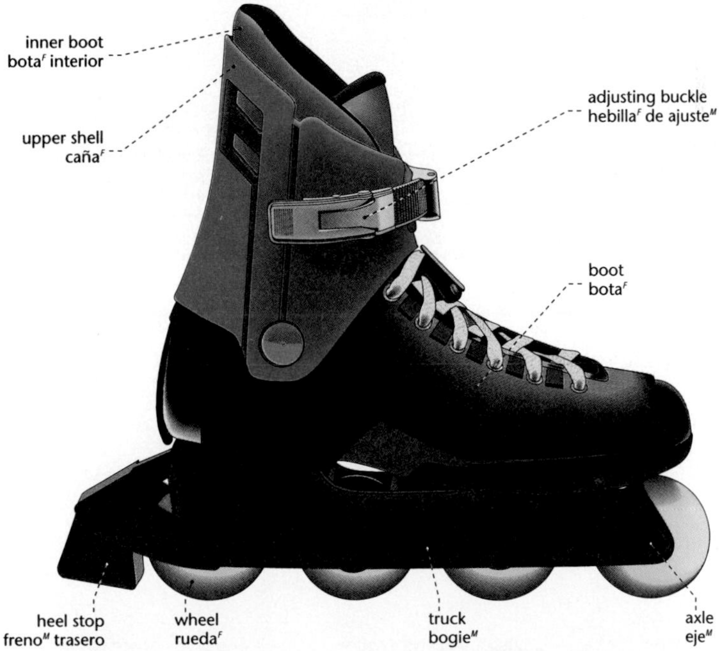

inner boot
bota^F interior

adjusting buckle
hebilla^F de ajuste^M

upper shell
caña^F

boot
bota^F

heel stop
freno^M trasero

wheel
rueda^F

truck
bogie^M

axle
eje^M

645

RIDING
EQUITACIÓN^F: CONCURSO^M DE SALTOS^M

COMPETITION RING
PISTA^F PARA PRUEBA^F DE OBSTÁCULOS^M

straight: post and rail
vertical de barras^F

oxer
óxer^M de barras^F

wall and rails
muro^M con barras^F

wall
muro^M

post and plank
poste^M con tablas^F

brush and rails
seto^M y barra^F

finish
llegada^F

gate
empalizada^F

water jump
ría^F

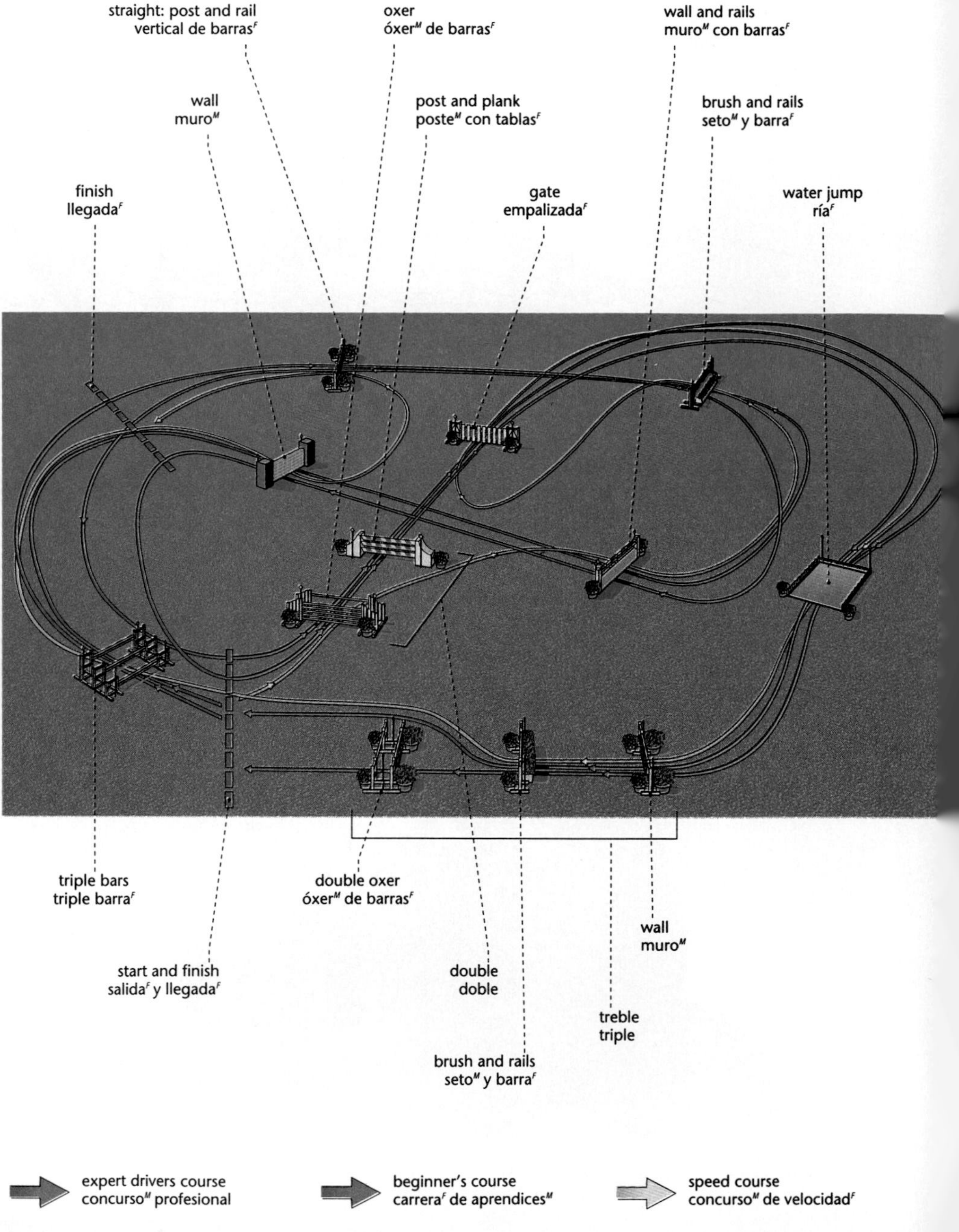

**EQUESTRIAN SPORTS
DEPORTES ECUESTRES**

triple bars
triple barra^F

double oxer
óxer^M de barras^F

wall
muro^M

start and finish
salida^F y llegada^F

double
doble

treble
triple

brush and rails
seto^M y barra^F

expert drivers course
concurso^M profesional

beginner's course
carrera^F de aprendices^M

speed course
concurso^M de velocidad^F

646

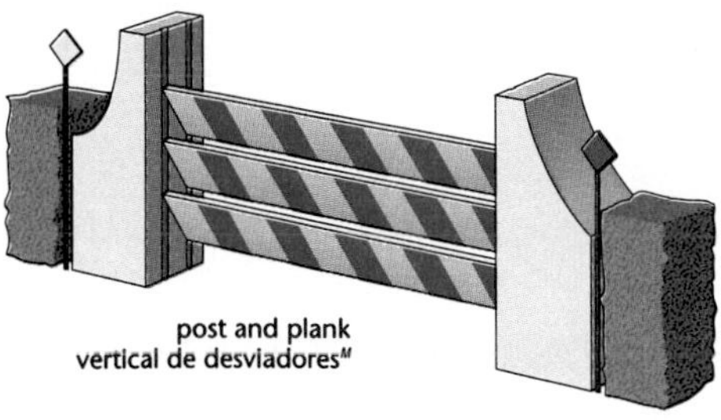

post and plank
vertical de desviadores^M

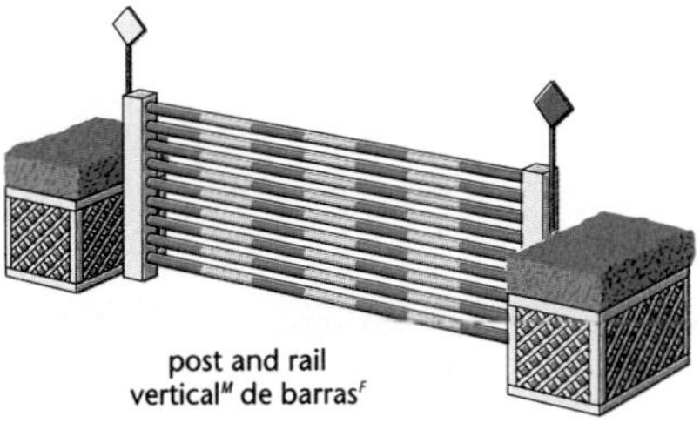

post and rail
vertical^M de barras^F

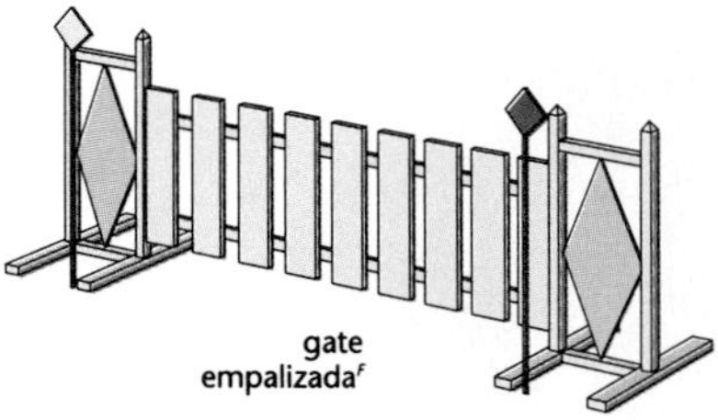

gate
empalizada^F

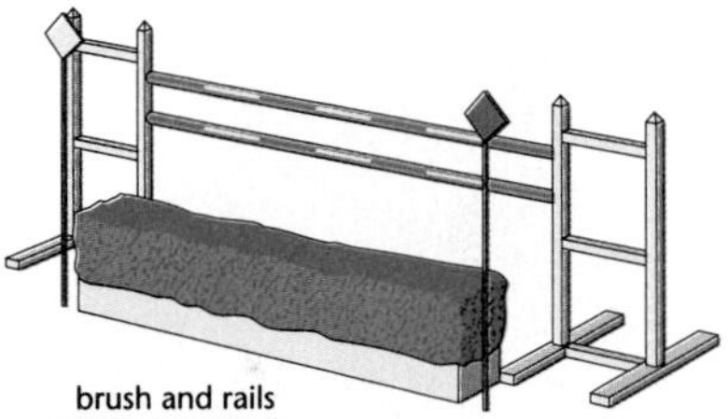

brush and rails
valla^F sobre seto^M

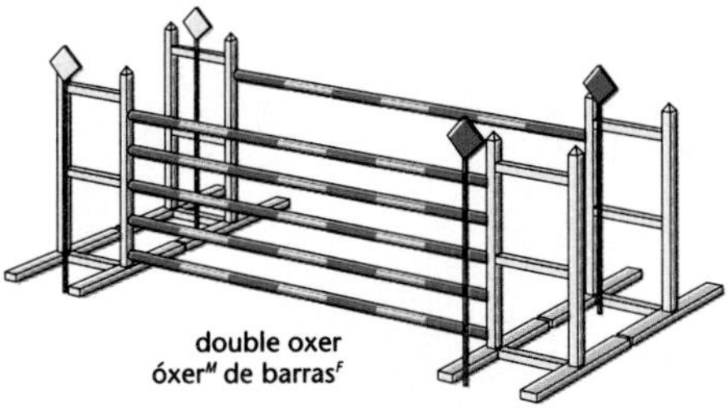

double oxer
óxer^M de barras^F

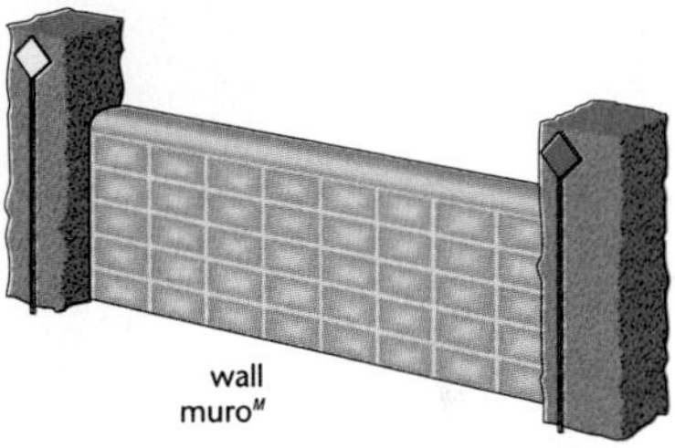

wall
muro^M

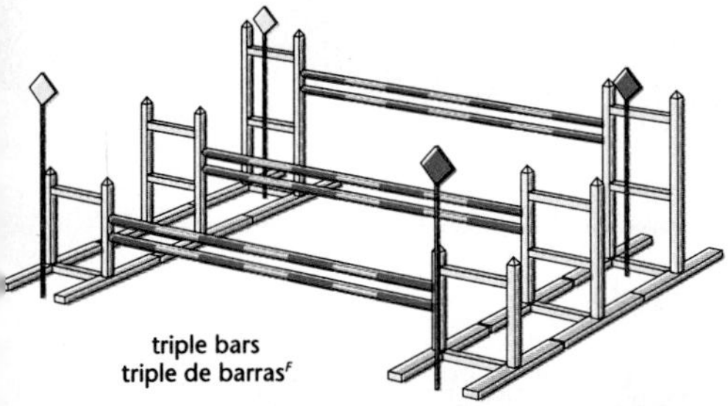

triple bars
triple de barras^F

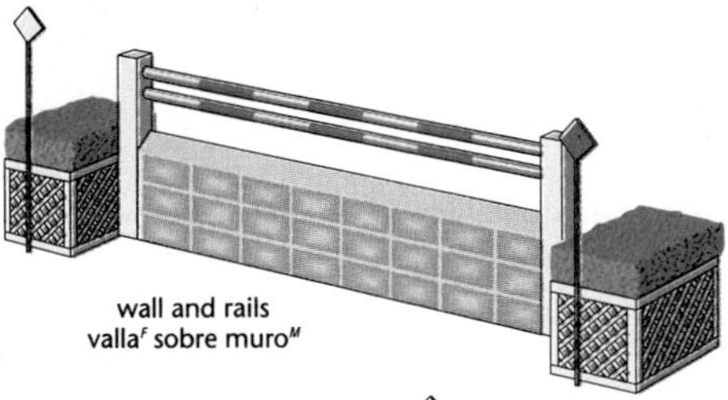

wall and rails
valla^F sobre muro^M

water jump
ría^F

EQUESTRIAN SPORTS
DEPORTES ECUESTRES

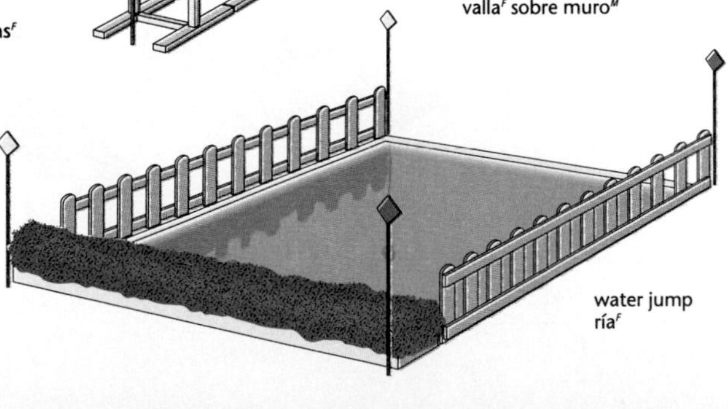

RIDER
JINETE^M

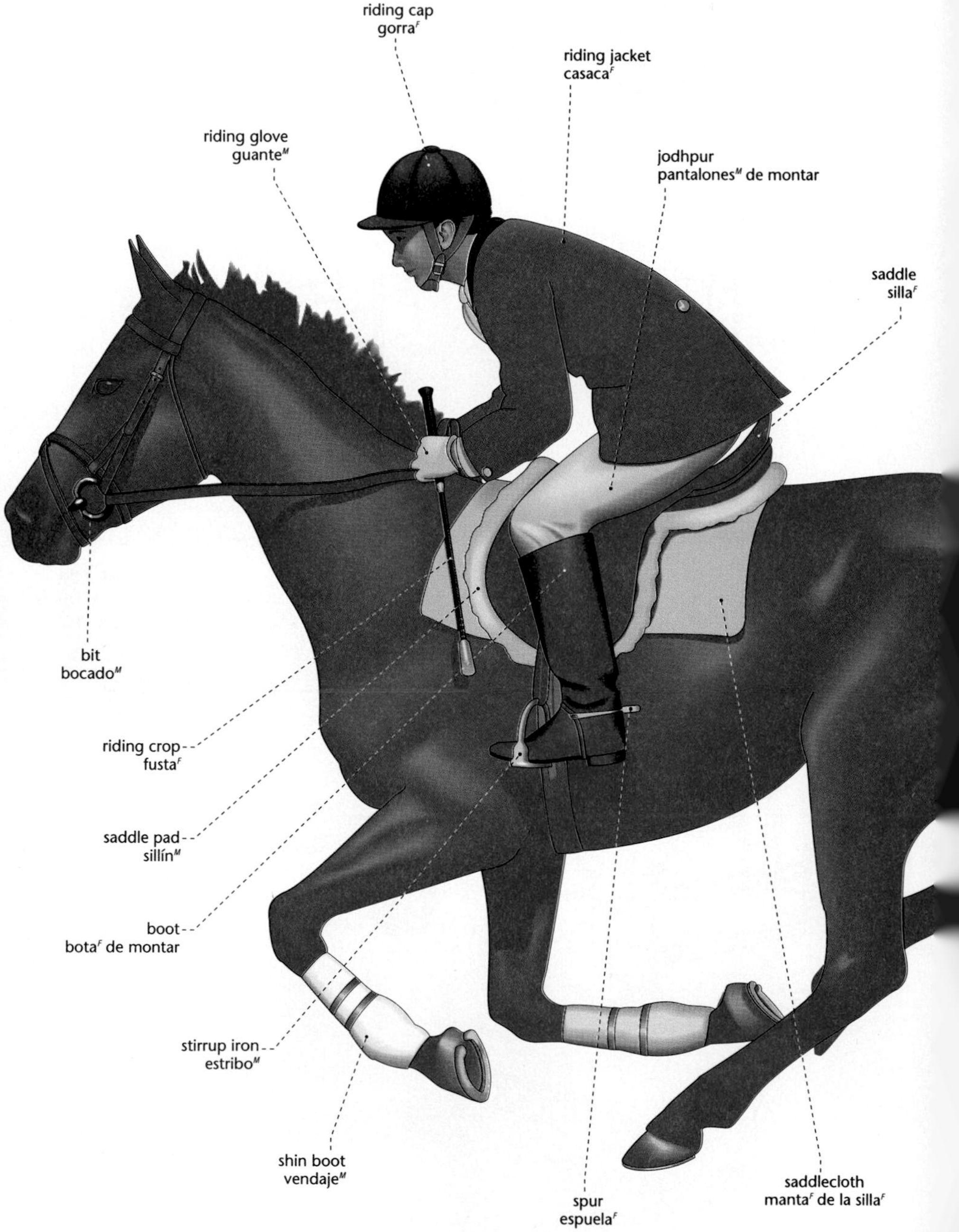

riding cap
gorra^F

riding jacket
casaca^F

riding glove
guante^M

jodhpur
pantalones^M de montar

saddle
silla^F

bit
bocado^M

riding crop
fusta^F

saddle pad
sillín^M

boot
bota^F de montar

stirrup iron
estribo^M

shin boot
vendaje^M

spur
espuela^F

saddlecloth
manta^F de la silla^F

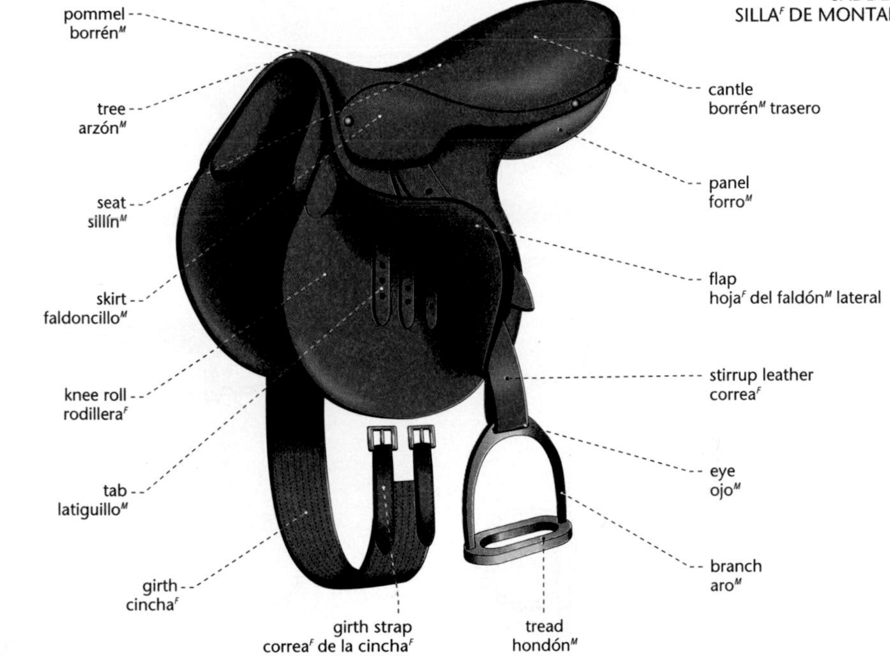

pommel
borrén^M

tree
arzón^M

seat
sillín^M

skirt
faldoncillo^M

knee roll
rodillera^F

tab
latiguillo^M

girth
cincha^F

girth strap
correa^F de la cincha^F

tread
hondón^M

cantle
borrén^M trasero

panel
forro^M

flap
hoja^F del faldón^M lateral

stirrup leather
correa^F

eye
ojo^M

branch
aro^M

BRIDLE
BRIDA^F

crownpiece
cabezada^F

throat latch
ahogadero^M

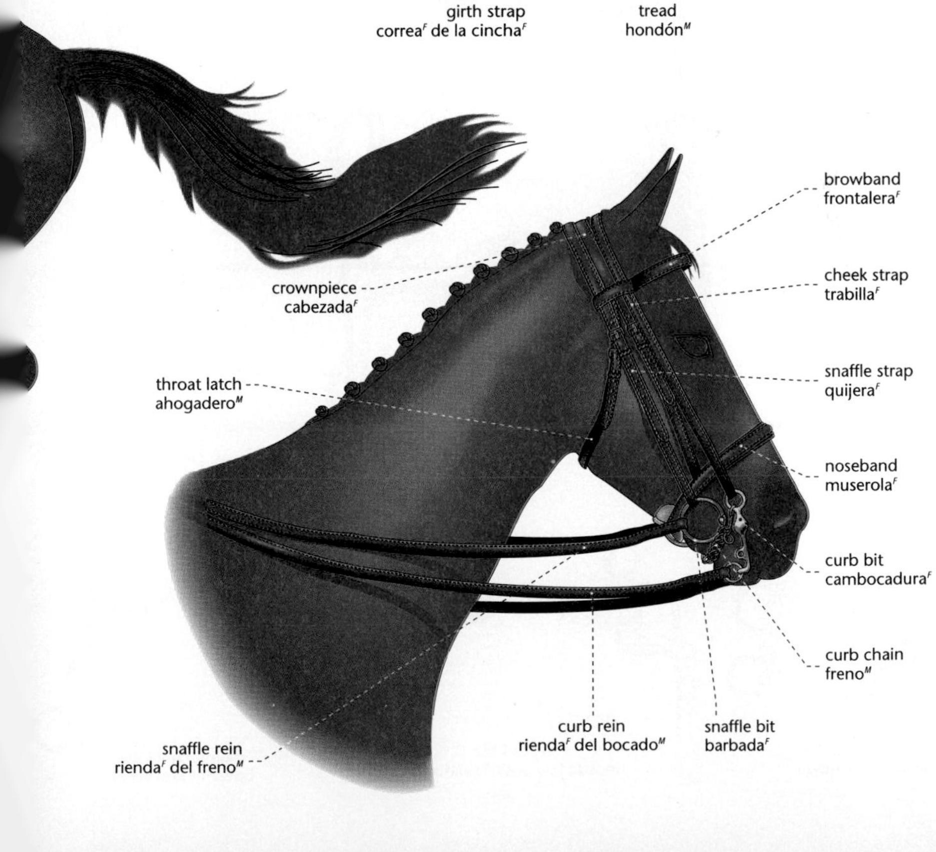

browband
frontalera^F

cheek strap
trabilla^F

snaffle strap
quijera^F

noseband
muserola^F

curb bit
cambocadura^F

curb chain
freno^M

snaffle rein
rienda^F del freno^M

curb rein
rienda^F del bocado^M

snaffle bit
barbada^F

TYPES OF BITS
BOCADOS^M

EQUESTRIAN SPORTS
DEPORTES ECUESTRES

SNAFFLE BIT
BOCADO^M ACODADO

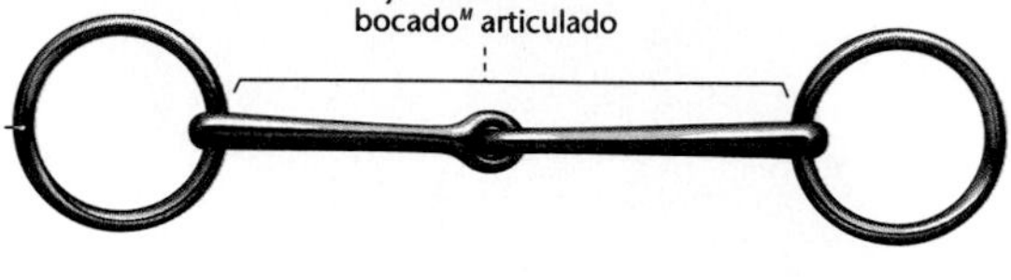

jointed mouth
bocado^M articulado

rein ring
anillo^M de las riendas^F

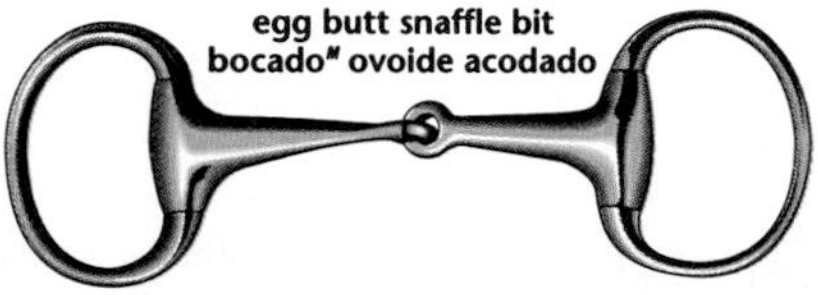

egg butt snaffle bit
bocado^M ovoide acodado

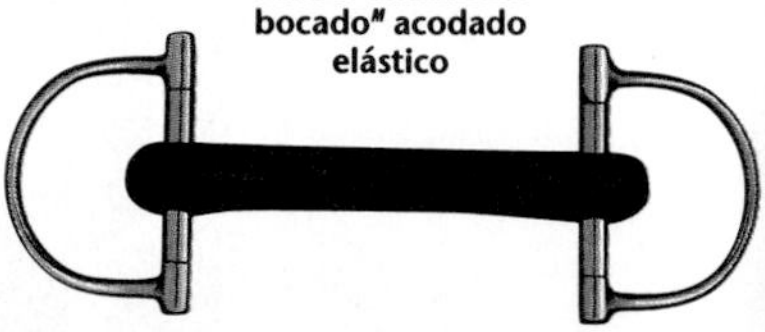

rubber snaffle bit
bocado^M acodado
elástico

full cheek snaffle bit
freno^M de quijada^F acodado

full cheek snaffle bit
bocado^M de quijada^F
acodado

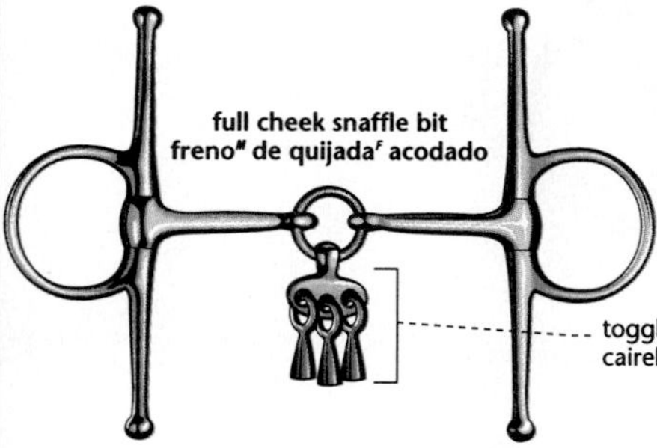

toggles
caireles^M

CURB BIT
BOCADO^M CON LA BARBADA^F

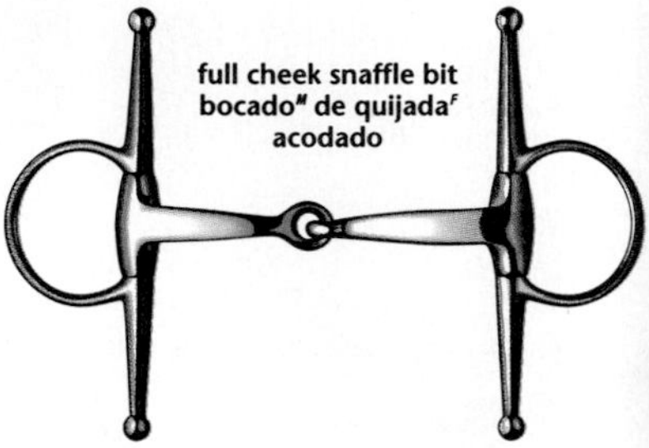

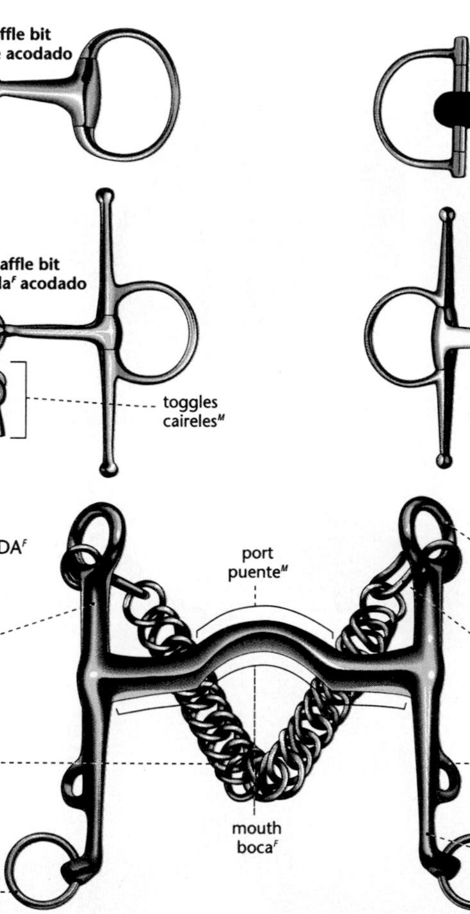

port
puente^M

cheek ring
anillo^M de quijada^F

upper cheek
quijada^F superior

curb hook
gancho^M de la barbada^F

curb chain
cadenilla^F de la barbada^F

lip strap ring
anillo^M de carrillera^F

mouth
boca^F

lower cheek
quijada^F inferior

rein ring
anillo^M de las riendas^F

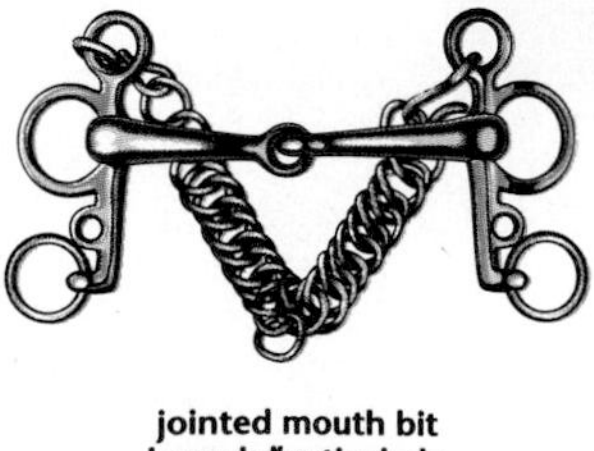

jointed mouth bit
bocado^M articulado

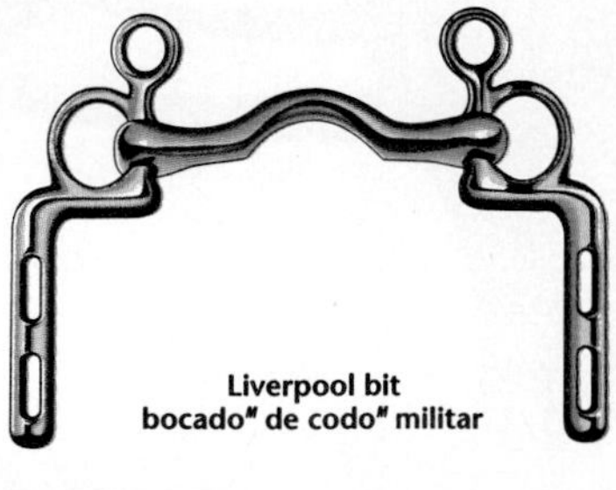

Liverpool bit
bocado^M de codo^M militar

sliding cheek bit
bocado^M corredizo

650

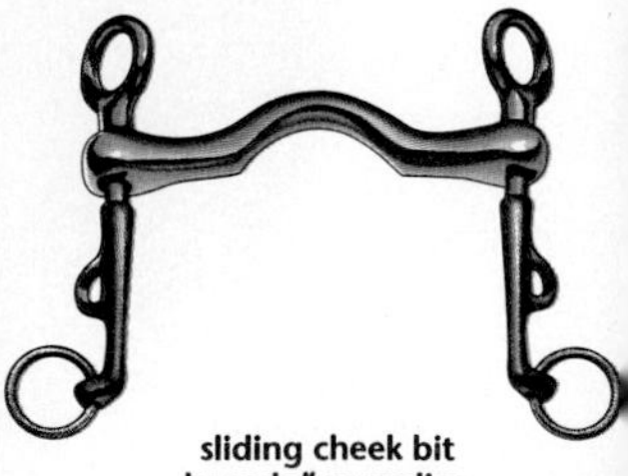

HORSE RACING
CARRERA^F DE CABALLOS^M

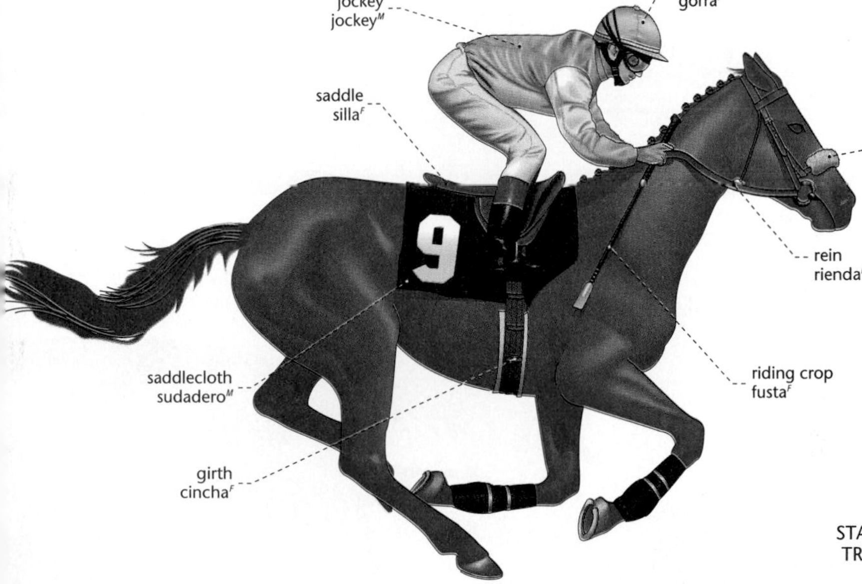

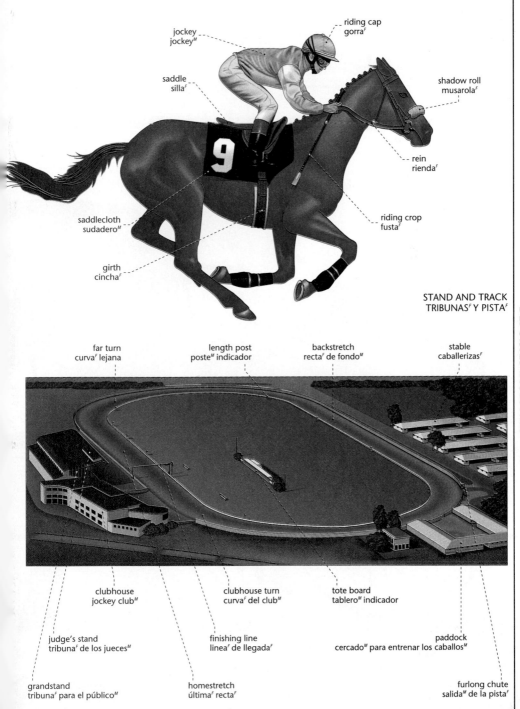

jockey
jockey^M

riding cap
gorra^F

saddle
silla^F

shadow roll
musarola^F

rein
rienda^F

saddlecloth
sudadero^M

riding crop
fusta^F

girth
cincha^F

STAND AND TRACK
TRIBUNAS^F Y PISTA^F

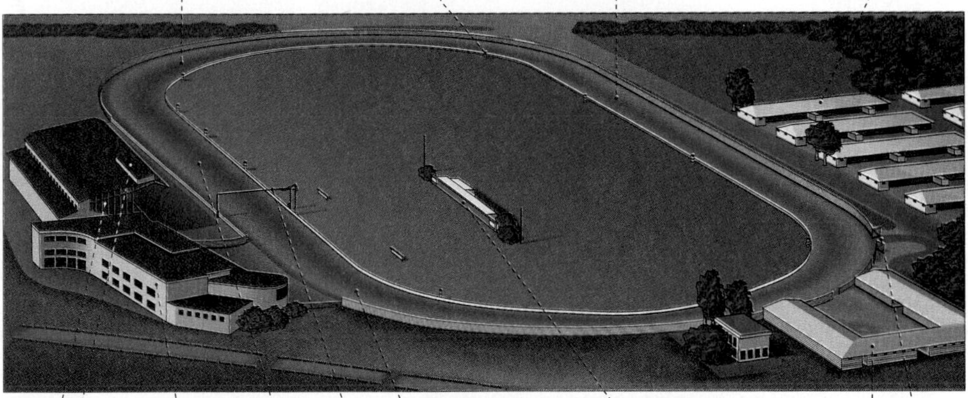

far turn
curva^F lejana

length post
poste^M indicador

backstretch
recta^F de fondo^M

stable
caballerizas^F

clubhouse
jockey club^M

clubhouse turn
curva^F del club^M

tote board
tablero^M indicador

judge's stand
tribuna^F de los jueces^M

finishing line
línea^F de llegada^F

paddock
cercado^M para entrenar los caballos^M

grandstand
tribuna^F para el público^M

homestretch
última^F recta^F

furlong chute
salida^M de la pista^F

651

STANDARDBRED PACER
ARNESES^M PARA TROTONES^M

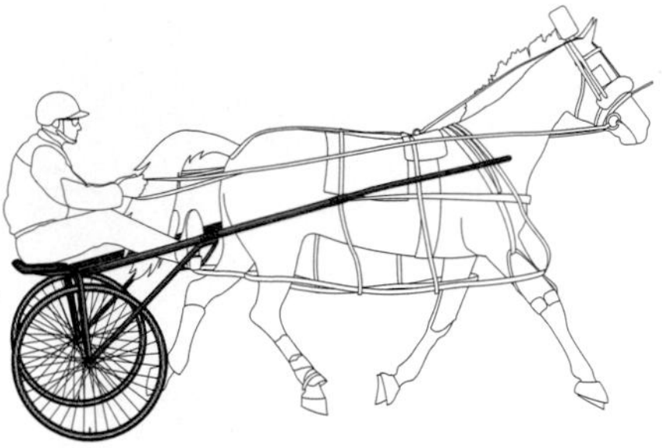

sulky
sulky^M

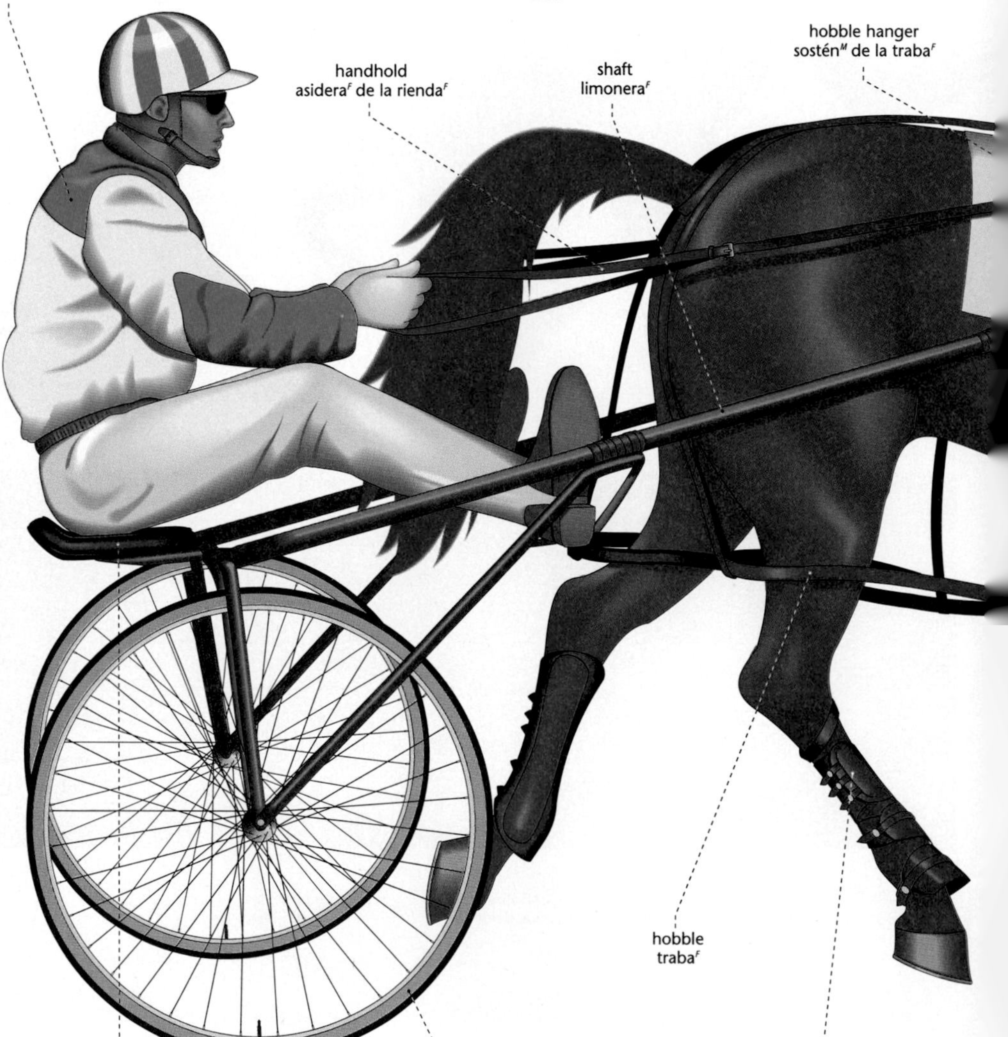

driver
conductor^M

handhold
asidera^F de la rienda^F

shaft
limonera^F

hobble hanger
sostén^M de la traba^F

hobble
traba^F

shin boot
polaina^F

seat
asiento^M

spoked wheel
rueda^F de rayos^M

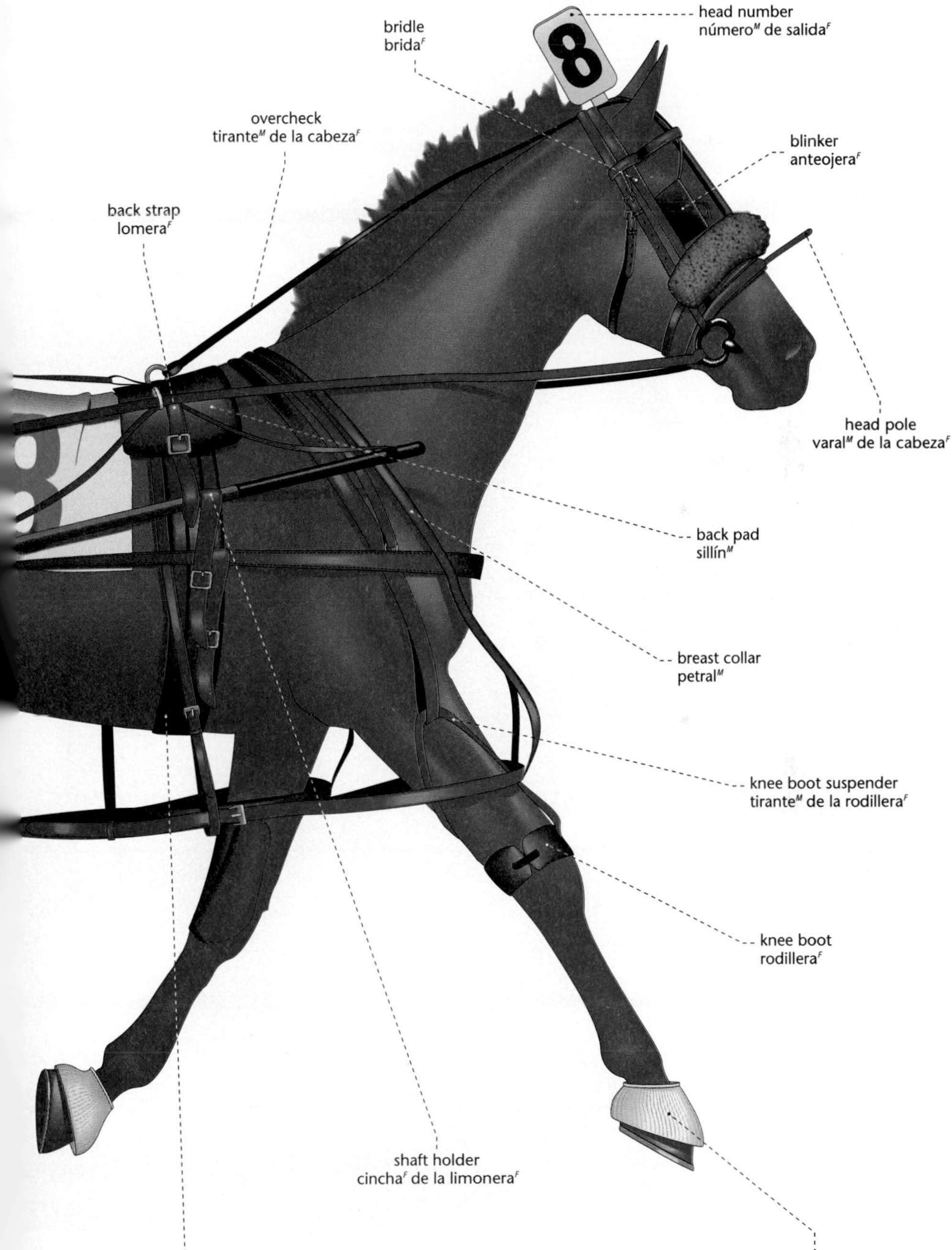

head number
número^M de salida^F

bridle
brida^F

overcheck
tirante^M de la cabeza^F

blinker
anteojera^F

back strap
lomera^F

head pole
varal^M de la cabeza^F

back pad
sillín^M

breast collar
petral^M

knee boot suspender
tirante^M de la rodillera^F

knee boot
rodillera^F

shaft holder
cincha^F de la limonera^F

scalper
bota^F de la corona^F del casco^M

surcingle
sobrecincha^F

ARENA
ESTADIO^M

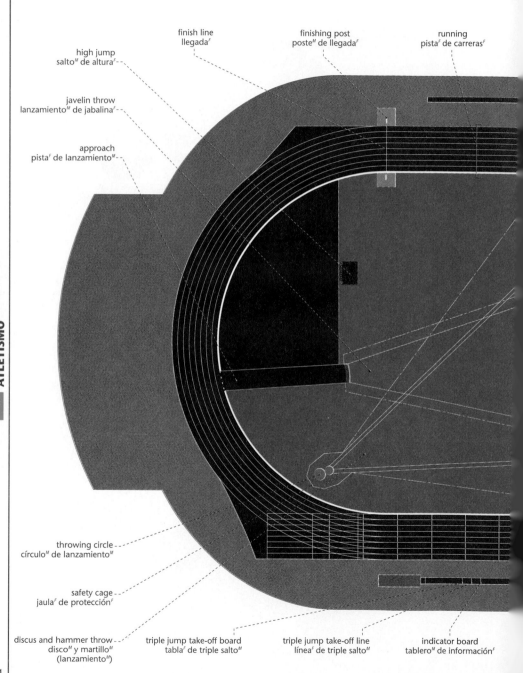

finish line
llegada^F

finishing post
poste^M de llegada^F

running
pista^F de carreras^F

high jump
salto^M de altura^F

javelin throw
lanzamiento^M de jabalina^F

approach
pista^F de lanzamiento^M

throwing circle
círculo^M de lanzamiento^M

safety cage
jaula^F de protección^F

discus and hammer throw
disco^M y martillo^M
(lanzamiento^M)

triple jump take-off board
tabla^F de triple salto^M

triple jump take-off line
línea^F de triple salto^M

indicator board
tablero^M de información^F

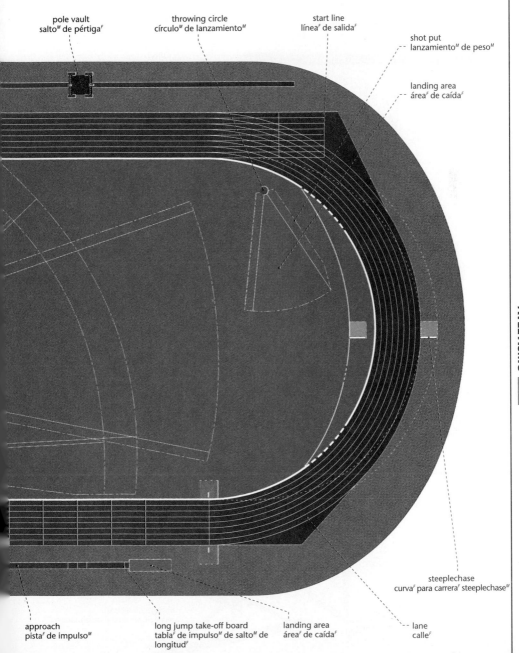

pole vault
salto^M de pértiga^F

throwing circle
círculo^M de lanzamiento^M

start line
línea^F de salida^F

shot put
lanzamiento^M de peso^M

landing area
área^F de caída^F

steeplechase
curva^F para carrera^F steeplechase^M

approach
pista^F de impulso^M

long jump take-off board
tabla^F de impulso^M de salto^M de longitud^F

landing area
área^F de caída^F

lane
calle^F

STARTING BLOCK
TACO^M DE SALIDA^F

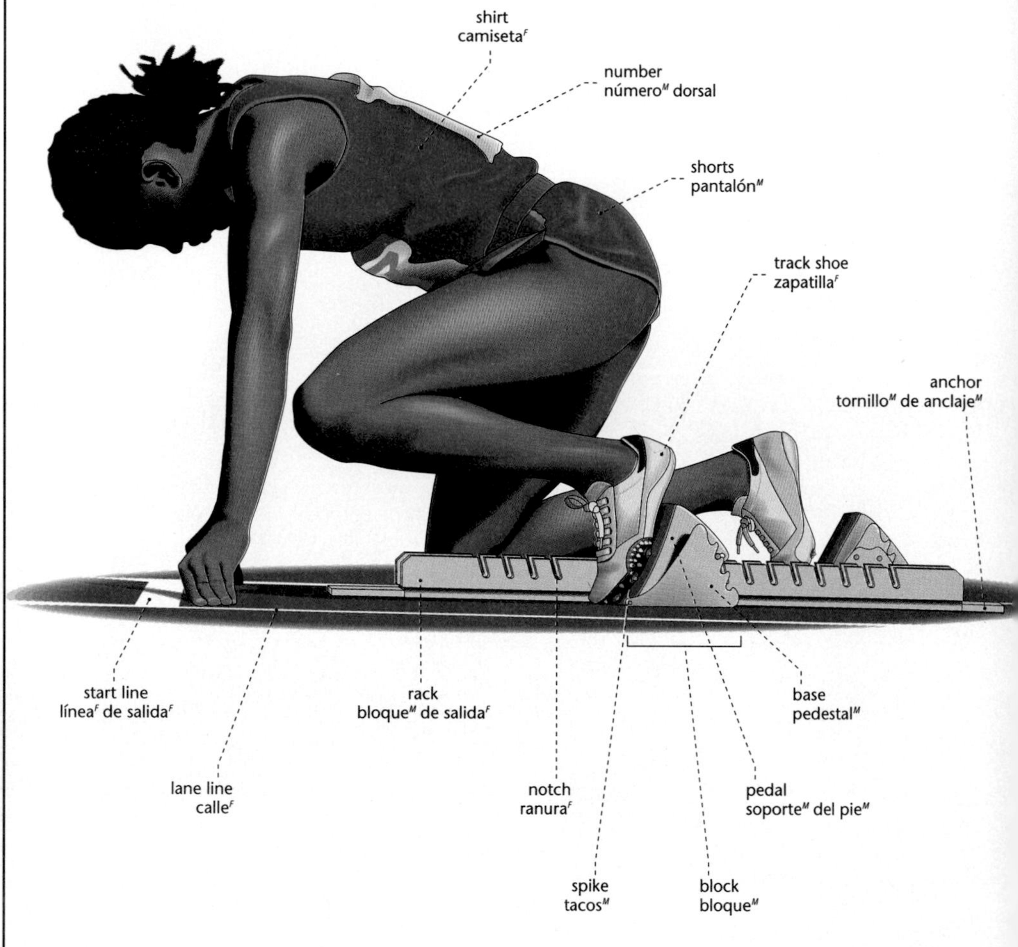

shirt
camiseta^F

number
número^M dorsal

shorts
pantalón^M

track shoe
zapatilla^F

anchor
tornillo^M de anclaje^M

start line
línea^F de salida^F

rack
bloque^M de salida^F

base
pedestal^M

lane line
calle^F

notch
ranura^F

pedal
soporte^M del pie^M

spike
tacos^M

block
bloque^M

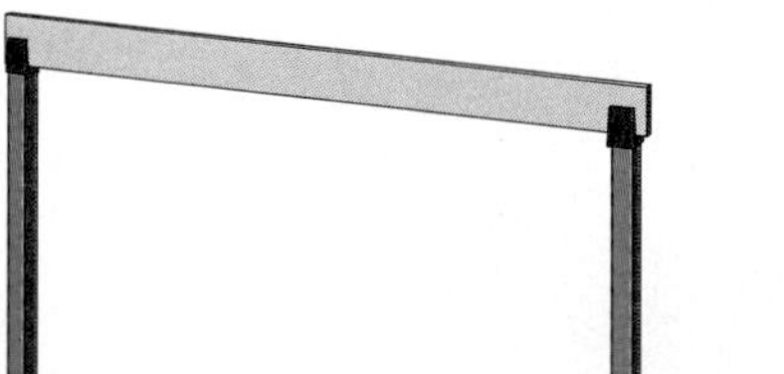

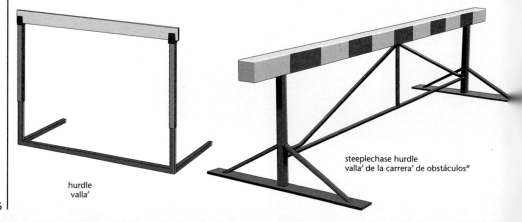

hurdle
valla^F

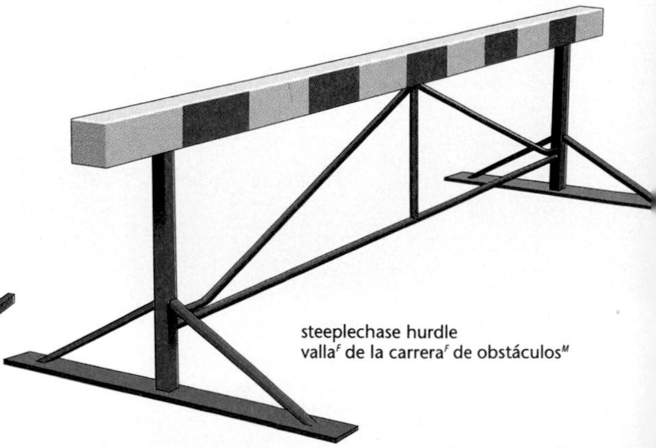

steeplechase hurdle
valla^F de la carrera^F de obstáculos^M

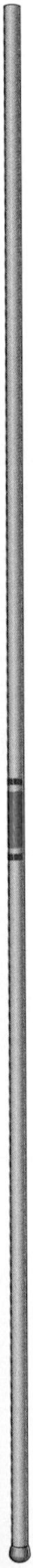

pole
pértiga^F

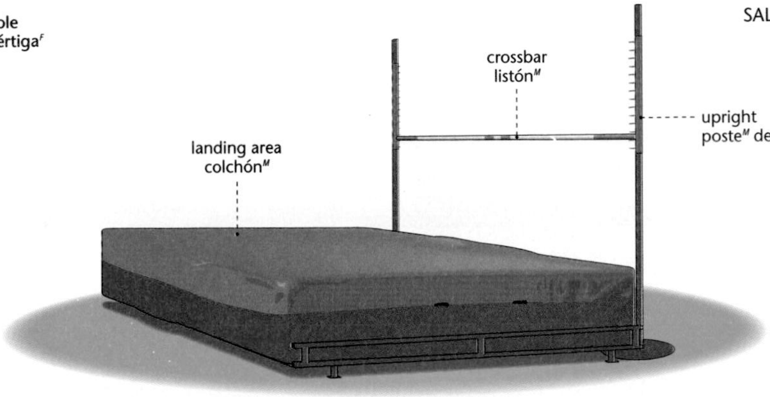

crossbar
listón^M

upright
poste^M de salto^M

landing area
colchón^M

POLE VAULT
SALTO^M DE PÉRTIGA^F

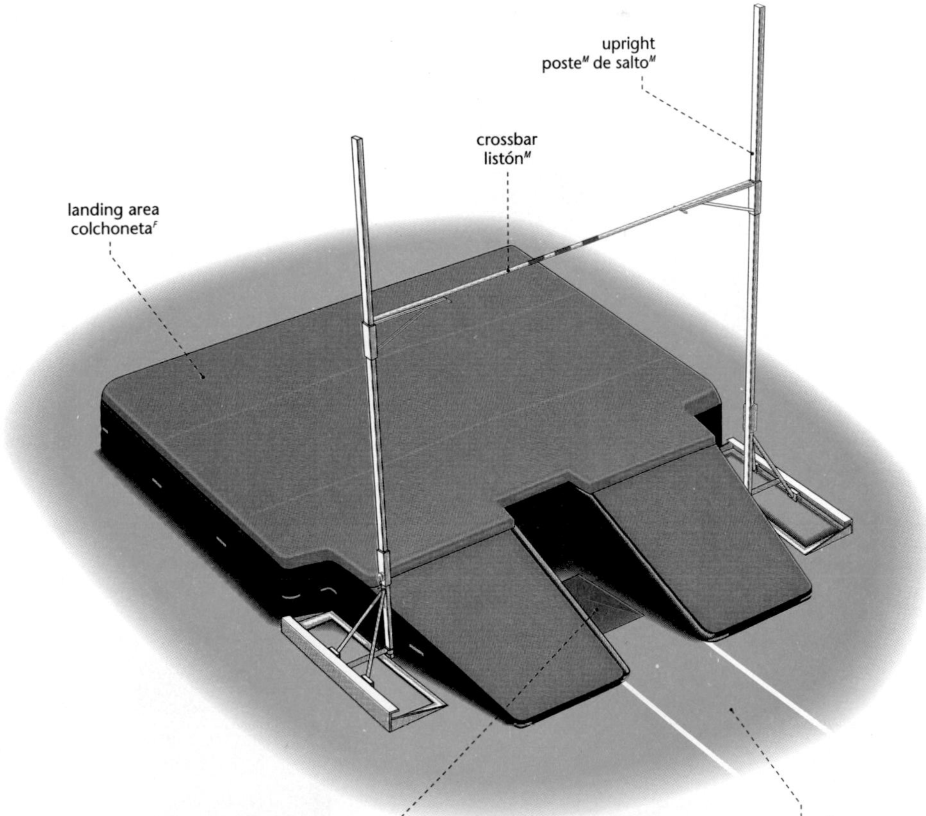

upright
poste^M de salto^M

crossbar
listón^M

landing area
colchoneta^F

planting box
cajón^M de batir

approach
pista^F de impulso^M

**ATHLETICS
ATLETISMO**

657

THROWINGS
LANZAMIENTOS*ᴹ*

hammer
martillo*ᴹ*

wire
cable*ᴹ*

handle
mango*ᴹ*

swivel
pivote*ᴹ*

head
cabeza*ᶠ* del martillo*ᴹ*

4 – 4 3/4 in

shot
peso*ᴹ*

♂

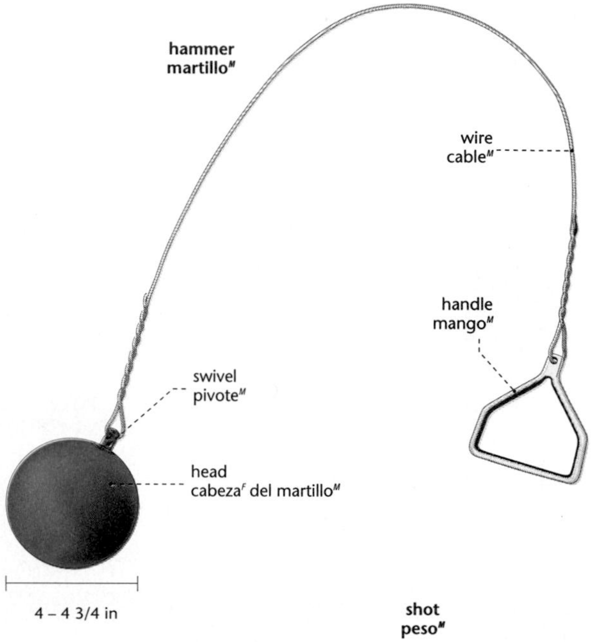

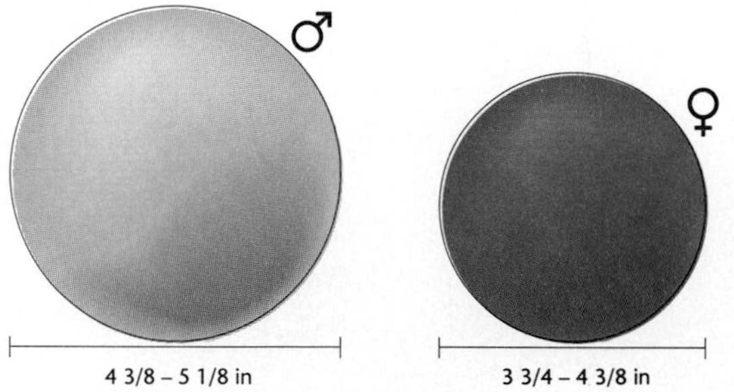

4 3/8 – 5 1/8 in

♀

3 3/4 – 4 3/8 in

javelins
jabalina*ᶠ*   ♂

tip
punta*ᶠ*

metal head
cabeza*ᶠ* de metal*ᴹ*

♀

shaft
fuste*ᴹ*

cord grip
empuñadura*ᶠ*

7 ft 2 in – 7 ft 6 in

8 ft 6 in – 8 ft 10 in

discus
disco*ᴹ*

♂

weight
peso*ᴹ*

rim
canto*ᴹ*

body
cuerpo*ᴹ*

8 5/8 – 8 3/4 in

♀

7 1/8 – 7 1/4 in

ATHLETICS
ATLETISMO

658

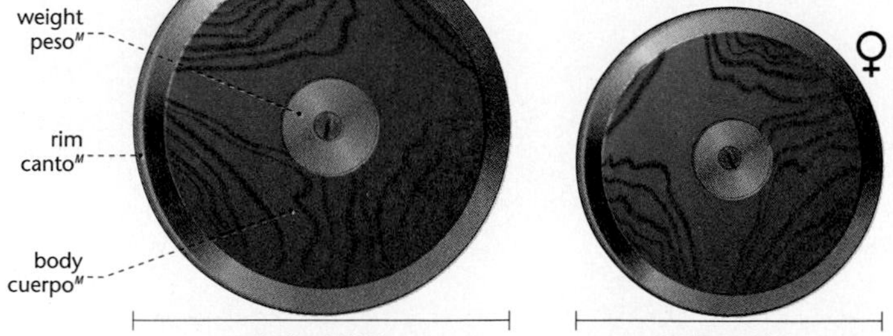

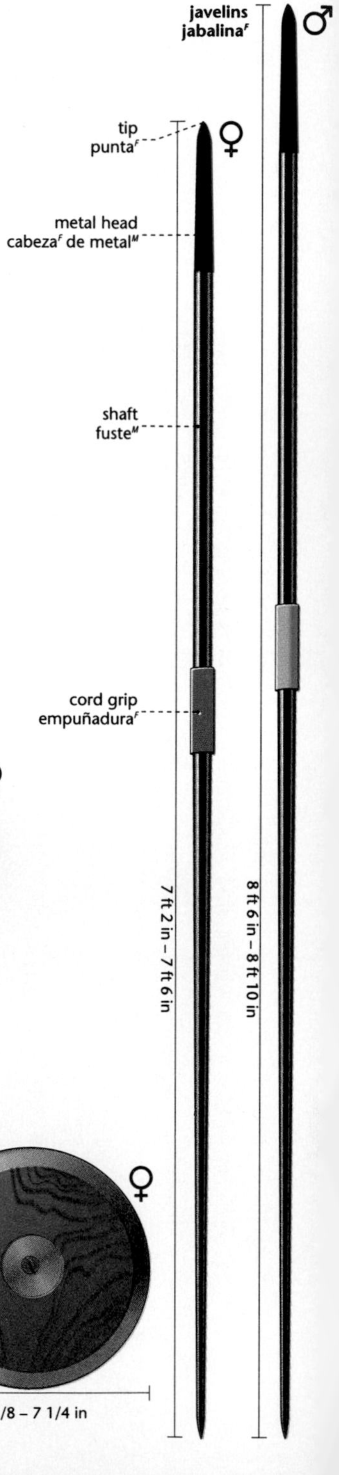

GYMNASTICS
GIMNASIA^F

vaulting horse
potro^M

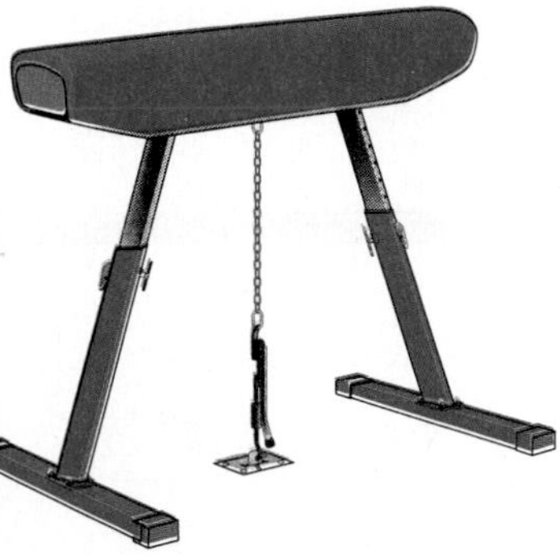

ASYMMETRICAL BARS
BARRAS^F ASIMÉTRICAS

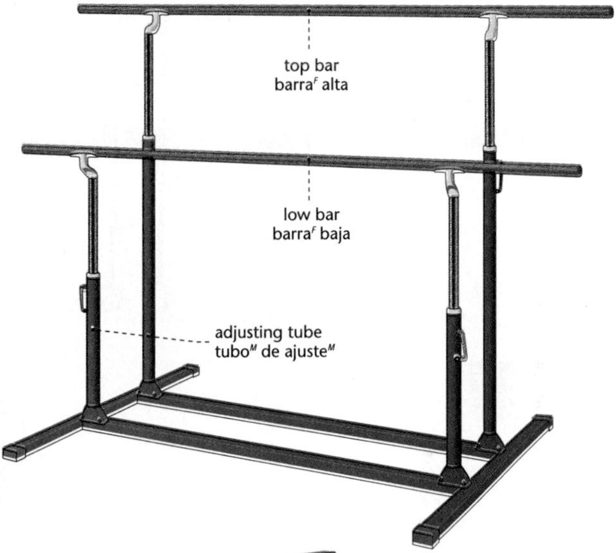

top bar
barra^F alta

low bar
barra^F baja

adjusting tube
tubo^M de ajuste^M

springboard
plancha^F de muelles^M

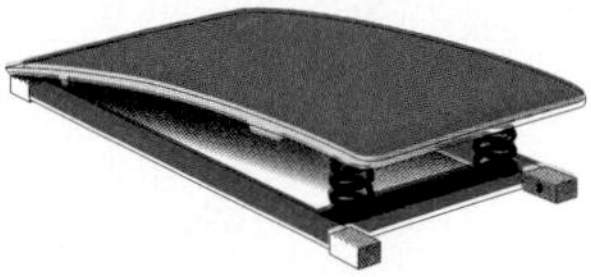

BALANCE BEAM
BARRA^F DE EQUILIBRIO^M

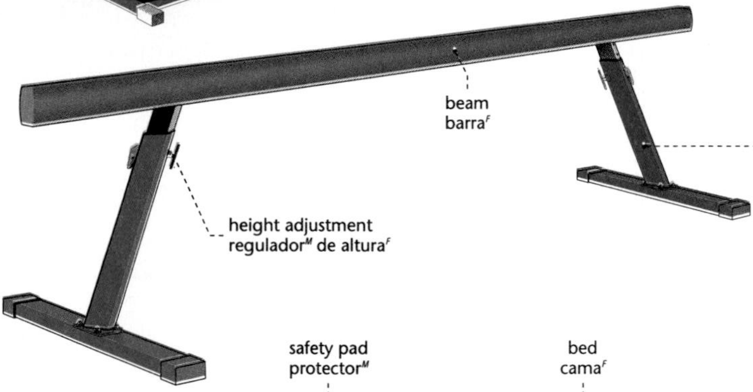

beam
barra^F

upright
montante^M

height adjustment
regulador^M de altura^F

TRAMPOLINE
CAMA^F ELÁSTICA

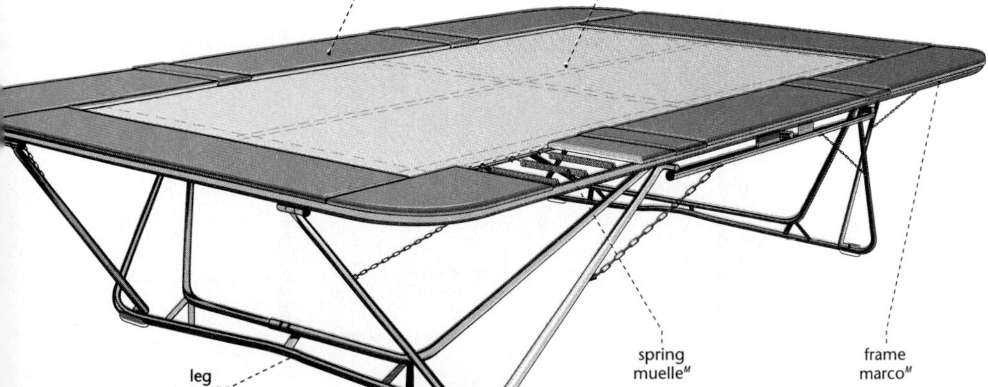

safety pad
protector^M

bed
cama^F

leg
pata^F

spring
muelle^M

frame
marco^M

RINGS
ANILLAS*M*

frame
bastidor*M*

cable
cable*M*

strap
correa*F*

guy cable
tensor*M*

ring
anilla*F*

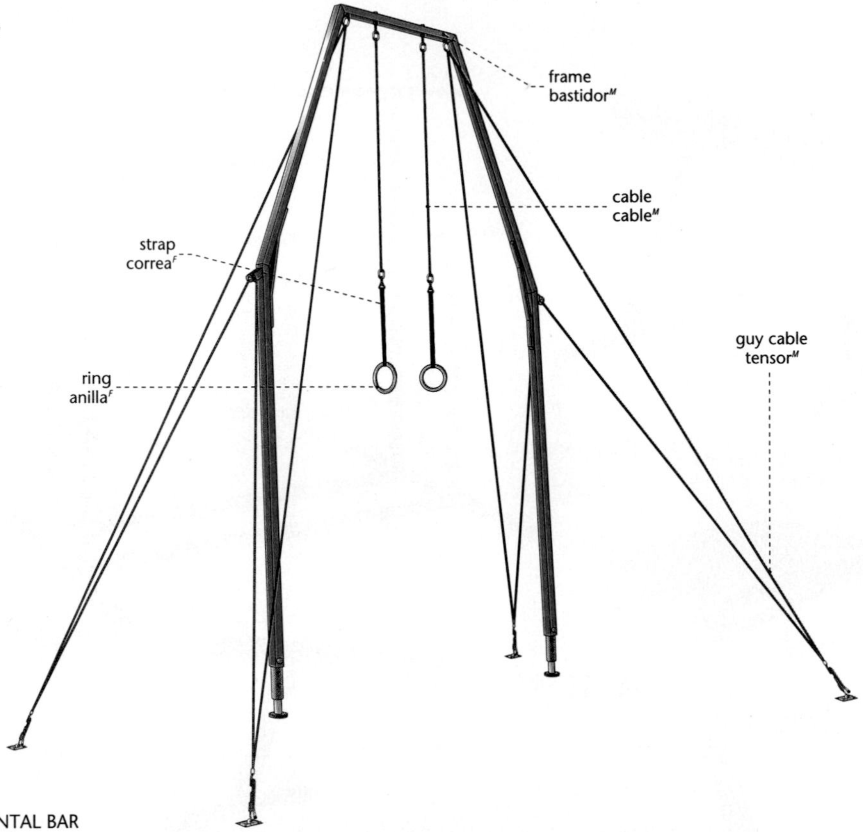

HORIZONTAL BAR
BARRA*F* FIJA

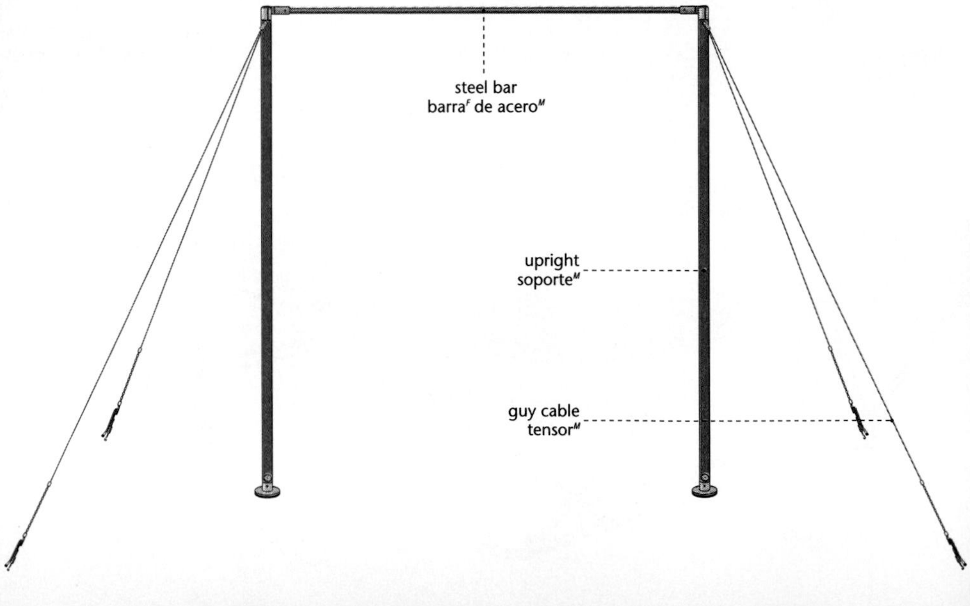

steel bar
barra*F* de acero*M*

upright
soporte*M*

guy cable
tensor*M*

POMMEL HORSE
CABALLO^M DE ARZÓN^M

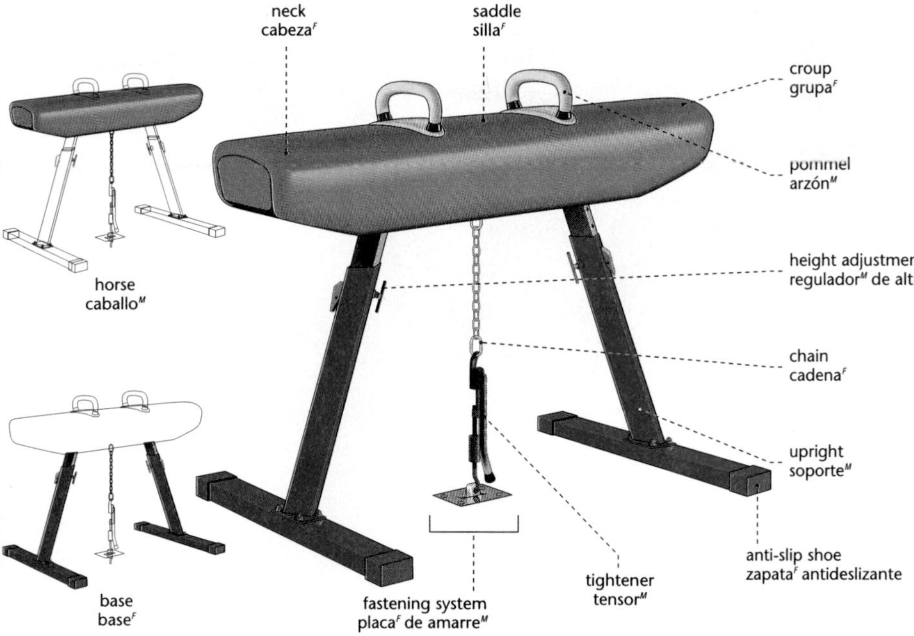

neck
cabeza^F

saddle
silla^F

croup
grupa^F

pommel
arzón^M

height adjustment
regulador^M de altura^F

chain
cadena^F

upright
soporte^M

anti-slip shoe
zapata^F antideslizante

tightener
tensor^M

fastening system
placa^F de amarre^M

base
base^F

horse
caballo^M

PARALLEL BARS
BARRAS^F PARALELAS

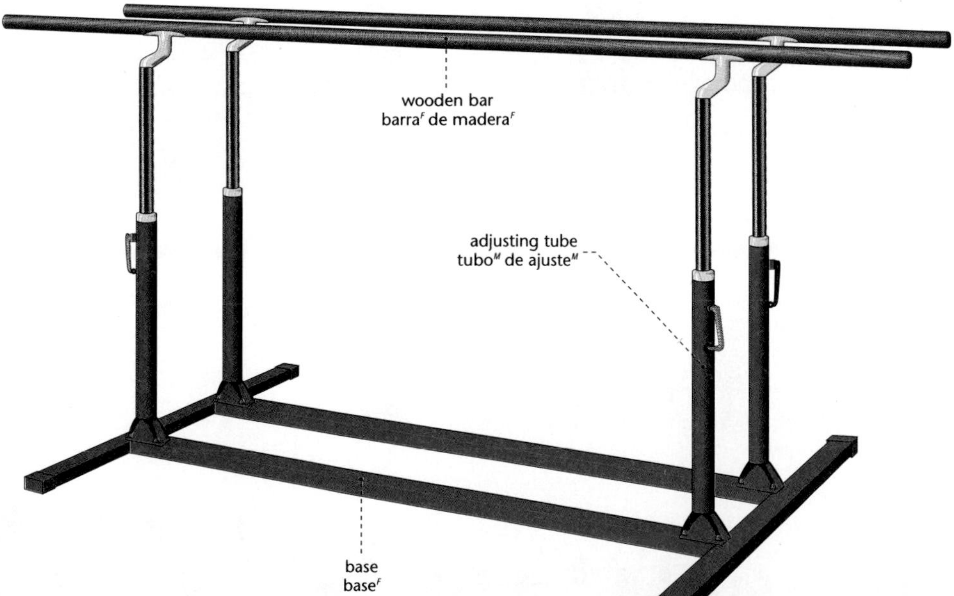

wooden bar
barra^F de madera^F

adjusting tube
tubo^M de ajuste^M

base
base^F

WEIGHTLIFTING
HALTEROFILIA^F

WEIGHTLIFTER
LEVANTADOR^M DE PESAS^F

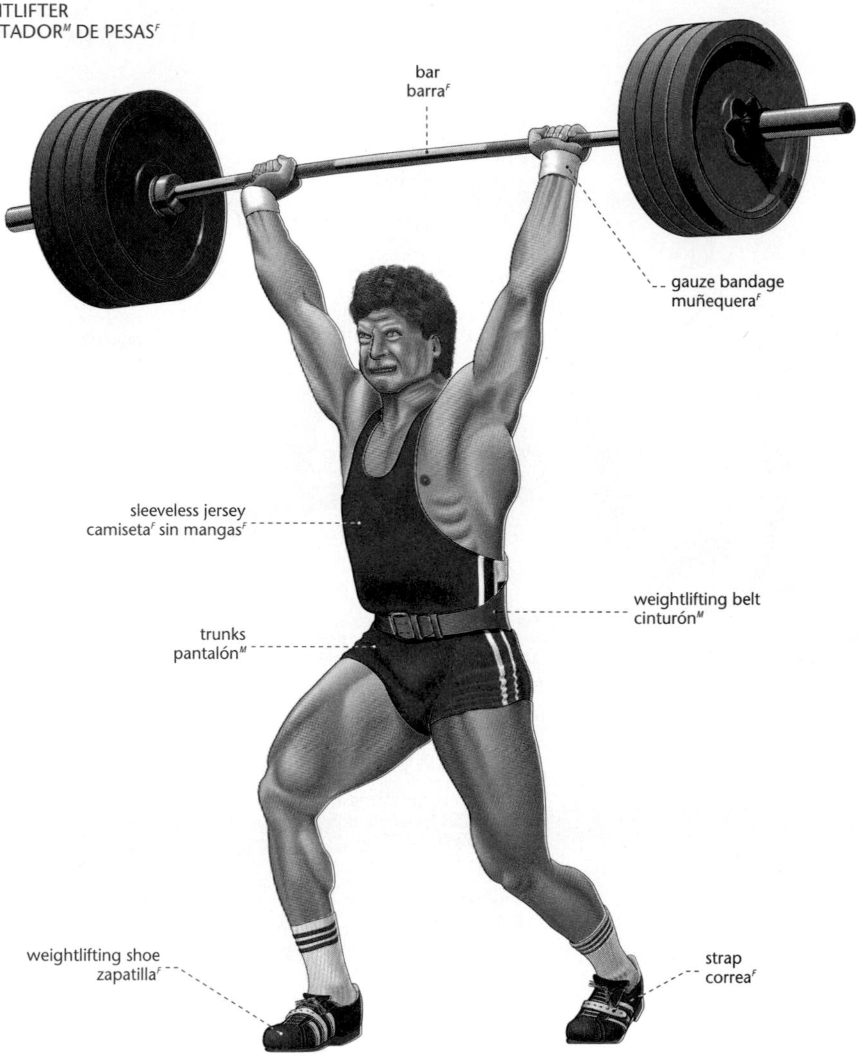

bar
barra^F

gauze bandage
muñequera^F

sleeveless jersey
camiseta^F sin mangas^F

weightlifting belt
cinturón^M

trunks
pantalón^M

weightlifting shoe
zapatilla^F

strap
correa^F

TWO-HAND SNATCH
MODALIDAD^F ARRANQUE^M

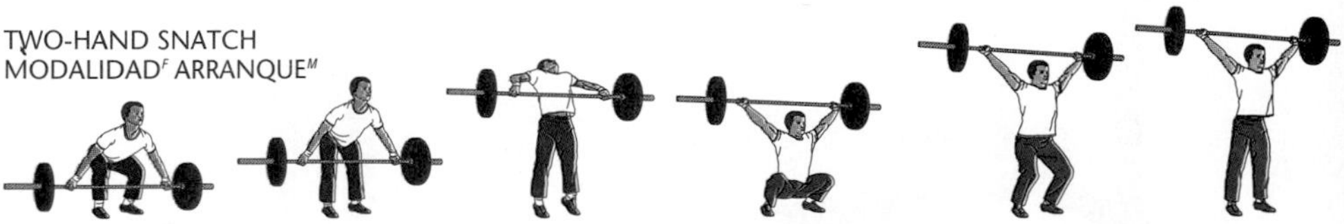

TWO-HAND CLEAN AND JERK
MODALIDAD^F CON IMPULSO^M EN DOS TIEMPOS^M

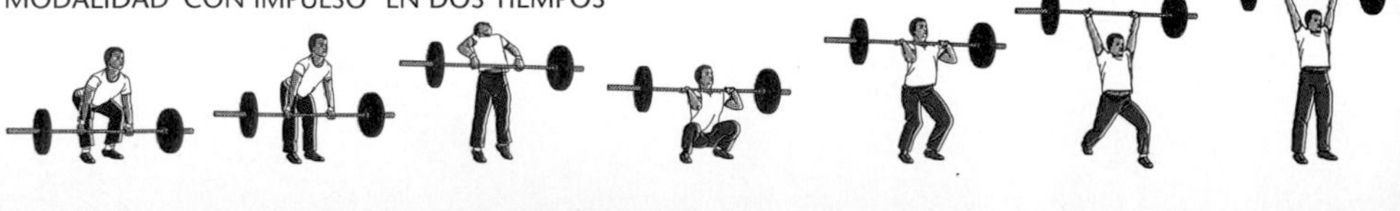

FITNESS EQUIPMENT
APARATOS^M DE EJERCICIOS^M

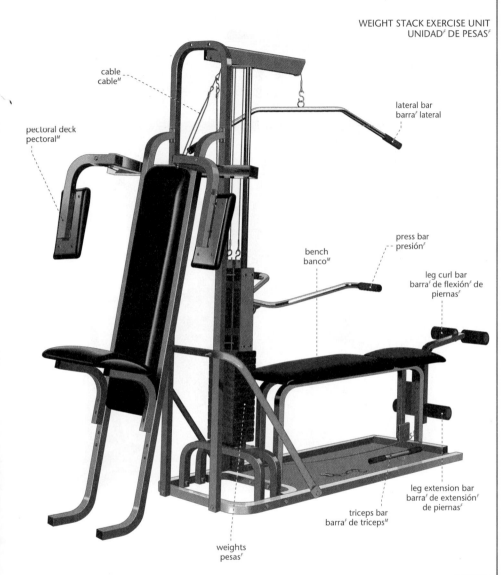

WEIGHT STACK EXERCISE UNIT
UNIDAD^F DE PESAS^F

cable
cable^M

lateral bar
barra^F lateral

pectoral deck
pectoral^M

press bar
presión^F

bench
banco^M

leg curl bar
barra^F de flexión^F de
piernas^F

leg extension bar
barra^F de extensión^F
de piernas^F

triceps bar
barra^F de triceps^M

weights
pesas^F

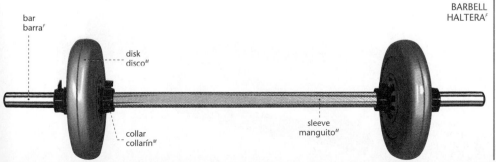

BARBELL
HALTERA^F

bar
barra^F

disk
disco^M

collar
collarín^M

sleeve
manguito^M

FITNESS EQUIPMENT
APARATOS^M DE EJERCICIOS^M

STATIONARY BICYCLE
BICICLETA^F ESTÁTICA

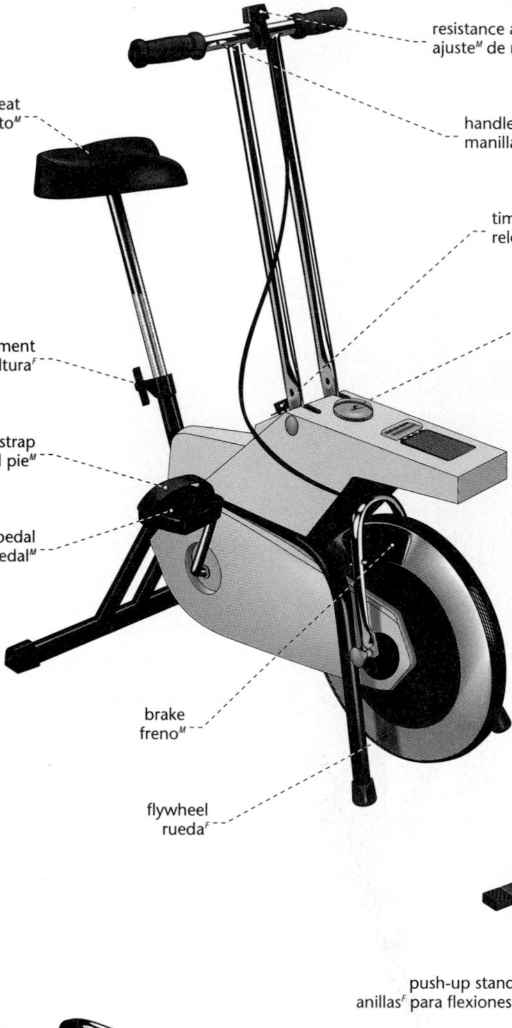

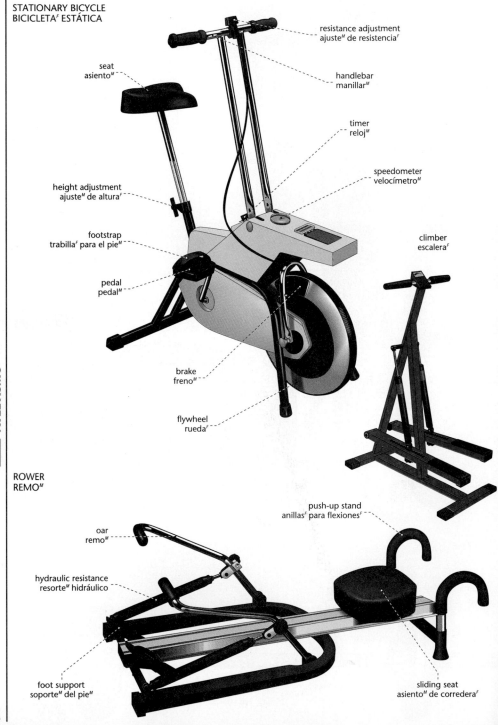

resistance adjustment
ajuste^M de resistencia^F

seat
asiento^M

handlebar
manillar^M

timer
reloj^M

speedometer
velocímetro^M

height adjustment
ajuste^M de altura^F

climber
escalera^F

footstrap
trabilla^F para el pie^M

pedal
pedal^M

brake
freno^M

flywheel
rueda^F

ROWER
REMO^M

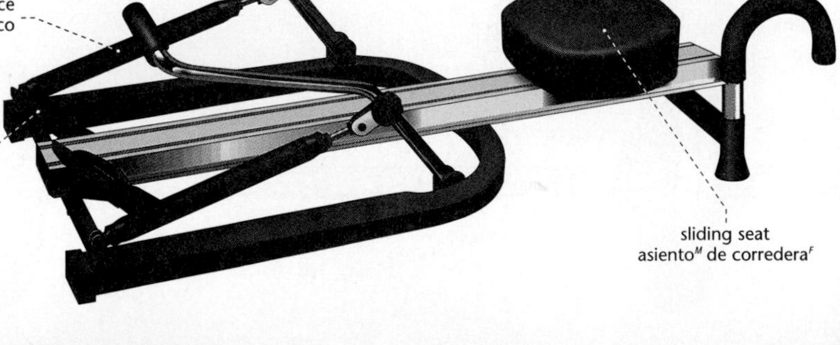

push-up stand
anillas^F para flexiones^F

oar
remo^M

hydraulic resistance
resorte^M hidráulico

foot support
soporte^M del pie^M

sliding seat
asiento^M de corredera^F

664

DUMBBELL
PESAS^F

handgrips
empuñaderas^F

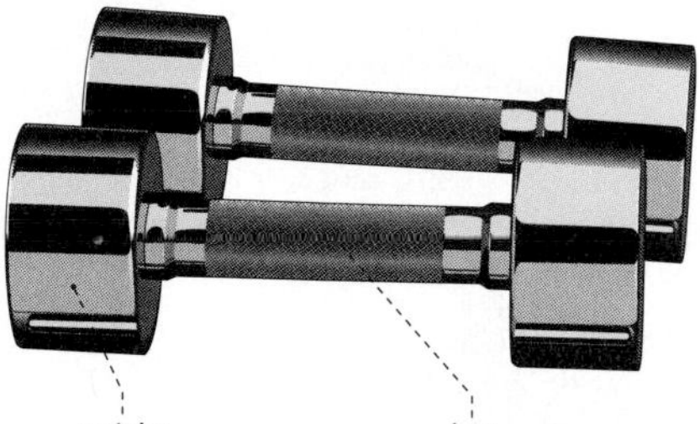

weight
pesas^F

bar
barra^F

ankle/wrist weight
pesas^F para muñecas^F y tobillos^M

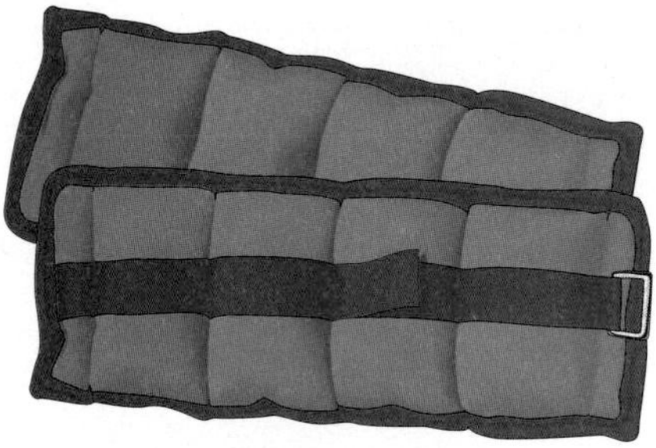

jump rope
cuerda^F

TWIST BAR
BARRA^F DE TORSIÓN^F

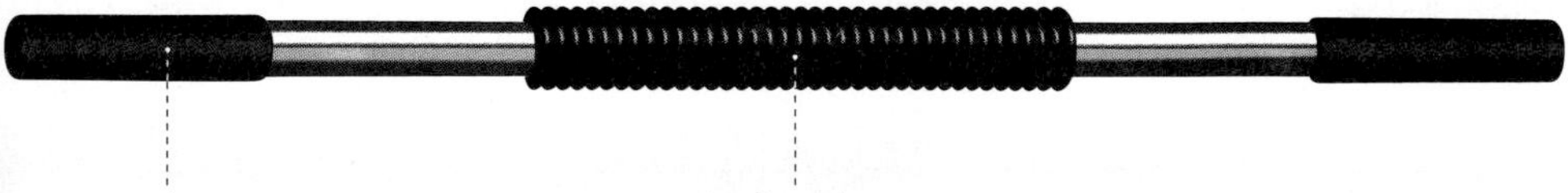

grip
empuñadura^F

tension spring
resorte^M de tensión^F

chest expander
tensores^M pectorales

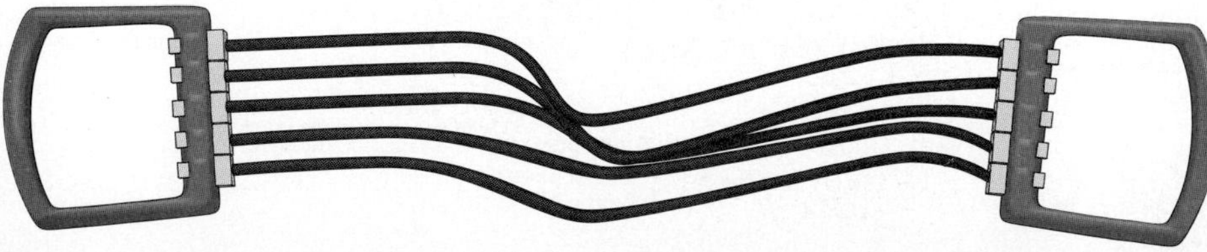

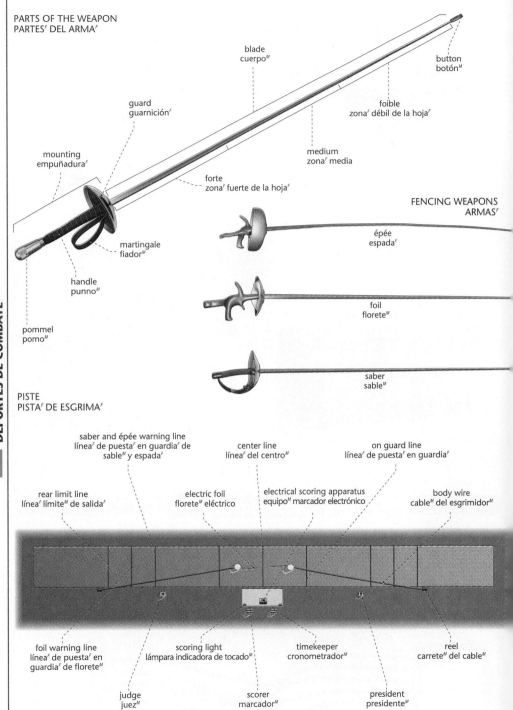

PARTS OF THE WEAPON
PARTES^F DEL ARMA^F

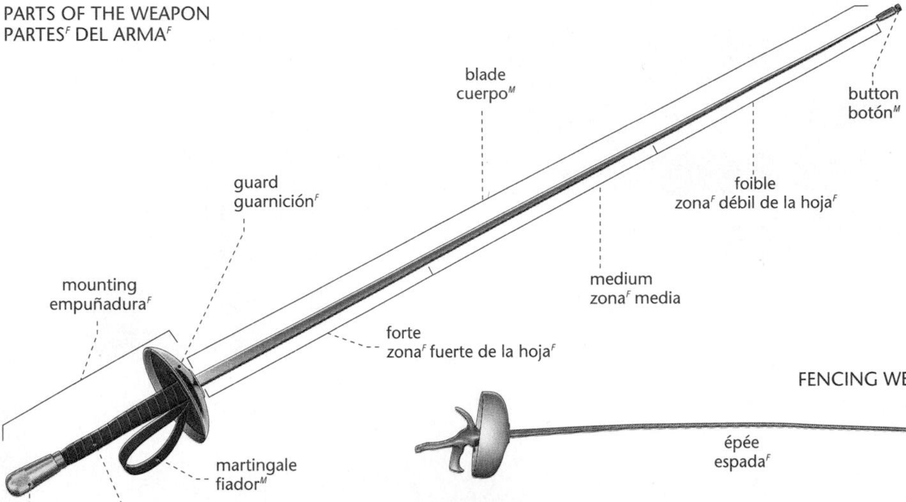

blade
cuerpo^M

button
botón^M

foible
zona^F débil de la hoja^F

guard
guarnición^F

medium
zona^F media

mounting
empuñadura^F

forte
zona^F fuerte de la hoja^F

FENCING WEAPONS
ARMAS^F

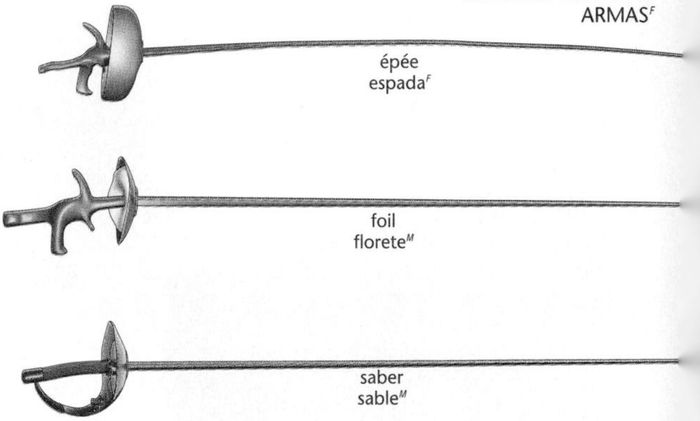

martingale
fiador^M

épée
espada^F

handle
punno^M

foil
florete^M

pommel
pomo^M

saber
sable^M

PISTE
PISTA^F DE ESGRIMA^F

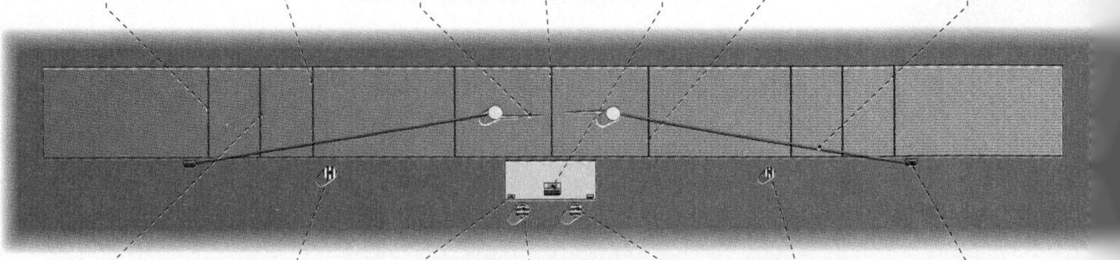

saber and épée warning line
línea^F de puesta^F en guardia^F de
sable^M y espada^F

center line
línea^F del centro^M

on guard line
línea^F de puesta^F en guardia^F

rear limit line
línea^F límite^M de salida^F

electric foil
florete^M eléctrico

electrical scoring apparatus
equipo^M marcador electrónico

body wire
cable^M del esgrimidor^M

foil warning line
línea^F de puesta^F en
guardia^F de florete^M

scoring light
lámpara indicadora de tocado^M

timekeeper
cronometrador^M

reel
carrete^M del cable^M

judge
juez^M

scorer
marcador^M

president
presidente^M

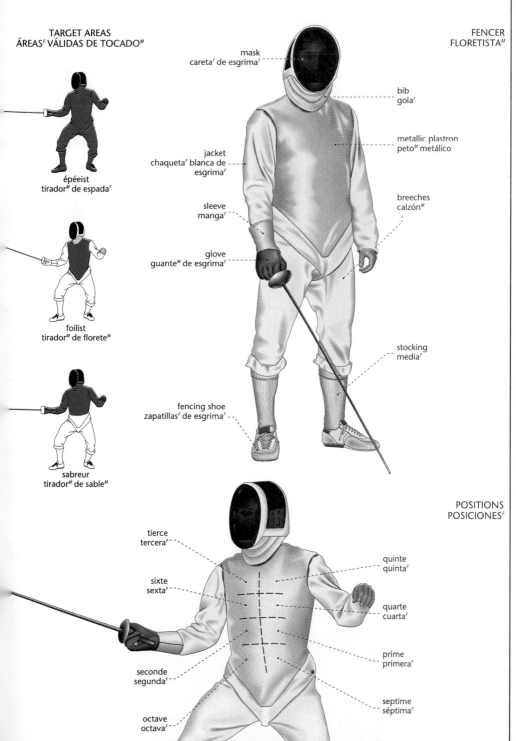

TARGET AREAS
ÁREAS^F VÁLIDAS DE TOCADO^M

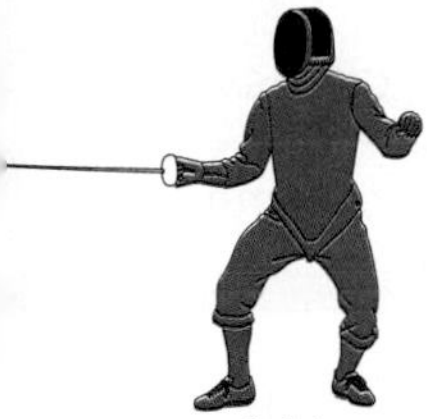

épéeist
tirador^M de espada^F

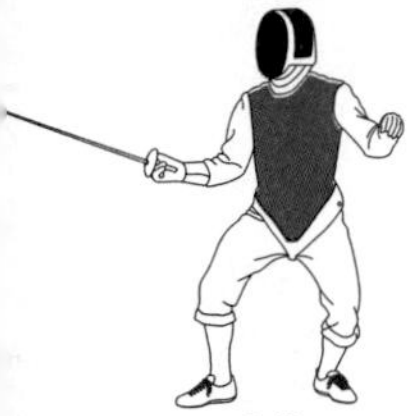

foilist
tirador^M de florete^M

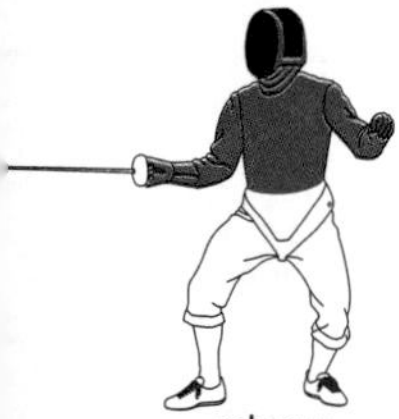

sabreur
tirador^M de sable^M

FENCER
FLORETISTA^M

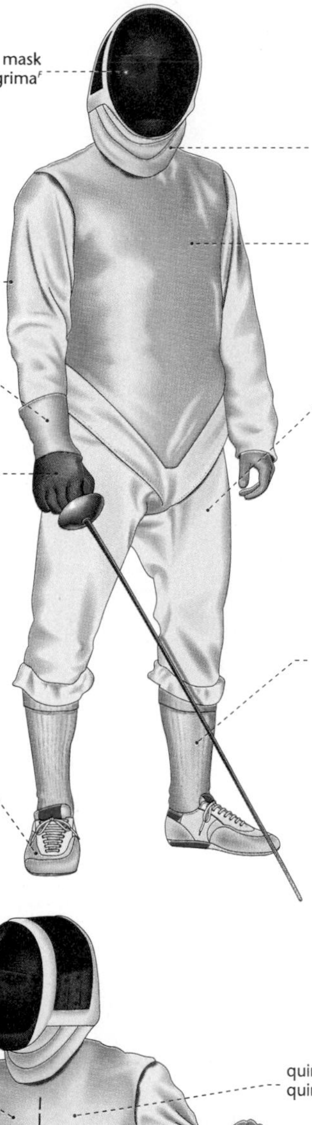

mask
careta^F de esgrima^F

bib
gola^F

metallic plastron
peto^M metálico

jacket
chaqueta^F blanca de
esgrima^F

sleeve
manga^F

glove
guante^M de esgrima^F

breeches
calzón^M

stocking
media^F

fencing shoe
zapatillas^F de esgrima^F

POSITIONS
POSICIONES^F

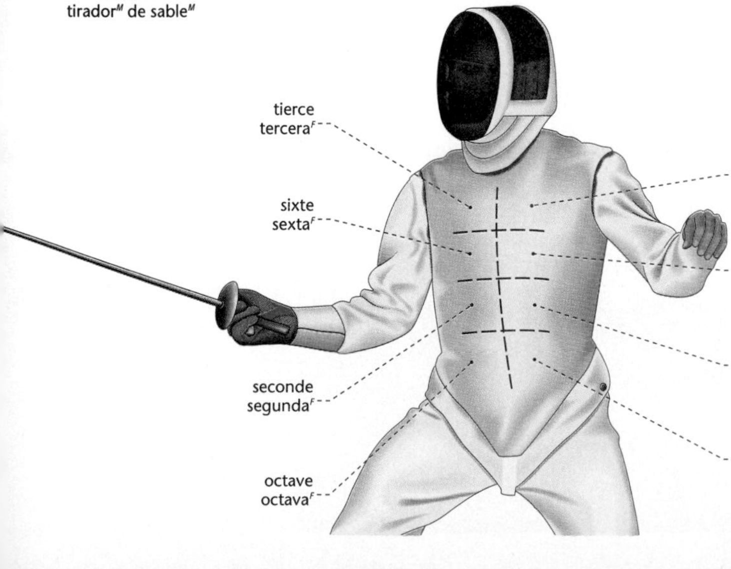

tierce
tercera^F

quinte
quinta^F

sixte
sexta^F

quarte
cuarta^F

prime
primera^F

seconde
segunda^F

septime
séptima^F

octave
octava^F

JUDO
JUDO^M

JUDO SUIT
JUDOKA^M

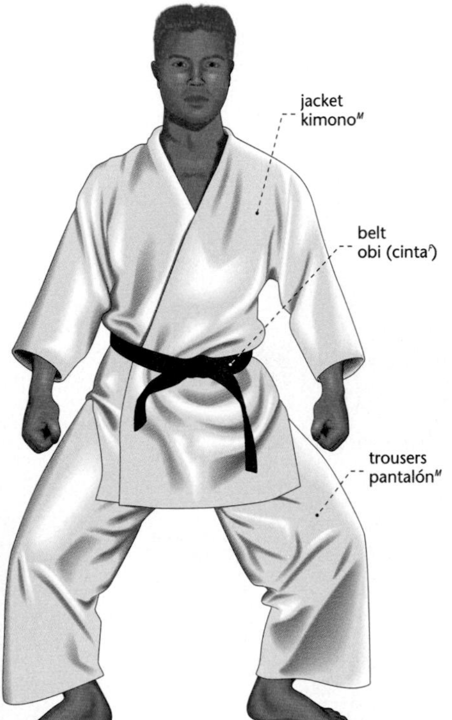

jacket
kimono^M

belt
obi (cinta^F)

trousers
pantalón^M

EXAMPLES OF HOLDS
EJEMPLOS^M DE LLAVES^F

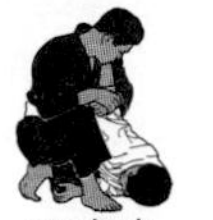

arm lock
presa^F de brazo^M

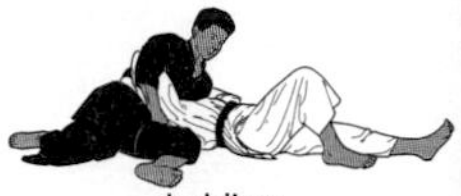

holding
presa^F

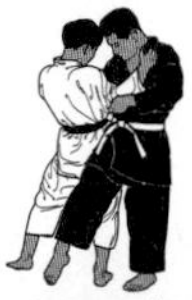

major outer reaping throw
osoto-gari (gran siega^F) exterior

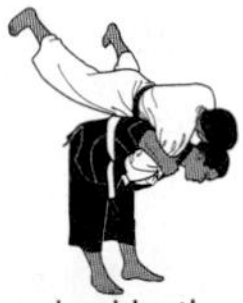

one-arm shoulder throw
ippon-seoi-nage (proyección^F)
por encima del hombro^M con
una mano^F

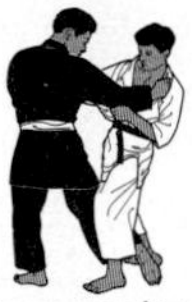

major inner reaping throw
o-uchi-gari (gran siega^F) interior

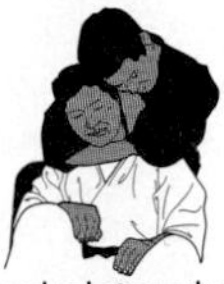

naked strangle
estrangulación^F

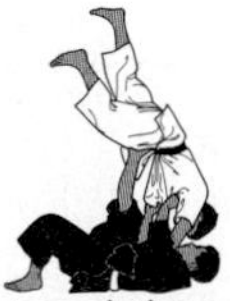

stomach throw
proyección^F en círculo^M

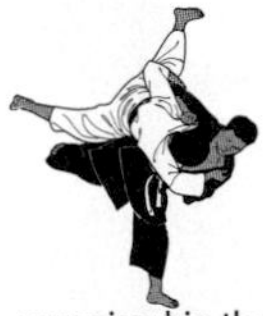

sweeping hip throw
proyección^F primera de
cadera^F

MAT
TATAMI^M

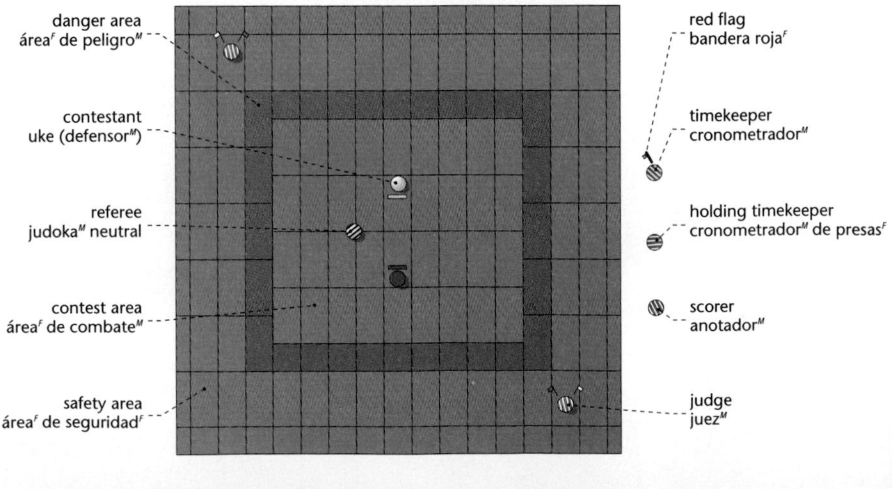

danger area
área^F de peligro^M

contestant
uke (defensor^M)

referee
judoka^M neutral

contest area
área^F de combate^M

safety area
área^F de seguridad^F

red flag
bandera roja^F

timekeeper
cronometrador^M

holding timekeeper
cronometrador^M de presas^F

scorer
anotador^M

judge
juez^M

668

BOXING
BOXEO^M

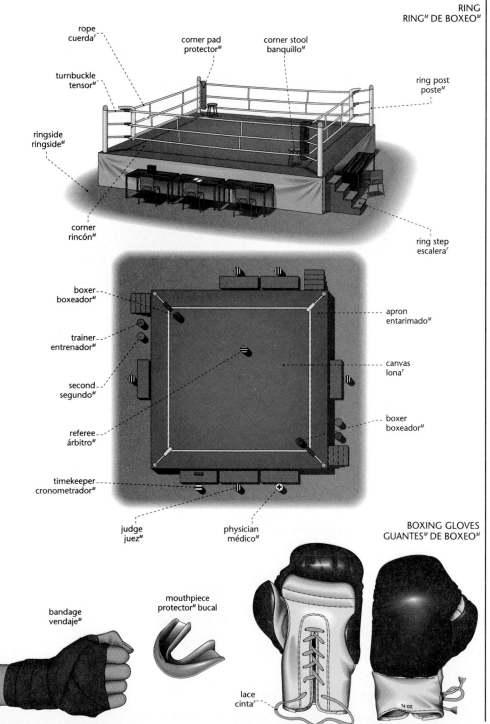

RING
RING^M DE BOXEO^M

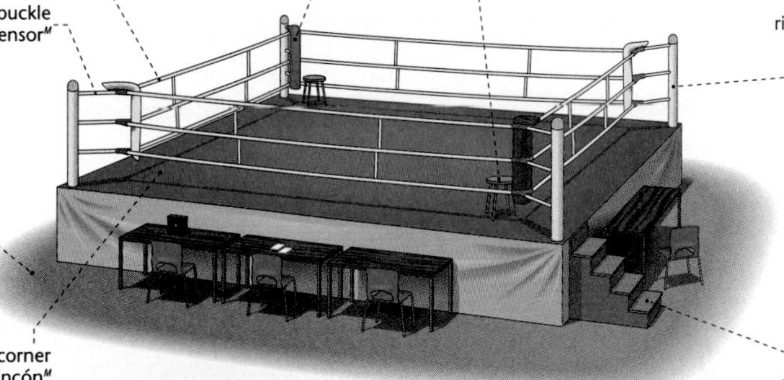

rope
cuerda^F

corner pad
protector^M

corner stool
banquillo^M

turnbuckle
tensor^M

ring post
poste^M

ringside
ringside^M

corner
rincón^M

ring step
escalera^F

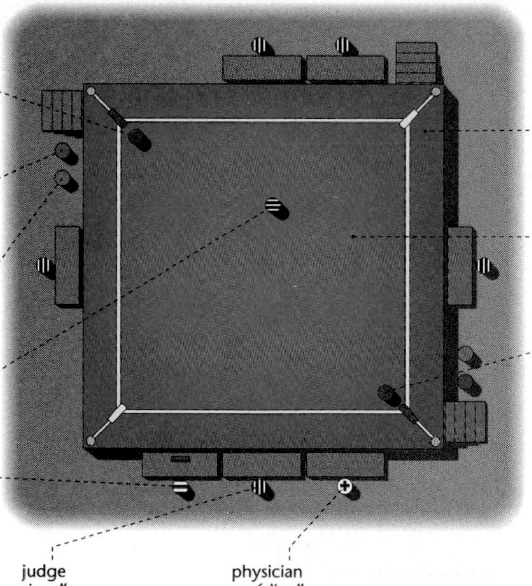

boxer
boxeador^M

apron
entarimado^M

trainer
entrenador^M

canvas
lona^F

second
segundo^M

referee
árbitro^M

boxer
boxeador^M

timekeeper
cronometrador^M

judge
juez^M

physician
médico^M

BOXING GLOVES
GUANTES^M DE BOXEO^M

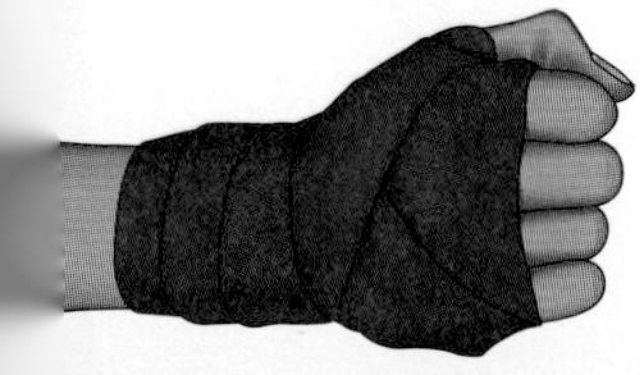

bandage
vendaje^M

mouthpiece
protector^M bucal

lace
cinta^F

14 OZ

669

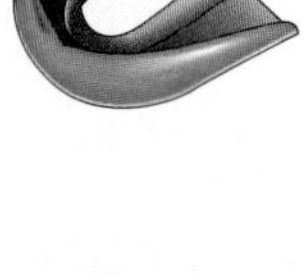

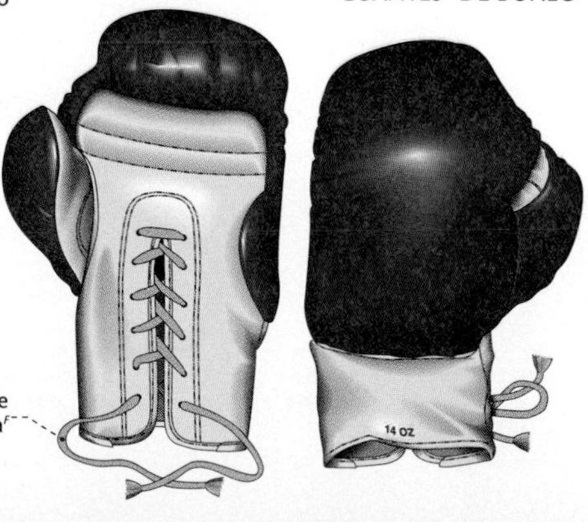

FISHING
PESCA^F

FLY ROD
CAÑA^F PARA MOSCA^F

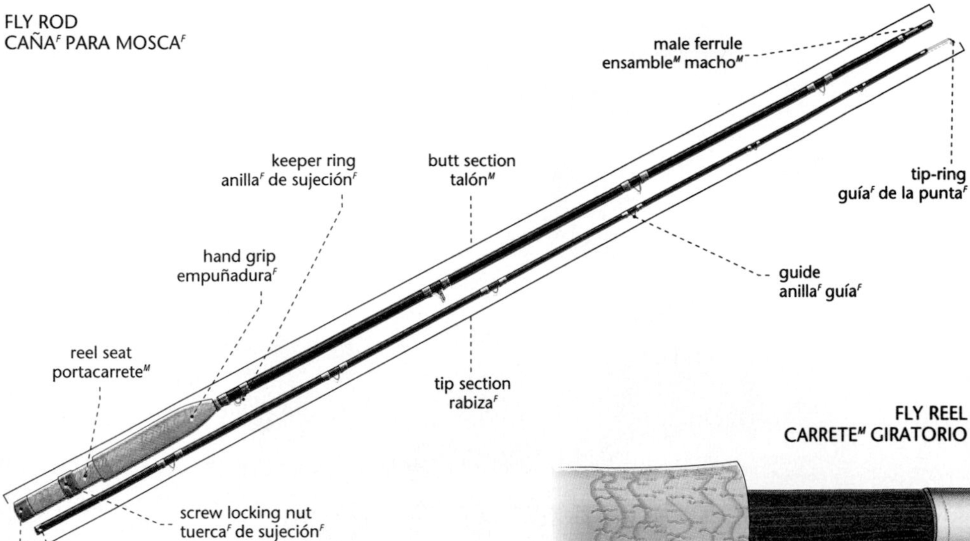

male ferrule
ensamble^M macho^M

keeper ring
anilla^F de sujeción^F

butt section
talón^M

tip-ring
guía^F de la punta^F

hand grip
empuñadura^F

guide
anilla^F guía^F

reel seat
portacarrete^M

tip section
rabiza^F

screw locking nut
tuerca^F de sujeción^F

female ferrule
ensamble^M hembra^F

butt cap
contera^F

FLY REEL
CARRETE^M GIRATORIO

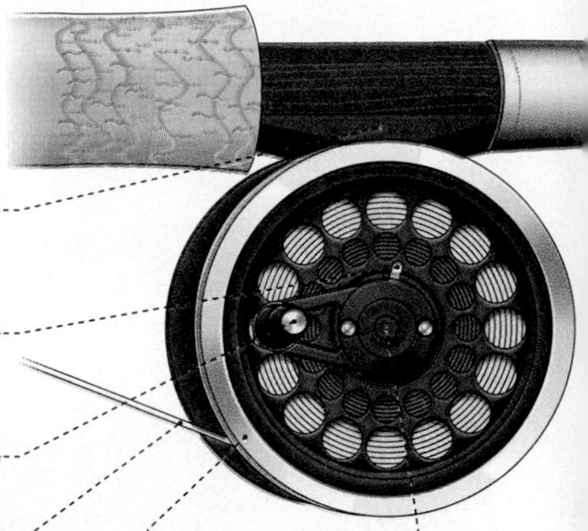

foot
pie^M

catch
matraca^F

handle
manivela^F

fly line
sedal^M

spool
bobina^F

drag
freno^M

ARTIFICIAL FLY
MOSCA^F ARTIFICIAL

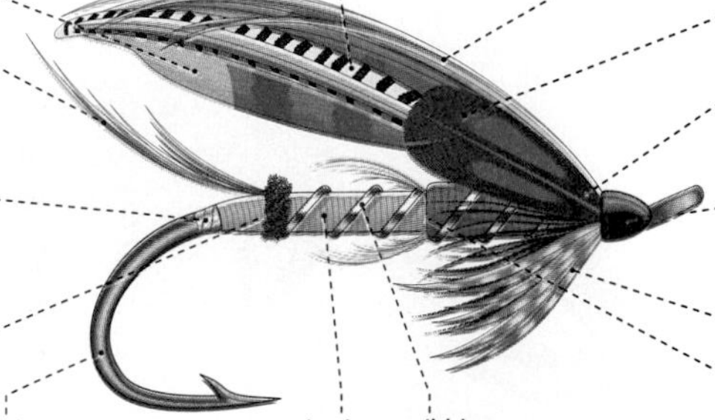

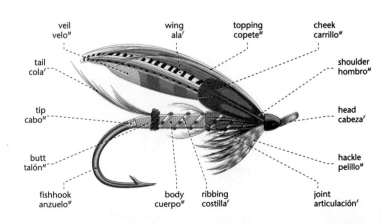

veil
velo^M

wing
ala^F

topping
copete^M

cheek
carrillo^M

tail
cola^F

shoulder
hombro^M

tip
cabo^M

head
cabeza^F

butt
talón^M

hackle
pelillo^M

fishhook
anzuelo^M

body
cuerpo^M

ribbing
costilla^F

joint
articulación^F

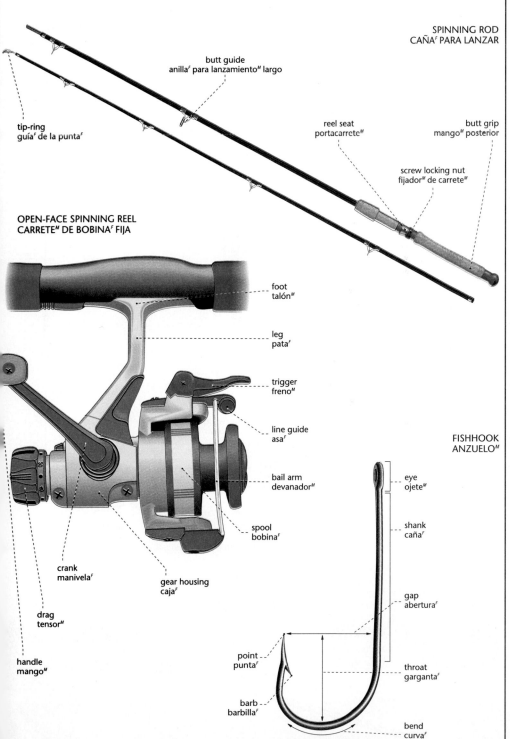

SPINNING ROD
CAÑA^F PARA LANZAR

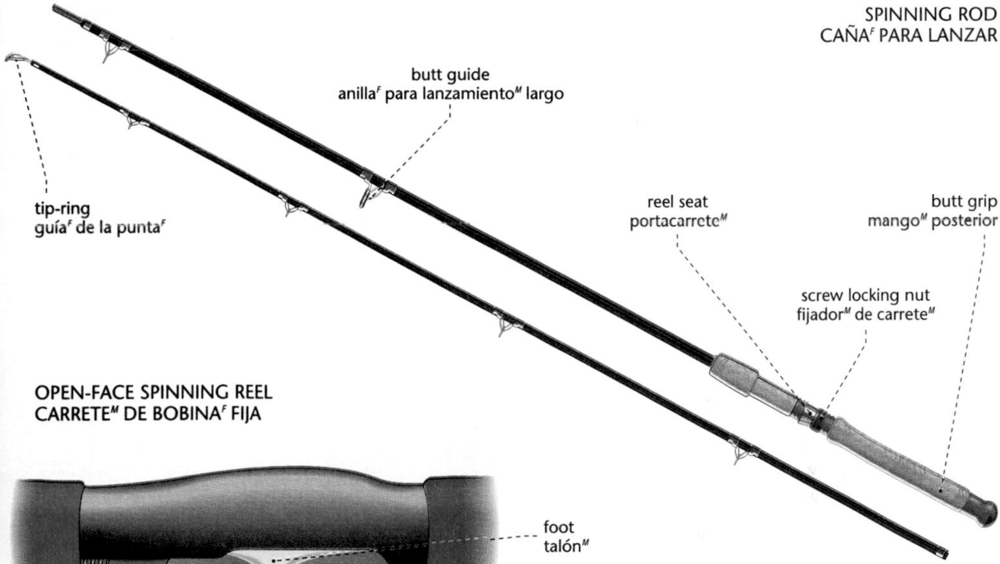

butt guide
anilla^F para lanzamiento^M largo

tip-ring
guía^F de la punta^F

reel seat
portacarrete^M

butt grip
mango^M posterior

screw locking nut
fijador^M de carrete^M

OPEN-FACE SPINNING REEL
CARRETE^M DE BOBINA^F FIJA

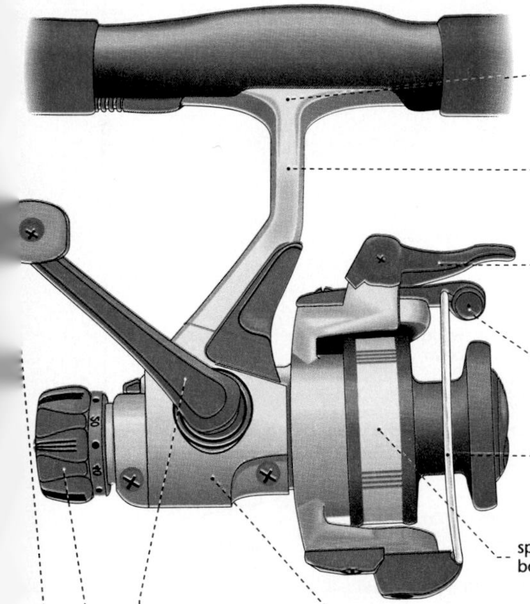

foot
talón^M

leg
pata^F

trigger
freno^M

line guide
asa^F

bail arm
devanador^M

spool
bobina^F

gear housing
caja^F

crank
manivela^F

drag
tensor^M

handle
mango^M

FISHHOOK
ANZUELO^M

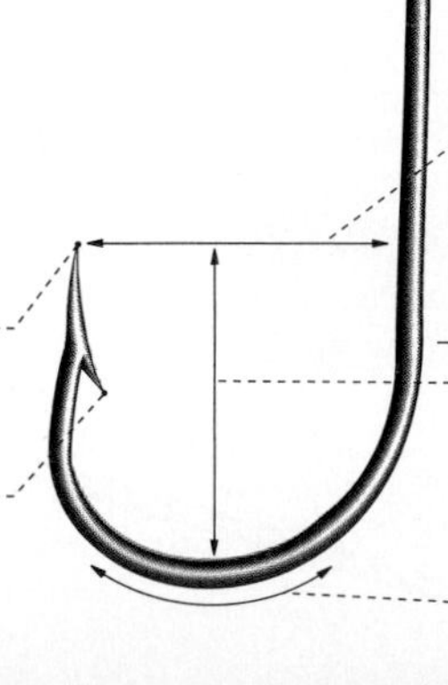

eye
ojete^M

shank
caña^F

gap
abertura^F

point
punta^F

throat
garganta^F

barb
barbilla^F

bend
curva^F

FISHING
PESCA^F

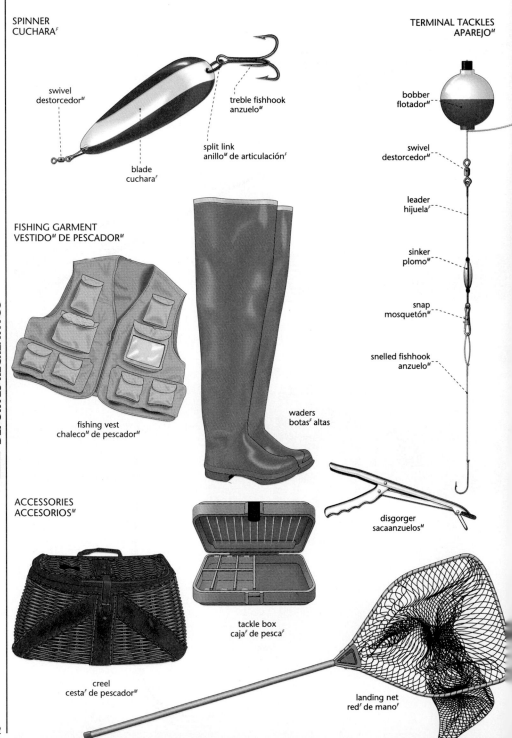

SPINNER
CUCHARA^F

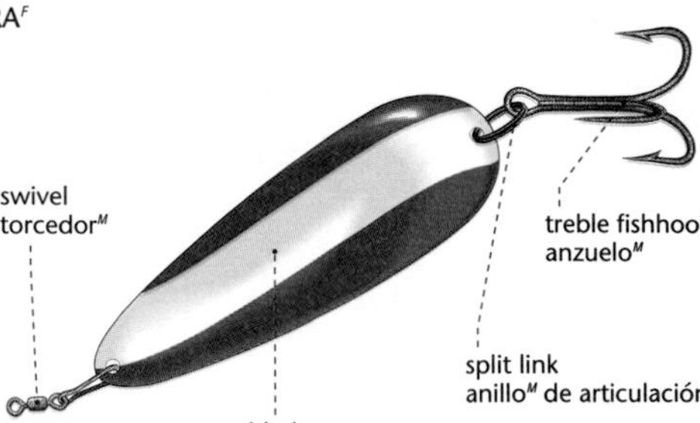

swivel
destorcedor^M

treble fishhook
anzuelo^M

split link
anillo^M de articulación^F

blade
cuchara^F

TERMINAL TACKLES
APAREJO^M

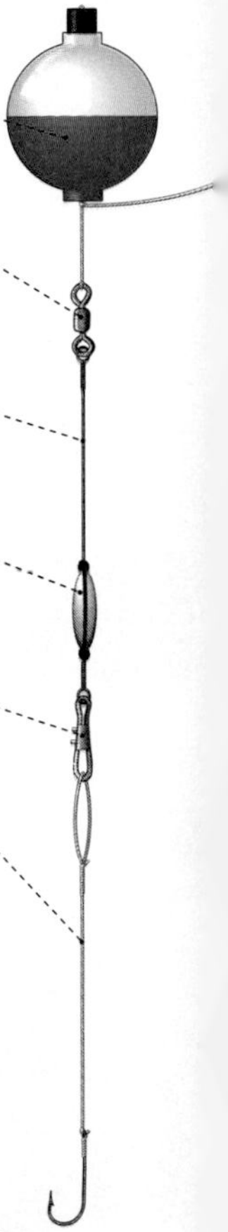

bobber
flotador^M

swivel
destorcedor^M

leader
hijuela^F

sinker
plomo^M

snap
mosquetón^M

snelled fishhook
anzuelo^M

FISHING GARMENT
VESTIDO^M DE PESCADOR^M

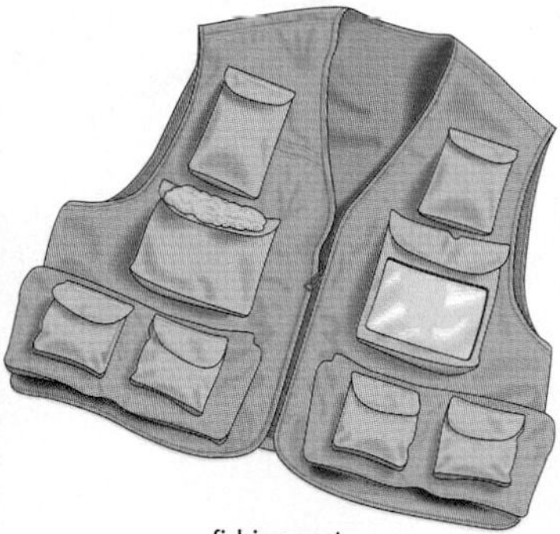

fishing vest
chaleco^M de pescador^M

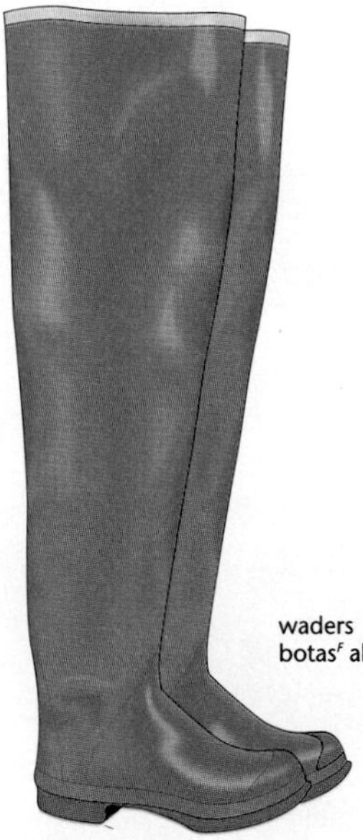

waders
botas^F altas

ACCESSORIES
ACCESORIOS^M

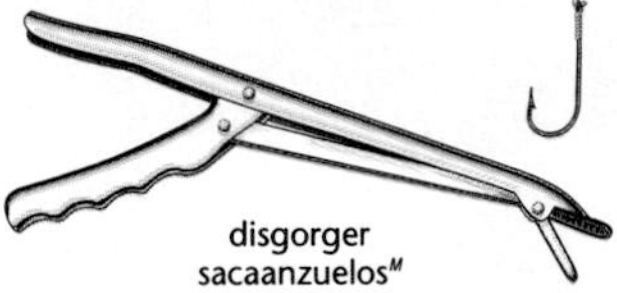

disgorger
sacaanzuelos^M

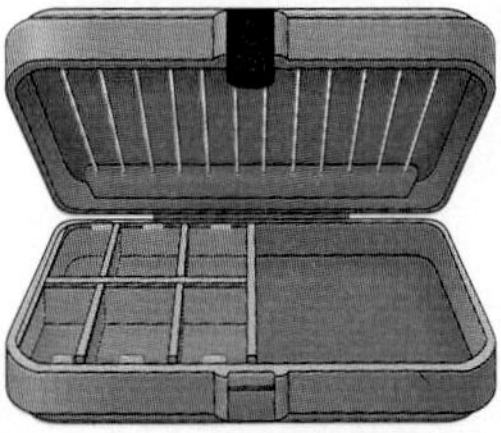

tackle box
caja^F de pesca^F

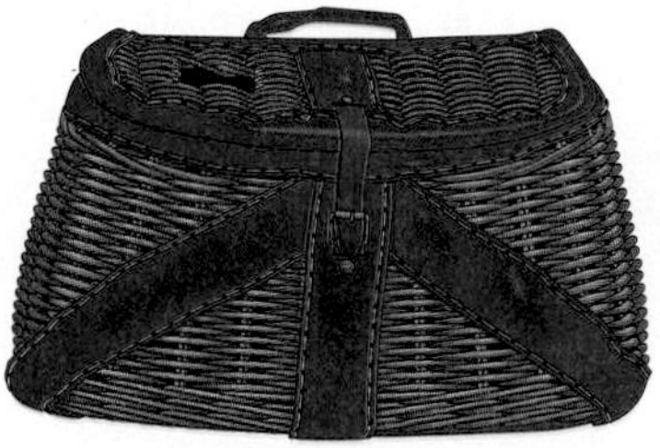

creel
cesta^F de pescador^M

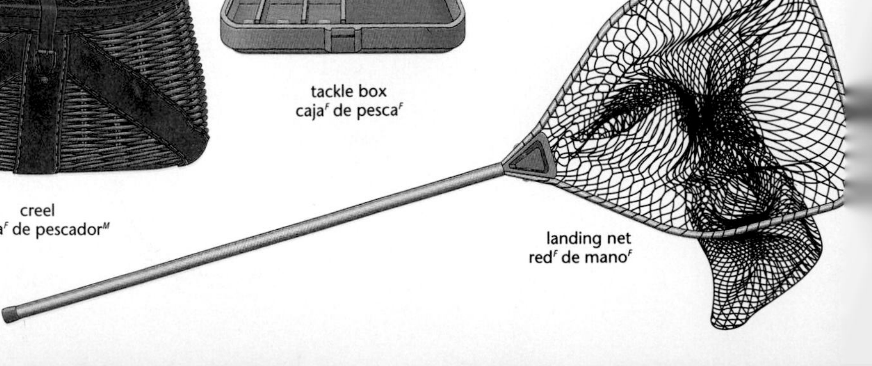

landing net
red^F de mano^F

BILLIARDS
BILLAR^M

CAROM BILLIARDS
CARAMBOLA^F

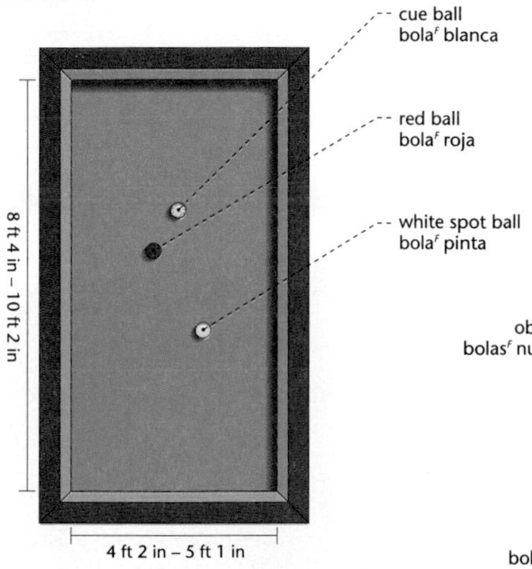

POOL
POOL^M

cue ball
bola^F blanca

red ball
bola^F roja

white spot ball
bola^F pinta

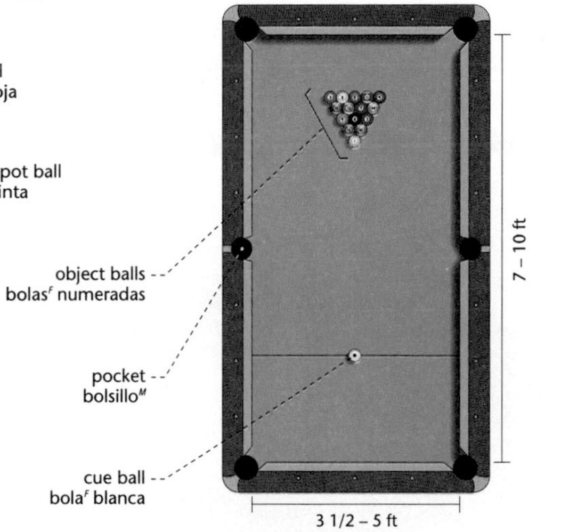

object balls
bolas^F numeradas

pocket
bolsillo^M

cue ball
bola^F blanca

8 ft 4 in – 10 ft 2 in

4 ft 2 in – 5 ft 1 in

7 – 10 ft

3 1/2 – 5 ft

ENGLISH BILLIARDS
BILLAR^M INGLÉS

SNOOKER
SNOOKER^M

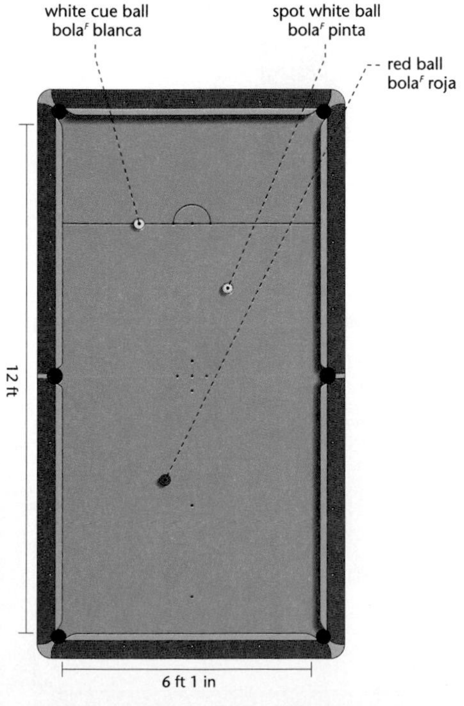

white cue ball
bola^F blanca

spot white ball
bola^F pinta

red ball
bola^F roja

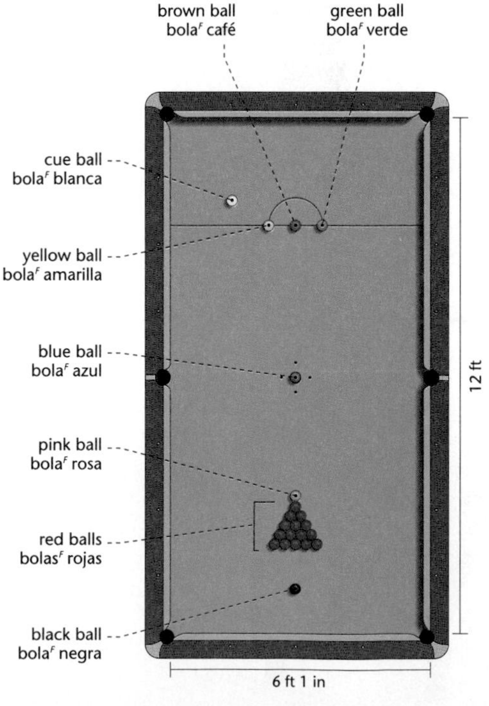

brown ball
bola^F café

green ball
bola^F verde

cue ball
bola^F blanca

yellow ball
bola^F amarilla

blue ball
bola^F azul

pink ball
bola^F rosa

red balls
bolas^F rojas

black ball
bola^F negra

12 ft

12 ft

6 ft 1 in

6 ft 1 in

TABLE
MESA^F

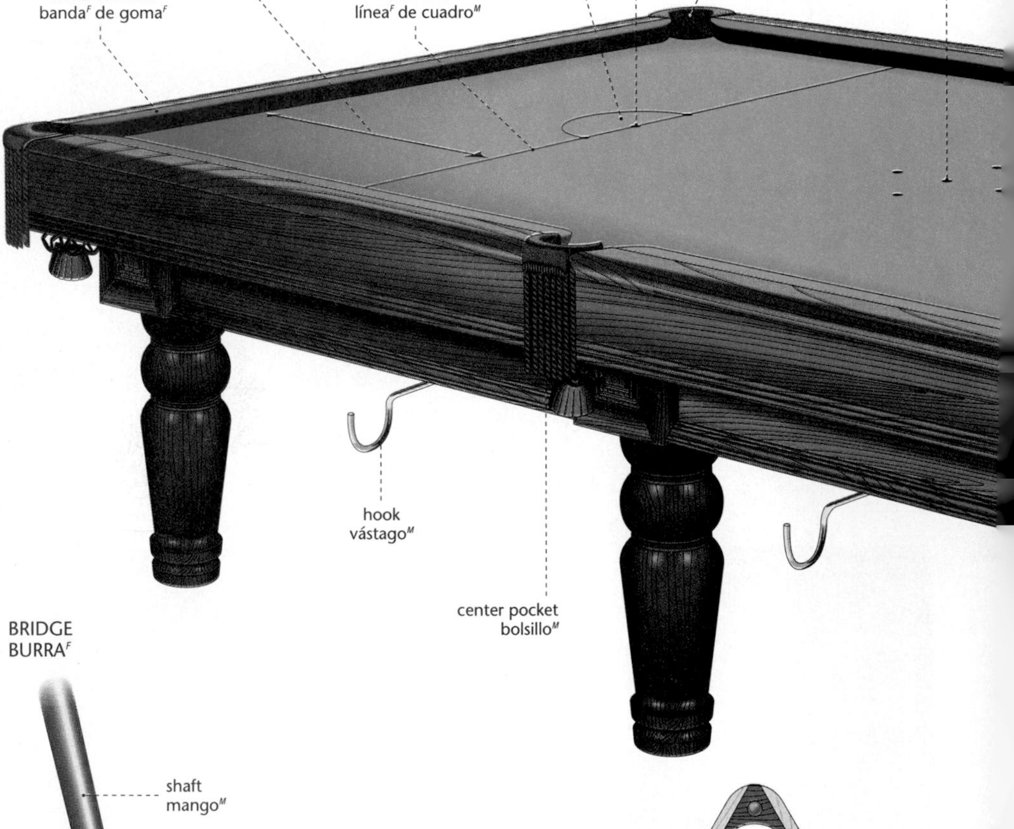

balk line spot
mosca^F de la línea^F de cuadro^M

center spot
mosca^F central

balk area
cuadro^M

«D»
semicírculo^M

bottom pocket
bolsillo^M

head cushion
banda^F de goma^F

balk line
línea^F de cuadro^M

hook
vástago^M

center pocket
bolsillo^M

BRIDGE
BURRA^F

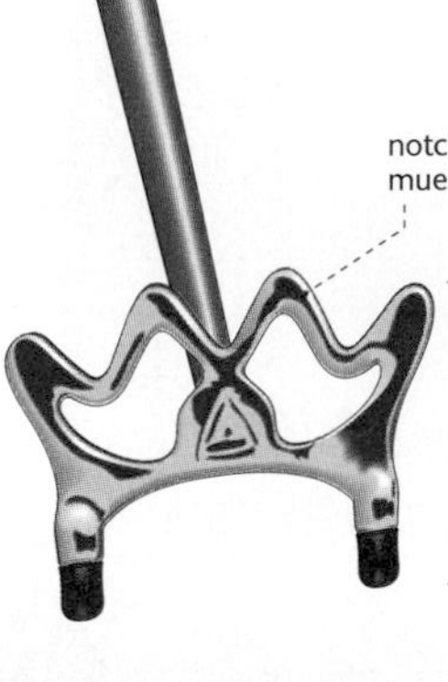

shaft
mango^M

notch
muesca^F

rack
triángulo^M

end-piece
cabeza^F

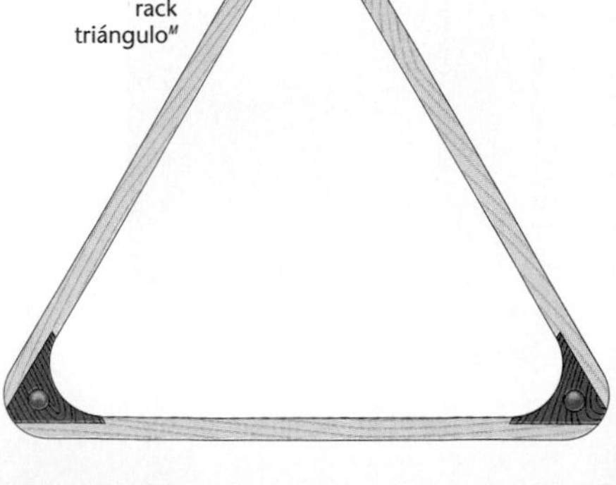

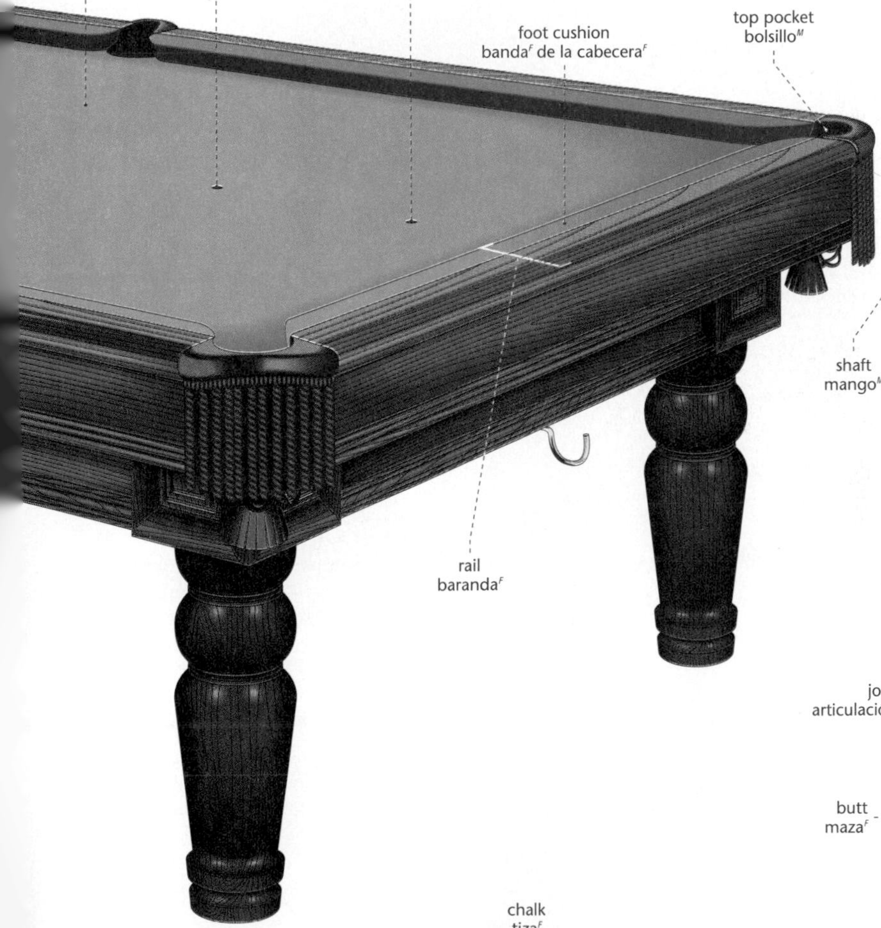

baize
tapete^M

pyramid spot
mosca^F superior

billiard spot
mosca^F

foot cushion
banda^F de la cabecera^F

top pocket
bolsillo^M

tip
suela^F

ferrule
casquillo^M

shaft
mango^M

rail
baranda^F

joint
articulación^F

butt
maza^F

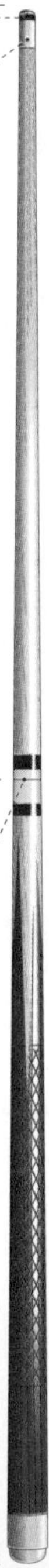

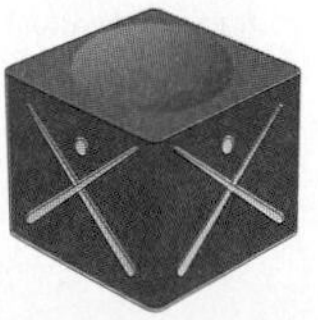

chalk
tiza^F

GOLF
ACCESORIOS^M DE GOLF^M

COURSE
CAMPO^M DE GOLF^M

cart path
vereda^F

putting green
césped^M

hole
zona^F del hoyo^M

clubhouse
casa^F club^M

practice green
green^M de entrenamiento^M

fairway
pista^F

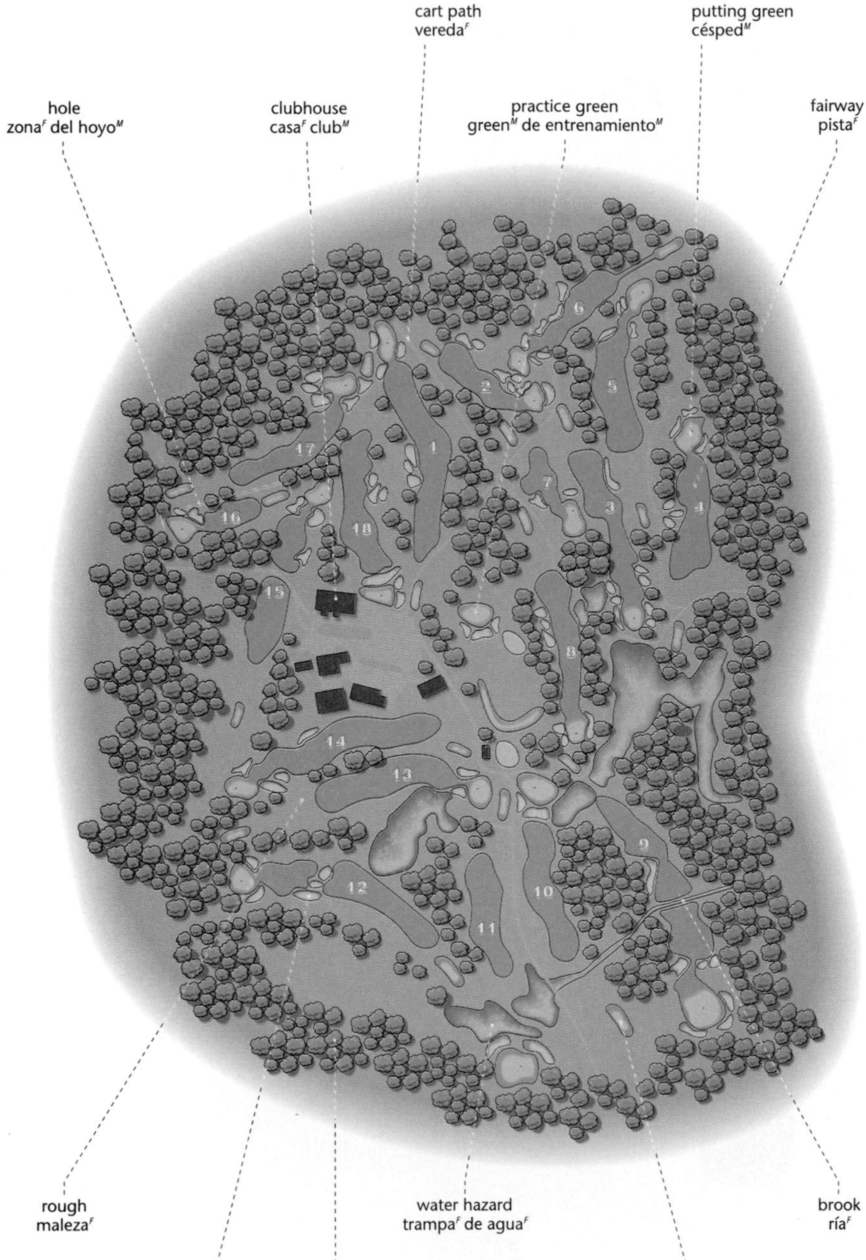

rough
maleza^F

water hazard
trampa^F de agua^F

brook
ría^F

bunker
trampa^F de arena^F

trees
árboles^M

teeing ground
punto^M de salida^F

CROSS SECTION OF A GOLF BALL
CORTE^M TRANSVERSAL DE UNA PELOTA^F DE GOLF^M

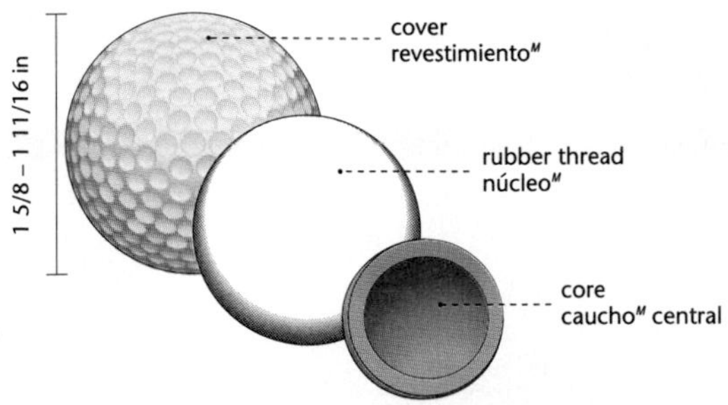

1 5/8 – 1 11/16 in

cover
revestimiento^M

rubber thread
núcleo^M

core
caucho^M central

GOLF BALL
PELOTA^F DE GOLF^M

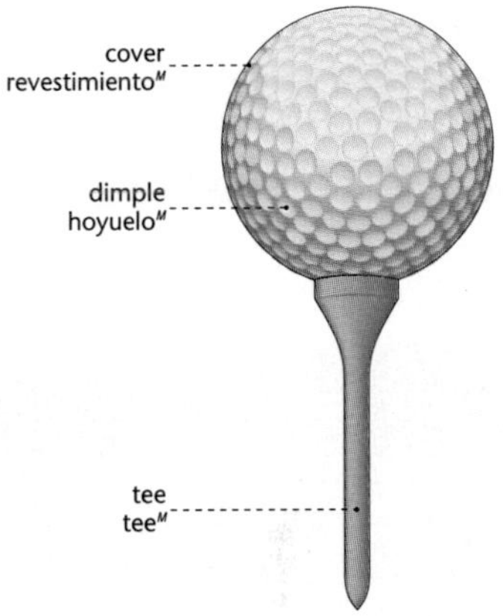

cover
revestimiento^M

dimple
hoyuelo^M

tee
tee^M

grip
empuñadura^F

TYPES OF GOLF CLUBS
BASTONES^M

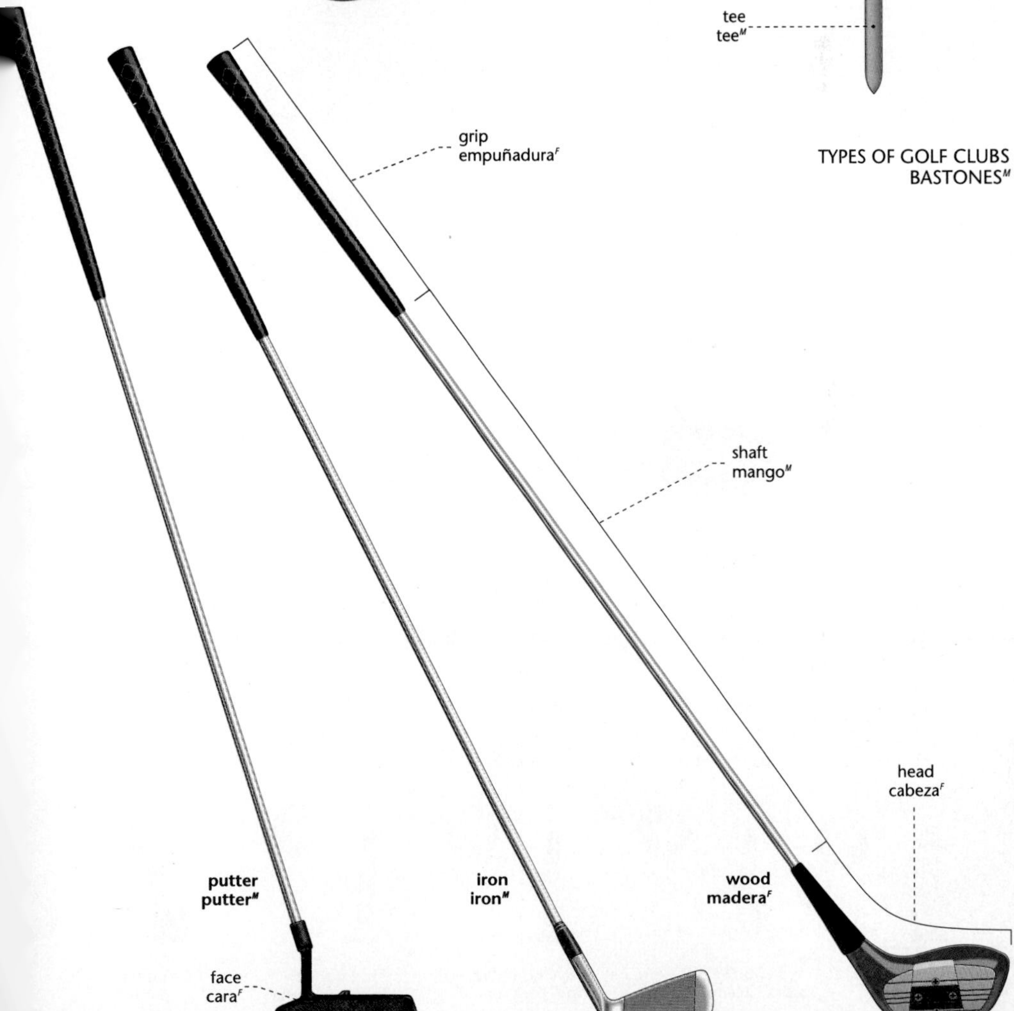

shaft
mango^M

head
cabeza^F

putter
putter^M

iron
iron^M

wood
madera^F

face
cara^F

677

WOOD
PALO^M

IRON
HIERRO^M

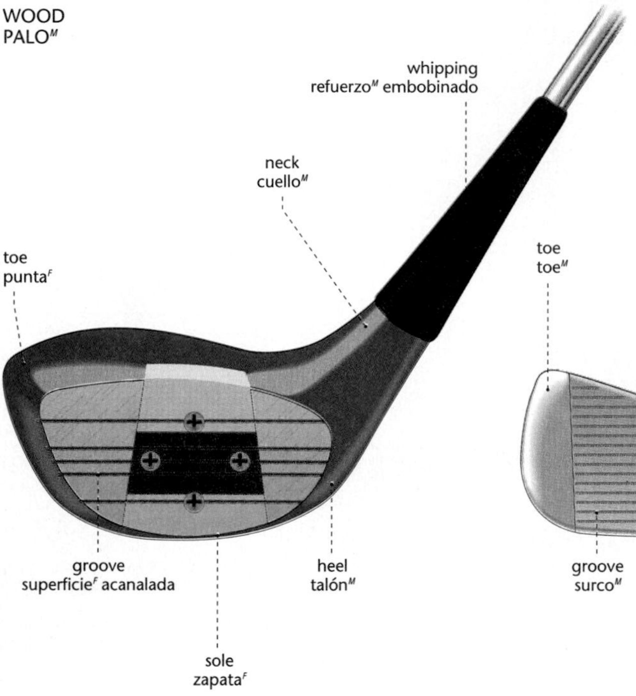

whipping
refuerzo^M embobinado

neck
cuello^M

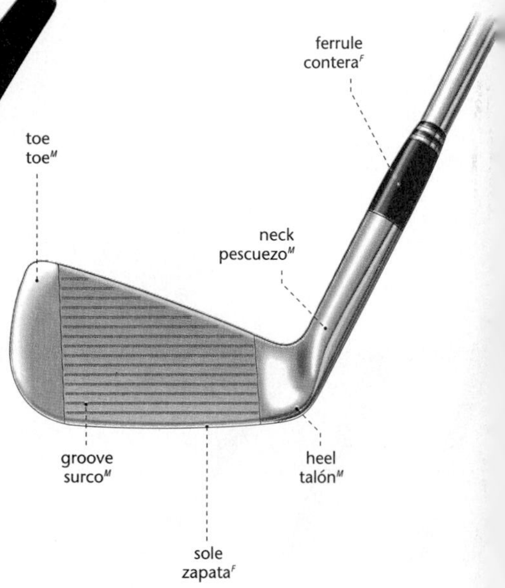

ferrule
contera^F

toe
punta^F

toe
toe^M

neck
pescuezo^M

groove
superficie^F acanalada

heel
talón^M

groove
surco^M

heel
talón^M

sole
zapata^F

sole
zapata^F

GOLF CLUBS
HIERROS^M Y PALOS^M

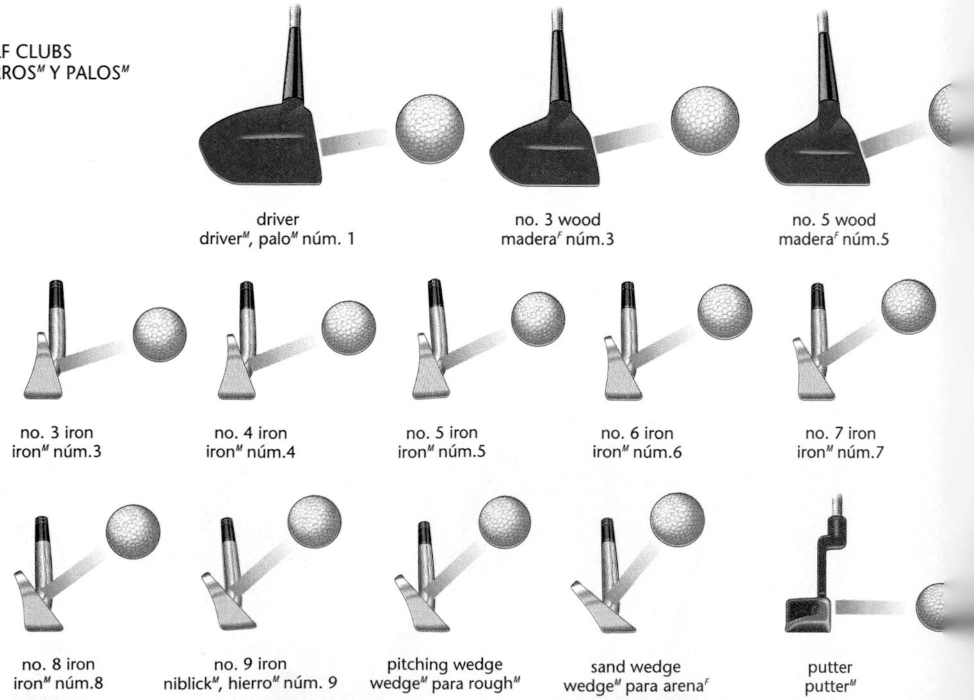

driver
driver^M, palo^M núm. 1

no. 3 wood
madera^F núm.3

no. 5 wood
madera^F núm.5

no. 3 iron
iron^M núm.3

no. 4 iron
iron^M núm.4

no. 5 iron
iron^M núm.5

no. 6 iron
iron^M núm.6

no. 7 iron
iron^M núm.7

no. 8 iron
iron^M núm.8

no. 9 iron
niblick^M, hierro^M núm. 9

pitching wedge
wedge^M para rough^M

sand wedge
wedge^M para arena^F

putter
putter^M

LEISURE SPORTS
DEPORTES RECREATIVOS

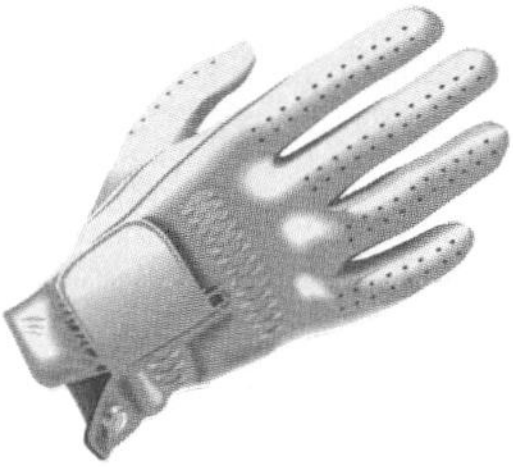

golf glove
guante^M de golf^M

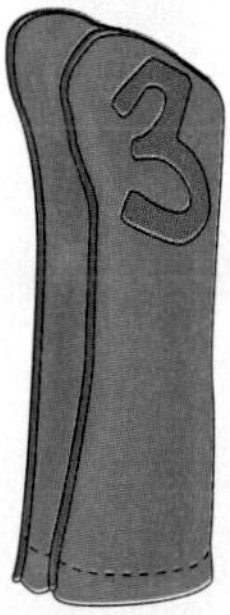

head cover
capuchón^M de bastones^M

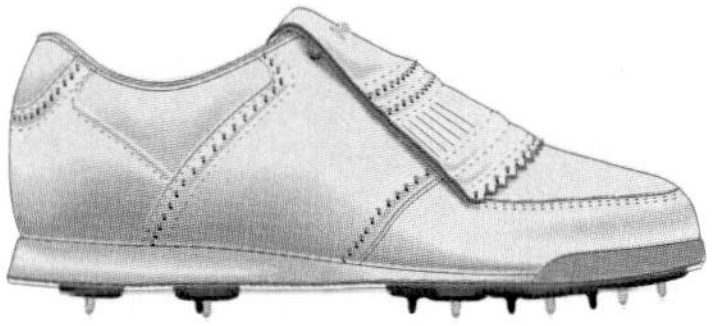

golf shoe
zapato^M de golf^M

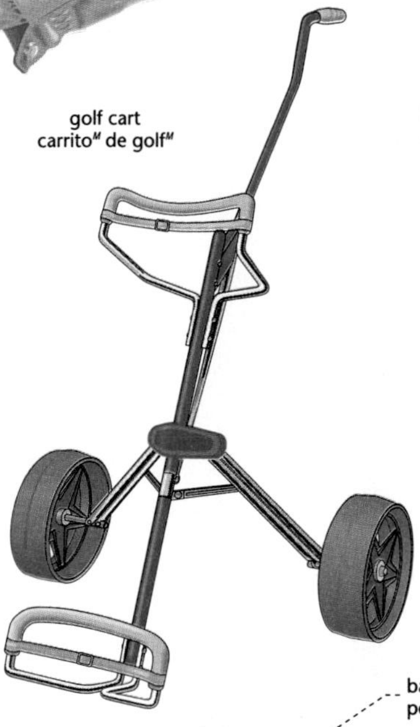

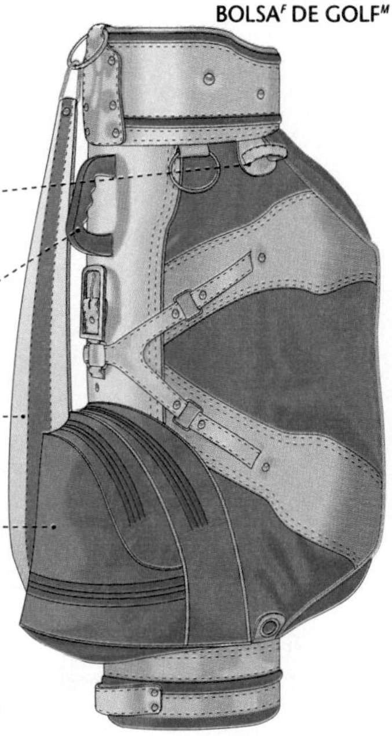

GOLF BAG
BOLSA^F DE GOLF^M

golf cart
carrito^M de golf^M

umbrella ring
portaparaguas^M

handle
empuñadura^F

shoulder strap
correa^F

pocket
bolsillo^M

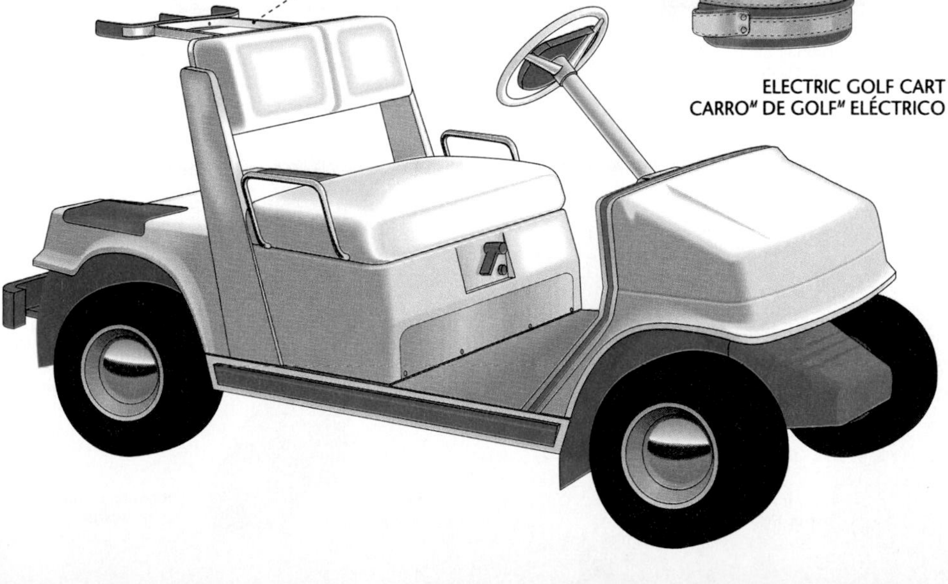

bag well
portabolsa^F

ELECTRIC GOLF CART
CARRO^M DE GOLF^M ELÉCTRICO

MOUNTAINEERING
ALPINISMO^M

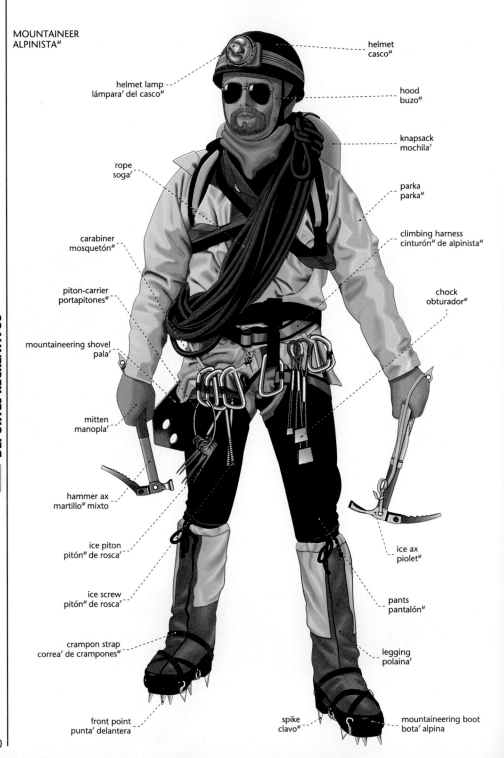

helmet
casco^M

helmet lamp
lámpara^F del casco^M

hood
buzo^M

knapsack
mochila^F

rope
soga^F

parka
parka^M

carabiner
mosquetón^M

climbing harness
cinturón^M de alpinista^M

piton-carrier
portapitones^M

chock
obturador^M

mountaineering shovel
pala^F

mitten
manopla^F

hammer ax
martillo^M mixto

ice piton
pitón^M de rosca^F

ice ax
piolet^M

ice screw
pitón^M de rosca^F

pants
pantalón^M

crampon strap
correa^F de crampones^M

legging
polaina^F

front point
punta^F delantera

spike
clavo^M

mountaineering boot
bota^F alpina

**LEISURE SPORTS
DEPORTES RECREATIVOS**

680

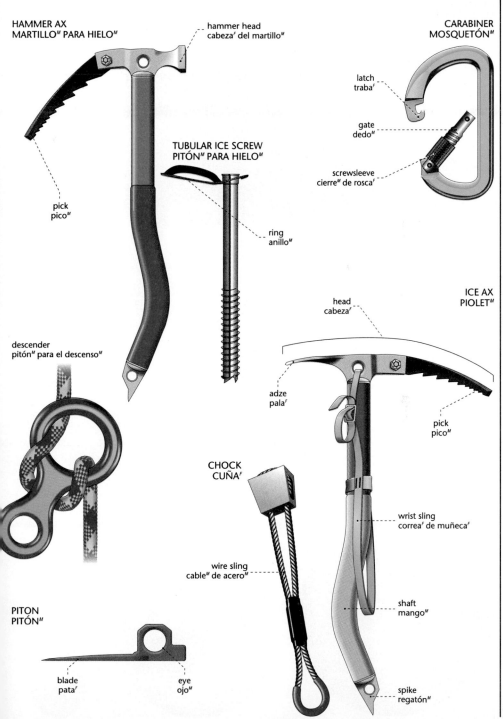

HAMMER AX
MARTILLO^M PARA HIELO^M

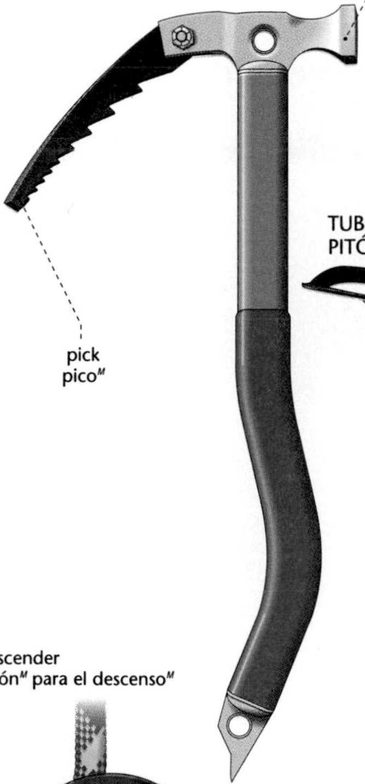

hammer head
cabeza^F del martillo^M

CARABINER
MOSQUETÓN^M

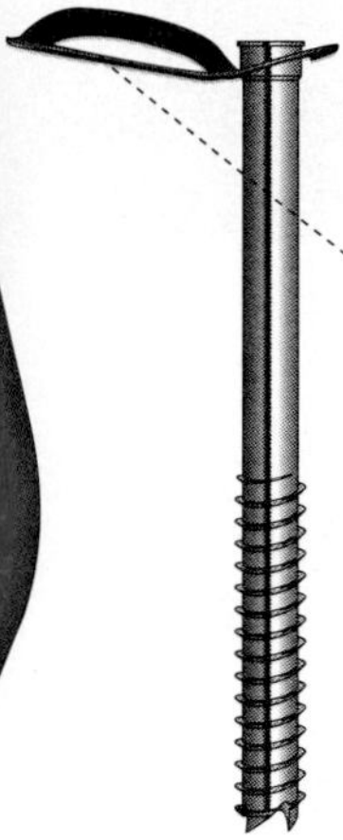

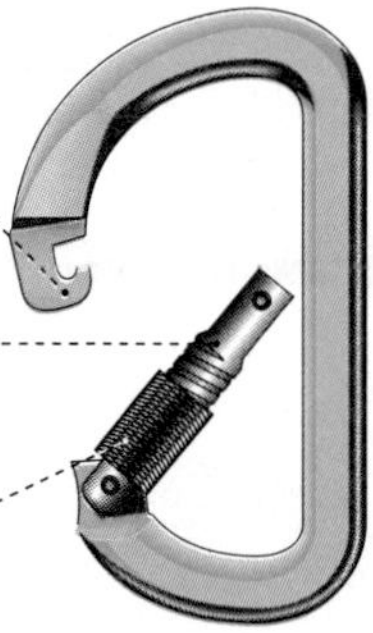

latch
traba^F

gate
dedo^M

screwsleeve
cierre^M de rosca^F

TUBULAR ICE SCREW
PITÓN^M PARA HIELO^M

pick
pico^M

ring
anillo^M

ICE AX
PIOLET^M

head
cabeza^F

descender
pitón^M para el descenso^M

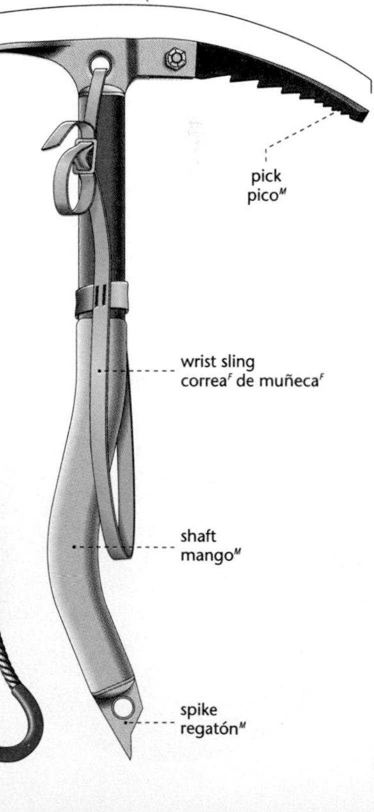

adze
pala^F

pick
pico^M

CHOCK
CUÑA^F

wrist sling
correa^F de muñeca^F

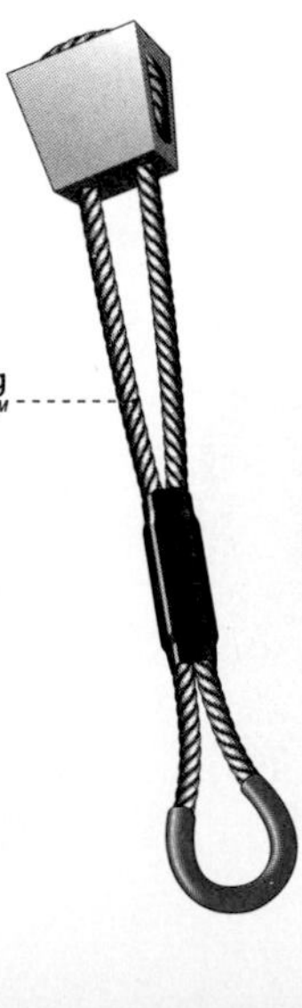

wire sling
cable^M de acero^M

shaft
mango^M

PITON
PITÓN^M

blade
pata^F

eye
ojo^M

spike
regatón^M

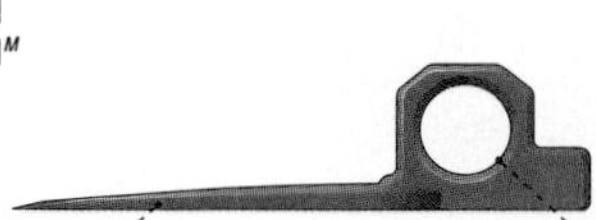

BOWLS AND PETANQUE
BOLOS^M Y PETANCA^F

GREEN
BOLERA^F EN EL CÉSPED^M

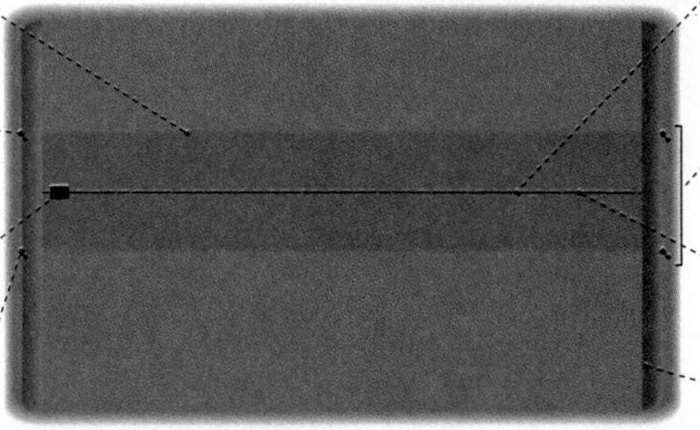

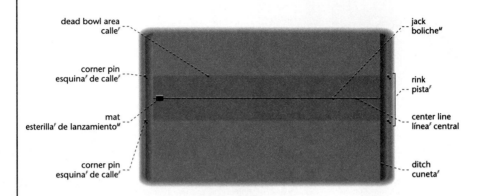

dead bowl area
calle^F

corner pin
esquina^F de calle^F

mat
esterilla^F de lanzamiento^M

corner pin
esquina^F de calle^F

jack
boliche^M

rink
pista^F

center line
línea^F central

ditch
cuneta^F

DELIVERY
LANZAMIENTO^M

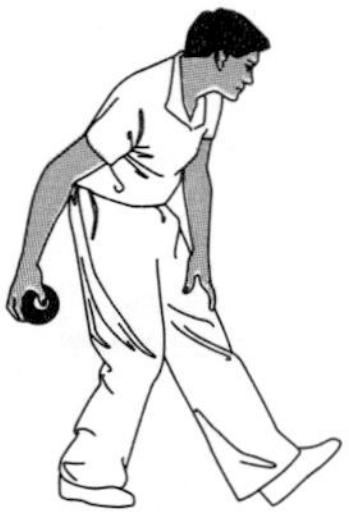

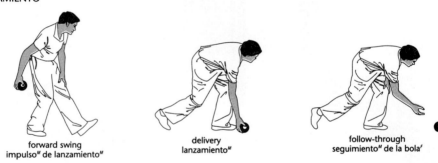

forward swing
impulso^M de lanzamiento^M

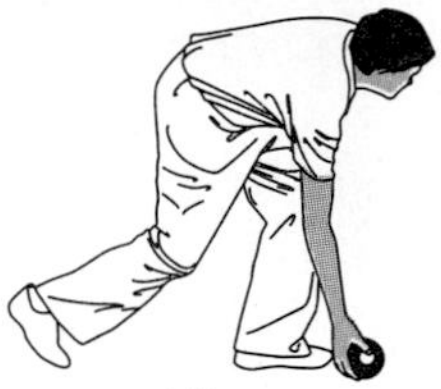

delivery
lanzamiento^M

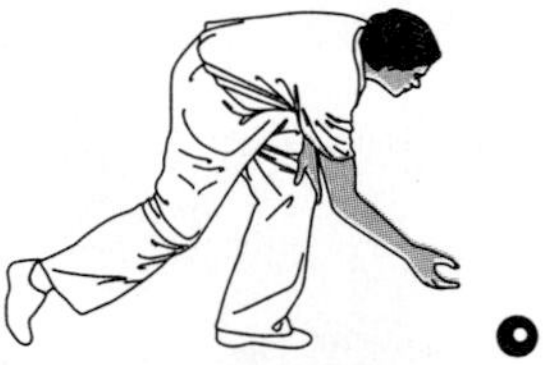

follow-through
seguimiento^M de la bola^F

bowl
bola^F

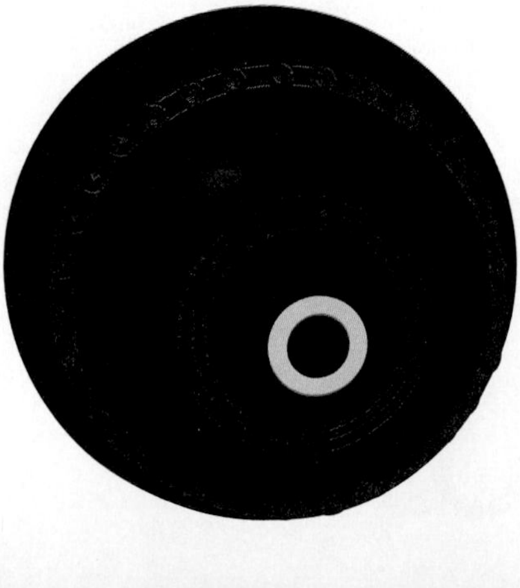

petanque bowl
bocha^F

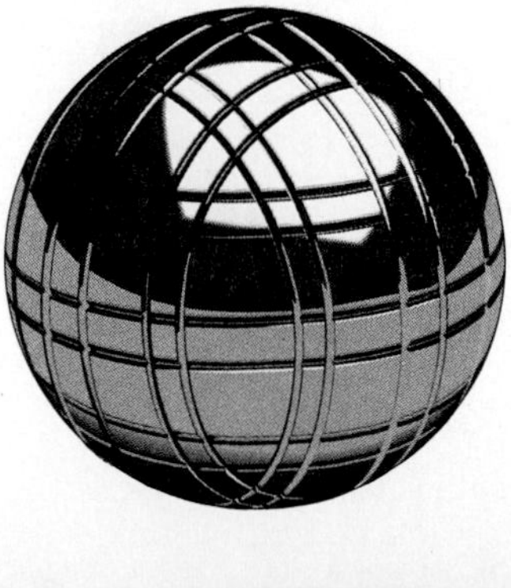

jack
boliche^M

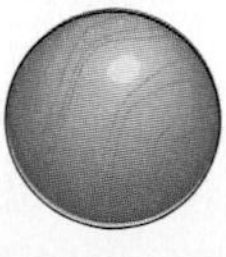

BOWLING
JUEGO^M DE BOLOS^M

BOWLING BALL
BOLA^F

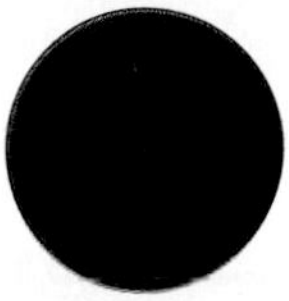

TYPES OF PINS
TIPOS^M DE BOLOS^M

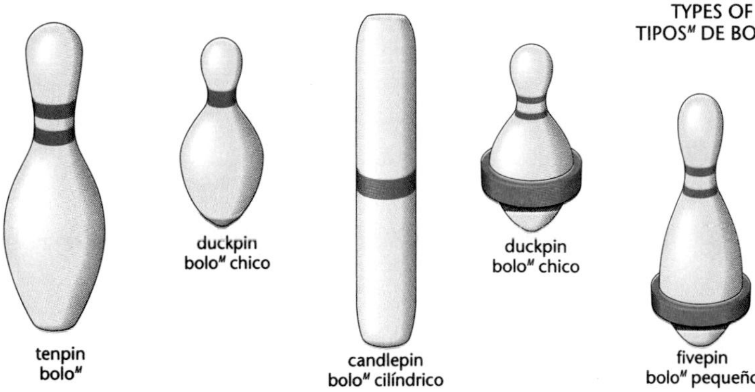

tenpin
bolo^M

duckpin
bolo^M chico

candlepin
bolo^M cilíndrico

duckpin
bolo^M chico

fivepin
bolo^M pequeño

SETUP
DISPOSICIÓN^F DE LOS BOLOS^M

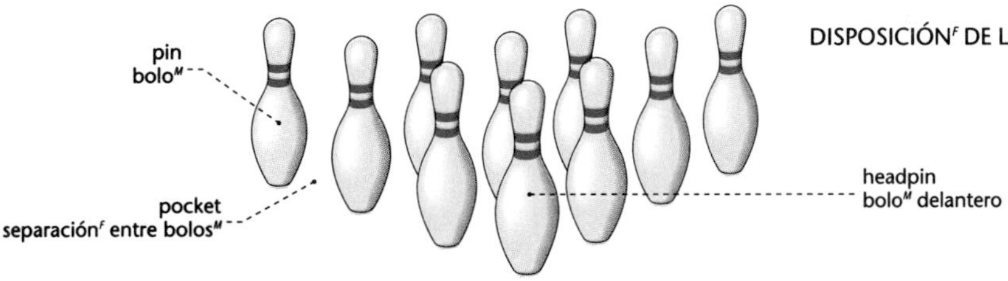

pin
bolo^M

pocket
separación^F entre bolos^M

headpin
bolo^M delantero

LANE
PISTA^F

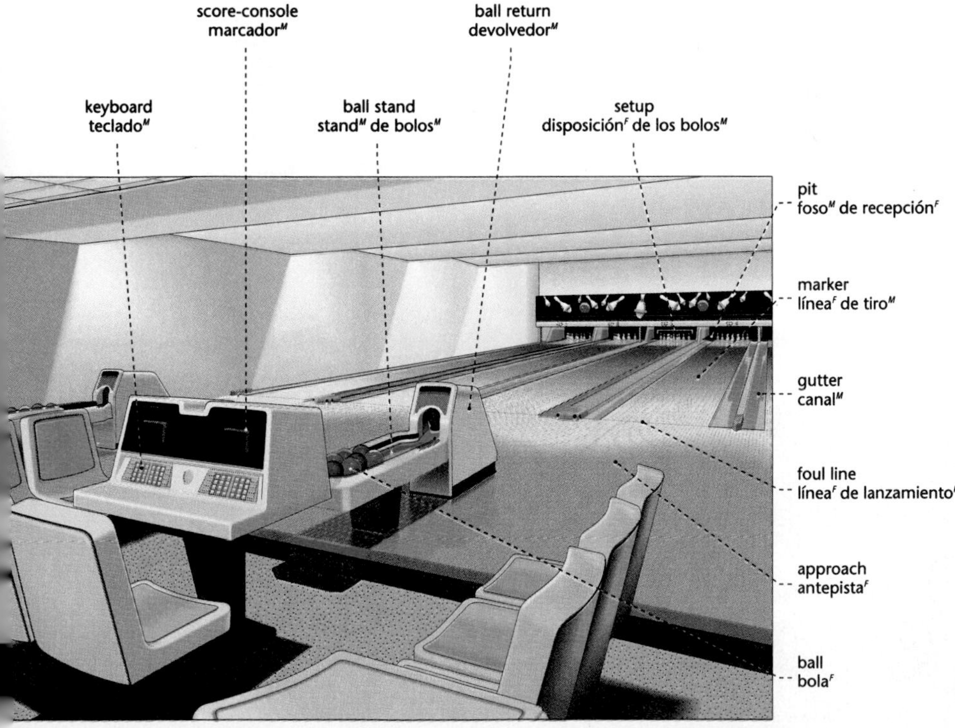

score-console
marcador^M

ball return
devolvedor^M

keyboard
teclado^M

ball stand
stand^M de bolos^M

setup
disposición^F de los bolos^M

pit
foso^M de recepción^F

marker
línea^F de tiro^M

gutter
canal^M

foul line
línea^F de lanzamiento^M

approach
antepista^F

ball
bola^F

ARCHERY
TIRO^M AL ARCO^M

ARROW
FLECHA^F

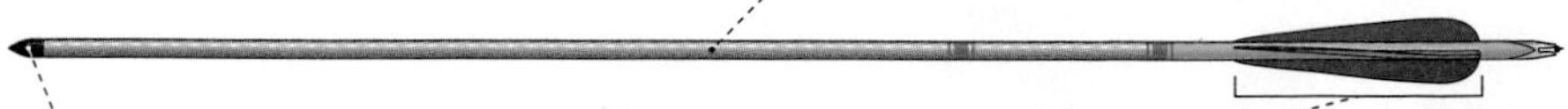

shaft
flecha^F

nock
muesca^F

point
punta^F

feathering
pluma^F de dirección^F

ARCHER
ARQUERO^M

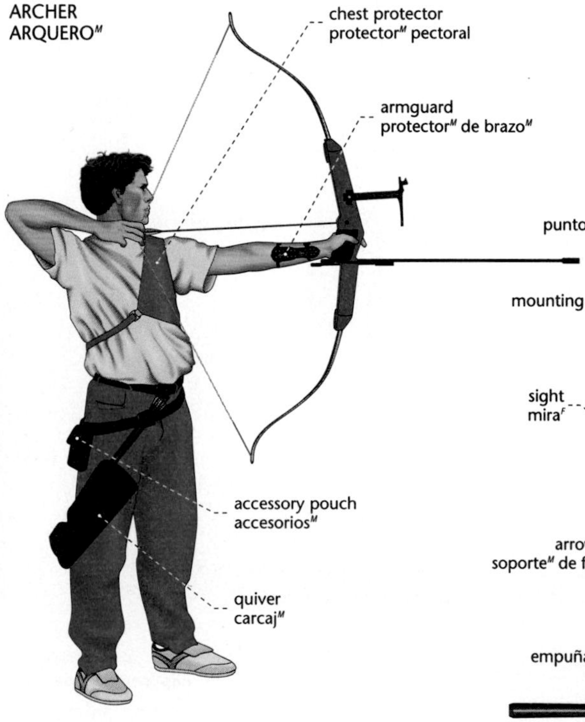

chest protector
protector^M pectoral

armguard
protector^M de brazo^M

COMPOUND BOW
ARCO^M DE COMPETICIÓN^F

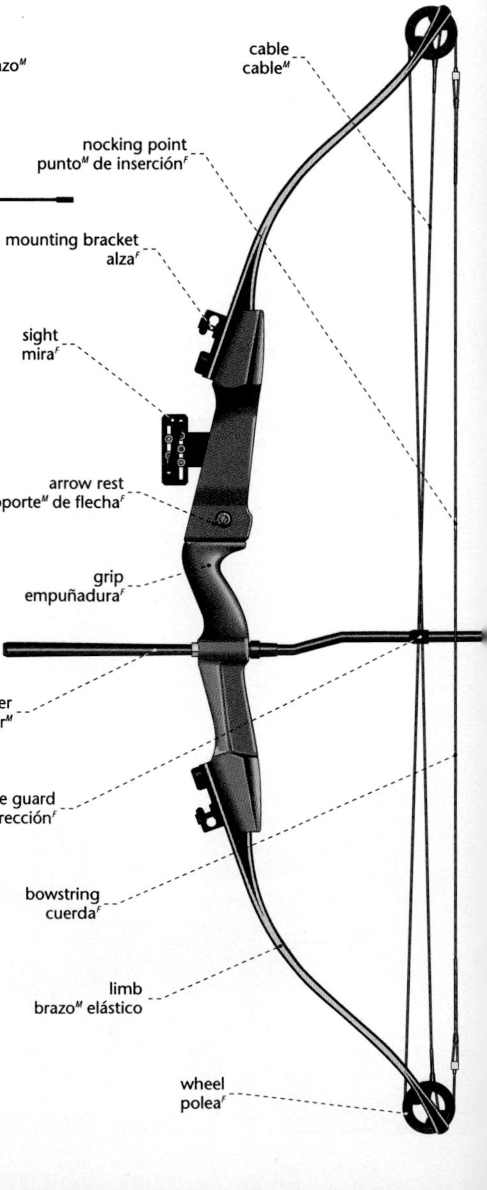

cable
cable^M

nocking point
punto^M de inserción^F

mounting bracket
alza^F

sight
mira^F

accessory pouch
accesorios^M

arrow rest
soporte^M de flecha^F

quiver
carcaj^M

grip
empuñadura^F

TARGET
BLANCO^M

stabilizer
estabilizador^M

cable guard
cable^M de dirección^F

bowstring
cuerda^F

bull's-eye
centro^M del blanco^M

limb
brazo^M elástico

wheel
polea^F

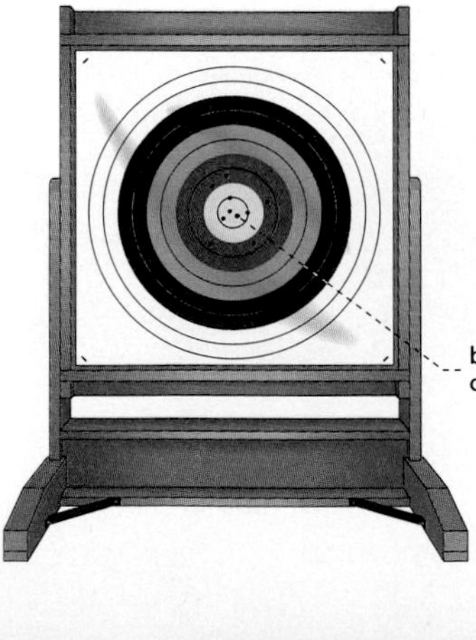

CAMPING
CAMPING^M

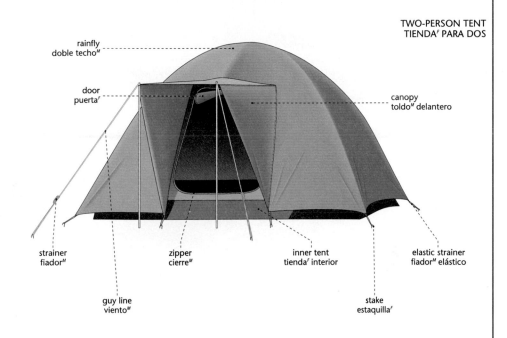

TWO-PERSON TENT
TIENDA^F PARA DOS

rainfly
doble techo^M

door
puerta^F

canopy
toldo^M delantero

strainer
fiador^M

zipper
cierre^M

inner tent
tienda^F interior

elastic strainer
fiador^M elástico

guy line
viento^M

stake
estaquilla^F

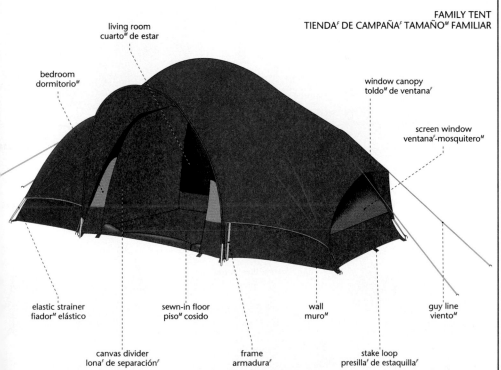

FAMILY TENT
TIENDA^F DE CAMPAÑA^F TAMAÑO^M FAMILIAR

living room
cuarto^M de estar

bedroom
dormitorio^M

window canopy
toldo^M de ventana^F

screen window
ventana^F-mosquitero^M

elastic strainer
fiador^M elástico

sewn-in floor
piso^M cosido

wall
muro^M

guy line
viento^M

canvas divider
lona^F de separación^F

frame
armadura^F

stake loop
presilla^F de estaquilla^F

685

PUP TENT
TIENDA^F DE CAMPAÑA^F CLÁSICA

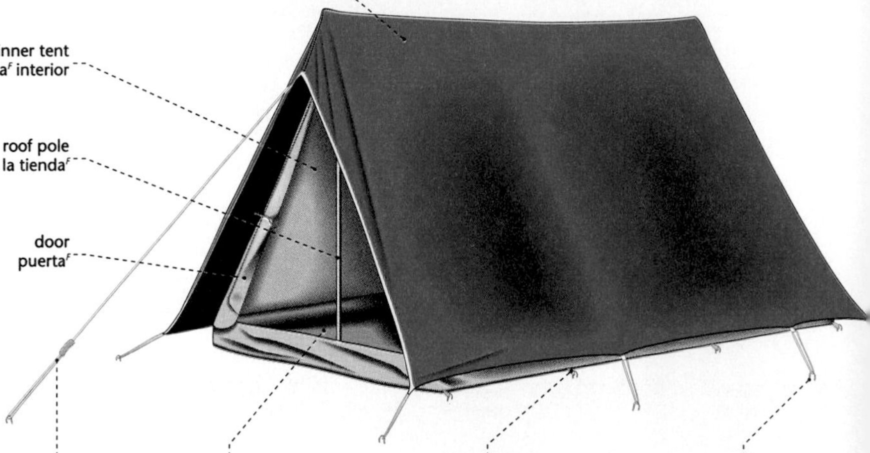

rainfly
doble toldo^M

inner tent
tienda^F interior

roof pole
palo^M de la tienda^F

door
puerta^F

elastic strainer
fiador^M elástico

sewn-in floor
piso^M cosido

stake loop
presilla^F de estaquilla^F

stake
estaquilla^F

MAJOR TYPES OF TENTS
TIPOS^M DE TIENDAS^F

wagon tent
tienda^F tipo^M vagón^M

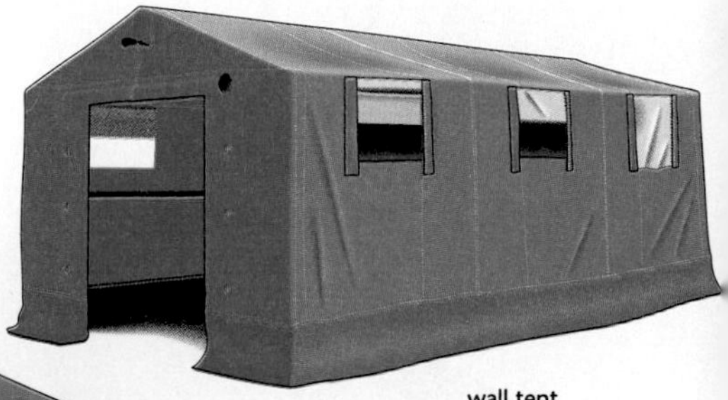

wall tent
tienda^F rectangular

dome tent
tienda^F tipo^M domo^M

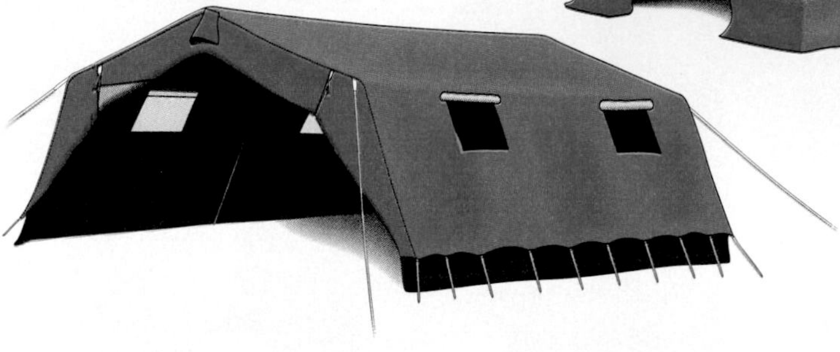

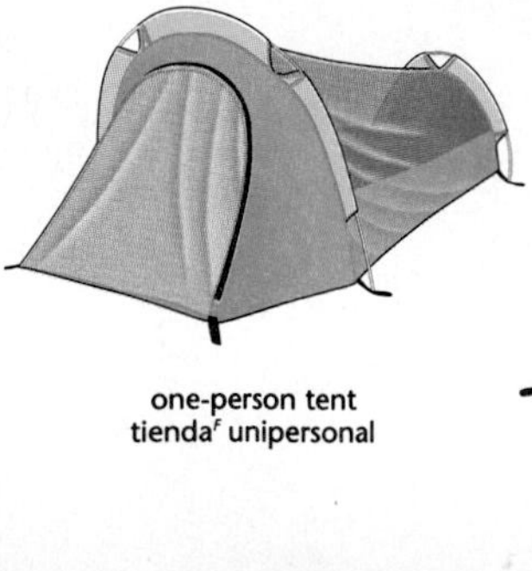

one-person tent
tienda^F unipersonal

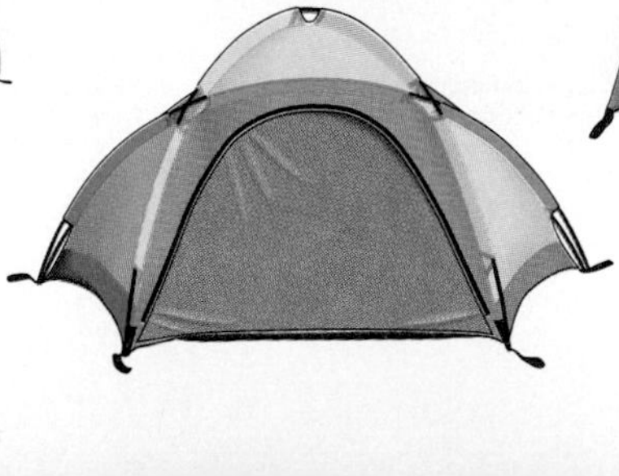

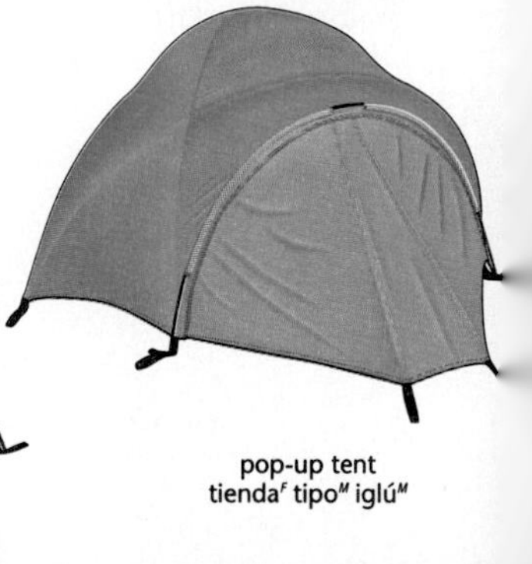

pop-up tent
tienda^F tipo^M iglú^M

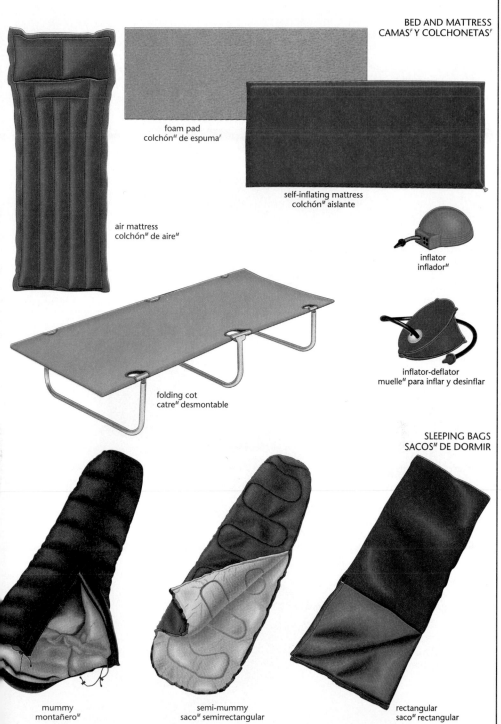

foam pad
colchón*M* de espuma*F*

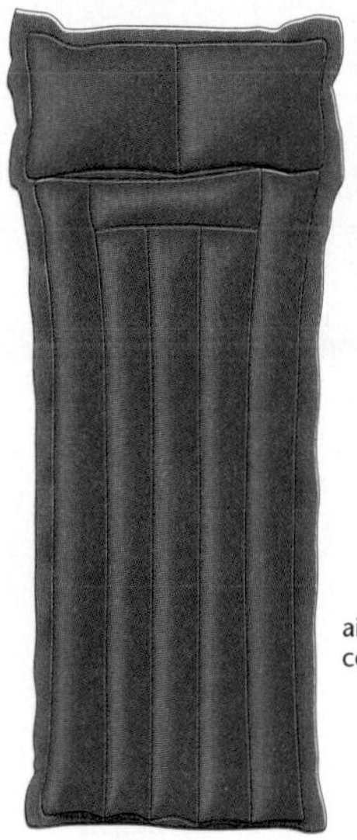

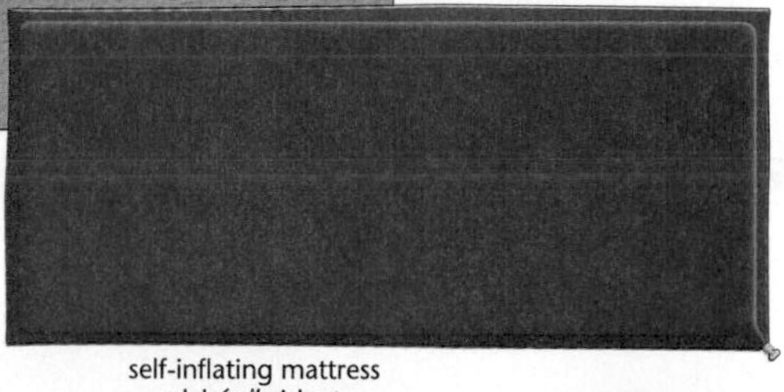

self-inflating mattress
colchón*M* aislante

air mattress
colchón*M* de aire*M*

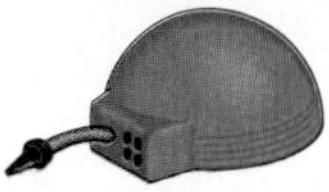

inflator
inflador*M*

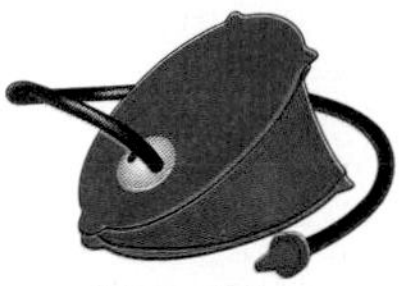

inflator-deflator
muelle*M* para inflar y desinflar

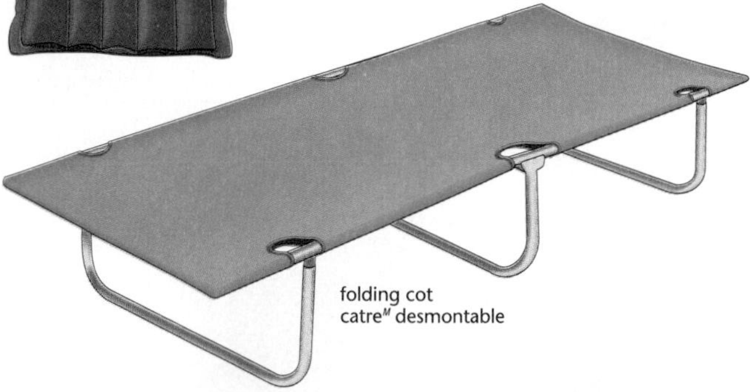

folding cot
catre*M* desmontable

SLEEPING BAGS
SACOS*M* DE DORMIR

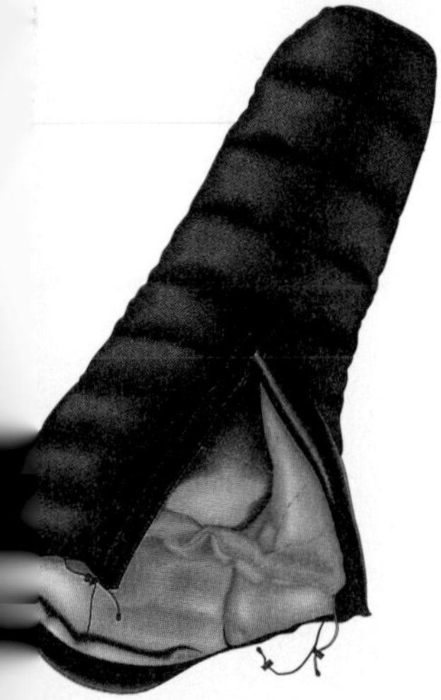

mummy
montañero*M*

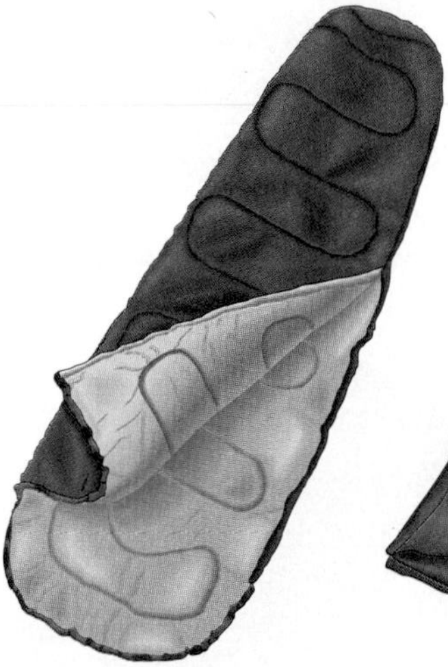

semi-mummy
saco*M* semirrectangular

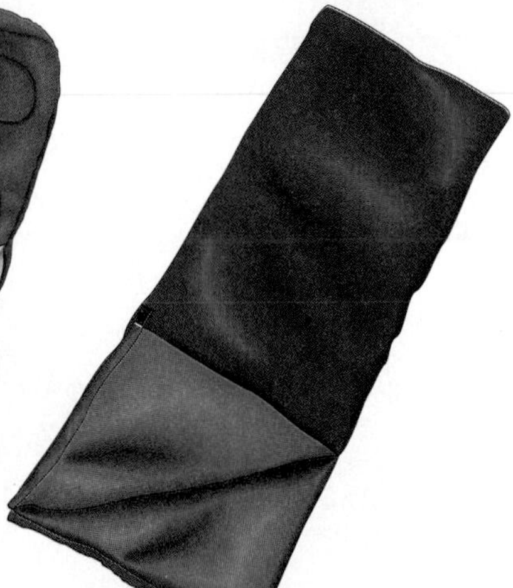

rectangular
saco*M* rectangular

CAMPING EQUIPMENT
EQUIPO^M PARA ACAMPAR

SWISS ARMY KNIFE
NAVAJA^F TIPO^M SUIZO

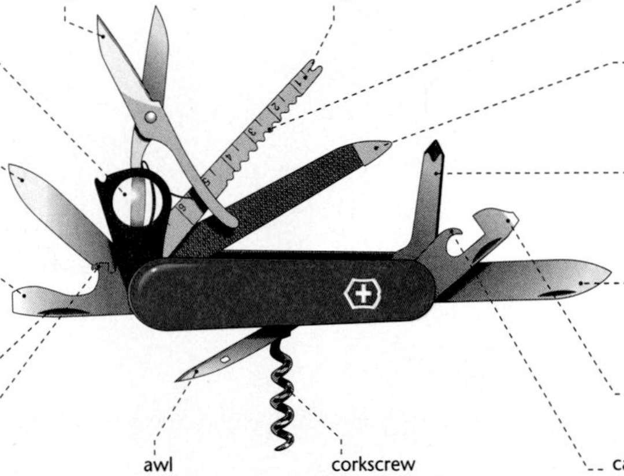

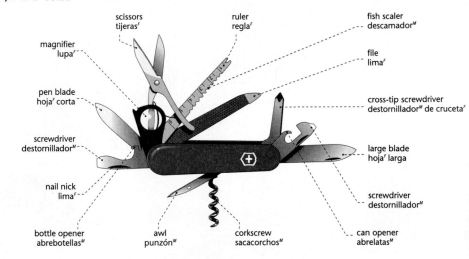

scissors
tijeras^F

ruler
regla^F

fish scaler
descamador^M

magnifier
lupa^F

file
lima^F

pen blade
hoja^F corta

cross-tip screwdriver
destornillador^M de cruceta^F

screwdriver
destornillador^M

large blade
hoja^F larga

nail nick
lima^F

screwdriver
destornillador^M

bottle opener
abrebotellas^M

awl
punzón^M

corkscrew
sacacorchos^M

can opener
abrelatas^M

COOKING SET
UTENSILIOS^M DE COCINA^F

cup
taza^F

coffee pot
cafetera^F

saucepan
olla^F

handle
mango^M

frying pan
sartén^F

plate
plato^M

CUTLERY SET
CUBERTERÍA^F

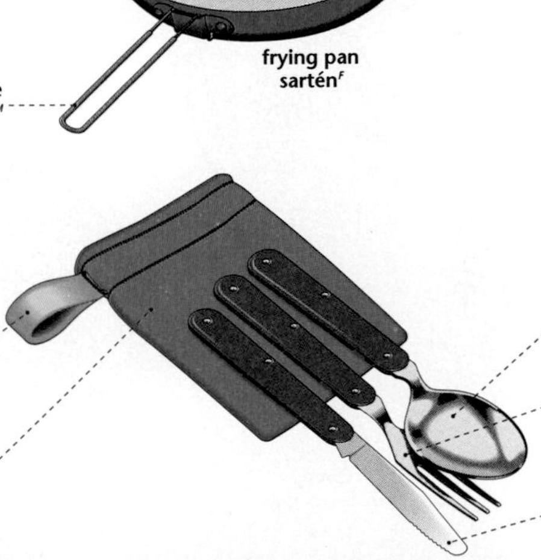

spoon
cuchara^F

belt loop
presilla^F

fork
tenedor^M

sheath
funda^F

knife
cuchillo^M

lantern
linterna^f

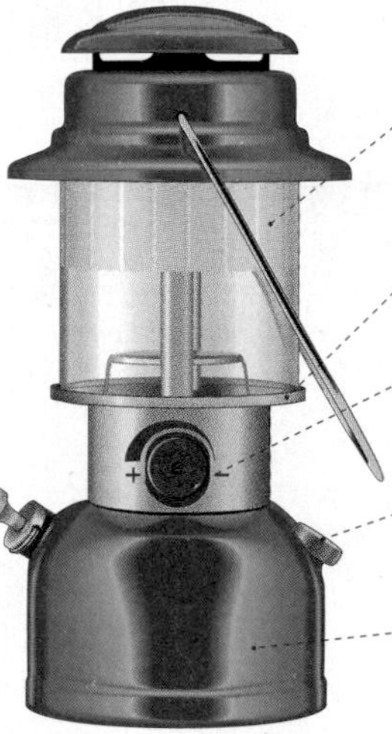

globe
globo^M

burner frame
armazón^M del quemador^M

pressure regulator
regulador^M de presión^F

leakproof cap
tapón^M hermético

tank
tanque^M

pump
bomba^f

heater
calentador^M

single-burner camp stove
camping^M gas^M

two-burner camp stove
cocina^f

burner
quemador^M

control valve
válvula^f de control^M

wire support
parrilla^f estabilizadora

tank
bombona^f de gas^M

CAMPING
CAMPING

689

CAMPING EQUIPMENT
EQUIPO^M PARA ACAMPAR

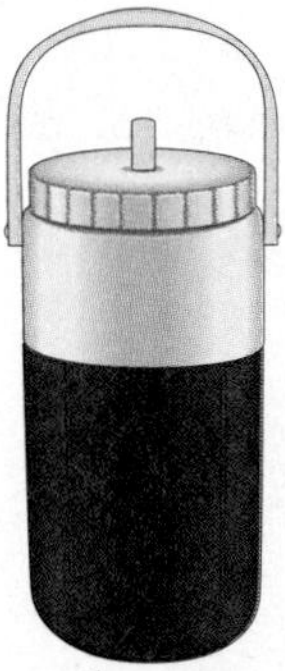

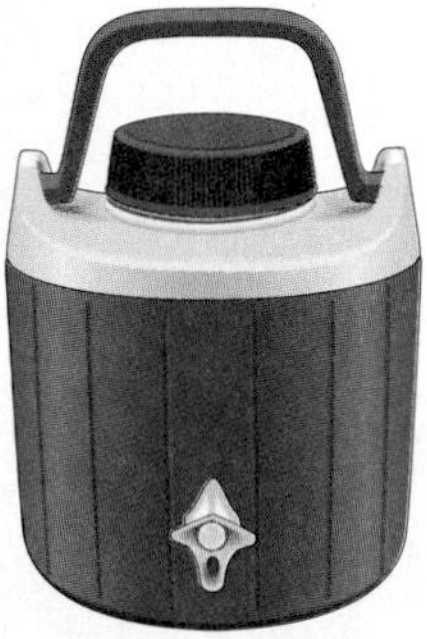

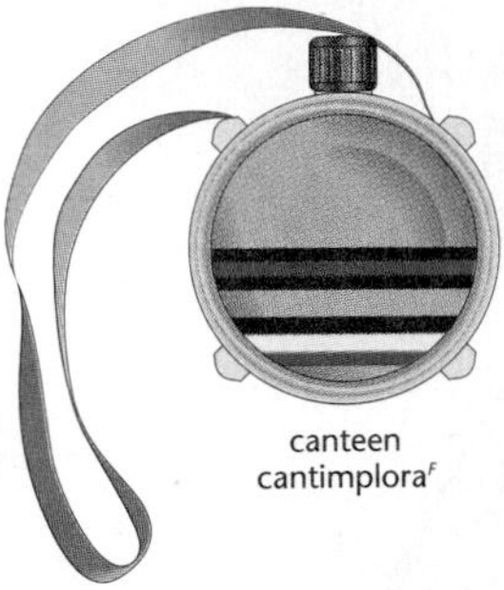

canteen
cantimplora^F

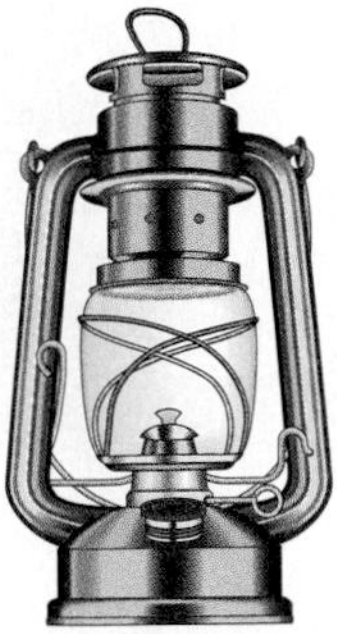

hurricane lamp
lámpara^F de petróleo^M

thermos
termos^M

water carrier
termos^M con llave^F de servicio^M

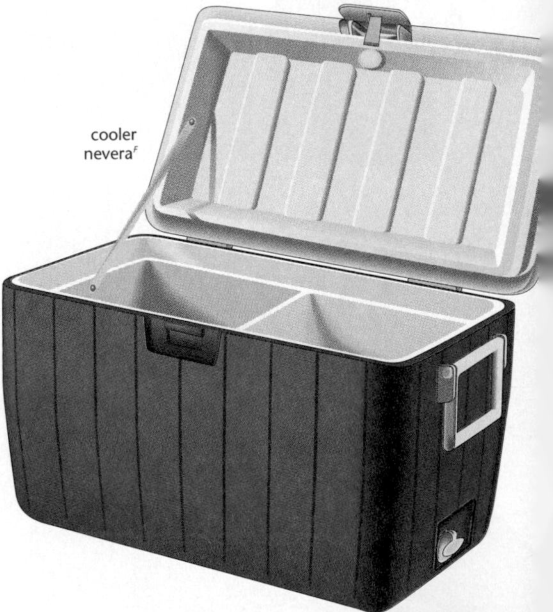

cooler
nevera^F

folding grill
parrilla^F plegable

TOOLS
HERRAMIENTAS^F

hatchet
hacha^F

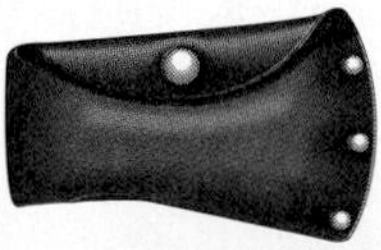

leather sheath
funda^F de cuero^M

sheath
funda^F

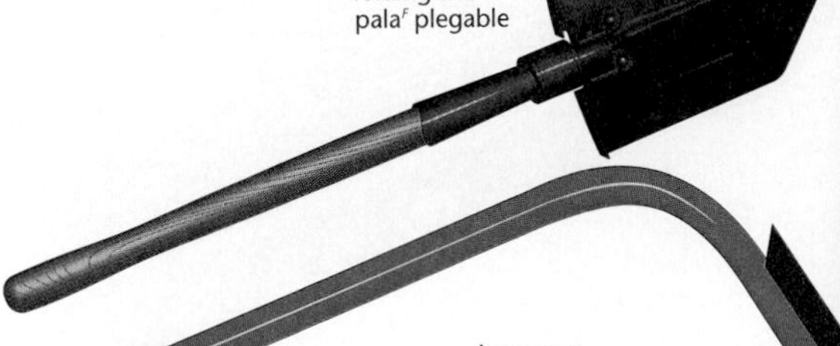

folding shovel
pala^F plegable

knife
cuchillo^M

bow saw
sierra^F de campo^M

square knot
nudo^M de rizo^M

overhand knot
nudo^M llano

granny knot
nudo^M de tejedor^M

running bowline
balso^M

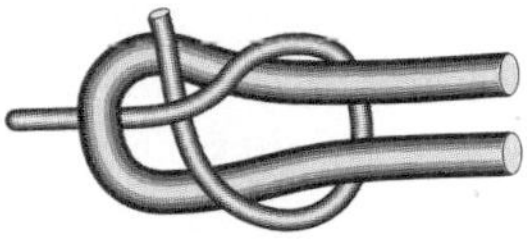

sheet bend
vuelta^F de escota^F

double sheet bend
vuelta^F de escota^F doble

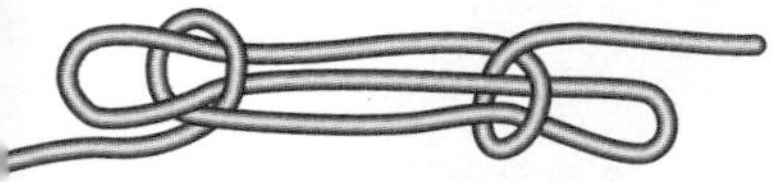

sheepshank
margarita^F

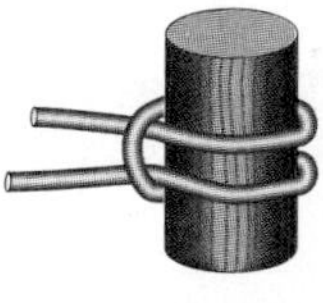

cow hitch
vuelta^F de cabo^M

heaving line knot
nudo^M de guía^M

fisherman's knot
nudo^M de pescador^M

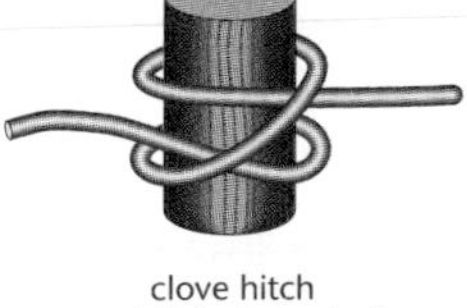

clove hitch
nudo^M de dos cotes^M

figure-eight knot
lasca^F doble

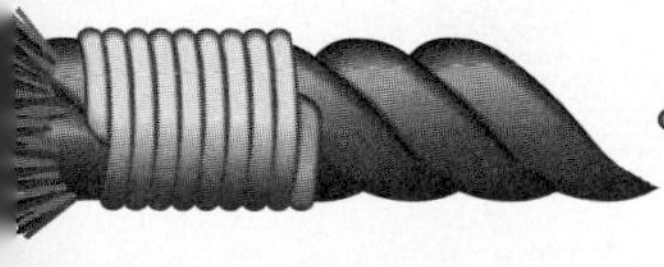

common whipping
sobrenudo^M

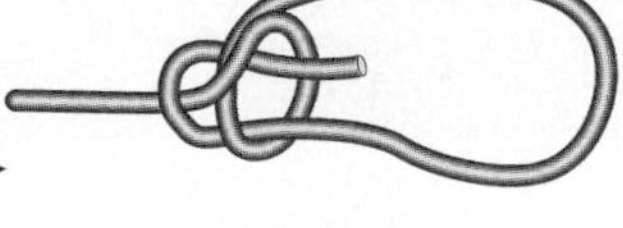

bowline
as^M de guía^F

bowline on a bight
as^M de guía^F de eslinga^F doble

SHORT SPLICE
EMPALMADURA^F

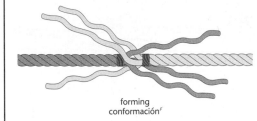

forming
conformación^F

completion
acabado^M

CABLE
CABLE^M

TWISTED ROPE
CABLE^M TORCIDO

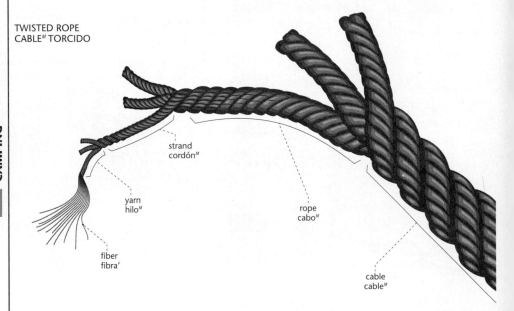

strand
cordón^M

yarn
hilo^M

rope
cabo^M

fiber
fibra^F

cable
cable^M

BRAIDED ROPE
CABLE^M TRENZADO

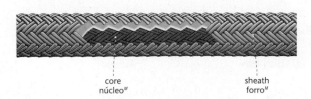

core
núcleo^M

sheath
forro^M

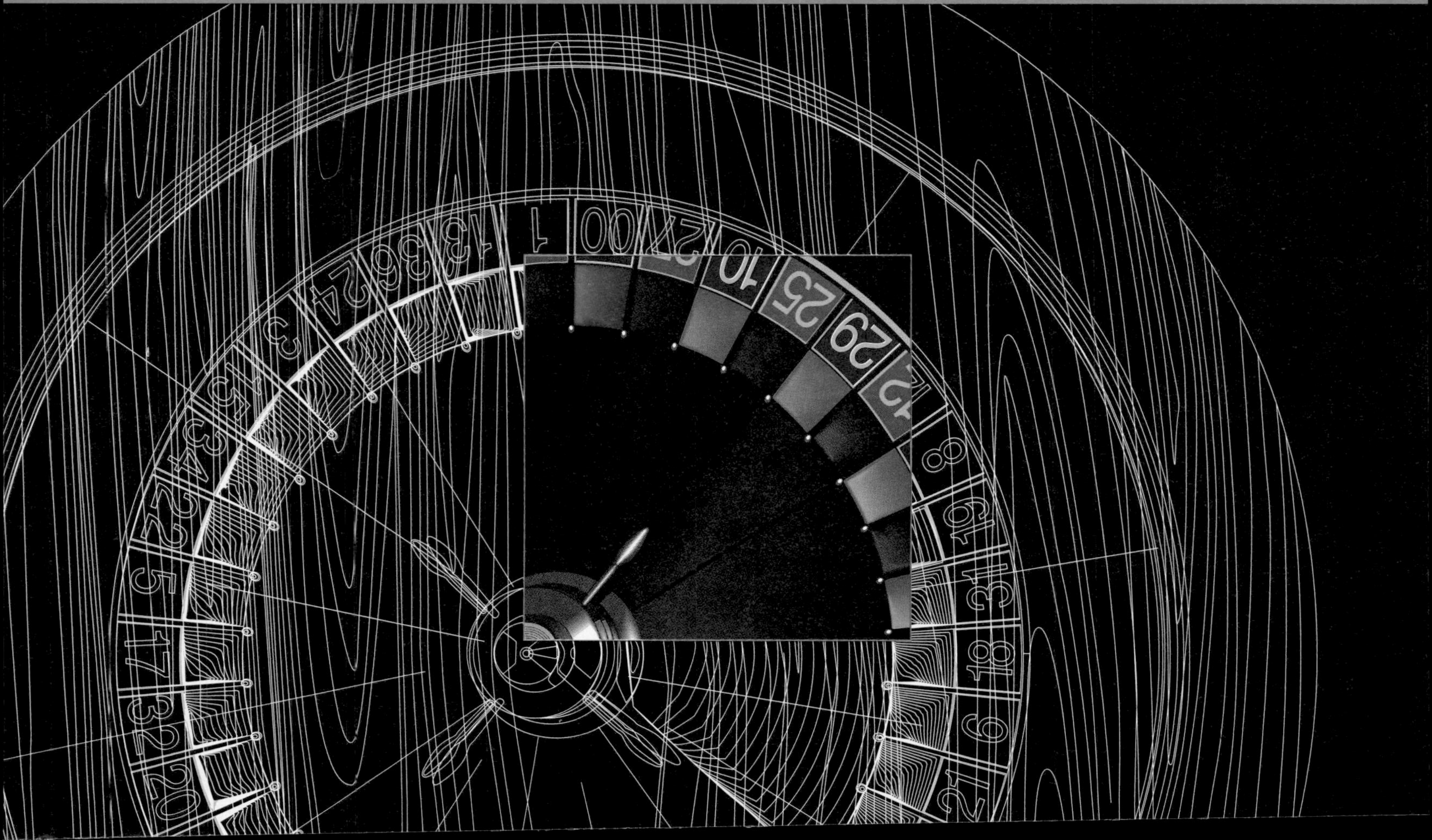

CONTENTS

INDOOR GAMES
JUEGOS DE INTERIOR

CARD GAMES
BARAJA^F

SYMBOLS
SÍMBOLOS^M

heart
corazón^M

diamond
diamante^M

club
trébol^M

spade
espada^F

Joker
comodín^M

Ace
as^M

King
rey^M

Queen
reina^F

Jack
jota^F

STANDARD POKER HANDS
MANOS^F DE PÓQUER^M

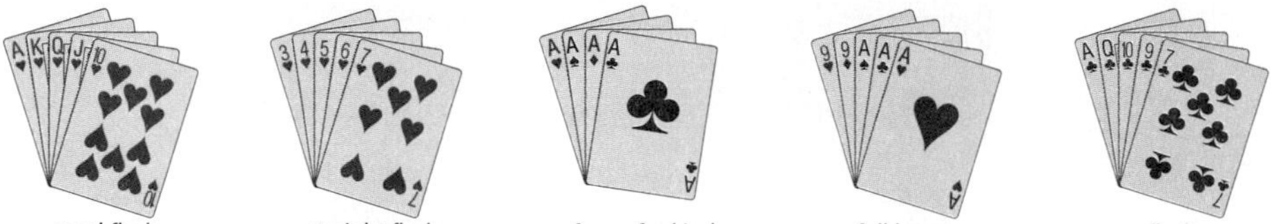

royal flush
escalera^F real

straight flush
escalera^F de color^M

four-of-a-kind
póquer^M

full house
full

flush
color^M

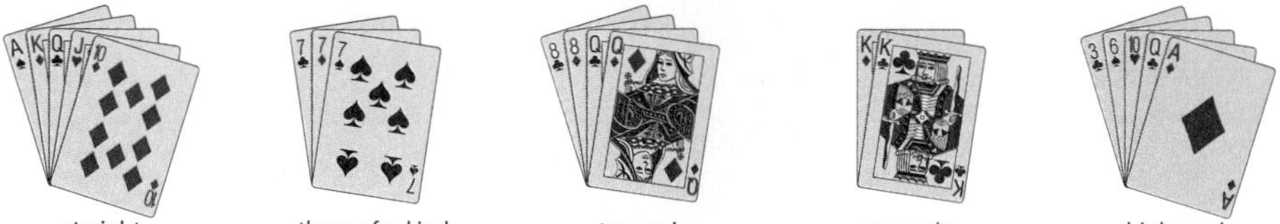

straight
escalera^F

three-of-a-kind
trío^M

two pairs
dos pares^M

one pair
un par^M

high card
cartas^F altas

**INDOOR GAMES
JUEGOS DE INTERIOR**

DOMINOES
DOMINÓ^M

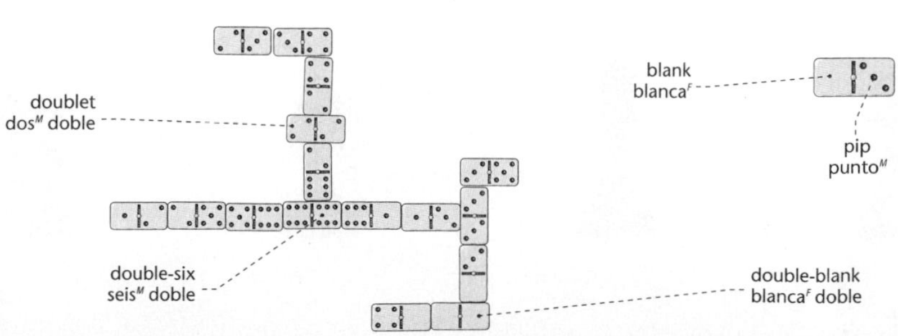

doublet
dos^M doble

blank
blanca^F

pip
punto^M

double-six
seis^M doble

double-blank
blanca^F doble

CHESS
AJEDREZ^M

CHESSBOARD
TABLERO^M DE AJEDREZ^M

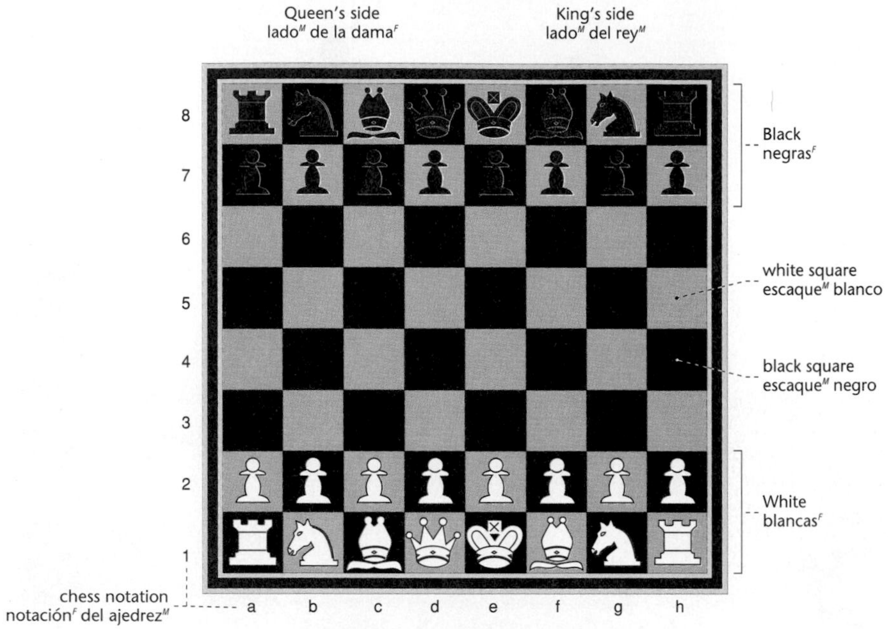

Queen's side
lado^M de la dama^F

King's side
lado^M del rey^M

Black
negras^F

white square
escaque^M blanco

black square
escaque^M negro

White
blancas^F

chess notation
notación^F del ajedrez^M

TYPES OF MOVEMENTS
TIPOS^M DE MOVIMIENTOS^M

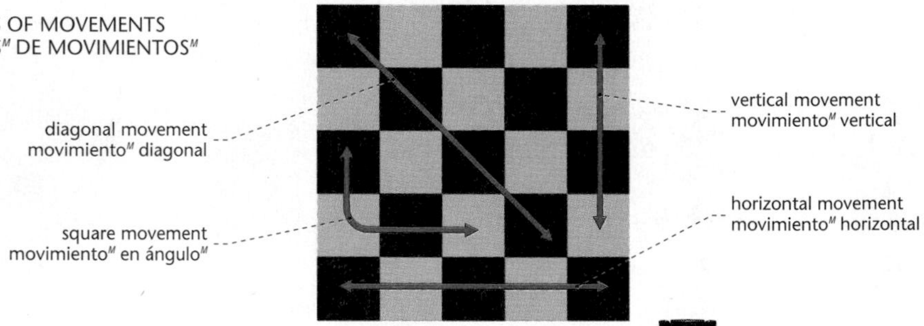

diagonal movement
movimiento^M diagonal

vertical movement
movimiento^M vertical

square movement
movimiento^M en ángulo^M

horizontal movement
movimiento^M horizontal

MEN
PIEZAS^F

Pawn
peón^M

Rook
torre^F

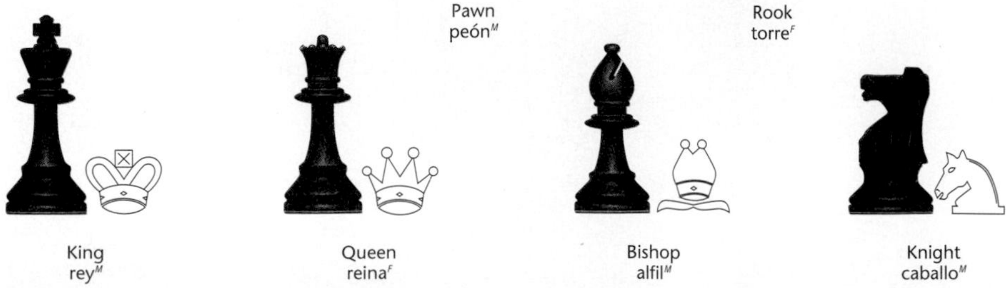

King
rey^M

Queen
reina^F

Bishop
alfil^M

Knight
caballo^M

BACKGAMMON
BACKGAMMON^M

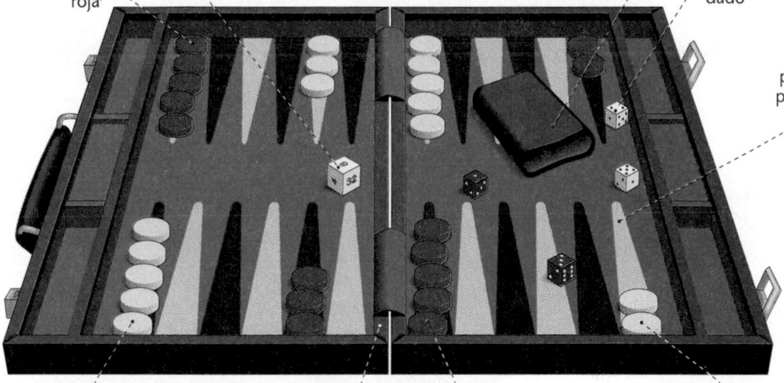

doubling die
dado^M doble

outer table
base^F exterior

inner table
base^F interior

dice cup
cubilete^M

Red
roja^F

die
dado^M

point
punta^F

White
blanca^F

bar
barra^F

men
dama^F

runner
jugador^M

GO
GO(SUN-TSE)

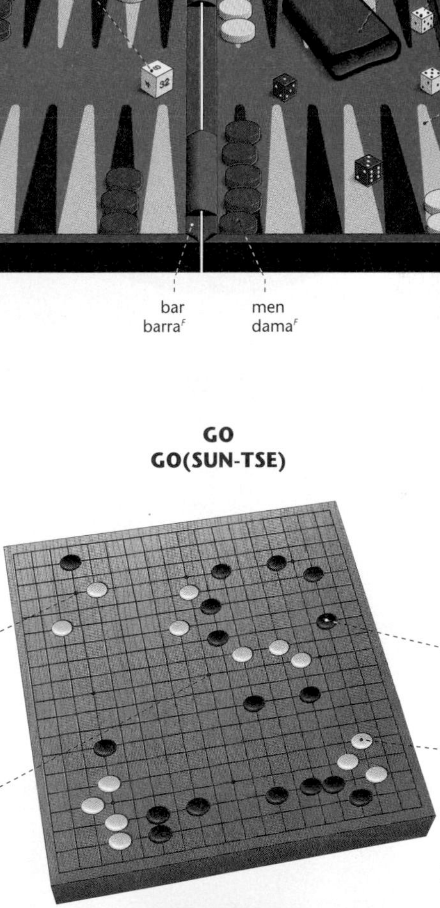

BOARD
TABLERO^M

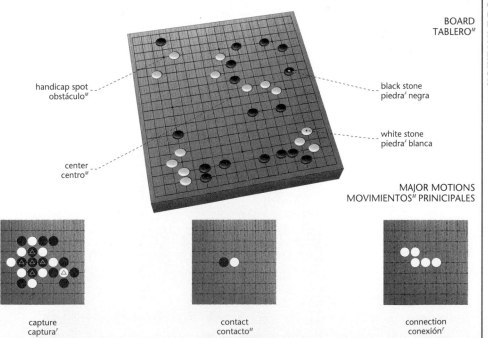

handicap spot
obstáculo^M

black stone
piedra^F negra

white stone
piedra^F blanca

center
centro^M

MAJOR MOTIONS
MOVIMIENTOS^M PRINICIPALES

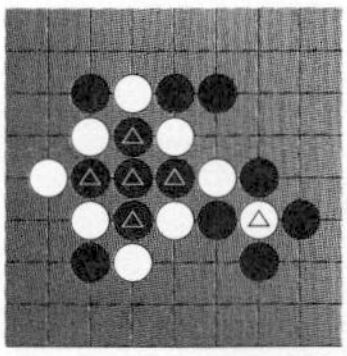

capture
captura^F

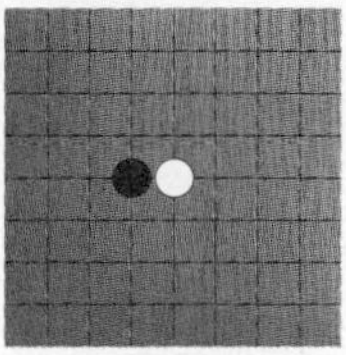

contact
contacto^M

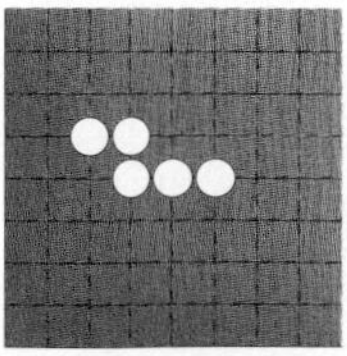

connection
conexión^F

GAME OF DARTS
JUEGO^M DE DARDOS^M

DARTBOARD
TABLERO^M DE TIRO^M

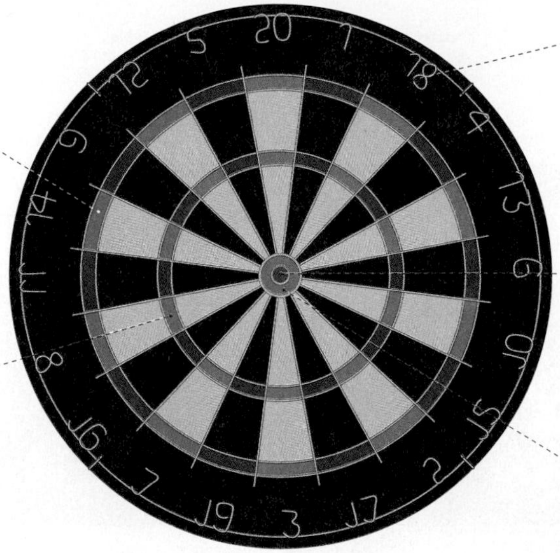

segment score number
segmento^M de marcas^F

double ring
círculo^M doble

bull's-eye
blanco^M

triple ring
círculo^M triple

25 ring
círculo^M 25

DART
DARDO^M

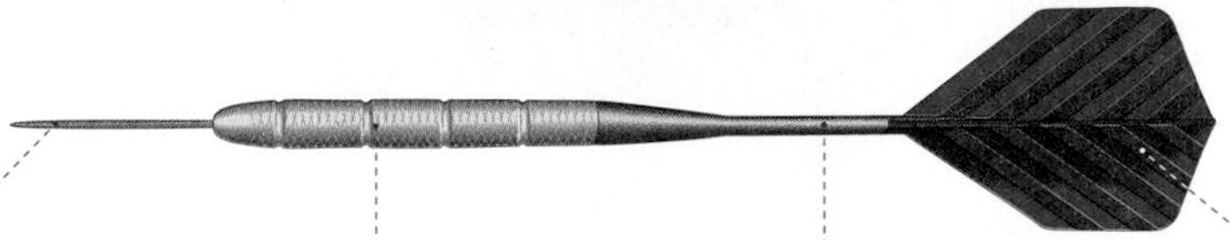

point
punta^F

barrel
cañón^M

shaft
asta^F

flight
volador^M

PLAYING AREA
ÁREA^F DE JUEGO^M

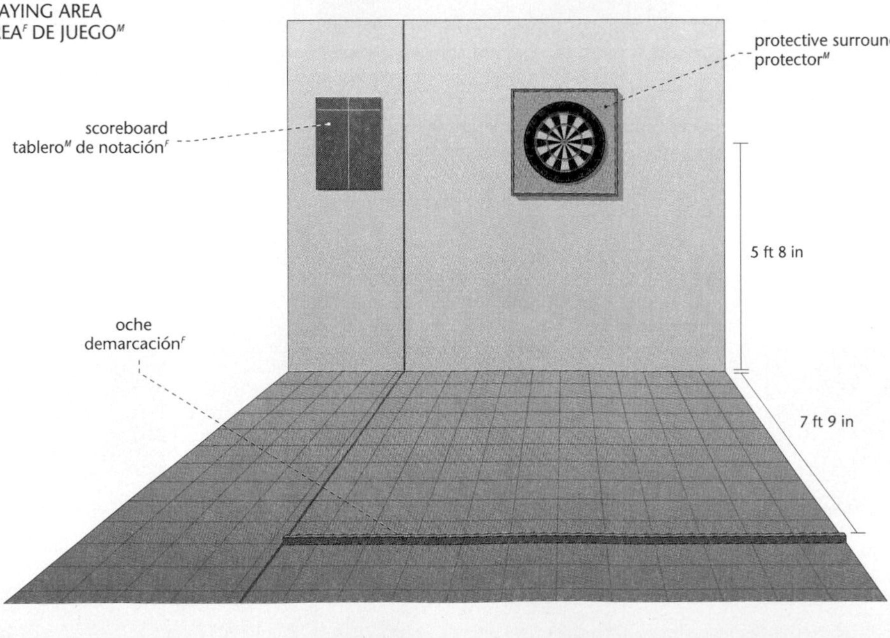

protective surround
protector^M

scoreboard
tablero^M de notación^F

5 ft 8 in

oche
demarcación^F

7 ft 9 in

VIDEO ENTERTAINMENT SYSTEM
SISTEMA^M DE VIDEO^M DE JUEGOS^M

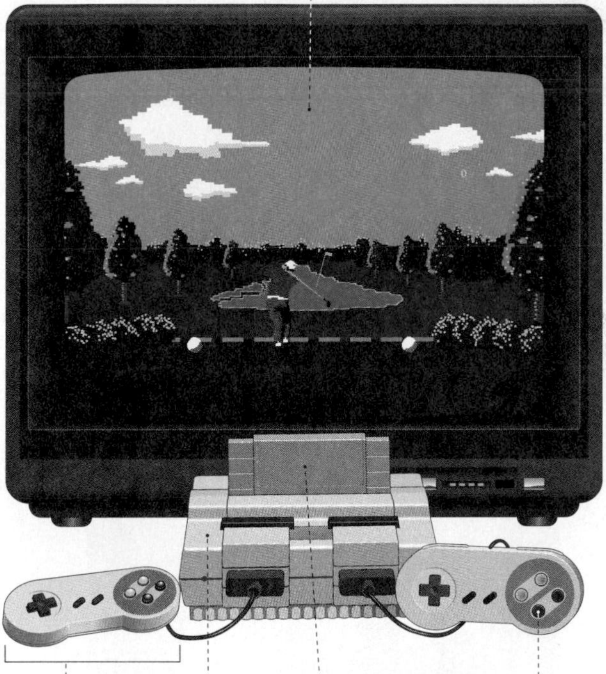

visual display
pantalla^F

control pad
mecanismo^M de control

function button
botón^M de funcionamiento^M

control deck
cubierta^F de control^M

game cartridge
casete^M de juego^M

DICE
DADOS^M

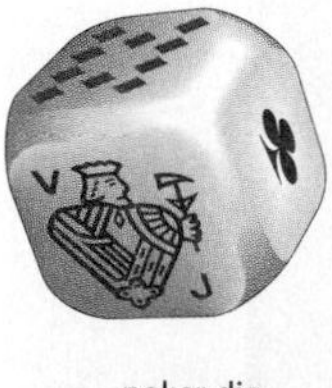

poker die
dado^M de póquer^M

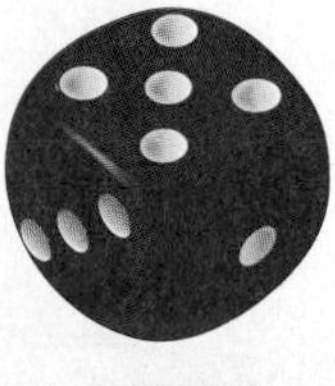

ordinary die
dado^M común

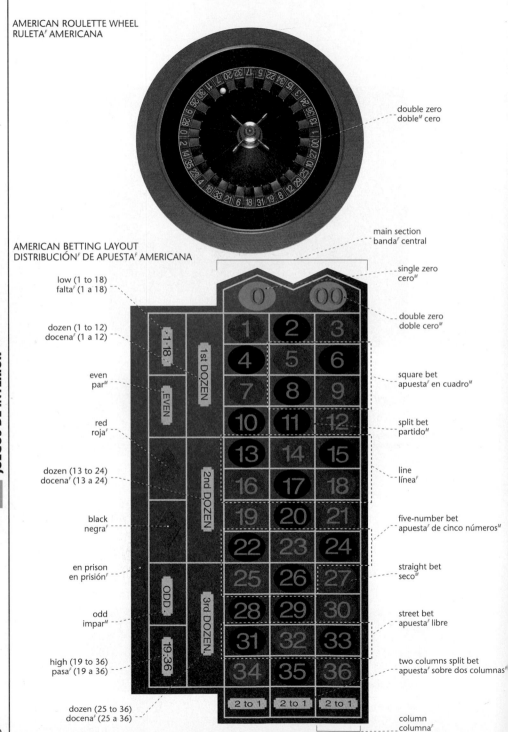

ROULETTE TABLE
MESA^F DE LA RULETA^F

AMERICAN ROULETTE WHEEL
RULETA^F AMERICANA

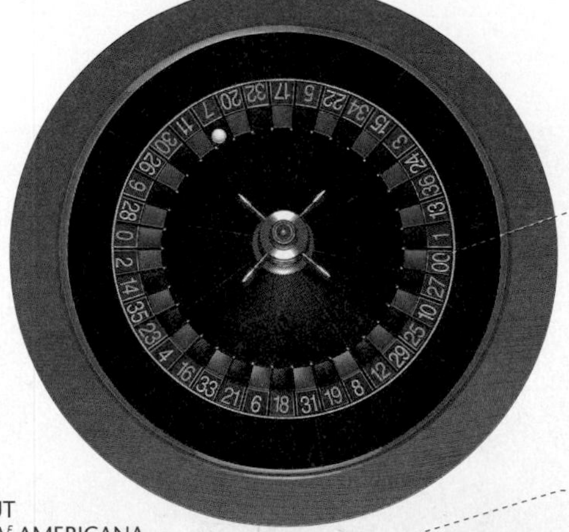

double zero
doble^M cero

AMERICAN BETTING LAYOUT
DISTRIBUCIÓN^F DE APUESTA^F AMERICANA

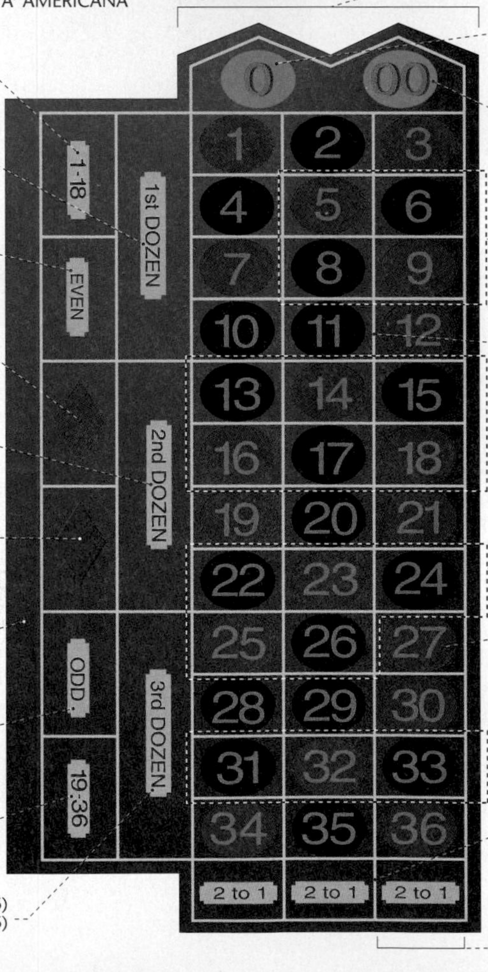

main section
banda^F central

single zero
cero^M

low (1 to 18)
falta^F (1 a 18)

double zero
doble cero^M

dozen (1 to 12)
docena^F (1 a 12)

even
par^M

square bet
apuesta^F en cuadro^M

red
roja^F

split bet
partido^M

dozen (13 to 24)
docena^F (13 a 24)

line
línea^F

black
negra^F

five-number bet
apuesta^F de cinco números^M

en prison
en prisión^F

straight bet
seco^M

odd
impar^M

street bet
apuesta^F libre

high (19 to 36)
pasa^F (19 a 36)

two columns split bet
apuesta^F sobre dos columnas^F

dozen (25 to 36)
docena^F (25 a 36)

column
columna^F

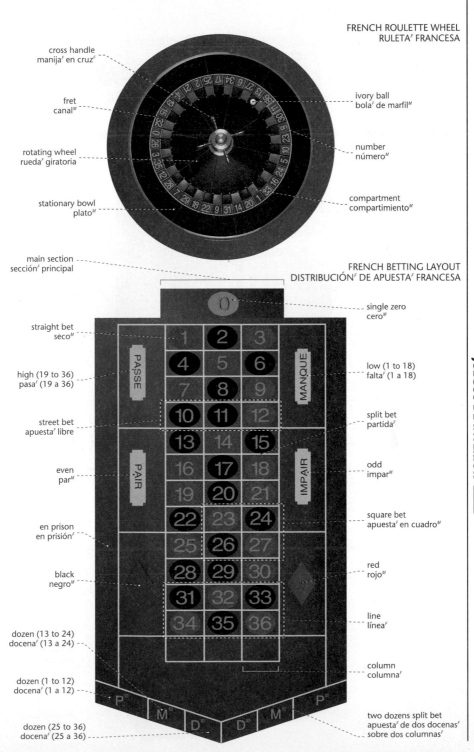

FRENCH ROULETTE WHEEL
RULETA^F FRANCESA

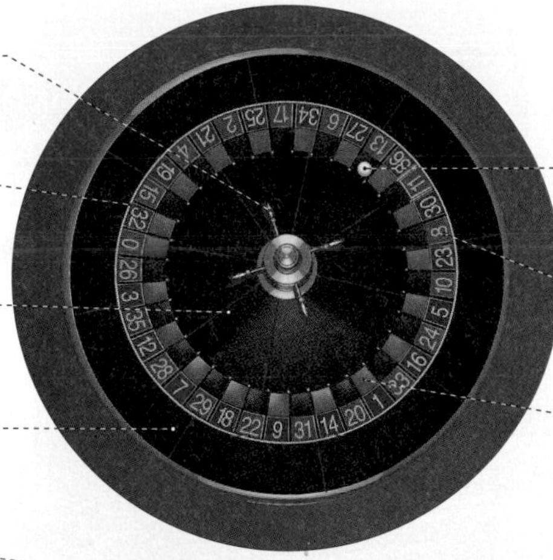

cross handle
manija^F en cruz^F

fret
canal^M

rotating wheel
rueda^F giratoria

stationary bowl
plato^M

ivory ball
bola^F de marfil^M

number
número^M

compartment
compartimiento^M

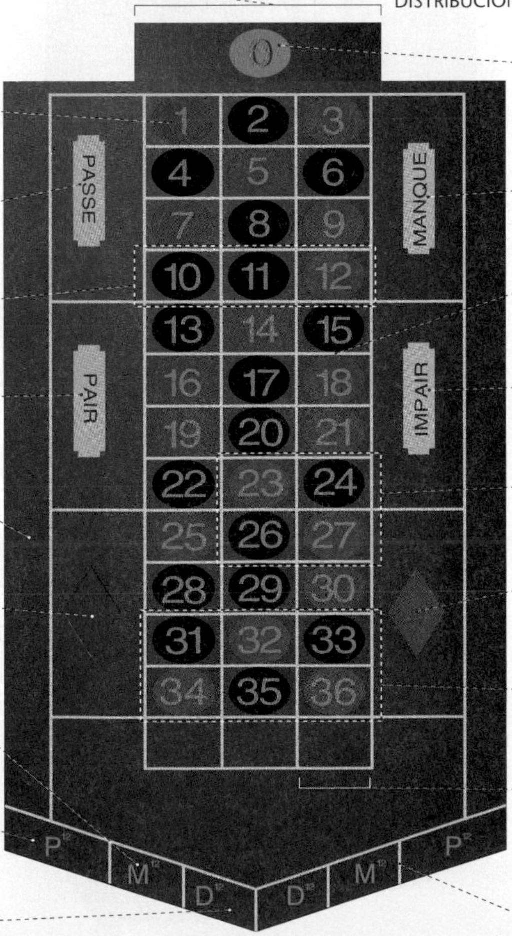

main section
sección^F principal

FRENCH BETTING LAYOUT
DISTRIBUCIÓN^F DE APUESTA^F FRANCESA

single zero
cero^M

straight bet
seco^M

high (19 to 36)
pasa^F (19 a 36)

low (1 to 18)
falta^F (1 a 18)

street bet
apuesta^F libre

split bet
partida^F

even
par^M

odd
impar^M

en prison
en prisión^F

square bet
apuesta^F en cuadro^M

black
negro^M

red
rojo^M

line
línea^F

dozen (13 to 24)
docena^F (13 a 24)

column
columna^F

dozen (1 to 12)
docena^F (1 a 12)

dozen (25 to 36)
docena^F (25 a 36)

two dozens split bet
apuesta^F de dos docenas^F
sobre dos columnas^F

PASSE   MANQUE   PAIR   IMPAIR

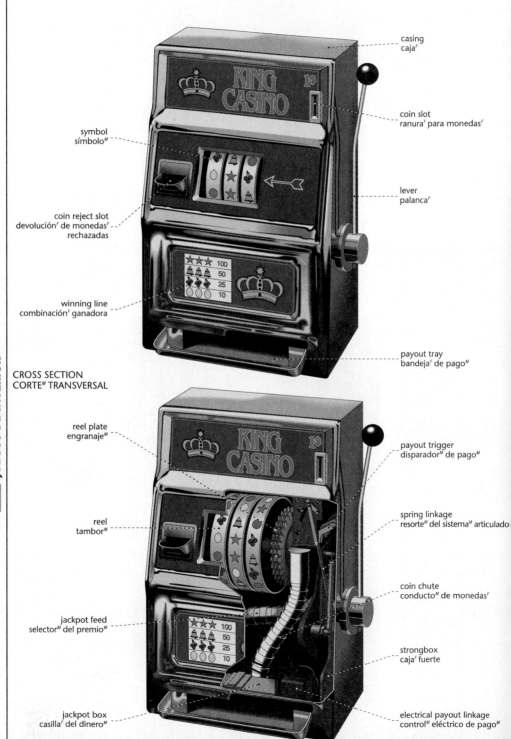

casing
caja^F

coin slot
ranura^F para monedas^F

symbol
símbolo^M

lever
palanca^F

coin reject slot
devolución^F de monedas^F
rechazadas

winning line
combinación^F ganadora

payout tray
bandeja^F de pago^M

CROSS SECTION
CORTE^M TRANSVERSAL

reel plate
engranaje^M

payout trigger
disparador^M de pago^M

reel
tambor^M

spring linkage
resorte^M del sistema^M articulado

coin chute
conducto^M de monedas^F

jackpot feed
selector^M del premio^M

strongbox
caja^F fuerte

jackpot box
casilla^F del dinero^M

electrical payout linkage
control^M eléctrico de pago^M

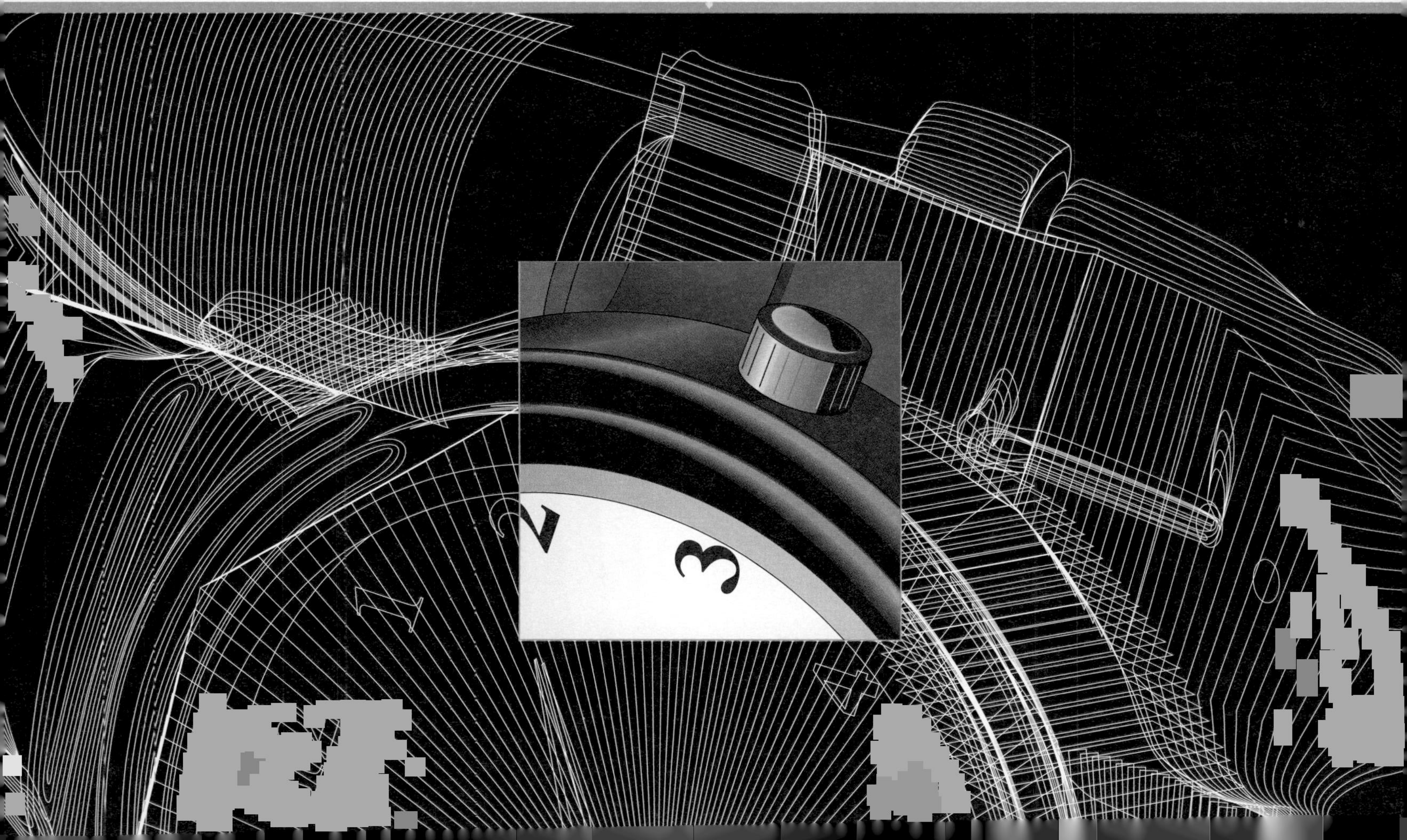

CONTENTS

MEASURING DEVICES
APARATOS DE MEDICIÓN

MEASURE OF TEMPERATURE
MEDICIÓN^F DE LA TEMPERATURA^F

THERMOMETER
TERMÓMETRO^M

CLINICAL THERMOMETER
TERMÓMETRO^M CLÍNICO

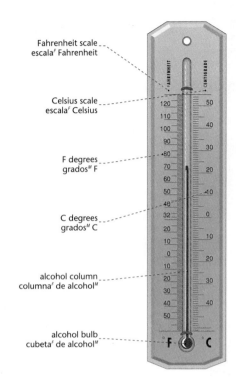

Fahrenheit scale
escala^F Fahrenheit

Celsius scale
escala^F Celsius

F degrees
grados^M F

C degrees
grados^M C

alcohol column
columna^F de alcohol^M

alcohol bulb
cubeta^F de alcohol^M

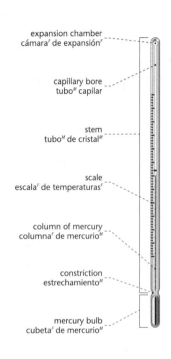

expansion chamber
cámara^F de expansión^F

capillary bore
tubo^M capilar

stem
tubo^M de cristal^M

scale
escala^F de temperaturas^F

column of mercury
columna^F de mercurio^M

constriction
estrechamiento^M

mercury bulb
cubeta^F de mercurio^M

BIMETALLIC THERMOMETER
TERMÓMETRO^M BIMETÁLICO

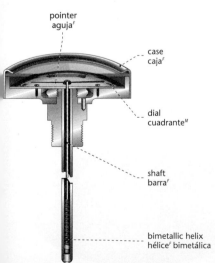

pointer
aguja^F

case
caja^F

dial
cuadrante^M

shaft
barra^F

bimetallic helix
hélice^F bimetálica

ROOM THERMOSTAT
TERMOSTATO^M AMBIENTAL

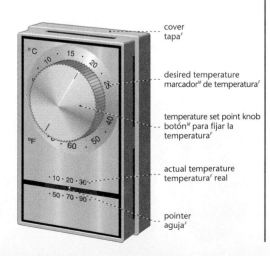

cover
tapa^F

desired temperature
marcador^M de temperatura^F

temperature set point knob
botón^M para fijar la
temperatura^F

actual temperature
temperatura^F real

pointer
aguja^F

MEASURE OF TIME
MEDICIÓN^F DEL TIEMPO^M

STOPWATCH
CRONÓMETRO^M

ring
anilla^F

start button
botón^M de inicio^M de marcha^F

reset button
botón^M de inicio^M del contador^M

second hand
segundero^M

stop button
botón^M de parada^F

1/10th second hand
segundero^M en décimas^F
de segundo^M

minute hand
minutero^M

case
estuche^M

MECHANICAL WATCH
RELOJ^M **MECÁNICO**

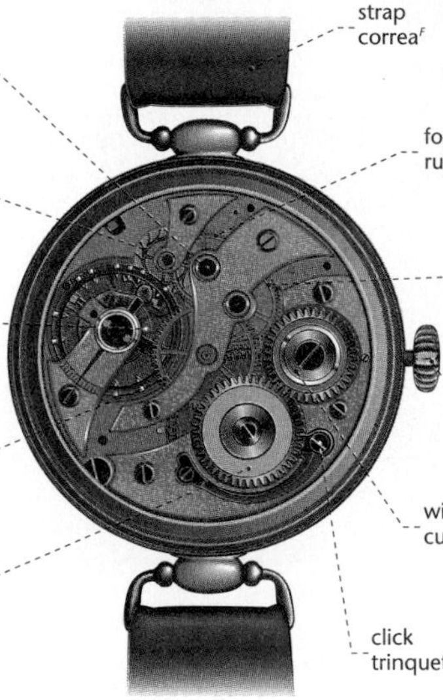

strap
correa^F

ANALOG WATCH
RELOJ^M **DE PULSERA**^F

jewel
rubí^M

fourth wheel
rueda^F de los segundos^M

escape wheel
rueda^F de escape^M

third wheel
rueda^F media

hairspring
espiral^M

crown
corona^F

center wheel
rueda^F central

winder
cuerda^F

ratchet wheel
rueda^F de trinquete^M

dial
cuadrante^M

click
trinquete^M

SUNDIAL
RELOJ^M **DE SOL**^M

DIGITAL WATCH
RELOJ^M **DIGITAL**

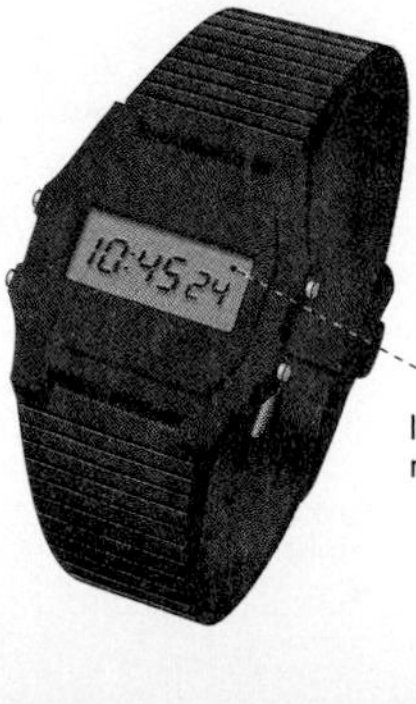

gnomon
estilo^M

dial
cuadrante^M

shadow
sombra^F

liquid-crystal display
registro^M de cristal^M líquido

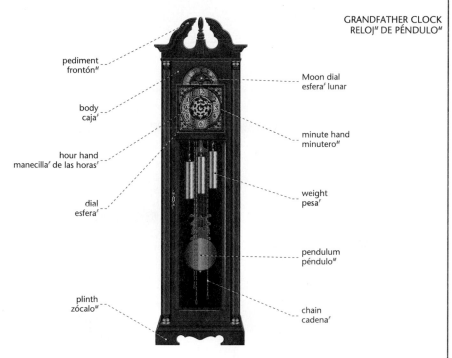

GRANDFATHER CLOCK
RELOJ^M DE PÉNDULO^M

pediment
frontón^M

body
caja^F

hour hand
manecilla^F de las horas^F

dial
esfera^F

plinth
zócalo^M

Moon dial
esfera^F lunar

minute hand
minutero^M

weight
pesa^F

pendulum
péndulo^M

chain
cadena^F

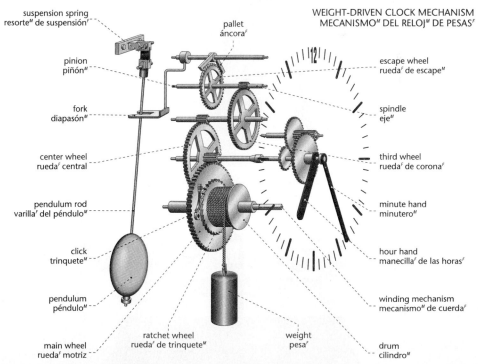

WEIGHT-DRIVEN CLOCK MECHANISM
MECANISMO^M DEL RELOJ^M DE PESAS^F

suspension spring
resorte^M de suspensión^F

pinion
piñón^M

fork
diapasón^M

center wheel
rueda^F central

pendulum rod
varilla^F del péndulo^M

click
trinquete^M

pendulum
péndulo^M

main wheel
rueda^F motriz

ratchet wheel
rueda^F de trinquete^M

weight
pesa^F

pallet
áncora^F

escape wheel
rueda^F de escape^M

spindle
eje^M

third wheel
rueda^F de corona^F

minute hand
minutero^M

hour hand
manecilla^F de las horas^F

winding mechanism
mecanismo^M de cuerda^F

drum
cilindro^M

707

MEASURE OF WEIGHT
MEDICIÓN^F DEL PESO^M

BEAM BALANCE
BALANZA^F DE ASTIL^M

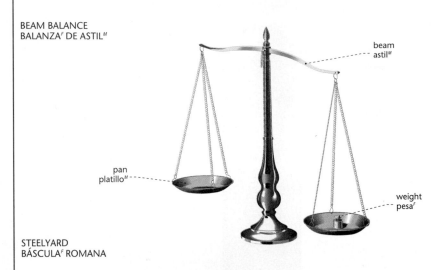

beam
astil^M

pan
platillo^M

weight
pesa^F

STEELYARD
BÁSCULA^F ROMANA

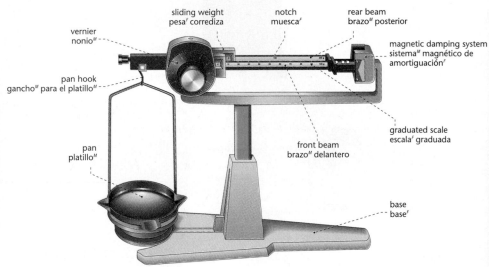

sliding weight
pesa^F corrediza

notch
muesca^F

rear beam
brazo^M posterior

vernier
nonio^M

magnetic damping system
sistema^M magnético de
amortiguación^F

pan hook
gancho^M para el platillo^M

graduated scale
escala^F graduada

pan
platillo^M

front beam
brazo^M delantero

base
base^F

ROBERVAL'S BALANCE
BALANZA^F DE ROBERVAL

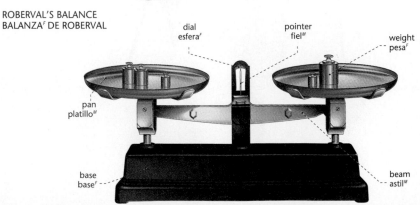

dial
esfera^F

pointer
fiel^M

weight
pesa^F

pan
platillo^M

base
base^F

beam
astil^M

SPRING BALANCE
DINAMÓMETRO*M*

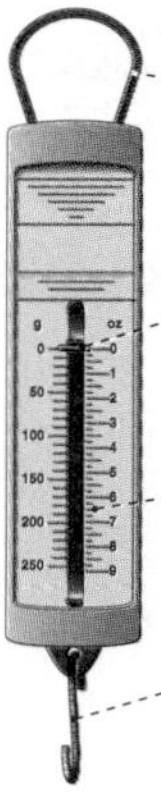

ring
anilla*F*

pointer
fiel*M*

graduated scale
escala*F* graduada

hook
gancho*M*

ELECTRONIC SCALES
BÁSCULA*F* ELECTRÓNICA

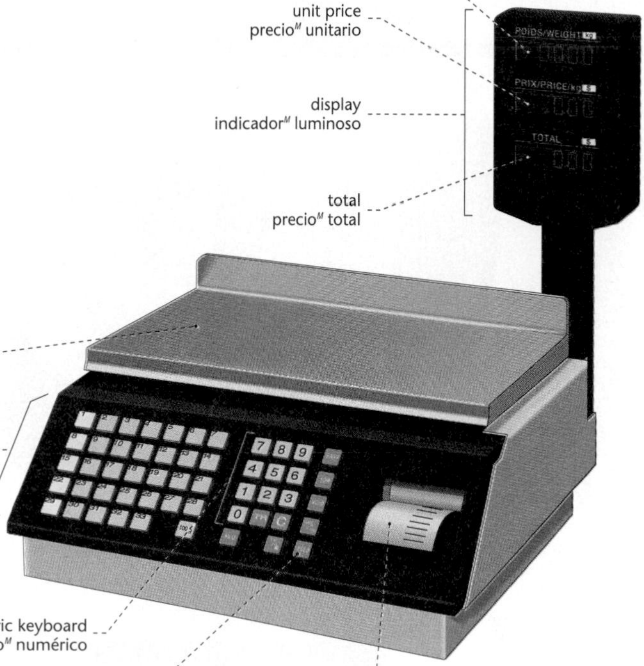

weight
peso*M*

unit price
precio*M* unitario

display
indicador*M* luminoso

total
precio*M* total

platform
platillo*M*

function keys
teclado*M* de funciones*F*

numeric keyboard
teclado*M* numérico

product code
código*M* del producto*M*

printout
recibo*M*

BATHROOM SCALES
BÁSCULA*F* DE BAÑO*M*

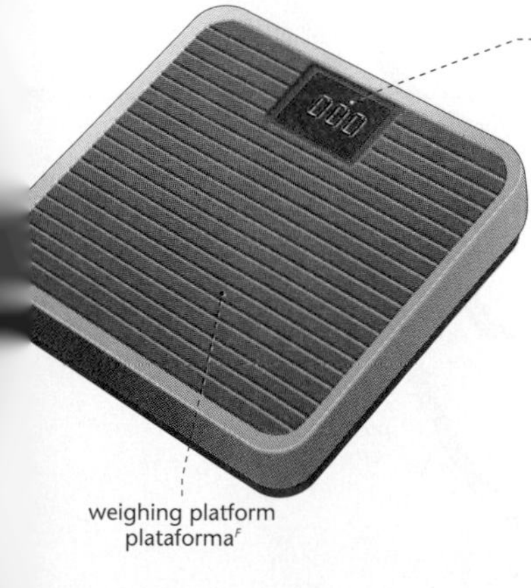

digital display
indicador*M* digital

weighing platform
plataforma*F*

ANALYTICAL BALANCE
BALANZA*F* DE PRECISIÓN*F*

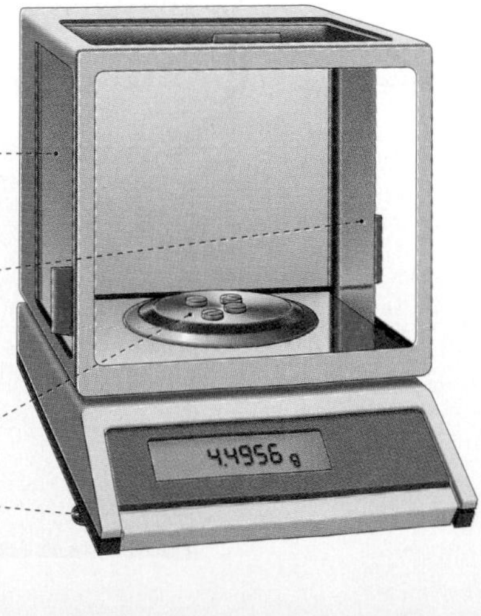

glass case
urna*F*

door access
puerta*F*

pan
platillo*M*

leveling screw
tornillo*M* nivelador

44956 g

MEASURE OF PRESSURE
MEDICIÓN^F DE LA PRESIÓN^F

BAROMETER/THERMOMETER
BARÓMETRO^M/TERMÓMETRO^M

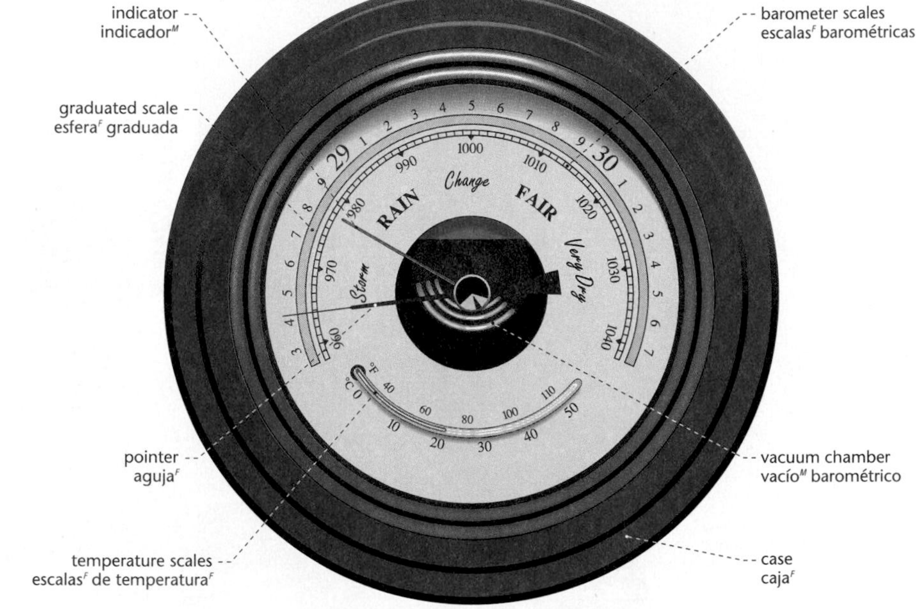

indicator
indicador^M

graduated scale
esfera^F graduada

barometer scales
escalas^F barométricas

pointer
aguja^F

temperature scales
escalas^F de temperatura^F

vacuum chamber
vacío^M barométrico

case
caja^F

MEASURING DEVICES
APARATOS DE MEDICIÓN

TENSIOMETER
TENSIÓMETRO^M

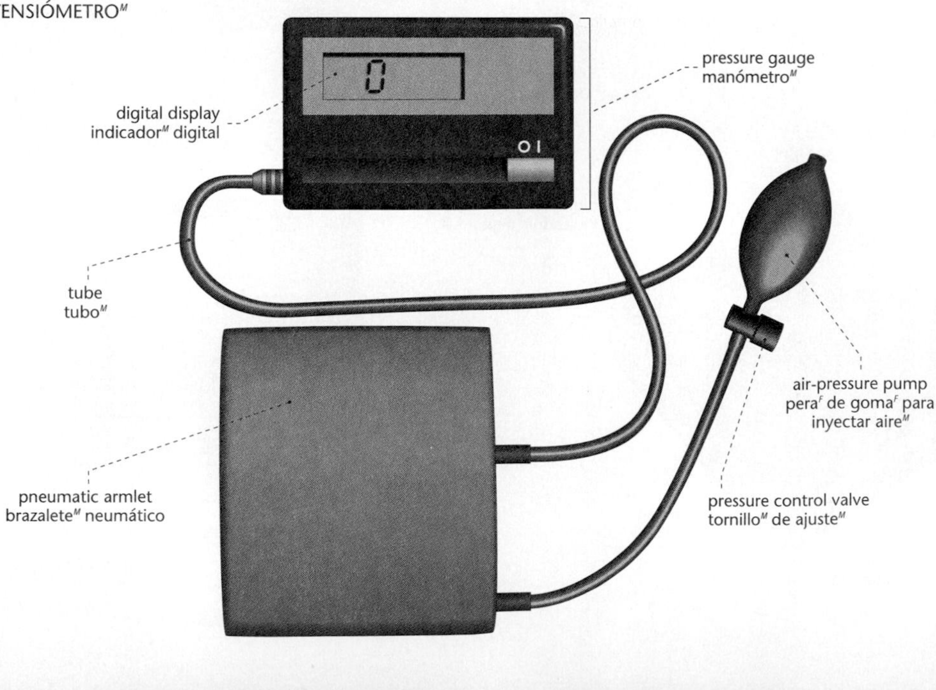

digital display
indicador^M digital

pressure gauge
manómetro^M

tube
tubo^M

pneumatic armlet
brazalete^M neumático

air-pressure pump
pera^F de goma^F para
inyectar aire^M

pressure control valve
tornillo^M de ajuste^M

MEASURE OF LENGTH
MEDICIÓN^F DE LA LONGITUD^F

TAPE MEASURE
CINTA^F MÉTRICA

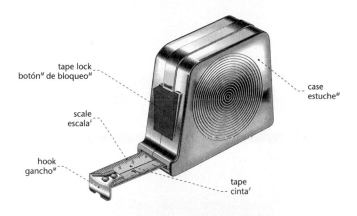

tape lock
botón^M de bloqueo^M

case
estuche^M

scale
escala^F

hook
gancho^M

tape
cinta^F

MEASURE OF DISTANCE
MEDICIÓN^F DE LA DISTANCIA^F

PEDOMETER
ODÓMETRO^M

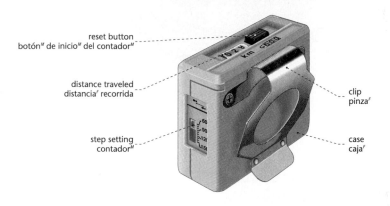

reset button
botón^M de inicio^M del contador^M

distance traveled
distancia^F recorrida

clip
pinza^F

step setting
contador^M

case
caja^F

MEASURE OF THICKNESS
MEDICIÓN^F DEL ESPESOR^M

MICROMETER CALIPER
MICRÓMETRO^M

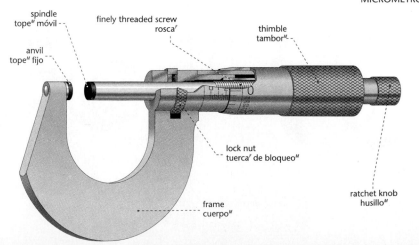

spindle
tope^M móvil

finely threaded screw
rosca^F

thimble
tambor^{ML}

anvil
tope^M fijo

lock nut
tuerca^F de bloqueo^M

frame
cuerpo^M

ratchet knob
husillo^M

711

WATT-HOUR METER
VATÍMETRO^M

EXTERIOR VIEW
VISTA^F EXTERIOR

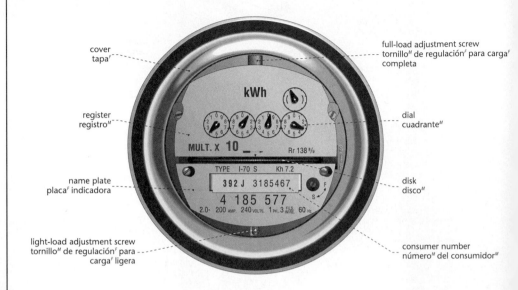

cover
tapa^F

full-load adjustment screw
tornillo^M de regulación^F para carga^F
completa

register
registro^M

dial
cuadrante^M

name plate
placa^F indicadora

disk
disco^M

light-load adjustment screw
tornillo^M de regulación^F para
carga^F ligera

consumer number
número^M del consumidor^M

MECHANISM
MECANISMO^M

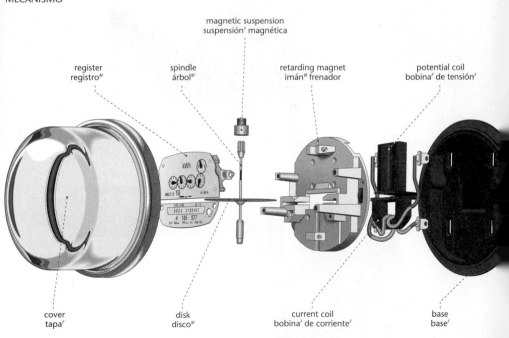

magnetic suspension
suspensión^F magnética

register
registro^M

spindle
árbol^M

retarding magnet
imán^M frenador

potential coil
bobina^F de tensión^F

cover
tapa^F

disk
disco^M

current coil
bobina^F de corriente^F

base
base^F

THEODOLITE
TEODOLITO^M

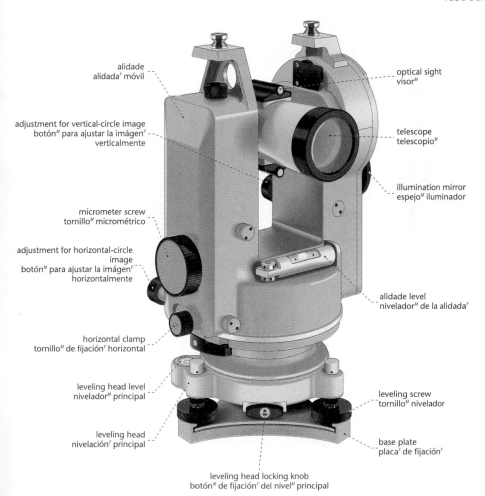

alidade
alidada^F móvil

optical sight
visor^M

adjustment for vertical-circle image
botón^M para ajustar la imágen^F
verticalmente

telescope
telescopio^M

illumination mirror
espejo^M iluminador

micrometer screw
tornillo^M micrométrico

adjustment for horizontal-circle
image
botón^M para ajustar la imágen^F
horizontalmente

alidade level
nivelador^M de la alidada^F

horizontal clamp
tornillo^M de fijación^F horizontal

leveling head level
nivelador^M principal

leveling screw
tornillo^M nivelador

leveling head
nivelación^F principal

base plate
placa^F de fijación^F

leveling head locking knob
botón^M de fijación^F del nivel^M principal

bevel square
falsa escuadra^F

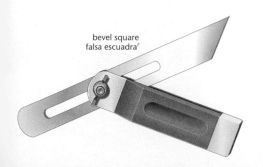

protractor
transportador^M

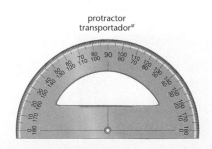

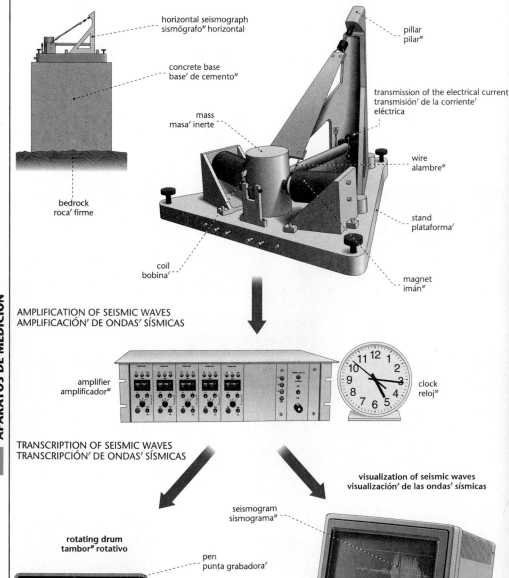

MEASURE OF SEISMIC WAVES
MEDICIÓN^F DE ONDAS^F SÍSMICAS

DETECTION OF SEISMIC WAVES
DETECCIÓN^F DE ONDAS^F SÍSMICAS

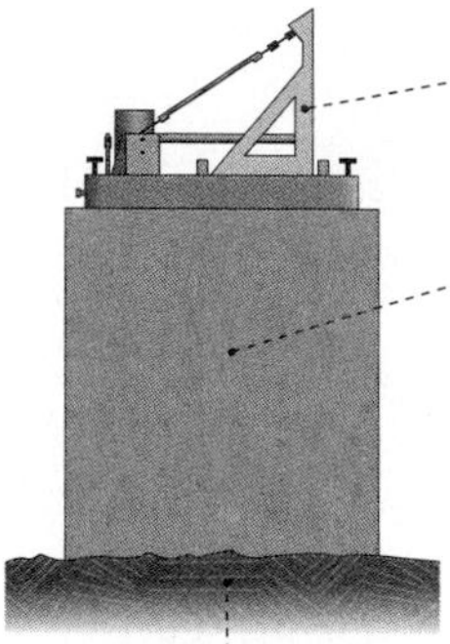

horizontal seismograph
sismógrafo^M horizontal

concrete base
base^F de cemento^M

mass
masa^F inerte

bedrock
roca^F firme

coil
bobina^F

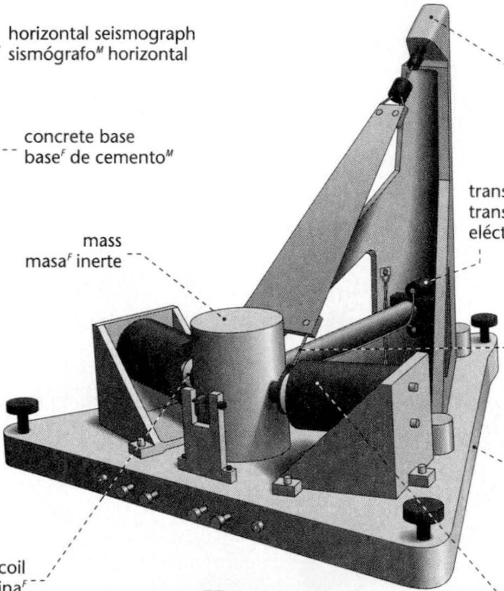

pillar
pilar^M

transmission of the electrical current
transmisión^F de la corriente^F
eléctrica

wire
alambre^M

stand
plataforma^F

magnet
imán^M

AMPLIFICATION OF SEISMIC WAVES
AMPLIFICACIÓN^F DE ONDAS^F SÍSMICAS

amplifier
amplificador^M

clock
reloj^M

TRANSCRIPTION OF SEISMIC WAVES
TRANSCRIPCIÓN^F DE ONDAS^F SÍSMICAS

visualization of seismic waves
visualización^F de las ondas^F sísmicas

seismogram
sismograma^M

rotating drum
tambor^M rotativo

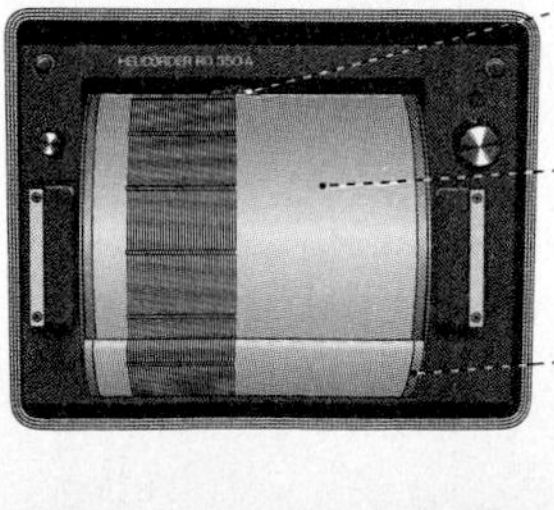

pen
punta grabadora^F

drum
tambor^M

sheet of paper
papel^M

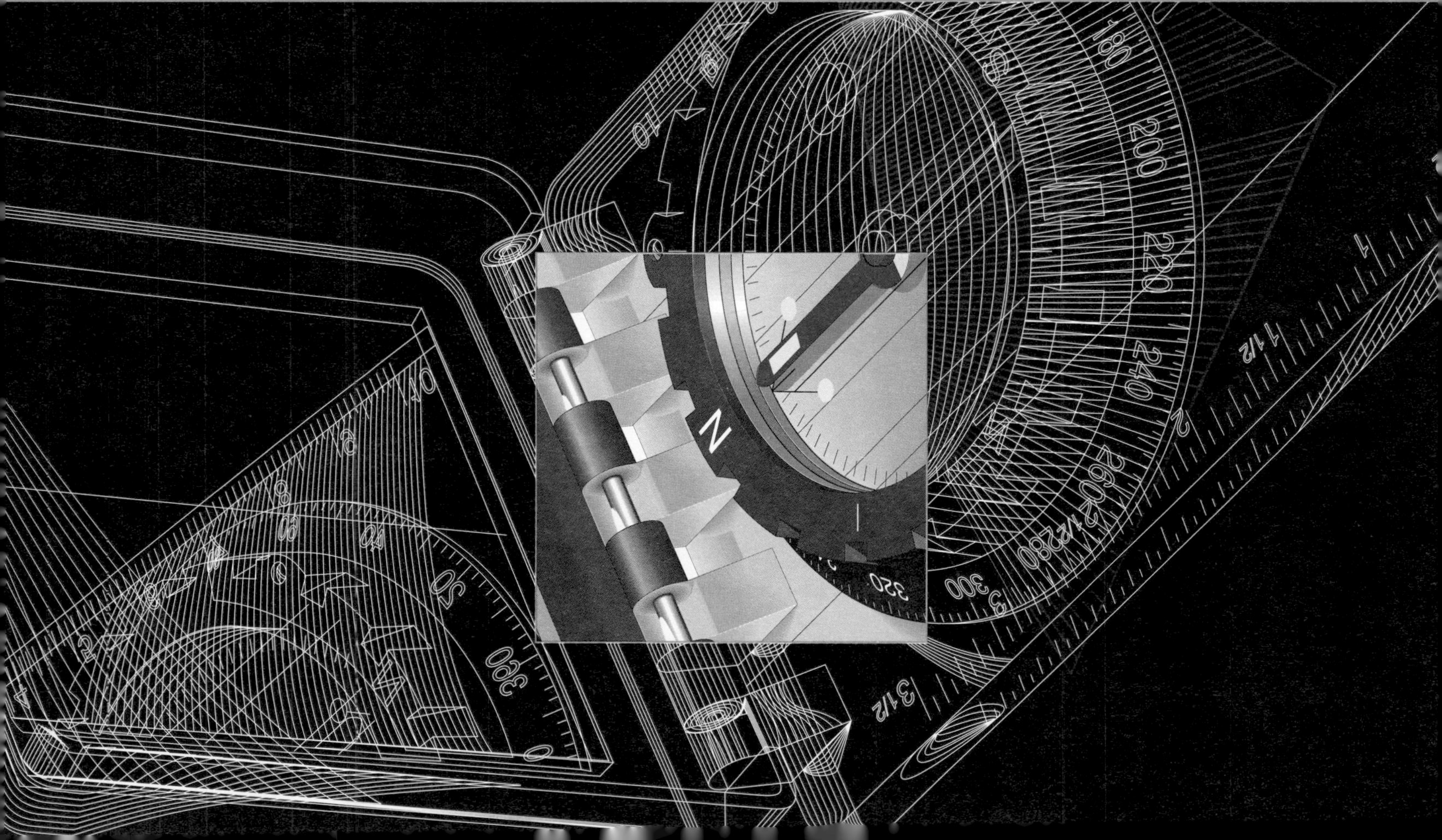

CONTENTS

**OPTICAL INSTRUMENTS
INSTRUMENTOS ÓPTICOS**

ELECTRON MICROSCOPE
MICROSCOPIO^M DE ELECTRONES

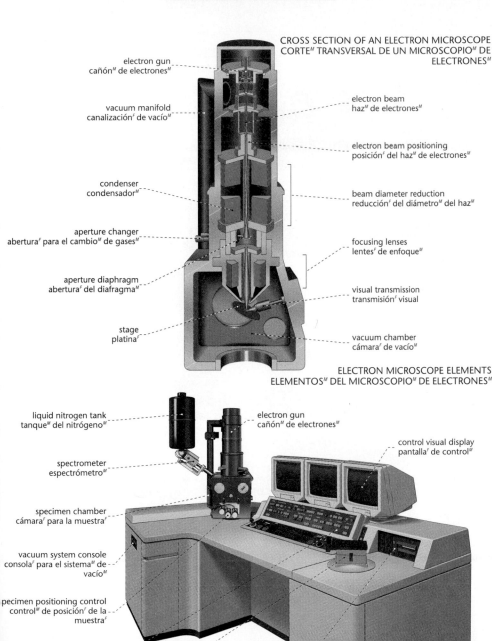

CROSS SECTION OF AN ELECTRON MICROSCOPE
CORTE^M TRANSVERSAL DE UN MICROSCOPIO^M DE
ELECTRONES^M

electron gun
cañón^M de electrones^M

vacuum manifold
canalización^F de vacío^M

condenser
condensador^M

aperture changer
abertura^F para el cambio^M de gases^M

aperture diaphragm
abertura^F del diafragma^M

stage
platina^F

electron beam
haz^M de electrones^M

electron beam positioning
posición^F del haz^M de electrones^M

beam diameter reduction
reducción^F del diámetro^M del haz^M

focusing lenses
lentes^F de enfoque^M

visual transmission
transmisión^F visual

vacuum chamber
cámara^F de vacío^M

ELECTRON MICROSCOPE ELEMENTS
ELEMENTOS^M DEL MICROSCOPIO^M DE ELECTRONES^M

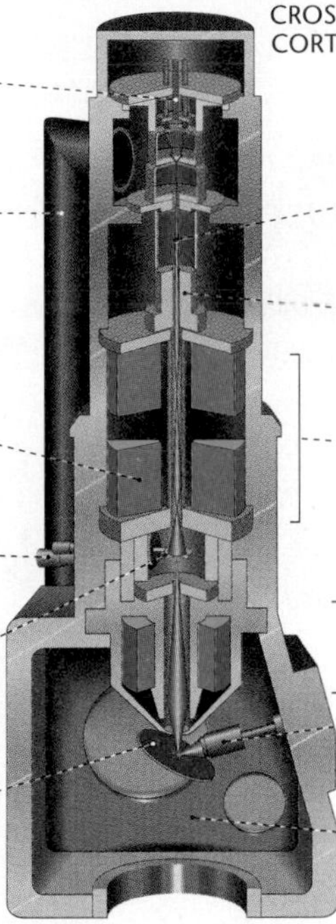

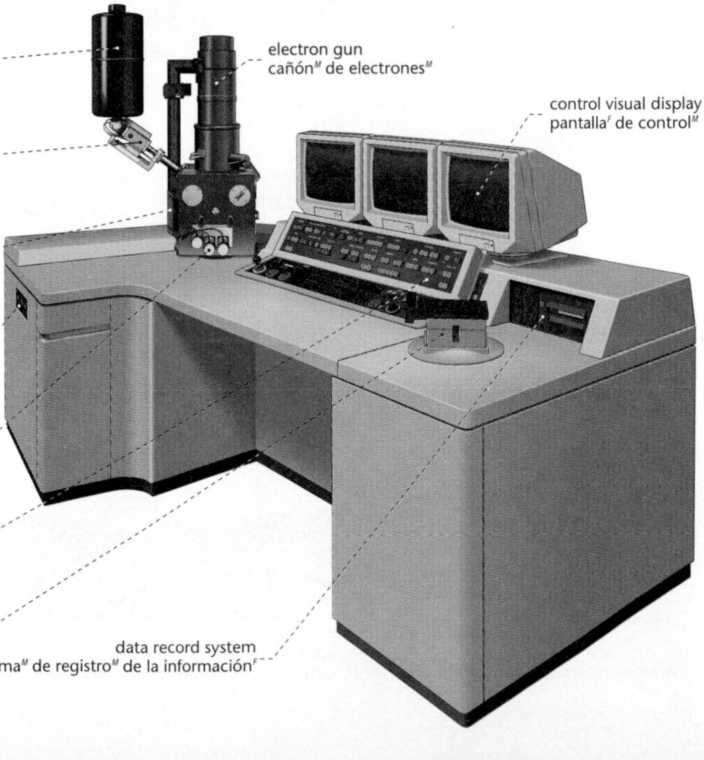

liquid nitrogen tank
tanque^M del nitrógeno^M

spectrometer
espectrómetro^M

specimen chamber
cámara^F para la muestra^F

vacuum system console
consola^F para el sistema^M de
vacío^M

pecimen positioning control
control^M de posición^F de la
muestra^F

control panel
tablero^M de control^M

photographic chamber
cámara^F de fotografía^F

electron gun
cañón^M de electrones^M

control visual display
pantalla^F de control^M

data record system
sistema^M de registro^M de la información^F

BINOCULAR MICROSCOPE
MICROSCOPIO^M BINOCULAR

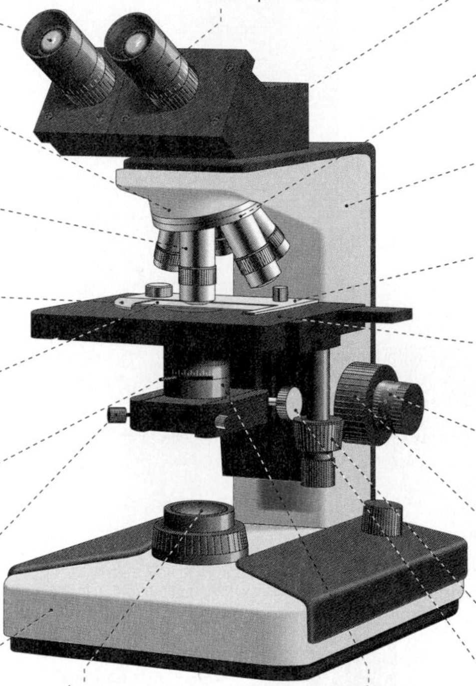

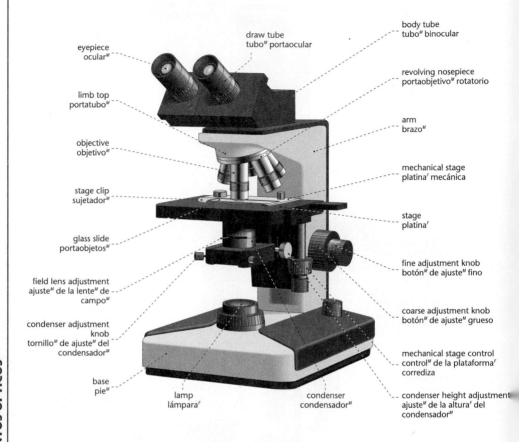

eyepiece
ocular^M

draw tube
tubo^M portaocular

body tube
tubo^M binocular

limb top
portatubo^M

revolving nosepiece
portaobjetivo^M rotatorio

objective
objetivo^M

arm
brazo^M

mechanical stage
platina^F mecánica

stage clip
sujetador^M

stage
platina^F

glass slide
portaobjetos^M

fine adjustment knob
botón^M de ajuste^M fino

field lens adjustment
ajuste^M de la lente^M de
campo^M

coarse adjustment knob
botón^M de ajuste^M grueso

condenser adjustment
knob
tornillo^M de ajuste^M del
condensador^M

mechanical stage control
control^M de la plataforma^F
corrediza

base
pie^M

lamp
lámpara^F

condenser
condensador^M

condenser height adjustment
ajuste^M de la altura^F del
condensador^M

TELESCOPIC SIGHT
VISOR^M TELESCÓPICO

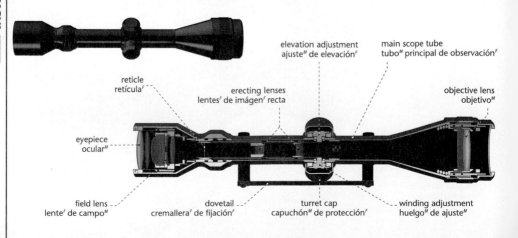

reticle
retícula^F

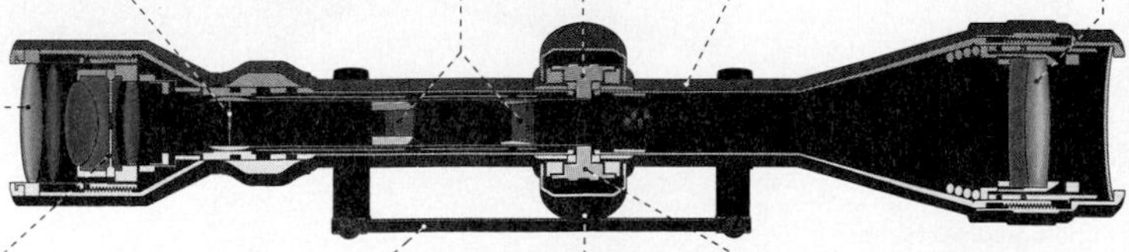

elevation adjustment
ajuste^M de elevación^F

main scope tube
tubo^M principal de observación^F

erecting lenses
lentes^F de imágen^F recta

objective lens
objetivo^M

eyepiece
ocular^M

field lens
lente^F de campo^M

dovetail
cremallera^F de fijación^F

turret cap
capuchón^M de protección^F

winding adjustment
huelgo^M de ajuste^M

PRISM BINOCULARS
PRISMÁTICOS^M BINOCULARES

eyepiece
ocular^M

lens system
sistema^M de lentes^F

Porro prism
prisma^M de Porro

hinge
bisagra^F

objective lens
objetivo^M

focusing ring
anillo^M de enfoque^M

central focusing wheel
rueda^F central de enfoque^M

bridge
puente^M

body
tubo^M

MAGNETIC COMPASS
BRÚJULA^F MAGNÉTICA

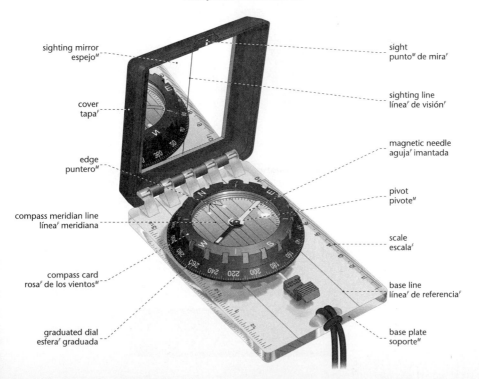

sighting mirror
espejo^M

cover
tapa^F

edge
puntero^M

compass meridian line
línea^F meridiana

compass card
rosa^F de los vientos^M

graduated dial
esfera^F graduada

sight
punto^M de mira^F

sighting line
línea^F de visión^F

magnetic needle
aguja^F imantada

pivot
pivote^M

scale
escala^F

base line
línea^F de referencia^F

base plate
soporte^M

REFLECTING TELESCOPE
TELESCOPIO^M REFLECTOR

support
soporte^M

finderscope
anteojo^M buscador

eyepiece
ocular^M

cradle
abrazadera^F

main tube
tubo^M principal

focusing knob
botón^M de enfoque^M

declination setting scale
disco^M de ajuste^M de declinación^F

right ascension setting scale
disco^M de ajuste^M de ascención^F recta

azimuth clamp
bloqueo^M del ajuste^M del acimut^M

azimuth fine adjustment
ajuste^M fino del acimut^M

altitude clamp
bloqueo^M del ajuste^M de la altura^F

altitude fine adjustment
ajuste^M fino de la altura^F

CROSS SECTION OF A REFLECTING TELESCOPE
CORTE^M TRANSVERSAL DE UN TELECOPIO^M REFLECTOR

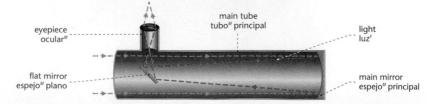

eyepiece
ocular^M

main tube
tubo^M principal

light
luz^F

flat mirror
espejo^M plano

main mirror
espejo^M principal

REFRACTING TELESCOPE
TELESCOPIO^M REFRACTOR

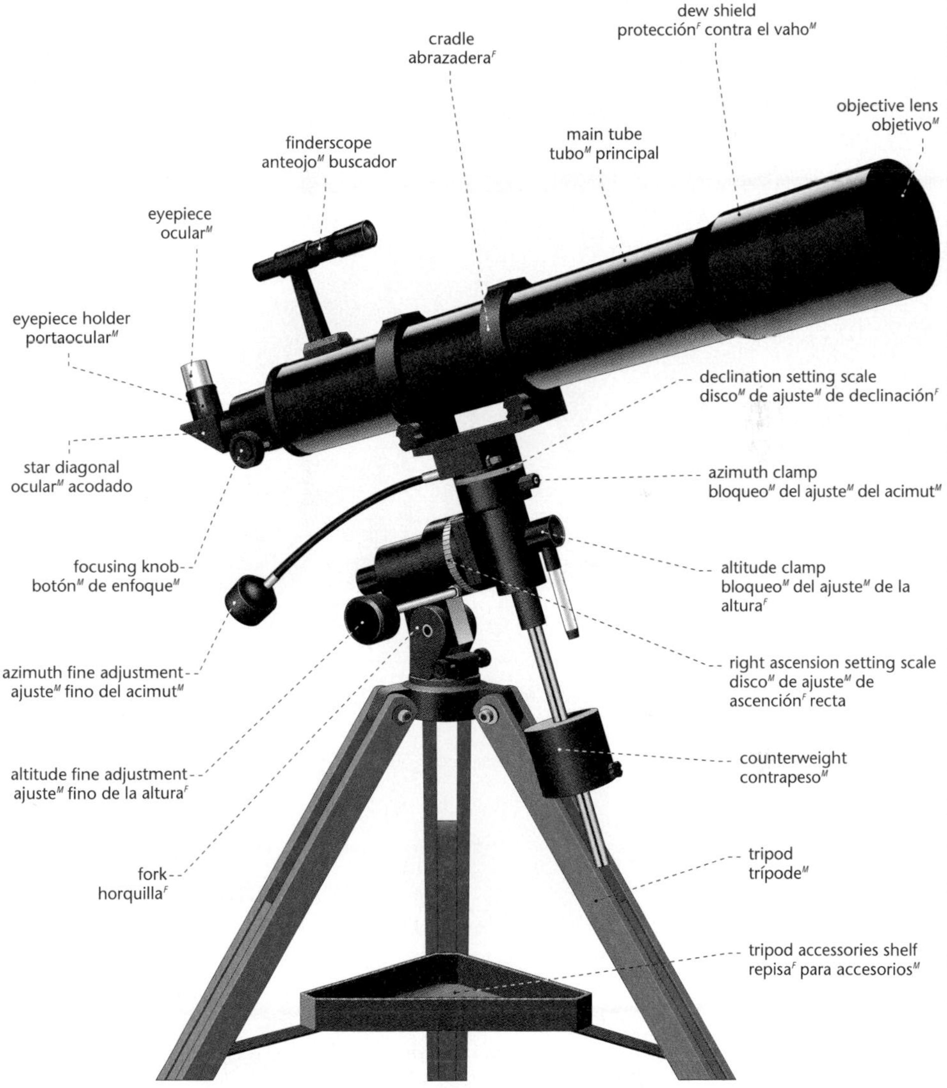

cradle
abrazadera^F

dew shield
protección^F contra el vaho^M

objective lens
objetivo^M

finderscope
anteojo^M buscador

main tube
tubo^M principal

eyepiece
ocular^M

eyepiece holder
portaocular^M

declination setting scale
disco^M de ajuste^M de declinación^F

star diagonal
ocular^M acodado

azimuth clamp
bloqueo^M del ajuste^M del acimut^M

focusing knob
botón^M de enfoque^M

altitude clamp
bloqueo^M del ajuste^M de la
altura^F

azimuth fine adjustment
ajuste^M fino del acimut^M

right ascension setting scale
disco^M de ajuste^M de
ascención^F recta

altitude fine adjustment
ajuste^M fino de la altura^F

counterweight
contrapeso^M

fork
horquilla^F

tripod
trípode^M

tripod accessories shelf
repisa^F para accesorios^M

CROSS SECTION OF A REFRACTING TELESCOPE
CORTE^M TRANSVERSAL DE UN TELESCOPIO^M REFRACTOR

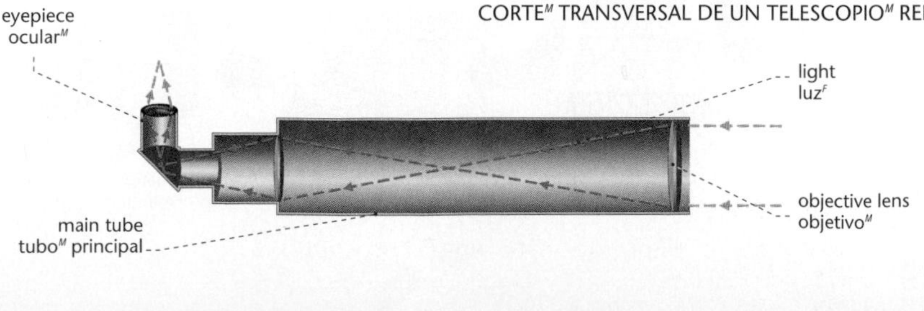

eyepiece
ocular^M

light
luz^F

objective lens
objetivo^M

main tube
tubo^M principal

721

LENSES
LENTES^F

CONVERGING LENSES
LENTES^F CONVERGENTES

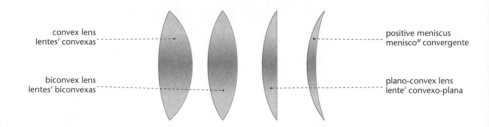

convex lens
lentes^F convexas

biconvex lens
lentes^F biconvexas

positive meniscus
menisco^M convergente

plano-convex lens
lente^F convexo-plana

DIVERGING LENSES
LENTES^F DIVERGENTES

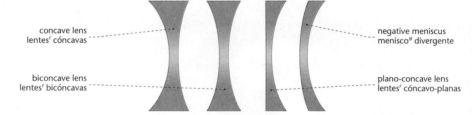

concave lens
lentes^F cóncavas

biconcave lens
lentes^F bicóncavas

negative meniscus
menisco^M divergente

plano-concave lens
lentes^F cóncavo-planas

RADAR
RADAR^M

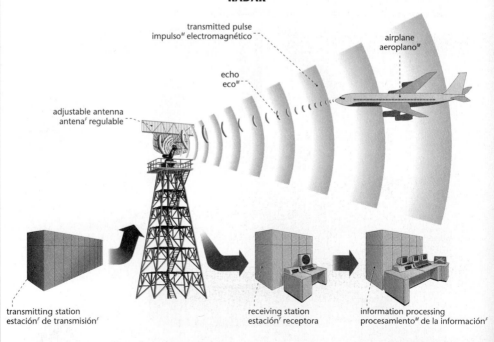

transmitted pulse
impulso^M electromagnético

echo
eco^M

airplane
aeroplano^M

adjustable antenna
antena^F regulable

transmitting station
estación^F de transmisión^F

receiving station
estación^F receptora

information processing
procesamiento^M de la información^F

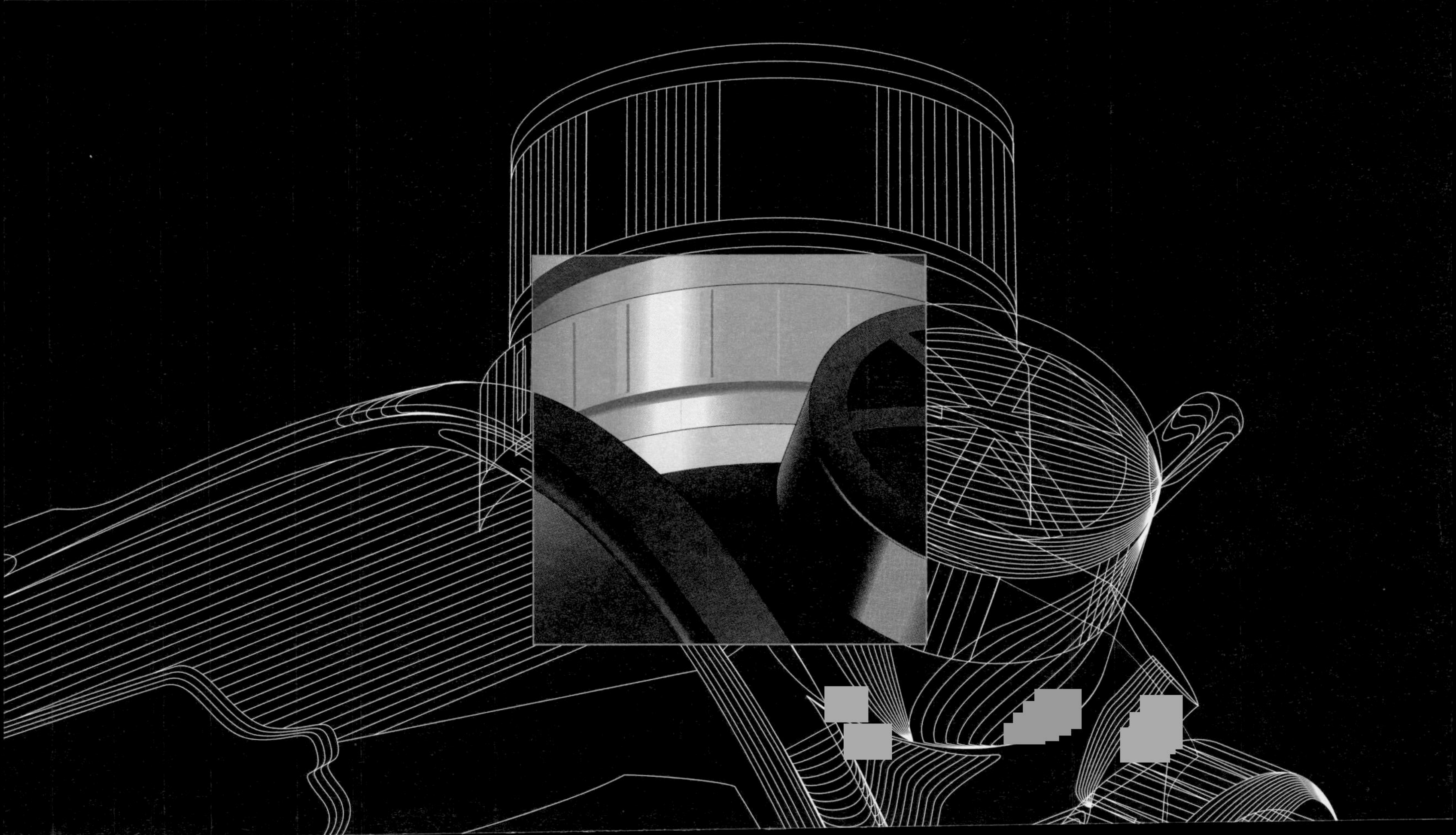

HEALTH AND SAFETY • SALUD Y SEGURIDAD

CONTENTS

HEALTH AND SAFETY
SALUD Y SEGURIDAD

FIRST AID KIT
BOTIQUÍN^M DE PRIMEROS AUXILIOS^M

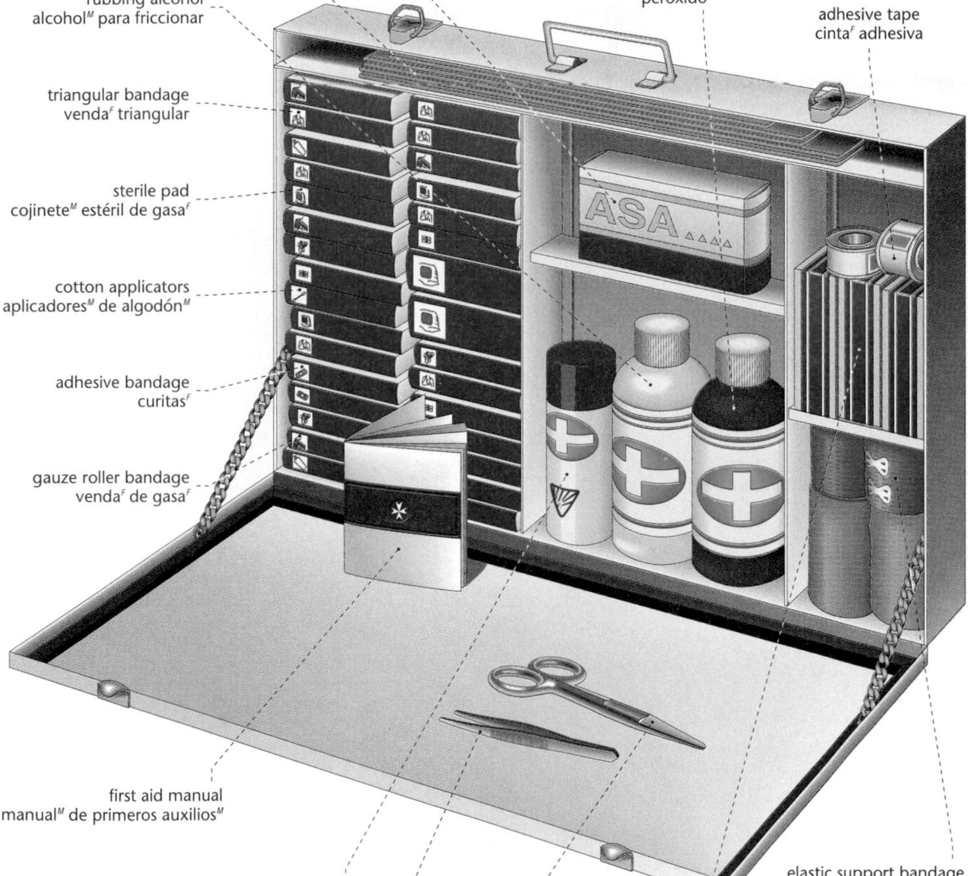

splints
tablillas^F

aspirin
aspirina^F

peroxide
peróxido^M

adhesive tape
cinta^F adhesiva

rubbing alcohol
alcohol^M para friccionar

triangular bandage
venda^F triangular

sterile pad
cojinete^M estéril de gasa^F

cotton applicators
aplicadores^M de algodón^M

adhesive bandage
curitas^F

gauze roller bandage
venda^F de gasa^F

first aid manual
manual^M de primeros auxilios^M

antiseptic
antiséptico^M

scissors
tijeras^F

elastic support bandage
venda^F elástica

absorbent cotton
algodón^M absorbente

tweezers
pinzas^F

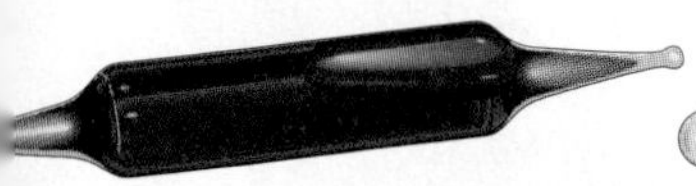

vial
ampolleta^F

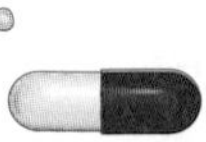

capsule
cápsula^F

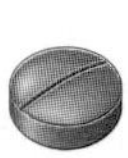

tablet
tableta^F

gelatin capsule
cápsula^F de gelatina^F

FIRST AID EQUIPMENT
EQUIPO^M DE PRIMEROS AUXILIOS^M

STETHOSCOPE
ESTETOSCOPIO^M

SYRINGE
JERINGA^F

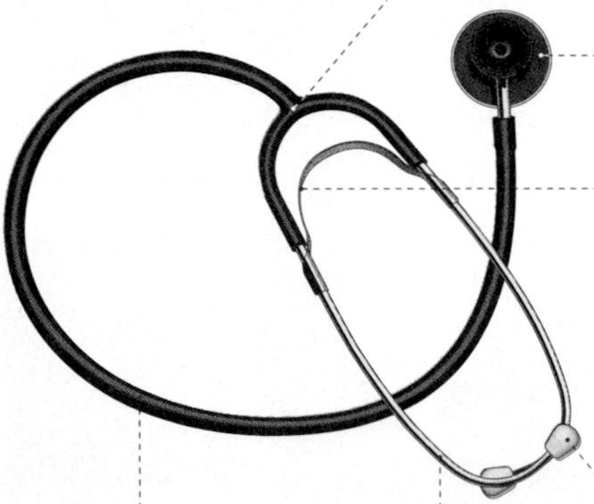

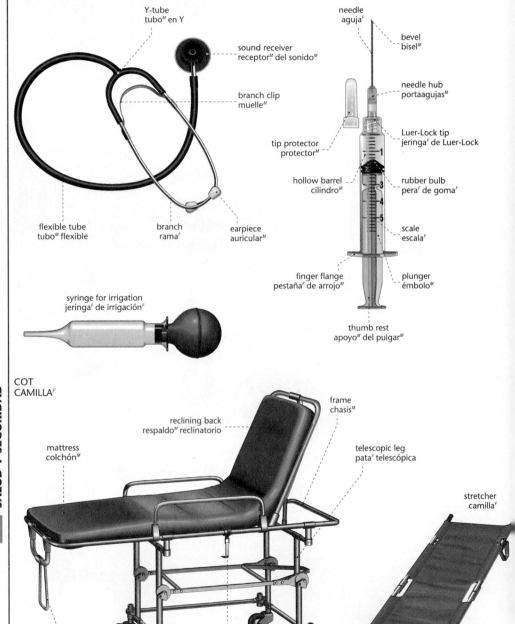

Y-tube
tubo^M en Y

sound receiver
receptor^M del sonido^M

branch clip
muelle^M

flexible tube
tubo^M flexible

branch
rama^F

earpiece
auricular^M

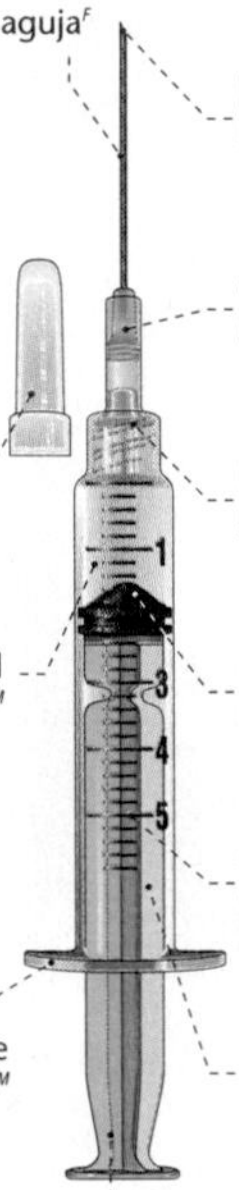

needle
aguja^F

bevel
bisel^M

needle hub
portaagujas^M

Luer-Lock tip
jeringa^F de Luer-Lock

tip protector
protector^M

hollow barrel
cilindro^M

rubber bulb
pera^F de goma^F

scale
escala^F

finger flange
pestaña^F de arrojo^M

plunger
émbolo^M

thumb rest
apoyo^M del pulgar^M

syringe for irrigation
jeringa^F de irrigación^F

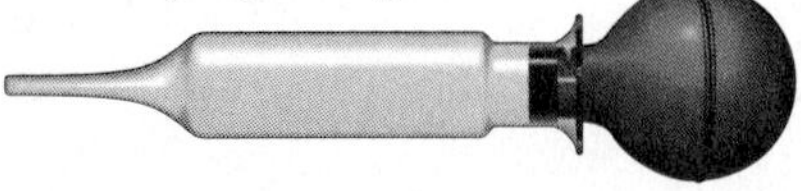

COT
CAMILLA^F

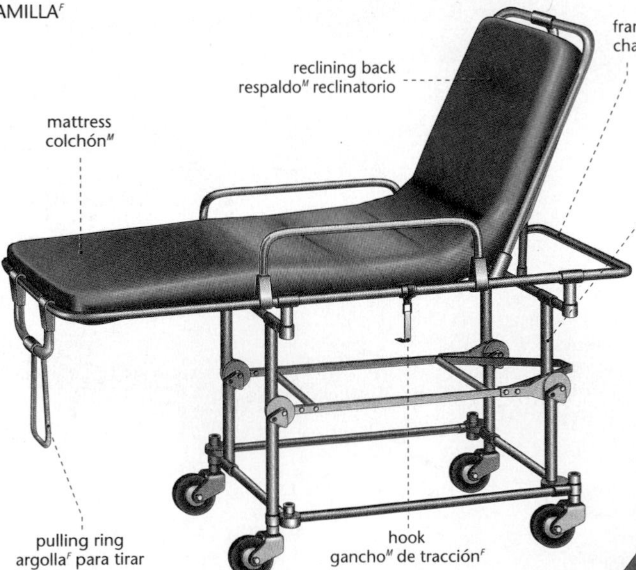

reclining back
respaldo^M reclinatorio

frame
chasis^M

mattress
colchón^M

telescopic leg
pata^F telescópica

stretcher
camilla^F

pulling ring
argolla^F para tirar

hook
gancho^M de tracción^F

726

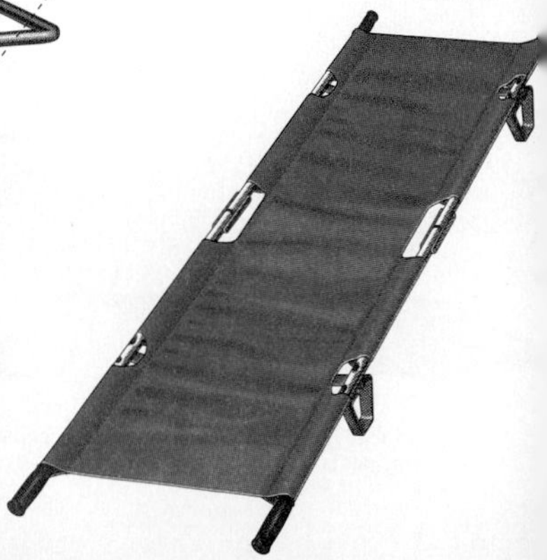

WHEELCHAIR
SILLA^F DE RUEDAS^F

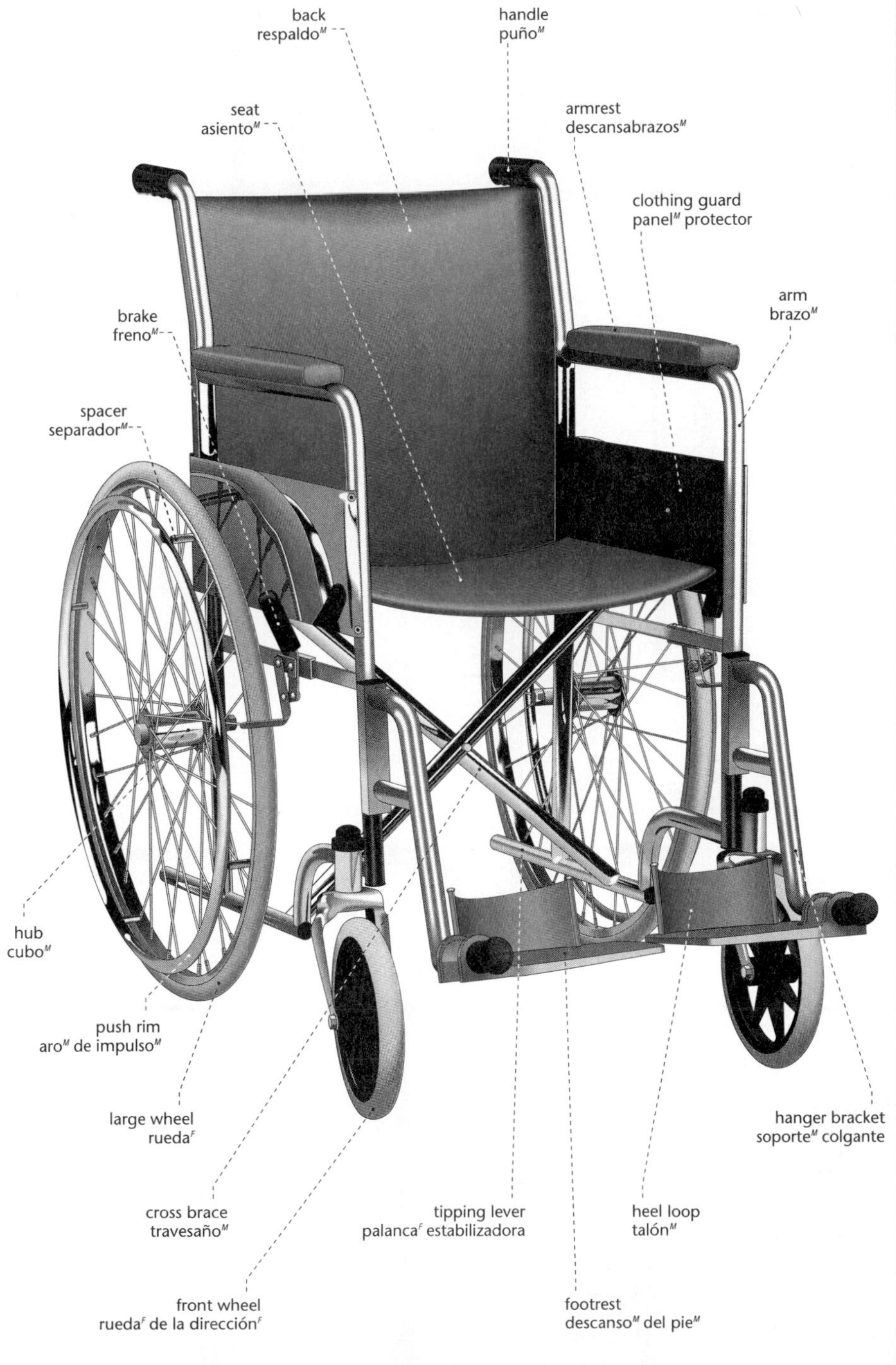

back
respaldo^M

handle
puño^M

seat
asiento^M

armrest
descansabrazos^M

clothing guard
panel^M protector

brake
freno^M

arm
brazo^M

spacer
separador^M

hub
cubo^M

push rim
aro^M de impulso^M

large wheel
rueda^F

hanger bracket
soporte^M colgante

cross brace
travesaño^M

tipping lever
palanca^F estabilizadora

heel loop
talón^M

front wheel
rueda^F de la dirección^F

footrest
descanso^M del pie^M

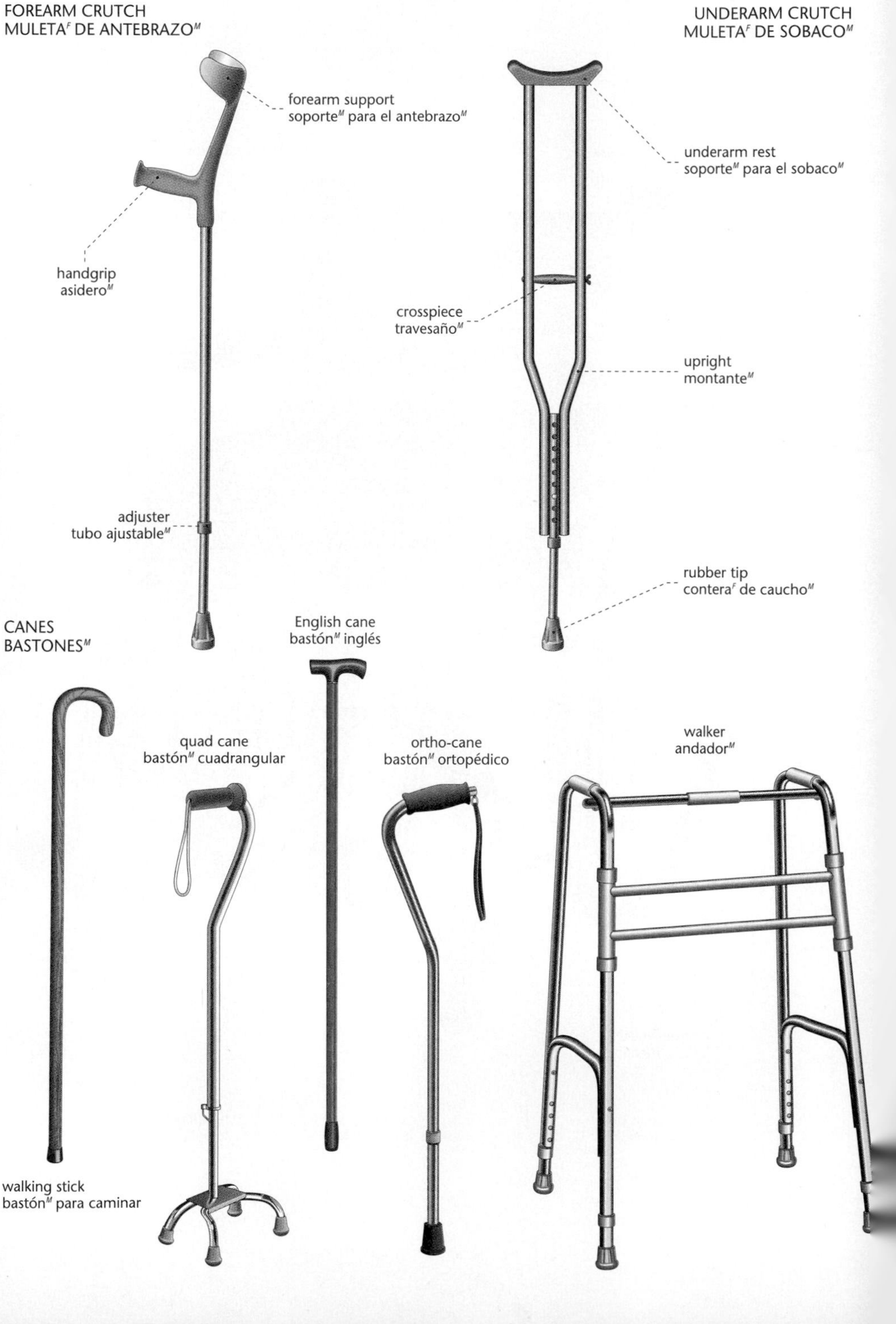

FOREARM CRUTCH
MULETA^F DE ANTEBRAZO^M

UNDERARM CRUTCH
MULETA^F DE SOBACO^M

forearm support
soporte^M para el antebrazo^M

underarm rest
soporte^M para el sobaco^M

handgrip
asidero^M

crosspiece
travesaño^M

upright
montante^M

adjuster
tubo ajustable^M

rubber tip
contera^F de caucho^M

CANES
BASTONES^M

English cane
bastón^M inglés

quad cane
bastón^M cuadrangular

ortho-cane
bastón^M ortopédico

walker
andador^M

walking stick
bastón^M para caminar

**HEALTH AND SAFETY
SALUD Y SEGURIDAD**

728

EAR PROTECTION
PROTECCIÓN*F* PARA LOS OÍDOS*M*

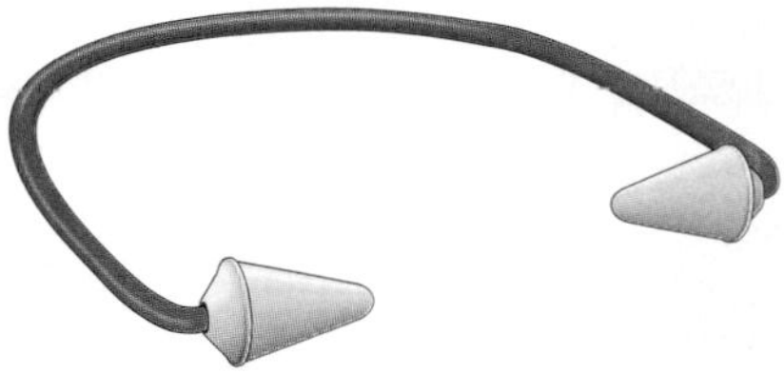

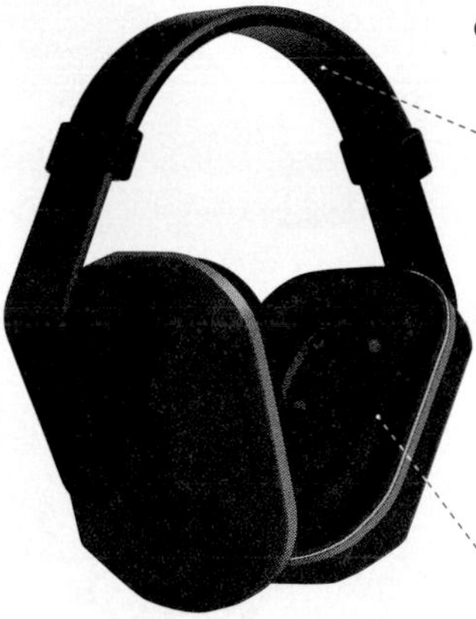

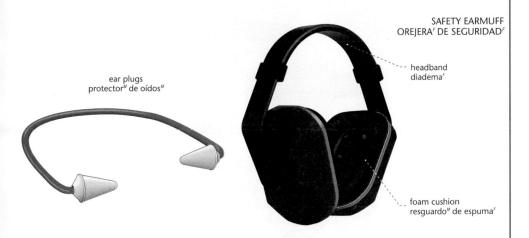

SAFETY EARMUFF
OREJERA*F* DE SEGURIDAD*F*

headband
diadema*F*

ear plugs
protector*M* de oídos*M*

foam cushion
resguardo*M* de espuma*F*

EYE PROTECTION
PROTECCIÓN*F* PARA LOS OJOS*M*

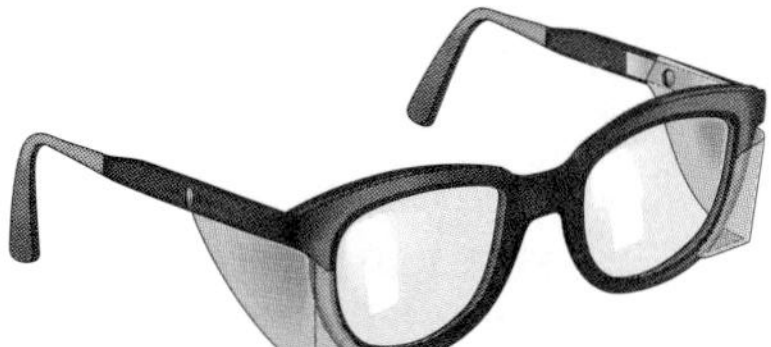

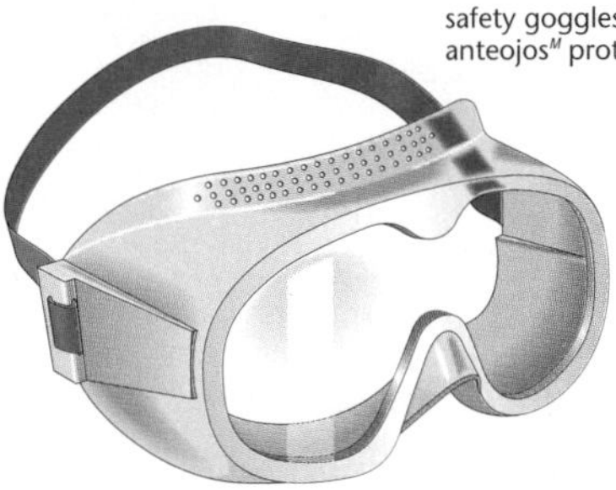

safety goggles
anteojos*M* protectores

safety glasses
anteojos*M* de seguridad*F*

HEAD PROTECTION
PROTECCIÓN*F* PARA LA CABEZA*F*

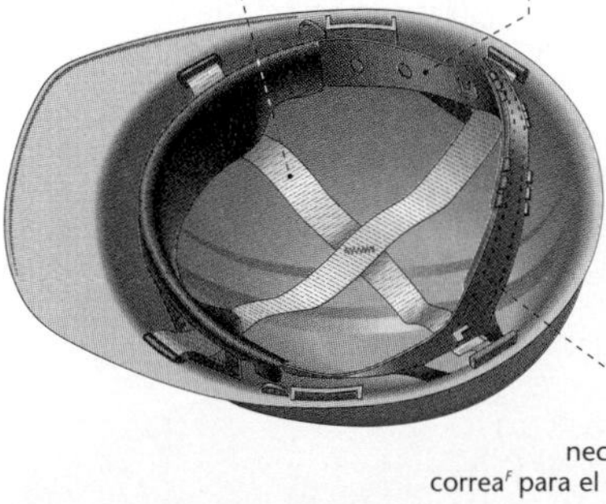

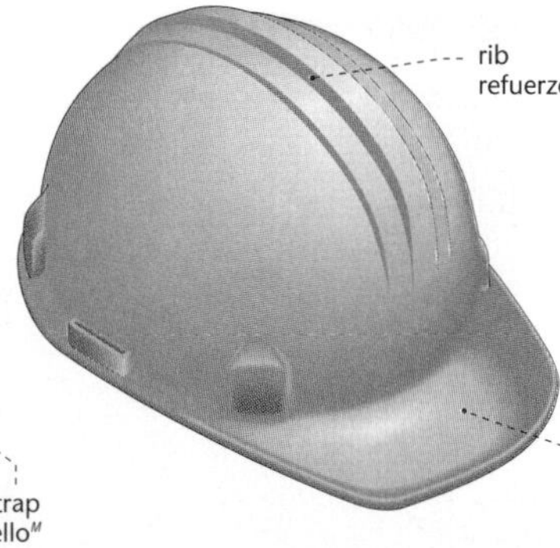

SAFETY CAP
CASCO*M* DE SEGURIDAD*F*

suspension band
banda*F* de suspensión*F*

headband
cinta*F*

rib
refuerzo*M*

neck strap
correa*F* para el cuello*M*

peak
visera*F*

RESPIRATORY SYSTEM PROTECTION
PROTECCIÓN^F PARA EL SISTEMA^M RESPIRATORIO^M

RESPIRATOR
MÁSCARA^F DE GAS^M

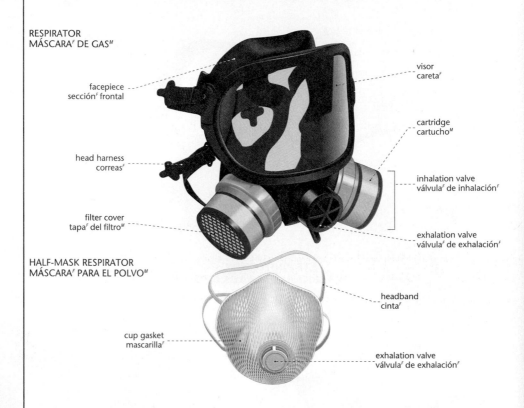

facepiece
sección^F frontal

visor
careta^F

head harness
correas^F

cartridge
cartucho^M

inhalation valve
válvula^F de inhalación^F

filter cover
tapa^F del filtro^M

exhalation valve
válvula^F de exhalación^F

HALF-MASK RESPIRATOR
MÁSCARA^F PARA EL POLVO^M

headband
cinta^F

cup gasket
mascarilla^F

exhalation valve
válvula^F de exhalación^F

SAFETY VEST
CHALECO^M DE SEGURIDAD^F

FEET PROTECTION
PROTECCIÓN^F PARA LOS PIES^M

toe guard
puntera^F protectora

SAFETY BOOT
BOTA^F DE SEGURIDAD^F

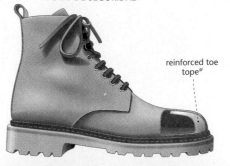

reinforced toe
tope^M

reflective stripe
banda^F reflectora

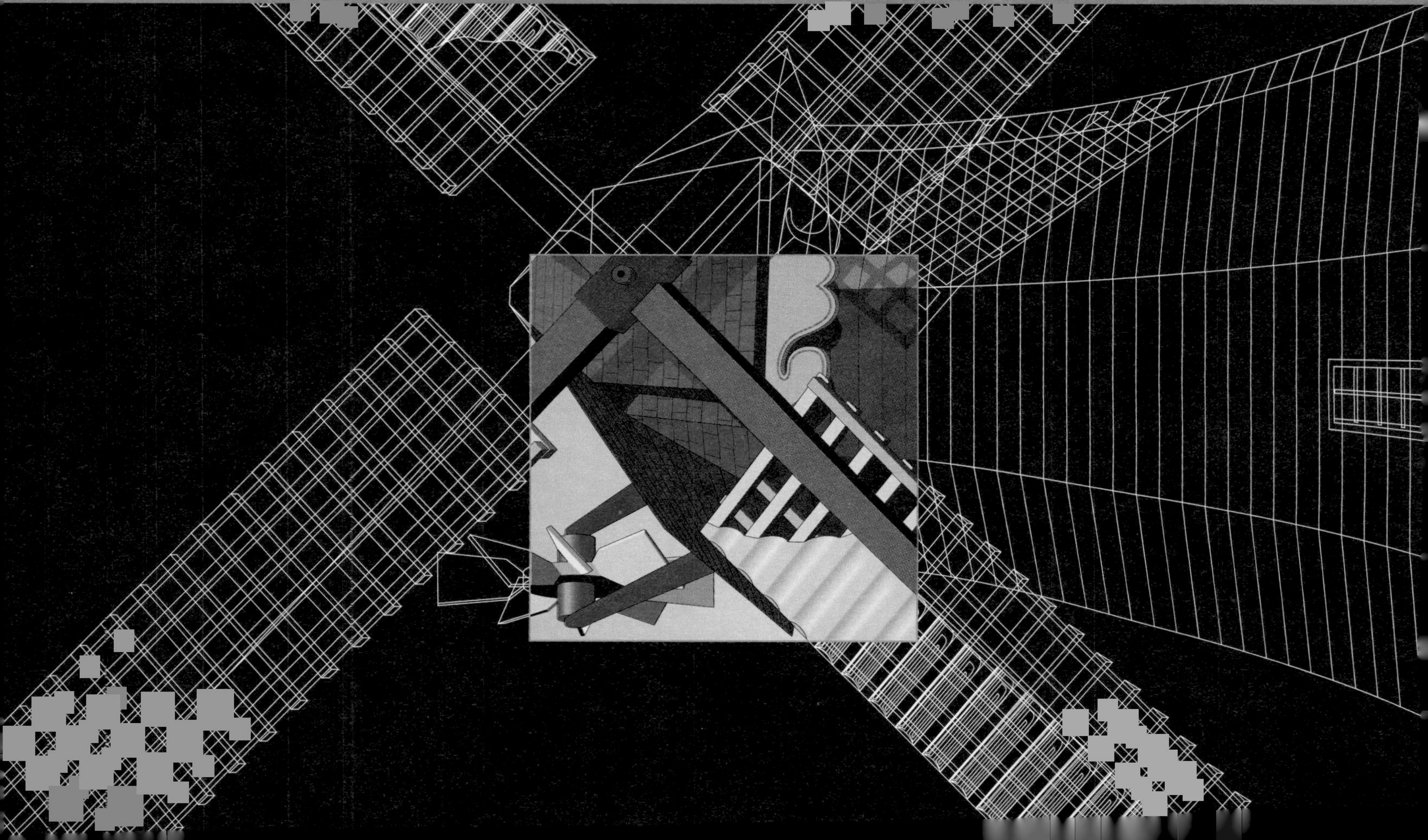

CONTENTS

COAL MINE
MINAS^F DE CARBÓN^M

OPEN-PIT MINE
MINA^F A CIELO^M ABIERTO

face
frente^M de corte^M

bench
antepecho^M

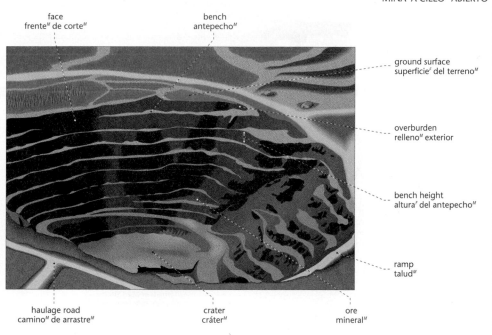

ground surface
superficie^F del terreno^M

overburden
relleno^M exterior

bench height
altura^F del antepecho^M

ramp
talud^M

haulage road
camino^M de arrastre^M

crater
cráter^M

ore
mineral^M

STRIP MINE
EXCAVACIÓN^F A CIELO^M ABIERTO

dump
basurero^M

conveyor
banda^F transportadora

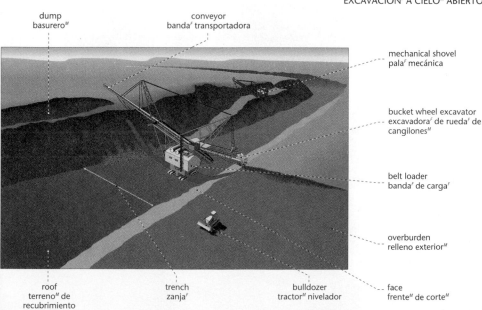

mechanical shovel
pala^F mecánica

bucket wheel excavator
excavadora^F de rueda^F de
cangilones^M

belt loader
banda^F de carga^F

overburden
relleno exterior^M

roof
terreno^M de
recubrimiento

trench
zanja^F

bulldozer
tractor^M nivelador

face
frente^M de corte^M

COAL MINE
MINA^F DE CARBÓN^M SUBTERRÁNEA

JACKLEG DRILL
TALADRO^M DE POSTE^M EXTENSIBLE

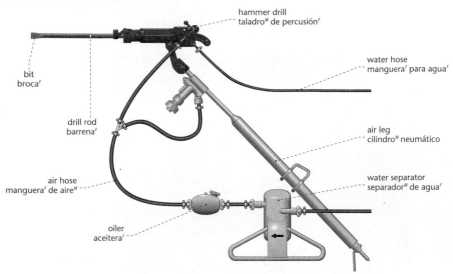

hammer drill
taladro^M de percusión^F

water hose
manguera^F para agua^F

bit
broca^F

drill rod
barrena^F

air leg
cilindro^M neumático

air hose
manguera^F de aire^M

water separator
separador^M de agua^F

oiler
aceitera^F

PITHEAD
PLANTA^F EXTERIOR

maintenance shop
taller^M de mantenimiento^M

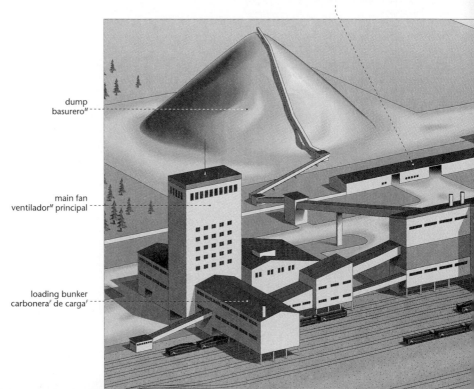

dump
basurero^M

main fan
ventilador^M principal

loading bunker
carbonera^F de carga^F

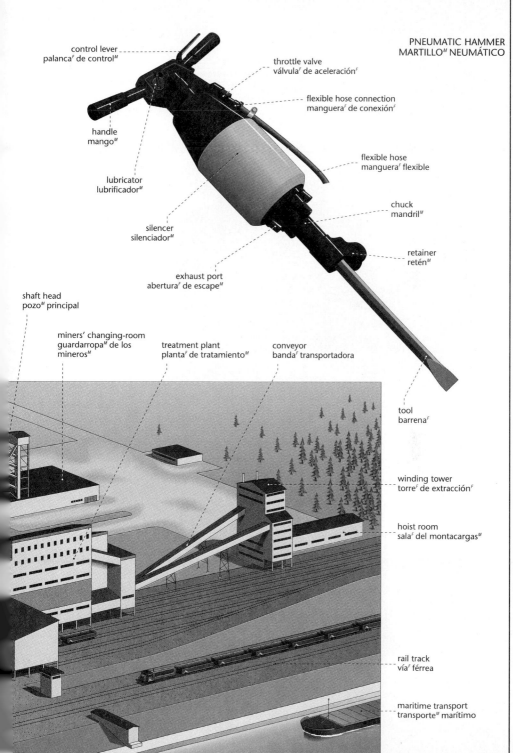

PNEUMATIC HAMMER
MARTILLO^M NEUMÁTICO

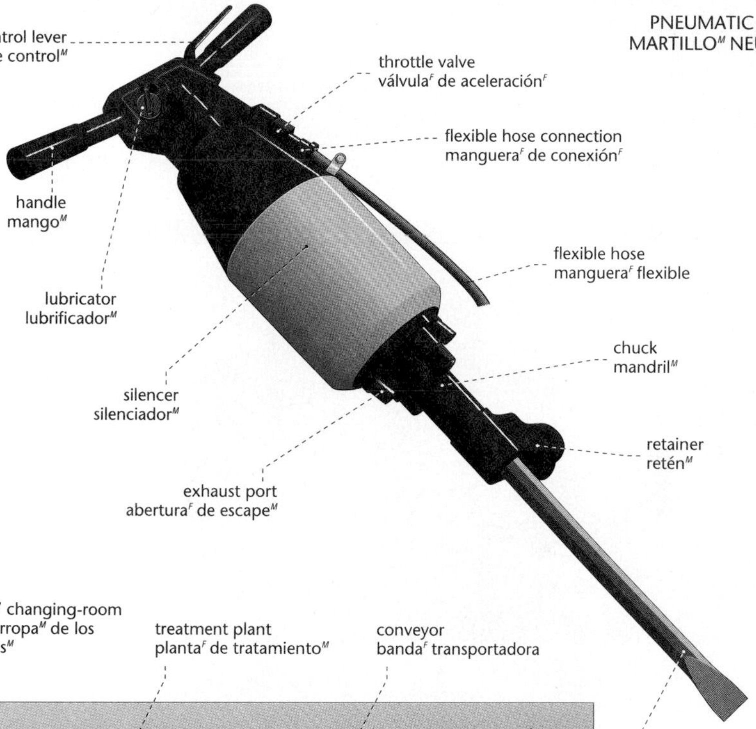

control lever
palanca^F de control^M

throttle valve
válvula^F de aceleración^F

flexible hose connection
manguera^F de conexión^F

handle
mango^M

flexible hose
manguera^F flexible

lubricator
lubrificador^M

chuck
mandril^M

silencer
silenciador^M

retainer
retén^M

exhaust port
abertura^F de escape^M

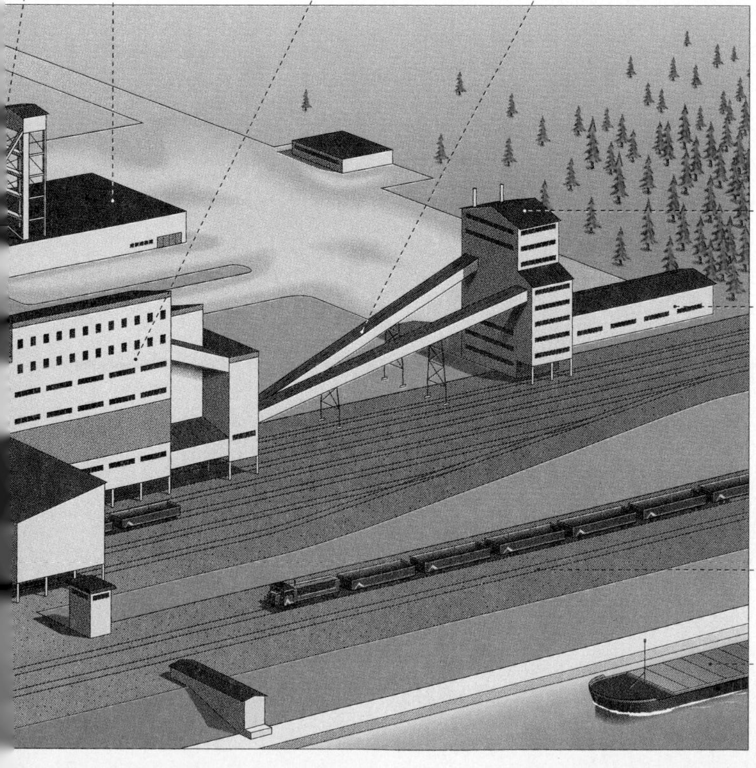

shaft head
pozo^M principal

miners' changing-room
guardarropa^M de los
mineros^M

treatment plant
planta^F de tratamiento^M

conveyor
banda^F transportadora

tool
barrena^F

winding tower
torre^F de extracción^F

hoist room
sala^F del montacargas^M

rail track
vía^F férrea

maritime transport
transporte^M marítimo

ENERGY
ENERGÍA

735

COAL MINE
MINA^F DE CARBÓN^M

UNDERGROUND MINE
MINA^F SUBTERRÁNEA

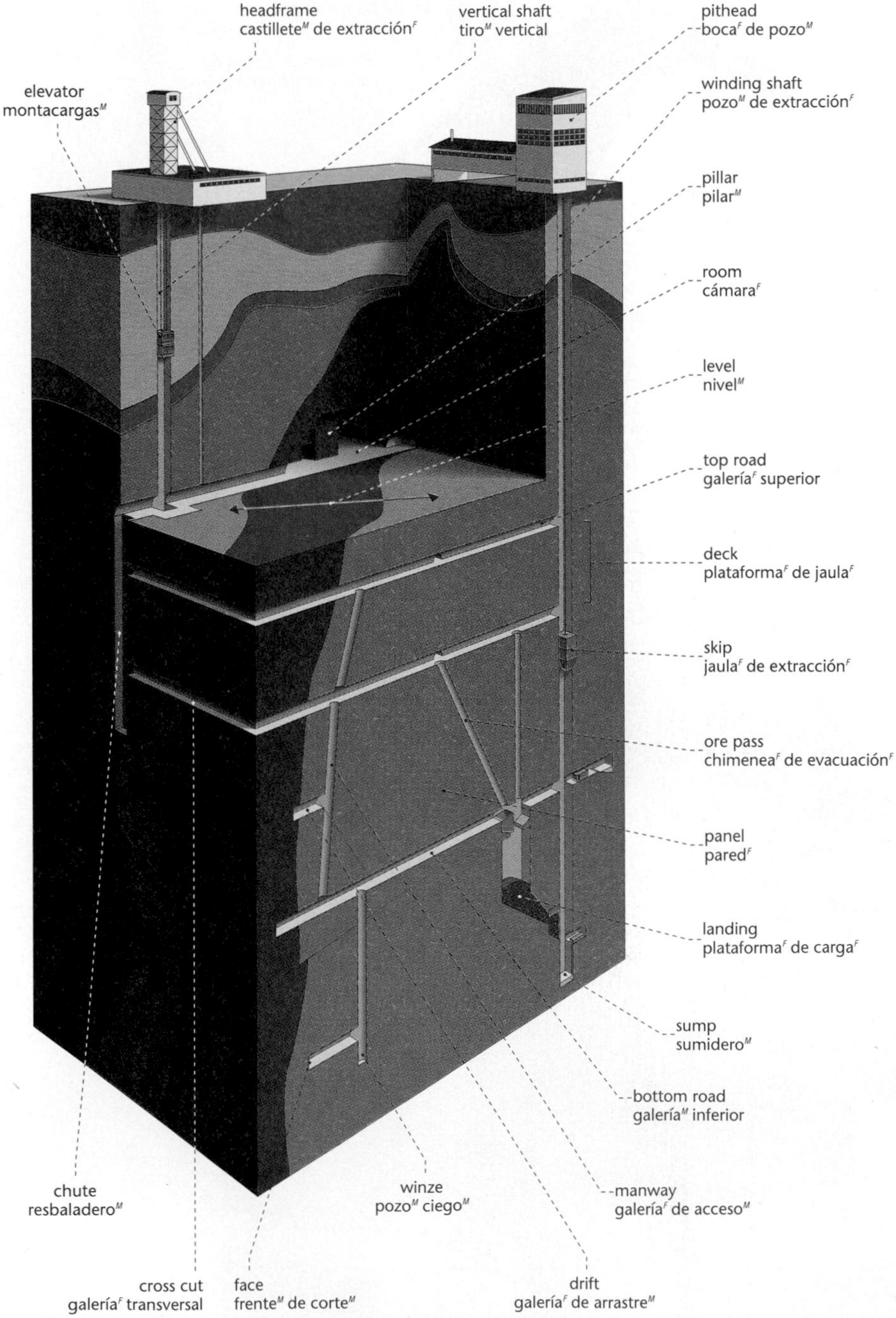

headframe
castillete^M de extracción^F

vertical shaft
tiro^M vertical

pithead
boca^F de pozo^M

elevator
montacargas^M

winding shaft
pozo^M de extracción^F

pillar
pilar^M

room
cámara^F

level
nivel^M

top road
galería^F superior

deck
plataforma^F de jaula^F

skip
jaula^F de extracción^F

ore pass
chimenea^F de evacuación^F

panel
pared^F

landing
plataforma^F de carga^F

sump
sumidero^M

bottom road
galería^M inferior

chute
resbaladero^M

winze
pozo^M ciego^M

manway
galería^F de acceso^M

cross cut
galería^F transversal

face
frente^M de corte^M

drift
galería^F de arrastre^M

ENERGY
ENERGÍA

736

OIL
PETRÓLEO^M

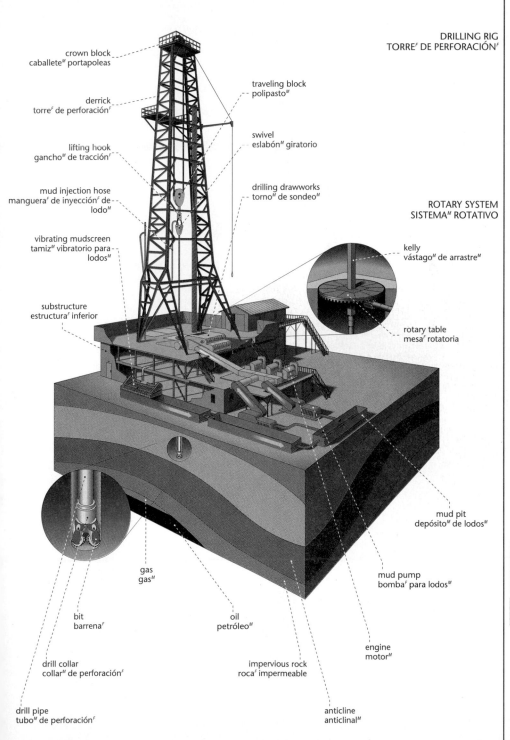

crown block
caballete^M portapoleas

derrick
torre^F de perforación^F

lifting hook
gancho^M de tracción^F

mud injection hose
manguera^F de inyección^F de
lodo^M

vibrating mudscreen
tamiz^M vibratorio para
lodos^M

substructure
estructura^F inferior

traveling block
polipasto^M

swivel
eslabón^M giratorio

drilling drawworks
torno^M de sondeo^M

ROTARY SYSTEM
SISTEMA^M ROTATIVO

kelly
vástago^M de arrastre^M

rotary table
mesa^F rotatoria

mud pit
depósito^M de lodos^M

gas
gas^M

mud pump
bomba^F para lodos^M

bit
barrena^F

oil
petróleo^M

drill collar
collar^M de perforación^F

engine
motor^M

impervious rock
roca^F impermeable

drill pipe
tubo^M de perforación^F

anticline
anticlinal^M

ENERGY
ENERGÍA

737

PRODUCTION PLATFORM
PLATAFORMA[F] DE PRODUCCIÓN[F]

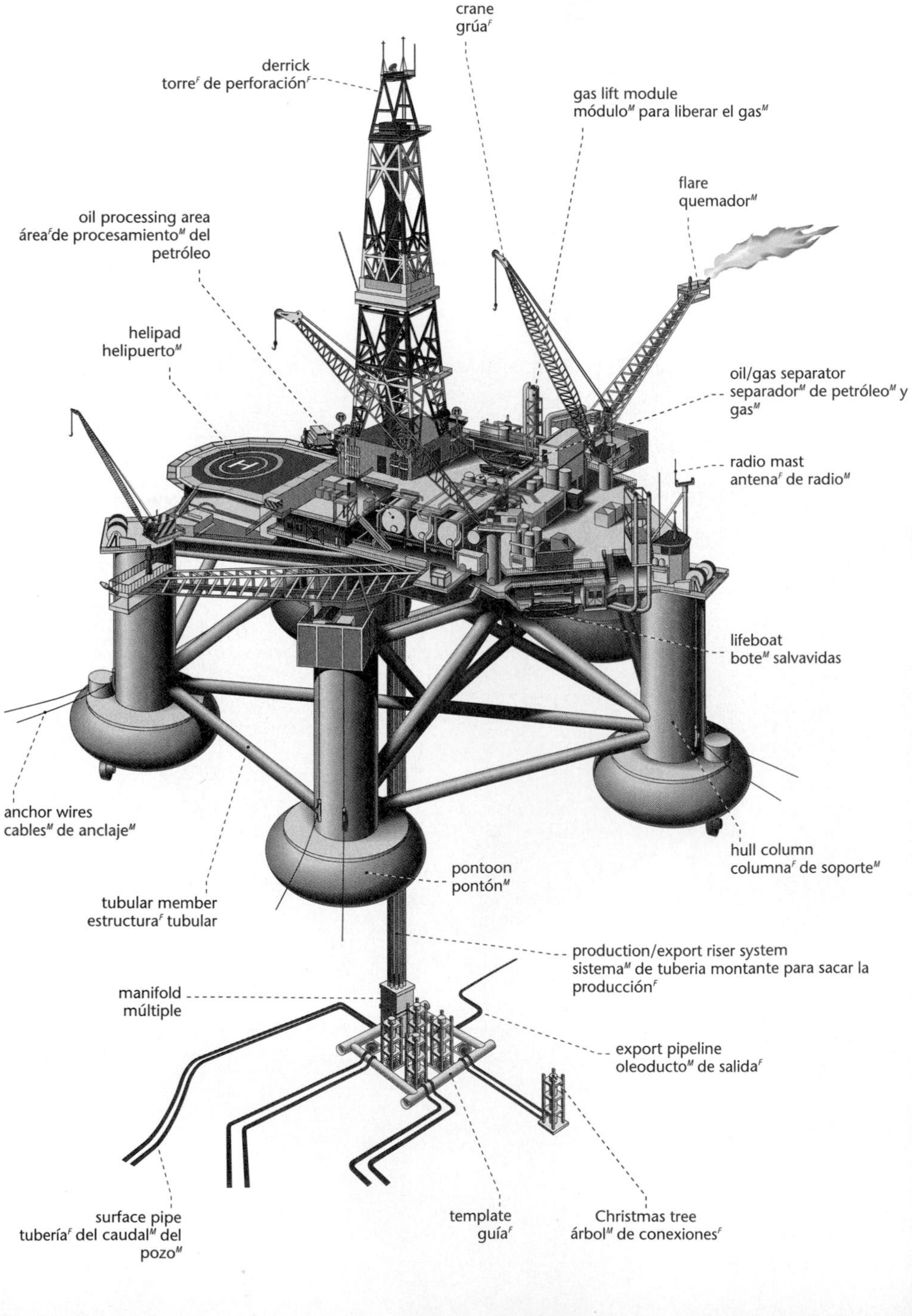

crane
grúa[F]

derrick
torre[F] de perforación[F]

gas lift module
módulo[M] para liberar el gas[M]

flare
quemador[M]

oil processing area
área[F] de procesamiento[M] del
petróleo

helipad
helipuerto[M]

oil/gas separator
separador[M] de petróleo[M] y
gas[M]

radio mast
antena[F] de radio[M]

lifeboat
bote[M] salvavidas

anchor wires
cables[M] de anclaje[M]

hull column
columna[F] de soporte[M]

tubular member
estructura[F] tubular

pontoon
pontón[M]

production/export riser system
sistema[M] de tubería montante para sacar la
producción[F]

manifold
múltiple

export pipeline
oleoducto[M] de salida[F]

surface pipe
tubería[F] del caudal[M] del
pozo[M]

template
guía[F]

Christmas tree
árbol[M] de conexiones[F]

pier
muelle^M saliente

emergency support vessel
embarcación^F de emergencia^F

jack-up platform
plataforma^F montada en gatos^M mecánicos

fixed platform
plataforma^F fija

semi-submersible platform
plataforma^F semisumergida

drill ship
barco^M perforador

OIL
PETRÓLEO^M

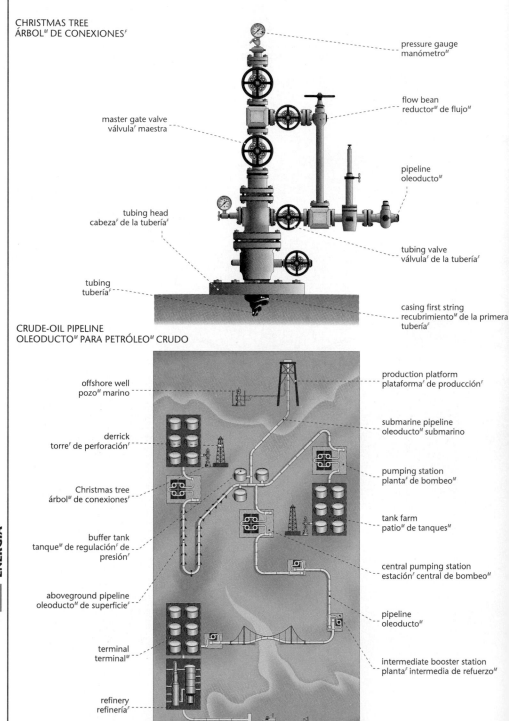

CHRISTMAS TREE
ÁRBOL^M DE CONEXIONES^F

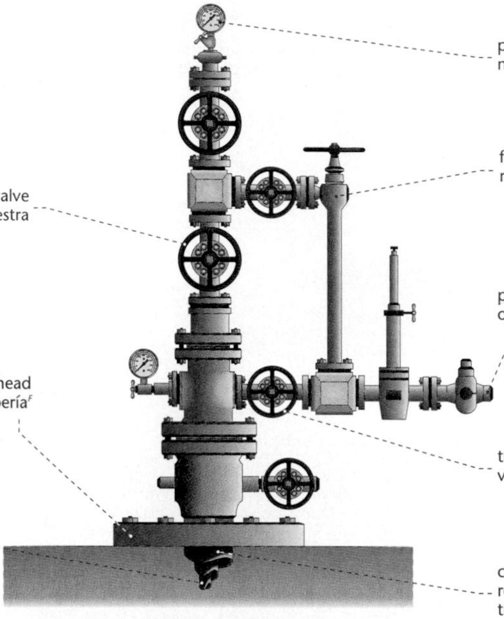

pressure gauge
manómetro^M

flow bean
reductor^M de flujo^M

master gate valve
válvula^F maestra

pipeline
oleoducto^M

tubing head
cabeza^F de la tubería^F

tubing valve
válvula^F de la tubería^F

tubing
tubería^F

casing first string
recubrimiento^M de la primera
tubería^F

CRUDE-OIL PIPELINE
OLEODUCTO^M PARA PETRÓLEO^M CRUDO

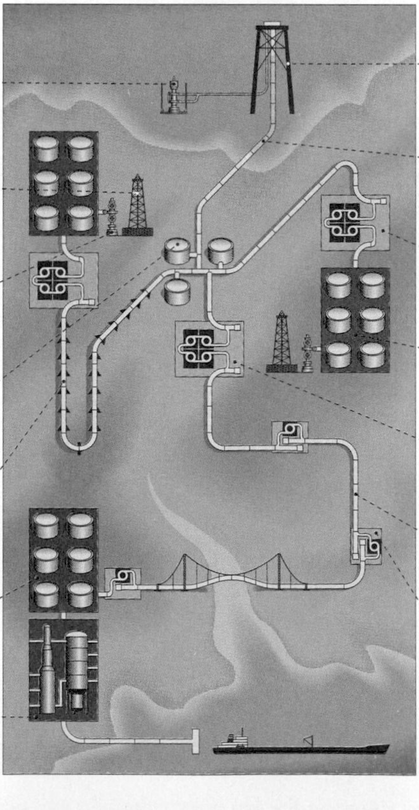

offshore well
pozo^M marino

production platform
plataforma^F de producción^F

derrick
torre^F de perforación^F

submarine pipeline
oleoducto^M submarino

pumping station
planta^F de bombeo^M

Christmas tree
árbol^M de conexiones^F

tank farm
patio^M de tanques^M

buffer tank
tanque^M de regulación^F de
presión^F

central pumping station
estación^F central de bombeo^M

aboveground pipeline
oleoducto^M de superficie^F

pipeline
oleoducto^M

terminal
terminal^M

intermediate booster station
planta^F intermedia de refuerzo^M

refinery
refinería^F

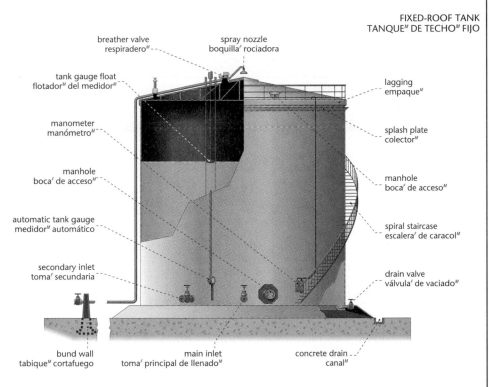

breather valve
respiradero*M*

spray nozzle
boquilla*F* rociadora

tank gauge float
flotador*M* del medidor*M*

lagging
empaque*M*

manometer
manómetro*M*

splash plate
colector*M*

manhole
boca*F* de acceso*M*

manhole
boca*F* de acceso*M*

automatic tank gauge
medidor*M* automático

spiral staircase
escalera*F* de caracol*M*

secondary inlet
toma*F* secundaria

drain valve
válvula*F* de vaciado*M*

bund wall
tabique*M* cortafuego

main inlet
toma*F* principal de llenado*M*

concrete drain
canal*M*

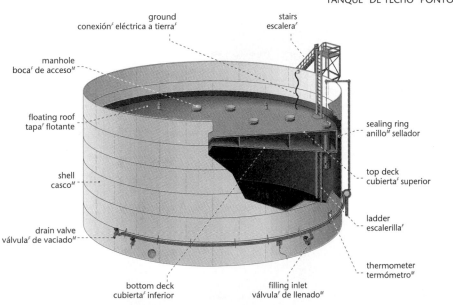

ground
conexión*F* eléctrica a tierra*F*

stairs
escalera*F*

manhole
boca*F* de acceso*M*

floating roof
tapa*F* flotante

sealing ring
anillo*M* sellador

shell
casco*M*

top deck
cubierta*F* superior

ladder
escalerilla*F*

drain valve
válvula*F* de vaciado*M*

thermometer
termómetro*M*

bottom deck
cubierta*F* inferior

filling inlet
válvula*F* de llenado*M*

**ENERGY
ENERGÍA**

OIL
PETRÓLEO^M

TANK TRAILER
CAMIÓN^M CISTERNA^F

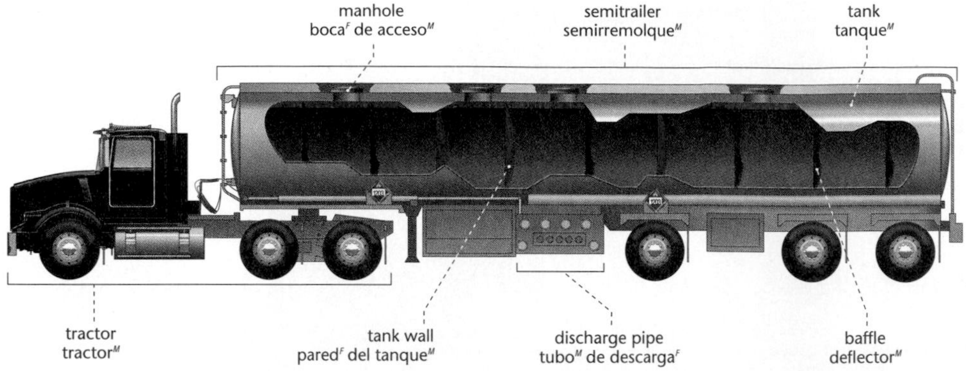

manhole
boca^F de acceso^M

semitrailer
semirremolque^M

tank
tanque^M

tractor
tractor^M

tank wall
pared^F del tanque^M

discharge pipe
tubo^M de descarga^F

baffle
deflector^M

TANKER
BARCO^M PETROLERO

radio antenna
antena^F de radio^F

separator
separador^M

gangway
pasarela^F

radar mast
poste^M del radar^M

davit
pescante^M

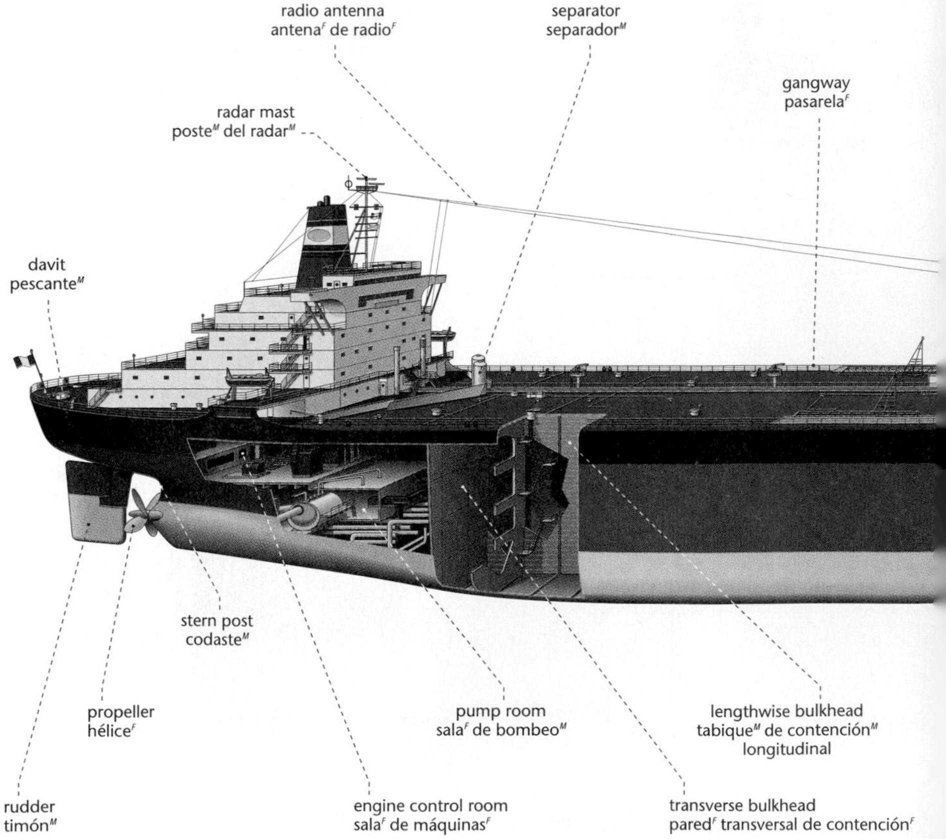

stern post
codaste^M

propeller
hélice^F

pump room
sala^F de bombeo^M

lengthwise bulkhead
tabique^M de contención^M
longitudinal

rudder
timón^M

engine control room
sala^F de máquinas^F

transverse bulkhead
pared^F transversal de contención^F

742

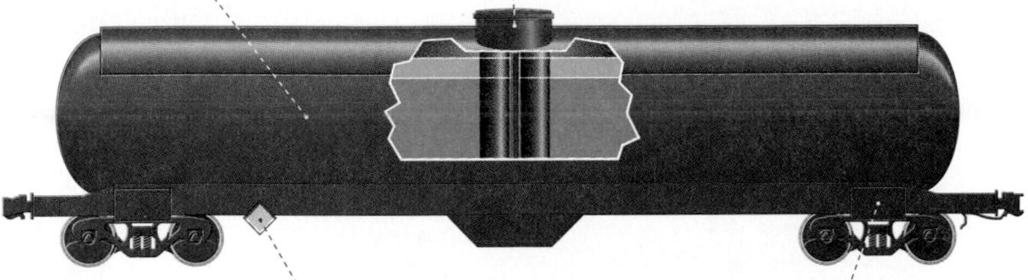

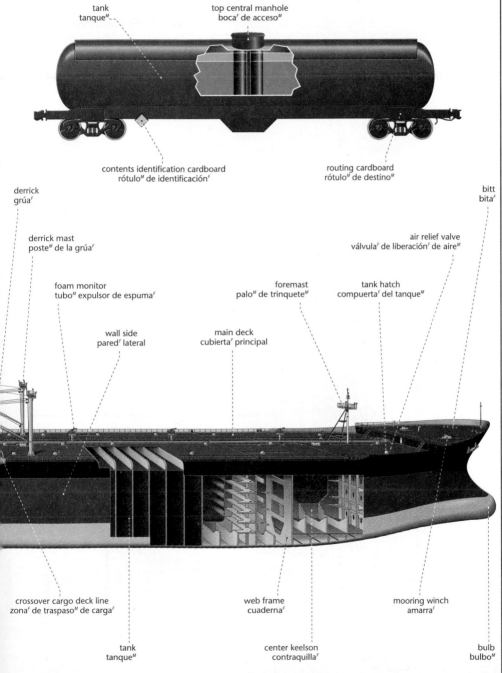

tank
tanque^M

top central manhole
boca^F de acceso^M

contents identification cardboard
rótulo^M de identificación^F

routing cardboard
rótulo^M de destino^M

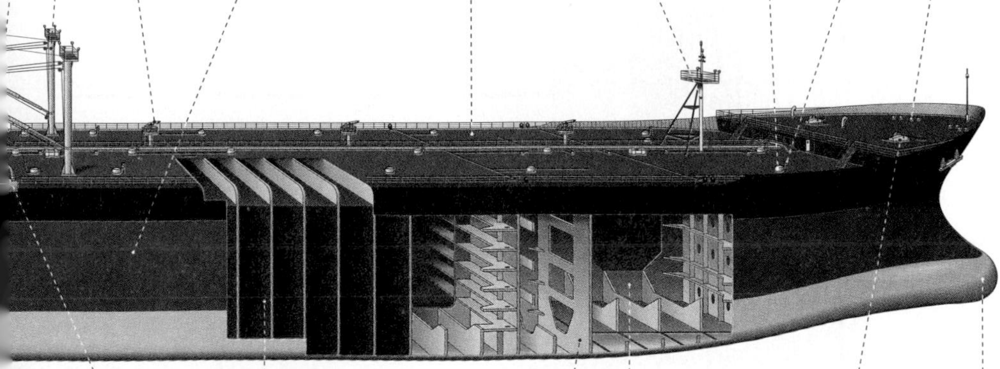

derrick
grúa^F

bitt
bita^F

derrick mast
poste^M de la grúa^F

air relief valve
válvula^F de liberación^F de aire^M

foam monitor
tubo^M expulsor de espuma^F

foremast
palo^M de trinquete^M

tank hatch
compuerta^F del tanque^M

wall side
pared^F lateral

main deck
cubierta^F principal

crossover cargo deck line
zona^F de traspaso^M de carga^F

web frame
cuaderna^F

mooring winch
amarra^F

tank
tanque^M

center keelson
contraquilla^F

bulb
bulbo^M

ENERGY
ENERGÍA

743

OIL
PETRÓLEO[M]

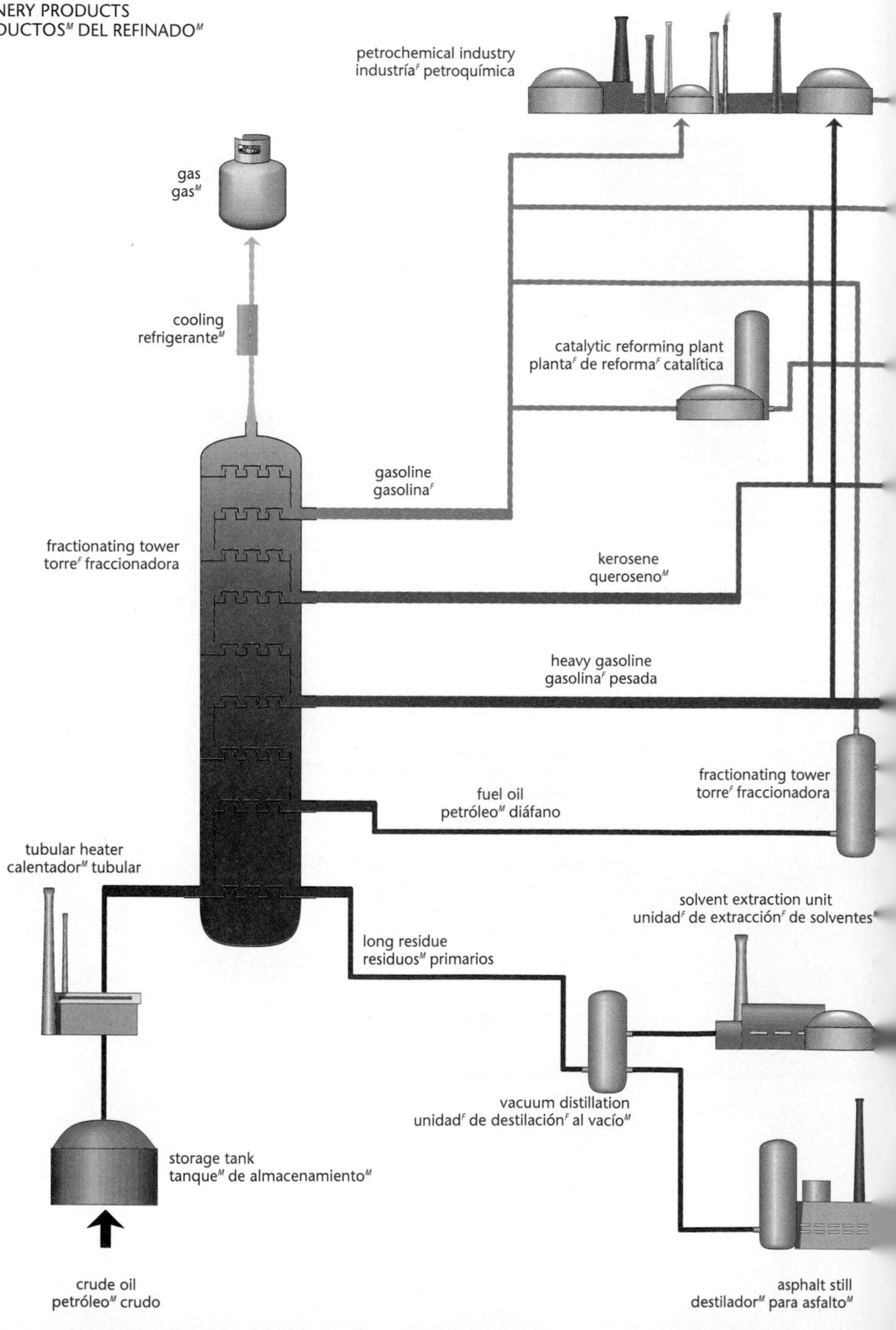

REFINERY PRODUCTS
PRODUCTOS[M] DEL REFINADO[M]

petrochemical industry
industría[F] petroquímica

gas
gas[M]

cooling
refrigerante[M]

catalytic reforming plant
planta[F] de reforma[F] catalítica

gasoline
gasolina[F]

fractionating tower
torre[F] fraccionadora

kerosene
queroseno[M]

heavy gasoline
gasolina[F] pesada

fractionating tower
torre[F] fraccionadora

fuel oil
petróleo[M] diáfano

tubular heater
calentador[M] tubular

solvent extraction unit
unidad[F] de extracción[F] de solventes[A]

long residue
residuos[M] primarios

storage tank
tanque[M] de almacenamiento[M]

vacuum distillation
unidad[F] de destilación[F] al vacío[M]

crude oil
petróleo[M] crudo

asphalt still
destilador[M] para asfalto[M]

ENERGY
ENERGÍA

744

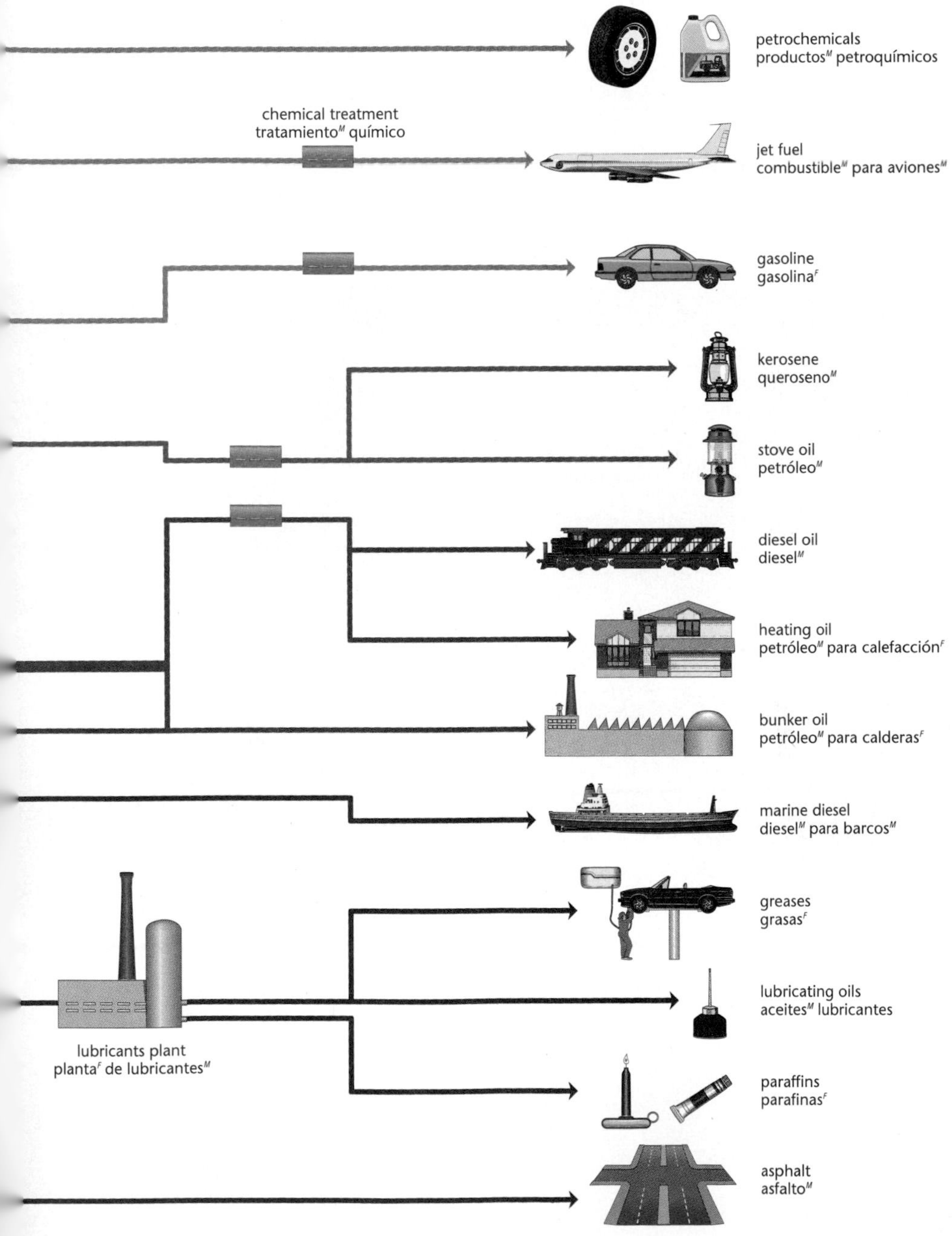

petrochemicals
productos^M petroquímicos

chemical treatment
tratamiento^M químico

jet fuel
combustible^M para aviones^M

gasoline
gasolina^F

kerosene
queroseno^M

stove oil
petróleo^M

diesel oil
diesel^M

heating oil
petróleo^M para calefacción^F

bunker oil
petróleo^M para calderas^F

marine diesel
diesel^M para barcos^M

greases
grasas^F

lubricating oils
aceites^M lubricantes

lubricants plant
planta^F de lubricantes^M

paraffins
parafinas^F

asphalt
asfalto^M

HYDROELECTRIC COMPLEX
COMPLEJO^M HIDROELÉCTRICO

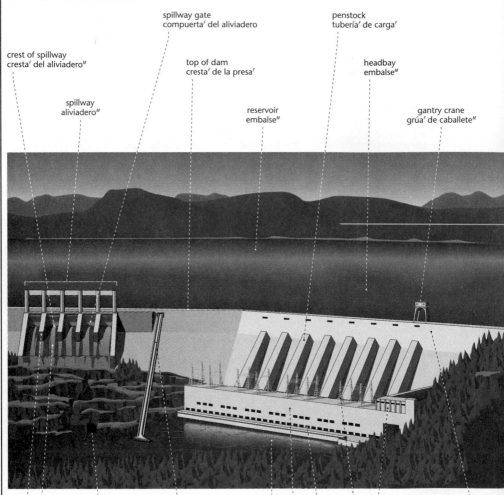

spillway gate
compuerta^F del aliviadero

penstock
tubería^F de carga^F

crest of spillway
cresta^F del aliviadero^M

top of dam
cresta^F de la presa^F

headbay
embalse^M

spillway
aliviadero^M

reservoir
embalse^M

gantry crane
grúa^F de caballete^M

log chute
rebosadero^M

control room
sala^F de control^M

diversion canal
canal^M de derivación^F

dam
presa^F

afterbay
cámara^F de salida^F

spillway chute
canal^M del aliviadero^M

bushing
boquilla^F reducidora

training wall
muro^M de encauzamiento^M

powerhouse
central^F hidroeléctrica

machine hall
sala^F de máquinas^F

gate
compuerta*F*

circuit breaker
interruptor*M* automático

gantry crane
grúa*F* de caballete*M*

bushing
boquilla*F* reducidora

transformer
transformador*M*

lightning arrester
pararrayos*M*

traveling crane
grúa*F* de puente*M*

machine hall
sala*F* de máquinas*F*

access gallery
galería*F* de acceso*M*

gantry crane
grúa*F* de caballete*M*

scroll case
caja*F* de caracol*M*

gate
compuerta*F*

afterbay
cámara*F* de salida*F*

tailrace
canal*M* de descarga*F*

generator unit
turbinas*F*

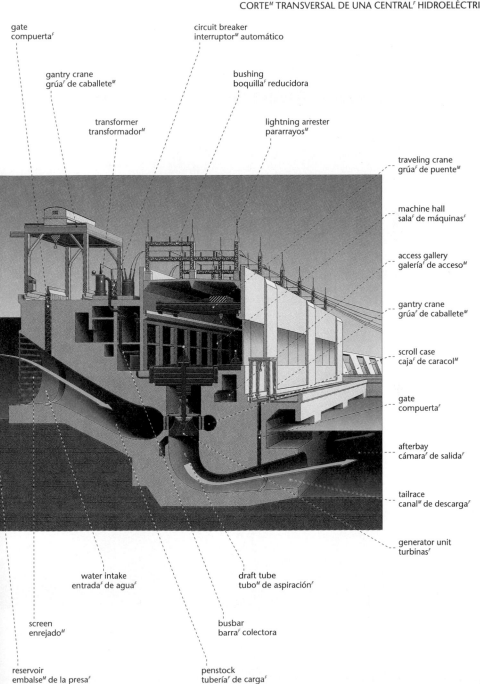

water intake
entrada*F* de agua*F*

draft tube
tubo*M* de aspiración*F*

screen
enrejado*M*

busbar
barra*F* colectora

reservoir
embalse*M* de la presa*F*

penstock
tubería*F* de carga*F*

EMBANKMENT DAM
DIQUE[M] DE TERRAPLÉN[M]

CROSS SECTION OF AN EMBANKMENT DAM
CORTE[M] TRANSVERSAL DE UN DIQUE[M] DE TERRAPLÉN[M]

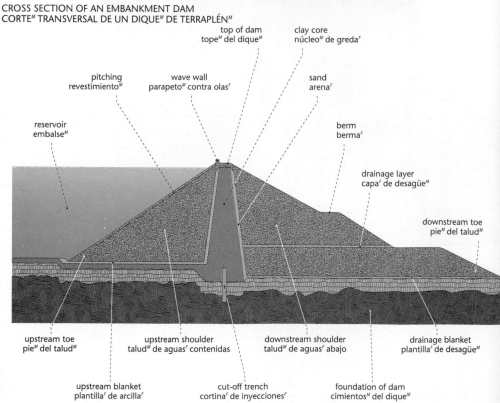

top of dam
tope[M] del dique[M]

clay core
núcleo[M] de greda[F]

pitching
revestimiento[M]

wave wall
parapeto[M] contra olas[F]

sand
arena[F]

reservoir
embalse[M]

berm
berma[F]

drainage layer
capa[F] de desagüe[M]

downstream toe
pie[M] del talud[M]

upstream toe
pie[M] del talud[M]

upstream shoulder
talud[M] de aguas[F] contenidas

downstream shoulder
talud[M] de aguas[F] abajo

drainage blanket
plantilla[F] de desagüe[M]

upstream blanket
plantilla[F] de arcilla[F]

cut-off trench
cortina[F] de inyecciones[F]

foundation of dam
cimientos[M] del dique[M]

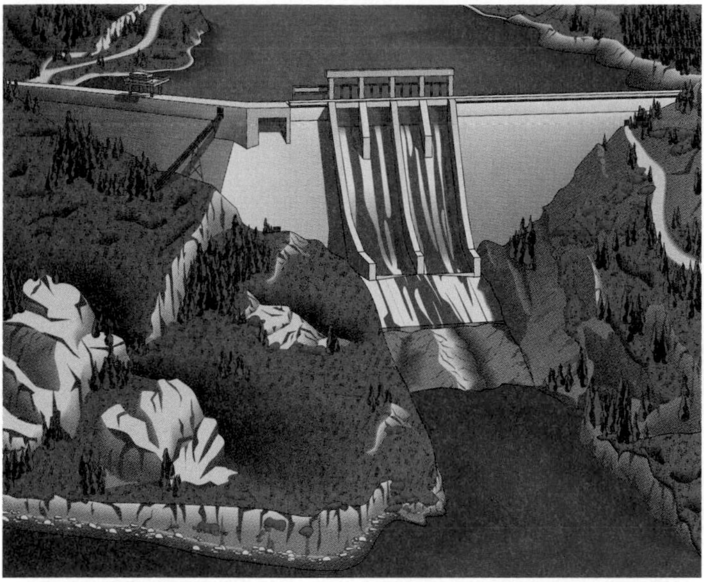

CROSS SECTION OF A GRAVITY DAM
CORTE^M TRANSVERSAL DE UNA PRESA^F

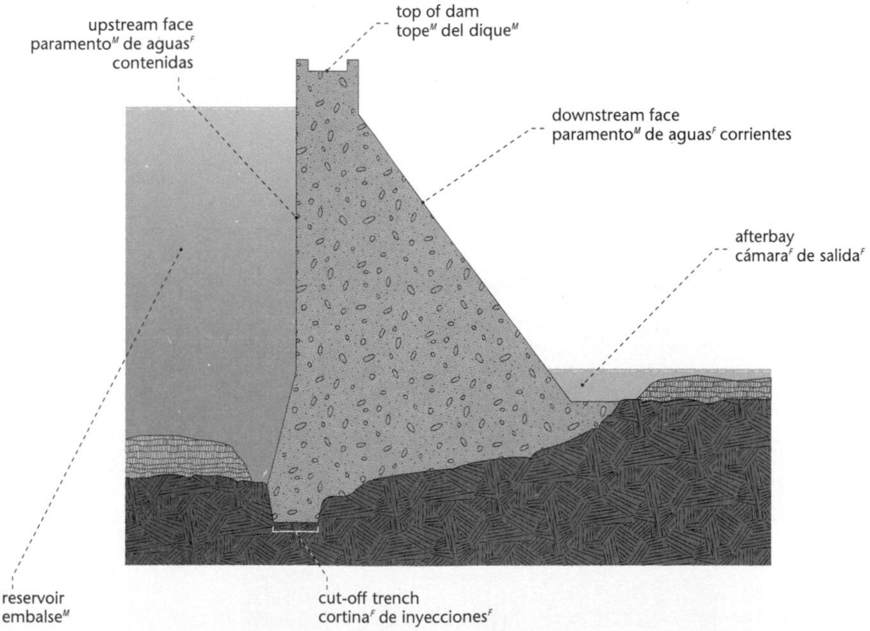

upstream face
paramento^M de aguas^F
contenidas

top of dam
tope^M del dique^M

downstream face
paramento^M de aguas^F corrientes

afterbay
cámara^F de salida^F

reservoir
embalse^M

cut-off trench
cortina^F de inyecciones^F

ENERGY
ENERGÍA

ARCH DAM
PRESA^F DE ARCO^M

CROSS SECTION OF AN ARCH DAM
CORTE^M TRANSVERSAL DE UNA PRESA^F DE ARCO^M

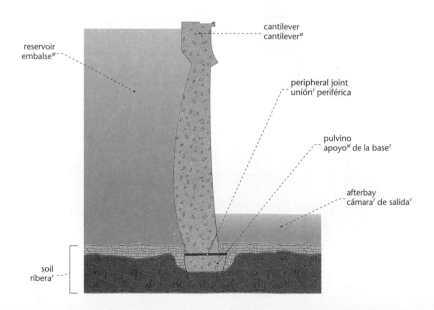

cantilever
cantilever^M

reservoir
embalse^M

peripheral joint
unión^F periférica

pulvino
apoyo^M de la base^F

afterbay
cámara^F de salida^F

soil
ribera^F

BUTTRESS DAM
DIQUE^M DE MACHONES^M

CROSS SECTION OF A BUTTRESS DAM
CORTE^M TRANSVERSAL DE UN DIQUE^M DE MACHONES^M

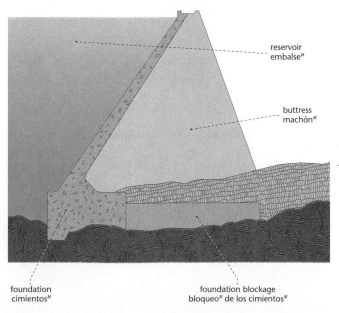

reservoir
embalse^M

buttress
machón^M

foundation
cimientos^M

foundation blockage
bloqueo^M de los cimientos^M

TIDAL POWER PLANT
CENTRAL^F MAREMOTRIZ

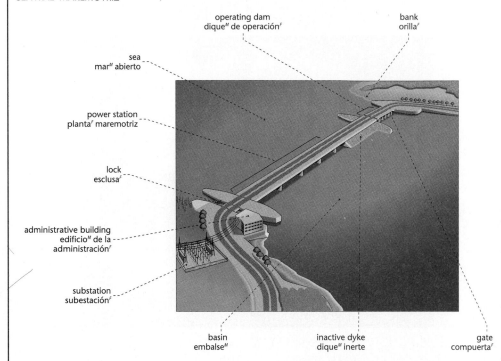

operating dam
dique^M de operación^F

bank
orilla^F

sea
mar^M abierto

power station
planta^F maremotriz

lock
esclusa^F

administrative building
edificio^M de la
administración^F

substation
subestación^F

basin
embalse^M

inactive dyke
dique^M inerte

gate
compuerta^F

CROSS SECTION OF POWER PLANT
CORTE^M TRANSVERSAL DE UNA PLANTA^F
MAREMOTRIZ

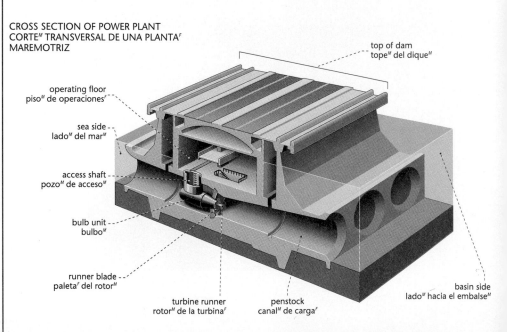

top of dam
tope^M del dique^M

operating floor
piso^M de operaciones^F

sea side
lado^M del mar^M

access shaft
pozo^M de acceso^M

bulb unit
bulbo^M

runner blade
paleta^F del rotor^M

turbine runner
rotor^M de la turbina^F

penstock
canal^M de carga^F

basin side
lado^M hacia el embalse^M

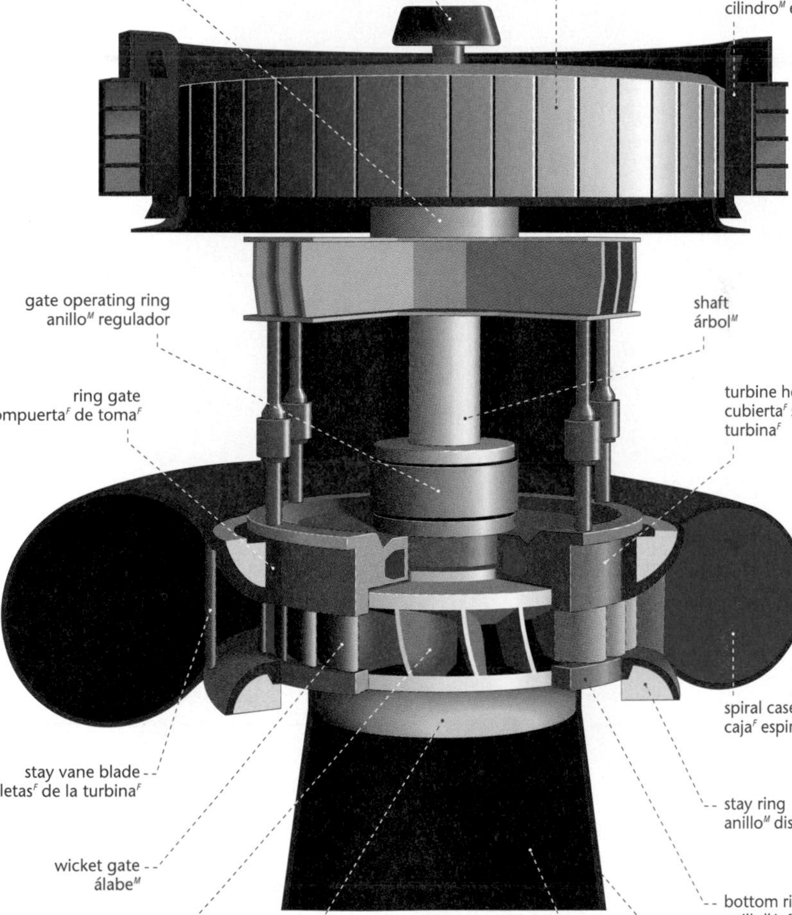

collector
colector^M

rotor
cilindro^M interno

thrust bearing
rodamiento^M

stator
cilindro^M externo

gate operating ring
anillo^M regulador

shaft
árbol^M

ring gate
compuerta^F de toma^F

turbine headcover
cubierta^F superior de la turbina^F

stay vane blade
paletas^F de la turbina^F

spiral case
caja^F espiral

wicket gate
álabe^M

stay ring
anillo^M distribuidor

runner blade
paleta^F de la turbina^F

runner
cojinete^M de rodamiento^M

draft tube
tubo^M de aspiración^F

bottom ring
anillo^M inferior

draft tube liner
calza^F de descarga^F

generator
generador^M

turbine
turbina^F

ENERGY
ENERGÍA

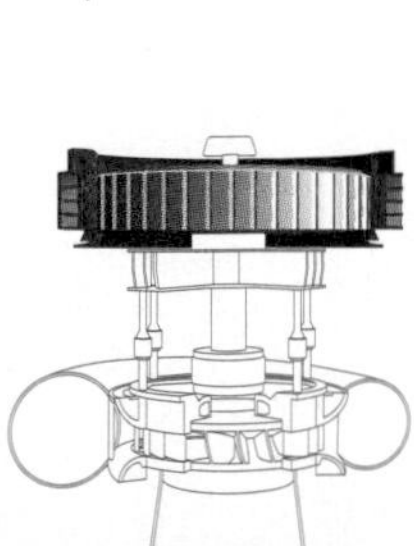

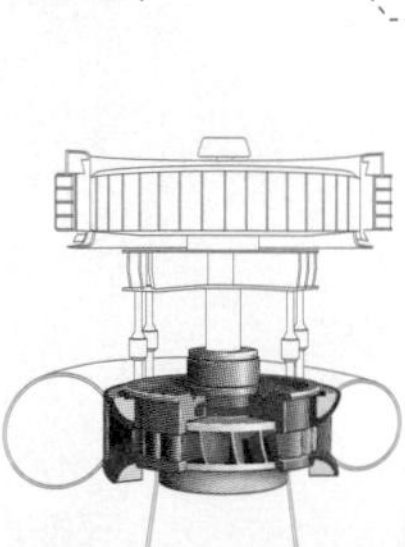

FRANCIS RUNNER
TURBINA^F FRANCIS

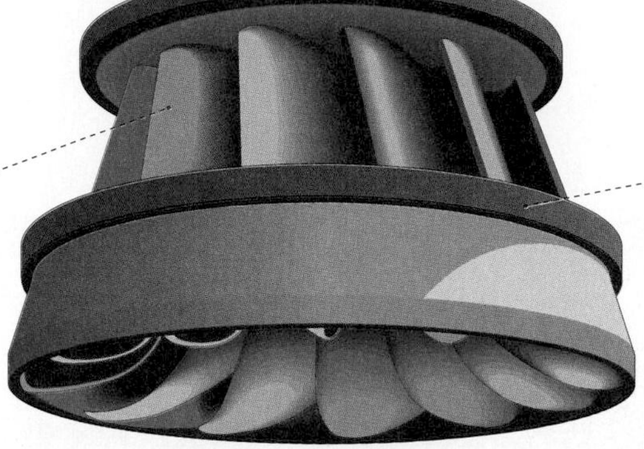

ring
anillo^M

blade
paleta^F

KAPLAN RUNNER
TURBINA^F KAPLAN

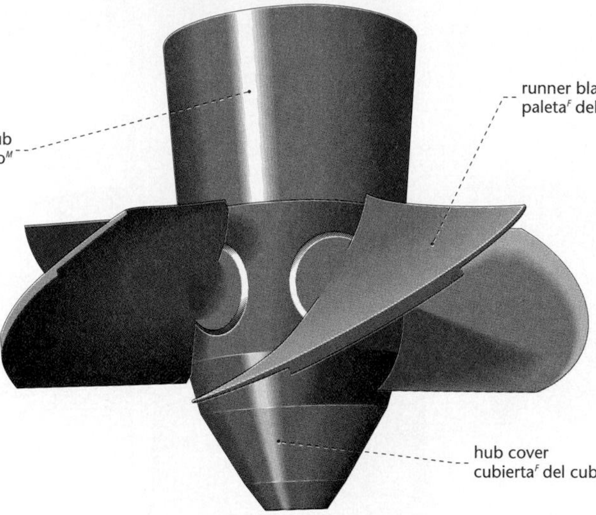

runner blade
paleta^F del rotor^M

hub
cubo^M

hub cover
cubierta^F del cubo^M

PELTON RUNNER
TURBINA^F PELTON

bucket ring
rueda^F de cangilones^M

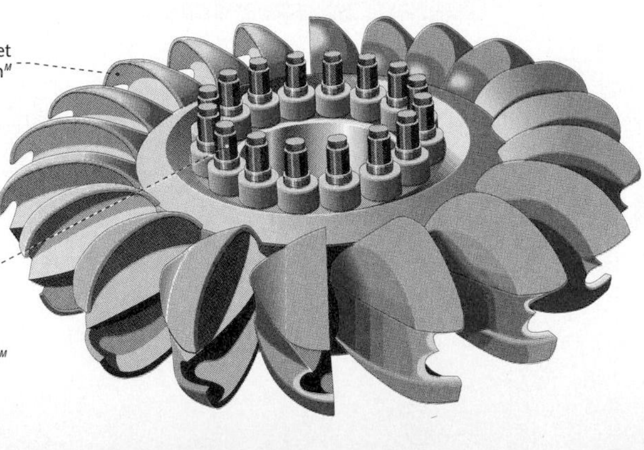

bucket
cangilón^M

coupling bolt
perno^M de acoplamiento^M

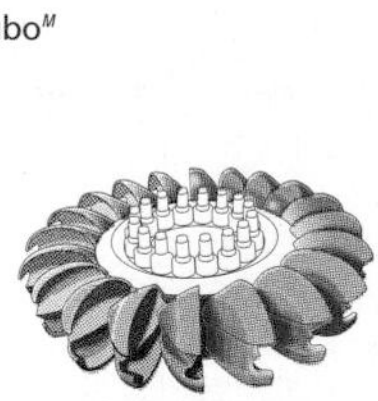

transmission to consumers
distribución[F] al consumidor[M]

voltage decrease
reductor[M] de voltaje[M]

high-tension electricity transmission
transmisión[F] de electricidad[F] de alto
voltaje[M]

energy integration to the transmission network
paso[M] de la energía[F] hacia la red[F] de transmisión[F]

energy transmission at the generator voltage
transmisión[F] de energía[F] al generador[M] de voltaje[M]

voltage increase
amplificador[M] de voltaje[M]

supply of water
suministro[M] de agua[F]

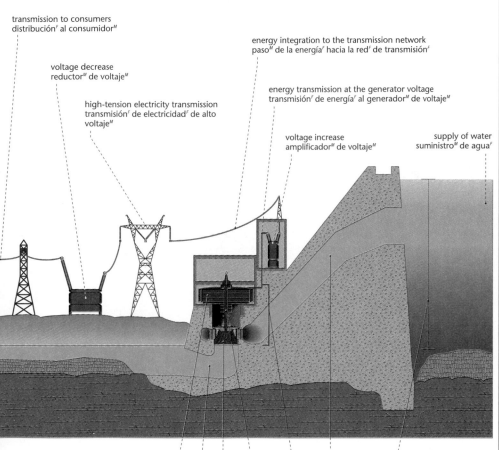

head of water
volumen[M] de agua[F]

production of electricity by the generator
producción[F] de electricidad[F] por generador[M]

water under pressure
agua[F] a presión[F]

turbined water draining
desagüe[M] de la turbina[F]

transformation of mechanical work into electricity
transformación[F] del trabajo[M] mecánico en
electricidad[F]

rotation of the turbine
rotación[F] de la turbina[F]

transmission of the rotative movement to the rotor
transmisión[F] del movimiento[M] hacia el rotor[M]

PYLON
TORRE^F DE ALTA TENSIÓN^F

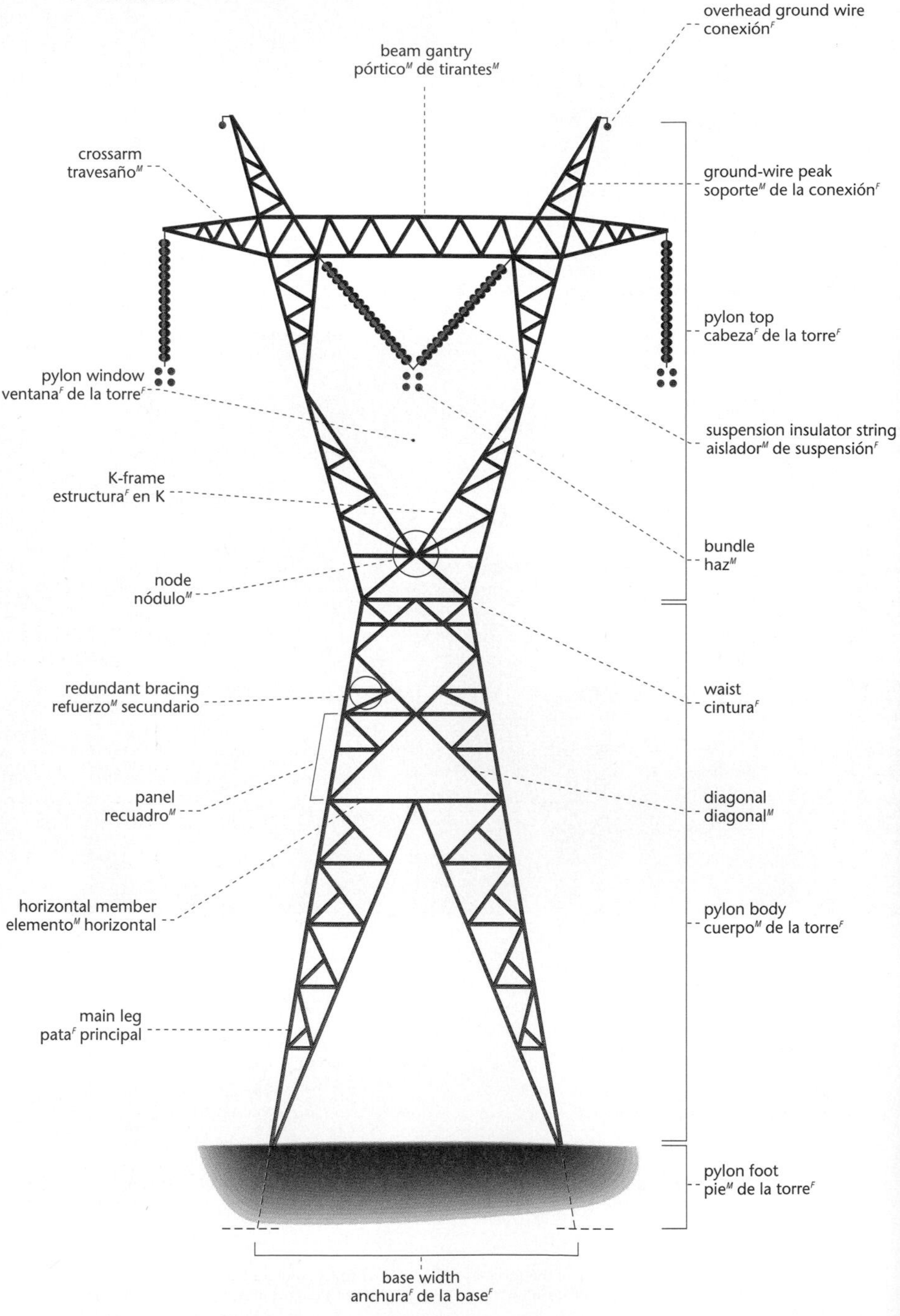

overhead ground wire
conexión^F

beam gantry
pórtico^M de tirantes^M

crossarm
travesaño^M

ground-wire peak
soporte^M de la conexión^F

pylon top
cabeza^F de la torre^F

pylon window
ventana^F de la torre^F

suspension insulator string
aislador^M de suspensión^F

K-frame
estructura^F en K

bundle
haz^M

node
nódulo^M

waist
cintura^F

redundant bracing
refuerzo^M secundario

panel
recuadro^M

diagonal
diagonal^M

horizontal member
elemento^M horizontal

pylon body
cuerpo^M de la torre^F

main leg
pata^F principal

pylon foot
pie^M de la torre^F

base width
anchura^F de la base^F

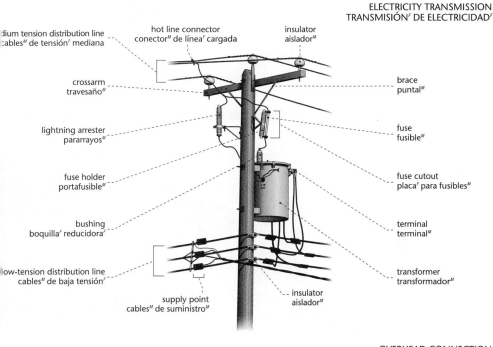

medium tension distribution line
cables^M de tensión^F mediana

hot line connector
conector^M de línea^F cargada

insulator
aislador^M

crossarm
travesaño^M

brace
puntal^M

lightning arrester
pararrayos^M

fuse
fusible^M

fuse holder
portafusible^M

fuse cutout
placa^F para fusibles^M

bushing
boquilla^F reducidora^F

terminal
terminal^M

low-tension distribution line
cables^M de baja tensión^F

transformer
transformador^M

supply point
cables^M de suministro^M

insulator
aislador^M

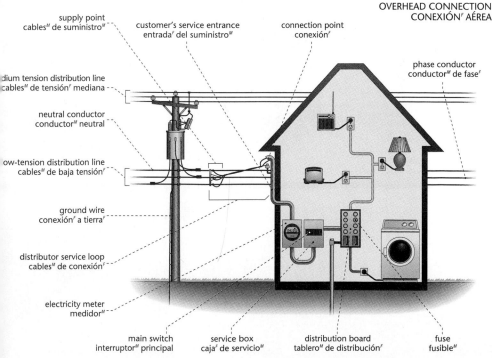

supply point
cables^M de suministro^M

customer's service entrance
entrada^F del suministro^M

connection point
conexión^F

phase conductor
conductor^M de fase^F

medium tension distribution line
cables^M de tensión^F mediana

neutral conductor
conductor^M neutral

low-tension distribution line
cables^M de baja tensión^F

ground wire
conexión^F a tierra^F

distributor service loop
cables^M de conexión^F

electricity meter
medidor^M

main switch
interruptor^M principal

service box
caja^F de servicio^M

distribution board
tablero^M de distribución^F

fuse
fusible^M

ENERGY
ENERGÍA

757

NUCLEAR GENERATING STATION
CENTRAL^F NUCLEAR

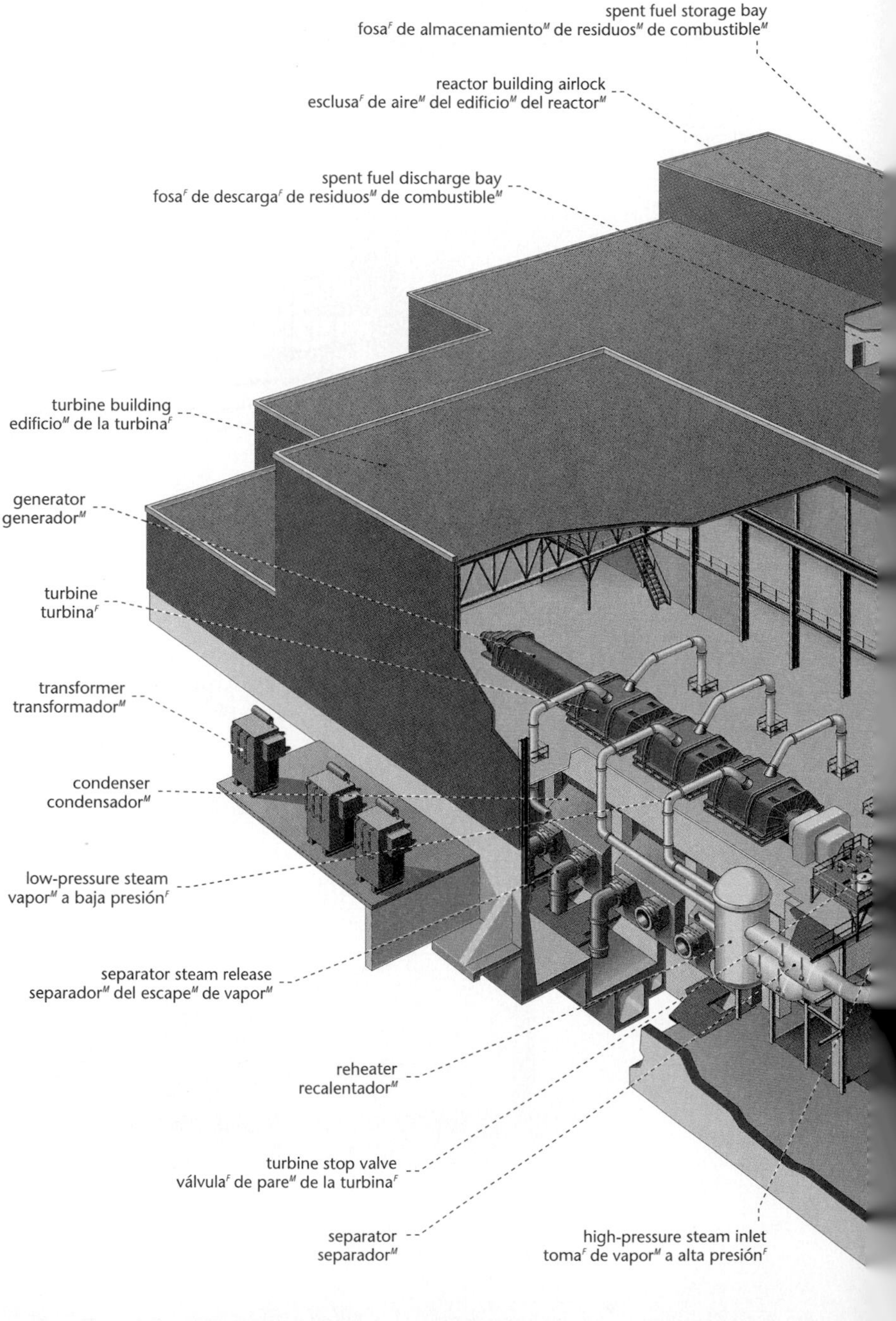

spent fuel storage bay
fosa^F de almacenamiento^M de residuos^M de combustible^M

reactor building airlock
esclusa^F de aire^M del edificio^M del reactor^M

spent fuel discharge bay
fosa^F de descarga^F de residuos^M de combustible^M

turbine building
edificio^M de la turbina^F

generator
generador^M

turbine
turbina^F

transformer
transformador^M

condenser
condensador^M

low-pressure steam
vapor^M a baja presión^F

separator steam release
separador^M del escape^M de vapor^M

reheater
recalentador^M

turbine stop valve
válvula^F de pare^M de la turbina^F

separator
separador^M

high-pressure steam inlet
toma^F de vapor^M a alta presión^F

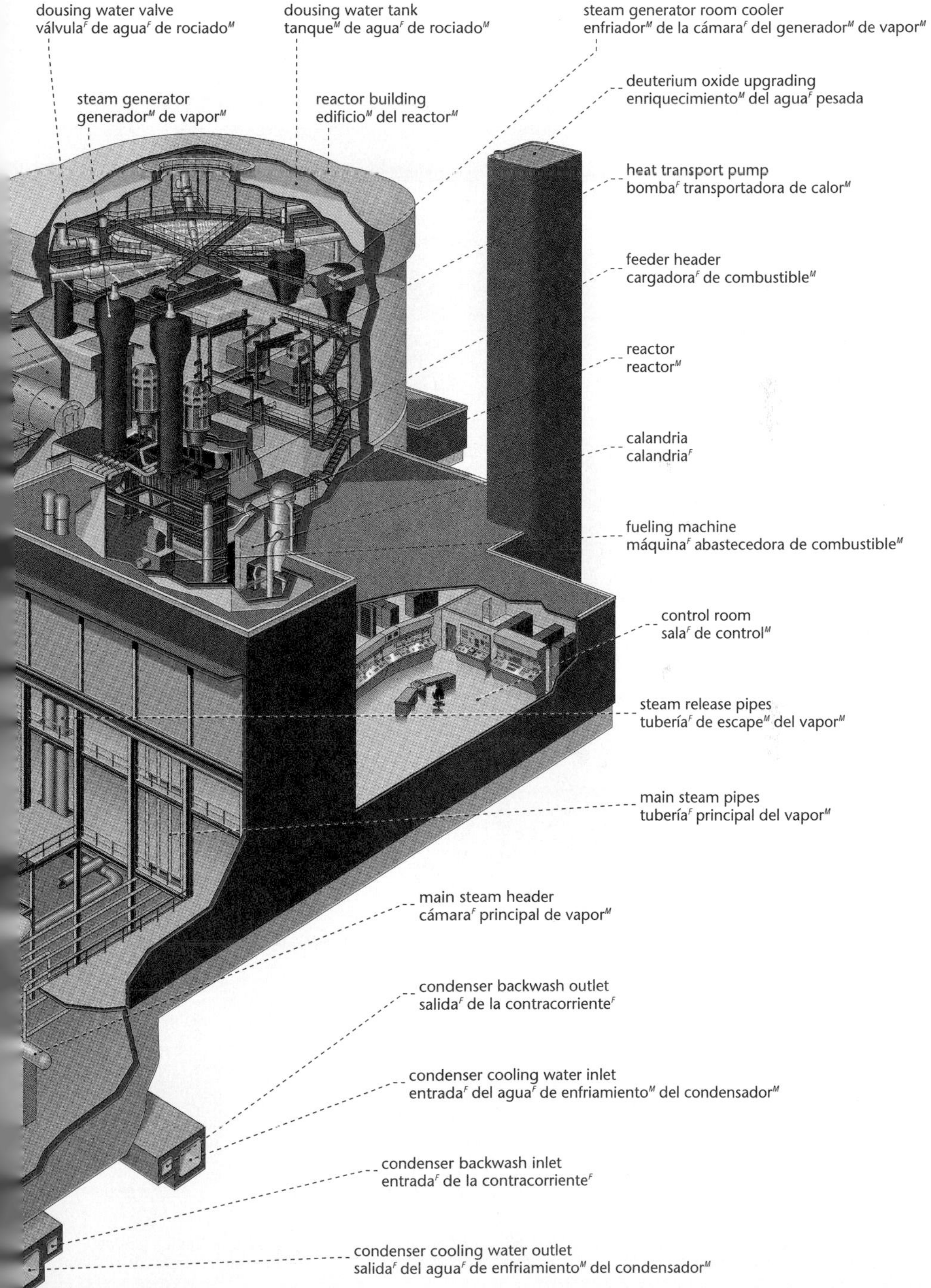

dousing water valve
válvula^F de agua^F de rociado^M

dousing water tank
tanque^M de agua^F de rociado^M

steam generator room cooler
enfriador^M de la cámara^F del generador^M de vapor^M

steam generator
generador^M de vapor^M

reactor building
edificio^M del reactor^M

deuterium oxide upgrading
enriquecimiento^M del agua^F pesada

heat transport pump
bomba^F transportadora de calor^M

feeder header
cargadora^F de combustible^M

reactor
reactor^M

calandria
calandria^F

fueling machine
máquina^F abastecedora de combustible^M

control room
sala^F de control^M

steam release pipes
tubería^F de escape^M del vapor^M

main steam pipes
tubería^F principal del vapor^M

main steam header
cámara^F principal de vapor^M

condenser backwash outlet
salida^F de la contracorriente^F

condenser cooling water inlet
entrada^F del agua^F de enfriamiento^M del condensador^M

condenser backwash inlet
entrada^F de la contracorriente^F

condenser cooling water outlet
salida^F del agua^F de enfriamiento^M del condensador^M

CARBON DIOXIDE REACTOR
REACTOR^M DE BIÓXIDO^M DE CARBONO^M

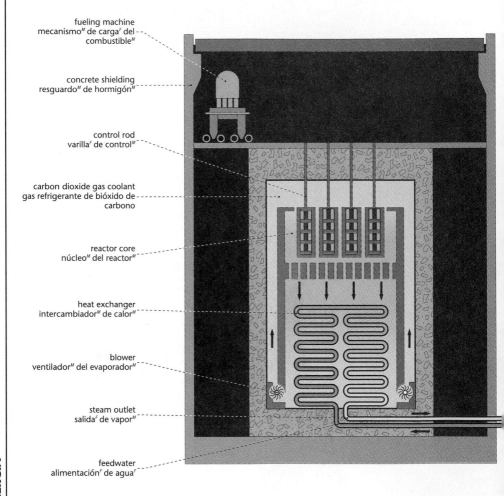

fueling machine
mecanismo^M de carga^F del
combustible^M

concrete shielding
resguardo^M de hormigón^M

control rod
varilla^F de control^M

carbon dioxide gas coolant
gas refrigerante de bióxido de
carbono

reactor core
núcleo^M del reactor^M

heat exchanger
intercambiador^M de calor^M

blower
ventilador^M del evaporador^M

steam outlet
salida^F de vapor^M

feedwater
alimentación^F de agua^F

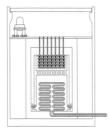

fuel: natural uranium
combustible^M: uranio^M natural

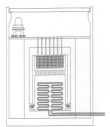

moderator: graphite
moderador^M: grafito^M

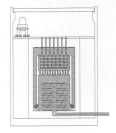

coolant: carbon dioxide
refrigerante^M: bióxido^M de carbono^M

HEAVY-WATER REACTOR
REACTOR^M DE AGUA^F PESADA

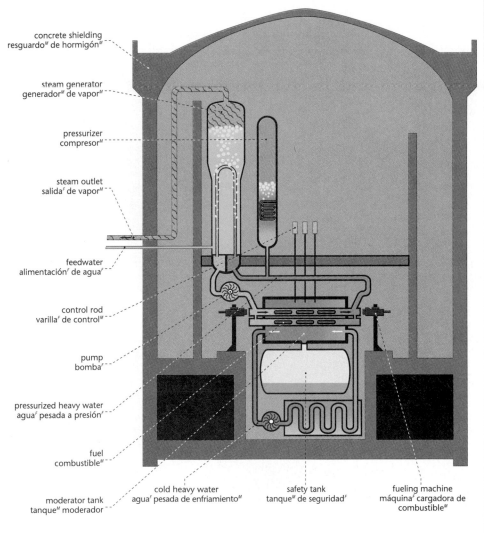

concrete shielding
resguardo^M de hormigón^M

steam generator
generador^M de vapor^M

pressurizer
compresor^M

steam outlet
salida^F de vapor^M

feedwater
alimentación^F de agua^F

control rod
varilla^F de control^M

pump
bomba^F

pressurized heavy water
agua^F pesada a presión^F

fuel
combustible^M

moderator tank
tanque^M moderador

cold heavy water
agua^F pesada de enfriamiento^M

safety tank
tanque^M de seguridad^F

fueling machine
máquina^F cargadora de
combustible^M

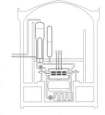

fuel: natural uranium
combustible^M: uranio^M natural

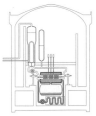

moderator: heavy water
moderador^M: agua^F pesada

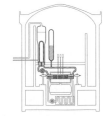

coolant: pressurized heavy water
refrigerante^M: agua^F pesada a presión^F

**ENERGY
ENERGÍA**

NUCLEAR ENERGY
ENERGÍA*F* NUCLEAR

PRESSURIZED-WATER REACTOR
REACTOR*M* DE AGUA*F* A PRESIÓN*F*

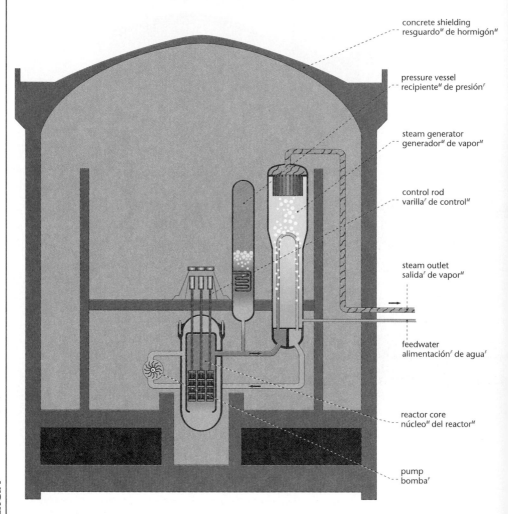

concrete shielding
resguardo*M* de hormigón*M*

pressure vessel
recipiente*M* de presión*F*

steam generator
generador*M* de vapor*M*

control rod
varilla*F* de control*M*

steam outlet
salida*F* de vapor*M*

feedwater
alimentación*F* de agua*F*

reactor core
núcleo*M* del reactor*M*

pump
bomba*F*

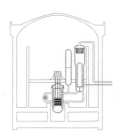

fuel: enriched uranium
combustible*M*: uranio*M* enriquecido

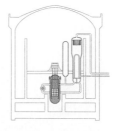

moderator: natural water
moderador*M*: agua*F* natural

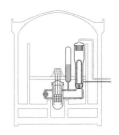

coolant: pressurized water
refrigerante*M*: agua*F* a presión*F*

BOILING-WATER REACTOR
REACTOR*M* DE AGUA*F* HIRVIENTE

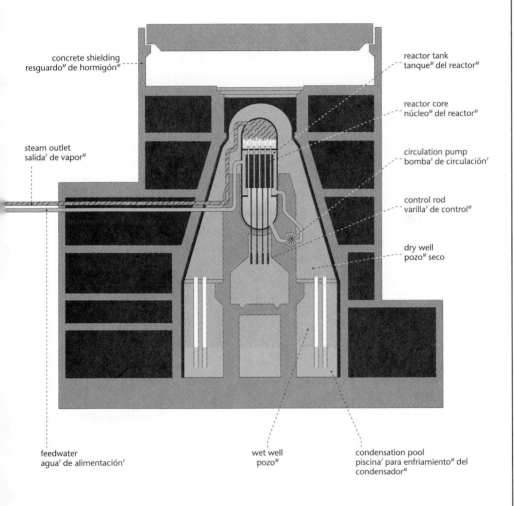

concrete shielding
resguardo*M* de hormigón*M*

reactor tank
tanque*M* del reactor*M*

reactor core
núcleo*M* del reactor*M*

steam outlet
salida*F* de vapor*M*

circulation pump
bomba*F* de circulación*F*

control rod
varilla*F* de control*M*

dry well
pozo*M* seco

feedwater
agua*F* de alimentación*F*

wet well
pozo*M*

condensation pool
piscina*F* para enfriamiento*M* del
condensador*M*

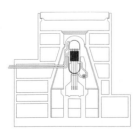

fuel: enriched uranium
combustible*M*: uranio*M* enriquecido

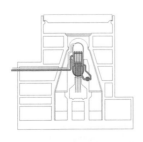

moderator: natural water
moderador*M*: agua*F* natural

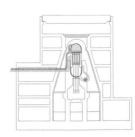

coolant: boiling water
refrigerante*M*: agua*F* hirviente

FUEL HANDLING SEQUENCE
SECUENCIA^F EN EL MANEJO^M DE COMBUSTIBLE^M

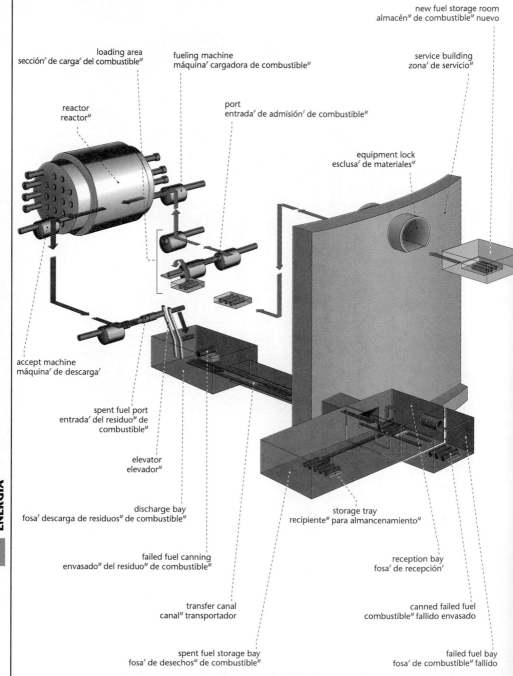

new fuel storage room
almacén^M de combustible^M nuevo

loading area
sección^F de carga^F del combustible^M

fueling machine
máquina^F cargadora de combustible^M

service building
zona^F de servicio^M

reactor
reactor^M

port
entrada^F de admisión^F de combustible^M

equipment lock
esclusa^F de materiales^M

accept machine
máquina^F de descarga^F

spent fuel port
entrada^F del residuo^M de
combustible^M

elevator
elevador^M

discharge bay
fosa^F descarga de residuos^M de combustible^M

storage tray
recipiente^M para almancenamiento^M

failed fuel canning
envasado^M del residuo^M de combustible^M

reception bay
fosa^F de recepción^F

transfer canal
canal^M transportador

canned failed fuel
combustible^M fallido envasado

spent fuel storage bay
fosa^F de desechos^M de combustible^M

failed fuel bay
fosa^F de combustible^M fallido

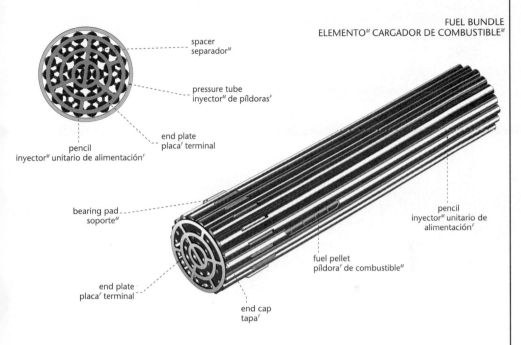

FUEL BUNDLE
ELEMENTO^M CARGADOR DE COMBUSTIBLE^M

spacer
separador^M

pressure tube
inyector^M de píldoras^F

end plate
placa^F terminal

pencil
inyector^M unitario de alimentación^F

bearing pad
soporte^M

end plate
placa^F terminal

end cap
tapa^F

fuel pellet
píldora^F de combustible^M

pencil
inyector^M unitario de
alimentación^F

NUCLEAR REACTOR
CARGA^F DEL REACTOR^M NUCLEAR

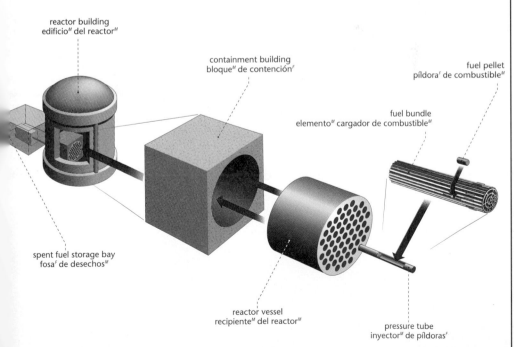

reactor building
edificio^M del reactor^M

containment building
bloque^M de contención^F

fuel pellet
píldora^F de combustible^M

fuel bundle
elemento^M cargador de combustible^M

spent fuel storage bay
fosa^F de desechos^M

reactor vessel
recipiente^M del reactor^M

pressure tube
inyector^M de píldoras^F

ENERGY
ENERGÍA

NUCLEAR ENERGY
ENERGÍA^F NUCLEAR

PRODUCTION OF ELECTRICITY FROM NUCLEAR ENERGY
PRODUCCIÓN^F DE ELECTRICIDAD^F POR MEDIO DE ENERGÍA^F NUCLEAR

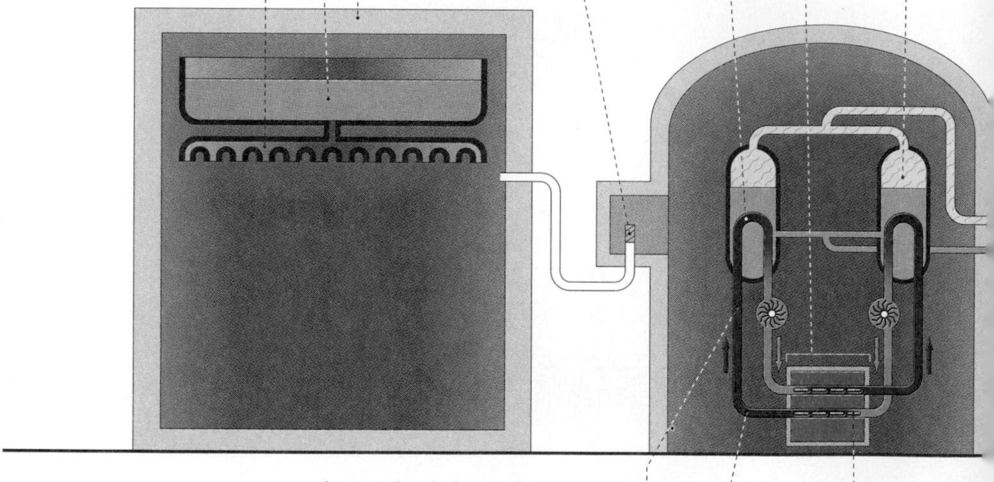

water turns into steam
conversión^F del agua^F en vapor^M

reactor
reactor^M

containment building
edificio^M

dousing water tank
tanque^M de agua^F de rociado^M

transfer of heat to water
transferencia^F de calor^M al agua^F

sprinklers
rociadores^M

safety valve
válvula^F de seguridad^F

coolant transfers the heat to the steam generator
el refrigerante^M transfiere el calor^M al generador^M de vapor^M

heat production
producción^F de calor^M

fission of uranium fuel
uranio^M en fisión^F

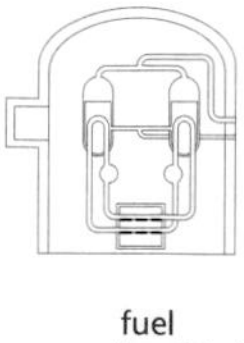

fuel
combustible^M

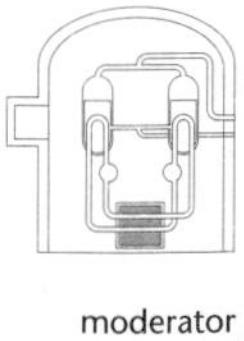

moderator
moderador^M

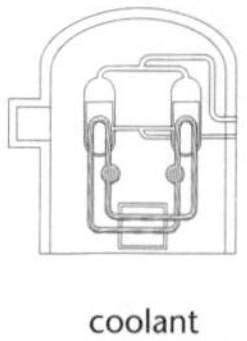

coolant
refrigerante^M

steam pressure drives turbine
la presión^F del vapor^M impulsa las turbinas^F

electricity transmission
transmisión^F de electricidad^F

voltage increase
ampliación^F del voltaje^M

turbine shaft turns generator
la flecha^F de la turbina^F hace girar el generador^M

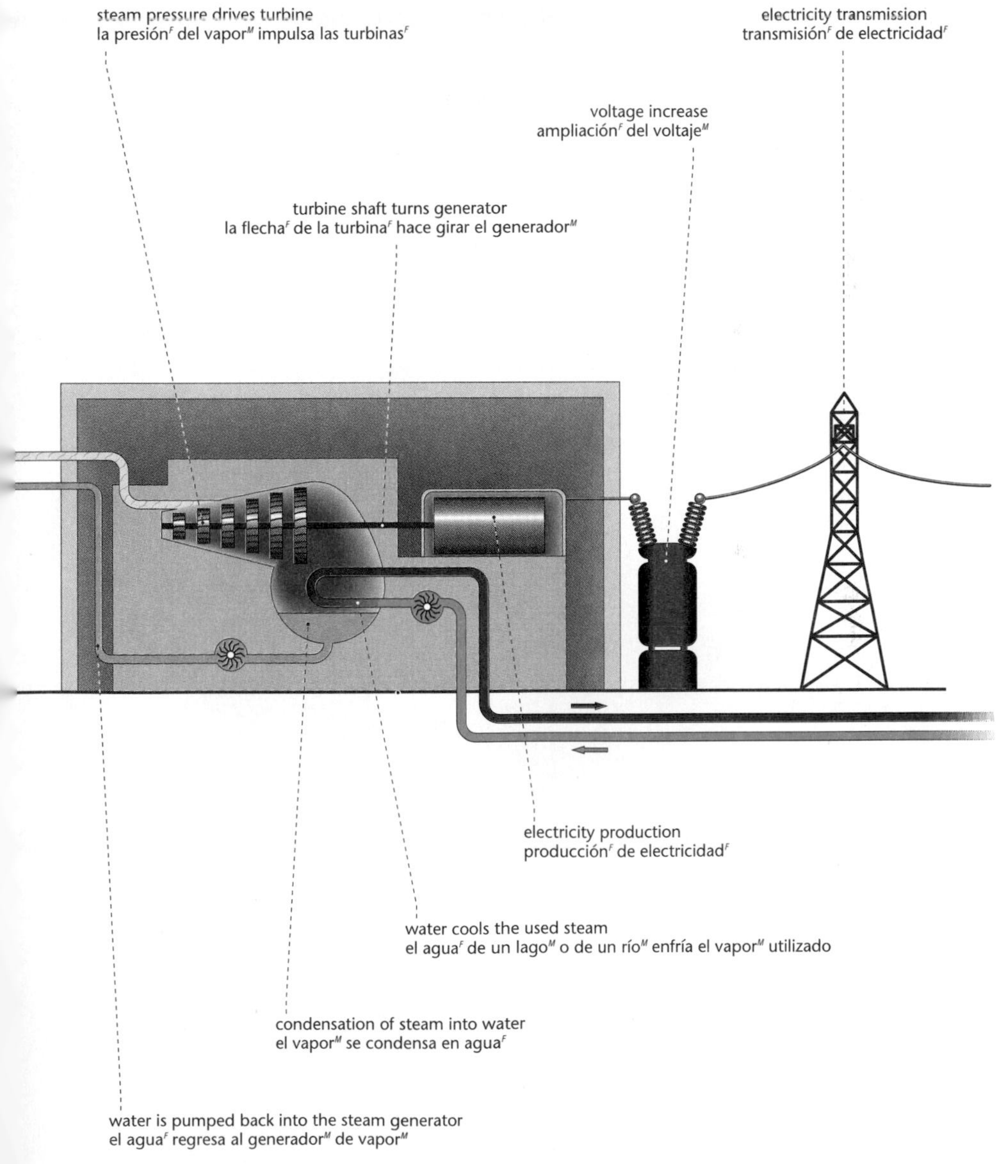

electricity production
producción^F de electricidad^F

water cools the used steam
el agua^F de un lago^M o de un río^M enfría el vapor^M utilizado

condensation of steam into water
el vapor^M se condensa en agua^F

water is pumped back into the steam generator
el agua^F regresa al generador^M de vapor^M

SOLAR CELL
CELDA^F SOLAR^F

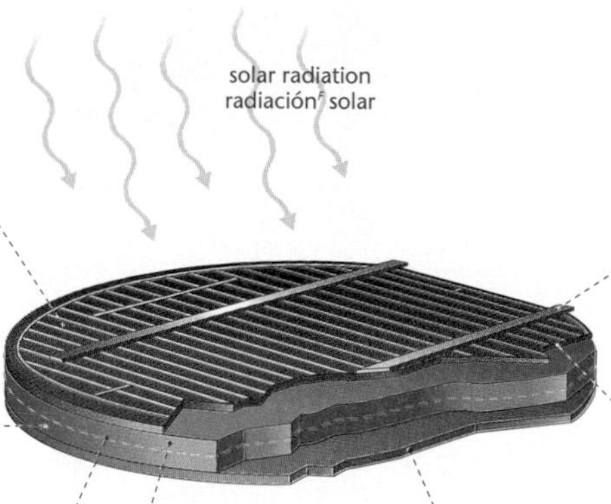

solar radiation
radiación^F solar

antireflection coating
recubrimiento^M antirreflectante

metallic contact grid
reja^F metálica de contacto^M

positive region
región^F positiva

positive/negative junction
junta^F

negative contact
contacto^M negativo

negative region
región^F negativa

positive contact
contacto^M positivo

FLAT-PLATE SOLAR COLLECTOR
COLECTOR^M SOLAR PLANO

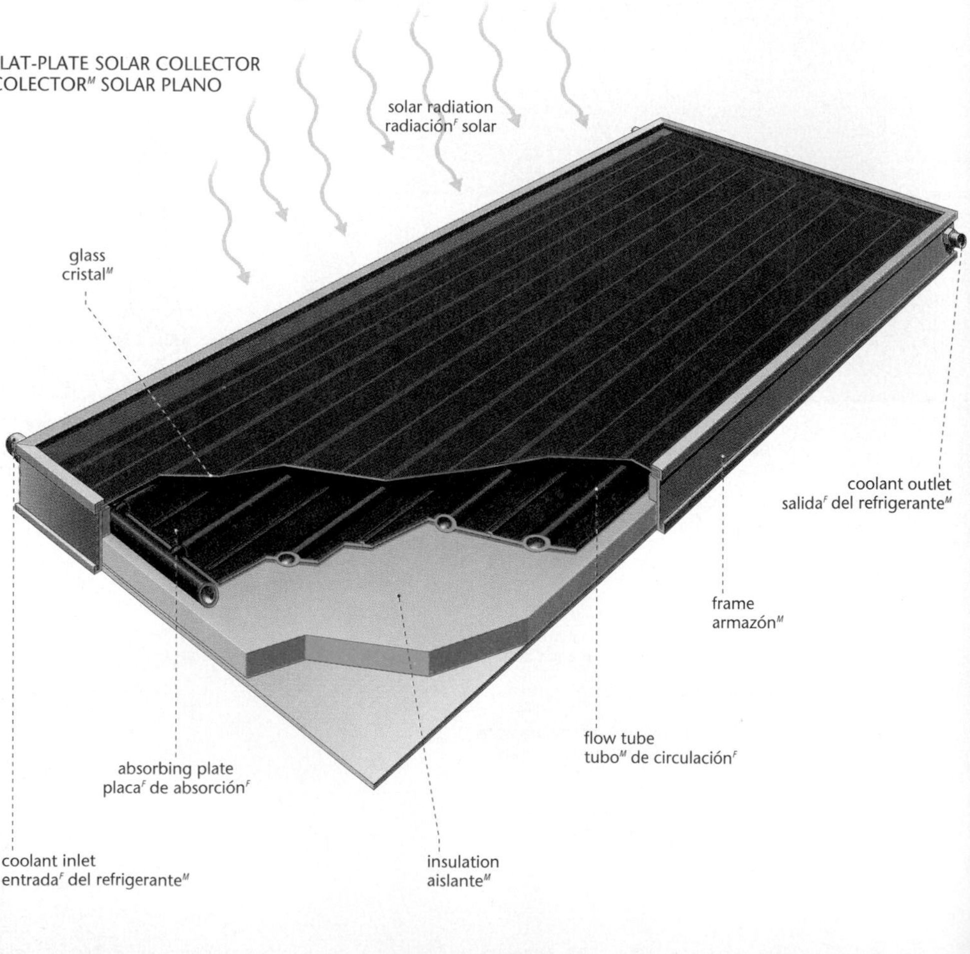

solar radiation
radiación^F solar

glass
cristal^M

coolant outlet
salida^F del refrigerante^M

frame
armazón^M

flow tube
tubo^M de circulación^F

absorbing plate
placa^F de absorción^F

coolant inlet
entrada^F del refrigerante^M

insulation
aislante^M

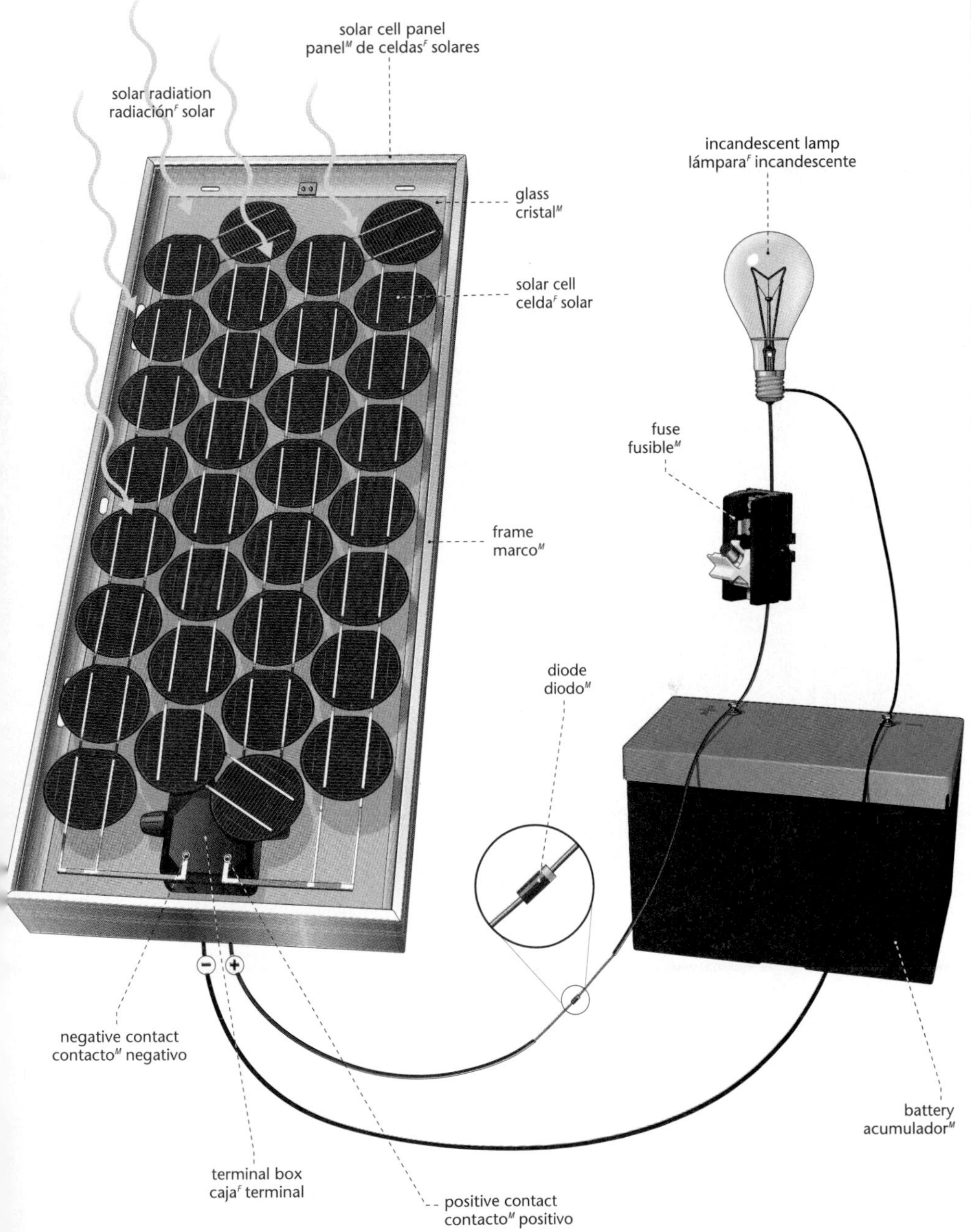

solar cell panel
panel^M de celdas^F solares

solar radiation
radiación^F solar

incandescent lamp
lámpara^F incandescente

glass
cristal^M

solar cell
celda^F solar

fuse
fusible^M

frame
marco^M

diode
diodo^M

negative contact
contacto^M negativo

battery
acumulador^M

terminal box
caja^F terminal

positive contact
contacto^M positivo

SOLAR FURNACE
HORNO^M SOLAR

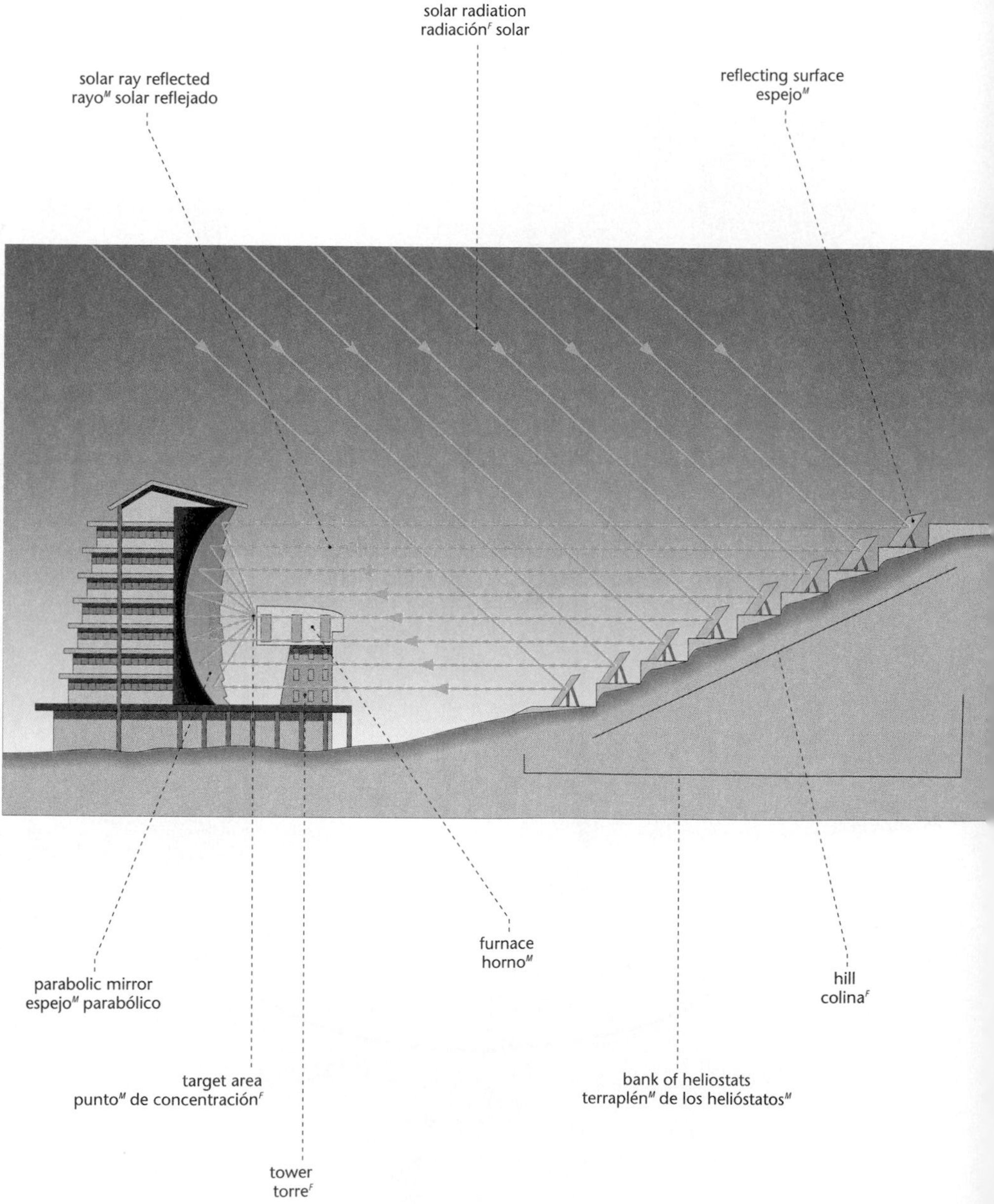

solar radiation
radiación^F solar

solar ray reflected
rayo^M solar reflejado

reflecting surface
espejo^M

parabolic mirror
espejo^M parabólico

target area
punto^M de concentración^F

tower
torre^F

furnace
horno^M

bank of heliostats
terraplén^M de los helióstatos^M

hill
colina^F

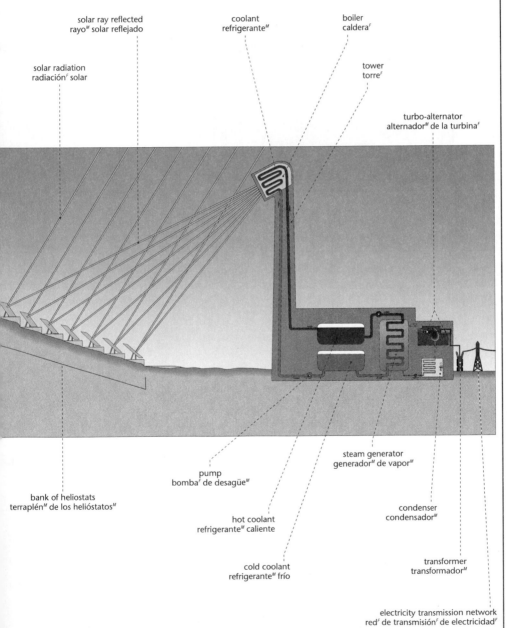

solar ray reflected
rayo^M solar reflejado

coolant
refrigerante^M

boiler
caldera^F

solar radiation
radiación^F solar

tower
torre^F

turbo-alternator
alternador^M de la turbina^F

steam generator
generador^M de vapor^M

pump
bomba^F de desagüe^M

bank of heliostats
terraplén^M de los helióstatos^M

hot coolant
refrigerante^M caliente

condenser
condensador^M

cold coolant
refrigerante^M frío

transformer
transformador^M

electricity transmission network
red^F de transmisión^F de electricidad^F

ENERGY
ENERGÍA

771

SOLAR ENERGY
ENERGÍA^F SOLAR

SOLAR HOUSE
CASA^F SOLAR

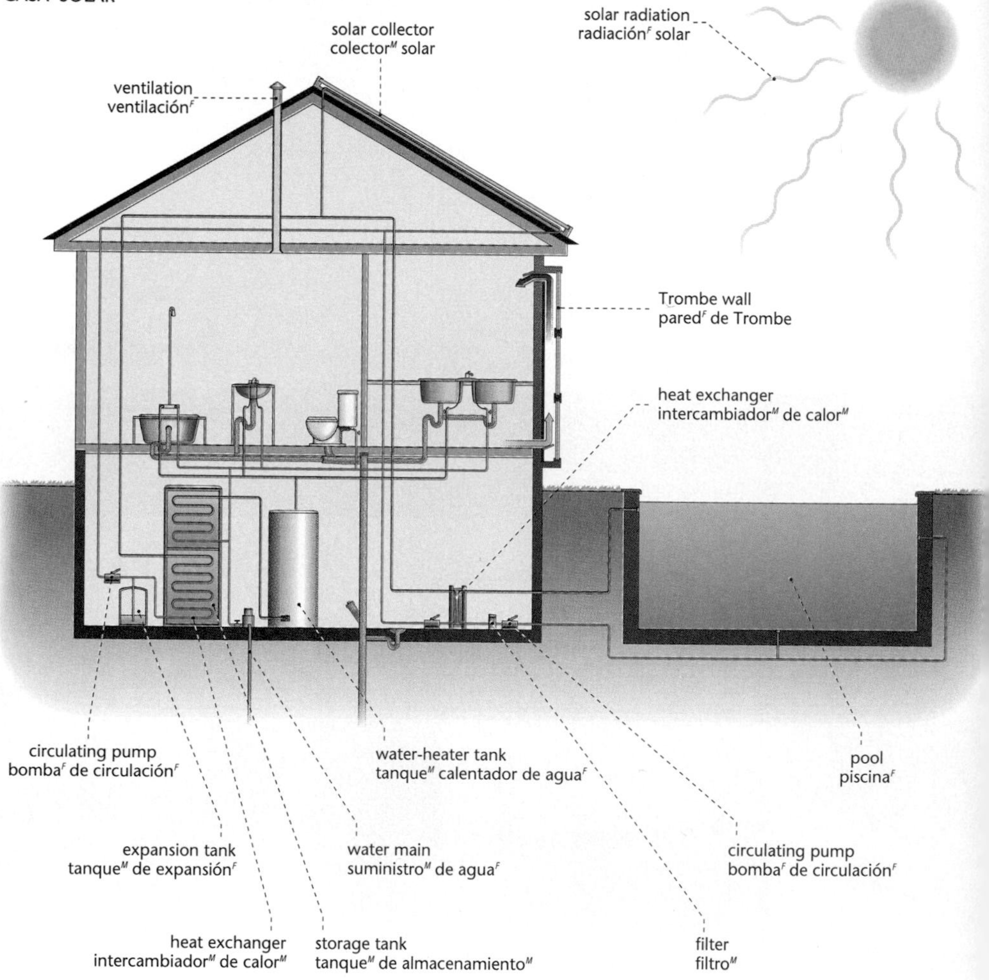

solar collector
colector^M solar

solar radiation
radiación^F solar

ventilation
ventilación^F

Trombe wall
pared^F de Trombe

heat exchanger
intercambiador^M de calor^M

circulating pump
bomba^F de circulación^F

water-heater tank
tanque^M calentador de agua^F

pool
piscina^F

expansion tank
tanque^M de expansión^F

water main
suministro^M de agua^F

circulating pump
bomba^F de circulación^F

heat exchanger
intercambiador^M de calor^M

storage tank
tanque^M de almacenamiento^M

filter
filtro^M

TROMBE WALL
PARED^F DE TROMBE

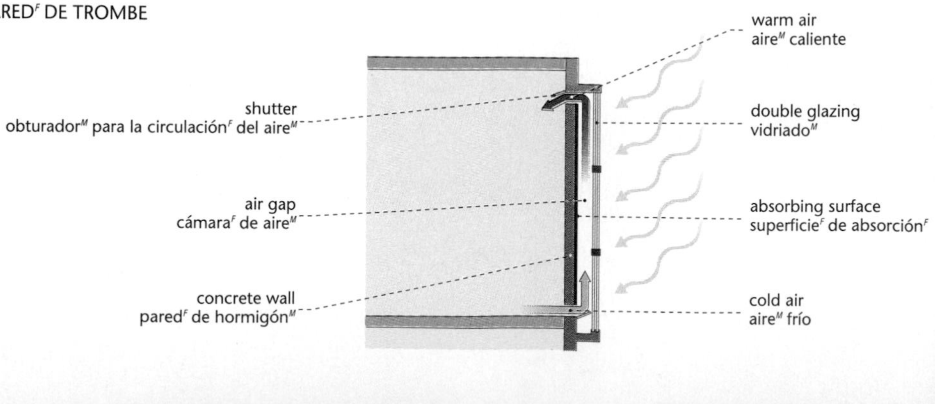

warm air
aire^M caliente

shutter
obturador^M para la circulación^F del aire^M

double glazing
vidriado^M

air gap
cámara^F de aire^M

absorbing surface
superficie^F de absorción^F

concrete wall
pared^F de hormigón^M

cold air
aire^M frío

WIND ENERGY
ENERGÍA^F EÓLICA

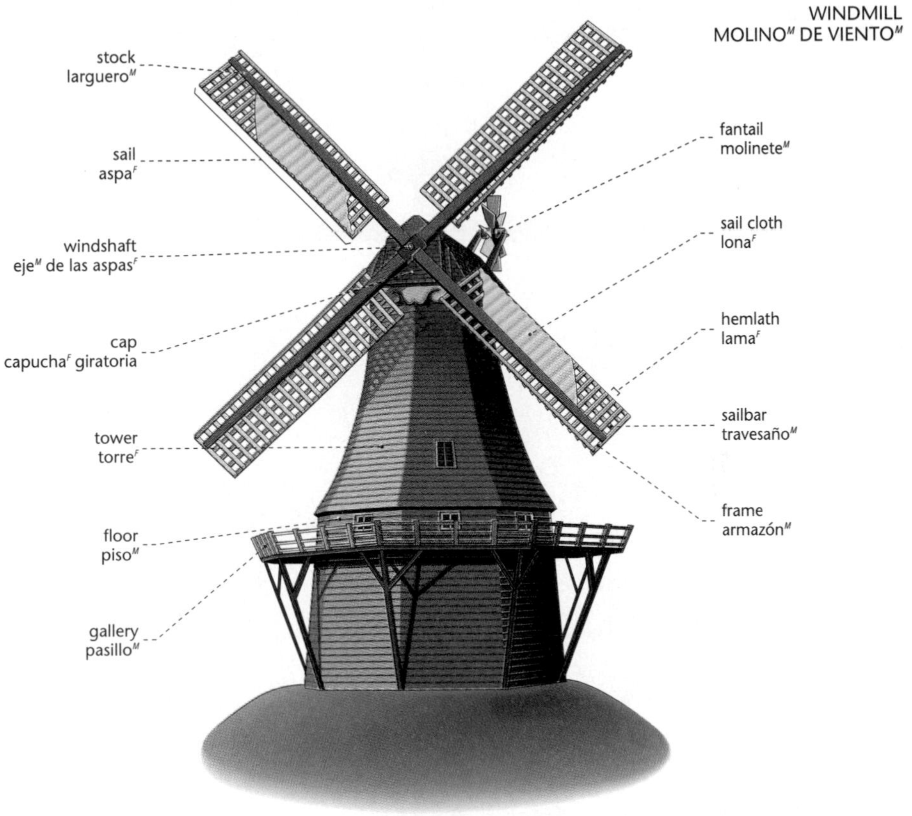

WINDMILL
MOLINO^M DE VIENTO^M

stock
larguero^M

sail
aspa^F

windshaft
eje^M de las aspas^F

cap
capucha^F giratoria

tower
torre^F

floor
piso^M

gallery
pasillo^M

fantail
molinete^M

sail cloth
lona^F

hemlath
lama^F

sailbar
travesaño^M

frame
armazón^M

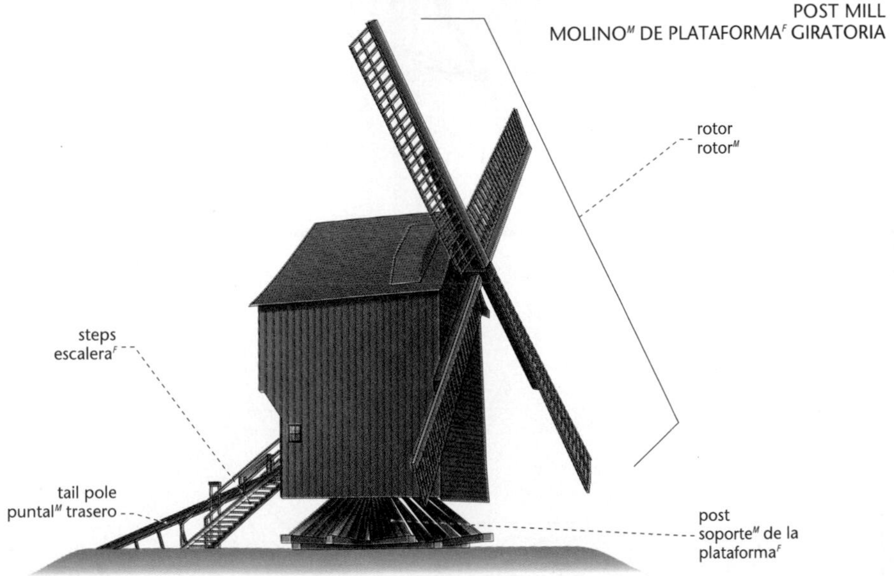

POST MILL
MOLINO^M DE PLATAFORMA^F GIRATORIA

rotor
rotor^M

steps
escalera^F

tail pole
puntal^M trasero

post
soporte^M de la
plataforma^F

773

WIND ENERGY
ENERGÍA^F EÓLICA

HORIZONTAL-AXIS WIND TURBINE
TURBINA^F DE VIENTO^M DE EJE^M HORIZONTAL

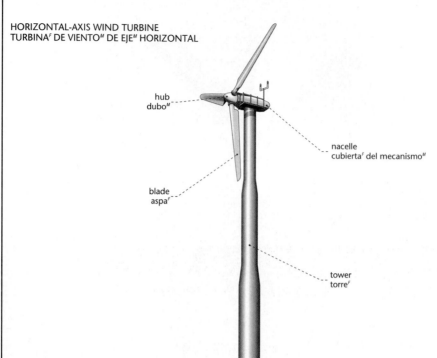

hub
dubo^M

nacelle
cubierta^F del mecanismo^M

blade
aspa^F

tower
torre^F

VERTICAL-AXIS WIND TURBINE
TURBINA^F DE VIENTO^M DE EJE^M VERTICAL

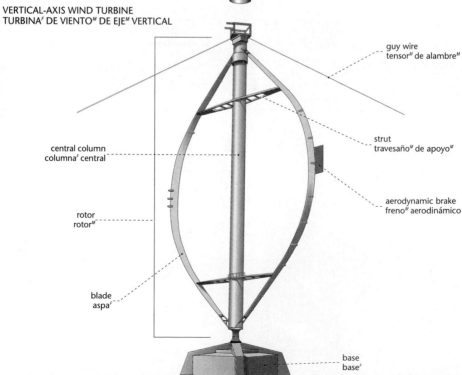

guy wire
tensor^M de alambre^M

strut
travesaño^M de apoyo^M

central column
columna^F central

aerodynamic brake
freno^M aerodinámico

rotor
rotor^M

blade
aspa^F

base
base^F

ENERGY
ENERGÍA

774

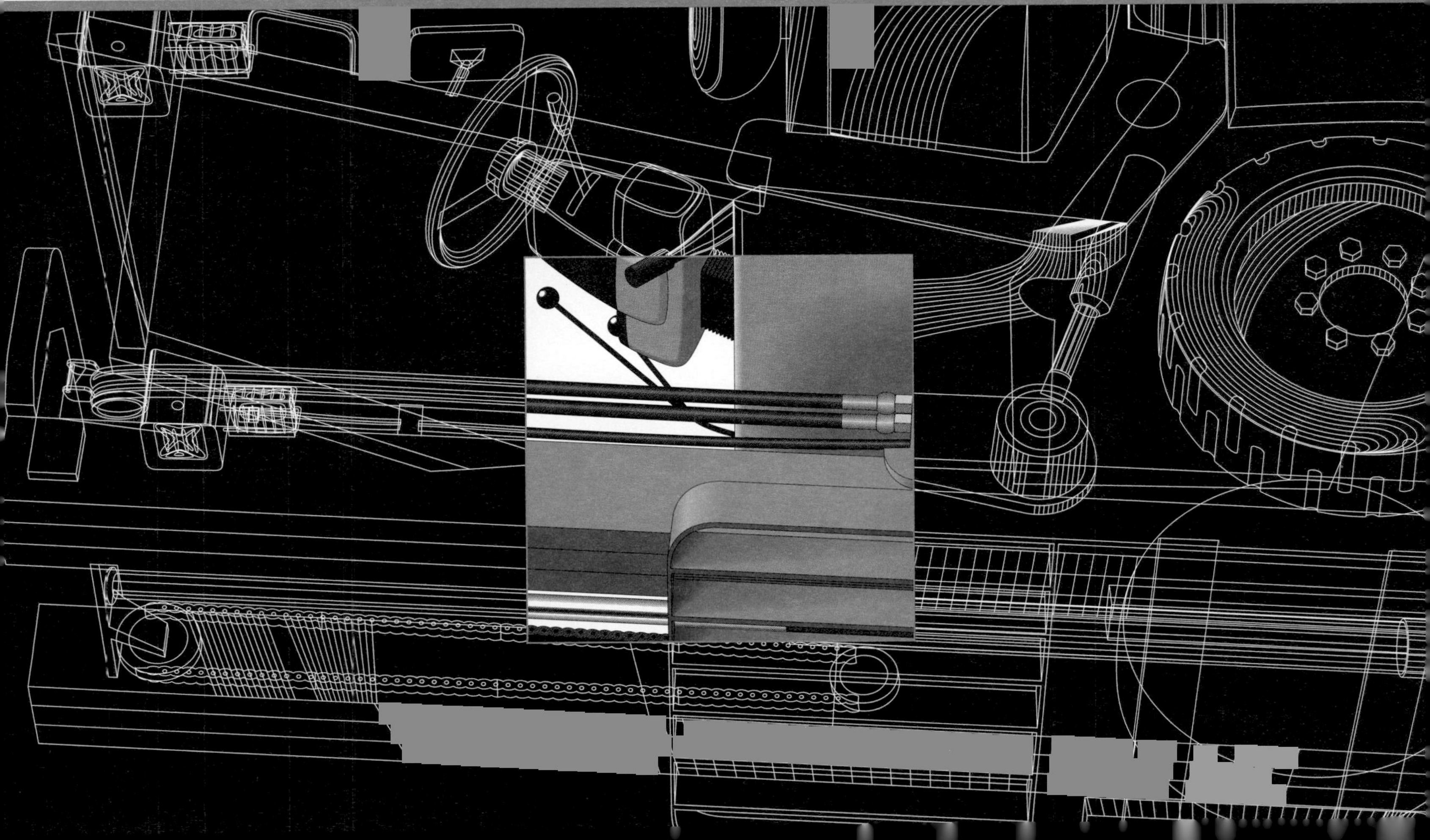

CONTENTS

**HEAVY MACHINERY
MAQUINARIA PESADA**

FIRE PREVENTION
PREVENCIÓN^F DE INCENDIOS^M

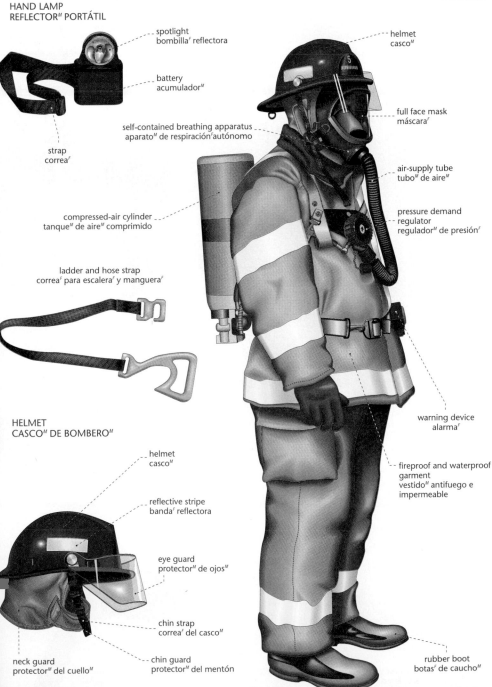

HAND LAMP
REFLECTOR^M PORTÁTIL

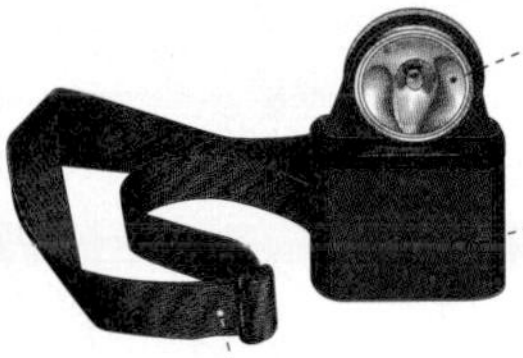

spotlight
bombilla^F reflectora

helmet
casco^M

battery
acumulador^M

full face mask
máscara^F

self-contained breathing apparatus
aparato^M de respiración^F autónomo

air-supply tube
tubo^M de aire^M

strap
correa^F

pressure demand
regulator
regulador^M de presión^F

compressed-air cylinder
tanque^M de aire^M comprimido

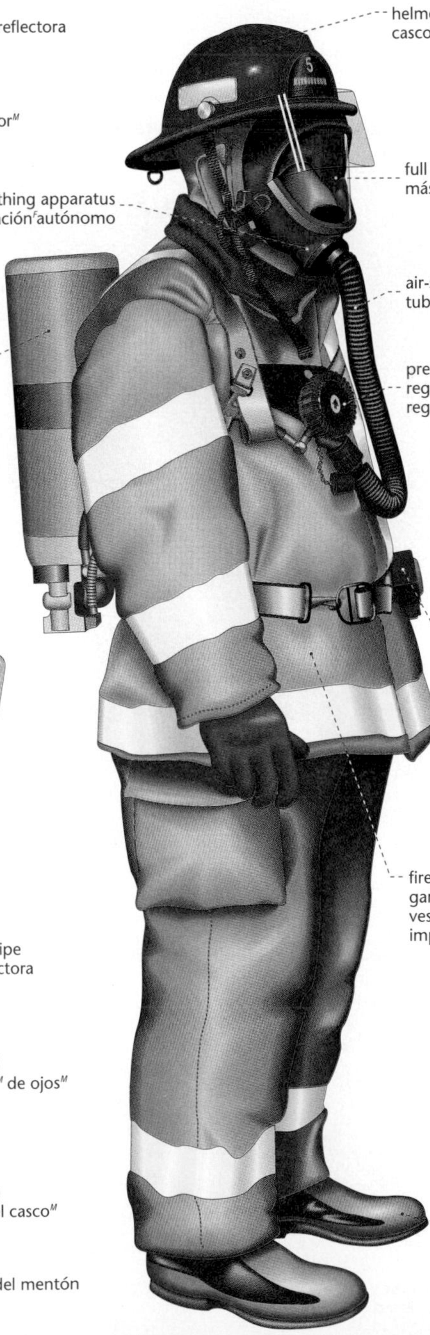

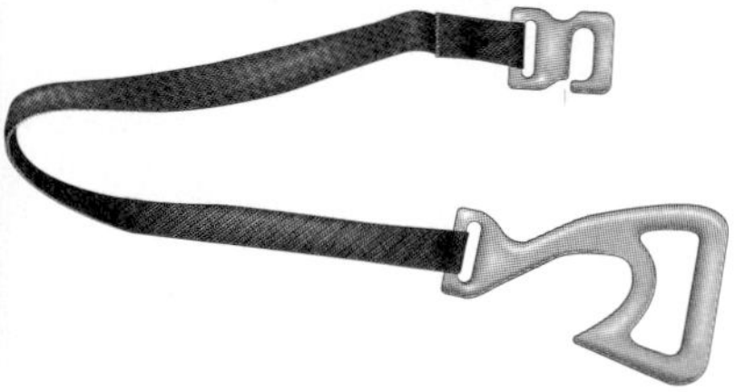

ladder and hose strap
correa^F para escalera^F y manguera^F

warning device
alarma^F

HELMET
CASCO^M DE BOMBERO^M

fireproof and waterproof
garment
vestido^M antifuego e
impermeable

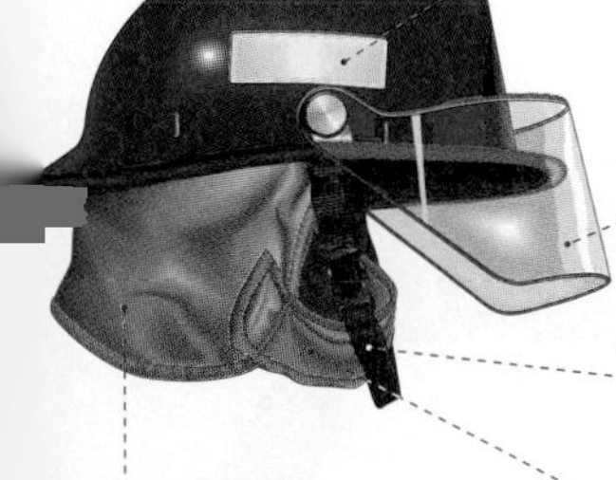

helmet
casco^M

reflective stripe
banda^F reflectora

eye guard
protector^M de ojos^M

chin strap
correa^F del casco^M

neck guard
protector^M del cuello^M

chin guard
protector^M del mentón

rubber boot
botas^F de caucho^M

**HEAVY MACHINERY
MAQUINARIA PESADA**

FIRE ENGINE
COCHE^M DE BOMBEROS^M

PUMPER
CAMIÓN^M BOMBA^F

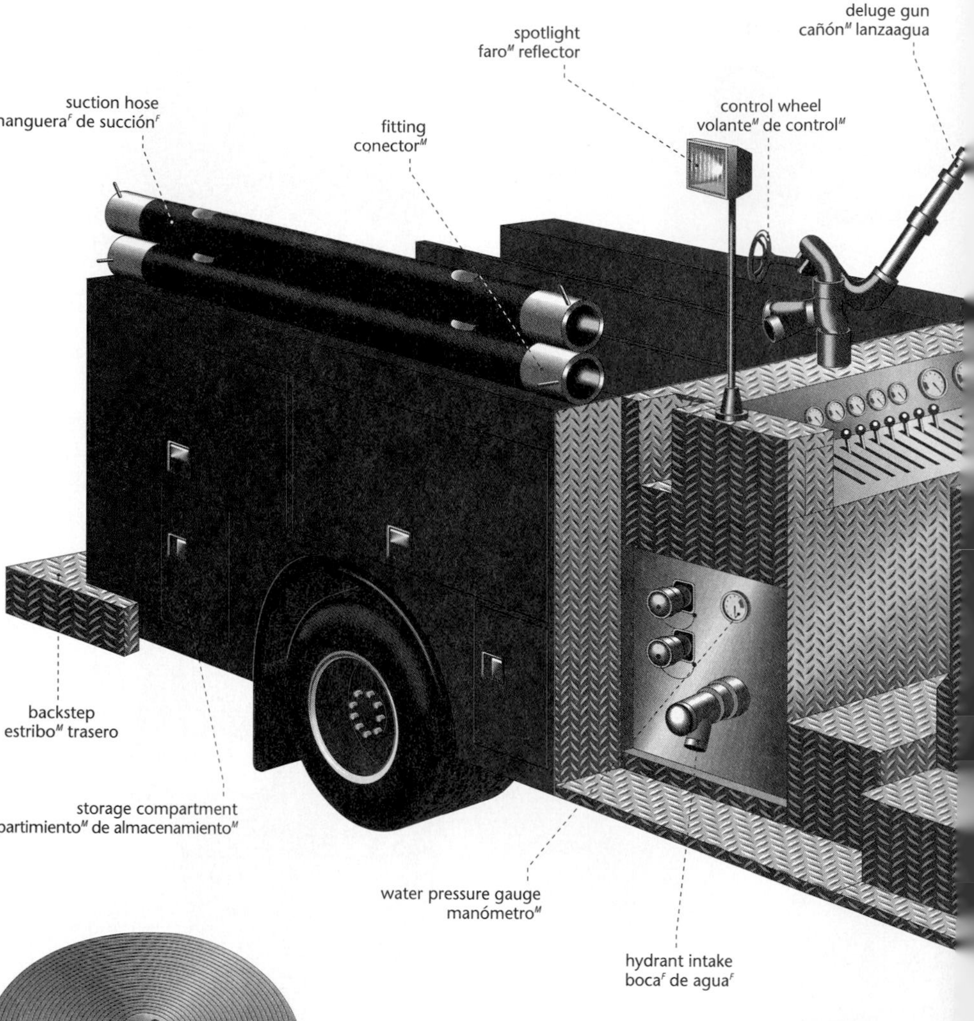

deluge gun
cañón^M lanzaagua

spotlight
faro^M reflector

control wheel
volante^M de control^M

suction hose
manguera^F de succión^F

fitting
conector^M

backstep
estribo^M trasero

storage compartment
compartimiento^M de almacenamiento^M

water pressure gauge
manómetro^M

hydrant intake
boca^F de agua^F

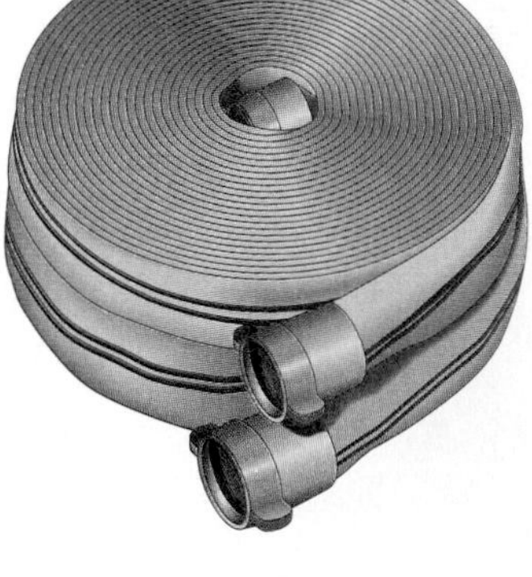

fire hose
manguera^F de incendios^M

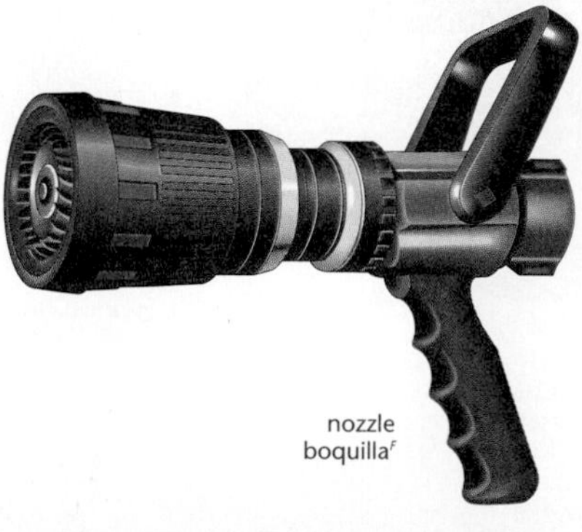

nozzle
boquilla^F

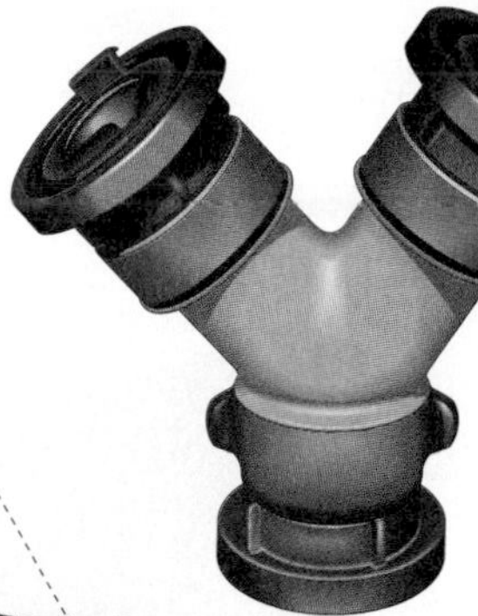

dividing breeching
separador^M de boca^F de agua^F

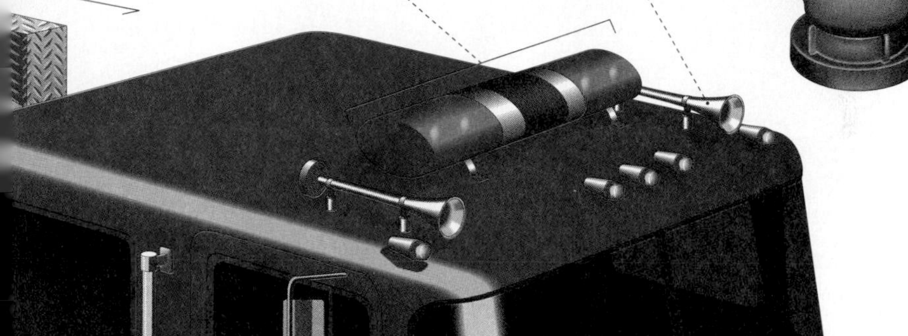

control panel
tablero^M de operaciónes^F

horn
bocina^F

light bar
luces^F de emergencia^F

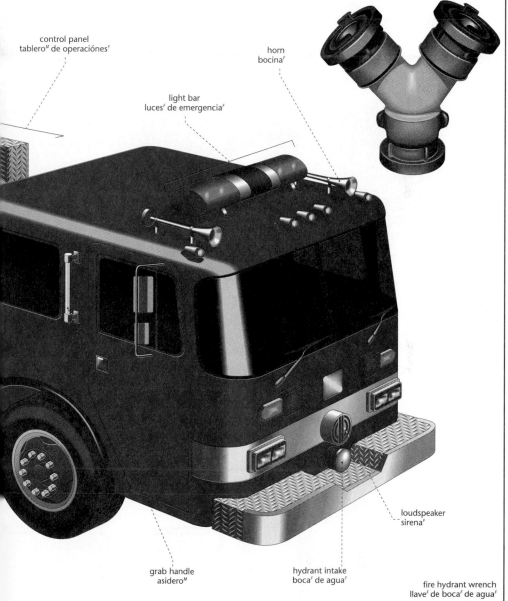

loudspeaker
sirena^F

grab handle
asidero^M

hydrant intake
boca^F de agua^F

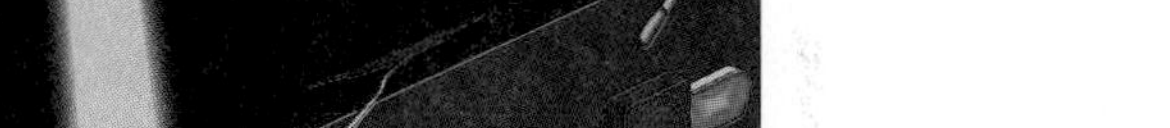

fire hydrant wrench
llave^F de boca^F de agua^F

FIRE ENGINE
COCHE^M DE BOMBEROS^M

AERIAL LADDER TRUCK
CAMIÓN^M DE ESCALELERA^F TELESCÓPICA

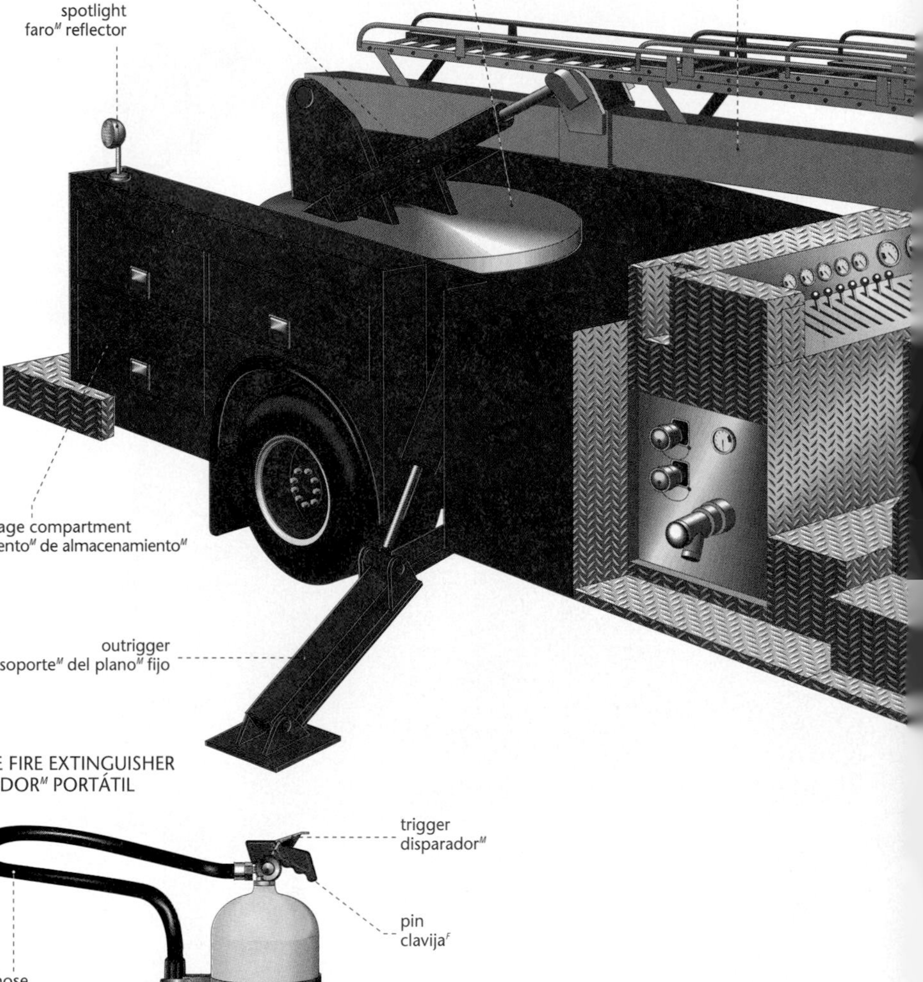

elevating cylinder
cilindro^M elevador

turntable mounting
plataforma^F giratoria

telescopic boom
elevador^M telescópico

spotlight
faro^M reflector

storage compartment
compartimiento^M de almacenamiento^M

outrigger
soporte^M del plano^M fijo

PORTABLE FIRE EXTINGUISHER
EXTINGUIDOR^M PORTÁTIL

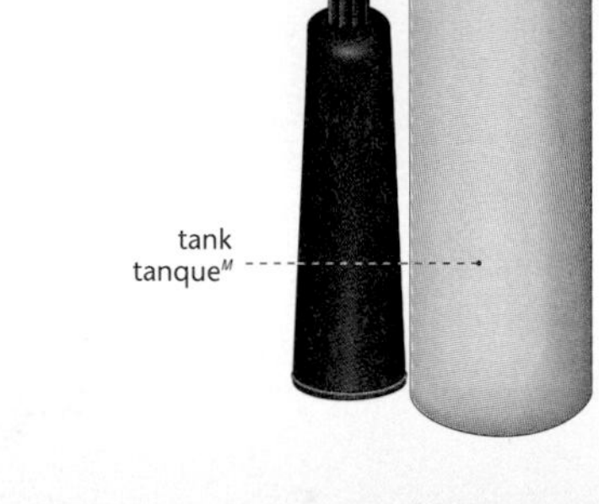

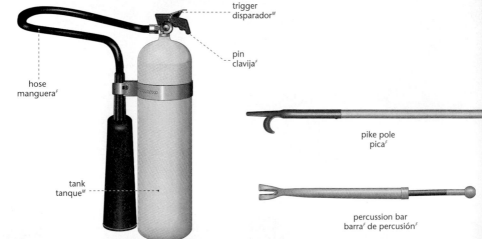

trigger
disparador^M

pin
clavija^F

hose
manguera^F

tank
tanque^M

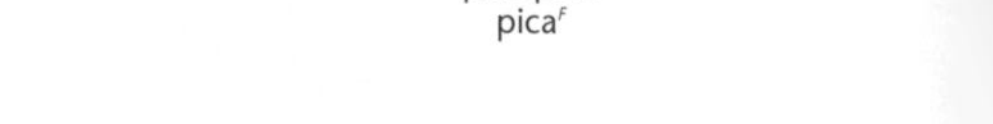

pike pole
pica^F

percussion bar
barra^F de percusión^F

780

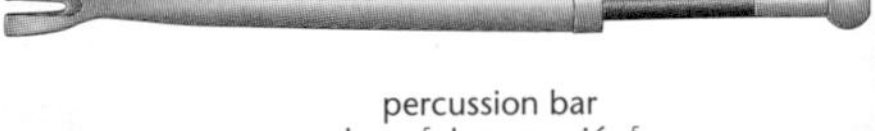

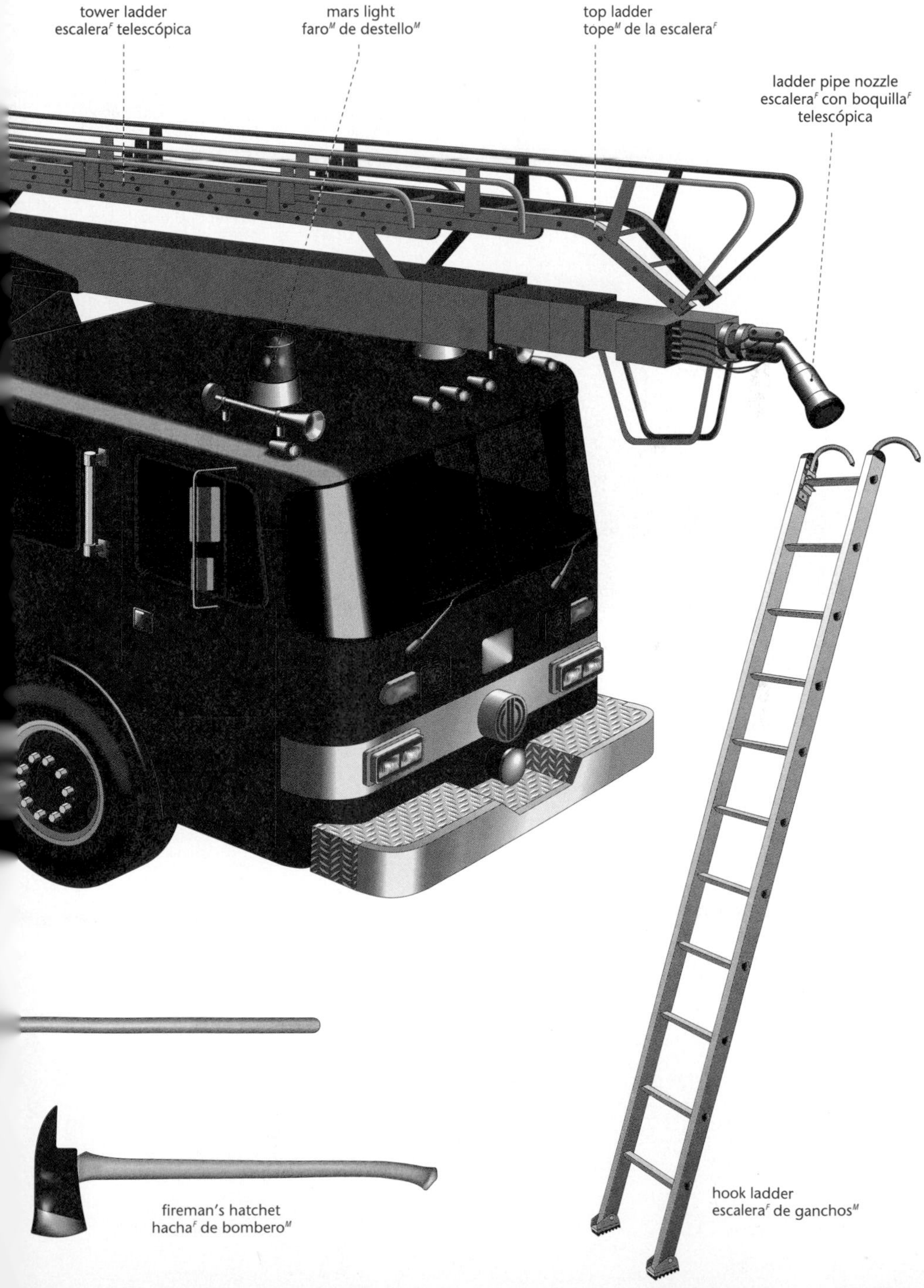

tower ladder
escalera^F telescópica

mars light
faro^M de destello^M

top ladder
tope^M de la escalera^F

ladder pipe nozzle
escalera^F con boquilla^F
telescópica

fireman's hatchet
hacha^F de bombero^M

hook ladder
escalera^F de ganchos^M

WHEEL LOADER
RETROEXCAVADORA^F CARGADORA^F

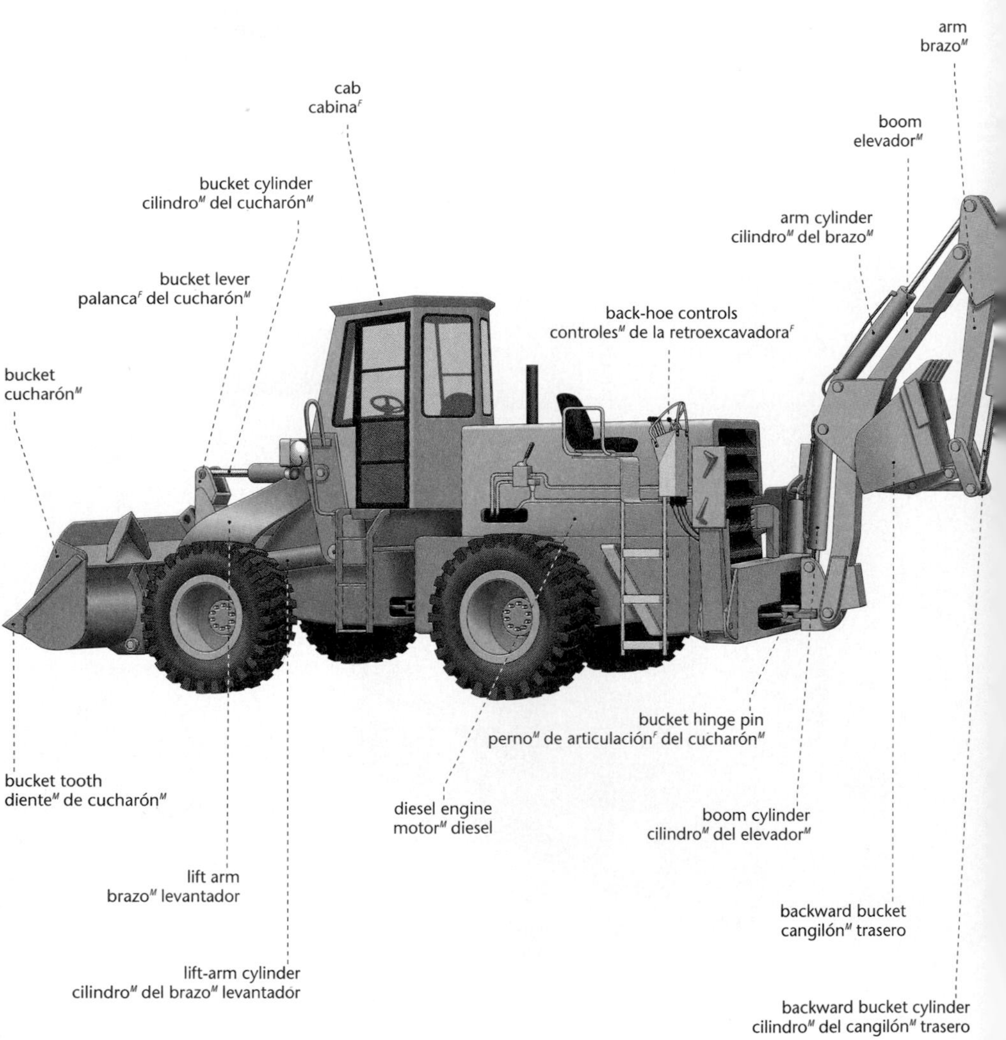

arm
brazo^M

cab
cabina^F

boom
elevador^M

bucket cylinder
cilindro^M del cucharón^M

arm cylinder
cilindro^M del brazo^M

bucket lever
palanca^F del cucharón^M

back-hoe controls
controles^M de la retroexcavadora^F

bucket
cucharón^M

bucket tooth
diente^M de cucharón^M

bucket hinge pin
perno^M de articulación^F del cucharón^M

diesel engine
motor^M diesel

boom cylinder
cilindro^M del elevador^M

lift arm
brazo^M levantador

backward bucket
cangilón^M trasero

lift-arm cylinder
cilindro^M del brazo^M levantador

backward bucket cylinder
cilindro^M del cangilón^M trasero

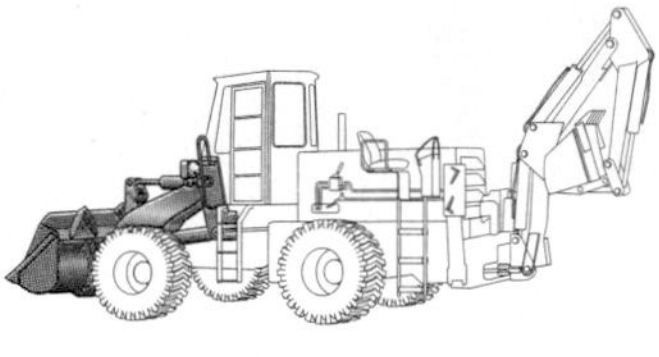

front-end loader
cargador^M delantero

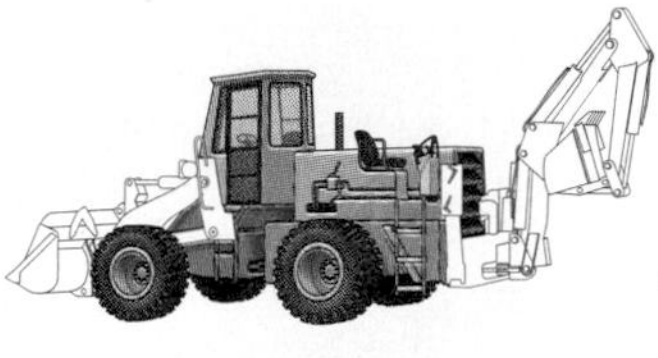

wheel tractor
tractor^M de ruedas^F

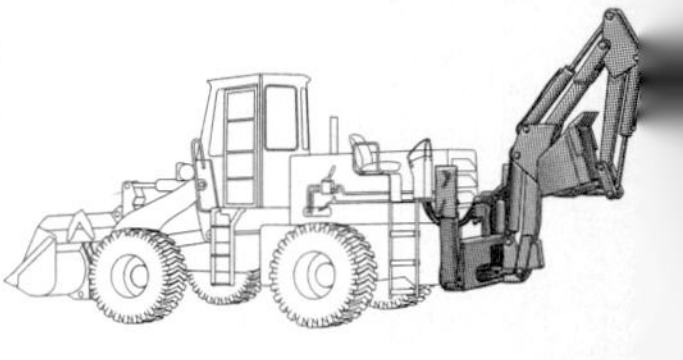

back-hoe
retroexcavadora^F

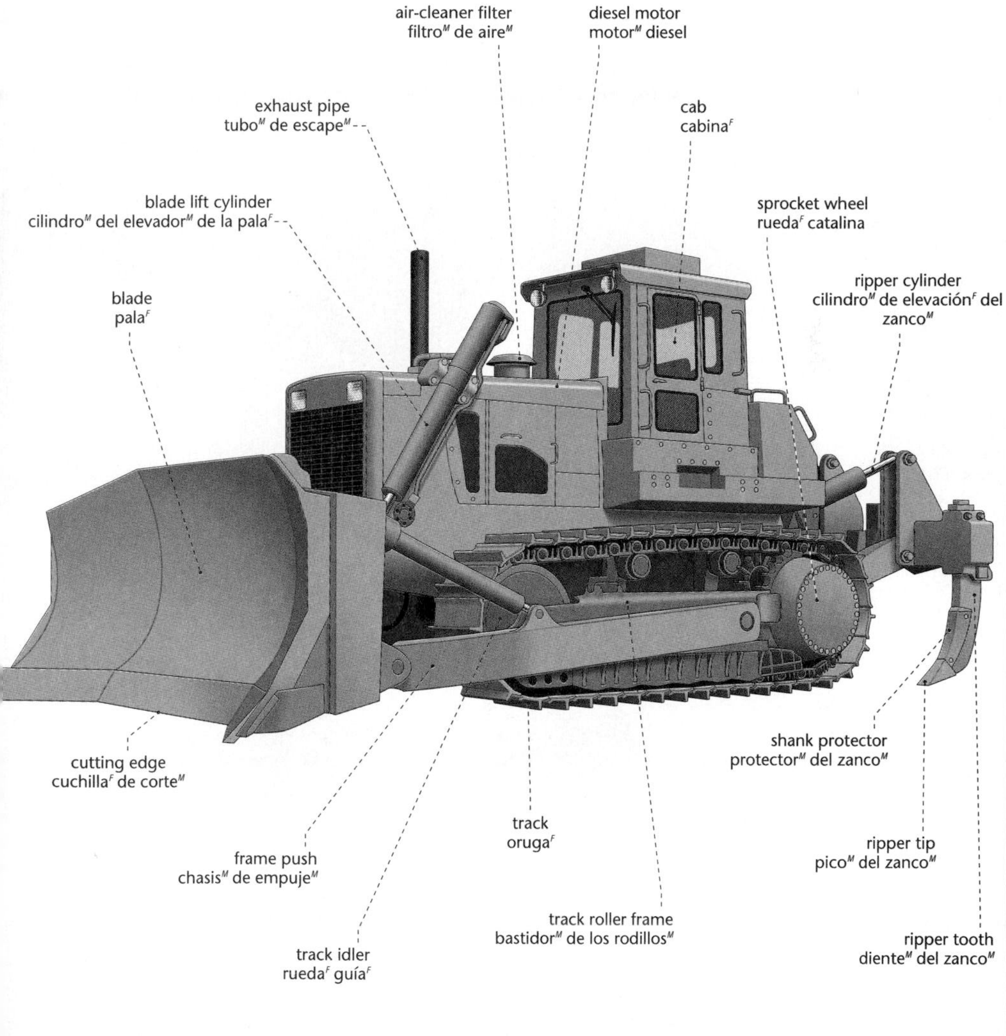

air-cleaner filter
filtro^M de aire^M

diesel motor
motor^M diesel

exhaust pipe
tubo^M de escape^M

cab
cabina^F

blade lift cylinder
cilindro^M del elevador^M de la pala^F

sprocket wheel
rueda^F catalina

blade
pala^F

ripper cylinder
cilindro^M de elevación^F del
zanco^M

cutting edge
cuchilla^F de corte^M

shank protector
protector^M del zanco^M

track
oruga^F

frame push
chasis^M de empuje^M

ripper tip
pico^M del zanco^M

track roller frame
bastidor^M de los rodillos^M

track idler
rueda^F guía^F

ripper tooth
diente^M del zanco^M

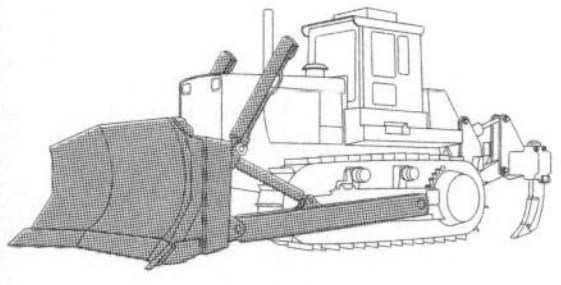

blade
pala^F

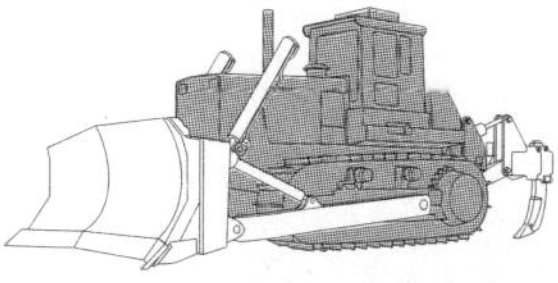

crawler tractor
tractor^M de orugas^F

ripper
zanco^M

HEAVY MACHINERY
MAQUINARIA PESADA

783

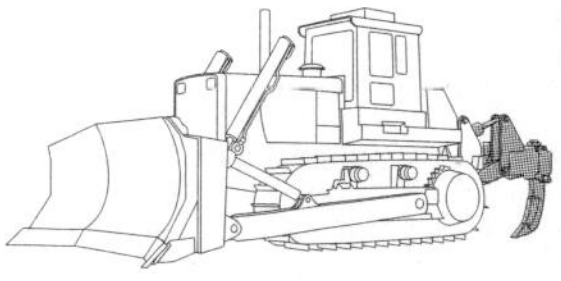

SCRAPER
RASPADOR*M*

steering cylinder
cilindro*M* de dirección*F*

gooseneck
cuello*M* de ganso*M*

ejector
eyector*M*

draft tube
barra*F* de arrastre*M*

draft arm
brazo*M* de arrastre*M*

bowl
contenedor*M*

cutting edge
cuchilla*F* de corte*M*

tractor engine
motor*M*

GRADER
NIVELADORA*F*

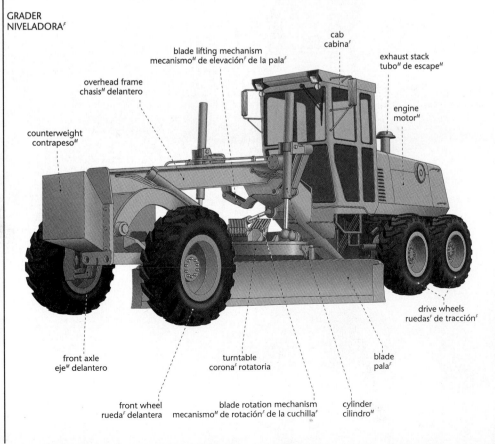

blade lifting mechanism
mecanismo*M* de elevación*F* de la pala*F*

cab
cabina*F*

exhaust stack
tubo*M* de escape*M*

overhead frame
chasis*M* delantero

engine
motor*M*

counterweight
contrapeso*M*

drive wheels
ruedas*F* de tracción*F*

front axle
eje*M* delantero

turntable
corona*F* rotatoria

blade
pala*F*

front wheel
rueda*F* delantera

blade rotation mechanism
mecanismo*M* de rotación*F* de la cuchilla*F*

cylinder
cilindro*M*

HEAVY MACHINERY
MAQUINARIA^F PESADA

DUMP TRUCK
CAMIÓN^M BASCULANTE

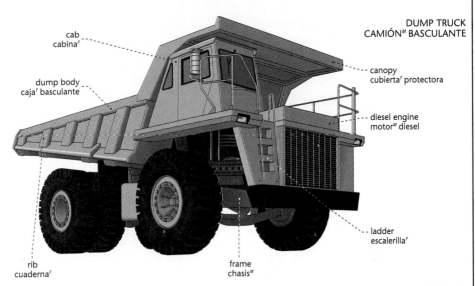

cab
cabina^F

dump body
caja^F basculante

canopy
cubierta^F protectora

diesel engine
motor^M diesel

ladder
escalerilla^F

rib
cuaderna^F

frame
chasis^M

HYDRAULIC SHOVEL
PALA^F HIDRÁULICA

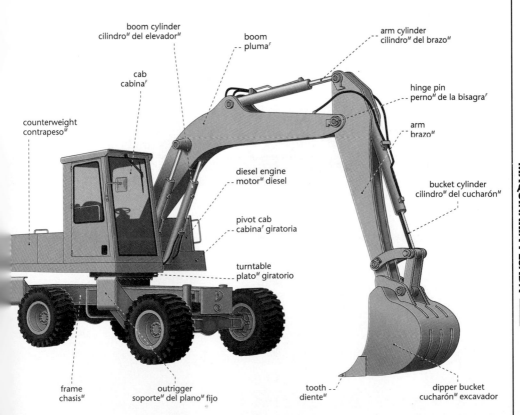

boom cylinder
cilindro^M del elevador^M

boom
pluma^F

arm cylinder
cilindro^M del brazo^M

cab
cabina^F

hinge pin
perno^M de la bisagra^F

counterweight
contrapeso^M

arm
brazo^M

diesel engine
motor^M diesel

bucket cylinder
cilindro^M del cucharón^M

pivot cab
cabina^F giratoria

turntable
plato^M giratorio

frame
chasis^M

outrigger
soporte^M del plano^M fijo

tooth
diente^M

dipper bucket
cucharón^M excavador

785

MATERIAL HANDLING
MANEJO^M DE MATERIALES^M

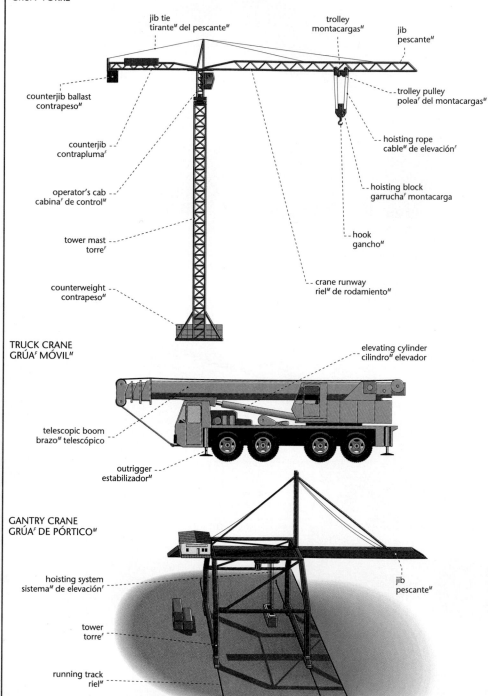

TOWER CRANE
GRÚA^F TORRE^F

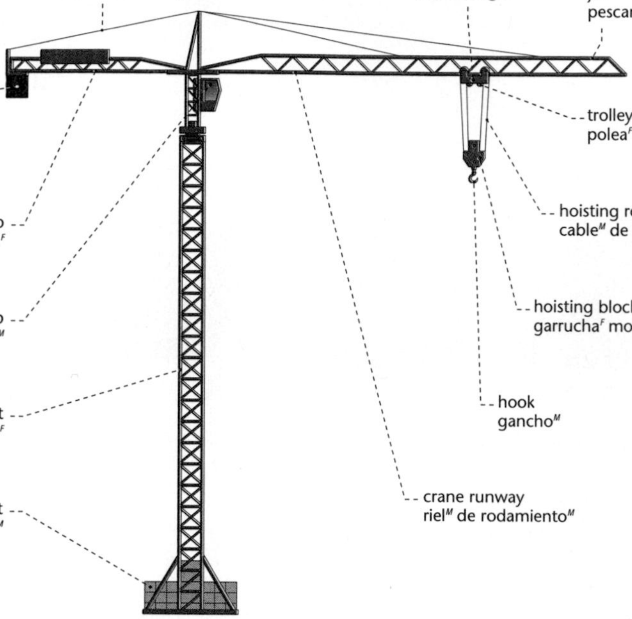

jib tie
tirante^M del pescante^M

trolley
montacargas^M

jib
pescante^M

counterjib ballast
contrapeso^M

trolley pulley
polea^F del montacargas^M

counterjib
contrapluma^F

hoisting rope
cable^M de elevación^F

operator's cab
cabina^F de control^M

hoisting block
garrucha^F montacarga

tower mast
torre^F

hook
gancho^M

counterweight
contrapeso^M

crane runway
riel^M de rodamiento^M

TRUCK CRANE
GRÚA^F MÓVIL^M

elevating cylinder
cilindro^M elevador

telescopic boom
brazo^M telescópico

outrigger
estabilizador^M

GANTRY CRANE
GRÚA^F DE PÓRTICO^M

hoisting system
sistema^M de elevación^F

jib
pescante^M

tower
torre^F

running track
riel^M

HEAVY MACHINERY
MAQUINARIA PESADA

786

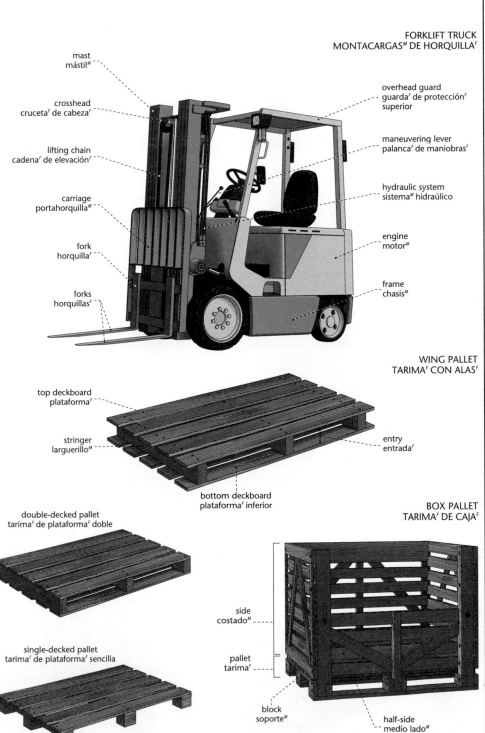

FORKLIFT TRUCK
MONTACARGAS[M] DE HORQUILLA[F]

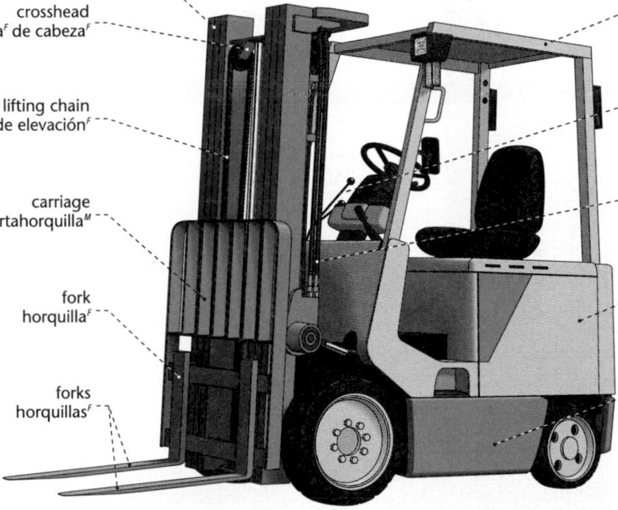

mast
mástil[M]

crosshead
cruceta[F] de cabeza[F]

lifting chain
cadena[F] de elevación[F]

carriage
portahorquilla[M]

fork
horquilla[F]

forks
horquillas[F]

overhead guard
guarda[F] de protección[F] superior

maneuvering lever
palanca[F] de maniobras[F]

hydraulic system
sistema[M] hidraúlico

engine
motor[M]

frame
chasis[M]

WING PALLET
TARIMA[F] CON ALAS[F]

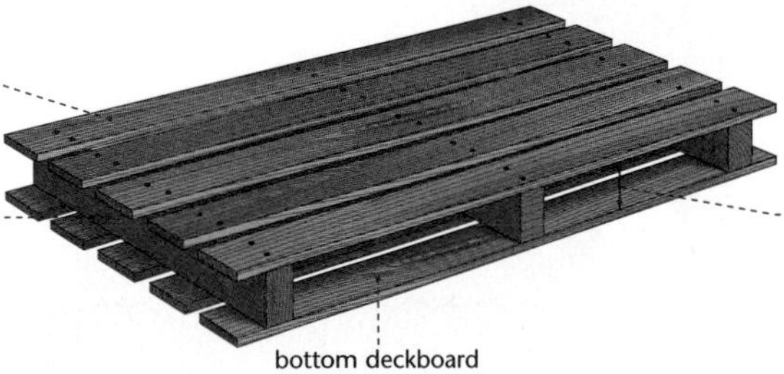

top deckboard
plataforma[F]

stringer
larguerillo[M]

entry
entrada[F]

bottom deckboard
plataforma[F] inferior

double-decked pallet
tarima[F] de plataforma[F] doble

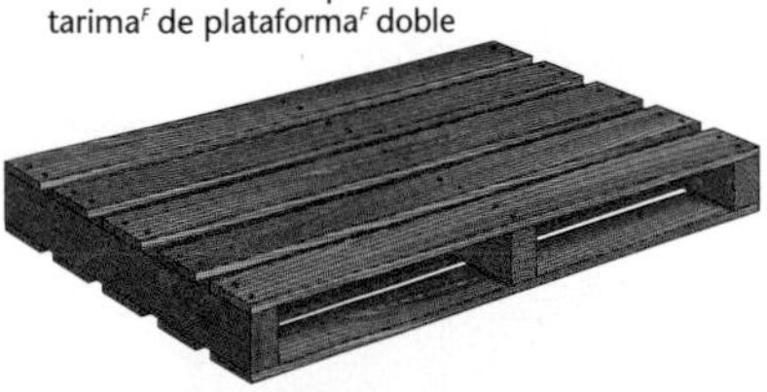

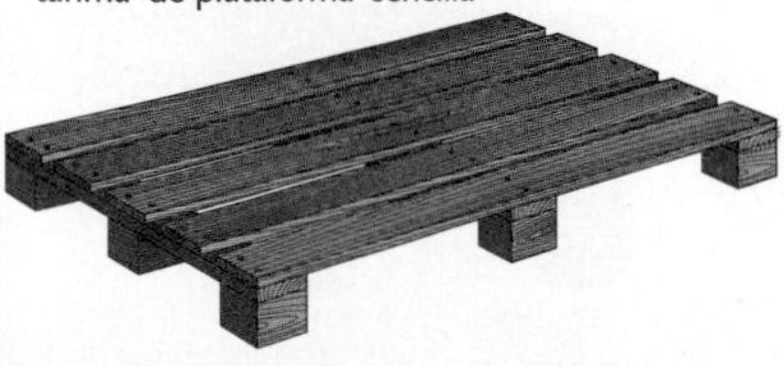

BOX PALLET
TARIMA[F] DE CAJA[F]

single-decked pallet
tarima[F] de plataforma[F] sencilla

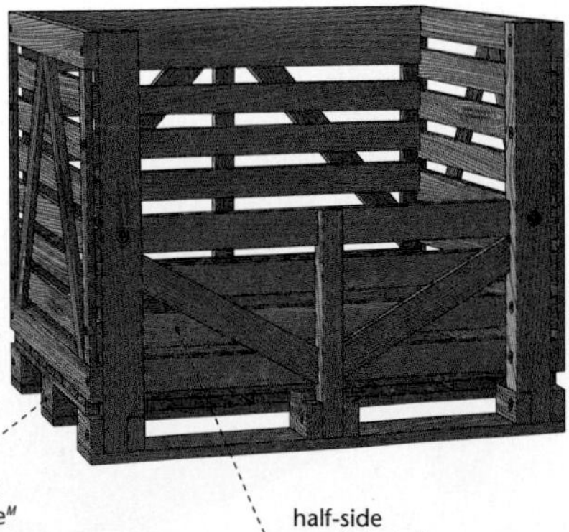

side
costado[M]

pallet
tarima[F]

block
soporte[M]

half-side
medio lado[M]

HEAVY MACHINERY
MAQUINARIA PESADA

787

HYDRAULIC PALLET TRUCK
MONTACARGAS^M HIDRÁULICO DE TARIMA^F

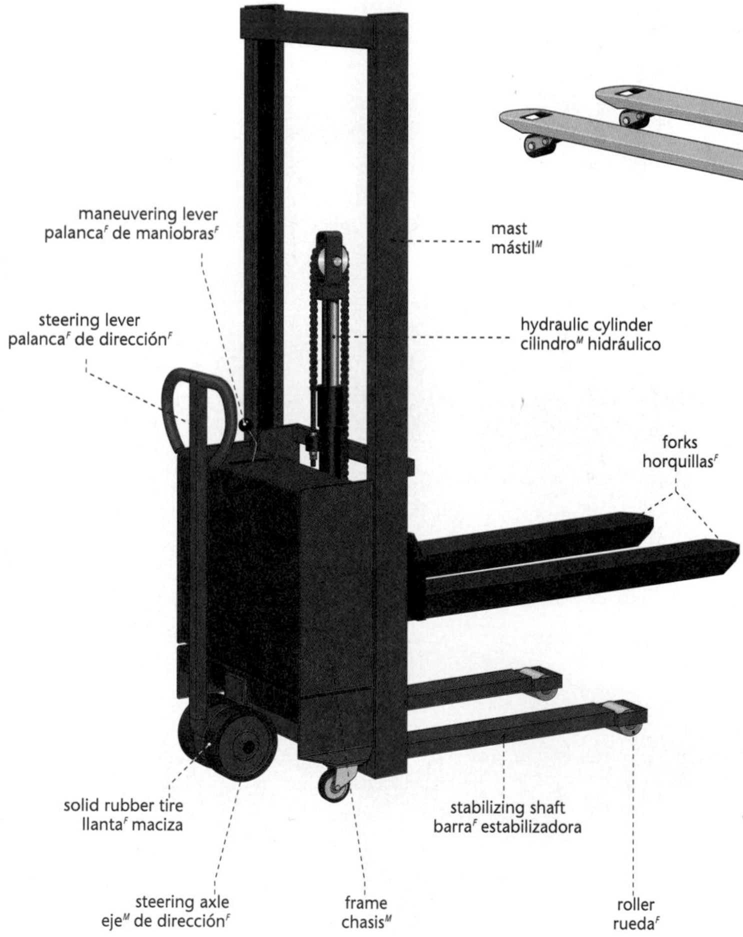

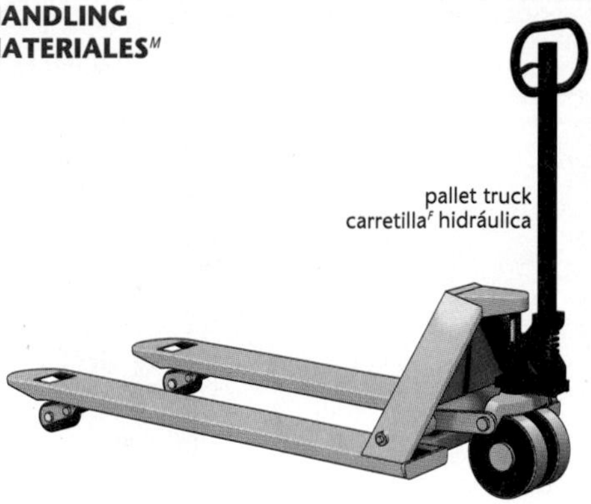

pallet truck
carretilla^F hidráulica

maneuvering lever
palanca^F de maniobras^F

mast
mástil^M

steering lever
palanca^F de dirección^F

hydraulic cylinder
cilindro^M hidráulico

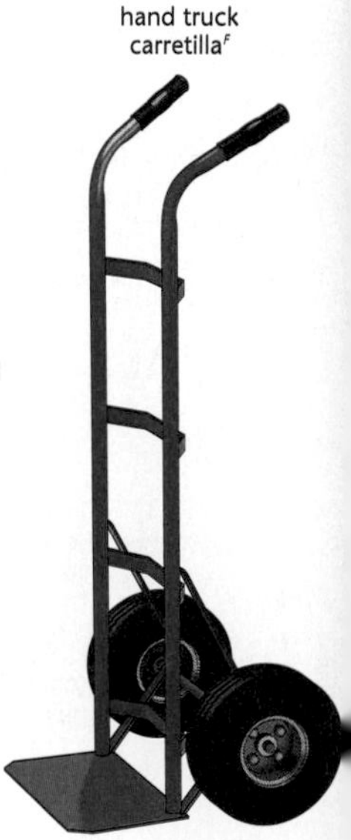

hand truck
carretilla^F

forks
horquillas^F

solid rubber tire
llanta^F maciza

stabilizing shaft
barra^F estabilizadora

steering axle
eje^M de dirección^F

frame
chasis^M

roller
rueda^F

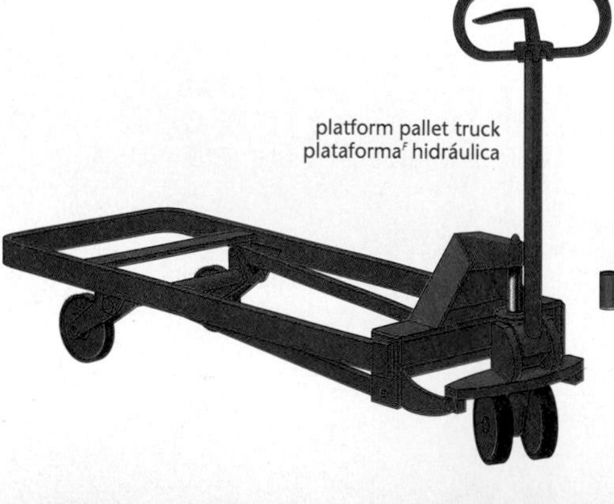

platform pallet truck
plataforma^F hidráulica

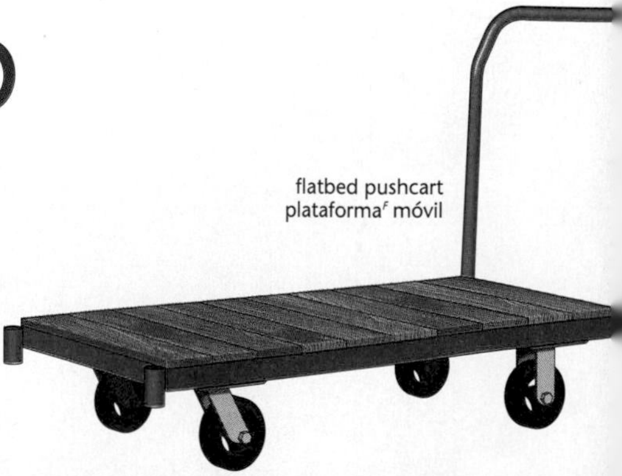

flatbed pushcart
plataforma^F móvil

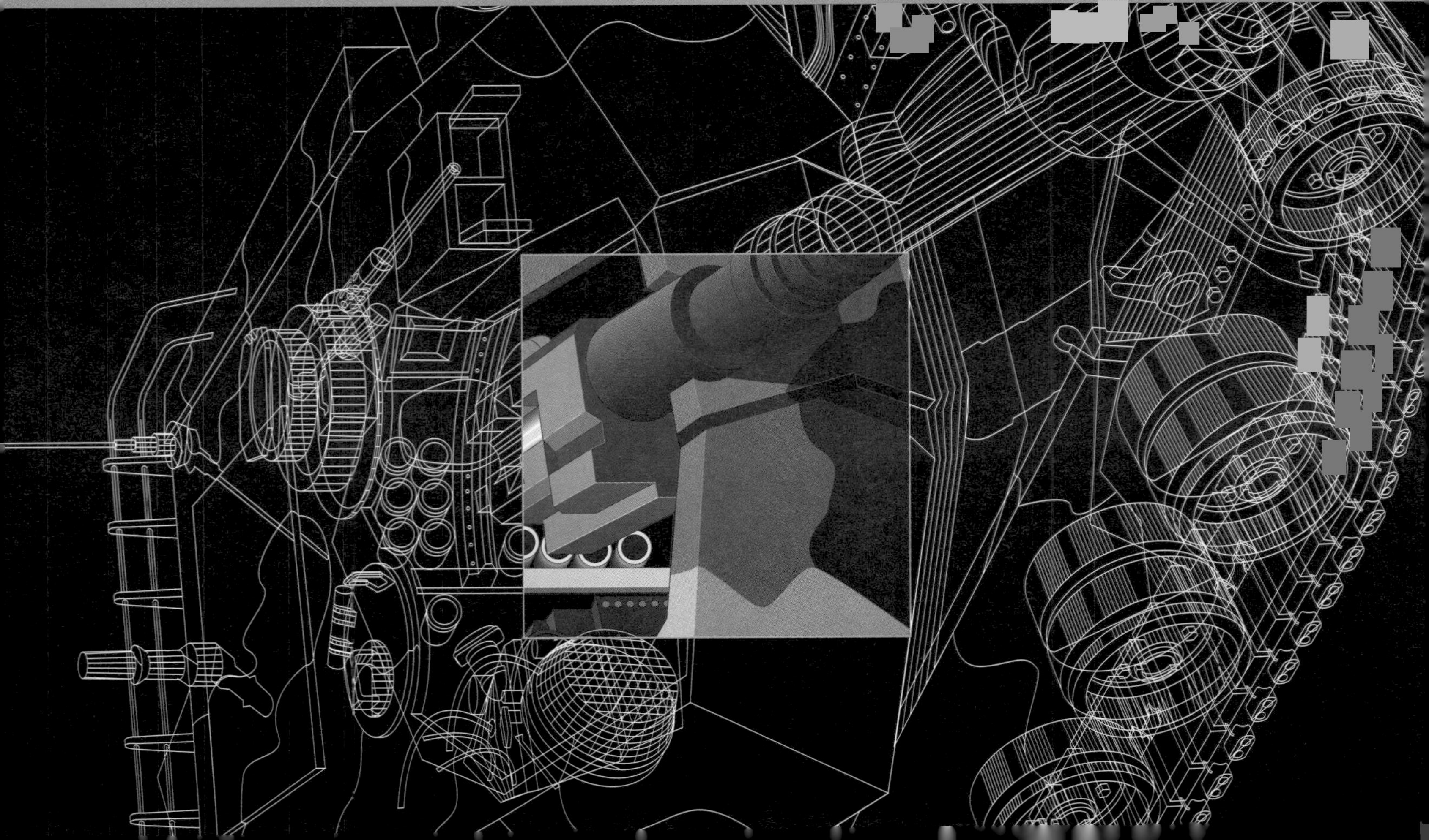

CONTENTS

WEAPONS
ARMAS

STONE AGE WEAPONS
ARMAS^F DE LA EDAD^F DE PIEDRA^F

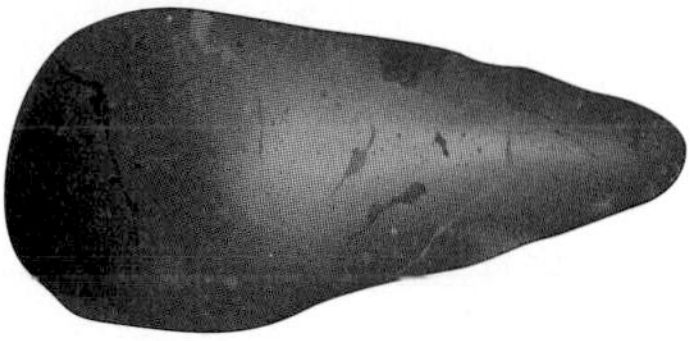

polished stone hand axe
hacha^F de piedra^F pulida

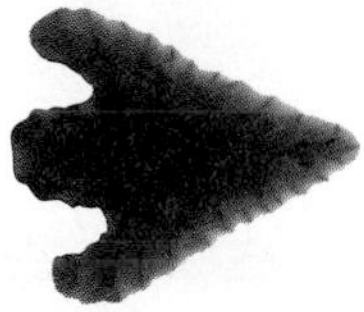

flint arrowhead
punta^F de flecha^F de pedernal^M

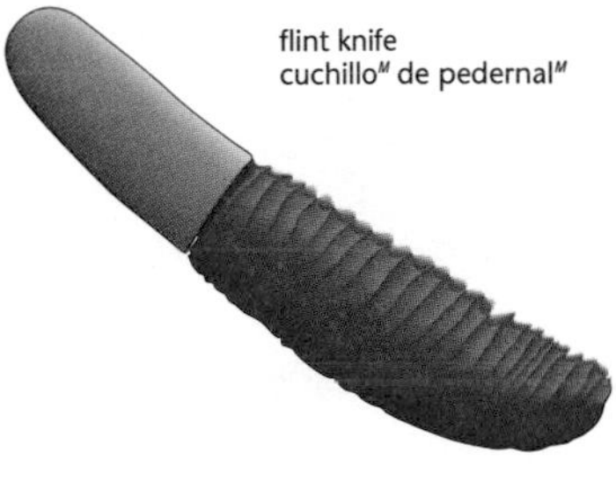

flint knife
cuchillo^M de pedernal^M

WEAPONS IN THE AGE OF THE ROMANS
ARMAS^F DEL IMPERIO^M ROMANO

GALLIC WARRIOR
GUERRERO^M GALO

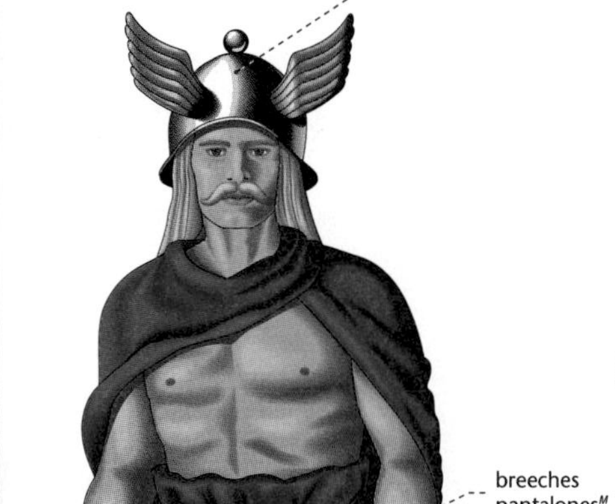

ROMAN LEGIONARY
LEGIONARIO^M ROMANO

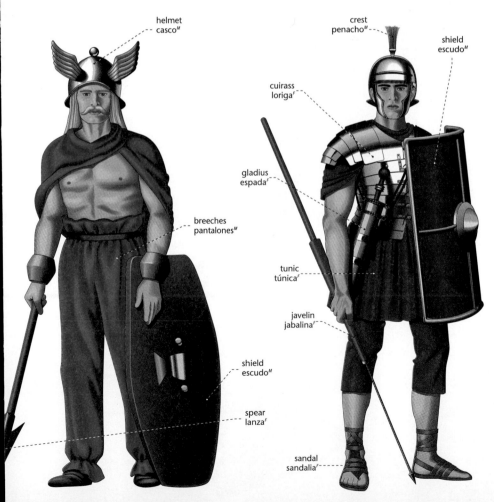

helmet
casco^M

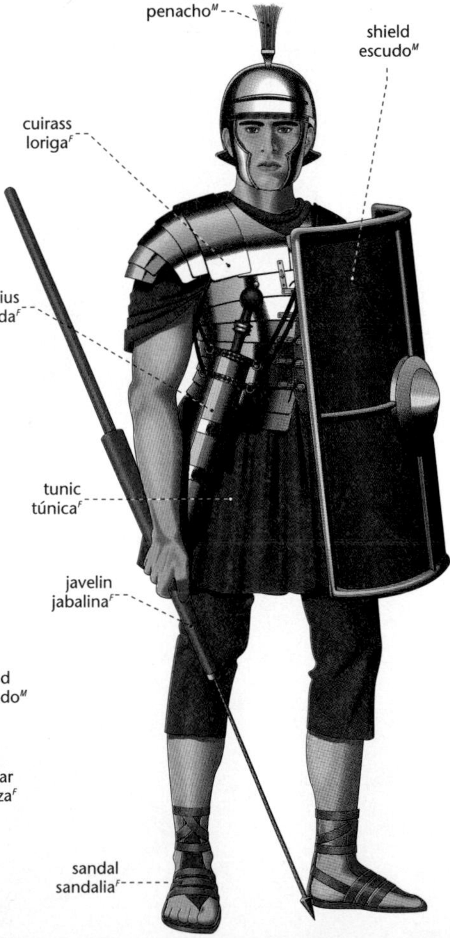

crest
penacho^M

shield
escudo^M

cuirass
loriga^F

gladius
espada^F

breeches
pantalones^M

tunic
túnica^F

javelin
jabalina^F

shield
escudo^M

spear
lanza^F

sandal
sandalia^F

ARMOR
ARMADURA^F

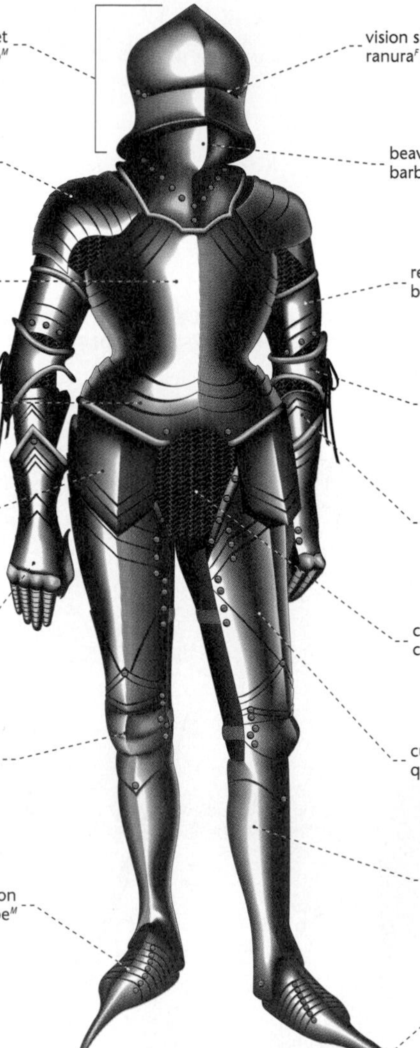

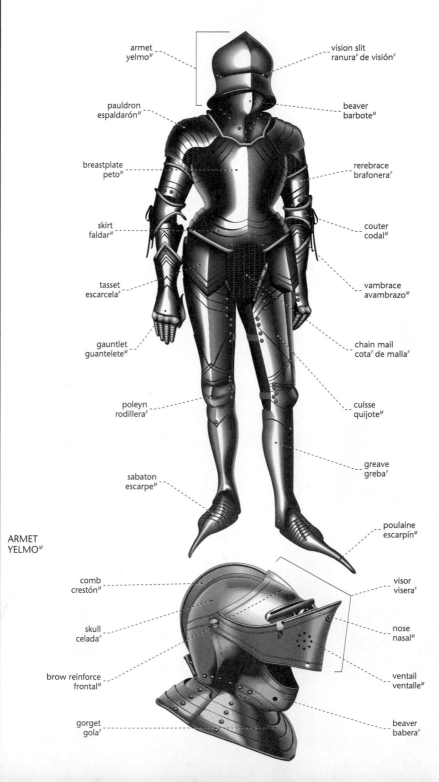

armet
yelmo^M

vision slit
ranura^F de visión^F

pauldron
espaldarón^M

beaver
barbote^M

breastplate
peto^M

rerebrace
brafonera^F

skirt
faldar^M

couter
codal^M

tasset
escarcela^F

vambrace
avambrazo^M

gauntlet
guantelete^M

chain mail
cota^F de malla^F

poleyn
rodillera^F

cuisse
quijote^M

sabaton
escarpe^M

greave
greba^F

poulaine
escarpín^M

ARMET
YELMO^M

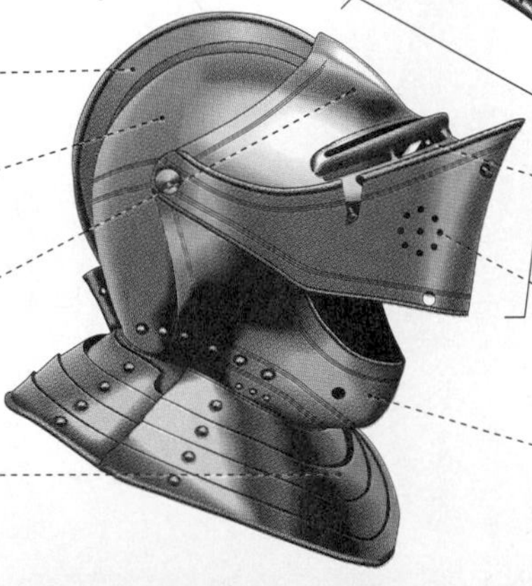

comb
crestón^M

visor
visera^F

skull
celada^F

nose
nasal^M

brow reinforce
frontal^M

ventail
ventalle^M

gorget
gola^F

beaver
babera^F

BOWS AND CROSSBOW
ARCOS^M Y BALLESTA^F

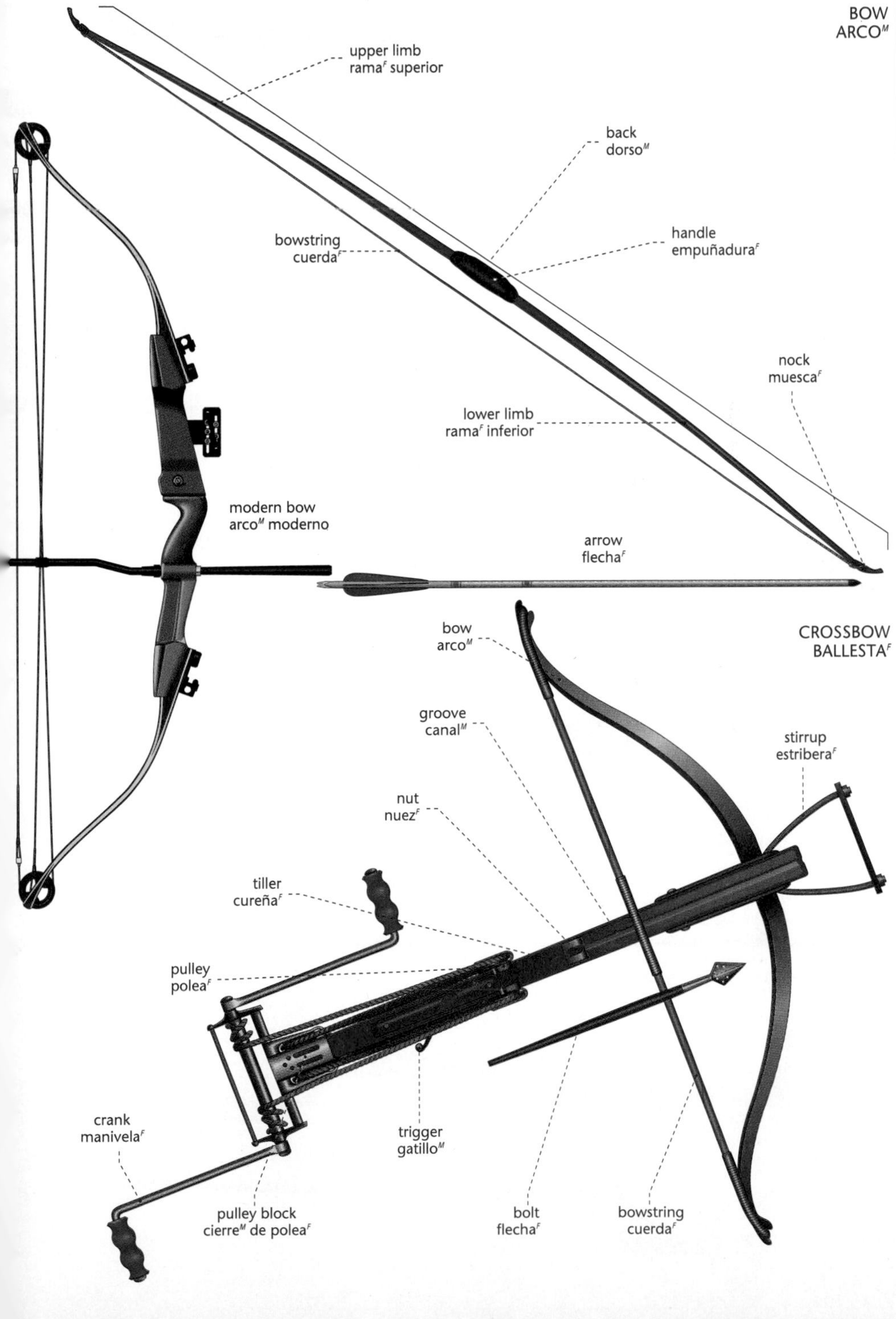

BOW
ARCO^M

upper limb
rama^F superior

back
dorso^M

bowstring
cuerda^F

handle
empuñadura^F

nock
muesca^F

lower limb
rama^F inferior

modern bow
arco^M moderno

arrow
flecha^F

CROSSBOW
BALLESTA^F

bow
arco^M

groove
canal^M

stirrup
estribera^F

nut
nuez^F

tiller
cureña^F

pulley
polea^F

crank
manivela^F

pulley block
cierre^M de polea^F

trigger
gatillo^M

bolt
flecha^F

bowstring
cuerda^F

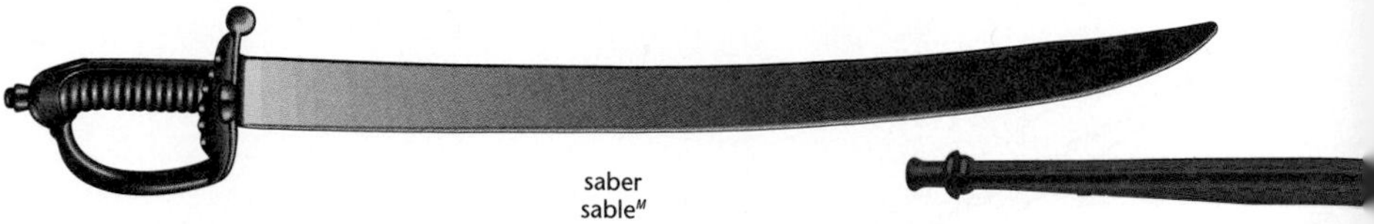

saber
sable^M

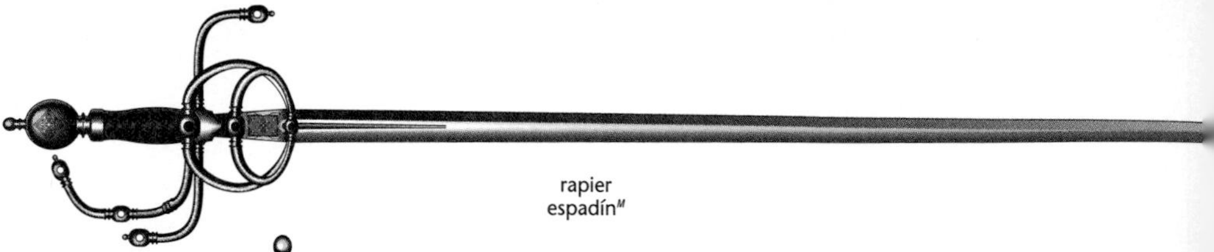

rapier
espadín^M

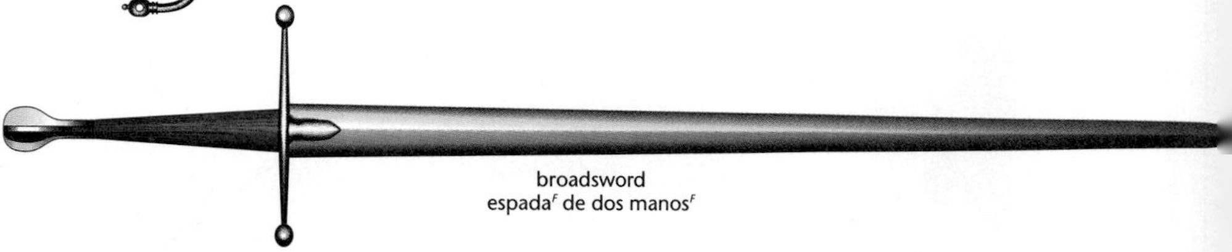

broadsword
espada^F de dos manos^F

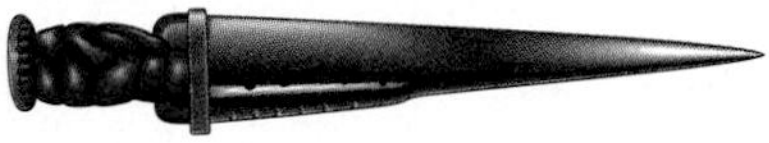

poniard
puñal^M

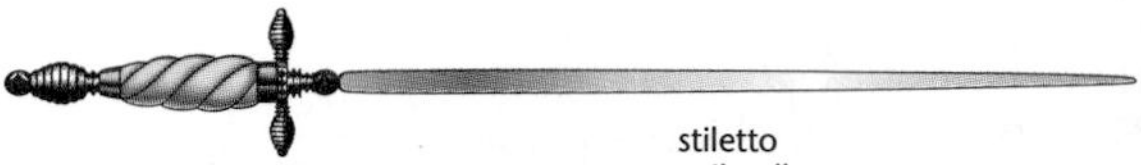

stiletto
estilete^M

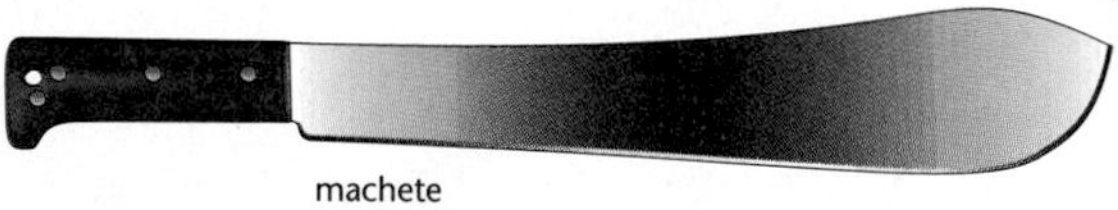

machete
machete^M

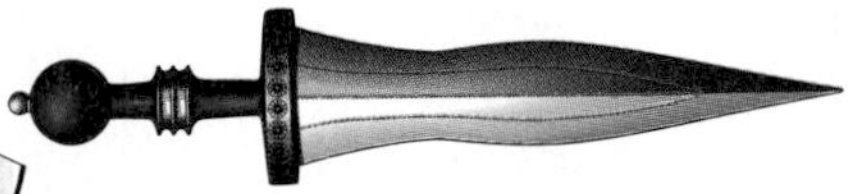

dagger
daga^F

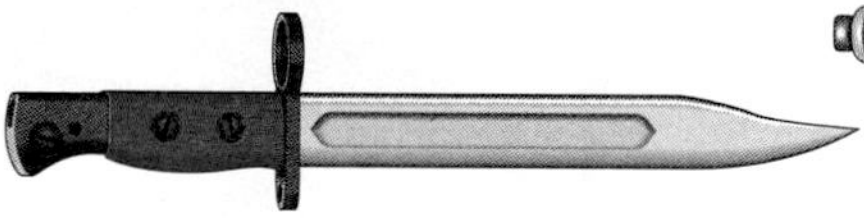

hilted bayonet
bayoneta^F con empuñadura^F

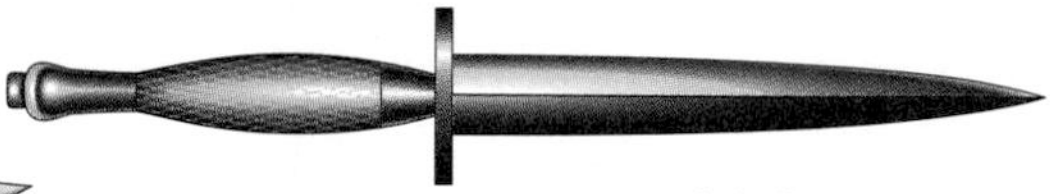

commando knife
cuchillo^M de combate^M

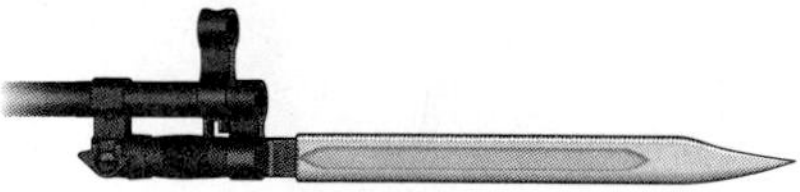

integral bayonet
bayoneta^F integral

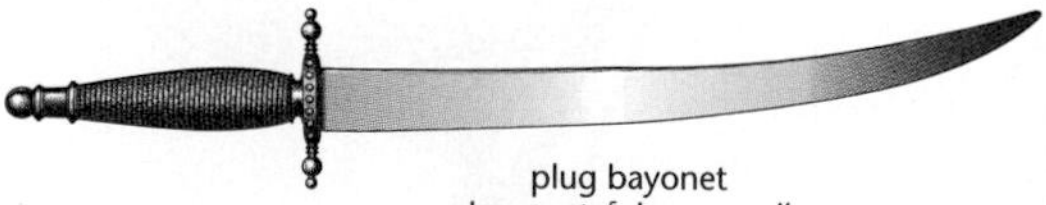

plug bayonet
bayoneta^F de mango^M

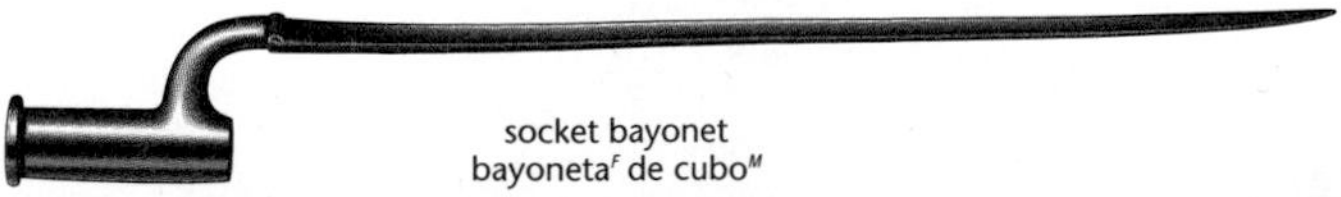

socket bayonet
bayoneta^F de cubo^M

HARQUEBUS
ARCABUZ^M

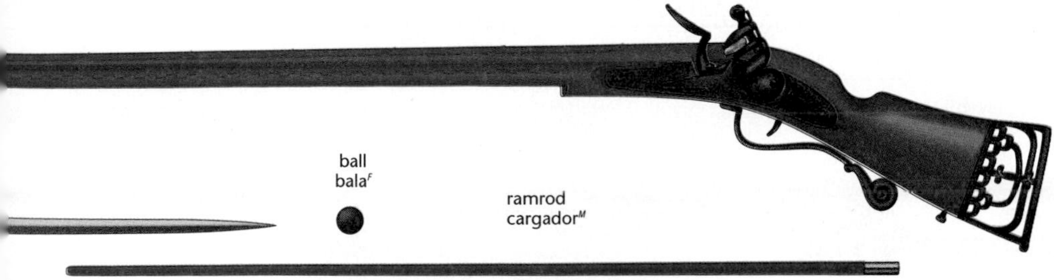

ball
bala^F

ramrod
cargador^M

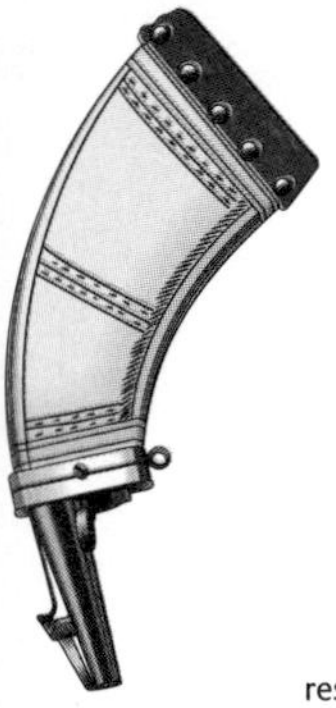

powder flask
cebador^M

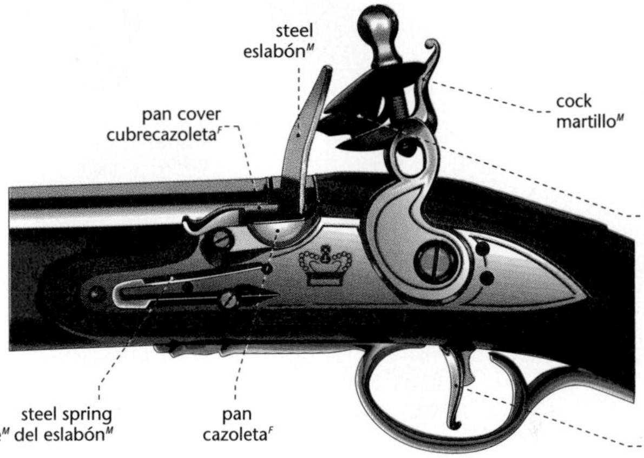

steel
eslabón^M

pan cover
cubrecazoleta^F

cock
martillo^M

flint
pedernal^M

steel spring
resorte^M del eslabón^M

pan
cazoleta^F

trigger
gatillo^M

SUBMACHINE GUN
METRALLETA^F

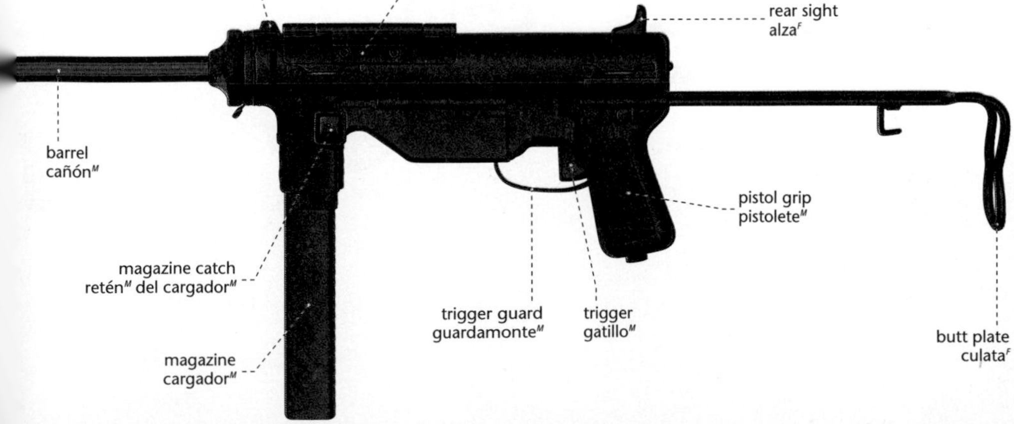

front sight
punto^M de mira^F

receiver
caja^F del cerrojo^M

rear sight
alza^F

barrel
cañón^M

pistol grip
pistolete^M

magazine catch
retén^M del cargador^M

trigger guard
guardamonte^M

trigger
gatillo^M

butt plate
culata^F

magazine
cargador^M

AUTOMATIC RIFLE
FUSIL^M AUTOMÁTICO

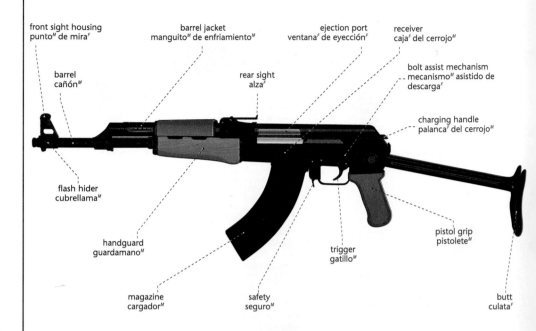

front sight housing
punto^M de mira^F

barrel jacket
manguito^M de enfriamiento^M

ejection port
ventana^F de eyección^F

receiver
caja^F del cerrojo^M

barrel
cañón^M

rear sight
alza^F

bolt assist mechanism
mecanismo^M asistido de
descarga^F

charging handle
palanca^F del cerrojo^M

flash hider
cubrellama^M

handguard
guardamano^M

pistol grip
pistolete^M

trigger
gatillo^M

butt
culata^F

magazine
cargador^M

safety
seguro^M

LIGHT MACHINE GUN
FUSIL^M AMETRALLADOR

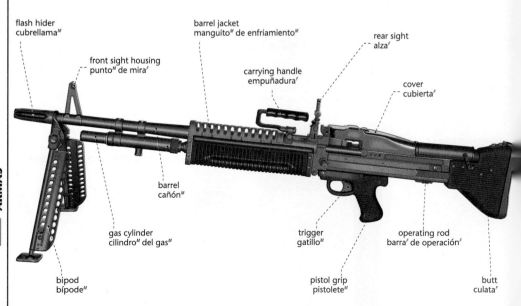

flash hider
cubrellama^M

barrel jacket
manguito^M de enfriamiento^M

rear sight
alza^F

front sight housing
punto^M de mira^F

carrying handle
empuñadura^F

cover
cubierta^F

barrel
cañón^M

gas cylinder
cilindro^M del gas^M

trigger
gatillo^M

operating rod
barra^F de operación^F

butt
culata^F

bipod
bípode^M

pistol grip
pistolete^M

REVOLVER
REVÓLVER^M

hammer
percutor^M

barrel
cañón^M

front sight
punto^M de mira^F

muzzle
boca^F

cylinder
tambor^M

trigger guard
guardamonte^M

butt
culata^F

trigger
gatillo^M

PISTOL
PISTOLA^F

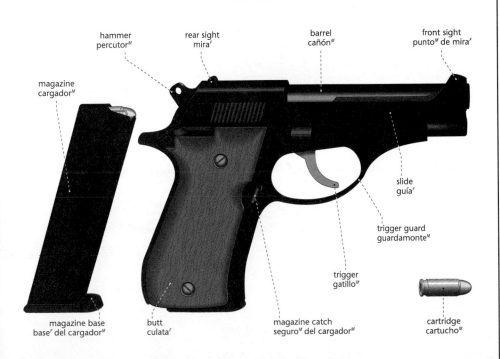

hammer
percutor^M

rear sight
mira^F

barrel
cañón^M

front sight
punto^M de mira^F

magazine
cargador^M

slide
guía^F

trigger guard
guardamonte^M

magazine base
base^F del cargador^M

butt
culata^F

magazine catch
seguro^M del cargador^M

trigger
gatillo^M

cartridge
cartucho^M

HUNTING WEAPONS
ARMAS^F DE CAZA^F

CARTRIDGE (RIFLE)
CARTUCHO^M DE RIFLE^M

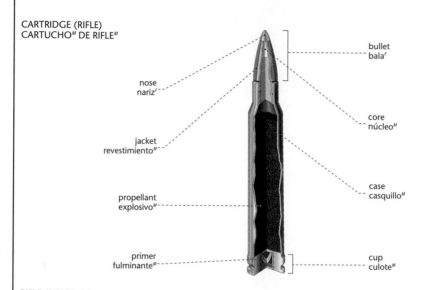

bullet
bala^F

nose
nariz^F

core
núcleo^M

jacket
revestimiento^M

case
casquillo^M

propellant
explosivo^M

primer
fulminante^M

cup
culote^M

RIFLE (RIFLED BORE)
RIFLE^M

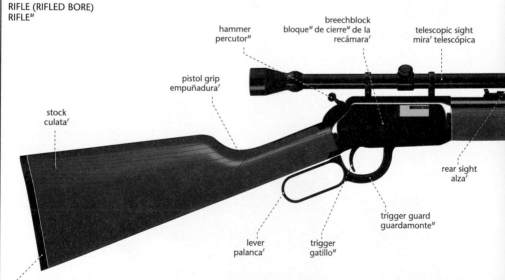

hammer
percutor^M

breechblock
bloque^M de cierre^M de la
recámara^F

telescopic sight
mira^F telescópica

pistol grip
empuñadura^F

stock
culata^F

rear sight
alza^F

trigger guard
guardamonte^M

lever
palanca^F

trigger
gatillo^M

butt plate
cantonera^F

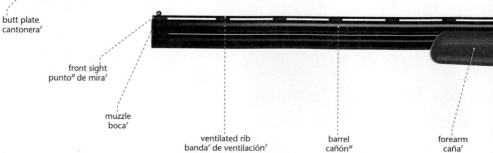

front sight
punto^M de mira^F

muzzle
boca^F

ventilated rib
banda^F de ventilación^F

barrel
cañón^M

forearm
caña^F

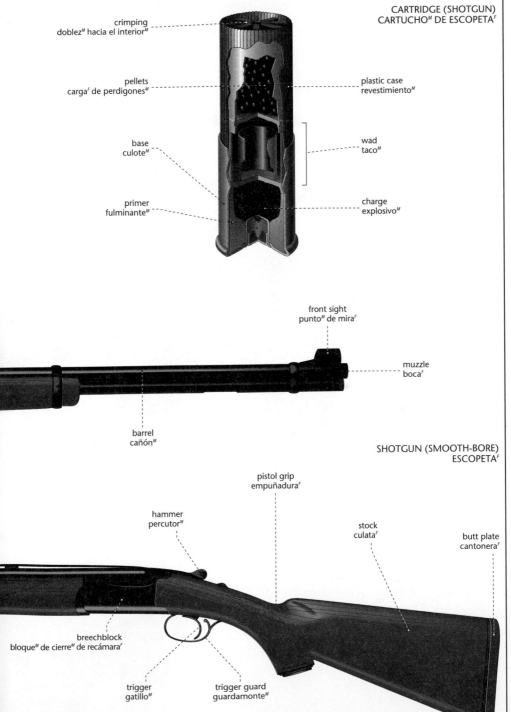

CARTRIDGE (SHOTGUN)
CARTUCHO^M DE ESCOPETA^F

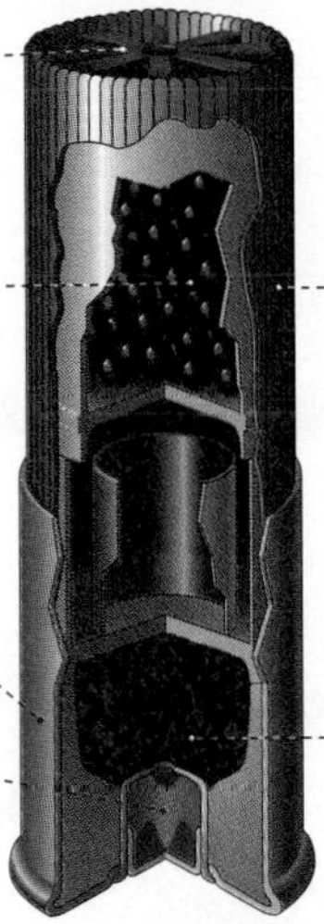

crimping
doblez^M hacia el interior^M

pellets
carga^F de perdigones^M

base
culote^M

primer
fulminante^M

plastic case
revestimiento^M

wad
taco^M

charge
explosivo^M

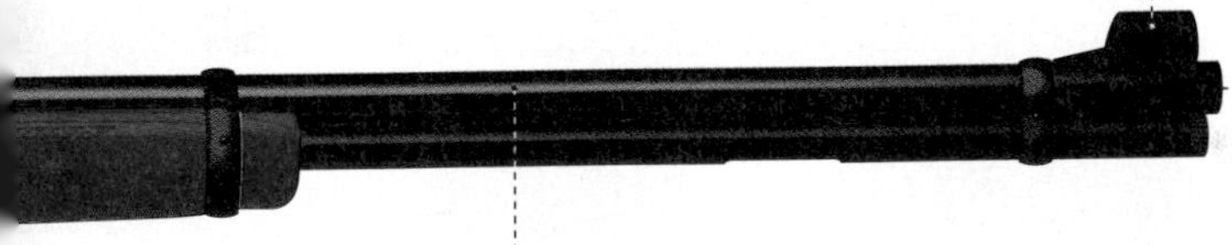

front sight
punto^M de mira^F

muzzle
boca^F

barrel
cañón^M

SHOTGUN (SMOOTH-BORE)
ESCOPETA^F

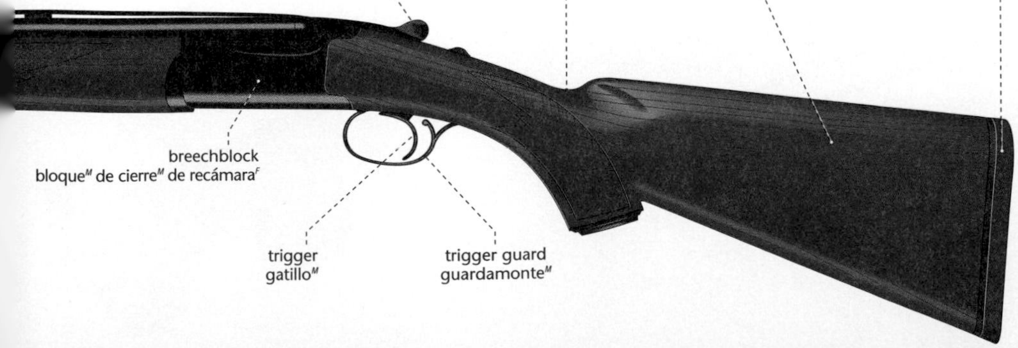

pistol grip
empuñadura^F

hammer
percutor^M

stock
culata^F

butt plate
cantonera^F

breechblock
bloque^M de cierre^M de recámara^F

trigger
gatillo^M

trigger guard
guardamonte^M

SEVENTEENTH CENTURY CANNON
CAÑON^M DEL SIGLO^M XVII

MUZZLE LOADING
CAÑON^M DE AVANCARGA^F

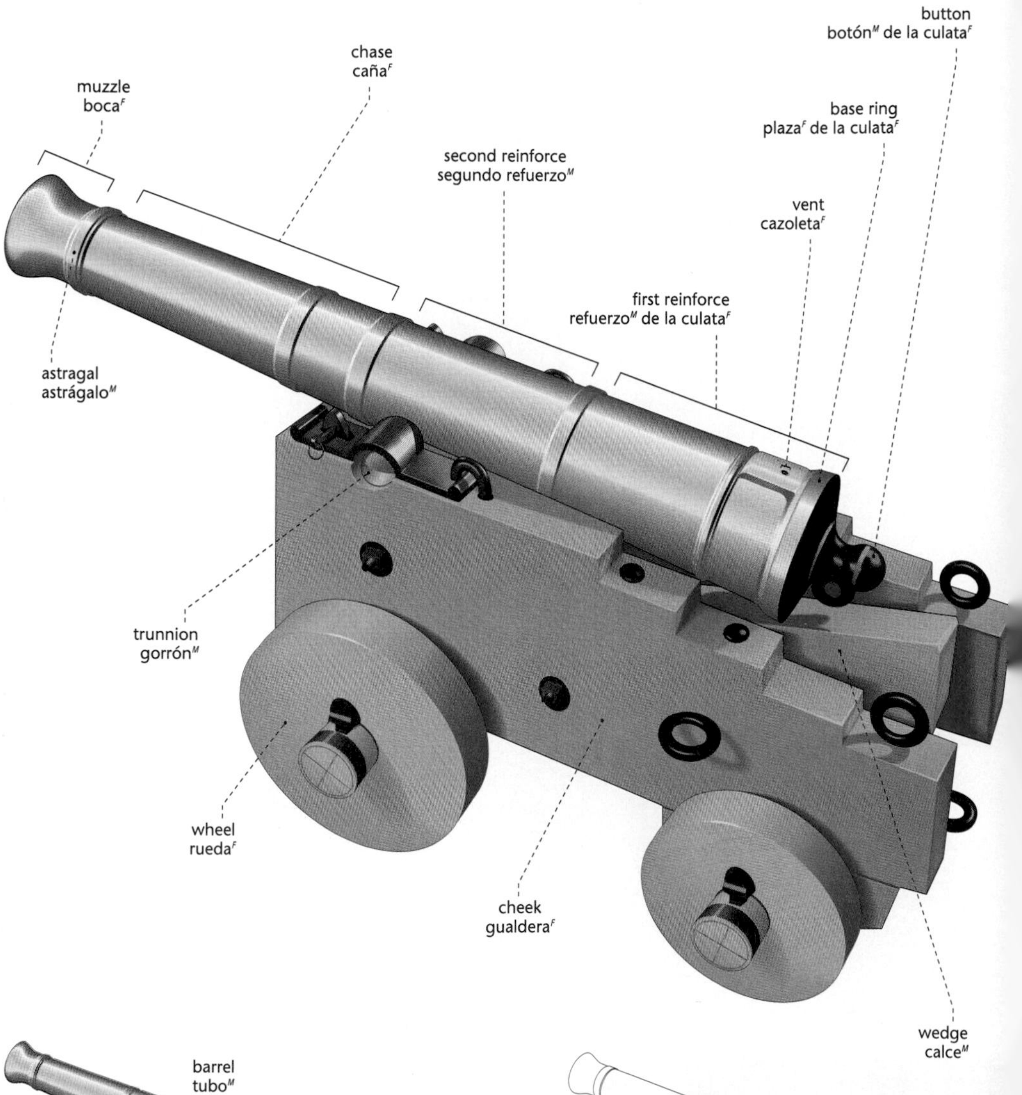

muzzle
boca^F

chase
caña^F

second reinforce
segundo refuerzo^M

first reinforce
refuerzo^M de la culata^F

vent
cazoleta^F

base ring
plaza^F de la culata^F

button
botón^M de la culata^F

astragal
astrágalo^M

trunnion
gorrón^M

wheel
rueda^F

cheek
gualdera^F

wedge
calce^M

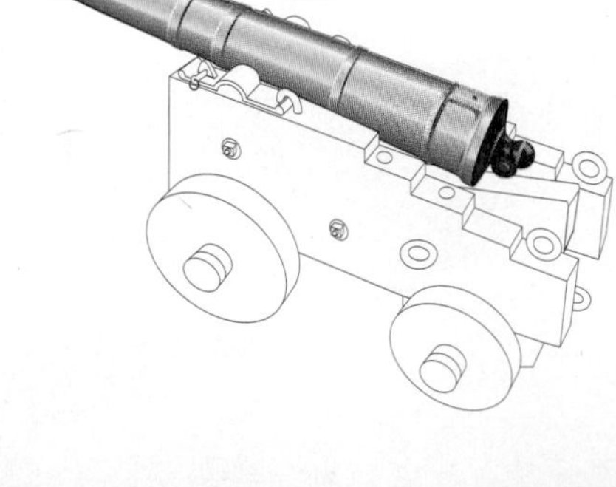

barrel
tubo^M

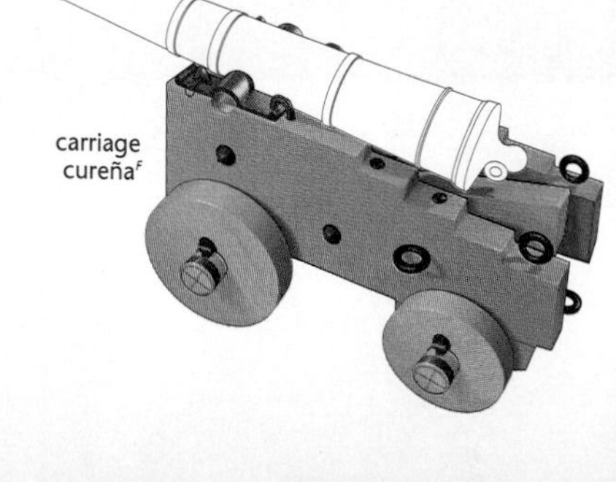

carriage
cureña^F

CROSS SECTION OF A MUZZLE LOADING
CORTE^M TRANSVERSAL DE UN CAÑÓN^M DE AVANCARGA^F

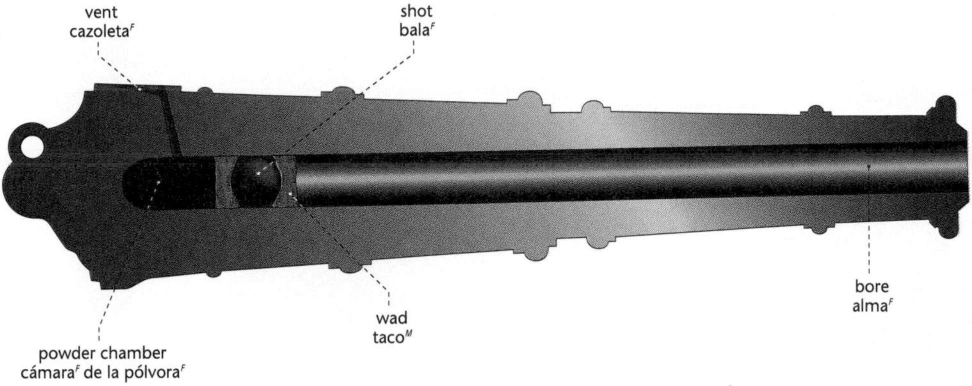

vent
cazoleta^F

shot
bala^F

bore
alma^F

wad
taco^M

powder chamber
cámara^F de la pólvora^F

FIRING ACCESSORIES
ACCESORIOS^M DE DISPARO^M

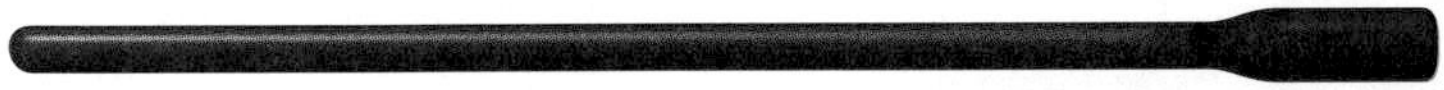

rammer
atacador^M

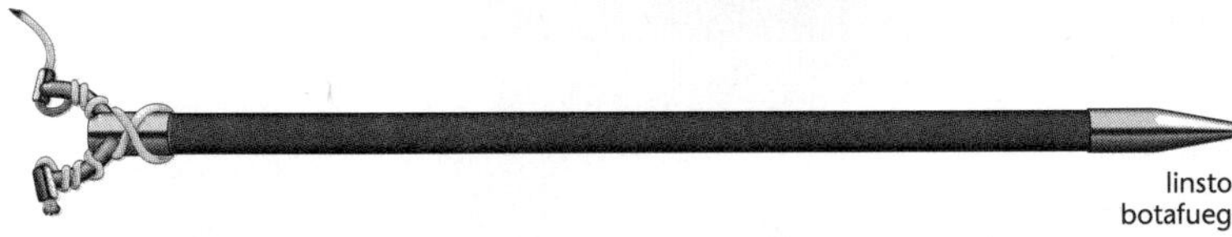

linstock
botafuego^M

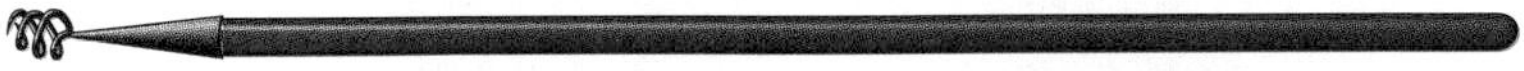

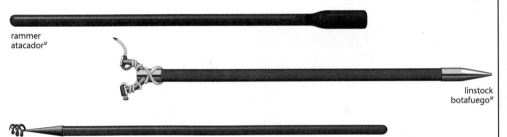

worm
sacatrapos^M

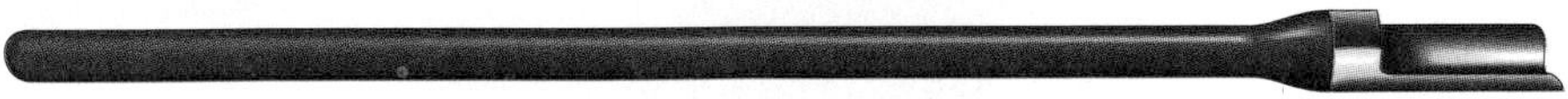

ladle
cucharón^M

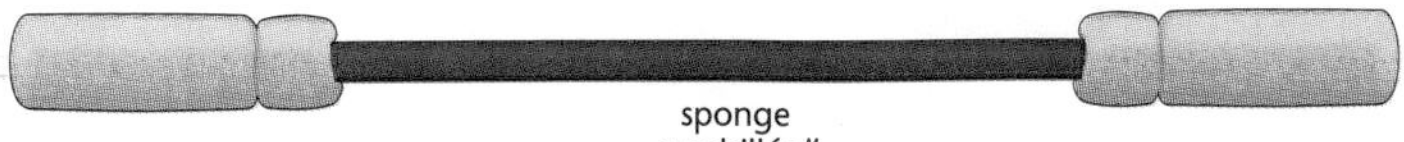

sponge
escobillón^M

PROJECTILES
PROYECTILES^M

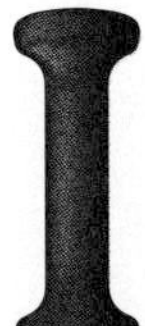

bar shot
bala^F de barra^F

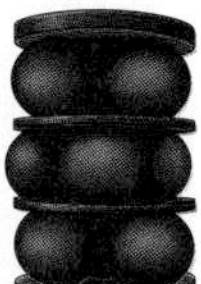

grapeshot
metralla^F

solid shot
bala^F sólida

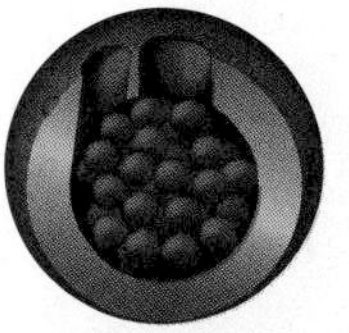

hollow shot
bala^F con perdigones^M

MODERN HOWITZER
OBÚS^M MODERNO

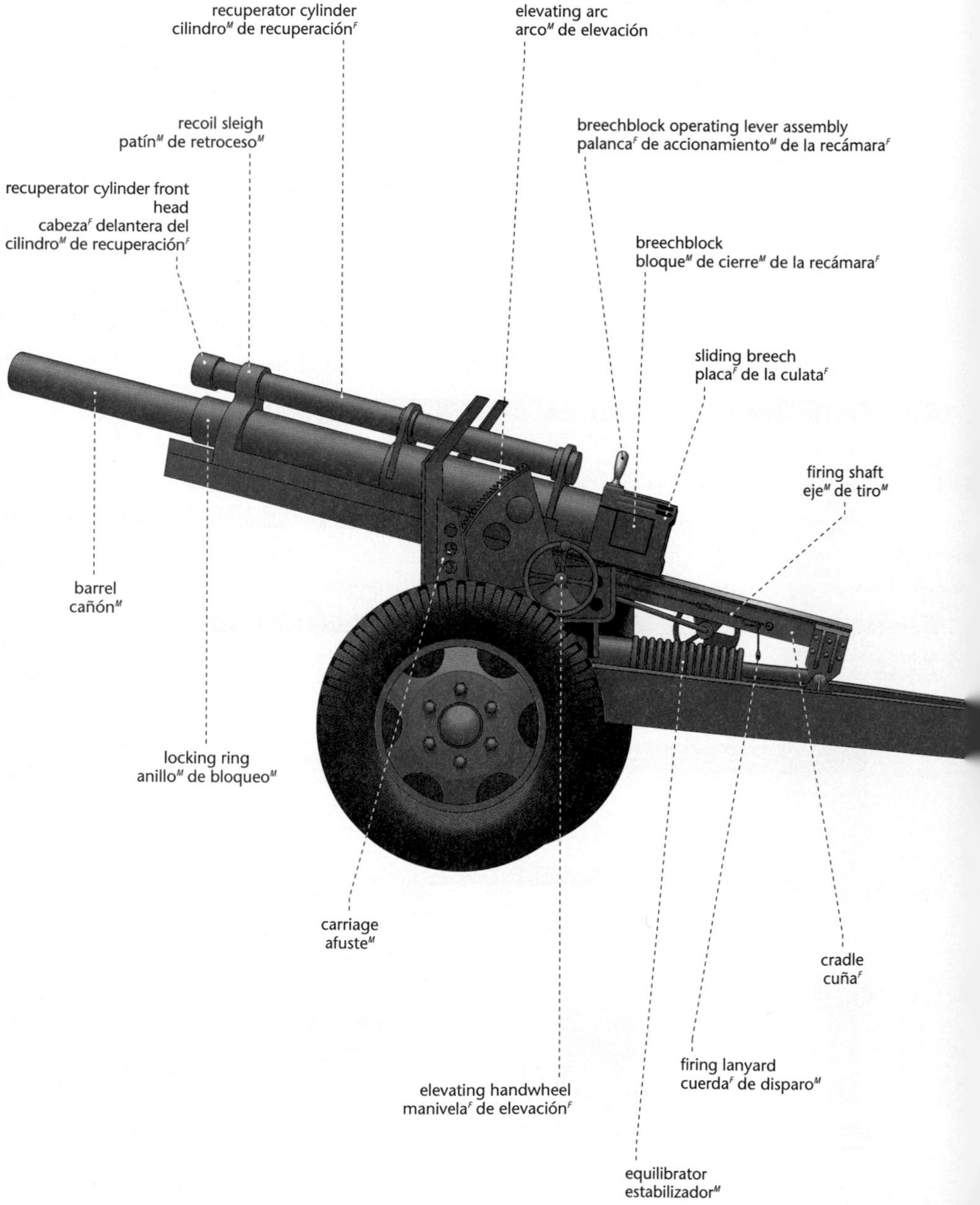

recuperator cylinder
cilindro^M de recuperación^F

elevating arc
arco^M de elevación

recoil sleigh
patín^M de retroceso^M

breechblock operating lever assembly
palanca^F de accionamiento^M de la recámara^F

recuperator cylinder front
head
cabeza^F delantera del
cilindro^M de recuperación^F

breechblock
bloque^M de cierre^M de la recámara^F

sliding breech
placa^F de la culata^F

barrel
cañón^M

firing shaft
eje^M de tiro^M

locking ring
anillo^M de bloqueo^M

carriage
afuste^M

cradle
cuña^F

firing lanyard
cuerda^F de disparo^M

elevating handwheel
manivela^F de elevación^F

equilibrator
estabilizador^M

MORTAR
MORTEROS^M

MODERN MORTAR
MORTERO^M MODERNO

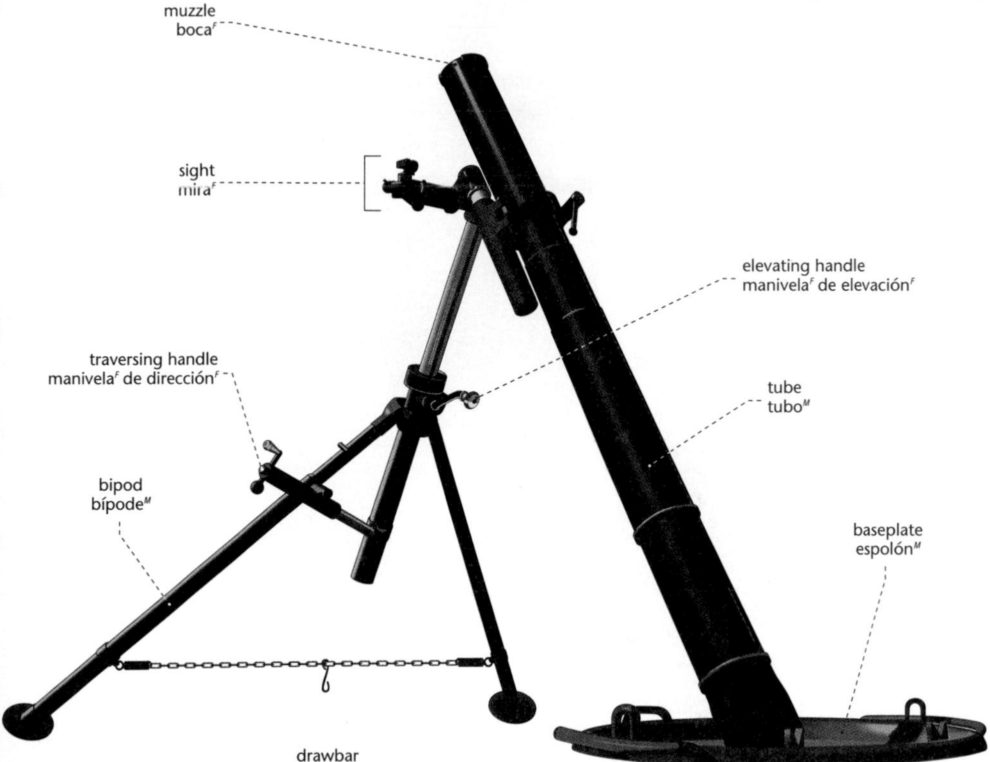

muzzle
boca^F

sight
mira^F

elevating handle
manivela^F de elevación^F

traversing handle
manivela^F de dirección^F

tube
tubo^M

bipod
bípode^M

baseplate
espolón^M

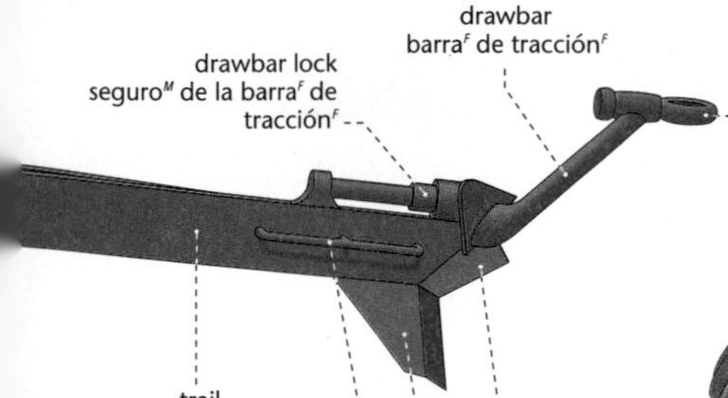

drawbar
barra^F de tracción^F

drawbar lock
seguro^M de la barra^F de
tracción^F

towing eye
argolla^F de remolque^M

SEVENTEENTH-CENTURY MORTAR
MORTERO^M DEL SIGLO^M XVII

trail
gualdera^F

lifting handle
asa^F de levantamiento^M

spade
pala^F

float
flotador^M

WEAPONS
ARMAS

803

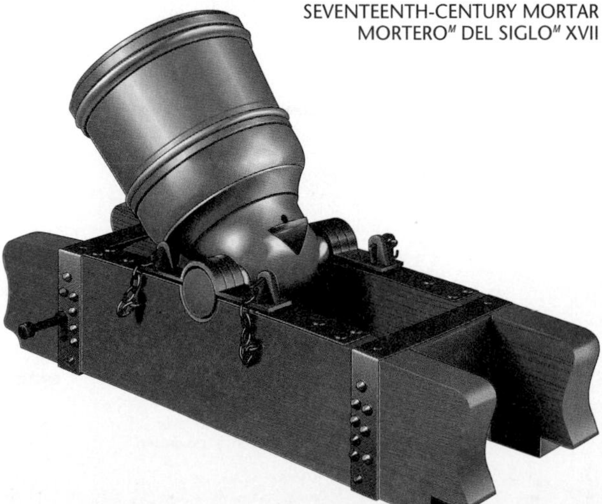

HAND GRENADE
GRANADA[F] DE MANO[F]

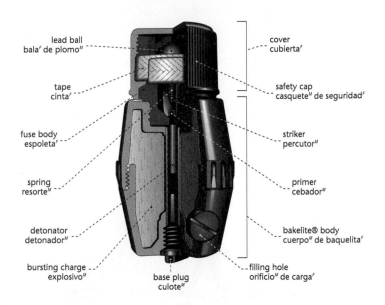

lead ball
bala[F] de plomo[M]

tape
cinta[F]

fuse body
espoleta[F]

spring
resorte[M]

detonator
detonador[M]

bursting charge
explosivo[M]

base plug
culote[M]

cover
cubierta[F]

safety cap
casquete[M] de seguridad[F]

striker
percutor[M]

primer
cebador[M]

bakelite® body
cuerpo[M] de baquelita[F]

filling hole
orificio[M] de carga[F]

BAZOOKA
BAZUCA[F]

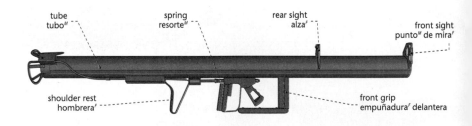

tube
tubo[M]

spring
resorte[M]

rear sight
alza[F]

front sight
punto[M] de mira[F]

shoulder rest
hombrera[F]

front grip
empuñadura[F] delantera

RECOILLESS RIFLE
FUSIL[M] SIN RETROCESO

barrel
cañón[M]

shoulder pad
hombrera[F]

firing mechanism
mecanismo[M] de disparo[M]

venturi fastening lever
palanca[F] de fijación[F] del
venturi[M]

front grip
empuñadura[F] delantera

trigger
gatillo[M]

cocking lever
palanca[F] de armar[F]

anti-tank rocket
bala[F] antitanque

venturi
venturi[M]

TANK
TANQUE^M

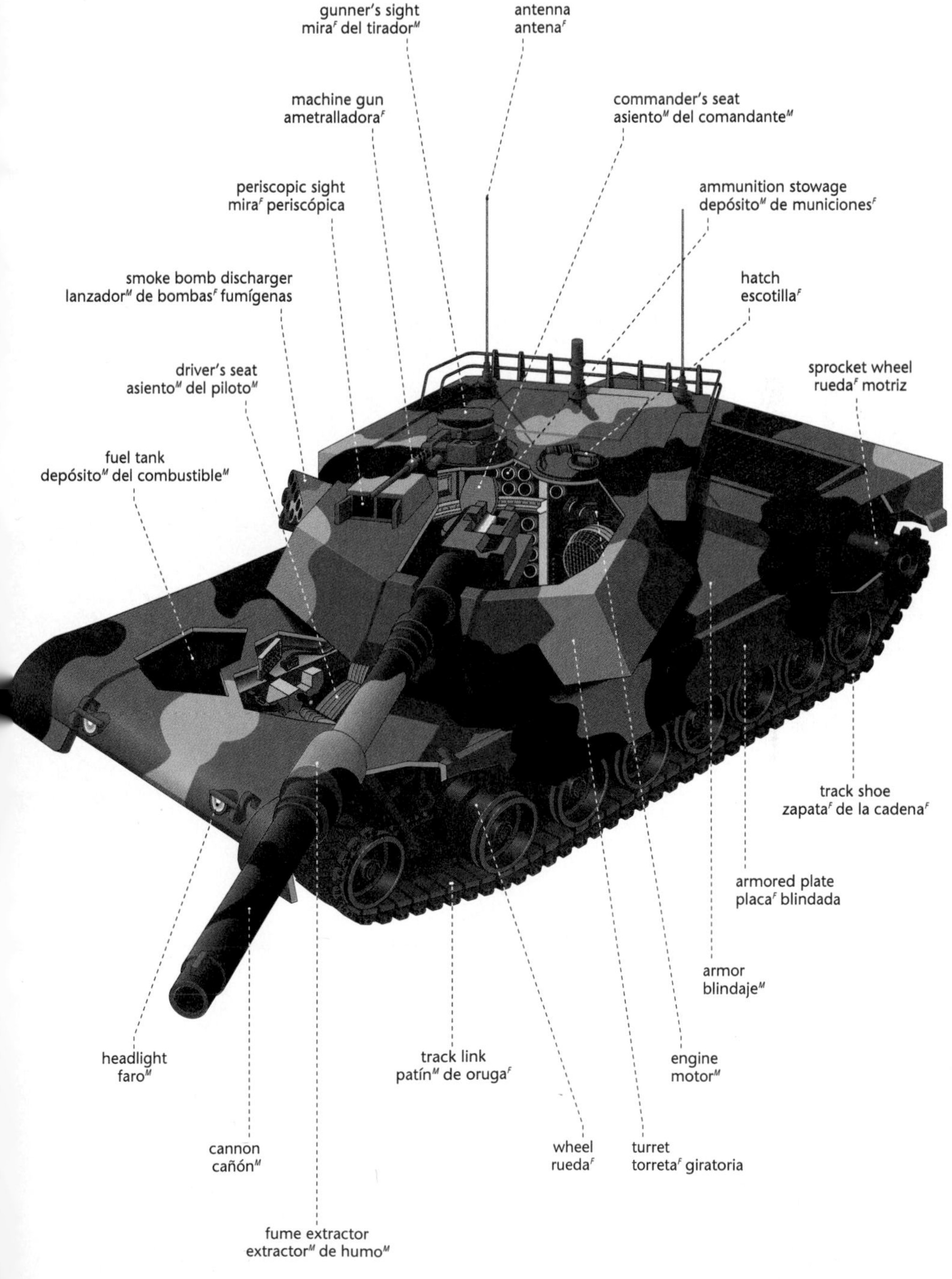

gunner's sight
mira^F del tirador^M

antenna
antena^F

machine gun
ametralladora^F

commander's seat
asiento^M del comandante^M

periscopic sight
mira^F periscópica

ammunition stowage
depósito^M de municiones^F

smoke bomb discharger
lanzador^M de bombas^F fumígenas

hatch
escotilla^F

driver's seat
asiento^M del piloto^M

sprocket wheel
rueda^F motriz

fuel tank
depósito^M del combustible^M

track shoe
zapata^F de la cadena^F

armored plate
placa^F blindada

armor
blindaje^M

headlight
faro^M

track link
patín^M de oruga^F

engine
motor^M

cannon
cañón^M

wheel
rueda^F

turret
torreta^F giratoria

fume extractor
extractor^M de humo^M

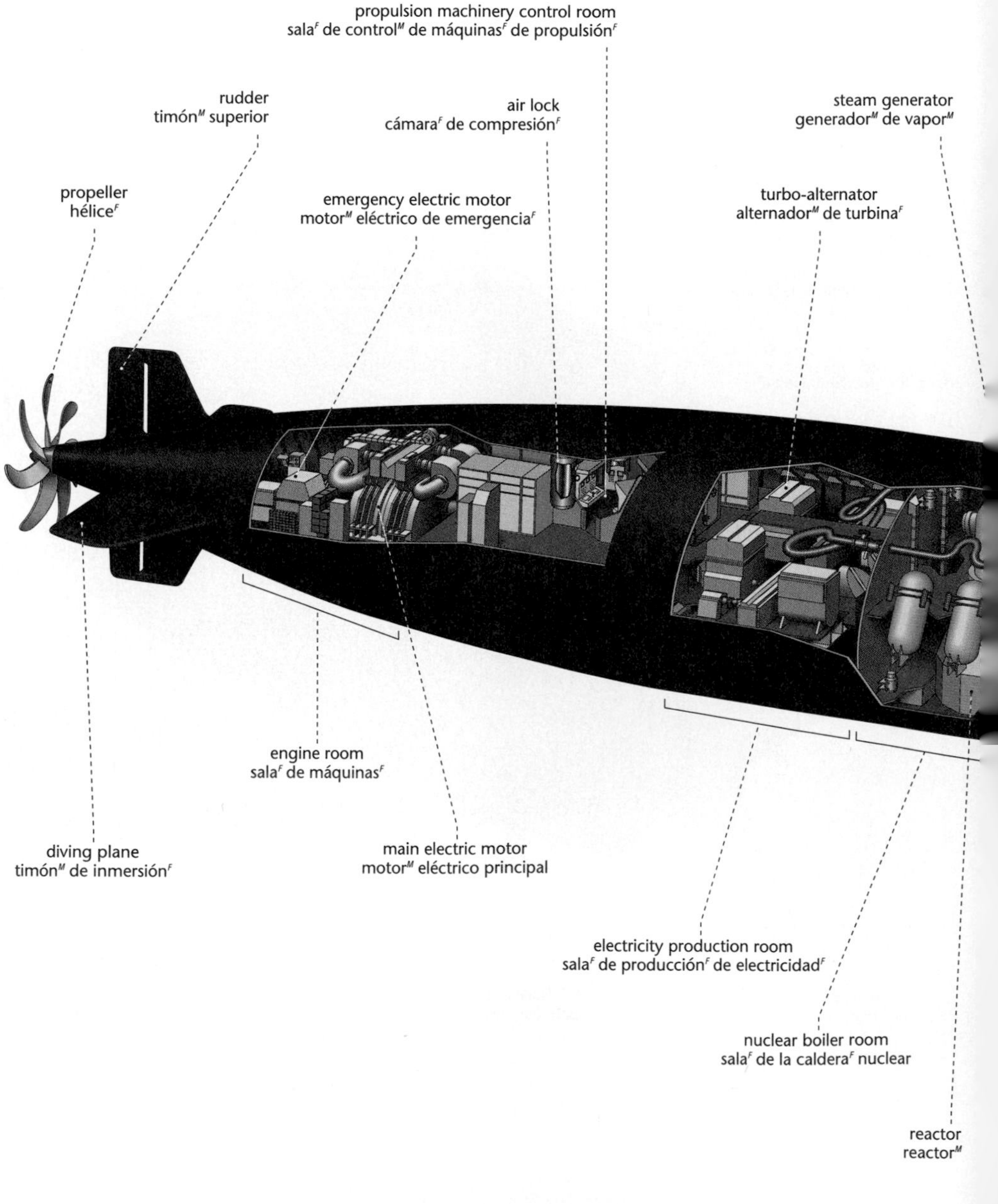

propulsion machinery control room
sala^F de control^M de máquinas^F de propulsión^F

rudder
timón^M superior

air lock
cámara^F de compresión^F

steam generator
generador^M de vapor^M

propeller
hélice^F

emergency electric motor
motor^M eléctrico de emergencia^F

turbo-alternator
alternador^M de turbina^F

engine room
sala^F de máquinas^F

diving plane
timón^M de inmersión^F

main electric motor
motor^M eléctrico principal

electricity production room
sala^F de producción^F de electricidad^F

nuclear boiler room
sala^F de la caldera^F nuclear

reactor
reactor^M

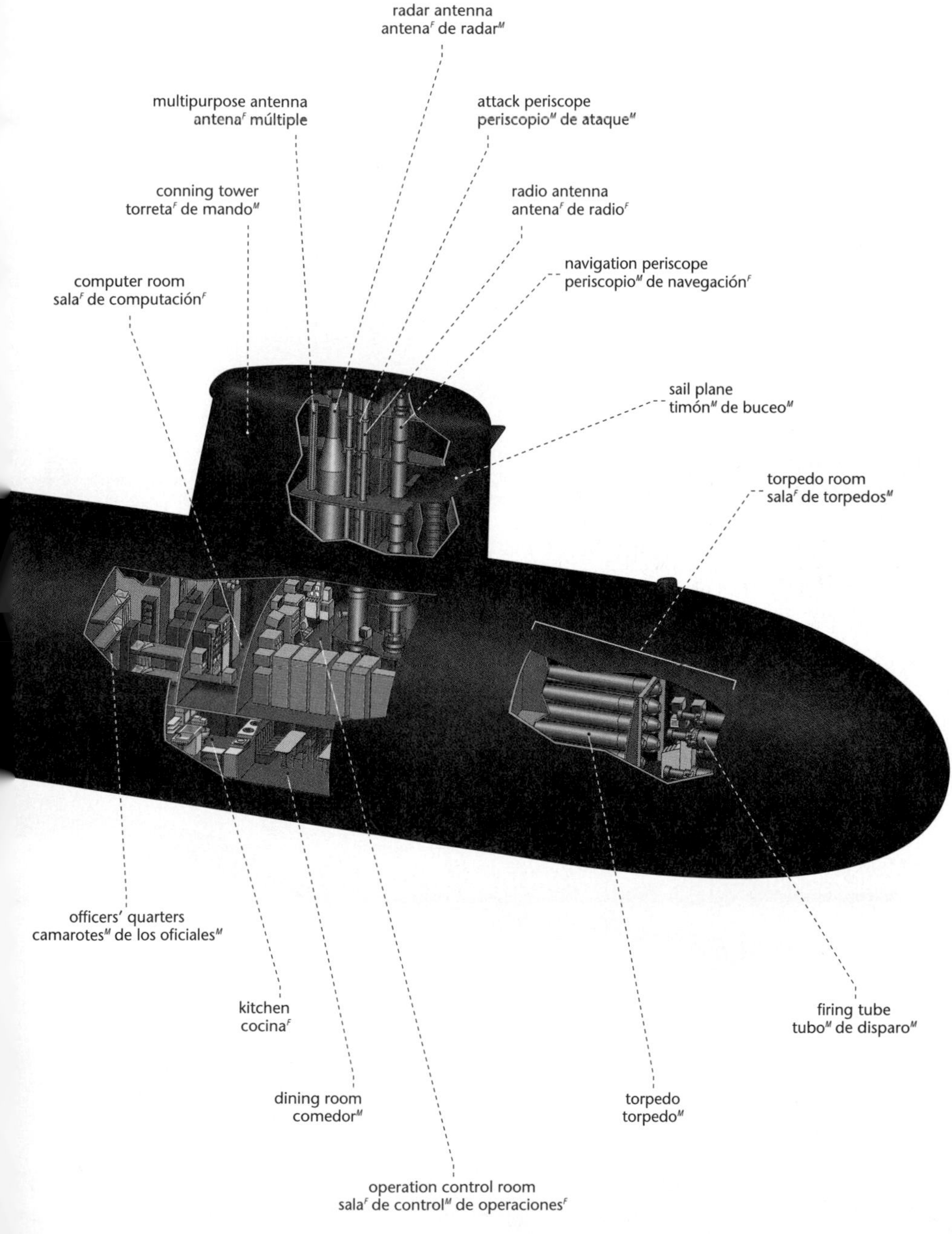

radar antenna
antena^F de radar^M

multipurpose antenna
antena^F múltiple

attack periscope
periscopio^M de ataque^M

conning tower
torreta^F de mando^M

radio antenna
antena^F de radio^F

computer room
sala^F de computación^F

navigation periscope
periscopio^M de navegación^F

sail plane
timón^M de buceo^M

torpedo room
sala^F de torpedos^M

officers' quarters
camarotes^M de los oficiales^M

kitchen
cocina^F

firing tube
tubo^M de disparo^M

dining room
comedor^M

torpedo
torpedo^M

operation control room
sala^F de control^M de operaciones^F

FRIGATE
FRAGATA[F]

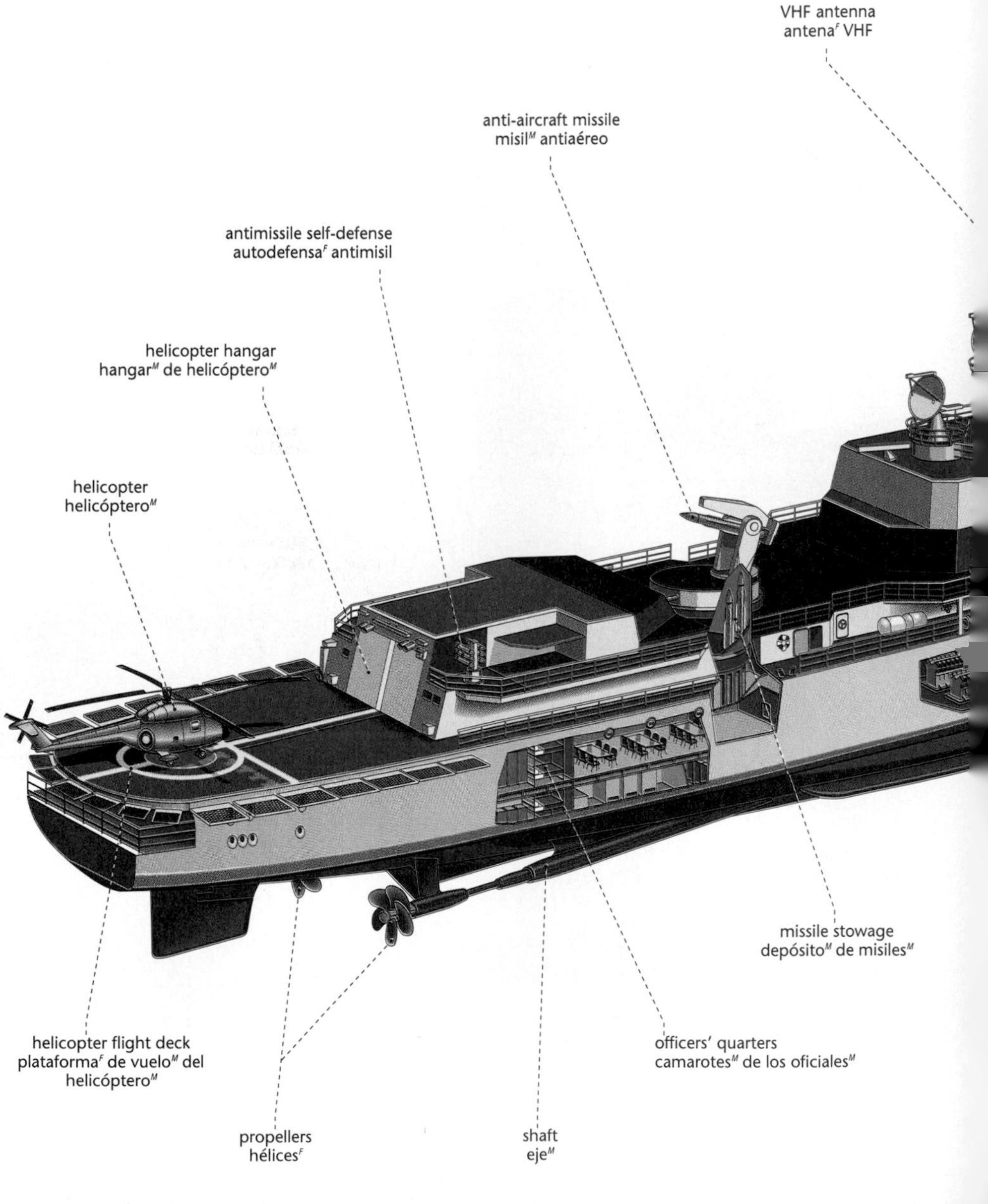

VHF antenna
antena[F] VHF

anti-aircraft missile
misil[M] antiaéreo

antimissile self-defense
autodefensa[F] antimisil

helicopter hangar
hangar[M] de helicóptero[M]

helicopter
helicóptero[M]

missile stowage
depósito[M] de misiles[M]

helicopter flight deck
plataforma[F] de vuelo[M] del
helicóptero[M]

officers' quarters
camarotes[M] de los oficiales[M]

propellers
hélices[F]

shaft
eje[M]

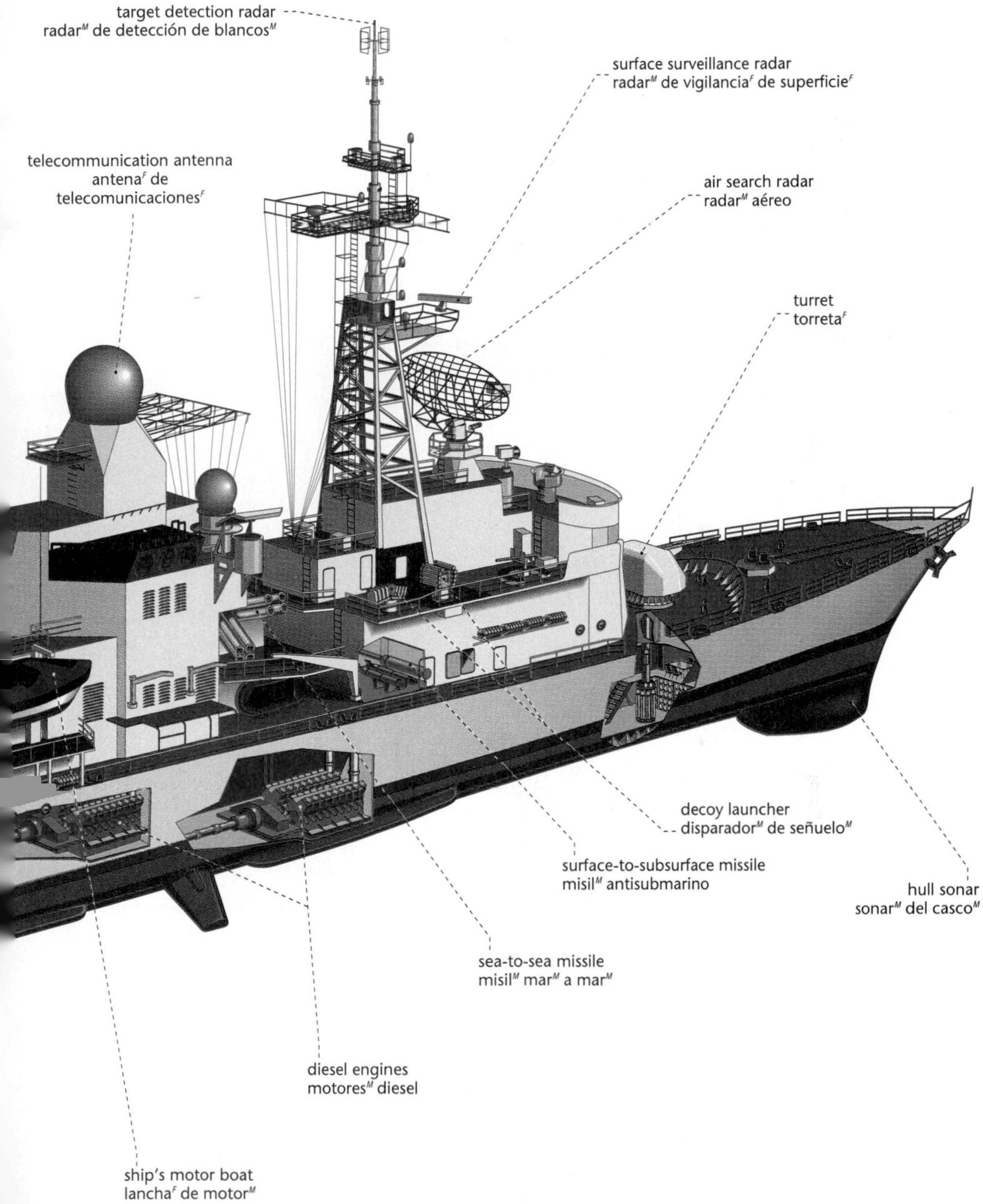

target detection radar
radar^M de detección de blancos^M

surface surveillance radar
radar^M de vigilancia^F de superficie^F

telecommunication antenna
antena^F de
telecomunicaciones^F

air search radar
radar^M aéreo

turret
torreta^F

decoy launcher
disparador^M de señuelo^M

surface-to-subsurface missile
misil^M antisubmarino

hull sonar
sonar^M del casco^M

sea-to-sea missile
misil^M mar^M a mar^M

diesel engines
motores^M diesel

ship's motor boat
lancha^F de motor^M

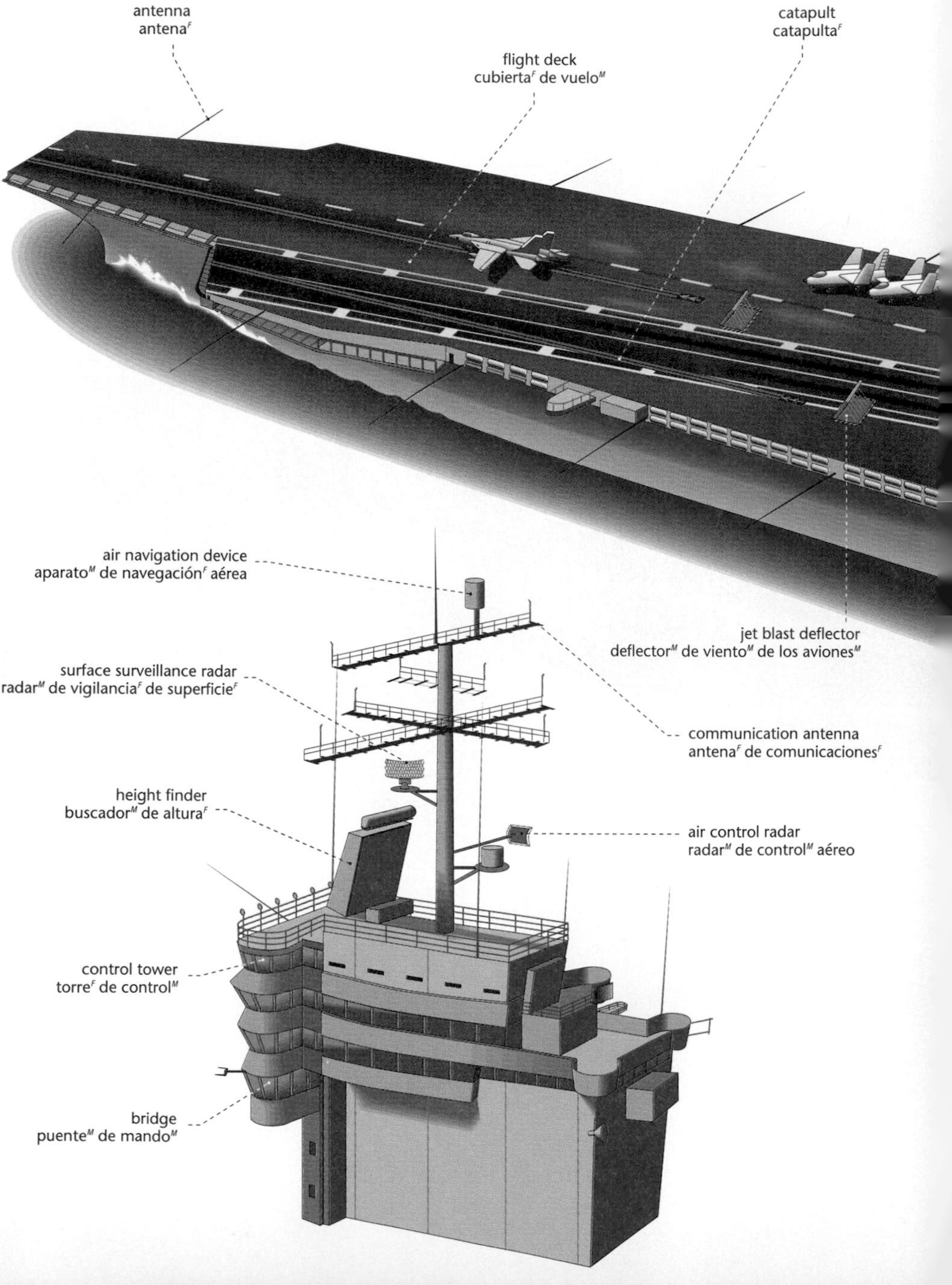

antenna
antena^F

flight deck
cubierta^F de vuelo^M

catapult
catapulta^F

air navigation device
aparato^M de navegación^F aérea

jet blast deflector
deflector^M de viento^M de los aviones^M

surface surveillance radar
radar^M de vigilancia^F de superficie^F

communication antenna
antena^F de comunicaciones^F

height finder
buscador^M de altura^F

air control radar
radar^M de control^M aéreo

control tower
torre^F de control^M

bridge
puente^M de mando^M

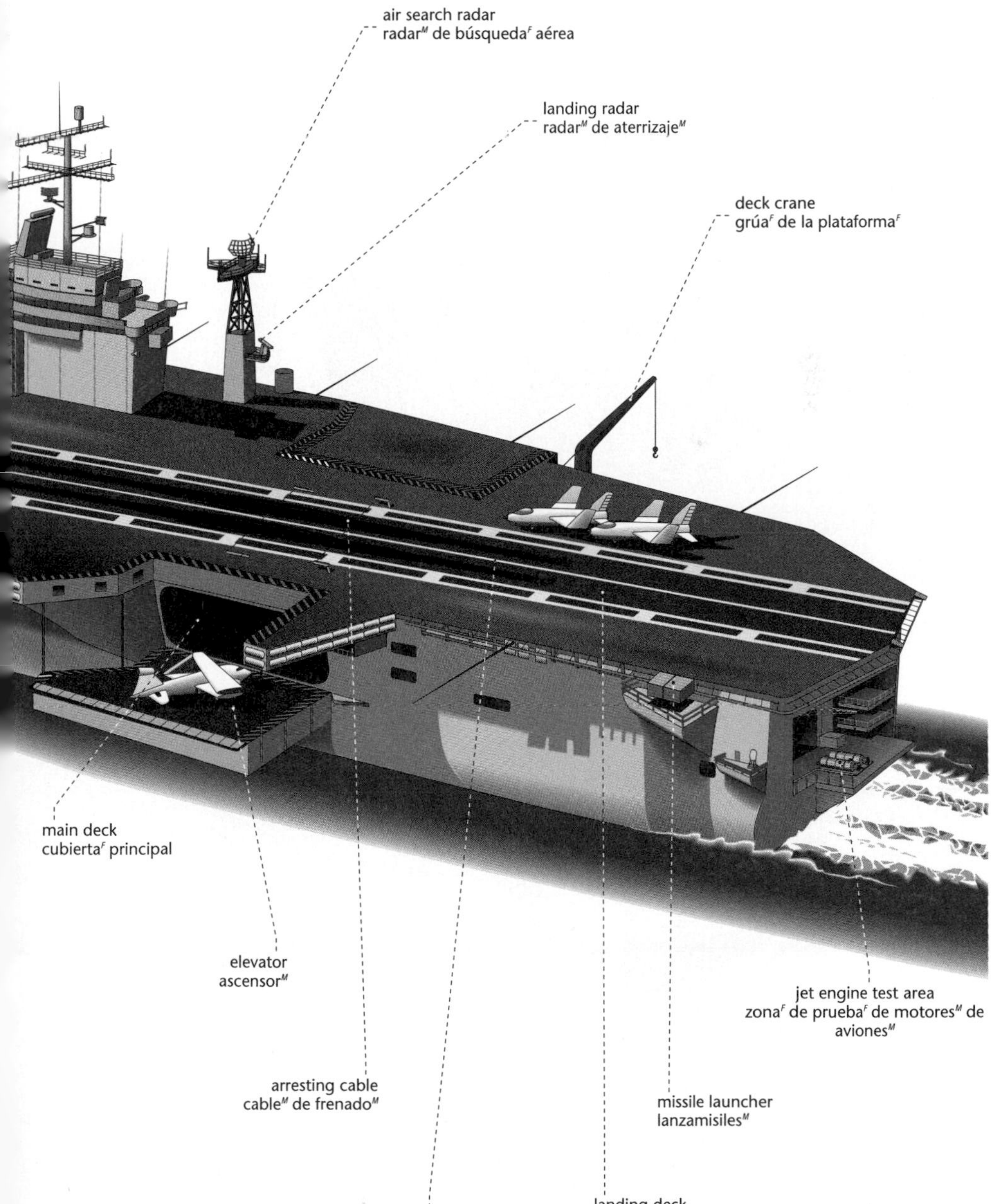

air search radar
radar^M de búsqueda^F aérea

landing radar
radar^M de aterrizaje^M

deck crane
grúa^F de la plataforma^F

main deck
cubierta^F principal

elevator
ascensor^M

jet engine test area
zona^F de prueba^F de motores^M de
aviones^M

arresting cable
cable^M de frenado^M

missile launcher
lanzamisiles^M

runway
pista^F

landing deck
cubierta^F de aterrizaje^M

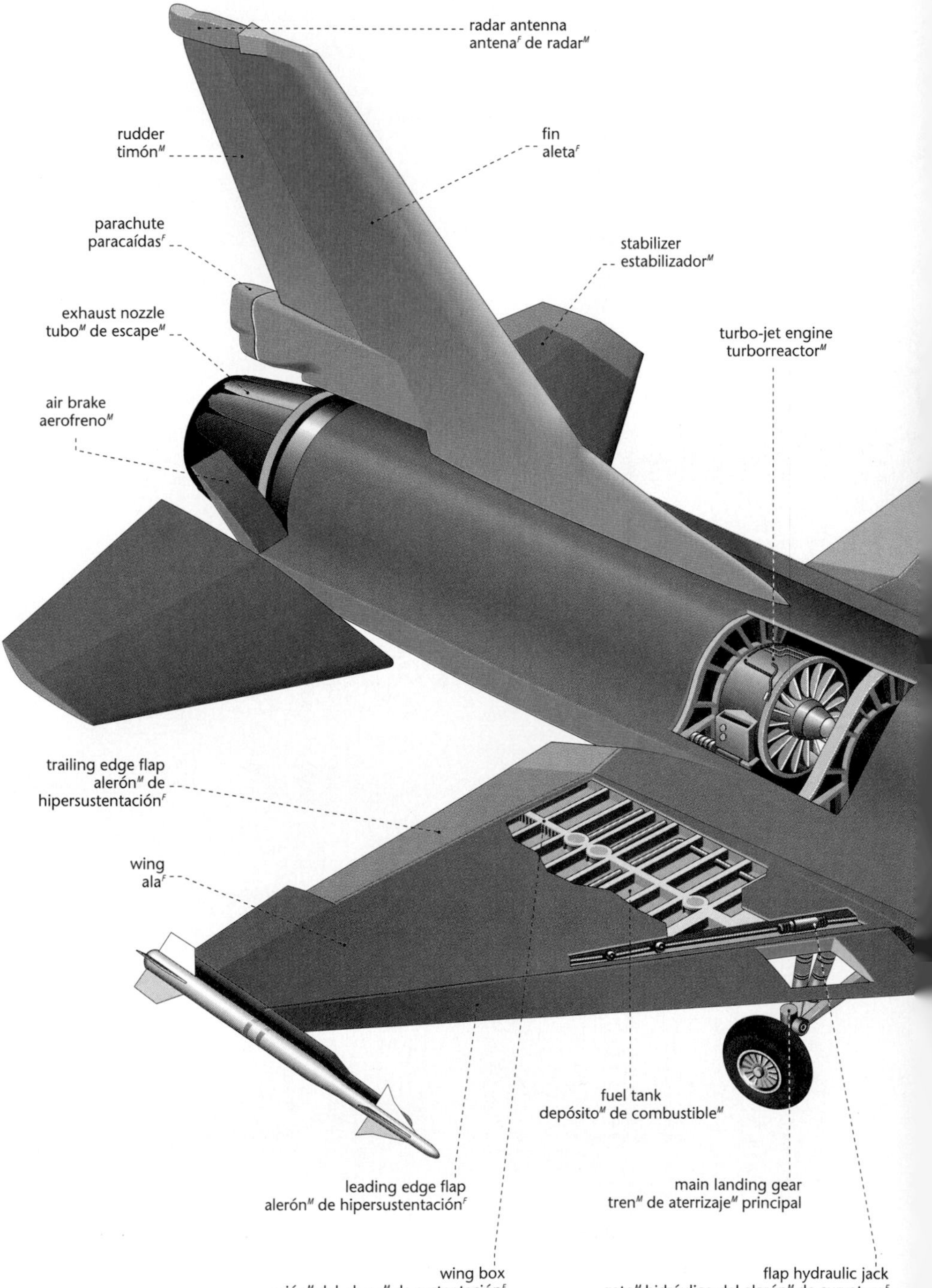

radar antenna
antena^F de radar^M

rudder
timón^M

fin
aleta^F

parachute
paracaídas^F

stabilizer
estabilizador^M

exhaust nozzle
tubo^M de escape^M

turbo-jet engine
turborreactor^M

air brake
aerofreno^M

trailing edge flap
alerón^M de
hipersustentación^F

wing
ala^F

fuel tank
depósito^M de combustible^M

leading edge flap
alerón^M de hipersustentación^F

main landing gear
tren^M de aterrizaje^M principal

wing box
cajón^M del plano^M de sustentación^F

flap hydraulic jack
gato^M hidráulico del alerón^M de curvatura^F

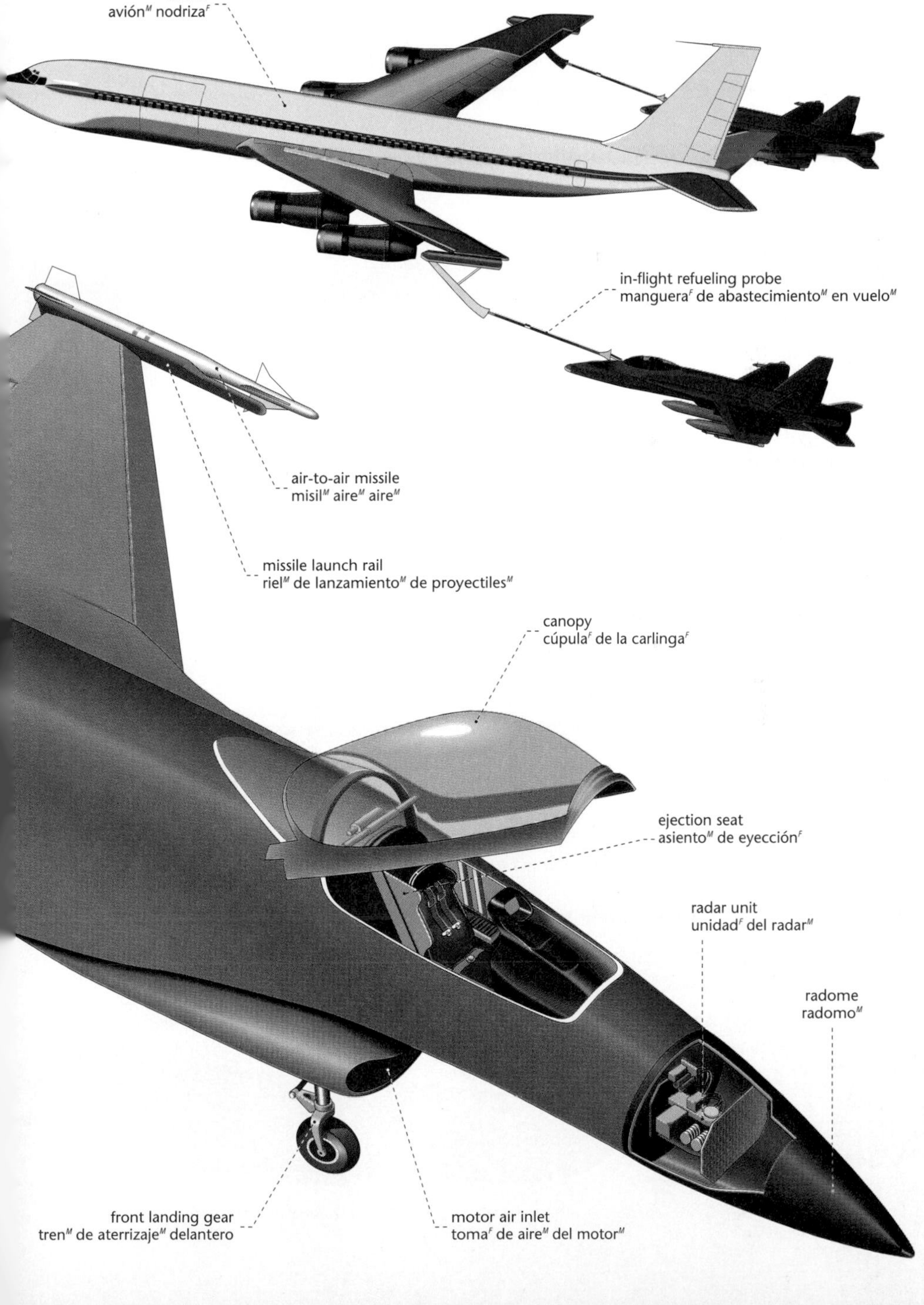

IN-FLIGHT REFUELING
REAPROVISIONAMIENTO^M DE COMBUSTIBLE^M EN VUELO^M

tanker
avión^M nodriza^F

in-flight refueling probe
manguera^F de abastecimiento^M en vuelo^M

air-to-air missile
misil^M aire^M aire^M

missile launch rail
riel^M de lanzamiento^M de proyectiles^M

canopy
cúpula^F de la carlinga^F

ejection seat
asiento^M de eyección^F

radar unit
unidad^F del radar^M

radome
radomo^M

front landing gear
tren^M de aterrizaje^M delantero

motor air inlet
toma^F de aire^M del motor^M

MISSILES
PROYECTILES[M]

STRUCTURE OF A MISSILE
ESTRUCTURA[F] DE UN MISIL[M]

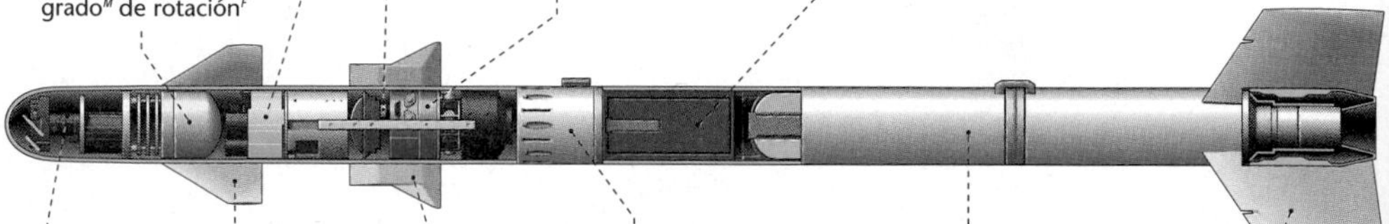

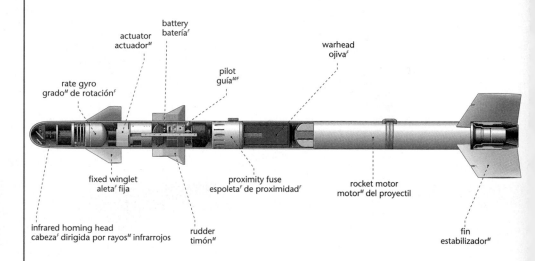

actuator
actuador[M]

battery
batería[F]

rate gyro
grado[M] de rotación[F]

pilot
guía[M/F]

warhead
ojiva[F]

fixed winglet
aleta[F] fija

proximity fuse
espoleta[F] de proximidad[F]

rocket motor
motor[M] del proyectil

infrared homing head
cabeza[F] dirigida por rayos[M] infrarrojos

rudder
timón[M]

fin
estabilizador[M]

MAJOR TYPES OF MISSILES
PRINCIPALES TIPOS[M] DE MISILES[M]

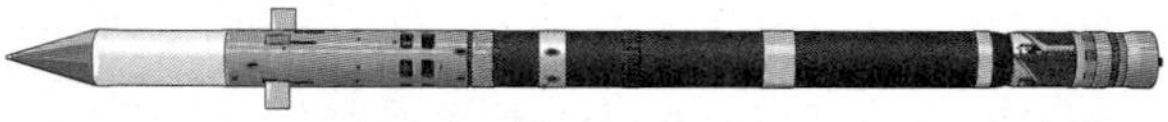

surface-to-air missile
misil[M] tierra[F] aire[M]

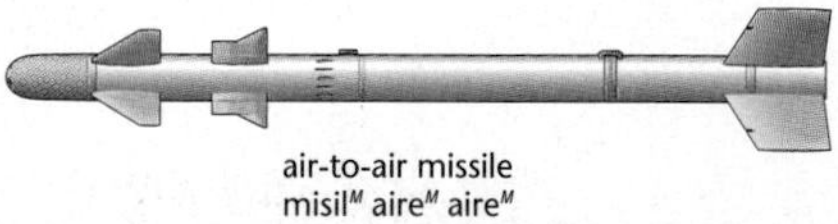

air-to-air missile
misil[M] aire[M] aire[M]

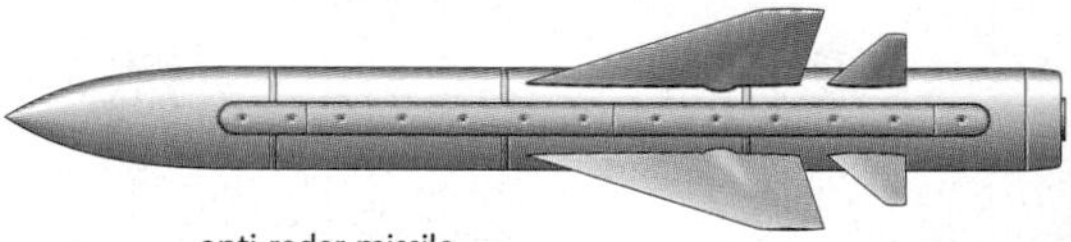

anti-radar missile
misil[M] antiradar

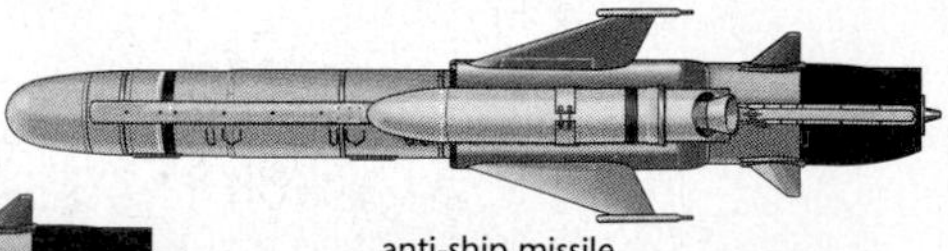

anti-ship missile
misil[M] antibuques

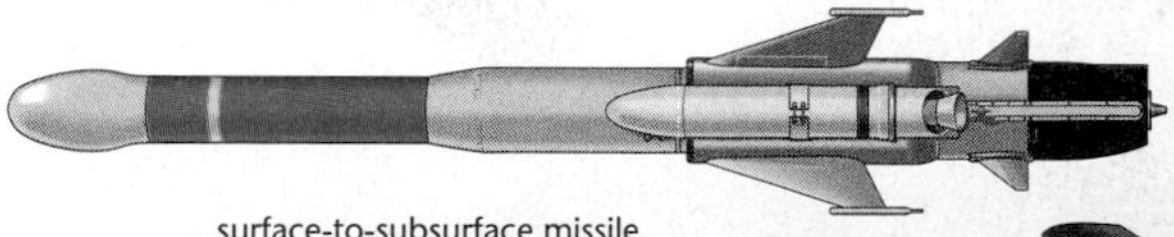

surface-to-subsurface missile
misil[M] antisubmarino

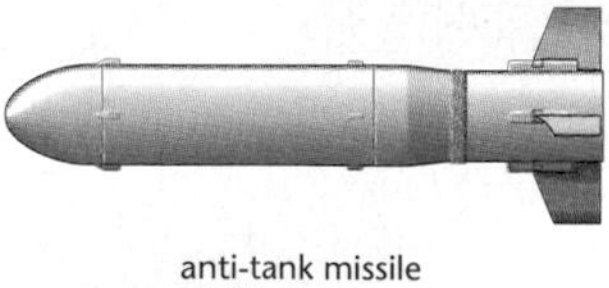

anti-tank missile
misil[M] antitanque

air-to-surface missile
misil[M] aire[M] tierra[F]

**WEAPONS
ARMAS**

814

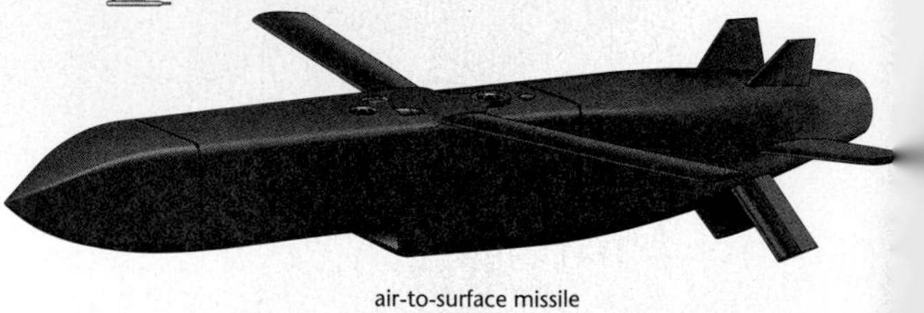

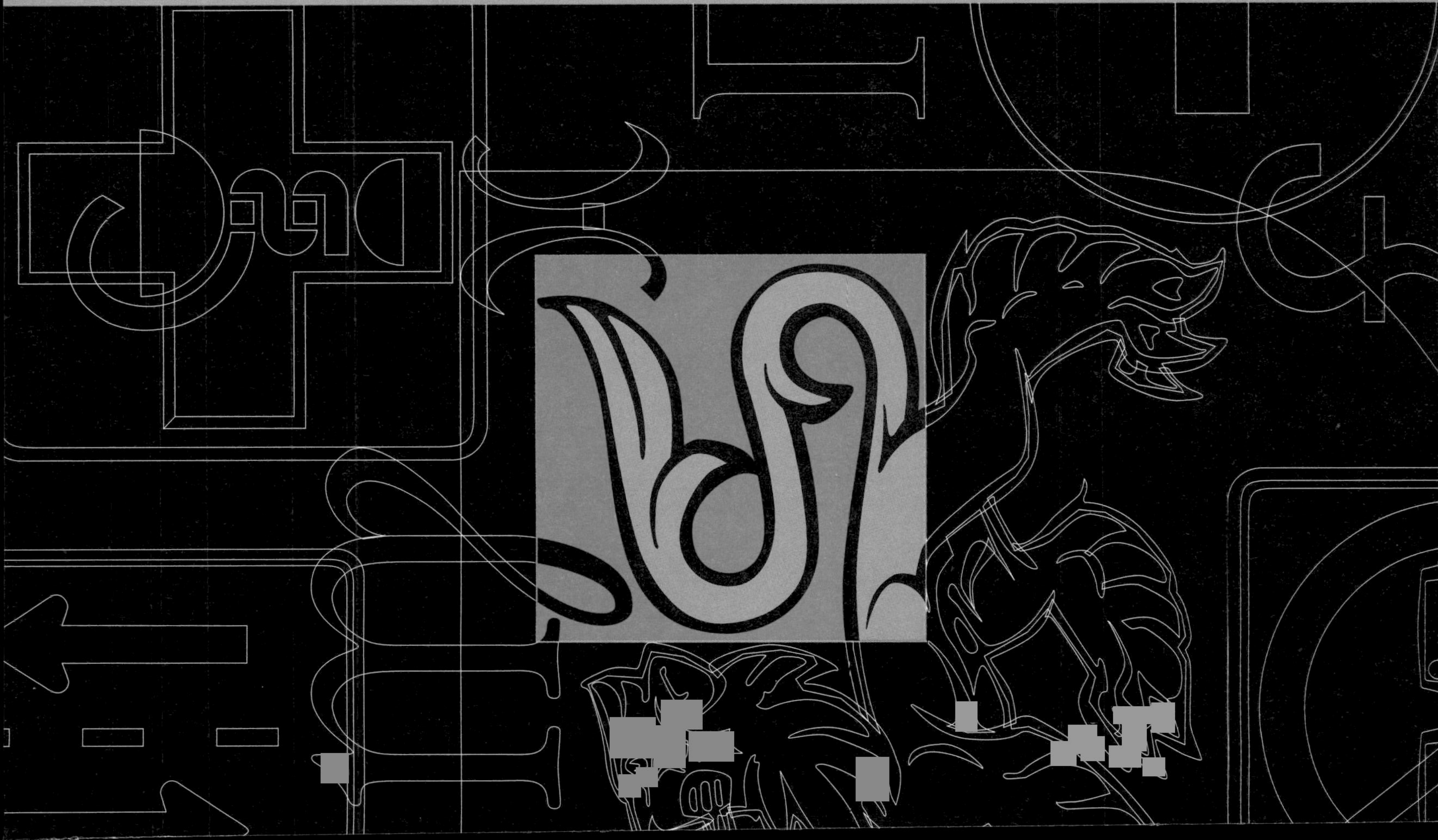

CONTENTS

SYMBOLS
SÍMBOLOS

HERALDRY
HERÁLDICA^F

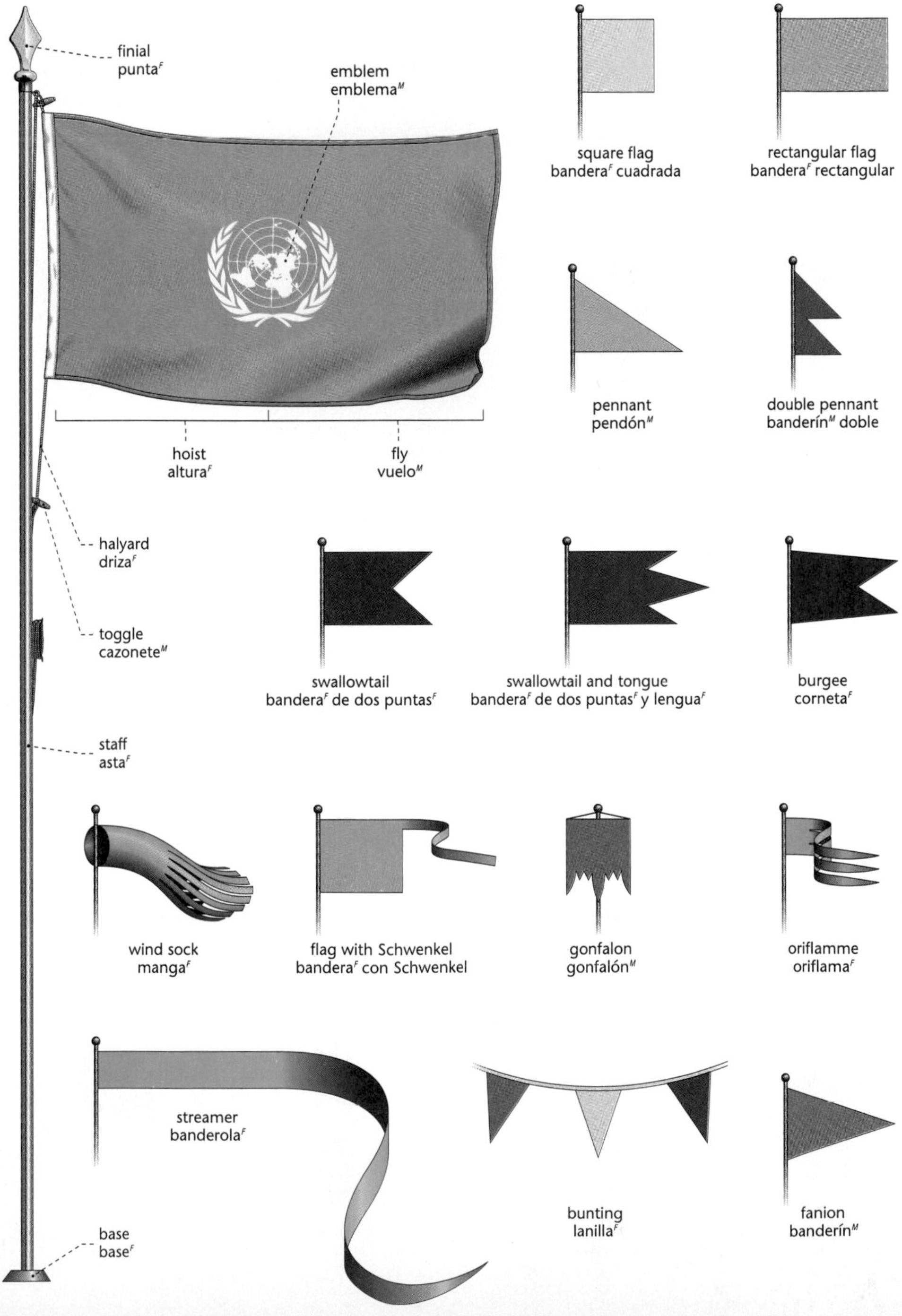

PARTS OF A FLAG
PARTES^F DE UNA BANDERA^F

finial
punta^F

emblem
emblema^M

hoist
altura^F

fly
vuelo^M

halyard
driza^F

toggle
cazonete^M

staff
asta^F

wind sock
manga^F

streamer
banderola^F

base
base^F

FLAG SHAPES
FORMAS^F DE BANDERAS^F

square flag
bandera^F cuadrada

rectangular flag
bandera^F rectangular

pennant
pendón^M

double pennant
banderín^M doble

swallowtail
bandera^F de dos puntas^F

swallowtail and tongue
bandera^F de dos puntas^F y lengua^F

burgee
corneta^F

flag with Schwenkel
bandera^F con Schwenkel

gonfalon
gonfalón^M

oriflamme
oriflama^F

bunting
lanilla^F

fanion
banderín^M

HERALDRY
HERÁLDICA^F

SHIELD DIVISIONS
DIVISIONES^F DE LOS ESCUDOS^M

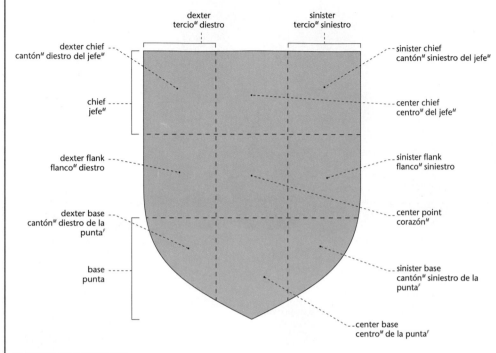

dexter
tercio^M diestro

sinister
tercio^M siniestro

dexter chief
cantón^M diestro del jefe^M

sinister chief
cantón^M siniestro del jefe^M

chief
jefe^M

center chief
centro^M del jefe^M

dexter flank
flanco^M diestro

sinister flank
flanco^M siniestro

dexter base
cantón^M diestro de la
punta^F

center point
corazón^M

base
punta

sinister base
cantón^M siniestro de la
punta^F

center base
centro^M de la punta^F

EXAMPLES OF PARTITIONS
EJEMPLOS^M DE PARTICIONES^F

per fess
escudo^M cortado

party
escudo^M partido

per bend
escudo^M tronchado

quarterly
escudo^M acuartelado

EXAMPLES OF ORDINARIES
EJEMPLOS^M DE PIEZAS^F HONORABLES

chief
jefe^M

chevron
cheurón^M

pale
palo^M

cross
cruz^F

EXAMPLES OF CHARGES
EJEMPLOS^M DE CARGAS^F

fleur-de-lis
flor^F de lis^F

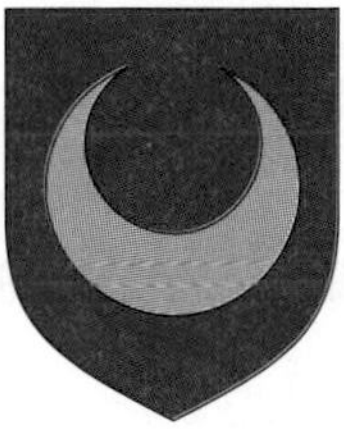

crescent
creciente^M

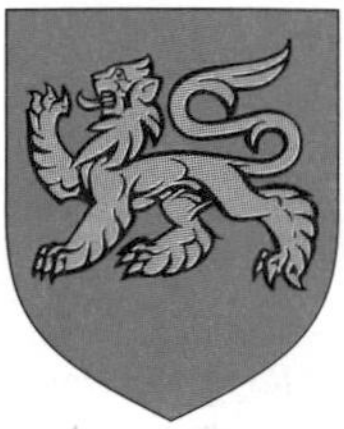

lion passant
león^M rampante

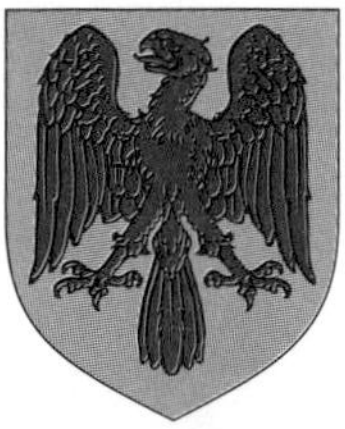

eagle
aguila^F

mullet
estrella^F

EXAMPLES OF METALS
EJEMPLOS^M DE METALES^M

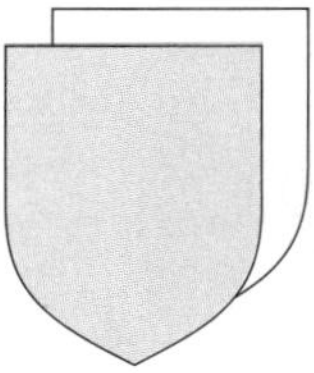

argent
plata^F

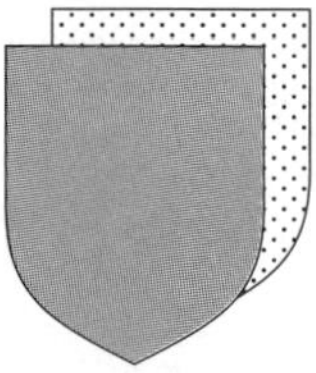

or
oro^M

EXAMPLES OF FURS
EJEMPLOS^M DE FORROS^M

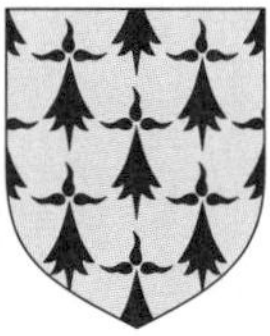

ermine
armiño^M

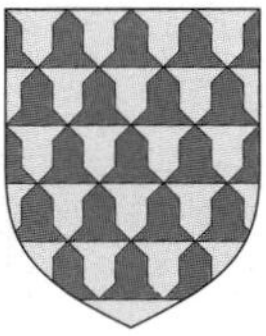

vair
cerros^M

EXAMPLES OF COLORS
EJEMPLOS^M DE COLORES^M

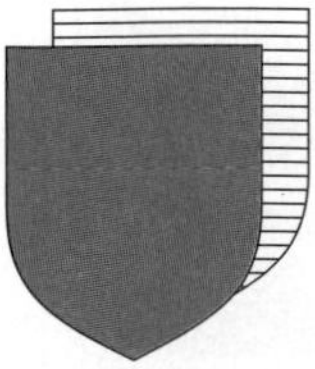

azure
azur^M

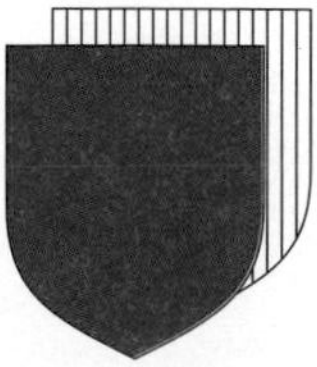

gules
gules^M

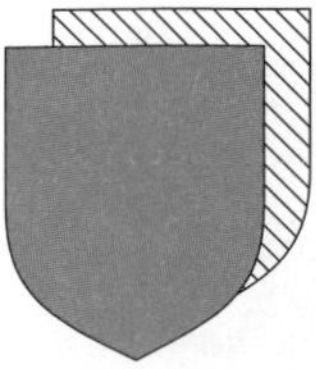

vert
sinople^M

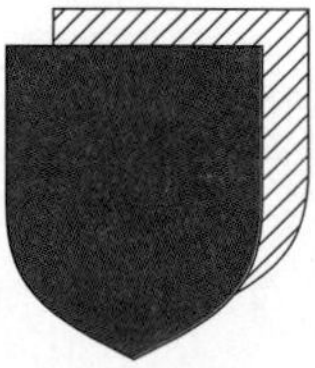

purpure
púrpura^M

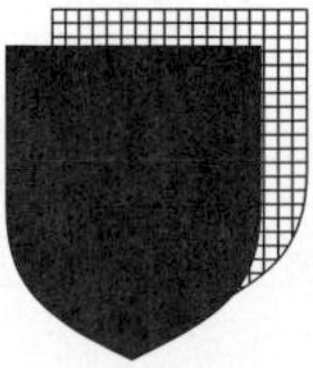

sable
sable^M

SIGNS OF THE ZODIAC
SIGNOS^M DEL ZODÍACO^M

FIRE SIGNS
SIGNOS^M DE FUEGO^M

Aries the Ram (March 21)
Aries, el Carnero (21 de marzo)

Leo the Lion (July 23)
Leo, el León (23 de julio)

Sagittarius the Archer (November 22)
Sagitario, el Arquero (22 de noviembre)

EARTH SIGNS
SIGNOS^M DE TIERRA^F

Taurus the Bull (April 20)
Tauro, el Toro (20 de abril)

Virgo the Virgin (August 23)
Virgo, la Virgen (23 de agosto)

Capricorn the Goat (December 22)
Capricornio, la Cabra (22 de diciembre)

AIR SIGNS
SIGNOS^M DE AIRE^M

Libra the Balance (September 23)
Libra, la Balanza (23 de septiembre)

Aquarius the Water Bearer (January 20)
Acuario, el Aguador (20 de enero)

Gemini the Twins (May 21)
Géminis, los Gemelos (21 de mayo)

WATER SIGNS
SIGNOS^M DE AGUA^F

Cancer the Crab (June 22)
Cáncer, el Cangrejo (22 de junio)

Scorpio the Scorpion (October 24)
Escorpio, el Escorpión (24 de octubre)

Pisces the Fishes (February 19)
Piscis, los peces (19 de febrero)

SAFETY SYMBOLS
SÍMBOLOS*M* DE SEGURIDAD*F*

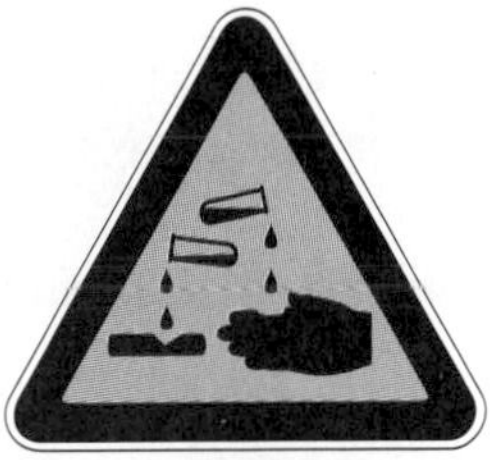

corrosive
corrosivo

electrical hazard
alto voltaje*M*

explosive
explosivo

flammable
inflamable

radioactive
radioactivo

poison
veneno*M*

PROTECTION
PROTECCIÓN*F*

eye protection
protección*F* de los ojos*M*

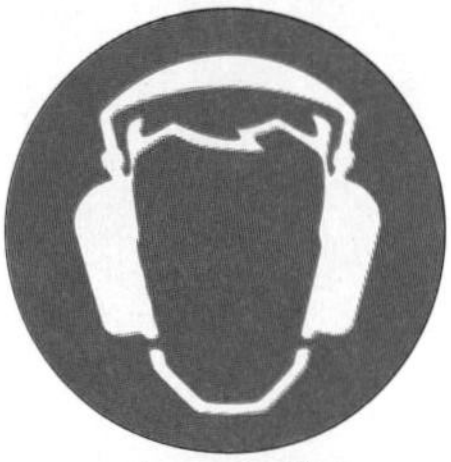

ear protection
protección*F* de los oidos*M*

head protection
protección*F* de la cabeza*F*

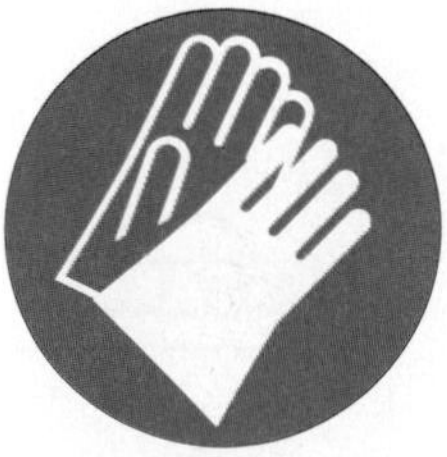

hand protection
protección*F* de las manos*F*

feet protection
protección*F* de los pies*M*

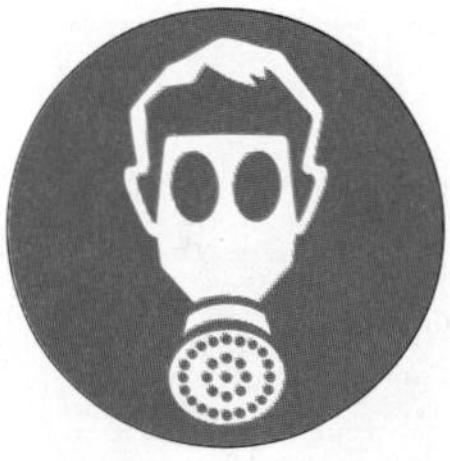

respiratory system protection
protección del sistema*M* respiratorio

COMMON SYMBOLS
SÍMBOLOS*ᴹ* DE USO*ᴹ* COMÚN

coffee shop
cafetería*ᶠ*

telephone
teléfono*ᴹ*

restaurant
restaurante*ᴹ*

men's rest room
Servicios*ᴹ* (Caballeros*ᴹ*)

women's rest room
Servicios*ᴹ* (Señoras*ᶠ*)

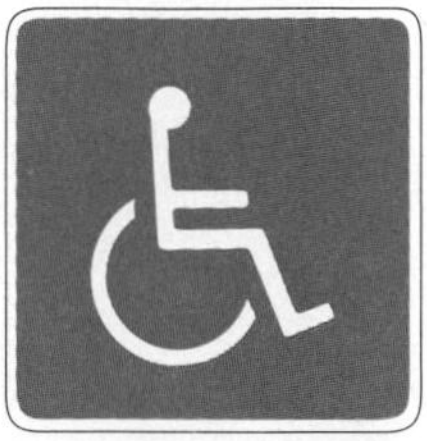

access for physically handicapped
acceso*ᴹ* para minusválidos*ᴹ*

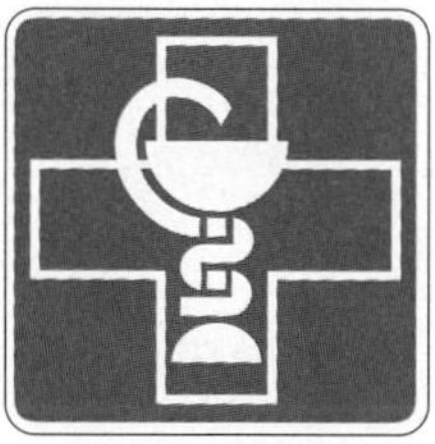

pharmacy
farmacia*ᶠ*

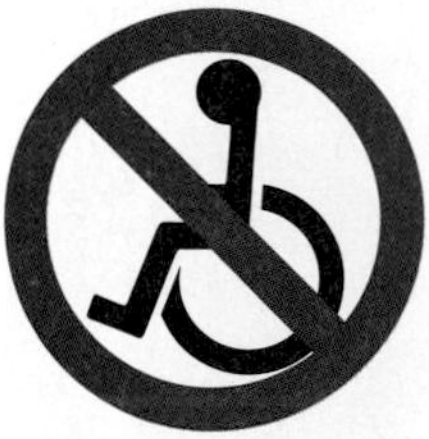

no access for wheelchairs
prohibido usar silla*ᶠ* de ruedas*ᶠ*

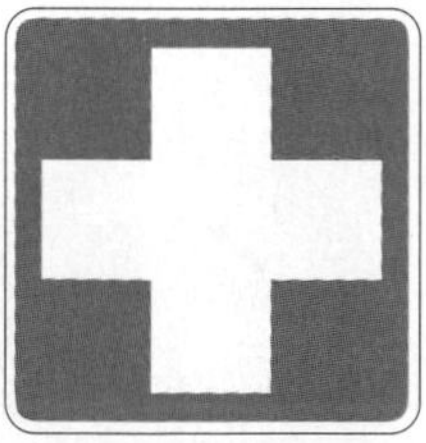

first aid
puesto*ᴹ* de socorro*ᴹ*

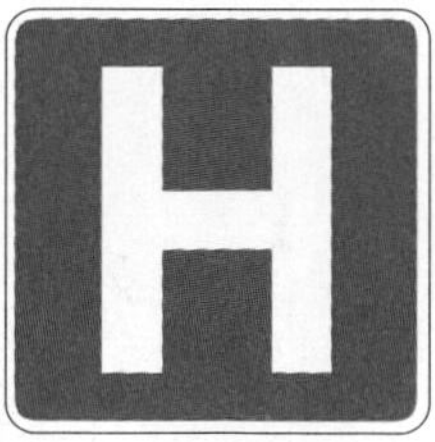

hospital
hospital*ᴹ*

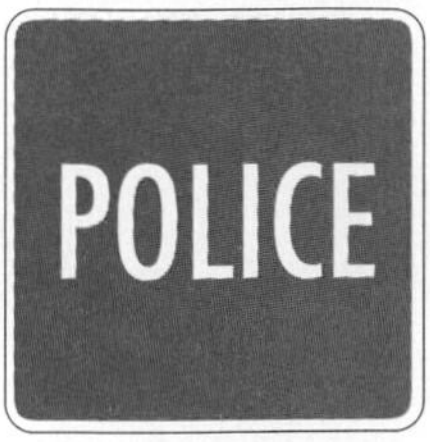

police
policía*ᶠ*

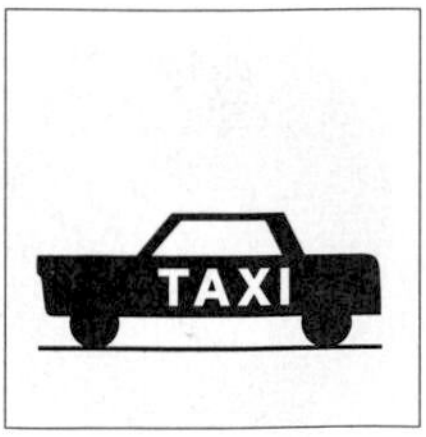

taxi transportation
servicio*ᴹ* de taxis*ᴹ*

camping (tent)
zona^f para acampar

camping prohibited
prohibido acampar

camping (trailer)
zona^f para casas^f rodantes

camping (trailer and tent)
zona^f para acampar y para casas^f rodantes

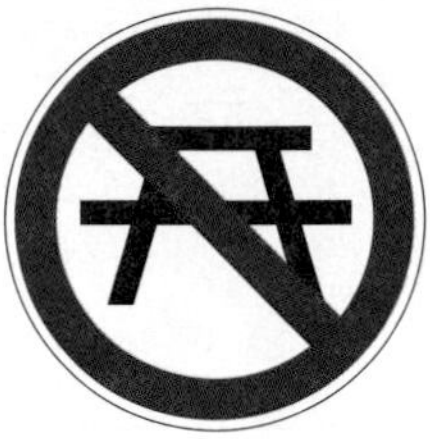

picnics prohibited
prohibido hacer comidas^f campestres

picnic area
zona^f de comidas^f campestres

service station
gasolinera^f

information
información^f

information
información^f

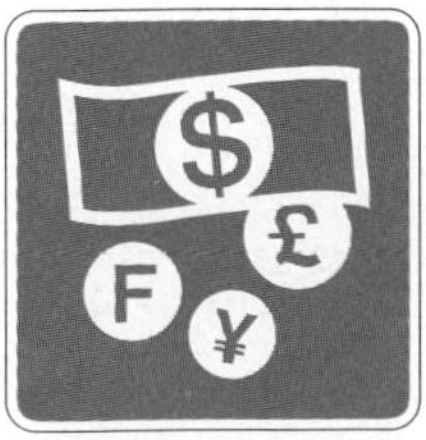

currency exchange
casa^f de cambio^M

lost and found articles
oficina^f de objetos^M perdidos

fire extinguisher
extintor^M de incendios^M

ROAD SIGNS
SEÑALES*F* DE TRANSITO*M*

MAJOR NORTH AMERICAN ROAD SIGNS
PRINCIPALES SEÑALES*F* DE TRANSITO*M* NORTEAMERICANAS

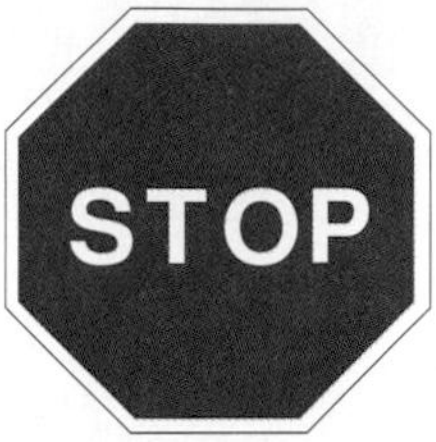

stop at intersection
alto

no entry
prohibido el paso*M*

yield
ceda el paso*M*

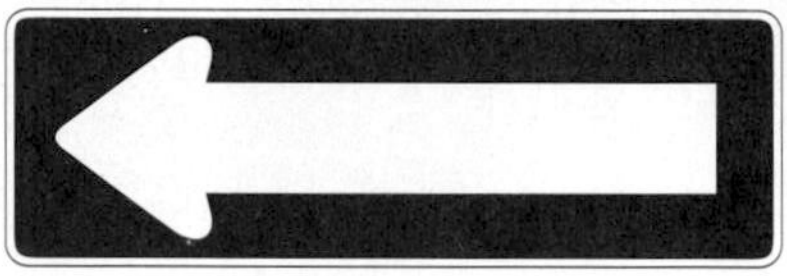

one-way traffic
una vía*F*

direction to be followed
dirección*F* obligatoria

direction to be followed
dirección*F* obligatoria

direction to be followed
dirección*F* obligatoria

direction to be followed
dirección*F* obligatoria

no U-turn
prohibido dar vuelta*F* en U

passing prohibited
prohibido adelantar

two-way traffic
doble vía*F*

merging traffic
señal*F* de unión*M*

SYMBOLS
SÍMBOLOS

stop at intersection
alto

no entry
prohibido el paso

yield
ceda el paso*M*

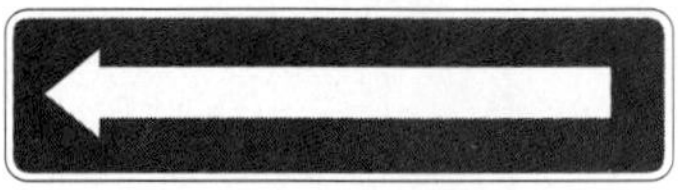

one-way traffic
una vía*F*

direction to be followed
dirección*F* obligatoria

direction to be followed
dirección*F* obligatoria

direction to be followed
dirección*F* obligatoria

direction to be followed
dirección*F* obligatoria

no U-turn
prohibido dar vuelta*F* en U

passing prohibited
prohibido adelantar

two-way traffic
doble vía*F*

priority intersection
cruce*M* con preferencia*F*

ROAD SIGNS
SEÑALES^F DE TRÁNSITO^M

MAJOR NORTH AMERICAN ROAD SIGNS
PRINCIPALES SEÑALES^F DE TRÁNSITO^M NORTEAMERICANAS

right bend
curva^F a la derecha^F

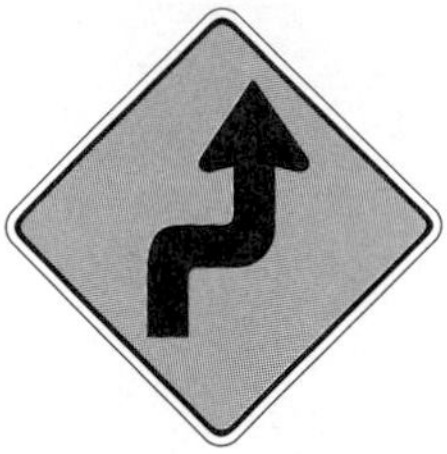

double bend
curva^F doble

roadway narrows
estrechamiento^M del camino^M

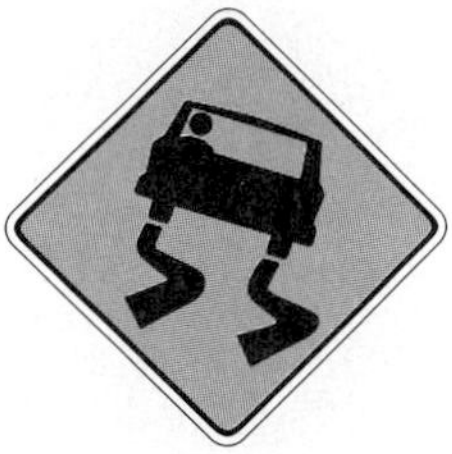

slippery road
camino^M resbaladizo

bumps
superficie^F irregular

steep hill
bajada^F pronunciada

falling rocks
zona^F de derrumbes^M

overhead clearance
altura^F máxima

signal ahead
semáforo^M

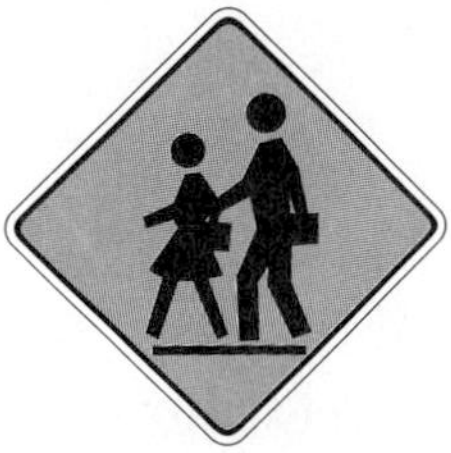

school zone
zona^F escolar

pedestrian crossing
paso^M de peatones^M

road work ahead
obras^F

right bend
curva*F* a la derecha*F*

double bend
curva*F* doble

roadway narrows
estrechamiento*M* del camino*M*

slippery road
camino*M* resbaladizo

bumps
badén*M*

steep hill
bajada*F* pronunciada

falling rocks
zona*F* de derrumbes*M*

overhead clearance
altura*F* máxima

signal ahead
semáforo*M*

school zone
zona*F* escolar

pedestrian crossing
paso*M* de peatones*M*

road work ahead
obras*F*

SYMBOLS
SÍMBOLOS

827

ROAD SIGNS
SEÑALES*F* DE TRÁNSITO*M*

MAJOR NORTH AMERICAN ROAD SIGNS
PRINCIPALES SEÑALES*F* DE TRÁNSITO*M* NORTEAMERICANAS

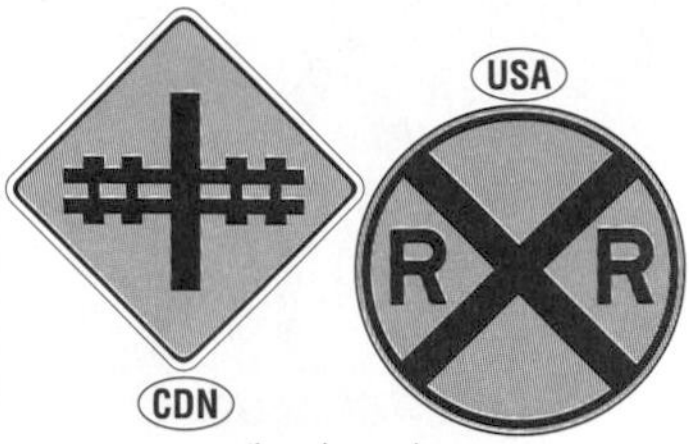

railroad crossing
paso*M* a nivel*M*

deer crossing
cruce*M* de animales*M* salvajes

closed to pedestrians
prohibido el paso*M* de peatones*M*

closed to bicycles
prohibido el paso*M* de bicicletas*F*

closed to motorcycles
prohibido el paso*M* de motocicletas*F*

closed to trucks
prohibido el paso*M* de camiones*M*

MAJOR INTERNATIONAL ROAD SIGNS
PRINCIPALES SEÑALES*F* DE TRÁNSITO*M* INTERNACIONALES

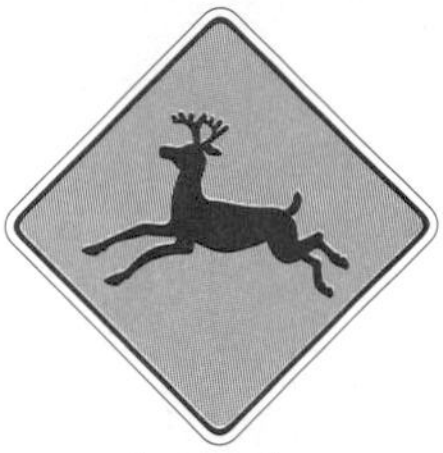

railroad crossing
paso*M* a nivel*M*

deer crossing
cruce*M* de animales*M* salvajes

closed to pedestrians
prohibido el paso*M* de peatones*M*

closed to bicycles
prohibido el paso*M* de bicicletas*F*

closed to motorcycles
prohibido el paso*M* de motocicletas*F*

closed to trucks
prohibido el paso*M* de camiones*M*

FABRIC CARE
CUIDADO^M DE TELAS^F

do not wash
no se lave

hand wash in lukewarm water
lávese a mano^F con agua^F tibia

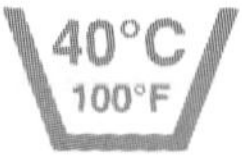

machine wash in lukewarm water at a gentle setting/reduced
agitation
lávese en lavadora^F con agua^F tibia en el ciclo^M para ropa^F
delicada

machine wash in warm water at a gentle setting/reduced
agitation
lávese en lavadora^F con agua^F caliente en el ciclo^M para ropa^F
delicada

machine wash in warm water at a normal setting
lávese en lavadora^F con agua^F caliente, en el ciclo^M normal

machine wash in hot water at a normal setting
lávese en lavadora^F con agua^F muy caliente, en el ciclo^M normal

do not use chlorine bleach
no use blanqueador^M de cloro^M

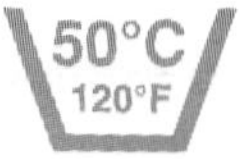

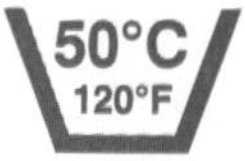

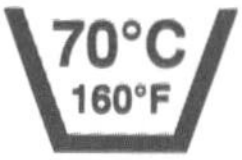

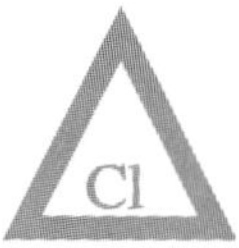

use chlorine bleach as directed
use blanqueador^M de cloro^M siguiendo las indicaciones^F

hang to dry
cuelgue al aire^M libre después de
escurrir

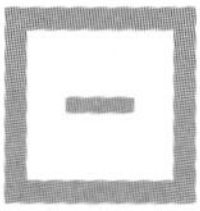

dry flat
seque extendido sobre una toalla^F después
de escurrir

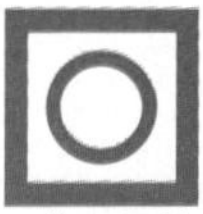

tumble dry at medium to high temperature
seque en secadora^F a temperatura^F de
mediana a alta

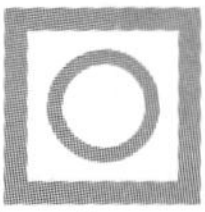

tumble dry at low temperature
seque en secadora^F a temperatura^F
baja

drip dry
cuelgue sin exprimir, dando forma^F a
mano^F

do not iron
no use plancha^F

iron at low setting
use plancha^F tibia

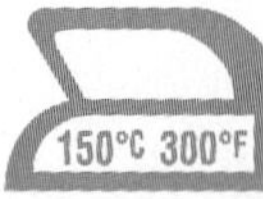

iron at medium setting
use plancha^F caliente

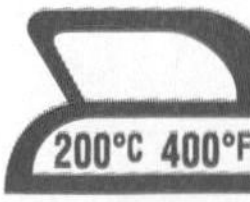

iron at high setting
use plancha^F muy
caliente

COMMON SCIENTIFIC SYMBOLS
SÍMBOLOS^M CIENTÍFICOS COMUNES

MATHEMATICS
MATEMÁTICAS^F

— subtraction menos^M	**+** addition más^M	**X** multiplication por^M	**÷** division entre^M
= is equal to igual a	**≠** is not equal to desigual a	**≋** is approximately equal to casi igual a	**∽** is equivalent to equivalente a
≡ is identical with idéntico a	**≢** is not identical with no es idéntico a	**±** plus or minus más^M o menos^M	**Ø** empty set conjunto^M vacío
> is greater than mayor que	**≥** is equal to or greater than igual o mayor que	**<** is less than menor que	**≤** is equal to or less than igual o menor que
∪ union unión^F	**∩** intersection intersección^F	**⊂** is contained in contenido en	**%** percent porcentaje^M
∈ belongs to pertenece a	**∉** does not belong to no pertenece a	**√** square root of raíz^F cuadrada de	**∑** sum suma^F
	∞ infinity infinito^M	**∫** integral integral	**!** factorial factorial

GEOMETRY
GEOMETRÍA^F

○ degree grado^M	**′** minute minuto^M	**″** second segundo^M	**π** pi pi	**⊥** perpendicular perpendicular
∠ acute angle ángulo^M agudo	**∟** right angle ángulo^M recto	**∠** obtuse angle ángulo^M obtuso	**∥** is parallel to es paralelo a	**∦** is not parallel to no es paralelo a

male
masculino^M

female
femenino^M

birth
nacimiento^M

blood factor positive
factor^MRH positivo

blood factor negative
factor^MRH negativo

death
muerte^F

CHEMISTRY
QUÍMICA^F

negative charge
elemento^M negativo

positive charge
elemento^M positivo

reversible reaction
reacción^F

reaction direction
dirección^F

MISCELLANEOUS
VARIOS

recycled
recuperado

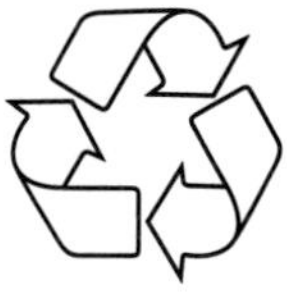

recyclable
recuperable

ampersand
y

registered trademark
marca^F registrada

copyright
copyright (derechos^M de
autor^M)

prescription
receta^F médica

pause/still
pausa^F

stop
paro^M

rewind
rebobinado^M

play
reproducción^F

fast forward
avance rápido

DIACRITIC SYMBOLS
SIGNOS^M DIACRÍTICOS

acute accent
acento^M agudo

umlaut
diéresis^F

grave accent
acento^M grave

circumflex accent
acento^M circunflejo

cedilla
cedilla^F

tilde
tilde^F

PUNCTUATION MARKS
SIGNOS^M DE PUNTUACIÓN^F

semicolon
punto^M y coma^F

period
punto^M

comma
coma^F

ellipses
puntos^M suspensivos

colon
dos puntos^M

*

asterisk
asterisco^M

《 》

quotation marks (French)
comillas^F

single quotation marks
comillas^F sencillas

quotation marks
comillas^F

dash
guión^M largo

( )

parentheses
paréntesis^M

/

virgule
diagonal^F

!

exclamation point
admiración^F

?

question mark
interrogación^F

[ ]

square brackets
corchetes^M

EXAMPLES OF CURRENCY ABBREVIATIONS
EJEMPLOS^M DE ABREVIACIONES^F DE MONEDAS^F

$

dollar
dólar^M

cent
centavo^M

pound
libras^F

¥

yen
yen^M

F

franc
franco^M

DM

deutsche mark
marco^M

Dr

drachma
dracma^M

L

lira
lira^F

Kr

krone
corona^F

IS

shekel
shekel^M

ECU

European Currency Unit
monedas^F de la Comunidad^F
Europea

Esc

escudo
escudo^M

Pta

peseta
peseta^F

Fl

florin
florín^M

Los términos en **negrita** corresponden a una ilustración; los que aparecen en MAYÚSCULAS indican un título.

ÍNDICE ESPAÑOL

Los términos en **negrita** corresponden a una ilustración; los que aparecen en MAYÚSCULAS indican un título.

Los términos en **negrita** corresponden a una ilustración; los que aparecen en MAYÚSCULAS indican un título.

Los términos en **negrita** corresponden a una ilustración; los que aparecen en MAYÚSCULAS indican un título.

Los términos en **negrita** corresponden a una ilustración; los que aparecen en MAYÚSCULAS indican un título.

ÍNDICE ESPAÑOL

Los términos en **negrita** corresponden a una ilustración; los que aparecen en MAYÚSCULAS indican un título.

Los términos en **negrita** corresponden a una ilustración; los que aparecen en MAYÚSCULAS indican un título.

Los términos en **negrita** corresponden a una ilustración; los que aparecen en MAYÚSCULAS indican un título.

Los términos en **negrita** corresponden a una ilustración; los que aparecen en MAYÚSCULAS indican un título.

Los términos en **negrita** corresponden a una ilustración; los que aparecen en MAYÚSCULAS indican un título.

INDICE ESPAÑOL

paraguas(m) de bastón(m) 375.
paraguas(m) plegable 375.
paragüero(m) 375.
paralelo(m) 47.
paramento(m) de aguas(f) contenidas
    749.
paramento(m) de aguas(f) corrientes
    749.
parapeto(m) 454.
parapeto(m) contra olas(f) 748.
pararrayos(m) 197, 747, 757.
parasol(m) 42, 430, 449.
parche(m) 283, 554.
parche(m) inferior 553.
parche(m) superior 552, 553.
pare(m) 411, 532.
pared(f) 104, 736.
pared(f) celulósica 115.
pared(f) de fondo(m) 621.
pared(f) de hormigón(m) 772.
pared(f) de rebote(m) 617.
pared(f) de Trombe 772.
pared(f) de Trombe 772.
pared(f) de viraje(m) 621, 622.
pared(f) del tanque(m) 742.
pared(f) frontal 616.
pared(f) lateral 104, 616, 617, 621,
    743.
pared(f) transversal de contención(f)
    742.
paréntesis(m) 832.
parietal(m) 123.
paripinnada 56.
parka(m) 321.
parka(m) 680.
paro(m) 831.
párpado(m) 97.
párpado(m) inferior 84, 107, 140.
párpado(m) interno 107.
párpado(m) superior 84, 107, 140.
parque(m) 52, 184.
parqué(m) 200.
parqué(m) alternado a la inglesa 200.
parqué(m) Arenberg 200.
parqué(m) Chantilly 200.
parqué(m) de cestería(f) 200.
parqué(m) entretejido 200.
parqué(m) espinapez(m) 200.
parqué(m) nacional 52.
parqué(f) sobre base(f) de
    cemento(m) 200.
parqué(m) sobrepuesto 200.
parqué(m) Versailles 200.
parqué(m), tipos(m) de 200.
parrilla(f) 253, 254.
parrilla(f) estabilizadora 689.
parrilla(f) plegable 690.
parte(f) plana 567.
parte(f) superior 302.
parteluz(m) 175, 203.
partes(f) 220, 223, 224.
partes(f) de un zapato(m) 354.
partes(f) del arma(f) 666.
partes(f) del oído(m) 138.
particiones(f), ejemplos(m) 818.
partida(f) 701.
partido(m) 700.
pasa(f) (19 a 36) 700, 701.
pasador(m) 289, 290, 323, 369, 566.
pasaje(m) subterráneo 464.
PASAJEROS(M), AVIÓN(M)
    TURBORREACTOR 498.
pasajeros(m), terminal(m) 504.
PASAJEROS(M), VAGONES(M) 460.
pasamanos(m) 201, 254.
pasapuré(m) 244.
pasarela(f) 180, 742.
pasarela(f) superior 475.
paseo(m) 263.
pasillo(m) 194, 773.
pasillo(m) central 460.
paso(m) 27.
paso(m) a nivel(m) 471.
paso(m) a nivel(m) 464, 828.
paso(m) de la energía(f) hacia la red(f)
    de transmisión(f) 755.
paso(m) de peatones(m) 186, 826,
    827.
paso(m) elevado 454.
paso(m) inferior 454.
pastel(m) 588.
pastel(m) de óleo(m) 588.
pastilla(f) de fricción(f) 432.
pata(f) 97, 112, 219, 223, 224, 225,
    232, 233, 270, 309, 376, 553, 574,
    659, 671, 681.
pata(f) anal 78.
pata(f) curvada 220.
pata(f) de ajuste(m) de altura(f) 397.
pata(f) de conexión(f) a tierra(f) 309.

pata(f) de gallo(m) 571.
pata(f) de la mesa(f) 619.
pata(f) de soporte(m) 156, 449.
pata(f) delantera 79, 80, 223.
pata(f) delantera (superficie(f)
    exterior) 80.
pata(f) media 79, 80.
pata(f) media (superficie(f)
    exterior) 80.
pata(f) móvil 219.
pata(f) posterior 78.
pata(f) posterior 78.
pata(f) principal 756.
pata(f) soporte 441.
pata(f) telescópica 393, 726.
pata(f) torácica 78.
pata(f) trasera 81, 223.
pata(f) trasera (superficie(f)
    interior) 81.
pata(f) ventosa 78.
patada(f) de crol(m) 622.
patada(f) de mariposa(f) 623.
patada(f) de rana(f) 622.
patas(f) de ganso(m) 634.
PATAS(F) DE UNGULADOS(M):
    TIPOS(M) MÁS COMUNES 99.
patas(f), principales tipos(m) de
    111.
patata(f) 71.
patín(m) 609, 643.
patín(m) de aterrizaje(m) 508.
patín(m) de cola(f) 508.
patín(m) de deslizamiento(m) 467.
patín(m) de oruga(f) 805.
patín(m) de retroceso(m) 802.
PATÍN(M) DE RUEDAS(F) 645.
patín(m) de velocidad(f) 644.
patín(m) delantero 643.
patín(m) para accesorios(m) 391, 409.
patín(m) para figuras(f) 644.
patín(m) trasero 643.
PATINAJE(M) 644.
patio(m) 172, 173, 263.
patio(m) de armas(f) 178, 180.
patio(m) de clasificación(m) 467.
patio(m) de lavado(m) de vagones(m)
    465.
patio(m) de recepción(f) 465.
patio(m) de tanques(m) 740.
pato(m) 150.
patrón(m) 565.
patrón(m) de prueba(f) 414.
pausa(f) 831.
pausa(f) \ imagen(f) fija 411.
pauta(f) A 539.
pavimento(m) 450, 451.
Pavo 13.
pavo(m) 150.
pecho(m) 100, 116, 118.
pechuga(f) 108.
pecíolo(m) 56.
pectén(m) 81.
pectoral(m) 602, 663.
pectoral(m) mayor 120.
pedal(m) 446, 448, 545, 552, 553,
    572, 664.
pedal(m) crescendo 542.
pedal(m) de ajuste(m) 591.
pedal(m) de amortiguación(f) 540.
pedal(m) de cambio(m) de
    velocidades(f) 444.
pedal(m) de expresión(f) 542.
pedal(m) de la sordina(f) 540, 555.
pedal(m) de los bajos(m) 555.
pedal(m) de los frenos(m) 430.
pedal(m) de velocidad(f) 561.
pedal(m) del acelerador(m) 430.
pedal(m) del embrague(m) 430.
pedal(m) del freno(m) 573.
pedal(m) del freno(f) trasero 444.
pedal(m) del timón(m) de mando(m)
    639.
pedal(m) delantero 443, 444.
pedal(m) eléctrico 561.
pedal(m) suave 540.
pedal(m) trasero 443, 444.
pedalero(m) 542.
pedernal(m) 795.
pedernal(m) 307, 795.
pedestal(m) 236, 283, 545, 656.
pedestal(m) de la cámara(f) 414.
pedio(m) 120.
pedúnculo(m) 60, 61, 62, 63, 64.
Pegaso 11.
PEINADO(M) 368, 370.
peinado(m), accesorios(m) 369.
peinazo(m) 225.
peinazo(m) de la cerradura(f) 225.
peinazo(m) inferior 202, 223, 225.

peinazo(m) superior 202, 223, 225.
peine(m) 572.
peine(m) combinado(m) 368.
peine(m) de mango(m) 368.
peine(m) de peluquero(m) 368.
peine(m) de tapicería(f) 574.
peine(m) metálico 368.
peine(m) para desenredar 368.
peine(m) tenedor(m) 368.
peine(m) y cuchilla(f) 374.
peines(m) 368.
pelacables(m) 311.
pelapatatas(m) 242.
peldaño(m) 147, 302.
peldaño(m) inferior 470.
pelele(m) 351.
película(f) 390.
película(f) de disco(m) 395.
película(f) de disco(m) para vídeo(m)
    fijo 395.
películas(f) 395.
peligro(m) 488.
pelillo(m) 670.
pelo(m) 117, 119, 136.
pelos(m) absorbentes 57.
pelos(m) absorbentes, zona(f) de 59.
pelota(f) 598, 599.
pelota(f) de cricket(m) 598.
pelota(f) de golf(m) 677.
pelota(f) de golf(m), corte(m)
    transversal de una 677.
pelota(f) de hockey(m) 607.
pelota(f) de ping pong(m) 619.
pelota(f) de raquetbol(m) 617.
pelota(f) de squash(m) 616.
pelota(f) de tenis(m) 615.
pelota(f), corte(m) transversal de
    la 596.
peltada 56.
Pelton, turbina(f) 754.
peluquero(m), tijeras(f) 369.
pelusa(f) de maíz(m) 72.
pelvis(f) 103.
pelvis(f) renal 132.
penacho(m) 109, 791.
penacho(m) de plumas(f) 618.
pendiente(m) 361.
pendientes(m) 361.
pendientes(m) de clip(m) 361.
pendientes(m) de espiga(f) 361.
pendientes(m) de tornillo(m) 361.
pendolón(m) 199.
pendón(m) 817.
péndulo(m) 539, 707.
péndulo(m), reloj(m) 707.
pene(m) 116, 127.
península(f) 51.
pentagrama(f) 537.
peón(m) 696.
pepino(m) 69.
pepita(f) 62, 64, 65.
peplo(m) 315.
pera(f) 64, 362.
pera(f) de goma(f) 726.
pera(f) de goma(f) para inyectar
    aire(m) 710.
peraltado(m) 174.
percha(f) 620.
perchero(m) 522.
perchero(m) de pared(f) 522.
perchero(m) de pie 522.
percolador(m) 247.
percusión(f), barra(f) 780.
PERCUSIÓN(F), INSTRUMENTOS(M)
    552, 554.
percutor(m) 797, 798, 799, 804.
perejil(m) 74.
perfil(m) 363.
perforación(f) 353, 395.
perforación(f) marina 739.
perforación(f), torre(f) 737.
perforaciones(f) 327, 355.
perforadora(f) 516.
pérgola(f) 263.
pericardio(m) 130.
pericarpio(m) 65, 66.
perifollo(m) 74.
perilla(f) 202, 277, 280, 284.
perilla(f) de registro(m) 543.
perilla(f) del rodillo(m) 531.
periodo(m) 489.
perioplo(m) 104.
periscopio(m) de ataque(m) 807.
periscopio(m) de navegación(f) 807.
peristilo(m) 168, 169, 171.
peritoneo(m) 127, 128.
perlas(f) 105.
perno(m) 279.
perno(m) 278, 282, 290.

perno(m) con collarín(m) 279.
perno(m) de acoplamiento(m) 754.
perno(m) de articulación(f) del
    cucharón(m) 782.
perno(m) de expansión(f) 276.
perno(m) de fijación(f) 432.
perno(m) de la bisagra(f) 785.
perno(m) de la eclisa(f) 466.
perno(m) difusor 264.
perno(m) maestro 441.
perno(m) para falso plafón(m)
    276.
peroné(m) 102.
peroneo(m) lateral corto 121.
peroneo(m) lateral largo 120.
peróxido(m) 725.
perpendicular 830.
PERRO(M) 106.
perro(m), pata(f) delantera 106.
Perseo 11.
persiana(f) enrollable 231.
persiana(f) veneciana 231.
persianas(f) romana 231.
personal(m) suplementario de
    producción(f) 412.
pertenece a 830.
pértiga(f) 657.
pértiga(f) de inclinación(f) 231.
pesa(f) 707, 708.
pesa(f) corrediza 708.
pesas(f) 665.
pesas(f) 663, 665.
pesas(f) para muñecas(f) y tobillos(m)
    665.
PESCA(F) 670, 672.
pescador(m), vestido(m) de 672.
pescadores(m) 336.
pescante(m) 478, 742, 786.
pescuezo(m) 678.
peseta(f) 832.
peso(m) 658.
peso(m) 658, 709.
peso(m) corredizo 539.
PESO(M), MEDICIÓN(F) 708.
pespunte(m) 571.
pespunteado(m) 352.
pestaña(f) 104, 140, 330, 565.
pestaña(f) de arrojo(m) 726.
pestaña(f) de la llanta(f) 433.
pestañas(f) 107.
pestillo(m) 203, 289, 290.
pestillo(m) de resorte(m) 375.
pétalo(m) 60.
PETANCA(F) Y BOLOS(M) 682.
petifoque(m) 481.
peto(m) 317, 350, 351, 595, 602, 609,
    792.
peto(m) metálico 667.
petral(m) 653.
PETRÓLEO(M) 737, 738, 740, 742,
    744.
petróleo(m) 737, 745.
petróleo(m) crudo 744.
petróleo(m) crudo, oleoducto(m)
    740.
petróleo(m) diáfano 744.
petróleo(m) para calderas(f) 745.
petróleo(m) para calefacción(f) 745.
Pez Austral 13.
Pez Dorado 13.
Pez Volador 13.
PEZ(M) 86, 88.
pezón(m) 116, 118, 129.
pi 830.
piano(m) 556.
piano(m) electrónico 555.
piano(m) vertical 540.
piano(m) vertical, mecanismo(m)
    541.
pica(f) 780.
picacho(m) 27.
picaporte(m) 289.
pico(m) 27, 108, 267, 681.
pico(m) de loro(m) 483.
pico(m) del zanco(m) 783.
pico(m) muesca(f) 565.
pícolo(m) 548, 557.
picos(m) (de aves) (f), principales
    tipos(m) de 111.
pie(m) 40, 83, 116, 117, 118, 119,
    232, 250, 542, 545, 670, 718.
pie(m) ajustable 257, 258, 259.
pie(m) de la cama(f) 224.
pie(m) de la torre(f) 756.
pie(m) de montura(f) 393.
pie(m) de voluta(f) 220.
pie(m) del electrodo(m) 232.
pie(m) del talud(m) 748.
pie(m) derecho 198.
pie(m), dedo(m) del 116, 118.

855

Los términos en **negrita** corresponden a una ilustración; los que aparecen en MAYÚSCULAS indican un título.

Los términos en **negrita** corresponden a una ilustración; los que aparecen en MAYÚSCULAS indican un título.

resorte(m) de retorno(m) 432.
resorte(m) de suspensión(f) 707.
resorte(m) de tensión(f) 562, 665.
resorte(m) de válvula(f) 543.
resorte(m) del eslabón(m) 795.
resorte(m) del martinete(m) 541.
resorte(m) del sistema(m) articulado 702.
resorte(m) del tensor(m) 569.
resorte(m) espiral 231.
resorte(m) hidráulico 664.
resorte(m) tensor 431.
respaldo(m) 220, 223, 386, 428, 445, 727.
respaldo(m) reclinatorio 726.
respiradero(m) 14, 82, 196, 197, 214, 385, 443, 741.
respiradero(m) lateral 449.
restador(m) 614, 616, 618.
restaurante(m) 185, 190, 494, 822.
retén(m) 735.
retén(m) de la esfera(f) 530.
retén(m) del cargador(m) 795.
retén(m) imantado 256.
retención(f) de datos(m) 310.
retenedor(m) de frecuencias(f) bajas 412.
retícula(f) 718.
Retículo 13.
retículo(m) endoplasmático 115.
retina(f) 140.
retoño(m) 59.
retorno(m) a la memoria(f) 523.
retrete(m) 293.
retrete(m) 215, 292.
retroexcavadora(f) 782.
retroexcavadora(f) cargadora(f) 782.
revelado(m), baños(m) 399.
revelado(m), tanque(m) 398.
revés(f) 567.
revestimiento(m) 432, 619, 635, 677, 748, 798, 799.
revestimiento(m) de fibra(f) de vidrio(m) 297.
revestimiento(m) de fósforo(m) 232.
revestimiento(m) interior 429, 433.
REVÓLVER(M) 797.
rey(m) 695, 696.
ría(f) 646, 647, 676.
ribera(f) 750.
ribete(m) 322, 328, 352, 354.
ribosoma(m) 115.
riel(m) 230.
riel(m) 230, 466, 476, 786.
riel(m) corredizo 630.
riel(m) de cierre(m) 467.
riel(m) de iluminación(f) 235.
riel(m) de lanzamiento(m) de proyectiles(m) 813.
riel(m) de retención(f) 467.
riel(m) de rodamiento(m) 786.
riel(m) de rotación(f) 15.
riel(m) deslizador 428.
riel(m) eléctrico 476.
riel(m) metálico 517.
riel(m) para las parrillas(f) 254.
rieles(m), empalme(m) 466.
rienda(f) 651.
rienda(f) del bocado(m) 649.
rienda(f) del freno(m) 649.
rifle(m) 798.
rifle(m), cartucho(m) 798.
rimaya(f) 26.
rímel(m) en pasta(f) 367.
rímel(m) líquido 367.
rincón(m) 669.
rinconera(f) 227.
ring(m) de boxeo(m) 669.
ringside(m) 669.
riñón(m) 89, 97, 124.
riñón(m) derecho 132.
riñón(m) izquierdo 132.
riñonera(f) 602.
riñones(m) 101.
río(m) 51, 52.
ripia(f) 286.
risco(m) 7.
ritmo(m) de las señales(f) nocturnas 489.
rizador(m) de mantequilla(f) 242.
rizador(m) de pestañas(f) 367.
Roberval, balanza(f) 708.
robot(m) de cocina(f) 251.
roca(f) 30.
roca(f) firme 714.
roca(f) impermeable 737.
rocas(f) ígneas 23.
rocas(f) intrusivas 23.

rocas(f) metamórficas 23.
rocas(f) sedimentarias 23.
rociador(m) 296.
rociadores(m) 766.
rocío(m) 37.
roda(f) 479.
rodamiento(m) 530, 753.
rodapié(m) 225.
rodete(m) 105.
rodilla(f) 100, 106, 116, 118.
rodillera(f) 595, 602, 609, 649, 653, 792.
rodillo(m) 584.
rodillo(m) 231, 245, 270, 304, 524, 531.
rodillo(m) de entrada(f) 160, 162.
rodillo(m) de pintor(m) 304.
rodillo(m) entintador 581.
rodillo(m) guía(f) 403.
rodillo(m) guía(f) de la película(f) 390.
rodillo(m) para barnizar 582.
rodillo(m) triturador 158.
rodrigón(m) 263.
roja(f) 697, 700.
rojo(f) 701.
rollo(m) de la película(f) 395.
rollo(m) para recubrimiento(m) impermeabilizante 287.
romero(m) 74.
rompiente(m) 30.
ropa(f) de cama(f) 224.
ROPA(F) DE HOMBRE(M) 319, 320, 322, 324.
ROPA(F) DE MUJER(F) 330, 332, 334, 336, 338, 340, 342, 344, 346, 348.
ROPA(F) DE NIÑOS(M) 349, 350.
ROPA(F) DEPORTIVA 352.
ropa(f) interior 325, 345, 346.
ropa(f) para ejercicio(m) 353.
ropero(m) 226.
rosa(f) de los vientos(m) 484, 719.
rosa(f) holandesa 362.
rosca(f) 276, 279, 294, 711.
roseta(f) 265, 289, 290, 546.
rosetón(m) 167, 175.
rostro(m) 90.
rotación(f) de la turbina(f) 755.
rotonda(f) 190.
rotor(m) 161, 290, 437, 508, 773, 774.
rotor(m) de cola(f) 508.
rotor(m) de la turbina(f) 752.
rótula(f) 103, 122.
rótula(f) de enganche(m) 471.
rotulador(m) 516, 588.
rótulo(m) de destino(m) 743.
rótulo(m) de identificación(f) 743.
rubí(m) 363, 706.
rubia(f) 425.
rubor(m) en polvo(m) 366.
rueda(f) 433.
rueda(f) 270, 427, 440, 563, 583, 645, 664, 727, 788, 800, 805.
rueda(f) catalina 783.
rueda(f) central 706, 707.
rueda(f) central de enfoque(m) 719.
rueda(f) compresora 158.
rueda(f) de cadena(f) 445.
rueda(f) de cangilones(m) 754.
rueda(f) de corona(f) 707.
rueda(f) de escape(m) 706, 707.
rueda(f) de la dirección(f) 727.
rueda(f) de los segundos(m) 706.
rueda(f) de modulación(f) 555.
rueda(f) de rayos(m) 652.
rueda(f) de transmisión(f) 445.
rueda(f) de trinquete(m) 706, 707.
rueda(f) de volante(m) 584.
rueda(f) delantera 147, 784.
rueda(f) giratoria 701.
rueda(f) guía(f) 783.
rueda(f) humedecedora 516.
rueda(f) libre 435.
rueda(f) media 706.
rueda(f) metálica de seguridad(f) 476.
rueda(f) motriz 147, 707, 805.
rueda(f) para ajustar el tono(m) 555.
ruedas(f) de tracción(f) 784.
RUEDAS(F), SILLA(F) 727.
ruedecilla(f) 260, 383, 553.
Ruffini, corpúsculo(m) de 136.
RUGBY(M) 606.
rugby(m), balón(m) de 606.
ruibarbo(m) 72.
ruleta(f) americana 700.
ruleta(f) estriada 582.
ruleta(f) francesa 701.
RULETA(F), MESA(F) 700.
ruta(f) circular 52.
ruta(f) de servicio(m) 502.
ruta(f) pintoresca 52.

sabana(f) 45.
sábana(f) 224.
sábana(f) ajustable 224.
sabañón(m) 55.
sable(m) 628, 631, 637, 666, 794, 819.
sabor(m) agrio 143.
sabor(m) amargo 143.
sabor(m) dulce 143.
sabor(m) salado 143.
sabores(m) 143.
sacaanzuelos(m) 672.
sacabotas(m) 358.
sacacorchos(m) 244, 688.
sacacorchos(m) con brazos(m) 244.
sacapuntas(m) 515, 516.
sacatrapos(m) 801.
saco(m) de marinero(m) 381.
saco(m) de piel(f) 536.
saco(m) de pilotaje(m) 637.
saco(m) de viaje(m) 380.
saco(m) rectangular 687.
saco(m) semirrectangular 687.
saco(m) uterovesical 128.
sacos(m) de dormir 687.
sacro(m) 122, 123.
Saeta 11.
Sagitario 13.
Sagitario, el Arquero (22 de noviembre) 820.
sala(f) 195.
sala(f) de bombeo(m) 742.
sala(f) de cine(m) 496.
sala(f) de computación(f) 807.
sala(f) de control(m) 14, 15, 189, 407, 746, 759.
sala(f) de control(m) de la producción(f) 415.
sala(f) de control(m) de luces(f) 412.
sala(f) de control(m) de máquinas(f) de propulsión(f) 806.
sala(f) de control(m) de operaciones(f) 807.
sala(f) de control(m) de producción(f) 413.
sala(f) de control(m) de sonido(m) 415.
SALA(F) DE CONTROL(M), ESTUDIO(M) DE RADIO(M) 407.
sala(f) de ensayo(m) 188.
sala(f) de equipajes(m) 462.
sala(f) de espera(f) para abordar 505.
sala(f) de instalaciones(f) auxiliares 412.
sala(f) de la caldera(f) nuclear 806.
sala(f) de máquinas(f) 496, 742, 746, 747, 806.
sala(f) de molinetes(m) del ancla(f) 495, 497.
sala(f) de navegación(f) 494.
sala(f) de oración(f) 172, 173.
sala(f) de producción(f) de electricidad(f) 806.
sala(f) de producción(f) y control(m) 412.
sala(f) de proyección(f) 16.
sala(f) de regulación(f) de luces 412.
sala(f) de torpedos(m) 807.
sala(f) del montacargas(m) 735.
sala(f) para el público(m) 189.
salamandra(f) 85.
salero(m) 238.
salida(f) 452.
salida(f) de agua(f) caliente 208, 296, 297.
salida(f) de agua(f) fría 296.
salida(f) de aire(m) caliente 204, 207, 438.
salida(f) de humo(m) 204.
salida(f) de la contracorriente(f) 759.
salida(f) de la pista(f) 505.
salida(f) de la pista(f) de alta velocidad(f) 502.
salida(f) de vapor(m) 760, 761, 762, 763.
salida(f) del agua(f) de enfriamiento(m) del condensador(m) 759.
salida(f) del refrigerante(m) 768.
salida(f) y llegada(f) 646.
salida(m) de la pista(f) 651.
salina(f) 30.
salón(m) de baile(m) 497.
salón(m) de pasajeros(m) 496.
salsera(f) 238.
salsifí(m) 71.
saltamontes(m) 77.
SALTO(M) 624.
salto(m) al frente(m) 624.

salto(m) al frente(m) en posición(f) A 625.
salto(m) atrás 624.
salto(m) atrás en posición(f) A 625.
salto(m) de altura(f) 657.
salto(m) de altura(f) 654.
salto(m) de cama(f) 348.
salto(m) de pértiga(f) 657.
salto(m) de pértiga(f) 655.
salto(m) de salida(f) 622.
salto(m) en equilibrio(m) 625.
salto(m) interior en posición(f) B 625.
salto(m) inverso en posición(f) B 625.
salto(m) tirabuzón(m) en posición(f) A 625.
saltos(m) 624.
salvavidas(m) 495.
salvia(f) 74.
sandalia(f) 356, 357, 791.
sandía(f) 69.
sapo(m) 85.
sarga(f) 576.
sarmiento(m) 61.
sarong(m) malayo 334.
sarta(f) 361.
sartén(f) 688.
sartén(f) 249.
sartén(f) honda 249.
sartén(f) para crepas(f) 249.
sartorio(m) 120.
satélite(m) 416.
satélite(m) artificial 19.
SATÉLITE(M) DE DETECCIÓN(F) A LARGA DISTANCIA(F) 48.
satélite(m) de órbita(f) polar 43.
SATÉLITE(M) DE TRANSMISIÓN(F), COMUNICACIÓN(F) 416.
satélite(m) geoestacionario 42.
SATÉLITE(M) METEOROLÓGICO 42.
satélite(m) Radarsat 49.
SATÉLITE(M), TELECOMUNICACIONES(F) 417.
SATÉLITES(M) DE TELECOMUNICACIONES(F) 418.
satélites(m), ejemplos(m) 418.
satélites(m), órbita(f) 43.
satén(m) 576.
Saturno 5.
saxofón(m) 548.
saxofón(m) 548.
Schwann, célula(f) de 135.
SEÑALES(F) DE TRÁNSITO(M) 826.
señales(f) de tránsito(m) internacionales, principales 825.
secado(m) 829.
secador(f) manual 370.
secadora(f) de ensalada(f) 243.
secadora(f) de pruebas(f) 399.
secadora(f) de ropa(f) 259.
sección(f) antirrotacional 42.
sección(f) de carga(f) del combustible(m) 764.
sección(f) de flotación(f) 486.
sección(f) del cañón(m) 205.
sección(f) frontal 730.
sección(f) para el equipo(m) 16.
sección(f) principal 701.
seco(m) 700, 701.
secretario(m) 612, 626.
sedal(m) 670.
sedán(m) de cuatro puertas(f) 425.
sedimento(m) 216.
segadora(f) 158.
segadora(f) 154.
segmento(m) abdominal 78.
segmento(m) de marcas(f) 698.
segmento(m) intermediario 127.
segmento(m) muscular 89.
segmento(m) terminal 127.
segueta(f) 277.
seguimiento(m) de la bola(f) 682.
segunda base(f) 597.
segunda etapa(f) 509.
segunda vía(f) de clasificación(f) 465.
segunda(f) 537, 667.
segundero(m) 706.
segundero(m) en décimas(f) de segundo(m) 706.
segundo árbitro(m) 613.
segundo espacio(m) 610.
segundo hueso(m) metacarpiano 112.
segundo jugador(m) 620.
segundo molar(m) 144.
segundo pistón(m) móvil 550.
segundo premolar(m) 144.
segundo recinto(m) focal 15.

Los términos en **negrita** corresponden a una ilustración; los que aparecen en MAYÚSCULAS indican un título.

Los términos en **negrita** corresponden a una ilustración; los que aparecen en MAYÚSCULAS indican un título.

Los términos en **negrita** corresponden a una ilustración; los que aparecen en MAYÚSCULAS indican un título.

Los términos en **negrita** corresponden a una ilustración; los que aparecen en MAYÚSCULAS indican un título.

Los términos en **negrita** corresponden a una ilustración; los que aparecen en MAYÚSCULAS indican un título.

The terms in **bold type** correspond to an illustration; those in CAPITALS indicate a title.

The terms in **bold type** correspond to an illustration; those in CAPITALS indicate a title.

The terms in **bold type** correspond to an illustration; those in CAPITALS indicate a title.

The terms in **bold type** correspond to an illustration; those in CAPITALS indicate a title.

ENGLISH INDEX

873

The terms in **bold type** correspond to an illustration; those in CAPITALS indicate a title.

The terms in **bold type** correspond to an illustration; those in CAPITALS indicate a title.

The terms in **bold type** correspond to an illustration; those in CAPITALS indicate a title.

The terms in **bold type** correspond to an illustration; those in CAPITALS indicate a title.

The terms in **bold type** correspond to an illustration; those in CAPITALS indicate a title.

The terms in **bold type** correspond to an illustration; those in CAPITALS indicate a title.

The terms in **bold type** correspond to an illustration; those in CAPITALS indicate a title.

keyboard port 528.
keystone 174, 177.
keyway 290.
kick pleat 335.
kickstand 443.
kidney 89, 97, 124.
kilt 335.
kimono 348.
kimono sleeve 340.
King 11, 695, 696.
king post 199, 637.
King's side 696.
kingpin 441.
kiosk 453, 475.
kitchen 171, 195, 460, 807.
kitchen knife 242.
kitchen knives, types 242.
kitchen scale 244.
kitchen timer 244.
KITCHEN UTENSILS 242, 244, 246.
kitchenette 195.
kiwi 68.
knapsack 680.
knee 100, 106, 116, 118.
knee boot 653.
knee boot suspender 653.
knee pad 595, 602, 609.
knee roll 649.
knee sock 642.
knee-high sock 344.
knickers 336.
knife 239.
knife 581, 587, 688, 690.
knife pleat 323, 335.
knife-blade cartridge fuse 312.
Knight 696.
knit cap 329.
knit shirt 326.
KNITTING 567.
KNITTING MACHINE 568.
knitting measure 567.
knitting needles 567.
knives, principal types 239.
knob 219, 596.
knob handle 284.
knockout 312.
knot 576.
knot stitches 571.
KNOTS 691, 692.
knurled bolt 304.
kohlrabi 71.
krone 832.
kumquat 65.

L

label 404.
label holder 517.
label maker 516.
labial palp 79, 81, 92.
labium majus 128, 129.
labium minus 128, 129.
laboratory 15.
laccolith 25.
lace 596, 644, 669.
lace carriage 568.
Lacerta 11.
lacing 645.
lacrimal duct 140.
lactiferous duct 129.
ladder 449, 487, 493, 741, 785.
ladder and hose strap 777.
ladder pipe nozzle 781.
ladder scaffold 303.
LADDERS 302.
ladle 244, 801.
Lady chapel 177.
Lady in the Chair 11.
ladybug 77.
lagging 741.
lagoon 30.
lake 7, 27, 51.
lam 572.
lamb 150.
laminboard 288.
lamp 718.
lamp base 486.
lamp socket 309.
lamphouse elevation control 399.
lamphouse head 399.
lanceolate 56.
lancet 17.
land 281.
landing 194, 201, 736.
landing area 655, 657.
landing deck 811.
landing gear lever 500.
landing light 508.
landing net 672.
landing radar 811.

landing window 508.
lane 683.
lane 621, 655.
lane line 656.
lane number 621.
lane rope 621.
lane timekeeper 621.
language display button 422.
languid 542.
lantern 689.
lantern 263, 486.
lantern pane 486.
lapel 322, 341.
lapiaz 24.
lapis lazuli 363.
larch 58.
large blade 688.
large intestine 131.
large wheel 727.
larger round 121.
larva 82.
larynx 130, 142.
laser beam 405.
laser printer 527.
last quarter 7.
latch 253, 257, 383, 568, 681.
latch bolt 289, 290.
latch lever 562.
latch needle 568.
latch needle 569.
lateen sail 482.
lateral bar 663.
lateral condyle of femur 123.
lateral cutaneous nerve of thigh 133.
lateral filing cabinet 520.
lateral great 120, 121.
lateral groove 104.
lateral incisor 144.
lateral line 87, 620.
lateral mark 489.
lateral moraine 27.
lateral rectus muscle 140.
lateral semicircular canal 139.
lateral-adjustment lever 277.
lath 231.
lath tilt device 231.
latitude 3.
latitude scale 40.
latrines 171.
launch escape system 509.
launcher/satellite separation 419.
launching into orbit 419.
launching orbit 48.
laundry room 194.
lava flow 25.
lava layer 25.
lavatory 195.
lavatory truck 506.
lawn 193, 263.
lawn aerator 266.
lawn edger 266.
lawn rake 267.
leach field 216.
lead 620.
lead ball 804.
lead pencil 389.
lead screw 281.
lead-in wire 232.
leader 672.
leading edge 341, 499, 636, 638.
leading edge flap 812.
leading edge tube 637.
leaf 56.
leaf 57, 72.
leaf axil 56.
leaf margin 56.
leaf node 57.
leaf vegetables 73.
leakproof cap 689.
lean-to roof 182.
leash rod 574.
leather end 323.
LEATHER GOODS 378.
leather sheath 632, 690.
leather skin 598.
LEAVES, TYPES 56.
leaves, types of 58.
ledger 198.
ledger line 537.
leech 631.
leek 70.
left atrium 124, 125.
left back 601, 607, 612, 613.
left center 606.
left channel 401.
left cornerback 603, 605.
left defense 608.
left defensive end 603, 605.
left defensive tackle 603, 605.
left field 597.

left fielder 597.
left forward 610, 613.
left guard 603, 605, 610.
left half 601, 607.
left halfback 603.
left inner 607.
left kidney 132.
left lung 124, 130.
left outside linebacker 605.
left pulmonary vein 125.
left safety 603.
left safety back 605.
left service court 614, 616.
left tackle 603, 605.
left valve, shell 95.
left ventricle 124, 125.
left wing 606, 607, 608.
left winger 612.
leg 97, 117, 119, 156, 219, 224, 270, 325, 553, 619, 659, 671.
leg curl bar 663.
leg extension bar 663.
leg position 625.
leg-of-mutton sleeve 340.
leg-warmer 353.
legging 680.
legume, section 67.
lemon 65.
length post 651.
lengthwise bulkhead 742.
lengthwise grain 565, 566.
lens 140, 390, 392.
lens accessories 392.
lens aperture scale 392.
lens cap 392.
lens hood 392, 409, 484.
lens mount 390.
lens release button 391.
lens system 719.
LENSES 722.
lenses 392.
lenticular galaxy 9.
lentils 72.
Leo 11.
Leo Minor 11.
Leo the Lion (July 23) 820.
leotard 353.
Lepus 13.
lesser covert 110.
letter opener 515.
letter scale 516.
leucoplast 115.
level 736.
level crossing 464.
leveling foot 257, 258, 259.
leveling head 713.
leveling head level 713.
leveling head locking knob 713.
leveling screw 40, 709, 713.
leveling-adjustment foot 397.
lever 252, 278, 295, 296, 365, 453, 583, 702, 798.
lever corkscrew 244.
lever cover 295.
levigator 583.
Libra 11.
Libra the Balance (September 23) 820.
license plate light 429.
lid 247, 248, 251, 252, 253, 256, 258, 398, 585.
lid brace 585.
lierne 177.
life buoy 495.
life raft 492.
life support system 512.
life support system controls 512.
lifeboat 478, 494, 496, 738.
lift 478.
lift arm 782.
lift bridge 457.
lift chain 293.
lift cord 231.
lift cord lock 231.
lift span 457.
lift-arm cylinder 782.
lift-fan air inlet 493.
lifting chain 787.
lifting handle 803.
lifting hook 737.
lifting lever 147.
lifting link 147.
ligament 95.
ligature 548.
light 477, 486, 487, 489, 720, 721.
light bar 779.
LIGHT MACHINE GUN 796.
light sensor 390.
light shield 16.
light signal 539.
light-load adjustment screw 712.

light-reading scale 396.
lightbox 398.
lighted mirror 368.
lighthouse 486.
lighthouse 491.
lighthouse lantern 486.
lighting 368, 500.
lighting board 412.
lighting board operator 412.
lighting cable 449.
lighting grid 414.
lighting grid access 412.
lighting technician 412.
lighting/camera control area 412.
lightning 36.
lightning arrester 747, 757.
lightning rod 197.
LIGHTS 232, 234, 236.
lights 429.
limb 59, 684.
limb top 718.
limousine 425.
limpet 83.
line 537, 700, 701.
line guide 671.
line hook 492.
line judge 603, 605.
line map 474.
line of scrimmage 603, 605.
linear 56.
lineman's pliers 311.
linen 224.
linen 460.
linen chest 226.
lines of latitude 47.
lines of longitude 47.
linesman 601, 605, 608, 613, 614, 618.
lingual papillae 143.
lingual tonsil 143.
lining 322, 324, 352, 354, 378, 565, 644.
linseed oil 592.
linstock 801.
lint filter 258.
lint trap 259.
lintel 175, 204.
lion 98.
Lion 11.
lion passant 819.
lip 100, 107.
lip makeup 366.
lip strap ring 650.
lipbrush 366.
lipid droplet 115.
lipliner 366.
lipstick 366.
liqueur glass 237.
liquid compass 484.
liquid compass, cross section 485.
liquid cooling and ventilation garment 512.
liquid eyeliner 367.
liquid foundation 366.
liquid hydrogen tank 509.
liquid mascara 367.
liquid nitrogen tank 717.
liquid oxygen tank 509.
liquid oxygen tank baffle 509.
liquid-crystal display 706.
liquid/gas separator 439.
lira 832.
listen button 420.
lists 181.
litchi 68.
litho crayon 583.
litho pencil 583.
lithographic press 583.
lithographic printing 580.
lithographic stone 583.
lithographic tusche 583.
LITHOGRAPHY 583.
lithography, equipment 583.
lithosphere 31.
Little Bear 11.
Little Dog 11.
little finger 137.
little finger hook 551.
Little Horse 11.
Little Lion 11.
liver 88, 97, 124, 131.
Liverpool bit 650.
livestock car 472.
living room 195, 685.
Lizard 11.
load support 635.
loading area 764.
loading bunker 734.
loading dock 190.
loading door 204.

The terms in **bold type** correspond to an illustration; those in CAPITALS indicate a title.

The terms in **bold type** correspond to an illustration; those in CAPITALS indicate a title.

The terms in **bold type** correspond to an illustration; those in CAPITALS indicate a title.

The terms in **bold type** correspond to an illustration; those in CAPITALS indicate a title.

The terms in **bold type** correspond to an illustration; those in CAPITALS indicate a title.

The terms in **bold type** correspond to an illustration; those in CAPITALS indicate a title.

The terms in **bold type** correspond to an illustration; those in CAPITALS indicate a title.

ROAD SIGNS 824, 826, 828.
ROAD SYSTEM 450, 452.
road transport 491.
road work ahead 826, 827.
road, cross section 450.
roadway 186, 450.
roadway narrows 826, 827.
roasting pans 248.
Roberval's balance 708.
rock 30.
rock basin 26.
rock garden 263.
rock step 26.
rocker arm 435.
ROCKET 509.
rocket motor 814.
rocking chair 221, 223.
rocking tool 582.
rocky desert 46.
rod 214, 539, 573.
rodent's jaw 98.
roll 341.
roll film 395.
roll-up blind 231.
roller 230, 231, 270, 369, 530, 583, 788.
roller board and arms 543.
roller cover 304.
roller frame 304.
roller shade 231.
ROLLER SKATE 645.
rolling ladder 303.
rolling pin 245.
romaine lettuce 73.
ROMAN HOUSE 170.
Roman legionary 791.
Roman metal pen 389.
roman shade 231.
Romanian couching stitch 571.
rompers 351.
roof 82, 171, 197, 205, 427, 470, 733.
roof pole 686.
roof truss 199.
roof vent 196, 215, 449.
ROOFS 182.
Rook 696.
room 736.
room air conditioner 214.
room thermostat 213, 705.
rooster 150.
root 70, 143, 144, 240.
root canal 144.
root cap 57.
root hairs 57.
root of nail 137.
root of nose 141.
root rib 498.
root system 57, 61.
root vegetables 71.
root-hair zone 59.
rope 361, 669, 680, 692.
rope ladder 303.
rose 265, 289, 290, 546.
rose cut 362.
rose window 175.
rosemary 74.
rosette 167.
rostrum 90.
rotary engine 437.
rotary film 516.
rotary hoe 157.
rotary system 737.
rotary table 737.
rotating auger 160, 162.
rotating dome 14.
rotating dome truck 14.
rotating drum 714.
rotating track 15.
rotating wheel 701.
rotation of the turbine 755.
rotor 161, 290, 437, 753, 773, 774.
rotor blade 508.
rotor head 508.
rotor hub 508.
rotunda 190.
rotunda roof 183.
rough 676.
roughing out 586.
roulette 582.
ROULETTE TABLE 700.
round brush 368.
round end pin 231.
round eye 566.
round head 276.
round ligament of uterus 129.
round neck 343.
round pronator 120.
router 283.
routing cardboard 471, 743.
row 373.

row counter 568.
row number display 569.
rower 664.
rowing (one oar) 632.
ROWING AND SCULLING 632.
rowing boats 632.
royal agaric 55.
royal antler 105.
royal flush 695.
rub rail 441.
rubber 355.
rubber boot 777.
rubber bulb 726.
rubber gasket 296.
rubber mat 404.
rubber snaffle bit 650.
rubber stamp 516.
rubber thread 677.
rubber tip 302, 728.
rubber wall 433.
rubbing alcohol 725.
rubbing strip 433.
ruby 363.
ruching 349.
rudder 492, 496, 499, 511, 628, 639, 742, 806, 812, 814.
rudder pedal 639.
Ruffini's corpuscle 136.
ruffle 228, 317.
ruffled rumba pants 349.
ruffled skirt 334.
rug and floor brush 260.
RUGBY 606.
rugby ball 606.
rugby, field 606.
ruler 578, 591, 688.
rump 109.
run 201, 599.
rung 302.
runner 643, 697, 753.
runner blade 752, 753, 754.
running 654.
running bowline 691.
running rail 476.
running shoe 352.
running surface 466.
running track 786.
runway 504.
runway 476, 811.
runway center line markings 504.
runway designation marking 504.
runway side stripe markings 504.
runway threshold markings 505.
runway touchdown zone marking 505.
Russian pumpernickel 153.
rutabaga 71.
rye 152.

S

S-band antenna 43.
S-band high gain antenna 42.
S-band omnidirectional antenna 42.
sabaton 792.
saber 666, 794.
saber and épée warning line 666.
sable 819.
sabreur 667.
sacral plexus 133.
sacral vertebrae 103.
sacrum 122, 123.
saddle 649.
saddle 397, 636, 648, 651, 661.
saddle pad 648.
saddlecloth 648, 651.
safari jacket 338.
safe water mark 489.
safelight 398.
safest water 488.
safety 796.
safety area 668.
safety binding 641.
safety boot 730.
safety cage 654.
safety cap 729.
safety cap 804.
safety chain 449.
safety earmuff 729.
safety glasses 729.
safety goggles 729.
safety handle 271.
safety line 475.
safety match 386.
safety pad 659.
safety pin 566.
safety rail 302, 468.
safety scissors 365.
safety suit connection 512.
SAFETY SYMBOLS 821.

safety tank 761.
safety tether 512.
safety thermostat 259.
safety thong 617.
safety valve 248, 766.
SAFETY VEST 730.
sage 74.
Sagitta 11.
sagittal section 127, 128, 129, 142.
Sagittarius 13.
Sagittarius the Archer (November 22) 820.
sail 631, 637, 773.
sail cloth 773.
sail panel 628.
sail plane 807.
sailbar 773.
SAILBOARD 631.
sailboat 628.
SAILING 628, 630.
sailing, points 629.
sailor collar 342.
sails 480.
SAILS, TYPES 482.
salad bowl 238.
salad dish 238.
salad fork 240.
salad plate 238.
salad spinner 243.
salamander 85.
salient angle 178.
saline lake 46.
salivary glands 131.
salsify 71.
salt marsh 30.
salt shaker 238.
salt taste 143.
sample 567.
sand 748.
sand bar 30.
sand island 30.
sand shoe 441.
sand wedge 678.
sandal 356, 357, 791.
sandbox 469.
sandstorm or dust storm 39.
sandy desert 46.
saphenous nerve 133.
sapphire 363.
sapwood 59.
sarong 334.
sartorius 120.
sash frame 203.
sash window 203.
satchel bag 380.
satellite 416.
satin weave 576.
Saturn 5.
saucepan 249, 688.
sauté pan 249.
savory 74.
sawing-in 578.
sawtooth roof 182.
saxhorn 551.
saxophone 548.
saxophone 548.
scale 537.
scale 87, 96, 97, 111, 705, 711, 719, 726.
scale leaf 70.
Scales 13.
scallion 70.
scallop 93.
scalper 653.
scampi 91.
Scandinavian crak bread 153.
scapula 102, 122, 123.
scapular 110.
scarp 178.
scatter cushion 224.
scattered sky 39.
scenery lift 188.
scenery storage 188.
scenic route 52.
schedules 463.
school zone 826, 827.
schooner 482.
sciatic nerve 133.
scientific air lock 511.
scientific instruments 16, 511.
scissors 564.
scissors 688, 725.
scissors crossing 464.
scissors cut 362.
scissors-glasses 377.
sclera 140.
scoop 385.
score-console 683.
scoreboard 698.

scorer 610, 613, 666, 668.
scoring light 666.
Scorpio the Scorpion (October 24) 820.
Scorpion 13.
Scorpius 13.
scotia 166, 167.
scraper 304, 784.
scraper 582, 583.
scraper bar holder 583.
screen 161, 374, 397, 410, 747.
screen case 397.
screen print 350.
screen window 685.
screw 276.
screw 544.
screw base 232.
screw earrings 361.
screw locking nut 670, 671.
screwdriver 276.
screwdriver 688.
screwsleeve 681.
scrimmage 603.
scrimmage in Canadian football 605.
script assistant 412.
scroll 544.
scroll case 747.
scroll foot 220.
scrotum 116, 127.
scrum half 606.
scuba diver 627.
SCUBA DIVING 627.
scuffle hoe 266.
sculling (two oars) 632.
sculling boats 632.
scythe 267.
sea 7, 51, 752.
sea anchor 483.
sea bag 381.
sea level 22, 28.
sea side 752.
sea-level pressure 38.
Sea-Serpent 13.
sea-to-sea missile 809.
seal 295.
sealed cell 82.
sealing ring 741.
seam 327, 384, 598.
seam allowance 565.
seam gauge 563.
seam line 565.
seam pocket 330, 339.
seaming 322.
seamount 29.
search-and-rescue antennas 43.
SEASONS OF THE YEAR 8.
seat 220, 223, 292, 293, 428, 445, 446, 584, 639, 649, 652, 664, 727.
seat belt 428.
seat cover 293.
seat post 446.
seat stay 446.
seat tube 446.
seat-belt warning light 431.
SEATS 222.
sebaceous gland 136.
second 537, 669, 830.
second base 597.
second baseman 597.
second classification track 465.
second dorsal fin 86.
second floor 194.
second floor 196.
second focal room 15.
second hand 706.
second molar 144.
second premolar 144.
second reinforce 800.
second space 610.
second stage 509.
second valve slide 550.
second violins 556.
secondaries 110.
secondary channel 489.
secondary consumers 31.
secondary inlet 741.
secondary mirror 16, 390.
secondary reflector 15.
secondary road 52.
secondary root 57.
seconde 667.
secretarial desk 521.
secretary 226, 612, 626.
section of a bulb 70.
security casing 271.
security check 504.
security trigger 272.
sedimentary rocks 23.
seed 62, 63, 64, 65, 66, 67.

The terms in **bold type** correspond to an illustration; those in CAPITALS indicate a title.

slip joint pliers 278.
slip-stitched seam 324.
slippery road 826, 827.
slit 576.
slope 451.
sloped turret 183.
sloping cornice 168.
slot 188, 240, 252, 276, 379, 578.
SLOT MACHINE 702.
slotback 605.
slow-burning stove 204.
slow-motion 411.
slower traffic 452.
sludge 216.
small decanter 237.
small hand cultivator 268.
small intestine 131.
smaller round 121.
SMELL 141.
smock 337.
smoke 39.
smoke baffle 204.
smoke bomb discharger 805.
SMOKING ACCESSORIES 384, 386.
smoking candle 582.
smoking-apparatus 582.
snaffle bit 650.
snaffle bit 649.
snaffle rein 649.
snaffle strap 649.
snail 83.
snail dish 246.
snail tongs 246.
snap 566.
snap 672.
snap fastener 321, 327.
snap shackle 630.
snap-fastening front 350.
snap-fastening tab 321.
snap-fastening waist 350.
snare 553.
snare drum 553.
snare drum 552, 557.
snare head 553.
snare strainer 553.
snelled fishhook 672.
snooker 673.
snorkel 627.
snout 84.
snow 34.
snow crystals, classification 36.
snow gauge 41.
snow guard 445.
snow pellet 37.
snow shower 39.
snowfall, measure 41.
snowmobile 445.
SNOWSHOE 645.
snowsuit 351.
soap dish 292.
SOCCER 600.
soccer ball 600.
soccer player 600.
soccer shoe 600.
soccer, playing field 601.
sock 344, 602, 615.
socket 309, 401, 566.
socket bayonet 794.
socket head 276.
socks 325.
sofa 221.
soft palate 141, 142.
soft pastel 588.
soft pedal 540, 555.
soft ray 87.
soft shell clam 93.
soft-drink dispenser 453.
soil 750.
solar array 42, 48, 418.
solar array deployment 48, 419.
solar array drive 42.
solar array extended 48.
solar cell 768.
solar cell 523, 769.
solar cell panel 769.
solar cells 42.
solar collector 772.
SOLAR ECLIPSE 8.
SOLAR ENERGY 768, 770, 772.
solar furnace 770.
solar house 772.
solar panel 16.
solar radiation 768, 769, 770, 771, 772.
solar ray reflected 770, 771.
solar reflectors 418.
solar shield 512.
SOLAR SYSTEM 4.
solar-cell system 769.
solder 307.
SOLDERING 305, 306, 308.

soldering gun 305.
soldering iron 305.
soldering torch 299, 307.
sole 104, 325, 641, 644, 678.
soleplate 256.
soleus 120.
solid body 547.
solid rubber tire 788.
solid shot 801.
solid-rocket booster 510.
solitaire ring 364.
solvent extraction unit 744.
sorghum 152.
sound alarm 485.
sound digitizing processor 528.
sound hole 544.
sound receiver 726.
SOUND REPRODUCING SYSTEM 400, 402, 404.
sound reproducing system, components 400.
sound signal 539.
soundboard 535, 540, 544, 545, 546.
soundbox 545.
soup bowl 238.
soup spoon 241.
soup tureen 238.
sour taste 143.
sources of pollution 34.
South 488.
South America 20.
South cardinal mark 489.
South celestial pole 3.
South Pole 3.
Southeast 488.
Southern Cross 13.
Southern Crown 13.
Southern Fish 13.
Southern hemisphere 3, 47.
Southern Triangle 13.
Southwest 488.
southwester 329.
sow 151.
soybeans 72.
space 537.
space bar 525, 530.
space probe 19.
SPACE SHUTTLE 510.
space shuttle at takeoff 510.
space shuttle in orbit 510.
spacelab 511.
spacer 727, 765.
SPACESUIT 512.
spade 632.
spade 266, 695, 803.
spading fork 266.
spadix 60.
spaghetti tongs 246.
spandrel 174.
spanker 480.
spar 498.
spar buoy 489.
spark 436.
spark plug 439.
spark plug 271, 435, 437.
spark plug body 439.
spark plug cable 435.
spark plug gap 439.
spark plug gasket 439.
spark plug terminal 439.
sparkling wine glass 237.
spatial dendrite 36.
spatula 244, 581, 589.
spatulate 56.
speaker 408, 420, 560.
speaker cover 401.
speaker selector 402.
spear 72, 791.
speargun 627.
special mark 489.
specimen chamber 717.
specimen positioning control 717.
spectrometer 717.
speed control 250, 271.
speed controller 561.
speed course 646.
speed selector 251, 404.
speed selector switch 370.
speed skate 644.
speedbrake lever 500.
speedometer 431, 445, 664.
spelling corrector 524.
spencer 338.
spent fuel discharge bay 758.
spent fuel port 764.
spent fuel storage bay 758, 764, 765.
spermatic cord 127.
spermatozoon 127.
sphenoidal sinus 141.
sphere support 40.
sphincter muscle of anus 131.

spicules 6.
SPIDER 77.
spider 77.
spike 60, 466, 656, 680, 681.
spiked shoe 595.
spillway 746.
spillway chute 746.
spillway gate 746.
spinach 73.
spinal cord 89, 134, 135.
spinal ganglion 135.
spinal nerve 135.
spindle 223, 251, 290, 294, 404, 707, 711, 712.
spine 577.
spine of scapula 123.
spine of the book 579.
spinner 672.
spinning rod 671.
spinous process 135.
spiny lobster 91.
spiny ray 86.
spiracle 78, 79.
spiral 276, 404.
spiral arm 9.
spiral beater 250.
spiral binder 519.
spiral case 753.
spiral galaxy 9.
spiral rib 94.
spiral screwdriver 276.
spiral staircase 741.
spiral-in groove 404.
spire 94, 175.
spirit level 291.
spit 30.
splash plate 741.
splat 220.
splay 175.
spleen 88, 124.
splenius muscle of head 121.
spline 439.
splints 725.
split bet 700, 701.
split end 603, 605.
split link 672.
spoiler 442, 498.
spoke 447.
spoked wheel 652.
sponge 801.
sponge-tipped applicator 367.
sponges 367.
spool 570, 670, 671.
spool pin 561.
spool rack 575.
spoon 241.
spoon 688.
spoon blade 587.
spoons, principal types 241.
spores 55.
sports car 425.
SPORTSWEAR 352.
spot 235.
spot white ball 673.
spotmeter 396.
spotlight 414, 777, 778, 780.
spout 162, 247, 252, 294, 295.
spout assembly 296.
spray 256.
spray arm 257.
spray button 256.
spray control 256.
spray head 296.
spray hose 292, 296.
spray nozzle 264, 741.
spray paint gun 304.
sprayer 264.
spread collar 324.
spreader 270, 375.
spreader adjustment screw 304.
spring 8, 234, 258, 278, 290, 294, 389, 469, 659, 804.
spring balance 709.
spring binder 519.
spring housing 230.
spring linkage 702.
spring wing 276.
spring-metal insulation 287.
springboard 659.
springer 174.
sprinkler hose 265.
sprinklers 766.
sprocket 445.
sprocket wheel 783, 805.
spur 27, 80, 281, 552, 648.
squall 39.
square 184, 577.
square bet 700, 701.
square brackets 832.
square flag 817.
square head plug 301.

square knot 691.
square movement 696.
square neck 343.
square root key 523.
square root of 830.
square sail 482.
square trowel 291.
square-headed tip 276.
SQUASH 616.
squash ball 616.
squash racket 616.
squash, court 616.
stabilizer 636, 684, 812.
stabilizer fin 496.
stabilizing fin 509.
stabilizing shaft 788.
stable 651.
stack 30, 494.
stacking chairs 223.
stadium 185.
staff 537.
staff 817.
stage 189.
stage 188, 717, 718.
stage clip 718.
stage curtain 188, 189.
stained glass 175.
STAIRS 201.
stairs 194, 474, 741.
stairwell 194.
stake 263, 685, 686.
stake loop 685, 686.
stake pocket 441.
stalactite 24.
stalagmite 24.
stalk 62, 63, 64, 72.
stalk vegetables 72.
stamen 60, 64.
stamp 384.
stamp pad 516.
stamp rack 516.
stanchion 644.
stand 651.
stand 236, 248, 250, 341, 370, 382, 552, 586, 714.
stand-off half 606.
stand-up collar 342.
standard A 539.
standard lens 392.
standardbred pacer 652.
standby airspeed indicator 500.
standby altimeter 500.
standby attitude indicator 500.
standing press 579.
standpipe 298.
staples 138.
staple remover 515.
stapler 515.
staples 515.
star anise 67.
star diagonal 721.
star facet (8) 363.
star tracker 16.
starboard hand 488, 489, 497.
starch 152.
starch granule 115.
start 532.
start and finish 646.
start button 706.
start key 421.
start line 655, 656.
start switch 259.
start wall 621.
start-up key 530.
starter 271, 272, 621.
starter handle 272.
starting bar (backstroke) 621.
starting block 621, 656.
starting block 621.
starting cable 270.
starting dive 622.
starting position 625.
starting step 201.
state 51.
station circle 38.
station entrance 474.
station name 474.
station platform 464.
station wagon 425.
stationary bicycle 664.
stationary bowl 701.
stationary front 39.
STATIONERY 515, 516, 518.
stationery cabinet 522.
stator 290, 294.
stay 479.
stay ring 753.
stay vane blade 753.
stays 456.
staysail-stay 479.
steak knife 239.

The terms in **bold type** correspond to an illustration; those in CAPITALS indicate a title.

T

The terms in **bold type** correspond to an illustration; those in CAPITALS indicate a title.

tackle box 672.
tadpole 84.
tail 91, 96, 97, 101, 106, 107, 112, 127, 499, 579, 633, 638, 641, 642, 643, 645, 670.
tail assembly 499.
tail boom 508.
tail comb 368.
tail edge 577.
tail feather 109.
tail of helix 139.
tail pipe 439.
tail pipe extension 439.
tail pole 773.
TAIL SHAPES, TYPES 498.
tail skid 508.
tail-out groove 404.
tailing auger 161.
taillight 147, 429, 441, 443, 444.
taillights 429.
tailored collar 330, 341.
tailored sleeve 340.
tailpiece 296, 544.
tailrace 747.
take-up handle 572.
take-up reel 403.
take-up spool 390.
talon 111.
talus 123.
tambourine 554.
tamper 385.
tandem disk harrow 157.
tandem disk harrow 154.
tandem tractor trailer 440.
tang 239, 242, 291.
TANK 805.
tank 216, 398, 399, 689, 742, 743, 780.
tank ball 293.
tank car 743.
tank car 472.
tank farm 740.
tank gauge float 741.
tank hatch 743.
tank lid 293.
tank sprayer 265.
tank top 351, 353.
tank trailer 742.
tank wall 742.
tanker 742.
tanker 491, 813.
tanks 511.
tap connector 265.
tape 566, 571, 607, 613, 711, 804.
tape counter 403.
tape dispenser 516.
tape lock 711.
tape measure 711.
tape measure 563.
tape selector 403.
tape-guide 403.
tapered wing 499.
tapestry bobbin 574.
taproot 59.
tar paper 286.
target 684.
target area 770.
target areas 667.
target detection radar 809.
tarlatan 582.
tarragon 74.
tarsus 78, 80, 103, 108, 122.
tassel 229, 231.
tasset 792.
taste sensations 143.
Taurus 11.
Taurus the Bull (April 20) 820.
taxi transportation 822.
taxiway 502.
taxiway line 503.
tea ball 246.
team bench 626.
team shirt 595, 600.
teapot 238.
tear tape 384.
tear-off calendar 518.
teaser comb 368.
teaspoon 241.
technical equipment compartment 415.
technical identification band 405.
technical producer 412, 415.
technical producer monitor 413.
technical specifications 433.
technical terms 62, 63, 64, 65.
TEDDING 159.
tedding 155.
teddy 345.
tee 298, 301, 620, 677.
teeing ground 676.
TEETH 144.

teeth 566.
tele-converter 392.
telecommunication antenna 494, 497, 809.
TELECOMMUNICATION SATELLITES 418.
telecommunication satellites, examples 418.
telecommunication terminal 422.
TELECOMMUNICATIONS BY SATELLITE 417.
telecommunications by telephone network 417.
telephone 413, 822.
telephone answering machine 420.
telephone cable 186.
telephone index 420, 516.
telephone network 417.
telephone set 420.
telephone set 415, 417.
TELEPHONE, COMMUNICATION 420, 422.
telephones, types 422.
telephoto lens 392.
teleport 417.
teleprompter 414.
telescope 14.
telescope 14, 42, 484, 713.
telescope base 14.
telescopic boom 780, 786.
telescopic corridor 503.
telescopic front fork 442.
telescopic leg 726.
TELESCOPIC SIGHT 718.
telescopic sight 798.
telescopic umbrella 375.
telescoping leg 393.
telescoping uncoupling rod 470.
TELEVISION 410, 412, 414.
television set 410.
television set 401.
telex 421.
telex 417.
telltale 616, 628.
telson 91.
temperate climates 45.
temperature 210.
temperature control 213, 252, 256, 297.
temperature control knob 585.
temperature indicator 431.
temperature of dew point 38.
temperature scale 19.
temperature scales 710.
temperature selector 253, 258, 259.
temperature set point knob 705.
temperature, measure 41.
template 738.
temple 116, 376, 573, 578.
tempo control 555.
tempo scale 539.
temporal bone 122.
tenaille 179.
tendon 107.
tendon guard 644.
tendril 61.
TENNIS 614.
tennis ball 615.
tennis player 615.
tennis racket 615.
tennis shoe 355, 615.
tennis, court 614.
tennis, net 614.
tenon saw 578.
tenor drum 553.
tenpin 683.
tensiometer 710.
tension block 562, 569.
tension block 561.
tension dial 562, 568, 569.
tension disk 562, 569.
tension guide 569.
tension pulley wheel 230.
tension rod 553.
tension screw 552.
tension spring 431, 562, 569, 665.
tensor of fascia lata 120.
tentacle 83.
tents, major types 686.
tepee 165.
terminal 422.
terminal 255, 309, 312, 740, 757.
terminal arborization 135.
terminal box 769.
terminal bronchiole 130.
terminal bud 57.
terminal filament 134.
terminal lobe 61.
terminal moraine 27.
terminal tackles 672.

terreplein 179.
terrestrial sphere 3.
tertial 110.
tertiary consumers 31.
test pattern 414.
testicle 127.
text 524.
text display 524.
THEATER 188.
theodolite 713.
theodolite 41.
thermal barrier 42.
thermal louver 43.
thermocouple 297.
thermocouple tube 297.
thermometer 705.
thermometer 627, 635, 741.
thermos 690.
thermosphere 19.
thermostat 210, 214, 252, 297.
thermostat control 254.
thigh 101, 106, 108, 117, 119, 127, 128.
thigh pad 602.
thigh-boot 357.
thigh-high stocking 344.
thimble 563, 711.
thinning razor 369.
third 537.
third base 597.
third baseman 597.
third finger 137.
third stage 509.
third valve slide 551.
third wheel 706, 707.
thirty-second note 538.
thirty-second rest 538.
thong 357.
thoracic legs 90.
thoracic vertebra (12) 123.
thoracic vertebrae 102.
thorax 78, 79, 80, 116, 118.
thread 276, 294.
thread guide 561, 562.
thread take-up lever 561.
thread trimmer 562.
threaded cap 301.
threaded rod 279.
three-four time 537.
three-hinged arch 455.
three-of-a-kind 695.
three-quarter coat 321.
three-quarter sleeve 339.
three-toed hoof 99.
threshing area 161.
threshold 202.
throat 108, 282, 483, 615, 671.
throat latch 649.
throat protector 595, 609.
throttle valve 735.
throttles 500.
through arch bridge 455.
throwing circle 654, 655.
throwings 658.
thrust 455.
thrust bearing 753.
thrust device 389.
thrust tube 389.
thruster 49, 512.
THRUSTING AND CUTTING WEAPONS 794.
thumb 112, 137, 327, 596.
thumb hook 550.
thumb piston 542.
thumb rest 549, 726.
thumb tacks 515.
thumbscrew 279.
thunderstorm 39.
thyme 74.
tibia 78, 80, 103, 112, 122.
tibial nerve 133.
ticket collector 463.
ticket collector's booth 474.
ticket control 463.
ticket counter 504.
tidal power plant 752.
tie 375, 466, 539.
tie bar 364.
tie beam 198.
tie closure 375.
tie plate 466.
tie rod 553.
tieback 228.
tiepin 364.
tierce 667.
tierceron 177.
tight end 603, 605.
tightener 661.
tightening band 40.
tilde 832.
tile 169, 170, 286, 511.

tiller 272.
tiller 628, 793.
tilt tube 231.
tilt-back head 250.
timber 168, 170.
time signatures 537.
timed outlet 255.
timekeeper 610, 612, 626, 666, 668, 669.
timer 252, 398, 585, 664.
timing belt 434.
timpani 557.
tine 157, 240, 272.
tip 57, 72, 239, 241, 275, 276, 284, 291, 305, 306, 323, 375, 633, 637, 640, 645, 658, 670, 675.
tip cleaners 307.
tip of nose 141.
tip protector 726.
tip section 670.
tip-ring 670, 671.
tipping lever 727.
tire 433.
tire 440, 447.
tire pump 446.
tire valve 447.
tissue holder 292.
Titan 5.
toad 85.
toaster 252.
tobacco 384.
tobacco hole 385.
tobacco pouch 385.
toe 104, 106, 111, 116, 118, 277, 325, 678.
toe binding 642.
toe box 644.
toe clip 104, 446, 448.
toe guard 595, 730.
toe hole 645.
toe pick 644.
toe piece 633, 640.
toe piston 542.
toe strap 633.
toe-piece 641.
toenail scissors 365.
toeplate 642.
toga 315.
toggle 817.
toggle bolt 276.
toggle fastening 320.
toggles 650.
toilet 293.
toilet 215, 292, 461.
toilet bowl 293.
toilet tank 292.
tom-tom 552.
tomato 69.
tombolo 30.
tone arm 404.
tone control 547.
tone leader generator 407.
tongs 246.
tongue 81, 88, 131, 142, 323, 352, 354, 536, 542, 566, 641, 644.
tongue sheath 96.
tongue, dorsum 143.
tonsil 142.
tool 735.
tool holder 283.
tool shelf 302.
tool tether 512.
TOOLS, CARPENTRY 275, 276, 278, 280, 282, 284.
tools, electricity 310.
tools, electricity 311.
tools, plumbing 299.
tools, wood carving 587.
tooth 96, 158, 159, 160, 162, 268, 277, 284, 369, 785.
toothbrush 373.
toothbrush 373.
toothbrush shaft 373.
toothbrush well 373.
toothed jaw 278.
toothpaste 373.
top 59, 219, 302, 478.
top bar 659.
top central manhole 743.
top coat 331.
top cylinder 581.
top deck 741.
top deckboard 787.
top edge 577.
top face 363.
top hat 328.
top ladder 781.
top lift 354.
top of dam 746, 748, 749, 752.
top plate 525.
top pocket 675.

ENGLISH INDEX

893

The terms in **bold type** correspond to an illustration; those in CAPITALS indicate a title.

The terms in **bold type** correspond to an illustration; those in CAPITALS indicate a title.

The terms in **bold type** correspond to an illustration; those in CAPITALS indicate a title.